CONCISE
WORLD
ATLAS

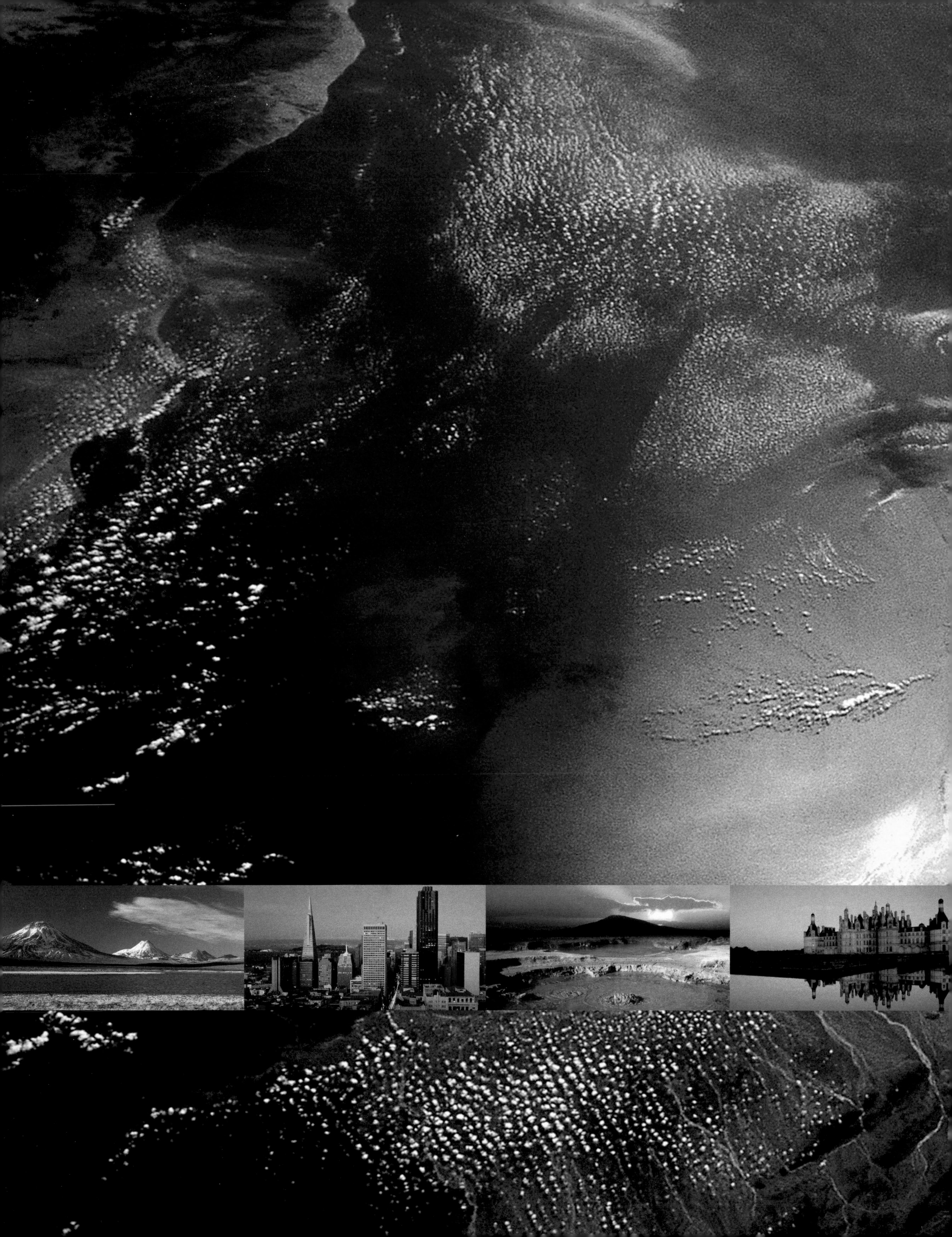

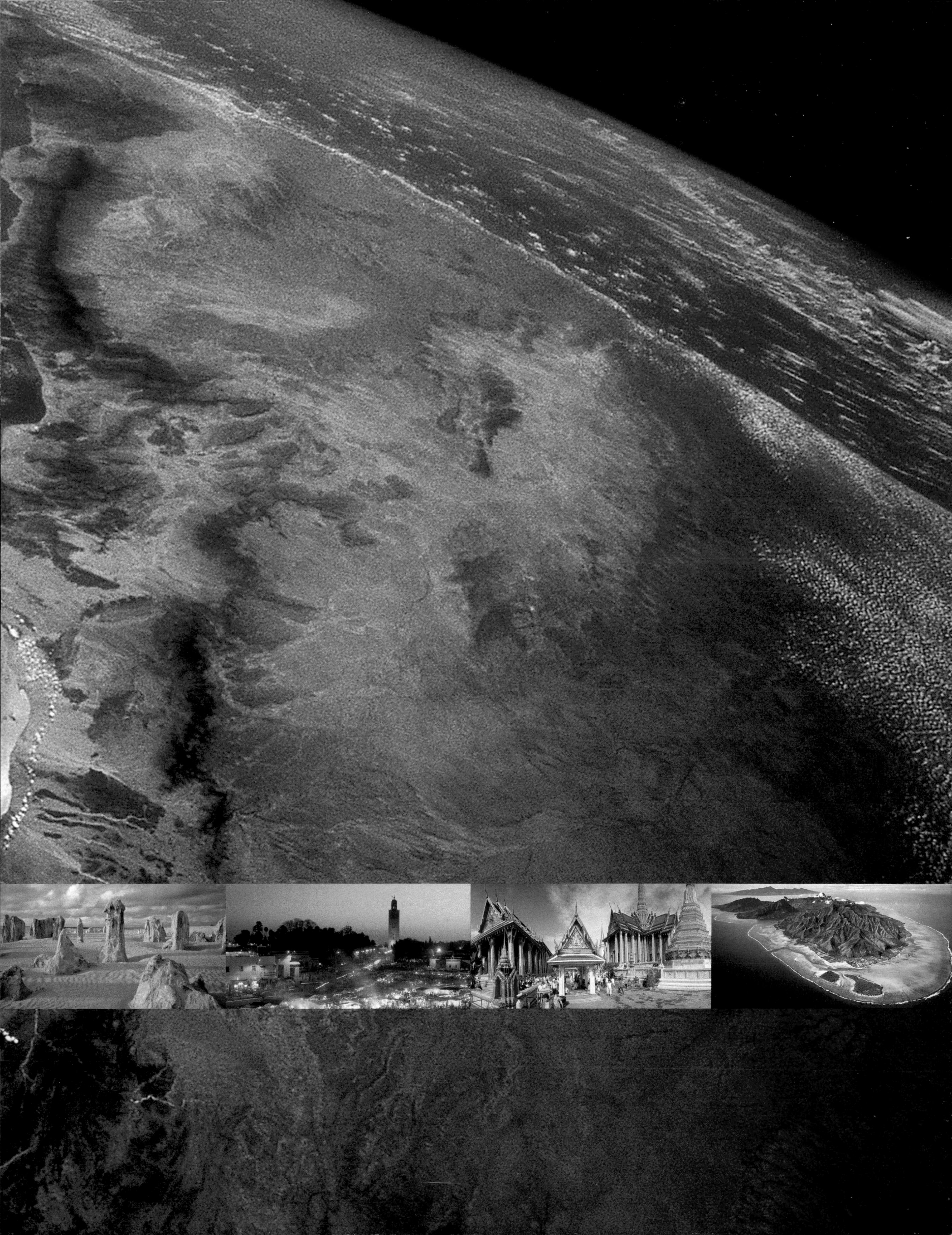

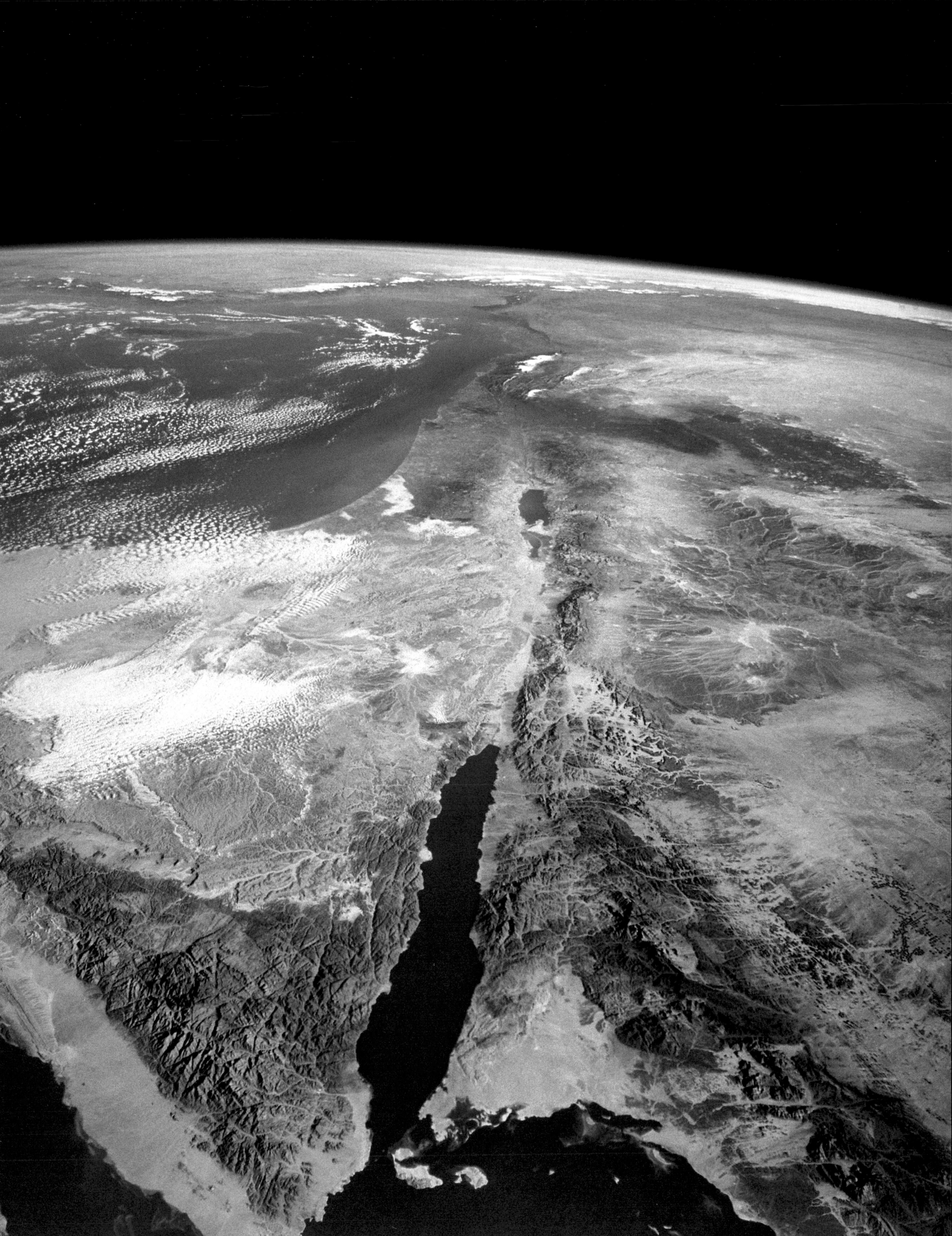

»The world is a beautiful book...«

Nothing sums up the new Concise World Atlas better than the words of Carlo Goldoni: "The world is a beautiful book, but of little use to him who cannot read it".

This groundbreaking atlas serves two functions: the first is to offer basic geographic knowledge of our planet, with detailed and clear cartography. The second is to serve as a comprehensive travel guide in which more than 16,000 fascinating attractions are highlighted – including landscapes, national parks, cities, cultural attractions, monuments, holiday destinations and travel routes.

Scientists and explorers have investigated every "terra incognita". Their pioneering work laid the foundations for the conquest of our planet. Now, thanks to increased mobility across countries and continents and the rapid developments in communications technology, many more of us can experience the great wonders of the earth. No major event can take place without awakening the attention of the global community. And yet, there is still much that remains unknown and foreign to us today. The landscapes of the southern Sahara, the sweeping expanses of Central Asia, the Andes Mountains: who can claim to possess exhaustive knowledge of these fascinating regions?

How the Atlas Works

The structure of the atlas follows that of "traditional" atlases. Physical and political maps of each continent are followed by overviews of their sub-continents, "zooming in" on detailed continental maps.

While traditional atlases constantly change their scales, the Concise World Atlas employs consistent scales for all areas of the world: Europe on a scale of 1:2.25 million, Asia, Australia, Africa and America on a scale of 1:4.5 million. Exceptions are the largely uninhabited regions in northern Canada, Greenland and Siberia. This design eliminates false impressions of dimensions and proportions, enabling a comparison of distances and facilitating planning.

The colouring reflects the ecological zones of the world, with their characteristic climates and vegetation. Where technically possible, the colours selected match the actual colours of the earth's surface.

The Concise World Atlas provides an overview of the world's main transport infrastructures including major continental connections, motorways, highways and roads, main rail networks, seaports and airports, and their ferry and shipping routes.

A new feature, unique in a world atlas, is the depiction and highlighting of outstanding natural landscapes and significant natural and cultural monuments. A specially developed system of over 120 symbols indicates the type of monument and its exact location. Green and blue symbols show the most interesting mountain, rock, sea, river, desert and coastal landscapes, fascinating volcanoes, gorges and canyons, caves, islands and coral reefs. Yellow symbols refer to the world's great metropolises and historical cityscapes, buildings and monuments of religious and cultural significance, reservations of indigenous peoples, and cultural landscapes and industrial monu-

ments. Monuments on the UNESCO World Heritage list are also marked.

In addition, the Concise World Atlas shows major sporting and holiday sites around the world, from famous mineral and thermal spas to great seaside resorts, from major sailing ports, surfing and diving areas to racetracks and amusement parks. Special markings are reserved for the world's legendary roads such as the Panamericana, world-famous railway lines such as the Eastern and Oriental Express, and world-renowned shipping routes, such as the Caribbean Sea or the Nile and Mississippi rivers.

May the Concise World Atlas enable us to know and understand our world better, as Goldoni intended. May our curiosity, fascination and wanderlust be aroused by its wealth of information. As the famous Indian writer and philosopher Rabindranath Tagore said: "We live in this world as long as we love it".

The Publisher

Table of Contents

Europe

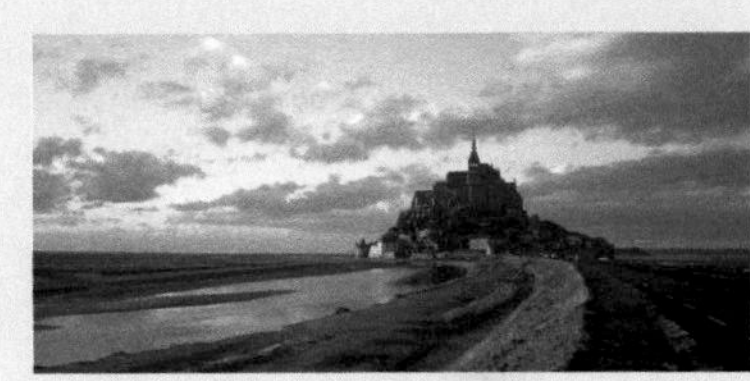

Asia

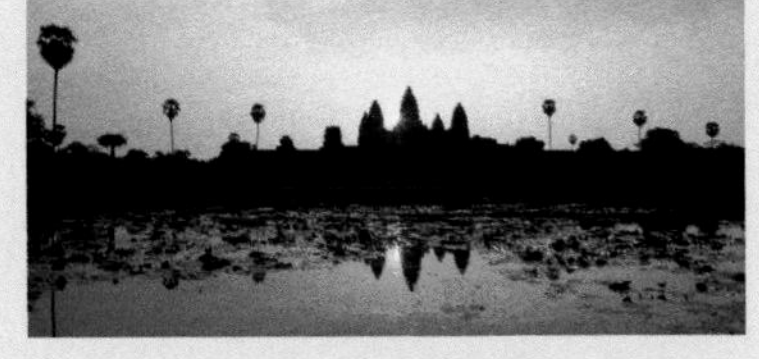

Australia/Oceania

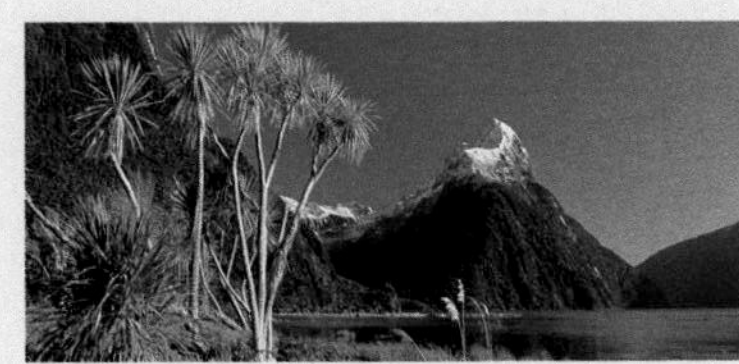

Africa

North and Central America

South America

Arctic Region, Antarctica, Oceans

Map locator

Europe

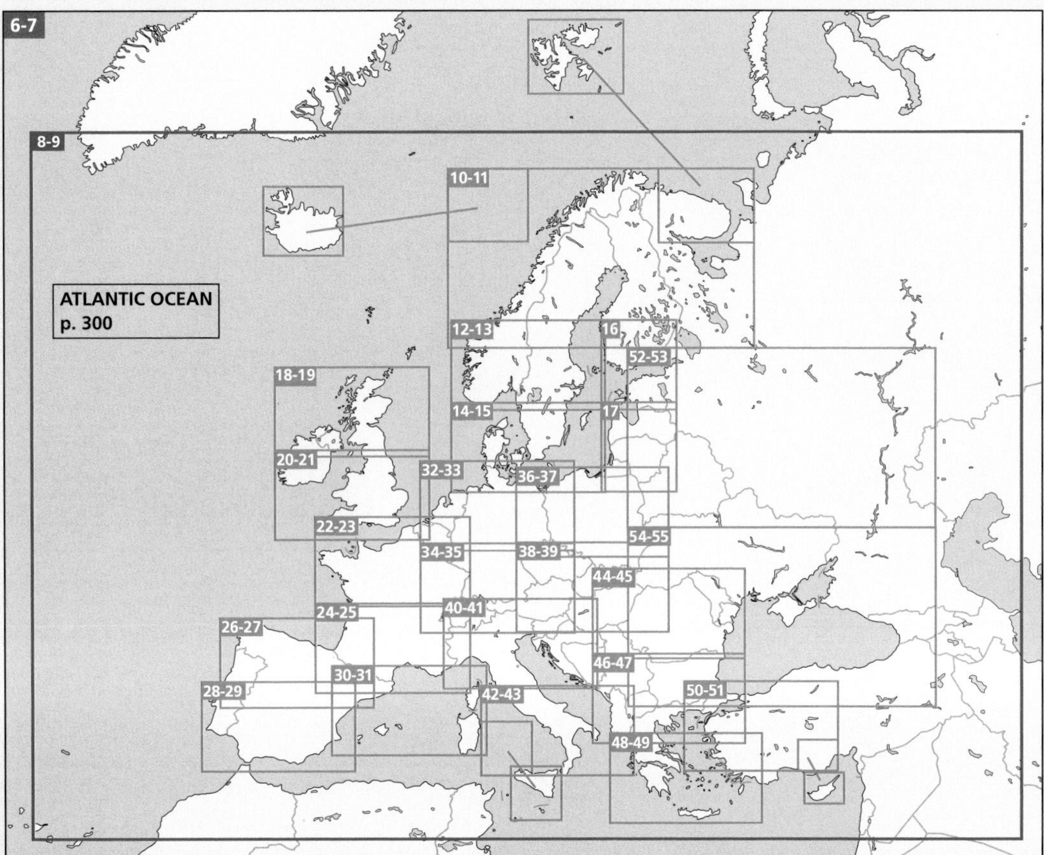

Southeastern Asia, Australia/Ocean

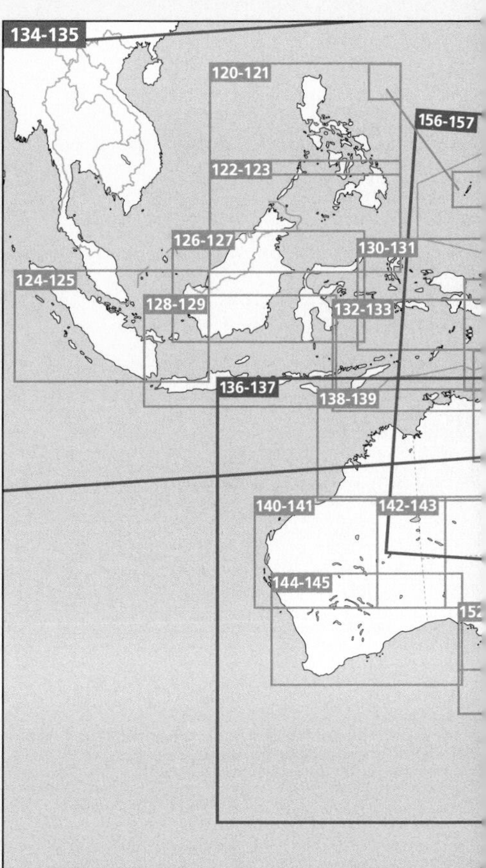

Near and Middle East, Northern Asia, Central Asia, Southern Asia

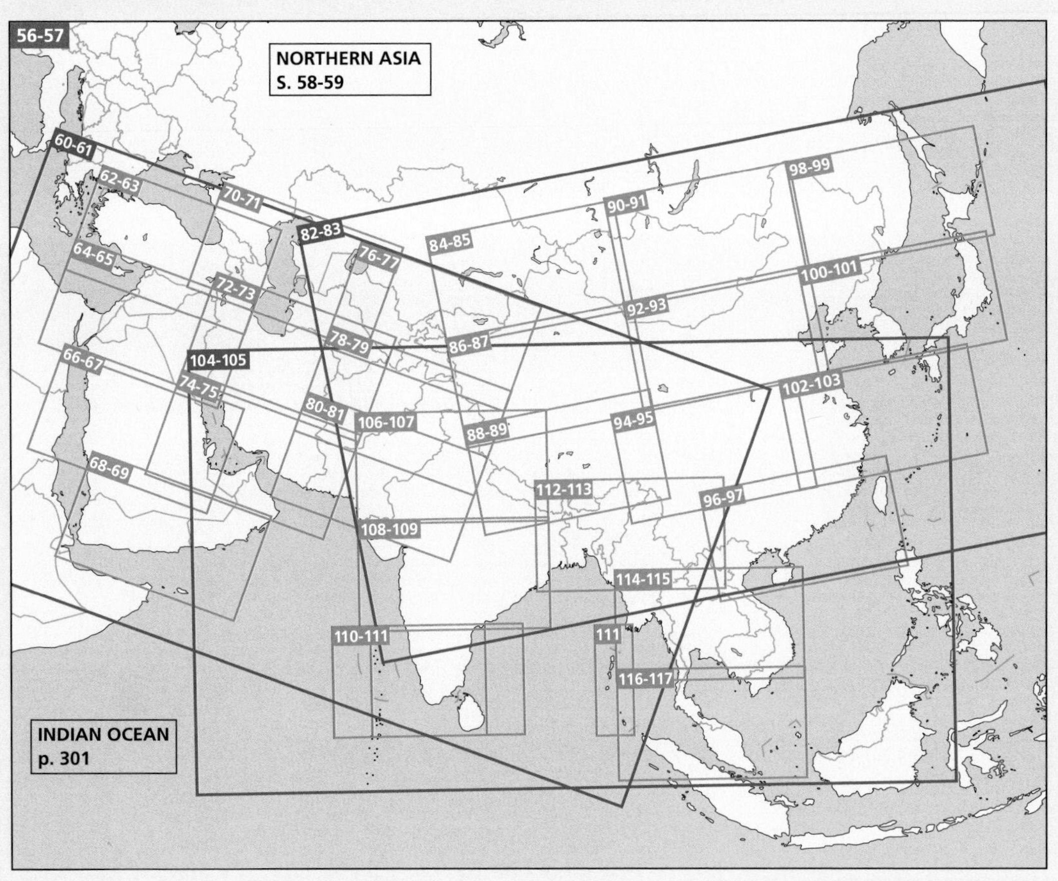

Africa

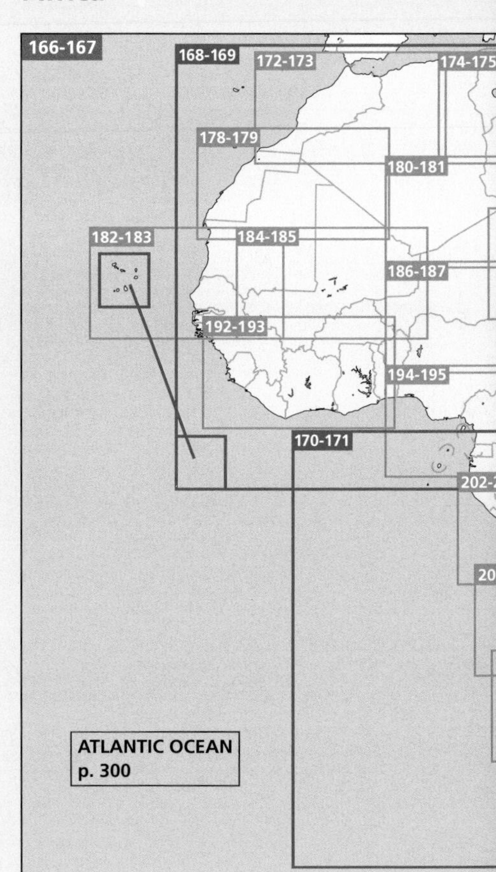

North and Central America

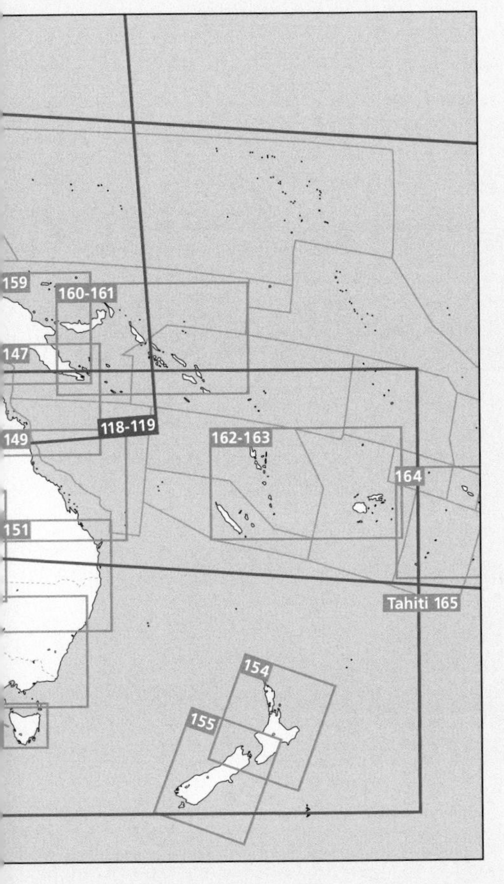
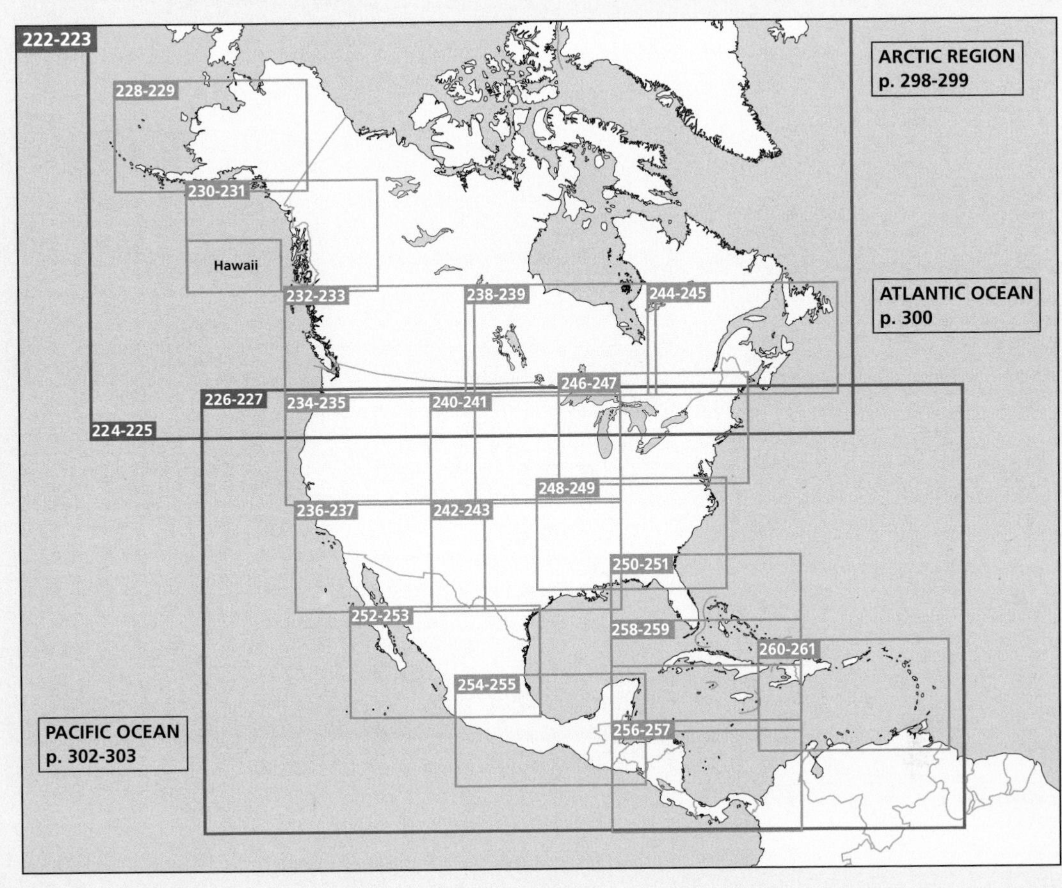

222-223

228-229

230-231

Hawaii

232-233

238-239

244-245

226-227

234-235

240-241

246-247

248-249

236-237

242-243

250-251

252-253

258-259

260-261

254-255

256-257

ARCTIC REGION
p. 298-299

ATLANTIC OCEAN
p. 300

PACIFIC OCEAN
p. 302-303

159
160-161
147
118-119
149
162-163
164
151
Tahiti 165
154
155

South America

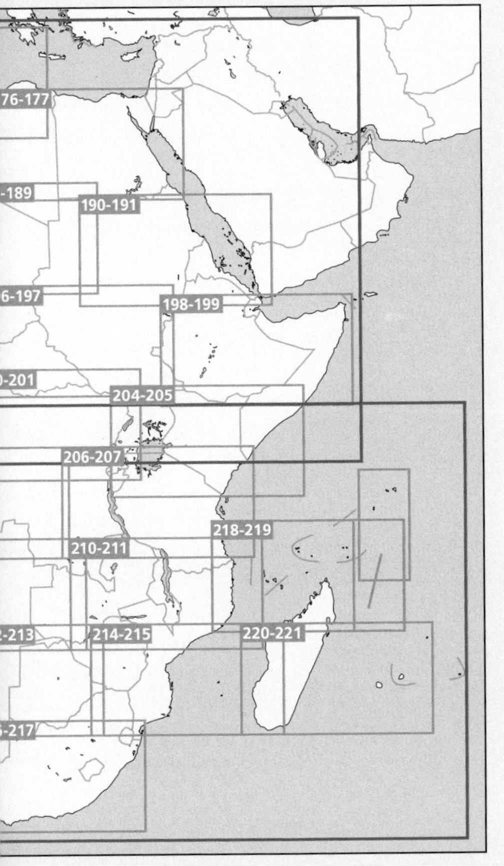
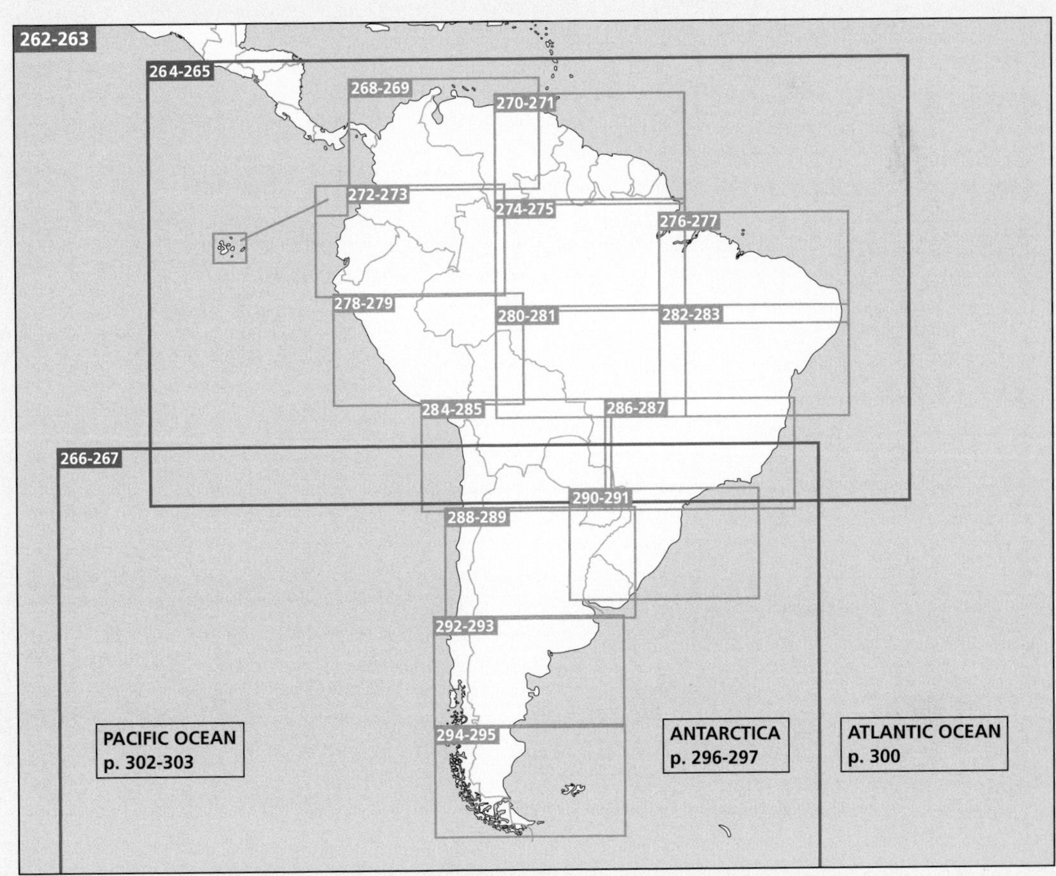

262-263

264-265

268-269

270-271

272-273

274-275

276-277

278-279

280-281

282-283

284-285

286-287

266-267

290-291

288-289

292-293

294-295

PACIFIC OCEAN
p. 302-303

ANTARCTICA
p. 296-297

ATLANTIC OCEAN
p. 300

76-177
189
190-191
6-197
198-199
0-201
204-205
206-207
218-219
210-211
213
214-215
220-221
217

Legend · Natural geographical features

Bodies of water

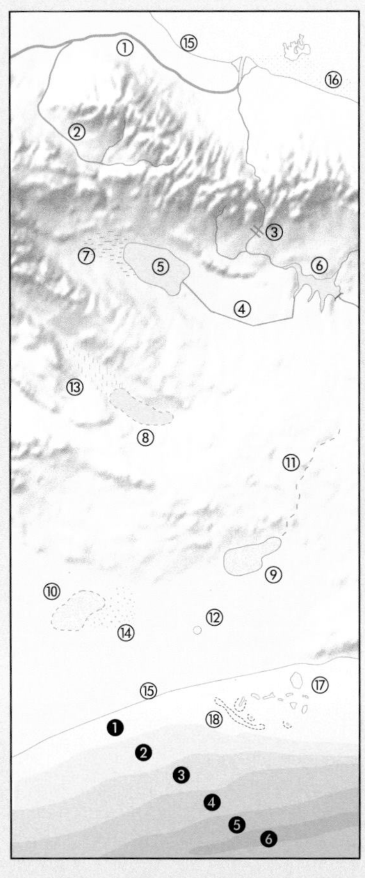

① Stream, river
② Tributary with headstreams
③ Waterfall, rapids
④ Canal
⑤ Lake
⑥ Reservoir with dam
⑦ Marsh, moor
⑧ Intermittent lake
⑨ Salt lake
⑩ Intermittent salt lake
⑪ Intermittent river (wadi)
⑫ Well, spring
⑬ Salt swamp
⑭ Salt pan
⑮ Shoreline
⑯ Mud flats
⑰ Island, archipelago
⑱ Coral reef

Depth tints

❶ 0 – 200 meters
❷ 200 – 2000 meters
❸ 2000 – 4000 meters
❹ 4000 – 6000 meters
❺ 6000 – 8000 meters
❻ below 8000 meters

Topography

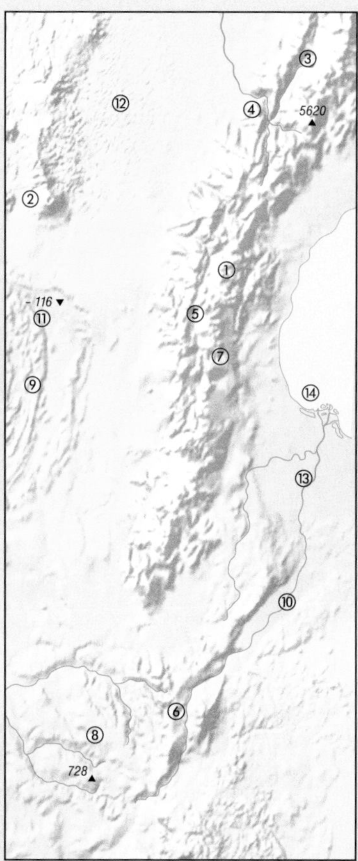

① High mountain region
② Volcano
③ V-shaped valley
④ Gorge
⑤ U-shaped valley
⑥ Canyon
⑦ Glacier in high mountain regions
⑧ Highland with valleys
⑨ Escarpment
⑩ Rift Valley
⑪ Depression
⑫ High dunes in arid areas
⑬ Lowland
⑭ Delta

Colour tints of climate and vegetation zones

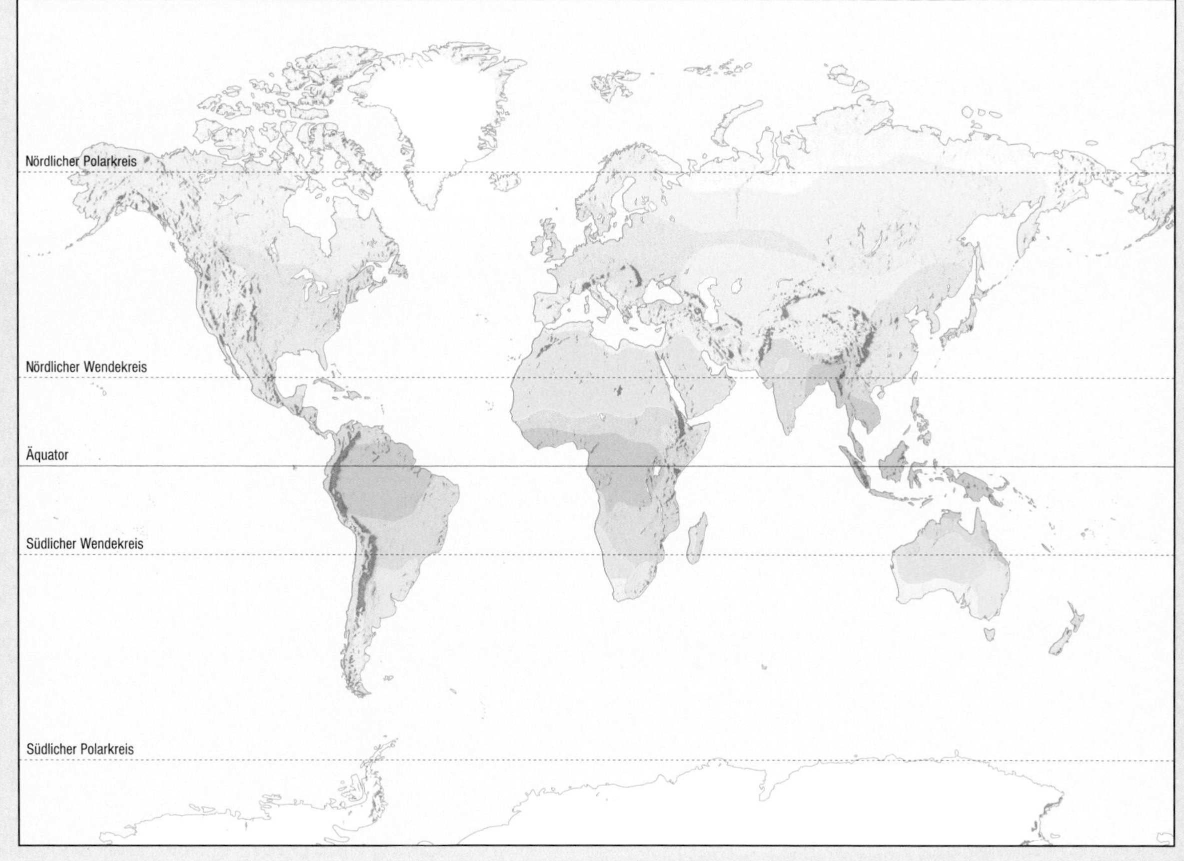

Polar and subpolar zone

Perpetual frost, all months below 0° C (32°F)

Arctic flora and Tundra (lichens, mosses, grasses, dwarf shrubs)

Boreal zone

Taiga, northern coniferous trees; pines, firs, larches, spruces

Temperate zones

Rainy climates with mild winters; deciduous broadleaf forests, mixed forests

Wintercold desert and semidesert climates; steppe, prairie, grasslands, semideserts

Subtropics

Mediterranean climate with dry summers and moist winters; broadleaved evergreen forests

Warm, humid moist climate; subtropical forests

Desert and semidesert climates; open shrub lands

Tropics

Humid and dry savannas with dry seasons; woody savannas

Tropical rainforest, rainy climate with no winter; high temperatures

Settlements and transportation routes

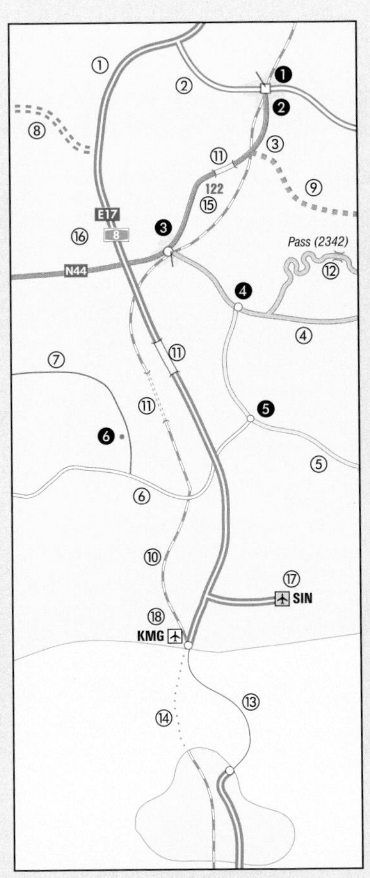

Transportation routes

① Interstate highway/motorway
② Multilane divided highway
③ Primary highway
④ Secondary highway
⑤ Main road
⑥ Secondary road
⑦ Unimproved road
⑧ Interstate highway/motorway under construction
⑨ Primary highway under construction
⑩ Railway
⑪ Tunnel
⑫ Pass with elevation in meters
⑬ Ferry, shipping route
⑭ Railway ferry
⑮ Distances in kilometers (within USA and UK in miles)
⑯ Road numbers
⑰ International Airport with IATA-code
⑱ Airport with IATA-code

Settlements

❶ Urban area
❷ Town over 1 million inhabitants
❸ Town 100,000 - 1 million inhabitants
❹ Town 10,000 - 100,000 inhabitants
❺ Town under 10,000 inhabitants
❻ Hamlet, research station

Type faces of cities and towns

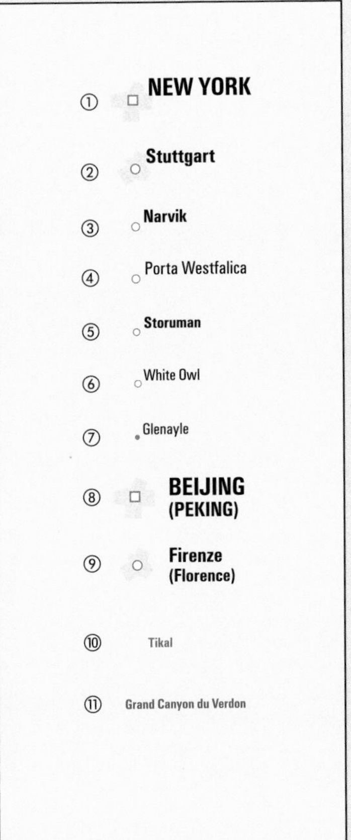

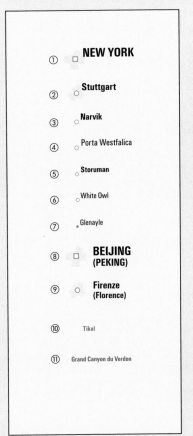

① Town over 1 million inhabitants
② Town 100,000 - 1 million inhabitants
③ Significant town 10,000 - 100,000 inhabitants
④ Town 10,000 - 100,000 inhabitants
⑤ Significant town under 10,000 inhabitants
⑥ Town under 10,000 inhabitants
⑦ Hamlet, research station
⑧ Town over 1 million inhabitants with translation
⑨ Town 100,000 - 1 million inhabitants with translation
⑩ Point of cultural interest
⑪ Point of natural interest

Political and other boundaries

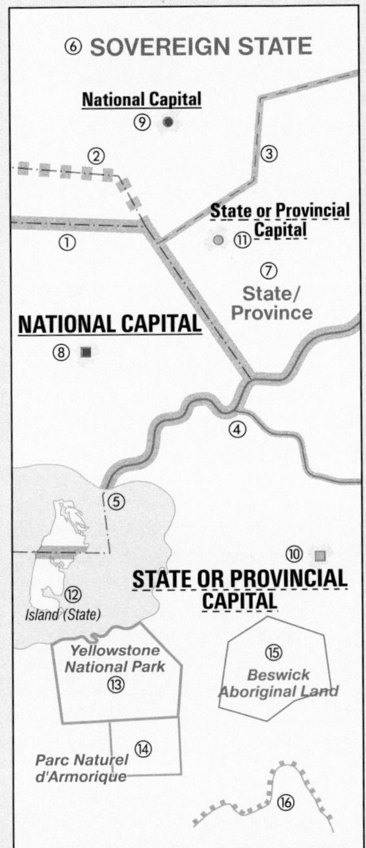

① International boundary
② Disputed international boundary
③ Administrative boundary
④ Boundary on rivers
⑤ Boundary in lake or sea
⑥ Country name
⑦ Administrative name
⑧ Capital with more than 1 million inhabitants
⑨ Capital below 1 million inhabitants
⑩ Administrative capital with more than 1 million inhabitants
⑪ Administrative capital with less than 1 million inhabitants
⑫ Dependent territory with administering country
⑬ National parks and biosphere reserves
⑭ Nature parks and other protected areas
⑮ Reservation
⑯ Walls (Great Wall of China, Hadrian's Wall)

Type faces of topographic features

① *PACIFIC OCEAN*

② *GULF OF MEXICO*

Gulf of Thailand

③ *Antalya Körfezi*

④ *Elbe   Rio Grande   Murray*

⑤ *White Nile   Suez Canal*

⑥ *H I M A L A Y A*

⑦ *Great Plains*

⑧ *Mt. Olympus*
▲
2424

⑨ *– 116 ▼   Danakil Depression*

⑩ *Tahiti*

⑪ *Cape of Good Hope*

⑫ *325*

⑬ *5425*

⑭ *Mexican Basin*

⑮ *Mariana Trench*

① Ocean
② Gulf, bay
③ Small bay, strait
④ River, lake, canal
⑤ River, lake, canal (translated)
⑥ Mountain name
⑦ Area name, landscape name
⑧ Mountain name with elevation above sea level in meters
⑨ Depression with depth below sea level in meters
⑩ Island name
⑪ Cape name
⑫ Elevation of lake above sea level
⑬ Depth in oceans and lakes
⑭ Undersea landscapes, mountains and trenches
⑮ Deepsea trench

XI

Explanation of symbols

Principal travel routes

Remarkable landscapes and natural monuments

Beautiful natural landscapes, fascinating wildlife, historic architecture, and vibrant cities – our world is rich in wonders. The modern cartography and layout of the Concise World Atlas highlights many of the world's attractions – unspoiled wilderness areas, the most famous and significant historic sites, culturally diverse urban areas, holiday resorts, as well as sporting venues. The system of pictograms developed specifically for this atlas gives the reader a clear impression of the diverse attractions in the world's regions. All of the pictograms featured on each map are listed and labeled in a legend at the bottom of the respective page.

The following pages offer an overview of the various pictograms used in the atlas. The pictograms are divided by color into two groups: green and blue pictograms represent natural attractions, while yellow pictograms represent cultural attractions and other man-made sites. The names of significant towns and cities are highlighted in yellow throughout the atlas. Blue pictograms represent sporting and recreational facilities. Important and well-known transportation routes, including highways and ship-ping routes, are also highlighted in the atlas. These routes are not only highlighted by picto-grams but also by distinctly-colored lines that identify each type of route.

Auto route
The maps display many of the world's most famous and historically significant roads and routes, such as the ancient Silk Road in Asia and historic Route 66 in the United States. The maps also feature important modern highways including the Pan-American Highway – which stretches from Alaska to Tierra del Fuego, the highway stretching between Bangkok in Thailand and Singapore, and the Stuart Highway, which traverses the fascinating landscapes in Australia's sparsely populated interior.

Rail road
The age of the railways started in 1804 when the world's first steam locomotive began operation in Wales. By the end of the 19th century it was possible to travel through most regions of Europe and North America and much of Asia and South America by train. The Orient Express, Europe's first long-distance luxury passenger line began operation in 1883 and traveled between Paris and Bucharest. The Trans-Siberian line was constructed between 1891 and 1916 with the goal of connecting Siberia to European Russia. The Trans-Siberian still runs between Moscow and Vladivostok on the Pacific Ocean almost 100 years after construction ended.

Highspeed train
The Eurostar trains travel at speeds up to 300 kilometers an hour and transports passengers between London and Brussels or Paris in less than three hours. Japan's Shinkansen line connects several of the major cities. In Europe, France and Germany maintain the most extensive networks of high speed trains.

Shipping route
Millions of passengers travel on cruise ships every year and experience one of the most leisurely and comfortable forms of long-distance travel. Thousands of cruise ships of vastly different sizes traverse the oceans, seas, and rivers of the world. The Caribbean Sea, Mediterranean Sea, Scandinavia, and Alaska are among the most popular locations for cruises on the open seas. Modern cruise ships offer an astounding variety of attractions including casinos, entertainment shows, fine restaurants, as well as side trips to attractive destinations on land.

UNESCO World Natural Heritage
Since 1972, UNESCO has compiled a growing list of specially designated natural sites that are deemed to be of outstanding importance and "universal" significance.

Mountain landscape
Mountain ranges are among the most scenic areas in the world. Many of the world's ancient low-mountain ranges including the Appalachians and the Central Massif feature heavily eroded and rounded peaks. Other younger mountain ranges feature jagged and high peaks that are often covered by snow.

Rock landscape
Many of the most interesting stone formations were shaped by wind and water erosion, including the natural attractions of Monument Valley National Park.

Ravine/canyon
Canyons and Gorges are narrow and often deep valleys created by rivers and wind erosion. The Grand Canyon in the American state of Arizona is the most famous and one of the most spectacular canyons on the planet.

Extinct volcano
Volcanoes are formed when solid, liquid, or gas-like materials from the Earth's interior rise to the planet's surface. Magma passes through the structure of a volcano and leaves its crater as lava, often accompanied by plumes of hot ash. An extinct volcanoe is a volcano that has not experienced an eruption in the last 10,000 years.

Active volcano
Geologists consider any volcano that has erupted in the last 10,000 years to be active. Most of the world's active volcanoes are concentrated in geologically active region such as areas near the boundaries of the world's tectonic plates or mid-ocean ridges. The Pacific Ring of Fire is an area of relatively frequent volcanic activity.

Geyser
Active geysers are hot springs that occasionally release plumes of water into the air. Geysers are located in volcanically active regions.

Cave
Caves are formed during the creation of stone formations (mountains, underground layers of stone, etc.) or emerge later due to the eroding effects of water that seeps into stone and often carves out entire networks of large caves containing lakes and rivers.

Glacier
Glaciers are large fields or rivers of ice that often migrate through mountain valleys. Glaciers are formed above the snow line in mountainous areas such as the Alps or in regions with cold climates such as Alaska, northern Canada, and Greenland.

River landscape
The eroding power of flowing water formed many of the world's valleys and canyons. Most of the world's earliest civilizations emerged in fertile river valleys. Many rivers in lowland areas have large branching deltas.

Waterfall/rapids
Waterfalls are formed when rivers flow over an area with a sudden drop in elevation. Waterfalls come in a variety of heights and lengths. Waterfalls are among the most stunning natural attractions on the planet.

Lake country
Most of the world's major lakes were created by glaciers during the ice ages. Several regions including southern Finland feature a large number of lakes, often interconnected and located one another. Other lakes formed as a result of tectonic activity.

Desert
Vast landscapes covered by sand dunes, sand fields, or stone with sparse rainfall. Deserts are the most arid regions on the earth and only a few types of plants and animals can survive in these harsh environments. Most deserts have major differences between night and daytime tem-peratures. Most of the world's deserts remain sparsely populated.

Oasis
Oases are fertile islands surrounded by barren, arid deserts or steppes. They are supplied with water by rivers, springs or underground ground-water repositories.

Remarkable cities and cultural monuments

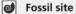 **Depression**
Depressions are small basins located on land but at significant depths below sea level. Many depressions were created through tectonic activity.

Fossil site
Fossils are ancient remnants and traces of animals and plants that have inhabited our planet during its long history.

Nature park
Conservation areas created to protect local flora and fauna. Most designated nature parks tend to be relatively small in size.

National park (landscape)
Large conservation areas created to protect areas of natural beauty and significant national or international importance. Development and industry are forbidden or heavily restricted in such area.

National park (flora)
This symbol designates national parks with interesting local flora.

National park (fauna)
This symbol designates national parks with unique local wildlife.

National park (culture)
National park with cultural attractions such as the Native American historic sites.

Biosphere reserve
Undeveloped conservation areas with pristine examples of distinct climate or vegetation zones. Many biosphere reserves exhibit high levels of biodiversity.

Wildlife reserve
Conservation areas created for the protection of endangered animals. Selous Game Reserve in Tanzania is home to large herds of protected elephants.

Whale watching
Boat tours providing the chance to observe whales or dolphins in their natural habitats.

Turtle conservation area
Several countries have specially designated coastal areas where endangered sea turtle species live or lay their eggs.

Protected area for sealions/seals
Coastal areas created especially for the protection of endangered seal and sea lion species.

Protected area for penguins
These areas were created to preserve threatened penguin colonies and to observe them in their habitats.

Zoo/safari park
Zoos are park-like areas that feature collections of animals mostly from a variety of regions. Safari parks are large properties open to tourists that feature wildlife in open wilderness.

Crocodile farm
Most alligator farms are commercial operations where animals are bred. Many are open to the public.

Coastal landscape
Coastal areas often feature diverse landscapes including beaches, cliffs, tidal flats, and large river deltas surrounded by marshlands and plains. Some coastal areas are flat with sand dunes and land spits, while others are lined by jagged-rock formations, stony beaches, and high cliffs.

Beach
Sand beaches are common in flat coastal areas. Many of the world's most famous beaches are now lined by large tourist and residential developments.

Coral reef
Coral Reefs are formed by small animals called coral in warm saltwater. Many of the largest coral reefs exhibit astonishing biodiversity. The world's largest coral reef is the Great Barrier Reef off the coast of Australia.

Island
Islands are land masses surrounded by water. Most islands are part of island groups. The islands on our planet have a combined land area of 10.5 million km². Many of the world's islands have become popular tourist destinations.

Underwater reserve
Underwater conservation areas created to protect local marine plants and animals.

UNESCO World Cultural Heritage
Since 1972, UNESCO has compiled a list of specially designated cultural sites that are deemed to be of outstanding importance. The list includes hundreds of cultural and historic sites around the world.

Remarkable city
Large and small cities of global importance or with an abundance of tourist attractions are highlighted in yellow on our maps.

Pre- and early history
Sites related to ancient human cultures and their ways of life during times before the emergence of written records. The most grandiose pre-historic sites include large megaliths created by different cultures, including the circle of stone pillars at Stonehenge in the United Kingdom.

Prehistoric rockscape
Prehistoric paintings, carvings and reliefs created by nomadic peoples during ancient times. Such sites have been found on all inhabited continents and often provide scientist with valuable information about life in the times before the first civilizations emerged on our planet.

The Ancient Orient
Sites related to the ancient cultures that developed in the region comprising modern Anatolia (Asia Minor), Syria, Iraq, Israel, Lebanon, Iran, and in some cases Egypt during the period between 7000 BC and the time of Alexander the Great (400 BC). The Sumerians developed one of the first urban civilizations on the planet. They also developed one of the first number systems. After 2000 BC, the first large empires emerged in the region including the kingdoms of the Babylonians, Assyrians, and Hittites. The region features temples, ziggurats, and palaces.

Ancient Egypt
One of the greatest ancient civilizations developed on the banks of the Nile River in Egypt. Around 3000 BC, Egypt was unified under the reign of one ruler for the first time. Between this time and the period of Alexander the Great's conquests, Egypt was ruled by more than 31 dynasties. The all-powerful pharaohs were considered living gods in Ancient Egypt. The ancient Egyptians developed

a writing system, a calendar, and eventually advanced building techniques. The greatest legacy of this fascinating culture is the spectacular pyramids. The arts of the ancient Egyptians were devoted primarily to religion and mythology.

Ancient Egyptian pyramids
The monumental pyramid tombs of Egyptian pharaohs were constructed during the Old Kingdom. The largest and most impressive pyramid is the 137-meter-high Great (Cheops) Pyramid at Giza.

Minoan culture
The advanced bronze-age culture of the Minoans flourished on Crete during ancient times. Minoan civilization first emerged during the 3rd millennium BC, after which the Minoans rapidly became the dominant power in the eastern Mediterranean. Modern Crete features the remnants of luxurious Minoan villas with impressive frescoes and interior design.

Phoenecian culture
During ancient times the area encompassing modern Israel, Lebanon, and Palestine was once the center of Phoenician culture. The Phoenicians were the dominant trading power in the Mediterranean and founded many colonies.

Early African culture
Ancient African civilizations include the cultures of the Kingdom of Ghana, Axum (Ethiopia), the Great Zimbabwe culture, and Kush, a complex and advanced society that developed south of Egypt.

Etruscan culture
The Etruscans probably originated in central Italy. During the 10th century BC, they conquered large sections of the Italian Peninsula before they were conquered by the Romans. Italy has numerous archeological and historic sites related to the culture of the ancient Etruscans.

Greek antiquity
No other civilization has had a greater influence on European culture than that of Ancient Greece. The city-state of Athens was one of the first basic democracies in history. The art, philosophy and architecture of Ancient Greece continue to inspire and shape our modern world. Ancient Greece was divided into city-states, many of which founded

Explanation of symbols

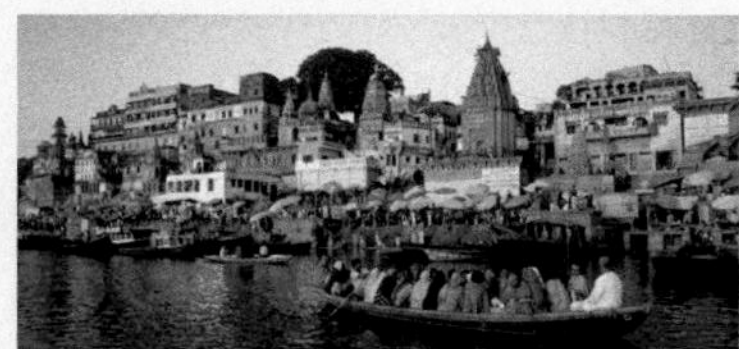

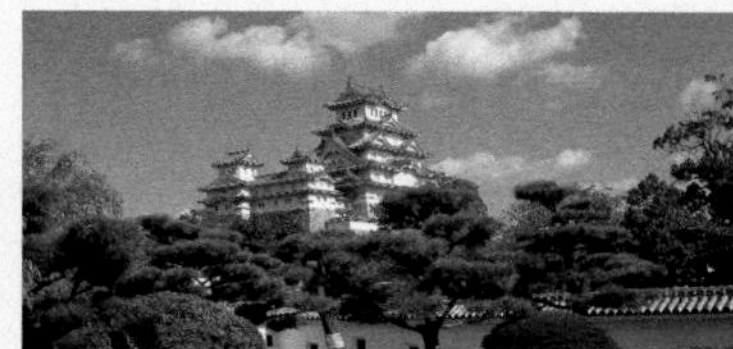

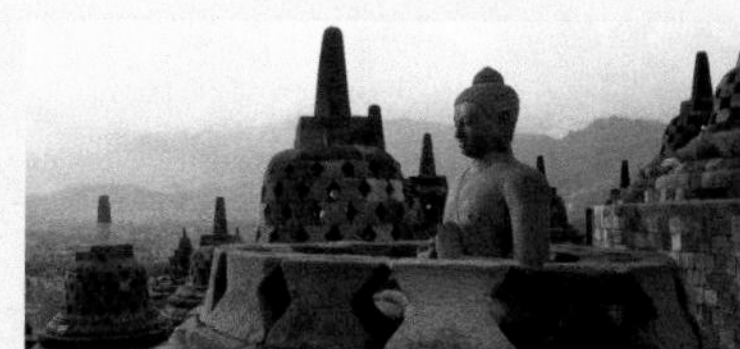

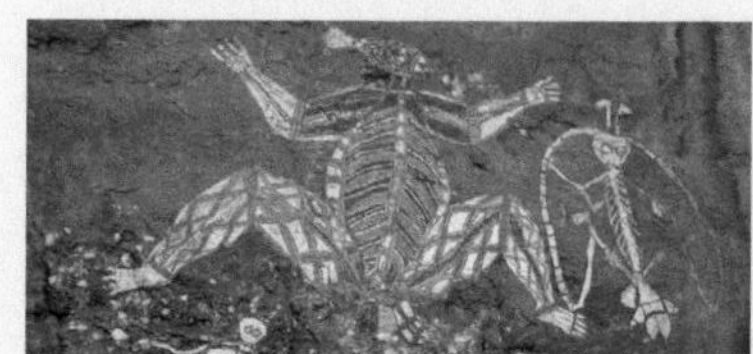

Remarkable cities and cultural monuments

distant colonies in Southern Europe, the Middle East, and North Africa. Ancient Greek art dealt mostly with subjects related to Greek mythology. The Greek city-states constructed many great structures including impressive temples and amphitheaters. During the Hellenistic period – after the death of Alexander the Great – Greek-speaking cities outside the mainland, including Alexandria in Egypt, replaced the city-states as the centers of Greek civilization.

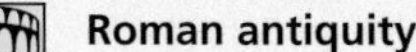

Roman antiquity
Over a period of centuries the once small city of Rome on the Tiber River emerged as the center of a vast and powerful empire. The Roman Empire was at its largest under the reign of the Emperor Trajan (98–117 BC) – during this period its borders extended from North Africa to Scotland and from Iberia to Mesopotamia. The Roman state that existed between 509 and 27 BC is referred to as the Roman Republic. The Roman state that was created after the reforms of Caesar Augustus is known as the Roman Empire. Roman art and culture was greatly influenced by other Mediterranean cultures. Roman historic sites can be found throughout Europe, the Middle East, and North Africa.

Nabatean culture
The ancient city of Petra (Jordan) was first settled by the Nabataeans in the 5th century BC. By the 1st century BC, the Nabateans ruled a powerful trading empire. The monumental ruins of Petra are the greatest remnant of this culture.

Vikings
Between the 9th and 11th centuries, Scandinavian Vikings conquered territories throughout Europe. During their centuries of conquest, the Vikings founded numerous settlements and trading posts in Russia, Western Europe, as well as in the British Isles.

Ancient India
India has a wealth of cultural and historic attractions. The Indus Valley civilization (2600–1400 BC) was one of the first urbanized civilizations to emerge on the planet. Indian culture reached one of its high points during the period between the 7th and 13th centuries. Many of India's greatest Buddhist and Hindu architectural masterpieces as well as artworks were created during these centuries. During the Mogul era (16th and 17th century), many impressive works of Islamic architecture were created throughout the country, including modern India's most famous structure, the Taj Mahal.

Ancient China
The oldest remnants of early Chinese culture date from the era between 5000–2000 BC. The Shang dynasty (1600–1000 BC) was the most influential and advanced bronze-age culture in China. Daoism and Confucian philosophy were both developed in China during the 5th century BC. The first great unified Chinese empire was forged around 220 BC by Ying Zheng, the king of Qin. After the emergence of the first Chinese empire, China was ruled by various dynasties and experienced many periods of cultural and technological advancement. The country's most impressive historic sites include the Great Wall of China, the tomb of Emperor Qin with its army of terracotta warriors in Xi'an, and the Forbidden City in Beijing.

Ancient Japan
The Yamato period of Japanese history began around 400 AD. During this period, the country was ruled by an imperial court in Nara. During the 5th century the Japanese adopted the Chinese writing system and in the 6th century Buddhism arrived in Japan. The Fujiwara clan dominated the country for more than 500 years starting in the 7th century. During this period the country's imperial capital was moved from Nara to Kyoto. Between 1192 and 1868, Japan was ruled by a series of shoguns (military rulers). The Meiji Era (1868–1912) saw the restoration of imperial power and the emergence of modern Japan.

Mayan culture
The Maya are an Amerindian people in southern Mexico and Central America. During pre-Columbian times, the Maya developed a powerful civilization that ruled over a vast territory. Mayan Civilization reached its cultural and technological peak around 300 AD and was eventually devastated by the arrival of Spanish conquistadors in the 16th century. Central America and Mexico are the sites of many grand Mayan ruins.

Inca culture
The Inca culture emerged around Cusco during the 12th century. By the 15th century, the Inca ruled a vast empire that encompassed parts of modern Peru, Bolivia, Ecuador, Chile, and Argentina. Although their empire was shortlived, the Inca left behind impressive stone monuments and structures throughout western South America. The Inca city Machu Picchu in Peru is one of the most impressive historic sites in South America.

Aztec culture
At some point during the 2nd millennium BC, the Aztec people migrated into Mexico where they eventually established a powerful empire. The Aztec capital Tenochtitlan (Mexico City) was founded in 1325 and was once one of the world's largest cities. The Aztecs constructed many grand temples and pyramids throughout their empire and made important cultural advances including the creation of a writing system and calendar. Central Mexico has numerous Aztec cultural sites.

Other ancient American cultures
Advanced Amerindian cultures appeared in both North America and the Andean regions of South America. Countless Amerindian historic sites including the remnants of ancient settlements can be found throughout the Americas.

Places of Jewish cultural interest
Judaism is the oldest of the world's major monotheist religions. The Jerusalem temple was a great achievement of early Jewish culture – now only a section of its walls remain. Historic synagogues can be found throughout the world, a legacy of the Jewish Diaspora.

Places of Christian cultural interest
Christianity is the world's most practiced and widespread religion. Christianity is based on the teachings in the old and new testaments of the Bible, and emerged in western Asia during the 1st century AD. Christian religious sites, including churches, cathedrals, and monasteries, can be found in most regions of the world.

Places of Islamic cultural interest
Islam, one of the world's major religions, was founded by Mohammed (570-632 AD). The teachings of the Koran are the basis for Islam. Muslims around the world pray in the direction of Mecca, the religion's holiest cities.

Places of Buddhist cultural interest
Buddhism is based on the teachings of Siddhartha Gautama (around 560–480 BC), also known as the Buddha. Buddhist sites include temples, pagodas, stupas, and monasteries.

Places of Hindu cultural interest
Most of the at least one billion followers of Hinduism, one of world's most practiced religions, live on the Indian subcontinent. Hinduism encompasses a variety of beliefs and practices, many of which are thousands of years old.

Places of Jainist cultural interest
Most followers of Jainism live in India. Jainism is based on the teachings of Mahavira, who lived in the 5th century BC. India features many Jainist sites including temples and monasteries.

Places of Sikh cultural interest
The Sikh philosophy emerged in 16th century India, as an attempt to merge the teachings of Islam and Hinduism. The "Golden Temple" in Amritsar is the most important Sikh religious center.

Places of Shinto cultural interest
Shinto, the indigenous religion of Japan, is based on the reverence of kami (nature) and ancestral spirits. Historic Shinto shrines can be seen throughout Japan.

Places of cultural interest to other religions
Sites related to other religions.

Places of cultural interest to indigenous peoples
Sites related to the culture or history of a region's indigenous inhabitants.

Aborigine reservation
The 500,000 Aborigines in Australia form only a small portion of the country's population. Many Aborigine communities control large land reserves.

Places of Aboriginal cultural interest
The cultural sites of the Aborigines are amongst the interesting attractions.

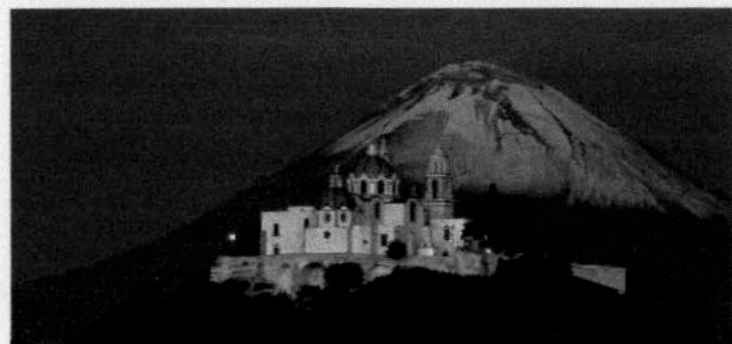 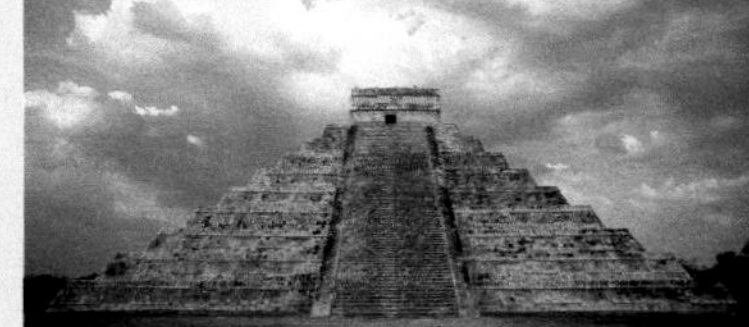 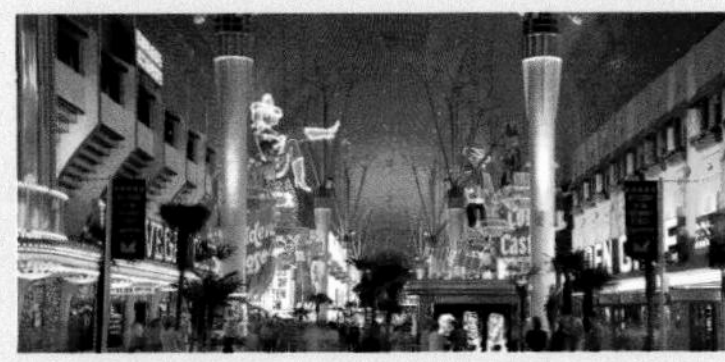 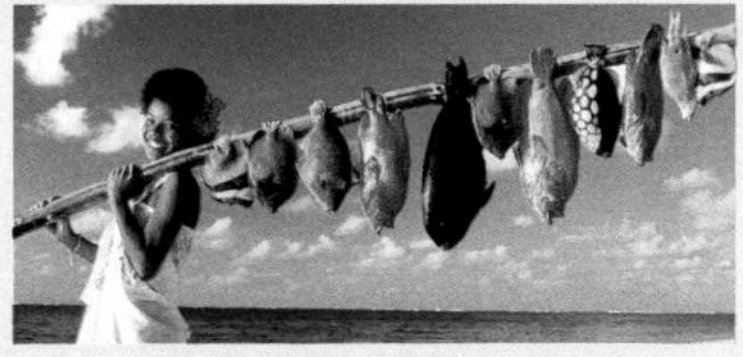

Sport and leisure sites

Indian reservation
Most of the Native American reservations in the United States and Canada were founded during the 19th century. Despite the history of low living standards on reservations, many Native American communities have successfully protected their culture and languages.

Pueblo Indian culture
The Pueblo Indians are a group of Native American communities who have lived in southwestern United States for centuries. Their traditional settlement consist of adobe buildings.

Places of Amerindian cultural interest
The different regions of North America feature hundreds of sites related to the history and cultures of Native Americans.

Amazonian Amerindians/ protected area
The rainforests of South America are home to many Amerindian communities. Land reserves have been created to protect the Amerindian cultures in the Amazon basin.

Cultural landscape
Areas with landscapes that have been shaped by human cultivation.

Historical cityscape
Historic cities and towns with well-preserved architectural attractions.

Impressive skyline
Cities featuring modern skylines, such as New York City and Hong Kong.

Castle/fortress/fort
Europe features the greatest concentration of these structures.

Caravanserai
Historic inns along the ancient routes of the Middle East and Northern Africa.

Palace
Grand castles and palaces that once housed nobility and royalty can be found in many different regions.

Technical/industrial monument
Man-made attractions related to the achievements of industrialization and modern technology.

Dam
The largest and most important dams and retaining walls on the planet.

Remarkable lighthouse
Many coastal areas feature beautiful or historic lighthouses.

Remarkable bridge
The world's ancient and modern great bridges.

Tomb/grave
Mausoleums, monuments, burial mounds, and other gravesites.

Theater of war/battlefield
Site where important battles occurred.

Monument
Sites dedicated to historic figures and important historical events.

Memorial
Site dedicated to the victims of wars and genocides, and disasters.

Space mission launch site
Landing and launch sites of manned and unmanned space missions.

Space telescope
Radio, X-ray, and gamma-ray telescopes are important tools of modern astronomy.

Market
Important and historic marketplaces around the world.

Festivals
Large celebrations of music and culture including Rio de Janeiro's Carnaval.

Museum
Important collections of man-made works, artifacts and natural relics.

Theater
Theaters – featuring opera, musicals, dramas, and avant-garde productions.

World exhibition/World's fair
Cities that have hosted a world's fair/ world exposition.

Olympics
Cities and towns that have hosted the modern summer or winter Olympic Games.

Arena/stadium
The largest sporting venues in the world – including venues for soccer, football, baseball, rugby, hockey, and other leading sports.

Race track
Auto and motorbike racing are popular sports in many of the world's regions. The atlas highlights many of the most famous auto-racing venues including Formula 1 and NASCAR race tracks in Daytona, Indianapolis, Melbourne, and numerous other cities around the world.

Golf
Golf has become an increasingly popular sport around the world in recent years. This atlas highlights many famous and beautiful golf courses as well as the areas that host important golf tournaments.

Horse racing
Several well-known racing courses and events are highlighted in the book. The Kentucky Derby is one of the most popular annual sporting events in the United States, while Hong Kong's Happy Valley draws thousands of visitors every week.

Skiing
The maps in the atlas point out the most important ski areas in the world including Chamonix in France, St. Moritz in Switzerland, and Aspen in Colorado. Many of these areas also offer facilities for other winter sports including snowboarding.

Sailing
Once a sport reserved for the wealthy, sailing is now enjoyed by millions of people. The atlas highlights areas with good conditions for recreational sailing.

Diving
Beautiful, colorful coral reefs, fascinating shipwrecks and close encounters with marine life – the atlas presents popular diving venues around the world.

Wind surfing
A mix of surfing and sailing, windsurfing has becomee a very popular aquatic sport in the last decades. The atlas points out coastal areas well suited to the sport.

Surfing
Popular coastal areas with adequate waves for surfing are highlighted – including well-known beaches in Australia, California, and Hawaii.

Canoeing/rafting
Adventurous and relaxing journeys along the world's rivers and lakes.

Seaport
Shipping remains vital for the global economy.

Deep-sea fishing
The atlas highlights several of the best and most well known locations on the world's seas and oceans for recreational fishing.

Waterskiing
Beaches and lakes with ideal conditions for waterskiing.

Beach resort
Many of the world's beachside communities feature excellent tourist facilities. The atlas highlights popular beaches and beach towns.

Mineral/thermal spa
The atlas presents several historic and beautiful towns with spas that have attracted visitors for centuries.

Amusement/theme park
Modern amusement parks offer diverse attractions. The parks highlighted in the atlas include Walt Disney World in Orlando, Sea World in California, Euro Disneyland in Paris, and Tivoli in Copenhagen.

Casino
Casinos including the historic casino of Monte Carlo in Monaco and the enormous resort-hotels of Las Vegas.

Hill resort
Exclusive resorts located in temperate highland areas. Mostly in Asia, hill resorts were once very popular destinations, especially for European colonial officials.

Lodge
Comfortable and in many cases luxurious camps or inns in pristine wilderness areas, mostly in Africa and North America.

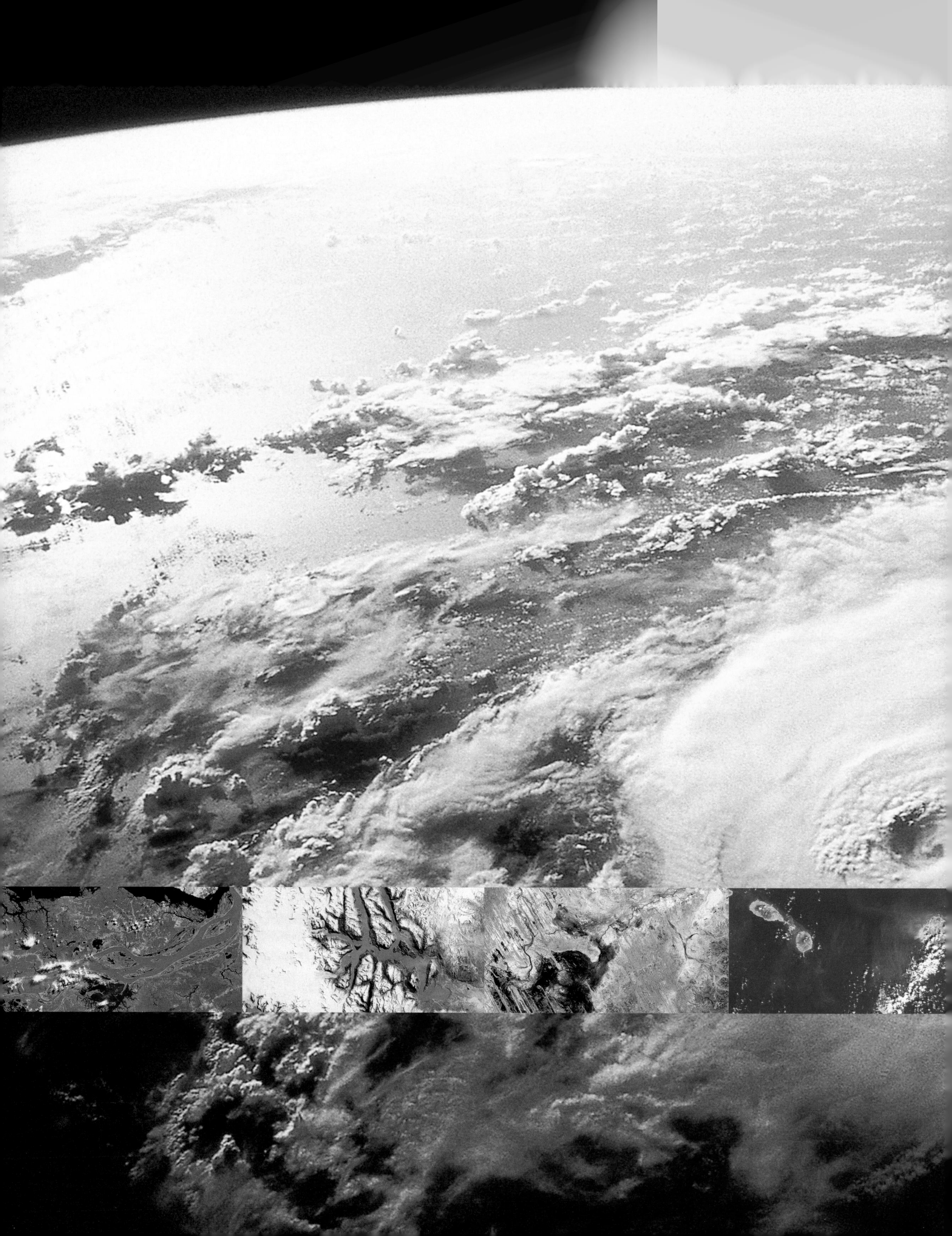

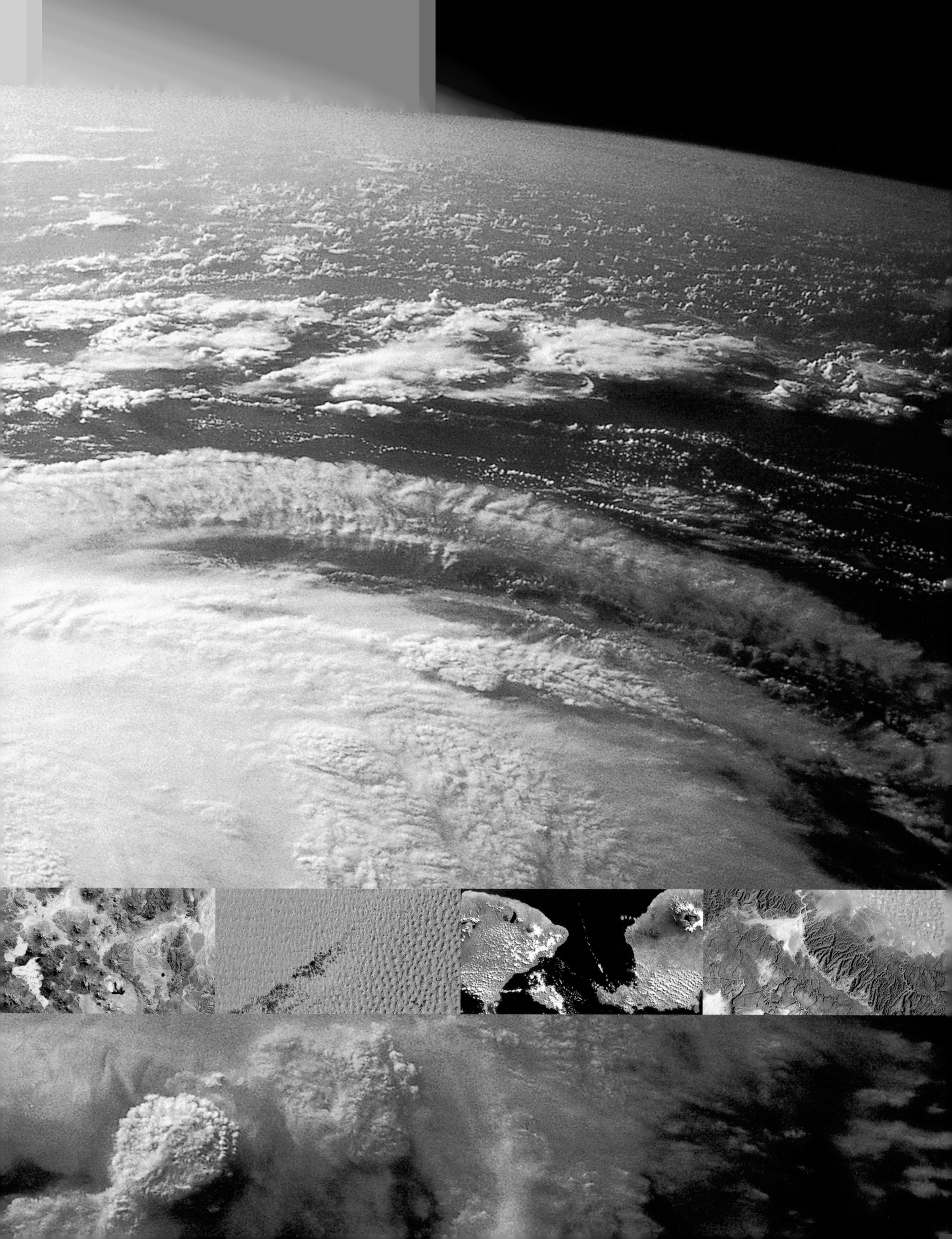

The world – physical map

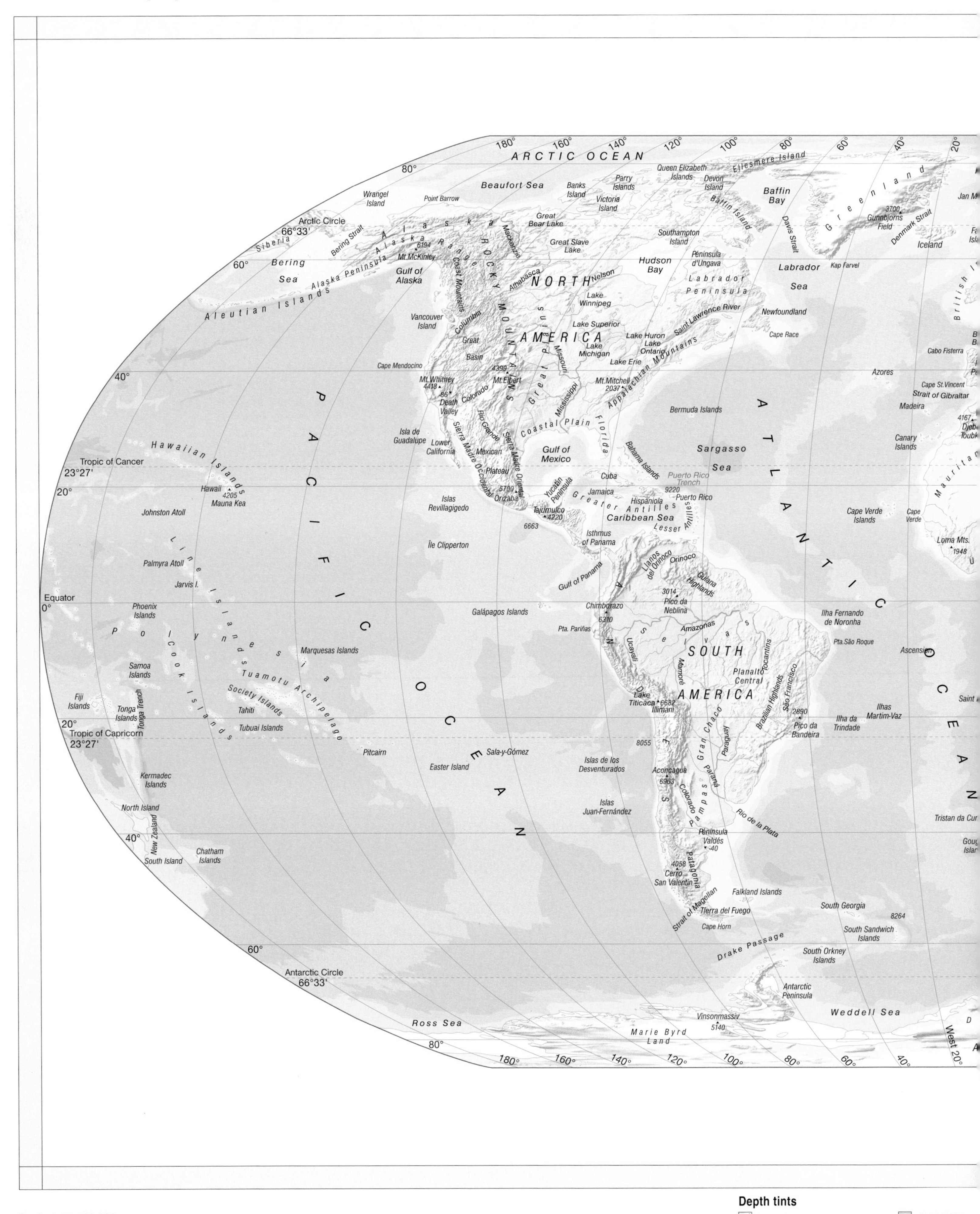

Scale 1:85,000,000

0   400   800 Kilometers

Depth tints

Shoreline	4000-6000 m
0-200 m	6000-8000 m
200-2000 m	> 8000 m
2000-4000 m	

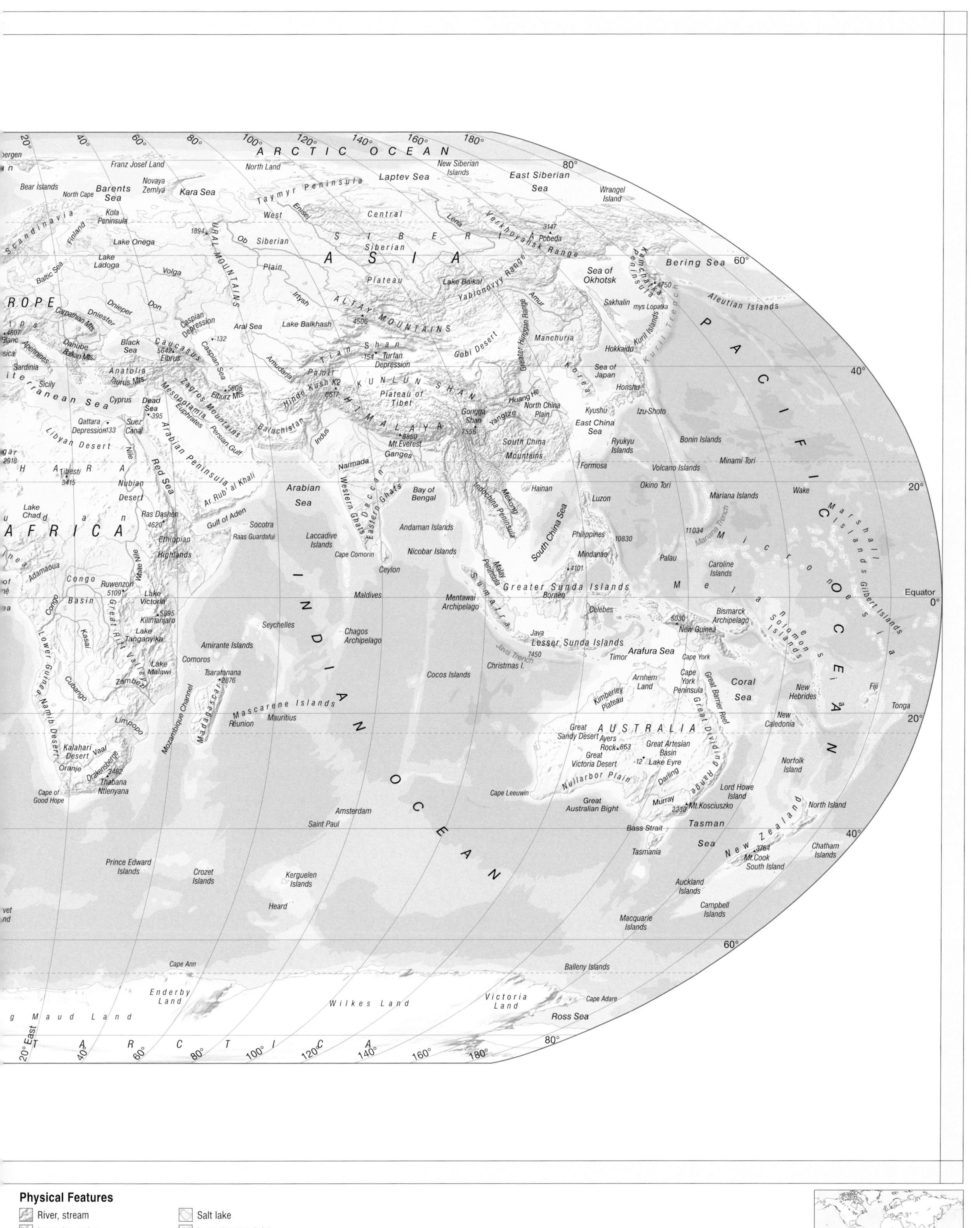

Physical Features

- River, stream
- Intermittent river
- Lake
- Intermittent lake
- Salt lake
- Intermittent salt lake
- Elevation above sea level in meters

The world – political map

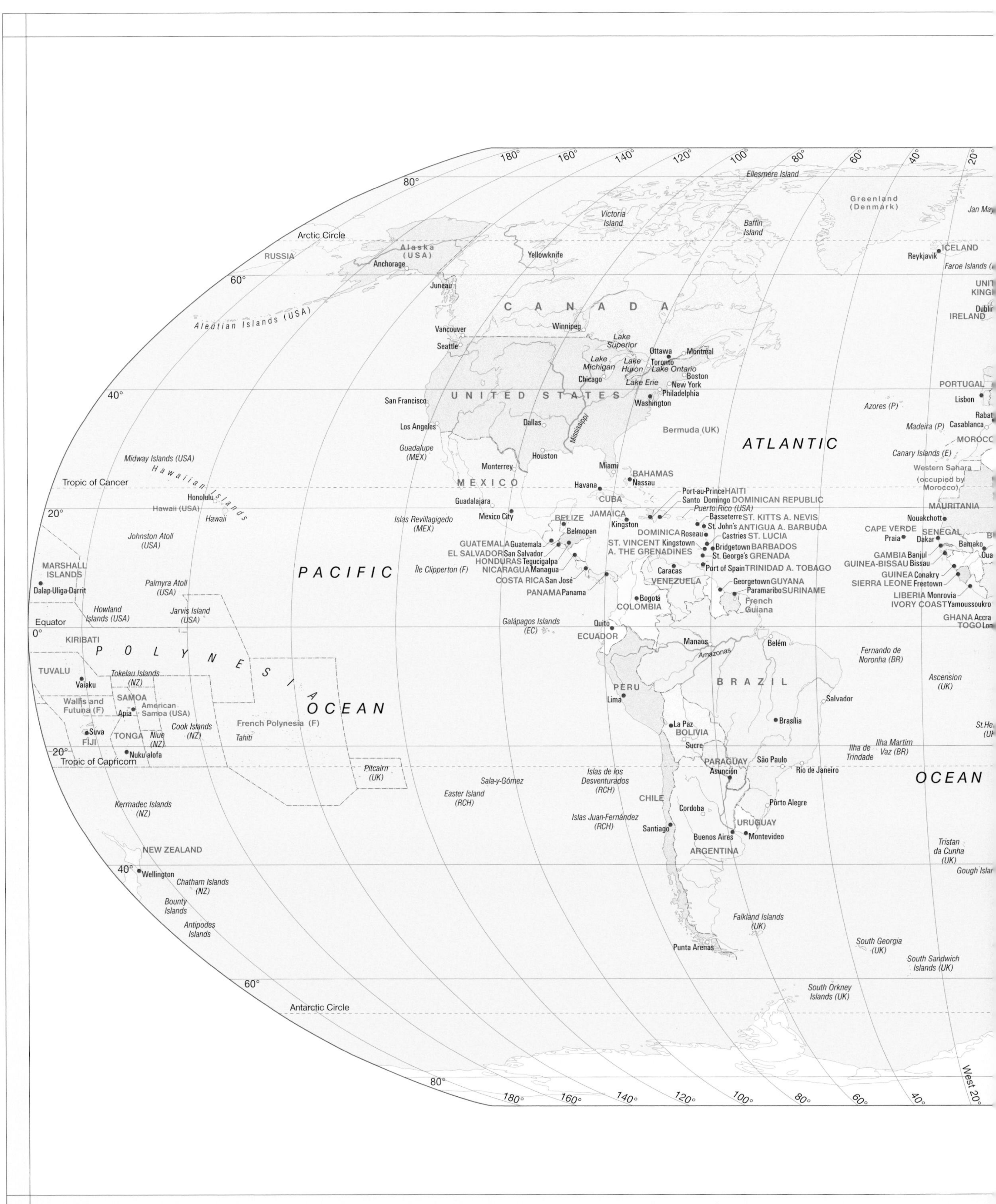

Scale 1:85,000,000

0   400 800 Kilometers

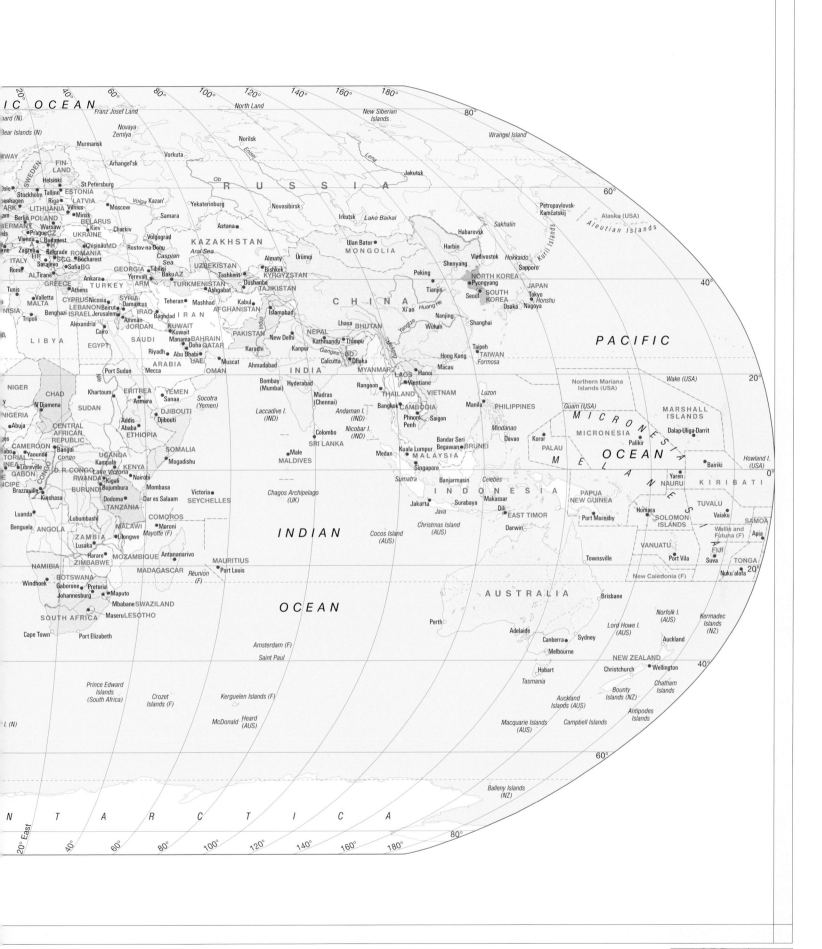

IC OCEAN

20° 40° 60° 80° 100° 120° 140° 160° 180°

North Land
New Siberian Islands
80°
Wrangel Island

Franz Josef Land
Bear Islands (N)
Novaya Zemlya
Norilsk
Murmansk
Vorkuta
Arhangel'sk
Ob
Enisej
Lena
Jakutsk
60°
RUSSIA
Petropavlovsk-Kamčatskij
Alaska (USA)
Aleutian Islands

NORWAY
SWEDEN
FINLAND
Helsinki
St.Petersburg
Yekaterinburg
Novosibirsk
Irkutsk
Lake Baikal
Sakhalin
Habarovsk

Oslo
Stockholm
Tallinn
ESTONIA
Riga
LATVIA
Volga
Kazan'
Samara
Astana
Hokkaido
Sapporo
Kuril Islands

openhagen
ARK
LITHUANIA
Vilnius
Moscow
KAZAKHSTAN
Ulan Bator
MONGOLIA
Harbin
Vladivostok
Sapporo

am
Berlin
POLAND
Minsk
BELARUS
Charkiv
Rostov-na-Donu
Aral Sea
Almaty
Ürümqi
Shenyang
40°
ne
GERMANY
Warsaw
Prague
CZ
Kiev
UKRAINE
Volgograd
Caspian Sea
Bishkek
KYRGYZSTAN
Peking
NORTH KOREA
Pyongyang
JAPAN
Tokyo
Honshu

Vienna
Budapest
Chişinău
MD
Tashkent
UZBEKISTAN
Tianjin
Seoul
SOUTH KOREA
Osaka
Nagoya

Zagreb
HR
Belgrade
ROMANIA
GEORGIA
Tbilisi
Baku
AZ
Dushanbe
TAJIKISTAN
Xi'an
Huang He
Nanjing
Shanghai

ITALY
Sarajevo
SCG
Bucharest
Sofia
BG
Yerevan
ARM
Ashgabat
TURKMENISTAN
CHINA
Yangtze
Wuhan

Rome
AL
Tirane
GREECE
Ankara
TURKEY
Athens
Baku
AZ
Teheran
Mashhad
Lhasa
BHUTAN
Hong Kong
Macau
Taipeh
TAIWAN
Formosa

Tunis
Valletta
MALTA
CYPRUS
Nicosia
SYRIA
Damascus
IRAN
Kabul
AFGHANISTAN
Islamabad
NEPAL
Kathmandu
Thimpu
BD
Calcutta
Dhaka

NISIA
Tripoli
Benghazi
LEBANON
Beirut
ISRAEL
Jerusalem
Baghdad
IRAQ
Amman
JORDAN
KUWAIT
Kuwait
Manama
BAHRAIN
Doha
QATAR
PAKISTAN
New Delhi
Kanpur
Karachi
Ganges
MYANMAR
Hanoi
PACIFIC

LIBYA
EGYPT
Alexandria
Cairo
SAUDI
Riyadh
Abu Dhabi
UAE
Muscat
OMAN
Ahmadabad
INDIA
Rangoon
LAOS
Vientiane
20°

NIGER
CHAD
N'Djamena
Khartoum
SUDAN
Mecca
ARABIA
Port Sudan
Nile
Bombay (Mumbai)
Hyderabad
Madras (Chennai)
THAILAND
VIETNAM
Luzon
Northern Mariana Islands (USA)
Wake (USA)

NIGERIA
Abuja
ERITREA
Asmara
YEMEN
Sanaa
Socotra (Yemen)
Laccadive I. (IND)
Andaman I. (IND)
Bangkok
CAMBODIA
Saigon
Manila
PHILIPPINES
Guam (USA)
MARSHALL ISLANDS
MICRONESIA

CENTRAL AFRICAN REPUBLIC
Addis Ababa
DJIBOUTI
Djibouti
ETHIOPIA
Colombo
Nicobar I. (IND)
Phnom Penh
Mindanao
Davao
Koror
MICRONESIA
Dalap-Uliga-Darrit
OCEAN

CAMEROON
Yaoundé
Bangui
SOMALIA
SRI LANKA
Bandar Seri Begawan
BRUNEI
PALAU
Bairiki

abo
TORIAL
Libreville
UGANDA
Kampala
KENYA
Nairobi
Male
MALDIVES
Medan
Kuala Lumpur
MALAYSIA
Yaren
NAURU
Howland I. (USA)

GABON
CONGO
D.R. CONGO
RWANDA
Kigali
Lake Victoria
Mombasa
Singapore
Sumatra
Banjarmasin
Celebes
KIRIBATI
0°

CIPE
Brazzaville
Kinshasa
BURUNDI
Bujumbura
Dodoma
Dar es Salaam
Chagos Archipelago (UK)
Jakarta
Java
Surabaya
Makassar
Dili
INDONESIA
PAPUA NEW GUINEA
TUVALU

Luanda
ANGOLA
Lubumbashi
TANZANIA
Victoria
SEYCHELLES
Christmas Island (AUS)
EAST TIMOR
Port Moresby
Honiara
SOLOMON ISLANDS
SAMOA
Apia

Benguela
ZAMBIA
MALAWI
COMOROS
Moroni
Mayotte (F)
INDIAN
Cocos Island (AUS)
Darwin
VANUATU
Wallis and Futuna (F)
FIJI

Lusaka
Harare
Lilongwe
Antananarivo
MAURITIUS
Port Vila
Suva
TONGA
20°

NAMIBIA
ZIMBABWE
MOZAMBIQUE
MADAGASCAR
Réunion (F)
Port Louis
New Caledonia (F)
Nuku'alofa

Windhoek
BOTSWANA
Gaborone
Pretoria
Maputo
OCEAN
AUSTRALIA
Brisbane
Norfolk I. (AUS)
Kermadec Islands (NZ)

SOUTH AFRICA
Johannesburg
Mbabane
SWAZILAND
Maseru
LESOTHO
Perth
Lord Howe I. (AUS)

Cape Town
Port Elizabeth
Amsterdam (F)
Saint Paul
Adelaide
Canberra
Sydney
Auckland

Prince Edward Islands (South Africa)
Crozet Islands (F)
Kerguelen Islands (F)
Melbourne
NEW ZEALAND
40°

I. (N)
McDonald
Heard (AUS)
Hobart
Tasmania
Christchurch
Wellington
Chatham Islands

Macquarie Islands (AUS)
Auckland Islands (AUS)
Bounty Islands (NZ)
Campbell Islands
Antipodes Islands

60°

Balleny Islands (NZ)

N T A R C T I C A

20° East 40° 60° 80° 100° 120° 140° 160° 180° 80°

5

Europe – physical map

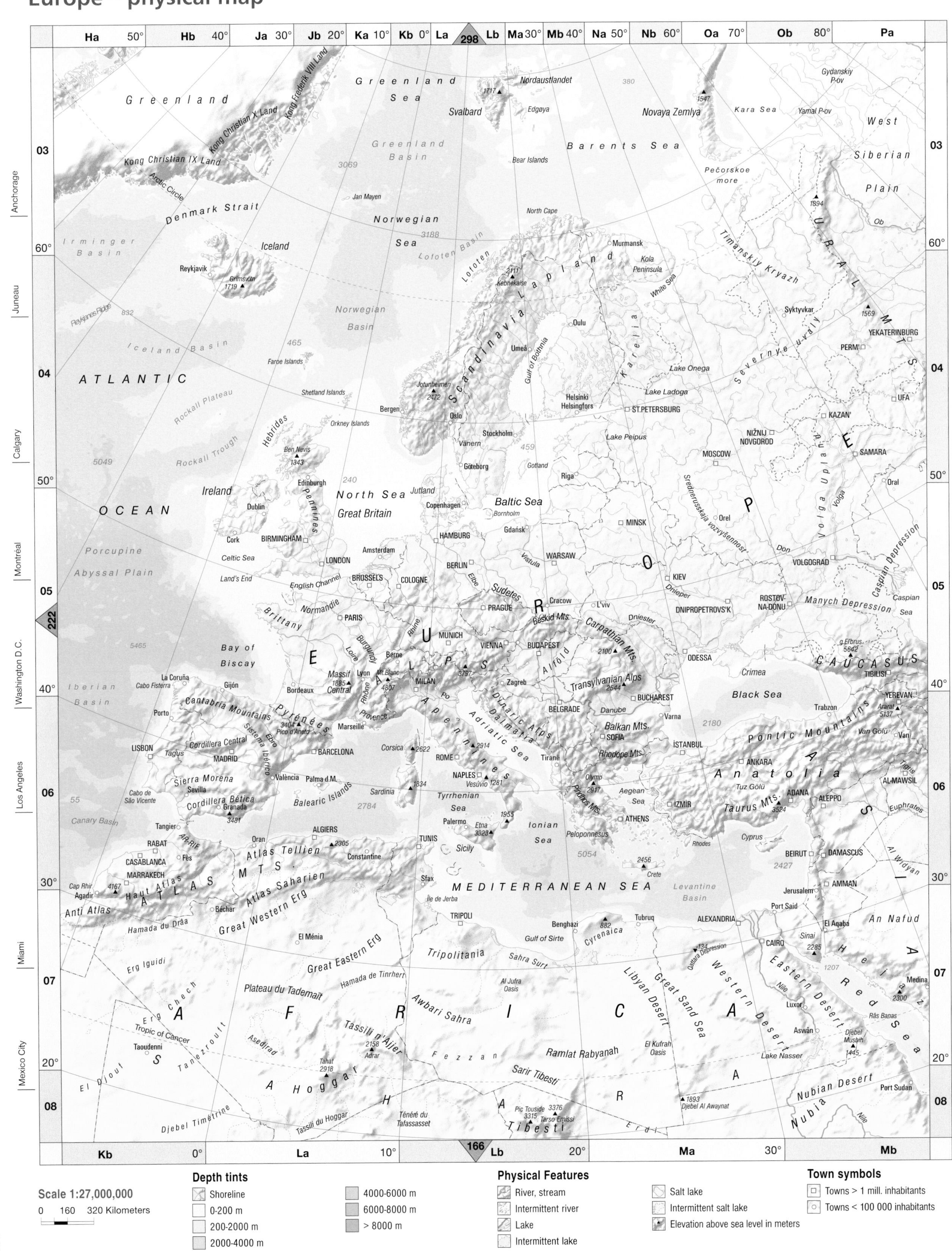

Scale 1:27,000,000

0   160   320 Kilometers

Depth tints

Shoreline
0-200 m
200-2000 m
2000-4000 m
4000-6000 m
6000-8000 m
> 8000 m

Physical Features

River, stream
Intermittent river
Lake
Intermittent lake
Salt lake
Intermittent salt lake
Elevation above sea level in meters

Town symbols

Towns > 1 mill. inhabitants
Towns < 100 000 inhabitants

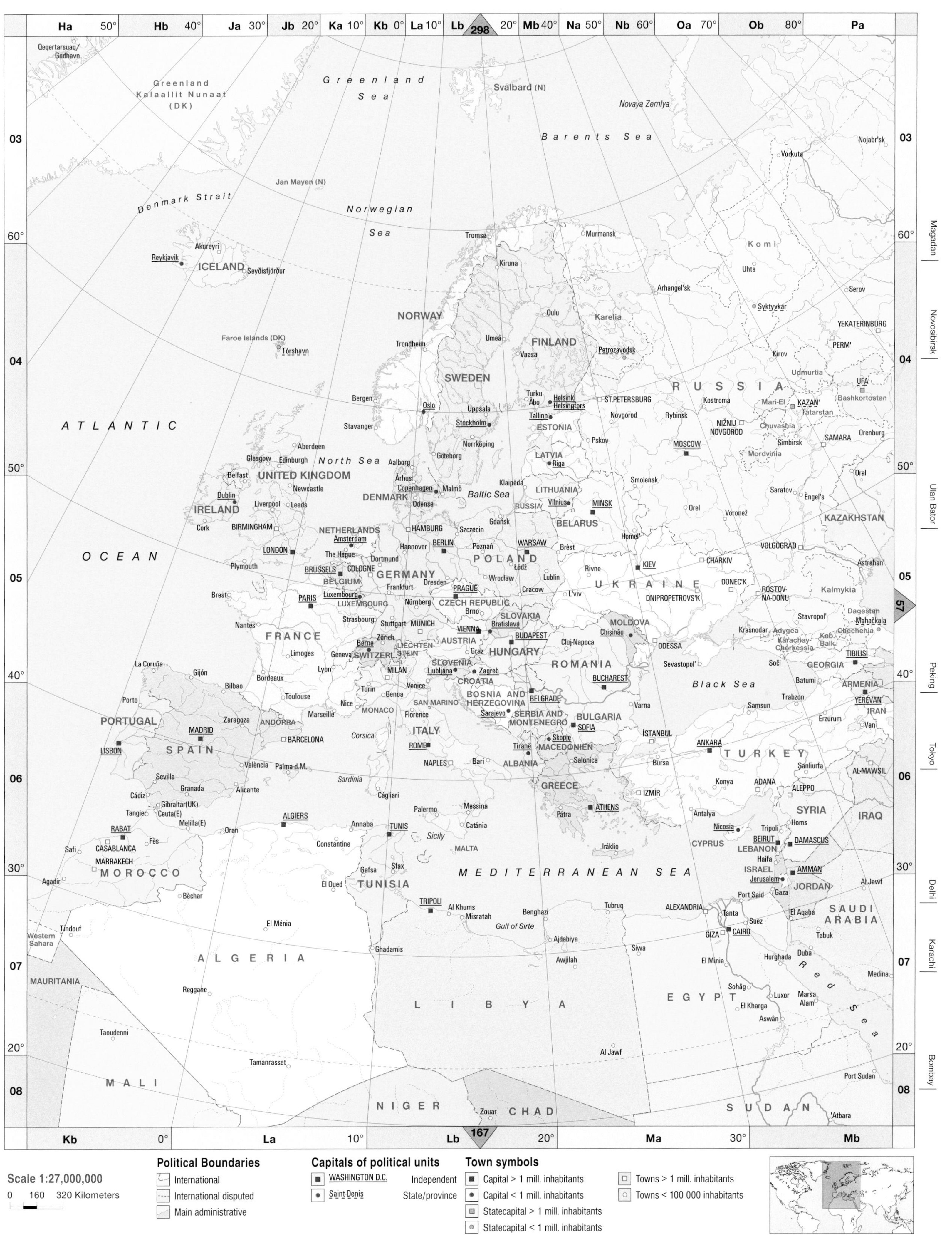

Europe – political map

Scale 1:27,000,000

0   160   320 Kilometers

Political Boundaries
— International
-·-·- International disputed
///// Main administrative

Capitals of political units
■ WASHINGTON D.C.   Independent
● Saint-Denis   State/province

Town symbols
■ Capital > 1 mill. inhabitants
● Capital < 1 mill. inhabitants
▣ Statecapital > 1 mill. inhabitants
◉ Statecapital < 1 mill. inhabitants
□ Towns > 1 mill. inhabitants
□ Towns < 100 000 inhabitants

Europe

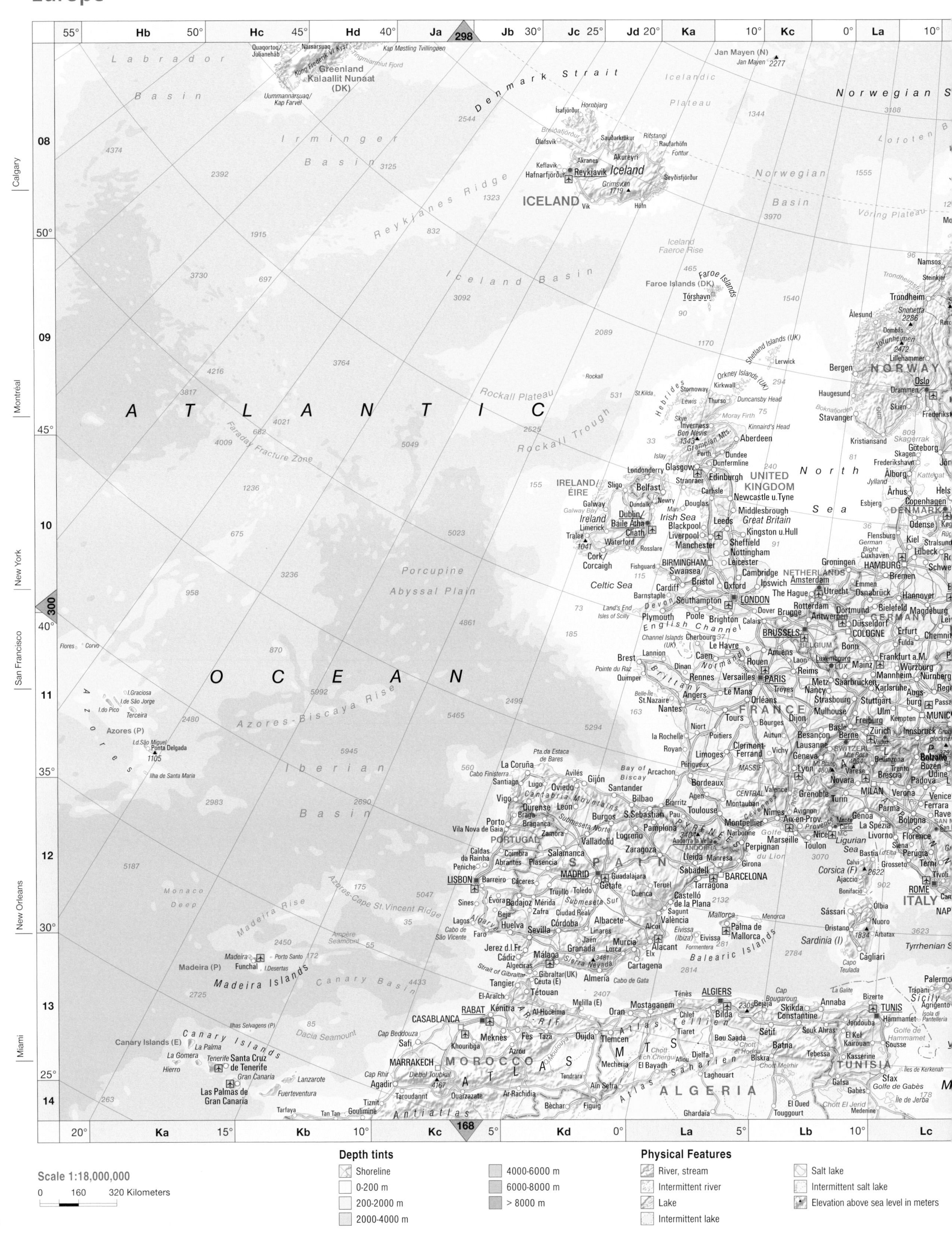

Scale 1:18,000,000

0   160   320 Kilometers

8

Depth tints

- ⊠ Shoreline
- ☐ 0-200 m
- ☐ 200-2000 m
- ☐ 2000-4000 m
- ☐ 4000-6000 m
- ☐ 6000-8000 m
- ☐ > 8000 m

Physical Features

- River, stream
- Intermittent river
- Lake
- Intermittent lake
- Salt lake
- Intermittent salt lake
- Elevation above sea level in meters

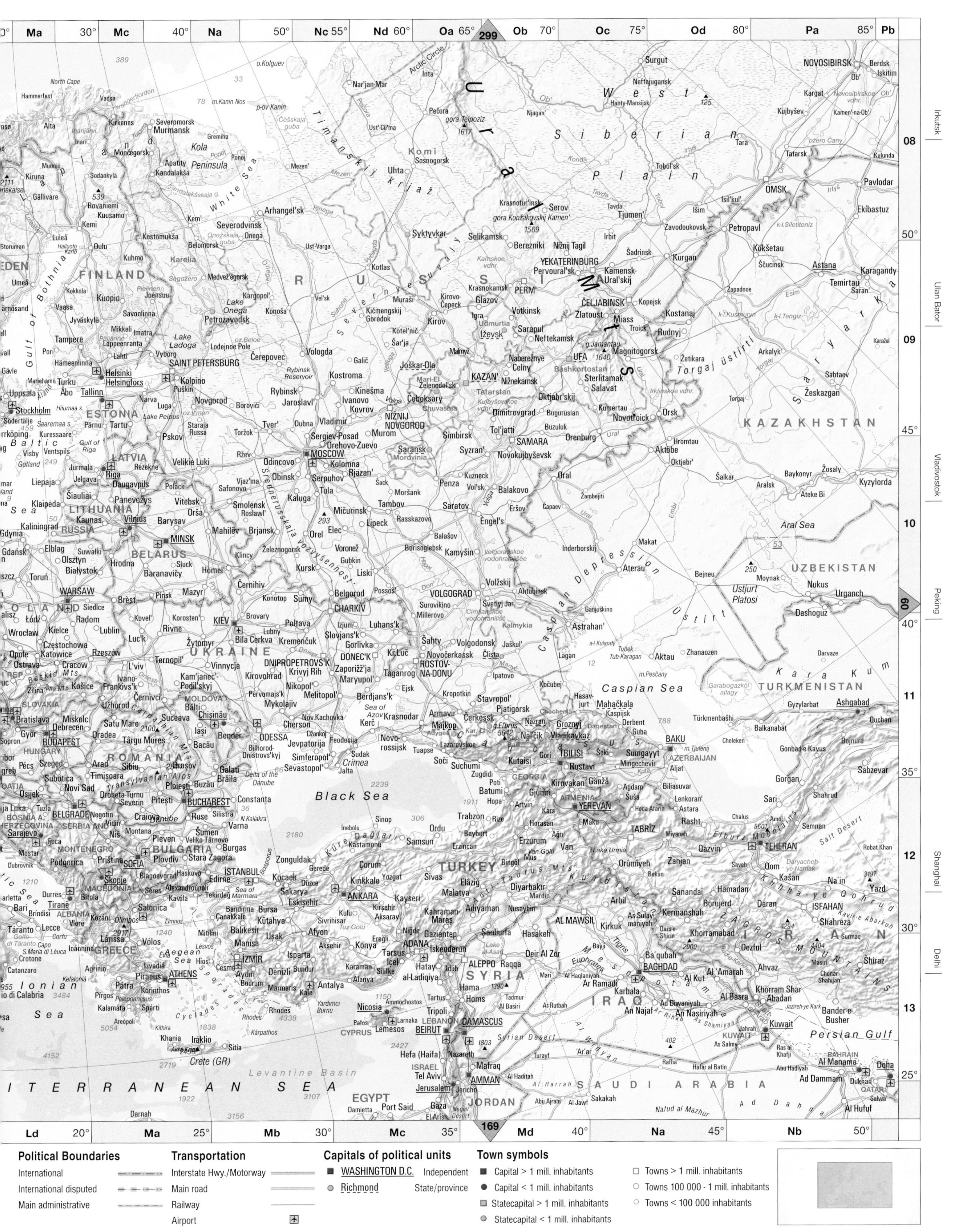

Irkutsk
08
50°
Ulan Bator
09
45°
Vladivostok
10
40°
Peking
11
Shanghai
12
Delhi
13
25°

Political Boundaries

International
International disputed
Main administrative

Transportation

Interstate Hwy./Motorway
Main road
Railway
Airport

Capitals of political units

■ WASHINGTON D.C. Independent
⊙ Richmond State/province

Town symbols

■ Capital > 1 mill. inhabitants
● Capital < 1 mill. inhabitants
▣ Statecapital > 1 mill. inhabitants
⊙ Statecapital < 1 mill. inhabitants

□ Towns > 1 mill. inhabitants
○ Towns 100 000 - 1 mill. inhabitants
○ Towns < 100 000 inhabitants

9

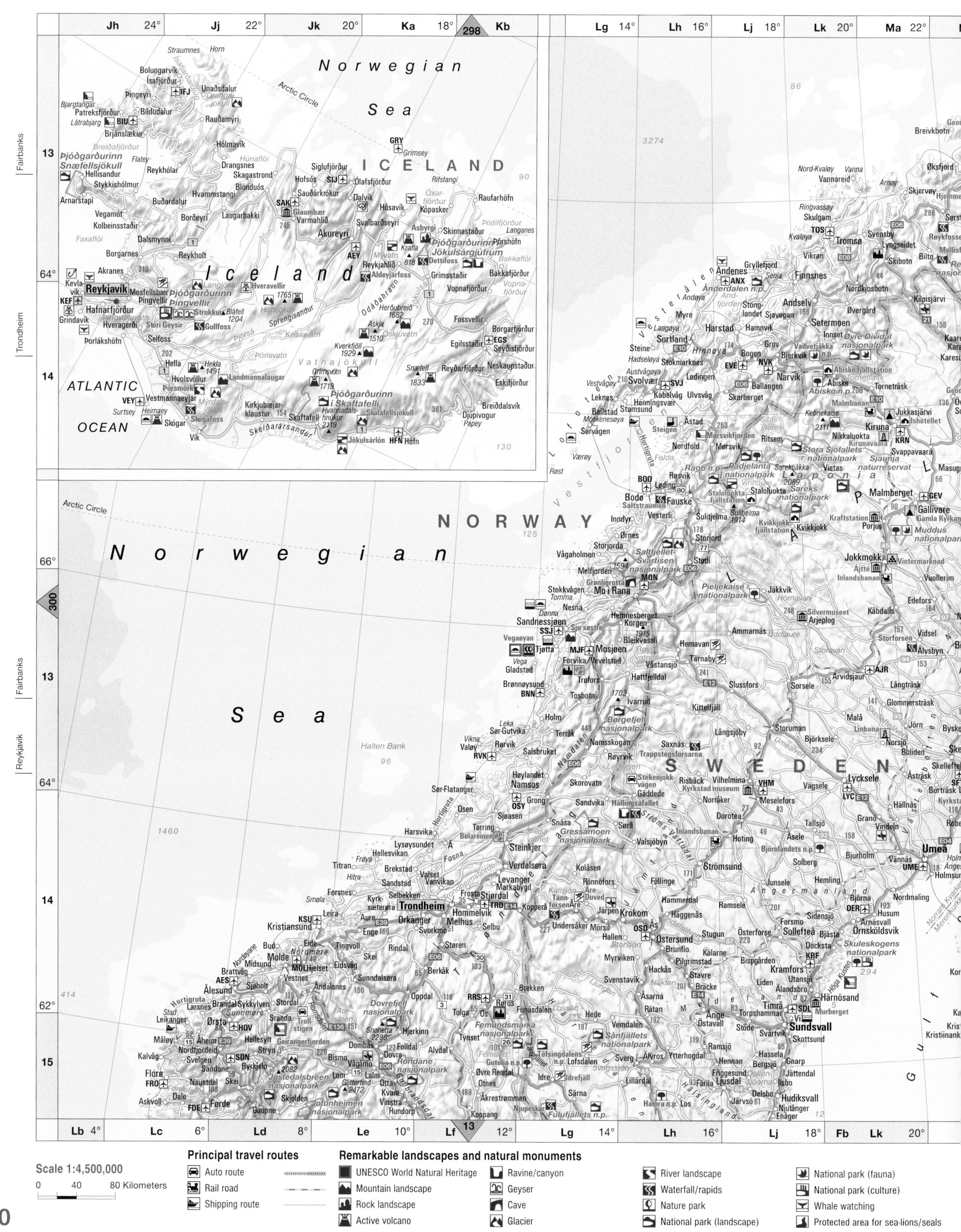

Scale 1:4,500,000

0   40   80 Kilometers

Principal travel routes

- 🚗 Auto route
- 🚆 Rail road
- ⛴ Shipping route

Remarkable landscapes and natural monuments

- ■ UNESCO World Natural Heritage
- ▲ Mountain landscape
- ▲ Rock landscape
- ▲ Active volcano
- ▪ Ravine/canyon
- Geyser
- Cave
- Glacier
- River landscape
- Waterfall/rapids
- Nature park
- National park (landscape)
- National park (fauna)
- National park (culture)
- Whale watching
- Protected area for sea-lions/seals

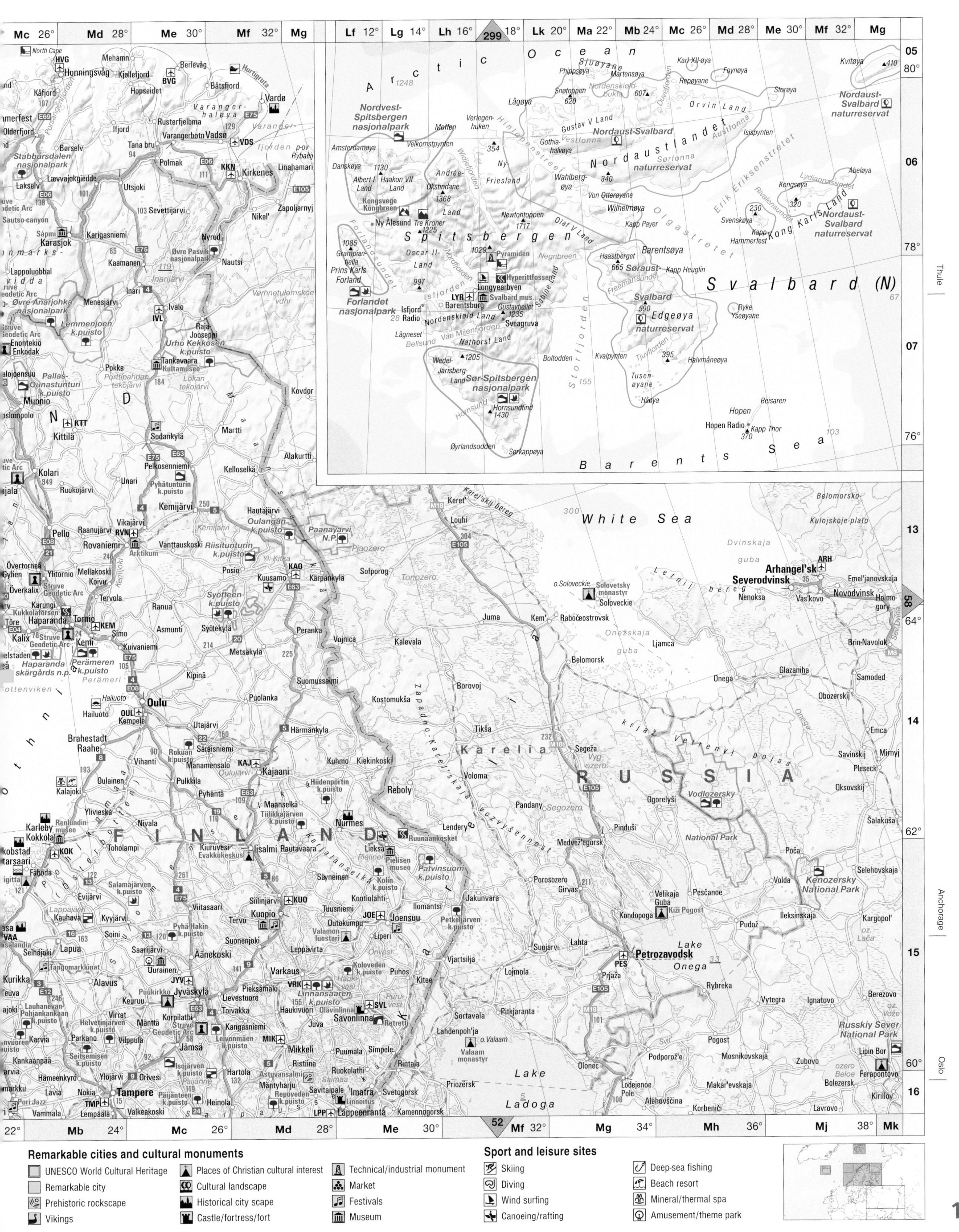

North Cape
HVG
Honningsvåg
Mehamn
Kjøllefjord
Berlevåg
Hurtigruta
Kåfjord
Hopseidet
Båtsfjord
Vardø
BVG
Varanger-haløa
Rusterfjelma
Varangerbotn Vadsø
VDS

Arctic Ocean
1248
Stuøyane
Phippsøya
Martensøya
Karl-XII-øya
Repøya
Foynøya
Kvitøya
410

Nordvest-
Spitsbergen
nasjonalpark
Lågøya
Snøtoppen
620
Nordenskiöld-
bukta
607
Orvin Land
Storøya
Nordaust-
Svalbard
naturreservat

Hammerfest
Olderfjord
Børselv
Polmak
94
E06
KKN
Kirkenes
Linahamari

Amsterdamøya
Danskøya
Albert I
Land
Haakon VII
Land
Moffen
Verlegen-
huken
Velkomstpynten
Andrée-
Land
1130
354
Ny-
Friesland
Okstindane
1368
Gustav V Land
Gothia-
halvøya
Vestfonna
Nordaust-Svalbard
Nordaustlandet
Sørfonna
naturreservat
Erik Eriksenstretet
Abeløya
Kongsøya
Lydlannasundet

Lakselv
E06
101
Utsjoki
Sevettijärvi
Nikel'
Zapoljarnyj
E105

Kongsvege
Kongbreen
Ny Ålesund
Tre Kroner
Oscar II-
Land
Grampian
fjella
1085
997
Land
1717
Newtontoppen
1029
Pyramiden
Olaf V Land
Von Otterøyane
Wilhelmøya
Kapp Payer
230
Kong Karls Land
320
Nordaust-
Svalbard
naturreservat

Sámpi
Karasjok
Karigasniemi
85
Kaamanen
Nautsi

Spitsbergen
Prins Karls
Forland
Isfjorden
Hyperittfossen
Longyearbyen
Barentsburg
LYR
Svalbard mus.
Gustavfjellet
1235
Barentsøya
Haasberget
665 Søraust-
Kapp Heuglin
Freemansundet
Edgeøya
naturreservat

Finn-
marks-
vidda
Lappluobbal
Inari
Ivalo
Menesjärvi
4

Forlandet
nasjonalpark
Isfjord
Radio
28
Barentsburg
Nordenskiöld Land
Van Mijenfjorden
Nathorst Land
590
Svalbard
67
Ryke
Yseøyane

Øvre Anarjohka
nasjonalpark
Enontekiö
Enkodak
Lemmenjoen
k.puisto
Urho Kekkosen
k.puisto
Raja
Joosephi
Tankavaara
Kultamuseo

Lågneset
Bellsund
Wedel-
Jarisberg-
Land
1205
Boltodden
155
Tusen-
øyane
395
Hopen
Beisaren

Pallas-
Ounastunturi
k.puisto
Muonio
N
KTT
Kittilä
Pokka
Porttipahdan
tekojärvi
184
Lokan
tekojärvi
Kovdor

Sør-Spitsbergen
nasjonalpark
Hornsund
Hornsundtind
1430
Øyrlandsodden
Sørkappøya
Hopen Radio
Kapp Thor
370
Barents
Sea
103

Kolari
349
Sodankylä
Martti
Alakurtti
Kelloselkä

Pelkosenniemi
Unari
Pyhätunturin
k.puisto
Kemijärvi
250

White Sea
Keret'
Louhi
304
E105
300
Belomorsko-
Kuloiskoje-plato

Pello
E08
Raanujärvi
RVN
Rovaniemi
Vikajärvi
246
Arktikum
Hautajärvi
Oulangan
k.puisto
Riisitunturin
k.puisto
Paanajärvi
N.P.
Piaozero
Tonozero
Dvinskaja
guba
Arhangel'sk
ARH
Severodvinsk
Emel'janovskaja
Novodvinsk
Holmo-
gory

Ylitornio
Mellakoski
Koivu
Tervola
Posio
KAO
Kuusamo
E63
Kärpänkylä
Sofporog
Kem'
Rabočeostrovsk
Soloveckie
o.Soloveckie
Solovetsky
monastyr
Nenoksa
Vas'kovo
Brin-Navolok
58
64°

Övertorneå
Ylitornio
Karungi
Struve
Geodetic Arc
Kukkolaforsen
Haparanda
Tornio
KEM
Simo
Kemi
E04
Ranua
Syötteen
k.puisto
Syötekylä
Asmunti
Peranka
Vojnica
Juma
Kalevala
Onežskaja
guba
Belomorsk
Ljamca
Glazaniha
Samoded
Emca

Haparanda
skärgårds n.p.
Perämeren
k.puisto
Perämeri
Hailuoto
OUL
Oulu
Kempele
E08
Kipinä
Puolanka
Suomussalmi
Borovoj
Kostomukša
Zapadno-Karel'skaja
Tikša
Onega
Obozerskij

Brahestadt
Raahe
Vihanti
Rokuan
k.puisto
Utajärvi
22
160
Säräisniemi
Härmänkylä
Kuhmo
Kiekinkoski
krjaž
Segeža
Vyg-
ozero
Velrenyj pojas
Savinskij
Plesck
Mirnyi
14

Oulainen
Pulkkila
193
Manamensalo
Oulujärvi
KAJ
Kajaani
Hiidenportin
k.puisto
Reboly
Pandany
Segozero
Karelia
RUSSIA
E105
Ogorelyši
Vodlozersky
Oksovskij

Kalajoki
Ylivieska
Nivala
Pyhäntä
E63
109
Maanselkä
Tiilikkajärven
k.puisto
Nurmes
Ruunaankosket
Lendery
Voloma
Medvež'egorsk
Porosozero
Pinduši
National Park
Šalakuša
Poča
62°

Karleby
Kokkola
KOK
Toholampi
19
110
Iisalmi
Rautavaara
Pielinen
Pielisen
museo
Patvinsuon
k.puisto
Girvas
211
Velikaja
Guba
Kenozersky
National Park
Selehovskaja

kobstad
Renlundin
museo
Evijärvi
122
Salamajärven
k.puisto
Kiuruvesi
Evakkokeskus
KUO
Kuopio
JOE
Joensuu
Ilomantsi
Petkeljärven
k.puisto
Jakunvara
Porosozero
Lahta
Kondopoga
Kiži Pogost
Lake
Onega
Pudož
Ileksinskaja
Kargopol'
oz.
Lača
15

VAA
Seinäjoki
Lapua
Saarijärvi
Viitasaari
261
Siilinjärvi
Tervo
Suonenjoki
Leppävirta
Valamon
luostari
Liperi
Orivesi
Suojarvi
Petrozavodsk
PES
Prjaža
Lake
Onega
33
Selivanovskaja

Kurikka
euva
Kauhava
Soini
163
Pyhä-Hakin
k.puisto
Äänekoski
141
Varkaus
Koloveden
k.puisto
Puhos
Kitee
Vjartsilja
Lojmola
Volda
Vytegra
Ignatovo
Berezovo

Kangasniemi
JYV
Jyväskylä
Pieksämäki
VRK
Linnansaaren
k.puisto
155
Olavinlinna
Savonlinna
Sortavala
Pitkjaranta
Lahdenpoh'ja
Priäža
E105
M18
101
Podporože
oz.
Beloe
Russkiy Sever
National Park

Kurikka
Parkano
Helvetinjärvi
Mänttä
Korpilahti
Struve
Geodetic Arc
Leivonmäen
k.puisto
MIK
Mikkeli
Juva
Puumala
Valaam
monastyr
Lake
Ladoga
Olonec
Lödejenoe
Pole
Lipin Bor
60°

Kankaanpää
Seitsemisen
k.puisto
Virrat
Vilppula
Jämsä
Isojärven
k.puisto
Orivesi
Hartola
Mäntyharju
Savitaipale
Imatra
Svetogorsk
Priozersk
108
Alehovščina
Makar'evskaja
Ferapontovo
Bolezersk

Nokia
Tampere
TMP
Lempäälä
Valkeakoski
Heinola
LPP
Lappeenranta
Kamennogorsk
Lake
Ladoga
Lavrovo
Korbeniči
Kirillov
16

Remarkable cities and cultural monuments

- UNESCO World Cultural Heritage
- Remarkable city
- Prehistoric rockscape
- Vikings
- Places of Christian cultural interest
- Cultural landscape
- Historical city scape
- Castle/fortress/fort
- Technical/industrial monument
- Market
- Festivals
- Museum

Sport and leisure sites

- Skiing
- Diving
- Wind surfing
- Canoeing/rafting
- Deep-sea fishing
- Beach resort
- Mineral/thermal spa
- Amusement/theme park

11

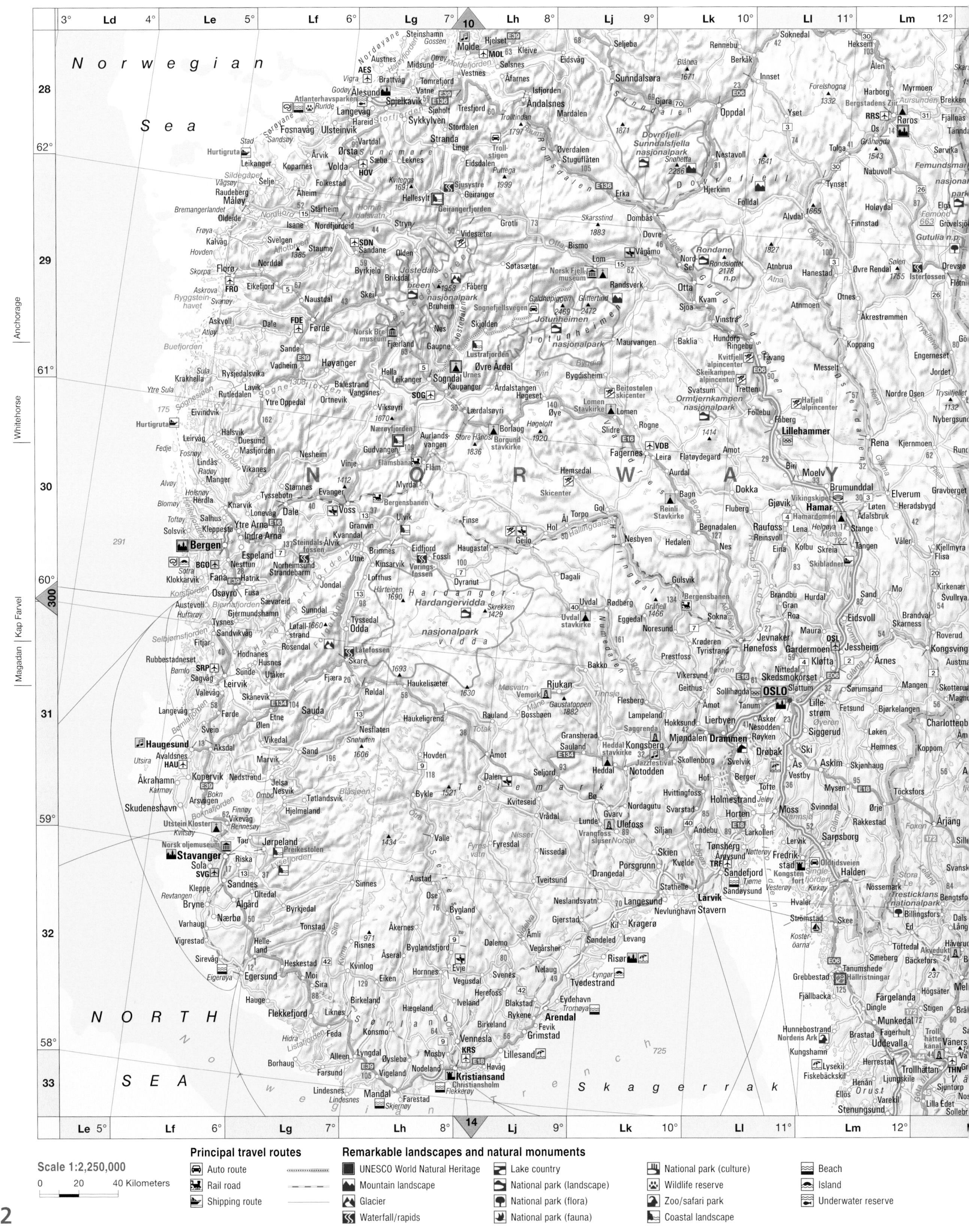

Scale 1:2,250,000

0   20   40 Kilometers

Principal travel routes

🚗 Auto route

🚂 Rail road

⛴ Shipping route

Remarkable landscapes and natural monuments

■ UNESCO World Natural Heritage

⛰ Mountain landscape

◩ Glacier

≋ Waterfall/rapids

▨ Lake country

◭ National park (landscape)

♣ National park (flora)

⬇ National park (fauna)

▨ National park (culture)

⬤ Wildlife reserve

▨ Zoo/safari park

▨ Coastal landscape

▨ Beach

▨ Island

▨ Underwater reserve

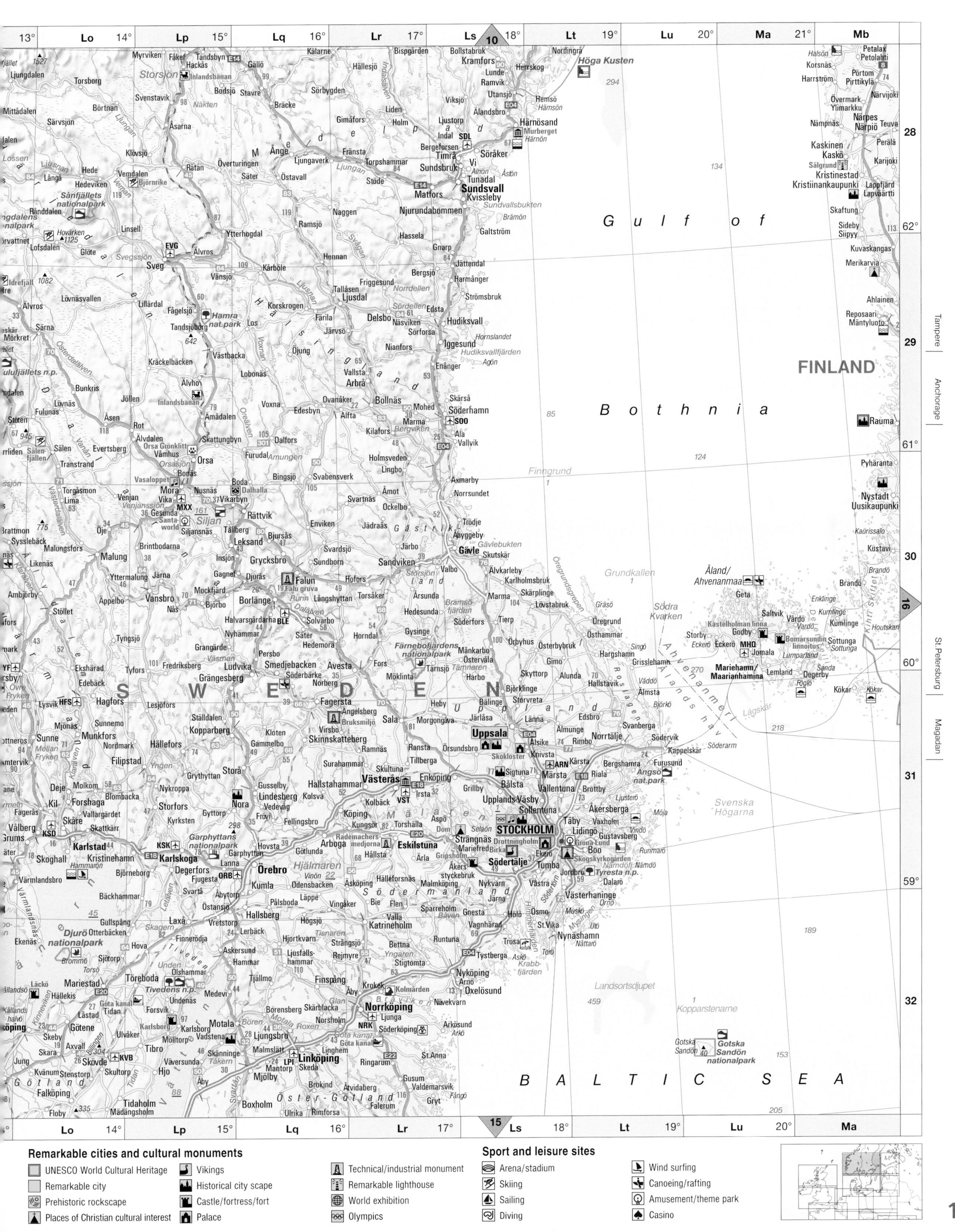

Remarkable cities and cultural monuments

- UNESCO World Cultural Heritage
- Remarkable city
- Prehistoric rockscape
- Places of Christian cultural interest
- Vikings
- Historical city scape
- Castle/fortress/fort
- Palace
- Technical/industrial monument
- Remarkable lighthouse
- World exhibition
- Olympics

Sport and leisure sites

- Arena/stadium
- Skiing
- Sailing
- Diving
- Wind surfing
- Canoeing/rafting
- Amusement/theme park
- Casino

Denmark, Southern Sweden

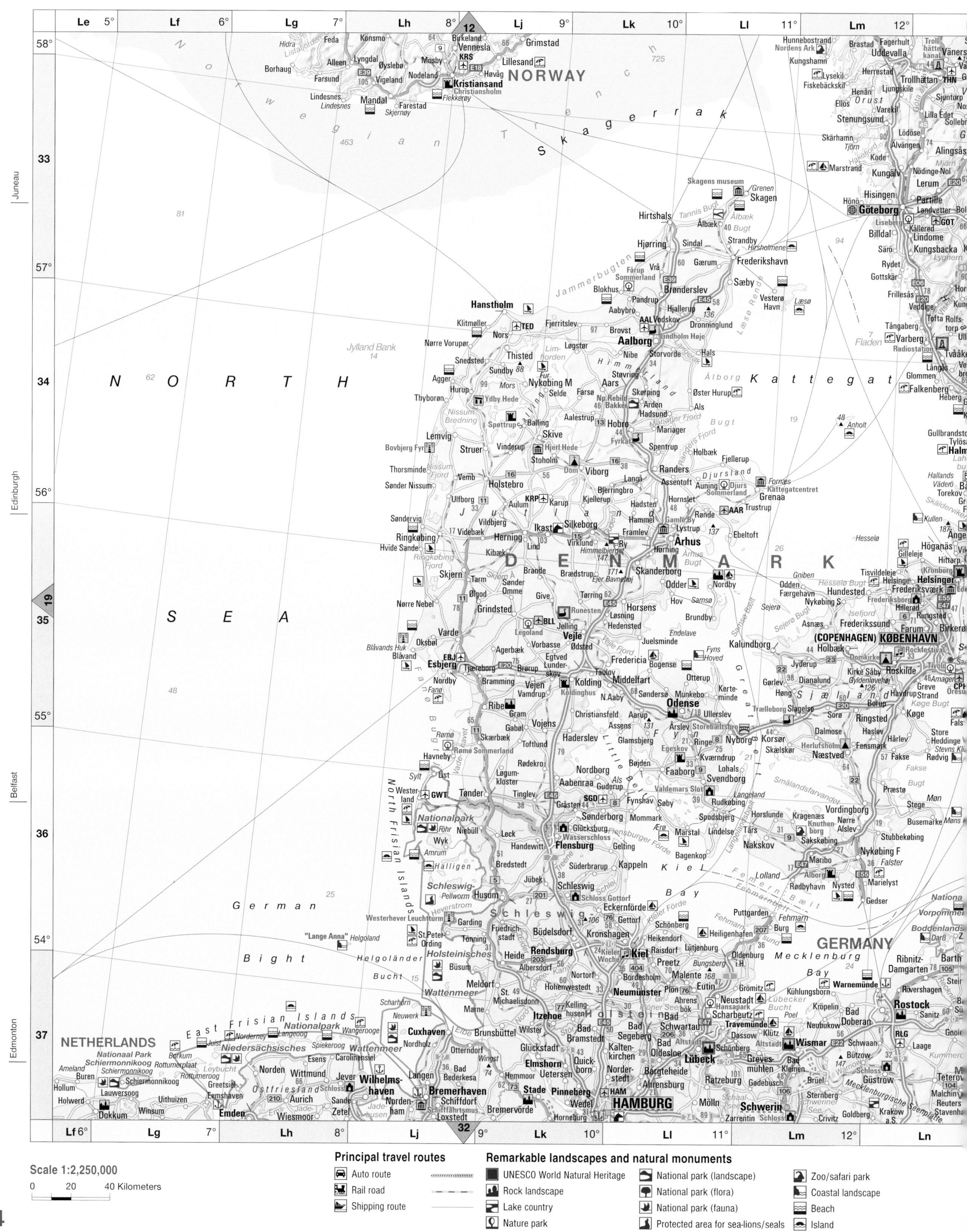

Scale 1:2,250,000

0   20   40 Kilometers

14

Principal travel routes
- Auto route
- Rail road
- Shipping route
- ·········· (dashed route line)
- ———— (route line)

Remarkable landscapes and natural monuments
- UNESCO World Natural Heritage
- Rock landscape
- Lake country
- Nature park
- National park (landscape)
- National park (flora)
- National park (fauna)
- Protected area for sea-lions/seals
- Zoo/safari park
- Coastal landscape
- Beach
- Island

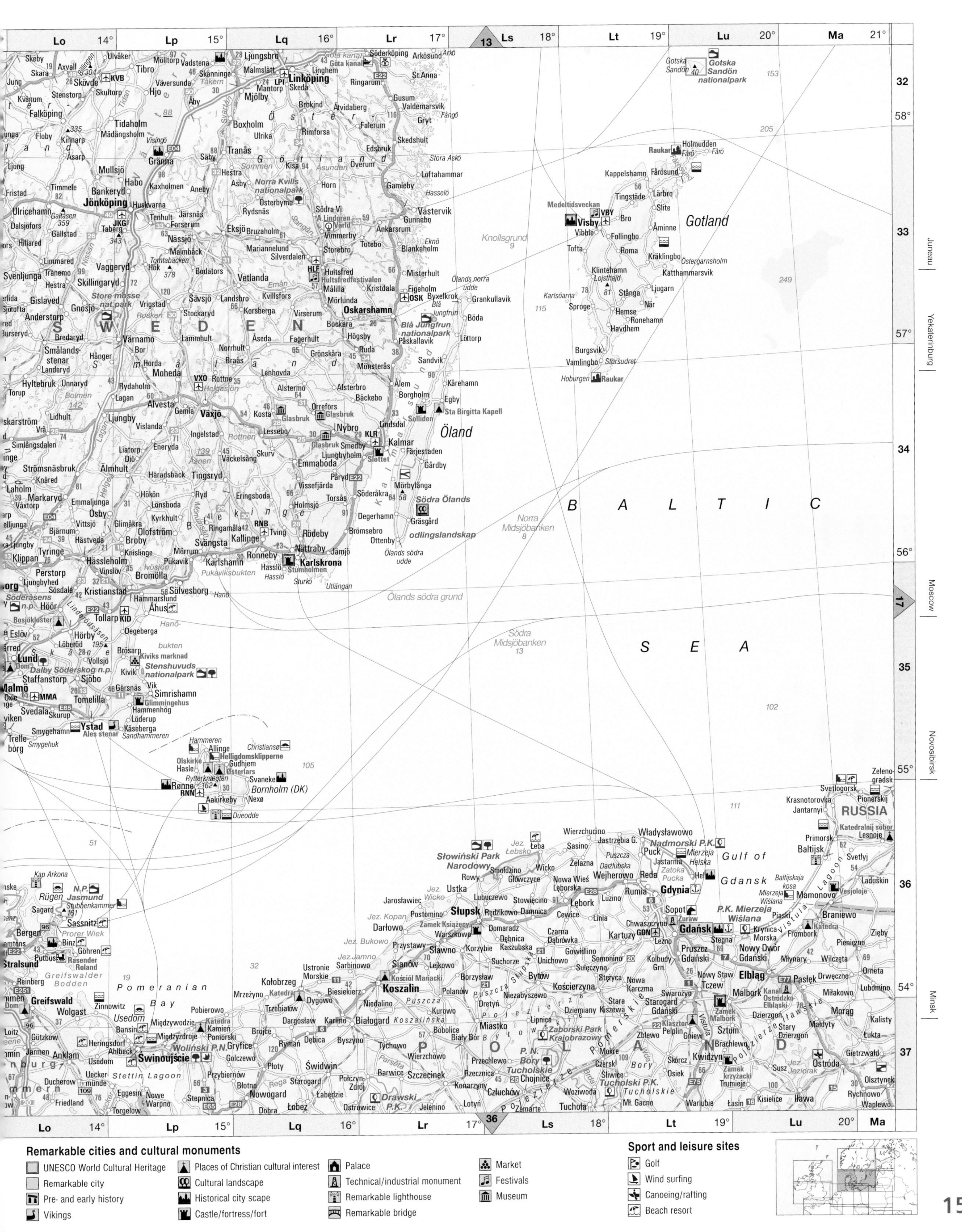

Remarkable cities and cultural monuments

- UNESCO World Cultural Heritage
- Remarkable city
- Pre- and early history
- Vikings
- Places of Christian cultural interest
- Cultural landscape
- Historical city scape
- Castle/fortress/fort
- Palace
- Technical/industrial monument
- Remarkable lighthouse
- Remarkable bridge
- Market
- Festivals
- Museum

Sport and leisure sites

- Golf
- Wind surfing
- Canoeing/rafting
- Beach resort

15

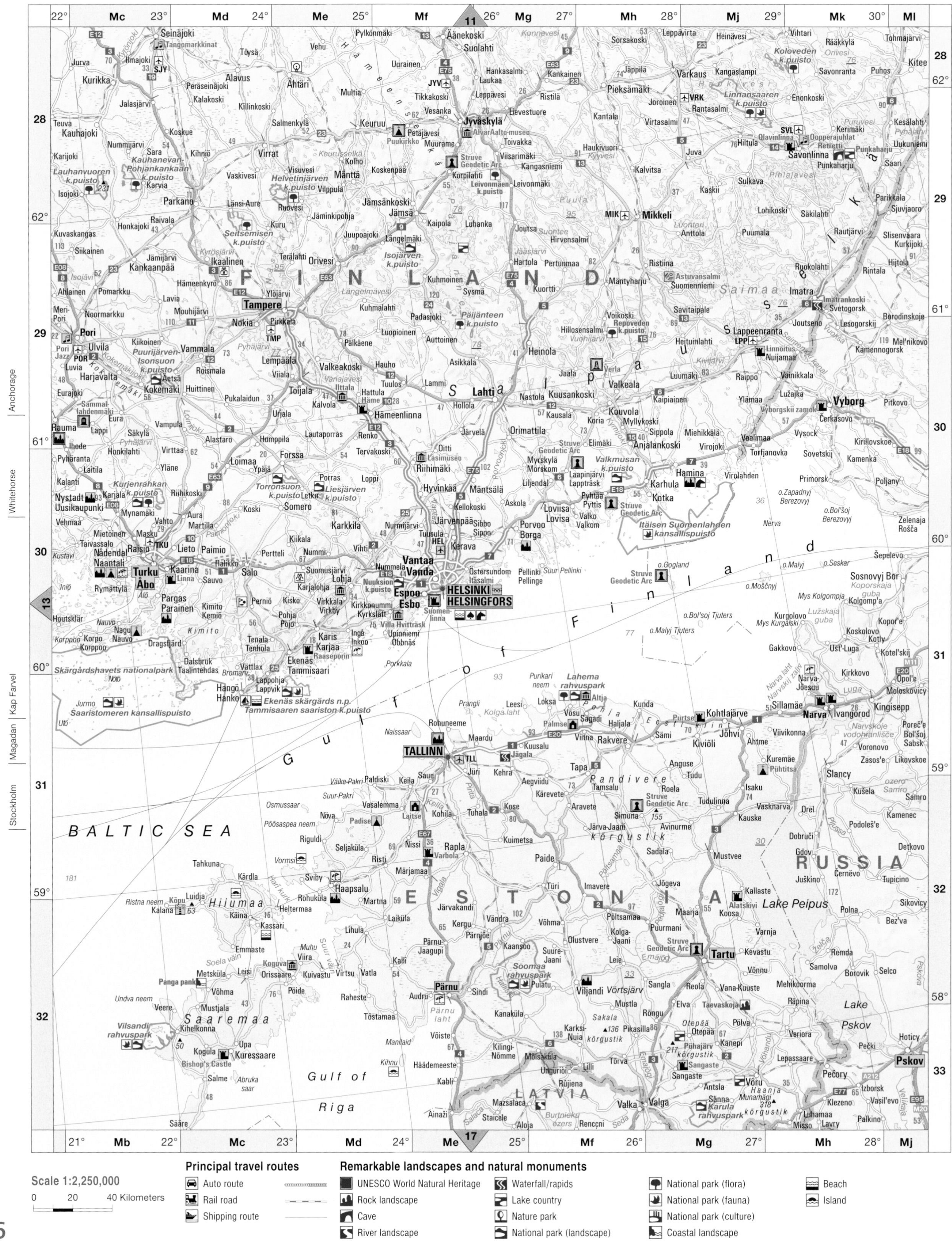

Scale 1:2,250,000

0   20   40 Kilometers

Principal travel routes
- 🚗 Auto route
- 🚂 Rail road
- ⛴ Shipping route

Remarkable landscapes and natural monuments
- ■ UNESCO World Natural Heritage
- Rock landscape
- Cave
- River landscape
- Waterfall/rapids
- Lake country
- Nature park
- National park (landscape)
- National park (flora)
- National park (fauna)
- National park (culture)
- Coastal landscape
- Beach
- Island

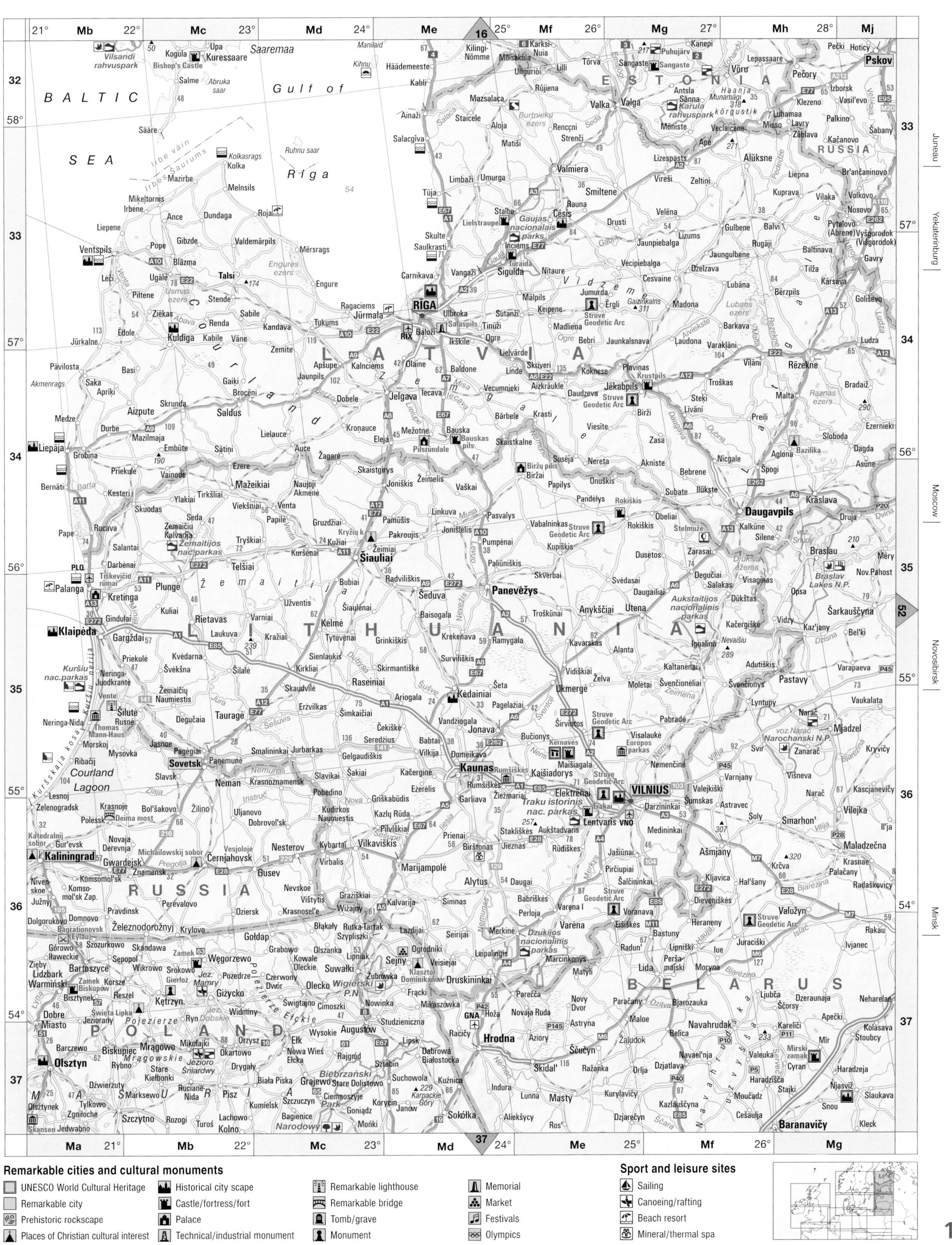

Remarkable cities and cultural monuments

- UNESCO World Cultural Heritage
- Remarkable city
- Prehistoric rockscape
- Places of Christian cultural interest
- Historical city scape
- Castle/fortress/fort
- Palace
- Technical/industrial monument
- Remarkable lighthouse
- Remarkable bridge
- Tomb/grave
- Monument
- Memorial
- Market
- Festivals
- Olympics

Sport and leisure sites

- Sailing
- Canoeing/rafting
- Beach resort
- Mineral/thermal spa

17

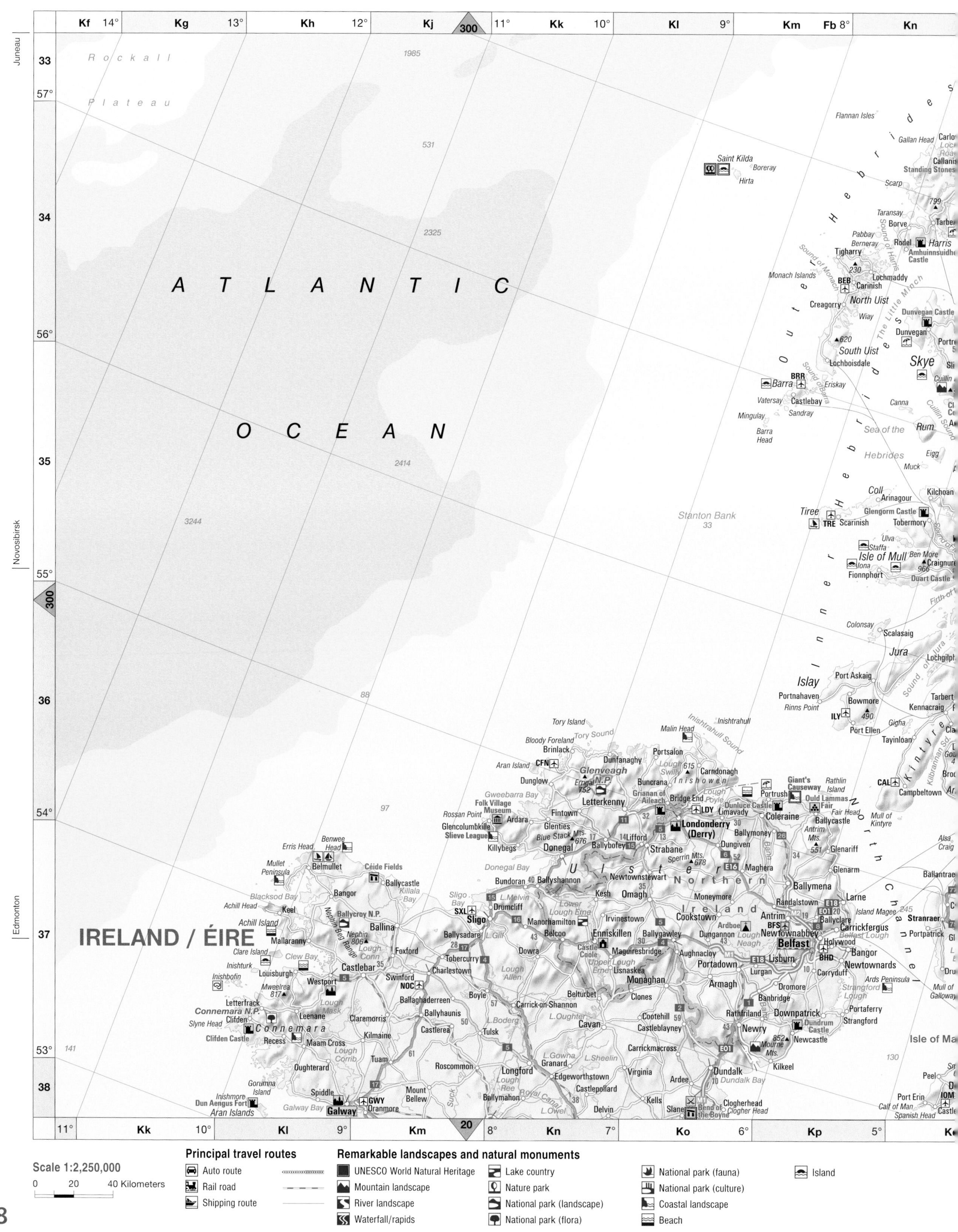

Kf 14° | Kg 13° | Kh 12° | Kj 300 11° | Kk 10° | Kl 9° | Km Fb 8° | Kn

Juneau
Novosibirsk
Edmonton

33 | 57°
34
56°
35
55° | 300
36 | 54°
37
53°
38

Rockall Plateau

A T L A N T I C

O C E A N

IRELAND / ÉIRE

1985
531
2325
2414
3244
88
97
141

Flannan Isles
Gallan Head
Standing Stones
Saint Kilda
Boreray
Hirta
Scarp
Taransay
Tarbert
Pabbay
Berneray
Tigharry
Rodel
Harris
Amhuinnsuidhe Castle
Monach Islands
BEB
Carinish
Lochmaddy
North Uist
Creagorry
Wiay
Dunvegan Castle
Dunvegan
Portree
South Uist
Lochboisdale
Skye
BRR
Barra
Eriskay
Cuillin
Vatersay
Castlebay
Canna
Mingulay
Sandray
Rum
Barra Head
Eigg
Muck
Sea of the
Hebrides
Coll
Arinagour
Kilchoan
Tiree
Glengorm Castle
TRE
Scarinish
Tobermory
Ulva
Staffa
Ben More
Isle of Mull
966
Craignure
Iona
Duart Castle
Fionnphort
Firth of
Colonsay
Scalasaig
Jura
Lochgilph
Islay
Port Askaig
Tarbert
Portnahaven
Bowmore
Kennacraig
Rinns Point
ILY
490
Gigha
Port Ellen
Tayinloan
Stanton Bank
33
Tory Island
Inishtrahull
Bloody Foreland
Tory Sound
Malin Head
Brinlack
Portsalon
Rathlin
Aran Island
CFN
Dunfanaghy
Lough Swilly
Carndonagh
Island
Giant's Causeway
Glenveagh N.P.
615
Inishowen
Ould Lammas Fair
Dunglow
Errigal
752
Buncrana
Portrush
Fair Head
Letterkenny
Grianan of Aileach
Bridge End
Dunluce Castle
Mull of Kintyre
Gweebarra Bay
Lough Foyle
Portstewart
Limavady
Coleraine
Folk Village Museum
32
LDY
Ballycastle
Rossan Point
Fintown
Londonderry (Derry)
Ballymoney
Antrim Mts.
Glencolumbkille
Ardara
Glenties
Strabane
Dungiven
551
Glenariff
Slieve League
676
Ballybofey
Maghera
Killybegs
Donegal
Sperrin Mts.
678
Newtownstewart
E16
Glenarm
Benwee Head
Bundoran
Ballyshannon
Kesh
Omagh
Northern
Ballymena
Erris Head
Killala Bay
Sligo Bay
L. Melvin
Lower Lough Erne
Moneymore
Larne
Mullet Peninsula
Belmullet
Céide Fields
Bangor
Drumcliff
Manorhamilton
Belcoo
Cookstown
Randalstown
E18
Bangor
Blacksod Bay
Ballina
SXL
Sligo
Enniskillen
Ballygawley
Ardboe
E01
Antrim
Island Magee
Achill Head
Keel
Ballycroy N.P.
Ballysadare
L. Gill
Dowra
Irvinestown
Dungannon
Lough Neagh
BFS
Carrickfergus
Achill Island
Nephin Beg Range
Foxford
Tobercurry
Maguiresbridge
Aughnacloy
Portadown
Belfast
Portpatrick
Clare Island
Mallaranny
Nephin
806
Charlestown
Castle Coole
Lisnaskea
Lurgan
BHD
Bangor
Inishturk
Louisburgh
Clew Bay
Westport
Castlebar
Swinford
Monaghan
Dromore
Newtownards
Inishbofin
Mweelrea
817
NOC
Ballaghaderreen
Boyle
Belturbet
Clones
Armagh
Corryduff
Ards Peninsula
Letterfrack
Claremorris
Castlerea
Carrick-on-Shannon
Banbridge
Strangford Lough
Connemara N.P.
Leenane
Ballyhaunis
L. Oughter
Cootehill
Rathfriland
Downpatrick
Clifden
C O N N E M A R A
Maam Cross
Tuam
Roscommon
Cavan
Castleblayney
Newry
Portaferry
Slyne Head
Recess
Lough Corrib
Tulsk
L. Gowna
Carrickmacross
Mourne Mts.
Dundrum Castle
Strangford
Clifden Castle
Oughterard
Maam
Granard
Longford
Virginia
Ardee
Kilkeel
Isle of Ma
Gorumna Island
Spiddle
Mount Bellew
Edgeworthstown
Kells
Newcastle
Peel
Inishmore
GWY
Oranmore
Ballymahon
Castlepollard
Dundalk
Port Erin
Dun Aengus Fort
Galway Bay
Suck
Delvin
Dundalk Bay
Call of Man
Aran Islands
Galway
L. Owel
Clogherhead
Spanish Head
Slane
Bend of the Boyne
Clogher Head

11° | Kk 10° | Kl 9° | Km 20 8° | Kn 7° | Ko 6° | Kp 5°

Scale 1:2,250,000

0   20   40 Kilometers

Principal travel routes

- Auto route
- Rail road
- Shipping route

······· (dotted line)
— · — (dash line)
— (plain line)

Remarkable landscapes and natural monuments

- UNESCO World Natural Heritage
- Mountain landscape
- River landscape
- Waterfall/rapids
- Lake country
- Nature park
- National park (landscape)
- National park (flora)
- National park (fauna)
- National park (culture)
- Coastal landscape
- Beach
- Island

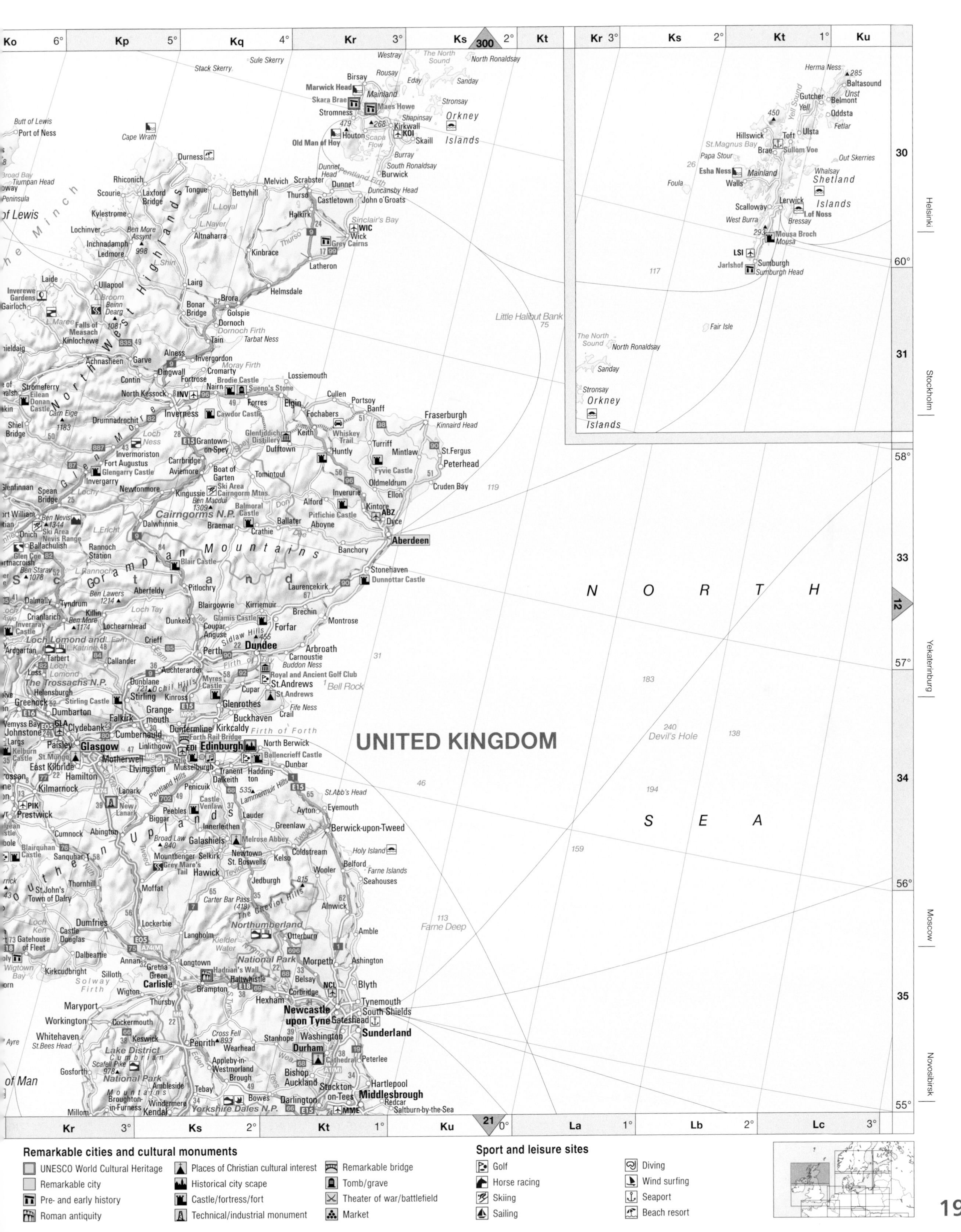

300

Westray
The North Sound
North Ronaldsay
Sule Skerry
Stack Skerry
Birsay
Rousay
Eday
Sanday
Herma Ness
▲285
Baltasound
Unst
Belmont
Marwick Head
Mainland
Stronsay
Orkney
450
Gutcher
Yell
Oddsta
Fetlar
Skara Brae
Maes Howe
Shapinsay
Islands
Ulsta
Stromness
Kirkwall
Hillswick
Toft
Sullom Voe
479
268
KOI
St.Magnus Bay
Brae
Old Man of Hoy
Houton
Skaill
Papa Stour
Out Skerries
Burray
Esha Ness
Mainland
Whalsay
South Ronaldsay
26
Walls
Shetland
Butt of Lewis
Cape Wrath
Durness
Dunnet Head
Scrabster
Burwick
Foula
Islands
Port of Ness
Broad Bay
Melvich
Dunnet
Duncansby Head
Scalloway
Lerwick
Tiumpan Head
Rhiconich
Bettyhill
Thurso
Castletown
John o'Groats
West Burra
Bressay
Peninsula
Scourie
Tongue
L.Loyal
Halkirk
293
L.of Noss
of Lewis
Laxford Bridge
Mousa Broch
Lochinver
Kylestrome
Altnaharra
L.Nayer
24
WIC
Mousa
Inchnadamph
Ben More Assynt
L.Shin
Wick
Jarlshof
LSI
Sumburgh
Ledmore
998
Kinbrace
Grey Cairns
117
Sumburgh Head
Laide
Ullapool
Lairg
Latheron
Inverewe Gardens
17 99
Little Halibut Bank
75
Gairloch
L.Broom
Brora
Helmsdale
The North Sound
North Ronaldsay
L.Maree
Beinn Dearg
Bonar Bridge
Golspie
Falls of Measach
1081
Dornoch
Fair Isle
Kinlochewe
835
49
Shin
Dornoch Firth
Sanday
Achnasheen
Garve
Tain
Tarbat Ness
Stromeferry
Eilean Donan Castle
Contin
Dingwall
Invergordon
Cromarty
Moray Firth
Lossiemouth
Stronsay
Shiel Bridge
Carn Eige
1183
Drumnadrochit
North Kessock
INV
Nairn
Brodie Castle
Sueno's Stone
Elgin
Cullen
Portsoy
Banff
Orkney
Inverness
Cawdor Castle
Forres
Fochabers
Fraserburgh
Islands
Glenfinnan
Spean Bridge
Invermoriston
Loch Ness
E15
Grantown-on-Spey
Keith
Whiskey Trail
Kinnaird Head
Fort Augustus
28
Dufftown
Huntly
Turriff
St.Fergus
Glengarry Castle
Aviemore
Glenfiddich Distillery
Mintlaw
Ben Nevis
Invergarry
Newtonmore
Boat of Garten
Tomintoul
Fyvie Castle
98
Peterhead
1344
Ski Area
Kingussie
56
Oldmeldrum
51
Onich
Nevis Range
Cairngorm Mtns.
Ellon
Cruden Bay
Ballachulish
Ben Macdui
Alford
Inverurie
119
Glen Coe
1309
Balmoral Castle
Pitfichie Castle
Kintore
ABZ
Dalwhinnie
Braemar
Ballater
Aboyne
Dyce
Ben Starav
Blair Castle
Crathie
1078
Rannoch Station
Banchory
Aberdeen
L.Ericht
Dalmally
Tyndrum
L.Rannoch
Aberfeldy
Pitlochry
Stonehaven
Ben Lawers
Kirriemuir
Laurencekirk
90
Dunnottar Castle
Cranlarich
Killin
1214
Loch Tay
Dunkeld
Blairgowrie
Brechin
67
Inveraray Castle
Ben More
1174
Glamis Castle
Montrose
Lochearnhead
Coupar Angus
Forfar
N O R T H
Ardgartan
Loch Lomond and
Earn
Crieff
85
Sidlaw Hills
456
Callander
Perth
22
Dundee
Carnoustie
31
The Trossachs N.P.
Auchterarder
90
Arbroath
Helensburgh
Dunblane
58
Buddon Ness
Greenock
Myres Castle
Cupar
Royal and Ancient Golf Club
Stirling Castle
Stirling
Kinross
St.Andrews
183
Dumbarton
Grangemouth
Glenrothes
St.Andrews
Bell Rock
Clydebank
E15
Buckhaven
Fife Ness
SLA
Falkirk
M90
Crail
Paisley
Cumbernauld
Dunfermline
Kirkcaldy
240
138
Kelburn Castle
Glasgow
Forth Rail Bridge
Firth of Forth
Devil's Hole
St.Mungo
Motherwell
EDI
Edinburgh
North Berwick
UNITED KINGDOM
East Kilbride
Livingston
Musselburgh
Ballencrieff Castle
Hamilton
Tranent
Haddington
Kilmarnock
Lanark
Dalkeith
Dunbar
New Lanark
Penicuik
535
E15
PIK
Peebles
68
St.Abb's Head
Prestwick
Biggar
Castle Venlaw
37
Eyemouth
46
Innerleithen
Lauder
Ayton
Cumnock
Broad Law
840
Galashiels
Greenlaw
Berwick-upon-Tweed
S E A
Abington
Sanquhar
78
Mounthenger
Melrose Abbey
Holy Island
Blairquhan Castle
Selkirk
Newtown St.Boswells
Kelso
194
St.John's Town of Dalry
Hawick
Coldstream
Wooler
159
Moffat
Jedburgh
815
Belford
Farne Islands
Thornhill
65
Seahouses
Dumfries
Lockerbie
Carter Bar Pass
62
113
Castle Douglas
Langholm
(418)
The Cheviot Hills
Alnwick
Farne Deep
Kirkcudbright
Dalbeattie
Northumberland
56°
Gatehouse of Fleet
Kielder Water
Otterburn
Amble
Wigtown Bay
National Park
696
Annan
Longtown
Morpeth
Ashington
Gretna Green
Hadrian's Wall
Belsay
1
Silloth
Carlisle
Brampton
Haltwhistle
Corbridge
Blyth
Maryport
Wigton
Thursby
Hexham
NCL
Workington
Cockermouth
Cross Fell
Stanhope
Washington
Newcastle upon Tyne
Tynemouth
South Shields
Whitehaven
Keswick
893
Wearhead
Gateshead
Sunderland
St.Bees Head
Penrith
38
Durham
Lake District
Scafell Pike
Appleby-in-Westmorland
Cathedral
Peterlee
of Man
978
Gosforth
Brough
Bishop Auckland
Stockton-on-Tees
Hartlepool
National Park
Tebay
Bowes
Darlington
Middlesbrough
Ayre
Broughton-in-Furness
Ambleside
34
Redcar
Millom
Kendal
Windermere
Yorkshire Dales N.P.
MME
Saltburn-by-the-Sea

Remarkable cities and cultural monuments

- UNESCO World Cultural Heritage
- Remarkable city
- Pre- and early history
- Roman antiquity
- Places of Christian cultural interest
- Historical city scape
- Castle/fortress/fort
- Technical/industrial monument
- Remarkable bridge
- Tomb/grave
- Theater of war/battlefield
- Market

Sport and leisure sites

- Golf
- Horse racing
- Skiing
- Sailing
- Diving
- Wind surfing
- Seaport
- Beach resort

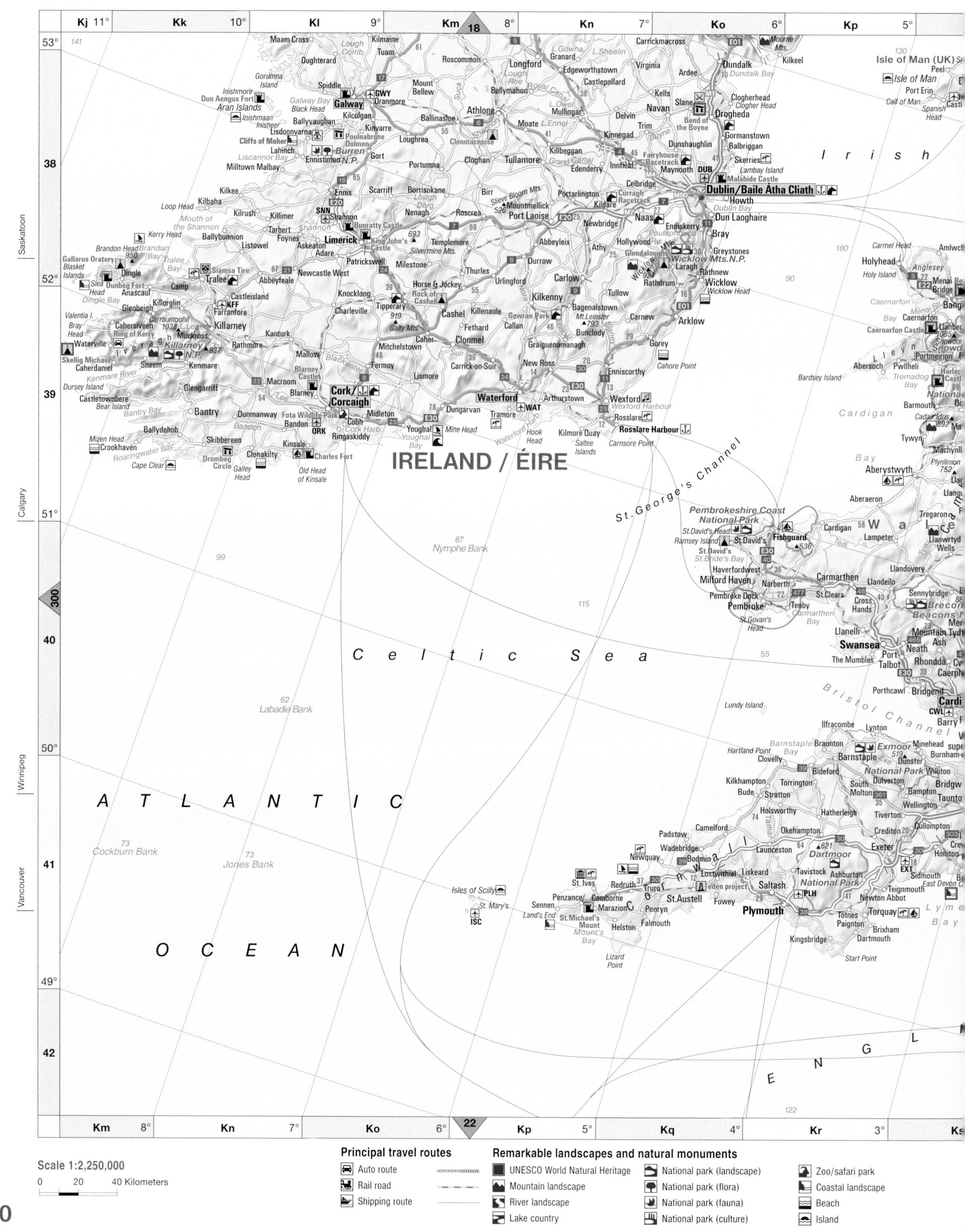

IRELAND / ÉIRE

ATLANTIC

OCEAN

Celtic Sea

St. George's Channel

Bristol Channel

Scale 1:2,250,000

0   20   40 Kilometers

Principal travel routes

🚗 Auto route
🚆 Rail road
🚢 Shipping route

Remarkable landscapes and natural monuments

■ UNESCO World Natural Heritage
▲ Mountain landscape
River landscape
Lake country

National park (landscape)
National park (flora)
National park (fauna)
National park (culture)

Zoo/safari park
Coastal landscape
Beach
Island

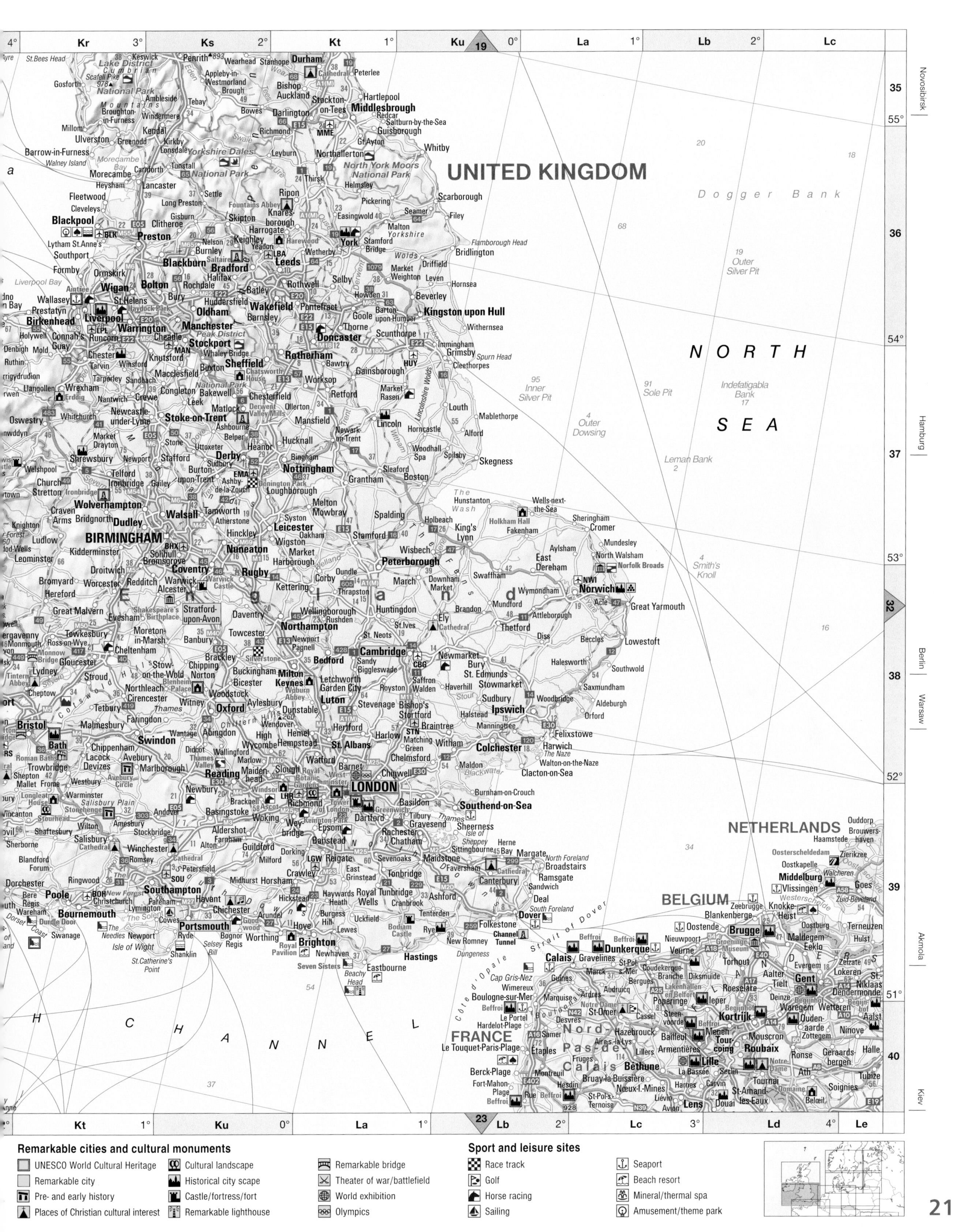

Remarkable cities and cultural monuments
- UNESCO World Cultural Heritage
- Remarkable city
- Pre- and early history
- Places of Christian cultural interest
- Cultural landscape
- Historical city scape
- Castle/fortress/fort
- Remarkable lighthouse
- Remarkable bridge
- Theater of war/battlefield
- World exhibition
- Olympics

Sport and leisure sites
- Race track
- Golf
- Horse racing
- Sailing
- Seaport
- Beach resort
- Mineral/thermal spa
- Amusement/theme park

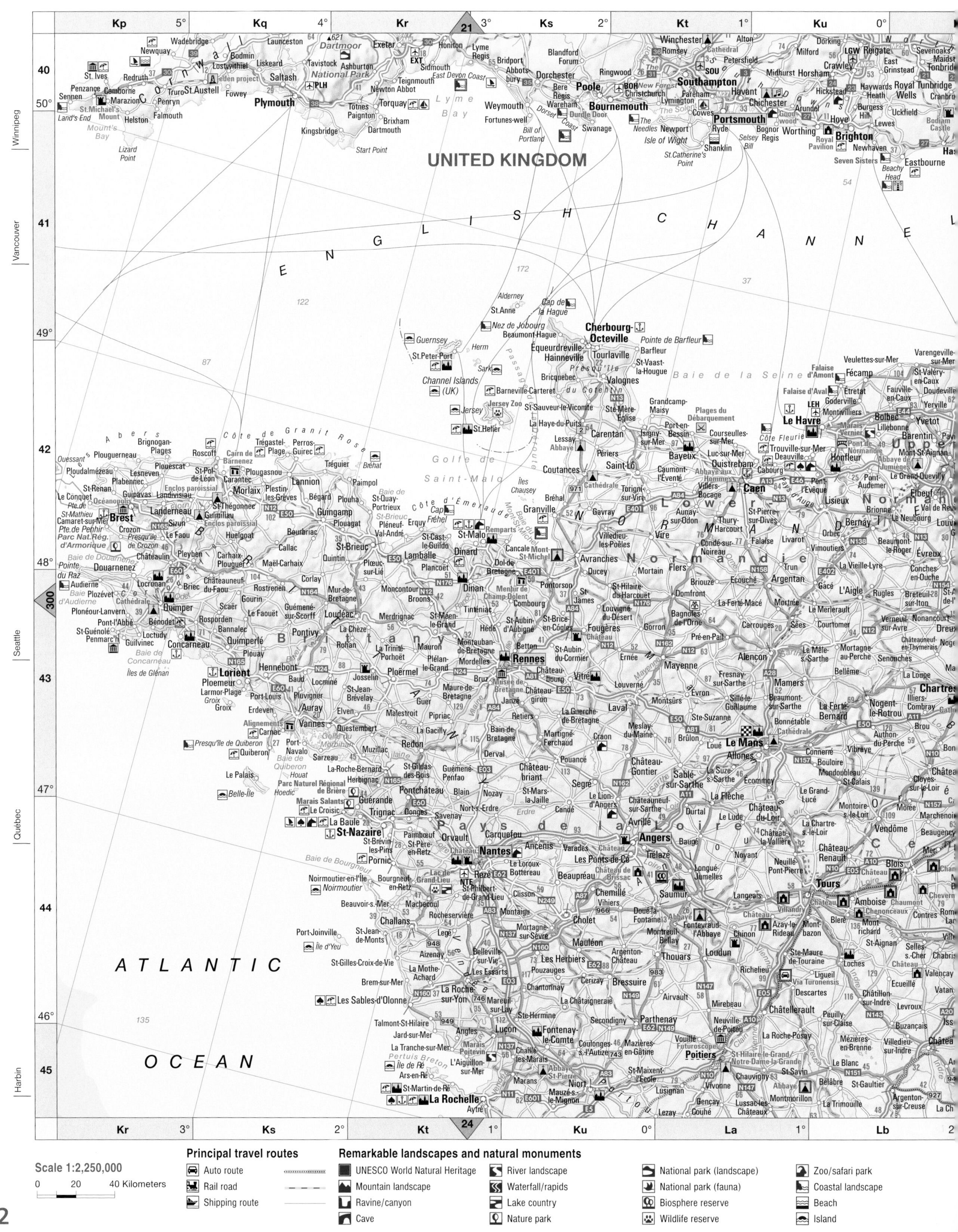

Scale 1:2,250,000

0   20   40 Kilometers

Principal travel routes
- Auto route
- Rail road
- Shipping route

Remarkable landscapes and natural monuments
- UNESCO World Natural Heritage
- Mountain landscape
- Ravine/canyon
- Cave
- River landscape
- Waterfall/rapids
- Lake country
- Nature park
- National park (landscape)
- National park (fauna)
- Biosphere reserve
- Wildlife reserve
- Zoo/safari park
- Coastal landscape
- Beach
- Island

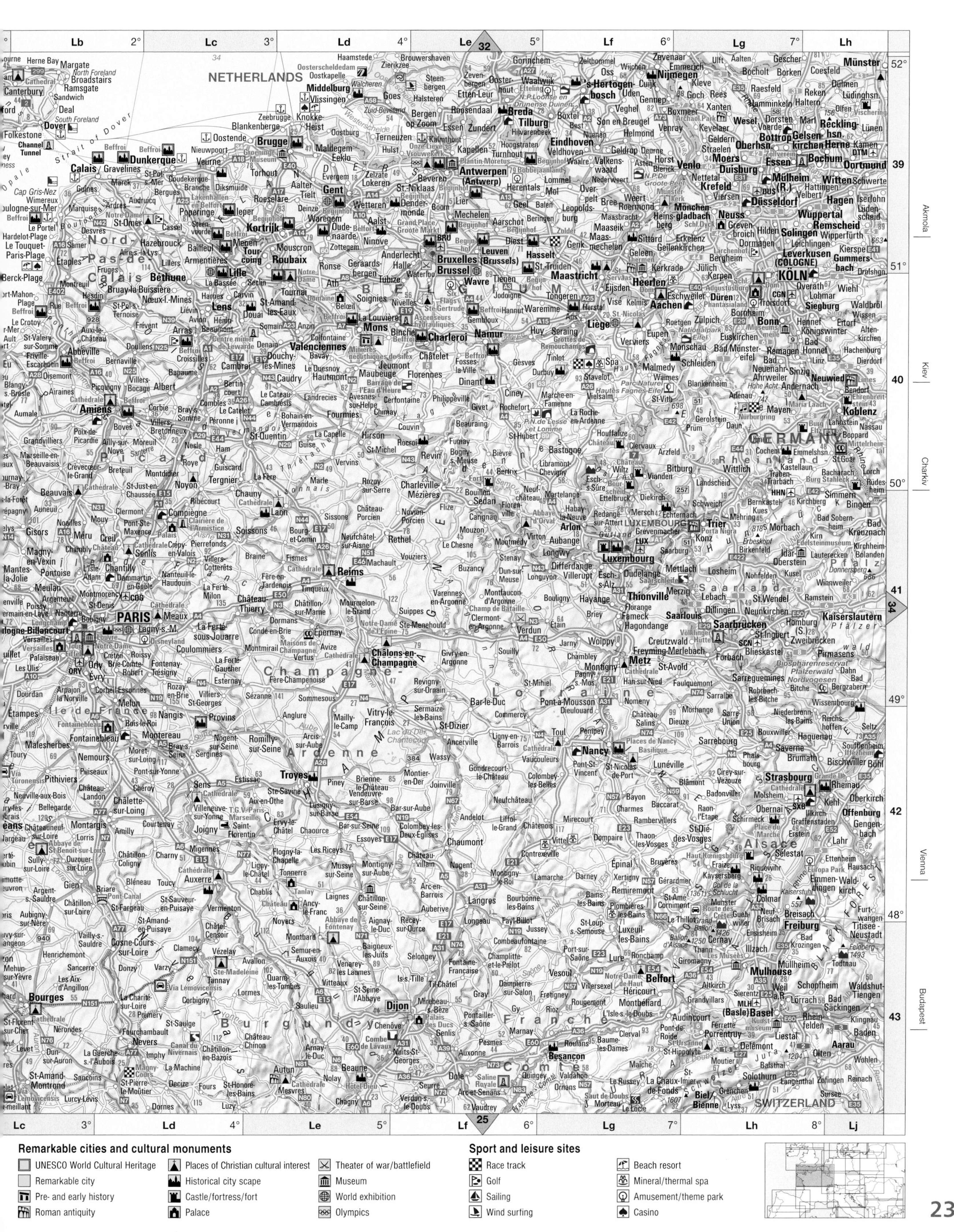

Lb 2° Lc 3° Ld 4° Le 32 5° Lf 6° Lg 7° Lh
52° 39 40 41 42 43 51° 50° 49° 48°
Lc 3° Ld 4° Le 5° Lf 25 6° Lg 7° Lh 8° Lj
Akmola
Kiev
Charkiv
Vienna
Budapest
NETHERLANDS
BELGIUM
LUXEMBOURG
GERMANY
SWITZERLAND
Champagne
Lorraine
Alsace
Bourgogne
Franche-Comté
Ardenne
Picardie
Ile de France
Nord-Pas-de-Calais
Strait of Dover
Canterbury
Dover
Calais
Dunkerque
Brugge
Gent
Antwerpen (Antwerp)
Bruxelles (Brussels)
Brussel
Lille
Amiens
PARIS
Reims
Châlons-en-Champagne
Troyes
Dijon
Besançon
Nancy
Metz
Strasbourg
Luxembourg
Liège
Maastricht
Aachen
KÖLN (COLOGNE)
Düsseldorf
Essen
Dortmund
Münster
Koblenz
Trier
Saarbrücken
Kaiserslautern
Freiburg
Mulhouse
Basel
Belfort
Bourges
Auxerre
Eindhoven
Nijmegen
's-Hertogen-bosch
Middelburg
Charleroi
Namur
Mons
Valenciennes
Verdun
Épinal
Colmar
Remarkable cities and cultural monuments
UNESCO World Cultural Heritage
Remarkable city
Pre- and early history
Roman antiquity
Places of Christian cultural interest
Historical city scape
Castle/fortress/fort
Palace
Theater of war/battlefield
Museum
World exhibition
Olympics
Sport and leisure sites
Race track
Golf
Sailing
Wind surfing
Beach resort
Mineral/thermal spa
Amusement/theme park
Casino

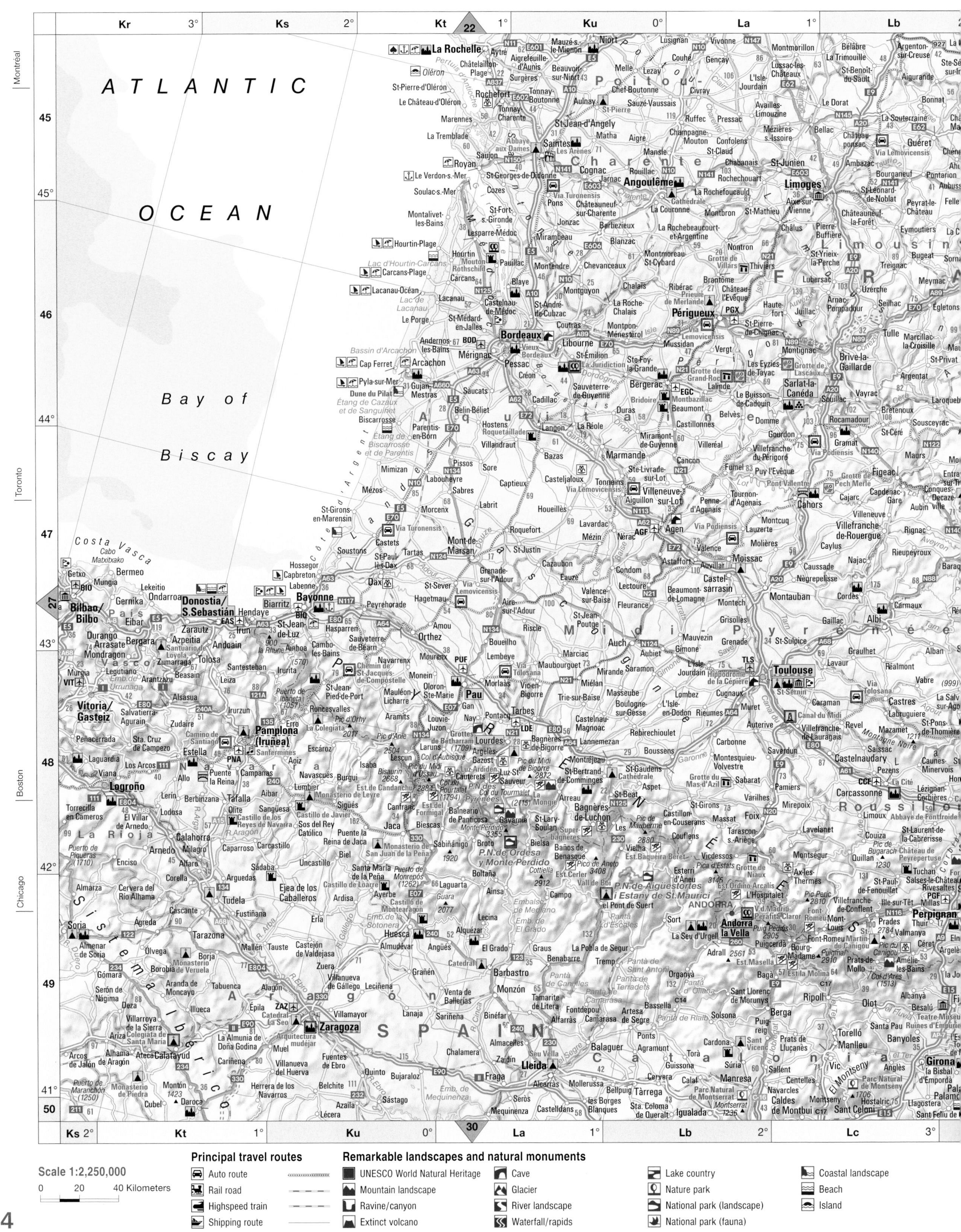

ATLANTIC

OCEAN

Bay of

Biscay

Costa Vasca

Principal travel routes

- 🚗 Auto route
- 🚂 Rail road
- 🚄 Highspeed train
- ⚓ Shipping route

Remarkable landscapes and natural monuments

- ■ UNESCO World Natural Heritage
- ▲ Mountain landscape
- Ravine/canyon
- Extinct volcano
- Cave
- Glacier
- River landscape
- Waterfall/rapids
- Lake country
- Nature park
- National park (landscape)
- National park (fauna)
- Coastal landscape
- Beach
- Island

Scale 1:2,250,000

0   20   40 Kilometers

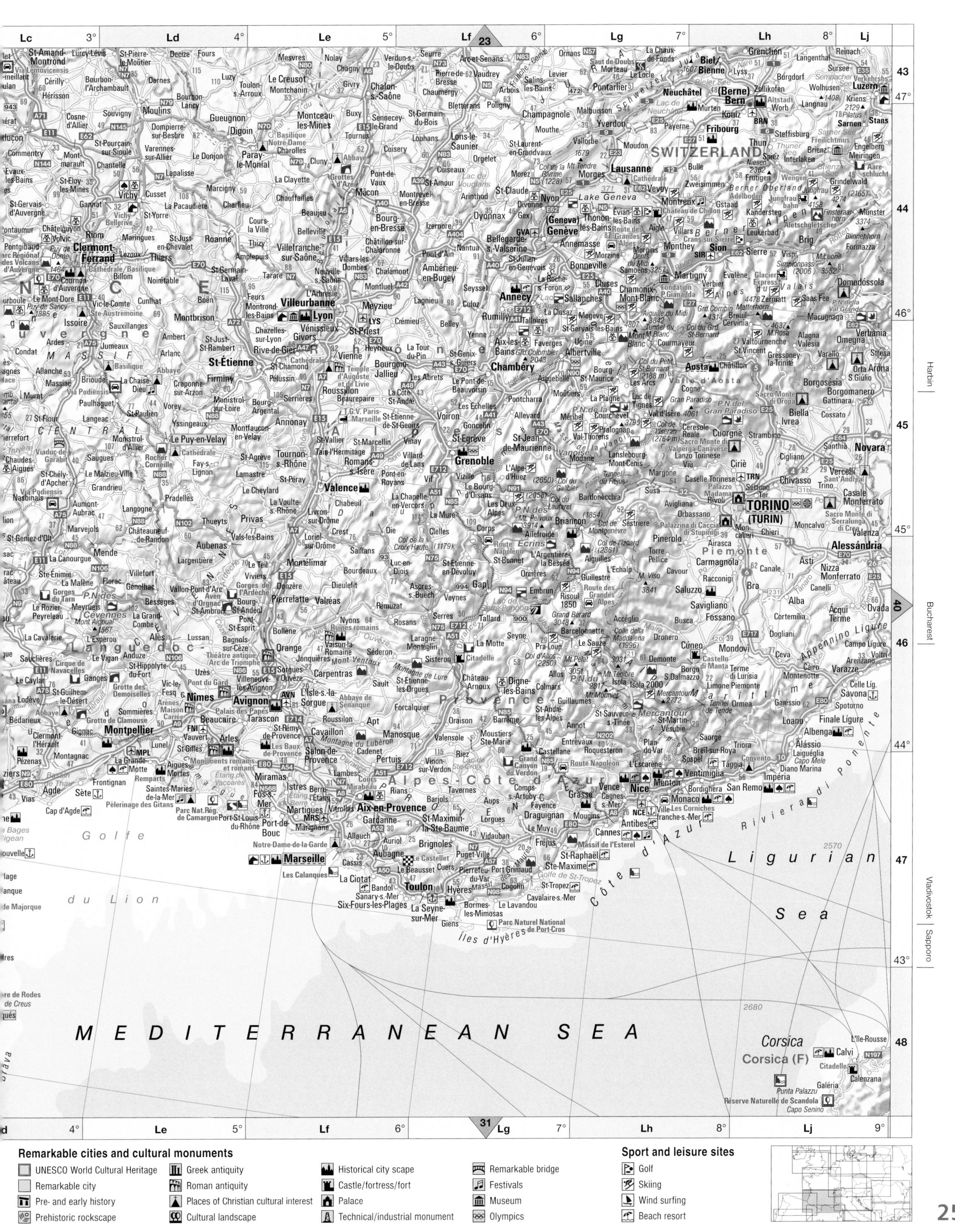

Remarkable cities and cultural monuments

- UNESCO World Cultural Heritage
- Remarkable city
- Pre- and early history
- Prehistoric rockscape
- Greek antiquity
- Roman antiquity
- Places of Christian cultural interest
- Cultural landscape
- Historical city scape
- Castle/fortress/fort
- Palace
- Technical/industrial monument
- Remarkable bridge
- Festivals
- Museum
- Olympics

Sport and leisure sites

- Golf
- Skiing
- Wind surfing
- Beach resort

25

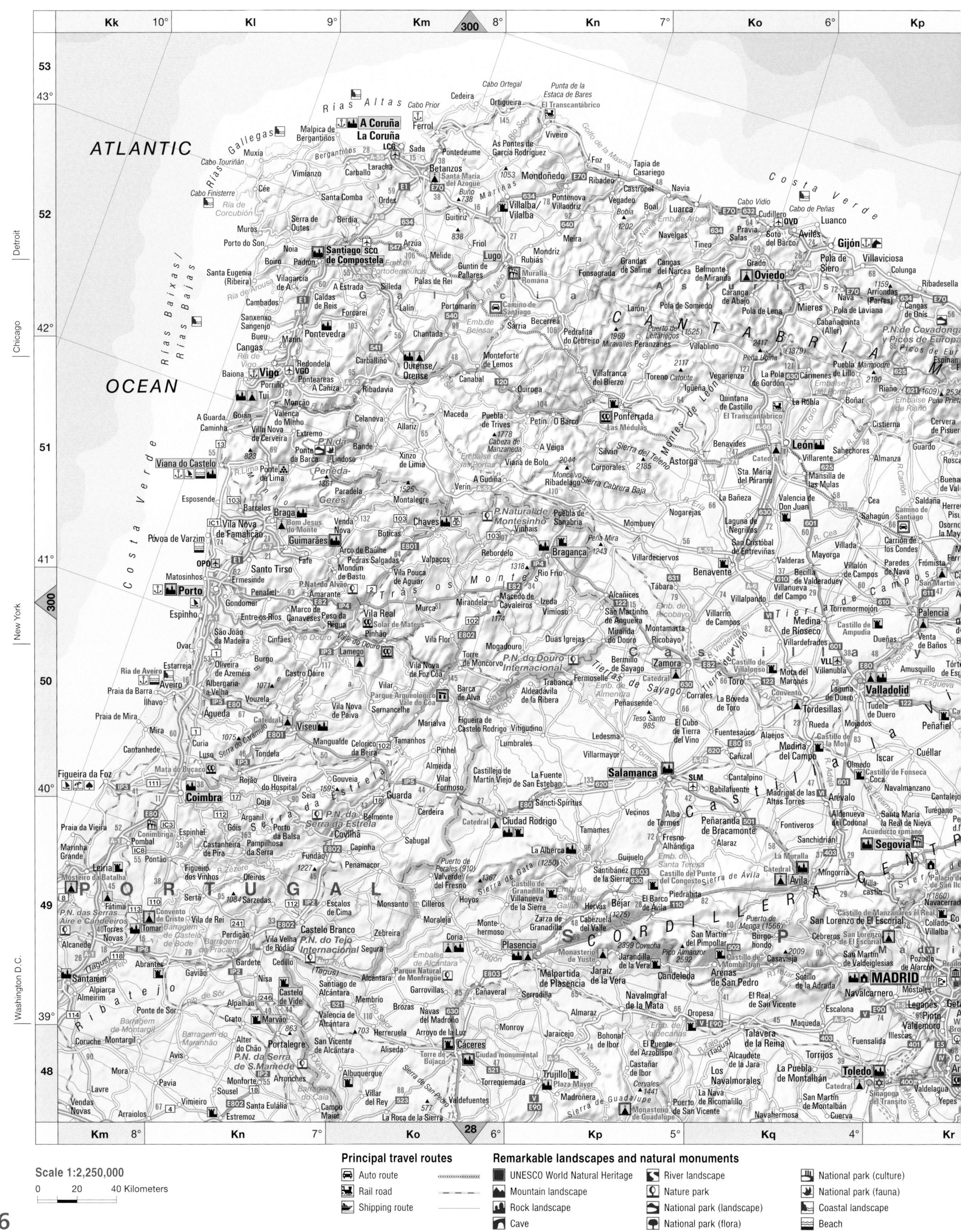

Scale 1:2,250,000

0   20   40 Kilometers

Principal travel routes

🚌 Auto route

🚂 Rail road

⚓ Shipping route

Remarkable landscapes and natural monuments

▣ UNESCO World Natural Heritage

⛰ Mountain landscape

▣ Rock landscape

🦇 Cave

🏞 River landscape

🌿 Nature park

▣ National park (landscape)

🌳 National park (flora)

🏛 National park (culture)

🦅 National park (fauna)

🏖 Coastal landscape

≋ Beach

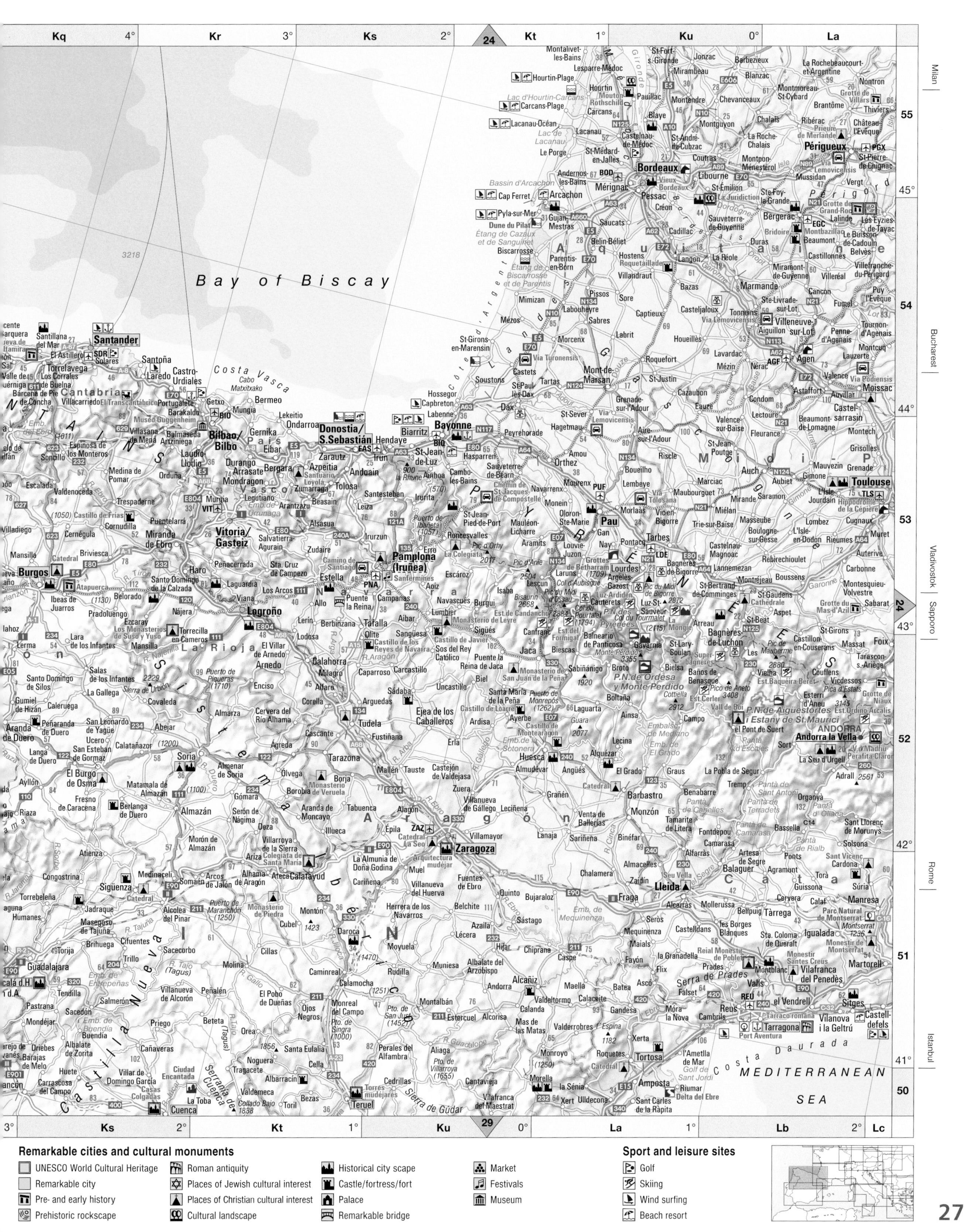

Bay of Biscay

MEDITERRANEAN SEA

Remarkable cities and cultural monuments

- ☐ UNESCO World Cultural Heritage
- ☐ Remarkable city
- 🏛 Pre- and early history
- 🗿 Prehistoric rockscape
- 🏛 Roman antiquity
- ✡ Places of Jewish cultural interest
- ✡ Places of Christian cultural interest
- ♋ Cultural landscape
- 🏭 Historical city scape
- 🏰 Castle/fortress/fort
- 🏛 Palace
- 🌉 Remarkable bridge
- ❀ Market
- 🎭 Festivals
- 🏛 Museum

Sport and leisure sites

- ⛳ Golf
- ⛷ Skiing
- 🏄 Wind surfing
- 🏖 Beach resort

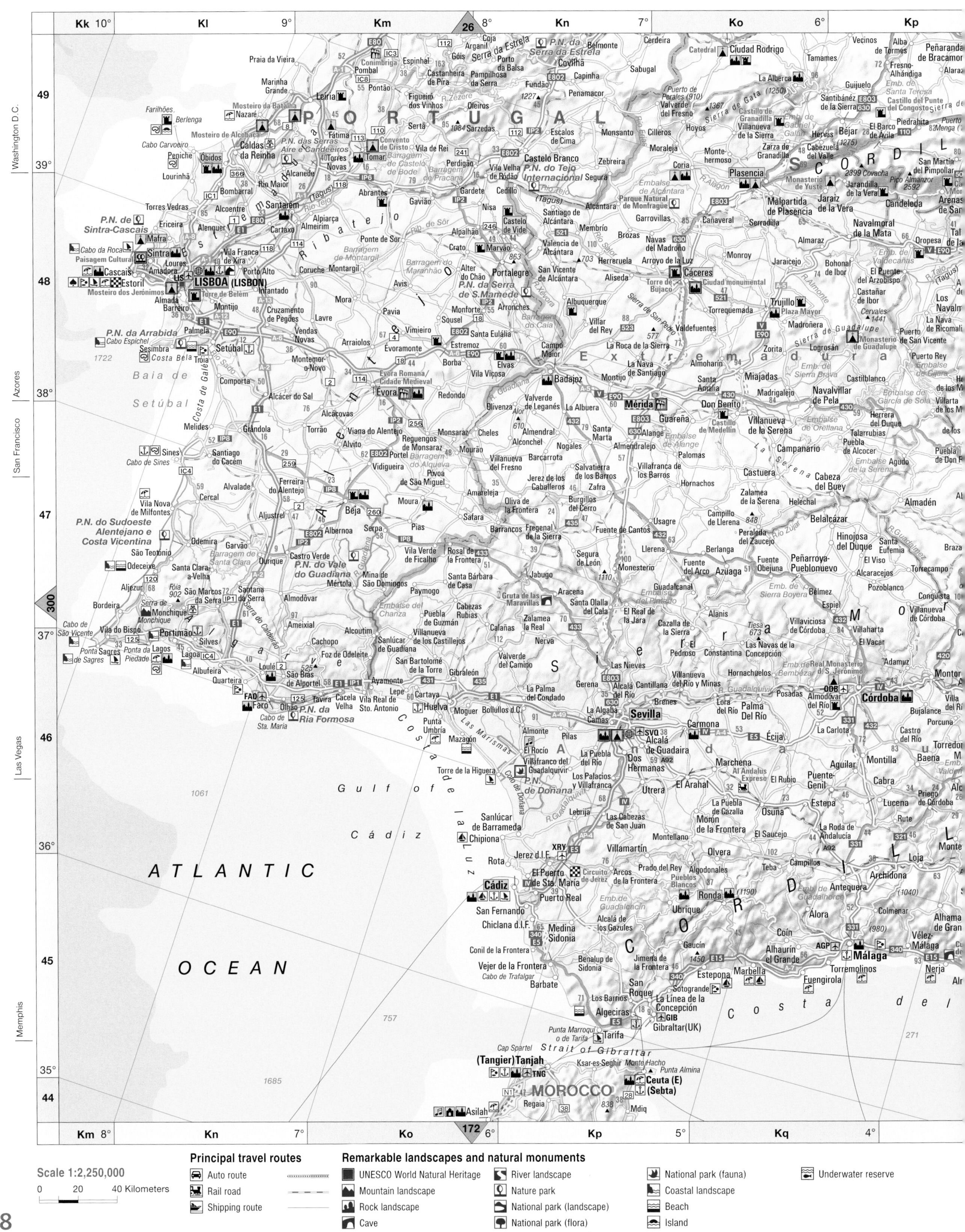

Scale 1:2,250,000

0   20   40 Kilometers

Principal travel routes
- Auto route
- Rail road
- Shipping route

Remarkable landscapes and natural monuments
- UNESCO World Natural Heritage
- Mountain landscape
- Rock landscape
- Cave
- River landscape
- Nature park
- National park (landscape)
- National park (flora)
- National park (fauna)
- Coastal landscape
- Beach
- Island
- Underwater reserve

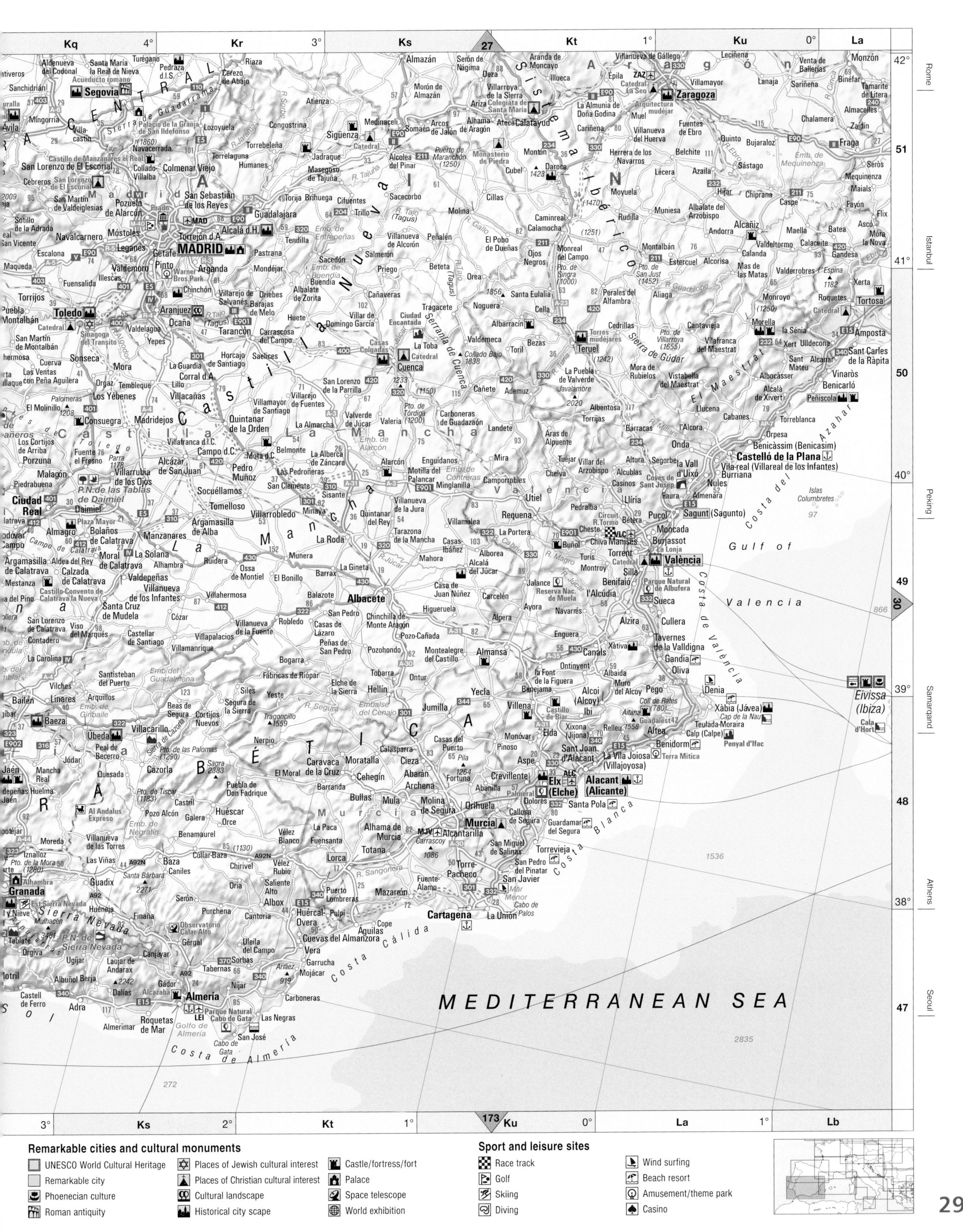

Kq
Kr
Ks
Kt
Ku
La
Lb
27
30
173
Rome
Istanbul
Peking
Samarqand
Athens
Seoul
42°
41°
40°
39°
38°
51
50
49
48
47
Segovia
Toledo
MADRID
Guadalajara
Alcalá d.H.
Aranjuez
Cuenca
Teruel
Zaragoza
Calatayud
Ciudad Real
Albacete
València
Castelló de la Plana
Vila-real (Villareal de los Infantes)
Sagunt (Sagunto)
Alacant (Alicante)
Elx (Elche)
Murcia
Cartagena
Lorca
Granada
Almería
Jaén
Úbeda
Baeza
Tortosa
Peñíscola
Eivissa (Ibiza)
Sistema Ibérico
Castilla La Mancha
Castilla-La Nueva
Aragón
Serranía de Cuenca
El Maestrat
Gulf of Valencia
Costa del Azahar
Costa de València
Costa Blanca
Costa Cálida
Costa de Almería
Sierra Nevada
MEDITERRANEAN SEA
Remarkable cities and cultural monuments
UNESCO World Cultural Heritage
Remarkable city
Phoenecian culture
Roman antiquity
Places of Jewish cultural interest
Places of Christian cultural interest
Cultural landscape
Historical city scape
Castle/fortress/fort
Palace
Space telescope
World exhibition
Sport and leisure sites
Race track
Golf
Skiing
Diving
Wind surfing
Beach resort
Amusement/theme park
Casino

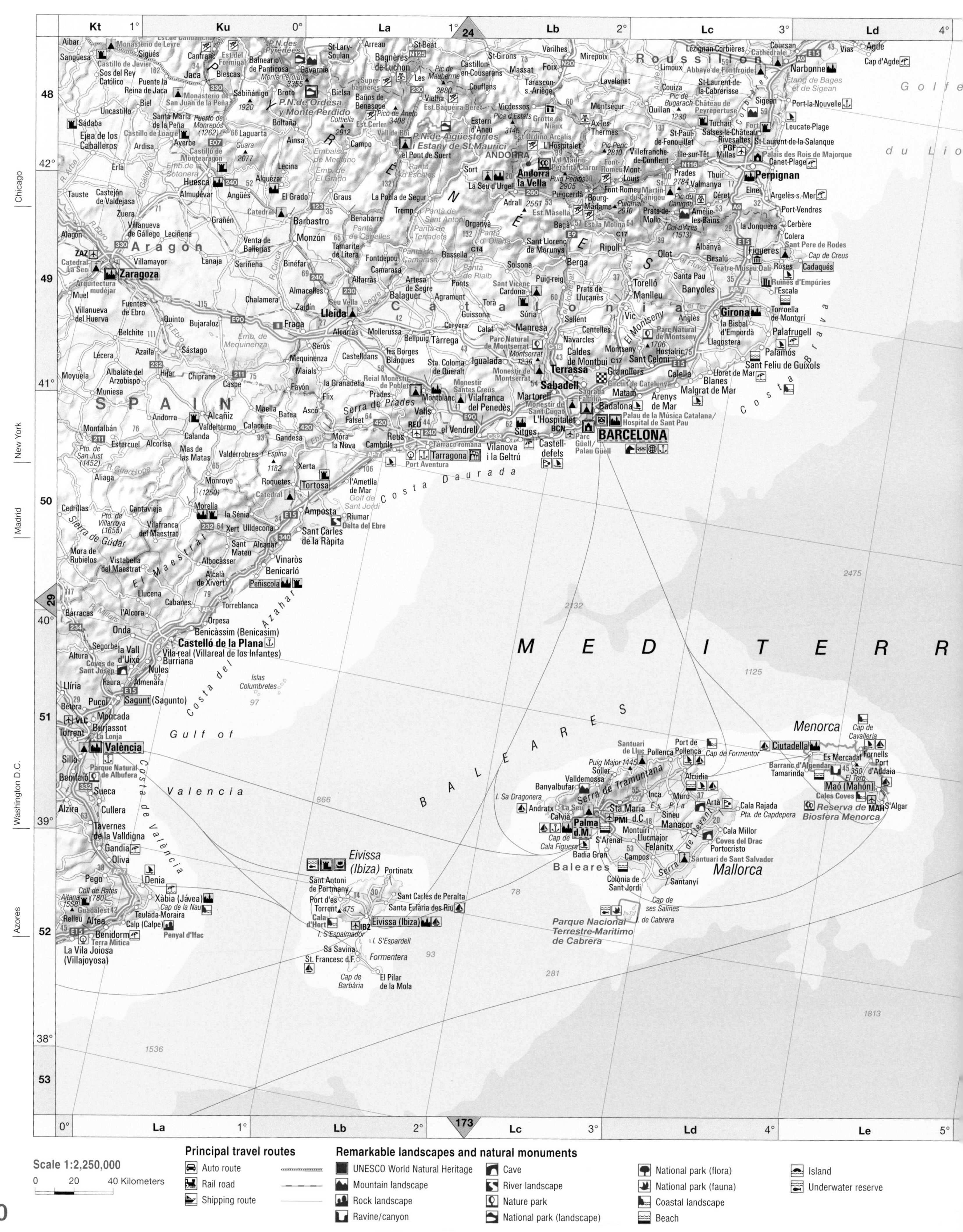

Scale 1:2,250,000

0   20   40 Kilometers

Principal travel routes

- Auto route
- Rail road
- Shipping route
- Gavarnie

Remarkable landscapes and natural monuments

- UNESCO World Natural Heritage
- Mountain landscape
- Rock landscape
- Ravine/canyon
- Cave
- River landscape
- Nature park
- National park (landscape)
- National park (flora)
- National park (fauna)
- Coastal landscape
- Beach
- Island
- Underwater reserve

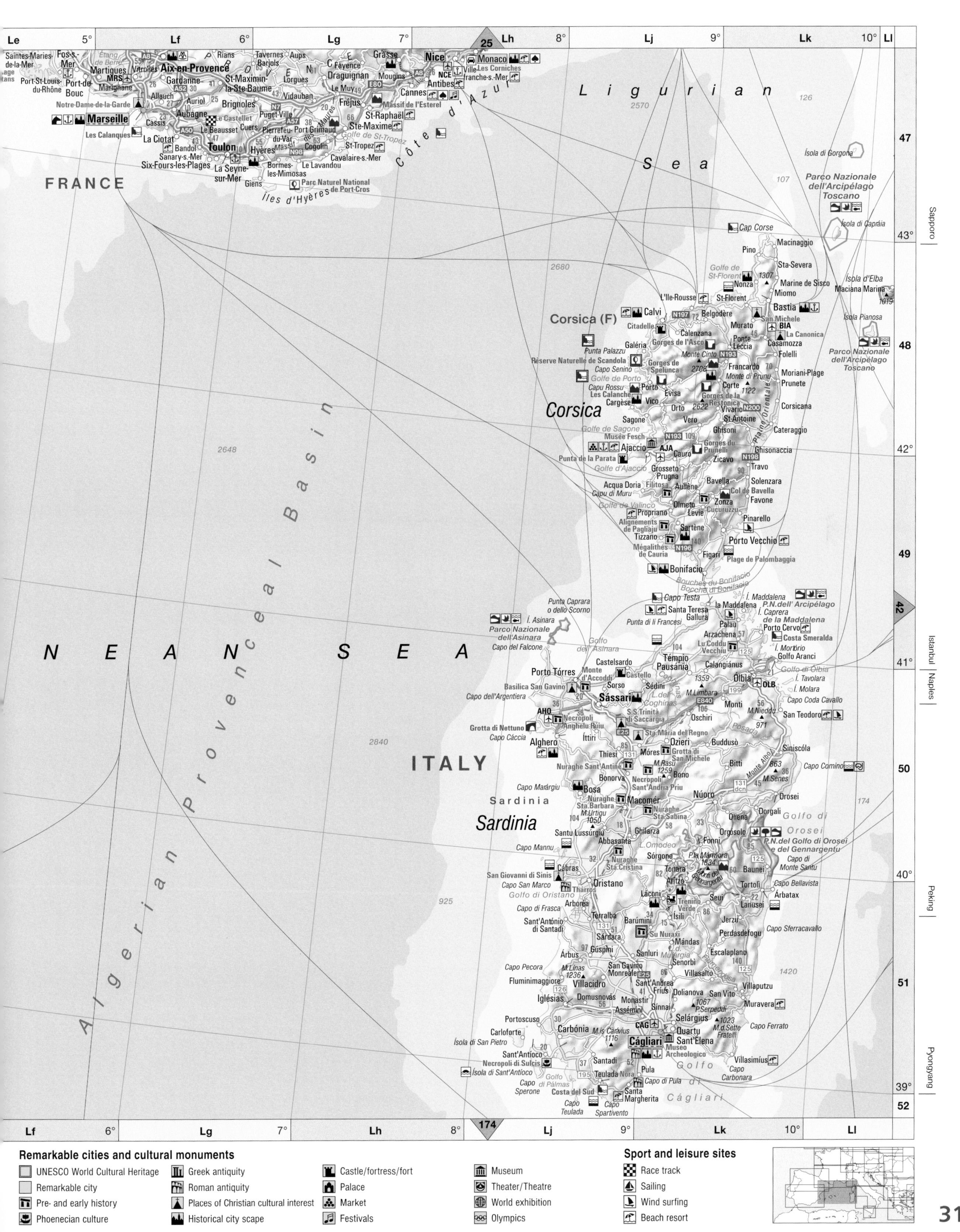

Map labels

Top border (longitude markers): Le 5° Lf 6° Lg 7° 25 Lh 8° Lj 9° Lk 10° Ll

Right border: 47 43° 48 42° 49 42 41° 50 40° 51 39° 52

Right margin labels: Sapporo | Istanbul | Naples | Pekíng | Pyongyang

Bottom border (longitude markers): Lf 6° Lg 7° Lh 8° 174 Lj 9° Lk 10° Ll

France / Côte d'Azur region

Saintes-Maries-de-la-Mer, Étang de Berre, Foss-s-Mer, Port-St-Louis-du-Rhône, Port-de-Bouc, Martigues, Vitrolles, Rians, Tavernes, Aups, Barjols, Lorgues, Fayence, Grasse, Nice, Monaco, Aix-en-Provence, Gardanne, St-Maximin-la-Ste-Baume, Vidauban, Draguignan, Mougins, Ville-franche-sur-Mer, Les Corniches, Antibes, Cannes, Allauch, Auriol, Brignoles, Le Muy, Fréjus, St-Raphaël, Massif de l'Esterel, Aubagne, Le Castellet, Pierrefeu-du-Var, Port Grimaud, Ste-Maxime, Marseille, Cassis, Cuers, Cogolin, St-Tropez, Golfe de St-Tropez, Les Calanques, La Ciotat, Bandol, Toulon, Hyères, Puget-Ville, Cavalaire-s-Mer, Notre-Dame-de-la-Garde, Sanary-s-Mer, Six-Fours-les-Plages, La Seyne-sur-Mer, Bormes-les-Mimosas, Le Lavandou, Giens, Îles d'Hyères, Parc Naturel National de Port-Cros

FRANCE

Côte d'Azur

Corsica (F)

Cap Corse, Macinaggio, Pino, Sta-Severa, Marine de Sisco, Miomo, Nonza, Golfe de St-Florent, L'Île-Rousse, St-Florent, Belgodère, Bastia, BIA, Calvi, Citadelle, Calenzana, San Michele, Murato, La Canonica, Casamozza, Punta Palazzu, Galéria, Gorges de l'Asco, Ponte-Leccia, Folelli, Réserve Naturelle de Scandola, Capo Senino, Gorges de Spelunca, Monte Cinto, Francardo, Moriani-Plage, Capu Rossu, Porto, Evisa, Monte di Prunu, Prunete, Les Calanche, Golfe de Porto, Vico, Orto, Gorges de la Restonica, Vivario, Corsicana, Cargèse, Sagone, Musée Fesch, Ghisoni, Cateraggio, Vero, St-Antoine, Musée Fesch, Ajaccio, AJA, Cauro, Gorges du Prunelli, Ghisonaccia, Punta de la Parata, Grosseto, Prugna, Zicavo, Travo, Golfe d'Ajaccio, Acqua Doria, Filitosa, Aullène, Solenzara, Capu di Muru, Bavella, Col de Bavella, Favone, Olmeto, Levie, Cucuruzzu, Zonza, Proprieno, Alignements de Pagliaju, Sartène, Pinarello, Tizzano, Mégalithes de Cauria, Porto Vecchio, Figari, Plage de Palombaggia, Bonifacio, Bouches de Bonifacio, Bocche di Bonifacio

Corsica

Sardinia (Italy)

Punta Caprara o dello Scorno, Î. Maddalena, P.N. dell'Arcipélago, Capo Testa, Santa Teresa Gallura, la Maddalena, Î. Caprera, de la Maddalena, Î. Asinara, Punta di li Francesi, Palau, Porto Cervo, Costa Smeralda, Parco Nazionale dell'Asinara, Capo del Falcone, Golfo dell'Asinara, Lu Coddu Vecchiu, Î. Mortorio, Golfo Aranci, Castelsardo, Monte d'Accodu, Témpio Pausánia, Calangiánus, Olbia, OLB, Golfo di Ólbia, Porto-Tórres, Sorso, Castello, Sédini, M.Limbara, Monti, Î. Tavolara, Capo Coda Cavallo, Basilica San Gavino, L.del Coghinas, Î. Molara, Sássari, S.S.Trinita di Saccargia, Oschiri, M.Nieddo, San Teodoro, AHQ, Necropoli Anghelu Ruju, Sta.María del Regno, Ozieri, Grotta di San Michele, Buddusò, Siniscóla, Grotta di Nettuno, Capo Cáccia, Alghero, Íttiri, Móres, M.Rasu, Bono, Bitti, Capo Comino, Thiesi, Nuraghe Sant'Antine, Necropoli Sant'Andría Priu, M.Senes, Bonorva, Núoro, Orosei, Capo Marárgiu, Bosa, Macomér, Oliena, Dorgali, Golfo di Orosei, Nuraghe Sta.Barbara, M.Urtigu, Nuraghe Sta.Sabina, Orgosolo, Ghilarza, Fonni, P.N.del Golfo di Orosei e del Gennargentu, Santu Lussúrgiu, Abbasanta, L.Omodeo, Pta.Marmora, Capo di Monte Santu, San Giovanni di Sinis, Cábras, Nuraghe Sta.Cristina, Sórgono, Tonara, Baunei, Oristano, Thárros, Aritzo, Capo Bellavista, Capo San Marco, Arborea, Láconi, Seui, Tortolì, Capo di Frasca, Terralba, Barúmini, Jerzu, Árbatax, Sant'António di Santadi, Su Nuraxi, Ísili, Lanusei, Sárdara, Mándas, Perdasdefogu, Capo Sferracavallo, Arbus, Gúspini, Sanluri, Senorbì, Villasalto, M.Linas, San Gavino Monreale, Escalaplano, Capo Pecora, Villacidro, Sant'Andrea Frius, Villaputzu, Fluminimaggiore, Iglésias, Domusnóvas, Monastir, Sinnai, Dolianova, San Vito, Muravera, Portoscuso, Assémini, P.Serpeddi, Carbónia, M.Is Cardius, Selárgius, M.d.Sette Fratelli, Capo Ferrato, Carloforte, Quartu, Ísola di San Pietro, CAG, Cágliari, Museo Archeologico, Sant'Élena, Villasimíus, Sant'Antíoco, Necrópoli di Sulcis, Santadi, Quartu, Ísola di Sant'Antíoco, Pula, Golfo di, Capo di Pula, Cágliari, Capo Spartivento, Teulada Nora, Santa Margherita, Costa del Súd, Capo Teulada, Capo Sperone, Golfo di Pálmas

ITALY

Sardinia

Seas

Ligurian Sea, Parco Nazionale dell'Arcipélago Toscano, Ísola di Gorgona, Ísola di Capráia, Ísola d'Elba, Maciana Marina, Ísola Pianosa, Algerian-Provençal Basin, MEDITERRANEAN SEA

Legend

Remarkable cities and cultural monuments

- ☐ UNESCO World Cultural Heritage
- ☐ Remarkable city
- ☐ Pre- and early history
- ☐ Phoenecian culture
- ☐ Greek antiquity
- ☐ Roman antiquity
- ☐ Places of Christian cultural interest
- ☐ Historical city scape
- ☐ Castle/fortress/fort
- ☐ Palace
- ☐ Market
- ☐ Festivals
- ☐ Museum
- ☐ Theater/Theatre
- ☐ World exhibition
- ☐ Olympics

Sport and leisure sites

- ☐ Race track
- ☐ Sailing
- ☐ Wind surfing
- ☐ Beach resort

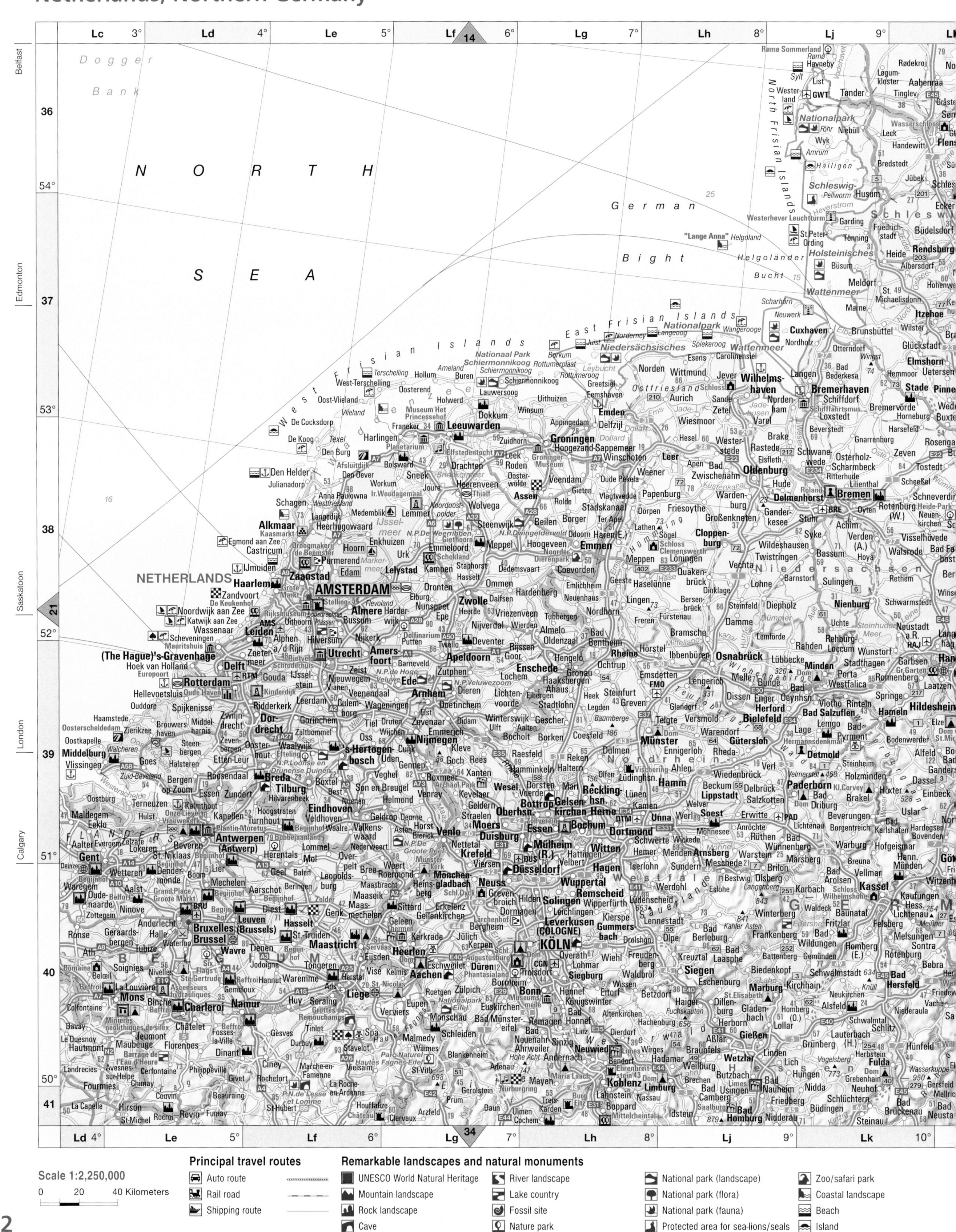

Scale 1:2,250,000

0   20   40 Kilometers

Principal travel routes

- 🚗 Auto route
- 🚂 Rail road
- ⋯⋯⋯ Shipping route

Remarkable landscapes and natural monuments

- ■ UNESCO World Natural Heritage
- ▲ Mountain landscape
- ▦ Rock landscape
- ⬤ Cave
- ▣ River landscape
- ▣ Lake country
- ◉ Fossil site
- ▣ Nature park
- ▣ National park (landscape)
- ▣ National park (flora)
- ▣ National park (fauna)
- ▣ Protected area for sea-lions/seals
- ▣ Zoo/safari park
- ▣ Coastal landscape
- ▦ Beach
- ▣ Island

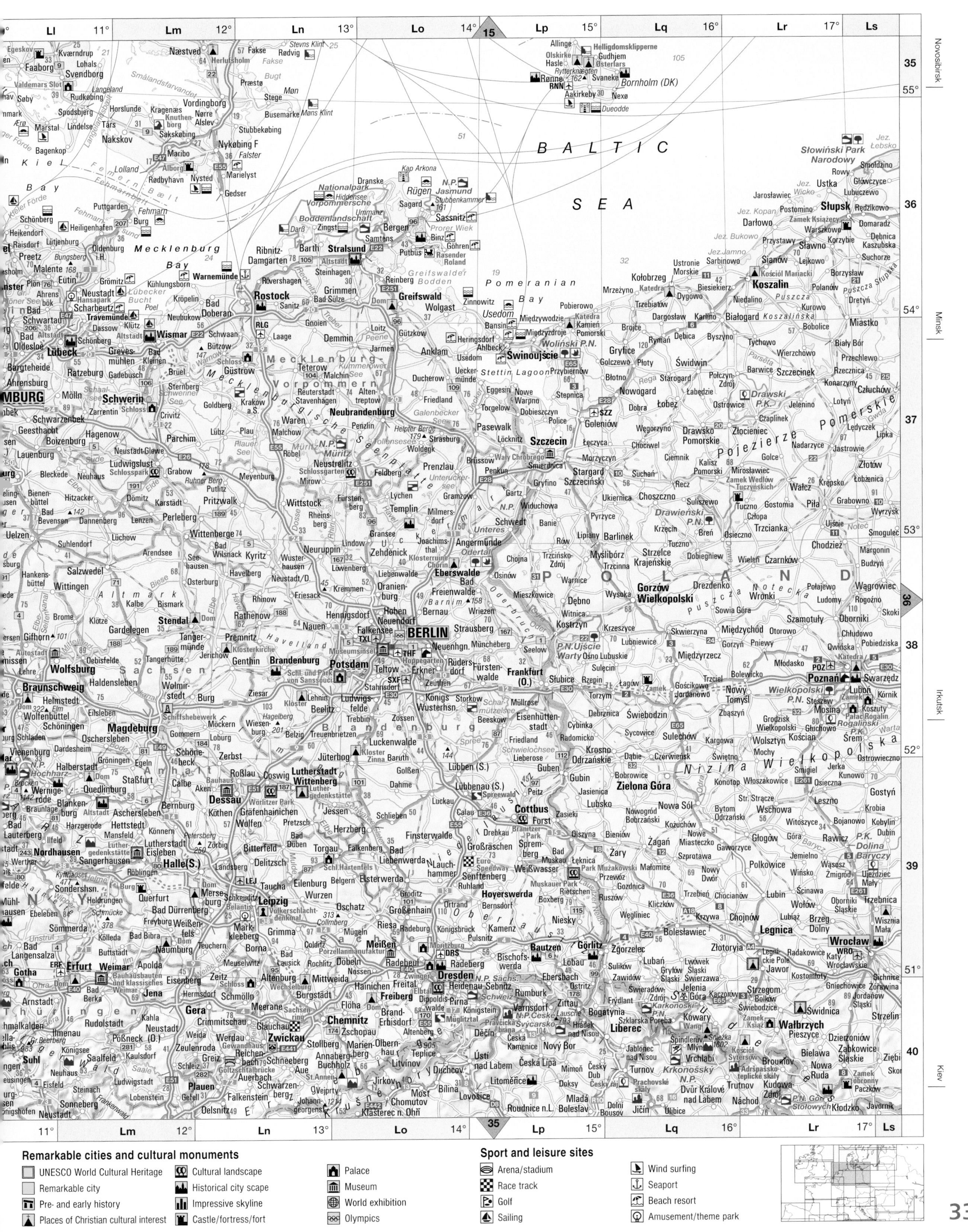

Remarkable cities and cultural monuments

- UNESCO World Cultural Heritage
- Remarkable city
- Pre- and early history
- Places of Christian cultural interest
- Cultural landscape
- Historical city scape
- Impressive skyline
- Castle/fortress/fort
- Palace
- Museum
- World exhibition
- Olympics

Sport and leisure sites

- Arena/stadium
- Race track
- Golf
- Sailing
- Wind surfing
- Seaport
- Beach resort
- Amusement/theme park

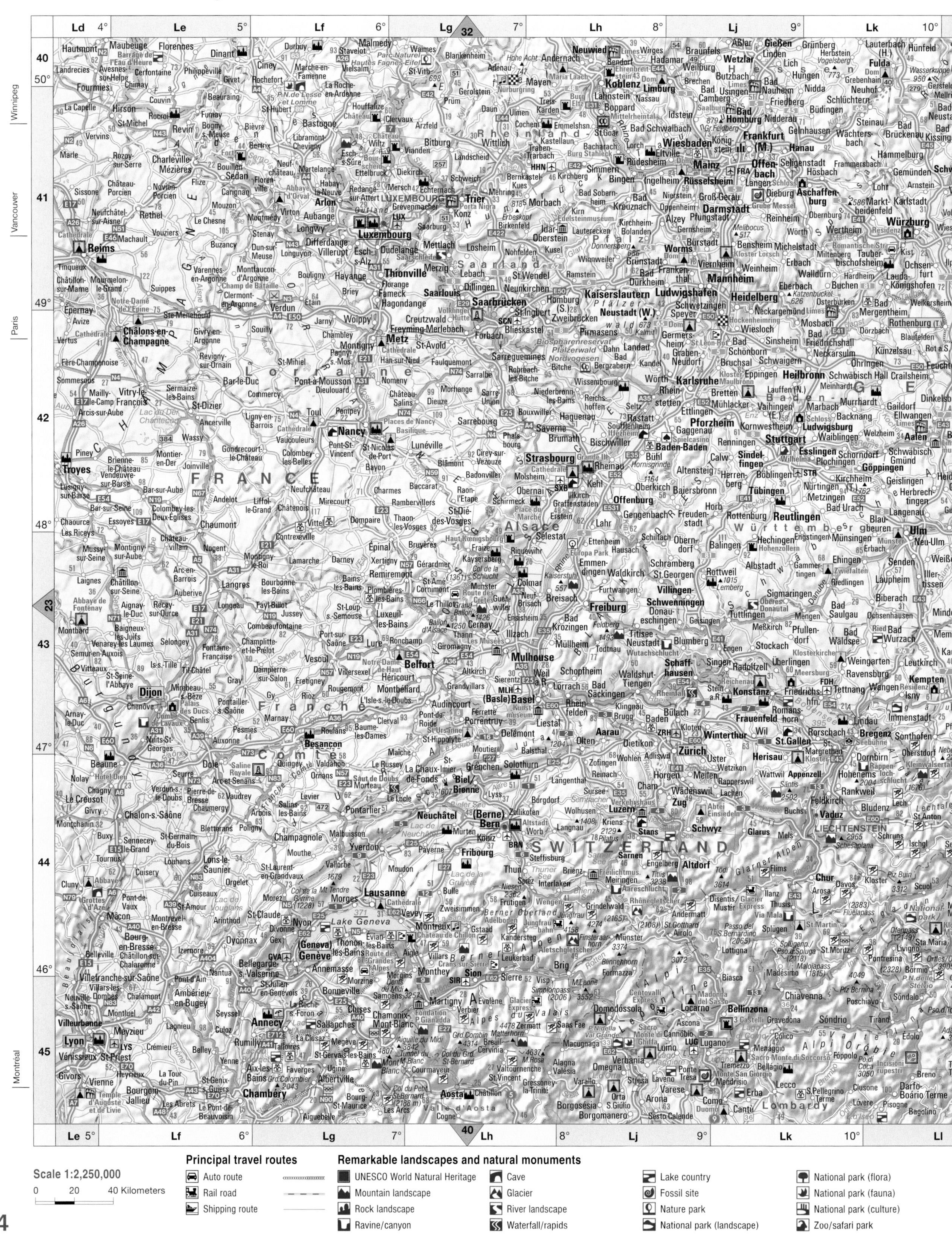

Scale 1:2,250,000

0   20   40 Kilometers

Principal travel routes

- 🚗 Auto route
- 🚃 Rail road
- 🚢 Shipping route

Remarkable landscapes and natural monuments

- ■ UNESCO World Natural Heritage
- ▲ Mountain landscape
- ▣ Rock landscape
- ▤ Ravine/canyon
- ● Cave
- ▲ Glacier
- ≈ River landscape
- ∿ Waterfall/rapids
- ▱ Lake country
- ⬡ Fossil site
- ⬢ Nature park
- ⬢ National park (landscape)
- ⬡ National park (flora)
- ⬡ National park (fauna)
- ⬡ National park (culture)
- ⬡ Zoo/safari park

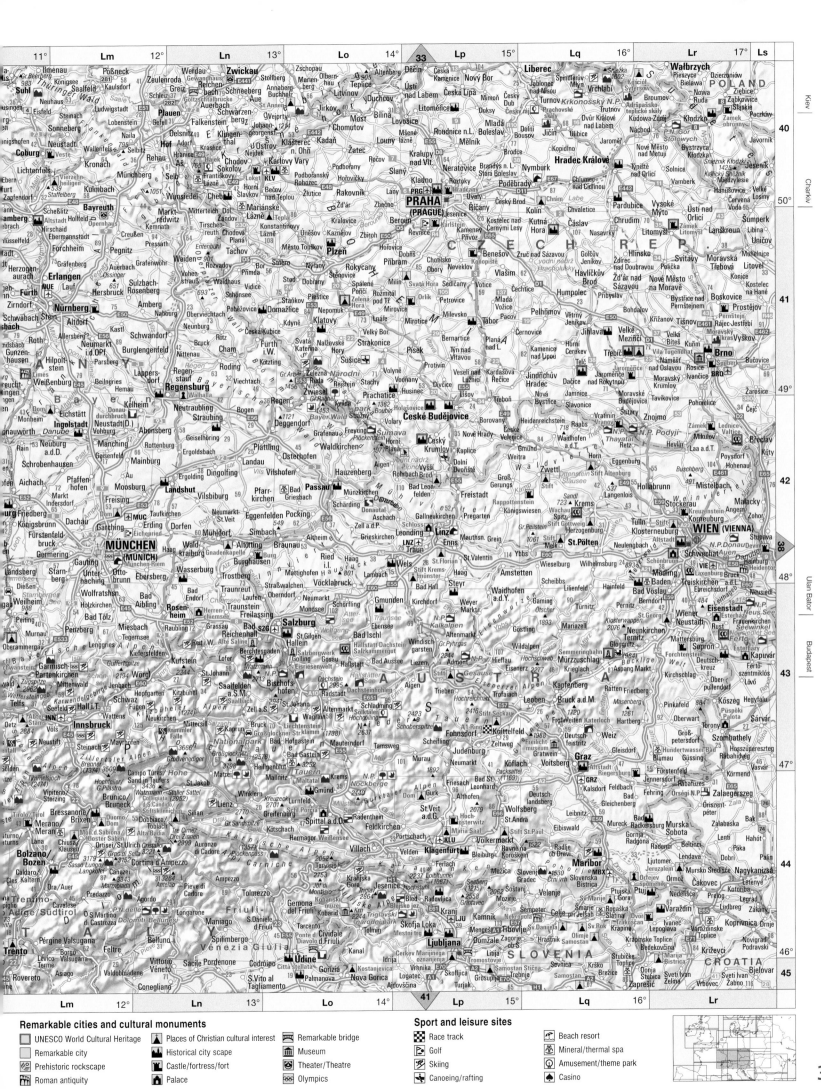

Remarkable cities and cultural monuments

- UNESCO World Cultural Heritage
- Remarkable city
- Prehistoric rockscape
- Roman antiquity
- Places of Christian cultural interest
- Historical city scape
- Castle/fortress/fort
- Palace
- Remarkable bridge
- Museum
- Theater/Theatre
- Olympics

Sport and leisure sites

- Race track
- Golf
- Skiing
- Canoeing/rafting
- Beach resort
- Mineral/thermal spa
- Amusement/theme park
- Casino

35

Poland

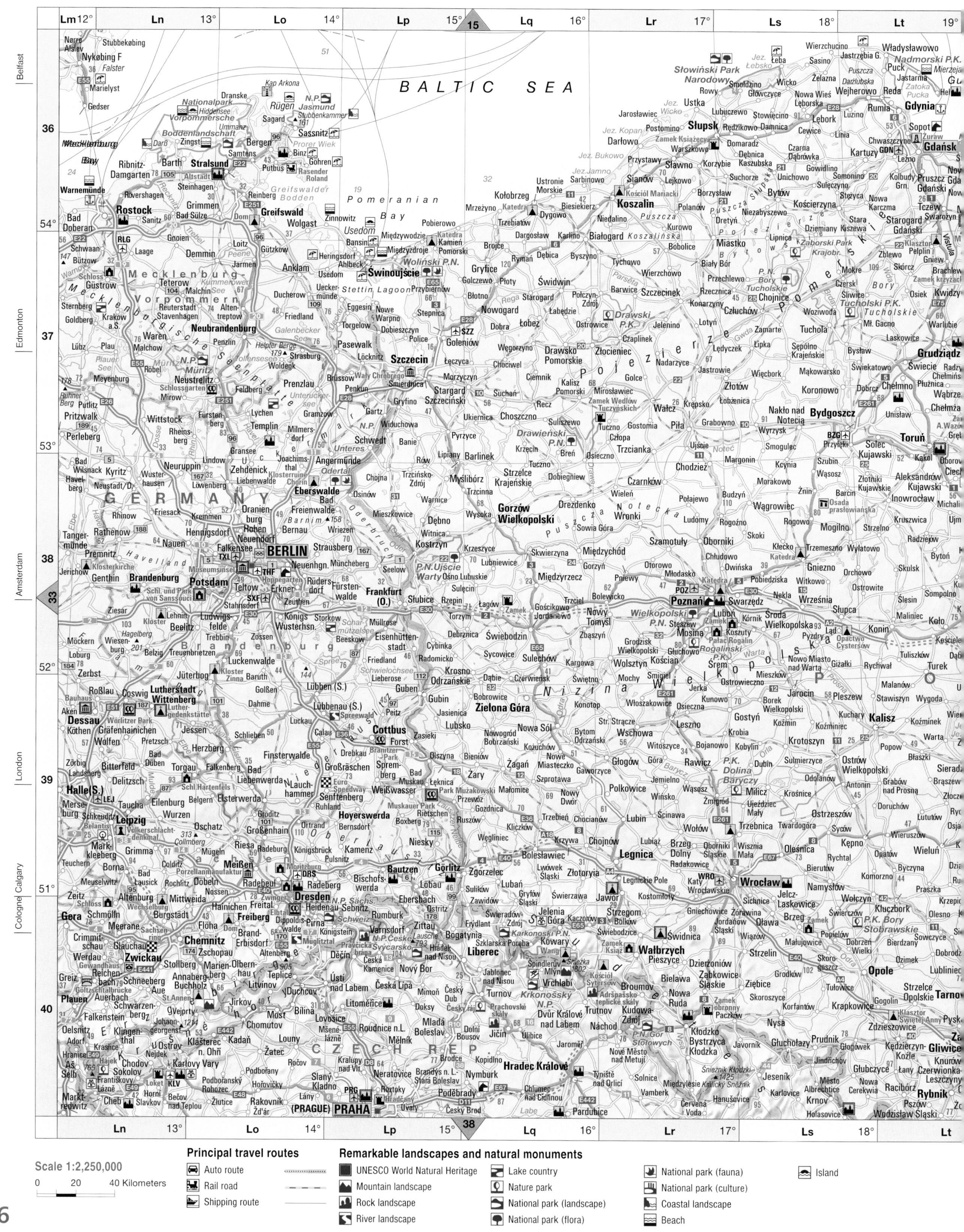

Scale 1:2,250,000

0   20   40 Kilometers

Principal travel routes
- 🚗 Auto route
- 🚃 Rail road
- ⛴ Shipping route

Remarkable landscapes and natural monuments
- UNESCO World Natural Heritage
- Mountain landscape
- Rock landscape
- River landscape
- Lake country
- Nature park
- National park (landscape)
- National park (flora)
- National park (fauna)
- National park (culture)
- Coastal landscape
- Beach
- Island

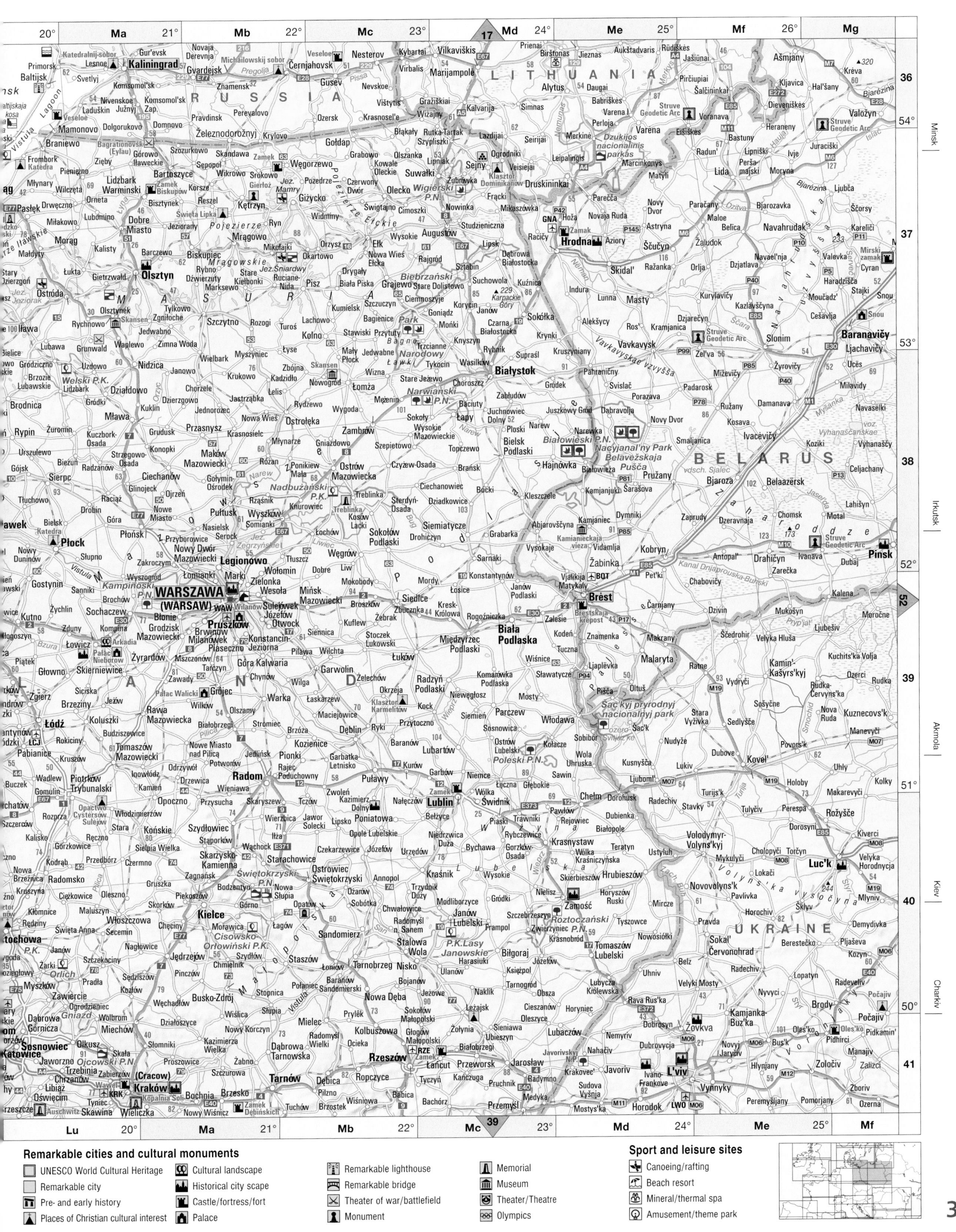

Remarkable cities and cultural monuments

☐ UNESCO World Cultural Heritage	✪ Cultural landscape	⌂ Remarkable lighthouse	⌂ Memorial
☐ Remarkable city	⌂ Historical city scape	⌂ Remarkable bridge	🏛 Museum
⌂ Pre- and early history	⌂ Castle/fortress/fort	✕ Theater of war/battlefield	⌂ Theater/Theatre
⌂ Places of Christian cultural interest	⌂ Palace	⌂ Monument	⌂ Olympics

Sport and leisure sites

- ⌂ Canoeing/rafting
- ⌂ Beach resort
- ⌂ Mineral/thermal spa
- ⌂ Amusement/theme park

Lu 20° Ma 21° Mb 22° Mc 39 23° Md 24° Me 25° Mf

Minsk
Irkutsk
Akmola
Kiev
Charkiv

37

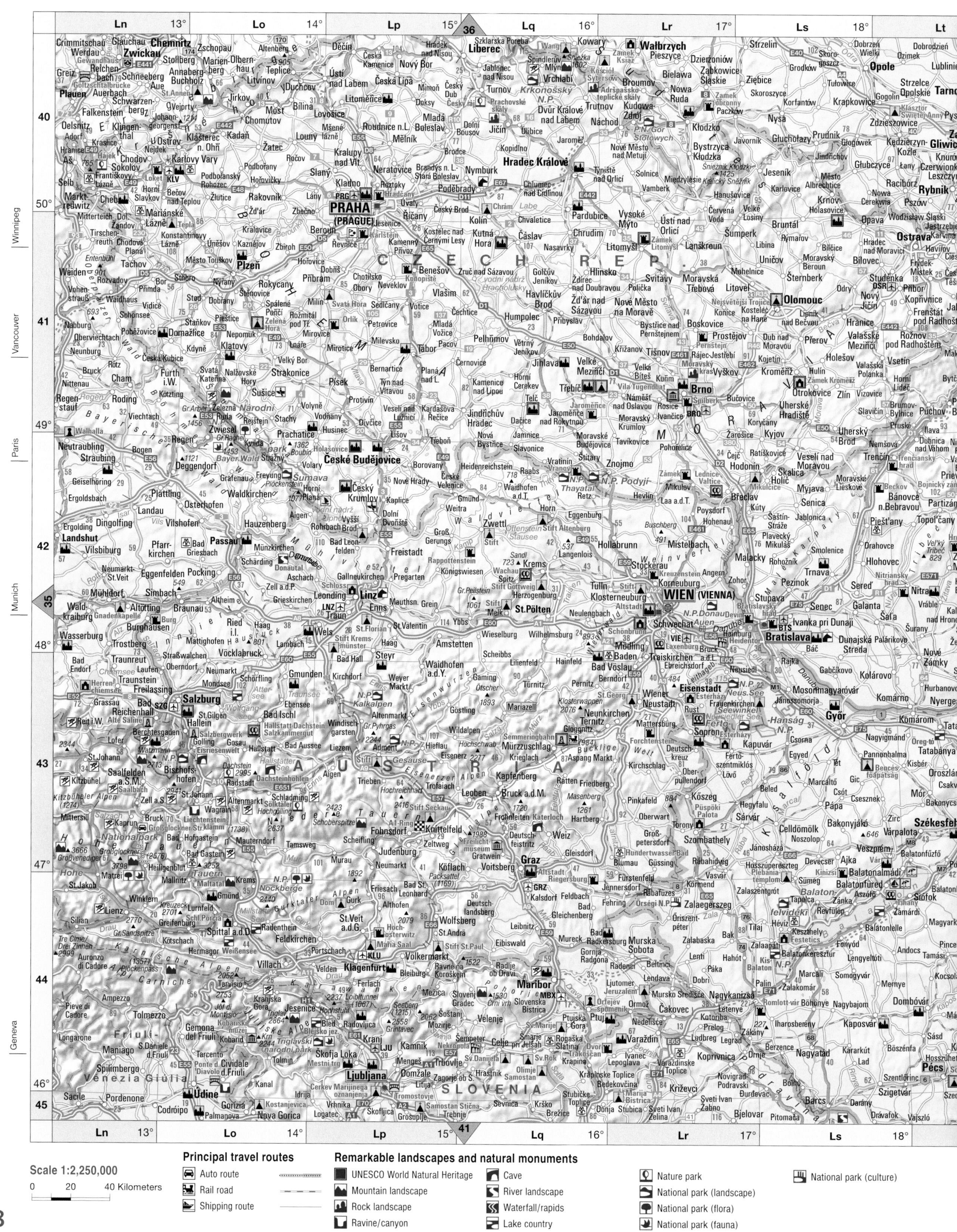

Scale 1:2,250,000

0   20   40 Kilometers

Principal travel routes

- Auto route
- Rail road
- Shipping route

Remarkable landscapes and natural monuments

- UNESCO World Natural Heritage
- Mountain landscape
- Rock landscape
- Ravine/canyon
- Cave
- River landscape
- Waterfall/rapids
- Lake country
- Nature park
- National park (landscape)
- National park (flora)
- National park (fauna)
- National park (culture)

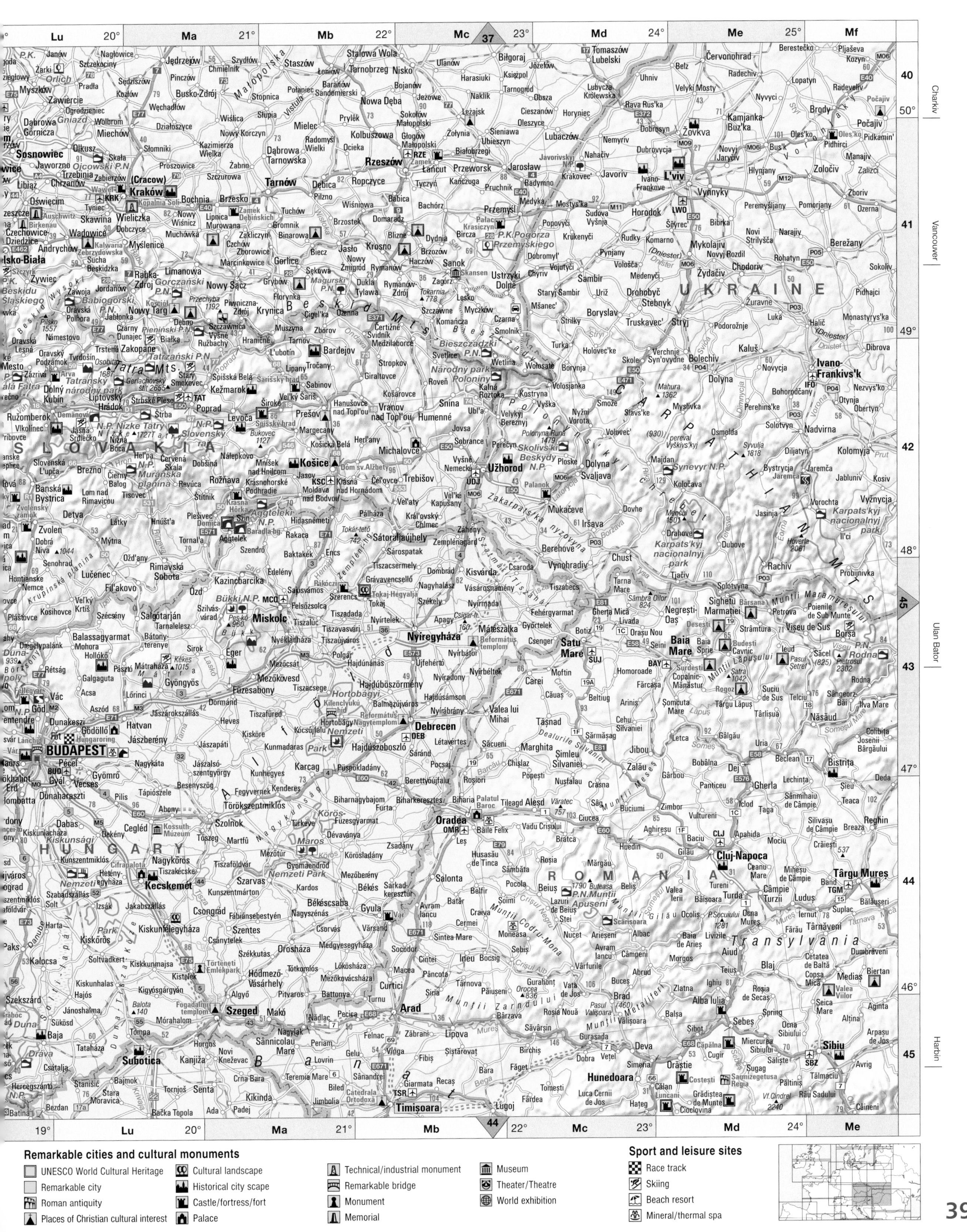

Remarkable cities and cultural monuments

- UNESCO World Cultural Heritage
- Remarkable city
- Roman antiquity
- Places of Christian cultural interest
- Cultural landscape
- Historical city scape
- Castle/fortress/fort
- Palace
- Technical/industrial monument
- Remarkable bridge
- Monument
- Memorial
- Museum
- Theater/Theatre
- World exhibition

Sport and leisure sites

- Race track
- Skiing
- Beach resort
- Mineral/thermal spa

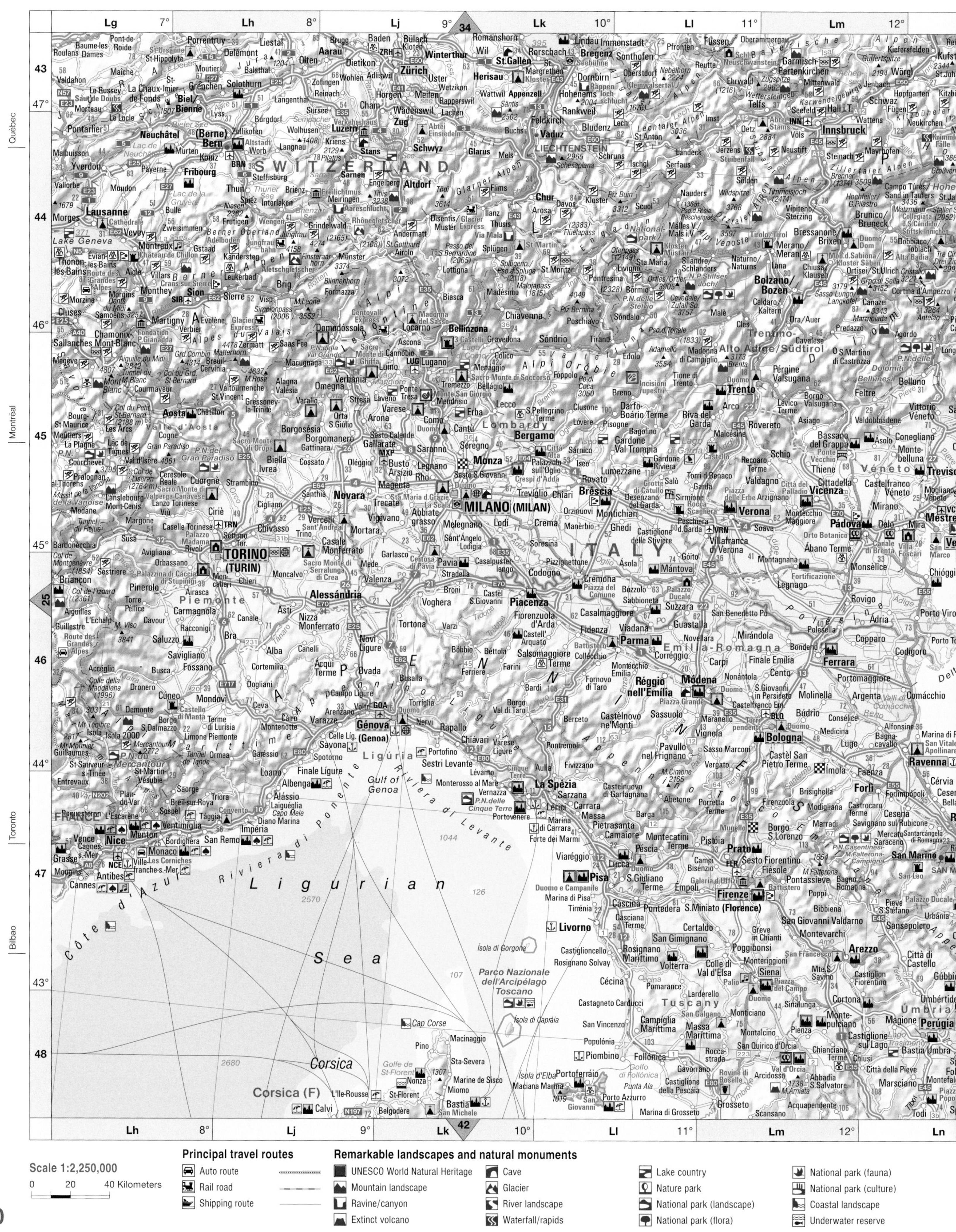

Scale 1:2,250,000

0   20   40 Kilometers

Principal travel routes

- Auto route
- Rail road
- Shipping route
- Principal travel routes (dotted)

Remarkable landscapes and natural monuments

- UNESCO World Natural Heritage
- Mountain landscape
- Ravine/canyon
- Extinct volcano
- Cave
- Glacier
- River landscape
- Waterfall/rapids
- Lake country
- Nature park
- National park (landscape)
- National park (flora)
- National park (fauna)
- National park (culture)
- Coastal landscape
- Underwater reserve

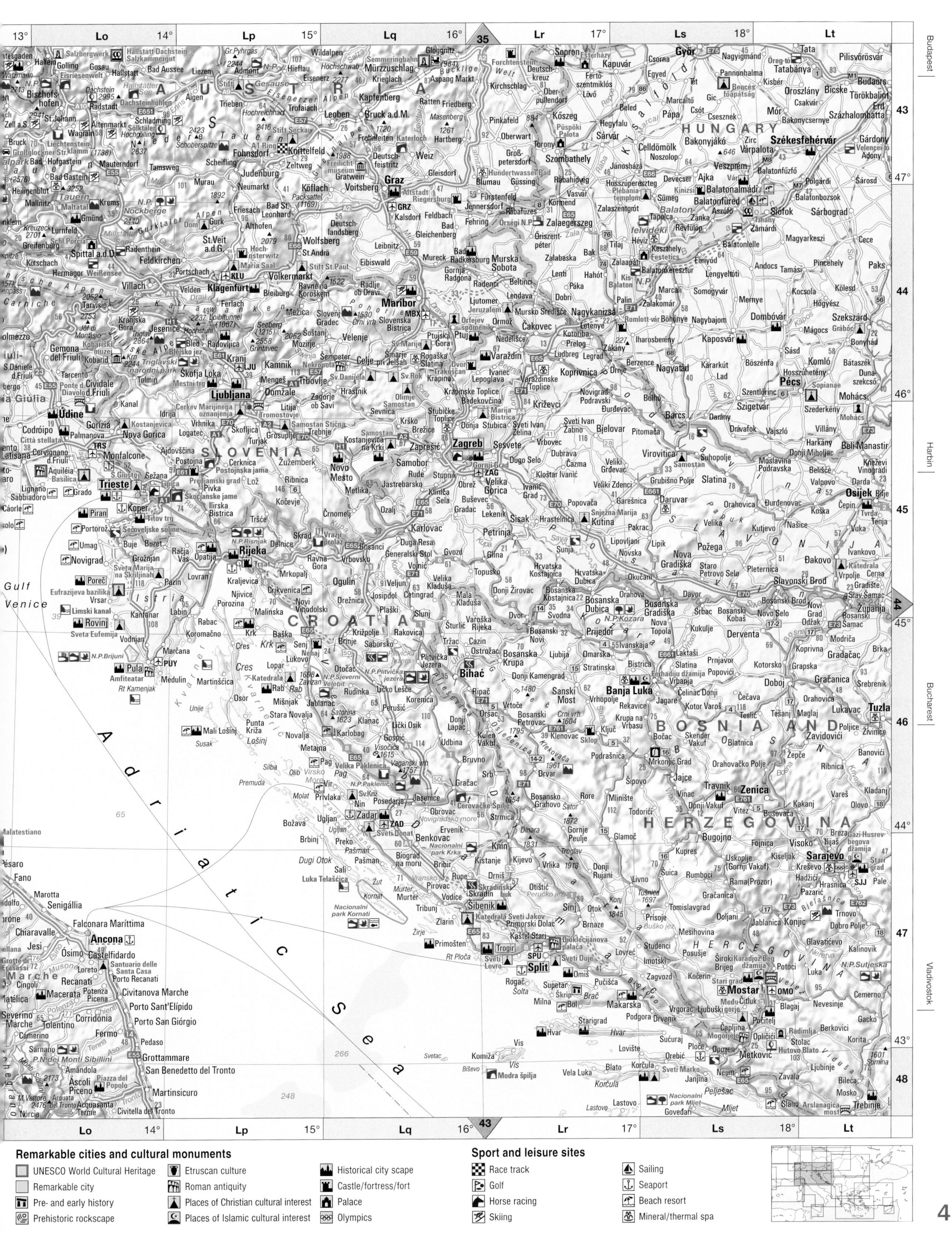

Remarkable cities and cultural monuments

- UNESCO World Cultural Heritage
- Remarkable city
- Pre- and early history
- Prehistoric rockscape
- Etruscan culture
- Roman antiquity
- Places of Christian cultural interest
- Places of Islamic cultural interest
- Historical city scape
- Castle/fortress/fort
- Palace
- Olympics

Sport and leisure sites

- Race track
- Golf
- Horse racing
- Skiing
- Sailing
- Seaport
- Beach resort
- Mineral/thermal spa

Southern Italy, Malta, Albania

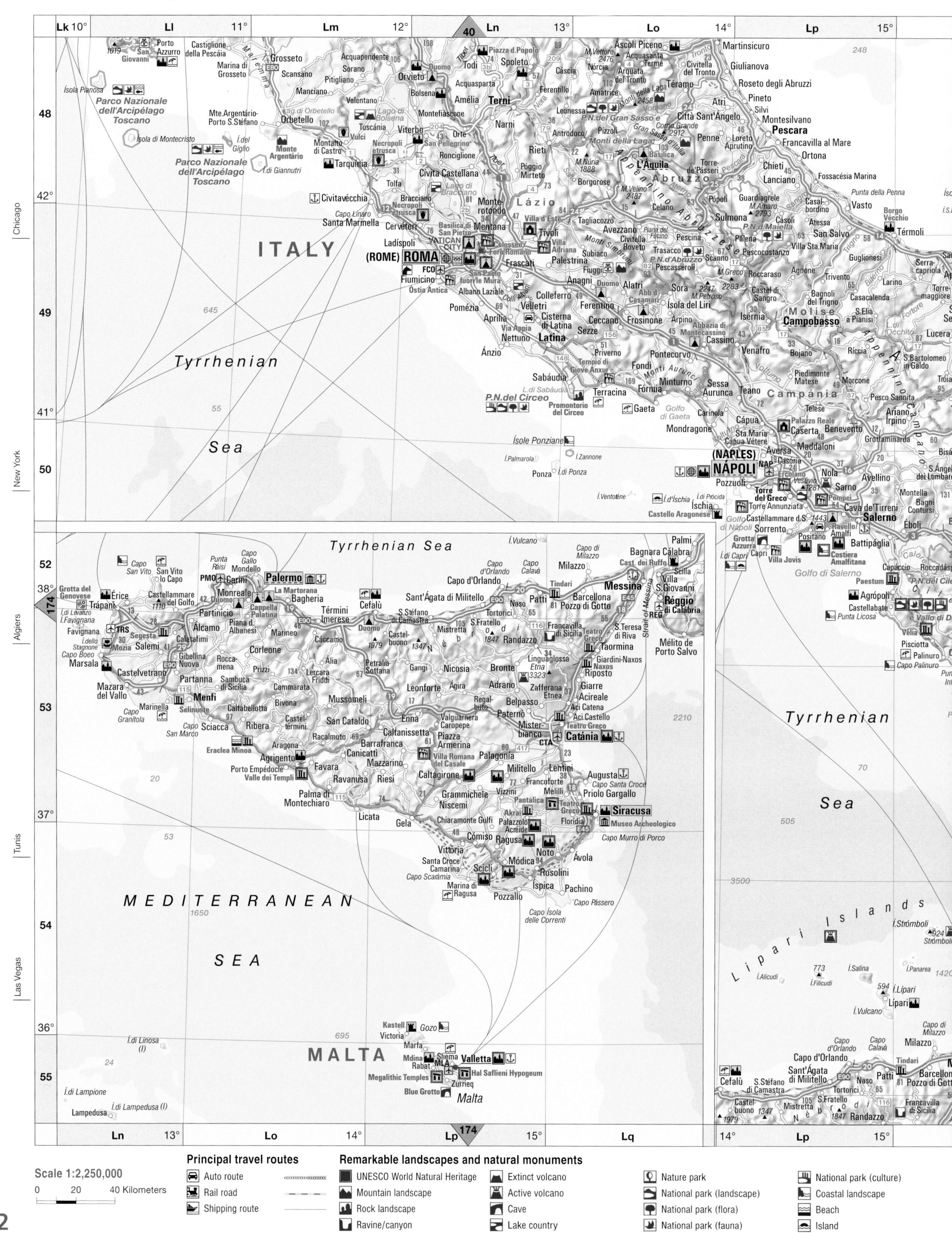

Scale 1:2,250,000

0   20   40 Kilometers

Principal travel routes

🚗 Auto route

🚂 Rail road

⚓ Shipping route

Remarkable landscapes and natural monuments

■ UNESCO World Natural Heritage

▲ Mountain landscape

▲ Rock landscape

⋀ Ravine/canyon

▲ Extinct volcano

▲ Active volcano

⛰ Cave

≋ Lake country

◊ Nature park

⌂ National park (landscape)

♣ National park (flora)

⌂ National park (fauna)

🏛 National park (culture)

▦ Coastal landscape

≈ Beach

≈ Island

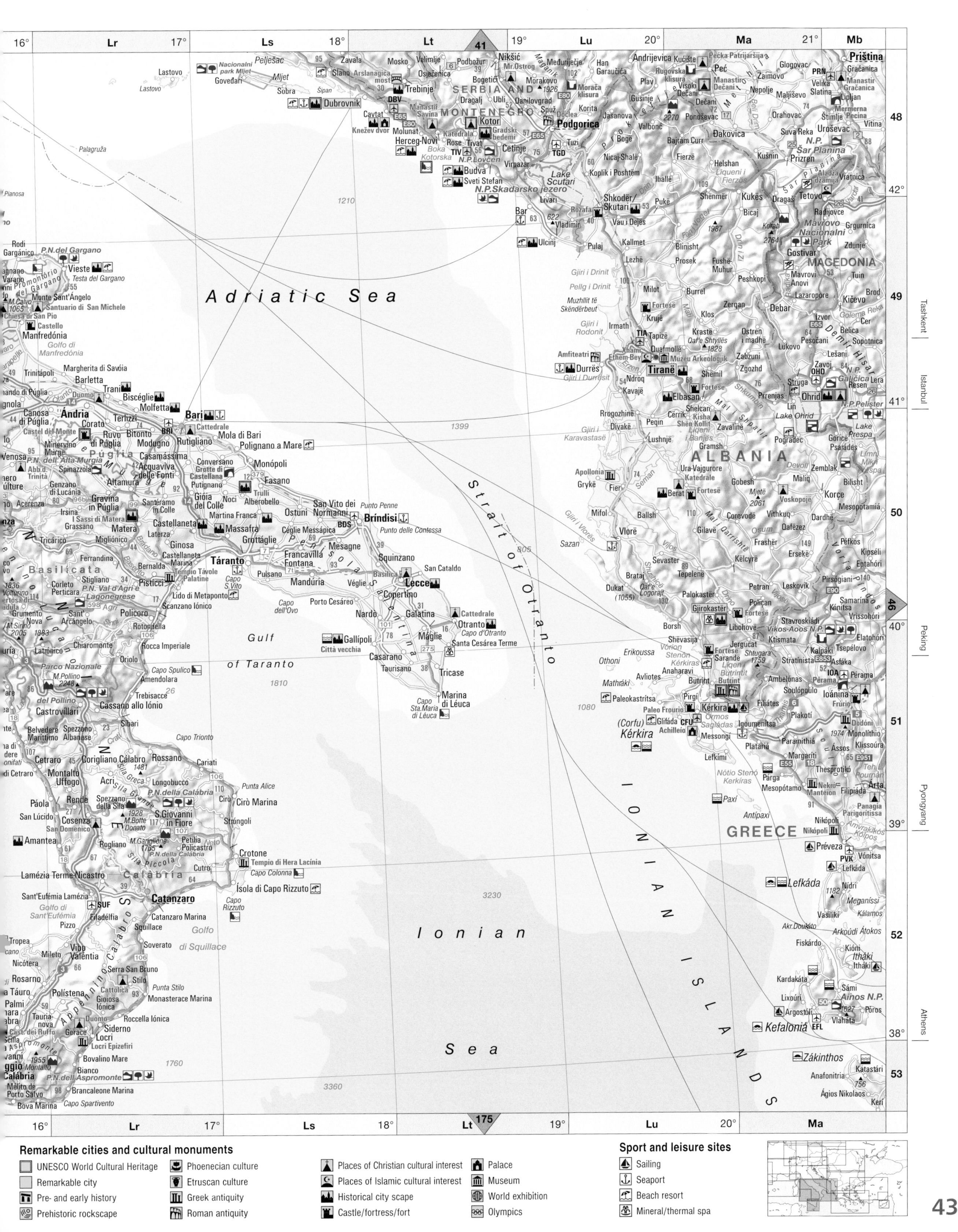

Remarkable cities and cultural monuments

- UNESCO World Cultural Heritage
- Remarkable city
- Pre- and early history
- Prehistoric rockscape

- Phoenecian culture
- Etruscan culture
- Greek antiquity
- Roman antiquity

- Places of Christian cultural interest
- Places of Islamic cultural interest
- Historical city scape
- Castle/fortress/fort

- Palace
- Museum
- World exhibition
- Olympics

Sport and leisure sites

- Sailing
- Seaport
- Beach resort
- Mineral/thermal spa

43

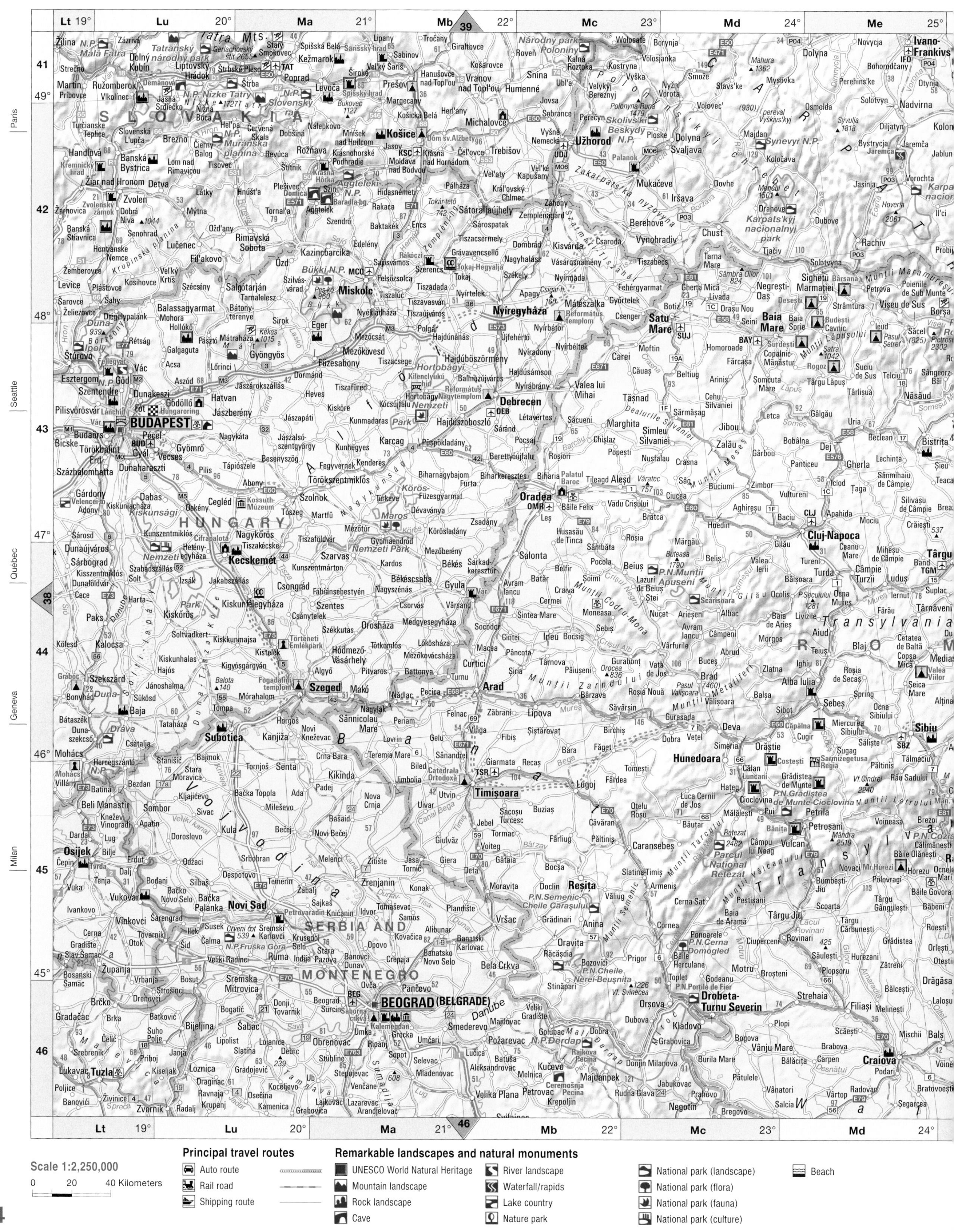

Scale 1:2,250,000

0   20   40 Kilometers

Principal travel routes
- Auto route
- Rail road
- Shipping route

Remarkable landscapes and natural monuments
- UNESCO World Natural Heritage
- Mountain landscape
- Rock landscape
- Cave
- River landscape
- Waterfall/rapids
- Lake country
- Nature park
- National park (landscape)
- National park (flora)
- National park (fauna)
- National park (culture)
- Beach

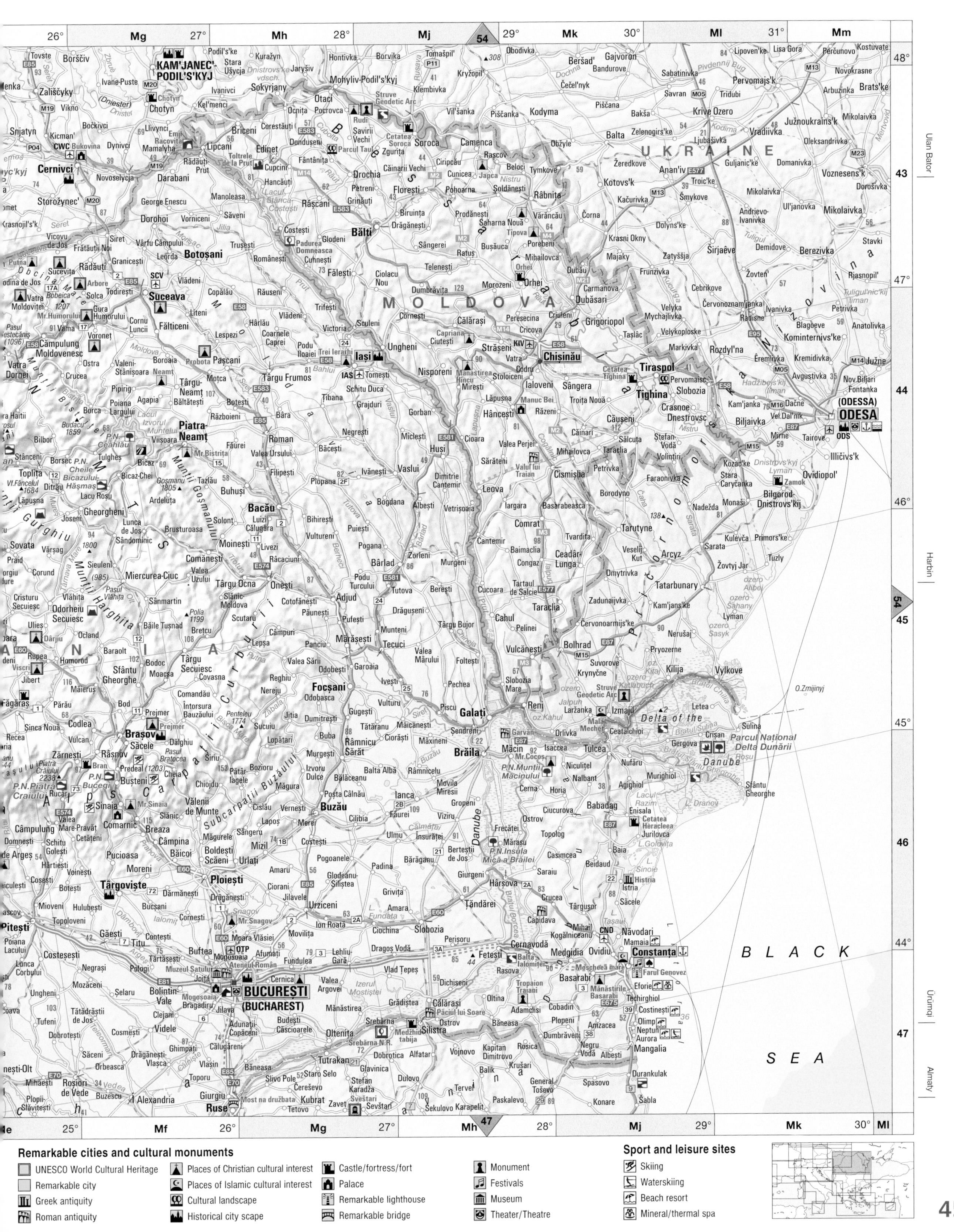

Remarkable cities and cultural monuments

- UNESCO World Cultural Heritage
- Remarkable city
- Greek antiquity
- Roman antiquity
- Places of Christian cultural interest
- Places of Islamic cultural interest
- Cultural landscape
- Historical city scape
- Castle/fortress/fort
- Palace
- Remarkable lighthouse
- Remarkable bridge
- Monument
- Festivals
- Museum
- Theater/Theatre

Sport and leisure sites

- Skiing
- Waterskiing
- Beach resort
- Mineral/thermal spa

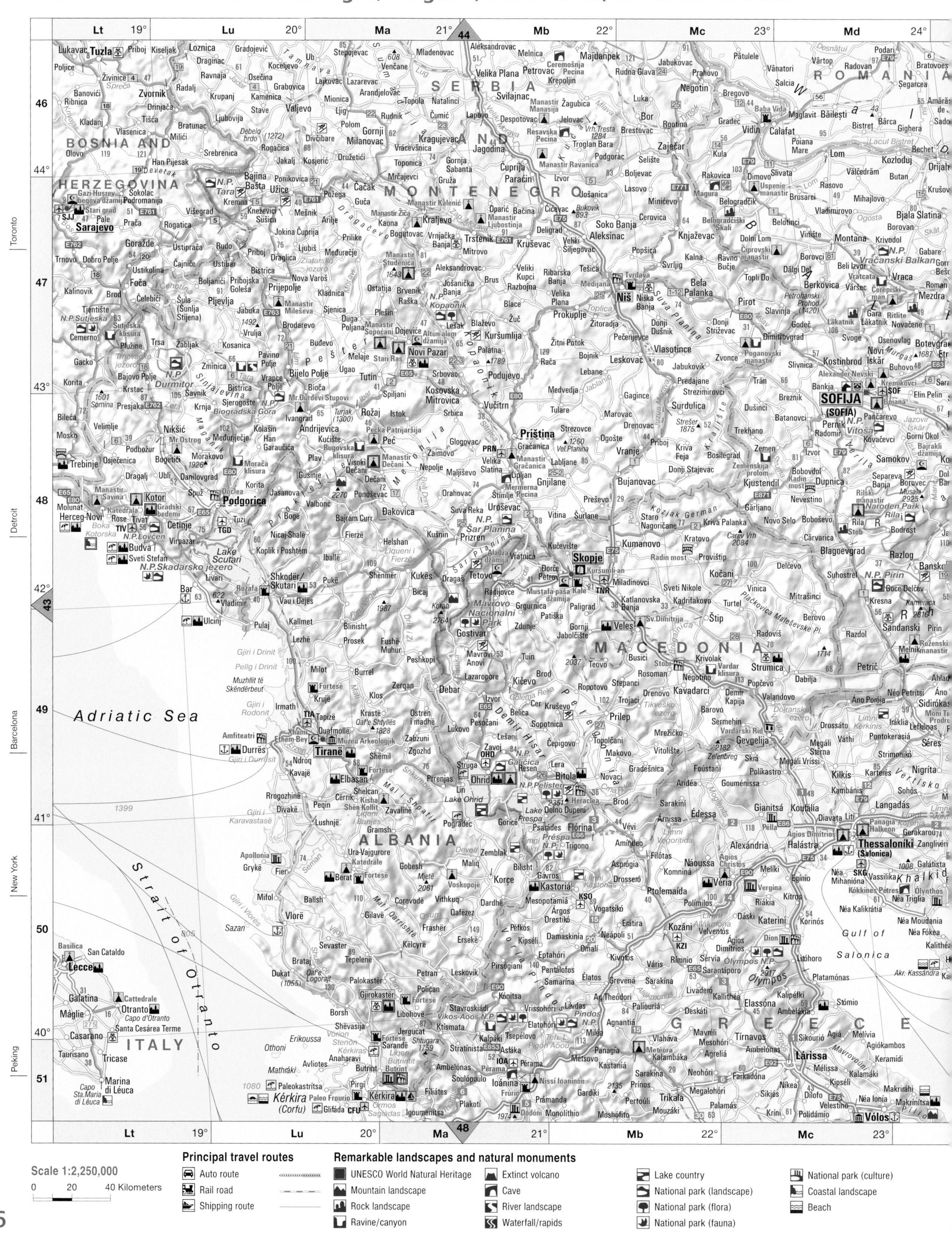

Scale 1:2,250,000

0   20   40 Kilometers

Principal travel routes
- Auto route
- Rail road
- Shipping route

Remarkable landscapes and natural monuments
- UNESCO World Natural Heritage
- Mountain landscape
- Rock landscape
- Ravine/canyon
- Extinct volcano
- Cave
- River landscape
- Waterfall/rapids
- Lake country
- National park (landscape)
- National park (flora)
- National park (fauna)
- National park (culture)
- Coastal landscape
- Beach

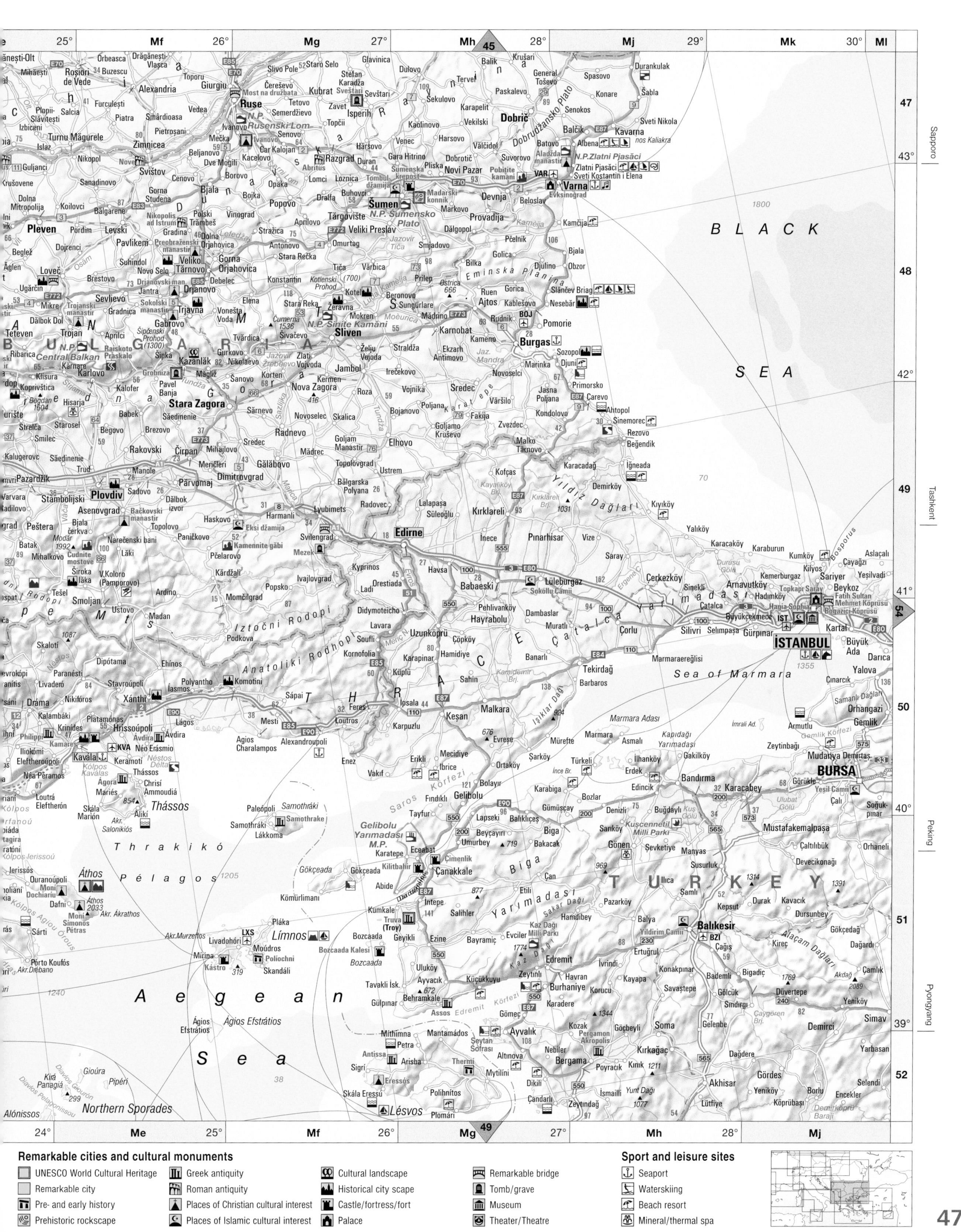

Sapporo

Tashkent

Peking

Pyongyang

B L A C K

S E A

Pleven

BULGARIA

Central Balkan N.P.

Plovdiv

Stara Zagora

Sliven

Burgas

Edirne

A E G E A N

T H R A C E

İSTANBUL

Sea of Marmara

BURSA

T U R K E Y

Balıkesir

A e g e a n

S e a

Thrakikó Pélagos

Northern Sporades

Remarkable cities and cultural monuments

- ▢ UNESCO World Cultural Heritage
- ▢ Remarkable city
- ⬚ Pre- and early history
- ⬚ Prehistoric rockscape
- ⌂ Greek antiquity
- ⌂ Roman antiquity
- ⌂ Places of Christian cultural interest
- ☪ Places of Islamic cultural interest
- ⬚ Cultural landscape
- ⬚ Historical city scape
- ⬚ Castle/fortress/fort
- ⬚ Palace
- ⬚ Remarkable bridge
- ⬚ Tomb/grave
- ⬚ Museum
- ⬚ Theater/Theatre

Sport and leisure sites

- ⬚ Seaport
- ⬚ Waterskiing
- ⬚ Beach resort
- ⬚ Mineral/thermal spa

47

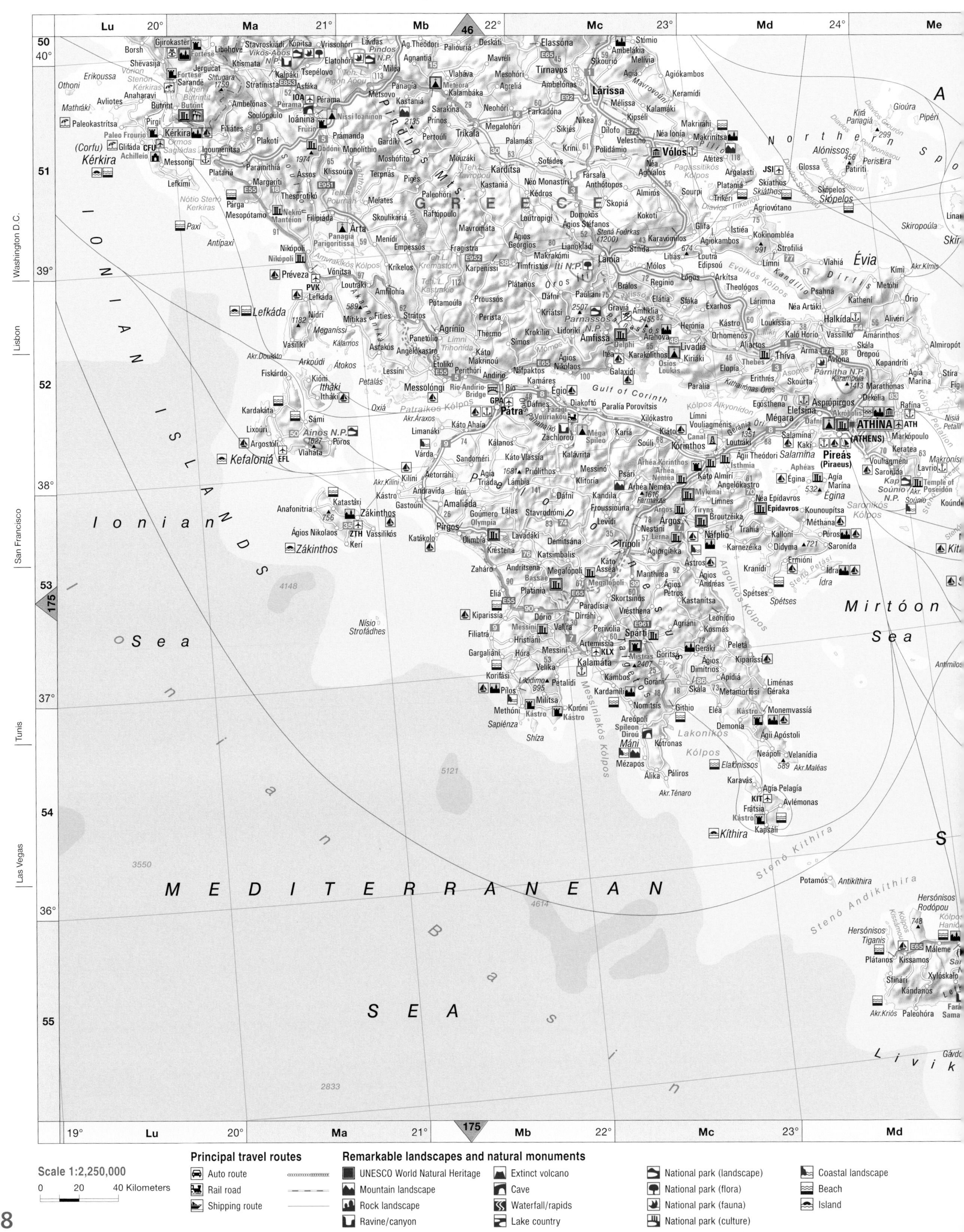

Scale 1:2,250,000

0   20   40 Kilometers

Principal travel routes

🚐 Auto route

🚃 Rail road

🚢 Shipping route

Remarkable landscapes and natural monuments

■ UNESCO World Natural Heritage

▲ Mountain landscape

▲ Rock landscape

▲ Ravine/canyon

▲ Extinct volcano

✖ Cave

✖ Waterfall/rapids

✖ Lake country

▲ National park (landscape)

▲ National park (flora)

▲ National park (fauna)

▲ National park (culture)

⬛ Coastal landscape

≋ Beach

⬛ Island

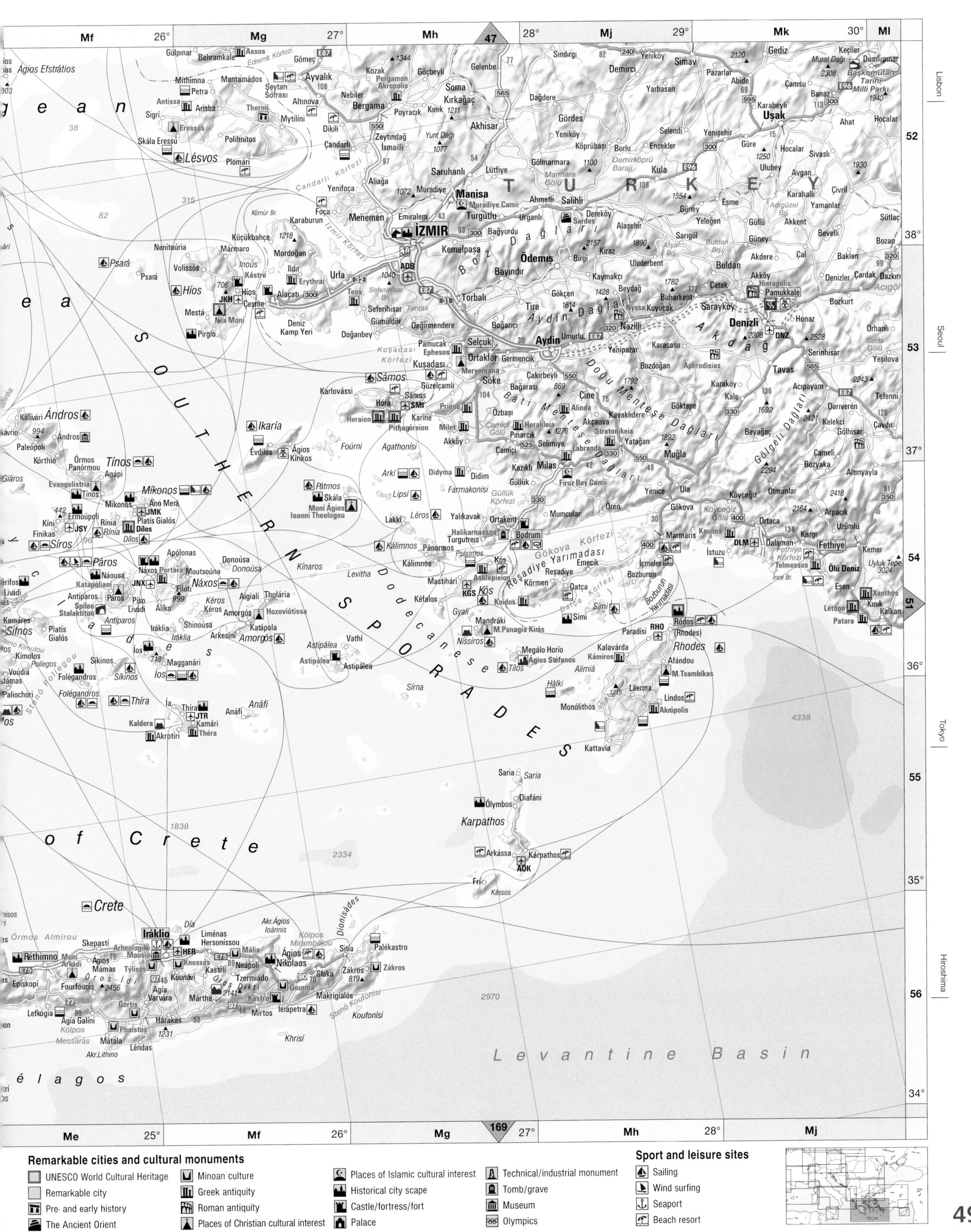

Remarkable cities and cultural monuments

- ☐ UNESCO World Cultural Heritage
- ☐ Remarkable city
- 🏛 Pre- and early history
- ⚐ The Ancient Orient
- ⛏ Minoan culture
- 🏛 Greek antiquity
- 🏛 Roman antiquity
- ▲ Places of Christian cultural interest
- ☪ Places of Islamic cultural interest
- 🏰 Historical city scape
- 🏯 Castle/fortress/fort
- 🏛 Palace
- 🅰 Technical/industrial monument
- ⚰ Tomb/grave
- 🏛 Museum
- ⚪ Olympics

Sport and leisure sites

- ⛵ Sailing
- 🏄 Wind surfing
- ⚓ Seaport
- 🏖 Beach resort

49

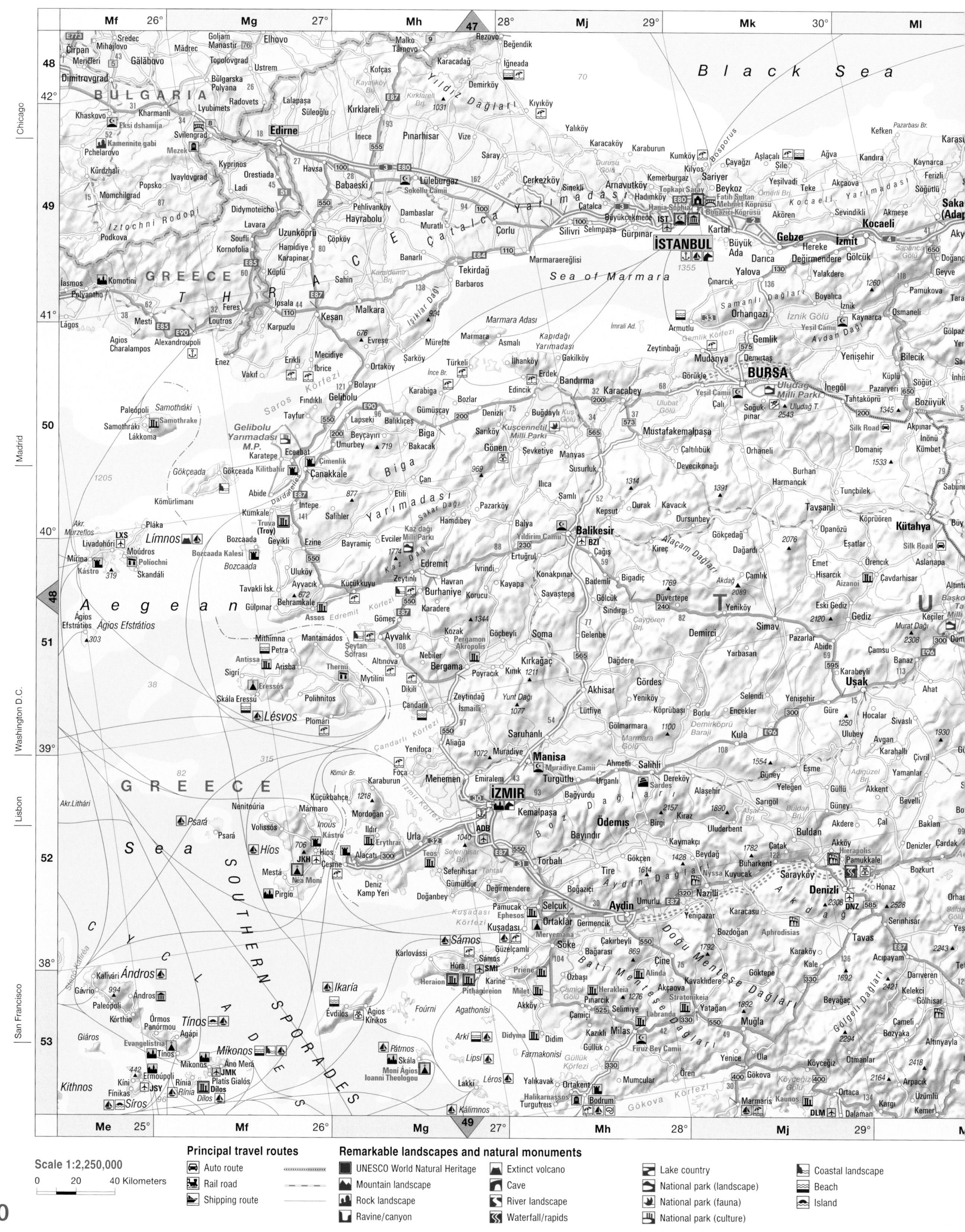

Scale 1:2,250,000

0   20   40 Kilometers

Principal travel routes

- Auto route
- Rail road
- Shipping route
- ·············· UNESCO World Natural Heritage
- Principal travel routes

Remarkable landscapes and natural monuments

- UNESCO World Natural Heritage
- Mountain landscape
- Rock landscape
- Ravine/canyon
- Extinct volcano
- Cave
- River landscape
- Waterfall/rapids
- Lake country
- National park (landscape)
- National park (fauna)
- National park (culture)
- Coastal landscape
- Beach
- Island

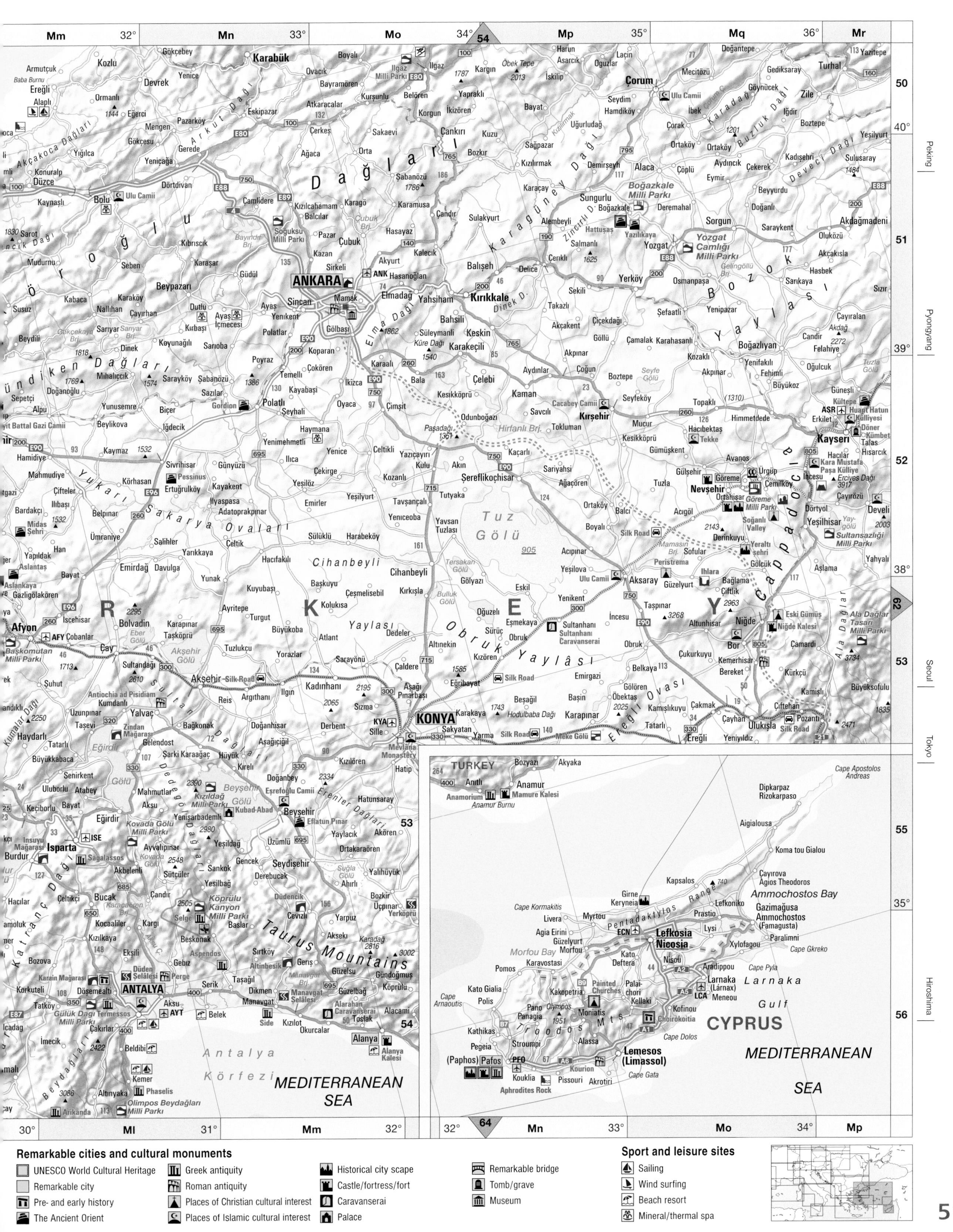

Peking

Pyongyang

Seoul

Tokyo

Hiroshima

Remarkable cities and cultural monuments

- UNESCO World Cultural Heritage
- Remarkable city
- Pre- and early history
- The Ancient Orient
- Greek antiquity
- Roman antiquity
- Places of Christian cultural interest
- Places of Islamic cultural interest
- Historical city scape
- Castle/fortress/fort
- Caravanserai
- Palace
- Remarkable bridge
- Tomb/grave
- Museum

Sport and leisure sites

- Sailing
- Wind surfing
- Beach resort
- Mineral/thermal spa

51

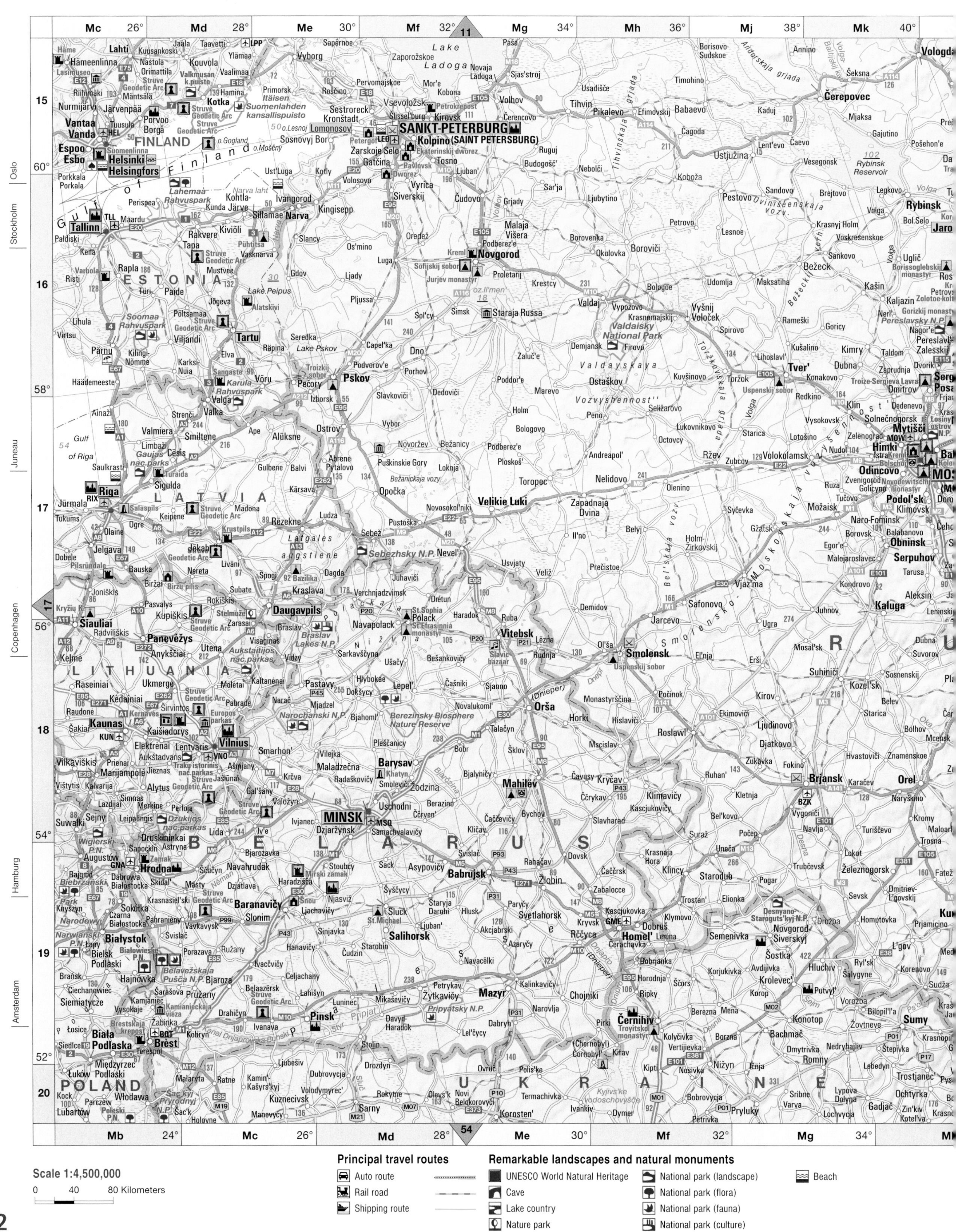

Scale 1:4,500,000

0   40   80 Kilometers

Principal travel routes

🚗 Auto route

🚂 Rail road

🚢 Shipping route

Remarkable landscapes and natural monuments

■ UNESCO World Natural Heritage

⌂ Cave

Lake country

Nature park

National park (landscape)

National park (flora)

National park (fauna)

National park (culture)

Beach

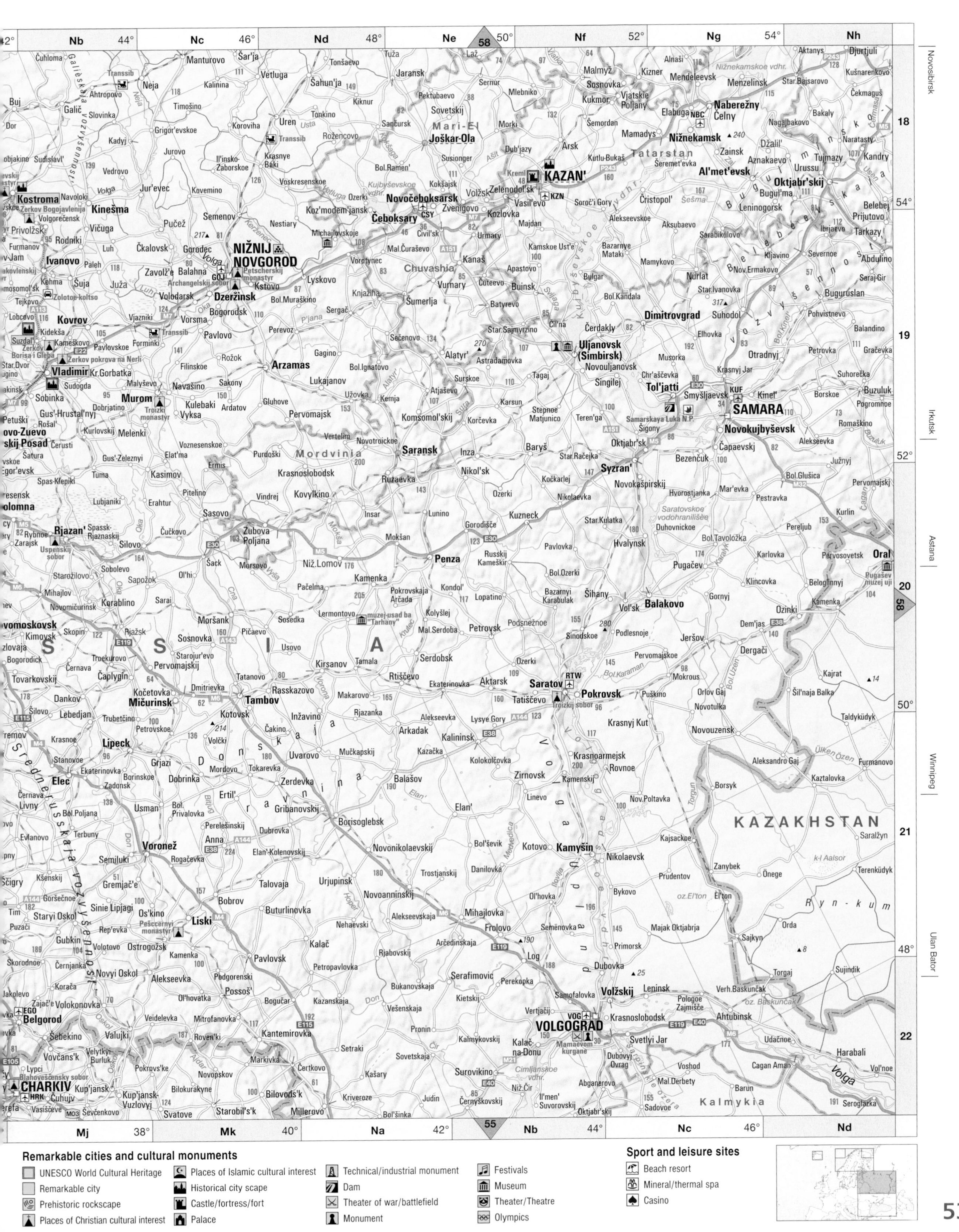

Remarkable cities and cultural monuments

- ▢ UNESCO World Cultural Heritage
- ▢ Remarkable city
- ▢ Prehistoric rockscape
- ▲ Places of Christian cultural interest
- ☾ Places of Islamic cultural interest
- ☷ Historical city scape
- ♜ Castle/fortress/fort
- ♟ Palace
- Ⓐ Technical/industrial monument
- ▣ Dam
- ✕ Theater of war/battlefield
- ⚥ Monument
- ♫ Festivals
- 血 Museum
- ☺ Theater/Theatre
- ⚭ Olympics

Sport and leisure sites

- ⛵ Beach resort
- ♨ Mineral/thermal spa
- ♠ Casino

53

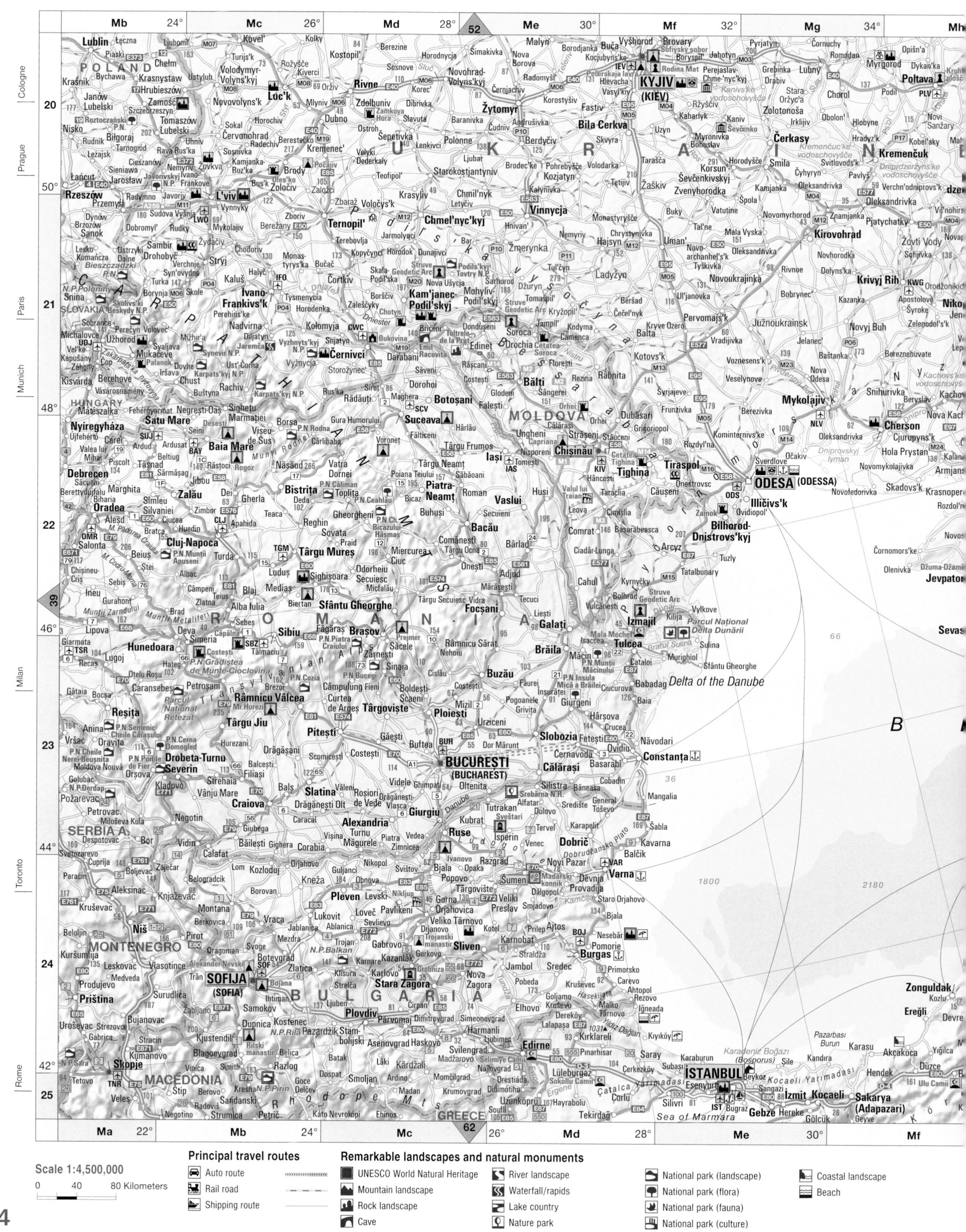

Scale 1:4,500,000

0   40   80 Kilometers

Principal travel routes
- Auto route
- Rail road
- Shipping route
- Auto route
- Rail road
- Shipping route

Remarkable landscapes and natural monuments
- UNESCO World Natural Heritage
- Mountain landscape
- Rock landscape
- Cave
- River landscape
- Waterfall/rapids
- Lake country
- Nature park
- National park (landscape)
- National park (flora)
- National park (fauna)
- National park (culture)
- Coastal landscape
- Beach

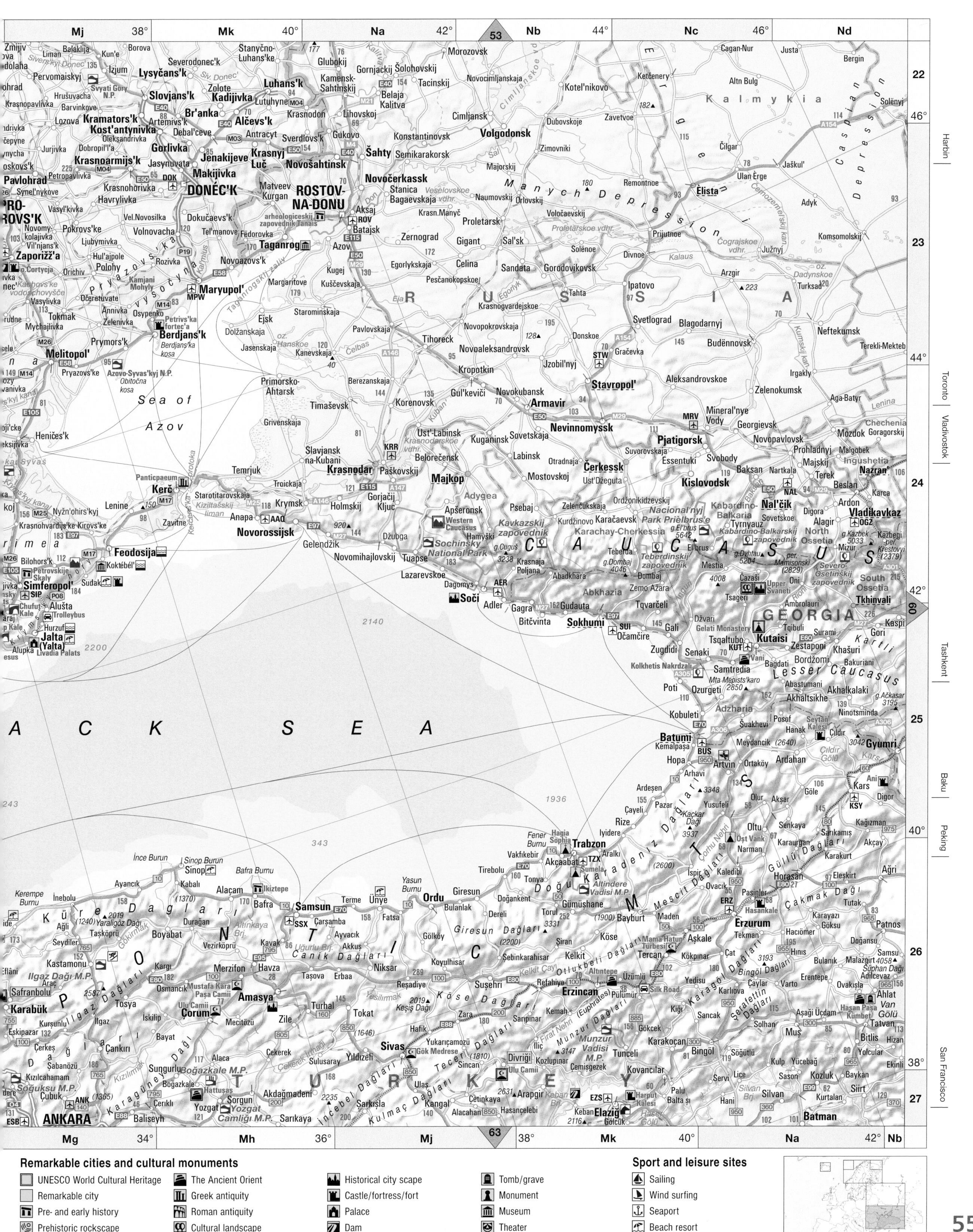

BLACK SEA

R U S S I A

C A U C A S U S

GEORGIA

T U R K E Y

ANKARA

Sea of Azov

Remarkable cities and cultural monuments

- ■ UNESCO World Cultural Heritage
- ■ Remarkable city
- ⛏ Pre- and early history
- 🗿 Prehistoric rockscape
- ⛵ The Ancient Orient
- 🏛 Greek antiquity
- 🏛 Roman antiquity
- ∞ Cultural landscape
- 🏰 Historical city scape
- 🏰 Castle/fortress/fort
- 🏰 Palace
- ⚒ Dam
- ▣ Tomb/grave
- ▣ Monument
- 🏛 Museum
- ◉ Theater

Sport and leisure sites

- ⛵ Sailing
- ⛵ Wind surfing
- ⚓ Seaport
- ⛱ Beach resort

Harbin
Toronto
Vladivostok
Tashkent
Baku
Peking
San Francisco

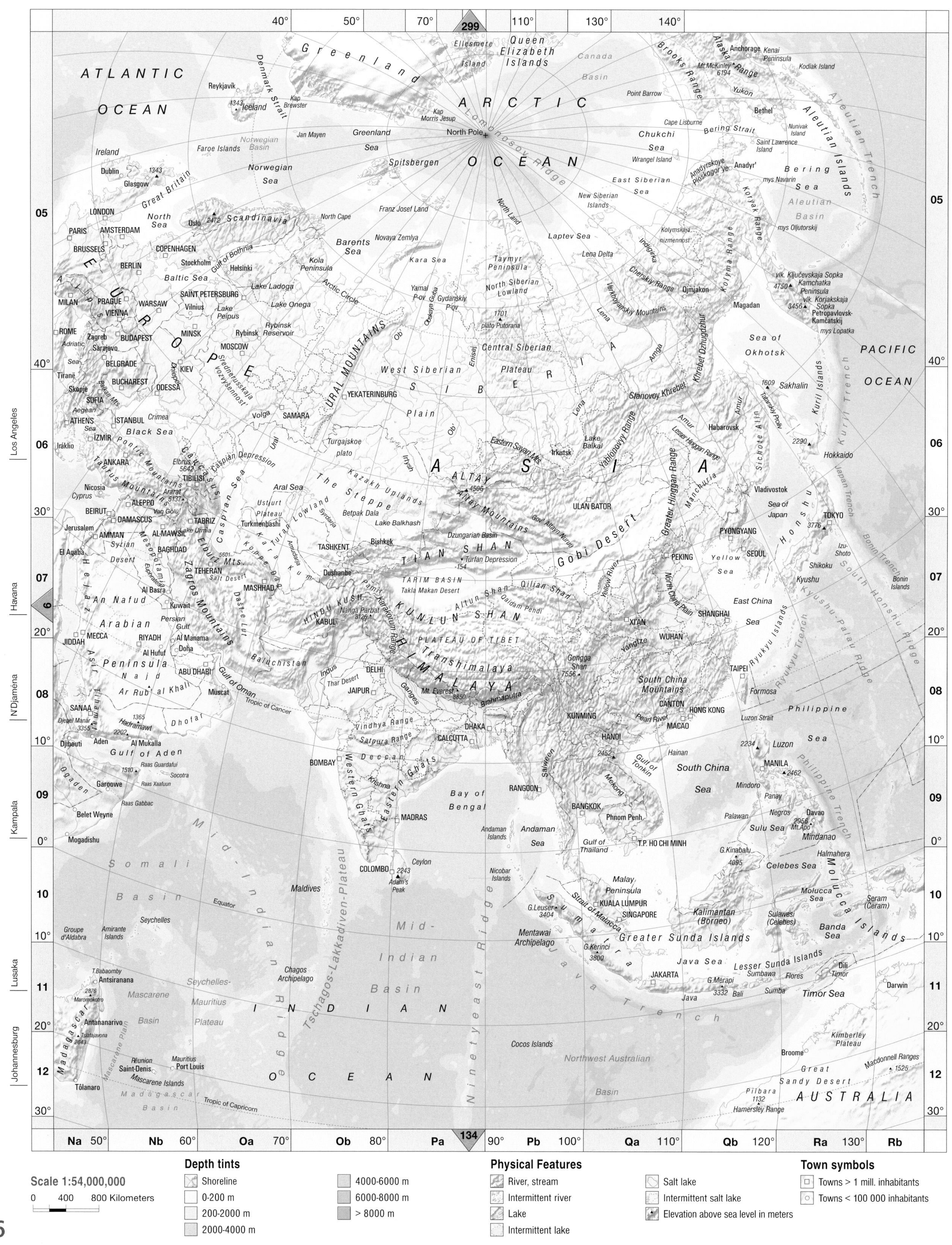

Scale 1:54,000,000

0   400   800 Kilometers

Depth tints

- Shoreline
- 0–200 m
- 200–2000 m
- 2000–4000 m
- 4000–6000 m
- 6000–8000 m
- > 8000 m

Physical Features

- River, stream
- Intermittent river
- Lake
- Intermittent lake
- Salt lake
- Intermittent salt lake
- Elevation above sea level in meters

Town symbols

- Towns > 1 mill. inhabitants
- Towns < 100 000 inhabitants

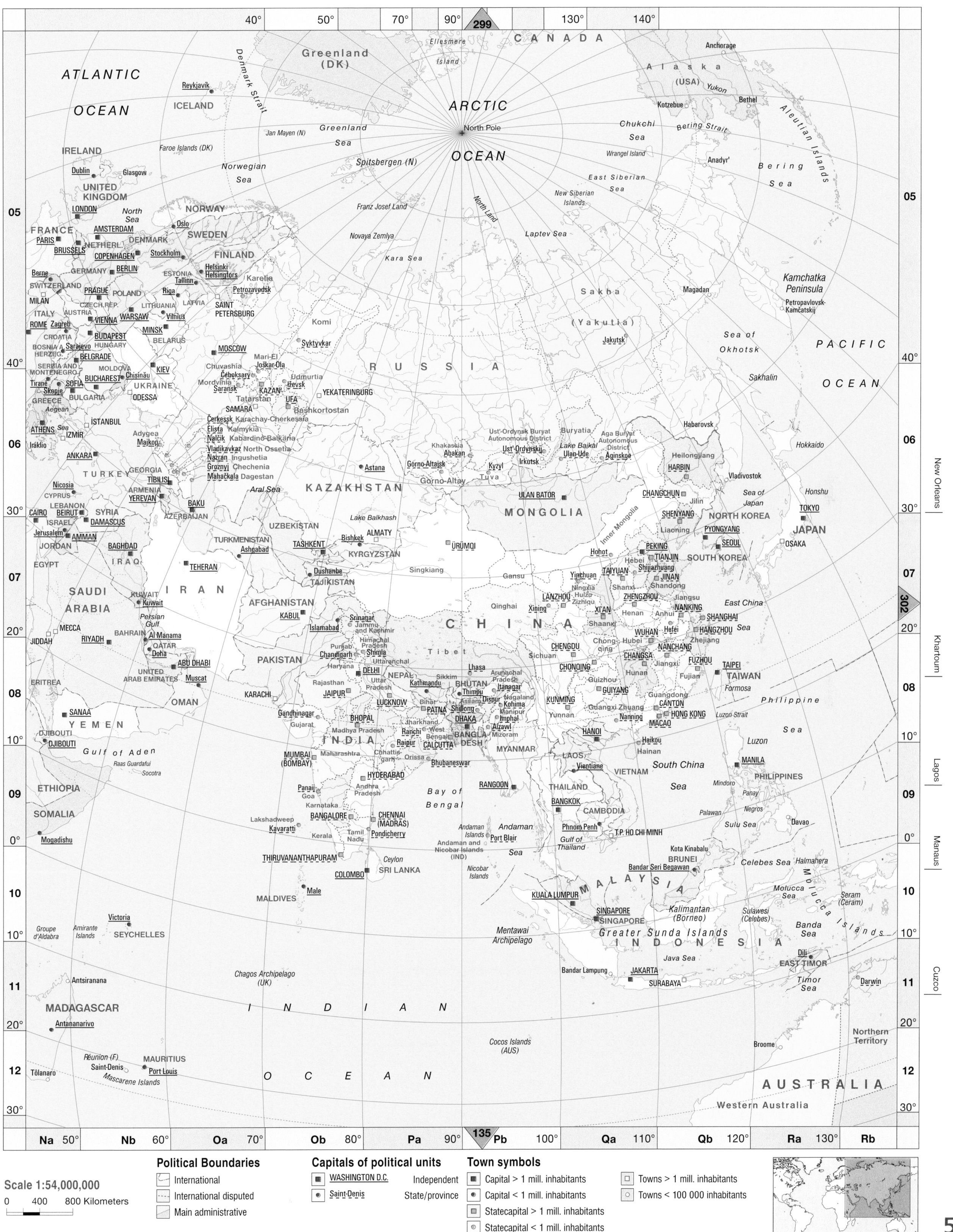

Scale 1:54,000,000

0   400   800 Kilometers

Political Boundaries
International
International disputed
Main administrative

Capitals of political units
WASHINGTON D.C.   Independent
Saint-Denis   State/province

Town symbols
Capital > 1 mill. inhabitants
Capital < 1 mill. inhabitants
Statecapital > 1 mill. inhabitants
Statecapital < 1 mill. inhabitants
Towns > 1 mill. inhabitants
Towns < 100 000 inhabitants

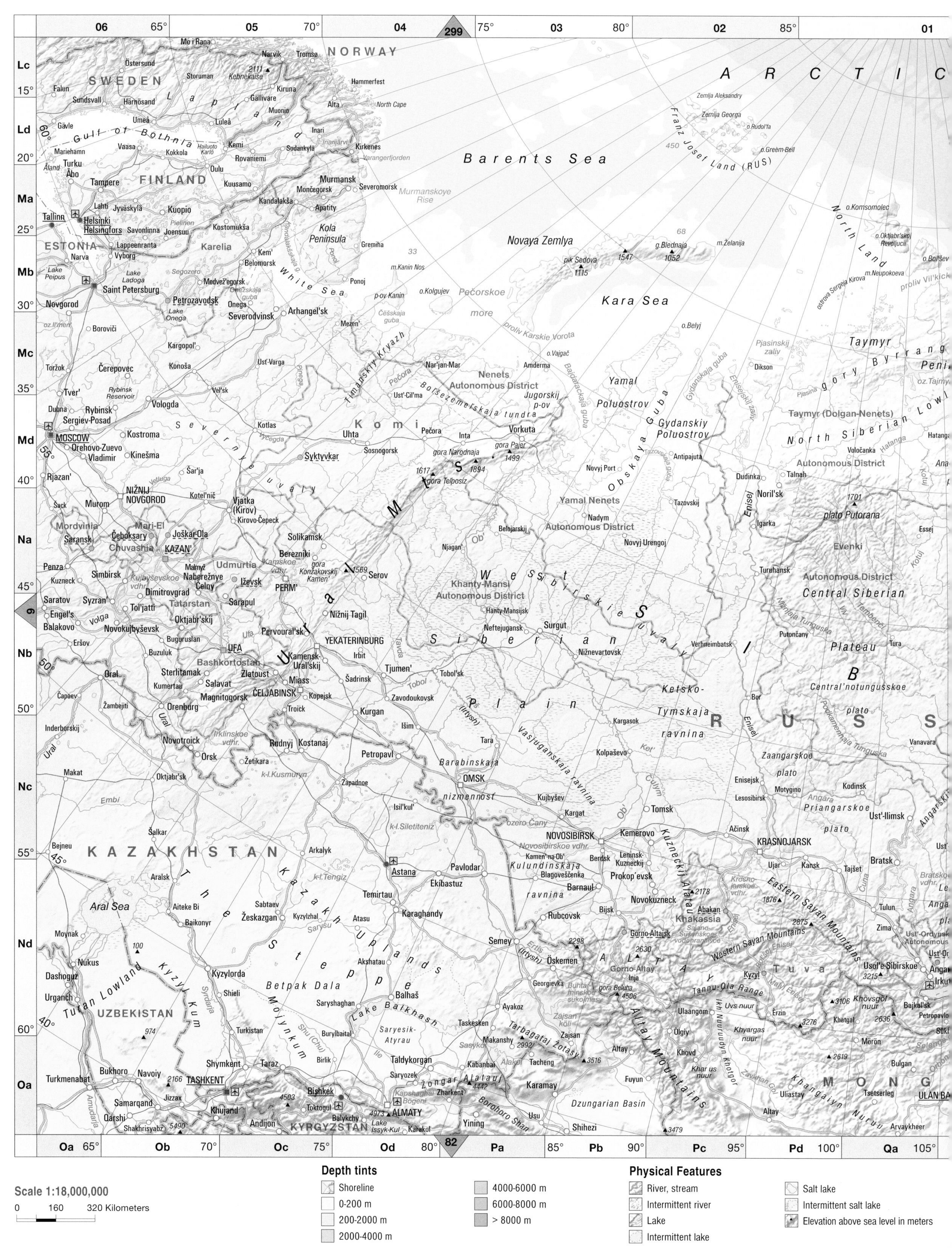

Scale 1:18,000,000

0   160   320 Kilometers

Depth tints

- Shoreline
- 0-200 m
- 200-2000 m
- 2000-4000 m
- 4000-6000 m
- 6000-8000 m
- > 8000 m

Physical Features

- River, stream
- Intermittent river
- Lake
- Intermittent lake
- Salt lake
- Intermittent salt lake
- Elevation above sea level in meters

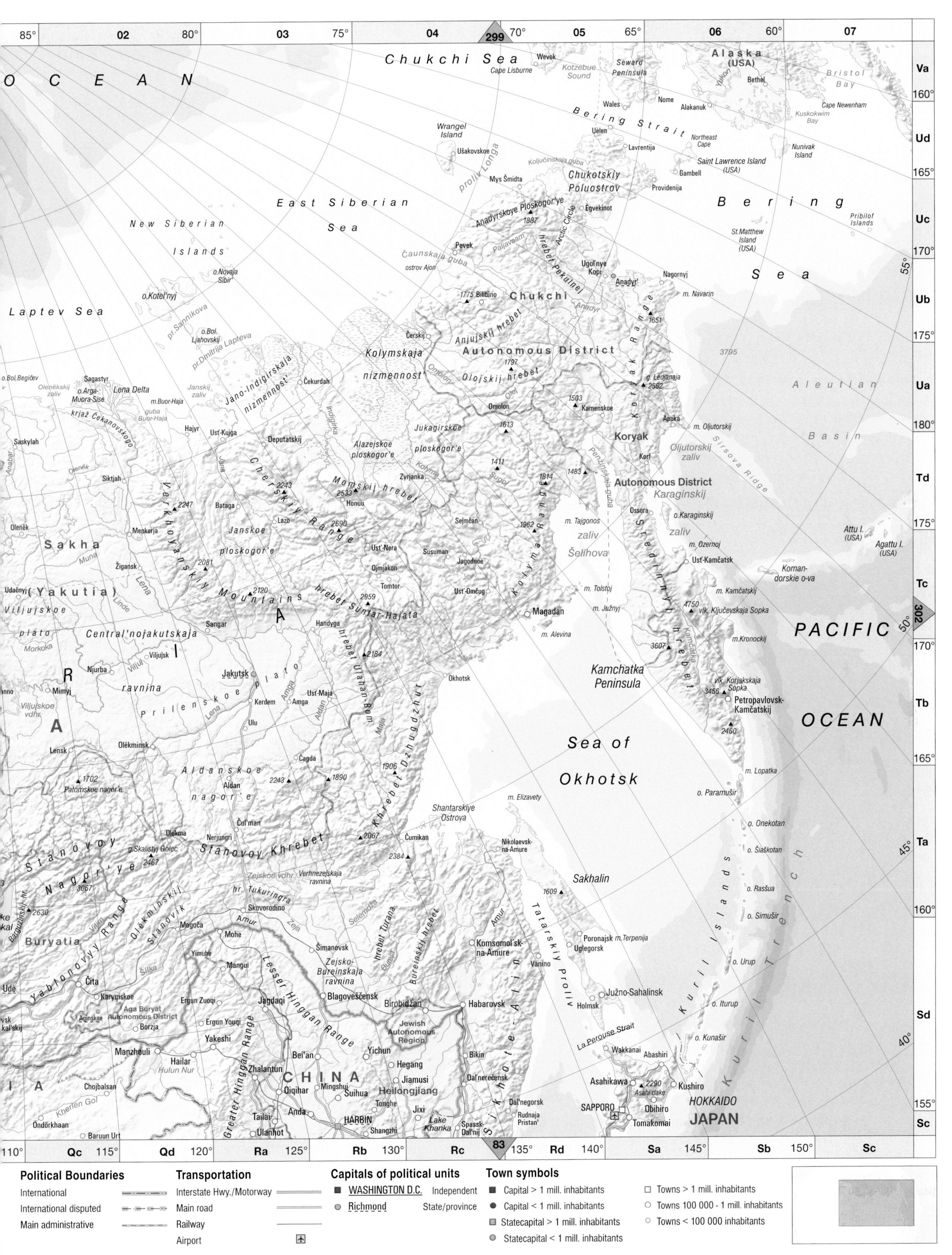

85°	02	80°	03	75°	04	299	70°	05	65°	06	60°	07

Va
160°
Ud
165°
Uc
170°
55°
Ub
175°
Ua
180°
Td
175°
Tc
50° 302
170°
Tb
165°
Ta
45°
Sd
40°
Sc
155°

OCEAN

Chukchi Sea

Wevok
Cape Lisburne
Kotzebue
Sound
Seward
Peninsula
Alaska (USA)
Bristol Bay

Wales
Nome
Alakanuk
Bethel
Cape Newenham
Kuskokwim
Bay

Bering Strait

Wrangel
Island
Ušakovskij
Uelen
Lavrentija
Northeast
Cape
Saint Lawrence Island
(USA)
Nunivak
Island

Proliv Longa
Koljučinskaja guba
Chukotskiy Poluostrov
Providenija
St.Matthew
Island
(USA)
Pribilof
Islands

East Siberian Sea

New Siberian Islands
o.Novaja
Sibir'

Anadyrskoye Ploskogor'ye
1887
Arctic Circle
Egvekinot
B e r i n g

Pevek
Pallavaam
Ugoľnye
Kopi
Nagornyj
m. Navarin

o.Kotel'nyj
pr.Sannikova

Laptev Sea

o.Bol.
Ljahovskij

1775 Bilibino
Chukchi
Anadyr'
1651

S e a

Čerskij
Anjujskij hrebet
hrebet Pekuľnej
3795

o.Bol.Begičev
Olenёkskij
zaliv
Sagastyr
krjaž Čekanovskogo
o.Arga-
Muora-Sise
guba
Buor-Haja
m.Buor-Haja
Janskij
zaliv
pr.Dmitrija Lapteva
Čekurdah

Kolymskaja nizmennost'
Autonomous District
1797
Olojskij hrebet
g. Ledjanaja
2562
A l e u t i a n

Saskylah
Hajyr
Ust'-Kujga
Deputatskij
Omolon
1503
Kamenskoe
Apuka
m. Oljutorskij
B a s i n

Sagastyr
Menkerja
Jukagirskoe ploskogor'e
1613
Koryak
Korf
Oljutorskij
zaliv
Sirsova Ridge

Olenёk
Siktjah
2243
Cherskiy Range
Zyrjanka
1411
Sugoj
1814
1485
Autonomous District
Karaginskij
Attu I.
(USA)
Agattu I.
(USA)

Sakha
Žigansk
Bataga
2533
Momskij hrebet
2690
Honuu
Sejmčan
1962
m. Tajgonos
Ossora
o.Karaginskij
m. Ozernoj

Udačnyj
2247
Lazo
Ust'-Nera
Susuman
Jagodnoe
zaliv
Šelihova
Ust'-Kamčatsk
Koman-
dorskie o-va

(Yakutia)
Viljujskoe
plato
Morkoka
2081
Sangar
hreber Suntar-Hajata
2120
Ojmjakon
Tomtor
Ust'-Omčug
m. Kamčatskij
4750
vlk. Ključevskaja Sopka

Sakha
A
2959
Magadan
m. Tolstoj
m. Južnyj
m. Kamčatskij
PACIFIC

Viljujskoe
vdhr.
Njurba
Central'nojakutskaja
Viljuj
2184
Handyga
Okhotsk
m. Alevina
3607
m.Kronockij

Mirnyj
ravnina
Jakutsk
Kerdem
Ust'-Maja
Amga
Kamchatka Peninsula
vlk. Korjakskaja
3456
Sopka
OCEAN

A
Lensk
Amga
Ulu
Aldan
Prilenskoe plato
hrebet Ulahan-Bom
Petropavlovsk-
Kamčatskij

R
A
1702
Patomskoe nagor'e
2243
Aldan
1890
1906
Sea of
2460

Aldanskoe nagor'e
Čagda
hrebet Dzhugdzhur
Čumikan
Okhotsk
m. Lopatka

Čul'man
2067
Šantarskiye
Ostrova
m. Elizavety
o. Paramušir

Stanovoy Nagor'ye
Olёkma
Nerjungri
2384
Nikolaevsk-
na-Amure
o. Onekotan

Skalistyj Golec
3067
Stanovoy Khrebet
Čumikan
o. Šiaškotan

Baduljachan
2630
2467
hr. Tukuringra
Zejskoe vdhr.
Verhnezejskaja
ravnina
1609
Sakhalin
o. Rassua

Buryatia
Mogoča
Skovorodino
hrebet Turana
Bureinskij hrebet
Poronajsk m. Terpenija
o. Simušir

Čita
Mohe
Šimanovsk
Uglegorsk
o. Urup

Karymskoe
Ergun Zuoqi
Zejsko-Bureinskaja ravnina
Komsomol'sk-
na-Amure
Vanino
Južno-Sahalinsk

Aginskoe
Aga Buryat
Autonomous District
Borzja
Jagdaqi
Blagoveščensk
Birobidžan
Habarovsk
Holmsk
o. Iturup

Yablonovyy Range
Yakeshi
Jewish
Autonomous
Region
Bikin
Wakkanai
Abashiri

Manzhouli
Hailar
Bei'an
Yichun
Dal'nerečensk
o. Kunašir
La Perouse Strait

Ondörhaan
Hulun Nur
Zhalantun
Hegang
Sikhote-Alin'
Dal'negorsk
Asahikawa
2290
Asahi dake
Kushiro

Chojbalsan
Mingshui
Suihua
Heilongjiang
Tonghe
Rudnaja
Pristan'
SAPPORO
Obihiro
HOKKAIDO

Kherlen Gol
Tailai
Anda
Jiamusi
Jixi
Spassk-
Dal'nij
JAPAN
Tomakomai

Baruun Urt
Ulanhot
HARBIN
Shangzhi
Lake
Khanka

Qiqihar
CHINA

Tatarskiy Proliv
Kuril Islands
Kuril Trench

Political Boundaries

International
International disputed
Main administrative

Transportation

Interstate Hwy./Motorway
Main road
Railway
Airport

Capitals of political units

WASHINGTON D.C. Independent
Richmond State/province

Town symbols

■ Capital > 1 mill. inhabitants
● Capital < 1 mill. inhabitants
▣ Statecapital > 1 mill. inhabitants
◉ Statecapital < 1 mill. inhabitants

□ Towns > 1 mill. inhabitants
○ Towns 100 000 - 1 mill. inhabitants
○ Towns < 100 000 inhabitants

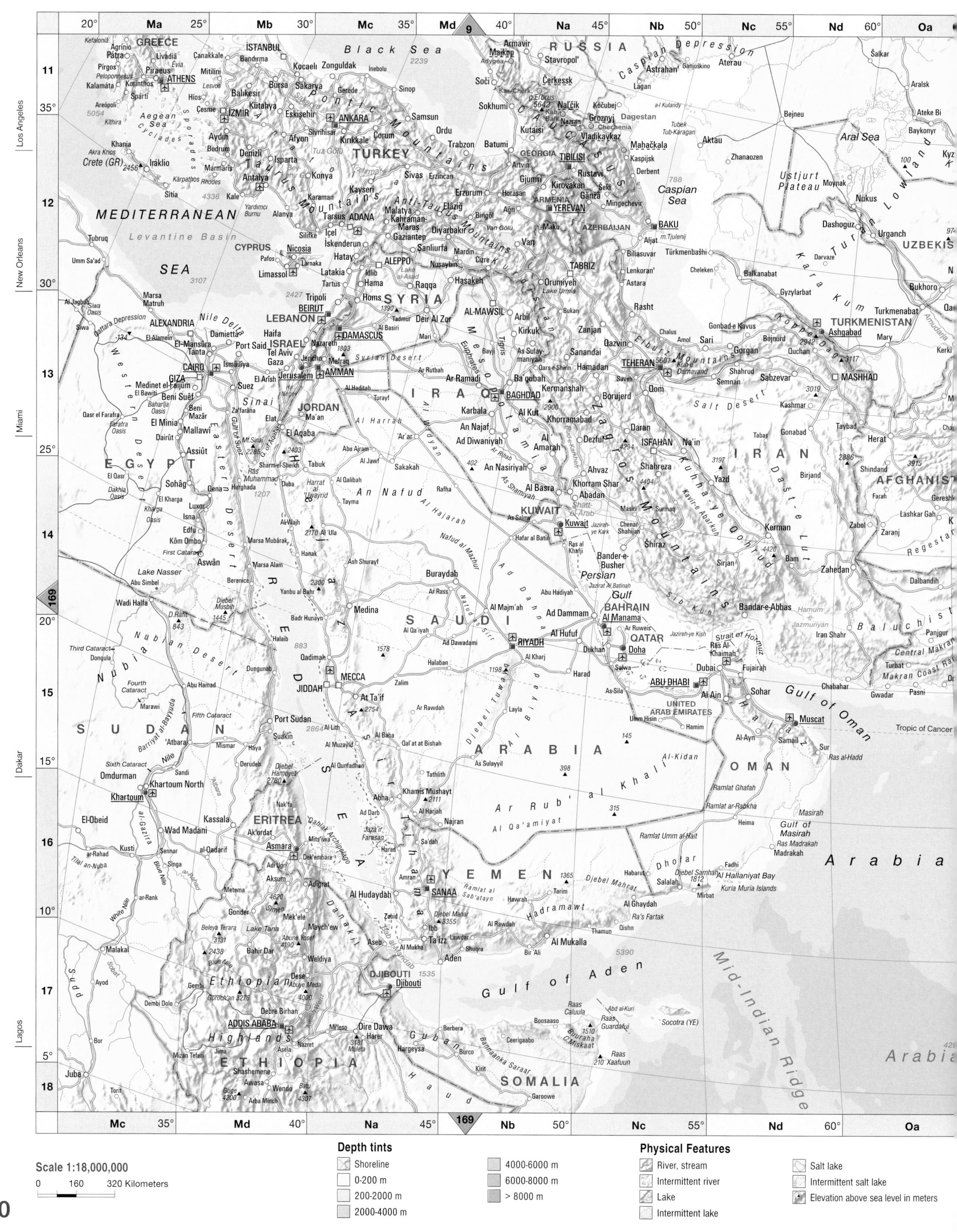

Scale 1:18,000,000

0   160   320 Kilometers

60

Depth tints

Shoreline
0–200 m
200–2000 m
2000–4000 m
4000–6000 m
6000–8000 m
> 8000 m

Physical Features

River, stream
Intermittent river
Lake
Intermittent lake
Salt lake
Intermittent salt lake
Elevation above sea level in meters

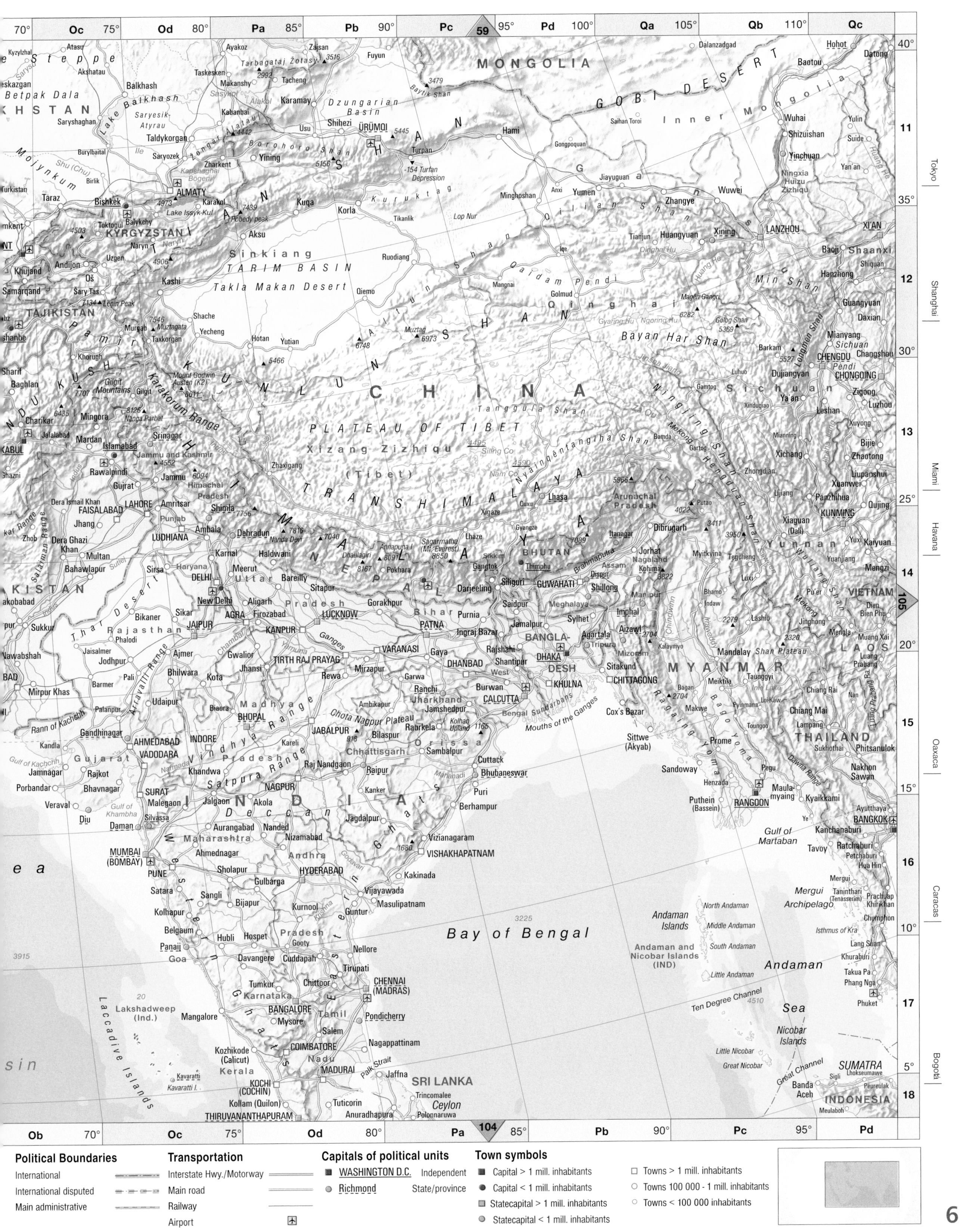

Political Boundaries

International

International disputed

Main administrative

Transportation

Interstate Hwy./Motorway

Main road

Railway

Airport

Capitals of political units

■ WASHINGTON D.C.   Independent

● Richmond   State/province

Town symbols

■ Capital > 1 mill. inhabitants

● Capital < 1 mill. inhabitants

■ Statecapital > 1 mill. inhabitants

● Statecapital < 1 mill. inhabitants

□ Towns > 1 mill. inhabitants

○ Towns 100 000 - 1 mill. inhabitants

○ Towns < 100 000 inhabitants

61

Turkey, Caucasus Region

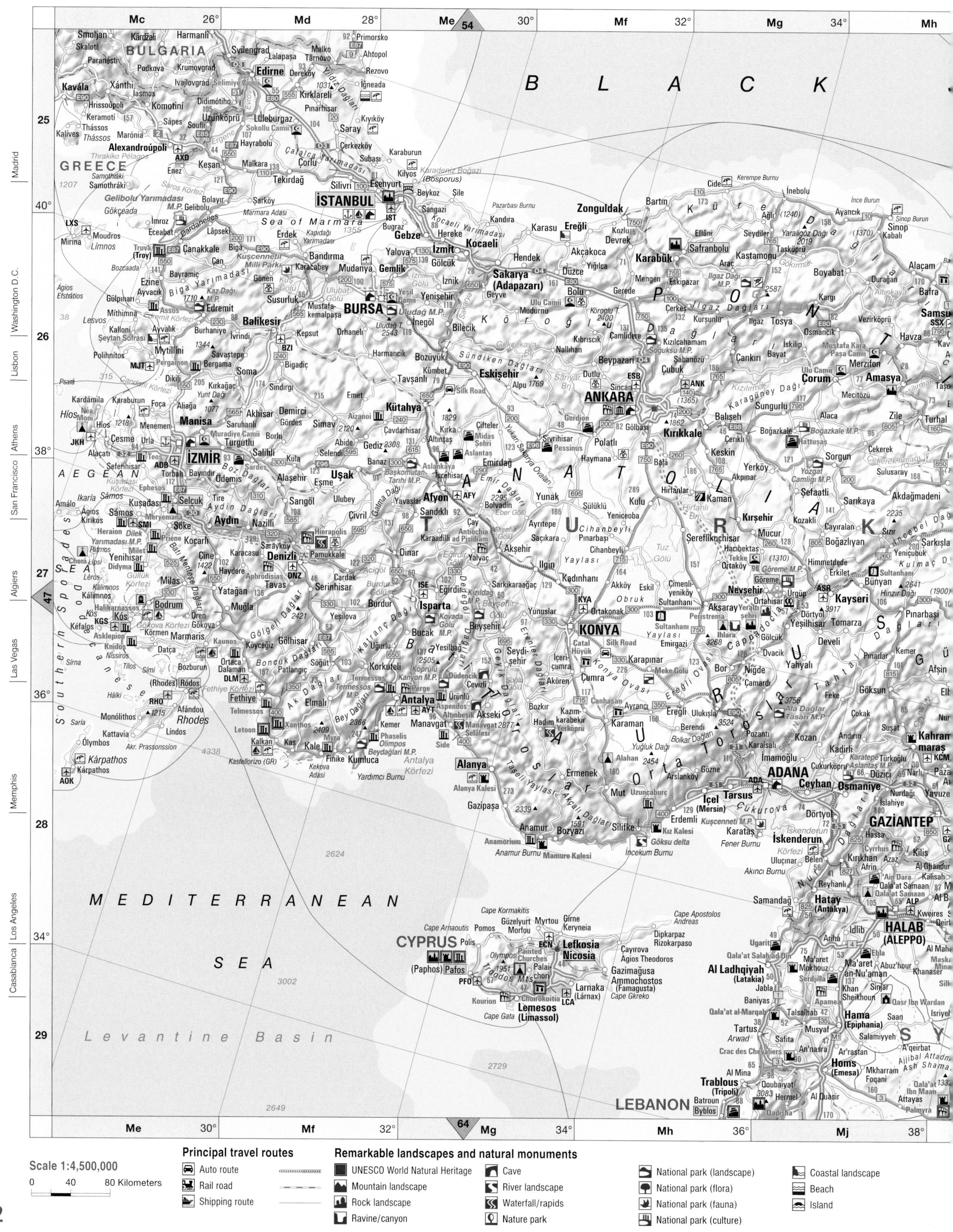

Scale 1:4,500,000

0   40   80 Kilometers

Principal travel routes

- Auto route
- Rail road
- Shipping route

Remarkable landscapes and natural monuments

- UNESCO World Natural Heritage
- Mountain landscape
- Rock landscape
- Ravine/canyon
- Cave
- River landscape
- Waterfall/rapids
- Nature park
- National park (landscape)
- National park (flora)
- National park (fauna)
- National park (culture)
- Coastal landscape
- Beach
- Island

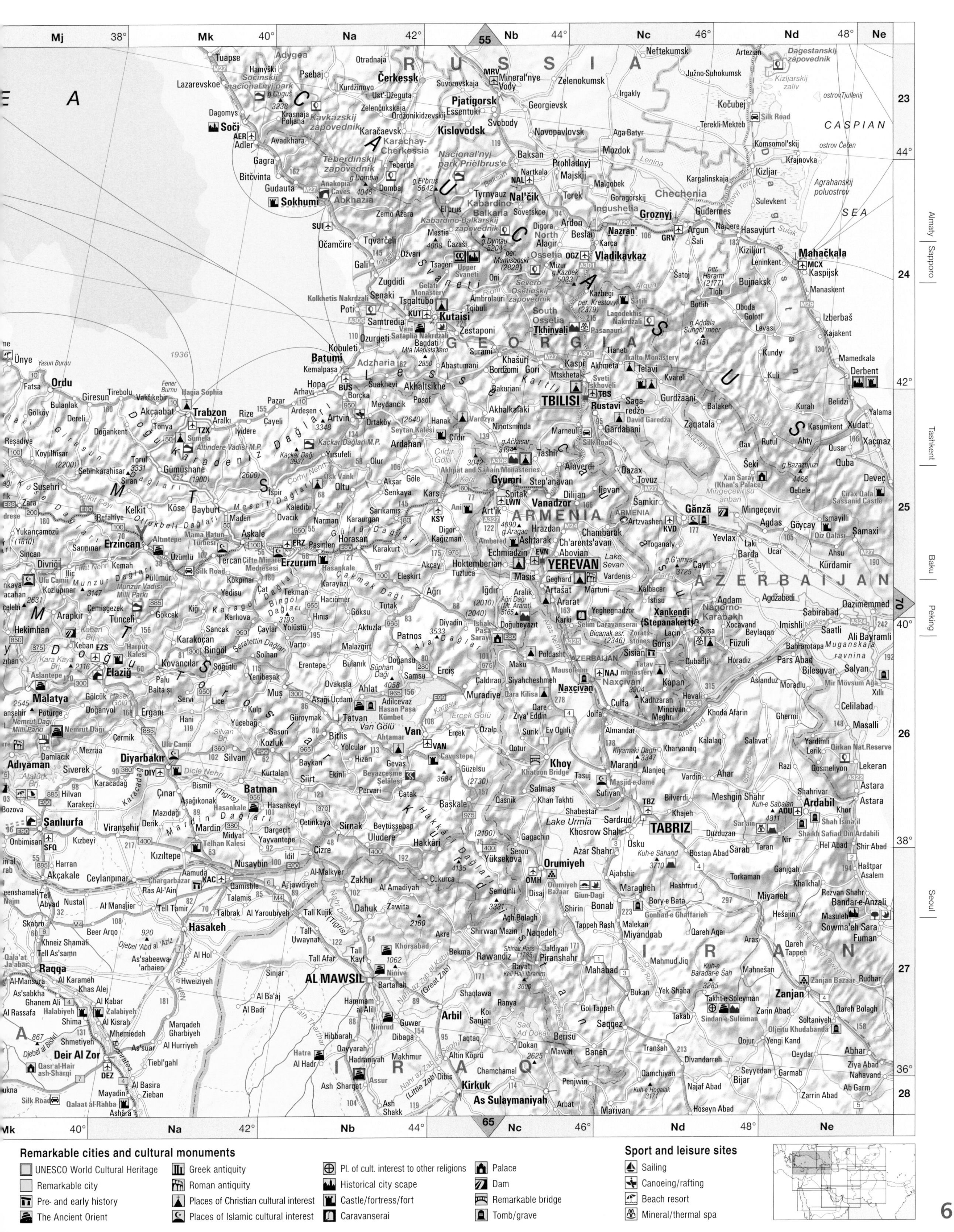

Remarkable cities and cultural monuments

- ▢ UNESCO World Cultural Heritage
- ▢ Remarkable city
- 🏛 Pre- and early history
- 🏛 The Ancient Orient
- 🏛 Greek antiquity
- 🏛 Roman antiquity
- 🏛 Places of Christian cultural interest
- ☪ Places of Islamic cultural interest
- ⊕ Pl. of cult. interest to other religions
- ▣ Historical city scape
- 🏰 Castle/fortress/fort
- 🏛 Caravanserai
- 🏰 Palace
- 🏞 Dam
- 🌉 Remarkable bridge
- 🪦 Tomb/grave

Sport and leisure sites

- ⛵ Sailing
- 🛶 Canoeing/rafting
- 🏖 Beach resort
- ♨ Mineral/thermal spa

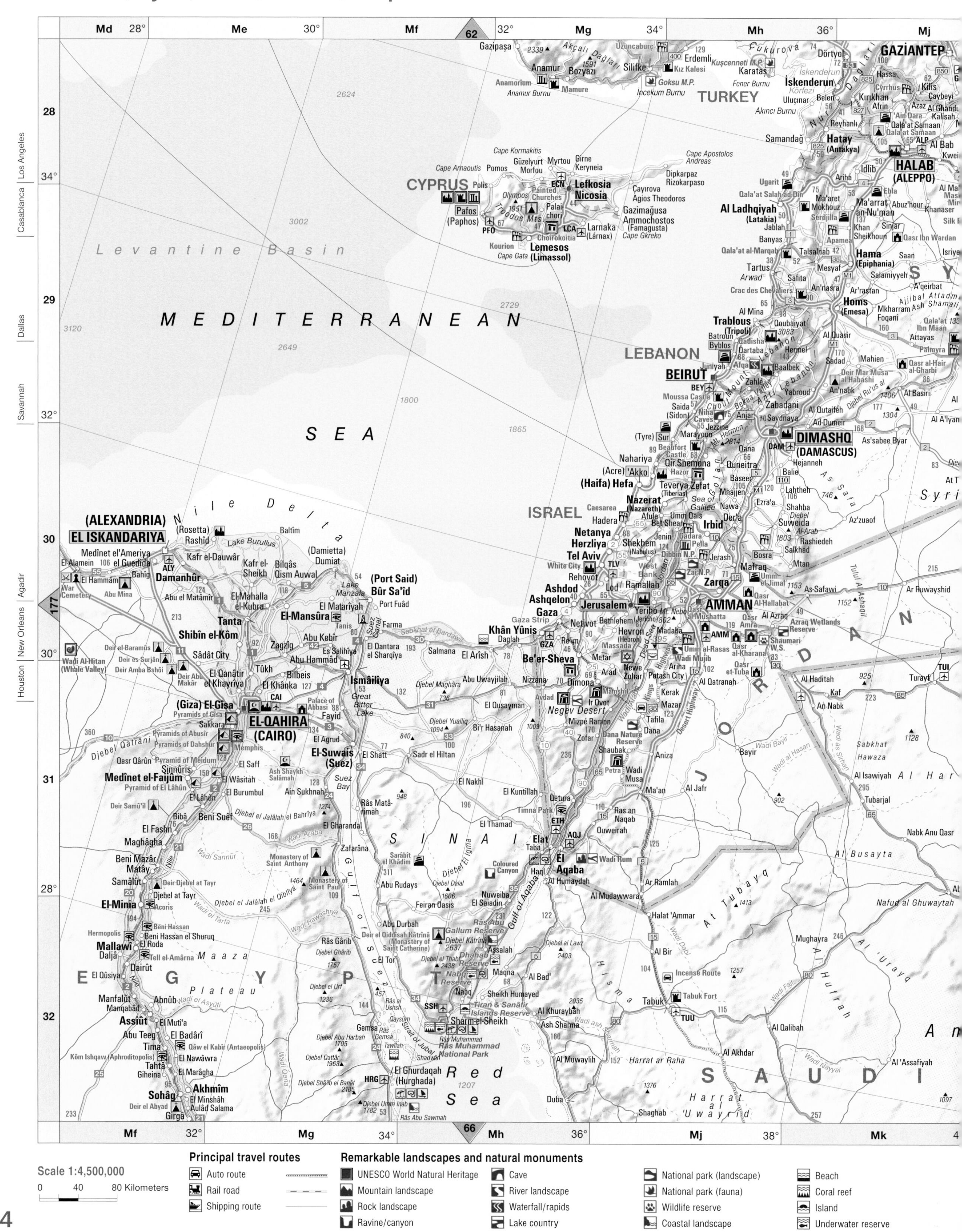

Scale 1:4,500,000

0   40   80 Kilometers

Principal travel routes
- Auto route
- Rail road
- Shipping route

Remarkable landscapes and natural monuments
- UNESCO World Natural Heritage
- Mountain landscape
- Rock landscape
- Ravine/canyon
- Cave
- River landscape
- Waterfall/rapids
- Lake country
- National park (landscape)
- National park (fauna)
- Wildlife reserve
- Coastal landscape
- Beach
- Coral reef
- Island
- Underwater reserve

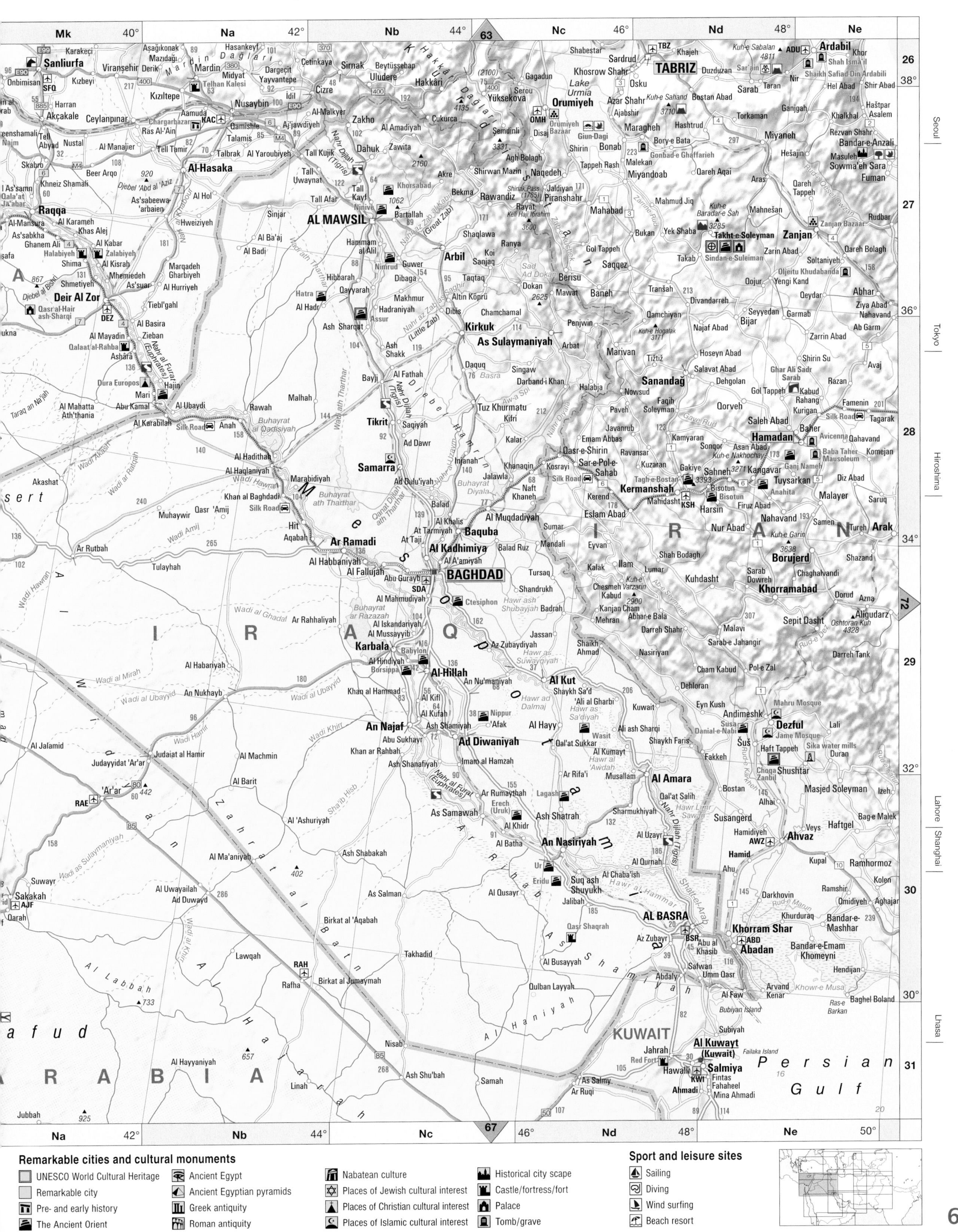

| Mk | 40° | Na | 42° | Nb | 44° | 63 | Nc | 46° | Nd | 48° | Ne |

Şanliurfa Onbinmisa SFO · Viranşehir Derik · Mardin · Midyat · Cizre · Hakkâri · Yüksekova · **Orumiyeh** · **TABRIZ** Duzduzan · Sardrud · Khosrow Shahr · Osku · Sarab · Taran · Hel Abad · Shir Abad · **Ardabil** Shah Isma'il

Akçakale · Ceylanpinar · Nusaybin · Al-Malkyer · Zakho · Al Amadiyah · Çukurca · Şemdinli · Disaj · Orumiyeh Bazaar · Giun-Dagi · Shabestan · Azar Shahr · Ajabshir · Maragheh · Bostan Abad · Sarab · Ganjah · Khalkhal · Hashpar · Asalem

Harran · Al-Hasaka · Tall Afar · Sinjar · Al Ba'aj · Al Badi · Akre · Shirwan Mazin · Naqedeh · Mahabad · Bukan · Saqqez · Zanjan · Rudbar

Deir Al Zor · **Al Mawsil** · **Arbil** · **Kirkuk** · **As Sulaymaniyah** · **Sanandaj** · **Hamadan** · **Kermanshah**

Samarra · **Tikrit** · **Baquba** · **BAGHDAD** · **Borujerd** · **Khorramabad** · **Arak**

Karbala · **Al-Hillah** · **Al Kut** · **Dezful** · **Ahvaz**

An Najaf · **Ad Diwaniyah** · **An Nasiriyah** · **Al Amara** · **Shushtar**

As Samawah · **Al Basra** · **Khorram Shahr** · **Abadan**

KUWAIT · **Al Kuwayt (Kuwait)** · **Salmiya** · *Persian Gulf*

Remarkable cities and cultural monuments

- UNESCO World Cultural Heritage
- Remarkable city
- Pre- and early history
- The Ancient Orient
- Ancient Egypt
- Ancient Egyptian pyramids
- Greek antiquity
- Roman antiquity
- Nabatean culture
- Places of Jewish cultural interest
- Places of Christian cultural interest
- Places of Islamic cultural interest
- Historical city scape
- Castle/fortress/fort
- Palace
- Tomb/grave

Sport and leisure sites

- Sailing
- Diving
- Wind surfing
- Beach resort

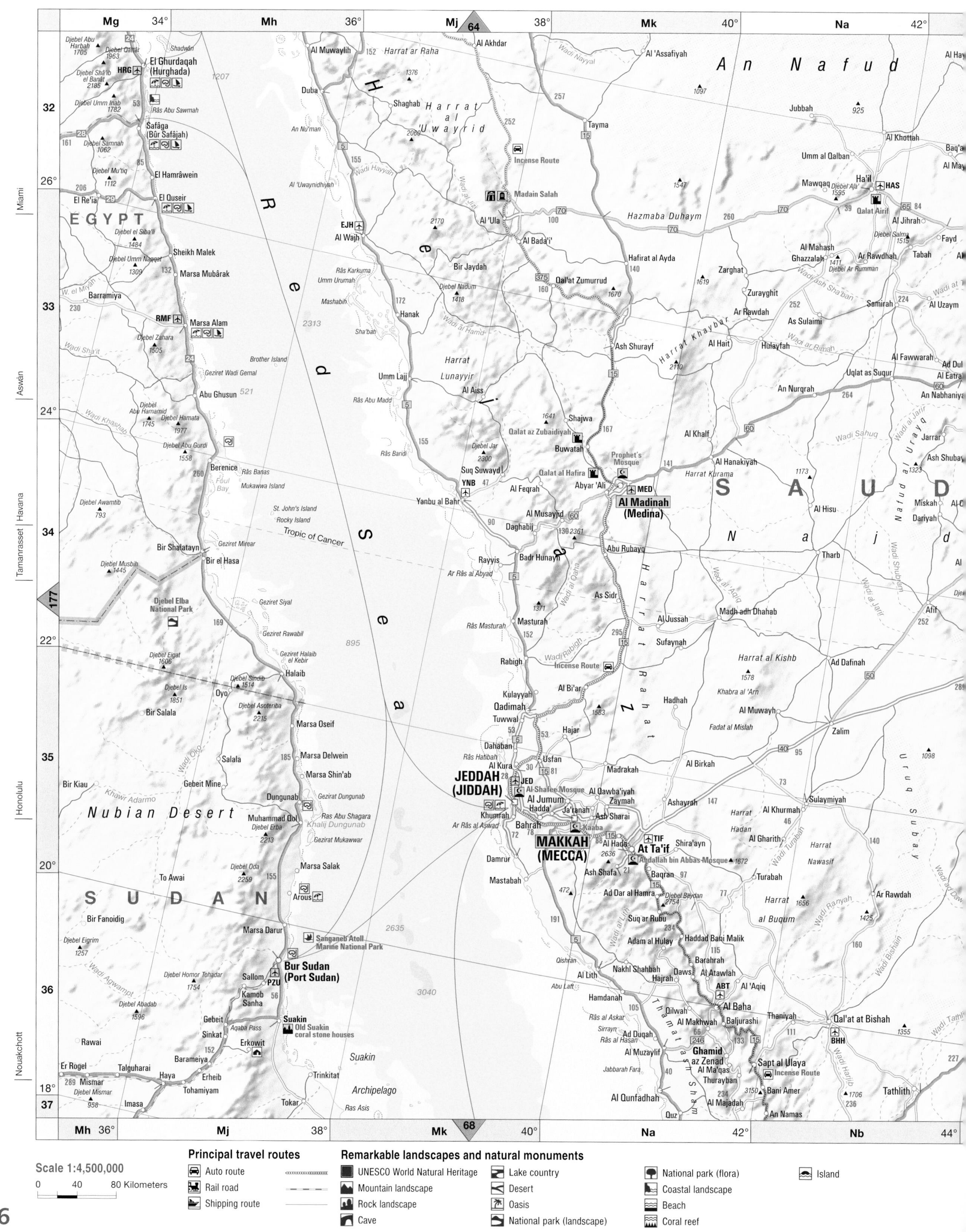

Scale 1:4,500,000

0   40   80 Kilometers

Principal travel routes

- 🚗 Auto route
- 🚆 Rail road
- 🚢 Shipping route

.... (dotted route)
— — — (dashed route)
——— (solid route)

Remarkable landscapes and natural monuments

- ■ UNESCO World Natural Heritage
- ▲ Mountain landscape
- ■ Rock landscape
- ■ Cave
- ■ Lake country
- ■ Desert
- 🕋 Oasis
- ■ National park (landscape)
- ▲ National park (flora)
- ■ Coastal landscape
- ■ Beach
- ≈ Coral reef
- ◩ Island

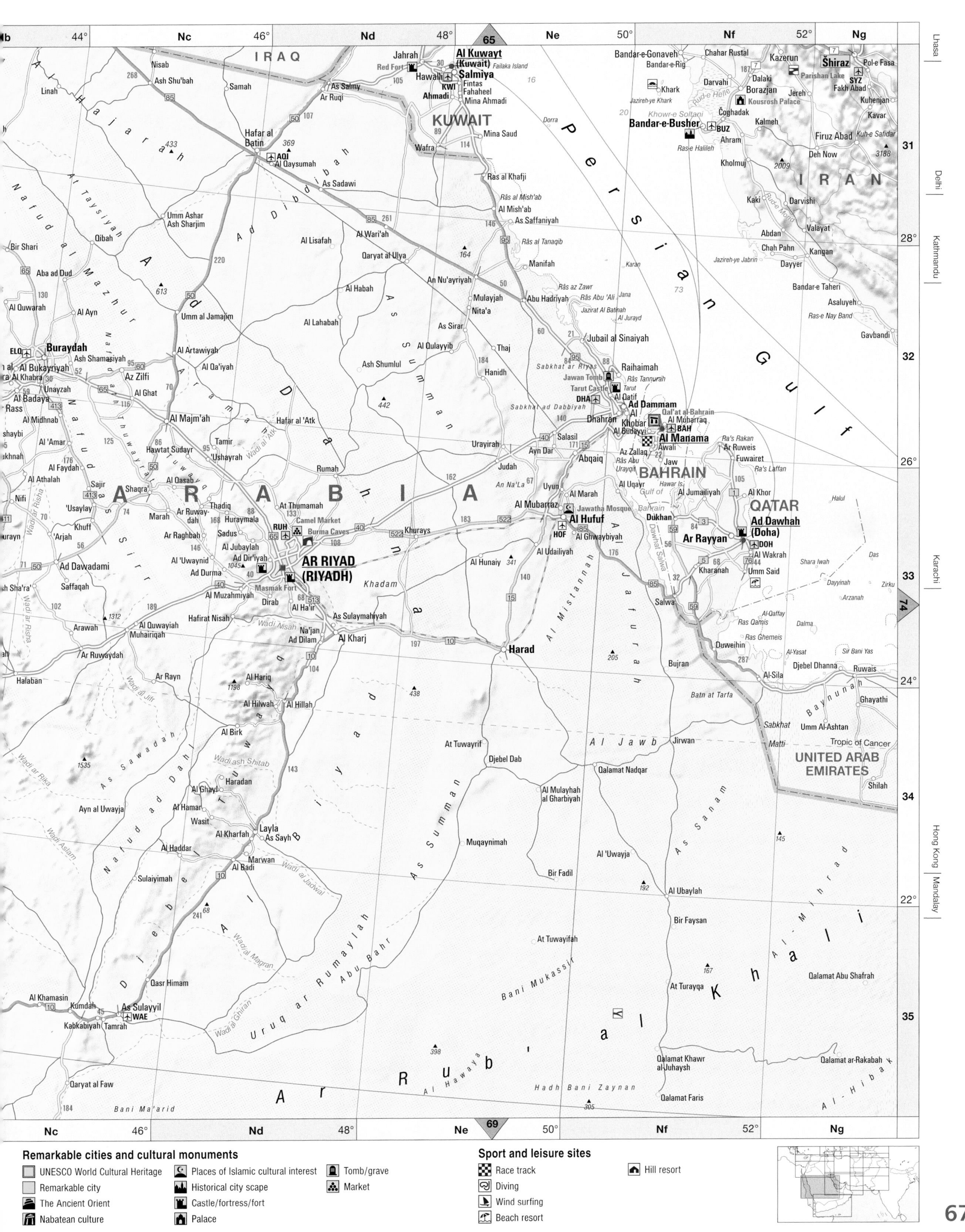

Nb		Nc		Nd		**65**	Ne		Nf		Ng
44°		46°		48°				50°		52°		

Lhasa

Delhi

Kathmandu

Karachi

Hong Kong

Mandalay

IRAQ

KUWAIT

Al Kuwayt (Kuwait)
Salmiya

Hafar al Batin

Buraydah

A R A B I A

AR RIYAD (RIYADH)

Harad

Persian Gulf

I R A N

Shiraz

Bandar-e-Busher

BAHRAIN
Al Manama

Ad Dammam
Dhahran

QATAR
Ad Dawhah (Doha)

UNITED ARAB EMIRATES

Tropic of Cancer

Ar Rub' al Khali

Nc		Nd		**69**	Ne		Nf		Ng
46°		48°				50°		52°		

67

Remarkable cities and cultural monuments

- UNESCO World Cultural Heritage
- Remarkable city
- The Ancient Orient
- Nabatean culture
- Places of Islamic cultural interest
- Historical city scape
- Castle/fortress/fort
- Palace
- Tomb/grave
- Market

Sport and leisure sites

- Race track
- Diving
- Wind surfing
- Beach resort
- Hill resort

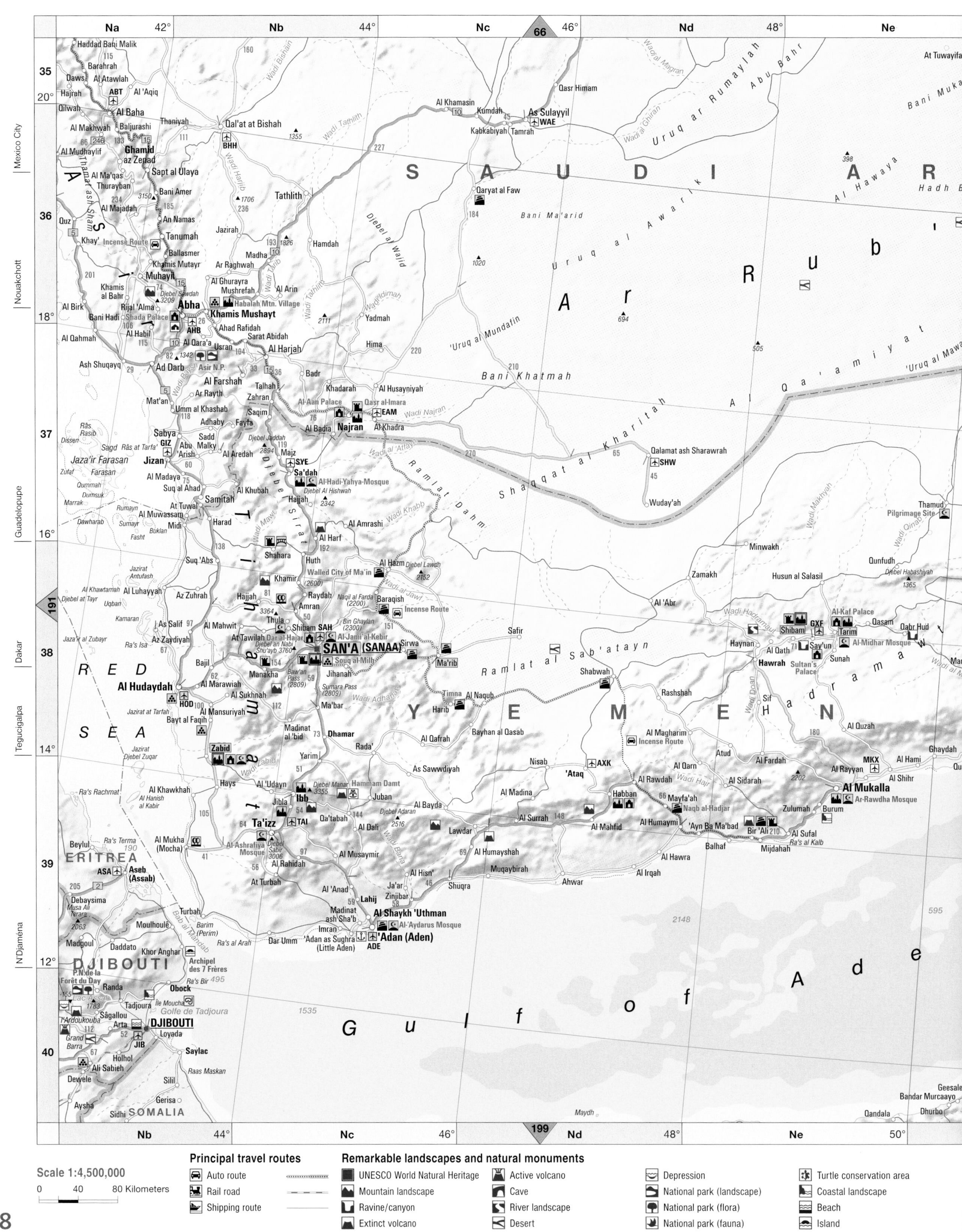

Scale 1:4,500,000

0   40   80 Kilometers

Principal travel routes
- 🚗 Auto route
- 🚂 Rail road
- 🚢 Shipping route
- ······ (auto route dotted)
- — — (shipping route)
- ——

Remarkable landscapes and natural monuments
- ■ UNESCO World Natural Heritage
- ▣ Mountain landscape
- ▣ Ravine/canyon
- ▣ Extinct volcano
- ▲ Active volcano
- ⌂ Cave
- ⌂ River landscape
- ⌂ Desert
- ⌂ Depression
- ⌂ National park (landscape)
- ⌂ National park (flora)
- ⌂ National park (fauna)
- ⌂ Turtle conservation area
- ⌂ Coastal landscape
- ⌂ Beach
- ⌂ Island

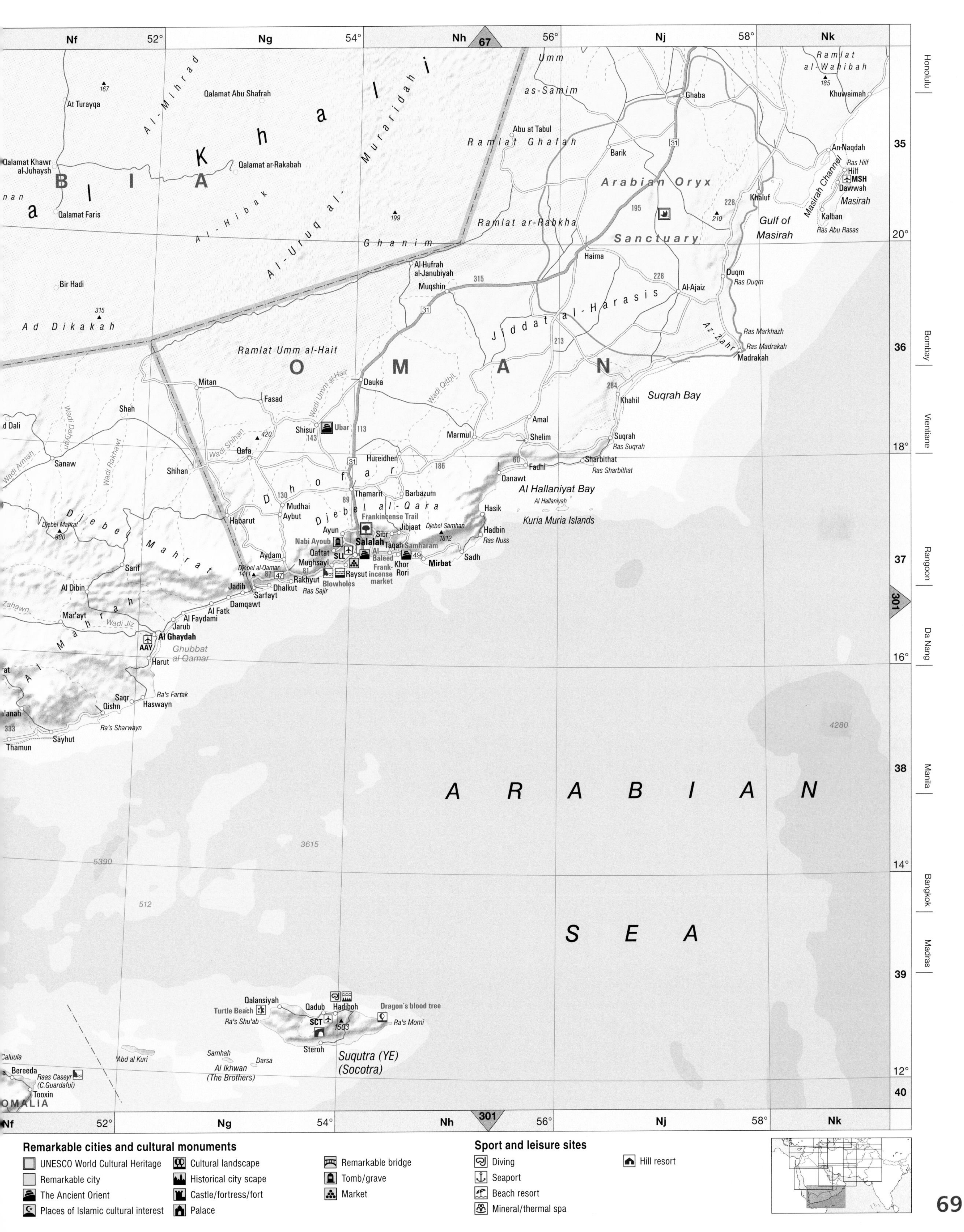

Al-Mibrad
At Turayqa
167
Qalamat Abu Shafrah
Umm
as-Samim
Ghaba
Ramlat
al-Wahibah
185
Khuwaimah

A B I A K h a l i
Qalamat Khawr al-Juhaysh
Qalamat ar-Rakabah
Muraridah
Abu at Tabul
Ramlat Ghafah
Barik
31
An-Naqdah
Ras Hilf
Hilf
MSH
Dawwah
Masirah

nan a
Qalamat Faris
Al-Hibak
Al-Uruq al-
199
Ramlat ar-Rabkha
Arabian Oryx
195
Khaluf
228
Gulf of Masirah
Kalban
Rás Abu Rasas
Sanctuary
210

Ghanim
Bir Hadi
Al-Hufrah al-Janubiyah
Haima
Duqm
Ras Duqm

Ad Dikakah
315
Muqshin
315
228
Al-Ajaiz
Az Zahr
Ras Markhazh
Ras Madrakah
Madrakah

Ramlat Umm al-Hait
O M A N
31
Jiddat al-Harasis
213

Mitan
Dauka
264
Khahil
Suqrah Bay

Wadi Daryan
Shah
Fasad
Wadi Umm al-Hait
Wadi Qitbit

Shisur
143
Ubar
113
Amal
Shelim
Marmul
Suqrah
Ras Suqrah

d Dali
Qafa
Hureidhen
31
186
Fadhl
60
Sharbithat
Ras Sharbithat

Sanaw
Shihan
420
Dhofar
Thamarit
89
Barbazum
Qanawt
Al Hallaniyat Bay

Djebel Mahrat
980
Mudhai
Aybut
Djebel al-Qara
Frankincense Trail
Hasik
Hadbin
Ras Nuss
Kuria Muria Islands

Habarut
Ayun
Nabi Ayoub
Sibr
Jibjaat
Djebel Samhan
1812
Al Hallaniyah

Al Dibin
Aydam
Qaftat
Mughsayl
SLL
Salalah
Al-Baleed
Taqah
Samharam
Sadh

Sarif
Djebel al-Qamar
1411
81 47
Rakhyut
81
Raysut
Frank-incense market
Khor Rori
Mirbat

Jadib
Dhalkut
Sarfayt
Blowholes
Ras Sajir
49
Hadbin

Mar'ayt
Damqawt
Al Fatk
Al Faydami
Jarub

Al Ghaydah
AAY
Ghubbat al Qamar

Zahawn
Wadi Jiz
Harut

Al Mahrah
Saqr
Qishn
Ra's Fartak
Haswayn
Ra's Sharwayn

333
Sayhut
Thamun

A R A B I A N

3615
4280

S E A

5390
512

Qalansiyah
Turtle Beach
Ra's Shu'ab
Qadub
Hadiboh
SCT
1503
Dragon's blood tree
Ra's Momi

Caluula
Bereeda
Tooxin
OMALIA
Abd al Kuri
Samhah
Al Ikhwan
(The Brothers)
Darsa
Steroh
Suqutra (YE)
(Socotra)

Raas Caseyr
(C.Guardafui)

Honolulu
Bombay
Vientiane
Rangoon
Da Nang
Manila
Bangkok
Madras
35
20°
36
18°
37
301
16°
38
14°
39
12°
40

Remarkable cities and cultural monuments

- UNESCO World Cultural Heritage
- Remarkable city
- The Ancient Orient
- Places of Islamic cultural interest
- Cultural landscape
- Historical city scape
- Castle/fortress/fort
- Palace
- Remarkable bridge
- Tomb/grave
- Market

Sport and leisure sites

- Diving
- Seaport
- Beach resort
- Mineral/thermal spa
- Hill resort

69

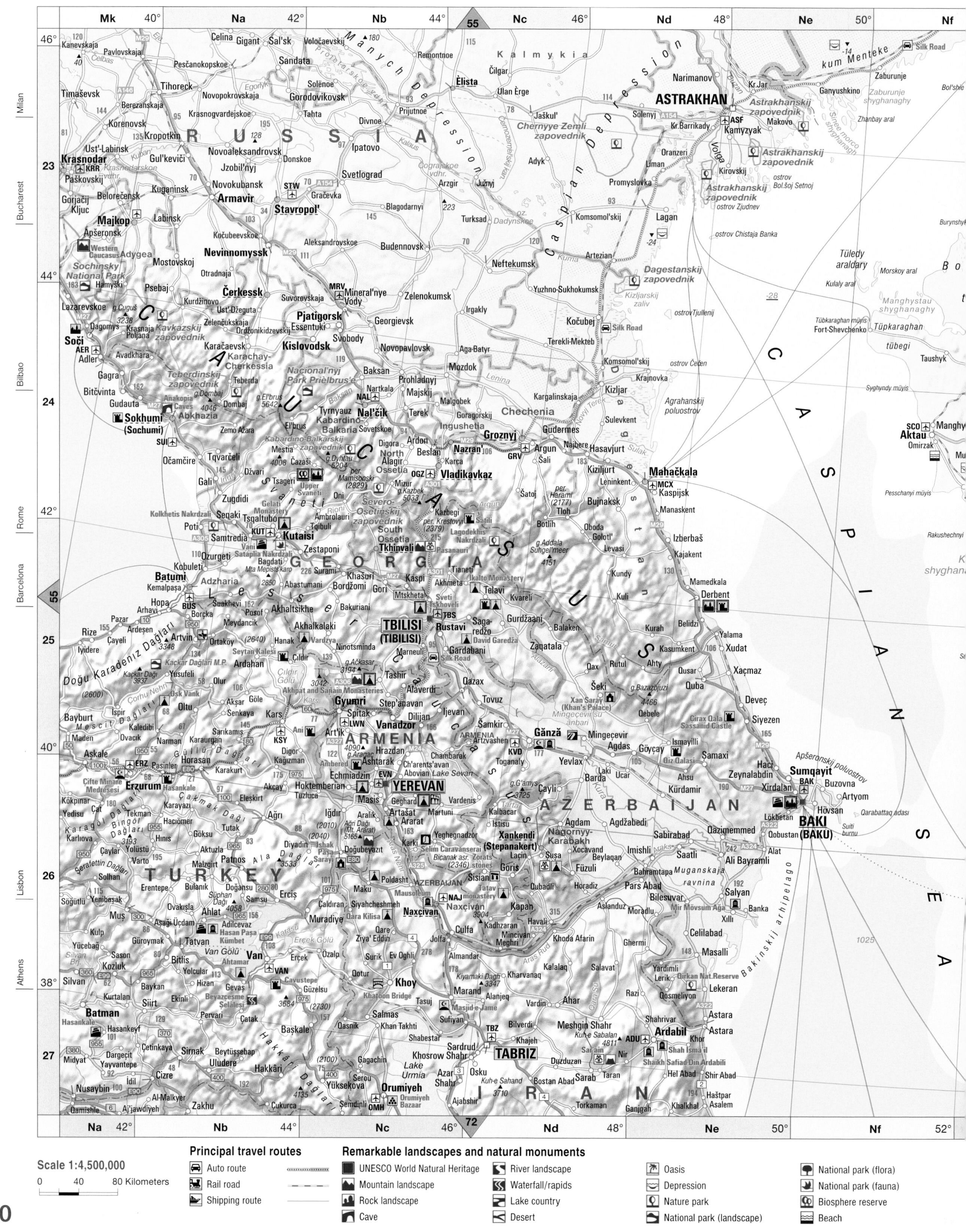

Scale 1:4,500,000

0   40   80 Kilometers

Principal travel routes

- Auto route
- Rail road
- Shipping route

Remarkable landscapes and natural monuments

- UNESCO World Natural Heritage
- Mountain landscape
- Rock landscape
- Cave

- River landscape
- Waterfall/rapids
- Lake country
- Desert

- Oasis
- Depression
- Nature park
- National park (landscape)

- National park (flora)
- National park (fauna)
- Biosphere reserve
- Beach

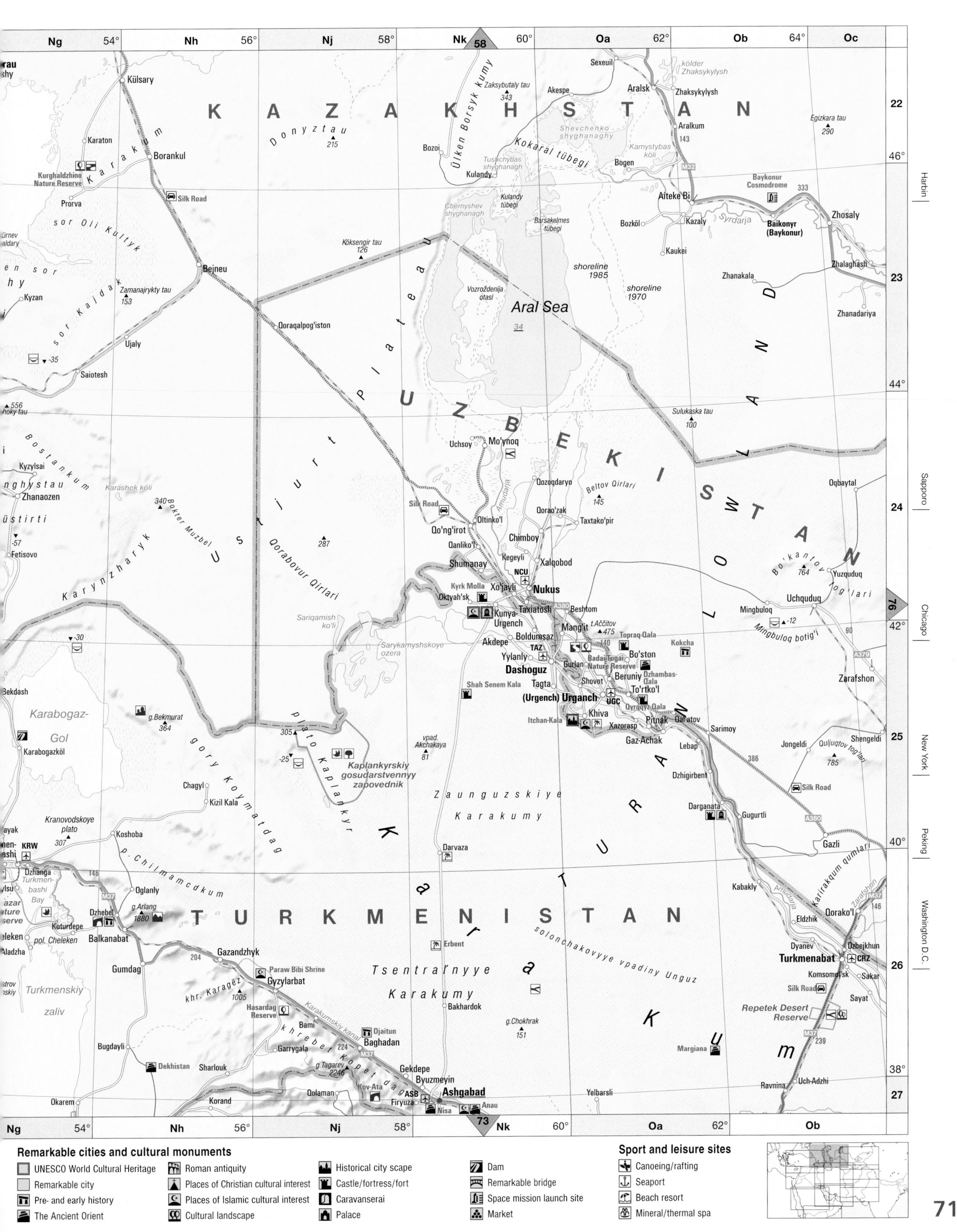

KAZAKHSTAN

Kürghaldzhino
Nature Reserve

Karaton
Borankul
Prorva

Külsary

Donyztau
215

sor Oli Kultyk

Silk Road

Bejneu

Köksengir tau
126

Shevchenko-
shyghanaghy

Sexeuil

Akespe

Aralsk
Zhaksykylysh

Aralkum
143

Zaksybutaly tau
343

Ülken Borsyk kumy

Kokaral tübegi

Bozoi

Kulandy

Tusshybas
shyghanagh

Kulandy
tübegi

Bärsakelmes
tübegi

kölder
Zhaksylysh

Kamystybas
köli

Bogen

Bozköl

Kazaly

Kaukei

Aiteke Bi

Baikonur
Cosmodrome

Baikonyr
(Baykonur)

333

Egizkara tau
290

Zhosaly

Zhalaghash

Syrdarja

Zhanakala

Zhanadariya

sor Oli Kultyk

ürnev
aldary

Kyzan

Zamanajrykty tau
153

Ujaly

Saiotesh

en sor
hy

Qoraqalpog'iston

Aral Sea
34

shoreline
1985

Vozroždenija
otasi

shoreline
1970

Chérnyshev
shyghanagh

556
hoky tau

Bostankum

Kyzylsai

Zhanaozen

Karashek köli

Uchsoy

Mo'ynoq

Beltov Qirlari
145

Sulukaska tau
100

Bo'kantov
tog'lari
764

Oqbaytal

Yuzquduq

Uchquduq

nghystau

üstirti

340
Bokter Muzbel

287

Qozoqdaryo

Qorao'zak

Taxtako'pir

Mingbuloq

-12

Zarafshon

90

-57
Fetisovo

Qanliko'f

Qo'ng'irot

Shumanay

Kyrk Molla

Xo'jayli

Oktyah'sk

NCU

Nukus

Chimboy

Xalqobod

Kegeyli

A380

Beshtom

Mingbuloq botig'i

A379

Zarafshon

Sariqamish
ko'li

Kunya-
Urgench

Taxiatosh

Mang'it

t.Aččitov
475

Topraq-Qala

Kokcha

Silk Road

-30

Sarykamyshskoye
ozera

Akdepe

Boldumsaz

TAZ

Yylanly

Dashoguz

Badai-Tugai
Nature Reserve
140

Gurlan

Shovot

Bo'ston

Beruniy

Dzhambas-
Qala

To'rtko'l

Xazorasp

Shengeldi

Bekdash

Karabogaz-
Gol

Karabogazköl

g.Bekmurat
364

305

-25

plato Kaplankyr

Kaplankyrskiy
gosudarstvennyy
zapovednik

Shah Senem Kala

Tagta

(Urgench) Urganch

UGC

Khiva

Itchan-Kala

Qyrqqyz-Qala

Pitnak

Gaz-Achak

Qaľatov

Sarimoy

Jongeldi

Quljuqtov tog'lari
785

786

Chagyl

Kizil Kala

gory Koymatdag

vpad.
Akchakaya
81

Zaunguzskiye
Karakumy

Lebap

Dzhigirbent

Darganata

Gugurtli

Silk Road

A380

Gazli

Kranovodskoye
plato
307

Koshoba

p. Chilmamcdkum

Darvaza

KURAN

Kabakly

kairakkum qumtari

Dyanev

Qorako'l

Eldzhik

Kaya
men-
ashi

KRW

Dzhanga
Turkmen-
bashi

146

Oglanly

g.Arlang
1880

TURKMENISTAN

solonchakovyye vpadiny Unguz

Turkmenabat

CRZ

Dzhebel

Koturdepe

Balkanabat

Gazandzhyk

Gumdag

Gyzylarbat

Paraw Bibi Shrine

khr. Karagēz
1005

Erbent

Tsentraľnyye
Karakumy

Bakhardok

g.Chokhrak
151

Komsomol'sk

Sakar

Silk Road

Karakumy

Repetek Desert
Reserve

M37

239

Sayat

azar
ature
eserve

Hasardag
Reserve

Bami

Djaitun
Baghadan

Karakumskiy kanal

khrebet Kopet dag

Margiana

Ravnina

Uch-Adzhi

Bugdayli

Garrygala

224

g.Tagarev
2246

Gekdepe

Byuzmeyin

M37

Dekhistan

Sharlouk

Kov-Ata

Qolaman

Firyuza

ASB

Ashgabad

Nisa

Anau

Yelbarsli

Okarem

Korand

Remarkable cities and cultural monuments

- □ UNESCO World Cultural Heritage
- ▢ Remarkable city
- Pre- and early history
- The Ancient Orient
- Roman antiquity
- Places of Christian cultural interest
- Places of Islamic cultural interest
- Cultural landscape
- Historical city scape
- Castle/fortress/fort
- Caravanserai
- Palace
- Dam
- Remarkable bridge
- Space mission launch site
- Market

Sport and leisure sites

- Canoeing/rafting
- Seaport
- Beach resort
- Mineral/thermal spa

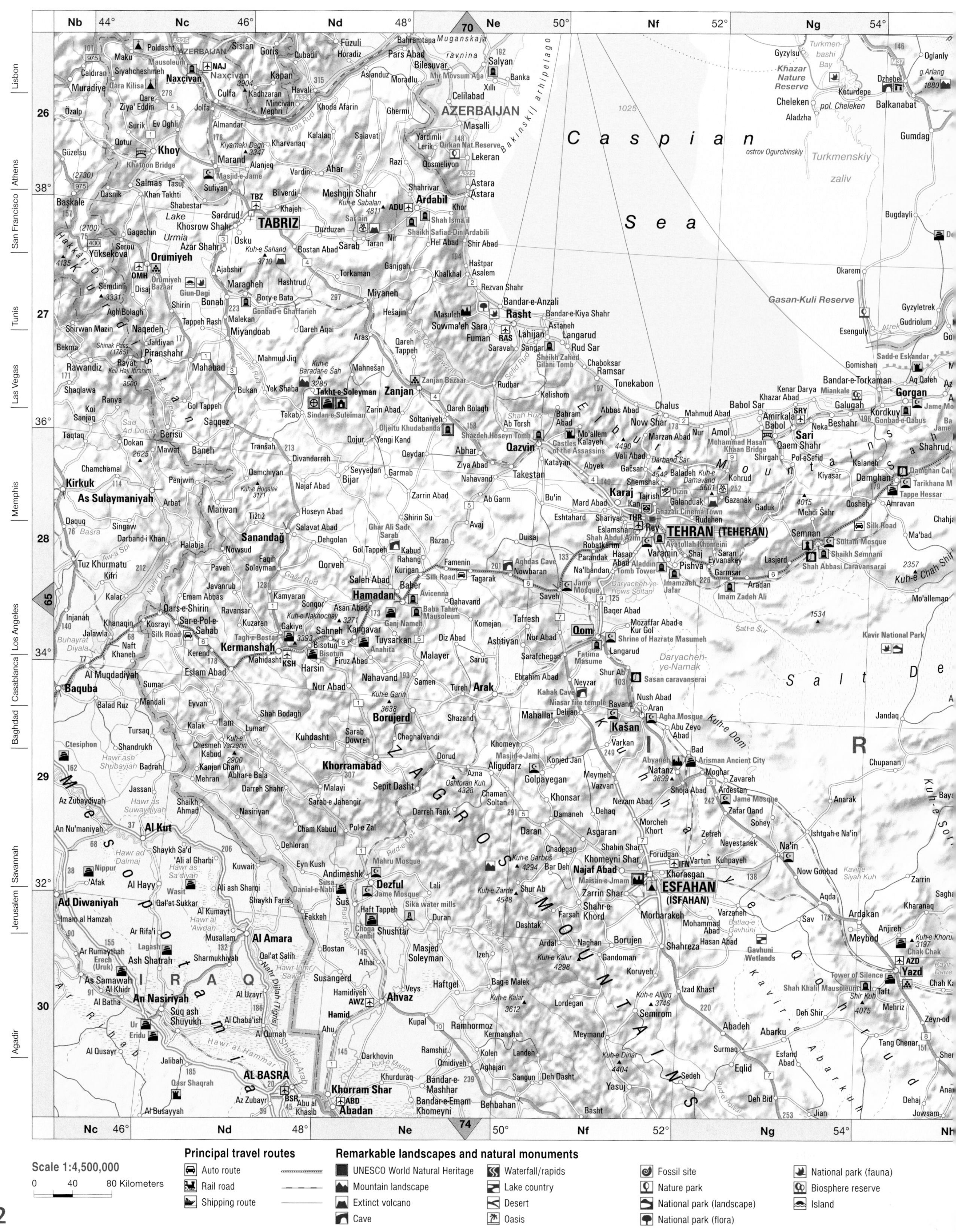

Scale 1:4,500,000

0   40   80 Kilometers

Principal travel routes
- Auto route
- Rail road
- Shipping route
....
– · – · –
———

Remarkable landscapes and natural monuments
- UNESCO World Natural Heritage
- Mountain landscape
- Extinct volcano
- Cave
- Waterfall/rapids
- Lake country
- Desert
- Oasis
- Fossil site
- Nature park
- National park (landscape)
- National park (flora)
- National park (fauna)
- Biosphere reserve
- Island

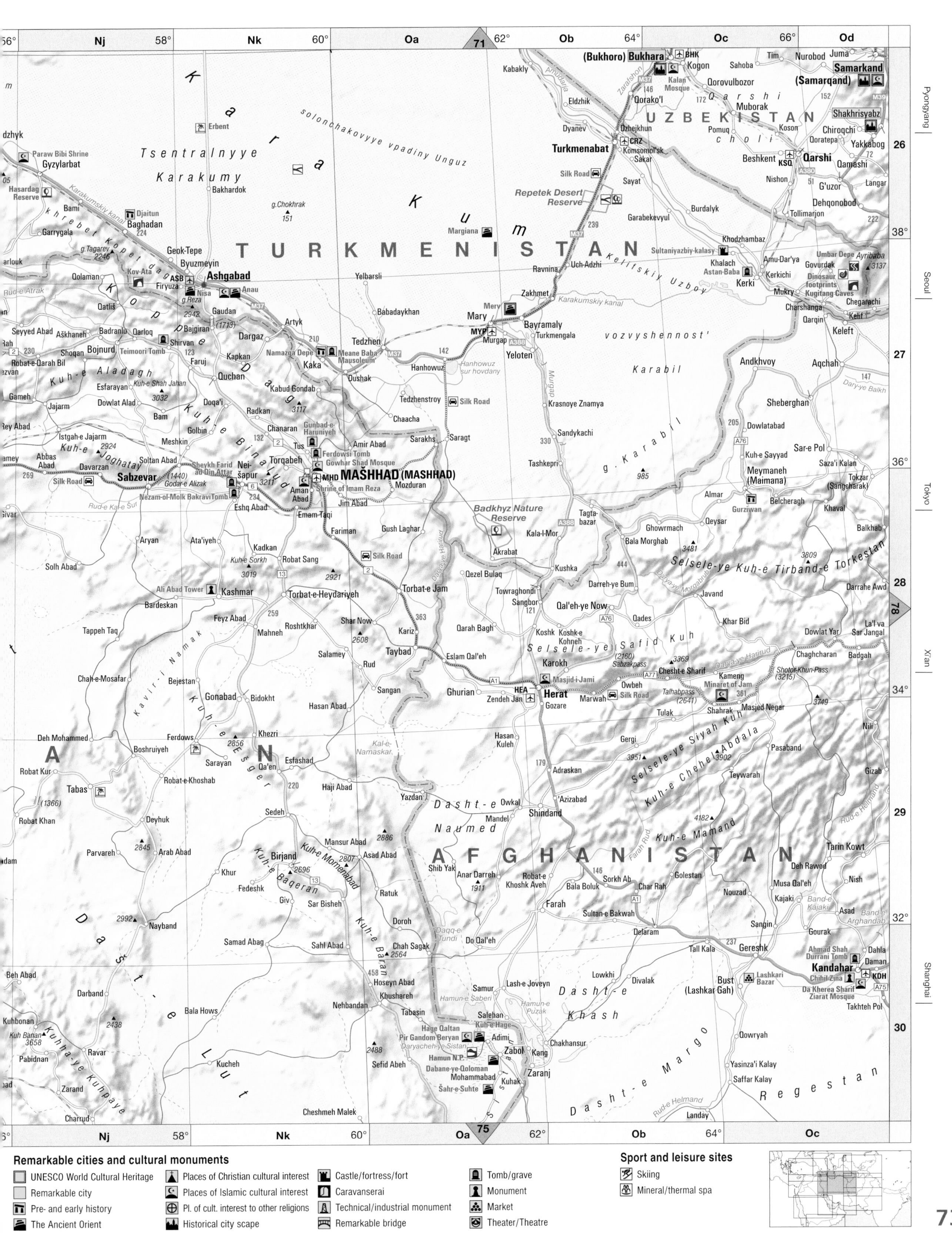

Remarkable cities and cultural monuments

- ⬜ UNESCO World Cultural Heritage
- ⬜ Remarkable city
- 🏛 Pre- and early history
- The Ancient Orient

- ▲ Places of Christian cultural interest
- ☪ Places of Islamic cultural interest
- ⊕ Pl. of cult. interest to other religions
- Historical city scape

- 🏰 Castle/fortress/fort
- Caravanserai
- Technical/industrial monument
- Remarkable bridge

- 🏛 Tomb/grave
- 🏛 Monument
- Market
- Theater/Theatre

Sport and leisure sites

- Skiing
- Mineral/thermal spa

Southern Iran, Persian Gulf

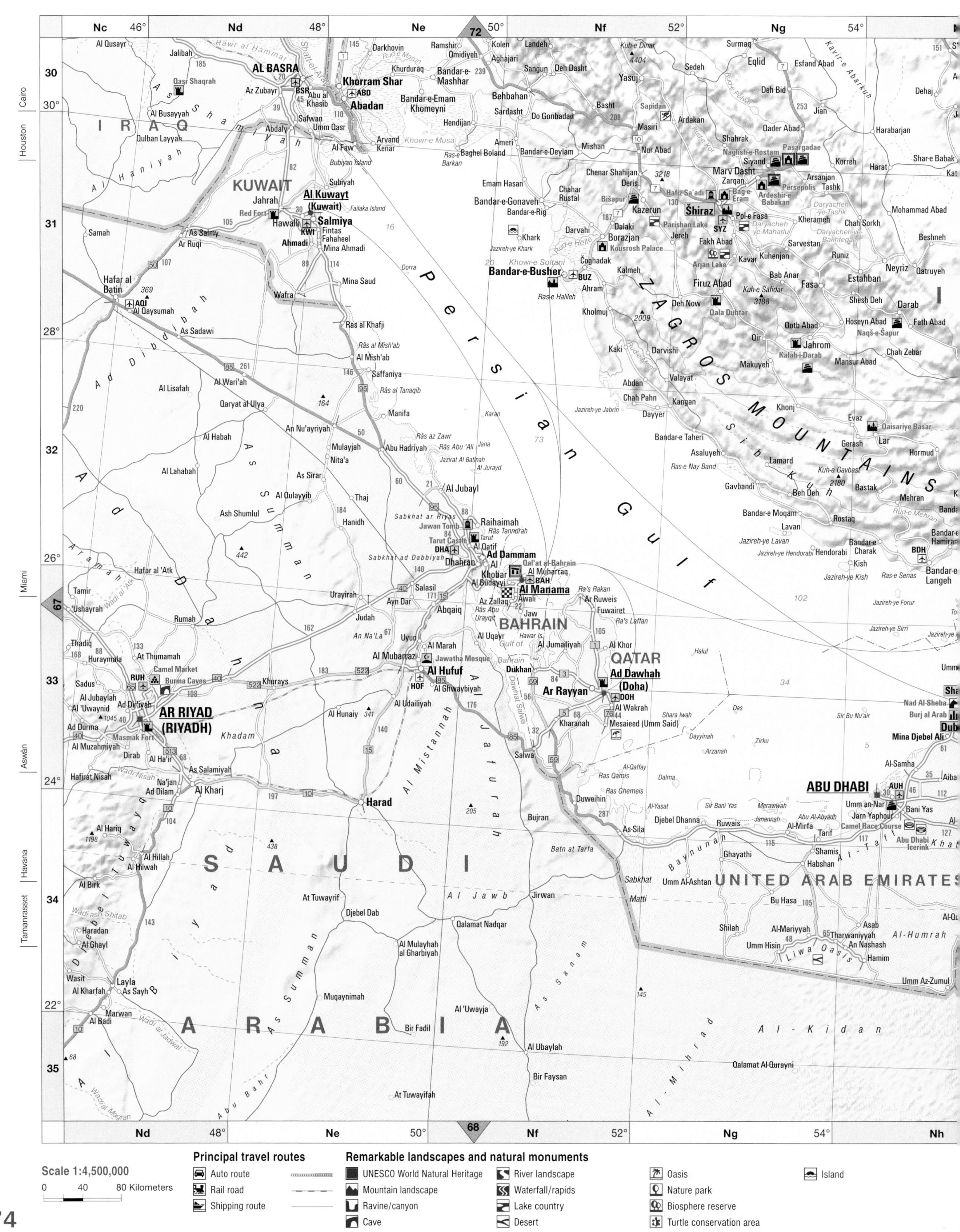

Scale 1:4,500,000

0   40   80 Kilometers

Principal travel routes

- 🚗 Auto route
- 🚌 Rail road
- ⛴ Shipping route

Remarkable landscapes and natural monuments

- ■ UNESCO World Natural Heritage
- Mountain landscape
- Ravine/canyon
- Cave
- River landscape
- Waterfall/rapids
- Lake country
- Desert
- Oasis
- Nature park
- Biosphere reserve
- Turtle conservation area
- Island

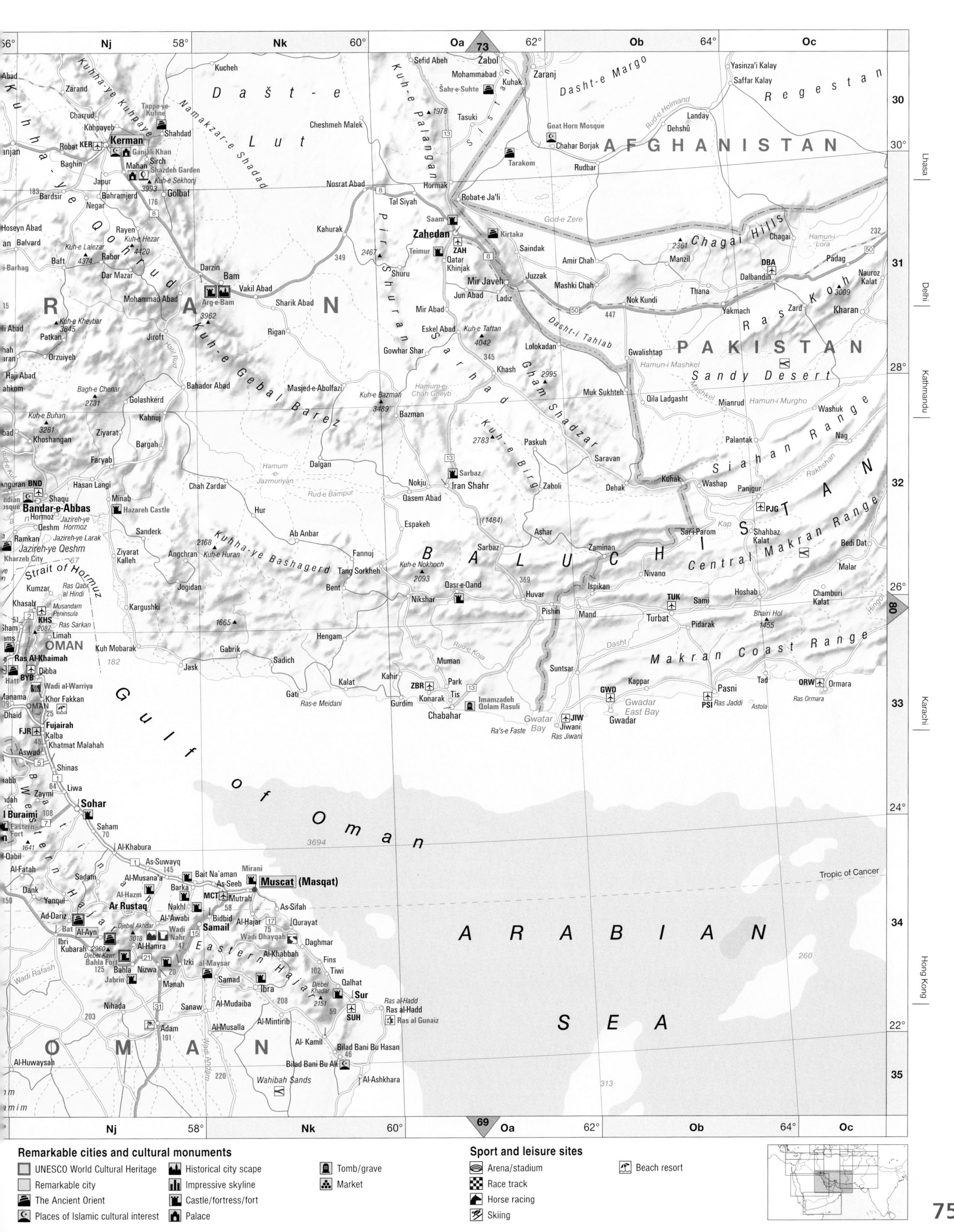
Nj
58°
Nk
60°
Oa
73
62°
Ob
64°
Oc
Dašt-e Lut
Dasht-e Margo
Regestan
AFGHANISTAN
PAKISTAN
IRAN
OMAN
BALUCHISTAN
Kerman
Zahedan
Bam
Bandar-e-Abbas
Zabol
Zaranj
Chagai Hills
Ras Koh
Sandy Desert
Siahan Range
Central Makran Range
Makran Coast Range
Kuh-e Gebal Barez
Kuhha-ye Bashagerd
Jazireh-ye Qeshm
Strait of Hormuz
Gulf of Oman
ARABIAN SEA
Tropic of Cancer
Muscat (Masqat)
Sohar
Ras Al-Khaimah
Fujairah
Khor Fakkan
Ar Rustaq
Samail
Nizwa
Ibra
Sur
Ras al-Hadd
Wahibah Sands
Eastern Hajar
Western Hajar
Chabahar
Gwadar
Jiwani
Pasni
Ormara
Turbat
Iran Shahr
Khash
Mir Javeh
Kharan
Dalbandin
Nok Kundi
Jask
Minab
Jiroft
Golbaf
Arg-e-Bam
Hazareh Castle
Lhasa
Delhi
Kathmandu
Karachi
Hong Kong
30
31
32
33
34
35
80
69
30°
28°
26°
24°
22°
Remarkable cities and cultural monuments
UNESCO World Cultural Heritage
Remarkable city
The Ancient Orient
Places of Islamic cultural interest
Historical city scape
Impressive skyline
Castle/fortress/fort
Palace
Tomb/grave
Market
Sport and leisure sites
Arena/stadium
Race track
Horse racing
Skiing
Beach resort

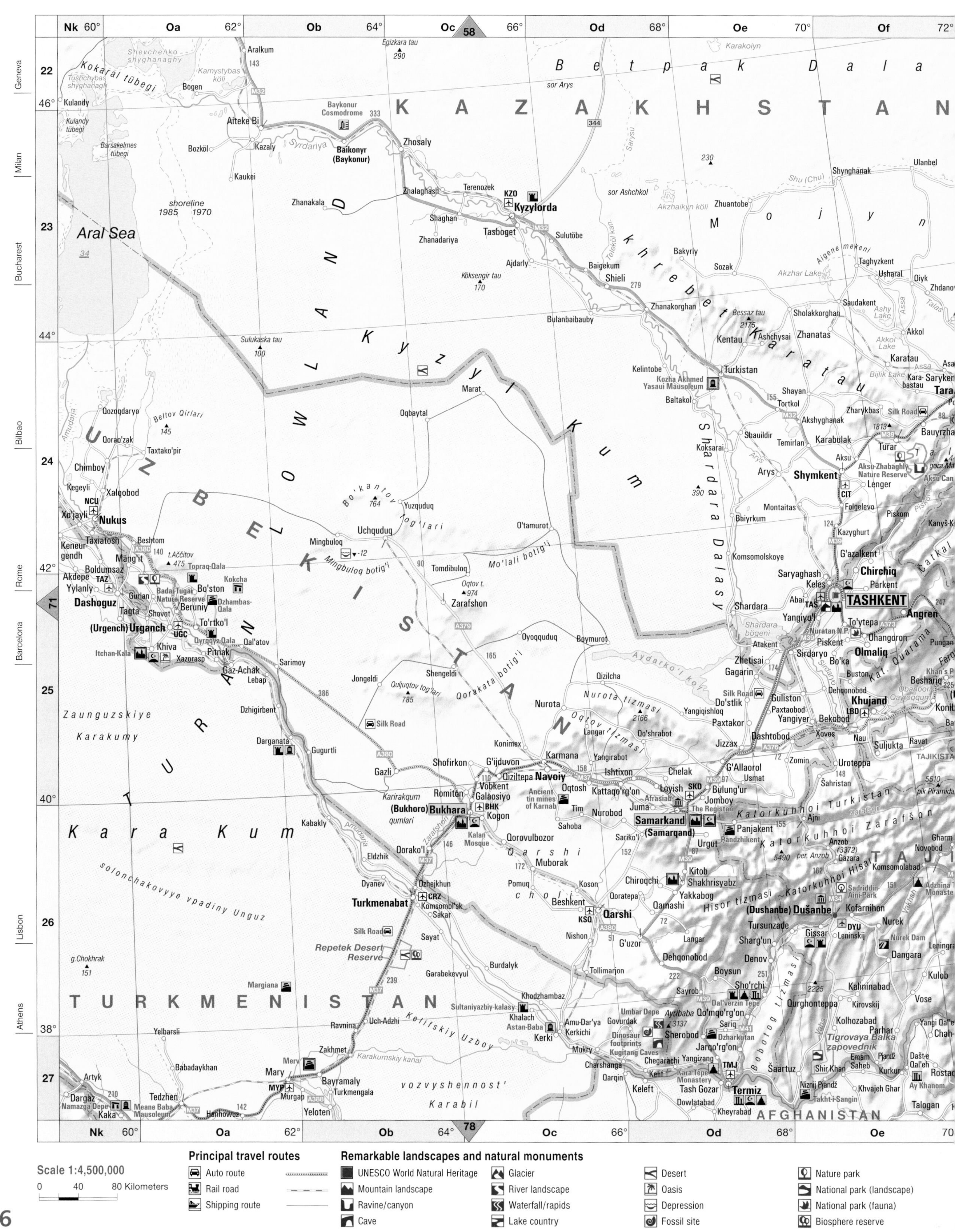

Scale 1:4,500,000

0   40   80 Kilometers

Principal travel routes
- Auto route
- Rail road
- Shipping route

Remarkable landscapes and natural monuments
- UNESCO World Natural Heritage
- Mountain landscape
- Ravine/canyon
- Cave
- Glacier
- River landscape
- Waterfall/rapids
- Lake country
- Desert
- Oasis
- Depression
- Fossil site
- Nature park
- National park (landscape)
- National park (fauna)
- Biosphere reserve

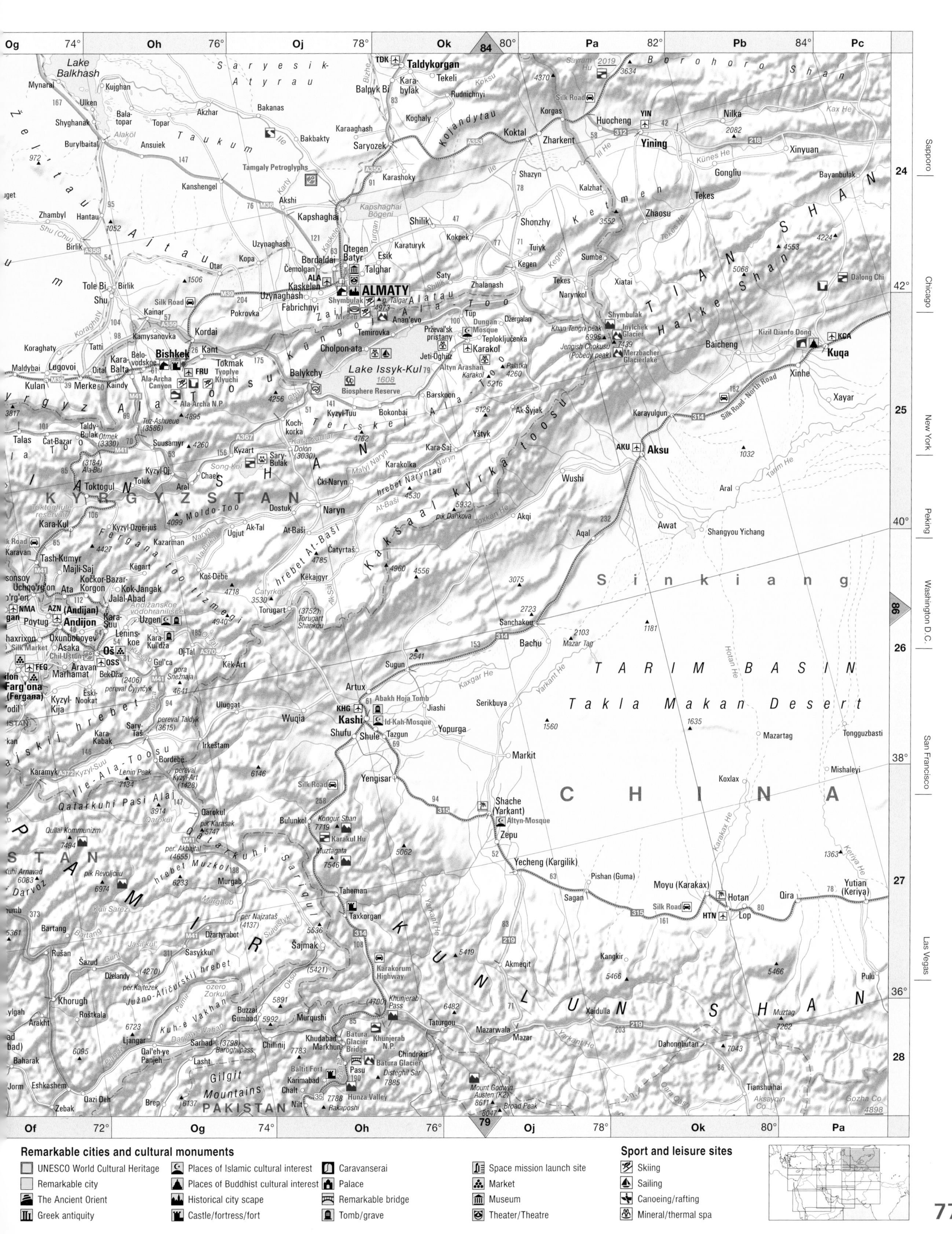

Lake Balkhash

Saryesik-Atyrau

Taukum

TDK Taldykorgan

Borohoro Shan

Mynaral
Kujghan
Ulken
Shyghanak
Bala-topar
Akzhar
Topar
Ansuiek
Bakanas
Kara-bylak
Tekeli
Rudnichnyi
Balpyk Bi
4370
Sayram 2019
3634
Silk Road

Burylbaital
972
Alaköl
Karaaghash
Saryozek
Koghaly
Korgas
Huocheng
YIN
Nilka
2082
Kax He

Zhambyl
Hantau
1052
Akshi
Kapshagai Bögeni
Karashoky
Shazyn
Kalzhat
312
42
Yining
Gongliu
Bayanbulak
Xinyuan

TIAN SHAN

KYRGYZSTAN

Bishkek

ALMATY

Lake Issyk-Kul

Kuqa
KQA

Aksu
AKU

Sinkiang

TARIM BASIN

Takla Makan Desert

CHINA

KUNLUN SHAN

PAKISTAN

Mount Godwin Austen (K2)
8611
Broad Peak
8047

Kashi
KHG

Remarkable cities and cultural monuments

- ☐ UNESCO World Cultural Heritage
- ☐ Remarkable city
- ⬛ The Ancient Orient
- ⬛ Greek antiquity
- ☾ Places of Islamic cultural interest
- ▲ Places of Buddhist cultural interest
- ⬛ Historical city scape
- ⬛ Castle/fortress/fort
- ⬛ Caravanserai
- ⬛ Palace
- ⬛ Remarkable bridge
- ⬛ Tomb/grave
- ⬛ Space mission launch site
- ⬛ Market
- 🏛 Museum
- ◉ Theater/Theatre

Sport and leisure sites

- ⛷ Skiing
- ⛵ Sailing
- 🛶 Canoeing/rafting
- ♨ Mineral/thermal spa

77

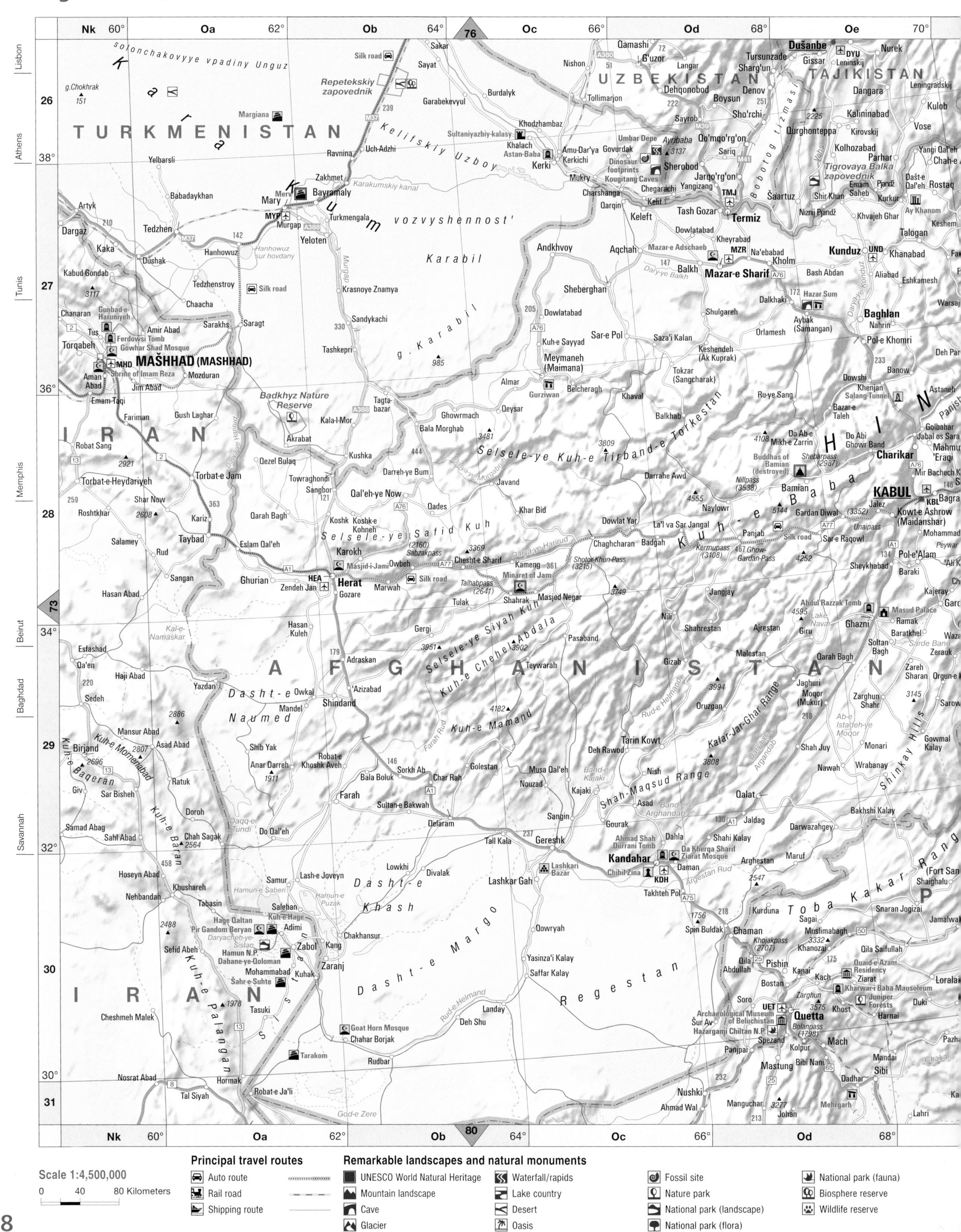

Scale 1:4,500,000

0   40   80 Kilometers

Principal travel routes
- Auto route
- Rail road
- Shipping route

Remarkable landscapes and natural monuments
- UNESCO World Natural Heritage
- Mountain landscape
- Cave
- Glacier
- Waterfall/rapids
- Lake country
- Desert
- Oasis
- Fossil site
- Nature park
- National park (landscape)
- National park (flora)
- National park (fauna)
- Biosphere reserve
- Wildlife reserve

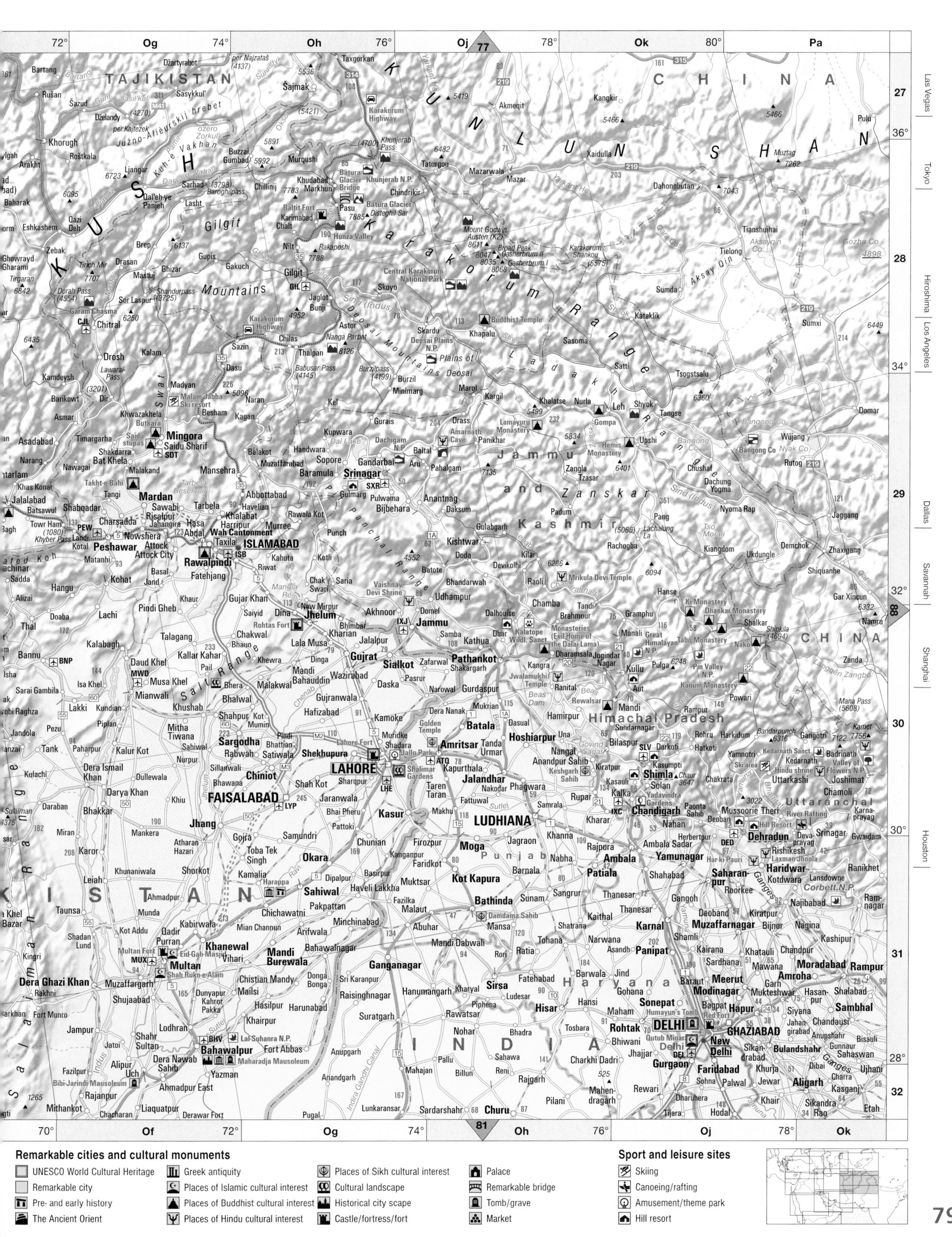

72°
Og
74°
Oh
76°
Oj
77
78°
Ok
80°
Pa
27
28
29
30
31
32
36°
34°
32°
30°
28°
70°
Of
72°
Og
74°
81
Oh
76°
Oj
78°
Ok
88
Las Vegas
Tokyo
Hiroshima
Los Angeles
Dallas
Savannah
Shanghai
Houston
TAJIKISTAN
CHINA
KUNLUN SHAN
HINDU KUSH
Karakorum Range
Ladakh Range
Jammu and Kashmir
Himachal Pradesh
Punjab
Haryana
Uttaranchal
INDIA
PAKISTAN
ISLAMABAD
Rawalpindi
Peshawar
LAHORE
FAISALABAD
LUDHIANA
DELHI
New Delhi
GHAZIABAD
Srinagar
Jammu
Amritsar
Chandigarh
Shimla
Dehradun
Multan
Bahawalpur
Gilgit
Leh
Kargil
Skardu
Mount Godwin Austen (K2) 8611
Nanga Parbat 8126
Salt Range
Pir Panjal Range
Sutlej
Indus
Remarkable cities and cultural monuments
UNESCO World Cultural Heritage
Remarkable city
Pre- and early history
The Ancient Orient
Greek antiquity
Places of Islamic cultural interest
Places of Buddhist cultural interest
Places of Hindu cultural interest
Places of Sikh cultural interest
Cultural landscape
Historical city scape
Castle/fortress/fort
Palace
Remarkable bridge
Tomb/grave
Market
Sport and leisure sites
Skiing
Canoeing/rafting
Amusement/theme park
Hill resort

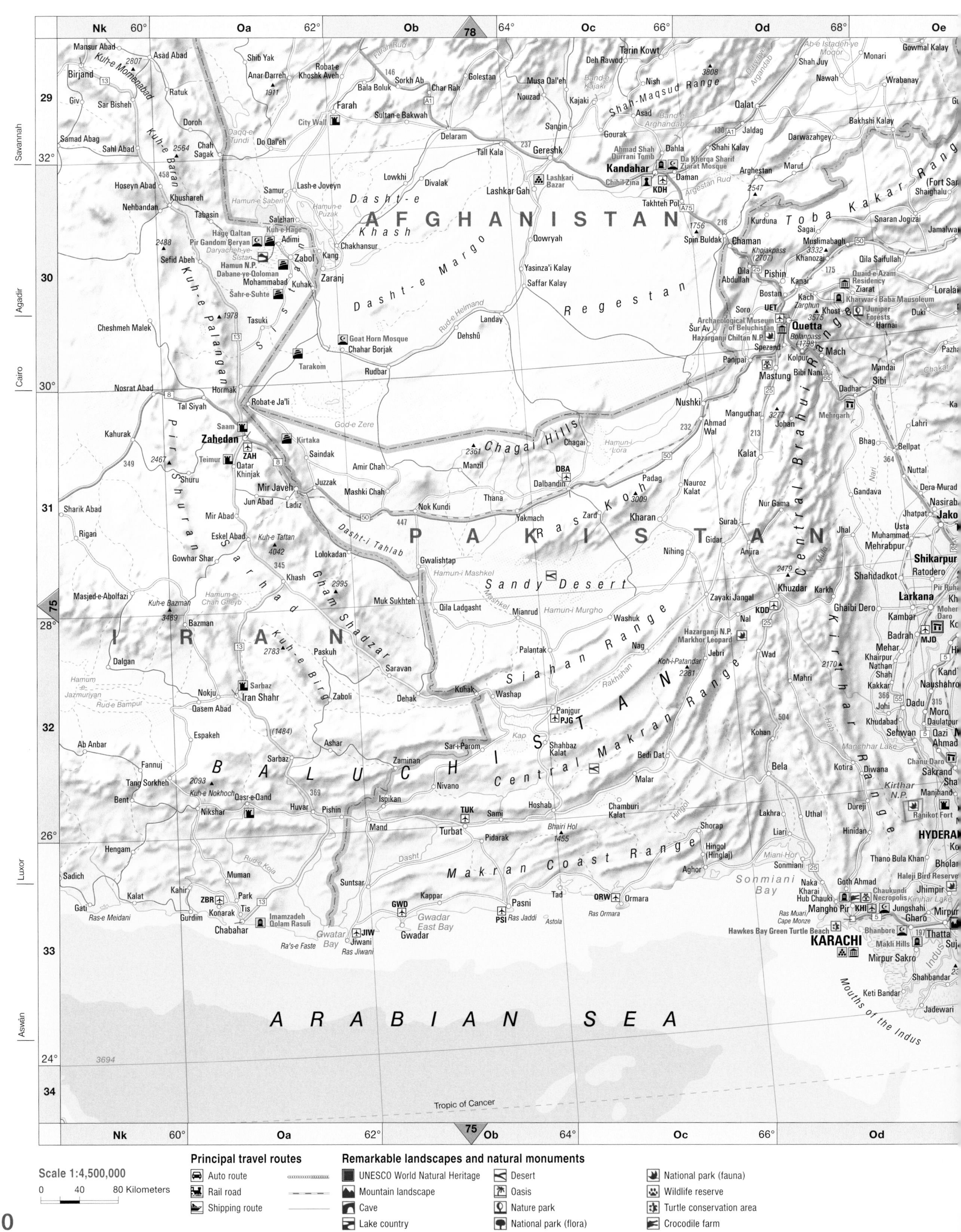

Scale 1:4,500,000

0   40   80 Kilometers

Principal travel routes
- 🚗 Auto route
- 🚂 Rail road
- 🚢 Shipping route
- ·········· (dotted route)
- –·–·–·– (dash-dot route)
- ——— (solid route)

Remarkable landscapes and natural monuments
- ■ UNESCO World Natural Heritage
- ■ Mountain landscape
- Cave
- Lake country
- ◁ Desert
- 🗻 Oasis
- Nature park
- ■ National park (flora)
- National park (fauna)
- Wildlife reserve
- Turtle conservation area
- Crocodile farm

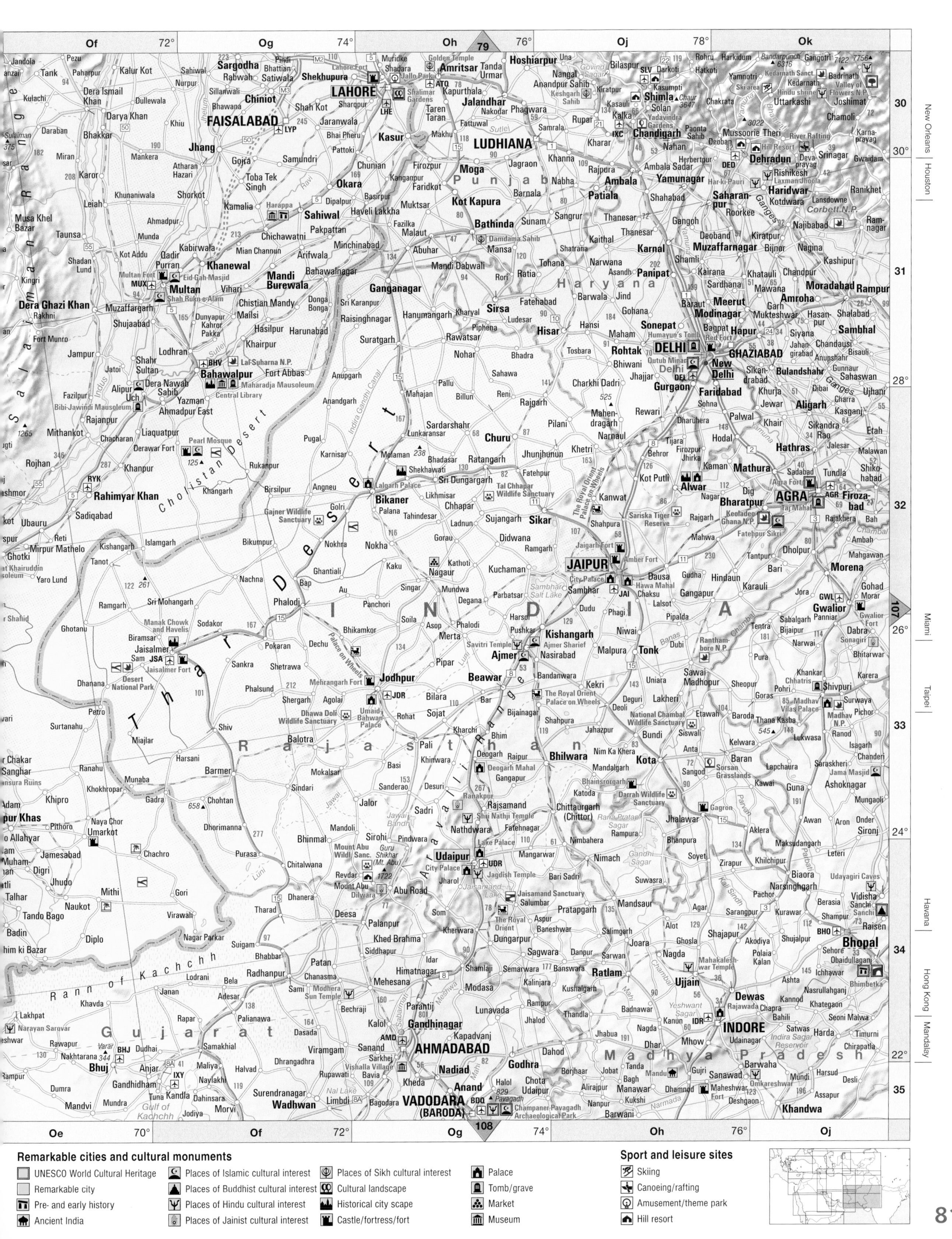

Of
72°
Og
74°
Oh
79
76°
Oj
78°
Ok
30
30°
31
28°
32
26°
33
24°
34
22°
35
Oe
70°
Of
72°
Og
108
74°
Oh
76°
Oj
107
New Orleans
Houston
Miami
Taipei
Havana
Hong Kong
Mandalay
LAHORE
FAISALABAD
Sargodha
Multan
Bahawalpur
Dera Ghazi Khan
Rahimyar Khan
Amritsar
Jalandhar
LUDHIANA
Shimla
Chandigarh
Dehradun
DELHI
New Delhi
GHAZIABAD
Meerut
AGRA
JAIPUR
Ajmer
Jodhpur
Bikaner
Jaisalmer
Udaipur
Kota
Gwalior
Bhopal
INDORE
Ujjain
AHMADABAD
Gandhinagar
VADODARA (BARODA)
Bhuj
Punjab
Haryana
Rajasthan
Gujarat
Madhya Pradesh
INDIA
Thar Desert
Cholistan Desert
Aravalli Range
Rann of Kachchh
Remarkable cities and cultural monuments
UNESCO World Cultural Heritage
Remarkable city
Pre- and early history
Ancient India
Places of Islamic cultural interest
Places of Buddhist cultural interest
Places of Hindu cultural interest
Places of Jainist cultural interest
Places of Sikh cultural interest
Cultural landscape
Historical city scape
Castle/fortress/fort
Palace
Tomb/grave
Market
Museum
Sport and leisure sites
Skiing
Canoeing/rafting
Amusement/theme park
Hill resort

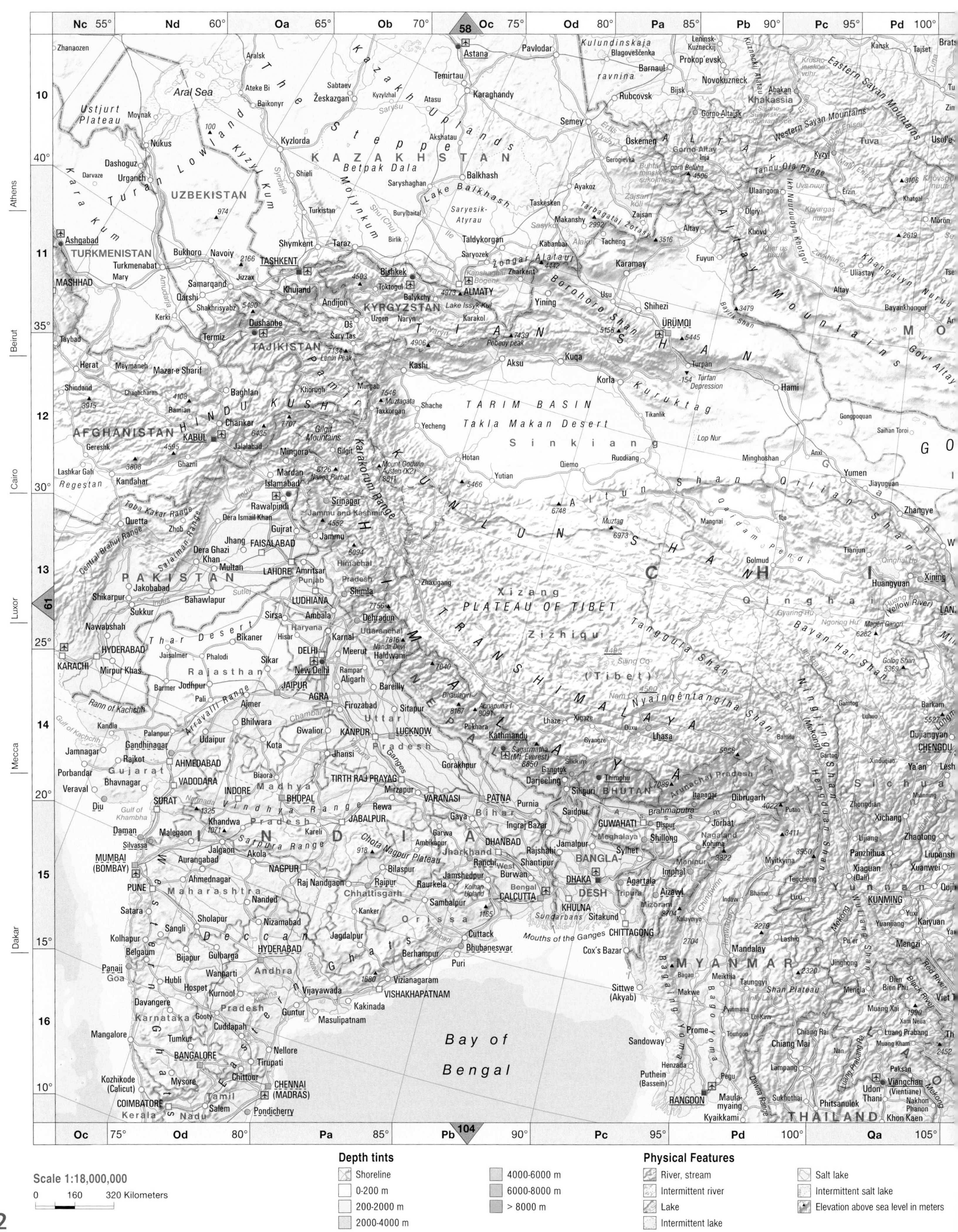

Athens
Beirut
Cairo
Luxor 61
Mecca
Dakar

Scale 1:18,000,000

0   160   320 Kilometers

82

Depth tints

⊠ Shoreline	▨ 4000-6000 m
☐ 0-200 m	▨ 6000-8000 m
☐ 200-2000 m	▨ > 8000 m
☐ 2000-4000 m	

Physical Features

River, stream	Salt lake
Intermittent river	Intermittent salt lake
Lake	Elevation above sea level in meters
Intermittent lake	

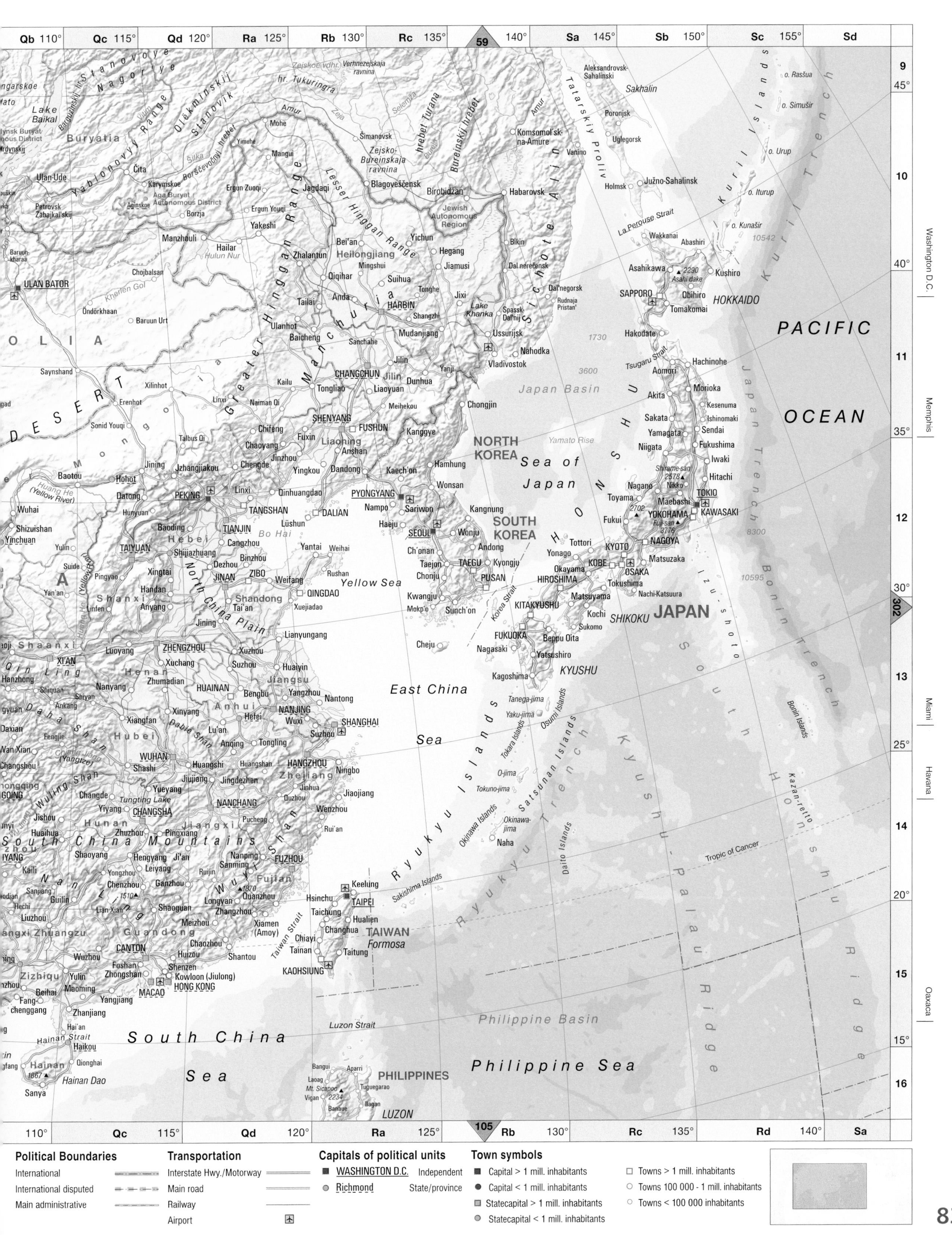

Stanovoye
Nagor'ye
Verhnezejskaja ravnina
9
45°

ngarskoe
Stanovik
hr. Tukuringra
Lake Baikal
Zejskoje vdhr.
Sakhalin
o. Rasšua

ato
Buryatia
Olёkminskij
Stanovik
hr. Tukuringra
Amur
Aleksandrovsk-Sahalinski
o. Simušir

lynsk Buryat
nous District
Borščёvočnyi hrebet
Silka
Yimuhe
Mohe
Zeja
Selenga
Burejinskij hrebet
Poronjsk
Tatarskij proliv
Južno-Sahalinsk
o. Urup
10

rdynskij
Čita
Karymskoe
Mangui
Amur
Simanovsk
Zejsko-Bureinskaja ravnina
Komsomol'sk-na-Amure
Vanino
Holmsk
Uglegorsk
o. Iturup

Ulan-Ude
Aga Buryat Autonomous District
Ergun Zuoqi
Jagdaqi
Blagoveščensk
Birobidžan
Habarovsk
Wakkanai
Abashiri
o. Kunašir
10542

Petrovsk Zabajkal'skij
Aginskoe
Borzja
Ergun Youqi
Bei'an
Yichun
Hegang
Jewish Autonomous Region
Bikin
Dal'nerečensk
Asahikawa
▲2290 Asahi dake
Kushiro
40°

Baruun-kharaa
Manzhouli
Hailar
Hulun Nur
Zhalantun
Heilongjiang
Mingshui
Suihua
Jiamusi
Jixi
Dal'negorsk
Rudnaja Pristan'
SAPPORO
Obihiro
HOKKAIDO
Tomakomai

ULAN BATOR
Chojbalsan
Qiqihar
Tailai
Anda
HARBIN
Shangzhi
Spassk-Dal'nij
Ussurijsk
Hakodate
PACIFIC

OLIA
Kherlen Gol
Baruun Urt
Ulanhot
Baicheng
Sanchahe
Mudanjiang
Lake Khanka
Nahodka
Tsugaru Strait
1730
Hachinohe
OCEAN
11

Saynshand
Öndörhaan
CHANGCHUN
Jilin
Dunhua
Yanji
Vladivostok
3600
Aomori
Morioka

Xilinhot
Erenhot
Tongliao
Liaoyuan
Meihekou
Chongjin
Japan Basin
Akita
Kesenuma
35°

A
Saynshand
Naiman Qi
Kailu
SHENYANG
FUSHUN
Kanggye
NORTH KOREA
Yamato Rise
Sakata
Ishinomaki
Sendai

Talbus Qi
Sonid Youqi
Chifeng
Chaoyang
Fuxin
Liaoning
Anshan
Hamhung
Sea of Japan
Niigata
Yamagata
Fukushima

Baotou
Hohhot
Zhangjiakou
Jinzhou
Chengde
Yingkou
Dandong
Kaech'on
Wonsan
Nagano
Nikko
Shirane-san ▲2578
Iwaki
Hitachi

Huang He (Yellow River)
Datong
Hunyuan
PEKING
Linxi
Qinhuangdao
PYONGYANG
Nampo
Sariwon
Kangnung
Toyama
Maebashi
Shirane-san 2702
TOKIO
12

Wuhai
Shizuishan
TANGSHAN
DALIAN
Lüshun
Haeju
Wonju
SOUTH KOREA
Fukui
YOKOHAMA
Fuji-san ▲3776
KAWASAKI

Yinchuan
Yulin
TAIYUAN
Baoding
TIANJIN
Cangzhou
Bo Hai
Yantai
Weihai
SEOUL
Ch'onan
Andong
Tottori
KYOTO
NAGOYA

Suide
Pingyao
Hebei
Shijiazhuang
Dezhou
Binzhou
Rushan
Taejon
TAEGU
Kyongju
Yonago
KOBE
Matsuzaka

Yan'an
Shanxi
Handan
Xingtai
JINAN
ZIBO
Weifang
QINGDAO
Chonju
PUSAN
OKAYAMA
HIROSHIMA
OSAKA

Linfen
North China Plain
Anyang
Tai'an
Shandong
Xuejiadao
Kwangju
Sunch'on
Mokp'o
JAPAN

Shaanxi
Jining
Lianyungang
Yellow Sea
Cheju
KITAKYUSHU
Matsuyama
Nachi-Katsuura
Tokushima
30°

XI'AN
Luoyang
ZHENGZHOU
Xuchang
Xuzhou
Suzhou
Huaiyin
Jiangsu
SHIKOKU
Kochi
302

Qin Ling
Nanyang
Henan
Zhumadian
Bengbu
Yangzhou
East China
FUKUOKA
Beppu Oita
Sukomo

Hanzhong
Xiangfan
HUAINAN
Xinyang
Lu'an
Hefei
Nantong
Sea
Nagasaki
KYUSHU
Yatsushiro

Daxian
Shiyan
Ankang
Anhui
NANJING
Wuxi
Kagoshima
Taneka-jima
Yaku-jima
13

Fengjie
Hubei
Huangshi
Huangshan
Anqing
Tongling
SHANGHAI
Suzhou
Osumi Islands

han Xian
Dabie Shan
WUHAN
Shashi
Jiujiang
Jingdezhen
HANGZHOU
Ningbo
Tokara Islands

Changsha
Wuling Shan
Yueyang
Tungting Lake
Zhejiang
Jinhua
Quzhou
Wenzhou
Jiaojiang
O-jima
Ryukyu Islands
25°

ngqing (Yangtze)
GOING
Changde
Yiyang
Pingxiang
NANCHANG
Pucheng
Rui'an
Tokuno-jima
Satsunan Islands

IYANG
South China Mountains
Hunan
Jishou
Zhuzhou
Jiangxi
Okinawa Islands
Okinawa-jima
Bonin Islands

Kaili
Shaoyang
Hengyang
Ji'an
Nanping
Sanming
Tropic of Cancer
14

Sanjiang
Chenzhou
Nan Ling
Yongzhou
Leiyang
Wuyi Shan
Fujian
Longyan
Quanzhou
Naha
Kazan-retto

gxi Zhuangzu
Guilin
Ganzhou
Ruijin
Zhangzhou
Xiamen (Amoy)
Keelung
Sakishima Islands
20°

Liuzhou
Wuzhou
Meizhou
Chaozhou
Shantou
Hsinchu
TAIPEI
Taichung
Hualien

Yulin
Guangdong
Huizou
Changhua
TAIWAN Formosa

CANTON
Foshan
Zhongshan
Shenzen
Chiayi
Tainan
15

Zizhiqu
Beihai
Maoming
MACAO
Kowloon (Jiulong)
HONG KONG
KAOHSIUNG
Taitung

Fang-chenggang
Yangjiang
Zhanjiang
South China
Luzon Strait
Philippine Basin
15°

Hainan Strait
Haikou
Qionghai
Sea
Bangui
Aparri
Philippine Sea

fang
Hainan Dao
Sanya
1867 ▲
PHILIPPINES
Mt. Sicapoo
Laoag
Tuguegarao
16

Vigan 2234 ▲
Ilagan
Banaue
LUZON

Political Boundaries

International
International disputed
Main administrative

Transportation

Interstate Hwy./Motorway
Main road
Railway
Airport ✈

Capitals of political units

■ WASHINGTON D.C. Independent
◉ Richmond State/province

Town symbols

■ Capital > 1 mill. inhabitants
● Capital < 1 mill. inhabitants
▣ Statecapital > 1 mill. inhabitants
◉ Statecapital < 1 mill. inhabitants

□ Towns > 1 mill. inhabitants
○ Towns 100 000 - 1 mill. inhabitants
○ Towns < 100 000 inhabitants

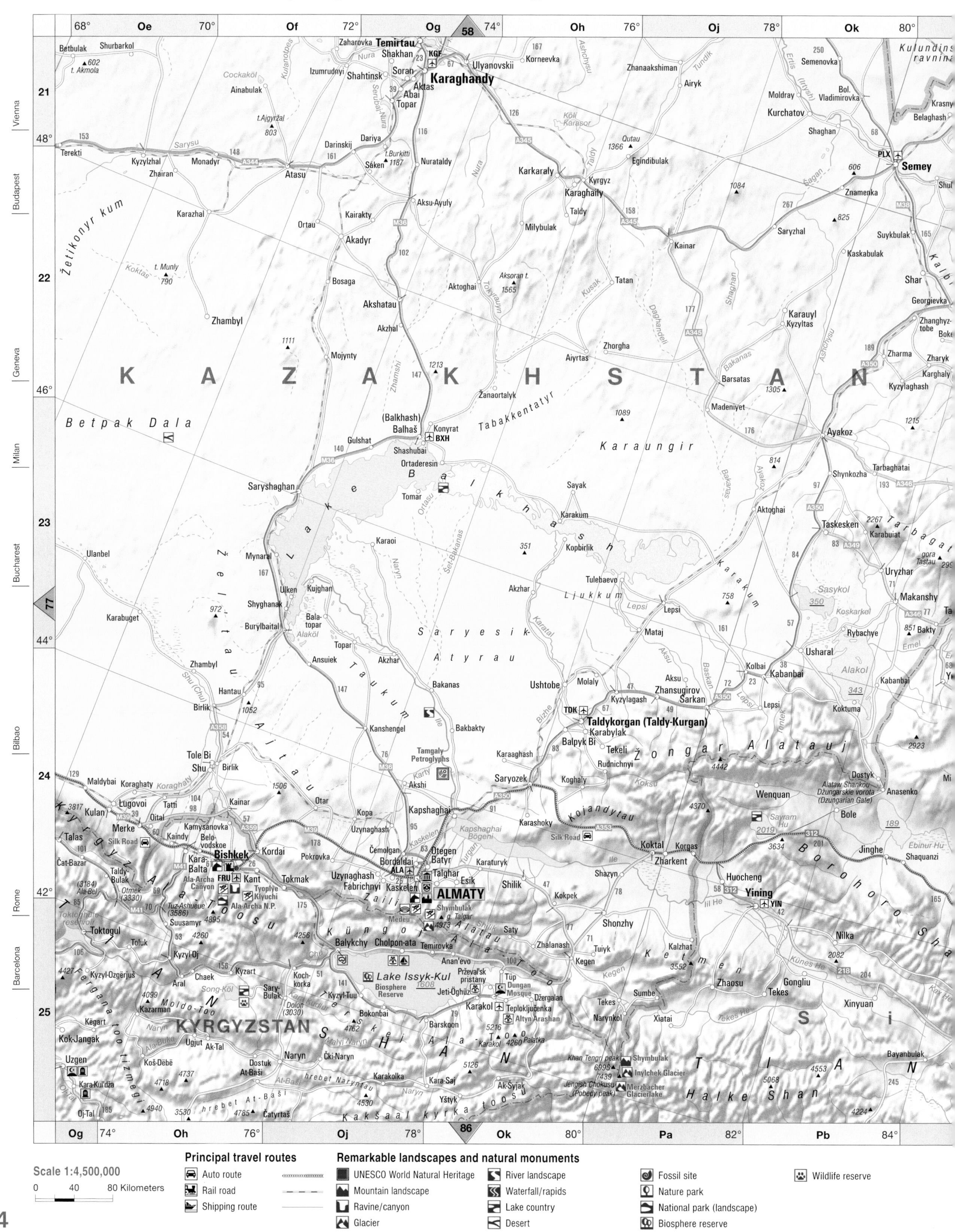

Scale 1:4,500,000

0   40   80 Kilometers

Principal travel routes
- Auto route
- Rail road
- Shipping route
- Auto route
- Mountain landscape
- Ravine/canyon
- Glacier

Remarkable landscapes and natural monuments
- UNESCO World Natural Heritage
- River landscape
- Waterfall/rapids
- Lake country
- Desert
- Fossil site
- Nature park
- National park (landscape)
- Biosphere reserve
- Wildlife reserve

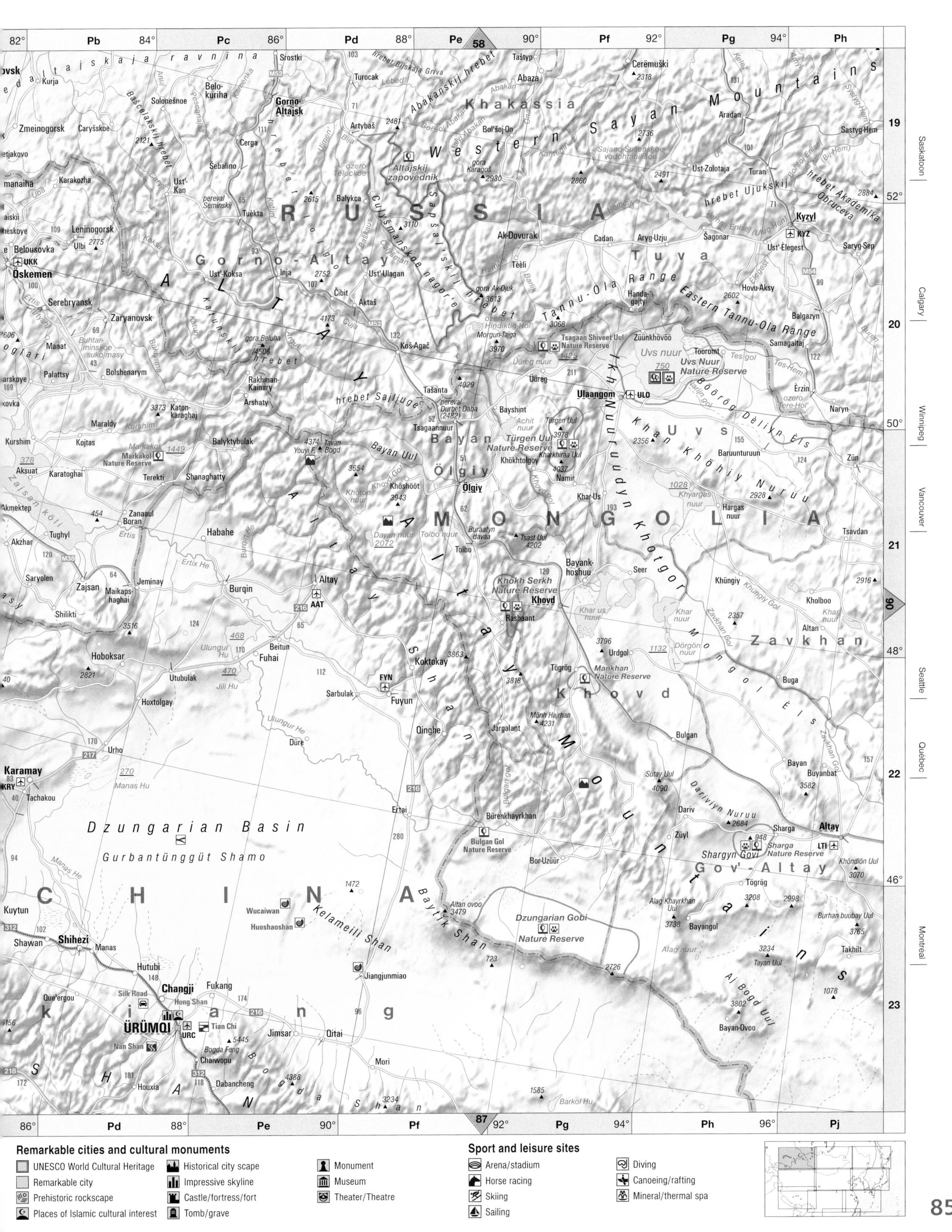

Remarkable cities and cultural monuments

- ⬛ UNESCO World Cultural Heritage
- ⬛ Remarkable city
- 🏞 Prehistoric rockscape
- ☪ Places of Islamic cultural interest
- 🏛 Historical city scape
- 📊 Impressive skyline
- 🏰 Castle/fortress/fort
- ⬛ Tomb/grave
- 🧍 Monument
- 🏛 Museum
- 🎭 Theater/Theatre

Sport and leisure sites

- 🤿 Arena/stadium
- 🐎 Horse racing
- ⛷ Skiing
- ⛵ Sailing
- 🤿 Diving
- 🛶 Canoeing/rafting
- ♨ Mineral/thermal spa

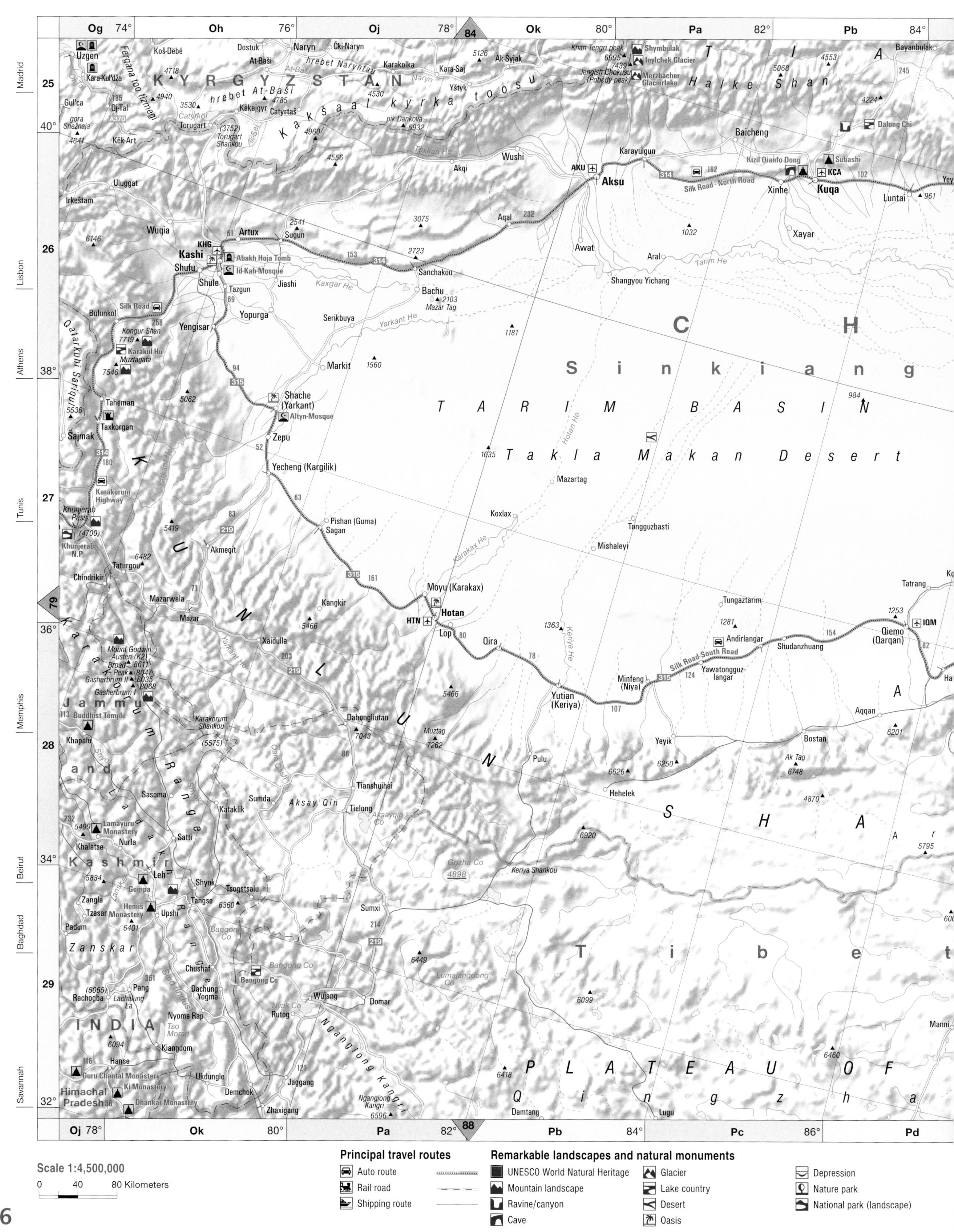

Scale 1:4,500,000

0   40   80 Kilometers

Principal travel routes

- Auto route
- Rail road
- Shipping route

Remarkable landscapes and natural monuments

- UNESCO World Natural Heritage
- Mountain landscape
- Ravine/canyon
- Cave
- Glacier
- Lake country
- Desert
- Oasis
- Depression
- Nature park
- National park (landscape)

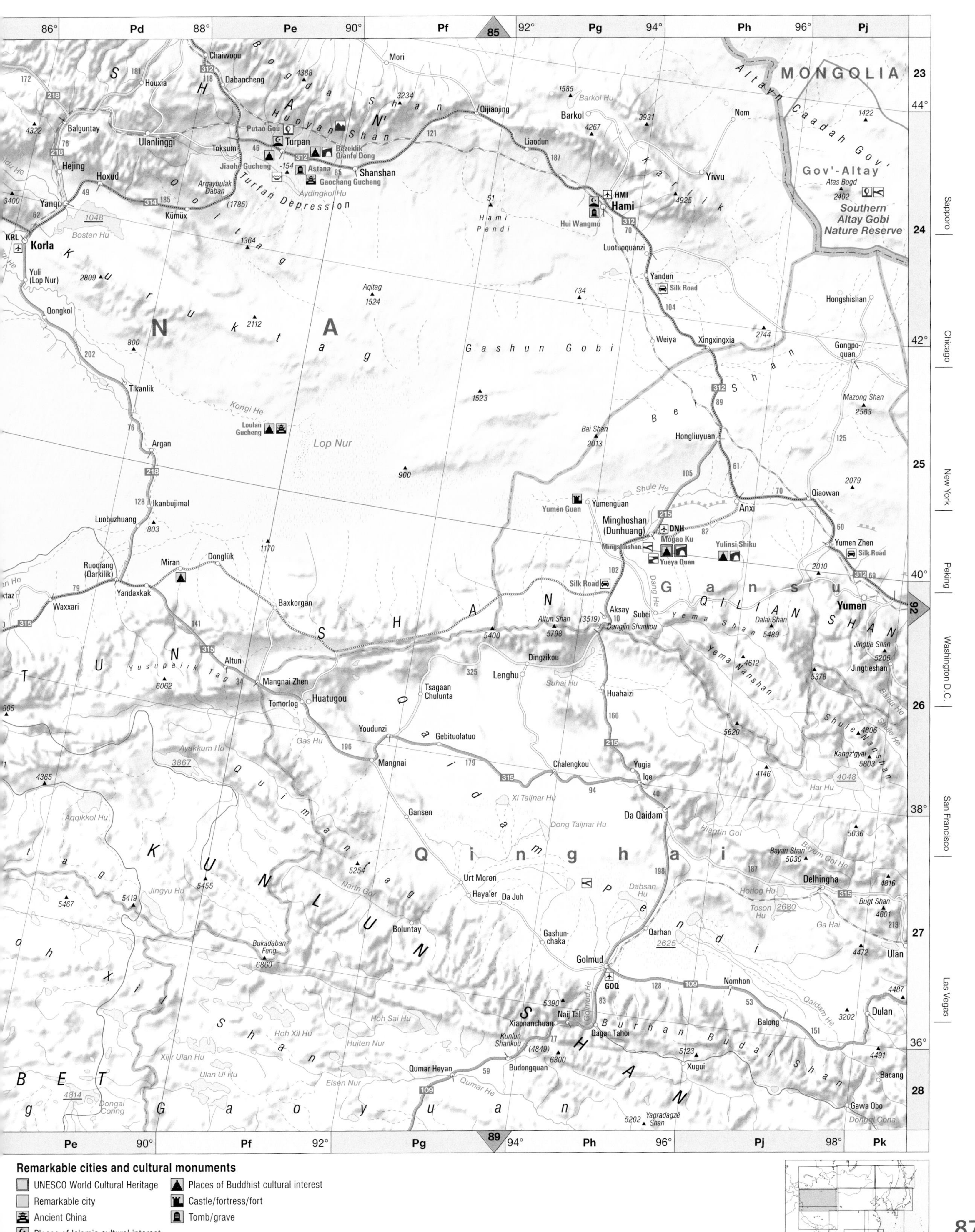

Remarkable cities and cultural monuments

- ☐ UNESCO World Cultural Heritage
- ☐ Remarkable city
- ⚜ Ancient China
- ☾ Places of Islamic cultural interest
- ▲ Places of Buddhist cultural interest
- ⚔ Castle/fortress/fort
- ⛪ Tomb/grave

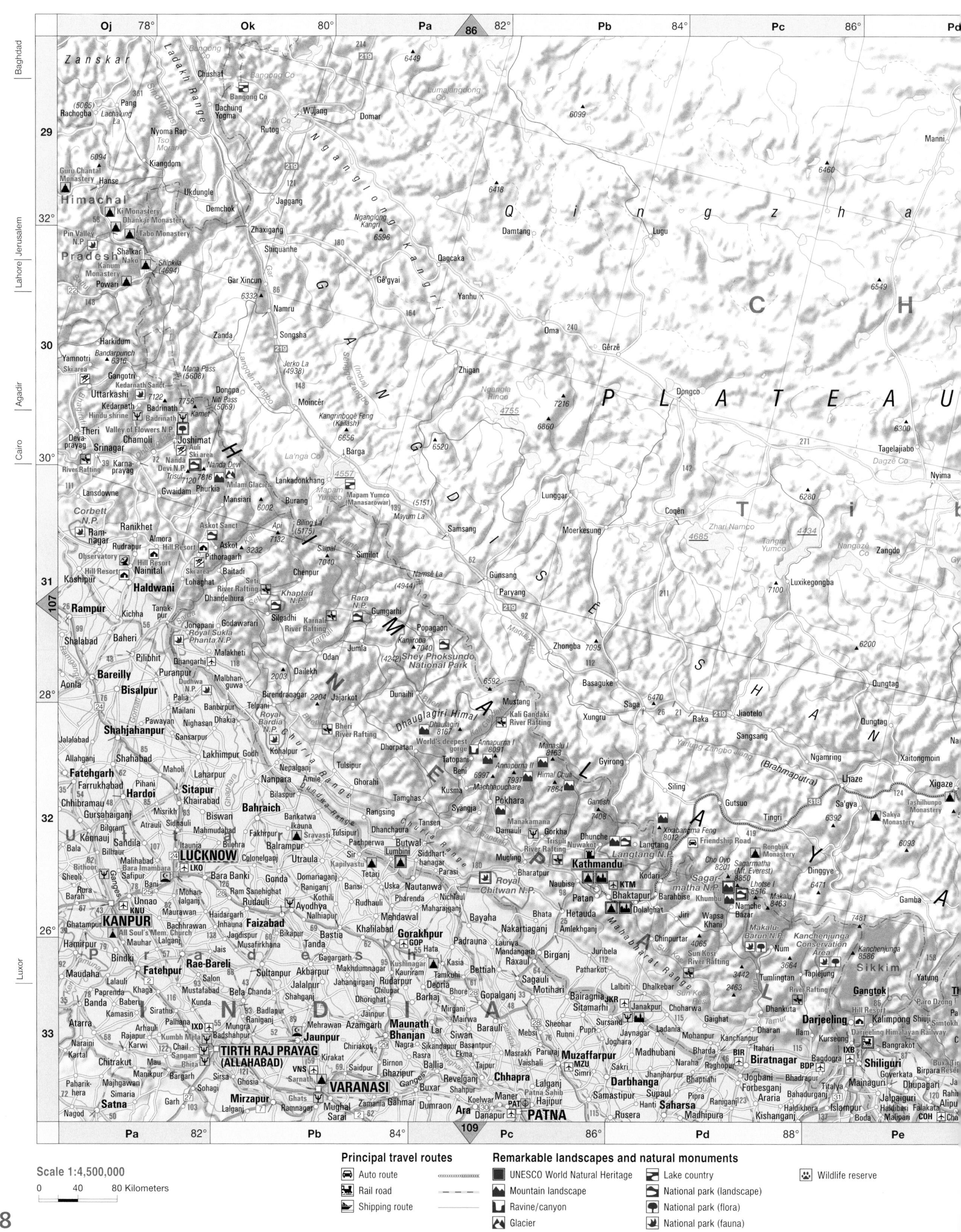

Scale 1:4,500,000

0   40   80 Kilometers

Principal travel routes

🚗	Auto route
🚂	Rail road
🚢	Shipping route

·········
— · — · —
————

Remarkable landscapes and natural monuments

■	UNESCO World Natural Heritage
▲	Mountain landscape
⌐	Ravine/canyon
◿	Glacier

◲	Lake country
⌂	National park (landscape)
♣	National park (flora)
⬇	National park (fauna)

✤	Wildlife reserve

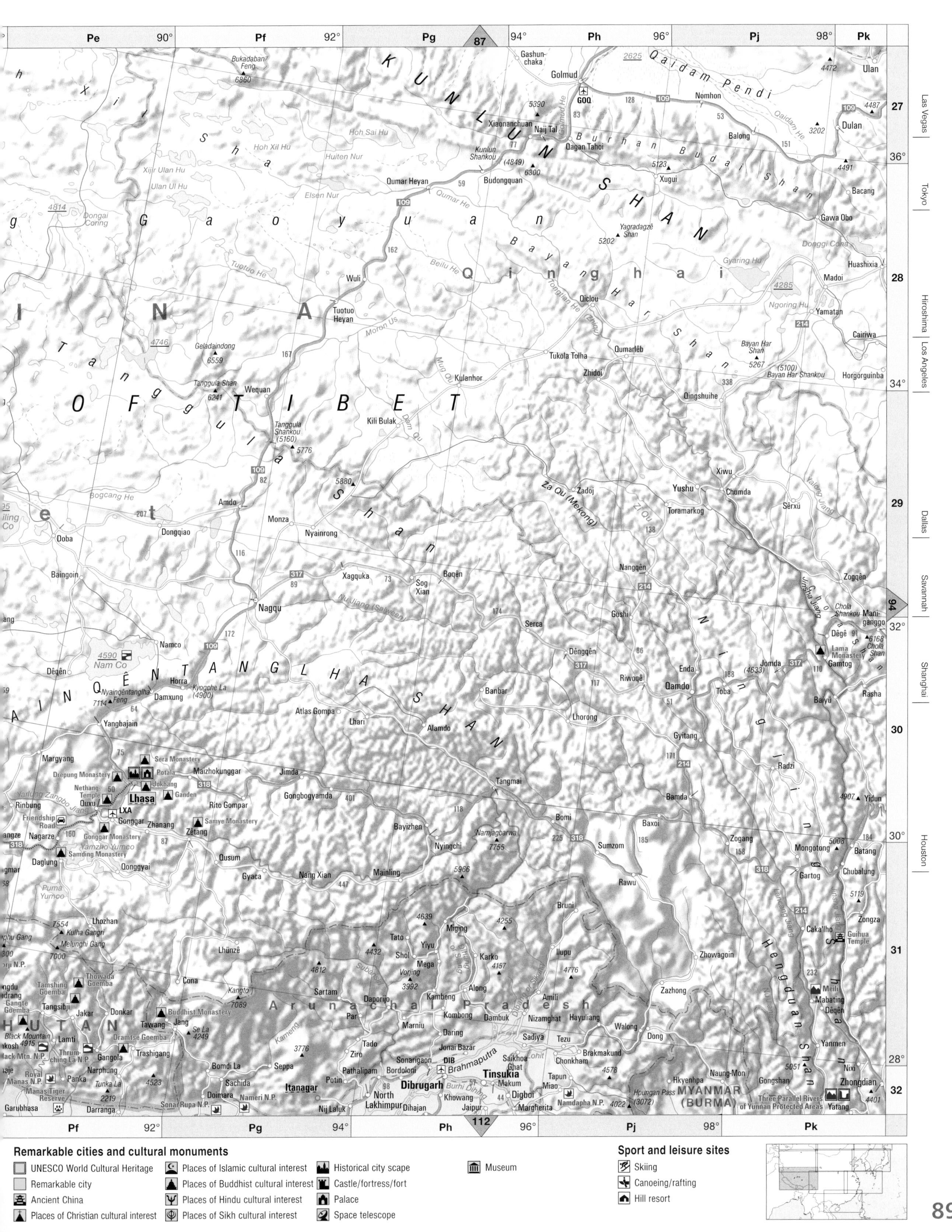
Pe 90° Pf 92° Pg 87 94° Ph 96° Pj 98° Pk
27 28 29 30 31 32
36° 34° 32° 30° 28°
Las Vegas
Tokyo
Hiroshima
Los Angeles
Dallas
Savannah
Shanghai
Houston
Pf 92° Pg 94° Ph 112 96° Pj 98° Pk
KUNLUN SHAN
Qaidam Pendi
Burhan Budai Shan
Bayan Har Shan
Qinghai
Tanggula Shan
Nyainqêntanglha Shan
Ningjing Shan
Hengduan Shan
Arunachal Pradesh
BHUTAN
MYANMAR (BURMA)
Golmud
Gashun-chaka
Nomhon
Ulan
Dulan
Balong
Xiaonanchuan
Naij Tal
Dagan Tahoi
Kunlun Shankou
Budongquan
Qumar Heyan
Xugui
Bacang
Gawa Obo
Huashixia
Madoi
Yamatan
Cairiwa
Horgorguinba
Wuli
Tuotuo Heyan
Qiclou
Qumarlêb
Tukola Tolha
Zhidoi
Kulanhor
Qingshuihe
Geladaindong 6559
Wequan
Kili Bulak
Xiwu
Yushu
Chumda
Toramarkog
Sêrxü
Zadoi
Amdo
Doba
Dongqiao
Monza
Nyainrong
Baingoin
Xagquka
Sog Xian
Boqên
Nangqên
Zogqên
Nagqu
Gushi
Serca
Namco
Nam Co
Dêqên
Dêngqên
Riwoqê
Enda
Jomda
Qamdo
Toba
Gamtog
Rasha
Baiyü
Horra
Damxung
Yangbajain
Atlas Gompa
Lhari
Alamdo
Banbar
Lhorong
Gyitang
Radzi
Margyang
Sera Monastery
Drepung Monastery
Potala
Jokhang
Ganden
Maizhokunggar
Jimda
Lhasa
LXA
Rinbung
Gonggar
Zhanang
Samye Monastery
Zêtang
Rito Gompar
Gongbogyamda
Tangmai
Bamda
Yidun
Bomi
Baxoi
Bayizhen
Nyingchi
Namjagbarwa 7755
Sumzom
Zogang
Mongotong
Batang
Qusum
Gyaca
Nang Xian
Mainling
Rawu
Gartog
Chubalung
Daglung
Qonggyai
Lhozhan
Kulha Gangri
Lhünzê
Bruni
Zongza
Cakalho
Tato
Yiyu
Shol
Mega
Karko
Ilupu
Zhowagoin
Cona
Sartam
Daporijo
Kambeng
Along
Amili
Zazhong
Meili
Mabating
Dêqên
Jakar
Donkar
Buddhist Monastery
Jang
Tawang
Kombong
Dambuk
Nizamghat
Hayuliang
Walong
Marniu
Daring
Sadiya
Tezu
Dong
Yanmen
Trashigang
Gangola
Tado
Ziro
Jonai Bazar
Brakmakund
Chonkham
Nixi
Bomdi La
Seppa
Itanagar
Potin
Pathalipam
Bordoloni
Dibrugarh
Tinsukia
Makum
Digboi
Margherita
Tapun
Miao
Namdapha N.P.
Hkyenhpa
Naung-Mon
Gongshan
Zhongdian
Yatang
Three Parallel Rivers of Yunnan Protected Areas
North Lakhimpur
Dihajan
Khowang
Jaipur
Nij Laluk
Nameri N.P.
Sonai Rupa N.P.
Darranga
Panka
Narphung
Manas N.P.
Manas Tiger Reserve
Garubhasa
Remarkable cities and cultural monuments
UNESCO World Cultural Heritage
Remarkable city
Ancient China
Places of Christian cultural interest
Places of Islamic cultural interest
Places of Buddhist cultural interest
Places of Hindu cultural interest
Places of Sikh cultural interest
Historical city scape
Castle/fortress/fort
Palace
Space telescope
Museum
Sport and leisure sites
Skiing
Canoeing/rafting
Hill resort

Southern Baykal Region, Northern Mongolia

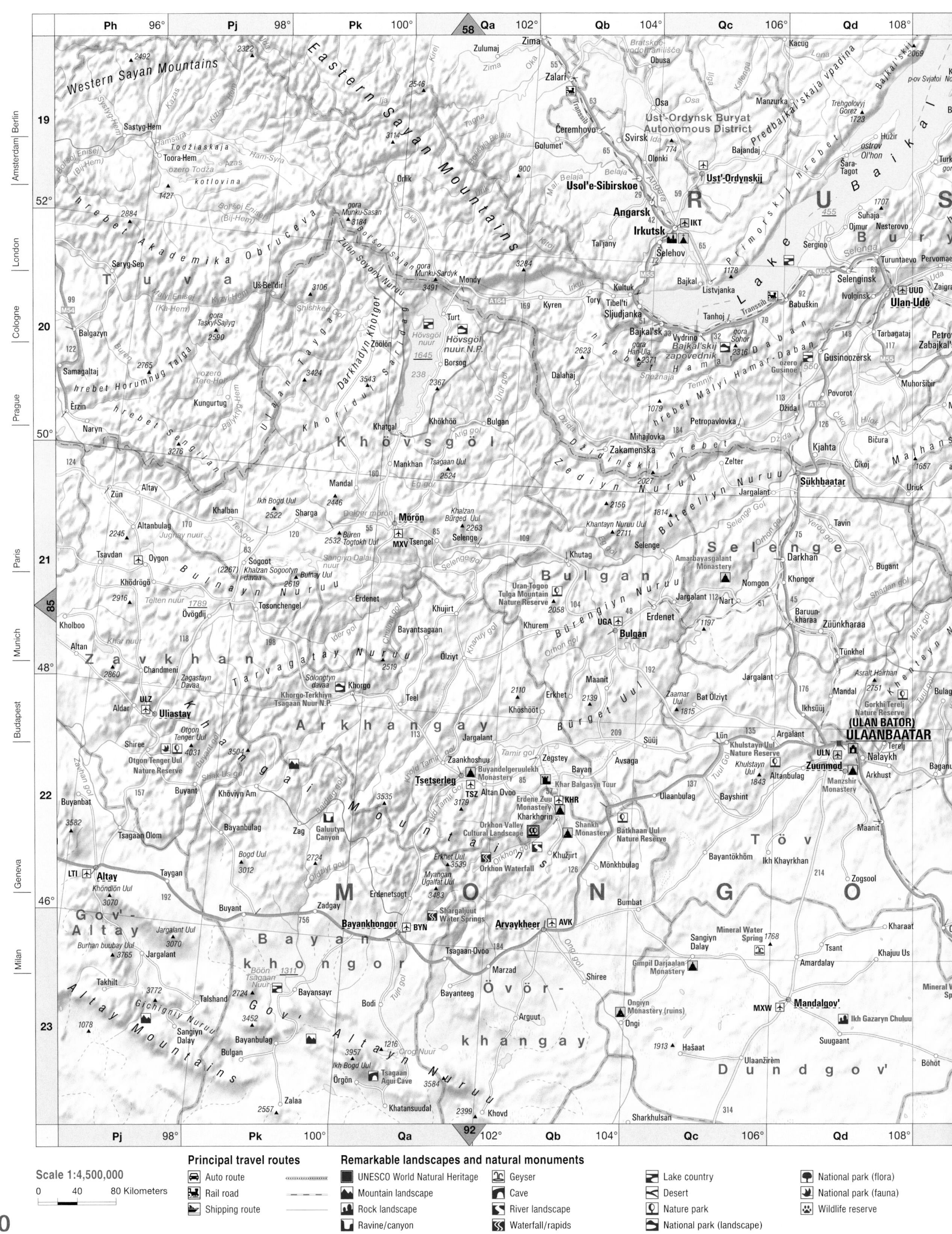

Scale 1:4,500,000

0   40   80 Kilometers

Principal travel routes

- Auto route
- Rail road
- Shipping route

Remarkable landscapes and natural monuments

- UNESCO World Natural Heritage
- Mountain landscape
- Rock landscape
- Ravine/canyon
- Geyser
- Cave
- River landscape
- Waterfall/rapids
- Lake country
- Desert
- Nature park
- National park (landscape)
- National park (flora)
- National park (fauna)
- Wildlife reserve

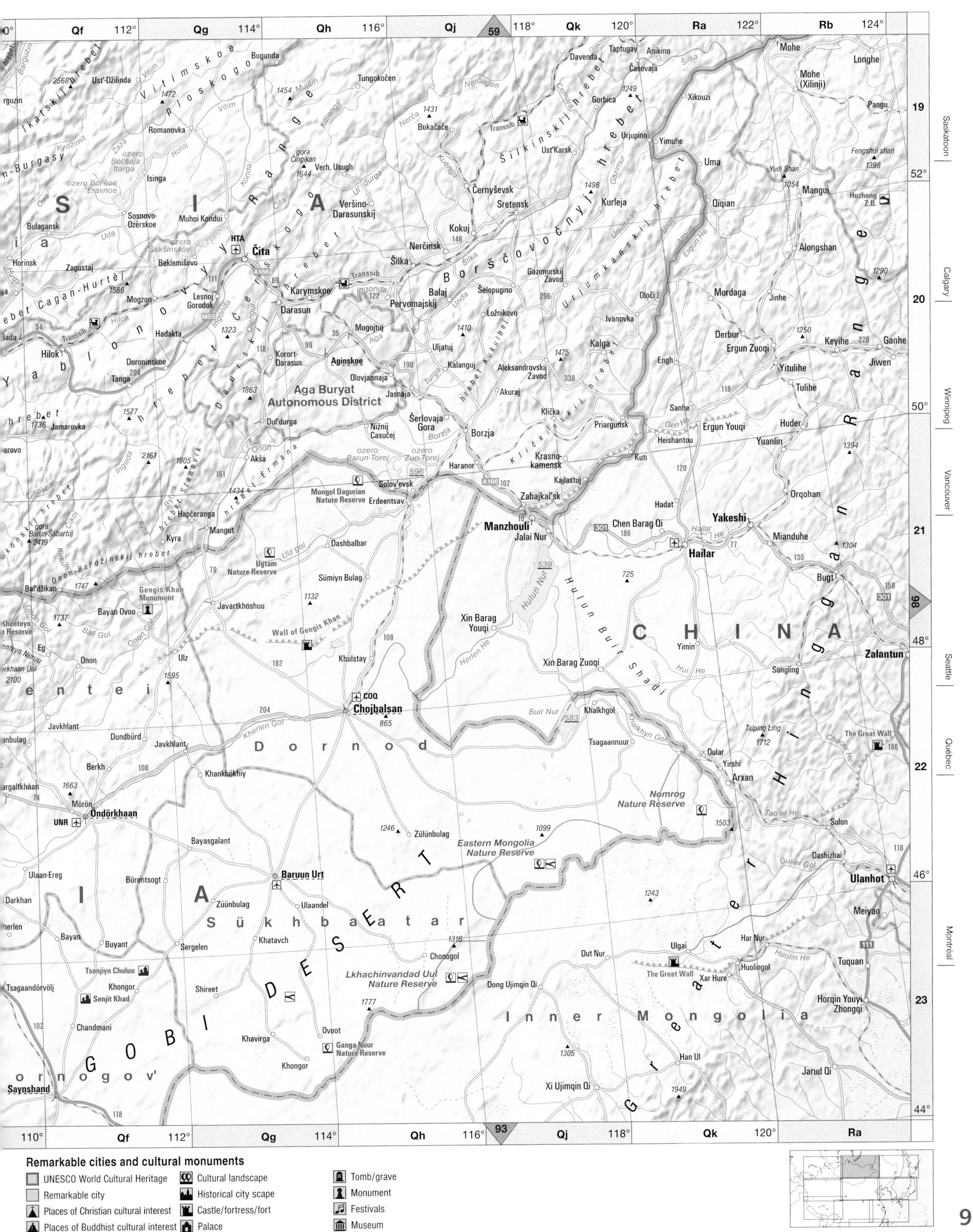

Remarkable cities and cultural monuments

- ⬜ UNESCO World Cultural Heritage
- ⬜ Remarkable city
- ▲ Places of Christian cultural interest
- ▲ Places of Buddhist cultural interest

- ⊙ Cultural landscape
- ▮ Historical city scape
- ♜ Castle/fortress/fort
- ⌂ Palace

- ⬛ Tomb/grave
- 👤 Monument
- ♫ Festivals
- 🏛 Museum

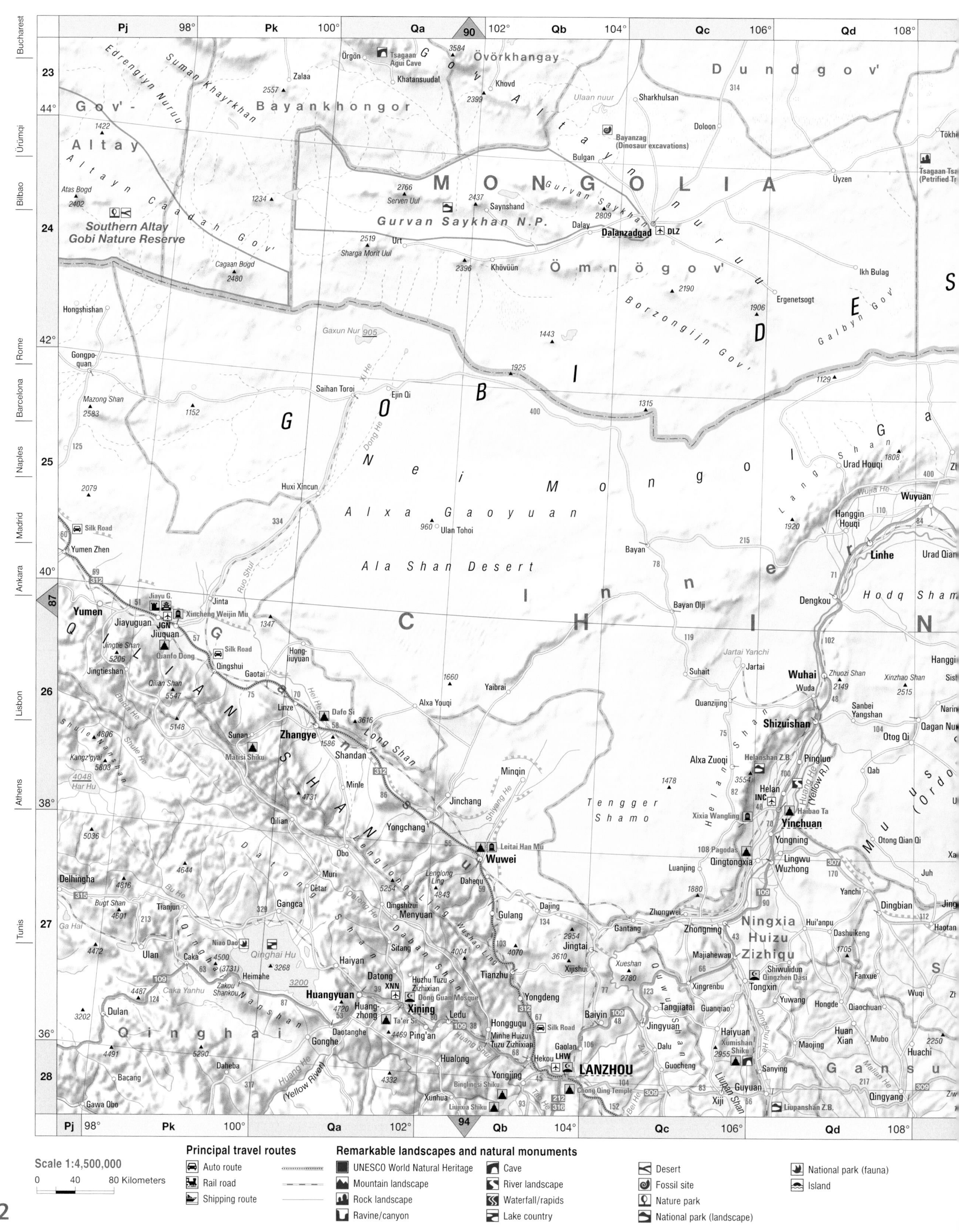

Scale 1:4,500,000

0   40   80 Kilometers

Principal travel routes

🚗 Auto route

🚆 Rail road

🚢 Shipping route

········ (dotted route)

Remarkable landscapes and natural monuments

■ UNESCO World Natural Heritage

⛰ Mountain landscape

🪨 Rock landscape

🏞 Ravine/canyon

🕳 Cave

🏞 River landscape

💦 Waterfall/rapids

🏞 Lake country

🏜 Desert

🦴 Fossil site

🏛 Nature park

🏕 National park (landscape)

🦌 National park (fauna)

🏝 Island

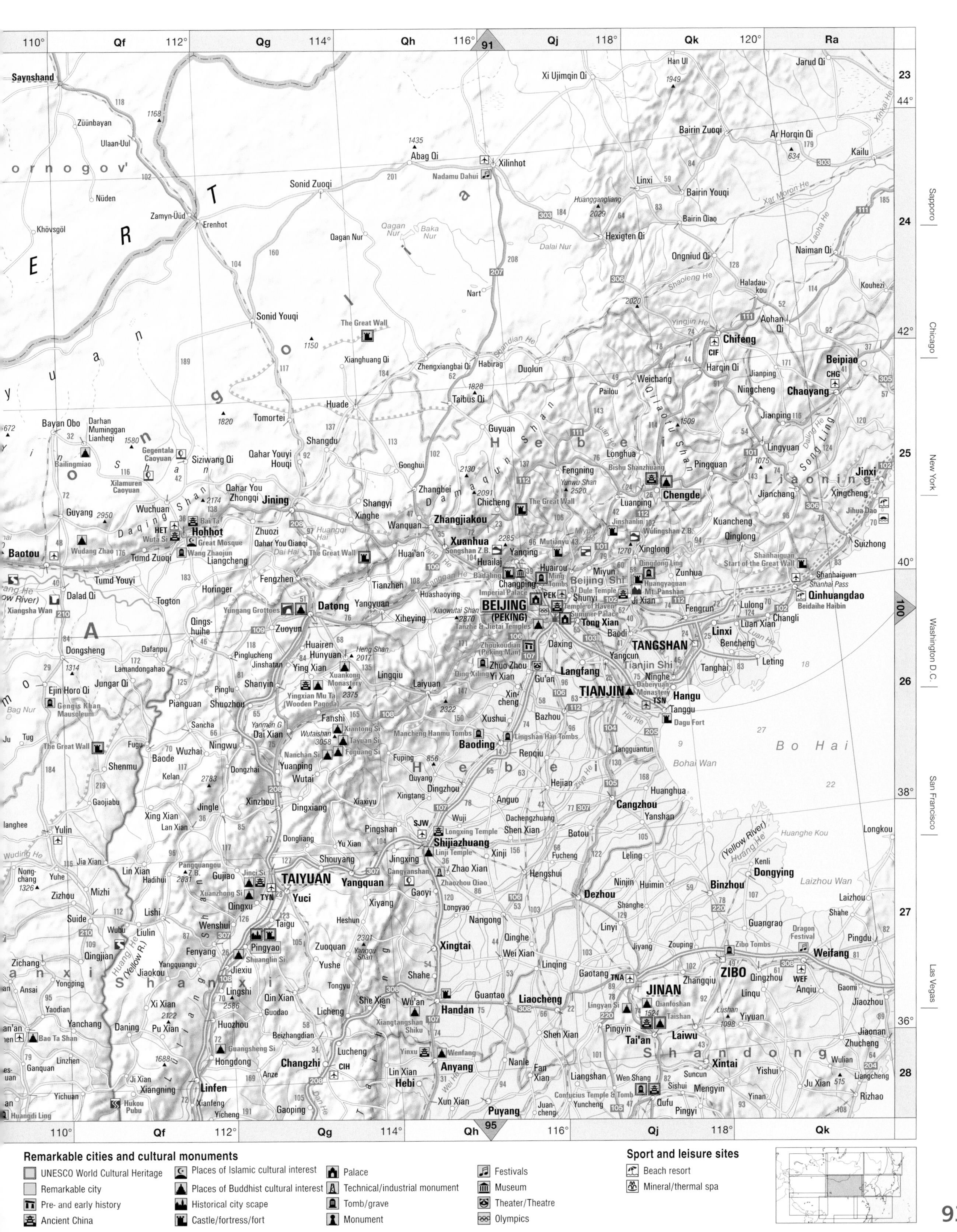

110°
Qf
112°
Qg
114°
Qh
116°
91
Qj
118°
Qk
120°
Ra
23
44°
24
42°
25
40°
26
38°
27
36°
28
100
95
Sapporo
Chicago
New York
Washington D.C.
San Francisco
Las Vegas
Saynshand
Züünbayan
Ulaan-Uul
Nüden
Zamyn-Üüd
Erenhot
Khövsgöl
Sonid Zuoqi
Abag Qi
Xilinhot
Nadamu Dahui
Xi Ujimqin Qi
Han Ul
Jarud Qi
Bairin Zuoqi
Ar Horqin Qi
Kailu
Linxi
Bairin Youqi
Xar Moron He
Huanggangliang
Bairin Qiao
Hexigten Qi
Dalai Nur
Ongniud Qi
Naiman Qi
Qagan Nur
Baka Nur
Nart
Sonid Youqi
The Great Wall
Shaoleng He
Haladau-kou
Kouhezi
Aohan Qi
Yingjin He
Chifeng
Xianghuang Qi
Zhengxiangbai Qi
Habirag
Duolun
Taibus Qi
Harqin Qi
Beipiao
Weichang
Pailou
Jianping
Ningcheng
Chaoyang
Huade
Tomortei
Bayan Obo
Darhan Muminggan Lianheqi
Shangdu
Guyuan
Gegentala Caoyuan
Siziwang Qi
Qahar Youyi Houqi
Gonghui
Fengning
Bishu Shanzhuang
Pingquan
Lingyuan
Jinxi
Bailingmiao
Xilamuren Caoyuan
Qahar You Zhongqi
Jining
Zhangbei
Chicheng
Chengde
Luanping
Jianchang
Xingcheng
Guyang
Wuchuan
Hohhot
Great Mosque
Wang Zhaojun
Shangyi
Xinghe
Wanquan
Zhangjiakou
Jinshanling
Kuancheng
Qinglong
Suizhong
Baotou
Wudang Zhao
Tumd Zuoqi
Zhuozi
Qahar You Qianqi
Dai Hai
Liangcheng
Xuanhua
Yanqing
Mutianyu
Huairou
Xinglong
Shanhaiguan
Start of the Great Wall
Tumd Youyi
Fengzhen
Huai'an
Badaling
Ming Tombs
Miyun
Zunhua
Qinhuangdao
Shanhai Pass
Dalad Qi
Horinger
Tianzhen
Changping
Beijing Shi
Huangyaguan
Mt. Panshan
Beidaihe Haibin
Togton
Yungang Grottoes
Datong
Yangyuan
Huashaoying
Imperial Palace
BEIJING (PEKING)
Shunyi
Temple of Heaven
Summer Palace
Ji Xian
Fengrun
Lulong
Changli
Xiangsha Wan
Qingshuihe
Zuoyun
Xiheying
Xiaowutai Shan
Tanzhe & Jietai Temples
Tong Xian
Baodi
Luan Xian
Linxi
Dongsheng
Dafanpu
Huairen
Hunyuan
Heng Shan
Zhoukoudian (Peking Man)
Daxing
TANGSHAN
Bencheng
Lamandongahao
Pinglucheng
Jinshatan
Ying Xian
Xuankong Monastery
Lingqiu
Zhuo Zhou
Yi Xian
Gu'an
Langfang
Yangcun
Tianjin Shi
Tanghai
Leting
Ejin Horo Qi
Jungar Qi
Shanyin
Yingxian Mu Ta (Wooden Pagoda)
Laiyuan
Xincheng
Ninghe
TIANJIN
Hangu
Genghis Khan Mausoleum
Pinglu
Pianguan
Shuozhou
Bazhou
Tanggu
Dagu Fort
Sancha
Yanmen G
Dai Xian
Fanshi
Xiantong Si
Wutaishan
Tayuan Si
Mancheng Hanmu Tombs
Baoding
Lingshan Han Tombs
Tug
The Great Wall
Fugu
Wuzhai
Baode
Ningwu
Nanchan Si
Foguang Si
Renqiu
Tangguantun
Bo Hai
Bohai Wan
Shenmu
Kelan
Dongzhai
Yuanping
Wutai
Fuping
Quyang
Hebei
Hejian
Dingzhou
Huanghua
Gaojiabu
Jingle
Xinzhou
Dingxiang
Xiaxiyu
Xingtang
Anguo
Cangzhou
Xing Xian
Lan Xian
Wuji
Dachengzhuang
Shen Xian
Yanshan
Yulin
Pingshan
Longxing Temple
Shijiazhuang
Botou
Longkou
Huanghe Kou
Dongliang
Yu Xian
Linji Temple
Xinji
Fucheng
Leling
Jia Xian
Shouyang
Jingxing
Cangyanshan
Zhao Xian
Hengshui
Kenli
Dongying
Laizhou Wan
Nongchang
Yuhe
Lin Xian
Gujiao
Jinci Si
TAIYUAN
Yangquan
Ningjin
Huimin
Binzhou
Zizhou
Mizhi
Xuanzhong Si
Yuci
Gaoyi
Zhaozhou Qiao
Dezhou
Qingxu
Xiyang
Longyao
Shanghe
Laizhou
Shahe
Suide
Lishi
Wenshui
Taigu
Heshun
Nangong
Linyi
Guangrao
Dragon Festival
Pingdu
Wubu
Liulin
Pingyao
Shuanglin Si
Zuoquan
Yangqu Shan
Xingtai
Qinghe
Jiyang
Zouping
Zibo Tombs
Weifang
Zichang
Qingjian
Fenyang
Yushe
Wei Xian
Linqing
Yangquangu
Jiexiu
Jiaokou
Shahe
Gaotang
ZIBO
Qingzhou
WEF
Anqiu
Gaomi
Ansai
Yongping
Shaanxi
Lingshi
Tongyu
She Xian
Wu'an
Guantao
Liaocheng
Zhangqiu
JINAN
Qianfoshan
Linqu
Jiaozhou
Yaodian
Xi Xian
Qin Xian
Guodao
Licheng
Handan
Lingyan Si
Taishan
Lushan
Yiyuan
Yan'an
Yanchang
Daning
Pu Xian
Huozhou
Beizhangdian
Xiangtangshan Shiku
Shen Xian
Pingyin
Tai'an
Laiwu
Jiaonan
Zhucheng
Bao Ta Shan
Guangsheng Si
Hongdong
Changzhi
Lucheng
Yinxu
Wenfang
Anyang
Nanle
Shandong
Xintai
Wulian
Ganquan
Linzhen
Ji Xian
Xiangning
Linfen
Anze
Lin Xian
Hebi
Fan Xian
Liangshan
Wen Shang
Suncun
Sishui
Mengyin
Yishui
Ju Xian
Liangcheng
Yichuan
Hukou Pubu
Xianfeng
Yicheng
Gaoping
Xun Xian
Puyang
Juancheng
Confucius Temple & Tomb
Yuncheng
Qufu
Pingyi
Yinan
Rizhao
Huangdi Ling
Remarkable cities and cultural monuments
UNESCO World Cultural Heritage
Remarkable city
Pre- and early history
Ancient China
Places of Islamic cultural interest
Places of Buddhist cultural interest
Historical city scape
Castle/fortress/fort
Palace
Technical/industrial monument
Tomb/grave
Monument
Festivals
Museum
Theater/Theatre
Olympics
Sport and leisure sites
Beach resort
Mineral/thermal spa

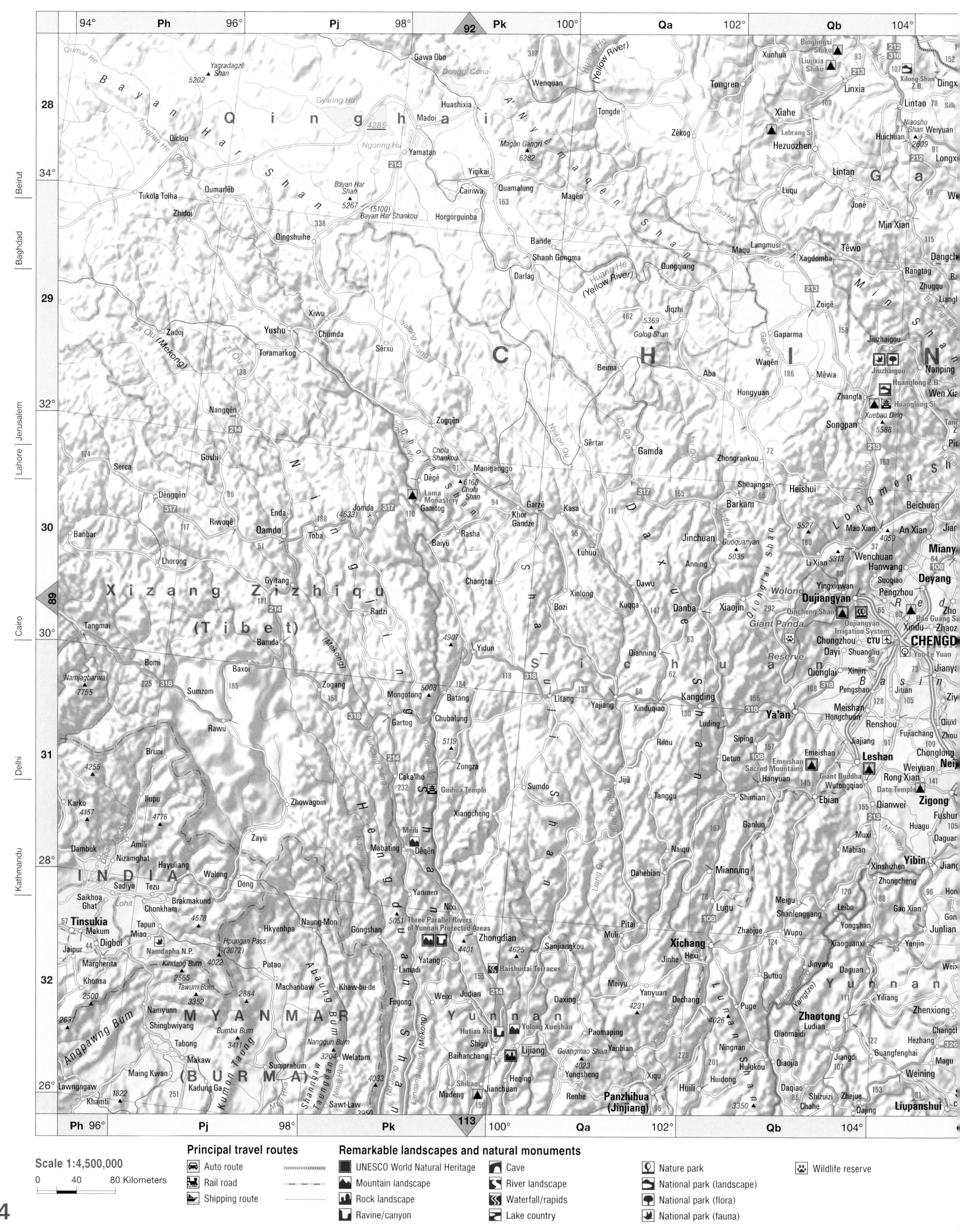

Principal travel routes

- 🚗 Auto route
- 🚆 Rail road
- 🚢 Shipping route

⸺ (dotted)
⸺ (dashed)

Remarkable landscapes and natural monuments

- ■ UNESCO World Natural Heritage
- ▮ Mountain landscape
- ▮ Rock landscape
- ▮ Ravine/canyon
- ▮ Cave
- ▮ River landscape
- ▮ Waterfall/rapids
- ▮ Lake country
- ▮ Nature park
- ▮ National park (landscape)
- ▮ National park (flora)
- ▮ National park (fauna)
- ▮ Wildlife reserve

Scale 1:4,500,000

0   40   80 Kilometers

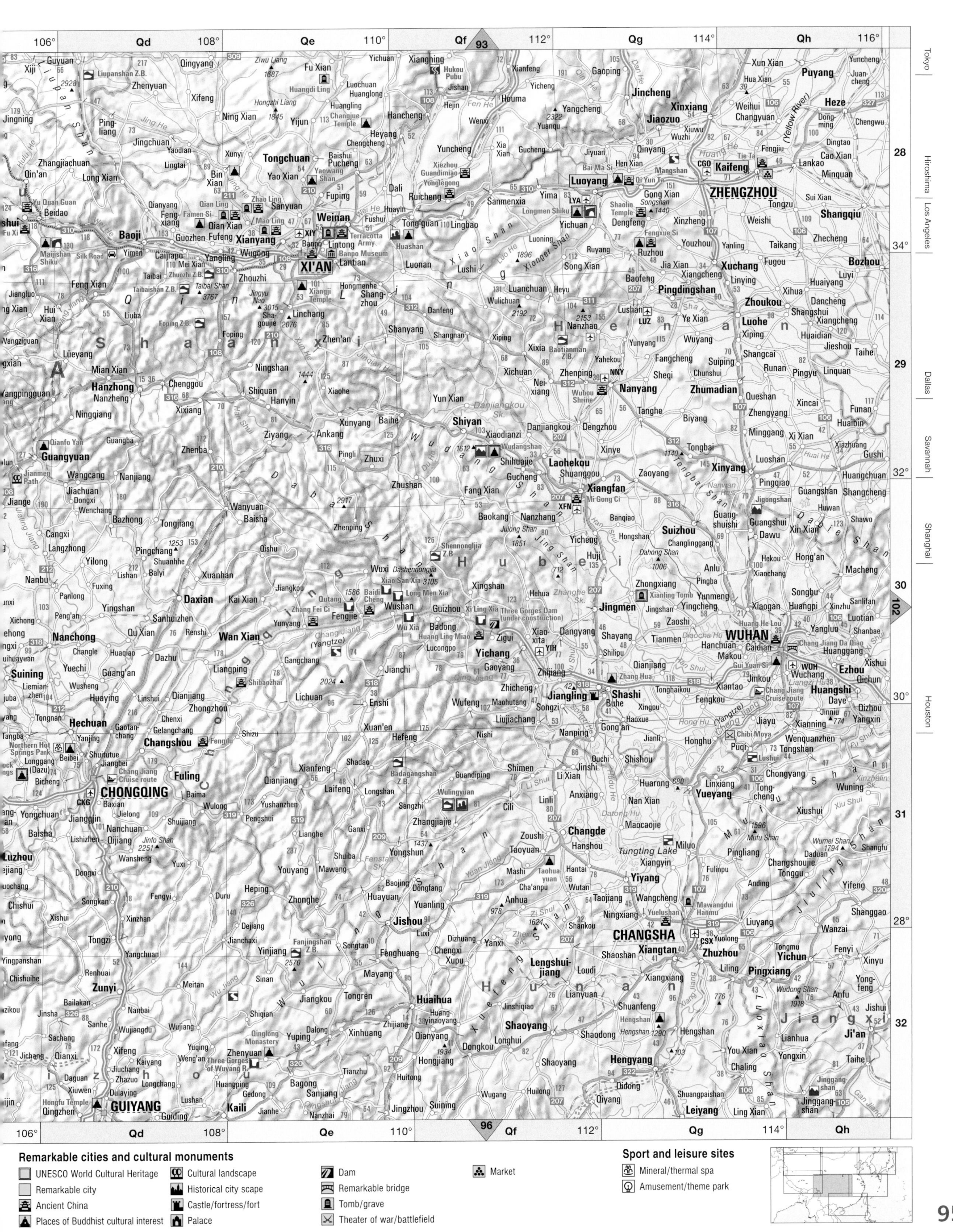

Remarkable cities and cultural monuments

▢ UNESCO World Cultural Heritage	∞ Cultural landscape	▨ Dam
▢ Remarkable city	▨ Historical city scape	▨ Remarkable bridge
▣ Ancient China	▨ Castle/fortress/fort	▨ Tomb/grave
▲ Places of Buddhist cultural interest	▥ Palace	⊠ Theater of war/battlefield
		♣ Market

Sport and leisure sites

♨ Mineral/thermal spa

Ⓐ Amusement/theme park

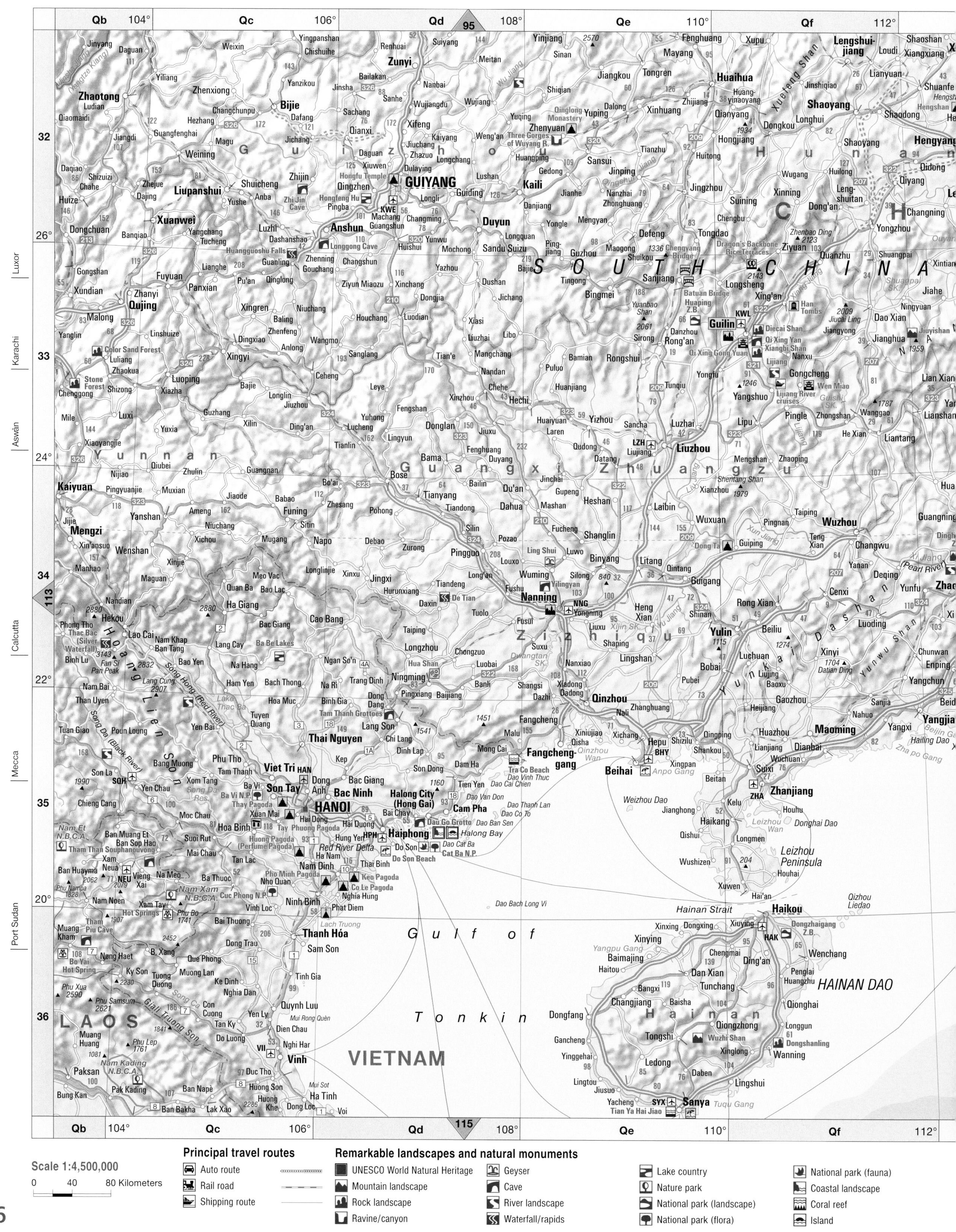

Scale 1:4,500,000

0   40   80 Kilometers

Principal travel routes

- Auto route
- Rail road
- Shipping route

Remarkable landscapes and natural monuments

- UNESCO World Natural Heritage
- Mountain landscape
- Rock landscape
- Ravine/canyon
- Geyser
- Cave
- River landscape
- Waterfall/rapids
- Lake country
- Nature park
- National park (landscape)
- National park (flora)
- National park (fauna)
- Coastal landscape
- Coral reef
- Island

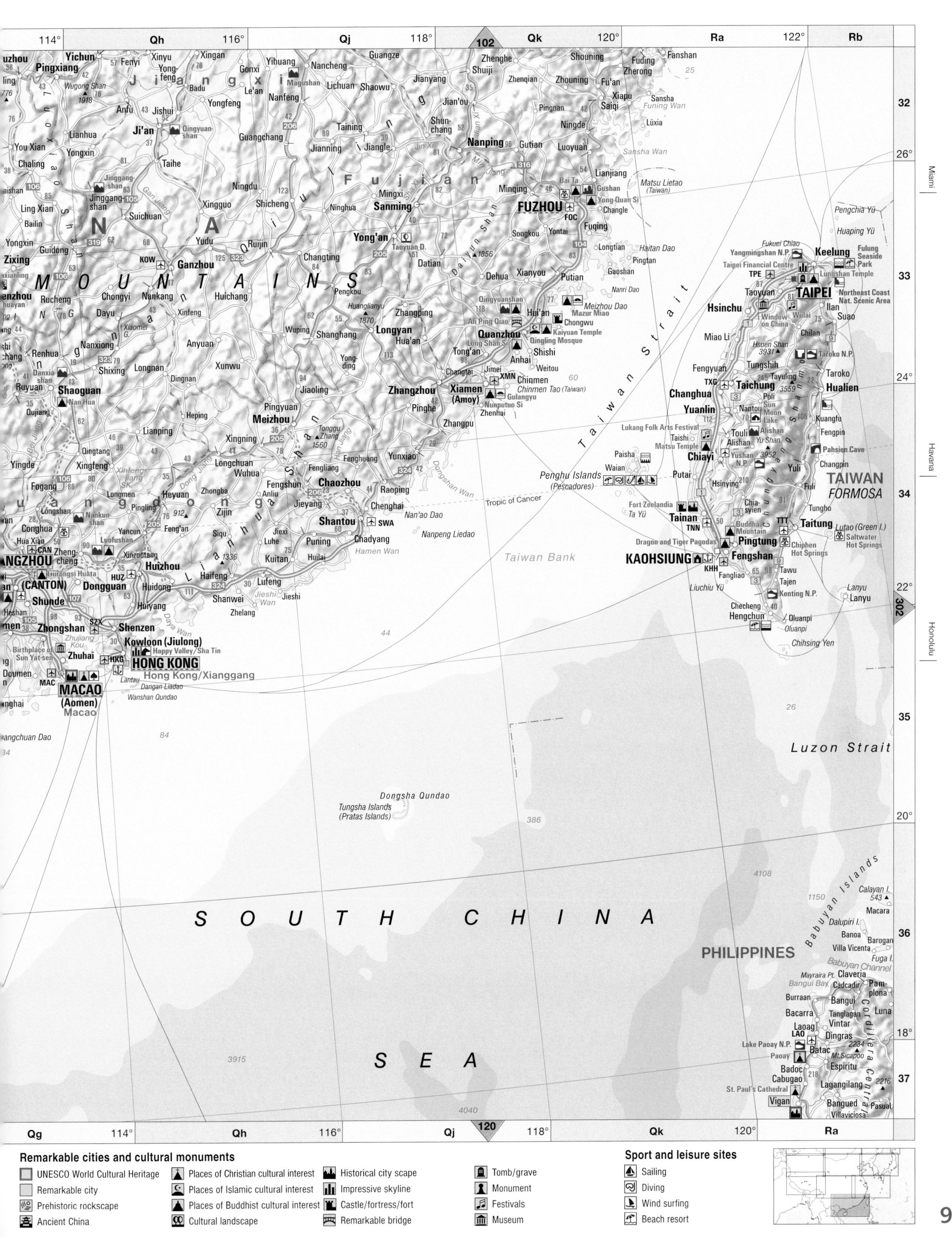

114°
Qh
116°
Qj
118°
102
Qk
120°
Ra
122°
Rb
32
26°
33
24°
34
22°
35
20°
36
18°
37
Miami
Havana
Honolulu
302
Qg
114°
Qh
116°
Qj
120
118°
Qk
120°
Ra
Yichun
Pingxiang
Xinyu
Xingan
Yongfeng
Gonxi
Yihuang
Nancheng
Guangze
Zhenghe
Shouning
Fuding
Zherong
Fanshan
Wugong Shan
1918
Badu
Le'an
Magushan
Lichuan
Shaowu
Jianyang
Shuiji
Zhenqian
Zhouning
Fu'an
Xiapu
Saiqi
Sansha
Funing Wan
Anfu
Jishui
Yongfeng
Nanfeng
Jian'ou
Pingnan
Ningde
Lüxia
Lianhua
Ji'an
Qingyuan-shan
Guangchang
Taining
Shun-chang
You Xian
Yongxin
Jianning
Jiangle
Nanping
Gutian
Luoyuan
Sansha Wan
Chaling
Taihe
Jinggang-shan
Lianjiang
Matsu Lietao
(Taiwan)
Ningdu
Mingxi
Minqing
Bai Ta
Gushan
Yong Quan Si
Ling Xian
Xingguo
Shicheng
Ninghua
Sanming
FUZHOU
FOC
Changle
Pengchia Yü
Suichuan
Huaping Yü
Bailin
Yong'an
Fuqing
Yongxin
Yudu
Ruijin
Taoyuan D.
Songkou
Yontai
Longtian
Haitan Dao
Pingtan
Fukuei Chiao
Zixing
Guidong
Ganzhou
KOW
Changting
Datian
Yangmingshan N.P.
Keelung
Fulung Seaside Park
Taipei Financial Centre
TPE
Lungshan Temple
Gaoshan
Dehua
Xianyou
Putian
Nanri Dao
M O U N T A I N S
Rucheng
Chongyi
Nankang
Huichang
Pengkou
Taoyuan
TAIPEI
Northeast Coast Nat. Scenic Area
Huanglianyu
1870
Qingyuanshan
Hsinchu
Ilan
Dayu
Xinfeng
Zhangping
Hui'an
Meizhou Dao
Mazur Miao
Window on China
Wulai
Suao
Xiaomei G.
An Ping Qiao
Chongwu
Nanxiong
Anyuan
Wuping
Shanghang
Longyan
Hua'an
Quanzhou
Kaiyuan Temple
Qingling Mosque
Miao Li
Chilan
Renhua
Long Shan Si
Tong'an
Anhai
Hsuen Shan
3931
Taroko N.P.
Shixing
Longnan
Xunwu
Yong-ding
Shishi
Fengyuan
Tungshih
Danxia-shan
Dingnan
Changtai
Jimei
XMN
Weitou
Chinmen
60
Chinmen Tao (Taiwan)
TXG
Taichung
Tayuling
Taroko
Ruyuan
Shaoguan
Jiaoling
Zhangzhou
Xiamen (Amoy)
Gulangyu
Nunputuo Si
3559
Hualien
Changhua
Nan Hua
Pingyuan
Pinghe
Zhenhai
Qujiang
Heping
Meizhou
Zhangpu
Yuanlin
Nantou
Sun Moon Lake
Kuangfu
Lianping
Tonggu Zhang
1560
Lukang Folk Arts Festival
Taishi
Touli
Alishan
Fengpin
Xingning
Matsu Temple
Qingtang
Xingfeng
Yushan N.P.
3952
Pahsien Cave
Longchuan
Wuhua
Fenghuang
Yunxiao
Paisha
Chiayi
Yingde
Fengliang
Dongshan Wan
Waian
Penghu Islands (Pescadores)
Putai
Changpin
Yuli
TAIWAN
FORMOSA
Fogang
Heyuan
Zhongba
Fengshun
Chaozhou
Raoping
Anliu
Hsinying
Fuli
Longmen
Tropic of Cancer
Longshan
Pingling
Jieyang
Chenghai
Nan'ao Dao
Fort Zeelandia
Ta Yü
Tunghpo
Nankun-shan
912
Zijin
Shantou
SWA
Chia-syien
Conghua
Feng'an
Tainan
TNN
Taitung
Lutao (Green I.)
Yancun
Siqu
Jiexi
Luhe
Puning
Chadyang
Nanpeng Liedao
Buddha Mountain
Luofushan
Saltwater Hot Springs
Hua Xian
CAN
Zheng-cheng
1336
Hamen Wan
Dragon and Tiger Pagodas
Pingtung
Chiphen Hot Springs
Xinzoutang
Taiwan Bank
ANGZHOU
Huizhou
Kuitan
Huilai
KAOHSIUNG
Fengshan
Liurongsi Huata
HUZ
Haifeng
KHH
(CANTON)
Dongguan
Huidong
Lufeng
Fangliao
Tawu
Tajen
Shunde
Jieshi Wan
Jieshi
Liuchiu Yü
Kenting N.P.
Lanyu
Heshan
Huiyang
Shanwei
Zhelang
Checheng
Hengchun
Oluanpi
Zhongshan
SZX
Shenzen
Daya Wan
44
Chihsing Yen
Zhujiang Kou
Kowloon (Jiulong)
Happy Valley/Sha Tin
Birthplace of Sun Yat-sen
Zhuhai
HKG
HONG KONG
Hong Kong/Xianggang
Doumen
MAC
Lantau
Dangan Liedao
MACAO
Wanshan Qundao
(Aomen)
Macao
26
Luzon Strait
84
Dongsha Qundao
Tungsha Islands (Pratas Islands)
386
Taiwan Strait
4108
Babuyan Islands
Calayan I.
543
1150
Macara
S O U T H C H I N A
Dalupiri I.
Banoa
Barogan
PHILIPPINES
Villa Vicenta
Fuga I.
Babuyan Channel
Mayraira Pt.
Claveria
Bangui Bay
Cadcadir
Pam-plona
Burraan
Bangui
Cordillera Central
Bacarra
Tanglagan
Luna
Vintar
Laoag
LAO
Dingras
Lake Paoay N.P.
Batac
2284
Paoay
Mt.Sicapoo
3915
S E A
Badoc
Espiritu
Cabugao
2216
St. Paul's Cathedral
Lagangilang
Vigan
Bangued
Pasual
Villaviciosa
4040
Remarkable cities and cultural monuments
UNESCO World Cultural Heritage
Remarkable city
Prehistoric rockscape
Ancient China
Places of Christian cultural interest
Places of Islamic cultural interest
Places of Buddhist cultural interest
Cultural landscape
Historical city scape
Impressive skyline
Castle/fortress/fort
Remarkable bridge
Tomb/grave
Monument
Festivals
Museum
Sport and leisure sites
Sailing
Diving
Wind surfing
Beach resort

Northeastern China, Southeastern Russia, Hokkaido (Northern Japan)

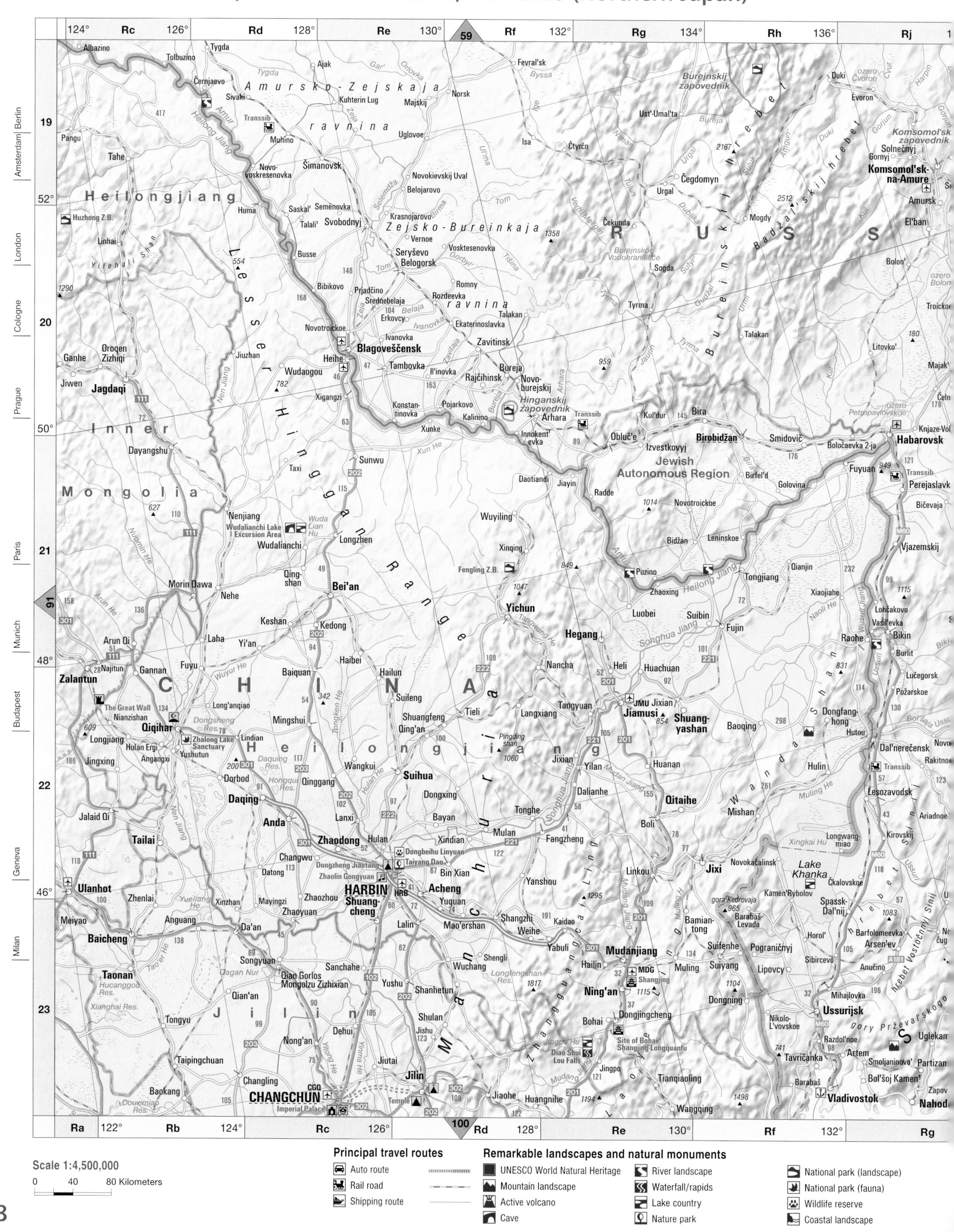

Scale 1:4,500,000

0   40   80 Kilometers

Principal travel routes

- Auto route
- Rail road
- Shipping route

Remarkable landscapes and natural monuments

- UNESCO World Natural Heritage
- Mountain landscape
- Active volcano
- Cave
- River landscape
- Waterfall/rapids
- Lake country
- Nature park
- National park (landscape)
- National park (fauna)
- Wildlife reserve
- Coastal landscape

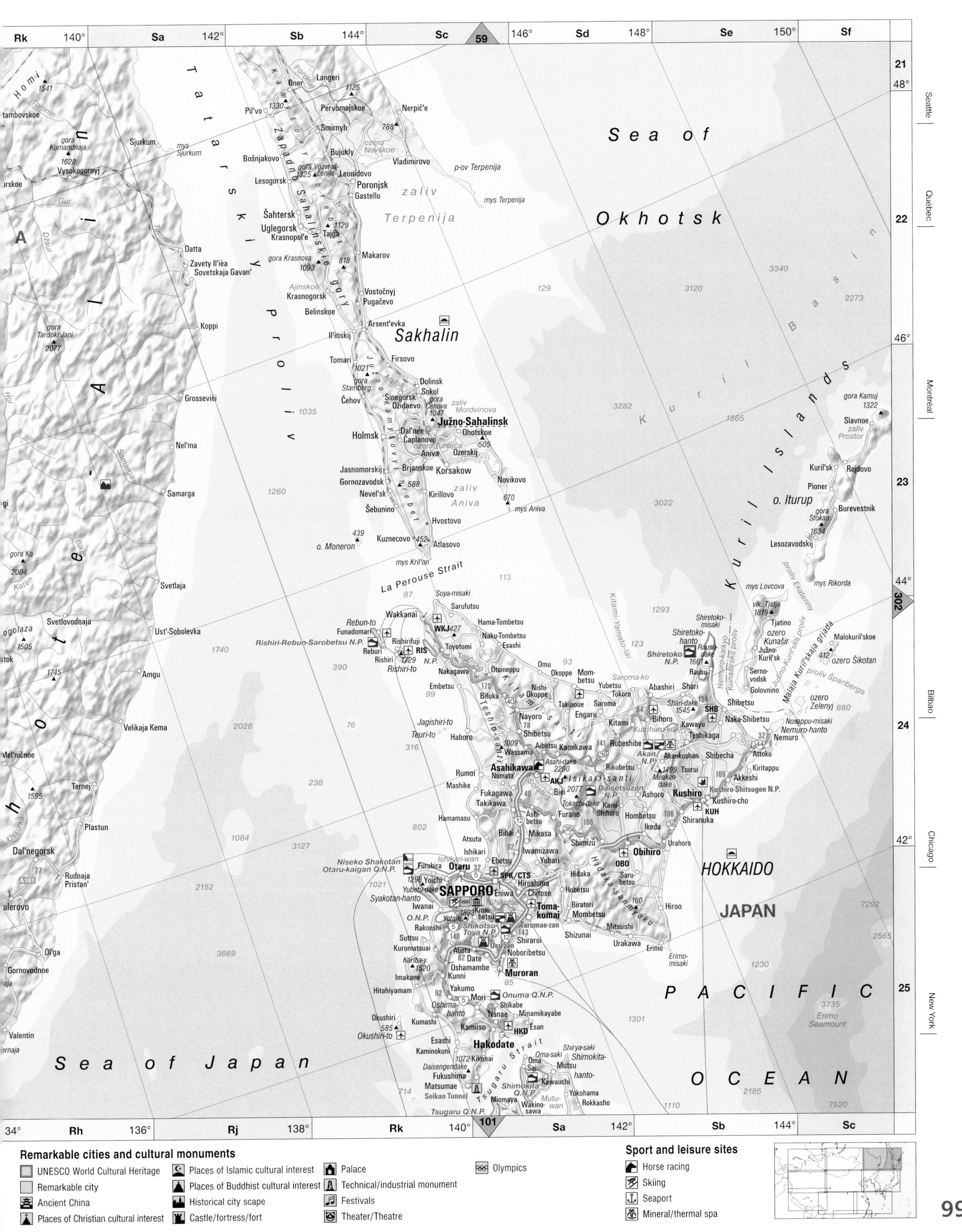
Rk
140°
Sa
142°
Sb
144°
Sc
59
146°
Sd
148°
Se
150°
Sf
21
48°
22
46°
23
44°
302
24
42°
25
Seattle
Québec
Montréal
Bilbao
Chicago
New York
Sea of Okhotsk
Tatarskiy proliv
Sakhalin
zaliv Terpenija
p-ov Terpenija
mys Terpenija
Kuril Basin
Kuril Islands
o. Iturup
La Perouse Strait
zaliv Aniva
zaliv Mordvinova
Južno-Sahalinsk
Korsakow
Holmsk
Nevel'sk
Poronjsk
Makarov
Dolinsk
Tomari
Uglegorsk
Šahtersk
Krasnogorsk
Il'inskij
Vostočnyj
Pugačevo
Langeri
Oner
Pervomajskoe
Smirnyh
Nerpič'e
Vladimirovo
Leonidovo
Gastello
Novikovo
mys Aniva
Kirillovo
Hvostovo
Atlasovo
Kuznecovo
o. Moneron
mys Kril'on
Soya-misaki
Wakkanai
Rebun-to
Rishiri-to
Rishiri-Rebun-Sarobetsu N.P.
Shiretoko N.P.
Akan N.P.
Daisetsuzan N.P.
Kushiro-Shitsugen N.P.
Niseko Shakotan Otaru-kaigan Q.N.P.
Shikotsu-Toya N.P.
Onuma Q.N.P.
Shimokita Q.N.P.
Tsugaru Q.N.P.
HOKKAIDO
JAPAN
SAPPORO
Asahikawa
Otaru
Obihiro
Kushiro
Abashiri
Nemuro
Muroran
Hakodate
Tomakomai
Chitose
Furano
Rumoi
Monbetsu
Erimo-misaki
Seikan Tunnel
Tsugaru Strait
Shimokita-hanto
Mutsu-wan
Okushiri-to
Oshima-hanto
Ishikari-wan
Shiretoko-hanto
Kunašir
ozero Kunašir
Malokuril'skoe
ozero Šikotan
Malaja Kuril'skaja grjada
Južno-Kuril'skij proliv
proliv Ekateriny
Kuril'sk
Rejdovo
Burevestnik
Slavnoe
Sea of Japan
PACIFIC OCEAN
Erimo Seamount
Samarga
Svetlaja
Amgu
Plastun
Ternej
Dal'negorsk
Rudnaja Pristan'
Ol'ga
Gornovodnoe
Valentin
Koppi
Datta
Zavety Il'iča
Sovetskaja Gavan'
Sjurkum
mys Sjurkum
Grosseviči
Nel'ma
Ust'-Sobolevka
Velikaja Kema
Svetlovodnaja
Vysokogornyj
34°
Rh
136°
Rj
138°
Rk
140°
101
Sa
142°
Sb
144°
Sc
Remarkable cities and cultural monuments
UNESCO World Cultural Heritage
Remarkable city
Ancient China
Places of Christian cultural interest
Places of Islamic cultural interest
Places of Buddhist cultural interest
Historical city scape
Castle/fortress/fort
Palace
Technical/industrial monument
Festivals
Theater/Theatre
Olympics
Sport and leisure sites
Horse racing
Skiing
Seaport
Mineral/thermal spa

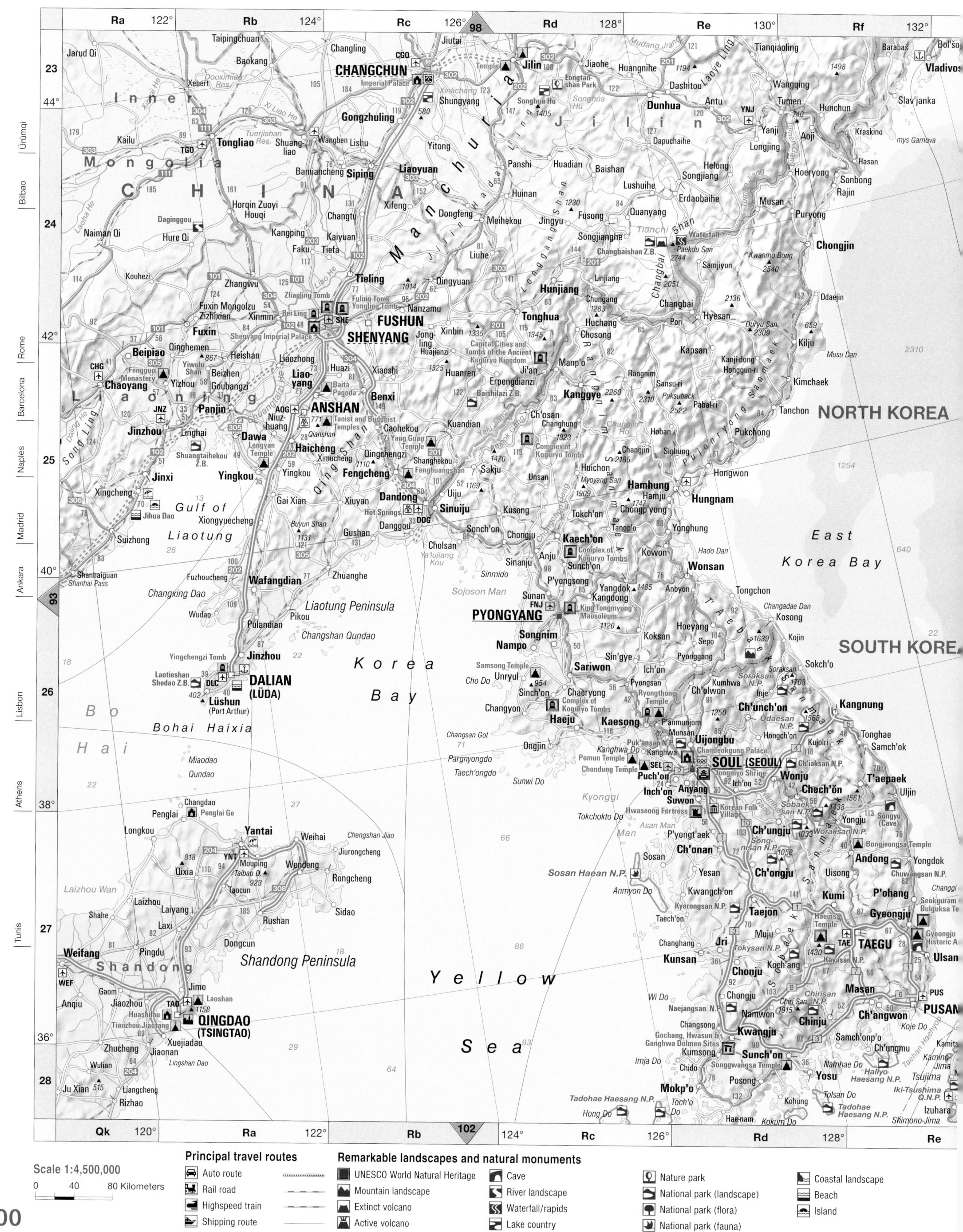

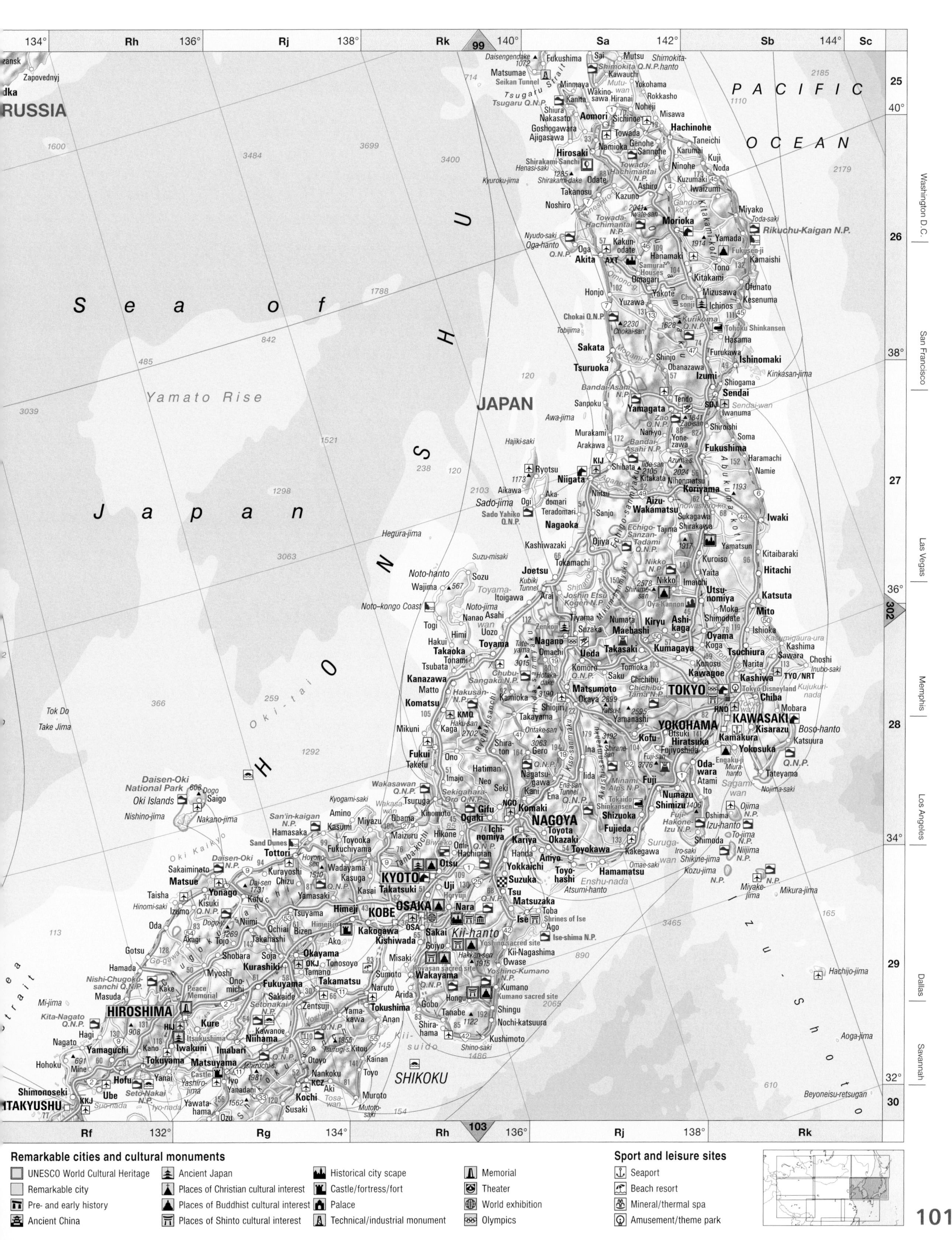

Remarkable cities and cultural monuments

- ⬜ UNESCO World Cultural Heritage
- ⬜ Remarkable city
- Pre- and early history
- Ancient China

- Ancient Japan
- Places of Christian cultural interest
- Places of Buddhist cultural interest
- Places of Shinto cultural interest

- Historical city scape
- Castle/fortress/fort
- Palace
- Technical/industrial monument

- Memorial
- Theater
- World exhibition
- Olympics

Sport and leisure sites

- Seaport
- Beach resort
- Mineral/thermal spa
- Amusement/theme park

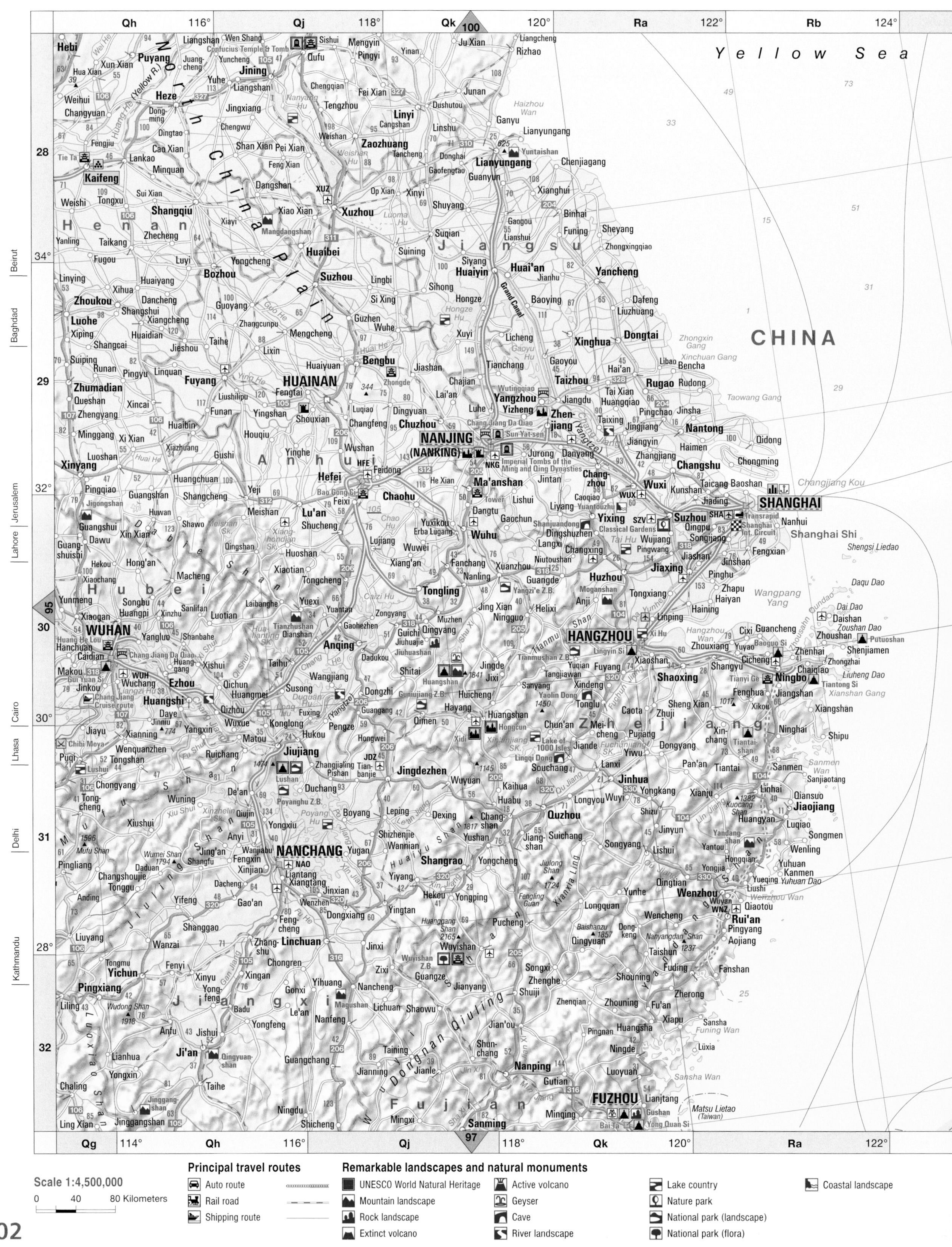

Scale 1:4,500,000

0   40   80 Kilometers

Principal travel routes
- 🚗 Auto route
- 🚆 Rail road
- ⛴ Shipping route

Remarkable landscapes and natural monuments
- ■ UNESCO World Natural Heritage
- ▲ Mountain landscape
- ▬ Rock landscape
- ▲ Extinct volcano
- ▲ Active volcano
- ⛲ Geyser
- ⌂ Cave
- ⚲ River landscape
- ⛱ Lake country
- ⚲ Nature park
- ⛺ National park (landscape)
- ⚑ National park (flora)
- ⛰ Coastal landscape

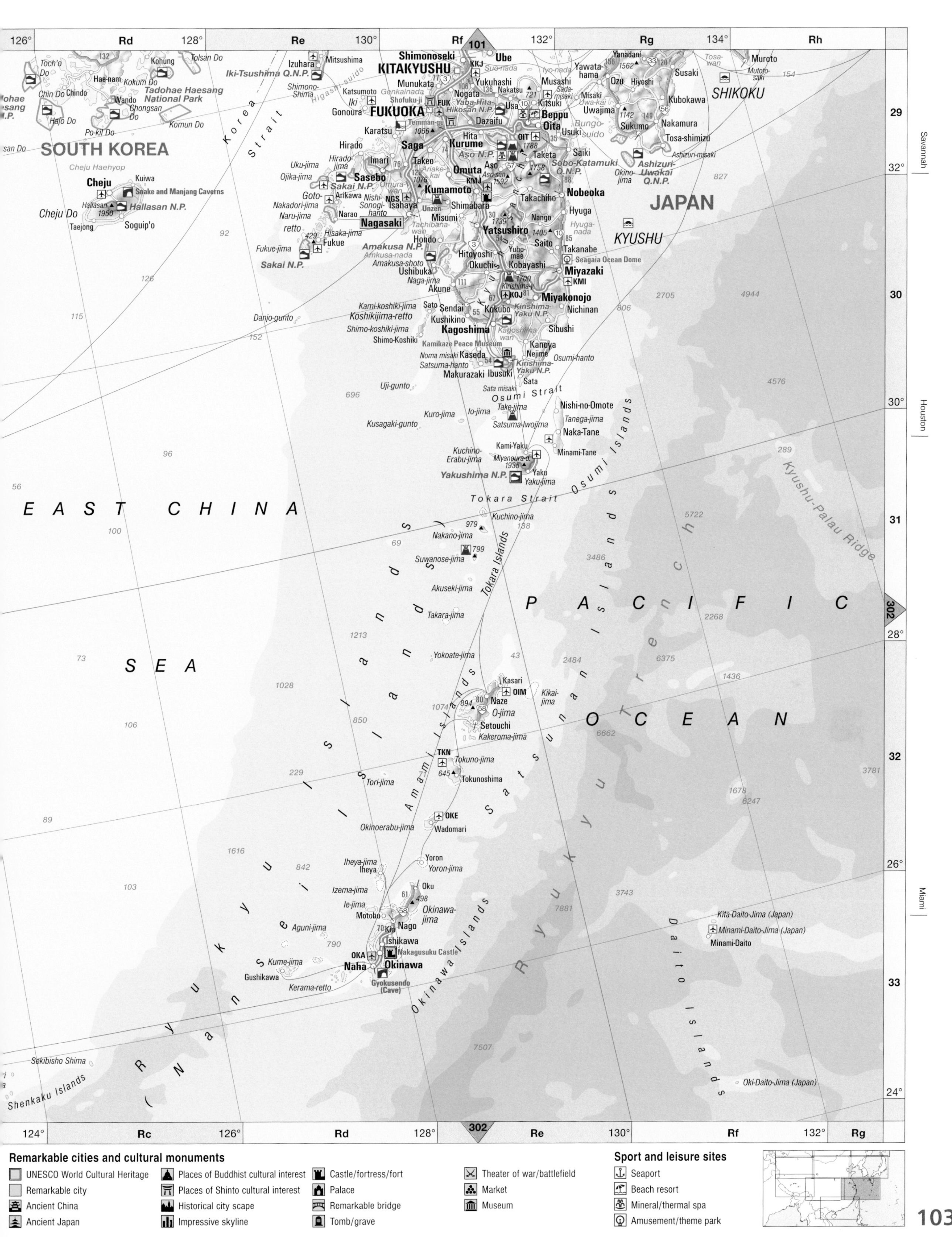

Remarkable cities and cultural monuments

- ☐ UNESCO World Cultural Heritage
- ☐ Remarkable city
- ☖ Ancient China
- ☖ Ancient Japan
- ▲ Places of Buddhist cultural interest
- ⛩ Places of Shinto cultural interest
- ⌗ Historical city scape
- ⊪ Impressive skyline
- ⛫ Castle/fortress/fort
- ⛪ Palace
- ⌂ Remarkable bridge
- ⛬ Tomb/grave
- ⚔ Theater of war/battlefield
- ⚘ Market
- 🏛 Museum

Sport and leisure sites

- ⚓ Seaport
- ⛱ Beach resort
- ♨ Mineral/thermal spa
- ⚲ Amusement/theme park

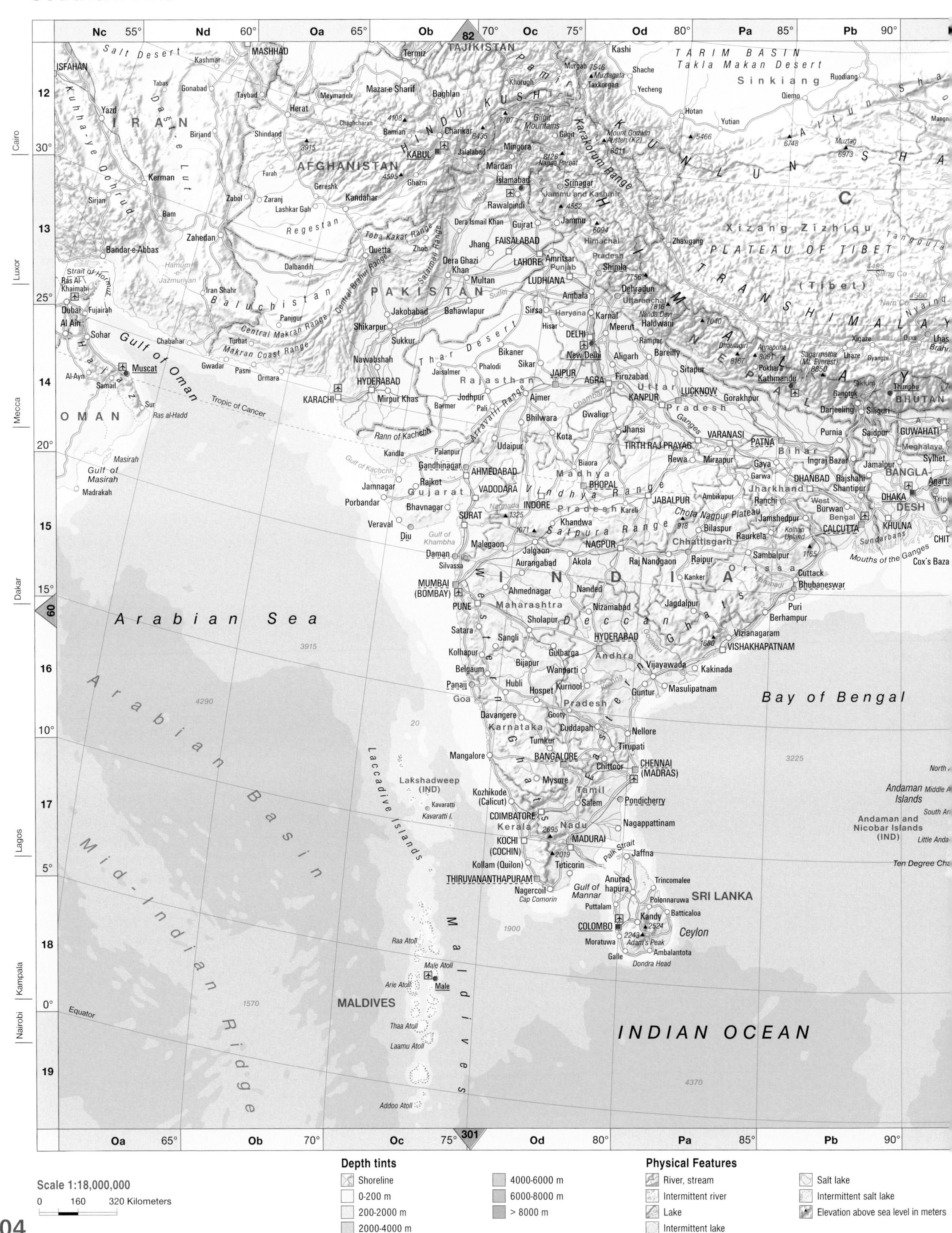

Scale 1:18,000,000

0   160   320 Kilometers

Depth tints

- Shoreline
- 0–200 m
- 200–2000 m
- 2000–4000 m
- 4000–6000 m
- 6000–8000 m
- > 8000 m

Physical Features

- River, stream
- Intermittent river
- Lake
- Intermittent lake
- Salt lake
- Intermittent salt lake
- Elevation above sea level in meters

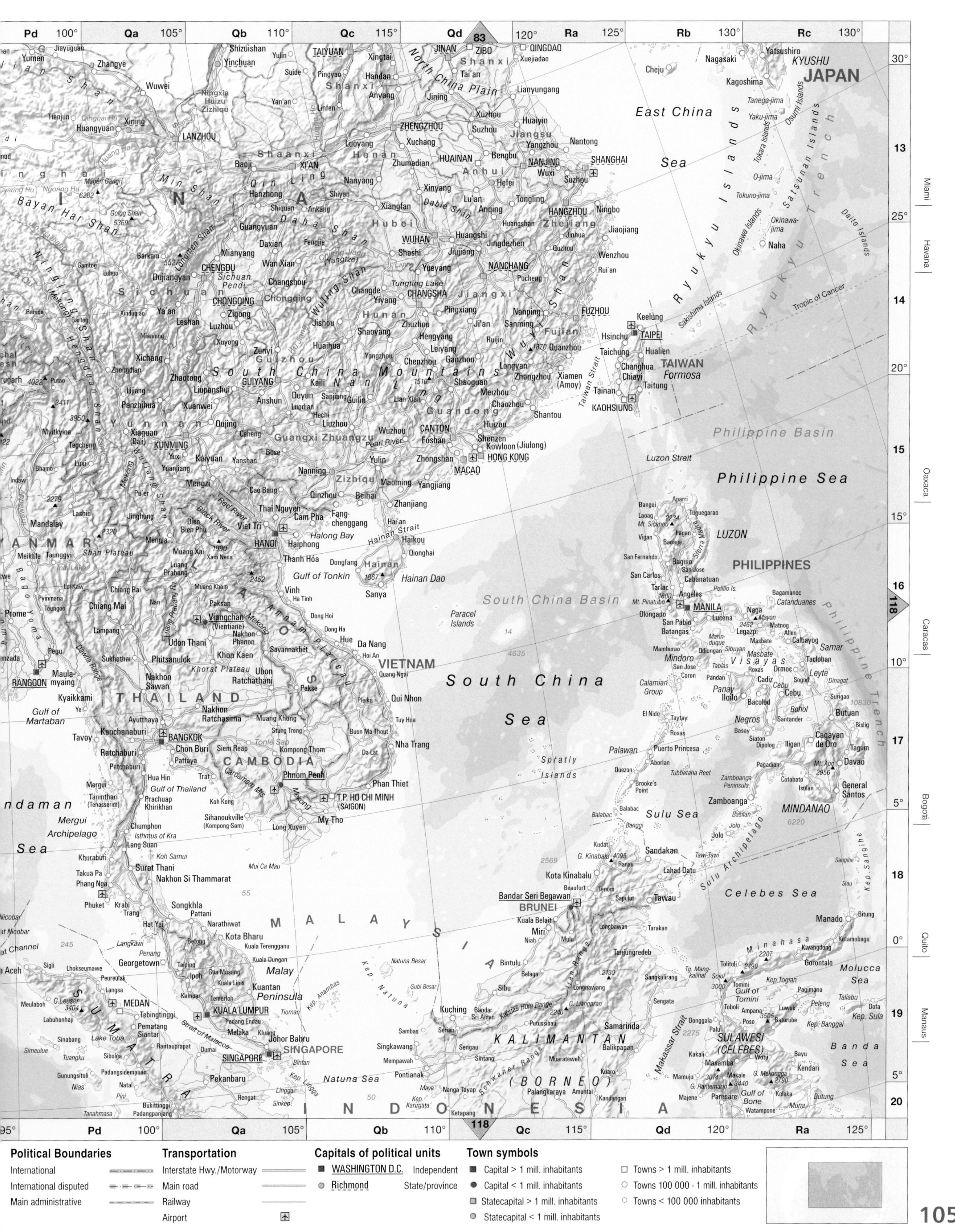

Political Boundaries

International
International disputed
Main administrative

Transportation

Interstate Hwy./Motorway
Main road
Railway
Airport

Capitals of political units

■ WASHINGTON D.C.   Independent
◎ Richmond   State/province

Town symbols

■ Capital > 1 mill. inhabitants   □ Towns > 1 mill. inhabitants
● Capital < 1 mill. inhabitants   ○ Towns 100 000 - 1 mill. inhabitants
■ Statecapital > 1 mill. inhabitants   ○ Towns < 100 000 inhabitants
◉ Statecapital < 1 mill. inhabitants

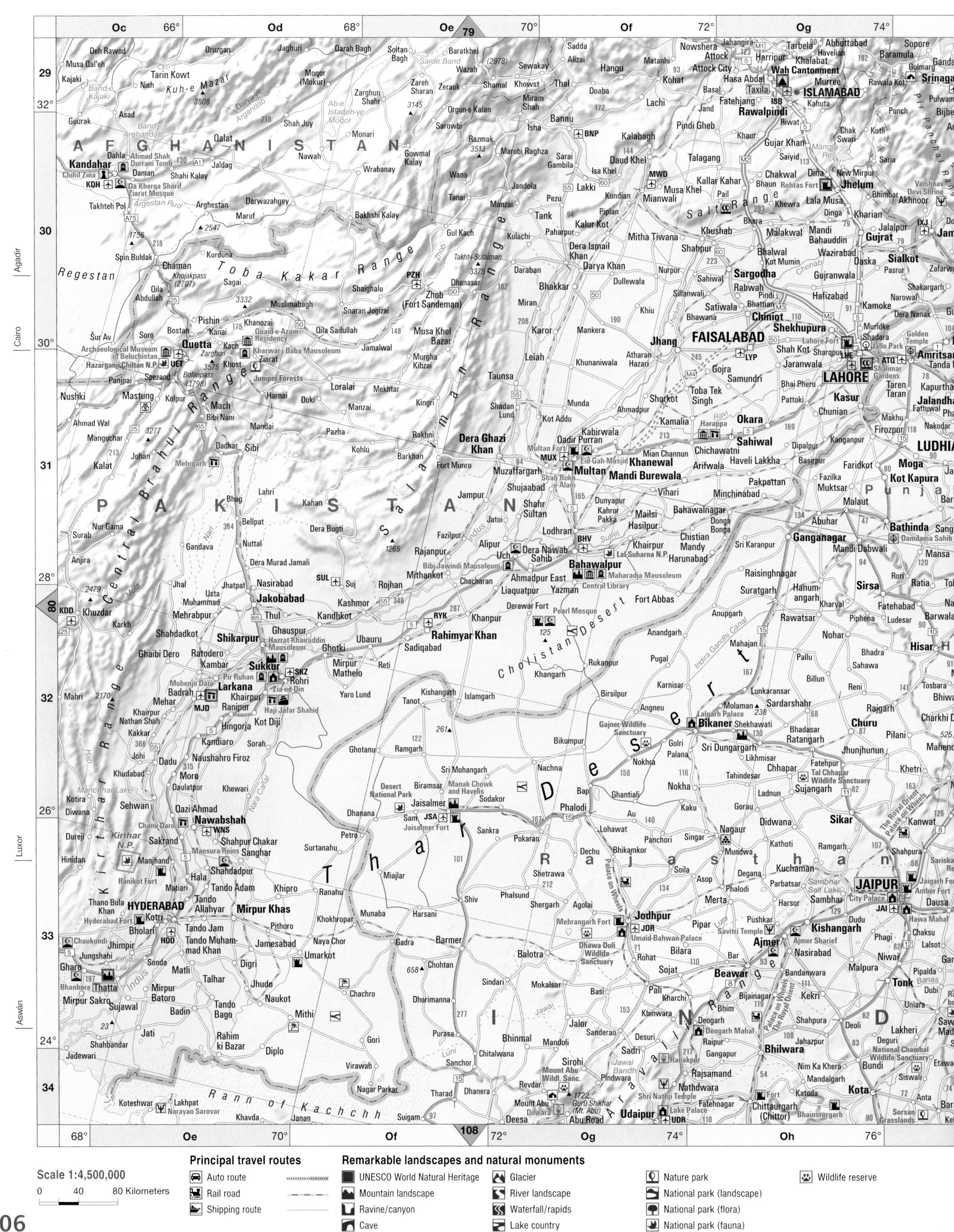

Scale 1:4,500,000

0   40   80 Kilometers

Principal travel routes
- 🚗 Auto route
- 🚂 Rail road
- 🚢 Shipping route

Remarkable landscapes and natural monuments
- ■ UNESCO World Natural Heritage
- 🏔 Mountain landscape
- 🝒 Ravine/canyon
- 🕳 Cave
- 🧊 Glacier
- 🏞 River landscape
- 💦 Waterfall/rapids
- 🏝 Lake country
- 🔭 Nature park
- 🏕 National park (landscape)
- 🌳 National park (flora)
- 🦌 National park (fauna)
- 🦋 Wildlife reserve

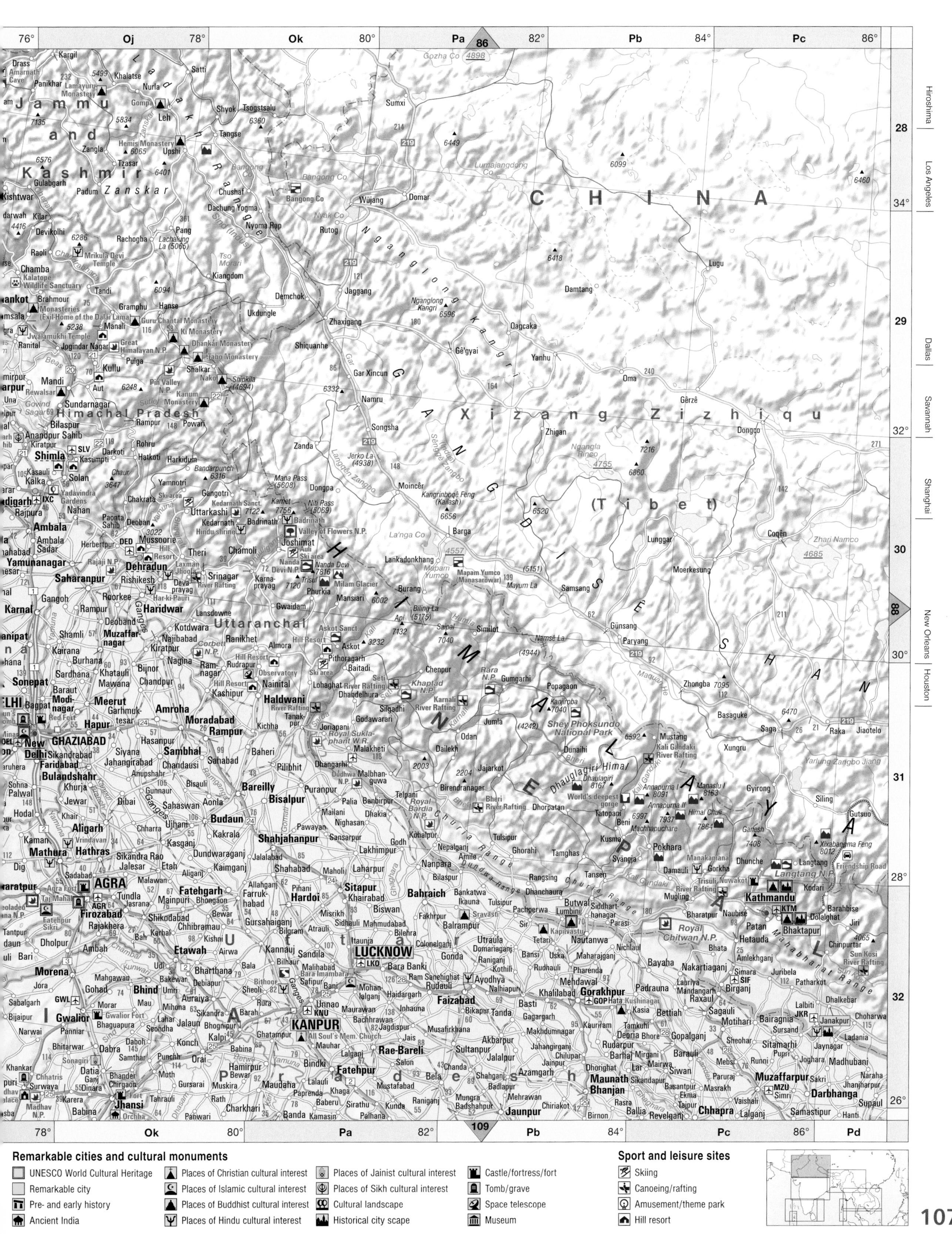

Remarkable cities and cultural monuments

- ▢ UNESCO World Cultural Heritage
- ▢ Remarkable city
- ⊓ Pre- and early history
- ▲ Ancient India
- ▲ Places of Christian cultural interest
- ☾ Places of Islamic cultural interest
- ▲ Places of Buddhist cultural interest
- Ψ Places of Hindu cultural interest
- ◉ Places of Jainist cultural interest
- ⊕ Places of Sikh cultural interest
- ☯ Cultural landscape
- ▰ Historical city scape
- ▮ Castle/fortress/fort
- ▯ Tomb/grave
- ▱ Space telescope
- ▦ Museum

Sport and leisure sites

- ⌇ Skiing
- ⤤ Canoeing/rafting
- ◎ Amusement/theme park
- ⌂ Hill resort

107

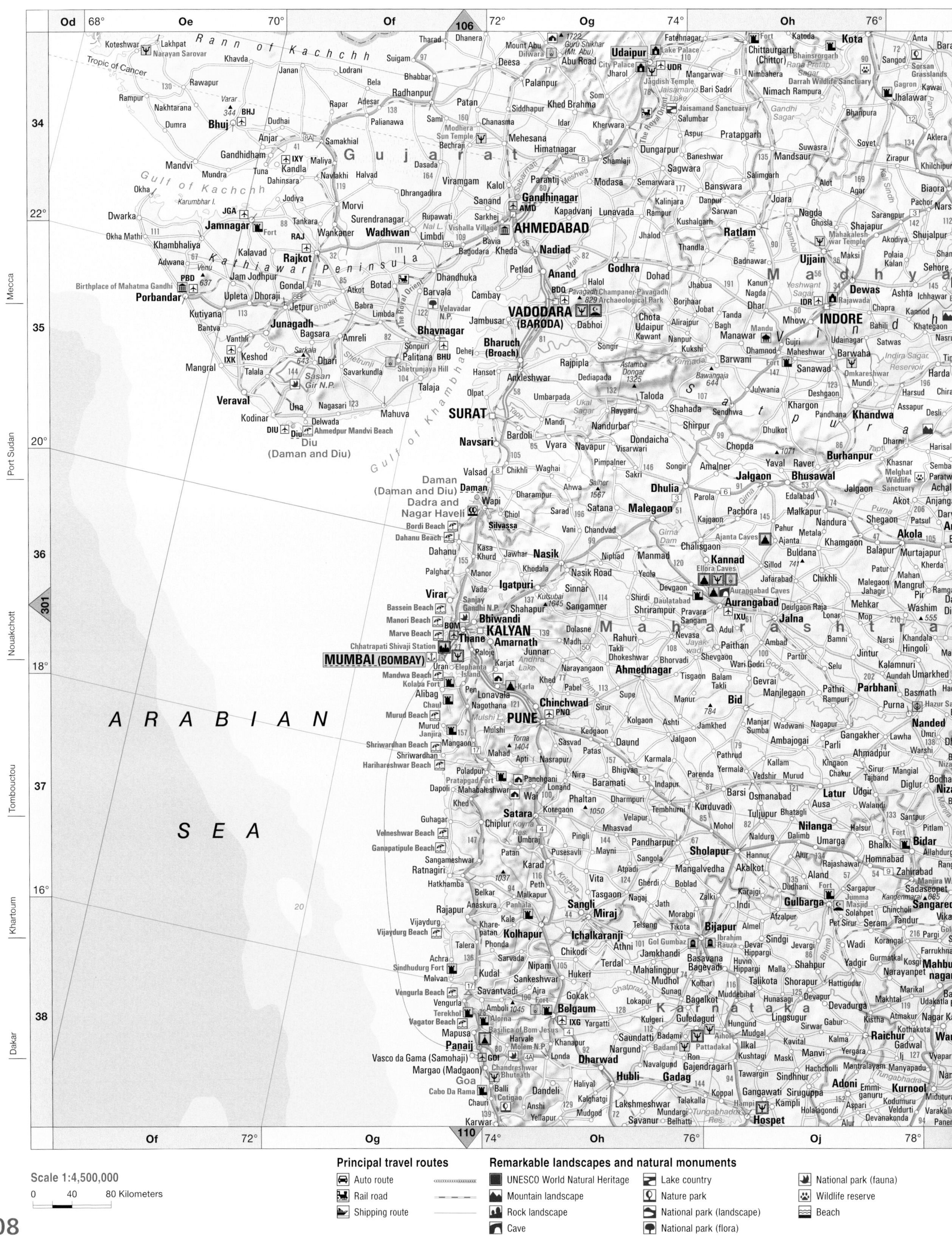

Scale 1:4,500,000

0   40   80 Kilometers

Principal travel routes

- Auto route
- Rail road
- Shipping route

Remarkable landscapes and natural monuments

- UNESCO World Natural Heritage
- Mountain landscape
- Rock landscape
- Cave
- Lake country
- Nature park
- National park (landscape)
- National park (flora)
- National park (fauna)
- Wildlife reserve
- Beach

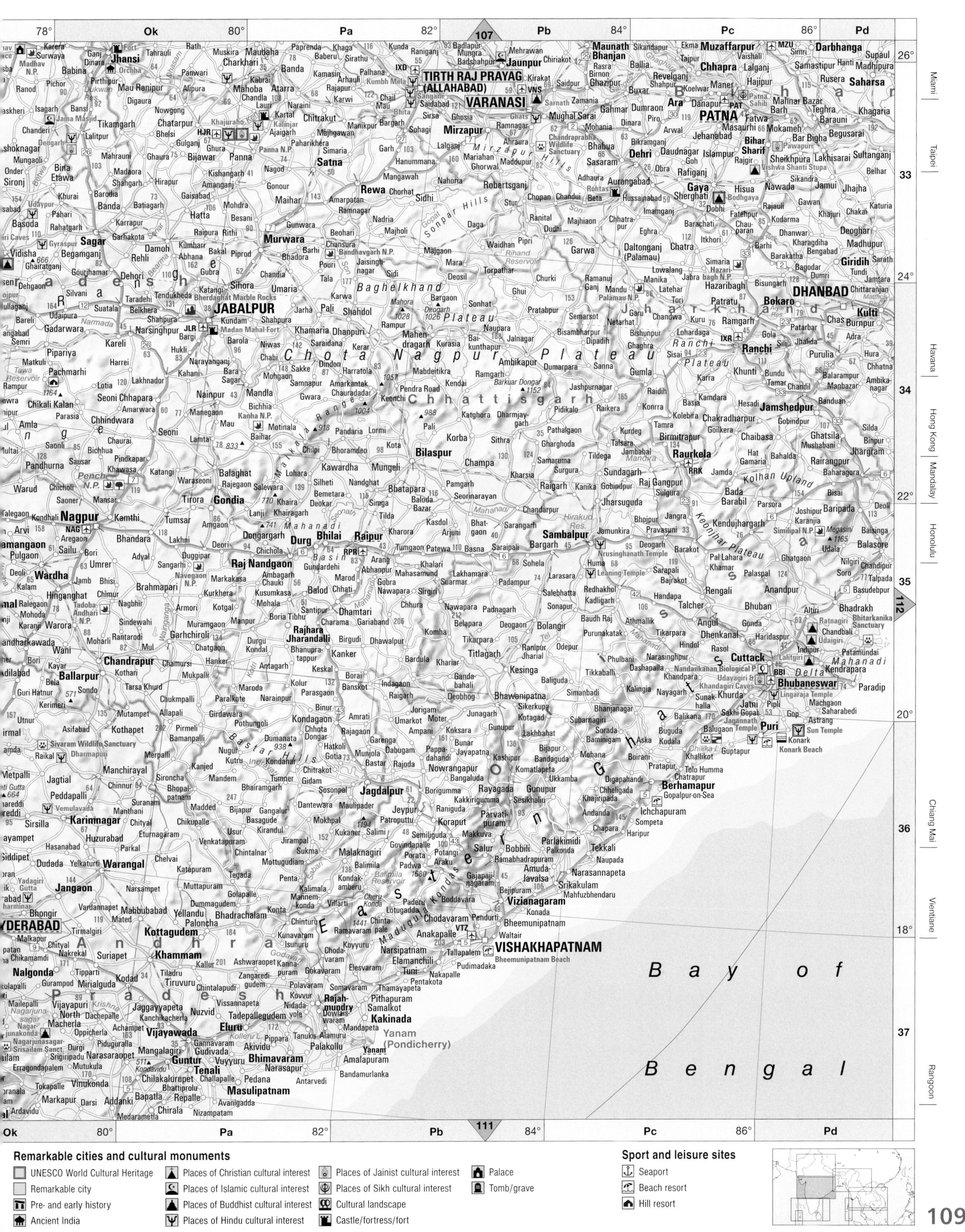

Remarkable cities and cultural monuments

- ▢ UNESCO World Cultural Heritage
- ▢ Remarkable city
- 🛕 Pre- and early history
- 🏛 Ancient India
- ▲ Places of Christian cultural interest
- ☪ Places of Islamic cultural interest
- ▲ Places of Buddhist cultural interest
- Ψ Places of Hindu cultural interest
- ◉ Places of Jainist cultural interest
- ⊕ Places of Sikh cultural interest
- ♨ Cultural landscape
- ▣ Castle/fortress/fort
- ▣ Palace
- ▣ Tomb/grave

Sport and leisure sites

- ⚓ Seaport
- 🏖 Beach resort
- 🏠 Hill resort

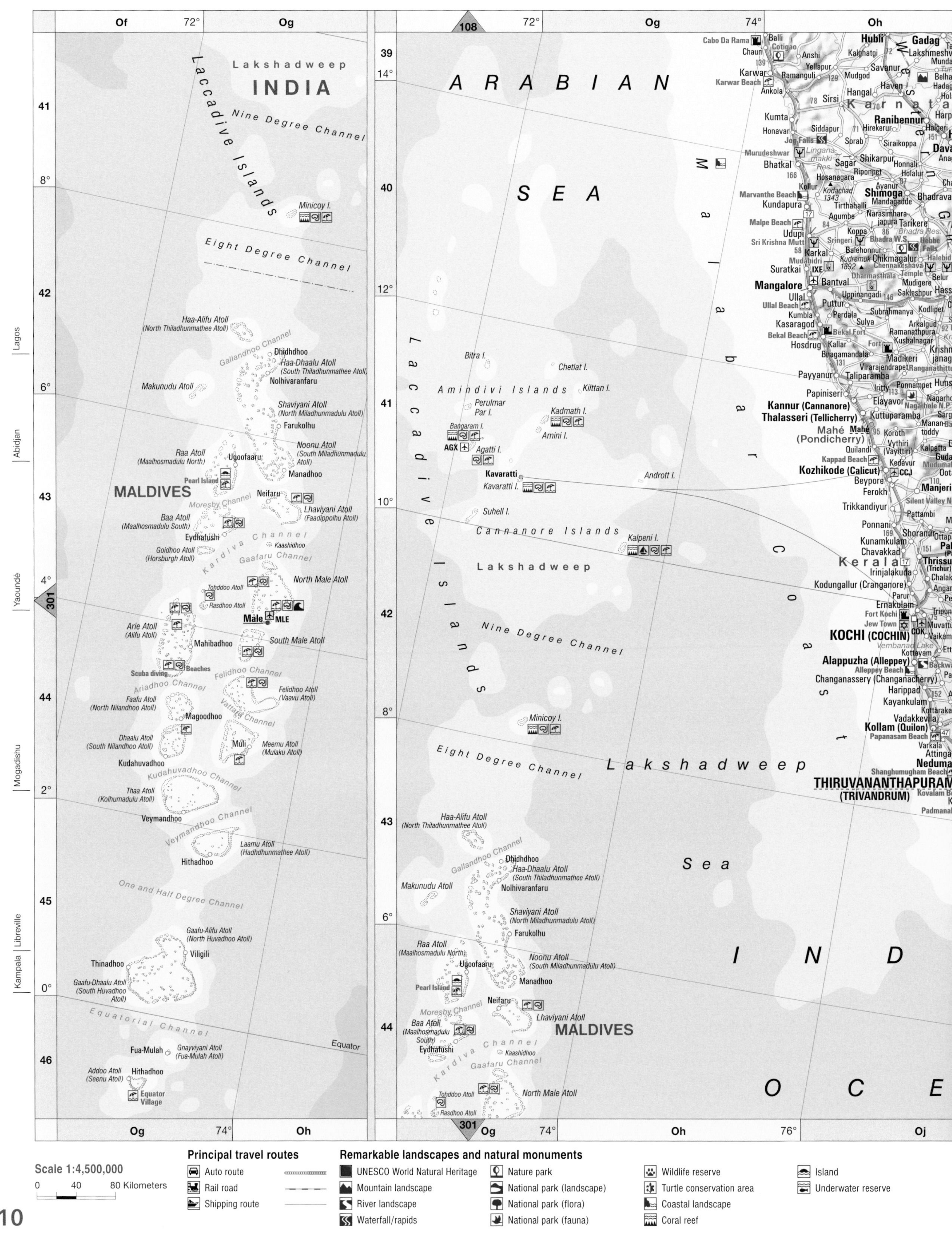

Scale 1:4,500,000

0 40 80 Kilometers

Principal travel routes

🚗 Auto route
🚉 Rail road
🚢 Shipping route

〜〜〜 (shipping route)
- - - (route)
—— (route)

Remarkable landscapes and natural monuments

◼ UNESCO World Natural Heritage
🏔 Mountain landscape
🏞 River landscape
💧 Waterfall/rapids

🌳 Nature park
🌲 National park (landscape)
🌿 National park (flora)
🦌 National park (fauna)

🐾 Wildlife reserve
🐢 Turtle conservation area
🏖 Coastal landscape
🪸 Coral reef

🏝 Island
🤿 Underwater reserve

110

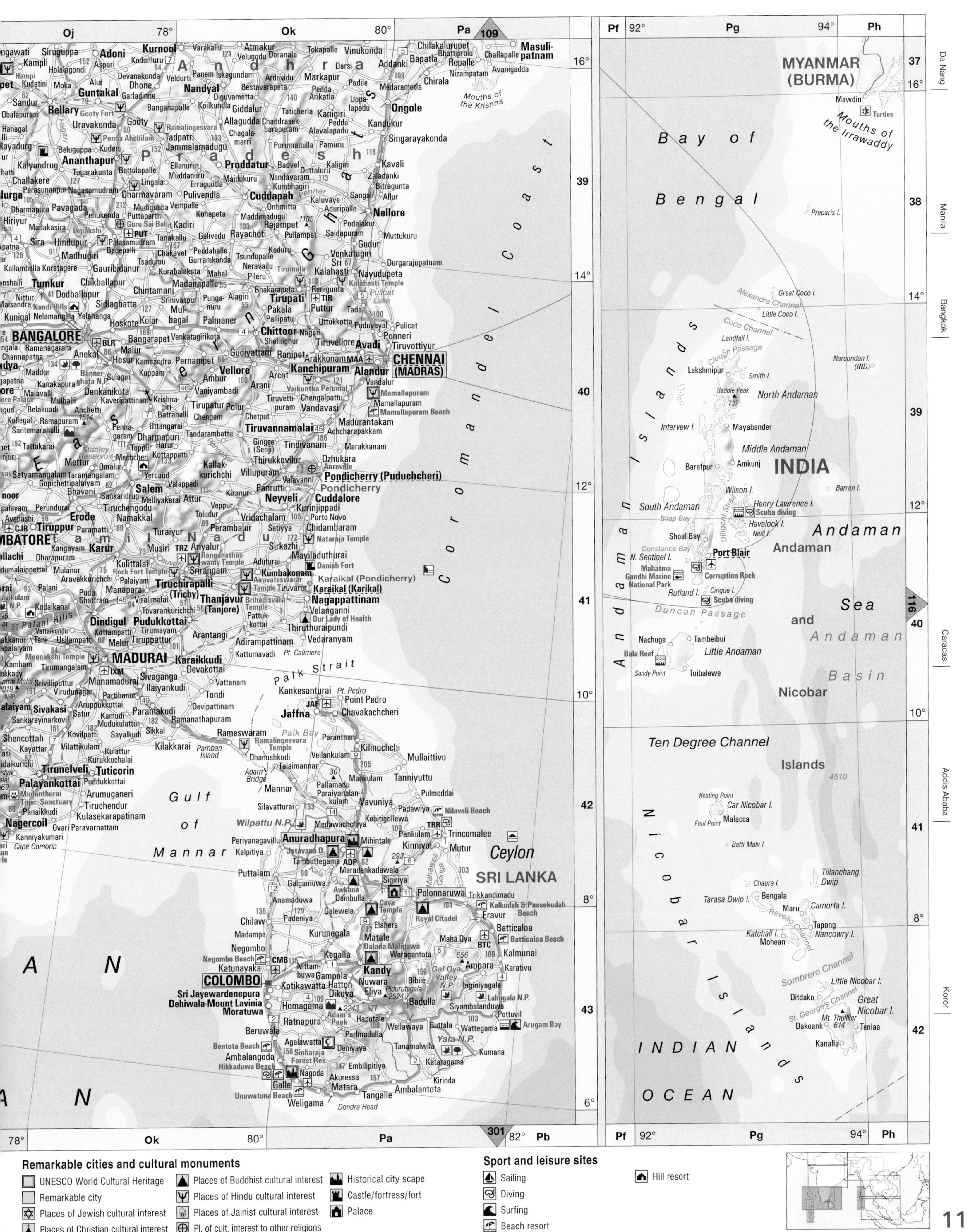

Oj
78°
Ok
80°
Pa
109
82°
Pb
Pf
92°
Pg
94°
Ph
16°
14°
12°
10°
8°
6°
39
40
41
42
43
37
38
116
Da Nang
Manila
Bangkok
Caracas
Addis Ababa
Koror
Andhra Pradesh
Eastern Ghats
Tamil Nadu
Kurnool
Adoni
Nandyal
Guntakal
Bellary
Ongole
Proddatur
Anantapur
Cuddapah
Nellore
Tirupati
Chittoor
Vellore
Kanchipuram
BANGALORE
BLR
CHENNAI
(MADRAS)
MAA
Mamallapuram
Mamallapuram Beach
Tiruvannamalai
Salem
Erode
Tiruppur
COIMBATORE
Pondicherry (Puduchcheri)
Pondicherry
Cuddalore
Neyveli
Karur
Tiruchirapalli
(Trichy)
Thanjavur
(Tanjore)
Kumbakonam
Karaikal (Karikal)
Karaikal (Pondicherry)
Nagappattinam
Danish Fort
Our Lady of Health
Dindigul
Pudukkottai
MADURAI
IXM
Meenakshi Temple
Karaikkudi
Tirunelveli
Tuticorin
Palayankottai
Nagercoil
Kanniyakumari
Cape Comorin
Rameswaram
Ramalingesvara Temple
Dhanushkodi
Adam's Bridge
Pamban Island
Coromandel Coast
Mouths of the Krishna
Palk Strait
Palk Bay
Pt. Calimere
Gulf of Mannar
Jaffna
JAF
Point Pedro
Kankesanturai
Kilinochchi
Mullaittivu
Mannar
Vavuniya
Trincomalee
TRR
Nilaveli Beach
Anuradhapura
Mihintale
Wilpattu N.P.
Puttalam
Sigiriya
Polonnaruwa
Dambulla
Kurunegala
Matale
Kandy
Batticaloa
Batticaloa Beach
Kalkudah & Passekudah Beach
Kalmunai
Negombo
Negombo Beach
CMB
Katunayaka
COLOMBO
Sri Jayewardenepura
Dehiwala-Mount Lavinia
Moratuwa
Kalutara
Ratnapura
Adam's Peak
Nuwara Eliya
Badulla
Gal Oya N.P.
Yala N.P.
Arugam Bay
Pottuvil
Beruwala
Bentota Beach
Ambalangoda
Hikkaduwa Beach
Galle
Unawatuna Beach
Weligama
Matara
Tangalle
Dondra Head
Ambalantota
Hambantota
Kirinda
Ceylon
SRI LANKA
INDIAN OCEAN
Bay of Bengal
MYANMAR
(BURMA)
Mawdin
Turtles
Mouths of the Irrawaddy
Preparis I.
Great Coco I.
Little Coco I.
Alexandra Channel
Coco Channel
Landfall I.
Cleugh Passage
Lakshmipur
Smith I.
Saddle Peak
737
North Andaman
Narcondan I.
(IND)
Interview I.
Mayabander
Middle Andaman
Baratpur
Amkunj
INDIA
Barren I.
Wilson I.
South Andaman
Henry Lawrence I.
Scuba diving
Havelock I.
Neill I.
Bilap Bay
Shoal Bay
Diligent Strait
Constance Bay
N. Sentinel I.
Port Blair
Mahatma Gandhi Marine National Park
Corruption Rock
Rutland I.
Cinque I.
Duncan Passage
Andaman Islands
Andaman Sea
Andaman and Nicobar
Andaman Basin
Nachuge
Tambeibui
Little Andaman
Bala Reef
Sandy Point
Toibalewe
Ten Degree Channel
Nicobar Islands
4510
Keating Point
Car Nicobar I.
Malacca
Foul Point
Batti Malv I.
Chaura I.
Bengala
Tillanchang Dwip
Tarasa Dwip I.
Revello Channel
Maru
Camorta I.
Tapong
Nancowry I.
Katchall I.
Mohean
Sombrero Channel
Little Nicobar I.
Ditdako
St. George's Channel
Great Nicobar I.
Mt. Thuillier
614
Dakoank
Tenlaa
Kanalla
301
Remarkable cities and cultural monuments
UNESCO World Cultural Heritage
Remarkable city
Places of Jewish cultural interest
Places of Christian cultural interest
Places of Buddhist cultural interest
Places of Hindu cultural interest
Places of Jainist cultural interest
Pl. of cult. interest to other religions
Historical city scape
Castle/fortress/fort
Palace
Sport and leisure sites
Sailing
Diving
Surfing
Beach resort
Hill resort

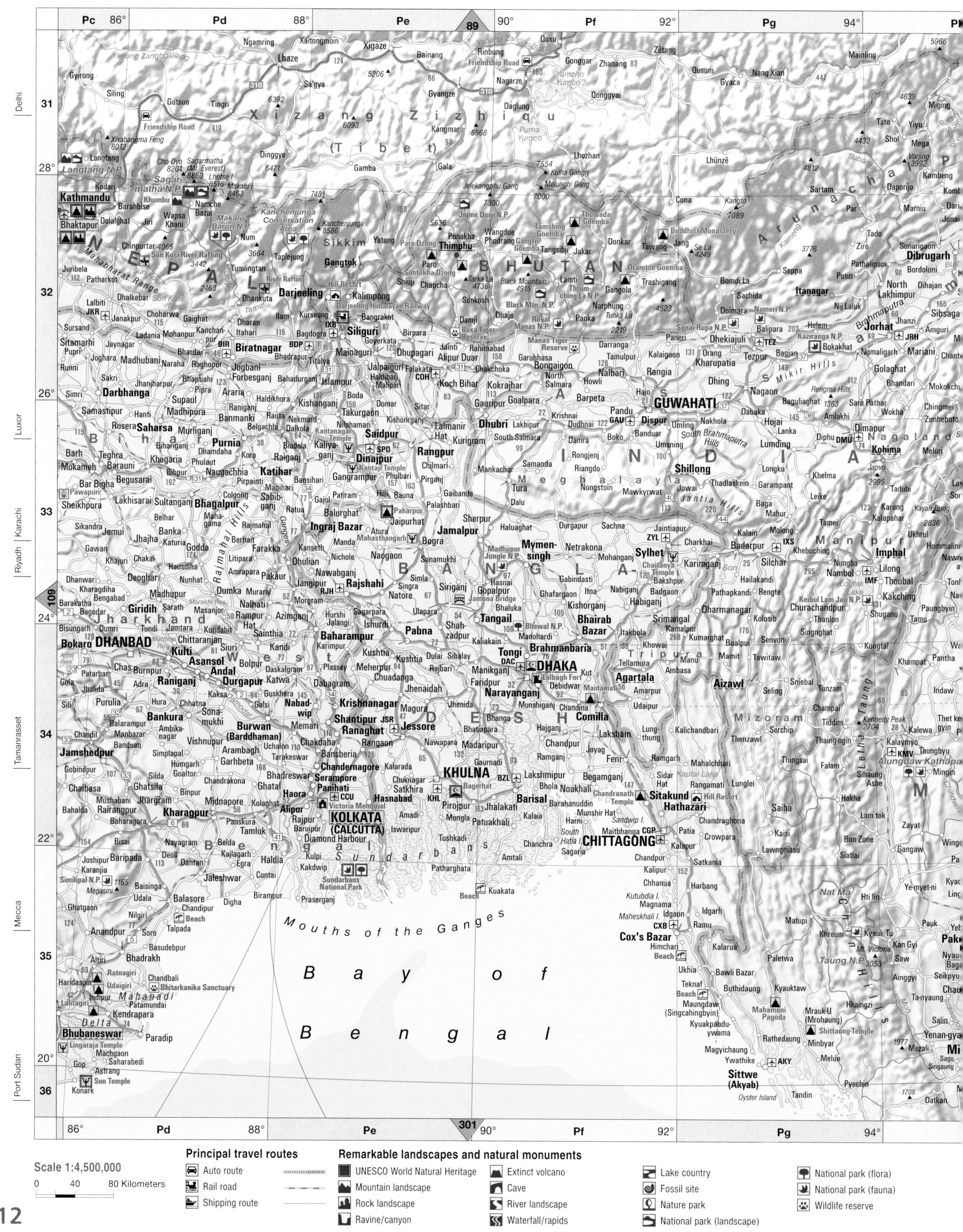

Scale 1:4,500,000

0   40   80 Kilometers

Principal travel routes

- Auto route
- Rail road
- Shipping route

Remarkable landscapes and natural monuments

- UNESCO World Natural Heritage
- Mountain landscape
- Rock landscape
- Ravine/canyon
- Extinct volcano
- Cave
- River landscape
- Waterfall/rapids
- Lake country
- Fossil site
- Nature park
- National park (landscape)
- National park (flora)
- National park (fauna)
- Wildlife reserve

Remarkable cities and cultural monuments

UNESCO World Cultural Heritage
Remarkable city
Ancient China
Places of Islamic cultural interest

Places of Buddhist cultural interest
Places of Hindu cultural interest
Places of Jainist cultural interest
Pl. of cult. interest to indig. peoples
Palace

Cultural landscape
Historical city scape
Castle/fortress/fort

Remarkable bridge
Theater of war/battlefield
Museum

Sport and leisure sites

Canoeing/rafting
Beach resort
Mineral/thermal spa
Hill resort

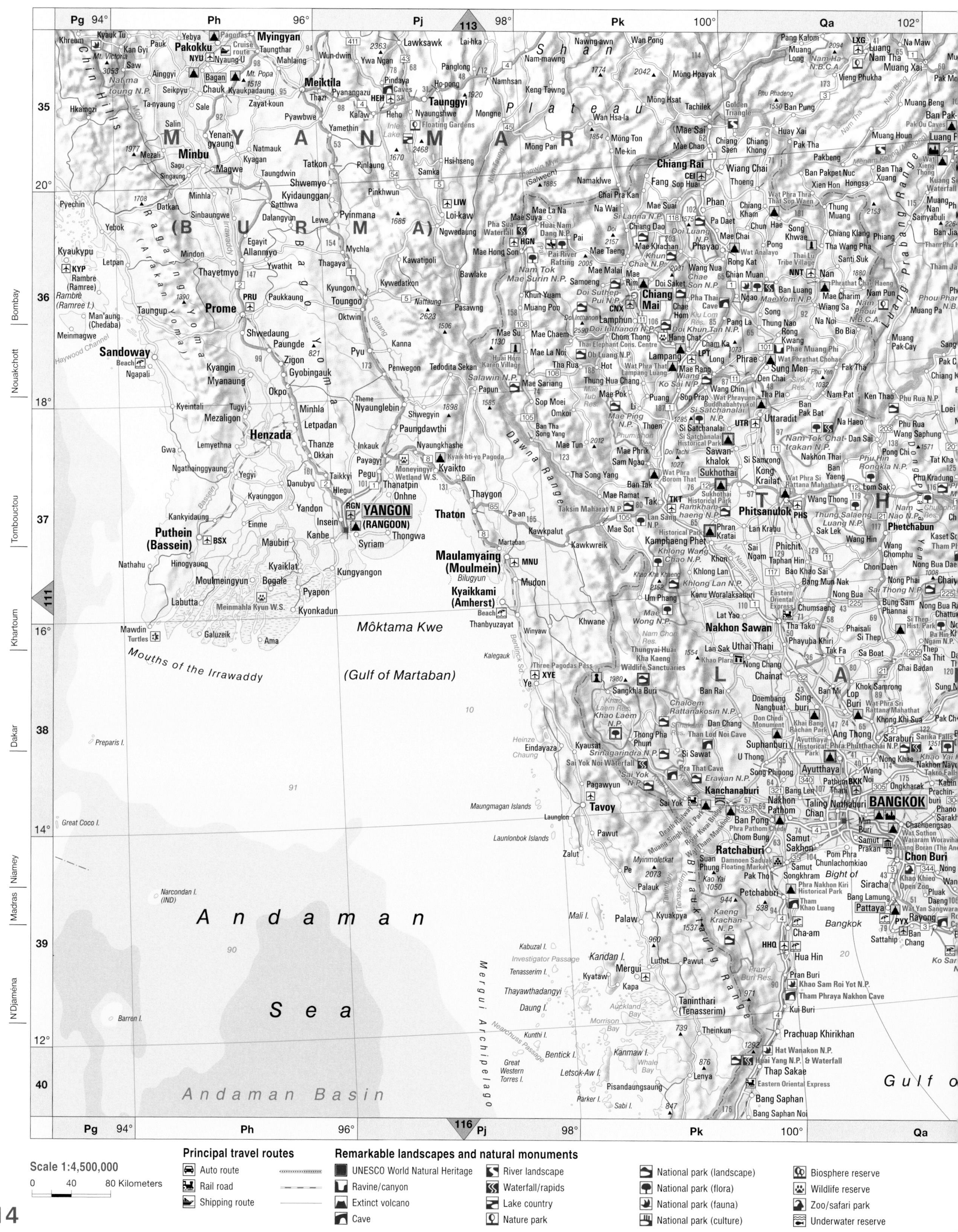

Scale 1:4,500,000

0   40   80 Kilometers

Principal travel routes

🚗 Auto route

🚂 Rail road

🚢 Shipping route

Remarkable landscapes and natural monuments

■ UNESCO World Natural Heritage

■ Ravine/canyon

■ Extinct volcano

■ Cave

■ River landscape

■ Waterfall/rapids

■ Lake country

■ Nature park

■ National park (landscape)

■ National park (flora)

■ National park (fauna)

■ National park (culture)

■ Biosphere reserve

■ Wildlife reserve

■ Zoo/safari park

■ Underwater reserve

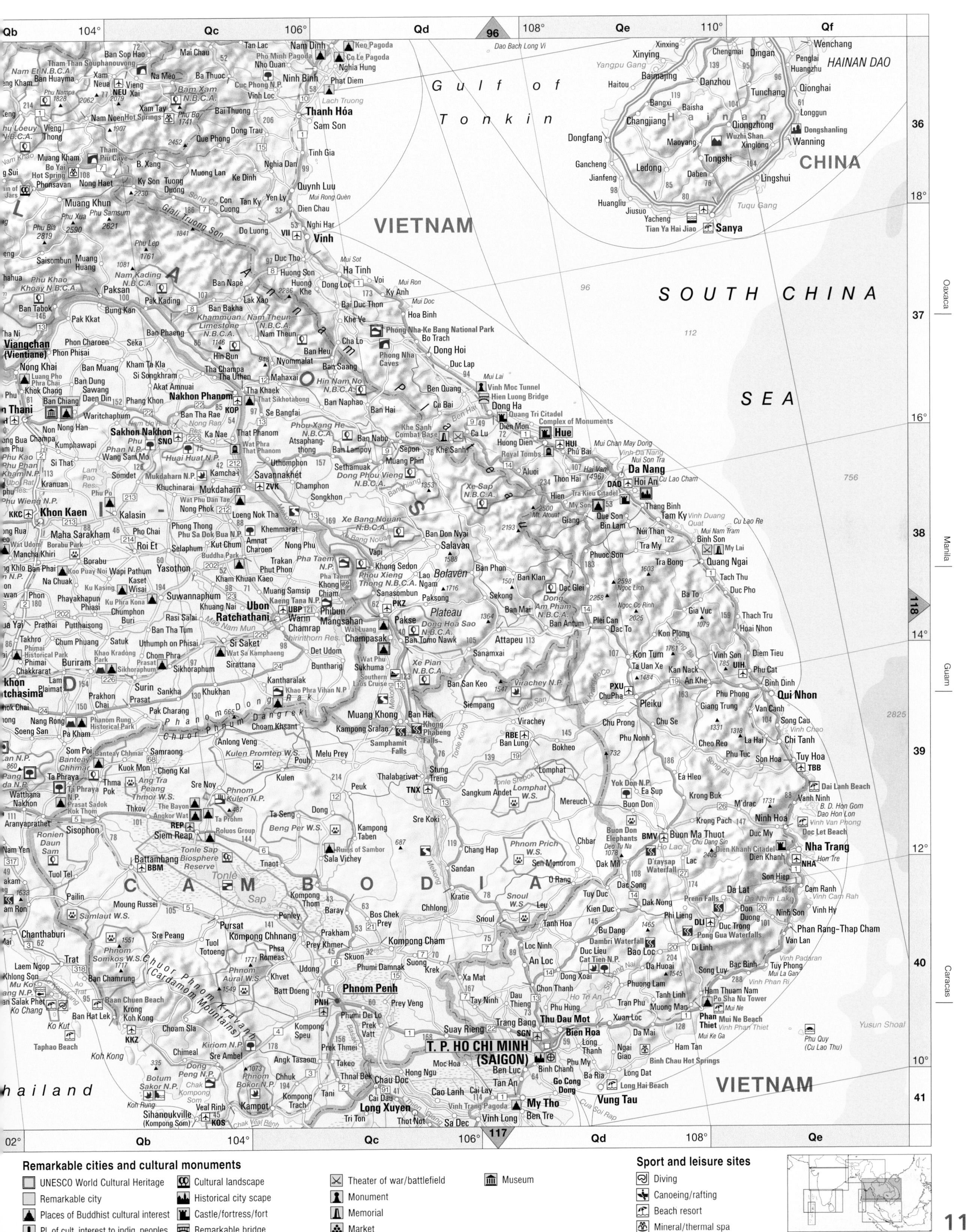

Remarkable cities and cultural monuments

- ▢ UNESCO World Cultural Heritage
- ▢ Remarkable city
- ▲ Places of Buddhist cultural interest
- ⬧ Pl. of cult. interest to indig. peoples
- ⊙ Cultural landscape
- ⬟ Historical city scape
- ⬟ Castle/fortress/fort
- ⬟ Remarkable bridge
- ⊠ Theater of war/battlefield
- ▮ Monument
- ⬛ Memorial
- ⬛ Market
- ⏛ Museum

Sport and leisure sites

- ⬚ Diving
- ⬚ Canoeing/rafting
- ⬚ Beach resort
- ⬚ Mineral/thermal spa

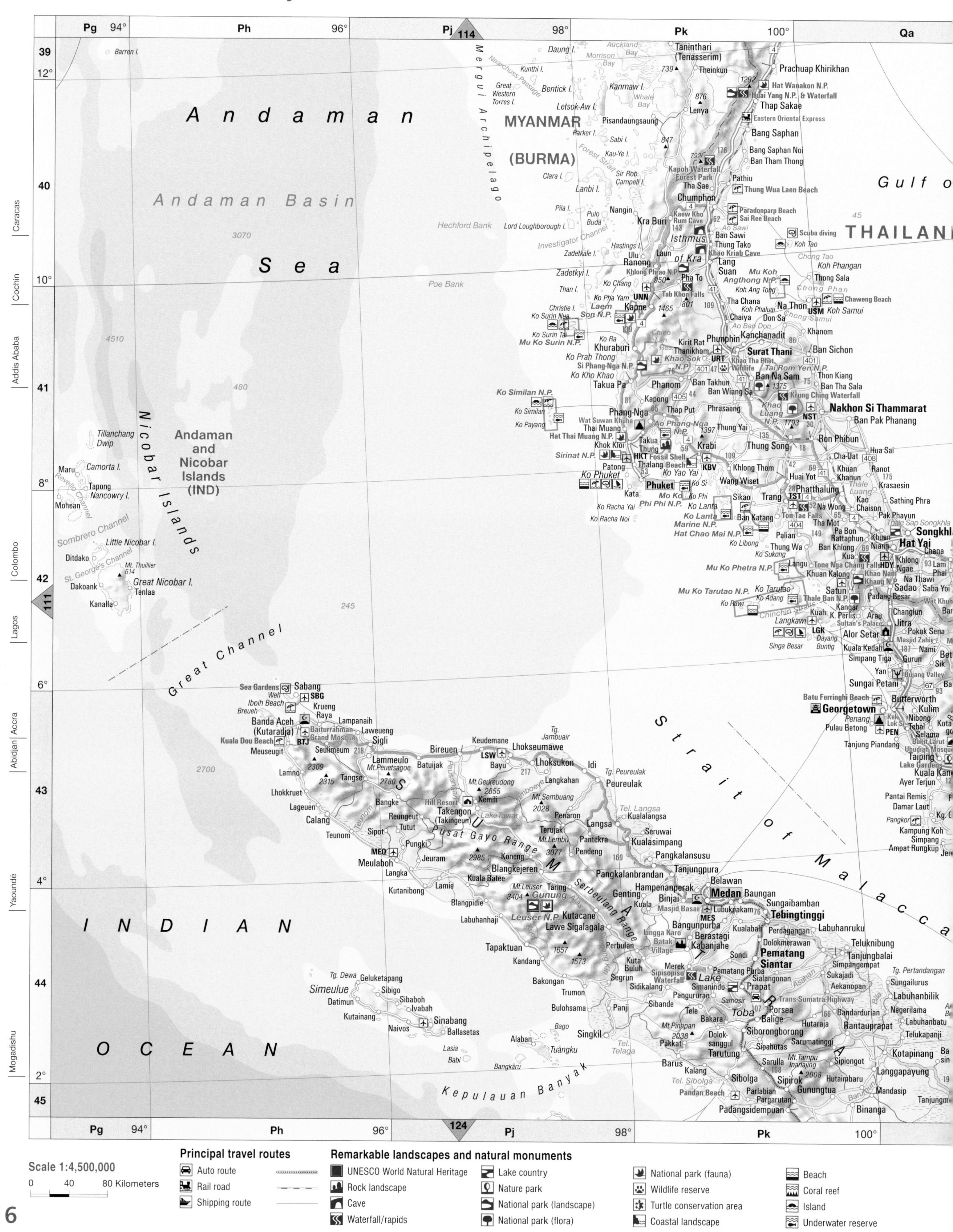

Southern Thailand, Malaysian Peninsula

Scale 1:4,500,000

0   40   80 Kilometers

Principal travel routes
- Auto route
- Rail road
- Shipping route

Remarkable landscapes and natural monuments
- UNESCO World Natural Heritage
- Rock landscape
- Cave
- Waterfall/rapids
- Lake country
- Nature park
- National park (landscape)
- National park (flora)
- National park (fauna)
- Wildlife reserve
- Turtle conservation area
- Coastal landscape
- Beach
- Coral reef
- Island
- Underwater reserve

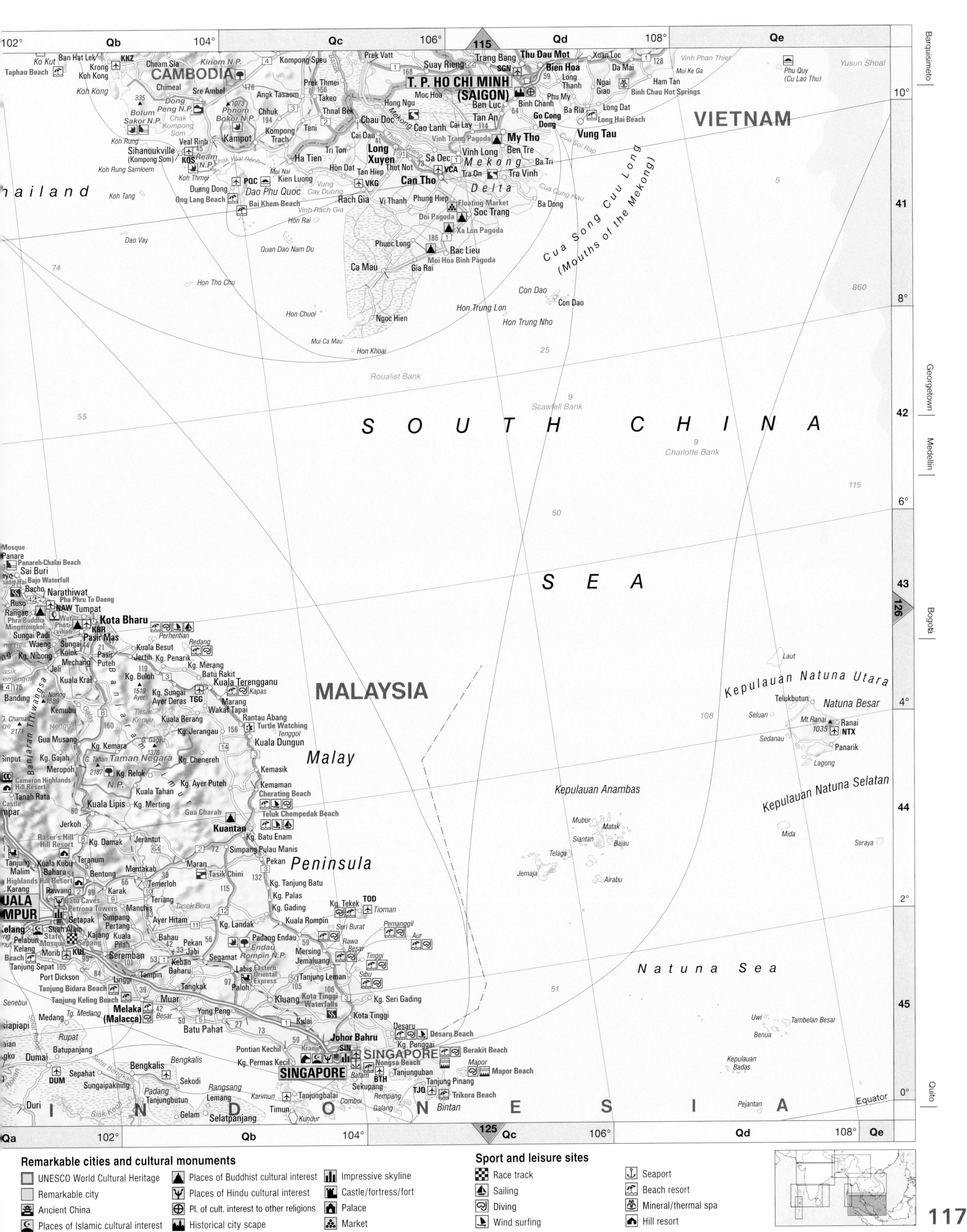

Remarkable cities and cultural monuments

- ⬚ UNESCO World Cultural Heritage
- ▪ Remarkable city
- 🏛 Ancient China
- ☪ Places of Islamic cultural interest
- ▲ Places of Buddhist cultural interest
- ▲ Places of Hindu cultural interest
- ☥ Pl. of cult. interest to other religions
- ▦ Historical city scape
- ▥ Impressive skyline
- ▣ Castle/fortress/fort
- ⌂ Palace
- ▦ Market

Sport and leisure sites

- 🏁 Race track
- ⛵ Sailing
- 🤿 Diving
- 🏄 Wind surfing
- ⚓ Seaport
- 🏖 Beach resort
- ♨ Mineral/thermal spa
- 🏠 Hill resort

117

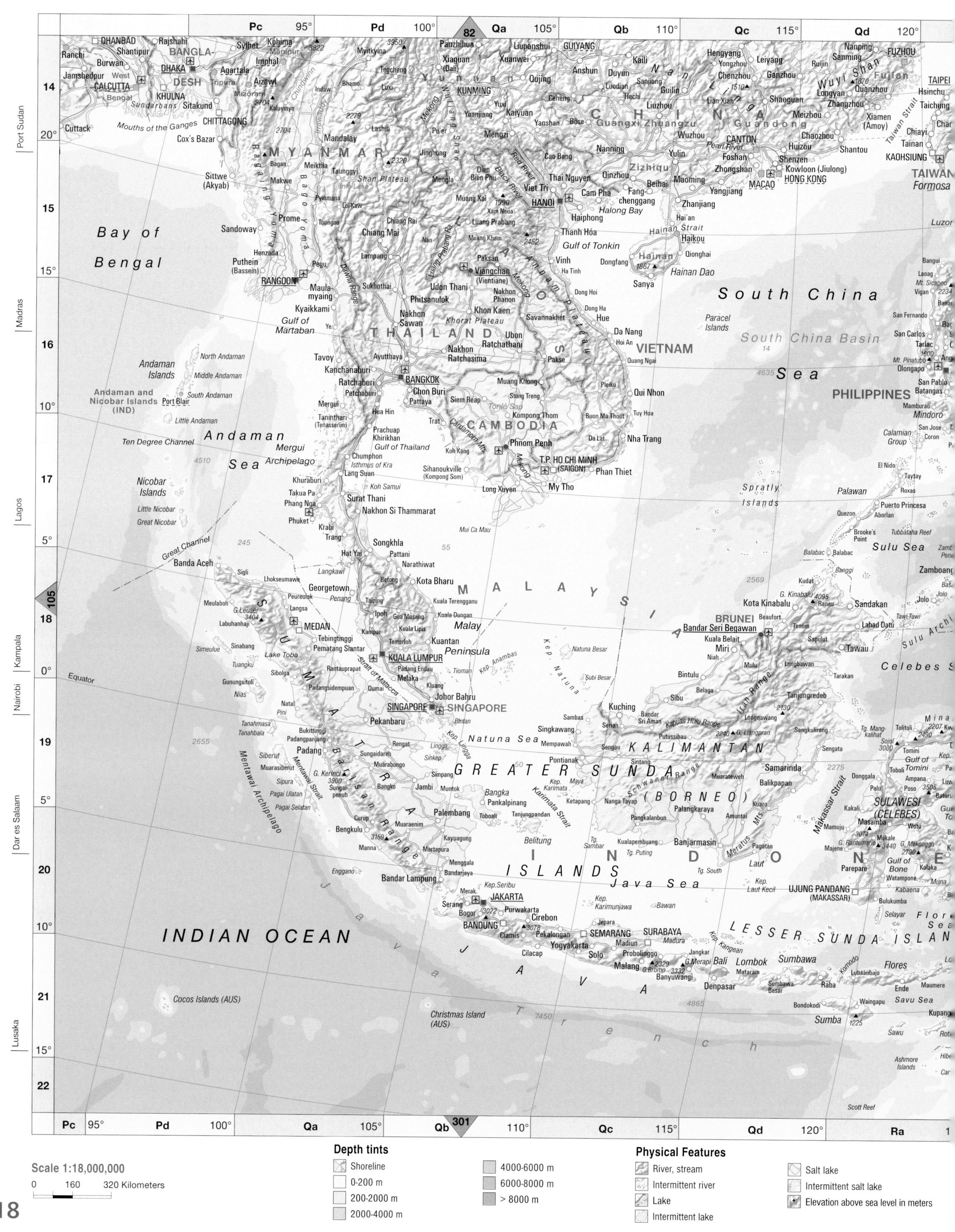

Scale 1:18,000,000

0   160   320 Kilometers

118

Depth tints

Shoreline		4000-6000 m
0-200 m		6000-8000 m
200-2000 m		> 8000 m
2000-4000 m		

Physical Features

River, stream		Salt lake
Intermittent river		Intermittent salt lake
Lake		Elevation above sea level in meters
Intermittent lake		

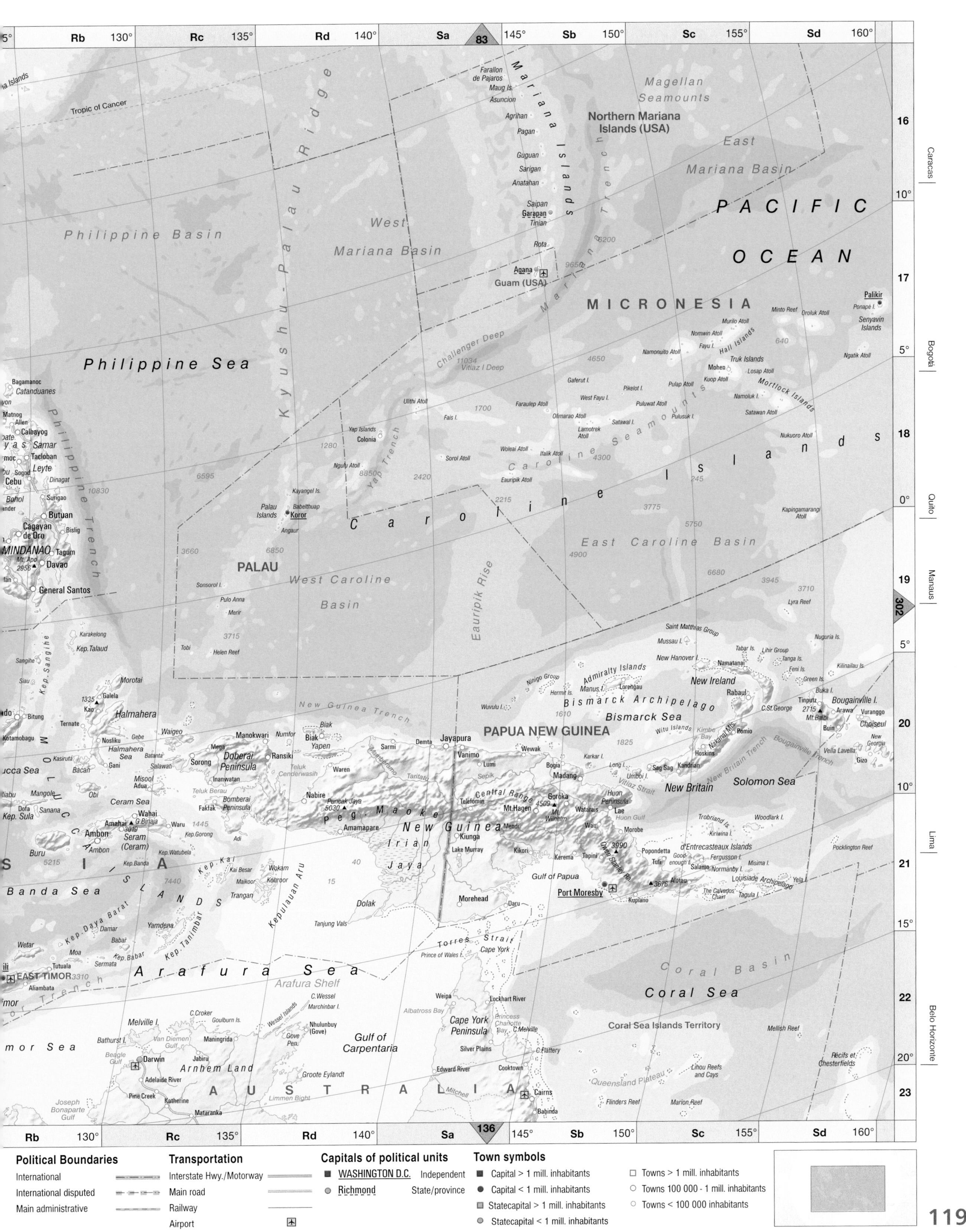

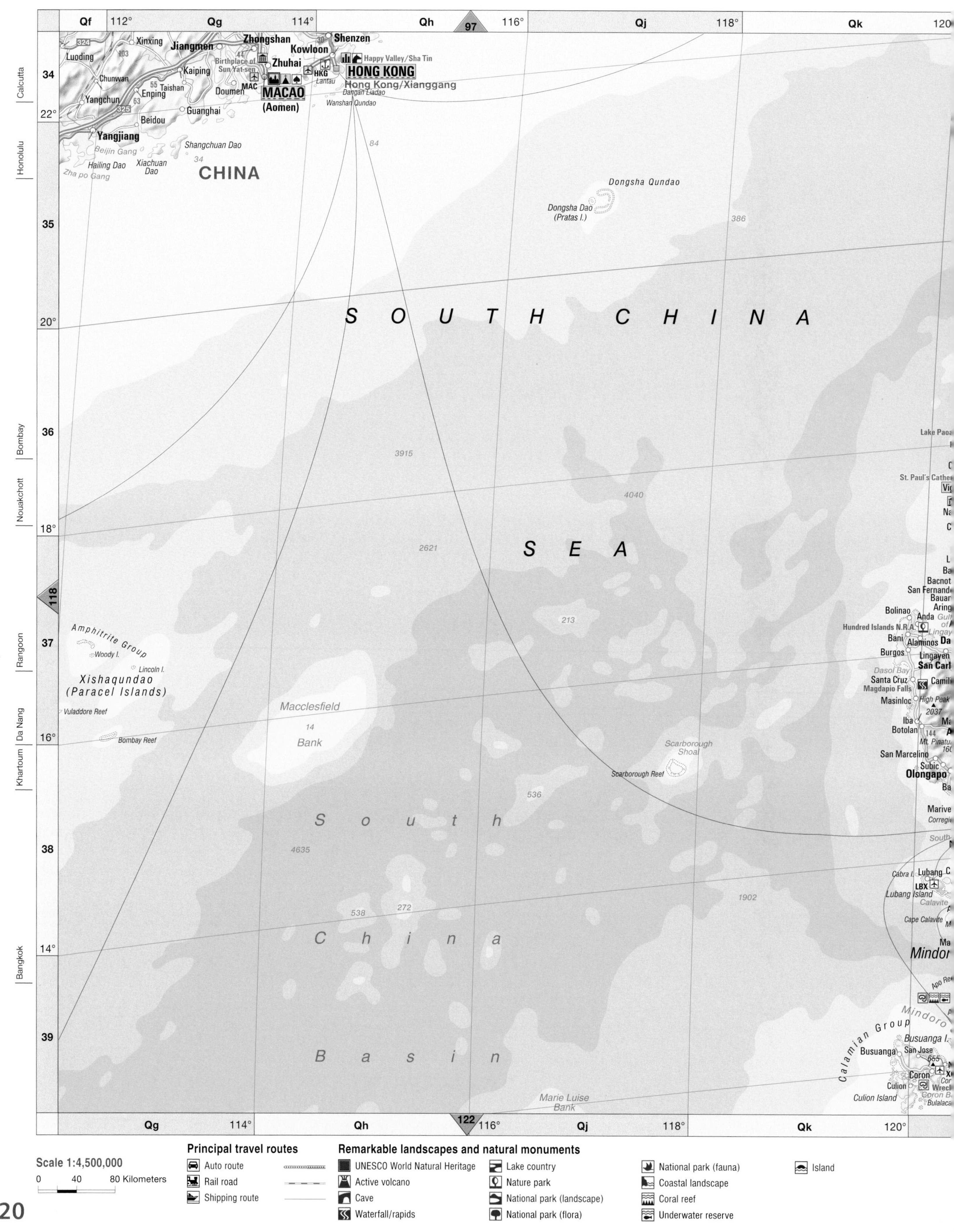

Qf 112° Qg 114° Qh 97 116° Qj 118° Qk 120

Calcutta

34

Luoding 324 Xinxing Jiangmen Zhongshan Kowloon Shenzen
103 44 Birthplace of Sha Tin
Chunwan Kaiping Sun Yat-sen Happy Valley/Sha Tin
55 Taishan MAC Zhuhai HKG HONG KONG
Yangchun Enping Doumen Lantau Hong Kong/Xianggang
63 MACAO Dangan Liadao
325 Beidou Guanghai (Aomen) Wanshan Qundao

Yangjiang

22°

Beijin Gang
Hailing Dao Shangchuan Dao 84
Zha po Gang Xiachuan 34
Dao

CHINA

Dongsha Qundao

Dongsha Dao
(Pratas I.)

35 386

SOUTH CHINA

20°

36 Lake Paoa

3915 St. Paul's Cather
4040 Vig
Na

18° 2621 SEA Ba
Bacnot
San Fernand
Bauar
Bolinao Aring
Anda Gul
213 Hundred Islands N.R.A. of
Bani Lingay
Amphitrite Group Alaminos Da
37 Burgos Lingayen San Carl
Woody I. Dasol Bay
Lincoln I. Santa Cruz Camil
Xishaqundao Magdapio Falls High Peak
(Paracel Islands) Masinloc 2037
Iba Ma
Vuladdore Reef Scarborough Botolan 144
Macclesfield Shoal Mt. Pinatu 160
16° Bombay Reef 14 San Marcelino
Bank Scarborough Reef Subic Ba
Olongapo

536

South Marive
Corregio
38 4635 South

Lubang C
Cabra I. LBX
538 272 1902 Lubang Island Calavite
China
Cape Calavite

14° Ma
Mindor
Calamian Group Mindoro

39 Busuanga I.
Busuanga San Jose
Basin Coron 655
Xa
Culion Cor
Marie Luise Culion Island Coron B.
Bank Bulalaca

Qg 114° Qh 122 116° Qj 118° Qk 120°

Scale 1:4,500,000

0   40   80 Kilometers

Principal travel routes

- Auto route
- Rail road
- Shipping route

- Cave
- Waterfall/rapids

Remarkable landscapes and natural monuments

- UNESCO World Natural Heritage
- Active volcano
- Cave
- Waterfall/rapids

- Lake country
- Nature park
- National park (landscape)
- National park (flora)

- National park (fauna)
- Coastal landscape
- Coral reef
- Underwater reserve

- Island

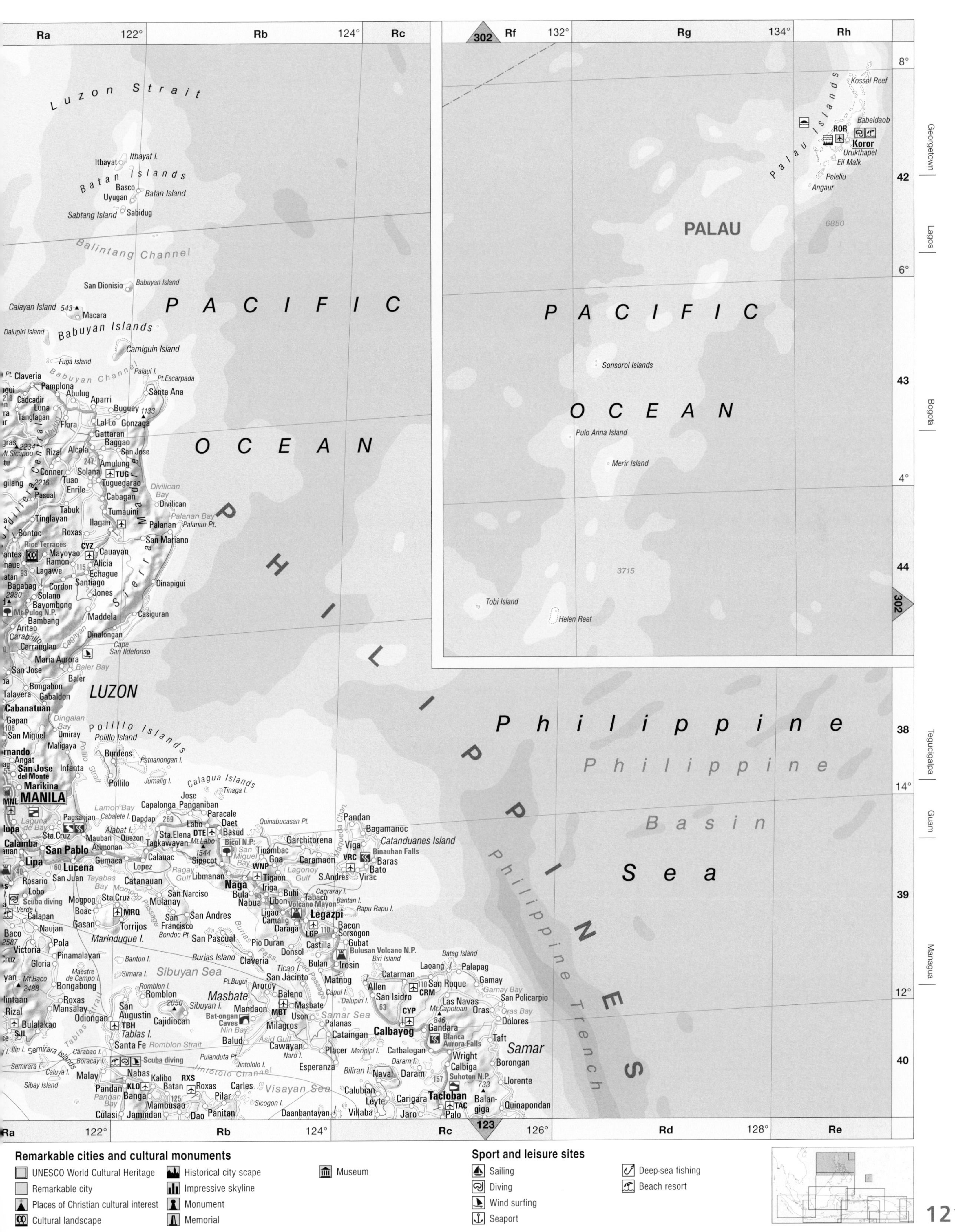

Remarkable cities and cultural monuments
- UNESCO World Cultural Heritage
- Remarkable city
- Places of Christian cultural interest
- Cultural landscape
- Historical city scape
- Impressive skyline
- Monument
- Memorial
- Museum

Sport and leisure sites
- Sailing
- Diving
- Wind surfing
- Seaport
- Deep-sea fishing
- Beach resort

121

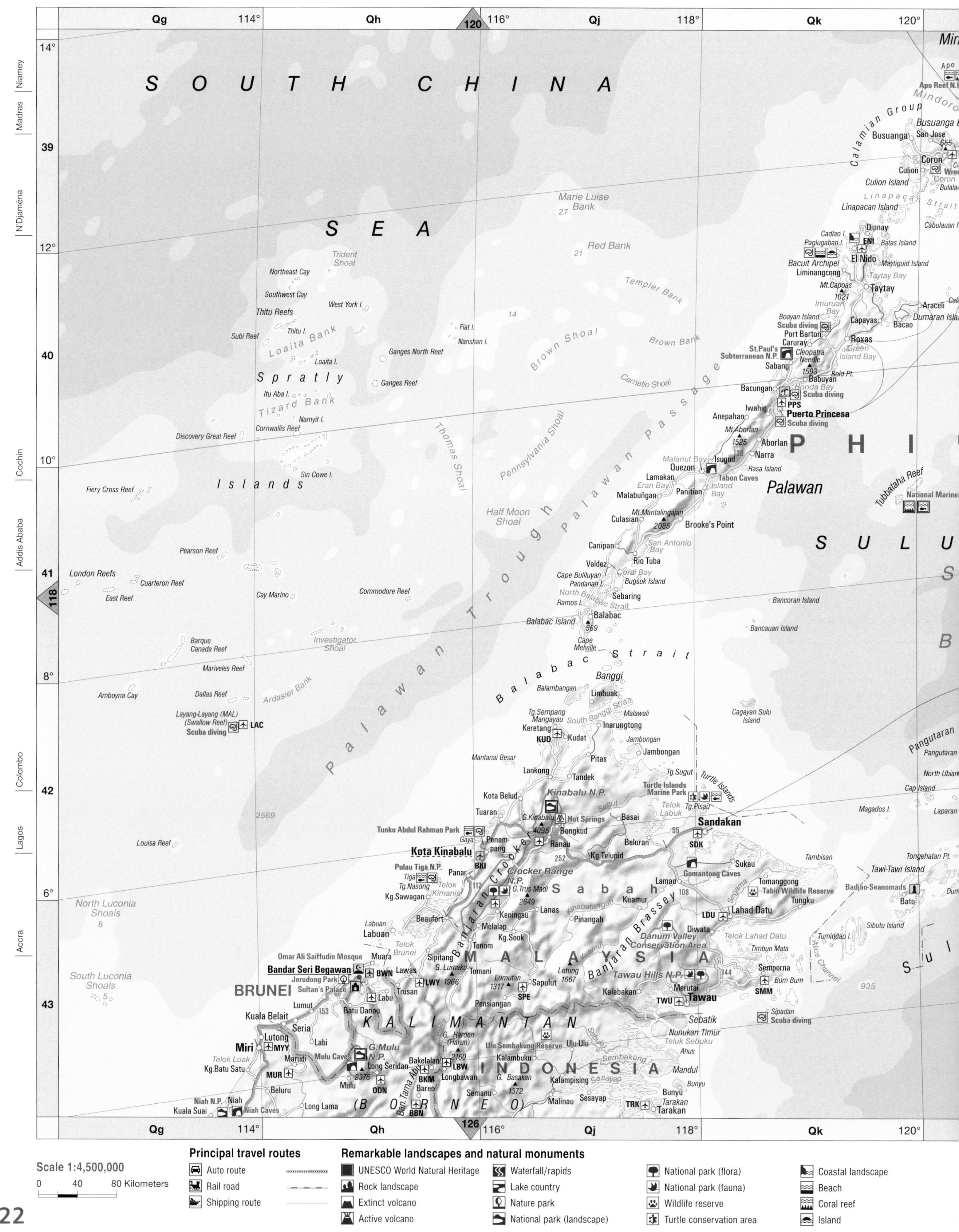

SOUTH CHINA

SEA

Marie Luise
Bank
27

Red Bank
21

Trident
Shoal

Northeast Cay

Southwest Cay

West York I.

Thitu Reefs

Thitu I.

Subi Reef

Nanshan I.

Flat I.

14

Brown Shoal

Brown Bank

Loaita Bank

Ganges North Reef

Loaita I.

Spratly

Ganges Reef

Carnatio Shoal

Itu Aba I.

Tizard Bank

Namyit I.

Discovery Great Reef

Cornwallis Reef

Sin Cowe I.

Islands

Fiery Cross Reef

Pennsylvania Shoal

Half Moon
Shoal

Pearson Reef

London Reefs

Cuarteron Reef

Commodore Reef

East Reef

Barque
Canada Reef

Investigator
Shoal

Cay Marino

Mariveles Reef

2569

Amboyna Cay

Dallas Reef

Ardasier Bank

Layang-Layang (MAL)
(Swallow Reef)
Scuba diving

LAC

Louisa Reef

North Luconia
Shoals
8

South Luconia
Shoals
5

Calamian Group

Busuanga

San Jose

655

Coron

Culion

Culion Island

Linapacan

Linapacan Island

Strait

Cadlao I.

Dipnay

Paglugaban I.

ENI

Batas Island

El Nido

Bacuit Archipel.

Maytiguid Island

Liminangcong

Taytay Bay

Mt.Capoas

1021

Taytay

Imuruan
Bay

Boayan Island

Scuba diving

Capayas

Araceli

Port Barton

Dumaran Isl.

Caruray

Bacao

St.Paul's
Subterranean N.P.

Cleopatra
Needle

Green
Island Bay

Roxas

Sabang

1593

Bold Pt.

Babuyan

Bacungan

Honda Bay

Scuba diving

Iwahig

PPS

Anepahan

Puerto Princesa

Scuba diving

Mt.Aborlan

1525

Aborlan

PHI

Malanut Bay

Isugod

Lamakan

138

Rasa Island

Eran Bay

Quezon

Island

Narra

Tabon Caves

Palawan

Malabuñgan

Panitian

Bay

SULU

Culasian

Mt.Mantalingajan

2085

Brooke's Point

Tubbataha Reef

National Marine

Canipan

San Antonio
Bay

Valdez

Rio Tuba

Cape Buliluyan

Coral Bay

Pandanan I.

Bugsuk Island

Sebaring

North Balabac Strait

Ramos I.

Bancoran Island

Balabac Island

Balabac

569

Bancauan Island

Cape
Melville

Strait

Bs

Banggi

Balabac

Limbuak

Balambangan

Cagayan Sulu
Island

Tg.Sempang

Banggi

Mangayau

South Banggi Strait

Malawali

Pangutaran

Keretang

Inarungtong

Pangutaran

KUD

Kudat

Jambongan

Mantanai Besar

Pitas

Tg.Sugut

North Ubian

Lankong

Tandek

Turtle Islands
Marine Park

Cap Island

Kota Belud

Kinabalu N.P.

Turtle Islands

Telok

Tg.Pisau

Magados I.

Sugut

Labuk

Laparan

Tuaran

G.Kinabalu

Hot Springs

Basai

Sandakan

4095

Bongkud

SDK

Tunku Abdul Rahman Park

Penam-

Ranau

Beluran

Sukau

Tambisan

Gaya

pang

Tongehatan I.

Kota Kinabalu

Crocker Range

Kg.Telupid

Gomantong Caves

Tomanggong

Tawi-Tawi Island

BKI

N.P.

Lamag

Tabin Wildlife Reserve

Badjao-Seanomads

Pulau Tiga N.P.

252

Sabah

Kuamur

Tungku

Bato

Tiga

Panar

112

G.Trus Madi

Lanas

Segama

Bum

Tg.Nasong

Telok

2649

Diwata

Lahad Datu

Sibutu Island

Kg.Sawagan

Kimanis

Keningau

Pinangah

LDU

SUL

Beaufort

Banjaran Crooker

Kuamur

Danum Valley

Tumindao I.

Labuan

Melalap

Kg.Soak

Conservation Area

108

Timbun Mata

Labuan

Tenom

MALAYSIA

Telok Lahad Datu

Omar Ali Saiffudin Mosque

Sipitang

Lumutan

Lotung

Banjaran Brassey

Semporna

935

Bandar Seri Begawan

Muara

G.Lumaku

Tomani

1317

1667

Tawau Hills N.P.

Bunyu

BWN

Lawas

Sapulut

144

Jerudong Park

Pensiangan

Kalabakan

Merutai

SMM

Sultan's Palace

LWY

1966

SPE

TWU

Tawau

BRUNEI

Labu

Trusan

Sebatik

Sipadan

Kuala Belait

Batu Danau

Scuba diving

Seria

153

KALIMANTAN

Nunukan Timur

Lumut

G.Harden

Teluk Sebuku

Miri

Labi

(Harun)

Ulu Sembakung Reserve

Ahus

MYY

G.Mulu
N.P.

Ulu-Ulu

Telok Loak

Marudi

Mulu Caves

2160

Kalambuku

Mandul

Kg.Batu Satu

Bakelalan

LBW

Sembakung

MUR

Long Seridan

Longbawan

Sesayap

Beluru

2376

G.Basakan

Kalampising

Bunyu

Mufu

BKM

Bareo

1372

Niah N.P.

Niah

ODN

BBN

Semanu

Malinau

Sesayap

TRK

Tarakan

Kuala Suai

Niah Caves

Long Lama

(B O R N E O)

INDONESIA

Tarakan

Principal travel routes

- Auto route
- Rail road
- Shipping route
- Extinct volcano
- Active volcano

Remarkable landscapes and natural monuments

- UNESCO World Natural Heritage
- Rock landscape
- Nature park
- National park (landscape)
- Waterfall/rapids
- Lake country
- National park (flora)
- National park (fauna)
- Wildlife reserve
- Turtle conservation area
- Coastal landscape
- Beach
- Coral reef
- Island

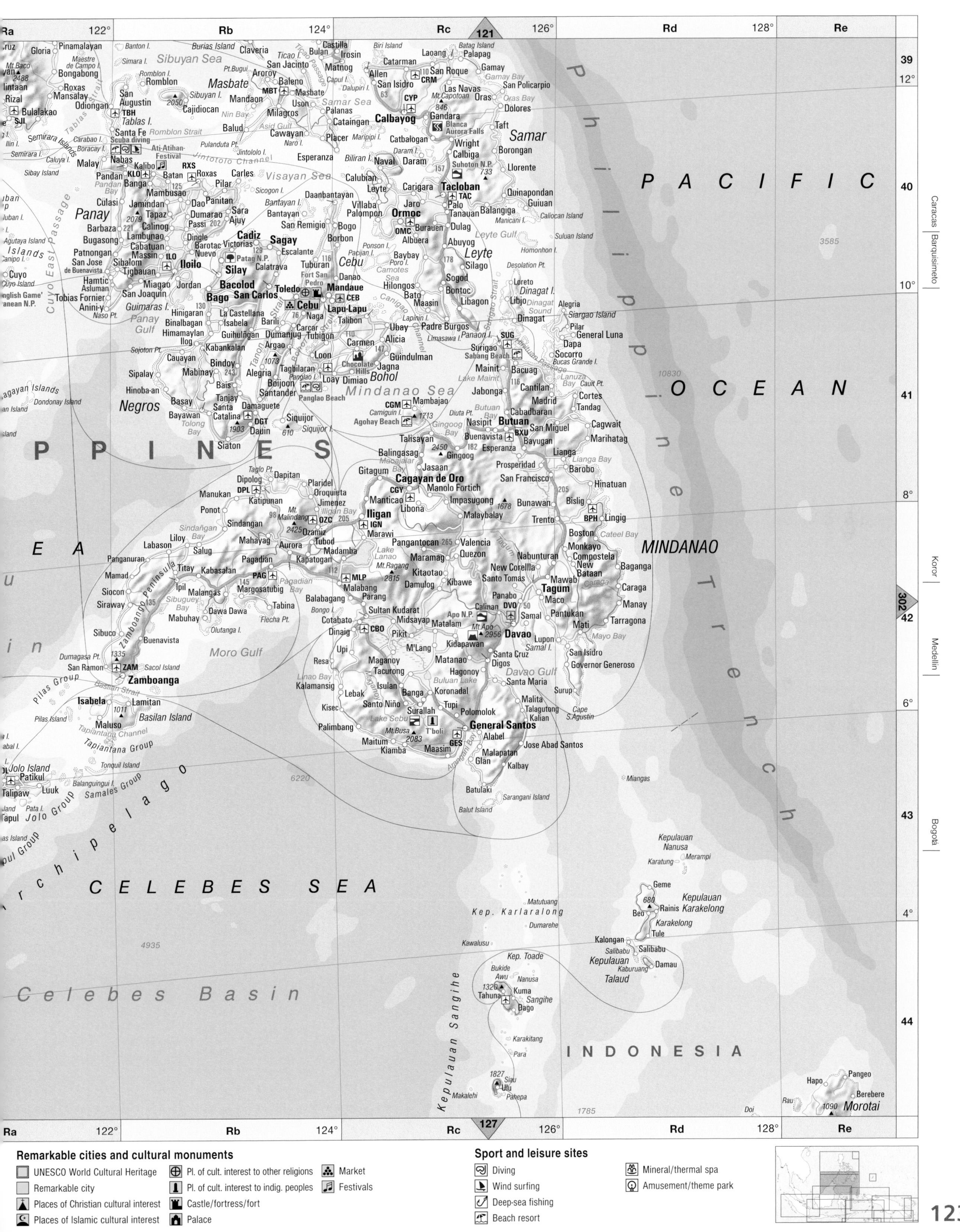

PACIFIC

OCEAN

Philippine Trench

Caracas | Barquisimeto

Koror

Medellin

Bogotá

39
12°

40

10°

41

8°

302
42

6°

43

4°

44

PPINES

Panay

Guimaras I.

Negros

EA

u

Cuyo East Passage

Moro Gulf

Zamboanga Peninsula

Sibuguey Bay

Basilan Island

Tapiantana Channel
Tapiantana Group

Pilas Group
Pilas Island

Jolo Island

Samales Group

Archipelago

Jolo Group

CELEBES SEA

Celebes Basin

MINDANAO

Davao Gulf

Caraga

Kepulauan Nanusa
Karatung Merampi

Geme
680 Rainis Karakelong
Beo Karakelong Tule
Kalongan
Salibabu Salibabu
Kep. Karlaralong Damau
Kalau Kepulauan Talaud
Kawalusu
Dumarehe Kabaruang

Kep. Toade
Bukide Nanusa
AWU
1326 Kuma Sangihe
Tahuna Siau Bago

Kepulauan Sangihe
Karakitang
Para

1827
Siau
Ulu
Makalehi Pahepa

INDONESIA

Hapo Pangeo
Rau Berebere
1090 Morotai
Doi
1785

Remarkable cities and cultural monuments

- ◻ UNESCO World Cultural Heritage
- ◻ Remarkable city
- ▲ Places of Christian cultural interest
- ☾ Places of Islamic cultural interest
- ⊕ Pl. of cult. interest to other religions
- ▲ Pl. of cult. interest to indig. peoples
- ⊞ Castle/fortress/fort
- ⊞ Palace
- ▲ Market
- ♪ Festivals

Sport and leisure sites

- ⊠ Diving
- ⊾ Wind surfing
- ⊠ Deep-sea fishing
- ⊠ Beach resort
- ⊠ Mineral/thermal spa
- ⊚ Amusement/theme park

123

Sumatra

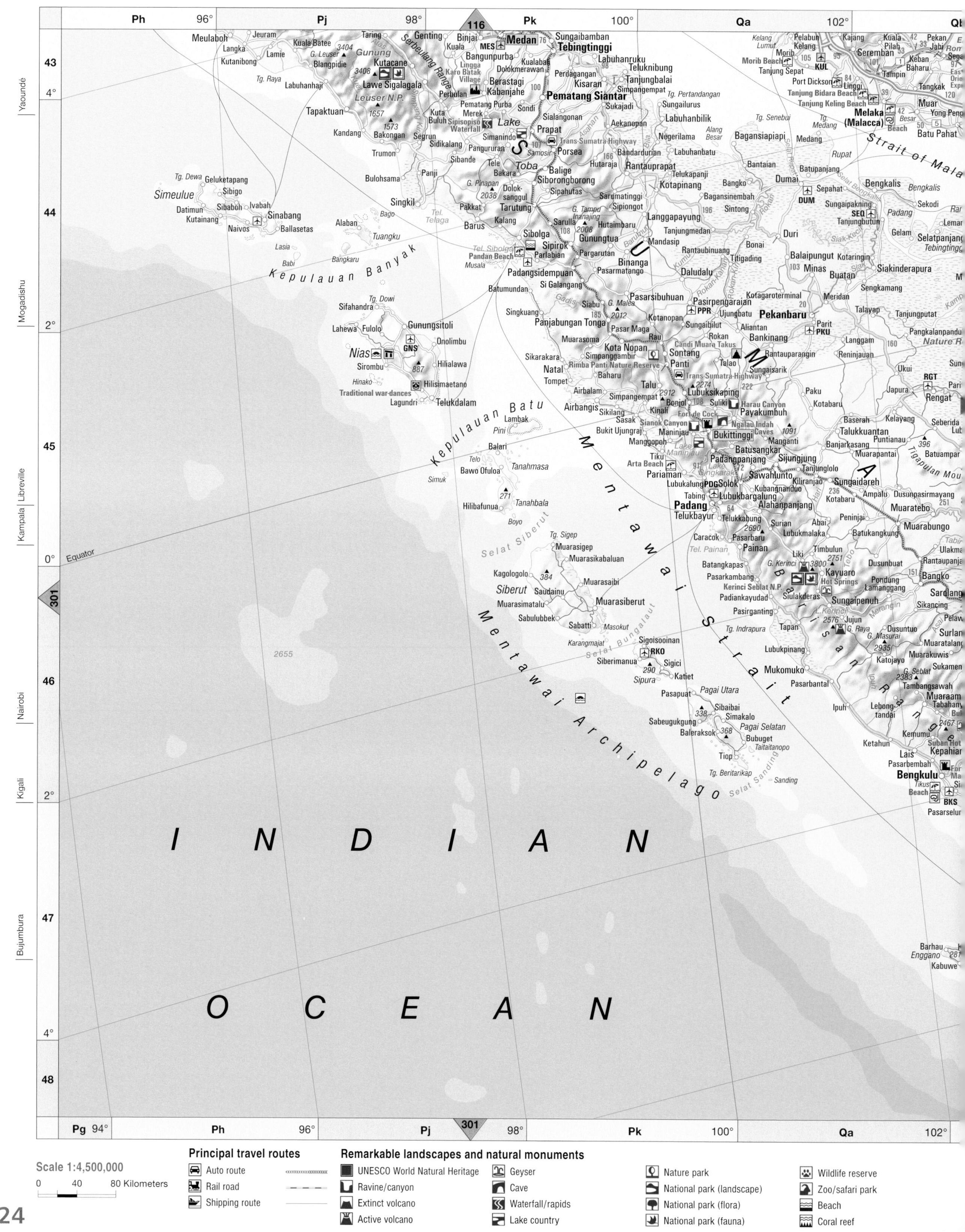

Scale 1:4,500,000

0   40   80 Kilometers

Principal travel routes
- 🚗 Auto route
- 🚂 Rail road
- ⛴ Shipping route

....
– · – · –
———

Remarkable landscapes and natural monuments
- ■ UNESCO World Natural Heritage
- ◤ Ravine/canyon
- ▲ Extinct volcano
- ▲ Active volcano
- 💧 Geyser
- Cave
- Waterfall/rapids
- Lake country
- Nature park
- National park (landscape)
- National park (flora)
- National park (fauna)
- Wildlife reserve
- Zoo/safari park
- Beach
- Coral reef

INDIAN

OCEAN

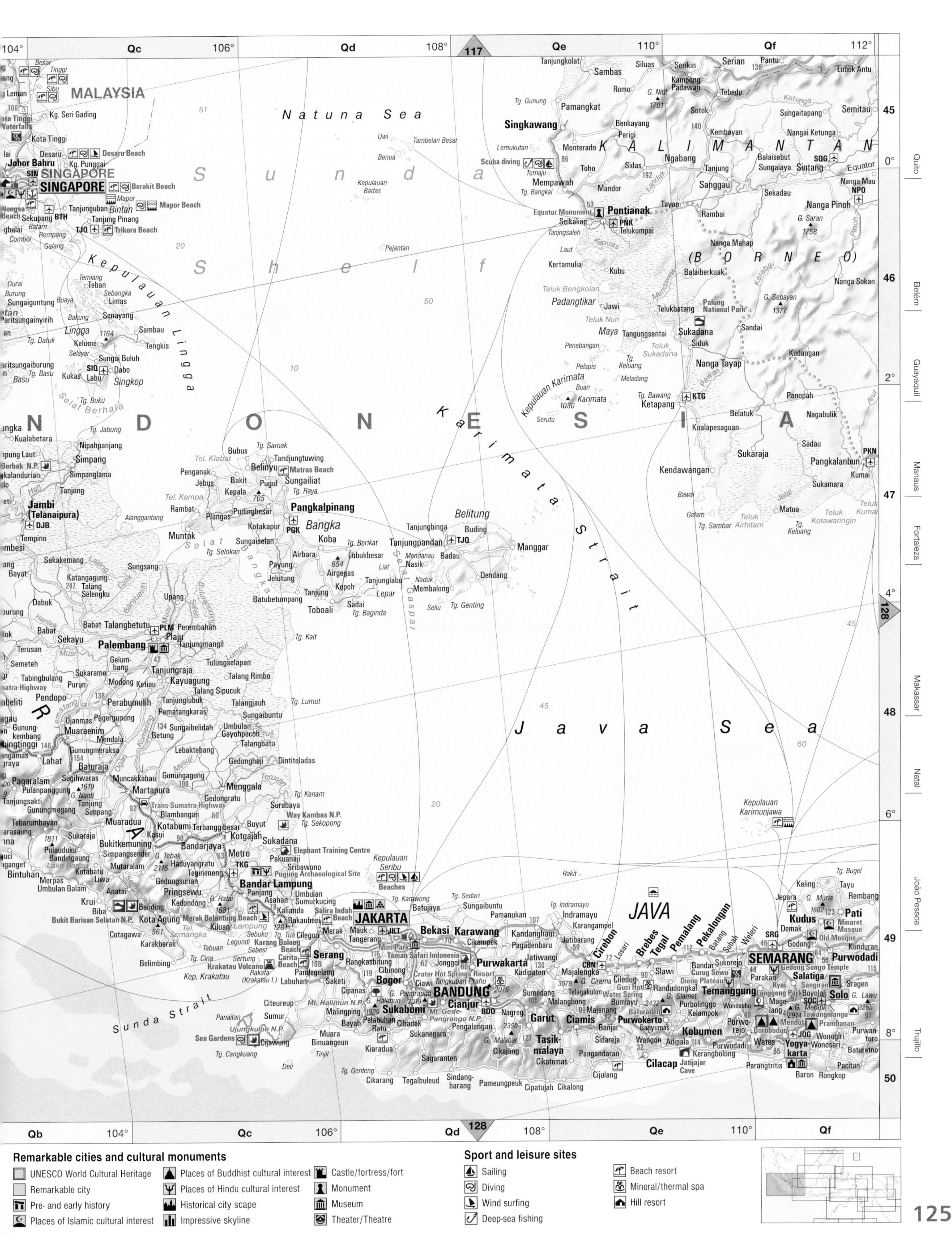

Remarkable cities and cultural monuments

- UNESCO World Cultural Heritage
- Remarkable city
- Pre- and early history
- Places of Islamic cultural interest
- Places of Buddhist cultural interest
- Places of Hindu cultural interest
- Historical city scape
- Impressive skyline
- Castle/fortress/fort
- Monument
- Museum
- Theater/Theatre

Sport and leisure sites

- Sailing
- Diving
- Wind surfing
- Deep-sea fishing
- Beach resort
- Mineral/thermal spa
- Hill resort

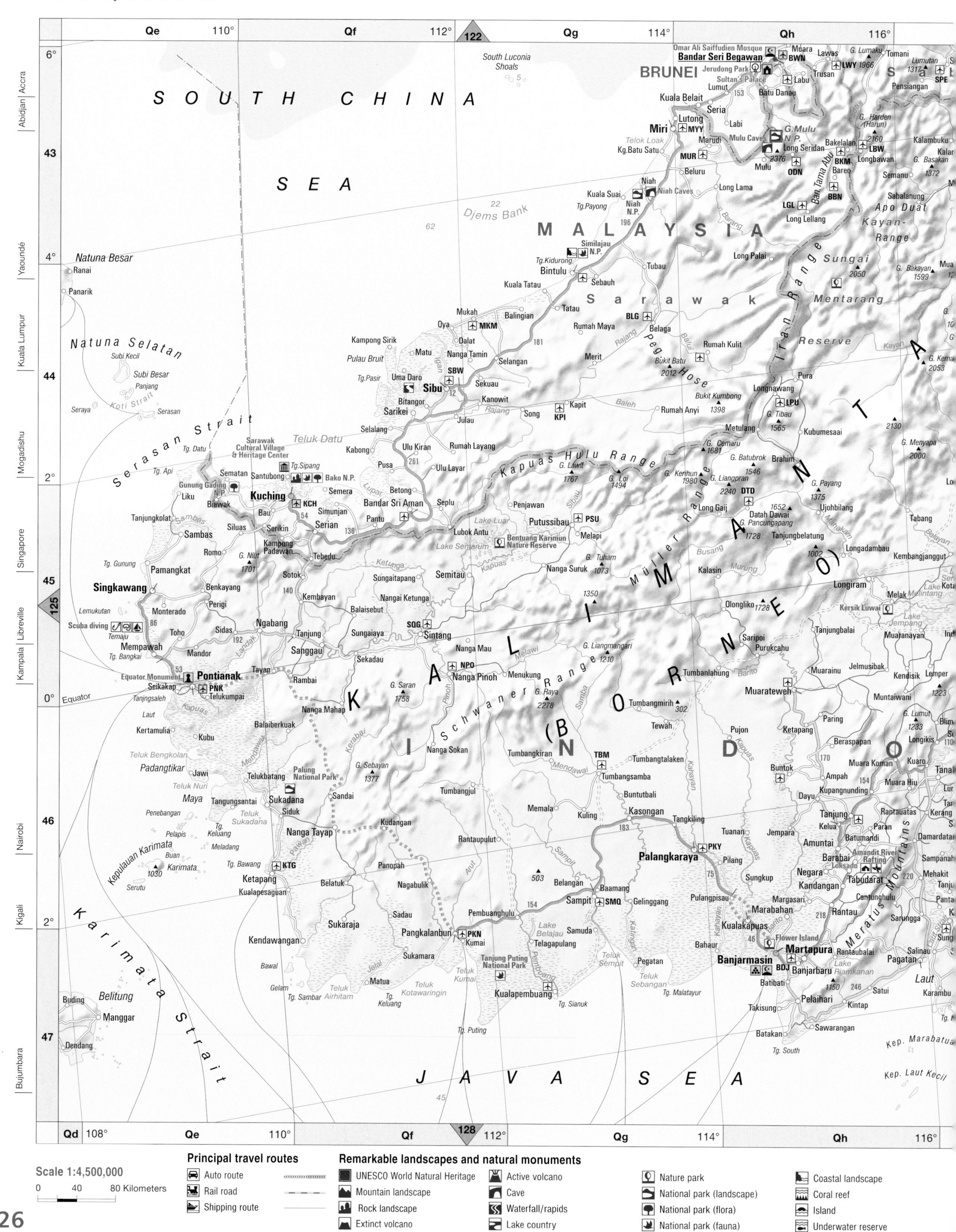

SOUTH CHINA

SEA

BRUNEI

MALAYSIA

Sarawak

KALIMANTAN (BORNEO)

JAVA SEA

Scale 1:4,500,000

0 40 80 Kilometers

Principal travel routes
- Auto route
- Rail road
- Shipping route

Remarkable landscapes and natural monuments
- UNESCO World Natural Heritage
- Mountain landscape
- Rock landscape
- Extinct volcano
- Active volcano
- Cave
- Waterfall/rapids
- Lake country
- Nature park
- National park (landscape)
- National park (flora)
- National park (fauna)
- Coastal landscape
- Coral reef
- Island
- Underwater reserve

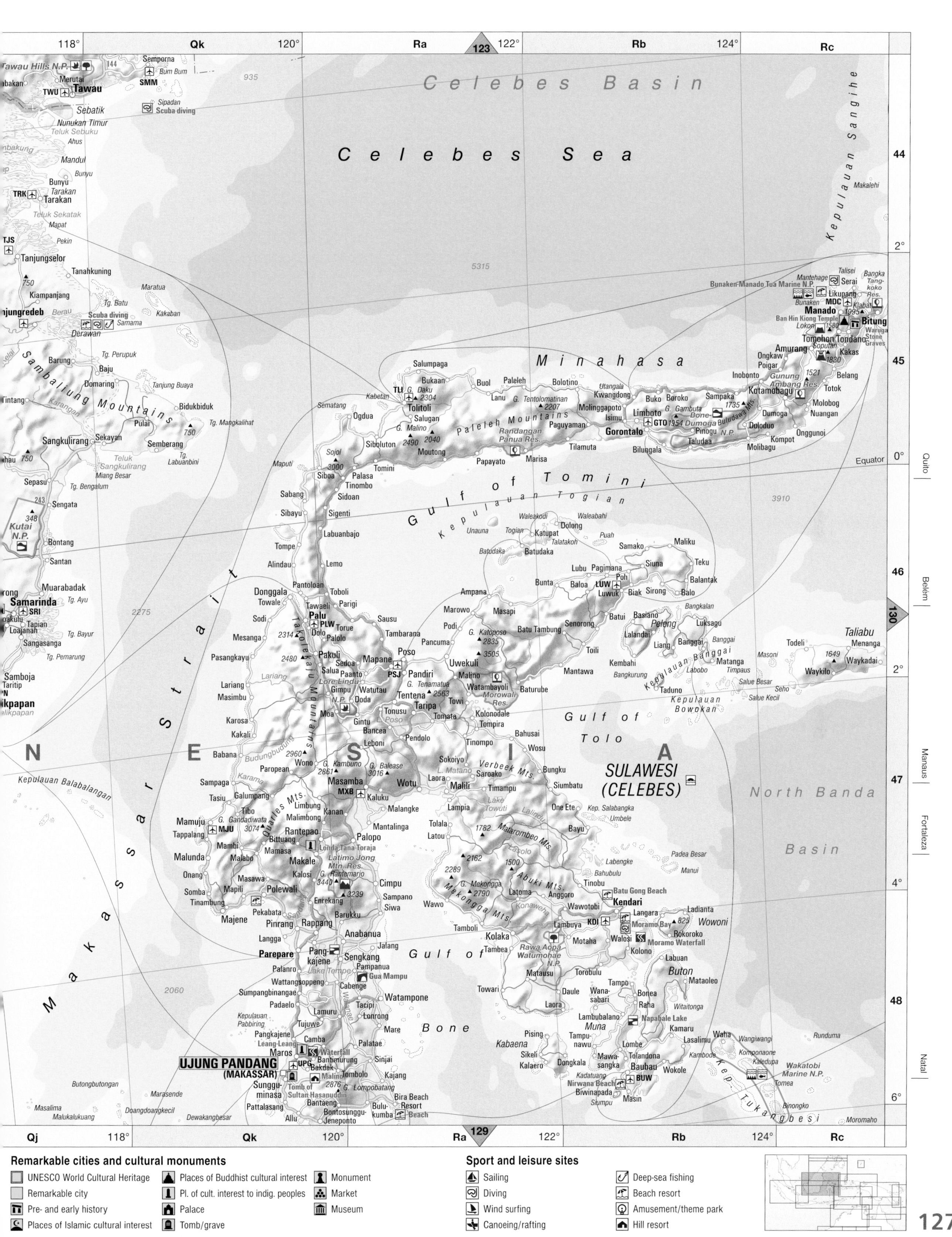

Celebes Basin
Celebes Sea
Kepulauan Sangihe
Minahasa
Gulf of Tomini
Kepulauan Togian
Gulf of Tolo
Gulf of Bone
North Banda Basin
Makassar Strait
Sambaliung Mountains
Paleleh Mountains
Takolekaju Mountains
Quarles Mts.
Verbeek Mts.
Mataronbeo Mts.
Abuki Mts.
Mekongga Mts.
SULAWESI (CELEBES)
Kepulauan Banggai
Kepulauan Bowokan
Kepulauan Balabalangan
Kep. Tukangbesi
Tawau
Tarakan
Tanjungselor
Samarinda
Palu
Poso
Manado
Bitung
Tomohon
Tondano
Kotamobagu
Gorontalo
Limboto
Tolitoli
Tomini
Ampana
Luwuk
Mamuju
Majene
Polewali
Rantepao
Makale
Palopo
Masamba
Parepare
Watampone
Kendari
Kolaka
Baubau
Raha
Muna
Buton
Wowoni
Kabaena
Taliabu
UJUNG PANDANG (MAKASSAR)
Maros
Sungguminasa
Pangkajene
Bulukumba
Jeneponto
Equator
Quito
Belém
Manaus
Fortaleza
Natal
Remarkable cities and cultural monuments
UNESCO World Cultural Heritage
Remarkable city
Pre- and early history
Places of Islamic cultural interest
Places of Buddhist cultural interest
Pl. of cult. interest to indig. peoples
Palace
Tomb/grave
Monument
Market
Museum
Sport and leisure sites
Sailing
Diving
Wind surfing
Canoeing/rafting
Deep-sea fishing
Beach resort
Amusement/theme park
Hill resort

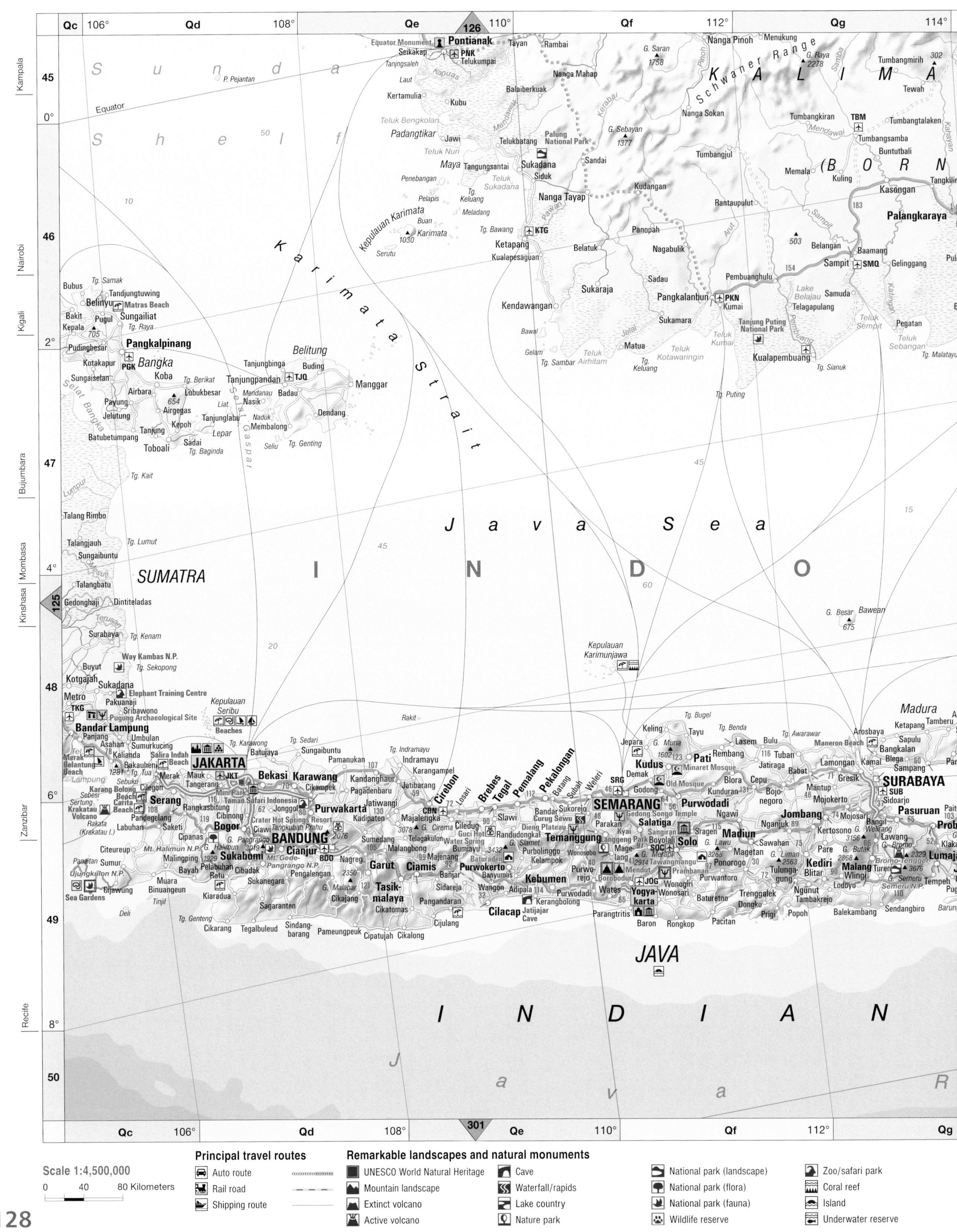

Scale 1:4,500,000

0   40   80 Kilometers

Principal travel routes
- Auto route
- Rail road
- Shipping route

Remarkable landscapes and natural monuments
- UNESCO World Natural Heritage
- Mountain landscape
- Extinct volcano
- Active volcano
- Cave
- Waterfall/rapids
- Lake country
- Nature park
- National park (landscape)
- National park (flora)
- National park (fauna)
- Wildlife reserve
- Zoo/safari park
- Coral reef
- Island
- Underwater reserve

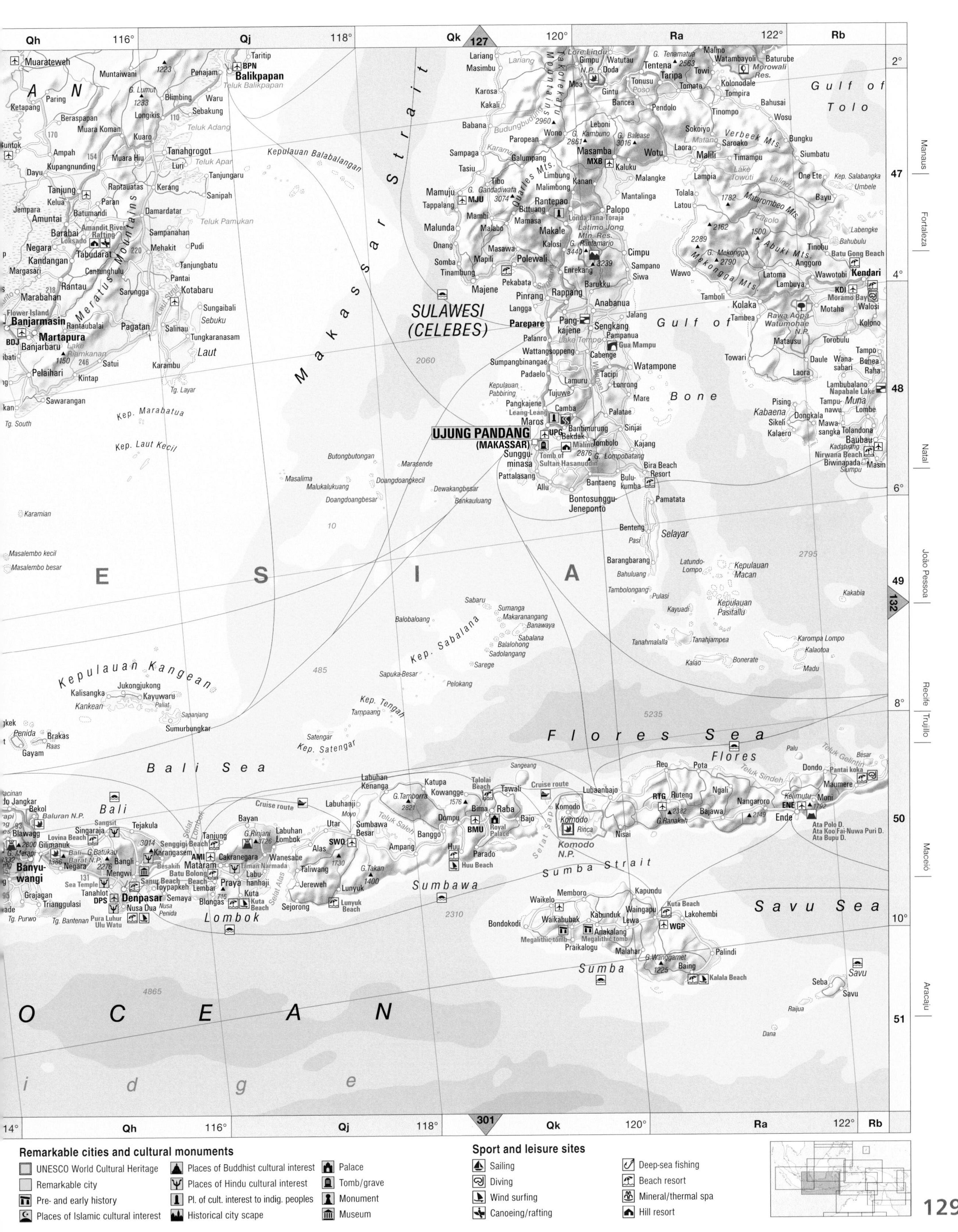

Remarkable cities and cultural monuments

- UNESCO World Cultural Heritage
- Remarkable city
- Pre- and early history
- Places of Islamic cultural interest
- Places of Buddhist cultural interest
- Places of Hindu cultural interest
- Pl. of cult. interest to indig. peoples
- Historical city scape
- Palace
- Tomb/grave
- Monument
- Museum

Sport and leisure sites

- Sailing
- Diving
- Wind surfing
- Canoeing/rafting
- Deep-sea fishing
- Beach resort
- Mineral/thermal spa
- Hill resort

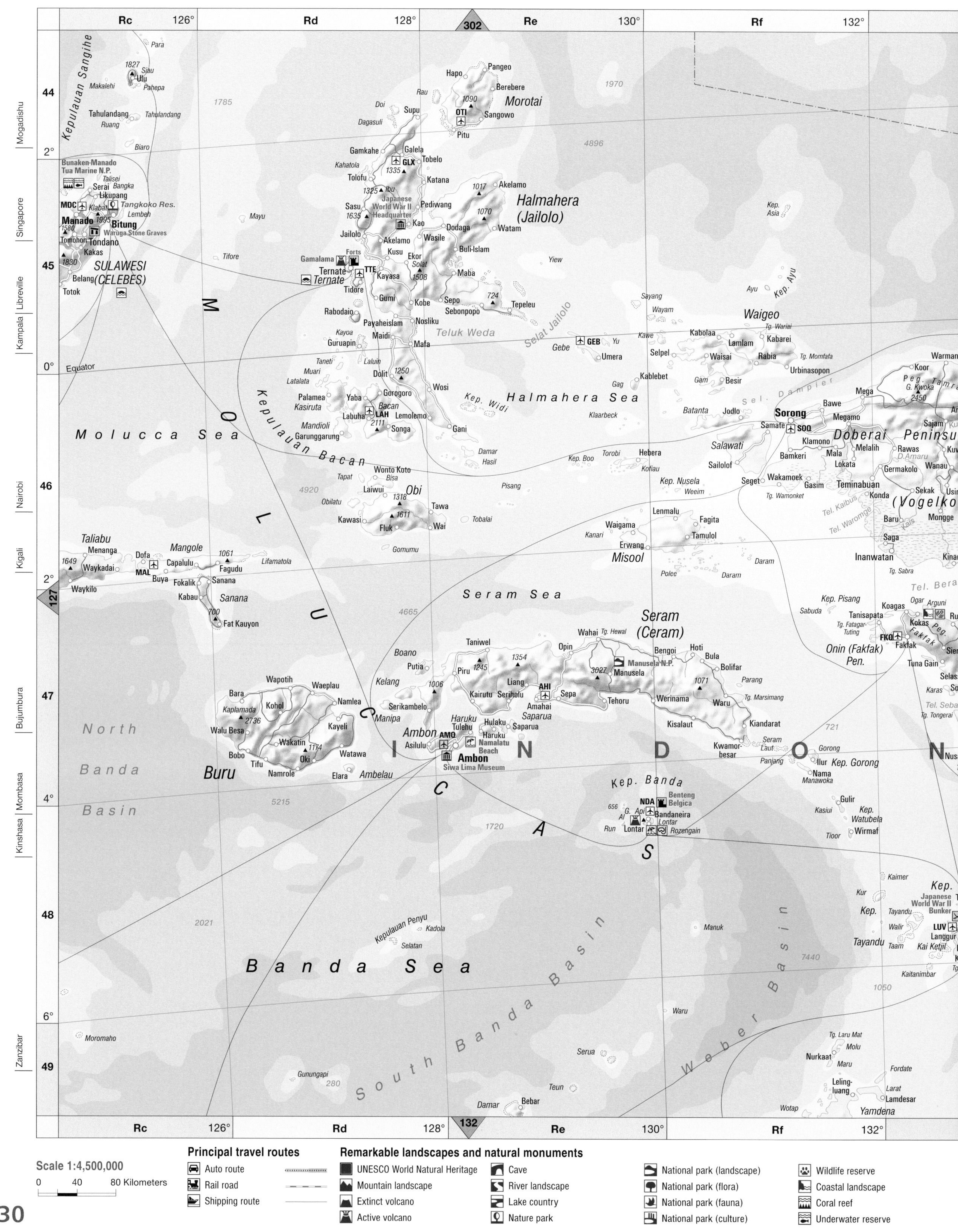

Scale 1:4,500,000

0   40   80 Kilometers

Principal travel routes

- Auto route
- Rail road
- Shipping route
- ·········· (dotted line)
- ─── (line)

Remarkable landscapes and natural monuments

- UNESCO World Natural Heritage
- Mountain landscape
- Extinct volcano
- Active volcano
- Cave
- River landscape
- Lake country
- Nature park
- National park (landscape)
- National park (flora)
- National park (fauna)
- National park (culture)
- Wildlife reserve
- Coastal landscape
- Coral reef
- Underwater reserve

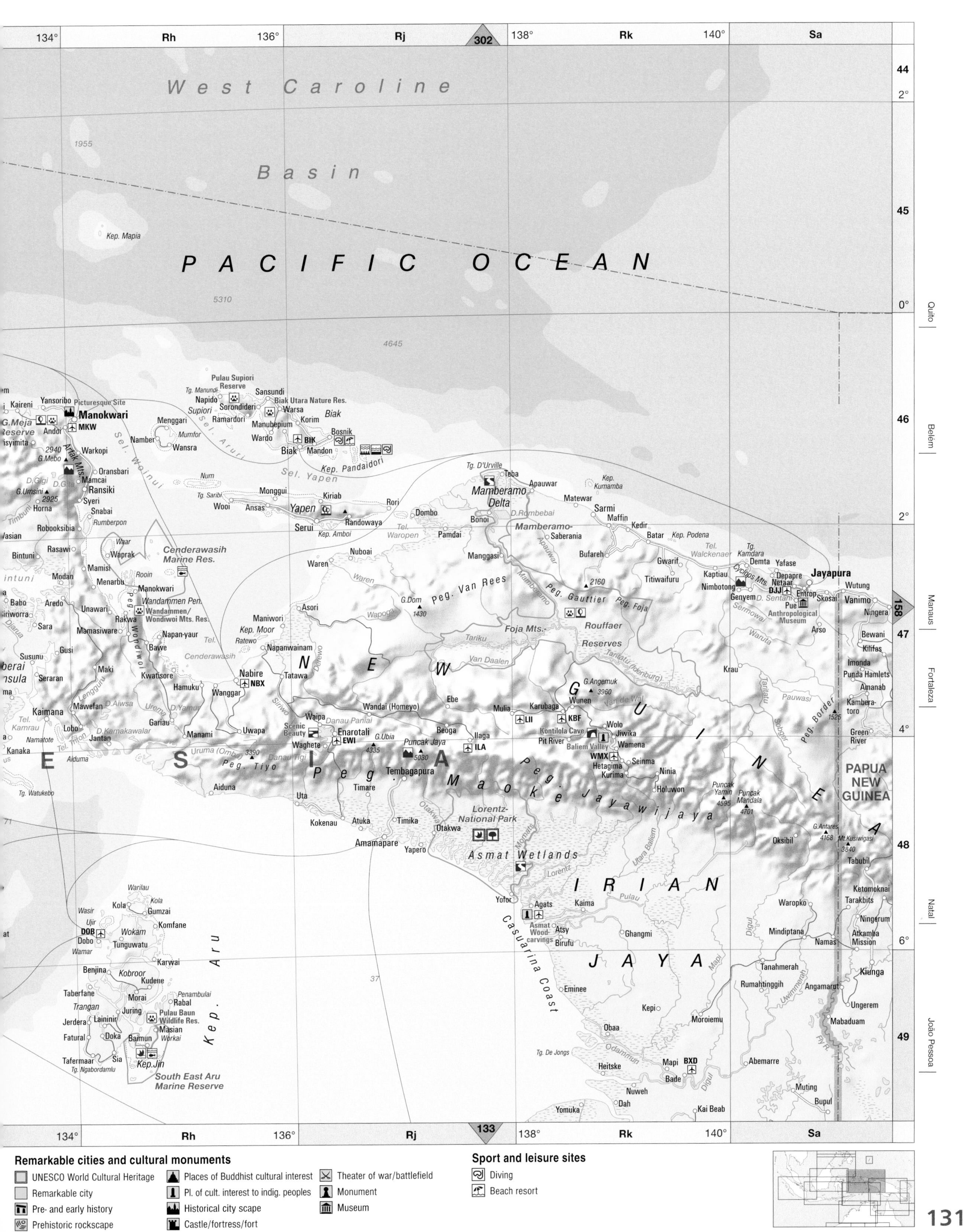
134°
Rh
136°
Rj
302
138°
Rk
140°
Sa
44
2°
45
0°
46
47
4°
48
6°
49
Quito
Belém
Manaus
Fortaleza
Natal
João Pessoa
158
133
West Caroline
Basin
1955
Kep. Mapia
PACIFIC OCEAN
5310
4645
Pulau Supiori Reserve
Tg. Manundi
Napido
Sansundi
Supiori
Sorondideri
Biak Utara Nature Res.
Warsa
Biak
Ramardori
Korim
Manubepium
Wardo
Bosnik
BIK
Biak
Mandon
Kep. Pandaidori
Sel. Yapen
Kaireni
Yansoribo
Picturesque Site
Manokwari
MKW
G.Meja Reserve
Andor
Isyimita
Arfak Mts.
2940
G.Mebo
Warkopi
Menggari
Namber
Mumfor
Wansra
Sel. Aruri
Sel. Woinui
Oransbari
Mamcai
Ransiki
D.Gigi
D.Gita
G.Umsini
2925
Syeri
Horna
Snabai
Rumberpon
Timbuni
Robooksibia
Num
Tg. Saribi
Wooi
Monggui
Ansas
Yapen
Kiriab
Rori
Serui
Randowaya
Kep. Amboi
Tg. D'Urville
Teba
Mamberamo Delta
Apauwar
Kep. Kumamba
Matewar
Sarmi
Maffin
Dombo
Bonoi
D.Rombebai
Mamberamo-
Saberania
Kedir
Batar
Kep. Podena
Tel. Waropen
Pamdai
Tel. Walckenaer
Bufareh
Tg. Kamdara
Demta
Yafase
Gwarif
Titiwaifuru
Kaptiau
Cyclops Mts.
Depapre
Jayapura
Netaar
Nimbotong
DJJ
Entrop
Wutung
Genyem
D. Sentani
Skosai
Vanimo
Pue
Anthropological Museum
Ningera
Arso
Sermowai
Waruta
Bewani
Kilifas
Imonda
Punda Hamlets
Amanab
Kambera-toro
1526
Green River
Peg. Border
Sobger
Pauwasi
Krau
Tariku
Tarita
Vasian
Bintuni
Rasawi
Waar
Waprak
Cenderawasih Marine Res.
Mamisi
Rooin
Menarbu
Manokwari
Modan
Wandammen Pen.
Wandammen/ Wondiwoi Mts. Res.
Babo
Aredo
Unawari
Rakwa
Iriworra
Sara
Mamasiware
Napan-yaur
Tel. Cenderawasih
Susunu
Gusi
Bawe
Maki
Kwatisore
Seraran
Hamuku
Peg. Wondiwoi
Kaimana
Mawefan
D.Aiwsa
Urema
D.Yamur
Gariau
Lobo
D.Kamakawalar
Jantan
Namatote
Tel. Kamrau
Tel. Triton
Kanaka
Alduma
Tg. Watukebo
Nuboai
Waren
Waren
Manggasi
Peg. Van Rees
Apauwar
Mamberamo
Peg. Gauttier
2160
Peg. Foja
Asori
G.Dom
1430
Wapoga
Maniwori
Kep. Moor
Ratewo
Foja Mts.
Rouffaer
Reserves
Tariku
Van Daalen
Taritatu (Idenburg)
Napanwainam
Dorewo
Nabire
NBX
Tatawa
Wanggar
NEW GUINEA
G.Angemuk
3960
Wunen
Van de Wal
Ebe
Wandai (Homeyo)
Mulia
Karubaga
Siriwo
Waipa
Danau Paniai
LII
KBF
Uwapa
Manami
Scenic Beauty
Enarotali
EWI
Beoga
Kontilola Cave
Wolo
Jiwika
Pit River
Baliem Valley
Wamena
Waghete
G.Ubia
4335
Puncak Jaya
5030
Ilaga
ILA
WMX
Seinma
Hetagima
Kurima
Ninia
Holuwon
Uruma (Omba)
3390
Danau Tigi
Peg. Tiyo
Peg. Maoke
Tembagapura
Timare
Peg. Jayawijaya
Puncak Yamin
4595
Puncak Mandala
4701
PAPUA NEW GUINEA
Aiduna
Uta
Kokenau
Atuka
Timika
Otakwa
Otakwa
Lorentz-National Park
Amamapare
Yapero
Asmat Wetlands
Momats
Utara Baliem
G.Antares
4168
Mt.Kusiwigasi
3840
Oksibil
Tabubil
Ketomoknai
Tarakbits
Lorentz
IRIAN JAYA
Yofor
Agats
Kaima
Pulau
Waropko
Asmat Wood-carvings
Atsy
Birufu
Casuarina Coast
Ghangmi
Digul
Mindiptana
Namas
Ningerum
Atkamba Mission
Tanahmerah
Kiunga
Mapi
Rumahtinggih
Uwimmerah
Angamarut
Emineee
Ungerem
Kepi
Moroiemu
Mabaduam
Fly R.
Obaa
Tg. De Jongs
Odammun
Heitske
Mapi
BXD
Bade
Digul
Abemarre
Muting
Nuweh
Dah
Bupul
Yomuka
Kai Beab
Warilau
Kola
Kola
Gumzai
Wasir
Ujir
Komfane
DOB
Dobo
Wokam
Tunguwatu
Wamar
Karwai
Benjina
Kobroor
Kudene
Taberfane
Penambulai
Trangan
Morai
Rabal
Juring
Pulau Baun Wildlife Res.
Jerdera
Lainingir
Masian
Fatural
Doka
Bamun
Workai
Tafermaar
Sia
Tg. Ngabordamlu
Kep.Jin
South East Aru Marine Reserve
Kep. Aru
37
71
Remarkable cities and cultural monuments
UNESCO World Cultural Heritage
Remarkable city
Pre- and early history
Prehistoric rockscape
Places of Buddhist cultural interest
Pl. of cult. interest to indig. peoples
Historical city scape
Castle/fortress/fort
Theater of war/battlefield
Monument
Museum
Sport and leisure sites
Diving
Beach resort

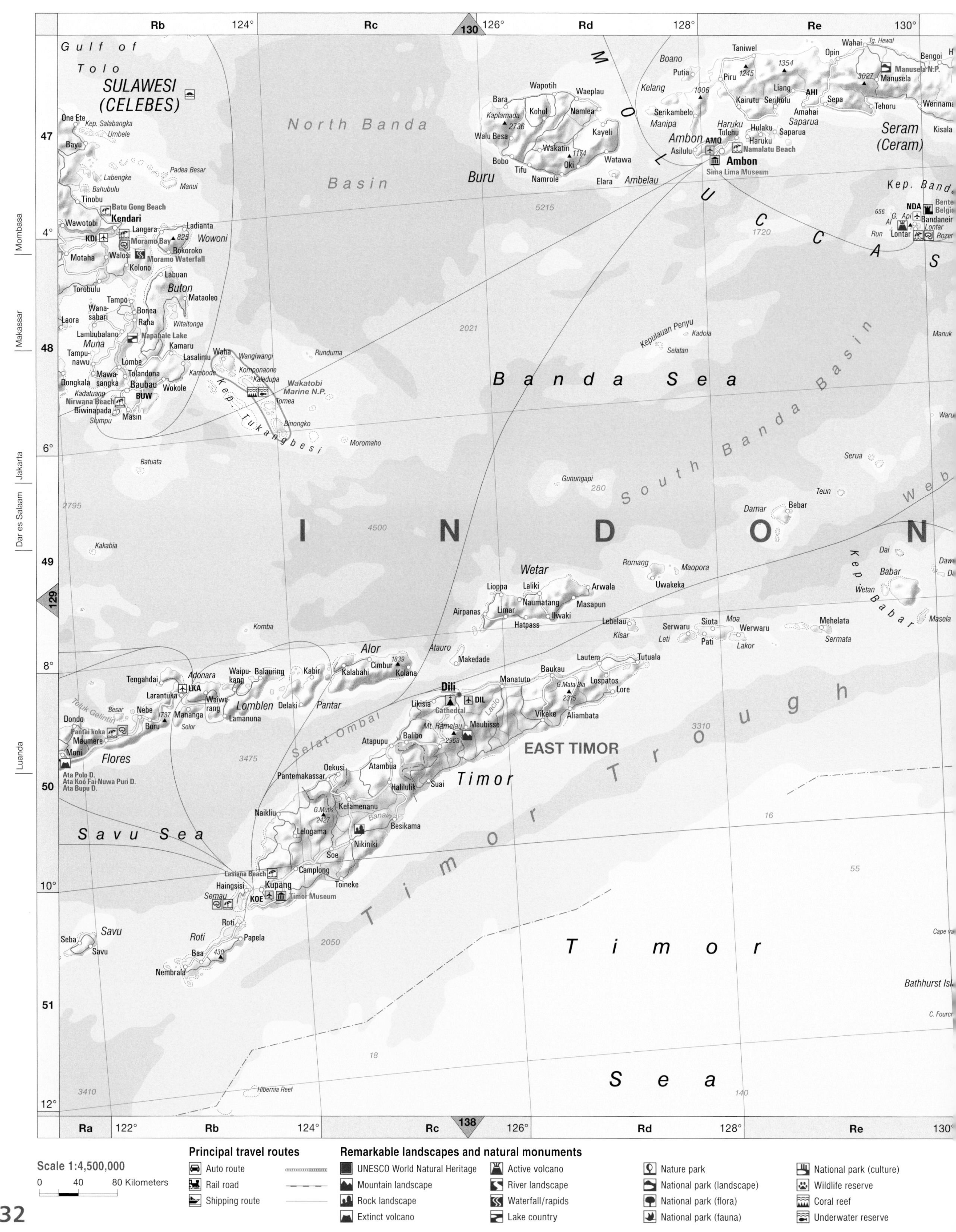

Gulf of
Tolo
**SULAWESI
(CELEBES)**

North Banda

Basin

Buru

MOLUCCAS

Taniwel
Boano
Putia   Piru 1245   1354   Opin   Wahai   Tg. Hewal
Kelang 1006 Liang **AHI**   3022 Manusela N.P.   Bengoi
Wapotih   Serikambelo Seriholu   Sepa   Manusela
Bara   Waeplau   Manipa   Kairutu   Amahai   Tehoru   Werinama
Kaplamada Kohol Namlea   Haruku Tulehu Hulaku   *Seram*
2736   Asilulu **AMQ** Haruku Saparua   *(Ceram)*
Walu Besa   Kayeli   **Ambon**
Bobo   Wakatin 1174   Sima Lima Museum   Namalatu Beach
Tifu   Oki   Watawa   Kep. Band
Namrole   Elara   *Ambeiau*   **NDA**   Bente
Belgi
656 G. Api   Bandaneir
1720   Lontar
Run Al   Lontar Rozer

5215

2021

Mombasa   *Banda Sea*   Kepulauan Penyu   Kadola   Manuk
Selatan   Kep. Penyu

Makassar   *South Banda*   Serua

Jakarta   Batuata   Gunungapi 280   Basin   Teun   Web
4500   Damar Bebar

Dar es Salaam   2795   Kakabia   *INDON*   Romang Maopora   Dai   Dawe
Kep. Babar   Babar   Di
Wetan   Masela
Komba   Wetar   Arwala   Uwakeka
Jakarta Lioppa Laliki   Mehelata
Limar Naumatang   Serwaru Siota Moa Werwaru   Sermata
129   Airpanas   Ilwaki   Lebelau   Leti Pati   Lakor
Hatpass   Kisar

Makedade   Lautem Tutuala
Adonara   Atauro   Baukau   Lospatos
Tengahdai   Kabir Cimbur 1839   Manatuto G.Mata Bia   Lore
Waipu- Balauring   Kalabahi Kolana   2315
Larantuka **LKA**   *Alor*   **Dili**   Manatuto   Vikeke Aliambata
Waiwe-   *Lomblen* Delaki *Pantar*   Likisia **DIL**   3310
Besar Nebe rang   Cathedral   Maubisse
Dondo 1737 Mananga   Lamanuna   Mt. Ramelau Maubisse
Pantai koka Boru Solor   Atapupu Balibo 2963   **EAST TIMOR**
Maumere   Atambua
Moni   Oekusi   Vikeke
Flores   Pantemakassar   *Timor*
Ata Polo D.   3475   16
Ata Koo Fai-Nuwa Puri D.   Naikliu Kefamenanu   Banain
Ata Bupu D.   G.Mutis   Besikama
2427   Halilulik
Savu Sea   Lelogama Nikiniki   Suai
Soe
Laslana Beach   Camplong   55
Haingsisi   Kupang Toineke
Semau **KOE** Timor Museum
Savu Roti   *Timor*
Seba   Roti Papela
Savu   Baa 430   2050
Nembrala

Savu

Timor

Bathhurst Isl

2050   140

18   C. Fourcr

3410   Hibernia Reef   *Sea*   Cape va

Scale 1:4,500,000

0   40   80 Kilometers

Principal travel routes

- Auto route
- Rail road
- Shipping route

Remarkable landscapes and natural monuments

- UNESCO World Natural Heritage
- Mountain landscape
- Rock landscape
- Extinct volcano
- Active volcano
- River landscape
- Waterfall/rapids
- Lake country
- Nature park
- National park (landscape)
- National park (flora)
- National park (fauna)
- National park (culture)
- Wildlife reserve
- Coral reef
- Underwater reserve

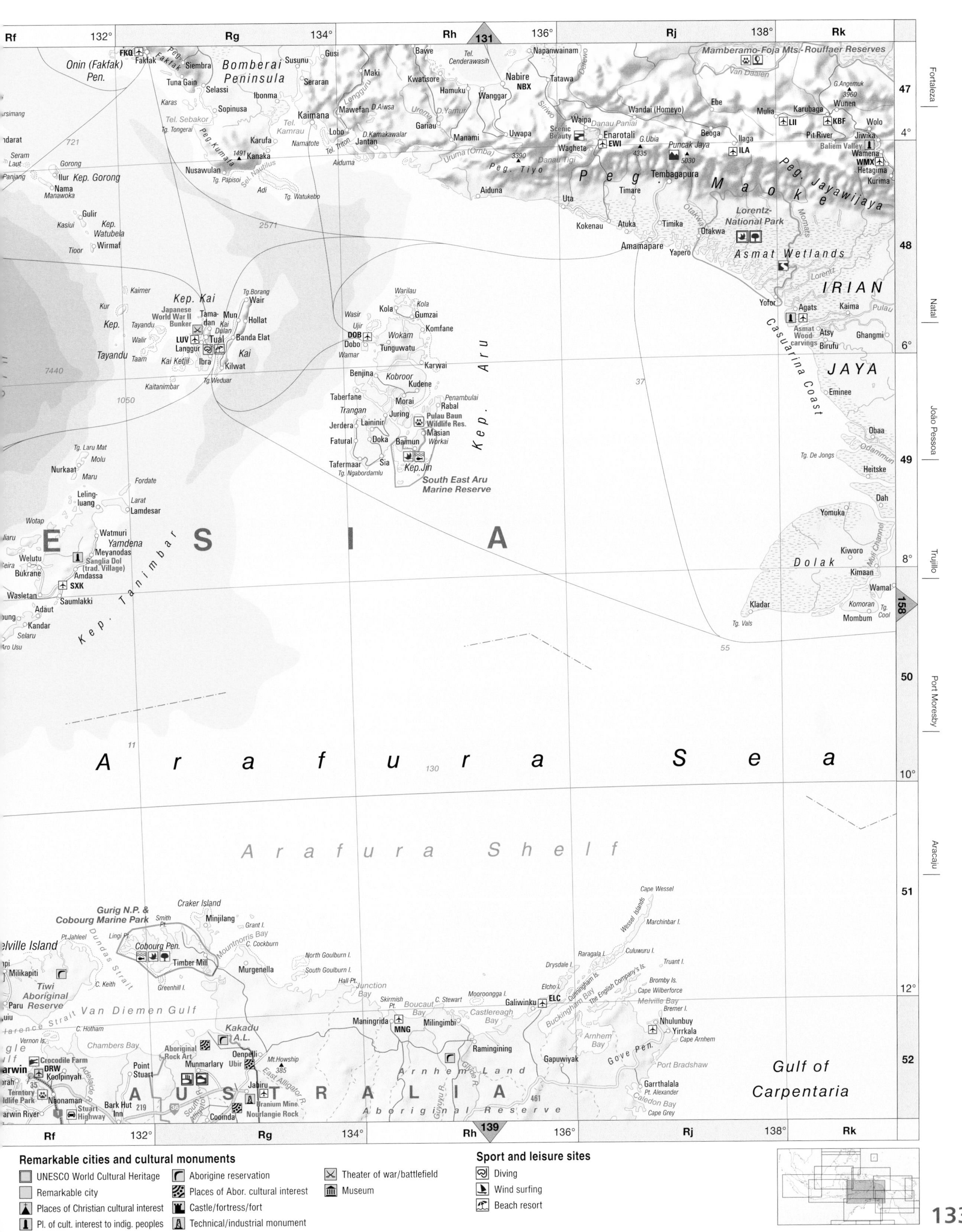

Remarkable cities and cultural monuments

- ⬜ UNESCO World Cultural Heritage
- ⬜ Remarkable city
- ▲ Places of Christian cultural interest
- 🏛 Pl. of cult. interest to indig. peoples
- ⛏ Aborigine reservation
- Places of Abor. cultural interest
- 🏰 Castle/fortress/fort
- 🏭 Technical/industrial monument
- ⚔ Theater of war/battlefield
- 🏛 Museum

Sport and leisure sites

- Diving
- Wind surfing
- Beach resort

133

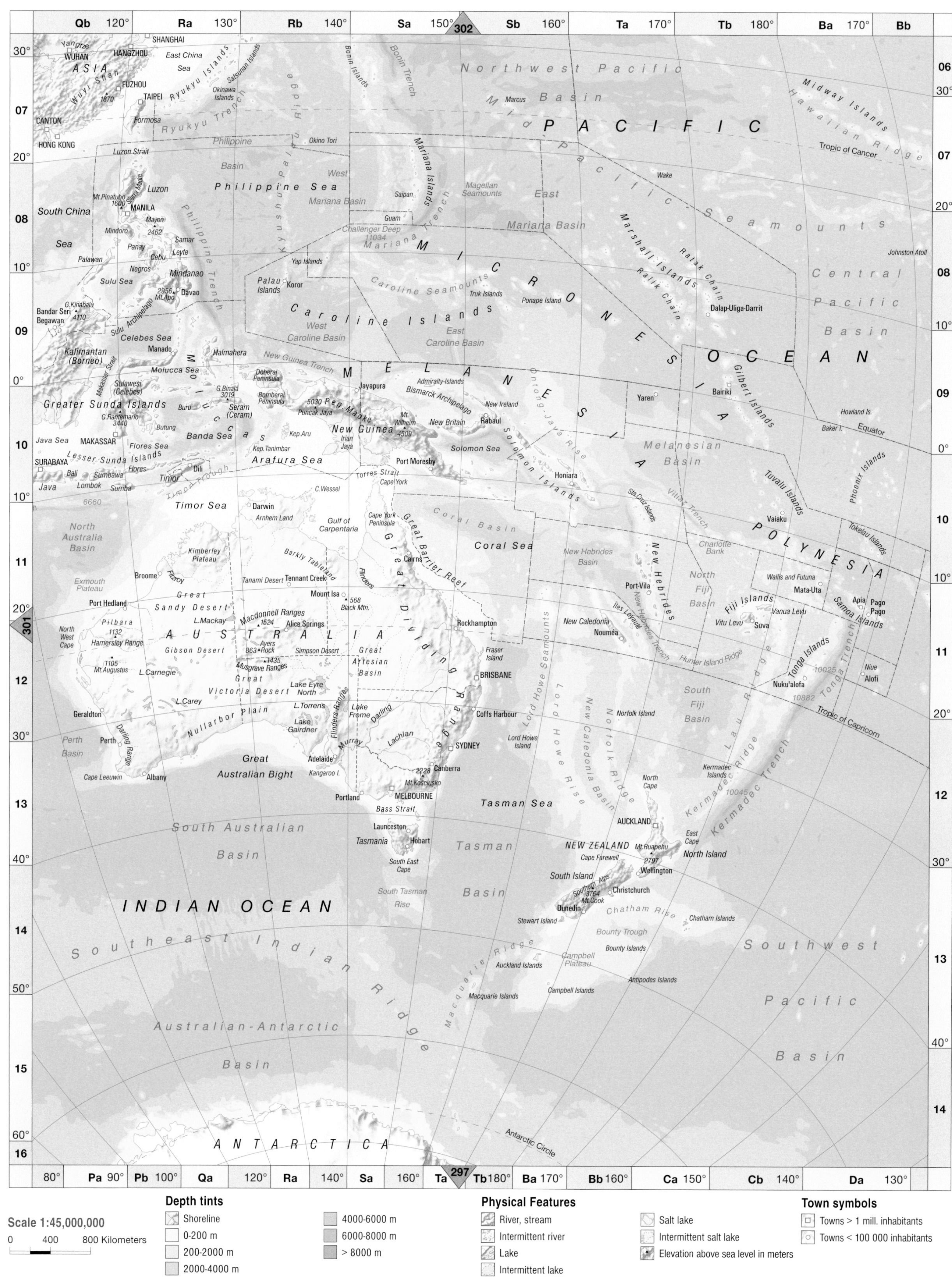

Scale 1:45,000,000

0   400   800 Kilometers

Depth tints

Shoreline	
0-200 m	
200-2000 m	
2000-4000 m	
4000-6000 m	
6000-8000 m	
> 8000 m	

Physical Features

River, stream
Intermittent river
Lake
Intermittent lake
Salt lake
Intermittent salt lake
Elevation above sea level in meters

Town symbols

Towns > 1 mill. inhabitants
Towns < 100 000 inhabitants

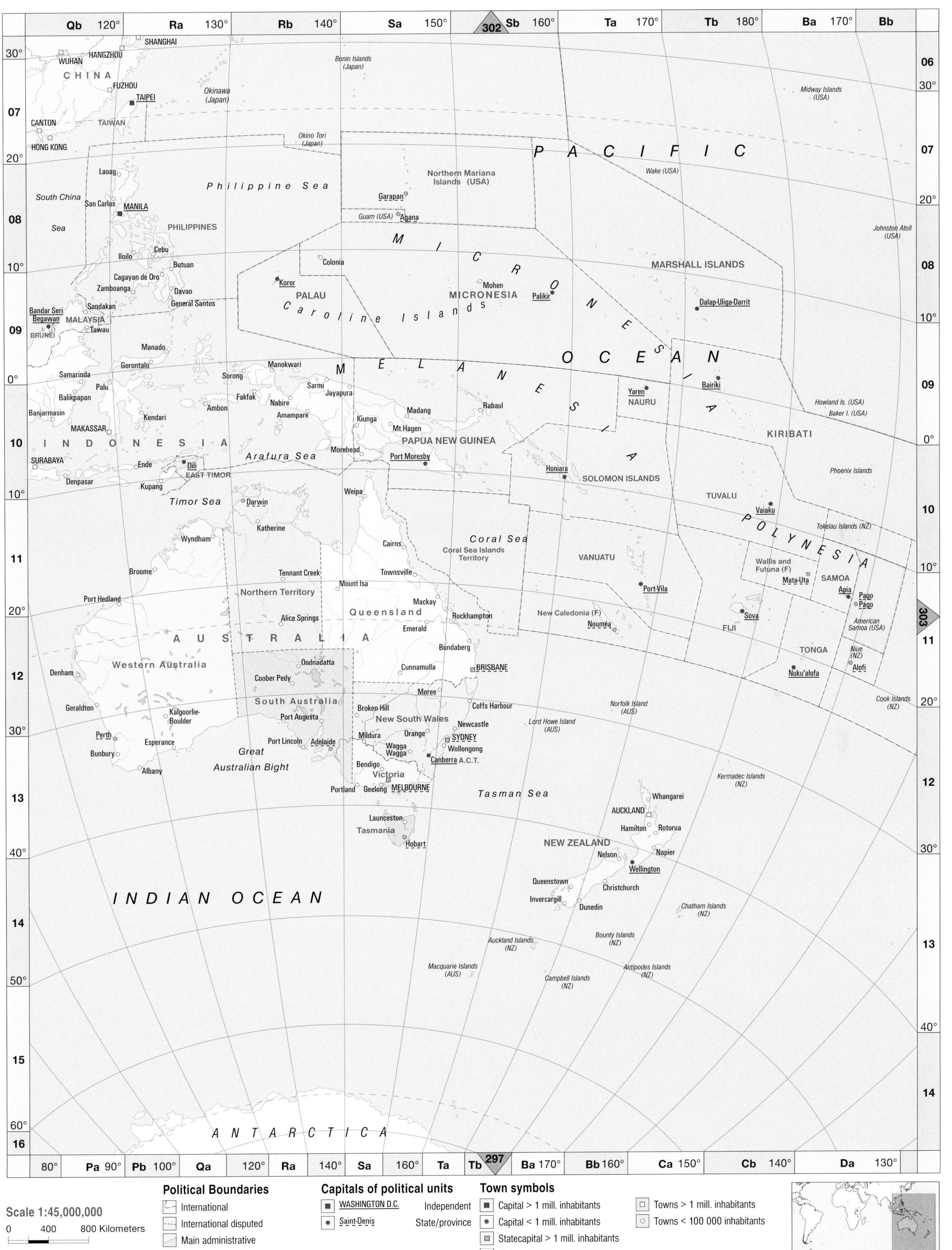

| Qb | 120° | Ra | 130° | Rb | 140° | Sa | 150° | 302 | Sb | 160° | Ta | 170° | Tb | 180° | Ba | 170° | Bb |

30°
SHANGHAI
WUHAN HANGZHOU
CHINA
06
30°
FUZHOU
07
Okinawa (Japan)
TAIPEI
Bonin Islands (Japan)
Midway Islands (USA)
CANTON
TAIWAN
HONG KONG
20°
Okino Tori (Japan)
P A C I F I C
07
Wake (USA)
Laoag
Philippine Sea
Northern Mariana Islands (USA)
20°
Johnston Atoll (USA)
San Carlos
MANILA
Garapan
M
08
Guam (USA) Agana
I
08
PHILIPPINES
Iloilo
Cebu
Colonia
C
MARSHALL ISLANDS
Butuan
R
Cagayan de Oro
Koror
Mohen
O
10°
Zamboanga
Davao
PALAU
MICRONESIA
Palikir
N
Dalap-Uliga-Darrit
10°
Bandar Seri Begawan
Sandakan
General Santos
Caroline Islands
E
MALAYSIA
09
Tawau
S
09
BRUNEI
Manado
Manokwari
M E L A N E S I A
Yaren
Bairiki
I
Samarinda
Gorontalo
Sorong
NAURU
A
Palu
Sarmi
Howland Is. (USA)
Balikpapan
Nabire Jayapura
Baker I. (USA)
Banjarmasin
Kendari
Ambon
Fakfak Amampare
Madang
Rabaul
KIRIBATI
0°
MAKASSAR
Kiunga
Mt.Hagen
0°
I N D O N E S I A
PAPUA NEW GUINEA
Phoenix Islands
SURABAYA
Morehead
Port Moresby
TUVALU
Dili
Arafura Sea
Vaiaku
10
EAST TIMOR
Tokelau Islands (NZ)
Denpasar
Weipa
Honiara
10°
Kupang
SOLOMON ISLANDS
P O L Y N E S I A
10°
Timor Sea
Darwin
Coral Sea
10°
Katherine
Coral Sea Islands Territory
VANUATU
Wallis and Futuna (F)
SAMOA
11
Wyndham
Cairns
Mata-Uta
Apia
Port-Vila
Pago Pago
Broome
Tennant Creek
Townsville
New Caledonia (F)
American Samoa (USA)
303
Port Hedland
Northern Territory
Mount Isa
Mackay
Nouméa
FIJI Suva
11
20°
Alice Springs
Queensland
Rockhampton
TONGA
Niue (NZ)
A U S T R A L I A
Emerald
Nuku'alofa
Alofi
Denham
Bundaberg
Norfolk Island (AUS)
20°
Oodnadatta
Cunnamulla
BRISBANE
Cook Islands (NZ)
12
Coober Pedy
Western Australia
Moree
Lord Howe Island (AUS)
Geraldton
South Australia
Broken Hill
Coffs Harbour
20°
Kalgoorlie-Boulder
Port Augusta
New South Wales
Newcastle
Kermadec Islands (NZ)
30°
Perth
Port Lincoln Adelaide
Mildura
Orange
SYDNEY
Whangarei
Esperance
Wagga Wagga
Wollongong
AUCKLAND
Bunbury
Great Australian Bight
Bendigo
Canberra A.C.T.
Hamilton Rotorua
12
Albany
Victoria
13
Portland Geelong MELBOURNE
Tasman Sea
NEW ZEALAND
Napier
30°
Launceston
Nelson Wellington
40°
Tasmania Hobart
Queenstown
Christchurch
I N D I A N   O C E A N
Invercargill
Chatham Islands (NZ)
14
Dunedin
13
Auckland Islands (NZ)
Bounty Islands (NZ)
50°
Macquarie Islands (AUS)
Campbell Islands (NZ)
Antipodes Islands (NZ)
40°
15
14
60°
16
A N T A R C T I C A

| 80° | Pa | 90° | Pb | 100° | Qa | 120° | Ra | 140° | Sa | 160° | Ta | Tb | 297 | Ba | 170° | Bb | 160° | Ca | 150° | Cb | 140° | Da | 130° |

Political Boundaries

Scale 1:45,000,000

0   400   800 Kilometers

~~~~ International
- - - - International disputed
░░░ Main administrative

Capitals of political units

■ WASHINGTON D.C.   Independent
● Saint-Denis   State/province

Town symbols

■ Capital > 1 mill. inhabitants
● Capital < 1 mill. inhabitants
▣ Statecapital > 1 mill. inhabitants
◉ Statecapital < 1 mill. inhabitants
□ Towns > 1 mill. inhabitants
○ Towns < 100 000 inhabitants

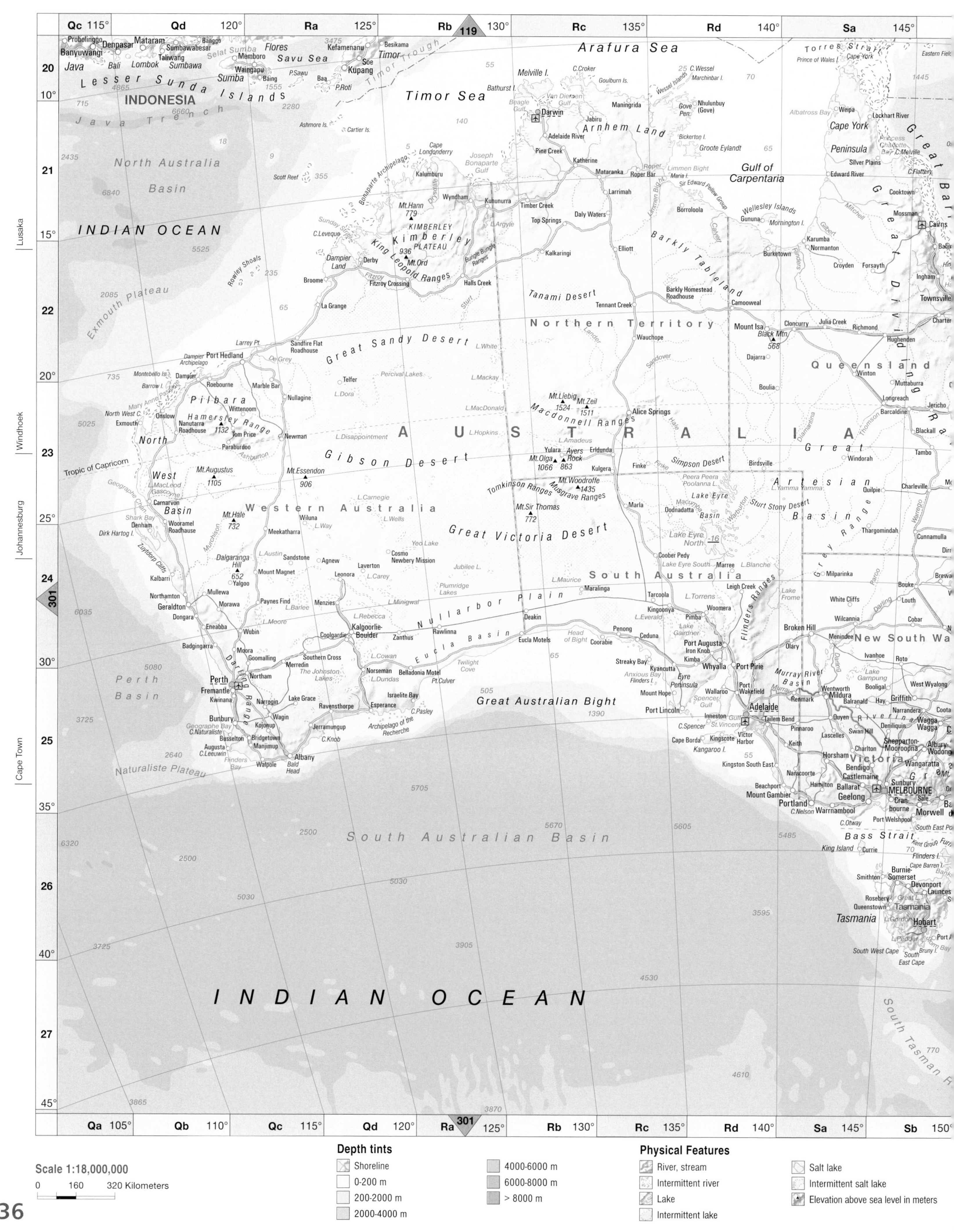

Scale 1:18,000,000

0   160   320 Kilometers

136

Depth tints

- Shoreline
- 0-200 m
- 200-2000 m
- 2000-4000 m
- 4000-6000 m
- 6000-8000 m
- > 8000 m

Physical Features

- River, stream
- Intermittent river
- Lake
- Intermittent lake
- Salt lake
- Intermittent salt lake
- Elevation above sea level in meters

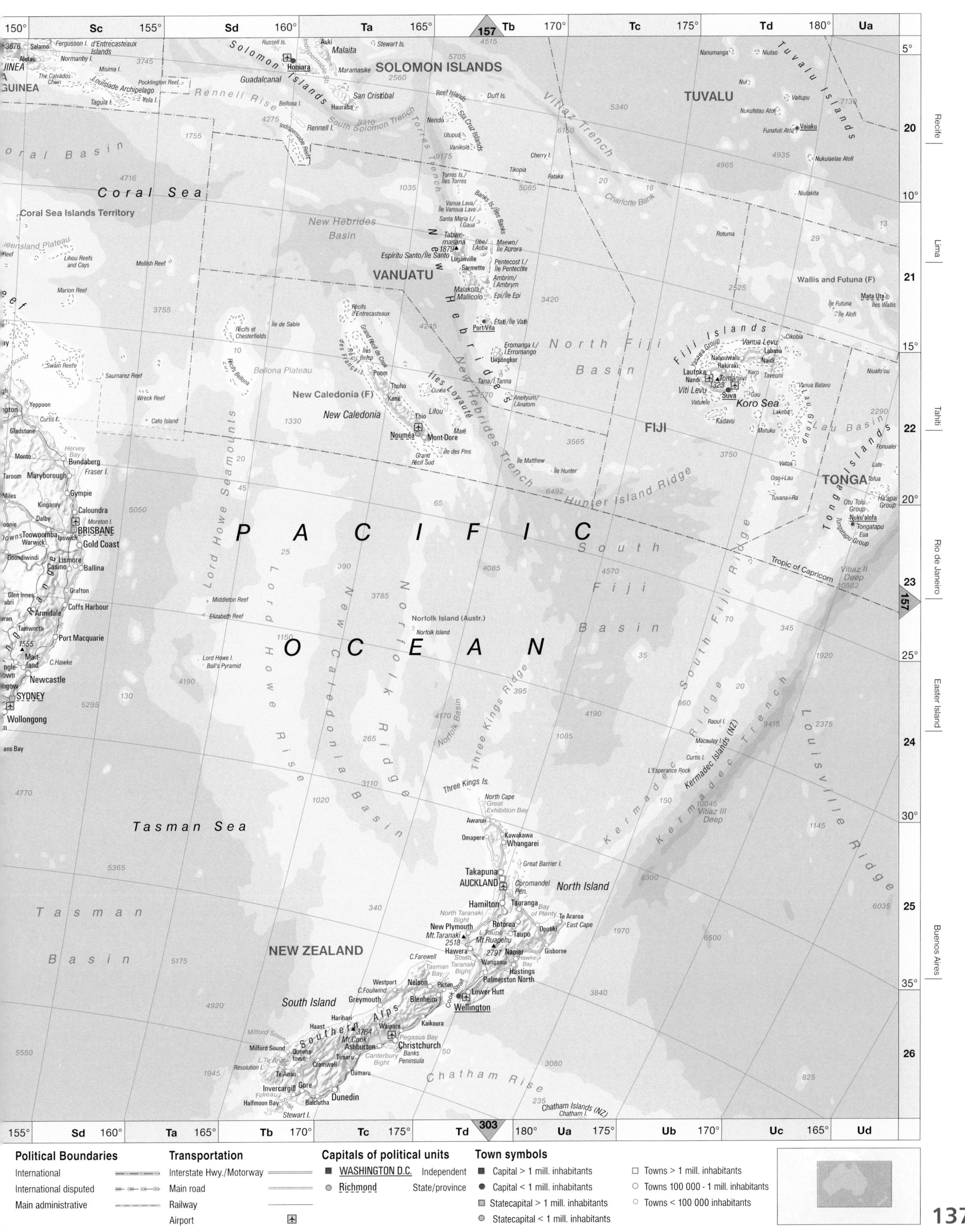

Map labels and geographic features

Recife · Lima · Tahiti · Rio de Janeiro · Easter Island · Buenos Aires

SOLOMON ISLANDS

Salamo · Fergusson I. d'Entrecasteaux Islands · Russell Is. · Auki · Malaita · Stewart Is. · Nanumanga · Niutao · Tuvalu Islands
Alotau · Normanby I. · 3745 · Honiara · Maramasike · 5705 · Reef Islands · Duff Is. · Vitiaz Trench · **TUVALU** · Nui · Vaitupu · 7130
GUINEA · Misima I. · Louisiade Archipelago · Pocklington Reef · Guadalcanal · 2560 · San Cristobal · Nendo · Utupua · 5340 · Nukufetau Atoll · Funafuti Atoll · Vaiaku
AGUINEA · The Calvados · Chain · Taguia I. · Yela I. · Rennell Rise · Bellona I. · San Cristobal · Haubara · 4275 · Vanikolo · 9175 · 6150 · 4935 · Nukulaelae Atoll
Coral Basin · 1755 · Indispensable Reefs · Rennell I. · 3310 · South Solomon Trench · Tikopia · Fataka · 4965 · Niulakita
4716 · Cherry I. · 5085 · Rotuma · 13 · 29

Coral Sea

Coral Sea Islands Territory · New Hebrides Basin · Vanua Lava/ Île Vanua Lava · Santa Maria I./ I. Gaua · **VANUATU**
Queensland Plateau · Lihou Reefs and Cays · Mellish Reef · Tabwe-masana 1879 · Obe/ I. Aoba · Maewo/ Île Aurora · Wallis and Futuna (F)
Marion Reef · 3755 · Espiritu Santo/Île Santo · Luganville · Sarmette · Pentecost I./ Île Pentecôte · Île Futuna · Îles Wallis · Mata Uta
Récifs d'Entrecasteaux · Île de Sable · Ambrim/ I.Ambrym · Malakula/ Mallicolo · Epi/Île Epi · 3420 · 2525 · Île Alofi
Récifs et Chesterfields · 10 · Récifs Bellona · Efaté/Île Vaté · Port-Vila · **North Fiji Basin** · Fiji Islands · Cikobia

New Caledonia (F) · Grand Récif des Cook · Poom · Eromanga I./ I.Erromango · Vanua Levu · Vanua Balavu
1330 · New Caledonia · Touho · Kone · Ouéna · Tana/I. Tanna · Unpongkor · Yasawa Group · Nabouwalu · Rakiraki · Naidi · Taveuni
Thio · Lifou · Aneityum/ I.Anatom · Lautoka · Nandi · Tomaniivi 1323 · Koro · Niuafo'ou
Nouméa · Mont-Dore · Maré · Viti Levu · Suva · **Koro Sea** · Lakeba · 2290
Grand Récif Sud · Île des Pins · Île Matthew · Vatulele · Kadavu · Matuku · Lau Basin

P A C I F I C

Île Hunter · **FIJI** · 3565 · 3750 · Vatoa · **TONGA**
Hervey Bay · Bundaberg · Fraser I. · Lord Howe Seamounts · Hunter Island Ridge · 6492 · Oog-i-Lau · Tuvana-i-Ra · Otu Tolu Group · Ha'apai Group · Tofua
Monto · Maryborough · 45 · 65 · South · Fiji · Nuku'alofa · Tongatapu · Eua
Gympie · Kingaroy · Caloundra · 5050 · Moreton I. · 25 · 390 · 4085 · 4570 · Tongatapu Group · Tongatapu · Fonualei · Ùate

O C E A N

Towns · Toowoomba · Ipswich · **BRISBANE** · Gold Coast · Lord Howe Rise · 3785 · Tropic of Capricorn · Vitiaz II Deep 10882
Goondiwindi · Warwick · Norfolk Basin · 4190 · Norfolk Island (Austr.) · South Fiji Ridge · 2290
Glen Innes · Casino · Lismore · Ballina · Middleton Reef · 1150 · Norfolk Island · Basin · 70 · 345
Armidale · Grafton · Elizabeth Reef · 1020 · 25 · 35 · 1920
Tamworth · Coffs Harbour · 1555 · Lord Howe I. Ball's Pyramid · 4170 · 4190 · 1085 · Raoul I. · Macauley Islands (NZ) · 9415 · 2375
Mait-land · C.Hawke · 5295 · 130 · 4190 · 265 · 395 · Curtis I. · Kermadec Islands (NZ) · 150 · 9415
ngle · Newcastle · 3110 · L'Esperance Rock · 860 · Kermadec Trench · 1145
town · **SYDNEY** · New Caledonia Basin · Three Kings Ridge · 150 · 10045 Vitiaz III Deep · Louisville Ridge
ngwo · Wollongong · Three Kings Is. · North Cape Great Exhibition Bay · 8300 · 6035
4770 · **Tasman Sea** · 1020 · Awanui · Kawakawa · Whangarei · 6500

Tasman · 5365 · Omapere · Takapuna · Great Barrier I. · Coromandel Pen. · North Island · 6035
Basin · 340 · **AUCKLAND** · Hamilton · Tauranga · Bay of Plenty · Te Araroa · East Cape
5175 · North Taranaki Bight · New Plymouth · Mt.Taranaki 2518 · Rotorua · Taupo · Te Araroa · 1970 · 6500
NEW ZEALAND · Hawera · Mt.Ruapehu 2797 · Napier · Gisborne · Hawke's Bay
C.Farewell · South Taranaki Bight · Wanganui · Hastings · Palmerston North · 3840
Westport · Nelson · Picton · Lower Hutt · Chatham Rise
South Island · C.Foulwind · Greymouth · Blenheim · Cook Strait · **Wellington** · Pegasus Bay · Banks Peninsula
4920 · Harihari · Southern Alps · Mt.Cook 3764 · Waipara · Kaikoura · 50
Haast · Milford Sound · L.Te Anau · Queenstown · Ashburton · **Christchurch** · Canterbury Bight · 3060 · 825
5550 · Resolution I. · Cromwell · Timaru · Oamaru · 1945
Invercargill · Gore · Balclutha · Dunedin · 235 · Chatham Islands (NZ) · Chatham I.
Foveaux · Halfmoon Bay · Stewart I.

Legend

Political Boundaries
- International
- International disputed
- Main administrative

Transportation
- Interstate Hwy./Motorway
- Main road
- Railway
- Airport

Capitals of political units
- ■ WASHINGTON D.C. — Independent
- ◉ Richmond — State/province

Town symbols
- ■ Capital > 1 mill. inhabitants
- ● Capital < 1 mill. inhabitants
- ▣ Statecapital > 1 mill. inhabitants
- ◉ Statecapital < 1 mill. inhabitants
- □ Towns > 1 mill. inhabitants
- ○ Towns 100 000 - 1 mill. inhabitants
- ○ Towns < 100 000 inhabitants

Northwestern Australia

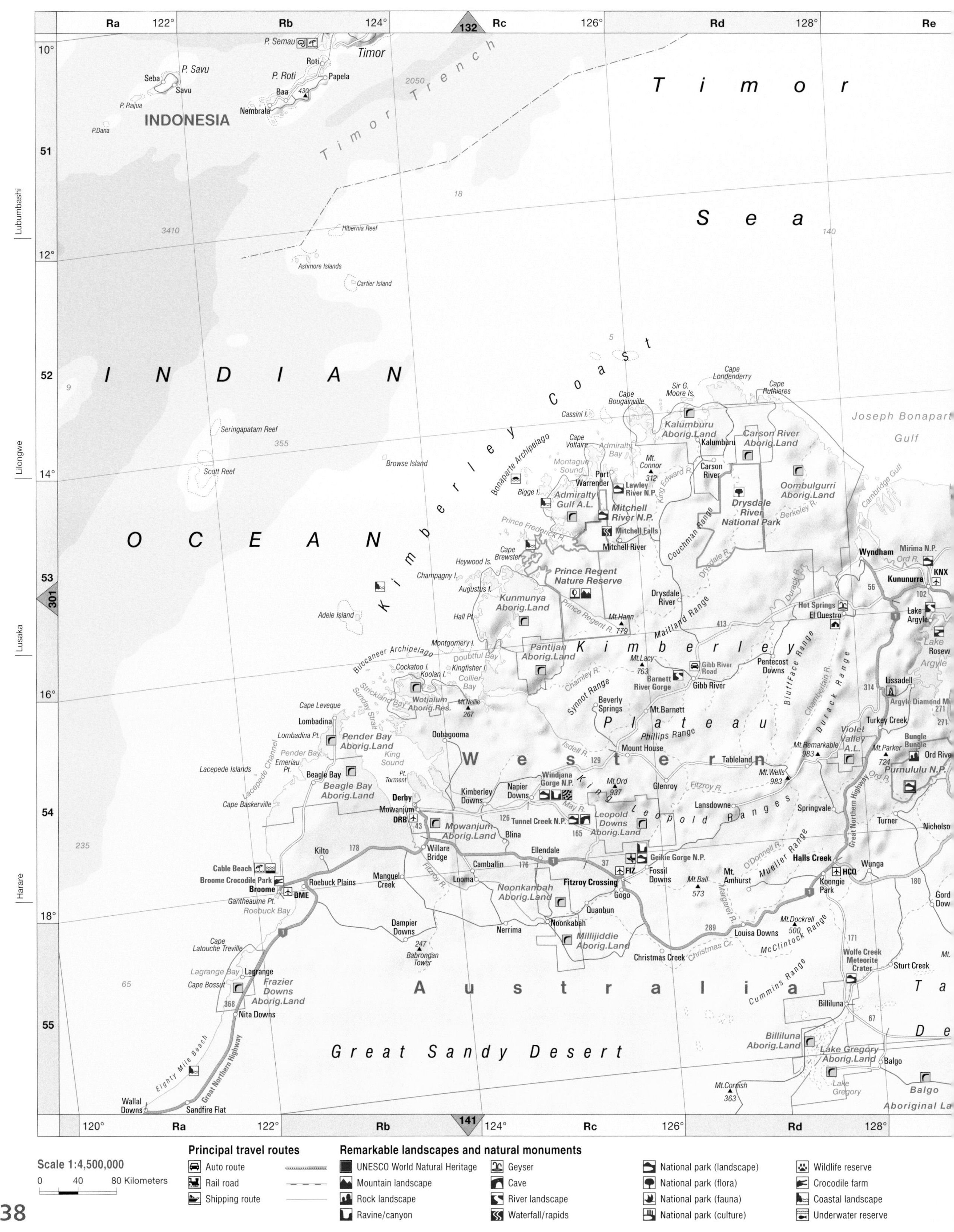

Ra 122° Rb 124° 132 Rc 126° Rd 128° Re

INDONESIA

P. Semau
Timor
P. Savu
Roti
Seba
P. Roti
Papela
Savu
Baa 430
Nembrala
P. Raijua
P.Dana

T i m o r

Timor Trench
2050

S e a

18

140

Hibernia Reef

Ashmore Islands
Cartier Island

I N D I A N

3410
9

Seringapatam Reef
355

Scott Reef

O C E A N

235

65

Kimberley Coast

Cape Londenderry
Cape Ruthieres
Sir G. Moore Is.
Cape Bougainville
Cassini I.
Kalumburu Aborig.Land
Kalumburu
Carson River Aborig.Land
Cape Voltaire
Admiralty Bay
Montague Sound
Mt. Connor 312
Carson River
Bigge I.
Port Warrender
Lawley River N.P.
Oombulgurri Aborig.Land
Admiralty Gulf A.L.
Mitchell River N.P.
Drysdale River National Park
Mitchell Falls
Mitchell River
Couchman Range
Berkeley R.
Cambridge Gulf
Joseph Bonaparte Gulf

Browse Island

Heywood Is.
Cape Brewster
Prince Regent Nature Reserve
Drysdale River
Wyndham
Mirima N.P.
Ord R.
Champagny I.
Augustus I.
Kunmunya Aborig.Land
Prince Frederick H.
Prince Regent R.
Maitland Range
Kununurra
KNX
Hall Pt.
Mt.Hann 779
Drysdale River
Durack R.
56
102
Hot Springs
El Questro
Lake Argyle
Adele Island
Lake Rosew Argyle

Buccaneer Archipelago
Montgomery I.
Doubtful Bay
Pantijan Aborig.Land
K i m b e r l e y
Mt.Lacy 763
Gibb River
Pentecost Downs
413
Cockatoo I.
Kingfisher I.
Collier Bay
Charnley R.
Barnett River Gorge
Gibb River Road
Bluttface Range
Chamberlain R.
Lissadell
314
Koolan I.
Beverly Springs
Mt.Barnett
Argyle Diamond Mi
271
Cape Leveque
Wotjalum Aborig.Res.
Mt.Nellie 267
P l a t e a u
Phillips Range
Turkey Creek
Lombadina
Synnot Range
Violet Valley A.L.
Bungle Bungle
Lombadina Pt.
Pender Bay Aborig.Land
Oobagooma
Mount House
Mt.Remarkable 983
Mt.Parker 724
Ord River
Emeriau Pt.
Isdell R.
W e s t e r n
129
Tableland
Purnululu N.P.
Beagle Bay
King Sound
Mt.Wells 983
Lacepede Islands
Pt. Torment
Windjana Gorge N.P.
Mt.Ord 937
Glenroy
Fitzroy R.
Beagle Bay Aborig.Land
Kimberley Downs
Napier Downs
May R.
L e o p o l d   R a n g e s
Cape Baskerville
Derby
126
Lansdowne
Springvale
Durack Range
Mowanjum
Tunnel Creek N.P.
Leopold Downs Aborig.Land
O'Donnell R.
Turner
Nicholso
DRB 43
Blina
165
Mueller Range
Kilto
Mowanjum Aborig.Land
Geikie Gorge N.P.
Halls Creek
Wunga
178
Willare Bridge
Ellendale
37
Mt. Amhurst
HCQ
Cable Beach
Camballin 176
FIZ
Fossil Downs
Koongie Park
180
Broome Crocodile Park
Roebuck Plains
Manguel Creek
Looma
Fitzroy Crossing
Mt.Ball 573
Margaret R.
Gord Dow
Broome
Gogo
BME
Gantheaume Pt.
Roebuck Bay
Dampier Downs
Nerrima
Noonkabah
Quanbun
289
Louisa Downs
Mt.Dockrell 500
McClintock Range
171
Cape Latouche Treville
Milljiddie Aborig.Land
Noonkanbah Aborig.Land
Christmas Creek
Christmas Cr.
Cummins Range
Wolfe Creek Meteorite Crater
Sturt Creek
Lagrange Bay
Lagrange
Babrongan Tower 247
A u s t r a l i a
Ta
Cape Bossut
Frazier Downs Aborig.Land
Billiluna
67
368
Nita Downs
Billiluna Aborig.Land
Balgo
55
Lake Gregory Aborig.Land
Mt.Cornish 363
Lake Gregory
Balgo Aboriginal La
Wallal Downs
G r e a t   S a n d y   D e s e r t
Eighty Mile Beach
Great Northern Highway
Sandfire Flat

120° Ra 122° Rb 141 124° Rc 126° Rd 128°

10° 51 12° 52 14° 53 301 16° 54 18° 55

Scale 1:4,500,000

0   40   80 Kilometers

138

Principal travel routes

- Auto route
- Rail road
- Shipping route
- ·········
- — — —
- ———

Remarkable landscapes and natural monuments

- UNESCO World Natural Heritage
- Mountain landscape
- Rock landscape
- Ravine/canyon
- Geyser
- Cave
- River landscape
- Waterfall/rapids
- National park (landscape)
- National park (flora)
- National park (fauna)
- National park (culture)
- Wildlife reserve
- Crocodile farm
- Coastal landscape
- Underwater reserve

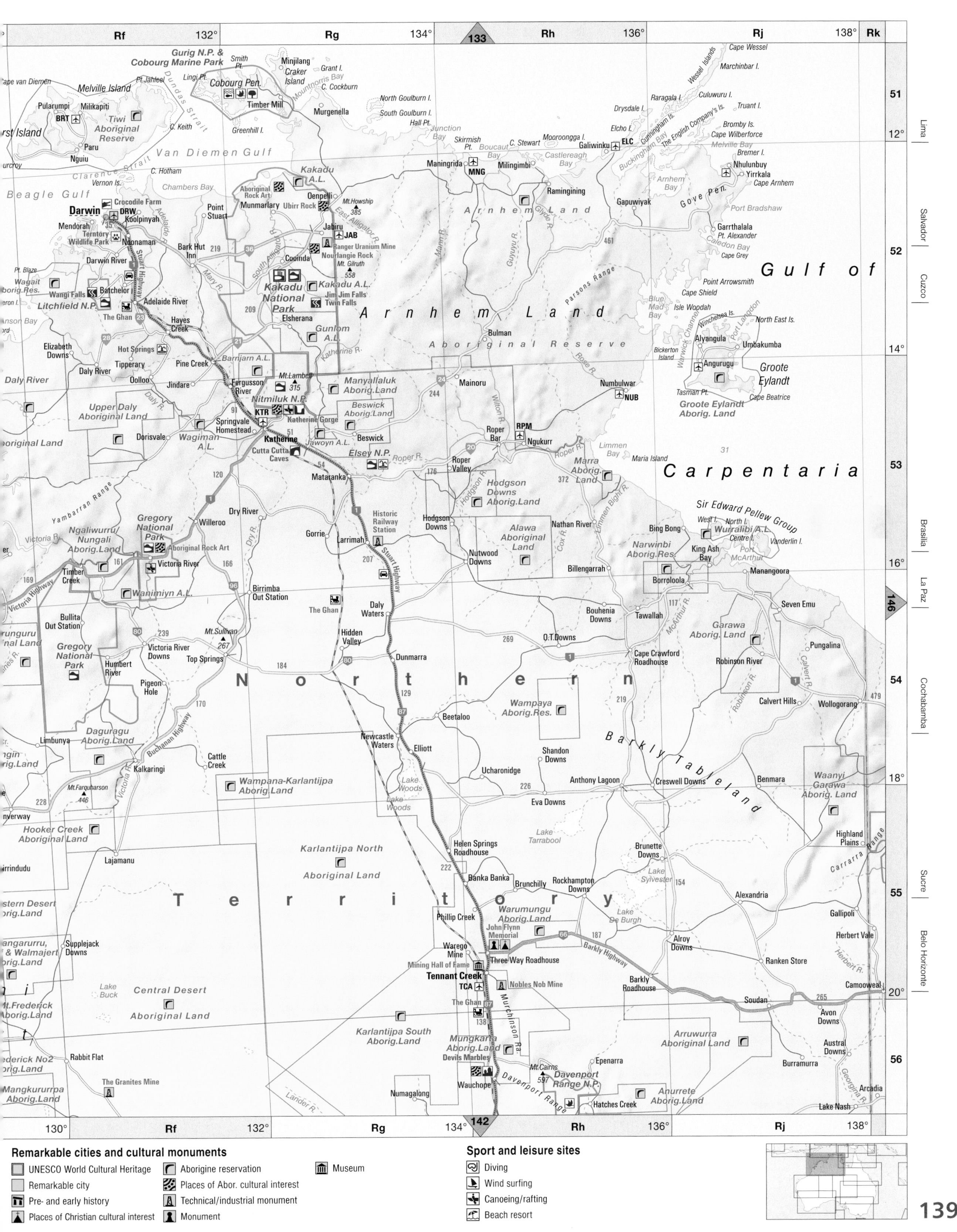

Map Labels

Lima
Salvador
Cuzco
Brasilia
La Paz
Cochabamba
Sucre
Belo Horizonte

51
12°
52
14°
53
16°
146
54
18°
55
20°
56

Gurig N.P. & Cobourg Marine Park
Smith Pt.
Minjilang
Craker Island
Grant I.
Cobourg Pen.
Lingi Pt.
C. Cockburn
Cape van Diemen
Melville Island
Pularumpi
Milikapiti
BRT
Tiwi Aboriginal Reserve
Paru
Nguiu
Timber Mill
Greenhill I.
Murgenella
North Goulburn I.
South Goulburn I.
Hall Pt.
Junction Bay
Skirmish Pt.
Boucaut Bay
C. Stewart
Mooroongga I.
Galiwinku
ELC
Cape Wessel
Wessel Islands
Marchinbar I.
Raragala I.
Culuwuru I.
Truant I.
Drysdale I.
Elcho I.
Bromby Is.
Cape Wilberforce
The English Company's Is.
Cunningham I.
Melville Bay
Nhulunbuy
Yirrkala
Cape Arnhem
Arnhem Bay
Gove Pen.
Port Bradshaw
Garrthalala
Pt. Alexander
Caledon Bay
Cape Grey
Point Arrowsmith
Cape Shield
Blue Mud Bay
Isle Woodah
North East Is.
Winchelsea Is.
Bickerton Island
Alyangula
Umbakumba
Groote Eylandt
Tasman Pt.
Angurugu
Groote Eylandt Aborig. Land
Cape Beatrice
Numbulwar
NUB

Gulf of Carpentaria

Beagle Gulf
Van Diemen Gulf
Clarence Strait
Chambers Bay
Point Stuart
Darwin
DRW
Koolpinyah
Crocodile Farm
Aboriginal Rock Art
Oenpelli
Munmarlary
Ubirr Rock
Mt.Howship 385
Kakadu A.L.
Maningrida
MNG
Milingimbi
Ramingining
Gapuwiyak
Mendorah
Terrnton Wildlife Park
Noonamah
Darwin River
Hayes Creek
Wangi Falls
Batchelor
Litchfield N.P.
The Ghan
Adelaide River
Jabiru
JAB
Ranger Uranium Mine
Nourlangie Rock
Mt. Gilruth 558
Cooinda
Kakadu National Park
Jim Jim Falls
Twin Falls
Kakadu A.L.
Elsherana
Gunlom A.L.
Bulman
Arnhem Land
Aboriginal Reserve
Main R.
Parsons Range
Mainoru
461
Wagait Aborig.Res.
Elizabeth Downs
Hot Springs
Pine Creek
Barnjarn A.L.
Mt.Lambell 315
Manyallaluk Aborig.Land
Mt. Howship
244
Wilton R.
Daly River
Tipperary
Oolloo
Jindare
Fergusson River
Nitmiluk N.P.
Beswick Aborig.Land
Springvale Homestead
KTR
Katherine Gorge
Beswick
Numbulwar
Upper Daly Aboriginal Land
Dorisvale
Wagiman A.L.
Katherine
Jawoyn A.L.
Elsey N.P.
Roper Bar
RPM
Ngukurr
Cutta Cutta Caves
Matarantka
Roper R.
Roper Valley
Marra Aborig. Land
Limmen Bight R.
Limmen Bight
Maria Island
31
Daly R.
Dry River
Willeroo
Historic Railway Station
Hodgson Downs Aborig.Land
Cox R.
372
Sir Edward Pellew Group
West I.
North I.
Wurralibi A.L.
Centre I.
Vanderlin I.
Yambarran Range
Gregory National Park
Gorrie
Larrimah
Hodgson Downs
Nathan River
Bing Bong
Narwinbi Aborig.Res.
King Ash Bay
Pt. McArthur
Manangoora
Ngaliwurru/ Nungali Aboriginal Land
Aboriginal Rock Art
Victoria River
161
166
207
Nutwood Downs
Alawa Aboriginal Land
Billengarrah
Borroloola
117
169
Timber Creek
Wahimiyn A.L.
96
Birrimba Out Station
The Ghan
Daly Waters
Bouhenia Downs
Tawallah
Seven Emu
Bullita Out Station
Mt.Sullivan 267
Hidden Valley
O.T.Downs
269
Cape Crawford Roadhouse
Robinson River
Pungalina
Gregory National Park
Humbert River
Victoria River Downs
Top Springs
184
Dunmarra
129
Wampaya Aborig.Res.
219
Calvert Hills
Wollogorang
479
Pigeon Hole
170
Beetaloo
Barkly Tableland
Daguragu Aborig.Land
Limbunya
Cattle Creek
Newcastle Waters
Elliott
Shandon Downs
Benmara
Kalkaringi
Mt.Farquharson 446
228
Lake Woods
Ucharonidge
Anthony Lagoon
Creswell Downs
Waanyi Garawa Aborig. Land
Hooker Creek Aboriginal Land
Lajamanu
Wampana-Karlantijpa Aboriginal Land
Lake Woods
Eva Downs
226
Highland Plains
Cararrra Range
Supplejack Downs
Karlantijpa North Aboriginal Land
Helen Springs Roadhouse
Lake Tarrabool
Brunette Downs
Alexandria
Mt.Frederick Aborig.Land
Banka Banka
Brunchilly
Rockhampton Downs
Lake Sylvester
154
Gallipoli
Mungarurru, & Walmajert Aborig.Land
222
Phillip Creek
Warumungu Aborig.Land
John Flynn Memorial
66
187
Alroy Downs
Herbert Vale
Central Desert Aboriginal Land
Lake Buck
Warego Mine
Three Way Roadhouse
Barkly Highway
Ranken Store
Camooweal
Mining Hall of Fame
Tennant Creek
TCA
Nobles Nob Mine
The Ghan
Barkly Roadhouse
Soudan
265
Frederick No2 Aborig.Land
Rabbit Flat
The Granites Mine
Karlantijpa South Aborig.Land
Mungkarta Aborig.Land
Devils Marbles
138
Mt.Cairns 597
Davenport Range N.P.
Arruwurra Aboriginal Land
Avon Downs
Austral Downs
Mangkururrpa Aborig.Land
Numagalong
Wauchope
Davenport Range
Epenarra
Anurrete Aboriginal Land
Burramurra
Hatches Creek
Lake Nash
Arcadia

Northern Territory

Lander R.
Davenport Ra.
Murchison Ra.
Buchanan Highway
Victoria Highway
Stuart Highway

Legend

Remarkable cities and cultural monuments

- ☐ UNESCO World Cultural Heritage
- ☐ Remarkable city
- 🛉 Pre- and early history
- ◼ Places of Christian cultural interest
- ◫ Aborigine reservation
- ▨ Places of Abor. cultural interest
- ⛏ Technical/industrial monument
- ♦ Monument
- 🏛 Museum

Sport and leisure sites

- 🤿 Diving
- 🏄 Wind surfing
- 🛶 Canoeing/rafting
- 🏖 Beach resort

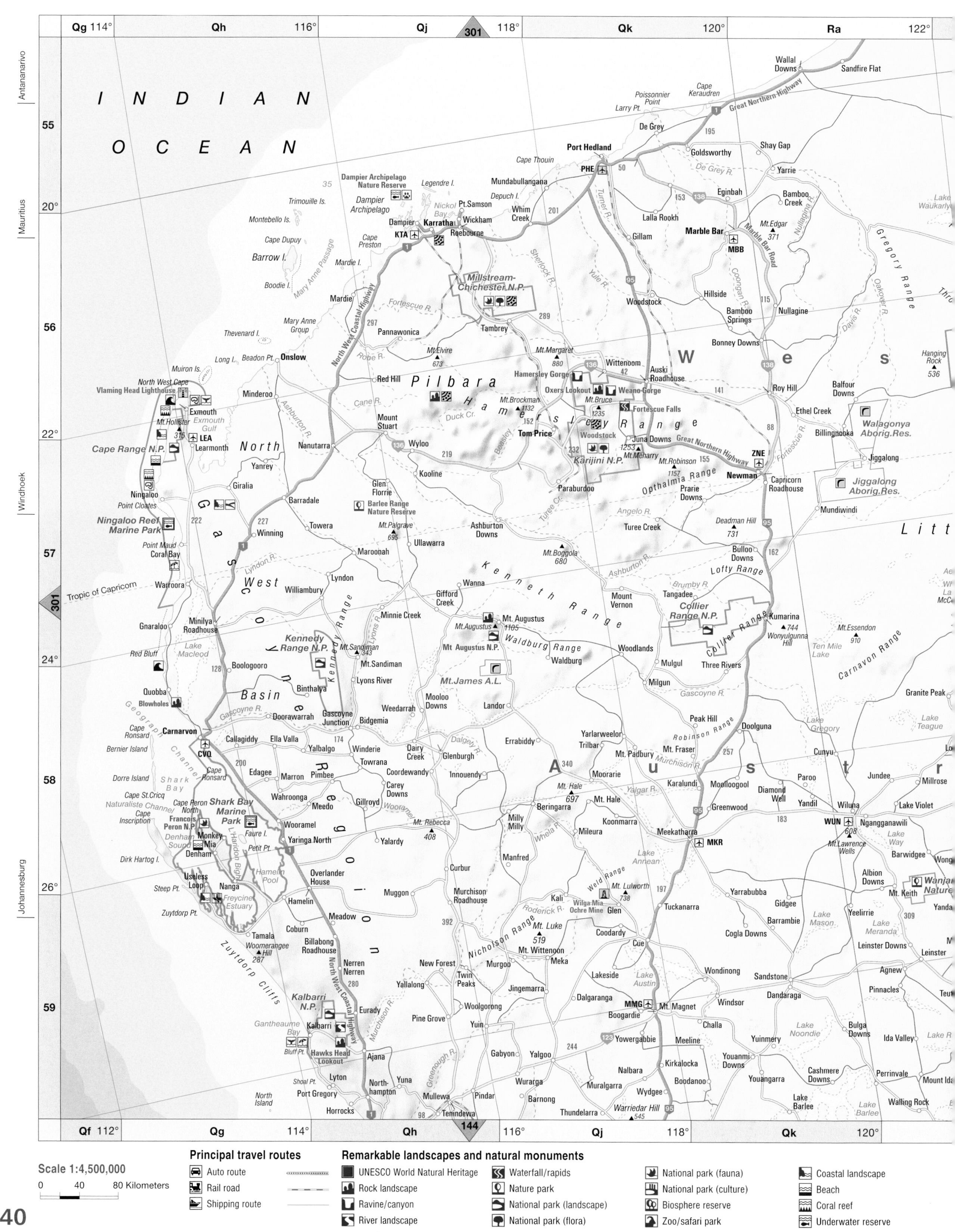

Scale 1:4,500,000

0   40   80 Kilometers

Principal travel routes

🚗 Auto route
🚃 Rail road
⚓ Shipping route

Remarkable landscapes and natural monuments

■ UNESCO World Natural Heritage
■ Rock landscape
■ Ravine/canyon
■ River landscape

■ Waterfall/rapids
■ Nature park
■ National park (landscape)
■ National park (flora)

■ National park (fauna)
■ National park (culture)
■ Biosphere reserve
■ Zoo/safari park

■ Coastal landscape
■ Beach
■ Coral reef
■ Underwater reserve

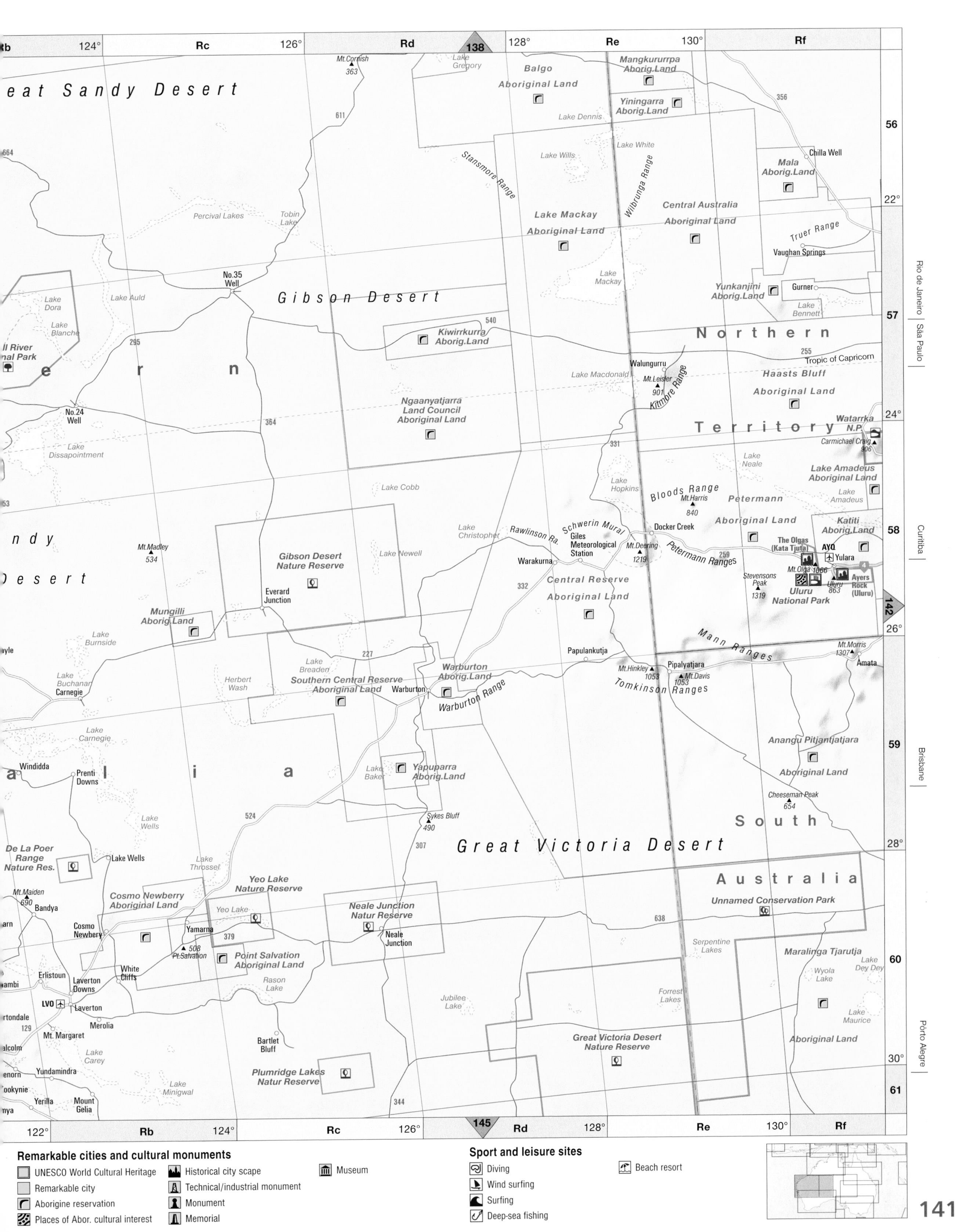

Great Sandy Desert
Gibson Desert
Great Victoria Desert
Western Australia
Northern Territory
South Australia
Balgo Aboriginal Land
Mangkururrpa Aborig.Land
Yiningarra Aborig.Land
Lake Gregory
Mt.Cornish 363
Lake Dennis
Lake White
Lake Wills
Stansmore Range
Wilbrunga Range
Mala Aborig.Land
Chilla Well
Central Australia Aboriginal Land
Lake Mackay Aboriginal Land
Lake Mackay
Truer Range
Vaughan Springs
Percival Lakes
Tobin Lake
No.35 Well
Lake Auld
Lake Dora
Lake Blanche
Yunkanjini Aborig.Land
Gurner
Lake Bennett
Kiwirrkurra Aborig.Land
Walungurru
Mt.Leisler 901
Kintore Range
Lake Macdonald
Tropic of Capricorn
Haasts Bluff Aboriginal Land
No.24 Well
Lake Dissapointment
Ngaanyatjarra Land Council Aboriginal Land
Watarrka N.P.
Carmichael Craig 906
Lake Neale
Lake Hopkins
Bloods Range
Mt.Harris 840
Petermann Aboriginal Land
Lake Amadeus Aboriginal Land
Lake Amadeus
Lake Cobb
Lake Christopher
Rawlinson Ra.
Schwerin Mural
Giles Meteorological Station
Docker Creek
Mt.Deering 1219
Petermann Ranges
Katiti Aborig.Land
The Olgas (Kata Tjuta)
AYQ
Yulara
Mt.Olga 1066
Uluru 863
Ayers Rock (Uluru)
Uluru National Park
Stevensons Peak 1319
Mt.Madley 534
Gibson Desert Nature Reserve
Lake Newell
Warakurna
Everard Junction
Central Reserve Aboriginal Land
Mungilli Aborig.Land
Lake Burnside
Mann Ranges
Mt.Morris 1307
Amata
Papulankutja
Lake Breaden
Herbert Wash
Lake Buchanan
Carnegie
Southern Central Reserve Aboriginal Land
Warburton
Warburton Aborig.Land
Warburton Range
Mt.Hinkley 1053
Pipalyatjara
Mt.Davis 1053
Tomkinson Ranges
Lake Carnegie
Anangu Pitjantjatjara Aboriginal Land
Windidda
Prenti Downs
Lake Baker
Yapuparra Aborig.Land
Cheeseman Peak 654
Lake Wells
Sykes Bluff 490
De La Poer Range Nature Res.
Lake Throssel
Yeo Lake Nature Reserve
Yeo Lake
Mt.Maiden 690
Bandya
Cosmo Newberry Aboriginal Land
Cosmo Newberry
Yamarna
Pt.Salvation 508
Point Salvation Aboriginal Land
Neale Junction Natur Reserve
Neale Junction
Unnamed Conservation Park
Serpentine Lakes
Maralinga Tjarutja Aboriginal Land
Lake Dey Dey
Wyola Lake
Lake Maurice
Erlistoun
Laverton Downs
White Cliffs
Rason Lake
Jubilee Lake
Forrest Lakes
LVO
Laverton
Merolia
Mt. Margaret
Bartlet Bluff
Great Victoria Desert Nature Reserve
Lake Carey
Yundamindra
Plumridge Lakes Natur Reserve
Lake Minigwal
Yerilla
Mount Gelia
Rio de Janeiro
São Paulo
Curitiba
Brisbane
Pôrto Alegre
Remarkable cities and cultural monuments
UNESCO World Cultural Heritage
Remarkable city
Aborigine reservation
Places of Abor. cultural interest
Historical city scape
Technical/industrial monument
Monument
Memorial
Museum
Sport and leisure sites
Diving
Wind surfing
Surfing
Deep-sea fishing
Beach resort

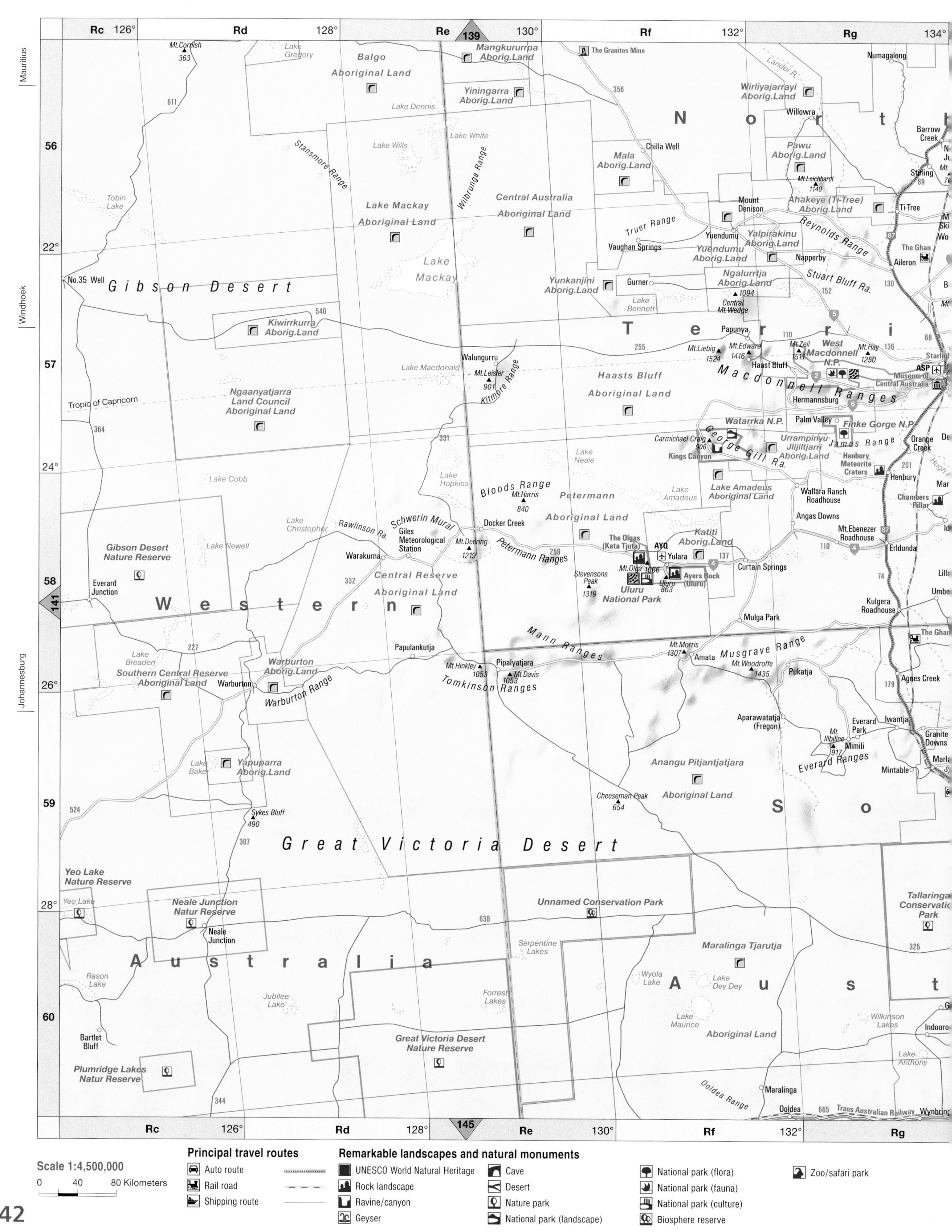

Scale 1:4,500,000

0   40   80 Kilometers

Principal travel routes

- Auto route
- Rail road
- Shipping route

.... UNESCO World Natural Heritage
— — — Rock landscape
——— Ravine/canyon
Geyser

Remarkable landscapes and natural monuments

- UNESCO World Natural Heritage
- Rock landscape
- Ravine/canyon
- Geyser
- National park (landscape)

- Cave
- Desert
- Nature park

- National park (flora)
- National park (fauna)
- National park (culture)
- Biosphere reserve

- Zoo/safari park

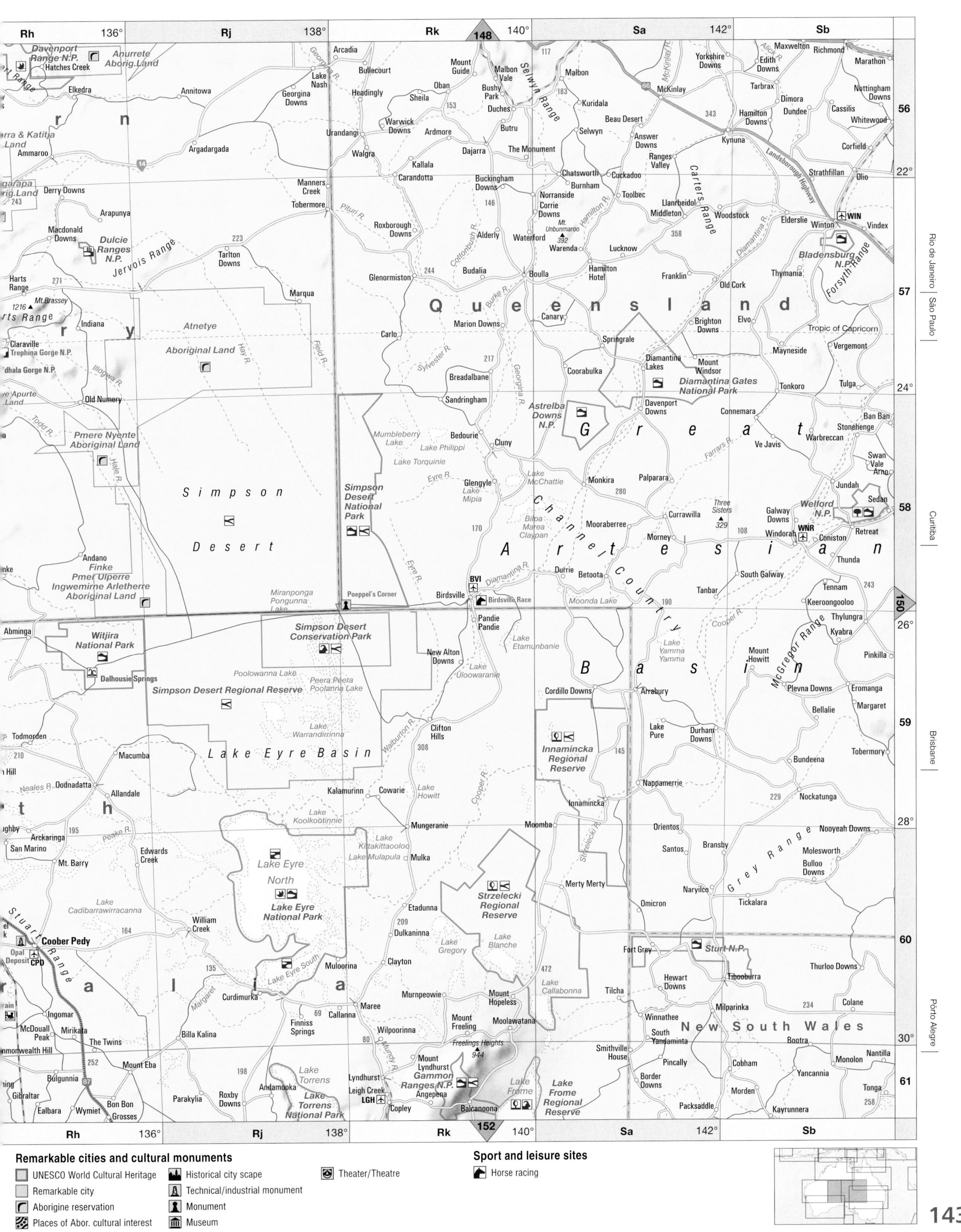

Davenport
Range N.P. Anurrete
Hatches Creek Aborig.Land

Elkedra Annitowa Lake Arcadia
Nash Bullecourt Mount Malbon Malbon 117 Yorkshire Maxwelton Richmond
Guide Vale Downs Edith Marathon
Georgina Headingly Oban Bushy 66 McKinlay Downs Tarbrax
Downs Sheila Park Duches McKinlay 183 Hamilton Dimora Nottingham
Ammaroo Argadargada Sheila 153 Duches Kuridala 343 Downs Dundee Downs
arra & Katitja Walgra Duches Selwyn Cassilis Whitewood
Land Urandangi Ardmore Dajarra The Monument Answer Beau Desert Strathfillan Olio
garapa Manners Carandotta Buckingham Downs Ranges Kynuna Corfield
rig.Land Derry Downs Creek Downs Norranside Valley Eldersie Winton WIN
243 Tobermore Roxborough Alderly Corrie Toolbec Middleton Woodstock Vindex
Arapunya Macdonald Downs Downs Waterford Mt. Llanrheidol Old Cork Bladensburg
Downs 223 Glenormiston Budalia Boulla Unbunmaroo 358 N.P. Forsyth Range
Harts 271 Tarlton Marqua 244 392 Hamilton Thymania
Range Jervois Range Downs Warenda Hotel Franklin
1216 Mt.Brassey Queensland Lucknow
rts Range Indiana Marion Downs Boulla Hamilton Brighton Elvo
Claraville Atnetye Carlo Hotel Downs Tropic of Capricorn
Trephina Gorge N.P. Aboriginal Land Canary Springrale Mayneside Vergemont
dhala Gorge N.P. Sylvester R. 217 Diamantina Mount
e Apurte Old Numery Breadalbane Coorabulka Lakes Windsor Tonkoro Tulga
Land Pmere Nyente Sandringham Georgina R. Diamantina Gates
Aboriginal Land Astrelba National Park Ban Ban
Mumbleberry Bedourie Downs Davenport Stonehenge
Simpson Lake Lake Philippi Cluny N.P. G Downs Connemara Warbreccan
Lake Torquinie Glengyle Lake Farrars R. Ve Javis Swan
Desert Eyre R. Glengyle McChattie Monkira Palparara Vale Arno
Simpson Lake Great Jundah
Desert Mipia Biloa Three Welford
Hale R. National Mooraberree Marea Sisters Galway N.P.
Andano Park Claypan 170 Currawilla 329 Downs Sedan
Finke 280 Morney Windorah WNR
Pmer Ulperre Eyre R. Glengyle 108 Coniston
Ingwemirne Arletherre Durrie Betoota South Galway Retreat
Aboriginal Land Miranponga BVI Thunda
Poeppel's Corner Birdsville Diamantina R. Tanbar Tennam 243
Abminga Pongunna Simpson Desert Birdsville Race Moonda Lake 190 Keeroongooloo
Lake Conservation Park Pandie Cooper R. Thylungra
Witjira Poolowanna Lake Pandie Lake McGregor Range Kyabra
National Park New Alton Etamunbanie Lake Pinkilla
Dalhousie Springs Downs Lake Yamma
Simpson Desert Regional Reserve Uloowaranie Yamma Mount
Peera Peeta Howitt Plevna Downs Eromanga
Todmorden Poolanna Lake Clifton B a s i n Bellalie Margaret
Macumba Lake Hills Cordillo Downs Arrabury
Warrandirrinna 308 Lake Durham Tobermory
Neales R. Oodnadatta Lake Eyre Basin Pure Downs
Allandale Walburton R. Innamincka Bundeena
Hill Kalamurinn Regional 145 Nappamerrie 229 Nockatunga
Arckaringa 195 Cowarie Lake Reserve
San Marino Peake R. Koolkootinnie Howitt Innamincka Orientos Nooyeah Downs
Mt. Barry Mungeranie Moomba Santos Bransby Molesworth
Edwards Lake Bulloo
Creek Kittakittaooloo Mulka Merty Merty Naryilco Downs
Lake Mulapula Tickalara
Lake Eyre Omicron
Lake North Etadunna
Cadibarrawirracanna Lake Eyre 209 Strzelecki
William National Park Dulkaninna Regional Fort Grey Sturt N.P.
Creek Reserve Hewart
Coober Pedy 164 Lake Thurloo Downs
Opal Gregory Lake Downs Tiboburra
Deposit CPD Muloorina Clayton Blanche Winnathee Colane
Lake Eyre South Maree Lake South
135 Curdimurka Callabonna Milparinka 234
Murnpeowie Mount Tilcha
Finniss 69 Callanna Hopeless Smithville
Ingomar Springs Wilpoorinna Moolawatana House New South Wales
McDouall Mirikata Murdy R. 472 Pincally Cobham
Peak The Twins Lake Mount Freelings Heights Lake Bootra
Mount Eba Torrens Freeling 944 Frome Border Monolon Nantilla
252 Andamooka Mount Downs Yancannia
Bulgunnia Lyndhurst Lyndhurst Lake Winnathee
Gibraltar Parakylia Roxby Leigh Creek Gammon Frome Packsaddle Morden
Ealbara Wymiet Downs Copley Ranges N.P. Regional Tonga 258
Bon Bon Lake Angepena Lake Reserve Kayrunnera
Grosses Torrens Balcanoona Frome

Remarkable cities and cultural monuments

⬚ UNESCO World Cultural Heritage ♜ Historical city scape 🎭 Theater/Theatre

⬚ Remarkable city 🅰 Technical/industrial monument

⌐ Aborigine reservation 🗿 Monument

🔲 Places of Abor. cultural interest 🏛 Museum

Sport and leisure sites

🏇 Horse racing

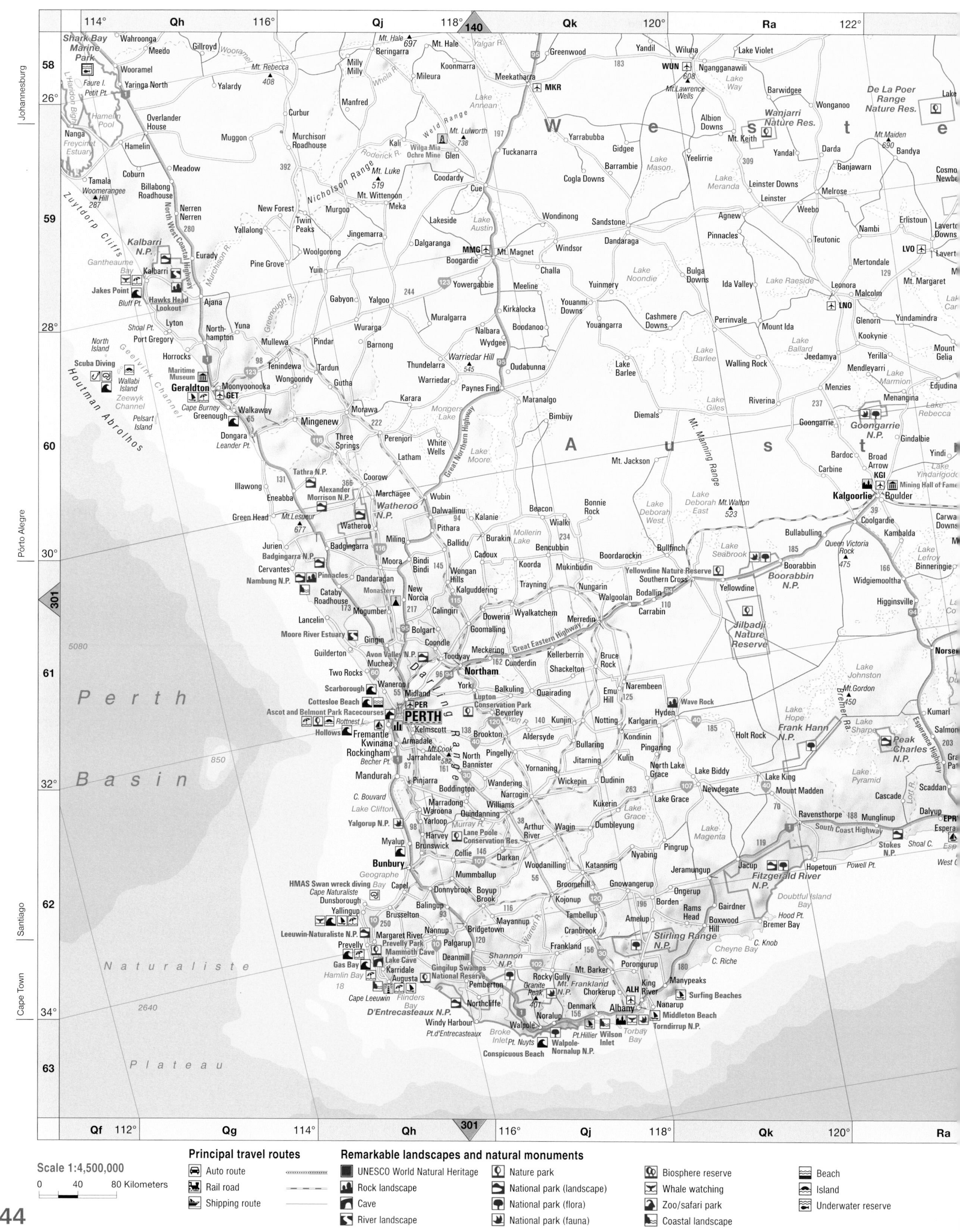

Scale 1:4,500,000

0   40   80 Kilometers

Principal travel routes
- Auto route
- Rail road
- Shipping route

Remarkable landscapes and natural monuments
- UNESCO World Natural Heritage
- Rock landscape
- Cave
- River landscape
- Nature park
- National park (landscape)
- National park (flora)
- National park (fauna)
- Biosphere reserve
- Whale watching
- Zoo/safari park
- Coastal landscape
- Beach
- Island
- Underwater reserve

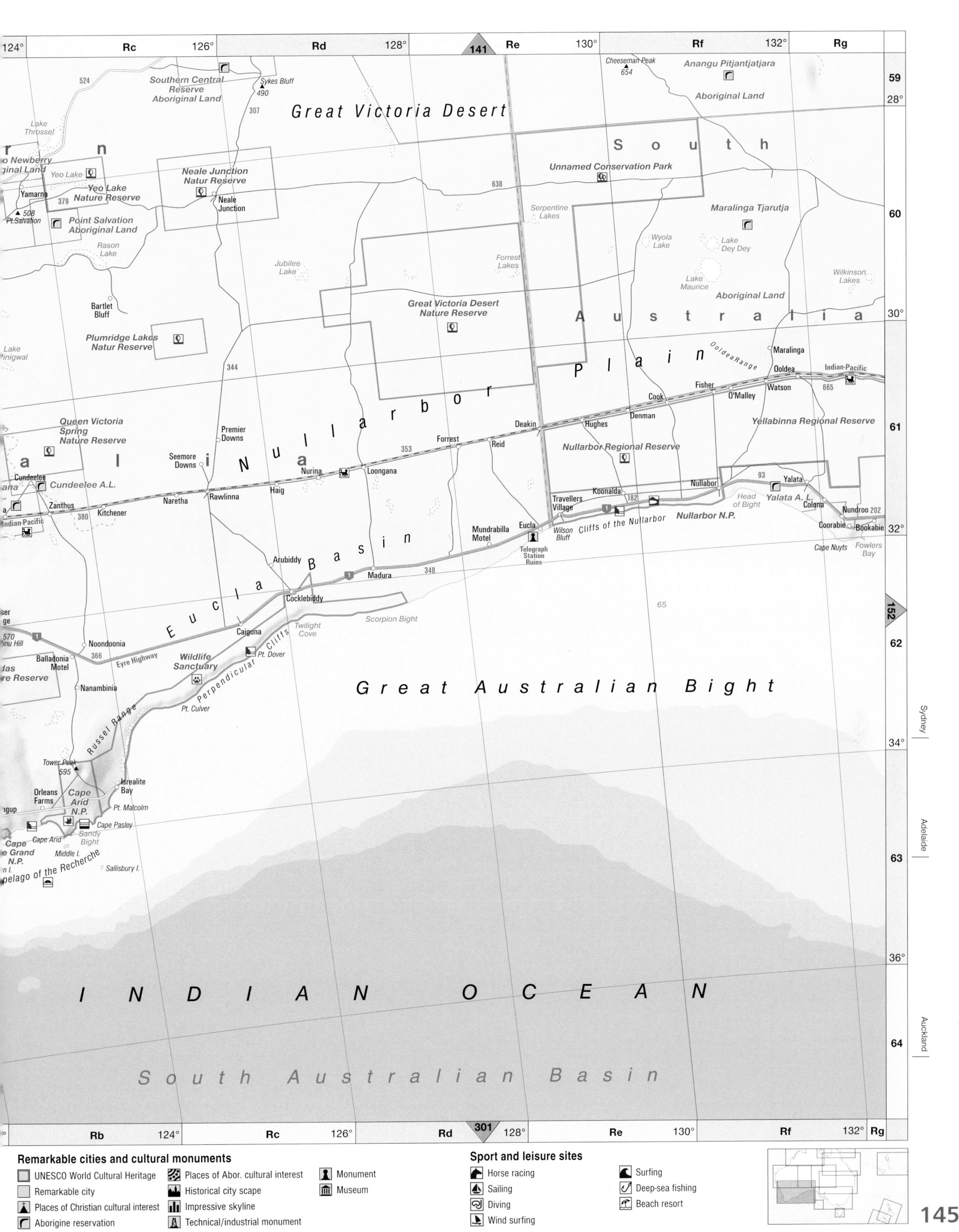

Cheeseman Peak
654

Anangu Pitjantjatjara

Southern Central
Reserve
Aboriginal Land

Sykes Bluff
490

524

307

59
28°

Great Victoria Desert

Aboriginal Land

S o u t h

Lake
Throssel

Newberry
ginal Land

Yeo Lake

Neale Junction
Natur Reserve

Unnamed Conservation Park

638

Serpentine
Lakes

Maralinga Tjarutja

60

Yamarna

Yeo Lake
Nature Reserve

379

Neale
Junction

508
Pt. Salvation

Point Salvation
Aboriginal Land

Rason
Lake

Jubilee
Lake

Forrest
Lakes

A u s t r a l i a

Wyola
Lake

Lake
Dey Dey

Aboriginal Land

Wilkinson
Lakes

Bartlet
Bluff

Great Victoria Desert
Nature Reserve

Lake
inigwal

Plumridge Lakes
Natur Reserve

344

P l a i n

Ooldea Range

Maralinga

Lake
Maurice

30°

Ooldea

Indian-Pacific

Queen Victoria
Spring
Nature Reserve

Premier
Downs

N u l l a r b o r

353

Forrest

Reid

Deakin

Fisher

O'Malley

Cook

Denman

Watson

665

Hughes

61

a

l

i

Seemore
Downs

Nurina

Loongana

Nullarbor Regional Reserve

Yellabinna Regional Reserve

Cundeelee

Cundeelee A.L.

Rawlinna

Haig

Naretha

93

Nullabor

Yalata

ana

Zanthus

Kitchener

Indian-Pacific

380

Travellers
Village

Koonalda

182

Yalata A. L.

Colona

Head
of Bight

Nundroo 202

Arubiddy

B a s i n

Mundrabilla
Motel

Eucla

Wilson
Bluff

Cliffs of the Nullarbor

Nullarbor N.P.

Coorabie

32°
Bookabie

Madura

348

Telegraph
Station
Ruins

Cape Nuyts

Fowlers
Bay

Cocklebiddy

E u c l a

65

◄**152**►

Scorpion Bight

Noondoonia

570
nu Hill

366

Caiguna

Twilight
Cove

62

Balladonia
Motel

Eyre Highway

Wildlife
Sanctuary

Pt. Dover

Perpendicular Cliffs

Nanambinia

Pt. Culver

Great   Australian   Bight

Russel Range

34°

Tower Peak
595

Isrealite
Bay

Orleans
Farms

Cape
Arid
N.P.

Pt. Malcolm

ngup

Cape Pasley

63

Cape
e Grand
N.P.

Cape Arid

Sandy
Bight

Middle I.

pelago of the Recherche

Sallisbury I.

I N D I A N   O C E A N

36°

South   Australian   Basin

64

Sydney

Adelaide

Auckland

Remarkable cities and cultural monuments

- ☐ UNESCO World Cultural Heritage
- ☐ Remarkable city
- ▲ Places of Christian cultural interest
- ⬓ Aborigine reservation
- ⬕ Places of Abor. cultural interest
- 🏰 Historical city scape
- 📊 Impressive skyline
- Ⓐ Technical/industrial monument
- 🧍 Monument
- 🏛 Museum

Sport and leisure sites

- 🏇 Horse racing
- ⛵ Sailing
- 🤿 Diving
- 🏄 Wind surfing
- 🏄 Surfing
- 🎣 Deep-sea fishing
- 🏖 Beach resort

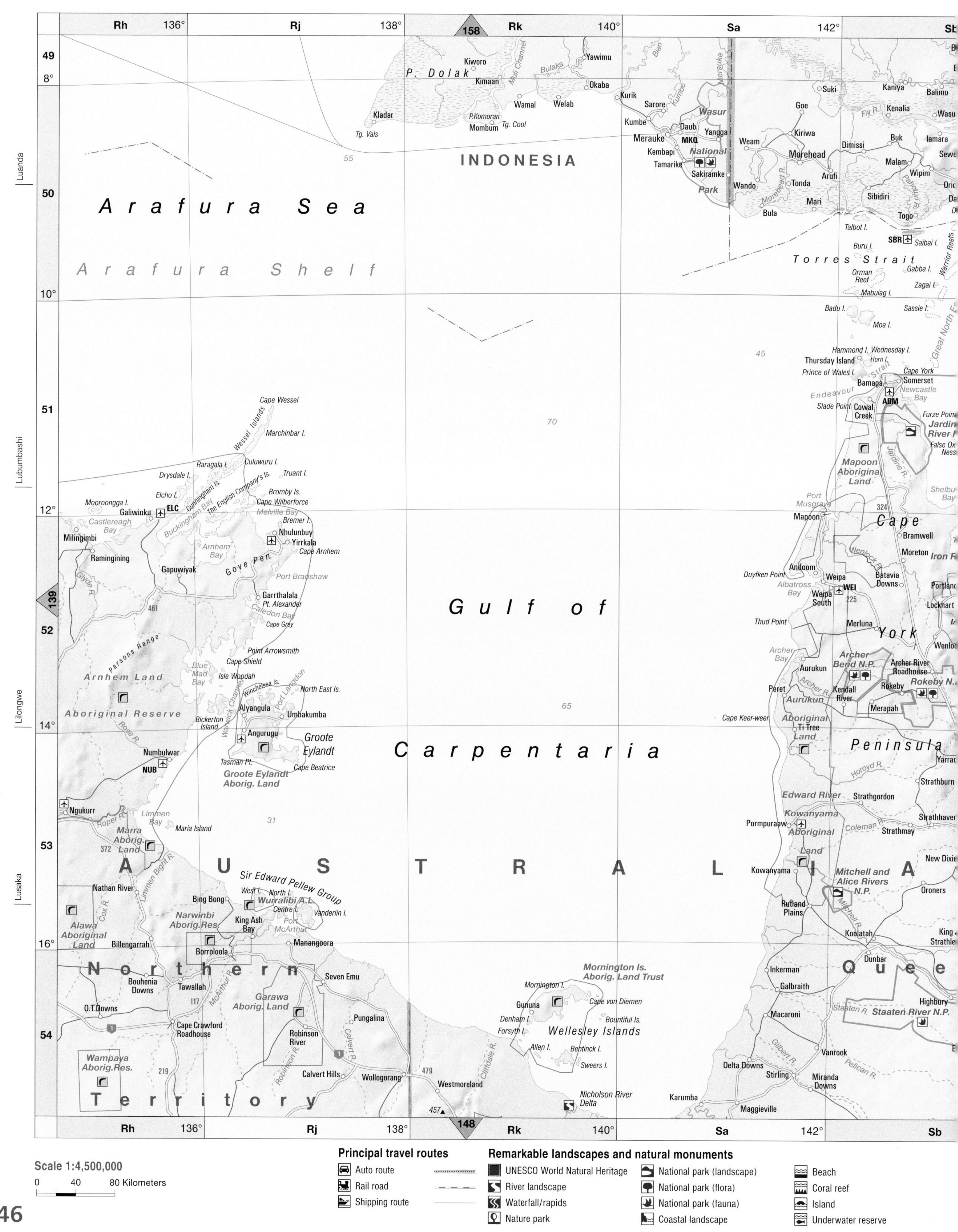

Northern Australia

| | Rh | 136° | | Rj | 138° | 158 | Rk | 140° | | Sa | 142° | Sb |

49
8°
Luanda

Arafura Sea

Arafura Shelf

P. Dolak
Kiworo
Kimaan
P.Komoran
Mombum
Tg. Cool
Kladar
Tg. Vals
Wamal
Welab
Okaba
Kurik
Sarore
Kumbe
Merauke
MKQ
Kembapi
Tamarike
Sakiramke
Wando
Bula
Daub
Yangga
National
Park
Weam
Mari
Tonda
Morehead R.
Bian
Kumbe
Wasur
Goe
Kiriwa
Morehead
Dimissi
Malam
Wipim
Arufi
Sibidiri
Togo
Suki
Kaniya
Balimo
Iamara
Sewe
Ori
D

INDONESIA

55

Torres Strait
Talbot I.
SBR
Saibai I.
Buru I.
Orman Reef
Gabba I.
Zagai I.
Mabuiag I.
Warrior Reefs

50

10°

45
70
65
31
479
457▲

Badu I.
Moa I.
Sassie I.
Hammond I.   Wednesday I.
Thursday Island   Horn I.
Prince of Wales I.
Endeavour
Slade Point
Cowal Creek
Bamaga
ABM
Cape York
Somerset
Newcastle Bay
Furze Point
Jardin
River N
False Ox
Ness

51
Lubumbashi

Cape Wessel
Marchinbar I.
Wessel Islands
Raragala I.   Culuwuru I.
Drysdale I.   Truant I.
Elcho I.   Bromby Is.
Galiwinku   ELC   Cape Wilberforce
Mooroongga I.   The English Company's Is.
Cunningham Is.   Melville Bay
Milingimbi   Buckingham Bay   Bremer I.
Castlereagh Bay   Nhulunbuy
Ramingining   Yirrkala
Gapuwiyak   Cape Arnhem
Arnhem Bay   Port Bradshaw
Gove Pen.
Garrthalala
Pt. Alexander
Caledon Bay
Cape Grey

Shelbu
Bay
Mapoon
Aboriginal
Land
Port
Musgrave
Mapoon
324
Cape
Bramwell
Moreton
Iron R
Portland
Lockhart
Merluna
Archer
Bay
Wenlo
Aurukun
Archer
Bend N.P.   Archer River Roadhouse
Kendall River   Rokeby   Rokeby N.
Peret
Aurukun
Merapah
Cape Keer-weer
Aboriginal
Ti Tree
Land
Peninsula
Yarrac
Strathburn

12°

Gulf of

Duyfken Point
Anidoom   Weipa   WEI
Albatross Bay   Weipa South   225
Thud Point

52
139

461

Parsons Range
Arnhem Land
Aboriginal Reserve
Blue Mud Bay
Isle Woodah
Cape Shield
Point Arrowsmith
Winchelsea Is.
North East Is.
Alyangula
Umbakumba
Bickerton Island
Angurugu
Groote Eylandt
Groote Eylandt
Aborig. Land
Tasman Pt.
Cape Beatrice
Numbulwar
NUB

York

Carpentaria

Glyde R.
Rose R.
Warwick Channel
Port Langdon

14°

Lilongwe

Ngukurr
Marra
Aborig.
Land   372
Roper R.
Limmen Bight R.
Cox R.
Limmen Bay
Maria Island
Nathan River
Alawa
Aboriginal
Land
Billengarrah
Bouhenia Downs
O.T.Downs
Cape Crawford
Roadhouse
Wampaya
Aborig.Res.   219
Borroloola
Bing Bong
West I.   North I.
Wuiralibi A.L.
Centre
Vanderlin I.
King Ash Bay
Port McArthur
Manangoora
Tawallah   117
Garawa
Aborig. Land
Robinson
River
Calvert Hills
Seven Emu
Pungalina
Wollogorang
McArthur R.
Robinson R.
Calvert R.
Clyde R.
Cliffdale R.

AUSTRALIA

Sir Edward Pellew Group

Mitchell and
Alice Rivers
N.P.
Rutland Plains
Kowanyama
Kowanyama
Aboriginal
Land
Pormpuraaw
Edward River
Strathgordon
Strathmay
Strathhaven
New Dixie
Oroners
Koolatah
Koorboora
Inkerman
Galbraith
Macaroni
Highbury
Staaten River N.P.
Dunbar
Delta Downs
Vanrook
Stirling
Karumba
Miranda Downs
Maggieville
Gilbert R.
Pelican R.
Staaten R.
Horoyd R.
Coleman R.
Mitchell R.

Queenslan

15
16°

Northern

Territory

53
54

Mornington Is.
Aborig. Land Trust
Mornington I.
Gununa
Denham I.
Forsyth I.
Wellesley Islands
Allen I.
Bentinck I.
Sweers I.
Nicholson River
Delta
Westmoreland
Cape von Diemen
Bountiful Is.

Lusaka

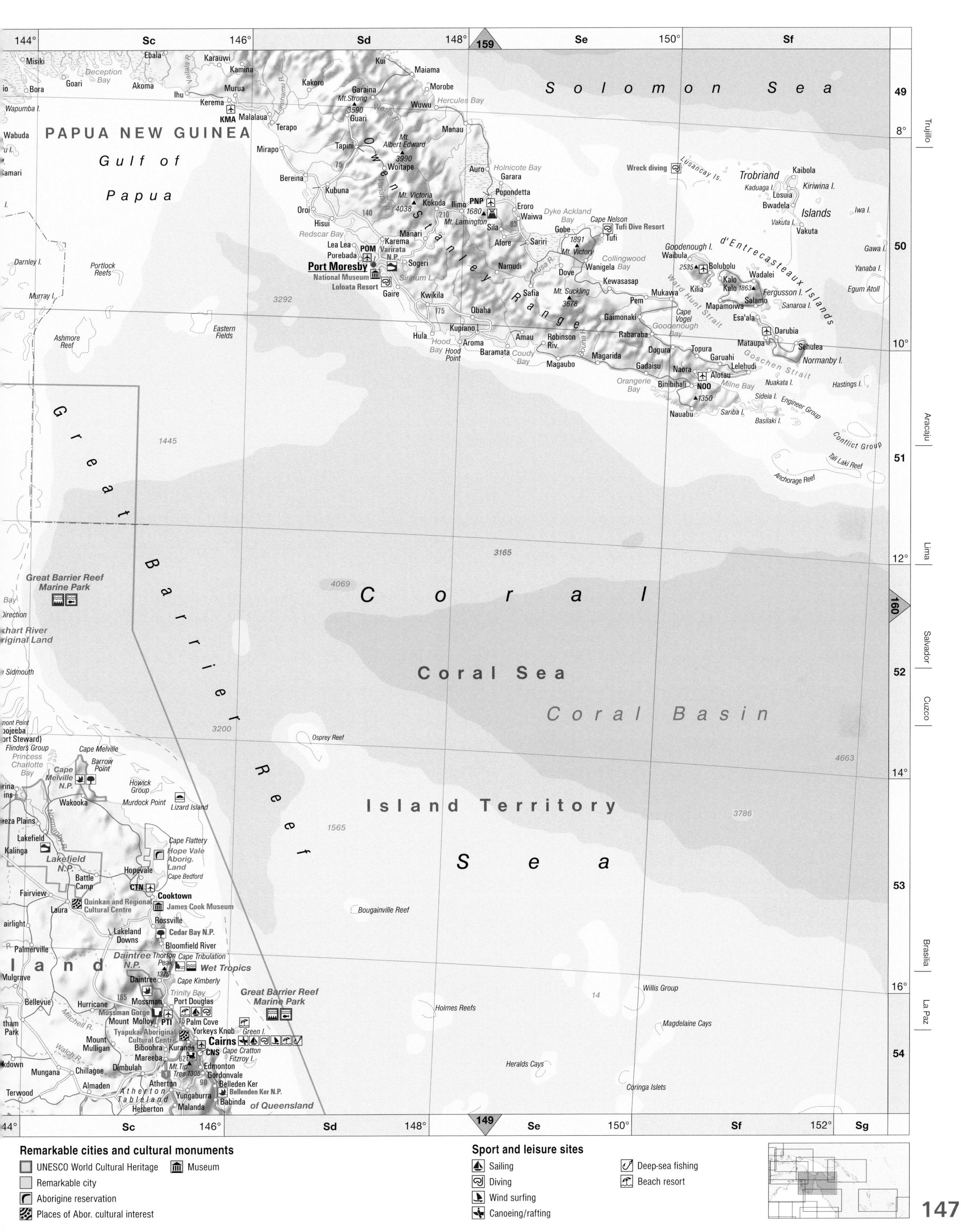

Remarkable cities and cultural monuments

- ▢ UNESCO World Cultural Heritage
- 🏛 Museum
- ▢ Remarkable city
- ⬕ Aborigine reservation
- ▨ Places of Abor. cultural interest

Sport and leisure sites

- ⛵ Sailing
- 🤿 Diving
- 🏄 Wind surfing
- 🛶 Canoeing/rafting
- 🎣 Deep-sea fishing
- 🏖 Beach resort

147

Northeastern Australia, Great Barrier Reef

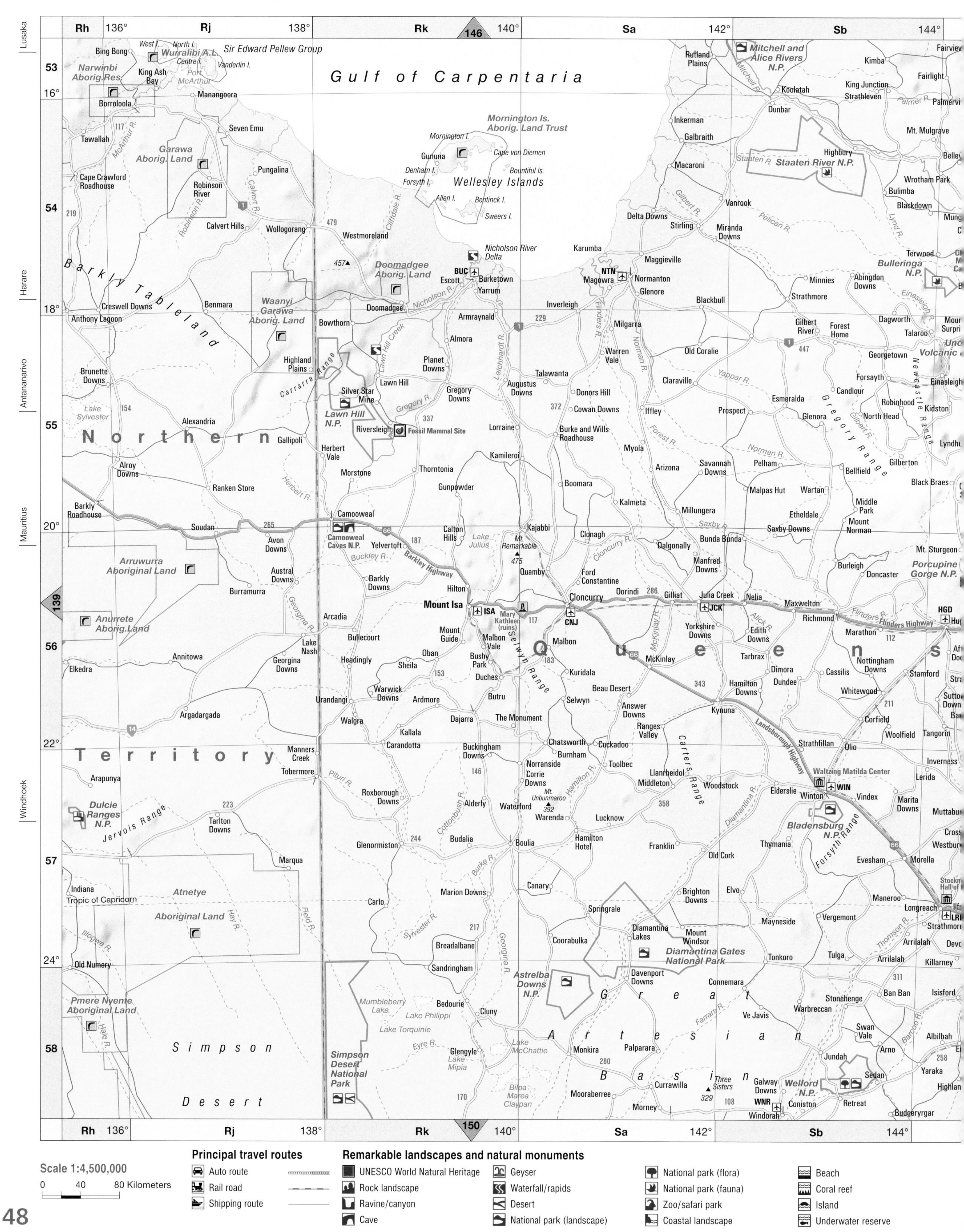

Scale 1:4,500,000

0   40   80 Kilometers

Principal travel routes

- Auto route
- Rail road
- Shipping route

Remarkable landscapes and natural monuments

- UNESCO World Natural Heritage
- Rock landscape
- Ravine/canyon
- Cave
- Geyser
- Waterfall/rapids
- Desert
- National park (landscape)
- National park (flora)
- National park (fauna)
- Zoo/safari park
- Coastal landscape
- Beach
- Coral reef
- Island
- Underwater reserve

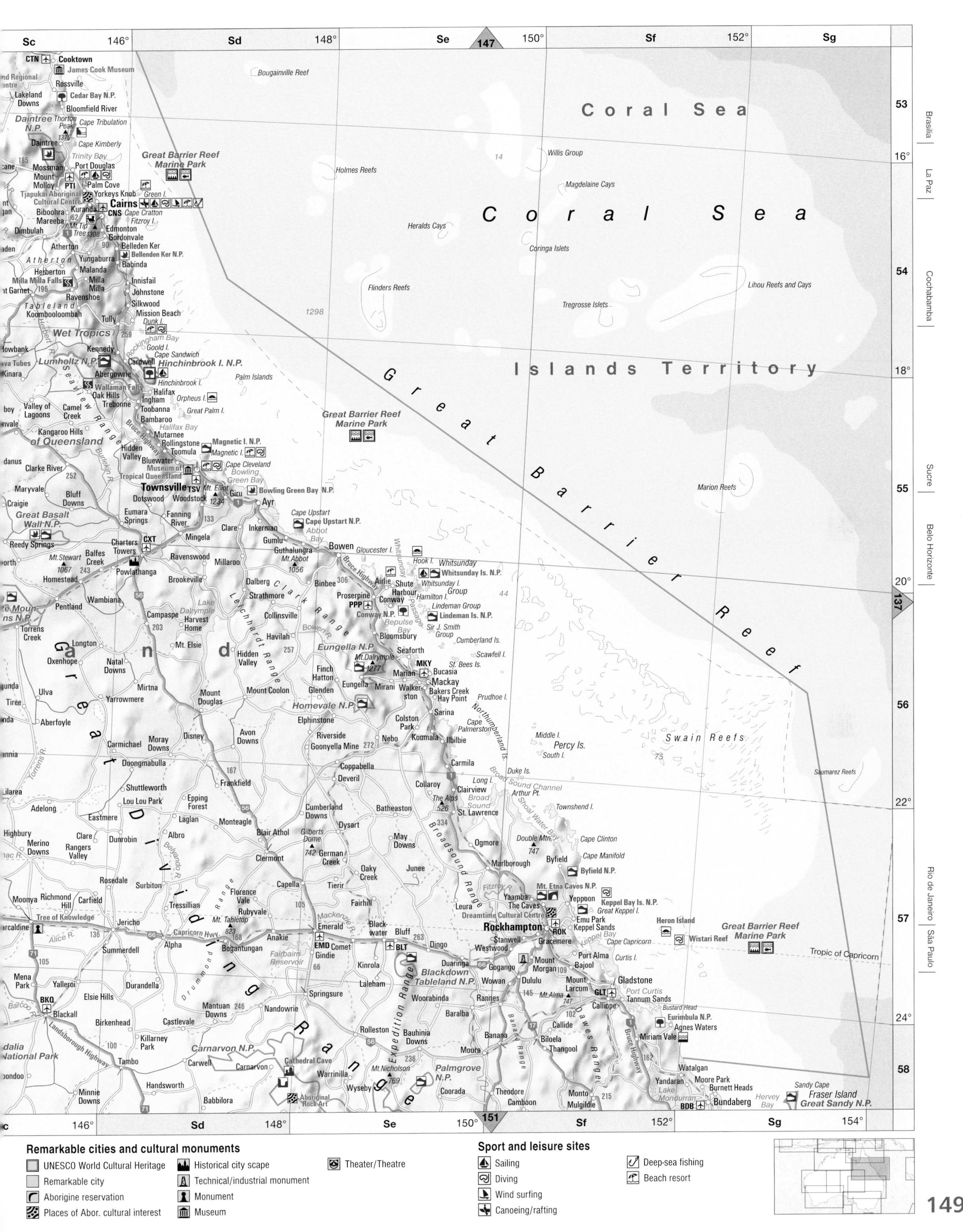

Sc
146°
Sd
148°
Se
147
150°
Sf
152°
Sg
Coral Sea
Coral Sea
Islands Territory
Great Barrier Reef
Great Barrier Reef Marine Park
Cooktown
James Cook Museum
Cairns
Port Douglas
Daintree
Mossman
Kuranda
Atherton
Innisfail
Tully
Cardwell
Hinchinbrook I. N.P.
Ingham
Townsville
Ayr
Bowen
Airlie
Proserpine
Whitsunday
Whitsunday Is. N.P.
Mackay
Sarina
Eungella N.P.
Homevale N.P.
Charters Towers
Great Basalt Wall N.P.
Great Dividing Range
Clermont
Emerald
Capella
Blackwater
Rockhampton
Yeppoon
Gladstone
Bundaberg
Fraser Island
Great Sandy N.P.
Blackdown Tableland N.P.
Carnarvon N.P.
Palmgrove N.P.
Expedition Range
Leichhardt Range
Clarke River
Broad Sound Channel
Percy Is.
Swain Reefs
Marion Reefs
Lihou Reefs and Cays
Flinders Reefs
Holmes Reefs
Willis Group
Magdelaine Cays
Heralds Cays
Coringa Islets
Tregrosse Islets
Bougainville Reef
Keppel Bay Is. N.P.
Tropic of Capricorn
Capricorn Hwy.
Bruce Highway
Landsborough Highway
53
54
55
56
57
58
16°
18°
20°
22°
24°
137
151
154°
Brasília
La Paz
Cochabamba
Sucre
Belo Horizonte
Rio de Janeiro
São Paulo
Remarkable cities and cultural monuments
UNESCO World Cultural Heritage
Remarkable city
Aborigine reservation
Places of Abor. cultural interest
Historical city scape
Technical/industrial monument
Monument
Museum
Theater/Theatre
Sport and leisure sites
Sailing
Diving
Wind surfing
Canoeing/rafting
Deep-sea fishing
Beach resort

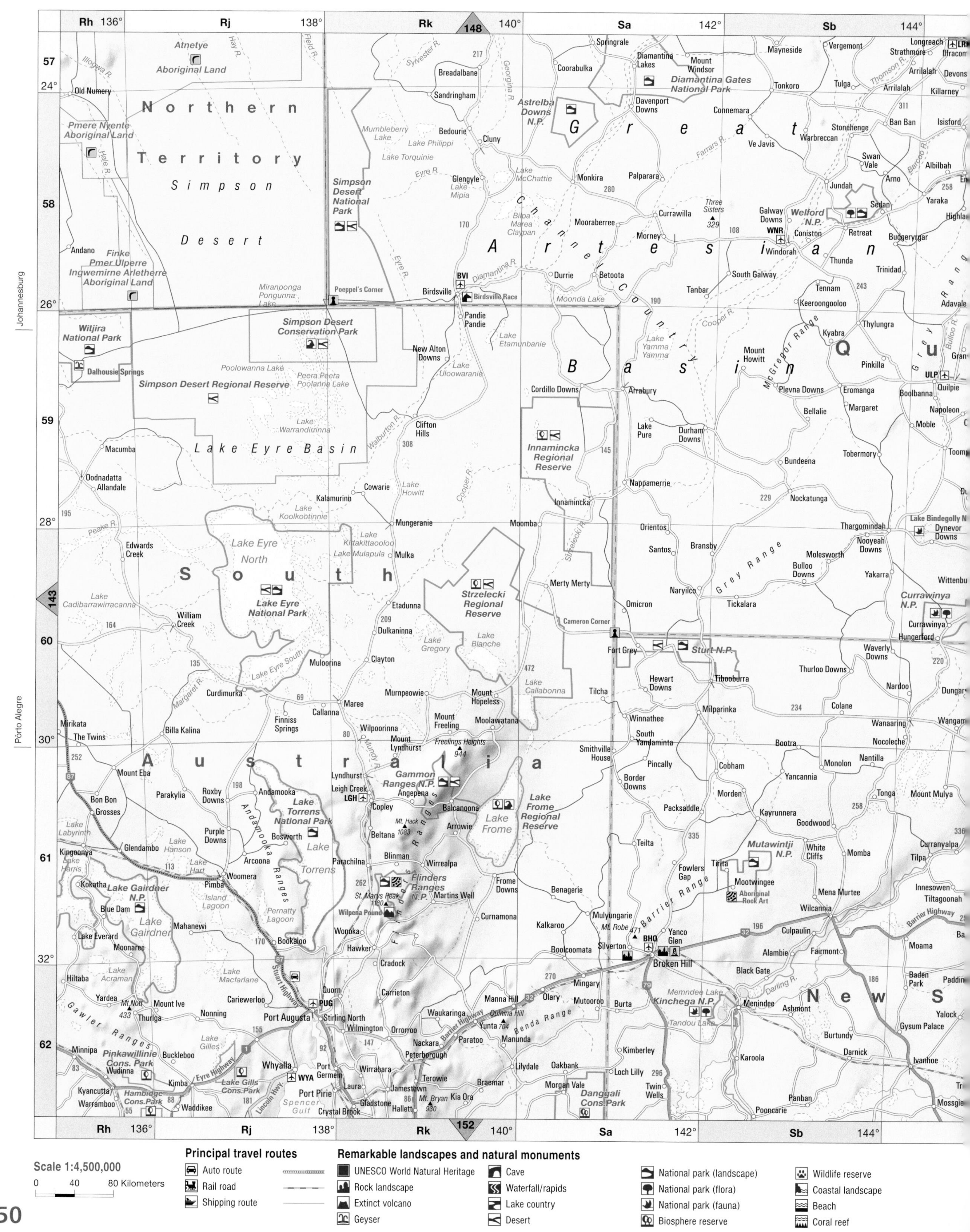

Scale 1:4,500,000

0   40   80 Kilometers

Principal travel routes

- Auto route
- Rail road
- Shipping route

Remarkable landscapes and natural monuments

- UNESCO World Natural Heritage
- Rock landscape
- Extinct volcano
- Geyser
- Cave
- Waterfall/rapids
- Lake country
- Desert
- National park (landscape)
- National park (flora)
- National park (fauna)
- Biosphere reserve
- Wildlife reserve
- Coastal landscape
- Beach
- Coral reef

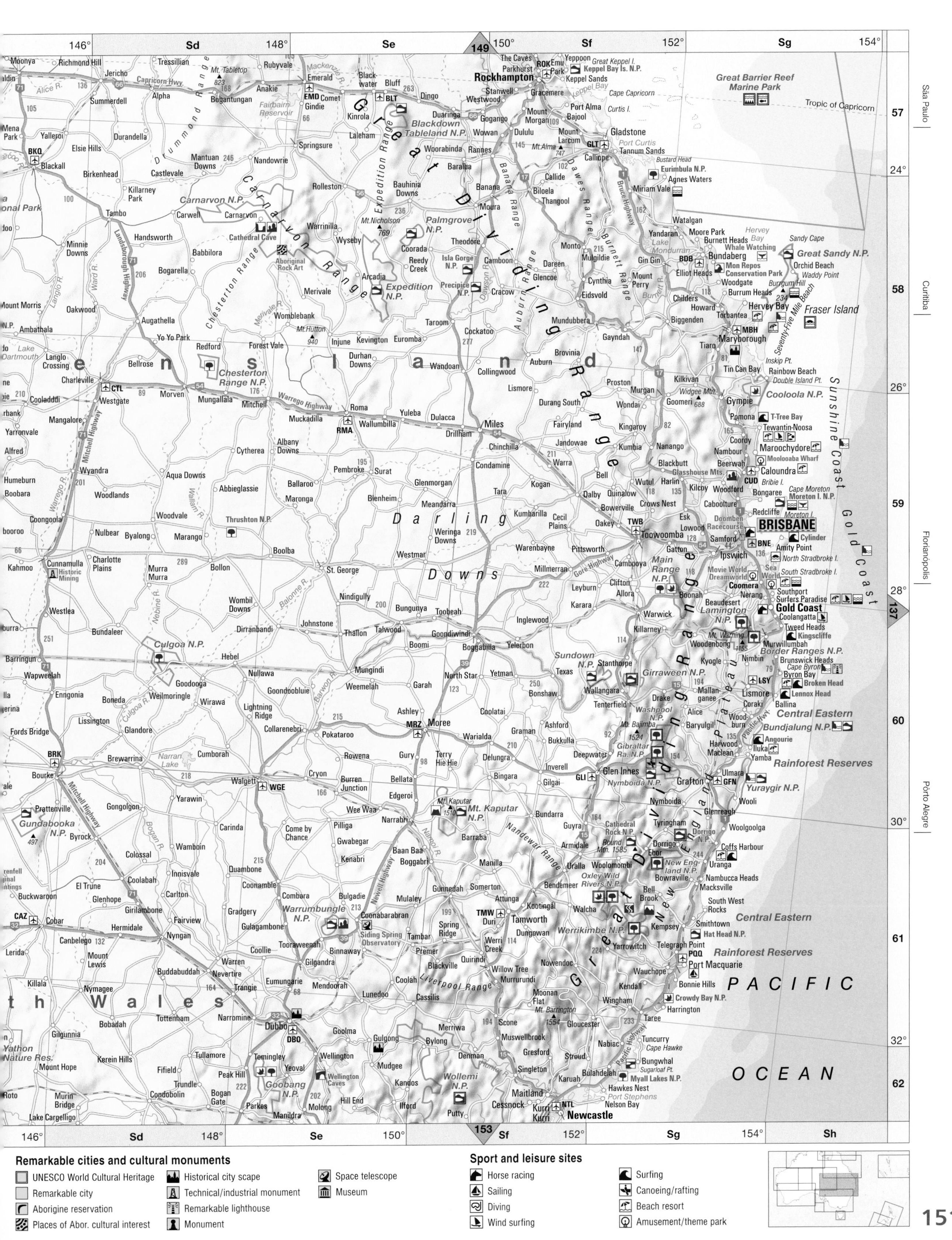

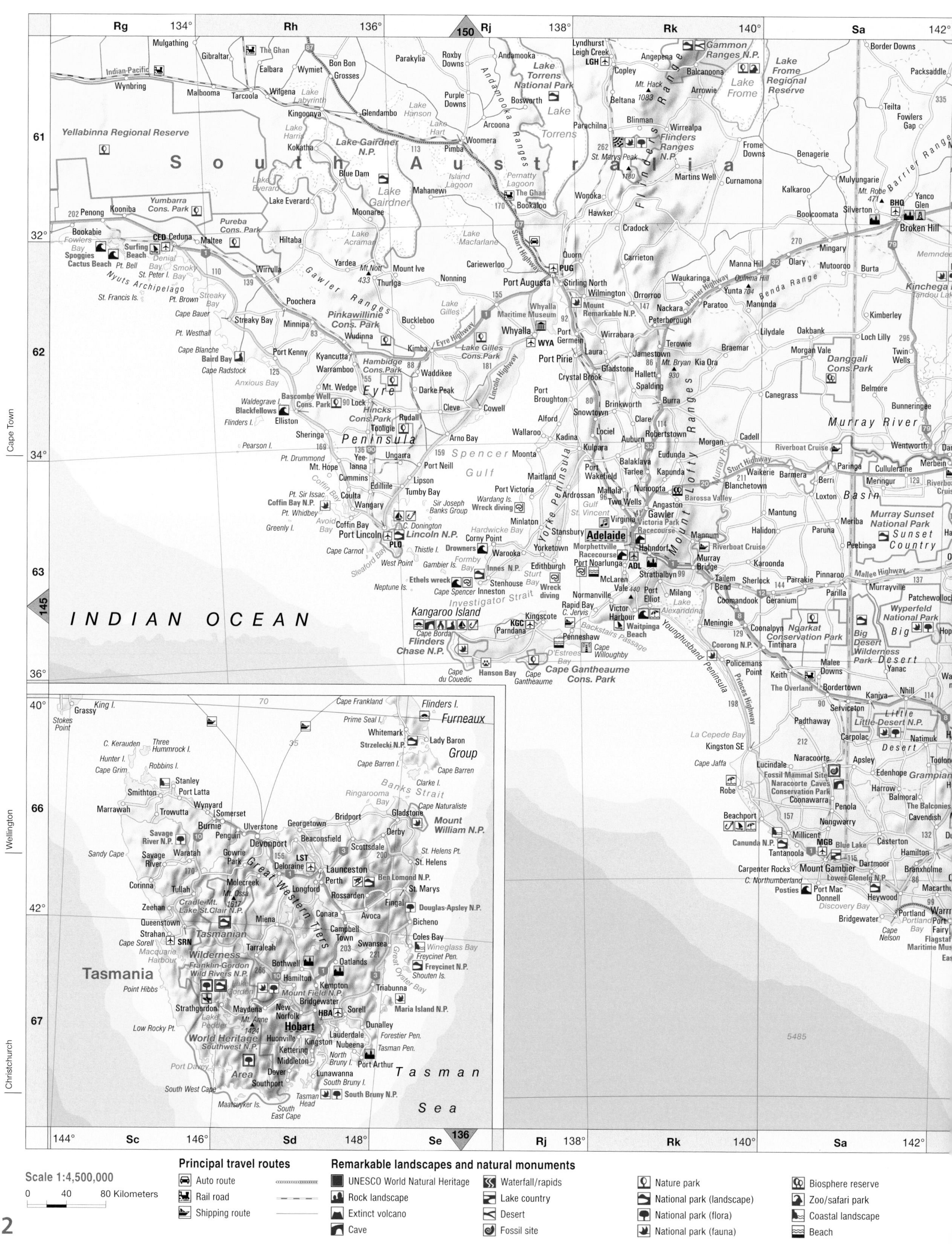

Scale 1:4,500,000

0   40   80 Kilometers

Principal travel routes
- Auto route
- Rail road
- Shipping route

Remarkable landscapes and natural monuments
- UNESCO World Natural Heritage
- Rock landscape
- Extinct volcano
- Cave
- Waterfall/rapids
- Lake country
- Desert
- Fossil site
- Nature park
- National park (landscape)
- National park (flora)
- National park (fauna)
- Biosphere reserve
- Zoo/safari park
- Coastal landscape
- Beach

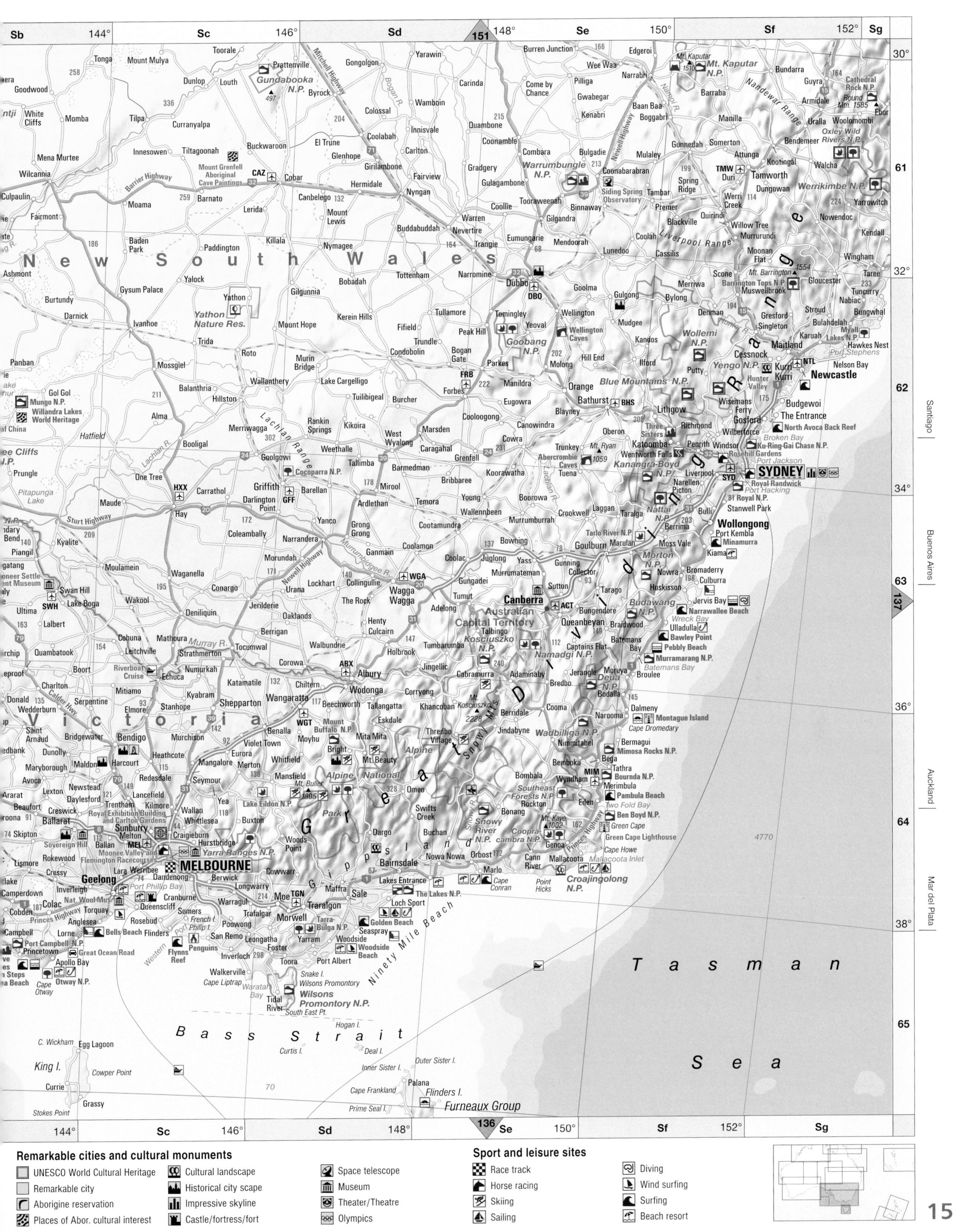

New South Wales

Tonga · Mount Mulya · Toorale · Yarawin · Burren Junction · Edgeroi
Goodwood · 258 · Dunlop · Louth · Gongolgon · Wee Waa · Narrabri · Mt. Kaputar · Mt. Kaputar N.P. · Bundarra · Guyra · 164 · Cathedral Rock N.P.
ntji · White Cliffs · Momba · Tilpa · Curranyalpa · Byrock · Gundabooka N.P. · Carinda · Come by Chance · Pilliga · Gwabegar · Kenabri · Baan Baa · Boggabri · Barraba · Manilla · Uralla · Round Mtn. 1585 · Ebor
Mena Murtee · Innesowen · Tiltagoonah · Buckwaroon · El Trune · Glenhope · Girilambone · Carlton · Innisvale · Quambone · Coonamble · Combara · Bulgadie · Gunnedah · Somerton · Attunga · Kootingal · Walcha · Woolombi · Oxley Wild Rivers N.P.
Wilcannia · Mount Grenfell Aboriginal Cave Paintings · CAZ · Cobar · Canbelego · Hermidale · Nyngan · Warren · Gilgandra · Coonabarabran · Warrumbungle N.P. · Siding Spring Observatory · Tambar Springs · Premer · TMW Duri · Tamworth · Werrikimbe N.P.
Culpaulin · Moama · Barnato · Lerida · Mount Lewis · Buddabuddah · Nevertire · Eumungarie · Mendooran · Blackville · Quirindi · Willow Tree · Nowendoc · Kendall
Fairmont · Baden Park · Paddington · Killala · Nymagee · Trangie · Narromine · Coolah · Cassilis · Murrurundi · Wingham

Remarkable cities and cultural monuments

- ▢ UNESCO World Cultural Heritage
- ▢ Remarkable city
- ▢ Aborigine reservation
- ▨ Places of Abor. cultural interest
- ◍ Cultural landscape
- ♨ Historical city scape
- ▥ Impressive skyline
- ▦ Castle/fortress/fort

- ◩ Space telescope
- ▤ Museum
- ▥ Theater/Theatre
- ▦ Olympics

Sport and leisure sites

- ▨ Race track
- ♞ Horse racing
- ▨ Skiing
- ◩ Sailing

- ◫ Diving
- ▨ Wind surfing
- ◪ Surfing
- ▨ Beach resort

153

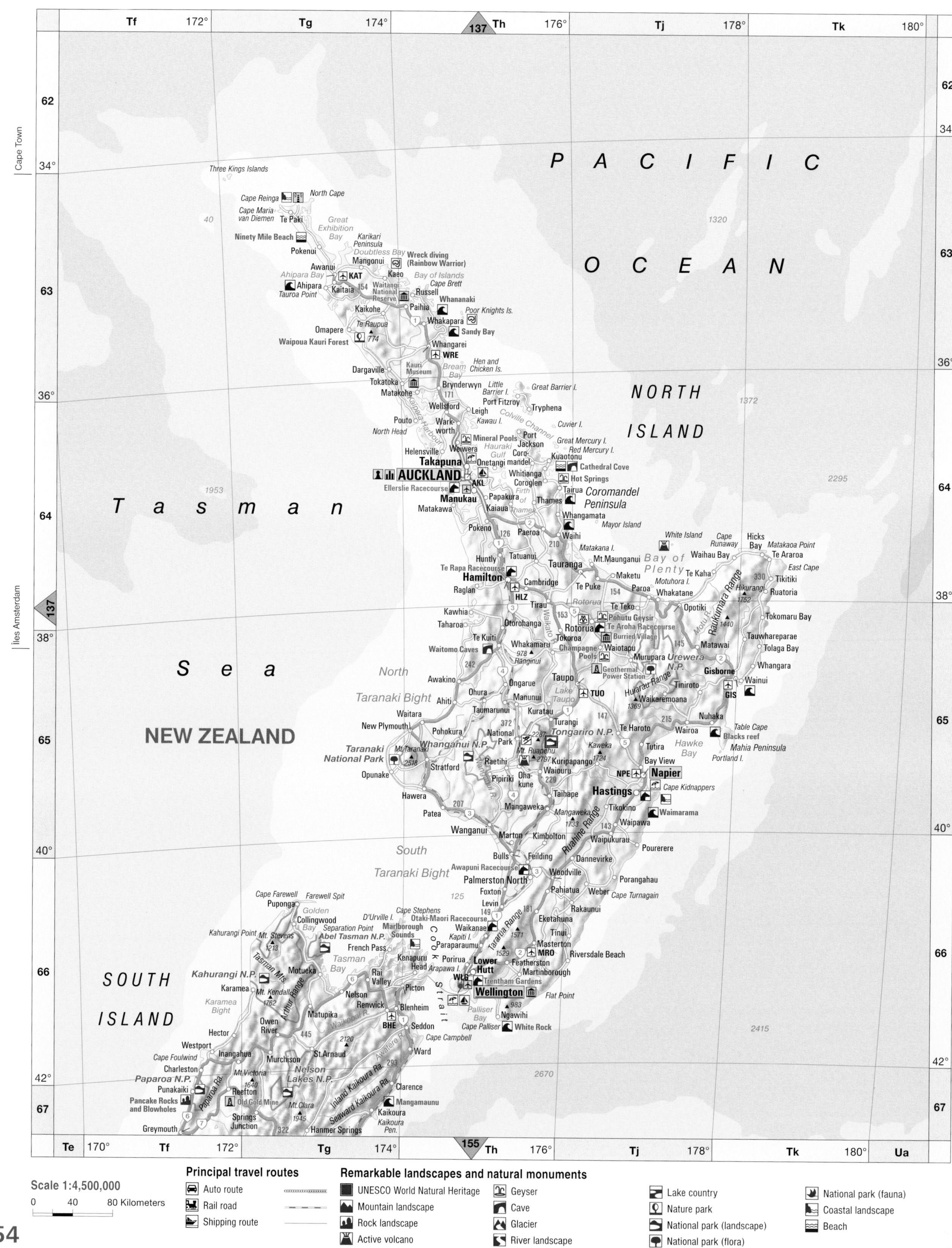

New Zealand

Tf 172°	**Tg** 174°	◆ 137 **Th** 176°	**Tj** 178°	**Tk** 180°	

P A C I F I C

O C E A N

N O R T H

I S L A N D

Three Kings Islands

Cape Reinga
North Cape
Cape Maria van Diemen
Te Paki
Great Exhibition Bay
Ninety Mile Beach
Pokenui
Awanui
Mangonui
Wreck diving (Rainbow Warrior)
Karikari Peninsula
Doubtless Bay
Kaeo
Bay of Islands
Cape Brett
KAT
Ahipara Bay
Ahipara
Kaitaia
Waitangi National Reserve
Russell
Paihia
Whananaki
Tauroa Point
Kaikohe
Te Raupua
774
Poor Knights Is.
Omapere
Sandy Bay
Waipoua Kauri Forest
Whangarei
WRE
Hen and Chicken Is.
Dargaville
Kauri Museum
Bream Bay
Tokatoka
Brynderwyn
Little Barrier I.
Great Barrier I.
Matakohe
Wellsford
Port Fitzroy
Tryphena
1372
Pouto
Warkworth
Leigh
Kawau I.
Colville Channel
Cuvier I.
North Head
Mineral Pools
Port Jackson
Great Mercury I.
Helensville
Weiwera
Coromandel
Red Mercury I.
Kuaotonu
Takapuna
Onetangi mandel
Whitianga
Cathedral Cove
2295
AUCKLAND
AKL
Coroglen
Hot Springs
Ellerslie Racecourse
Papakura
Whenuapai
Tairua
Coromandel Peninsula
Manukau
Thames
Matakawa
Firth of Thames
Whangamata
Kaiaua
Mayor Island
Pokeno
126
Paeroa
210
Waihi
White Island
Cape Runaway
Hicks Bay
Matakaoa Point
Huntly
Tatuanui
Mt.Maunganui
Waihau Bay
Te Araroa
Bay of Plenty
East Cape
Tasman
Te Rapa Racecourse
Hamilton
Cambridge
Tauranga
Maketu
Te Kaha
Motuhora I.
330
Tikitiki
Ruatoria
Raglan
HLZ
Tirau
Te Puke
154
Paroa
Whakatane
Raukumara Range
Hikurangi 1752
Sea
Kawhia
153
Otorohanga
L.Rotorua
Te Teko
Opotiki
Tokomaru Bay
Taharoa
Pohutu Geysir
Te Aroha Racecourse
Matawai
Tauwhareparae
Te Kuiti
Rotorua
145
Tolaga Bay
Waitomo Caves
Whakamaru
Burried Village
Urewera N.P.
Whangara
978
Champagne Pools
Waiotapu
Murupara
Gisborne
North
Ranginui
Geothermal Power Station
GIS
242
Tokoroa
Wainui
Awakino
Ongarue
Taupo
Huiarau Range
Table Cape
Taranaki Bight
Ohura
Manunui
Lake Taupo
TUO
Tiniroto
Waikaremoana
Blacks reef
Ahiti
Taumarunui
Kuratau
1369
Nuhaka
Mahia Peninsula
Waitara
372
Turangi
147
Te Haroto
Wairoa
Portland I.
New Plymouth
National Park
2237
Tongariro N.P.
215
Tutira
Hawke Bay
Pohokura
Mt.Ruapehu
Kaweka
NEW ZEALAND
Taranaki National Park
Mt.Taranaki
2518
Whanganui N.P.
2797
Kuripapango
1724
Bay View
Opunake
Stratford
Raetihi
Oha-kune
Waiouru
229
NPE
Napier
Pipiriki
Cape Kidnappers
Hawera
Taihape
Hastings
Waimarama
Patea
207
Mangaweka
Tikokino
133
Waipawa
Wanganui
143
Waipukurau
Marton
Kimbolton
Ruahine Range
Pourerere
South Taranaki Bight
Bulls
Feilding
Dannevirke
Woodville
Porangahau
Awapuni Racecourse
Palmerston North
Cape Turnagain
125
Foxton
Pahiatua
Weber
Levin
149
Rakaunui
Cape Farewell
Farewell Spit
Cape Stephens
Eketahuna
Cape Stephens
Otaki-Maori Racecourse
Tinui
Puponga
Golden Bay
D'Urville I.
Waikanae
181
Masterton
Collingwood
Separation Point
Marlborough Sounds
1571
MRO
Kahurangi Point
Mt. Stevens
Abel Tasman N.P.
Kapiti I.
Riversdale Beach
1213
French Pass
Paraparaumu
1529
Featherston
Karamea
Motueka
Kenepuru Head
Porirua
Martinborough
Flat Point
Kahurangi N.P.
Rai Valley
Arapawa I.
Lower Hutt
Tasman Bay
Nelson
Picton
WLG
Trentham Gardens
Karamea
Tasman Mts
Renwick
983
Wellington
Karamea Bight
Mt.Kendall
Matupika
Blenheim
Palliser Bay
Flat Point
SOUTH
1752
Arthur Range
BHE
Ngawihi
Hector
Owen River
Seddon
Cape Palliser
White Rock
ISLAND
445
Cape Campbell
Westport
Nelson Lakes N.P.
Ward
Inangahua
Mt.Victoria
2120
2415
Cape Foulwind
Murchison
Mt.Clara
St.Arnaud
Charleston
1640
1945
Inland Kaikoura Ra.
293
Paparoa N.P.
Reefton
Clarence
Punakaiki
Old Gold Mine
Mangamaunu
Pancake Rocks and Blowholes
Seaward Kaikoura Ra.
Kaikoura
322
Kaikoura Pen.
Springs Junction
Hanmer Springs
2670
Greymouth

T a s m a n

S e a

1953

1320

40

Cape Town	Iles Amsterdam	

Te 170°	**Tf** 172°	**Tg** 174°	◆ 155 **Th** 176°	**Tj** 178°	**Tk** 180° **Ua**

Scale 1:4,500,000

0   40   80 Kilometers

154

Principal travel routes
- Auto route
- Rail road
- Shipping route

Remarkable landscapes and natural monuments
- UNESCO World Natural Heritage
- Mountain landscape
- Rock landscape
- Active volcano
- Geyser
- Cave
- Glacier
- River landscape
- Lake country
- Nature park
- National park (landscape)
- National park (flora)
- National park (fauna)
- Coastal landscape
- Beach

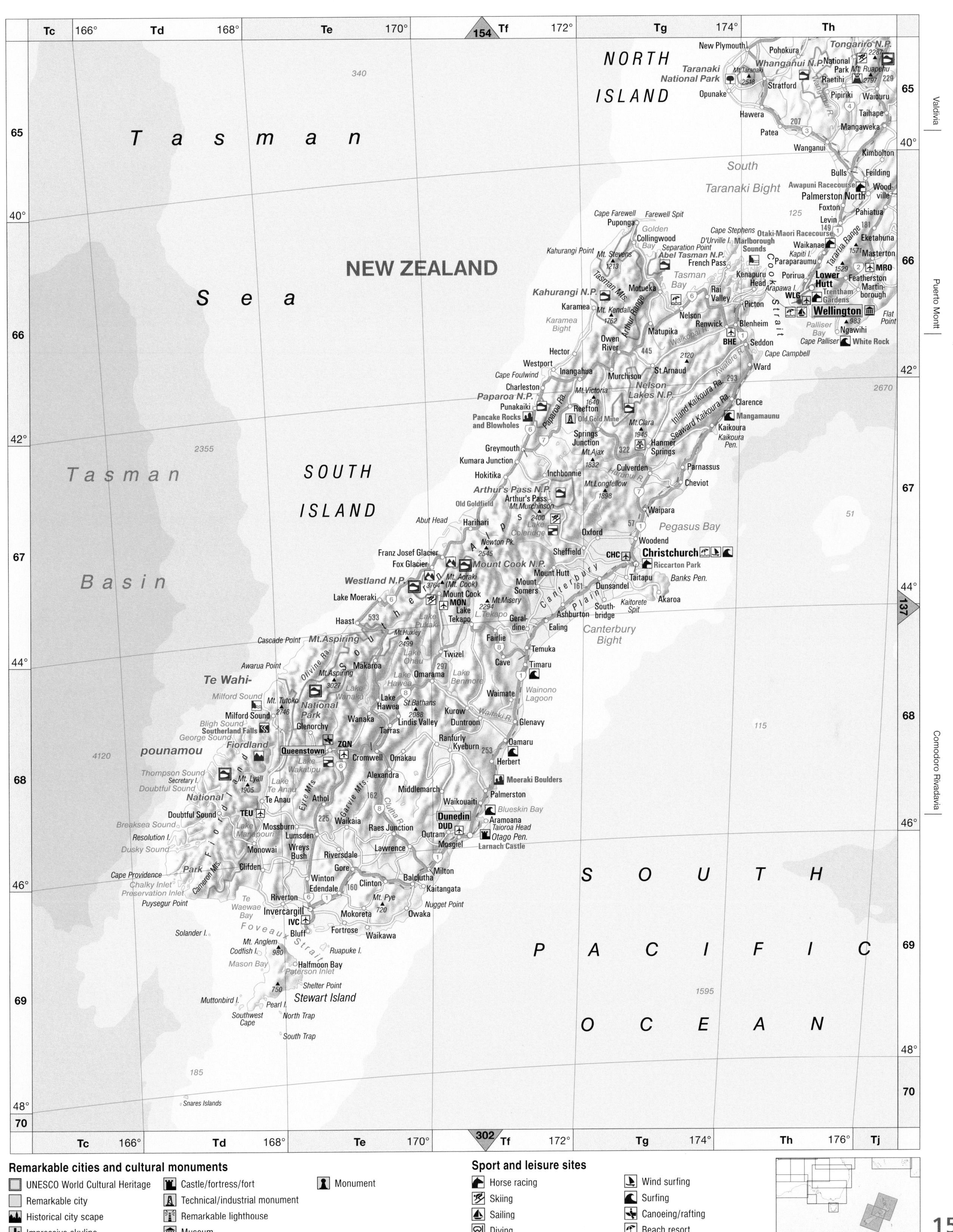

NORTH
ISLAND

T a s m a n

NEW ZEALAND

S e a

New Plymouth
Pohokura
Tongariro N.P.
National
Park
2287
Mt. Ruapehu
2757 229
Taranaki
National Park
Mt. Taranaki
2518
Stratford
Waitara
Raetihi
Pipiriki
Waiouru
Opunake
Taihape
Hawera
Mangaweka
207
Patea
Kimbolton
Wanganui

South
Taranaki Bight
Bulls
Feilding
125
Awapuni Racecourse
Palmerston North
Wood-ville
Foxton
Cape Farewell
Farewell Spit
Puponga
149
Levin
181
Golden
Bay
Otaki-Maori Racecourse
Cape Stephens
Pahiatua
Collingwood
D'Urville I.
Marlborough
Eketahuna
Kahurangi Point
Mt. Stevens
Abel Tasman N.P.
1213
Sounds
Kapiti I.
1571
Masterton
French Pass
Paraparaumu
1529
2
MRO
Motueka
Tasman
Porirua
Lower
Featherston
Kenapuru
Head
Bay
6
Hutt
Martin-
Karamea
Rai
Valley
Picton
WLG
Trentham
borough
Arapawa I.
Gardens
Karamea
Mt. Kendall
Nelson
Renwick
Wellington
Bight
1762
Blenheim
Palliser
983
Flat
Owen
River
Bay
Point
Hector
445
2120
Seddon
Ngawihi
Cape Campbell
Cape Palliser
White Rock
Inangahua
BHE
Ward
Westport
Murchison
St.Arnaud
Cape Foulwind
Nelson
2670
Charleston
Mt. Victoria
Lakes N.P.
Clarence
Paparoa N.P.
1640
Mangamaunu
Punakaiki
Reefton
Old Gold Mine
Mt.Clara
Seaward Kaikoura Ra.
Pancake Rocks
1945
Kaikoura
and Blowholes
6
Springs
Hanmer
Kaikoura
Greymouth
Junction
Springs
Pen.
Kumara Junction
Mt.Ajax
326
1832
Culverden
Parnassus
Hokitika
Inchbonnie
Cheviot
Arthur's Pass N.P.
Mt.Longfellow
Old Goldfield
1898
Waipara
SOUTH
Arthur's Pass
57
2400
Pegasus Bay
ISLAND
Abut Head
Harihari
Oxford
51
Newton Pk.
Woodend
2545
Sheffield
CHC
Christchurch
Franz Josef Glacier
Riccarton Park
Fox Glacier
Mount Cook N.P.
Mount Hutt
Westland N.P.
Mt. Aoraki
Mount
Banks Pen.
(Mt. Cook)
Somers
Akaroa
3764
Canterbury
Lake Moeraki
Mount Cook
Taitapu
161
MON
Lake
2294
Dunsandel
Mt.Misery
South-
Haast
533
Tekapo
Geral-
bridge
Kaitorete
L.Tekapo
dine
Spit
Mt.Huxley
Plain
Cascade Point
Mt.Aspiring
2499
Fairlie
8
Canterbury
Awarua Point
3027
Twizel
Temuka
Bight
Te Wahi-
Makaroa
Lake
297
Cave
Timaru
Milford Sound
Ohau
Lake
Omarama
Waimate
Mt. Tutoko
Wanaka
Lake
Wainono
2746
National
Benmore
Lagoon
Milford Sound
Park
Glenorchy
Lake
St.Bathans
Waitaki R.
Bligh Sound
Hawea
2088
Kurow
Southerland Falls
Tarras
Glenavy
George Sound
Fiordland
Lindis Valley
Duntroon
Oamaru
pounamou
ZQN
Cromwell
Ranfurly
253
Thompson Sound
Queenstown
Omakau
Kyeburn
Herbert
Secretary I.
Mt. Lyall
Lake
Alexandra
Moeraki Boulders
Doubtful Sound
1905
Wakatipu
Middlemarch
Palmerston
National
162
Waikouaiti
Athol
Blueskin Bay
Te Anau
Aramoana
Breaksea Sound
TEU
Dunedin
Taiaroa Head
Resolution I.
225
Waikaia
DUD
Otago Pen.
Dusky Sound
Lake
Mossburn
Raes Junction
Outram
Larnach Castle
Manapouri
Lumsden
Mosgiel
Park
Wreys
Lawrence
Cape Providence
Bush
Riverdale
Chalky Inlet
Clifden
Gore
Milton
Preservation Inlet
Monowai
Winton
Clinton
Balclutha
Puysegur Point
Edendale
160
Mt. Pye
Kaitangata
Te
Riverton
720
Waewae
Bluff
Mokoreta
Nugget Point
Bay
Invercargill
Waikawa
Foveaux
IVC
Fortrose
Owaka
Solander I.
Mt. Anglem
Codfish I.
980
Ruapuke I.
Strait
Mason Bay
Halfmoon Bay
Paterson Inlet
Muttonbird I.
750
Shelter Point
Pearl I.
Stewart Island
Southwest
North Trap
Cape
South Trap
Snares Islands

B a s i n

T a s m a n

S O U T H

P A C I F I C

O C E A N

Remarkable cities and cultural monuments

- ☐ UNESCO World Cultural Heritage
- ▨ Remarkable city
- ⏶ Historical city scape
- 📊 Impressive skyline
- 🏰 Castle/fortress/fort
- 🅰 Technical/industrial monument
- 🏛 Remarkable lighthouse
- 🏛 Museum
- 🧍 Monument

Sport and leisure sites

- 🏇 Horse racing
- ⛷ Skiing
- ⛵ Sailing
- 🤿 Diving
- 🏄 Wind surfing
- 🏄 Surfing
- 🚣 Canoeing/rafting
- ⛱ Beach resort

Islands of the South Pacific

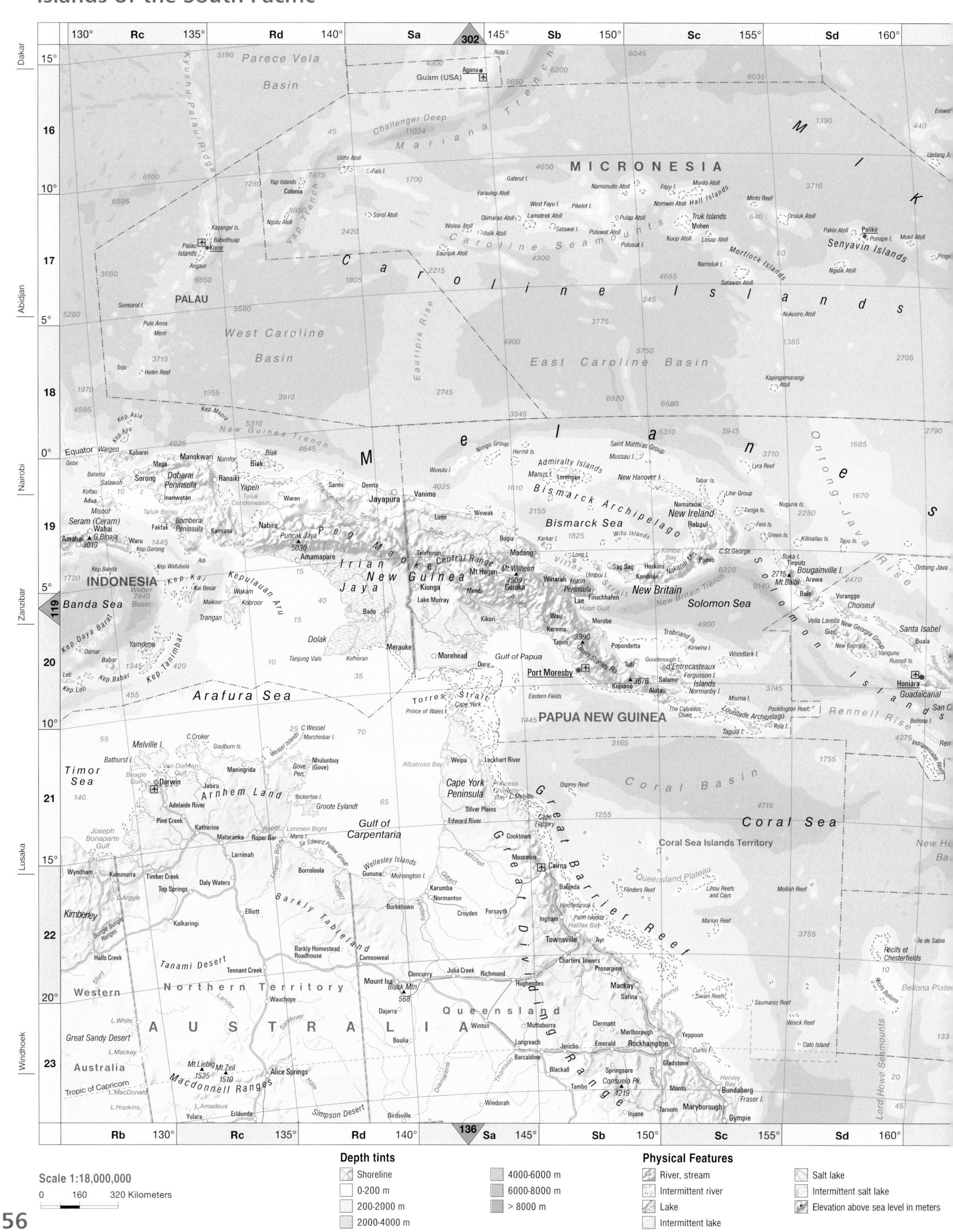

Scale 1:18,000,000

0   160   320 Kilometers

Depth tints

- ⬡ Shoreline
- 0-200 m
- 200-2000 m
- 2000-4000 m
- 4000-6000 m
- 6000-8000 m
- > 8000 m

Physical Features

- River, stream
- Intermittent river
- Lake
- Intermittent lake
- Salt lake
- Intermittent salt lake
- ▲ Elevation above sea level in meters

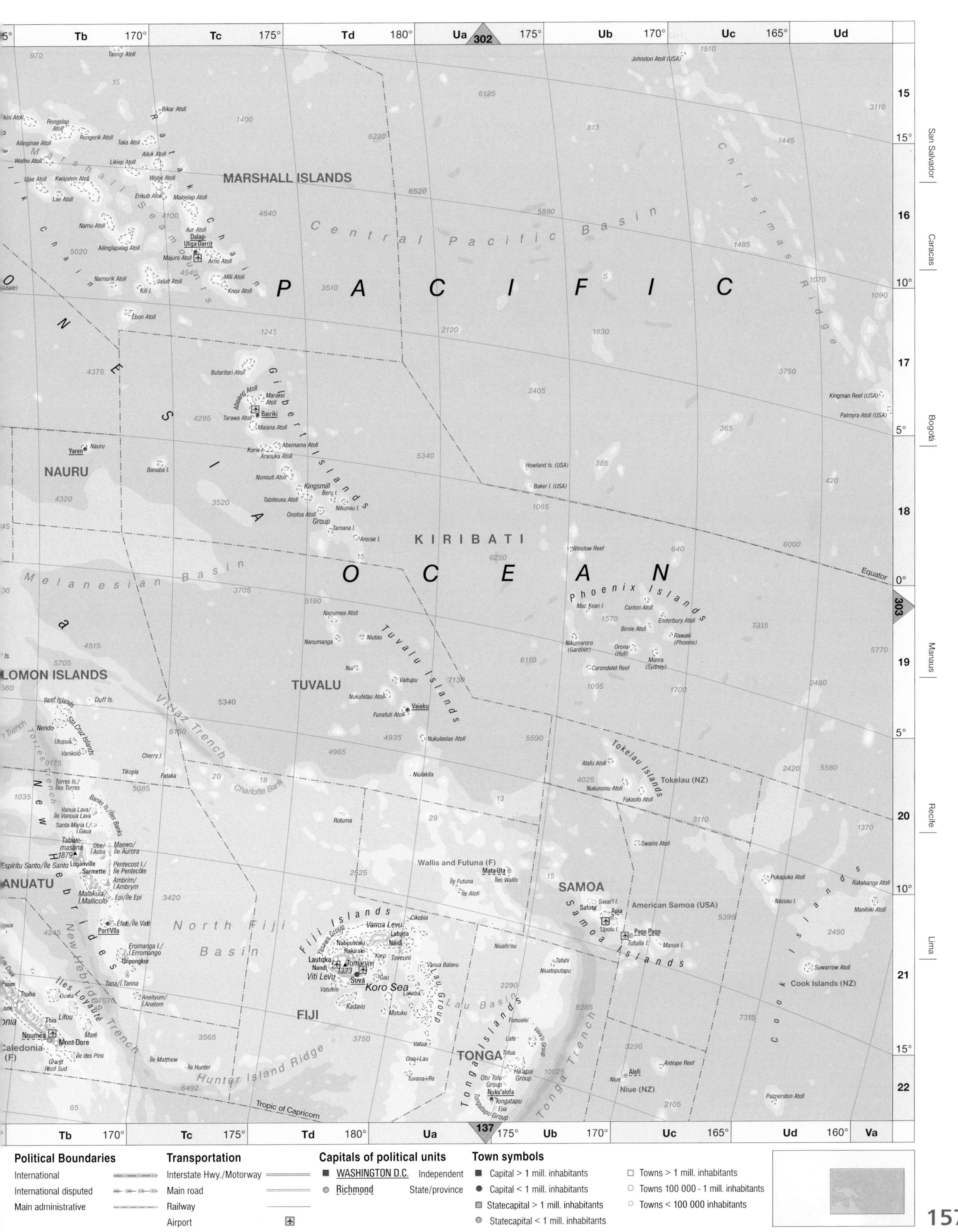

970

Taongi Atoll

15

Bikar Atoll

15

6125

3110

'kini Atoll
Rongelap
Atoll

Ailinginae Atoll

Rongerik Atoll

Taka Atoll

Johnston Atoll (USA)

1510

15°

Wotho Atoll
Likiep Atoll
Ailuk Atoll

1400

1445

15°

San Salvador

Ujae Atoll
Kwajalein Atoll

Wotje Atoll

6220

MARSHALL ISLANDS

Erikub Atoll
Maloelap Atoll

Lae Atoll

4840

6520

5890

1070

Caracas

Namu Atoll

Aur Atoll
**Dalap-
Uliga-Darrit**

16

4100

5020

Ailinglapalag Atoll

Majuro Atoll ✈
Arno Atoll

P   A   C   I   F   I   C

1485

1090

Narmorik Atoll

Jaluit Atoll
Mili Atoll

4540

5

3110

(susaie)

Kili I.

Knox Atoll

3510

10°

Ebon Atoll

1245

2120

1830

Caracas

N

4375

Butaritari Atoll

17

3750

Bogotá

S

Marakei
Atoll

Abaiang Atoll

4295

Tarawa Atoll
✈ **Bairiki**

Maiana Atoll

Kingman Reef (USA)

Palmyra Atoll (USA)

Yaren ▲ Nauru

Abemama Atoll

Kuria I.
Aranuka Atoll

365

5°

NAURU

Banaba I.

Nonouti Atoll

Howland Is. (USA)

385

420

18

4320

3520

Kingsmill
Beru I.
Tabiteuea Atoll

Baker I. (USA)

Nikunau I.

1065

6000

Onotoa Atoll
Group

Tamana I.

15

K I R I B A T I

6250

640

Equator 0°

Arorae I.

Winslow Reef

Melanesian   Basin

3705

O   C   E   A   N

Mac Kean I.
Canton Atoll

Phoenix Islands

7315

5770

303

Manaus

5190

Nanumea Atoll

1570
Birnie Atoll

Enderbury Atoll

4515

Nikumaroro
(Gardner)

Orona
(Hull)

Rawaki
(Phoenix)

19

'LOMON ISLANDS

Niutao

Nanumanga

Carondelet Reef

Manra
(Sydney)

2480

Reef Islands
Duff Is.

Tuvalu Islands

6110

1095

1700

5705

Nui

Vaitupu

7130

5340

TUVALU

5°

Nendo
Sta. Cruz Islands

Nukufetau Atoll

Tokelau Islands

5580

Utupua
Vanikolo

Funafuti Atoll ✈ **Vaiaku**

4935

5590

Atafu Atoll

2420

9175

6150

Cherry I.

4965

Nukulaelae Atoll

4025

Tokelau (NZ)

Tikopia
Fataka

18

Niulakita

Nukunonu Atoll

New

Torres Is./
Iles Torres

Charlotte Bank

20

Fakaofo Atoll

1035

Banks Is./Iles Banks
Santa Maria I./
I. Gaua

5085

13

3110

1370

Vanua Lava/
Ile Vanua Lava

Rotuma

29

Espíritu Santo/Ile St. Santo
Luganville
Sarmette

Obe/
I.Aoba
Maewo/
Ile Aurora

Swains Atoll

Recife

Tabwe-
masana
▲1879

Pentecost I./
Ile Pentecôte

2525

Wallis and Futuna (F)

Mata-Uta

Pukapuka Atoll

Rakahanga Atoll

'ANUATU

Malakula/
Ile Mallicolo

Ambrim/
I.Ambrym
Epi/Ile Epi

3420

Ily Futuna
Iles Wallis

15

SAMOA

Savai'i I.

Nassau I.

Manihiki Atoll

10°

aux

Efaté/Ile Vaté

Ile Alofi

Satofu

Apia

American Samoa (USA)

5395

North   Fiji

2450

4245

Port-Vila

Fiji Islands

Cikobia

✈ Upolu I.

Pago Pago

Basin

Vanua Levu

Niuafo'ou

Tutuila I.
Manua Is.

aux

Ouvéa

Yasava Group
Labasa
Nabouwalu
Naidi

Suwarrow Atoll

Touho

Eromanga /
I.Erromango

Rakiraki
Koro
Taveuni

Niuatoputapu

Lima

7570

Lifou

Unpongkor

Lautoka
Nandi ✈Tomaniivi
1323

Vanua Balavu

Tafahi

Cook Islands (NZ)

21

re
Thio

Tana/I.Tanna

Viti Levu
▲Suva
Vatulele

Gau
Lakeba

2290

8285

7315

' onia

Nouméa ✈

Aneityum/
I.Anatom

Maré

Koro Sea

Kadavu

Lau Group

Fonualei

Mont-Dore

3565

Kadavu

Matuku

Vatoa

Late

3290

Antiope Reef

15°

Caledonia
(F)

Ile des Pins

Ile Matthew
Ile Hunter

3750

FIJI

Ono-i-Lau

TONGA

Tofua

Ha'apai
Group

Alofi

Niue (NZ)

Palmerston Atoll

22

65

6492

Hunter Island Ridge

Tuvana-i-Ra

Otu Tolu
Group

Nuku'alofa

Niue

2105

Tropic of Capricorn

Tongatapu
Eua Group

Political Boundaries

International
International disputed
Main administrative

Transportation

Interstate Hwy./Motorway
Main road
Railway
Airport ✈

Capitals of political units

■ WASHINGTON D.C. Independent
◉ Richmond State/province

Town symbols

■ Capital > 1 mill. inhabitants
● Capital < 1 mill. inhabitants
▪ Statecapital > 1 mill. inhabitants
● Statecapital < 1 mill. inhabitants

□ Towns > 1 mill. inhabitants
○ Towns 100 000 - 1 mill. inhabitants
○ Towns < 100 000 inhabitants

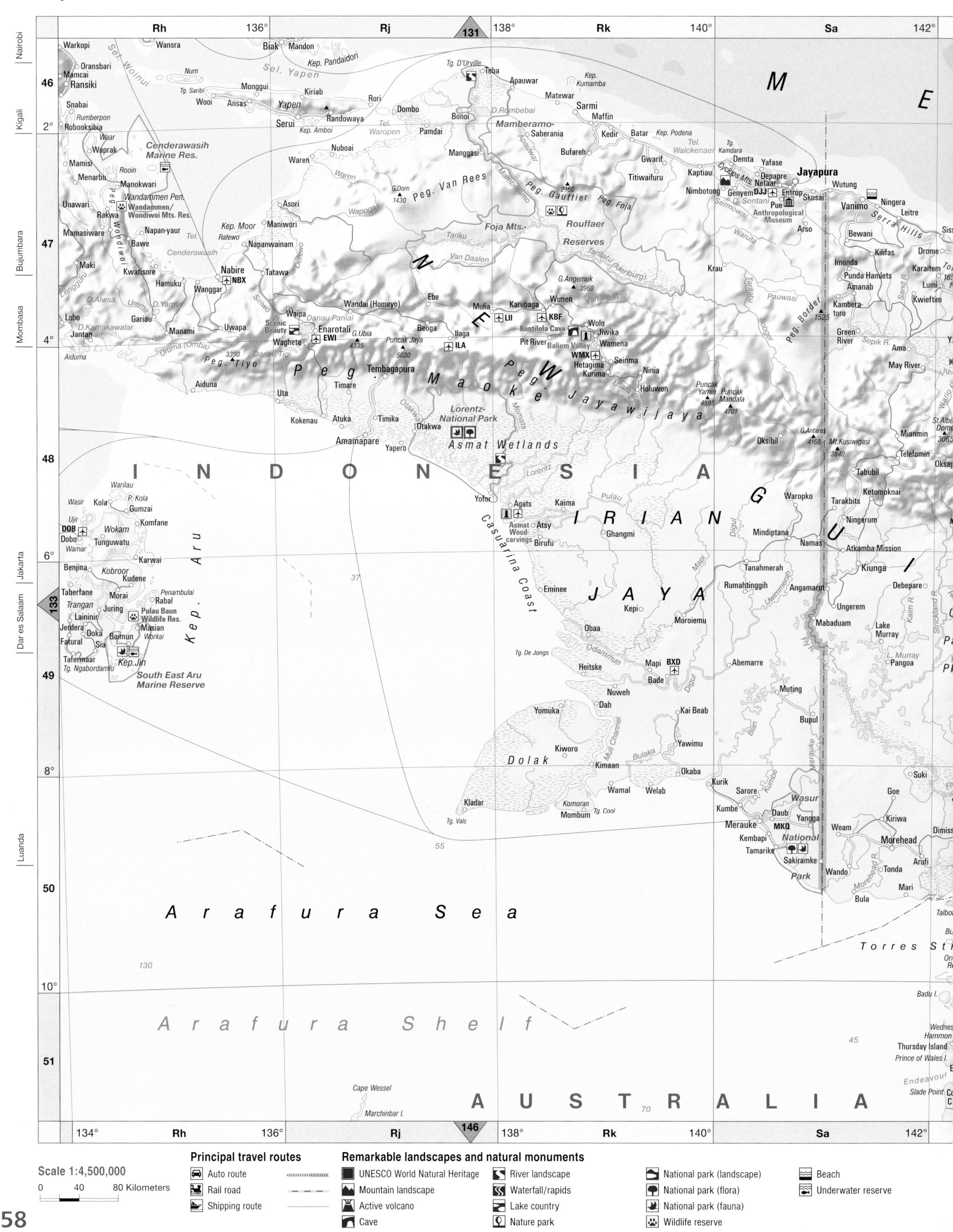

Nairobi
Kigali
Bujumbara
Mombasa
Jakarta
Dar es Salaam
Luanda

Scale 1:4,500,000

0   40   80 Kilometers

158

Principal travel routes

Auto route
Rail road
Shipping route

Remarkable landscapes and natural monuments

UNESCO World Natural Heritage
Mountain landscape
Active volcano
Cave

River landscape
Waterfall/rapids
Lake country
Nature park

National park (landscape)
National park (flora)
National park (fauna)
Wildlife reserve

Beach
Underwater reserve

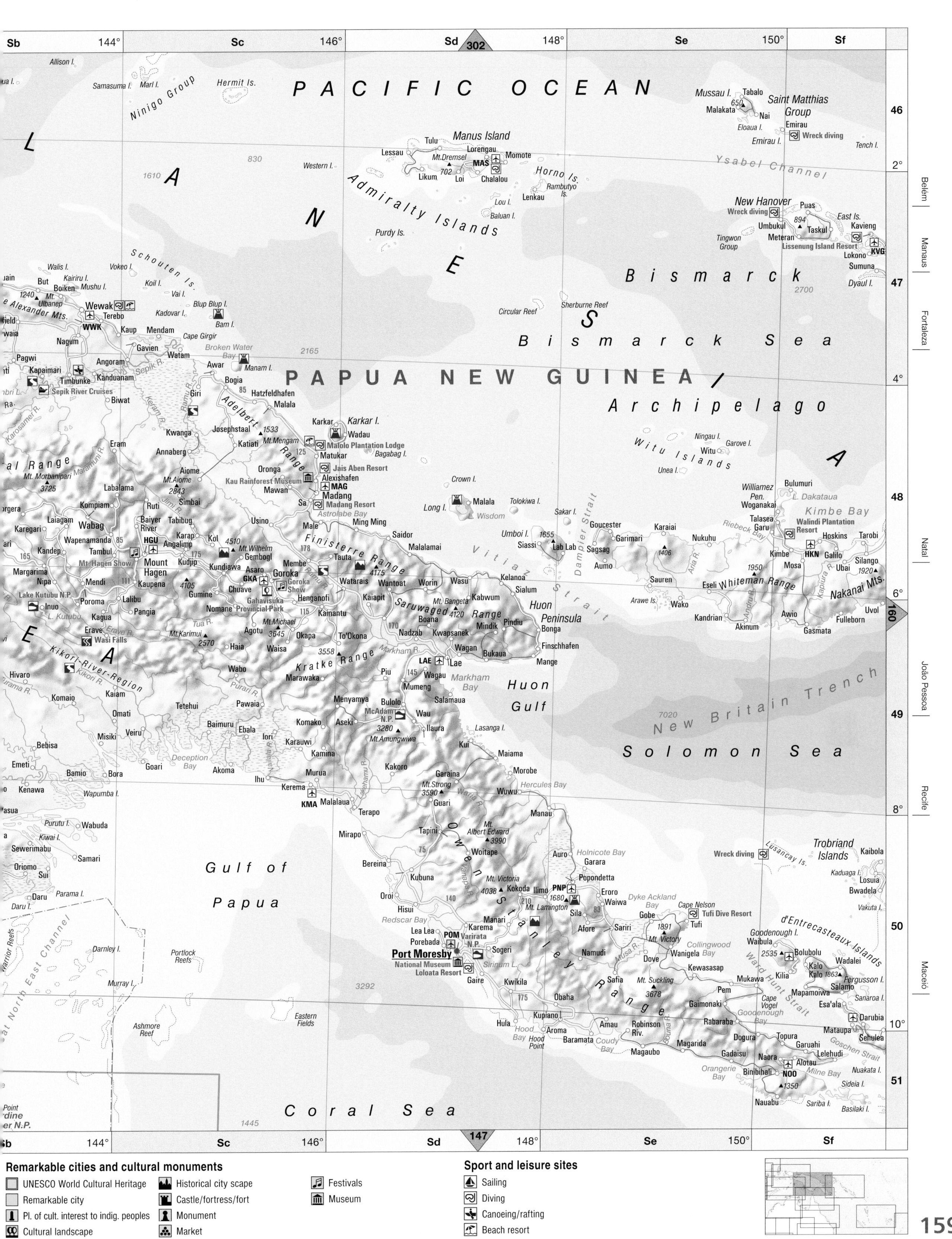
PACIFIC OCEAN
Manus Island
Admiralty Islands
Bismarck Sea
Bismarck Archipelago
PAPUA NEW GUINEA
MELANESIA
Saint Matthias Group
Mussau I.
Emirau
Wreck diving
Tench I.
Ysabel Channel
New Hanover
Kavieng
Lissenung Island Resort
Schouten Is.
Ninigo Group
Hermit Is.
Wewak
Alexander Mts.
Sepik River Cruises
Sepik R.
Ramu R.
Adelbert Range
Karkar I.
Malolo Plantation Lodge
Jais Aben Resort
Madang
Madang Resort
Kau Rainforest Museum
Long I.
Witu Islands
Kimbe Bay
Walindi Plantation Resort
Hoskins
Whiteman Range
Nakanai Mts.
Dampier Strait
Vitiaz Strait
Finisterre Range
Mt.Wilhelm 4510
Mount Hagen
Mt. Hagen Show
Goroka
Goroka Show
Lake Kutubu N.P.
Wasi Falls
Kikori River-Region
Huon Peninsula
Saruwaged Range
Lae
Huon Gulf
Markham Bay
Kratke Range
McAdam N.P.
New Britain Trench
Solomon Sea
Owen Stanley Range
Mt. Victoria 4038
Kokoda
Gulf of Papua
Port Moresby
National Museum
Loloata Resort
Varirata N.P.
Trobriand Islands
Lusancay Is.
d'Entrecasteaux Islands
Goodenough I.
Fergusson I.
Ward Hunt Strait
Tufi Dive Resort
Milne Bay
Alotau
Goschen Strait
Coral Sea
Sb Sc Sd Se Sf
144° 146° 148° 150°
2° 4° 6° 8° 10°
46 47 48 49 50 51
302 160 147
Belém
Manaus
Fortaleza
Natal
João Pessoa
Recife
Maceió
Remarkable cities and cultural monuments
UNESCO World Cultural Heritage
Remarkable city
Pl. of cult. interest to indig. peoples
Cultural landscape
Historical city scape
Castle/fortress/fort
Monument
Market
Festivals
Museum
Sport and leisure sites
Sailing
Diving
Canoeing/rafting
Beach resort

Bismarck Archipelago, Solomon Islands

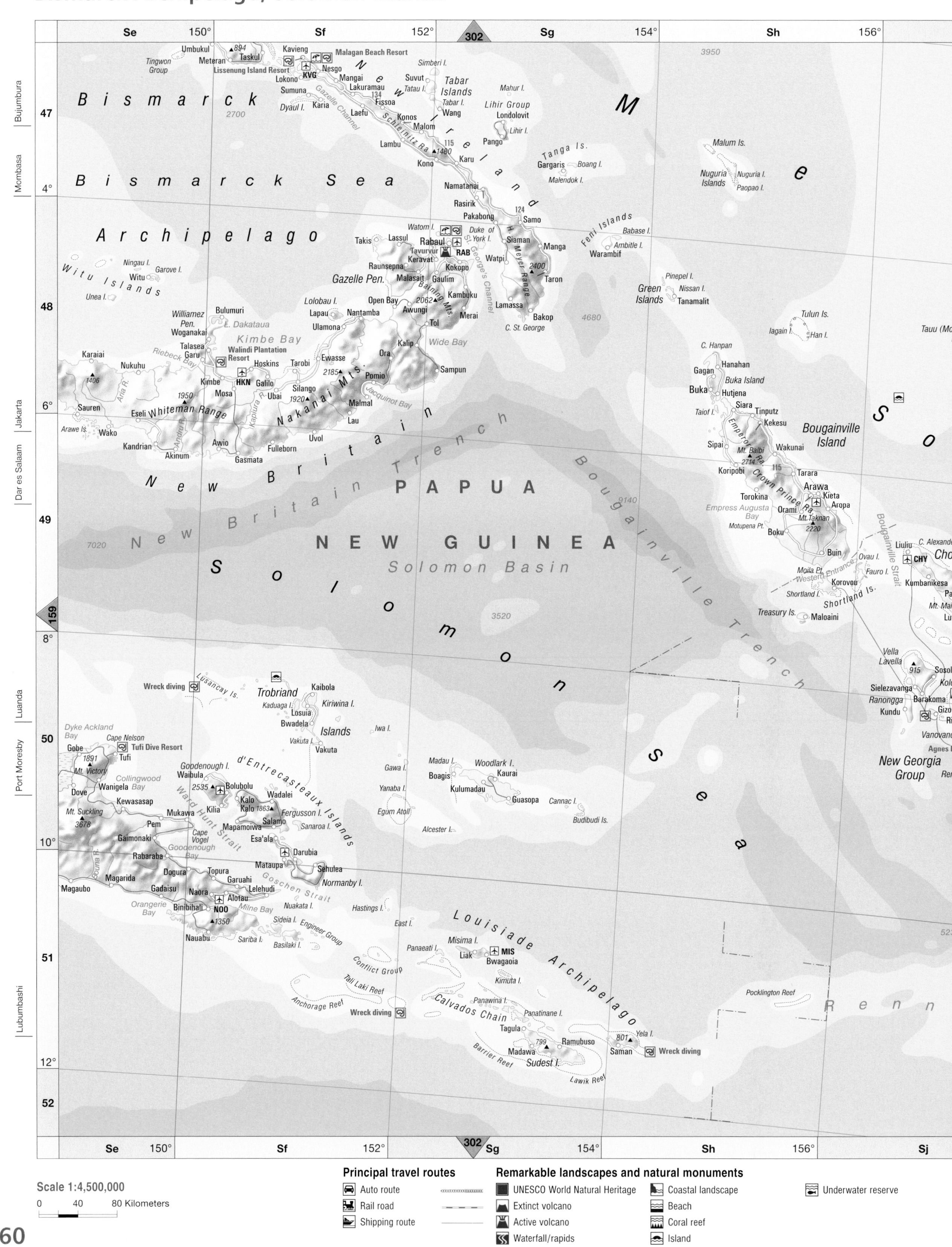

Scale 1:4,500,000

0   40   80 Kilometers

Principal travel routes
- Auto route
- Rail road
- Shipping route

- Waterfall/rapids

Remarkable landscapes and natural monuments
- UNESCO World Natural Heritage
- Extinct volcano
- Active volcano

- Coastal landscape
- Beach
- Coral reef
- Island

- Underwater reserve

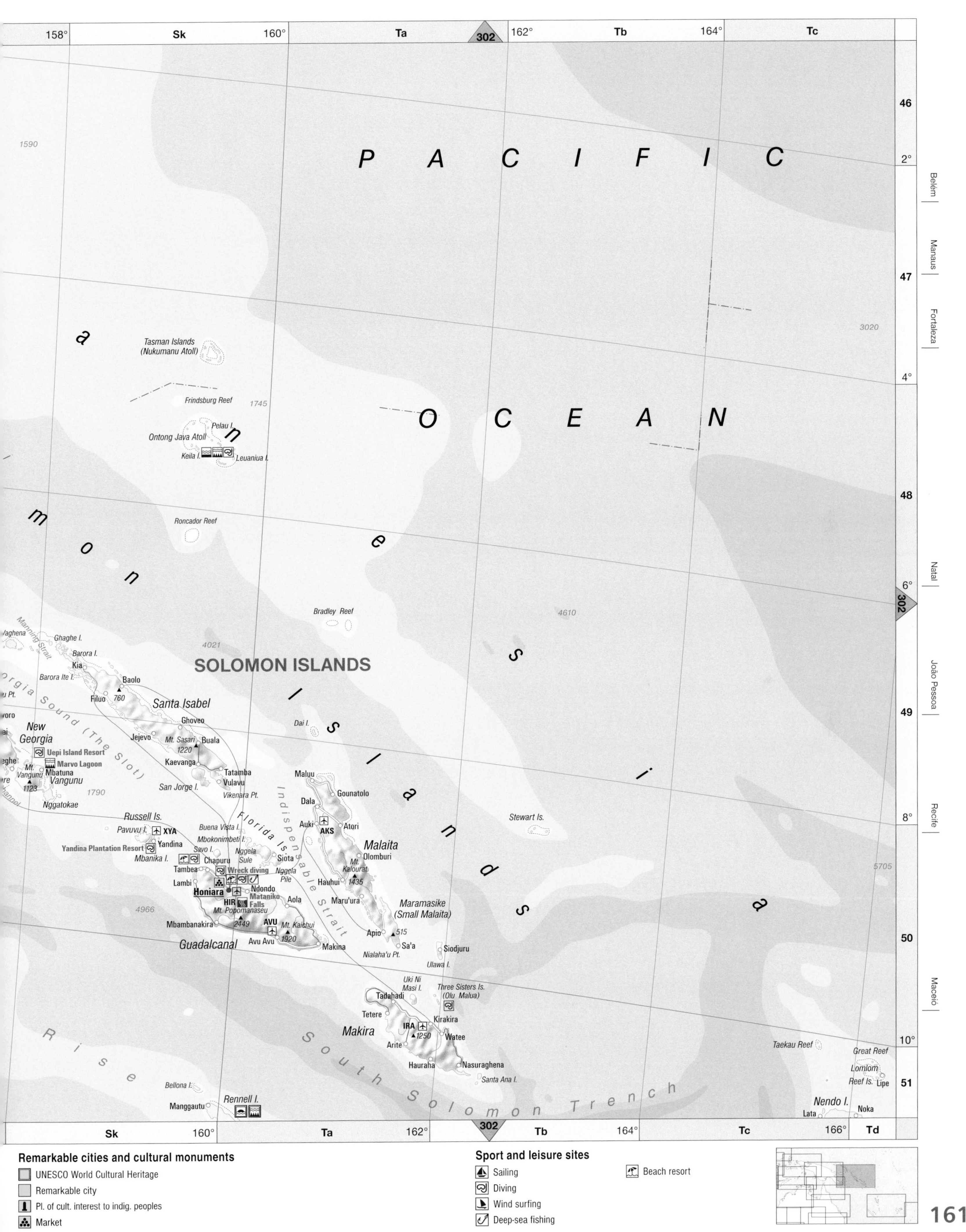

46

2°

47

3020

4°

P A C I F I C

O C E A N

48

6°   302

1590

a

Tasman Islands
(Nukumanu Atoll)

Frindsburg Reef   *1745*

Ontong Java Atoll   Pelau I.

Keila I.   Leuaniua I.

n

Roncador Reef

e

4610

Bradley Reef

4021

SOLOMON ISLANDS

Belém

Manaus

Fortaleza

Natal

João Pessoa

49

o r g i a Sound (The Slot)

Vaghena   Ghaghe I.

Barora I.

Kia

Barora Ite I.

Pt.

Filuo   *760*

Santa Isabel

Ghoveo

Jejevo

Mt. Sasari
1220

Buala

Dai I.

Kaevanga

voro

New
Georgia

Uepi Island Resort

Marvo Lagoon

eghe

*Mt.
Vangunu
1123*

Mbatuna

Vangunu

Tatamba

Vulavu

Maluu

Gounatolo

I

s

l

Dala

Auki

Atori

San Jorge I.

Vikenara Pt.

1790

Nggatokae

Russell Is.

Pavuvu I.

XYA

Buena Vista I.

Mbokonimbeti I.

Stewart Is.

a

n

d

s

Yandina Plantation Resort   Yandina

Mbanika I.

Savo I.

Nggela

Siota

Chapuru

Sule

Nggela
Pile

Tambea

Wreck diving

Hauhui

Malaita

Olomburi

*Mt.
Kalourat
1435*

50

4966

Lambi

Honiara

HIR   Mataniko
Falls

Ndondo

Aola

Maru'ura

Mbambanakira

Mt. Popomanaseu
2449

AVU   Mt. Kaichui
1920

Avu Avu

Makina

Nialaha'u Pt.

Maramasike
(Small Malaita)

Apio   *515*

Sa'a

Siodjuru

Ulawa I.

Guadalcanal

Uki Ni
Masi I.

Tadahadi

Three Sisters Is.
(Olu Malua)

Tetere

IRA

Kirakira

Rise

Makira

Arite

1250

Watee

Hauraha

Nasuraghena

Santa Ana I.

Recife

5705

Macelió

10°

Taekau Reef

Great Reef

Lomlom
Reef Is.   Lipe

Bellona I.

Manggautu   Rennell I.

South Solomon Trench

Nendo I.

Lata   Noka

51

Remarkable cities and cultural monuments

- ▢ UNESCO World Cultural Heritage
- ▢ Remarkable city
- ▲ Pl. of cult. interest to indig. peoples
- ⛰ Market

Sport and leisure sites

- ⛵ Sailing
- Diving
- Wind surfing
- Deep-sea fishing
- Beach resort

161

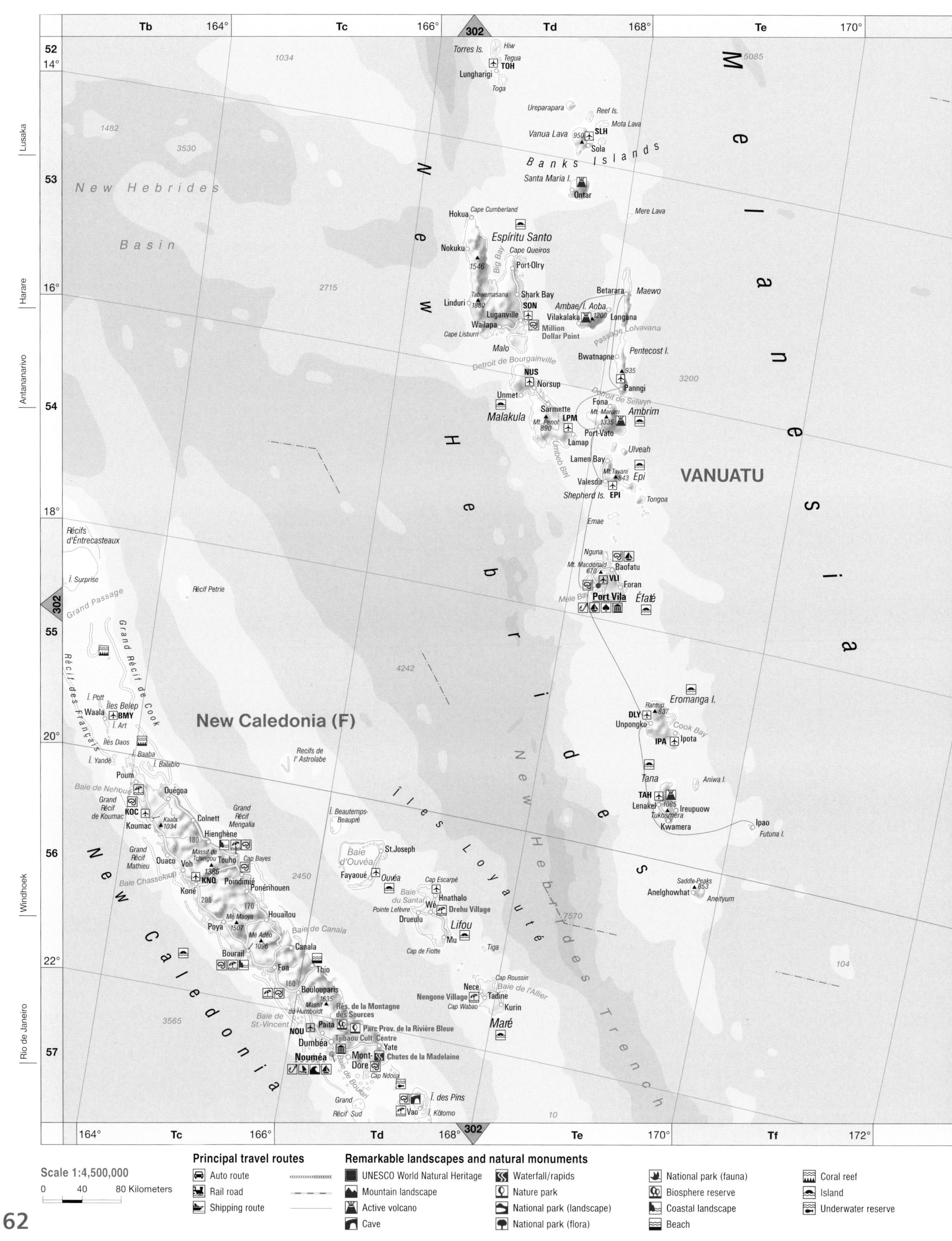

Tb	164°	**Tc**	166°	**302**	**Td**	168°	**Te**	170°

52 14°
302
Torres Is. Hiw
Tegua
TOH Toga
Lungharigi
Toga

Lusaka

1034
Ureparapara
Reef Is.
Mota Lava
Vanua Lava 950 SLH
1482
3530
Sola
Banks Islands
Mere Lava

53
New Hebrides
Santa Maria I.
Ontar
Basin
Hokua Cape Cumberland
Mere Lava

Harare
Espíritu Santo
Nokuku Cape Queiros
1546 Port-Olry
2715
Tabwemasana Shark Bay
Linduri 1880 SON Betarara Maewo
Luganville Ambae/I. Aoba 1200 Longana
16° Wailapa Vilakalaka
Million Dollar Point

Antananarivo
Cape Lisburn
Malo Pentecost I.
Detroit de Bougainville Bwatnapne
935
NUS Panngi
Norsup 3200
Unmet Détroit de Selwyn
Sarmette Fona
Malakula LPM Mt. Marum Ambrim
54 Mt. Penot 1335
890 Port-Vato
Lamap
Lamen Bay Ulveah
Mt. Tavani **VANUATU**
Valesdir 643 Epi
Shepherd Is. EPI Tongoa

18°
Récifs Emae
d'Éntrecasteaux
Nguna
Mt. Macdonald Baofatu
Î. Surprise 670 VLI
302 Foran
Récif Petrie Mele Bay **Port Vila** Éfaté
Grand Passage

55
4242
Eromanga I.
Rantop 837
DLY
New Caledonia (F) Unpongko Cook Bay
IPA Ipota
Î. Pott
Îles Belep
Waala BMY Tana
Î. Art Aniwa I.
20° Îles Daos TAH
Î. Baaba Lenakel 1085 Ireupuow
Î. Yandé Tukosmera
Poum Î. Balabio Kwamera
Baie de Nehoué Ipao
Grand Futuna I.
Récif Ouégoa
de Koumac KOC Î. Beautemps-
Koumac Colnett Beaupré Saddle-Peaks
Kaala 1034 853
Hienghène St.Joseph Anelghowhat
Grand Baie Aneityum
Massif de d'Ouvéa
Grand Tchingou Cap Bayes Ouvéa
Récif Mathieu Voh 1356 Fayaoué
56 Quaco KNQ Baie
Koné Poindimié du Santal
Baie Chasseloup Ponérihouen Pointe Lefèvre Wé Hnathalo
205 170 Drueulu Drehu Village
Mé Maoya Houaïlou Lifou
Poya 1507 Mu
Mé Adéo Baie de Canala Tiga
1096
Bourail Canala
22° Foa Cap de Fiotte
Thio
160 Bouloupatis Cap Roussin
1635 Nece Baie de l'Allier
Massif Rés. de la Montagne Nengone Village Tadine
du Humboldt des Sources Kurin
Baie de Parc Prov. de la Rivière Bleue Cap Wabao
St-Vincent **NOU** Paita Maré
3565 Dumbéa Tjibaou Cult. Centre
57 Mont- Yate
Nouméa Doré Chutes de la Madeleine
Cap Ndoua
Grand Î. des Pins
Récif Sud Vao Î. Kotomo
10

164°	**Tc**	166°	**Td**	168°	**302**	**Te**	170°	**Tf**	172°

Windhoek

Rio de Janeiro

Principal travel routes | **Remarkable landscapes and natural monuments**

Scale 1:4,500,000

0 40 80 Kilometers

Principal travel routes	Remarkable landscapes and natural monuments		
Auto route	UNESCO World Natural Heritage	Waterfall/rapids	National park (fauna)	Coral reef
Rail road	Mountain landscape	Nature park	Biosphere reserve	Island
Shipping route	Active volcano	National park (landscape)	Coastal landscape	Underwater reserve
	Cave	National park (flora)	Beach	

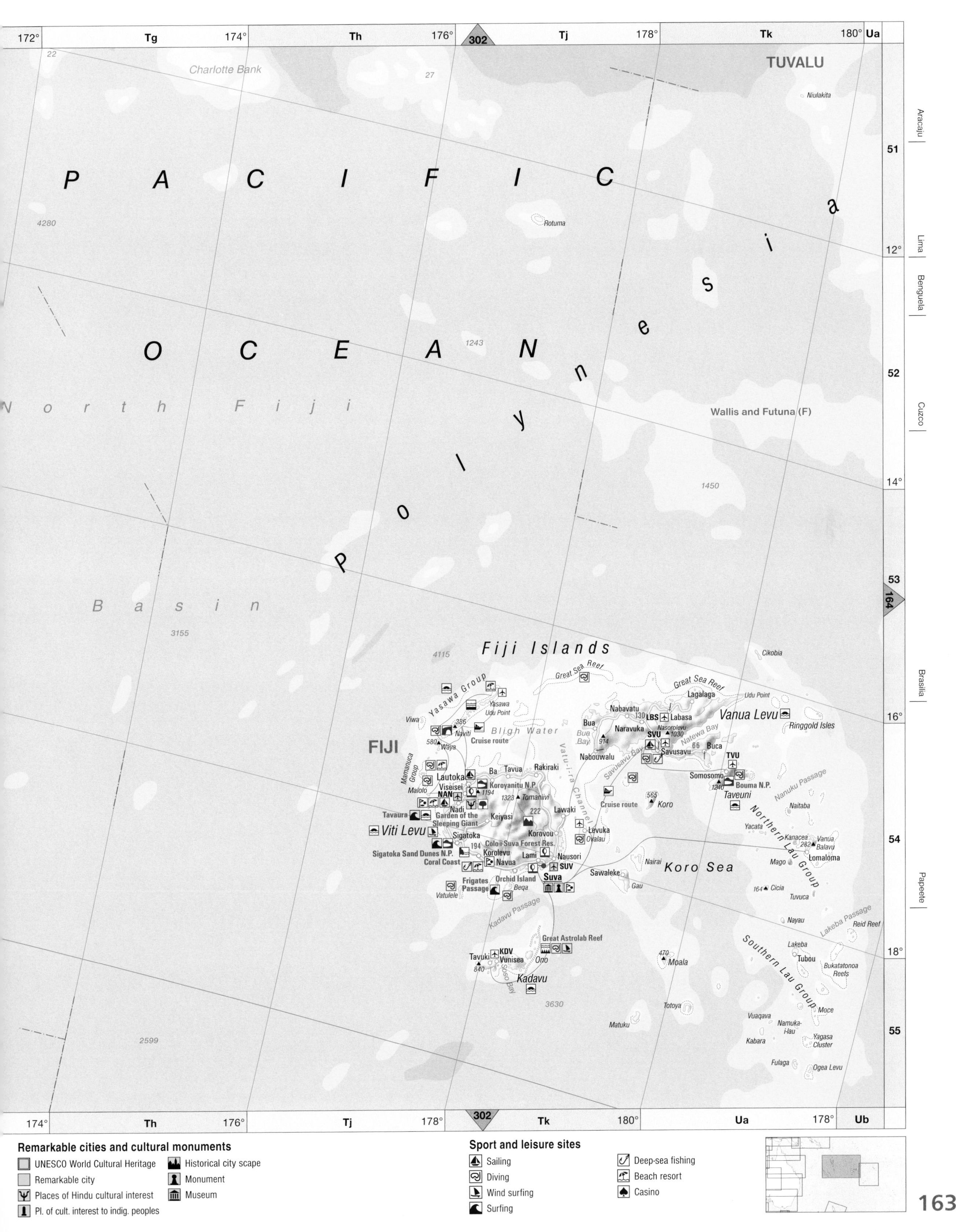

Remarkable cities and cultural monuments
- UNESCO World Cultural Heritage
- Remarkable city
- Places of Hindu cultural interest
- Pl. of cult. interest to indig. peoples
- Historical city scape
- Monument
- Museum

Sport and leisure sites
- Sailing
- Diving
- Wind surfing
- Surfing
- Deep-sea fishing
- Beach resort
- Casino

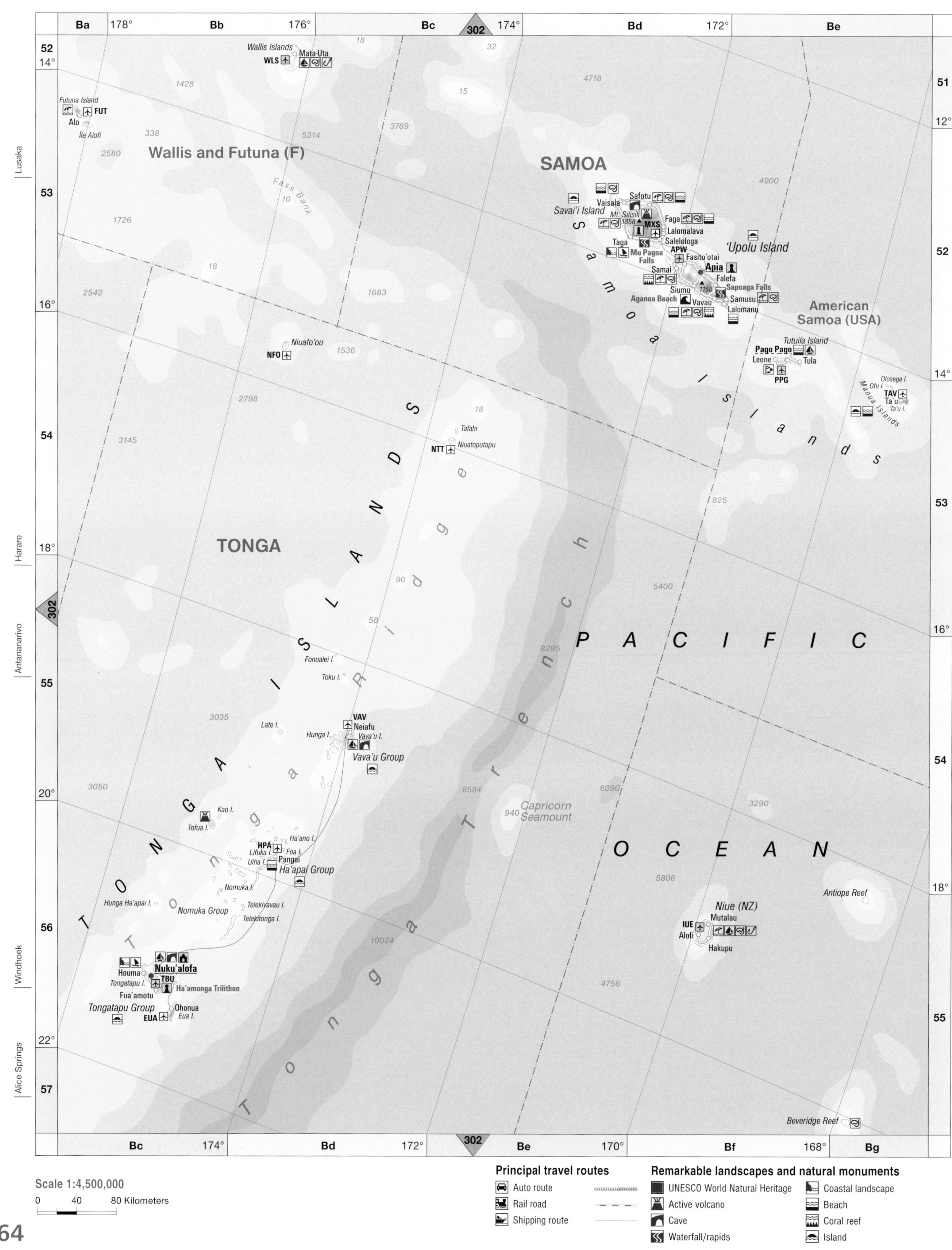

| Ba | 178° | Bb | 176° | Bc | **302** | 174° | Bd | 172° | Be |

52
14° Wallis Islands · Mata-Uta
WLS 18 32

1428 15 4718

Lusaka

Futuna Island 338 5314 3769 4900
FUT
Alo
Île Alofi 1726 **Wallis and Futuna (F)** **SAMOA**
2580 10 Vaisala Safotu
53 Fass Bank Savai'i Island Faga
1858 Mt. Silisili Lalomalava
MXS Salelologa
Taga APW 'Upolu Island
Mu Pagoa APW Fasito'otai
Falls Apia
Samai Falefa
Siumu 1156 Sapoaga Falls American
16° 2542 1683 Aganoa Beach Vavau Samusu Samoa (USA)
Lalomanu

Harare

Niuafo'ou Tutuila Island Ofu I.
NFO 1536 Pago Pago Olosega I.
Leone Tula Ta'u I.
PPG **TAV** Ta'u I.
Manua Islands
2798 18 14°
54 Tafahi
3145 **NTT** Niuatoputapu 825

Antananarivo

18° **TONGA** 90 5400 16°

58
302 Fonualei I. 8285 **PACIFIC**
55 Toku I. 940 Capricorn
Seamount
3035
Late I. **VAV** 6584 6090 3290
Hunga I. Neiafu
Vava'u I.
Vava'u Group 5806 Antiope Reef
20° 3050
Kao I. Niue (NZ)
Tofua I. Mutalau **OCEAN**
Ha'ano I. **IUE** 18°
HPA Foa I. Alofi
Lifuka I. Pangai Hakupu
Uiha I. Ha'apai Group
Nomuka I. 10024 4756
Telekivavau I.
Hunga Ha'apai I. Telekitonga I.
56 Nomuka Group
Houma
TBU Nuku'alofa
Tongatapu I. Ha'amonga Trilithon
Fua'amotu
Ohonua
EUA Eua I.
Tongatapu Group Beveridge Reef
22° 57

| Bc | 174° | Bd | 172° | Be | 170° | Bf | 168° | Bg |

Windhoek

Alice Springs

Scale 1:4,500,000

0   40   80 Kilometers

Principal travel routes

- Auto route
- Rail road
- Shipping route

Remarkable landscapes and natural monuments

- UNESCO World Natural Heritage
- Active volcano
- Cave
- Waterfall/rapids
- Coastal landscape
- Beach
- Coral reef
- Island

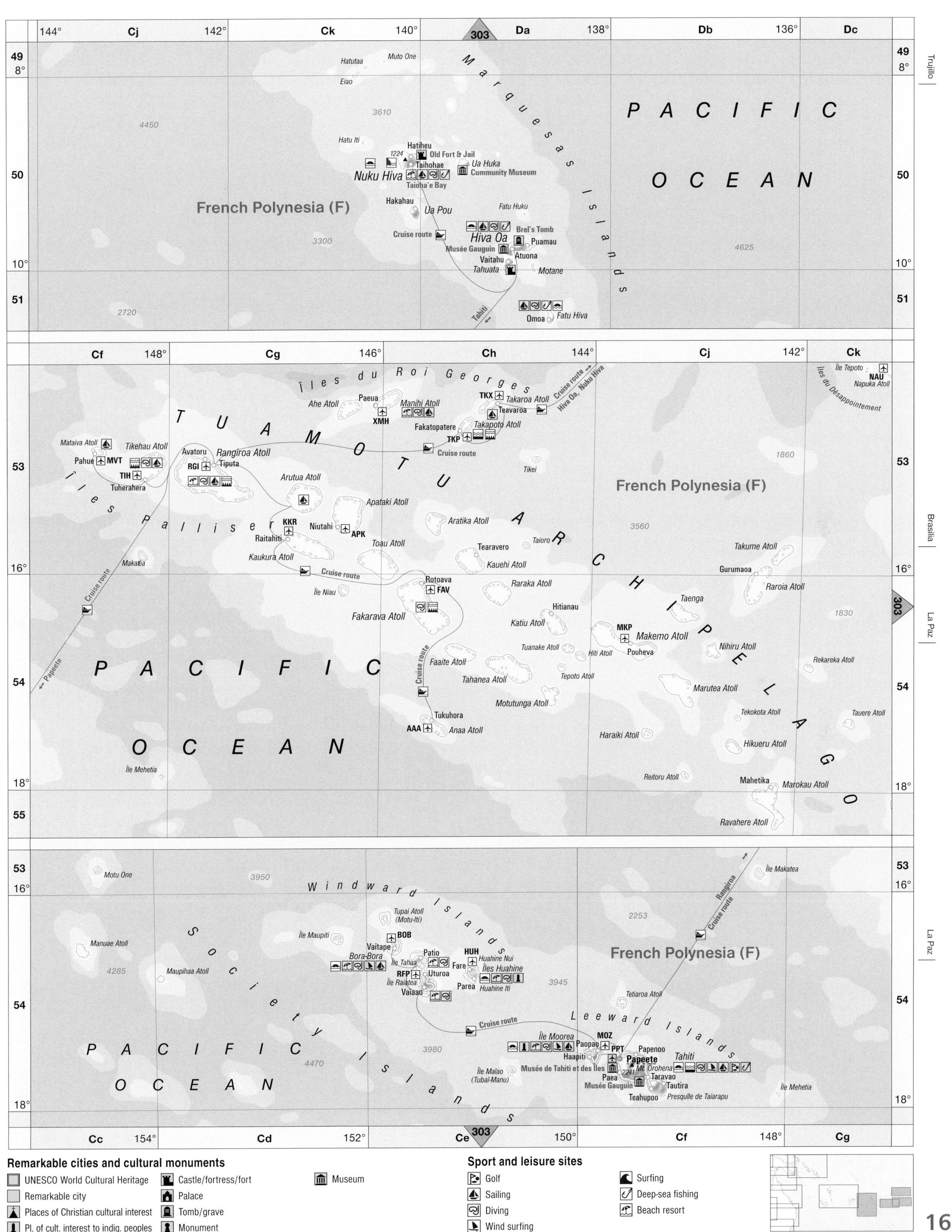

Africa – physical map

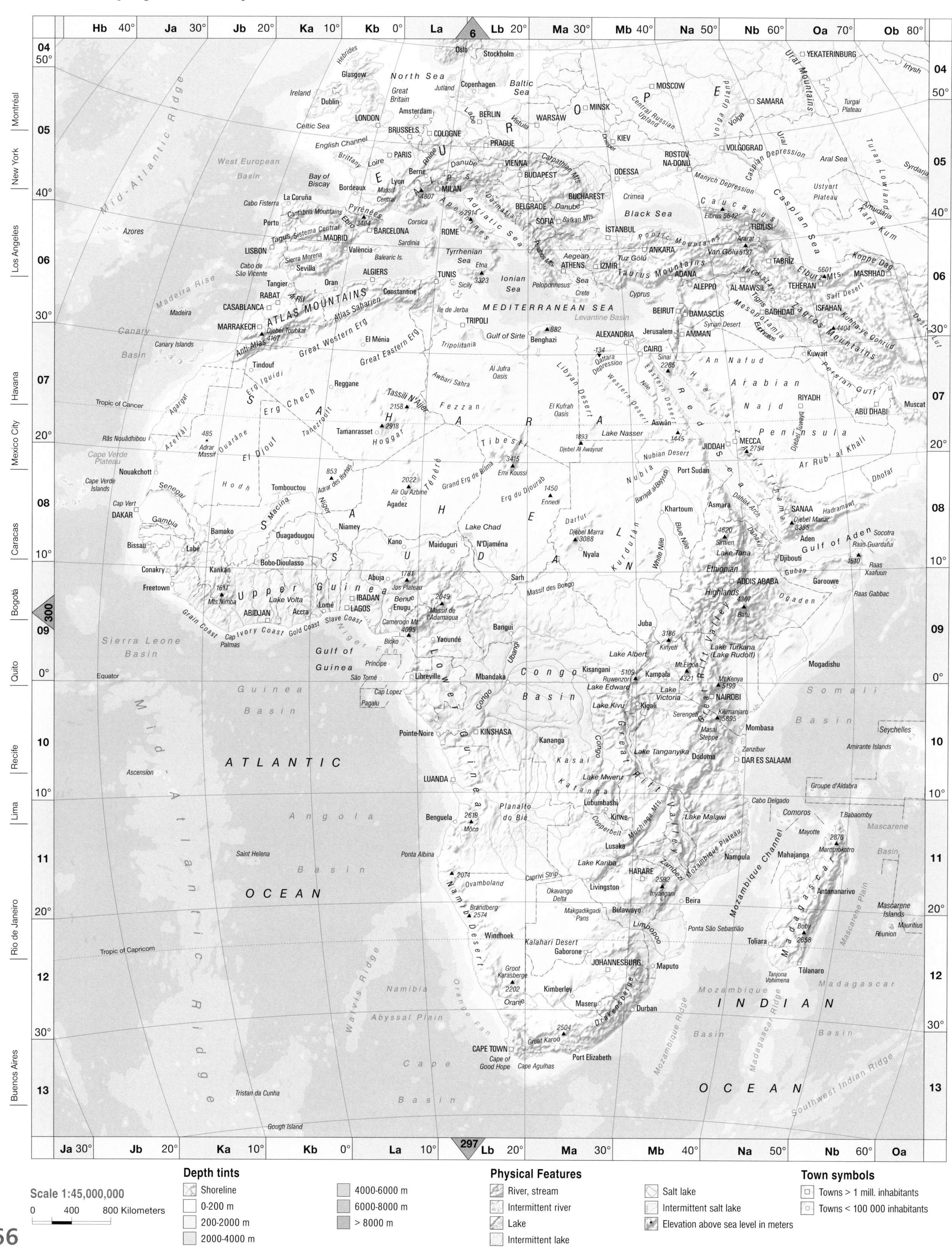

Scale 1:45,000,000

0   400   800 Kilometers

Depth tints

- Shoreline
- 0-200 m
- 200-2000 m
- 2000-4000 m
- 4000-6000 m
- 6000-8000 m
- > 8000 m

Physical Features

- River, stream
- Intermittent river
- Lake
- Intermittent lake
- Salt lake
- Intermittent salt lake
- Elevation above sea level in meters

Town symbols

- Towns > 1 mill. inhabitants
- Towns < 100 000 inhabitants

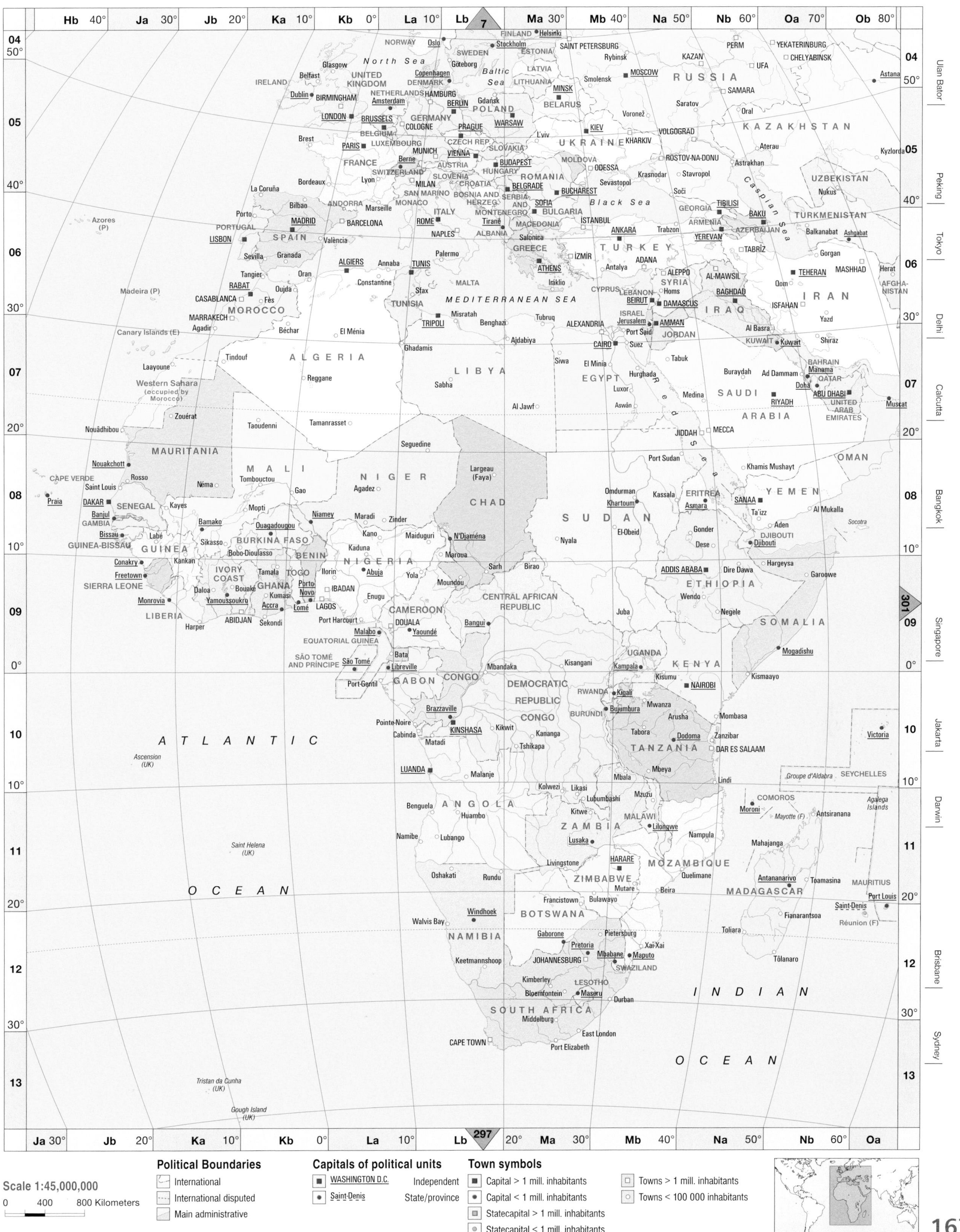

Hb 40°
Ja 30°
Jb 20°
Ka 10°
Kb 0°
La 10°
Lb
7
Ma 30°
Mb 40°
Na 50°
Nb 60°
Oa 70°
Ob 80°
04
05
06
07
08
09
10
11
12
13
50°
40°
30°
20°
10°
0°
Ulan Bator
Peking
Tokyo
Delhi
Calcutta
Bangkok
Singapore
Jakarta
Darwin
Brisbane
Sydney
301
297
FINLAND
Helsinki
NORWAY
Oslo
SWEDEN
Stockholm
ESTONIA
SAINT PETERSBURG
PERM
YEKATERINBURG
CHELYABINSK
Rybinsk
KAZAN
UFA
Astana
North Sea
Glasgow
Göteborg
Baltic Sea
LATVIA
LITHUANIA
Smolensk
MOSCOW
RUSSIA
SAMARA
Belfast
UNITED KINGDOM
Copenhagen
DENMARK
IRELAND
Dublin
BIRMINGHAM
NETHERLANDS
HAMBURG
Amsterdam
MINSK
BELARUS
Saratov
Oral
LONDON
BRUSSELS
BERLIN
Gdańsk
POLAND
Voronež
GERMANY
COLOGNE
PRAGUE
WARSAW
KIEV
VOLGOGRAD
KAZAKHSTAN
Brest
BELGIUM
LUXEMBOURG
CZECH REP.
SLOVAKIA
L'viv
UKRAINE
KHARKIV
PARIS
MUNICH
VIENNA
Aterau
Kyzlorda
FRANCE
Berne
AUSTRIA
BUDAPEST
MOLDOVA
ROSTOV-NA-DONU
Astrakhan
SWITZERLAND
HUNGARY
ODESSA
Lyon
SLOVENIA
ROMANIA
Krasnodar
Stavropol
UZBEKISTAN
MILAN
CROATIA
Sevastopol
Nukus
Bordeaux
SAN MARINO
BOSNIA AND HERZEG.
BELGRADE
BUCHAREST
Caspian Sea
La Coruña
MONACO
SERBIA AND
SOFIA
Black Sea
Soči
Bilbao
ANDORRA
Marseille
MONTENEGRO
BULGARIA
GEORGIA
TBILISI
Porto
ITALY
BAKU
TURKMENISTAN
MADRID
BARCELONA
ROME
Tiranë
MACEDONIA
ISTANBUL
ARMENIA
PORTUGAL
ALBANIA
ANKARA
Trabzon
AZERBAIJAN
Balkanabat
Ashgabat
Azores (P)
LISBON
SPAIN
València
NAPLES
Salonica
YEREVAN
TURKEY
TABRIZ
Gorgan
Sevilla
Granada
Palermo
GREECE
IZMIR
ADANA
Herat
ALGIERS
Annaba
TUNIS
ATHENS
Antalya
ALEPPO
AL-MAWSIL
TEHERAN
MASHHAD
Tangier
Oran
Constantine
MALTA
Iráklio
SYRIA
Qom
AFGHANISTAN
RABAT
Oujda
Sfax
CYPRUS
LEBANON
Homs
BAGHDAD
IRAN
Madeira (P)
CASABLANCA
Fès
TUNISIA
MEDITERRANEAN SEA
BEIRUT
DAMASCUS
IRAQ
ISFAHAN
MARRAKECH
MOROCCO
Misratah
Tubruq
ISRAEL
Jerusalem
AMMAN
Yazd
Agadir
Béchar
El Ménia
TRIPOLI
Benghazi
ALEXANDRIA
Port Said
JORDAN
Al Basra
Canary Islands (E)
CAIRO
Suez
KUWAIT
Kuwait
Shiraz
Ghadamis
Ajdabiya
Tindouf
ALGERIA
Siwa
Tabuk
BAHRAIN
Laayoune
El Minia
Buraydah
Ad Dammam
Manama
LIBYA
Hurghada
QATAR
Western Sahara (occupied by Morocco)
Reggane
EGYPT
Doha
ABU DHABI
Sabha
Luxor
SAUDI
RIYADH
UNITED ARAB EMIRATES
Medina
Muscat
Red Sea
Aswân
Al Jawf
ARABIA
Zouérat
Taoudenni
Tamanrasset
JIDDAH
MECCA
Nouâdhibou
Seguedine
MAURITANIA
Port Sudan
OMAN
Largeau (Faya)
Khamis Mushayt
Nouakchott
MALI
CAPE VERDE
Rosso
NIGER
Saint Louis
Tombouctou
YEMEN
Néma
Agadez
Omdurman
Kassala
ERITREA
Praia
DAKAR
Gao
Khartoum
Asmara
SANAA
SENEGAL
Kayes
CHAD
Ta'izz
Al Mukalla
Banjul
GAMBIA
Mopti
SUDAN
Niamey
Maradi
Zinder
Aden
Bamako
Ouagadougou
El-Obeid
Gonder
Socotra
Bissau
Labé
Kano
DJIBOUTI
BURKINA FASO
Maiduguri
N'Djaména
Nyala
Dese
Djibouti
GUINEA-BISSAU
GUINEA
Sikasso
Kaduna
Bobo-Dioulasso
BENIN
Maroua
Hargeysa
Conakry
Kankan
NIGERIA
ADDIS ABABA
Dire Dawa
Freetown
IVORY COAST
Tamale
TOGO
Ilorin
Abuja
Sarh
Birao
Garoowe
SIERRA LEONE
GHANA
Porto-Novo
IBADAN
Yola
ETHIOPIA
Daloa
Bouaké
Moundou
Wendo
Monrovia
Yamoussoukro
Kumasi
Enugu
CENTRAL AFRICAN REPUBLIC
Accra
Lomé
LAGOS
Juba
Negele
LIBERIA
ABIDJAN
Sekondi
CAMEROON
Harper
Port Harcourt
DOUALA
Bangui
SOMALIA
Malabo
Yaoundé
EQUATORIAL GUINEA
SÃO TOMÉ AND PRÍNCIPE
São Tomé
Bata
Libreville
UGANDA
Mogadishu
Mbandaka
Kisangani
Kampala
KENYA
GABON
CONGO
Kismaayo
Port-Gentil
DEMOCRATIC REPUBLIC CONGO
Kisumu
NAIROBI
RWANDA
Kigali
Brazzaville
BURUNDI
Bujumbura
Mwanza
Arusha
Mombasa
Pointe-Noire
KINSHASA
Kikwit
Cabinda
Matadi
Kananga
Tabora
Dodoma
Zanzibar
Victoria
ATLANTIC
Tshikapa
TANZANIA
DAR ES SALAAM
Ascension (UK)
LUANDA
Malanje
Mbeya
SEYCHELLES
Groupe d'Aldabra
Mbala
Lindi
Kolwezi
Likasi
Benguela
ANGOLA
Lubumbashi
Mzuzu
COMOROS
Agalega Islands
Huambo
Kitwe
MALAWI
Moroni
Mayotte (F)
Antsiranana
ZAMBIA
Lilongwe
Namibe
Lubango
Nampula
Lusaka
Mahajanga
Saint Helena (UK)
HARARE
Livingstone
MOZAMBIQUE
Oshakati
Rundu
Quelimane
Antananarivo
Toamasina
MAURITIUS
ZIMBABWE
Mutare
Beira
OCEAN
MADAGASCAR
Port Louis
Francistown
Bulawayo
Saint-Denis
Windhoek
BOTSWANA
Fianarantsoa
Walvis Bay
Réunion (F)
NAMIBIA
Gaborone
Pietersburg
Toliara
Pretoria
Xai-Xai
Mbabane
Maputo
Keetmanshoop
JOHANNESBURG
SWAZILAND
Tôlanaro
Kimberley
LESOTHO
INDIAN
Bloemfontein
Maseru
Durban
SOUTH AFRICA
Middelburg
East London
CAPE TOWN
Port Elizabeth
OCEAN
Tristan da Cunha (UK)
Gough Island (UK)
Ja 30°
Jb 20°
Ka 10°
Kb 0°
La 10°
Lb 20°
Ma 30°
Mb 40°
Na 50°
Nb 60°
Oa
Scale 1:45,000,000
0 400 800 Kilometers
Political Boundaries
International
International disputed
Main administrative
Capitals of political units
WASHINGTON D.C. Independent
Saint-Denis State/province
Town symbols
Capital > 1 mill. inhabitants
Capital < 1 mill. inhabitants
Statecapital > 1 mill. inhabitants
Statecapital < 1 mill. inhabitants
Towns > 1 mill. inhabitants
Towns < 100 000 inhabitants

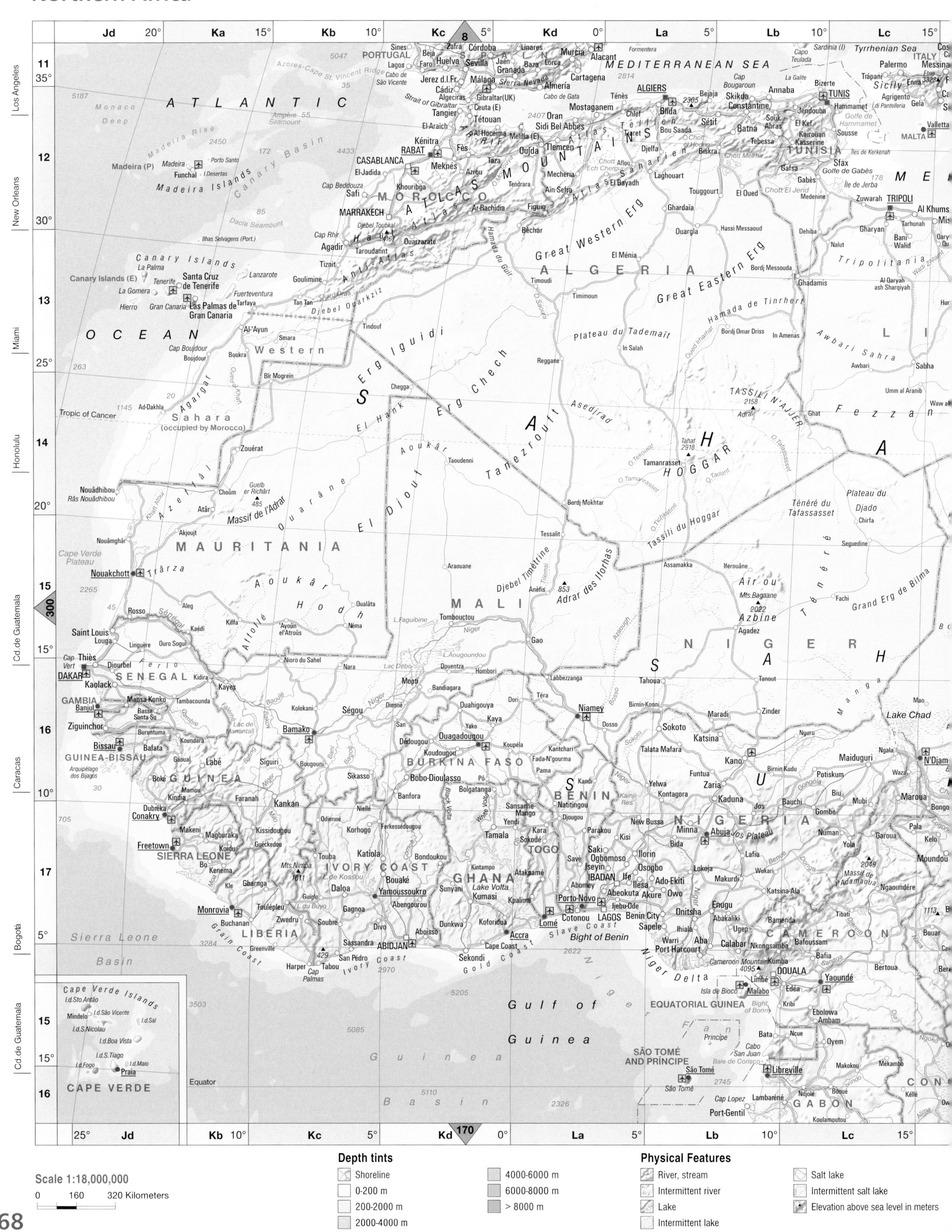

Scale 1:18,000,000

0   160   320 Kilometers

Depth tints

- Shoreline
- 0-200 m
- 200-2000 m
- 2000-4000 m
- 4000-6000 m
- 6000-8000 m
- > 8000 m

Physical Features

- River, stream
- Intermittent river
- Lake
- Intermittent lake
- Salt lake
- Intermittent salt lake
- Elevation above sea level in meters

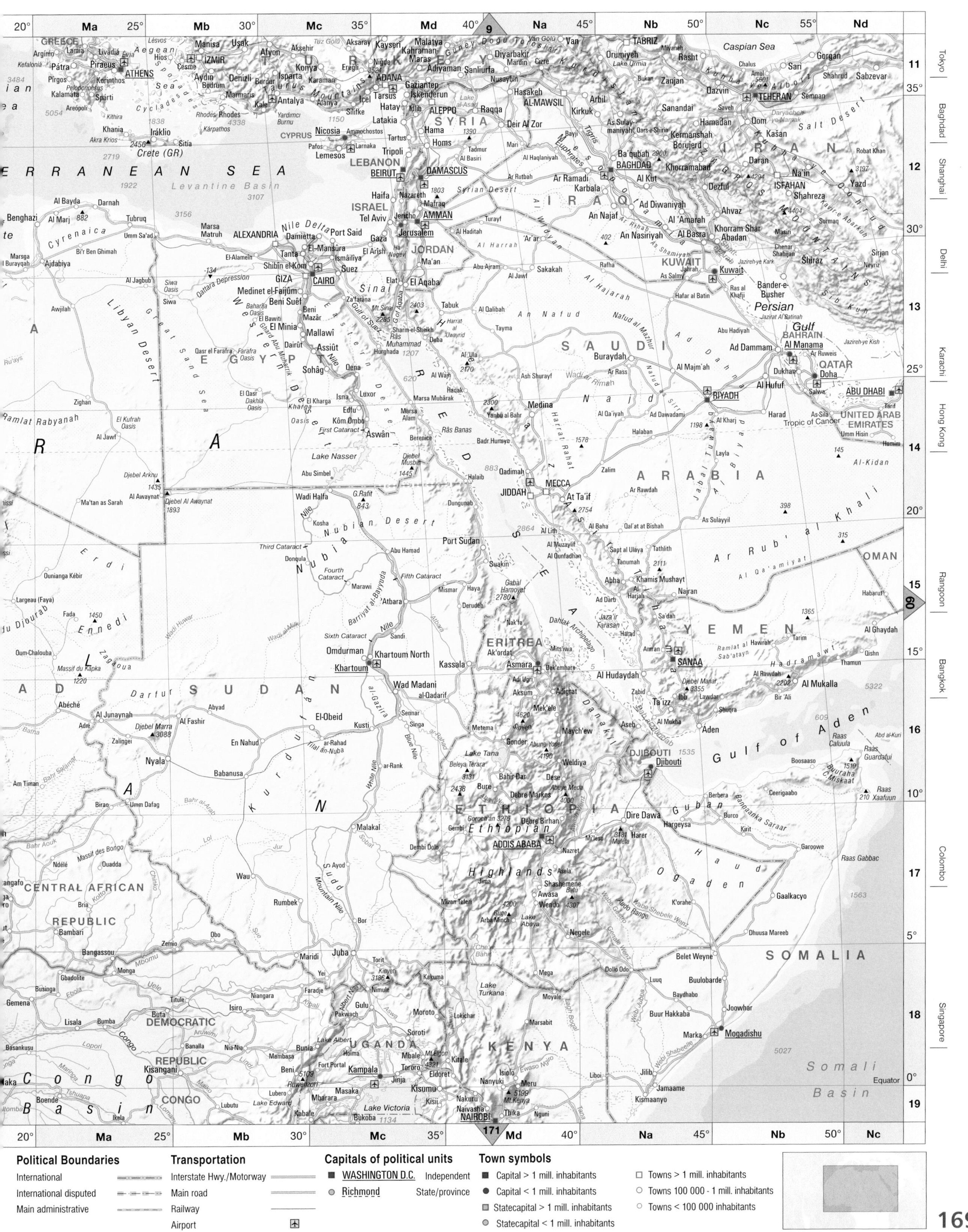

Tokyo

Baghdad

Shanghai

Delhi

Karachi

Hong Kong

Rangoon

Bangkok

Colombo

Singapore

Political Boundaries

International

International disputed

Main administrative

Transportation

Interstate Hwy./Motorway

Main road

Railway

Airport

Capitals of political units

■ WASHINGTON D.C. Independent

● Richmond State/province

Town symbols

■ Capital > 1 mill. inhabitants

● Capital < 1 mill. inhabitants

▣ Statecapital > 1 mill. inhabitants

⊙ Statecapital < 1 mill. inhabitants

□ Towns > 1 mill. inhabitants

○ Towns 100 000 - 1 mill. inhabitants

○ Towns < 100 000 inhabitants

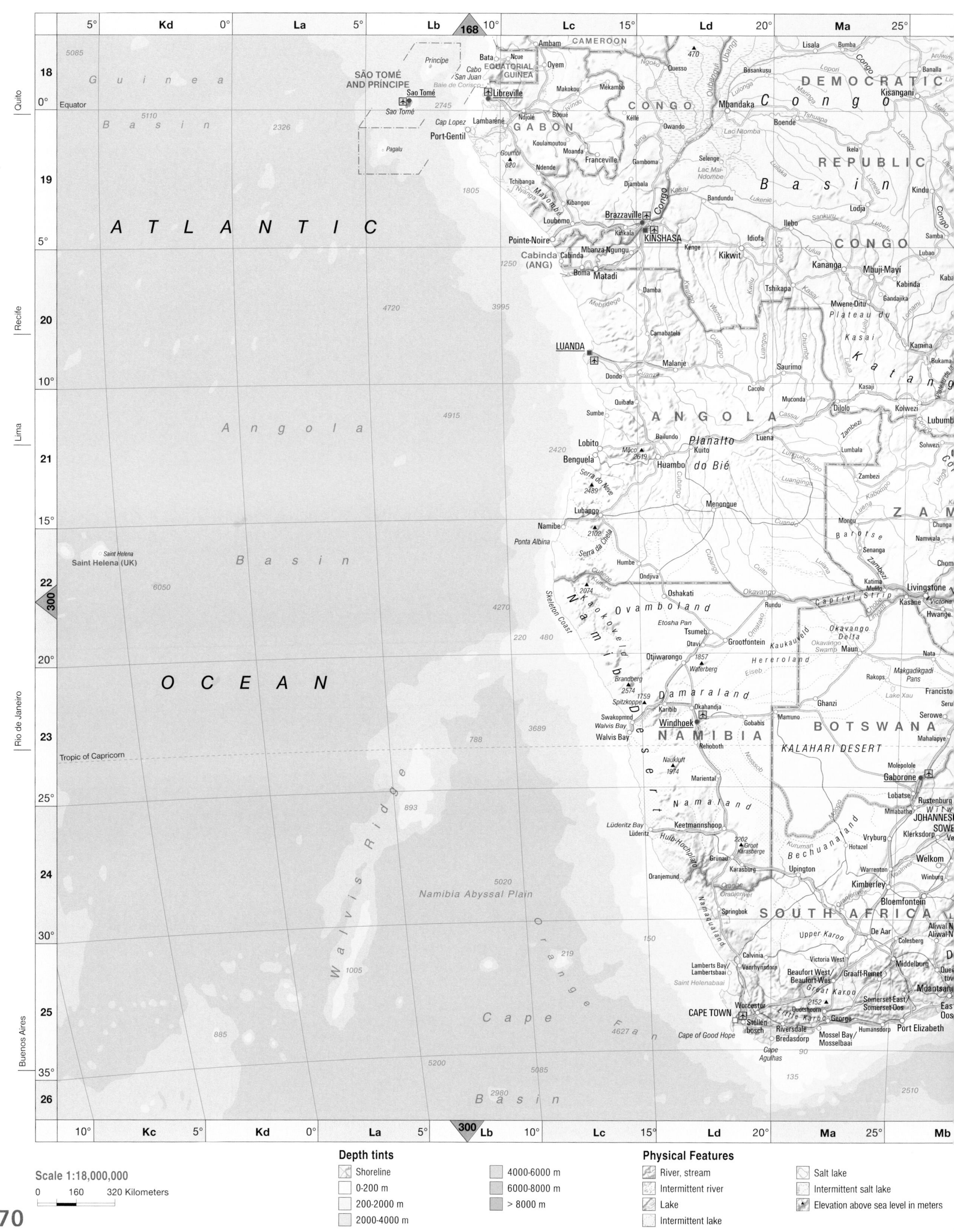

Map labels

Top scale: 5° Kd 0° La 5° Lb 168 10° Lc 15° Ld 20° Ma 25°

18
0° Quito
Equator

19

ATLANTIC
5°
20
21
15°
22
300
20°
OCEAN
Tropic of Capricorn
23
25°
24
30°
25
35°
26

Left margin labels: Quito, Recife, Lima, Rio de Janeiro, Buenos Aires

Bottom scale: 10° Kc 5° Kd 0° La 5° 300 Lb 10° Lc 15° Ld 20° Ma 25° Mb

Ocean labels
G u i n e a
B a s i n
5085
5110
2326
Sao Tomé
SÃO TOMÉ AND PRÍNCIPE
Príncipe
2745
Pagalu
1805
A n g o l a
4720
3995
4915
B a s i n
Saint Helena
Saint Helena (UK)
6050
4270
220 480
2074
Walvis Ridge
3689
788
893
Namibia Abyssal Plain
5020
1005
219
885
Cape
4627
B a s i n
5200
5085
2980
2510
90
135
150
Orange Fan

Land features
CAMEROON
Ambam
Ngoko
Ouesso
Basankusu
Lisala
Bumba
Banalia
Aruwimi
470
DEMOCRATIC
Kisangani
Bata
Ncue
Oyem
EQUATORIAL GUINEA
Cabo San Juan
Baie de Corisco
Libreville
Makokou
Mékambo
Mbandaka
C o n g o
Boende
Ikela
Tshuapa
Lomela
Kindu
REPUBLIC
Lopori
Lulonga
Ngoko
Cap Lopez
Lambaréné
Ndjolé
Booué
Kéllé
Owando
Lac Ntomba
B a s i n
Lubefu
GABON
Port-Gentil
Koulamoutou
Moanda
Franceville
Gamboma
Selenge
Lac Mai-Ndombe
Djambala
Bandundu
Lukenie
Lodja
Lukuru
Congo
Samba
Goumbi
620
Ndende
Nyanga
Mayumba
Kibangou
Loubomo
Brazzaville
Pointe-Noire
KINSHASA
Kinkala
Kasai
Sankuru
Ilebo
Idiofa
CONGO
Lubao
Mbanza-Ngungu
Kenge
Kikwit
Lua
Luilu
Cabinda (ANG)
Cabinda
1250
Boma
Matadi
Damba
Kwango
Kwilu
Tshikapa
Kasai
Kananga
Mbuji-Mayi
Kabinda
Mebridege
Mwene-Ditu
Gandajika
Plateau du Kasai
Kamina
LUANDA
Camabatela
Malanje
Saurimo
Kasaji
Katanga
Dondo
Cacolo
Muconda
Dilolo
Kolwezi
Lubumbashi
Quibala
Sumbe
A N G O L A
Cassai
Zambezi
Lumbala
Solwezi
Lobito
Bailundo
Planalto do Bié
Luena
Lunda-Bungo
Zambezi
Benguela
Moco 2619
Kuito
Huambo
Luanginga
Z A M
Serra do Neve
2489
Menongue
Cuando
Cuango
Mongu
B a r o t s e
Namwala
Lubango
Namibe
2102
Cuito
Cuando
Katima Mulilo
Livingstone
Victoria
Ponta Albina
Serra da Chela
Humbe
Ondjiva
Okavango
Caprivi Strip
Kasane
Hwange
Skeleton Coast
Kunene
Oshakati
Rundu
Naokoveld
Ovamboland
Etosha Pan
Tsumeb
Grootfontein
Okavango Delta
Okavango Swamp
Maun
Nata
Otavi
Kaukauveld
Hereroland
Makgadikgadi Pans
Francistown
Otjiwarongo
1857
Waterberg
Eiseb
Rakops
Lake Xau
Serule
N a m i b
Brandberg 2574
Damaraland
Karibib
Okahandja
Ghanzi
B O T S W A N A
Mahalapye
Spitzkoppe 1759
Swakopmund
Walvis Bay
Windhoek
Gobabis
Mamuno
Molepolole
Gaborone
Rehoboth
KALAHARI DESERT
Lobatse
Rustenburg
Nauuluft 1974
Mariental
JOHANNESBURG
SOWE
N a m a l a n d
Klerksdorp
Lüderitz Bay
Lüderitz
Keetmannshoop
Vryburg
Welkom
Hotazel
B e c h u a n a l a n d
Warrenton
Winburg
2202 Groot Karasberge
Karasburg
Upington
Kimberley
Grünau
N a m a q u a l a n d
Oranjemund
Springbok
SOUTH AFRICA
Bloemfontein
Upper Karoo
De Aar
Colesberg
Aliwal-N
Calvinia
Victoria West
Middelburg
Lamberts Bay/Lambertsbaai
Beaufort West/Beaufort-Wes
Great Karoo
Graaff-Reinet
Mdantsane
Saint Helenabaai
2152
Somerset East/Somerset-Oos
East
Worcester
Oudtshoorn
Little Karoo
George
Humansdorp
Port Elizabeth
CAPE TOWN
Stellenbosch
Riversdale
Mossel Bay
Cape of Good Hope
Bredasdorp
Cape Agulhas

Scale

Scale 1:18,000,000

0   160   320 Kilometers

Depth tints

Shoreline		4000-6000 m	
0-200 m		6000-8000 m	
200-2000 m		> 8000 m	
2000-4000 m			

Physical Features

River, stream	Salt lake
Intermittent river	Intermittent salt lake
Lake	Elevation above sea level in meters
Intermittent lake	

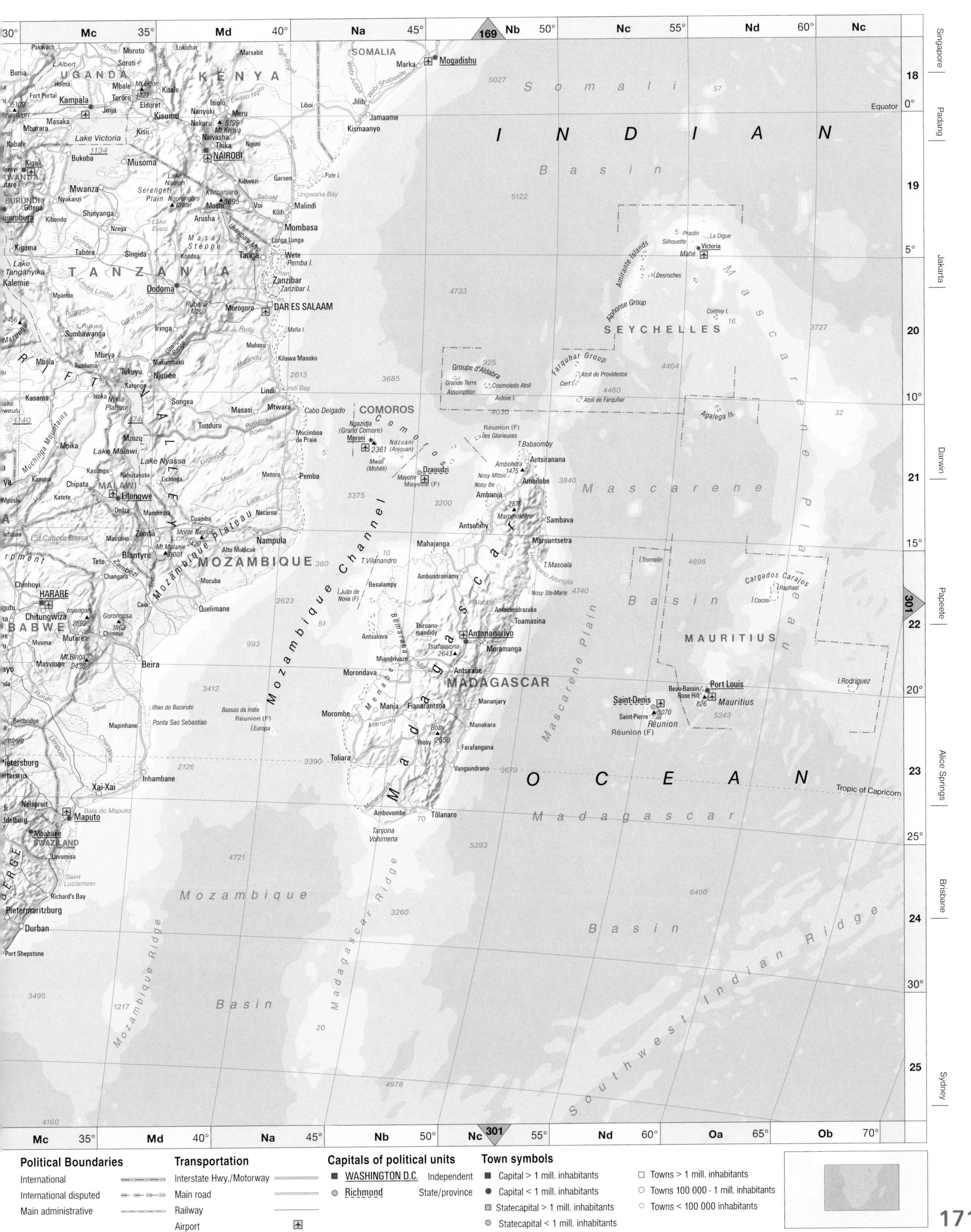

Mc 35° Md 40° Na 45° ◈ 169 Nb 50° Nc 55° Nd 60° Nc
Singapore
Padang
Jakarta
Darwin
Papeete
Alice Springs
Brisbane
Sydney

Political Boundaries

International
International disputed
Main administrative

Transportation

Interstate Hwy./Motorway
Main road
Railway
Airport

Capitals of political units

■ WASHINGTON D.C. Independent
● Richmond State/province

Town symbols

■ Capital > 1 mill. inhabitants
● Capital < 1 mill. inhabitants
▣ Statecapital > 1 mill. inhabitants
◉ Statecapital < 1 mill. inhabitants

□ Towns > 1 mill. inhabitants
○ Towns 100 000 - 1 mill. inhabitants
○ Towns < 100 000 inhabitants

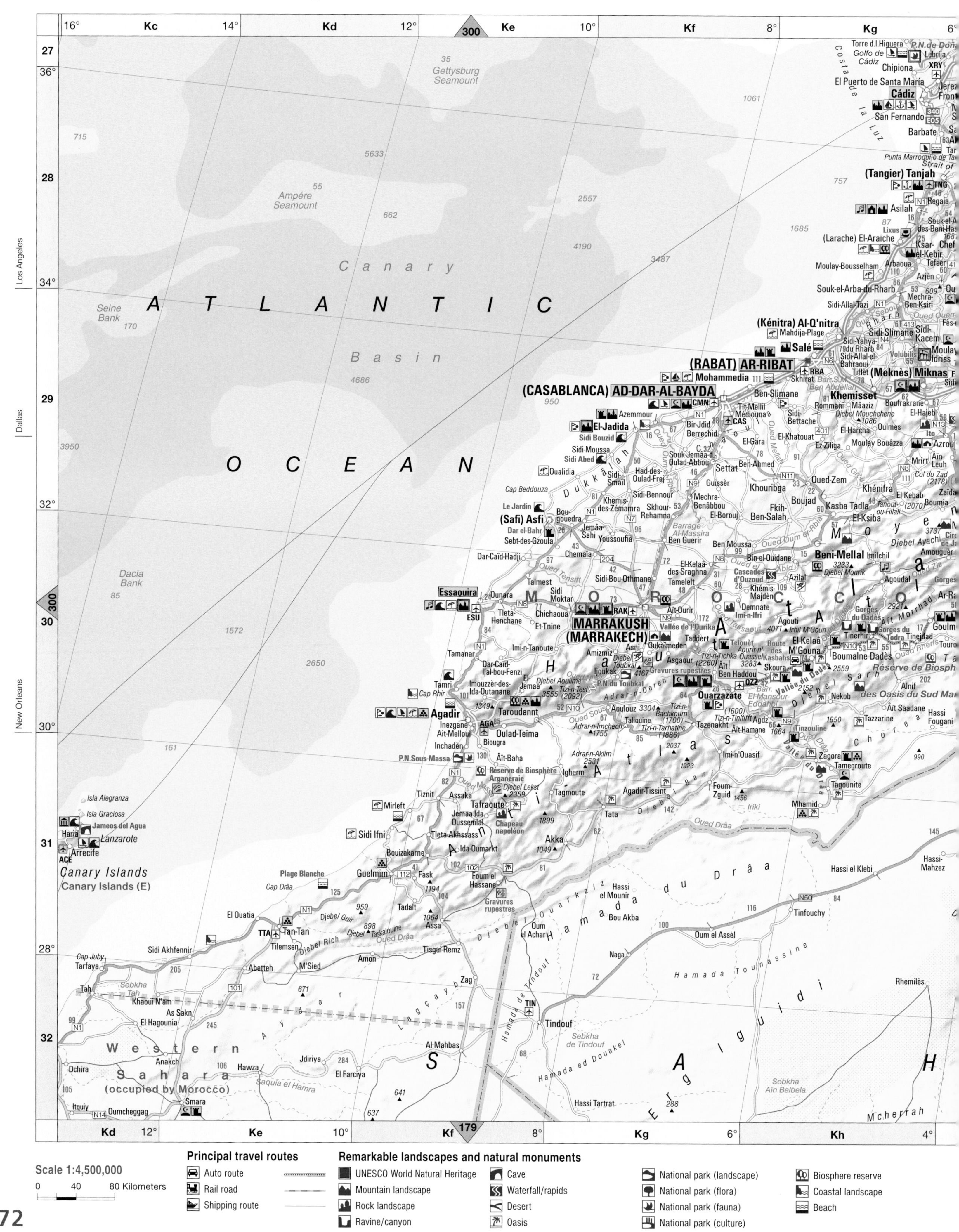

Scale 1:4,500,000

0   40   80 Kilometers

Principal travel routes
- Auto route
- Rail road
- Shipping route

Remarkable landscapes and natural monuments
- UNESCO World Natural Heritage
- Mountain landscape
- Rock landscape
- Ravine/canyon
- Cave
- Waterfall/rapids
- Desert
- Oasis
- National park (landscape)
- National park (flora)
- National park (fauna)
- National park (culture)
- Biosphere reserve
- Coastal landscape
- Beach

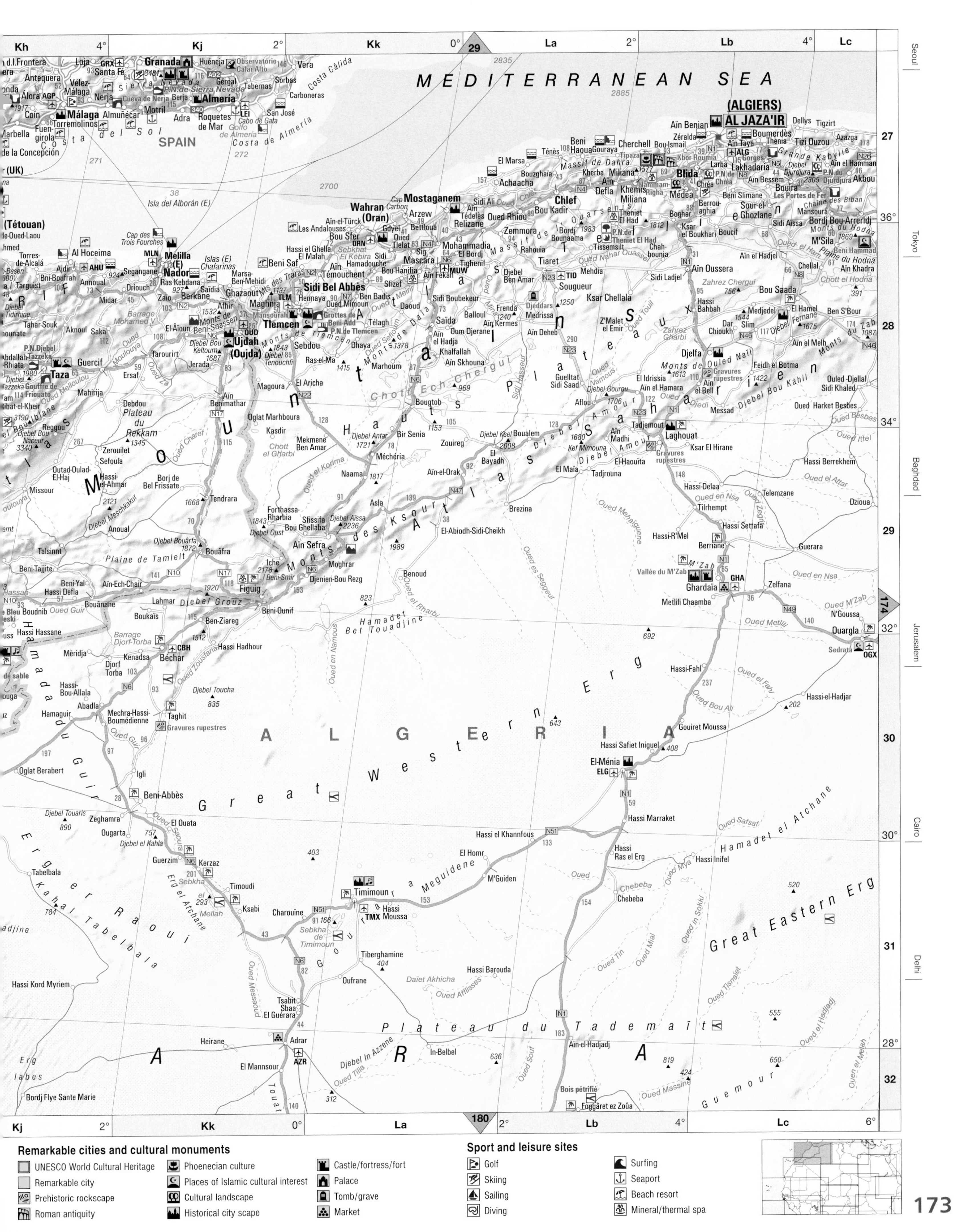
MEDITERRANEAN SEA
SPAIN
(ALGIERS)
AL JAZA'IR
ALGERIA
Great Western Erg
Great Eastern Erg
Plateau du Tademaït
Hamada du Guir
Erg er Raoui
Hamadet el Atchane
Chott Ech Chergui
Remarkable cities and cultural monuments
UNESCO World Cultural Heritage
Remarkable city
Prehistoric rockscape
Roman antiquity
Phoenecian culture
Places of Islamic cultural interest
Cultural landscape
Historical city scape
Castle/fortress/fort
Palace
Tomb/grave
Market
Sport and leisure sites
Golf
Skiing
Sailing
Diving
Surfing
Seaport
Beach resort
Mineral/thermal spa

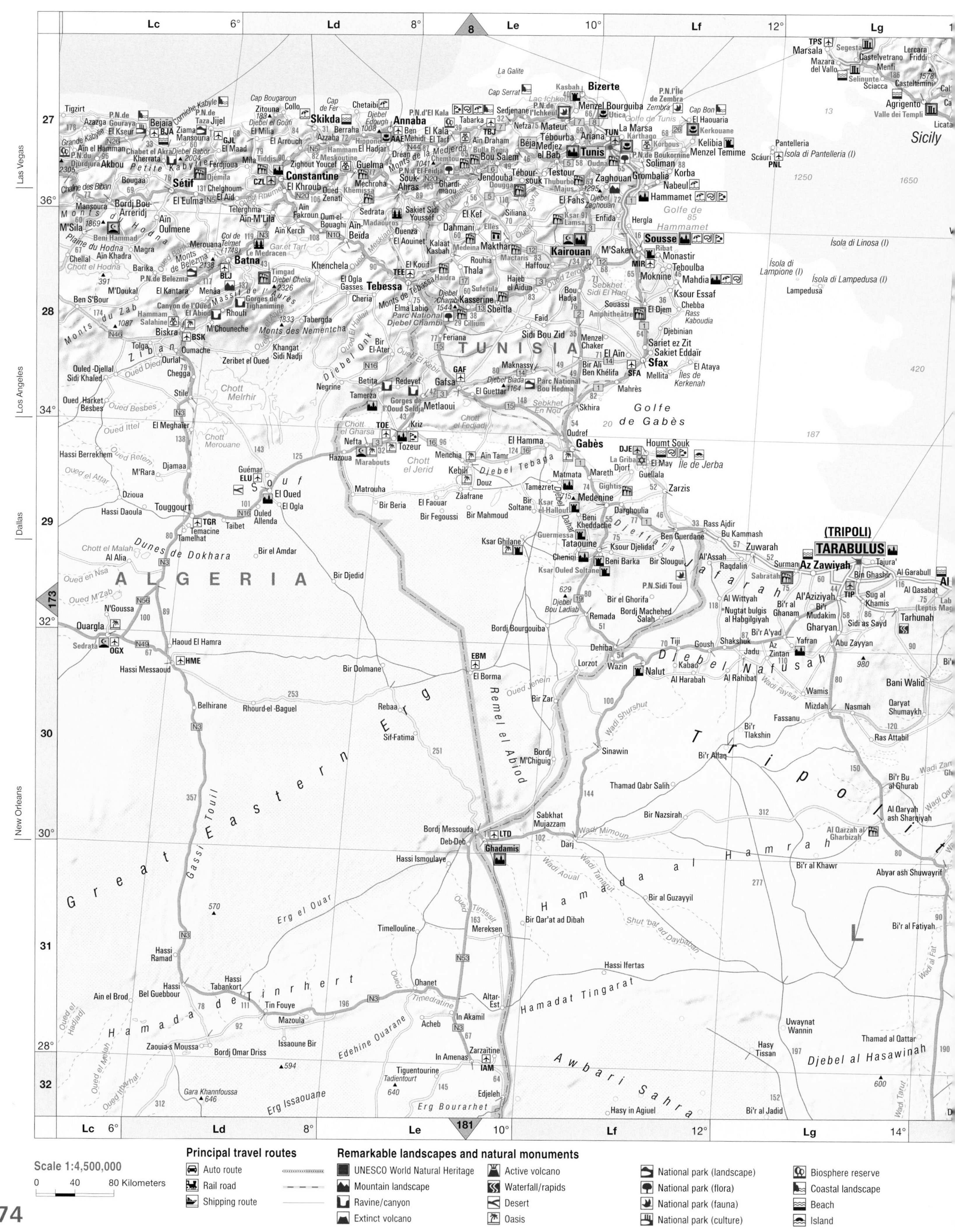

Scale 1:4,500,000

0   40   80 Kilometers

Principal travel routes

🚗 Auto route
🚂 Rail road
🚢 Shipping route

Remarkable landscapes and natural monuments

⬛ UNESCO World Natural Heritage
⬛ Mountain landscape
⬛ Ravine/canyon
⬛ Extinct volcano

🌋 Active volcano
🏞 Waterfall/rapids
🏜 Desert
🌴 Oasis

🏕 National park (landscape)
🌲 National park (flora)
🦌 National park (fauna)
🏛 National park (culture)

🌐 Biosphere reserve
🏖 Coastal landscape
🏖 Beach
🏝 Island

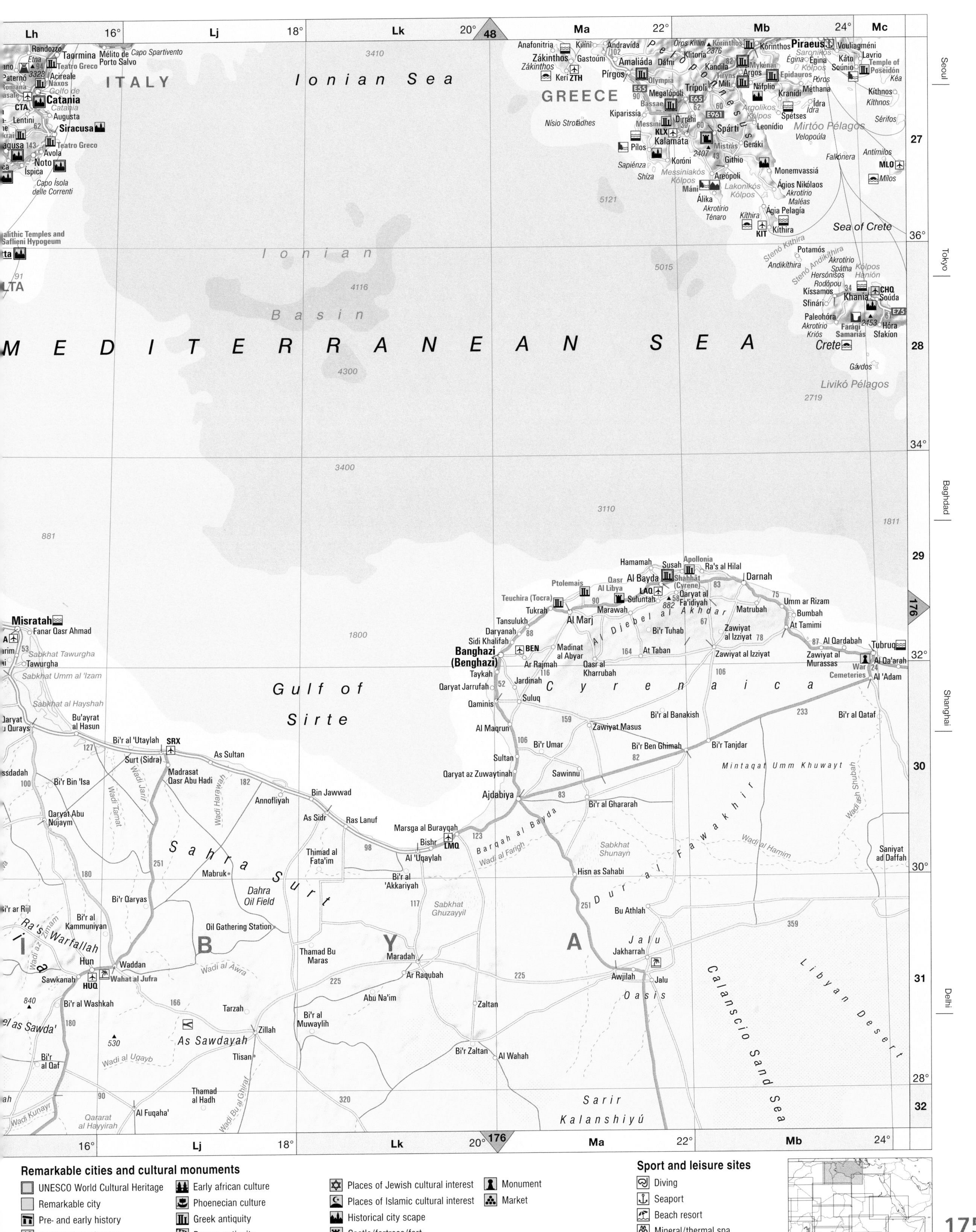

Column headers (top): Lh 16° Lj 18° Lk 20° 48 Ma 22° Mb 24° Mc

Right margin: Seoul · Tokyo · Baghdad · Shanghai · Delhi
27 · 36° · 28 · 34° · 29 · 176 · 32° · Shanghai · 30 · 31 · 28° · 32

Sicily / Italy (upper left):
Randozzo, Mélito de Capo Spartivento, Porto Salvo, Taormina, Etna, 3329, Teatro Greco, Paternò, Acireale, Naxos, Golfo di, Catania, CTA, Catania, Lentini, Augusta, Siracusa, Avola, Ispica, Noto, Teatro Greco, Avola, 143, ...ugusta, ...agusa, Capo Ísola delle Correnti

Megalithic Temples and Saflieni Hypogeum, ...ta, ...91, ...LTA

ITALY — **Ionian Sea**

GREECE (upper right):
Anafonitria, Kilíni, Andravída, Oros Killíni, Korinthos, Piraeus, Vouliagméni, Zákinthos, Gastoúni, Amaliáda, Klitória, 2376, Korinthos, Káto, Lavrio, Temple of Poseidon, Zákinthos, Pírgos, Olympia, Trípoli, Mykénai, Argos, Epidauros, Kéa, Kerí, ZTH, Megalópoli, Bassae, Tríyns, Náfplio, Kranídi, Methana, Kíthnos, Kiparissía, Dírahi, Spárti, Leonídio, Idra, Sérifos, Messíni, Kalamáta, 2407, Mistrás, Geráki, Mirtóo Pélagos, Pílos, Koróni, Githio, Falkónera, Antímilos, MLO, Sapiénza, Shíza, Messiniakós Kólpos, Areópoli, Ágios Nikólaos, Mílos, Máni, Lakonikós Kólpos, Akrotírio Maléas, Álika, Akrotírio Ténaro, Agia Pelagía, Kíthira, KIT, Kíthira, Stenó Kíthira

Potamós, Andikíthira, Stenó Andikíthira, Akrotírio Spátha, Kólpos Hanión, Kíssamos, Khaniá, CHQ, Soúda, Sfinári, Hersónisos, Rodópou, 34, Paleohóra, Akrotírio Kríós, Farági Samariás, 2453, Hóra Sfakíon, Crete, Gávdos, Livikó Pélagos, 2719

Sea numbers (Mediterranean): 3410, 4116, 4300, 3400, 3110, 1811, 5121, 5015, 4300, 1800, 881

MEDITERRANEAN SEA · **Ionian Sea** · **Ionian Basin**

Libya (lower portion):
Misratah, Fanar Qasr Ahmad, A, 53, Sabkhat Tawurgha, Tawurgha, Sabkhat Umm al 'Izam, Sabkhat al Hayshah, Bu'ayrat al Hasun, Jaryat al Qurays, 127, Bi'r al 'Utaylah, SRX, As Sultan, Surt (Sidra), Madrasat Qasr Abu Hadi, 182, Bi'r Bin 'Isa, ...ssaddadah, 100, Qaryat Abu Nujaym, Bi'r Qaryas, Sahra Surt, Annofliyah, Bin Jawwad, As Sidr, Ras Lanuf, Mabruk, Dahra Oil Field, Thimad al Fata'im, 98, Bishr, LMQ, Marsga al Burayqah, 123, Al 'Uqaylah, Oil Gathering Station, Bi'r al 'Akkariyah, 117, Sabkhat Ghuzayyil, Thamad Bu Maras, Maradah, Abu Na'im, Zaltan, Ar Raqubah, Bi'r al Muwaylih, Tarzah, Zillah, Tlisan, As Sawdayah, 530, Wadi al Ugayb, Thamad al Hadh, 320, Al Fuqaha', Qararat al Hayyirah

Ra's az Zimam, Warfallah, Hun, Sawkanah, Waddan, Wahat al Jufra, HUQ, Bi'r al Washkah, 166, Bi'r al Qaf, ...el as Sawda', 840, 180, 90

Cyrenaica region:
Hamamah, Susah, Apollonia, Ra's al Hilal, Ptolemais, Qasr, Al Bayda, Shahhat (Cyrene), Darnah, Teuchira (Tocra), Al Libya, LAQ, Qaryat al Fa'idiyah, 83, 75, Umm ar Rizam, Tukrah, Suluntah, 882, Al Djebel al Akhdar, Matrubah, Bumbah, Marawah, At Tamimi, Tansulukh, 88, Zawiyat al Izziyat, 78, Al Qardabah, Tubruq, Daryanah, Bi'r Tuhab, 67, 87, Sidi Khalifah, BEN, Madinat al Abyar, 164, At Taban, Zawiyat al Izziyat, Zawiyat al Murassas, Ai Qa'arah, Banghazi (Benghazi), Ar Rajmah, Qasr al Kharrubah, 116, 106, War Cemeteries, 24, Al 'Adam, Taykah, Jardinah, 52, Qaryat Jarrufah, Suluq, Cyrenaica, 233, Bi'r al Qataf, Qaminis, Bi'r al Banakish, Bi'r al Qatar, Al Maqrun, 159, Zawiyat Masus, Bi'r Umar, 106, Bi'r Ben Ghimah, Bi'r Tanjdar, Mintaqat Umm Khuwayt, Sultan, 82, Qaryat az Zuwaytinah, Sawinnu, Wadah al Shubah, Ajdabiya, 83, Bi'r al Ghararah, Dur al Fawakhir, Wadi al Hamim, Hisn as Sahabi, Saniyat ad Daffah, Bu Athlah, 251, Jalu, Jakharron, Jalu, 359, Awjilah, Jalu, Calanscio Sand Sea, Libyan Desert, Oasis

LIBYA (spread across: i B Y A)

Gulf of Sirte

Sarir Kalanshiyú

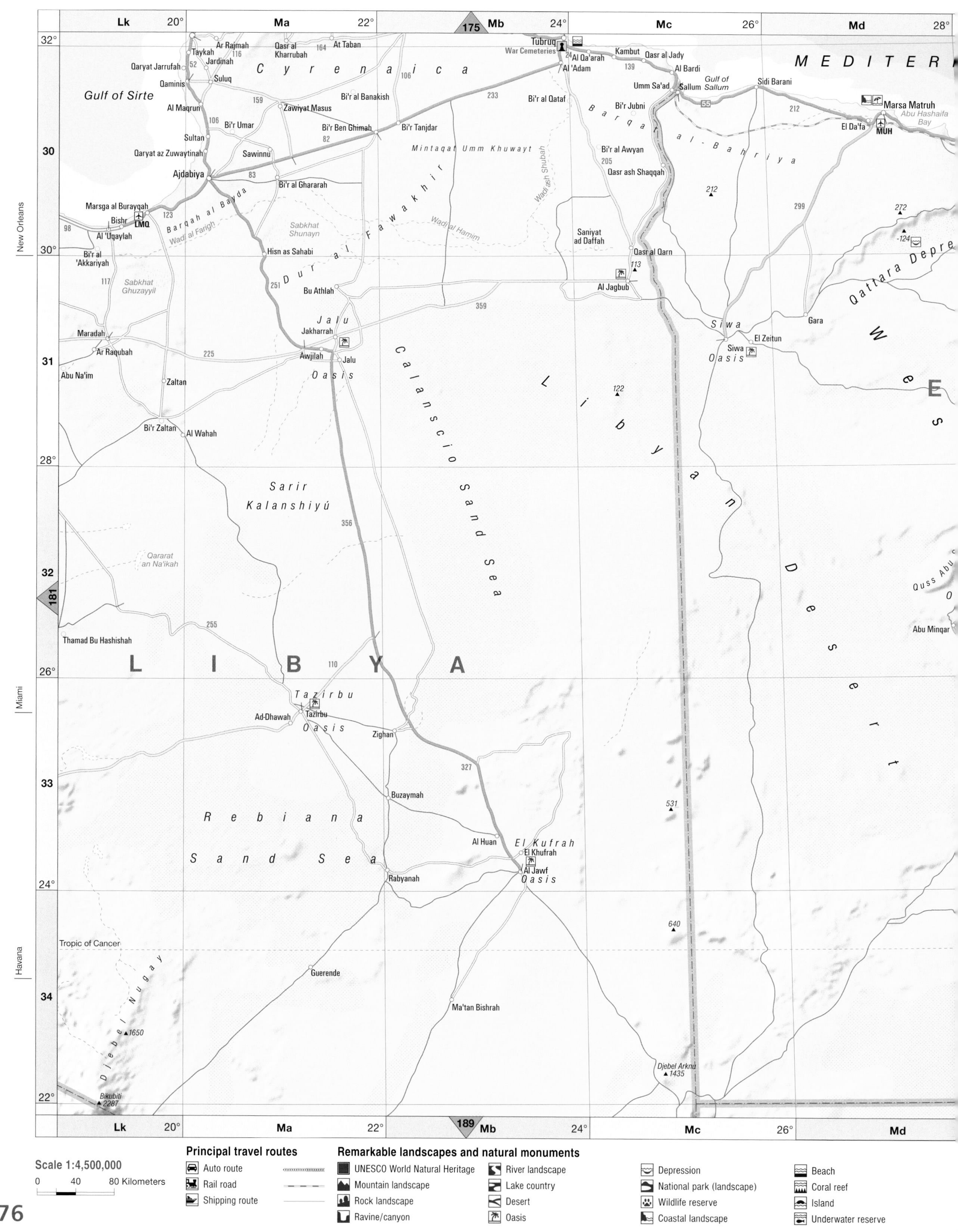

Scale 1:4,500,000

0   40   80 Kilometers

Principal travel routes

- Auto route
- Rail road
- Shipping route

Remarkable landscapes and natural monuments

- UNESCO World Natural Heritage
- Mountain landscape
- Rock landscape
- Ravine/canyon
- River landscape
- Lake country
- Desert
- Oasis
- Depression
- National park (landscape)
- Wildlife reserve
- Coastal landscape
- Beach
- Coral reef
- Island
- Underwater reserve

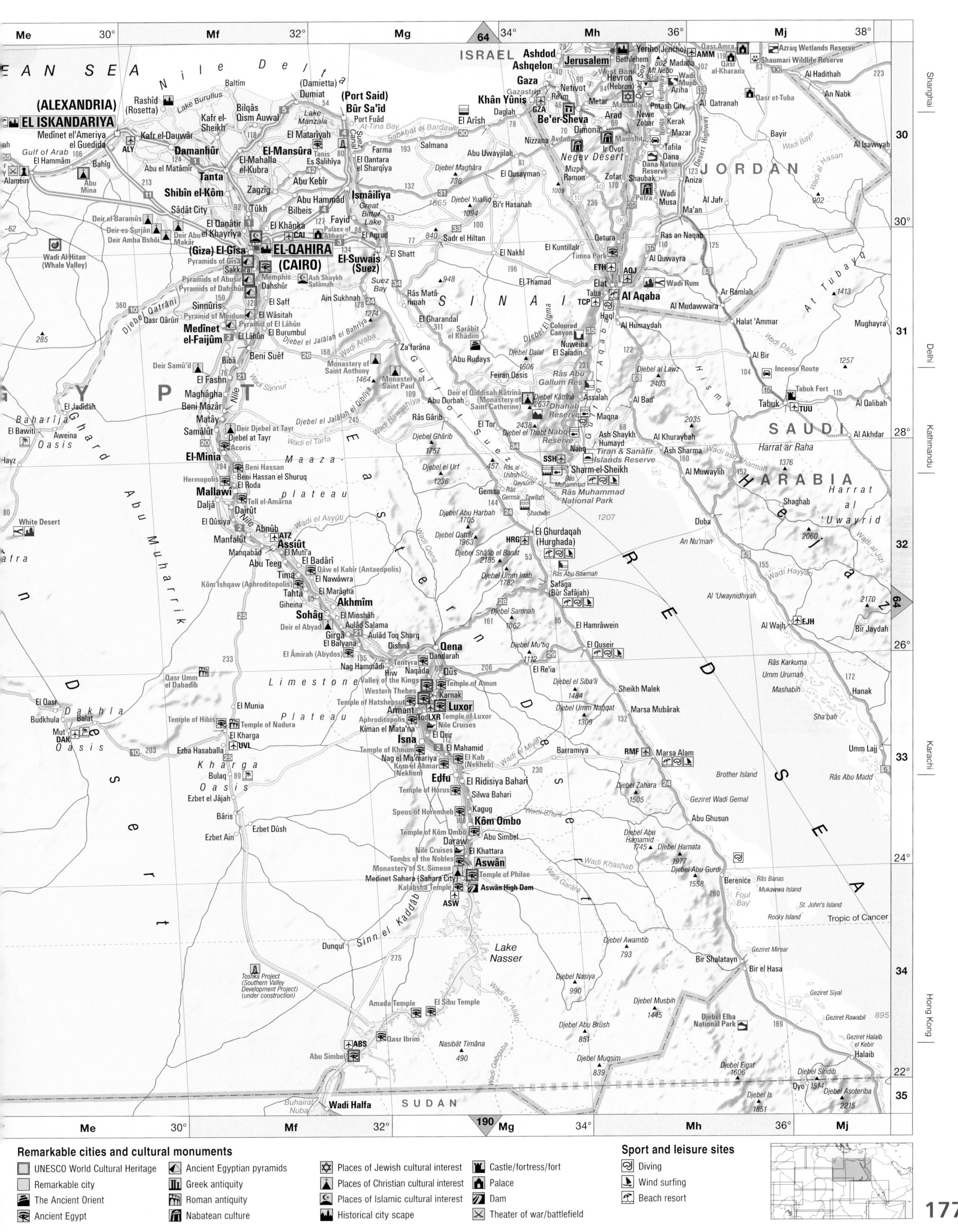

Remarkable cities and cultural monuments

- ◻ UNESCO World Cultural Heritage
- ◻ Remarkable city
- ⬛ The Ancient Orient
- ⬛ Ancient Egypt
- ⬛ Ancient Egyptian pyramids
- ⬛ Greek antiquity
- ⬛ Roman antiquity
- ⬛ Nabatean culture
- ✡ Places of Jewish cultural interest
- ▲ Places of Christian cultural interest
- ☪ Places of Islamic cultural interest
- ⬛ Historical city scape
- ⬛ Castle/fortress/fort
- ⬛ Palace
- ⬛ Dam
- ⬛ Theater of war/battlefield

Sport and leisure sites

- ⬛ Diving
- ⬛ Wind surfing
- ⬛ Beach resort

177

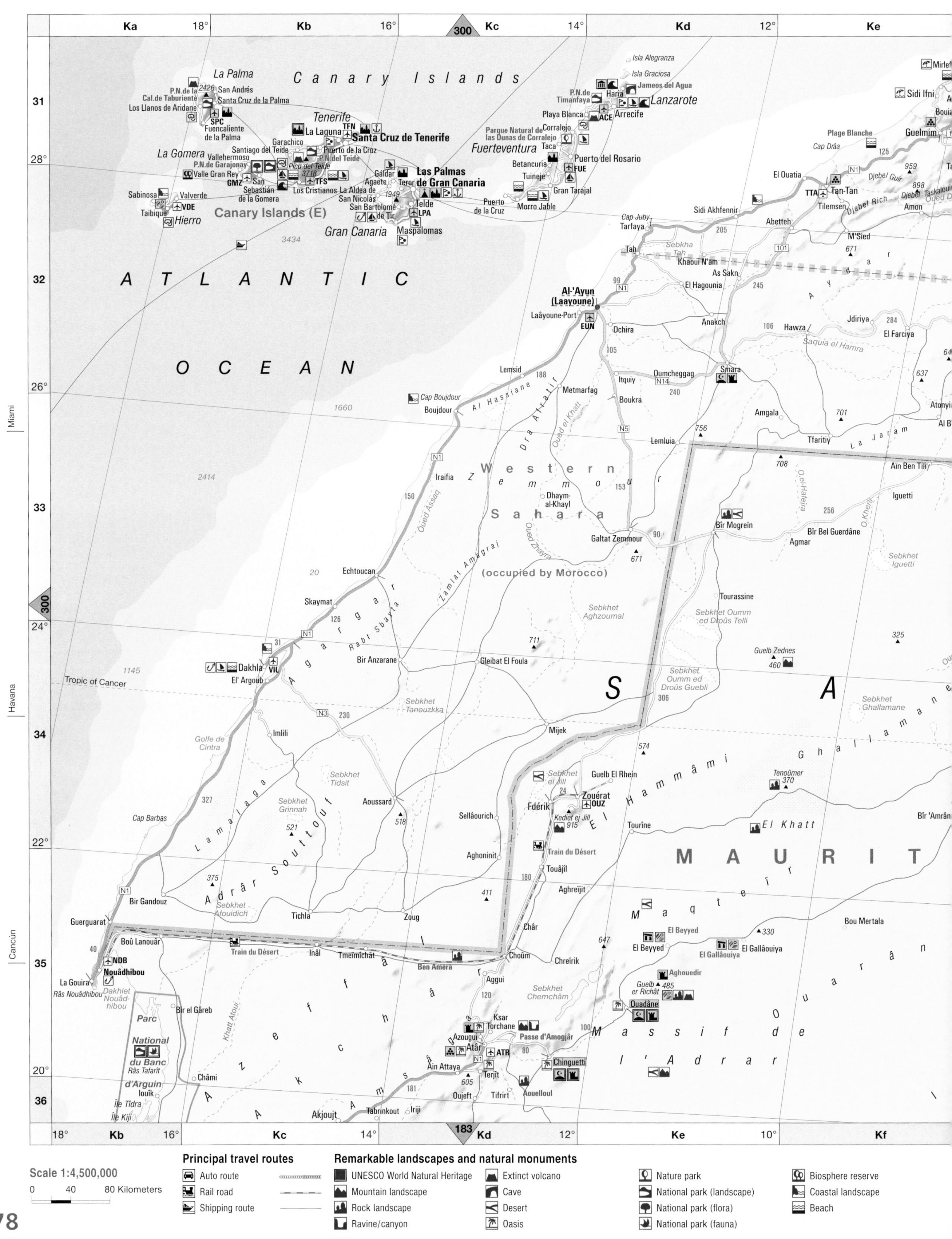

Scale 1:4,500,000

0   40   80 Kilometers

Principal travel routes
- Auto route
- Rail road
- Shipping route

Remarkable landscapes and natural monuments
- UNESCO World Natural Heritage
- Mountain landscape
- Rock landscape
- Ravine/canyon
- Extinct volcano
- Cave
- Desert
- Oasis
- Nature park
- National park (landscape)
- National park (flora)
- National park (fauna)
- Biosphere reserve
- Coastal landscape
- Beach

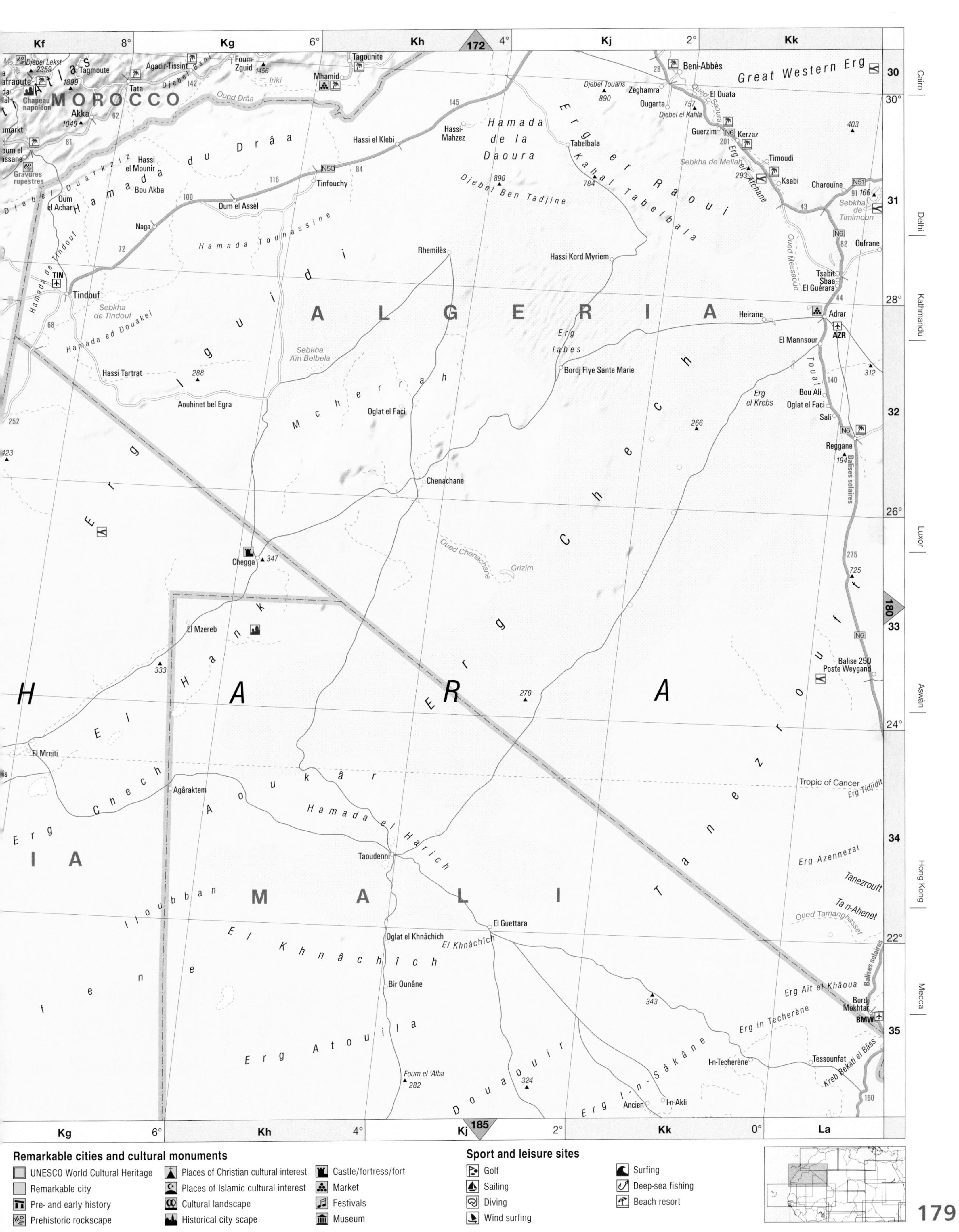

Cairo

Djebel Lekst 2359
Tagmoute
Afraoute
1899
Agadir-Tissint
Foum Zguid 1456
Tagounite
Beni-Abbès
28
Great Western Erg
30

afraoute
Djebel Ban 142
Iriki
Mhamid
Djebel Touaris 890
Zeghamra
Ougarta
757
El Ouata
30°

M O R O C C O
Akka
62
1049
Oued Drâa
Hassi el Klebi
Hassi-Mahzez
145
Hamada de la Daoura
Tabelbala
Djebel el Kahla
Guerzim N6 Kerzaz
201
Timoudi
403

Delhi

oum el assane
Gravures rupestres
Hassi el Mounir
Bou Akba
100
N50 84
Tinfouchy
116
Djebel Ben Tadjine
890
784
Sebkha de Mellah
293 Méhane
Ksabi
Charouïne N51
91 166
Sebkha de Timimoun
31

Oum el Achar
Naga
Oum el Assel
72
Hamada Tounassine
Rhemilès
Hassi Kord Myriem
43
N6
82
Oufrane

A L G E R I A
Heirane
Tsabit
Sbaa
El Guérara
44
28°

Kathmandu

de Tindouf
TIN
Tindouf
68
Sebkha de Tindouf
Hamada ed Douakel
Hassi Tartrat
288
Sebkha Aïn Belbela
Erg Iabes
Bordj Flye Sante Marie
El Mannsour
Adrar
AZR
312

252
423
Aouhinet bel Egra
Mcherrah
Oglat el Faci
266
Erg el Krebs
Bou Ali
Oglat el Faci
Sali
N6
Reggane
194
140
32

Chenachane
Chech
Luxor

Chegga
347
Oued Chenachane
Grizim
275
725
26°

El Mzereb
333
270
Balise 250
Poste Weygand
N6
180

H
El Mreiti
A
Erg
180
33

El Chech
Agâraktem
Aoukâr
Hamada el Harich
Tropic of Cancer
Erg Tidjidit
Aswän

I A
Erg
Taoudenni
M A L I
Erg Azennezal
Tanezrouft
24°

lIjoubban
El Khnâchîch
El Guettara
Oglat el Khnâchich
El Khnâchîch
Ta n-Ahenet
Oued Tamanghasset
Hong Kong

Bir Ounâne
343
Erg Aït el Khâoua
Bordj Mekhtar
BMW
22°

f e n e
Erg Atouïla
Douaouir
Foum el 'Alba
282
324
Ancien
I-n-Akli
Erg in Techerène
Erg I-n-Sâkâne
I-n-Techerène
Tessounfat
Kreb Bekati el Bâss
160
Mecca
35

Remarkable cities and cultural monuments

- ◻ UNESCO World Cultural Heritage
- ◻ Remarkable city
- ⌂ Pre- and early history
- ⌂ Prehistoric rockscape
- ▲ Places of Christian cultural interest
- ☾ Places of Islamic cultural interest
- ▥ Cultural landscape
- ▦ Historical city scape
- ▦ Castle/fortress/fort
- ▦ Market
- ♫ Festivals
- ▥ Museum

Sport and leisure sites

- ▣ Golf
- ⊿ Sailing
- ◈ Diving
- ⏚ Wind surfing
- ◣ Surfing
- ✓ Deep-sea fishing
- ◿ Beach resort

179

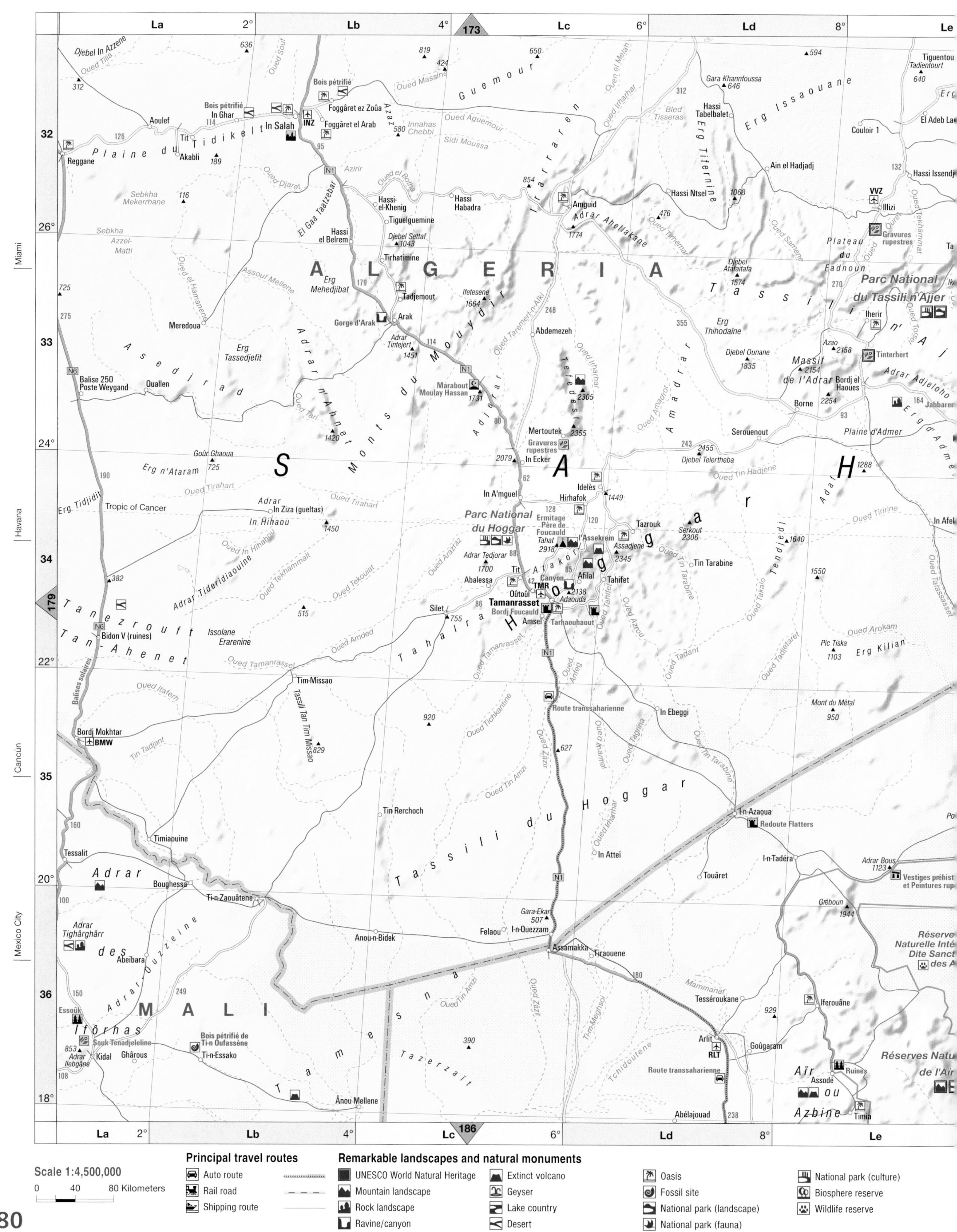

Central Sahara

Scale 1:4,500,000

0   40   80 Kilometers

180

Principal travel routes
- Auto route
- Rail road
- Shipping route

Remarkable landscapes and natural monuments
- UNESCO World Natural Heritage
- Mountain landscape
- Rock landscape
- Ravine/canyon
- Extinct volcano
- Geyser
- Lake country
- Desert
- Oasis
- Fossil site
- National park (landscape)
- National park (fauna)
- National park (culture)
- Biosphere reserve
- Wildlife reserve

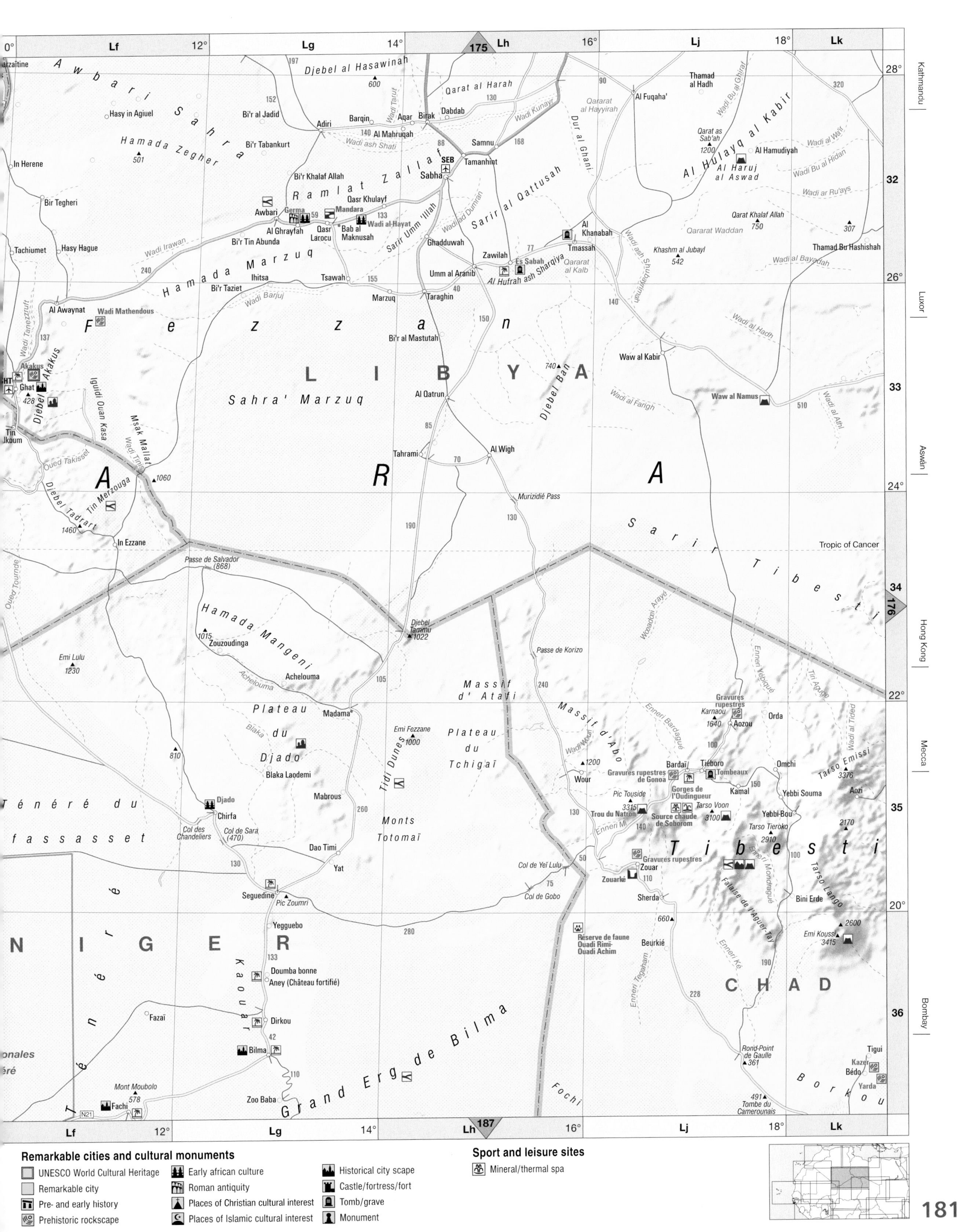

Remarkable cities and cultural monuments

- UNESCO World Cultural Heritage
- Remarkable city
- Pre- and early history
- Prehistoric rockscape
- Early african culture
- Roman antiquity
- Places of Christian cultural interest
- Places of Islamic cultural interest
- Historical city scape
- Castle/fortress/fort
- Tomb/grave
- Monument

Sport and leisure sites

- Mineral/thermal spa

Cape Verde Islands, Senegal, Gambia

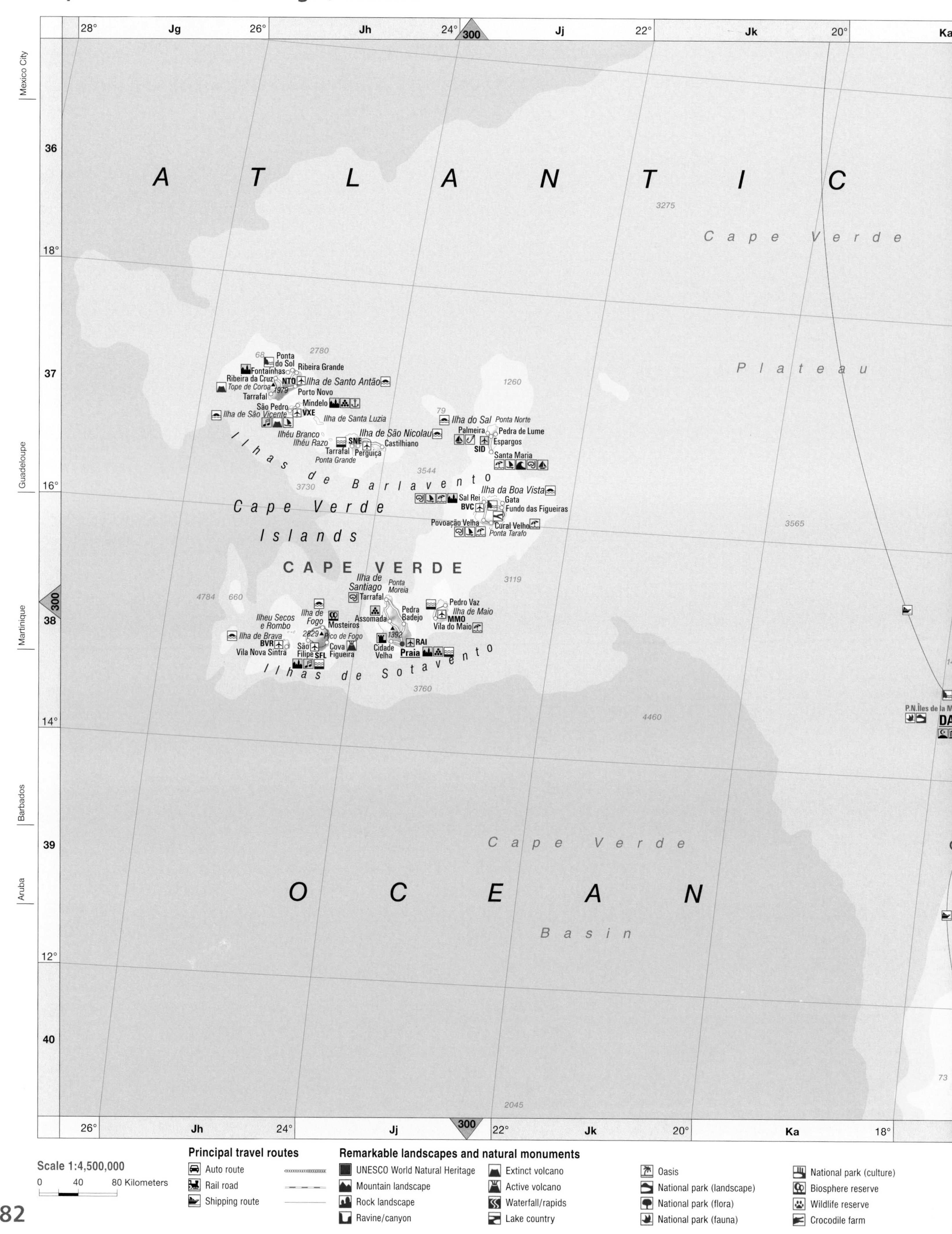

Scale 1:4,500,000

0   40   80 Kilometers

Principal travel routes

- 🚗 Auto route
- 🚆 Rail road
- 🚢 Shipping route

Remarkable landscapes and natural monuments

- ■ UNESCO World Natural Heritage
- ▲ Mountain landscape
- ■ Rock landscape
- ▨ Ravine/canyon
- ▲ Extinct volcano
- ▲ Active volcano
- ≋ Waterfall/rapids
- ▨ Lake country
- 🌴 Oasis
- National park (landscape)
- National park (flora)
- National park (fauna)
- National park (culture)
- Biosphere reserve
- Wildlife reserve
- Crocodile farm

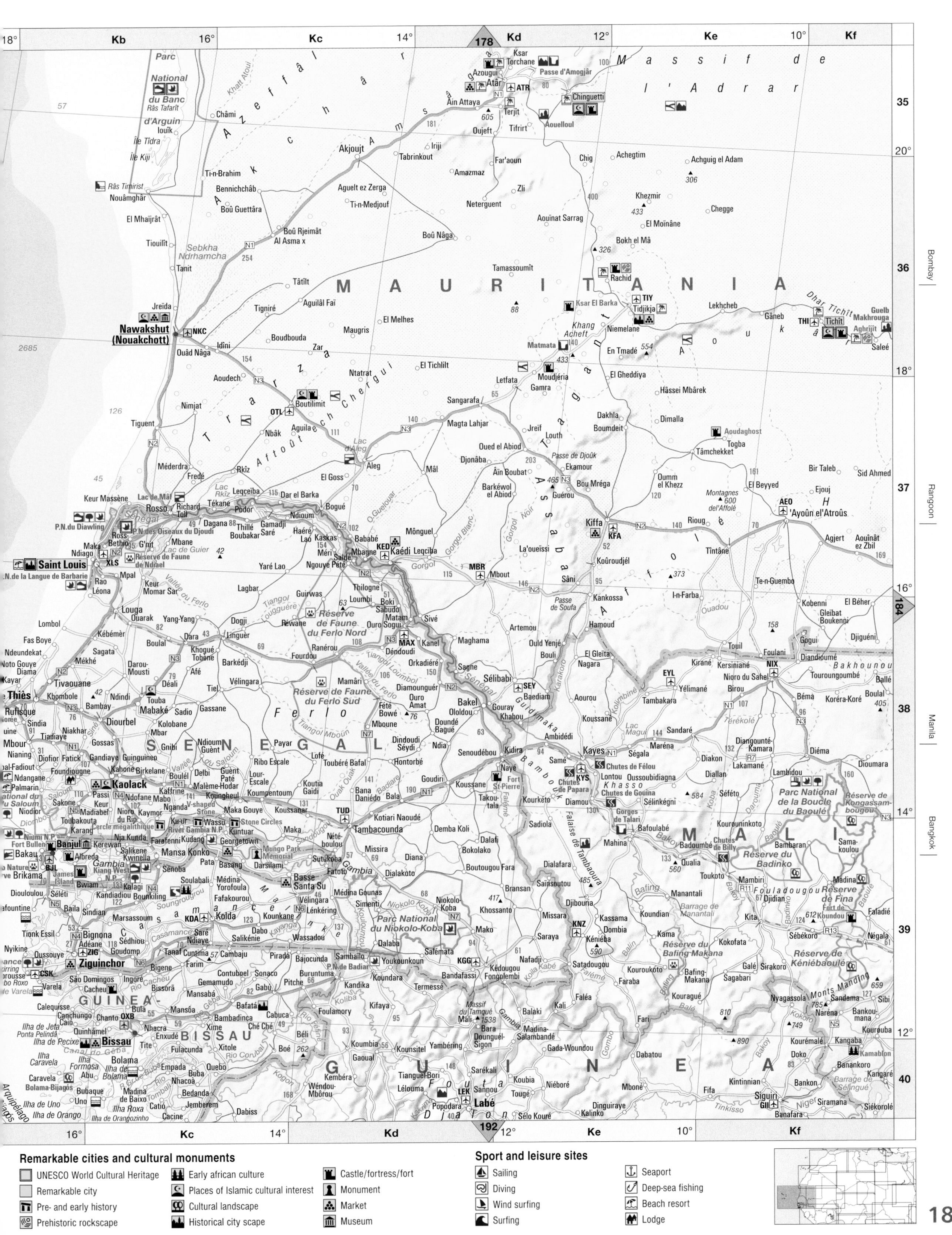

Parc
National
du Banc
d'Arguin
Râs Tafarît

Châmi

Île Tidra
Île Kiji

Râs Tinirirst
Nouâmghâr

MAURITANIA

Massif de
l'Adrar

Ksar
Torchane
Azougui   Passe d'Amogjâr
Atâr   **ATR**
Aïn Attaya
Chinguetti
Terjit
Aouelloul
Tifrirt

Akjoujt
Irìji
Tabrinkout
Far'aoun
Achegtim   Achguig el Adam
Amazmaz
Zli   Chig
306

Ti-n-Brahim
Bennichchâb
Boû Guettâra
Aguelt ez Zerga
Tin-Medjouf
Neterguent   Khezmir
433
Chegge

El Mhaïjrât

Tiouilît
Boû Rjeimât
Al Asma x   **N1**
254   Boû Nâga
Aouînat Sarrag   El Moînâne

Sebkha
Ndrhamcha

Tanit
Tamassoumît   Bokh el Mâ
326

Jreida
Tignirè   88   Ksar El Barka   **TIY**
Tidjikja   Lekhcheb   Gâneb   Guelb
Makhrouga
Aghrijît   Aghrijît
THI
Tichît
Salée

Nawakshut (Nouakchott)   **NKC**
Idîni
Ouâd Nâga
Maugris   El Melhes   Khang
Acheft   Niemelane
En Tmadé   554
Aoudaghost
Togba   Tâmchekket

2685

Boudbouda
Zara   El Tichilt
Gamra   Letfata   El Gheddiya   Hâssei Mbârek

Aoudech   Ntatrat
Sangarafa   65   Moudjéria   Dakhla
Boumdeit   Dimalla   Bir Taleb   Sid Ahmed

Nimjat   Boutilimit   **OTL**   Magta Lahjar   **N3**   Djonâba   Oued el Abiod   Jreif   Louth
Bir Taleb   Ejouj   169

Tiguent   Nbâk   Aguila   Mâl   Barkéwol   Guérou
203   Bou Mréga   Ekamour   Oumm   el Khezz   El Beyyed   Montagnes   600   del'Affolé   120   Rioug   70   **AEO**   'Ayoûn el'Atroûs   H

Méderdra   Fredé   Aleg   .O.Guelouar   Gorgol Noir   Passe de Djoûk   Koûroudjél   Tintâne

Keur Massène   Lac de Mâl   Richard   Toll   Podor   Bogué   Kiffa   **KFA**   **N3**   140   Agjert   Aouînât   ez Zbil

Saint Louis   **XLS**   Mbane   Saldé   Mbagne   Leqceïba   La'ouessi   Sâni   373   Te-n-Guembo

Rao   Léona   Ngouye Paté   Thilogne   Boki   Matam   Passe de Soufa   Kankossa   I-n-Farba   Ouadou   Kobenni   El Béher   Gleibat   Boukenni   158   Gogui

Remarkable cities and cultural monuments

	UNESCO World Cultural Heritage		Early african culture		Castle/fortress/fort
	Remarkable city		Places of Islamic cultural interest		Monument
	Pre- and early history		Cultural landscape		Market
	Prehistoric rockscape		Historical city scape		Museum

Sport and leisure sites

	Sailing		Seaport
	Diving		Deep-sea fishing
	Wind surfing		Beach resort
	Surfing		Lodge

183

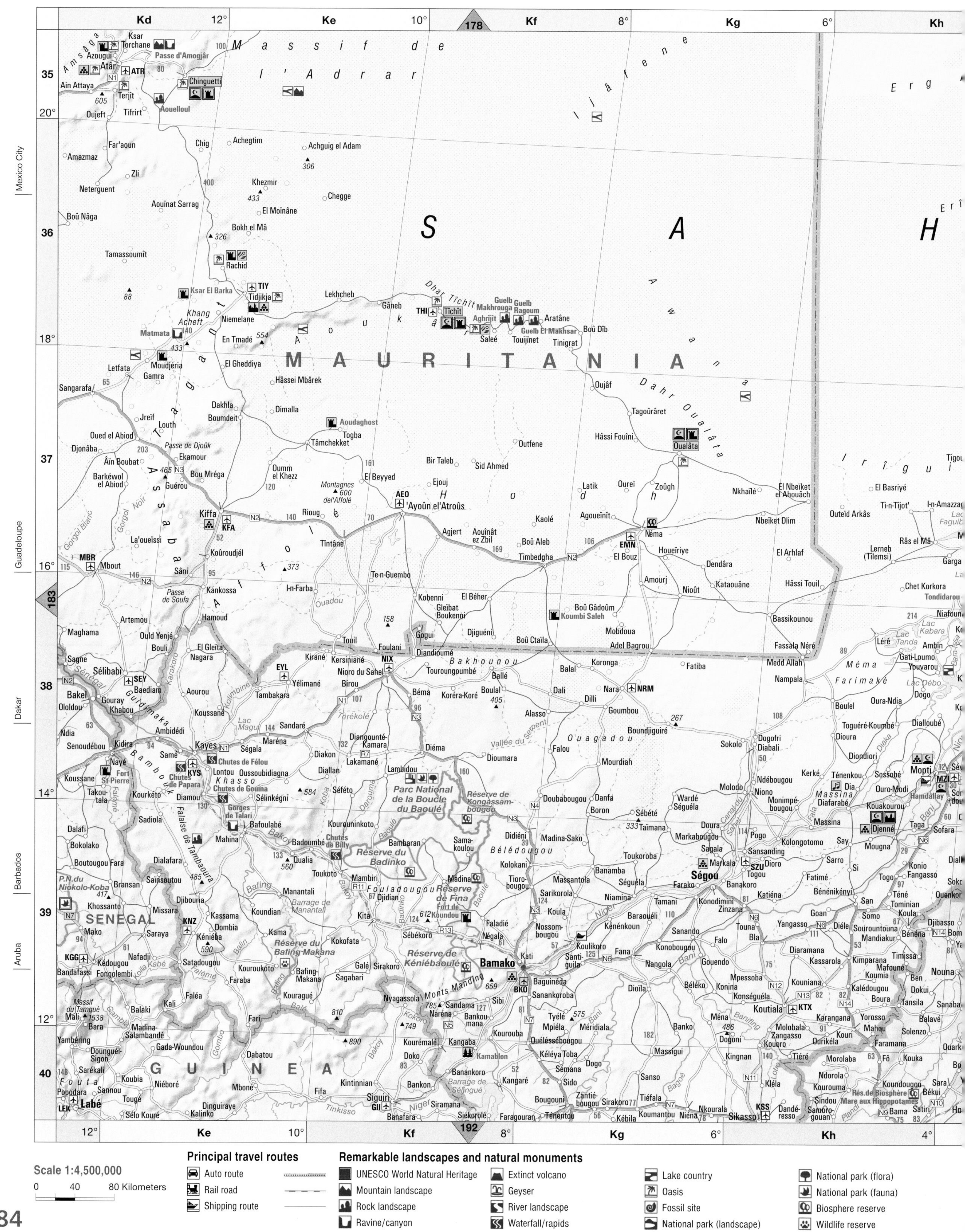

Mali

Massif de l'Adrar

SAHARA

MAURITANIA

Scale 1:4,500,000

0 40 80 Kilometers

184

Principal travel routes

- Auto route
- Rail road
- Shipping route

Remarkable landscapes and natural monuments

- UNESCO World Natural Heritage
- Mountain landscape
- Rock landscape
- Ravine/canyon
- Extinct volcano
- Geyser
- River landscape
- Waterfall/rapids
- Lake country
- Oasis
- Fossil site
- National park (landscape)
- National park (flora)
- National park (fauna)
- Biosphere reserve
- Wildlife reserve

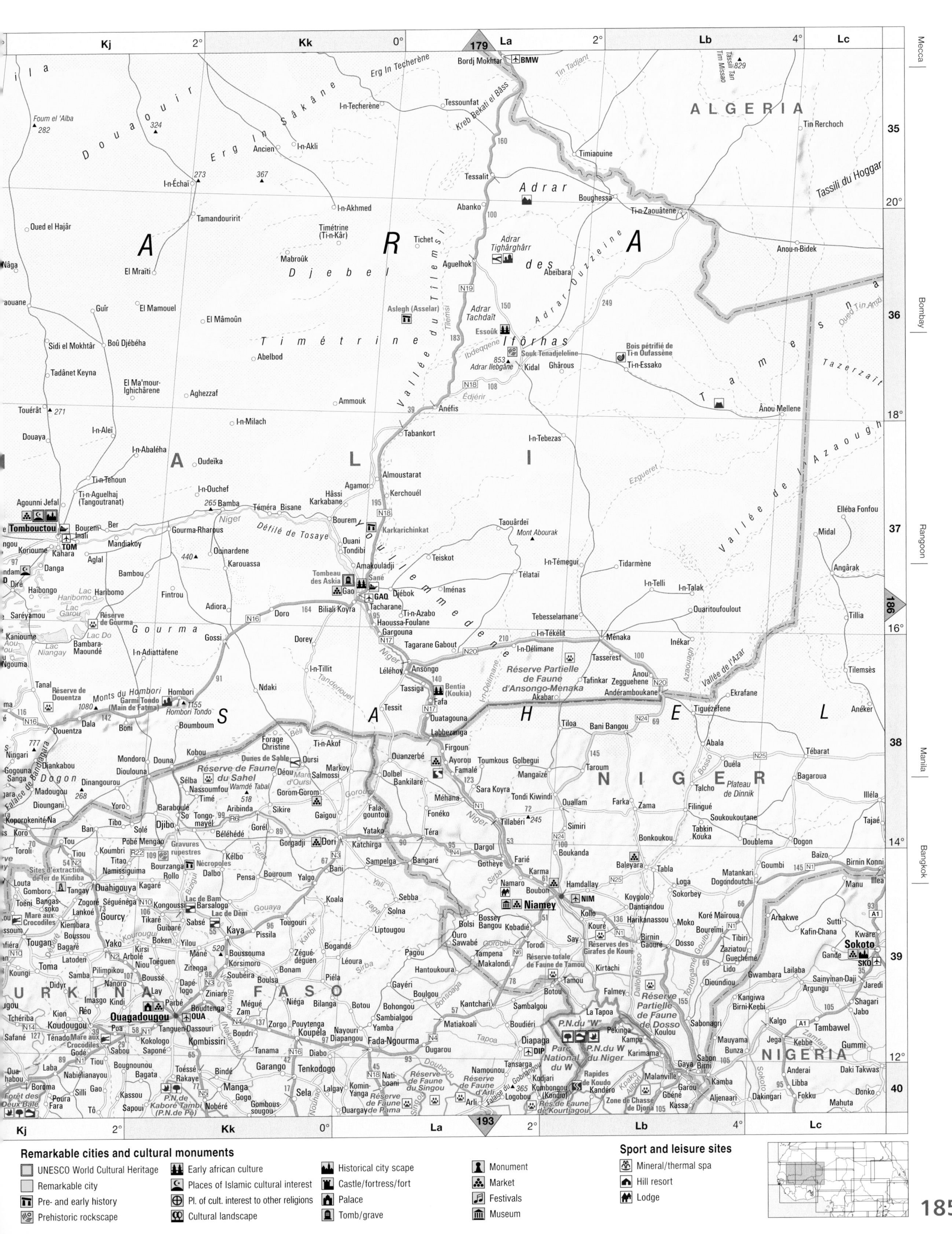

Remarkable cities and cultural monuments

- UNESCO World Cultural Heritage
- Remarkable city
- Pre- and early history
- Prehistoric rockscape
- Early african culture
- Places of Islamic cultural interest
- Pl. of cult. interest to other religions
- Cultural landscape
- Historical city scape
- Castle/fortress/fort
- Palace
- Tomb/grave
- Monument
- Market
- Festivals
- Museum

Sport and leisure sites

- Mineral/thermal spa
- Hill resort
- Lodge

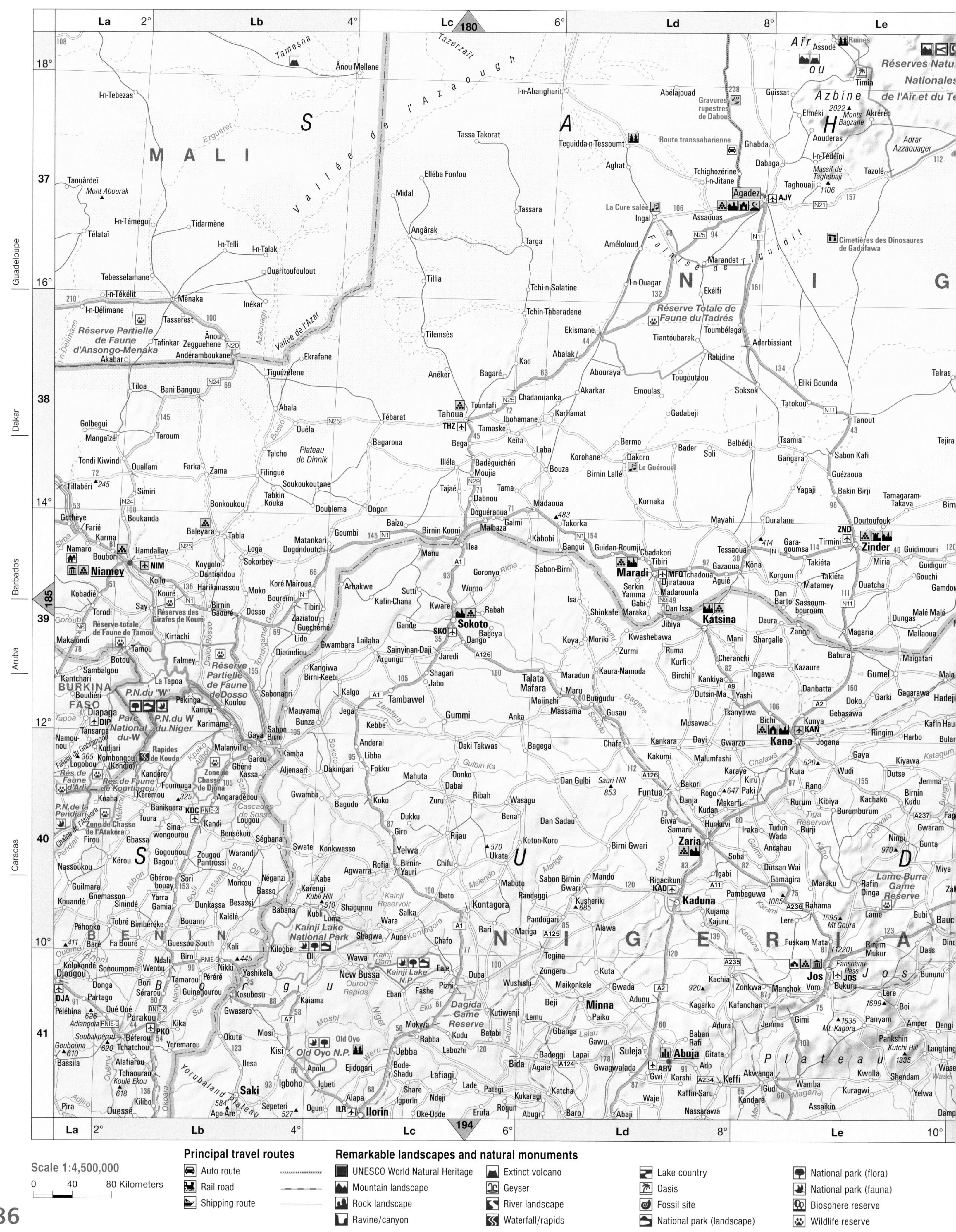

Scale 1:4,500,000

0   40   80 Kilometers

Principal travel routes

- Auto route
- Rail road
- Shipping route

- UNESCO World Natural Heritage
- Mountain landscape
- Rock landscape
- Ravine/canyon

Remarkable landscapes and natural monuments

- Extinct volcano
- Geyser
- River landscape
- Waterfall/rapids

- Lake country
- Oasis
- Fossil site
- National park (landscape)

- National park (flora)
- National park (fauna)
- Biosphere reserve
- Wildlife reserve

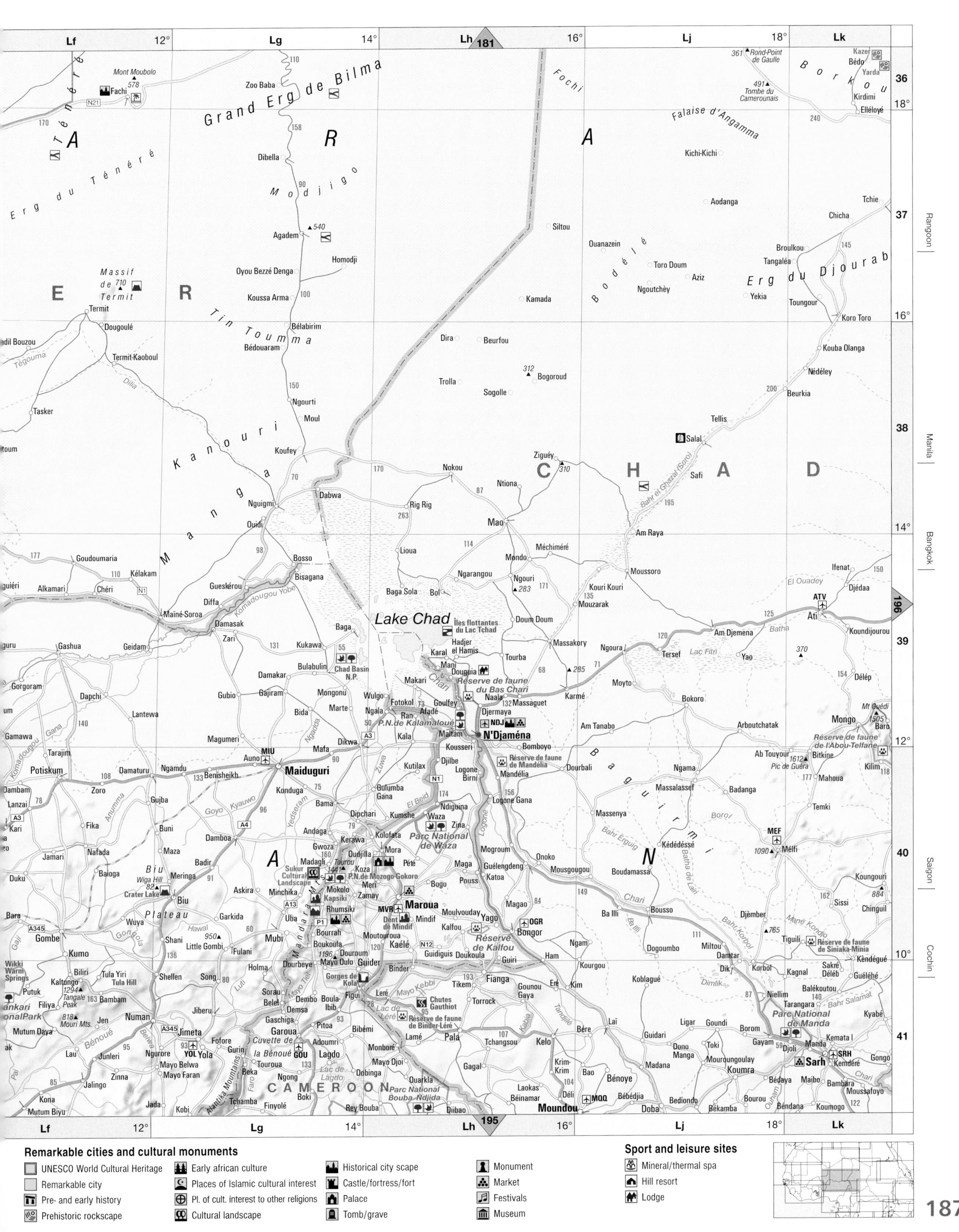

Remarkable cities and cultural monuments

- ⬛ UNESCO World Cultural Heritage
- ⬜ Remarkable city
- 🔝 Pre- and early history
- ⬚ Prehistoric rockscape
- 🔄 Early african culture
- ☪ Places of Islamic cultural interest
- ⊕ Pl. of cult. interest to other religions
- ⚭ Cultural landscape
- 🏛 Historical city scape
- 🏰 Castle/fortress/fort
- 🏛 Palace
- 🪦 Tomb/grave
- 🧍 Monument
- ♣ Market
- 🎵 Festivals
- 🏛 Museum

Sport and leisure sites

- ♨ Mineral/thermal spa
- 🏠 Hill resort
- 🏔 Lodge

187

Northern Chad

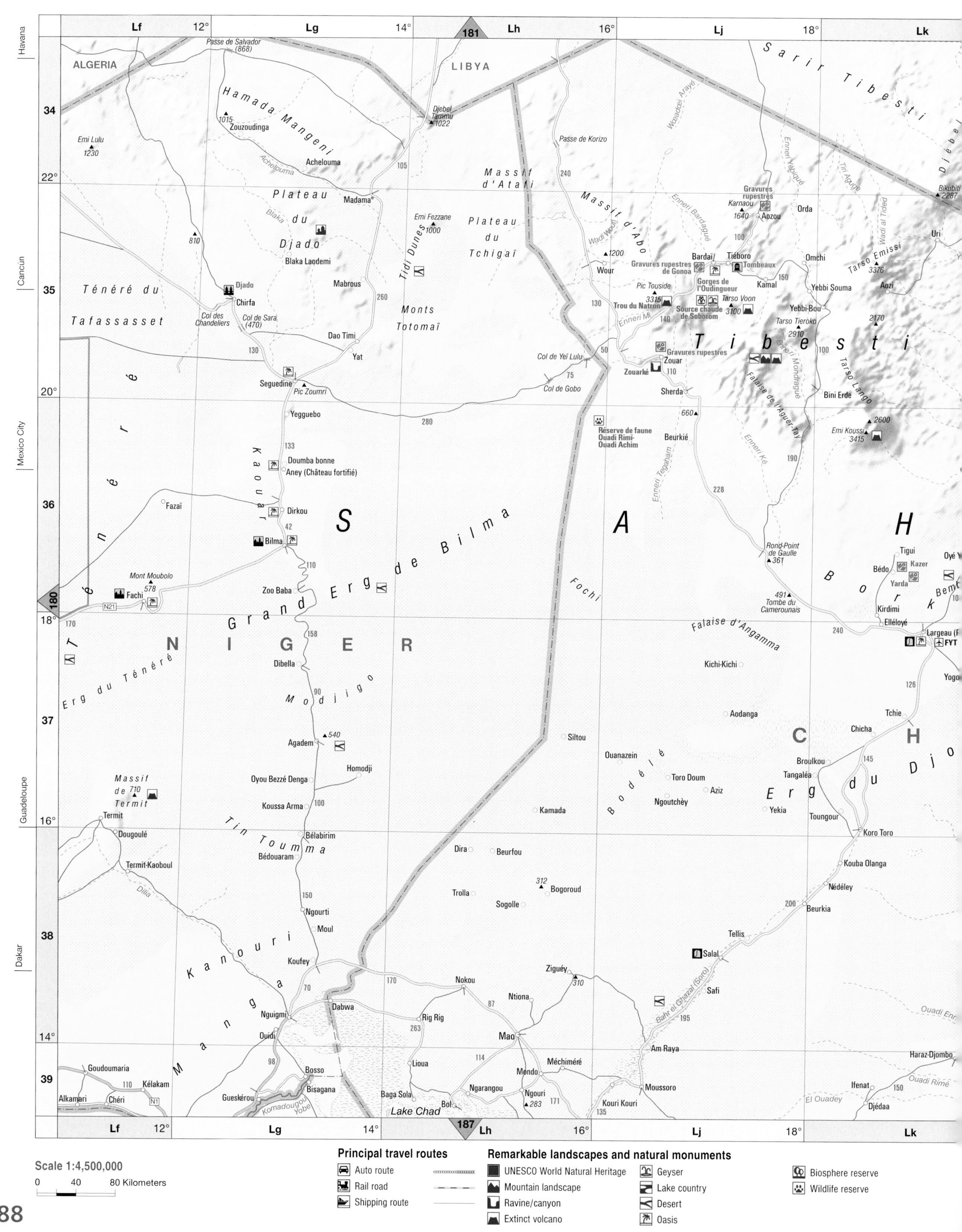

ALGERIA

LIBYA

Passe de Salvador (868)

Emi Lulu 1230

Zouzoudinga

1015

Hamada Mangeni

Achedouma

Acheluoma

105

Madama

Plateau du Djado

Blaka

810

Blaka Laodemi

Mabrous

Djado

Chirfa

Ténéré du Tafassasset

Col des Chandeliers

Col de Sara (470)

260

130

Dao Timi

Yat

Monts Totomaï

Séguédine

Pic Zoumri

Yegguebo

133

Doumba bonne

Aney (Château fortifié)

Fazaï

Dirkou

42

Bilma

110

Grand   Erg   de   Bilma

Zoo Baba

S

A

H

Mont Moubolo 578

Fachi

N21

Ténéré

170

158

Erg du Ténéré

N   I   G   E   R

Dibella

Modjigo

90

Agadem

540

Homodji

Oyou Bezzé Denga

Massif de 710 Termit

Koussa Arma

100

Termit

Dougoulé

Bélabirim

Tin Toumma

Termit-Kaboul

Bédouaram

Dilia

150

Ngourti

Moul

Kanouri

Koufey

M   a   n   g   a

70

Nguigmi

Dabwa

Ouidi

Rig Rig

263

98

Goudoumaria

110

Kélakam

Bosso

Bisagana

Alkamari

Chéri

N1

Gueskérou

Baga Sola

Lake Chad

Komadougou Yobe

Bol

Djebel Tarmu 1022

Passe de Korizo

240

Massif d'Atafi

Plateau du Tchigaï

Emi Fezzane 1000

Tidi Dunes

260

75

Col de Yeï Lulu

Col de Gobo

280

Massif d'Abo

1200

Wour

Gravures rupestres de Gonoa

Bardaï

Tiéboro

Pic Touside 3315

Trou du Natron

Source chaude de Sobórom

Gorges de l'Oudingueur

Tarso Voon 3100

130

140

50

Gravures rupestres

Zouar

Zouarké

110

Sherda

660

T   i   b   e   s   t   i

Kamal

Karnaou 1640

Aozou

Orda

Omchi

Yebbi Souma

Tarso Emissi 3376

Aozi

2170

Yebbi-Bou

Tarso Tieroko 2910

Bini Erde

2600

Emi Koussi 3415

Réserve de faune Ouadi Rimi-Ouadi Achim

Beurkié

190

228

Rond-Point de Gaulle 361

Fochi

491 Tombe du Camerounais

Kichi-Kichi

Falaise d'Angamma

240

Siltou

Aodanga

Ouanazein

Bodélé

Toro Doum

Ngoutchèy

Aziz

Erg du Djourab

C   H

Tigui

Bédo

Kazer

Yarda

Kirdimi

Elléloyé

Largeau (F

FYT

126

Yogo

Tchie

Chicha

Broulkou

Tangaléa

145

Yekia

Toungour

Koro Toro

Kouba Olanga

Nédéley

200

Beurkia

Kamada

Dira

Beurfou

Trolla

Bogoroud 312

Sogolle

Bahr el Ghazal (Soro)

Tellis

Salal

195

Ziguéy

310

Safi

Nokou

Ntiona

87

Mao

Am Raya

Haraz-Djombo

Lioua

114

Mondo

Méchiméré

Moussoro

Ngarangou

Ngouri

171 283

Kouri Kouri

135

El Ouadey

Ifenat

150

Ouadi Rimé

Djédaa

Ouadi Enr

Scale 1:4,500,000

0   40   80 Kilometers

Principal travel routes

- Auto route
- Rail road
- Shipping route

  Remarkable landscapes and natural monuments

- UNESCO World Natural Heritage
- Mountain landscape
- Ravine/canyon
- Extinct volcano

- Geyser
- Lake country
- Desert
- Oasis

- Biosphere reserve
- Wildlife reserve

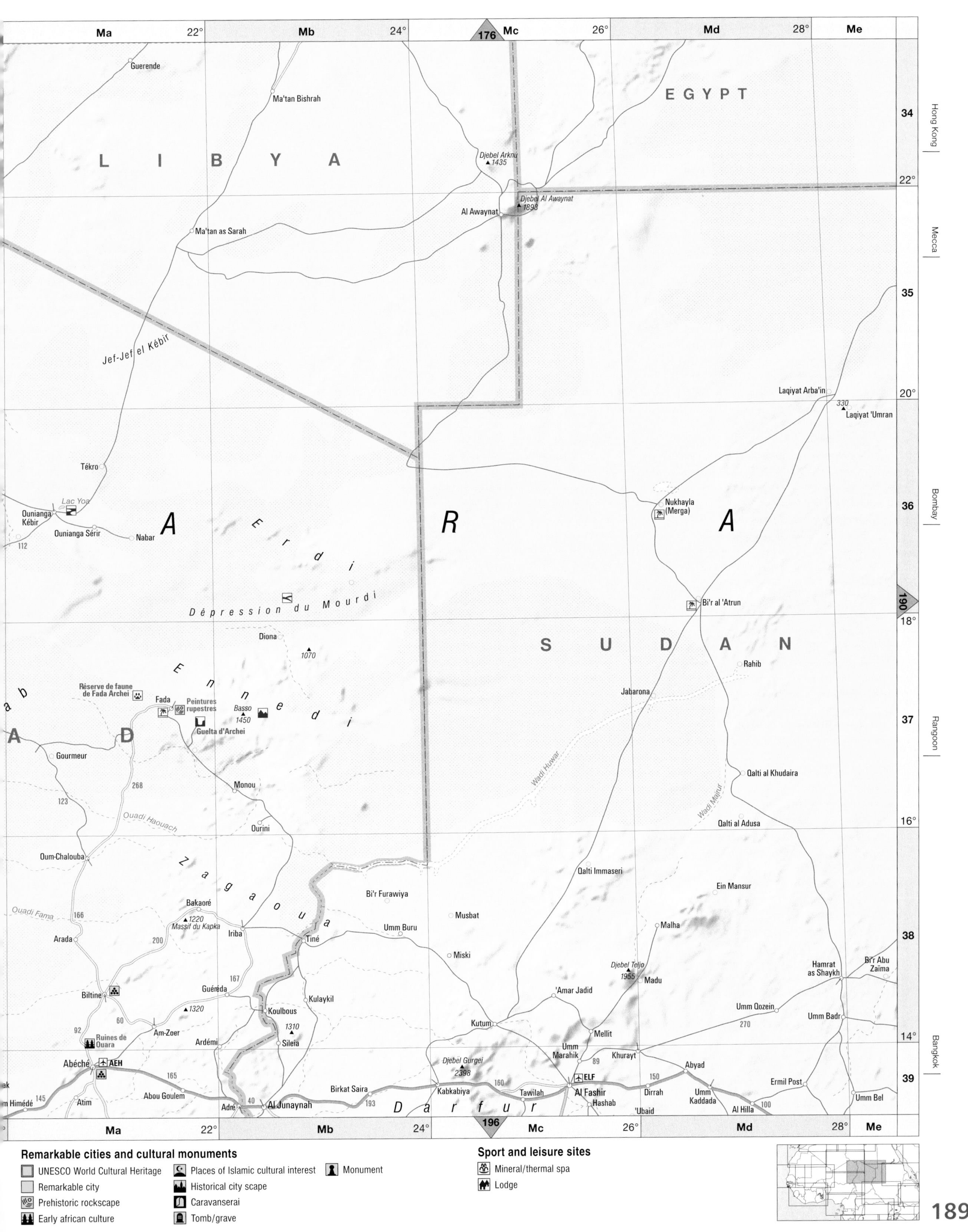

EGYPT

LIBYA

Guerende

Ma'tan Bishrah

Djebel Arknu
▲1435

34

22°

Djebel Al Awaynat
▲1898

Al Awaynat

35

Ma'tan as Sarah

Jef-Jef el Kébir

Laqiyat Arba'in

20°

330
Laqiyat 'Umran

Tékro

A

Lac Yoa

Ounianga
Kébir

Ounianga Sérir   Nabar

Nukhayla
(Merga)

36

112

R

A

E   r   d   i

Dépression du Mourdi

Bi'r al 'Atrun

190

18°

Diona

1070

SUDAN

Rahib

Réserve de faune
de Fada Archei

Fada   Peintures
rupestres

E
n
n
e
d
i

Basso
▲1450

Jabarona

37

A   D

Guelta d'Archei

Qalti al Khudaira

Gourmeur

Monou

Wadi Huwar

A

Ourini

268

Wadi Majrur

Qalti al Adusa

123

Ouadi Haouach

16°

Oum-Chalouba

Z
a
g
a
o
u
a

Qalti Immaseri

Ein Mansur

Ouadi Fama   166

Bakaoré

Bi'r Furawiya

Musbat

Malha

▲1220
Massif du Kapka

Arada

200

Iriba   Tiné

Umm Buru

38

167

Guéréda

Kulaykil

Miski

Djebel Teljo
1955   Madu

Hamrat
as Shaykh

Bi'r Abu
Zaima

Biltine

▲1320

Koulbous

'Amar Jadid

92   Ruines de
Ouara

Am-Zoer

1310

Umm Qozein

Umm Badr

60

Kutum   Mellit

Ardémi   Sileia

270

14°

Abéché   AEH

Umm
Marahik   Khurayt

89

Djebel Gurgei
2398

Abyad

Ermil Post

150

145

Atim

165

Abou Goulem

Birkat Saira   Kabkabiya

ELF

39

Adré   40

Al Junaynah   193

D a r f u r   160   Tawilah   Al Fashir   Dirrah   Umm
Kaddada   100   Umm Bel

'Ubaid   Hashab   Al Hilla

Remarkable cities and cultural monuments

- UNESCO World Cultural Heritage
- Remarkable city
- Prehistoric rockscape
- Early african culture
- Places of Islamic cultural interest
- Historical city scape
- Caravanserai
- Tomb/grave
- Monument

Sport and leisure sites

- Mineral/thermal spa
- Lodge

Hong Kong
Mecca
Bombay
Rangoon
Bangkok

189

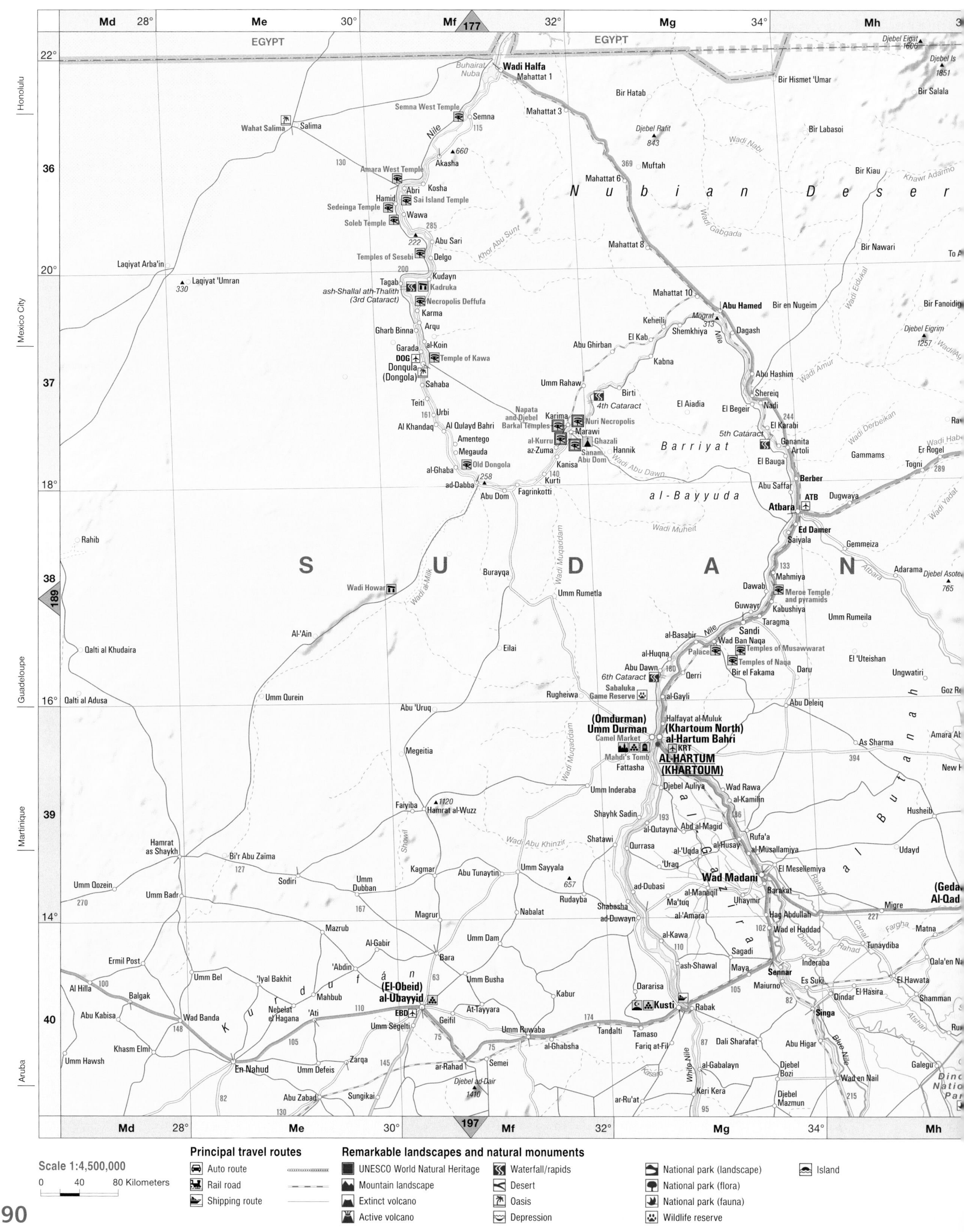

EGYPT   EGYPT

Honolulu

Mexico City

Guadeloupe

Martinique

Aruba

Scale 1:4,500,000

0   40   80 Kilometers

190

Principal travel routes

- Auto route
- Rail road
- Shipping route

Remarkable landscapes and natural monuments

- UNESCO World Natural Heritage
- Mountain landscape
- Extinct volcano
- Active volcano
- Waterfall/rapids
- Desert
- Oasis
- Depression
- National park (landscape)
- National park (flora)
- National park (fauna)
- Wildlife reserve
- Island

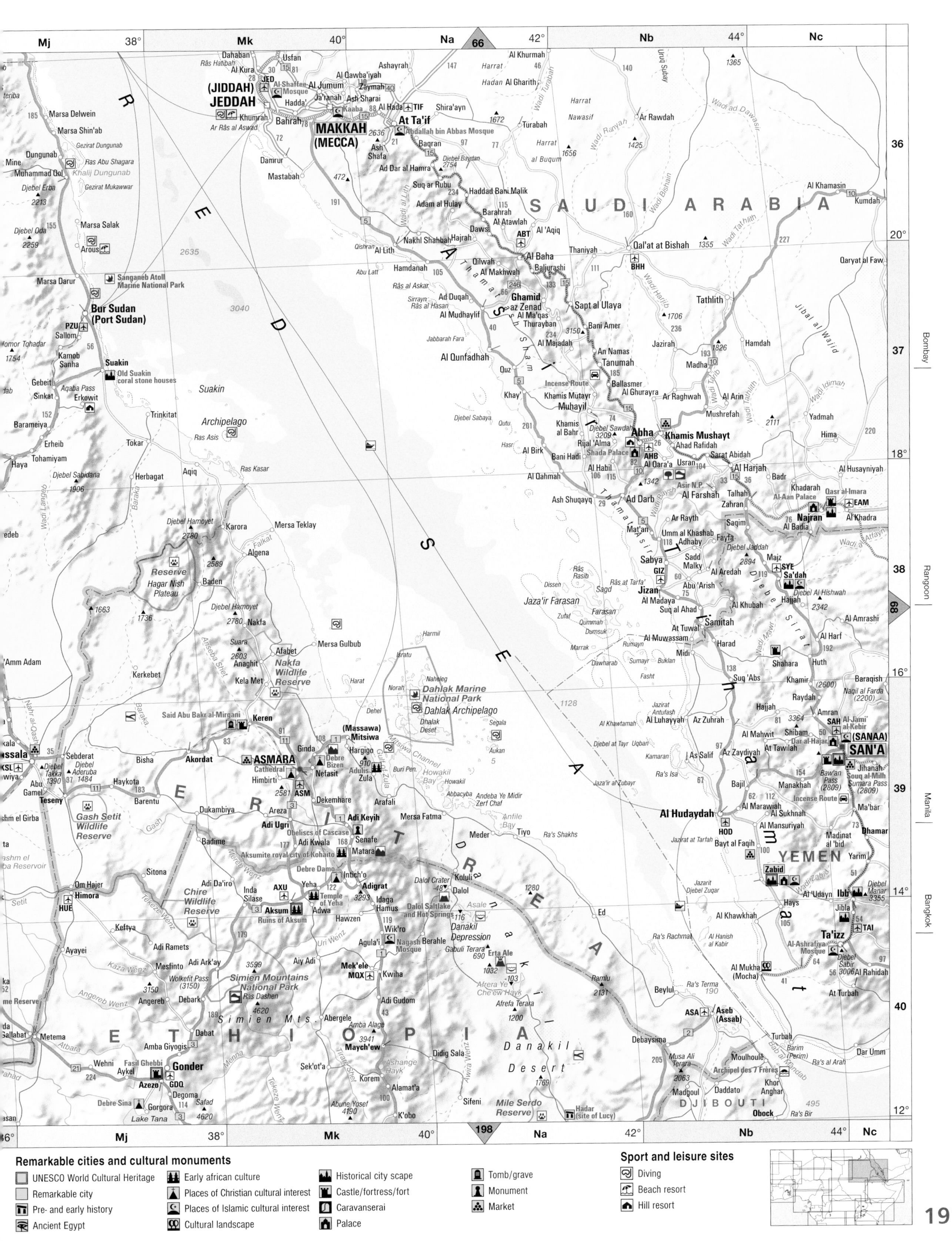

Remarkable cities and cultural monuments

▢ UNESCO World Cultural Heritage	Early african culture	Historical city scape
▢ Remarkable city	Places of Christian cultural interest	Castle/fortress/fort
Pre- and early history	Places of Islamic cultural interest	Caravanserai
Ancient Egypt	Cultural landscape	Palace

Tomb/grave	
Monument	
Market	

Sport and leisure sites

Diving
Beach resort
Hill resort

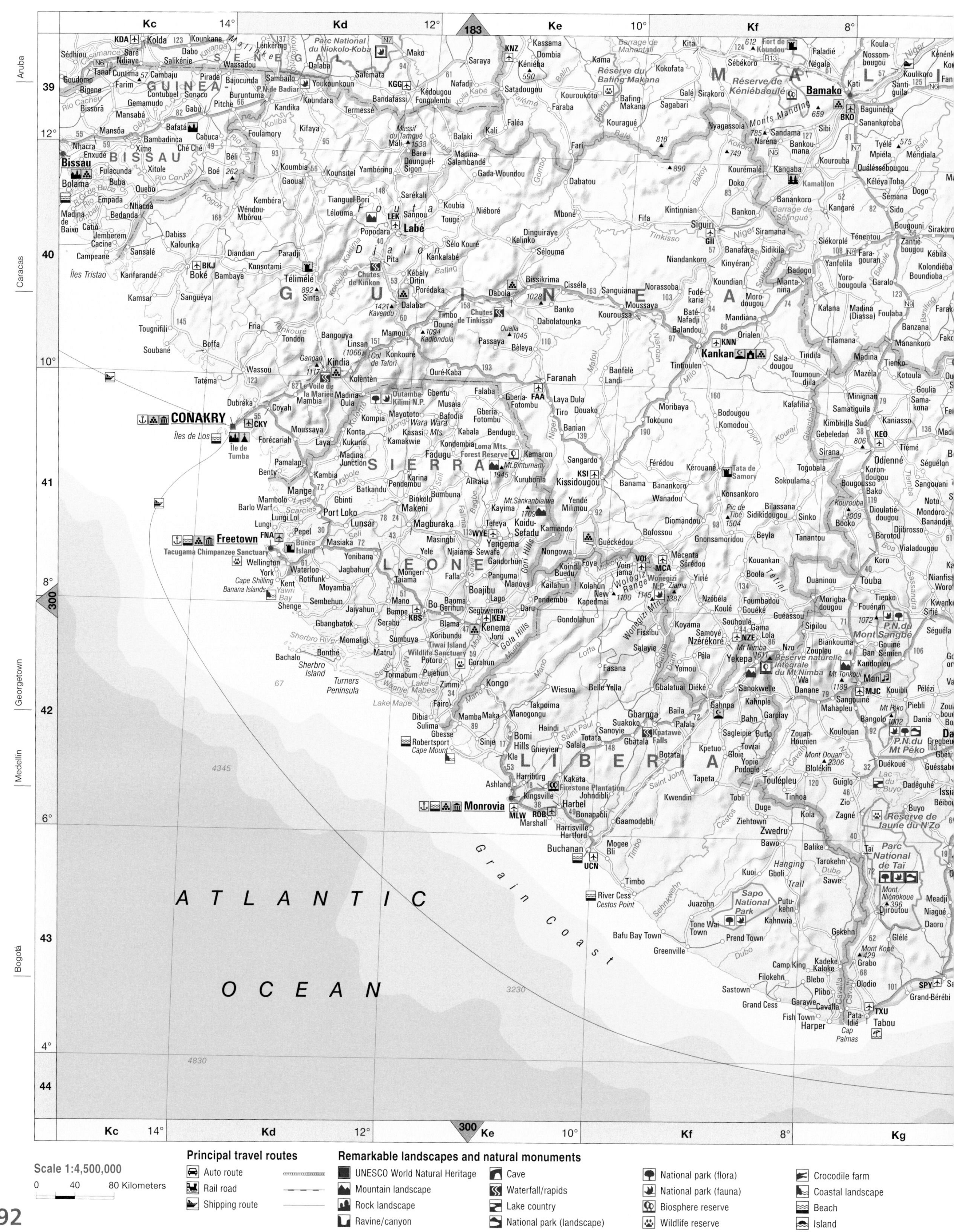

ATLANTIC

OCEAN

Scale 1:4,500,000

0   40   80 Kilometers

Principal travel routes		Remarkable landscapes and natural monuments					
✈ Auto route		■ UNESCO World Natural Heritage	✦ Cave	✿ National park (flora)	✦ Crocodile farm
▭ Rail road		▲ Mountain landscape	✦ Waterfall/rapids	✦ National park (fauna)	≈ Coastal landscape
⛴ Shipping route		■ Rock landscape	✦ Lake country	❀ Biosphere reserve	≈ Beach
		■ Ravine/canyon	✦ National park (landscape)	✿ Wildlife reserve	▭ Island

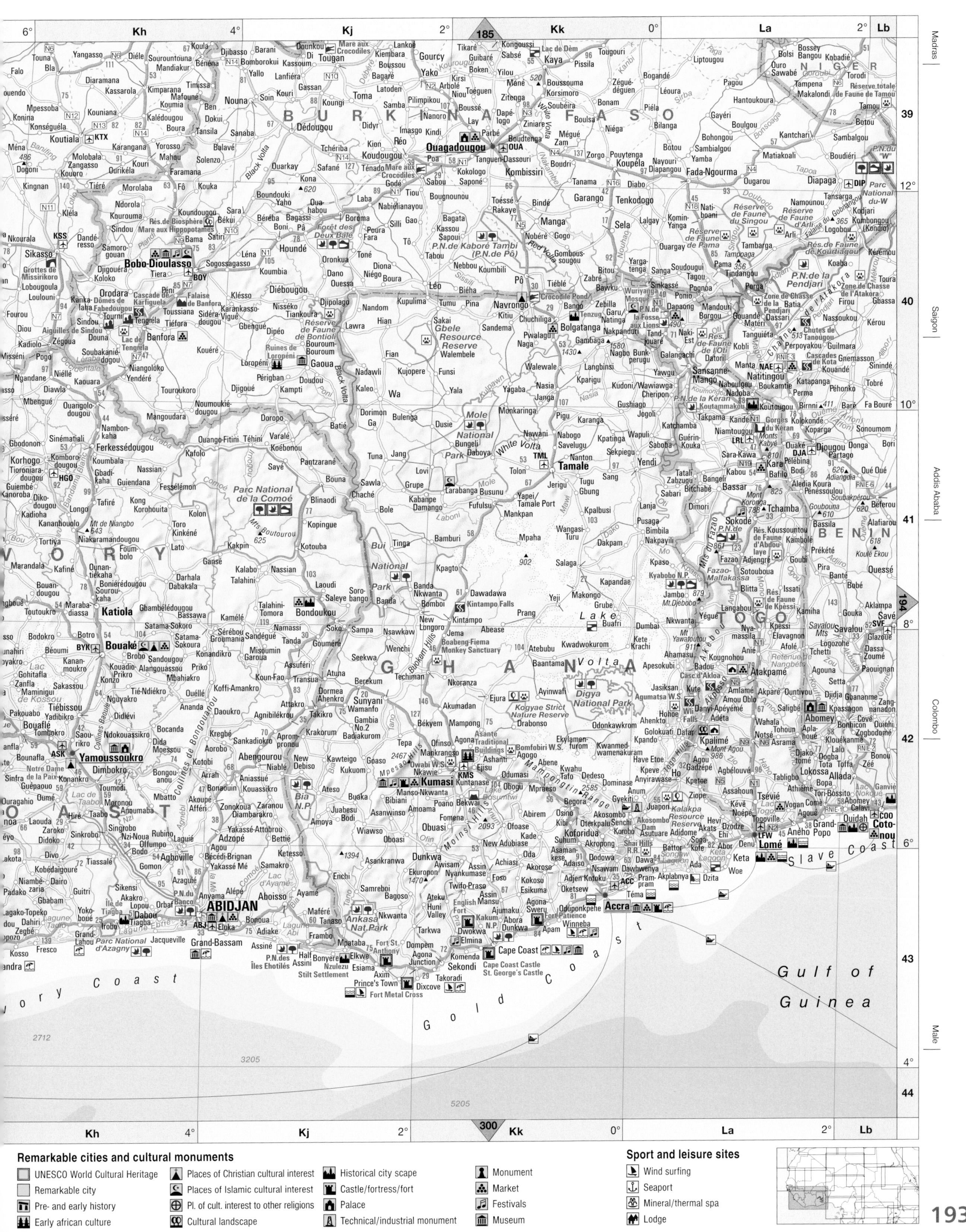

Remarkable cities and cultural monuments

- UNESCO World Cultural Heritage
- Remarkable city
- Pre- and early history
- Early african culture
- Places of Christian cultural interest
- Places of Islamic cultural interest
- Pl. of cult. interest to other religions
- Cultural landscape
- Historical city scape
- Castle/fortress/fort
- Palace
- Technical/industrial monument
- Monument
- Market
- Festivals
- Museum

Sport and leisure sites

- Wind surfing
- Seaport
- Mineral/thermal spa
- Lodge

193

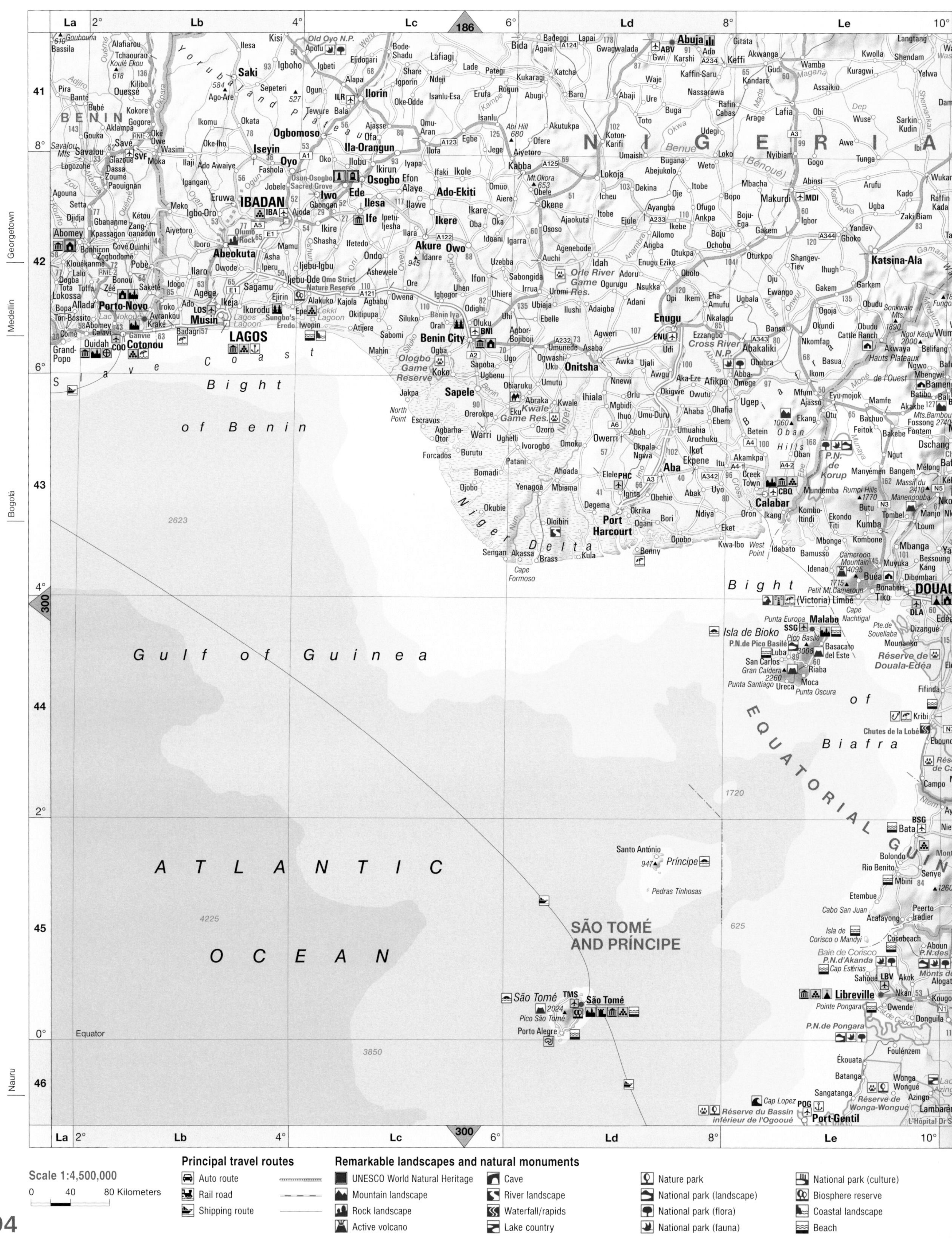

Scale 1:4,500,000

0   40   80 Kilometers

Principal travel routes
- Auto route
- Rail road
- Shipping route

Remarkable landscapes and natural monuments
- UNESCO World Natural Heritage
- Mountain landscape
- Rock landscape
- Active volcano
- Cave
- River landscape
- Waterfall/rapids
- Lake country
- Nature park
- National park (landscape)
- National park (flora)
- National park (fauna)
- National park (culture)
- Biosphere reserve
- Coastal landscape
- Beach

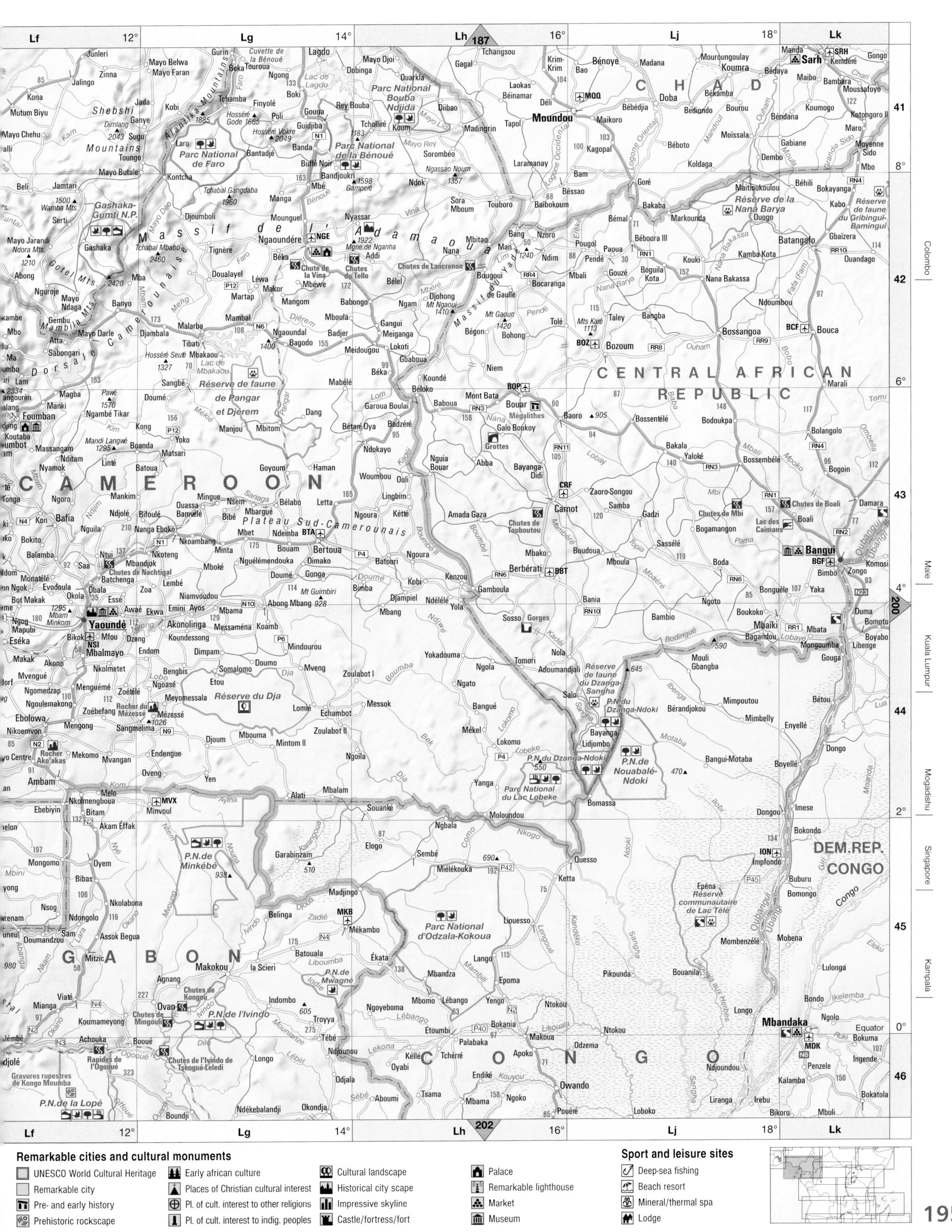

Remarkable cities and cultural monuments

- UNESCO World Cultural Heritage
- Remarkable city
- Pre- and early history
- Prehistoric rockscape
- Early african culture
- Places of Christian cultural interest
- Pl. of cult. interest to other religions
- Pl. of cult. interest to indig. peoples
- Cultural landscape
- Historical city scape
- Impressive skyline
- Castle/fortress/fort
- Palace
- Remarkable lighthouse
- Market
- Museum

Sport and leisure sites

- Deep-sea fishing
- Beach resort
- Mineral/thermal spa
- Lodge

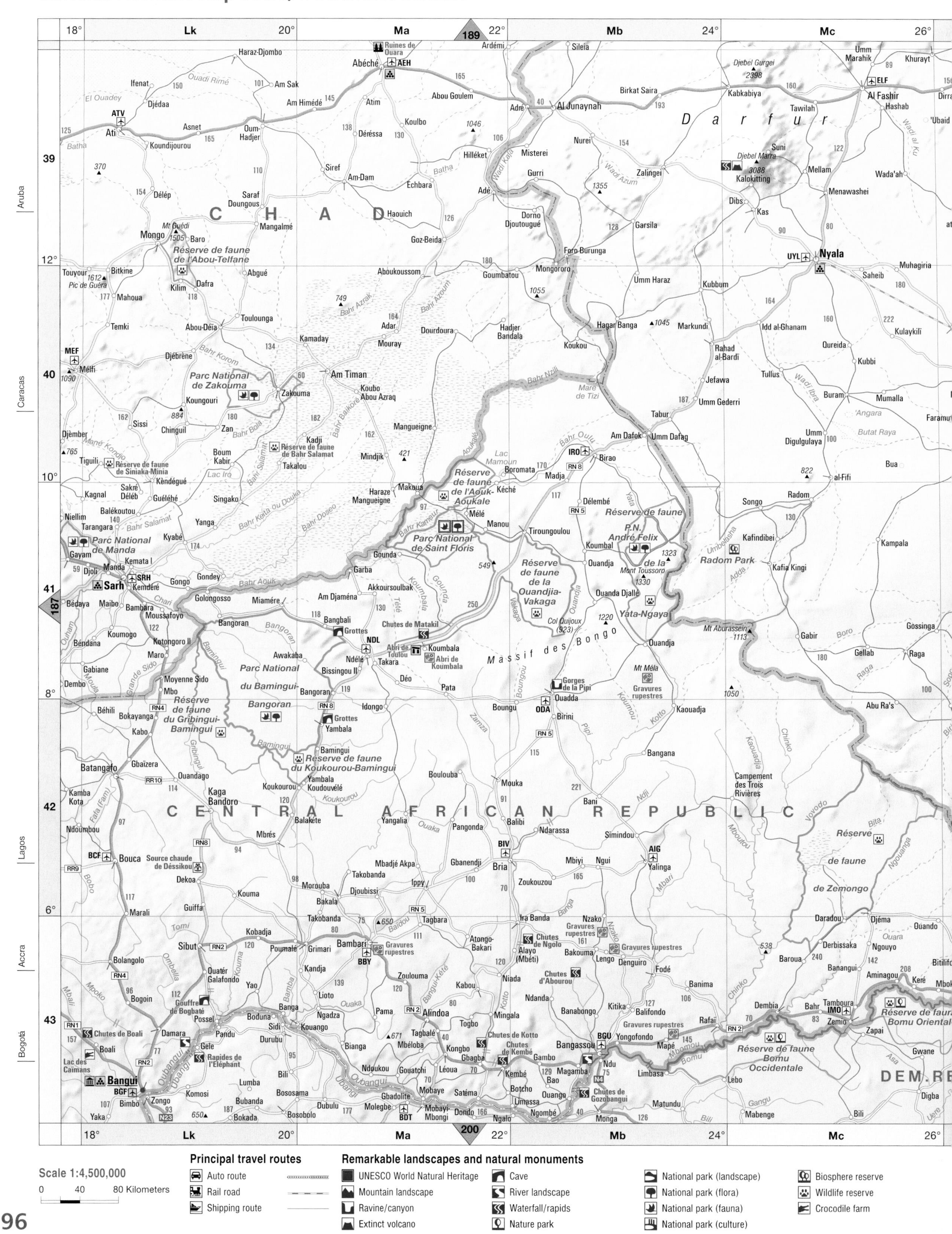

Principal travel routes

- Auto route
- Rail road
- Shipping route

Remarkable landscapes and natural monuments

- UNESCO World Natural Heritage
- Mountain landscape
- Ravine/canyon
- Extinct volcano
- Cave
- River landscape
- Waterfall/rapids
- Nature park
- National park (landscape)
- National park (flora)
- National park (fauna)
- National park (culture)
- Biosphere reserve
- Wildlife reserve
- Crocodile farm

Scale 1:4,500,000

0   40   80 Kilometers

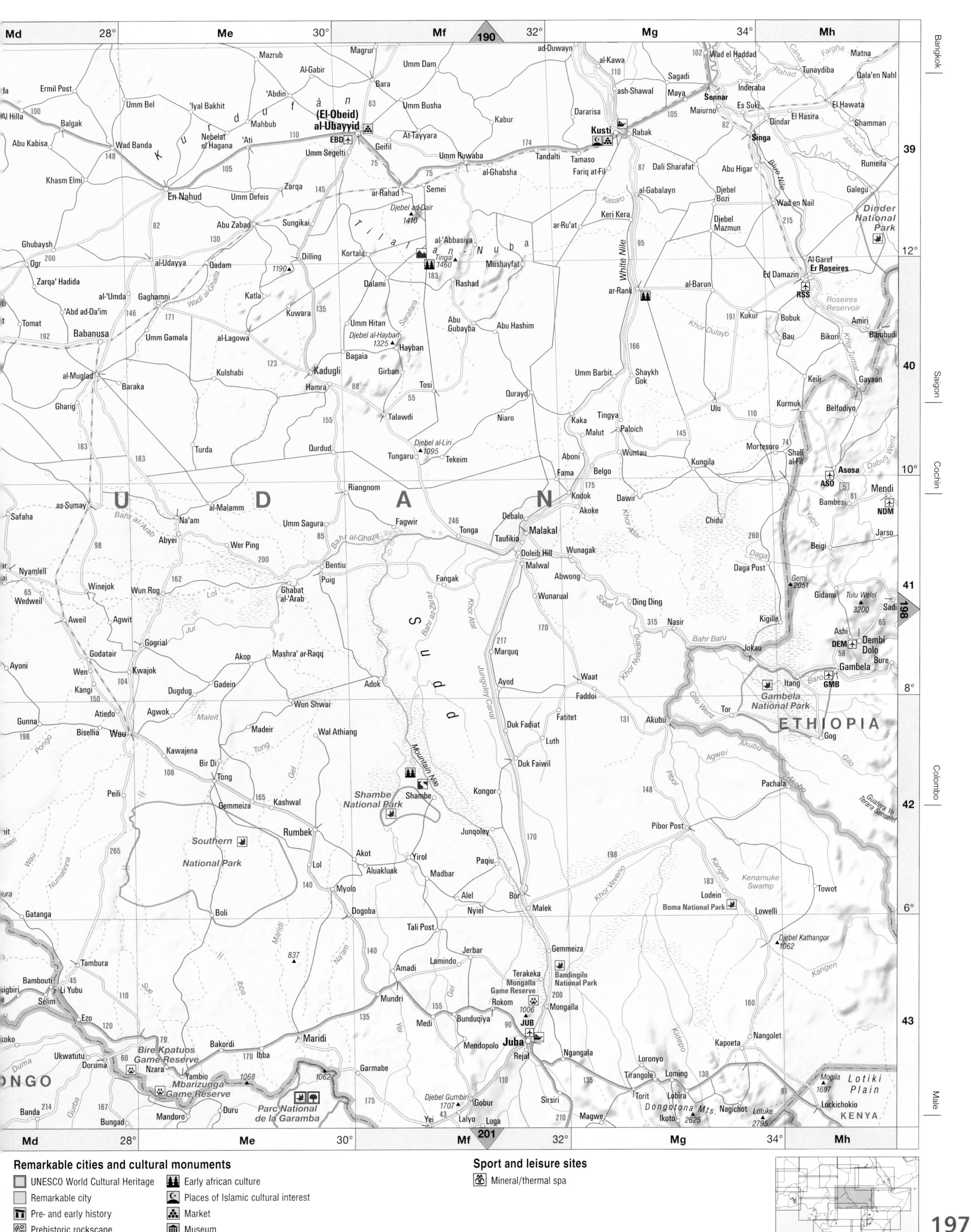

Remarkable cities and cultural monuments

- ▢ UNESCO World Cultural Heritage
- ▢ Remarkable city
- ⬚ Pre- and early history
- ◎ Prehistoric rockscape
- ⏶ Early african culture
- ☽ Places of Islamic cultural interest
- ⛏ Market
- ⛫ Museum

Sport and leisure sites

- ♨ Mineral/thermal spa

197

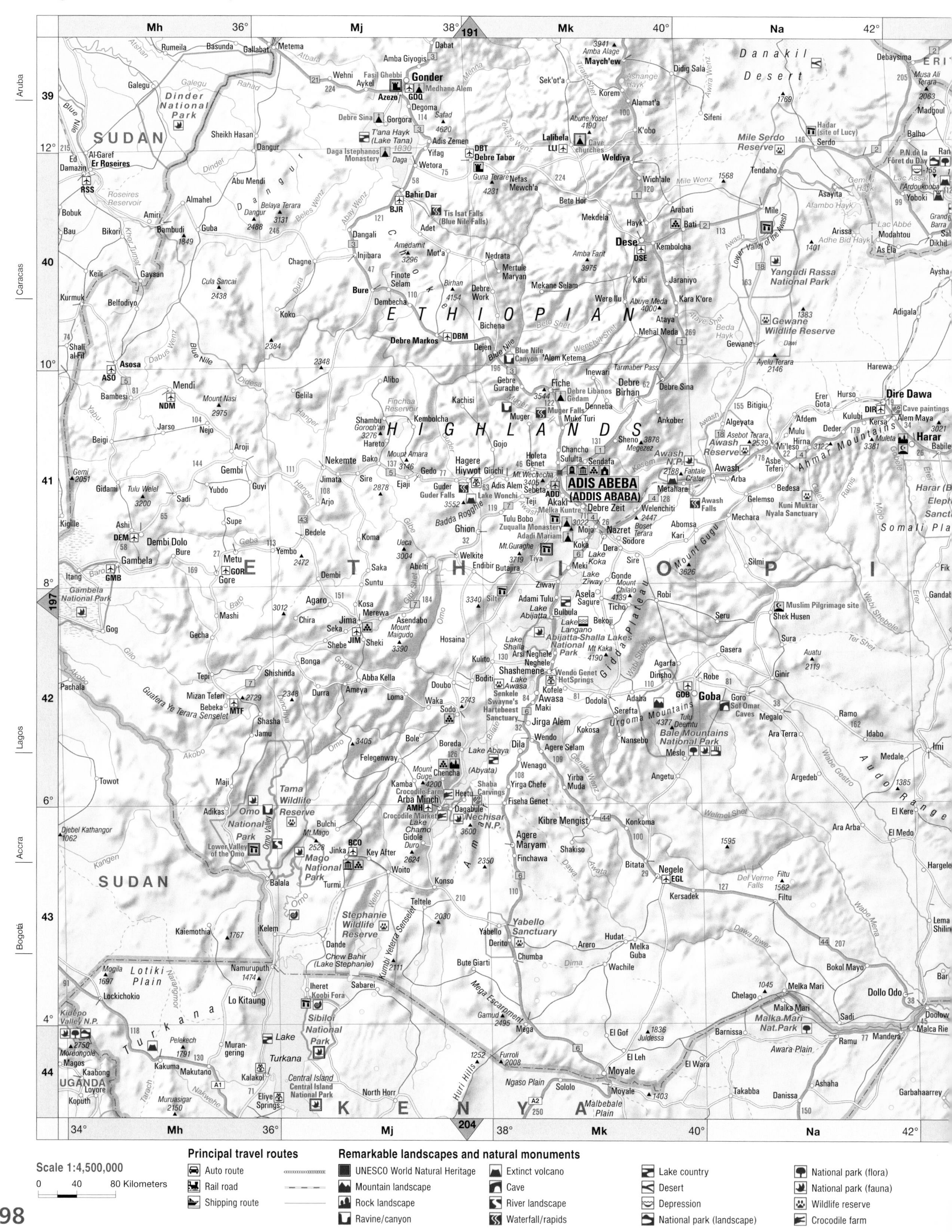

Scale 1:4,500,000

0   40   80 Kilometers

198

Principal travel routes
- Auto route
- Rail road
- Shipping route

Remarkable landscapes and natural monuments
- UNESCO World Natural Heritage
- Mountain landscape
- Rock landscape
- Ravine/canyon
- Extinct volcano
- Cave
- River landscape
- Waterfall/rapids
- Lake country
- Desert
- Depression
- National park (landscape)
- National park (flora)
- National park (fauna)
- Wildlife reserve
- Crocodile farm

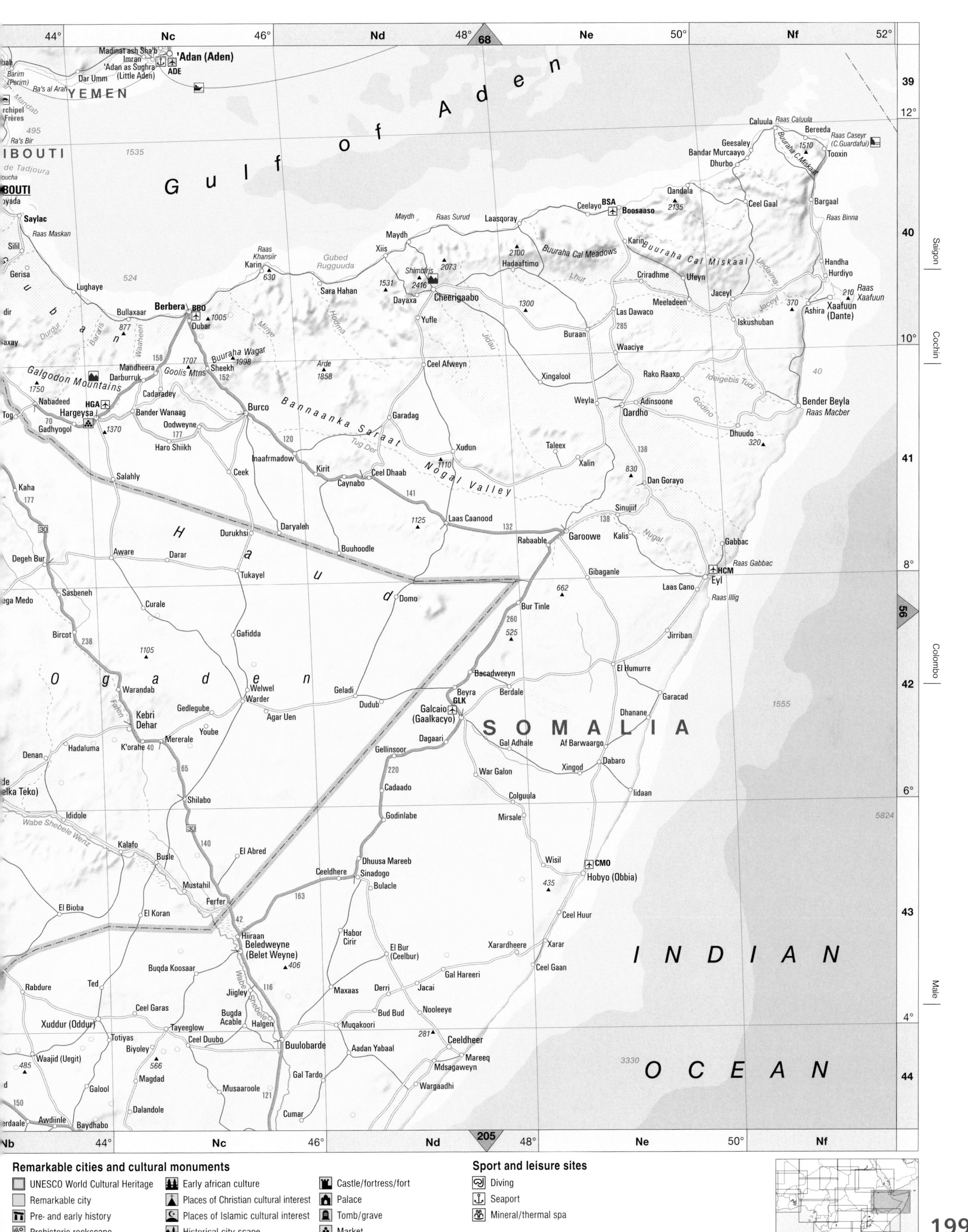

Remarkable cities and cultural monuments

- UNESCO World Cultural Heritage
- Remarkable city
- Pre- and early history
- Prehistoric rockscape
- Early african culture
- Places of Christian cultural interest
- Places of Islamic cultural interest
- Historical city scape
- Castle/fortress/fort
- Palace
- Tomb/grave
- Market

Sport and leisure sites

- Diving
- Seaport
- Mineral/thermal spa

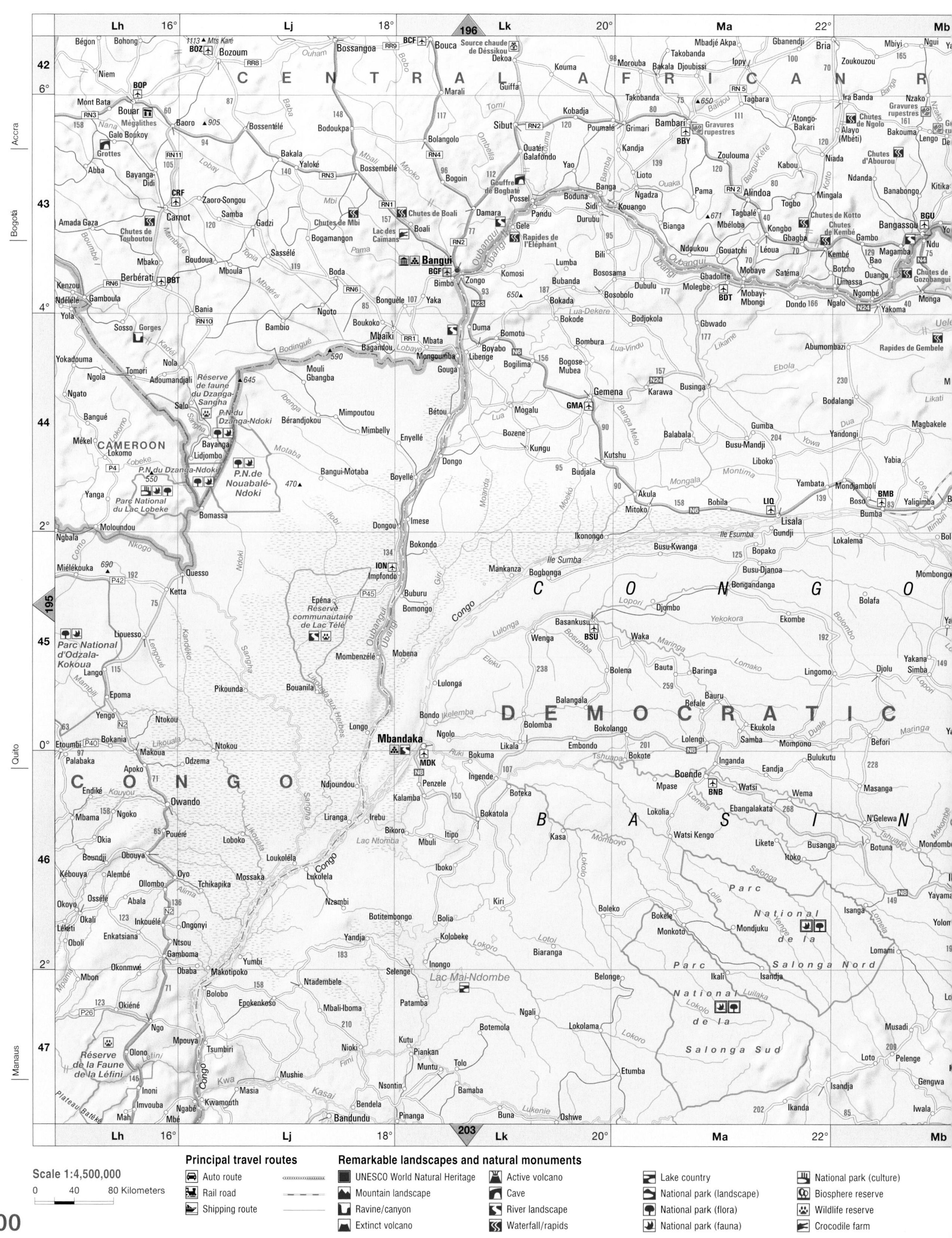

Scale 1:4,500,000

0   40   80 Kilometers

Principal travel routes

- Auto route
- Rail road
- Shipping route
- UNESCO World Natural Heritage
- Mountain landscape
- Ravine/canyon
- Extinct volcano

Remarkable landscapes and natural monuments

- Active volcano
- Cave
- River landscape
- Waterfall/rapids
- Lake country
- National park (landscape)
- National park (flora)
- National park (fauna)
- National park (culture)
- Biosphere reserve
- Wildlife reserve
- Crocodile farm

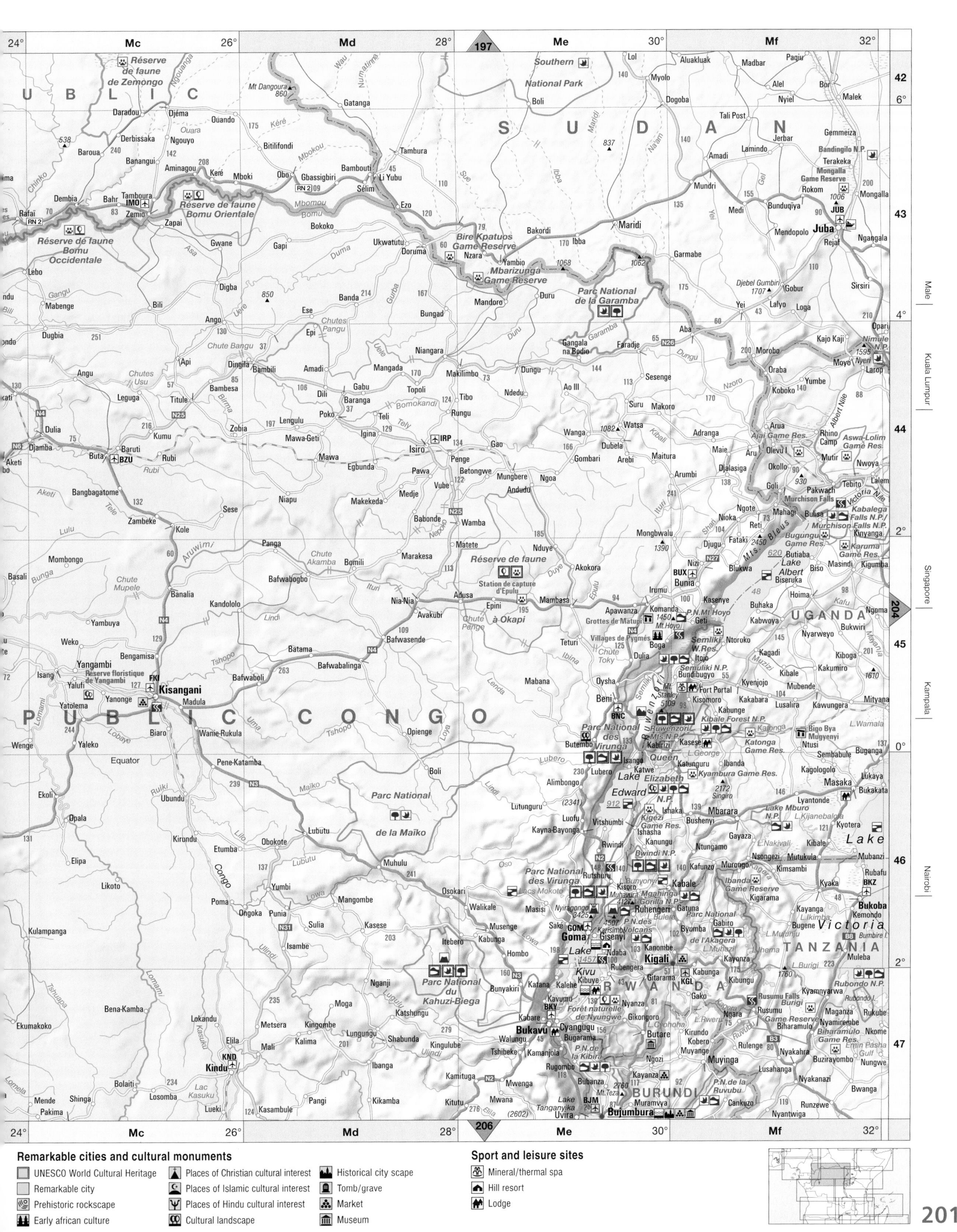

Remarkable cities and cultural monuments

- UNESCO World Cultural Heritage
- Remarkable city
- Prehistoric rockscape
- Early african culture
- Places of Christian cultural interest
- Places of Islamic cultural interest
- Places of Hindu cultural interest
- Cultural landscape
- Historical city scape
- Tomb/grave
- Market
- Museum

Sport and leisure sites

- Mineral/thermal spa
- Hill resort
- Lodge

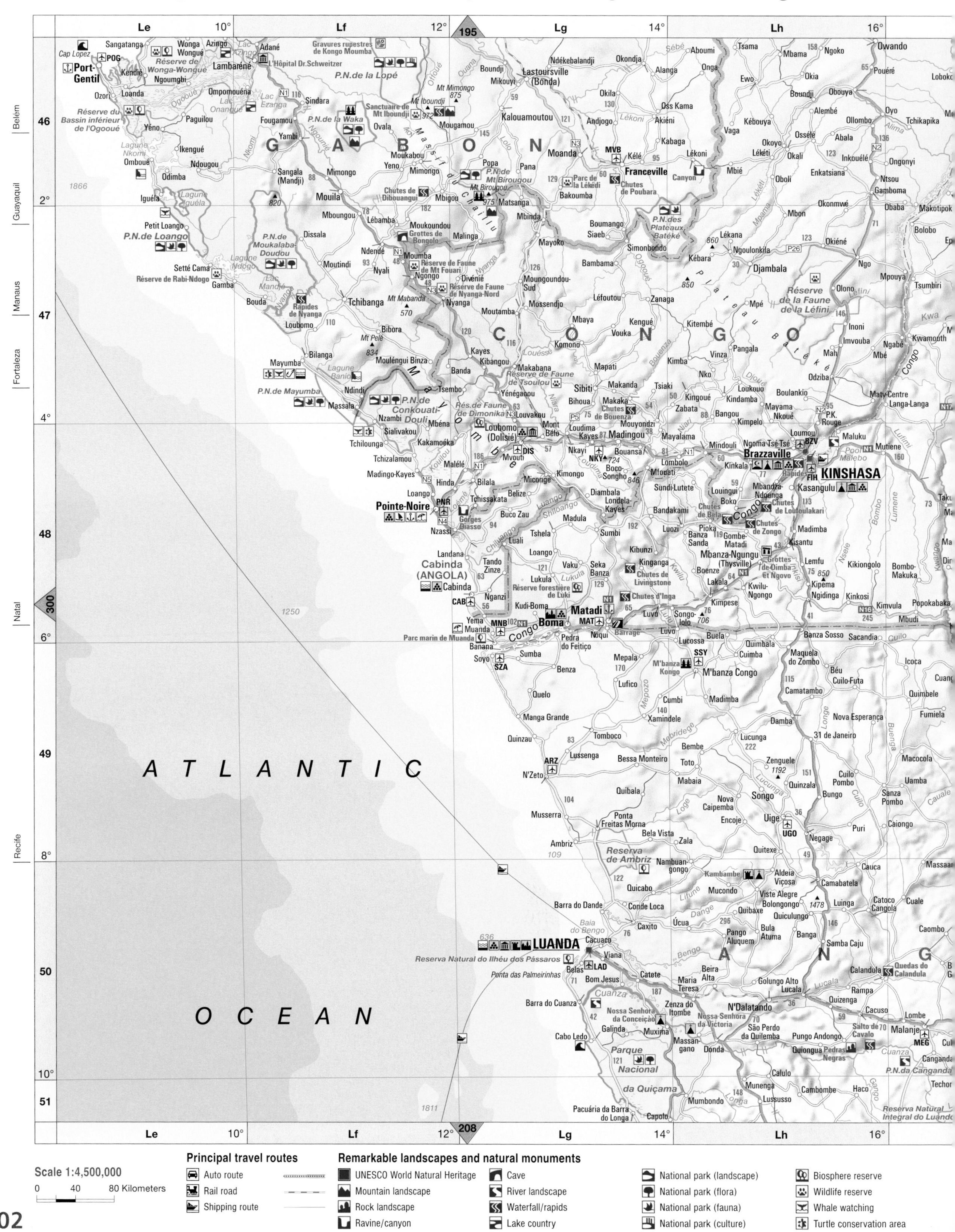

A T L A N T I C

O C E A N

Scale 1:4,500,000
0   40   80 Kilometers

Principal travel routes
- Auto route
- Rail road
- Shipping route

Remarkable landscapes and natural monuments
- UNESCO World Natural Heritage
- Mountain landscape
- Rock landscape
- Ravine/canyon
- Cave
- River landscape
- Waterfall/rapids
- Lake country
- National park (landscape)
- National park (flora)
- National park (fauna)
- National park (culture)
- Biosphere reserve
- Wildlife reserve
- Whale watching
- Turtle conservation area

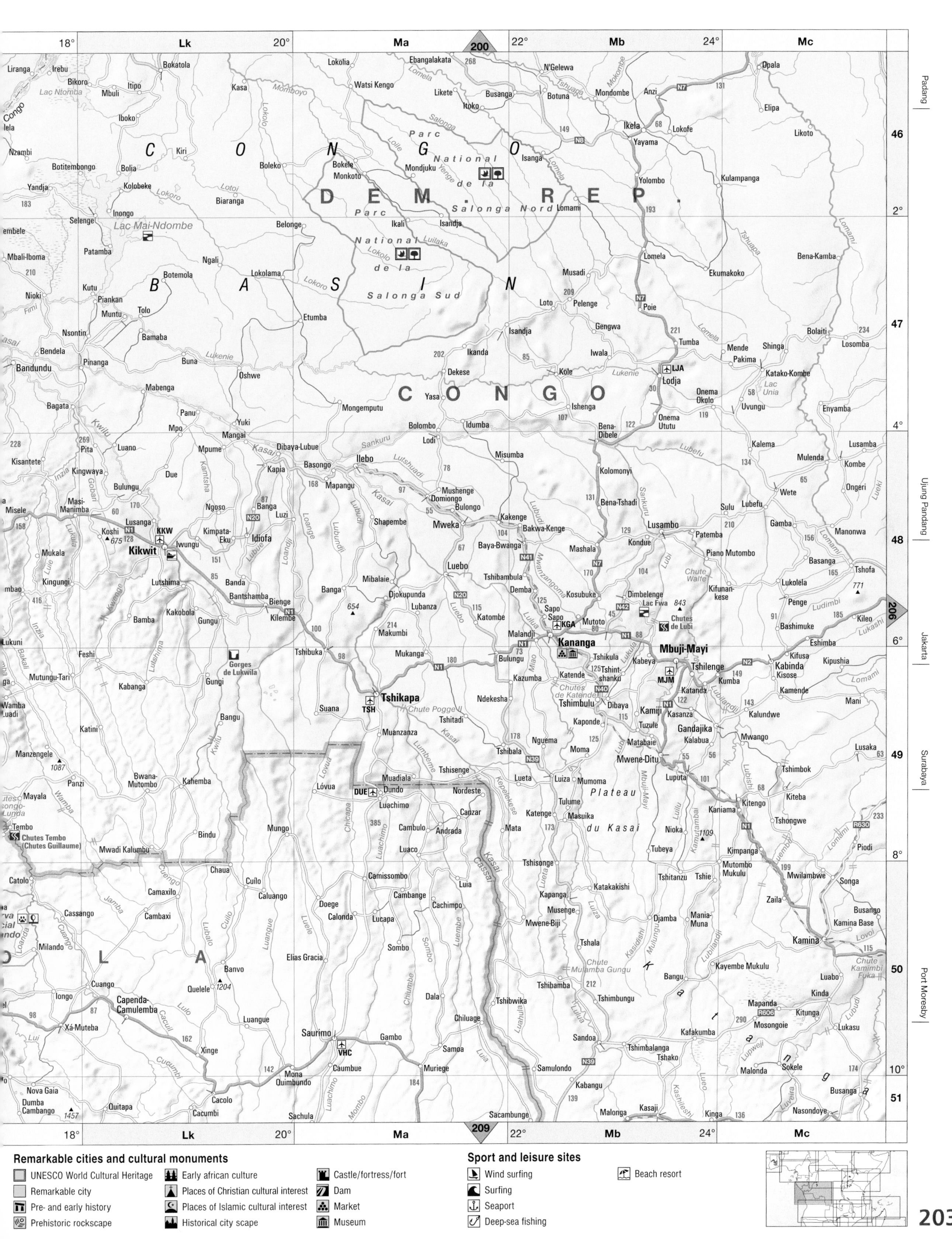

18°
Lk
20°
Ma
200
22°
Mb
24°
Mc
46
2°
47
4°
48
6°
49
8°
50
10°
51
209
206
Padang
Ujung Pandang
Jakarta
Surabaya
Port Moresby
DEM. REP. CONGO
CONGO BASIN
Parc National de la Salonga Nord
Parc National de la Salonga Sud
Plateau du Kasai
Katanga
Lac Mai-Ndombe
Bandundu
Kikwit
Idiofa
Ilebo
Mweka
Luebo
Tshikapa
Kananga
Mbuji-Mayi
Mwene-Ditu
Kamina
Lodja
Lusambo
Saurimo
Dundo
Kabinda
Gandajika
Tshimbulu
Kasai
Sankuru
Lukenie
Kwilu
Lomami
Lulua
Remarkable cities and cultural monuments
UNESCO World Cultural Heritage
Remarkable city
Pre- and early history
Prehistoric rockscape
Early african culture
Places of Christian cultural interest
Places of Islamic cultural interest
Historical city scape
Castle/fortress/fort
Dam
Market
Museum
Sport and leisure sites
Wind surfing
Surfing
Seaport
Deep-sea fishing
Beach resort

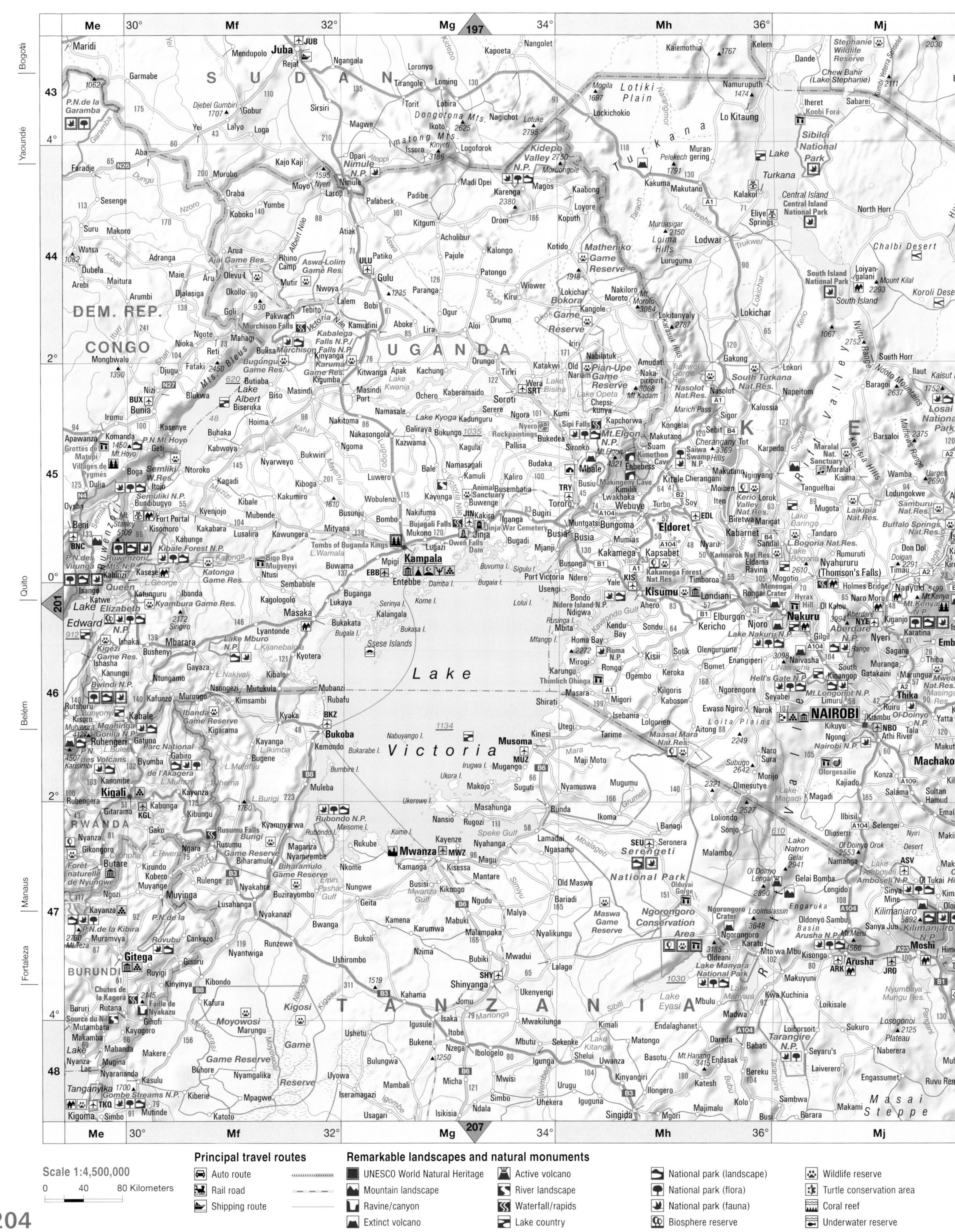

Scale 1:4,500,000

0   40   80 Kilometers

Principal travel routes

- 🚗 Auto route
- 🚂 Rail road
- ⚓ Shipping route

Remarkable landscapes and natural monuments

- ◾ UNESCO World Natural Heritage
- ▲ Mountain landscape
- Ravine/canyon
- ▰ Extinct volcano
- ▲ Active volcano
- River landscape
- Waterfall/rapids
- Lake country

- National park (landscape)
- National park (flora)
- National park (fauna)
- Biosphere reserve

- Wildlife reserve
- Turtle conservation area
- Coral reef
- Underwater reserve

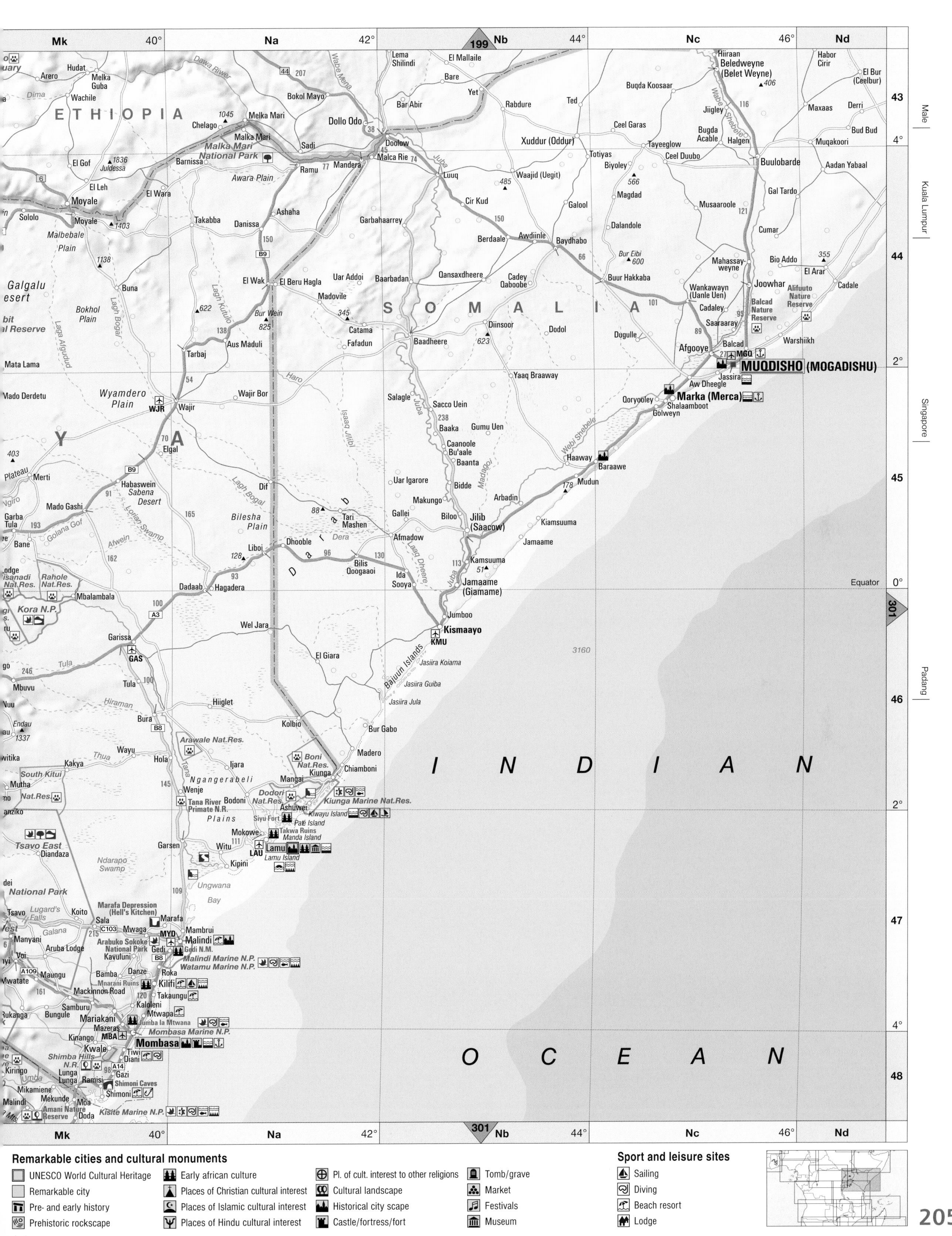

Mk
40°
Na
42°
199
Nb
44°
Nc
46°
Nd
43
44
45
46
47
48
4°
2°
0°
Equator
Male
Kuala Lumpur
Singapore
Padang
301
ETHIOPIA
SOMALIA
INDIAN
OCEAN
MUQDISHO (MOGADISHU)
Marka (Merca)
Kismaayo
Beledweyne (Belet Weyne)
Jamaame (Giamame)
Jilib (Saacow)
Mombasa
Malindi
Lamu
Kilifi
Garissa
Moyale
Mandera
Dollo Odo
Luuq
Baardheere
Buulobarde
Joowhar
Afgooye
Xuddur (Oddur)
Baraawe
Wajir
Malka Mari National Park
Kora N.P.
Tsavo East National Park
Arawale Nat.Res.
Boni Nat.Res.
Dodori Nat.Res.
Tana River Primate N.R.
Kiunga Marine Nat.Res.
Malindi Marine N.P.
Watamu Marine N.P.
Mombasa Marine N.P.
Kisite Marine N.P.
Shimba Hills N.R.
Balcad Nature Reserve
Alifuuto Nature Reserve
Arabuko Sokoke National Park
Gedi N.M.
Shimoni Caves
Takwa Ruins
Mnarani Ruins
Jumba la Mtwana
Marafa Depression (Hell's Kitchen)
Lamu Island
Pate Island
Manda Island
Kiwayu Island
Bajuun Islands
Jasiira Koiama
Jasiira Guiba
Jasiira Jula
Ungwana Bay
Juba
Webi Shebele
Wabe Shebele
Tana
Galana
Dawa River
Lagh Bogal
Lorian Swamp
Wyamdero Plain
Bilesha Plain
Awara Plain
Malbebale Plain
Bokhol Plain
Habaswein Sabena Desert
Ngangerabeli Plains
3160
Remarkable cities and cultural monuments
UNESCO World Cultural Heritage
Remarkable city
Pre- and early history
Prehistoric rockscape
Early african culture
Places of Christian cultural interest
Places of Islamic cultural interest
Places of Hindu cultural interest
Pl. of cult. interest to other religions
Cultural landscape
Historical city scape
Castle/fortress/fort
Tomb/grave
Market
Festivals
Museum
Sport and leisure sites
Sailing
Diving
Beach resort
Lodge

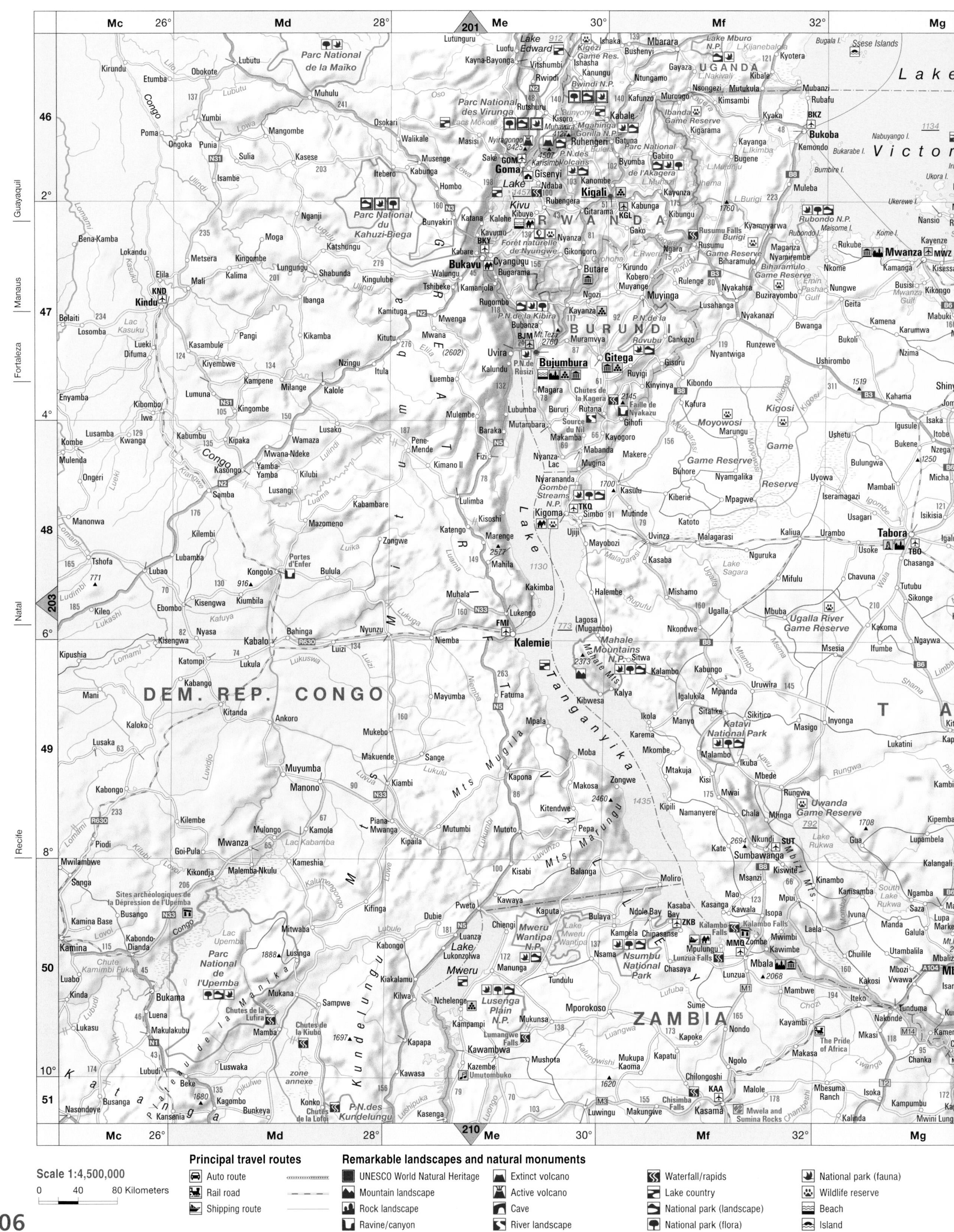

Scale 1:4,500,000

0   40   80 Kilometers

Principal travel routes
- Auto route
- Rail road
- Shipping route

Remarkable landscapes and natural monuments
- UNESCO World Natural Heritage
- Mountain landscape
- Rock landscape
- Ravine/canyon
- Extinct volcano
- Active volcano
- Cave
- River landscape
- Waterfall/rapids
- Lake country
- National park (landscape)
- National park (flora)
- National park (fauna)
- Wildlife reserve
- Beach
- Island

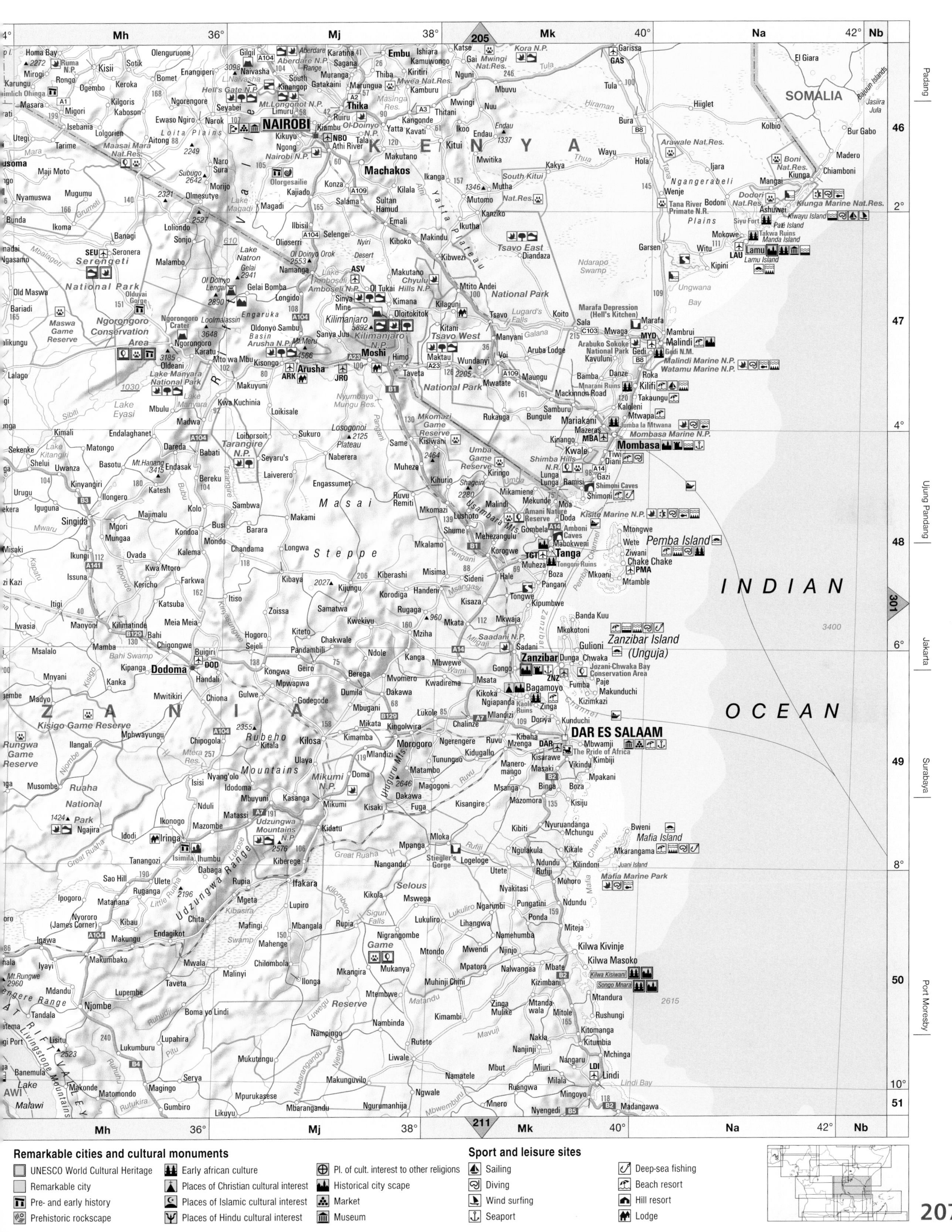

Mh
Mj
Mk
Na
Nb
36°
38°
40°
42°
205
211
301
46
47
48
49
50
51
2°
4°
6°
8°
10°
Padang
Ujung Pandang
Jakarta
Surabaya
Port Moresby
KENYA
SOMALIA
INDIAN OCEAN
NAIROBI
DAR ES SALAAM
Mombasa
Dodoma
Zanzibar
Tanga
Arusha
Moshi
Machakos
Lamu
Malindi
Kilimanjaro 5892
Serengeti National Park
Ngorongoro Conservation Area
Tsavo East National Park
Tsavo West National Park
Masai Steppe
Pemba Island
Zanzibar Island (Unguja)
Mafia Island
Selous Game Reserve
Ruaha National Park
Rubeho Mountains
Udzungwa Range
Remarkable cities and cultural monuments
UNESCO World Cultural Heritage
Remarkable city
Pre- and early history
Prehistoric rockscape
Early african culture
Places of Christian cultural interest
Places of Islamic cultural interest
Places of Hindu cultural interest
Pl. of cult. interest to other religions
Historical city scape
Market
Museum
Sport and leisure sites
Sailing
Diving
Wind surfing
Seaport
Deep-sea fishing
Beach resort
Hill resort
Lodge

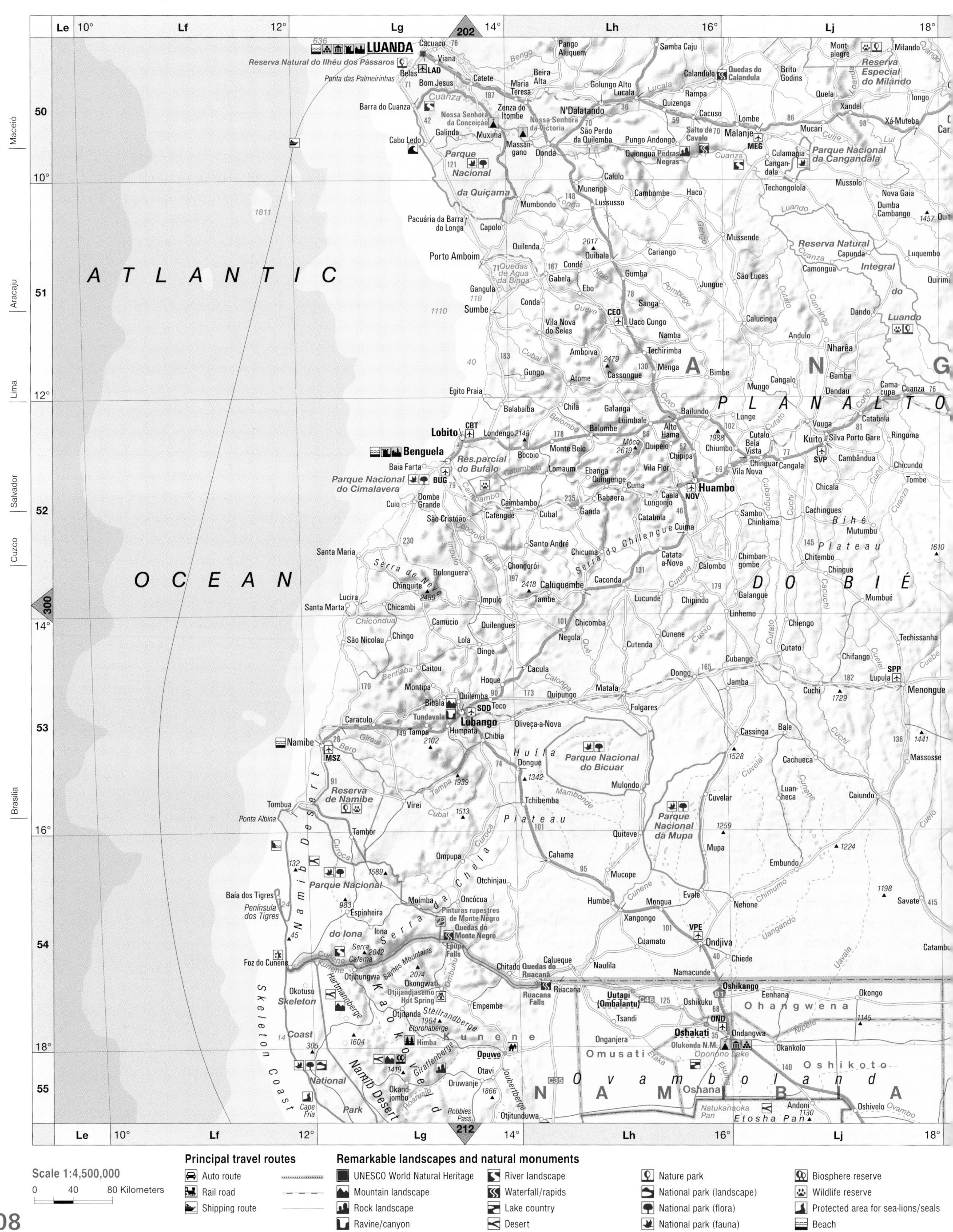

Scale 1:4,500,000

0   40   80 Kilometers

Principal travel routes

- Auto route
- Rail road
- Shipping route

Remarkable landscapes and natural monuments

- UNESCO World Natural Heritage
- Mountain landscape
- Rock landscape
- Ravine/canyon
- River landscape
- Waterfall/rapids
- Lake country
- Desert
- Nature park
- National park (landscape)
- National park (flora)
- National park (fauna)
- Biosphere reserve
- Wildlife reserve
- Protected area for sea-lions/seals
- Beach

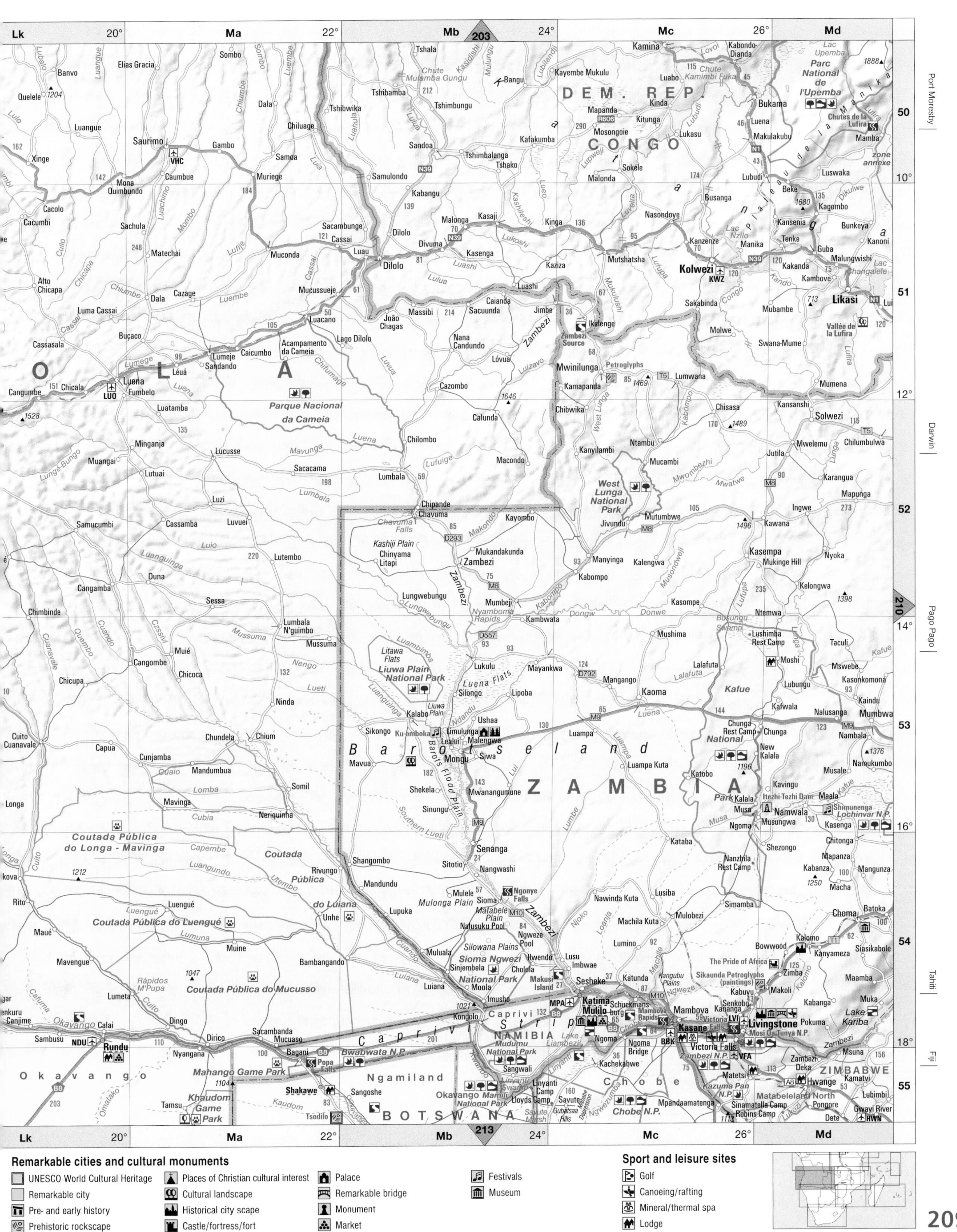

Remarkable cities and cultural monuments

- ⬜ UNESCO World Cultural Heritage
- ⬜ Remarkable city
- 🔲 Pre- and early history
- 🔲 Prehistoric rockscape
- 🔺 Places of Christian cultural interest
- 🔲 Cultural landscape
- 🔲 Historical city scape
- 🔲 Castle/fortress/fort
- 🔲 Palace
- 🔲 Remarkable bridge
- 🔲 Monument
- 🔲 Market
- 🔲 Festivals
- 🏛 Museum

Sport and leisure sites

- 🔲 Golf
- 🔲 Canoeing/rafting
- 🔲 Mineral/thermal spa
- 🔲 Lodge

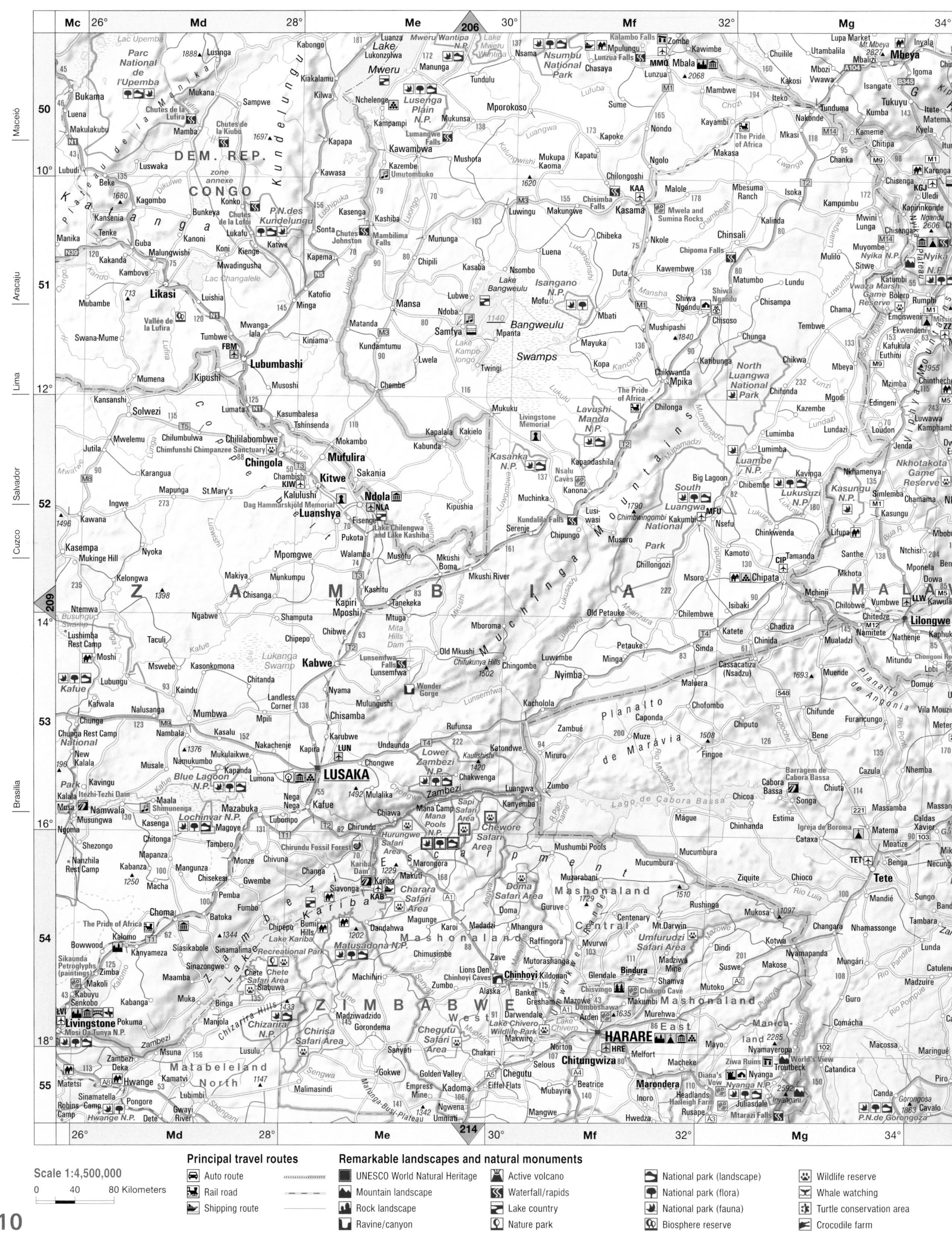

Scale 1:4,500,000

0   40   80 Kilometers

Principal travel routes

- Auto route
- Rail road
- Shipping route
- Auto route (dotted)
- Rail line (dashed)
- Ordinary road

Remarkable landscapes and natural monuments

- UNESCO World Natural Heritage
- Mountain landscape
- Rock landscape
- Ravine/canyon
- Active volcano
- Waterfall/rapids
- Lake country
- Nature park
- National park (landscape)
- National park (flora)
- National park (fauna)
- Biosphere reserve
- Wildlife reserve
- Whale watching
- Turtle conservation area
- Crocodile farm

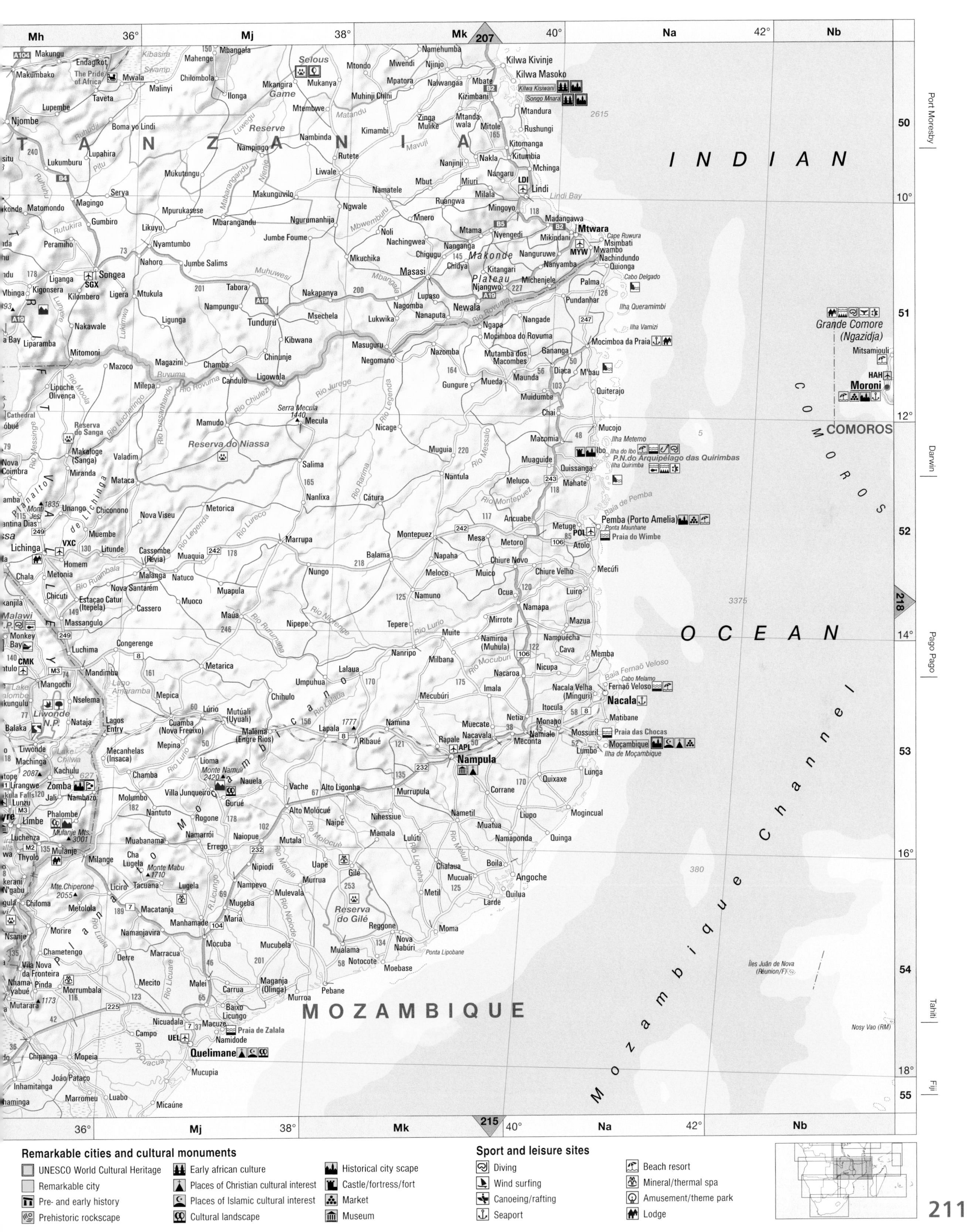

TANZANIA

A104 Makungu
Endagikot
The Pride
of Africa
Makumbako
Taveta
Malinyi
Njombe
Lupembe
Mwala
Kibasira
Swamp
Mahenge
Chilombola
Mbangala
Selous
Mkangira Game
Mukanya
Reserve
Mtondo
Mwendi Njinjo
Mpatora Nalwangaa
Kilwa Kivinje
Kilwa Masoko
Mbate
Kizimbani
Kilwa Kisiwani B2
Songo Mnara

INDIAN

OCEAN

MOZAMBIQUE

COMOROS

Moroni

Grande Comore
(Ngazidja)
Mitsamiouli
HAH

211

Remarkable cities and cultural monuments

- UNESCO World Cultural Heritage
- Remarkable city
- Pre- and early history
- Prehistoric rockscape
- Early african culture
- Places of Christian cultural interest
- Places of Islamic cultural interest
- Cultural landscape
- Historical city scape
- Castle/fortress/fort
- Market
- Museum

Sport and leisure sites

- Diving
- Wind surfing
- Canoeing/rafting
- Seaport
- Beach resort
- Mineral/thermal spa
- Amusement/theme park
- Lodge

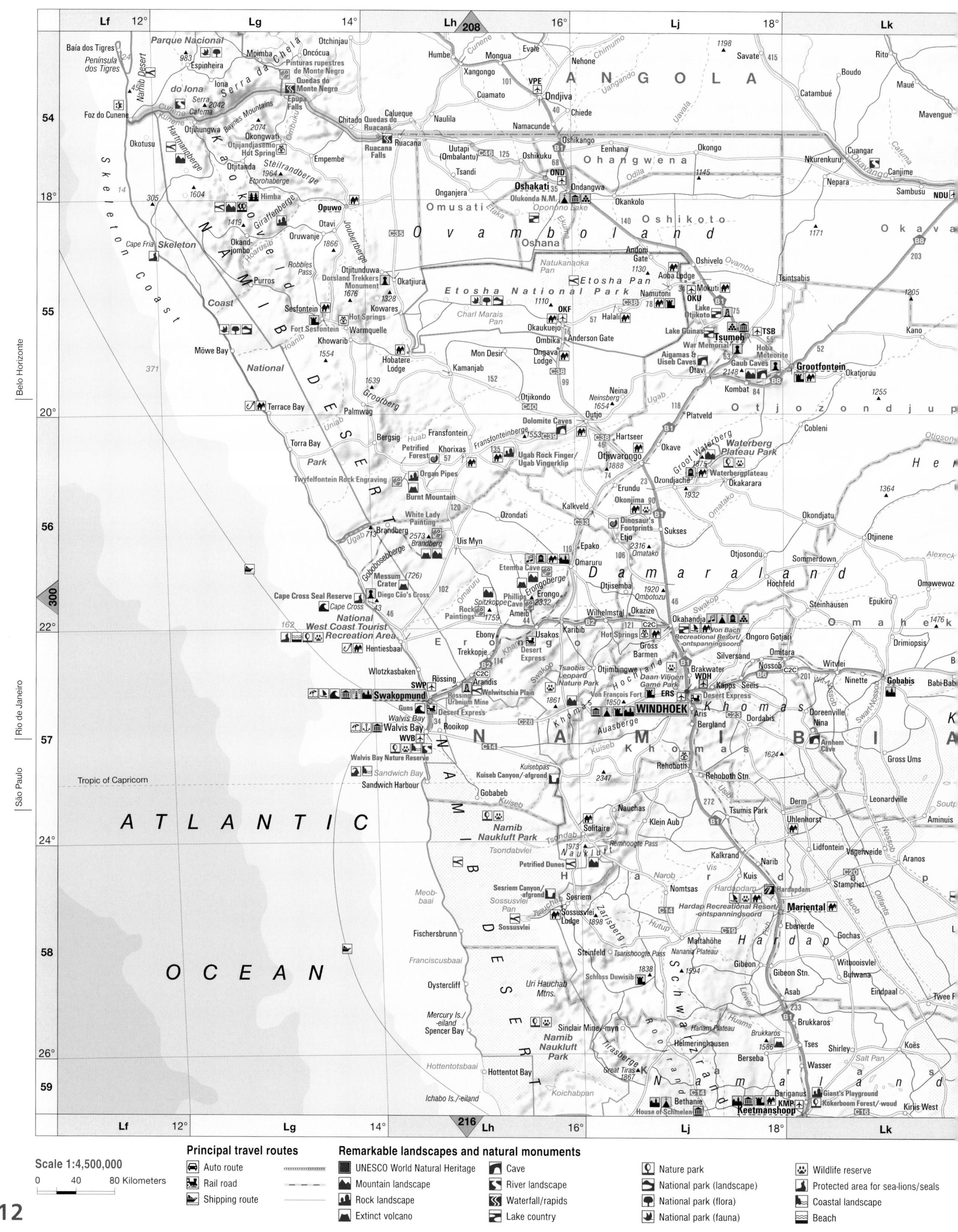

Scale 1:4,500,000

0   40   80 Kilometers

Principal travel routes

- Auto route
- Rail road
- Shipping route

Remarkable landscapes and natural monuments

- UNESCO World Natural Heritage
- Mountain landscape
- Rock landscape
- Extinct volcano
- Cave
- River landscape
- Waterfall/rapids
- Lake country
- Nature park
- National park (landscape)
- National park (flora)
- National park (fauna)
- Wildlife reserve
- Protected area for sea-lions/seals
- Coastal landscape
- Beach

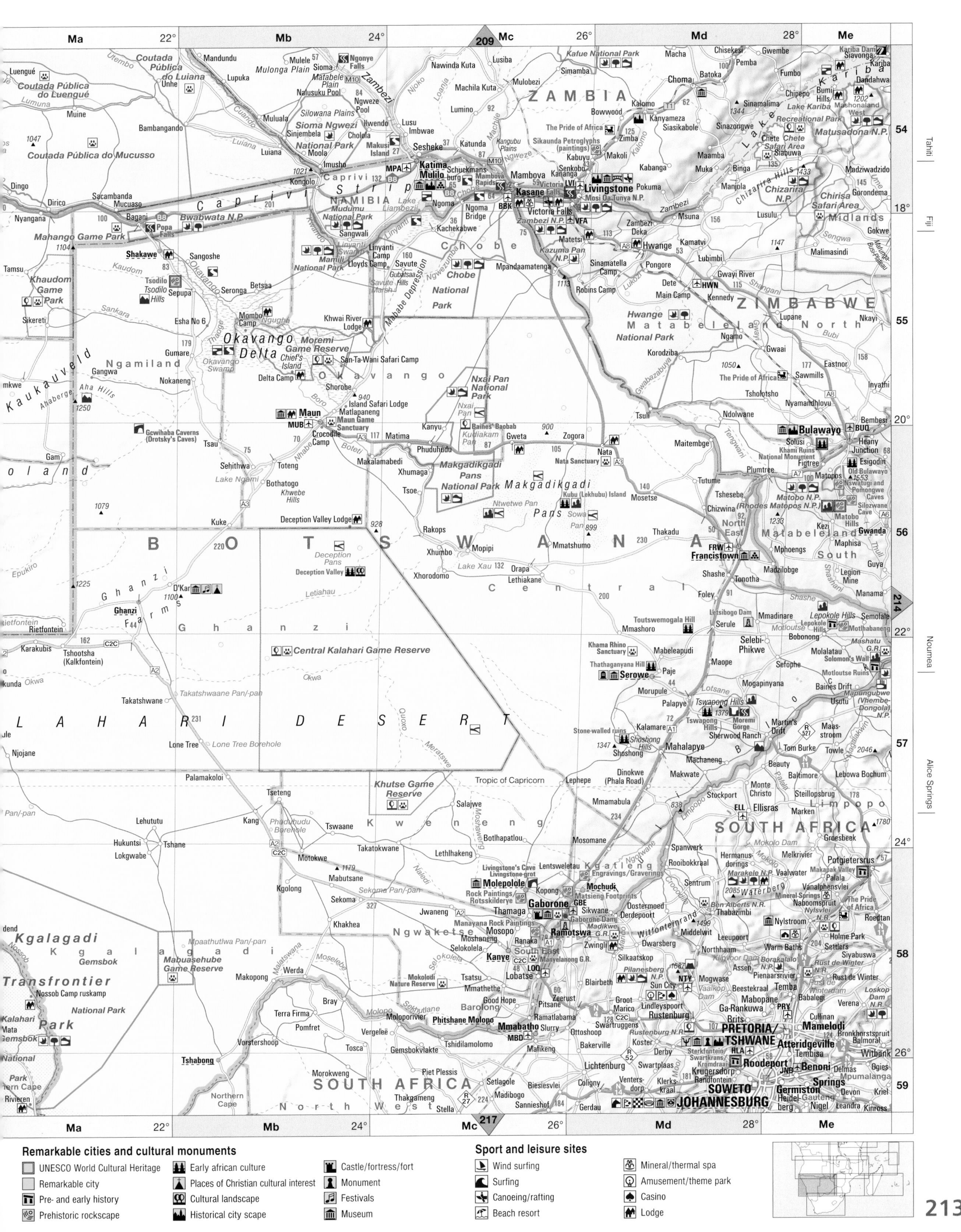

Ma
22°
Mb
24°
209
Mc
26°
Md
28°
Me
ZAMBIA
Kafue National Park
Livingstone
Mosi Oa Tunya N.P.
Victoria Falls
Zambezi N.P.
Kasane
Katima Mulilo
Caprivi Strip
NAMIBIA
Mudumu National Park
Mamili National Park
Bwabwata N.P.
Mahango Game Park
Coutada Pública do Luiana
Coutada Pública do Luengué
Coutada Pública do Mucusso
Sioma Ngwezi National Park
Chobe National Park
Hwange National Park
Matabeleland North
ZIMBABWE
Lake Kariba
Matusadona N.P.
Chizarira N.P.
Chirisa Safari Area
Midlands
Bulawayo
Matobo N.P.
Matabeleland South
Francistown
Okavango Delta
Moremi Game Reserve
Okavango
Ngamiland
Kaukauveld
Khaudom Game Park
Tsodilo Hills
Maun
Nxai Pan National Park
Makgadikgadi Pans National Park
Makgadikgadi Pans
Central
BOTSWANA
Ghanzi
Ghanzi Farms
Central Kalahari Game Reserve
Deception Pans
KALAHARI DESERT
Tropic of Capricorn
Khutse Game Reserve
Kweneng
Kgatleng
Molepolole
Gaborone
Ramotswa
Kanye
Lobatse
Ngwaketse
Kgalagadi
Mabuasehube Game Reserve
Kgalagadi Transfrontier National Park
Tshabong
Mmabatho
Mafikeng
SOUTH AFRICA
North West
Northern Cape
Limpopo
Waterberg
Rustenburg
PRETORIA/TSHWANE
SOWETO
JOHANNESBURG
Roodepoort
Germiston
Benoni
Springs
Mpumalanga
Gauteng
Serowe
Palapye
Mahalapye
Selebi-Phikwe
Lephepe
Kang
Tshane
Lehututu
Hukuntsi
Werda
Tsabong
Mc
217
26°
Md
28°
Me
54
55
56
57
58
59
18°
20°
22°
24°
26°
214
Tahiti
Fiji
Noumea
Alice Springs
Remarkable cities and cultural monuments
UNESCO World Cultural Heritage
Remarkable city
Pre- and early history
Prehistoric rockscape
Early african culture
Places of Christian cultural interest
Cultural landscape
Historical city scape
Castle/fortress/fort
Monument
Festivals
Museum
Sport and leisure sites
Wind surfing
Surfing
Canoeing/rafting
Beach resort
Mineral/thermal spa
Amusement/theme park
Casino
Lodge

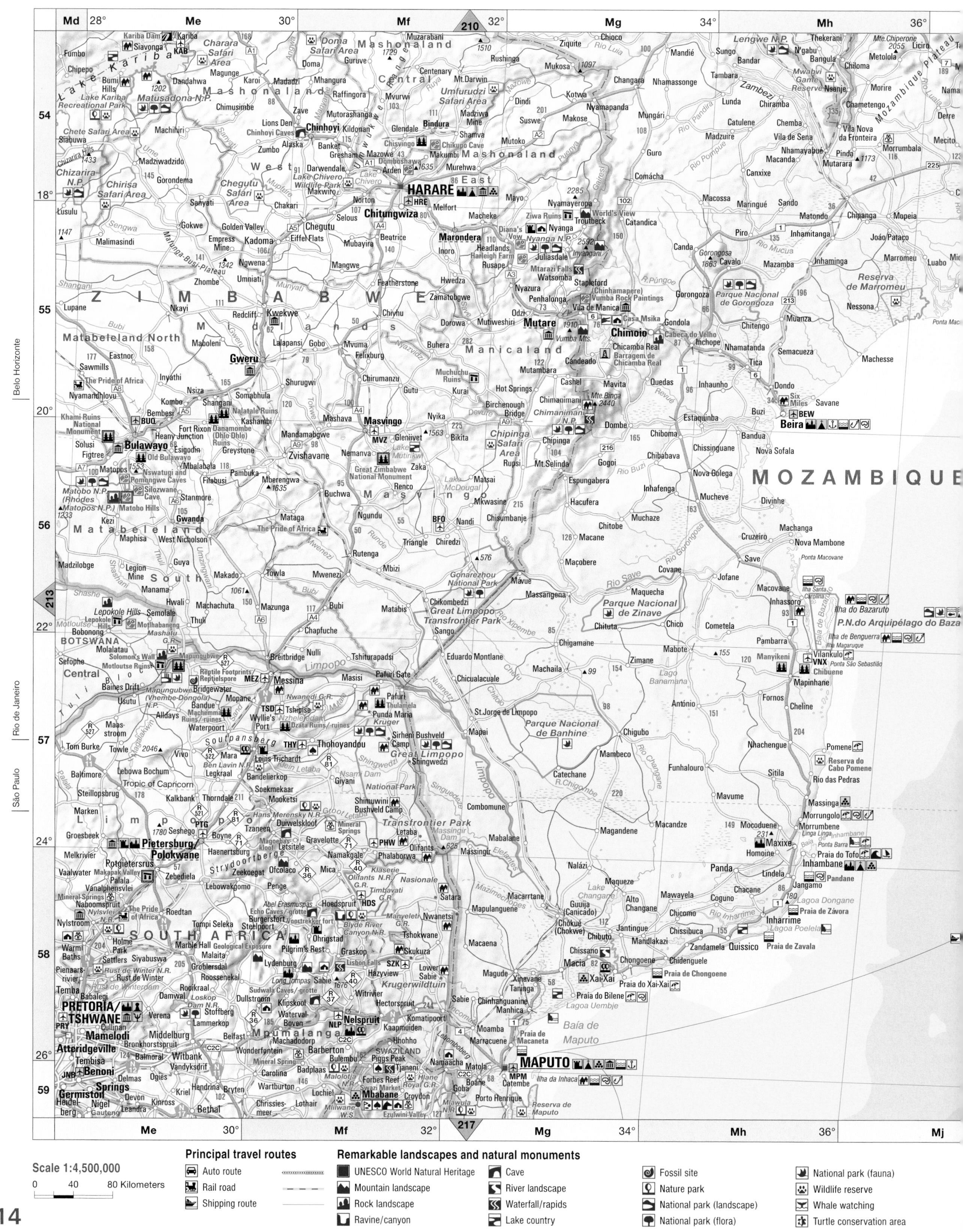

Principal travel routes

- Auto route
- Rail road
- Shipping route

Remarkable landscapes and natural monuments

- UNESCO World Natural Heritage
- Mountain landscape
- Rock landscape
- Ravine/canyon
- Cave
- River landscape
- Waterfall/rapids
- Lake country
- Fossil site
- Nature park
- National park (landscape)
- National park (flora)
- National park (fauna)
- Wildlife reserve
- Whale watching
- Turtle conservation area

Scale 1:4,500,000

0   40   80 Kilometers

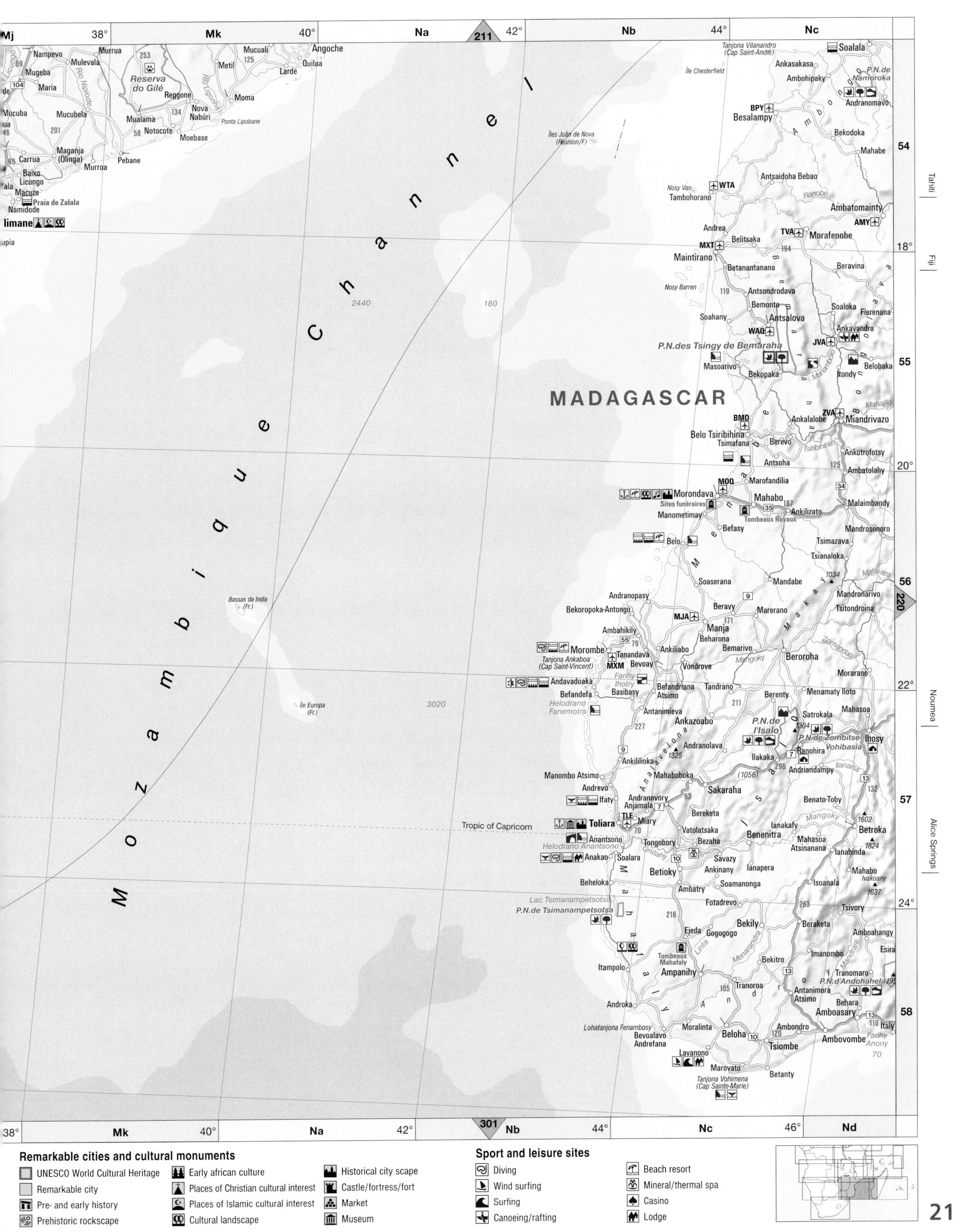

Murrua
Nampevo Mulevala Angoche
Mugeba Murraia Metil Mucuali
Maria Reserva 253 Mucuali
do Gilé Larde Quilua
104 Reggone Moma
Notocote 134 Nova Moebase
Mualama Nabúri Ponta Lipobane
58
Maganja 201
Carrua (Olinga) Pebane
Baixo
Licungo Murroa
Macuze Praia de Zalala
Namidode
limane

Tanjona Vilanandro
(Cap Saint-André) Soalala
Île Chesterfield Ankasakasa P.N. de
Ambohipaky Namoroka
BPY Andranomavo
Besalampy
Bekodoka
Mahabe
54

Antsaidoha Bebao
WTA Nosy Vao
Tambohorano Ranobe Ambatomainty
Andrea **TVA** Morafenobe **AMY**
MXT Belitsaka **18°**
Maintirano 194
Betanantanana Beravina
Nosy Barren 119 Antsondrodava
Bemonte Soaloka Fierenana
Soahany Antsalova Ankavandra
WAQ **JVA**
P.N. des Tsingy de Bemaraha Itondy Belobaka
Masoarivo **55**
Bekopaka

MADAGASCAR

BMD
Ankalalobe **ZVA** Mahajilo Miandrivazo
Belo Tsiribihina Berevo Ankotrofotsy
Tsimafana Antsoha Tsiribihina **20°**
125 Ambatolahy
MOQ Marofandilia 34
Morondava Mahabo
Sites funéraires Ankilizato Malaimbandy
Manometimay 35 187
Tombeaux Royaux
Befasy Tsimazava
Belo Mandrosonoro
Soaserana Mandabe Tsianaloka
Andranopasy 1034
Beravy Marerano Mandronarivo
Bekoropoka-Antongo 9 Tsitondroina
MJA Manja 171
55 79 Beharona
Ambahikily Ankiliabo Bemarivo Beroroha
Tanandava Vondrove Morarano
Morombe Bevoay **MXM**
Tanjona Ankaboa **22°**
(Cap Saint-Vincent) Befandriana Tandrano
Andavadoaka Atsimo Berenty Menamaty Iloto
Befandefa Basibasy P.N. de Satrokala Mahasoa
Helodrano Antanimieva l'Isalo 904
Fanemotra Ankazoabo Andranolava P.N. de Zombitse- Ihosy
227 Vohibasia
 Île Europa Ranohira **57**
(Fr.) 9 1325 Ilakaka 7 Andriandampy
3020 Ankililioka (1056) 298 13
Manombo Atsimo Mahaboboka Sakaraha 132
Andrevo Andranovory 63 Benato-Toby
Ifaty Anjamala 7 Bereketa
TLE Miary Ianakafy 1602
Toliara Vatolatsaka Benenitra Mahasoa
70 Tongobory Bezaha Atsinanana 1824
Anantsono Ianabinda
Helodrano Anantsono Ankinany Ianapera Isoanala
Anakao 10 Savazy Mahabo
Soalara Betioky Soamanonga Ivakoany
Beheloka Ambatry 1637
Fotadrevo Tsivory
Lac Tsimanampetsotsa 263 Beraketa
P.N. de Tsimanampetsotsa 216 Bekily Amboahangy
Ejeda Gogogogo Imanombo Esira
Bekitro P.N. d'Andohahela 195
Itampolo 13 Tranomaro
Tombeaux Antanimora
Mahafaly Tranoroa 105 Atsimo Behara
Ampanihy 13 Amboasary
Androka Ambondro
Lohatanjona Fenambosy Beloha Italy
Bevoalavo Moralinta 10 110
Andrefana Lavanono Tsiombe Ambovombe Farihy
Marovato Anony
Tanjona Vohimena 70
(Cap Sainte-Marie) Betanty

Remarkable cities and cultural monuments

- UNESCO World Cultural Heritage
- Remarkable city
- Pre- and early history
- Prehistoric rockscape
- Early african culture
- Places of Christian cultural interest
- Places of Islamic cultural interest
- Cultural landscape
- Historical city scape
- Castle/fortress/fort
- Market
- Museum

Sport and leisure sites

- Diving
- Wind surfing
- Surfing
- Canoeing/rafting
- Beach resort
- Mineral/thermal spa
- Casino
- Lodge

215

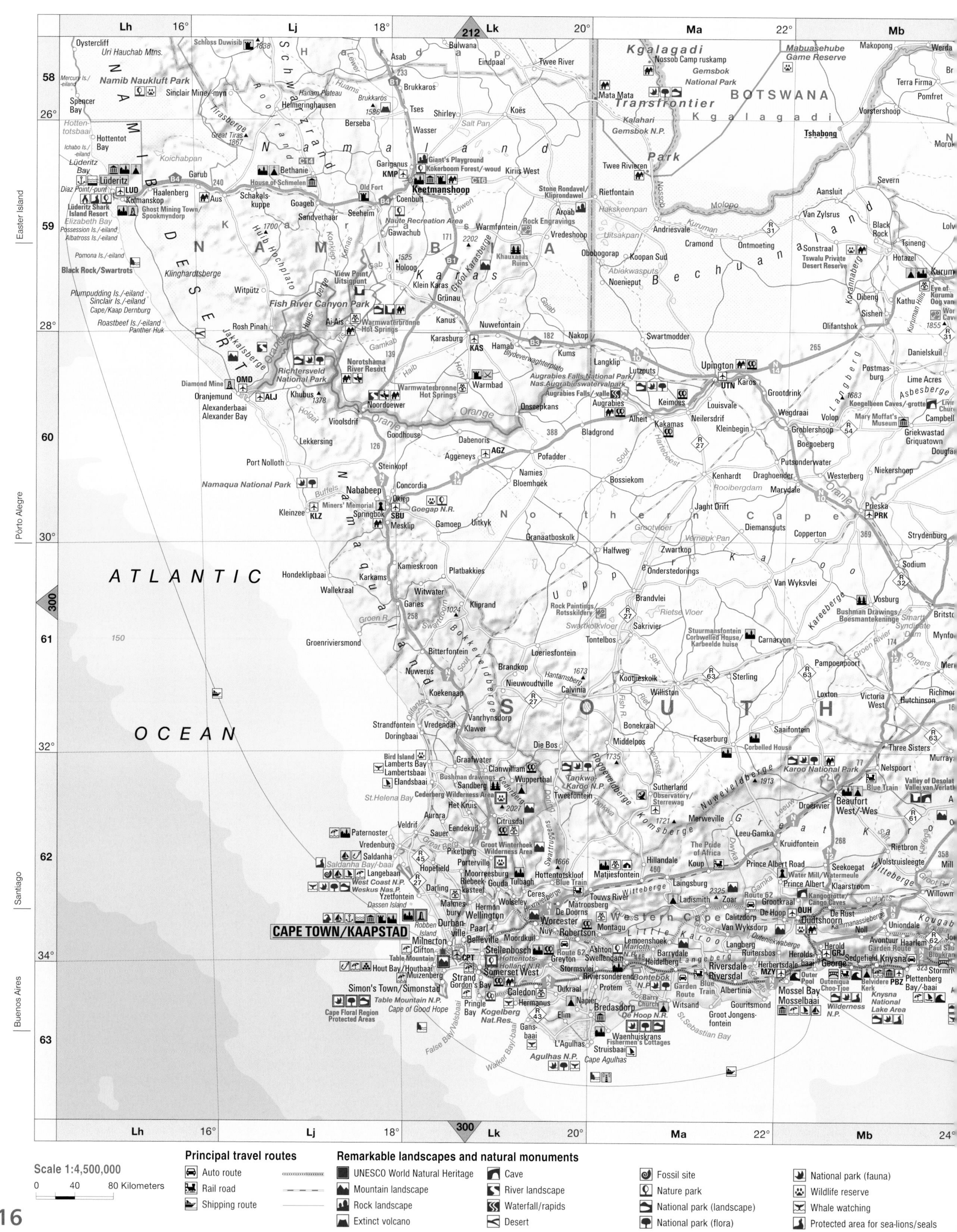

Scale 1:4,500,000

0   40   80 Kilometers

Principal travel routes

- Auto route
- Rail road
- Shipping route

Remarkable landscapes and natural monuments

- UNESCO World Natural Heritage
- Mountain landscape
- Rock landscape
- Extinct volcano
- Cave
- River landscape
- Waterfall/rapids
- Desert
- Fossil site
- Nature park
- National park (landscape)
- National park (flora)
- National park (fauna)
- Wildlife reserve
- Whale watching
- Protected area for sea-lions/seals

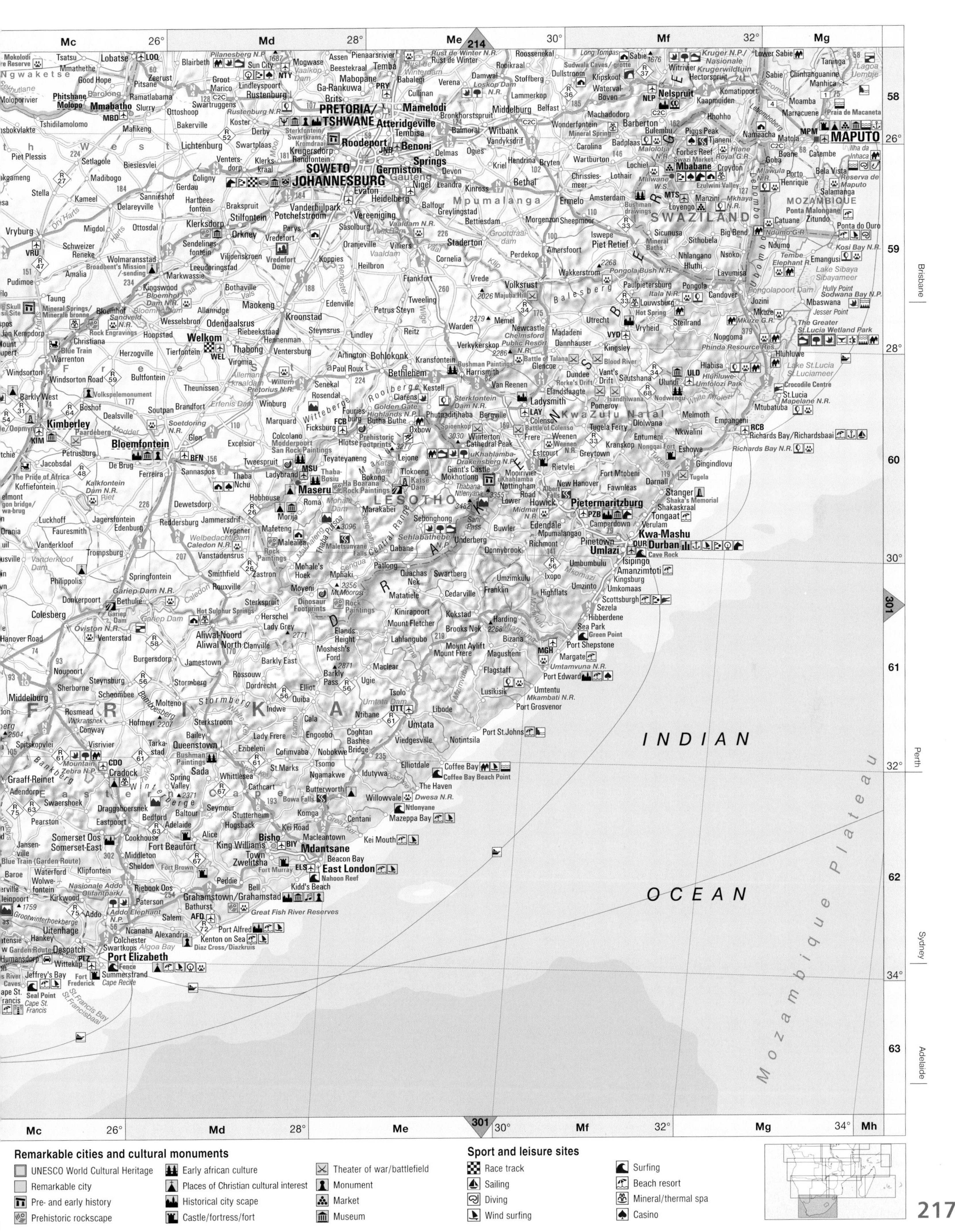

Remarkable cities and cultural monuments

- UNESCO World Cultural Heritage
- Remarkable city
- Pre- and early history
- Prehistoric rockscape
- Early african culture
- Places of Christian cultural interest
- Historical city scape
- Castle/fortress/fort
- Theater of war/battlefield
- Monument
- Market
- Museum

Sport and leisure sites

- Race track
- Sailing
- Diving
- Wind surfing
- Surfing
- Beach resort
- Mineral/thermal spa
- Casino

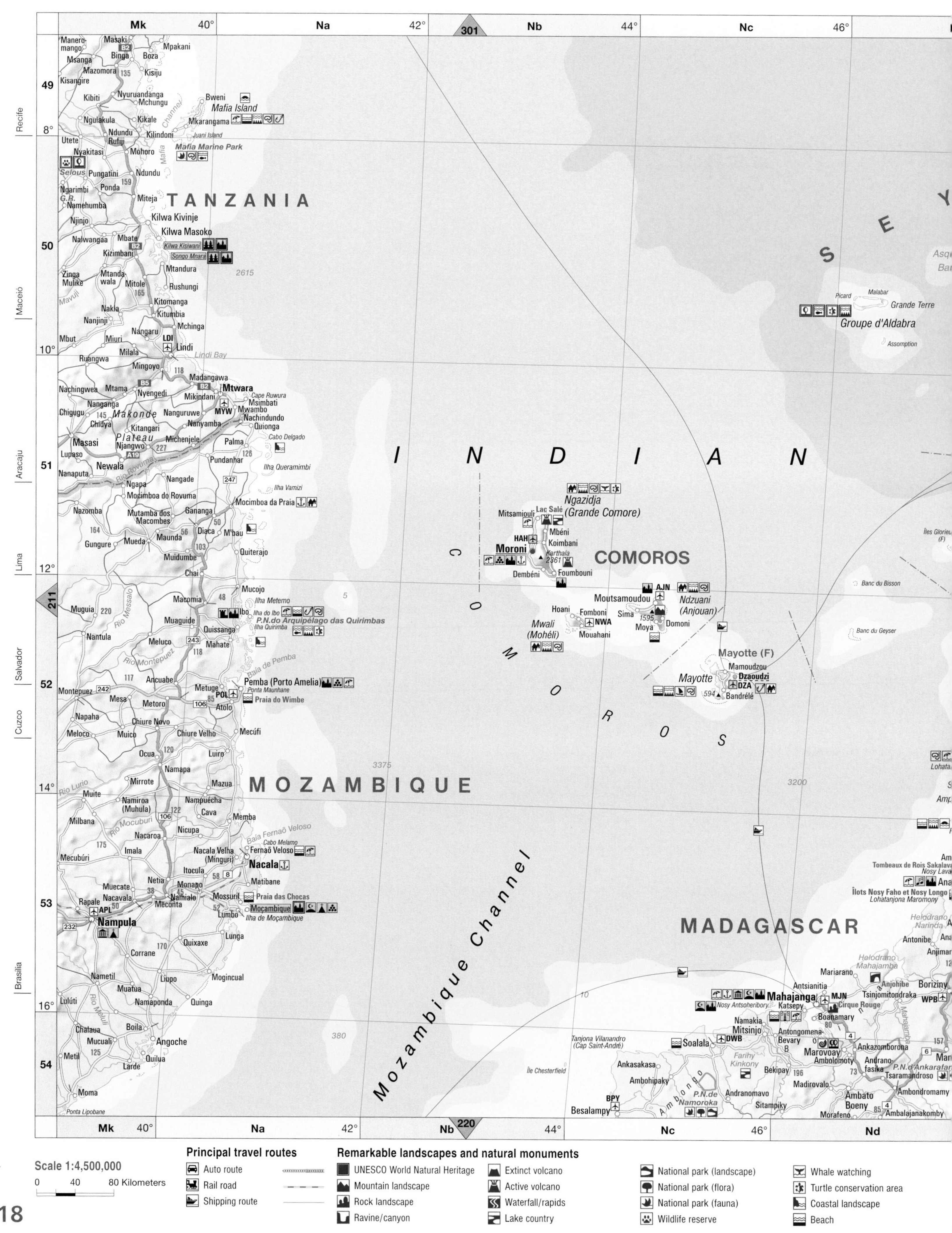

Comoros, Seychelles, Northern Madagascar

TANZANIA

INDIAN

MOZAMBIQUE

MADAGASCAR

Mozambique Channel

COMOROS

SEY...

Ngazidja (Grande Comore)

Moroni

Ndzuani (Anjouan)

Mwali (Mohéli)

Mayotte (F)

Groupe d'Aldabra

Scale 1:4,500,000

0   40   80 Kilometers

218

Principal travel routes

- 🚗 Auto route
- 🚂 Rail road
- ⚓ Shipping route

Remarkable landscapes and natural monuments

- ■ UNESCO World Natural Heritage
- ■ Mountain landscape
- ■ Rock landscape
- ■ Ravine/canyon
- ■ Extinct volcano
- ■ Active volcano
- ■ Waterfall/rapids
- ■ Lake country
- ■ National park (landscape)
- ■ National park (flora)
- ■ National park (fauna)
- ■ Wildlife reserve
- ■ Whale watching
- ■ Turtle conservation area
- ■ Coastal landscape
- ■ Beach

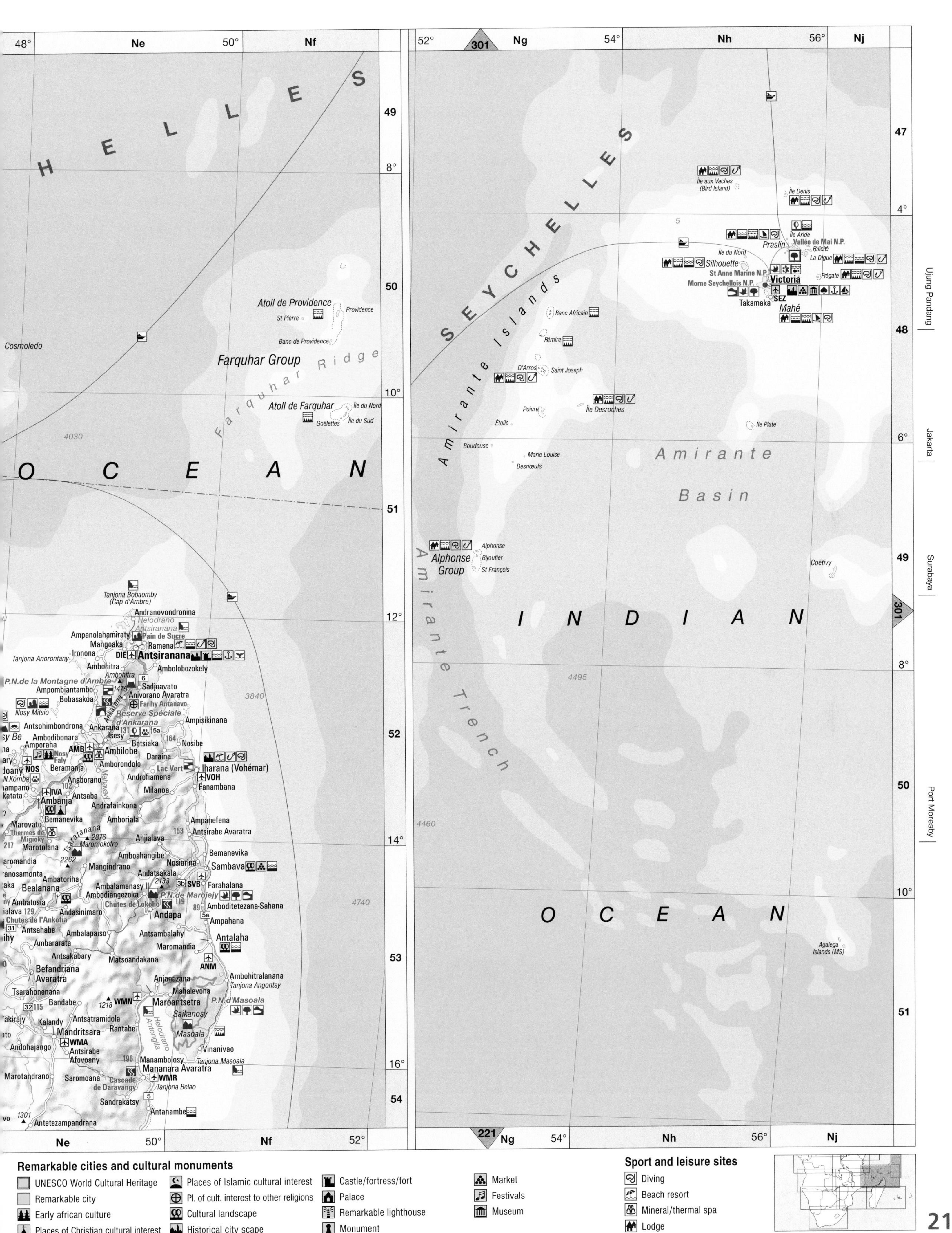

H E L L E S

S E Y C H E L L E S

49

8°

47

4°

Île aux Vaches (Bird Island)

Île Denis

Île Aride
Praslin   Vallée de Mai N.P.
Île du Nord   Félicité
La Digue
Silhouette
St Anne Marine N.P.   Frégate
Morne Seychellois N.P.
Victoria
SEZ
Takamaka   *Mahé*

50

Atoll de Providence

St Pierre   Providence

Banc de Providence

Cosmoledo

Farquhar Group

Farquhar Ridge

Banc Africain

Rémire

48

Amirante Islands

O C E A N

4030

Farquhar Group

Atoll de Farquhar   Île du Nord
Goëlettes   Île du Sud

10°

D'Arros   Saint Joseph

Poivre   Île Desroches

Étoile   Île Plate

6°

Farquhar Trench

Boudeuse

Marie Louise
Desnœufs

Amirante Basin

Amirante

Basin

51

Alphonse
Bijoutier
**Alphonse
Group**   St François

Coëtivy

49

301

Amirante Trench

Tanjona Bobaomby
(Cap d'Ambre)

I N D I A N

12°

8°

Andranovondronina
Helodrano
Antsiranana
Ampanolahamiraty   Pain de Sucre
Mangoaka   Ramena
Irontoka   **DIE**   **Antsiranana**
Tanjona Anorontany   Ambolobozokely
Ambohitra
Ambohitra
P.N.de la Montagne d'Ambre
Ampombiantambo   6
Bobasakoa   Sadjoavato
Aniviorano Avaratra
Nosy Mitsio   Farihy Antanavo
Reserve Spéciale
Antsohimbondrona   d'Ankarana
Ambodibonara   Isesy   Ampisikinana
Amporaha   Betsiaka   164   Nosibe
sy Be   **AMB**   Ambilobe
loany **NOS**   Amborondolo   Daraina   **Iharana (Vohémar)**
N.Komba   Anaborano   Androfiamena   **VOH**
ampano   Lac Vert   Fanambana
katata   **IVA**   Antsaba
Ambanja   Milanoa
Bemanevika   Amoriala   Ampanefabe
Antsirabe Avaratra
Marovato   Anjialava   153
Thermes de   2876   Bemanevika
Migiokv   Marotolana   Maromokotro
217   Amboahangibe
aromandia   2262   Mangindrano   Nosiarina   **Sambava**
anosamonta   Andatsakala
Ambatoriha   2133   3b   **SVB**   Farahalana
aka   **Bealanana**   Ambalamanasy II
Ambodiangezoka   P.N.de Marojejy   119
ialava 129   Chutes de Lokoho
my   Ambatosia   Andasinimaro   **Andapa**   Amboditetezana-Sahana
Chutes de l'Ankofia   5a
31   Antsahabe   Ampahana
ihy   Ambalapaiso   Antsambalahy
Ambararata   Maromandia   **Antalaha**
Antsakabary
Befandriana   Matsoandakana
Avaratra   Anjanazana   Ambohitralanana
Tanjona Angontsy
32 115   Bandabe   1218   **WMN**   Mahalevona
akirajy   Kalandy   Antsatramidola   **Maroantsetra**
Rantabe   Saikanosy
ato   Andohajango   **WMA**   *Masoala*
Antsirabe   196   Manambolosy   Tanjona Masoala
ihy   Afovoany   Vinanivao
Marotandrano   Saromoana   **Mananara Avaratra**
Cascade   **WMR**
de Daravangy   Tanjona Belao
Sandrakatsy
vo   1301   Antetezampandrana   Antanambe

4495

**Agalega
Islands (MS)**

4460

O C E A N

Amirante Basin

10°

52

53

14°

50

16°

51

3840

*Nosy
Faly*

N.Komba

Tsaratanana

Antongila

Helodrano
Antongila

54°

56°

Nj

Nh

Ng

48°

50°

52°

54°

56°

Ujung Pandang

Jakarta

Surabaya

301

Port Moresby

Remarkable cities and cultural monuments

- ▢ UNESCO World Cultural Heritage
- ▢ Remarkable city
- ▲▲ Early african culture
- ▲ Places of Christian cultural interest
- ☾ Places of Islamic cultural interest
- ⊕ Pl. of cult. interest to other religions
- ▥ Cultural landscape
- ▥ Historical city scape
- ▣ Castle/fortress/fort
- ▣ Palace
- ▣ Remarkable lighthouse
- ▣ Monument
- ▦ Market
- ♫ Festivals
- ▥ Museum

Sport and leisure sites

- ▣ Diving
- ▣ Beach resort
- ▣ Mineral/thermal spa
- ▣ Lodge

219

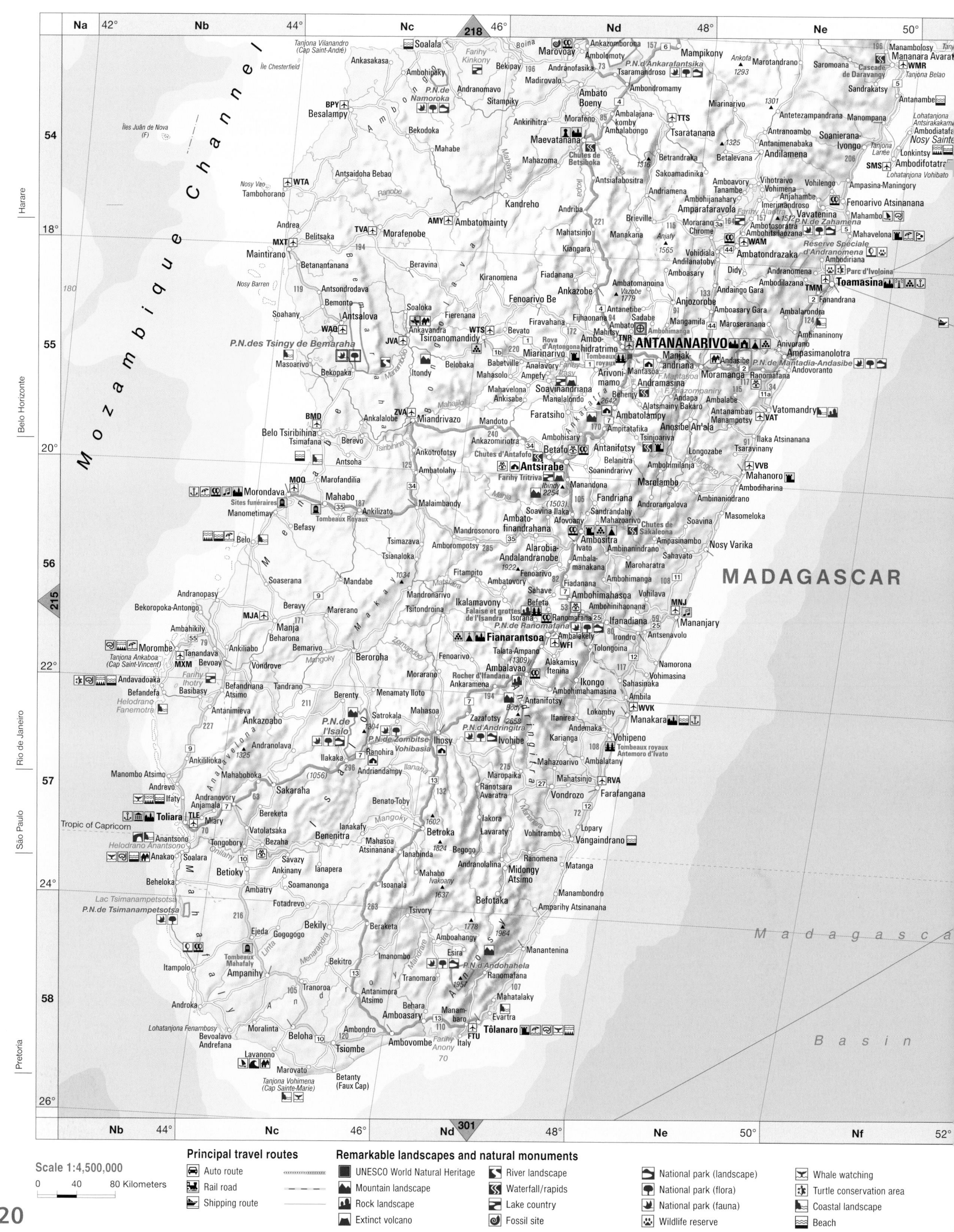

Scale 1:4,500,000

0   40   80 Kilometers

Principal travel routes
- Auto route
- Rail road
- Shipping route

Remarkable landscapes and natural monuments
- UNESCO World Natural Heritage
- Mountain landscape
- Rock landscape
- Extinct volcano
- River landscape
- Waterfall/rapids
- Lake country
- Fossil site
- National park (landscape)
- National park (flora)
- National park (fauna)
- Wildlife reserve
- Whale watching
- Turtle conservation area
- Coastal landscape
- Beach

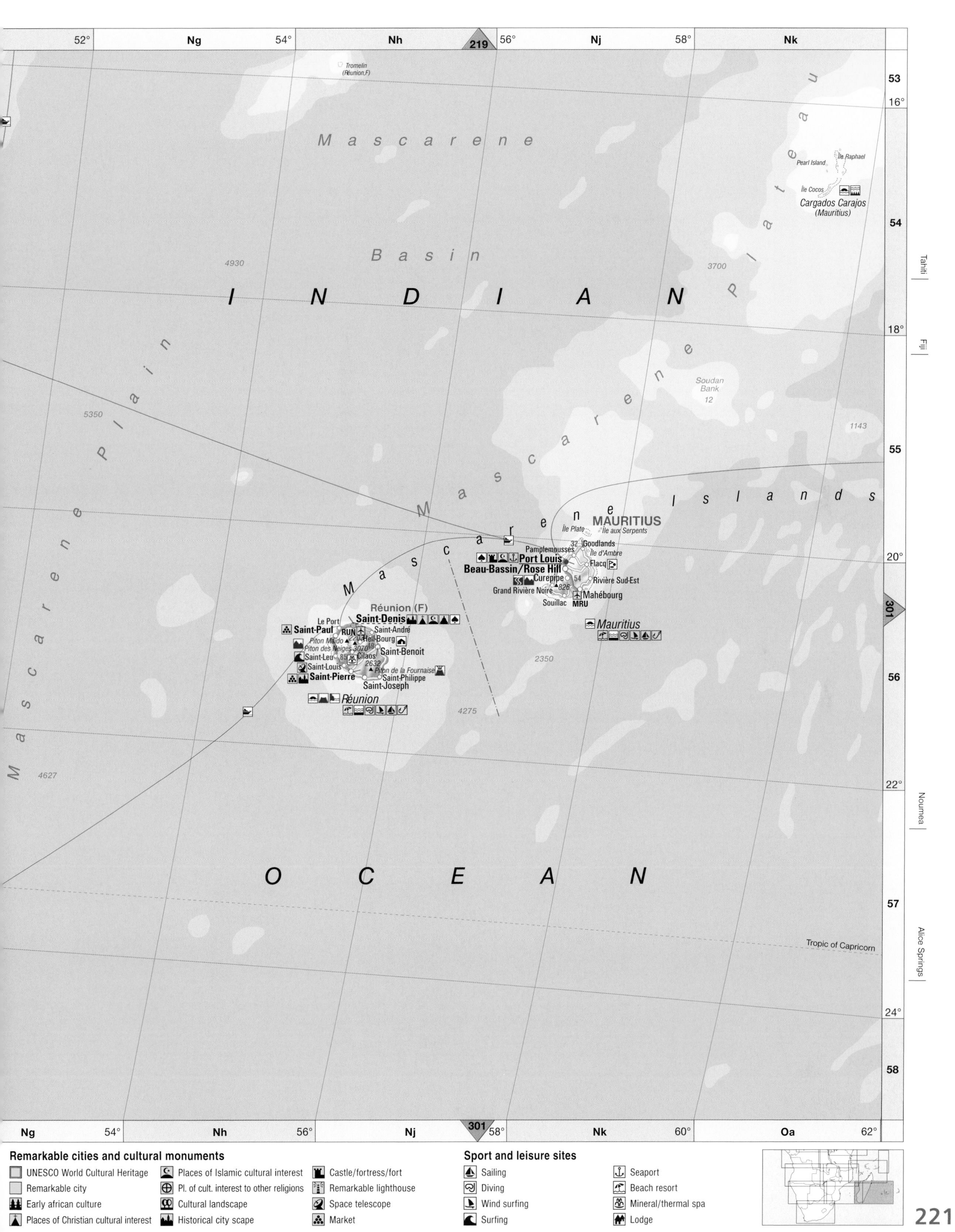

Tromelin
(Réunion, F)

Pearl Island
Île Raphael
Île Cocos
Cargados Carajos
(Mauritius)

Mascarene

Basin

I N D I A N

4930

3700

Mascarene Plateau

Soudan
Bank
12

5350

1143

Mascarene Plain

Mascarene

Islands

Île Plate
MAURITIUS
Île aux Serpents

Pamplemousses
32 Goodlands
Île d'Ambre
Port Louis
Flacq
Beau-Bassin/Rose Hill
Curepipe 54
Rivière Sud-Est
826
Grand Rivière Noire
Mahébourg
Souillac MRU

Mauritius

Réunion (F)
Le Port Saint-Denis
Saint-Paul RUN Saint-André
Piton Maïdo Hell-Bourg
Piton des Neiges 3070 Saint-Benoit
Saint-Leu Cilaos
2632
Saint-Louis
Piton de la Fournaise
Saint-Pierre Saint-Philippe
Saint-Joseph

Réunion

2350

4275

4627

O C E A N

Tropic of Capricorn

Tahiti
Fiji
Noumea
Alice Springs

Remarkable cities and cultural monuments

- UNESCO World Cultural Heritage
- Remarkable city
- Early african culture
- Places of Christian cultural interest
- Places of Islamic cultural interest
- Pl. of cult. interest to other religions
- Cultural landscape
- Historical city scape
- Castle/fortress/fort
- Remarkable lighthouse
- Space telescope
- Market

Sport and leisure sites

- Sailing
- Diving
- Wind surfing
- Surfing
- Seaport
- Beach resort
- Mineral/thermal spa
- Lodge

221

North and Central America – physical map

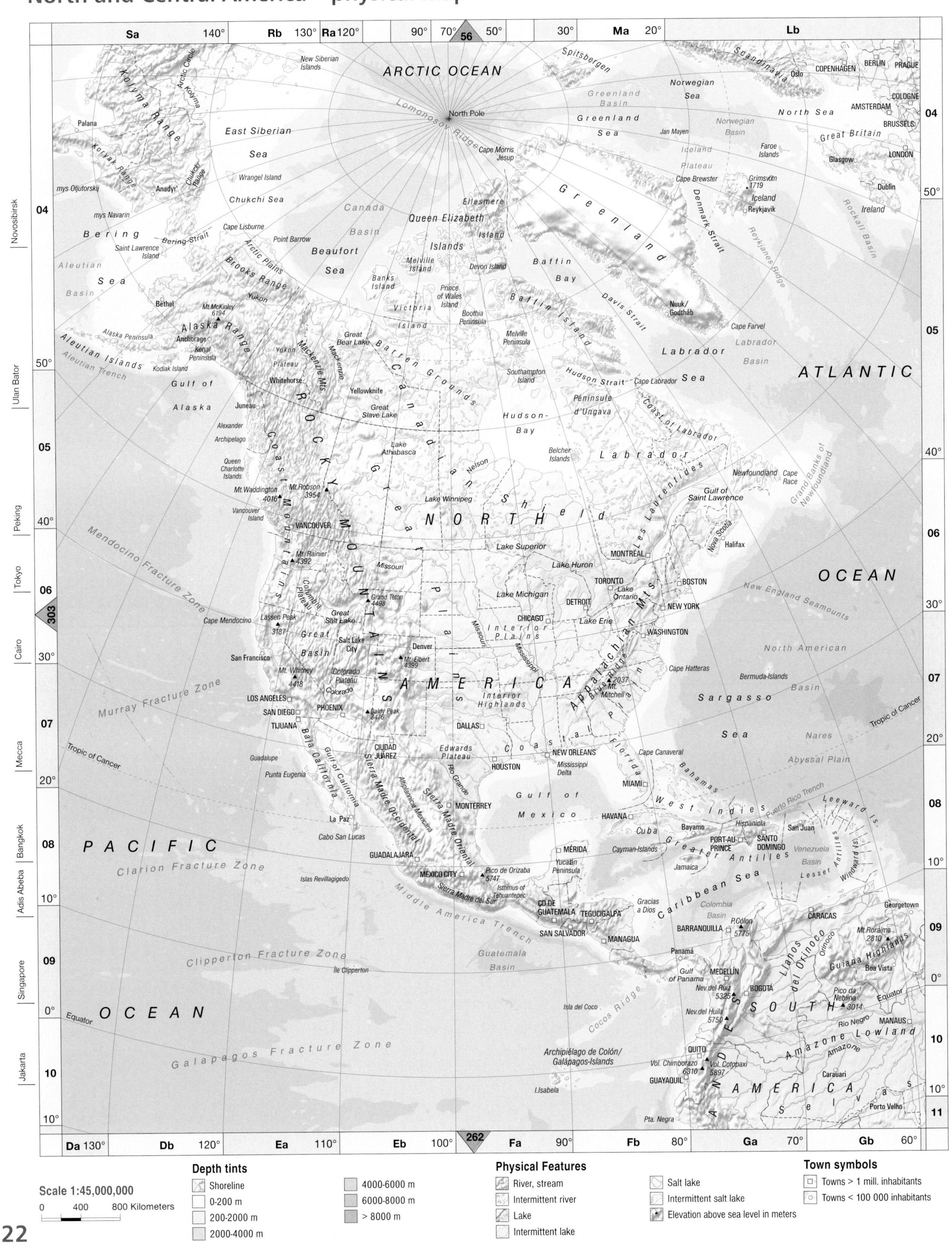

Depth tints

- Shoreline
- 0–200 m
- 200–2000 m
- 2000–4000 m
- 4000–6000 m
- 6000–8000 m
- > 8000 m

Physical Features

- River, stream
- Intermittent river
- Lake
- Intermittent lake
- Salt lake
- Intermittent salt lake
- Elevation above sea level in meters

Town symbols

- Towns > 1 mill. inhabitants
- Towns < 100 000 inhabitants

Scale 1:45,000,000

0   400   800 Kilometers

North and Central America – political map

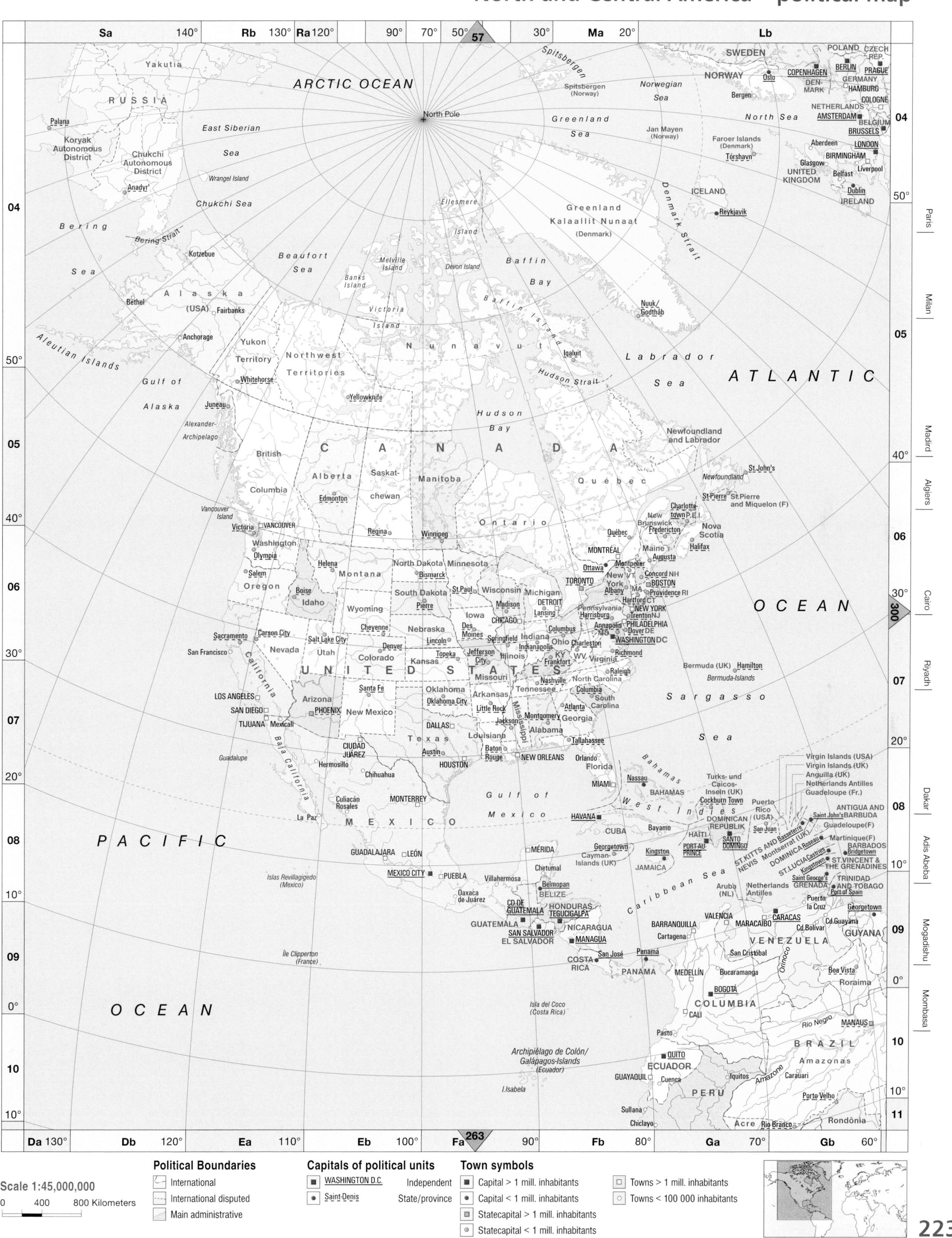

Scale 1:45,000,000

0   400   800 Kilometers

Political Boundaries
- ⌐ International
- ┈ International disputed
- ▨ Main administrative

Capitals of political units
- ■ WASHINGTON D.C.   Independent
- ● Saint-Denis   State/province

Town symbols
- ■ Capital > 1 mill. inhabitants
- ● Capital < 1 mill. inhabitants
- ▣ Statecapital > 1 mill. inhabitants
- ◉ Statecapital < 1 mill. inhabitants
- □ Towns > 1 mill. inhabitants
- ○ Towns < 100 000 inhabitants

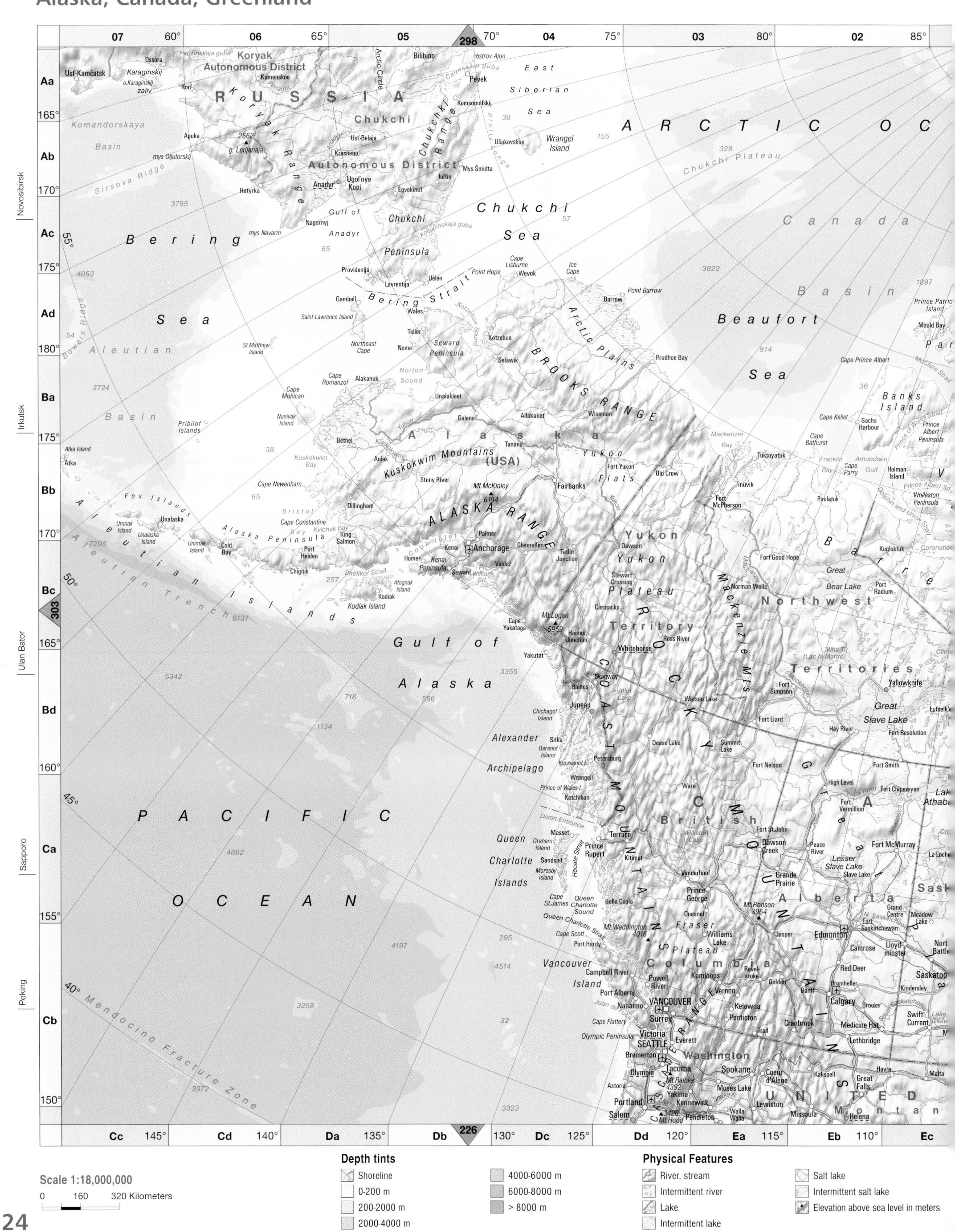

Scale 1:18,000,000

0   160   320 Kilometers

Depth tints

- ⊠ Shoreline
- ☐ 0-200 m
- ☐ 200-2000 m
- ☐ 2000-4000 m
- ☐ 4000-6000 m
- ☐ 6000-8000 m
- ☐ > 8000 m

Physical Features

- River, stream
- Intermittent river
- Lake
- Intermittent lake
- Salt lake
- Intermittent salt lake
- ▲ Elevation above sea level in meters

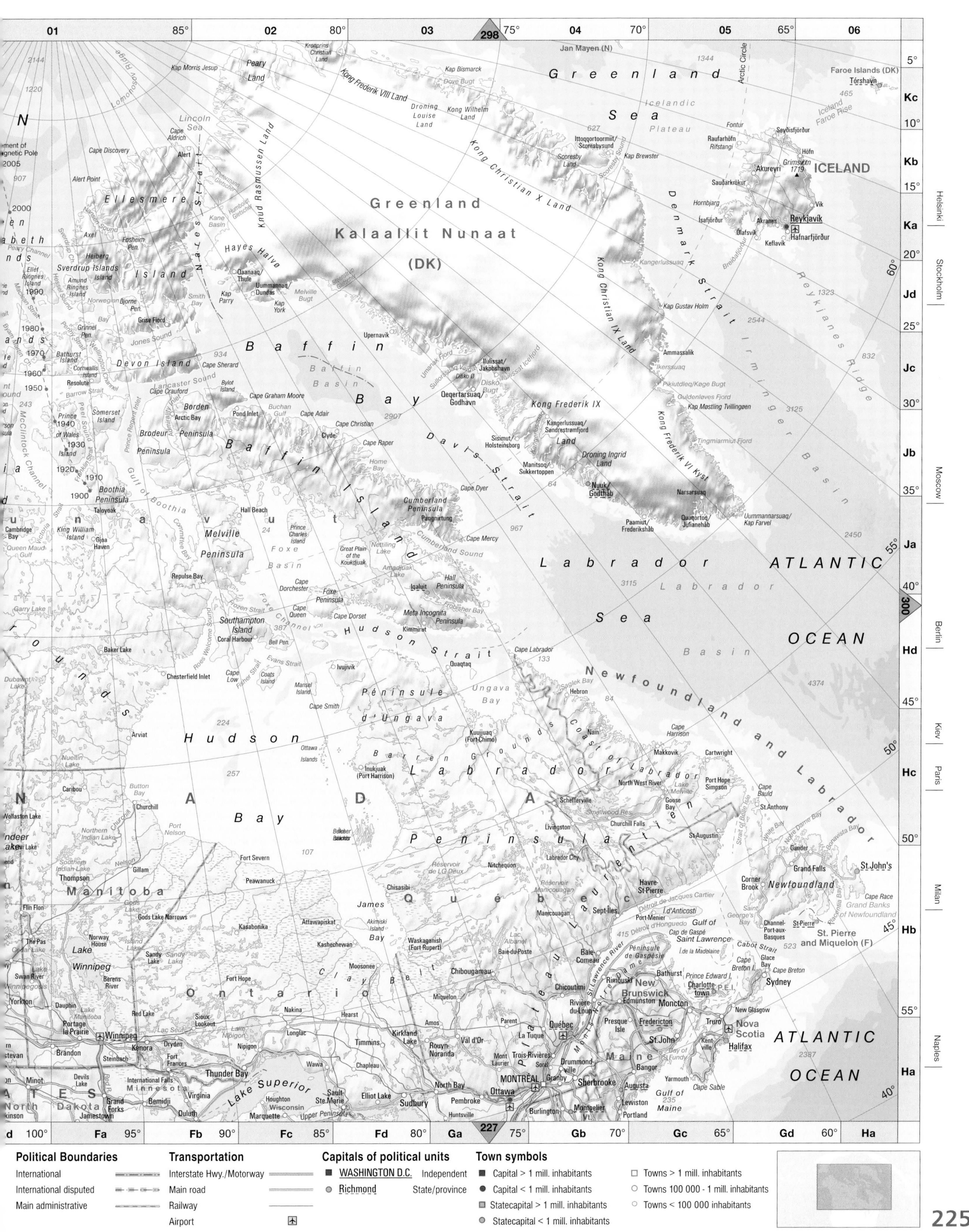

Greenland

Kalaallit Nunaat

(DK)

Greenland Sea

Icelandic Plateau

ICELAND

Denmark Strait

Baffin Bay

Baffin Basin

Davis Strait

Baffin Island

Cumberland Peninsula

ATLANTIC

Labrador Sea

Labrador Basin

OCEAN

Hudson Strait

Péninsule d'Ungava

Ungava Bay

Newfoundland and Labrador

Hudson Bay

Labrador

Coast of Labrador

C A N A D A

Labrador Peninsula

Manitoba

Québec

Ontario

Newfoundland

St. John's

Gulf of Saint Lawrence

St. Pierre and Miquelon (F)

Winnipeg

New Brunswick

Charlottetown P.E.I.

Sydney

Nova Scotia

Halifax

MONTRÉAL

Ottawa

Maine

ATLANTIC OCEAN

Gulf of Maine

Minnesota

Wisconsin

North Dakota

Political Boundaries

International

International disputed

Main administrative

Transportation

Interstate Hwy./Motorway

Main road

Railway

Airport ✈

Capitals of political units

■ WASHINGTON D.C. Independent

● Richmond State/province

Town symbols

■ Capital > 1 mill. inhabitants

● Capital < 1 mill. inhabitants

■ Statecapital > 1 mill. inhabitants

● Statecapital < 1 mill. inhabitants

□ Towns > 1 mill. inhabitants

○ Towns 100 000 - 1 mill. inhabitants

○ Towns < 100 000 inhabitants

225

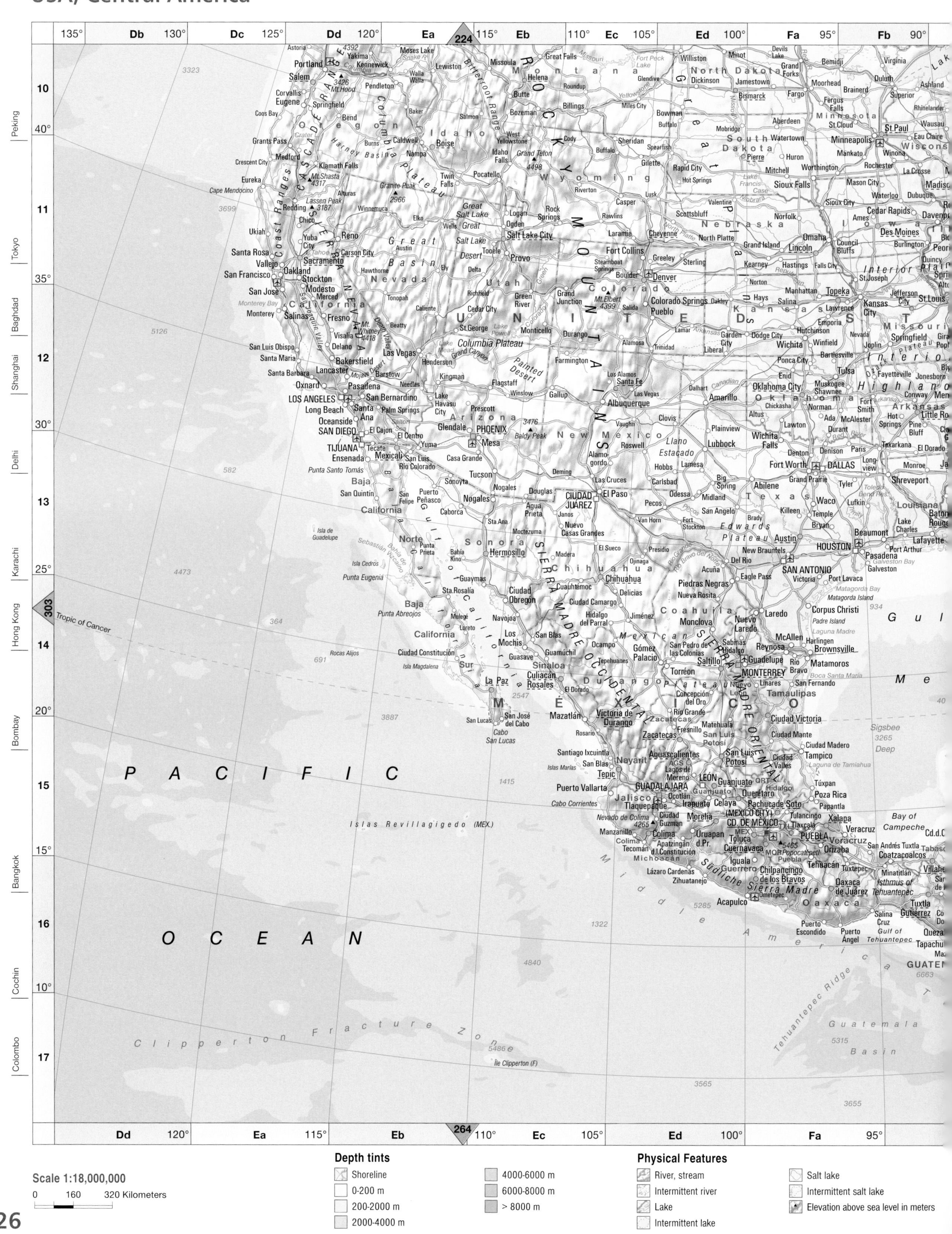

Scale 1:18,000,000

0   160   320 Kilometers

Depth tints

- Shoreline
- 0-200 m
- 200-2000 m
- 2000-4000 m
- 4000-6000 m
- 6000-8000 m
- > 8000 m

Physical Features

- River, stream
- Intermittent river
- Lake
- Intermittent lake
- Salt lake
- Intermittent salt lake
- Elevation above sea level in meters

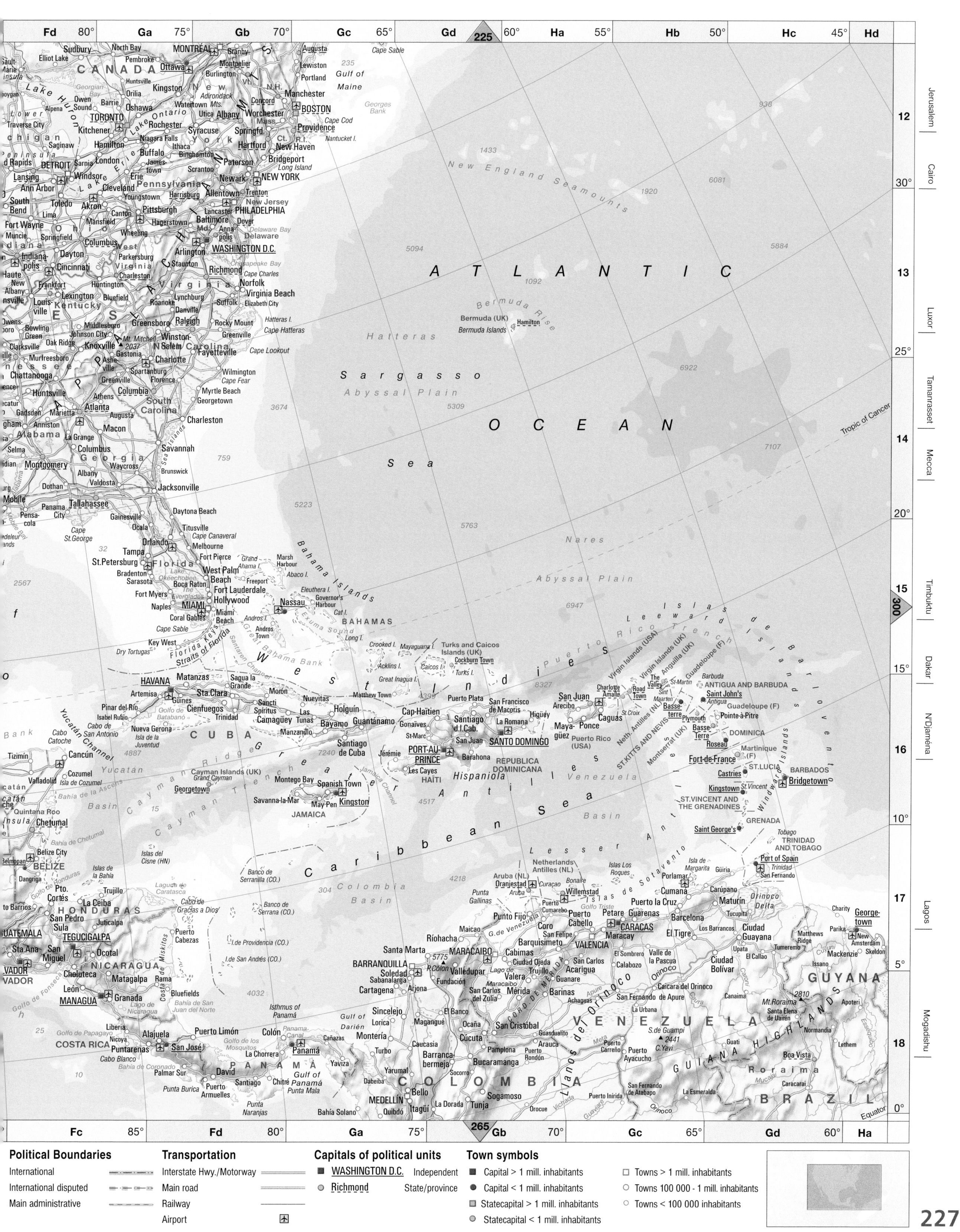

Fd 80° Ga 75° Gb 70° Gc 65° Gd 225 60° Ha 55° Hb 50° Hc 45° Hd
Fc 85° Fd 80° Ga 75° 265 Gb 70° Gc 65° Gd 60° Ha
12 13 14 15 16 17 18
30° 25° 20° 15° 10° 5° 0°
Jerusalem
Cairo
Luxor
Tamanrasset
Mecca
Timbuktu
Dakar
N'Djaména
Lagos
Mogadishu
300
ATLANTIC OCEAN
Sargasso Sea
Sargasso Abyssal Plain
Hatteras Abyssal Plain
Nares Abyssal Plain
New England Seamounts
Bermuda Rise
Bermuda (UK)
Bermuda Islands
Hamilton
Tropic of Cancer
Gulf of Maine
Georges Bank
Cape Sable
Cape Cod
Nantucket I.
CANADA
Sudbury
North Bay
MONTRÉAL
Ottawa
Toronto
Lake Huron
Lake Ontario
Lake Erie
Buffalo
Rochester
Syracuse
Albany
BOSTON
Providence
Hartford
New Haven
Bridgeport
Long Island
NEW YORK
Newark
Trenton
PHILADELPHIA
Baltimore
Dover
Annapolis
WASHINGTON D.C.
Delaware Bay
Chesapeake Bay
Richmond
Norfolk
Virginia Beach
Cape Hatteras
Cape Lookout
Cape Fear
Raleigh
Greensboro
Charlotte
Columbia
Charleston
Savannah
Atlanta
Montgomery
Jacksonville
Tallahassee
Orlando
Tampa
St.Petersburg
Cape Canaveral
West Palm Beach
Fort Lauderdale
Hollywood
MIAMI
Key West
Straits of Florida
Florida Keys
DETROIT
Cleveland
Pittsburgh
Columbus
Cincinnati
Indianapolis
Frankfort
Lexington
Nashville
Knoxville
Chattanooga
Huntsville
Birmingham
Alabama
Georgia
Florida
Kentucky
Tennessee
Virginia
West Virginia
North Carolina
South Carolina
Pennsylvania
New York
New Jersey
APPALACHIAN MTS.
Mt. Mitchell 2037
Bahama Islands
BAHAMAS
Nassau
Freeport
Andros I.
Exuma Sound
Great Bahama Bank
Turks and Caicos Islands (UK)
Cockburn Town
West Indies
Greater Antilles
Lesser Antilles
CUBA
HAVANA
Matanzas
Santa Clara
Cienfuegos
Camagüey
Holguín
Santiago de Cuba
Guantánamo
Cayman Islands (UK)
Georgetown
Cayman Trench
JAMAICA
Kingston
Montego Bay
Spanish Town
Hispaniola
HAÏTI
PORT-AU-PRINCE
Cap-Haïtien
REPUBLICA DOMINICANA
SANTO DOMINGO
Santiago d.l.Cab.
Puerto Rico (USA)
San Juan
Ponce
Mayagüez
Puerto Rico Trench
Virgin Islands (USA)
Virgin Islands (UK)
Anguilla (UK)
Guadeloupe (F)
ANTIGUA AND BARBUDA
Saint John's
ST.KITTS AND NEVIS
Basseterre
Montserrat (UK)
DOMINICA
Roseau
Martinique (F)
Fort-de-France
ST.LUCIA
Castries
BARBADOS
Bridgetown
ST.VINCENT AND THE GRENADINES
Kingstown
GRENADA
Saint George's
TRINIDAD AND TOBAGO
Port of Spain
Leeward Islands
Windward Islands
Islas de Barlovento
Caribbean Sea
Colombia Basin
Venezuela Basin
Yucatán Basin
Yucatán Channel
Cancún
Cozumel
BELIZE
Belize City
Belmopan
Golfo de Honduras
HONDURAS
TEGUCIGALPA
San Pedro Sula
GUATEMALA
EL SALVADOR
NICARAGUA
MANAGUA
COSTA RICA
San José
Puerto Limón
PANAMA
Panamá
Colón
Isthmus of Panamá
Gulf of Panamá
Aruba (NL)
Oranjestad
Curaçao
Netherlands Antilles (NL)
Willemstad
Bonaire
COLOMBIA
BARRANQUILLA
Cartagena
Santa Marta
MEDELLÍN
Bucaramanga
Cúcuta
VENEZUELA
CARACAS
Maracaibo
Lago de Maracaibo
Valencia
Barquisimeto
Maracay
Barcelona
Cumaná
Ciudad Guayana
Ciudad Bolívar
Orinoco
Orinoco Delta
Llanos del Orinoco
GUIANA HIGHLANDS
Mt.Roraima 2810
GUYANA
Georgetown
BRAZIL
Equator
Political Boundaries
International
International disputed
Main administrative
Transportation
Interstate Hwy./Motorway
Main road
Railway
Airport
Capitals of political units
WASHINGTON D.C. Independent
Richmond State/province
Town symbols
Capital > 1 mill. inhabitants
Capital < 1 mill. inhabitants
Statecapital > 1 mill. inhabitants
Statecapital < 1 mill. inhabitants
Towns > 1 mill. inhabitants
Towns 100 000 - 1 mill. inhabitants
Towns < 100 000 inhabitants

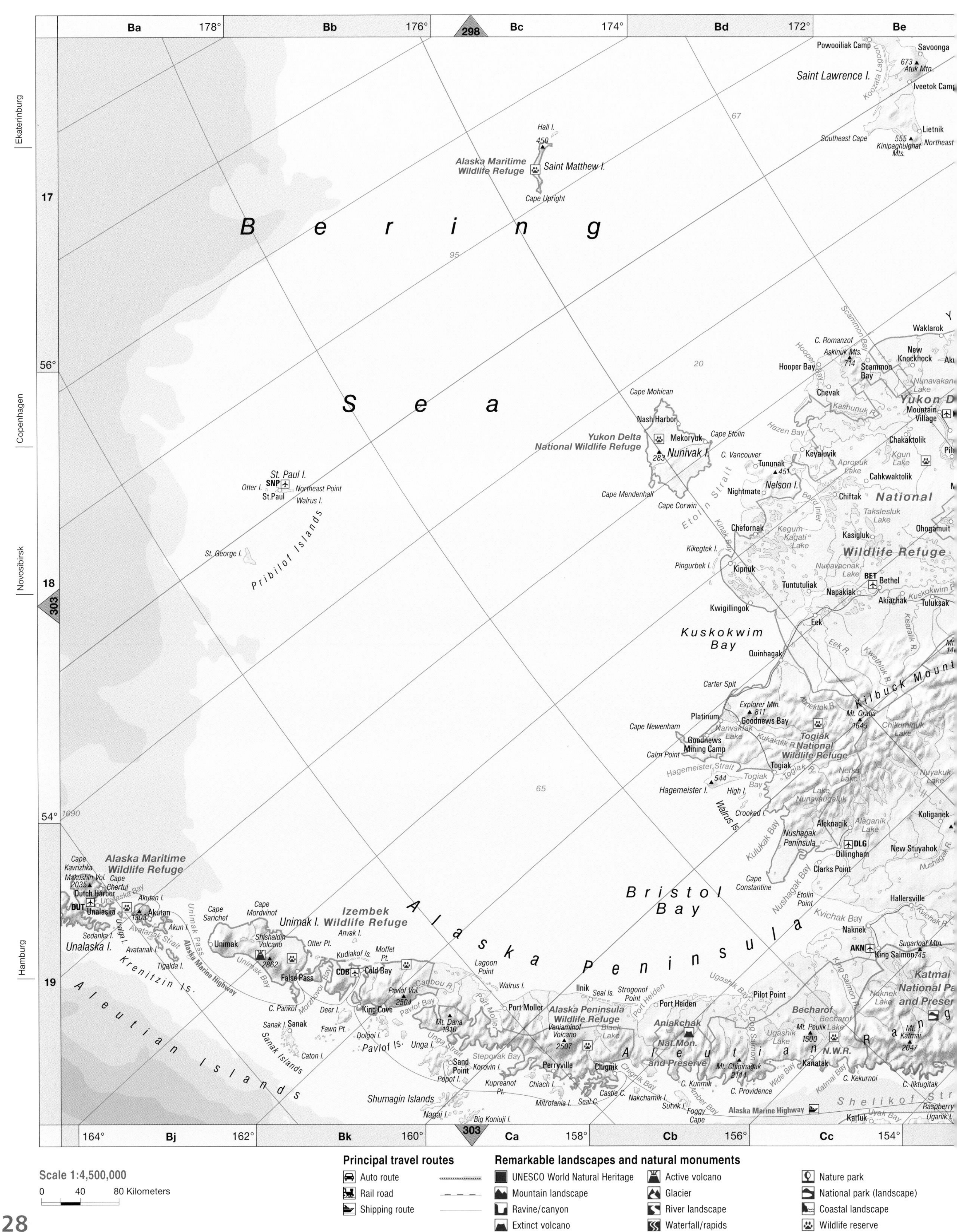

| Ba | 178° | Bb | 176° | **298** | Bc | 174° | Bd | 172° | Be |

Ekaterinburg

Copenhagen

Novosibirsk

303

Hamburg

17

56°

18

54°

19

Powooiliak Camp
Savoonga
673 ▲ Atuk Mtn.
Saint Lawrence I.
Iveetok Camp
Koozata Lagoon
67
Southeast Cape
555 ▲ Lietnik
Kinipaghulghat
Mts.
Northeast

Hall I.
450 ▲
Alaska Maritime
Wildlife Refuge
Saint Matthew I.
Cape Upright

B e r i n g
95

S e a
20

Cape Mohican
Nash Harbor
Yukon Delta
National Wildlife Refuge
Mekoryuk
283 ▲ *Nunivak I.*
Cape Etolin
C. Vancouver
Cape Mendenhall
Cape Corwin

C. Romanzof
Askinuk Mts.
714 ▲ Scammon
Bay
Hooper Bay
Chevak
Nunavakan
Lake
Keyalivik
Tununak
Nightmate
451 ▲
Chefornak
Nelson I.

Waklarok
New
Knockhock
Aku
Yukon D
Mountain
Village
Chakaktolik
Pile
Kgun
Lake
Cahkwaktolik
Chiftak
National
Takslesluk
Lake
Ohogamuit
Kasigluk
Wildlife Refuge
BET ◉ Bethel
Napakiak
Kuskokwim
Akiachak
Tuluksak

St. Paul I.
Otter I. SNP ◉ Northeast Point
St.Paul Walrus I.
St. George I.
Pribilof Islands

Etolin Strait
Knik Bay
Kwethluk
Nunavacnak
Lake
Kipnuk
Tuntutuliak
Kwigillingok
Eek
*Kuskokwim
Bay*
Quinhagak

Kikegtek I.
Pingurbek I.
Eek R.
Kisaralik R.

1090

65

Cape
Kavrizhka
Makushin Vol. Cape
2035 ▲ Chertul
Dutch Harbor
DUT ◈ Akutan I.
Unalaska 1303 ▲ Akutan
Sedanka I.
Unalga I.
Unalaska I. Avatanak I.
Tigalda I.

Carter Spit
Platinum Explorer Mtn.
811 ▲ Goodnews Bay
Cape Newenham
Goodnews
Manokotak
Mining Camp
Lake
Calm Point
Hagemeister Strait
544 ▲ Togiak
Hagemeister I.
High I.
Crooked I.
Walrus Is.
Kilbuck Mount
Mt. Oratia
1645 ▲
Chikuminuk
Lake
*Togiak National
Wildlife Refuge*
Togiak
Togiak Bay
Togiak R.
Nelka
Lake
Nuyakuk
Lake

Aleutian
Islands

Cape
Sarichef
Cape
Mordvinof
Unimak
Shishaldin
Volcano
2862 ▲
Unimak I. Wildlife Refuge
Anvak I.
Otter Pt.
Kudiakof Is.
Moffet
Pt.
False Pass
CDB ◈ Cold Bay
Izembek
Alaska Marine Highway

A l a s k a   P e n i n s u l a

Kulukak Bay
Nushagak
Peninsula
Aleknagik
Nushagak
Lake
Nunavaugaluk
Cape
Constantine
Nushagak R.
Nushagak Bay
Clarks Point
DLG ◉ Dillingham
New Stuyahok
Koliganek
Alaganik
Lake

*Bristol
Bay*

Krenitzin Is.
Avatanak Strait
Unimak Pass
Unimak
Bay
C. Pankof
Morzhovoi Bay
Deer I.
King Cove
Pavlof Vol.
2504 ▲
Caribou R.
Pavlof Bay
Unga Strait
Mt. Dana
1310 ▲
Pavlof Is.
Sanak I. Sanak
Fawn Pt.
Dolgoi I.
Unga I.
Sanak Islands
Caton I.
Popof I.
Sand
Point
Korovin I.
Kupreanof
Pt.
Chiach I.
Shumagin Islands
Nagai I. Big Koniuji I.

Lagoon
Point
Walrus I.
Ilnik
Port
Moller
Port Moller
*Alaska Peninsula
Wildlife Refuge*
Veniaminof
Volcano
2507 ▲
Perryville
Stepovak Bay
Mitrofania I. Seal C.
Seal Is.
Strogonof
Point
Port Heiden
Black
Lake
Aniakchak
Nat.Mon.
and Preserve
Mt. Chiginagak
2144 ▲
Chignik
C. Kunmik
C. Providence
Nakchamik I.
Sutvik I. Foggy
Cape

Pilot Point
Ugashik Bay
Ugashik
Lake
Becharof
Lake
Mt. Peulik
1500 ▲
Becharof
N.W.R.
Wide Bay
Kvichak Bay
King Salmon 745 ▲
AKN ◈
Naknek
Naknek
Lake
Sugarloaf Mtn.
Hallersville
Kvichak R.
*Katmai
National Pa
and Preser*
Mt.
Katmai
2047 ▲
Aleutian
Ugashik
Kejulik R.
C. Kekurnoi
Alaska Marine Highway
Shelikof Str
Karluk
Uyak Bay
C. Ilktugitak
Raspberry
Uganik I.

Mi
14

Kwe...
Etolin
Point

| 164° | Bj | 162° | Bk | 160° | **303** | Ca | 158° | Cb | 156° | Cc | 154° |

Scale 1:4,500,000

0   40   80 Kilometers

Principal travel routes

🚌 Auto route

🚂 Rail road

🚢 Shipping route

Remarkable landscapes and natural monuments

■ UNESCO World Natural Heritage

▲ Mountain landscape

◣ Ravine/canyon

▲ Extinct volcano

🌋 Active volcano

◭ Glacier

≋ River landscape

〰 Waterfall/rapids

◉ Nature park

⊞ National park (landscape)

⊞ Coastal landscape

⊞ Wildlife reserve

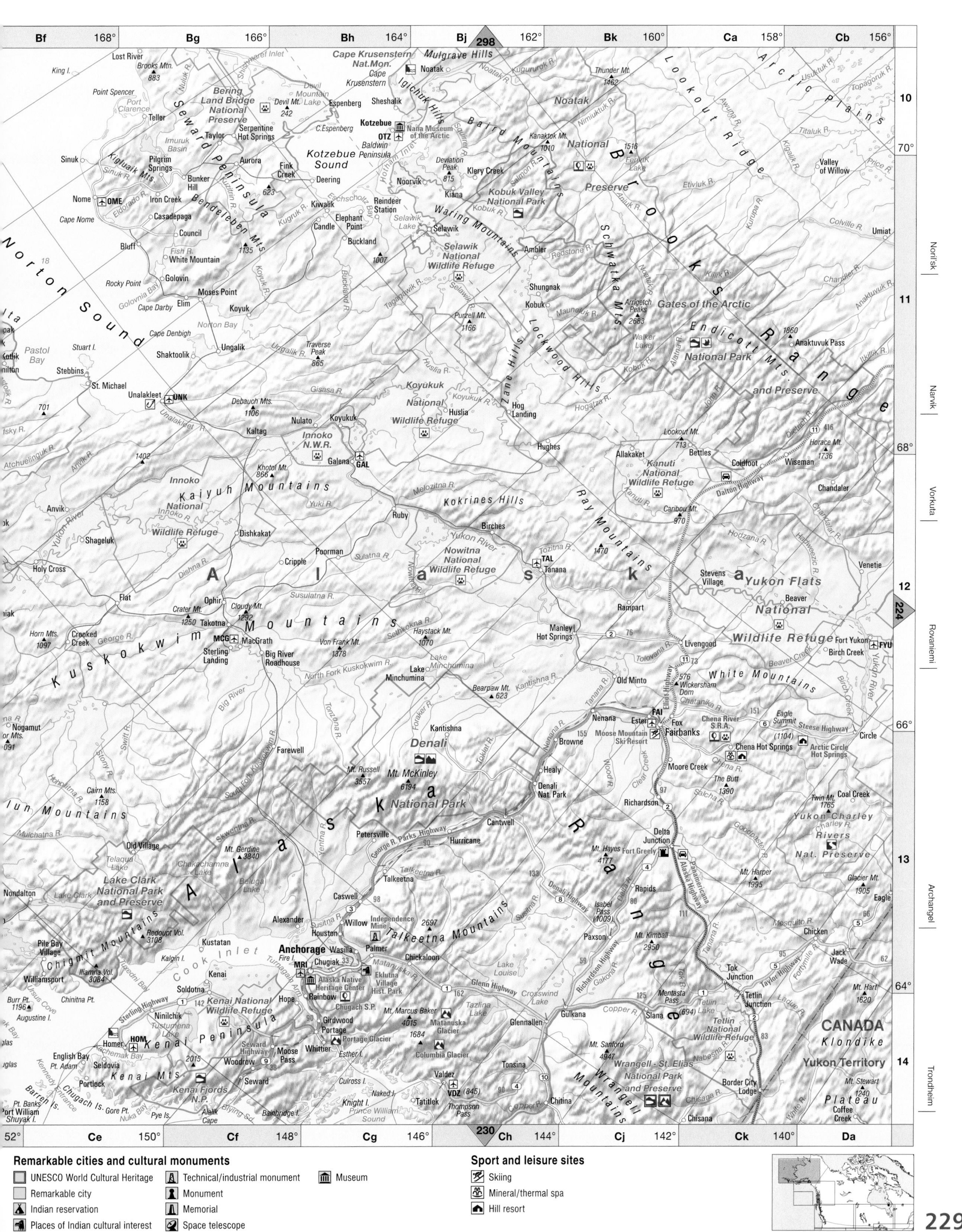

Bf 168° Bg 166° Bh 164° Bj 298 162° Bk 160° Ca 158° Cb 156°
10 11 12 13 14
70° 68° 66° 64°
Noril'sk
Narvik
Vorkuta
Rovaniemi
Archangel
Trondheim
224
52° Ce 150° Cf 148° Cg 146° 230 Ch 144° Cj 142° Ck 140° Da
Lost River
King I.
Brooks Mtn. 883
Point Spencer
Port Clarence
Teller
Bering Land Bridge National Preserve
Seward Peninsula
Devil Mt. 242
Devil Mountain Lakes
Espenberg
C.Espenberg
Serpentine Hot Springs
Imuruk Basin
Taylor
Sinuk
Kigluaik Mts.
Pilgrim Springs
Aurora
Bunker Hill
Nome
OME
Iron Creek
Cape Nome
Casadepaga
Council
Bendeleben Mts.
1135
Bluff
Fish R.
White Mountain
Golovin
Rocky Point
Norton Sound
Moses Point
Elim
Cape Darby
Koyuk
Norton Bay
Cape Denbigh
Stuart I.
Pastol Bay
Shaktoolik
Ungalik
Stebbins
St. Michael
Unalakleet
UNK
701
Cape Krusenstern Nat.Mon.
Cape Krusenstern
Mulgrave Hills
Noatak
Sheshalik
Igichuk Hills
Kotzebue
OTZ
Nana Museum of the Arctic
Baldwin Peninsula
Kotzebue Sound
Fink Creek
Deering
623
Kiwalik
Candle
Elephant Point
Reindeer Station
Buckland
1007
Selawik Lake
Selawik
Noorvik
Kiana
Deviation Peak 815
Klery Creek
Baird Mountains
Waring Mountains
Selawik National Wildlife Refuge
Kobuk Valley National Park
Noatak National Preserve
Thunder Mt. 1462
Kanaktok Mt. 1010
Lookout Ridge
Arctic Plains
Brooks Range
Valley of Willow
Umiat
Ambler
Shungnak
Kobuk
Schwatka Mts.
Arrigetch Peaks 2683
Gates of the Arctic National Park and Preserve
Endicott Mts.
1860
Anaktuvuk Pass
Walker Lake
Purzell Mt. 1166
Traverse Peak 865
Zane Hills
Lockwood Hills
Hog Landing
Koyukuk National Wildlife Refuge
Huslia
Koyukuk
Nulato
Kaltag
Debauch Mts. 1106
Innoko N.W.R.
Galena
GAL
Hughes
Allakaket
Kanuti National Wildlife Refuge
Bettles
Lookout Mt. 713
Coldfoot
Wiseman
Horace Mt. 1736
Chandalar
Dalton Highway
Caribou Mt. 970
1402
Khotol Mt. 866
Innoko National Wildlife Refuge
Kaiyuh Mountains
Kokrines Hills
Ray Mountains
Ruby
Birches
Anvik
Shageluk
Dishkakat
Yukon River
Poorman
Cripple
Nowitna National Wildlife Refuge
TAL
Tanana
1470
Holy Cross
Alaska
Stevens Village
Yukon Flats National Wildlife Refuge
Venetie
Beaver
Rampart
Fort Yukon
FYU
Birch Creek
Flat
Ophir
Crater Mt. 1250
Cloudy Mt. 1292
Takotna
McGrath
MCG
Sterling Landing
Big River Roadhouse
Kuskokwim Mountains
Horn Mts. 1097
Crooked Creek
Von Frank Mt. 1378
Haystack Mt. 1070
Manley Hot Springs
Livengood
Lake Minchumina
Bearpaw Mt. 623
White Mountains
Old Minto
Wickersham Dome
Nenana
Ester
FAI
Fox
Fairbanks
Moose Mountain Ski Resort
Chena River S.R.A.
Chena Hot Springs
Eagle Summit
Steese Highway
Circle
Arctic Circle Hot Springs
Nogamut
Farewell
Kantishna
Denali
Mt. Russell 3557
Mt. McKinley 6194
Denali National Park
Healy
Denali Nat. Park
Browne
Moore Creek
The Butt 1390
Richardson
Twin Mt. 1765
Coal Creek
Yukon-Charley Rivers Nat. Preserve
Cairn Mts. 1158
Alaska Range
Cantwell
Petersville
George R. Parks Highway
Hurricane
Delta Junction
Fort Greely
Mt. Hayes 4177
Old Village
Mt. Gerdine 3840
Talkeetna
Lake Clark National Park and Preserve
Nondalton
Caswell
Denali Highway
Isabel Pass (1009)
Rapids
Mt. Harper 1995
Glacier Mt. 1905
Eagle
Alexander
Willow
Independence Mine
Talkeetna Mountains
Paxson
Mt. Kimball 2950
Chicken
Redoubt Vol. 3108
Houston
Wasilla
Palmer
Chickaloon
Chigmit Mountains
Pile Bay Village
Kustatan
Cook Inlet
Anchorage
MRI
Chugiak
Alaska Native Heritage Center
Eklutna Village Hist. Park
Iliamna Vol. 3084
Williamsport
Kenai
Soldotna
Glenn Highway
Lake Louise
Tok Junction
Jack Wade
Tetlin Junction
Taylor Highway
Mt. Hart 1620
Chinitna Pt.
Burr Pt. 1196
Augustine I.
Kenai National Wildlife Refuge
Hope
Rainbow
Chugach S.P.
Mt. Marcus Baker 4015
Matanuska Glacier
Crosswind Lake
Mentasta Pass
Slana
Tetlin National Wildlife Refuge
CANADA
Klondike
Sterling Highway
Ninilchik
Kenai Peninsula
Girdwood
Portage
Portage Glacier
Glennallen
Gulkana
HOM
Homer
Kachemak Bay
Seward Highway
Moose Pass
Whittier
1684
Columbia Glacier
Mt. Sanford 4947
Wrangell-St. Elias National Park and Preserve
Wrangell Mountains
Tonsina
English Bay
Pt. Adam
Seldovia
Kenai Mts.
Woodrow
Seward
Kenai Fjords N.P.
Valdez
VDZ
Thompson Pass
Chitina
Border City Lodge
Chisana
Yukon Territory
Mt. Stewart 1240
Plateau
Coffee Creek
Portlock
Chugach Is.
Gore Pt.
Pye Is.
Pt. Banks
Port William
Shuyak I.
Barren Is.
Kennedy Entrance
Culross I.
Naked I.
Knight I.
Tatitlek
Prince William Sound
Bainbridge I.
Aialik Cape
Remarkable cities and cultural monuments
UNESCO World Cultural Heritage
Remarkable city
Indian reservation
Places of Indian cultural interest
Technical/industrial monument
Monument
Memorial
Space telescope
Museum
Sport and leisure sites
Skiing
Mineral/thermal spa
Hill resort

Southern Alaska, Northwestern Canada, Hawaiian Islands

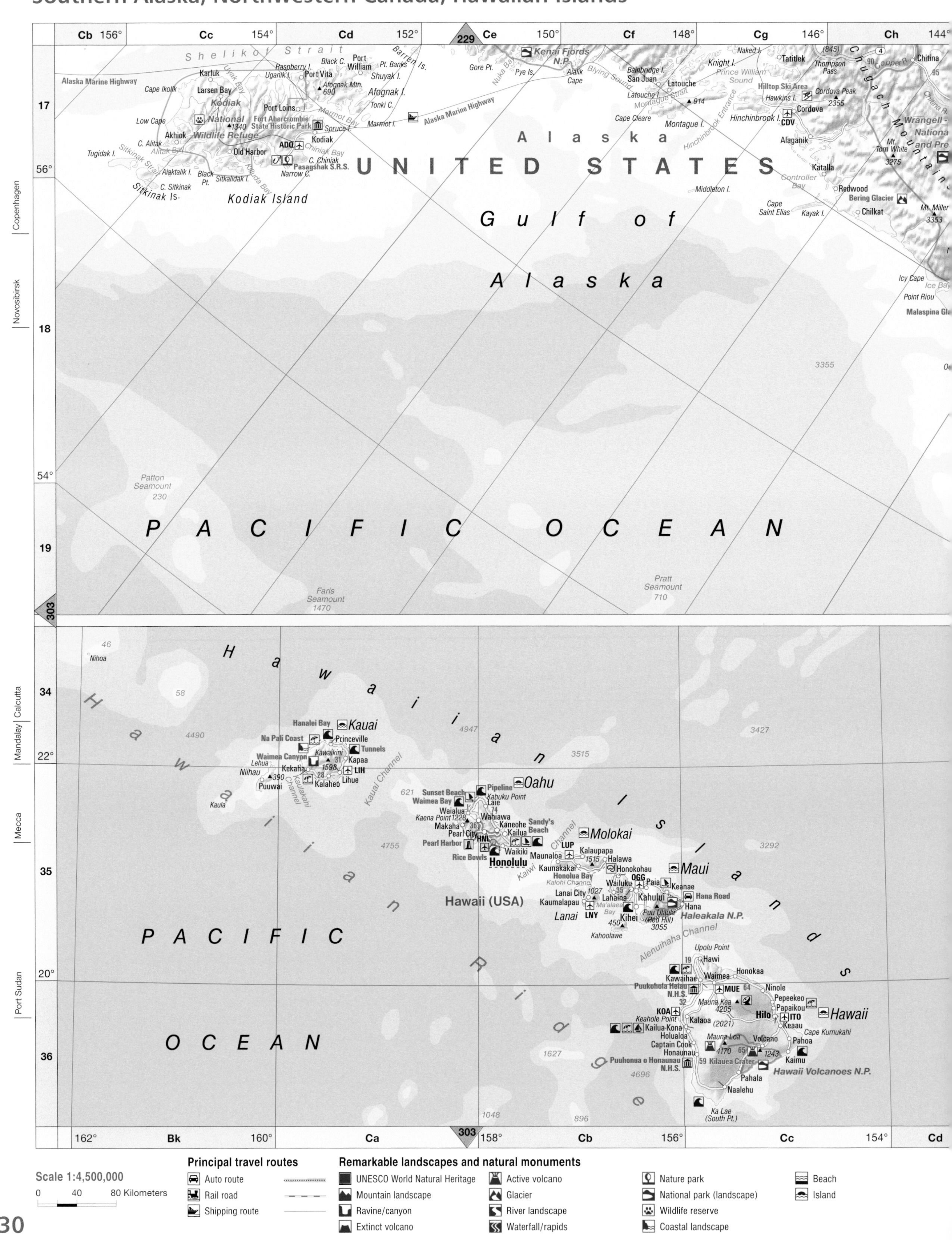

Scale 1:4,500,000

0   40   80 Kilometers

Principal travel routes

🚗 Auto route

🚆 Rail road

🚢 Shipping route

Remarkable landscapes and natural monuments

UNESCO World Natural Heritage

Mountain landscape

Ravine/canyon

Extinct volcano

Active volcano

Glacier

River landscape

Waterfall/rapids

Nature park

National park (landscape)

Wildlife reserve

Coastal landscape

Beach

Island

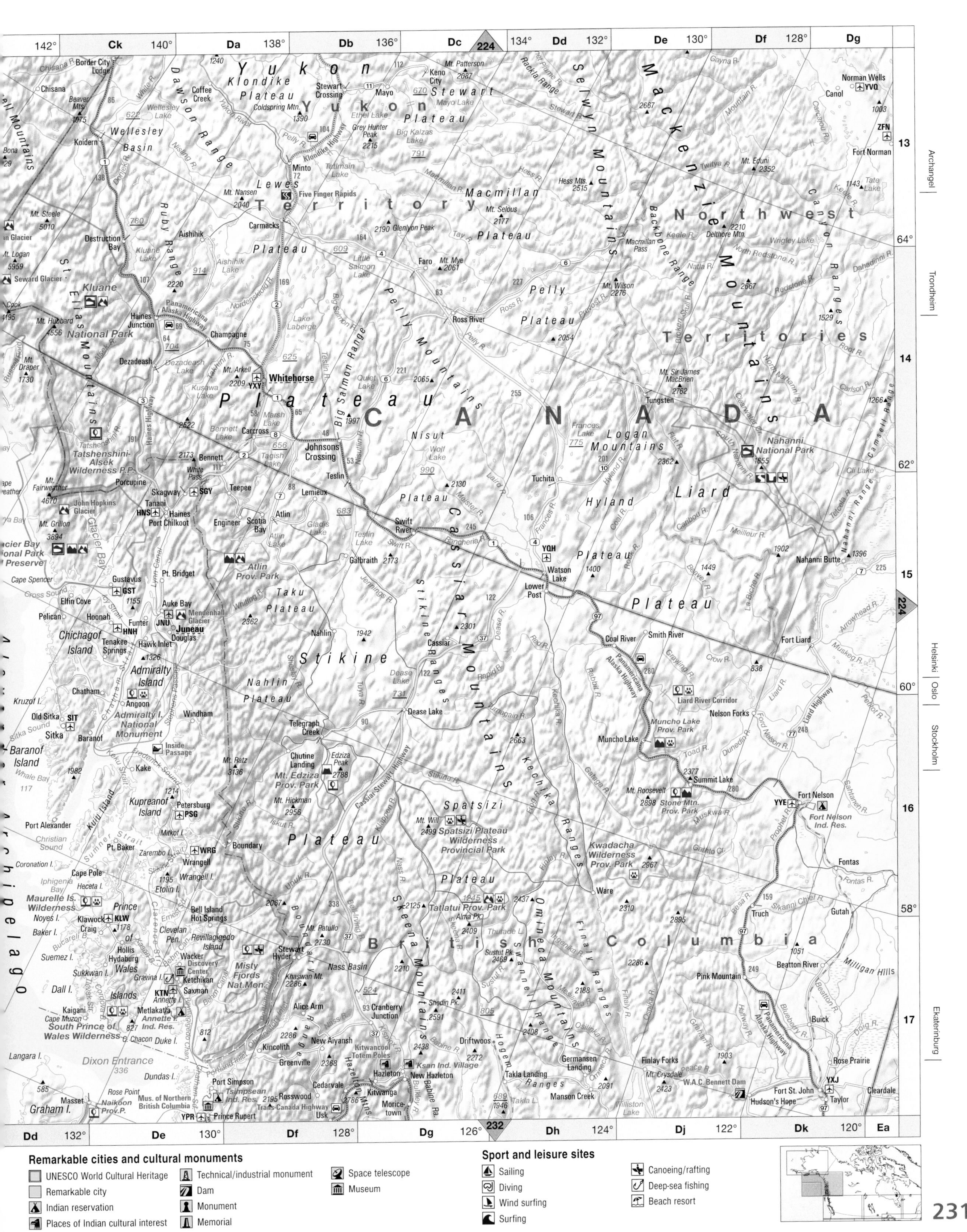

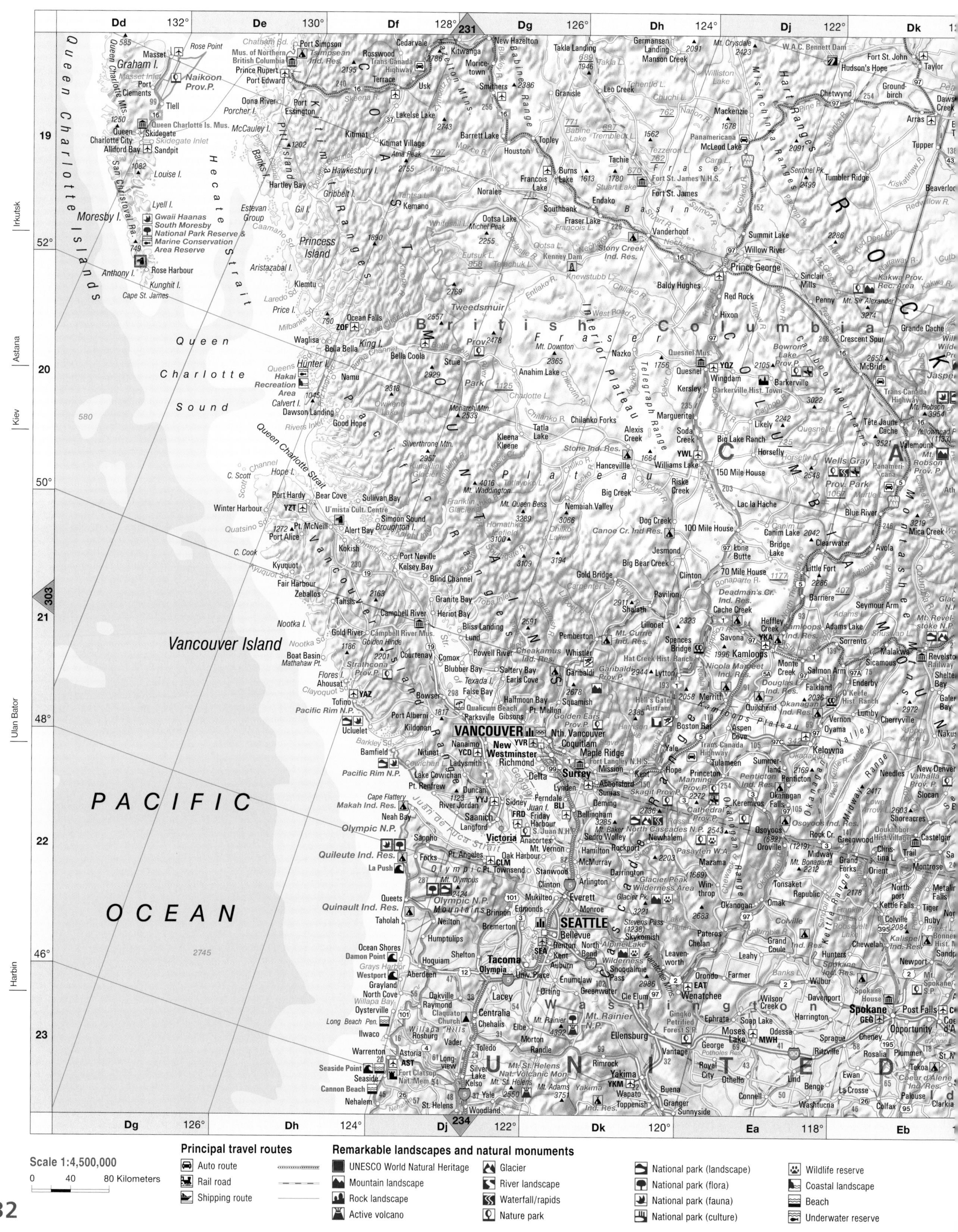

Scale 1:4,500,000

0   40   80 Kilometers

Principal travel routes

- Auto route
- Rail road
- Shipping route

Remarkable landscapes and natural monuments

- UNESCO World Natural Heritage
- Mountain landscape
- Rock landscape
- Active volcano
- Glacier
- River landscape
- Waterfall/rapids
- Nature park
- National park (landscape)
- National park (flora)
- National park (fauna)
- National park (culture)
- Wildlife reserve
- Coastal landscape
- Beach
- Underwater reserve

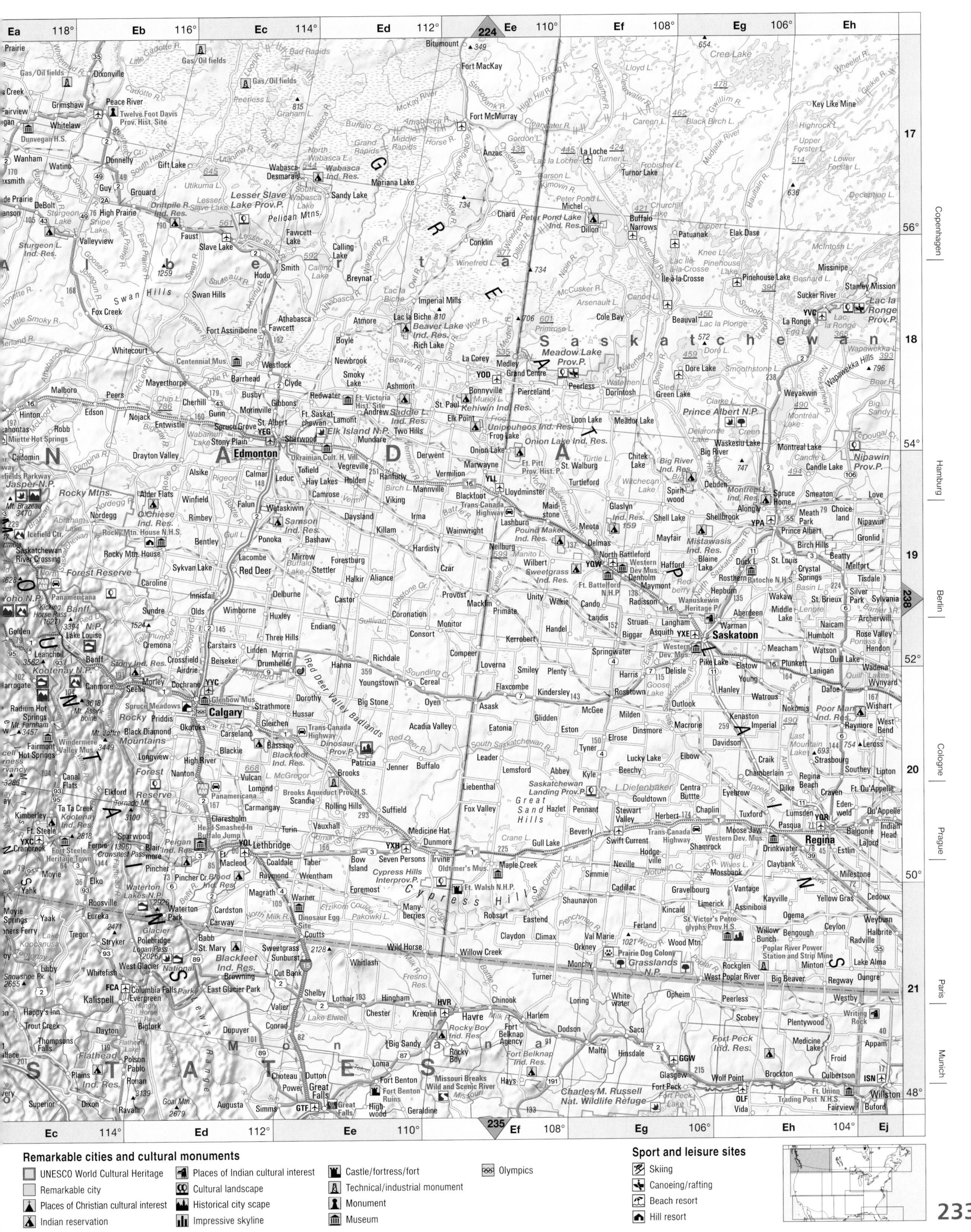

Copenhagen
17
56°
Hamburg
18
54°
Berlin 238
19
Cologne
52°
20
Prague
50°
Paris
21
Munich
48°

Remarkable cities and cultural monuments

- UNESCO World Cultural Heritage
- Remarkable city
- Places of Christian cultural interest
- Indian reservation
- Places of Indian cultural interest
- Cultural landscape
- Historical city scape
- Impressive skyline
- Castle/fortress/fort
- Technical/industrial monument
- Monument
- Museum
- Olympics

Sport and leisure sites

- Skiing
- Canoeing/rafting
- Beach resort
- Hill resort

233

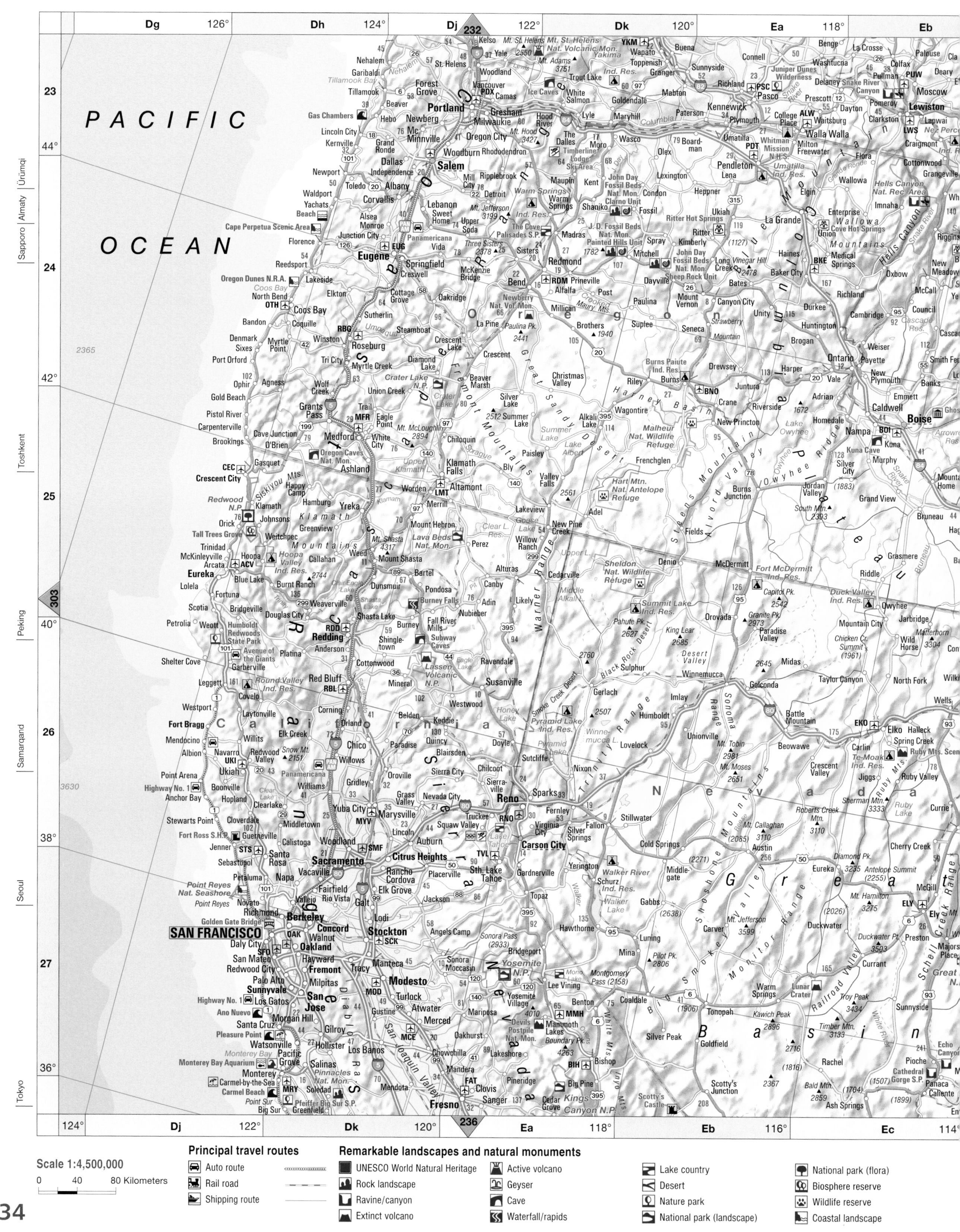

PACIFIC

OCEAN

Scale 1:4,500,000

0   40   80 Kilometers

| Dj | | | Dk | 120° | Ea | 118° | Eb | 116° | Ec | 114° |

Principal travel routes

- 🚗 Auto route
- 🚆 Rail road
- 🚢 Shipping route

⋯⋯ (rail road line)

Remarkable landscapes and natural monuments

- ■ UNESCO World Natural Heritage
- ▪ Rock landscape
- ▪ Ravine/canyon
- ▪ Extinct volcano
- ▲ Active volcano
- ▲ Geyser
- ▲ Cave
- ▲ Waterfall/rapids
- ▪ Lake country
- ▪ Desert
- ▪ Nature park
- ▪ National park (landscape)
- ▪ National park (flora)
- ▪ Biosphere reserve
- ▪ Wildlife reserve
- ▪ Coastal landscape

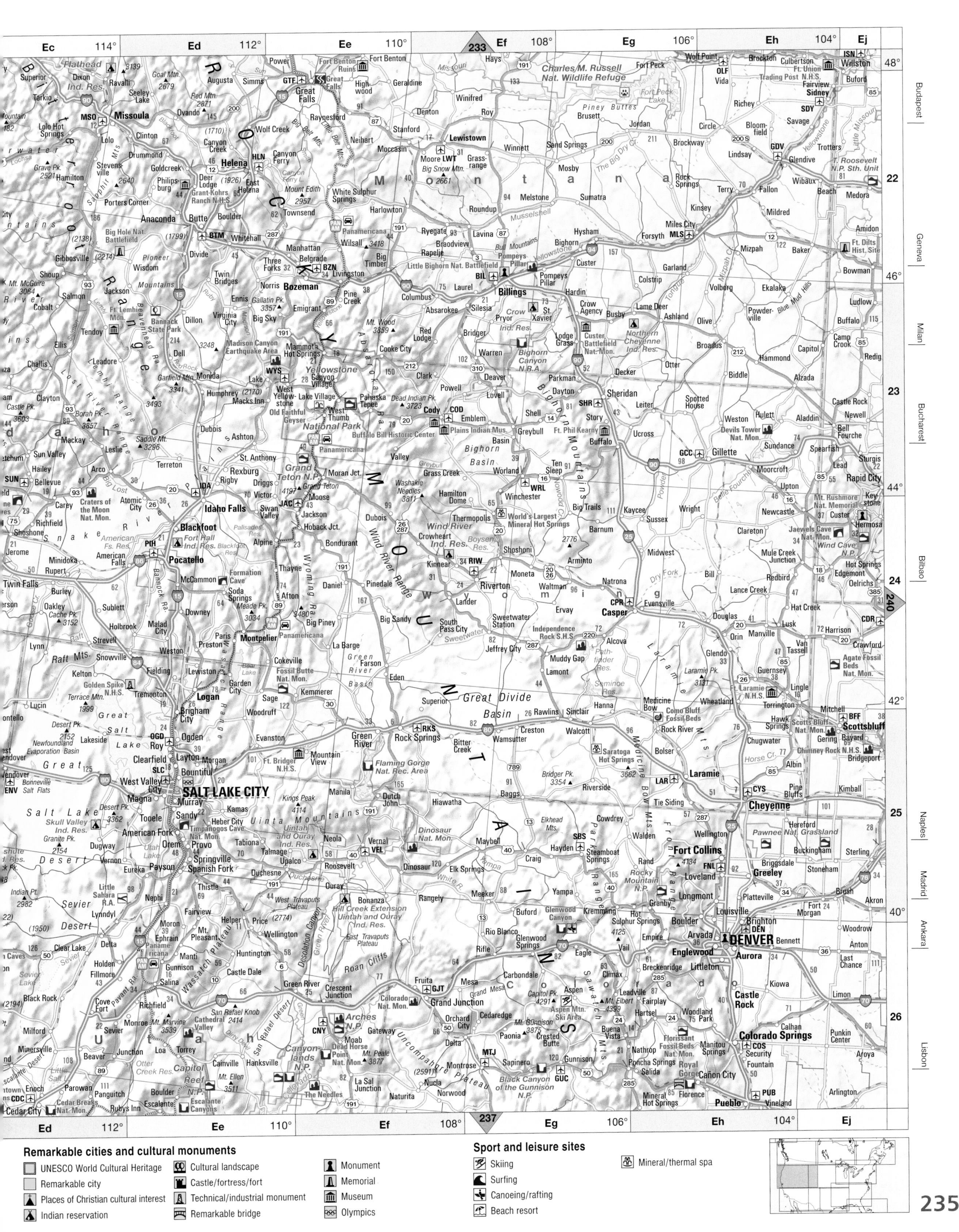

Remarkable cities and cultural monuments

- ▢ UNESCO World Cultural Heritage
- ▢ Remarkable city
- ▲ Places of Christian cultural interest
- ▲ Indian reservation
- ◉ Cultural landscape
- ⌂ Castle/fortress/fort
- ⚒ Technical/industrial monument
- ⌂ Remarkable bridge
- 🏛 Monument
- 🏛 Memorial
- 🏛 Museum
- ⚬ Olympics

Sport and leisure sites

- 🎿 Skiing
- 🏄 Surfing
- 🛶 Canoeing/rafting
- 🏖 Beach resort
- ♨ Mineral/thermal spa

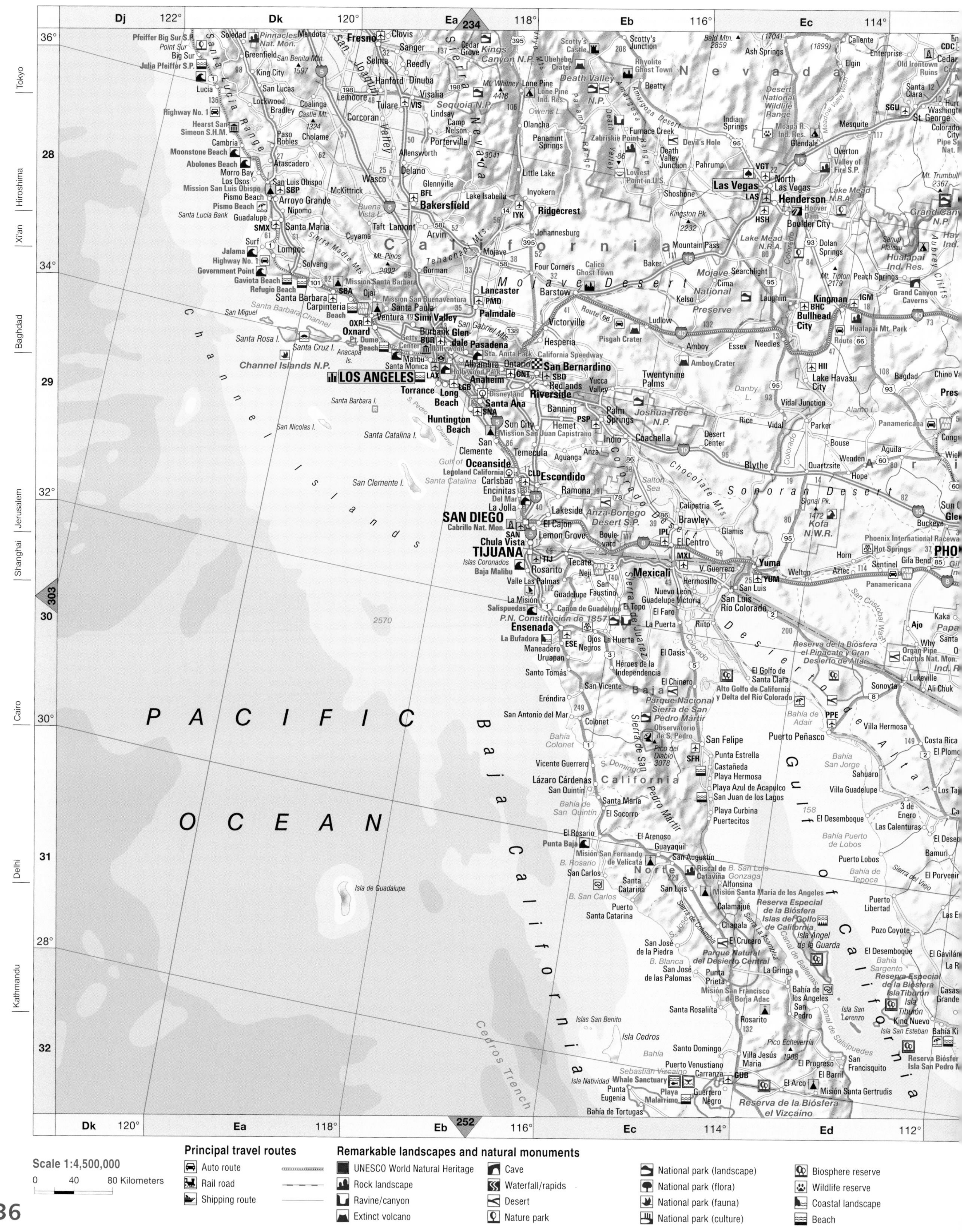

| Dj | 122° | Dk | 120° | Ea | 234 | 118° | Eb | 116° | Ec | 114° |

Tokyo | Hiroshima | Xi'an | Baghdad | Shanghai | Jerusalem | Cairo | Delhi | Kathmandu

36°
28°
34°
29°
32°
303
30°
30°
31°
28°
32°

| Dk | 120° | Ea | 118° | Eb | 252 | 116° | Ec | 114° | Ed | 112° |

PACIFIC

OCEAN

Scale 1:4,500,000

0   40   80 Kilometers

Principal travel routes

- Auto route
- Rail road
- Shipping route

Remarkable landscapes and natural monuments

- UNESCO World Natural Heritage
- Rock landscape
- Ravine/canyon
- Extinct volcano
- Cave
- Waterfall/rapids
- Desert
- Nature park
- National park (landscape)
- National park (flora)
- National park (fauna)
- National park (culture)
- Biosphere reserve
- Wildlife reserve
- Coastal landscape
- Beach

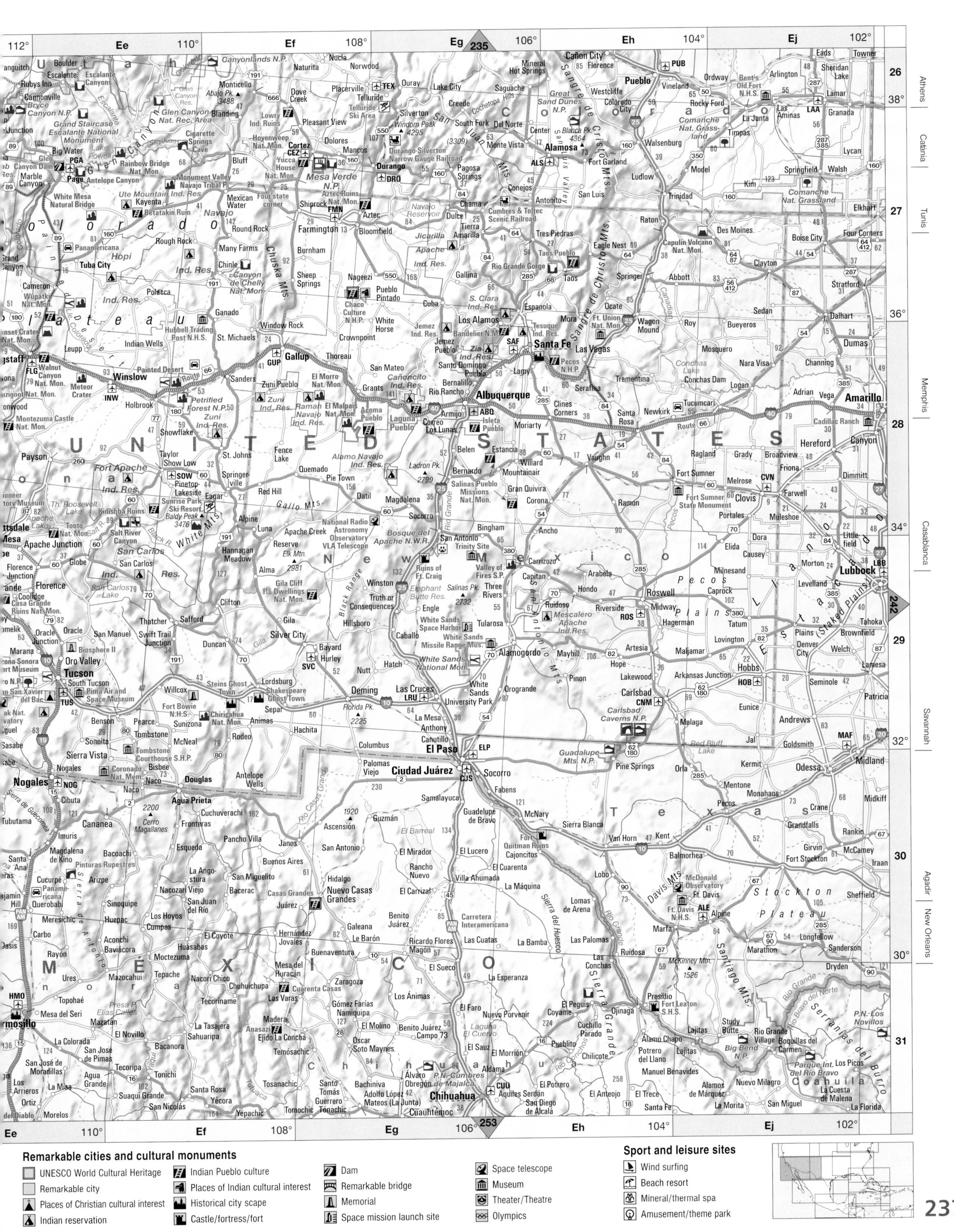

Athens
Catania
Tunis
Memphis
Casablanca
Savannah
Agadir
New Orleans

Remarkable cities and cultural monuments

- UNESCO World Cultural Heritage
- Remarkable city
- Places of Christian cultural interest
- Indian reservation
- Indian Pueblo culture
- Places of Indian cultural interest
- Historical city scape
- Castle/fortress/fort
- Dam
- Remarkable bridge
- Memorial
- Space mission launch site
- Space telescope
- Museum
- Theater/Theatre
- Olympics

Sport and leisure sites

- Wind surfing
- Beach resort
- Mineral/thermal spa
- Amusement/theme park

237

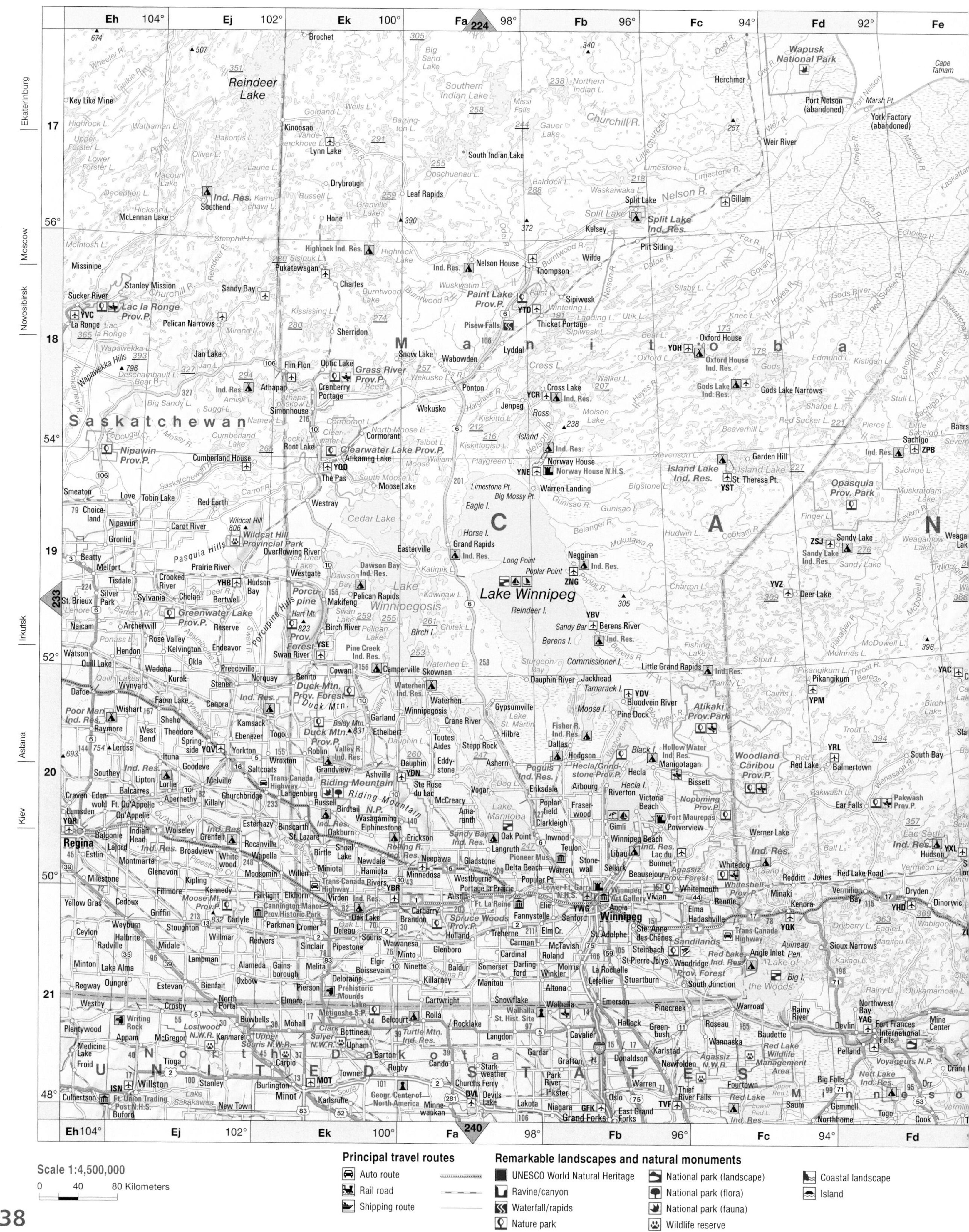

Scale 1:4,500,000

0   40   80 Kilometers

Principal travel routes

- Auto route
- Rail road
- Shipping route
- ▦ Waterfall/rapids
- Nature park

Remarkable landscapes and natural monuments

- UNESCO World Natural Heritage
- Ravine/canyon
- Waterfall/rapids
- Nature park
- National park (landscape)
- National park (flora)
- National park (fauna)
- Wildlife reserve
- Coastal landscape
- Island

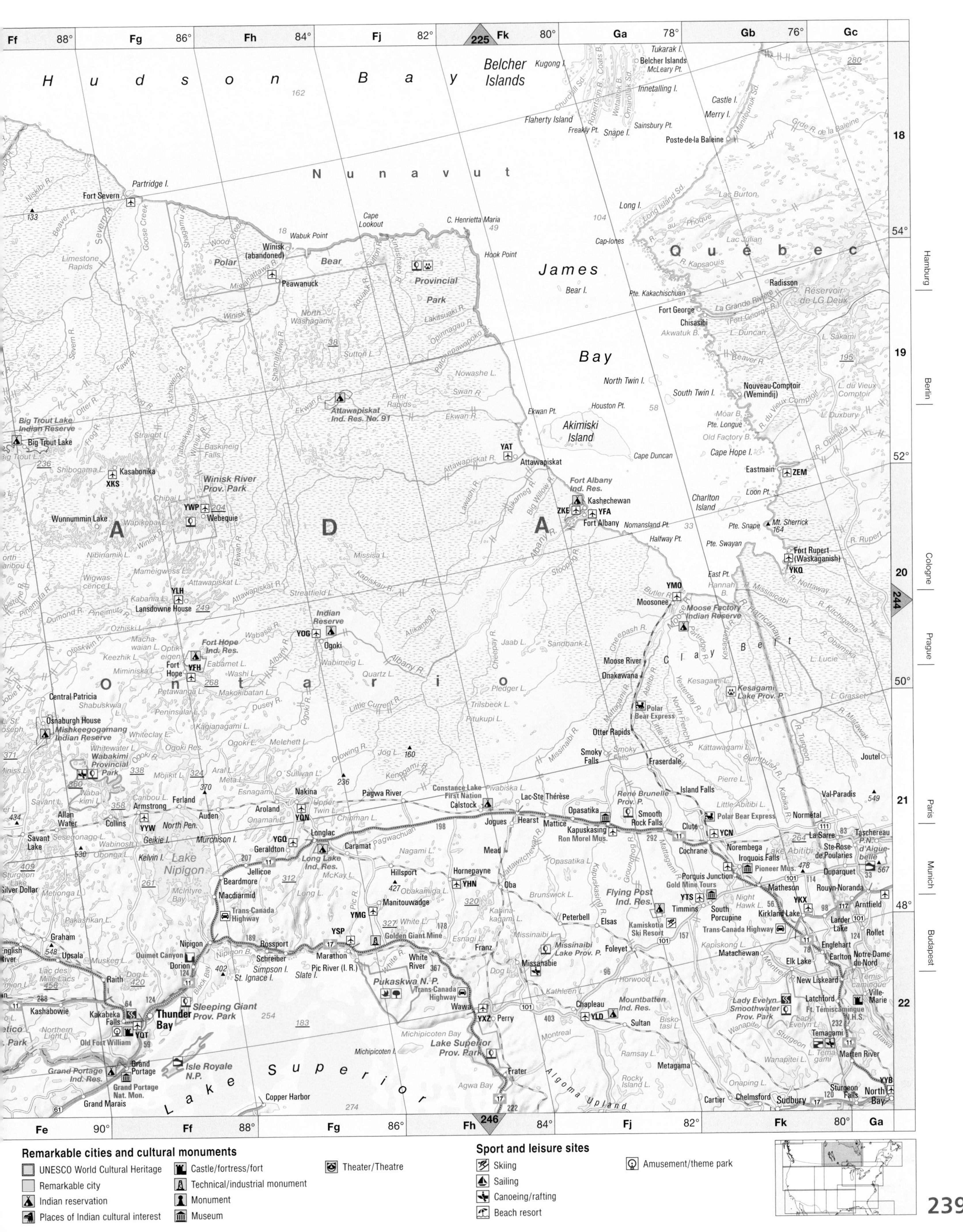

Hudson Bay

162

Belcher Islands

Kugong I.
Tukarak I.
Belcher Islands 280
McLeary Pt.
Churchill Sd.
Robertson B.
Wetwilek B.
Omarolluk Sd.
Innetalling I.
Castle I.
Merry I.
Flaherty Island
Freakly Pt. Snape I.
Sainsbury Pt.
Poste-de-la-Baleine
Gde R. de la Baleine

18

Nunavut

Fort Severn
Partridge I.
133
Beaver R.
Niskibi R.
Severn R.
Goose Creek
Sachigo R.
Wood Creek
Shagamu R.
Wabuk Point 18
Cape Lookout
C. Henrietta Maria 49
Hook Point

James

Long I.
Long Island Sd.
au Phoque
Lac Burton
Cap-Jones
104

Québec

L. Kapsaouis

54°

Limestone Rapids
Winisk (abandoned)
Polar
Peawanuck
Bear
Winisk R.
North Washagami
Provincial Park
Bear I.
Pte. Kakakischuan
Radisson
Réservoir de LG Deux
Fort George (Fort George R.)
Chisasibi
La Grande Rivière
Akwatuk B.
L. Duncan
Beaver R.

Bay

North Twin I.
South Twin I.
Houston Pt. 58
Ekwan Pt.
Môar B.
Pte. Longue
Old Factory B.
Nouveau-Comptoir (Wemindij)
L. du Vieux Comptoir
L. Duxbury
R. du Vieux Comptoir
L. Opinaca
L. Sakami

19

195

Big Trout Lake Indian Reserve
Big Trout Lake ▲
XKS Kasabonika
236
Shibogama L.
Otter R.
Fawn R.
Straight L.
Baskineig Falls
Attawapiskat Ind. Res. No. 91
Ekwan R.
Swan R.
Ekwan R.
Akimiski Island
Cape Duncan
Cape Hope I.
Eastmain ZEM
Charlton Island
Loon Pt.
Pte. Snape ▲Mt. Sherrick 164
Fort Rupert (Waskaganish)
YKQ

52°

Wunnummin Lake
Wapikopa L.
YWP 204
Webequie
Chipal L.
Winisk River Prov. Park
Nibinamik L.
Mameigwess L.
Attawapiskat L.
Missisa L.
Kapiskau R.
Fort Albany Ind. Res.
ZKE Kashechewan
YFA
Fort Albany
Nomansland Pt. 33
Halfway Pt.
Pte. Swayan
East Pt.
Hannah
Mt. Mississicabi
R. Nottaway
R. Kitchigama
R. Obamsca

A   D   A

20

244

Lansdowne House 249
YLH
Pineimuta R.
Dumont R.
Ozhiski L.
Machawaian L.
Keezhik L.
Optikeigen L.
Indian Reserve
YOG
Ogoki
Wabassi R.
Eabamet L.
Streatfield L.
Albany R.
Butler R.
YMO
Moosonee
Moose Factory Indian Reserve
L. Lucie
L. Sakami
Kesagami Lake Prov. P.
L. Grasset
R. Miskawak

Central Patricia
Shabuskwia L.
Osnaburgh House
Mishkeegogamang Indian Reserve
Whitclay L.
Fort Hope Ind. Res.
Fort Hope YFH 268
Washi L.
Ogoki Res.
Makokibatan L.
Dusey L.
Little Current R.
Trilsbeck L.
Pitukupi L.
Cheepash R.
Jaab L.
Sandbank L.
Moose River
Onakawana
Kesagami L.
Otter Rapids
Kattawagami R.
Pierre L.

50°

Wabakimi Provincial Park
338 324
Mojikit L. 370
Meta L.
O'Sullivan L.
Jog L. 160
Kenogami R.
Missinaibi R.
Smoky Falls
Fraserdale
Island Falls
Little Abitibi L.
Quinibush L.
Val-Paradis 549
Normétal

Ontario

21

Wabakimi 860
Waba kimi L. 358
Savant L. 434
Caribou L.
Armstrong
North Pen.
YYW
Collins
Allan Water
Geikie L.
Murchison I.
Nakina
YGQ
236
Pagwa River
Constance Lake First Nation
Calstock
Lac-Ste Thérèse
Pivabiska L.
René Brunelle Prov. P.
Opasatika
Smooth Rock Falls
Clute
YCN
Cochrane
Polar Bear Express
La Sarre 83
Ste-Rose-de-Poularies
Duparquet 567
111
264

Savant Lake
Wabinosh L.
Geraldton
Esnagami L.
Upper Twin L.
YQN
Aroland
Onamani L.
Jellicoe
Longlac
Caramat
198
Chipman L.
Jogues
Hearst
Mattice
Kapuskasing
Ron Morel Mus.
Opasatika R.
Groundhog R. 292
11
Norembega
Iroquois Falls
Gold Mine Tours
Porquis Junction
Pioneer Mus. 478
Matheson
Rouyn-Noranda
Tascherau P.N.
d'Aiguebelle
33
114

48°

Silver Dollar
Metionga L.
Kelvin L.
530
Onbonga L. 261
Lake Nipigon
207
Beardmore
Macdiarmid
McIntyre Bay
Long L.
312
McKay L.
Obakamiga L.
320
Brunswick L.
Flying Post Ind. Res.
Kabinakagami L.
Elsas
Kapuskasing R.
Matichewan
Night Hawk L. 56
South Porcupine
Timmins
YTS
Kamiskotia Ski Resort 157
Kirkland Lake
YKX
Larder Lake
Arntfield 117
Rollet
Kirkland Lake 98
101

Lake Nipigon

Graham 548
Upsala
Lac des Mille Lacs 456
Raith 288
Nipigon
Dorion
Ouimet Canyon 124
402
Schreiber
Terrace Bay
Rossport
Simpson I.
St. Ignace I.
Slate I.
YSP
Marathon
Pic River (I. R.)
YMG
Manitouwadge
327 White L.
White River 367
Peterbell
Franz
Missanabie
Missinaibi Lake Prov. P.
Foleyet
Dog L.
Horwood L. 96
Kapiskong L.
Matachewan
Elk Lake
Englehart
Earlton
Notre-Dame-du-Nord
New Liskeard
124 78

Kakabeka Falls
YQT 59
Thunder Bay
Old Fort William
254
183
Pukaskwa N.P.
Trans-Canada Highway
Wawa
YXZ Perry
403
Chapleau
YLD
Sultan
Mountbatten Ind. Res.
Biskotasi L.
Lady Evelyn Smoothwater Prov. Park
Latchford
Ville-Marie
Temagami
22

Grand Portage Ind. Res.
Grand Portage
Grand Portage Nat. Mon.
Isle Royale N.P.
Copper Harbor
274
Michipicoten Bay
Michipicoten I.
Lake Superior Prov. Park
Agwa Bay
Frater
17 222
Montreal R.
Algoma Upland
Rocky Island L.
Ramsay L.
Metagama
Wanapitei L.
Cartier
Chelmsford
Sudbury
17 120
North Bay
YYB
Sturgeon Falls
Marten River

61
Grand Marais
Lake Superior

Remarkable cities and cultural monuments

- ☐ UNESCO World Cultural Heritage
- ☐ Remarkable city
- ⛊ Indian reservation
- ⛏ Places of Indian cultural interest
- ⛫ Castle/fortress/fort
- ⛩ Technical/industrial monument
- ⛳ Monument
- 🏛 Museum
- ◉ Theater/Theatre

Sport and leisure sites

- 🎿 Skiing
- ⛵ Sailing
- 🚣 Canoeing/rafting
- 🏖 Beach resort
- ⊚ Amusement/theme park

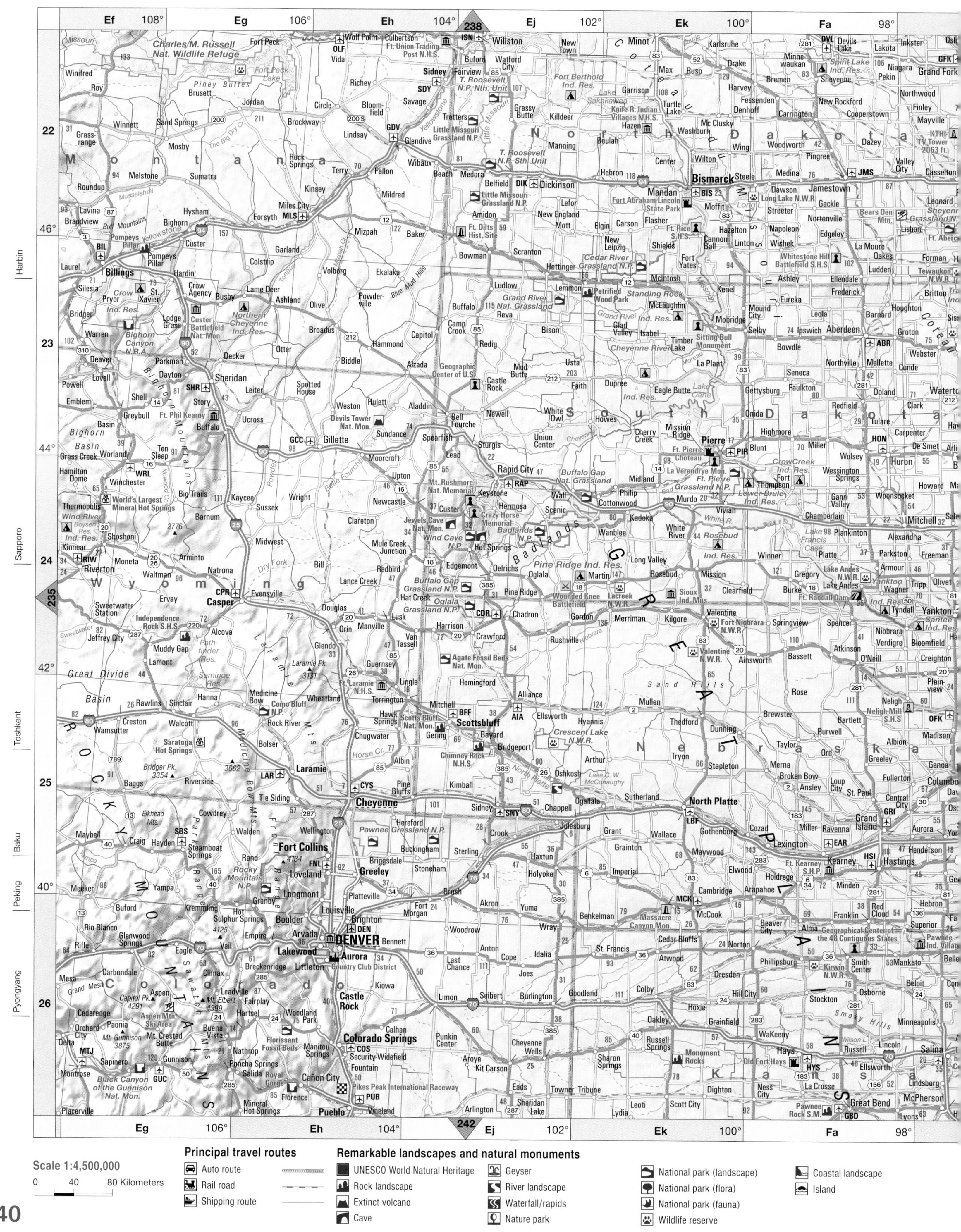

Scale 1:4,500,000

0   40   80 Kilometers

Principal travel routes

- Auto route
- Rail road
- Shipping route

Remarkable landscapes and natural monuments

- UNESCO World Natural Heritage
- Rock landscape
- Extinct volcano
- Cave
- Geyser
- River landscape
- Waterfall/rapids
- Nature park
- National park (landscape)
- National park (flora)
- National park (fauna)
- Wildlife reserve
- Coastal landscape
- Island

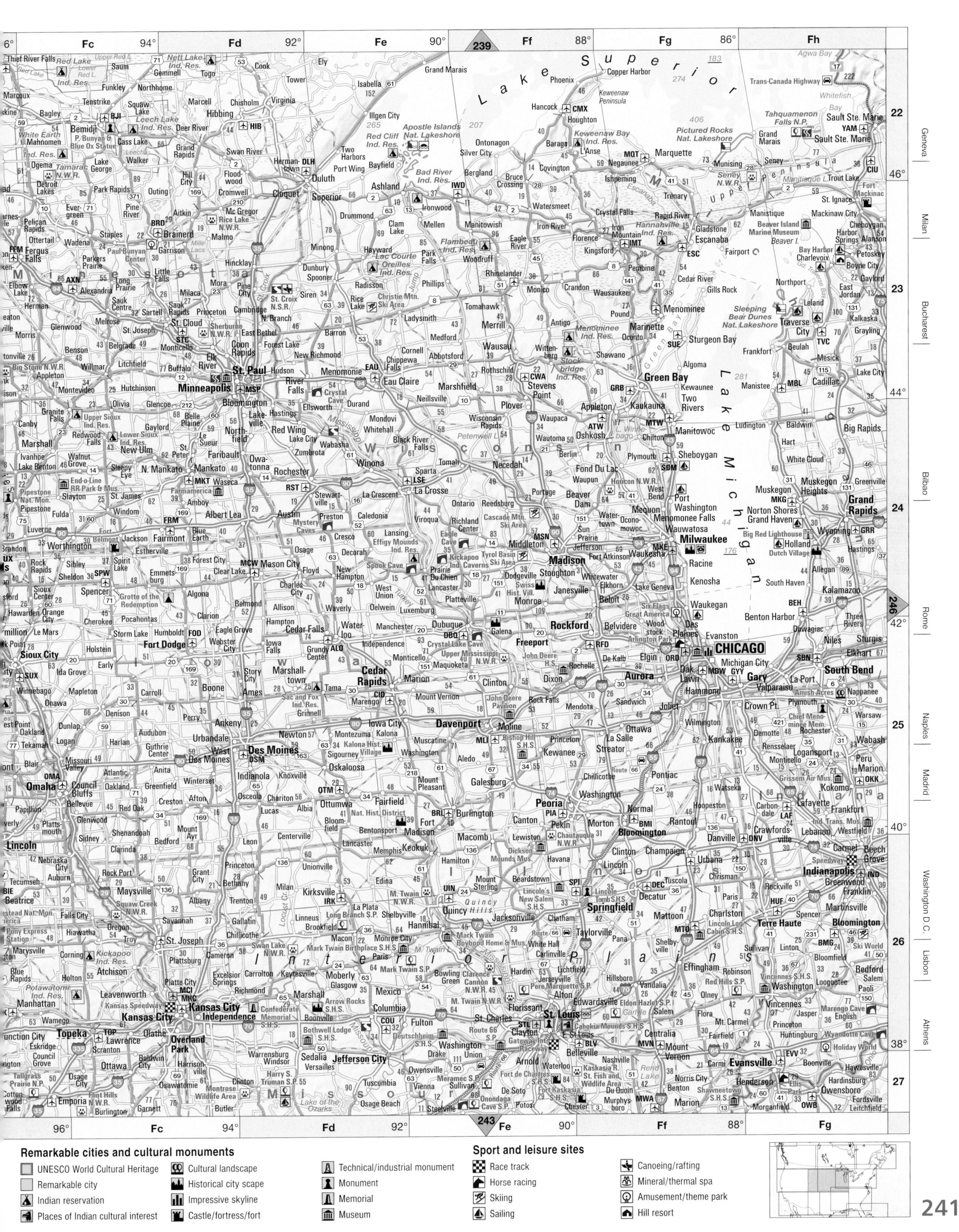

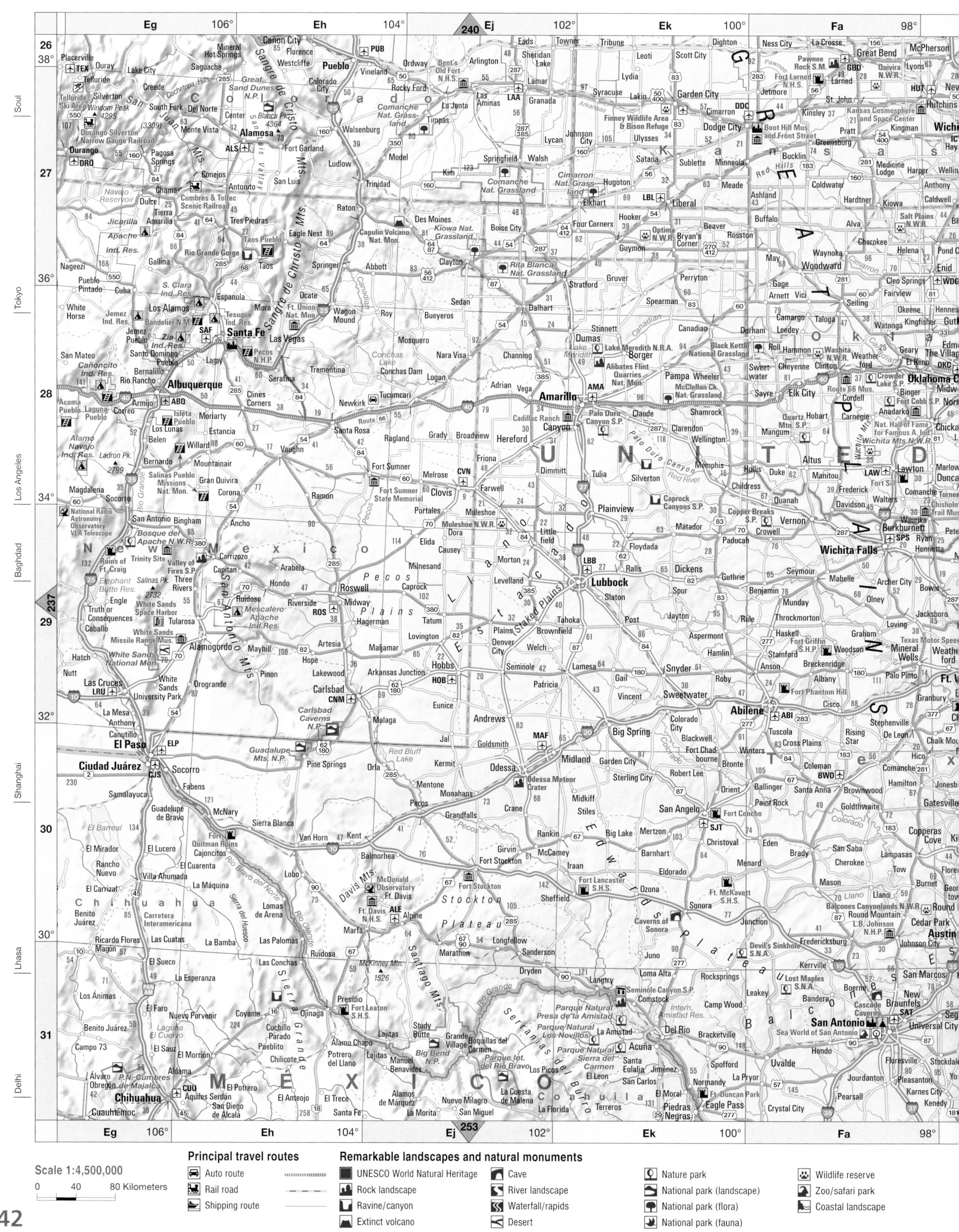

Scale 1:4,500,000

0   40   80 Kilometers

Principal travel routes

- Auto route
- Rail road
- Shipping route

Remarkable landscapes and natural monuments

- UNESCO World Natural Heritage
- Rock landscape
- Ravine/canyon
- Extinct volcano
- Cave
- River landscape
- Waterfall/rapids
- Desert
- Nature park
- National park (landscape)
- National park (flora)
- National park (fauna)
- Wildlife reserve
- Zoo/safari park
- Coastal landscape

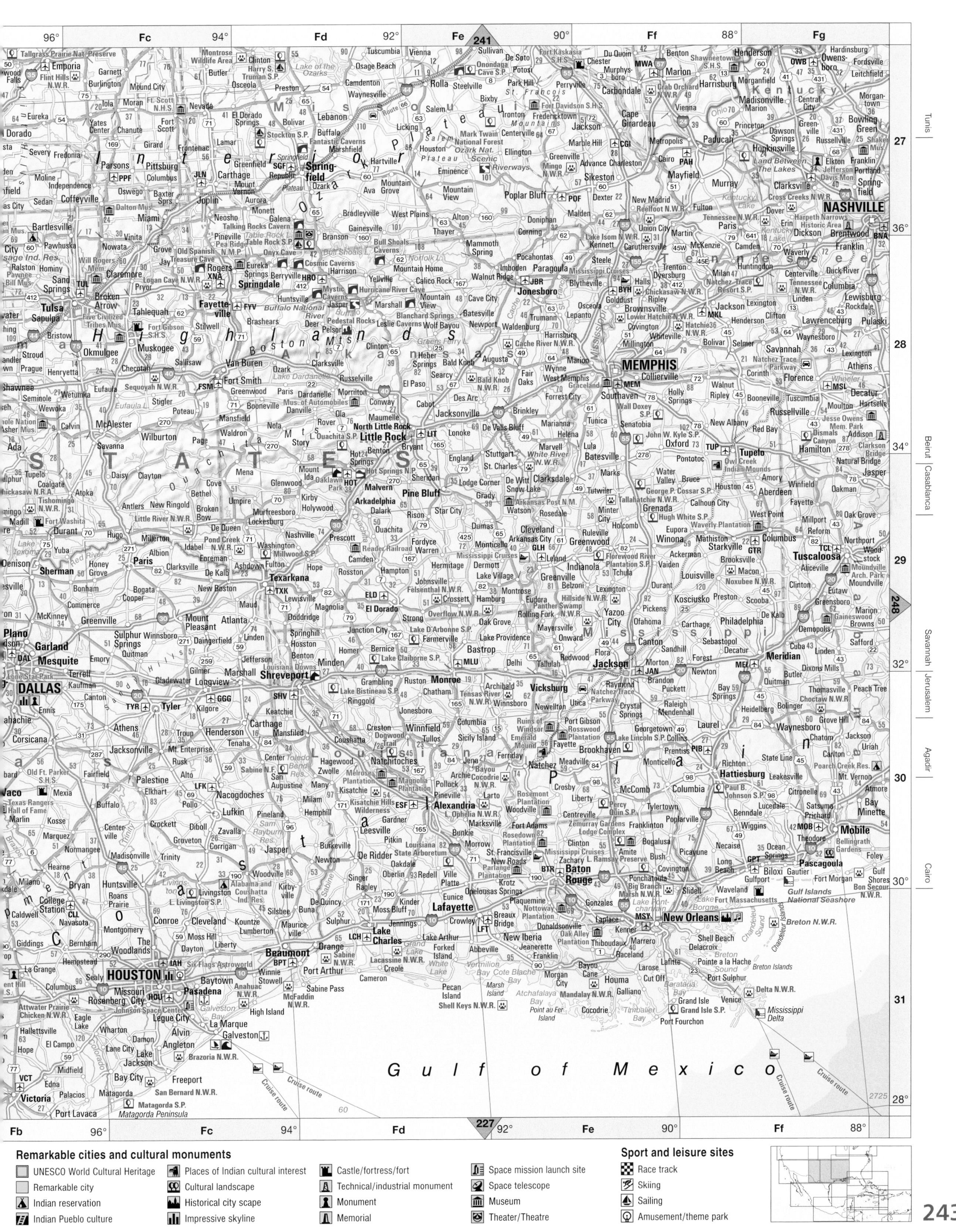
Gulf of Mexico
DALLAS
HOUSTON
MEMPHIS
NASHVILLE
New Orleans
Little Rock
Shreveport
Jackson
Baton Rouge
Tulsa
Remarkable cities and cultural monuments
UNESCO World Cultural Heritage
Remarkable city
Indian reservation
Indian Pueblo culture
Places of Indian cultural interest
Cultural landscape
Historical city scape
Impressive skyline
Castle/fortress/fort
Technical/industrial monument
Monument
Memorial
Space mission launch site
Space telescope
Museum
Theater/Theatre
Sport and leisure sites
Race track
Skiing
Sailing
Amusement/theme park

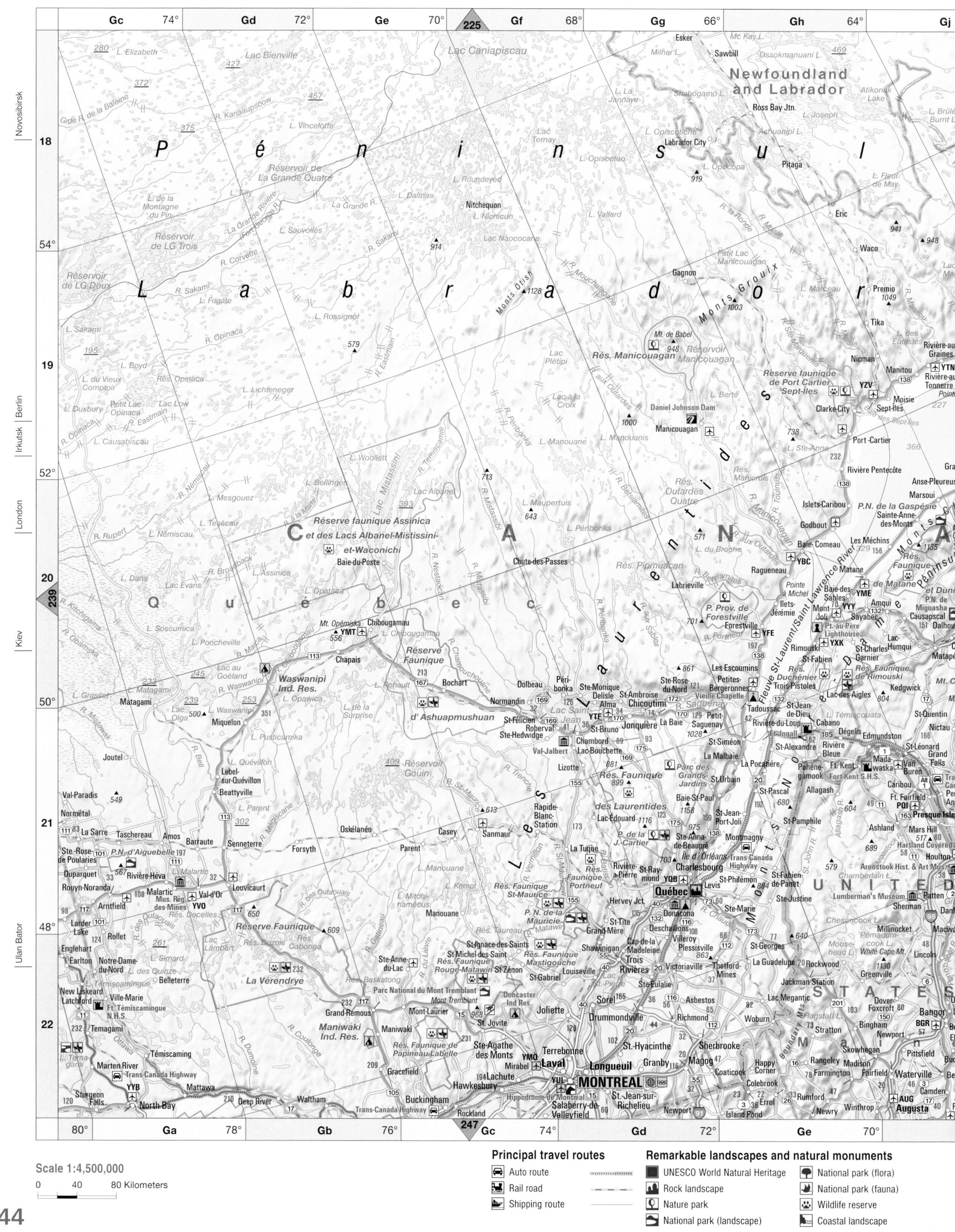

Principal travel routes

- Auto route
- Rail road
- Shipping route

Remarkable landscapes and natural monuments

- UNESCO World Natural Heritage
- Rock landscape
- Nature park
- National park (landscape)
- National park (flora)
- National park (fauna)
- Wildlife reserve
- Coastal landscape

Scale 1:4,500,000

0   40   80 Kilometers

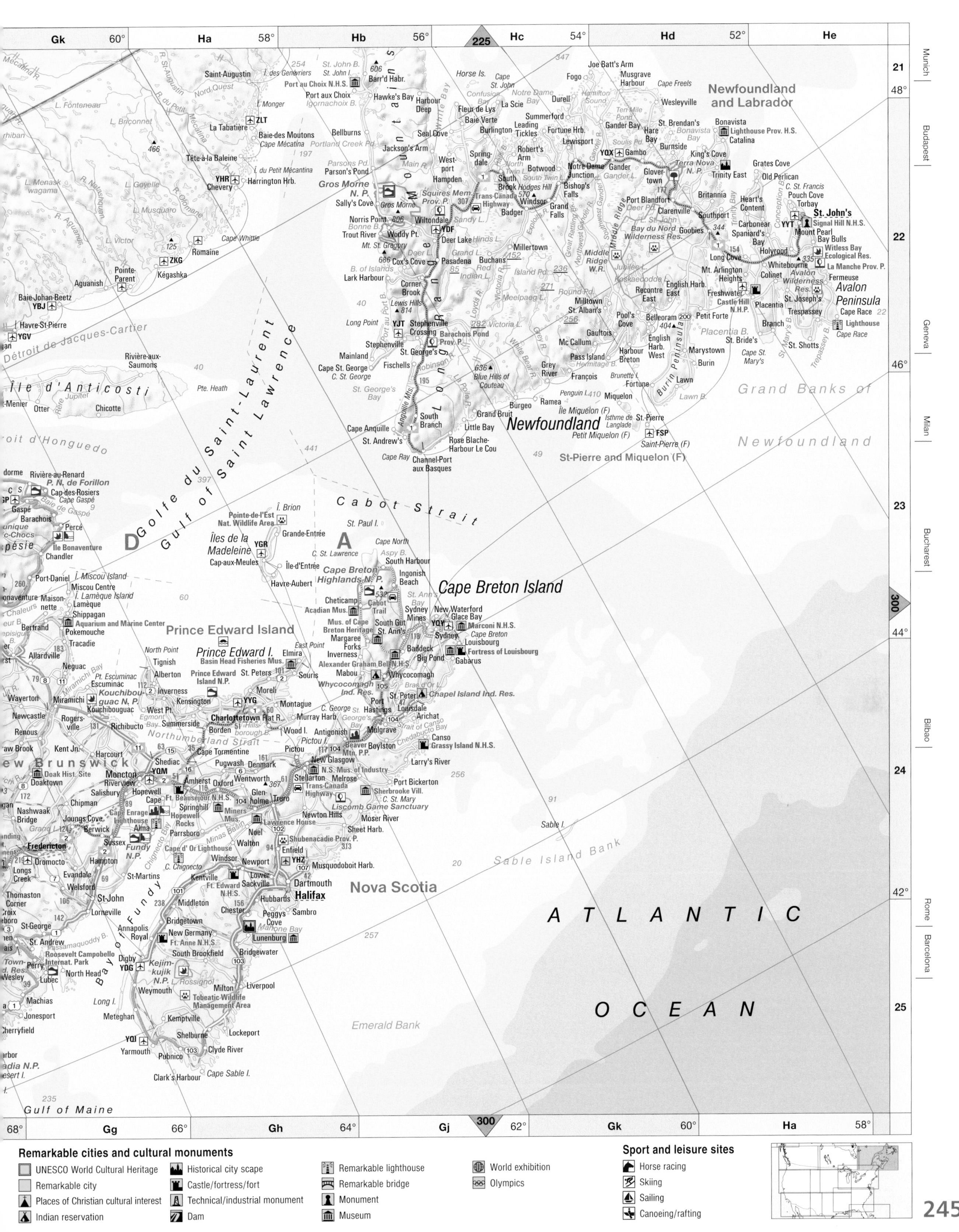

Gk 60° Ha 58° Hb 56° 225 Hc 54° Hd 52° He
Munich
Budapest
Geneva
Milan
Bucharest
Bilbao
Rome
Barcelona
21 22 23 24 25
48° 46° 44° 42°
Newfoundland and Labrador
Newfoundland
Avalon Peninsula
St. John's
Grand Banks of Newfoundland
St-Pierre and Miquelon (F)
Golfe du Saint-Laurent
Gulf of Saint Lawrence
Cabot Strait
Île d'Anticosti
Détroit de Jacques-Cartier
Îles de la Madeleine
Cape Breton Island
Prince Edward Island
Prince Edward I.
Charlottetown
New Brunswick
Fredericton
Moncton
St-John
Nova Scotia
Halifax
Sydney
Truro
Yarmouth
Bay of Fundy
Gulf of Maine
Sable I.
Sable Island Bank
Emerald Bank
ATLANTIC OCEAN
Long Range Mountains
Gros Morne N. P.
Corner Brook
Stephenville
Gander
Channel-Port aux Basques
Cape Race
68° Gg 66° Gh 64° Gj 300 62° Gk 60° Ha 58°
300
Remarkable cities and cultural monuments
UNESCO World Cultural Heritage
Remarkable city
Places of Christian cultural interest
Indian reservation
Historical city scape
Castle/fortress/fort
Technical/industrial monument
Dam
Remarkable lighthouse
Remarkable bridge
Monument
Museum
World exhibition
Olympics
Sport and leisure sites
Horse racing
Skiing
Sailing
Canoeing/rafting

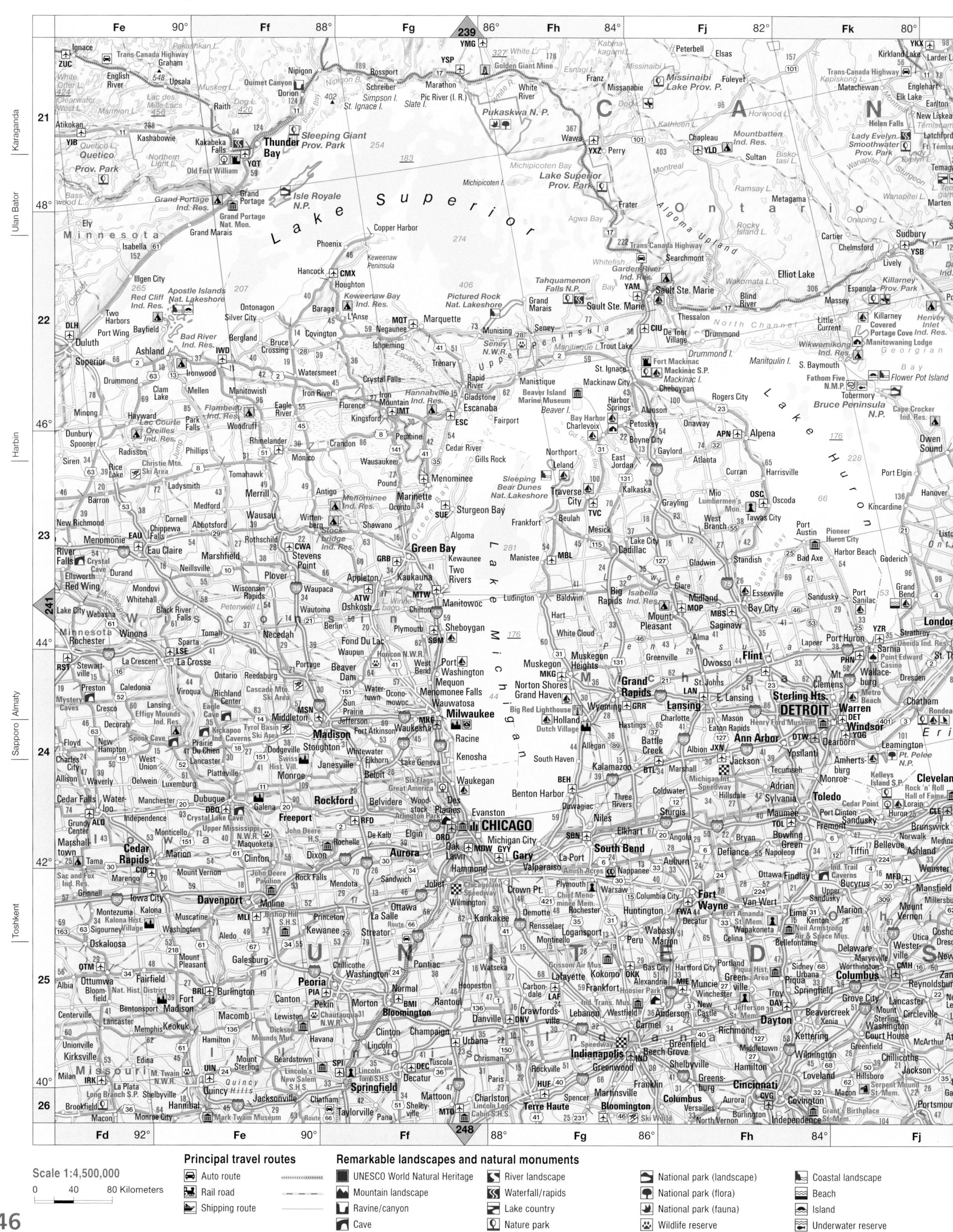

Scale 1:4,500,000

0   40   80 Kilometers

Principal travel routes
- Auto route
- Rail road
- Shipping route

Remarkable landscapes and natural monuments
- UNESCO World Natural Heritage
- Mountain landscape
- Ravine/canyon
- Cave
- River landscape
- Waterfall/rapids
- Lake country
- Nature park
- National park (landscape)
- National park (flora)
- National park (fauna)
- Wildlife reserve
- Coastal landscape
- Beach
- Island
- Underwater reserve

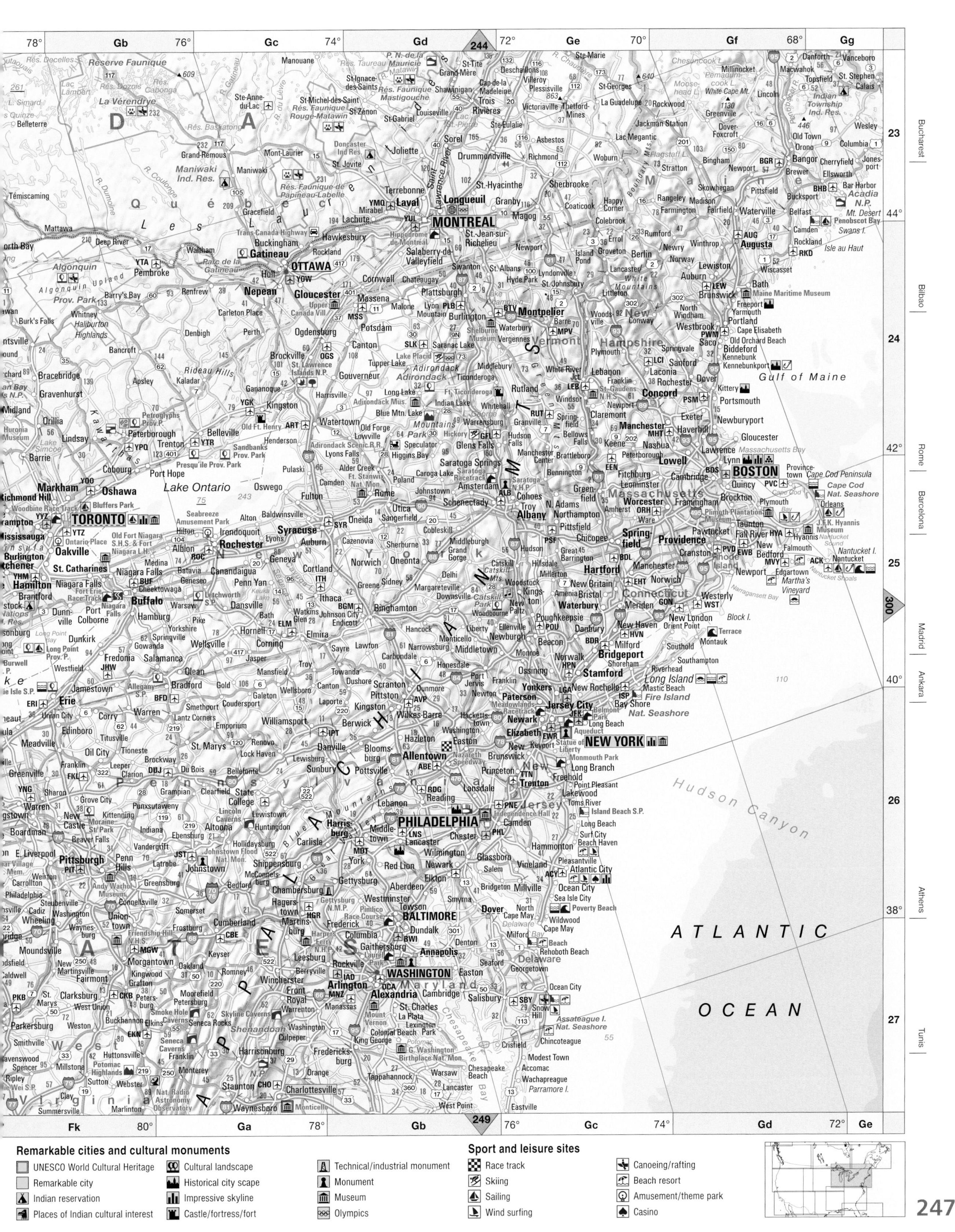

78° Gb 76° Gc 74° Gd 244 72° Ge 70° Gf 68° Gg
Fk 80° Ga 78° Gb 249 76° Gc 74° Gd 72° Ge
23
24
25
26
27
300
Bucharest
Bilbao
Rome
Barcelona
Madrid
Ankara
Athens
Tunis
MONTREAL
OTTAWA
TORONTO
BOSTON
NEW YORK
PHILADELPHIA
BALTIMORE
WASHINGTON
ATLANTIC
OCEAN
Lake Ontario
Gulf of Maine
Hudson Canyon
Remarkable cities and cultural monuments
UNESCO World Cultural Heritage
Remarkable city
Indian reservation
Places of Indian cultural interest
Cultural landscape
Historical city scape
Impressive skyline
Castle/fortress/fort
Technical/industrial monument
Monument
Museum
Olympics
Sport and leisure sites
Race track
Skiing
Sailing
Wind surfing
Canoeing/rafting
Beach resort
Amusement/theme park
Casino

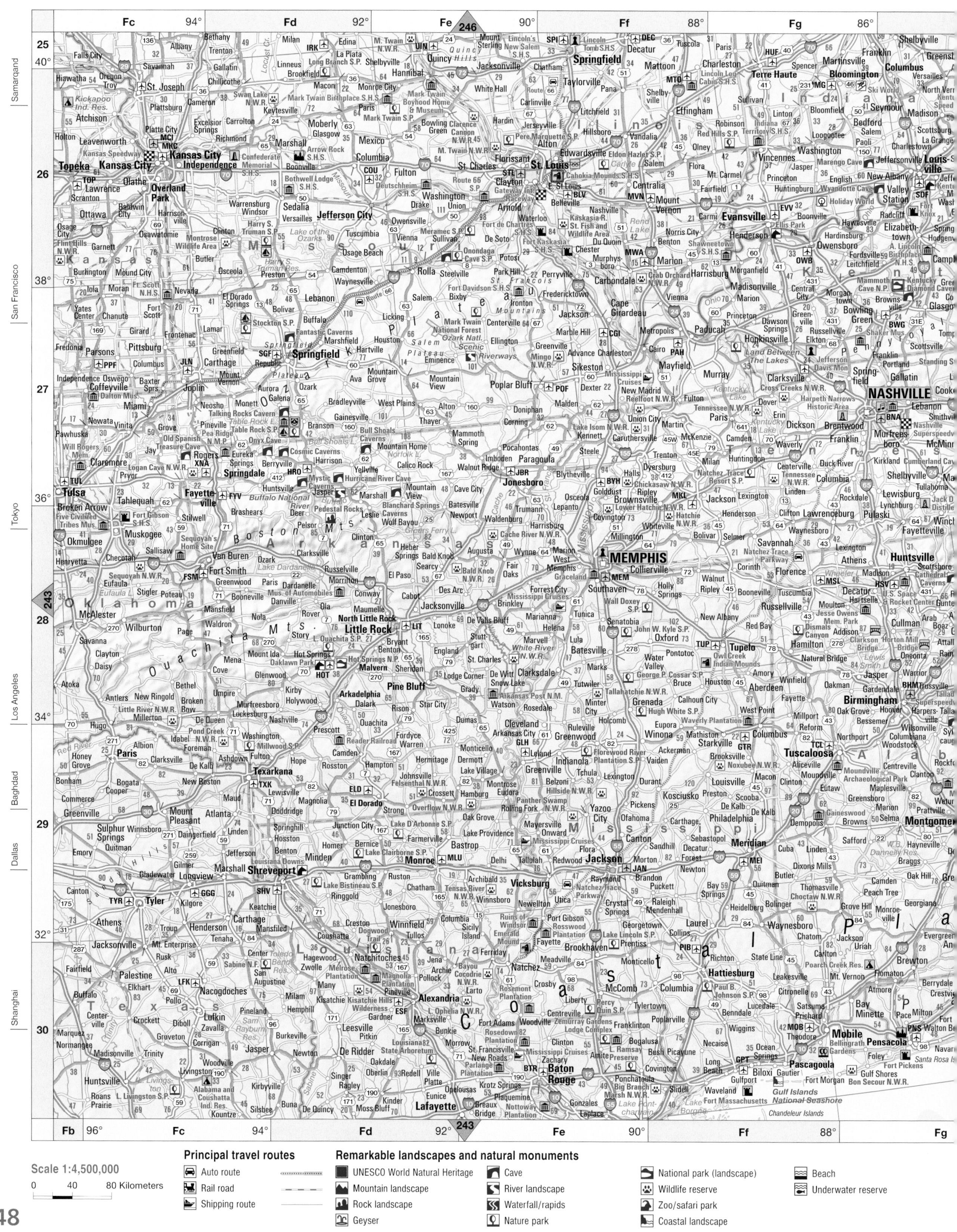

Scale 1:4,500,000

0   40   80 Kilometers

Principal travel routes

- Auto route
- Rail road
- Shipping route

Remarkable landscapes and natural monuments

- UNESCO World Natural Heritage
- Mountain landscape
- Rock landscape
- Geyser
- Cave
- River landscape
- Waterfall/rapids
- Nature park
- National park (landscape)
- Wildlife reserve
- Zoo/safari park
- Coastal landscape
- Beach
- Underwater reserve

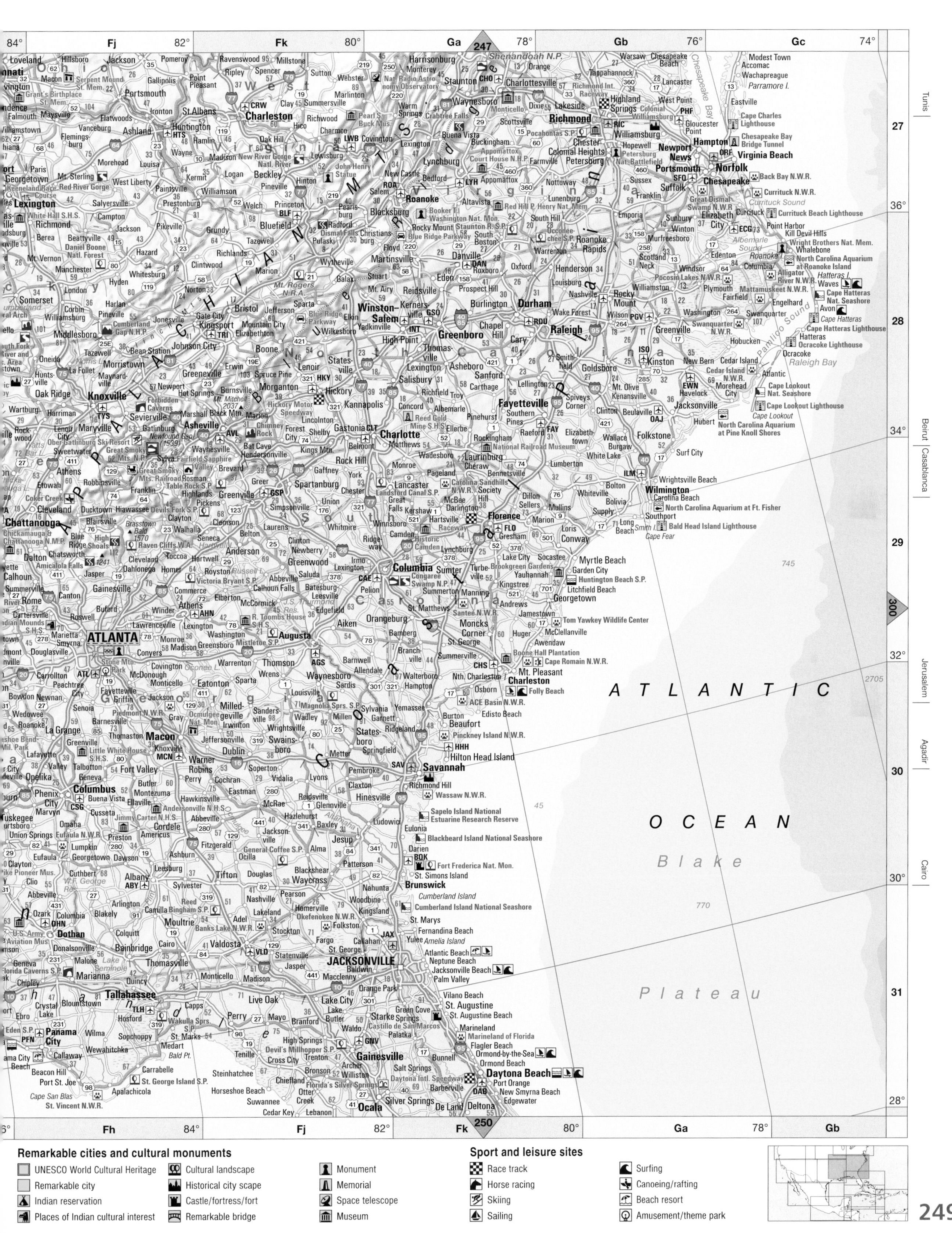

84° Fj 82° Fk 80° Ga 78° Gb 76° Gc 74°
247
250
300
27
28
29
30
31
36°
34°
32°
30°
28°
Fh 84° Fj 82° Fk 80° Ga 78° Gb
Tunis
Beirut
Casablanca
Jerusalem
Agadir
Cairo
ATLANTIC
OCEAN
Blake
Plateau
ATLANTA
JACKSONVILLE
Charleston
Richmond
Raleigh
Columbia
Charlotte
Savannah
Norfolk
Knoxville
Chattanooga
Tallahassee
Remarkable cities and cultural monuments
UNESCO World Cultural Heritage
Remarkable city
Indian reservation
Places of Indian cultural interest
Cultural landscape
Historical city scape
Castle/fortress/fort
Remarkable bridge
Monument
Memorial
Space telescope
Museum
Sport and leisure sites
Race track
Horse racing
Skiing
Sailing
Surfing
Canoeing/rafting
Beach resort
Amusement/theme park

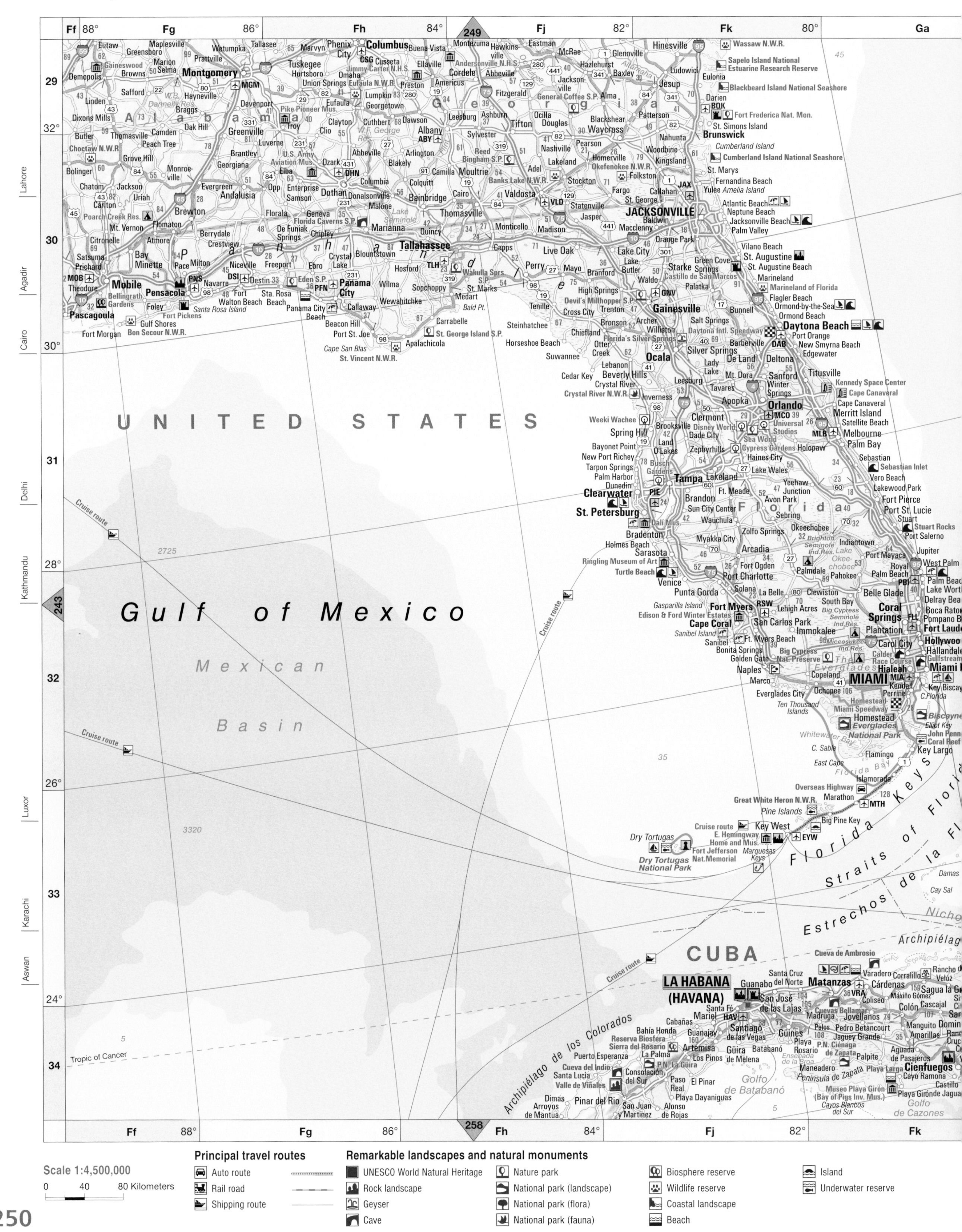

Scale 1:4,500,000

0   40   80 Kilometers

Principal travel routes
- Auto route
- Rail road
- Shipping route

Remarkable landscapes and natural monuments
- UNESCO World Natural Heritage
- Rock landscape
- Geyser
- Cave
- Nature park
- National park (landscape)
- National park (flora)
- National park (fauna)
- Biosphere reserve
- Wildlife reserve
- Coastal landscape
- Beach
- Island
- Underwater reserve

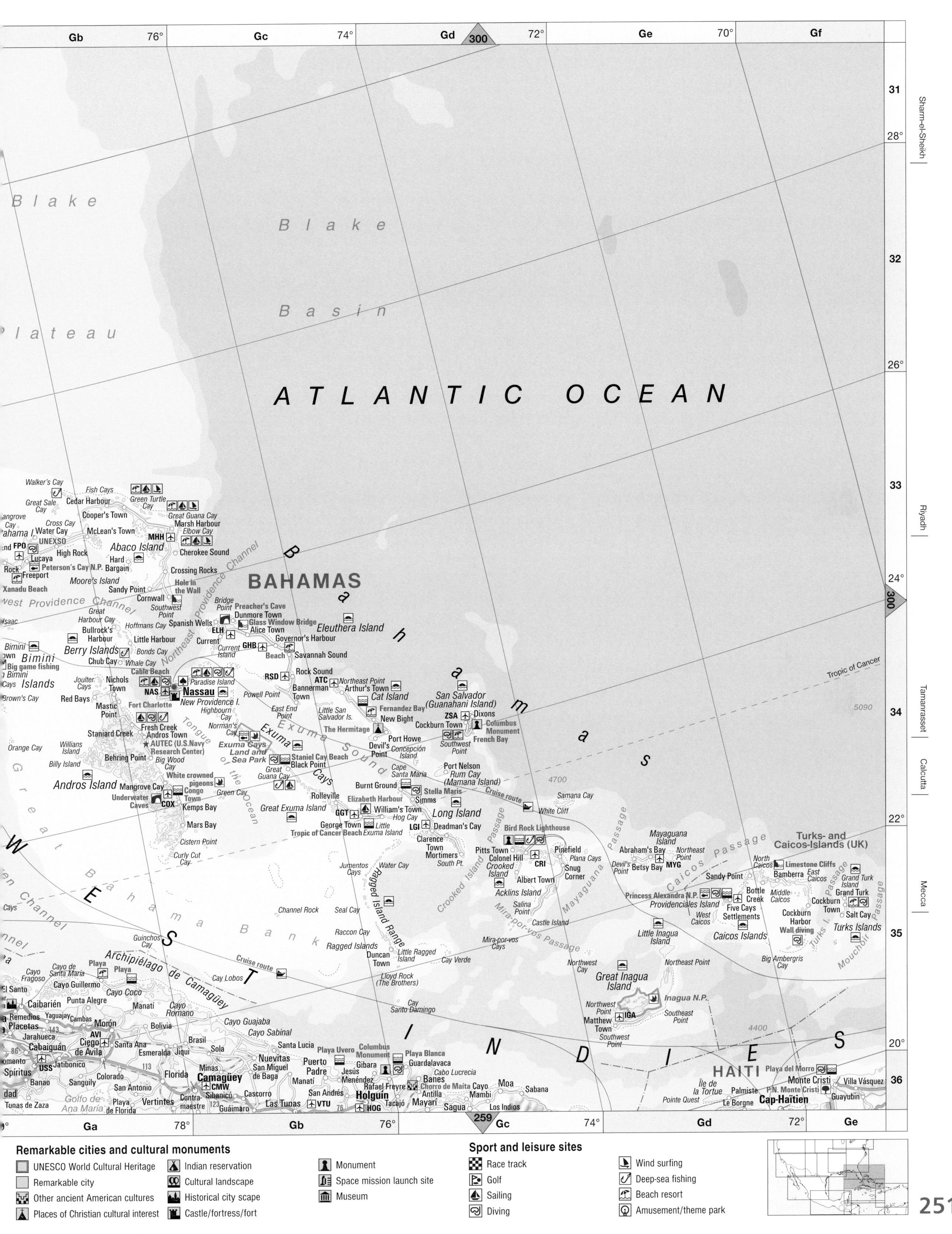

Remarkable cities and cultural monuments

- UNESCO World Cultural Heritage
- Remarkable city
- Other ancient American cultures
- Places of Christian cultural interest
- Indian reservation
- Cultural landscape
- Historical city scape
- Castle/fortress/fort
- Monument
- Space mission launch site
- Museum

Sport and leisure sites

- Race track
- Golf
- Sailing
- Diving
- Wind surfing
- Deep-sea fishing
- Beach resort
- Amusement/theme park

251

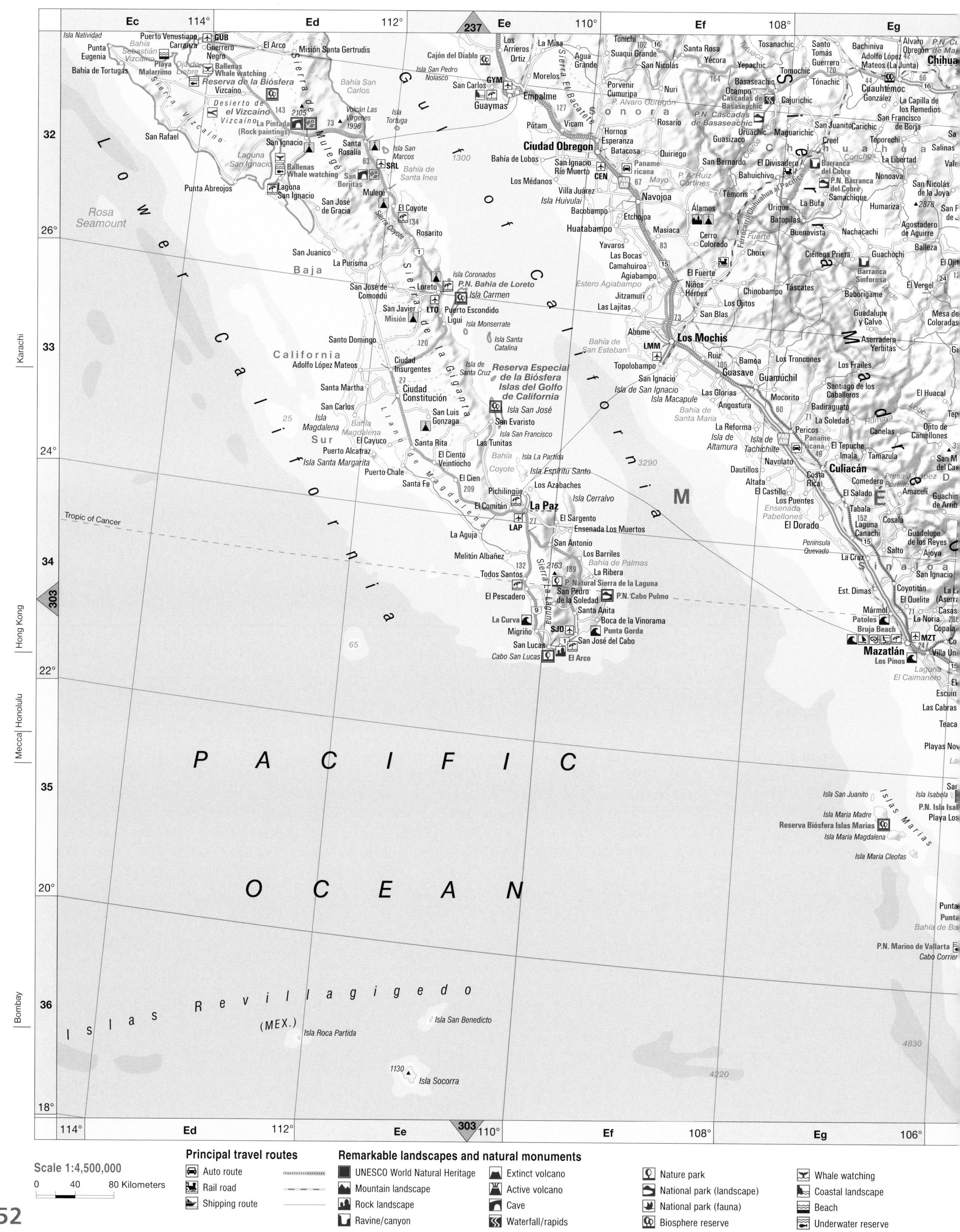

Scale 1:4,500,000

0   40   80 Kilometers

Principal travel routes
- Auto route
- Rail road
- Shipping route

Remarkable landscapes and natural monuments
- UNESCO World Natural Heritage
- Mountain landscape
- Rock landscape
- Ravine/canyon
- Extinct volcano
- Active volcano
- Cave
- Waterfall/rapids
- Nature park
- National park (landscape)
- National park (fauna)
- Biosphere reserve
- Whale watching
- Coastal landscape
- Beach
- Underwater reserve

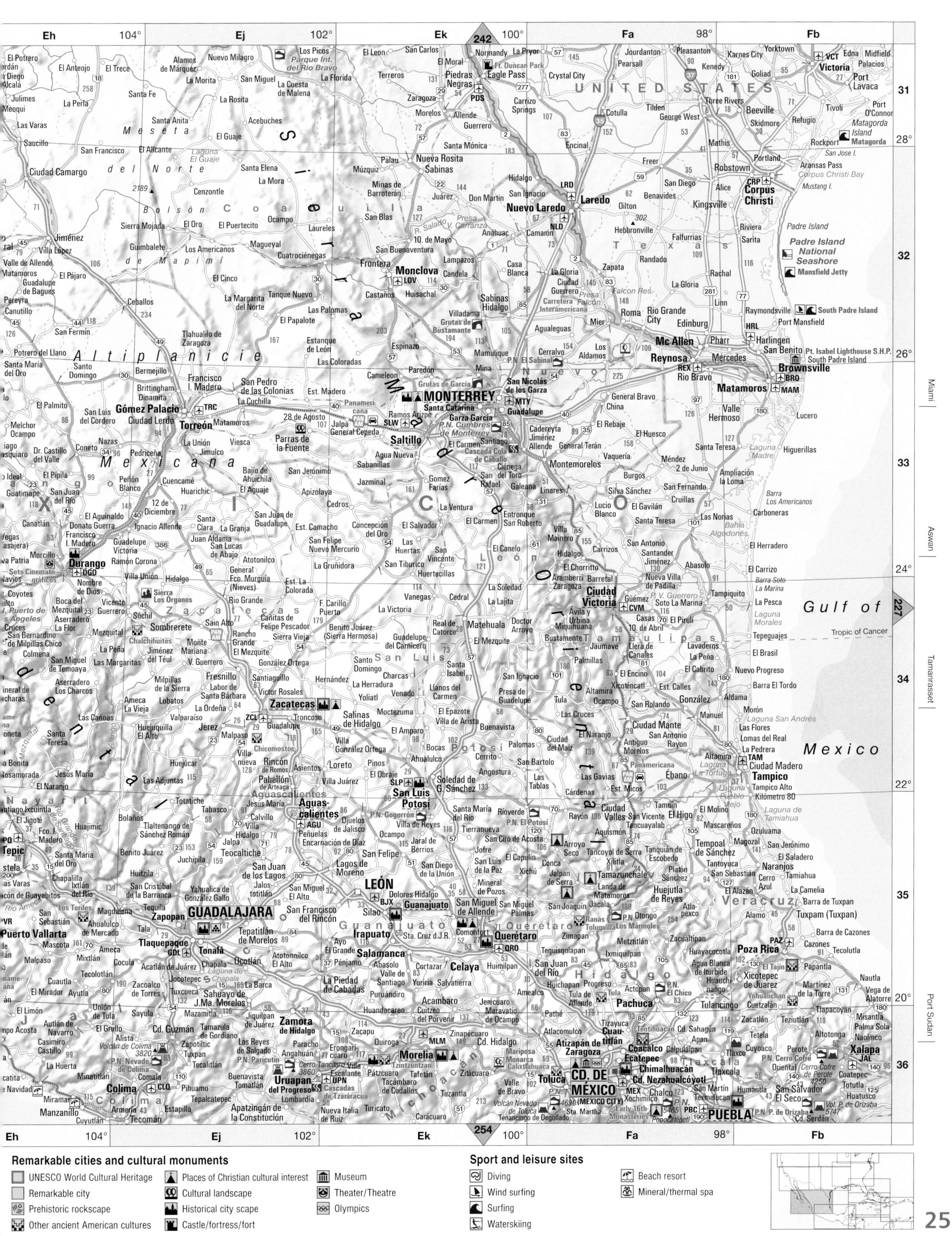
Remarkable cities and cultural monuments
UNESCO World Cultural Heritage
Remarkable city
Prehistoric rockscape
Other ancient American cultures
Places of Christian cultural interest
Cultural landscape
Historical city scape
Castle/fortress/fort
Museum
Theater/Theatre
Olympics
Sport and leisure sites
Diving
Wind surfing
Surfing
Waterskiing
Beach resort
Mineral/thermal spa
Gulf of Mexico
Tropic of Cancer
UNITED STATES
MONTERREY
CD. DE MÉXICO
GUADALAJARA
PUEBLA
Miami
Aswan
Tamanrasset
Port Sudan

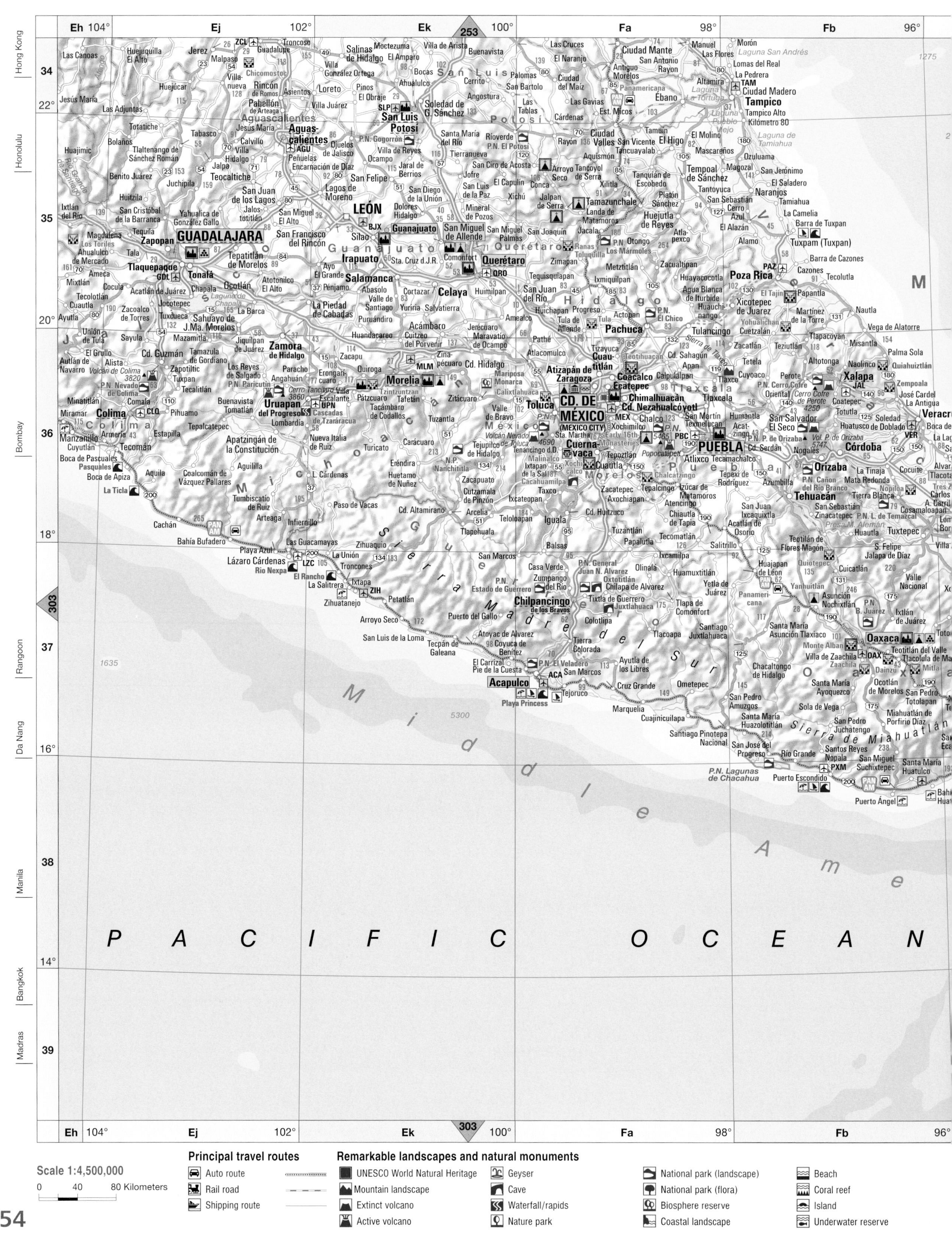

Scale 1:4,500,000

0   40   80 Kilometers

Principal travel routes
- Auto route
- Rail road
- Shipping route

Remarkable landscapes and natural monuments
- UNESCO World Natural Heritage
- Mountain landscape
- Extinct volcano
- Active volcano
- Geyser
- Cave
- Waterfall/rapids
- Nature park
- National park (landscape)
- National park (flora)
- Biosphere reserve
- Coastal landscape
- Beach
- Coral reef
- Island
- Underwater reserve

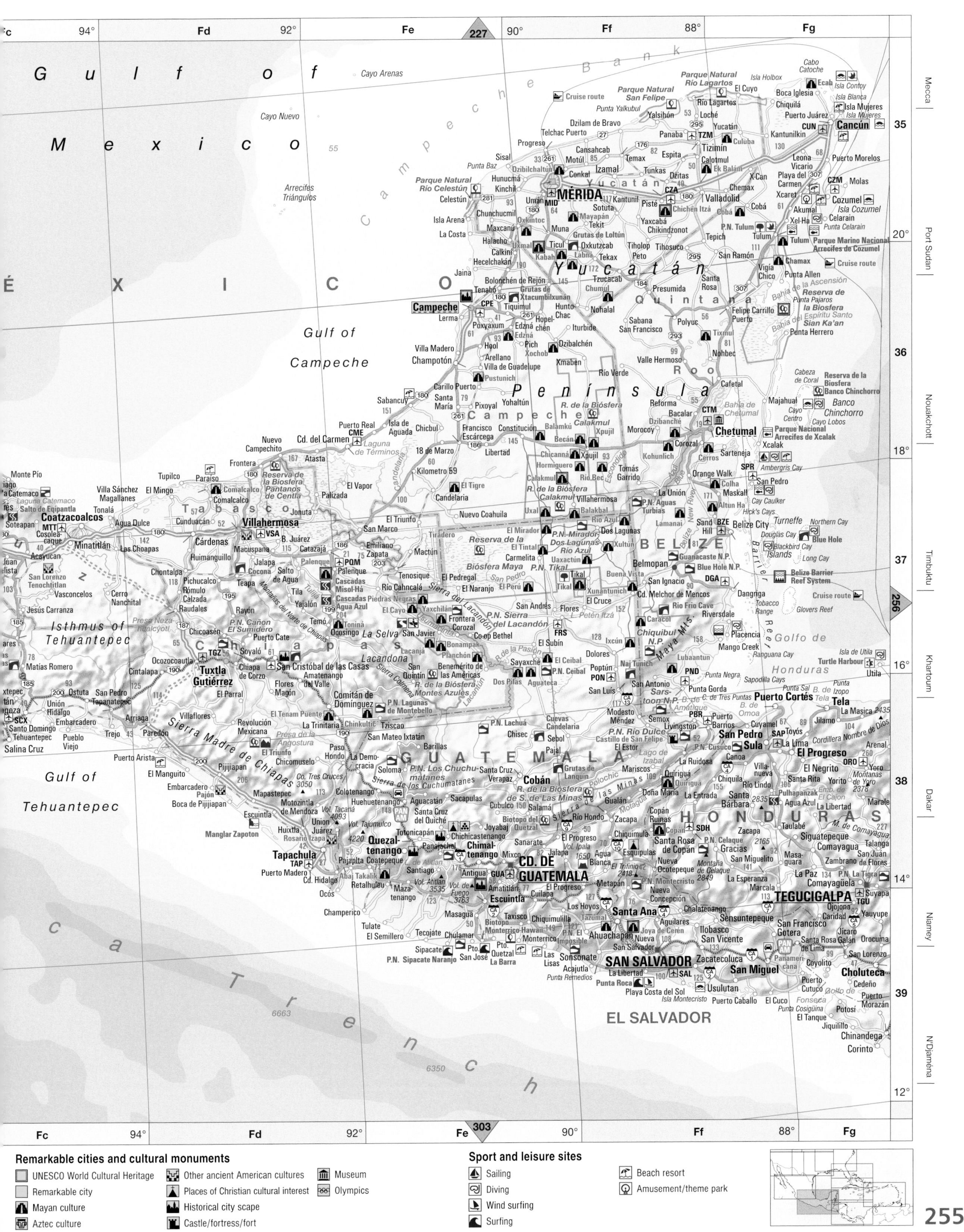

Remarkable cities and cultural monuments

- ☐ UNESCO World Cultural Heritage
- ☐ Remarkable city
- ▲ Mayan culture
- ⊠ Aztec culture
- ✠ Other ancient American cultures
- ▲ Places of Christian cultural interest
- ⛰ Historical city scape
- ⛫ Castle/fortress/fort
- 🏛 Museum
- ⚜ Olympics

Sport and leisure sites

- ⛵ Sailing
- ⊠ Diving
- 🏄 Wind surfing
- 🏄 Surfing
- 🏖 Beach resort
- ☉ Amusement/theme park

255

Honduras, El Salvador, Nicaragua, Costa Rica, Panama

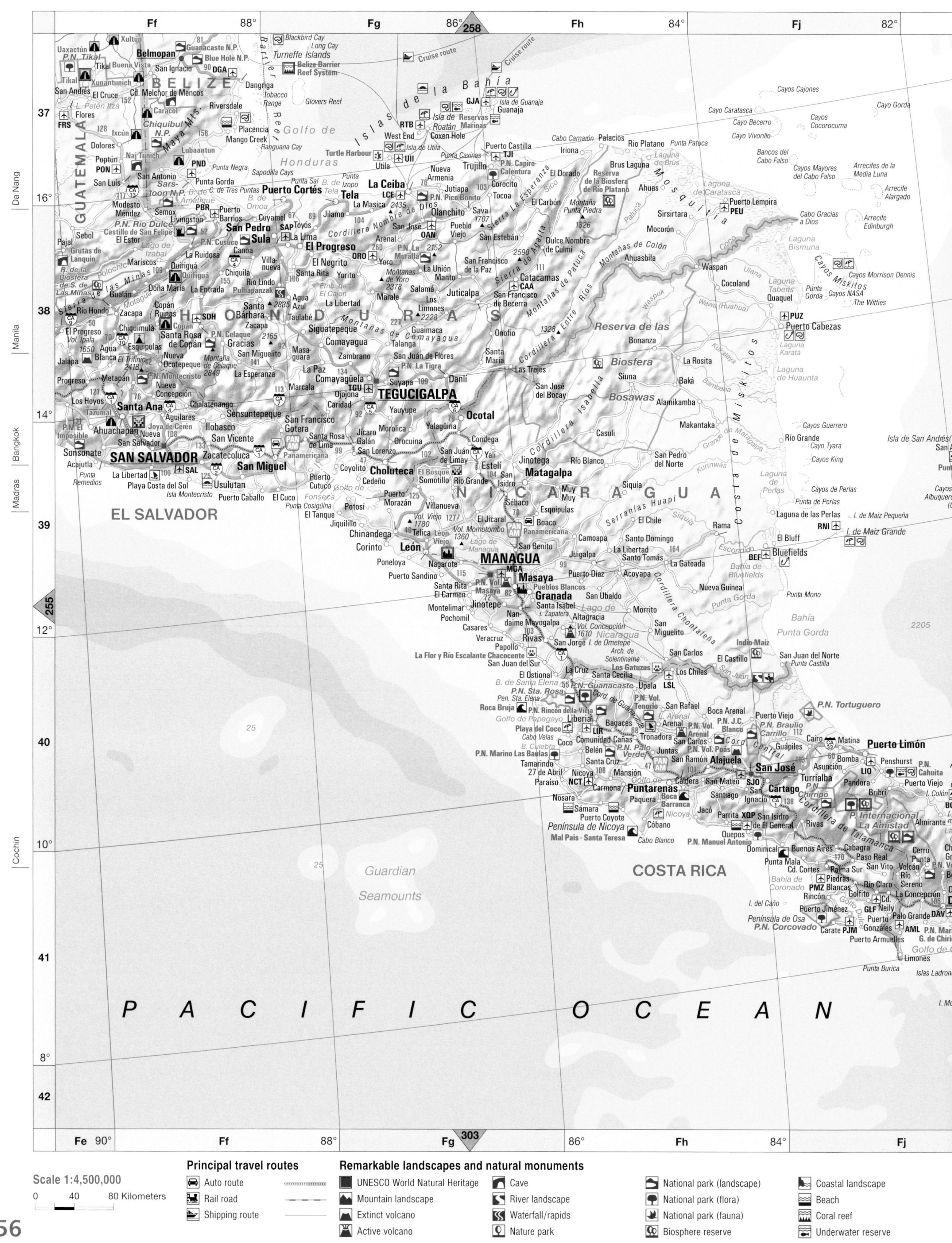

Scale 1:4,500,000

0   40   80 Kilometers

Principal travel routes

- Auto route
- Rail road
- Shipping route
- Cruise route
- Mountain landscape
- Extinct volcano
- Active volcano

Remarkable landscapes and natural monuments

- UNESCO World Natural Heritage
- Mountain landscape
- Extinct volcano
- Active volcano
- Cave
- River landscape
- Waterfall/rapids
- Nature park
- National park (landscape)
- National park (flora)
- National park (fauna)
- Biosphere reserve
- Coastal landscape
- Beach
- Coral reef
- Underwater reserve

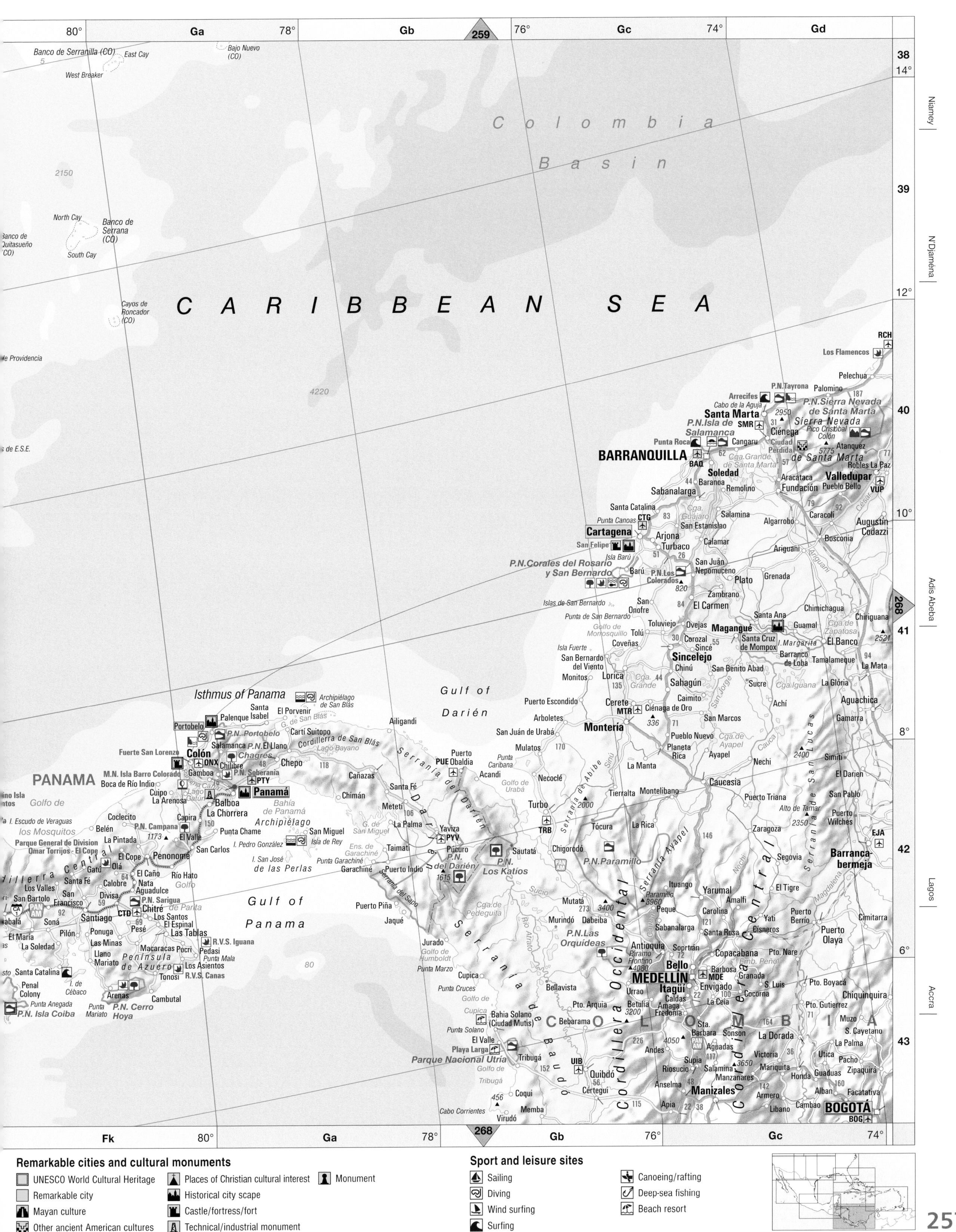

Remarkable cities and cultural monuments

- ⬚ UNESCO World Cultural Heritage
- ⬚ Remarkable city
- ⬛ Mayan culture
- ⬛ Other ancient American cultures
- ▲ Places of Christian cultural interest
- ⬛ Historical city scape
- ⬛ Castle/fortress/fort
- Ⓐ Technical/industrial monument
- ♟ Monument

Sport and leisure sites

- ⛵ Sailing
- ▨ Diving
- ⛵ Wind surfing
- 🌊 Surfing
- ✈ Canoeing/rafting
- ◪ Deep-sea fishing
- ⛱ Beach resort

257

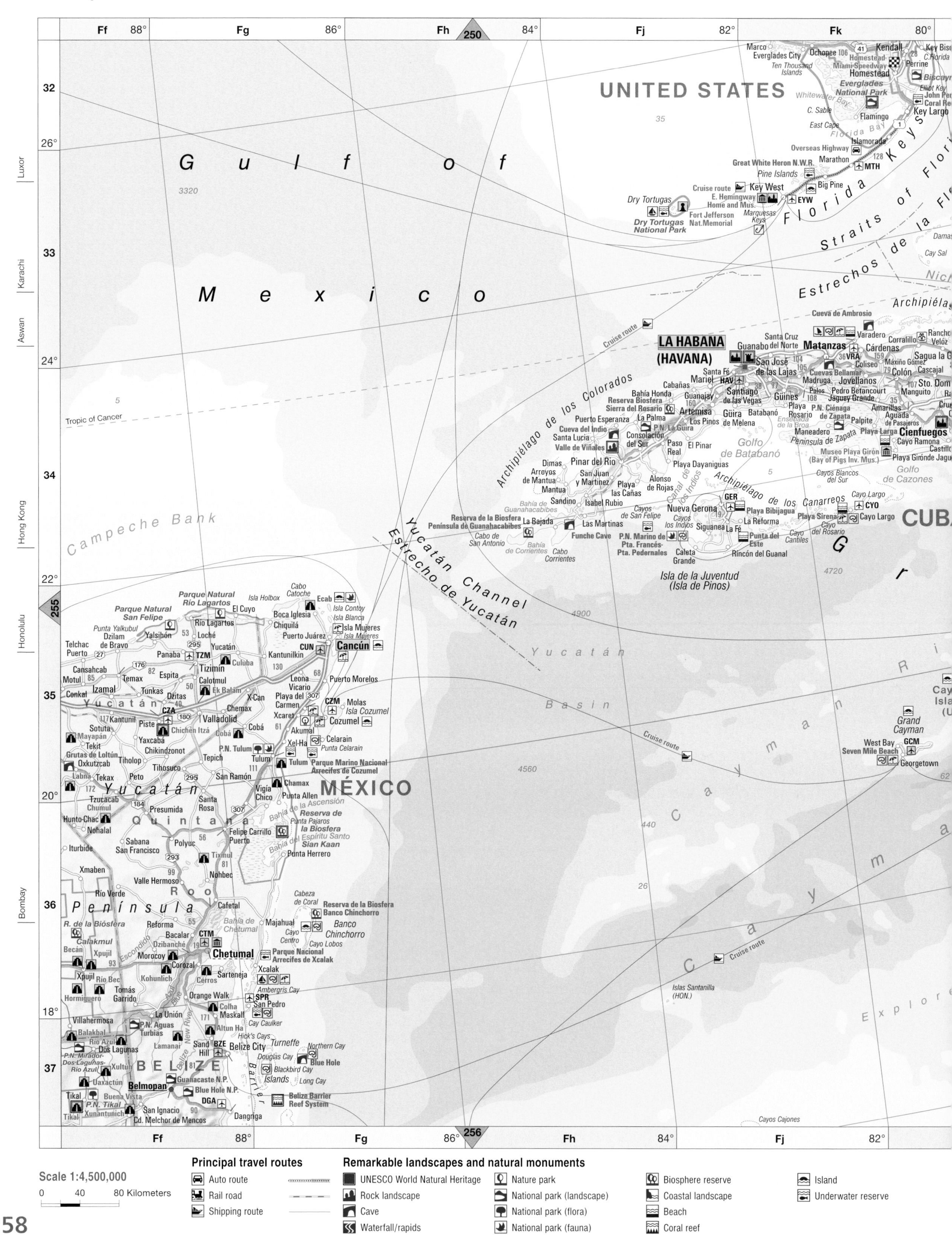

Scale 1:4,500,000

0   40   80 Kilometers

Principal travel routes
- Auto route
- Rail road
- Shipping route

Remarkable landscapes and natural monuments
- UNESCO World Natural Heritage
- Rock landscape
- Cave
- Waterfall/rapids
- Nature park
- National park (landscape)
- National park (flora)
- National park (fauna)
- Biosphere reserve
- Coastal landscape
- Beach
- Coral reef
- Island
- Underwater reserve

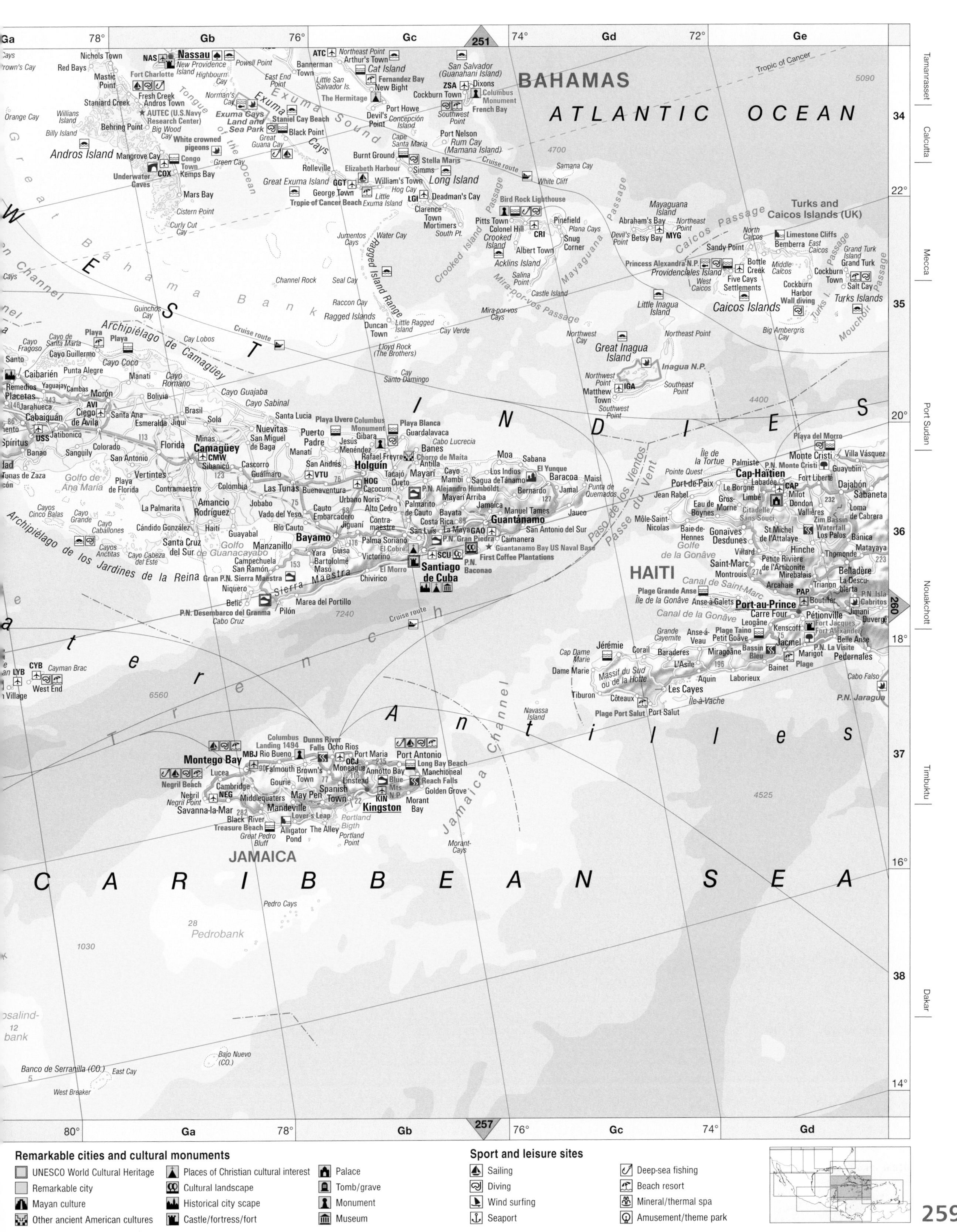

BAHAMAS

ATLANTIC OCEAN

WEST INDIES

Greater Antilles

CARIBBEAN SEA

HAITI

JAMAICA

Remarkable cities and cultural monuments

- ▢ UNESCO World Cultural Heritage
- ▢ Remarkable city
- ▲ Mayan culture
- ▣ Other ancient American cultures
- ▲ Places of Christian cultural interest
- ✿ Cultural landscape
- ▦ Historical city scape
- ▣ Castle/fortress/fort
- ▥ Palace
- ▥ Tomb/grave
- ▯ Monument
- ▥ Museum

Sport and leisure sites

- ⛵ Sailing
- ▧ Diving
- ▽ Wind surfing
- ⚓ Seaport
- ▱ Deep-sea fishing
- ▱ Beach resort
- ▨ Mineral/thermal spa
- ◉ Amusement/theme park

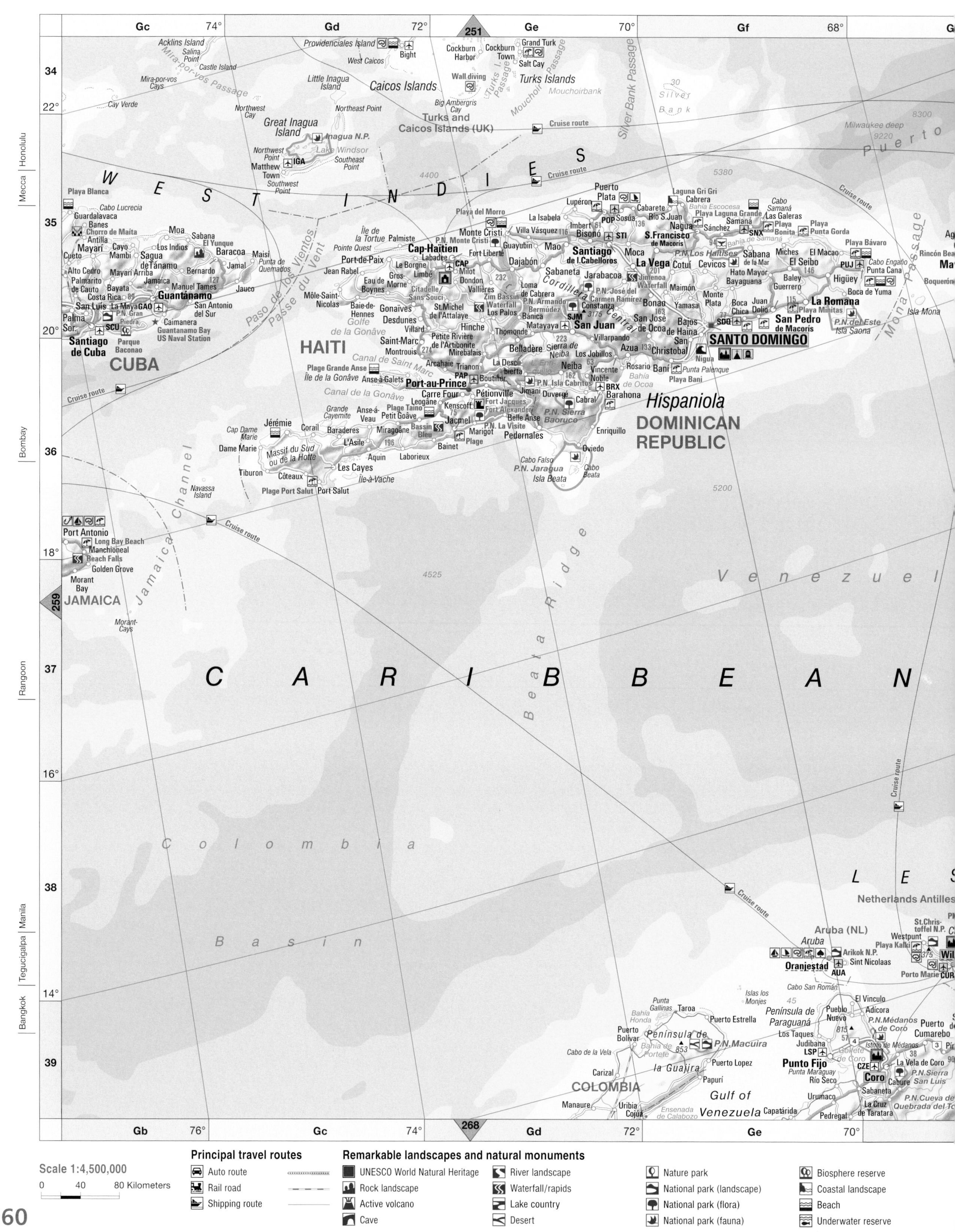

Scale 1:4,500,000

0   40   80 Kilometers

Principal travel routes

- 🚗 Auto route
- 🚂 Rail road
- ⚓ Shipping route

Remarkable landscapes and natural monuments

- ⬛ UNESCO World Natural Heritage
- Rock landscape
- Active volcano
- Cave
- River landscape
- Waterfall/rapids
- Lake country
- Desert
- Nature park
- National park (landscape)
- National park (flora)
- National park (fauna)
- Biosphere reserve
- Coastal landscape
- Beach
- Underwater reserve

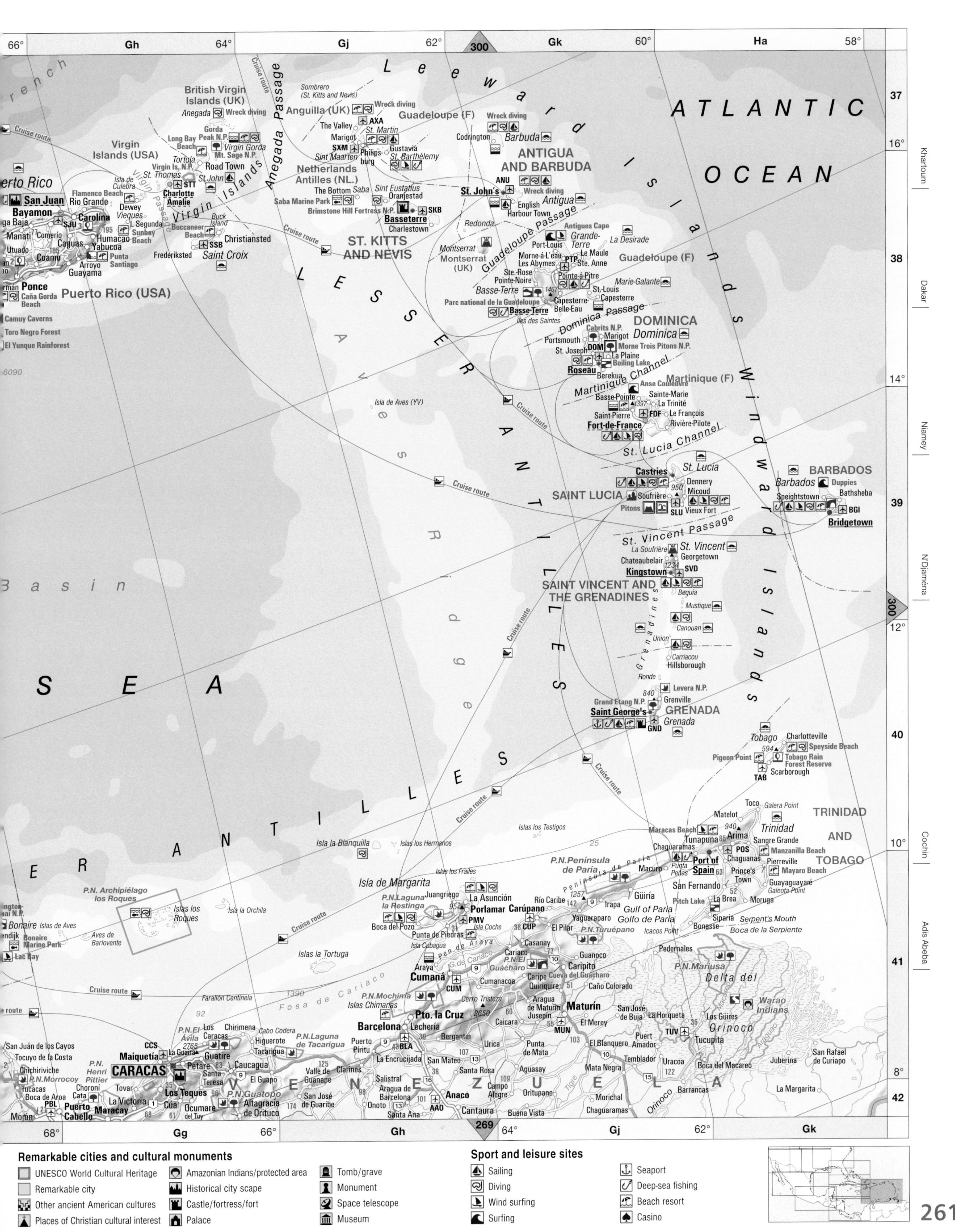

66° Gh 64° Gj 62° 300 Gk 60° Ha 58°
37
38
39
40
41
42
16°
14°
12°
10°
8°
Khartoum
Dakar
Niamey
N'Djaména
Cochin
Adis Abeba
ATLANTIC OCEAN
Leeward Islands
Windward Islands
LESSER ANTILLES
Aves Ridge
Basin
SEA
Anegada Passage
Virgin Islands
Virgin Passage
Guadeloupe Passage
Dominica Passage
Martinique Channel
St. Lucia Channel
St. Vincent Passage
Cruise route
British Virgin Islands (UK)
Anegada
Wreck diving
Virgin Islands (USA)
Gorda Peak N.P.
Virgin Gorda
Mt. Sage N.P.
Long Bay Beach
Tortola
Road Town
Virgin Is. N.P.
St. Thomas
St. John
Isla de Culebra
STT
Charlotte Amalie
Buck Island
Buccaneer Beach
Christiansted
Frederiksted
Saint Croix
SSB
Puerto Rico
San Juan
Bayamon
Flamenco Beach
Rio Grande
Carolina
SJU
Dewey
Vieques
I. Segunda
Sunbay Beach
Manatí
Comerío
Caguas
Humacao
Yabucoa
Utuado
Coamo
Punta Santiago
Arroyo
Guayama
Ponce
Caña Gorda Beach
Puerto Rico (USA)
Camuy Caverns
Toro Negro Forest
El Yunque Rainforest
6090
Sombrero (St. Kitts and Nevis)
Anguilla (UK)
The Valley
AXA
St. Martin
Marigot
SXM
Sint Maarten
Philipsburg
Gustavia
St. Barthélemy
Guadeloupe (F)
Netherlands Antilles (NL.)
The Bottom
Saba
Sint Eustatius
Oranjestad
Saba Marine Park
Brimstone Hill Fortress N.P.
SKB
Basseterre
Charlestown
ST. KITTS AND NEVIS
Codrington
Barbuda
ANTIGUA AND BARBUDA
ANU
St. John's
English Harbour Town
Antigua
Redonda
Montserrat
Montserrat (UK)
Antigues Cape
Grande-Terre
Port-Louis
La Desirade
Morne-à-L'eau
PTP
Le Maule
Les Abymes
Ste. Anne
Guadeloupe (F)
Ste.-Rose
Pointe-Noire
Pointe-à-Pitre
Marie-Galante
Basse-Terre
St.-Louis
Capesterre
Parc national de la Guadeloupe
Capesterre-Belle-Eau
Îles des Saintes
1467
DOMINICA
Cabrits N.P.
Marigot
Dominica
Portsmouth
DOM
Morne Trois Pitons N.P.
St. Joseph
La Plaine
Boiling Lake
Roseau
Berekua
Martinique (F)
Anse Couleuvre
Sainte-Marie
Basse-Pointe
1397
La Trinité
Saint-Pierre
FDF
Le François
Fort-de-France
Rivière-Pilote
Isla de Aves (YV)
Castries
St. Lucia
Dennery
Micoud
SAINT LUCIA
Soufrière
950
Pitons
SLU
Vieux Fort
BARBADOS
Barbados
Duppies
Bathsheba
Speightstown
BGI
Bridgetown
St. Vincent
La Soufrière
Georgetown
Chateaubelair
1234
Kingstown
SVD
SAINT VINCENT AND THE GRENADINES
Bequia
Mustique
Canouan
Union
Carriacou
Hillsborough
Grenadines
Ronde
Levera N.P.
840
Grand Etang N.P.
Grenville
Saint George's
GRENADA
Grenada
GND
Tobago
Charlotteville
Speyside Beach
594
Pigeon Point
Tobago Rain Forest Reserve
TAB
Scarborough
Toco
Galera Point
Matelot
TRINIDAD AND TOBAGO
Maracas Beach
940
Trinidad
Tunapuna
Arima
Sangre Grande
Chaguaramas
POS
Port of Spain
Manzanilla Beach
Chaguanas
Pierreville
Mayaro Beach
Prince's Town
San Fernando
Guayaguayare
Galeota Point
Pitch Lake
La Brea
Moruga
Siparia
Serpent's Mouth
Bonasse
Boca de la Serpiente
Islas los Testigos
Isla la Blanquilla
Islas los Hermanos
Islas los Frailes
P.N. Peninsula de Paria
Peninsula de Paria
Macuro
Punta Peñas
Isla de Margarita
Juangriego
La Asunción
P.N. Laguna la Restinga
957
Porlamar
Carúpano
PMV
Río Caribe
1257
Güiria
Irapa
Gulf of Paria
Golfo de Paria
Yaguaraparo
Boca del Pozo
Isla Coche
CUP
El Pilar
P.N. Turuépano
Icacos Point
Punta de Piedras
Isla Cubagua
Pen. de Araya
Casanay
Cariaco
Pedernales
P.N. Archipiélago los Roques
Islas los Roques
Isla la Orchila
Bonaire
Islas de Aves
Aves de Barlovente
Bonaire Marine Park
Lac Bay
Islas la Tortuga
Araya
Cumaná
CUM
G. de Cariaco
P.N. El Guácharo
Cumanacoa
Caripito
Guanoco
Caripe
Cueva del Guácharo
Quiriquire
Caño Colorado
P.N. Mariusa
Delta del Orinoco
Warao Indians
Farallón Centinela
1390
Fosa de Cariaco
P.N. Mochima
Islas Chimanas
Cerro Tristeza
2650
Aragua de Maturín
Maturín
Jusepín
MUN
El Merey
San José de Buja
La Horqueta
Los Güires
TUV
Tucupita
Barcelona
Lechería
Pto. la Cruz
Caicara
92
P.N. El Ávila
2765
Los Caracas
Chirimena
Cabo Codera
Higuerote
Tacarigua
P.N. Laguna de Tacarigua
Puerto Píritu
BLA
Bergantín
Urica
Punta de Mata
El Blanquero
Puert Amador
CCS
Maiquetía
La Guaira
Guatire
CARACAS
Petare
Caucagua
Santa Teresa
El Guapo
Los Teques
Tovar
Cúa
Ocumare del Tuy
P.N. Guatopo
Altagracia de Orituco
La Victoria
Maracay
Puerto Cabello
PBL
Morón
Cata
Choroní
P.N. Henri Pittier
Boca de Aroa
Tucacas
Chichiriviche
P.N. Morrocoy
Tocuyo de la Costa
San Juán de los Cayos
Valle de Guanape
Clarines
San José de Guaribe
Salistral
Aragua de Barcelona
Onoto
La Encrucijada
San Mateo
Santa Rosa
Santa Ana
Anaco
AAO
Cantaura
Campo Alegre
Oritupano
Buena Vista
Aguasay
Mata Negra
Temblador
Uracoa
Boca del Macareo
Juberina
San Rafael de Curiapo
La Margarita
Barrancas
Morichal
Chaguaramas
Orinoco
Tigre
VENEZUELA
68° Gg 66° Gh 269 64° Gj 62° Gk
Remarkable cities and cultural monuments
UNESCO World Cultural Heritage
Remarkable city
Other ancient American cultures
Places of Christian cultural interest
Amazonian Indians/protected area
Historical city scape
Castle/fortress/fort
Palace
Tomb/grave
Monument
Space telescope
Museum
Sport and leisure sites
Sailing
Diving
Wind surfing
Surfing
Seaport
Deep-sea fishing
Beach resort
Casino

South America – physical map

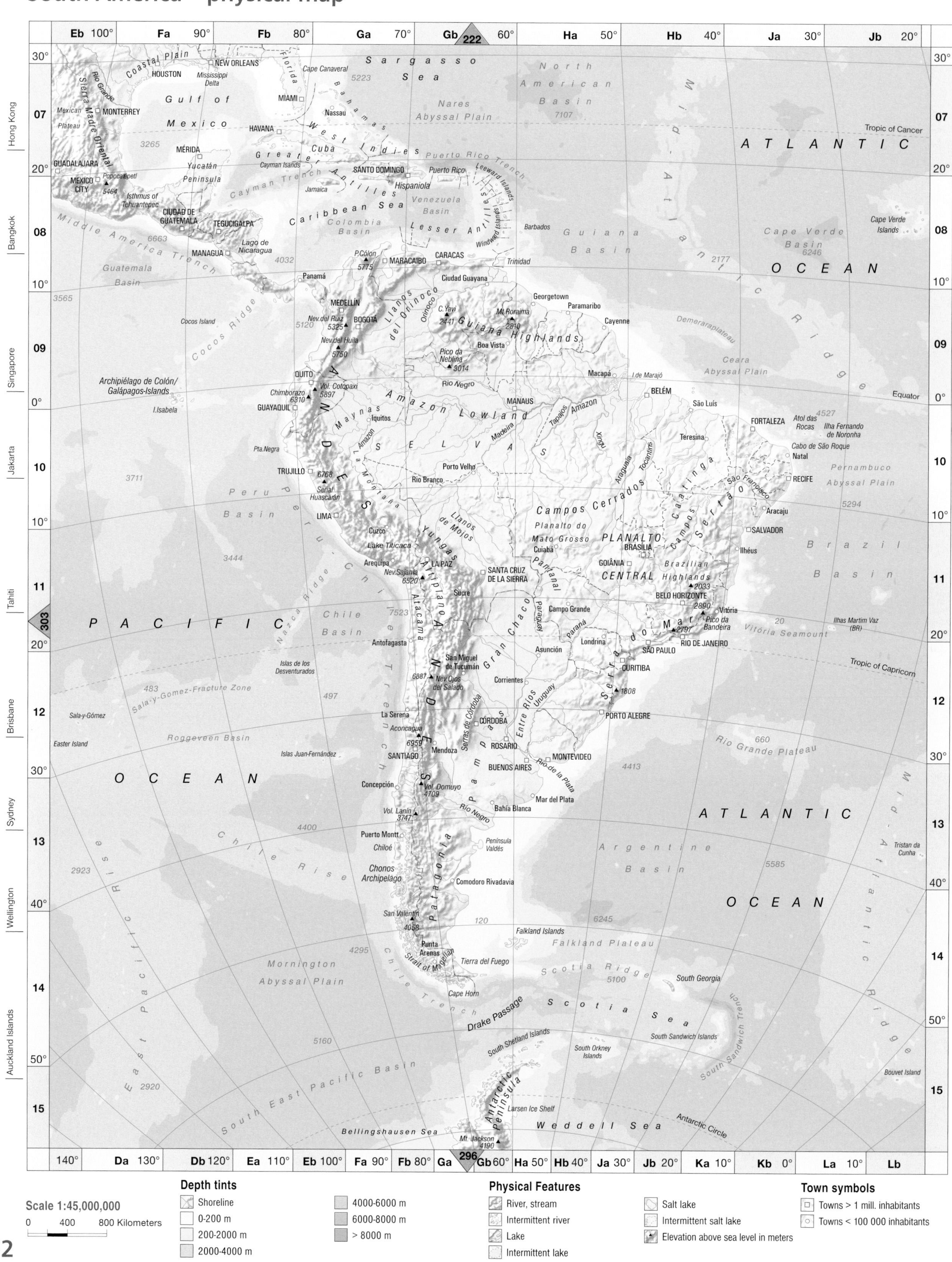

Scale 1:45,000,000

0   400   800 Kilometers

Depth tints
- Shoreline
- 0–200 m
- 200–2000 m
- 2000–4000 m
- 4000–6000 m
- 6000–8000 m
- > 8000 m

Physical Features
- River, stream
- Intermittent river
- Lake
- Intermittent lake
- Salt lake
- Intermittent salt lake
- Elevation above sea level in meters

Town symbols
- Towns > 1 mill. inhabitants
- Towns < 100 000 inhabitants

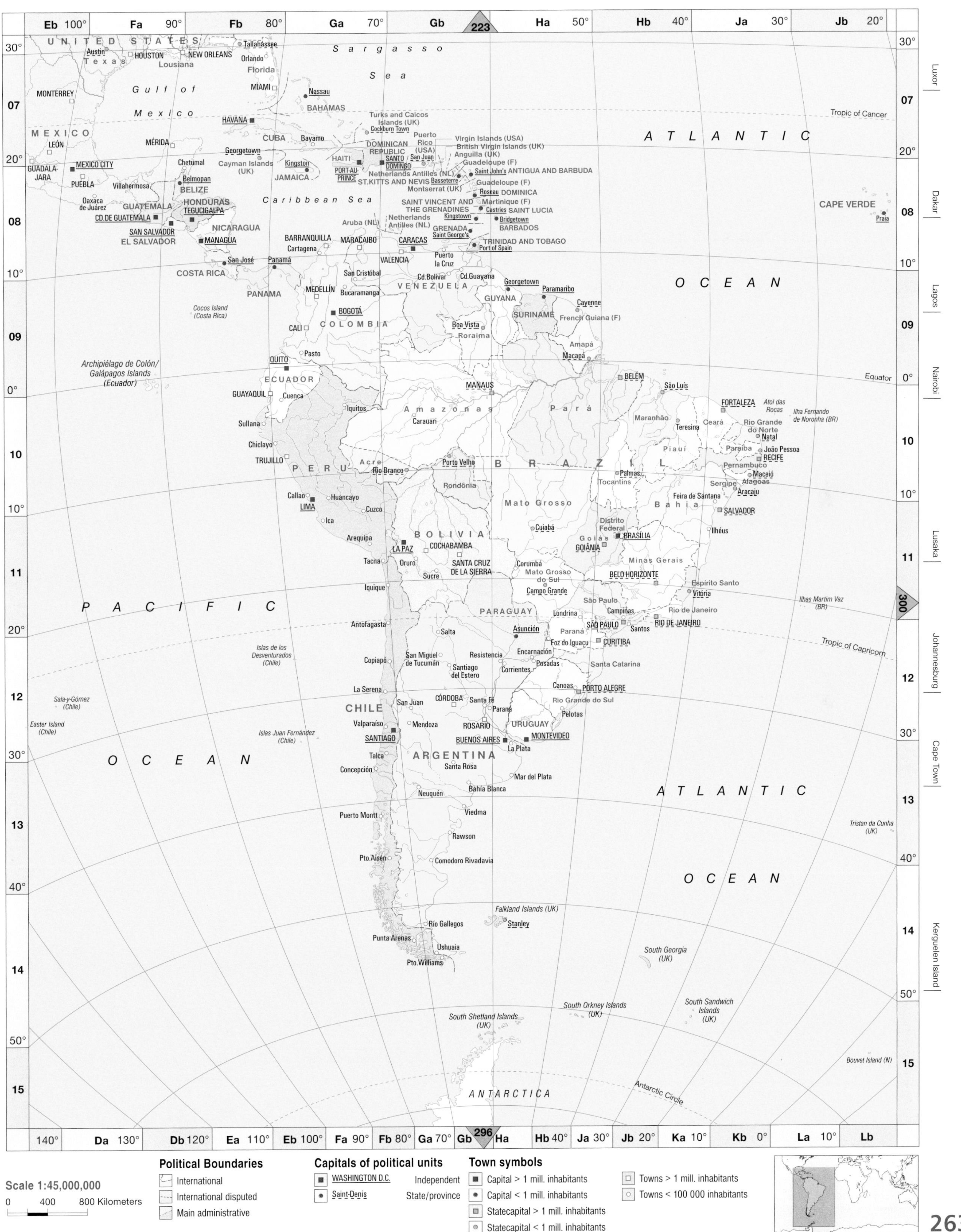

Scale 1:45,000,000

0   400   800 Kilometers

Political Boundaries
- International
- International disputed
- Main administrative

Capitals of political units
- ■ WASHINGTON D.C.   Independent
- ⊙ Saint-Denis   State/province

Town symbols
- ■ Capital > 1 mill. inhabitants
- ● Capital < 1 mill. inhabitants
- □ Statecapital > 1 mill. inhabitants
- ⊙ Statecapital < 1 mill. inhabitants
- □ Towns > 1 mill. inhabitants
- ○ Towns < 100 000 inhabitants

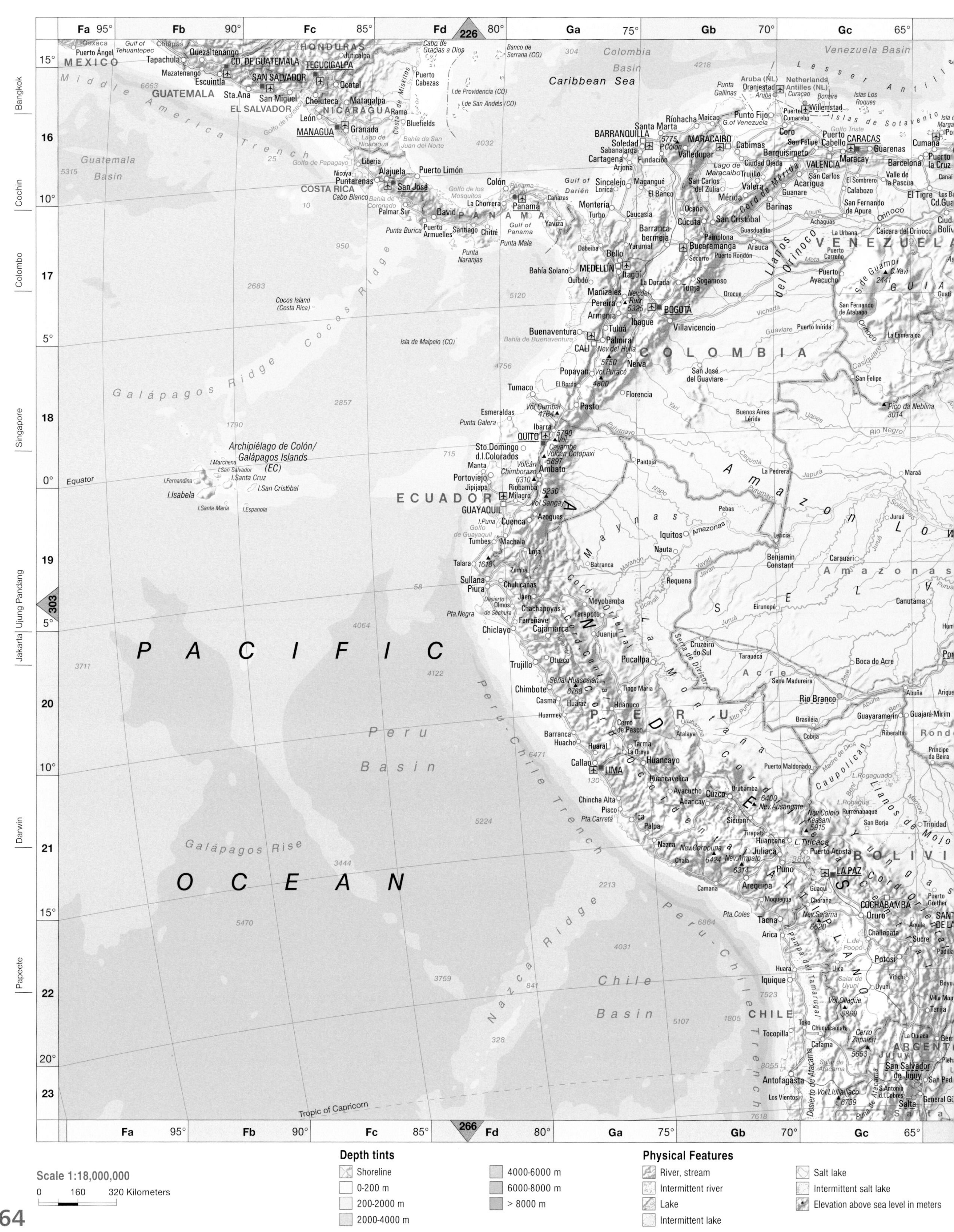

Bangkok | Cochin | Colombo | Singapore | Jakarta | Ujung Pandang | Darwin | Papeete

MEXICO

HONDURAS

Caribbean Sea

GUATEMALA

EL SALVADOR   NICARAGUA

MANAGUA

COSTA RICA

PANAMA

COLOMBIA

VENEZUELA

GUIA

P A C I F I C

Peru Basin

O C E A N

Galápagos Rise

Archipiélago de Colón/
Galápagos Islands
(EC)

Equator

E C U A D O R

GUAYAQUIL

QUITO

P E R U

LIMA

BOLIVI

LA PAZ

COCHABAMBA

CHILE

Nazca Ridge

Peru-Chile Trench

Chile Basin

Tropic of Capricorn

Scale 1:18,000,000

0   160   320 Kilometers

Depth tints

- Shoreline
- 0–200 m
- 200–2000 m
- 2000–4000 m
- 4000–6000 m
- 6000–8000 m
- > 8000 m

Physical Features

- River, stream
- Intermittent river
- Lake
- Intermittent lake
- Salt lake
- Intermittent salt lake
- ▲ Elevation above sea level in meters

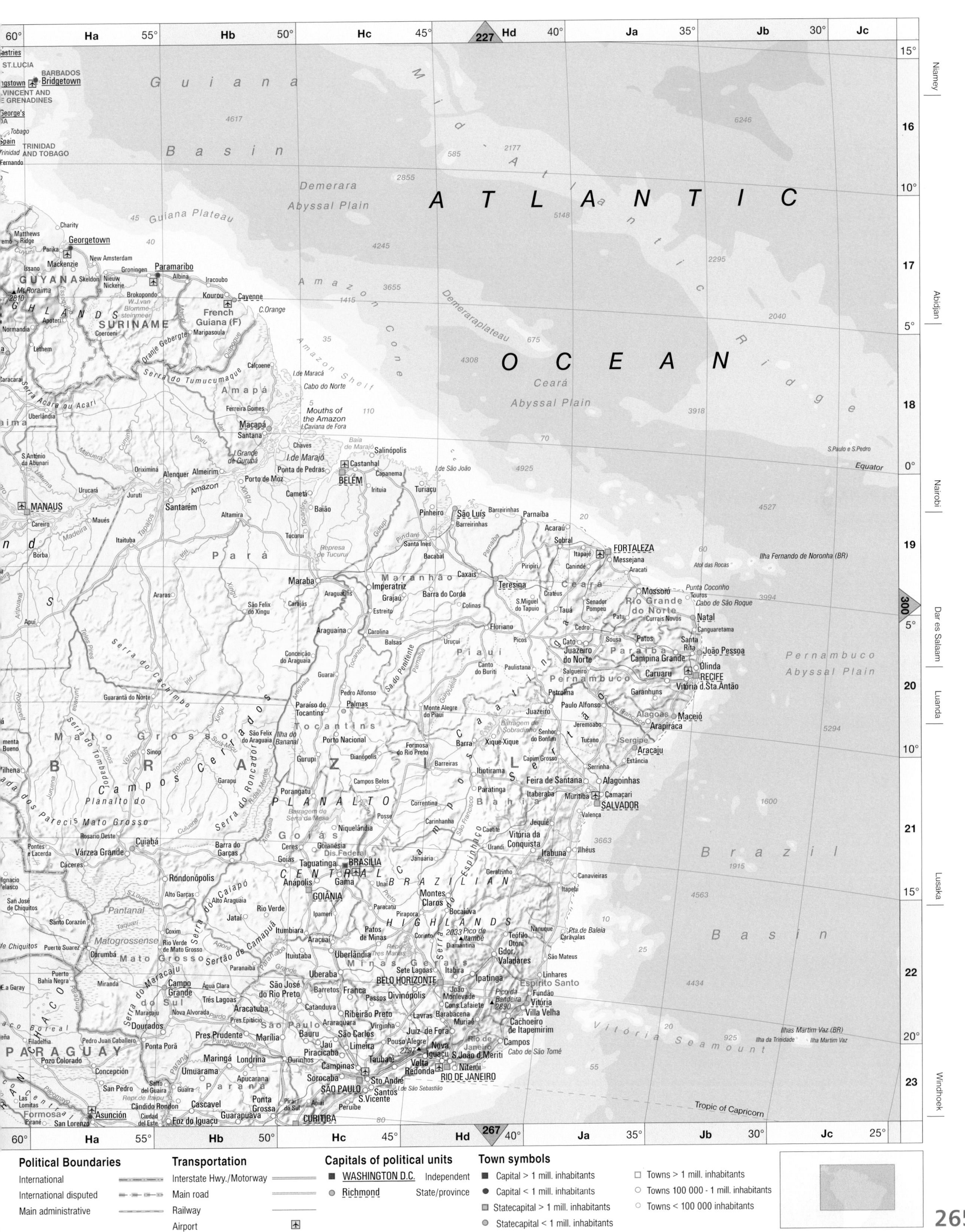

ATLANTIC

OCEAN

Niamey

Abidjan

Nairobi

Dar es Salaam

Luanda

Lusaka

Windhoek

GUIANA
SURINAME
French Guiana (F)
Georgetown
Paramaribo
Cayenne

ST.LUCIA
BARBADOS
Bridgetown
VINCENT AND
GRENADINES
TRINIDAD AND TOBAGO

B R A Z I L

MANAUS
Pará
Maranhão
Ceará
FORTALEZA
Teresina
Rio Grande do Norte
Natal
Paraíba
João Pessoa
Pernambuco
RECIFE
Maceió
Sergipe
Aracaju
Bahia
SALVADOR

Piauí
Tocantins
Goiás
BRASÍLIA
GOIÂNIA
Minas Gerais
BELO HORIZONTE
Espírito Santo
Vitória
RIO DE JANEIRO
SÃO PAULO
CURITIBA

PARAGUAY
Asunción

Tropic of Capricorn

Political Boundaries
International
International disputed
Main administrative

Transportation
Interstate Hwy./Motorway
Main road
Railway
Airport ✈

Capitals of political units
■ WASHINGTON D.C. Independent
◉ Richmond State/province

Town symbols
■ Capital > 1 mill. inhabitants
● Capital < 1 mill. inhabitants
▣ Statecapital > 1 mill. inhabitants
◉ Statecapital < 1 mill. inhabitants
□ Towns > 1 mill. inhabitants
○ Towns 100 000 - 1 mill. inhabitants
○ Towns < 100 000 inhabitants

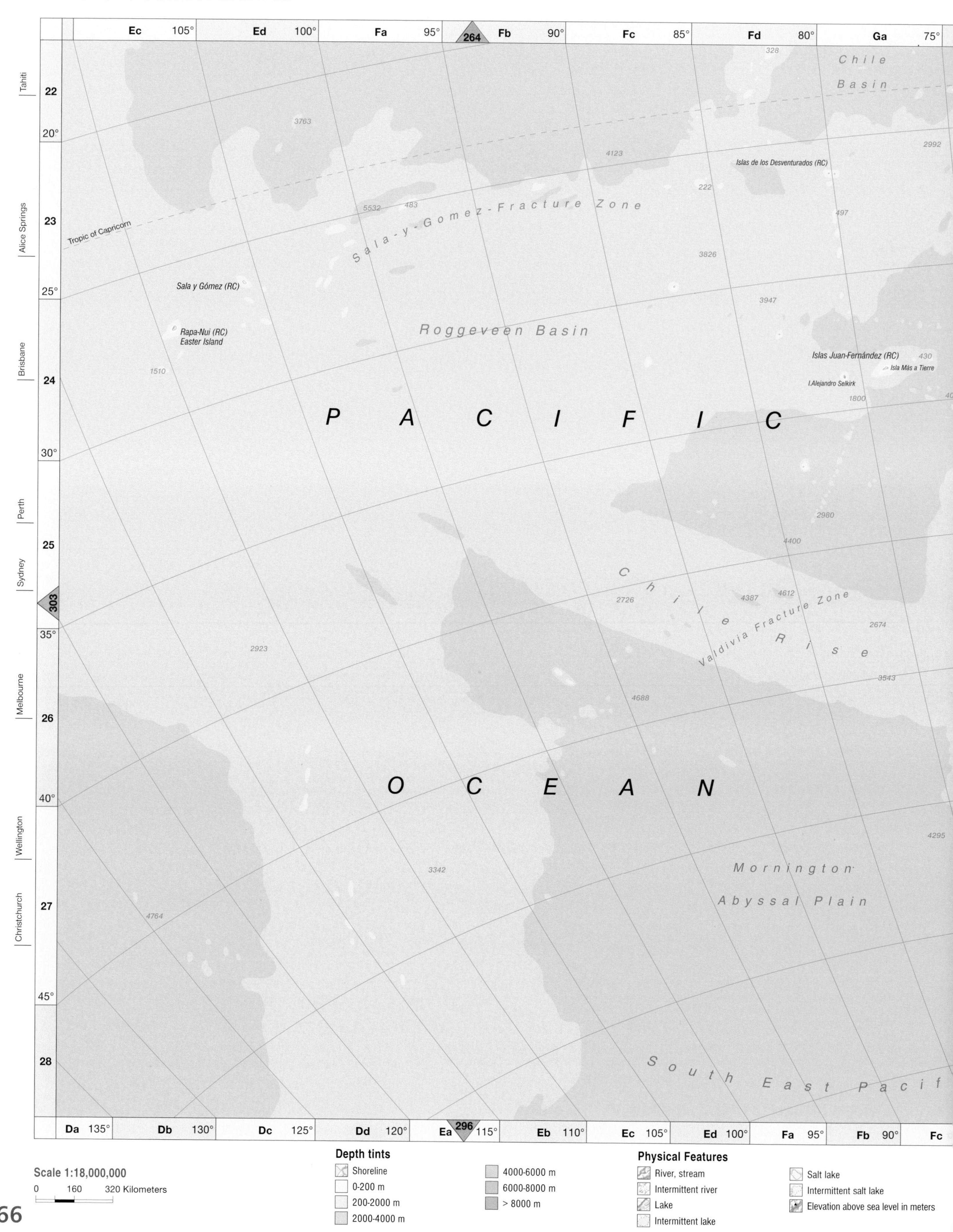

| | Ec 105° | Ed 100° | Fa 95° | ◆264 Fb 90° | Fc 85° | Fd 80° | Ga 75° |

Chile Basin

328

Tahiti
22
20°
3763
4123
2992

Alice Springs
23
Tropic of Capricorn
5532 483
Sala-y-Gomez-Fracture Zone
222
Islas de los Desventurados (RC)
497
3826

25°
Sala y Gómez (RC)
3947

Brisbane
24
Rapa-Nui (RC)
Easter Island
Roggeveen Basin
Islas Juan-Fernández (RC) 430
Isla Más a Tierre
1510
I.Alejandro Selkirk
1800
40

30°

P A C I F I C

Perth
2980
4400

Sydney
25
◆303
Chile
2726
4387 4612
Valdivia Fracture Zone
2674
Rise

35°
2923
3543

Melbourne
26
4688

O C E A N

Wellington
40°
4295

3342
Mornington
Abyssal Plain

Christchurch
27
4764

45°

28
South East Pacif

| Da 135° | Db 130° | Dc 125° | Dd 120° | Ea ◆296 115° | Eb 110° | Ec 105° | Ed 100° | Fa 95° | Fb 90° | Fc |

Scale 1:18,000,000

0   160   320 Kilometers

Depth tints

- ⊠ Shoreline
- ☐ 0-200 m
- ☐ 200-2000 m
- ☐ 2000-4000 m
- ☐ 4000-6000 m
- ☐ 6000-8000 m
- ☐ > 8000 m

Physical Features

- River, stream
- Intermittent river
- Lake
- Intermittent lake
- Salt lake
- Intermittent salt lake
- Elevation above sea level in meters

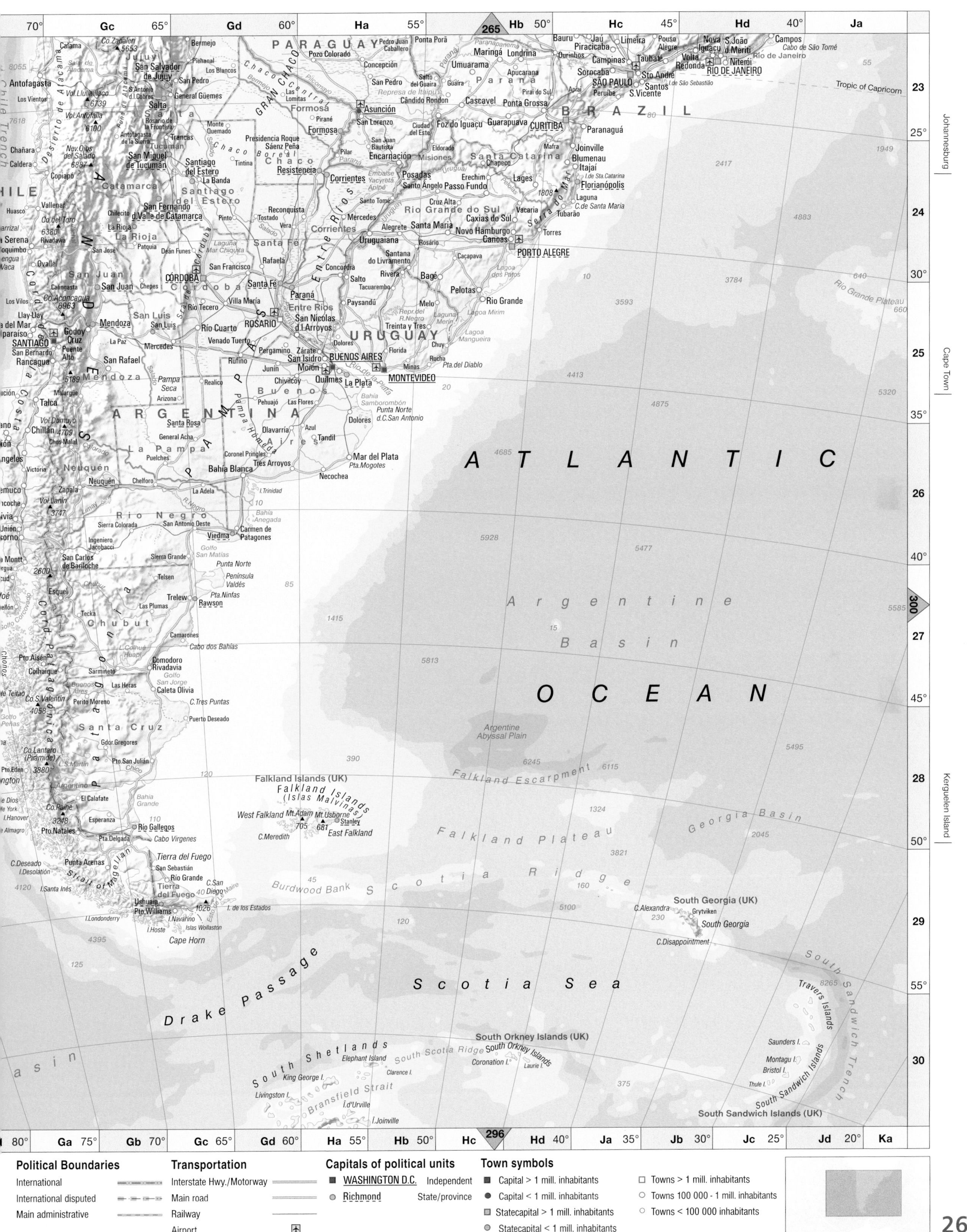

PARAGUAY

BRAZIL

A T L A N T I C

O C E A N

Argentine

Basin

Argentine
Abyssal Plain

Falkland Escarpment

Georgia Basin

Falkland Islands (UK)
Falkland Islands
(Islas Malvinas)

West Falkland   East Falkland

Falkland Plateau

Scotia Ridge

South Georgia (UK)
South Georgia
Grytviken

South Sandwich Trench

Burdwood Bank

Scotia Sea

Drake Passage

South Orkney Islands (UK)
South Orkney Islands

South Sandwich Islands (UK)

South Shetlands

Johannesburg

Cape Town

Kerguelen Island

Political Boundaries	
International	
International disputed	
Main administrative	

Transportation	
Interstate Hwy./Motorway	
Main road	
Railway	
Airport	✈

Capitals of political units

◼ WASHINGTON D.C.   Independent

◉ Richmond   State/province

Town symbols

◼ Capital > 1 mill. inhabitants
● Capital < 1 mill. inhabitants
▢ Statecapital > 1 mill. inhabitants
◉ Statecapital < 1 mill. inhabitants

☐ Towns > 1 mill. inhabitants
○ Towns 100 000 - 1 mill. inhabitants
○ Towns < 100 000 inhabitants

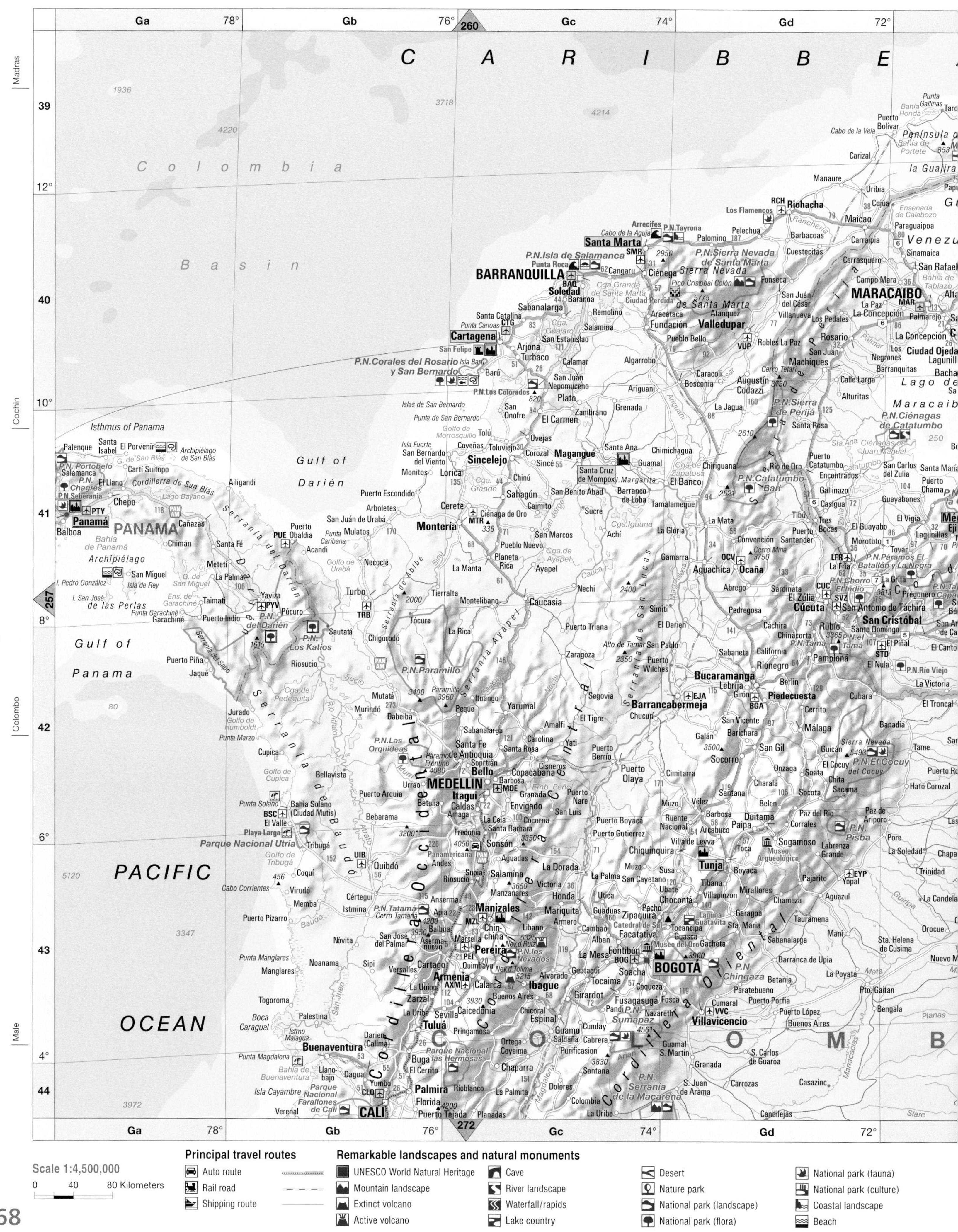

Principal travel routes

- Auto route
- Rail road
- Shipping route

Remarkable landscapes and natural monuments

- UNESCO World Natural Heritage
- Mountain landscape
- Extinct volcano
- Active volcano
- Cave
- River landscape
- Waterfall/rapids
- Lake country
- Desert
- Nature park
- National park (landscape)
- National park (flora)
- National park (fauna)
- National park (culture)
- Coastal landscape
- Beach

Scale 1:4,500,000

0   40   80 Kilometers

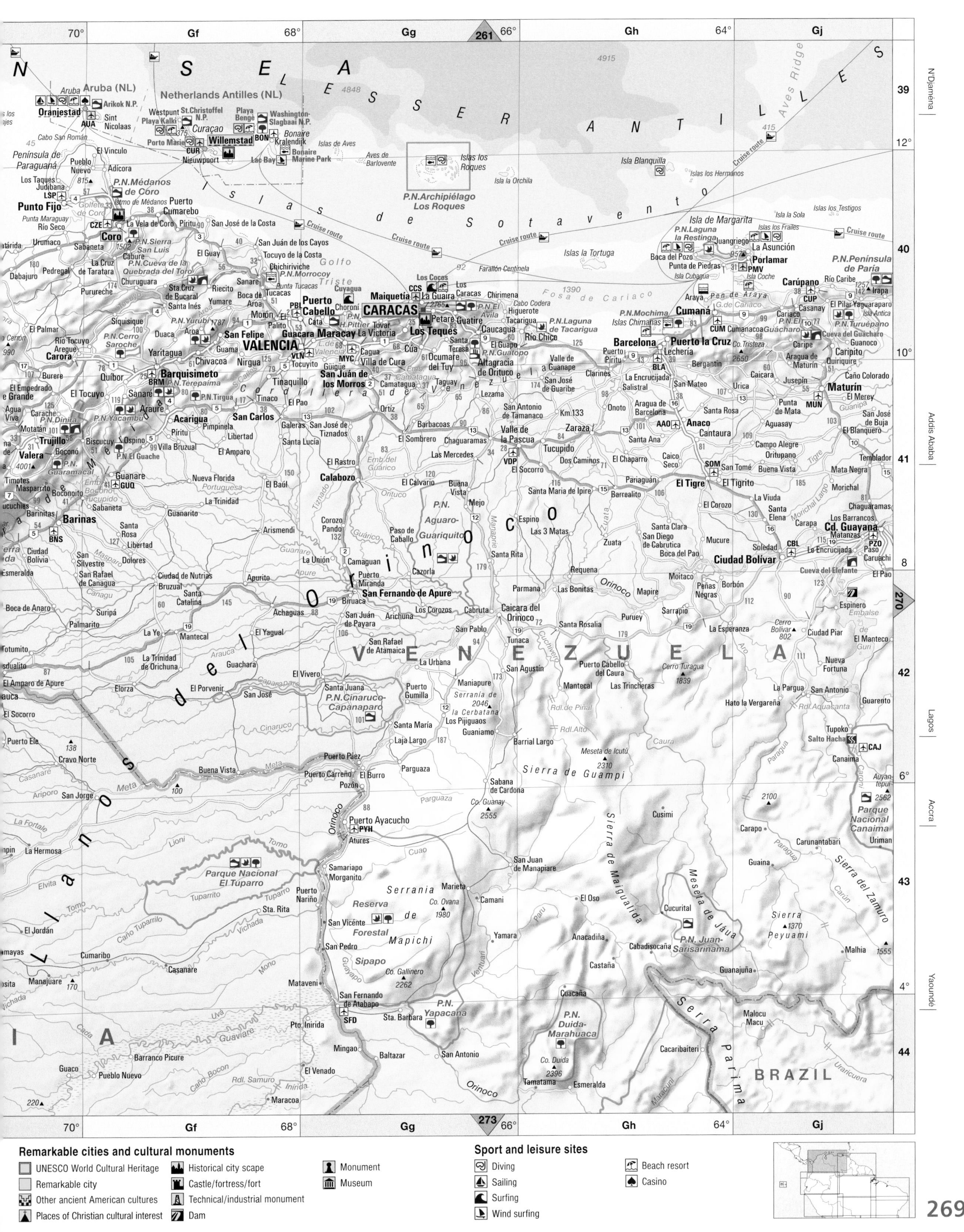

Remarkable cities and cultural monuments

- ☐ UNESCO World Cultural Heritage
- ☐ Remarkable city
- Other ancient American cultures
- ▲ Places of Christian cultural interest
- Historical city scape
- Castle/fortress/fort
- Technical/industrial monument
- Dam
- Monument
- 🏛 Museum

Sport and leisure sites

- Diving
- Sailing
- Surfing
- Wind surfing
- Beach resort
- Casino

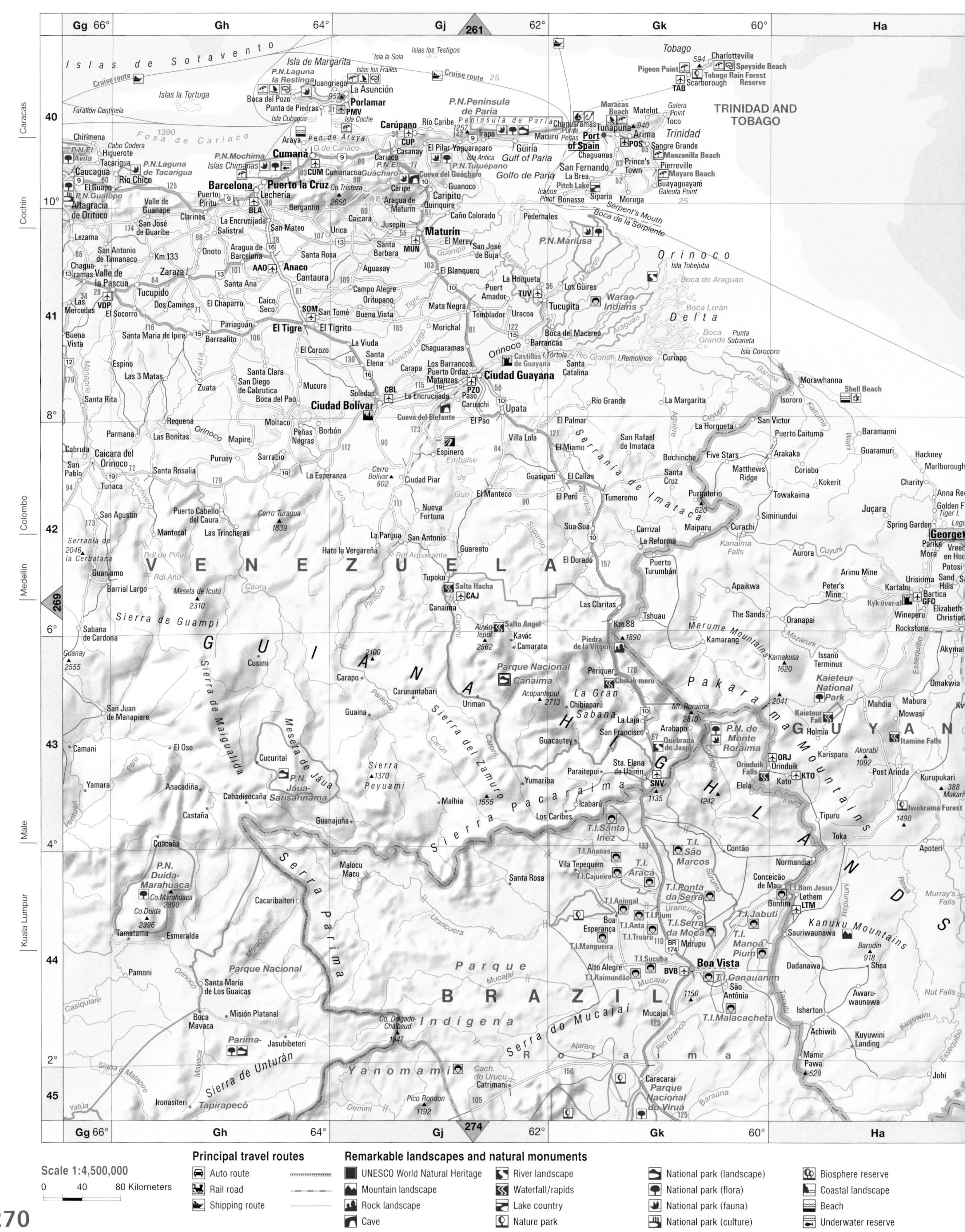

Scale 1:4,500,000

0   40   80 Kilometers

Principal travel routes
- Auto route
- Rail road
- Shipping route

Remarkable landscapes and natural monuments
- UNESCO World Natural Heritage
- Mountain landscape
- Rock landscape
- Cave
- River landscape
- Waterfall/rapids
- Lake country
- Nature park
- National park (landscape)
- National park (flora)
- National park (fauna)
- National park (culture)
- Biosphere reserve
- Coastal landscape
- Beach
- Underwater reserve

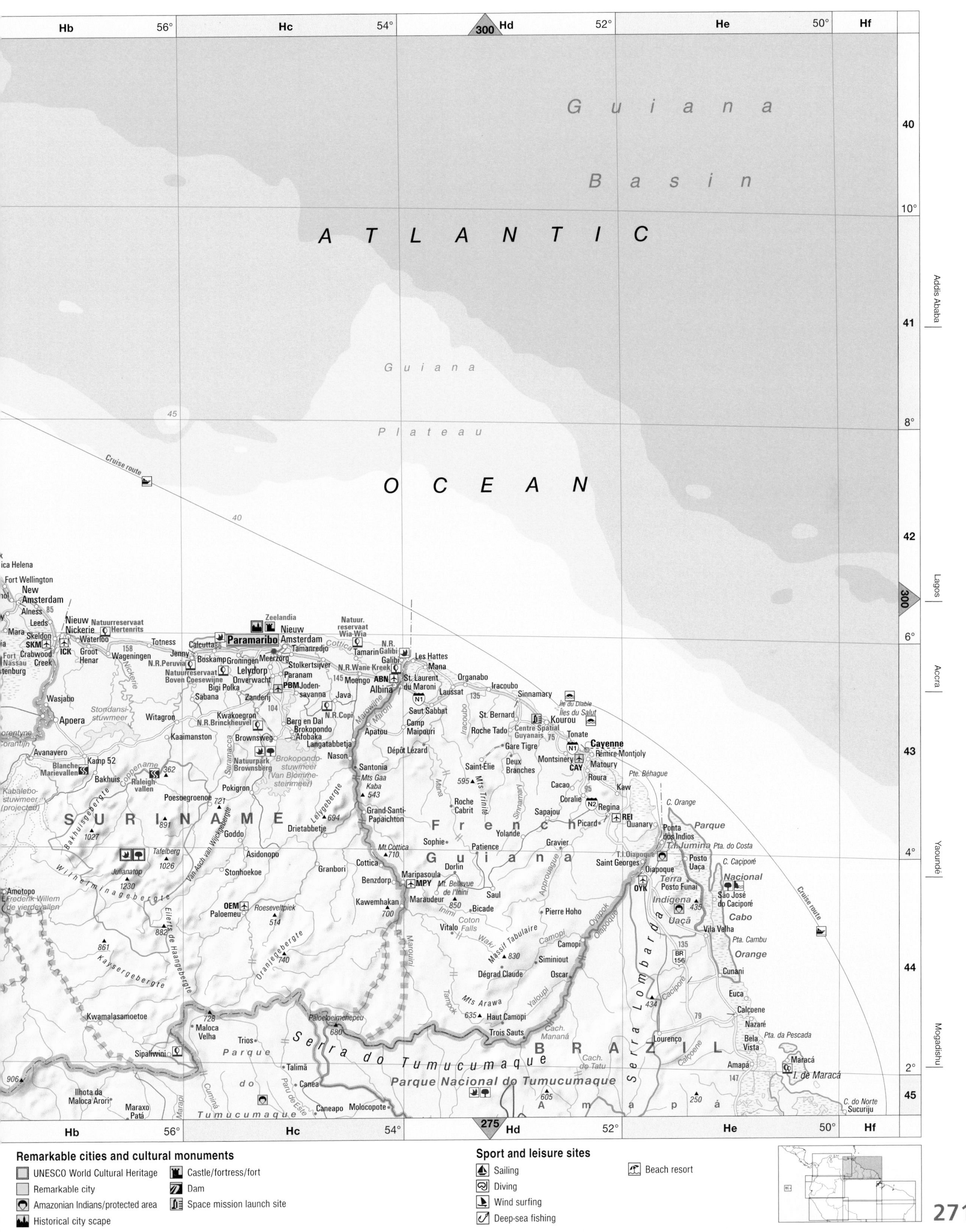

Remarkable cities and cultural monuments
- UNESCO World Cultural Heritage
- Remarkable city
- Amazonian Indians/protected area
- Historical city scape
- Castle/fortress/fort
- Dam
- Space mission launch site

Sport and leisure sites
- Sailing
- Diving
- Wind surfing
- Deep-sea fishing
- Beach resort

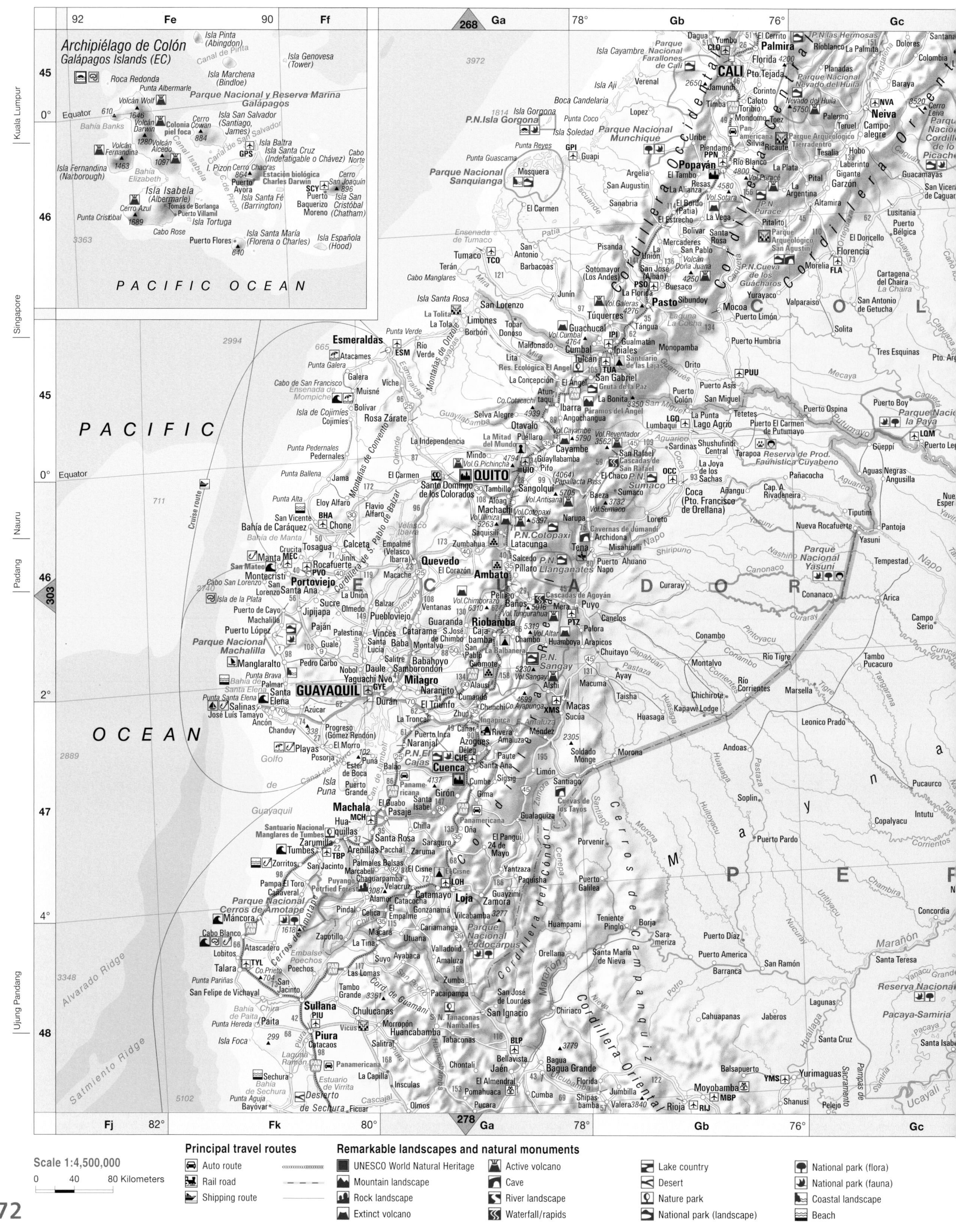

Archipiélago de Colón
Galápagos Islands (EC)

Parque Nacional y Reserva Marina Galápagos

PACIFIC OCEAN

PACIFIC

OCEAN

Scale 1:4,500,000

0   40   80 Kilometers

Principal travel routes
- 🚗 Auto route
- 🚃 Rail road
- 🚢 Shipping route

Remarkable landscapes and natural monuments
- ■ UNESCO World Natural Heritage
- ▲ Mountain landscape
- ■ Rock landscape
- ▲ Extinct volcano
- ▲ Active volcano
- Cave
- River landscape
- Waterfall/rapids
- Lake country
- Desert
- Nature park
- National park (landscape)
- National park (flora)
- National park (fauna)
- Coastal landscape
- Beach

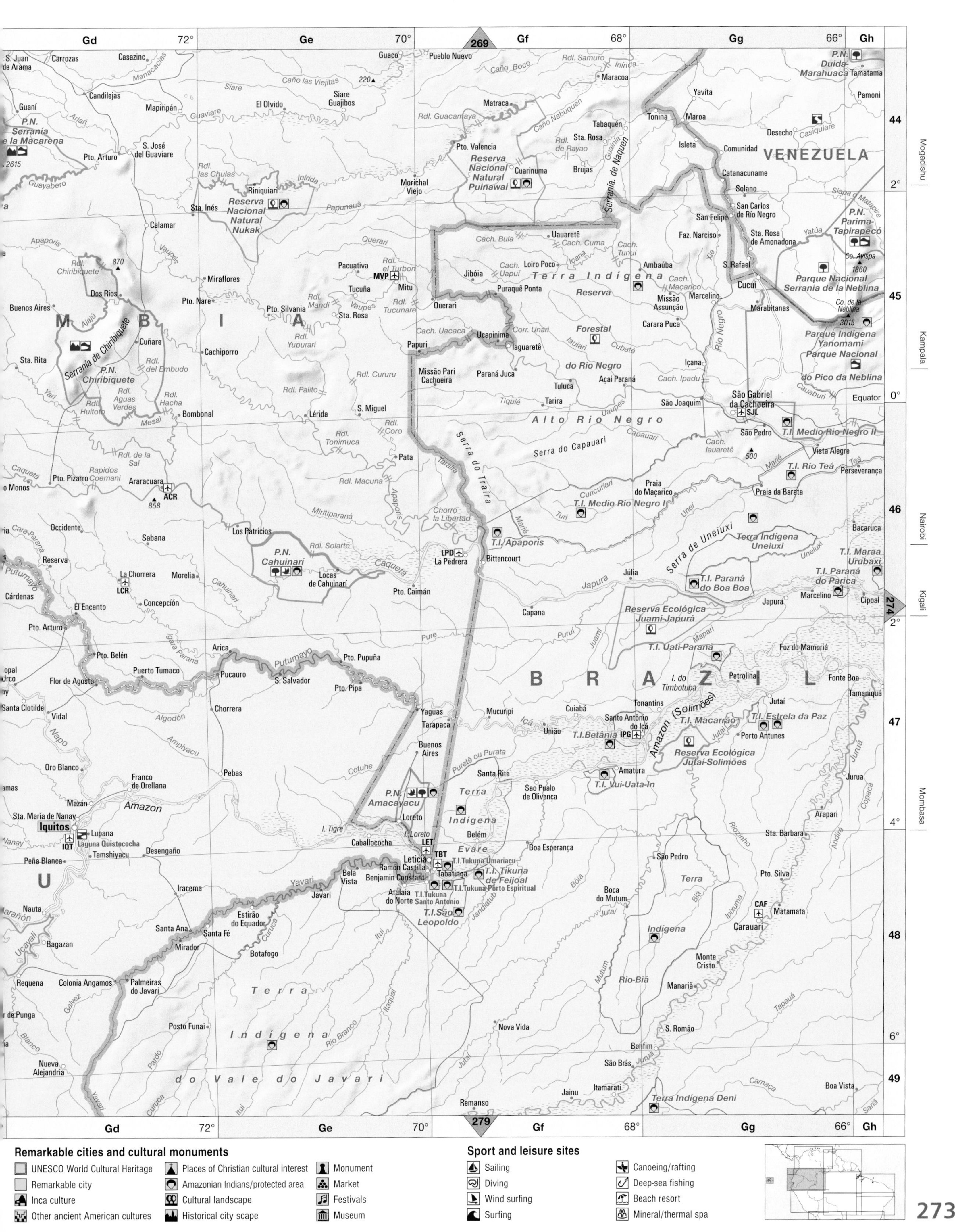

Gd
72°
Ge
70°
269
Gf
68°
Gg
66°
Gh
44
45
46
47
48
49
2°
0°
Equator
4°
6°
Mogadishu
Kampala
Nairobi
Kigali
Mombasa
274
279
VENEZUELA
B R A Z I L
Amazon
Amazon (Solimões)
Japura
Putumayo
Caquetá
Yavari
Iquitos
Leticia
Tabatinga
Benjamin Constant
São Gabriel da Cachoeira
Mitu
Araracuara
Parque Nacional Serrania de la Neblina
Parque Indígena Yanomami
Parque Nacional do Pico da Neblina
Alto Rio Negro
Serra do Traíra
Serra do Capauari
Serra de Uneiuxi
Terra Indígena Evare
Terra Indígena do Vale do Javari
Reserva Nacional Natural Puinawai
Reserva Nacional Natural Nukak
Reserva Ecológica Juami-Japurá
Reserva Ecológica Jutaí-Solimões
P.N. Amacayacu
P.N. Cahuinarí
P.N. Chiribiquete
Serrania de Chiribiquete
Terra Indígena Deni
Remarkable cities and cultural monuments
UNESCO World Cultural Heritage
Remarkable city
Inca culture
Other ancient American cultures
Places of Christian cultural interest
Amazonian Indians/protected area
Cultural landscape
Historical city scape
Monument
Market
Festivals
Museum
Sport and leisure sites
Sailing
Diving
Wind surfing
Surfing
Canoeing/rafting
Deep-sea fishing
Beach resort
Mineral/thermal spa

Amazonian Lowlands

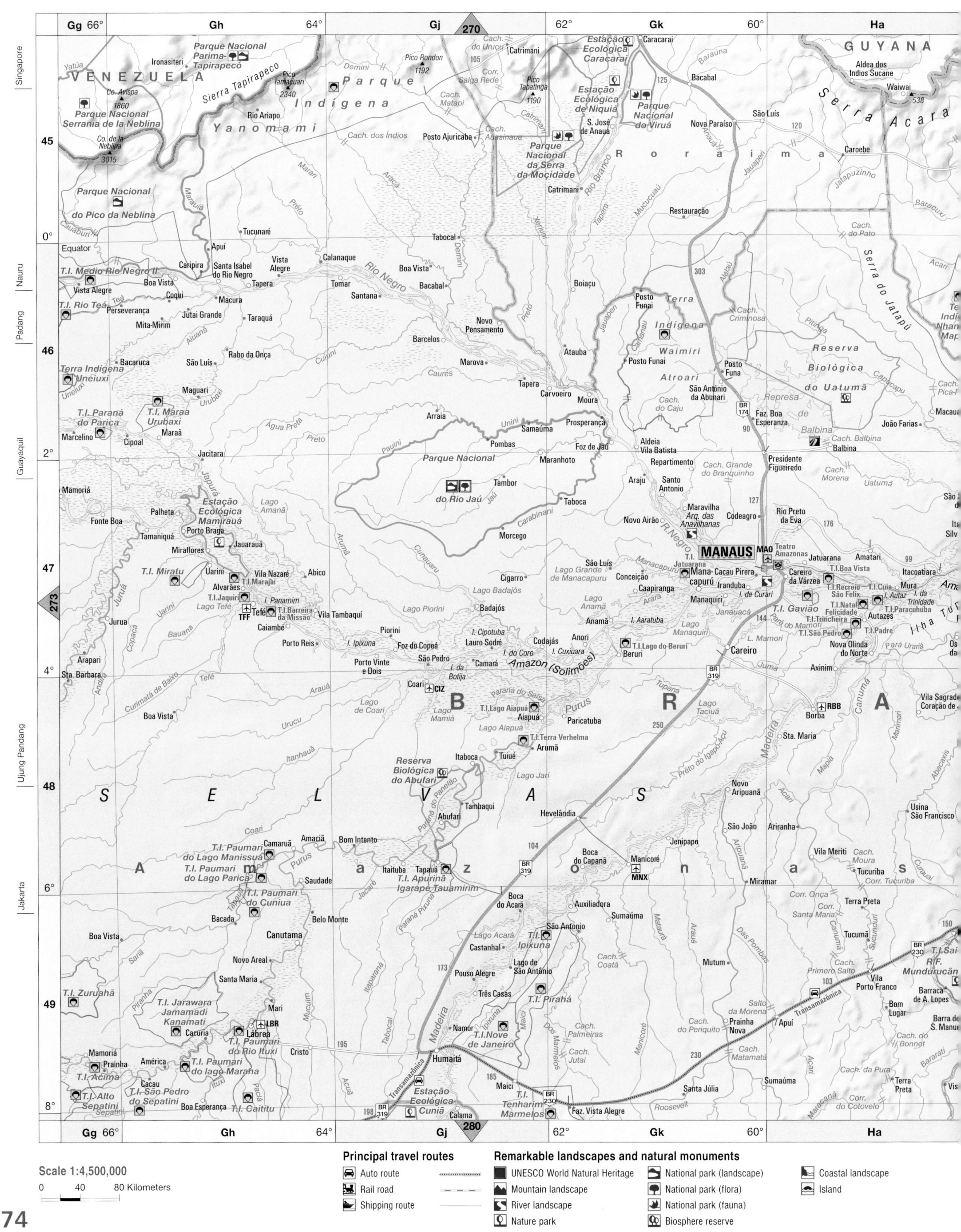

Scale 1:4,500,000

0   40   80 Kilometers

274

Principal travel routes

- Auto route
- Rail road
- Shipping route

...... Auto route
— — — Mountain landscape
——— River landscape

Nature park

Remarkable landscapes and natural monuments

- UNESCO World Natural Heritage
- Mountain landscape
- River landscape
- Nature park

- National park (landscape)
- National park (flora)
- National park (fauna)
- Biosphere reserve

- Coastal landscape
- Island

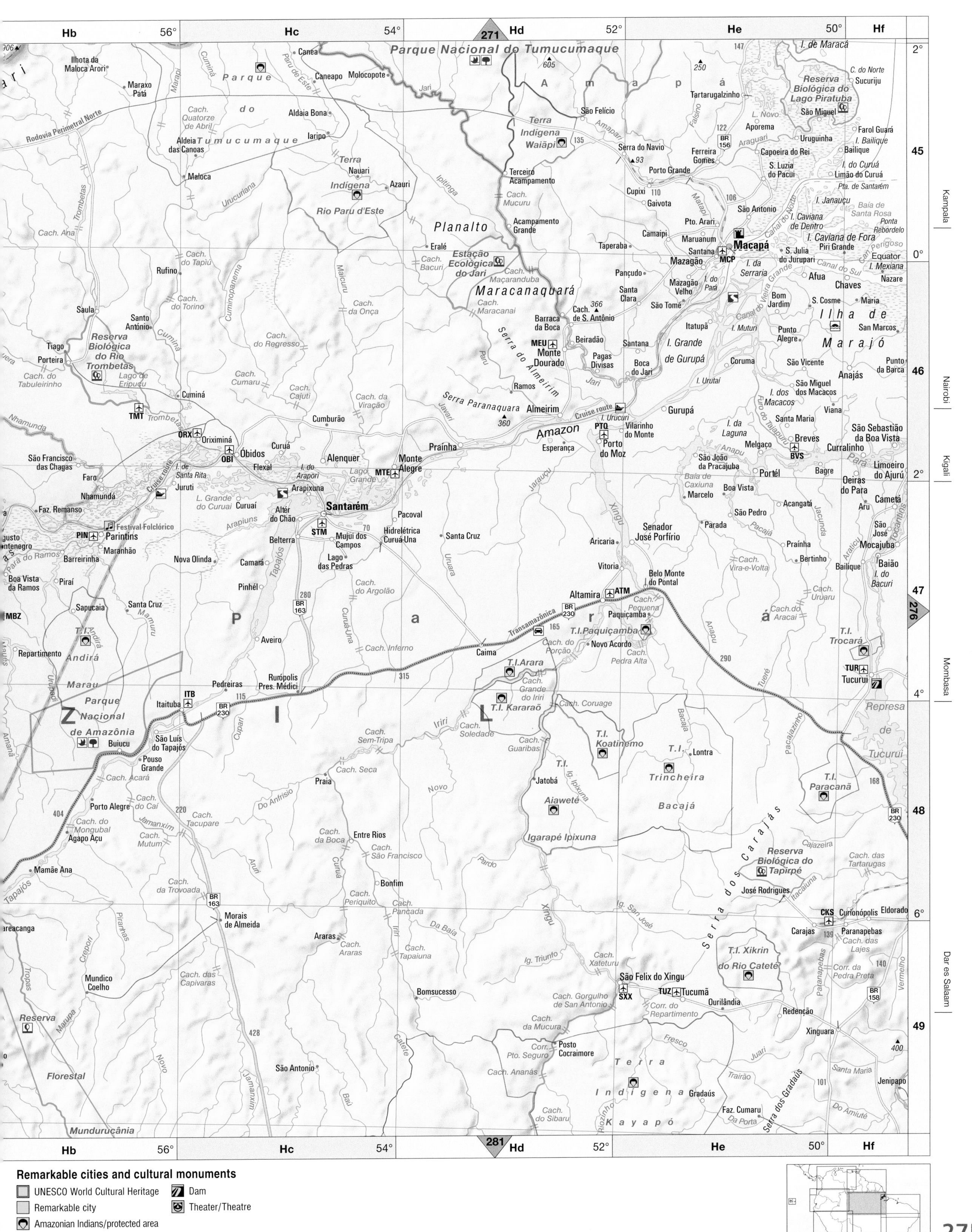

Parque Nacional do Tumucumaque

Parque do

Planalto

Estação Ecológica do Jari

Maracanaquará

Reserva Biológica do Rio Trombetas

Reserva Biológica do Lago Piratuba

Macapá

Ilha de Marajó

Amazon

Santarém

Parintins

Parque Nacional de Amazônia

Altamira

Tucuruí

Reserva Biológica do Tapirpé

Reserva Biológica do

São Felix do Xingu

Terra Indígena Kayapó

Remarkable cities and cultural monuments

- ☐ UNESCO World Cultural Heritage
- ☐ Remarkable city
- ◉ Amazonian Indians/protected area
- ♜ Castle/fortress/fort
- ⚙ Dam
- ◉ Theater/Theatre

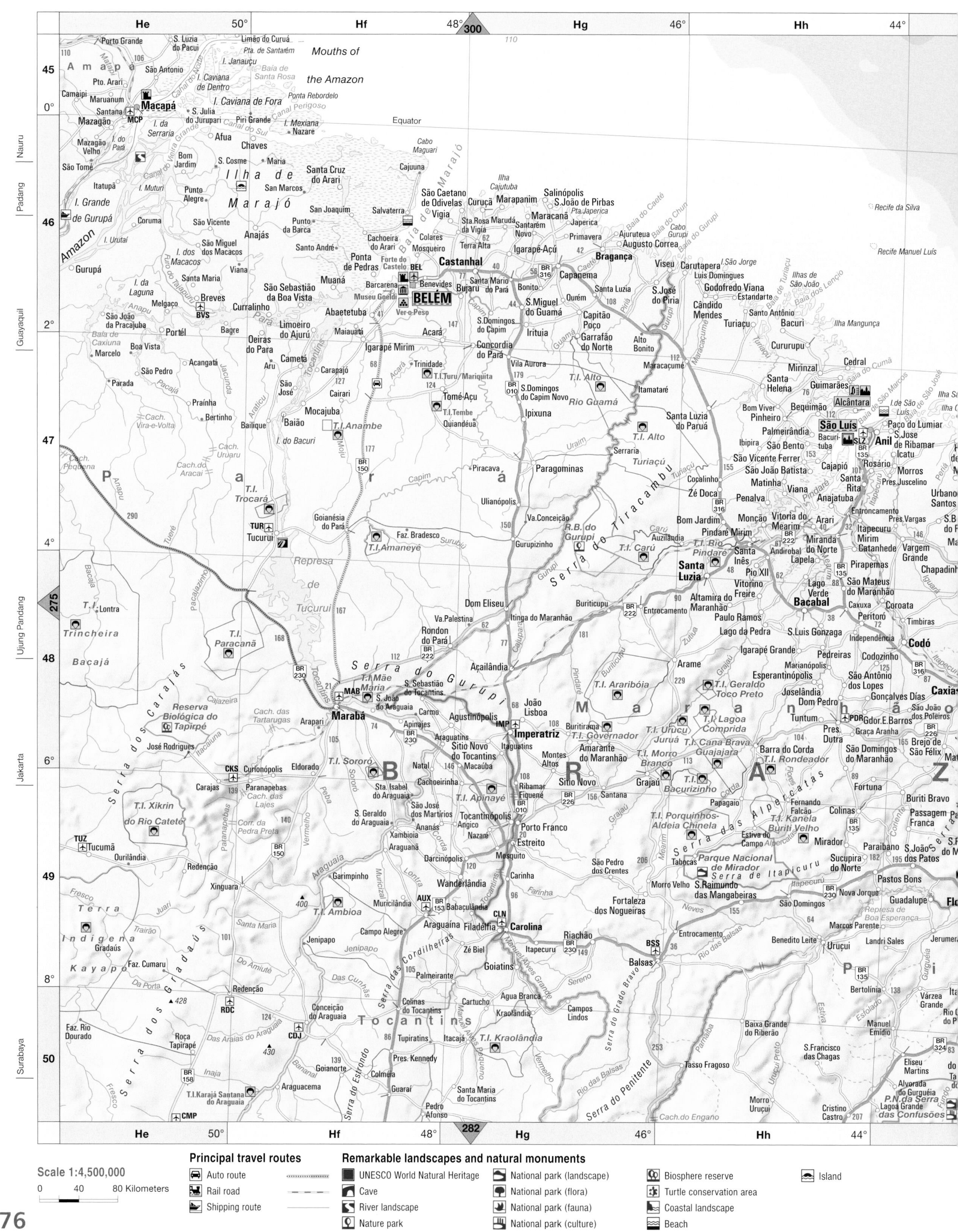

Scale 1:4,500,000

0   40   80 Kilometers

Principal travel routes

- Auto route
- Rail road
- Shipping route

Remarkable landscapes and natural monuments

- UNESCO World Natural Heritage
- Cave
- River landscape
- Nature park
- National park (landscape)
- National park (flora)
- National park (fauna)
- National park (culture)
- Biosphere reserve
- Turtle conservation area
- Coastal landscape
- Beach
- Island

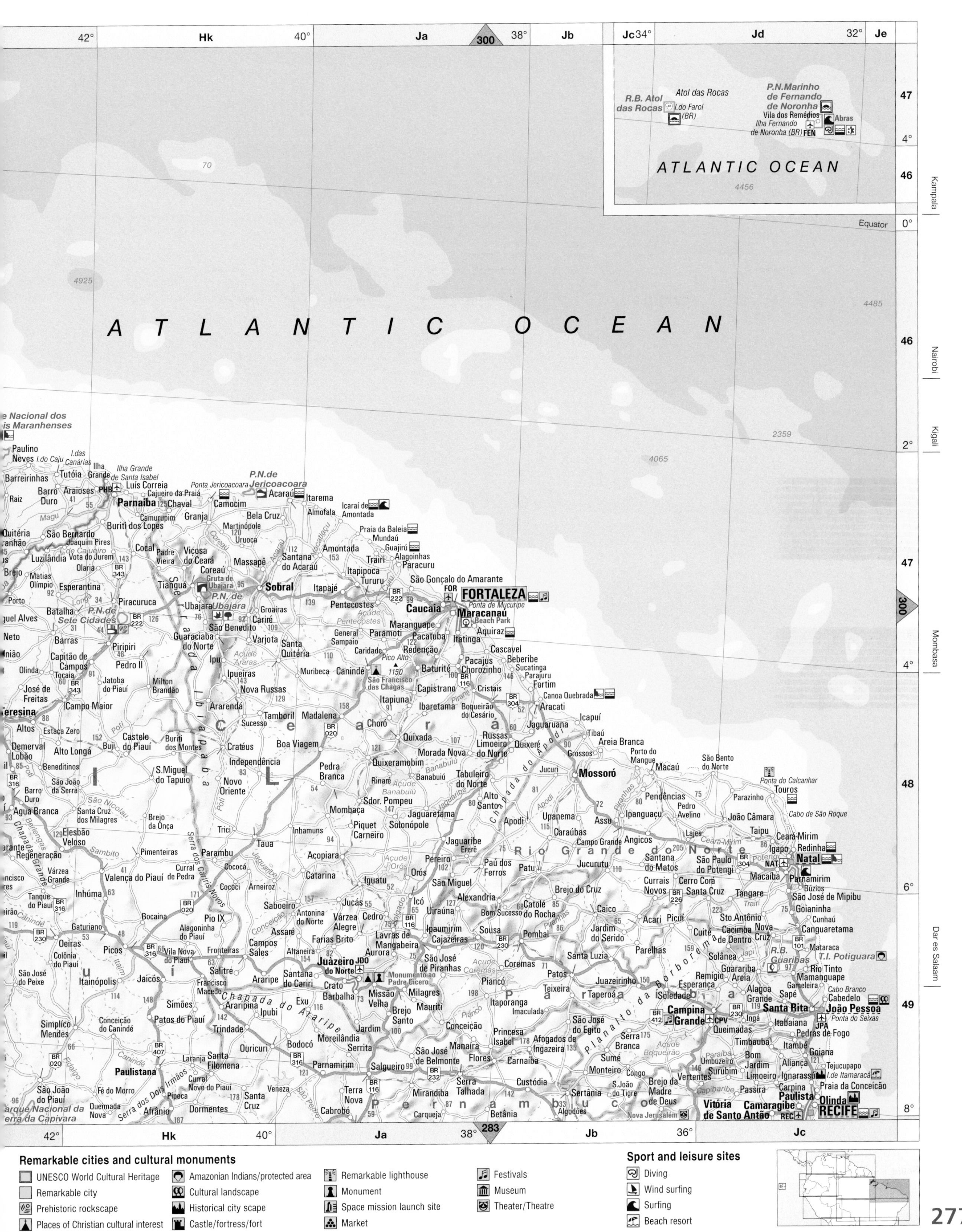

Remarkable cities and cultural monuments

- UNESCO World Cultural Heritage
- Remarkable city
- Prehistoric rockscape
- Places of Christian cultural interest
- Amazonian Indians/protected area
- Cultural landscape
- Historical city scape
- Castle/fortress/fort
- Remarkable lighthouse
- Monument
- Space mission launch site
- Market
- Festivals
- Museum
- Theater/Theatre

Sport and leisure sites

- Diving
- Wind surfing
- Surfing
- Beach resort

277

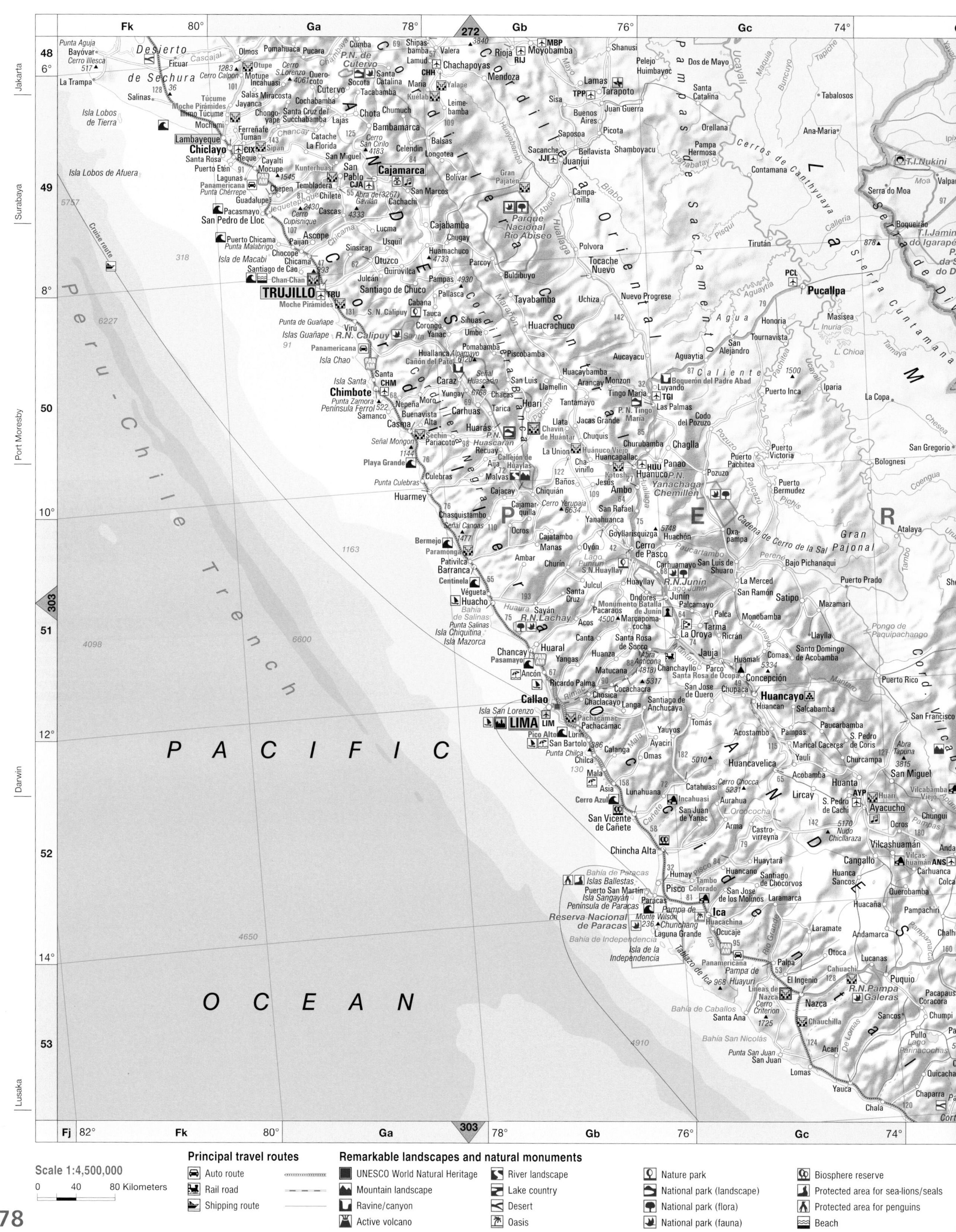

Principal travel routes

- Auto route
- Rail road
- Shipping route

----- S.Lorenzo -----

Remarkable landscapes and natural monuments

- UNESCO World Natural Heritage
- Mountain landscape
- Ravine/canyon
- Active volcano

- River landscape
- Lake country
- Desert
- Oasis

- Nature park
- National park (landscape)
- National park (flora)
- National park (fauna)

- Biosphere reserve
- Protected area for sea-lions/seals
- Protected area for penguins
- Beach

Scale 1:4,500,000

0   40   80 Kilometers

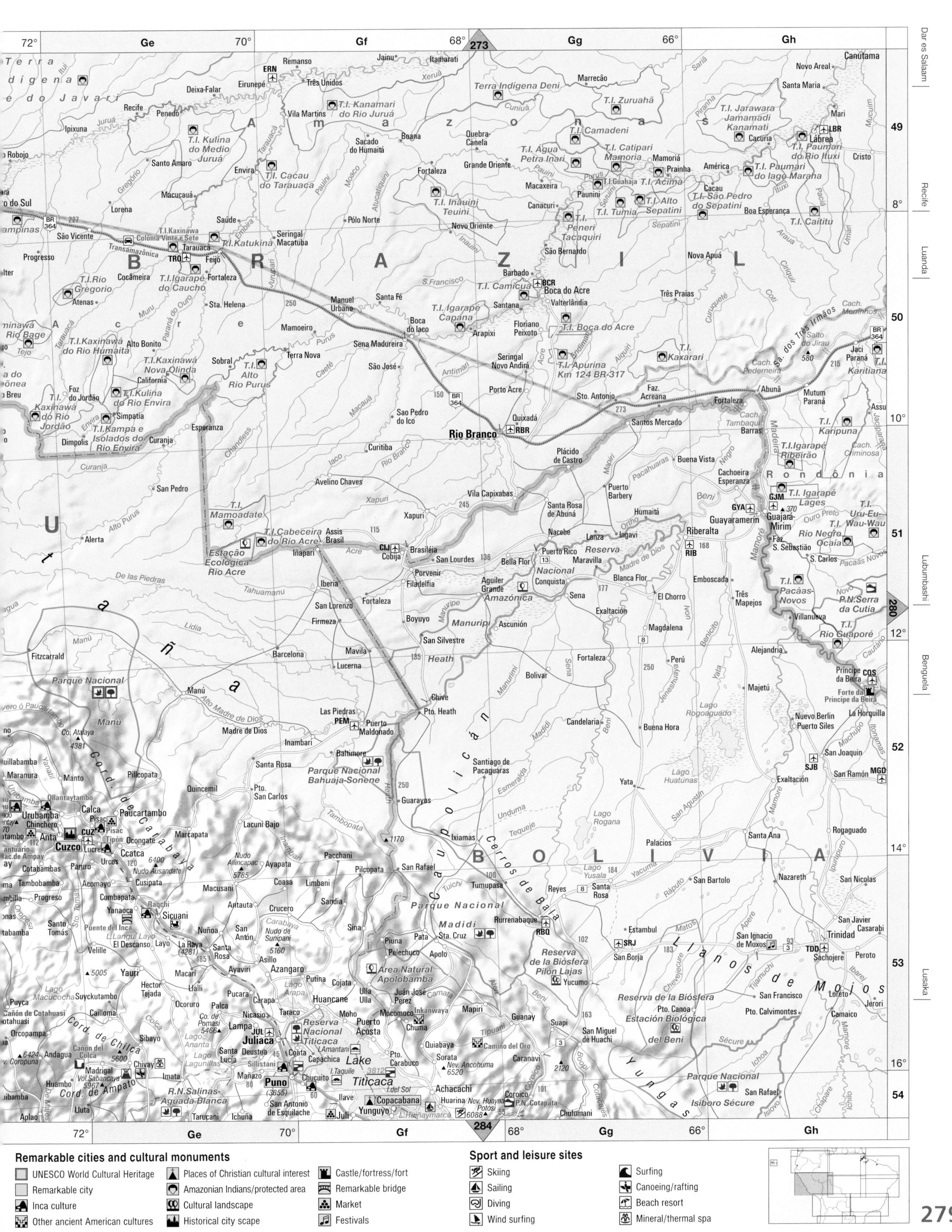

Remarkable cities and cultural monuments

- UNESCO World Cultural Heritage
- Remarkable city
- Inca culture
- Other ancient American cultures
- Places of Christian cultural interest
- Amazonian Indians/protected area
- Cultural landscape
- Historical city scape
- Castle/fortress/fort
- Remarkable bridge
- Market
- Festivals

Sport and leisure sites

- Skiing
- Sailing
- Diving
- Wind surfing
- Surfing
- Canoeing/rafting
- Beach resort
- Mineral/thermal spa

279

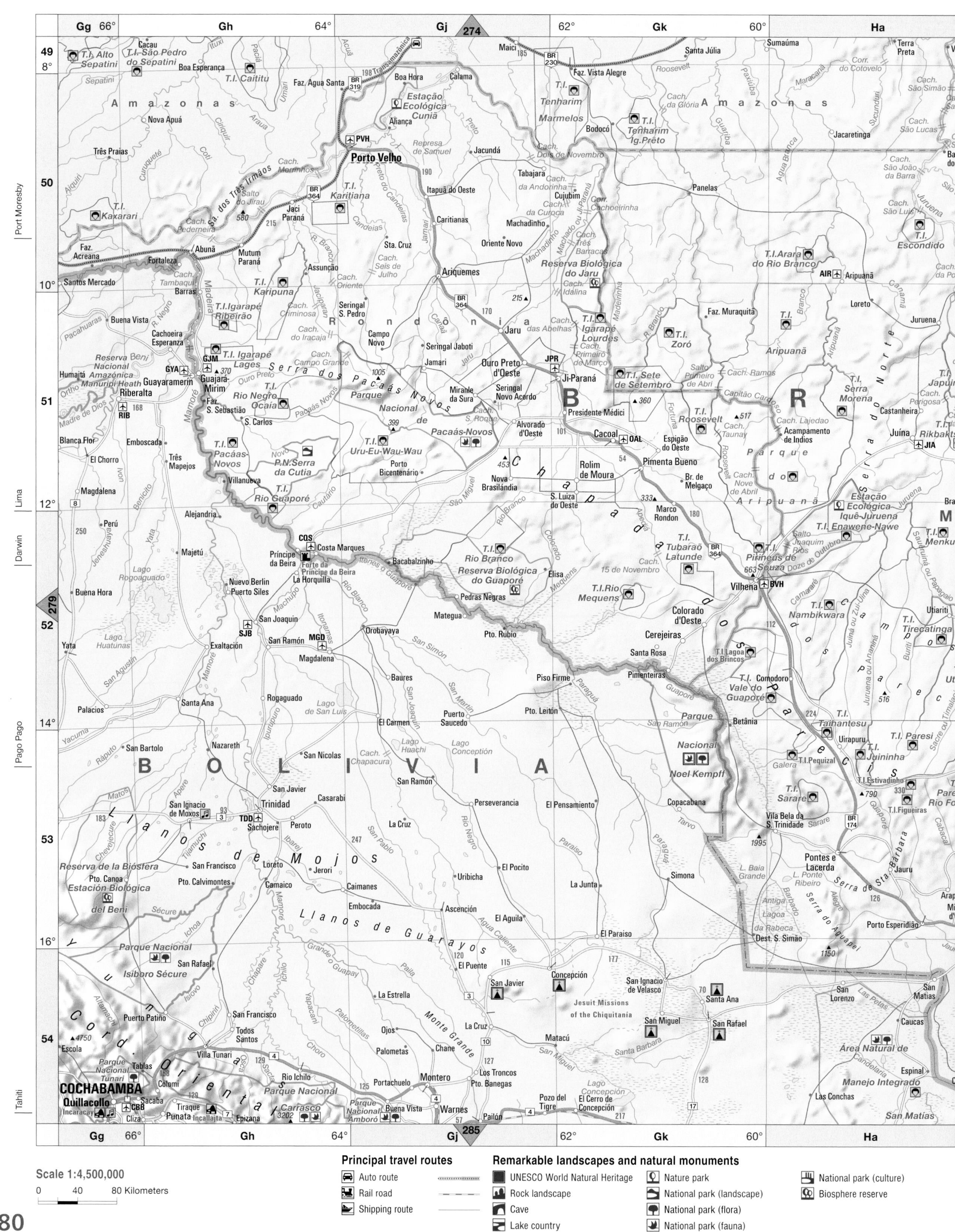

Scale 1:4,500,000

0   40   80 Kilometers

Principal travel routes

- Auto route
- Rail road
- Shipping route

Remarkable landscapes and natural monuments

- UNESCO World Natural Heritage
- Rock landscape
- Cave
- Lake country
- Nature park
- National park (landscape)
- National park (flora)
- National park (fauna)
- National park (culture)
- Biosphere reserve

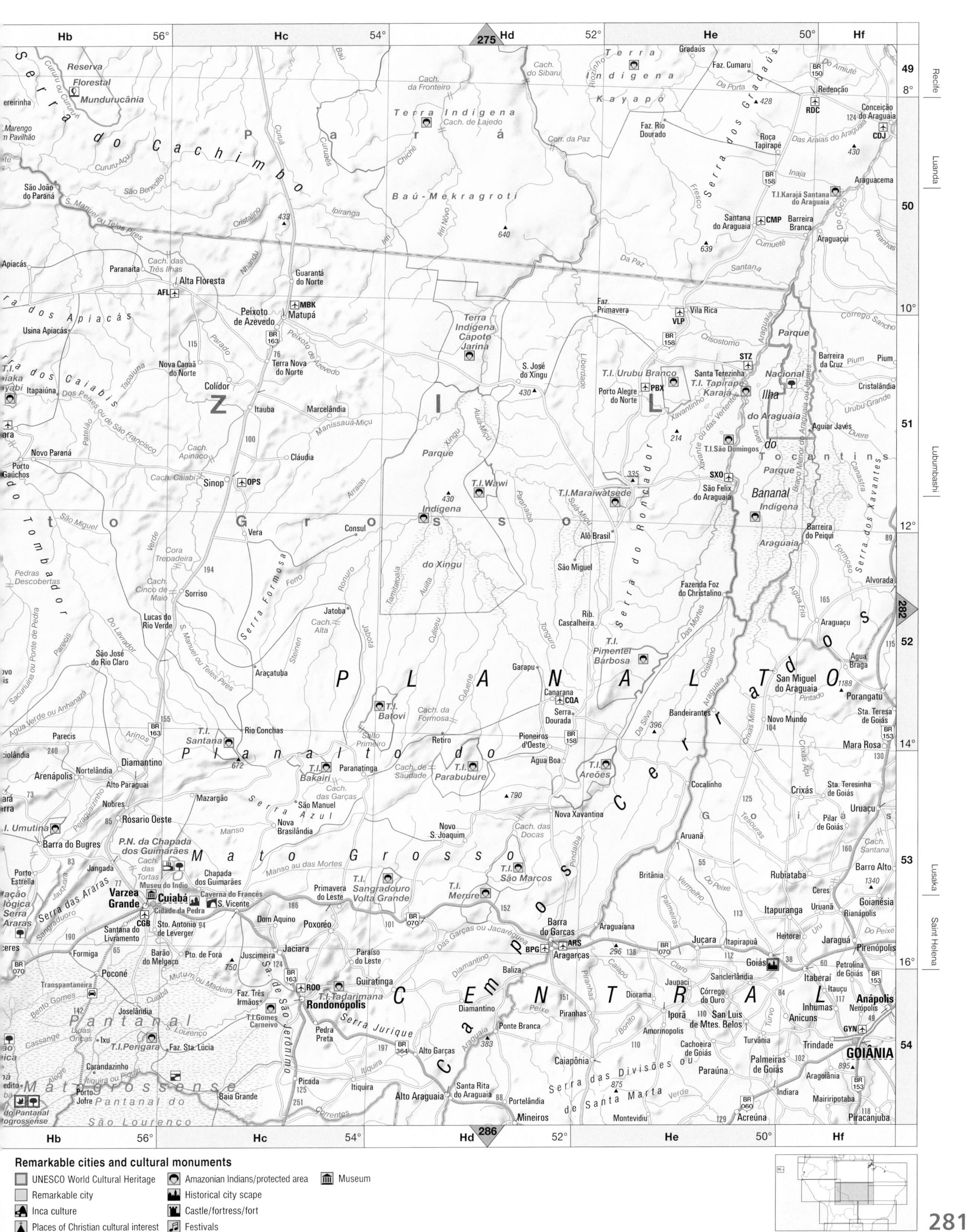

Serra

Reserva
Florestal
Mundurucânia

do Cachimbo

Terra Indígena
Pará

Baú-Mekragroti

Terra
Indígena Kayapó

Terra
Indígena
Capoto
Jarina

Z I N

T.I. Urubu Branco

Parque
Nacional
Ilha do Araguaia

Parque Indígena
do Xingu

Parque
Indígena do Tocantins

Bananal

MATO GROSSO

PLANALTO DO

Planalto do

P L A N A L T O   D O S   C E R R A D O S

P.N. da Chapada
dos Guimarães

Pantanal

Pantanal do
São Lourenço

C A M P O S   G E R A I S

C E N T R A L

GOIÂNIA

Anápolis

Remarkable cities and cultural monuments

- ▫ UNESCO World Cultural Heritage
- ▫ Remarkable city
- ▲ Inca culture
- ▲ Places of Christian cultural interest
- ◉ Amazonian Indians/protected area
- ⛰ Historical city scape
- ⛫ Castle/fortress/fort
- ♫ Festivals
- 🏛 Museum

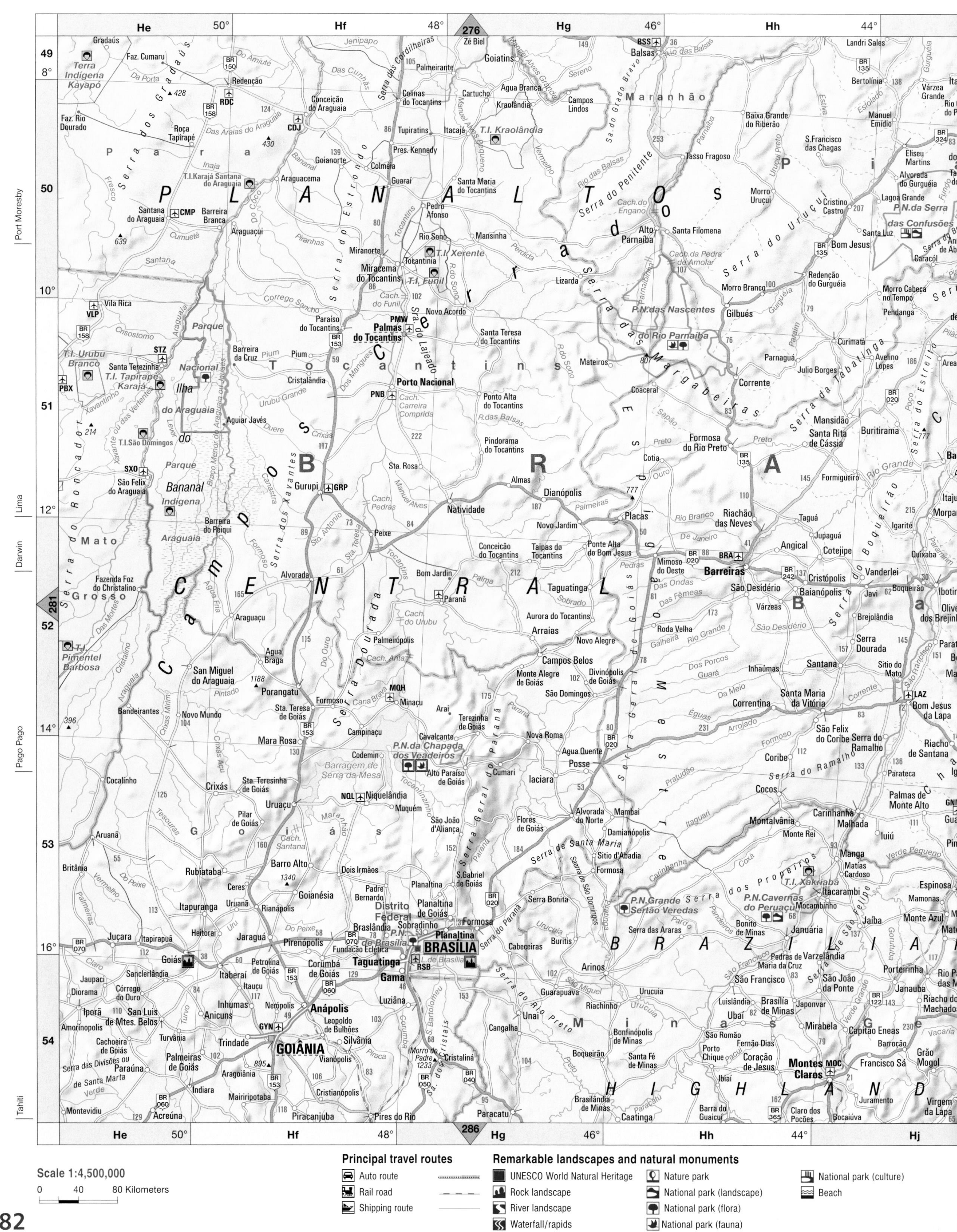

Scale 1:4,500,000

0   40   80 Kilometers

Principal travel routes

🚗 Auto route

🚃 Rail road

🚢 Shipping route

Remarkable landscapes and natural monuments

⬛ UNESCO World Natural Heritage

◾ Rock landscape

◾ River landscape

◾ Waterfall/rapids

◻ Nature park

◻ National park (landscape)

◻ National park (flora)

◻ National park (fauna)

▣ National park (culture)

▨ Beach

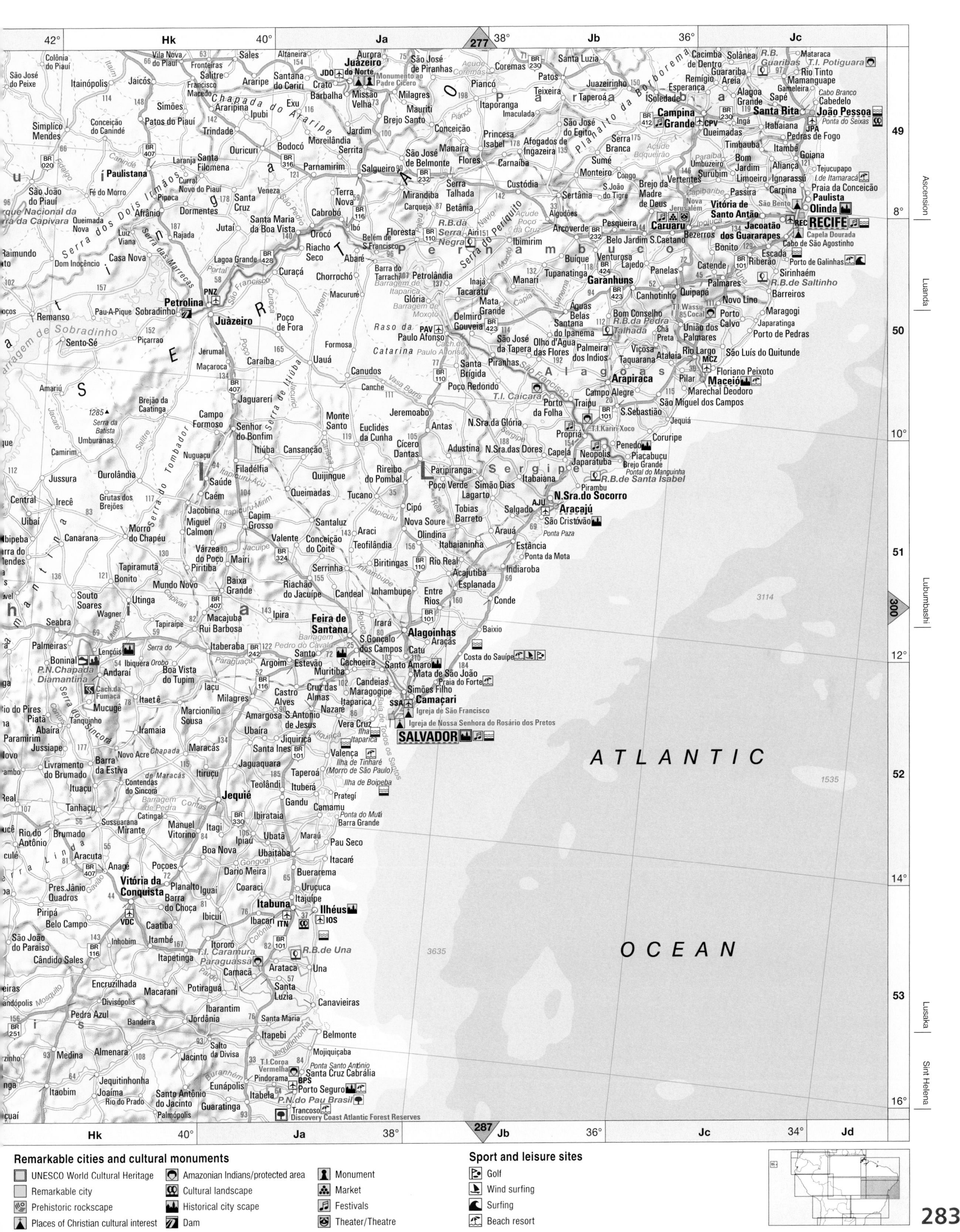

Remarkable cities and cultural monuments

- ☐ UNESCO World Cultural Heritage
- ☐ Remarkable city
- ☐ Prehistoric rockscape
- ▲ Places of Christian cultural interest
- ⊛ Amazonian Indians/protected area
- ⊠ Cultural landscape
- ⛰ Historical city scape
- 🏛 Monument
- 🏪 Market
- 🎵 Festivals
- 🎭 Theater/Theatre
- ☷ Dam

Sport and leisure sites

- ⛳ Golf
- 🏄 Wind surfing
- 🏄 Surfing
- 🏖 Beach resort

283

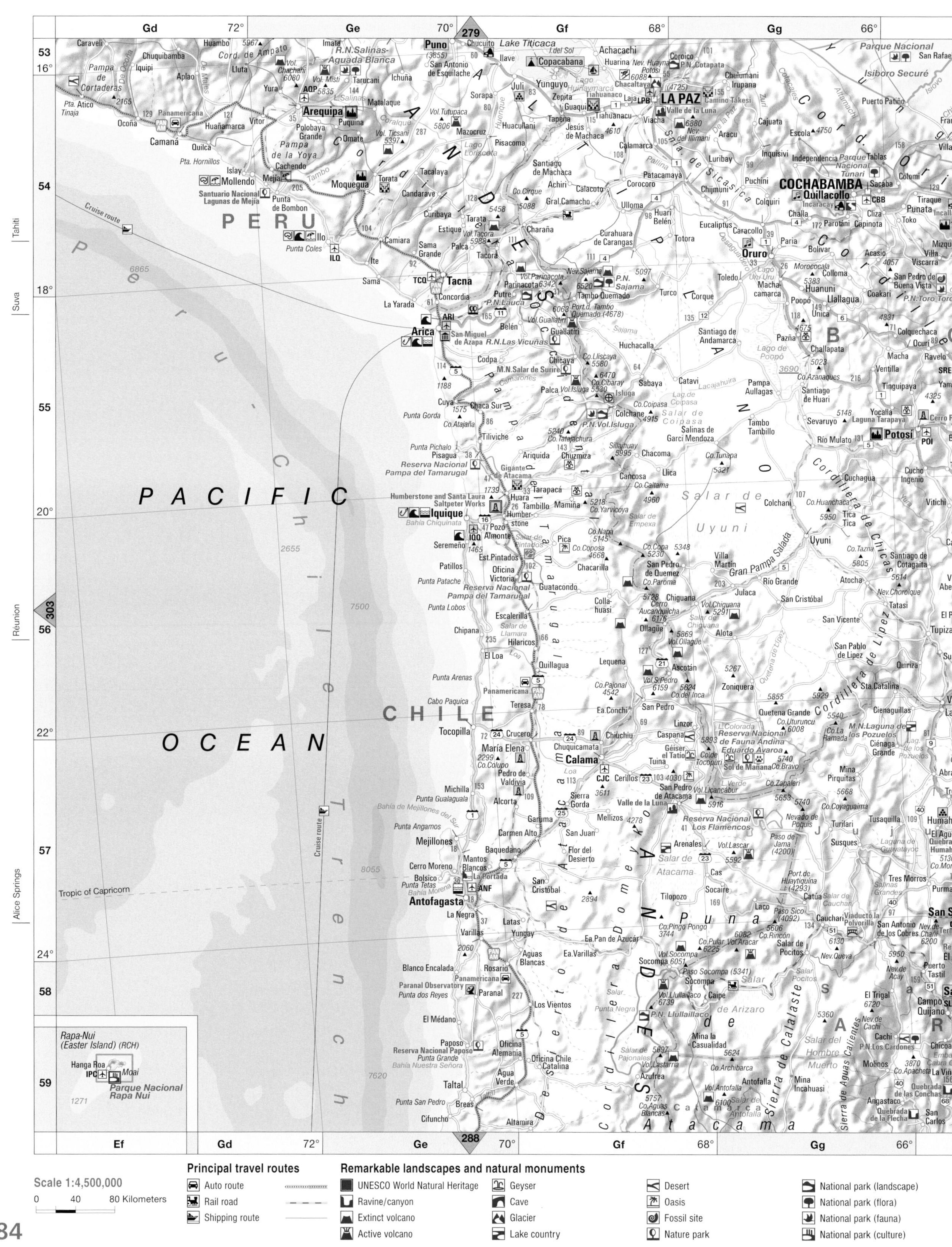

Scale 1:4,500,000

0   40   80 Kilometers

Principal travel routes

- 🚗 Auto route
- 🚂 Rail road
- 🚢 Shipping route
- ·········· UNESCO World Natural Heritage
- ✈ (cruise route)

Remarkable landscapes and natural monuments

- 🏛 UNESCO World Natural Heritage
- 🏔 Ravine/canyon
- 🌋 Extinct volcano
- 🌋 Active volcano
- 💨 Geyser
- 🕳 Cave
- ❄ Glacier
- 🏞 Lake country
- 🏜 Desert
- 🌴 Oasis
- 🦴 Fossil site
- ✿ Nature park
- 🏞 National park (landscape)
- 🌸 National park (flora)
- 🦌 National park (fauna)
- 🏛 National park (culture)

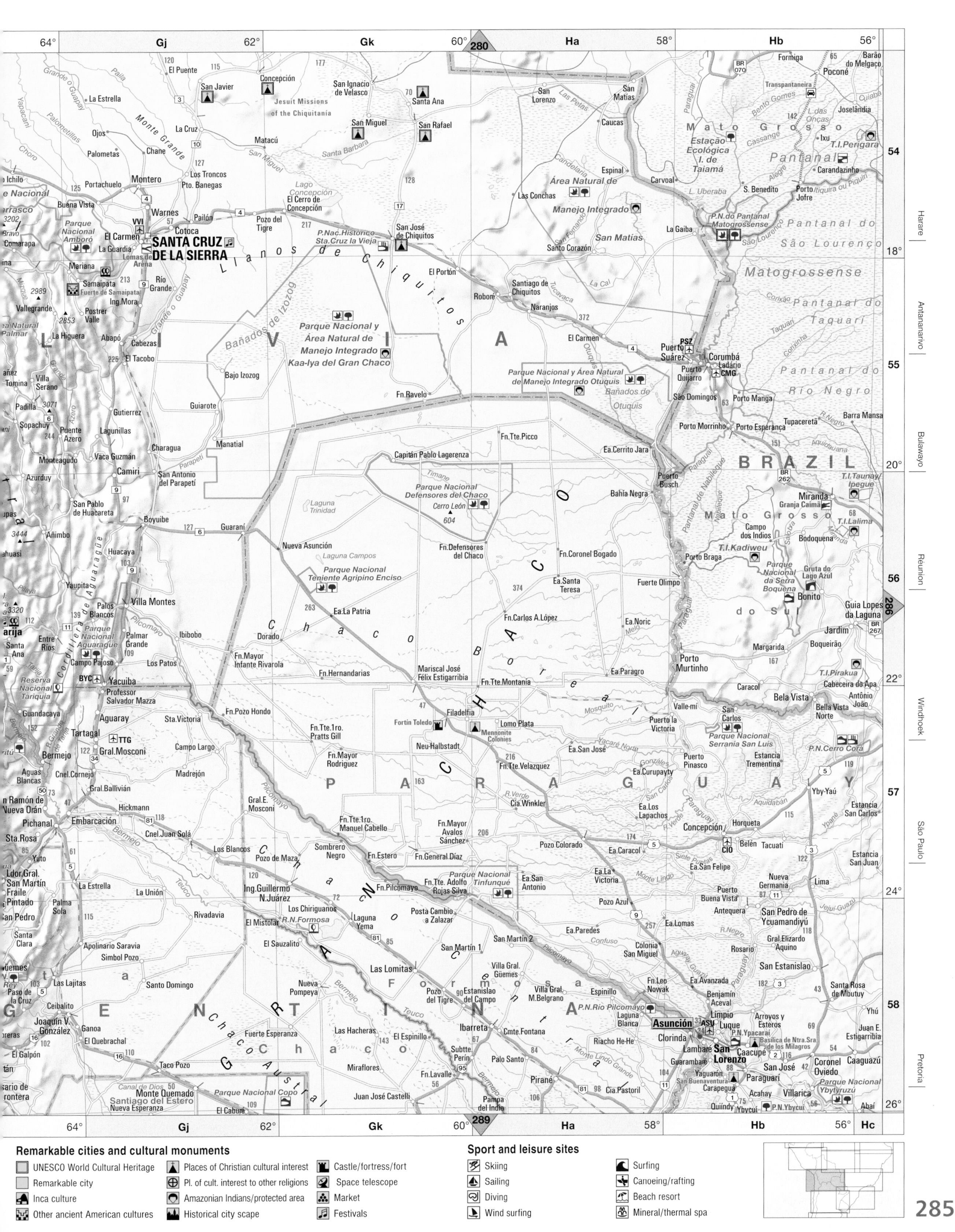

Harare

Antananarivo

Bulawayo

Réunion

Windhoek

São Paulo

Pretoria

54

18°

55

20°

286

22°

57

24°

58

26°

El Puente 115
San Javier
Concepción
La Estrella
San Ignacio de Velasco
177
San Ignacio
San Lorenzo
San Matías
Formiga 65 Barão do Melgaço
BR 070
Poconé
Transpantaneira
Joselândia

La Cruz
San Miguel
San Rafael
70 Santa Ana
Caucas
142 das Onças
T.I. Perigara
Ixu

Matacú
San Barbara
Área Natural de
Espinal
Carvoal
Estação Ecológica I. de Taiamá
Carandazinho

Los Troncos
Pto. Banegas
128
Las Conchas
Manejo Integrado
S. Benedito
L. Uberaba
Porto Jofre

Montero
217
El Cerro de Concepción
San José de Chiquitos
Santo Corazón
San Matías
La Gaiba
P.N. do Pantanal Matogrossense
Pantanal do São Lourenço

SANTA CRUZ DE LA SIERRA
Llanos de Chiquitos
El Portón
Santiago de Chiquitos
La Cal

Mariana
Samaipata
Robore
Naranjos
El Carmen
Puerto Suárez PSZ
Corumbá

La Higuera
372
Ladário
CMG
Puerto Quijarro

Remarkable cities and cultural monuments

Sport and leisure sites

285

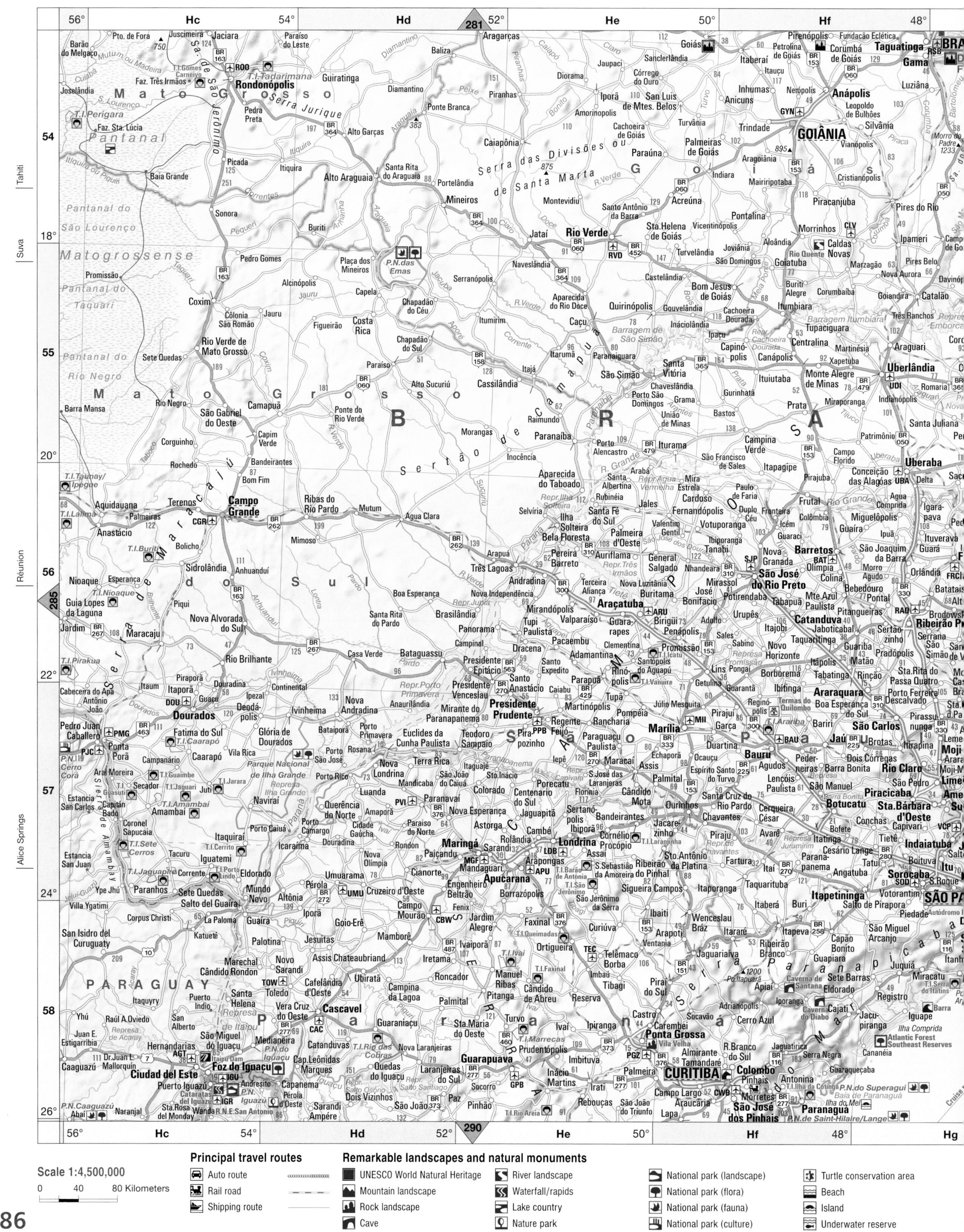

Scale 1:4,500,000

0   40   80 Kilometers

Principal travel routes

🚗 Auto route
🚂 Rail road
⚓ Shipping route

Remarkable landscapes and natural monuments

■ UNESCO World Natural Heritage
▲ Mountain landscape
▬ Rock landscape
◗ Cave

🏞 River landscape
🌊 Waterfall/rapids
≋ Lake country
📷 Nature park

🏞 National park (landscape)
🌸 National park (flora)
🐾 National park (fauna)
🏛 National park (culture)

🐢 Turtle conservation area
≈ Beach
🏝 Island
≈ Underwater reserve

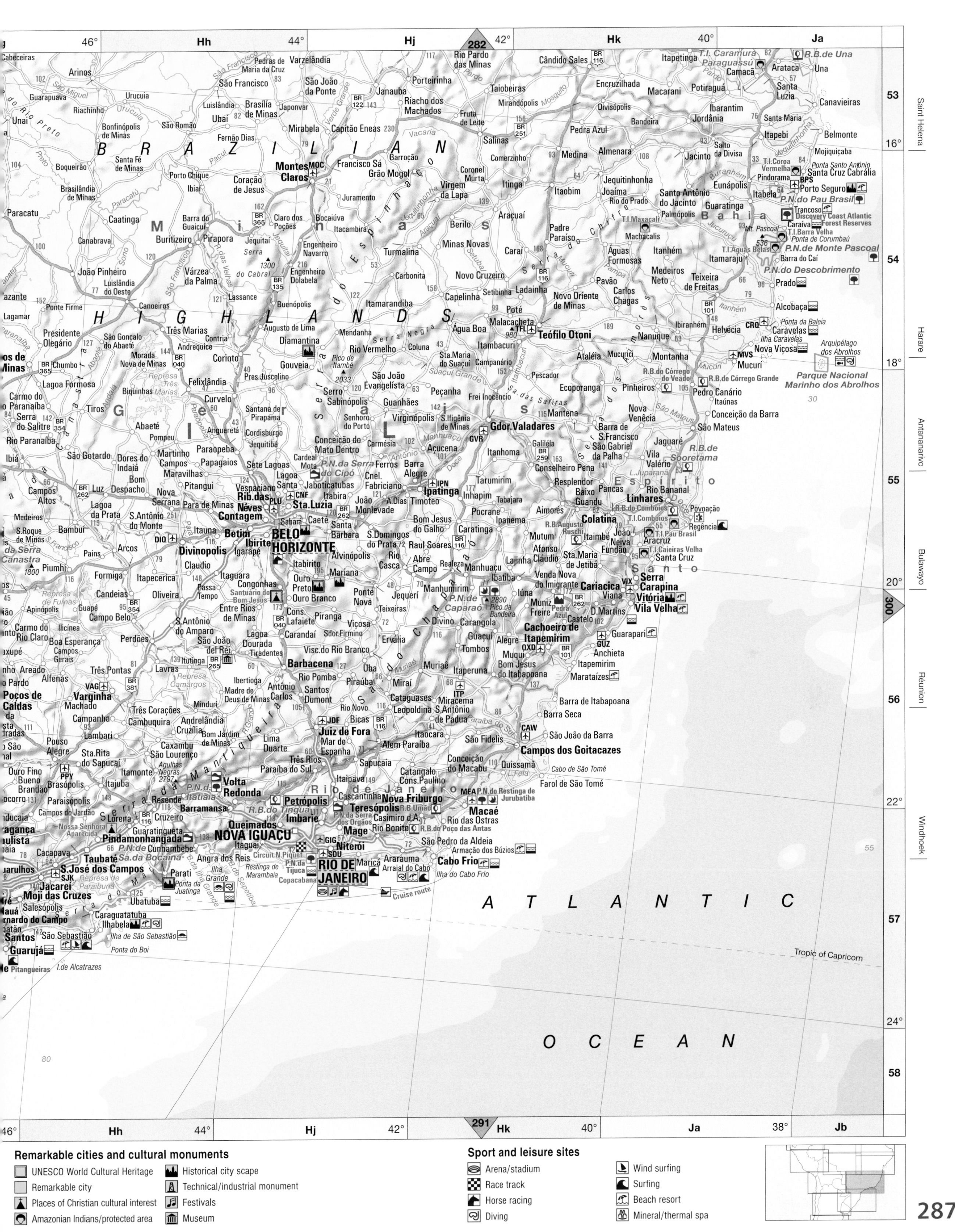

Remarkable cities and cultural monuments

- UNESCO World Cultural Heritage
- Remarkable city
- Places of Christian cultural interest
- Amazonian Indians/protected area
- Historical city scape
- Technical/industrial monument
- Festivals
- Museum

Sport and leisure sites

- Arena/stadium
- Race track
- Horse racing
- Diving
- Wind surfing
- Surfing
- Beach resort
- Mineral/thermal spa

287

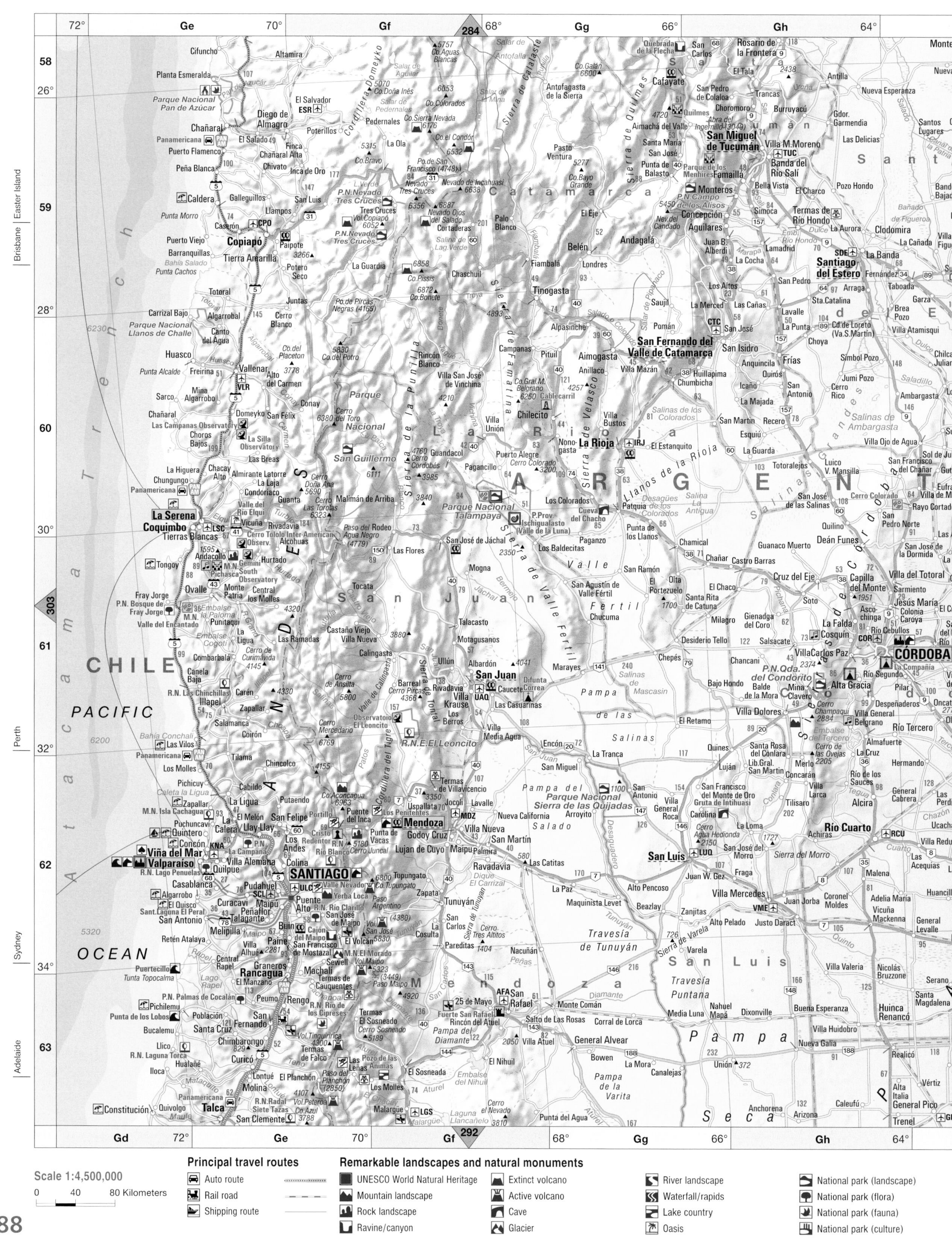

Scale 1:4,500,000

0   40   80 Kilometers

Principal travel routes

- 🚗 Auto route
- 🚂 Rail road
- ⚓ Shipping route

.... (dotted line)
— — — (dashed line)
——— (solid line)

Remarkable landscapes and natural monuments

- ■ UNESCO World Natural Heritage
- ▲ Mountain landscape
- ■ Rock landscape
- ▲ Ravine/canyon

- ▲ Extinct volcano
- ▲ Active volcano
- ■ Cave
- ■ Glacier

- ■ River landscape
- ■ Waterfall/rapids
- ■ Lake country
- ■ Oasis

- ■ National park (landscape)
- ■ National park (flora)
- ■ National park (fauna)
- ■ National park (culture)

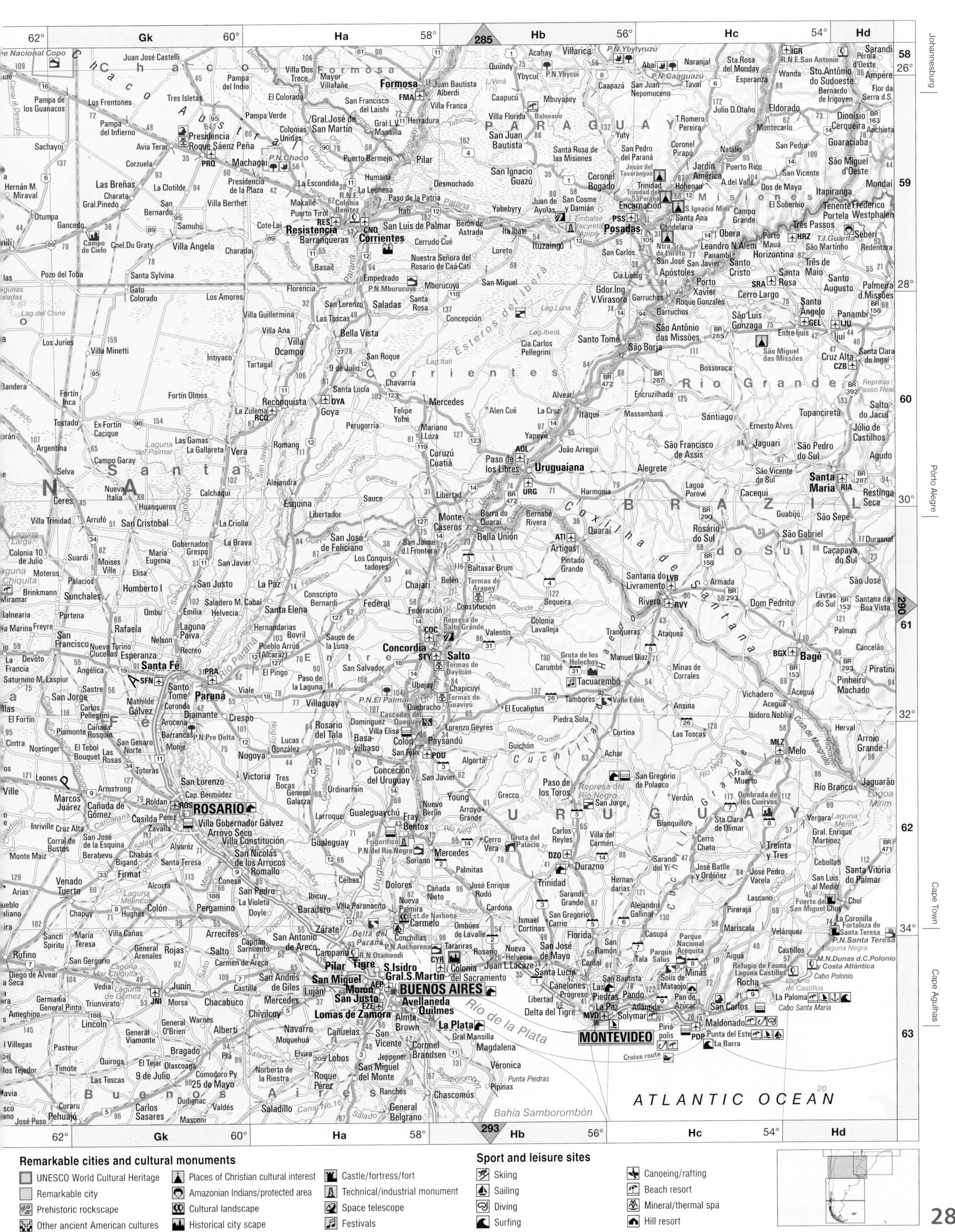

Remarkable cities and cultural monuments

- ☐ UNESCO World Cultural Heritage
- ☐ Remarkable city
- ⬡ Prehistoric rockscape
- ⬢ Other ancient American cultures
- ▲ Places of Christian cultural interest
- ⬤ Amazonian Indians/protected area
- ⬡ Cultural landscape
- ⬛ Historical city scape
- ⬛ Castle/fortress/fort
- ▲ Technical/industrial monument
- ⬛ Space telescope
- ♫ Festivals

Sport and leisure sites

- Skiing
- Sailing
- Diving
- Surfing
- Canoeing/rafting
- Beach resort
- Mineral/thermal spa
- Hill resort

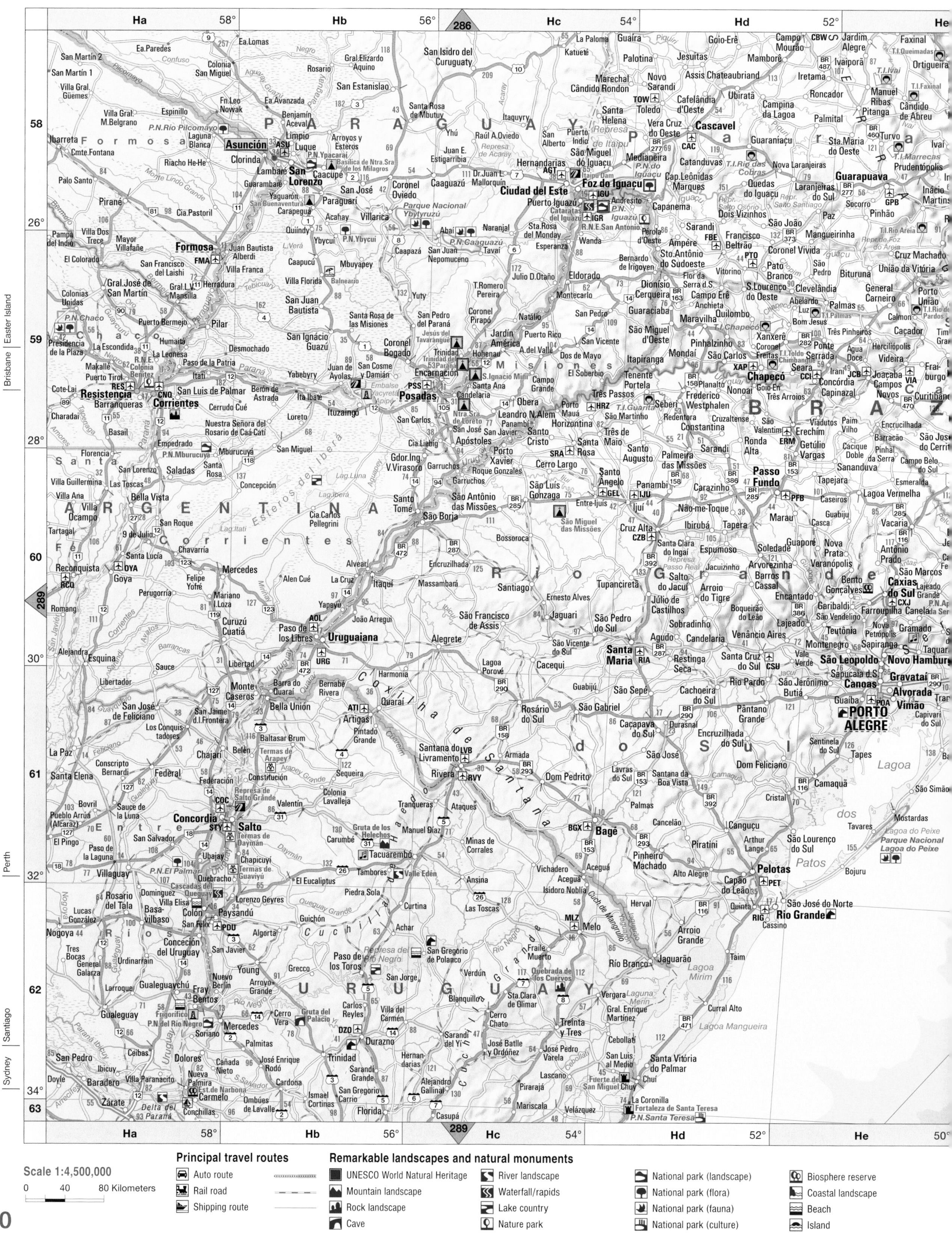

Scale 1:4,500,000

0   40   80 Kilometers

Principal travel routes

- Auto route
- Rail road
- Shipping route

Remarkable landscapes and natural monuments

- UNESCO World Natural Heritage
- Mountain landscape
- Rock landscape
- Cave
- River landscape
- Waterfall/rapids
- Lake country
- Nature park
- National park (landscape)
- National park (flora)
- National park (fauna)
- National park (culture)
- Biosphere reserve
- Coastal landscape
- Beach
- Island

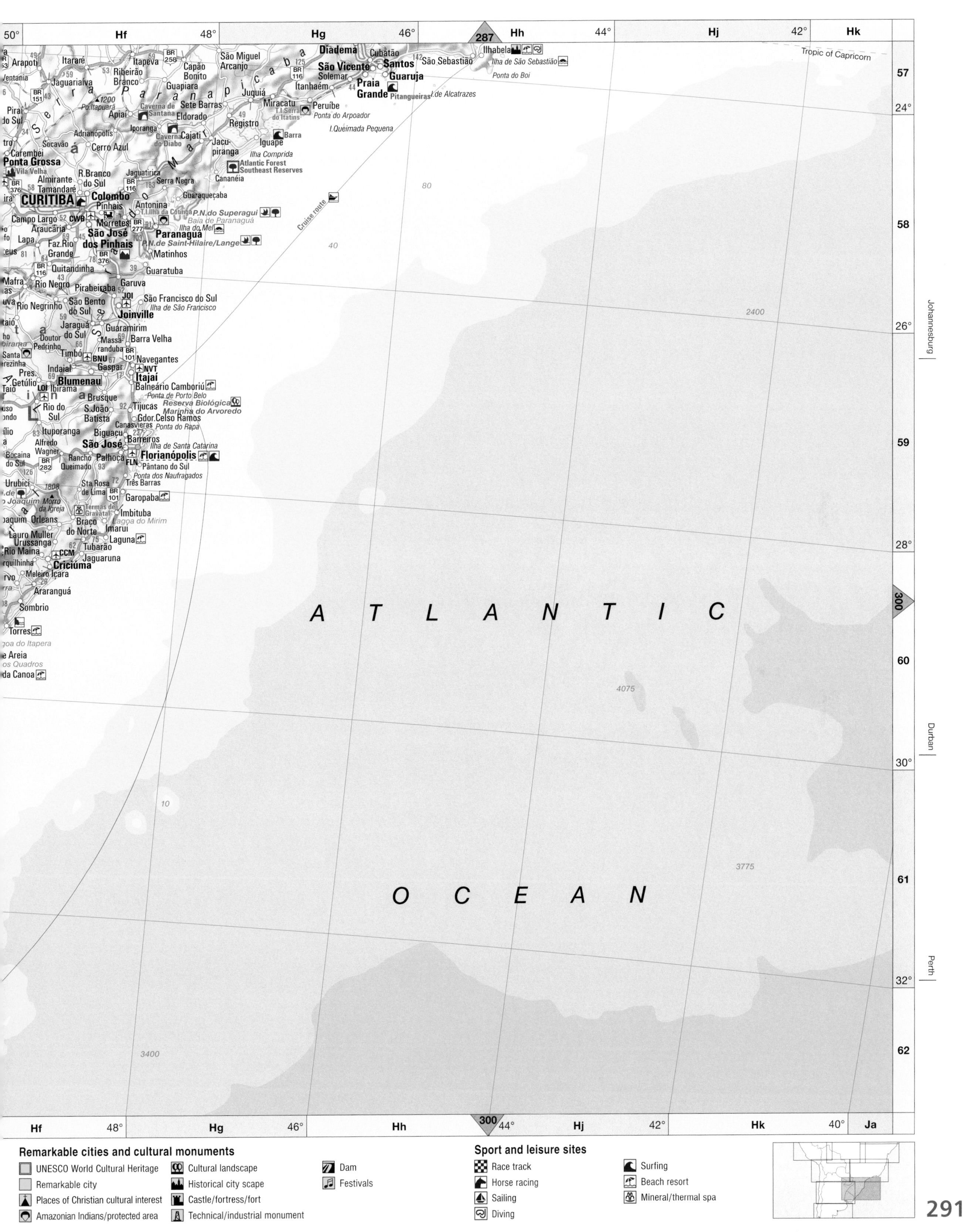

ATLANTIC

OCEAN

Tropic of Capricorn

Remarkable cities and cultural monuments

- ☐ UNESCO World Cultural Heritage
- ☐ Remarkable city
- 🅰 Places of Christian cultural interest
- ◩ Amazonian Indians/protected area
- ⊕ Cultural landscape
- ◩ Historical city scape
- ◪ Castle/fortress/fort
- 🅰 Technical/industrial monument
- ▨ Dam
- 🎵 Festivals

Sport and leisure sites

- ▨ Race track
- 🐎 Horse racing
- ⛵ Sailing
- ◲ Diving
- 🏄 Surfing
- 🏖 Beach resort
- ♨ Mineral/thermal spa

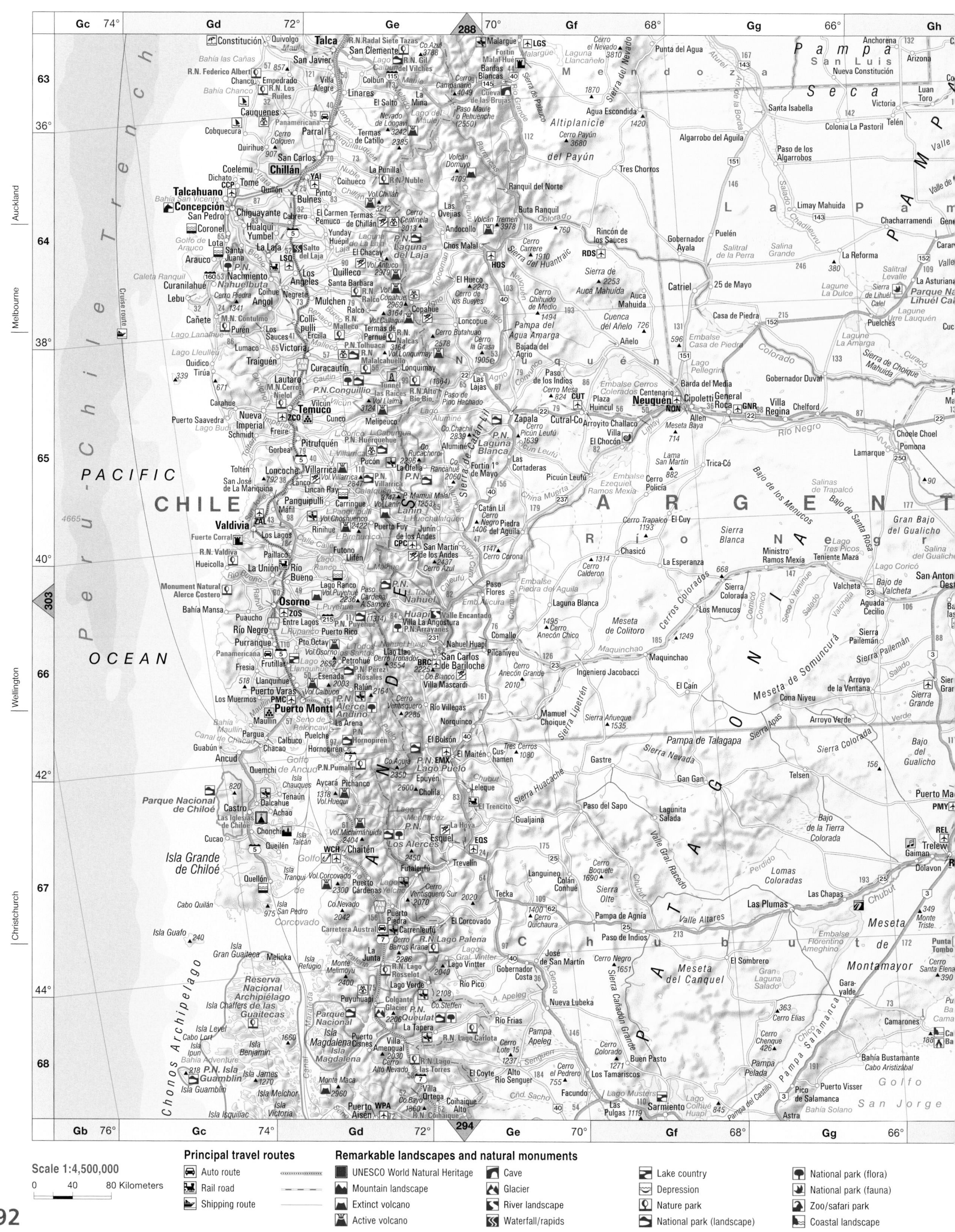

Scale 1:4,500,000

0   40   80 Kilometers

Principal travel routes

🚗 Auto route
🚂 Rail road
⚓ Shipping route

Remarkable landscapes and natural monuments

⬛ UNESCO World Natural Heritage
🏔 Mountain landscape
🌋 Extinct volcano
🌋 Active volcano

🕳 Cave
❄ Glacier
🏞 River landscape
💧 Waterfall/rapids

🏞 Lake country
🔽 Depression
🏕 Nature park
🏔 National park (landscape)

🌳 National park (flora)
🦅 National park (fauna)
🦓 Zoo/safari park
🏖 Coastal landscape

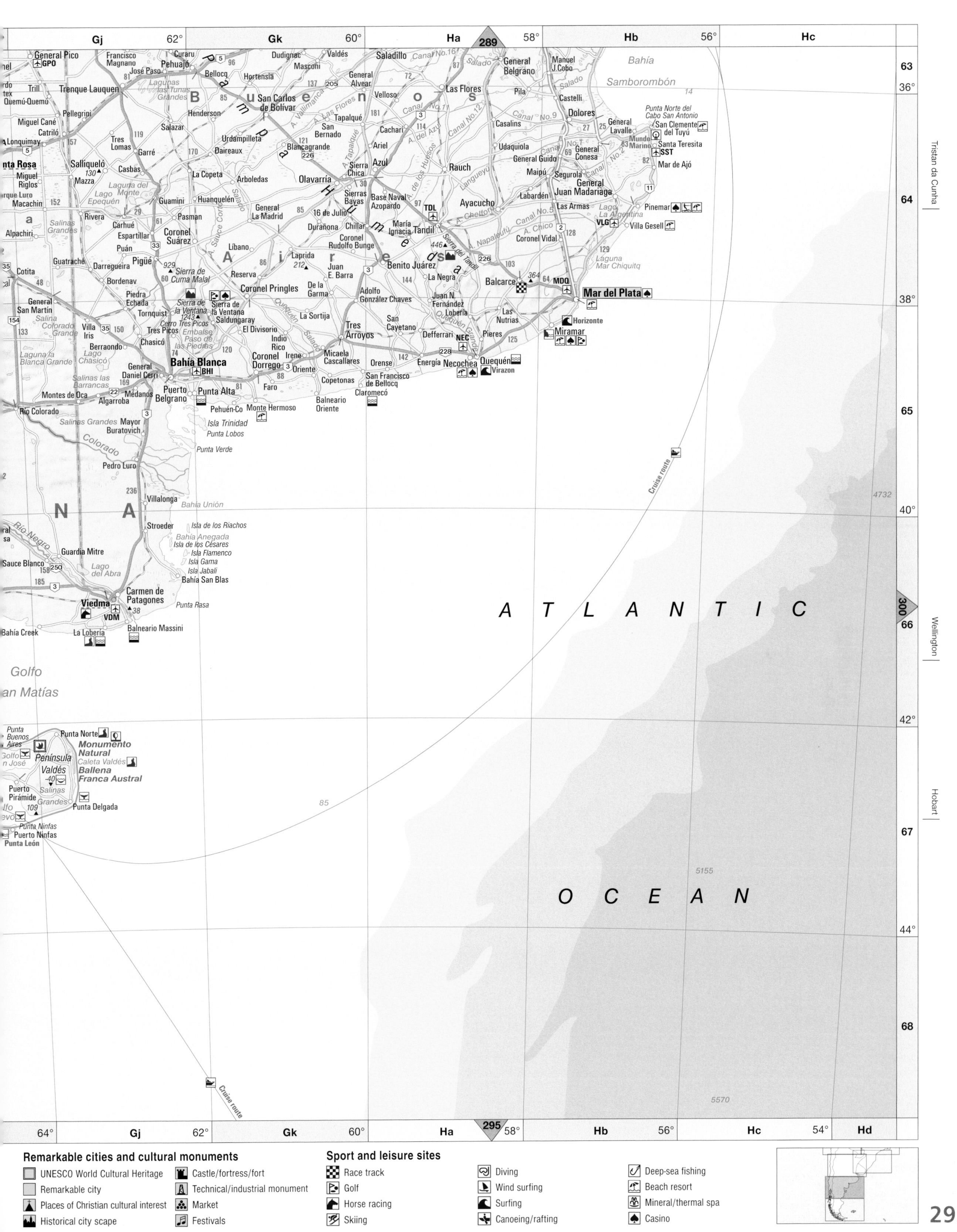

Remarkable cities and cultural monuments

- UNESCO World Cultural Heritage
- Remarkable city
- Places of Christian cultural interest
- Historical city scape
- Castle/fortress/fort
- Technical/industrial monument
- Market
- Festivals

Sport and leisure sites

- Race track
- Golf
- Horse racing
- Skiing
- Diving
- Wind surfing
- Surfing
- Canoeing/rafting
- Deep-sea fishing
- Beach resort
- Mineral/thermal spa
- Casino

293

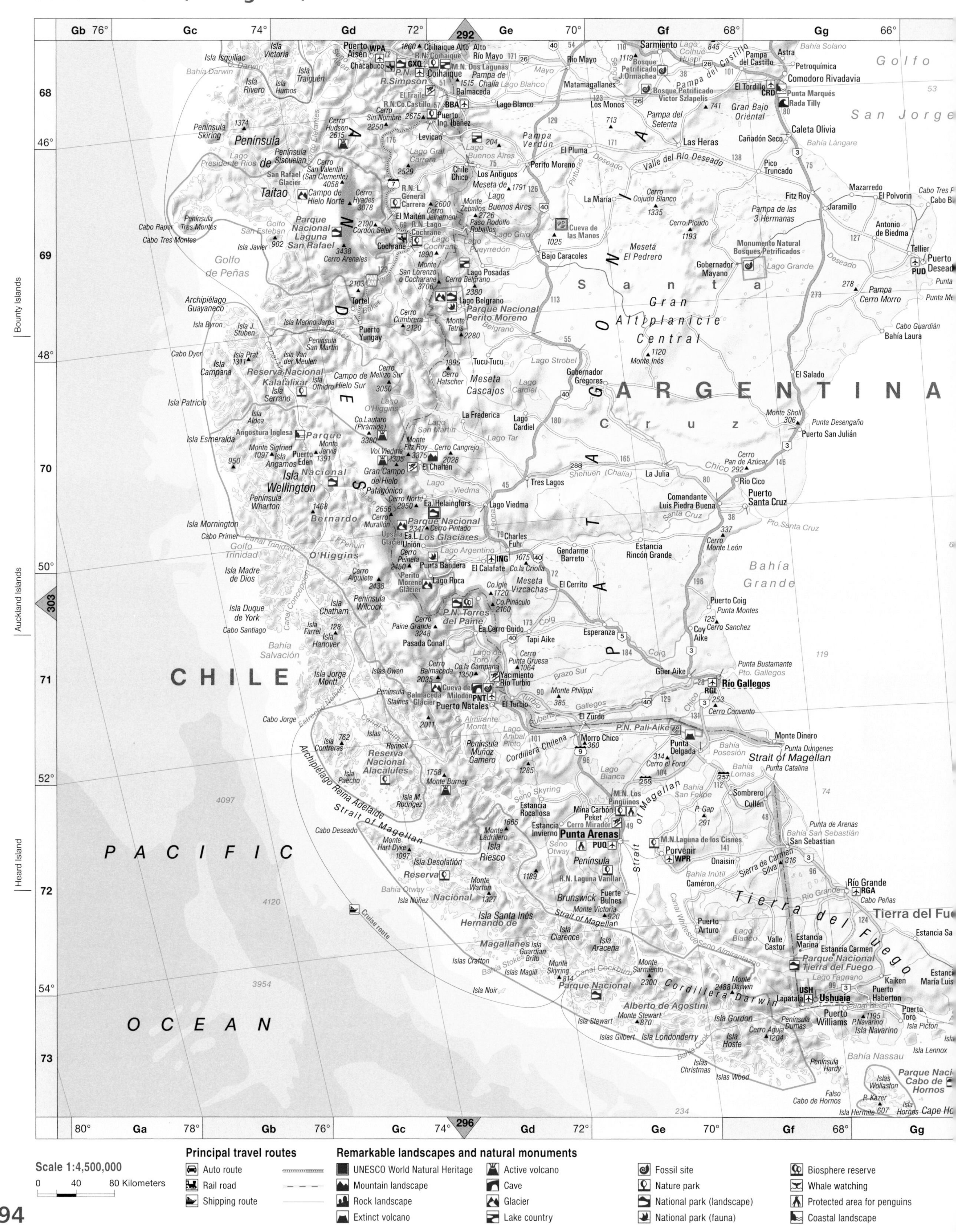

Scale 1:4,500,000

0   40   80 Kilometers

Principal travel routes

- Auto route
- Rail road
- Shipping route

Remarkable landscapes and natural monuments

- UNESCO World Natural Heritage
- Mountain landscape
- Rock landscape
- Extinct volcano
- Active volcano
- Cave
- Glacier
- Lake country
- Fossil site
- Nature park
- National park (landscape)
- National park (fauna)
- Biosphere reserve
- Whale watching
- Protected area for penguins
- Coastal landscape

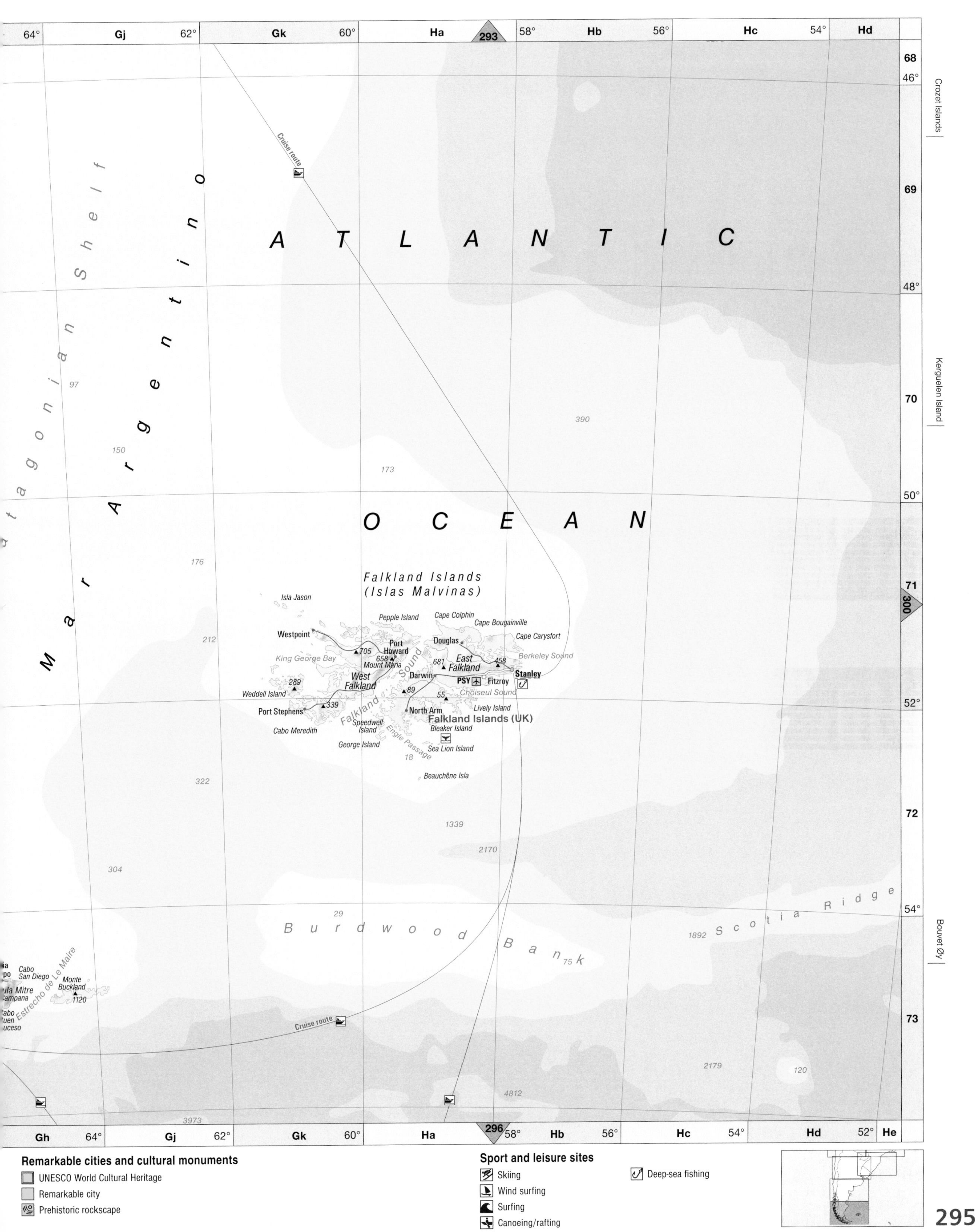

68
46°

Crozet Islands

Cruise route

A T L A N T I C

69

48°

Mar Argentino *Patagonian Shelf*

97

Kerguelen Island

70

150

173

390

O C E A N

176

50°

Falkland Islands *(Islas Malvinas)*

Isla Jason

212

71
300

Pepple Island *Cape Colphin* *Cape Bougainville*
Cape Carysfort

Westpoint *Berkeley Sound*

Douglas

▲705 **Port Howard** *East Falkland* 458▲

King George Bay ▲658 *Mount Maria* 681▲ **Stanley**
Darwin 458 **PSY** ✈ *Fitzroy*

West Falkland ▲289 ▲89 55▲ *Choiseul Sound*
Weddell Island

North Arm *Lively Island*

Port Stephens ▲339 **Falkland Islands (UK)**

322 *Speedwell Island* *Bleaker Island*

Cabo Meredith *Sea Lion Island*

George Island 18 *Engle Passage*

Beauchêne Isla

1339

2170

304

Scotia Ridge

54°

29

B u r d w o o d   B a n 75 *k* 1892

Cabo San Diego *Monte Buckland*
Estrecho de Le Maire 1120

73

2179 120

Cruise route

3973 4812

52°

72

Bouvet Øy

Remarkable cities and cultural monuments

⬜ UNESCO World Cultural Heritage

⬜ Remarkable city

Prehistoric rockscape

Sport and leisure sites

Skiing

Wind surfing

Surfing

Canoeing/rafting

Deep-sea fishing

295

Antarctica

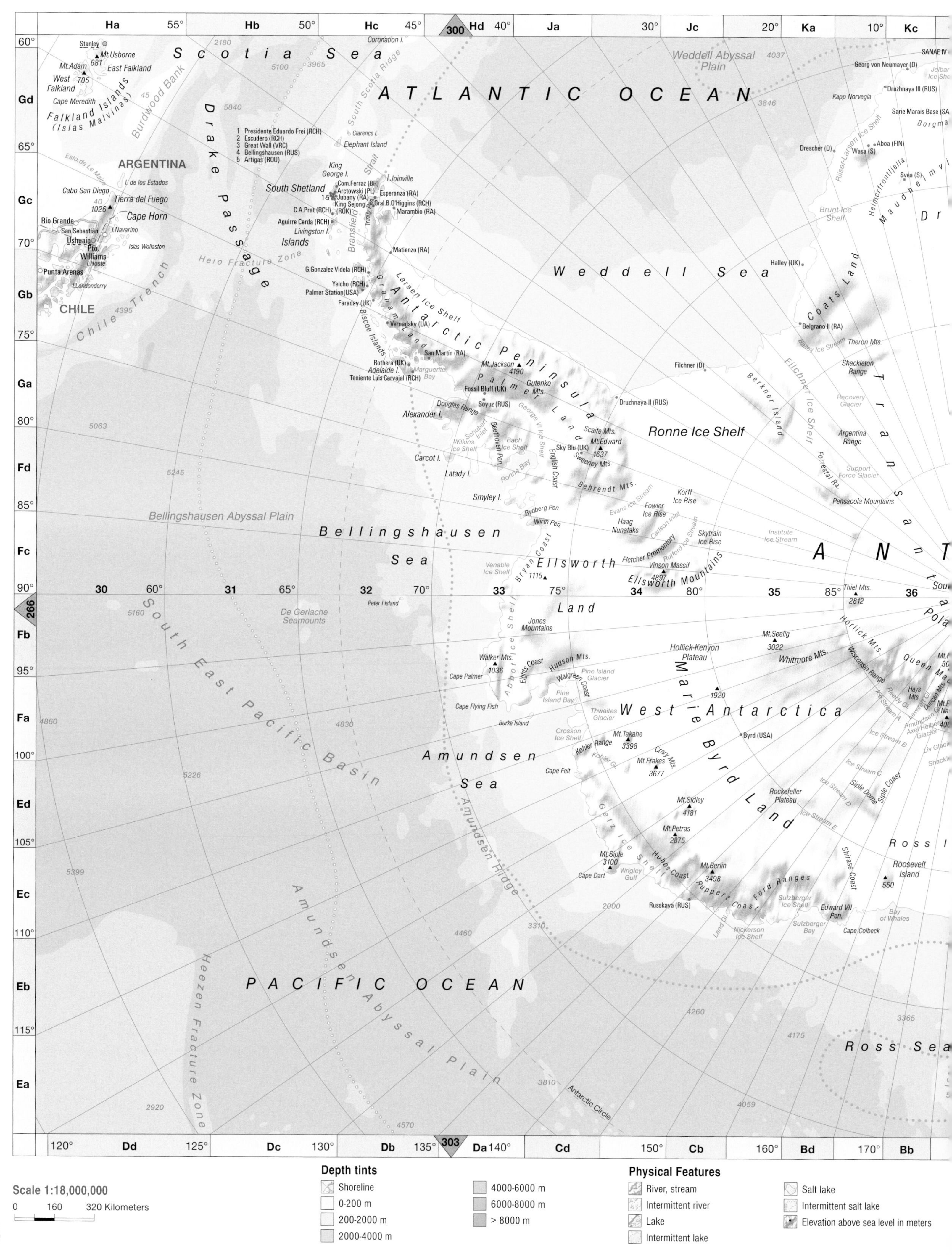

Scale 1:18,000,000

0   160   320 Kilometers

Depth tints

- Shoreline
- 0-200 m
- 200-2000 m
- 2000-4000 m
- 4000-6000 m
- 6000-8000 m
- > 8000 m

Physical Features

- River, stream
- Intermittent river
- Lake
- Intermittent lake
- Salt lake
- Intermittent salt lake
- Elevation above sea level in meters

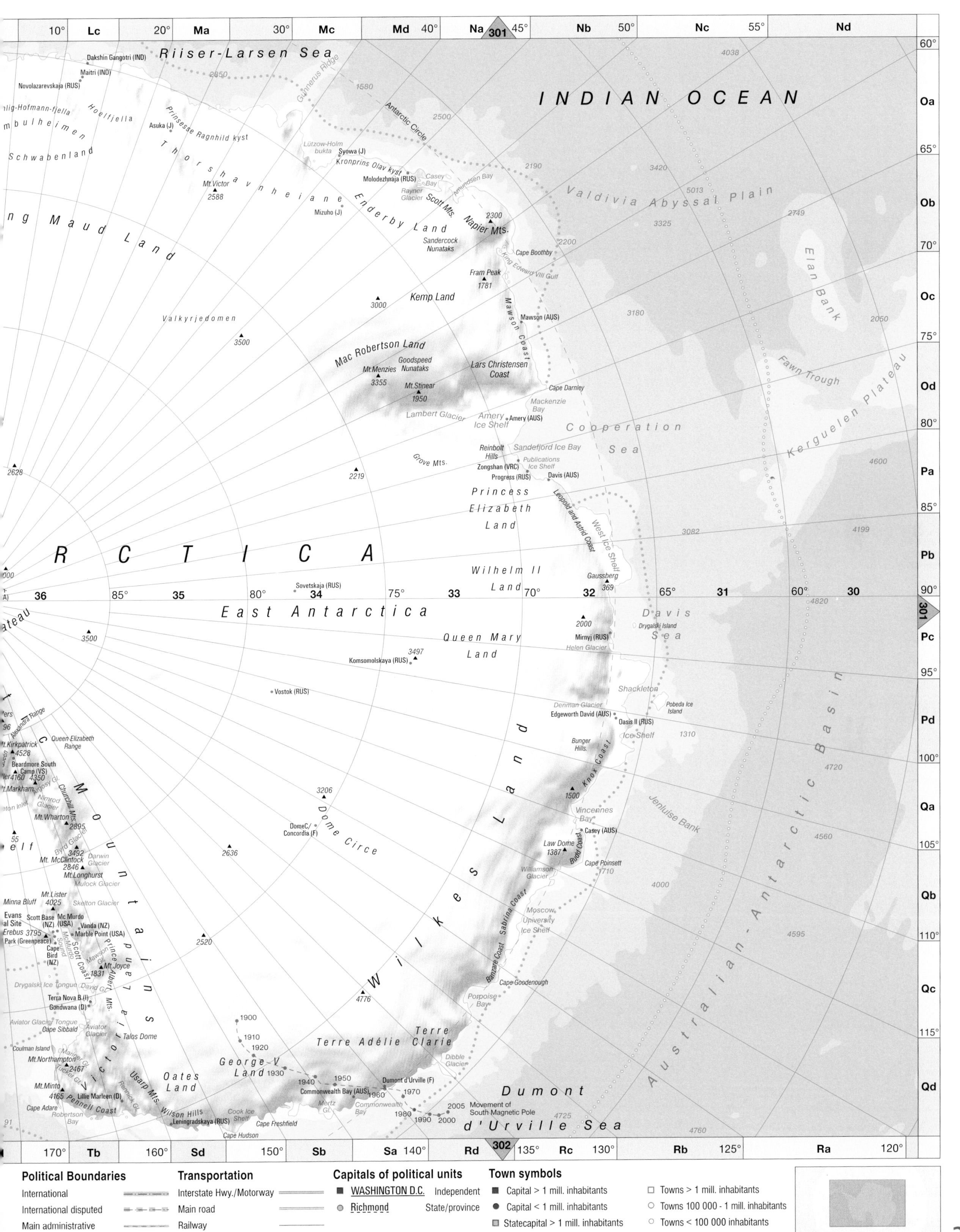

Riiser-Larsen Sea

INDIAN OCEAN

Dakshin Gangotri (IND)
Maitri (IND)
Novolazarevskaya (RUS)

Gunnerus Ridge
Antarctic Circle

lig-Hofmann-fjella
mbuheimen
Hoelfjella

Schwabenland

Thorshavnheiane

Prinsesse Ragnhild kyst

Asuka (J)

Mt.Victor
2588

Valdivia Abyssal Plain

Lützow-Holm bukta

Syowa (J)

Kronprins Olav kyst

Molodezhnaja (RUS)

Casey Bay

Rayner Glacier

Scott Mts.

Mizuho (J)

Napier Mts.

2300

Amundsen Bay

Enderby Land

ng Maud Land

Elan Bank

Cape Boothby

Sandercock Nunataks

King Edward VIII Gulf

Fram Peak
1781

Valkyrjedomen

Kemp Land

3000

Mawson (AUS)

Mawson Coast

Mac Robertson Land

3500

Goodspeed Nunataks

Mt.Menzies
3355

Lars Christensen Coast

Mt.Stinear
1950

Cape Darnley

Lambert Glacier

Mackenzie Bay

Fawn Trough

Kerguelen Plateau

Amery Ice Shelf

Amery (AUS)

Co o p e r a t i o n

Grove Mts.

Reinbolt Hills

Sandefjord Ice Bay

S e a

2219

Zongshan (VRC)

Publications Ice Shelf

Progress (RUS)

Davis (AUS)

Princess Elizabeth Land

Leopold and Astrid Coast

West Ice Shelf

Wilhelm II Land

Gaussberg
369

R C T I C A

Sovetskaja (RUS)

E a s t A n t a r c t i c a

D a v i s
S e a

Drygalski Island

3500

2000

Mirnyj (RUS)

Queen Mary Land

Helen Glacier

Komsomolskaya (RUS)

3497

Vostok (RUS)

Shackleton

Denman Glacier

Edgeworth David (AUS)

Pobeda Ice Island

Oasis II (RUS)
Ice Shelf

Bunger Hills.

1310

Knox Coast

Vincennes Bay

3206

1500

Dome C./Concordia (F)

Dome Circe

Casey (AUS)

Law Dome
1387

2636

Budd Coast

Cape Poinsett

Williamson Glacier

Moscow University Ice Shelf

Sabrina Coast

2520

W i l k e s L a n d

Banzare Coast

Cape Goodenough

Porpoise Bay

1900

Terre Adélie

1910

Clarie

1920

George V Land

Dibble Glacier

Terra Nova B.(I)

1930

Gondwana (D)

Aviator Glacier Tongue

Talos Dome

Cape Sibbald

Coulman Island

Mt.Northampton

2467

Oates Land

1940

Wilson Hills

1950

Commonwealth Bay (AUS)

Dumont d'Urville (F)

Mt.Minto
4165

Lillie Marleen (D)

Leningradskaya (RUS)

Cape Freshfield

Cape Hudson

D u m o n t

1960

1970

Mertz Gl.

Commonwealth Bay

1980

1990

2000

2005

Movement of South Magnetic Pole

d ' U r v i l l e S e a

Political Boundaries

International

International disputed

Main administrative

Transportation

Interstate Hwy./Motorway

Main road

Railway

Airport

Capitals of political units

■ WASHINGTON D.C. Independent
◉ Richmond State/province

Town symbols

■ Capital > 1 mill. inhabitants
● Capital < 1 mill. inhabitants
▣ Statecapital > 1 mill. inhabitants
◉ Statecapital < 1 mill. inhabitants

□ Towns > 1 mill. inhabitants
◌ Towns 100 000 - 1 mill. inhabitants
○ Towns < 100 000 inhabitants

Arctic Region

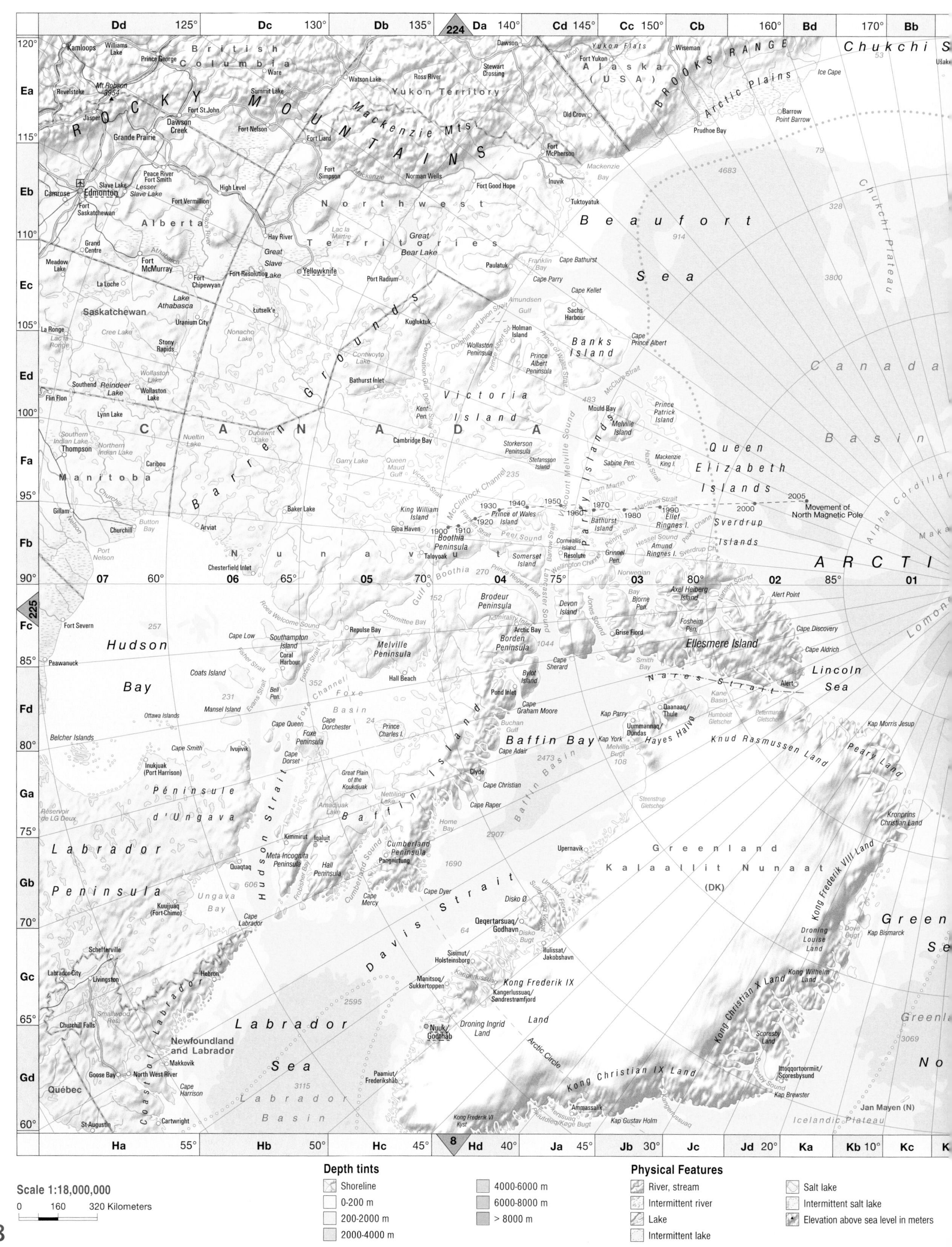

| | Dd | 125° | Dc | 130° | Db | 135° | 224 Da | 140° | Cd | 145° | Cc | 150° | Cb | | 160° | Bd | | 170° | Bb |

Scale 1:18,000,000

0   160   320 Kilometers

Depth tints

- Shoreline
- 0–200 m
- 200–2000 m
- 2000–4000 m
- 4000–6000 m
- 6000–8000 m
- > 8000 m

Physical Features

- River, stream
- Intermittent river
- Lake
- Intermittent lake
- Salt lake
- Intermittent salt lake
- Elevation above sea level in meters

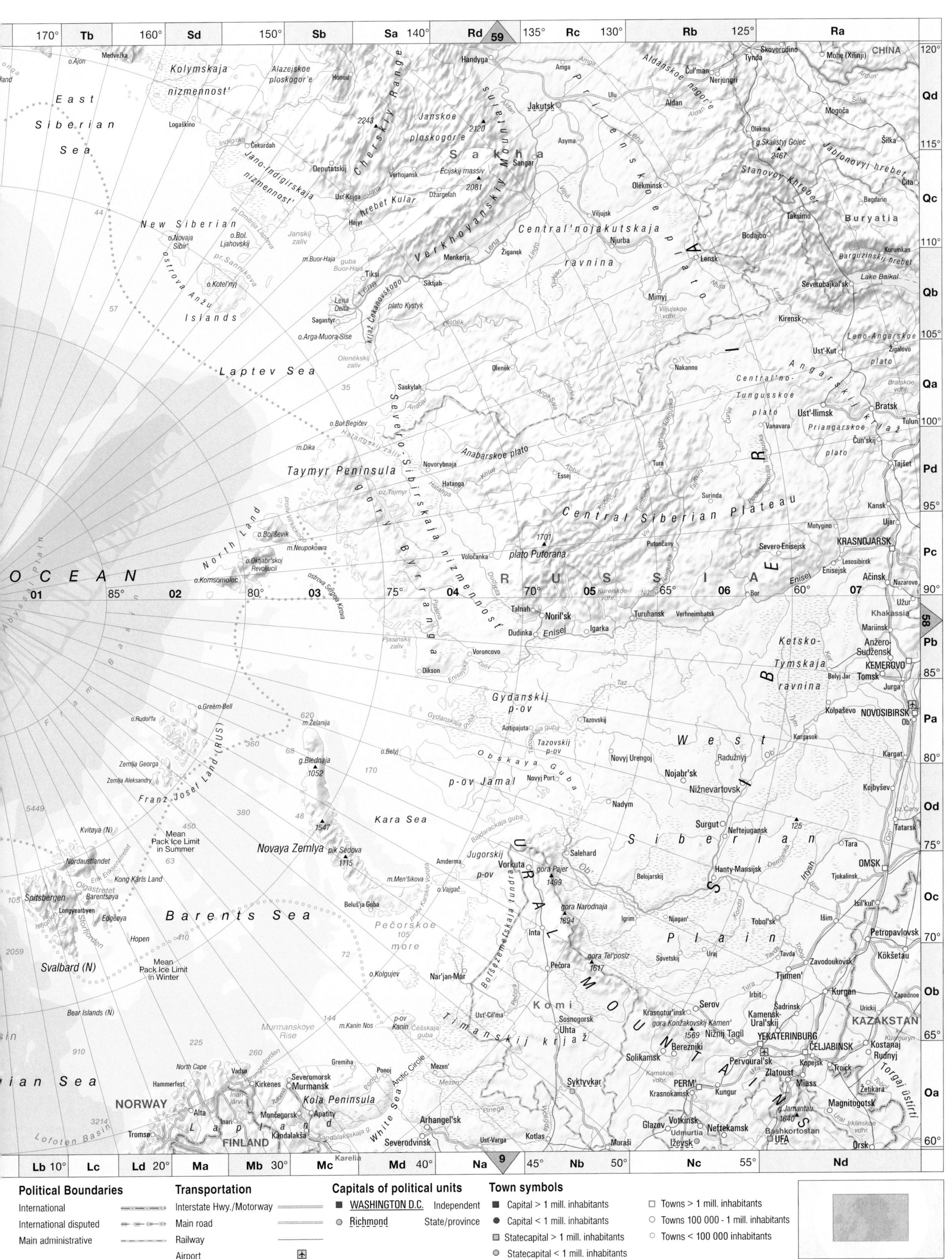

170°
Tb
160°
Sd
150°
Sb
Sa 140°
Rd 59
135°
Rc
130°
Rb
125°
Ra
120°
Qd
115°
Qc
110°
Qb
105°
Qa
100°
Pd
95°
Pc
90°
58
Pb
85°
Pa
80°
Od
75°
Oc
70°
Ob
65°
Oa
60°
Lb 10°
Lc
Ld 20°
Ma
Mb 30°
Mc
Md 40°
Na 9
45°
Nb
50°
Nc
55°
Nd
01
85°
02
80°
03
75°
04
70°
05
65°
06
60°
07
CHINA
Skovorodino
Tynda
Molie (Xilinji)
Čul'man
Nerjungri
Aldanskoe nagor'e
Aldan
Mogoča
Handyga
Amga
Jakutsk
Ulu
Asyma
Prilenskoe plato
Olëkma
g.Skalistyj Golec
2467
Stanovoy Khrebet
Jablonovyj hrebet
Šilka
Čita
Bagdarin
Buryatia
Taksimo
Bodajbo
Kurumkan
Barguzinskij hrebet
Lake Baikal
Severobajkal'sk
Olëkminsk
Viljujsk
Central'nojakutskaja ravnina
Njurba
Lensk
Mirnyj
Kirensk
Ust'-Kut
Leno-Angarskoe plato
Žigalovo
Angarskij krjaž
Central'no-Tungusskoe plato
Nakanno
Vanavara
Ust'-Ilimsk
Bratsk
Tulun
Priangarskoe plato
Čun'skij
Tajšet
Kansk
Ujar
Motygino
KRASNOJARSK
Lesosibirsk
Enisejsk
Severo-Enisejsk
Ačinsk
Nazarovo
Užur
Khakassia
Mariinsk
Anžero-Sudžensk
KEMEROVO
Tomsk
Belyj Jar
Jurga
Kolpaševo
NOVOSIBIRSK
Kargasok
Kargat
Kujbyšev
Tatarsk
Tara
OMSK
Tjukalinsk
Isil'kul'
Išim
Petropavlovsk
Kökšetau
Zavodoukovsk
Tjumen'
Kurgan
KAZAKSTAN
Kostanaj
Rudnyj
Torgai üstirti
Žetikara
Magnitogorsk
Orsk
Bashkortostan
UFA
Miass
Zlatoust
Troick
ČELJABINSK
Kopejsk
YEKATERINBURG
Kamensk-Ural'skij
Šadrinsk
Irbit
Nižnij Tagil
Serov
Krasnotur'insk
gora Konžakovskij Kamen'
1569
Berezniki
Solikamsk
Pervoural'sk
PERM'
Krasnokamsk
Kungur
Votkinsk
Glazov
Udmurtia
Iževsk
Neftekamsk
Muraši
Kotlas
Syktyvkar
Ust'-Vaga
Arhangel'sk
Severodvinsk
Mezen'
Kola Peninsula
Murmansk
Severomorsk
Kirkenes
Apatity
Mončegorsk
Kandalakša
Lapland
FINLAND
NORWAY
Alta
Hammerfest
Vadsø
Tromsø
Inari
Karelia
White Sea
Arctic Circle
Lofoten Basin
Barents Sea
Svalbard (N)
Spitsbergen
Longyearbyen
Barentsøya
Edgeøya
Hopen
Kong Karls Land
Nordaustlandet
Kvitøya (N)
Bear Islands (N)
Mean Pack Ice Limit in Summer
Mean Pack Ice Limit in Winter
Franz Josef Land (RUS)
Zemlja Georga
Zemlja Aleksandry
o.Rudol'fa
o.Greem-Bell
m.Želanija
g.Blednaja
1052
Novaya Zemlya
pik Sedova
1115
1547
Kara Sea
Belus'ja Guba
m.Men'šikova
o.Vajgač
Amderma
Jugorskij p-ov
Pečorskoe more
o.Kolgujev
Nar'jan-Mar
Kanin Nos
Murmanskoe Rise
Timanskij krjaž
Komi
Uhta
Sosnogorsk
Ust'-Cil'ma
Pečora
gora Tel'posiz
1617
Inta
gora Narodnaja
1894
Vorkuta
gora Pajer
1499
URAL MOUNTAINS
Salehard
Labytnangi
Bol'šezemel'skaja tundra
West Siberian Plain
Hanty-Mansijsk
Beloiarskij
Igrim
Njagan'
Sovetskij
Uraj
Tobol'sk
Surgut
Neftejugansk
Nižnevartovsk
Nojabr'sk
Raduž nyj
Novyj Urengoj
Nadym
p-ov Jamal
Obskaja Guba
Novyj Port
Tazovskij p-ov
Tazovskij
Antipajuta
Gydanskij p-ov
o.Belyj
Dikson
Voroncovo
Dudinka
Noril'sk
Talnah
Igarka
Turuhansk
Verhneimbatsk
Ketsko-Tymskaja ravnina
RUSSIA
SIBERIA
Bor
Putorana
plato Putorana
1701
Voločanka
Central Siberian Plateau
Surinda
Tura
Essej
Hatanga
Novorybnaja
Anabarskoe plato
Taymyr Peninsula
Severo-Sibirskaja nizmennost'
gory Byrranga
o.Bol'ševik
m.Neupokoeva
o.Oktjabr'skoj Revoljucii
o.Komsomolec
North Land
ostrova Sergeja Kirova
m.Dika
o.Bol.Begičev
Saskylah
Olenëk
Laptev Sea
Olenëkskij zaliv
o.Arga-Muora-Sise
Sagastyr
Lena Delta
plato Kystyk
Tiksi
Siktjah
Menkerja
Žigansk
Verkhoyansk Mountains
hrebet Kular
Džargelah
Ust'-Kujga
Verhojansk
Batagaj
Sangar
Sakha
Ečijskij massiv
2081
Suntar-Hajata
2120
Janskoe ploskogor'e
Cherskiy Range
2243
Deputatskij
Jano-Indigirskaja nizmennost'
Čokurdah
Logaškino
Kolymskaja nizmennost'
Alazejskoe ploskogor'e
Medvežka
Honuu
o.Ajon
East Siberian Sea
New Siberian Islands
o.Novaja Sibir'
o.Bol. Ljahovskij
o.Kotel'nyj
ostrova Anžu
Janskij zaliv
m.Buor-Haja
guba Buor-Haja
OCEAN
Abyssal Plain
Fram Basin

Political Boundaries
International
International disputed
Main administrative
Transportation
Interstate Hwy./Motorway
Main road
Railway
Airport
Capitals of political units
WASHINGTON D.C. Independent
Richmond State/province
Town symbols
Capital > 1 mill. inhabitants
Capital < 1 mill. inhabitants
Statecapital > 1 mill. inhabitants
Statecapital < 1 mill. inhabitants
Towns > 1 mill. inhabitants
Towns 100 000 - 1 mill. inhabitants
Towns < 100 000 inhabitants

Atlantic Ocean

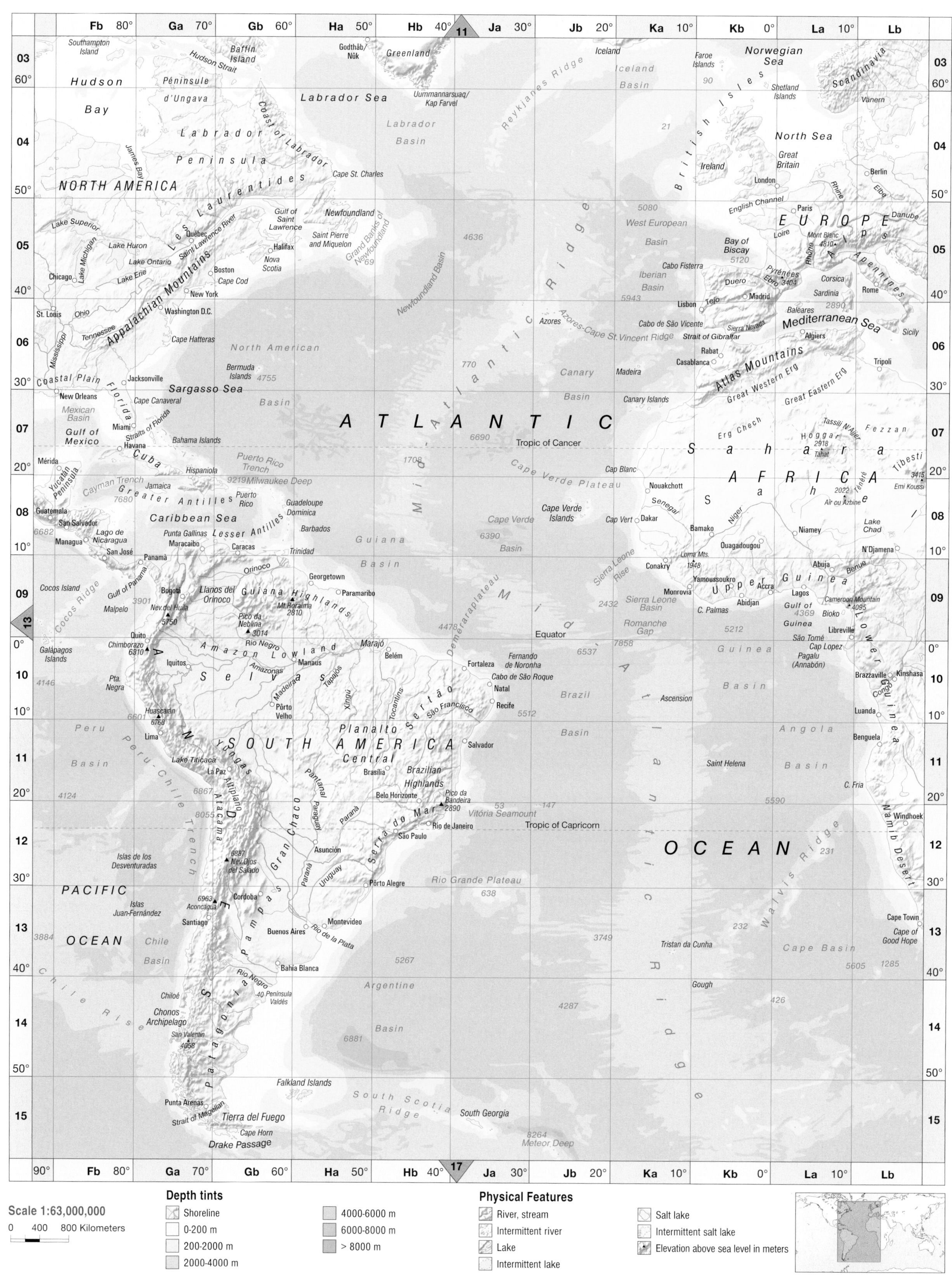

Scale 1:63,000,000

0   400   800 Kilometers

Depth tints

- Shoreline
- 0–200 m
- 200–2000 m
- 2000–4000 m
- 4000–6000 m
- 6000–8000 m
- > 8000 m

Physical Features

- River, stream
- Intermittent river
- Lake
- Intermittent lake
- Salt lake
- Intermittent salt lake
- ▲ Elevation above sea level in meters

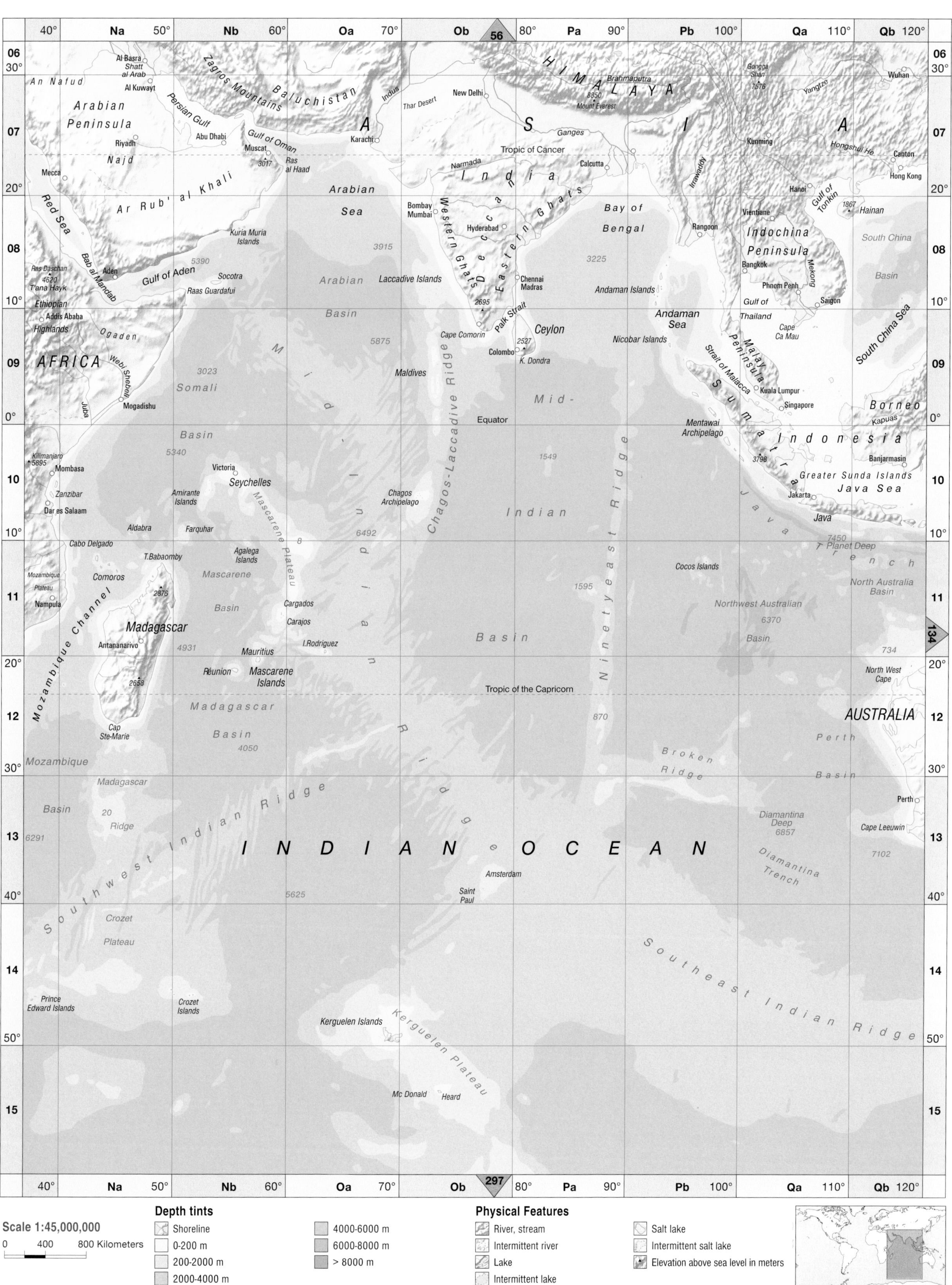

Scale 1:45,000,000

0   400   800 Kilometers

Depth tints

- Shoreline
- 0-200 m
- 200-2000 m
- 2000-4000 m
- 4000-6000 m
- 6000-8000 m
- > 8000 m

Physical Features

- River, stream
- Intermittent river
- Lake
- Intermittent lake
- Salt lake
- Intermittent salt lake
- Elevation above sea level in meters

Pacific Ocean

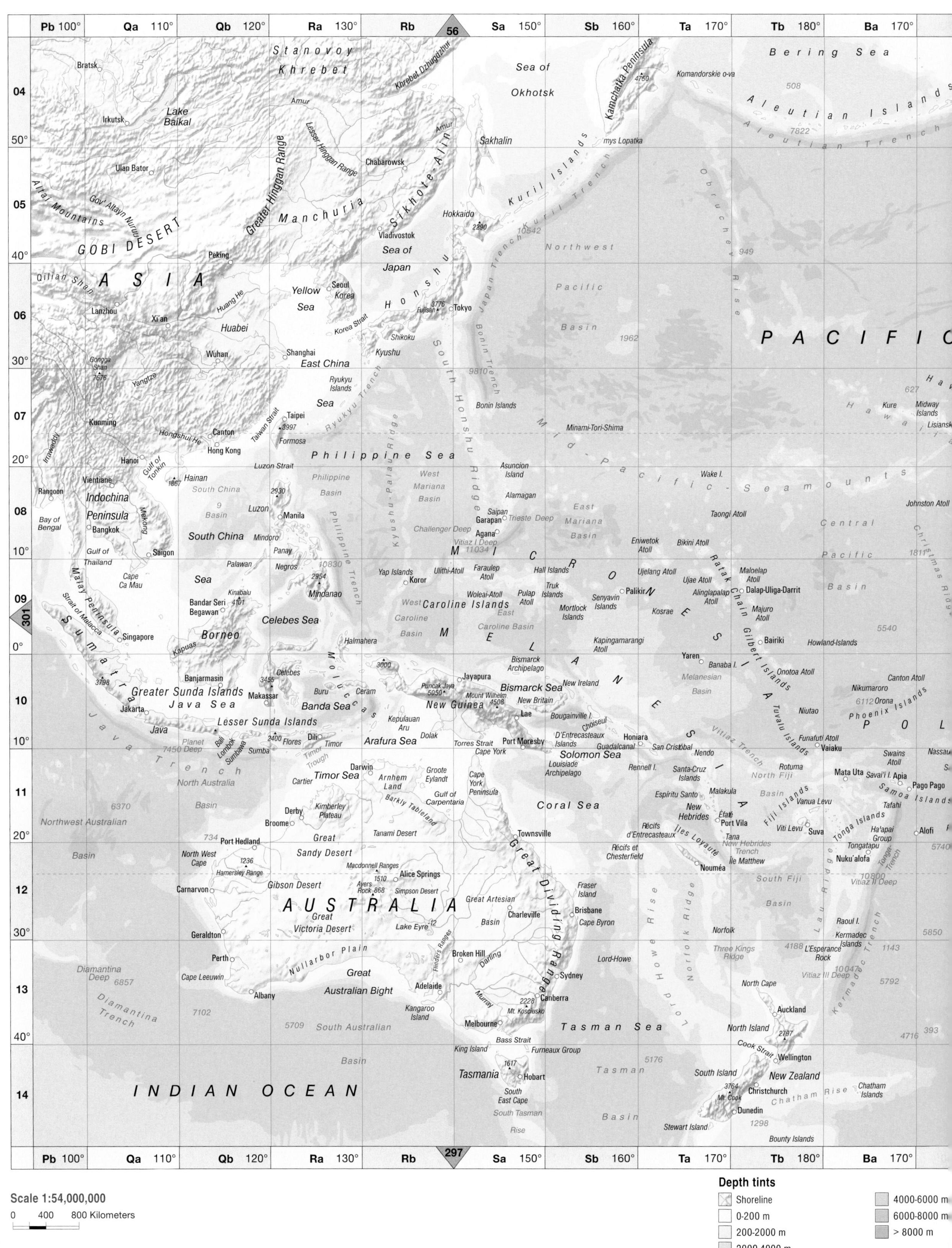

Stanovoy Khrebet
Bering Sea
Bratsk
Sea of Okhotsk
Kamchatka Peninsula
4750
Komandorskie o-va
508
Aleutian Islands
Irkutsk
Lake Baikal
Amur
Khrebet Dzhugdzhur
Aleutian Trench
7822
Ulan Bator
Lesser Hinggan Range
Sakhalin
Kuril Islands
mys Lopatka
Gov. Altayn Nuruu
Manchuria
Chabarowsk
Amur
Kuril Trench
Obruchev Rise
949
Altai Mountains
Greater Hinggan Range
Sikhote-Alin
Hokkaido
2590
10542
Northwest
GOBI DESERT
Peking
Vladivostok
Sea of Japan
Pacific
Qilian Shan
A S I A
Honshu
Basin
Lanzhou
Yellow Sea
Seoul Korea
3776
Tokyo
Japan Trench
Bonin Trench
1962
P A C I F I C
Xi'an
Huabei
Wuhan
Shanghai
Korea Strait
Fujisan
Shikoku
East China
Kyushu
South Honshu Ridge
9810
Mid-Pacific
627
Hawa
Gongga Shan 7576
Yangtze
Ryukyu Islands
Sea
Bonin Islands
Minami-Tori-Shima
Kure
Midway Islands
Hawai
Lisianski
Kunming
Canton
Taipei 3997
Taiwan Strait
Ryukyu Trench
Philippine Sea
Asuncion Island
Wake I.
Pacific-Seamounts
Hongshui He
Hong Kong
Formosa
Kyushu-Palau Ridge
West Mariana Basin
Alamagan
East Mariana Basin
Taongi Atoll
Central
Johnston Atoll
Hainan 1867
Philippine Basin
Saipan
Garapan
Trieste Deep
Eniwetok Atoll
Bikini Atoll
Pacific
Christmas Ridge
Bangkok
South China
Luzon 2930
Manila
Challenger Deep
Agana
Vitiaz I Deep
11034
M I C R O
Ujelang Atoll
Ujae Atoll
Maloelap Atoll
1811
Saigon
Palawan
Mindoro
Panay
Yap Islands
Ulithi-Atoll
Faraulep Atoll
Hall Islands
Alinglapalap Atoll
Dalap-Uliga-Darrit
Basin
Cape Ca Mau
Sea
Negros 2954
Mindanao
10830
Philippine Trench
Koror
Woleai-Atoll
Pulap Atoll
Truk Islands
Palikir
N
Majuro Atoll
5540
Strait of Malacca
Kinabalu 4101
Bandar Seri Begawan
Caroline Islands
Mortlock Islands
Senyavin Islands
Kosrae
Bairiki
Howland-Islands
Singapore
Borneo
Celebes Sea
West Caroline Basin
East Caroline Basin
M E L
Kapingamarangi Atoll
Yaren
Banaba I.
Onotoa Atoll
Kapuas
Halmahera
Bismarck Archipelago
A N
Melanesian Basin
Canton Atoll
3798
Banjarmasin
Celebes
3455
Molucca
3000
Jayapura
New Ireland
E S
Nikumaroro
6112 Orona
Greater Sunda Islands
Makassar
Buru
Ceram
Puncak Jaya 5050
Mount Wilhelm 4508
Bismarck Sea
New Britain
I
Niutao
Phoenix Islands
Jakarta
Java Sea
Banda Sea
New Guinea
Lae
Bougainville I.
Choiseul
A
Tuvalu Islands
Funafuti Atoll
Swains Atoll
Nassau
Java
Lesser Sunda Islands
Kepulauan Aru
Dolak
Torres Strait
Port Moresby
D'Entrecasteaux Islands
Honiara
Guadalcanal
San Cristobal
North Fiji
Rotuma
Vaiaku
Mata Uta
Savai'i I. Apia
Pago Pago
Bali
Lombok
Sumbawa
2400 Flores
Dili Timor
Arafura Sea
Cape York
Solomon Sea
Louisiade Archipelago
Rennell I.
Santa-Cruz Islands
Nendo
Vitiaz Trench
Samoa Islands
Planet Deep 7450
Sumba
Timor Sea
Darwin
Arnhem Land
Groote Eylandt
Cape York Peninsula
Coral Sea
Espíritu Santo
Malakula
Vanua Levu
Tafahi
Timor Trough
Cartier
Kimberley Plateau
Gulf of Carpentaria
New Hebrides
Été
Port Vila
Viti Levu
Suva
Ha'apai Group
Alofi
North Australia Basin
6370
Derby
Broome
Barkly Tableland
Townsville
Récifs d'Entrecasteaux
Îles Loyauté
Tana
New Hebrides Trench
Lau Ridge
Tonga Islands
Tongatapu
Northwest Australian
734 Port Hedland
Great Sandy Desert
Tanami Desert
Récifs et Chesterfield
Île Matthew
Nouméa
South Fiji
Nuku'alofa
5740
Vitiaz II Deep
North West Cape
1236
Macdonnell Ranges
Alice Springs
1510
Fraser Island
Lord-Howe Rise
Norfolk Ridge
Basin
70900
Carnarvon
Gibson Desert
Ayers Rock 868
Simpson Desert
A U S T R A L I A
Great Artesian Basin
Brisbane
Cape Byron
Norfolk
Three Kings Ridge
Raoul I.
Kermadec Islands
4188 L'Esperance Rock
1143
5850
Geraldton
Great Victoria Desert
Lake Eyre -12
Charleville
Lord-Howe
Kermadec Trench
5792
Perth
Nullarbor Plain
Broken Hill
Darling
Sydney
North Cape
Vitiaz III Deep 10047
Diamantina Deep 6857
Cape Leeuwin
Great
Flinders Ranges
Canberra
Great Dividing Range
Auckland
Albany
Australian Bight
Adelaide
Murray
2228
Mt. Kosciusko
North Island 2797
Diamantina Trench
7102
Kangaroo Island
Melbourne
South Australian Basin
Tasman Sea
Christchurch
Chatham Rise
Chatham Islands
5709
Bass Strait
South Island
New Zealand
4716
393
King Island
Furneaux Group
5176
Tasman
Wellington
I N D I A N   O C E A N
Tasmania
1617
Hobart
Cook Strait
3764 Mt. Cook
Basin
Dunedin
South East Cape
South Tasman Rise
Stewart Island
1298
Bounty Islands

Scale 1:54,000,000

0   400   800 Kilometers

302

Depth tints

⊠ Shoreline		▢ 4000-6000 m
▢ 0-200 m		▢ 6000-8000 m
▢ 200-2000 m		▢ > 8000 m
▢ 2000-4000 m		

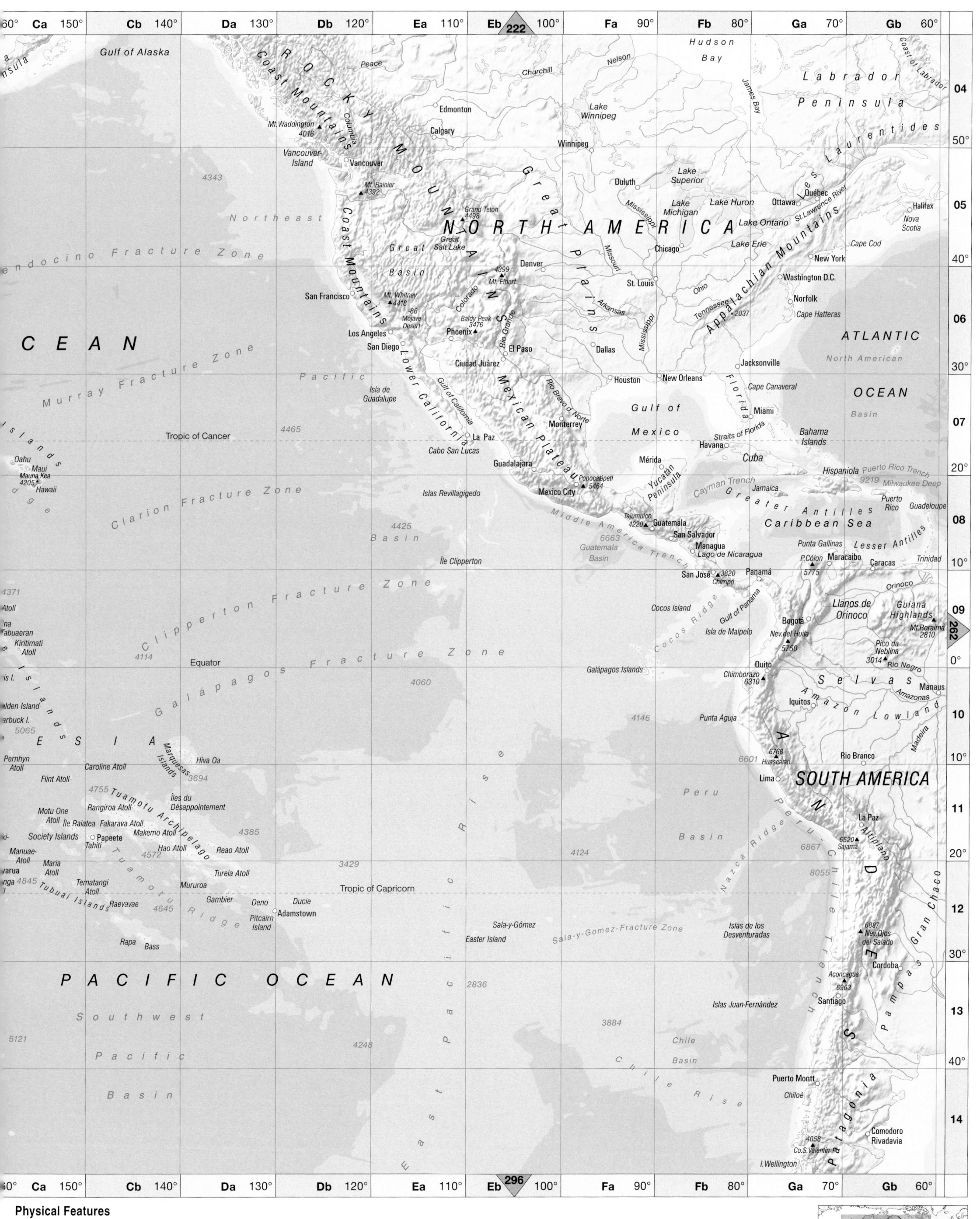

Gulf of Alaska
ROCKY
Coast Mountains
Peace
Hudson
Bay
Labrador
Peninsula
Coast of Labrador
04
Edmonton
Calgary
Lake
Winnipeg
Churchill
Nelson
James Bay
Laurentides
50°
Mt. Waddington
4016
Columbia
Winnipeg
Vancouver
Island
Vancouver
MOUNTAINS
Great
Plains
Lake
Superior
Duluth
Lake
Michigan
Lake Huron
Ottawa
Québec
St. Lawrence River
Halifax
Nova
Scotia
05
4343
Mt. Rainier
4392
Northeast
NORTH AMERICA
Lake Ontario
Appalachian Mountains
Cape Cod
40°
Grand Teton
4498
Chicago
Lake Erie
New York
Great
Basin
Great
Salt Lake
Denver
4399
Missouri
St. Louis
Ohio
Washington D.C.
06
Mt. Elbert
4399
Mt. Whitney
4418
San Francisco
Colorado
Coast Mountains
-86
Mojave
Desert
Baldy Peak
3476
Arkansas
Mississippi
Norfolk
2037
Cape Hatteras
ATLANTIC
OCEAN
CEAN
Mendocino Fracture Zone
Los Angeles
Phoenix
San Diego
Rio Grande
Ciudad Juárez
El Paso
Dallas
Jacksonville
North American
30°
Murray Fracture Zone
Pacific
Lower California
Gulf of California
Mexican Plateau
Rio Bravo del Norte
Houston
New Orleans
Florida
Cape Canaveral
Miami
OCEAN
Basin
07
Isla de
Guadalupe
Monterrey
Gulf of
Mexico
Straits of Florida
Havana
Bahama
Islands
Tropic of Cancer
4465
La Paz
Cabo San Lucas
Cuba
Hispaniola
Puerto Rico Trench
9219
Milwaukee Deep
20°
Oahu
Maui
Mauna Kea
4205
Hawaii
Islas Revillagigedo
Guadalajara
Mérida
Yucatán
Peninsula
Cayman Trench
Jamaica
Greater Antilles
Puerto
Rico
Guadeloupe
Mexico City
Popocatepetl
5464
Caribbean Sea
Lesser Antilles
08
Clarion Fracture Zone
4425
Basin
Tajumulco
4220
Guatemala
San Salvador
Managua
Lago de Nicaragua
Punta Gallinas
P. Colón
Maracaibo
Caracas
Trinidad
Île Clipperton
6663
Guatemala
Basin
5775
10°
4371
Atoll
Clipperton Fracture Zone
San José
3820
Chirripó
Panamá
Orinoco
Llanos de
Orinoco
Guiana
Highlands
Mt. Roraima
2810
262
09
na
Tabuaeran
Kiritimati
Atoll
4114
Cocos Island
Gulf of Panama
Cocos Ridge
Isla de Malpelo
Bogotá
Nev. del Huila
5750
Pico da
Neblina
3014
Rio Negro
0°
Equator
4060
Galápagos Islands
Quito
Chimborazo
6310
Selvas
Manaus
10
is I.
alden Island
arbuck I.
5065
ESIA
Galápagos Fracture Zone
Punta Aguja
Iquitos
Amazon Lowland
Amazonas
Madeira
Pernhyn
Atoll
Caroline Atoll
Marquesas
Islands
Hiva Oa
3694
4146
6768
Huascarán
Rio Branco
10°
Flint Atoll
4755 Tuamotu Archipelago
6601
Lima
SOUTH AMERICA
Motu One
Atoll
Rangiroa Atoll
Île Raiatea
Fakarava Atoll
Makemo Atoll
Peru
A
11
Society Islands
Papeete
Tahiti
Hao Atoll
Reao Atoll
4385
Basin
La Paz
6520
Sajama
Altiplano
Manuae
Atoll
4572
Tureia Atoll
3429
6867
20°
varua
4845
Tematangi
Atoll
Mururoa
Tubuai Island
Raevavae
Tropic of Capricorn
4124
Nazca Ridge
8055
Nev. Ojos
del Salado
Gran Chaco
12
Rapa
Bass
4645
Gambier
Pitcairn
Island
Oeno
Ducie
Adamstown
Sala-y-Gómez
Easter Island
Sala-y-Gomez Fracture Zone
Islas de los
Desventuradas
6887
Córdoba
30°
PACIFIC OCEAN
2836
Aconcagua
6963
Santiago
Pampas
13
Southwest
Islas Juan-Fernández
Chile
Basin
5121
Pacific
3884
Chile Rise
40°
Basin
4248
Puerto Montt
Chiloé
Patagonia
14
4058
Co. S. Valentín
Comodoro
Rivadavia
I. Wellington

Physical Features

River, stream
Intermittent river
Lake
Intermittent lake

Salt lake
Intermittent salt lake
Elevation above sea level in meters

The index explained

All of the places named on the maps in the atlas are listed in the atlas index. The place names are listed alphabetically. Special symbols and letters including accents and umlauts are ignored in the order of the index. For example, the letters Á, Ä, Å are all categorized under A, and è, °, Î are all treated as the standard Latin letter Z. Written characters consisting of two letters joined together (ligatures) are treated as two separate characters in the index: for example, words beginning with the character Æ would be indexed under AE.

The most commonly used abbreviations in the atlas – including N.P. for national park or N.W.R. for national wildlife refuge – are also used in the index. These abbreviations are listed and explained on this page (below). Generic geographic terms (sea, bay, etc.) and word articles (the, le, el, etc.) were used in the order of the index: for example, the Gulf of Mexico is listed under G and Le Havre, France is listed under L.

A special aspect of the atlas is the detailed and specially developed system of pictograms it features. These pictograms highlight famous travel routes, scenic landscapes, natural attractions, man-made attractions, cultural sites, as well as sporting, vacation, and recreation facilities. These pictograms also appear in the index (up to three per place name). The pictograms provide a basic overview of the attractions featured in a particular area. The meanings of all of the pictograms featured in the atlas are explained on the following page. In addition to these pictograms, the index also features special symbols to provide information about the political status of certain places including states, provinces, and capital cities. Virtually all of the places listed in the atlas have a country reference; these nations are identified by their international license (registration) plate codes. The various international license codes are identified on this page. In the case of communities and areas that are located on or between the borders of two nations, the license plate codes of both nations are listed and separated by a backslash.

The names of areas and geographic features that cannot be assigned to specific states, such as the Atlantic Ocean, are followed by the page number of a map featuring the area and the number of the map grid box in which the area is depicted on the map.

Niue	⬛ ⬛ ⬛	NZ	164	Bf55
Place name	Pictograms	Nation	Page	Map grid

Abbreviations

Abb.	Abbey, abbaye (French), abbadia (Span.), abbazia (Ital.)
Abor.	Aboriginal (indigenous inhabitants of Australia)
Aborig.	Aboriginal (indigenous inhabitants of Australia)
Ad.	Adas (Turkish) = Island
Ág.	Ági -os, -a, -i (Greek) = Saint
A.L.	Aboriginal Land = Aboriginal land reserve in Australia
Ban.	Banjaran (Malaysian) = mountain range
Bol'.	Bol'-šoj, -šaja, -šoe (Russian) = large-
C.	Cape, cap (French), cabo (Span./Port.), capo (Ital.)
Can.	Canal
Cast.	Castle, castel (French), castillo (Span.), castelo (Port.), castello (Ital.)
Cd.	Ciudad (Span.), cidade (Port.) = city
Co.	Cerro (Span.) = mountain, hill
Conv.	Convento (Span.) = monastery
Cord.	Cordillera (Span.) = mountain range
Corr.	Corrente (Port.), corriente (Ital./Span.) = river
Cr.	Creek
D.	Dake (Jap.) = mountain
D.	Danau (Indonesian) = lake
Dağ.	Dağlar, dağlari (Turkish) = mountain range
Ea.	Estancia (Span.) = estate
Emb.	Embalse (Span.), embassament (catalonian) = reservoir
Ens.	Ensenada (Span./Port.) = small bay
Erm.	Ermita (Span.) = hermitage
Est.	Estación (Span.) = rail station
Faz.	Fazenda (Port.) = estate
Fl.	Fleuve (French) = river
Fs.	waterfalls
g.	gawa (Jap.) = river
G.	Gora (Russian), góra (Polish), gunung (Indonesian) = mountain
Gde.	Grande (Span./French) = large
Geb.	Gebirge (German), gebergte (Dutch) = mountain range
Grd.	Grand (French) = large
Gt.	Great-
Hist.	Historic, historical
Hr.	Hrebet (Russian) = high
Ht.	Haut (French) = high-
Hte.	Haute (French) = high-
Hts.	Haut -s, -es (French) = high-
Hwy.	Highway
I.	Isla (Span.), ilha (Port.) = island

Î.	Île (French) = island
Ind.	Indian/ Native Americans
Ind.Res.	Indian Reservation = Native American land reserves in North America
Is.	Islands
Îs.	Îles (French) = islands
Jaz.	Jazovir (Bulg.) = reservoir
Jct.	Junction
Jez.	Jezioro (Pol.), jezero (Czech/Slovak./Serb./Croat./Slov.) = lake
Kan.	Kanal (Turk./Rus.), kanaal (Dutch), kanał (Pol.) = canal
Kep.	Kepulauan (Malaysian) = archipelago
Kg.	Kampong (Malaysian), kampung (Khmer) = village
Kör.	Körfezi (Turk.) = gulf, bay
L.	Lake, lac (French), lago (Ital./Span./Port.), loch, lough (Gaelic)
M.	Mys (Rus./Ukr.) = cape
Mal.	Malo, -yj, -aja, -oe (Rus.) = small
Mem.	Memorial
Mon.	Monastery, monastère (French), monasterio (Span.), monastero (Ital.)
M.P.	Milli Parki (Turk.) = national park
Mt.	Mount, mont (French)
Mta.	Montagna (Ital.), montaña (Span.) = mountain range
Mte.	Monte (Ital./Span./Port.), montagne (French) = mountain
Mtes.	Montes (Span./Port.), montagnes (French) = mountains
Mți.	Munţii (Romanian) = mountain range
Mti.	Monti (Ital.) = mountain range
Mtn.	Mountain
Mtns.	Mountains
Mts.	Mountains, Monts (French)
Mus.	Musée (French), museo (Span.), museu (Port.) = museum
N.	North, Northern, Norte (Ital./Span./Port.), Norra (Swedish), Nørdre (Norwegian), Nørre (Danish), Nord (German)
Nac.	Nacional (Span.), Nacional'-nyj, -aja, -oe (Russian) = national
Naz.	Nazionale (Ital.) = national
N.B.C.A.	National Biodiversity and Conservation Area = protected natural area
Nev.	Nevado (Span.) = snow-covered mountain peaks
N.H.P.	National Historic Park

N.H.S.	National Historic Site
Niž.	Niž-e, -nij, -naja, -neje (Russian) = lower-
Nižm.	Nižmennost' (Rus.) = plain
N.M.P.	National Military Park
N.P.	National Park, Nationalpark (Swedish), nasjonal park (Norwegian), Nemzeti Park (Hungarian)
N.R.	Nature Reserve, Natuurreservaat (Dutch)
N.R.A.	National Recreation Area
N.S.	National Seashore
N.Sra.	Nossa Senhora (Port.) = our lady (Mary, the mother of Jesus)
Nva.	Nueva (Span.) = new-
Nvo.	Nuevo (Span.) = new-
N.W.R.	National Wildlife Refuge
o.	Ostrov (Rus.) = island
P.	Port (English and French), puerto (Span./Port.), porto (Ital.) = harbor
Peg.	Pegunungan (Indonesian) = mountain
Pen.	Peninsula, péninsule (franz.), península (Span.), penisola (Ital.)
Pk.	Peak
P.N.	Parc National (French), parque nacional (Span./Port.), parco nazionale (Ital.) = national park
p-ov.	Poluostrov (Rus.) = peninsula
Pres.	Presidente (Span./Port.) = president
Prov.	Provincial, Province
Pse.	Passe (French) = Pass
Pso.	Paso (Span.), passo (Ital.) = Pass
Pt.	Point
Pta.	Punta (Span./Port.) = point
Pte.	Pointe (French) = point
Pto.	Punto (Ital.) = point
Q.N.P.	Quasi National Park (Jap.) = national park
R.	River, rivière (French), río (Span.), ribeiro, rio (Port.), ríu (Romanian), reka (Bulgarian)
Ra.	Range
Rep.	Republic, république (French), república (Span./Port.), republicca (Ital.)
Repr.	Represa (Port.) = dam
Res.	Reserva (Span.), réserve (French) = nature reserve
Res.	Reservoir, réservoir (French)
Resp.	Respublika (Russian) = Republik
s.	San (Jap.) = mountain

S.	San (Span./Ital.), são (Port.) = saint
Sanc./Sanct.	Sanctuary
Sd.	Sound, sund (German, Danish, Norwegian, Swedish)
Sel.	Selat (Indonesian) = strait
Sg.	Song (Vietnamese) = river
S.H.P.	State Historic Park
S.H.S.	State Historic Site
Sk.	Shuiku (Chinese) = reservoir
S.M.	State Monument
S.P.	State Park
Sr.	Sredn -e, -ij, -jaja (Russian) = central, middle
Sra.	Sierra (Span.), serra (Port./Ital.) = mountain range
St./St	Saint (English and French), sankt (German, Dutch)
Sta.	Santa (Span./Port./Ital.) = saint
Star.	Star -o, -yj, -aja, -oe (Russian) = old-
Ste	Sainte (French) = saint
Sth.	South, southern
St.Mem.	State Memorial
Sto.	Santo (Span./Port.) = Saint
Str.	Street, Strait, stretto (Italian), strӕde (Danish), stret (Norwegian)
t.	tau (Kaz.) = mountain
T.	Take (Jap.) = peak, summit
T.	Temple
Tel.	Teluk (Indonesian) = bay
Tg.	Tanjung (Indonesian) = cape
T.I.	Terra Indígena (Port.), territorio indigena (Span.) = indigenous land reservation in Latin America
Vdhr.	Vodohranilišče (Russian) = reservoir
Vel.	Velik -o, -ij, -yki, -oe (Rus.) = large-
Verh.	Verhn -ee, -ie, -ij, -jaja (Rus.) = mountain
Vill.	Village
vlk.	Vulkan (Rus.) = volcano
Vol.	Volcano, volcan (French), volcán (Span.)
Vul.	Vulkan (German.), Vulcano (Ital./Romanian) = volcano
W.A.	Wilderness Area
Wildl.	Wildlife
W.S.	Wildlife Sanctuary
Y.	Yama (Jap.) = mountain, mountain range
Zal.	Zaliv (Russian), zalew (Polish) = bay
Zap.	Zapovednik (Russian) = nature reserve
Z.B.	Nature reserve in the People's Republic of China
Zp.	Zapadn -e, -ji, -aja, -noe (Russian) = west, western

International license (registration) plate code

A	Austria	CV	Cape Verde	HN	Honduras	MOC	Mozambique	RIM	Mauritania	TO	Tonga
AFG	Afghanistan	CY	Cyprus	HR	Croatia	MS	Mauritius	RL	Lebanon	TR	Turkey
AG	Antigua and Barbuda	CZ	Czech Republic	I	Italy	MV	Maldives	RM	Madagascar	TT	Trinidad and Tobago
AL	Albania	D	Germany	IL	Israel	MW	Malawi	RMM	Mali	TUV	Tuvalu
AND	Andorra	DARS	Western Sahara	IND	India	MYA	Burma	RN	Niger	UA	Ukraine
ANG	Angola	DJI	Djibouti	IR	Iran	N	Norway	RO	Romania	UAE	United Arab Emirates
ARM	Armenia	DK	Denmark	IRL	Ireland	NAM	Namibia	ROK	Korea, South	USA	United States of America
AUS	Australia	DOM	Dominican Republic	IRQ	Iraq	NAU	Nauru	ROU	Uruguay		
AZ	Azerbaijan	DY	Benin	IS	Iceland	NEP	Nepal	RP	Philippines	UZ	Uzbekistan
B	Belgium	DZ	Algeria	J	Japan	NIC	Nicaragua	RSM	San Marino	V	Vatican City
BD	Bangladesh	E	Spain	JA	Jamaica	NL	Netherlands	RUS	Russia	VN	Vietnam
BDS	Barbados	EAK	Kenya	JOR	Jordan	NZ	New Zealand	RWA	Rwanda	VU	Vanuatu
BF	Burkina Faso	EAT	Tanzania	K	Cambodia	OM	Oman	S	Sweden	WAG	Gambia
BG	Bulgaria	EAU	Uganda	KIR	Kiribati	P	Portugal	SD	Swaziland	WAL	Sierra Leone
BH	Belize	EC	Ecuador	KNA	Saint Kitts and Nevis	PA	Panama	SGP	Singapore	WAN	Nigeria
BHT	Bhutan	ER	Eritrea	KS	Kyrgyzstan	PAL	Palau	SCG	Serbia and Montenegro	WD	Dominica
BIH	Bosnia and Herzegovina	ES	El Salvador	KSA	Saudi Arabia	PE	Peru			WG	Grenada
BOL	Bolivia	EST	Estonia	KWT	Kuwait	PK	Pakistan	SK	Slovakia	WL	Saint Lucia
BR	Brazil	ET	Egypt	KZ	Kazakhstan	PL	Poland	SLO	Slovenia	WS	Samoa
BRN	Bahrain	ETH	Ethiopia	L	Luxembourg	PNG	Papua New Guinea	SME	Suriname	WV	Saint Vincent and the Grenadines
BRU	Brunei	F	France	LAO	Laos	PRK	Korea, North	SN	Senegal		
BS	Bahamas	FIN	Finland	LAR	Libya	PY	Paraguay	SOL	Solomon Islands	YE	Yemen
BU	Burundi	FJI	Fiji	LB	Liberia	Q	Qatar	SP	Somalia	YV	Venezuela
BY	Belarus	FL	Liechtenstein	LS	Lesotho	RA	Argentina	STP	São Tomé and Príncipe	Z	Zambia
C	Cuba	FSM	Micronesia	LT	Lithuania	RB	Botswana			ZA	South Africa
CAM	Cameroon	G	Gabon	LV	Latvia	RC	Taiwan	SUD	Sudan	ZW	Zimbabwe
CDN	Canada	GB	Great Britain	M	Malta	RCA	Central African Republic	SY	Seychelles		
CH	Switzerland	GCA	Guatemala	MA	Morocco			SYR	Syria		
CHN	China	GE	Georgia	MAL	Malaysia	RCB	Republic of the Congo	TCH	Chad		
CI	Cote d'Ivoire	GH	Ghana	MC	Monaco	RCH	Chile	TG	Togo		
CL	Sri Lanka	GNB	Guinea-Bissau	MD	Moldova	RDC	Democratic Republic of the Congo	THA	Thailand		
CO	Colombia	GQ	Equatorial Guinea	MEX	Mexico			TJ	Tajikistan		
COM	Comoros	GR	Greece	MH	Marshall Islands	RG	Guinea	TLS	East Timor		
CR	Costa Rica	GUY	Guyana	MK	Macedonia	RH	Haiti	TM	Turkmenistan		
		H	Hungary	MNG	Mongolia	RI	Indonesia	TN	Tunisia		

Symbols used in the index

City
State
Capital
Province
Provincial Capital

Principal travel routes

Auto route
Rail road
Highspeed train
Shipping route

Remarkable landscapes and natural monuments

UNESCO World Natural Heritage
Mountain landscape
Rock landscape
Ravine/canyon
Extinct volcano
Active volcano
Geyser
Cave
Glacier
River landscape
Waterfall/rapids
Lake country
Desert
Oasis
Fossil site
Depression
Nature park
National park (landscape)
National park (flora)
National park (fauna)

National park (culture)
Biosphere reserve
Wildlife reserve
Whale watching
Turtle conservation area
Protected area for sea-lions/seals
Protected area for penguins
Zoo/safari park
Crocodile farm
Coastal landscape
Beach
Coral reef
Island
Underwater reserve

Remarkable cities and cultural monuments

UNESCO World Cultural Heritage
Pre- and early history
Prehistoric rockscape
The Ancient Orient
Ancient Egypt
Ancient Egyptian pyramids
Minoan culture
Phoenecian culture
Early African culture
Etruscan culture
Greek antiquity
Roman antiquity
Nabatean culture
Vikings
Ancient India
Ancient China
Ancient Japan
Mayan culture
Inca culture

Aztec culture
Other ancient American cultures
Places of Jewish cultural interest
Places of Christian cultural interest
Places of Islamic cultural interest
Places of Buddhist cultural interest
Places of Hindu cultural interest
Places of Jainist cultural interest
Places of Sikh cultural interest
Places of Shinto cultural interest
Places of cultural interest to other religions
Places of cultural interest to indigenous peoples (native peoples)
Aborigine reservation
Places of Aboriginal cultural interest
Indian reservation
Indian Pueblo culture
Places of Indian cultural interest
Amazonian Indians/protected area
Cultural landscape
Historical city scape
Impressive skyline
Castle/fortress/fort
Caravanserai
Palace
Technical/industrial monument
Dam
Remarkable lighthouse
Remarkable bridge
Tomb/grave
Theater of war/battlefield
Monument
Memorial
Space mission launch site
Space telescope
Market
Festivals

Museum
Theater
World exhibition
Olympics

Sport and leisure sites

Stadiums and Arenas
Race Tracks
Golf Course
Horse Racing
Ski Resorts/Areas
Sailing
Diving areas
Windsurfing
Surfing
Canoeing/Rafting
Harbors
Deep Sea Fishing
Waterskiing
Beaches
Spas and Hot Springs
Amusement Parks
Casinos
Hill Resorts
Lodges

Special index pictograms

Bodies of Water
Canal
Other physical names
Pass
Underwater topography

305

2 de Junio – Agua Blanca de Iturbide

2 de Junio MEX (TM) 253 Fa33
3 Castelli CH 34 Lk44
2 de Enero MEX (SO) 236 Ed30
9 de Julio RA (BA) 289 Gk63
9 de Julio RA (CR) 289 Ha60
10. de Abril MEX (TM) 253 Fa34
10. de Mayo MEX (COH) 253 Ek32
12 de Diciembre MEX (DGO) 253 Ej33
16 de Julio RA (BA) 293 Gk64
18 de Marzo MEX (CAM) 255 Fe36
24 de Mayo EC 272 Ga47
25 de Mayo RA (BA) 289 Gk63
25 de Mayo RA (LP) 292 Gg64
25 de Mayo RA (MD) 288 Gf63
27 de Abril CR 256 Fh40
27 de Enero MEX (BC) 236 Eb30
28 de Agosto MEX (COH) 253 Ej33
31 de Janeiro ANG 202 Lh49
70 Mile House CDN (BC) 232 Dk20
100 Mile House CDN (BC) 232 Dk20
108 Pagodas CHN 92 Qd26
150 Mile House CDN (BC) 232 Dk19

A

Å N 10 Lf14
A1-Ring A 35 Lp43
Aabenraa DK 14 Lk35
Aabybro DK 14 Lk33
Aachen D 32 Lg40
Aadan Yabaal SP 199 Nd44
Aakirkeby DK 15 Lp35
Aalborg DK 14 Lk33
Aalen D 34 Ll42
Aalestrup DK 14 Lk34
Aalst B 23 Le40
Aalten NL 32 Lg39
Aalter B 23 Ld39
Aamuda SYR 65 Na27
Äänekoski FIN 16 Mf28
Aansluit ZA 216 Mb59
Aarau CH 34 Lj43
Aare CH 34 Lh43
Aareschlucht CH 34 Lj44
Aars DK 14 Lk34
Aarschot B 23 Le40
Aarup DK 14 Ll35
Aba CHN (SCH) 94 Qa29
Aba RDC 201 Mf44
Aba WAN 194 Ld43
Aba ad Dud KSA 67 Nc32
Abacaxis BR 274 Ha48
Abaco Island BS 251 Gb32
Abadan IR 74 Ne30
Abadla DZ 173 Kj30
Abaeté BR (MG) 287 Hh55
Abaeté BR 287 Hh55
Abaetetuba BR (PA) 276 Hf46
Abag Qi CHN (NMZ) 93 Qh23
Abai KZ 76 Oe25
Abai KZ 84 Og21
Abai PY 289 Hc58
Abai RI 124 Qa46
Abaiang Atoll KIR 157 Tc18
Abaira BR (BA) 283 Hk52
Abaji WAN 186 Ld41
Abajo Peak USA 237 Ef27
Abaj Takalik GCA 255 Fe38
Abak WAN 194 Ld43
Abakaliki WAN 194 Le42
Abakan RUS 58 Pc08
Abakan RUS 85 Pe19
Abakanskij hrebet RUS 85 Pe19
Abakh Hoja Tomb CHN 86 Oj26
Abala RCB 202 Lh46
Abala RN 185 Lb38
Abalak RN 186 Ld38
Abalessa DZ 180 Lc34
Ab Anbar IR 75 Nk32
Abancay PE 279 Gd52
Abanga G 195 Lf45
Abanilla E 29 Kt48
Abanko RMM 185 La36
Ábano Terme I 40 Lm45
Abapó BOL 285 Gj55
Abarán E 29 Kt48
Abaré BR (BA) 283 Ja50
Abashiri J 99 Sc23
Abasolo MEX (GJT) 254 Ek35
Abasolo MEX (TM) 253 Fa33
Abastumani GE 70 Nb25
Abatan RP 121 Ra37
Abava LV 17 Mc33
Abay Wenz ETH 198 Mj40
Abaza RUS (CHK) 85 Pf19
Abba RCA 195 Lh43
Abbacyba ER 191 Na39
Abbadia San Salvatore I 40 Lm48
Abba Kella ETH 198 Mj42
Abba-Omege WAN 194 Le42
Abbas Abad IR 72 Nf27
Abbas Abad IR 73 Nj27
Abbas Abad IR 73 Nh30
Abbasanta I 31 Lj50
Abbaye aux Dames de Saintes F 24 Ku45
Abbaye aux Hommes de Caen F 22 Ku41
Abbaye de Fontenay F 23 Le43
Abbaye de Fontfroide F 24 Lc47
Abbaye de Jumièges F 22 La41
Abbaye de la Chaise-Dieu F 25 Ld45
Abbaye de Saint-Benoit-sur-Loire F 23 Lc43
Abbaye de Saint-Guilhem-le-Désert F 25 Ld47
Abbaye de Sénanque F 25 Lf47
Abbaye d'Orval B 23 Lf41
Abbaye Sainte-Foy F 24 Lc46
Abbaye Saint-Pierre F 22 Ku44
Abbazia della Trinità di Venosa I 43 Lq50
Abbazia di Casamari I 42 Lo49
Abbazia di Montecassino I 42 Lo49
Abbeville F 23 Lb40
Abbeville USA (AL) 249 Fh30
Abbeville USA (GA) 249 Fj30
Abbeville USA (LA) 243 Fd31
Abbeville USA (SC) 249 Fj28
Abbey CDN (SK) 233 Ef20
Abbeyfeale IRL 20 Kl38
Abbeyleix IRL 20 Kn38
Abbiategrasso I 40 Lj45
Abbieglassie AUS (QLD) 151 Sd59
Abbot Bay AUS (QLD) 149 Sd55
Abbot Ice Shelf 296 Fa33
Abbot, Mount AUS (QLD) 149 Sd56
Abbotsbury GB 21 Ks40
Abbotsford CDN (BC) 232 Dj21
Abbotsford USA (WI) 241 Fe23
Abbott USA (NM) 237 Eh27
Abbottabad PK 79 Og28
'Abd ad-Da'im SUD 197 Md40
'Abd al Kuri YE 69 Ng39
Abdallah bin Abbas Mosque KSA 66 Na35
Abd al-Magid SUD 190 Mg39
Abdaly KWT 74 Nd30
Abdan IR 74 Nf31
Abdemezeh DZ 180 Lc33
'Abdin SUD 197 Me39
Abdulino RUS 53 Ng19
Abdul Razzak Tomb AFG 78 Oe29
Abease GH 193 Kk41
Abéché TCH 196 Ma39
Abeïbara RMM 185 La36
Ab-e Istadeh-ye Moqor AFG 78 Od29
Abejar E 27 Ks51
Abejukolo WAN 194 Ld42
Abélajouad RN 186 Ld37
Abelardo Luz BR (SC) 290 Hd59
Abelbod RMM 185 Kk36
Abel Erasmuspas ZA 214 Mf58
Abeløya N 11 Mf06
Abel Tasman N.P. NZ 155 Tg66
Abelti ETH 198 Mj41
Abemama Atoll KIR 157 Tc18
Abemarre RI 158 Sa49
Abene GH 193 Kk42
Abengourou CI 193 Kj42
Abenójar E 28 Kq48
Abensberg D 35 Lm42
Abeokuta WAN 194 Lb42
Aberaeron GB 20 Kq38
Abercrombie Caves AUS (NSW) 153 Se62
Aberdare N.P. EAK 204 Mj46
Aberdare Range EAK 204 Mj46
Aberdeen CDN (SK) 233 Eg19
Aberdeen GB 19 Ks33
Aberdeen USA (MD) 247 Gb26
Aberdeen USA (MS) 243 Ff29
Aberdeen USA (SD) 240 Fa23
Aberdeen USA (WA) 232 Dj22
Aberdeen ZA 217 Mc62
Aberdeen Road ZA 217 Mc62
Aberfeldy GB 19 Kr34
Aberfoyle AUS (QLD) 149 Sc56
Abergavenny GB 21 Ks39
Abergele ETH 191 Mk40
Abergele GB 21 Kr37
Abergowrie AUS (QLD) 149 Sc55
Abernethy CDN (SK) 238 Ej20
Abersoch GB 20 Kq38
Aberystwyth GB 20 Kq38
Ab-e Seymareh IR 72 Nd29
Abetone I 40 Ll46
Abetteh MA 172 Ke31
Abganerovo RUS 53 Nc21
Ab Garm IR 72 Ne28
Abgué TCH 196 Lk40
Abha KSA 68 Nb36
Abhana IND (MPH) 109 Ok34
Abhanpur IND (CGH) 109 Pa35
Abhar IR 72 Ne27
Abhar-e Bala IR 72 Nd29
Abico BR (AM) 274 Gh47
Abide TR 50 Mg50
Abide TR 50 Mk52
Abidjan CI 193 Kj43
Abiekwasputs ZA 216 Ma59
Abi Hill WAN 194 Ld42
Abijatta-Shalla Lakes N.P. ETH 198 Mk42
Abilene USA (KS) 240 Fb26
Abilene USA (TX) 242 Fa29
Abingdon = Isla Pinta EC 272 Fe45
Abingdon GB 21 Kt39
Abingdon Downs AUS (QLD) 148 Sb54
Abington GB 19 Kr35
Abinsi WAN 194 Le42
Abirem GH 193 Kk42
Abiseo PE 278 Gb49
Abisko S 10 Lk11
Abisko fjällstation S 10 Lk11
Abisko n.p. S 10 Lk11
Abitibi River CDN 239 Fk20
Abjarovščyna BY 37 Md38
Abkhazia GE 63 Na24
Abminga AUS (SA) 143 Rh59
Abnûb ET 177 Mf32
Åbo = Turku FIN 16 Mc30
Aboa ANT (FIN) 296 Kb33
Aboh WAN 194 Ld43
Aboine WAN 194 Ld42
Aboisso CI 193 Kj43
Aboke EAU 204 Mg44
Abolones Beach USA (CA) 236 Dk28
Abomey DY 193 La42
Abomey Calavi DY 194 Lb42
Abomsa ETH 198 Na41
Abong WAN 195 Lf42
Abong Mbang CAM 195 Lg44
Aboni SUD 197 Mg40
Abony H 39 Lu43
Abor GH 193 La42
Abora Dunkwa GH 193 Kk43
Aboriginal Rock Art AUS (NSW) 151 Se58
Aboriginal Rock Art AUS 150 Sb61
Aborlan RP 122 Qk41
Aborlan, Mount RP 122 Qk41
Abou-Déïa TCH 196 Lk40
Abou Goulem TCH 196 Ma39
Aboukoussom TCH 196 Ma40
Aboumi G 195 Lh46
Aboun G 194 Le45
Abouraya RN 186 Ld38
Abovian ARM 70 Nc25
Aboyne GB 19 Ks33
Abqaiq KSA 67 Ne33
Abra Anticona PE 278 Gb51
Abra de Gavilán PE 278 Ga49
Abra de Ilog RP 121 Ra39
Abra del Ingenillo RA 288 Gh59
Abraham Lake CDN 233 Eb19
Abraham's Bay BS 251 Gd34
Abra Huashuaccasa PE 278 Gd53
Abraka WAN 194 Ld43
Abrantes P 28 Km49
Abra Pampa RA (PJ) 284 Gh57
Abras BR 277 Jd47
Abra Tapuna PE 278 Gd52
Abre Campo BR (MG) 287 Hj56
Abrego CO 268 Gd41
Abrene = Pytalovo RUS 17 Mh33
Abrene Pytalovo RUS 52 Md17
Abreu MOC 214 Mj55
Abri SUD 190 Mf36
Abri de Koumbala RCA 196 Ma41
Abri de Toulou RCA 196 Ma41
Abritus BG 47 Mg47
Abrud RO 44 Md44
Abruka saar EST 16 Mc32
Abruzzo I 42 Lo48
Abruzzo, P.N. d' I 42 Lo49
Absaroka Range USA 235 Ee23
Absarokee USA (MT) 235 Ef23
Abtei Einsiedeln CH 34 Lj43
Abtei Stams A 35 Lm43
Ab Torsh IR 72 Ne27
Ab Touyour TCH 196 Lk40
Abu GNB 183 Kc40
Abu Ajram KSA 64 Mk31
Abu al-Abyadh UAE 74 Ng33
Abu al Khasib IRQ 65 Nd30
Abu 'Arish KSA 68 Nb37
Abu at Tabul OM 69 Nh35
Abu Bahr KSA 67 Nd35
Abu Dawn SUD 190 Mg38
Abu Deleiq SUD 190 Mg39
Abu Dhabi UAE 74 Nh33
Abu Dhabi Icerink UAE 74 Nh33
Abu Dom SUD 190 Mf38
Abu Durbah ET 177 Mg31
Abu el Matâmir ET 177 Mf30
Abufari BR (AM) 274 Gj48
Abu Gabra SUD 197 Md40
Abu Gamel SUD 191 Mj39
Abu Ghirban SUD 190 Mg37
Abu Ghusun ET 177 Mh33
Abugi WAN 186 Ld41
Abu Gubayba SUD 197 Mf40
Abu Gurayb IRQ 65 Nc29
Abu Hadriyah KSA 67 Ne32
Abu Hamed SUD 190 Mg37
Abu Hammâd ET 177 Mf30
Abuhar IND (PJB) 106 Oh30
Abu Hashaifa Bay ET 176 Md30
Abu Hashim SUD 190 Mg37
Abu Hashim SUD 197 Mf40
Abu Higar SUD 190 Mg40
Abuja WAN 186 Ld41
Abu Kabisa SUD 197 Md39
Abu Kamal SYR 65 Na28
Abu Kebir ET 177 Mf30
Abuki Mountains RI 127 Ra47
Abuko Nature Reserve WAG 183 Kb39
Abukuma-koti J 101 Sa27
Abu Latt KSA 66 Na36
Abulug RP 121 Ra36
Abulug RP 121 Ra36
Abu Maztariq SUD 196 Md40
Abu Mendi ETH 198 Mh40
Abu Mina ET 177 Me30
Abu Minqar ET 176 Md32
Abumombazi RDC 200 Mb44
Abu, Mount = Guru Shikhar IND 106 Og33
Abunã BR (RO) 280 Gh50
Abu Na'im LAR 175 Lk31
Abune Yosef ETH 191 Mk40
Abu Ra's SUD 196 Mc42
Abu Road IND (RJT) 108 Og33
Abu Rubayq KSA 66 Mk34
Abu Rudays ET 177 Mg31
Abu Saffar SUD 190 Mg38
Abu Sari SUD 190 Mf36
Abu Simbel ET 177 Mf34
Abu Simbel ET 177 Mg33
Abu Sukhayr IRQ 65 Nc30
Abuta J 99 Sa24
Abu Teeg ET 177 Mf32
Abut Head NZ 155 Tf67
Abu Tunaytin SUD 190 Mf39
Abu 'Uruq SUD 190 Mf39
Abu Uwayjilah ET 177 Mh30
Abuye Meda ETH 198 Mk40
Abuyog RP 123 Rc40
Abu Zabad SUD 197 Me39
Abu Zayyan LAR 174 Lg29
Abu Zeyo Abad IR 72 Nf29
Abuz'hour SYR 64 Mj28
Abwong SUD 197 Mg41
Åby S 13 Lp32
Åby S 13 Lr32
Abyad SUD 196 Md39
Abyaneh IR 72 Nf29
Abyar 'Ali KSA 66 Mk33
Abyar ash Shuwayrif LAR 174 Lh31
Abyata ETH 198 Mj42
Abydos = El Âmirah ET 177 Mf32
Abyei SUD 197 Me41
Abyek IR 72 Nf27
Åbyggeby S 13 Ls30
Åbytorp S 13 Lq31
Acadian Museum CDN 245 Gk22
Acadia N.P. USA 245 Gf23
Acadia Valley CDN (AB) 233 Ee20
Acahay PY 285 Hb58
Açailândia BR (MA) 276 Hg48
Açai Paraná BR (AM) 273 Gf45
Acajutiba BR (BA) 283 Ja51
Acajutla ES 255 Ff39
Acalayong GQ 194 Le45
Acambaro MEX (GJT) 254 Ek35
Acampamento da Cameia ANG 209 Ma51
Acampamento de Indios BR (MT) 280 Ha51
Acampamento Grande BR (AP) 275 Hd45
Acandi CO 268 Gb41
Acangatá BR (PA) 275 He47
A Cañiza E 26 Km52
Acaponeta MEX (NYT) 253 Eh34
Acapulco MEX (GUR) 254 Fa37
Acará BR (PA) 276 Hf46
Acará BR 276 Hf47
Acarauú BR (CE) 277 Hk47
Acaraú BR 277 Hk47
Acaray PY 286 Hc58
Acari BR (RN) 277 Jb49
Acari BR 274 Ha46
Acari BR 274 Ha49
Acari PE 278 Gc53
Acarigua YV 269 Gf41
Acasio BOL 284 Gg55
Acatlán de Juárez MEX (JLC) 254 Ej35
Acatlán de Osorio MEX (PUE) 254 Fa36
Acat zingo MEX (PUE) 254 Fb36
Acay, Nevado de RA 284 Gg58
Acayucan MEX (VC) 255 Fc37
Accéglio I 40 Lh46
Accomac USA (VA) 247 Gc27
Accra GH 193 Kk43
ACE Basin N.W.R. USA 249 Fk29
Acebuches MEX (COH) 253 Ej31
Aceguá BR (RS) 290 Hc61
Aceguá ROU 289 Hc61
Acerenza I 43 Lq50
Achaacha DZ 173 La27
Achacachi BOL 284 Gf54
Achaguas YV 269 Gf42
Achalpur IND (MHT) 108 Oj35
Achampet IND (APH) 109 Pa37
Achao RCH 292 Gd67
Achar ROU 289 Hb62
Achcharapakkam IND (TNU) 111 Ok40
Acheb DZ 174 Le31
Achegtim RIM 183 Ke36
Achelouma RN 181 Lg34
Achelouma RN 181 Lg34
Acheng CHN (HLG) 98 Rd23
Achensee A 35 Lm43
Achguig el Adam RIM 183 Ke36
Achi CO 268 Gc41
Achiasi GH 193 Kk43
Achilleio GR 48 Lu51
Achill Head IRL 18 Kk37
Achill Island IRL 18 Kk37
Achim D 32 Lk38
Achiras RA (CD) 288 Gh62
Achiri BOL 284 Gf54
Achit nuur MNG 85 Pf21
Achiwib GUY 270 Ha44
Achnasheen GB 19 Kp33
Acholibur EAU 204 Mg44
Achouka G 195 Lf46
Achra IND (MHT) 108 Og37
Aci Castello I 42 Lq53
Aci Catena I 42 Lq53
Acıgöl TR 50 Mk53
Acıgöl TR 51 Mp52
Acima, T.I. BR 279 Gg49
Ačinsk RUS 58 Pc07
Acıpayam TR 50 Mk53
Acıpınar TR 51 Mo52
Acireale I 42 Lq53
Ackerman USA (MS) 243 Ff29
Acklins Island BS 251 Gc34
Acle GB 21 Lb38
Acobamba PE 278 Gc52
Acoma Pueblo USA 237 Eg28
Acomayo PE 279 Ge52
Aconcagua, Cerro RA 288 Ge62
Aconchi MEX (SO) 237 Ee31
Acopantepui YV 270 Gj43
Acoplara BR (CE) 277 Ja49
Acoris ET 177 Mf31
A Coruña E 26 Km53
Acos PE 278 Gb51
Acostambo PE 278 Gc52
Acoyapa NIC 256 Fh40
Acqua Doria F 31 Lj49
Acquapendente I 40 Lm48
Acquasanta Terme I 42 Lo48
Acquasparta I 42 Ln48
Acquaviva delle Fonti I 43 Lr50
Acqui Terme I 40 Lj46
Acre BOL/BR 279 Gf51
Acre BR 264 Gb20
Acre IL 64 Mh29
Acreúna BR (GO) 286 He54
Acri I 43 Lr51
Acsa H 39 Lu43
Acton S.H.S. USA 242 Fb29
Actopan MEX (HDG) 254 Fa35
Acuã BR 274 Gj49
Açucena BR (MG) 287 Hj55
Açude Araras BR 277 Hk48
Açude Banabuiú BR 277 Ja48
Açude Boqueirão BR 277 Jb49
Açude Coremas BR 277 Ja49
Açude Orós BR 277 Ja49
Açude Pentecostes BR 277 Ja47
Açude Poço da Cruz BR 283 Jb50
Acueducto romano de Segovia E 26 Kq50
Acuña MEX (COH) 242 Ek31
Acurenam GQ 195 Lf45
Ada GH 193 La43
Ada SCG 44 Ma45
Ada USA (MN) 241 Fb22
Ada USA (OK) 243 Fb28
Adaba ETH 198 Mk42
Adadi Mariam ETH 198 Mk41
Adaf DZ 180 Le34
Adaigba WAN 194 Ld42
Adaiso GH 193 Kk43
Ådalsbruk N 12 Lm30
Ådalselv N 12 Ll30
Adam OM 75 Nj34
Adam al Hulay KSA 66 Na35
Adamantina BR (SP) 286 He56
Adámas GR 49 Me54
Adamclisi RO 45 Mh46
Adamello I 40 Ll44
Adaminaby AUS (NSW) 153 Se63
Adami Tulu ETH 198 Mk42
Adam's Bridge IND/CL 111 Ok42
Adams Lake CDN (BC) 232 Ea20
Adams Lake CDN 232 Ea20
Adams, Mount USA 232 Dk22
Adam's Peak CL 111 Pa43
Adams River CDN 232 Ea20
Adamstown 303 Db12
Adamuz E 28 Kq48
'Adan YE 68 Nc39
Adana TR 62 Mh27
Adan as Sughra YE 68 Nc39
Adané G 194 Lf46
Adani WAN 194 Ld42
Adaouda DZ 180 Lc34
Adapazarı = Sakarya TR 50 Ml50
Adar TCH 196 Ma40
Adarama SUD 190 Mh38
Adare IRL 20 Km38
Adatoprakpınar TR 51 Mm51
Adaut RI 133 Rf50
Adavale AUS (QLD) 150 Sc58
Adda I 40 Lk45
Adda SUD 196 Mc41
ad-Dabba SUD 190 Mf37
Ad Dafinah KSA 66 Nb34
Ad Dahna KSA 67 Nc32
Ad Dali YE 69 Nf36
Ad Dammam KSA 67 Nf32
Addanki IND (APH) 111 Ok39
Ad-dar-al-Bayda MA 172 Kg29
Ad Dar al Hamra KSA 66 Na35
Ad Darb KSA 68 Nb37
Ad-Dariz OM 75 Nj34
Ad Dawadami KSA 67 Nc33
Ad Dawhah Q 74 Nf33
Ad Dawr IRQ 65 Nb28
Ad-Dhaid UAE 75 Nh33
Ad-Dhawah LAR 176 Ma33
Addi CAM 195 Lh42
Ad Dibdibah KSA 67 Nc32
Ad Dikakah KSA 69 Nf36
Ad Dilam KSA 67 Nd33
Ad Dir'iyah KSA 67 Nd33
Addis Ababa ETH 198 Mk41
Addison USA (AL) 248 Fg28
Ad Diwaniyah IRQ 65 Nc30
Addo ZA 217 Mc62
Addo Elephant N.P. ZA 217 Mc62
Addoo Atoll MV 110 Og46
ad-Dubasi SUD 190 Mg39
ad-Du'hayn SUD 196 Md40
Ad Dulaymiyah KSA 66 Nb32
Ad Dulu'iyah IRQ 65 Nc28
Ad-Dumeir SYR 64 Mj29
Ad Duqah KSA 66 Na36
Ad Durma KSA 67 Nd33
Ad Duwayd KSA 65 Nb30
ad-Duwayn SUD 190 Mg40
Adé TCH 196 Ma39
Adéane SN 183 Kb39
Adel USA (GA) 249 Fj30
Adel USA (OR) 234 Ea24
Adelaide AUS (SA) 152 Rk63
Adelaide ZA 217 Md62
Adelaide Island 296 Gc32
Adelaide River AUS (NT) 139 Rf52
Adelaide River AUS 139 Rf52
Adel Bagrou RIM 184 Kg38
Adelbert Range PNG 159 Sc48
Adelboden CH 34 Lh44
Adele Island AUS 138 Rb53
Adelia María RA (CD) 288 Gh62
Adelong AUS (NSW) 153 Se63
Adelong AUS (QLD) 149 Sc57
Ademuz E 29 Kt50
Aden YE 68 Nc39
Adenau D 32 Lg40
Adendorp ZA 217 Mc62
Aderbissinat RN 186 Ld38
Adesar IND (GUJ) 108 Of34
Adet ETH 198 Mj40
Adéta TG 193 La42
Adhaby KSA 68 Nb37
Adhaura IND (BIH) 109 Pb33
Adhe Bid Hayk ETH 198 Na40
Adi RI 131 Rg48
Adiake CI 193 Kj43
Adiangdia DY 193 La41
Adi Ark'ay ETH 191 Mj40
Adicora YV 269 Gf40
Adi Da'iro ETH 191 Mk39
Adidome GH 193 La42
Adigala ETH 198 Nb40
Adige = Etsch I 40 Ln45
Adigrat ETH 191 Mk39
Adi Gudom ETH 191 Mk40
Adıgüzel Baraj TR 50 Mk52
Adikas ETH 197 Mh43
Adi Keyih ER 191 Mk39
Adi Kwala ER 191 Mk39
Adilabad IND (APH) 109 Ok36
Adilcevaz TR 63 Nb26
Adimi IR 73 Oa30
Adin USA (CA) 234 Dk25
Adinsoone SP 199 Ne41
Adiora RMM 185 Kk37
Adipala RI 128 Qe49
Adi Ramets ETH 191 Mj40
Adirampattinam IND (TNU) 111 Ok41
Adiri LAR 181 Lg32
Adirondack Mountains USA 247 Gc24
Adirondack Museum USA 247 Gc24
Adirondack Park USA 247 Gc24
Adirondack Scenic R.R. USA 247 Gc24
Adis Abeba ETH 198 Mk41
Adis Alem ETH 198 Mk41
Adis Zemen ETH 198 Mj39
Adi Ugri ER 191 Mk39
Adıyaman TR 63 Mk27
Adjengré TG 193 La41
Adjen Kotoku GH 193 Kk43
Adjerar DZ 180 Lc33
Adjiro TG 186 La41
Adjud RO 45 Mh44
Adler RUS 55 Mk24
Adliswil CH 34 Lj43
Admirality Inlet CDN 225 Fc04
Admiralty Bay AUS 138 Rc53
Admiralty Gulf A.L. AUS 138 Rc53
Admiralty I. National Monument USA 231 Dc17
Admiralty Islands PNG 159 Sd47
Admiralty Island USA 231 Dc17
Admjany BY 17 Mf36
Admont A 35 Lp43
Ado WAN 186 Ld41
Ado WAN 194 Lb42
Ado Awaiye WAN 194 Lb42
Ado-Ekiti WAN 194 Lc42
Adok SUD 197 Mf41
Adolfo BR (SP) 286 Hf56
Adolfo González Chaves RA (BA) 293 Gk65
Adolfo López Mateos MEX (BCS) 252 Ed33
Adolfo López Mateos (La Junta) MEX (CHH) 252 Eg31
Adonara RI 132 Rb50
Adoni IND (APH) 111 Oj39
Adony H 39 Lt43
Adorf D 35 Ln40
Adoru WAN 194 Ld42
Adoumandjali RCA 195 Lh44
Adoumri CAM 187 Lg41
Adour F 24 Ku47
Adra E 29 Kr46
Adra IND (WBG) 112 Pd34
Adrall E 30 Lb48
Adranga RDC 201 Mf44
Adrano I 42 Lp53
Adrar DZ 179 Kk32
Adrar Adjeloho DZ 180 Le33
Adrar Ahellakane DZ 180 Lc32
Adrar Azzaouager RN 186 Le37
Adrar Bous RN 180 Le35
Adrar des Ifôrhas RMM 185 La36
Adrar Ikohahoène DZ 180 Le32
Adrar Ilebgâne RMM 180 La36
Adrar In Hihaou DZ 180 Lb34
Adrar Mariaou DZ 181 Le34
Adrar n'Ahnet DZ 180 Lb33
Adrar-n-Aklim MA 172 Kg30
Adrar-n-Deren MA 172 Kg30
Adrar-n-Imchech MA 172 Kg30
Adrar-Ouzzeine RMM 180 La36
Adrar Souttouf DARS 178 Kc34
Adrar Tachdait RMM 185 La36
Adrar Tedjorar DZ 180 Lc34
Adrar Tideridiaouine DZ 180 La34
Adrar Tighârghârr RMM 185 La36
Adrar Tintejert DZ 180 Lb33
Adraskan AFG 78 Ob29
Adré TCH 196 Mb39
Adria I 40 Ln45
Adrian USA (MI) 246 Fh25
Adrian USA (OR) 234 Eb24
Adrian USA (TX) 237 Ej28
Adrianópolis BR (PR) 286 Hf58
Adriatic Sea 6 Lb05
Adršpašsko- teplické skály CZ 38 Lq40
Adul IND (MHT) 108 Oh36
Adulis ER 191 Mk39
Adunaţii-Copăceni RO 45 Mg46
Adunguar Daban CHN 84 Pc24
Adunu WAN 186 Ld41
Adur IND (KER) 110 Oj42
Adura WAN 186 Ld41
Aduripalle IND (APH) 111 Ok39
Adusa RDC 201 Me45
Adustina BR (BA) 283 Ja51
Adutiškis LT 17 Mg35
Aduturai IND (TNU) 111 Ok41
Advance USA (MO) 243 Ff27
Adwa ETH 191 Mk39
Adwana IND (GUJ) 108 Oe35
Adyal IND (MHT) 109 Ok35
Adygea RUS 5 Md10
Adyk RUS (KAL) 70 Nc23
Adzharia GE 63 Na25
Adzhina Tepe Monastery TJ 76 Oe26
Adzopé CI 193 Kj42
Aegean Sea 9 Ma11
Aegviidu EST 16 Mf31
Aekanopan RI 116 Pk44
Ærø DK 14 Ll36
A Estrada E 26 Km52
Aetorráhi GR 48 Mb53
Äetsä FIN 16 Mc29
Afabet ER 191 Mk38
Afadé CAM 187 Lh39
,Afak IRQ 65 Nc29
Afambo Hayk ETH 198 Na40
Afándou GR 49 Mj54
Åfarnes N 12 Lh28
Af Barwaargo SP 199 Ne42
Afdem ETH 198 Na41
Afé SN 183 Kc38
Aféfes GR 48 Md51
Afféri CI 193 Kj42
Affolé RIM 183 Ke37
Affon = Ouémé DY 193 La41
Afghanistan AFG 57 Oa06
Afgooye SP 205 Nc44
Afhir MA 173 Kj28
Afif KSA 66 Nb34
Afikpo WAN 194 Ld43
Afilal DZ 180 Lc34
Aflou DZ 173 Lb28
Afmadow SP 205 Nb45
Afobaka SME 271 Hc43
Afogados de Ingazeira BR (PE) 283 Jb49
Afognak Island USA 230 Ce16
Afognak Mtn. USA 230 Cd16
Afolé TG 193 La42
Afonso Cláudio BR (ES) 287 Hk56
Afore PNG 159 Se50
Afqa RL 64 Mh28
Afrânio BR (PE) 283 Hk50
Afrasiab UZ 76 Od26
Afrefa Terara ETH 191 Na40
Afrera Ye Che'ew Hayk ETH 191 Na40
Africa
Afrin SYR 64 Mj27
Afşar Baraj TR 50 Mj52
Afşin TR 62 Mj26
Afsluitdijk NL 32 Lf37
Afton USA (IA) 241 Fc25
Afton USA (WY) 235 Ee24
Aftor Doons AUS (QLD) 148 Sc56
Aftoût ech Chergui RIM 183 Kc37
Afua BR (PA) 275 He46
Afula IL 64 Mh29
Afumaţi RO 45 Mg46
Afwein EAK 205 Mk45
Afyon TR 51 Ml52
Afzalpur IND (KTK) 108 Oj37
Aga RUS 91 Qh20
Aga-Batyr RUS 70 Nc24
Aga Buryat Autonomous District RUS 59 Qd08
Ağaca TR 51 Mn50
Ağaçören TR 51 Mo52
Agadem RN 187 Lg37
Agadez RN 186 Ld37
Agadir MA 172 Kf30
Agadir-Tissint MA 172 Kg31
Agaete E 178 Kc31
Agaie WAN 186 Ld41
Agalawatta CL 111 Pa43
Agalega Islands MS 219 Nj51
Agamor RMM 185 La37
Agana USA 156 Sa16
Aganoa Beach WS 164 Be53
Agano-gawa J 101 Rk27
Agápi GR 49 Mf53
Agapia RO 45 Mg43
Agapo Açu BR (PA) 275 Hb48
Agar IND (MPH) 108 Oh34
Agâraktem RMM 179 Kg34
Agarfa ETH 198 Mk42
Agargar DARS 178 Kc33
Agaro ETH 198 Mj42
Agartala IND (TRP) 112 Pf34
Agar Uen ETH 199 Nc42
Agassiz Prov. Forest CDN 238 Fc20
Agastya Malai IND 111 Oj42
Agate Fossil Beds Nat. Mon. USA 240 Ej24
Agathonisi GR 49 Mg53
Agats RI 131 Rk48
Agatti Island IND 110 Og41
Agattu Island USA 59 Tc08
Agbabu WAN 194 Lc42
Agbarha-Otor WAN 194 Lc43
Agbélouvé TG 193 La42
Agbor-Bojiboji WAN 194 Ld42
Agboville CI 193 Kh43
Agdam AZ 70 Nd25
Agdas AZ 70 Nd25
Agde F 25 Ld47
Agdz MA 172 Kg30
Agdžabedi AZ 70 Nd25
Agege WAN 194 Lb42
Agen F 24 La46
Agenebode WAN 194 Ld42
Agerbæk DK 14 Lj35
Agere Maryam ETH 198 Mk43
Agere Selam ETH 198 Mk42
Ageneys ZA 216 Lk60
Agger DK 14 Lj34
Aggtelek H 39 Ma42
Aggteleki N.P. H 39 Ma42
Aggui RIM 178 Kd35
Aghajari IR 72 Ne30
Agha Mosque IR 72 Nf28
Aghat RN 186 Ld37
Agh Bolagh IR 72 Nc27
Aghdas Cave IR 72 Ne28
Aghezzaf RMM 185 Kk36
Aghireşu RO 44 Md44
Aghoninit DARS 178 Kd34
Aghor PK 80 Oc33
Aghouedir RIM 178 Ke35
Aghreijit RIM 178 Kf35
Aghrijit RIM 184 Kf36
Agiá GR 46 Mc51
Agiabampo MEX (SO) 252 Ef32
Agia Eirini CY 51 Mn55
Agia Galini GR 49 Me55
Agia Marina GR 48 Md53
Agía Marina GR 48 Me52
Agia Pelagia GR 48 Mc54
Agia Triáda GR 48 Mb53
Agia Varvára GR 49 Mf55
Aghiol RO 45 Mj45
Agii Apóstoli GR 48 Md54
Agii Theódori GR 46 Mb51
Agii Theódori GR 48 Md53
Aginskoe RUS (AGB) 91 Qh20
Aginta RO 44 Me45
Agiókambos GR 46 Mc51
Agiókambos GR 48 Md52
Agiorgitika GR 48 Mc53
Ágios Andréas GR 48 Mc53
Ágios Charalampos GR 47 Mf50
Ágios Christós GR 46 Mc50
Ágios Dimitrios GR 46 Mc50
Ágios Dimitrios GR 46 Mc50
Ágios Dimitrios GR 48 Mc54
Ágios Efstrátios GR 47 Me51
Ágios Efstrátios GR 47 Mf51
Ágios Geórgios GR 48 Mb52
Ágios Kírikos GR 49 Mg53
Ágios Mámas GR 49 Me55
Ágios Nikolaos GR 48 Ma53
Ágios Nikólaos GR 48 Mc52
Ágios Nikólaos GR 49 Mf55
Ágios Pétros GR 48 Mc53
Ágios Stéfanos GR 48 Mc51
Ágios Stéfanos GR 49 Mh54
Ágios Theodoros = Çayırova CY 51 Mp55
Agira I 42 Lp53
Agjert RIM 184 Kf37
Aglal RMM 185 Kj37
Aglen BG 47 Me47
Ağlı TR 62 Mg25
Aglona LV 17 Mg34
Agmar RIM 178 Ke33
Agnang G 195 Lg45
Agnantiá GR 46 Mb51
Agnébi CI 193 Kh42
Agnes Creek AUS (SA) 142 Rg59
Agnes Lodge SOL 160 Sj50
Agness USA (OR) 234 Dh24
Agnes Waters AUS (QLD) 151 Sf58
Agnew AUS (WA) 144 Ra60
Agnibilékrou CI 193 Kj42
Agnone I 42 Lp49
Ago J 101 Rj28
Agogo-Are WAN 186 Lb41
Agogo GH 193 Kk42
Agohay Beach RP 123 Rc41
Agolai IND (RJT) 106 Og32
Agön S 13 Ls29
Agona GH 193 Kk42
Agona Junction GH 193 Kk43
Agona-Sweru GH 193 Kk43
Agoo RP 120 Ra37
Agora GR 47 Me50
Agordo I 40 Ln44
Agostadero de Aguirre MEX (CHH) 252 Eg32
Agotu PNG 159 Sc49
Agou CI 193 Kj43
Agoudal MA 172 Kh30
Agoué TG 193 La42
Agoueinit RIM 184 Kg37
Agoua Gadzépé TG 193 La42
Agouna DY 193 La42
Agounni Jefal RMM 185 Kj37
Agout F 24 Lc47
Agouti MA 172 Kg30
Agra IND (UPH) 107 Ok32
Agra Fort IND 107 Oj32
Agrahanskij poluostrov RUS 70 Nd24
Agramunt E 30 Lb49
Agreda E 27 Kt51
Agreliá GR 46 Mb51
Agri I 43 Lr50
Ağrı TR 63 Nb26
Agriáni GR 48 Mc53
Ağrı Dağı TR 63 Nc26
Agrigento I 42 Lo53
Agrihan USA 119 Sb15
Agrinio GR 48 Mb52
Agrio RA 292 Ge65
Agriovótano GR 48 Md51
Agrópoli I 42 Lp50
Agua Azul HN 256 Fg38
Agua Blanca GCA 255 Ff38
Agua Blanca de Iturbide MEX (HDG) 254 Fa35

Água Boa – Aldan

Água Boa BR (MG) 287 Hj54
Agua Boa BR (MT) 281 Hd53
Agua Braga BR (GO) 282 Hf52
Agua Branca BR (MA) 276 Hg49
Agua Branca BR (PI) 277 Hj48
Agua Branca BR 280 Ha50
Agua Caliente BOL 280 Gj53
Agua Caliente PE 278 Gc50
Aguacatán GCA 255 Fe38
Aguachica CO 268 Gd41
Agua Clara BR (MS) 286 Hd56
Agua Comprida BR (SP) 286 Hf56
Aguada Cecilio RA (RN) 292 Gh66
Aguada de Pasajeros C 258 Fk34
Aguadas CO 268 Gc43
Aguadilla USA (PR) 260 Gg36
Água Doce BR (SC) 290 He59
Agua Dulce MEX (VC) 255 Fc36
Aguadulce PA 257 Fk41
Agua Escondida RA (MD) 292 Gf64
Agua Fria BR 281 He52
Agua Grande MEX (SO) 252 Ee31
Agua Hedionda, Cerro RA 288 Gg62
Aguaí BR (SP) 286 Hg57
Agualeguas MEX (NL) 253 Fa32
Aguanga USA (CA) 236 Eb29
Aguanish CDN (QC) 245 Gj20
Agua Nueva MEX (COH) 253 Ek33
Aguapeí BR 286 He56
Água Petra Inari, T.I. BR 279 Gg49
Aguapey RA 289 Hb60
Água Preta BR 274 Gh46
Agua Prieta MEX (SO) 237 Ef30
Agua Quente BR (GO) 282 Hg52
Aguaragüe, P.N. BOL 285 Gj56
Aguaray RA (SA) 285 Gj57
Aguaray Guazú PY 285 Hb58
A Guarda E 26 Km51
Aguarico EC 272 Gc46
Aguaro-Guariquito, P.N. YV 269 Gg41
Aguasay YV 270 Gj41
Águas Belas BR (PE) 283 Jb50
Águas Belas, T.I. BR 287 Ja54
Aguas Blancas PE 284 Gf58
Aguas Blancas RA (SA) 285 Gh57
Aguas Blancas, Cerro RA/RCH 284 Gf58
Aguascalientes MEX (AGS) 254 Ej35
Aguascalientes MEX 253 Ej34
Águas Formosas BR (MG) 287 Hk54
Aguas Negras PE 272 Gc46
Aguas Turbias, P.N. BH 255 Ff37
Aguateca GCA 255 Fe37
Agua Verde PE 284 Gf58
Agua Verde ou Anhanazá BR 281 Hb52
Agua Viva YV 269 Ge41
Aguaytía PE 278 Gc50
Aguaytia PE 278 Gc50
Aguazul CO 268 Gd43
A Gudiña E 26 Kn52
Agudo BR (RS) 290 Hd60
Agudo E 28 Kq48
Agudos BR (SP) 286 Hf57
Águeda P 26 Km50
Aguelhok RMM 185 La36
Aguelt ez Zerga RIM 183 Kc36
Aguga EAU 204 Mg44
Aguiar Javés BR (TO) 282 Hf51
Aguié RN 186 Ld39
Aguila RIM 183 Kc37
Aguila USA (AZ) 236 Ed29
Aguilâl Faï RIM 183 Kc36
Aguilar E 28 Kq47
Aguilar de Campóo E 27 Kq52
Aguilares ES 255 Ff39
Aguilares RA (TU) 288 Gh59
Águilas E 29 Kt47
Aguiler Grande BOL 279 Gf51
Aguililla MEX (MHC) 254 Ej36
Aguirre YV 270 Gk42
Aguirre Cerda ANT (RCH) 296 Gd31
Aguja, Cerro RA/RCH 292 Ge67
Aguja, Cerro RCH 294 Gf73
Agula'i ETH 191 Mk40
Agulhas Negras BR 287 Hh57
Agulhas N.P. ZA 216 Lk63
Agumatsa W.S. GH 193 La42
Agumbe IND (KTK) 110 Oh40
Aguni-jima J 103 Rd32
Agustinópolis BR (TO) 276 Hf48
Agutaya Island RP 123 Ra40
Ağva TR 50 Mk49
Agwa Bay CDN 239 Fh22
Agwarra WAN 186 Lc40
Agwei SUD 197 Mg42
Agweri WAN 194 Ld42
Agwit SUD 197 Md41
Agwok SUD 197 Me42
Ahaba WAN 194 Ld43
Ahaberge NAM 213 Ma55
Ahad Rafidah KSA 68 Nb36
Aha Hills RB 213 Ma55
Ahakeye (Ti-Tree) A.L. AUS 142 Rg57
Ahamasu GH 193 La42
Ahar IR 72 Nd26
Ahat TR 50 Mk52
Ahaus D 32 Lh38
Ahe Atoll F 165 Cg53
Åheim N 12 Lf28
Ahelóos GR 48 Mb51
Ahenkto GH 193 La42
Ahero EAK 204 Mh46
Ahipara NZ 154 Tg63
Ahipara Bay NZ 154 Tg63
Ahırlı TR 51 Mm53
Ahiti NZ 154 Th65
Ahklun Mountains USA 229 Cc15
Ahladiá GR 47 Me49
Ahladohóri GR 46 Md49
Ahlainen FIN 13 Mb29
Ahlainen FIN 16 Mb29
Ahlat TR 63 Nb26
Ahlbeck D 33 Lp37
Ahlen D 32 Lh39
Ahmadi KWT 74 Ne31
Ahmadpur IND (MHT) 108 Oj36
Ahmadpur PK 79 Of30
Ahmadpur East PK 81 Of31
Ahmad Shah Durrani Tomb AFG 78 Oc30
Ahmad Wal PK 80 Oc31
Ahmar Mountains ETH 198 Na41
Ahmedabad IND (GUJ) 108 Og34
Ahmednagar IND (MHT) 108 Oh36
Ahmedpur Mandvi Beach IND 108 Of35
Ahmetli TR 49 Mh52
Ahoada WAN 194 Ld43
Ahome MEX (SL) 252 Ef33
Ahousat CDN (BC) 232 Dg21
Ahram IR 74 Nf31
Ahraura IND (UPH) 109 Pb33
Ahrensbök D 33 Ll36
Ahrensburg D 33 Ll37
Ahsu AZ 70 Ne25
Ahtamar TR 63 Nb26
Ähtäri FIN 16 Me28
Ahtme EST 16 Mh31
Ahtopol BG 47 Mh48
Ahtropovo RUS 53 Nb16
Ahtubinsk RUS 53 Nd21
Ahty RUS (DAG) 70 Nd25
Ahu IR 72 Ne30
Ahuachapan ES 255 Ff39
Ahualulco MEX (SLP) 253 Ek34
Ahualulco de Mercado MEX (JLC) 254 Ej35
Ahuano EC 272 Gb46
Ahuas HN 256 Fh38
Ahuasbila HN 256 Fh38
Ahun F 24 Lc44
Ahus RI 127 Qj44
Åhus S 15 Lp35
Ahvaz IR 72 Ne30
Ahvenanmaa = Åland FIN 13 Lu30
Ahvenanmeri FIN 13 Lu30
Ahwa IND (GUJ) 108 Og35
Ahwar YE 68 Nd39
Ai-Ais NAM 216 Lj59
Ai-Ais Hot Springs NAM 216 Lj59
Ai-Ais Warmwaterbronne NAM 216 Lj59
Aiaktalik Island USA 230 Cd17
Aialik Cape USA 229 Cf16
Aiapuá BR (AM) 274 Gj48
Aiaweté Igarapé Ipixuna , T.I. BR 275 Hd48
Aiban UAE 74 Nh33
Aibar E 27 Kt52
Aibetsu J 99 Sb24
Aichach D 35 Lm42
Aiduma RI 131 Rh48
Aiduna RI 131 Rh48
Aiema River PNG 158 Sb49
Aiere WAN 194 Ld42
Aigamas Caves NAM 212 Lj55
Aigen A 35 Lp43
Aigen A 35 Lo42
Aigene mekeni KZ 76 Oe23
Aigiali GR 49 Mf54
Aigialousa CY 51 Mp55
Aigle CH 34 Lg44
Aignay-le-Duc F 23 Le43
Aigre F 24 La45
Aigrefeuille-d'Aunis F 24 Ku44
Aiguá ROU 289 Hc63
Aiguebelle F 25 Lg45
Aiguebelle, P.N. d' CDN 244 Ga21
Aigues F 25 Le46
Aigues-Mortes F 25 Le47
Aigüestortes i Estany de Sant Maurici, P.N. de E 30 La48
Aiguilete, Cerro RCH 294 Gd71
Aiguille du Midi F 25 Lg45
Aiguilles F 25 Lg46
Aiguilles de Sindou BF 193 Kh40
Aiguillon F 24 La46
Aigurande F 24 Lb44
Aihole IND 108 Oh38
Aija PE 278 Gb50
Aikawa J 101 Rk26
Aiken USA (SC) 249 Fk29
Ailao Shan CHN 113 Qa33
Ailefroide F 25 Lg46
Aileron AUS (NT) 142 Rg57
Ailigandi PA 257 Ga41
Ailinginae Atoll MH 157 Tb16
Ailinglapalag Atoll MH 157 Tb17
Ailly-sur-Noye F 23 Lc41
Ailuk Atoll MH 157 Tb16
Aimachá del Valle RA (TU) 288 Gh59
Aimogasta RA (LR) 288 Gg60
Aimorés BR (MG) 287 Hk55
Ainabulak KZ 84 Of21
Ain al Arab SYR 65 Mk27
Ain Attaya RIM 178 Kd35
Ainaži LV 17 Me33
Aïn-Beïda DZ 174 Ld28
Aïn Benian DZ 173 Lb27
Aïn Benimathar MA 173 Kj28
Aïn Ben Tili RIM 178 Kf33
Aïn Bessem DZ 173 Lb27
Âïn Boubat RIM 183 Kd37
Ain Dara SYR 64 Mj27
Aïn Defla DZ 173 La27
Aïn Deheb DZ 173 La28
Aïn Draham TN 174 Le27
Aïn-Ech-Chair MA 173 Kj29
Aïn el Bell DZ 173 Lb28
Ain el Brod DZ 174 Lc31
Aïn el Hadja DZ 173 La28
Aïn-el-Hadjadj DZ 173 Lb31
Ain el Hadjadj DZ 180 Ld32
Aïn el Hadjel DZ 173 Lb28
Aïn el Hamara DZ 173 Lb28
Aïn el Hamman DZ 173 Lc27
Aïn el Melh DZ 173 Lc28
Aïn-el-Orak DZ 173 La29
Aïn-el-Türck DZ 173 Kk28
Aïn Fakroun DZ 174 Ld28
Aïn Fekan DZ 173 La28
Ainggyi MYA 112 Ph35
Ainhoa F 24 Kt47
Aïn Kerch DZ 174 Ld28
Aïn Kermes DZ 173 La28
Aïn Khadra DZ 173 Lc28
Âïn-Leuh MA 172 Kh29
Aïn Madhi DZ 173 Lb29
Aïn-M'Lila DZ 174 Ld27
Ainos N.P. GR 48 Ma52
Aïn Oulmene DZ 174 Lc28
Aïn Oussera DZ 173 Lb28
Ainsa E 30 La48
Aïn Sefra DZ 173 Kk29
Aïn Skhouna DZ 173 La28
Ain Sukhnah ET 177 Mg31
Ainsworth USA (NE) 240 Fa24
Aïn Tamr TN 174 Le29
Aïn Taya DZ 173 Lb27
Aïn Tédelès DZ 173 La28
Aïn Témouchent DZ 173 Kk28
Aintree GB 21 Ks37
Aiome PNG 159 Sc48
Aiome, Mount PNG 159 Sc48
Aiquile BOL 284 Gh55
Aiquiri BR 279 Gg50
Airabu RI 117 Qd44
Airaines F 23 Lb41
Airasca I 40 Lh46
Airavateswarar Temple IND (TNU) 111 Ok41
Airbalam RI 124 Pk45
Airbangis RI 124 Pk45
Airbara RI 125 Qd47
Airdrie CDN (AB) 233 Ec20
Aire-sur-l'Adour F 24 Ku47
Aire-sur-la-Lys F 23 Lc40
Airgegas RI 125 Qd47
Airi BR (PE) 283 Ja50
Airlie AUS (QLD) 149 Se56
Airolo CH 34 Lj44
Aïr ou Azbine RN 180 Le36
Airpanas RI 132 Rc49
Airvault F 22 Ku44
Airwa IND (UPH) 107 Ok32
Airyk KZ 84 Oj20
Aisch D 35 Ll41
Aishihik CDN (YT) 231 Db15
Aishihik Lake CDN 231 Db15
Aisne F 23 Ld41
Aitana E 29 Ku48
Aitape PNG 158 Sb47
Âït-Baha MA 172 Kf30
Âït Ben Haddou MA 172 Kg30
Aiteke Bi KZ 76 Ob23
Âït-Hamane MA 172 Kg30
Aitkin USA (MN) 241 Fd22
Ait-Melloul MA 172 Kf30
Âït Morrhad MA 172 Kh30
Aitong EAK 204 Mh46
Âït-Ourir MA 172 Kg30
Âït Saadane MA 172 Kh30
Aiuanã BR 274 Gh46
Aiud RO 44 Md44
Aiuiá-Miçu BR 281 Hd51
Aiviekste LV 17 Mg34
Aix-en-Othe F 23 Ld42
Aix-en-Provence F 25 Lf47
Aixe-sur-Vienne F 24 Lb45
Aix-les-Bains F 25 Lf45
Aiy Adi ETH 191 Mk40
Aiyar Reservoir IND 109 Pc34
Aiyetoro WAN 194 Lb42
Aiyetoro WAN 194 Lc42
Aiyrtas KZ 84 Oj21
Aizanoi TR 50 Mk51
Aizawl IND (MZR) 112 Pg34
Aizenay F 22 Kt44
Aizkrāukle LV 17 Mf34
Aizpute LV 17 Mb34
Aizu-Wakamatsu J 101 Rk27
Ajabshir IR 72 Nc27
Ajaccio F 31 Lj49
Ajai Game Reserve EAU 204 Mf44
Ajaigarh IND (MPH) 109 Pa33
Ajajú CO 273 Gd45
Ajak RUS 98 Rd19
Ajana AUS (WA) 140 Qh59
Ajanta IND (MHT) 108 Oh35
Ajanta Caves IND 108 Oh35
Ajaokuta WAN 194 Ld42
Ajarani BR 270 Gk44
Ajasse WAN 194 Lc41
Ajasso WAN 194 Le43
Ajax, Mount NZ 155 Tg67
Aj Bogd Uul MNG 85 Ph23
Ajdabiya LAR 175 Ma30
Ajdar UA 53 Mk21
Ajdarly KZ 76 Oc23
Ajdir MA 173 Kj28
Ajdovščina SLO 41 Lo45
Ajigasawa J 101 Sa25
Ajinskoe RUS 99 Sb21
Aj'jawdiyeh SYR 65 Na27
Ajjibal Attadmur lych SYR 64 Mj28
Ajka H 38 Ls43
Ajman UAE 74 Nh33
Ajmer IND (RJT) 106 Oh32
Ajmer Sharief IND 106 Oh32
Ajni TJ 76 Oe26
Ajo USA (AZ) 236 Ed29
Ajoda WAN 194 Lc42
Ajoya MEX (SL) 252 Eg33
Ajra IND (MHT) 108 Oh37
Ajrestan AFG 78 Od29
Ajtos BG 47 Mh48
Ájtte S 10 Lk12
Ajumaku GH 193 Kk43
Ajuruteua BR (PA) 276 Hg46
Ajuy RP 123 Rb40
Akabar RMM 185 La38
Akabli DZ 180 La32
Akadomari J 101 Rk27
Akadyr KZ 84 Og21
Aka-Eze WAN 194 Ld43
Akagera, P.N. de l' RWA 206 Mf46
Akagi J 101 Rg28
Akaishi-sanmyahku J 101 Rk28
Akakbe CAM 194 Le43
Akaki ETH 198 Mk41
Akakro CI 193 Kh43
Akakus LAR 181 Lf33
Akala SUD 191 Mj39
Akalkot IND (MHT) 108 Oj37
Akam Éffak G 195 Lf45
Akamkpa WAN 194 Le43
Akanda, P.N. d' G 194 Le45
Akankoshan J 99 Sc24
Akan N.P. J 99 Sc24
Akarkar RN 186 Ld38
Akarnaniká GR 48 Mb52
Akaroa NZ 155 Tg67
Akasame PNG 159 Sb49
Akasha SUD 190 Mf36
Akashat IRQ 65 Mk29
Akassa WAN 194 Ld43
Akat Amnuai THA 115 Qb37
Akats GH 193 La42
Akbado DY 193 Lb42
Akbarpur IND (UPH) 107 Pb32
Akbelenli TR 51 Ml53
Akbou DZ 173 Lc27
Akçaabat TR 63 Mk25
Akçakale TR 63 Mk27
Akçakent TR 51 Mp51
Akçakısla TR 51 Mq51
Akçakoca TR 51 Mm49
Akçakoca Dağları TR 51 Mm50
Akçalar TR 62 Mj27
Akçalı Dağları TR 62 Mg27
Akçaova TR 50 Mj53
Akçaova TR 50 Mk49
Akçay TR 51 Mk54
Akçay TR 63 Nb25
Akchâr RIM 178 Kc35
Akcjabrski BY 52 Me19
Akdağ TR 50 Mj51
Akdağ TR 50 Mj53
Akdağ TR 51 Mq51
Ak Dağlar TR 51 Mk54
Akdağmadeni TR 51 Mq51
Akdepe TM 71 Nk24
Akdere TR 50 Mk52
Ak-Dovurak RUS (TUV) 85 Pf20
Akébou TG 193 La42
Akelamo RI 130 Rd45
Akelamo RI 130 Re45
Aken D 33 Ln39
Åkernes N 12 Lh32
Åkersberga S 13 Lt31
Åkers styckebruk S 13 Ls31
Akespe KZ 71 Oa22
Aketi RDC 201 Mc44
Aketi RDC 201 Mb44
Akhalkalaki GE 70 Nb25
Akhaltsikhe GE 70 Nb25
Akhiok USA (AK) 230 Cc17
Akhisar TR 49 Mh52
Akhmeta GE 70 Nc25
Akhmîm ET 177 Mf32
Akhnoor 79 Oh29
Akhpat and Sanain Monasteries ARM 70 Nc25
Aki J 101 Rg29
Akiachak USA (AK) 228 Bk15
Akiéni G 202 Lg46
Akimiski Island CDN 239 Fk19
Akın TR 51 Mo51
Akıncı Burnu TR 62 Mh27
Akinum PNG 159 Se49
Akita J 101 Sa26
Akividu IND (APH) 109 Pa37
Akjoujt RIM 183 Kc36
Akka MA 172 Kf31
Akkajaure S 10 Lj12
Akkent TR 50 Mk52
Akkeshi J 99 Sc24
'Akko IL 64 Mh29
Akkol KZ 76 Of24
Akkol Lake KZ 76 Of24
Akkoursoulbak RCA 196 Ma41
Akköy TR 49 Mh53
Akköy TR 50 Mk53
Akköy TR 62 Mg26
Akkum KZ 76 Of24
Ak Kuprak = Keshendeh AFG 78 Od27
Akkuş TR 63 Mj25
Aklampa DY 194 Lb41
Aklera IND (RJT) 108 Oj33
Akmektep KZ 85 Pb22
Akmenrags LV 17 Mb34
Akmeqit CHN (XUZ) 86 Oj27
Akmeşe TR 50 Ml50
Aknīste LV 17 Mf34
Aknoul MA 173 Kj28
Ako J 101 Rh28
Akobo ETH 197 Mg42
Akodiya IND (MPH) 108 Oj34
Akok G 194 Le45
Akoke SUD 197 Mg41
Akokora RDC 201 Me45
Akola IND (MHT) 108 Oj35
Akoma PNG 159 Sc49
Akom II CAM 195 Lf44
Akono CAM 195 Lf44
Akonolinga CAM 195 Lg44
Akop SUD 197 Me41
Akorabi GUY 270 Ha43
Akordat ER 191 Mj39
Akören TR 51 Mn53
Akören TR 62 Mg27
Akoroso GH 193 Kk43
Akosombo GH 193 La42
Akosombo Dam GH 193 La42
Akot IND (MHT) 108 Oj35
Akot SUD 197 Mf42
Akoupé CI 193 Kj42
Akparé TG 193 La42
Akpınar TR 50 Ml51
Akpınar TR 51 Mo51
Akpınar TR 51 Ml51
Akpınar TR 51 Mp51
Akplabnya GH 193 La43
Akposso TG 193 La42
Akqi CHN (XUZ) 86 Ok25
Akrabat TM 73 Oa28
Åkrahamn N 12 Lf31
Akrai I 42 Lp53
Akranes IS 10 Jj13
Akre IRQ 65 Nb27
Akréréb RN 186 Le37
Åkrestrømmen N 12 Lm29
Akron USA (CO) 240 Ej25
Akron USA (IA) 241 Fb24
Akron USA (OH) 247 Fk25
Akrópolis GR 48 Md53
Akrópolis GR 49 Mj54
Akropong GH 193 Kk42
Akrotiri CY 51 Mn56
Akrotíri GR 49 Mf54
Akrotíri Ágios Ioánnis GR 49 Mf55
Akrotíri Ákrathos GR 47 Me50
Akrotíri Áraxos GR 48 Mb52
Akrotíri Doukáto GR 48 Ma52
Akrotíri Drébano GR 47 Md51
Akrotíri Kassándra GR 46 Md51
Akrotíri Kilíni GR 48 Mb53
Akrotíri Kímis GR 48 Me52
Akrotíri Kriós GR 48 Md55
Akrotíri Lithári GR 49 Me52
Akrotíri Lithino GR 49 Me56
Akrotíri Maléas GR 48 Md54
Akrotíri Murzeflos GR 47 Mf51
Akrotíri Palioúri GR 47 Md51
Akrotíri Salonikiós GR 47 Me50
Akrotíri Soúnio GR 48 Me53
Akrotíri Ténaro GR 48 Mc54
Akša RUS 91 Qg20
Ak-Saj KS 77 Oh25
Aksaj RUS 55 Mk22
Akşar TR 63 Nb25
Aksaray TR 51 Mp52
Aksay CHN (GSU) 87 Ph26
Aksay Qin 79 Ok28
Aksayqin Co 79 Ok28
Aksdal N 12 Lf31
Akşehir TR 51 Mm52
Akşehir Gölü TR 51 Mm52
Aksekı TR 51 Mm53
Akshatau KZ 84 Og22
Akshi KZ 84 Oj23
Akshyghanak KZ 76 Oe24
Aksoran tau KZ 84 Oh21
Aksu CHN (XUZ) 86 Pa25
Aksu KZ 76 Oe24
Aksu KZ 84 Ok23
Aksu KZ 84 Ok23
Aksu TR 51 Ml54
Aksu TR 51 Mm53
Aksuat KZ 84 Pb22
Aksuat KZ 85 Pb21
Aksu-Ayuly KZ 84 Og21
Aksubaevo RUS (TAR) 53 Nf18
Aksu Canyon KZ 76 Of24
Aksu Çay TR 51 Ml53
Aksum ETH 191 Mk39
Aksumite royal city of Kohaito ER 191 Mk39
Aksu-Zhabaghly Nature Reserve KZ 76 Of24
Ak-Šyjak KS 77 Ok25
Ak Tag CHN 86 Pc27
Ak-Tal KS 77 Oh25
Aktanys RUS (TAR) 53 Nh18
Aktarsk RUS 53 Nc20
Aktas KZ 84 Og21
Aktaš RUS (ALT) 85 Pd20
Aktau KZ 70 Nf24
Aktaz CHN (XUZ) 87 Pd26
Aktoghai KZ 84 Oh21
Aktoghai KZ 84 Ok22
Aktuzla TR 63 Nb26
Akubu SUD 197 Mg42
Akubu SUD 197 Mg42
Akula RDC 200 Ma44
Akulurak USA (AK) 228 Bh14
Akumadan GH 193 Kk42
Akumal MEX (QTR) 255 Fg35
Akune J 103 Rf29
Akun Island USA 228 Bh18
Akuraj RUS 91 Qj20
Akure WAN 194 Lc42
Akuressa CL 111 Pa43
Akureyri IS 10 Ka13
Akuseki-jima J 103 Re31
Akutan USA (AK) 228 Bh18
Akutan Island USA 228 Bg18
Akutukpa WAN 194 Ld41
Håverud Akvedukt S 12 Ln32
Akvinu River CDN 233 Ec18
Akwanga WAN 186 Le41
Akwatuk Bay CDN 239 Ga19
Akwaya CAM 194 Le42
Akyab = Sittwe MYA 112 Pg35
Akyaka TR 51 Mo54
Akyazı TR 50 Ml50
Akyma GUY 270 Ha43
Akyurt TR 51 Mo50
Akzhaikyn köli KZ 76 Od23
Akzhal KZ 84 Oh22
Akzhar KZ 84 Oh23
Akzhar KZ 84 Oj23
Akzhar KZ 85 Pb22
Akzhar Lake KZ 76 Oe23
Ål N 12 Lj30
Al RI 130 Re48
Ala S 13 Ls29
Al A'amiyah IRQ 65 Nc29
Al-Aan Palace KSA 68 Nc37
Ala-Archa Canyon KS 77 Oh24
Ala-Archa N.P. KS 77 Oh24
Alabama USA 227 Fc12
Alabama and Coushatta Ind. Res. USA 243 Fc30
Alaban RI 116 Pj44
Alabat Island RP 121 Rb38
al-'Abbasiya SUD 197 Mf39
Ala-Bel KS 77 Og24
Alabel RP 123 Rc42
Al 'Abr YE 68 Nd37
Ala-Buka KS 77 Of25
Ala-Buka KS 77 Oh25
Alaca TR 51 Mp50
Alacahan TR 63 Mj26
Alacalı TR 50 Mk49
Alaçam TR 62 Mh25
Alaçam Dağları TR 50 Mj51
Alacami TR 51 Mn54
Alacant E 29 Ku48
Alaçatı TR 49 Mg52
Ala Dağlar TR 51 Mq53
Ala Dağlar TR 63 Nb26
Ala DağlarTasarı Milli Parkı TR 51 Mq53
Al 'Adam LAR 175 Mb30
Aladdin USA (WY) 235 Eh23
Aladdin Tomb Tower IR 72 Nf28
Aladža džamija MK 46 Ma48
Aladžda manastir BG 47 Mh47
Aladzha TM 71 Ng26
Alaejos E 26 Kp51
Alafiarou DY 186 Lb41
Alaganik USA (AK) 230 Ch15
Alaganik Lake USA 228 Ca16
Alagir RUS (SOA) 70 Nc24
Alagiri IND (APH) 111 Ok40
Alag Khayrkhan Uul MNG 85 Ph23
Alagna Valésia I 40 Lh45
Alag nuur MNG 85 Ph23
Alagoa Grande BR (PB) 277 Jc49
Alagoas BR 265 Ja20
Alagoinhas BR (BA) 283 Ja52
Alagoinhas BR (CE) 277 Ja47
Alagón E 27 Kt51
Alagoninha do Piauí BR (PI) 277 Hk49
Alahan TR 62 Mg27
Alahanpanjang RI 124 Qa46
Al-'Ain SUD 190 Me38
Al Ain UAE 75 Nh33
Al Aiss KSA 66 Mk33
Al-Ajaiz OM 69 Nj36
Alajärvi FIN 16 Md28
Alajskij hrebet KS 77 Of26
Alajuela CR 256 Fh40
Alakamisy Itenina RM 220 Nd56
Alakanuk USA (AK) 228 Bh14
Al Akhdar KSA 64 Mj31
Alaköl KZ 84 Oh23
Alakol KZ 84 Pa22
Alakuko WAN 194 Lc42
Alakurtti RUS 11 Mf12
Alalaú BR 274 Gk46
Al Alia DZ 174 Lc29
Al A'lyaneh SYR 64 Mk28
Al Amadiyah IRQ 65 Nb27
Al 'Amar KSA 67 Nc33
Al Amara IRQ 65 Nd30
al-'Amara SUD 190 Mg39
Alamat'a ETH 191 Mk40
Alambie AUS (NSW) 150 Sb61
Alamdo CHN (TIB) 89 Ph30
Alameda CDN (SK) 238 Ej21
Alamikamba NIC 256 Fh39
Alaminos RP 120 Qk37
Alamo MEX (VC) 254 Fb35
Álamo Chapo MEX (CHH) 237 Eh31
Alamogordo USA (NM) 237 Eh29
Alamo Lake USA 236 Ed28
Alamo Navajo Ind. Res. USA 237 Eg28
Alamor EC 272 Fk47
Álamos MEX (SO) 252 Ef32
Alamosa USA (CO) 237 Eh27
Alamos de Márquez MEX (COH) 237 Ej31
Al Amrashi YE 68 Nc37
Alamuru IND (APH) 109 Pa37
Al ,Anad YE 68 Nc39
Åland = Ahvenanmaa FIN 13 Lu30
Aland IND (KTK) 108 Oj37
Al Andalus Expreso E 29 Kr47
Älandsbro S 13 Ls28
Ålands hav S 13 Lu30
Alandur IND (TNU) 111 Pa40
Alanga G 202 Lg46
Alang Besar RI 116 Qa44
Alange E 28 Ko48
Alanggantang RI 125 Qc46
Alangouassou CI 193 Kh42
Alanis E 28 Kp48
Alanjeq IR 72 Nd26
Alanson USA (MI) 246 Fh23
Alanta LT 17 Mf35
Alantika Mountains WAN 195 Lg41
Alanya TR 51 Mm54
Alanya Kalesi TR 51 Mm54
Alapa WAN 186 Lc41
Alaplı TR 51 Mm49
Alappuzha IND (KER) 110 Oj41
Al ,Aqiq KSA 66 Na35
Alarahan Caravanserai TR 51 Mm54
Alaraz E 26 Kp50
Alarcón E 29 Ks49
Al Aredah KSA 68 Nb37
Al Arin KSA 68 Nb36
Alarobia-Andalandranobe RM 220 Nd56
Al Artawiyah KSA 67 Nc32
Alas RI 116 Pj44
Alas RI 129 Qj50
Alaşehir TR 50 Mj52
Al-Ashkhara OM 75 Nk35
Al-Ashrafiya Mosque YE 68 Nb39
Al 'Ashuriyah IRQ 65 Nb30
Alaska USA 224 Ca06
Alaska ZW 210 Mf54
Alaska Highway USA 229 Ch14
Alaska Marine Highway USA (AK) 228 Cb17
Alaska Maritime Wildlife Refuge USA (AK) 228 Bg18
Alaska Peninsula USA 224 Bd07
Alaska Peninsula Wildlife Refuge USA 228 Ca17
Alaska Range USA 229 Ce14
Al Asma x RIM 183 Kc36
Alassa CY 51 Mn56
Al 'Assafiyah KSA 64 Mk31
Al'Assah LAR 174 Lf29
Alássio I 40 Lj47
Alasso RMM 184 Kf38
Alastaro FIN 16 Mc30
Alat AZ 70 Ne26
Al Atawlah KSA 66 Na35
Alataw Shankou KZ/CHN 84 Pb23
Al Athalah KSA 67 Nb33
Alati CAM 195 Lg44
Alatna River USA 229 Cd12
Alatri I 42 Lo49
Alatsinainy Bakaro RM 220 Nd55
Alatskivi EST 16 Mh32
Alatyr' RUS (CHU) 53 Nd18
Alatyr' RUS 53 Nc18
Alausí EC 272 Ga47
Alaverdi ARM 70 Nc25
Alavus FIN 16 Md28
Alawa WAN 186 Ld40
Alawa A.L. AUS 139 Rh53
Al-'Awabi OM 75 Nj34
Al Awaynat LAR 181 Lf33
Al Awaynat LAR 189 Mc35
Al-'Awir UAE 74 Nh33
Al-'Aydarus Mosque YE 68 Nc39
Al Ayn KSA 67 Nc32
Al-Ayn OM 75 Nj34
Alayo RCA 200 Mb43
Al-'Ayun MA/DARS 178 Kd32
Alazani AZ/GE 70 Nd25
Alazejskoe ploskogor'e RUS 59 Sb05
Al'Aziziyah LAR 174 Lg29
Al Azraq JOR 64 Mj30
Alb CH 34 Lj43
Alba I 40 Lj46
Al Ba'aj IRQ 65 Na27
Al Bab SYR 64 Mj27
Albac RO 44 Mc44
Albacete E 29 Kt48
Al Bad' KSA 64 Mh31
Al Bada'i' KSA 66 Mk32
Al Badaya KSA 67 Nb33
Alba de Tormes E 26 Kp50
Al Badi IRQ 65 Na28
Al Badi KSA 67 Nd35
Al Badia KSA 68 Nc37
Ålbæk DK 14 Ll33
Ålbæk Bugt DK 14 Ll33
Al Baha KSA 66 Na36
Albaida E 29 Ku48
Alba Iulia RO 44 Md44
Albalate del Arzobispo E 27 Ku51
Albalate de Zorita E 29 Ks50
Al Baleed OM 69 Nh37
Alban CO 268 Gc43
Alban = San José CO 272 Gb45
Alban F 24 Lc47
Albania AL 46 Lu50
Albano Laziale I 42 Ln49
Albany AUS (WA) 144 Qj63
Albany USA (GA) 249 Fh30
Albany USA (KY) 249 Fh27
Albany USA (MO) 241 Fc25
Albany USA (NY) 247 Gd24
Albany USA (OR) 234 Dj23
Albany USA (TX) 242 Fa29
Albanyà E 30 Lc48
Albany Downs AUS (QLD) 151 Se59
Albany River CDN 239 Fh20
Al Bardi LAR 176 Mc30
Albardón RA (SJ) 288 Gf61
Al Barit IRQ 65 Nb30
Albarracín E 29 Kt50
al-Barun SUD 197 Mg40
al-Basabir SUD 190 Mg38
Al Basira SYR 65 Na28
Al Basiri SYR 64 Mj28
Al Basra IRQ 65 Nd30
Al Basra IRQ 65 Nd30
Al Batha IRQ 65 Nc30
Albatross Bay AUS 146 Sa52
Albatross-eiland NAM 216 Lh59
Albatross Island NAM 216 Lh59
Al Bayda LAR 175 Ma29
Al Bayda YE 68 Nc38
Albazino RUS 98 Rc19
Albemarle USA (NC) 249 Fk28
Albemarle Sound USA 249 Gb27
Albena BG 47 Mj47
Albenga I 40 Lj46
Albentosa E 29 Ku50
Albergaria-a-Velha P 26 Km50
Alberga River AUS 143 Rh59
Albermarle = Isla Isabela EC 272 Fe46
Albernoa P 28 Kn47
Alberobello I 43 Ls50
Albersdorf D 32 Lk36
Albert F 23 Lc40
Alberta CDN 224 Ea08
Albert Edward, Mount PNG 159 Sd50
Albert Falls ZA 217 Mf60
Alberti RA (BA) 289 Gk63
Albert I Land N 11 Lf06
Albertinia ZA 216 Ma63
Albert Lea USA (MN) 241 Fd24
Albert Nile EAU 169 Mc18
Alberto de Agostini, P.N. RCH 294 Ge73
Alberton CDN (PE) 245 Gh22
Albert Town BS 251 Gc34
Albertville F 25 Lg45
Albertville USA (AL) 248 Fg28
Albeşti RO 45 Mj47
Albeşti RO 45 Mh44
Albi F 24 Lc47
Albia USA (IA) 241 Fd25
Al Bi'ar KSA 66 Mk34
Albilbah AUS (QLD) 150 Sc58
Albin USA (WY) 235 Eh25
Albina SME 271 Hc43
Albion USA (CA) 234 Dj26
Albion USA (MI) 246 Fh24
Albion USA (NY) 247 Ga24
Albion USA (TX) 243 Fc29
Albion Downs AUS (WA) 140 Ra59
Al Bir KSA 64 Mj31
Al Birk KSA 67 Nd34
Al Birk KSA 68 Na36
Al Birkah KSA 66 Na34
Al Bîr Lahlou DARS 178 Kf32
Al Biyad KSA 67 Nd35
Albocàsser E 30 La50
Alborea E 29 Kt49
Ålborg DK 14 Lm36
Ålborg Bugt DK 14 Ll34
Albox E 29 Ks47
Albreda WAG 183 Kb39
Albro AUS (QLD) 149 Sd57
Albstadt D 34 Lk42
Al Budayyi BRN 74 Nf32
Albuera RP 123 Rc40
Albufeira P 28 Km47
Al Bukayriyah KSA 67 Nb32
Albuñol E 29 Kr46
Albuquerque E 28 Kn49
Albuquerque USA (NM) 237 Eg28
Al Buraimi OM 75 Nh33
Albury AUS (NSW) 153 Sd64
Al Busayta KSA 64 Mk30
Al Busayyah IRQ 65 Nd30
al Butanah SUD 190 Mh39
Alcácer do Sal P 28 Km48
Alcáçovas P 28 Km48
Alcala RP 121 Ra37
Alcalá de Guadaira E 28 Kp47
Alcalá de Henares E 29 Kr50
Alcalá del Júcar E 29 Kt49
Alcalá de los Gazules E 28 Kp46
Alcalá del Río E 28 Kp47
Alcalà de Xivert E 30 La50
Alcalá la Real E 28 Kr47
Álcamo I 42 Ln53
Alcanar E 30 La50
Alcanede P 28 Km49
Alcañices E 26 Ko51
Alcañiz E 27 Ku51
Alcântara BR (MA) 276 Hh47
Alcántara E 28 Ko49
Alcántara I 42 Lq53
Alcantarilla E 29 Kt47
Alcaracejos E 28 Kq48
Alcaraz = Pueblo Arrúa RA (ER) 289 Ha61
Alcarràs E 30 La49
Alcaudete E 28 Kq47
Alcaudete de la Jara E 28 Kq49
Alcazaba de Almería E 29 Ks46
Alcázar de San Juan E 29 Kr49
Alcedo, Volcán EC 272 Fe46
Alcester GB 21 Kt38
Alcester Island PNG 160 Sg50
Alčevs'k UA 55 Mk21
Al Chaba'ish IRQ 65 Nd30
Alcinópolis BR (MS) 286 Hd55
Alcira RA (CD) 288 Gh62
Alcobaça BR (BA) 287 Ja54
Alcoba de los Montes E 28 Kq49
Alcoentre P 28 Km49
Alcohuas RCH 288 Ge61
Alcoi E 29 Ku48
Alcolea del Pinar E 29 Ks51
Alconchel E 28 Kn48
Alcoota AUS (NT) 143 Rh57
Alcorisa E 29 Ku50
Alcorta RA (SF) 289 Gk62
Alcorta RCH 284 Gf57
Alcoutim P 28 Kn47
Alcova USA (WY) 235 Eg24
Alcoy = Alcoi E 29 Ku48
Alcublas E 29 Ku49
Alcúdia E 30 Ld51
Aldaia Bona BR (PA) 275 Hc45
Al Dali YE 68 Nc39
Aldama MEX (CHH) 237 Eh31
Aldama MEX (TM) 253 Fa34
Aldan RUS 59 Rb07

Aldan – Amaculí

Aldan RUS 59 Rc07
Aldanskoe nagor'e RUS 59 Ra07
Aldar MNG 90 Pj22
Aldeadávila de la Ribera E 26 Ko51
Aldea del Rey E 29 Kr48
Aldea dos Indios Sucane GUY 274 Ha45
Aldeburgh GB 21 Lb38
Aldeia das Canoas BR (PA) 275 Hc45
Aldeia Viçosa ANG 202 Lh50
Aldeia Vila Batista BR (AM) 274 Gk46
Aldenueva del Codonal E 26 Kq51
Alder Creek USA (NY) 247 Gc24
Alder Flats CDN (AB) 233 Ec19
Alderly AUS (QLD) 148 Rk57
Alderney GB 22 Ks41
Aldershot GB 21 Ku39
Aldersyde AUS (WA) 144 Qj62
Aldeyjarfoss IS 10 Kb13
Al Dibin YE 69 Nf37
Al Djebel al Akhdar LAR 175 Ma29
Al Eatrah KSA 66 Nb33
Åled S 15 Ln34
Aledia Koura DY 193 La41
Aledo USA (IL) 241 Fe25
Aleg RIM 183 Kd37
Alegre BR (ES) 287 Hk56
Alegre BR (MG) 287 Hg55
Alegre BR 280 Ha53
Alegre BR 281 Hb54
Alegrete BR (RS) 290 Hc60
Alegria RP 123 Rb41
Alegria RP 123 Rd40
Alëhovščina RUS 11 Mg15
Alej RUS 85 Pa20
Alejandra RA (SF) 289 Ha60
Alejandria BOL 280 Gh52
Alejandro Gallinal ROU 289 Hc62
Alejandro Humboldt, P.N. C 259 Gc35
Aleknagik USA (AK) 228 Ca16
Aleksandro Gaj RUS 53 Ne20
Aleksandrov RUS 52 Mk17
Aleksandrovac SCG 44 Mb46
Aleksandrovac SCG 46 Mb47
Aleksandrovskoe RUS 70 Nb23
Aleksandrów Kujawski PL 36 Lt38
Aleksandrów Łódzki PL 37 Lu39
Alekseevka RUS 53 Mk20
Alekseevka RUS 53 Nb20
Alekseevka RUS 53 Nf19
Alekseevskaja RUS 53 Nb20
Alekseevskoe RUS (TAR) 53 Nf18
Aleksin RUS 52 Mj18
Aleksinac SCG 46 Mb47
Alekšycy BY 17 Md37
Alel SUD 197 Mf42
Ålem S 15 Lr34
Alémbé G 195 Lf46
Alembé RCB 202 Lh46
Alembeyli TR 51 Mp50
'Alem Ketema ETH 198 Mk40
Alem Maya ETH 198 Na41
Alem Paraiba BR (MG) 287 Hj56
Ålen N 12 Lm28
Alençon F 22 La42
Alen Cué RA (CR) 289 Hb60
Alenquer BR (PA) 275 Hc46
Alenquer P 28 Km48
Alentejo P 28 Kn48
Alenuihaha Channel USA 230 Cb35
Alépé CI 193 Kj43
Aleppo SYR 64 Mj28
Alerce Andino, P.N. RCH 292 Gd66
Alert CDN 225 Gd02
Alerta PE 279 Ge51
Alert Bay CDN (BC) 232 Dg20
Alert Point CDN 225 Fb02
Alès F 25 Le46
Alešd RO 44 Mc43
Alessándria I 40 Lj46
Ales stenar S 15 Lp35
Ålesund N 12 Lg28
Aletschgletscher CH 34 Lh44
Aleutian Basin USA 224 Ba07
Aleutian Islands USA 224 Bc08
Aleutian Range USA 228 Cb17
Aleutian Trench USA 224 Bc08
Alexander USA (AK) 229 Ce15
Alexander Archipelago USA 224 Da07
Alexanderbaai ZA 216 Lj60
Alexander Bay ZA 216 Lj60
Alexander City USA (AL) 249 Fh29
Alexander Graham Bell N.H.S. CDN 245 Gk22
Alexander Island 296 Ga32
Alexander Morrison N.P. AUS 144 Qh60
Alexander-Nevski BG 46 Md48
Alexandra NZ 155 Te68
Alexandra Channel MYA 111 Pg38
Alexandria AUS (NT) 139 Rj55
Alexandria BR (RN) 277 Ja49
Alexandria ET 177 Me30
Alexandria GR 46 Mc50
Alexandria RO 47 Mf47
Alexandria USA (IN) 246 Fh25
Alexandria USA (LA) 243 Fd30
Alexandria USA (MN) 241 Fc23
Alexandria USA (SD) 240 Fa24
Alexandria USA (VA) 247 Gb26
Alexandria ZA 217 Md62
Alexandroupoli GR 47 Mf50
Aleksandrovskij Zavod RUS 91 Qj20
Alexeck NAM 212 Lk56
Alexis Creek CDN (BC) 232 Dj19
Alexishafen PNG 159 Sc48
Al Faid Majir LAR 174 Lh29
Alfalfa USA (OR) 234 Dk23
Al Fallujah IRQ 65 Nb29
Al Fardah YE 68 Ne38
Alfaro E 27 Kt52
Alfarràs E 30 La49
Al Farshah KSA 68 Nb37
Al Fashir SUD 196 Mc39
Al-Fatah OM 75 Nj34
Alfatar BG 45 Mh47
Al Fathah IRQ 65 Nb28
Al Fatk YE 69 Ng37
Al Faw IRQ 65 Nc31
Al Fawwarah KSA 66 Nb32
Al Faydah KSA 67 Nc33
Al Faydami YE 69 Ng37
Alfeld D 32 Lk39
Alfenas BR (MG) 287 Hh56
Al Feqrah KSA 66 Mk33
al-Fifi SUD 196 Mc40
Alfioó GR 48 Mb53
Alföld H 39 Ma43
Alfonsina MEX (BC) 236 Ec31
Alfonsine I 40 Ln46
Alford AUS (SA) 152 Rj62
Alford GB 19 Ks33
Alford GB 21 La37
Ålfotbreen N 12 Lf29
Alfredo Wagner BR (SC) 291 Hf59
Alfta S 13 Lr29
Al Fuqaha' LAR 181 Lj32
al-Gabalayn SUD 190 Mg40
Al-Gabir SUD 197 Me39
Al Garabull LAR 174 Lg29
Ålgård N 14 Lf32
Al-Garef SUD 197 Mh40
Algarroba RA (BA) 293 Gj65
Algarrobal RCH 288 Ge60
Algarrobal RCH 288 Ge60
Algarrobo CO 268 Gc40
Algarrobo RCH 288 Ge62
Algarrobo del Aguila RA (LP) 292 Gg64
Algarve P 28 Km47
al-Gayli SUD 190 Mg38
al-Gazira SUD 190 Mg39
Algeciras E 28 Kp46
Algena ER 191 Mk38
Algeria DZ 167 Kb07
Algerian Provenceal Basin 31 Lf51
Algeyata ETH 198 Na41
al-Ghaba SUD 190 Mf37
al-Ghabsha SUD 190 Mf39
Al Ghandura SYR 64 Mj27
Al Gharith KSA 66 Na35
Al Ghat KSA 67 Nc32
Al Ghaydah YE 69 Ng37
Al Ghayl KSA 67 Nd34
Alghero I 31 Lj50
Al Ghrayfah LAR 181 Lg32
Al Ghuraya KSA 68 Nb36
Al Ghwaybiyah KSA 67 Ne33
Algiers DZ 173 Lb27
Algoa Bay ZA 217 Md62
Algodões BR (PE) 283 Jb50
Algodón PE 273 Gd47
Algodonales E 28 Kp46
Algoma USA (WI) 246 Fg23
Algoma Upland CDN 239 Fj22
Algona USA (IA) 241 Fc24
Algonquin Prov. Park CDN 247 Ga23
Algonquin Upland CDN 247 Ga23
Algorta ROU 289 Hb62
Algyő H 39 Ma44
Al Habah KSA 67 Nd32
Al Habariyah IRQ 65 Nb29
Al Habbaniyah IRQ 65 Nb29
Al Habil KSA 68 Nb36
Al Hada KSA 66 Na35
Al Haddar KSA 67 Nc34
Al Haditah KSA 64 Mj30
Al Hadithah IRQ 65 Nb28
Al-Hadi-Yahya-Mosque YE 68 Nb37
Al Hadr IRQ 65 Nb28
Alhai IR 72 Ne30
Al Ha'ir KSA 67 Nd33
Al Hait KSA 66 Na33
Al-Hajar OM 75 Nk34
Al Hajarah KSA 65 Nb31
Al Halbeh SYR 64 Mk28
Al Hallaniyah OM 69 Nh37
Al Hallaniyat Bay OM 69 Nh37
Al Hamad KSA 65 Mk30
Alhama de Aragón E 27 Kt51
Alhama de Granada E 28 Kr46
Alhama de Murcia E 29 Kt47
Al Hamar KSA 67 Nd34
Alhambra E 29 Kr47
Alhambra E 29 Kr48
Alhambra USA (CA) 236 Ea28
Al Hami YE 68 Ne38
Al-Hamra OM 75 Nj34
Al Hamudiyah LAR 181 Lj32
Al Hanakiyah KSA 66 Na33
Al Hanish al Kabir YE 68 Nb39
Al Haniyah KSA 65 Nc31
Al Haqlaniyah IRQ 65 Nb28
Al Harabah LAR 174 Lf30
Al Harf YE 68 Nc37
Al Hariq KSA 67 Nd34
Al Harjah KSA 68 Nb36
Al Harrah KSA 64 Mk30
Al-Hartum SUD 190 Mg39
al-Hartum Bahri SUD 190 Mg39
Al Haruj al Aswad LAR 181 Lj32
Al-Hasaka SYR 65 Na27
Al Hassiane DARS 178 Kc32
Alhaurin el Grande E 28 Kq46
Al Hawaya KSA 67 Ne35
Al Hawra YE 68 Nd39
Al Hayy IRQ 65 Nc29
Al Hayyaniyah KSA 65 Nb31
Al-Hazm OM 75 Nj34
Al Hazm YE 68 Nc37
Alheit ZA 216 Ma60
Al-Hibak KSA 69 Ng35
Al Hilla SUD 197 Md39
Al-Hillah IRQ 65 Nc29
Al-Hillah KSA 67 Nd34
Al Hilwah KSA 67 Nd34
Al Hindiyah IRQ 65 Nc29
Al Hisn' YE 68 Nc39
Al Hisu KSA 66 Na33
Al Hoceima MA 173 Kj28
Al Hol SYR 65 Na27
Al Huan LAR 176 Mb33
Al Hudaydah YE 68 Nb38
Al Hufrah KSA 64 Mk31
Al-Hufrah al-Janubiyah OM 69 Nh36
Al Hufrah ash Sharqiya LAR 181 Lh32
Al Hufuf KSA 67 Ne33
Al Hulayq al Kabir LAR 181 Lj32
Al Humaydah KSA 64 Mh31
Al Humaymi YE 68 Nd38
Al Humayshah YE 68 Nc39
Al-Humrah UAE 74 Nh34
Al Hunaiy KSA 67 Ne33
al-Huqna SUD 190 Mg38
Al Hurriyeh SYR 65 Na28
al-Husay SUD 190 Mg39
Al Husayniyah KSA 68 Nc37
Al-Huwaysah OM 75 Nj35
Ália I 42 Lo53
Aliabad AFG 78 Oe27
Ali Abad IR 72 Nh27
Ali Abad IR 75 Nh31
Ali Abad Tower IR 73 Nk28
Aliaga E 29 Ku50
Aliağa TR 49 Mg52
Aliákmonas GR 46 Mb50
'Ali al Gharbi IRQ 65 Nd29
Aliambata TLS 132 Rd50
Aliança BR (PE) 283 Jc49
Aliança BR (RO) 280 Gj50
Aliance CDN (AB) 233 Ee19
Aliantan RI 124 Qa45
Aliartos GR 48 Md52
Ali ash Sharqi IRQ 65 Nd29
Alibag IND (MHT) 108 Og36
Alibates Flint Quarries Nat. Mon. USA 242 Ek28
Ali Bayramli AZ 70 Ne26
Alibo ETH 198 Mj41
Alibori DY 185 Lb40
Alibunar SCG 44 Ma45
Alicante = Alacant E 29 Ku48
Alice AUS (NSW) 151 Sg60
Alice USA (TX) 253 Fa32
Alice ZA 217 Md62
Alice Arm CDN (BC) 231 Df18
Alice Channel MAL/RP 122 Qk43
Alice River AUS (QLD) 149 Sc57
Alice Springs AUS (NT) 142 Rg57
Alice Town BS 251 Ga33
Alice Town BS 251 Gb33
Aliceville USA (AL) 243 Ff29
Ali Chuk USA (AZ) 236 Ed30
Alicia RP 121 Ra37
Alicia RP 123 Rc41
Alick River AUS (QLD) 148 Sb56
Alifu Atoll = Arie Atoll MV 110 Og44
Alifuato Nature Reserve SP 205 Nc44
Aliganj IND (UPH) 107 Ok32
Aligarh IND (UPH) 107 Ok32
Alignements de Pagliaju F 31 Lj49
Aligudarz IR 72 Ne29
Álika GR 48 Mc54
Alikalia WAL 192 Ke41
,Ali Kheyl AFG 78 Oe29
Al Ikhwan YE 69 Ng39
Aliki GR 47 Me50
Aliko GR 49 Mf54
Alima RCB 200 Lj46
Alimbongo RDC 201 Me46
Alimiá GR 49 Mh54
Alinda TR 49 Mh53
Alindau RI 127 Qk46
Alindoa RCA 200 Ma43
Alingsås S 14 Ln33
Alipur IND (WBG) 112 Pe34
Alipur PK 81 Of31
Alipura IND (MPH) 109 Ok33
Alipur Duar IND (WBG) 112 Pe32
Alirajpur IND (MPH) 108 Oh34
Al Irqah YE 68 Nd39
Ali Sabieh DJI 198 Nb40
Al Isawiyah KSA 64 Mk30
Aliseda E 28 Ko49
Alishan RC 97 Ra34
Alishan RC 97 Ra34
Al Iskandariyah IRQ 65 Nc29
Alista MEX (JLC) 254 Ej36
Alitak Bay USA 230 Cc17
Alivéri GR 48 Me52
Aliwal-Noord ZA 217 Md61
Aliwal North ZA 217 Md61
Alizai PK 79 Of29
Al Jafr JOR 64 Mj30
Al Jafurah KSA 67 Nf33
Al Jagbub LAR 176 Mc31
Al Jalamid KSA 65 Na30
Al-Jami'al-Kebir YE 68 Nc38
Al Jawb KSA 67 Nf34
Al Jawf KSA 65 Mk31
Al Jawf LAR 176 Mb33
Al Jaza'ir DZ 173 Lb27
Aljenaari WAN 186 Lb40
Aljezur P 28 Km47
Al Jihrah KSA 66 Nb32
Al Jubaylah KSA 67 Nd33
Al Jufra Oasis 168 Ld13
Al Jumailiyah Q 74 Nf33
Al Jumum KSA 66 Mk35
Al Junaynah SUD 196 Mb39
Al Jurayd KSA 67 Ne32
Al Jussah KSA 66 Na34
Aljustrel P 28 Km47
Al Kabar SYR 65 Mk28
Al Kadhimiya IRQ 65 Nc29
Al-Kaf Palace YE 68 Ne37
Alkali Lake USA (OR) 234 Ea24
Alkamari RN 187 Lf39
Al- Kamil OM 75 Nk34
Al-Kamilin SUD 190 Mg39
Al Karabilah IRQ 65 Na28
Al Karameh SYR 65 Mk28
Al Kararim LAR 175 Lh29
al-Kawa SUD 190 Mg40
Al-Khabb UAE 75 Nh33
Al-Khabbah OM 75 Nk34
Al Khabra KSA 67 Nb32
Al-Khabura OM 75 Nj34
Al Khadra KSA 68 Nc37
Al Khafah KSA 66 Nb32
Al Khalf KSA 66 Na33
Al Khalis IRQ 65 Nc29
Al Khamasin KSA 67 Nc35
Al Khanabah LAR 181 Lh32
Al Khandaq SUD 190 Mf37
Al Kharfah KSA 67 Nd34
Al Kharj KSA 67 Nd33
Al Khawkhah YE 68 Nb39
Al-Khawrah UAE 74 Nh33
Al Khawtamah YE 68 Nb38
Al Khidr IRQ 65 Nc30
Al Khobar KSA 67 Nf32
Al Khor Q 74 Nf33
Al Khottah KSA 66 Na32
Al Khubah KSA 68 Nb37
Al Khums LAR 174 Lh29
Al Khuraybah KSA 64 Mh31
Al Khurmah KSA 67 Nb35
Al Khushaybi KSA 67 Nb33
Al-Kidan KSA 74 Ng34
Al Kifl IRQ 65 Nc29
Al Kisrah SYR 65 Mk28
Alkmaar NL 32 Le38
al-Koin SUD 190 Mf37
Al Kufah IRQ 65 Nc29
Al Kumayt IRQ 65 Nd29
Al Kura KSA 66 Mk35
al-Kurru SUD 190 Mf37
Al Kut IRQ 65 Nc29
Al Kuwayt KWT 74 Nd31
Al Kuwayt KWT 74 Nd31
Al Labbah KSA 65 Na31
Allada DY 194 Lb42
Al Ladhqiyah SYR 62 Mh28
Allagash USA (MA) 244 Gf22
Allagash River USA 244 Gf22
al-Lagowa SUD 197 Me40
Allagudda IND (APH) 111 Ok39
Allahabad = Tirth Raj Prayag IND (UPH) 109 Pa33
Al Lahabah KSA 67 Nd32
Allahdurg IND (APH) 108 Oj37
Allahganj IND (UPH) 107 Ok32
Allakaket USA (AK) 229 Cd12
Allanche F 25 Lc45
Allandale AUS (SA) 143 Rh59
Allanmyo MYA 114 Ph36
Allanridge ZA 217 Md59
Allansford AUS (VIC) 153 Sb65
Allan Water CDN (ON) 239 Fe20
Allapalli IND (MHT) 109 Pa36
Allardville CDN (NB) 245 Gh22
Allariz E 26 Kn52
Allauch F 25 Lf47
Alldays ZA 214 Me57
Alleen N 12 Lh32
Allegan USA (MI) 246 Fh24
Allegany S.P. USA 247 Ga24
Allemanskraaldam ZA 217 Md60
Allen RA (RN) 292 Gg65
Allen RP 121 Rc39
Allendale USA (SC) 249 Fk29
Allende MEX (COH) 253 Ek31
Allende MEX (NL) 253 Ek33
Allen Island AUS (QLD) 148 Rk54
Allensworth USA (CA) 236 Ea28
Allentown USA (PA) 247 Gc25
Alleppey = Alappuzha IND (KER) 110 Oj41
Alleppey Beach IND 110 Oj42
Aller D 33 Ll38
Aller = Cabañaquinta E 26 Kp53
Allersberg D 35 Lm41
Allevard F 25 Lg45
Allgäu D 34 Ll43
Allgäuer Alpen D/A 34 Ll43
Alliance USA (NE) 240 Ej24
Alliance USA (OH) 247 Fk25
Allier F 25 Ld44
Alliford Bay CDN (BC) 232 De19
Alligator Pond JA 259 Gb37
Alligator River N.W.R. USA 249 Gc28
Allinge DK 15 Lp35
Al Lisafah KSA 67 Nd32
Allison USA (IA) 241 Fd24
Allison Island PNG 159 Sb46
Al Lith KSA 66 Na35
Allo E 27 Ks52
Allomo WAN 194 Ld42
Allones F 22 La43
Allora AUS (QLD) 151 Sf60
Allos F 25 Lg46
All Soul's Memorial Church (Kanpur) IND 107 Pa32
Allu RI 129 Ra48
Al Luhayyah YE 68 Nb38
Allur IND (APH) 111 Pa39
Alma AUS (NSW) 153 Sc62
Alma CDN (NB) 245 Gh23
Alma CDN (QC) 244 Ge21
Alma USA (GA) 249 Fj30
Alma USA (MI) 246 Fh24
Alma USA (NE) 240 Fa25
Alma USA (NM) 237 Ef29
Al Ma'aniyah IRQ 65 Nb30
Almacelles E 30 La49
Al Machmin IRQ 65 Nb30
Almada P 28 Kl48
Al Madaya KSA 68 Nb37
Almaden AUS (QLD) 149 Sc54
Almadén E 28 Kq48
Al Madina YE 68 Nd38
Al Madinah KSA 66 Mk33
Almafuerte RA (CD) 288 Gh62
Al Magharim YE 68 Nd38
Almagro E 29 Kr48
Al Mahash KSA 66 Na32
Al Mahatta Ath'thania SYR 65 Na28
Al Mahbas DARS 179 Kf32
Al Mahdoom SYR 64 Mj27
Almahel ETH 198 Mh40
Al Mahfid YE 68 Nd38
Al Mahmudiyah IRQ 65 Nc29
Al Mahrah YE 69 Nf38
Al Mahruqah LAR 181 Lh32
Al Mahwit YE 68 Nb38
Al Majadah KSA 68 Na36
Al Majm'ah KSA 67 Nc33
Al Makhwah KSA 66 Na36
Al-Malamm SUD 197 Me41
Al-Malkyer SYR 65 Nb27
Alma, Mount AUS 151 Sf58
Al Manajier SYR 65 Na27
Al Manama BRN 74 Nf32
Al Manama UAE 75 Nh33
al-Manaqil SUD 190 Mg39
Almandar IR 72 Nc26
Almansa E 29 Kt48
Al-Mansura SYR 65 Mk28
Al Mansuriyah YE 68 Nb38
Almanza E 26 Kp52
Alma Peak CDN 231 Dg17
Al Ma'qas KSA 66 Na36
Al Maqrun LAR 175 Ma30
Almar AFG 78 Oc28
Al Marah KSA 67 Nc33
Al Marawiah YE 68 Nb38
Almaraz E 28 Kp49
Al-Mariyyah UAE 74 Ng34
Al Marj LAR 175 Ma29
Almarza E 27 Ks51
Almas BR (TO) 282 Hg51
Almaty KZ 77 Oj24
Al Mawsil IRQ 65 Nb27
Al-Mawsil IRQ 65 Nb27
Al Mayadin SYR 65 Na28
al-Maysar OM 75 Nk34
Al Mayyah KSA 66 Nb32
Almazán E 27 Ks51
Almeida P 26 Ko50
Almeirim BR (PA) 275 Hd46
Almeirim P 28 Km49
Almel IND (KTK) 108 Oj37
Almelo NL 32 Lg38
Almenara BR (MG) 287 Hk54
Almenara E 29 Ku49
Almenar de Soria E 27 Ks51
Almendo MW 211 Mh54
Almendral E 28 Ko48
Almendralejo E 28 Ko48
Almere NL 32 Lf38
Almeria E 29 Ks46
Almerimar E 29 Ks46
Al'met'evsk RUS (TAR) 53 Ng18
Älmhult S 15 Lp34
Al-Midhar Mosque (Tarim) YE 68 Ne38
Al Midhnab KSA 67 Nc33
Al-Mihrad KSA 74 Ng35
Al Mina RL 64 Mh28
Al-Mintirib OM 75 Nk34
Almirante PA 256 Fj41
Almirante Brown RA (BA) 289 Ha63
Almirante Latorre RCH 288 Ge60
Almirante Tamandaré BR (PR) 286 Hf58
Al-Mirfa UAE 74 Ng33
Almiropótamos GR 48 Me52
Almirós GR 48 Mc51
Al Mish'ab KSA 67 Ne31
Al Mistannah KSA 67 Ne33
Almodôvar P 28 Km47
Almodóvar del Campo E 29 Kq48
Almodóvar del Río E 28 Kp47
Almofala BR (CE) 277 Ja47
Almoharin E 28 Ko49
Almonte E 28 Ko47
Almora AUS (QLD) 148 Rk55
Almora IND (UTT) 107 Ok31
Almoustarat RMM 185 La37
Älmsta S 13 Lt31
Al Mubarraz KSA 67 Ne33
Al-Mudaiba OM 75 Nk34
Al Mudawwara JOR 64 Mh31
Almudévar E 27 Ku52
al-Muglad SUD 197 Md40
Al Muharraq BRN 74 Nf32
Al Mukalla YE 68 Ne38
Al Mukha YE 68 Nb39
Al Mulayhah al Gharbiyah KSA 67 Ne34
Almuñécar E 28 Kr46
Almunge S 13 Lt31
Al Muqdadiyah IRQ 65 Nc29
Al-Musalla OM 75 Nk34
al-Musallamiya SUD 190 Mg39
Al-Musana'a OM 75 Nj34
Al Musayjid KSA 66 Mk33
Al Musaymir YE 68 Nc39
Al Mussayyib IRQ 65 Nc29
Al Muwassam KSA 68 Nb37
Al Muwayh KSA 66 Na34
Al Muwaylih KSA 66 Mh32
Al Muzahmiyah KSA 67 Nd33
Al Muzaylif KSA 66 Na36
Al Naqub YE 68 Nc38
Alnaši RUS 53 Ng17
Alness GB 19 Kq33
Alness GUY 271 Hb42
Alnif MA 172 Kh30
Alnön S 13 Ls28
Alnwick GB 19 Kt35
Alo F 164 Ba53
Ålö FIN 16 Mc30
Alóag EC 272 Ga46
Aloândia BR (GO) 286 Hf54
Aló Brasil BR (MT) 281 He52
Alofi NZ 164 Bf55
Alogtina G 194 Lf45
Aloi EAU 204 Mg44
Aloja LV 17 Me33
Aloja LV 17 Mc33
Aloma WAN 194 Le42
Alon IND (ARP) 112 Ph31
Alongly CDN (SK) 233 Eh19
Alongshan CHN (NMZ) 91 Rb20
Alónissos GR 48 Md51
Alonso de Rojas C 258 Fj34
Alor E 28 Kn48
Alor RI 132 Rc50
Álora E 28 Kq46
Alorna IND 108 Og38
Alor Setar MAL 116 Qa42
Alot IND (MPH) 108 Oh34
Alota BOL 284 Gg56
Alotau PNG 160 Sf51
Alpachiri RA (LP) 293 Gj64
Alpalhão P 28 Kn49
Alpamayo PE 278 Gb50
Alpasinche RA (LR) 288 Gg60
Alpena USA (MI) 246 Fj23
Alpera E 29 Kt48
Alpercatas BR 276 Hh49
Alpes du Valais CH 34 Lh44
Alpha AUS (QLD) 149 Sd57
Alpha Cordillera 298 Ec01
Alphen a/d Rijn NL 32 Le38
Alphonse SY 219 Ng49
Alphonse Group SY 219 Ng49
Alplarça P 28 Km49
Alpi Carniche I 41 Lo44
Alpi Lepontine I/CH 34 Lj44
Alpi Marittime I 40 Lh46
Alpine USA (AZ) 237 Ef29
Alpine USA (TX) 237 Ej30
Alpine USA (WY) 235 Ee24
Alpine Lake Wilderness USA 232 Dk22
Alpine N.P. AUS 153 Sd64
Alpi Orobie I 40 Lk44
Alpi Venoste I 40 Ll44
Alpouro DY 186 Lb41
Alps 8 Lb09
Alpu TR 51 Mi51
Alpujarras E 29 Kr46
Al Qa'amiyat KSA 68 Ne36
Al Qa'arah LAR 176 Mc30
Al-Qabil OM 75 Nk34
Al-Qadarif SUD 190 Mh39
Al-Qaffay UAE 74 Nf33
Al Qafrah YE 68 Nc38
Al Qahmah KSA 68 Na37
Al Qa'iyah KSA 66 Nb33
Al Qa'iyah KSA 67 Nc32
Al Qala'a LAR 174 Lh30
Al Qalibah KSA 64 Mj31
Al Qara'a KSA 66 Nb36
Al Qardabah LAR 175 Mb29
Al Qarn YE 68 Nd38
Al Qaryah ash Sharqiyah LAR 174 Lg30
Al Qaryah al Gharbiyah LAR 174 Lg30
Al Qasab KSA 67 Nc33
Al Qasabat LAR 175 Lh29
Al Qath YE 68 Ne38
Al Qatif KSA 67 Nf32
Al Qatranah JOR 64 Mj30
Al Qatrun LAR 181 Lh33
Al Qawba'iyah KSA 66 Mk35
Al Qaysumah KSA 67 Nd31
Al-Q'nitra MA 172 Kg28
Al-Qua'a UAE 74 Nh34
Al Quasir SYR 64 Mj28
Alquézar E 30 La48
Al Qulayd Bahri SUD 190 Mf37
Al Qulayyib KSA 67 Ne32
Al Qunfadhah KSA 66 Na36
Al Qurayn KSA 67 Nb33
Al Qurayyah KSA 66 Nb33
Al Qurnah IRQ 65 Nd30
Al Qusayr IRQ 65 Nd30
Al Qutaifeh SYR 64 Mj29
al-Qutayna SUD 190 Mg39
Al Quwarah KSA 67 Nb32
Al Quwayiyah KSA 67 Nc33
Al Quzah YE 68 Ne38
Al Rahibat LAR 174 Lf30
Al Rahidah YE 68 Nc39
Al Rassafa SYR 65 Mk28
Al Rawdah YE 68 Nd38
Al Rayyan YE 68 Ne38
Alroy Downs AUS (NT) 139 Rj55
Als DK 14 Lk35
Als DK 14 Ll34
Alsace F 23 Lh42
Alsace F 23 Lh43
Alsa Craig GB 18 Kp35
Al-Samha UAE 74 Nh33
Alsasua E 27 Ks52
Alsea USA (OR) 234 Dj23
Alsek River CDN 231 Da15
Alsfeld D 32 Lk40
Al-Shafee Mosque KSA 66 Mk35
Al Shaykh 'Uthman YE 68 Nc39
Alshi EC 272 Ga47
Al Shihr YE 68 Ne38
Al Sidarah YE 68 Ne38
Alsike CDN (AB) 233 Ec19
Alsike S 13 Ls31
Alsterbro S 15 Lq34
Alstermo S 15 Lq34
Al Sufal YE 68 Ne38
Al Sukhnah YE 68 Nb38
Al Surrah YE 68 Nd39
Alta N 11 Mb11
Alta Badia I 40 Lm44
Alta Floresta BR (MT) 281 Hc50
Altagracia NIC 256 Fh40
Alta Gracia RA (CD) 288 Gh61
Altagracia YV 268 Ge40
Altagracia de Orituco YV 269 Gg41
Alta Italia RA (LP) 288 Gh63
Altajskij zapovednik RUS 85 Pe20
Altamachi BOL 280 Gg54
Altamaha USA 249 Fk30
Altamira BR (PA) 275 Hd47
Altamira CO 272 Gc44
Altamira MEX (TM) 253 Fa34
Altamira MEX (TM) 253 Fb34
Altamira PE 284 Gf58
Altamira do Maranhão BR (MA) 276 Hh48
Altamont USA (OR) 234 Dk24
Altamura I 43 Lr50
Altamura, P.N. dell' I 43 Lr50
Altan MNG 85 Pf21
Altanbulag MNG 90 Pj21
Altanbulag MNG 90 Qd22
Altaneira BR (CE) 277 Ja49
Altan ovoo CHN/MNG 85 Pf23
Altan Ovoo MNG 90 Qa22
Altar MEX (SO) 236 Ee30
Altar-Est DZ 174 Le31
Altar, Volcán EC 272 Ga46
Altata MEX (SL) 252 Eg33
Altavista USA (VA) 249 Ga27
Altay CHN (XUZ) 85 Pe22
Altay MNG 90 Pj21
Altay MNG 90 Pj22
Altay RUS 58 Pb08
Altay Mountains MNG 82 Pc09
Altayn Caadah Gov' MNG 92 Pj24
Altay Shan CHN 85 Pd21
Altdorf CH 34 Lj44
Altdorf D 35 Lm41
Altea E 29 Ku48
Altenberg D 33 Lo40
Altenburg D 33 Ln40
Altenkirchen D 32 Lh40
Altenmarkt A 35 Lo43
Altenmarkt A 35 Lp43
Altensteig D 34 Lj42
Altentreptow D 33 Lo37
Altér do Chão P 28 Kn49
Alter do Chão BR (PA) 275 Hc47
Alte Saline Bad Reichenhall D 35 Ln43
Al Thaura SYR 65 Mk28
Altheim A 35 Lo42
Althofen A 35 Lp44
Altîna RO 44 Me45
Altınbesik TR 51 Mm54
Altındere Vadisi Milli Parkı TR 63 Mk25
Altınekin TR 51 Mn52
Altınhisar TR 51 Mp52
Altınkaya Baraj TR 62 Mh25
Altın Köprü IRQ 65 Nc28
Altinópolis BR (SP) 286 Hg56
Altınova TR 50 Mg51
Altıntaş TR 50 Ml51
Altıntepe TR 63 Mk26
Altınyaka TR 51 Ml54
Altınyayla TR 50 Mk53
Altiplanicie del Payún RA 292 Gf64
Altiplano BOL 284 Gf54
Altiri IND (ORS) 112 Pd35
Altja EST 16 Mf31
Altkirch F 23 Lh43
Altmark D 33 Lm38
Altmühl D 35 Lm42
Altnaharra GB 19 Kq32
Altn Bulg RUS (KAL) 55 Nc22
Alto USA (TX) 243 Fc30
Alto Alegre BR (RR) 270 Gk44
Alto Alegre BR (RS) 290 Hd61
Alto Araguaia BR (MT) 286 Hd54
Alto Bonito BR (AC) 279 Ge50
Alto Bonito BR (PA) 276 Hg46
Alto Cedro C 259 Gc35
Alto Changane MOC 214 Mg58
Alto Chicapa ANG 209 Lk51
Alto del Carmen RCH 288 Ge60
Alto de Tamar CO 268 Gd42
Alto Garças BR (MT) 286 Hd54
Alto Golfo de California y Delta del Río Colorado MEX (BC) 236 Ec30
Alto Hama ANG 208 Lh52
Alto Ligonha MOC 211 Mk53
Alto Longá BR (PI) 277 Hj48
Alto Madre de Dios PE 279 Ge52
Alto Molócuè MOC 211 Mj53
Alton GB 21 Ku39
Alton USA (IL) 241 Fe26
Alton USA (MO) 243 Fe27
Alton USA (NY) 247 Gb24
Altona CDN (MB) 238 Fb21
Alto Nevado, Cerro RCH 292 Gd68
Altônia BR (PR) 286 Hd57
Altoona USA (PA) 247 Ga25
Alto Paraguai BR (MT) 281 Hb53
Alto Paraíso de Goiás BR (GO) 282 Hg53
Alto Parnaíba BR (MA) 282 Hh50
Alto Pelado RA (SL) 288 Gg62
Alto Pencoso RA (SL) 288 Gg62
Alto Purus PE 279 Ge51
Alto Rio Guamá, T.I. BR 276 Hg47
Alto Río Mayo RA (CB) 294 Ge68
Alto Rio Negro, T.I. BR 273 Gf45
Alto Rio Purus, T.I. BR 279 Ge50
Alto Río Senguer RA (CB) 292 Ge68
Altos BR (PI) 277 Hj48
Alto Santo BR (CE) 277 Ja48
Alto Sepatini, T.I. BR 279 Gg49
Alto Sucuriú BR (MS) 286 Hd55
Altotonga MEX (VC) 254 Fb36
Altötting D 35 Ln42
Alto Turiaçu, T.I. BR 276 Hg47
Altun CHN (XUZ) 87 Pe26
Altun-alem džamija SCG 46 Ma47
Altun Ha BH 255 Ff37
Altun Shan CHN 87 Pg26
Altun Shan CHN 87 Pc27
Altura E 29 Ku49
Alturas USA (CA) 234 Dk25
Alturitas YV 268 Gd41
Altus USA (OK) 242 Fa28
Altyn Arashan KS 77 Ok24
Altyn-Mosque CHN 86 Oj26
Aluakluak SUD 197 Mf42
Al Ubaydi IRQ 65 Na28
Al Ubaylah KSA 67 Nf34
al-Ubayyid SUD 197 Mf39
Al Udailiyah KSA 67 Ne33
Al 'Udayn YE 68 Nb39
al-Udayya SUD 197 Me39
Alu Grottos CHN 113 Pk33
Alüksne LV 17 Mh33
Al ,Ula KSA 66 Mj32
al-'Umda SUD 197 Md40
Aluminé RA (NE) 292 Ge65
Aluminé RA 292 Ge65
Alunda S 13 Lt30
Alungdaw Kathapa National Park MYA 112 Ph34
Aluoi VN 115 Qd37
Alupka UA 55 Mh23
Al 'Uqaylah LAR 175 Lk30
Al Uqayr KSA 67 Nf33
al-'Uqda SUD 190 Mg39
Alur IND (APH) 111 Oj39
Alur IND (MHT) 108 Oj37
Al 'Urayq KSA 64 Mk31
Al-Uruq al-Muraridah KSA 69 Ng36
Alušta UA 55 Mh23
Al Uwayailah KSA 65 Nb30
Al 'Uwayja KSA 67 Nf34
Al 'Uwaynid KSA 67 Nc33
Al 'Uwaynidhiyah KSA 66 Mh32
Al Uzaym KSA 66 Nb32
Al Uzayr IRQ 65 Nd30
Alva USA (OK) 242 Fa27
Alvalade P 28 Km47
Älvängen S 14 Ln33
AlvarAalto-museo FIN 16 Mf28
Alvarado CO 268 Gc43
Alvarado MEX (VC) 254 Fc36
Alvarães BR (AM) 274 Gh47
Alvaréz RA (SF) 289 Gk62
Álvaro Obregón MEX (CHH) 237 Eg31
Alvaro Obregón MEX 252 Ef32
Ålvdal N 12 Ll28
Älvdalen S 13 Lp29
Älvdalen S 13 Lo30
Alvear RA (CR) 289 Hb60
Alvesta S 15 Lp34
Älvho S 13 Lp29
Ålvik N 12 Lg30
Alvin USA (TX) 243 Fc31
Alvinópolis BR (MG) 287 Hj56
Alvito P 28 Kn48
Älvkarleby S 13 Ls30
Alvorada BR (RS) 290 He61
Alvorada BR (TO) 282 Hf52
Alvorada do Gurguéia BR (PI) 282 Hj50
Alvorada do Norte BR (GO) 282 Hg53
Alvorada d'Oeste BR (RO) 280 Gj51
Alvord Valley USA 234 Ea24
Alvøy N 12 Le30
Älvros S 13 Lp28
Älvros S 13 Ln29
Älvsbyn S 10 Ma13
Älvsered S 15 Ln33
Al Wahah LAR 175 Lk31
Al Wajh KSA 66 Mj32
Al Wakrah Q 74 Nf33
Alwar IND (RJT) 106 Oj32
Al Wari'ah KSA 67 Nd32
Al Widyan IRQ/KSA 65 Na29
Al Wigh LAR 181 Lh33
Al Wittyah LAR 174 Lf29
Alxa Gaoyuan CHN 92 Qa25
Alxa Youqi CHN (NMZ) 92 Qa26
Alxa Zuoqi CHN (NMZ) 92 Qc26
Alyangula AUS (NT) 139 Rj52
Al Yarubiyeh SYR 65 Nb27
Al-Yasat UAE 74 Ng33
Alyawarra & Katitja A.L. AUS 143 Rh56
Alytus LT 17 Me36
Alz D 35 Ln42
Alzada USA (MT) 235 Eh23
Alzey D 34 Lj41
Alzira E 29 Ku49
Ama MYA 114 Ph38
Ama PNG 158 Sa48
Amacayacu, P.N. CO 273 Gf47
Amaciá BR (AM) 274 Gh48
Amaculí MEX (DGO) 252 Eg33

Amacuro – Annoual

Amacuro YV 270 Gk41
Amada Gaza RCA 195 Lh43
Åmådalen S 13 Lp29
Amada Temple ET 177 Mg34
Amadi BD 112 Pe34
Amadi RDC 201 Md44
Amadi RDC 201 Me44
Amadi SUD 201 Mf43
Amadjuak Lake CDN 224 Gb05
Amadora P 28 Kl48
Amadrar DZ 180 Ld33
Amaga CO 268 Gc42
Amager DK 14 Ln35
Amahai RI 130 Re47
Amakouladji RMM 185 Kk37
Amakusa N.P. J 103 Re29
Amakusa-shoto J 103 Re29
Amal OM 69 Nh36
Åmål S 13 Ln31
Amalapuram IND (APH) 109 Pb37
Amalfi CO 268 Gc42
Amalfi I 42 Lp50
Amalia ZA 217 Mc59
Amaliáda GR 48 Mb53
Amalner IND (MHT) 108 Oh35
Amaluza EC 272 Ga47
Amaluza EC 272 Ga48
Amamá RA (SE) 288 Gj59
Amamapare RI 131 Rj48
Amambai BR (MS) 286 Hc57
Amambai, T.I. BR 286 Hc57
Amami Islands J 103 Re32
Amanã BR 275 Hb48
Amanab PNG 158 Sa47
Aman Abad IR 73 Nk27
Amancio Rodríguez C 259 Gb35
Amandit River Rafting RI 126 Qh47
Amándola I 41 Lo48
Amaneyé, T.I. BR 276 Hf47
Amanganj IND (MPH) 109 Pa33
Amani Nature Reserve EAT 207 Mk48
Amantea I 43 Lr51
Amanzimtoti ZA 217 Mf61
Amapá BR (AP) 271 He44
Amapá BR 265 Hb18
Amapari BR 275 Hd45
Amaporã BR (PR) 286 Hd57
Amar ETH 198 Mj43
Amara RO 45 Mh46
Amara Abu Sin SUD 190 Mh39
Amaradia RO 44 Md46
Amara, Mount ETH 198 Mj41
Amarante BR (PI) 277 Hj49
Amarante P 26 Km51
Amarante do Maranhão BR (MA) 276 Hg48
Amaranth CDN (MB) 238 Fa20
Amărăştii de Jos RO 46 Me47
Amara West Temple SUD 190 Mf36
Amarbayasgalant Monastery MNG 90 Qc21
Amardalay MNG 90 Qd22
Amareleja P 28 Kn48
Amargosa BR (BA) 283 Ja52
Amargosa Desert USA 236 Eb27
Amargosa Range USA 236 Eb27
Amarillas C 258 Fk34
Amarillo USA (TX) 242 Ek28
Amárinthos GR 48 Md52
Amariú BR (BA) 283 Hk51
'Amar Jadid SUD 189 Mc38
Amarkantak IND (MPH) 109 Pa34
Amarnath IND (MHT) 108 Og36
Amarnath Cave PK 79 Oh28
Amarpatan IND (MPH) 109 Pa33
Amarpur IND (TRP) 112 Pf34
Amaru RO 45 Mg46
Amarwara IND (MPH) 109 Ok34
Amasya TR 62 Mh25
Amata AUS (SA) 142 Rf59
Amatari BR (AM) 274 Ha47
Amatenango del Valle MEX (CHP) 255 Fd37
Amatitlán GCA 255 Fe38
Amatrice I 42 Lo48
Amatura BR (AM) 273 Gf47
Amau PNG 159 Se51
Amaya E 27 Kq52
Amazmaz RIM 183 Kd36
Amazon 265 Hb19
Amazonas BR 264 Gc20
Amazon Cone 265 Hc17
Amazônia, P.N. de BR 275 Hb48
Amazon Shelf 265 Hc18
Amba Alage ETH 191 Mk40
Ambad IND (MHT) 108 Oh36
Ambae VU 162 Td53
Amba Farit ETH 198 Mk40
Ambagarh Chauki IND (CGH) 109 Pa35
Amba Giyogis ETH 191 Mj40
Ambah IND (MPH) 107 Ok32
Ambahikily RM 220 Nb56
Ambajogai IND (MHT) 108 Oj36
Ambala IND (HYA) 107 Oj30
Ambalabe RM 220 Ne55
Ambalabongo RM 220 Nd54
Ambalajanakomby RM 220 Nd54
Ambalakely RM 220 Nd56
Ambalakirajy RM 219 Ne53
Ambalamanakana RM 220 Nd56
Ambalamanasy II RM 219 Ne53
Ambalangoda CL 111 Pa43
Ambalantota CL 111 Pa43
Ambalapaiso RM 219 Ne53
Ambalarondra RM 220 Ne55
Ambala Sadar IND (HYA) 107 Oj30
Ambalatany RM 220 Nd57
Ambalavao RM 220 Nd56
Ambam CAM 195 Lf44
Ambanja RM 219 Ne52
Ambar PE 278 Gb51
Ambararata RM 219 Ne53
Ambargasta RA (SE) 288 Gj60
Ambasa IND (TRP) 112 Pf34
Ambathala AUS (QLD) 151 Sc58
Ambato EC 272 Ga46
Ambato RM 220 Nd55
Ambato Boeny RM 220 Nd54
Ambatofinandrahana RM 220 Nd56
Ambatolahy RM 220 Nc56
Ambatolampy RM 220 Nd55
Ambatomainty RM 220 Nc54
Ambatomanoina RM 220 Nd55
Ambatondrazaka RM 220 Ne54
Ambatoriha RM 219 Ne53
Ambatosia RM 219 Ne53
Ambatovory RM 220 Nd56
Ambatry RM 220 Nc57
Ambaúba BR (AM) 273 Gg45
Ambazac F 24 Lb45
Ambelákia GR 46 Mc51
Ambelau RI 130 Rd47
Ambelónas GR 46 Mc51
Ambelónas GR 48 Ma51
Amber Bay USA 228 Cb17
Ambered ARM 70 Nc25
Amber Fort IND 106 Oh32
Amberg D 35 Lm41
Ambergris Cay BH 255 Fg36
Ambérieu-en-Bugey F 25 Lf45
Ambert F 25 Ld45
Ambidédi RMM 183 Ke38
Ambikanagar IND (WBG) 112 Pd34
Ambikapur IND (CGH) 109 Pb34
Ambila RM 220 Nd56
Ambil Island RP 120 Ra39
Ambilobe RM 219 Ne52
Ambin RMM 184 Kh38
Ambinanindrano RM 220 Nd56
Ambinanindrano RM 220 Ne56
Ambinaninony RM 220 Ne55
Amboa, T.I. BR 276 Hf49
Ambitle Island PNG 160 Sg48
Ambjörby S 13 Lo30
Amble GB 19 Kt35
Ambler USA (AK) 229 Cb12
Ambleside GB 21 Ks36
Ambo PE 278 Gb51
Amboahangibe RM 219 Ne53
Amboahangy RM 220 Nd58
Amboasary RM 220 Nd55
Amboasary RM 220 Nd58
Amboasary Gara RM 220 Ne55
Amboavory RM 220 Ne54
Ambodiangezoka RM 219 Ne53
Ambodiatafana RM 220 Ne54
Ambodibonara RM 219 Ne52
Ambodifotatra RM 220 Ne54
Ambodiharina RM 220 Ne55
Ambodilazana RM 220 Ne55
Ambodiriana RM 220 Ne54
Ambodisetezana-Sahana RM 219 Nf53
Ambohidratrimo RM 220 Nd55
Ambohijanahary RM 220 Ne54
Ambohimahamasina RM 220 Nd56
Ambohimahasoa RM 220 Nd56
Ambohimanga RM 220 Nd55
Ambohimanga RM 220 Nd56
Ambohimilanja RM 220 Nd55
Ambohinihaonana RM 220 Nd56
Ambohipaky RM 220 Nc54
Ambohisary RM 220 Nd55
Ambohitra RM 219 Ne52
Ambohitra RM 219 Ne52
Ambohitralanana RM 219 Nf53
Ambohitsilaozana RM 220 Ne54
Amboise F 22 Lb43
Amboiva ANG 208 Lh51
Amboli IND (MHT) 108 Og38
Ambolobozo RM 218 Nd53
Ambolobozokely RM 219 Ne52
Ambolomoty RM 220 Nd54
Ambon RI 130 Rd47
Ambon RI 130 Re47
Ambondro RM 220 Nc58
Ambondromamy RM 220 Nd54
Ambongo RM 218 Nc54
Amboni Caves EAT 207 Mk48
Amboriala RM 219 Ne52
Amborompotsy RM 220 Nd56
Amborondolo RM 219 Ne52
Amboró, P.N. BOL 285 Gj54
Amboseli N.P. EAK 204 Mj47
Ambositra RM 220 Nd56
Ambotosoratra RM 220 Ne54
Ambovombe RM 220 Nd58
Amboy USA (CA) 236 Ec28
Amboy USA (MN) 241 Fc24
Amboy Crater USA 236 Ec28
Amboyna Cay 122 Qg42
Ambrim VU 162 Te54
Ambriz ANG 202 Lg49
Ambrolauri GE 70 Nb24
Ambuaki RI 130 Rg46
Ambulong Island RP 121 Ra39
Ambunten RI 128 Qg49
Ambunti PNG 159 Sb48
Ambur IND (TNU) 111 Ok40
Am Dafok RCA 196 Mb40
Am-Dam TCH 196 Ma39
Amdassa RI 133 Rf49
Amderma RUS 58 Oa05
Am Djaména RCA 196 Ma41
Am Djemena TCH 187 Lj39
Amdo CHN (TIB) 89 Pf29
Amealco MEX (QRT) 254 Ek35
Ameca MEX (JLC) 253 Eh35
Ameca La Vieja MEX (ZCT) 253 Eh34
Amedamit ETH 198 Mj40
Ameghino RA (BA) 289 Gj63
Ameib NAM 212 Lh56
Ameixial P 28 Kn47
Ameland NL 32 Lf37
Amélia I 42 Ln48
Amelia Island USA 249 Fk30
Amélie-les-Bains F 24 Lc48
Amelinghausen D 33 Ll37
Améloloud RN 186 Ld37
Amelup AUS (WA) 144 Qk63
Amendolara I 43 Lr51
Ameng CHN (YUN) 96 Qc34
Amenia USA (NY) 247 Gd25
Amentego SUD 190 Mf37
Ameri IR 74 Nf30
América BR (AM) 274 Gh49
Americana BR (SP) 286 Hg57
American Falls USA (ID) 235 Ed24
American Fork USA (UT) 235 Ee25
American Fs. Res. USA 235 Ed24
American Samoa USA 135 Bb11
Americus USA (GA) 249 Fh29
Amersfoort NL 32 Lf38
Amersfoort ZA 217 Me59
Amery ANT (AUS) 297 Oc32
Amery Ice Shelf 297 Oc32
Ames USA (IA) 241 Fd24
Amesbury GB 21 Kt39
Ameya ETH 198 Mj42
Amfíklia GR 48 Mc52
Amfilohía GR 48 Mb52
Ámfissa GR 48 Mc52
Amfiteatri AL 46 Lu49
Amga RUS 59 Rc06
Amga RUS 59 Rc06
Amgala DARS 178 Ke32
Amgaon IND (MHT) 109 Pa35
Amgu RUS 99 Rj23
Amguid DZ 180 Lc32
Amgun' RUS 98 Rh20
Amguri IND (ASM) 112 Ph32
Amherst CDN (NS) 245 Gh23
Amherst = Kyaikkami MYA 114 Pj37
Amherst USA (MA) 247 Gd24
Amhertsburg CDN (ON) 246 Fj24
Am Himédé TCH 196 Ma39
Amhuinnsuidhe Castle GB 18 Ko33
Amicalola Falls USA 249 Fh28
Amidon USA (ND) 240 Ej22
Amiens F 23 Lc41
Amile NEP 88 Pb32
Amili IND (ARP) 113 Ph31
Amilly F 23 Lc43
Aminagou RCA 201 Mc43
Amíndeo GR 46 Mb50
Amindivi Islands IND 110 Og41
Amini Island IND 110 Og41
Åminne S 15 Lt33
Amino J 101 Rh28
Aminuis NAM 212 Lk57
Amir Abad IR 73 Oa27
Amirante Basin 219 Nh49
Amirante Islands SY 219 Ng48
Amirante Trench 219 Ng49
Amir Chah PK 80 Ob31
Amiri SUD 197 Mh40
Amirkala IR 72 Ng27
Amish Acres USA 246 Fg25
Amisk Lake CDN 238 Ej18
Amite USA (LA) 243 Fe30
Amity Point AUS (QLD) 151 Sg59
Amizmiz MA 172 Kf30
Amkunj IND (AAN) 111 Pg39
Amkusa-nada J 103 Re29
Amla IND (MPH) 109 Ok35
Amlakhi IND (ASM) 112 Pg33
Amlamé TG 193 La42
Amlekhganj NEP 88 Pc32
Åmli N 12 Lj32
Amlwch GB 20 Kq37
'Amm Adam SUD 191 Mj38
Amman JOR 64 Mh30
Ammarnäs S 10 Lj13
Ammaroo AUS (NT) 143 Rh56
Ammassalik DK 225 Ja05
Ammersee D 35 Lm43
Ammochostos CY 51 Mo55
Ammochostos Bay CY 51 Mp55
Ammouk RMM 185 Kk36
Amnat Charoen THA 115 Qc38
Amnok Gang PRK/CHN 100 Rd25
Amoama GH 193 Kj42
Amol IR 72 Ng27
Amoliani GR 47 Md50
Amon MA 172 Ke31
Amontada BR (CE) 277 Ja47
Amores RA 289 Ha59
Amorgós GR 49 Mf54
Amorgós GR 49 Mf54
Amorinopolis BR (GO) 286 He54
Amory USA (MS) 243 Ff29
Amos CDN (QC) 244 Ga21
Åmot N 12 Lj31
Åmot N 12 Lk31
Åmot N 12 Ll29
Åmot S 13 Lr30
Amotape, Cerros de PE 272 Fk48
Åmotfors S 12 Ln31
Amotopo SME 271 Hb44
Amou F 24 Ku47
Amou TG 193 La42
Amouguèr MA 172 Kh29
Amou Oblo TG 193 La42
Amourj RIM 184 Kg37
Amoy = Xiamen CHN (FJN) 97 Qk33
Amoya GH 193 Kj42
Ampah RI 126 Qh46
Ampahana RM 219 Nf53
Ampalu RI 124 Qa46
Ampana RI 127 Ra46
Ampanefena RM 219 Ne52
Ampang RI 129 Qj50
Ampani IND (ORS) 109 Pb36
Ampanihy RM 220 Nc58
Ampanolahamiraty RM 219 Ne52
Ampara CL 111 Pa43
Amparafaravola RM 220 Ne54
Amparihy Atsinanana RM 220 Nd57
Amparo BR (SP) 287 Hg57
Ampasimanolotra RM 220 Ne55
Ampasimatera RM 218 Nd53
Ampasina-Maningory RM 220 Ne54
Ampasinambo RM 220 Ne56
Ampefy RM 220 Nd55
Amper D 35 Lm42
Amper WAN 186 Le41
Ampère BR (PR) 290 Hd58
Ampère Seamount 168 Kb12
Ampezzo I 41 Ln44
Amphitheâtre d'El Djem TN 174 Lf28
Amphitrite Group RP 120 Qg37
Ampisikinana RM 219 Ne52
Ampitatafika RM 220 Nd55
Ampiyacu PE 273 Gd47
Amplepuis F 25 Le45
Ampliación la Loma MEX (TM) 253 Fa33
Ampombiantambo RM 219 Ne52
Amporaha RM 219 Ne52
Amposta E 30 La50
Amqui CDN (QC) 244 Gg21
Amrabad IND (APH) 109 Ok37
Amran YE 68 Nb38
Amrapara IND (JKD) 112 Pd33
Amrati IND (CGH) 109 Pa36
Amravan IR 72 Nh28
Amravati IND (MHT) 108 Oj35
Am Raya TCH 187 Lj38
Amreli IND (GUJ) 108 Of35
Amritsar IND (PJB) 106 Oh30
Amroha IND (UPH) 107 Ok31
Amrum D 32 Lj36
Amsâga RIM 178 Kd35
Am Sak TCH 196 Lk39
Amsel DZ 180 Lc34
Amsterdam NL 32 Le38
Amsterdam USA (NY) 247 Gc24
Amsterdam ZA 217 Mf59
Amsterdam 301 Ob13
Amsterdamøya N 11 Lf06
Amstetten A 35 Lp42
Amtali BD 112 Pf34
Am Tanabo TCH 187 Lj39
Am Timan TCH 196 Ma40
Amudalavalsa IND (APH) 109 Pb36
Amudarja TM 71 Ob26
Amudarjo UZ 71 Nk24
Amu-Dar'ya TM 73 Oc27
Amudat EAU 204 Mh45
Amulung RP 121 Ra37
Amund Ringnes Island CDN 225 Fa03
Amundsen Bay 297 Nc32
Amundsen Glacier 296 Ca36
Amundsen Gulf CDN 224 Dd04
Amundsen Ridge ANT 296 Eb32
Amundsen Sea ANT 296 Ec32
Amungen S 13 Lq29
Amungwiwa, Mount PNG 159 Sd49
Amuntai RI 126 Qh47
Amur RUS/CHN 83 Ra08
Amurang RI 127 Rc45
Amursk RUS 98 Rj20
Amursko-Zejskaja ravnina RUS 98 Rd19
Amusquillo E 26 Kq51
Amvrakikós Kólpos GR 48 Ma51
Amyl RUS 85 Ph19
Amzacea RO 45 Mj47
Am-Zoer TCH 189 Ma38
Anaa Atoll F 165 Ch54
Anabanua RI 127 Ra47
Anabar RUS 59 Qc04
Anabarskoe plato RUS 58 Qb04
Anaborano RM 219 Ne52
Anacadiña YV 269 Gh43
Anacapa Is. USA 236 Ea29
Anaco YV 269 Gh41
Anaconda USA (MT) 235 Ed22
Anacortes USA (WA) 232 Dj21
Anadarko USA (OK) 243 Fb28
Anadyr RUS 59 Tc05
Anadyr' RUS 59 Td06
Anadyrskoye Ploskogor'ye RUS 59 Tc05
Anáfi GR 49 Mf54
Anáfi GR 49 Mf54
Anafonitria GR 48 Ma53
Anagé BR (BA) 283 Hk53
Anaghit ER 191 Mk38
Anagni I 42 Lo49
Anagodu IND (KTK) 110 Oj39
Anah IRQ 65 Na28
Anaharavi GR 48 Lu51
Anaheim USA (CA) 236 Eb29
Anahidrano RM 218 Nd53
Anahim Lake CDN (BC) 232 Dh19
Anahita IR 72 Ne28
Anáhuac MEX (NL) 253 Ek32
Anahuac N.W.R. USA 243 Fc31
Anai Mudi IND 111 Oj41
Anajás BR (PA) 276 Hf46
Anajatuba BR (MA) 276 Hh47
Anakalang RI 129 Qk50
Anakao RM 220 Nb57
Anakapalle IND (APH) 109 Pb37
Anakch DARS 178 Kd32
Anakie AUS (QLD) 149 Sd57
Anakopia Caves GE 70 Na24
Anaktuvuk Pass USA (AK) 229 Ce11
Anaktuvuk River USA 229 Ce11
Analalava RM 218 Nd53
Analavelona RM 220 Nc57
Analavory RM 220 Nd55
Anamã BR (AM) 274 Gk47
Anamaduwa CL 111 Pa43
Ana-Maria PE 278 Gc49
Anambe, T.I. BR 276 Hf47
Anambra WAN 194 Ld42
Anamorium TR 62 Mg27
Anamur TR 51 Mn54
Anamur TR 62 Mg27
Anamur Burnu TR 62 Mg27
Anan J 101 Rh29
Ananás BR (TO) 276 Hf49
Ananas, T.I. BR 270 Gk44
Anand IND (GUJ) 108 Og34
Ananda CI 193 Kh42
Anandgarh IND (RJT) 106 Og31
Anandpur IND (ORS) 112 Pd35
Anandpur Sahib IND (PJB) 107 Oj30
Anan'evo KS 77 Oj24
Añangu EC 272 Gb46
Anangu Pitjantjatjara A.L. AUS 142 Rf59
Anan'iv UA 45 Mk43
Ananthapur IND (APH) 111 Oj39
Anantnag 79 Oh29
Anantsono RM 220 Nb57
Anapa RUS 55 Mj23
Anápolis BR (GO) 286 Hf54
Anapu BR 275 He46
Anapu BR 275 He47
Anapurus BR (MA) 277 Hj47
Anar IR 72 Nh30
Anarak IR 72 Ng29
Anar Darreh AFG 78 Oa29
Anasazi MEX 237 Ef31
Anascaul IRL 20 Kk38
Anasenko CHN (XUZ) 84 Pb23
Anaskura IND (MHT) 108 Og37
Anastácio BR (MS) 286 Hc56
Anatahan USA 119 Sb15
Anatai RI 125 Qc48
Anatolia TR 62 Mf26
Anatoliki Rodhopi GR 47 Mf49
Anatolivka UA 45 Mm44
Añatuya RA (SE) 289 Gj60
Anau TM 73 Nk27
Anauá BR 274 Gk45
Anaurilândia BR (MS) 286 Hd57
Anba CHN (GZH) 96 Qc32
Anban CHN (YUN) 113 Qa34
Anbyon PRK 100 Rd26
Ancahau WAN 186 Le40
Ance LV 17 Mc33
Ancenis F 22 Kt43
Ancerville F 23 Lf42
Anchetti IND (TNU) 111 Oj40
Anchieta BR (ES) 287 Hk56
Anchieta BR (SC) 290 Hd59
Ancho USA (NM) 237 Eh29
Anchorage USA (AK) 229 Cf15
Anchorage Reef PNG 160 Sf51
Anchor Bay USA (CA) 234 Dj26
Anchorena RA (SE) 288 Gh63
Anchorena, P.N. ROU 289 Hb63
Ancien RMM 179 Kk35
Ancient tin mines of Karnab UZ 76 Oc26
Ancohuma, Nevado BOL 279 Gf53
Ancón EC 272 Fk47
Ancón PE 278 Gb51
Ancona I 41 Lo47
Ancuabe MOC 211 Mk52
Ancud RCH 292 Gd66
Ancy-le-Franc F 23 Le43
Anda CHN (HLG) 98 Rc22
Anda RP 120 Qk37
Andacollo RCH 288 Ge61
Andaga WAN 187 Lg40
Andagalá RA (CA) 288 Gg59
Andagua PE 279 Gd53
Andahuaylas PE 278 Gd52
Andaiá BR 287 Hh55
Andaingo Gara RM 220 Ne55
Andal IND (WBG) 112 Pd34
Åndalsnes N 12 Lh28
Andalucía E 28 Ko47
Andalusia USA (AL) 248 Fg30
Andaman and Nicobar Islands IND 111 Pg40
Andaman and Nicobar Islands IND 104 Pb16
Andaman Basin 116 Ph40
Andaman Islands IND 104 Pc16
Andaman Sea IND 105 Pd16
Andamarca PE 278 Gc53
Andamooka AUS (SA) 152 Rj61
Andamooka Ranges AUS 152 Rj61
Andanda IND (ORS) 109 Pc36
Andano AUS (NT) 143 Rh58
Andapa RM 219 Ne53
Andapa RM 220 Nd55
Andarai BR (BA) 283 Hk52
Andasibe RM 220 Ne55
Andasinimaro RM 219 Ne53
Andatsakala RM 219 Ne53
Andavadoaka RM 220 Nb57
Andeba Ye Midir Zerf Chaf ER 191 Na39
Andebu N 12 Ll31
Andelot F 23 Lf42
Andemaka RM 220 Nd57
Andenes N 10 Lj11
Anderai WAN 186 Lc40
Andéramboukane RMM 185 Lb38
Ånderdalen n.p. N 10 Lj11
Anderlecht B 23 Le40
Andermatt CH 34 Lj44
Andernach D 32 Lh40
Andernos-les-Bains F 24 Kt46
Anderson USA (CA) 234 Dj25
Anderson USA (IN) 246 Fh25
Anderson USA (SC) 249 Fj28
Anderson Gate NAM 212 Lh55
Andersonville N.H.S. USA 249 Fh29
Anderstorp S 15 Lo33
Andes CO 268 Gc43
Andes 262 Ga10
Andfjorden N 10 Lj11
Andhra Lake IND 108 Og36
Andhra Pradesh IND 104 Od15
Andijan UZ 77 Og25
Andijon UZ 77 Og25
Andilamena RM 220 Ne54
Andilana RM 219 Ne52
Andilanatoby RM 220 Ne54
Andimeshk IR 72 Ne29
Anding CHN (HUN) 95 Qg31
Andirá BR 273 Gg48
Andirá BR 275 Hb47
Andirá Marau, T.I. BR 275 Hb47
Andırın TR 62 Mj27
Andírio GR 48 Mb52
Andirlangar CHN (XUZ) 86 Pb27
Andirobal BR (MA) 276 Hh47
Andižanskoe vodohranilišče KS 77 Og25
Andjogo G 202 Lg46
Andkhvoy AFG 78 Oc27
Andoain E 27 Ks53
Andoany RM 219 Ne52
Andoas PE 272 Gb47
Andocollo RA (NE) 292 Ge64
Andocs H 38 Ls44
Andohahela, P.N. d' RM 220 Nd58
Andohajango RM 219 Ne53
Andoi RI 131 Rg46
Andong ROK 100 Re27
Andoni Gate NAM 212 Lj55
Andoom AUS (QLD) 146 Sa52
Andorra AND 24 Lb48
Andorra E 29 Ku50
Andorra la Vella AND 30 Lb48
Andorskaja grjada RUS 52 Mj16
Andover GB 21 Kt39
Andovoranto RM 220 Ne55
Andøya N 10 Lh11
Andrada ANG 203 Ma49
Andradas BR (MG) 287 Hg57
Andradina BR (SP) 286 He56
Andrafainkona RM 219 Ne52
Andramasina RM 220 Nd55
Andranofasika RM 220 Nd54
Andranolalina RM 220 Nd57
Andranolava RM 220 Nc57
Andranomavo RM 220 Nc54
Andranomena RM 220 Ne55
Andranopasy RM 220 Nb56
Andranosamonta RM 219 Ne53
Andranovondronina RM 219 Ne52
Andranovory RM 220 Nc57
Andratx E 30 Lc51
Andravida GR 48 Mb53
Andrea RM 220 Nc54
Andreafsky River USA 229 Bj14
Andreapol' RUS 52 Mg17
Andrée-Land N 11 Lh06
André Felix, P.N. RCA 196 Mb41
Andrelândia BR (MG) 287 Hh56
Andrequice BR (MG) 287 Hh55
Andresito RA (MI) 286 Hc58
Andrevo RM 220 Nb57
Andrew CDN (AB) 233 Ed19
Andrews USA (SC) 249 Ga29
Andrews USA (TX) 237 Ej29
Ándria I 43 Lr49
Andriamena RM 220 Nd54
Andriandampy RM 220 Nc57
Andriba RM 220 Nd54
Andriesvale ZA 216 Ma59
Andrievo-Ivanivka UA 45 Ml43
Andrijevica SCG 46 Lu48
Andrijivka UA 55 Mj22
Andringitra RM 220 Nd57
Andringitra, P.N. d' RM 220 Nd57
Andritsena GR 48 Mb53
Androfiamena RM 219 Ne52
Androka RM 220 Nc58
Androrangalova RM 220 Nd56
Ándros GR 49 Me53
Ándros GR 49 Me53
Andros Island BS 251 Ga33
Andros Town BS 251 Gb33
Andrott Island IND 110 Og41
Androy RM 220 Nc58
Andru River PNG 159 Se49
Andrušivka UA 54 Me20
Andrychów PL 39 Lu41
Andselv N 10 Lk11
Andújar E 28 Kq48
Andulo ANG 208 Lj51
Anduze F 25 Ld46
Andy Warhol Museum USA 247 Ga25
Aneby S 15 Lp33
Anecón Chico, Cerro RA 292 Gf66
Anecón Grande, Cerro RA 292 Ge66
Anéfis RMM 185 La36
Anegada GB 261 Gh36
Anegada Passage 261 Gj36
Aného TG 193 La42
Aneityum VU 162 Te56
Anekal IND (KTK) 111 Oj40
Anéker RN 186 Lc38
Anelghowhat VU 162 Te56
Añelo RA (NE) 292 Gf65
Anepahan RP 122 Qk41
Aney RN 188 Lg36
Anfile Bay ER 191 Na39
Anfu CHN (JGX) 102 Qh32
Angahuán MEX (MHC) 254 Ej36
Angalimp PNG 159 Sc48
Angamali IND (KER) 110 Oj41
Angamarut PNG 158 Sa49
Angangxi CHN (HLG) 98 Rb22
Angara RUS 58 Qa08
‚Angara SUD 196 Mc40
Angaradébou DY 186 Lb40
Angårak RN 186 Lc37
Angarapa A.L. AUS 143 Rh57
Angarsk RUS 90 Qb19
Angarskij krjaž RUS 58 Qa07
Angas Downs AUS (NT) 142 Rg58
Angastaco RA (SA) 284 Gg58
Angaston AUS (SA) 152 Rk63
Angat RP 121 Ra38
Angatuba BR (SP) 286 Hf57
Angaur PAL 121 Rh42
Angba WAN 194 Ld42
Angchran IR 75 Nj32
Ånge S 13 Lq28
Angeles RP 120 Ra38
Ängelholm S 14 Ln34
Angélica RA (SF) 289 Gk61
Angelókastro GR 48 Md53
Angelókastro GR 48 Mb52
Angelo River AUS 140 Qk57
Ängelsberg S 13 Lq31
Angels Camp USA (CA) 234 Dk26
Angemuk, Gunung RI 131 Rk47
Angepena AUS (SA) 143 Rk61
Angereb ETH 191 Mj40
Angereb Wenz ETH 191 Mj40
Angermanland S 10 Lj14
Angermünde D 33 Lo37
Angern A 35 Lr42
Angers F 22 Ku43
Angerville F 23 Lb42
Ängesön S 10 Ma14
Angetu ETH 198 Mk42
Anggoro RI 127 Ra47
Angical BR (BA) 282 Hh51
Angico BR (TO) 276 Hg49
Angicos BR (BA) 282 Hj51
Angicos BR (RN) 277 Jb48
Angkor Wat K 115 Qb39
Angk Tasaom K 115 Qc40
Angle Inlet USA (MN) 238 Fc21
Anglem, Mount NZ 155 Td69
Anglès E 30 Lc49
Angles F 22 Kt44
Anglesea AUS (VIC) 153 Sc65
Anglesey GB 20 Kq37
Angleton USA (TX) 243 Fc31
Anglure F 23 Ld42
Angneu IND (RJT) 106 Og31
Ango RDC 201 Mc43
Angochangua EC 272 Ga45
Angoche MOC 211 Mk54
Angol RCH 292 Gd64
Angola ANG 167 Lb11
Angola USA (IN) 246 Fh25
Angola Basin 170 La21
Angoon USA (AK) 231 Dc17
Angoram PNG 159 Sc48
Angostura MEX (SL) 252 Ef33
Angostura MEX (SLP) 253 Ek34
Angostura Inglesa RCH 294 Gc70
Angoulême F 24 La45
Angourie AUS 151 Sg60
Angpawing Bum MYA 113 Ph32
Angra dos Reis BR (RJ) 287 Hh57
Angren KS 76 Of25
Ängsö n.p. S 13 Lt31
Ang Thong THA 114 Qa38
Ang Tra Peang Thmor W.S. K 115 Qb39
Angu RDC 201 Mc44
Anguang CHN (JLN) 98 Rb23
Anguereta BR (MG) 287 Hh55
Angües E 27 Ku52
Anguilla GB 261 Gj36
Anguilla GB 261 Gj36
Anguilla Cays BS 251 Ga34
Anguille Mts. CDN 245 Ha21
Angul IND (ORS) 109 Pc35
Anguo CHN (HBI) 93 Qh26
Anguran IR 75 Nh32
Angurugu AUS (NT) 139 Rj53
Anguse EST 16 Mg31
Angusilla PE 272 Gc46
Angwa ZW 210 Me54
Anhai CHN (FJN) 97 Qk33
Anholt DK 14 Lm34
Anhua CHN (HUN) 95 Qf31
Anhuanduí BR (MS) 286 Hc56
Anhuanduí BR 286 Hc56
Anhui CHN 83 Qd12
Ani TR 63 Nb25
Aniak USA (AK) 229 Ca15
Aniakchak Nat.Mon. and Preserve USA 228 Ca17
Aniassué CI 193 Kj42
Anicuns BR (GO) 286 Hf54
Anié TG 193 La41
Anié TG 193 La42
Anikino RUS 91 Ra19
Anil BR (MA) 276 Hh47
Anillaco RA (LR) 288 Gg60
Animas USA (NM) 237 Ef30
Animbo BOL 285 Gh56
Anina RO 44 Mb45
Aningal, T.I. BR 270 Gk44
Anini-y RP 123 Ra40
Anisio de Abreu BR (PI) 282 Hj50
Anita USA (IA) 241 Fc25
Anıtkaya TR 51 Ml52
Anıtlı TR 51 Mn54
Aniuk River USA 229 Cb11
Aniva RUS 99 Sb22
Anivorano RM 220 Ne55
Anivorano Avaratra RM 219 Ne52
Aniwa Island VU 162 Te55
Aniyo J 101 Rj28
Aniza JOR 64 Mh30
Anjafy RM 220 Nd54
Anjahambe RM 220 Ne54
Anjalankoski FIN 16 Mg30
Anjamala RM 220 Nb57
Anjanazana RM 219 Ne53
Anjangaon IND (MHT) 108 Oj35
Anjar IND (GUJ) 108 Of34
Anjar RL 64 Mh29
Anji CHN (ZJG) 102 Qk30
Anjialava RM 219 Ne53
Anjialava RM 219 Ne53
Anjimangirana RM 218 Nd53
Anjira PK 80 Od31
Anjireh IR 72 Nh29
Anjohibe RM 218 Nd53
Anjoman AFG 79 Of28
Anjou F 22 Ku42
Anjouan = Ndzuani COM 218 Nc52
Anjozorobe RM 220 Nd55
Anju PRK 100 Rc26
Anjuba CHN (SCH) 95 Qc30
Anjuj RUS 99 Rj21
Anjujskij hrebet RUS 59 Ta05
Anka WAN 186 Lc39
Ankalabe RM 220 Ne55
Ankang CHN (SAA) 95 Qe29
Ankara TR 51 Mn51
Ankarafantsika, P.N. d' RM 218 Nd54
Ankaramena RM 220 Nd56
Ankaramy RM 219 Ne52
Ankarana RM 219 Ne52
Ankarana RM 219 Ne52
Ankaratra RM 220 Nd55
Ankarsrum S 15 Lr33
Ankasakasa RM 220 Nc54
Ankasa Nature Park GH 193 Kj43
Ankatata RM 219 Ne52
Ankavandra RM 220 Nc55
Ankazoabo RM 220 Nc57
Ankazobe RM 220 Nd55
Ankazomborona RM 220 Nd54
Ankazomiriotra RM 220 Nd55
Ankeny USA (IA) 241 Fd25
Ankerika RM 218 Nd53
An Khe VN 115 Qe39
Ankiliabo RM 220 Nb56
Ankililioka RM 220 Nb57
Ankilizato RM 220 Nc56
Ankinany RM 220 Nc57
Ankirihitra RM 220 Nd54
Ankisabe RM 220 Nd55
Anklam D 33 Lo37
Ankleshwar IND (GUJ) 108 Og35
Ankober ETH 198 Mk41
Ankofa RM 219 Ne54
Ankola IND (KTK) 110 Oh39
Ankoro RDC 206 Md49
Ankotrofotsy RM 220 Nc55
Ankpa WAN 194 Ld42
Anlejie CHN (YUN) 113 Qa33
Anliu CHN (GDG) 97 Qh34
An Loc VN 115 Qd40
Anlong CHN (GZH) 96 Qc33
Anlong Veng K 115 Qc38
Anlu CHN (HUB) 95 Qg30
Anmyon Do ROK 100 Rd27
Anna RUS 53 Na20
Annaba DZ 174 Ld27
Annaberg PNG 159 Sc48
Annaberg-Buchholz D 33 Ln40
An Nabhaniyah KSA 66 Nb33
An Nabk KSA 64 Mj30
An'nabk SYR 64 Mj28
An Nafud KSA 65 Mk31
An Najaf IRQ 65 Nc29
An Na'La KSA 67 Ne33
An Namas KSA 68 Nb36
Annam Plateau LAO/VN 115 Qc36
Annan GB 19 Kr36
Anna Paulowna NL 32 Le38
Annapolis USA (MD) 247 Gb26
Annapolis Royal CDN (NS) 245 Gh23
Annapurna I NEP 88 Pb31
Annapurna II NEP 88 Pc31
An-Naqdah OM 69 Nk35
Ann Arbor USA (MI) 246 Fj24
Anna Regina GUY 270 Ha42
An Nashash UAE 74 Nh34
An Nasiriyah IRQ 65 Nd30
An'nasra SYR 64 Mj28
Annecy F 25 Lg45
Annemasse F 25 Lg44
Anne, Mount AUS (TAS) 152 Sd67
Annette Island USA 231 De18
Annette Island Ind. Res. USA 231 De18
Anning CHN (SCH) 94 Qa30
Anning CHN (YUN) 113 Qb33
Annino RUS 52 Mj16
Anniston USA (AL) 249 Fh29
Annitowa AUS (NT) 143 Rj56
Annofliyah LAR 175 Lj30
Annonay F 25 Le45
Annopol PL 37 Mb40
Annot F 25 Lg47
Annotto Bay JA 259 Gb36
Annoual MA 173 Kj28

Armant – Auckland

Armant ET 177 Mg33
Armavir RUS 55 Na23
Armenia ARM 63 Nc25
Armenia CO 268 Gc43
Armeniş RO 44 Mc45
Armentières F 23 Lc40
Armeria MEX (COL) 254 Ej36
Armero CO 268 Gc43
Armidale AUS (NSW) 151 Sf61
Armijo USA (NM) 237 Eg28
Arminto USA (WY) 235 Eg24
Armjans'k UA 54 Mg22
Armori IND (MHT) 109 Ok35
Armour USA (SD) 240 Fa24
Armraynald AUS (QLD) 148 Rk55
Arm River CDN 233 Eh20
Armstrong CDN (ON) 239 Ff20
Armstrong RA (SF) 289 Gk62
Armur IND (APH) 109 Ok36
Armutçuk TR 51 Mm49
Armutlu TR 50 Mj50
Armutova TR 50 Mg51
Arnac-Pompadour F 24 Lb45
Arnäsvall S 10 Lk14
Arnavutköy TR 50 Mj49
Arnay-le-Duc F 23 Le43
Arnéa GR 46 Md50
Arnedo E 27 Ks52
Arneiroz BR (CE) 277 Hk49
Årnes N 12 Lm30
Arnett USA (OK) 242 Fa27
Arnhem NL 32 Lf39
Arnhem Bay AUS 139 Rj52
Arnhem Cave NAM 212 Lk57
Arnhem Land AUS 136 Rc21
Arnhem Land Aboriginal Reserve AUS 139 Rh52
Arni IND (MHT) 109 Oj35
Árnissa GR 46 Mb50
Arno AUS (QLD) 150 Sb58
Arno I 40 Ll47
Arnö S 13 Ls32
Arno Atoll MH 157 Tc17
Arno Bay AUS (SA) 152 Rj62
Arnold USA (MO) 241 Fe26
Arnøy N 10 Ma10
Arnsberg D 32 Lj39
Arnstadt D 33 Ll40
Arnstein D 34 Lk41
Arntfield CDN (QC) 239 Ga21
Aro YV 269 Gj42
Aroa YV 269 Gf40
Aroa YV 269 Gf40
Aroab NAM 216 Lk59
Arocena RA (SF) 289 Gk62
Arochuku WAN 194 Ld43
Aroji ETH 197 Mh41
Aroland CDN (ON) 239 Fg20
Aroma PNG 159 Se51
Aroma SUD 191 Mj39
Aron IND (MPH) 109 Oj33
Arona I 40 Lj45
Aroostock River USA 244 Gf22
Aroostook Hist. & Art Mus. USA 244 Gf22
Arop PNG 160 Sh49
Arorae Island KIR 157 Td19
Aroroy RP 121 Rb39
Arosa CH 34 Lk44
Arosbaya RI 128 Qg49
Arous SUD 191 Mj36
Aroya USA (CO) 240 Ej26
Arøysund N 12 Ll31
Arpacık TR 49 Mk54
Arpajon la Norville F 23 Lc42
Arpașu de Jos RO 44 Me45
Arpino I 42 Lo49
Arqu SUD 190 Mf37
Arquata del Tronto I 42 Lo48
Arquillos E 29 Kr48
Arquipélago das Anavilhanas BR 274 Gk47
Arquipélago das Quirimbas, P.N. do MOC 211 Na52
Arquipélago do Bazaruto, P.N. do MOC 214 Mh56
Arquipélago dos Abrolhos BR 287 Ja54
Arquipélago dos Bijagós GNB 183 Kb40
Arquitectura mudéjar de Zaragoza E 27 Ku51
Arrabury AUS (QLD) 150 Sa59
Ar-Rachidia MA 172 Kh30
Arráez E 29 Kt47
Arraga RA (SE) 288 Gh60
Ar Raghbah KSA 67 Nc33
Ar Raghwah KSA 68 Nb36
Arrah CI 193 Kj42
ar-Rahad SUD 197 Mf39
Ar Rahhaliyah IRQ 65 Nb29
Arraia BR (AM) 274 Gj46
Arraial do Cabo BR (RJ) 287 Hj57
Arraias BR (TO) 282 Hg52
Arraias BR 281 Hc51
Arraiolos P 28 Kn48
Ar Rajmah LAR 175 Ma29
Ar Ramadi IRQ 65 Nb29
Ar Ramlah JOR 64 Mh31
Arran GB 18 Kp35
ar-Rank SUD 197 Mg40
Ar Raqubah LAR 175 Lk31
Arras CDN (BC) 232 Dk18
Arras F 23 Lc40
Ar Râs al Abyad KSA 66 Mk34
Ar Râs al Aswad KSA 66 Mk35
Arrasate Mondragon E 27 Ks53
Ar Rass KSA 67 Nb33
Ar'rastan SYR 64 Mj28
Arrats F 24 La47
Ar Rawdah KSA 66 Na32
Ar Rawdah KSA 67 Nb35
Ar Rawdhah KSA 66 Na32
Ar-Rawdha Mosque YE 68 Ne38
Arrayanes, P.N. RA 292 Ge66
Ar Rayn KSA 67 Nc34
Ar Rayth KSA 68 Nb37
Ar Rayyan BRN 74 Nf33
Arreau F 24 La48
Arrecife E 178 Kd31
Arrecife Alargado HN 256 Fj38
Arrecife Alargado HN 256 Fj38
Arrecife Edinburgh HN 256 Fj38
Arrecife Edinburgh HN 256 Fj38
Arrecifes CO 268 Gc40
Arrecifes CO 268 Gc40
Arrecifes RA (BA) 289 Gk63
Arrecifes RA 289 Ha62
Arrecifes de la Media Luna HN 256 Fj38
Arrecifes de la Media Luna HN 256 Fj38
Arrecifes Triángulos MEX 255 Fd35
Arriaga MEX (CHP) 255 Fd37
Ar-Ribat MA 172 Kg29
Ar-Rif MA 172 Kh28
Ar Rifa'i IRQ 65 Nd30
Arrigetch Peaks USA 229 Cc12
Ar Rihab IRQ 65 Nc30
Arrilalah AUS (QLD) 148 Sb57
Arriondas E 26 Kp53
Ar Riyad KSA 66 Nd33
Arroio do Tigre BR (RS) 290 Hd60
Arroio Grande BR (RS) 290 Hd62
Arrojado BR 282 Hh52
Arronches P 28 Kn49
Arrovo Seco RA (SF) 289 Gk62
Arrowhead River CDN 231 Dj15
Arrowie AUS (SA) 152 Rk61
Arrowrock Reservoir USA 234 Ec24
Arrow Rocks S.H.S. USA 241 Fd26
Arroyito RA (CD) 288 Gj61
Arroyito RA (MD) 288 Gg62
Arroyito Challaco RA (NE) 292 Gf65
Arroyo USA (PR) 261 Gg37
Arroyo Apeleg RA 292 Ge68
Arroyo Chelforo RA 293 Ha64
Arroyo Chico RA 293 Ha64
Arroyo de la Borda RA 292 Gg64
Arroyo de la Luz E 28 Ko49
Arroyo de la Ventana RA (RN) 292 Gg66
Arroyo del Azul RA 293 Ha64
Arroyo de los Huesos RA 293 Ha64
Arroyo Genoa RA 292 Ge68
Arroyo Grande ROU 289 Hb62
Arroyo Grande USA (CA) 236 Dk28
Arroyo Las Flores RA 293 Gk64
Arroyo Napaleufú RA 293 Ha64
Arroyo Sauce Corto RA 293 Gk64
Arroyos de Mantua C 258 Fh34
Arroyo Seco MEX (GUR) 254 Ek37
Arroyo Seco MEX 253 Fa35
Arroyos y Esteros PY 285 Hb58
Arroyo Tapalqué RA 293 Gk64
Arroyo Vallimanca RA 293 Gk64
Arroyo Verde RA (RN) 292 Gg66
ar-Ru'at SUD 190 Mg40
Ar Rub' al Khali KSA 68 Ne36
Arrufó RA (SF) 289 Gk61
Ar Rumaythah IRQ 65 Nc30
Ar Ruqi KSA 67 Nd31
Ar Rustaq OM 75 Nj34
Ar Rutbah IRQ 65 Na29
Ar Ruwaydah KSA 67 Nc33
Ar Ruwaydah KSA 67 Nc34
Ar Ruwayshid JOR 64 Mk29
Ar Ruweis Q 74 Nf32
Arruwurra A.L. AUS 139 Rj56
Arsanjan IR 74 Ng31
Arsen'ev RUS 98 Rg23
Ars-en-Ré F 22 Kt44
Arsent'evka RUS 99 Sb22
Arshaty KZ 85 Pd21
Arsikere IND (KTK) 110 Oj40
Arsi Neghele ETH 198 Mk42
Arsk RUS (TAR) 53 Ne17
Arslanagića most BIH 46 Lt48
Arslanköy TR 62 Mh27
Årslev DK 14 Ll35
Arso RI 131 Sa47
Årsunda S 13 Lr30
Arsvågen N 12 Lf31
Arta DJI 198 Nb40
Arta E 30 Ld51
Árta GR 48 Ma51
Arta Beach RI 124 Qa46
Artašat ARM 70 Nc26
Arteaga MEX (MHC) 254 Ej36
Artem RUS 98 Rg24
Artemisa C 258 Fj34
Artemissia GR 48 Mc53
Artemivs'k UA 55 Mk21
Artemou RIM 183 Kd38
Artenay F 23 Lb42
Artesa de Segre E 30 Lb49
Artesia USA (NM) 237 Eh29
Artezian RUS (KAL) 70 Nd23
Arthur USA (ND) 240 Fb22
Arthur USA (NE) 240 Ek25
Arthur Lange BR (RS) 290 Hd61
Arthur Point AUS 149 Sf57
Arthur Range NZ 155 Tg66
Arthur River AUS (WA) 144 Qj62
Arthur's Pass NZ 155 Tf67
Arthur's Pass N.P. NZ 155 Tf67
Arthur's Town BS 251 Gc33
Arthurstown IRL 20 Ko38
Artigas ROU 289 Hb61
Artigas ANT (ROU) 296 Ha30
Art'ik ARM 70 Nb25
Artin Jelow AFG 78 Of27
Artois F 23 Lc40
Artoli SUD 190 Mg37
Artux CHN (XUZ) 86 Oj26
Artvin TR 63 Na25
Artybaš RUS (ALT) 85 Pd20
Artyk TM 73 Nk27
Artyom AZ 70 Nf25
Artziniega E 27 Kr53
Artzvashen ARM 70 Nc25
Aru BR (PA) 276 Hf47
Aru RDC 201 Mf44
Aru 79 Oh28
Arua EAU 201 Mf44
Aruanã BR (GO) 281 He53
Aruba NL 269 Ge39
Aruba NL 260 Gf39
Aruba 260 Ge39
Aruba Lodge EAK 207 Mk47
Arubiddy AUS (WA) 145 Rd61
Arufi PNG 158 Sa50
Arufu WAN 194 Le42
Arugam Bay CL 111 Pa43
Arumã BR (AM) 274 Gj48
Arumã BR 274 Gj47
Arumbi RDC 201 Mf44
Arumuganeri IND (TNU) 111 Ok42
Arun NEP 88 Pd32
Arunachal Pradesh IND 105 Pc13
Arundel GB 21 Ku40
Arun He CHN 98 Rb21
Arun Qi CHN (NMZ) 98 Rb21
Aruppukkottai IND (TNU) 111 Ok42
Aruri BR 275 Hc48
Arusan IR 72 Nh28
Arusha EAT 207 Mj47
Arusha N.P. EAT 207 Mj47
Arutua Atoll F 165 Cg53
Aruwimi RDC 201 Mc45
Arva SK 39 Lu41
Arvada USA (CO) 235 Eh26
Arvand Kenar IR 74 Ne30
Arvaykheer MNG 90 Qb22
Arvi IND (MHT) 109 Ok35
Arviat CDN 225 Fb06
Arvidsjaur S 10 Lk13
Årvik N 12 Lf28
Arvika S 12 Ln31
Arvin USA (CA) 236 Ea28
Arvorezinha BR (RS) 290 Hd60
Arwad SYR 64 Mh28
Arwal IND (BIH) 109 Pc33
Arwala RI 132 Rd49
Arxan CHN (NMZ) 91 Qk22
Aryan IR 73 Nj28
Aryg-Uzju RUS (TUV) 85 Pg20
Arys KZ 76 Oe24
Arys KZ 76 Oe24
Arzachena I 31 Lk49
Arzamas RUS 53 Nb18
Arzanah UAE 74 Ng33
Arzew DZ 173 Kk28
Arzfeld D 34 Lg40
Arzgir RUS 70 Nc23
Arzignano I 40 Lm45
Arzúa E 26 Km52
Aš CZ 38 Ln40
Ås N 12 Ll31
Ås S 10 Lh14
Asa KZ 76 Of24
Asa RDC 196 Mc43
Asab NAM 212 Lj58
Asab UAE 74 Nh34
Asaba WAN 194 Ld42
Asad AFG 78 Oc29
Asadabad AFG 79 Of28
Asad Abad IR 73 Oa29
Aşağıçiğil TR 51 Mm52
Aşağıkonak TR 63 Na27
Aşağıpınar TR 51 Mn52
Aşağı Üçdam TR 63 Na26
Asahan RI 116 Pk44
Asahan RI 125 Qc48
Asahi J 101 Rj27
Asahi-dake J 99 Sb24
Asahikawa J 99 Sb24
Asai RI 124 Qb47
Asaka UZ 77 Og25
Asale ETH 191 Na39
Asalem IR 72 Ne27
Asaluyeh IR 74 Ng32
Asamankese GH 193 Kk43
Asan Abad IR 72 Ne28
Asandh IND (HYA) 107 Oj31
Asandi IND (KTK) 110 Oj40
Asankranwa GH 193 Kj43
Asan Man PRK 100 Rd27
Asansol IND (WBG) 112 Pd34
Asanwinso GH 193 Kj42
Asarcık TR 51 Mp50
Åsarna S 13 Lp28
Asaro PNG 159 Sc49
Åsarp S 15 Lo32
Asask CDN (SK) 233 Ef20
Asayita ETH 198 Na40
Asbesberge ZA 216 Mb60
Asbestos CDN (QC) 247 Ge23
Asbe Teferi ETH 198 Na41
Asby S 15 Lq33
Åsbyrgi IS 10 Kb13
Ascención BOL 280 Gj53
Ascension GB 167 Ka10
Ascensión MEX (CHH) 237 Eg30
Aschach A 35 Lp42
Aschaffenburg D 34 Lk41
Aschersleben D 33 Lm39
Ascó E 30 La49
Ascochinga RA (CD) 288 Gh61
Ascoli Piceno I 41 Lo48
Ascoli Satriano I 43 Lq49
Ascona CH 34 Lj44
Ascope PE 278 Ga49
Ascot GB 21 Ku39
Ascotán RCH 284 Gf56
Ascot Racecourse AUS (WA) 144 Qh61
Ascunión BOL 279 Gg51
Aseb ER 191 Nb40
Asebot Terara ETH 198 Na41
Åseda S 15 Lq33
Asedjrad DZ 180 La33
Aseki PNG 159 Sd49
As Éla DJI 198 Nb40
Asela ETH 198 Mk42
Åsele S 10 Lj13
Åsen S 13 Lo29
Asendabo ETH 198 Mj42
Asenovgrad BG 47 Me48
Åseral N 12 Lh32
Asermanuevo CO 268 Gb43
Aserradero La Flor MEX (DGO) 253 Eh34
Aserradero Los Charcos MEX (DGO) 253 Eh34
Aserradero Yerbitas MEX (CHH) 252 Eg32
Asfáka GR 48 Ma51
Asfi MA 172 Kf29
Asgaour MA 172 Kg30
Asgaran IR 72 Nf29
Asha WAN 194 Lb42
Ashaha EAK 205 Na44
Ashange Hayk ETH 191 Mk40
Ashanti GH 193 Kk42
Ashar IR 75 Oa32
Ashârâ SYR 65 Na28
Ashayrah KSA 66 Na35
Ashbourne GB 21 Kt37
Ashburn USA (GA) 249 Fj30
Ashburton GB 20 Kr40
Ashburton NZ 155 Tf67
Ashburton Downs AUS (WA) 140 Qj57
Ashburton River AUS 140 Qh57
Ashby-de-la-Zouch GB 21 Kt38
Ashchysai KZ 76 Oe24
Ashchysu KZ 84 Pa21
Ashchysu KZ 84 Oh20
Ashdod IL 64 Mh30
Asheboro USA (NC) 249 Ga28
Asher USA (OK) 243 Fb28
Ashern CDN (MB) 238 Fa20
Asheville USA (NC) 249 Fj28
Asheweig River CDN 239 Fg18
Ashewele WAN 194 Lc42
Ashford AUS (NSW) 151 Sf60
Ashford GB 21 La39
Ash Fork USA (AZ) 236 Ed28
Ashgabad TM 73 Nk27
Ashi ETH 197 Mh41
Ashibetsu J 99 Sb24
Ashikaga J 101 Rk27
Ashington GB 19 Kt35
Ashira SP 199 Nf40
Ashiro J 101 Sa25
Ashizuri-misaki J 103 Rg29
Ashizuri-Uwakai Q.N.P. J 103 Rg29
Ashland LB 192 Ke42
Ashland USA (AL) 249 Fh29
Ashland USA (KS) 242 Fa27
Ashland USA (KY) 249 Fj26
Ashland USA (MA) 244 Gf22
Ashland USA (MT) 235 Eg23
Ashland USA (OH) 246 Fj25
Ashland USA (OR) 234 Dj24
Ashland USA (WI) 241 Fe22
Ashley AUS (NSW) 151 Se60
Ashley USA (ND) 240 Fa22
Ashmont AUS (NSW) 153 Sb62
Ashmont CDN (AB) 233 Ee18
Ashmore Islands AUS 138 Rb52
Ashmore Reef PNG 159 Sc51
Ashoknagar IND (MPH) 109 Oj33
Ashoro J 99 Sb24
Ashqelon IL 64 Mh30
Ash Shabakah IRQ 65 Nb30
Ash Shafa KSA 66 Na35
Ash Shakk IRQ 65 Nb28
ash-Shallal ath-Thalith SUD 190 Mf37
Ash-Sham UAE 75 Nj32
Ash Shamaliyeh SYR 64 Mj28
Ash Shamasiyah KSA 67 Nc32
Ash Shamiyah IRQ 65 Nc30
Ash Shanafiyah IRQ 65 Nc30
Ash Sha'ra' KSA 67 Nc33
Ash Sharai KSA 66 Mk35
Ash Sharma KSA 64 Mh31
Ash Sharqat IRQ 65 Nb28
Ash Shatrah IRQ 65 Nd30
ash-Shawal SUD 190 Mg40
Ash Shaykh Salâmah ET 177 Mf31
Ash Shu'bah KSA 65 Nc31
Ash Shubaykiyah KSA 66 Nb33
Ash Shumlul KSA 67 Nd32
Ash Shuqayq KSA 68 Na37
Ash Shurayf KSA 66 Mk33
Ash Springs USA (NV) 234 Ec27
Ashta IND (MPH) 108 Oj34
Ashtabula USA (OH) 247 Fk25
Ashtarak ARM 70 Nc25
Ashti IND (MHT) 108 Oh36
Ashtiyan IR 72 Ne28
Ashton USA (ID) 235 Ee23
Ashton ZA 216 Ma62
Ashuanipi Lake CDN 244 Gg19
Ashuwei EAK 205 Na46
Ashville CDN (MB) 238 Ek20
Ashville USA (AL) 248 Fg29
Ashwaraopet IND (APH) 109 Pa37
Ashy Lake KZ 76 Of24
Asia PE 278 Gb52
Asia
Asiago I 40 Lm45
Asid Gulf RP 121 Rb39
Asidonopo SME 271 Hc44
Asientos MEX (AGS) 253 Ej34
Asifabad IND (APH) 109 Ok36
Asikkala FIN 16 Mf29
Asilah MA 172 Kg28
Asillo PE 279 Ge53
Asilulu RI 130 Rd47
Asinara, P.N. dell' I 31 Lj49
Asipovičy BY 52 Me19
Asir KSA 68 Na36
Asir N.P. KSA 68 Nb37
Ašit RUS 53 Ne17
Aska IND (ORS) 109 Pc36
Aşkale TR 63 Na26
Askeaton IRL 20 Km38
Asker N 12 Ll31
Askersund S 13 Lp32
Aškhaneh IR 73 Nj27
Askim N 12 Lm31
Askinuk Mts. USA 228 Bg15
Askira WAN 187 Lg40
Askja IS 10 Kb13
Asklepieion GR 49 Mh54
Askö S 13 Ls32
Askola FIN 16 Mf30
Äsköping S 13 Lr31
Askot IND (UTT) 107 Pa31
Askot Sanctuary IND 107 Pa31
Askrova N 12 Le29
Askvoll N 12 Lf29
Asla DZ 173 Kk29
Aşlama TR 51 Mq52
Aslanapa TR 50 Mk51
Aslanduz IR 72 Nd26
Aslankaya TR 51 Ml51
Aslantaş TR 51 Ml51
Aslantepe TR 63 Mk26
Aslegh RMM 185 La36
Asluman RP 123 Rb40
Asmali TR 50 Mh50
Asmar AFG 79 Of28
Asmat Wetlands RI 131 Rj48
Asmat Woodcarvings RI 131 Rk48
Asmunti FIN 11 Md13
Asnæs DK 14 Lm35
Åsnen S 15 Lp34
Asnet TCH 196 Lk39
Asni MA 172 Kg30
Aso I 41 Lo47
Aso J 103 Rf29
Asola I 40 Ll45
Asolo I 40 Lm45
Aso N.P. J 103 Rf29
Asop IND (RJT) 106 Og32
Asopós P. GR 48 Md52
Asori RI 131 Rj47
Asosa ETH 197 Mh40
Aso-san J 103 Rf29
Aspang Markt A 35 Lr43
Aspari IND (APH) 111 Oj39
Aspe E 29 Ku48
Aspen USA (CO) 235 Eg26
Aspen Cove CDN (BC) 232 Dk21
Aspendos TR 51 Mm53
Aspen Mtn. Ski Area USA 235 Eg26
Aspermont USA (TX) 242 Ek29
Aspet F 24 La47
Aspiring, Mount NZ 155 Te68
Aspö S 13 Lr31
As Pontes de García Rodríguez E 26 Kn53
Aspres-sur-Buëch F 25 Lf46
Asprógia GR 46 Mb50
Aspromonte I 43 Lq52
Aspromonte, P.N. dell I 43 Lr52
Asprópirgos GR 48 Md52
Aspur IND (RJT) 108 Oh34
Aspy Bay CDN 245 Gk22
Asquith CDN (SK) 233 Eg19
Asquith Bank SY 218 Nd50
Asralt Hairhan MNG 90 Qd21
Asrama TG 193 La42
Assa KZ 76 Of24
Assa MA 172 Kf31
Assab = Aseb ER 191 Nb40
Assaba RIM 183 Ke37
As'sabee Byar SYR 64 Mj29
As'sabeewa'arbaien SYR 65 Na27
As'sabkha SYR 65 Mk28
As Sadawi KSA 67 Nd31
Assadjene DZ 180 Ld34
As Safa SYR 64 Mj29
As-Safawi JOR 64 Mj29
As Saffaniyah KSA 67 Ne31
Assahoun TG 193 La42
Assai BR (PR) 286 He57
Assaikio WAN 186 Le41
Assaka MA 172 Kf31
As Sakn DARS 178 Ke32
Assalah ET 177 Mh31
As Salif YE 68 Nb38
As Salman IRQ 65 Nc30
As Salmy KSA 67 Nd31
Assam IND 104 Pc13
Assamakka RN 180 Lc36
As Samawah IRQ 65 Nc30
As Sanam KSA 67 Nf34
Assaouas RN 186 Ld37
Assapur IND (MPH) 108 Oj35
Assaré BR (CE) 277 Ja49
Assateague I. Nat. Seashore USA 247 Gc26
As Sawadah KSA 67 Nc34
As Sawdayah LAR 175 Lj31
As Sawwdiyah YE 68 Nc38
As Sayh KSA 67 Nd34
Assdadah LAR 175 Lh30
As-Seeb OM 75 Nk34
Asselar = Aslegh RMM 185 La36
Assémini I 31 Lj51
Assen NL 32 Lg38
Assen ZA 213 Md58
Assens DK 14 Lk35
Assentoft DK 14 Ll34
As Shamiyah IRQ/KWT 65 Nd30
As Sharma SUD 190 Mh39
As Sidr KSA 66 Mk34
As Sidr LAR 175 Lk30
As-Sifah OM 75 Nk34
As-Sila UAE 74 Nf33
Assiné CI 193 Kj43
Assiniboia CDN (SK) 233 Eh21
Assiniboine, Mount CDN 232 Ec20
Assiniboine River CDN 238 Ej20
Assin Mansu GH 193 Kk43
Assin Nyankumase GH 193 Kk43
As Sirar KSA 67 Ne32
Assis BR (SP) 286 He57
Assis Brasil BR (AC) 279 Gf51
Assis Chateaubriand BR (PR) 286 Hd58
Assisi I 40 Ln47
Assiût ET 177 Mf32
Aßlar D 32 Lj40
Assodé RN 180 Le36
Assok Begua G 195 Lf45
Assomada CV 182 Jj38
Assomption SY 218 Nd50
Assos GR 48 Ma51
Assos TR 50 Mg51
Assouf Mellene DZ 180 Lb33
Assu BR (RN) 277 Jb48
As'suar SYR 65 Na28
Assuféri CI 193 Kj42
As Sulaimi KSA 66 Na32
As Sulaymahiyah KSA 67 Nd33
As Sulaymaniyah IRQ 65 Nc28
As Sulayyil KSA 67 Nc35
As Sultan LAR 175 Lj30
as-Sumay SUD 197 Md41
As Summan KSA 67 Nd32
As Summan KSA 67 Ne34
Assunção BR (RO) 280 Gh50
Assur IRQ 65 Nb28
As-Suwayq OM 75 Nj34
Åstad N 10 Lh12
Astaffort F 24 La46
Astakós GR 48 Mb52
Astamba Dongar IND 108 Oh35
Astana CHN 87 Pe24
Astana KZ 58 Oc08
Astan-Baba TM 73 Oc27
Astaneh AFG 78 Oe28
Astaneh IR 72 Ne27
Astara AZ 70 Ne26
Astara IR 72 Ne26
Asten NL 32 Lf39
Asti I 40 Lj46
Astipálea GR 49 Mg54
Astipálea GR 49 Mg54
Astola PK 80 Ob33
Astön S 13 Ls28
Astor 79 Oh28
Astorga BR (PR) 286 He57
Astorga E 26 Ko52
Astoria USA (OR) 232 Dj22
Astove SY 219 Nd51
Astra RA (CB) 294 Gg68
Astradamovka RUS 53 Nd18
Astrakhan RUS 70 Ne22
Astrakhanskij zapovednik RUS 70 Nd23
Astrakhanskij zapovednik RUS 70 Ne22
Astrakhanskij zapovednik RUS 70 Ne23
Astrang IND (ORS) 112 Pd36
Åsträsk S 10 Lk13
Astravec BY 17 Mf36
Astrelba Downs N.P. AUS 150 Sa58
Astrid Lindgren Värld S 15 Lq33
Astrolabe Bay PNG 159 Sc48
Ástros GR 48 Mc53
Astryna BY 17 Me37
Astudillo E 26 Kq52
Asturias E 26 Ko53
Astuvansalmi FIN 16 Mh29
Asuka ANT (J) 297 Ma33
Asunción CR 256 Fj41
Asunción PY 285 Hb58
Asuncion USA 119 Sb15
Asunción Nochixtlán MEX (OAX) 254 Fb37
Åsunden S 15 Lq33
Asūne LV 17 Mh34
Asutuare GH 193 La42
Aswa EAU 204 Mg44
Aswad OM 75 Nj33
Aswa-Lolim Game Reserve EAU 204 Mf44
Aswân ET 177 Mg33
Aswân ET 177 Mg33
Aswân High Dam ET 177 Mg34
Aszód H 39 Lu43
Aszófő H 38 Ls44
Ata KS 77 Og25
Atabey TR 51 Ml53
Ata Bupu D. RI 129 Ra50
Atacama Trench 264 Gb22
Atacames EC 272 Ga45
Atafu Atoll NZ 157 Ub20
Ata'iyeh IR 73 Nk28
Atajaña, Cerro RCH 284 Ge55
Atakent KZ 76 Oe25
Ata Koo Fai-Nuwa Puri D. RI 129 Ra50
Atakor DZ 180 Lc34
Atakpamé TG 193 La42
Atalaia BR (AL) 283 Jb50
Atalaia do Norte BR (AM) 273 Ge48
Atalaya, Cerro PE 279 Ge52
Atalaya PE 278 Gd51
Ataléia BR (MG) 287 Hk55
Atambua RI 132 Rc50
Atami J 101 Rk28
Atanquez CO 268 Gd40
Ata Polo D. RI 129 Ra50
Atapuerca E 27 Kr52
Atapupu RI 132 Rc50
'Ataq YE 68 Nd38
Ataques ROU 289 Hc61
Atâr RIM 178 Kd35
Atarra IND (UPH) 109 Pa33
Atarte E 29 Kr47
Atas Bogd MNG 92 Pj24
Atascadero PE 272 Fk48
Atascadero USA (CA) 236 Dk28
Atasta MEX (CAM) 255 Fd36
Atasu KZ 84 Of21
Atatürk Baraji TR 63 Mk27
Atauba BR (RR) 274 Gk46
Atauro TLS 132 Rc50
Ataya ETH 198 Mk40
Ataye Shet ETH 198 Na40
Atbara SUD 190 Mg38
Atbara SUD 190 Mh38
At-Baši KS 77 Oh25
At-Baši KS 77 Oj25
Atchafalaya Bay USA 243 Fe31
Atchison USA (KS) 241 Fc26
Atchuelinguk River USA 229 Bk14
Atebubu GH 193 Kk42
Ateca E 27 Kt51
Ateku GH 193 Kk43
Aten BOL 279 Gf53
Atenas BR (AC) 279 Ge50
Atencingo MEX (PUE) 254 Fa36
Ateneul Român RO 45 Mg46
Atengo MEX 253 Eh34
Aterno I 42 Lo48
Ateso GH 193 Kj42
Atessa I 42 Lp48
Ath B 23 Ld40
Athabasca CDN (AB) 233 Ed18
Athabasca Falls CDN 232 Ea19
Athapap CDN (MB) 238 Ek18
Athapapuskow Lake CDN 238 Ek18
Atharan Hazari PK 79 Og30
Athens GR 48 Md53
Athens USA (AL) 248 Fg28
Athens USA (GA) 249 Fj29
Athens USA (OH) 246 Fj26
Athens USA (TN) 249 Fh28
Athens USA (TX) 243 Fc29
Atherstone GB 21 Kt38
Atherton AUS (QLD) 149 Sc54
Atherton Tableland AUS (QLD) 149 Sc54
Athi EAK 204 Mj46
Athiémè DY 193 La42
Athina GR 48 Md53
Athi River EAK 204 Mj46
Athlone IRL 20 Kn37
Athmallik IND (ORS) 109 Pc35
Athni IND (KTK) 108 Oh37
Athol NZ 155 Te68
Athol USA (ID) 232 Eb22
Áthos GR 47 Me50
Áthos GR 47 Me50
Athy IRL 20 Ko38
'Ati SUD 197 Me39
Ati TCH 196 Lj39
Atiak EAU 204 Mg44
Ati-Atihan-Festival (Kalibo) RP 123 Rb40
Atibaia BR (SP) 287 Hg57
Atico PE 284 Gd54
Atiedo SUD 197 Md42
Atienza E 29 Ks51
Atijere WAN 194 Lc42
Atikaki Prov. Park CDN 238 Fc20
Atikameg Lake CDN (MB) 238 Ek18
Atikameg River CDN 239 Fj19
Atikokan CDN (ON) 239 Fe21
Atikonak Lake CDN 244 Gh19
Atim TCH 196 Lk39
Atimonan RP 121 Ra39
Atitlan, Volcán GCA 255 Fe38
Atizapán de Zaragoza MEX (MEX) 254 Fa36
Atjaševo RUS (MOR) 53 Nd18
Atkamba Mission PNG 158 Sa48
Atkaracalar TR 51 Mo50
Atkinson USA (NE) 240 Fa24
Atkot IND (GUJ) 108 Of35
Atlacomulco MEX (MEX) 254 Fa36
Atlant TR 51 Mn52
Atlanta USA (GA) 249 Fh29
Atlanta USA (MI) 246 Fh23
Atlanta USA (TX) 243 Fc29
Atlanterhavsparken N 12 Lf28
Atlantic USA (IA) 241 Fc25
Atlantic USA (NC) 249 Gb28
Atlantic Beach USA (FL) 249 Fk30
Atlantic City USA (NJ) 247 Gc26
Atlantic Forest Southeast Reserves BR 286 Hg58
Atlantic Ocean 300 Ha07
Atlántida ROU 289 Hc63
Atla pexco MEX (HDG) 254 Fa35
Atlas Gompa CHN (TIB) 89 Pg30
Atlas Mountains MA 168 Kc12
Atlasovo RUS 99 Sb22
Atlas Saharien DZ 173 La29
Atlas Tellien DZ 173 Kk28
Atlin CDN (BC) 231 Dd16
Atlin Lake CDN 231 Dd16
Atlin Prov. Park CDN 231 Dd16
Atlixco MEX (PUE) 254 Fa36
Atløy N 12 Le29
Atmakur IND (APH) 108 Oj37
Atmakur IND (APH) 109 Ok38
Atmore CDN (AB) 233 Ed18
Atmore USA (AL) 248 Fg30
Atna N 12 Ll29
Atna Peak CDN 232 Df19
Atnbrua N 12 Ll29
Atnetye A.L. AUS 143 Rj57
Atnmoen N 12 Ll29
Atocha BOL 284 Gg56
Atog CAM 195 Lf44
Atoka USA (OK) 243 Fb28
Átokos GR 48 Ma52
Atol das Rocas BR 277 Jd47
Atoll de Cosmoledo SY 219 Nd50
Atoll de Farquhar SY 219 Nf51
Atoll de Providence SY 219 Nf50
Atolo MOC 211 Na52
Atome ANG 208 Lh51
Atomic City USA (ID) 235 Ed24
Atongo-Bakari RCA 200 Ma43
Atonyia DARS 178 Kf32
Atori SOL 161 Ta50
Atotonilco MEX (ZCT) 253 Ej33
Atotonnilco El Alto MEX (JLC) 254 Ej35
Atouat, Mount VN 115 Qd38
Atoyac de Alvarez MEX (GUR) 254 Ek37
Atpadi IND (MHT) 108 Oh37
Ätran S 15 Ln33
Ätran S 15 Ln33
Atrato CO 268 Gb43
Atrauli IND (UPH) 107 Pa32
Atri I 42 Lo48
Atsaphangthong LAO 115 Qc37
Atshan SUD 190 Mh40
Atsumi-hanto J 101 Rj28
Atsuta J 99 Sa24
Atsy RI 131 Rk48
Atta CAM 195 Lf42
At Taban LAR 175 Ma29
At-Taff UAE 74 Nh34
At Ta'if KSA 66 Na35
At Taji IRQ 65 Nc29
Attakro CI 193 Kj42
Attalla USA (AL) 248 Fg29
At Tamimi LAR 175 Mb29
At Tanf SYR 64 Mk29
Attapeu LAO 115 Qd38
At Tarmiyah IRQ 65 Nc29
Attawapiskat CDN (ON) 239 Fj19
Attawapiskat Ind. Res. No. 91 CDN 239 Fh19
Attawapiskat Lake CDN 239 Fg19
Attawapiskat River CDN 239 Fj19
At Tawilah YE 68 Nb38
Attayas SYR 64 Mj28
At Taysiyah KSA 67 Nc32
At-Tayyara SUD 197 Mf39
Atteridgeville ZA 213 Me58
Attersee A 35 Lo43
At Thumamah KSA 67 Nd33
At-Tina Bay ET 177 Mg30
Attingal IND (KER) 110 Oj42
Attleborough GB 21 Lb38
Attock PK 79 Og29
Attock City PK 79 Og29
Attoko J 99 Sc24
At Tubayq KSA 64 Mj31
Attu Island USA 59 Tc08
Attunga AUS (NSW) 151 Sf61
Attur IND (TNU) 111 Ok41
At Turayqa KSA 67 Ne35
At Turbah YE 68 Nc39
At Tuwal KSA 68 Nb37
At Tuwayifah KSA 67 Ne35
At Tuwayrif KSA 67 Ne34
at Tuwaysha SUD 196 Md39
Attwater Prairie Chicken N.W.R. USA 243 Fb31
Atucatiquini BR 279 Gf49
Atud YE 68 Ne38
Atuka RI 131 Rj48
Atuk Mountain USA 228 Be14
Atuna GH 193 Kj42
Atuntaqui EC 272 Ga45
Atuona F 165 Da50
Atura BD 112 Pe33
Aturel RA 288 Gf63
Atures YV 269 Gg43
Åtvidaberg S 15 Lq32
Atwater USA (CA) 234 Dk27
Atwood USA (KS) 240 Ek26
Atyrau KZ 71 Ng22
Au D 35 Lm42
Au IND (RJT) 106 Og32
Aua Island PNG 159 Sb46
Auasberge NAM 212 Lj57
Auatu ETH 198 Na42
Aubagne F 25 Lf47
Aubange B 23 Lf41
Aube F 23 Ld42
Aubenas F 25 Le46
Aubergenville F 23 Lb42
Auberive F 23 Lf43
Aubiet F 24 La47
Aubigny-sur-Nère F 23 Lc43
Aubin F 24 Lc46
Aubrey Cliffs USA 236 Ed28
Auburn AUS (QLD) 151 Sf58
Auburn AUS (SA) 152 Rk62
Auburn USA (AL) 249 Fh29
Auburn USA (CA) 234 Dk26
Auburn USA (IN) 246 Fh25
Auburn USA (ME) 247 Ge23
Auburn USA (NE) 241 Fc25
Auburn USA (NY) 247 Gb24
Auburn USA (WA) 232 Dj22
Auburn Range AUS 151 Sf58
Aubusson F 24 Lc45
Auca Mahuida RA (NE) 292 Gf64
Aucanquilcha, Cerro RCH 284 Gf56
Aucayacu PE 278 Gb50
Auce LV 17 Mc34
Auch F 24 La47
Auche MYA 113 Pj33
Auchi WAN 194 Ld42
Auchterarder GB 19 Kr34
Auckland NZ 154 Th64

B

Bahía Inútil – Ban Dung

Bahía Inútil RCH 294 Gf72
Bahía Kino MEX (SO) 236 Ee31
Bahía Lángare RA 294 Gg69
Bahía las Cañas RCH 292 Gd63
Bahía Laura RA (SC) 294 Gg70
Bahía Lomas RCH 294 Gf72
Bahía Magdalena MEX 252 Ed33
Bahía Mansa RCH 292 Gd66
Bahía Maullín RCH 292 Gd66
Bahía Morena RCH 284 Ge57
Bahía Nassau RCH 294 Gg73
Bahía Negra PY 285 Ha56
Bahía Nuestra Señora RCH 284 Ge58
Bahía Otway RCH 294 Gc72
Bahía Posesión RCH 294 Gf72
Bahía Puerto de Lobos MEX 236 Ed30
Bahía Punta Gorda NIC 256 Fj40
Bahía Rosario MEX 236 Ec31
Bahía Salado RCH 288 Ge59
Bahía Salvación RCH 294 Gc71
Bahía Samborombón RA 293 Hb63
Bahía San Blas RA (BA) 293 Gj66
Bahía San Carlos MEX 236 Ec31
Bahía San Carlos MEX 252 Ed32
Bahía San Felipe RCH 294 Gf72
Bahía San Jorge MEX 236 Ed30
Bahía San Luis Gonzaga MEX 236 Ec31
Bahía San Nicolás PE 278 Gc53
Bahía San Sebastián RA 294 Gf72
Bahía San Vicente RCH 292 Gd64
Bahía Sargento MEX 236 Ed31
Bahías de Huatulco MEX (OAX) 254 Fb38
Bahía Sebastián Vizcaíno MEX 236 Ec31
Bahía Solano CO 268 Gb42
Bahía Solano RA 292 Gg68
Bahía Stokes RCH 294 Gd73
Bahía Unión RA 293 Gj65
Bahía Vera RA 292 Gh68
Bahig ET 177 Me30
Bahili IND (MPH) 108 Oj34
Bahinga RDC 206 Md48
Bahir Dar ETH 198 Mj40
Bahi Swamp EAT 207 Mh49
Bahla OM 75 Nj34
Bahla Fort OM 75 Nj34
Bahlui RO 45 Mh43
Bahn LB 192 Kf42
Bahr RCA 201 Mc43
Bahrah KSA 66 Mk35
Bahraich IND (UPH) 107 Pa32
Bahrain BRN 74 Nf33
Bahr al-Arab SUD 197 Me41
Bahr al-Ghazal SUD 197 Me41
Bahram Abad IR 72 Nf27
Bahramjerd IR 75 Nj31
Bahramtapa AZ 70 Nd26
Bahr Aouk RCA/TCH 196 Lk41
Bahr Azoum TCH 196 Ma40
Bahr Azrak TCH 196 Ma40
Bahr az-Zaraf SUD 197 Mf41
Bahr Baïkoré TCH 196 Ma40
Bahr Baru ETH/SUD 197 Mg41
Bahr Bola TCH 196 Lk40
Bahr Doseo TCH 196 Ma41
Bahr el Ghazal TCH 187 Lj38
Bahr Erguig TCH 187 Lj40
Bahr Kameur RCA 196 Ma41
Bahr Keïta ou Douka TCH 196 Lk41
Bahr Korbol TCH 187 Lj40
Bahr Korom TCH 196 Lk40
Bahr Nzili RCA/TCH 196 Mb40
Bahr Oulu RCA 196 Mb40
Bahr Salamat TCH 187 Lk41
Bahsili TR 51 Mo51
Bahuaja-Sonene, P.N. PE 279 Gf52
Bahubulu RI 127 Rb47
Bahuichivo MEX (CHH) 252 Ef32
Bahuluang RI 129 Ra49
Bahusai RI 127 Ra47
Baia RO 45 Mj46
Baia de Aramă RO 44 Mc45
Baia de Arieş RO 44 Md44
Baía de Bazaruto MOC 214 Mh56
Baía de Caxiuna BR 275 He47
Baía de Inhambane MOC 214 Mh57
Baía de Maputo MOC 214 Mg58
Baía de Marajó BR 276 Hf46
Baía de Paranaguá BR 286 Hf58
Baía de Pemba MOC 211 Na52
Baía de Santa Rosa BR 275 Hf45
Baía de São José BR 276 Hj47
Baía de São Marcos BR 276 Hh47
Baía de Setúbal P 28 Kl48
Baía de Todos os Santos BR 283 Ja52
Baía de Turiaçu BR 276 Hh46
Baía de Varela GNB 183 Kb39
Baía do Bengo ANG 202 Lg50
Baía do Caeté BR 276 Hg46
Baía do Chun BR 276 Hg46
Baía do Cumã BR 276 Hh47
Baía do Gurupi BR 276 Hg46
Baía dos Lençios BR 276 Hh46
Baía dos Tigres ANG 208 Lf54
Baía Farta ANG 208 Lg52
Baía Fernaõ Veloso MOC 211 Na53
Baía Grande BR (MT) 286 Hc54
Baia Mare RO 44 Md43
Baianópolis BR (BA) 282 Hh52
Baião BR (PA) 276 Hf47
Baia Sprie RO 44 Md43
Baibokoum TCH 195 Lh42
Bai Chay VN 96 Qd35
Baicheng CHN (JLN) 98 Rb23
Baicheng CHN (XUZ) 86 Pa25
Băicoi RO 45 Mf45
Băiculeşti RO 45 Me45
Baidi He CHN 92 Pk26
Baidi Cheng CHN 95 Qe30
Baidou RCA 196 Ma43
Bai Duc Thon VN 115 Qc36
Baie Chasseloup F 162 Tc56
Baie-Comeau CDN (QC) 244 Gf21
Baie d'Audierne F 22 Kq43
Baie de Boulari F 162 Td57
Baie de Bourgneuf F 22 Ks43
Baie de Canala F 162 Tc56
Baie de Concarneau F 22 Kq43
Baie de Corisco G/GQ 194 Le45
Baie de Douarnenez F 22 Kq42
Baie de Gaspé CDN 245 Gh21
Baie-deHenne RH 260 Gd36
Baie de l'Allier F 162 Te56
Baie de la Seine F 22 Ku41
Baie de Nehoué F 162 Tc56
Baie de Quiberon F 22 Ks43
Baie de Saint-Brieuc F 22 Ks42
Baie de Saint-Vincent F 162 Td57
Baie des Chaleurs CDN 245 Gh22
Baie-des Moutons CDN (QC) 245 Ha20
Baie-desSables CDN (QC) 244 Gg21
Baie d'Ouvéa F 162 Td56
Baie du Mont-Saint-Michel F 22 Kt42
Baie-du-Poste CDN (QC) 244 Gd20
Baie du Santal F 162 Td56
Baie-Johan-Beetz CDN (QC) 245 Gj20
Baiersbronn D 34 Lj42
Baie-Saint-Paul CDN (QC) 244 Ge22
Baie Verte CDN (NF) 245 Hb21
Baigekum KZ 76 Od23
Baigneux-les-Juifs F 23 Le43
Baihanchang CHN (YUN) 113 Qa32
Baihar IND (MPH) 109 Pa34
Baihe CHN (SAA) 95 Qf29
Baijiahe CHN (GSU) 94 Qc29
Baijiang CHN (GZG) 96 Qd34
Bai Khem Beach VN 117 Qc40
Baikonyr KZ 76 Ob23
Baikunthapur IND (CGH) 109 Pb34
Baila LB 192 Kf42
Baila SN 183 Kb39
Bailakan CHN (GZH) 96 Qd32
Baile Átha Cliath = Dublin IRL 20 Ko37
Băile Felix RO 44 Mb43
Băile Govora RO 44 Me45
Băile Herculane RO 44 Mc46
Bailén E 29 Kr48
Băile Olăneşti RO 44 Me45
Băileşti RO 46 Md46
Băile Tuşnad RO 45 Mf44
Bailey ZA 217 Md61
Bailey Ice Stream 296 Jb35
Bailin CHN (GZG) 96 Qd34
Bailin CHN (HUN) 97 Qg32
Bailingmiao CHN 93 Qf25
Bailique BR (AP) 275 He45
Bailique BR (PA) 276 Hf47
Bailleul F 23 Lc40
Ba Illi TCH 187 Lj40
Ba Illi TCH 187 Lj40
Bailong Jiang CHN 94 Qc29
Bailundo ANG 208 Lh52
Baima CHN (CGQ) 95 Qd31
Baimaclia MD 45 Mj44
Baimajing CHN (HAN) 96 Qe36
Bai Ma Si CHN 95 Qg28
Baimun RI 131 Rh49
Baimuru PNG 159 Sc49
Bainang CHN (TIB) 88 Pe31
Bainbridge USA (GA) 249 Fh30
Bainbridge Island USA 229 Cf15
Bain-de-Bretagne F 22 Kt43
Baines' Baobab RB 213 Mc56
Baines Drift RB 214 Me57
Bainet RH 260 Gd36
Baing RI 129 Ra51
Baingoin CHN (TIB) 89 Pf30
Baining Mountains PNG 160 Sf48
Bains-les-Bains F 23 Lg42
Baioga WAN 187 Lf40
Baiona E 26 Km52
Baiquan CHN (HLG) 98 Rd22
Bairagnia IND (BIH) 107 Pc32
Baird Inlet USA 228 Bj15
Baird Mountains USA 229 Bk12
Bairiki KIR 157 Tc18
Bairin Qiao CHN (NMZ) 93 Qk24
Bairin Youqi CHN (NMZ) 93 Qk24
Bairin Zuoqi CHN (NMZ) 93 Qk24
Bairnsdale AUS (VIC) 153 Sd64
Bais RP 123 Rb41
Baïse F 24 La46
Baisha CHN (CGQ) 95 Qd31
Baisha CHN (HAN) 96 Qe36
Baisha CHN (SCH) 95 Qe30
Baishan CHN (JLN) 100 Rd24
Bai Shan CHN 87 Pg25
Baishanzu CHN 102 Qk32
Baishilazi Z.B. CHN 100 Rc25
Baishui CHN (SAA) 95 Qe28
Baishuijiang Z.B. CHN 95 Qc29
Baishuitai Terraces CHN 113 Pk32
Baisinga IND (ORS) 112 Pd35
Băişoara RO 44 Md44
Baisogala LT 17 Md35
Baissa WAN 195 Lf42
Bai Ta CHN 93 Qf25
Bai Ta CHN 102 Qk32
Baitadi NEP 88 Pa31
Baita Pagoda CHN 100 Rb25
Bai Thuong VN 115 Qc36
Bait Na'aman OM 75 Nj34
Baiturrahman Grand Mosque RI 116 Ph43
Baixa Grande BR (BA) 283 Hk51
Baixa Grande do Riberão BR (PI) 282 Hh50
Bai Xang VN 115 Qc36
Baixio BR (BA) 283 Jb52
Baixo Guandu BR (ES) 287 Hk55
Baixo Licungo MOC 211 Mj54
Baixo Longa ANG 209 Lk53
Baiyer River PNG 159 Sc48
Baiyin CHN (GSU) 92 Qc27
Baiyrkum KZ 76 Oe24
Baiyü CHN (SCH) 94 Pk30
Baïzo RN 186 Lc39
Baja H 39 Lt44
Baja California MEX 226 Eb13
Baja California Norte MEX 226 Ea12
Baja California Sur MEX 226 Eb13
Bajada del Agrio RA (NE) 292 Gf65
Baja Malibu MEX 236 Eb29
Bajandaj RUS (UOB) 90 Qc19
Bajau RI 117 Qd44
Bajawa RI 129 Ra50
Bajdarackaja guba RUS 58 Oa04
Bajdrag gol MNG 90 Pk22
Bajgiran IR 73 Nk27
Bajie CHN (GZG) 96 Qc33
Bajie CHN (GZH) 96 Qe33
Bajil YE 68 Nb38
Bajimba, Mount AUS 151 Sg60
Bajina Bašta SCG 46 Lu47
Bajio de Ahuichila MEX (COH) 253 Ej33
Bajkal RUS 90 Qc20
Bajkal'sk RUS 90 Qc20
Bajkal'skij RUS 90 Qd19
Bajkal'skij zapovednik RUS 90 Qc20
Bajmok SCG 44 Lu45
Bajo RI 129 Qk50
Bajo Caracoles RA (SC) 294 Ge69
Bajocunda GNB 183 Kc39
Bajo de la Tierra Colorada RA 292 Gg67
Bajo del Gualicho RA 292 Gh67
Bajo de los Menucos RA 292 Gg65
Bajo de Santa Rosa RA 292 Gg66
Bajo de Valcheta RA 292 Gh66
Bajo Hondo RA (LR) 288 Gh61
Bajo Izozog BOL 285 Gj55
Bajo Nuevo CO 257 Ga38
Bajool AUS (QLD) 149 Sf57
Bajo Pichanaqui PE 278 Gc51
Bajos de Haina DOM 260 Ge36
Bajovo Polje SCG 46 Lt47
Bajo Waterfall THA 117 Qa42
Bajrakli džamija BG 46 Md48
Bajrakot IND (ORS) 109 Pc35
Bajram Curr AL 46 Ma48
Baju RI 127 Qk45
Bajuun Islands SP 205 Nb46
Bak H 38 Lr44
Baká NIC 256 Fh39
Bakaba TCH 195 Lj42
Bakacak TR 50 Mh50
Bakairi, T.I. BR 281 Hc53
Bakal IND (UPH) 109 Ok34
Bakala RCA 195 Lj43
Bakala RCA 196 Ma42
Bakali RDC 203 Lj49
Bakaly RUS 53 Ng18
Bakanas KZ 84 Oj23
Bakanas KZ 84 Ok21
Baka Nur CHN 93 Qh24
Bakaoré TCH 196 Ma38
Bakara RI 116 Pk44
Bakau WAG 183 Kb39
Bakauheni RI 125 Qc48
Bakayan, Gunung RI 126 Qj44
Bakbakty KZ 84 Oj23
Bakdak RI 129 Ra48
Bakebe CAM 194 Le43
Bakel SN 183 Kd38
Bakelalan MAL 126 Qh44
Baker RCH 294 Gd69
Baker USA (CA) 236 Eb28
Baker USA (MT) 235 Eh22
Baker City USA (OR) 234 Eb23
Baker Creek CDN 232 Dj19
Baker Island USA 231 Dc18
Baker Island USA 157 Ua18
Baker Lake CDN 225 Fb06
Baker, Mount USA 232 Dk21
Bakers Creek AUS (QLD) 149 Se56
Bakersfield USA (CA) 236 Ea28
Bakerville ZA 213 Md58
Bakewar IND (UPH) 107 Ok32
Bakewell GB 21 Kt37
Bakhardok TM 71 Nk26
Bakhounou RMM 183 Kf38
Bakhshi Kalay AFG 78 Oe30
Bakhuis SME 271 Hb43
Bakhuisgebergte SME 271 Hb43
Baki AZ 70 Ne25
Bakin Birji RN 186 Le38
Bakinskij arhipelago AZ 70 Ne26
Bakit RI 125 Qc46
Bakkafjörður IS 10 Kc12
Bakkaflói IS 10 Kc12
Bakkagerði IS 10 Kd13
Bakko N 12 Lj31
Baklan TR 50 Mk52
Baklia N 12 Lk29
Bako CI 192 Kg41
Bako ETH 198 Mj41
Bakongan RI 116 Pj44
Bako N.P. MAL 126 Qf45
Bakonycsernye H 38 Lt43
Bakonyjákó H 38 Ls43
Bakop PNG 160 Sg48
Bakordi SUD 201 Me43
Bakori WAN 186 Ld40
Bakouma RCA 200 Mb43
Bakoumba G 202 Lg46
Bakoy RMM 183 Ke39
Bakša UA 45 Mk42
Baksan RUS (KBA) 70 Nb24
Baksan RUS 70 Nb24
Bakshpur BD 112 Pf33
Baktakék H 39 Mb42
Bakty PK 84 Pb22
Baku AZ 70 Ne25
Bakung RI 125 Qc45
Bakuriani GE 70 Nb25
Bakwa-Kenge RDC 203 Mb48
Bakyrly KZ 76 Od23
Bala, Cerros de BOL 279 Gg53
Bala GB 21 Kr38
Bala IND (UPH) 107 Ok32
Bala SN 183 Kd38
Balâ TR 51 Mo51
Bala WAN 194 Lc41
Balabac RP 122 Qj42
Balabac Island RP 122 Qj42
Balabac Strait 122 Qj42
Balabagang RP 123 Rc42
Balabaiba ANG 208 Lg52
Balabala RDC 200 Ma44
Balabanovo RUS 52 Mj18
Bala Boluk AFG 78 Ob29
Bălăceanu RO 45 Mh45
Bălăciţa RO 44 Md46
Balad IRQ 65 Nc28
Baladeh IR 72 Nf27
Balad Ruz IRQ 65 Nc29
Balaghat IND (MPH) 109 Pa35
Balaguer E 30 La49
Balahna RUS 53 Nb17
Bala Hows IR 73 Nk30
Balaiberkuak RI 126 Qf46
Balaipungut RI 124 Qa45
Balaisebut RI 126 Qf45
Balaj RUS 91 Qj20
Balaka MW 211 Mh53
Balakbal MEX 255 Ff37
Balaken AZ 70 Nd25
Balakéte RCA 196 Lk42
Balaki RG 183 Ke39
Balaklava AUS (SA) 152 Rk63
Balaklija UA 54 Mj21
Balakot PK 79 Og28
Balakovo RUS 53 Nd20
Balal RMM 184 Kg38
Balala ETH 197 Mh43
Balalohong RI 129 Qk49
Balama MOC 211 Mk52
Balamba CAM 195 Lf43
Balambangan MAL 122 Qj42
Balamkú MEX 255 Ff36
Bala Morghab AFG 78 Ob28
Balam Takli IND (MHT) 108 Oh36
Balanced Rock USA 234 Ec24
Balandino RUS 53 Ng19
Balandou RG 192 Kf40
Balanga RDC 206 Mc50
Balangala RDC 200 Lk45
Balangiga RP 123 Rc40
Balaño RP 120 Ra38
Balanguingui Island RP 123 Ra43
Balantak RI 127 Rb46
Balanthria AUS (NSW) 153 Sc62
Balao EC 272 Ga47
Balaoan RP 120 Ra37
Balapur IND (MHT) 108 Oj35
Balarampur IND (WBG) 112 Pd34
Balarampuram IND (TNU) 111 Oj42
Bala Reef IND 111 Pg40
Balari RI 124 Pk46
Balašiha RUS 52 Mj18
Balasore IND (ORS) 112 Pd35
Balašov RUS 53 Nb20
Balassagyarmat H 39 Lu42
Balat ET 177 Me33
Balaton H 38 Ls44
Balatonalmádi H 38 Ls43
Balatonbozsok H 38 Kq35
Balaton-felvidéki N.P. H 38 Ls44
Balatonfüred H 38 Ls44
Balatonfűzfő H 38 Lt43
Balatonkeresztúr H 38 Ls44
Balatonlelle H 38 Ls44
Balatopar KZ 84 Oh23
Balauring RI 132 Rb50
Bălăuşeri RO 44 Me44
Balavé BF 184 Kh39
Balazote E 29 Ks48
Balbi, Mount PNG 160 Sh48
Balbina BR (AM) 274 Ha46
Balboa CO 268 Gc43
Balboa PA 257 Ga41
Balbriggan IRL 20 Ko37
Balcad SP 205 Nc44
Balcad Nature Reserve SP 205 Nc44
Balcanoona AUS (SA) 152 Rk61
Balcarce RA (BA) 293 Ha64
Balcarres CDN (SK) 238 Ej20
Bălceşti RO 44 Md46
Balcı TR 51 Mp52
Balčik BG 47 Mj47
Balcılar TR 51 Mn50
Balclutha NZ 155 Te69
Balcones Canyonlands N.W.R. USA 242 Fa30
Balcones Escarpment USA 242 Fa31
Balde de la Mora RA (CD) 288 Gh61
Bald Head Island Lighthouse USA 249 Gb29
Bald Knob USA (AR) 243 Fe28
Bald Knob N.W.R. USA 248 Fe28
Bald Mtn. USA 234 Ec27
Baldock Lake CDN 238 Fb17
Baldone LV 17 Me34
Bald Pt. USA 249 Fh31
Baldur CDN (MB) 238 Fa21
Baldwin USA (FL) 249 Fk30
Baldwin USA (MI) 246 Fh24
Baldwin City USA (KS) 241 Fc26
Baldwin Peninsula USA 229 Bj12
Baldwinsville USA (NY) 247 Gb24
Baldy Hughes CDN (BC) 232 Dj19
Baldy Mtn. CDN 238 Ek20
Baldy Peak USA 237 Ef29
Bal'dzikan RUS 91 Qf21
Bale ANG 208 Lj53
Bale EAU 204 Mg45
Bale RMM 192 Kf40
Balé RMM/SN 183 Ke39
Baleares E 30 Lc51
Balearic Islands E 30 Lb51
Balease, Gunung RI 127 Ra47
Baleh MAL 126 Qg45
Balehonnur IND (KTK) 110 Oh40
Balekambang RI 128 Qg50
Balékoutou TCH 196 Lk41
Bale Mountains N.P. ETH 198 Mk42
Balen B 23 Lf39
Baleno RP 121 Rb39
Baler RP 121 Ra38
Baleraksok RI 124 Qa47
Baler Bay RP 121 Ra38
Balesang RI 127 Ra46
Balesberg ZA 217 Mf59
Baleyara RN 185 Lb39
Baley Guerrero DOM 260 Gf36
Balfes Creek AUS (QLD) 149 Sc56
Balfour CDN (BC) 232 Eb21
Balfour ZA 217 Me59
Balfour Downs AUS (WA) 140 Ra57
Balgak SUD 197 Md39
Bålgarene BG 47 Mf47
Bălgarska Polyana BG 47 Mg48
Balgazyn RUS (TUV) 85 Ph20
Balgo AUS (WA) 138 Rd56
Balgo A.L. AUS 141 Re56
Balgonie CDN (SK) 233 Eh20
Balguntay CHN (XUZ) 87 Pd24
Balhaf YE 68 Ne38
Balhaš KZ 84 Oh22
Balho DJI 199 Nb39
Bali CAM 194 Lf43
Bali RI 129 Qh49
Bali Barat N.P. RI 129 Qh50
Balibi RCA 196 Ma42
Balibo TLS 132 Rc50
Balie SYR 64 Mj29
Baliem Valley RI 131 Rk48
Balifondo RCA 200 Mb43
Balige RI 116 Pk44
Baliguda IND (ORS) 109 Pb35
Balik BG 45 Mh47
Balik BG 47 Mh47
Balikana IND (ORS) 109 Pc36
Balike LB 192 Kg43
Balıkesir TR 50 Mh51
Balıklıçeşme TR 50 Mh50
Balikpapan RI 127 Qj46
Balimila IND (ORS) 109 Pb36
Balimila Reservoir IND 109 Pb36
Balimo PNG 159 Sb50
Balin RMM 183 Ke39
Baling CHN (GZH) 96 Qc33
Baling MAL 116 Qa43
Balingasag RP 123 Rc41
Bälinge S 13 Ls31
Balingen D 34 Lj42
Balingian MAL 126 Qg44
Balingup AUS (WA) 144 Qh62
Balintang Channel RP 121 Ra36
Balintang Island RP 121 Rb36
Balipara IND (ASM) 112 Pg32
Balise 250 Poste Weygand DZ 180 La33
Bali Sea RI 129 Qh49
Balışeyh TR 51 Mo51
Baliuag RP 121 Ra38
Baliza BR (GO) 286 Hd54
Baljaga RUS 90 Qe20
Balj Gol MNG 91 Qf21
Baljurashi KSA 66 Na36
Balkanabat TM 71 Nh26
Balkan Mountains BG 46 Mc47
Balkh AFG 78 Od27
Balkhab AFG 78 Od28
Balkhash KZ 84 Oh22
Balkuling AUS (WA) 144 Qj61
Ballachulish GB 19 Kp34
Balladonia Motel AUS (WA) 145 Rb62
Ballaghaderreen IRL 18 Km37
Ballan AUS (VIC) 153 Sc64
Ballangen N 10 Lj11
Ballantrae GB 18 Kq35
Ballarat AUS (VIC) 153 Sb64
Ballaroo AUS (QLD) 151 Se59
Ballarpur IND (MHT) 109 Ok36
Ballasetas RI 116 Pj44
Ballasmer KSA 68 Nb36
Ballater GB 19 Ks33
Ballé RMM 184 Kf38
Ballenas Whale watching MEX 252 Ed32
Ballencrieff Castle GB 19 Ks33
Balleny Islands 3
Ballesreros RA (CD) 289 Gj62
Balleza MEX (CHH) 252 Eg32
Balli IND (GOA) 108 Oh38
Ballia IND (UPH) 109 Pc33
Ballidu AUS (WA) 144 Qj61
Ballina AUS (NSW) 151 Sg60
Ballina IRL 18 Kl36
Ballinasloe IRL 20 Km37
Balling DK 14 Lj34
Ballinger USA (TX) 242 Fa30
Ball Lake CDN 238 Fd20
Ball, Mount AUS 138 Rd55
Ballon d'Alsace F 23 Lg43
Balloul DZ 173 La28
Ballsh AL 46 Lu50
Ball's Pyramid AUS 137 Sd25
Ballstad N 10 Lg11
Ballybofey IRL 18 Kn36
Ballybunnion IRL 20 Kl38
Ballycastle GB 18 Ko35
Ballycastle IRL 18 Kl36
Ballyclare GB 18 Kp36
Ballycroy N.P. IRL 18 Kl36
Ballydehob IRL 20 Kl39
Ballygawley GB 18 Kn36
Ballyhaunis IRL 18 Km37
Ballymahon IRL 20 Kn37
Ballymena GB 18 Ko36
Ballymoney GB 18 Ko35
Ballysadare IRL 18 Km36
Ballyshannon IRL 18 Km36
Ballyvaughan IRL 20 Kl37
Balmaceda, Cerro RCH 294 Gd71
Balmaceda RCH 294 Ge68
Balmaceda Glacier RCH 294 Gd71
Balmaseda E 27 Kr53
Balmazújváros H 39 Mb43
Balmertown CDN (ON) 238 Fd20
Balmoral AUS (VIC) 152 Sa64
Balmoral ZA 213 Me58
Balmoral Castle GB 19 Kr33
Balmorhea USA (TX) 237 Ej30
Balnearia RA (CD) 289 Gj61
Balneario PY 289 Hb59
Balneário Camboriú BR (SC) 291 Hf59
Balneario del Sol C 259 Gc36
Balneario de Panticosa E 27 Ku52
Balneario las Grutas RA (RN) 292 Gh66
Balneario Massini RA (RN) 293 Gj66
Balneario Oriente RA (BA) 293 Gk65
Balo RI 127 Rb46
Baloa RI 127 Rb46
Balobaloang RI 129 Qk49
Balod IND (CGH) 109 Pa35
Baloda Bazar IND (CGH) 109 Pb35
Balombe ANG 208 Lh52
Balombo ANG 208 Lh52
Balong CHN (QHI) 87 Pj27
Balonne River AUS 151 Se60
Balota H 39 Lu44
Balotra IND (RJT) 106 Og33
Baloži LV 17 Me34
Balpyk Bi KZ 84 Ok23
Balrampur IND (UPH) 107 Pb32
Balş RO 44 Me46
Balşa RO 44 Md44
Balsapuerto PE 272 Gb48
Balsas BR (MA) 276 Hg49
Balsas EC 272 Ga47
Balsas MEX (GUR) 254 Fa36
Balsas PE 278 Gb49
Bålsta S 13 Ls31
Balsthal CH 34 Lh43
Balta UA 45 Mk43
Balta Albă RO 45 Mh45
Balta Ialomiţei RO 45 Mh46
Baltakol KZ 76 Od24
Baltai 79 Oh28
Baltanás E 26 Kq51
Baltasar Brum ROU 289 Hb61
Balta şı TR 63 Mk26
Baltasound GB 19 Ku30
Bălăteşti RO 45 Mg43
Baltazar YV 269 Gg44
Bălţi MD 45 Mh43
Baltic Sea 6 Lb04
Baltijsk RUS 37 Lu36
Baltim ET 177 Mf30
Baltimore PE 279 Gf52
Baltimore USA (MD) 247 Gb26
Baltimore ZA 214 Me57
Baltinava LV 17 Mh34
Baltit Fort PK 79 Oh27
Baltour ZA 217 Md62
Baluan Island PNG 159 Sd47
Baluarte de Santiago MEX (CAM) 255 Fe36
Baluchistan IR/PK 80 Oa32
Balud RP 121 Rb39
Balugaon IND (ORS) 109 Pc36
Balui MAL 126 Qh44
Baluran N.P. RI 129 Qh49
Balurghat IND (WBG) 112 Pe33
Balut Island RP 123 Rc43
Balvard IR 75 Nj31
Balvi LV 17 Mh33
Balya TR 50 Mh51
Balyi CHN (SCH) 95 Qd30
Balykca RUS (ALT) 85 Pd20
Balykchy KS 77 Oj24
Balykshy KZ 71 Nf22
Balyktybulak KZ 85 Pd21
Balyktyg-Hem RUS 90 Pj20
Balzar EC 272 Ga46
Bam IR 73 Nj27
Bam IR 75 Nk31
Bam TCH 195 Lj41
Bama BF 193 Kh40
Bama CHN (GZG) 96 Qd33
Bama WAN 187 Lg40
Bamaba RDC 203 Lk47
Bamaga AUS (QLD) 146 Sb51
Bamaji Lake CDN 238 Fe20
Bamako RMM 184 Kf39
Bamanpalli IND (MHT) 109 Pa36
Bamba EAK 207 Mk47
Bamba RCA 196 Lk43
Bamba RDC 203 Lk48
Bamba RMM 185 Kk37
Bambadinca GNB 183 Kc39
Bambalang CAM 195 Lf43
Bambam WAN 187 Lf41
Bambama RCB 202 Lg47
Bambamarca PE 278 Ga49
Bambana NIC 256 Fh39
Bambang RP 121 Ra37
Bambangando ANG 209 Mb54
Bambara TCH 196 Lk41
Bambara-Maoundé RMM 185 Kj38
Bambaran RMM 184 Kf39
Bambari RCA 200 Ma43
Bambaroo AUS (QLD) 149 Sd55
Bambay SN 183 Kb38
Bambaya RG 192 Kd40
Bamberg D 35 Ll41
Bamberg USA (SC) 249 Fk29
Bamberra GB 251 Ge35
Bambesa RDC 201 Mc44
Bambesi ETH 197 Mh41
Bambili RDC 201 Md44
Bambili RDC 201 Me44
Bambio RCA 195 Lj44
Bamboesberg ZA 217 Md61
Bamboo Creek AUS (WA) 140 Ra56
Bamboo Springs AUS (WA) 140 Qk57
Bamboo Temple CHN 113 Qb33
Bambou RMM 185 Kj37
Bambouk RMM 183 Ke38
Bambouti RCA 201 Md43
Bambudi ETH 197 Mh40
Bambuí BR (MG) 287 Hh56
Bambui CAM 194 Lf42
Bamburi GH 193 Kk41
Bamda CHN (TIB) 89 Pj30
Bamenda CAM 194 Lf43
Bamendjing CAM 195 Lf43
Bamfield CDN (BC) 232 Dh21
Bami TM 71 Nj26
Bamian AFG 78 Od28
Bamian CHN (GZG) 96 Qe33
Bamiancheng CHN (LNG) 100 Rb24
Bamiantong CHN (HLG) 98 Rf23
Bamingui RCA 196 Ma42
Bamingui TCH 196 Lk41
Bamingui-Bangoran, P.N. du RCA 196 Lk42
Baminigam IND (ORS) 109 Pc36
Bamio PNG 159 Sb49
Bam Island PNG 159 Sc47
Bamkeri RI 130 Rf46
Bamni IND (MHT) 108 Oj36
Bamoa MEX (SL) 252 Ef33
Bampton GB 20 Kr40
Bamuri MEX (SO) 236 Ed30
Bamusso CAM 194 Le43
Ban BF 185 Kj38
Bana CAM 194 Lf43
Banaba Island KIR 157 Tb19
Banabongo RCA 200 Mb43
Banabuiú BR (CE) 277 Ja48
Banabuiú BR 277 Ja48
Bana Daniédo SN 183 Kd38
Banadia CO 268 Ge42
Bañado de Figueroa RA 288 Gj59
Bañados de Izozog BOL 285 Gj55
Bañados de Otuquis BOL 285 Ha55
Banafara RG 192 Kf40
Banagi EAT 207 Mh47
Banaïn TLS 132 Rc50
Banakoro RMM 184 Kg39
Banalia RDC 201 Mc45
Banama RG 192 Kf41
Banamba RMM 184 Kg39
Banana AUS (QLD) 151 Sf58
Banana RDC 202 Lg49
Banana Islands WAL 192 Kd41
Bananal BR 276 Hf50
Banana Range AUS 151 Sf58
Banandje CI 192 Kg41
Banangui RCA 201 Mc43
Banankoro RG 192 Kf41
Banankoro RMM 192 Kf40
Ban Antum LAO 115 Qd38
Banao C 259 Ga35
Ban Aranyaprathet THA 115 Qb39
Banarlı TR 50 Mh49
Banas IND 106 Oj32
Banat RO 44 Ma45
Banatski Karlovac SCG 44 Mb45
Banatsko Novo Selo SCG 44 Ma46
Banaue RP 121 Ra37
Banavar IND (KTK) 110 Oj40
Banawaya RI 129 Qk49
Banaz TR 50 Mk52
Ban Bakha LAO 115 Qc36
Ban Ban AUS (QLD) 150 Sb58
Banbar CHN (TIB) 89 Ph30
Banbirpur IND (UPH) 107 Pa31
Ban Boun Tai LAO 113 Qa35
Banbridge GB 18 Ko36
Ban Bua Yai THA 115 Qb38
Banbury GB 21 Kt38
Banc Africain SY 219 Ng48
Bancauan Island RP 122 Qk42
Banc d'Arguin, P.N. du RIM 178 Kb35
Banc du Bisson RM 218 Nd51
Banc du Geyser RM 218 Nd52
Banc du Leven 219 Nd52
Bancea RI 127 Ra47
Ban Chamrung THA 115 Qb39
Ban Chang THA 114 Qa39
Ban Chiang THA 115 Qb37
Banchory GB 19 Ks33
Banco Chinchorro MEX 255 Fg36
Banco de Quitasueño CO 257 Fk38
Banco de Serrana CO 257 Fk38
Banco de Serranilla CO 257 Ga38
Banco, P.N. du CI 193 Kh43
Bancoran Island RP 122 Qk42
Bancos del Cabo Falso HN 256 Fj38
Bancos del Cabo Falso HN 256 Fj38
Bancroft CDN (ON) 247 Gb23
Band RO 44 Me44
Banda CAM 195 Lg41
Banda GH 193 Kj41
Banda IND (MPH) 109 Ok33
Banda IND (UPH) 109 Pa33
Banda RCB 202 Lf47
Banda RDC 201 Md43
Banda RDC 203 Lk48
Banda Aceh RI 116 Ph43
Bandabe RM 219 Ne53
Banda del Río Salí RA (TU) 288 Gh59
Banda Elat RI 131 Rg48
Bandafassi SN 183 Kd39
Bandaguda IND (ORS) 109 Pb36
Bandai-Asahi N.P. J 101 Rk26
Bandai-Asahi N.P. J 101 Rk27
Bandakami RDC 202 Lg48
Banda Kuu EAT 207 Mk48
Bandama Blanc CI 193 Kh41
Bandama Rouge CI 192 Kg41
Bandamurlanka IND (APH) 109 Pb37
Bandaneira RI 130 Re48
Banda Nkwanta GH 193 Kj41
Bandanwara IND (RJT) 106 Oh32
Bandar MOC 210 Mh54
Bandar RI 128 Qe49
Bandardurian RI 116 Pk44
Bandar-e-Abbas IR 75 Nj32
Bandar-e-Anzali IR 72 Ne27
Bandar-e-Busher IR 74 Nf31
Bandar-e-Charak IR 74 Nh32
Bandar-e-Deylam IR 74 Nf30
Bandar-e-Emam Khomeyni IR 74 Ne30
Bandar-e-Gonaveh IR 74 Nf31
Bandar-e Hamiran IR 74 Nh32
Bandar-e-Khamir IR 75 Nh32
Bandar-e-Kiya Shahr IR 72 Ne27
Bandar-e-Langeh IR 74 Nh32
Bandar-e-Mashhar IR 74 Ne30
Bandar-e-Moqam IR 74 Ng32
Bandar-e-Rig IR 74 Nf31
Bandar-e-Taheri IR 74 Ng32
Bandar-e-Torkaman IR 72 Nh27
Bandarjaya RI 125 Qc48
Bandar Lampung RI 125 Qc48
Bandar Murcaayo SP 199 Nf40
Bandarpunch IND 107 Ok30
Bandar Seri Begawan BRU 122 Qh43
Bandar Sri Aman MAL 126 Qf45
Banda Sea RI 132 Rc48
Bande CHN (QHI) 94 Pk29
Bande E 26 Kn52
Band-e Arghandab AFG 78 Oc29
Bandeira BR (MG) 283 Hk53
Bandeirantes BR (GO) 281 He52
Bandeirantes BR (MS) 286 Hc55
Bandeirantes BR (PR) 286 He57
Band-e Kajaki AFG 78 Oc29
Bandelierkop ZA 214 Me57
Bandelier N.M. USA 237 Eg28
Bandera RA (SE) 289 Gj60
Bandera USA (TX) 242 Fa31
Bandera Bajada RA (SE) 288 Gj59
Bander Wanaag SP 199 Nc41
Bandhavgarh N.P. IND 109 Pa34
Bandiagara RMM 185 Kj38
Bandiagara RMM 185 Kj38
Bandialit RI 128 Qg50
Banding RI 125 Qc48
Bandingaung RI 125 Qb48
Bandingilo N.P. SUD 197 Mf43
Bandipur N.P. IND 110 Oj41
Bandırma TR 50 Mh50
Bandjoukri CAM 195 Lg41
Bandjoun CAM 195 Lf43
Bandol F 25 Lf47
Bandon IRL 20 Kl39
Bandon IRL 20 Km39
Bandon USA (OR) 234 Dh24
Ban Don Nyai LAO 115 Qd38
Bandrélé F 218 Nc52
Bandua MOC 214 Mh56
Banduan IND (WBG) 112 Pd34
Banduar IND (MGA) 112 Pf33
Bandue ZA 214 Me57
Bandundu RDC 203 Lj47
Bandung RI 128 Qd49
Ban Dung THA 115 Qb37

Bandurove UA 45 Mk42
Bandya AUS (WA) 141 Rb59
Bane EAK 205 Mk45
Băneasa RO 45 Mg46
Băneasa RO 45 Mh46
Baneh IR 72 Nc27
Banemula EAT 207 Mh50
Banes C 259 Gc35
Baneshwar IND (RJT) 108 Oh34
Banfèlè RG 192 Ke40
Banff CDN (AB) 233 Ec20
Banff GB 19 Ks33
Banff N.P. CDN 233 Ec20
Banfora BF 193 Kh40
Bang RCA 195 Lh42
Banga ANG 202 Lh50
Banga RCA 196 Mb42
Banga RCA 200 Lk43
Banga RDC 203 Lk48
Banga RDC 203 Ma48
Banga RP 123 Rb40
Banga RP 123 Rc42
Bangalore IND (KTK) 111 Oj40
Bangaluda IND (ORS) 109 Pb36
Banga Melo RDC 200 Ma44
Bangana RCA 196 Mb42
Banganapalle IND (APH) 111 Oj39
Bangangté CAM 195 Lf43
Bangar RP 120 Ra37
Bangaram Island IND 110 Og41
Bangarapet IND (KTK) 111 Ok40
Bangaré RN 185 La39
Bangassoko BF 185 Kj39
Bangassou RCA 200 Mb43
Bangba RCA 195 Lj42
Bangbagatome RDC 201 Mc44
Bangbali RCA 196 Ma41
Bangeli TG 193 La41
Bangem CAM 194 Le43
Bangeta, Mount PNG 159 Sd49
Banggai RI 127 Rb46
Banggai RI 127 Rb46
Banggi MAL 122 Qj42
Banggo RI 129 Qk50
Banghazi LAR 175 Ma29
Banghiang LAO 115 Qd37
Bangil RI 128 Qg49
Bangka RI 125 Qd47
Bangka RI 127 Rc45
Bangkalan RI 127 Rb46
Bangkalan RI 128 Qg49
Bangkaru RI 116 Pj44
Bangke RI 116 Pj43
Bangko RI 124 Qa45
Bangko RI 124 Qb47
Bangkok THA 114 Qa39
Bangkurung RI 127 Rb46
Bangladesh BD 104 Pb14
Bang Lamung THA 114 Qa39
Bang Lang Reservoir THA 117 Qa42
Bang Len THA 114 Qa38
Bangli RI 129 Qh50
Bangma Shan CHN 113 Pk34
Bang Mun Nak THA 114 Qa37
Bang Muong VN 96 Qc35
Bang Nang Sata THA 117 Qa42
Bango GH 193 Kk40
Bangolo CI 192 Kg42
Bangong Co CHN 88 Ok29
Bangong Co 79 Ok29
Bangor GB 18 Kp36
Bangor GB 20 Kq37
Bangor IRL 18 Kl36
Bangor USA (MA) 247 Gf23
Bangoran RCA 196 Lk41
Bangoran RCA 196 Ma41
Bangoran TCH 196 Lk41
Bangou RCB 202 Lh47
Bangourèn CAM 195 Lf43
Bangouya RG 192 Kd40
Bangrakot IND (WBG) 112 Pe32
Bang Saphan THA 116 Pk40
Bang Saphan Noi THA 116 Pk40
Bangu RDC 203 Lk49
Bangu RDC 203 Mb50
Bangué CAM 195 Lh44
Bangued RP 121 Ra37
Bangui RCA 200 Lk43
Bangui RN 186 Ld39
Bangui RP 121 Ra36
Bangui Bay RP 121 Ra36
Bangui-Kété RCA 196 Ma43
Bangui-Motaba RCB 195 Lj44
Bangula MW 211 Mh54
Bangunpurba RI 116 Pk44
Bangweulu Swamps Z 210 Mf51
Bangxi CHN (HAN) 96 Qe36
Ban Hai LAO 115 Qd37
Ban Hat LAO 115 Qc38
Ban Hat Lek THA 115 Qb40
Ban Heu LAO 115 Qc37
Banhine, P.N. de MOC 214 Mg57
Ban Hin Kiong Temple RI 127 Rc45
Ban Huayma LAO 113 Qb35
Bani BF 185 Kk39
Bani DOM 260 Ge36
Bani IND (UPH) 107 Pa32
Bani RCA 196 Mb42
Bani RMM 184 Kh38
Bani RP 120 Qk37
Bania RCA 195 Lj43
Bani Amer KSA 68 Nb36
Banian RG 192 Ke41
Bani Bangou RN 185 Lb38
Bánica DOM 260 Ge36
Banie PL 36 Lp37
Banifing RMM 184 Kh39
Bani Hadi KSA 68 Na36
Banikane RMM 185 Kj37
Bani Khatmah KSA 68 Nc36
Banikoara DY 186 Lb40
Banima RCA 201 Mb43
Bani Ma'arid KSA 68 Nc36
Bani Mukassir KSA 67 Ne35
Băniţa RO 44 Md45
Bani Walid LAR 174 Lg30
Bani Yas UAE 74 Nh33
Banja Luka BIH 41 Ls46
Banjar RI 128 Qe49
Banjaram Timur MAL 117 Qb43
Banjaran Bintang MAL 116 Qa43
Banjaran Brassey MAL 122 Qj43
Banjaran Crocker MAL 122 Qh43
Banjaran Tama Abu MAL 126 Qh44
Banjaran Titiwangsa MAL 117 Qa43
Banjarbaru RI 126 Qh47
Banjarkasang RI 124 Qa46
Banjarmasin RI 126 Qh47
Banjawarn AUS (WA) 141 Ra59
Ban Jiang LAO 114 Qb36
Banjul WAG 183 Kb39
Banka AZ 70 Ne26
Banka IND (BIH) 112 Pd33
Banka Banka AUS (NT) 139 Rh55
Bankass RMM 185 Kj38
Ban Katang THA 116 Pk42
Bankatwa IND (UPH) 107 Pb32
Bankauluang RI 129 Qk48
Bankberg ZA 217 Mc62
Bankeryd S 15 Lp33
Banket ZW 210 Mf54
Ban Khlong Kua THA 116 Qa42
Ban Khlong Son THA 115 Qb39
Bankilaré RN 185 La38
Bankinang RI 124 Qa45
Bankja BG 46 Md48
Ban Klan LAO 115 Qd38
Banko RG 192 Ke40
Banko RMM 184 Kg39
Bankon RG 192 Kf40
Bankou mana RMM 184 Kf39
Banks USA (ID) 234 Eb23
Banks Island CDN 232 De19
Banks Island CDN 224 Dd04
Banks Islands VU 162 Td53
Banks Lake USA 232 Ea22
Banks Lake N.W.R. USA 249 Fj30
Banks Peninsula NZ 155 Tg67
Banks Providence SY 219 Nf50
Banks Strait AUS 152 Se66
Bankura IND (WBG) 112 Pd34
Ban Lampoy LAO 115 Qc37
Banli CHN (GZG) 96 Qd34
Ban Luang THA 114 Qa36
Ban Lung K 115 Qd39
Ban Mai LAO 115 Qd38
Banmanki IND (BIH) 112 Pd33
Ban Mi THA 114 Qa38
Ban Muang THA 115 Qb37
Ban Muang Et LAO 96 Qc35
Bann GB 18 Ko36
Bannaanka Saraat SP 199 Nd41
Ban Nabo LAO 115 Qd37
Bannalec F 22 Kr43
Ban Napè LAO 115 Qc36
Ban Naphao LAO 115 Qc37
Ban Na Sam THA 116 Pk41
Bannerghata N.P. IND 111 Oj40
Bannerman Town BS 251 Gb33
Banning USA (CA) 236 Eb29
Bannock Range USA 235 Ed24
Bannu PK 79 Of29
Baños EC 272 Ga46
Baños PE 278 Gb51
Baños de Benasque E 30 La48
Bánovce nad Bebravou SK 38 Lt42
Banovci Dunav SCG 44 Ma46
Banovići BIH 41 Lt46
Banovići BIH 44 Lt46
Banow AFG 78 Oe28
Ban Pak Bat THA 114 Qa37
Ban Pak-ou LAO 113 Qb35
Ban Pakpet Nuc LAO 114 Qa36
Ban Pak Phanang THA 116 Qa41
Ban Phaeng THA 115 Qc37
Ban Phai THA 115 Qb37
Ban Phe THA 114 Qa39
Ban Phon LAO 115 Qd38
Ban Phu THA 115 Qb37
Banpo CHN (SAA) 95 Qe28
Banpo Museum CHN 95 Qe28
Ban Pong THA 114 Pk39
Ban Pung LAO 113 Qa35
Ban Sichon THA 116 Pk41
Bansberia IND (WBG) 112 Pe34
Bansi IND (UPH) 107 Pb32
Bansi IND (UPH) 109 Ok33
Bansihari IND (WBG) 112 Pe33
Bansin D 33 Lp37
Ban Sinxa LAO 113 Qb35
Banská Bystrica SK 39 Lu42
Banská Štiavnica SK 39 Lt42
Bansko BG 46 Md49
Banskot IND (ORS) 109 Pb36
Ban Sop Hao LAO 96 Qc35
Banstead GB 21 Ku39
Banswada IND (APH) 108 Oj36
Banswara IND (RJT) 108 Oh34
Ban Tabok LAO 115 Qb36
Bantadjé CAM 195 Lg41
Bantaeng RI 129 Ra48
Bantaian RI 124 Qa45
Ban Tak THA 114 Pk37
Ban Takhun THA 116 Pk41
Bantan Island RP 121 Rc39
Bantayan RP 123 Rb40
Bantayan Island RP 123 Rb40
Banté DY 193 La41
Banteay Chhmar K 115 Qb38
Banteay Chhmar K 115 Qb39
Ban Thahua LAO 115 Qb36
Ban Tham Thong THA 116 Pk40
Ban Tha Rae THA 115 Qc37
Ban Tha Sala THA 116 Pk41
Ban Tha Song Yang THA 114 Pj37
Ban Tha Tum THA 115 Qb38
Ban Tha Xuang LAO 114 Qa36
Bantimurung RI 129 Ra48
Ban Tomo Nawk LAO 115 Qc38
Banton Island RP 121 Rb39
Bantry IRL 20 Kl39
Bantry Bay IRL 20 Kl39
Bantshamba RDC 203 Lk48
Bantva IND (GUJ) 108 Of35
Bantval IND (KTK) 110 Oh40
Ban Un Mai LAO 113 Qa35
Banvo ANG 203 Lk50
Ban Wiang Sa THA 116 Pk41
Ban Yaeng THA 114 Qa37
Banyalbufar E 30 Lc51
Banyas SYR 64 Mh28
Banyo CAM 195 Lf42
Banyoles E 30 Lc48
Banyuasin RI 125 Qc47
Banyumas RI 128 Qe49
Banyuwangi RI 129 Qh50
Banzana RMM 192 Kg40
Banzare Coast 297 Rb32
Banza Sanda RDC 202 Lh48
Banza Sosso ANG 202 Lh48
Bao RCA 200 Mb43
Bao TCH 187 Lj41
Baode CHN (SAX) 93 Qf26
Baodi CHN (TJN) 93 Qj26
Baoding CHN (HBI) 93 Qh26
Baofatu VU 162 Te54
Baofeng CHN (HNN) 95 Qg29
Bao Gong Ci CHN 102 Qj30
Bao Guang Si CHN 94 Qc30
Baoguo Si CHN 102 Ra30
Baoji CHN (SAA) 95 Qd28
Baojing CHN (HUN) 95 Qe31
Baokang CHN (HUB) 95 Qf30
Baokang CHN (NMZ) 98 Rb23
Bao Khao Sai THA 114 Qa37
Bao Lac VN 96 Qc34
Baolo SOL 161 Sk49
Bao Loc VN 115 Qd40
Baolun CHN (SCH) 95 Qc29
Baoma WAL 192 Ke41
Baoqing CHN (HLG) 98 Rg22
Baoro RCA 195 Lh43
Baoshan CHN (SHG) 102 Ra30
Baoshan CHN (YUN) 113 Pk33
Bao Ta Shan CHN 93 Qe27
Baotianman Z.B. CHN 95 Qf29
Baotou CHN (NMZ) 93 Qe25
Baoulé RMM 183 Kf39
Baoxu CHN (GDG) 96 Qf34
Bao Yen VN 96 Qc34
Baoying CHN (JGS) 102 Qk29
Bap IND (RJT) 106 Og32
Bapatla IND (APH) 111 Pa39
Bapaume F 23 Lc40
Baq'a KSA 66 Nb32
Baqer Abad IR 72 Nf28
Baqran KSA 66 Na35
Baquba IRQ 65 Nc29
Baquedano RCH 284 Gf57
Bar IND (RJT) 106 Oh32
Bar SCG 46 Lu48
Bar UA 54 Md21
Bara RG 183 Kd39
Bara RI 130 Rd47
Bara RO 44 Mb45
Băra RO 45 Mh43
Bara SUD 197 Mf39
Bara WAN 187 Lf40
Baraawe SP 205 Nc45
Barabai RI 126 Qh47
Bara Banki IND (UPH) 107 Pa32
Barabaš RUS 100 Rf24
Barabaš-Levada RUS 98 Rf23
Barabinskaja nizmennost' RUS 58 Oc07
Bara Bir ETH 198 Nb43
Baraboulé BF 185 Kk38
Barachati IND (BIH) 109 Pc33
Barachois CDN (QC) 245 Gh21
Barachois Pond Prov. Park CDN 245 Ha21
Baracoa C 259 Gc35
Baracuxi BR 274 Ha45
Baraderes RH 260 Gd36
Baradero RA (BA) 289 Ha62
Baradla-barlang H 39 Ma42
Baraga USA (MI) 246 Ff22
Bărăganu RO 45 Mh46
Baragoi EAK 204 Mj45
Barah IND (UPH) 107 Pa32
Barahanuddin BD 112 Pf34
Barahbise NEP 88 Pc32
Barahona DOM 260 Ge36
Barahrah KSA 66 Na35
Bara Imambara IND 107 Pa32
Bara-Issa RMM 184 Kh38
Barajas de Melo E 29 Ks50
Baraka ER 191 Mj39
Baraka RDC 206 Me48
Baraka SUD 191 Mj38
Baraka SUD 197 Md40
Barakaldo E 27 Ks53
Barakat SUD 190 Mg39
Barakatha IND (JKD) 109 Pc33
Baraki AFG 78 Oe29
Barakoma SOL 160 Sj49
Barakot IND (ORS) 109 Pc35
Baralba AUS (QLD) 151 Se58
Baramanni GUY 270 Ha42
Baramata PNG 159 Se51
Baramati IND (MHT) 108 Oh36
Barameiya SUD 191 Mj37
Baramula 79 Oh28
Baran IND (RJT) 108 Oj33
Baranavičy BY 17 Mg37
Barang MAL 126 Qh44
Baranga RDC 201 Md44
Baranga RDC 201 Me44
Barangbarang RI 129 Ra49
Barani BF 184 Kj39
Baranivka UA 54 Md20
Baranoa CO 268 Gc40
Baranof USA (AK) 231 Dc17
Baranof Island USA 231 Dc17
Baranów PL 37 Mc39
Baranów Sandomierski PL 37 Mb40
Barão de Antonia, T.I. BR 286 He57
Barão de Grajaú BR (MA) 276 Hj49
Barão de Melgaço BR (RO) 280 Gk51
Barão do Melgaço BR (MT) 286 Hc54
Baraolt RO 45 Mf44
Baraouéli RMM 184 Kg39
Baraqish YE 68 Nc38
Baraqueville F 24 Lc46
Barara EAT 207 Mj48
Bararati BR 274 Ha49
Bararis SP 199 Nc40
Baras RP 121 Rc39
Bara Sagar IND (MPH) 109 Pa34
Barataria Bay USA 243 Ff31
Barate CI 193 Kh42
Baratkhel AFG 78 Oe29
Baratpur IND (AAN) 111 Pg39
Barauli IND (BIH) 107 Pc32
Baraúna BR 274 Gk45
Barauni IND (BIH) 112 Pd33
Baraut IND (UPH) 107 Oj31
Baray K 115 Qc39
Baraya CO 272 Gc44
Barbacena BR (MG) 287 Hj56
Barbacoas CO 268 Gd40
Barbacoas CO 272 Ga45
Barbacoas YV 269 Gg41
Barbado BR (AM) 279 Gg50
Barbados BR 280 Ha53
Barbados BDS 261 Ha39
Barbados 261 Ha39
Barbalha BR (CE) 277 Ja49
Barbaros TR 50 Mh50
Barbastro E 30 La48
Barbate E 28 Kp46
Barbaza RP 123 Rb40
Barbazum OM 69 Nh37
Bărbele LV 17 Me34
Barberton ZA 214 Mf58
Barberville USA (FL) 250 Fk31
Barbezieux F 24 Ku45
Bar Bigha IND (BIH) 109 Pc33
Barbosa CO 268 Gc42
Barbosa CO 268 Gd42
Barbuda AG 261 Gk37
Bârca RO 46 Md47
Barca de Alva P 26 Ko51
Barcaldine AUS (QLD) 149 Sc57
Barcarena BR (PA) 276 Hf46
Barcarrota E 28 Ko48
Barcău RO 44 Mc43
Barcellona Pozzo di Gotto I 42 Lq52
Barcelona E 30 Lc49
Barcelona PE 279 Gf51
Barcelona YV 269 Gh40
Barcelonnette F 25 Lg46
Barcelos BR (AM) 274 Gj46
Barcelos P 26 Km51
Bárcena de Pie de Concha E 27 Kq53
Barcin PL 36 Ls38
Barcoo River AUS 150 Sb58
Barcs H 41 Ls45
Barczewo PL 37 Ma37
Barda AZ 70 Nd25
Barda del Medio RA (RN) 292 Gf65
Bardaï TCH 181 Lj35
Bardakçı TR 51 Ml51
Bardas Blancas RA (MD) 288 Gf63
Barddhaman = Burwan IND (WBG) 112 Pd34
Bar Deh IR 72 Nf29
Bardejov SK 39 Mb41
Bardeskan IR 73 Nj28
Bardi I 40 Lk46
Bardoc AUS (WA) 144 Ra61
Bardoli IND (GUJ) 108 Og35
Bardonècchia I 40 Lg45
Bardsey Island GB 20 Kq38
Bardsir IR 75 Nj30
Bardstown USA (KY) 248 Fh27
Bardula IND (CGH) 109 Pb35
Baré DY 193 La41
Bare ETH 198 Nb43
Bareilly IND (UPH) 107 Ok31
Bareli IND (MPH) 109 Ok34
Barellan AUS (NSW) 153 Sd63
Barentin F 22 La41
Barentsburg N 11 Lh06
Barentsøya N 11 Mb06
Barents Sea 6 Mb02
Barentu ER 191 Mj39
Barenya AUS (QLD) 148 Sc56
Bareo MAL 126 Qh44
Barfleur F 22 Kt41
Barfolomeevka RUS 98 Rg23
Barga CHN (TIB) 88 Pa30
Barga I 40 Ll46
Bargaal SP 199 Nf40
Bargah IR 75 Nj32
Bargaon IND (CGH) 109 Pb34
Bargarh IND (ORS) 109 Pb35
Bargarh IND (UPH) 109 Pa33
Bargi IND (MPH) 109 Ok34
Bargteheide D 33 Ll37
Barguzin RUS (BUR) 91 Qe19
Barguzin RUS 91 Qf19
Barguzinskij Hrebet RUS 59 Qb08
Barguzinskij hrebet RUS 91 Qe19
Barh IND (BIH) 109 Pc33
Barhaj IND (UPH) 107 Pb32
Bar Harbor USA (MA) 247 Gf23
Barhau RI 124 Qb48
Barhi IND (JKD) 109 Pc33
Barhi IND (MPH) 109 Pa34
Bari I 43 Lr49
Bari IND (RJT) 107 Oj32
Bari WAN 186 Lc40
Ba Ria VN 115 Qd40
Bariadi EAT 207 Mg47
Barichara CO 268 Gd42
Barik OM 69 Nj35
Barika DZ 174 Lc28
Barikowt AFG 79 Of28
Barili RP 123 Ra40
Barillas GCA 255 Fe38
Barim YE 68 Nb39
Barima YV 270 Gk41
Barinas YV 269 Ge41
Baringa RDC 200 Ma45
Barinitas YV 269 Ge41
Baripada IND (ORS) 112 Pd35
Bariri BR (SP) 286 Hf57
Bâris ET 177 Mf33
Bari Sadri IND (RJT) 108 Oh33
Barisal BD 112 Pf34
Barisan Range RI 124 Qa46
Barisan Range RI 124 Qa46
Barito RI 126 Qh46
Barítú RA (SA) 285 Gh57
Barítú, P.N. RA 285 Gh57
Barjols F 25 Lg47
Barka OM 75 Nj34
Barkam CHN (SCH) 94 Qb30
Barkava LV 17 Mg34
Barkédji SN 183 Kc38
Barkerville CDN (BC) 232 Dk19
Barkerville Hist. Town CDN 232 Dk19
Barkéwo el Abiod RIM 183 Kd37
Barkhan PK 81 Oe31
Bark Hut Inn AUS (NT) 139 Rf52
Barkley Sound CDN 232 Dh21
Barkly Downs AUS (QLD) 148 Rk56
Barkly East ZA 217 Md61
Barkly Highway AUS (QLD) 148 Rk56
Barkly Highway AUS 139 Rh55
Barkly Pass ZA 217 Md61
Barkly Roadhouse AUS (NT) 139 Rh55
Barkly Tableland AUS 139 Rh54
Barkly West ZA 217 Mc60
Barkol CHN (XUZ) 87 Pg24
Barkol Hu CHN 87 Pg24
Barkuar Dongar IND 109 Pb34
Bârlad RO 45 Mh44
Bârlad RO 45 Mh44
Bar-le-Duc F 23 Lf42
Barlee Range Nature Reserve AUS (WA) 140 Qh57
Barletta I 43 Lr49
Barlik RUS 85 Pf20
Barlinek PL 36 Lq37
Barlo Warf WAL 192 Kd41
Barma RI 130 Rg46
Barmedman AUS (NSW) 153 Sd63
Barmer IND (RJT) 106 Of33
Barmera AUS (SA) 152 Sa63
Barmouth GB 20 Kq38
Barnala IND (PJB) 106 Oh30
Barnard USA (SD) 240 Fa23
Barnato AUS (NSW) 150 Sc61
Barnaul RUS 58 Pa08
Barnesville USA (GA) 249 Fh29
Barnesville USA (MN) 241 Fb22
Barnet GB 21 Ku39
Barnett River Gorge AUS 138 Rd54
Barneveld NL 32 Lf38
Barneville-Carteret F 22 Kt41
Barnhart USA (TX) 242 Ek30
Barnim D 33 Lo38
Barnissa EAK 205 Na44
Barnjarn A.L. AUS 139 Rg52
Barnong AUS (WA) 144 Qj60
Barnsley GB 21 Kt37
Barnstaple GB 20 Kq39
Barnstaple Bay GB 20 Kq39
Barnstorf D 32 Lj38
Barnum USA (WY) 235 Eg24
Barnwell USA (SC) 249 Fk29
Baro ETH 197 Mh41
Baro TCH 196 Lk39
Baro WAN 186 Ld41
Barobo RP 123 Rd41
Baroda = Vadodara IND (GUJ) 108 Og34
Baroda IND (MPH) 106 Oj33
Barodia IND (MPH) 109 Ok33
Baroe ZA 217 Mc62
Baroghilpass AFG/PK 79 Og27
Barola IND (MPH) 109 Pa34
Barolong RB 213 Mc58
Baron RI 128 Qf50
Barora Island SOL 161 Sk49
Barora Ite Island SOL 161 Sk49
Barossa Valley AUS 152 Rk63
Barotac Nuevo RP 123 Rb40
Barotseland Z 209 Mb53
Barots Flood Plain Z 209 Mb53
Baroua RCA 201 Mc43
Barovo MK 46 Mc49
Barpeta IND (ASM) 112 Pf32
Barqah al Bayda LAR 175 Ma30
Barqat al-Bahriya ET/RN 176 Mc30
Barqin LAR 181 Lg32
Barque Canada Reef 122 Qg41
Barquisimeto YV 269 Gf40
Barra BR (BA) 282 Hj51
Barra BR 286 Hg58
Barra BR 286 Hg58
Barra GB 18 Kn34
Barra Alegre BR (MG) 287 Hj55
Barraba AUS (NSW) 151 Sf61
Barra Bonita BR (SP) 286 Hf57
Barraca da Boca BR (AP) 275 Hd46
Barraca de A.Lopes BR (PA) 274 Ha49
Barracão BR (RS) 290 He59
Barracão do Barreto BR (MT) 280 Ha50
Barracas E 29 Ku50
Barra da Estiva BR (BA) 283 Hk52
Barradale AUS (WA) 140 Qh57
Barra de Cazones MEX (VC) 254 Fb35
Barra de Itabapoana BR (RJ) 287 Hk56
Barra de Navidad MEX (JLC) 253 Eh36
Barra de São Francisco BR (ES) 287 Hk55
Barra de São Manuel BR (AM) 274 Ha49
Barra de Tuxpan MEX (VC) 254 Fb35
Barra do Bugres BR (MT) 281 Hb53
Barra do Cai BR (BA) 287 Ja54
Barra do Choça BR (BA) 283 Hk53
Barra do Corda BR (MA) 276 Hh48
Barra do Cuanza ANG 202 Lg50
Barra do Dande ANG 202 Lg50
Barra do Garças BR (MT) 281 Hd53
Barra do Guaicui BR (MG) 287 Hh54
Barra do Mendes BR (BA) 283 Hj51
Barra do Quaraí BR (RS) 290 Hb61
Barra do Tarrachi BR (BA) 283 Ja50
Barra El Tordo MEX (TM) 253 Fb34
Barrafranca I 42 Lp53
Barrage Al-Massira MA 172 Kg29
Barrage de l'Eau d'Heure B 23 Le40
Barrage de Manantali RMM 183 Ke39
Barrage de Matadi RDC 202 Lg48
Barrage de Sélingué RMM 183 Kf40
Barrage Djorf-Torba DZ 173 Kj30
Barrage El-Mansour-Eddahbi MA 172 Kg30
Barrage Hassan-Addakhil MA 173 Kh29
Barragem de Cabora Bassa MOC 210 Mg53
Barragem de Castelo de Bode P 28 Km49
Barragem de Chicamba Real MOC 214 Mg55
Barragem de Itaparica BR 283 Ja50
Barragem de Montargil P 28 Km49
Barragem de Moxotó BR 283 Ja50
Barragem de Pedra BR 283 Hk52
Barragem de Pracana P 28 Kn49
Barragem de Santa Clara P 28 Km47
Barragem de São Simão BR 286 He55
Barragem de Serra da Mesa BR 282 Hf53
Barragem de Sobradinho BR 283 Hj50
Barragem do Alqueva P 28 Kn48
Barragem do Caia P 28 Kn49
Barragem do Maranhão P 28 Kn49
Barragem Itumbiara BR 286 Hf55
Barrage Mohamed V MA 173 Kj28
Barragem Pedro do Cavalo BR 283 Ja52
Barrage S.M. Ben Abdellah MA 172 Kg29
Barra Grande BR (BA) 283 Ja52
Barra Head GB 18 Kn34
Barra Los Americanos MEX 253 Fb33
Barra Mansa BR (MS) 285 Hb55
Barramansa BR (RJ) 287 Hh57
Barrambie AUS (WA) 140 Qj59
Barramiya ET 177 Mg33
Barranca PE 272 Gb48
Barranca PE 278 Gb51
Barrancabermeja CO 268 Gd42
Barranca del Cobre MEX 252 Eg32
Barranca del Cobre, P.N. MEX 252 Eg32
Barranca de Upia CO 268 Gd43
Barrancas RA (SF) 289 Gk62
Barrancas RA 289 Ha60
Barrancas RA 292 Ge64
Barrancas YV 270 Gj41
Barranca Sinforosa MEX 252 Eg32
Barranc d'Algendar E 30 Ld51
Barranco de Loba CO 268 Gd41
Barranco Picure CO 269 Gf44
Barrancos P 28 Ko48
Barranda E 29 Kt48
Barranqueras RA (CH) 289 Ha59
Barranquilla CO 268 Gc40
Barranquillas RCH 288 Ge59
Barranquitas YV 268 Gd40
Barras BR (PI) 277 Hj48
Barras BR (RO) 280 Gh51
Barra Seca BR (RJ) 287 Hk56
Barra Soto La Marina MEX 253 Fb34
Barraute CDN (QC) 244 Gb21
Barra Velha BR (SC) 291 Hf59
Barra Velha, T.I. BR 287 Ja54
Barrax E 29 Ks49
Barr'd Harbour CDN (NF) 245 Hb20
Barre USA (VT) 247 Gd23
Barreal RA (SJ) 288 Gf61
Barrealito YV 269 Gh41
Barreira Branca BR (PA) 281 He50
Barreira da Cruz BR (TO) 282 Hf51
Barreira da Missão, T.I. BR 274 Gh47
Barreira do Peiqui BR (TO) 282 Hf52
Barreiras BR (BA) 282 Hh52
Barreirinha BR (AM) 275 Hb47
Barreirinhas BR (MA) 277 Hj47
Barreiro P 28 Kl48
Barreiros BR (PE) 283 Jc50
Barreiros BR (SC) 291 Hf59
Barrême F 25 Lg47
Barren Grounds CDN 225 Gb07
Barren Grounds CDN 224 Dd05
Barren Is. USA 229 Cd16
Barren Island IND 111 Pg39
Barretal MEX (TM) 253 Fa33
Barretos BR (SP) 286 Hf56
Barrett Lake CDN (BC) 232 Dg18
Barrhead CDN (AB) 233 Ec18
Barrial Largo YV 269 Gg42
Barrie CDN (ON) 247 Ga23
Barriere CDN (BC) 232 Dk20
Barrier Highway AUS 150 Sc61
Barrier Range AUS 150 Sa61
Barrier Reef BH 255 Fg37
Barrier Reef PNG 160 Sg51
Barrier River CDN 233 Eh19
Barrington = Isla Santa Fé EC 272 Fe46
Barrington Lake CDN 238 Ek17
Barrington, Mount AUS (NSW) 153 Sf62
Barrington Tops N.P. AUS (NSW) 153 Sf62
Barringun AUS (NSW) 151 Sc60
Barriyat al-Bayyuda SUD 190 Mg37
Barro Alto BR (GO) 282 Hf53
Barroção BR (MG) 287 Hj54
Barro Duro BR (MA) 277 Hj47
Barro Duro BR (PI) 277 Hj48
Barron USA (WI) 241 Fe23
Barros Arana, Cerro RCH 292 Gd67
Barros Cassal BR (RS) 290 Hd60
Barrow IRL 20 Ko38
Barrow USA 224 Cb04
Barrow Creek AUS (NT) 142 Rg56
Barrow-in-Furness GB 21 Kr36
Barrow Island AUS 140 Qh56
Barrow Point AUS 147 Sc53
Barrow Strait CDN 225 Fa04
Barruelo de Santullán E 27 Kq52
Barry GB 20 Kr39
Barry Church ZA 216 Ma63
Barrydale ZA 216 Ma62
Barry's Bay CDN (ON) 247 Gb23
Barsakelmes tübegi KZ 71 Nk23
Barsalogo BF 185 Kk39
Barsaloi EAK 204 Mj45
Bârsana RO 44 Me43
Barsatas KZ 84 Ok21
Barsi IND (MHT) 108 Oh36
Barskoon KS 77 Oj24
Barstow USA (CA) 236 Eb28
Bar-sur-Aube F 23 Le42
Bar-sur-Seine F 23 Le42
Barta LV 17 Mb34
Bartallah IRQ 65 Nb27
Bartang TJ 77 Of26
Bartang TJ 77 Of26
Bartel USA (CA) 234 Dk25
Barth D 33 Ln36
Bartica GUY 270 Ha42
Bartın TR 62 Mg25
Bartlesville USA (OK) 243 Fb27
Bartlet Bluff AUS (WA) 145 Rc60
Bartlett USA (NE) 240 Fa25
Bartolomé Masó C 259 Gb35
Barton USA (ND) 238 Ek21
Barton-upon-Humber GB 21 Ku37
Bartoszyce PL 37 Ma36
Barú CO 268 Gc40
Baru RI 124 Qb48
Baru RI 130 Rg46
Barudin GUY 270 Ha44
Barueri BR (SP) 286 Hg57
Baruipur IND (WBG) 112 Pe34
Barukku RI 127 Ra47
Barúmini I 31 Lk51
Barumun RI 124 Pk45
Barun RUS (KAL) 53 Nc22
Barung RI 127 Qj45
Barung RI 128 Qg50
Baruth D 33 Lo38
Baruti RDC 201 Mc44
Baruunkharaa MNG 90 Qd21
Baruunturuun MNG 85 Ph21
Baruun Urt MNG 91 Qg22
Barvala IND (GUJ) 108 Of34
Barvas GB 19 Ko32
Barvinkove UA 55 Mj21
Barwaha IND (MPH) 108 Oj34
Barwala IND (HYA) 106 Oh31
Barwani IND (MPH) 108 Oh35
Barwice PL 36 Lr37
Barwidgee AUS (WA) 140 Ra59
Barwidgi AUS (QLD) 148 Sc54
Barwon River AUS 151 Se60
Barycz PL 36 Lr39
Baryš RUS 53 Nd19
Barysav BY 52 Me18
Baryulgil AUS (NSW) 151 Sg60
Bărzava RO 44 Mb44
Bârzava RO 44 Mb45
Basacato del Este GQ 194 Le44
Basagude IND (CGH) 109 Pa36
Basaguke CHN (TIB) 88 Pc31
Basai MAL 122 Qj42
Bašaid SCG 44 Ma45
Basaidu IR 74 Nh32
Basail RA (CH) 289 Ha59
Basak K 115 Qc40
Basakan, Gunung RI 126 Qj44
Basal PK 79 Og29
Basali RDC 201 Mc45
Basang WAG 183 Kc39
Basanga RDC 203 Mc48
Basankusu RDC 200 Lk45
Basantpur IND (BIH) 107 Pc32
Basar IND (APH) 108 Oj36
Basarabeasca MD 45 Mj44
Basarabi RO 45 Mj46
Basaseachic MEX (CHH) 252 Ef31
Basavana Bagevadi IND (KTK) 108 Oh37
Basavilbaso RA (ER) 289 Ha62
Basay RP 123 Rb41
Bašcelakskij hrebet RUS 85 Pb20
Basco RP 121 Ra35
Bascombe Well Conservation Park AUS 152 Rh62
Bascov RO 45 Me46
Baseer SYR 64 Mj29
Basel CH 34 Lh43
Base Naval Azopardo RA (BA) 293 Ha64
Basento I 43 Lr50
Baserah RI 124 Qa46
Bash Abdan AFG 78 Oe27
Bashaw CDN (AB) 233 Ed19
Bashee ZA 217 Me62
Bashee Bridge ZA 217 Me61
Bashimuke RDC 203 Mc48
Bashkortostan 9 Nd08
Basht IR 74 Nf30
Basi IND (RJT) 106 Og33
Basi LV 17 Mb34
Basia IND (JKD) 109 Pc34
Basiano RI 127 Rb46
Basibasy RM 220 Nb57
Basilaki Island PNG 160 Sf51
Basilan Island RP 123 Rb42
Basilan Strait RP 123 Ra42
Basildon GB 21 La39
Basilica d'Aquila I 42 Lo48
Basilica d'Aquileia I 41 Lo45
Basílica de Nuestra Señora de los Milagros PY 285 Hb58
Basilica di Lecce I 43 Lt50
Basilica di San Francesco d'Assisi I 40 Ln47
Basilica di San Pietro I 42 Ln49
Basilica of Bom Jesus IND 108 Og38
Basilica San Gavino I 31 Lj50
Basilicata I 43 Lr50
Basilique de Saint-Nicolas-de-Port F 23 Lg42
Basilique Notre-Dame de Paray-le-Monial F 25 Le44
Basilique Notre Dame de Port de Clermont-Ferrand F 25 Ld45
Başın TR 51 Mo53
Basin USA (WY) 235 Ef23
Basingstoke GB 21 Kt39
Basin Head Fisheries Mus. CDN 245 Gj22
Basin Lake CDN 233 Eh19
Basirka WAN 187 Lf40
Basirpur PK 79 Og30
Baška HR 41 Lp46
Başkale TR 63 Nb26
Baskan KZ 84 Ok23
Baškaus RUS 85 Pd20
Baskineig Falls CDN 239 Fg19
Başkomutan Milli Parkı TR 51 Ml52
Başkomutan Tarihi Milli Parkı TR 50 Mk52
Başkuyu TR 51 Mn52
Baslar TR 51 Mm53
Basle CH 34 Lh43
Başmakçı TR 51 Ml53
Basmath IND (MHT) 108 Oj36
Basna IND (CGH) 109 Pb35
Basoda IND (MPH) 109 Oj34
Basoko RDC 201 Mb45
Basongo RDC 203 Ma48
Basotu EAT 207 Mh48
Basra IRQ 65 Nd30
Bassa CI 192 Kg43
Bassae GR 48 Mb53
Bassano CDN (AB) 233 Ed20
Bassano del Grappa I 40 Lm45

Bassar TG 193 La41
Bassas da India F 215 Mk56
Bassaula WAN 195 Lf42
Bassawa CI 193 Kh41
Basse Casamance, P.N. du SN 183 Kb39
Bassein MYA 114 Ph37
Bassein = Puthein MYA 114 Ph37
Bassein Beach IND 108 Og36
Bassella E 30 Lb48
Basse-Pointe F 261 Gk38
Basse Santa Su WAG 183 Kc39
Basse-Terre F 261 Gk37
Basse Terre F 261 Gk37
Basseterre KNA 261 Gj37
Bassett USA (NE) 240 Fa24
Bassikounou RIM 184 Kh38
Bassila DY 193 La41
Bassin Bleu RH 260 Gd36
Bassin d'Arcachon F 24 Kt46
Bassin de Thau F 25 Ld47
Basso DY 186 Lb40
Basso TCH 189 Mb37
Bass Strait AUS 136 Sa26
Bassum D 32 Lj38
Basswood Lake USA 238 Fd21
Båstad S 14 Ln34
Bastak IR 74 Nh32
Bastam Jame Mosque IR 72 Nh27
Baštanka UA 54 Mg22
Bastar IND (CGH) 109 Pa36
Bastar Hills IND 109 Pa36
Basti IND (UPH) 107 Pb32
Bastia F 31 Lk48
Bastia Umbra I 40 Ln47
Bastogne B 23 Lf41
Bastos BR (MG) 286 Hf55
Bastrop USA (LA) 243 Fe29
Bastrop USA (TX) 243 Fb30
Bastuny BY 17 Mf36
Basu RI 125 Qb46
Basua WAN 194 Le42
Basud RP 121 Rb38
Basudebpur IND (ORS) 112 Pd35
Basunda SUD 191 Mh40
Bat OM 75 Nj34
Båta BG 47 Me48
Bata GQ 194 Le45
Batabanó C 258 Fj34
Batabi WAN 186 Lc41
Batac RP 121 Ra37
Batacosa MEX (SO) 252 Ef32
Bataga RUS 59 Rc05
Batag Island RP 121 Rc39
Bataguassu BR (MS) 286 Hd56
Bataiporã BR (MS) 286 Hd57
Batajsk RUS 55 Mk22
Batak BG 47 Me49
Batakan RI 126 Qh48
Batala IND (PJB) 106 Oh30
Batalha BR (PI) 277 Hj48
Batam RI 125 Qb45
Batama RDC 201 Md45
Batan RP 123 Rb40
Batang CHN (SCH) 94 Pk31
Batang RI 128 Qe49
Batanga G 194 Le46
Batangafo RCA 196 Lk42
Batangas RP 121 Ra39
Batangkapas RI 124 Qa46
Batan Island RP 121 Rb35
Batan Islands RP 121 Ra35
Batanovci BG 46 Mc48
Batanta RI 130 Rf46
Batar RI 131 Rk47
Batăr RO 44 Mb44
Batas Island RP 122 Qk40
Bátaszék H 39 Lt44
Batatais BR (SP) 286 Hg56
Batavia USA (NY) 247 Ga24
Batavia Downs AUS (QLD) 146 Sb52
Bat Cave USA (NC) 249 Fj28
Batcham CAM 194 Lf43
Batchelor AUS (NT) 139 Rf52
Batchenga CAM 195 Lf43
Batea E 30 La49
Batemans Bay AUS (NSW) 153 Sf63
Batemans Bay AUS 153 Sf63
Baté-Nafadji RG 192 Kf40
Bates USA (OR) 234 Ea23
Batesburg Leesville USA (SC) 249 Fk29
Batesville USA (AR) 243 Fe28
Batesville USA (MS) 243 Ff28
Bath GB 21 Ks39
Bath USA (MA) 247 Gf24
Bath USA (NY) 247 Gb24
Batha TCH 187 Lj39
Batha de Laïri TCH 187 Lj40
Batheaston AUS (QLD) 149 Se57
Bathhurst Island AUS 139 Rf51
Bathinda IND (PJB) 106 Oh30
Bathsheba BDS 261 Ha39
Ba Thuoc VN 96 Qc35
Bathurst AUS (NSW) 153 Se62
Bathurst CDN (NB) 245 Gh22
Bathurst ZA 217 Md62
Bathurst Inlet CDN 224 Ec05
Bathurst Island CDN 225 Fa03
Bati ETH 198 Na40
Batia DY 193 La40
Batiagarh IND (MPH) 109 Ok33
Batibati RI 126 Qh47
Batibo CAM 194 Le43
Batié BF 193 Kj41
Bati Menteşe Dağları TR 49 Mh53
Batina HR 44 Lt45
Batinah OM 75 Nj33
Bati Toroslar TR 62 Mf27
Batkandu WAL 192 Kd41
Batken UZ 76 Of25
Batkhaan Uul Nature Reserve MNG 90 Qb22
Bat Khela PK 79 Of28
Batković BIH 44 Lu46
Batlaq-e Gavhuni IR 72 Nf29
Batley GB 21 Kt37
Batman TR 63 Na27
Batna DZ 174 Ld28
Batn at Tarfa KSA 67 Nf34
Bato RP 121 Rc39
Bato RP 122 Qk43
Bato RP 123 Rc40
Ba To VN 115 Qe38
Batoche N.H.S. CDN 233 Eg19
Batoka Z 210 Md54
Bat Ölziyt MNG 90 Qc21
Bat-ongan Caves RP 121 Rb39
Baton Rouge USA (LA) 243 Fe30
Bátonyterenye H 39 Lu43
Batopilas MEX (CHH) 252 Eg32
Batote 79 Oh29
Batoua CAM 195 Lg43
Batouala G 195 Lg45
Batouri CAM 195 Lh43
Batovi, T.I. BR 281 Hd52
Batovo BG 47 Mh47
Batrahalli IND (TNU) 111 Ok40
Batroun RL 64 Mh28
Batsawul AFG 79 Of28
Båtsfjord N 11 Me10
Battambang K 115 Qb39
Batt Doeng K 115 Qc40
Battenberg D 32 Lj39
Batticaloa CL 111 Pa43
Batticaloa Beach CL 111 Pa43
Batti Malv Island IND 111 Pg41
Battipáglia I 42 Lp50
Battistero di Firenze I 40 Lm47
Battistero di Parma I 40 Ll46
Battle Camp AUS (QLD) 147 Sc53
Battle Creek USA (MI) 246 Fh24
Battle Creek USA 233 Ef21
Battle Mountain USA (NV) 234 Eb25
Battle of Colenso ZA 217 Me60
Battle of Talana ZA 217 Mf60
Battle River CDN 233 Ed19
Battonya H 39 Mb44
Battor GH 193 La42
Battulapalle IND (APH) 111 Oj39
Batuampar RI 124 Qb46
Batuan Bridge CHN 96 Qe33
Batuata RI 132 Rb49
Batubetumpang RI 125 Qd47
Batu Bolong Beach RI 129 Qj50
Batubrok, Gunung RI 126 Qh45
Batu Caves MAL 117 Qa44
Batudaka RI 127 Ra46
Batudaka RI 127 Ra46
Batu Danau MAL 122 Qh43
Batu Ferringhi Beach MAL 116 Qa43
Batu Gong Beach RI 127 Rb47
Batui RI 127 Rb46
Batuijak RI 116 Pj43
Batujaya RI 128 Qd49
Batukangkung RI 124 Qa46
Batukau, Gunung RI 129 Qh50
Batulaki RP 123 Rc43
Batulintang RI 125 Qb47
Batumandi RI 126 Qh47
Batumi GE 70 Na25
Batumi GE 63 Na25
Batumundan RI 124 Pk45
Batu Pahat MAL 117 Qb45
Batupanjang RI 124 Qa45
Baturaden RI 128 Qe49
Batura Glacier PK 79 Oh27
Batura Glacier Bridge PK 79 Oh27
Baturaja RI 125 Qc48
Batu Rakit MAL 117 Qb43
Baturetno RI 128 Qf50
Baturité BR (CE) 277 Ja48
Baturube RI 127 Ra46
Batuša SCG 44 Mb46
Batusangkar RI 124 Qa46
Batu Tambung RI 127 Rb46
Batyrevo RUS (CHU) 53 Nd18
Baú BR 275 Hc49
Bau MAL 126 Qf45
Bau SUD 197 Mh40
Bauana BR 274 Gh47
Bauang RP 120 Ra37
Baubau RI 127 Rb48
Bauchi WAN 186 Le40
Baud F 22 Kr43
Baudette USA (MN) 238 Fc21
Baudh Raj IND (ORS) 109 Pc35
Baudo CO 268 Gb43
Baugé F 22 Ku43
Bauhaus D 33 Ln39
Bauhausbauten und klassisches Weimar D 33 Lm40
Bauhinia Downs AUS (QLD) 151 Se58
Baukau TLS 132 Rd50
Baumberge D 32 Lh39
Baú-Mekragroti, T.I. BR 281 Hd50
Baume-les-Dames F 23 Lg43
Bauna BD 112 Pe33
Baunatal D 32 Lk39
Baunei I 31 Lk50
Baungan RI 116 Pk44
Baures BOL 280 Gj52
Bauru BR (SP) 286 Hf57
Bauru RDC 200 Ma45
Bauska LV 17 Me34
Bauskas pils LV 17 Me34
Bauta RDC 200 Ma45
Băuţar RO 44 Mc45
Bautzen D 33 Lp39
Bauyrzhan KZ 76 Of24
Bavaria = Bayern D 35 Lm42
Bavay F 23 Ld40
Bavella F 31 Lk49
Båven S 13 Lr31
Ba Vi VN 96 Qc35
Bavia IND (GUJ) 108 Og34
Baviaanskloof ZA 217 Mc62
Baviácora MEX (SO) 237 Ee31
Ba Vi N.P. VN 96 Qc35
Bawal RI 126 Qf47
Bawangaja IND 108 Oh35
Baw'an Pass YE 68 Nb38
Bawe RI 130 Rf46
Bawe RI 131 Rh47
Bawean RI 128 Qg48
Bawku GH 193 Kk40
Bawlake MYA 114 Pj36
Bawley Point AUS 153 Sf63
Bawli Bazar MYA 112 Pg35
Bawo LB 192 Kf43
Bawo Ofuloa RI 124 Pk46
Bawtry GB 21 Kt37
Baxian CHN (CGQ) 95 Qd31
Baxkorgan CHN (XUZ) 87 Pf26
Baxley USA (GA) 249 Fj30
Baxoi CHN (TIB) 89 Pj30
Baxter Springs USA (KS) 243 Fc27
Bay RMM 185 Kj39
Baya-Bwanga RDC 203 Mb48
Bayaguana DOM 260 Gf36
Bayah RI 128 Qd49
Bayaha IND (BIH) 107 Pc32
Bayamo C 259 Gb35
Bayamon USA (PR) 261 Gg36
Bayan CHN (HLG) 98 Rd22
Bayan CHN (NMZ) 92 Qc25
Bayan MNG 85 Ph22
Bayan MNG 90 Qb22
Bayan MNG 91 Qf22
Bayan RI 129 Qj50
Bayanbulag MNG 90 Pk22
Bayanbulag MNG 90 Pk23
Bayanbulag MNG 91 Qe22
Bayanbulak CHN (XUZ) 84 Pc24
Bayanga RCA 195 Lj44
Bayanga-Didi RCA 195 Lh43
Bayangol MNG 85 Ph23
Bayan Har Shan CHN 89 Ph28
Bayan Har Shan CHN 89 Pj28
Bayan Har Shankou CHN 89 Pj28
Bayankhongor MNG 90 Qa22
Bayankhongor MNG 90 Pk23
Bayankhoshuu MNG 85 Pg21
Bayan Obo CHN (NMZ) 93 Qe25
Bayan Ölgiy MNG 85 Pe21
Bayan Oljii CHN (NMZ) 92 Qc25
Bayan-Ovoo MNG 85 Ph23
Bayan-Ovoo MNG 91 Qf21
Bayansayr MNG 90 Pk23
Bayan Shan CHN 87 Pj27
Bayanteeg MNG 90 Qa23
Bayantökhöm MNG 90 Qc22
Bayantsagaan MNG 90 Qa21
Bayan Uul MNG 85 Pf21
Bayanzag (Dinosaur excavations) MNG 92 Qb23
Bayard USA (NE) 240 Ej25
Bayard USA (NM) 237 Ef29
Bayasgalant MNG 91 Qg22
Bayat RI 125 Qb47
Bayat TR 50 Mk52
Bayat TR 51 Mp50
Bayat TR 51 Ml52
Bayat TR 51 Ml53
Bayata C 259 Gc35
Bayawan RP 123 Rb41
Bayaz IR 74 Nh30
Bayaziyeh IR 72 Nj29
Baybay RP 123 Rc40
Bay Bulls CDN (NF) 245 Hd22
Bayburt TR 63 Na25
Bay City USA (MI) 246 Fj24
Bay City USA (TX) 243 Fc31
Baydhabo SP 205 Nb44
Bay du Nord Wilderness Res. CDN 245 Hc21
Bayerische Alpen D 35 Lm43
Bayerischer Wald D 35 Ln41
Bayerischer Wald, N.P. D 35 Lo42
Bayern D 35 Lm42
Bayeux F 22 Ku41
Bayfield USA (WI) 241 Fe22
Bayhan al Qasab YE 68 Nc38
Bay Harbor USA 246 Fh23
Bayındır TR 49 Mh52
Bayındır Baraj TR 51 Mn50
Bayir JOR 64 Mj30
Bayizhen CHN (TIB) 89 Ph31
Bayji IRQ 65 Nb28
Baykan TR 63 Na26
Baykonur KZ 76 Ob23
Baykonur Cosmodrome KZ 76 Ob23
Baylamören TR 51 Mo50
Bay Minette USA (AL) 248 Fg30
Baynes Mountains NAM 208 Lg54
Baynunah UAE 74 Ng34
Bayo, Cerro RCH 292 Gd68
Bay of Bengal 104 Pb15
Bay of Biscay F/E 24 Ks46
Bay of Campeche MEX 255 Fd36
Bay of Fundy CDN 245 Gg23
Bay of Islands CDN 245 Ha21
Bay of Islands NZ 154 Th63
Bay of Plenty NZ 154 Tj64
Bay of Whales 296 Bd34
Bayo Grande, Cerro RA 288 Gg59
Bayombong RP 121 Ra37
Bayon F 23 Lg42
Bayonet Point USA (FL) 250 Fj31
Bayonne F 24 Kt47
Bayou Cane USA (LA) 243 Fe31
Bayou Cocodrie N.W.R. USA 243 Fe30
Bayóvar PE 278 Fk48
Bayramaly TM 73 Ob27
Bayramiç TR 50 Mg51
Bayreuth D 35 Lm41
Bayshint MNG 85 Pf21
Bayshint MNG 90 Qc22
Bay Shore USA (NY) 247 Gd25
Bay Springs USA (MS) 243 Ff30
Bayt al Faqih YE 68 Nb38
Baytik Shan CHN/MNG 85 Pf23
Baytown USA (TX) 243 Fc31
Bay Tree CDN (AB) 232 Ea18
Bayu RI 116 Pj43
Bayu RI 127 Rb47
Bayugan RP 123 Rc41
Bayum Gol He CHN 87 Pj27
Bay View NZ 154 Tj65
Baza E 29 Ks47
Bazar-e Taleh AFG 78 Oe28
Bazarnye Mataki RUS (TAR) 53 Nf18
Bazarnyi Karabulak RUS 53 Nd19
Bazas F 24 Ku46
Bazhong CHN (SCH) 95 Qd30
Bazhou CHN (HBI) 93 Qj26
Bazman IR 75 Oa32
Beach USA (ND) 240 Ej22
Beach Haven USA (NJ) 247 Gc26
Beach Park BR 277 Ja47
Beachport AUS (SA) 152 Sa64
Beachy Head GB 21 La40
Beacon AUS (WA) 144 Qj61
Beacon USA (NY) 247 Gd25
Beacon Bay ZA 217 Md62
Beacon Hill USA (FL) 249 Fh31
Beaconsfield AUS (TAS) 152 Sd66
Beadon Point AUS 140 Qh56
Beagle Bay AUS (WA) 138 Rb54
Beagle Bay A.L. AUS 138 Rb54
Beagle Gulf AUS 139 Rf52
Bealanana RM 219 Ne53
Bean Station USA (TN) 249 Fj27
Bear Cove CDN (BC) 232 Dg20
Beardmore CDN (ON) 239 Fg21
Beardmore Glacier 297 Tc35
Beardmore South Camp USA 297 Ta35
Beardstown USA (IL) 241 Fe25
Bearhead River CDN 233 Eb17
Bear Island CDN 239 Fk18
Bear Island IRL 20 Kl39
Bear Islands N 6 Ma02
Bear Lake CDN 238 Fb18
Bear Lake CDN 235 Ee25
Bearma IND 109 Ok34
Bearpaw Mount USA 229 Ce13
Bear River CDN 233 Eh18
Bears Den Mtn. USA 240 Fa22
Beas IND 106 Oh30
Beasain E 27 Ks53
Beas Dam IND 107 Oj30
Beas de Segura E 29 Ks48
Beasley AUS 140 Qj57
Beata Ridge 260 Gd38
Beatrice USA (NE) 241 Fb25
Beatrice ZW 214 Mf55
Beatton River CDN (BC) 231 Dk17
Beatton River CDN 231 Dk17
Beatty CDN (SK) 233 Eh19
Beatty USA (NV) 236 Eb27
Beattyville CDN (QC) 244 Gb21
Beattyville USA (KY) 249 Fj27
Beau-Bassin MS 221 Nj56
Beaucaire F 25 Le47
Beauce F 22 Lb42
Beauchêne Isla GB 295 Ha72
Beau Desert AUS (QLD) 148 Sa56
Beaudesert AUS (QLD) 151 Sg60
Beaufort AUS (VIC) 153 Sb64
Beaufort MAL 122 Qj43
Beaufort USA (SC) 249 Fk29
Beaufort Castle RL 64 Mh29
Beaufort Sea 224 Cd04
Beaufort Wes ZA 216 Mb62
Beaufort-West ZA 216 Mb62
Beaugency F 22 Lb43
Beaujeu F 25 Le44
Beaujolais F 25 Le44
Beaumaris Castle GB 20 Kq37
Beaumont F 24 La46
Beaumont USA (TX) 243 Fc30
Beaumont-de-Lomagne F 24 La47
Beaumont-Hague F 22 Kt41
Beaumont-le-Roger F 22 La41
Beaumont-sur-Sarthe F 22 La42
Beaune F 23 Le43
Beaupréau F 22 Ku43
Beauraing B 23 Le40
Beaurepaire F 25 Lf45
Beausejour CDN (MB) 238 Fb20
Beauty ZA 213 Md57
Beauvais F 23 Lc41
Beauval CDN (SK) 233 Eg18
Beauvoir-sur-Mer F 22 Ks44
Beauvoir-sur-Niort F 24 Ku44
Beavenhead Range USA 235 Ed23
Beaver USA (AK) 229 Cg12
Beaver USA (OK) 242 Ek27
Beaver USA (OR) 234 Dj23
Beaver USA (UT) 235 Ed26
Beaver City USA (NE) 240 Fa25
Beavercreek USA (OH) 246 Fh26
Beaver Creek USA 229 Cg13
Beaver Dam USA (WI) 246 Ff24
Beaver Falls USA (PA) 247 Fk25
Beaverhill Lake CDN 238 Fc18
Beaver Island USA 241 Fh23
Beaver Island Marine Museum USA 246 Fh23
Beaver Lake Ind. Res. CDN 233 Ee18
Beaverlodge CDN (AB) 232 Ea18
Beaver Marsh USA (OR) 234 Dk24
Beaver Mountain Provincial Park CDN 245 Gk23
Beaver Mts. CDN 231 Ck14
Beaver River CDN 231 Dg15
Beaver River CDN 233 Ee18
Beaver River CDN 233 Eg18
Beaver River CDN 239 Ff18
Beaver River CDN 239 Ga19
Beawar IND (RJT) 106 Oh32
Beazlay RA (SL) 288 Gg62
Bebar RI 132 Re49
Bebarama CO 268 Gb42
Bebédjia TCH 187 Lj41
Bebedouro BR (SP) 286 Hf56
Bebeka ETH 197 Mh42
Beberibe BR (CE) 277 Ja48
Bebisa PNG 159 Sb49
Bébéto TCH 195 Lj41
Béboura III RCA 195 Lj42
Bebra D 32 Lk40
Bebrene LV 17 Mg34
Bebri LV 17 Mf34
Becán MEX 255 Ff36
Beccles GB 21 Lb38
Bécédi-Brignan CI 193 Kh43
Bečej SCG 44 Ma45
Becerreá E 26 Kn52
Béchar DZ 173 Kj30
Becharof Lake USA 228 Cb17
Becharof N.W.R. USA 228 Cb17
Becher Point AUS 144 Qh62
Bechet RO 46 Md47
Bechraji IND (GUJ) 108 Og34
Bechuanaland ZA 216 Ma59
Becilla de Valderaduey E 26 Kp52
Beckley USA (WV) 249 Fk27
Beckov SK 38 Ls42
Beckum D 32 Lj39
Beclean RO 44 Me43
Bečov nad Teplou CZ 38 Ln40
Bečva CZ 38 Ls41
Beda Hayk ETH 198 Na40
Bedanda GNB 183 Kc40
Bédarieux F 25 Ld47
Bédaya TCH 187 Lj41
Bedekovčina HR 41 Lq44
Bedele ETH 198 Mj41
Bedessa ETH 198 Na41
Bedford GB 21 Ku38
Bedford USA (IA) 241 Fc25
Bedford USA (IN) 248 Fg26
Bedford USA (PA) 247 Ga26
Bedford USA (VA) 249 Ga27
Bedford ZA 217 Md62
Bedi Dat PK 80 Oc32
Bediondo TCH 187 Lj41
Bednja HR 41 Lr44
Bédo TCH 188 Lk36
Bédouaram RN 187 Lg38
Bedourie AUS (QLD) 150 Rk58
Beech Grove USA (IN) 246 Fg26
Beechworth AUS (VIC) 153 Sd64
Beechy CDN (SK) 233 Eg20
Beelitz D 33 Ln38
Beer Arqo SYR 65 Mk27
Be'er-Sheva IL 64 Mh30
Beerwah AUS (QLD) 151 Sg59
Beeskow D 33 Lp38
Beestekraal ZA 213 Md58
Beetaloo AUS (NT) 139 Rg54
Beethoven Peninsula 296 Gb33
Beeville USA (TX) 253 Fb31
Befale RDC 200 Ma45
Befandefa RM 220 Nb57
Befandriana Atsimo RM 220 Nb57
Befandriana Avaratra RM 219 Ne53
Befasy RM 220 Nc56
Béferou DY 186 Lb41
Befeta RM 220 Nd56
Befori RDC 200 Mb45
Befotaka RM 219 Nd53
Befotaka RM 220 Nd57
Bega AUS (NSW) 153 Se64
Bega RN 186 Lc38
Bega RO 44 Mb45
Begamganj BD 112 Pf34
Begamganj IND (MPH) 109 Ok34
Bégard F 22 Kr42
Beğendik TR 50 Mj49
Beglež BG 47 Me47
Begna N 12 Lk30
Begnadalen N 12 Lk30
Begogo RM 220 Nd57
Bégon RCA 195 Lh42
Begora GH 193 Kk42
Begovo BG 47 Me48
Begusarai IND (BIH) 112 Pd33
Beh Abad IR 72 Nj30
Behara RM 220 Nd58
Beharona RM 220 Nc56
Behbahan IR 74 Nf30
Beh Deh IR 74 Ng32
Beheloka RM 220 Nb57
Behenjy RM 220 Nd55
Béhili RCA 196 Lk42
Behm Canal USA 231 De18
Behramkale TR 50 Mg51
Behrendt Mountains 296 Gb34
Behring Point BS 251 Gb33
Behror IND (RJT) 106 Oj32
Bei'an CHN (HLG) 98 Rd21
Beibei CHN (CGQ) 95 Qd31
Béïbouo CI 192 Kg42
Beichuan CHN (SCH) 94 Qc30
Beidaihe Haibin CHN 93 Qk26
Beidao CHN (GSU) 95 Qc28
Beidaud RO 45 Mj46
Beidou CHN (GDG) 96 Qg35
Beigi ETH 197 Mh41
Beihai CHN (GZG) 96 Qe35
Bei He CHN 94 Qc28
Bei Jiang CHN 97 Qg33
Beijing CHN (BJG) 93 Qj26
Beijing CHN 93 Qj26
Beijin Gang CHN 96 Qg35
Beijing Shi CHN 93 Qj25
Beilen NL 32 Lg38
Bei Ling CHN 100 Rb25
Beiliu CHN (GZG) 96 Qf34
Beilngries D 35 Lm41
Beilu He CHN 89 Pg28
Beima CHN (QHI) 94 Qa29
Béinamar TCH 187 Lh41
Beinn Dearg GB 19 Kq33
Beipiao CHN (LNG) 100 Ra25
Beira MOC 214 Mh55
Beira P 26 Km50
Beira Alta ANG 202 Lh50
Beiradão BR (AP) 275 Hd46
Beirut RL 64 Mh29
Beisaren N 11 Mc07
Beiseker CDN (AB) 233 Ed20
Bei Shan CHN 87 Ph25
Beitan CHN (GZG) 96 Qe35
Beitostølen skicenter N 12 Lj29
Beitun CHN (XUZ) 85 Pd22
Beiuş RO 44 Mc44
Beizhangdian CHN (SAX) 93 Qg27
Beizhen CHN (LNG) 100 Ra25
Beja P 28 Kn47
Béja TN 174 Le27
Bejaïa DZ 174 Lc27
Béjar E 26 Kp50
Bejestan IR 73 Nk28
Beji WAN 186 Ld41
Bejipuram IND (APH) 109 Pb36
Bejneu KZ 58 Nc09
Bejneu KZ 71 Nh23
Bek CAM 195 Lh44
Beka CAM 187 Lg41
Béka CAM 195 Lg42
Béka CAM 195 Lh42
Bekaa Valley RL 64 Mh29
Bekal Beach IND 110 Oh40
Bekal Fort IND 110 Oh40
Békamba TCH 187 Lj41
Bekasi RI 128 Qd49
Bekdash TM 71 Ng25
Bek-Džar KS 77 Og25
Beke RDC 206 Md50
Békés H 39 Mb44
Békéscsaba H 39 Mb44
Bekily RM 220 Nc58
Bekipay RM 220 Nd54
Bekitro RM 220 Nc58
Beklemiševo RUS 91 Qg19
Bekma IRQ 65 Nc27
Bekobod UZ 76 Oe25
Bekodoka RM 220 Nc54
Bekoji ETH 198 Mk42
Bekol RI 129 Qh49
Bekopaka RM 220 Nc55
Bekoropoka-Antongo RM 220 Nb56
Békuí BF 193 Kj40
Bekwai GH 193 Kk42
Békyem GH 193 Kj42
Bela IND (APH) 109 Ok36
Bela IND (GUJ) 108 Of34
Bela IND (UPH) 107 Pa33
Bela PK 80 Od32
Belaazërsk BY 37 Mf38
Bélabirim RN 187 Lg38
Bélabo CAM 195 Lg43
Bélâbre F 22 Lb44
Bela Crkva SCG 44 Mb46
Bela Cruz BR (CE) 277 Hk47
Bela Floresta BR (SP) 286 He56
Belaga MAL 126 Qg44
Belaghash KZ 84 Pa20
Belaja RUS 90 Qb19
Belaja RUS 98 Re20
Belaja Kalitva RUS 55 Na21
Belakuadi IND (KTK) 111 Oj40
Belalcázar E 28 Kp48
Belang RI 127 Rc45
Belangan RI 126 Qg47
Belanger River CDN 238 Fb19
Belanitra RM 220 Nd55
Belantis D 33 Ln39
Bela Palanka SCG 46 Mc47
Belapara IND (ORS) 109 Pb35
Belarus BY 52 Mc19
Belas ANG 202 Lg50
Belatuk RI 126 Qf47
Belaveżskaja Pušča, N.P. BY 37 Me38
Bela Vista ANG 202 Lg49
Bela Vista ANG 208 Lj52
Bela Vista BR (AM) 273 Ge48
Bela Vista BR (AP) 271 He44
Bela Vista BR (MS) 285 Hb57
Bela Vista MOC 217 Mg59
Belawan RI 116 Pk44
Belayan RI 126 Qj45
Belaya Terara ETH 198 Mj40
Belbédji RN 186 Ld38
Bełchatów PL 37 Lu39
Belcheragh AFG 78 Oc28
Belcher Islands CDN 239 Fk17
Belchite E 27 Ku51
Belcoo GB 18 Kn36
Belcourt USA (ND) 238 Fa21
Belda IND (WBG) 112 Pd34
Belďca BY 17 Mf37
Belden USA (CA) 234 Dk25
Beldibi TR 51 Ml54
Belebej RUS 53 Nh18
Beled H 38 Ls43
Belédougou RMM 184 Kf39
Beledweyne SP 199 Nc43
Béléhédé BF 185 Kk38
Belek TR 51 Mm54
Béléko RMM 184 Kg39
Bélel CAM 195 Lh42
Belel WAN 187 Lg41
Belém BR (AM) 273 Gf47
Belém BR (PA) 276 Hf46
Belém de São Francisco BR (PE) 283 Ja50
Belen CO 268 Gd42
Belén CO 256 Fh40
Belén PA 257 Fk41
Belén PY 285 Hb57
Belén RA (CA) 288 Gg59
Belén RCH 284 Gf55
Belén ROU 289 Hb61
Belen TR 62 Mj27
Belen USA (NM) 237 Eg28
Beles Wenz ETH 198 Mj40
Belet Weyne SP 199 Nc43
Belev RUS 52 Mj19
Beleya RG 192 Ke40
Belezma, P.N. de DZ 174 Lc28
Belfast GB 18 Kp36
Belfast USA (MA) 247 Gf23
Belfast ZA 214 Mf58
Belfast Lough GB 18 Kp36
Belfield USA (ND) 240 Ej22
Belfir RO 44 Mb44
Belfodiyo ETH 197 Mh40
Belford GB 19 Kt35
Belfort F 23 Lg43
Belgachhi IND (BIH) 112 Pd33
Belgaum IND (KTK) 108 Oh38
Belgaum Fort IND (KTK) 108 Oh38
Belgern D 33 Lo39
Belgium B 23 Le40
Bel'go RUS 98 Rj20
Belgo SUD 197 Mg40
Belgodère F 31 Lk48
Belgorod RUS 55 Mj20
Belgrade SCG 44 Ma46
Belgrade USA (MN) 241 Fc23
Belgrade USA (MT) 235 Ee23
Belgrano RA 294 Ge70
Belgrano, Cerro RA 294 Ge69
Belgrano II ANT (RA) 296 Jb34
Belhar IND (BIH) 112 Pd33
Belhatti IND (KTK) 110 Oh39
Belhirane DZ 174 Ld30
Béli BF 185 Kk38
Béli GNB 192 Kd40
Beli WAN 195 Lf42
Belic C 259 Gb36
Belica MK 46 Ma49
Beli Drim SCG 46 Ma48
Belidzi RUS (DAG) 70 Ne25
Belifang CAM 195 Lf42
Beli Izvor BG 46 Md47
Beli Manastir HR 44 Lt45
Belimbing RI 125 Qc48
Belin-Béliet F 24 Ku46
Belinga G 195 Lg45
Belinskoe RUS 99 Sb21
Belinyu RI 125 Qd46
Beliş RO 44 Md44
Belišće HR 41 Lt45
Belitsaka RM 220 Nc54
Belitung RI 125 Qd47
Belize ANG 202 Lg48
Belize BH 255 Ff37
Belize Barrier Reef System BH 255 Fg37
Belize City BH 255 Ff37
Belize New River BH 255 Ff37
Beljanovo BG 47 Mf47
Belkar IND (MHT) 108 Og37
Belkaya TR 51 Mo53
Belkhera IND (MPH) 109 Ok34
Bel'ki BY 17 Mh35
Bel'kovo RUS 52 Mg19
Bell AUS (QLD) 151 Sf59
Bell ZA 217 Md62
Bella CAM 194 Lf44
Bella Bella CDN (BC) 232 Df19
Bellac F 24 Lb44
Bella Coola CDN (BC) 232 Dg19
Bella Copla River CDN 232 Dg19
Belladère DOM 260 Ge36
Bella Flor BOL 279 Gg51
Bellágio I 40 Lk45
Bellalie AUS (QLD) 150 Sb59
Bellária-Igea Marina I 40 Ln46
Bellary IND (KTK) 111 Oj39
Bellata AUS (NSW) 151 Se60
Bella Unión ROU 289 Hb61
Bellavista CO 268 Gb42
Bellavista PE 272 Ga48
Bellavista PE 278 Gb49
Bella Vista RA (CR) 289 Ha60
Bella Vista RA (TU) 288 Gh59
Bella Vista Norte PY 285 Hb57
Bell Brook AUS (NSW) 151 Sg61
Bellburns CDN (NF) 245 Hb20
Belle Anse RH 260 Gd36
Belleden Ker AUS (QLD) 149 Sc54
Bellefontaine USA (OH) 246 Fj25
Bellefonte USA (PA) 247 Gb25
Belle Fourche USA 235 Eh23
Bellegarde F 23 Lc43
Bellegarde-sur-Valserine F 25 Lf44
Belle Glade USA (FL) 250 Fk32
Belle-Île F 22 Kr43
Bellême F 22 La42
Bellenden Ker N.P. AUS (QLD) 149 Sd54
Belleoram CDN (NF) 245 Hc22
Belle Plaine USA (MN) 241 Fd23
Belleterre CDN (QC) 247 Ga22
Belleville CDN (ON) 247 Gb23
Belleville F 25 Le44
Belleville USA (IL) 241 Fe26
Belleville USA (KS) 240 Fb26
Belleville ZA 216 Lk62
Belleville-sur-Vie F 22 Kt44
Bellevue AUS (QLD) 148 Sc54
Bellevue USA (ID) 235 Ec24
Bellevue USA (NE) 241 Fc25
Bellevue USA (OH) 246 Fj25
Bellevue USA (WA) 232 Dj22
Belley F 25 Lf45
Belle Yella LB 192 Kf42
Bellfield AUS (QLD) 148 Sb55
Bell Fourche USA (SD) 240 Ej23
Bellingham USA (WA) 232 Dj21
Bellingrath Gardens USA 248 Ff30
Bellingshausen ANT (RUS) 296 Ha30
Bellingshausen Sea ANT 296 Fd32
Bellinzona CH 34 Lk44
Bell-Irving River CDN 231 Df17
Bell Island Hot Springs USA (AK) 231 De18
Bello CO 268 Gc42
Bellocq RA (BA) 293 Gk63
Bellona Plateau 137 Ta23
Bellows Falls USA (VT) 247 Gd24
Bellpat PK 80 Od31
Bell Peninsula CDN 225 Fd06
Bellpuig E 30 Lb49
Bell Rock 19 Ks34
Bellrose AUS (QLD) 151 Sd59
Bells Beach AUS (VIC) 153 Sc65
Bellsund N 11 Lg07
Belluno I 40 Ln44
Bell Ville RA (CD) 289 Gj62
Belly River CDN 233 Ed21
Bélmez E 28 Kp48
Belmond USA (IA) 241 Fd24
Belmont GB 19 Ku30
Belmont USA (NC) 249 Fk28
Belmont ZA 217 Mc60
Belmonte BR (BA) 283 Ja53
Belmonte E 29 Ks49
Belmonte P 26 Kn50
Belmonte de Miranda E 26 Ko53
Belmont Park USA (NY) 247 Gd25
Belmont Park Racecourse AUS (WA) 144 Qh61
Belmopan BH 255 Ff37
Belmopan BH 255 Ff37
Belmore AUS (NSW) 152 Sa62
Belmullet IRL 18 Kl36
Belo RM 220 Nc56
Belobaka RM 220 Nc55
Belo Campo BR (BA) 283 Hk53
Beloci MD 45 Mj43
Belœil B 23 Ld40
Beloglinnyj RUS 53 Nf20
Belogorsk RUS 98 Re20
Belogradčik BG 46 Mc47
Belogradčiški Skali BG 46 Mc47
Beloha RM 220 Nc58
Belo Horizonte BR (MG) 287 Hj55
Beloit USA (KS) 240 Fa26
Beloit USA (WI) 246 Ff24
Belo Jardim BR (PE) 283 Jb50
Belojarovo RUS 98 Re20
Belojarskij RUS 58 Ob06
Béloko RCA 195 Lh43
Belokuriha RUS 85 Pc20
Belo Monte BR (AM) 274 Gh49
Belo Monte do Pontal BR (PA) 275 He47
Belomorsk RUS (KAR) 11 Mh13
Belomorsko-Kulojskoje-plato RUS 11 Na13
Belonge RDC 203 Ma47
Belorado E 27 Kr52
Belorečensk RUS 55 Mk23
Belören TR 51 Mo50
Beloslav BG 47 Mh47
Belotinci BG 46 Mc47
Belo Tsiribihina RM 220 Nc55
Belousovka KZ 85 Pb20
Belovodskoe KS 77 Oh24
Belpasso I 42 Lp53
Belper GB 21 Kt37
Belpınar TR 51 Mm51
Belpre USA (OH) 247 Fk26
Belsay GB 19 Kt35
Bel'skaja vozvyšennost' RUS 52 Mg18
Beltana AUS (SA) 152 Rk61
Belterra BR (PA) 275 Hc47
Beltinci SLO 41 Lr44
Beltiug RO 44 Mc43
Belton USA (SC) 249 Fj28
Belton USA (TX) 242 Fb30
Beltov Qirlari UZ 71 Oa24
Belturbet IRL 18 Kn36
Beluga Lake USA 229 Ce15
Beluguppa IND (APH) 111 Oj39
Belur IND (KTK) 110 Oh40
Beluran MAL 122 Qj43
Beluru MAL 126 Qh44
Belvedere Marittimo I 43 Lq51
Belvès F 24 La46
Belvidere USA (IL) 246 Ff24
Belvidere Kerk ZA 216 Mb63
Belwa WAN 187 Lf41
Belyando River AUS 149 Sd57
Belyj RUS 52 Mg18
Belz UA 37 Me40
Belzig D 33 Ln38
Belzoni USA (MS) 243 Fe29

Bełżyce – Bilad Bani Bu Hasan

Bełżyce PL 37 Mc39
Béma RMM 184 Kf38
Bémal RCA 195 Lj42
Bemanevika RM 219 Ne52
Bemanevika RM 219 Nf53
Bemaraha RM 220 Nc55
Bemarivo RM 220 Nc56
Bembe ANG 202 Lh49
Bembeche TCH 188 Lk36
Bembesi ZW 214 Me56
Bemboka AUS (NSW) 153 Se64
Bemetara IND (CGH) 109 Pa35
Bemidji USA (MN) 241 Fc22
Bemonto RM 220 Nc55
Ben BF 184 Kh39
Bena WAN 186 Lc40
Benabarre E 30 La48
Bena-Dibele RDC 203 Mb48
Benagerie AUS (SA) 152 Sa61
Ben-Ahmed MA 172 Kg29
Bena-Kamba RDC 203 Mc47
Ben Alberts Nature Reserve ZA 213 Md58
Benalla AUS (VIC) 153 Sc64
Benalup de Sidonia E 28 Kp46
Benamaurel E 29 Ks47
Ben Amera RIM 178 Kd35
Benato-Toby RM 220 Nc57
Bena-Tshadi RDC 203 Mb48
Benavente E 26 Kp51
Benavides E 26 Kp52
Benavides USA (TX) 253 Fa32
Ben Badis DZ 173 Kk28
Ben Boyd N.P. AUS (NSW) 153 Se64
Bencés főapátság H 38 Ls43
Bencha CHN (JGS) 102 Ra29
Bencheng CHN (HBI) 93 Qk26
Bencubbin AUS (WA) 144 Qj61
Bend USA (OR) 234 Dk23
Béndana TCH 196 Lk41
Benda Range AUS 152 Sa62
Bendela RDC 203 Lj47
Bendeleben Mts. USA 229 Bj13
Bendemeer AUS (NSW) 151 Sf61
Bender Beyla SP 199 Nf41
Bendigo AUS (VIC) 153 Sc64
Bend of the Boyne IRL 20 Ko37
Bendorf D 32 Lh40
Bendugu WAL 192 Ke41
Bene MOC 210 Mg53
Beneditinos BR (PI) 277 Hj48
Benedito Leite BR (MA) 276 Hh49
Benejama E 29 Ku48
Benemérito de las Américas MEX (CHP) 255 Fe37
Bénéna RMM 184 Kh39
Bénéninkényi RMM 184 Kh39
Benenitra RM 220 Nc57
Benešov CZ 38 Lp41
Benevento I 42 Lp49
Benevides BR (PA) 276 Hf46
Benga MOC 210 Mg54
Benga MW 210 Mh52
Bengabad IND (JKD) 112 Pd33
Bengala CO 268 Gd43
Bengala IND (AAN) 111 Pg41
Bengamisa RDC 201 Mc45
Bengbis CAM 195 Lg44
Bengbu CHN (AHU) 102 Qj29
Benge USA (WA) 232 Ea22
Benghazi LAR 175 Ma29
Bengkalis RI 124 Qb45
Bengkalis RI 124 Qb45
Bengkulu RI 124 Qb47
Bengo ANG 202 Lh50
Bengoi RI 130 Rf47
Bengough CDN (SK) 233 Eh21
Beng Per W.S. K 115 Qc39
Bengtsfors S 12 Ln31
Benguela ANG 208 Lg52
Ben Guerdane TN 174 Lf29
Ben Guerir MA 172 Kg29
Ben Hai VN 115 Qd37
Beni BOL 279 Gh51
Beni NEP 88 Pb31
Beni RDC 201 Me45
Beni-Abbès DZ 173 Kj30
Beni Barka TN 174 Lf29
Benicarló E 30 La50
Benicasim = Benicàssim E 30 La50
Benicàssim E 30 La50
Benicito BOL 279 Gh51
Benidorm E 29 Ku48
Benifaió E 29 Ku49
Beni Hammad DZ 174 Lc28
Beni Haoua DZ 173 La27
Beni Hassan ET 177 Mf32
Beni Hassan el Shuruq ET 177 Mf32
Beni Kheddache TN 174 Lf29
Beni Mazâr ET 177 Mf31
Beni-Mellal MA 172 Kg29
Benin WAN 194 Lc43
Benin 167 La08
Benin City WAN 194 Lc42
Benin Iya WAN 194 Lc42
Beni-Ounif DZ 173 Kk29
Beni Saf DZ 173 Kk28
Benisheikh WAN 187 Lg40
Beni Slimane DZ 173 Lb27
Beni-Smir DZ/MA 173 Kk29
Beni-Suef ET 177 Mf31
Beni-Tajjite MA 173 Kj29
Benito CDN (MB) 238 Ek20
Benito Juárez MEX (CHH) 237 Eg30
Benito Juárez MEX (CHH) 237 Eg31
Benito Juárez MEX (TB) 255 Fd37
Benito Juárez MEX (ZCT) 254 Ej35
Benito Juárez RA (BA) 293 Ha64
Benito Juárez, P.N. MEX 254 Fb37
Benito Juárez (Sierra Hermosa) MEX (ZCT) 253 Ek34
Beni-Yal MA 173 Kj29
Benjamin USA (TX) 242 Fa29
Benjamín Aceval PY 285 Hb58
Benjamin Constant BR (AM) 273 Ge48
Benjamin Hill MEX (SO) 237 Ee30
Benjina RI 131 Rh49
Benkayang RI 126 Qe45
Benkelman USA (NE) 240 Ek25
Benkovac HR 41 Lq46
Ben Lavin Nature Reserve ZA 214 Me57
Ben Lawers GB 19 Kq34
Ben Lomond N.P. AUS (TAS) 152 Sd66
Ben Luc VN 115 Qd40
Ben Macdui GB 19 Kr33
Benmara AUS (NT) 139 Rj54
Ben Mehidi DZ 174 Ld27
Ben More GB 18 Ko34
Ben More GB 19 Kq34
Ben More Assynt GB 19 Kq32
Ben Moussa MA 172 Kg29
Benndale USA (MS) 243 Ff30
Bennetsville USA (SC) 249 Ga28
Bennett CDN (BC) 231 Dc16
Bennett USA (CO) 235 Eh26
Bennett Dam, W.A.C. CDN 232 Dj17
Bennett Lake CDN 231 Dc15
Ben Nevis GB 19 Kq34
Bennichchâb RIM 183 Kc36
Bennington USA (VT) 247 Gd24
Bénodet F 22 Kq43
Benoni ZA 217 Me59
Benoud DZ 173 La29
Bénoué = Benue WAN 194 Le42
Bénoué, P.N. de la CAM 195 Lg41
Bénoye TCH 187 Lj41
Ben Quang VN 115 Qd37
Ben S'Bour DZ 173 Lc28
Bensékou DY 186 Lb40
Bensheim D 34 Lj41
Ben-Slimane MA 172 Kg29
Benson USA (AZ) 237 Ee30
Benson USA (MN) 241 Fc23
Ben Starav GB 19 Kp34
Bent IR 75 Nk32
Benteng RI 129 Ra49
Benteng Belgica RI 130 Rf48
Bentia RMM 185 La38
Bentiaba ANG 208 Lg53
Benda Range AUS 152 Sa62
Bentick Island MYA 116 Pj40
Bentinck Island AUS (QLD) 148 Rk54
Bentinck Sound MYA 114 Pj38
Bentiu SUD 197 Me41
Bentley CDN (AB) 233 Ec19
Bento Gomes BR 281 Hb54
Bento Gonçalves BR (RS) 290 He60
Benton USA (AR) 243 Fd28
Benton USA (CA) 234 Ea27
Benton USA (IL) 243 Ff27
Benton USA (LA) 243 Fd29
Bentong MAL 117 Qa44
Benton Harbor USA (MI) 246 Fg24
Bentonsport USA (MO) 241 Fe25
Bentonsport Nat. Hist. District USA (MO) 241 Fe25
Bentota Beach CL 111 Ok43
Bentuang Karimun Nature Reserve RI 126 Qg45
Benty RG 192 Kd41
Benua RI 117 Qd45
Benue WAN 194 Ld41
Benwee Head IRL 18 Kl36
Benxi CHN (LNG) 100 Rb25
Benza ANG 202 Lg49
Benzdorp SME 271 Hc44
Ben-Zlareg DZ 173 Kk30
Beo RI 123 Rd43
Beoga RI 131 Rj47
Beograd SCG 44 Ma46
Beograd-Surcin SCG 44 Ma46
Beohari IND (MPH) 109 Pa33
Béoumi CI 193 Kh42
Beowawe USA (NV) 234 Eb25
Beppu J 103 Rf29
Beqa FJI 163 Tk55
Bequia WV 261 Gk39
Bequimão BR (MA) 276 Hh47
Ber RMM 185 Kj37
Berabevu RA (SF) 289 Gk62
Berahle ETH 191 Mk40
Beraketa RM 220 Nc58
Berakit Beach RI 125 Qc45
Beramanja RM 219 Ne52
Bérandjokou RCB 195 Lj44
Berangang RI 125 Qb46
Berasia IND (MPH) 109 Oj34
Beraspapan RI 126 Qh46
Berastagi RI 116 Pk44
Berat AL 46 Lu50
Berat Fortesë AL 46 Lu50
Berau RI 127 Qj44
Beravina RM 220 Nc55
Beravy RM 220 Nc56
Berazino BY 52 Me19
Berbak National Park RI 125 Qb46
Berber SUD 190 Mg37
Berbera SP 199 Nc40
Berbérati RCA 195 Lh43
Berbice GUY 270 Ha43
Berbinzana E 27 Kt52
Berceto I 40 Lk46
Berchtesgaden D 35 Ln43
Berchtesgaden, N.P. D 35 Ln43
Berck-Plage F 23 Lb40
Berdaale SP 205 Nb44
Berdale SP 199 Nd42
Berdía E 26 Km52
Berdjans'k UA 55 Mj22
Berdjans'ka kosa UA 55 Mj22
Berdsk RUS 58 Pa08
Berdyčiv UA 54 Me21
Bére TCH 187 Lj41
Berea USA (KY) 249 Fh27
Béréba BF 193 Kj40
Berebere RI 130 Re44
Bereeda SP 199 Nf40
Berega EAT 207 Mj49
Berehomet UA 45 Mf42
Berehove UA 39 Mc42
Bereina PNG 159 Sd50
Bereket TR 51 Mp53
Bereketa RM 220 Nc57
Bereku EAT 207 Mh48
Berekua WD 261 Gk38
Berekum GH 193 Kj42
Berendi TR 62 Mh27
Berenice ET 177 Mh34
Berens Island CDN 238 Fb19
Berens River CDN (MB) 238 Fb19
Berens River CDN 238 Fb19
Berenty RM 220 Nc57
Bere Regis GB 21 Ks40
Beresford USA (SD) 241 Fb24
Berestečko UA 37 Mf40
Berești RO 45 Mh44
Berettyóújfalu H 39 Mb43
Berevo RM 220 Nc55
Berezanka UA 45 Ml43
Berezanskaja RUS 55 Mk23
Berežany UA 39 Me41
Berezinsky Biosphere Nature Reserve BY 52 Me18
Berezna UA 52 Mf20
Berezne UA 54 Md20
Bereznehuvate UA 54 Mg22
Berezniki RUS 58 Nd07
Berezovo RUS 11 Mk15
Berga E 30 Lb48
Bergama TR 50 Mh51
Bergamo I 40 Lk45
Bergantin YV 269 Gh41
Bergantiños E 26 Km53
Bergara E 27 Ks53
Bergeforsen S 13 Ls28
Bergen D 32 Lk38
Bergen D 33 Lo36
Bergen N 12 Lf30
Berg en Dal SME 271 Hc43
Bergen op Zoom NL 32 Le39
Bergensbanen N 12 Lg30
Berger N 12 Ll31
Bergerac F 24 La46
Bergheim D 32 Lg40
Bergin RUS (KAL) 55 Nd22
Bergland CDN (ON) 238 Fc21
Bergland NAM 212 Lj57
Bergland USA (MI) 246 Ff22
Bergshamra S 13 Lt31
Bergsig NAM 212 Lh56
Bergsjö S 13 Ls29
Bergstadens Ziir N 12 Lm28
Bergues F 23 Lc40
Bergviken S 13 Lr29
Bergville ZA 217 Me60
Berhait IND (JKD) 112 Pd33
Berhampur IND (ORS) 109 Pc36
Berheci RO 45 Mh44
Berilo BR (MG) 287 Hj54
Beringarra AUS (WA) 140 Qj59
Beringen B 23 Lf39
Bering Glacier USA 230 Cj15
Bering Land Bridge National Preserve USA 229 Bh13
Bering Sea USA/RUS 224 Ad07
Bering Strait USA/RUS 224 Bc05
Berisu IR 72 Nc27
Berja E 29 Ks46
Berkåk N 12 Lk28
Berkane MA 173 Kj28
Berkeley USA (CA) 234 Dj27
Berkeley River AUS 138 Rd53
Berkeley Sound GB 295 Hb71
Berkh MNG 91 Qf22
Berkner Island 296 Hc34
Berkovica BG 46 Md47
Berkovici BIH 41 Lt47
Berland River CDN 233 Eb19
Berlanga E 28 Kp48
Berlanga de Duero E 27 Ks51
Berlenga P 28 Kl49
Berlengas BR 277 Hj49
Berlevåg N 11 Me10
Berlin CO 268 Gd42
Berlin D 33 Lo38
Berlin USA (NH) 247 Ge23
Berlin USA (WI) 246 Ff24
Berlin, Mount 296 Da34
Bermagui AUS (NSW) 153 Sf64
Bermejillo MEX (DGO) 253 Ej33
Bermejo BOL 285 Gh57
Bermejo BOL/RA 285 Gh57
Bermejo PE 278 Gb51
Bermejo PE 278 Gb51
Bermejo RA 288 Gf61
Bermeo E 27 Ks53
Bermillo de Sayago E 26 Ko51
Bermo RN 186 Ld38
Bermuda GB 227 Gc12
Bermuda Islands GB 227 Gc12
Bermuda Rise 227 Gd12
Bern CH 34 Lh44
Bernabé Rivera ROU 289 Hb61
Bernalda I 43 Lr50
Bernalillo USA (NM) 237 Eg28
Bernardo C 259 Gc35
Bernardo USA (NM) 237 Eg28
Bernardo de Irigoyen RA (MI) 289 Hd59
Bernardo O'Higgins, P.N. RCH 294 Gc70
Bernartice CZ 38 Lp41
Bernāti LV 17 Ma34
Bernau D 33 Lo38
Bernaville F 23 Lc40
Bernay F 22 La41
Bernburg D 33 Lm39
Berndorf A 35 Lr43
Berne CH 34 Lh44
Berner Alpen CH 34 Lh44
Berneray GB 18 Kn33
Berner Oberland CH 34 Lg44
Bernham USA (TX) 243 Fb30
Bernice USA (LA) 243 Fd29
Bernier Island AUS 140 Qg58
Bernkastel-Kues D 34 Lh41
Bernsdorf D 33 Lp39
Bero ANG 208 Lg53
Berón de Astrada RA (CR) 289 Hb59
Beronovo BG 47 Mg48
Beroroha RM 220 Nc56
Beroun CZ 38 Lp41
Berounka CZ 38 Lo41
Berovo MK 46 Mc49
Berraha DZ 174 Ld27
Berrahal DZ 174 Ld27
Berraondo RA (BA) 293 Gj65
Berrechid MA 172 Kg29
Berre-l'Étang F 25 Lf47
Berri AUS (SA) 152 Sa63
Berriane DZ 173 Lb29
Berridale AUS (NSW) 153 Se64
Berrigan AUS (NSW) 153 Sc63
Berrima AUS (NSW) 153 Sf63
Berrouaghia DZ 173 Lb27
Berrydale USA (FL) 248 Fg30
Berry Islands BS 251 Gb33
Berryville USA (AR) 243 Fd27
Berryville USA (VA) 247 Gb26
Beršad' UA 45 Mk42
Berseba NAM 216 Lj59
Bersenbrück D 32 Lh38
Berteştii de Jos RO 45 Mh46
Bertincourt F 23 Ld40
Bertinho BR (PA) 275 He47
Bertolínia BR (PI) 277 Hj49
Bertoua CAM 195 Lg43
Bertrand CDN (NB) 245 Gh22
Bertrix B 23 Lf41
Berwell CDN (SK) 238 Ej19
Beru Island KIR 157 Td19
Beruniy UZ 71 Oa25
Beruri BR (AM) 274 Gk47
Beruwala CL 111 Ok43
Berwick AUS (VIC) 153 Sc64
Berwick CDN (NB) 245 Gh23
Berwick USA (PA) 247 Gb25
Berwick-upon-Tweed GB 19 Ks35
Beryslav UA 54 Mg22
Berzence H 38 Ls44
Berzo LV 17 Md34
Bērzpils LV 17 Mh34
Beşağil TR 51 Mo53
Besakih RI 129 Qh50
Besalampy RM 220 Nc54
Besalú E 30 Lc48
Besançon F 23 Lg43
Besani IND (MPH) 109 Pa33
Bešankovičy BY 52 Me18
Besar MAL 117 Qb44
Besar MAL 117 Qc44
Besar RI 129 Rb50
Besar, Gunung RI 128 Qg48
Besa River CDN 231 Dj17
Besassi DY 186 Lb40
Beschoky tau KZ 71 Ng23
Besedino RUS 53 Mj20
Besenyszög H 39 Ma43
Beshahr IR 72 Ng27
Besham PK 79 Og28
Beshariq UZ 76 Of25
Beshkent UZ 76 Oc26
Beshneh IR 74 Nh31
Beshtom UZ 71 Oa24
Besikama RI 132 Rc50
Besir RI 130 Rf46
Beskid Mountains PL/SK 39 Mb41
Beskid Wysoki PL 39 Lu41
Beşkonak TR 51 Mm53
Beslan RUS (SOA) 70 Nc24
Besnard Lake CDN 233 Eh18
Besni TR 63 Mj27
Bessa Monteiro ANG 202 Lg49
Béssao TCH 195 Lh42
Bessarabia MD 54 Me22
Bessaz tau KZ 76 Oe24
Bessèges F 25 Le46
Bessemer USA (AL) 248 Fg29
Bessoung Kang CAM 194 Le43
Best NL 32 Lf39
Bestavarapeta IND (APH) 111 Ok39
Bestwig D 32 Lj39
Besuki RI 128 Qg49
Beswick AUS (NT) 139 Rg53
Beswick A.L. AUS 139 Rg53
Beta IND (BIH) 109 Pb33
Betafo RM 220 Nd55
Betalevana RM 220 Ne54
Betanantanana RM 220 Nc55
Betancuria E 178 Kc31
Betânia BR (MT) 280 Gk53
Betânia BR (PE) 283 Ja50
Betania CO 268 Gd43
Betânia, T.I. BR 273 Gf47
Betanty RM 220 Nc58
Betanzos BOL 284 Gh55
Betanzos E 26 Km53
Betarara VU 162 Te53
Bétaré Oya CAM 195 Lh43
Betatakin Ruin USA 237 Ee27
Betbulak KZ 84 Oe21
Bete Hor ETH 198 Mk40
Betein WAN 194 Le43
Bétera E 29 Ku49
Betera E 29 Ks50
Bethal ZA 217 Me59
Bethanie NAM 216 Lj59
Bethany USA (MO) 241 Fc25
Bethel USA (AK) 228 Bk15
Bethel USA (OK) 243 Fc28
Bethlehem IL 64 Mh30
Bethlehem ZA 217 Me60
Bethulie ZA 217 Mc61
Béthune F 23 Lc40
Betim BR (MG) 287 Hh55
Betioky RM 220 Nc57
Betita DZ 174 Ld28
Betong MAL 126 Qf45
Betong THA 117 Qa43
Betoota AUS (QLD) 150 Sa58
Beto Shet ETH 198 Mk40
Bétou RCB 200 Lk44
Betpak Dala KZ 58 Ob09
Betrandraka RM 220 Nd54
Betroka RM 220 Nd57
Betsaa RB 213 Mb55
Bet Shean IL 64 Mh29
Betsiaka RM 219 Ne52
Betsiboka RM 220 Nd54
Betsy Bay BS 251 Gd34
Bettiah IND (BIH) 107 Pc32
Bettié CI 193 Kj42
Bettiesdam ZA 217 Me59
Bettles USA (AK) 229 Ce12
Bettioua DZ 173 Kk28
Bettna S 13 Lr32
Bèttola I 40 Lk46
Betton F 22 Kt42
Bettyhill GB 19 Kq32
Betul IND (MPH) 109 Oj35
Betulia CO 268 Gd42
Betung RI 125 Qc47
Betwa IND 109 Ok33
Betws-y-Coed GB 20 Kr37
Betzdorf D 32 Lh40
Béu ANG 202 Lh49
Beulah AUS (VIC) 152 Sb63
Beulah USA (MI) 246 Fg23
Beulah USA (ND) 240 Ek22
Beulaville USA (NC) 249 Gb28
Beurfou TCH 187 Lh38
Beurkia TCH 187 Lj38
Beurkié TCH 188 Lj36
Bevato RM 220 Nd55
Bevelli TR 50 Mk52
Beveren B 23 Le39
Beveridge Reef NZ 164 Bg56
Beverley AUS (WA) 144 Qj62
Beverley GB 21 Ku37
Beverly CDN (SK) 233 Ef20
Beverly Hills USA (FL) 250 Fj31
Beverly Springs AUS (WA) 138 Rc54
Beverstedt D 32 Lj37
Beverungen D 32 Lk39
Bevoalavo Andrefana RM 220 Nc58
Bevoay RM 220 Nb56
Bewani PNG 158 Sa47
Bewar IND (UPH) 107 Ok32
Bewar IND (UPH) 107 Ok33
Beyağaç TR 50 Mj53
Beyazçeşme Şelâlesi TR 63 Nb26
Beyçayırı TR 50 Mg50
Beydağ TR 50 Mj52
Bey Dağları TR 51 Ml54
Beydili TR 51 Ml50
Beykoz TR 50 Mk49
Beyla RG 192 Kf41
Beylaqan AZ 70 Nd26
Beylikova TR 51 Mm51
Beylul ER 191 Nb40
Beyoneisu-retsugan J 101 Rk30
Beypazarı TR 51 Mm50
Beypore IND (KER) 110 Oh41
Beyra SP 199 Nd42
Beyşehir TR 51 Mm53
Beyşehir Gölü TR 51 Mm53
Beytüşşebap TR 63 Nb27
Beyyurdu TR 51 Mq51
Bezaha RM 220 Nc57
Bežanickaja vozvyšennost' RUS 52 Me17
Bežanicy RUS 52 Me17
Bezanson CDN (AB) 233 Ea18
Bezas E 29 Kt50
Bezdan SCG 44 Lt45
Bežeck RUS 52 Mj17
Bežeckij verhnij RUS 52 Mj17
Bezeklik Qianfo Dong CHN 87 Pe24
Bezenčuk RUS 53 Ne19
Bezerros BR (PE) 283 Jc50
Béziers F 25 Ld47
Bez'va RUS 16 Mj32
Bhabbar IND (GUJ) 108 Of33
Bhabua IND (BIH) 109 Pb33
Bhadar IND 108 Of35
Bhadasar IND (RJT) 106 Oh31
Bhadora IND (MPH) 109 Pa34
Bhadra IND (RJT) 106 Oh31
Bhadrachalam IND (APH) 109 Pa37
Bhadrakh IND (ORS) 112 Pd35
Bhadrapur NEP 88 Pe32
Bhadra Reservoir IND 110 Oh40
Bhadravati IND (KTK) 110 Oh40
Bhadra W.S. IND 110 Oh40
Bhadreswar IND (WBG) 112 Pe34
Bhag PK 80 Od31
Bhagalpur IND (BIH) 112 Pd33
Bhagamandala IND (KTK) 110 Oh40
Bhagirafi IND 107 Ok30
Bhaguapura IND (MPH) 107 Ok32
Bhainsrorgarh IND 106 Oh33
Bhai Pheru PK 79 Og30
Bhairab Bazar BD 112 Pf33
Bhairamgarh IND (CGH) 109 Pa36
Bhairi Hol PK 80 Oc33
Bhaisa IND (APH) 108 Oj36
Bhakarapeta IND (APH) 111 Ok40
Bhakkar PK 79 Of30
Bhaktapur NEP 88 Pc32
Bhalki IND (KTK) 108 Oj37
Bhaluka BD 112 Pf33
Bhalwal PK 79 Og29
Bhamo MYA 113 Pj33
Bhanbore PK 80 Od33
Bhandara IND (MHT) 109 Ok35
Bhandari IND (NGL) 112 Ph32
Bhandarwah 79 Oh29
Bhander IND (MPH) 107 Ok33
Bhanga BD 112 Pf34
Bhanjanagar IND (ORS) 109 Pc36
Bhanpura IND (MPH) 108 Oj33
Bhanupratappur IND (CGH) 109 Pa35
Bhaptiahi IND (BIH) 112 Pd32
Bharatpur IND (RJT) 107 Oj32
Bharatpur NEP 88 Pc32
Bharatpur National Park = Keoladeo National Park IND 107 Oj32
Bharda NEP 88 Pd32
Bharthana IND (UPH) 107 Ok32
Bharuch IND (GUJ) 108 Og35
Bhata NEP 88 Pc32
Bhatagli IND (MHT) 108 Oj36
Bhatapara IND (CGH) 109 Pa35
Bhatgaon IND (CGH) 109 Pb35
Bhatiapara BD 112 Pe34
Bhatkal IND (KTK) 110 Oh40
Bhattiprolu IND (APH) 109 Pa37
Bhaun PK 79 Og29
Bhavani IND (TNU) 111 Oj41
Bhavnagar IND (GUJ) 108 Og35
Bhawal N.P. BD 112 Pf33
Bhawana PK 79 Og30
Bhawanipatna IND (ORS) 109 Pb36
Bhawra IND (MPH) 108 Oj34
Bheemunipatnam IND (APH) 109 Pb37
Bheemunipatnam Beach IND 109 Pb37
Bhelsi IND (MPH) 109 Ok33
Bhera PK 79 Og29
Bherdaghat Marble Rocks IND 109 Ok34
Bheri NEP 88 Pa31
Bheri River Rafting NEP 88 Pb31
Bhigvan IND (MHT) 108 Oh36
Bhikamkor IND (RJT) 106 Og32
Bhilai IND (CGH) 109 Pa35
Bhilwara IND (RJT) 106 Oh33
Bhim IND (RJT) 106 Oh33
Bhima IND 108 Oj37
Bhimavaram IND (APH) 109 Pa37
Bhimbar PK 79 Oh29
Bhimbetka IND 108 Oj34
Bhimpur IND (MPH) 108 Oj35
Bhind IND (MPH) 107 Ok32
Bhinmal IND (RJT) 106 Og33
Bhisi IND (MHT) 109 Ok35
Bhita IND 109 Pa33
Bhitarkanika Sanctuary IND 109 Pd35
Bhitarwar IND (MPH) 107 Ok33
Bhiwandi IND (MHT) 108 Og36
Bhiwani IND (HYA) 106 Oj31
Bhognipur IND (UPH) 107 Ok32
Bhojpur IND (ORS) 109 Pc35
Bhojpur IND 109 Oj34
Bhokar IND (MHT) 108 Oj36
Bhola BD 112 Pf34
Bholari PK 80 Oe33
Bhongaon IND (UPH) 107 Ok32
Bhongir IND (APH) 109 Ok37
Bhopal IND (MPH) 108 Oj34
Bhopalpatnam IND (CGH) 109 Pa36
Bhoramdeo IND (CGH) 109 Pa34
Bhore IND (BIH) 107 Pc32
Bhorvadi IND (MHT) 108 Oh36
Bhuban IND (ORS) 109 Pc35
Bhubaneswar IND (ORS) 109 Pc35
Bhuj IND (GUJ) 108 Oe34
Bhusawal IND (MHT) 108 Oh35
Bhutan BHT 104 Pb13
Biá BR 273 Gg48
Bia CI 193 Kj43
Biabo PE 278 Gb49
Biadola IND (WBG) 112 Pe33
Biafra WAN 194 Le43
Biak RI 127 Rb46
Biak RI 131 Rj46
Biak RI 131 Rj46
Biak Utara Nature Reserve RI 131 Rh46
Biała Piska PL 37 Mc37
Biała Podlaska PL 37 Md38
Białka PL 39 Ma41
Białobrzegi PL 37 Ma39
Białobrzegi PL 37 Mc40
Białogard PL 36 Lq36
Białopole PL 37 Md40
Białowieski P.N. PL 37 Md37
Białowieża PL 37 Md38
Biały Bór PL 36 Lr37
Białystok PL 37 Md37
Bian RI 158 Sa49
Bianco I 43 Lr52
Bianga RCA 200 Ma43
Biankouma CI 192 Kg42
Bia N.P. GH 193 Kj42
Biaora IND (MPH) 108 Oj34
Biaranga RDC 200 Lk46
Biaro RDC 201 Mc45
Biaro RI 130 Rc44
Biarritz F 24 Kt47
Biasca CH 34 Lj44
Biawak MAL 126 Qe45
Bibā ET 177 Mf31
Biba RI 125 Qc48
Bibai J 99 Sa24
Bibala ANG 208 Lg53
Bibas G 195 Lf45
Bibbiena I 40 Lm47
Bibé CAM 195 Lg43
Bibémi CAM 187 Lg41
Biberach D 34 Lk42
Bibiani GH 193 Kj42
Bibi-Jawindi Mausoleum PK 81 Of31
Bibikovo RUS 98 Rd20
Bibile CL 111 Pa43
Bibi Nani PK 80 Od31
Biboohra AUS (QLD) 149 Sc54
Bibora G 202 Lf47
Bibrka UA 39 Me41
Bicade F 271 Hd44
Bicaj AL 46 Ma49
Bicanak asr. ARM/AZ 70 Nc26
Bicas BR (MG) 287 Hj56
Bicaz RO 45 Mg44
Bicaz-Chei RO 45 Mf44
Biçer TR 51 Mm51
Bicester GB 21 Kt39
Bičevaja RUS 98 Rh22
Bichena ETH 198 Mk40
Bicheng CHN (CGQ) 95 Qd31
Bicheno AUS (TAS) 152 Se66
Bichhia IND (MPH) 109 Pa34
Bichhua IND (MPH) 109 Ok35
Bichi WAN 186 Le39
Bickerton Island AUS 139 Rj52
Bicol N.P. RP 121 Rb39
Bicske H 38 Lt43
Bicuar, P.N. do ANG 208 Lh53
Bičura RUS (BUR) 90 Qd20
Bid IND (MHT) 108 Oh36
Bida WAN 186 Ld41
Bida WAN 187 Lg39
Bidar IND (KTK) 108 Oj37
Bidar Fort IND 108 Oj37
Bidbid OM 75 Nk34
Bidde SP 205 Nb45
Biddeford USA (ME) 247 Ge24
Biddle USA (MT) 235 Eh23
Bideford GB 20 Kq39
Bidgemia AUS (WA) 140 Qh58
Bidokht IR 73 Nk28
Bidon V DZ 180 La34
Bidor MAL 117 Qa43
Bidukbiduk RI 127 Qk45
Bidžan RUS (YAO) 98 Rf22
Bie S 13 Lr31
Biebrzański Park Narodowy PL 37 Mc37
Biecz PL 39 Mb41
Biedenkopf D 32 Lj40
Biéha BF 193 Kk40
Biei J 99 Sb24
Biel = Bienne CH 34 Lh43
Biel E 27 Ku52
Bielawa PL 36 Lr40
Bielefeld D 32 Lj38
Bieler See CH 34 Lh43
Bielice PL 37 Lu37
Biella I 40 Lj45
Biélou CI 193 Kg41
Bielsa E 30 La48
Bielsk PL 37 Lu38
Bielsko-Biała PL 39 Lu41
Bielsk Podlaski PL 37 Md38
Bienenbüttel D 33 Ll37
Bienfait CDN (SK) 238 Ej21
Bienge RDC 203 Ma48
Bien Hoa VN 115 Qd40
Bieniów PL 36 Lq39
Bienne = Biel CH 34 Lh43
Bierbank AUS (QLD) 151 Sc59
Bierdzany PL 36 Lt40
Biertan RO 44 Me44
Bierutów PL 36 Ls39
Biescas E 27 Ku52
Biese D 33 Lm38
Biesiekierz PL 36 Lr36
Biesiesvlei ZA 217 Mc59
Bieszczady PL 39 Mc41
Bieszczadzki P.N. PL 39 Mc41
Bièvre B 23 Lf41
Bieżuń PL 37 Lu38
Biferno I 42 Lp49
Bifoulé CAM 195 Lg43
Bifoun G 194 Lf46
Bifuka J 99 Sb23
Biga TR 50 Mh50
Bigadiç TR 50 Mj51
Big Ambergris Cay GB 251 Ge35
Bigand RA (SF) 289 Gk62
Biga Yarımadası TR 50 Mg50
Big Baldy USA 235 Ec23
Big Bay VU 162 Td53
Big Bear Creek CDN (BC) 232 Dj20
Big Beaver CDN (SK) 233 Eh21
Big Belt Mts. USA 235 Ee22
Big Bend SD 217 Mf59
Big Bend N.P. USA 237 Ej31
Big Branch Marsh N.W.R. USA 243 Fe30
Big Creek CDN (BC) 232 Dj20
Big Creek USA (ID) 235 Ec23
Big Cypress Seminole Ind. Res. USA 250 Fk32
Big Desert AUS 152 Sa63
Big Desert Wilderness Park AUS 152 Sa63
Bigene GNB 183 Kc39
Big Falls USA (MN) 238 Fd21
Bigfork USA (MT) 233 Ec21
Biggar CDN (SK) 233 Eg19
Biggar GB 19 Kr35
Bigge Island AUS 138 Rc53
Biggenden AUS (QLD) 151 Sg58
Biggleswade GB 21 Ku38
Big Hole ZA 217 Mc60
Big Hole Nat. Battlefield USA 235 Ed23
Bighorn USA (MT) 235 Eg22
Bighorn Basin USA 235 Ef23
Bighorn Canyon N.R.A. USA 235 Ef23
Bighorn Mountains USA 235 Eg23
Bight of Bangkok T 114 Qa39
Bight of Benin 194 Lb43
Bight of Biafra 194 Ld43
Bigi Polka SME 271 Hc43
Big Island CDN 238 Fc21
Big Kalzas Lake CDN 231 Dc14
Big Koniuji Island USA 228 Ca18
Big Lagoon Z 210 Mg52
Big Lake USA (TX) 242 Ek30
Big Lake Ranch CDN (BC) 232 Dk19
Big Lost USA 235 Ed24
Big Mossy Pt. CDN 238 Fa19
Bignona SN 183 Kb39
Bigo Bya Mugyenyi EAU 204 Mf45
Bigoray River CDN 233 Ec19
Big Pine USA (CA) 234 Ea27
Big Pine USA (FL) 250 Fk33
Big Piney USA (WY) 235 Ee24
Big Pond CDN (NS) 245 Gk23
Big Rapids USA (MI) 246 Fh24
Big Red Lighthouse USA 246 Fg24
Big River CDN (SK) 233 Eg19
Big River CDN 233 Eg19
Big River CDN 239 Cc14
Big River Ind. Res. CDN 233 Eg19
Big River Roadhouse USA (AK) 229 Cc14
Big Rock USA (CA) 236 Eb29
Big Salmon Range CDN 231 Dd15
Big Salmon River CDN 231 Dc15
Big Sand Lake CDN 238 Fa17
Big Sandy USA (MT) 233 Ee21
Big Sandy USA (WY) 235 Ef24
Big Sandy Lake CDN 233 Eh18
Big Sky USA (MT) 235 Ee23
Big Smokey Valley USA 234 Eb26
Big Snow Mtn. USA 235 Ef22
Big South Fork Nat. River and Rec. Area USA 249 Fh27
Big Spring USA (TX) 242 Ek29
Big Stone CDN (AB) 233 Ee20
Bigstone Lake CDN 238 Fb19
Big Stone N.W.R. USA 241 Fb23
Big Sur USA (CA) 236 Dk27
Big Timber USA (MT) 235 Ef23
Big Trails USA (WY) 235 Eg24
Big Trout Lake CDN (ON) 239 Ff19
Big Trout Lake CDN 239 Fe19
Big Trout Lake Indian Reserve CDN 239 Ff19
Biguaçu BR (SC) 291 Hf59
Big Water USA (UT) 237 Ee27
Big Willow River CDN 239 Fj19
Big Wood Cay BS 251 Gb33
Bihać BIH 41 Lq46
Bihar IND 104 Pb13
Biharamulo EAT 206 Mf47
Biharamulo Game Reserve EAT 206 Mf47
Biharia RO 44 Mb43
Bihariganj IND (BIH) 112 Pd33
Biharkeresztes H 39 Mb43
Biharnagybajom H 39 Mb43
Bihar Sharif IND (BIH) 109 Pc33
Bihé Plateau ANG 208 Lj52
Bihireşti RO 45 Mh44
Bihoro J 99 Sc24
Bihoua RCB 202 Lg47
Bihpur IND (BIH) 112 Pd33
Bija RUS 85 Pd20
Bijainagar IND (RJT) 106 Oh33
Bijaipur IND (MPH) 107 Oj32
Bijapur IND (CGH) 109 Pa36
Bijapur IND (KTK) 108 Oh37
Bijapur IND (ORS) 109 Pb36
Bijar IR 72 Nd28
Bijawar IND (MPH) 109 Ok33
Bijbehara 79 Oh29
Bijeljina BIH 44 Lu46
Bijelo Polje SCG 46 Lu47
Bij-Hem = Bol'šoj Enisej RUS 85 Ph19
Bijie CHN (GZH) 96 Qc32
Bijlik Lake KZ 76 Of24
Bijnapalli IND (APH) 108 Ok37
Bijnor IND (UPH) 107 Ok31
Bijoutier SY 219 Ng49
Bijsk RUS 58 Pb08
Bikaner IND (RJT) 106 Og31
Bikapur IND (UPH) 107 Pb32
Bikar Atoll MH 157 Tc16
Bikin RUS 98 Rh22
Bikin RUS 98 Rh22
Bikini Atoll MH 157 Tb16
Bikita ZW 214 Mf56
Bikok CAM 195 Lf44
Bikori SUD 197 Mh40
Bikoro RDC 200 Lk46
Bikou CHN (GSU) 95 Qc29
Bikramganj IND (BIH) 109 Pc33
Bikubiti LAR/TCH 176 Lk34
Bikumpur IND (RJT) 106 Og32
Bila RI 116 Qa44
Bila Cerkva UA 54 Mf21
Bilad Bani Bu Ali OM 75 Nk34
Bilad Bani Bu Hasan OM 75 Nk34

Boumerdès – Buenavista de Valdavia

Boumerdès DZ 173 Lb27
Bou Mertala RIM 178 Kf35
Boumia MA 172 Kh29
Boum Kabir TCH 196 Lk40
Bou Mréga RIM 183 Ke37
Bouna CI 193 Kj41
Bounafla CI 193 Kh42
Boû Nâga RIM 183 Kd36
Boû Nâga RMM 185 Kj36
Bouna River PNG 159 Se51
Boundary CDN (BC) 231 De17
Boundary Bend AUS (VIC) 153 Sb63
Boundary Mts. USA 244 Ge23
Boundary Peak USA 234 Ea27
Boundary Range CDN 231 Df18
Boundiali CI 192 Kg41
Boundioba RMM 192 Kg40
Boundji G 195 Lg46
Boundji RCB 202 Lh46
Boundjiguiré RMM 184 Kg38
Boundouki BF 193 Kj40
Boungou RCA 196 Mb41
Boungu RCA 196 Mb42
Bounkiling SN 183 Kc39
Bountiful USA (UT) 235 Ee25
Bountiful Islands AUS (QLD) 148 Rk54
Bounty Islands 134 Tb14
Bounty Trough 134 Tb14
Bouquet RA (SF) 289 Gk62
Boura BF 193 Kj40
Boura RMM 184 Kh39
Bourail F 162 Tc56
Bourbon-Lancy F 25 Ld44
Bourbon-l'Archambault F 25 Ld44
Bourbonne-les-Bains F 23 Lf43
Bourbriac F 22 Kr42
Bourdeaux F 25 Lf46
Boureïmi RN 185 Lb39
Bourem RMM 185 Kk37
Bourem-Inali RMM 185 Kj37
Bourganeuf F 24 Lb45
Bourg-Argental F 25 Le45
Bourg-en-Bresse F 25 Lf44
Bourges F 23 Lc43
Bourg-et-Comin F 23 Ld41
Bourg-Madame F 24 Lb48
Bourgneuf-en-Retz F 22 Kt43
Bourgoin-Jallieu F 25 Lf45
Bourg-Saint-Andéol F 25 Le46
Bourg-Saint-Maurice F 25 Lg45
Boû Rjeimât RIM 183 Kc36
Bourke AUS (NSW) 151 Sc61
Bournda N.P. AUS (NSW) 153 Se64
Bournemouth GB 21 Kt40
Bourou TCH 187 Lj41
Bouroum BF 185 Kk39
Bouroum-Bouroum BF 193 Kj40
Bourrah CAM 187 Lg40
Bourscheid L 23 Lg41
Bourzanga BF 185 Kk39
Bou Saada DZ 173 Lc28
Bou Salem TN 174 Le27
Bouse USA (AZ) 236 Ed29
Bou Sfer DZ 173 Kk28
Boussac F 24 Lc44
Boussé BF 185 Kk39
Boussens F 24 La47
Bousso TCH 187 Lj40
Boussou BF 185 Kj39
Boussouma BF 185 Kk39
Boutilimit RIM 183 Kc37
Boutiller RH 260 Gd36
Boutougou Fara SN 183 Kd39
Bouvet Island 262 La15
Bouxwiller F 23 Lh42
Bouza RN 186 Ld38
Bouzghaïa DZ 173 La27
Bovalino Marina I 43 Lr52
Bova Marina I 43 Lq53
Bovbjerg Fyr DK 14 Lj34
Bovenden D 32 Lk39
Boves F 23 Lc41
Bovino I 42 Lq49
Bovril RA (ER) 289 Ha61
Bowa Falls ZA 217 Md62
Bowbells USA (ND) 238 Ej21
Bowdle USA (SD) 240 Fa23
Bowdon USA (GA) 249 Fh29
Bowen AUS (QLD) 149 Se56
Bowen RA (MD) 288 Gg63
Bowen River AUS (QLD) 149 Sd56
Bowerville AUS (QLD) 151 Sf59
Bowes GB 21 Kt36
Bowie USA (TX) 243 Fb29
Bow Island CDN (AB) 233 Ee21
Bowling Green USA (KY) 248 Fg27
Bowling Green USA (MO) 241 Fe26
Bowling Green USA (OH) 246 Fj25
Bowling Green Bay AUS (QLD) 149 Sd55
Bowling Green Bay N.P. AUS (QLD) 149 Sd55
Bowman USA (ND) 240 Ej22
Bowmore GB 18 Ko35
Bowning AUS (NSW) 153 Se63
Bowraville AUS (NSW) 151 Sg61
Bow River CDN 233 Ed20
Bowron Lake Prov. Park CDN 232 Dk19
Bowser CDN (BC) 232 Dh21
Bowthorn AUS (QLD) 148 Rk55
Bowwood Z 210 Md54
Boxberg D 33 Lp39
Boxholm S 15 Lq32
Boxmeer NL 32 Lg39
Boxtel NL 32 Lf39
Boxwood Hill AUS (WA) 144 Qk63
Boyabat TR 62 Mh25
Boyabo RDC 200 Lk44
Boyaca CO 268 Gd43
Bo Yai Hot Spring LAO 115 Qb36
Boyakro CI 193 Kh42
Boyalı TR 51 Mo49
Boyalı TR 51 Mo52
Boyalıca TR 50 Mk50
Boyang CHN (JGX) 102 Qj31
Boyellé RCB 200 Lk44
Boyle CDN (AB) 233 Ed18
Boyle IRL 18 Km37
Boylston CDN (NS) 245 Gk23
Boymurot UZ 76 Od25
Boyne IRL 20 Ko37
Boyne ZA 214 Me57
Boyne City USA (MI) 246 Fh23
Boyo RI 124 Pk46
Boyolali RI 128 Qf49
Boysen Res. USA 235 Ef24
Boysun UZ 76 Od26
Boyuibe BOL 285 Gj56
Boyup Brook AUS (WA) 144 Qj62
Boyuyo BOL 279 Gf51
Boza EAT 207 Mk48
Boza EAT 207 Mk49
Bozan TR 50 Mk53
Bozanbai KZ 85 Pb21
Bozashchy tübegi KZ 70 Nf23
Božava HR 41 Lp46
Bozburun TR 49 Mj54
Bozburun Yarımadası TR 49 Mj54
Bozcaada TR 50 Mg51
Bozcaada TR 50 Mg51
Boz Dağları TR 49 Mh52
Bozdoğan TR 50 Mj53
Bozeman USA (MT) 235 Ee23
Bozen = Bolzano I 40 Lm44
Bozene RDC 200 Lk44
Bozhou CHN (AHU) 102 Qh29
Bozi CHN (SCH) 94 Qa30
Bozier TR 50 Mh50
Bozioru RO 45 Mg45
Bozkır TR 51 Mn53
Bozkır TR 51 Mo50
Bozköl KZ 71 Oa23
Bozkurt TR 50 Mk53
Bozoi KZ 71 Nk22
Bozok Yaylası TR 51 Mq51
Bozouls F 25 Lc46
Bozoum RCA 195 Lj42
Bozova TR 51 Mi53
Bozova TR 63 Mk27
Bozovici RO 44 Mb46
Boztepe TR 51 Mp51
Boztepe TR 51 Mq50
Bozüyük TR 50 Ml51
Bozyaka TR 50 Mk53
Bozyazı TR 51 Mn54
Bozyazı TR 62 Mg27
Bózzolo I 40 Ll45
Bra I 40 Lh46
Braås S 15 Lq33
Brabova RO 44 Md46
Brač HR 41 Lr47
Bracciano I 42 Ln48
Bracebridge CDN (ON) 247 Ga23
Brachlewo PL 36 Lt37
Bräcke S 13 Lq28
Brackettville USA (TX) 242 Ek31
Brackley GB 21 Kt38
Bracknell GB 21 Ku39
Braço do Norte BR (SC) 291 Hf60
Braço Menor do Araguaia ou Jauaés BR 281 He51
Brad RO 44 Mc44
Brádano I 43 Lr50
Brădeni RO 45 Me44
Bradenton USA (FL) 250 Fj32
Bradford GB 21 Kt37
Bradford USA (PA) 247 Ga25
Bradley USA (CA) 236 Dk28
Bradley Reef SOL 161 Ta49
Bradleyville USA (MO) 243 Fd27
Brady USA (TX) 242 Fa30
Brae GB 19 Kt30
Brædstrup DK 14 Lk35
Braemar AUS (SA) 152 Rk62
Braemar GB 19 Kr33
Braga P 26 Km51
Bragadiru RO 45 Mf46
Bragado RA (BA) 289 Gk63
Bragança BR (PA) 276 Hg46
Bragança P 26 Ko51
Bragança Paulista BR (SP) 287 Hg57
Braggs USA (AL) 248 Fg29
Brahestadt FIN 11 Mc13
Brahim RI 126 Qh45
Brahmanbaria BD 112 Pf34
Brahmapari IND (MHT) 109 Ok35
Brahmaputra IND 112 Pg32
Brahmour IND (HPH) 107 Oj29
Braidwood AUS (NSW) 153 Se63
Brăila RO 45 Mh45
Braine F 23 Ld41
Brainerd USA (MN) 241 Fc22
Braintree GB 21 La39
Brak ZA 214 Me57
Brakas RI 129 Qh49
Brake D 32 Lj37
Brakel D 32 Lk39
Brakmakund IND (ARP) 113 Pj32
Brakspruit ZA 217 Md59
Brakwater NAM 212 Lj57
Brålanda S 12 Ln32
Brálos GR 48 Mc52
Bramming DK 14 Lj35
Brämön S 13 Ls28
Brampton CDN (ON) 247 Ga24
Brampton GB 19 Ks36
Brampton Island AUS 149 Se56
Bramsche D 32 Lj38
Bramsöfjärden S 13 Ls30
Bramwell AUS (QLD) 146 Sb52
Bran RO 45 Mf45
Branäs S 13 Ln30
Brancaleone Marina I 43 Lr53
Branch CDN (NF) 245 Hd22
Branchville USA (SC) 249 Fk29
Brandberg NAM 212 Lh56
Brandberg NAM 212 Lh56
Brandbu N 12 Ll30
Brande DK 14 Lk35
Brandenburg D 33 Ln38
Brandenburg D 33 Lo38
Brand-Erbisdorf D 33 Lo40
Brandfort ZA 217 Md60
Brandkop ZA 216 Lk61
Brandö FIN 13 Mb30
Brandö FIN 13 Mb30
Brandon CDN (MB) 238 Fa21
Brandon GB 21 La38
Brandon USA (FL) 250 Fj32
Brandon USA (MS) 243 Ff29
Brandon USA (SD) 241 Fb24
Brandon Bay IRL 20 Kk38
Brandon Head IRL 20 Kk38
Brandval N 12 Lm30
Brandvlei ZA 216 Ma61
Brandýs nad Labem-Stará Boleslav CZ 38 Lp40
Branford USA (FL) 250 Fj31
Braniewo PL 37 Lu36
Branitzer Park D 33 Lp39
Bränna S 12 Ln32
Bransan SN 183 Kd39
Bransby AUS (QLD) 150 Sa60
Bransfield Strait 296 Ha31
Brańsk PL 37 Mc38
Branson USA (MO) 243 Fd27
Brantford CDN (ON) 247 Fk24
Brantôme F 24 La45
Branxholme AUS (VIC) 152 Sa64
Braodview USA (MT) 235 Ef22
Brás BR (AM) 274 Ha46
Bras d'Or Lake CDN 245 Gk23
Brashears USA (AR) 243 Fd28
Brasil C 259 Gb35
Brasilândia BR (MS) 286 Hd56
Brasilândia de Minas BR (MG) 287 Hh54
Brasiléia BR (AC) 279 Gf51
Brasília BR (DF) 282 Hg53
Brasília de Minas BR (MG) 287 Hh54
Brasília, P.N. de BR 282 Hg53
Braslândia BR (DF) 282 Hf53
Braslav BY 17 Mh35
Braslav Lakes N.P. BY 17 Mh35
Brasnorte BR (MT) 280 Ha51
Brasópolis BR (MG) 287 Hh57
Brașov RO 45 Mf45
Brass WAN 194 Ld43
Brasschaat B 23 Le39
Brassey, Mount AUS 143 Rh57
Brasstown Bald USA 249 Fj28
Brastad S 12 Lm32
Brąszewice PL 36 Lt39
Brataj AL 46 Lu50
Bratca RO 44 Mc44
Bratislava SK 38 Ls42
Bratislavský hrad SK 38 Ls42
Bratovoești RO 44 Md46
Bratsk RUS 58 Qa07
Brats'ke UA 45 Mm43
Bratskoe-vodohranilišče RUS 58 Qa07
Brattfjället S 13 Ln29
Brattleboro USA (VT) 247 Gd24
Brattmon S 13 Ln30
Brattvåg N 12 Lg28
Bratul Borcea RO 45 Mh46
Bratul Chilia RO 45 Mk45
Bratul Sfântu Gheorghe RO 45 Mk45
Bratul Sulina RO 45 Mk45
Bratunac BIH 46 Lu46
Braulio Carrillo, P.N. CR 256 Fj40
Braunau A 35 Lo42
Braunfels D 32 Lj40
Braunlage D 33 Ll39
Braunschweig D 33 Ll38
Braunton GB 20 Kq39
Bråviken S 13 Lr32
Brawley USA (CA) 236 Ec29
Bray IRL 20 Ko37
Bray ZA 213 Mb58
Bray Head IRL 20 Kk39
Bray-sur-Seine F 23 Ld42
Bray-sur-Somme F 23 Lc41
Brazatortas E 28 Kq48
Brazeau, Mount CDN 232 Eb19
Brazeau River CDN 233 Eb19
Brazil 263 Ha10
Brazil Basin 265 Jb21
Brazilian Highlands BR 265 Hd22
Brazoria N.W.R. USA 243 Fc31
Brazos USA 243 Fb30
Brazo Sur del Rio RA 294 Ge71
Brazzaville RCB 202 Lh48
Brbinj HR 41 Lp46
Brčko BIH 44 Lt46
Brda PL 36 Ls37
Breadalbane AUS (QLD) 148 Rk57
Breaksea Sound NZ 155 Td68
Bream Bay NZ 154 Th63
Brea Pozo RA (SE) 288 Gj60
Breas PE 284 Ge58
Breaux Bridge USA (LA) 243 Fe30
Breaza RO 44 Me44
Breaza RO 45 Mf45
Brebes RI 128 Qe49
Brechen D 32 Lj40
Brechin GB 19 Ks34
Breckenridge USA (CO) 235 Eh26
Breckenridge USA (MN) 241 Fb22
Breckenridge USA (TX) 242 Fa29
Břeclav CZ 38 Lr42
Brecon GB 20 Kr39
Brecon Beacons N.P. GB 20 Kr39
Breda NL 32 Le39
Bredaryd S 15 Lo33
Bredasdorp ZA 216 Ma63
Bredbo AUS (NSW) 153 Se63
Bredstedt D 32 Lj36
Bree B 23 Lf39
Breede ZA 216 Ma63
Breeza Plains AUS (QLD) 147 Sc53
Bregalnica MK 46 Mb49
Bregenz A 34 Lk43
Bregovo BG 46 Mc46
Bréhal F 22 Kt42
Bréhat F 22 Ks42
Breiðafjörður IS 10 Jj13
Breiðdalsvík IS 10 Kd13
Breil-sur-Roya F 25 Lh47
Breisach D 34 Lh42
Breitbridge ZW 214 Mf57
Breivikbotn N 10 Mb10
Brejão da Caatinga BR (BA) 283 Hk51
Brejo BR (MA) 277 Hj47
Brejo da Madre de Deus BR (PE) 283 Jb50
Brejo da Onça BR (PI) 277 Hk48
Brejo de São Félix BR (MA) 276 Hj48
Brejo do Cruz BR (PB) 277 Jb49
Brejo Grande BR (SE) 283 Jb51
Brejolândia BR (BA) 282 Hj52
Brejo Santo BR (CE) 277 Ja49
Brejtovo RUS 52 Mj16
Brekken N 12 Lm28
Brekstad N 10 Le14
Brel's Tomb F 165 Da50
Bremangerlandet N 12 Le29
Brembo I 40 Lk45
Bremen D 32 Lj37
Bremen USA (ND) 240 Fa22
Bremer Bay AUS (WA) 144 Qk63
Bremerhaven D 32 Lj37
Bremer Island AUS 139 Rj52
Bremer Range AUS 144 Ra62
Bremerton USA (WA) 232 Dj22
Bremervörde D 32 Lk37
Brem-sur-Mer F 22 Kt44
Breň PL 36 Lq37
Brenes E 28 Kp47
Brenner A/I 35 Lm43
Breno I 40 Ll45
Brenta I 40 Ll44
Brenta I 40 Lm45
Brentley USA (AL) 248 Fg30
Brentwood USA (TN) 248 Fg27
Brep PK 79 Og27
Bréscia I 40 Ll45
Bressanone = Brixen I 40 Lm44
Bressay GB 19 Kt30
Bressuire F 22 Ku44
Brest BY 37 Md38
Brest F 22 Kq42
Brestovac SCG 46 Mc46
Brestovo BG 47 Me47
Bretaña PE 273 Gc48
Bretcu RO 45 Mg44
Bretenoux F 24 Lb46
Breteuil F 23 Lc41
Breteuil-sur-Iton F 22 La42
Breton N.W.R. USA 243 Ff31
Breton Sound USA 243 Ff31
Bretten D 34 Lj41
Breueh RI 116 Ph43
Breuil-Cervinia I 40 Lh45
Breuna D 32 Lk39
Brevard USA (NC) 249 Fj28
Breves BR (PA) 275 He46
Brewarrina AUS (NSW) 151 Sd60
Brewer USA (MA) 247 Gf23
Brewster USA (NE) 240 Fa25
Brewton USA (AL) 248 Fg30
Breynat CDN (AB) 233 Ed18
Breza BIH 41 Lt46
Brežice SLO 41 Lq45
Brezina DZ 173 La29
Breznik BG 46 Mc48
Brezno SK 39 Lu42
Brezoi RO 44 Me45
Brezovo BG 47 Mf48
Bria RCA 196 Ma42
Briançon F 25 Lg46
Briare F 23 Lc43
Bribbaree AUS (NSW) 153 Sd63
Bribie Island AUS 151 Sg59
Bribir HR 41 Lq47
Bribri CR 256 Fj41
Briceni MD 45 Mh42
Bricquebec F 22 Kt41
Bridge End IRL 18 Kn35
Bridge Lake CDN (BC) 232 Dk20
Bridgend GB 20 Kr39
Bridge Point BS 251 Gb33
Bridgeport USA (CA) 234 Ea26
Bridgeport USA (CT) 247 Gd25
Bridgeport USA (NE) 240 Ej25
Bridger USA (MT) 235 Ef23
Bridger Peak USA 235 Eg25
Bridgeton USA (NJ) 247 Gc26
Bridgetown AUS (WA) 144 Qj62
Bridgetown BDS 261 Ha39
Bridgetown CDN (NS) 245 Gh23
Bridgeville USA (CA) 234 Dj25
Bridgewater AUS (TAS) 152 Sd67
Bridgewater AUS (VIC) 152 Sa65
Bridgewater AUS (VIC) 153 Sb64
Bridgewater CDN (NS) 245 Gh23
Bridgewater ZA 214 Me57
Bridgnorth GB 21 Ks38
Bridgwater GB 20 Ks39
Bridlington GB 21 Ku36
Bridoire F 24 La46
Bridport AUS (TAS) 152 Sd66
Bridport GB 20 Ks40
Brie F 23 Ld42
Briec F 22 Kr42
Brie-Comte-Robert F 23 Lc42
Brienne-le-Château F 23 Le42
Brienz CH 34 Lj44
Brienzer See CH 34 Lj44
Brieville RM 220 Nd54
Briey F 23 Lf41
Brig CH 34 Lh44
Brigde River CDN 232 Dj20
Briggsdale USA (CO) 235 Eh25
Brigham City USA (UT) 235 Ee25
Bright AUS (VIC) 153 Sd64
Brighton GB 21 Ku40
Brighton USA (CO) 235 Eh26
Brighton Downs AUS (QLD) 148 Sa57
Brighton Seminole Ind. Res. USA 250 Fk32
Brignogan-Plages F 22 Kq42
Brignoles F 25 Lg47
Brihadisvara Temple IND 111 Ok41
Brihuega E 29 Ks50
Brijuni, N.P. HR 41 Lo46
Brikama WAG 183 Kb39
Briksdal N 12 Lg29
Brilhante BR 286 Hc56
Brilon D 32 Lj39
Brimnes N 12 Lg30
Brimstone Hill Fortress N.P. KNA 261 Gj37
Brindisi I 43 Ls50
Brinje HR 41 Lq46
Brinkley USA (AR) 243 Fe28
Brinkmann RA (CD) 289 Gj61
Brinkworth AUS (SA) 152 Rk62
Brinlack IRL 18 Km35
Brin-Navolok RUS 11 Na14
Brinnon USA (WA) 232 Dj22
Brintbodarna S 13 Lp30
Brionne F 22 La41
Brioude F 25 Ld45
Briouze F 22 Ku42
Brisbane AUS (QLD) 151 Sg59
Brisighella I 40 Lm46
Bristol CDN (NB) 244 Gg22
Bristol GB 21 Ks39
Bristol USA (CT) 247 Gd25
Bristol USA (VA) 249 Fj27
Bristol Bay USA 228 Ca17
Bristol Channel GB 20 Kr39
Bristow USA (OK) 243 Fb28
Britânia BR (GO) 281 He53
Britannia CDN (NF) 245 Hd21
British Columbia CDN 224 Dc07
British Virgin Islands USA 261 Gh36
Brito Godins ANG 202 Lj50
Brits ZA 213 Md58
Britstown ZA 216 Mb61
Brittany F 22 Kr43
Brittany F 22 Kr42
Brittingham MEX (DGO) 253 Ej33
Britton USA (SD) 240 Fb23
Brive-la-Gaillarde F 24 Lb45
Briviesca E 27 Kr52
Brixen = Bressanone I 40 Lm44
Brixham GB 20 Kr40
Brjanka UA 55 Mk21
Brjansk RUS 52 Mh19
Brjanskoe RUS 99 Sb22
Brjánslækur IS 10 Jj13
Brka BIH 44 Lt46
Brnaze HR 41 Lr47
Brno CZ 38 Lr41
Bro S 15 Lt33
Broach = Bharuch IND (GUJ) 108 Og35
Broad Arrow AUS (WA) 144 Ra61
Broad Bay GB 19 Ko32
Broadbent's Mission ZA 217 Mc59
Broadbent's Sending ZA 217 Mc59
Broadford GB 18 Kp33
Broad Law GB 19 Kr35
Broad Peak 79 Oj28
Broad Sound AUS 149 Se57
Broad Sound Channel AUS 149 Sf57
Broadsound Range AUS 149 Se57
Broadstairs GB 21 Lb39
Broadus USA (MT) 235 Eh23
Broadview CDN (SK) 238 Ej20
Broadview USA (NM) 237 Ej28
Brobo CI 193 Kh42
Broby S 15 Lp34
Brocěni LV 17 Mc34
Brochet CDN (MB) 238 Ek17
Brochów PL 37 Ma38
Brocken D 33 Ll39
Brockman, Mount AUS 140 Qj57
Brockton USA (MA) 247 Ge24
Brockton USA (MT) 233 Eh21
Brockville CDN (ON) 247 Gc23
Brockway USA (MT) 235 Eh22
Brockway USA (PA) 247 Ga25
Brod BIH 46 Lt47
Brod MK 46 Mb49
Brod MK 46 Mb50
Brodaiži LV 17 Mh34
Brodarevo SCG 46 Lu47
Brodce CZ 38 Lp40
Brodec'ke UA 54 Me21
Brodeur Peninsula CDN 225 Fc04
Brodick GB 18 Kp35
Brodie Castle GB 19 Kr33
Brodina de Jos RO 45 Mf43
Brodnica PL 37 Lu37
Brodowski BR (SP) 286 Hg56
Brody UA 37 Mf40
Brogan USA (OR) 234 Eb23
Brojce PL 36 Lq37
Broke Inlet AUS 144 Qj62
Broken Arrow USA (OK) 243 Fc27
Broken Bay AUS (NSW) 153 Sf62
Broken Bow USA (NE) 240 Fa25
Broken Bow USA (OK) 243 Fc28
Broken Head AUS 151 Sg60
Broken Hill AUS (NSW) 150 Sa61
Broken Ridge 301 Pb13
Broken Skull River CDN 231 Df14
Broken Water Bay PNG 159 Sc47
Brokind S 15 Lq32
Brokopondo SME 271 Hc43
Brokopondostuwmeer SME 271 Hc43
Brokoyo CI 192 Kg43
Bromaderry AUS (NSW) 153 Sf63
Bromarv FIN 16 Mc31
Bromby Islands AUS 139 Rj51
Brome D 33 Ll38
Brommö S 13 Lo32
Bromo, Gunung RI 128 Qg49
Bromölla S 15 Lp34
Bromo-Tengger-Semeru N.P. RI 128 Qg50
Brömsebro S 15 Lr34
Bromsgrove GB 21 Ks38
Bromyard GB 21 Ks38
Brønderslev DK 14 Lk33
Broni I 40 Lk45
Bronkhorstspruit ZA 213 Me58
Brønnøysund N 10 Lg13
Bronson USA (FL) 250 Fj31
Bronte I 42 Lp53
Bronte USA (TX) 242 Ek30
Brooke's Point RP 122 Qj41
Brookeville AUS (QLD) 149 Sd56
Brookfield USA (MO) 241 Fd26
Brookgreen Gardens USA 249 Ga29
Brookhaven USA (MS) 243 Fe30
Brookings USA (OR) 234 Dh24
Brookings USA (SD) 240 Fb23
Brooks CDN (AB) 233 Ee20
Brooks Aqueduct Prov. H.S. CDN 233 Ee20
Brooks Mtn. USA 229 Bg13
Brooks Nek ZA 217 Me61
Brooks Range USA 229 Cc11
Brooksville USA (FL) 250 Fj31
Brooksville USA (MS) 243 Ff29
Brookton AUS (WA) 144 Qj62
Broome AUS (WA) 138 Rb54
Broome Crocodile Park AUS 138 Rb54
Broomehill AUS (WA) 144 Qj62
Broons F 22 Ks42
Brora GB 19 Kr32
Brørup DK 14 Lk35
Brösarp S 15 Lp35
Broșteni RO 44 Mc46
Broszków PL 37 Mc38
Brotas BR (SP) 286 Hf57
Brotas de Macaúbas BR (BA) 283 Hj52
Brother Island ET 177 Mh33
Brothers USA (OR) 234 Dk24
Broto E 27 Ku52
Brottby S 13 Lt31
Brou F 22 Lb42
Brough GB 19 Ks36
Broughton-in-Furness GB 21 Kr36
Broughton Island CDN 232 Dg20
Broulee AUS (NSW) 153 Sf63
Broulkou TCH 188 Lk37
Broumov CZ 38 Lr40
Broutzéika GR 48 Mc53
Brouwershaven NL 32 Ld39
Brovary UA 54 Mf20
Brovinia AUS (QLD) 151 Sf58
Brovst DK 14 Lk33
Brown Bank 122 Qj40
Browne USA (AK) 229 Cf13
Brownfield USA (TX) 237 Ej29
Browning USA (MT) 233 Ed21
Browns USA (AL) 248 Fg29
Brown's Cay BS 251 Ga33
Brown Shoal 122 Qj40
Brown's Town JA 259 Gb36
Brownsville USA (KY) 248 Fg27
Brownsville USA (TN) 243 Ff28
Brownsville USA (TX) 253 Fb33
Brownsweg SME 271 Hc43
Brownwood USA (TX) 242 Fa30
Browse Island AUS 138 Rb53
Brozas E 28 Ko49
Bruay-la-Buissière F 23 Lc40
Bruce USA (MS) 243 Ff29
Bruce Crossing USA (MI) 246 Ff22
Bruce Highway AUS (QLD) 149 Sd55
Bruce, Mount AUS 140 Qk57
Bruce Peninsula N.P. CDN 246 Fk23
Bruce Rock AUS (WA) 144 Qk61
Bruchsal D 34 Lj41
Bruck A 35 Ln43
Bruck A 35 Ln41
Bruck an der Leitha A 35 Lr42
Bruck an der Mur A 35 Lq43
Brüel D 33 Lm37
Brugg CH 34 Lj43
Brugge B 23 Ld39
Bruheim N 12 Lh29
Bruja Beach MEX 252 Eg34
Brujas CO 273 Gf44
Brukkaros NAM 212 Lj58
Brukkaros NAM 212 Lk58
Bruksmiljö S 13 Lq31
Brûlon F 22 Ku43
Brumado BR (BA) 283 Hk53
Brumath F 23 Lh42
Brumby River AUS 140 Qk58
Brumov-Bylnice CZ 38 Lt41
Brumunddal N 12 Ll30
Brunchilly AUS (NT) 139 Rh55
Brundby DK 14 Ll35
Bruneau USA (ID) 234 Ec24
Bruneau USA 234 Ec24
Bruneck = Brunico I 40 Lm44
Brunei BRU 118 Qc17
Brunette Downs AUS (NT) 139 Rh55
Brunette Island CDN 245 Hb22
Brunflo S 10 Lh14
Bruni IND (ARP) 113 Pj31
Brunico = Bruneck I 40 Lm44
Brunsbüttel D 32 Lk37
Brunswick AUS (WA) 144 Qh62
Brunswick USA (GA) 249 Fk30
Brunswick USA (ME) 247 Ge24
Brunswick USA (OH) 246 Fk25
Brunswick Heads AUS (NSW) 151 Sg60
Brunswick Lake CDN 239 Fj21
Bruntál CZ 38 Ls41
Brunt Ice Shelf 296 Jd34
Brus SCG 46 Mb47
Brusarci BG 46 Md47
Brusett USA (MT) 235 Eg22
Brush USA (CO) 240 Ej25
Brus Laguna HN 256 Fh38
Brusque BR (SC) 291 Hf59
Brussel B 23 Le40
Brussels B 23 Le40
Brusselton AUS (WA) 144 Qh62
Brüssow D 33 Lp37
Brusturoasa RO 45 Mg44
Brusvino HR 41 Lq46
Bruxelles B 23 Le40
Bruyères F 23 Lg42
Bruz F 22 Kt42
Bruzaholm S 15 Lq33
Bruzual YV 269 Gf41
Brvenik SCG 46 Ma47
Brwinów PL 37 Ma38
Bryan USA (OH) 246 Fh25
Bryan USA (TX) 243 Fb30
Bryan Coast 296 Fd33
Bryan, Mount AUS 152 Rk62
Bryan's Corner USA (OK) 242 Ek27
Bryant USA (AR) 243 Fd28
Bryce Canyon N.P. USA 237 Ed27
Brynderwyn NZ 154 Th64
Bryne N 12 Lf32
Bryten ZA 217 Mf59
Brzeg PL 36 Ls40
Brzeg Dolny PL 36 Lr39
Brześć Kujawski PL 36 Lt38
Brzesko PL 39 Ma41
Brzeszcze PL 37 Lu40
Brzeszcze PL 39 Lu41
Brzeziny PL 37 Lu39
Brzostek PL 39 Mb41
Brzóza PL 37 Mb39
Brzozie Lubawskie PL 37 Lu37
Brzozów PL 39 Mc41
Bua FJI 163 Tk54
Bua SUD 196 Mc40
Bu'aale SP 205 Nb45
Bua Bay FJI 163 Tk54
Buafri GH 193 Kk41
Buaka GH 193 Kj42
Buala SOL 161 Sk50
Bualpui IND (MZR) 112 Pg33
Buan RI 126 Qe46
Bua River Z 210 Mg52
Buatan RI 124 Qa45
Bu Athlah LAR 175 Ma31
Buaya RI 125 Qc45
Bu'ayrat al Hasun LAR 175 Lh30
Buba GNB 183 Kc40
Buba RO 45 Mg45
Bubanda RDC 200 Lk43
Bubanza BU 206 Me47
Bubaque GNB 183 Kc40
Bubi ZW 213 Me55
Bubi ZW 214 Mf56
Bubiai LT 17 Md35
Bubiki EAT 206 Mg47
Bubiyan Island KWT 74 Ne31
Bubu EAT 204 Mh48
Bubuget RI 124 Qa47
Buburu RDC 200 Lk45
Bubus RI 125 Qc46
Buca FJI 163 Tk54
Buča UA 54 Mf20
Bučač UA 54 Mc21
Buçaco ANG 209 Ma51
Bucak TR 51 Ml53
Bucalemu RCH 288 Gd63
Bucaramanga CO 268 Gd42
Bucareli Bay USA 231 Dd18
Bucas Grande Island RP 123 Rd41
Bucasia AUS (QLD) 149 Se56
Buccaneer Archipelago AUS 138 Rb53
Buccaneer Beach USA 261 Gh37
Buccino I 42 Lq50
Bucegi, P.N. RO 45 Mf45
Bucerias MEX (NYT) 253 Eh35
Buceș RO 44 Mc44
Buchan AUS (VIC) 153 Se64
Buchanan LB 192 Ke43
Buchanan Highway AUS 139 Rf54
Buchan Gulf CDN 225 Gb04
Buchans CDN (NF) 245 Hb21
Bucharest RO 45 Mg46
Buchen D 34 Lk41
Buchholz D 32 Lk37
Buchloe D 35 Ll42
Buchs CH 34 Lk43
Buchwa ZW 214 Mf56
Buchy F 23 Lb41
Bučionys LT 17 Me35
Buciumi RO 44 Md43
Buckeye USA (AZ) 236 Ed29
Buckhannon USA (WV) 247 Fk26
Buckhaven GB 19 Kr34
Buckingham CDN (QC) 247 Gc23
Buckingham GB 21 Ku39
Buckingham USA (CO) 240 Ej25
Buckingham USA (VA) 249 Ga27
Buckingham Bay AUS 139 Rh52
Buckingham Downs AUS (QLD) 148 Rk57
Buck Island USA 261 Gh37
Buckland USA (AK) 229 Bk13
Buckland River USA 229 Bk13
Buckleboo AUS (SA) 152 Rj62
Buckley River AUS (QLD) 148 Rk56
Bucklige Welt A 35 Lq43
Bucklin USA (KS) 242 Fa27
Bucksport USA (MA) 247 Gf23
Buckwaroon AUS (NSW) 151 Sc61
Bučovice CZ 38 Lr41
Buco Zau ANG 202 Lg48
Bucșani RO 45 Mf46
București RO 45 Mg46
Bucyrus USA (OH) 246 Fj25
Buczek PL 37 Lu39
Bud N 10 Ld14
Budacu RO 45 Mf43
Budaka EAU 204 Mg45
Budalia AUS (QLD) 148 Rk57
Budalin MYA 113 Ph34
Bu Dang VN 115 Qd40
Budaörs H 39 Lt43
Budapest H 39 Lu43
Buðardalur IS 10 Jk13
Budaun IND (UPH) 107 Ok31
Budawang N.P. AUS 153 Sf63
Bud Bud SP 199 Nd43
Buddabuddah AUS (NSW) 151 Sd61
Budd Coast 297 Qc32
Buddha Mountain RC 97 Ra34
Buddha Park THA 115 Qc38
Buddhas of Bamian AFG 78 Od28
Buddhist Monastery IND 112 Pf32
Buddhist Temple PK 79 Oj28
Buddon Ness GB 19 Ks34
Buddusò I 31 Lk50
Bude GB 20 Kq40
Büdelsdorf D 32 Lk36
Budennovsk RUS 70 Nc23
Budești RO 44 Md43
Budești RO 44 Me45
Budești RO 45 Mg46
Budevo SCG 46 Ma47
Budgerygar AUS (QLD) 150 Sb58
Budgewoi AUS (NSW) 153 Sf62
Budibudi Islands PNG 160 Sg50
Buding RI 125 Qd47
Büdingen D 34 Lk40
Budjala RDC 200 Lk44
Budkhula ET 177 Me33
Budogošč' RUS 52 Mg16
Budongquan CHN (QHI) 89 Pg28
Búdrio I 40 Lm46
Budungbudung RI 127 Qk47
Budva SCG 46 Lt48
Budziszewice PL 37 Lu39
Budzyń PL 36 Lr38
Buéa CAM 194 Le43
Buëch F 25 Lf46
Buedu WAL 192 Ke41
Buefjorden N 12 Le29
Buela ANG 202 Lh48
Buena USA (WA) 232 Dk22
Buena Esperanza RA (SL) 288 Gh63
Buena Hora BOL 279 Gg52
Buenaventura C 259 Gb35
Buenaventura CO 268 Gb44
Buenaventura MEX (CHH) 237 Eg31
Buena Vista BOL 285 Gj54
Buena Vista BOL 279 Gg51
Buena Vista GCA 255 Ff37
Buenavista MEX (CHH) 252 Eg32
Buenavista MEX (SLP) 253 Ek34
Buenavista RP 123 Rb42
Buenavista RP 123 Rc41
Buena Vista USA (CO) 235 Eg26
Buena Vista USA (GA) 249 Fh29
Buena Vista USA (VA) 249 Ga27
Buena Vista YV 269 Gg42
Buena Vista YV 269 Gj41
Buena Vista YV 270 Gj41
Buenavista Alta PE 278 Ga50
Buenavista de Valdavia E 26 Kq52

Caramura Paraguassa, T.I. BR 283 Ja53
Caramut AUS (VIC) 152 Sb64
Caranavi BOL 279 Gg53
Carancho RA (LP) 292 Gh64
Carandai BR (MG) 287 Hj56
Carandazinho BR (MT) 285 Hb54
Carandotta AUS (QLD) 148 Rk56
Caranga de Abajo E 26 Ko53
Carangola BR (MG) 287 Hj56
Caransebeș RO 44 Mc45
Carantec F 22 Kr42
Carapa PE 279 Ge53
Carapa YV 270 Gj41
Carapajó BR (PA) 276 Hf47
Cara-Paraná CO 273 Gd46
Carapeguá PY 285 Hb58
Carapelle I 43 Lq49
Carapina BR (ES) 287 Hk56
Carapo YV 270 Gj43
Carare Puca BR (AM) 273 Gg45
Carate CR 256 Fj41
Caratinga BR (MG) 287 Hj55
Carauari BR (AM) 273 Gg48
Caraúbas BR (RN) 277 Jb48
Caravaca de la Cruz E 29 Kt48
Caravela GNB 183 Kb40
Caraveli PE 278 Gd53
Caraz PE 278 Gb50
Carazinho BR (RS) 290 Hd60
Carballiño E 26 Km52
Carballo E 26 Km53
Carberry CDN (MB) 238 Fa21
Carbine AUS (WA) 144 Ra61
Carbo MEX (SO) 237 Ee31
Carbondale USA (CO) 235 Eg26
Carbondale USA (IL) 243 Ff27
Carbondale USA (IN) 246 Fg25
Carbondale USA (PA) 247 Gc25
Carbonear CDN (NF) 245 Hd22
Carboneras E 29 Kt46
Carboneras MEX (TM) 253 Fb33
Carboneras de Guadazaón E 29 Kt49
Carbónia I 31 Lj51
Carbonita BR (MG) 287 Hj54
Carbonne F 24 Lb47
Carcajou River CDN 231 Dg13
Carcans F 24 Kt45
Carcans-Plage F 24 Kt45
Carcar RP 123 Rb40
Carcarañá RA 289 Gk62
Carcassonne F 24 Lc47
Carcastillo E 27 Kt52
Carcelén E 29 Kt49
Carcot Island 296 Ga32
Carcross CDN (YT) 231 Dc15
Çardak TR 50 Mk53
Cardal ROU 289 Hb63
Cardamom Mountains K 115 Qb39
Cardeal Mota BR (MG) 287 Hj55
Cardeña E 28 Kq48
Cárdenas C 258 Fk34
Cárdenas MEX (SLP) 253 Fa34
Cárdenas MEX (TB) 255 Fd37
Cardiff GB 20 Kr39
Cardigan GB 20 Kq38
Cardigan Bay GB 20 Kq38
Cardinal CDN (MB) 238 Fa21
Cardona E 30 Lb49
Cardona ROU 289 Hb62
Cardoso BR (SP) 286 Hf56
Cardwell AUS (QLD) 149 Sd55
Careen Lake CDN 233 Ef17
Carei RO 44 Mc43
Careiro BR (AM) 274 Gk47
Careiro da Várzea BR (AM) 274 Ha47
Carembei BR (PR) 286 He58
Carén RCH 288 Ge61
Carentan F 22 Kt41
Carevo BG 47 Mh48
Carev Vrh MK 46 Mc48
Carey USA (ID) 235 Ed24
Carey Downs AUS (WA) 140 Qh58
Carfield AUS (QLD) 149 Sc57
Cargados Carajos MS 221 Nk54
Cargèse F 31 Lj48
Carhaix-Plouguer F 22 Kr42
Carhuamayo PE 278 Gb51
Carhuanca PE 278 Gd52
Carhuas PE 278 Gb50
Carhué RA (BA) 293 Gj64
Caraiça BR 283 Ja51
Cariacica BR (ES) 287 Hk56
Cariaco YV 270 Gj40
Cariamanga EC 272 Ga48
Cariango ANG 208 Lh51
Cariati I 43 Lr51
Caribbean Sea 227 Ga15
Cariboo Mountains CDN 232 Dk19
Cariboo River CDN 232 Dk19
Caribou CDN 225 Fa07
Caribou USA (MA) 244 Gf22
Caribou Lake CDN 239 Ff20
Caribou Mount USA 229 Ce12
Caribou River CDN 231 Dg15
Caribou River USA 228 Bk18
Carichic MEX (CHH) 252 Eg32
Caridad HN 256 Fg39
Caridade BR (CE) 277 Ja48
Cariewerloo AUS (SA) 152 Rj62
Carigara RP 123 Rc40
Carignan F 23 Lf41
Carillo Puerto MEX (CAM) 255 Fe36
Carinda AUS (NSW) 151 Sd61
Cariñena E 27 Kt51
Carinhanha BR (MA) 276 Hg49
Carinhanha BR (BA) 282 Hj53
Carinhanha BR 282 Hh53
Carini I 42 Lo52
Carinish GB 18 Kn33
Carinola I 42 Lo49
Caripe YV 270 Gj40
Caripira BR (AM) 274 Gh46
Caripito YV 270 Gj40
Cariré BR (CE) 277 Hk47
Carita Beach RI 128 Qc49
Caritianas BR (RO) 280 Gj50
Carizal CO 268 Gd39
Car Kalojan BG 47 Mg47
Carles RP 123 Rb40
Carleton, Mount CDN 244 Gg22
Carleton Place CDN (ON) 247 Gb23
Cârlibaba RO 45 Mf43
Carlin USA (NV) 234 Eb25
Carlisle GB 19 Ks36
Carlisle USA (PA) 247 Gb25
Carlo AUS (QLD) 148 Rk57
Carloforte I 31 Lj51
Carlos A. Carrillo MEX (VC) 254 Fc36
Carlos Chagas BR (MG) 287 Hk54
Carlos Pellegrini RA (SF) 289 Gk62
Carlos Reyles ROU 289 Hb62
Carlos Sasares RA (BA) 289 Gk63
Carlos Tejedor RA (BA) 289 Gj63
Carlow IRL 20 Ko38
Carloway GB 18 Ko32
Carlsbad USA (CA) 236 Eb29
Carlsbad USA (NM) 237 Eh29
Carlsbad Caverns N.P. USA (NM) 237 Eh29
Carlson Inlet 296 Ga34
Carlson River CDN 231 Dh14
Carlton AUS (NSW) 151 Sd61
Carlton USA (AL) 248 Fg30
Carlyle CDN (SK) 238 Ej21
Carlyle Lake USA 241 Ff26
Carmacks CDN (YT) 231 Db14
Carmagnola I 40 Lh46
Carman CDN (MB) 238 Fb21
Carmangay CDN (AB) 233 Ed20
Carmanova MD 45 Mk43
Carmarthen GB 20 Kq39
Carmarthen Bay GB 20 Kq39
Carmaux F 24 Lc46
Carmel USA (IN) 246 Fg26
Carmel Beach USA (CA) 234 Dk27
Carmel Head GB 20 Kq37
Carmelita GCA 255 Fe37
Carmelo ROU 289 Ha62
Carmen RCH 288 Ge60
Carmen RP 123 Rc41
Carmen Alto RCH 284 Gf57
Carmen de Areco RA (BA) 289 Ha63
Carmen de Patagones RA (BA) 293 Gj66
Cármenes E 26 Kp52
Carmésia BR (MG) 287 Hj55
Carmichael AUS (QLD) 149 Sd56
Carmichael Craig AUS 142 Rf58
Carmila AUS (QLD) 149 Se56
Carmo BR (TO) 276 Hf48
Carmo do Paranaíba BR (MG) 287 Hg55
Carmo do Rio Claro BR (MG) 287 Hg56
Carmona CR 256 Fh40
Carmona E 28 Kp47
Carnac F 22 Kr43
Carnaíba BR (PE) 283 Jb49
Carnarvon AUS (QLD) 151 Sd58
Carnarvon AUS (WA) 140 Qg58
Carnarvon ZA 216 Mb61
Carnarvon N.P. AUS (QLD) 151 Sd58
Carnarvon Range AUS 140 Ra58
Carnatio Shoal 122 Qj40
Carnarvon Range AUS 151 Se58
Carndonagh IRL 18 Kn35
Carnegie AUS (WA) 141 Rb58
Carnegie USA (OK) 242 Fa28
Carn Eige GB 19 Kp33
Carnew IRL 20 Ko38
Carnforth GB 21 Ks36
Car Nicobar Island IND 111 Pg41
Carnikava LV 17 Me33
Čarnjany BY 37 Me39
Carnot RCA 195 Lh43
Carnoustie GB 19 Ks34
Carnsore Point IRL 20 Ko38
Caroebe BR (RR) 274 Ha45
Caroga Lake USA (NY) 247 Gc24
Carolina BR (MA) 276 Hg49
Carolina CO 268 Gc42
Carolina RA (SL) 288 Gg62
Carolina USA (PR) 261 Gh36
Carolina ZA 217 Mf59
Carolina Beach USA (NC) 249 Gb29
Carolina Sandhills N.W.R. USA 249 Fk28
Caroline CDN (AB) 233 Ec19
Caroline Atoll KIR 303 Cb11
Caroline Islands 134 Rb09
Carolinensiel D 32 Lh37
Caroline Seamounts 156 Sa17
Carondelet Reef KIR 157 Ub20
Caroni YV 270 Gj43
Carora YV 269 Ge40
Carot River CDN (SK) 238 Ej19
Carpathian Mountains UA 39 Md42
Carpathian Mountains 54 Mb21
Carpathian Mountains = Carpații Orientali RO 45 Mf43
Carpații Curburii RO 45 Mf45
Carpații Orientali RO 45 Mf43
Carpen RO 44 Md46
Carpenter USA (SD) 240 Fb23
Carpenter Lake CDN 232 Dj20
Carpenter Rocks AUS (SA) 152 Sa64
Carpenterville USA (OR) 234 Dh24
Carpentras F 25 Lf46
Carpi I 40 Ll46
Carpina BR (PE) 283 Jc49
Carpinteria USA (CA) 236 Ea28
Carpio USA (ND) 238 Ek21
Carp Lake CDN 232 Dj18
Carpolac AUS (VIC) 152 Sa64
Carquefou F 22 Kt43
Carqueja BR (PE) 283 Ja50
Carrabelle USA (FL) 249 Fh31
Carrabin AUS (WA) 144 Qk61
Carraipia CO 268 Gd40
Carranglan RP 121 Ra37
Carrara I 40 Ll46
Carrara Range AUS 139 Rj55
Carrasco, P.N. BOL 285 Gh54
Carrascosa del Campo E 29 Ks50
Carrascoy E 29 Kt47
Carrasquero YV 268 Gd40
Carrathol AUS (NSW) 153 Sc63
Carrauntoohil IRL 20 Kl38
Carrbridge GB 19 Kr33
Carre Four RH 260 Gd36
Carrenleufú RCH 292 Ge67
Carrere, Cerro RA 292 Gf64
Carretera Austral RCH 292 Gd67
Carriacou WV 261 Gk39
Carrickfergus GB 18 Kp36
Carrickmacross IRL 18 Ko37
Carrick-on-Shannon IRL 18 Km37
Carrick-on-Suir IRL 20 Kn38
Carrieton AUS (SA) 152 Rk62
Carrington USA (ND) 240 Fa22
Carringue RCH 292 Ge65
Carrión de los Condes E 26 Kq52
Carrizal YV 270 Gk42
Carrizal Bajo RCH 288 Ge60
Carrizos MEX (TM) 253 Fa33
Carrizo Springs USA (TX) 253 Fa31
Carrizozo USA (NM) 237 Eh29
Carroll USA (IA) 241 Fc24
Carrollton USA (GA) 249 Fh29
Carrollton USA (OH) 247 Fk25
Carrolton USA (MO) 241 Fd26
Carrot River CDN 238 Ej19
Carrouges F 22 Ku42
Carrozas CO 268 Gd44
Carrua MOC 211 Mj54
Carryduff GB 18 Kp36
Çarşamba TR 62 Mj25
Carseland CDN (AB) 233 Ed20
Carson USA (ND) 240 Ek22
Carson City USA (NV) 234 Ea26
Carson River AUS (WA) 138 Rd53
Carson River A.L. AUS 138 Rd53
Carstairs CDN (AB) 233 Ec20
Cartagena CO 268 Gc40
Cartagena E 29 Ku47
Cartagena del Chaira CO 272 Gc45
Cartago CO 268 Gc43
Cartago CR 256 Fj41
Cartaxo P 28 Km49
Cartaya E 28 Kn47
Carter Bar Pass GB 19 Ks35
Carter, Mount AUS 146 Sb52
Carter Spit USA 228 Bj16
Carters Range AUS (QLD) 148 Sa57
Cartersville USA (GA) 249 Fh28
Carthage USA (MO) 243 Fc27
Carthage USA (MS) 243 Ff29
Carthage USA (NC) 249 Ga28
Carthage USA (TX) 243 Fc29
Cartier CDN (ON) 246 Fk22
Cartier Island AUS 138 Rb52
Carti Suitopo PA 257 Ga41
Cartucho BR (TO) 282 Hg50
Cartwright CDN (MB) 238 Fa21
Cartwright CDN 225 Ha08
Carú BR 276 Hg47
Caruaru BR (PE) 283 Jc50
Carumbé ROU 289 Hb61
Carún YV 269 Gj43
Carunantabari YV 270 Gj43
Carúpano YV 270 Gj40
Caruray RP 122 Qk40
Carutapera BR (MA) 276 Hh46
Caruthersville USA (MO) 243 Ff27
Carú, T.I. BR 276 Hg47
Cărvarica BG 46 Mc48
Caravelas BR 287 Ja54
Carver USA (NV) 234 Eb26
Carvin F 23 Lc40
Carvoal BR (MT) 285 Hb54
Carvoeiro BR (AM) 274 Gk46
Carwarna Downs AUS (WA) 144 Rb61
Carway CDN (AB) 233 Ed21
Carwell AUS (QLD) 151 Sd58
Cary USA (NC) 249 Ga28
Caryš RUS 85 Pc20
Caryškoe RUS 85 Pb20
Cas RCH 284 Gg57
Casablanca MA 172 Kg29
Casa Blanca MEX (NL) 253 Ek32
Casablanca RCH 288 Ge62
Casa Branca BR (SP) 286 Hg56
Casacalenda I 42 Lp49
Casa de Juan Núñez E 29 Kt49
Casadepaga USA (AK) 229 Bh13
Casa de Piedra RA (LP) 292 Gg65
Casa Grande USA (AZ) 237 Ee29
Casa Grande Ruins Nat. Mon. USA 237 Ee29
Casalbordino I 42 Lp48
Casale Monferrato I 40 Lj45
Casalins RA (BA) 293 Ha64
Casalmaggiore I 40 Ll46
Casalpusterlengo I 40 Lk45
Casamance SN 183 Kc39
Casamance SN 183 Kc39
Casamássima I 43 Lr50
Casamozza F 31 Lk48
Casa Msika MOC 214 Mg55
Casanare CO 269 Ge42
Casanare CO 269 Gf43
Casanay YV 270 Gj40
Casa Nova BR (BA) 283 Hk50
Casarabi BOL 280 Gh53
Casarano I 43 Lt50
Casares NIC 256 Fg40
Casas MEX (TM) 253 Fa34
Casas Colgadas de Cuenca E 29 Ks50
Casas de Lázaro E 29 Ks48
Casas del Puerto E 29 Kt48
Casas Grandes MEX (SO) 236 Ee31
Casas Grandes MEX 237 Eg30
Casas-Ibáñez E 29 Kt49
Casas Viejas MEX (DGO) 253 Eh34
Casa Verde BR (MS) 286 Hd56
Casa Verde MEX (GUR) 254 Fa37
Casavieja E 26 Kq50
Casazinc CO 268 Gd44
Casbas RA (BA) 293 Gj64
Casca BR (RS) 290 He60
Cascada Cola de Caballo MEX 253 Ek33
Cascadas Agua Azul MEX 255 Fd37
Cascadas de Agoyán EC 272 Ga46
Cascadas de Basaseachic MEX 252 Ef31
Cascadas de Basaseachic, P.N. MEX 252 Ef32
Cascadas del Queguay ROU 289 Ha62
Cascadas de San Rafael EC 272 Gb46
Cascadas de Tzaráracua MEX 254 Ej36
Cascadas Misol-Há MEX 255 Fd37
Cascade AUS (WA) 144 Ra62
Cascade USA (ID) 234 Ec23
Cascade Caverns USA 242 Fa31
Cascade d'Akloa TG 193 La42
Cascade de Daravangy RM 219 Ne54
Cascade de Karfiguela BF 193 Kh40
Cascade de Vierges MA 172 Kh29
Cascade Mtn. Ski Area USA 246 Ff24
Cascade Point NZ 155 Te68
Cascade Range CDN 232 Dk21
Cascade Range USA 234 Dj24
Cascade Res. USA 234 Eb23
Cascades de Kota DY 193 La40
Cascades de Sosso DY 186 Lb40
Cascades d'Ouzoud MA 172 Kg29
Cascais P 28 Kl48
Cascajal C 258 Fk34
Cascajal PE 272 Fk48
Cascante E 27 Kt51
Cascantinha BR (RJ) 287 Hj57
Cascas PE 278 Ga49
Cascavel BR (CE) 277 Ja48
Cascavel BR (PR) 286 Hd58
Càscia I 42 Lo48
Casciana Terme I 40 Ll47
Càscina I 40 Ll47
Căscioarele RO 45 Mg46
Cascorro C 259 Gb35
Caseiros BR (RS) 290 He60
Caselle Torinese I 40 Lh45
Casentinesi-Monte Falterona-Campigna, P.N. I 40 Lm47
Caserón RCH 288 Ge59
Caserta I 42 Lp49
Casey CDN (QC) 244 Gc22
Casey ANT (AUS) 297 Qc32
Casey Bay 297 Nb32
Cashel IRL 20 Kn38
Cashel ZW 214 Mg55
Cashmere Downs AUS (WA) 144 Qk60
Casigua YV 268 Gd41
Casiguran RP 121 Rb37
Casilda RA (SF) 289 Gk62
Casimcea RO 45 Mj46
Casimiro Castillo MEX (JLC) 253 Eh36
Casimiro de Abreu BR (RJ) 287 Hj57
Casinos E 29 Ku49
Casiquiare YV 270 Gg44
Casiquiare YV 273 Gg45
Čáslav CZ 38 Lq41
Casma PE 278 Ga50
Čašniki BY 52 Me18
Càsoli I 42 Lp48
Casória I 42 Lp50
Časovaja RUS 91 Qk19
Caspana RCH 284 Gf57
Caspe E 27 Ku51
Casper USA (WY) 235 Eg24
Caspian Depression 60 Nb10
Caspian Sea 60 Nc10
Cassacatiza MOC 210 Mg53
Cassai ANG 209 Ma51
Cassai ANG/RDC 203 Ma50
Cassamba ANG 209 Ma52
Cassange BR 281 Hb54
Cassango ANG 203 Lj50
Cassano allo Iónio I 43 Lr51
Cassasala ANG 209 Lk51
Cassel F 23 Lc40
Casselton USA (ND) 240 Fb22
Cassembe MOC 211 Mj52
Cassero MOC 211 Mj52
Cássia BR (MG) 287 Hg56
Cassiar CDN (BC) 231 Df16
Cassiar Mountains CDN 231 Df16
Cassiar-Stewart Highway CDN 231 Df17
Cassilândia BR (MS) 286 He55
Cassilis AUS (QLD) 148 Sb56
Cassinga ANG 208 Lj53
Cassini Island AUS 138 Rc52
Cassino BR (RS) 290 Hd62
Cassino I 42 Lo49
Cassis F 25 Lf47
Cass Lake USA (MN) 241 Fc22
Cassongue ANG 208 Lh51
Castagneto Carducci I 40 Ll47
Castaña YV 269 Gh43
Castañar de Ibor E 28 Kp49
Castañeda MEX (BC) 236 Ec30
Castanhal BR (AM) 274 Gj49
Castanhal BR (PA) 276 Hg46
Castanheira BR (MT) 280 Ha51
Castanheira de Pira P 28 Km49
Castaños MEX (COH) 253 Ek32
Castaño Viejo RA (SJ) 288 Gf61
Castejón de Valdejasa E 27 Ku51
Castelândia BR (GO) 286 He55
Castelbuono I 42 Lp53
Castel del Monte I 43 Lr49
Castèl di Sangro I 42 Lp49
Castelfidardo I 41 Lo47
Castelfranco Emilia I 40 Lm46
Castelfranco Vèneto I 40 Lm45
Castelgar CDN (BC) 232 Eb21
Casteljaloux F 24 La46
Castellabate I 42 Lp50
Castellammare del Golfo I 42 Ln52
Castellammare di Stábia I 42 Lp50
Castellane F 25 Lg47
Castellaneta I 43 Lr50
Castellaneta Marina I 43 Lr50
Castellar de Santiago E 29 Kr48
Castell'Arquato I 40 Lk46
Castelldans E 30 La49
Castelldefels E 30 Lb49
Castell de Ferro E 29 Kr46
Castelli RA (BA) 293 Hb64
Castello Aragonese d'Ìschia I 42 Lo50
Castello dei Ruffo I 43 Lq52
Castelló de la Plana E 29 Ku49
Castello di Castelsardo I 31 Lj50
Castello di Manfredónia I 43 Lq49
Castello di Manta I 40 Lh46
Castelnaudary F 24 Lb47
Castelnau-de-Médoc F 24 Ku45
Castelnau-Magnoac F 24 La47
Castèlnovo ne'Monti I 40 Ll46
Castelnuovo di Garfagnana I 40 Ll46
Castelo BR (ES) 287 Hk56
Castelo Branco P 28 Kn49
Castelo de Vide P 28 Kn49
Castelo do Piauí BR (PI) 277 Hk48
Castèl San Giovanni I 40 Lk45
Castèl San Pietro Terme I 40 Lm46
Castelsardo I 31 Lj50
Castelsarrasin F 24 Lb46
Casteltérmini I 42 Lo53
Castelvetrano I 42 Ln53
Casterton AUS (VIC) 152 Sa64
Castets F 24 Kt47
Castiglioncello I 40 Ll47
Castiglione della Pescáia I 40 Ll48
Castiglione delle Stiviere I 40 Ll45
Castiglione sul Lago I 40 Ln47
Castiglion Fiorentino I 40 Lm47
Castilblanco E 28 Kp49
Castilhiano CV 182 Jh37
Castilla RA (BA) 289 Ha63
Castilla RP 121 Rb39
Castilla - La Mancha E 29 Kr49
Castilla la Vieja E 26 Kp50
Castilla Nueva E 29 Kr49
Castilla y León E 26 Kp51
Castillejo de Martín Viejo E 26 Ko50
Castillo-Convento de Calatrava la Nueva E 29 Kr48
Castillo de Ampudia E 26 Kq51
Castillo de Biar E 29 Ku48
Castillo de Fonseca E 26 Kq51
Castillo de Frías E 27 Kr52
Castillo de Granadilla E 28 Ko50
Castillo de Jagua C 258 Fk34
Castillo de Javier E 27 Kt52
Castillo de la Mota E 26 Kq51
Castillo de Loarre E 27 Ku52
Castillo de los Reyes de Navarra E 27 Kt52
Castillo del Puente del Congosto E 26 Kp50
Castillo de Manzanares el Real E 29 Kr50
Castillo de Medellín E 28 Kp48
Castillo de Mombeltrán E 26 Kp50
Castillo de Montearagón E 27 Ku52
Castillo de Peñafiel E 26 Kq51
Castillo de San Felipe GCA 255 Ff38
Castillo de San Marcos USA 250 Fk31
Castillo de Villalonso E 26 Kp51
Castillon-en-Couserans F 24 Lb48
Castillonnès F 24 La46
Castillos ROU 289 Hd63
Castillos de Guayana YV 270 Gj41
Castlebar IRL 18 Kl37
Castlebay GB 18 Kn34
Castleblayney IRL 18 Ko36
Castle C. USA 228 Ca17
Castle Coole GB 18 Kn36
Castle Dale USA (UT) 235 Ee26
Castle Douglas GB 19 Kr36
Castle Hill N.H.P. CDN 245 Hd22
Castle Island BS 251 Gc34
Castle Island CDN 239 Gb18
Castleisland IRL 20 Kl38
Castle Mount USA 236 Dk28
Castle Peak USA 235 Ec23
Castlepollard IRL 18 Kn37
Castlerea IRL 18 Km37
Castlereagh Bay AUS 139 Rh52
Castle Rock USA (CO) 235 Eh26
Castle Rock USA (SD) 240 Ej23
Castles of the Assassins IR 72 Nf27
Castletown GB 18 Kq36
Castletown GB 19 Kr32
Castletownbere IRL 20 Kl39
Castlevale AUS (QLD) 151 Sd58
Castle Venlaw GB 19 Kr35
Castor CDN (AB) 233 Ee19
Castres F 24 Lc47
Castricum NL 32 Le38
Castries WL 261 Gk38
Castril E 29 Ks47
Castro BR (PR) 286 He58
Castro RCH 292 Gd67
Castro Alves BR (BA) 283 Ja52
Castro Barras RA (LR) 288 Gh61
Castrocaro Terme I 40 Lm46
Castro Daire P 26 Kn50
Castro del Río E 28 Kq47
Castrojeriz E 26 Kq52
Castropol E 26 Kn53
Castro-Urdiales E 27 Kr53
Castro Verde P 28 Km47
Castro Viejo RA 288 Gf61
Castrovillari I 43 Lr51
Castrovirreyna PE 278 Gc52
Castuera E 28 Kp48
Casuarina Coast RI 158 Rk49
Casuarina Coast RI 158 Rj48
Casuli NIC 256 Fh39
Casupá ROU 289 Hc63
Caswell USA (AK) 229 Ce15
Çat TR 63 Na26
Cata YV 269 Gg40
Catabola ANG 208 Lh52
Catabola ANG 208 Lj52
Cataby Roadhouse AUS (WA) 144 Qh61
Catacamas HN 256 Fh38
Catacaos PE 272 Fk48
Catache PE 278 Ga49
Catacocha EC 272 Ga48
Cataguases BR (MG) 287 Hj56
Catahuasi PE 278 Gc52
Cataingan RP 121 Rb39
Çatak TR 50 Mj52
Çatak TR 51 Ml50
Çatak TR 63 Nb26
Catalão BR (GO) 286 Hg55
Çatalca TR 50 Mj49
Çatalca Yarımadası TR 50 Mh49
Çatal Hüyük TR 62 Mg27
Catalina CDN (NF) 245 Hd21
Catalina PE 284 Gf58
Catalonia E 30 La49
Catama SP 205 Na44
Catamarca RA 267 Gc24
Catamayo EC 272 Ga47
Catambué ANG 208 Lk54
Catanacuname YV 273 Gg44
Catanauan RP 121 Rb39
Catandica MOC 214 Mg55
Catanduanes Island RP 121 Rc39
Catanduva BR (SP) 286 Hf56
Catanduvas BR (PR) 286 Hd58
Catangalo BR (RJ) 287 Hj57
Catanhede BR (MA) 276 Hh47
Catània I 42 Lq53
Catán Lil RA (NE) 292 Ge65
Catanzaro I 43 Lr52
Catanzaro Marina I 43 Lr52
Catarama EC 272 Ga46
Cataratas del Iguazú BR/RA 286 Hc58
Catarina BR (CE) 277 Ja49
Catarman RP 121 Rc39
Catata-a-Nova ANG 208 Lh52
Catatumbo YV 268 Gd41
Catatumbo-Bari, P.N. CO 268 Gd41
Catavi BOL 284 Gf55
Cataxa MOC 210 Mg53
Catazajá MEX (CHP) 255 Fd37
Catbalogan RP 123 Rc40
Cat Ba N.P. VN 96 Qd35
Čat-Bazar KS 77 Og24
Cat Cays BS 251 Ga33
Catechane MOC 214 Mg57
Catedral de Ávila E 26 Kq50
Catedral de Barbastro E 30 La48
Catedral de Burgos E 27 Kr52
Catedral de Ciudad Rodrigo E 26 Ko50
Catedral de Cuenca E 29 Ks50
Catedral de León E 26 Kp52
Catedral de Sal CO 268 Gd43
Catedral de Sigüenza E 29 Ks51
Catedral de Toledo E 29 Kq49
Catedral de Tortosa E 30 La50
Catedral de València E 29 Ku49
Catedral de Viseu P 26 Kn50
Catedral de Zamora E 26 Kp51
Catedral La Seo de Zaragoza E 27 Ku51
Cateel Bay RP 123 Rd42
Catemaco MEX (VC) 255 Fc36
Catembe MOC 217 Mg59
Catende BR (PE) 283 Jc50
Catengue ANG 208 Lg52
Cateraggio F 31 Lk48
Catete ANG 202 Lg50
Catete BR 275 Hd49
Cathcart ZA 217 Md62
Cathedral Cave AUS (QLD) 151 Sd58
Cathedral Caverns USA 248 Fg28
Cathedral Cove NZ 154 Th64
Cathédrale de Clermont-Ferrand F 25 Ld45
Cathédrale de Lausanne CH 34 Lg44
Cathédrale de Narbonne F 25 Lc47
Cathédrale de Reims F 23 Le41
Cathédrale de Saint-Bertrand-de-Comminges F 24 La47
Cathédrale de Strasbourg F 23 Lh42
Cathédrale de Vienne F 25 Le45
Cathédrale d'Orléans F 23 Lb43
Cathédrale du Puy-en-Velay F 25 Ld45
Cathedral Gorge S.P. USA 234 Ec27
Cathedral Peak ZA 217 Me60
Cathedral Prov. Park CDN 232 Dk21
Cathedral Rock N.P. AUS 151 Sg61
Cathedral Valley USA 235 Ee26
Catingal BR (BA) 283 Hk53
Catió GNB 183 Kc40
Catipari Mamoria, T.I. BR 279 Gg49
Cat Island BS 251 Gc33
Catkal KS 76 Of25
Čatkal kyrka toosu KS 76 Of25
Cat Lake CDN (ON) 238 Fe20
Cat Lake CDN 238 Fe20
Catoco Cangola ANG 202 Lh50
Cato Island AUS 137 Sd23
Catolé do Rocha BR (PB) 277 Jb49
Catolo ANG 203 Lj50
Caton Island USA 228 Bj18
Catoute E 26 Ko52
Catriel RA (RN) 292 Gg64
Catriló RA (LP) 293 Gj64
Catrimani BR (RR) 274 Gj45
Catrimani BR (RR) 274 Gk45
Catrimani BR 274 Gj45
Catskill USA (NY) 247 Gd24
Catskill Mts. USA 247 Gc24
Catskill Park USA 247 Gc25
Cattedrale di Bari I 43 Lr49
Cattedrale d'Otranto I 43 Lt50
Cat Tien N.P. VN 115 Qd40
Cattle Creek AUS (NT) 139 Rf54
Cattólica I 41 Ln47
Cattolica di Stilo I 43 Lr52
Catu BR (BA) 283 Ja52
Catúa RA (PJ) 284 Gg57
Catuane MOC 217 Mg59
Catulene MOC 210 Mh54
Catumbela ANG 208 Lh52
Cátura MOC 211 Mk52
Caturama BR (BA) 283 Hj52
Čatyrköl KS 77 Oh25
Čatyrtaš KS 77 Oj25
Cauaburi BR 273 Gg45
Cauale ANG 202 Lj49
Căuaș RO 44 Mc43
Cauayan RP 121 Ra37
Cauayan RP 123 Rb41
Cauca ANG 202 Lh50
Cauca CO 268 Gc42
Caucagua YV 269 Gg40
Caucaia BR (CE) 277 Ja47
Caucas BOL 285 Ha54
Caucasia CO 268 Gc41
Caucasus RUS/GE 60 Na10
Caucete RA (SJ) 288 Gf61
Cauchari RA (PJ) 284 Gg58
Caudry F 23 Ld40
Cauit Point RP 123 Rd41
Caumbue ANG 203 Ma50
Caumont-l'Eventé F 22 Ku41
Caunes-Minervois F 24 Lc47
Čaunskaja guba RUS 59 Tb04
Caupolicán BOL 279 Gf52
Cauquenes RCH 292 Gd63
Caura YV 269 Gh42
Caurés BR 274 Gj46
Cauro F 31 Lj49
Causapscal CDN (QC) 244 Gg21
Căușeni MD 45 Mk44
Causey USA (NM) 237 Ej29
Caussade F 24 Lb46
Cautário BR 279 Gh52
Cauterets F 24 Ku48
Cautín RCH 292 Gd65
Cauto Embarcadero C 259 Gb35
Cauvery IND 111 Ok41
Cava MOC 211 Na53
Cava de'Tirreni I 42 Lp50
Cavaillon F 25 Lf47
Cavalaire-sur-Mer F 25 Lg47
Cavalcante BR (GO) 282 Hg52
Cavalese I 40 Lm44
Cavalier USA (ND) 238 Fb21
Cavalla LB 192 Kg43
Cavalla LB 192 Kg43
Cavally CI 192 Kg43
Cavalo MOC 214 Mh55
Cavan IRL 18 Kn37
Căvăran RO 44 Mc45
Çavdarhisar TR 50 Mk51
Çavdır TR 50 Mk53
Cave NZ 155 Tf68
Cave City USA (AR) 243 Fe28
Cave Junction USA (OR) 234 Dj24
Cavendish AUS (VIC) 152 Sb64
Cave paintings (Alem Maya) ETH 198 Na41
Caverna de Santana BR 286 Hf58
Caverna do Diabo BR 286 Hf58
Caverna do Francês BR 281 Hc53
Cavernas de Júmandi EC 272 Gb46
Cavernas do Peruaçu, P.N. BR 282 Hh53
Caverns of Sonora USA 242 Ek30
Cave Rock ZA 217 Mf61
Cave Temple (Dambulla) CL 111 Pa43
Cavili Island RP 123 Ra41
Cavite RP 121 Ra38
Cavnic RO 44 Md43
Cavour I 40 Lh46
Cavtat HR 43 Lt48
Çavuştepe TR 63 Nb26
Čavusy BY 52 Mf19
Cawayan RP 123 Rb40
Cawdor Castle GB 19 Kr33
Caxambu BR (MG) 287 Hh56
Caxias BR (MA) 276 Hj48
Caxias do Sul BR (RS) 290 He60
Caxito ANG 202 Lg50
Caxuxa BR (MA) 276 Hh48
Çay TR 51 Mm52
Çayağzı TR 50 Mk49
Cayalti PE 278 Ga49
Cayambe EC 272 Ga45
Cayambe, Volcán EC 272 Ga45
Cayapas EC 272 Ga45
Çaybeyi TR 62 Mj27
Cay Caulker BH 255 Fg37
Çayeli TR 63 Na25
Cayenne F 271 Hd43
Cayeux-sur-Mer F 23 Lb40
Çaygören Baraj TR 50 Mj51
Çayhan TR 51 Mp53
Çayıralan TR 51 Mq51
Çayırhan TR 51 Mm50
Çayırova = Agios Theodoros CY 51 Mp55
Çayırözü TR 51 Mq52
Çaylar TR 63 Na26
Çayli AZ 70 Nd25
Cay Lobos C 259 Gb34
Caylus F 24 Lb46
Cayman Brac GB 259 Ga36
Cayman Islands GB 258 Fk36
Cayman Ridge 258 Fj36
Cayman Trench 258 Fj37
Cay Marino 122 Qh41
Cayanabo SP 199 Nd41
Cayo Arenas MEX 255 Fe34
Cayo Becerro HN 256 Fj38
Cayo Becerro HN 256 Fj38
Cayo Caballones C 259 Ga35
Cayo Cabeza del Este C 259 Ga35
Cayo Cantiles C 258 Fj35
Cayo Caratasca HN 256 Fj37
Cayo Caratasca HN 256 Fj37
Cayo Centro MEX 255 Fg36
Cayo Coco C 259 Ga34
Cayo del Rosario C 259 Fj35
Cayo de Santa María C 259 Ga34
Cayo Fragoso C 259 Ga34
Cayo Gorda HN 256 Fj38
Cayo Gorda HN 256 Fj38
Cayo Grande C 259 Ga35
Cayo Guajaba C 259 Gb35
Cayo Guillermo C 259 Ga34
Cayo Largo C 258 Fk35
Cayo Largo C 258 Fj35
Cayo Lobos MEX 255 Fg36
Cayo Mambi C 259 Gc35
Cayo Nuevo MEX 255 Fd35
Cayo Ramona C 258 Fk34
Cayo Romano C 259 Gb34
Cayo Sabinal C 259 Gb35
Cayos Anclitas C 259 Ga35
Cayos Blancos del Sur C 258 Fk34
Cayos Cajones HN 256 Fj37
Cayos Cajones HN 256 Fj37
Cayos Cinco Balas C 259 Ga35
Cayos Cocorocuma HN 256 Fj38
Cayos Cocorocuma HN 256 Fj38
Cayos de Albuquerque CO 256 Fk39
Cayos de E.S.E. CO 257 Fk39
Cayos de Perlas NIC 256 Fj39
Cayos de Roncador CO 257 Fk39
Cayos de San Felipe C 258 Fj35
Cayos Guerrero NIC 256 Fj39
Cayos King NIC 256 Fj39
Cayos los Indios C 258 Fj35
Cayos Mayores del Cabo Falso HN 256 Fj38
Cayos Mayores del Cabo Falso HN 256 Fj38

Chipping Norton GB 21 Kt39
Chiprana E 27 Ku51
Chipungo Z 210 Mf52
Chiputo MOC 210 Mg53
Chiquián PE 278 Gb51
Chiquibul N.P. BH 255 Ff37
Chiquila HN 255 Ff38
Chiquilá MEX (QTR) 255 Fg35
Chiquimula GCA 255 Ff38
Chiquimulilla GCA 255 Fe38
Chiquinquira CO 268 Gd43
Chira ETH 198 Mj42
Chira PE 272 Fk48
Chirala IND (APH) 111 Pa39
Chiramba MOC 210 Mh54
Chirapatla IND (MPH) 108 Oj34
Chirchiq UZ 76 Oe25
Chiredzi ZW 214 Mf56
Chire Wildlife Reserve ETH 191 Mj39
Chirfa RN 181 Lg35
Chirgaon IND (UPH) 107 Ok33
Chiriaco PE 272 Ga48
Chiriakot IND (UPH) 109 Pb33
Chiribiquete, P.N. CO 273 Gd45
Chiricahua Nat. Mon. USA 237 Ef29
Chiriguana CO 268 Gd41
Chirimena YV 269 Gg40
Chiriqui Grande PA 256 Fj41
Chiri San ROK 100 Rd28
Chirisan N.P. ROK 100 Rd28
Chirisa Safari Area ZW 210 Me54
Chirivel E 29 Ks47
Chiroqchi UZ 76 Od26
Chirripó, P.N. CR 256 Fj41
Chirumanzu ZW 214 Mf55
Chirundu Z 210 Me53
Chirundu Fossil Forest Z 210 Me54
Chisamba Z 210 Me53
Chisampa Z 210 Mg51
Chisana USA (AK) 231 Ck14
Chisana River USA 229 Ck14
Chisanga Z 210 Md52
Chisasa Z 209 Mc52
Chisasibi CDN (QC) 239 Ga19
Chisec GCA 255 Fe38
Chisekesi Z 210 Md54
Chisenga MW 206 Mg50
Chisenga MW 210 Mg51
Chisholm USA (MN) 241 Fd22
Chisholm Trail Mus. USA 242 Fb28
Chishui CHN (GZH) 95 Qc31
Chishuihe CHN (SCH) 96 Qc32
Chisimba Falls Z 210 Mf51
Chişinău MD 45 Mj43
Chişlaz RO 44 Mc43
Chisone I 40 Lh46
Chisoso Z 210 Mf51
Chissano MOC 214 Mg58
Chissibuca MOC 214 Mh58
Chissinguane MOC 214 Mh56
Chistian Mandy PK 81 Og31
Chisumbanje ZW 214 Mg56
Chisvingo ZW 210 Mf54
Chita CO 268 Gd42
Chita EAT 207 Mh50
Chitado ANG 208 Lg54
Chitalwana IND (RJT) 106 Of33
Chitanda Z 210 Md53
Chi Tanh VN 115 Qe39
Chitedze MW 210 Mg52
Chitek Lake CDN (SK) 233 Eg19
Chitek Lake CDN 238 Fa19
Chitembo ANG 208 Lj52
Chitengo MOC 214 Mh55
Chitina USA (AK) 230 Ch15
Chitina River USA 230 Cj15
Chitipa MW 206 Mg50
Chitobe MOC 214 Mg56
Chitolo MOC 214 Mg57
Chitonga Z 210 Md54
Chitose J 99 Sa24
Chitradurga IND (KTK) 111 Oj39
Chitrakot IND (CGH) 109 Pa36
Chitrakut IND (UPH) 109 Pa33
Chitral PK 79 Of28
Chitré PA 257 Fk42
Chittagong BD 112 Pf34
Chittaranjan IND (JKD) 112 Pd34
Chittaurgarh IND (RJT) 106 Oh33
Chittaurgarh Fort IND (RJT) 106 Oh33
Chittoor IND (APH) 111 Ok40
Chittor = Chittaurgarh IND (RJT) 106 Oh33
Chitungwiza ZW 214 Mf55
Chituta MOC 214 Mg56
Chityal IND (APH) 109 Ok36
Chityal IND (APH) 109 Ok37
Chiuchiu RCH 284 Gf57
Chium ANG 209 Ma53
Chiumbe ANG 203 Ma50
Chiumbo ANG 208 Lj52
Chiure Novo MOC 211 Mk52
Chiure Velho MOC 211 Mk52
Chiusa = Klausen I 40 Lm44
Chiusi I 40 Lm47
Chiuta MOC 210 Mg53
Chiva E 29 Ku49
Chivacoa YV 269 Gf40
Chivasso I 40 Lh45
Chivato RCH 288 Ge59
Chivay PE 279 Ge53
Chive BOL 279 Gf52
Chivhu ZW 214 Mf55
Chivilcoy RA (BA) 289 Ha63
Chivirico C 259 Gb36
Chivuna Z 210 Md54
Chizarira Hills ZW 210 Md54
Chizarira N.P. ZW 210 Md54
Chizu J 101 Rh28
Chizwina RB 213 Md56
Chlef DZ 173 La27
Chłudowo PL 36 Lr38
Chlumec nad Cidlinou CZ 38 Lq40
Chmel'nyc'kyj UA 54 Md21
Chmielnik PL 37 Ma40
Chmil'nyk UA 54 Md21
Choam Khsant K 115 Qc38
Choam Sla K 115 Qb40
Choapa RCH 288 Ge61
Chobe RB 213 Mc55
Chobe RB/NAM 213 Mc54
Chobe N.P. RB 213 Mc55
Chocca, Cerro PE 278 Gc52
Chocianów PL 36 Lq39
Chociwel PL 36 Lq37
Chocolate Hills RP 123 Rc41
Chocolate Mts. USA 236 Ec29
Chocontá CO 268 Gd43
Chocope PE 278 Ga49
Choctaw N.W.R. USA 248 Ff30
Chodavaram IND (APH) 109 Pa37
Chodavaram IND (APH) 109 Pb37
Cho Do PRK 100 Rc26
Chodoriv UA 39 Me41
Chodov CZ 38 Ln40
Chodová Planá CZ 38 Ln41
Chodzież PL 36 Lr38
Choele Choel RA (RN) 292 Gh65
Chofombo MOC 210 Mf53
Choharwa NEP 88 Pd32
Chohtan IND (RJT) 106 Of33
Choiceland CDN (SK) 233 Eh19
Choirokoitia CY 51 Mo56
Choiseul SOL 160 Sj49
Choiseul Sound GB 295 Ha71
Choix MEX (SL) 252 Ef32
Chojbalsan MNG 91 Qh21
Chojna PL 36 Lp38
Chojnice PL 36 Ls37
Chojniki BY 52 Me20
Chojnów PL 36 Lq39
Chokai Q.N.P. J 101 Rk26
Chokai-san J 101 Sa26
Chok Chai THA 115 Qb38
Choke ETH 198 Mj40
Chókué MOC 214 Mg58
Chokwe = Chókué MOC 214 Mg58
Cholame USA (CA) 236 Dk28
Chola Shan CHN 94 Pk30
Chola Shankou CHN 94 Pk30
Cholchol RCH 292 Gd65
Cholet F 22 Ku43
Cholila RA (CB) 292 Ge67
Cholistan Desert PK 81 Of31
Cholola Z 209 Mb54
Cholopyči UA 37 Me40
Cholpon-ata KS 77 Oj24
Cholsan PRK 100 Rc26
Choluteca HN 256 Fg39
Ch'olwon ROK 100 Rd26
Choma Z 210 Md54
Chom Bung THA 114 Pk39
Chom Phra THA 115 Qb38
Chomsk BY 37 Mf38
Chom Thong THA 114 Pk36
Chomutov CZ 38 Lo40
Chona EAT 207 Mg48
Ch'onan ROK 100 Rd27
Chon Buri THA 114 Qa39
Chonchi RCH 292 Gd67
Chon Daen THA 114 Qa37
Chondung Temple ROK 100 Rd27
Chone EC 272 Fk46
Chongchon Gang PRK 100 Rc26
Chongjin PRK 100 Re25
Chongju PRK 100 Rc26
Ch'ongju ROK 100 Rd27
Chongju ROK 100 Rd28
Chong Kal K 115 Qb39
Chonglong CHN (SCH) 94 Qc31
Chongming CHN (JGS) 102 Ra30
Chongoene MOC 214 Mg58
Chongoni Rock Art MW 210 Mh53
Chongoroi ANG 208 Lg52
Chongoyape PE 278 Ga49
Chong Phan THA 116 Pk41
Chongp'yong PRK 100 Rd26
Chongqing CHN (CGQ) 95 Qd31
Chongqing CHN 83 Qb13
Chong Qing-Temple CHN 92 Qb28
Chongren CHN (JGX) 102 Qj32
Chong Samui THA 116 Pk41
Chongsan Do ROK 103 Rd28
Chongshen Monastery CHN 113 Qa33
Chong Tao THA 116 Pk41
Chongwe Z 210 Me53
Chongwe Z 210 Me53
Chongwu CHN (FJN) 97 Qk33
Chongyang CHN (HUB) 102 Qh31
Chongyi CHN (JGX) 97 Qh33
Chongzhou CHN (SCH) 94 Qb30
Chongzuo CHN (GZG) 96 Qd34
Chonju ROK 100 Rd28
Chonkham IND (ARP) 113 Pj32
Chonogol MNG 91 Qh23
Chonos Archipelago RCH 292 Gc68
Chontali PE 272 Ga48
Chontalpa MEX (TB) 255 Fd37
Chon Thanh VN 115 Qd40
Cho Oyo NEP/CHN 88 Pd31
Chopan IND (UPH) 109 Pb33
Chopda IND (MHT) 108 Oh35
Chopim BR 290 Hd59
Choqa Zanbil IR 72 Ne29
Chorea MA 172 Kh30
Chorhat IND (MPH) 109 Pa33
Chorkerup AUS (WA) 144 Qj63
Choro BOL 280 Gh54
Choró BR (CE) 277 Ja48
Chorol UA 54 Mg21
Chorolque, Nevado BOL 284 Gh56
Choromoro RA (TU) 288 Gh59
Choroni YV 269 Gg40
Choros Bajos RCH 288 Ge60
Choroszcz PL 37 Mc37
Chorozinho BR (CE) 277 Ja48
Chorrera PE 273 Ge47
Chorrochó BR (BA) 283 Ja50
Chorro de Maita C 259 Gc35
Chorro El Indio, P.N. YV 268 Gd41
Chorro la Libertad CO 273 Gf46
Chorzele PL 37 Ma37
Chorzów PL 37 Lt40
Ch'osan PRK 100 Rc25
Choshi J 101 Sa28
Choshuenco, Volcán RCH 292 Gd65
Chosica PE 278 Gb51
Chos Malal RA (NE) 292 Ge64
Chosong PRK 100 Rd25
Choszczno PL 36 Lq37
Chota PE 278 Ga49
Chota Nagpur Plateau IND 109 Pa34
Chota Udaipur IND (GUJ) 108 Oh34
Choteau USA (MT) 233 Ed22
Chotilsko CZ 38 Lp41
Chott Ech Chergui DZ 173 La28
Chott el Fedjadj TN 174 Le28
Chott el Gharbi DZ 173 Kk29
Chott el Gharsa TN 174 Ld28
Chott el Hodna DZ 173 Lc28
Chott el Jerid TN 174 Le29
Chott el Malah DZ 174 Lc29
Chott Melrhir DZ 174 Ld28
Chott Merouane DZ 174 Ld29
Chotyn UA 45 Mg42
Chouf RL 64 Mh29
Choûm RIM 178 Kd35
Chowchilla USA (CA) 234 Dk27
Choya RA (SE) 288 Gh60
Choyr MNG 90 Qe22
Chozi Z 206 Mf50
Chrám CZ 38 Lq40
Chr'aščevka RUS 53 Ne19
Chréa DZ 173 Lb27
Chréa, P.N. de DZ 173 Lb27
Chreïrik RIM 178 Kd35
Chrisí Ammoudiá GR 47 Me50
Chrisman USA (IL) 246 Fg26
Chrissiesmeer ZA 217 Mf59
Christchurch GB 21 Kt40
Christchurch NZ 155 Tg67
Christiana ZA 217 Mc59
Christianburg GUY 270 Ha42
Christiansburg USA (VA) 249 Fk27
Christiansfeld DK 14 Lk35
Christiansholm N 12 Lh32
Christianso DK 15 Lq35
Christian Sound USA 231 Dc17
Christiansted USA (VI) 261 Gh37
Christie Island MYA 116 Pj41
Christie Mtn. Ski Area USA 246 Fe23
Christina Lake CDN (BC) 232 Eb21
Christina River CDN 233 Ee17
Christmas Creek AUS (WA) 138 Rc55
Christmas Creek AUS 138 Rd55
Christmas Island AUS 118 Qb21
Christmas Ridge 302 Bb08
Christmas Valley USA (OR) 234 Dk24
Christoval USA (TX) 242 Ek30
Chrudim CZ 38 Lq41
Chrystynivka UA 54 Me21
Chrzanów PL 37 Lu40
Chu RUS 77 Oh24
Chu = Shu KZ 76 Oe23
Chuadanga BD 112 Pe34
Chuave PNG 159 Sc49
Chubalung CHN (SCH) 94 Pk31
Chub Cay BS 251 Gb33
Chubu-Sangaku N.P. J 101 Rj27
Chubut RA 292 Gg67
Chubut RA 267 Gc27
Chuchi Lake CDN 232 Dh18
Chuchiliga GH 193 Kk40
Chucuito PE 279 Gf53
Chucuma RA (SJ) 288 Gg61
Chucuri CO 268 Gc42
Chuka EAK 204 Mj46
Chukchi Autonomous District RUS 59 Tb05
Chukchi Plateau 298 Bd03
Chukchi Sea RUS 59 Uc04
Chukmpalli IND (MHT) 109 Pa36
Chuknagar BD 112 Pe34
Chukotskiy Poluostrov RUS 59 Ua05
Chulamar GCA 255 Fe39
Chulaphon Reservoir THA 114 Qa37
Chula Vista USA (CA) 236 Eb29
Chulluncani, Cerro BOL 285 Gh55
Chulucanas PE 272 Fk48
Chulumani BOL 284 Gg54
Chuluut gol MNG 90 Qa21
Chuma BOL 279 Gf53
Chumba ETH 198 Mk43
Chumbicha RA (CA) 288 Gg60
Chumbo BR (MG) 287 Hg55
Chumda CHN (QHI) 89 Pj29
Chumphae THA 114 Qb37
Chumphon THA 116 Pk40
Chumphon Buri THA 115 Qb38
Chum Phuang THA 115 Qb38
Chumpi PE 278 Gd53
Chumsaeng THA 114 Qa38
Chumuch PE 278 Ga49
Chumul MEX 255 Ff36
Chun THA 114 Qa36
Chun'an CHN (ZJG) 102 Qk31
Chunchi EC 272 Ga47
Ch'unch'on ROK 100 Rd27
Chunchucmil MEX (YT) 255 Fe35
Chundela ANG 209 Ma53
Chunga Z 209 Mc53
Chunga Z 210 Mg51
Chungang PRK 100 Rd25
Chunga Rest Camp Z 209 Mc53
Ch'ungju ROK 100 Rd27
Ch'ungmu ROK 100 Rd28
Chungui PE 278 Gd52
Chungungo RCH 288 Ge60
Chungyang Shanmo RC 97 Ra34
Chunian PK 79 Og30
Chunshui CHN (HNN) 95 Qg29
Chunwan CHN (GDG) 96 Qf34
Chunya EAT 206 Mg50
Chuor Phnom Kravanh K 115 Qb39
Chuor Phnum Dangrek K 115 Qb38
Chupaca PE 278 Gc52
Chupanan IR 72 Nh29
ChuPha VN 115 Qd39
Chu Prong VN 115 Qd39
Chuquibamba PE 279 Gd53
Chuquibambilla PE 279 Gd53
Chuquicamata RCH 284 Gf57
Chuquis PE 278 Gb50
Chur CH 34 Lk44
Churachandpur IND (MNP) 112 Pg33
Churcampa PE 278 Gc52
Churchbridge CDN (SK) 238 Ek20
Churchill CDN 225 Fb07
Churchill CDN 225 Fa07
Churchill Falls CDN 225 Gd08
Churchill Lake CDN 233 Ef17
Churchill Mountains 297 Sc35
Churchill River CDN 233 Ef18
Churchill Sound CDN 239 Ga17
Churchs Ferry USA (ND) 238 Fa21
Church Stretton GB 21 Ks38
Churia Range NEP 88 Pa31
Churia Range NEP 88 Pb32
Churin PE 278 Gb51
Churki IND (CGH) 109 Pb34
Churu IND (RJT) 106 Oh31
Churubamba PE 278 Gb50
Churuguara YV 269 Gf40
Chu Se VN 115 Qe39
Chushaf 79 Ok29
Chuska Mts. USA 237 Ef27
Chu-sonji J 101 Sa26
Chust UA 39 Md42
Chust UZ 76 Of25
Chute Akamba RDC 201 Md45
Chute Bangu RDC 201 Mc44
Chute de la Vina CAM 195 Lg42
Chute-des-Passes CDN (QC) 244 Ge21
Chute Kamimbi Fuka RDC 203 Mc50
Chute Mulamba Gungu RDC 203 Mb50
Chute Mupele RDC 201 Mc45
Chute Penge RDC 201 Me45
Chute Pogge II RDC 203 Ma49
Chutes d'Abourou RCA 196 Mb43
Chutes d'Antafofo RM 220 Nd55
Chutes de Béla RCB/RDC 202 Lh48
Chutes de Betsiboka RM 220 Nd54
Chutes de Billy RMM 184 Kf39
Chutes de Boali RCA 196 Lk43
Chutes de Bouenza RCB 202 Lg47
Chutes de Dibouangui G 202 Lf46
Chutes de Félou RMM 183 Ke38
Chutes de Gouina RMM 183 Ke38
Chutes de Gozobangui RDC 200 Mb43
Chutes de Katende RDC 203 Mb49
Chutes de Kembé RCA 196 Ma43
Chutes de Kinkon RG 192 Kd40
Chutes d'Ekom CAM 194 Lf43
Chutes de Kongou G 195 Lg45
Chutes de Kotto RCA 196 Ma43
Chutes de la Kagera BU 206 Me47
Chutes de la Kiubo RDC 206 Md50
Chutes de la Lobé CAM 194 Le44
Chutes de la Lofoi RDC 210 Md51
Chutes de la Lufira RDC 206 Md50
Chutes de la Madelaine F 162 Td57
Chutes de Lancrenon CAM 195 Lh42
Chutes de l'Ankofia RM 219 Ne53
Chutes de l'Ivindo de Tsengué Leledi G 195 Lg46
Chutes de Livingstone RDC 202 Lg48
Chutes de Lokoho RM 219 Ne53
Chutes de Loufoulakari RCB/RDC 202 Lh48
Chutes de Lubi RDC 203 Mb49
Chutes de Matakil RCA 196 Ma41
Chutes de Mbi RCA 195 Lj43
Chutes de Mingouli G 195 Lg45
Chutes de Nachtigal CAM 195 Lf43
Chutes de Ngolo RCA 196 Mb43
Chutes de Papara RMM 183 Ke38
Chutes de Poubara G 202 Lg46
Chutes de Sakaleona RM 220 Nd56
Chutes de Tanougou DY 193 La40
Chutes de Tinkisso RG 192 Ke40
Chutes de Touboutou RCA 195 Lh43
Chutes de Zongo RCB/RDC 202 Lh48
Chutes d'Inga RDC 202 Lg48
Chutes du Tello CAM 195 Lg42
Chutes Gauthiot TCH 187 Lh41
Chutes Guillaume = Chutes Tembo RDC 203 Lj49
Chutes Johnston RDC 210 Me51
Chutes Kasongo-Lunda RDC 203 Lj49
Chutes Pangu RDC 201 Md44
Chutes Tembo RDC 203 Lj49
Chutes Usu RDC 201 Mc44
Chute Toky RDC 201 Me45
Chute Walfe RDC 203 Mb48
Chutine Landing CDN (BC) 231 De17
Chuvashia RUS 53 Nd18
Chuwangsan N.P. ROK 100 Re27
Chuxiong CHN (YUN) 113 Qa33
Chuy ROU 289 Hd62
Chuzhou CHN (AHU) 102 Qk29
Chuzmiza RCH 284 Gf55
Chvaletice CZ 38 Lq40
Chwaka EAT 207 Mk49
Chwałowice PL 37 Mb40
Chwaszczyno PL 36 Lt36
Chynów PL 37 Mb39
Chynthiana USA (KY) 249 Fh26
Chyriv UA 39 Mc41
Chyulu Hills N.P. EAK 204 Mj47
Ciadâr-Lunga MD 45 Mj44
Ciamis RI 128 Qe49
Cianjur RI 128 Qd49
Cianorte BR (PR) 286 Hd57
Ciawi RI 128 Qd49
Cibadak RI 128 Qd49
Cibaray, Cerro BOL 284 Gf55
Cibinong RI 128 Qd49
Cibit RUS (ALT) 85 Pd20
Cibuta MEX (SO) 237 Ee30
Çiçekdağı TR 51 Mp51
Cicero Dantas BR (BA) 283 Ja51
Ćićevac SCG 46 Mb47
Cicheng CHN (ZJG) 102 Ra31
Cicia FJI 163 Ua54
Cidade da Pedra BR 281 Hc53
Cidade Gaúcha BR (PR) 286 Hd57
Cidade Medieval de Évora P 28 Kn48
Cidade Velha CV 182 Jj38
Cide TR 62 Mg25
Ciechanów PL 37 Ma38
Ciechanowiec PL 37 Mc38
Ciechocinek PL 36 Lt38
Ciego de Ávila C 259 Ga34
Ciego de Ávila C 259 Ga35
Ciemnik PL 36 Lq37
Ciemnoszyje PL 37 Mc37
Ciénaga de Ayapel CO 268 Gc43
Ciénaga de Oro CO 268 Gc41
Ciénaga de Pedeguita CO 268 Gb42
Ciénaga de Zapata, P.N. C 258 Fk34
Ciénaga de Zapatosa CO 268 Gd41
Ciénaga Grande CO 268 Gc41
Ciénaga Grande RA (PJ) 284 Gg57
Ciénaga Grande de Santa Marta CO 268 Gc40
Ciénaga Guájaro CO 268 Gc40
Ciénaga Iguana CO 268 Gc41
Ciénagas de Catatumbo, P.N. YV 268 Ge41
Ciénagas de Juan Manual YV 268 Gd41
Cienaguillas RA (PJ) 284 Gh57
Ciénega CO 268 Gc40
Ciénega del Toro MEX (NL) 253 Ek33
Ciénega Prieta MEX (CHH) 252 Eg32
Cienfuegos C 258 Fk34
Čierny Balog SK 39 Lu42
Cieszanów PL 37 Md40
Cieszyn PL 38 Lt41
Cieza E 29 Kt48
Ciężkowice PL 37 Lu40
Cifrapalota H 39 Lu44
Çiftehan TR 51 Mp53
Çifteler TR 51 Mm51
Çifte Minare Medresesi TR 63 Na26
Çiftlik TR 51 Mp52
Cifuentes C 258 Fk34
Cifuentes E 29 Ks50
Cifuncho PE 284 Ge58
Cigarette Springs Cave USA 237 Ee27
Cigarro BR (AM) 274 Gj47
Cigel'ka SK 39 Mb41
Cigliano I 40 Lj45
Cihanbeyli TR 51 Mn52
Cihanbeyli Yaylası TR 51 Mn52
Cijawung RI 128 Qc49
Cijulang RI 128 Qe49
Cikajang RI 128 Qd49
Cikalong RI 128 Qe49
Cikampek RI 128 Qd49
Cikarang RI 128 Qd49
Cikatomas RI 128 Qe49
Cikobia FJI 163 Ua53
Čikoj MNG 91 Qf21
Čikoj RUS (BUR) 90 Qd20
Čikokon RUS 91 Qf20
Cilacap RI 128 Qe49
Cilaos F 221 Nh56
Çıldır TR 63 Nb25
Çıldır Gölü TR 63 Nb25
Ciledug RI 128 Qe49
Cilegon RI 128 Qd49
Cilento I 42 Lq50
Cilento e Vallo di Diano, P.N. del I 42 Lq50
Çilgar RUS (KAL) 55 Nc22
Cili CHN (HUN) 95 Qf31
Cilibia RO 45 Mh45
Çilimli TR 51 Mm50
Cillas E 29 Kt50
Cilleros E 28 Ko50
Cillium TN 174 Le28
Čil'na RUS 53 Ne18
Cima USA (CA) 236 Ec28
Cimalavera, P.N. do ANG 208 Lg52
Cimarron USA (KS) 242 Ek27
Cimarron USA 242 Ek27
Cimarron Nat. Grassland USA 242 Ek27
Cimbur RI 132 Rc50
Çimenlik TR 50 Mg50
Çimenliyeniköy TR 62 Mg26
Cimetières des Dinosaures de Gadafawa RN 186 Le37
Cimitarra CO 268 Gd42
Cimljansk RUS 55 Nb22
Cimljanskoe Vodohranilišće RUS 53 Nb21
Cimoszki PL 37 Mc37
Cimpu RI 127 Ra47
Çimşit TR 51 Mn51
Çınar TR 63 Na27
Çınarcık TR 50 Mk50
Cinaruco YV 269 Gf42
Cinaruco-Capanaparo, P.N. YV 269 Gg42
Cincinnati USA (OH) 246 Fh26
Çine TR 50 Mj53
Ciney B 23 Lf40
Cinfães P 26 Km51
Cingoli I 41 Lo47
Cinque Island IND 111 Pg40
Cinque Terre I 40 Lk46
Cinque Terre, P.N. delle I 40 Lk46
Cintalapa MEX (CHP) 255 Fd37
Cintei RO 44 Mb44
Cintra RA (CD) 289 Gj62
Cioara MD 45 Mj44
Ciocănești RO 45 Mf43
Ciochina RO 45 Mh46
Ciocloivina RO 44 Md45
Ciolacu Nou MD 45 Mh43
Ciorani RO 45 Mg46
Ciorăști RO 45 Mh45
Cipanas RI 128 Qd49
Cipatujah RI 128 Qe49
Cipó BR (BA) 283 Ja51
Cipoal BR (AM) 274 Gh46
Cipoletti RA (RN) 292 Gg65
Čiprovski manastir BG 46 Mc47
Čir RUS 53 Nb21
Çirax Qala Sassanid Castle AZ 70 Ne25
Circeo, P.N. del I 42 Ln49
Circle USA (AK) 229 Cj13
Circle USA (MT) 235 Eh22
Circleville USA (OH) 246 Fj26
Circuit de Catalunya E 30 Lc49
Circuit Nelson Piquet BR 287 Hj57
Circuito de Jerez E 28 Kp46
Circuito Ricardo Tormo E 29 Ku49
Circular Reef PNG 159 Sd47
Cirebon RI 128 Qe49
Cirema, Gunung RI 128 Qe49
Cirencester GB 21 Kt39
Cirey-sur-Vezouze F 23 Lg42
Ciriè I 40 Lh45
Ciripču MD 45 Mj43
Ciriquiri BR 279 Gh50
Cir Kud SP 205 Nb44
Cirò I 43 Ls51
Cirò Marina I 43 Ls51
Čirpan BG 47 Mf48
Cirque, Cerro BOL 284 Gf54
Cirque de Jaffar MA 172 Kh29
Cirque de Navacelles F 25 Ld47
Cirque Rouge RM 218 Nd53
Cisco USA (TX) 242 Fa29
Cislău RO 45 Mg45
Cismișlia MD 45 Mj44
Cisneros CO 268 Gc42
Cisowsko-Orłowiński Park Krajobrazowy PL 37 Ma40
Cisséla RG 192 Ke40
Cisterna di Latina I 42 Ln49
Cistern Point BS 251 Gb34
Cistierna E 26 Kp52
Čita RUS 91 Qg19
Čita RUS 91 Qh19
Citadelle/Sans Souci RH 259 Gd36
Citadelle de Calvi F 31 Lj48
Citeureup RI 128 Qc49
Čitluk BIH 41 Ls47
Citronelle USA (AL) 243 Ff30
Citrusdal ZA 216 Lk62
Citrus Heights USA (CA) 234 Dk26
Città Alta di Bergamo I 40 Lk45
Cittadella I 40 Lm45
Città della Pieve I 40 Ln48
Città del Palladio I 40 Lm45
Città di Castello I 40 Ln47
Città Sant'Angelo I 42 Lp48
City Palace (Jaipur) IND 106 Oh32
City Palace (Udaipur) IND 108 Og33
Ciucea RO 44 Mc44
Ciucurova RO 45 Mj46
Ciudad Altamirano MEX (GUR) 254 Ek36
Ciudad Bolívar YV 270 Gj41
Ciudad Bolivia YV 269 Ge41
Ciudad Camargo MEX (CHH) 253 Eh32
Ciudad Constitución MEX (BCS) 252 Ee33
Ciudad Cortes CR 256 Fj41
Ciudad de Guatemala GCA 255 Fe38
Ciudad del Carmen MEX (CAM) 255 Fe36
Ciudad del Este PY 286 Hc58
Ciudad del Maíz MEX (SLP) 253 Fa34
Ciudad de Loreto RA (SE) 288 Gh60
Ciudad de México MEX (MEX) 254 Fa36
Ciudad de México MEX (MEX) 254 Fa36
Ciudad de Nutrias YV 269 Gf41
Ciudad Encantada E 29 Ks50
Ciudad Guayana YV 270 Gj41
Ciudad Guerrero MEX (TM) 253 Fa32
Ciudad Guzmán MEX (JLC) 254 Ej36
Ciudad Hidalgo MEX (CHP) 255 Fd38
Ciudad Hidalgo MEX (MHC) 254 Ek36
Ciudad Huitzuco MEX (GUR) 254 Fa36
Ciudad Insurgentes MEX (BCS) 252 Ee33
Ciudad Ixtepec MEX (OAX) 255 Fc37
Ciudad Juárez MEX (CHH) 237 Eg30
Ciudad Lerdo MEX (DGO) 253 Ej33
Ciudad Lerdo de Tejada MEX (VC) 255 Fc36
Ciudad Madero MEX (TM) 253 Fb34
Ciudad Mante MEX (TM) 253 Fa34
Ciudad Melchor de Mencos GCA 255 Ff37
Ciudad monumental de Cáceres E 28 Ko49
Ciudad Mutis = Bahía Solano CO 268 Gb42
Ciudad Neily CR 256 Fj41
Ciudad Nezahualcóyotl MEX (MEX) 254 Fa36
Ciudad Obregón MEX (SO) 252 Ef32
Ciudad Ojeda YV 268 Ge40
Ciudad Perdida CO 268 Gd40
Ciudad Piar YV 270 Gj42
Ciudad Real E 29 Kr48
Ciudad Rodrigo E 26 Ko50
Ciudad Sahagún MEX (HDG) 254 Fa36
Ciudad Serdán MEX (PUE) 254 Fb36
Ciudad Valles MEX (SLP) 254 Fa35
Ciudad Victoria MEX (TM) 253 Fa34
Ciuperceni RO 44 Md46
Ciutadella E 30 Ld50
Ciutești MD 45 Mj43
Cividale del Friuli I 41 Lo44
Civil'sk RUS (CHU) 53 Nd18
Civita Castellana I 42 Ln48
Civitanova Marche I 41 Lo47
Civitavécchia I 42 Lm48
Civitella del Tronto I 42 Lo48
Civitella Roveto I 42 Lo49
Çivray F 24 La44
Çivril TR 50 Mk52
Cixi CHN (ZJG) 102 Ra30
Cizre TR 63 Nb27
Cjurupyns'k UA 54 Mg22
Čkalovsk RUS 53 Nb17
Čkalovskoe RUS 98 Rg23
Čki-Naryn KS 77 Oj25
Clacton-on-Sea GB 21 Lb39
Clain F 22 La44
Clair Engle Lake USA 234 Dj25
Clairview AUS (QLD) 149 Se57
Clamecy F 23 Ld43
Clam Lake USA (WI) 241 Fe22
Clan Donald Centre GB 18 Kp33
Clanton USA (AL) 248 Fg29
Clanville ZA 217 Md61
Clanwilliam ZA 216 Lk62
Claonaig GB 18 Kp35
Claquato Church USA 232 Dj22
Clara Island MYA 116 Pj40
Clara, Mount NZ 155 Tg67
Claraville AUS (NT) 143 Rh57
Claraville AUS (QLD) 148 Sa55
Clare AUS (QLD) 149 Sd55
Clare AUS (QLD) 149 Sc57
Clare AUS (SA) 152 Rk62
Clare USA (MI) 246 Fh24
Clare Island IRL 18 Kk37
Claremont USA (NH) 247 Gd24
Claremont Point AUS 147 Sb52
Claremore USA (OK) 243 Fc27
Claremorris IRL 18 Km37
Clarence NZ 155 Tg67
Clarence Cannon N.W.R. USA 241 Fe26
Clarence Island 296 Ha31
Clarence Strait AUS 139 Rf52
Clarence Strait USA 231 Dd18
Clarence Town BS 251 Gc34
Clarendon USA (TX) 242 Ek28
Clarens ZA 217 Me60
Clarenville CDN (NF) 245 Hc21
Claresholm CDN (AB) 233 Ed20
Clareton USA (WY) 235 Eh24
Clarinda USA (IA) 241 Fc25
Clarines YV 269 Gh41
Clarion USA (IA) 241 Fd24
Clarion USA (PA) 247 Ga25
Clarion Fracture Zone 303 Cb08
Clark USA (SD) 240 Fb23
Clark USA (WY) 235 Ef23
Clarke-City CDN (QC) 244 Gg20
Clarke Island AUS 152 Se66
Clarke Lake CDN 233 Eg18
Clarke River AUS (QLD) 149 Sc55
Clarkia USA (ID) 232 Eb22
Clarkleigh CDN (MB) 238 Fa20
Clark Range AUS (QLD) 149 Sd56
Clarksburg USA (WV) 247 Fk26
Clarksdale USA (MS) 243 Fe28
Clark's Harbour CDN (NS) 245 Gh24
Clarkson ZA 217 Mc63
Clarkson Bridge USA 248 Fg28
Clarks Point USA (AK) 228 Ca16
Clarkston USA (WA) 234 Eb22
Clarksville USA (AR) 243 Fd28
Clarksville USA (TN) 248 Fg27
Clarksville USA (TX) 243 Fc29
Claro BR 281 He54
Claro BR 286 He54
Claro dos Poções BR (MG) 287 Hh54
Claromecó RA (BA) 293 Gk65
Classical Gardens CHN 102 Ra30
Claude USA (TX) 242 Ek28
Cláudia BR (MT) 281 Hc51
Claudio BR (MG) 287 Hh56
Clausthal-Zellerfeld D 33 Ll39
Claveria RP 121 Ra36
Claveria RP 121 Rb39
Claxton USA (GA) 249 Fk29
Clay USA (WV) 249 Fk26
Claybank CDN (SK) 233 Eh20
Clay Belt CDN 239 Fk20
Clay Center USA (KS) 240 Fb26
Claydon CDN (SK) 233 Ef21
Clayoquot Sound CDN 232 Dg21
Clayton AUS (SA) 143 Rk60
Clayton USA (AL) 249 Fh30
Clayton USA (GA) 249 Fj28
Clayton USA (ID) 235 Ec23
Clayton USA (MO) 241 Fe26
Clayton USA (NM) 237 Ej27
Clayton USA (OK) 243 Fc28
Clear Creek USA 229 Cg13
Clear Creek CDN (AB) 233 Ea17
Clearfield USA (PA) 247 Ga25
Clearfield USA (SD) 240 Ek24
Clearfield USA (UT) 235 Ed25
Clearlake USA (CA) 234 Dj26
Clear Lake USA (IA) 241 Fd24
Clear Lake USA (SD) 241 Fb23
Clear Lake USA (UT) 235 Ed26
Clear Lake USA 234 Dj26
Clear Lake Reservoir USA 234 Dk25
Clear Prairie CDN (AB) 233 Ea17
Clearwater CDN (BC) 232 Dk20
Clearwater USA (FL) 250 Fj32
Clearwater USA 234 Eb22
Clearwater Creek CDN 231 Dg14
Clearwater Lake CDN 238 Ek18
Clearwater Lake Prov. Park CDN 238 Ek18
Clearwater Mountains USA 235 Ec22
Clearwater River CDN 233 Ee17
Clearwater West Lake CDN 238 Fd21
Cleburne USA (TX) 242 Fb29
Cle Elum USA (WA) 232 Dk22
Cleethorpes GB 21 Ku37
Clejani RO 45 Mf46
Clelles F 25 Lf46
Clementina BR (SP) 286 He56
Clemson USA (SC) 249 Fj28
Cleopatra Needle RP 122 Qk40
Cleo Springs USA (OK) 242 Fa27
Clermont AUS (QLD) 149 Sd57
Clermont F 23 Lc41
Clermont USA (FL) 250 Fk31

Clermont-en-Argonne – Coral Harbour

Clermont-en-Argonne F 23 Lf41
Clermont-Ferrand F 25 Ld45
Clermont-l'Hérault F 25 Ld47
Clerval F 23 Lg43
Clervaux L 23 Lg40
Cles I 40 Lm44
Cleugh Passage IND 111 Pg39
Cleve AUS (SA) 152 Rj62
Clevedon GB 21 Ks39
Cleveland USA (GA) 249 Fj28
Cleveland USA (MS) 243 Fe29
Cleveland USA (OH) 246 Fk25
Cleveland USA (TN) 249 Fh28
Cleveland USA (TX) 243 Fc30
Clevelândia BR (PR) 290 Hd59
Clevelan Pen. USA 231 Dd18
Cleveleys GB 21 Kr37
Clew Bay IRL 18 Kl37
Clewiston USA (FL) 250 Fk32
Clifden IRL 18 Kk36
Clifden NZ 155 Td69
Clifden Castle IRL 18 Kk36
Cliffdale River AUS (QLD) 148 Rk54
Cliffs of Moher IRL 20 Kl38
Cliffs of the Nullarbor AUS 145 Re61
Clifton AUS (QLD) 151 Sf59
Clifton USA (AZ) 237 Ef29
Clifton USA (TN) 248 Fg28
Clifton ZA 216 Lk62
Clifton Bridge GB 21 Ks39
Clifton Hills AUS (SA) 143 Rk59
Cli Lake CDN 231 Dj15
Climax CDN (SK) 233 Ef21
Climax USA (CO) 235 Eg26
Climax USA (MN) 240 Fb22
Clinch Mts. USA 249 Fj27
Clines Corners USA (NM) 237 Eh28
Clinton CDN (BC) 232 Dk20
Clinton NZ 155 Te69
Clinton USA (AL) 248 Fg29
Clinton USA (AR) 243 Fd28
Clinton USA (IA) 241 Fe25
Clinton USA (IL) 246 Ff25
Clinton USA (LA) 243 Fe30
Clinton USA (MO) 241 Fd26
Clinton USA (MT) 235 Ed22
Clinton USA (NC) 249 Ga28
Clinton USA (OK) 242 Fa28
Clinton USA (SC) 249 Fk28
Clinton USA (WA) 232 Dj21
Clintwood USA (VA) 249 Fj27
Clio USA (AL) 249 Fh30
Clipperton Fracture Zone 303 Cb09
Clisson F 22 Kt43
Clitheroe GB 21 Ks37
Cliza BOL 284 Gg54
Clodomira RA (SE) 288 Gh59
Cloghan IRL 20 Kn37
Clogher Head IRL 20 Ko37
Clogherhead IRL 20 Ko37
Clonagh AUS (QLD) 148 Sa56
Clonakilty IRL 20 Km39
Clonbrook GUY 271 Hb42
Cloncurry AUS (QLD) 148 Sa56
Cloncurry River AUS (QLD) 148 Sa56
Clones IRL 18 Kn36
Clonmacnoise IRL 20 Kn37
Clonmel IRL 20 Kn38
Cloppenburg D 32 Lj38
Cloquet USA (MN) 241 Fd22
Cloquet USA 241 Fd22
Clorindorme CDN (QC) 245 Gh21
Clorinda RA (FO) 285 Hb58
Cloudy Mount USA 229 Cb14
Clovelly GB 20 Kq40
Cloverdale USA (CA) 234 Dj26
Clovis USA (CA) 234 Ea27
Clovis USA (NM) 237 Ej28
Cloyes-sur-le-Loir F 22 Lb43
Cl'ton RUS 53 Nd21
Clucellas RA (SF) 289 Gk61
Cluj-Napoca RO 44 Md44
Cluny AUS (QLD) 150 Rk58
Cluny F 25 Le44
Cluses F 25 Lg44
Clusone I 40 Lk45
Clute CDN (ON) 239 Fk21
Clutha River NZ 155 Te68
Clyde CDN (AB) 233 Ed18
Clyde CDN 225 Gc04
Clyde GB 19 Kr35
Clydebank GB 19 Kq35
Clyde River CDN (NS) 245 Gh24
Cna RUS 53 Na19
Coacalco MEX (MEX) 254 Fa36
Coaceral BR (BA) 282 Hh51
Coachella USA (CA) 236 Eb29
Coahuila MEX 226 Ed13
Coakari BOL 284 Gg55
Coalcomán de Vázquez Pallares MEX (MHC) 254 Ej36
Coal Creek USA (AK) 229 Cj13
Coaldale CDN (AB) 233 Ed21
Coaldale USA (NV) 234 Eb26
Coalgate USA (OK) 243 Fb28
Coalinga USA (CA) 236 Dk27
Coal River CDN (BC) 231 Dg16
Coal River CDN 231 Dg15
Coamo USA (PR) 261 Gg36
Coaraci BR (BA) 283 Ja53
Coari BR (AM) 274 Gj48
Coari BR 274 Gh48
Coarnele Caprei RO 45 Mh43
Coasa PE 279 Ge53
Coastal Plain USA 222 Fa06
Coast Mountains CDN/USA 222 Db04
Coast of Labrador CDN 225 Gd07
Coast Ranges USA 234 Dj23
Coata PE 279 Gf53
Coatepec MEX (VC) 254 Fb36
Coatepeque GCA 255 Fe38
Coaticook CDN (QC) 247 Ge23
Coats Bay CDN 239 Ga17
Coats Island CDN 225 Fd06
Coats Land ANT 296 Jb34
Coatzacoalcos MEX (VC) 255 Fc36
Cobá MEX (QTR) 255 Fg35
Cobá MEX 255 Fg35
Cobadin RO 45 Mj46
Cobalt USA (ID) 235 Ec23
Cobán GCA 255 Fe38
Çobanlar TR 51 Ml52
Cobano CR 256 Fh41
Cobar AUS (NSW) 151 Sc61
Cobblestones AUS 144 Qh62
Cobden AUS (VIC) 153 Sb65
Cobh IRL 20 Km39
Cobham AUS (NSW) 150 Sb61
Cobham River CDN 238 Fc19
Cobija BOL 279 Gf51
Cobleni NAM 212 Lk56
Cobleskill USA (NY) 247 Gc24
Cobos RA (SA) 285 Gh58
Cobourg CDN (ON) 247 Ga24
Cobourg Peninsula AUS 139 Rg51
Cobquecura RCH 292 Gd64
Cóbué MOC 211 Mh52
Coburg D 35 Ll40
Coburn AUS (WA) 140 Qh59
Coca E 26 Kq51
Coca EC 272 Gb46
Coca EC 272 Gb46
Cocachacra PE 278 Gb51
Cocal BR (PI) 277 Hk47
Cocalinho BR (MA) 276 Hh47
Cocalinho BR (MT) 281 He53
Cocameira BR (AC) 279 Ge50
Cochabamba BOL 284 Gg54
Cochabamba PE 278 Ga49
Cochem D 34 Lh40
Cochetopa Hills USA 237 Eg27
Cochin = Kochi IND (KER) 110 Oj42
Cochran USA (GA) 249 Fj29
Cochrane CDN (AB) 233 Ec20
Cochrane CDN (ON) 239 Fk21
Cochrane RCH 294 Gd69
Cockaköl KZ 84 Of21
Cockatoo AUS (QLD) 151 Sf58
Cockatoo Island AUS 138 Rb54
Cockburn Bank 20 Km41
Cockburn Harbor GB 251 Ge35
Cockburn Town BS 251 Gc33
Cockburn Town GB 251 Ge35
Cockermouth GB 19 Kr36
Cocklebiddy AUS (WA) 145 Rd62
Coclecito PA 257 Fk41
Coco CR 256 Fh40
Coco HN/NIC 256 Fj38
Cocobeach G 194 Le45
Cococá BR (CE) 277 Hk49
Coco Channel IND 111 Pg39
Cococi BR (CE) 277 Hk49
Cocodrie USA (LA) 243 Fe31
Cocoland NIC 256 Fj38
Cocona MEX 255 Fd37
Cocoparra N.P. AUS (NSW) 153 Sd63
Cocorna CO 268 Gc42
Cocos BR (BA) 282 Hh53
Cocos Island CR 264 Fc17
Cocos Islands AUS 118 Pd21
Cocos Ridge 264 Fc18
Cocuite MEX (VC) 254 Fb36
Cocula MEX (JLC) 254 Ej35
Codajás BR (AM) 274 Gj47
Codeagro BR (AM) 274 Gk47
Codemin BR (GO) 282 Hf53
Codfish Island NZ 155 Td69
Codigoro I 40 Ln46
Codlea RO 45 Mf45
Codó BR (MA) 276 Hj48
Codo del Pozuzo PE 278 Gc50
Codogno I 40 Lk45
Codozinho BR (MA) 276 Hh48
Codpa RCH 284 Gf55
Codrington AG 261 Gk37
Codróipo I 41 Ln45
Codru MD 45 Mj44
Cody USA (WY) 235 Ef23
Coelemu RCH 292 Gd64
Coelho Neto BR (MA) 277 Hj48
Coenbult NAM 216 Lk59
Coengua PE 278 Gd51
Coeur d'Alene Ind. Res. USA 232 Eb22
Coeur d'Alene Lake USA 232 Eb22
Coesfeld D 32 Lh39
Coëtivy SY 219 Nj49
Coeur d'Alene USA (ID) 232 Eb22
Coevorden NL 32 Lg38
Coffee Bay ZA 217 Me62
Coffee Bay Beach Point ZA 217 Me62
Coffee Creek CDN (YT) 231 Da14
Coffeyville USA (KS) 243 Fc27
Coffin Bay AUS (SA) 152 Rh63
Coffin Bay AUS 152 Rh63
Coffin Bay N.P. AUS 152 Rh63
Coffs Harbour AUS (NSW) 151 Sg61
Cofimvaba ZA 217 Md61
Cofre de Perote, Cerro MEX 253 Fb36
Cogâlnic MD 45 Mj44
Çoghadak IR 74 Nf31
Coghinas I 31 Lk50
Coghtan ZA 217 Me61
Cogla Downs AUS (WA) 140 Qj59
Cognac F 24 Ku45
Cogne I 40 Lh45
Cogolin F 25 Lg47
Čograjskoe vodohranilišče RUS 70 Nc23
Çoğun TR 51 Mp51
Coguno MOC 214 Mh58
Cohoes USA (NY) 247 Gd24
Cohuna AUS (VIC) 153 Sc63
Coig RA 294 Gf71
Coihaique RCH 294 Gd68
Coihaique Alto RCH 292 Ge68
Coihue RCH 292 Gd64
Coihueco RCH 292 Ge64
Coimbatore IND (TNU) 111 Oj41
Coimbra P 26 Km50
Coin E 28 Kq46
Coipasa, Cerro BOL 284 Gf55
Coirón RCH 288 Ge61
Coja P 26 Kn50
Cojata PE 279 Gf53
Cojimies EC 272 Fk45
Cojúa YV 268 Ge40
Cojudo Blanco, Cerro RA 294 Gf69
Çokak TR 62 Mj27
Coker Creek USA 249 Fh28
Cokeville USA (WY) 235 Ee24
Çokören TR 51 Mn51
Colac AUS (VIC) 153 Sb65
Colán Conhué RA (CB) 292 Gf67
Colane AUS (NSW) 150 Sb60
Colares BR (PA) 276 Hf46
Colatina BR (ES) 287 Hk55
Colazolo RA (CD) 288 Gj61
Colbún RCH 292 Ge63
Colby USA (KS) 240 Ek26
Colca PE 279 Ge53
Colcabamba PE 278 Gd52
Colchane RCH 284 Gf55
Colchani BOL 284 Gg56
Colchester GB 21 La39
Colchester ZA 217 Mc62
Colcolano ZA 217 Md60
Col d'Allos F 25 Lg46
Col d'Ares F 24 Lc48
Col d'Aubisque F 24 Ku48
Cold Bay USA (AK) 228 Bj18
Col de Bavella F 31 Lk49
Col de Gobo RN 181 Lh35
Col de la Croix Haute F 25 Lf46
Col de la Givrine CH 34 Lg44
Col de la Schlucht F 23 Lh42
Col de l'Iseran F 25 Lh45
Col de l'Izoard F 25 Lg46
Col de Montgenèvre F 25 Lg46
Col de Sara RN 181 Lg35
Col des Chandeliers RN 181 Lg35
Col de Tafori RG 192 Kd40
Col de Telmet DZ 174 Ld28
Col de Yeï Lulu RN 181 Lh35
Colditz D 33 Ln39
Cold Lake CDN 233 Ef18
Coldspring Mtn. CDN 231 Db14
Cold Springs USA (NV) 234 Eb26
Coldstream GB 19 Ks35
Col du Galibier F 25 Lg45
Col du Grand Saint-Bernard I/CH 34 Lh45
Col du Lautaret F 25 Lg45
Col du Petit St-Bernard F/I 25 Lg45
Col du Pourtalet F 24 Ku48
Col du Tourmalet F 24 La48
Col du Zad MA 172 Kh29
Coldwater USA (KS) 242 Fa27
Coldwater USA (MI) 246 Fh25
Coleambally AUS (NSW) 153 Sc63
Cole Bay CDN (SK) 233 Ef18
Colebrook USA (NH) 247 Ge23
Colegiata de Santa María de Calatayud E 27 Kt51
Colekeplaas ZA 217 Mc62
Coleman USA (TX) 242 Fa30
Coleman River AUS 146 Sb53
Colenso ZA 217 Me60
Co Le Pagoda VN 96 Qd35
Colera E 30 Ld48
Coleraine GB 18 Ko35
Coles Bay AUS (TAS) 152 Se67
Colesberg ZA 217 Mc61
Colfax USA (ND) 240 Fb22
Colfax USA (WA) 234 Eb22
Colfontaine B 23 Ld40
Colgante Glacier RCH 292 Gd68
Colgong IND (BIH) 112 Pd33
Colguila SP 199 Nd42
Colha BH 255 Ff37
Colibita RO 44 Me43
Cólico I 40 Lk44
Colidor BR (MT) 281 Hc51
Coligny ZA 217 Md59
Colima MEX (COL) 254 Ej36
Colima MEX 254 Ej36
Colima, Volcán de MEX 254 Ej36
Colina BR (SP) 286 Hf56
Colina RCH 288 Ge62
Colinas BR (MA) 276 Hh49
Colinas do Tocantins BR (TO) 282 Hf50
Colinet CDN (NF) 245 Hd22
Colintraive GB 19 Kp35
Coliseo C 258 Fk34
Coll GB 18 Ko34
Collado Bajo E 29 Kt50
Collado-Villalba E 29 Kr50
Collahuasi RCH 284 Gf56
Collarenebri AUS (NSW) 151 Se60
Collaroy AUS (QLD) 149 Se57
Coll de Rates E 29 Ku48
Collécchio I 40 Ll46
Collector AUS (NSW) 153 Se63
Colle della Maddalena F/I 40 Lg46
Colle di Val d'Elsa I 40 Lm47
Colleferro I 42 Lo49
College Place USA (WA) 234 Ea22
College Station USA (TX) 243 Fb30
Collegiata di San Càndido I 40 Ln44
Colli Albani I 42 Ln49
Collie AUS (WA) 144 Qj62
Collie Bay AUS 138 Rc54
Collier Range AUS 140 Qk58
Collier Range N.P. AUS 140 Qk58
Collierville USA (TN) 243 Ff28
Collines Baoulé CI 193 Kh42
Collines de Bongouanou CI 193 Kh42
Collingullie AUS (NSW) 153 Sd63
Collingwood AUS (QLD) 151 Sf59
Collingwood CDN (ON) 247 Fk23
Collingwood NZ 155 Tg66
Collingwood Bay PNG 159 Se50
Collins CDN (ON) 239 Ff20
Collins USA (MS) 243 Ff30
Collinsville AUS (QLD) 149 Sd56
Collipulli RCH 292 Gd64
Collmberg D 33 Lo39
Collo DZ 174 Ld27
Colloma BOL 284 Gg55
Collón Cura RA 292 Ge66
Colmar F 23 Lh42
Colmars F 25 Lg46
Colméia BR (TO) 282 Hf50
Colmena MEX (DGO) 253 Eh34
Colmenar E 28 Kq46
Colmenar Viejo E 29 Kr50
Colnett C 162 Tc56
Cologne D 32 Lg40
Colo-i-Suva Forest Reserve FJI 163 Tk54
Colombey-les-Belles F 23 Lf42
Colombey-les-Deux-Églises F 23 Le42
Colômbia BR (SP) 286 Hf56
Colombia C 259 Gb35
Colombia CO 268 Gc44
Colombia MEX 263 Ga09
Colombia Basin 260 Gc38
Colombo BR (PR) 286 Hf58
Colombo CL 111 Ok43
Colomi BOL 284 Gh54
Colón C 258 Fk34
Colón PA 257 Ga41
Colón RA (BA) 289 Gk62
Colón RA (ER) 289 Ha62
Colona AUS (SA) 145 Rg61
Colonelganj IND (UPH) 107 Pa32
Colonel Hill BS 251 Gc34
Colonet MEX (BC) 236 Eb30
Colônia BR 283 Ja53
Colonia FSM 156 Rd17
Colonia 10 de Julio RA (CD) 289 Gj61
Colonia Angamos PE 273 Gd48
Colonia Carlos Pellegrini RA (CR) 289 Hb60
Colonia Caroya RA (CD) 288 Gj61
Colonia del Sacramento ROU 289 Hb63
Colònia de Sant Jordi E 30 Lc51
Colônia do Piauí BR (PI) 277 Hj49
Colonia Dora RA (SE) 288 Gj60
Colonia La Pastoril RA (LP) 292 Gg64
Colonia Lavalleja ROU 289 Hb61
Colonial Beach USA (VA) 247 Gb26
Colonial Heights USA (VA) 249 Gb27
Colonia Liebig RA (CR) 289 Hc59
Colonial Williamsburg USA (VA) 249 Gb27
Colonia Marina RA (CD) 289 Gj61
Colonia Pastoril RA (FO) 285 Ha58
Colonia piel foca EC 272 Fe46
Colonia San Miguel PY 285 Ha58
Colônia São Romão BR (MS) 286 Hc55
Colonias Unidas RA (CH) 289 Ha59
Colonia Winkler PY 285 Ha57
Colonsay GB 18 Ko34
Colorado BR (PR) 286 He57
Colorado BR 280 Gj52
Colorado C 259 Ga35
Colorado, Cerro RA 288 Gg60
Colorado RA 292 Gg65
Colorado, Cerro RA 292 Gf68
Colorado USA 237 Ee27
Colorado USA 242 Fa30
Colorado USA 226 Ec11
Colorado City USA (AZ) 236 Ed27
Colorado City USA (CO) 237 Eh27
Colorado City USA (TX) 242 Ek29
Colorado Desert USA 236 Ec29
Colorado d'Oeste BR (RO) 280 Gk52
Colorado Nat. Mon. USA 235 Ef26
Colorado Plateau USA 237 Ee27
Colorados, Cerro RA/RCH 288 Gf59
Colorado Springs USA (CO) 235 Eh26
Color Sand Forest CHN 113 Qb33
Colossal AUS (NSW) 151 Sd61
Colosseo I 42 Ln49
Colotenango GCA 255 Fe38
Colotlipa MEX (GUR) 254 Fa37
Coloured Canyon ET 177 Mh31
Colquechaca BOL 284 Gh55
Colquen, Cerro RCH 292 Gd64
Col Quijoux RCA 196 Mb41
Colquiri BOL 284 Gg54
Colquitt USA (GA) 249 Fh30
Colston Park AUS (QLD) 149 Se56
Colstrip USA (MT) 235 Eg23
Columbia USA (AL) 249 Fh30
Columbia USA (KY) 248 Fh27
Columbia USA (LA) 243 Fd29
Columbia USA (MD) 247 Gb26
Columbia USA (MO) 241 Fd26
Columbia USA (MS) 243 Ff30
Columbia USA (NC) 249 Gb28
Columbia USA (SC) 249 Fk29
Columbia USA (TN) 248 Fg28
Columbia USA 234 Dk23
Columbia City USA (IN) 246 Fh25
Columbia Falls USA (MT) 233 Ec21
Columbia Glacier USA 229 Cg15
Columbia Icefield CDN 233 Eb20
Columbia, Mount CDN 232 Eb19
Columbia Mountains CDN 232 Ea20
Columbiana USA (AL) 248 Fg29
Columbia Plateau USA 234 Eb24
Columbia Reach CDN 232 Ea20
Columbia River CDN 232 Ea20
Columbia River USA 232 Ea21
Columbus USA (GA) 249 Fh29
Columbus USA (KS) 243 Fc27
Columbus USA (MS) 243 Ff29
Columbus USA (MT) 235 Ef23
Columbus USA (NM) 237 Eg30
Columbus USA (OH) 246 Fj26
Columbus USA (IN) 248 Fh26
Columbus Landing 1494 JA 259 Gb36
Columbus Monument BS 251 Gc33
Columbus Monument C 259 Gb35
Columbus USA (NE) 240 Fb25
Columbus USA (TX) 243 Fb31
Coluna BR (MG) 287 Hj55
Colunga E 26 Kp53
Colupo, Cerro RCH 284 Ge57
Colville USA (WA) 232 Eb21
Colville Channel NZ 154 Th64
Colville Ind. Res. USA 232 Ea21
Colville River USA 229 Cd11
Colwyn Bay GB 21 Kr37
Comácchio I 40 Ln46
Comácha MOC 210 Mg54
Comala MEX (COL) 254 Ej36
Comalcalco MEX (TB) 255 Fd36
Comalcalco MEX 255 Fd36
Comallo RA (RN) 292 Ge66
Comallo RA 292 Ge66
Comanche USA (OK) 242 Fb28
Comanche USA (TX) 242 Fa30
Comanche Nat. Grassland USA 237 Ej27
Comandante Fontana RA (FO) 285 Ha58
Comandante Luis Piedra Buena RA (SC) 294 Gf70
Comandău RO 45 Mg45
Comănești RO 45 Mg44
Comarapa BOL 285 Gh54
Comarnic RO 45 Mf45
Comas PE 278 Gc51
Comayagua HN 256 Fg38
Comayagüela HN 256 Fg38
Combapata PE 279 Ge53
Combara AUS (NSW) 151 Se61
Combarbalá RCH 288 Ge61
Combeaufontaine F 23 Lf43
Combe de Lavaux F 23 Le43
Combles F 23 Lc41
Comboi RI 125 Qb45
Comboios, T.I. BR 287 Hk55
Combomune MOC 214 Mg57
Combourg F 22 Kt42
Comè DY 193 La42
Come by Chance AUS (NSW) 151 Se61
Comedero MEX (SL) 252 Eg33
Comerio USA (PR) 261 Gg36
Comerzinho BR (MG) 287 Hk54
Comet AUS (QLD) 149 Se57
Comet AUS (SA) 143 Rh60
Cometela MOC 214 Mh56
Comicó RA 292 Gg66
Comilla BD 112 Pf34
Cómiso I 42 Lp54
Comitán de Domínguez MEX (CHP) 255 Fd37
Commentry F 25 Lc44
Commerce USA (GA) 249 Fj28
Commerce USA (TX) 243 Fc29
Commercy F 23 Lf42
Commissioner Island CDN 238 Fb19
Committee Bay CDN 224 Fc05
Commodore Reef 122 Qh41
Commonwealth Bay ANT (AUS) 297 Sa32
Commonwealth Bay 297 Sa32
Commonwealth Hill AUS (SA) 143 Rh60
Como I 40 Lk45
Como RCB 195 Lh45
Como Bluff Fossil Beds USA 235 Eh25
Comodoro BR (MT) 280 Ha52
Comodoro Py RA (BA) 289 Gk63
Comodoro Rivadavia RA (CB) 294 Gg68
Comoé CI 193 Kj43
Comoé, P.N. de la CI 193 Kj41
Comonfort MEX (GJT) 254 Ek35
Comoros COM 218 Nb51
Comoros 167 Na11
Comox CDN (BC) 232 Dh21
Compeer CDN (AB) 233 Ee20
Compiègne F 23 Lc41
Complex of Monuments (Hue) VN 115 Qd37
Comporta P 28 Km48
Compostela MEX (NYT) 253 Eh35
Compostela RP 123 Rd42
Comps-sur-Artuby F 25 Lg47
Comrat MD 45 Mj44
Comstock USA (TX) 242 Ek31
Comunidad CR 256 Fh40
Comunidad YV 273 Gg44
Cona CHN (TIB) 89 Pf32
Conakry RG 192 Kd41
Conambo EC 272 Gb46
Conambo EC 272 Gb46
Conanaco EC 272 Gc46
Cona Niyeu RA (RN) 292 Gg66
Conara AUS (TAS) 152 Sd66
Conargo AUS (NSW) 153 Sc63
Conay RCH 288 Ge60
Conay RCH 288 Ge60
Conca MEX (HDG) 254 Fa35
Concarán RA (SL) 288 Gh62
Concarneau F 22 Kr43
Concepción del Uruguay RA (ER) 289 Ha62
Conceição BR (AM) 274 Gk47
Conceição BR (PB) 277 Ja49
Conceição BR 277 Hk49
Conceição da Barra BR (ES) 287 Ja55
Conceição das Alagoas BR (MG) 286 Hf55
Conceição de Mau BR (RR) 270 Ha44
Conceição do Araguaia BR (PA) 281 Hf50
Conceição do Canindé BR (PI) 277 Hk49
Conceição do Coite BR (BA) 283 Ja51
Conceição do Macabu BR (RJ) 287 Hk57
Conceição do Mato Dentro BR (MG) 287 Hj55
Conceição do Tocantins BR (TO) 282 Hg52
Concepción BOL 285 Gj54
Concepción CO 273 Gd46
Concepción PE 278 Gc51
Concepción PY 285 Hb57
Concepción RA (CR) 289 Hb60
Concepción RA (TU) 288 Gh59
Concepción RCH 292 Gd64
Concepción del Oro MEX (ZCT) 253 Ek33
Concepción Island BS 251 Gc34
Concepción, Volcán NIC 256 Fh40
Conception Bay CDN 245 Hd22
Conchas BR (SP) 286 Hf57
Conchas Dam USA (NM) 237 Eh28
Conchas Lake USA 237 Eh28
Conches-en-Ouche F 22 La42
Conchillas ROU 289 Ha63
Conchos MEX 252 Eg32
Concón RCH 288 Ge62
Concord USA (CA) 234 Dk27
Concord USA (NC) 249 Fk28
Concord USA (NH) 247 Ge24
Concórdia BR (SC) 290 Hd59
Concordia MEX (SL) 252 Eg34
Concordia PE 272 Gc48
Concordia PE 284 Ge55
Concordia RA (ER) 289 Ha61
Concordia USA (KS) 240 Fb26
Concordia ZA 216 Lj60
Concordia do Pará BR (PA) 276 Hg46
Con Cuong VN 115 Qc36
Conda ANG 208 Lh51
Condamine AUS (QLD) 151 Sf59
Con Dao VN 117 Qd41
Con Dao VN 117 Qd41
Condat F 25 Lc45
Condé ANG 208 Lh51
Conde BR (BA) 283 Ja51
Conde USA (SD) 240 Fa23
Condé-en-Brie F 23 Ld42
Condega NIC 256 Fg39
Conde Loca ANG 202 Lg50
Condé-sur-Noireau F 22 Ku42
Condeúba BR (BA) 283 Hk53
Condingup AUS (WA) 145 Rb62
Condobolin AUS (NSW) 153 Sd62
Condom F 24 La47
Condon USA (OR) 234 Dk23
Condór, Cerro el RA 288 Gf59
Condoriaco RCH 288 Ge60
Conegliano I 40 Ln45
Conejos USA (CO) 237 Eg27
Conesa RA (BA) 289 Gk62
Coneto MEX (DGO) 253 Eh33
Confederate Memorial Park USA 248 Fg29
Confederate Memorial S.H.S. USA 241 Fd26
Conflict Group PNG 160 Sf51
Confolens F 24 La44
Confucius Temple & Tomb CHN 93 Qj28
Confusion Bay CDN 245 Hc20
Confuso PY 285 Ha58
Congaree Swamp N.P. USA 249 Fk29
Congaz MD 45 Mj44
Congerenge MOC 211 Mh53
Conghua CHN (GDG) 97 Qg34
Congleton GB 21 Ks37
Congo BR (PB) 277 Jb49
Congo RDC 200 Mb45
Congo 167 Lb10
Congo Basin RDC 200 Ma45
Congonhas BR (MG) 287 Hj56
Congostrina E 29 Ks51
Congo Town BS 251 Gb33
Congress USA (AZ) 236 Ed28
Conguillio, P.N. RCH 292 Ge65
Conhelo RA (LP) 292 Gh64
Conil de la Frontera E 28 Ko46
Conimbriga P 26 Km50
Coniston AUS (QLD) 150 Sb58
Conjo ANG 208 Lj51
Conjuboy AUS (QLD) 149 Sc55
Conkal MEX (YT) 255 Ff35
Conklin CDN (AB) 233 Ee18
Conkouati-Douli, P.N. de RCB 202 Lf47
Conlara RA 288 Gh62
Connah's Quay GB 21 Kr37
Conneaut USA (OH) 247 Fk25
Connecticut USA 247 Gd25
Connel GB 19 Kp34
Connell USA (WA) 232 Ea22
Connellsville USA (PA) 247 Ga25
Connemara AUS (QLD) 150 Sb58
Connemara IRL 18 Kl37
Connemara N.P. IRL 18 Kl37
Conner RP 121 Ra37
Connerré F 22 La42
Connor, Mount AUS 138 Rd53
Conques F 24 Lc46
Conquista BOL 279 Gg51
Conquista E 28 Kq48
Conrad USA (MT) 233 Ee21
Conroe USA (TX) 243 Fc30
Conscripto Bernardi RA (ER) 289 Ha61
Conselheiro Lafaiete BR (MG) 287 Hj56
Conselheiro Paulino BR (RJ) 287 Hj57
Conselheiro Pena BR (MG) 287 Hk55
Consélice I 40 Lm46
Consolación del Sur C 258 Fj34
Consort CDN (AB) 233 Ee20
Conspicuous Beach AUS 144 Qj63
Constance Bay IND 111 Pg40
Constance Lake First Nation CDN 239 Fj21
Constanța RO 45 Mj46
Constantina BR (RS) 290 Hd59
Constantina E 28 Kp47
Constantine DZ 174 Ld27
Constanza DOM 260 Ge36
Constitución MEX (CAM) 255 Fe36
Constitución RCH 292 Gd63
Constitución ROU 289 Hb61
Constitución de 1857, P.N. MEX 236 Eb29
Consuegra E 29 Kr49
Consul BR (MT) 281 Hc52
Contact USA (NV) 234 Ec25
Contadero E 29 Kr48
Contagem BR (MG) 287 Hh55
Contai IND (WBG) 112 Pd35
Contamana PE 278 Gc49
Contão BR (RR) 270 Gk44
Contas BR 283 Hk52
Contendas do Sincorá BR (BA) 283 Hk52
Contești RO 45 Mf46
Contin GB 19 Kq33
Continental BR (MS) 286 Hc56
Contramaestre C 259 Gb35
Contramaestre C 259 Gb35
Contres F 22 Lb43
Contrexéville F 23 Lf42
Contria BR (MG) 287 Hh55
Controller Bay USA 230 Ch15
Contuboel GNB 183 Kc39
Contumaza PE 278 Ga49
Convención CO 268 Gd41
Convento, Cerro RA 294 Gf71
Convento de Cristo de Tomar P 28 Km49
Convento de Tordesillas E 26 Kp51
Conversano I 43 Ls50
Convuno RA 292 Gf65
Conway AUS (QLD) 149 Se56
Conway USA (AR) 243 Fd28
Conway USA (NH) 247 Ge24
Conway USA (SC) 249 Ga29
Conway ZA 217 Mc61
Conway N.P. AUS 149 Se56
Conwy Castle GB 20 Kr37
Conyers USA (GA) 249 Fj29
Coober Pedy AUS (SA) 143 Rh60
Coodardy AUS (WA) 140 Qj59
Cooinda AUS (NT) 139 Rg52
Cook AUS (SA) 145 Rf61
Cook USA (MN) 241 Fd22
Cook Bay VU 162 Te55
Cooke City USA (MT) 235 Ef23
Cookeville USA (TN) 248 Fh27
Cookhouse ZA 217 Mc62
Cook Ice Shelf 297 Sc32
Cook Inlet USA 229 Ce15
Cook Islands NZ 157 Ud21
Cook, Mount AUS 144 Qj62
Cook, Mount CDN 231 Ck15
Cookstown GB 18 Ko36
Cook Strait NZ 154 Th66
Cooktown AUS (QLD) 147 Sc53
Coolabah AUS (NSW) 151 Sd61
Coolac AUS (NSW) 153 Se63
Cooladdi AUS (QLD) 151 Sc59
Coolah AUS (NSW) 151 Se61
Coolamon AUS (NSW) 153 Sd63
Coolangatta AUS (QLD) 151 Sg60
Coolatai AUS (NSW) 151 Sf60
Coolgardie AUS (WA) 144 Ra61
Coolidge USA (AZ) 237 Ee29
Coollie AUS (NSW) 151 Se61
Cooloogong AUS (NSW) 153 Se62
Cooloola N.P. AUS 151 Sg59
Cooma AUS (NSW) 153 Se64
Coomandook AUS (SA) 152 Rk63
Coomera AUS (QLD) 151 Sg59
Coonabarabran AUS (NSW) 151 Se61
Coonalpyn AUS (SA) 152 Rk63
Coonamble AUS (NSW) 151 Se61
Coonana AUS (WA) 145 Rb61
Coonana A.L. AUS 145 Rb61
Coonawarra AUS (SA) 152 Sa64
Coondle AUS (WA) 144 Qj61
Coongan River AUS 140 Qk56
Coongoola AUS (QLD) 151 Sc59
Coonoor IND (TNU) 111 Oj41
Coon Rapids USA (MN) 241 Fd23
Co-op Bethel GCA 255 Fe37
Cooper USA (TX) 243 Fc29
Cooperation Sea 297 Od32
Cooper River AUS 150 Sa59
Cooper's Town BS 251 Gb32
Cooperstown USA (ND) 240 Fa22
Coopracambra N.P. AUS 153 Se64
Coorabie AUS (SA) 145 Rg61
Coorabulka AUS (QLD) 148 Sa57
Coorada AUS (QLD) 151 Se58
Coordewandy AUS (WA) 140 Qh58
Coorong N.P. AUS 152 Rk63
Coorow AUS (WA) 144 Qj60
Cooroy AUS (QLD) 151 Sg59
Coos Bay USA (OR) 234 Dh24
Coos Bay USA 234 Dh24
Cootamundra AUS (NSW) 153 Se63
Cootehill IRL 18 Kn36
Copa, Cerro BOL/RCH 284 Gf56
Copacá BR 273 Gh47
Copacabana BOL 280 Gf53
Copacabana BOL 284 Gf54
Copacabana BR 287 Hj57
Copacabana CO 268 Gc42
Copahue RA (NE) 292 Ge64
Copahue, Volcán RA/RCH 292 Ge64
Copala MEX (SL) 252 Eh34
Copălău RO 45 Mg43
Copalnic-Mănăștur RO 44 Md43
Copal Urco PE 273 Gd47
Copalyacu PE 272 Gc47
Copán HN 255 Ff38
Copán Ruinas HN 255 Ff38
Cope, Cabo E 29 Kt47
Cope USA (CO) 240 Ej26
Copeland USA (FL) 250 Fk33
Copenhagen DK 14 Ln35
Copertino I 43 Lt50
Copetonas RA (BA) 293 Gk65
Copiapó RCH 288 Ge59
Copiapó, Volcán RCH 288 Gf59
Çöpköy TR 50 Mg49
Copley AUS (SA) 143 Rk61
Çöplü TR 51 Mp50
Copo, P.N. RA 285 Gk58
Coporolo ANG 208 Lg52
Coposa, Cerro RCH 284 Gf56
Coppabella AUS (QLD) 149 Se56
Copparo I 40 Lm46
Coppename SME 271 Hb43
Copperas Cove USA (TX) 242 Fb30
Copperbelt Z 210 Md52
Copper Breaks S.P. USA 242 Fa28
Copper Harbor USA (MI) 246 Fg22
Copper River USA 229 Ch14
Copperton ZA 216 Mb60
Copșa Mică RO 44 Me44
Coqen CHN (TIB) 88 Pc30
Coqui BR (AM) 274 Gh46
Coqui CO 268 Gb43
Coquille USA (OR) 234 Dh24
Coquimbo RCH 288 Ge60
Coquitlam CDN (BC) 232 Dj21
Corabia RO 47 Me47
Coração de Jesus BR (MG) 287 Hh54
Coracora PE 278 Gd53
Corail RH 260 Gd36
Coraki AUS (NSW) 151 Sg60
Coral Basin 137 Sb21
Coral Bay AUS (WA) 140 Qg57
Coral Bay RP 122 Qj41
Coral City USA (FL) 250 Fk32
Coral Coast FJI 163 Tj55
Corales del Rosario y San Bernardo, P.N. CO 268 Gc40
Coral Harbour CDN 225 Fd06

Cugir – Dar el-Bahr

Cugir RO 44 Md45
Cugnaux F 24 Lb47
Čuhloma RUS 53 Nb16
Cuhnești MD 45 Mh43
Čuhujiv UA 53 Mj21
Cuiabá BR (AM) 273 Gf47
Cuiabá BR (MT) 281 Hb53
Cuiabá BR 281 Hb54
Cuia, T.I. BR 274 Ha47
Cuicatlán MEX (OAX) 254 Fb37
Cuije ANG 203 Lj50
Cuijk NL 32 Lf39
Cuilapa GCA 255 Fe38
Cuillin Hills GB 18 Ko33
Cuillin Sound GB 18 Ko33
Cuilo ANG 202 Lh49
Cuilo ANG 203 Lk50
Cuilo ANG 203 Lk50
Cuilo-Futa ANG 202 Lh49
Cuilo Pombo ANG 202 Lh49
Cuima ANG 208 Lh52
Cuimba ANG 202 Lh49
Cuio ANG 208 Lg52
Cuipo PA 257 Fk41
Cuira o Monos CO 273 Gd46
Cuiriri ANG 209 Lk53
Cuiseaux F 25 Lf44
Cuisery F 25 Lf44
Cuité BR (PB) 277 Jb49
Cuito ANG 209 Lk54
Cuito Cuanavale ANG 209 Lk53
Cuitzeo del Porvenir MEX (MHC) 254 Ek36
Cuiuni BR 274 Gh46
Cuiyun Lang CHN 95 Qc29
Cuja RUS 85 Pd20
Cujubim BR (RO) 280 Gk50
Çukurca TR 63 Nb27
Çukurköprü TR 62 Mh27
Çukurkuyu TR 51 Mp53
Çukurova TR 62 Mh27
Culamagia ANG 202 Lj50
Culan F 25 Lc44
Cu Lao Cham VN 115 Qe38
Cu Lao Re VN 115 Qe38
Cu Lao Thu = Phu Quy VN 115 Qe40
Cula Sancai ETH 198 Mh40
Culasi RP 123 Rb40
Culasian RP 122 Qj41
Culbertson USA (MT) 233 Eh21
Culburra AUS (NSW) 153 Sf63
Culcairn AUS (NSW) 153 Sd63
Culebras PE 278 Ga50
Culemborg NL 32 Lf39
Culfa AZ 70 Nc26
Culgoa N.P. AUS 151 Sd60
Culgoa River AUS 151 Sd60
Culiacán MEX (SL) 252 Eg33
Culion RP 122 Ra40
Culion Island RP 122 Qk40
Culiseu BR 281 Hd52
Cúllar-Baza E 29 Ks47
Cullen GB 19 Ks33
Cullén RCH 294 Gf72
Cullera E 29 Ku49
Cullinan ZA 213 Me58
Cullman USA (AL) 248 Fg28
Cullompton GB 20 Kr40
Culluleraine AUS (VIC) 152 Sa63
Čul'man RUS 59 Rb07
Culoz F 25 Lf45
Culpaulin AUS (NSW) 150 Sb61
Culpeper USA (VA) 247 Ga26
Culpina BOL 285 Gh56
Culross Island USA 229 Cg15
Culuba MEX 255 Fg35
Culuene BR 281 Hd52
Culuwuru Island AUS 139 Rj51
Culverden NZ 155 Tg67
Čulym RUS 58 Pa07
Culyšman RUS 85 Pe20
Culyšmanskoe nagor'e RUS 85 Pe20
Culzean Castle GB 19 Kq35
Cuma ANG 208 Lh52
Cumaná YV 269 Gh40
Cumanacoa YV 270 Gj40
Cumanayagua C 258 Fk34
Cumandá EC 272 Ga47
Cumar SP 205 Nc44
Cumaral CO 268 Gd43
Cumari BR (GO) 282 Hg53
Cumaribo CO 269 Gf43
Cumba PE 272 Ga48
Cumbal CO 272 Gb45
Cumbal, Volcán CO 272 Gb45
Cumbe EC 272 Ga47
Cumberland USA (MD) 247 Ga26
Cumberland Caverns USA 248 Fh28
Cumberland Downs AUS (QLD) 149 Sd57
Cumberland Gap N.H.P. USA 249 Fj27
Cumberland House CDN (SK) 238 Ej19
Cumberland Island USA 249 Fk30
Cumberland Island National Seashore USA 249 Fk30
Cumberland Islands AUS 149 Se56
Cumberland Lake CDN 238 Ek18
Cumberland Peninsula CDN 224 Gd05
Cumberland Sound CDN 224 Gc05
Cumbernauld GB 19 Kr35
Cumbi ANG 202 Lg49
Cumborah AUS (NSW) 151 Sd60
Cumbrera, Cerro RCH 294 Gd69
Cumbres de Majalca, P.N. MEX 237 Eg31
Cumbres de Monterrey, P.N. MEX 253 Ek33
Cumbres & Toltec Scenic Railroad USA 237 Eg27
Cumbrian Mountains GB 19 Kr36
Cumburão BR (PA) 275 Hc46
Čumerna BG 47 Mf48
Čumić SCG 46 Ma46
Čumikan RUS 59 Rd08
Cuminá BR (PA) 275 Hb46
Cuminá BR 275 Hb46
Cuminopanema BR 275 Hc46
Cummins AUS (SA) 152 Rh63
Cummins Range AUS 138 Rd55
Community Museum F 165 Da50
Cumnock GB 19 Kq35
Cumpas MEX (SO) 237 Ef31
Çumra TR 62 Mg27
Cumuetè BR 281 He50
Čuna RUS 58 Pd07
Cunani BR (AP) 271 He44
Cuñare CO 273 Gd45
Cunauaru BR 274 Gj47
Cunco RCH 292 Gd65
Cund ANG 208 Lj52
Cunday CO 268 Gc43
Cundeelee AUS (WA) 145 Rb61
Cundeelee A.L. AUS 145 Rb61
Cunderdin AUS (WA) 144 Qj61
Cunduacán MEX (TB) 255 Fd36
Cunene ANG 208 Lg54
Cunene ANG 208 Lh53
Cunene ANG 208 Lj53
Cúneo I 40 Lh46
Cunhambebe BR (RJ) 287 Hh57
Cunhaú BR (RN) 277 Jc49
Cunhinga ANG 208 Lj51
Cunicea MD 45 Mj43
Cuniuá BR 279 Gg49
Cunjamba ANG 209 Ma53
Cunlhat F 25 Ld45
Cunnamulla AUS (QLD) 151 Sc60
Cunningham Islands AUS 139 Rj51
Cuntima GNB 183 Kc39
Cunyu AUS (WA) 140 Ra59
Cuorgnè I 40 Lh45
Cupar GB 19 Kr34
Cupari BR 275 Hc48
Cupcini MD 45 Mh42
Cupica CO 257 Gb42
Cupica CO 268 Gb42
Cupisnique, Cerro PE 278 Ga49
Cupixi BR (AP) 275 He45
Ćuprija SCG 46 Mb47
Curaçá BR (BA) 283 Ja50
Curaça BR 283 Ja50
Curaçao NL 269 Gf39
Curacautin RCH 292 Ge65
Curacaví RCH 288 Ge62
Curachi GUY 270 Gk42
Curacó RA 292 Gh65
Curahuara de Carangas BOL 284 Gf54
Curale ETH 199 Nc42
Cural Velho CV 182 Jj37
Curanilahué RCH 292 Gd64
Curanja PE 279 Ge51
Curanja PE 279 Ge50
Curaray EC 272 Gb46
Curaray EC 272 Gb46
Curaray PE 273 Gc47
Curaru RA (BA) 289 Gj63
Curauai BR 274 Ha48
Curbur AUS (WA) 140 Qh59
Curdimurka AUS (SA) 143 Rj60
Curepipe MS 221 Nj56
Curia P 26 Km50
Curiapo YV 270 Gk41
Curibaya PE 284 Ge54
Curicó RCH 288 Ge63
Curicuriari BR 273 Gf46
Curi Leuvú RA 292 Ge64
Curimatá BR (PI) 282 Hh51
Curimatá de Baixo BR 274 Gh48
Curimávida, Cerro de RCH 288 Ge61
Curionópolis BR (PA) 276 Hf48
Curitiba BR (AC) 279 Gf51
Curitiba BR (PR) 286 Hf58
Curitibanos BR (SC) 290 He59
Curiúva BR (PR) 286 He58
Curly Cut Cay BS 251 Gb34
Curnamona AUS (SA) 152 Rk61
Curoca ANG 208 Lg54
Curragh Racetrack IRL 20 Ko37
Currais BR (PI) 282 Hj50
Currais Novos BR (RN) 277 Jb49
Curral Alto BR (RS) 290 Hd62
Curral de Pedra BR (PI) 277 Hk49
Curralinho BR (PA) 276 Hf46
Curral Novo do Piauí BR (PI) 283 Hk50
Curran USA (MI) 246 Fj23
Currant USA (NV) 234 Ec26
Curranyalpa AUS (NSW) 150 Sc61
Currawilla AUS (QLD) 150 Sa58
Currawinya AUS (QLD) 150 Sc60
Currawinya N.P. AUS 150 Sc60
Current BS 251 Gb33
Current Island BS 251 Gb33
Currie AUS (TAS) 153 Sb65
Currie USA (NV) 234 Ec25
Currituck USA (NC) 249 Gb27
Currituck Beach Lighthouse USA 249 Gc27
Currituck N.W.R. USA 249 Gc27
Currituck Sound USA 249 Gc27
Curtain Springs AUS (NT) 142 Rf58
Curtea de Argeș RO 45 Me45
Curtici RO 44 Mb44
Curtina ROU 289 Hb62
Curtis Island AUS (VIC) 153 Sd65
Curtis Island AUS 149 Sf57
Curtis Island NZ 137 Ua25
Curu BR 277 Ja47
Curuá BR (PA) 275 Hc46
Curuá BR 275 Hc48
Curuaés BR 281 Hc50
Curuai BR (PA) 275 Hc47
Curuá-Una BR 275 Hc47
Curuçá BR (PA) 276 Hg46
Curuca BR 273 Ge48
Curucay PE 272 Gc47
Curug Sewu RI 128 Qe49
Curup RI 124 Qb47
Curuqueté BR 279 Gh50
Cururu-Açu BR 281 Hb50
Cururu ou Cururu-ri BR 281 Hb50
Cururupu BR (MA) 276 Hh46
Curuzú Cuatiá RA (CR) 289 Ha60
Curvelo BR (MG) 287 Hh55
Cushabatay PE 278 Gc49
Cushamen RA (CB) 292 Ge67
Cushing USA (OK) 243 Fb28
Cusimi YV 269 Gh43
Cusipata PE 279 Ge52
Cusset F 25 Ld44
Cusseta USA (GA) 249 Fh29
Cusso ANG 208 Lh53
Custer USA (MT) 235 Eg22
Custer USA (SD) 240 Ej24
Custer Battlefield Nat. Mon. USA 235 Eg23
Custódia BR (PE) 283 Jb50
Cusuco, P.N. HN 255 Ff38
Cutalo ANG 208 Lj52
Cutato ANG 208 Lj53
Cutato ANG 208 Lj53
Cut Bank USA (MT) 233 Ed21
Cutbank River CDN 232 Ea18
Čuteevo RUS (TAR) 53 Nd18
Cutenda ANG 208 Lh53
Cutervo PE 278 Ga49
Cutervo, P.N. de PE 278 Ga49
Cuthbert USA (GA) 249 Fh30
Cut Off USA (LA) 243 Fe31
Čutove UA 54 Mh21
Cutral-Co RA (NE) 292 Gf65
Cutro I 43 Lr51
Cuttack IND (ORS) 109 Pc35
Cutta Cutta Caves AUS 139 Rg53
Cutzamala de Pinzón MEX (GUR) 254 Ek36
Cuvelai ANG 208 Lj53
Cuvelar ANG 208 Lh53
Cuvette de Doany RM 219 Nd53
Cuvette de la Bénoué CAM 187 Lg41
Cuvier Island NZ 154 Th64
Cuvo ANG 208 Lh51
Cuxhaven D 32 Lj37
Cuya RCH 284 Ge55
Cuyagua YV 269 Gg40
Cuyagua YV 269 Gg40
Cuyahoga Valley N.P. USA 247 Fk25
Cuyama USA (CA) 236 Ea28
Cuyamel HN 255 Ff38
Cuyo RP 123 Ra40
Cuyoaco MEX (PUE) 254 Fb36
Cuyo East Passage RP 123 Ra40
Cuyo ‚English Game' Subterranean N.P. RP 123 Ra40
Cuyo Island RP 123 Ra40
Cuyo Islands RP 123 Ra40
Cuyo West Passage RP 122 Ra40
Cuyuni GUY 270 Ha42
Cuyupini YV 270 Gk41
Cuyutlán MEX (COL) 253 Eh36
Cuzco PE 279 Ge52
Čvur RUS 98 Rj20
Cwmcarn GB 20 Kr39
Cyangugu RWA 206 Me47
Cybinka PL 36 Lp38
Cyclades GR 48 Md53
Cyclops Mountains RI 131 Sa47
Čyhyryn UA 54 Mg21
Cylinder AUS 151 Sg59
Cynthia AUS (QLD) 151 Sf58
Cypress Gardens USA 250 Fk31
Cypress Hills CDN 233 Ef21
Cypress Hills Interprov. Park CDN 233 Ee21
Cyprus CY 51 Mo55
Cyran BY 17 Mg37
Cyrenaica LAR 175 Ma31
Cyrene = Shahhat LAR 175 Ma29
Cyrrhus SYR 64 Mj27
Cytherea AUS (QLD) 151 Sd59
Czaplinek PL 36 Lr37
Czar CDN (AB) 233 Ee19
Czarna PL 39 Mc41
Czarna Białostocka PL 37 Md37
Czarna Dąbrówka PL 36 Ls36
Czarnków PL 36 Lr38
Czarny Dunajec PL 39 Lu41
Czchów PL 39 Ma41
Czechowice-Dziedzice PL 39 Lu41
Czech Republic CZ 38 Lp41
Czekarzewice PL 37 Mb39
Czermno PL 37 Ma39
Czersk PL 36 Ls37
Czerwieńsk PL 36 Lq38
Czerwionka-Leszczyny PL 36 Lt40
Czerwony Dwór PL 37 Mc36
Częstochowa PL 37 Lu40
Człopa PL 36 Lr37
Człuchów PL 36 Ls37
Czssivi ANG 209 Ma53
Czyżew-Osada PL 37 Mc38

D

Da'an CHN (JLN) 98 Rc23
Daanbantayan RP 123 Rc40
Daan Viljoen Game Park NAM 212 Lj57
Dabaga EAT 207 Mh50
Dabaga RN 186 Le37
Dabagram IND (WBG) 112 Pe34
Dabai WAN 186 Lc40
Da Baia BR 275 Hd49
Dabajuro YV 269 Ge40
Dabaka IND (ASM) 112 Pg32
Dabakala CI 193 Kh41
Dabancheng CHN (XUZ) 85 Pe24
Dabane-ye-Qoloman IR 73 Oa30
Daban Shan CHN 92 Qa27
Dabaro SP 199 Ne42
Dabas H 39 Lu43
Daba Shan CHN 95 Qe29
Dabat ETH 191 Mj40
Dabatou RG 192 Ke40
Dabdab LAR 181 Lh32
Dabeiba CO 268 Gb42
Dabeiyuan Monastery CHN 93 Qj26
Daben CHN (HAN) 96 Qe36
Dabenoris ZA 216 Lk60
Dabhoi IND (GUJ) 108 Og34
Dąbie PL 36 Lq38
Dąbie PL 36 Lt38
Dabie Shan CHN 102 Qh30
Dabilja MK 46 Mc49
Dabiss RG 183 Kc40
Dabnou RN 186 Lc38
Dabo RI 125 Qc46
Dabo SN 183 Kc39
Daboh IND (MPH) 107 Ok33
Dabola RG 192 Ke40
Dabolatounka RG 192 Ke40
Dabou CI 193 Kh43
Daboya GH 193 Kk41
Dabra IND (MPH) 107 Ok33
Dabravolja BY 37 Me38
Dąbrowa Białostocka PL 37 Md37
Dąbrowa Górnicza PL 37 Lu40
Dąbrowa Tarnowska PL 37 Ma40
Dabryn' BY 52 Me20
Dabsan Hu CHN 87 Ph27
Dabugam IND (ORS) 109 Pb36
Dabuk RI 125 Qb47
Dăbuleni RO 46 Me47
Dabus Wenz ETH 197 Mh40
Dabwa TCH 187 Lg38
Dac Glei VN 115 Qd38
Dachau D 35 Lm42
Dacheng CHN (JGX) 102 Qh31
Dachengzhuang CHN (HBI) 93 Qj26
Dachepalle IND (APH) 109 Ok37
Dachigam N.P. PK 79 Oh28
Dachstein A 35 Lo43
Dachsteinhöhlen A 35 Lo43
Dachung Yogma 79 Ok29
Dacia Seamount 168 Kb12
Dačice CZ 38 Lq41
Dačne UA 45 Ml44
Dac Song VN 115 Qd39
Dac To VN 115 Qd38
Dadaab EAK 205 Na45
Dadanawa GUY 270 Ha44
Daddato DJI 191 Nb40
Dade City USA (FL) 250 Fj31
Dadéguhé CI 192 Kg42
Dadeville USA (AL) 249 Fh29
Dadhar PK 80 Od31
Dadong CHN (GZG) 96 Qe34
Dadra and Nagar Haveli IND 108 Og35
Dadra and Nagar Haveli IND 108 Og35
Dadu PK 80 Od32
Daduan CHN (JGX) 102 Qh31
Dadu He CHN 94 Qb30
Dadukou CHN (AHU) 102 Qj30
Daet RP 121 Rb38
Dafang CHN (GZH) 96 Qc32
Dafanpu CHN (NMZ) 93 Qf26
Dafar GH 193 La42
Dafeng CHN (JGS) 102 Ra29
Dáfnes GR 48 Mb52
Dáfni GR 47 Me50
Dáfni GR 48 Md53
Dáfni GR 48 Mc52
Dáfni GR 48 Mc53
Dafoe CDN (SK) 233 Eh20
Dafoe River CDN 238 Fc18
Dafo Si CHN 92 Qa26
Dafra TCH 196 Lk40
Daga IND (MPH) 109 Pb33
Daga SUD 197 Mg41
Dagaari SP 199 Nd42
Dagabule ETH 198 Mj43
Daga Istephanos Monastery ETH 198 Mj40
Dagali N 12 Lj30
Dagana SN 183 Kc37
Daga Post SUD 197 Mg41
Dağardı TR 50 Mj51
Dagash SUD 190 Mg37
Dagasuli RI 130 Rd44
Dagda LV 17 Mh34
Dağdere TR 50 Mj52
Dagestan RUS 63 Nd24
Dagestanskij zapovednik RUS 70 Nd23
Daghabij KSA 66 Mk34
Dag Hammarskjöld Memorial Z 210 Me52
Daghandeli KZ 84 Oj21
Daghmar OM 75 Nk34
Dagida Game Reserve WAN 186 Lc41
Daginggou CHN 100 Ra24
Daglah ET 177 Mh31
Daglung CHN (TIB) 89 Pf31
Dago RI 123 Rc44
Dagomys RUS 55 Mk24
Dagua CO 268 Gb44
Daguan CHN (GZH) 96 Qd32
Daguan CHN (SCH) 94 Qc31
Daguan CHN (YUN) 113 Qb32
Dagu Fort CHN 93 Qj26
Dagupan RP 120 Ra37
Daguragu A.L. AUS 139 Rf54
Dagworth AUS (QLD) 148 Sb54
Dagzê Co CHN 88 Pd30
Dah RI 158 Rk49
Dahaban KSA 66 Mk35
Dahadinni River CDN 231 Dh14
Dahanu IND (MHT) 108 Og36
Dahanu Beach IND 108 Og35
Daheba CHN (QHI) 92 Pk28
Dahebian CHN (SCH) 94 Qa31
Dahequ CHN (GSU) 92 Qb27
Dahinsara IND (GUJ) 108 Of34
Dahiri CI 193 Kh43
Dahla AFG 78 Oc30
Dahlak Archipelago ER 191 Na39
Dahlak Marine N.P. ER 191 Na39
Dahlonega USA (GA) 249 Fj28
Dahmani TN 174 Le28
Dahme D 33 Lo39
Dahn D 34 Lh41
Dahongliutan 79 Ok27
Dahong Shan CHN 95 Qg30
Dahra Oil Field LAR 175 Lj31
Dahr Oualâta RIM 184 Kg37
Dahshûr ET 177 Mf31
Dahua CHN (GZG) 96 Qe34
Dahuk IRQ 65 Nb27
Da Huoai VN 115 Qd40
Dai RI 132 Re49
Dai Dao CHN 102 Rb30
Daïet Akhicha DZ 173 La31
Dai Hai CHN 93 Qg25
Dai Island SOL 161 Ta49
Dai Lanh Beach VN 115 Qe39
Dailekh NEP 88 Pa31
Daimiel E 29 Kr49
Daingerfield USA (TX) 243 Fc29
Daintree AUS (QLD) 149 Sc54
Daintree N.P. AUS (QLD) 149 Sc54
Dainzü MEX 254 Fb37
Daireaux RA (BA) 293 Gk64
Dairo CI 193 Kh43
Dairût ET 177 Mf32
Dairy Creek AUS (WA) 140 Qh58
Dai-sen J 101 Rg28
Daisengendake J 99 Sa25
Daisen-Oki N.P. J 101 Rf27
Daisen-Oki N.P. J 101 Rg28
Daisetsuzan N.P. J 99 Sb24
Daishan CHN (ZJG) 102 Rb30
Daisy USA (OK) 243 Fc28
Daito Islands J 103 Rf33
Dai Xian CHN (SAX) 93 Qg26
Daiyun Shan CHN 97 Qk33
Dajabón DOM 260 Ge36
Dajarra AUS (QLD) 148 Rk56
Dajing CHN (GSU) 92 Qb27
Dajing CHN (YUN) 113 Qb32
Da Juh CHN (QHI) 87 Pg27
Dakar SN 183 Kb38
Dakawa EAT 207 Mj49
Dakawa EAT 207 Mj49
Daketa ETH 198 Nb42
Da Kherqa Sherif Ziarat Mosque AFG 78 Oc30
Dakhla DARS 178 Kc34
Dakhla RIM 183 Ke37
Dakhla Oasis ET 177 Me33
Dakhlet Nouâdhibou RIM 178 Kb35
Dakingari WAN 186 Lc40
Daki Takwas WAN 186 Lc40
Dak Mil VN 115 Qd39
Dak Nong VN 115 Qd40
Dako GH 193 Kk41
Dakoank IND (AAN) 111 Pg42
Dakoro RN 186 Ld38
Đakovica SCG 46 Ma48
Đakovo HR 41 Lt45
Katedrala u Đakovu HR 41 Lt45
Dakpam GH 193 Kk41
Dakshin Gangotri ANT (IND) 297 Lc32
Daksum 79 Oh29
Daku, Gunung RI 127 Ra45
Dala ANG 203 Ma50
Dala ANG 209 Ma51
Dala RMM 185 Kj38
Dala SOL 161 Ta50
Dalaba SN 183 Kd39
Dalabar RG 192 Kd40
Dalada Maligawa (Kandy) CL 111 Pa43
Dalad Qi CHN (NMZ) 93 Qf25
Dalafi SN 183 Kd39
Dalahaj RUS (BUR) 90 Qb20
Dalai Nur CHN 93 Qj24
Dalai Shan CHN 87 Pj26
Dalaki IR 74 Nf31
Dalälven S 13 Lq30
Dalaman TR 49 Mj54
Dalami SUD 197 Mf40
Dalandole SP 205 Nc44
Dalangyun MYA 114 Ph36
Dalanzadgad MNG 92 Qc24
Dalap-Uliga-Darrit MH 157 Tc17
Dalark USA (AR) 243 Fd29
Dalarna S 13 Lo29
Dalarö S 13 Lt31
Dalat MAL 126 Qf44
Da Lat VN 115 Qe40
Dalay MNG 92 Qb24
Dalbandin PK 80 Ob31
Dalbeattie GB 19 Kr36
Dalberg AUS (QLD) 149 Sd56
Dalbo BF 185 Kk39
Dålbok Dol BG 47 Me48
Dålbok izvor BG 47 Mf48
Dalbosjön S 13 Ln32
Dalby AUS (QLD) 151 Sf59
Dalby Söderskog n.p. S 15 Lo35
Dalcahue RCH 292 Gd67
Dale N 12 Lf29
Dale N 12 Lf30
Dalen N 12 Lj31
Dalfors S 13 Lq29
Dalfsen NL 32 Lg38
Dalgan IR 75 Nk32
Dalgaranga AUS (WA) 140 Qj59
Dalgety River AUS 140 Qj58
Dălghiu RO 45 Mf45
Dălgi Del BG 46 Mc47
Dalgonally AUS (QLD) 148 Sa56
Dălgopol BG 47 Mh47
Dalhalla S 13 Lq30
Dalhart USA (TX) 237 Ej27
Dalhousie IND (HPH) 107 Oj29
Dalhousie CDN (NB) 244 Gg21
Dalhousie Springs AUS (SA) 143 Rh59
Dali CHN (SAA) 95 Qe28
Dali = Xiaguan CHN (YUN) 113 Qa33
Dali RMM 184 Kg38
Dalian CHN (LNG) 100 Ra26
Dalianhe CHN (HLG) 98 Re22
Dalias E 29 Ks46
Dalimb IND (MHT) 108 Oj37
Dali Museum (Saint Petersburg) USA 250 Fj32
Daling He CHN 93 Qk25
Dali Sharafat SUD 190 Mg40
Dalj HR 44 Lt45
Daljā ET 177 Mf32
Dalkeith GB 19 Kr35
Dalkhaki AFG 78 Od27
Dalkola IND (WBG) 112 Pd33
Dal Lake 79 Oh28
Dallas CDN (MB) 238 Fb20
Dallas USA (OR) 234 Dj23
Dallas USA (TX) 243 Fb29
Dallas Reef 122 Qg42
Dalli WAN 195 Lf41
Dall Island USA 231 Dd18
Dallol Bosso RN 185 Lb39
Dalma UAE 74 Ng33
Dalmacija HR 41 Lq46
Dalmally GB 19 Kq34
Dalmatia 6 Lb05
Dalmeny AUS (NSW) 153 Sf64
Dalmose DK 14 Lm35
Dal'nee RUS 99 Sb22
Dal'negorsk RUS 99 Rh23
Dal'nerečensk RUS 98 Rg23
Daloa CI 192 Kg42
Dalol ETH 191 Na39
Dalol Crater ER 191 Na39
Dalol Saltlake and Hot Springs ETH 191 Na39
Dalong CHN (HUN) 96 Qe32
Dalong Chi CHN 86 Pb24
Dalrymple, Mount AUS 149 Se56
Dalsbruk = Taalintehdas FIN 16 Mc30
Dalsjöfors S 15 Lo33
Dals Långed S 12 Ln32
Dalton USA (GA) 249 Fh28
Daltonganj IND (JKD) 109 Pc33
Dalton Mus. USA 243 Fc27
Dalu CHN (GSU) 92 Qc27
Dalu IND (MGA) 112 Pf33
Daludalu RI 124 Qa45
Dalupiri Island RP 121 Ra36
Dalupiri Island RP 121 Rc39
Dal'verzin Tepe UZ 76 Od27
Dalvík IS 10 Ka13
Dalwallinu AUS (WA) 144 Qj61
Dalwhinnie GB 19 Kq34
Daly City USA (CA) 234 Dj27
Daly River AUS (NT) 139 Rf52
Daly River AUS 139 Rf53
Daly River A.L. AUS 139 Rf53
Dalyup AUS (WA) 144 Ra62
Daly Waters AUS (NT) 139 Rg54
Damaguete RP 123 Rb41
Da Mai VN 115 Qd40
Damakar WAN 187 Lg39
Daman AFG 78 Oc30
Daman IND (DAD) 108 Og35
Daman IND 108 Og35
Damanava BY 37 Mf38
Damaneh IR 72 Nf29
Damango GH 193 Kk41
Damanhûr ET 177 Mf30
Damaqun Shan CHN 93 Qh25
Damar RI 130 Re46
Damar RI 132 Re49
Damara RCA 200 Lk43
Damaraland NAM 212 Lj56
Damardatar RI 126 Qh47
Damar Laut MAL 116 Qa43
Damasak WAN 187 Lg39
Damas Cays BS 250 Fk34
Damascus SYR 64 Mj29
Damaskinia GR 46 Mb50
Damaturu WAN 187 Lf40
Damau RI 123 Rd44
Damauli NEP 88 Pc32
Damba ANG 202 Lh49
Damba KZ 71 Nf22
Damba Island EAU 204 Mg46
Dambam WAN 187 Lf40
Dambaslar TR 50 Mh49
Damboa WAN 187 Lg40
Dâmbovita RO 45 Mf46
Dambri Waterfall VN 115 Qd40
Dambuk IND (ARP) 113 Ph31
Dambulla CL 111 Pa43
Damdama Sahib IND 106 Oh31
Da Meio BR 282 Hh52
Dame Marie RH 260 Gc36
Damenge CHN (YUN) 113 Pk34
Damghan IR 72 Nh27
Damghan Caravansaraī IR 72 Nh27
Dam Ha VN 96 Qd35
Damianópolis BR (GO) 282 Hg53
Damietta ET 177 Mf30
Damji BHT 112 Pe32
Damlacık TR 63 Mk27
Dammartin-en-Goële F 23 Lc41
Damme D 32 Lj38
Damnica PL 36 Ls36
Damnoen Saduak Floating Market THA 114 Pk39
Damodar IND 112 Pd34
Damoh IND (MPH) 109 Ok34
Damon USA (TX) 243 Fc31
Damon Point USA (WA) 232 Dh22
Dampar WAN 186 Lf41
Dampier AUS (WA) 140 Qj56
Dampier Archipelago AUS 140 Qj56
Dampier Archipelago Nature Reserve AUS 140 Qj56
Dampier Downs AUS (WA) 138 Rb55
Dampierre-sur-Salon F 23 Lf43
Dampier Strait PNG 159 Se48
Damqawt YE 69 Ng37
Dam Qu CHN 89 Pg29
Damra IND (MGA) 112 Pf33
Damrur KSA 66 Mk35
Damtang CHN (TIB) 88 Pb29
Damtar TCH 187 Lj40
Damulog RP 123 Rc42
Damwal ZA 214 Me58
Damxung CHN (TIB) 89 Pf30
Dana JOR 64 Mh30
Dana RI 129 Ra51
Danakil ETH 191 Na40
Danakil Depression ETH 191 Na40
Danakil Desert ETH 191 Na40
Danamombe (Dhlo Dhlo) Ruins ZW 214 Me56
Dana, Mount USA 228 Bk18
Dana Nature Reserve JOR 64 Mh30
Danane CI 192 Kf42
Da Nang VN 115 Qe37
Danao RP 123 Rc40
Danapur IND (BIH) 109 Pc33
Danau Aiwsa RI 131 Rh47
Danau Amaru RI 130 Rg46
Danau Gigi RI 131 Rg46
Danau Gita RI 131 Rg46
Danau Kamakawalar RI 131 Rh47
Danau Paniai RI 131 Rj47
Danau Rombebai RI 131 Rj46
Danau Sentani RI 131 Sa47
Danau Tigi RI 131 Rj48
Danau Yamur RI 131 Rh47
Danba CHN (SCH) 94 Qa30
Dan Barto RN 186 Le39
Danbatta WAN 186 Le39
Danbury USA (CT) 247 Gd25
Danby Lake USA 236 Ec28
Dan Chang THA 114 Pk38
Dancheng CHN (HNN) 102 Qh29
Dandahwa ZW 210 Me54
Dandaraga AUS (WA) 144 Qk60
Dandaragan AUS (WA) 144 Qh61
Dandarah ET 177 Mg32
Dandau ANG 208 Lj51
Dande ETH 198 Mj43
Dandeli IND (KTK) 108 Oh38
Dandenong AUS (VIC) 153 Sc64
Dandéresso RMM 193 Kh40
Dando ANG 208 Lj51
Dandong CHN (LNG) 100 Rc25
Danfa RMM 184 Kg38
Danfeng CHN (SAA) 95 Qf29
Danforth USA (ME) 244 Gg23
Danga CAM 195 Lg43
Danga RMM 185 Kj37
Dangali ETH 198 Mj40
Dangan Liedao CHN 97 Qh34
Dangara TJ 76 Oe26
Dangchang CHN (GSU) 94 Qc28
Dange ANG 202 Lh50
Danggali Conservation Park AUS 152 Sa62
Danggou CHN (LNG) 100 Rc26
Dang He CHN 87 Ph26
Dangjin Shankou CHN 87 Ph26
Dango WAN 186 Lc39
Dan Gorayo SP 199 Ne41
Dangriga BH 255 Ff37
Dangriga BH 255 Ff37
Dangshan CHN (AHU) 102 Qj28
Dangtu CHN (AHU) 102 Qk30
Dan Gulbi WAN 186 Ld40
Dangur ETH 197 Mh39
Dangur ETH 198 Mj40
Dangur ETH 198 Mj40
Dangyang CHN (HUB) 95 Qf30
Dan He CHN 95 Qg28
Da Nhim Lake VN 115 Qe40
Dania CI 192 Kg42
Daniel USA (WY) 235 Ee24
Daniel Boone Natl. Forest USA 249 Fj27
Daniel Johnson Dam CDN 244 Gf20
Danielskuil ZA 216 Mb60
Danilov RUS 52 Na16
Danilovgrad SCG 46 Lu48
Danilovka RUS 53 Nc20
Daning CHN (SAX) 93 Qf27
Danish Fort IND 111 Ok41
Danissa EAK 205 Na44
Dan Issa RN 186 Ld39
Danja WAN 186 Ld40
Danjiang CHN (GZH) 96 Qe32
Danjiangkou CHN (HUB) 95 Qf29
Danjiangkou Shuiku CHN 95 Qf29
Danjo-gunto J 103 Re29
Dank OM 75 Nj34
Dan Khun Thot THA 114 Qa38
Dankov RUS 53 Mk19
Danlí HN 256 Fg38
Dannelly Res. USA 248 Fg29
Dannenberg D 33 Lm37
Dannevirke NZ 154 Tj66
Dannhauser ZA 217 Mf60
Dano BF 193 Kj40
Danpur IND (RJT) 108 Oh34
Dan Sadau WAN 186 Ld40
Dan Sai THA 114 Qa37
Danskøya N 11 Lf06
Dansville USA (NY) 247 Gb24
Dantan IND (WBG) 112 Pd35
Dante = Xaafuun SP 199 Nf40
Dantewara IND (CGH) 109 Pa36
Dantiandou RN 185 Lb39
Danube 6 Ma05
Danubyu MYA 114 Ph37
Danum Valley Conservation Area MAL 122 Qj43
Danville USA (AR) 243 Fd28
Danville USA (IL) 246 Fg25
Danville USA (KY) 249 Fh27
Danville USA (PA) 247 Gb25
Danville USA (VA) 249 Ga27
Dan Xian CHN (HAN) 96 Qe36
Danxiashan CHN 97 Qg33
Danyang CHN (JGS) 102 Qk29
Danyi-Apéyémé TG 193 La42
Danze EAK 207 Mk47
Danzhou CHN (GZG) 96 Qe33
Dao RP 123 Rb40
Dao Bach Long Vi VN 96 Qd35
Dao Ban Sen VN 96 Qd35
Dao Cai Chien VN 96 Qd35
Dao Cat Ba VN 96 Qd35
Dao Co To VN 96 Qd35
Dao Hon Lon VN 115 Qe39
Dao Phu Quoc VN 117 Qc40
Daoro CI 192 Kg43
Daotanghe CHN (QHI) 92 Qa27
Dao Thanh Lan VN 96 Qd35
Daotiandi CHN (HLG) 98 Rf21
Dao Timi RN 181 Lg35
Daoud DZ 173 Kk28
Daoukro CI 193 Kj42
Dao Van Don VN 96 Qd35
Dao Vay VN 117 Qb41
Dao Vinh Thuc VN 96 Qd35
Dao Xian CHN (HUN) 96 Qf33
Dapa RP 123 Rd41
Dapaong TG 193 La40
Da Paz BR 281 He50
Dapchi WAN 187 Lf39
Dapdap RP 121 Rb38
Dapélogo BF 185 Kk39
Dapitan RP 123 Rb41
Dapoli IND (MHT) 108 Og37
Daporijo IND (ARP) 112 Ph31
Da Porta BR 275 He49
Dapuchaihe CHN (JLN) 100 Re24
Da Qaidam CHN (QHI) 87 Ph27
Daqiao CHN (YUN) 113 Qb32
Daqing CHN (HLG) 98 Rc22
Daqing Shan CHN 93 Qf25
Daqq-e Tundi AFG 78 Oa29
Daqu Dao CHN 102 Rb30
Daquing Reservoir CHN 98 Rc22
Daquq IRQ 65 Nc28
Dara SN 183 Kc38
Darab IR 74 Nh31
Darab SP 205 Na45
Daraban PK 79 Of30
Darabani RO 45 Mg42
Daradou RCA 201 Mc43
Daraga RP 121 Rb39
Daraina RM 219 Ne52
Dar al-Hajar YE 68 Nc38
Daram RI 130 Rf47
Daram RP 123 Rc40
Daram Island RP 123 Rc40
Daran IR 72 Nf29
Darány H 41 Ls45
Darar ETH 199 Nc41
Dararisa SUD 190 Mg40
Darasun RUS 91 Qg20
Daraw ET 177 Mg33
Darazo WAN 187 Lf40
Darband IR 73 Nj30
Darband-i Khan IRQ 65 Nc28
Darband Sar IR 72 Nf27
Darbėnai LT 17 Mb34
Darbhanga IND (BIH) 107 Pc32
Darburruk SP 199 Nc41
Dar-Caïd-Hadji MA 172 Kf30
Dar-Caïd-Ilal-bou-Fenzi MA 172 Kf30
Dar Chioukh DZ 173 Lb28
Darcinópolis BR (TO) 276 Hg49
Darda AUS (WA) 140 Ra59
Darda HR 44 Lt45
Dardanelle USA (AR) 243 Fd28
Dardanelles TR 50 Mg50
Dardesheim D 33 Ll39
Dardhë AL 46 Ma50
Dareda EAT 207 Mh48
Dareen AUS (QLD) 151 Sf58
Dar el-Bahr MA 172 Kf29

Dar el Barka – Devils Tower

Dar el Barka RIM 183 Kc37
Darende TR 62 Mj26
Dar es Salaam EAT 207 Mk49
Dareton AUS (NSW) 152 Sb63
Darfo-Boário Terme I 40 Ll45
Darfur SUD 189 Mc39
Darganata TM 71 Ob25
Dargaville NZ 154 Tg63
Dargaz IR 73 Nk27
Dargeçit TR 63 Na27
Darghoulia TN 174 Lf29
Dargo AUS (VIC) 153 Sd64
Dargol RN 185 La39
Dargosław PL 36 Lq36
Darhala CI 193 Kh41
Darhan Muminggan Lianheqi CHN (NMZ) 93 Qf25
Darıca TR 50 Mk50
Darıca TR 63 Mj26
Darien CO 268 Gb44
Darién PA 257 Ga42
Darien USA (GA) 249 Fk30
Darién, P.N. del PA 257 Gb42
Daring IND (ARP) 112 Ph32
Darinskij KZ 84 Og21
Dario Meira BR (BA) 283 Ja53
Dariv MNG 85 Ph22
Darıveren TR 50 Mk53
Dariviyn Nuruu MNG 85 Ph22
Dariya KZ 84 Og21
Dariyah KSA 66 Nb33
Darj LAR 174 Lf30
Darjeeling IND (WBG) 112 Pe32
Darjeeling Himalayan Railway IND 112 Pe32
Dârjiu RO 45 Mf44
Darkan AUS (WA) 144 Qj62
Darke Peak AUS (SA) 152 Rj62
Darkhadyn Khotgor MNG 90 Pk20
Darkhan MNG 90 Qd21
Darkhan MNG 91 Qe22
Darkhovin IR 74 Ne30
Darkoti IND (HPH) 107 Oj30
Darlag CHN (QHI) 94 Pk29
Darling ZA 216 Lk62
Darling Downs AUS 151 Se59
Darlingford CDN (MB) 238 Fb21
Darling Range AUS 144 Qj61
Darling River AUS 153 Sc62
Darlington GB 21 Kt36
Darlington USA (SC) 249 Ga28
Darlington Point AUS (NSW) 153 Sd63
Darlington Raceway USA 249 Ga28
Darłowo PL 36 Lr36
Dărmănești RO 45 Mf46
Dar Mazar IR 75 Nj31
Darmstadt D 34 Lj41
Darnah LAR 175 Mb29
Darnall ZA 217 Mf60
Darney F 23 Lg42
Darnick AUS (NSW) 153 Sb62
Darnley Island AUS 147 Sb50
Daroca E 27 Kt51
Darouma RMM 183 Kf38
Darou-Mousti SN 183 Kb38
Darrahe Awd AFG 78 Od28
Darrah Wildlife Sanctuary IND 108 Oh33
Darranga IND (ASM) 112 Pf32
Darregueira RA (BA) 293 Gj64
Darreh Shahr IR 72 Nd29
Darreh Tank IR 72 Ne29
Darreh-ye Bum AFG 78 Ob28
Darrington USA (WA) 232 Dk21
D'Arros SY 219 Ng48
Darsa YE 69 Ng39
Darsi IND (APH) 111 Ok39
Darsilami WAG 183 Kc39
Darß D 33 Ln36
Dartford GB 21 La39
Dartmoor AUS (VIC) 152 Sa64
Dartmoor N.P. GB 20 Kr40
Dartmouth CDN (NS) 245 Gj23
Dartmouth GB 20 Kr40
Daru PNG 159 Sb50
Daru SUD 190 Mg38
Daru WAL 192 Ke42
Darubia PNG 160 Sf50
Daru Island PNG 159 Sb50
Dar Umm YE 68 Nc39
Daruntah AFG 79 Of28
Daruvar HR 41 Ls45
Darvahi IR 74 Nf31
Darvaza TM 71 Nk25
Darvishi IR 74 Nf31
Darwazahgey AFG 78 Od30
Darwendale ZW 210 Mf54
Darwha IND (MHT) 108 Oj35
Darwin AUS (NT) 139 Rf52
Darwin GB 295 Ha71
Darwin Glacier 297 Sd34
Darwin River AUS (NT) 139 Rf52
Darwin, Volcán EC 272 Fe46
Daryacheh-ye-Bakhtegan IR 74 Ng31
Daryacheh-ye-Hows Soltan IR 72 Nf28
Daryacheh-ye-Maharlu IR 74 Ng31
Daryacheh-ye-Namak IR 72 Nf28
Daryacheh-ye-Sistan IR 73 Oa30
Daryacheh-ye-Tashk IR 74 Ng31
Darya Khan PK 79 Of30
Daryaleh SP 199 Nc41
Daryanah LAR 175 Ma29
Daryapur IND (MHT) 108 Oj35
Darya-ye Argandab AFG 78 Od29
Darya-ye Harirud AFG 78 Oc28
Darya-ye Kabul AFG 78 Oe28
Darya-ye Konduz AFG 78 Oe27
Darya-ye Morgabrub AFG 78 Ob28
Darya-ye Pang AFG/TJ 78 Of27
Darya-ye Vahan AFG 79 Og27
Dary-ye Balkh AFG 78 Od27
Darzin IR 75 Nk31
Darzininkai LT 17 Mf36
Das UAE 74 Ng33
Dasada IND (GUJ) 108 Of34
Das Araias do Araguaia BR 276 Hf50
Das Cunhãs BR 276 Hf49
Das Fêmeas BR 282 Hh52
Das Garças ou Jacaréguea BR 281 Hd53
Dashanshao CHN (GZH) 96 Qc32
Dashapalla IND (ORS) 109 Pc35
Dashbalbar MNG 91 Qh21
Dashennongjia CHN 95 Qf30
Dashitou CHN (JLN) 100 Re24
Dashizhai CHN (NMZ) 91 Ra22
Dashoguz TM 71 Nk25
Dasht PK 80 Ob33
Dashtak IR 72 Nf29
Dasht-e Khash AFG 78 Ob30
Dasht-e Margo AFG 78 Oc30
Dasht-e Naumed AFG 78 Oa29
Dasht-i Tahlab PK 80 Oa31
Dashtobod UZ 76 Oe25
Dashuikeng CHN (NHZ) 92 Qd27
Da Silva BR 281 He52
Daska PK 79 Oh29
Daskalgram IND (WBG) 112 Pd34
Dáski GR 46 Mc50
Das Mortes BR 281 He52
Dasol Bay RP 120 Qk38
Das Ondas BR 282 Hh52
Das Pombas BR 274 Gk49
Dass WAN 186 Le40
Dassari DY 193 La40
Dassa Zoumé DY 194 Lb42
Dassel D 32 Lk39
Dassen Island ZA 216 Lj62
Dassow D 33 Ll37
Dašt-e Lut IR 60 Nd12
Dašt-e Qal'eh AFG 78 Oe27
Dasu PK 79 Og28
Dasual IND (PJB) 106 Oh30
Datah Dawai RI 126 Qh45
Datang CHN (GZG) 96 Qe33
Datça TR 49 Mh54
Datça Körfezi TR 49 Mh54
Date J 99 Sa24
Datia IND (MPH) 107 Ok33
Datian CHN (FJN) 97 Qj33
Datian Ding CHN 96 Qf34
Datil USA (NM) 237 Eg28
Datimun RI 116 Ph44
Datkan MYA 114 Ph36
Datong CHN (HLG) 98 Rc23
Datong CHN (QHI) 92 Qa27
Datong CHN (SAX) 93 Qg25
Datong He CHN 92 Qa27
Datong Hu CHN 95 Qg31
Datong Shan CHN 92 Qa27
Datori DY 193 La40
Dato Temple CHN 94 Qc31
Datta RUS 99 Sa21
Daub RI 158 Sa50
Daud Khel PK 79 Of29
Daudnagar IND (BIH) 109 Pc33
Daudzeva LV 17 Mf34
Daugai LT 17 Me36
Daugailiai LT 17 Mf35
Daugava LV 17 Mg34
Daugavpils LT 17 Mg35
Dau Go Grotto VN 96 Qd35
Dauin RP 123 Rb41
Dauka OM 69 Nh36
Daulatabad IND 108 Oh36
Daulatpur PK 80 Od32
Daule EC 272 Fk46
Daule EC 272 Ga46
Daule RI 127 Rb48
Daun D 32 Lg40
Daund IND (MHT) 108 Oh36
Daung Island MYA 114 Pj39
Dauphin CDN (MB) 238 Ek20
Dauphiné F 25 Lf46
Dauphin Lake CDN 238 Ek20
Dauphin River CDN (MB) 238 Fa20
Daura WAN 186 Le39
Daurskij hrebet RUS 91 Qg20
Dausa IND (RJT) 106 Oj32
Dau Thieng VN 115 Qd40
Dautillos MEX (SL) 252 Eg33
Davangere IND (KTK) 110 Oh39
Davao RP 123 Rc42
Davao Gulf RP 123 Rc42
Davarzan IR 73 Nj27
Davenda RUS 91 Qk19
Davenport USA (AL) 248 Fg29
Davenport USA (MO) 241 Fe25
Davenport USA (WA) 232 Ea22
Davenport Downs AUS (QLD) 150 Sa58
Davenport Range AUS 143 Rh56
Davenport Range N.P. AUS 143 Rh56
Daventry GB 21 Kt38
David PA 256 Fj41
David City USA (NE) 240 Fb25
David Garedža GE 70 Nc25
David Glacier 297 Ta34
Davidson CDN (SK) 233 Eh20
Davidson USA (OK) 242 Fa28
Davinópolis BR (GO) 286 Hg55
Davis USA (OK) 243 Fb28
Davis ANT (AUS) 297 Od32
Davis, Mount AUS 142 Re59
Davis Mts. USA 237 Eh30
Davis River AUS 140 Ra57
Davis Sea 297 Pc31
Davis Strait 225 Ha05
Davo CI 193 Kg43
Davor HR 41 Ls45
Davos CH 34 Lk44
Davulga TR 51 Mm52
Davyd-Haradok BY 52 Md19
Dawa CHN (LNG) 100 Rb25
Dawa ETH 198 Mk43
Dawa GH 193 La43
Dawab SUD 190 Mg38
Dawadawa GH 193 Kk41
Dawa Dawa RP 123 Rb42
Dawa River ETH 198 Na43
Daweloor RI 132 Rf49
Dawera RI 132 Rf49
Dawes Range AUS 151 Sf58
Dawharab YE 68 Na37
Dawhat Salwa KSA 67 Nf33
Dawhwenya GH 193 La43
Dawi ETH 198 Na40
Dawir SUD 197 Mg41
Dawna Range MYA 114 Pj37
Daws KSA 66 Na35
Dawson CDN 224 Da06
Dawson USA (GA) 249 Fh30
Dawson USA (ND) 240 Fa22
Dawson Bay CDN 238 Ek19
Dawson Bay Ind. Res. CDN 238 Ek19
Dawson Creek CDN (BC) 232 Dk18
Dawson Landing CDN (BC) 232 Dg20
Dawson Range CDN 231 Da14
Dawson River AUS 151 Sf58
Dawson Springs USA (KY) 248 Fg27
Dawu CHN (HUB) 102 Qh30
Dawu CHN (SCH) 94 Qa30
Dawwah OM 69 Nk35
Dax F 24 Kt47
Daxian CHN (SCH) 95 Qd30
Daxin CHN (GZG) 96 Qd34
Daxing CHN (BJG) 93 Qj26
Daxing CHN (YUN) 113 Qa32
Daxue Shan CHN 94 Qa30
Dayang Buntig MAL 116 Pk42
Dayangshu CHN (NMZ) 98 Rc21
Dayan nuur MNG 85 Pe21
Dayao CHN (YUN) 113 Qa33
Daya Wan CHN 97 Qh34
Dayaxa SP 199 Nd40
Daye CHN (HUB) 102 Qh30
Dayi CHN (SCH) 94 Qb30
Dayi WAN 186 Ld40
Daying Jiang MYA/CHN 113 Pj33
Daylesford AUS (VIC) 153 Sc64
Daymán ROU 289 Hb61
Daysland CDN (AB) 233 Ed19
Dayton USA (MT) 233 Ec22
Dayton USA (OH) 246 Fh26
Dayton USA (TN) 249 Fh28
Dayton USA (TX) 243 Fc30
Dayton USA (WA) 234 Eb22
Dayton USA (WY) 235 Eg23
Daytona Beach USA (FL) 250 Fk31
Daytona Intl. Speedway USA 250 Fk31
Dayu CHN (JGX) 97 Qh33
Dayu RI 126 Qh46
Da Yunhe CHN 102 Ra30
Dayville USA (OR) 234 Ea23
Dayyer IR 74 Nf32
Dayyinah UAE 74 Ng33
Dazaifu J 103 Rf29
Dazey USA (ND) 240 Fa22
Dazhi CHN (GZG) 96 Qe34
Dazhu CHN (SCH) 95 Qd30
Dazkırı TR 50 Mk53
Dazu = Longgang CHN (CGQ) 95 Qc31
Dazu Rock Carvings CHN 95 Qc31
Dchira DARS 178 Kd32
De Aar ZA 217 Mc61
Dead Horse Point Nat. Mon. USA 235 Ef26
Dead Indian Peak USA 235 Ef23
Deadman Hill AUS 140 Qk57
Deadman's Cay BS 251 Gc34
Deadman's Cr. Ind. Res. CDN 232 Dk20
Dead Sea IL 64 Mh30
Deakin AUS (WA) 145 Re61
Deal GB 21 Lb39
Déali SN 183 Kc38
Deal Island AUS (VIC) 153 Sd65
Dealsville ZA 217 Mc60
Dealurile Silvaniei RO 44 Mc43
De'an CHN (JGX) 102 Qh31
Dean Channel CDN 232 Dg19
Deán Funes RA (CD) 288 Gh61
Deanmill AUS (WA) 144 Qj63
Dearborn USA (MI) 246 Fj24
Deary USA (ID) 234 Eb22
Dease Lake CDN (BC) 231 Df16
Dease Lake CDN 231 De16
Dease River CDN 231 Df16
Dease Strait CDN 224 Ec05
Death Railway THA 114 Pk38
Death Valley USA (CA) 236 Eb27
Death Valley USA 236 Eb27
Death Valley Junction USA (CA) 236 Eb27
Death Valley N.P. USA 236 Eb27
Deauville F 22 La41
Deaver USA (WY) 235 Ef23
Debal'ceve UA 55 Mk21
Debalo SUD 197 Mf41
Debao CHN (GZG) 96 Qd34
Debar MK 46 Ma49
Debark ETH 191 Mj40
Debauch Mts. USA 229 Ca13
Debaysima ER 191 Nb40
Deb-Deb DZ 174 Le30
Debden CDN (SK) 233 Eg19
Debdou MA 173 Kj29
Debelec BG 47 Mf47
Debelo brdo SCG 46 Lu46
Debepare PNG 158 Sa49
Débéré BF 185 Kj39
Debiapur IND (UPH) 107 Ok32
Dębica PL 36 Lq37
Dębica PL 37 Mb40
Debidwar BD 112 Pf34
Dęblin PL 37 Mb39
Dębnica Kaszubska PL 36 Ls36
Dębno PL 36 Lp38
Dębno PL 39 Ma41
DeBolt CDN (AB) 233 Eb18
Debrc SCG 44 Lu46
Debre Birhan ETH 198 Mk41
Debre Bizen ER 191 Mk39
Debrecen H 39 Mb43
Debre Damo ETH 191 Mk39
Debre Libanos Gedam ETH 198 Mk41
Debre Markos ETH 198 Mj40
Debre Sina ETH 198 Mj39
Debre Sina ETH 198 Mk41
Debre Tabor ETH 198 Mk40
Debre Work ETH 198 Mk40
Debre Zeit ETH 198 Mk41
De Brug ZA 217 Mc60
Debrznica PL 36 Lq38
Dečani SCG 46 Ma48
Decatur USA (AL) 248 Fg28
Decatur USA (IL) 241 Ff26
Decatur USA (IN) 246 Fh25
Decatur USA (MS) 243 Ff29
Decatur USA (TX) 242 Fb29
Decazeville F 24 Lc46
Deccan IND 104 Od15
Deception Bay PNG 159 Sc49
Deception Lake CDN 233 Eh17
Deception Pans RB 213 Mb56
Deception Valley RB 213 Mb56
Deception Valley Lodge RB 213 Mb56
Dechang CHN (SCH) 113 Qb32
Dechu IND (RJT) 106 Og32
Děčín CZ 38 Lp40
Deciolândia BR (MT) 281 Hb53
Decize F 23 Ld44
Decker USA (MT) 235 Eg23
De Cocksdorp NL 32 Le37
Decorah USA (IA) 241 Fe24
Deda RO 45 Me44
Dedegöl Dağları TR 51 Mm53
Dedeler TR 51 Mn52
Dedemsvaart NL 32 Lg38
Dedenevo RUS 52 Mj17
Deder ETH 198 Na41
Dedeso GH 193 Kk42
Dediapada IND (GUJ) 108 Og35
De Doorns ZA 216 Lk62
Dédougou BF 185 Kj39
Dedoviči RUS 52 Me17
Dedza MW 210 Mh53
Dee GB 19 Ks33
Dee GB 21 Ks37
Deep River CDN (ON) 244 Gb22
Deepwater AUS (NSW) 151 Sf60
Deep Well AUS (NT) 142 Rh58
Deer USA (AR) 243 Fd28
Deering USA (AK) 229 Bj12
Deering, Mount AUS 141 Re58
Deer Island USA 228 Bj18
Deer Lake CDN (NF) 245 Hb21
Deer Lake CDN (ON) 238 Fc19
Deer Lake CDN 245 Hb21
Deer Lodge USA (MT) 235 Ed22
Deer Pd. CDN 245 Hc21
Deer River CDN 238 Fc17
Deer River USA (MN) 241 Fd22
Deesa IND (GUJ) 108 Og33
Defeng CHN (GZH) 96 Qe32
Defensores del Chaco, P.N. PY 285 Gk56
Defferrari RA (BA) 293 Ha65
Defiance USA (OH) 246 Fh25
Défilé de Tosaye RMM 185 Kk37
De Funiak Springs USA (FL) 249 Fg30
Dega Medo ETH 199 Nb42
Degana IND (RJT) 106 Oh32
De Gaulle RCA 195 Lh42
Dêgê CHN (SCH) 94 Pk30
Degeberga S 15 Lp35
Degeh Bur ETH 199 Nb41
Dégelis CDN (QC) 244 Gf22
Degema WAN 194 Ld43
Degerby FIN 13 Ma30
Degerfors S 13 Lp31
Degerhamn S 15 Lr34
De Gerlache Seamounts Fb31
Deggendorf D 35 Ln42
Değirmendere TR 49 Mh52
Değirmendere TR 50 Mk50
Degoma ETH 191 Mj40
Dégrad Claude F 271 Hd44
De Grey AUS (WA) 140 Qk56
De Grey River AUS 140 Qk56
De Groote Peel, N.P. NL 32 Lf39
Degučiai LT 17 Mb35
Degučiai LT 17 Mg35
Deguri IND (RJT) 106 Oh33
Dehaj IR 74 Nh30
Dehak IR 75 Ob32
Dehaq IR 72 Nf29
Deh Bid IR 74 Ng30
Deh Dasht IR 72 Nf30
Dehej IND (GUJ) 108 Og35
Dehel ER 191 Mk39
Dehgaon IND (MPH) 109 Ok34
Dehgolan IR 72 Nd28
Dehiba TN 174 Lf30
Dehiwala-Mount Lavinia CL 111 Ok43
Dehloran IR 72 Nd29
Deh Mohammed IR 73 Nj28
Deh Now IR 74 Ng31
De Hoop ZA 216 Mb62
De Hoop Nature Reserve ZA 216 Ma63
Dehori IND (MPH) 109 Ok34
Deh Parian AFG 78 Oe28
Dehqonobod UZ 76 Od26
Dehqonobod UZ 76 Oe25
Dehradun IND (UTT) 107 Ok30
Deh Rawod AFG 78 Oc29
Dehri IND (BIH) 109 Pc33
Deh Shir IR 72 Ng30
Deh Shir IR 72 Ng30
Deh Shu AFG 78 Ob30
Dehua CHN (FJN) 97 Qk33
Dehui CHN (JLN) 98 Rc23
Deima most RUS 17 Mb36
Deim Bukhit SUD 197 Md42
Deinze B 23 Ld40
Deir Abu Makâr ET 177 Mf30
Deir Al Zor SYR 65 Na28
Deir Amba Bshôi ET 177 Mf30
Deir Djebel at Tayr ET 177 Mf31
Deir el Abyad ET 177 Mf32
Deir el-Baramûs ET 177 Mf30
Deir el Qiddîsah Kâtrînâ ET 177 Mg31
Deir es-Surjân ET 177 Mf30
Deirhafer SYR 64 Mj27
Deir Mar Musa al-Habashi SYR 64 Mj28
Deir Samû'il ET 177 Mf31
Deixa-Falar BR (AM) 279 Ge49
Dej RO 44 Md43
De Janeiro BR 282 Hh51
Deje S 13 Lo31
Dejen ETH 198 Mk40
Dejiang CHN (GZH) 95 Qe31
De Kalb USA (IL) 246 Ff25
De Kalb USA (MS) 243 Ff29
De Kalb USA (TX) 243 Fc29
Dekélia GR 48 Md52
Dekemhare ER 191 Mk39
Dekese RDC 203 Ma47
De Keukenhof NL 32 Le38
Dekhistan TM 71 Nh26
Dekina WAN 194 Ld42
Dekoa RCA 196 Lk42
De Koog NL 32 Le37
Delacroix USA (LA) 243 Ff31
De la Garma RA (BA) 293 Gk64
Delaki RI 132 Rc50
De Land USA (FL) 250 Fk31
Delaney USA (WA) 234 Eb22
Delano USA (CA) 236 Ea28
De la Paz BOL 284 Gg54
De La Poer Range Nature Reserve AUS 141 Rb59
Delaram AFG 78 Ob29
Delareyville ZA 217 Mc59
Delaronde Lake CDN 233 Eg18
De las Piedras PE 279 Ge51
Delaware USA (OH) 246 Fj25
Delaware USA 247 Gc26
Delaware Bay USA 247 Gc26
Delbi SN 183 Kc38
Delbrück D 32 Lj39
Delburne CDN (AB) 233 Ed19
Delčevo MK 46 Mc49
Deleau CDN (MB) 238 Ek21
Déleg EC 272 Ga47
Délembé RCA 196 Mb41
Delémont CH 34 Lh43
De Leon USA (TX) 242 Fa29
Délép TCH 196 Lk39
Delet Teili FIN 13 Ma30
Delfinópolis BR (MG) 287 Hg56
Delft NL 32 Le39
Delfzijl NL 32 Lg37
Delgado-Chalbaud, Cerro BR/YV 270 Gj44
Delgerkhaan Uul MNG 91 Qe21
Delger mörön MNG 90 Pk21
Delgo SUD 190 Mf36
Delhi IND (DEL) 107 Oj31
Delhi IND 107 Oj31
Delhi USA (LA) 243 Fe29
Delhi USA (NY) 247 Gc24
Delhingha CHN (QHI) 87 Pj27
Deli RI 128 Qc49
Déli TCH 187 Lh41
Delice TR 51 Mo51
Delicias CO 273 Gc46
Delicias MEX (CHH) 253 Eh31
Deligrad SCG 46 Mb47
Delijan IR 72 Nf29
Delisle CDN (QC) 244 Ge21
Delisle CDN (SK) 233 Eg20
Delitzsch D 33 Ln39
Dell USA (MT) 235 Ed23
Dell Rapids USA (SD) 241 Fb24
Dellys DZ 173 Lb27
Del Mar USA (CA) 236 Eb29
Delmas CDN (SK) 233 Ef19
Delmas ZA 217 Me59
Delmenhorst D 32 Lj37
Delmiro Gouveia BR (AL) 283 Jb50
Delnice HR 41 Lp45
Del Norte USA (CO) 237 Eg27
De Lomas PE 278 Gc53
Deloraine AUS (TAS) 152 Sd66
Deloraine CDN (MB) 238 Ek21
Delphí GR 48 Mc52
Delray Beach USA (FL) 250 Fk32
Del Rio USA (TX) 242 Ek31
Delsbo S 13 Lr29
Delta BR (MG) 286 Hg55
Delta CDN (BC) 232 Dj21
Delta USA (CO) 235 Ef26
Delta USA (UT) 235 Ed26
Delta Beach CDN (MB) 238 Fa20
Delta Camp RB 213 Mb55
Delta del Ebre E 30 La50
Delta del Paraná RA 289 Ha62
Delta del Po I 40 Ln46
Delta del Río Colorado, Alto Golfo de California y MEX (BC) 236 Ec30
Delta del Tigre ROU 289 Hb63
Delta Downs AUS (QLD) 148 Sa54
Delta Dunării, P.N. RO 45 Mk45
Delta du Saloum, P.N. du SN 183 Kb39
Delta Junction USA (AK) 229 Ch13
Delta N.W.R. USA 243 Ff31
Delta of the Danube RO 45 Mk45
Delta River USA 229 Ch14
Delthore Mtn. CDN 231 Df14
Deltona USA (FL) 250 Fk31
Delungra AUS (NSW) 151 Sf60
Del Verme Falls ETH 198 Na43
Delvin IRL 20 Kn37
Delwada IND (GUJ) 108 Of35
De Majes PE 279 Gd53
Demak RI 128 Qf49
Demänová SK 39 Lu41
Demba RDC 203 Mb48
Demba Koli SN 183 Kd39
Dembecha ETH 198 Mj40
Dembéni COM 218 Nb51
Dembi ETH 198 Mj41
Dembia RCA 201 Mc43
Dembi Dolo ETH 197 Mh41
Dembo CAM 187 Lg41
Dembo TCH 195 Lj41
Demchok 79 Ok29
Demerara Abyssal Plain 265 Hc17
Demeraraplateau 265 Hd18
Demerval Lobão BR (PI) 277 Hj48
Demidov RUS 52 Mf18
Demidove UA 45 Ml43
Deming USA (NM) 237 Eg29
Deming USA (WA) 232 Dj21
Demini BR 274 Gj46
Demirci TR 50 Mj51
Demir Hisar MK 46 Ma49
Demir Kapija MK 46 Mc49
Demirköprü Baraji TR 50 Mj52
Demirköy TR 50 Mh49
Demirşeyh TR 51 Mp50
Demırtaş TR 50 Mk50
Demitsána GR 48 Mc53
Demjansk RUS 52 Mg17
Dem'jas RUS 53 Ne20
Demmin D 33 Lo37
Demnate MA 172 Kg30
Democratic Republic Congo 167 Ma10
Demonía GR 48 Mc54
Demonte I 40 Lh46
de Monte Roraima, P.N. BR 270 Gk43
Demopolis USA (AL) 248 Fg29
Demotte USA (IN) 246 Fg25
Dempo, Gunung RI 125 Qb47
Demsa CAM 187 Lg41
Demta RI 131 Sa47
Demydivka UA 37 Mf40
Denain F 23 Ld40
Denali Highway USA 229 Cg14
Denali National Park USA (AK) 229 Cf14
Denali National Park USA 229 Ce14
Denan ETH 199 Nb42
Denbigh CDN (ON) 247 Gb23
Denbigh GB 21 Kr37
Den Burg NL 32 Le37
Den Chai THA 114 Qa37
Dendang RI 125 Qd47
Dendâra RIM 184 Kg37
Dendermonde B 23 Le39
Déndoudi SN 183 Kd38
Dengchuan CHN (YUN) 113 Qa33
Dengfeng CHN (HNN) 95 Qg28
Dengi WAN 186 Le41
Dengkou CHN (NMZ) 92 Qd25
Dêngqên CHN (TIB) 89 Ph30
Denguiro RCA 200 Mb43
Dengzhou CHN (HNN) 95 Qg29
Denham AUS (WA) 140 Qg58
Denham Island AUS (QLD) 148 Rk54
Denham Sound AUS 140 Qg58
Den Helder NL 32 Le38
Denhoff USA (ND) 240 Ek22
Denholm CDN (SK) 233 Eg19
Denia E 29 La48
Denial Bay AUS 152 Rg62
Deniliquin AUS (NSW) 153 Sc63
Denio USA (NV) 234 Ea25
Denison USA (IA) 241 Fc24
Denison USA (TX) 243 Fb29
Deni, T.I. BR 279 Gg49
Deniyaya CL 111 Pa43
Deniz Kamp Yeri TR 49 Mg52
Denizler TR 50 Mk53
Denizli TR 50 Mh50
Denizli TR 50 Mk53
Denkanikota IND (TNU) 111 Oj40
Denman AUS (NSW) 153 Sf62
Denman AUS (SA) 145 Rf61
Denman Glacier 297 Qa32
Denmark AUS (WA) 144 Qj63
Denmark CDN (NS) 245 Gj23
Denmark DK 14 Lj35
Denmark USA (OR) 234 Dh24
Denmark Strait 6 Jb03
Denneba ETH 198 Mk41
Dennery WL 261 Gk39
Den Oever NL 32 Lf38
Denov UZ 76 Od26
Denpasar RI 129 Qh50
Dent de Mindif CAM 187 Lh40
Denton USA (MD) 247 Gc26
Denton USA (MT) 235 Ef22
Denton USA (TX) 243 Fb29
d'Entrecasteaux Islands PNG 160 Sf50
D'Entrecasteaux N.P. AUS 144 Qh63
Dents du Midi CH 34 Lg44
Denu GH 193 La42
Denver USA (CO) 235 Eh26
Denver City USA (TX) 237 Ej29
Déo RCA 196 Ma41
Deoban IND (UTT) 107 Oj30
Deoband IND (UPH) 107 Oj31
Deobhog IND (CGH) 109 Pb36
De Ocoña PE 279 Gd53
Deodápolis BR (MS) 286 Hc57
Deogaon IND (ORS) 109 Pb35
Deogarh IND (ORS) 109 Pc35
Deogarh IND (RJT) 106 Og33
Deogarh IND 109 Ok33
Deogarh IND 109 Pb34
Deogarh Mahal IND 106 Og33
Deoghar IND (JKD) 112 Pd33
Deokar IND (CGH) 109 Pa35
Deoli IND (MHT) 109 Ok35
Deoli IND (ORS) 112 Pd34
Deoli IND (RJT) 106 Oh33
Deori IND (MHT) 109 Pa35
Deoria IND (UPH) 107 Pb32
Deosai Mountains 79 Oh28
Deosai Plains N.P. PK 79 Oh28
Deosil IND (CGH) 109 Pb34
Deo Tu Na VN 115 Qd39
Déou BF 185 Kk38
Dep WAN 194 Le41
de Pacaás-Novos, P.N. BR 280 Gj51
Depapre RI 131 Sa47
Dépôt Lézard F 271 Hd43
Dépression du Mourdi TCH 189 Mb36
Depuch Island AUS 140 Qj56
Deputatskij RUS 59 Sa05
Dêqên CHN (TIB) 89 Pf30
Dêqên CHN (YUN) 94 Pk31
Deqing CHN (GDG) 96 Qf34
De Queen USA (AR) 243 Fc28
De Quincy USA (LA) 243 Fd30
Dera ETH 198 Mk41
Dera SP 205 Na45
Der'a SYR 64 Mj29
Dera Bugti PK 81 Oe31
Dera Ghazi Khan PK 79 Of30
Dera Ismail Khan PK 79 Of30
Dera Murad Jamali PK 80 Oe31
Dera Nanak IND (PJB) 106 Oh29
Dera Nawab PK 81 Of31
Derawan RI 127 Qk44
Derawar Fort PK 81 Of31
Derbent RUS (DAG) 70 Ne24
Derbent TR 51 Mn52
Derbissaka RCA 201 Mc43
Derbur CHN (NMZ) 91 Ra20
Derby AUS (TAS) 152 Sd66
Derby AUS (WA) 138 Rb54
Derby GB 21 Kt38
Derby USA (KS) 242 Fb27
Derby ZA 213 Md58
Đerdap, N.P. SCG 44 Mb46
Derdepoort ZA 213 Md58
Derebucak TR 51 Mm53
Dereköy TR 50 Mj52
Dereli TR 63 Mk25
Deremahal TR 51 Mp51
Déréssa TCH 196 Ma39
Derewo RI 131 Rj47
Dergači RUS 53 Ne20
Derhači UA 53 Mj20
De Ridder USA (LA) 243 Fd30
Derik TR 63 Na27
Derinkuyu TR 51 Mp52
Deris IR 74 Nf31
Derito ETH 198 Mk43
Derm NAM 212 Lk57
Dermott USA (AR) 243 Fe29
Derre MOC 211 Mj54
Derri SP 199 Nd43
Derry = Londonderry GB 18 Kn36
Derry Downs AUS (NT) 143 Rh57
De Rust ZA 216 Mb62
Derval F 22 Kt43
Derventa BIH 41 Ls46
Derwent CDN (AB) 233 Ee19
Derwent GB 21 Ku37
Derwent Valley Mills GB 21 Kt37
Desaguadero BOL 284 Gg54
Desaguadero RA 288 Gg62
Desagües de los Colorados RA 288 Gg60
Des Arc USA (AR) 243 Fe28
Desaru MAL 117 Qc45
Desaru Beach MAL 117 Qc45
Descalvado BR (SP) 286 Hg56
Descartes F 22 La44
Deschaillons CDN (QC) 244 Gd22
Deschambault Lake CDN 238 Ej18
Descharme River CDN 233 Ef17
Descobrimento, P.N. do BR 287 Ja54
Desdunes RH 260 Gd36
Dese ETH 198 Mk40
Deseado RA 294 Gg69
Desecho YV 273 Gg44
Desembarco del Granma, P.N. C 259 Gb36
Desengaño PE 273 Gd47
Desenzano del Garda I 40 Ll45
Desert Center USA (CA) 236 Ec29
Desert Express NAM 212 Lh57
Desert Highway JOR 64 Mj30
Desert Island, Mount USA 245 Gf23
Desert National Wildlife Range USA 236 Ec27
Desert N.P. IND 106 Of32
Desert Peak USA 235 Ed25
Desert Peak USA 235 Ed25
Desert Valley USA 234 Ea25
Desești RO 44 Md43
Deshgaon IND (MPH) 108 Oj35
Desiderio Tello RA (LR) 288 Gg61
Desierto de Altar MEX 236 Ed30
Desierto de Atacama RCH 284 Gf57
Desierto de Sechura PE 272 Fk48
Desierto de Vizcaíno MEX 252 Ed32
Deskáti GR 46 Mb51
Desli IND (MPH) 108 Oj35
De Smet USA (SD) 240 Fb23
Desmochado PY 289 Ha59
Des Moines USA (IA) 241 Fd25
Des Moines USA (NM) 237 Ej27
Desna RUS 52 Mh19
Desna UA 52 Mf20
Desnățui RO 44 Md46
Desnœufs SY 219 Ng49
Desnyano-Staroguts'kyj N.P. UA 52 Mg19
Desolation Canyon USA 235 Ee26
Desolation Point RP 123 Rc40
De Soto USA (MO) 241 Fe26
DeSoto Caverns Park USA 248 Fg29
Despatch ZA 217 Mc62
Despeñaderos RA (CD) 288 Gh61
Des Plaines USA (IL) 246 Ff24
Despotovac SCG 46 Mb46
Despotovo SCG 44 Lu45
Dessau D 33 Ln39
Destacamento São Simão BR (MT) 280 Gk53
Destin USA (FL) 248 Fg30
D'Estrees Bay AUS 152 Rj63
Destruction Bay CDN (YT) 231 Da15
Desuri IND (RJT) 106 Og33
Desvres F 23 Lb40
Deta RO 44 Mb45
Dete ZW 213 Md55
De Tian CHN 96 Qd34
Detkovo RUS 16 Mj32
Detmold D 32 Lj39
De Tour Village USA (MI) 246 Fj23
Detroit USA (MI) 246 Fj24
Detroit USA (OR) 234 Dj23
Detroit de Bougainville VU 162 Td53
Détroit de Jacques-Cartier CDN 245 Gj21
Detroit de Selwyn VU 162 Te54
Détroit d'Honguedo CDN 245 Gh21
Detroit Lakes USA (MN) 241 Fc22
Dettifoss IS 10 Kb13
Det Udom THA 115 Qc38
Detuo CHN (SCH) 94 Qb31
Detva SK 39 Lu42
Deua N.P. AUS (NSW) 153 Se63
de Ubajara, P.N. BR 277 Hk47
Deukeskenkala TM 71 Nk24
Deulgaon Raja IND (MHT) 108 Oj35
Deurne NL 32 Lf39
Deustua PE 279 Ge53
Deutschfeistritz A 35 Lq43
Deutschheim S.H.S. USA 241 Fe26
Deutschkreuz A 35 Lr43
Deutschlandsberg A 35 Lq44
Deux Branches F 271 Hd43
Deva RO 44 Mc45
Devadurga IND (KTK) 108 Oj37
Devakottai IND (TNU) 111 Ok42
De Valls Bluff USA (AR) 243 Fe28
Devanakonda IND (APH) 111 Oj39
Devaprayag IND (UTT) 107 Ok30
Devapur IND (KTK) 108 Oj37
Devar Hippargi IND (KTK) 108 Oj37
Devarshola IND (TNU) 110 Oj41
Dévaványa H 39 Ma43
Deveç AZ 70 Ne25
Deveci Dağı TR 51 Mq51
Devecikonağı TR 50 Mj51
Devecser H 38 Ls43
Develi TR 51 Mq52
Deventer NL 32 Lg38
Deveril AUS (QLD) 149 Se57
Devetak BIH 46 Lt46
Devgaon IND (MHT) 108 Oh36
Deviation Peak USA 229 Bk12
Devikolhi IND (HPH) 107 Oj29
Devil Mount USA 229 Bh12
Devil Mountain Lake USA 229 Bh12
Devils Fork S.P. USA 249 Fj28
Devil's Hole USA 236 Eb27
Devil's Hole 19 La34
Devils Lake USA (ND) 238 Fa21
Devils Marbles AUS 139 Rh56
Devil's Millhopper S.P. USA 250 Fj31
Devil's Point BS 251 Gc33
Devil's Point BS 251 Gd34
Devils Postpile Nat. Mon. USA 234 Ea27
Devil's Sinkhole S.N.A. USA 242 Ek30
Devils Tower Nat. Mon. USA 235 Eh23

Devín – Doi Suthep-Pui

Devín SK 38 Lr42
Devipattinam IND (TNU) 111 Ok42
Devizes GB 21 Kt39
Devlin CDN (ON) 238 Fd21
Devnja BG 47 Mh47
Devoll AL 46 Ma50
Devon ZA 217 Me59
Devon Island CDN 225 Fc03
Devonport AUS (TAS) 152 Sd66
Devonshire AUS (QLD) 148 Sc57
Devoto RA (CD) 289 Gj61
Devrek TR 51 Mm49
Devure ZW 214 Mf55
Dewakangbesar RI 129 Qk48
Dewas IND (MPH) 108 Oj34
De Weerribben, N.P. NL 32 Lf38
Dewele ETH 198 Nb40
Dewetsdorp ZA 217 Md60
Dewey USA (OK) 261 Gh36
De Witt USA (AR) 243 Fe28
Dexing CHN (JGX) 102 Qj31
Dexter USA (MO) 243 Ff27
Deyang CHN (SCH) 94 Qc30
Deyhuk IR 73 Nj29
Deza E 27 Ks51
Dezadeash CDN (YT) 231 Db15
Dezadeash Lake CDN 231 Db15
Dezful IR 72 Ne29
Dezhou CHN (SDG) 93 Qj27
Dhaalu Atoll MV 110 Og44
Dhahab Reserve ET 177 Mh31
Dhahran KSA 67 Nf32
Dhaje BHT 112 Pf32
Dhakia IND (UPH) 107 Pa31
Dhalak Deset ER 191 Na39
Dhalkebar NEP 88 Pd32
Dhalkut OM 69 Ng37
Dhamangaon IND (MHT) 109 Oj35
Dhamar YE 68 Nc38
Dhamdaha IND (BIH) 112 Pd33
Dhamnod IND (MPH) 108 Oh34
Dhamtari IND (CGH) 109 Pa35
Dhanana IND (RJT) 106 Of32
Dhanane SP 199 Ne42
Dhanasar PK 79 Oe30
Dhanbad IND (JKD) 112 Pd34
Dhanchaura NEP 88 Pb32
Dhandelhura NEP 88 Pa31
Dhandhuka IND (GUJ) 108 Of34
Dhanera IND (GUJ) 108 Of33
Dhangarhi NEP 88 Pa31
Dhankar Monastery IND 107 Ok29
Dhankuta NEP 88 Pd32
Dhanpuri IND (MPH) 109 Pa34
Dhanushkodi IND (TNU) 111 Ok42
Dhanwar IND (JKD) 112 Pd33
Dhar IND (MPH) 108 Oh34
Dhar IND (PJB) 107 Oh29
Dhar IND 108 Oj35
Dharampur IND (GUJ) 108 Og35
Dharamsala IND (HPH) 107 Oj29
Dharan NEP 88 Pd32
Dharapuram IND (TNU) 111 Oj41
Dhari IND (GUJ) 108 Of35
Dharmabad IND (MHT) 108 Oj36
Dharmanagar IND (TRP) 112 Pg33
Dharmapura IND (KTK) 111 Oj39
Dharmapuri IND (TNU) 111 Ok40
Dharmapuri IND 109 Ok36
Dharmasthala IND 110 Oh40
Dharmavaram IND (APH) 111 Oj39
Dharmjaygarh IND (CGH) 109 Pb34
Dharmpuri IND (MHT) 108 Oh37
Dharni IND (MHT) 108 Oj35
Dhar Tichit RIM 183 Kf36
Dharuhera IND (HYA) 107 Oj31
Dharwad IND (KTK) 108 Oh38
Dhasam IND 107 Ok33
Dhasam IND 109 Ok33
Dhauglagiri Himal NEP 88 Pb31
Dhaulagiri NEP 88 Pb31
Dhaulagiri Himal NEP 88 Pb31
Dhauliganga IND 107 Ok30
Dhawa Doli Wildlife Sanctuary IND 106 Og32
Dhawalpur IND (CGH) 109 Pb35
Dhaya DZ 173 Kk28
Dhaym-al-Khayl DARS 178 Kd33
Dhekiajuli IND (ASM) 112 Pg32
Dhenkanal IND (ORS) 109 Pc35
Dhidhdhoo MV 110 Og42
Dhing IND (ASM) 112 Pg32
Dhofar OM 69 Ng37
Dholpur IND (RJT) 107 Oj32
Dhone IND (APH) 111 Oj39
Dhooble SP 205 Na45
Dhoraji IND (GUJ) 108 Of35
Dhorighat IND (UPH) 107 Pb32
Dhorimanna IND (RJT) 106 Of33
Dhorpatan NEP 88 Pb31
Dhrangadhra IND (GUJ) 108 Of34
Dhubri IND (ASM) 112 Pe32
Dhulia IND (MHT) 108 Oh35
Dhulian IND (WBG) 112 Pd33
Dhulkot IND (MPH) 108 Oh35
Dhunche NEP 88 Pc31
Dhupagari IND (WBG) 112 Pe32
Dhurbo SP 199 Nf40
Dhuudo SP 199 Nf41
Dhuusa Mareeb SP 199 Nd43
Di BF 185 Kj39
Dia GR 49 Mf55
Dia RMM 184 Kh38
Diabali RMM 184 Kh38
Diablo Range USA 234 Dk27
Diabo BF 185 Kk39
Diaca MOC 211 Na51
Diadema BR (SP) 286 Hg57
Diafani GR 49 Mh55
Diafarabé RMM 184 Kh38
Diaka RMM 184 Kh38
Diakofto GR 48 Mc52
Diakon RMM 183 Ke38
Dialafara RMM 183 Ke39
Dialakoto SN 183 Kd39
Diallan RMM 183 Ke38
Diallassagou RMM 184 Kj39
Dialloubé RMM 184 Kh38
Diamante I 43 Lq51
Diamante RA (ER) 289 Gk62
Diamante RA 288 Gf63
Diamantina BR (MG) 287 Hj55
Diamantina Deep 301 Qa13
Diamantina Gates N.P. AUS (QLD) 148 Sa57
Diamantina Lakes AUS (QLD) 148 Sa57
Diamantina River AUS (QLD) 148 Sb57
Diamantina Trench 301 Qa13
Diamantino BR (MT) 281 Hb53
Diamantino BR (MT) 286 Hd54
Diamantino BR 281 Hd54
Diambala RCB 202 Lg48
Diambarakro CI 193 Kj42
Diamond Harbour IND (WBG) 112 Pe34
Diamond Lake USA (OR) 234 Dj24
Diamond Mine NAM 216 Lj60
Diamond Peak USA 234 Ec26
Diamond Well AUS (WA) 140 Qj59
Diamou RMM 183 Ke38
Diamounguér SN 183 Kd38
Diana SN 183 Kd39
Dianalund DK 14 Lm35
Diana's Vow ZW 214 Mg55
Dianbai CHN (GDG) 96 Qf35
Dian Chi CHN 113 Qb33
Dianda LB 192 Kf42
Diandaza EAK 207 Mk47
Diandian RG 192 Kd40
Diandioumé RMM 184 Kf38
Dianfa CI 193 Kg41
Diangounté-Kamara RMM 184 Kf38
Diani EAK 207 Mk48
Diani RG 192 Kf42
Dianjiang CHN (CGQ) 95 Qd30
Diankabou RMM 185 Kj38
Diano Marina I 40 Lj47
Dianópolis BR (TO) 282 Hg51
Dianra CI 193 Kg41
Diaocha Hu CHN 95 Qg30
Diao Shui Lou Falls CHN 98 Re23
Diapaga BF 185 La39
Diapangou BF 185 La39
Diaramana RMM 184 Kh39
Diassa = Madina RMM 192 Kg40
Diavata GR 46 Mc50
Diavlos Alonissou GR 48 Md51
Diavlos Giourón GR 48 Me51
Diavlos Pelagonissou GR 48 Md51
Diavlos Skopélou GR 48 Md51
Diavlos Trikeriou GR 48 Md51
Diawla CI 193 Kh40
Diawling, P.N. du RIM 183 Kb37
Diaz Cross ZA 217 Md62
Diazkruis ZA 217 Md62
Diaz Point NAM 216 Lh59
Diazpunt NAM 216 Lh59
Dibaga IRQ 65 Nb28
Dibai IND (UPH) 107 Ok31
Dibang IND 113 Ph31
Dibaya RDC 203 Mb49
Dibaya-Lubue RDC 203 Lk48
Dibba UAE 75 Nj33
Dibbin N.P. JOR 64 Mh29
Dibble Glacier 297 Rc32
Dibella RN 187 Lg37
Dibeng ZA 216 Mb59
Dibia WAL 192 Ke42
Dibis IRQ 65 Nb28
Diboll USA (TX) 243 Fc30
Dibombari CAM 194 Le43
Dibrova UA 39 Mf42
Dibrugarh IND (ASM) 112 Ph32
Dibs SUD 196 Mc39
Dichato RCH 292 Gd64
Dichiseni RO 45 Mh46
Dickens USA (TX) 242 Ek29
Dickinson USA (ND) 240 Ej22
Dickson USA (TN) 248 Fg27
Dickson Mounds Mus. USA 246 Fe25
Dicle Nehri TR 63 Na27
Dida Galgalu Desert EAK 205 Mk44
Didam NL 32 Lg39
Dida Moessou CI 193 Kh42
Didcot GB 21 Kt39
Didesa ETH 198 Mh41
Didiéni RMM 184 Kf39
Didiévi CI 193 Kh42
Didig Sala ETH 191 Mk40
Didoko CI 193 Kh42
Didwana IND (RJT) 106 Oh32
Didy RM 220 Ne55
Didyma GR 48 Md53
Didyma TR 49 Mh53
Didymoteicho GR 47 Mg49
Didyr BF 185 Kj39
Die F 25 Lf46
Die Bos ZA 216 Lk61
Diébougou BF 193 Kj40
Dieburg D 34 Lj41
Diecai Shan CHN 96 Qf33
Diego Cão's Cross NAM 212 Lg56
Diego de Almagro RCH 288 Ge59
Diego de Alvear RA (BA) 289 Gj63
Diéké RG 192 Kf42
Diekirch L 23 Lg41
Diéle RMM 184 Kh39
Diéma RMM 184 Kf38
Diemals AUS (WA) 144 Qk60
Diemansputs ZA 216 Ma60
Diemel D 32 Lj39
Diem Tieu VN 115 Qe38
Dien Bien Phu VN 113 Qb35
Dien Chau VN 115 Qc36
Dieng Plateau RI 128 Qe49
Dien Khanh VN 115 Qe39
Dien Khanh Citadel VN 115 Qe39
Dien Mon VN 115 Qd37
Diepholz D 32 Lj38
Dieppe F 22 Lb41
Dierdorf D 32 Lh40
Dieren NL 32 Lg38
Dießen D 35 Lm43
Diest B 23 Lf40
Dietikon CH 34 Lj43
Dietrich River USA 229 Ce12
Dieulefit F 25 Lf46
Dieulouard F 23 Lg42
Dieuze F 23 Lg42
Dievenišķės LT 17 Mf36
Die Wies D 35 Ll43
Dif EAK 205 Na45
Diffa RN 187 Lg39
Differdange L 23 Lf41
Difuma RDC 206 Mc47
Difunta Correa RA 288 Gg61
Dig IND (RJT) 107 Oj32
Digapahandi IND (ORS) 109 Pc36
Digaura IND (MPH) 109 Ok33
Digba RDC 201 Mc43
Digboi IND (ASM) 113 Ph32
Digby CDN (NS) 245 Gh23
Digha IND (WBG) 112 Pd35
Dighton USA (KS) 240 Ek26
Diglur IND (MHT) 108 Oj36
Digne-les-Bains F 25 Lg46
Digoin F 25 Ld44
Digor TR 63 Nb25
Digora RUS (SOA) 70 Nc24
Digos RP 123 Rc42
Digras IND (MHT) 108 Oj35
Digri PK 81 Oe33
Digul RI 158 Rk49
Diguvametta IND (APH) 111 Ok39
Digya N.P. GH 193 Kk42
Dihajan IND (ASM) 112 Ph32
Dihang IND 112 Ph31
Diibao CAM 187 Lh41
Diinsoor SP 205 Nb44
Dijon F 23 Lf43
Dijon RG 192 Kf41
Dik TCH 187 Lj41
Dikhil DJI 198 Nb40
Dikili TR 50 Mg51
Dikmen TR 51 Mm54
Dikodougou CI 193 Kh41
Diksmuide B 23 Lc39
Dikson RUS 58 Pa04
Dikulwe RDC 206 Md51
Dikwa WAN 187 Lg40
Dila ETH 198 Mk42
Dili RDC 201 Md44
Dili RDC 201 Me44
Dili TLS 132 Rc50
Dilia RN 187 Lf38
Diligent Strait IND 111 Pg40
Dilijan ARM 70 Nc25
Di Linh VN 115 Qe40
Diljatyn UA 39 Me42
Dilke CDN (SK) 233 Eh20
Dillenburg D 32 Lj40
Dilli RMM 184 Kg38
Dilling SUD 197 Me39
Dillingen D 34 Lg41
Dillingen D 34 Ll42
Dillingham USA (AK) 228 Ca16
Dillon CDN (SK) 233 Ef18
Dillon USA (MT) 235 Ed23
Dillon USA (SC) 249 Ga28
Dillon River CDN 233 Ee18
Dilo G 195 Lg46
Dilofo GR 46 Mc51
Dilolo RDC 209 Mb51
Dilolo RDC 209 Mb51
Dilos GR 49 Mf53
Dilos GR 49 Mf53
Dilwara IND 108 Og33
Dima ETH 198 Mh43
Dimako CAM 195 Lg43
Dimalla RIM 183 Ke37
Dimapur IND (ASM) 112 Pg33
Dimas C 258 Fh34
Dimashq SYR 64 Mj29
Dimbelenge RDC 203 Mb48
Dimbokro CI 193 Kh42
Dimbulah AUS (QLD) 149 Sc54
Dimiao RP 123 Rc41
Dimissi PNG 158 Sb50
Dimitrie Cantemir RO 45 Mj44
Dimitrovgrad BG 47 Mf48
Dimitrovgrad RUS 53 Ne18
Dimitrovgrad SCG 46 Mc47
Dimlang WAN 195 Lf41
Dimlik TCH 187 Lj41
Dimmitt USA (TX) 237 Ej28
Dimnycja UA 39 Me42
Dimona IL 64 Mh30
Dimora AUS (QLD) 148 Sb56
Dimori TG 193 La41
Dimovo BG 46 Mc47
Dimpam CAM 195 Lg44
Dimpolis BR (AC) 279 Ge50
Dina PK 79 Og29
Dinagat RP 123 Rc41
Dinagat Island RP 123 Rc40
Dinagat Sound RP 123 Rc40
Dinaig RP 123 Rc42
Dinajpur BD 112 Pe33
Dinalongan RP 121 Ra37
Dinamita MEX (DGO) 253 Ej33
Dinan F 22 Ks42
Dinangourou RMM 185 Kj38
Dinant B 23 Le40
Dinapigui RP 121 Rb37
Dinar TR 51 Ml52
Dinara HR 41 Lr46
Dinara IND (BIH) 109 Pc33
Dinard F 22 Ks42
Dinaric Alps 6 Lb05
Dinchiya ETH 198 Mj42
Dindar SUD 190 Mg40
Dindar SUD 190 Mh40
Dinder ETH 198 Mh40
Dinder N.P. SUD 198 Mh39
Dindi ZW 210 Mg54
Dindigul IND (TNU) 111 Oj41
Dindima WAN 186 Lf40
Dindon IND (MPH) 109 Pa34
Dindoudi Séydi SN 183 Kd38
Dinek TR 51 Mm51
Dinek Dağı TR 51 Mo51
Dinga PK 79 Og29
Dinga RDC 202 Lj48
Dingalan Bay RP 121 Ra38
Ding'an CHN (GZG) 96 Qc33
Ding'an CHN (HAN) 96 Qf36
Dingbian CHN (SAA) 92 Qd27
Ding Ding SUD 197 Mg41
Dinge ANG 208 Lg53
Dinggye CHN (TIB) 88 Pd31
Dinghushan Z.B. CHN 96 Qg34
Dingila RDC 201 Md44
Dingila RDC 201 Me44
Dingle IRL 20 Kk38
Dingle RP 123 Rb40
Dingle S 12 Lm32
Dingle Bay IRL 20 Kk38
Dingnan CHN (JGX) 97 Qh33
Dingo ANG 209 Ma54
Dingo AUS (QLD) 149 Se57
Dingolfing D 35 Ln42
Dingras RP 121 Ra36
Dingshuzhen CHN (JGS) 102 Qk30
Dingtao CHN (SDG) 102 Qh28
Dinguiraye RG 192 Ke40
Dingwall GB 19 Kq33
Dingxi CHN (GSU) 94 Qc28
Dingxiang CHN (SAX) 93 Qg26
Dingxiao CHN (GZH) 96 Qc33
Dingyuan CHN (AHU) 102 Qj29
Dingzhou CHN (HBI) 93 Qh26
Dingzikou CHN (QHI) 87 Pg26
Dinh Lap VN 96 Qd35
Dinira, P.N. YV 269 Ge41
Dinkelsbühl D 34 Ll41
Dinklage D 32 Lj38
Dinokwe RB 213 Md57
Dinorwic CDN (ON) 238 Fd21
Dinosaur USA (CO) 235 Ef25
Dinosaur Egg Site CDN 233 Ed21
Dinosaur footprints TM 73 Od27
Dinosaur Footprints (Moyeni) LS 217 Md61
Dinosaur Nat. Mon. USA 235 Ef25
Dinosaur Prov. Park CDN 233 Ee20
Dinosaur's Footprints NAM 212 Lj56
Dinsho ETH 198 Mk42
Dinsmore CDN (SK) 233 Eg20
Dintiteladas RI 125 Qc48
Dinuba USA (CA) 236 Ea27
Diö S 15 Lp34
Diofior SN 183 Kb38
Dioïla RMM 184 Kg39
Dioklecijanova palača HR 41 Lr47
Diomandou RG 192 Kf41
Diombos SN 183 Kb39
Dion GR 46 Mc50
Diona BF 193 Kj40
Diona TCH 189 Mb37
Diondiori RMM 184 Kh38
Dionisádes GR 49 Mg55
Dionisio Cerqueira BR (SC) 290 Hd59
Diorama BR (GO) 286 He54
Dioro RMM 184 Kh39
Dioşti RO 44 Me46
Diou RMM 193 Kh40
Dioulatiédougou CI 192 Kg41
Diouloulou SN 183 Kb39
Dioulouna RMM 185 Kk38
Dioumara RMM 184 Kf38
Dioundiou RN 185 Lb39
Dioungani RMM 185 Kj38
Dioura RMM 184 Kh38
Diourbel SN 183 Kb38
Dipadih IND (CGH) 109 Pb34
Dipalpur PK 79 Og30
Dipchari WAN 187 Lg40
Dipéo BF 193 Kj40
Diphu IND (ASM) 112 Pg33
Dipkarpaz = Rizokarpaso CY 51 Mp55
Diplo PK 81 Oe33
Dipnay RP 122 Qk40
Dipolog RP 123 Rb41
Dipótama GR 47 Me49
Dipper Lake CDN 233 Eg18
Dippoldis walde D 33 Lo40
Dique El Carrizal RA 288 Gf62
Dir PK 79 Og28
Dira TCH 187 Lh38
Dirab KSA 67 Nd33
Diré RMM 185 Kj37
Dire Dawa ETH 198 Na41
Dirfis GR 48 Md52
Dirico ANG 209 Ma54
Dirk Hartog Island AUS 140 Qg58
Dirkou RN 188 Lg36
Dirrah SUD 196 Md39
Dirráhi GR 48 Mc53
Dirranbandi AUS (QLD) 151 Se60
Dirty Devil USA 235 Ee26
Disaj IR 72 Nc27
Discovery Bay AUS 152 Sa65
Discovery Center (Ketchikan) USA 231 De18
Discovery Coast Atlantic Forest Reserves BR 287 Ja54
Discovery Great Reef 122 Qg40
Disentis = Mustér CH 34 Lj44
Dishkakat USA (AK) 229 Cb14
Dishná ET 177 Mg32
Dishna River USA 229 Cb14
Disko Bugt DK 225 Hb05
Disko Ø DK 225 Hb05
Dismal Falls USA 249 Fk27
Dismals Canyon USA 248 Fg28
Disney AUS (QLD) 149 Sd56
Disneyland F 23 Lc42
Disneyland USA 236 Eb29
Disney World USA 250 Fk31
Dispur IND (ASM) 112 Pf32
Diss GB 21 Lb38
Dissala G 202 Lf47
Dissen D 32 Lj38
Dissen KSA 68 Na37
Disteghil Sar PK 79 Oh27
Distrito Federal BR 265 Hc22
Ditdako IND (AAN) 111 Pg42
Ditin RG 192 Kd40
Ditrău RO 45 Mf44
Diu IND (DAD) 108 Of35
Diu IND 108 Of35
Diuta Point RP 123 Rc41
Divaké AL 46 Lu50
Divalak AFG 78 Ob30
Divandarreh IR 72 Nd28
Divčibare SCG 46 Ma46
Divčice CZ 38 Lp41
Divénié RCB 202 Lg47
Divide USA (MT) 235 Ed23
Divilican RP 121 Rb37
Divilican Bay RP 121 Rb37
Divinhe MOC 214 Mh56
Divino BR (MG) 287 Hj56
Divinópolis BR (MG) 287 Hh56
Divinópolis de Goiás BR (GO) 282 Hg52
Divisa PA 257 Fk41
Divisópolis BR (MG) 283 Hk53
Divnoe RUS 70 Nb23
Divo CI 193 Kh43
Divonne F 25 Lg44
Divriği TR 63 Mk26
Divuma RDC 209 Mb51
Diwana PK 80 Od32
Diwata MAL 122 Qk43
Dixcove GH 193 Kk43
Dixie AUS (QLD) 146 Sb53
Dixie USA (ID) 235 Ec23
Dixie USA (VA) 249 Ga27
Dixon USA (IL) 246 Ff25
Dixon USA (MT) 235 Ec22
Dixon Entrance CDN 231 Dd18
Dixons BS 251 Gc33
Dixons Mills USA (AL) 248 Fg29
Dixonville CDN (AB) 233 Eb17
Dixonville RA (SL) 288 Gh63
Diyadin TR 63 Nb26
Diyarbakır TR 63 Na27
Diz Abad IR 72 Ne28
Dizangué CAM 194 Le44
Dizhuang CHN (HUN) 95 Qf31
Dizin IR 72 Nf28
Dja CAM 195 Lh44
Djado RN 181 Lg35
Djaitun TM 71 Nj26
Djakotomé DY 193 La42
Djalasiga RDC 201 Mf44
Djamaa DZ 174 Lc29
Djamandjary RM 219 Ne52
Djamba RDC 201 Mc44
Djamba RDC 203 Mb50
Djambala CAM 195 Lg42
Djambala RCB 202 Lh47
Djampiel CAM 195 Lh43
Djanet DZ 180 Le33
Djarua RI 131 Rg47
Djat'kovo RUS 52 Mh19
Djebel Ababab SUD 191 Mj37
Djebel 'Abd al 'Aziz SYR 64 Na27
Djebel Abu Brûsh ET 177 Mg34
Djebel Abu Gurdi ET 177 Mh33
Djebel Abu Hamamid ET 177 Mh33
Djebel Abu Harbah ET 177 Mg32
Djebel Adaran YE 68 Nc39
Djebel ad-Dair SUD 190 Mf40
Djebel Aderuba ER 191 Mj39
Djebel Aïssa MA 173 Kk29
Djebel Aja' KSA 66 Na32
Djebel Akakus LAR 181 Lf33
Djebel Akhdar OM 75 Nj34
Djebel Al-Arab SYR 64 Mj29
Djebel Al Awaynat LAR/SUD 189 Mc35
Djebel al Bishri SYR 65 Mk28
Djebel al Hasawinah LAR 174 Lg31
Djebel al-Hayban SUD 197 Mf40
Djebel Al Hishwah YE 68 Nc37
Djebel al Lawz KSA 64 Mh31
Djebel al-Liri SUD 197 Mf40
Djebel al-Qamar OM 69 Ng37
Djebel al-Qara OM 69 Ng37
Djebel al Wajid KSA 68 Nc36
Djebel Amour DZ 173 La29
Djebel an Nabi Shu'ayb YE 68 Nb38
Djebel an Nir KSA 66 Nb33
Djebel Antar MA 173 Kk29
Djebel Aoulime MA 172 Kg30
Djebel Arknu LAR 176 Mc34
Djebel Ar Rumman KSA 66 Na32
Djebel Asoteriba SUD 177 Mj35
Djebel Asoteriba SUD 190 Mh38
Djebel as Sawda' LAR 175 Lh31
Djebel Atafaitafa DZ 180 Ld33
Djebel at Tanf SYR 64 Mk29
Djebel at Tayr ET 177 Mf31
Djebel at Tayr YE 68 Na38
Djebel Auliya SUD 190 Mg39
Djebel Awamtib ET 177 Mh34
Djebel Ayachi MA 172 Kh29
Djebel Babor DZ 174 Lc27
Djebel Ban Ghanimah LAR 181 Lh33
Djebel Bani DZ 172 Kg31
Djebel Baydan KSA 66 Na35
Djebel Ben Amar DZ 173 La28
Djebel Ben Tadjine DZ 173 Kj31
Djebel Biada TN 174 Le28
Djebel Bouârfa MA 173 Kj29
Djebel Bou Iblane MA 173 Kh29
Djebel Bou Kahil DZ 173 Lc28
Djebel Bou Keltoum MA 173 Kj28
Djebel Bou Ladiab TN 174 Lf29
Djebel Bou Naceur MA 173 Kh29
Djebel Bozi SUD 190 Mg40
Djebel Chambi TN 174 Le28
Djebel Chambi, P.N. TN 174 Le28
Djebel Chelia DZ 174 Ld28
Djebel Dab KSA 67 Ne34
Djebel Dahar TN 174 Lf29
Djebel Dalal ET 177 Mg31
Djebel Dhanna UAE 74 Ng33
Djebel Djurdjura DZ 173 Lc27
Djebel Edough DZ 174 Ld27
Djebel Eigat SUD 177 Mh34
Djebel Eigrim SUD 190 Mh37
Djebel Elba N.P. SUD 177 Mh34
Djebel el Goûfi DZ 174 Ld27
Djebel El Igma ET 177 Mh31
Djebel el Jalâlah el Bahriya ET 177 Mf31
Djebel el Jalâlah el Qibliya ET 177 Mf31
Djebel el Kahla DZ 173 Kj31
Djebel el Siba'i ET 177 Mh33
Djebel el Thabt ET 177 Mg31
Djebel el Urf ET 177 Mg32
Djebel Erba SUD 191 Mj36
Djebel Fernane DZ 173 Lc28
Djebel Ghârib ET 177 Mg31
Djebel Gourou DZ 173 Lb28
Djebel Grouz DZ/MA 173 Kk29
Djebel Guir MA 172 Ke31
Djebel Gumbiri SUD 197 Mf43
Djebel Gurgei SUD 189 Mc39
Djebel Habashiyah YE 68 Ne37
Djebel Hafit OM/UAE 75 Nh33
Djebel Hamata ET 177 Mh33
Djebel Hamoyet ER 191 Mk38
Djebel Hamoyet SUD 191 Mk38
Djebel Hamrin IRQ 65 Nb28
Djebel Homor Tohadar SUD 191 Mj37
Djebel In Azzene DZ 173 La32
Djebel Is SUD 177 Mh34
Djebel Jaddah YE 68 Nb37
Djebel Jar KSA 66 Mk33
Djebel Kathangor SUD 197 Mh43
Djebel Kâtrînâ ET 177 Mh31
Djebel Kawr OM 75 Nj34
Djebel Khadar OM 75 Nk34
Djebel Ksel DZ 173 La29
Djebel Lawdh YE 68 Nc37
Djebel Lekst MA 172 Kf31
Djebel Maghâra ET 177 Mg30
Djebel Mahrat YE 69 Nf37
Djebel Manar YE 68 Nc38
Djebel Marra SUD 196 Mc39
Djebel Mazmun SUD 190 Mg40
Djebel Meschkakur MA 173 Kj29
Djebel Mismar SUD 190 Mh37
Djebel Mouchchene MA 172 Kg29
Djebel Mourik MA 172 Kh29
Djebel Muqsim ET 177 Mh34
Djebel Musbih ET 177 Mh34
Djebel Mu'tiq ET 177 Mg32
Djebel Nadum KSA 66 Mj33
Djebel Nafusah LAR 174 Lg30
Djebel Nasiya ET 177 Mg34
Djebel Nugay LAR 176 Lk34
Djebel Oda SUD 191 Mj36
Djebel Onk DZ 174 Ld28
Djebel Ouarkziz DZ/MA 172 Kf31
Djebel Ounane DZ 180 Ld33
Djebel Qatrâni ET 177 Me32
Djebel Qattâr ET 177 Mg32
Djebel Rafit SUD 190 Mg36
Djebel Rich MA 172 Ke31
Djebel Ru'us al Tiwal SYR 64 Mj29
Djebel Sabidana SUD 191 Mj37
Djebel Sabir YE 68 Nc39
Djebel Salma KSA 66 Nb32
Djebel Samhan OM 69 Nh37
Djebel Samnah ET 177 Mg32
Djebel Sarhro MA 172 Kh30
Djebel Sawdah KSA 68 Nb36
Djebel Settaf DZ 180 Lb32
Djebel Shâ'ib el Banât ET 177 Mg32
Djebel Sindib SUD 177 Mj34
Djebel Sirat YE 68 Nb37
Djebel Tadrart DZ 181 Lf34
Djebel Takka SUD 191 Mj39
Djebel Tammu LAR/RN 181 Lh34
Djebel Taskalouine MA 172 Ke31
Djebel Tazzeka MA 173 Kh28
Djebel Tazzeka, P.N. MA 173 Kh28
Djebel Tebaga TN 174 Le29
Djebel Telertheba DZ 180 Ld33
Djebel Teljo SUD 189 Mc38
Djebel Tenouchfi DZ 173 Kk28
Djebel Tidirhine MA 173 Kh28
Djebel Timétrine RMM 185 Kk36
Djebel Touaris DZ 173 Kj31
Djebel Toubkal MA 172 Kg30
Djebel Toucha DZ 173 Kk30
Djebel Tuwayq KSA 67 Nc35
Djebel Umm Inab ET 177 Mg32
Djebel Umm Naqqat ET 177 Mh33
Djebel Yualliq ET 177 Mg30
Djebel Zaghouan TN 174 Lf27
Djebel Zahara ET 177 Mh33
Djebinian TN 174 Lf28
Djebobo, Mount GH/TG 193 La41
Djébok RMM 185 La37
Djébrène TCH 196 Lk40
Djédaa TCH 196 Lk39
Djeddars DZ 173 La29
Djeffara TN 174 Lf29
Djelfa DZ 173 Lb28
Djéma RCA 196 Mc42
Djember TCH 187 Lj40
Djémila DZ 174 Lc27
Djems Bank MAL 126 Qg44
Djenien-Bou Rezg DZ 173 Kk29
Djenné RMM 184 Kh39
Djérem CAM 195 Lg42
Djermaya TCH 187 Lh39
Djibasso BF 184 Kh39
Djibo BF 185 Kk38
Djibouria RMM 183 Ke39
Djibouti DJI 199 Nb40
Djibouti 167 Na08
Djibrosso CI 192 Kg41
Djidian RMM 184 Kf39
Djidja DY 193 La42
Djigoué BF 193 Kj40
Djiguéra BF 193 Kh40
Djiguéni RIM 184 Kf38
Djilbe CAM 187 Lh40
Djipologo BF 193 Kj40
Djirataoua RN 186 Ld39
Djiroutou CI 192 Kg43
Djohong CAM 195 Lh42
Djokupunda RDC 203 Ma48
Djoli TCH 196 Lk41
Djolu RDC 200 Mb45
Djombo RDC 200 Ma45
Djonâba RIM 183 Kd37
Djorf TN 174 Lf29
Djorf Torba DZ 173 Kj30
Djoua G 195 Lg45
Djoubissi RCA 196 Ma42
Djoué RCB 202 Lh47
Djougou DY 193 La41
Djoum CAM 195 Lg44
Djoumboli CAM 195 Lg42
Djugu RDC 201 Mf45
Djulino BG 47 Mh48
Djuni BG 47 Mh48
Djúpivogur IS 10 Kc13
Djurås S 13 Lq30
Djurdjura, P.N. du DZ 173 Lc27
Djurö n.p. S 13 Lo32
Djursland DK 14 Ll34
Djurs Sommerland DK 14 Ll34
Djurtjuli RUS 53 Nh18
D'Kar RB 213 Ma56
Dlolwana ZA 217 Mf60
Dmitrievka RUS 53 Na19
Dmitriev-L'govskij RUS 52 Mh19
Dmitrov RUS 52 Mj17
Dmytrivka UA 45 Mj45
Dmytrivka UA 52 Mg20
Dnepr 52 Mf19
Dnestrovsc MD 45 Mk44
Dnieper 52 Mf19
Dniester UA/MD 45 Mg42
Dniprdzeržyns'ke vodoschovyšče UA 54 Mg21
Dnipro UA 54 Mg22
Dniprodzeržyns'k UA 54 Mh21
Dnipropetrovs'k UA 55 Mh21
Dniprorudne UA 55 Mh22
Dniprovs'kyj lyman UA 54 Mf22
Dnistrovs'ke vodoschovyšče UA 45 Mh42
Dnistrovs'kyj Lyman UA 45 Ml44
Dnjapro BY 52 Mf19
Dnjestr UA/MD 45 Mj42
Dno RUS 52 Me17
Doaba PK 79 Of29
Do Ab-e Mikh-e Zarrin AFG 78 Od28
Do Abi Ghowr Band AFG 78 Oe28
Doak Hist. Site CDN 245 Gh22
Doaktown CDN (NB) 245 Gg22
Do Amiuté BR 275 Hf48
Do Anfrísio BR 275 Hc48
Doangdoangbesar RI 129 Qj48
Doangdoangkecil RI 129 Qj48
do Araguaia, P.N. BR 281 He51
Doba CHN (TIB) 89 Pe30
Doba TCH 187 Lj41
Dobbiaco = Toblach I 40 Ln44
Dobczyce PL 39 Ma41
Dobele LV 17 Md34
Döbeln D 33 Lo39
Doberai Peninsula RI 130 Rf46
Dobhi IND (BIH) 109 Pc33
Dobiegniew PL 36 Lq38
Dobie River CDN 239 Fe20
Dobiesczcyn PL 36 Lp37
Dobinga CAM 187 Lg41
Dobo RI 131 Rh48
Doboj BIH 41 Lt46
Dobra PL 36 Lq37
Dobra RO 44 Mc45
Dobra SCG 44 Mb46
Dobrá Niva SK 39 Lu42
Dobřany CZ 38 Lo41
Dobrcz PL 36 Lt37
Dobre PL 37 Mb38
Dobre Miasto PL 37 Ma37
Dobri H 38 Lr44
Dobrič BG 47 Mh47
Dobrinka RUS 53 Na19
Dobříš CZ 38 Lp41
Dobrjanka UA 52 Mf19
Dobrjatino RUS 53 Na18
Dobrodzień PL 36 Lt40
Dobromyl' UA 39 Mc41
Dobropillja UA 55 Mj21
Dobro Polje BIH 41 Lt47
Dobrosyn UA 37 Md40
Dobroteşti RO 45 Me46
Dobrotić BG 47 Mh47
Dobrotica BG 45 Mh47
Dobrotica BG 47 Mh47
Dobrovol'sk RUS 17 Mc36
Dobruči RUS 16 Mh32
Dobrudžansko Plato BG 47 Mh47
Dobruja RO 45 Mj46
Dobruš BY 52 Mf19
Dobrzeń Wielki PL 36 Ls40
Dobšiná SK 39 Ma42
Doce BR 286 He54
Doce BR 287 Ja55
Dochna UA 45 Mk42
Docker Creek AUS (NT) 142 Re58
Dockrell, Mount AUS 138 Rd55
Docksta S 10 Lk14
Doclea SCG 46 Lu48
Doc Let Beach VN 115 Qe39
Doclin RO 44 Mb45
Do Côco BR 281 Hf50
Doctor Arroyo MEX (NL) 253 Ek34
Doctor Juan L.Mallorquín PY 286 Hc58
Doda EAT 207 Mk48
Doda RI 127 Ra46
Doda 79 Oh29
Dodaga RI 130 Re45
Dodballapur IND (KTK) 111 Oj40
Doddridge USA (AR) 243 Fd29
Dodecanese GR 49 Mg54
Dodge City USA (KS) 242 Ek27
Dodgeville USA (WI) 241 Fe24
Dodol SP 205 Nb44
Dodola ETH 198 Mk42
Dodoma EAT 207 Mh49
Dodóni GR 48 Ma51
Dodori National Reserve EAK 205 Na46
Dodowa GH 193 Kk43
Dodson USA (MT) 233 Ef21
Doege ANG 203 Ma50
Doembang Nangbuat THA 114 Qa38
Doetinchem NL 32 Lg39
Dofa RI 130 Rc46
Doğanbey TR 49 Mg52
Doğanbey TR 51 Mm53
Doğançay TR 50 Ml50
Doğanhisar TR 51 Mm52
Doğankent TR 63 Mk25
Doğanlı TR 51 Mq51
Doğanoğlu TR 51 Mm51
Doğanşehir TR 63 Mj26
Doğansu TR 63 Nb26
Doğantepe TR 51 Mq50
Doğanyol TR 63 Mk26
Dogba Tota DY 193 La42
Dog Creek CDN (BC) 232 Dj20
Döger TR 51 Ml51
Dogger Bank 21 Lb36
Dogji SN 183 Kc38
Dog Lake CDN 238 Fa20
Dog Lake CDN 239 Ff21
Dog Lake CDN 239 Fh21
Dogliani I 40 Lh46
Dogo J 101 Rg27
Dogo RMM 184 Kh38
Dogo RMM 192 Kg40
Dogoba SUD 197 Me42
Dogofri RMM 184 Kh38
Dogon RN 186 Lc38
Do Gonbadan IR 74 Nf30
Dogondoutchi RN 186 Lc39
Dogoni RMM 184 Kh39
Dogoumbo TCH 187 Lj40
Dogo-yama J 101 Rg28
Dogpound Creek CDN 233 Ec20
Dog Salmon River USA 228 Cb17
Doğubeyazıt TR 63 Nc26
Doguéraoua RN 186 Lc39
Doğu Karadeniz Dağları TR 63 Mk25
Doğu Menteşe Dağları TR 50 Mj53
Dogura PNG 160 Sf51
Dogwalo WAN 186 Le40
Dogwood Trail USA 243 Fd30
Doha Q 74 Nf33
Dohad IND (GUJ) 108 Oh34
Doi RI 130 Rd44
Doi THA 114 Pk36
Doigan EAK 204 Mj45
Doig River CDN 231 Dk17
Doi Inthanon THA 114 Pk36
Doi Inthanon N.P. THA 114 Pk36
Doi Khun Tan N.P. THA 114 Pk36
Doi Luang N.P. THA 114 Pk36
Doimara IND (ARP) 112 Pg32
Doi Pagoda VN 117 Qc41
Doi Saket THA 114 Pk36
Dois Córregas BR (SP) 286 Hf57
Dois Irmãos BR (GO) 282 Hf53
Doi Suthep-Pui N.P. THA 114 Pk36

Dois Vizinhos – Dumraon

Dois Vizinhos **BR** (PR) 290 Hd58
Doi Tachi **THA** 114 Pk37
Dojeviće **SCG** 46 Ma47
Dojransko ezero **MK** 46 Mc49
Dojrenci **BG** 47 Me47
Doka **RI** 131 Rh49
Doka **SUD** 191 Mh40
Dokan **IRQ** 65 Nc28
Dokis Ind. Res. **CDN** 246 Fk22
Dokka **N** 12 Ll30
Dokkum **NL** 32 Lg37
Doko **RG** 192 Kf40
Doko **WAN** 186 Le39
Doksy **CZ** 38 Lp40
Dokšycy **BY** 52 Md18
Dokučajevs'k **UA** 55 Mj22
Dokui **BF** 184 Kh39
Dolak **RI** 158 Rk49
Dolalghat **NEP** 88 Pc32
Doland **USA** (SD) 240 Fa23
Dolan Springs **USA** (AZ) 236 Ec28
Dolasne **IND** (MHT) 108 Oh36
Dolavon **RA** (CB) 292 Gh67
Do Lavrador **BR** 281 Hb52
Dolbeau **CDN** (QC) 244 Gd21
Dolbel **RN** 185 La38
Dol-de-Bretagne **F** 22 Kt42
Dole **F** 23 Lf43
Dolega **PA** 256 Fj41
Doleib Hill **SUD** 197 Mf41
Dølemo **N** 12 Lj32
Dolfinarium **NL** 32 Lf38
Dolgellau **GB** 20 Kr38
Dolgoi Island **USA** 228 Bk18
Dolgorukovo **RUS** 17 Ma36
Dolianova **I** 31 Lk51
Dolinsk **RUS** 99 Sb22
Dolisie = Loubomo **RCB** 202 Lg48
Dolišnij Šepit **UA** 45 Mf42
Dolit **RI** 130 Rd46
Doljani **BIH** 41 Ls47
Dollard **NL** 32 Lh37
Dollart **D** 32 Lh37
Dollo Odo **ETH** 198 Na43
Dolna Banja **BG** 46 Md48
Dolna Mitropolija **BG** 47 Me47
Dolna Orjahovica **BG** 47 Mf47
Dolni Bousov **CZ** 38 Lq40
Dolni Dăbnik **BG** 47 Me47
Dolní Dvořiště **CZ** 38 Lp42
Dolni Lom **BG** 46 Mc47
Dolní Žandov **CZ** 38 Ln40
Dolno Dupeni **MK** 46 Mb50
Dolný Kubín **SK** 39 Lu41
Dolo **I** 40 Ln45
Dolo **RI** 127 Qk46
Dolokmerawan **RI** 116 Pk44
Doloksanggul **RI** 116 Pk44
Dolomite Caves **NAM** 212 Lh56
Dolomiti **I** 40 Lm44
Dolomiti Bellunesi, P.N. delle **I** 40 Ln44
Dolon **KS** 77 Oh25
Dolong **RI** 127 Rb46
Doloon **MNG** 92 Qc23
Dolores **CO** 268 Gc44
Dolores **E** 29 Ku48
Dolores **GCA** 255 Ff37
Dolores **RA** (BA) 293 Hb64
Dolores **ROU** 289 Ha62
Dolores **RP** 121 Rc39
Dolores **USA** (CO) 237 Ef27
Dolores **YV** 269 Gf41
Dolores Hidalgo **MEX** (GJT) 254 Ek35
Dolores Hidalgo **MEX** (OAX) 255 Fc37
Dolphin and Union Strait **CDN** 224 Ea05
Do Luong **VN** 115 Qc36
Dolyna **UA** 39 Md42
Dolyna **UA** 39 Me42
Dolyns'ka **UA** 54 Mg21
Dolyns'ke **UA** 45 Mk43
Dolžanskaja **RUS** 55 Mj22
Doma **EAT** 207 Mj49
Doma **ZW** 210 Mf54
Domaniç **TR** 50 Mk51
Domanivka **UA** 45 Ml43
Domar Aquino **BR** (MT) 281 Hc53
Domar **BD** 112 Pe32
Domar **CHN** (TIB) 88 Pa29
Domaradz **PL** 36 Ls36
Domaradz **PL** 39 Mb41
Domariaganj **IND** (UPH) 107 Pb32
Domaring **RI** 127 Qk45
Doma Safari Area **ZW** 210 Mf54
Domažlice **CZ** 38 Ln41
Dombaj **RUS** (KCH) 70 Na24
Dombås **N** 12 Lk28
Dombe **MOC** 214 Mg55
Dombe Grande **ANG** 208 Lg52
Dombia **RMM** 183 Ke39
Dombo **RI** 131 Rj46
Domboshawa **ZW** 210 Mf54
Dombóvár **H** 38 Lt44
Dombrád **H** 39 Mb42
DomeC/ Concordia **ANT** (F) 297 Ra34
Dome Circe 297 Ra33
Domeikava **LT** 17 Md36
Domel 79 Oh29
Dom Eliseu **BR** (PA) 276 Hg48
Domérat **F** 25 Lc44
Dômes de Fabedougou **BF** 193 Kh40
Domeyko **RCH** 288 Ge60
Dom Feliciano **BR** (RS) 290 Hd61
Domfront **F** 22 Ku42
Dom, Gunung **RI** 131 Rj47
Domica **SK** 39 Ma42
Dominase **GH** 193 Kk42
Domingos Martins **BR** (ES) 287 Hk56
Dominguez **RA** (ER) 289 Ha62
Dominica **WD** 261 Gk38
Dominica 261 Gk38
Dominical **CR** 256 Fj41
Dominican Republic **DOM** 260 Ge37
Dominica Passage 261 Gk38
Dom Inocêncio **BR** (PI) 282 Hj50
Domiongo **RDC** 203 Ma48
Dömitz **D** 33 Lm37
Domme **F** 24 Lb46
Domnești **RO** 45 Me45
Domnovo **RUS** 17 Ma36
Domo **ETH** 199 Nd42
Domodedovo **RUS** 52 Mj18
Domodóssola **I** 40 Lj44
Domokós **GR** 48 Mc51
Domoni **COM** 218 Nc52
Dompaire **F** 23 Lg42
Dom Pedrito **BR** (RS) 290 Hc61
Dom Pedro **BR** (MA) 276 Hh48
Dompem **GH** 193 Kj43
Dompierre-sur-Besbre **F** 25 Ld44
Dompu **RI** 129 Qk50
Domué **MOC** 210 Mg53
Dom und Sankt Michael in Hildesheim **D** 32 Lk38
Domusnovás **I** 31 Lj51
Domuyo, Volcán **RA** 292 Ge64
Domžale **SLO** 41 Lp44
Dom zu Aachen **D** 32 Lg40
Dom zu Braunschweig **D** 33 Ll38
Dom zu Eichstätt **D** 35 Lm42
Dom zu Erfurt **D** 33 Lm40
Dom zu Freiberg **D** 33 Lo40
Dom zu Freising **D** 35 Lm42
Dom zu Fulda **D** 32 Lk40
Dom zu Greifswald **D** 33 Lo36
Dom zu Gurk **A** 35 Lp44
Dom zu Halberstadt **D** 33 Lm39
Dom zu Köln **D** 32 Lg40
Dom zu Limburg **D** 32 Lj40
Dom zu Mainz **D** 34 Lj40
Dom zu Merseburg **D** 33 Lm39
Dom zu Minden **D** 32 Lj38
Dom zu Münster **D** 32 Lh39
Dom zu Naumburg **D** 33 Lm39
Dom zu Paderborn **D** 32 Lj39
Dom zu Speyer **D** 34 Lj41
Dom zu Stendal **D** 33 Lm38
Dom zu Worms **D** 34 Lj41
Don **GB** 19 Kr33
Don' **RUS** 9 Na09
Doña Ana, Cerro **RCH** 288 Ge60
Donacona **CDN** (QC) 244 Ge22
Doña Inés, Cerro **RCH** 288 Gf59
Doña Juana, Volcán **CO** 272 Gb45
Donald **AUS** (VIC) 153 Sb64
Donald **CDN** (BC) 233 Eb20
Donaldson **USA** (MN) 238 Fb21
Donaldsonville **USA** (LA) 243 Fe30
Donalsonville **USA** (GA) 249 Fh30
Doña María **GCA** 255 Ff38
Doñana, P.N. de **E** 28 Ko47
Donato Guerra **MEX** (DGO) 253 Eh33
Donau Auen, N.P. **A** 35 Lr42
Donaudurchbruch **D** 35 Lm42
Donaueschingen **D** 34 Lj43
Donautal **A** 35 Lo42
Donauwörth **D** 35 Ll42
Don Benito **E** 28 Kp48
Doncaster **AUS** (QLD) 148 Sb56
Doncaster **GB** 21 Kt37
Doncaster Ind Res. **CDN** 244 Gc22
Don Chedi Monument **THA** 114 Qa38
Donda **ANG** 202 Lh50
Dondaicha **IND** (MHT) 108 Oh35
Dondo **MOC** 214 Mh55
Dondo **RDC** 200 Ma43
Dondo **RI** 129 Ra50
Don Dol **EAK** 204 Mj45
Dondon **RH** 260 Gd36
Dondonay Island **RP** 123 Ra41
Dondra Head **CL** 111 Pa44
Don Duong **VN** 115 Qe40
Donduşeni **MD** 45 Mh42
Donec'k **UA** 55 Mj22
Donegal **IRL** 18 Km36
Donegal Bay **IRL** 18 Km36
Döner Kümbet **TR** 51 Mq52
Dong **IND** (ARP) 113 Pj31
Dong **K** 115 Qc39
Donga **DY** 193 La41
Donga **WAN** 194 Lf42
Donga **WAN** 195 Lf42
Donga Bonga **PK** 81 Og31
Dongai Coring **CHN** 89 Pe28
Dong Am Pham N.B.C.A. **LAO** 115 Qd38
Dong'an **CHN** (HUN) 96 Qf32
Dong Anh **VN** 96 Qc35
Dongara **AUS** (WA) 144 Qh60
Dongargarh **IND** (CGH) 109 Pa35
Dongbeihu Linyuan **CHN** 98 Rd23
Dongchuan **CHN** (YUN) 113 Qb32
Dongco **CHN** (TIB) 88 Pc29
Dongcun **CHN** (SDG) 100 Ra27
Dong Dang **VN** 96 Qd35
Donges **F** 22 Ks43
Dongfang **CHN** (HAN) 96 Qe36
Dongfang **CHN** (HUN) 95 Qf31
Dongfanghong **CHN** (HLG) 98 Rg22
Dongfeng **CHN** (JLN) 100 Rc24
Donggala **RI** 127 Qk46
Donggi Cona **CHN** 94 Pk28
Dongguan **CHN** (GDG) 97 Qg34
Dong Guan Mosque **CHN** 92 Qa27
Dong Ha **VN** 115 Qd37
Donghae Rf26
Donghai **CHN** (JGS) 102 Qk28
Donghai Dao **CHN** 96 Qf35
Dong He **CHN** 92 Qa25
Dong Hoa Sao N.B.C.A. **LAO** 115 Qd38
Dong Hoi **VN** 115 Qd37
Dongjia **CHN** (GZH) 96 Qd33
Dong Jiang **CHN** 97 Qh34
Dongjingcheng **CHN** (HLG) 98 Re23
Dongkala **RI** 127 Rb48
Dongkeng **CHN** (ZJG) 102 Qk32
Dongko **RI** 128 Qf50
Dongkou **CHN** (HUN) 96 Qf32
Donglan **CHN** (GZG) 96 Qd33
Dongliang **CHN** (SAX) 93 Qg26
Dong Ling = Fuling Tomb **CHN** 100 Rb25
Dong Loc **VN** 115 Qc36
Donglük **CHN** (XUZ) 87 Pe26
Dongming **CHN** (SDG) 102 Qh28
Dongnan Qiuling **CHN** 96 Qg33
Dongnan Qiuling **CHN** 102 Qj32
Dongning **CHN** (HLG) 98 Rf23
Dongo **ANG** 208 Lh53
Dongo **RDC** 200 Lk44
Dongola = Donqula **SUD** 190 Mf37
Dongotona Mountains **SUD** 204 Mg43
Dongou **RCB** 200 Lk44
Dongpa **CHN** (TIB) 88 Pa30
Dong Peng N.P. **K** 115 Qb40
Dong Phaya Yen **THA** 114 Qa37
Dong Phou Vieng N.B.C.A. **LAO** 115 Qd37
Dongqiao **CHN** (TIB) 89 Pf30
Dongshanling **CHN** 96 Qf36
Dongshan Wan **CHN** 97 Qj34
Dongsha Qundao **CHN** 97 Qj35
Dongsheng **CHN** (NMZ) 93 Qf26
Dongsheng Reservoir **CHN** 98 Rc22
Dong Ta **CHN** 96 Qf34
Dongtai **CHN** (JGS) 102 Ra29
Dong Taijnar Hu **CHN** 87 Ph27
Dong Trau **VN** 115 Qc36
Dongue **ANG** 208 Lh53
Donguila **G** 194 Le45
Dong Ujimqin Qi **CHN** (NMZ) 91 Qj23
Dongw **Z** 209 Mc52
Dongxi **CHN** (CGQ) 95 Qd31
Dongxi **CHN** (SCH) 95 Qd29
Dongxiang **CHN** (JGX) 102 Qj31
Dongxing **CHN** (HAN) 96 Qe36
Dongxing **CHN** (HLG) 98 Rd22
Dong Xoai **VN** 115 Qd40
Dongyang **CHN** (ZJG) 102 Ra31
Dongying **CHN** (SDG) 93 Qk27
Dongzhai **CHN** (SAX) 93 Qg26
Dongzhaigang Z.B. **CHN** 96 Qf36
Dongzheng Jiaotang **CHN** 98 Rd23
Dongzhi **CHN** (AHU) 102 Qj30
Donington Park **GB** 21 Kt38
Doniphan **USA** (MO) 243 Fe27
Donja Stubica **HR** 41 Lr45
Donji Dušnik **SCG** 46 Mc47
Donji Kamengrad **BIH** 41 Lr46
Donji Lapac **HR** 41 Lq46
Donji Miholjac **HR** 41 Lt45
Donjin Milanova **SCG** 44 Mc46
Donji Rujani **BIH** 41 Lr47
Donji Stajevac **SCG** 46 Mc48
Donji Striževac **SCG** 46 Mc47
Donji Tovarnik **SCG** 44 Lu46
Donji Vakuf **BIH** 41 Ls46
Donji Vakuf **BIH** 41 Ls46
Donji Žirovac **HR** 41 Lr45
Donkar **BHT** 112 Pf32
Donkerpoort **ZA** 217 Mc61
Donko **WAN** 186 Lc40
Don Martin **MEX** (COH) 253 Ek32
Donna **N** 10 Lg12
Donnelly **CDN** (AB) 233 Eb18
Donnersberg **D** 34 Lh41
Donnybrook **AUS** (WA) 144 Qh62
Donnybrook **ZA** 217 Me60
Dono Manga **TCH** 187 Lj41
Donors Hill **AUS** (QLD) 148 Sa55
Donostia = San Sebastián **E** 27 Ks53
Donoúsa **GR** 49 Mf53
Donoúsa **GR** 49 Mf53
Donqula **SUD** 190 Mf37
Don Sa **THA** 116 Pk41
Donskaja ravnina **RUS** 53 Na19
Donskoe **RUS** 55 Na23
Donsol **RP** 121 Rb39
Donwe **Z** 209 Mc52
Donyztau **KZ** 71 Nj22
Donzère **F** 25 Le46
Donzy **F** 23 Ld43
Doolguna **AUS** (WA) 140 Qk58
Doolow **SP** 198 Nb43
Doomadgee **AUS** (QLD) 148 Rk54
Doomadgee A.L. **AUS** (QLD) 148 Rk54
Doomben Racecourse **AUS** (QLD) 151 Sg59
Doongmabulla **AUS** (QLD) 149 Sd57
Doorawarrah **AUS** (WA) 140 Qh58
Do Ouro **BR** 282 Hf52
Do Peixe **BR** 281 He53
Doqa'i **IR** 73 Nk27
Do Qal'eh **AFG** 78 Oa29
Do Qu **CHN** 94 Qa29
Dor **RUS** 53 Na16
Dora **USA** (NM) 237 Ej29
Dorado **PY** 285 Gk56
Dorah Pass **AFG/PK** 79 Of27
Doranala **IND** (APH) 111 Ok39
Dorbod **CHN** (HLG) 98 Rc22
Đorče Petrov **MK** 46 Mb48
Dorchester **GB** 21 Ks40
Dordabis **NAM** 212 Lj57
Dordogne **F** 24 Ku46
Dordrecht **NL** 32 Le39
Dordrecht **ZA** 217 Md61
Doreenville **NAM** 212 Lk57
Dore Lake **CDN** (SK) 233 Eg18
Doré Lake **CDN** 233 Eg18
Dores do Indaiá **BR** (MG) 287 Hh55
Dorey **RMM** 185 Kk38
Dorfen **D** 35 Ln42
Dorgali **I** 31 Lk50
Dörgön nuur **MNG** 85 Pg22
Dori **BF** 185 Kk38
Dorimon **GH** 193 Kj41
Doring **ZA** 216 Lk62
Doringbaai **ZA** 216 Lk61
Dorintosh **CDN** (SK) 233 Ef18
Dório **GR** 48 Mb53
Dorion **CDN** (ON) 239 Ff21
Dorisvale **AUS** (NT) 139 Rf53
Doriya **EAT** 207 Mk49
Dorking **GB** 21 Ku39
Dorlin **F** 271 Hd44
Dormagen **D** 32 Lg39
Dormánd **H** 39 Ma43
Dormans **F** 23 Ld41
Dormea Ahenkro **GH** 193 Kj42
Dormentes **BR** (PE) 283 Hk50
Dornbirn **A** 34 Lk43
Dornes **F** 25 Ld44
Dornoch **GB** 19 Kq33
Dornoch Firth **GB** 19 Kr33
Dornod **MNG** 91 Qg22
Dorno Djoutougué **TCH** 196 Mb39
Dornogov' **MNG** 91 Qg23
Doro **RMM** 185 Kk37
Doroh **IR** 73 Oa29
Dorohoi **RO** 45 Mg43
Dorohusk **PL** 37 Md39
Doroninskoe **RUS** 91 Qg20
Doropo **CI** 193 Kj41
Dorošivka **UA** 45 Mm43
Doroslovo **SCG** 44 Lu45
Dorosyni **UA** 37 Mf40
Dorotea **S** 10 Lj13
Dorothy **CDN** (AB) 233 Ed20
Dorowa **ZW** 214 Mf55
Dörpen **D** 32 Lh38
Dorra **KWT** 74 Ne31
Dorre Island **AUS** 140 Qg58
Dorrigo **AUS** (NSW) 151 Sg61
Dorrigo N.P. **AUS** 151 Sg61
Dorsale Camerounaise **CAM** 195 Lf42
Dorset Coast **GB** 21 Ks40
Dorsland Trekkers Monument **NAM** 212 Lh55
Dorsten **D** 32 Lg39
Dörtdivan **TR** 51 Mn50
Dortmund **D** 32 Lh39
Dörtyol **TR** 51 Mq53
Dörtyol **TR** 62 Mj27
Doruchów **PL** 36 Lt39
Dorud **IR** 72 Ne29
Doruma **RDC** 201 Md43
Dörzbach **D** 34 Lk41
Do Sangue **BR** 280 Ha51
Dos Caminos **YV** 269 Gh41
Dos de Mayo **PE** 278 Gc49
Dos de Mayo **RA** (MI) 289 Hc59
Döşemealti **TR** 51 Ml53
Dos Hermanas **E** 28 Kp47
Dos Lagunas **GCA** 255 Ff37
Dos Mangues **BR** 282 Hf51
Dos Marmelos **BR** 274 Gk49
Do Son **VN** 96 Qd35
Do Son Beach **VN** 96 Qd35
Dospat **BG** 47 Me49
Dos Peixes ou de São Francisco **BR** 281 Hb51
Dos Pilas **GCA** 255 Ff37
Dos Porcos **BR** 282 Hh52
Dos Ríos **CO** 273 Gd45
Dosse **D** 33 Ln37
Dosso **RN** 185 Lb39
Do'stlik **UZ** 76 Oe25
Dostuk **KS** 77 Oh25
Dostyk **KZ** 84 Pb23
Dothan **USA** (AL) 249 Fh30
Dotswood **AUS** (QLD) 149 Sd55
Douai **F** 23 Ld40
Douako **RG** 192 Ke41
Douala **CAM** 194 Le43
Doualayel **CAM** 195 Lg42
Douaouir **RMM** 179 Kj35
Douarnenez **F** 22 Kq42
Douaya **RMM** 185 Kj37
Doubabougou **RMM** 184 Kg38
Double Island Point **AUS** 151 Sg58
Doublema **RN** 185 Lb38
Double Mountain **AUS** 149 Sf57
Doubo **ETH** 198 Mj42
Douboudo **BF** 185 La40
Doubtful Bay **AUS** 138 Rc54
Doubtful Island Bay **AUS** 144 Qk62
Doubtful Sound **NZ** 155 Td68
Doubtful Sound **NZ** 155 Td68
Doubtless Bay **NZ** 154 Tg63
Douchy-les-Mines **F** 23 Ld40
Doudeville **F** 22 La41
Doudou **BF** 193 Kj40
Doué-la-Fontaine **F** 22 Ku43
Douentza **RMM** 185 Kj38
Dougga **TN** 174 Le27
Douglas **GB** 18 Kq36
Douglas **GB** 295 Ha71
Douglas **USA** (AK) 231 Dc16
Douglas **USA** (AZ) 237 Ef30
Douglas **USA** (GA) 249 Fj30
Douglas **USA** (WY) 235 Eh24
Douglas **ZA** 216 Mb60
Douglas-Apsley National Park **AUS** 152 Se66
Douglas Cay **BH** 255 Fg37
Douglas Channel **CDN** 232 Df19
Douglas City **USA** (CA) 234 Dj25
Douglas L. Ind. Res. **CDN** 232 Dk20
Douglas, Mount **USA** 229 Cd16
Douglas Range 296 Gb32
Douglasville **USA** (GA) 249 Fh29
Dougoulé **RN** 187 Lf38
Douguia **TCH** 187 Lh39
Doukhobor Hist. Village **CDN** 232 Eb21
Doukoula **CAM** 187 Lh40
Doullens **F** 23 Lc40
Doumandzou **G** 195 Lf45
Doumba bonne **RN** 188 Lg36
Doum Doum **TCH** 187 Lh39
Doumé **CAM** 195 Lh43
Doumé **CAM** 195 Lg43
Doumé **CAM** 195 Lg43
Doumen **CHN** (GDG) 97 Qg34
Doumo **CAM** 195 Lg44
Douna **BF** 193 Kh40
Douna **RMM** 185 Kh38
Doundé Bagué **SN** 183 Kd38
Douné **RG** 192 Ke40
Dounguél-Sigon **RG** 192 Kd40
Dounkou **BF** 185 Kj39
Doura **RMM** 184 Kg39
Douradina **BR** (MS) 286 Hc57
Douradina **BR** (PR) 286 Hd57
Dourados **BR** (MS) 286 Hc57
Dourados **BR** 286 Hc57
Dourbali **TCH** 187 Lh40
Dourbeye **CAM** 187 Lg41
Dourdan **F** 23 Lc42
Dourdoura **TCH** 196 Ma40
Douro **RMM** 185 Kj38
Douroum **CAM** 187 Lg40
Doutor Pedrinho **BR** (SC) 291 Hf59
Doutoufouk **RN** 186 Le39
Douximiao Reservoir **CHN** 100 Rb23
Douz **TN** 174 Le29
Douze **F** 24 Ku47
do Vale do Javari, T.I. **BR** 273 Ge48
Dove **GB** 21 Kt38
Dove **PNG** 159 Se50
Dove Bugt **DK** 225 Ka03
Dove Creek **USA** (CO) 237 Ef27
Dover **AUS** (TAS) 152 Sd67
Dover **GB** 21 Lb39
Dover **USA** (DE) 247 Gc26
Dover **USA** (NH) 247 Ge24
Dover **USA** (OH) 247 Fk25
Dover **USA** (TN) 248 Fg27
Dover Foxcroft **USA** (MA) 247 Gf23
Dovhe **UA** 39 Md42
Dovre **N** 12 Lk29
Dovrefjell **N** 12 Lk28
Dovrefjell-Sunndalsfjella n.p. **N** 12 Lj28
Dovsk **BY** 52 Mf19
Dowa **MW** 210 Mg52
Dowagiac **USA** (MI) 246 Fg25
Dowerin **AUS** (WA) 144 Qj61
Dowlaiswaram **IND** (APH) 109 Pa37
Dowlatabad **AFG** 78 Oc27
Dowlatabad **AFG** 78 Od27
Dowlat Alad **IR** 73 Nj27
Dowlat Yar **AFG** 78 Oc28
Downey **USA** (ID) 235 Ed24
Downham Market **GB** 21 La38
Downpatrick **GB** 18 Kp36
Downsville **USA** (NY) 247 Gc24
Downton, Mount **CDN** 232 Dh19
Dowra **IRL** 18 Km36
Dowshi **AFG** 78 Oe28
Doyle **RA** (BA) 289 Ha62
Doyle **USA** (CA) 234 Dk26
Doze de Outubro **BR** 280 Ha52
Dra Afratir **DARS** 178 Kd32
Drabiv **UA** 54 Mg21
Drabonso **GH** 193 Kk42
Drac **F** 25 Lf46
Dracena **BR** (SP) 286 He56
Drachten **NL** 32 Lg37
Dragačevo **SCG** 46 Ma47
Dragalj **SCG** 46 Lt48
Drăgănești **MD** 45 Mj43
Drăgănești **RO** 45 Mg46
Drăgănești-Olt **RO** 45 Me46
Drăgănești-Vlașca **RO** 45 Mf46
Dragaš **SCG** 46 Ma48
Drăgășani **RO** 44 Me46
Draggaboersnek **ZA** 217 Mc62
Draghoender **ZA** 216 Mb60
Draginac **SCG** 44 Lu46
Draglica **SCG** 46 Lu47
Dragon and Tiger Pagodas **RC** 97 Ra34
Dragon Festival **CHN** 93 Qk27
Dragon's Backbone Rice Terraces **CHN** 96 Qf33
Dragon's blood tree **YE** 69 Nh39
Dragoș Vodă **RO** 45 Mh46
Dragsfjärd **FIN** 16 Mc30
Draguignan **F** 25 Lg47
Drăgușeni **RO** 45 Mh45
Drahičyn **BY** 37 Mf38
Drahovce **SK** 38 Ls42
Drahove **UA** 39 Md42
Drake **AUS** (NSW) 151 Sg60
Drake **USA** (MO) 241 Fe26
Drake **USA** (ND) 240 Ek22
Drakensberge **ZA** 217 Me61
Drakensberge **ZA** 217 Me61
Drake Passage 267 Gc30
Dralfa **BG** 47 Mg47
Dráma **GR** 47 Me49
Drammen **N** 12 Ll31
Dramtse Goemba **BHT** 112 Pf32
Drangajökull **IS** 10 Jj12
Drangedal **N** 12 Lk31
Drangsnes **IS** 10 Jk13
Dranske **D** 33 Lo36
Draper, Mount **USA** 231 Da16
Drasan **PK** 79 Og27
Drass 79 Oh28
Drau **A** 35 Lp44
Drava **SLO** 41 Lq44
Drávafok **H** 41 Ls45
Drawa **PL** 36 Lq38
Drawieński P.N. **PL** 36 Lq37
Drawski Park Krajobrazowy **PL** 36 Lr37
Drawsko Pomorskie **PL** 36 Lq37
D'raysap Waterfall **VN** 115 Qd39
Drayton Valley **CDN** (AB) 233 Ec19
Dr. Castillo del Valle **MEX** (DGO) 253 Eh33
Dreamtime Cultural Centre **AUS** 149 Sf57
Dreamworld **AUS** 151 Sg59
Dréan **DZ** 174 Ld27
Drebkau **D** 33 Lp39
Drégelypalánk **H** 39 Lu42
Drehu Village **F** 162 Td56
Dreikikir **PNG** 159 Sb49
Drei Zinnen **I** 40 Ln44
Dremsel, Mount **PNG** 159 Sd47
Drenovac **SCG** 46 Mb48
Drenovci **HR** 44 Lt46
Drenovo **MK** 46 Mb49
Drepung Monastery **CHN** 89 Pf31
Drescher **ANT** (D) 296 Ka33
Dresden **CDN** (ON) 246 Fj24
Dresden **D** 33 Lo39
Dresden **USA** (KS) 240 Ek26
Dresden **USA** (OH) 246 Fj25
Drètun' **BY** 52 Me18
Dretyń **PL** 36 Lr36
Dreux **F** 22 Lb42
Drevsjø **N** 12 Ln29
Drewsey **USA** (OR) 234 Ea24
Drezdenko **PL** 36 Lq38
Drežnica **HR** 41 Lq45
Driebes **E** 29 Kr50
Drietabbetje **SME** 271 Hc43
Driffield **GB** 21 Ku37
Driftpile R. Ind. Res. **CDN** 233 Ec18
Driftwood **CDN** (BC) 231 Dg18
Driggs **USA** (ID) 235 Ee24
Drillham **AUS** (QLD) 151 Se59
Drimiopsis **NAM** 212 Lk57
Drin **AL** 46 Lu48
Drina **BIH** 46 Lt47
Drin i Zi **AL** 46 Ma49
Drinjača **BIH** 46 Lu46
Drinkwater **CDN** (SK) 233 Eh20
Drino **AL** 46 Ma50
Driouch **MA** 173 Kj28
Drjanovo **BG** 47 Mf48
Drjanovski manastir **BG** 47 Mf47
Drniš **HR** 41 Lr47
Drnje **HR** 41 Lr44
Drøbak **N** 12 Ll31
Drobeta-Turnu Severin **RO** 44 Md46
Drobin **PL** 37 Lu38
Drochia **MD** 45 Mh42
Droërivier **ZA** 216 Mb62
Drogheda **IRL** 20 Ko37
Drohiczyn **PL** 37 Mc38
Drohobyč **UA** 39 Md41
Droitwich **GB** 21 Ks38
Drolshagen **D** 32 Lh39
Drombeg Circle **IRL** 20 Kl39
Drome **PNG** 158 Sb47
Dromore **GB** 18 Ko36
Dronero **I** 40 Lh46
Droning Ingrid Land **DK** 225 Hc06
Droning Louise Land **DK** 225 Jc03
Dronninglund **DK** 14 Ll33
Dronning Maud Land **ANT** 296 Kc34
Dronten **NL** 32 Lf38
Droogmakerij de Beemster **NL** 32 Le38
Dropt **F** 24 La46
Drosh **PK** 79 Of28
Droskovo **RUS** 53 Mj19
Drossáto **GR** 46 Mc49
Drosseró **GR** 46 Mb50
Drotsky's Caves = Gcwihaba Caverns **RB** 213 Ma56
Drottningholm **S** 13 Ls31
Drowing River **CDN** 239 Fh20
Drowners **AUS** 152 Rj63
Drozdyn' **UA** 52 Md20
Drueulu **F** 162 Td56
Druja **BY** 17 Mh35
Drukšiu ežeras **LT** 17 Mg35
Drumcliff **IRL** 18 Km36
Drumheller **CDN** (AB) 233 Ed20
Drummond **USA** (MI) 246 Fj23
Drummond **USA** (MT) 235 Ed22
Drummond **USA** (WI) 241 Fe22
Drummond Island **USA** 246 Fj23
Drummond Range **AUS** (QLD) 151 Sd58
Drummond Range **AUS** 149 Sd57
Drummondville **CDN** (QC) 247 Gd23
Drummore **GB** 18 Kq36
Drumnadrochit **GB** 19 Kq33
Druskininkai **LT** 17 Md36
Drusti **LV** 17 Mf33
Druten **NL** 32 Lf39
Družba **UA** 52 Mg19
Družetići **SCG** 46 Ma46
Družnaja II **ANT** (RUS) 296 Gc33
Družnaja III **ANT** (RUS) 296 Kb33
Drvar **BIH** 41 Lr46
Drvenik **HR** 41 Ls47
Drwęczno **PL** 37 Ma36
Dry Bay **USA** 231 Da16
Dryberry Lake **CDN** 238 Fd21
Drybrough **CDN** (MB) 238 Ek17
Dryden **CDN** (ON) 238 Fd21
Dryden **USA** (TX) 237 Ej31
Dry Fork **USA** 235 Eg24
Drygalski Ice Tongue 297 Tb34
Drygalski Island 297 Pc32
Drygały **PL** 37 Mc37
Dry Harts **ZA** 217 Mc59
Dry River **AUS** (NT) 139 Rg53
Dry River **AUS** 139 Rg53
Drysdale Island **AUS** 139 Rh51
Drysdale River **AUS** (WA) 138 Rd53
Drysdale River **AUS** 138 Rd53
Drysdale River N.P. **AUS** 138 Rd53
Dry Tortugas **USA** 250 Fj33
Dry Tortugas National Park **USA** 250 Fj33
Drzewica **PL** 37 Ma39
Dschang **CAM** 194 Lf43
Dua **RDC** 200 Mb44
Duaca **YV** 269 Gf40
Duale **RDC** 200 Ma45
Dualla **CI** 192 Kg41
Du'an **CHN** (GZG) 96 Qe34
Duaringa **AUS** (QLD) 149 Se57
Duart Castle **GB** 18 Kp34
Duartina **BR** (SP) 286 Hf57
Duas Igrejas **P** 26 Ko51
Duba **KSA** 66 Mh32
Duba **WAN** 186 Lc41
Dubai **UAE** 74 Nh33
Dubaj **BY** 37 Mf38
Dubar **SP** 199 Nc40
Dubăsari **MD** 45 Mk43
Dubău **MD** 45 Mk43
Dubawnt Lake **CDN** 225 Ed06
Dubbo **AUS** (NSW) 153 Se62
Dube **LB** 192 Kg43
Dubi **IND** (RJT) 106 Oj32
Dubie **RDC** 206 Me50
Dubienka **PL** 37 Md39
Dubin **PL** 36 Ls39
Dub'jazy **RUS** (TAR) 53 Ne17
Dublikan **RUS** 98 Rg20
Dublin = Baile Átha Cliath **IRL** 20 Ko37
Dublin **USA** (GA) 249 Fj29
Dublin Bay **IRL** 20 Ko37
Dubna **LV** 17 Mg34
Dubna **RUS** 52 Mj17
Dubna **RUS** 52 Mj18
Dub nad Moravou **CZ** 38 Ls41
Dubnica nad Váhom **SK** 38 Lt42
Dubno **UA** 54 Mc20
Dubo **LB** 192 Kf43
Dubois **USA** (ID) 235 Ed23
Du Bois **USA** (PA) 247 Ga25
Dubois **USA** (WY) 235 Ef24
Dubova **RO** 44 Mc46
Dubove **UA** 37 Me39
Dubove **UA** 39 Md42
Dubovka **RUS** 53 Nc21
Dubovskoje **RUS** 55 Nb22
Dubovyj Ovrag **RUS** 53 Nc21
Dubrava **HR** 41 Ls45
Dubréka **RG** 192 Kd41
Dubrivka **UA** 54 Md20
Dubrovka **RUS** 53 Na20
Dubrovnik **HR** 43 Lt48
Dubrovycja **UA** 39 Md41
Dubrovycja **UA** 52 Md20
Dubulu **RDC** 200 Ma43
Dubuque **USA** (IA) 241 Fe24
Dubysa **LT** 17 Md35
Ducey **F** 22 Kt42
Duchang **CHN** (JGX) 102 Qj31
Duchcov **CZ** 38 Lo40
Ducherow **D** 33 Lo37
Duches **AUS** (QLD) 148 Rk56
Duchesne **USA** (UT) 235 Ee25
Duchesne **USA** 235 Ee25
Ducie 303 Db12
Duck Creek **AUS** 140 Qj57
Duck Lake **CDN** (SK) 233 Eg19
Duck Mtn. Prov. Park **CDN** 238 Ek20
Duck Mtn. Prov. Forest **CDN** 238 Ek20
Duck Mtn. Prov. Park **CDN** 238 Ek20
Duck River **USA** (TN) 248 Fg28
Ducktown **USA** (TN) 249 Fh28
Duck Valley Ind. Res. **USA** 234 Eb25
Duckwater **USA** (NV) 234 Ec26
Duckwater Pt. **USA** 234 Ec26
Duc Lap **VN** 115 Qd37
Duc Lieu **VN** 115 Qd40
Duc My **VN** 115 Qe39
Duc Pho **VN** 115 Qe38
Duc Tho **VN** 115 Qc36
Duc Trong **VN** 115 Qe40
Duda **CO** 272 Gc44
Dudada **IND** (APH) 109 Ok37
Dudelange **L** 23 Lg41
Düdencik **TR** 51 Mm53
Düden Şelâlesi **TR** 51 Ml53
Duderstadt **D** 33 Ll39
Dudhai **IND** (GUJ) 108 Of34
Dudhani **IND** (MHT) 108 Oj37
Dudhi **IND** (UPH) 109 Pb33
Dudhnai **IND** (ASM) 112 Pf33
Dudhwa N.P. **IND** 107 Pa31
Dudignac **RA** (BA) 289 Gk63
Dudinin **AUS** (WA) 144 Qk62
Dudinka **RUS** 58 Pb05
Dudley **GB** 21 Ks38
Dudu **IND** (RJT) 106 Oh32
Dudub **ETH** 199 Nd42
Due **RDC** 203 Lk48
Duékoué **CI** 192 Kg42
Dueñas **E** 26 Kq51
Dueodde **DK** 15 Lq35
Duere **BR** 281 Hf51
Duesund **N** 12 Lf30
Duff Islands **SOL** 157 Tb20
Dufftown **GB** 19 Kr33
Duga Poljana **SCG** 46 Ma47
Duga Resa **HR** 41 Lq45
Dugbia **RDC** 201 Mc44
Dugdug **SUD** 197 Me41
Duge **LB** 192 Kf42
Duggipar **IND** (MHT) 109 Pa35
Dugi Otok **HR** 41 Lq47
Dugo Selo **HR** 41 Lr45
Duguan Hu **CHN** 102 Qj30
Dugulle **SP** 205 Nc44
Dugway **USA** (UT) 235 Ed25
Dugwaya **SUD** 190 Mh38
Du He **CHN** 95 Qf29
Duhovnickoe **RUS** 53 Ne19
Duida, Cerro **YV** 269 Gh44
Duida-Marahuaca, P.N. **YV** 269 Gh45
Duisaj **IR** 72 Ne28
Duisburg **D** 32 Lg39
Duitama **CO** 268 Gd43
Duiwelskloof **ZA** 214 Mf57
Dujiangyan **CHN** (SCH) 94 Qb30
Dujiangyan Irrigation System **CHN** 94 Qb30
Dukambiya **ER** 191 Mj39
Dukat **AL** 46 Lu50
Duke **USA** (OK) 242 Fa28
Duke Island **USA** 231 De18
Duke Islands **AUS** 149 Sf56
Duke of York Island **PNG** 160 Sg48
Duk Fadiat **SUD** 197 Mf42
Duk Faiwil **SUD** 197 Mf42
Dukhan **Q** 74 Nf33
Dukhnah **KSA** 67 Nb33
Duki **PK** 78 Oe30
Duki **RUS** 98 Rh20
Duki **RUS** 98 Rh20
Dukkālah **MA** 172 Kf29
Dukku **WAN** 186 Lc40
Dukla **PL** 39 Mb41
Dūkštas **LT** 17 Mg35
Duku **WAN** 187 Lf40
Dukwan Reservoir **IND** 109 Ok33
Dulacca **AUS** (QLD) 151 Se59
Dulag **RP** 123 Rc40
Dulai **BD** 112 Pe34
Dulan **CHN** (QHI) 92 Pk27
Dular **CHN** (NMZ) 91 Qk22
Dulaying **CHN** (GZH) 96 Qd32
Dulce **RA** 288 Gj60
Dulce **USA** (NM) 237 Eg27
Dulce Nombre de Culmi **HN** 256 Fh38
Dulcie Ranges N.P. **AUS** 143 Rh57
Dul'durga **RUS** (AGB) 91 Qg20
Dule Temple **CHN** 93 Qj25
Dulia **RDC** 201 Me45
Dulia **RDC** 201 Mc44
Dulkaninna **AUS** (SA) 143 Rk60
Dullewala **PK** 79 Of30
Dullstroom **ZA** 214 Mf58
Dülmen **D** 32 Lh39
Duloduo **RI** 127 Rb45
Dulovo **BG** 47 Mh47
Dululu **AUS** (QLD) 149 Sf57
Duluth **USA** (MN) 241 Fd22
Dulverton **GB** 20 Kr39
Duma **RDC** 197 Md43
Duma **RDC** 200 Lk44
Dumagasa Point **RP** 123 Ra42
Dumai **RI** 124 Qa45
Dumanata **IND** (CGH) 109 Pa36
Dumanjug **RP** 123 Rb40
Dumaran Island **RP** 122 Qk40
Dumarao **RP** 123 Rb40
Dumarehe **RI** 123 Rc43
Dumarpara **IND** (CGH) 109 Pb34
Dumas **USA** (AR) 243 Fe29
Dumas **USA** (TX) 242 Ek28
Dumba Cambango **ANG** 208 Lj51
Dumbai **GH** 193 La41
Dumbarton **GB** 19 Kq35
Dumbéa **F** 162 Td57
Dumbleyung **AUS** (WA) 144 Qj62
Dumbo **CAM** 195 Lf42
Dumbrăveni **RO** 44 Me44
Dumbrăveni **RO** 45 Mh47
Dumbrăvița **MD** 45 Mj43
Dumfries **GB** 19 Kr35
Dumiat **ET** 177 Mf30
Dumila **EAT** 207 Mj49
Dumitrești **RO** 45 Mg45
Dumka **IND** (JKD) 112 Pd33
Dumlupınar **TR** 50 Mk52
Dummagudem **IND** (APH) 109 Pa37
Dümmer **D** 32 Lj38
Dumoga **RI** 127 Rc45
Dumond River **CDN** 239 Ff19
Dumont d'Urville **ANT** (F) 297 Rd32
Dumont d'Urville Sea 297 Rc31
Dumra **IND** (GUJ) 108 Oe34
Dumraon **IND** (BIH) 109 Pc33

El Carmen – Engures ezers

El Carmen RA (PJ) 284 Gh58
El Carmen RCH 292 Ge64
El Carrizal MEX (CHH) 237 Eg30
El Carrizal MEX (GUR) 254 Ek37
El Carrizo MEX (TM) 253 Fb33
El Castillo MEX (SL) 252 Eg33
El Cayo MEX 255 Fe37
El Cayuco MEX (BCS) 252 Ee33
El Ceibal GCA 255 Ff37
El Centro USA (CA) 236 Ec29
El Cerrito CO 268 Gb44
El Cerrito RA (SC) 294 Gc71
El Cerro de Concepción BOL 285 Gk54
El Chacay RA 288 Gf63
El Chacay RCH 292 Ge64
El Chaco EC 272 Gb46
El Chaco RA (CD) 288 Gh61
El Chaltén RA (SC) 294 Gd70
El Chaparro YV 269 Gh41
El Charco RA (SE) 288 Gh59
Elche = Elx E 29 Ku48
Elche de la Sierra E 29 Ks48
El Chico, P.N. MEX 254 Fa35
El Chile NIC 256 Fh39
El Chinero MEX (BC) 236 Ec30
Elcho Island AUS 139 Rh51
El Chorrito MEX (TM) 253 Fa33
El Chorro BOL 279 Gg51
El Cien MEX (BCS) 252 Ee33
El Ciento Veintiocho MEX (BCS) 252 Ee33
El Cinco MEX (COH) 253 Ej32
El Cisne EC 272 Ga47
El Cisne EC 272 Ga47
El Cobre C 259 Gb35
El Cocuy CO 268 Gd42
El Cocuy, P.N. CO 268 Gd42
El Colorado RA (FO) 289 Ha59
El Comitán MEX (BCS) 252 Ee33
El Cope PA 257 Fk41
El Corazón EC 272 Ga46
El Corcovado RA (CB) 292 Ge67
El Corozo YV 269 Gh41
El Coyote MEX (BCS) 252 Ee32
El Coyote MEX (SO) 237 Ef31
El Coyte RA (CB) 292 Ge68
El Crispín RA (CD) 288 Gj61
El Cruce GCA 255 Ff37
El Crucero MEX (BC) 236 Ec31
El Cuarenta MEX (CHH) 237 Eg30
El Cubo de Tierra del Vino E 26 Kp51
El Cuco ES 255 Ff39
El Cuy RA (RN) 292 Gf65
El Cuyo MEX (YT) 255 Fg35
Elda E 29 Ku48
El Dab'ah ET 177 Me30
El Da'fa ET 176 Md30
Eldama Ravina EAK 204 Mh45
El Darien CO 268 Gd42
Elde D 33 Lm37
El Deir ET 177 Mg33
Elderslie AUS (QLD) 148 Sb57
El Descanso PE 279 Ge53
El Desemboque MEX (SO) 236 Ed30
El Desemboque MEX (SO) 236 Ed31
El Deseo MEX (SO) 236 Ed30
El Divisadero MEX (CHH) 252 Eg32
El Divisorio RA (BA) 293 Gk65
El Djem TN 174 Lf28
El Doncello CO 272 Gc45
Eldon Hazlet S.P. USA 241 Ff26
Eldorado BR (MS) 286 Hc57
Eldorado BR (PA) 276 Hf48
Eldorado BR (SP) 286 Hf58
El Dorado HN 256 Fh38
El Dorado MEX (SL) 252 Eg33
Eldorado RA (MI) 289 Hc59
El Dorado USA (AR) 243 Fd29
El Dorado USA (KS) 243 Fb27
Eldorado USA (TX) 242 Ek30
El Dorado YV 270 Gk42
Eldorado River USA 229 Bh13
El Dorado Springs USA (MO) 243 Fc27
Eldoret EAK 204 Mh45
Eldzhik TM 71 Ob26
Eléa GR 48 Mc54
Elec RUS 53 Mk19
Elefantes MOC 214 Mg57
Elefsína GR 48 Md52
Eleftheroúpoli GR 47 Me50
Élegest RUS 85 Ph20
Eleja LV 17 Md34
El Eje RA (CA) 288 Gg59
Élektostal' RUS 52 Mk18
Elektrėnai LT 17 Me36
Eleku RDC 195 Lk45
Elela BR (RR) 270 Gk43
Elele WAN 194 Ld43
El Empalme EC 272 Ga46
El Empedrado YV 269 Ge41
Elena BG 47 Mf48
El Encanto CO 273 Gd46
El Encino MEX (TM) 253 Fa34
El Epazote MEX (SLP) 253 Ek34
Elephanta Island IND 108 Og36
Elephant Butte Res. USA 237 Eg29
Elephant Island 296 Hb31
Elephant Point USA (AK) 229 Bk12
Elephant Training Centre RI 125 Qc48
Elesbão Veloso BR (PI) 277 Hj49
Eleşkirt TR 63 Nb26
El Espinal PA 257 Fk42
El Espinillo RA (CH) 285 Gk58
El Estanquito RA (LR) 288 Gg60
El Estor GCA 255 Ff38
El Estrecho CO 272 Gb45
Elesvaram IND (APH) 109 Pb37
El Eucaliptus ROU 289 Hb61
El Eulma DZ 174 Lc27
Eleuthera Island BS 251 Gb33
El Fahs TN 174 Le27
El Faouar TN 174 Le29
El Farciya DARS 178 Ke32
El Faro MEX (BC) 236 Ec29
El Faro MEX (CHH) 237 Eg31
El Fashn ET 177 Mf31
El Feidja, P.N. d' TN 174 Le27
Elfin Cove USA (AK) 231 Db16
el Fluvià E 30 Lc48
El Fortín RA (CD) 289 Gj61
El Fraile RCH 294 Gd68
Elfstedentocht NL 32 Lf37
El Fud ETH 199 Nb42
El Fuerte MEX (SL) 252 Ef32
Elgå N 12 Lm28
El Gaa Taatzebar DZ 180 Lb32
Elgal EAK 205 Mk45
El Gallâouiya RIM 178 Ke35
El Gallâouiya RIM 178 Ke35
El Galpón RA (SA) 285 Gh58
El-Gara MA 172 Kg29
El Gavilán MEX (SO) 236 Ee31
El Gavilán MEX (TM) 253 Fa33
El Gharandal ET 177 Mg31
El Gheddiya RIM 183 Ke37
El Ghurdaqah ET 177 Mg32
El Giara SP 205 Na46
Elgin GB 19 Kr33
Elgin USA (IL) 246 Ff25
Elgin USA (ND) 240 Ek22
Elgin USA (NV) 236 Ec27
Elgin USA (OR) 234 Eb23
Elgir CDN (MB) 238 Ek21
El-Gîsa ET 177 Mf31
El Gîsa ET 177 Mf30
El Gleïta RMM 183 Ke38
El Gof ETH 205 Mk44
El Golfo de Santa Clara MEX (SO) 236 Ec30
Elgon, Mount EAU/EAK 204 Mh45
El Goss RIM 183 Kc37
El Grado E 30 La48
El Grullo MEX (JLC) 253 Eh36
El Guabo EC 272 Ga47
El Guácharo, P.N. YV 269 Gj40
El Guache, P.N. YV 269 Gf41
El Guaje MEX (COH) 253 Ej31
El Guapo YV 269 Gh40
El Guay YV 269 Gf40
El Guayabo YV 268 Gd41
El Guérara DZ 173 Kk31
El Guettar TN 174 Le28
El Guettara RMM 179 Kj34
El Hadjar DZ 174 Ld27
El Hagounia DARS 178 Kd32
El-Hajeb MA 172 Kh29
El Hamel DZ 173 Lc28
El Hamma TN 174 Le29
El Hammâm ET 177 Me30
El Hammâmi RIM 178 Ke34
El Hamrâwein ET 177 Mh32
El Hank RIM/RMM 179 Kg33
El Haouaria TN 174 Lf27
El-Haouïta DZ 173 Lb29
El-Harcha MA 172 Kg29
El Hasira SUD 190 Mh40
El Hawata SUD 190 Mh40
El Hayz ET 177 Me31
El Herradero MEX (TM) 253 Fb33
El Higo MEX (VC) 254 Fa35
El Homr DZ 173 La31
Elhovka RUS 53 Nf19
Elhovo BG 47 Mg48
El Huacal MEX (DGO) 252 Eg33
El Hueco RA (NE) 292 Ge64
El Huesco MEX (NL) 253 Fa33
El Humurre SP 199 Ne42
Eliá GR 48 Mb53
Elias, Cerro RA 292 Gg68
Eliase RI 133 Rf50
Elias Gracia ANG 203 Ma50
Elida USA (NM) 237 Ej29
El Idrissia DZ 173 Lb28
Elie CDN (MB) 238 Fb21
Eliki Gounda RN 186 Le38
Elila RDC 201 Me47
Elila RDC 206 Mc47
Elim USA (AK) 229 Bj13
Elim ZA 216 Lk63
Elimäki FIN 16 Mg30
El Imposible, P.N. ES 255 Ff39
El Ingenio PE 278 Gc53
Elin Pelin BG 46 Md48
Elionka RUS 52 Mg19
Elipa RDC 201 Mc46
Elisa BR (RO) 280 Gj52
Elisa RA (SF) 289 Gk61
Eliseu Martins BR (PI) 282 Hj50
El Iskandariya ET 177 Me30
Elista RUS (KAL) 55 Nc22
Eliye Springs EAK 204 Mj44
Elizabeth GUY 270 Ha42
Elizabeth USA (NJ) 247 Gc25
Elizabeth Bay NAM 216 Lh59
Elizabeth City USA (NC) 249 Gb27
Elizabeth Downs AUS (NT) 139 Rf52
Elizabeth Harbour BS 251 Gc34
Elizabeth Reef AUS 137 Sd24
Elizabethton USA (TN) 249 Fj27
Elizabethtown USA (KY) 248 Fh27
Elizabethtown USA (NC) 249 Ga28
El Jacuixtle MEX (DGO) 253 Eh34
El-Jadida MA 172 Kf29
El Jadidah ET 177 Me31
El-Jemaa MA 172 Kf30
El Jicaral NIC 256 Fg39
El Jigoté MEX (NYT) 253 Eh35
El Jordán CO 269 Ge43
Elk PL 37 Mc37
El Kab SUD 190 Mg37
El Kab (Nekheb) ET 177 Mg33
El Kala DZ 174 Le27
El Kala, P.N. d' DZ 174 Le27
El Kantara DZ 174 Lc28
El Karabi SUD 190 Mg37
Elk City USA (ID) 235 Ec23
Elk City USA (OK) 242 Fa28
Elk Creek USA (CA) 234 Dj26
El Kebab MA 172 Kh29
Elkedra AUS (NT) 143 Rh56
El Kef TN 174 Le27
El-Kelaâ-des-Sraghna MA 172 Kg29
El-Kelaâ M'Gouna MA 172 Kg30
El Kere ETH 199 Nb43
Elkford CDN (BC) 233 Ec20
Elk Grove USA (CA) 234 Dk26
El Khânka ET 177 Mf30
El Kharga ET 177 Mf33
Elkhart USA (IN) 246 Fh25
Elkhart USA (KS) 242 Ek27
Elkhart USA (TX) 243 Fc30
El-Khatouat MA 172 Kg29
El Khatt RIM 178 Ke34
El Khattara ET 177 Mg33
Elkhead Mts. USA 235 Eg25
El Khnâchich RMM 179 Kh35
Elkhorn CDN (MB) 238 Ek21
Elkhorn USA (WI) 246 Ff24
El Khroub DZ 174 Ld27
El Khufrah LAR 176 Mb33
Elkin USA (NC) 249 Fk27
Elkins USA (WV) 247 Ga26
Elk Island N.P. CDN 233 Ed19
Elk Lake CDN (ON) 246 Fk22
Elk Mtn. USA 237 Ef29
Elko CDN (BC) 233 Ec21
Elko USA (NV) 234 Ec25
El Koran ETH 199 Nc43
El Kouif DZ 174 Le28
Elk Point CDN (AB) 233 Ee19
Elk Point USA (SD) 241 Fb24
Elk River USA (ID) 234 Eb22
Elk River USA (MN) 241 Fd23
El Kseur DZ 174 Lc27
El-Ksiba MA 172 Kh29
Elk Springs USA (CO) 235 Ef25
Elkton USA (KY) 248 Fg27
Elkton USA (MD) 247 Gc26
Elkton USA (OR) 234 Dj24
El Kufrah Oasis LAR 176 Mb33
El Kuntillah ET 177 Mh31
Elkwe GH 193 Kj43
El Lâhûn ET 177 Mf31
Ellanuru IND (APH) 111 Ok39
Ella Valla AUS (WA) 140 Qh58
Ellaville USA (GA) 249 Fh29
Elléba Fonfou RN 186 Lc37
Ellef Ringnes Island CDN 225 Ed03
El Leh ETH 205 Mk44
Elléloyé TCH 188 Lk37
Ellendale AUS (WA) 138 Rc54
Ellendale USA (ND) 240 Fa23
Ellen, Mount USA 235 Ee26
Ellensburg USA (WA) 232 Dk22
Ellenville USA (NY) 247 Gc25
El Leon MEX (COH) 242 Ek31
Ellerbe USA (NC) 249 Ga28
Ellerslie Racecourse NZ 154 Th64
Ellès TN 174 Le28
Ellesmere Island CDN 225 Fd02
El Limón MEX (JLC) 253 Eh36
Ellington USA (MO) 243 Fe27
Elliot ZA 217 Md61
Elliotdale ZA 217 Me62
Elliot Heads AUS (QLD) 151 Sg58
Elliot Key USA 250 Fk33
Elliot Lake CDN (ON) 246 Fj22
Elliot, Mount AUS (QLD) 149 Sd55
Elliott AUS (NT) 139 Rg54
Ellis USA (ID) 235 Ec23
Ellis Park USA (KY) 248 Fg27
Ellisras ZA 213 Md57
Elliston AUS (SA) 152 Rh62
El Llano PA 257 Ga41
el Llobregat E 30 Lb49
El Loa RCH 284 Ge56
Ellon GB 19 Ks33
Ellora Caves IND 108 Oh35
Ellös S 14 Lm32
Ellsworth USA (KS) 240 Fa26
Ellsworth USA (MA) 247 Gf23
Ellsworth USA (NE) 240 Ej25
Ellsworth USA (WI) 241 Fd23
Ellsworth Land ANT 296 Fc33
Ellsworth Mountains 296 Fc34
El Lucero MEX (CHH) 237 Eg30
Ellwangen D 34 Ll42
Elm D 33 Lk38
Elma CDN (MB) 238 Fc21
El Maad DZ 174 Lc27
El Macao DOM 260 Gf36
Elmadağ TR 51 Mo51
Elma Dağı TR 51 Mn51
El Maestrat E 29 Ku50
El-Mahalla el-Kubra ET 177 Mf30
El Mahamid ET 177 Mg33
El Maïa DZ 173 Lb29
El Maitén RA (CB) 292 Ge67
El Maitén RCH 294 Gd69
Elma Labio DZ 174 Le28
El Malah DZ 173 Kk28
Elmalı TR 51 Mk54
El Mallaile ETH 199 Nb43
El Malpais Nat. Mon. USA 237 Eg28
El Mamouel RMM 185 Kj36
El Mâmoûn RMM 185 Kk36
El Ma'mour-Ighichârene RMM 185 Kj36
Elmancık Dağı TR 51 Mi50
El Manguito MEX (CHP) 255 Fd38
El Mannsour DZ 179 Kk32
El-Mansûra ET 177 Mf30
El Manteco YV 270 Gj42
El Manzano RCH 288 Ge63
El Marâgha ET 177 Mf32
El Maria PA 257 Fk41
El Marsa DZ 173 La27
El Matariyah ET 177 Mf30
El May TN 174 Lf29
Elm Creek CDN (MB) 238 Fb21
El Médano PE 284 Ge58
El Medo ETH 198 Na43
El Meghaïer DZ 174 Lc29
Elméki RN 186 Le37
El Melhes RIM 183 Kd36
El Melón RCH 288 Ge62
El-Ménia DZ 173 Lb30
El Merey YV 270 Gj41
El Mesellemiya SUD 190 Mg39
El Mezquite MEX (SLP) 253 Ek34
El Mezquite MEX (ZCT) 253 Ej34
El Mhaïjrât RIM 183 Kb36
El Miamo YV 270 Gk42
El Milia DZ 174 Ld27
Elmina GH 193 Kk43
El Mingo MEX (TB) 255 Fd36
El-Minia ET 177 Mf31
El Minshâh ET 177 Mf32
Elmira CDN (PE) 245 Gj22
Elmira USA (NY) 247 Gb24
El Mirador GCA 255 Ff37
El Mirador MEX (CHH) 237 Eg30
El Mirador MEX (JLC) 253 Eh35
El Mistolar RA (FO) 285 Gk58
El Moïnâne RIM 183 Ke36
El Molinillo E 29 Kk49
El Molino MEX (CHH) 237 Eg31
El Molino MEX (VC) 254 Fa35
El Montseny E 30 Lc49
El Moral E 29 Ks47
El Moral MEX (COH) 242 Ek31
Elmore AUS (VIC) 153 Sc64
Elmore CDN (SK) 238 Ek21
El Morrión MEX (CHH) 237 Eh31
El Morro CO 272 Fk47
El Morro Nat. Mon. USA 237 Ef28
El Morro = San Pedro de la Roca Castle C 259 Gc35
El Mraïti RMM 185 Kj36
El Mreïti RIM 179 Kg34
Elmshorn D 32 Lk37
El Munia ET 177 Mf33
El Muti'a ET 177 Mg31
El Mzereb RMM 179 Kg33
El Nakhl ET 177 Mg31
El Naranjo GCA 255 Fe37
El Naranjo MEX (NYT) 253 Eh34
El Naranjo MEX (SLP) 253 Fa34
El Nawâwra ET 177 Mf32
El Nbeïket el Ahouâch RIM 184 Kh37
Elne F 24 Lc48
El Negrito HN 256 Fg38
El Nido RP 122 Qk40
El Nihuil RA (MD) 288 Gf63
El'nja RUS 52 Mg18
El Novillo MEX (SO) 237 Ef31
El Nula YV 268 Ge42
El Oasis MEX (BC) 236 Ec30
El Oasis MEX (SO) 237 Ee31
Eloaua Island PNG 159 Se46
El-Obeid SUD 197 Mf39
El Obraje MEX (ZCT) 253 Ek34
Elogbatindi CAM 194 Lf44
El Ogla DZ 174 Ld29
El Ogla Gasses DZ 174 Ld28
Elogo RCB 195 Lh45
El Ojito MEX (DGO) 252 Eg32
Eloka CI 193 Kj43
El Olvido CO 273 Ge44
Elopia GR 48 Md52
Elorn F 22 Kq42
El Oro MEX (COH) 253 Ej32
Elorza YV 269 Gf42
El Oso YV 269 Gh43
El Ostional NIC 256 Fh40
El Ouadey TCH 187 Lk39
El Ouata DZ 173 Kk31
El Ouatia MA 172 Ke31
El Oued DZ 174 Ld29
Eloy USA (AZ) 237 Ee29
Eloy Alfaro EC 272 Fk46
El Pájaro MEX (CHH) 253 Eh32
El Palito YV 269 Gf40
El Palmar YV 269 Ge40
El Palmar YV 270 Gk41
El Palmar, P.N. RA 289 Ha61
El Palmito MEX (DGO) 253 Eh33
El Pangui EC 272 Ga47
El Pao YV 269 Gf41
El Pao YV 270 Gj41
El Papalote MEX (COH) 253 Ej32
El Paraíso BOL 280 Gk53
El Parral MEX (CHP) 255 Fd37
El Paso USA (AR) 243 Fd28
El Paso USA (TX) 237 Eg30
El Pedregal MEX (TB) 255 Fe37
El Pedroso E 28 Kp47
El Pensamiento BOL 280 Gk53
El Perú GCA 255 Fe37
El Perú YV 270 Gk42
El Pescadero MEX (BCS) 252 Ee34
Elphinestone CDN (MB) 238 Ek20
Elphinstone AUS (QLD) 149 Se56
El Pilar YV 270 Gj40
El Pilar de la Mola E 30 Lb52
El Pinal CO 268 Ge43
El Piñal YV 268 Ge42
El Pinar C 258 Fj34
El Pingo RA (ER) 289 Ha61
El Pipila MEX (DGO) 253 Eh33
El Piruli MEX (TM) 253 Fa34
El Planchón RCH 288 Ge63
El Plomo MEX (SO) 236 Ed30
El Pluma RA (SC) 294 Ge69
El Pobo de Dueñas E 29 Kt50
El Pocito BOL 280 Gj53
El Polvorín RA (SC) 294 Gg69
el Pont de Suert E 30 La48
El Portezuelo RA (LR) 288 Gg61
El Portón BOL 285 Gk55
El Porvenir MEX (SO) 236 Ee30
El Porvenir PA 257 Ga41
El Porvenir YV 269 Gf42
El Potosí, P.N. MEX 254 Fa35
El Potrero MEX (CHH) 237 Eh31
El Progreso GCA 255 Fe38
El Progreso GCA 255 Ff38
El Progreso HN 256 Fg38
El Progreso MEX (BC) 236 Ed31
El Puente BOL 285 Gj54
El Puente BOL 284 Gh56
El Puente del Arzobispo E 28 Kp49
El Puertecito MEX (COH) 253 Ej32
El Puerto de Santa María E 28 Ko46
El-Qahira ET 177 Mf30
El Qanâtir el Khayriya ET 177 Mf30
El Qantara el Sharqiya ET 177 Mg30
El Qasr ET 177 Me33
El Quebrachal RA (SA) 285 Gh58
El Quelite MEX (SL) 252 Eg34
El Questro AUS (WA) 138 Rd53
Elqui RCH 288 Ge60
El Quisco RCH 288 Ge62
El Qusayman ET 177 Mh30
El Quseir ET 177 Mh32
El Qûsiya ET 177 Mf32
El Rancho MEX 254 Ek37
El Rastro YV 269 Gg41
El Real de la Jara E 28 Ko47
El Real de San Vicente E 29 Kq50
El Rebaje MEX (NL) 253 Fa33
El Re'ia ET 177 Mg33
El Reno USA (OK) 243 Fb28
El Retamo RA (SL) 288 Gg62
El Rey, P.N. RA 285 Gh58
El Ridisiya Bahari ET 177 Mg33
El Rocío E 28 Ko47
El Roda ET 177 Mf32
El Rosario MEX (BC) 236 Ec30
El Rosario MEX (SL) 252 Eh34
Elrose CDN (SK) 233 Eg20
El Rubio E 28 Kq47
El Sabinal, P.N. MEX 253 Fa32
El Saff ET 177 Mf31
El Saiadin ET 177 Mh31
El Saladero MEX (VC) 254 Fb35
El Salado MEX (SL) 252 Eg33
El Salado RA (SC) 294 Gg70
El Salado RCH 288 Ge59
El Salitre MEX (CHH) 252 Eg31
El Salto MEX (DGO) 253 Eh34
El Salto RCH 292 Ge63
El Salvador MEX (ZCT) 253 Ek33
El Salvador RCH 288 Gf59
El Salvador 255 Ff39
El Santo C 259 Ga34
El Sargento MEX (BCS) 252 Ef33
Elsas CDN (ON) 239 Fj21
El Sasabe MEX (SO) 237 Ee30
El Saucejo E 28 Kp47
El Sauz MEX (CHH) 237 Eg31
El Sauzalito RA (CH) 285 Gk58
el Segre E 30 La49
El Seibo DOM 260 Gf36
El Semillero GCA 255 Fe38
Elsen Nur CHN 89 Pg28
Elsey N.P. AUS 139 Rg53
Elsfleth D 32 Lj37
El Shatt ET 177 Mg31
Elsherana AUS (NT) 139 Rg52
El Sibu Temple ET 177 Mg34
Elsie Hills AUS (QLD) 151 Sc58
El Soberbio RA (MI) 289 Hc59
El Socorro CO 269 Ge42
El Socorro MEX (BC) 236 Ec30
El Socorro YV 269 Gh41
El Sombrero RA (CB) 292 Gf68
El Sombrero YV 269 Gg41
El Sosneada RA (MD) 288 Gf63
Elst NL 32 Lf39
Elsterwerda D 33 Lo39
Elstow CDN (SK) 233 Eg20
El Subin GCA 255 Fe37
El Sueco MEX (CHH) 237 Eg31
El-Suwais = Suez ET 177 Mg31
El-Suwais ET 177 Mg31
El Tacobo BOL 285 Gj55
El Tajín MEX 254 Fb35
El Tala RA (SA) 288 Gh59
el Tamá, P.N. YV 268 Gd42
El Tambo CO 272 Gb44
El Tanque NIC 256 Fg39
El Tarf DZ 174 Le27
El Tebol RA (SF) 289 Gk62
El Tejar RA (BA) 289 Gk63
El Tenam Puente MEX 255 Fd37
El Tepuche MEX (SL) 252 Eg33
el Ter E 30 Lc48
El Thamad ET 177 Mh31
El Tichlit RIM 183 Kd37
El Tigre CO 268 Gc42
El Tigre MEX 255 Fe36
El Tigre YV 269 Gh41
El Tigrito YV 269 Gh41
El Tintal GCA 255 Fe37
El Tío RA (CD) 289 Gj61
Eltmann D 35 Ll41
El Toba RA 289 Gk60
El Tocuyo YV 269 Gf41
El Topo MEX (BC) 236 Ec29
El Tor ET 177 Mg31
El Tordillo RA (CB) 294 Gg68
El Toro E 30 Le51
El Transcantábrico E 27 Kr53
El Trece MEX (CHH) 237 Eh31
El Trencito RA 292 Ge67
El Trifinio ES/GCA/HN 255 Ff38
El Trigal RA (SA) 284 Gg58
El Triunfo EC 272 Ga47
El Triunfo MEX (TB) 255 Fe37
El Triunfo MEX 255 Fd38
El Troncal CO 268 Ge42
El Trune AUS (NSW) 151 Sd61
El Tuito MEX (JLC) 253 Eh35
El Tuparro, P.N. CO 269 Gf43
El Turbio RA (SC) 294 Gd71
Eltville D 34 Lj40
Eluru IND (APH) 109 Pa37
El 'Uteishan SUD 190 Mh38
Elva EST 16 Mg32
El Vacar E 28 Kq48
El Valle CO 268 Gb42
El Valle PA 257 Fk41
El Vapor MEX (CAM) 255 Fe36
Elvas P 28 Kn48
El Veladero, P.N. MEX 254 Fa37
Elven F 22 Ks43
El Venado CO 269 Gg44
el Vendrell E 30 Lb49
El Vergel MEX (CHH) 252 Eg32
Elverum N 12 Lm30
El Vigía YV 268 Ge41
El Villar de Arnedo E 27 Ks52
El Vinculo YV 269 Gf39
Elvira RA (BA) 289 Ha63
Elvire, Mount AUS 140 Qj56
El Viso E 28 Kq48
Elvita CO 269 Ge43
El Vivero YV 269 Gg42
Elvo AUS (QLD) 148 Sb57
El Volcán RCH 288 Ge62
El Wak EAK 205 Na44
El Wara EAK 205 Mk44
El Wâsitah ET 177 Mf31
Elwood USA (NE) 240 Fa25
Elx E 29 Ku48
Ely GB 21 La38
Ely USA (MN) 241 Fe22
Ely USA (NV) 234 Ec26
El Yagual YV 269 Gf42
El Yunque C 259 Gc35
El Yunque Rainforest USA 261 Gh36
Elze D 32 Lk38
El Zeitun ET 176 Mc31
El Zúlia CO 268 Gd42
El Zurdo RA (SC) 294 Ge71
Emae VU 162 Te54
Emajõgi EST 16 Mg32
Emali EAK 207 Mj47
Emam Abbas IR 72 Nc28
Emam Hasan IR 74 Nf31
Emam Saheb AFG 78 Oe27
Emam Taqi IR 73 Nk27
Emån S 15 Lq33
Emangusi ZA 217 Mg59
Emas, P.N. das BR 286 Hd55
Embalse Alicura RA 292 Ge66
Embalse Amaluza EC 272 Ga47
Embalse Boconó Tucupido YV 269 Gf41
Embalse Cabra Corral RA 284 Gh58
Embalse Camatagua YV 269 Gg41
Embalse Casa de Piedra RA 292 Gg65
Embalse Cerros Colorados RA 292 Gf65
Embalse Cogoti RCH 288 Ge61
Embalse de Aguilar de Campóo E 26 Kq52
Embalse de Alange E 28 Ko48
Embalse de Alarcón E 29 Ks49
Embalse de Alcántara E 28 Ko49
Embalse de Almendra E 26 Ko51
Embalse de Arbón E 26 Ko53
Embalse de Belesar E 26 Kn52
Embalse de Bembézar E 28 Kp47
Embalse de Buendía E 29 Ks50
Embalse de Cíjara E 28 Kq49
Embalse de Contreras E 29 Kt49
Embalse de El Cajon HN 255 Fg38
Embalse de El Grado E 30 La48
Embalse de Entrepeñas E 29 Ks50
Embalse de Gabriel y Galán E 28 Ko50
Embalse de García de Sola E 28 Kp49
Embalse de Giribaile E 29 Kr48
Embalse de Guadalcacín E 28 Kp46
Embalse de Guadalhorce E 28 Kq46
Embalse de Guri YV 269 Gj42
Embalse de Jándula E 29 Kr48
Embalse de la Serena E 28 Kp48
Embalse de la Sotonera E 27 Ku52
Embalse de las Portas E 26 Kn52
Embalse del Cenajo E 29 Kt48
Embalse del Chanza E 28 Kn47
Embalse del Ebro E 27 Kr53
Embalse del Guárico YV 269 Gg41
Embalse del Nihuil RA 288 Gf63
Embalse del Pintado E 28 Kp47
Embalse del Porma E 26 Kp52
Embalse del Rumblar E 29 Kr48
Embalse del Tercero RA 288 Gh62
Embalse de Mediano E 30 La48
Embalse de Mequinenza E 30 La49
Embalse de Negratín E 29 Ks47
Embalse de Orellana E 28 Kp48
Embalse de Portodemouros E 26 Km52
Embalse de Riaño E 26 Kp52
Embalse de Ricobayo E 26 Kp51
Embalse de Santa Teresa E 26 Kp50
Embalse de Sierra Boyera E 28 Kp48
Embalse de Sierra Brava E 28 Kp49
Embalse de Urrunaga E 27 Ks52
Embalse de Valdecañas E 28 Kp49
Embalse de Valdemojón E 28 Kq47
Embalse Ezequiel Ramos Mexía RA 292 Gf65
Embalse Florentino Ameghino RA 292 Gg67
Embalse la Paloma RCH 288 Ge61
Embalse Paso de las Piedras RA 293 Gk65
Embalse Peñol CO 268 Gc42
Embalse Piedra del Aguila RA 292 Ge66
Embalse Poechos PE 272 Fk48
Embalse Río Hondo RA 288 Gh59
Embalse Yacyretá Apipé PY/RA 289 Hb59
Embarcación RA (SA) 285 Gh57
Embarcadero MEX (CHP) 255 Fd38
Embarcadero MEX (OAX) 255 Fc37
Emb del Guadalmena E 29 Ks48
Embetsu J 99 Sa23
Embi KZ 58 Nd09
Embilipitiya CL 111 Pa43
Embira BR 279 Ge49
Emblem USA (WY) 235 Ef23
Embocada BOL 280 Gj53
Embondo RDC 200 Lk45
Emboscada BOL 279 Gh51
Embrun F 25 Lg46
Embu EAK 204 Mj46
Embundo ANG 208 Lj54
Embûte LV 17 Mb34
Emca RUS 11 Na14
Emciswení MW 210 Mg51
Emden D 32 Lh37
Emecik TR 49 Mh54
Emeishan CHN (SCH) 94 Qb31
Emeishan Sacred Mountains CHN 94 Qb31
Emel KZ 84 Pb22
Emel'janovskaja RUS 11 Na13
Emerald AUS (QLD) 149 Se57
Emerald Bank Gj24
Emerald Mound USA 243 Fe30
Emeriau Point AUS 138 Rb54
Emerson CDN (MB) 238 Fb21
Emesa SYR 64 Mj28
Emet TR 50 Mk51
Emeti PNG 159 Sb49
Emi Fezzane RN 181 Lh35
Emigrant USA (MT) 235 Ee23
Emi Koussi TCH 188 Lk36
Emilia RA (SF) 289 Gk61
Emiliano Zapata MEX (CHP) 255 Fe37
Emilia-Romagna I 40 Ll46
Emil Racovita MD 45 Mg42
Emi Lulu RN 181 Lf34
Emin CHN (XUZ) 85 Pb22
Eminee RI 158 Rk49
Eminence USA (MO) 243 Fe27
Emin He CHN 84 Pa22
Emini CAM 195 Lg44
Emin Pasha Gulf EAT 201 Mf47
Eminska Planina BG 47 Mh48
Emiralem TR 49 Mh52
Emirau PNG 159 Se46
Emirau Island PNG 159 Se46
Emirdağ TR 51 Mf52
Emir Dağları TR 62 Mf26
Emirgazi TR 51 Mo53
Emirler TR 51 Mn51
Emlichheim D 32 Lg38
Emmaboda S 15 Lq34
Emmaljunga S 15 Lo34
Emmaste EST 16 Mc32
Emmel AUS (QLD) 150 Sc58
Emmeloord NL 32 Lf38
Emmelshausen D 34 Lh40
Emmen NL 32 Lg38
Emmendingen D 34 Lh42
Emmerich D 32 Lg39
Emmetsburg USA (IA) 241 Fc24
Emmett USA (ID) 234 Eb24
Emmiganuru IND (APH) 108 Oj38
Emmonak USA (AK) 229 Bh14
Emory USA (TX) 243 Fc29
Emoulas RN 186 Ld38
Empada GNB 183 Kc40
Empalmé EC 272 Ga46
Empalme MEX (SO) 252 Ee32
Empangeni ZA 217 Mf60
Empedrado RA (CR) 289 Ha59
Empedrado RCH 292 Gd63
Empembe NAM 208 Lg54
Emperor Range PNG 160 Sh48
Empessós GR 48 Mb51
Empire USA (CO) 235 Eh26
Empoli I 40 Ll47
Emporia USA (KS) 241 Fb26
Emporia USA (VA) 249 Gb27
Emporium USA (PA) 247 Ga25
Empress Augusta Bay PNG 160 Sh49
Empress Mine ZW 214 Me55
Ems D 32 Lh38
Emsdetten D 32 Lh38
Ems-Jade-Kanal D 32 Lh37
Emu Hill AUS (WA) 144 Qk62
Emu Park AUS (QLD) 149 Sf57
Ena J 101 Rj28
Ena Lake CDN (SK) Ef16
Enånger S 13 Lr29
Enangiperi EAK 204 Mh46
Enarotali RI 131 Rj47
Ena-san Tunnel J 101 Rj28
Enawene-Nawe, T.I. BR 280 Ha52
Enbebess EAK 204 Mh45
Encantado BR (RS) 290 He60
Encarnación PY 289 Hc59
Encarnación de Díaz MEX (JLC) 254 Ej35
Encekler TR 50 Mj52
Enchi GH 193 Kj43
Encinal USA (TX) 253 Fa31
Encinitas USA (CA) 236 Eb29
Enciso E 27 Ks52
Encoje ANG 202 Lh49
Encón RA (SJ) 288 Gg62
Encontrados YV 268 Gd41
Encruzilhada BR (SC) 290 He59
Encruzilhada BR (BA) 283 Hk53
Encruzilhada BR (RS) 290 Hc60
Encruzilhada do Sul BR (RS) 290 Hd61
Encs H 39 Mb42
Enda CHN (TIB) 89 Pj30
Endagikot EAT 207 Mh50
Endako CDN (BC) 232 Dh18
Endalaghanet EAT 207 Mh48
Endasak EAT 207 Mh48
Endau EAK 205 Mk46
Endau EAK 205 Mk46
Endau Rompin N.P. MAL 117 Qb44
Ende RI 129 Ra50
Endeavor CDN (SK) 238 Ej19
Endeavour Strait AUS 146 Sb51
Endelave DK 14 Ll35
Endengue CAM 195 Lg44
Enderbury Atoll KIR 157 Ub19
Enderby CDN (BC) 232 Ea20
Enderbyland ANT 297 Na32
Endiang CDN (AB) 233 Ed20
Endibir ETH 198 Mj41
Endicott USA (NY) 247 Gb24
Endicott Mountains USA 229 Cd12
Endiké RCB 195 Lh46
Endimari BR 279 Gg50
End-o-Line RR Park & Mus. USA 241 Fc23
Endom CAM 195 Lg44
Eneabba AUS (WA) 144 Qh60
Energía RA (BA) 293 Ha65
Enerhodar UA 54 Mh22
Eneryda S 15 Lp34
Enez TR 50 Mg50
Enfida TN 174 Lf27
Enfield CDN (NS) 245 Gj23
Engadin CH 34 Ll44
Engaku-ji J 101 Rk28
Engaru J 99 Sb23
Engaruka Basin EAT 204 Mj47
Engassumet EAT 207 Mj48
Enge N 10 Le14
Engelberg CH 34 Lj44
Engelhard USA (NC) 249 Gc28
Engen D 34 Lj43
Engenheiro Beltrão BR (PR) 286 Hd57
Engenheiro Dolabela BR (MG) 287 Hh54
Engenheiro Navarro BR (MG) 287 Hj54
Enger D 32 Lj38
Engerneset N 12 Ln29
Enggano RI 124 Qb48
Engh CHN (NMZ) 91 Qk20
Engineer CDN (BC) 231 Dc16
Engineer Group PNG 160 Sf51
England GB 21 Ks38
England USA (AR) 243 Fe28
Engle USA (NM) 237 Eg29
Englee CDN Hb20
Englehart CDN (ON) 247 Ga22
Engle Passage GB 295 Ha72
English USA (IN) 248 Fg26
English Bay USA (AK) 229 Ce16
English Channel 22 Kr41
English Coast 296 Gb33
English Fort GH 193 Kk43
English Harbour East CDN (NF) 245 Hc22
English Harbour Town AG 261 Gk37
English Harbour West CDN (NF) 245 Hc22
English River CDN (ON) 239 Fe21
Engoobo ZA 217 Md61
Engravings RB 213 Md58
Engre Rios = Malema MOC 211 Mj53
Engstingen D 34 Lk42
Enguera E 29 Ku48
Enguidanos E 29 Kt49
Engure LV 17 Md33
Engures ezers LV 17 Md33

Enid – Faille de Nyakazu

Enid USA (OK) 242 Fb27
Enisala RO 45 Mj46
Enisej RUS 58 Pb05
Enisejsk RUS 58 Pc07
Enisejskij zaliv RUS 58 Od04
Eniwa J 99 Sa24
Eniwetok Atoll MH 156 Ta16
Enjil MA 173 Kh29
Enkatsiana RCB 202 Lh46
Enkhuizen NL 32 Lf38
Enklinge FIN 13 Ma30
Enkodak FIN 11 Mb11
Enköping S 13 Ls31
Enna I 42 Lp53
En Nahud SUD 197 Me39
Ennedi TCH 189 Mb37
Enneri Bardagué TCH 181 Lj35
Enneri Ké TCH 181 Lj36
Enneri Mi TCH 181 Lj35
Enneri Mondragué TCH 181 Lj35
Enneri Tegaham TCH 181 Lj36
Enneri Yébiqué TCH 181 Lj34
Engonia AUS (NSW) 151 Sc60
Enniberg DK
Ennigerloh D 32 Lj39
Ennis IRL 20 Km38
Ennis USA (MT) 235 Ee23
Ennis USA (TX) 243 Fb29
Enniscorthy IRL 20 Ko38
Enniskerry IRL 20 Ko37
Enniskillen GB 18 Kn36
Ennistimon IRL 20 Kl38
Enns A 35 Lp43
Enns A 35 Lp42
Enoch USA (UT) 235 Ed27
Enonkoski FIN 16 Mj28
Enontekiö FIN 11 Mb11
Enping CHN (GDG) 96 Qg34
Enrekang RI 127 Qk47
Enrile RP 121 Ra37
Enriquillo DOM 260 Ge37
Enschede NL 32 Lg38
Ensenada MEX (BC) 236 Eb30
Ensenada de Calabozo YV 268 Ge40
Ensenada de Garachiné PA 257 Ga41
Ensenada de la Broa C 258 Fj34
Ensenada de Mompiche EC 272 Fk45
Ensenada de Tumaco CO 272 Ga45
Ensenada Los Muertos MEX (BCS) 252 Ef34
Ensenada Pabellones MEX 252 Eg33
Enshi CHN (HUB) 95 Qe30
Enshu-nada J 101 Rj28
Ensisheim F 23 Lh43
Entebbe EAU 204 Mg45
Entenbühl D 35 Ln41
Enterprise USA (AL) 249 Fh30
Enterprise USA (OR) 234 Eb23
Enterprise USA (UT) 234 Ed27
Entiako River CDN 232 Dh19
En Tmadé RIM 183 Ke36
Entrance CDN (AB) 233 Eb19
Entraygues-sur-Truyère F 24 Lc46
Entre-Ijuís BR (RS) 290 Hc60
Entre Lagos RCH 292 Gd66
Entre-os-Rios P 26 Km51
Entre Rios BOL 285 Gh56
Entre Rios BR (BA) 283 Ja51
Entre Rios BR (PA) 275 Hc48
Entre Rios RA 267 Ha25
Entre Rios de Minas BR (MG) 287 Hh56
Entrevaux F 25 Lg47
Entrocamento BR (MA) 276 Hg48
Entrocamento BR (MA) 276 Hh49
Entroncamento BR (MA) 276 Hh47
Entronque San Roberto MEX (NL) 253 Ek33
Entrop RI 131 Sa47
Entumeni ZA 217 Mf60
Entwistle CDN (AB) 233 Ec19
Enugu WAN 194 Ld42
Enugu Ezike WAN 194 Le42
Enumclaw USA (WA) 232 Dj22
Envermeu F 23 Lb41
Envigado CO 268 Gc42
Enviken S 13 Lq30
Envira BR (AM) 279 Ge49
Envira BR 279 Ge50
Enxudé GNB 183 Kc40
Enyamba RDC 203 Mc47
Enyellé RCB 200 Lk44
Enz D 34 Lj42
Enza I 40 Ll46
Epako NAM 212 Lj56
Epe NL 32 Lg38
Epe WAN 194 Lb42
Epéna RCB 195 Lj45
Epenarra AUS (NT) 139 Rh56
Épernay F 23 Ld41
Ephesos TR 49 Mh53
Ephrain USA (UT) 235 Ee26
Ephrata USA (WA) 232 Ea22
Epi RDC 201 Md44
Epi RDC 201 Me44
Epi VU 162 Te54
Epidavros GR 48 Md53
Épila E 27 Kt51
Épinal F 23 Lg42
Epini RDC 201 Me45
Epiphania SYR 64 Mj28
Episkopí GR 49 Me55
Epizana BOL 284 Gh54
Epokenkoso RDC 202 Lj47
Epoma RCB 195 Lh45
Eppingen D 34 Lj41
Epping Forest AUS (QLD) 149 Sd57
Epsom GB 21 Ku39
Eptahóri GR 46 Mb50
Epukiro NAM 212 Lk56
Epukiro NAM 213 Ma56
Epulu RDC 201 Me45
Epupa Falls NAM 212 Lg54
Epuyén RA (CB) 292 Ge67
Equatorial Channel MV 110 Og46
Equatorial Guinea 167 La09
Equator Monument RI 126 Qe45
Equator Village MV 110 Og46
Équeurdreville-Hainneville F 22 Kt41
Eraballi IND (KTK) 111 Oj39
Eraclea Minoa I 42 Lo53
Erahtur RUS 53 Na18
Eralé BR (PA) 275 Hd45
Eram PNG 159 Sb48
Eran Bay RP 122 Qj41
Erátira GR 46 Mb50
Erave PNG 159 Sb49
Erave River PNG 159 Sb49
Eravikulam N.P. IND 111 Oj41
Eravur CL 111 Pa43
Erawan Cave THA 114 Qb37
Erawan N.P. THA 114 Pk38
Erba I 40 Lk45
Erbaa TR 62 Mj25
Erbach D 34 Lj41
Erbach D 34 Lk42
Erba Lugang CHN (AHU) 102 Qk30
Erbent TM 71 Nk26
Erbeskopf D 34 Lh41
Erçek TR 63 Nb26
Erçek Gölü TR 63 Nb26
Ercilla RCH 292 Gd65
Erciş TR 63 Nb26
Erciyes Dağı TR 51 Mq52
Ercolano I 42 Lp50
Erd H 39 Lt43
Erdaobaihe CHN (JLN) 100 Re24
Erddig GB 21 Ks37
Erdeentsav MNG 91 Qh21
Erdek TR 50 Mh50
Erdemli TR 62 Mh27
Erdenet MNG 90 Pk21
Erdenet MNG 90 Qc21
Erdenetsogt MNG 90 Qa22
Erdene Zuu Monastery MNG 90 Qb22
Erdeven F 22 Kr43
Erdi TCH 189 Mb36
Erding D 35 Lm42
Erdre F 22 Kt43
Erdut HR 44 Lu45
Eré TCH 187 Lh41
Erebus, Mount 297 Tc34
Erech IRQ 65 Nc30
Erechim BR (RS) 290 Hd59
Ereğli TR 51 Mm49
Ereğli TR 51 Mp53
Ereğli Ovası TR 51 Mo53
Eréké RCA 195 Lj42
Eremiivka UA 45 Ml44
Eremitu RO 45 Me44
Eréndira MEX (BC) 236 Eb30
Eréndira MEX (MHC) 254 Ek36
Erenhot CHN (NMZ) 93 Qg24
Erenler Dağlari TR 51 Mn53
Erentepe TR 63 Na26
Erer ETH 198 Nb42
Ereré BR (CE) 277 Ja48
Erer Gota ETH 198 Na41
Eressós GR 49 Mf51
Erfenis Dam ZA 217 Md60
Erfoud MA 173 Kh30
Erft D 32 Lg40
Erfurt D 33 Lm40
Erg Aït el Khâoua DZ/RMM 179 La35
Ergani TR 63 Mk26
Erg Atouila RMM 179 Kh35
Erg Azennezal DZ 179 La34
Erg Bourarhet DZ 174 Le32
Erg Chech DZ 179 Kj33
Erg Chech RIM 179 Kg34
Erg d'Admer DZ 180 Le33
Erg du Djourab TCH 187 Lk37
Erg du Ténéré RN 187 Lf37
Ergel MNG 93 Qe24
Erg el Atchane DZ 173 Kk31
Erg el Ouar DZ 174 Ld31
Ergene Çay TR 50 Mh49
Ergenetsogt MNG 92 Qd24
Ergeni RUS 55 Nc22
Erg er Raoui DZ 173 Kj31
Erg labes DZ 173 Kj32
Erg Iguidi DZ 172 Kg32
Erg I-n-Sâkâne RMM 179 Kk35
Erg in Techerène RMM 179 Kk35
Erg Issaouane DZ 174 Ld32
Erg Kilian DZ 180 Le34
Ergli LV 17 Mf34
Erg Mehedjibat DZ 180 Lb33
Erg n'Ataram DZ 180 La34
Ergolding D 35 Ln42
Ergoldsbach D 35 Ln42
Erg Tassedjefit DZ 180 Lb33
Erg Thihodaïne DZ 180 Ld33
Erg Tidjidit DZ 179 La34
Erg Tifernine DZ 180 Ld32
Ergun He CHN/RUS 91 Ra20
Ergun Youqi CHN (NMZ) 91 Ra20
Ergun Zuoqi CHN (NMZ) 91 Ra20
Er Hai CHN 113 Qa33
Erheib SUD 191 Mj37
Eri WAN 186 Lb41
Eriba SUD 191 Mj38
Eric CDN (QC) 244 Gh20
Érice I 42 Ln52
Ericeira P 28 Kl48
Erickson CDN (MB) 238 Fa20
Eridu IRQ 65 Nd30
Erie USA (PA) 247 Fk24
Erigât RMM 184 Kh36
Erik Eriksenstretet N 11 Mc06
Erikli TR 50 Mg50
Erikoussa GR 48 Lu51
Eriksdale CDN (MB) 238 Fa20
Erikub Atoll MH 157 Tb17
Erimitage Père de Foucauld DZ 180 Lc34
Erimo J 99 Sb24
Erimo-misaki J 99 Sb25
Erimo Seamount J 99 Sc25
Erin USA (TN) 248 Fg27
Eringsboda S 15 Lq34
Eriskay GB 18 Kn33
Erithrés GR 48 Md52
Eritrea ER 167 Mb08
Erka N 12 Lj28
Erkelenz D 32 Lg39
Erkhet MNG 90 Qb21
Erkhet Uul MNG 90 Qa22
Erkilet TR 51 Mq52
Erkner D 33 Lo38
Erkovcy RUS 98 Re20
Erkowit SUD 191 Mj37
Erla E 27 Ku52
Erlangen D 35 Lm41
Erldunda AUS (NT) 142 Rg58
Erlistoun AUS (WA) 144 Rb60
Ermelo ZA 217 Mf59
Ermenek TR 62 Mg27
Ermesinde P 26 Km51
Ermil Post SUD 197 Md39
Ermióni GR 48 Md53
Ermiš RUS 53 Nb18
Ermoúpoli GR 49 Me53
Ernakulam IND (KER) 110 Oj42
Erne IRL/GB 18 Km36
Ernée F 22 Ku42
Ernesto Alves BR (RS) 290 Hc60
Ernest Sound USA 231 Dd18
Erode IND (TNU) 111 Oj41
Eromanga AUS (QLD) 150 Sb59
Eromanga Island VU 162 Te55
Erongari cuaro MEX (MHC) 254 Ek36
Erongo NAM 212 Lh56
Erongo NAM 212 Lh57
Erongoberge NAM 212 Lh56
Eroro PNG 159 Se50
Erpengdianzi CHN (LNG) 100 Rc25
Erquy F 22 Ks42
Errabiddy AUS (WA) 140 Qj58
Erragondapalem IND (APH) 109 Ok37
Erraguntla IND (APH) 111 Ok39
Errego MOC 211 Mj54
Errigal IRL 18 Km35
Erris Head IRL 18 Kk36
Erro E 27 Kt52
Er Rogel SUD 190 Mh37
Errol USA (NH) 247 Ge23
Er Roseires SUD 197 Mh40
Ersaf MA 173 Kj28
Ersekë AL 46 Ma50
Erši RUS 52 Mh18
Erskine USA (MN) 241 Fb22
Erstein F 23 Lh42
Erta Ale ETH 191 Na40
Ertai CHN (XUZ) 85 Pf22
Ërtil' RUS 53 Na20
Ertis 58 Pa08
Ertix He CHN 85 Pd22
Ertuğrul TR 50 Mh51
Ertuğrulköy TR 51 Mm51
Erufa WAN 186 Lc41
Erundu NAM 212 Lj56
Eruwa WAN 194 Lb42
Ervália BR (MG) 287 Hj56
Ervay USA (WY) 235 Eg24
Ervenik HR 41 Lq46
Ervy-le-Châtel F 23 Ld42
Erwang RI 130 Re46
Erwin USA (TN) 249 Fj27
Erwitte D 32 Lj39
Erythrai TR 49 Mg52
Erzen AL 46 Lu49
Erzgebirge D/CZ 35 Ln40
Erzin RUS (TUV) 85 Ph20
Erzincan TR 63 Mk26
Erzurum TR 63 Na26
Eržvilkas LT 17 Mc35
Esa'ala PNG 160 Sf50
Esan J 99 Sa25
Esashi J 99 Sa25
Esashi J 99 Sb23
Eşatlar TR 50 Mk51
Esbjerg DK 14 Lj35
Esbo = Espoo FIN 16 Me30
Escada BR (PE) 283 Jc50
Escalada E 27 Kr52
Escalante RP 123 Rb40
Escalante RP 123 Rc41
Escalante USA (UT) 237 Ee27
Escalante USA 237 Ee27
Escalante Canyons USA 237 Ee27
Escalante Desert USA 235 Ed27
Escalaplano I 31 Lk51
Escalerilla RCH 284 Gf56
Escalona E 29 Kq50
Escalos de Cima P 28 Kn49
Escanaba USA (MI) 246 Fg23
Escanaba USA 241 Fg22
Escároz E 27 Kt52
Eschede D 33 Ll38
Eschenburg D 32 Lj40
Esch-s-Alzette L 23 Lf41
Eschscholtz Bay USA 229 Bk12
Esch-s-Sûre L 23 Lf41
Eschwege D 32 Ll39
Eschweiler D 32 Lg40
Escola BOL 284 Gg54
Escondido MEX 255 Ff36
Escondido NIC 256 Fh39
Escondido USA (CA) 236 Eb29
Escondido, T.I. BR 280 Ha50
Escott AUS (QLD) 148 Rk54
Escoumins CDN (QC) 244 Gf21
Escravos WAN 194 Ld43
Escudero ANT (RCH) 296 Ha30
Escuinapa MEX (SL) 252 Eh34
Escuintla GCA 255 Fe38
Escuintla MEX (CHP) 255 Fd38
Escuminac CDN (NB) 245 Gh22
Escus BG 47 Me47
Ese RDC 201 Md43
Eséka CAM 195 Lf44
Eseli PNG 159 Se49
Eşen TR 49 Mk54
Esenada RCH 292 Gd66
Esens D 32 Lh37
Esenyurt TR 62 Me25
Esfahan IR 72 Nf29
Esfand Abad IR 72 Ng30
Esfand Abad IR 72 Ng30
Esfarayan IR 73 Nj27
Esfashad IR 73 Nk29
Esfolado BR 276 Hh49
Eshan CHN (YUN) 113 Qb33
Esha Ness GB 19 Kt30
Esha No 6 RB 213 Mb55
Eshimba RDC 203 Mc48
Eshkamesh AFG 78 Oe27
Eshkashem AFG 79 Of27
Eshowe ZA 217 Mf60
Eshq Abad IR 73 Nk27
Eshtehard IR 72 Nf28
Esiama GH 193 Kj43
Esigodini ZW 214 Me56
Esik KZ 77 Oj24
Esikuma GH 193 Kk43
Esino I 41 Lo47
Esira RM 220 Nd58
Esk AUS 151 Sg59
Eskdale AUS (VIC) 153 Sd64
Eskel Abad IR 75 Oa31
Esker CDN (NF) 244 Gg19
Eskifjörður IS 10 Kd13
Eski Gediz TR 50 Mk51
Eski Gümüş TR 51 Mp53
Eskil TR 51 Mo52
Eskilstuna S 13 Lr31
Eski-Nookat KS 77 Og25
Eskipazar TR 51 Mn50
Eskişehir TR 51 Ml51
Eskridge USA (KS) 241 Fb26
Eslam Abad IR 72 Nd28
Eslam Qal'eh AFG 78 Oa28
Eslamsham IR 72 Nf28
Eslohe D 32 Lj39
Eslöv S 15 Lo35
Eşme TR 50 Mj52
Esmekaya TR 51 Mo52
Esmeralda AUS (QLD) 148 Sb55
Esmeralda BOL 279 Gg52
Esmeralda BR (RS) 290 He60
Esmeralda C 259 Ga35
Esmeralda YV 270 Gh44
Esmeraldas EC 272 Ga45
Esmeraldas EC 272 Ga45
Es Mercadal E 30 Le50
Esnagami Lake CDN 239 Fg20
Esnagi Lake CDN 239 Fh21
Espakeh IR 75 Oa32
Espalion F 25 Lc46
Espanola CDN (ON) 246 Fk22
Espanola USA (NM) 237 Eg28
Espargos CV 182 Jj37
Espartillar RA (BA) 293 Gj64
Espeland N 12 Lf30
Espenberg USA (AK) 229 Bj12
Esperança BR (MS) 286 Hc56
Esperança BR (PA) 275 Hd46
Esperança BR (PB) 277 Jc49
Esperance AUS (WA) 144 Ra62
Esperance Bay AUS 144 Ra62
Esperance Highway AUS 144 Ra62
Esperantina BR (PI) 277 Hj47
Esperantinópolis BR (MA) 276 Hh48
Esperanza MEX (SO) 252 Ef32
Esperanza PE 279 Ge50
Esperanza RA (MI) 289 Hc59
Esperanza RA (SC) 294 Ge71
Esperanza RA (SF) 289 Gk61
Esperanza RP 123 Rc40
Esperanza RP 123 Rc41
Esperanza ANT (RA) 296 Ha31
Espiel E 28 Kp48
Espigão do Oeste BR (RO) 280 Gk51
Espigão Mestre BR 282 Hh52
Espina, l' E 30 La50
Espinal BOL 285 Ha54
Espinal CO 268 Gc43
Espinama E 26 Kq53
Espinazo MEX (NL) 253 Ek32
Espinero YV 270 Gj42
Espinhal P 26 Km50
Espinheira ANG 208 Lg54
Espinho P 26 Km51
Espinillo RA (FO) 285 Ha58
Espino YV 269 Gh41
Espinosa BR (MG) 282 Hj53
Espinosa de los Monteros E 27 Kr53
Espírito Santo BR 265 Hd22
Espírito Santo do Turvo BR (SP) 286 Hf57
Espírito São do Pinhal BR (SP) 287 Hg57
Espiritu RP 121 Ra37
Espiritu Santo VU 162 Td53
Espita MEX (YT) 255 Ff35
Es Pla E 30 Ld51
Esplanada BR (BA) 283 Jb51
Espoo = Esbo FIN 16 Me30
Esposende P 26 Km51
Espumoso BR (RS) 290 Hd60
Espungabera MOC 214 Mg56
Esqueda MEX (SO) 237 Ef30
Esquel RA (CB) 292 Ge67
Esquina RA (CR) 289 Ha60
Esquipulas GCA 255 Ff38
Esquipulas NIC 256 Fh39
Esquiú RA (CA) 288 Gh60
Eşrefoğlu Camii TR 51 Mm53
Es Sabah LAR 181 Lh32
Es Salihiya ET 177 Mg30
Essaouira MA 172 Kf30
Essé CAM 195 Lf43
Essej RUS 58 Qa05
Essen B 23 Le39
Essen D 32 Lh39
Essendon, Mount AUS 140 Ra58
Essentuki RUS 70 Nb23
Essequibo GUY 270 Ha43
Essex USA (CA) 236 Ec28
Essexville USA (MI) 246 Fj24
Esslingen D 34 Lk42
Essoûk RMM 185 La36
Essoyes F 23 Le42
Es Suki SUD 190 Mg40
Estaçao Catur MOC 211 Mh52
Estação de Narbona ROU 289 Ha62
Estação Ecológica Caracaraí BR 274 Gk45
Estação Ecológica Cuniã BR 280 Gj50
Estação Ecológica da Serra das Araras BR 281 Hb53
Estação Ecológica de Niquiá BR 274 Gk45
Estação Ecológica do Jari BR 275 Hd46
Estação Ecológica Ilha de Taiamã BR 281 Hb54
Estação Ecológica Ilhas Maracá e Jipióca BR 271 He44
Estação Ecológica Iquê-Juruena BR 280 Ha52
Estação Ecológica Mamirauá BR 274 Gh47
Estação Ecológica Maracá BR 270 Ha44
Estação Ecológica Rio Acre BR 279 Ge51
Estaca Zero BR (PI) 277 Hj48
Estación Baquéira-Beret E 30 La48
Estación biológica Charles Darwin EC 272 Fe45
Estación Calles MEX (TM) 253 Fa34
Estación Camacho MEX (ZCT) 253 Ej33
Estación Cerler E 30 La48
Estación Coyotes MEX (DGO) 253 Eh34
Estación de Candanchú E 27 Ku52
Estación del Formigal E 27 Ku52
Estación Dimas MEX (SL) 252 Eg34
Estación La Colorada MEX (ZCT) 253 Ej34
Estación la Molina E 30 Lb48
Estación Madero MEX (COH) 253 Ej33
Estación Masella E 30 Lb48
Estación Micos MEX (SLP) 253 Fa34
Estación Ordino-Arcalís AND 30 Lb48
Estación Pintados RCH 284 Gf56
Estación Sierra Nevada E 29 Kr47
Estado de Guerrero, P.N. MEX 254 Fa37
Estahban IR 74 Nh31
Estaing F 25 Lc46
Estambul BOL 279 Gg53
Estância BR (SE) 283 Jb51
Estancia USA (NM) 237 Eg28
Estancia Avanzada PY 285 Hb58
Estancia Caracol PY 285 Ha57
Estancia Carmen RA (TF) 294 Gf73
Estancia Cerrito Jara PY 285 Ha55
EstanciaCerro Guido RCH 294 Gd71
Estancia Conchi RCH 284 Gf57
Estancia Curupayty PY 285 Ha57
Estancia Helaingfors RA (SC) 294 Gd70
Estancia Invierno RCH 294 Ge72
Estancia La Patria PY 285 Gk56
Estancia La Victoria PY 285 Ha57
Estancia Lomas PY 285 Ha58
Estancia los Lapachos PY 285 Ha57
Estancia L.Unión RA (SC) 294 Gd71
Estancia María Luisa RA (TF) 294 Gg73
Estancia Marina RA (TF) 294 Gf73
Estancia Noric PY 285 Ha56
Estancia Pan de Azucár PE 284 Gf58
Estancia Paragro PY 285 Ha56
Estancia Paredes PY 285 Ha58
Estancia Policarpo RA (TF) 295 Gh73
Estancia Rincón Grande RA (SC) 294 Ge71
Estancia Rocallosa RCH 294 Ge72
Estancia San Antonio PY 285 Ha57
Estancia San Carlos PY 286 Hc57
Estancia San Felipe PY 285 Hb57
Estancia San José PY 285 Ha57
Estancia San Juan PY 286 Hc57
Estancia San Pablo RA (TF) 294 Gg73
Estancia Santa Teresa PY 285 Ha56
Estancia Trementina PY 285 Hb57
Estancia Varillas PE 284 Gf58
Estandarte BR (MA) 276 Hh46
Estanislao del Campo RA (FO) 285 Gk58
Estanque de León MEX (COH) 253 Ej32
Estapilla MEX (COL) 254 Ej36
Estaquinha MOC 214 Mh55
Estarreja P 26 Km50
Estcourt ZA 217 Me60
Estelí NIC 256 Fg39
Estella E 27 Ks52
Estepa E 28 Kq47
Este, P.N. del DOM 260 Gf36
Estepona E 28 Kp46
Ester USA (AK) 229 Cg13
Estercuel E 29 Ku50
Ester de Boca EC 272 Fk47
Esterhazy CDN (SK) 238 Ej20
Esterházy H 38 Lr43
Esternay F 23 Ld42
Estero Agiabampo MEX 252 Ef32
Esteros del Iberá RA 289 Hb60
Esterri d'Àneu E 30 Lb48
Estevan CDN (SK) 238 Ej21
Estevan Group CDN 232 Df19
Esther Island USA 229 Cf15
Estherville USA (IA) 241 Fc24
Estill USA (SC) 249 Fk29
Estima MOC 210 Mg53
Estique PE 284 Ge54
Estirão do Equador BR (AM) 273 Ge48
Estirão do Robojo BR (AM) 279 Gd49
Estissac F 23 Ld42
Estiva BR 276 Hh49
Estivadinho, T.I. BR 280 Ha53
Estiva do Campo BR (MA) 276 Hh49
Estlin CDN (SK) 233 Eh20
Eston CDN (SK) 233 Ef20
Estonia EST 16 Me32
Estoril P 28 Kl48
Estrecho de Le Maire RA 295 Gh73
Estrecho de Yucatán 258 Fh35
Estrecho Nelson RCH 294 Gc71
Estrechos de la Florida 251 Fk34
Estreito BR (MA) 276 Hg49
Estrela da Paz, T.I. BR 273 Gg47
Estremadura P 28 Kl48
Estremoz P 28 Kn48
Estuario de Virrita PE 272 Fk48
Esztergom H 39 Lt43
Etadunna AUS (SA) 143 Rk60
Etah IND (UPH) 107 Ok32
Étain F 23 Lf41
Etaka NAM 208 Lh55
Étampes F 23 Lc42
Étang de Bages et de Sigean F 25 Ld47
Étang de Berre F 25 Lf47
Étang de Biscarrosse et de Parentis F 24 Kt46
Étang de Cazaux et de Sanguinet F 24 Kt46
Étang de Vaccarès F 25 Le47
Étaples F 23 Lb40
Etawah IND (RJT) 106 Oj33
Etawah IND (UPH) 107 Ok32
Etchojoa MEX (SO) 252 Ef32
Etembue GQ 194 Le45
Etemba Cave NAM 212 Lh56
Ethelbert CDN (MB) 238 Ek20
Ethel Creek AUS (WA) 140 Ra57
Etheldale AUS (QLD) 148 Sb55
Ethel Lake CDN 231 Db14
Ethels wreck AUS 152 Rj63
Ethiopia ETH 167 Mb09
Ethiopian Highlands ETH 198 Mj40
Etili TR 50 Mg51
Etivluk River USA 229 Cb11
Etjo NAM 212 Lj56
Etna I 42 Lp53
Etne N 12 Lf31
Étoile SY 219 Ng48
Etolikó GR 48 Mb52
Etolin Island USA 231 Dd17
Etolin Point USA 228 Ca16
Etolin Strait USA 228 Bh15
Etorohaberge NAM 208 Lg54
Etosha N.P. NAM 212 Lh55
Etosha Pan NAM 212 Lj55
Etou CAM 195 Lg44
Etoumbi RCB 195 Lh45
Etowah USA (TN) 249 Fh28
Étrépagny F 23 Lb41
Étretat F 22 La41
Etropole BG 46 Md48
Etropolski manastir BG 47 Me48
Etsch = Ädige I 40 Ll44
Ettelbruck L 23 Lg41
Ettenheim D 34 Lh42
Etten-Leur NL 32 Le39
Et-Tleta-de-Oued-Laou MA 173 Kh28
Ettlingen D 34 Lj42
Et-Tnine MA 172 Kf30
Ettumanur IND (KER) 110 Oj42
Etumba RDC 201 Mc46
Etumba RDC 203 Ma47
Eturnagaram IND (APH) 109 Pa36
Etzikom Coulée CDN 233 Ee21
Eu F 23 Lb40
Eua Island TO 164 Bc56
Euca BR (AP) 271 He44
Eucaliptus BOL 284 Gg54
Eucla AUS (WA) 145 Re61
Eucla Basin AUS 145 Rc62
Euclid USA (OH) 246 Fk25
Euclides da Cunha BR (BA) 283 Ja51
Euclides da Cunha Paulista BR (SP) 286 Hd57
Eudora USA (AR) 243 Fe29
Eudunda AUS (SA) 152 Rk63
Eufaula USA (AL) 249 Fh30
Eufaula USA (OK) 243 Fc28
Eufaula Lake USA 243 Fc28
Eufaula N.W.R. USA 249 Fh29
Eufrasio Loza RA (CD) 288 Gj60
Eufrazijeva bazilika HR 41 Lo45
Eugene USA (OR) 234 Dj23
Eugowra AUS (NSW) 153 Se62
Eulo AUS (QLD) 151 Sc60
Eulonia USA (GA) 249 Fk30
Eumara Springs AUS (QLD) 149 Sd55
Eumungerie AUS (NSW) 151 Se61
Eunápolis BR (BA) 287 Ja54
Eungella AUS (QLD) 149 Se56
Eungella N.P. AUS 149 Se56
Eunice USA (LA) 243 Fd30
Eunice USA (NM) 237 Ej29
Eupen B 23 Lg40
Euphrates IRQ 60 Na12
Eupora USA (MS) 243 Ff29
Eura FIN 16 Mc29
Eurady AUS (WA) 140 Qh59
Eurajoki FIN 16 Mb29
Eureka USA (CA) 234 Dh25
Eureka USA (KS) 243 Fb27
Eureka USA (MT) 233 Ec21
Eureka USA (NV) 234 Ec26
Eureka USA (SD) 240 Fa23
Eureka USA (UT) 235 Ed26
Eureka Springs USA (AR) 243 Fd27
Eurimbula N.P. AUS 151 Sf58
Euromba AUS (QLD) 151 Se58
Europa Park D 34 Lh42
Europe
Europoort NL 32 Ld39
Europos parkas LT 17 Mf36
Eurora AUS (VIC) 153 Sc64
Euro Speedway D 33 Lo39
Euskirchen D 32 Lg40
Euston AUS (NSW) 153 Sb63
Eutaw USA (AL) 248 Fg29
Euthini MW 210 Mg51
Eutin D 33 Ll36
Eutsuk Lake CDN 232 Dg19
Eva Downs AUS (NT) 139 Rh55
Evakkokeskus FIN 11 Md14
Evale ANG 208 Lh54
Evandale CDN (NB) 245 Gg23
Evangelístria GR 49 Mf53
Evanger N 12 Lg30
Evans Ice Stream 296 Ga34
Evans Strait CDN 225 Fd06
Evanston USA (IL) 246 Fg24
Evanston USA (WY) 235 Ee25
Evansville USA (IN) 248 Fg27
Evare, T.I. BR 273 Gf47
Evartra RM 220 Nd58
Evaton ZA 217 Md59
Evaux-les-Bains F 25 Lc44
Evaz IR 74 Ng32
Evciler TR 50 Mg51
Évdilos GR 49 Mg53
Evenki Autonomous District RUS 58 Pc05
Evensville USA (WY) 235 Eg24
Everard Junction AUS (WA) 141 Rc58
Everard Park AUS (SA) 142 Rg59
Everard Ranges AUS 142 Rg59
Everest, Mount NEP/CHN 88 Pd31
Everett USA (WA) 232 Dj22
Evergem B 23 Ld39
Everglades City USA (FL) 250 Fk33
Everglades National Park USA 250 Fk33
Evergreen USA (AL) 248 Fg30
Evergreen USA (MN) 241 Fc22
Evergreen USA (MT) 233 Ec21
Evertsberg S 13 Lo29
Evesham AUS (QLD) 148 Sb57
Evesham GB 21 Kt38
Évia GR 48 Md52
Évia GR 48 Me52
Évian-les-Bains F 25 Lg44
Evijärvi FIN 11 Mb14
Evinayong GQ 195 Lf45
Evisa F 31 Lj48
Evje N 12 Lh32
Evksinograd BG 47 Mh47
Evlanovo RUS 53 Mj19
Evodoula CAM 195 Lf43
Ev Oghli IR 72 Nc26
Evoikós Kólpos GR 48 Md52
Evolène CH 34 Lh44
Évora P 28 Kn48
Évoramonte P 28 Kn48
Évora Romana P 28 Kn48
Évoron RUS 98 Rj20
Évreux F 22 Lb41
Évron F 22 Ku42
Évros GR 47 Mg49
Evrótas GR 48 Mc54
Évry F 23 Lc42
Ewan USA (WA) 232 Eb22
Ewango WAN 194 Le42
Ewaso Ngiro EAK 204 Mh46
Ewaso Ngiro EAK 205 Mk45
Ewasse PNG 160 Sf48
Ewo RCB 202 Lh46
Exaltación BOL 279 Gg51
Exaltación BOL 280 Gh52
Exarhos GR 48 Mc52
Excelsior ZA 217 Md60
Excelsior Springs USA (MO) 241 Fc26
Exe GB 20 Kr39
Exeter GB 20 Kr40
Exeter USA (NH) 247 Ge24
Ex-Fortin Cacique RA (SF) 289 Gk60
Exil-Home of the Dalai Lama IND 107 Oj29
Exmoor N.P. GB 20 Kr39
Exmouth AUS (WA) 140 Qh56
Exmouth Gulf AUS 140 Qh57
Exmouth Plateau AUS 136 Qc22
Expedition N.P. AUS 151 Se58
Expedition Range AUS 151 Se58
Exploits River CDN 245 Hb21
Explorerbank 258 Fk37
Explorer Mtn. USA 228 Bk16
Extremadura E 28 Ko49
Extremo P 26 Km51
Exu BR (PE) 283 Ja49
Exuma Cays BS 251 Gb33
Exuma Cays Land and Sea Park BS 251 Gb33
Exuma Sound BS 251 Gb33
Eydehavn N 12 Lj32
Eydhafushi MV 110 Og43
Eyebrow CDN (SK) 233 Eg20
Eyehill Creek CDN 233 Ef19
Eyemouth GB 19 Ks35
Eye of Kuruman ZA 216 Mb59
Eye Peninsula GB 19 Ko32
Eygurande F 25 Lc45
Eyl SP 199 Ne42
Eylau = Bagrationovsk PL 37 Ma36
Eymir TR 51 Mq50
Eymoutiers F 24 Lb45
Eyn Kush IR 72 Nd29
Eyre Highway AUS 145 Rc62
Eyre Mountains NZ 155 Te68
Eyre Peninsula AUS 152 Rh62
Eyre River AUS 150 Rk58
Eyu-mojok CAM 194 Le43
Eyvan IR 72 Nd29
Eyvanakey IR 72 Ng28
Ezba Hasaballa ET 177 Mf33
Ezbet Ain ET 177 Mf33
Ezbet Dûsh ET 177 Mf33
Ezbet el Jâjah ET 177 Mf33
Ezcaray E 27 Ks52
Ezere LV 17 Mc34
Ežerėlis LT 17 Md36
Ezernieki LV 17 Mh34
Ezgueret RMM 185 Lb37
Ezhou CHN (HUB) 102 Qh30
Ezibeleni ZA 217 Md61
Ezine TR 50 Mg51
Ezo SUD 201 Md43
Ezra'a SYR 64 Mj29
Ezulwini Valley SD 217 Mf59
Ezzangbo WAN 194 Ld42
Ez-Ziliga MA 172 Kg29

F

Faaborg DK 14 Ll35
Faadippolhu Atoll = Lhaviyani Atoll MV 110 Og43
Faafu Atoll MV 110 Og44
Faaite Atoll F 165 Ch54
Fabens USA (TX) 237 Eg30
Fåberg N 12 Ll29
Fåberg N 12 Lh29
Fábiánsebestyén H 39 Ma44
Fåboda FIN 11 Mb14
Fa Bouré DY 186 Lb40
Fabriano I 41 Ln47
Fábricas de Riópar E 29 Ks48
Fabrichnyi KZ 77 Oj24
Facatativa CO 268 Gc43
Fachi RN 181 Lf36
Facundo RA (CB) 292 Gf68
Fada TCH 189 Ma37
Fada-Ngourma BF 185 La39
Fadat al Mislah KSA 66 Na34
Faddoi SUD 197 Mg41
Fadhi OM 69 Nh37
Fadiadougou CI 192 Kg41
Fadugu WAL 192 Ke41
Faenza I 40 Lm46
Fafa RCA 195 Lk42
Fafa RMM 185 La38
Fafadun SP 205 Na44
Fafakourou SN 183 Kc39
Fafe P 26 Km51
Fafen ETH 199 Nb41
Faga BF 185 La39
Faga WS 164 Bd52
Făgăraș RO 45 Me45
Fägelsjö S 13 Lp29
Fagerås S 13 Lo31
Fagerhult S 12 Lm32
Fagerhult S 15 Lq33
Fagernes N 12 Lk30
Fagersta S 13 Lq30
Făget RO 44 Mc45
Faggo WAN 186 Le40
Fagita RI 130 Rf46
Fagne B 23 Le40
Fagrinkotti SUD 190 Mf38
Fagudu RI 130 Rd46
Fagwir SUD 197 Mf41
Fahaheel KWT 74 Ne31
Faïd TN 174 Le28
Failaka Island KWT 74 Ne31
Faille de Nyakazu BU 206 Mf47

Fairbairn Reservoir – Florence Junction

Fairbairn Reservoir AUS 149 Sd57
Fairbanks USA (AK) 229 Cg13
Fairbury USA (NE) 240 Fb25
Fairfield USA (CA) 234 Dj26
Fairfield USA (ID) 235 Ec24
Fairfield USA (MA) 247 Gf23
Fairfield USA (MO) 241 Fe25
Fairfield USA (NC) 249 Gb28
Fairfield USA (TX) 243 Fb30
Fairfield Sapphire Valley USA 249 Fj28
Fair Harbour CDN (BC) 232 Dg20
Fair Head GB 18 Ko35
Fairhill AUS (QLD) 149 Se57
Fair Isle GB 19 Kt31
Fairlie NZ 155 Tf68
Fairlight AUS (QLD) 147 Sc53
Fairlight CDN (SK) 238 Ek21
Fairmont AUS (NSW) 150 Sb61
Fairmont USA (MN) 241 Fc24
Fairmont USA (WV) 247 Fk26
Fairmont Hot Springs CDN (BC) 233 Ec20
Fairo WAL 192 Ke42
Fair Oaks USA (AR) 243 Fe28
Fairplay USA (CO) 235 Eh26
Fairport USA (MI) 246 Fg23
Fairview AUS (NSW) 151 Sd61
Fairview AUS (QLD) 147 Sc53
Fairview CDN (AB) 233 Ea17
Fairview USA (MT) 235 Eh22
Fairview USA (OK) 242 Fa27
Fairview USA (UT) 235 Ee26
Fairweather, Mount CDN 231 Db16
Fairyhouse Racetrack IRL 20 Ko37
Fairyland AUS (QLD) 151 Sf59
Faisalabad PK 79 Og30
Fais Island FSM 156 Sa17
Faith USA (SD) 240 Ej23
Faiyiba SUD 190 Mf39
Faizabad AFG 79 Of27
Faizabad IND (UPH) 107 Pb32
Faje WAN 186 Lc41
Fakaofo Atoll NZ 157 Ub20
Fakarava Atoll F 165 Ch54
Fakatopatere F 165 Ch53
Fakenham GB 21 La38
Fåker S 13 Lp27
Fakfak = Onin Peninsula RI 130 Rf47
Fakfak RI 130 Rg47
Fakh Abad IR 74 Ng31
Fakhrpur IND (UPH) 107 Pa32
Fakija BG 47 Mh48
Fakkeh IR 72 Nd29
Fakola RMM 192 Kg40
Fakse DK 14 Ln35
Fakse Bugt DK 14 Ln35
Fak Tha THA 114 Qa37
Faku CHN (LNG) 100 Rb24
Fala RMM 184 Kh38
Falaba WAL 192 Ke41
Faladié RMM 184 Kf39
Falagountou BF 185 La38
Falaise F 22 Ku42
Falaise d'Amont F 22 La41
Falaise d'Angamma TCH 187 Lj37
Falaise d'Aval F 22 La41
Falaise de Bandiagara RMM 185 Kj38
Falaise de Banfora BF 193 Kh40
Falaise de l'Aguer-Tay TCH 181 Lj35
Falaise de Tambaoura RMM 183 Ke39
Falaise de Tiguidit RN 186 Ld37
Falaise du Gobnangou BF 185 La40
Falaise et grottes de l'Isandra RM 220 Nd56
Falakata IND (WBG) 112 Pe32
Falam MYA 112 Pg34
Falconara Marittima I 41 Lo47
Falcon Reservoir USA 253 Fa32
Faléa RMM 183 Ke39
Falefa WS 164 Be52
Falémé SN 183 Kd38
Falerum S 15 Lr32
Fălești MD 45 Mh43
Falfurrias USA (TX) 253 Fa32
Falima WAL 192 Ke41
Fali Mountains WAN 195 Lf42
Falkat ER 191 Mk38
Falkenberg D 33 Lo39
Falkenberg S 14 Ln34
Falkensee D 33 Lo38
Falkenstein D 35 Ln40
Falkirk GB 19 Kr34
Falkland CDN (BC) 232 Ea20
Falkland Escarpment 267 Hb28
Falkland Islands GB 267 Gd29
Falkland Islands GB 267 Gd29
Falkland Plateau 267 Hb29
Falkland Sound GB 295 Ha71
Falköping S 15 Lo32
Falla WAL 192 Ke41
Fallenumber Creek CDN 233 Ec20
Fallingbostel D 32 Lk38
Fallon USA (MT) 235 Eh22
Fallon USA (NV) 234 Ea26
Fall River USA (MA) 247 Ge25
Fall River Mills USA (CA) 234 Dk25
Falls City USA (NE) 241 Fc25
Falls of Measach GB 19 Kp33
Falmey RN 185 Lb39
Falmouth GB 20 Kp40
Falmouth JA 259 Gb36
Falmouth USA (KY) 249 Fh26
Falmouth USA (MA) 247 Ge25
Falo RMM 184 Kg39
Falou RMM 184 Kg38
False Bay CDN (BC) 232 Dh21
False Bay ZA 216 Lk63
False Oxford Ness AUS 146 Sb51
False Pass USA (AK) 228 Bj18
Falset E 30 La49
Falsino BR 275 He45
Falso Cabo de Hornos RCH 294 Gf73
Falster DK 14 Ln36
Falsterbo S 14 Ln35
Fălticeni RO 45 Mg43
Falu gruva S 13 Lq30
Falun CDN (AB) 233 Ed19
Falun S 13 Lq30
Fam = Fafa RCA 195 Lk42
Fama SUD 197 Mf40
Famagusta CY 51 Mo55
Famaillá RA (TU) 288 Gh59
Famalé RN 185 La38
Fameck F 23 Lg41
Famenin IR 72 Ne28
Famen Si CHN 95 Qd28
Family Lake CDN 238 Fc20
Fana N 12 Lf30
Fana RMM 184 Kg39
Fanambana RM 219 Ne52
Fanandrana RM 220 Ne55
Fanar Qasr Ahmad LAR 175 Lh29
Fanchang CHN (AHU) 102 Qk30
Fandriana RM 220 Nd56
Fang THA 114 Pk36
Fangak SUD 197 Mf41
Fangasso RMM 184 Kh39
Fangcheng CHN (GZG) 96 Qe35
Fangcheng CHN (HNN) 95 Qg29
Fangchenggang CHN (GZG) 96 Qe35
Fangliao RC 97 Ra34
Fångö S 15 Lr32
Fang Xian CHN (HUB) 95 Qf29
Fangzheng CHN (HLG) 98 Re23
Fan i Vogel AL 46 Ma49
Fanjingshan Z.B. CHN 95 Qe31
Fanning River AUS (QLD) 149 Sd55
Fannuj IR 75 Nk32
Fannystelle CDN (MB) 238 Fb21
Fanø DK 14 Lj35
Fano I 41 Lo47
Fanø Bugt DK 14 Lj35
Fanshan CHN (ZJG) 102 Ra32
Fanshi CHN (SAX) 93 Qg26
Fansipan VN 113 Qb34
Fantale Crater ETH 198 Mk41
Fântânița MD 45 Mh42
Fantastic Caverns USA 243 Fd27
Fan Xian CHN (HNN) 93 Qh28
Fanxue CHN (SAA) 92 Qd27
Faom Lake CDN (SK) 238 Ej20
Faqih Soleyman IR 72 Nd28
Fara BF 193 Kj40
Faraba RMM 183 Ke39
Farache RMM 185 Kj37
Faraday ANT (UK) 296 Gd32
Faraday Fracture Zone 8 Jb09
Farafangana RM 220 Nd57
Farafenni WAG 183 Kc39
Farafra Oasis ET 177 Me32
Farági Samariás GR 48 Md55
Farági Vouriakoú GR 48 Mc52
Farah AFG 78 Ob29
Farahalana RM 219 Nf53
Farah Rud AFG 78 Ob29
Farakka IND (WBG) 112 Pd33
Farako RMM 184 Kg39
Farako RMM 192 Kg40
Farallón Centinela YV 269 Gg40
Farallon de Pajaros USA 119 Sa14
Farallones de Cali, P.N. CO 268 Gb44
Faramana BF 184 Kh39
Faramuti SUD 196 Md40
Faranah RG 192 Ke40
Faraonivka UA 45 Mk44
Far'aoun RIM 183 Kd36
Farasan KSA 68 Na37
Faratsiho RM 220 Nd55
Fărău RO 44 Me44
Faraulep Atoll FSM 156 Sa17
Fărcașa RO 44 Md43
Fărdea RO 44 Mc45
Fare F 165 Ce54
Fareham GB 21 Kt40
Farestad N 12 Lh33
Farewell USA (AK) 229 Cd14
Farewell Spit NZ 155 Tg66
Färgelanda S 12 Lm32
Fargha SUD 190 Mh40
Fargo USA (GA) 249 Fj30
Fargo USA (ND) 240 Fb22
Farg'ona UZ 77 Of25
Fari RMM 183 Ke39
Farias Brito BR (CE) 277 Ja49
Faribault USA (MN) 241 Fd23
Faridabad IND (HYA) 107 Oj31
Faridkot IND (PJB) 106 Oh30
Faridpur BD 112 Pe34
Farié RN 185 La39
Farihy Alaotra RM 220 Ne54
Farihy Anony RM 220 Nd58
Farihy Antanavo RM 219 Ne52
Farihy Ihotry RM 220 Nb57
Farihy Itasy RM 220 Nd55
Farihy Kinkony RM 218 Nc54
Farihy Mantasoa RM 220 Ne55
Farihy Tritriva RM 220 Nd56
Farihy Tsiazompaniry RM 220 Ne55
Färila S 13 Lq29
Farilhões P 28 Kl49
Farim GNB 183 Kc39
Farimān IR 73 Nk28
Faringdon GB 21 Kt39
Farinha BR 276 Hg49
Farini I 40 Lk46
Fariq at-Fil SUD 190 Mg40
Faris Seamount 230 Cg18
Färjestaden S 15 Lr34
Farka RN 185 Lb38
Farkadóna GR 46 Mc51
Farkhar AFG 78 Oe27
Farkwa EAT 207 Mh48
Fårliug RO 44 Mb45
Farma ET 177 Mg30
Farmakas GR 48 Mc53
Farmakonisi GR 49 Mh53
Farmamerica USA 241 Fd24
Farmer USA (WA) 232 Ea22
Farmerville USA (LA) 243 Fd29
Farmington USA (ME) 247 Ge23
Farmington USA (NM) 237 Ef27
Farmville USA (VA) 249 Ga27
Färnebofjärdens n.p. S 13 Lr30
Farne Deep GB 19 Ku35
Farne Islands GB 19 Kt35
Farnham GB 21 Ku39
Farnham, Mount CDN 232 Eb20
Faro BR (PA) 275 Hb47
Faro CAM 195 Lg41
Faro CDN (YT) 231 Dd14
Faro P 28 Kn47
Faro RA (BA) 293 Gk65
Fårö S 15 Lu33
Faroe Islands DK 8 Kc06
Farol de São Tomé BR (RJ) 287 Hk57
Farol Guará BR (AP) 275 Hf45
Faro, P.N. de CAM 195 Lg41
Fårösund S 15 Lu33
Fårösund S 15 Lu33
Farquhar Group SY 219 Nf50
Farquhar Ridge SY 219 Nf50
Farquharson, Mount AUS 139 Rf54
Farranfore IRL 20 Kl38
Farrars River AUS 150 Sa58
Farroupilha BR (RS) 290 He60
Farrukhabad IND (UPH) 107 Ok32
Farrukhnagar IND (APH) 108 Ok37
Farsah IR 72 Nf29
Fársala GR 48 Mc51
Farsø DK 14 Lk34
Farson USA (WY) 235 Ef24
Farsund N 12 Lg32
Fartura BR (SP) 286 Hf57
Faruj IR 73 Nk27
Farukolhu MV 110 Og42
Farul Genovez RO 45 Mj46
Farum DK 14 Ln35
Fårup Sommerland DK 14 Lk33
Farwell USA (TX) 237 Ej28
Faryab IR 75 Nj32
Fasa IR 74 Ng31
Fasad OM 69 Ng36
Fasana LB 192 Kf42
Fasano I 43 Ls50
Fas Boye SN 183 Kb38
Fashe WAN 186 Lc41
Fashola WAN 194 Lb42
Fasht YE 68 Nb37
Fasil Ghebbi ETH 198 Mj39
Fasito'otai WS 164 Be52
Fask MA 172 Kf31
Fassala Néré RIM 184 Kh38
Fassanu LAR 174 Lg30
Fass Bank F 164 Bc53
Fastiv UA 54 Me20
Fataki RDC 201 Mf44
Fatehabad IND (HYA) 106 Oh31
Fatehgarh IND (UPH) 107 Ok32
Fatehjang PK 79 Og29
Fatehnagar IND (RJT) 106 Oh33
Fatehpur IND (BIH) 109 Pc33
Fatehpur IND (RJT) 106 Oh32
Fatehpur IND (UPH) 107 Pa33
Fatehpur Sikri IND 107 Oj32
Fatež RUS 52 Mh19
Fath Abad IR 74 Nh31
Fathom Five N.M.P. CDN 246 Fk23
Fatiba RMM 184 Kg38
Fatick SN 183 Kb38
Fatih Sultan Mehmet Köprüsü TR 50 Mk49
Fátima P 28 Km49
Fatima do Sul BR (MS) 286 Hc57
Fatima Masume IR 72 Nf28
Fatimé RMM 184 Kh39
Fatitet SUD 197 Mf42
Fat Kauyon RI 130 Rd47
Fatoto WAG 183 Kd39
Fatsa TR 63 Mj25
Fattasha SUD 190 Mg39
Fattuwal IND (PJB) 106 Oh30
Fatu Hiva F 165 Da51
Fatu Huku F 165 Da50
Fatuma RDC 206 Me49
Fatunda RDC 203 Lj48
Fatural RI 131 Rh49
Fatutaka SOL 157 Tc21
Fatwa IND (BIH) 109 Pc33
Faulkton USA (SD) 240 Fa23
Faulquemont F 23 Lg41
Faura E 29 Ku49
Făurei RO 45 Mh45
Făurei RO 45 Mg44
Faure Island AUS 140 Qg58
Fauresmith ZA 217 Mc60
Fauro Island SOL 160 Sj49
Fauske N 10 Lh12
Faust CDN (AB) 233 Ec18
Fauville-en-Caux F 22 La41
Faux Cap = Betanty RM 220 Nc58
Fåvang N 12 Ll29
Favara I 42 Lo53
Faverges F 25 Lg45
Faversham GB 21 La39
Favignana I 42 Ln53
Favone F 31 Lk49
Fawcett CDN (AB) 233 Ec18
Fawcett Lake CDN (AB) 233 Ed18
Fawnleas ZA 217 Mf60
Fawn Pt. USA 228 Bj18
Fawn River CDN 239 Ff18
Fawn Trough 297 Oc30
Faxaflói IS 10 Jj13
Faxinal BR (PR) 286 He58
Faxinal, T.I. BR 286 He58
Faya = Largeau TCH 188 Lk37
Fayala RDC 203 Lj47
Fayaoué F 162 Td56
Fayd KSA 66 Nb32
Fayence F 25 Lg47
Fayette USA (AL) 248 Fg29
Fayette USA (MS) 243 Fe30
Fayetteville USA (AR) 243 Fc27
Fayetteville USA (GA) 249 Fh29
Fayetteville USA (NC) 249 Ga28
Fayetteville USA (TN) 248 Fg28
Fayfa KSA 68 Nb37
Fayid ET 177 Mg30
Fayl-Billot F 23 Lf43
Fayón E 30 La49
Fay-sur-Lignon F 25 Le46
Fayu Island FSM 156 Sc17
Faz MA 172 Kh28
Fazai RN 181 Lf36
Fazao TG 193 La41
Fazao-Malfakassa, P.N. de TG 193 La41
Fazenda Acurauá BR (RO) 280 Gg50
Fazenda Agua Santa BR (AM) 280 Gj50
Fazenda Boa Esperanza BR (AM) 274 Gk46
Fazenda Bradesco BR (PA) 276 Hf47
Fazenda Cumaru BR (PA) 275 He49
Fazenda Foz do Christalino BR (MT) 281 He52
Fazenda Itanorte BR (MT) 280 Hb53
Fazenda Muraquitã BR (MT) 280 Gk51
Fazenda Narciso BR (AM) 273 Gg45
Fazenda Primavera BR (MT) 281 Hd51
Fazenda Remanso BR (AM) 275 Hb47
Fazenda Rio Dourado BR (PA) 281 He50
Fazenda Rio Grande BR (PR) 291 Hf58
Fazenda Santa Lúcia BR (MT) 286 Hc54
Fazenda São Sebastião BR (RO) 280 Gh51
Fazenda Três Irmãos BR (MT) 286 Hc54
Fazenda Vista Alegre BR (AM) 280 Gk50
Fazilka IND (PJB) 106 Oh30
Fazilpur PK 81 Of31
F. Carillo Puerto MEX (ZCT) 253 Ej34
Fdérik RIM 178 Kd34
Featherston NZ 154 Th66
Featherstone ZW 214 Mf55
Fécamp F 22 La41
Feda N 12 Lg32
Federación RA (ER) 289 Hb61
Federal RA (ER) 289 Ha61
Fedeshk IR 73 Nk29
Fedje N 12 Le30
Fé do Morro BR (PI) 283 Hk50
Fëdorovka RUS 55 Mk22
Fegyvernek H 39 Ma43
Fehérgyarmat H 39 Mc43
Fehimli TR 51 Mq51
Fehmarn D 33 Lm36
Fehmarnbelt D 33 Lm36
Fehmarnsund D 33 Ll36
Fehring A 35 Lr44
Feidh el Botma DZ 173 Lb28
Feidong CHN (AHU) 102 Qj30
Feijó BR (AC) 279 Ge50
Feilding NZ 154 Th66
Feira de Santana BR (BA) 283 Ja52
Feiran Oasis ET 177 Mg31
Feistritz A 35 Lq43
Feitok CAM 194 Le43
Feixi CHN (AHU) 102 Qj30
Fei Xian CHN (SDG) 102 Qj28
Feke TR 62 Mh27
Felahiye TR 51 Mq51
Felanitx E 30 Ld51
Felaou DZ 180 Lc36
Feldbach A 35 Lq44
Feldberg D 33 Lo37
Feldberg D 34 Lj43
Feldkirch A 34 Lk43
Feldkirchen A 35 Lp44
Felegenway ETH 198 Mj42
Feliciano RA 289 Ha61
Félicité SY 219 Nh48
Felidhoo Atoll MV 110 Og44
Felidhoo Channel MV 110 Og44
Felipe Carrillo Puerto MEX (QTR) 255 Ff36
Felipe Yofré RA (CR) 289 Ha60
Felixburg ZW 214 Mf55
Felixlândia BR (MG) 287 Hh55
Felixstowe GB 21 Lb39
Fellegvár H 39 Lt43
Felletin F 24 Lc45
Fellingsbro S 13 Lq31
Felnac RO 44 Mb44
Felsberg D 32 Lk39
Felsenthal N.W.R. USA 243 Fd29
Felsőzsolca H 39 Ma42
Feltre I 40 Lm44
Femern Bælt DK 14 Lm36
Femund N 12 Lm28
Femundsmarka n.p. N 12 Ln28
Fence ZA 217 Mc63
Fence Lake USA (NM) 237 Ef28
Fener Burnu TR 62 Mh27
Fener Burnu TR 63 Mk25
Feng'an CHN (GDG) 97 Qh34
Fengcheng CHN (JGX) 102 Qh31
Fengcheng CHN (LNG) 100 Rc25
Fengdu CHN 95 Qd31
Fengelo CI 192 Kg41
Fengguo Monastery CHN 100 Ra25
Fenghua CHN (ZJG) 102 Ra31
Fenghuang CHN (GDG) 97 Qj34
Fenghuang CHN (GZG) 96 Qd33
Fenghuang CHN (HUN) 96 Qe32
Fenghuangshan CHN 100 Rc25
Fengjie CHN (CGQ) 95 Qe30
Fengjiu CHN (HNN) 102 Qh28
Fengkou CHN (HUB) 95 Qg30
Fengliang CHN (GDG) 97 Qj34
Fengling Guan CHN 102 Qk31
Fengling Z.B. CHN 98 Re21
Fengning CHN (HBI) 93 Qj25
Fengpin RC 97 Ra34
Fengpo CHN (YUN) 113 Qa34
Fengqing CHN (YUN) 113 Pk33
Fengrun CHN (HBI) 93 Qk26
Fengshan CHN (GZG) 96 Qd33
Fengshan RC 97 Ra34
Fengshui shan CHN 91 Rb19
Fengshun CHN (GDG) 97 Qj34
Fengtai CHN (AHU) 102 Qj29
Feng Xian CHN (JGS) 102 Qj28
Feng Xian CHN (SAA) 95 Qd29
Fengxian CHN (SHG) 102 Ra30
Fengxiang CHN (SAA) 95 Qd28
Fengxin CHN (JGX) 102 Qh31
Fengxue Si CHN 95 Qg28
Fengyi CHN (GZH) 95 Qd31
Fengyuan RC 97 Ra33
Fengzhen CHN (NMZ) 93 Qg25
Fen He CHN 95 Qf28
Feni BD 112 Pf34
Feniak Lake USA 229 Ca11
Feni Islands PNG 160 Sg48
Fenix BR (PR) 286 He57
Fenoarivo RM 220 Nd56
Fenoarivo RM 220 Nd56
Fenoarivo Atsinanana RM 220 Ne54
Fenoarivo Be RM 220 Nd55
Fensmark DK 14 Lm35
Fenstan Shuiku CHN 95 Qe31
Fenyang CHN (SAX) 93 Qf27
Fenyi CHN (JGX) 102 Qh32
Feodosija UA 55 Mh23
Ferapontovo RUS 11 Mk16
Ferdjioua DZ 174 Lc27
Ferdows IR 73 Nk29
Ferdowsi Tomb IR 73 Nk27
Fère-Champenoise F 23 Ld42
Férédou RG 192 Kf41
Fère-en-Tardenois F 23 Ld41
Ferentillo I 42 Ln48
Ferentino I 42 Lo49
Feres GR 47 Mg50
Ferfer ETH 199 Nc43
Fergana UZ 77 Of25
Fergana too tizmegi KS 77 Og25
Ferganskaja dolina UZ 76 Of25
Fergus Falls USA (MN) 241 Fb22
Fergusson Island PNG 160 Sf50
Fergusson River AUS (NT) 139 Rf53
Ferhadiju džamija BIH 41 Ls46
Feriana TN 174 Le28
Ferizli TR 50 Ml50
Ferkessédougou CI 193 Kh41
Ferlach A 35 Lp44
Ferland CDN (ON) 239 Ff20
Ferland CDN (SK) 233 Eg21
Ferlo SN 183 Kc38
Fermo I 41 Lo47
Fermoselle E 26 Ko51
Fermoy IRL 20 Km38
Fernández RA (SE) 288 Gj59
Fernandez Bay BS 251 Gc33
Fernandina Beach USA (FL) 249 Fk30
Fernandina, Volcán EC 272 Fe46
Fernando Falcão BR (MA) 276 Hh48
Fernandópolis BR (SP) 286 He56
Fernão Dias BR (MG) 287 Hh54
Fernão Veloso MOC 211 Na53
Ferndale USA (WA) 232 Dj21
Fernie CDN (BC) 233 Ec21
Fernley USA (NV) 234 Ea26
Ferokh IND (KER) 110 Oh41
Ferrandina I 43 Lr50
Ferrara I 40 Lm46
Ferraz, Com. ANT (BR) 296 Ha31
Ferreira ZA 217 Md60
Ferreira do Alentejo P 28 Km48
Ferreira Gomes BR (AP) 275 He45
Ferreñafe PE 278 Ga49
Ferrette F 23 Lh43
Ferriday USA (LA) 243 Fe30
Ferriere I 40 Lk46
Ferro BR 281 Hc52
Ferrocarril Chihuahua al Pacifico MEX 252 Ef32
Ferrol E 26 Km53
Ferros BR (MG) 287 Hj55
Fertő-Hanság N.P. H 38 Lr43
Fertőszentmiklós H 38 Lr43
Fès MA 172 Kh28
Fès-el-Bali MA 172 Kh28
Feshi RDC 203 Lk49
Fessélémon CI 193 Kh41
Fessenden USA (ND) 240 Fa22
Festetics H 38 Ls44
Festival Folclórico (Parintins) BR (AM) 275 Hb47
Fété Bowé SN 183 Kd38
Fetești RO 45 Mh46
Fethard IRL 20 Kn38
Fethiye TR 49 Mk54
Fethiye Körfezi TR 49 Mj54
Fetisovo KZ 71 Ng24
Fetlar GB 19 Ku30
Fetsund N 12 Lm31
Feuchtwangen D 34 Ll41
Feurs F 25 Le45
Fevik N 12 Lj32
Fevral'sk RUS 98 Rf19
Feyzabad = Faizabad AFG 79 Of27
Feyz Abad IR 73 Nk28
Fezna MA 172 Kh30
Fezzan LAR 181 Lg33
Ffestiniog GB 20 Kr38
Fiadanana RM 220 Nd55
Fiadanana RM 220 Nd56
Fiambalá RA (CA) 288 Gg59
Fiambalá RA 288 Gg59
Fian GH 193 Kj40
Fianarantsoa RM 220 Nd56
Fianga TCH 187 Lh41
Fibiș RO 44 Mb45
Fiche ETH 198 Mk41
Fichtelgebirge D 35 Lm40
Ficksburg ZA 217 Md60
Ficuar PE 278 Fk48
Fidalgo BR 277 Hk50
Fidenza I 40 Ll46
Fielding USA (UT) 235 Ed25
Field River AUS 143 Rj57
Fields USA (OR) 234 Ea24
Fier AL 46 Lu50
Fierenana RM 220 Nc55
Fiery Cross Reef 122 Qg41
Fierzë AL 46 Ma48
Fiésole I 40 Lm47
Fifa RG 192 Kf40
Fife Ness GB 19 Ks34
Fifield AUS (NSW) 153 Sd62
Fifinda CAM 194 Lf44
Figari F 31 Lk49
Figeac F 24 Lc46
Figeholm S 15 Lr33
Figias GR 48 Me52
Figtree ZW 214 Me56
Figueira da Foz P 26 Km50
Figueira de Castelo Rodrigo P 26 Ko50
Figueirão BR (MS) 286 Hd55
Figueiras, T.I. BR 280 Ha53
Figueiró dos Vinhos P 28 Km49
Figueres E 32 Lc48
Figui CAM 187 Lg41
Figuig MA 173 Kk29
Fijhaonana RM 220 Nd55
Fiji 135 Tb11
Fiji Islands 137 Td22
Fik ETH 198 Nb41
Fika WAN 187 Lf40
Filabusi ZW 214 Me56
Filadelfia BOL 279 Gf51
Filadélfia BR (BA) 283 Hk51
Filadélfia BR (TO) 276 Hg49
Filadelfia I 43 Lr52
Filadelfia PY 285 Gk57
Fil'akovo SK 39 Lu42
Filamana RMM 192 Kg40
Filchner ANT (D) 296 Hb33
Filchner Ice Shelf 296 Hd35
Filer USA (ID) 235 Ec24
Filey GB 21 Ku36
Filiași RO 44 Md46
Filiátes GR 48 Ma51
Filiatrá GR 48 Mb53
Filingué RN 185 Lb38
Filinskoe RUS 53 Nb18
Filipești RO 45 Mg44
Filipiáda GR 48 Ma51
Filipstad S 13 Lp31
Filitosa F 31 Lj49
Filiya WAN 187 Lf41
Fillmore CDN (SK) 238 Ej21
Fillmore USA (UT) 235 Ed26
Filokehn LB 192 Kf43
Filótas GR 46 Mb50
Filóti GR 49 Mf53
Fils D 34 Lk42
Filtu ETH 198 Na43
Filtu ETH 198 Na43
Filuo SOL 161 Sk49
Fimbulheimen 297 Lb33
Fimbul Ice Shelf 296 Kd33
Fimi RDC 200 Lj47
Fin IR 75 Nh32
Finale Emilia I 40 Lm46
Finale Ligure I 40 Lj46
Finaly Ranges CDN 231 Dh17
Finaly River CDN 231 Dh17
Finaña E 29 Ks47
Finca Chañaral Alta RCH 288 Gf59
Finchaa Reservoir ETH 198 Mj41
Finchawa ETH 198 Mk43
Finch Hatton AUS (QLD) 149 Se56
Fındıklı TR 50 Mg50
Findlay USA (OH) 246 Fj25
Fingal AUS (TAS) 152 Sd66
Finger Lake CDN 238 Fd19
Fingoe MOC 210 Mf53
Finikas GR 49 Me53
Finike TR 62 Mf27
Finisterre Range PNG 159 Sc48
Fink Creek USA (AK) 229 Bj13
Finke AUS (NT) 143 Rh58
Finke Gorge N.P. AUS 142 Rg58
Finke Pmer Ulperre Ingwemirne Arletherre A.L. AUS 143 Rh58
Finkolo RMM 193 Kg40
Finland 7 Ma03
Finlay Forks CDN (BC) 231 Dj17
Finlay River CDN 231 Dg17
Finley USA (ND) 240 Fb22
Finnerödja S 13 Lp32
Finney Wildlife Area & Bison Refuge USA 242 Ek27
Finngrund 13 Ls29
Finniss Springs AUS (SA) 143 Rj60
Finnmarksvidda N 11 Mb11
Finnoy N 12 Lf31
Finnsnes N 10 Lk11
Finnstad N 12 Lm28
Finote Selam ETH 198 Mj40
Fins OM 75 Nk34
Finschhafen PNG 159 Sd49
Finse N 12 Lh30
Finskij zaliv 16 Md31
Finspång S 13 Lq32
Finsteraarhorn CH 34 Lj44
Finsterwalde D 33 Lo39
Fintas KWT 74 Ne31
Fintown IRL 18 Km36
Fintrou RMM 185 Kk37
Finyolé CAM 187 Lg41
Fionnphort GB 18 Ko34
Fiordland NZ 155 Td68
Fiordland N.P. NZ 155 Td68
Fiordo Falcón RCH 294 Gd70
Fiordo Penuin RCH 294 Gc71
Fiorenzuola d'Arda I 40 Lk46
Firat Nehri TR 63 Mk26
Firavahana RM 220 Nd55
Fire Island USA 229 Ce15
Fire Island Nat. Seashore USA 247 Gd25
Firenze I 40 Lm47
Firenzuola I 40 Lm46
Firestone Plantation LB 192 Ke42
Firgoun RN 185 La38
Firmat RA (SF) 289 Gk62
Firmeza PE 279 Gf51
Firminy F 25 Le45
Firou DY 193 La40
Firovo RUS 52 Mg17
Firozabad IND (UPH) 107 Ok32
Firozpur IND (PJB) 106 Oh30
Firozpur Jhirka IND (HYA) 106 Oj32
Firsovo RUS 99 Sb22
First Coffee Plantations C 259 Gc36
Firth of Clyde GB 19 Kq35
Firth of Forth GB 19 Ks34
Firth of Lorne GB 18 Kp34
Firth of Tay GB 19 Kr34
Firth of Thames NZ 154 Th64
Firuz Abad IR 72 Ne28
Firuz Abad IR 74 Ng31
Firuz Bey Camii TR 49 Mh53
Firyuza TM 73 Nk27
Fischells CDN (NF) 245 Ha21
Fischersbrunn NAM 212 Lh58
Fiseha Genet ETH 198 Mk42
Fisenge Z 210 Me52
Fish Cays BS 251 Gb32
Fisher AUS (SA) 145 Rf61
Fishermen's Cottages ZA 216 Ma63
Fisher R. Ind. Res. CDN 238 Fb20
Fisher Strait CDN 225 Fd06
Fishguard GB 20 Kq39
Fishing Lake CDN 238 Fc19
Fish River NAM 212 Lj58
Fish River USA 229 Bj13
Fish River ZA 216 Ma61
Fish River Canyon Park NAM 216 Lj59
Fish Town LB 192 Kg43
Fiskárdo GR 48 Ma52
Fiskebäckskil S 12 Lm32
Fismes F 23 Ld41
Fissibu LB 192 Kf42
Fissoa PNG 160 Sf47
Fitampito RM 220 Nd56
Fitchburg USA (MA) 247 Ge24
Fities GR 48 Mb52
Fitjar N 12 Lf31
Fitzcarrald PE 279 Gd51
Fitzgerald USA (GA) 249 Fj30
Fitzgerald River N.P. AUS 144 Qk62
Fitzroy GB 295 Ha71
Fitz Roy RA (SC) 294 Gg69
Fitzroy Crossing AUS (WA) 138 Rc55
Fitzroy Island AUS (QLD) 149 Sd54
Fitzroy River AUS 138 Rb54
Fitzroy River AUS 149 Se57
Fiuggi I 42 Lo49
Fiumendosa I 31 Lk51
Fiumicino I 42 Ln49
Five Cays Settlements GB 251 Gd35
Five Civilized Tribes Mus. USA 243 Fc28
Five Finger Rapids CDN 231 Db14
Five Stars GUY 270 Gk42
Fivizzano I 40 Ll46
Fizi RDC 206 Me48
Fjæra N 12 Lg31
Fjærland N 12 Lg29
Fjällbacka S 12 Lm32
Fjällnäs S 12 Ln28
Fjellerup DK 14 Ll34
Fjerritslev DK 14 Lk33
Fjordo Elefantes RCH 294 Gd69
Fjugesta S 13 Lp31
Fkih-Ben-Salah MA 172 Kg29
Flacq MS 221 Nj56
Fladen 14 Lm33
Fladungen D 34 Ll40
Flagler Beach USA (FL) 250 Fk31
Flagstaff USA (AZ) 237 Ee28
Flagstaff ZA 217 Me61
Flagstaff Hill Maritime Museum AUS 152 Sb65
Flagstaff Lake USA 244 Ge23
Flaherty Island CDN 239 Fk18
Flåm N 12 Lh30
Flambeau Ind. Res. USA 246 Ff23
Flamborough Head GB 21 Ku36
Flamenco Beach USA 261 Gh36
Fläming D 33 Ln38
Flaming Gorge Nat. Rec. Area USA 235 Ef25
Flamingo USA (FL) 250 Fk33
Flåmsbana N 12 Lh30
Flanagan River CDN 238 Fd19
Flanders B 23 Lc40
Flannan Isles GB 18 Kn32
Flasher USA (ND) 240 Ek22
Flat USA (AK) 229 Ca14
Flatey IS 10 Jj13
Flathead USA 233 Ed22
Flathead Ind. Res. USA 233 Ec22
Flathead Lake USA 233 Ec22
Flathead River CDN 233 Ec21
Flat Island 122 Qh40
Flatøydegard N 12 Lk30
Flat Point NZ 154 Th66
Flat River CDN (PE) 245 Gj22
Flat River CDN 231 Dg15
Flatwoods USA (KY) 249 Fj26
Flavio Alfaro EC 272 Ga46
Flaxcombe CDN (SK) 233 Ef20
Flé RG 192 Kf40
Flecha Point RP 123 Rb42
Fleetwood GB 21 Kr37
Flekkefjord N 12 Lg32
Flekkeroy N 12 Lh32
Flemingsburg USA (KY) 249 Fj26
Flemington Racecourse AUS (VIC) 153 Sc64
Flen S 13 Lr31
Flensburg D 32 Lk36
Flensburger Förde D 33 Ll36
Flers F 22 Ku42
Flesberg N 12 Lk31
Fletcher Promontory 296 Fd34
Fleurance F 24 La47
Fleur de Lys CDN (NF) 245 Hb20
Fleury-les-Aubrais F 23 Lb43
Fleuve Saint-Laurent CDN 244 Gf21
Flevoland NL 32 Lf38
Flexal BR (PA) 275 Hc46
Flims CH 34 Lk44
Flinders AUS (VIC) 153 Sc65
Flinders Bay AUS 144 Qh62
Flinders Chase N.P. AUS 152 Rj63
Flinders Group AUS 147 Sc53
Flinders Highway AUS (QLD) 148 Sb56
Flinders Island AUS 152 Rh62
Flinders Island AUS 152 Se65
Flinders Ranges AUS 152 Rk61
Flinders Ranges N.P. AUS 152 Rk61
Flinders Reefs AUS 149 Se54
Flinders River AUS (QLD) 148 Sa54
Flin Flon CDN (MB) 238 Ek18
Flint USA (MI) 246 Fj24
Flint USA 249 Fh30
Flint Atoll KIR 303 Ca11
Flint Hills USA 243 Fb27
Flint Hills N.W.R. USA 241 Fc26
Flint Rapids CDN 239 Fh19
Flisa N 12 Lm30
Flisa N 12 Lm30
Flix E 30 La49
Flize F 23 Le41
Floating Gardens MYA 113 Pj35
Floating Market (Phung Hiep) VN 117 Qc41
Floby S 15 Lo32
Flogny-la-Chapelle F 23 Ld43
Flöha D 33 Lo40
Flomaton USA (AL) 248 Fg30
Floodwood USA (MN) 241 Fd22
Flora RP 121 Ra36
Flora USA (MS) 243 Fe29
Flora USA (OR) 234 Eb23
Florac F 25 Ld46
Florala USA (AL) 248 Fg30
Florange F 23 Lg41
Flor da Serra do Sul BR (SC) 290 Hd59
Flor de Agosto PE 273 Gd47
Flor del Desierto RCH 284 Gf57
Flor de Punga PE 273 Gc48
Florena o Charles = Isla Santa María EC 272 Fe46
Florence I 40 Lm47
Florence USA (AL) 248 Fg28
Florence USA (AZ) 237 Ee29
Florence USA (CO) 235 Eh26
Florence USA (SC) 249 Ga28
Florence USA (SD) 241 Fb23
Florence USA (WI) 246 Ff23
Florence Junction USA (AZ) 237 Ee29

Florence Vale – Frøya

Florence Vale AUS (QLD) 149 Sd57
Florencia CO 272 Gc45
Florencia RA (SF) 289 Ha60
Florennes B 23 Le40
Florenville B 23 Lf41
Flores BR (PE) 283 Jb49
Flores BR 276 Hh48
Flores GCA 255 Ff37
Flores P 8 Jb11
Flores RI 129 Ra50
Flores de Goiás BR (GO) 282 Hg53
Flores do Piauí BR (PI) 277 Hj49
Flores Island CDN 232 Dg21
Flores Magón MEX (CHP) 255 Fd37
Flores Sea RI 129 Qk49
Floresta BR (PE) 283 Ja50
Floreşti MD 45 Mj43
Floresville USA (TX) 242 Fa31
Florewood River Plantation S.P. USA 248 Fe29
Floriano BR (PI) 276 Hj49
Floriano Peixoto BR (AL) 283 Jc50
Floriano Peixoto BR (AM) 279 Gg50
Florianópolis BR (SC) 291 Hf59
Florida C 259 Ga35
Florida CO 268 Gb44
Florida PE 272 Gb48
Florida ROU 289 Hb63
Florida USA 227 Fd13
Florida USA 227 Fd13
Florida Bay USA 250 Fk33
Florida Caverns S.P. USA 250 Fh30
Florida Islands SOL 161 Ta50
Florida Keys USA 250 Fk33
Florida Peak USA 237 Eg29
Florida's Silver Springs USA 250 Fj31
Florídia I 42 Lq53
Flórina GR 46 Mb50
Florínia BR (SP) 286 He57
Florissant USA (MO) 241 Fe26
Florissant Fossil Beds Nat. Mon. USA 235 Eh26
Florø N 12 Lf29
Florynka PL 39 Ma41
Flötningen S 12 Ln29
Flower Island RI 126 Qh47
Flower Pot Island CDN 246 Fk23
Floyd USA (IA) 241 Fd24
Floyd USA (VA) 249 Fk27
Floydada USA (TX) 242 Ek29
Fluberg N 12 Ll30
Flüelapass CH 34 Lk44
Fluk RI 130 Rd46
Fluminimaggiore I 31 Lj51
Flying Post Ind. Res. CDN 239 Fj21
Flynns Reef AUS (VIC) 153 Sc65
Fly River PNG 158 Sb50
Fô BF 193 Kh40
Foa F 162 Tc56
Foa Island TO 164 Bc55
Foča BIH 46 Lt47
Foça TR 49 Mg52
Fochabers GB 19 Kr33
Fochi TCH 181 Lh36
Focşani RO 45 Mh45
Fodé RCA 200 Mb43
Fodékaria RG 192 Kf40
Fofore WAN 187 Lg41
Fogadalmi templom H 39 Ma44
Fogang CHN (GDG) 97 Qg34
Foggåret el Arab DZ 180 Lb32
Foggåret ez Zoûa DZ 173 Lb32
Fóggia I 42 Lq49
Foggy Cape USA 228 Cb17
Föglia I 40 Ln47
Föglö FIN 13 Ma31
Fogo CDN (NF) 245 Hc21
Foguang Si CHN 93 Qg26
Fohnsdorf A 35 Lp43
Föhr D 32 Lj36
Fóia P 28 Km47
Foix F 24 Lb48
Fojnica BIH 41 Ls47
Fokalik RI 130 Rc47
Fokino RUS 52 Mh19
Fokku WAN 186 Lc40
Folda N 10 Lh12
Folégandros GR 49 Me54
Folégandros GR 49 Me54
Folelli F 31 Lk48
Foley RB 213 Md56
Foley USA (AL) 248 Fg30
Foleyet CDN (ON) 239 Fj21
Folgares ANG 208 Lh53
Folgefonna N 12 Lg30
Folgelevo KZ 76 Oe24
Foligno I 40 Ln48
Folkestad N 12 Lg28
Folkestone GB 21 Lb39
Folkston USA (GA) 249 Fk30
Folkstone USA (NC) 249 Gb28
Folk Village Museum IRL 18 Km35
Folldal N 12 Lk28
Follebu N 12 Ll29
Follingbo S 15 Lt33
Föllinge S 10 Lh14
Follónica I 40 Ll48
Folly Beach USA 249 Ga29
Folteşti RO 45 Mj45
Fomboni COM 218 Nb52
Fomena GH 193 Kk42
Fomento C 259 Ga34
Fominki RUS 53 Nb18
Fona VU 162 Te54
Fondation P.Gianadda in Martigny CH 34 Lh44
Fond Du Lac USA (WI) 246 Ff24
Fondi I 42 Lo49
Fonéko RN 185 La38
Fongolembi SN 183 Ke39
Fonni I 31 Lk50
Fonsagrada E 26 Kn53
Fonseca CO 268 Gd40
Fontainebleau F 23 Lc42
Fontaine-Française F 23 Lf43
Fontainhas CV 182 Jh37
Fontanka UA 45 Ml44
Fontas CDN (BC) 231 Dk16
Fontas River CDN 231 Dk16
Fontdepou E 30 La49
Fonte Avellana I 40 Ln47
Fonte Boa BR (AM) 273 Gg47
Fontenay-le-Comte F 22 Ku44
Fontenay-Trésigny F 23 Lc42
Fontevraud-l'Abbaye F 22 La43
Fontibón CO 268 Gc43
Fontiveros E 26 Kq50
Font-Romeu F 24 Lc48
Font-Romeu F 24 Lc48
Fonualei Island TO 164 Bc55
Fonyód H 38 Ls44
Foping CHN (SAA) 95 Qd29
Foping Z.B. CHN 95 Qd29
Föppolo I 40 Lk44
Forage Christine BF 185 Kk38
Foraker River USA 229 Ce14
Foran VU 162 Te54
Forbach F 23 Lg41
Forbes AUS (NSW) 153 Se62
Forbesganj IND (BIH) 112 Pd32
Forbes Reef SD 217 Mf59
Forbidden Caverns USA 249 Fj28
Forcados WAN 194 Lc43
Forcalquier F 25 Lf47
Forcarei E 26 Km52
Forchheim D 35 Lm41
Forchtenstein A 35 Lr43
Ford, Cerro el RCH 294 Ge72
Fordate RI 133 Rg49
Ford Constantine AUS (QLD) 148 Sa56
Førde N 12 Lf29
Førde N 12 Lf31
Ford Nelson River CDN 231 Dj16
Ford Ranges 296 Cc34
Fords Bridge AUS (NSW) 151 Sc60
Fordsville USA (KY) 248 Fg27
Fordyce USA (AR) 243 Fd29
Forécariah RG 192 Kd41
Forelshogna N 12 Ll28
Foreman USA (AR) 243 Fc29
Foremost CDN (AB) 233 Ee21
Forest USA (MS) 243 Ff29
Forestburg CDN (AB) 233 Ed19
Forest City USA (IA) 241 Fd24
Forest City USA (NC) 249 Fk28
Forest Grove USA (OR) 234 Dj23
Forest Home AUS (QLD) 148 Sb55
Forestier Peninsula AUS 152 Se67
Forest Lake USA (MN) 241 Fd23
Forest River AUS (QLD) 148 Sa55
Forest Strait MYA 116 Pk40
Forest Vale AUS (QLD) 151 Sd58
Forestville CDN (QC) 244 Gf21
Forêt des Deux Balé BF 193 Kj40
Forêt du Day, P.N. de la DJI 198 Nb40
Forêt naturelle de Nyungwe RWA 206 Me47
Forfar GB 19 Ks34
Forges-les-Eaux F 23 Lb41
Forillon, P.N. de CDN 245 Gh21
Forked Island USA (LA) 243 Fd31
Forks USA (WA) 232 Dh22
Forlandet n.p. N 11 Lf06
Forlandsundet N 11 Lf06
Forlì I 40 Ln46
Forlimpópoli I 40 Ln46
Forman USA (ND) 240 Fb22
Formation Cave USA 235 Ee24
Formazza I 40 Lj44
Formby GB 21 Kr37
Formby Bay AUS 152 Rj63
Formentera E 30 Lb52
Fórmia I 42 Lo49
Formiga BR (MG) 287 Hh56
Formiga BR (MT) 285 Hb54
Formigueiro BR (RS) 282 Hh51
Formosa BR (BA) 283 Ja50
Formosa BR (GO) 282 Hg53
Formosa BR (MG) 282 Hg53
Formosa RA (FO) 289 Ha59
Formosa RA 267 Ha24
Formosa 83 Ra14
Formosa do Rio Preto BR (BA) 282 Hh51
Formoso BR (GO) 282 Hf52
Formoso BR 281 Hf52
Formoso BR 282 Hh52
Fornæs DK 14 Ll34
Fornells E 30 Le50
Fornos MOC 214 Mh57
Fornovo di Taro I 40 Ll46
Foro Burunga SUD 196 Mb39
Foro Romano I 42 Ln49
Forquilhinha BR (SC) 291 Hf60
Forres GB 19 Kr33
Forrest AUS (WA) 145 Re61
Forrestal Range 296 Hb35
Forrest City USA (AR) 243 Fe28
Forrest Lakes AUS 145 Re60
Fors S 13 Lr30
Forsayth AUS (QLD) 148 Sb55
Forserum S 15 Lp33
Forshaga S 13 Lo31
Förslöv S 14 Ln34
Forsmo S 10 Lj14
Forsnes N 10 Le14
Forssa FIN 16 Md30
Forst D 33 Lp39
Forsvik S 13 Lp32
Forsyth CDN (QC) 244 Gb21
Forsyth USA (MT) 235 Eg22
Forsyth Island AUS (QLD) 148 Rk54
Forsyth Range AUS (QLD) 148 Sb57
Fort (Maheshwar) IND (MPH) 108 Oh34
Fort Abbas PK 81 Og31
Fort Abercrombie S.H.S. USA 240 Fb22
Fort Abercrombie State Historic Park USA 230 Cd17
Fort Adams USA (MS) 243 Fe30
Fort Albany CDN (ON) 239 Fk19
Fort Albany Ind. Res. CDN 239 Fk19
Fort Alexander RH 260 Gd36
Fortaleza BOL 279 Gf51
Fortaleza BOL 279 Gh50
Fortaleza BOL 279 Gg52
Fortaleza BR (AC) 279 Ge50
Fortaleza BR (AM) 274 Ha47
Fortaleza BR (AM) 279 Gf49
Fortaleza BR (CE) 277 Ja47
Fortaleza de Santa Teresa ROU 289 Hd62
Fortaleza dos Nogueiras BR (MA) 276 Hg49
Fort Amanda St. Mem. USA 246 Fh25
Fort Anne N.H.S. CDN 245 Gh23
Fort Apache Ind. Res. USA 237 Ee29
Fort Assiniboine CDN (AB) 233 Ec18
Fort Atkinson USA (WI) 246 Ff24
Fort Augustus GB 19 Kq33
Fort Battleford N.H.P. CDN 233 Ef19
Fort Beaufort ZA 217 Md62
Fort Beauséjour N.H.S. CDN 245 Gh23
Fort Belknap Agency USA (MT) 233 Ef21
Fort Belknap Ind. Res. USA 233 Ef21
Fort Benham USA 241 Fc24
Fort Benton USA (MT) 233 Ee22
Fort Benton Ruins USA 233 Ee22
Fort Berthold Ind. Res. USA 240 Ej22
Fort Bowie N.H.S. USA 237 Ef29
Fort Bragg USA (CA) 234 Dj26
Fort Bridger N.H.S. USA 235 Ee25
Fort Brown ZA 217 Md62
Fort Bullen WAG 183 Kb39
Fort Chadbourne USA (TX) 242 Ek29
Fort Charlotte BS 251 Gb33
Fort-Chimo = Kuujjuaq CDN 225 Gc07
Fort Chipewyan CDN 224 Eb07
Fort Clatsop National Memorial USA (WA) 232 Dj22
Fort Cobb S.P. USA 242 Fa28
Fort Collins USA (CO) 235 Eh25
Fort Concho USA 242 Ek30
Fort Davidson S.H.S. USA 248 Fe27
Fort Davis USA (TX) 237 Ej30
Fort Davis N.H.S. USA 237 Eh30
Fort de Chartres S.H.S. USA 241 Fe26
Fort de Chartres S.H.S. USA 248 Fe26
Fort de Cock RI 124 Qa46
Fort-de-France F 261 Gk38
Fort de Koundou RMM 184 Kf39
Fort Dilts Hist. Site USA 240 Ej22
Fort Dodge USA (IA) 241 Fc24
Fort Duncan Park USA 242 Ek31
Forte da Principe da Beira BR 280 Gh52
Forte dei Marmi I 40 Ll47
Forte do Castelo (Belém) BR (PA) 276 Hf46
Fort Edward N.H.S. CDN 245 Gh23
Fort Erie Race Track CDN (ON) 247 Ga24
Fortescue Falls AUS 140 Qk57
Fortescue River AUS 140 Qj56
Fort Fairfield USA (ME) 244 Gg22
Fort Frances CDN (ON) 238 Fd21
Fort Frederica Nat. Mon. USA 249 Fk30
Fort Frederick ZA 217 Mc63
Fort Garland USA (CO) 237 Eh27
Fort George CDN (QC) 239 Ga19
Fort George River = La Grande Rivière CDN 239 Ga19
Fort Gibson S.H.S. USA 243 Fc28
Fort Good Hope CDN 224 Dc05
Fort Greely USA 229 Ch14
Fort Grey AUS (NSW) 150 Sa60
Fort Griffin S.H.P. USA 242 Fa29
Fort Hall Ind. Res. USA 235 Ed24
Forthassa-Rharbia DZ 173 Kk29
Fort Hope CDN (ON) 239 Ff20
Fort Hope Ind. Res. CDN 239 Fg20
Forth Rail Bridge GB 19 Kr34
Fortim BR (CE) 277 Jb48
Fortín 1° de Mayo RA (NE) 292 Ge65
Fortín Carlos A.López PY 285 Ha56
Fortín Coronel Bogado PY 285 Ha56
Fortín Defensores del Chaco PY 285 Ha56
Fortín Estero PY 285 Gk57
Fort Ingall CDN 244 Gf22
Fortín General Díaz PY 285 Gk57
Fortín Hernandarias PY 285 Gk56
Fortín Inca RA (SF) 289 Gk60
Fortín Lavalle RA (CH) 285 Gk58
Fortín Leo Nowak PY 285 Ha58
Fortín Malal-Hué RA 292 Gf63
Fortín Mayor Avalos Sánchez PY 285 Gk57
Fortín Mayor Infante Rivarola PY 285 Gj56
Fortín Mayor Rodriguez PY 285 Gk57
Fortín Olmos RA (SF) 289 Gk60
Fortín Pilcomayo RA (FO) 285 Gk57
Fortín Pozo Hondo PY 285 Gj57
Fortín Ravelo BOL 285 Gk55
Fortín Teniente 1ro.Manuel Cabello PY 285 Gk57
Fortín Teniente 1ro.Pratts Gill PY 285 Gk57
Fortín Teniente Adolfo Rojas Silva PY 285 Gk57
Fortín Teniente Montanía PY 285 Ha57
Fortín Teniente Picco PY 285 Ha55
Fortín Teniente Velazquez PY 285 Ha57
Fortín Toledo PY 285 Gk57
Fort Jacques RH 260 Gd36
Fort Jefferson National Park USA 250 Fj33
Fort Jefferson St. Mem. USA 246 Fh25
Fort Kaskasia S.H.S. USA 248 Fe26
Fort Kearney S.H.P. USA 240 Fa25
Fort Kent USA (MA) 244 Gf22
Fort Kent S.H.S. USA 244 Gf22
Fort Knox USA 248 Fh27
Fort Kochi IND 110 Oj42
Fort Lancaster S.H.S. USA 242 Ek30
Fort Langley N.H.S. CDN 232 Dj21
Fort Laramie N.H.S. USA 235 Eh24
Fort La Reine CDN 238 Fa21
Fort Larned N.H.S. USA 242 Fa26
Fort Lauderdale USA (FL) 250 Fk32
Fort Leaton S.H.S. USA 237 Eh31
Fort Lemhi Mon. USA 235 Ed23
Fort Liard CDN (NWT) 231 Dj15
Fort Liberté RH 260 Ge36
Fort MacKay CDN (AB) 233 Ee17
Fort Mackinac USA 246 Fh23
Fort Macleod CDN (AB) 233 Ed21
Fort Madison USA (MO) 241 Fe25
Fort-Mahon-Plage F 23 Lb40
Fort Malborough RI 124 Qb47
Fort Massachusetts USA 243 Ff30
Fort Maurepas CDN 238 Fb20
Fort McDermitt Ind. Res. USA 234 Eb25
Fort McKavett S.H.S. USA 242 Ek30
Fort McMurray CDN (AB) 233 Ee17
Fort McPherson CDN 224 Db05
Fort Meade USA (FL) 250 Fk32
Fort Metal Cross GH 193 Kj43
Fort Morgan USA (CO) 240 Ej25
Fort Mtobeni ZA 217 Mf60
Fort Munro PK 81 Oe31
Fort Murray ZA 217 Md62
Fort Myers USA (FL) 250 Fk32
Fort Nassau GUY 271 Hb43
Fort Nelson CDN (BC) 231 Dj16
Fort Nelson Ind. Res. CDN 231 Dj16
Fort Niobrara N.W.R. USA 240 Ek24
Fort Ogden USA (FL) 250 Fk32
Fortore I 42 Lq49
Fort Patience GH 193 Kk43
Fort Payne USA (AL) 249 Fh28
Fort Peck USA (MT) 235 Eg22
Fort Peck Ind. Res. USA 233 Eh21
Fort Peck Lake USA 235 Eg22
Fort Phantom Hill USA 242 Fa29
Fort Phil Kearny USA 235 Eg23
Fort Pickens USA 250 Fg30
Fort Pierce USA (FL) 250 Fk32
Fort Pierre Choteau USA 240 Ek23
Fort Pierre Grassland N.P. USA 240 Ek23
Fort Portal EAU 201 Mf45
Fort Qu'Appelle CDN (SK) 238 Ej20
Fort Quitman Ruins USA 237 Eh30
Fort Randall Dam USA 240 Fa24
Fort Resolution CDN 224 Eb06
Fortress of Louisbourg CDN 245 Gk23
Fort Rice S.H.S. USA 240 Ek22
Fort Rixon ZW 214 Me56
Fortrose GB 19 Kq33
Fortrose NZ 155 Te69
Fort Ross S.H.P. USA 234 Dj26
Fort Rupert (Waskaganish) CDN (QC) 239 Ga20
Fort Saint Anthony GH 193 Kj43
Fort Saint James CDN (BC) 232 Dh18
Fort Saint James N.H.S. CDN 232 Dh18
Fort Saint John CDN (BC) 231 Dk17
Fort Saint-Pierre SN 183 Kd38
Fort Sandeman = Zhob PK 78 Oe30
Fort San Pedro RP 123 Rb40
Fort Saskatchewan CDN (AB) 233 Ed19
Fort Scott USA (KS) 243 Fc27
Fort Scott N.H.S. USA 243 Fc27
Fort Sesfontein NAM 212 Lg55
Fort Severn CDN (ON) 239 Fg17
Fort-Shevchenko KZ 70 Nf23
Fort Simpson CDN 224 Dd06
Fort Smith CDN 224 Eb07
Fort Smith USA (AR) 243 Fc28
Fort Stanwix Nat. Mon. USA 247 Gc24
Fort Steele CDN (BC) 233 Ec21
Fort Steele Heritage Town CDN 233 Ec21
Fort Stockton USA (TX) 237 Ej30
Fort Stockton USA (TX) 242 Ej30
Fort Sumner USA (NM) 237 Eh28
Fort Sumner State Monument USA 237 Eh28
Fort Témiscamingue N.H.S. CDN 246 Ga22
Fort Thompson USA (SD) 240 Fa23
Fort Ticonderoga USA 247 Gd24
Fortuna BR (MA) 276 Hh48
Fortuna BR 280 Gk51
Fortuna E 29 Kt48
Fortuna USA (CA) 234 Dh25
Fortune CDN (NF) 245 Hc22
Fortune Harbour CDN (NF) 245 Hc21
Fortuneswell GB 21 Ks40
Fort Union Nat. Mon. USA 237 Eh28
Fort Union Trading Post N.H.S. USA 233 Eh21
Fort Valley USA (GA) 249 Fj29
Fort Vermillion CDN 224 Ea07
Fort Victoria Hist. Site CDN 233 Ed18
Fort Walsh N.H.P. CDN 233 Ef21
Fort Walton Beach USA (FL) 248 Fg30
Fort Washita USA 243 Fb28
Fort Wayne USA (IN) 246 Fh25
Fort Wellington GUY 271 Hb42
Fort William GB 19 Kp34
Fort Worth USA (TX) 242 Fb29
Fort Yates USA (ND) 240 Ek22
Fortymile River USA 229 Ck14
Fort Yukon USA (AK) 229 Ch12
Fort Zeelandia RC 97 Ra34
Fort Zeelandia SME 271 Hc43
Forudgan IR 72 Nf29
Forvika N 10 Lg13
Fosa de Cariaco YV 269 Gh40
Fosca CO 268 Gd43
Foshan CHN (GDG) 97 Qg34
Fosheim Peninsula CDN 225 Fd03
Fosna N 10 Lf14
Fosnavåg N 12 Lf28
Fosnøy N 12 Le30
Foso GH 193 Kk43
Fossacésia Marina I 42 Lp48
Fossano I 40 Lh46
Fosse aux Lions, P.N. de la TG 193 La40
Fosses-la-Ville B 23 Le40
Fossil USA (OR) 234 Dk23
Fossil Bluff ANT (UK) 296 Gc33
Fossil Butte Nat. Mon. USA 235 Ee25
Fossil Downs AUS (WA) 138 Rc55
Fossil Mammal Site (Naracoorte) AUS 152 Sa64
Fossil Mammal Site (Riversleigh) AUS (QLD) 148 Rk55
Fossil Shell Beach THA 116 Pk41
Fossli N 12 Lh30
Fossombrone I 41 Ln47
Fossong Fontem CAM 194 Le43
Fos-sur-Mer F 25 Le47
Foster AUS (VIC) 153 Sd65
Fót H 39 Lu43
Fotadrevo RM 220 Nc58
Fota Wildlife Park IRL 20 Km39
Fotokol CAM 187 Lh39
Fouénan CI 192 Kg41
Fougamou G 202 Lf46
Fougères F 22 Kt42
Foula GB 19 Ks30
Foulaba RMM 192 Kg40
Fouladougou RMM 183 Kf39
Foulamory RG 183 Kd39
Foulani RIM 184 Kf38
Foul Bay ET 177 Mh34
Foulénzem G 194 Le46
Foul Point IND 111 Pg41
Foumbadou RG 192 Kf41
Foumban CAM 195 Lf43
Foumbolo CI 193 Kh41
Foumbot CAM 195 Lf43
Foumbouni COM 218 Nb51
Foum el 'Alba RMM 179 Kj35
Foum el Hassane MA 172 Kf31
Foum-Zguid MA 172 Kg30
Foundiougne SN 183 Kb38
Founouga DY 186 Lb40
Fountain USA (CO) 235 Eh26
Fountains Abbey GB 21 Kt36
Fourchambault F 23 Ld43
Four Corners USA (CA) 236 Eb28
Four Corners USA (OK) 242 Ek27
Fourdou SN 183 Kc38
Fourfouras GR 49 Me55
Fouriesburg ZA 217 Me60
Fourmies F 23 Le40
Foúrni GR 49 Mg53
Fourou RMM 193 Kg40
Fours F 23 Ld44
Fourtown USA (MN) 238 Fc21
Foúrstani GR 46 Mc49
Fouta Djalon RG 192 Kd40
Foveaux Strait NZ 155 Td69
Fowey GB 20 Kq40
Fowler Ice Rise 296 Ga34
Fowlers Bay AUS 152 Rg62
Fowlers Gap AUS (NSW) 150 Sa61
Fox USA (AK) 229 Cg13
Fox Creek CDN (AB) 233 Eb18
Foxe Basin CDN 224 Ga05
Foxe Channel CDN 224 Fd06
Foxen S 12 Lm31
Foxe Peninsula CDN 224 Ga06
Foxford IRL 18 Kl37
Fox Glacier NZ 155 Tf67
Fox River CDN 238 Fc18
Foxton NZ 154 Th66
Fox Valley CDN (SK) 233 Ef20
Foya LB 192 Ke41
Foyle IRL/GB 18 Kn36
Foynes IRL 20 Kl38
Foynøya N 11 Md05
Foz E 26 Kn53
Foz de Jaú BR (AM) 274 Gk46
Foz de Odeleite P 28 Kn47
Foz do Breu BR (AC) 279 Gd50
Foz do Copeá BR (AM) 274 Gj47
Foz do Cunene ANG 208 Lf54
Foz do Iguaçu BR (PR) 286 Hc58
Foz do Jordão BR (AC) 279 Ge50
Foz do Mamoriá BR (AM) 273 Gg47
Frąckí PL 37 Md37
Fraga E 30 La49
Fraga RA (SL) 288 Gh62
Fragistra GR 48 Mb52
Fraiburgo BR (SC) 290 He59
Fraile Muerto ROU 289 Hc62
Fraile Pintado RA (PJ) 285 Gh57
Fraize F 23 Lg42
Frakes, Mount 296 Ea34
Fram Basin 299 Mc02
Frambo CI 193 Kj43
Framingham USA (MA) 247 Ge24
Framlev DK 14 Lk34
Frammersbach D 34 Lk40
Fram Peak 297 Nd32
Frampol PL 37 Mc40
Franca BR (SP) 286 Hg56
Francardo F 31 Lk48
Francavilla al Mare I 42 Lp48
Francavilla di Sicilia I 42 Lq53
Francavilla Fontana I 43 Ls50
France 7 La05
Frances Lake CDN 231 Df15
Frances River CDN 231 Df15
Franceville G 202 Lg46
Franche - Comté F 23 Lg43
Franche-Comté F 23 Lf43
Franciscan Missions in the Sierra Gorda de Querétaro = Arroyo Seco, Jalpan de Serra, Landa de Matamoros = Misiones franciscanas de la Sierra Gorda de Querétaro = Arroyo Seco, Jalpan de Serra, Landa de Matamoros MEX 253 Fa35
Francisco Ayres BR (PI) 277 Hj49
Francisco Beltrão BR (PR) 290 Hd59
Francisco Escárcega MEX (CAM) 255 Fe36
Francisco I. Madero MEX (DGO) 253 Eh33
Francisco I. Madero MEX (NYT) 253 Eh35
Francisco I. Madero MEX (COH) 253 Ej33
Francisco Macedo BR (PI) 277 Hk49
Francisco Magnano RA (BA) 289 Gj63
Francisco Morato BR (SP) 287 Hg57
Francisco Sá BR (MG) 287 Hj54
Franciscusbaai NAM 212 Lh58
Francistown RB 213 Md56
Franco de Orellana PE 273 Gd47
Francoforte I 42 Lp53
François CDN (NF) 245 Hb22
Francois Lake CDN (BC) 232 Dh18
Francois Lake CDN 232 Dh19
Francois Peron N.P. AUS 140 Qg58
Franeker NL 32 Lf37
Frankenberg D 32 Lj39
Frankenthal D 34 Lj41
Frankenwald D 35 Lm40
Frankfield AUS (QLD) 149 Sd57
Frankfort USA (IN) 246 Fg25
Frankfort USA (KY) 249 Fh26
Frankfort USA (MI) 246 Fg23
Frankfort USA (WI) 246 Fg23
Frankfort ZA 217 Me59
Frankfurt (Main) D 34 Lj40
Frankfurt (Oder) D 33 Lp38
Frank Hann N.P. AUS 144 Ra62
Frankincense market OM 69 Nh37
Frankincense Trail OM 69 Nh37
Fränkische Alb D 35 Lm41
Frankland AUS (WA) 144 Qj63
Franklin AUS (QLD) 148 Sa57
Franklin USA (IN) 246 Fg26
Franklin USA (KY) 248 Fg27
Franklin USA (LA) 243 Fe31
Franklin USA (NC) 249 Fj28
Franklin USA (NE) 240 Fa25
Franklin USA (NH) 247 Ge24
Franklin USA (NJ) 247 Gc25
Franklin USA (PA) 247 Ga25
Franklin USA (TN) 248 Fg28
Franklin USA (VA) 249 Gb27
Franklin USA (WV) 247 Ga26
Franklin ZA 217 Me61
Franklin Bay CDN 224 Dc04
Franklin Delano Roosevelt Lake USA 232 Ea21
Franklin Glacier CDN 232 Dh20
Franklin-Gordon Wild Rivers N.P. AUS 152 Sc67
Franklin Strait CDN 225 Fa04
Franklinton USA (LA) 243 Fe30
Fransfontein NAM 212 Lh56
Fransfonteinberge NAM 212 Lh56
Fränsta S 13 Lr28
Františkovy Lázně CZ 38 Ln40
Franz CDN (ON) 239 Fh21
Franz Josef Glacier NZ 155 Tf67
Franz Josef Land RUS 58 Nb03
Frascati I 42 Ln49
Fraser Basin CDN 232 Dj18
Fraserburg ZA 216 Ma61
Fraserburgh GB 19 Ks33
Fraserdale CDN (ON) 239 Fk21
Fraser Island AUS 151 Sg58
Fraser Lake CDN (BC) 232 Dh18
Fraser Plateau CDN 232 Dh19
Fraser Range AUS (WA) 145 Rb62
Fraser River CDN 232 Dk19
Fraser River CDN 232 Dk21
Fraser's Hill Hill Resort MAL 117 Qa44
Fraserwood CDN (MB) 238 Fb20
Frashër AL 46 Ma50
Frătăuţii Noi RO 45 Mf43
Frater CDN (ON) 246 Fh22
Frátsia GR 48 Mc54
Frauenfeld CH 34 Lj43
Frauenkirchen A 35 Lr43
Fray Bentos ROU 289 Ha62
Fray Jorge RCH 288 Ge61
Frazier Downs A.L. AUS 138 Ra55
Freakly Pt. CDN 239 Ga18
Frebag River CDN 233 Ee17
Frecăţei RO 45 Mj46
Fredé RIM 183 Kc37
Fredericia DK 14 Lk35
Frederick USA (MD) 247 Gb26
Frederick USA (OK) 242 Fa28
Frederick USA (SD) 240 Fa23
Fredericksburg USA (TX) 242 Fa30
Fredericksburg USA (VA) 247 Gb26
Frederick Sound USA 231 Dd17
Fredericktown USA (MO) 243 Fe27
Frederico Westphalen BR (RS) 290 Hd59
Fredericton CDN (NB) 245 Gg23
Frederiksborg DK 14 Ln35
Frederikshåb = Paamiut DK 225 Hb06
Frederikshavn DK 14 Ll33
Frederikssund DK 14 Ln35
Frederiksted USA (VI) 261 Gh37
Frederiksværk DK 14 Ln35
Frederik Willem de vierdevallen SME 271 Hb44
Fredonia CO 268 Gc43
Fredonia USA (AZ) 237 Ed27
Fredonia USA (KS) 243 Fc27
Fredonia USA (NY) 247 Ga24
Fredriksberg S 13 Lp30
Fredrikstad N 12 Ll31
Freehold USA (NJ) 247 Gc25
Freelings Heights AUS 143 Rk61
Freeman USA (SD) 240 Fb24
Freeman River CDN 233 Ec18
Freemansundet N 11 Ma06
Freeport BS 251 Ga32
Freeport USA (FL) 249 Fg30
Freeport USA (IL) 246 Ff24
Freeport USA (TX) 243 Fc31
Freer USA (TX) 253 Fa32
Free State ZA 217 Mc60
Freetown WAL 192 Kd41
Frégate SY 219 Nj48
Fregenal de la Sierra E 28 Ko48
Fregon = Aparawatatja AUS (SA) 142 Rh59
Freiberg D 33 Lo40
Freiburg D 34 Lh43
Frei Inocêncio BR (MG) 287 Hk55
Freilassing D 35 Ln43
Freilichtmuseum Ballenberg CH 34 Lj44
Freilichtmuseum Stübing A 35 Lp43
Freire RCH 292 Gd65
Freirina RCH 288 Ge60
Freising D 35 Lm42
Freistadt A 35 Lp42
Freital D 33 Lo40
Fréjus F 25 Lg47
Fremantle AUS (WA) 144 Qh62
Fremont USA (CA) 234 Dk27
Fremont USA (NE) 241 Fb25
Fremont USA (OH) 246 Fj25
Fremont Mountains USA 234 Dk24
French Bay BS 251 Gc34
Frenchglen USA (OR) 234 Ea24
French Guiana 263 Ha09
French Island AUS 153 Sc65
Frenchman River CDN 233 Ef21
French Pass NZ 155 Tg66
French Polynesia F 165 Cf54
Frenda DZ 173 La28
Frenštát pod Radhoštěm CZ 38 Lt41
Frere ZA 217 Me60
Freren D 32 Lh38
Fresco BR 275 He49
Fresco CI 193 Kh43
Freshwater CDN (NF) 245 Hc22
Fresia RCH 292 Gd66
Fresnay-sur-Sarthe F 22 La42
Fresnillo MEX (ZCT) 253 Ej34
Fresno USA (CA) 234 Ea27
Fresno-Alhándiga E 26 Kp50
Fresno de Caracena E 27 Kr51
Fresno Reservoir USA 233 Ee21
Fretigney F 23 Lf43
Freudenberg D 32 Lh40
Freudenstadt D 34 Lj42
Frévent F 23 Lc40
Freyburg D 33 Lm39
Freycinet Estuary AUS 140 Qg59
Freycinet N.P. AUS 152 Se67
Freycinet Peninsula AUS 152 Se67
Freyming-Merlebach F 23 Lg41
Freyre RA (CD) 289 Gj61
Freyung D 35 Lo42
Fri GR 49 Mg55
Fria RG 192 Kd40
Frias RA (SE) 288 Gh60
Fribourg CH 34 Lh44
Friday Harbour USA (WA) 232 Dj21
Fridtjof Nansen, Mount 296 Bd36
Friedberg A 35 Lr43
Friedberg D 34 Lj40
Friedberg D 35 Lm42
Friedewald D 32 Lk40
Friedland D 32 Lk39
Friedland D 33 Lo37
Friedland D 33 Lp38
Friedrichshafen D 34 Lk43
Friedrichstadt D 32 Lk36
Friendship Hill N.H.S. USA 247 Ga26
Friendship Road CHN 89 Pf31
Friesach A 35 Lp44
Friesack D 33 Ln38
Friesoythe D 32 Lh37
Frigates Passage FJI 163 Tj55
Friggesund S 13 Lr29
Frigorífico ROU 289 Ha62
Frillesås S 14 Ln33
Frindsburg Reef SOL 161 Sk48
Friol E 26 Kn53
Friona USA (TX) 237 Ej28
Fristad S 15 Lo33
Fritsla S 15 Ln33
Fritz Hugh Sound CDN 232 Dg20
Fritzlar D 32 Lk39
Friuli-Venezia Giúlia I 41 Ln44
Friville-Escarbotin F 23 Lb40
Frjanovo RUS 52 Mk17
Frobisher Bay CDN 225 Gc06
Frobisher Lake CDN 233 Ef17
Frog Lake CDN (AB) 233 Ee19
Frog Lake CDN 233 Ee19
Frog River CDN 231 Dg16
Frog River CDN 239 Ff19
Frohnleiten A 35 Lq43
Froid USA (MT) 233 Eh21
Frolovo RUS 53 Nb21
Frombork PL 37 Lu36
Frome GB 21 Ks39
Frome Downs AUS (SA) 152 Rk61
Frómista E 26 Kq52
Fronteira BR (SP) 286 Hf56
Fronteiras BR (PI) 277 Hk49
Frontenac USA (KS) 243 Fc27
Frontera MEX (COH) 253 Ek32
Frontera MEX (TB) 255 Fd36
Frontera Corozal MEX (CHP) 255 Fe37
Fronteras MEX (SO) 237 Ef30
Frontignan F 25 Ld47
Front Range USA 235 Eh25
Front Royal USA (VA) 247 Ga26
Frosinone I 42 Lo49
Frosta N 10 Lf14
Frostburg USA (MD) 247 Ga26
Froussioúna GR 48 Mc53
Frövi S 13 Lq31
Frøya N 10 Le14
Frøya N 12 Le29

Frozen Strait – Gayam

Frozen Strait CDN 224 Fd05
Fruges F 23 Lc40
Fruita USA (CO) 235 Ef26
Frunzivka UA 45 Mk43
Frúrio GR 48 Ma51
Fruška Gora, N.P. SCG 44 Lu45
Fruta de Leite BR (MG) 287 Hj54
Frutal BR (SP) 286 Hf56
Frutigen CH 34 Lh44
Frutillar RCH 292 Gd66
Frýdek-Místek CZ 38 Lt41
Frýdlant CZ 36 Lq40
Fua'amotu TO 164 Bc56
Fua-Mulah MV 110 Og46
Fua-Mulah Atoll = Gnayviyani Atoll MV 110 Og46
Fu'an CHN (FJN) 102 Qk32
Fucheng CHN (GZG) 96 Qe34
Fucheng CHN (HBI) 93 Qj27
Fuchskauten D 32 Lj40
Fuchun Jiang CHN 102 Qk31
Fuchunjiang Shuiku CHN 102 Qk31
Fuding CHN (FJN) 102 Ra32
Fuego, Volcán de GCA 255 Fe38
Fuencaliente de la Palma E 178 Kb31
Fuengirola E 28 Kq46
Fuensalida E 29 Kq50
Fuensanta E 29 Kt47
Fuente-Álamo E 29 Kt47
Fuente de Cantos E 28 Ko48
Fuente del Arco E 28 Kp48
Fuente el Fresno E 29 Kr49
Fuente Obejuna E 28 Kp48
Fuentesaúco E 26 Kp51
Fuentes de Ebro E 27 Ku51
Fuerte MEX 252 Ef32
Fuerte Bulnes RCH 294 Ge72
Fuerte Corral RCH 292 Gd65
Fuerte de Samaipata BOL 285 Gj55
Fuerte de San Miguel ROU 289 Hd62
Fuerte Esperanza RA (CH) 285 Gk58
Fuerte Olimpo PY 285 Hb56
Fuerte San Lorenzo PA 257 Fk41
Fuerte San Rafael RA 288 Gf63
Fufeng CHN (SAA) 95 Qd28
Fufulsu GH 193 Kk41
Fuga EAT 207 Mj49
Fuga Island RP 121 Ra36
Fügen A 35 Lm43
Fuggerei D 35 Ll42
Fugong CHN (YUN) 113 Pk32
Fugou CHN (HNN) 102 Qh28
Fugu CHN (SAA) 93 Qf26
Fuhai CHN (XUZ) 85 Pd22
Fu He CHN 102 Qj31
Fujairah UAE 75 Nj33
Fuji J 101 Rk28
Fujiachang CHN (SCH) 94 Qc31
Fujian CHN 83 Qd13
Fu Jiang CHN 94 Qc29
Fujieda J 101 Rk28
Fuji-Hakone-Izu N.P. J 101 Rk28
Fujin CHN (HLG) 98 Rg22
Fuji-san J 101 Rk28
Fujiyoshida J 101 Rk28
Fukagawa J 99 Sb24
Fukang CHN (XUZ) 85 Pd23
Fukuchiyama J 101 Rh28
Fukue J 103 Re29
Fukuei Chiao RC 97 Ra33
Fukue-jima J 103 Re29
Fukui J 101 Rj27
Fukuoka J 103 Rf29
Fukusen-ji J 101 Sa26
Fukushima J 99 Sa25
Fukushima J 101 Sa27
Fukuyama J 101 Rg28
Fulacunda GNB 183 Kc40
Fulaga FJI 163 Ua55
Fulani WAN 187 Lg40
Fulda D 32 Lk40
Fulda D 32 Lk40
Fulda USA (MN) 241 Fc24
Fuli RC 97 Ra34
Fuling CHN (CQG) 95 Qd31
Fuling Tomb CHN 100 Rb25
Fulinpu CHN (HUN) 95 Qg31
Fulleborn PNG 160 Sf49
Fullers USA (CA) 236 Dk27
Fulolo RI 124 Pj45
Fulton USA (AR) 243 Fd29
Fulton USA (KY) 243 Ff27
Fulton USA (MO) 241 Fe26
Fulton USA (NY) 247 Gb24
Fulufjällets n.p. S 13 Ln29
Fulula RDC 202 Lj48
Fulunäs S 13 Lo29
Fulung Seaside Park RC 97 Ra33
Fuman IR 72 Ne27
Fumay F 23 Le41
Fumba EAT 207 Mk49
Fumbelo ANG 209 Lk51
Fumbo Z 210 Md54
Fumel F 24 La46
Fumiela ANG 202 Lj49
Funadomari J 99 Sa23
Funafuti Atoll TUV 157 Td20
Funan CHN (AHU) 102 Qh29
Funäsdalen S 13 Ln28
Funchal P 8 Ka12
Funche Cave C 258 Fh35
Fundacão Eclética BR (GO) 282 Hf53
Fundación CO 268 Gc40
Fundão BR (ES) 287 Hk55
Fundão P 26 Kn50
Fundición, Cerro RA 284 Gh57
Fundo BR 276 Hj50
Fundo das Figueiras CV 182 Jj37
Fundong CAM 194 Lf42
Fundulea RO 45 Mg46
Fundy N.P. CDN 245 Gh23
Fungom WAN 194 Le42
Funhalouro MOC 214 Mh57
Funil, T.I. BR 282 Hf50
Funing CHN (JGS) 102 Qk29
Funing CHN (YUN) 96 Qc34
Funing Wan CHN 102 Ra32
Funkley USA (MN) 241 Fc22
Funsi GH 193 Kk40
Funter USA (AK) 231 Dc16
Funtua WAN 186 Ld40
Fuping CHN (HBI) 93 Qh26
Fuping CHN (SAA) 95 Qe28
Fuqing CHN (FJN) 97 Qk33
Fur DK 14 Lk34
Furancungo MOC 210 Mg53
Furano J 99 Sb24
Furcești RO 47 Mf47
Furcy RH 260 Gd36
Furk IR 74 Nh31
Furmanov RUS 53 Na17
Furmanovo KZ 53 Ne21
Furneaux Group AUS 152 Se66
Furo do Tajapuru BR 275 He46
Furroli EAK/ETH 198 Mk44
Fürstenau D 32 Lh38
Fürstenberg D 33 Lo37
Fürstenfeld A 35 Lr43
Fürstenfeldbruck D 35 Lm42
Fürstenwalde D 33 Lp38
Furta H 39 Mb43
Fürth D 35 Ll41
Furth im Wald D 35 Ln41
Furtwangen D 34 Lj42
Furubira J 99 Sa24
Furudal S 13 Lq29
Furukawa J 101 Sa26
Furusund S 13 Lt31
Furze Point AUS 146 Sb51
Fusa N 12 Lf30
Fusagasugá CO 268 Gc43
Fushë-Muhur AL 46 Ma49
Fushu CHN (GZG) 96 Qd34
Fushui CHN (SAA) 95 Qe28
Fu Shui CHN 102 Qh31
Fushun CHN (LNG) 100 Rb25
Fushun CHN (SCH) 94 Qc31
Fuskam Mata WAN 186 Le40
Fusong CHN (JLN) 100 Rd24
Füssen D 35 Ll43
Fustiñana E 27 Kt52
Fusui CHN (GZG) 96 Qd34
Futaleufú RCH 292 Ge67
Futong RCH 292 Gd66
Futuna Island F 164 Ba53
Futuna Island VU 162 Tf55
Futuroscope F 22 La44
Fuwairet Q 74 Nf32
Fu Xi CHN 95 Qc28
Fu Xian CHN (SAA) 95 Qe28
Fuxian Hu CHN 113 Qb33
Fuxin CHN (LNG) 100 Ra24
Fuxing CHN (AHU) 102 Qj31
Fuxing CHN (SCH) 95 Qd30
Fuxin Mongolzu Zizhixian CHN (LNG) 100 Ra24
Fuyang CHN (AHU) 102 Qh29
Fuyang CHN (ZJG) 102 Qk30
Fuyong CHN (YUN) 113 Pk34
Fuyu CHN (HLG) 98 Rc22
Fuyuan CHN (HLG) 98 Rh21
Fuyuan CHN (YUN) 96 Qc33
Fuyun CHN (XUZ) 85 Pe22
Füzesabony H 39 Ma43
Füzesgyarmat H 39 Mb43
Fuzhou CHN (FJN) 102 Qk32
Fuzhoucheng CHN (LNG) 100 Ra26
Füzuli AZ 70 Nd26
Fyllinge S 15 Ln34
Fyn DK 14 Ll35
Fynshav DK 14 Lk36
Fyns Hoved DK 14 Ll35
Fyresdal N 12 Lj31
Fyresvatn N 12 Lj31
Fyrkat DK 14 Lk34
Fyvie Castle GB 19 Ks33

G

Ga GH 193 Kj41
Gaafaru Channel MV 110 Og43
Gaafu-Alifu Atoll MV 110 Og45
Gaafu-Dhaalu Atoll MV 110 Og45
Gaa Kaba Montagnes F 271 Hc43
Gaalkacyo = Galcaio SP 199 Nd42
Gaamodebli LB 192 Kf42
Gab NAM 216 Lj59
Gaba ETH 198 Nb42
Gabaldon RP 121 Ra38
Gabare BG 46 Md47
Gabarus CDN (NS) 245 Gk23
Gabbac SP 199 Ne41
Gabba Island AUS 146 Sb50
Gabbs USA (NV) 234 Eb26
Gabčíkovo SK 38 Ls43
Gabela ANG 208 Lh51
Gabès TN 174 Lf29
Gabi RN 186 Ld39
Gabia RDC 203 Lj48
Gabiane TCH 196 Lk41
Gabindasti BD 112 Pf33
Gabir SUD 196 Mc41
Gabiro RWA 201 Mf46
Gabøl DK 14 Lk35
Gabon 167 Lb10
Gabon, Estuaire de G 194 Le45
Gaborone RB 213 Mc58
Gaborone Dam RB 213 Mc58
Gabras SUD 196 Md40
Gabrik IR 75 Nk33
Gabrovo BG 47 Mf48
Gabú GNB 183 Kc39
Gabu RDC 201 Md44
Gabu RDC 201 Me44
Gabuli Terara ETH 191 Na40
Gabur IND (KTK) 108 Oj37
Gabyon AUS (WA) 144 Qj60
Gacé F 22 La42
Gacheta CO 268 Gd43
Gackle USA (ND) 240 Fa22
Gacko BIH 41 Lt47
Gačsar IR 72 Nf27
Gadabeji RN 186 Ld38
Gadag IND (KTK) 108 Oh38
Gadaisu PNG 159 Se51
Gadara JOR 64 Mh29
Gadarwara IND (MPH) 109 Ok34
Gada-Woundou RG 192 Ke40
Gäddede S 10 Lh13
Gadebusch D 33 Lm37
Gadein SUD 197 Me41
Gadhyogol SP 199 Nb41
Gading N.P., Gunung MAL 126 Qe45
Gadis RI 124 Pk45
Gádor E 29 Ks46
Gadra PK 81 Of33
Gadsden USA (AL) 248 Fh29
Gaduk IR 72 Ng28
Gadwal IND (APH) 108 Oj37
Gadzi RCA 195 Lj43
Gærum DK 14 Ll33
Găești RO 45 Mf46
Gaeta I 42 Lo49
Gaferut Island FSM 156 Sb17
Gaffney USA (SC) 249 Fk28
Gafidda ETH 199 Nc42
Gafsa TN 174 Le28
Gag RI 130 Re46
Gagachin IR 72 Nc27
Gagal TCH 187 Lh41
Gagan PNG 160 Sh48
Gagarawa WAN 186 Le39
Gagargarh IND (UPH) 107 Pb32
Gagarin UZ 76 Oe25
Gagau, Gunung MAL 117 Qb43
Gage USA (OK) 242 Fa27
Gagere WAN 186 Ld39
Gaggenau D 34 Lj42
Gaghamni SUD 197 Me40
Gagince SCG 46 Mb48
Gagino RUS 53 Nc18
Gagnef S 13 Lq30
Gagnoa CI 193 Kh42
Gagra GE 70 Na24
Gagron IND 108 Oj33
Ga Hai CHN 87 Pj27
Gahavisuka Provincial Park PNG 159 Sc49
Gahkom IR 75 Nh31
Gahmar IND (UPH) 109 Pb33
Gahnpa LB 192 Kf42
Gai EAK 205 Mk46
Gaiab NAM 216 Lk59
Gaibanda BD 112 Pe33
Gaighat NEP 88 Pd32
Gaigou BF 185 Kk38
Gaiki LV 17 Mc34
Gail A 35 Ln44
Gail USA (TX) 242 Ek29
Gaildorf D 34 Lk42
Gailey GB 21 Ks38
Gaillac F 24 Lb47
Gaillon F 22 Lb41
Gaiman RA (CB) 292 Gh67
Gaimonaki PNG 159 Se50
Gainesville USA (FL) 250 Fj31
Gainesville USA (GA) 249 Fj28
Gainesville USA (MO) 243 Fd27
Gainesville USA (TX) 243 Fb29
Gaineswood USA 248 Fg29
Gainsborough CDN (SK) 238 Ek21
Gainsborough GB 21 Ku37
Gairdner AUS (WA) 144 Qk63
Gaire PNG 159 Sd50
Gairesi ZW 210 Mg54
Gairloch GB 19 Kp33
Gaisabad IND (MPH) 109 Ok33
Gaithersburg USA (MD) 247 Gb26
Gaivota BR (AP) 275 He45
Gai Xian CHN (LNG) 100 Rb25
Gaizinkalns LV 17 Mf34
Gajapajinagaram IND (APH) 109 Pb36
Gajendragarh IND (KTK) 108 Oh38
Gaji WAN 187 Lf40
Gajiram WAN 187 Lg39
Gajner Wildlife Sanctuary IND 106 Og32
Gajol IND (WBG) 112 Pe33
Gajutino RUS 52 Mk16
Gajvoron UA 45 Mk42
Gakem WAN 194 Le42
Gakem WAN 194 Le42
Gakilköy TR 50 Mj50
Gakiye IR 72 Nd28
Gakkovo RUS 16 Mj31
Gako RWA 206 Mf47
Gakona USA (AK) 229 Ch14
Gakona River USA 229 Ch14
Gakong EAK 204 Mh44
Gakuch 79 Og27
Gala CHN (TIB) 88 Pe31
Gălăbovo BG 47 Mf48
Gal Adhale SP 199 Nd42
Galán CO 268 Gd42
Galán, Cerro RA 288 Gg59
Galana EAK 205 Mk47
Galanduak IR 72 Nf28
Galang RI 125 Qc45
Galanga ANG 208 Lh52
Galangachi TG 193 La40
Galangue ANG 208 Lj52
Galanta SK 38 Ls42
Galaosiyo UZ 76 Oc26
Galápagos Fracture Zone 303 Cb10
Galápagos Islands EC 272 Fe45
Galas MAL 117 Qb43
Galashiels GB 19 Ks35
Galați RO 45 Mj45
Galatina I 43 Lt50
Galátista GR 46 Md50
Galax USA (VA) 249 Fk27
Galaxidi GR 48 Mc52
Galbraith AUS (QLD) 148 Sa54
Galbraith CDN (BC) 231 Dd16
Galbyn Gov' MNG 92 Qd24
Galcaio SP 199 Nd42
Gáldar E 178 Kc31
Galdhøpiggen N 12 Lj29
Galé RMM 184 Kf39
Galeana MEX (CHH) 237 Eg30
Galeana MEX (NL) 253 Ek33
Galegu SUD 190 Mh40
Galegu SUD 190 Mh40
Galela RI 130 Rd45
Galena USA (AK) 229 Cb13
Galena USA (MO) 243 Fd27
Galena Bay CDN (BC) 232 Eb20
Galenbecker See D 33 Lo37
Galeota Point TT 270 Gk40
Galera BR 280 Ha53
Galera E 29 Ks47
Galera EC 272 Fk45
Galera Point TT 270 Gk40
Galeras YV 269 Gf41
Galeras, Volcán CO 272 Gb45
Galéria F 31 Lj48
Galeria degli Uffizi I 40 Lm47
Galesburg USA (IL) 241 Fe25
Galeti ETH 198 Na41
Galeton USA (PA) 247 Gb25
Galewela CL 111 Pa43
Galgaguta H 39 Lu43
Galgamuwa CL 111 Pa43
Gălgău RO 44 Md43
Galgodon Mountains SP 199 Nb41
Gal Hareeri SP 199 Nd43
Galheirã BR 282 Hb52
Gali GE 70 Na24
Galibi SME 271 Hc43
Galič RUS 53 Nb16
Galicia E 26 Km52
Galičica, N.P. MK 46 Ma49
Galičskaja vozvyšennost' RUS 53 Nb16
Galiléia BR (MG) 287 Hk55
Gallio PNG 160 Sf48
Galim CAM 194 Lf43
Galinda ANG 202 Lg50
Galiraya EAU 204 Mg45
Galiwadu IND (APH) 111 Ok40
Galiwinku AUS (NT) 139 Rh52
Gallabat SUD 191 Mj40
Gallandhoo Channel MV 110 Og42
Gallan Head GB 18 Kn32
G'Allaorol UZ 76 Od26
Gallarate I 40 Lj45
Gallarus Oratory IRL 20 Kk38
Gallatin USA (MO) 241 Fd26
Gallatin USA (TN) 248 Fg27
Gallatin Peak USA 235 Ee23
Galle CL 111 Pa43
Gallegos RA 294 Ge71
Galleguillos RCH 288 Ge59
Gallei SP 205 Nb45
Galley Head IRL 20 Km39
Galliano USA (LA) 243 Fe31
Gallina USA (NM) 237 Eg27
Gallinazo YV 268 Gd41
Gallinero, Cerro YV 269 Gg43
Gallipoli AUS (NT) 139 Rj55
Gallipoli I 43 Ls50
Gallipolis USA (OH) 249 Fj26
Gällivare S 10 Ma12
Gallneukirchen A 35 Lp42
Gällö S 13 Lq28
Gallo Mts. USA 237 Ef28
Gällstad S 15 Lo33
Gallup USA (NM) 237 Ef28
Galma WAN 186 Le40
Galmi RN 186 Lc39
Galo Boukoy RCA 195 Lh43
Galool SP 205 Nb44
Gal Oya Valley N.P. CL 111 Pa43
Galsi IND (WBG) 112 Pd34
Galt USA (CA) 234 Dk26
Gal Tardo SP 205 Nc44
Galtåsen S 15 Lo33
Galtat Zemmour DARS 178 Kd33
Galtström S 13 Ls28
Galty Mountains IRL 20 Km38
Galugah IR 72 Ng27
Galula EAT 206 Mg50
Galumpang RI 127 Qk47
Galuutyn Canyon MNG 90 Pk22
Galuzeik MYA 114 Ph38
Galveston USA (TX) 243 Fc31
Galveston Bay USA 243 Fc31
Galvez PE 273 Gd48
Gálvez RA (SF) 289 Gk62
Galway IRL 20 Kl37
Galway Bay IRL 20 Kl37
Galway Downs AUS (QLD) 150 Sb58
Gam NAM 213 Ma56
Gam RI 130 Rf46
Gama BR (DF) 282 Hf54
Gama RG 192 Kf42
Gamadji Saré SN 183 Kc37
Gamagira WAN 186 Le40
Gamalama RI 130 Rd45
Gamana WAN 194 Le42
Gamarra CO 268 Gd41
Gamawa WAN 187 Lf39
Gamay RP 121 Rc39
Gamay Bay RP 121 Rc39
Gamba ANG 208 Lj51
Gamba CHN (TIB) 88 Pe31
Gamba G 202 Le47
Gamba RDC 203 Mc48
Gambaga GH 193 Kk40
Gambela ETH 197 Mh41
Gambela N.P. ETH 197 Mg42
Gambell USA 224 Bb06
Gambia WAG 183 Kb39
Gambia 167 Ka08
Gambia No.2 GH 193 Kj42
Gambier 303 Da12
Gambier Islands AUS 152 Rj63
Gambo ANG 203 Ma50
Gambo CDN (NF) 245 Hc21
Gambo RCA 200 Mb43
Gamboa PA 257 Ga41
Gamboma RCB 202 Lh46
Gamboula RCA 195 Lh43
Gambuta, Gunung RI 127 Rb45
Gamda CHN (SCH) 94 Qa29
Gamdou RN 186 Le39
Gameh IR 73 Nj27
Gameleira BR (PB) 277 Jc49
Gamia DY 186 Lb40
Gaming A 35 Lq43
Gamka ZA 216 Ma62
Gamkab NAM 216 Lj60
Gamkahe RI 130 Rd45
Game Bay DK 14 Ll34
Gamleby S 15 Lr33
Gammams SUD 190 Mh37
Gammelbo S 13 Lq31
Gammelstaden S 10 Mb13
Gammertingen D 34 Lk42
Gammon Ranges N.P. AUS 143 Rk61
Gamoep ZA 216 Lk60
Gamperé CAM 195 Lh42
Gampola CL 111 Pa43
Gamra RIM 183 Kd37
Gamtog CHN (SCH) 94 Pk30
Gamud ETH 198 Mk43
Gan CI 192 Kg42
Gan F 24 Ku47
Ganado USA (AZ) 237 Ef28
Gananga MOC 211 Na51
Gananita SUD 190 Mg37
Gananoque CDN (ON) 247 Gb23
Ganapatipule Beach IND 108 Og37
Gancedo RA (CH) 289 Gk59
Gancheng CHN (HAN) 96 Qe36
Ganda ANG 208 Lh52
Gandaba ETH 198 Nb42
Gandabahali IND (ORS) 109 Pb35
Gandadiwata, Gunung RI 127 Qk47
Gandajika RDC 203 Mb49
Gandak IND 107 Pc32
Gandara RP 121 Rc39
Gandara RP 123 Rc40
Gandarbal PK 79 Oh28
Gandava PK 80 Od31
Gande WAN 186 Lc39
Ganden CHN 89 Pf31
Gander CDN (NF) 245 Hc21
Gander Bay CDN (NF) 245 Hc21
Ganderkesee D 32 Lj37
Gander Lake CDN 245 Hc21
Gander River CDN 245 Hc21
Gandesa E 30 La49
Gandhidham IND (GUJ) 108 Of34
Gandhinagar IND (GUJ) 108 Og34
Gandhi Sagar IND 108 Oh33
Gandia E 29 Ku48
Gandiaye SN 183 Kb38
Gando-ko J 101 Sa26
Gandoman IR 72 Nf30
Gandorhun WAL 192 Ke41
Gandu BR (BA) 283 Ja52
Gâneb RIM 183 Ke36
Ganesh NEP/CHN 88 Pc31
Gangakher IND (MHT) 108 Oj36
Gangalur IND (CGH) 109 Pa36
Gan Gan RA (CB) 292 Gf67
Gangan RG 192 Kd40
Ganganagar IND (RJT) 106 Og31
Ganga Nuur Nature Reserve MNG 91 Qg23
Gangapur IND (RJT) 106 Oh33
Gangapur IND (RJT) 106 Oj32
Gangara RN 186 Le38
Gangaw MYA 112 Ph34
Gangawati IND (KTK) 111 Oj39
Gangca CHN (QHI) 92 Qa27
Gangchang CHN (CGQ) 95 Qe30
Gangdisê Shan CHN 88 Pa29
Ganges F 25 Ld47
Ganges IND 107 Ok31
Ganges North Reef 122 Qh40
Ganges Reef 122 Qh40
Ganghwa Dolmen Site ROK 100 Rd28
Gangi I 42 Lp53
Gango ANG 208 Lh51
Gangoh IND (UPH) 107 Oj31
Gangola BHT 112 Pf32
Gangotri IND (UTT) 107 Ok30
Gangrampur IND (WBG) 112 Pe33
Gangte Goemba BHT 112 Pf32
Gangtok IND (SIK) 112 Pe32
Gangu CHN (GSU) 95 Qc28
Gangu RDC 196 Mc43
Gangui CAM 195 Lh42
Gangula ANG 208 Lg51
Gangwa RB 213 Ma55
Ganhe CHN (NMZ) 91 Rb20
Gani RI 130 Re46
Ganjali Khan IR 75 Nj30
Ganj Dinara IND (MPH) 107 Ok33
Ganjgah IR 72 Ne27
Gan Jiang CHN 97 Qh32
Ganj Nameh IR 72 Ne28
Ganlanba CHN (YUN) 113 Qa35
Ganluo CHN (SCH) 94 Qb31
Ganmain AUS (NSW) 153 Sd63
Gannan CHN (HLG) 98 Rb22
Gannat F 25 Ld44
Gannavaram IND (APH) 109 Pa37
Gann Valley USA (SD) 240 Fa23
Ganoa RA (SA) 285 Gh58
Ganquan CHN (SAA) 93 Qe27
Gansbaai ZA 216 Lk63
Gansé CI 193 Kj41
Gansen CHN (QHI) 87 Pg27
Gansu CHN 82 Pd10
Gantang CHN (NHZ) 92 Qc27
Gantheaume Bay AUS 140 Qg59
Gantheaume Point AUS 138 Rb55
Ganvié DY 194 Lb42
Ganxi CHN (HUN) 95 Qe31
Ganye WAN 195 Lg41
Ganyesa ZA 217 Mc59
Ganyu CHN (JGS) 102 Qk28
Ganyushkino KZ 70 Ne22
Gänzä AZ 70 Nd25
Ganzhou CHN (JGX) 97 Qh33
Gao BF 193 Kj40
Gao RMM 185 Kk37
Gao'an CHN (JGX) 102 Qh31
Gaochang Gucheng CHN 87 Pe24
Gaochun CHN (JGS) 102 Qk30
Gaofengtao CHN (SDG) 102 Qk28
Gaogou CHN (JGS) 102 Qk28
Gaohezhen CHN (AHU) 102 Qj30
Gaojiabu CHN (SAA) 93 Qf26
Gaolan CHN (GSU) 92 Qb27
Gaomi CHN (SDG) 93 Qk27
Gaoping CHN (SAX) 95 Qg28
Gaoshan CHN (FJN) 97 Qk33
Gaotai CHN (GSU) 92 Pk26
Gaotanchang CHN (SCH) 95 Qd30
Gaotang CHN (SDG) 93 Qj27
Gaoua BF 193 Kj40
Gaoual RG 192 Kd40
Gao Xian CHN (SCH) 94 Qc31
Gaoyang CHN (HUB) 95 Qf30
Gaoyi CHN (HBI) 93 Qh27
Gaoyou CHN (JGS) 102 Qk29
Gaoyou Hu CHN 102 Qk29
Gaozhou CHN (GDG) 96 Qf35
Gap F 25 Lg46
Gapan RP 121 Ra38
Gaparma CHN (SCH) 94 Qb29
Gapi RDC 201 Mc43
Gapuwiyak AUS (NT) 139 Rh52
Gar CHN 88 Pa29
Gar' RUS 98 Re19
Gara I 176 Md31
Garabekevyul TM 73 Oc26
Garabinzam RCB 195 Lg45
Garacad SP 199 Ne42
Garachico E 178 Kb31
Garachiné PA 257 Ga41
Garada SUD 190 Mf37
Garadag SP 199 Nd41
Gara-Ekar DZ 180 Lc36
Garagoa CO 268 Gd43
Garagoumsa RN 186 Le39
Garah AUS (NSW) 151 Se60
Gara Hitrino BG 47 Mg47
Garaina PNG 159 Sd49
Garajonay, P.N. de E 178 Kb31
Gara Khannfoussa DZ 174 Ld32
Gara Lăkatnik BG 46 Md47
Garalo RMM 192 Kg40
Garamba RDC 201 Me44
Garamba, P.N. de la RDC 201 Me43
Garam Chasma PK 79 Of27
Garampant IND (ASM) 112 Pg33
Garango BF 193 Kk40
Garanhuns BR (PE) 283 Jb50
Ga-Rankuwa ZA 213 Md58
Garapan USA 119 Sb15
Garapu BR (MT) 281 Hd52
Garara PNG 159 Se50
Garawa A.L. AUS 139 Rj54
Garawe LB 192 Kg43
Garayalde RA (CB) 292 Gg68
Garba RCA 196 Ma41
Garbahaarrey SP 205 Nb44
Garbatka-Letnisko PL 37 Mb39
Garba Tula EAK 205 Mk45
Garberville USA (CA) 234 Dj25
Gârbou RO 44 Md43
Garbów PL 37 Mc39
Garbsen D 32 Lk38
Garça BR (SP) 286 Hf57
Garching D 35 Lm42
Garchitorena RP 121 Rb39
Garda I 40 Ll45
Gardabani GE 70 Nc25
Gardan Diwal AFG 78 Oe28
Gardanne F 25 Lf47
Gardar USA (ND) 238 Fb21
Gårdby S 15 Lr34
Gardelegen D 33 Lm38
Garden City USA (KS) 242 Ek27
Garden City USA (SC) 249 Ga29
Garden City USA (TX) 242 Ek30
Garden City USA (UT) 235 Ee25
Gardendale USA (AL) 248 Fg29
Garden Hill CDN (MB) 238 Fc19
Garden of the Sleeping Giant FJI 163 Tj54
Garden Route ZA 216 Ma63
Gardermoen N 12 Lm30
Gardete P 28 Kn49
Gardez AFG 78 Oe29
Gardiki GR 48 Mb51
Garding D 32 Lj36
Gardner = Nikumaroro KIR 157 Ub19
Gardner USA (LA) 243 Fd30
Gardnerville USA (NV) 234 Ea26
Gardone Riviera I 40 Ll45
Gardone Val Trompia I 40 Ll45
Gárdony H 39 Lt43
Garenga IND (CGH) 109 Pb36
Garešnica HR 41 Lr45
Garéssio I 40 Lj46
Gare Tigre F 271 Hd43
Gar et Tarf DZ 174 Ld28
Garfield Mtn. USA 235 Ed23
Garford AUS (SA) 142 Rg60
Gargaliáni GR 48 Mb53
Gargango RMM 184 Kh37
Gargano, P.N. del I 43 Lr49
Gargaris PNG 160 Sg47
Gargouna RMM 185 La38
Gargždai LT 17 Mb35
Garh IND (MPH) 109 Pa33
Garhakota IND (MPH) 109 Ok34
Garhbeta IND (WBG) 112 Pd34
Garhchiroli IND (MHT) 109 Ok35
Garhmuktesar IND (UPH) 107 Ok31
Gariaband IND (CGH) 109 Pb35
Gariau RI 131 Rh47
Garibaldi BR (RS) 290 He60
Garibaldi CDN (BC) 232 Dj20
Garibaldi USA (OR) 234 Dj23
Garibaldi Prov. Park CDN 232 Dj21
Gariep Dam ZA 217 Mc61
Gariep Dam Nature Reserve ZA 217 Mc61
Garies ZA 216 Lk61
Gariganus NAM 216 Lk59
Garigliano I 42 Lo49
Garimari PNG 159 Se48
Garimpinho BR (TO) 276 Hf49
Garin Shehu WAN 186 Lf41
Garissa EAK 205 Mk46
Garkem WAN 194 Le42
Garki WAN 186 Le39
Garkida WAN 187 Lg40
Garladinne IND (APH) 111 Oj39
Garland CDN (MB) 238 Ek20
Garland USA (MT) 235 Eh22
Garland USA (TX) 243 Fb29
Garlasco I 40 Lj45
Garliava LT 17 Md36
Gărljano BG 46 Mc48
Garmab IR 72 Ne28
Garmabe SUD 201 Mf43
Garmisch-Partenkirchen D 35 Lm43
Garmi Tondo (Main de Fatma) RMM 185 Kk38
Garmsar IR 72 Ng28
Garnett USA (KS) 243 Fc26
Garnett USA (SC) 249 Fk29
Garoaia RO 45 Mh45
Garonne F 24 Ku46
Garoowe SP 199 Ne41
Garopaba BR (SC) 291 Hf60
Garou DY 186 Lb40
Garoua CAM 187 Lg41
Garoua CI 193 Kj42
Garoua Boulaï CAM 195 Lh43
Garove Island PNG 159 Se48
Garphyttan S 13 Lp31
Garphyttans n.p. S 13 Lp31
Garplay LB 192 Kf42
Gar Qu CHN 94 Qb29
Garrafão do Norte BR (PA) 276 Hg46
Garré RA (BA) 293 Gj64
Garrison USA (MN) 241 Fd22
Garrison USA (ND) 240 Ek22
Garrison USA (UT) 235 Ed26
Garrovillas E 28 Ko49
Garrthalala AUS (NT) 139 Rj52
Garrucha E 29 Kt47
Garruchos BR (RS) 290 Hc60
Garruchos RA (CR) 289 Hc60
Garrygala TM 71 Nj26
Garry Lake CDN 224 Ed05
Garsen EAK 207 Na47
Garsila SUD 196 Mb39
Gärsnäs S 15 Lp35
Garson Lake CDN 233 Ef17
Gartempe F 24 La44
Gartog CHN (TIB) 94 Pk31
Gartz D 33 Lp37
Garu GH 193 Kk40
Garu IND (JKD) 109 Pc34
Garu PNG 159 Se48
Garuahi PNG 160 Sf51
Garub NAM 216 Lj59
Garubhasa IND (ASM) 112 Pf32
Garuma RCH 284 Gf57
Garunggarung RI 130 Rd46
Garut RI 128 Qd49
Garuva BR (SC) 291 Hf59
Garvăn RO 45 Mj45
Garvão P 28 Km47
Garve GB 19 Kq33
Garvie Mountains NZ 155 Te68
Garwa IND (JKD) 109 Pb33
Garwolin PL 37 Mb39
Gar Xincun CHN (TIB) 88 Pa29
Gary USA (IN) 246 Fg25
Garza RA (SE) 288 Gj60
Garza Garcia MEX (NL) 253 Ek33
Garzê CHN (SCH) 94 Pk30
Garzón CO 272 Gc44
Gasan RP 121 Ra39
Gas Bay AUS 144 Qh63
Gas Chambers USA (OR) 234 Dh23
Gaschiga CAM 187 Lg41
Gas City USA (IN) 246 Fh25
Gascogne F 24 Ku47
Gascogne F 24 Ku47
Gascoyne Region AUS (WA) 140 Qh57
Gascoyne Junction AUS (WA) 140 Qh58
Gascoyne River AUS 140 Qg58
Gasera ETH 198 Na42
Gash ER 191 Mj39
Gashaka WAN 195 Lf42
Gashaka-Gumti N.P. WAN 195 Lf42
Gasherbrum I PK 79 Oj28
Gasherbrum II PK 79 Oj28
Gasherbrum II 79 Oj28
Gash Setit Wildlife Reserve ER 191 Mj39
Gas Hu CHN 87 Pf27
Gashua WAN 187 Lf39
Gashunchaka CHN (QHI) 87 Ph27
Gashun Gobi CHN 87 Pg25
Gasim RI 130 Rf46
Gasmata PNG 160 Sf49
Gaspar BR (SC) 291 Hf59
Gasparilla Island USA 250 Fj32
Gaspé CDN (QC) 245 Gh21
Gaspésie, P.N. de la CDN 244 Gg21
Gasquet USA (CA) 234 Dj25
Gassan BF 185 Kj39
Gassane SN 183 Kc38
Gassi Touil DZ 174 Ld30
Gassol WAN 187 Lf41
Gastello RUS 99 Sb21
Gastonia USA (NC) 249 Fk28
Gastoúni GR 48 Mb53
Gastre RA (CB) 292 Gf67
Gästrikland S 13 Lr30
Gata CV 182 Jj37
Gataga River CDN 231 Dg16
Gătaia RO 44 Mb45
Gatakaini EAK 204 Mj46
Gatanga SUD 197 Me41
Gatčina RUS 52 Mf16
Gatčina dvorec RUS 52 Mf16
Gate City USA (VA) 249 Fj27
Gatehouse of Fleet GB 19 Kq36
Gateshead GB 19 Kt36
Gates of the Arctic National Park and Preserve USA 229 Cc12
Gatesville USA (TX) 242 Fb30
Gateway USA (CO) 235 Ef26
Gateway International Raceway USA (IL) 248 Fe26
Gatho Creek CDN 231 Dh16
Gati IR 75 Nk33
Gati-Loumo RMM 184 Kh38
Gatineau CDN (QC) 247 Gc23
Gatlinburg USA (TN) 249 Fj28
Gatma Dağı TR 62 Me26
Gato Colorado RA (SF) 289 Gk60
Gattaran RP 121 Ra36
Gattinara I 40 Lj45
Gatton AUS (QLD) 151 Sg59
Gatú PA 257 Fk41
Gatuna RWA 201 Mf46
Gaturiano BR (PI) 277 Hk49
Gau FJI 163 Tk55
Gaub Caves NAM 212 Lj55
Gaucín E 28 Kp46
Gaudan TM 73 Nk27
Gauer Lake CDN 238 Fb17
Gauja LV 17 Me33
Gaujas n.p. LV 17 Mf33
Gaulim PNG 160 Sg48
Gaultois CDN (NF) 245 Hc22
Gaupne N 12 Lh29
Gauribidanur IND (KTK) 111 Oj40
Gauripur IND (ASM) 112 Pe32
Gaurnadi BD 112 Pf34
Gaussberg 297 Pb32
Gaustatoppen N 12 Lj31
Gauteng ZA 217 Me59
Gautier USA (MS) 243 Ff30
Gauting D 35 Lm42
Gavarnie F 24 Ku48
Gavbandi IR 74 Ng32
Gavdopoúla GR 48 Md56
Gávdos GR 49 Me56
Gave Rud IR 72 Nd28
Gavhuni Wetlands IR 72 Ng29
Gavião BR 283 Hk53
Gavião P 28 Kn49
Gavião, T.I. BR 274 Ha47
Gavien PNG 159 Sc49
Gaviota Beach USA 236 Dk28
Gävle S 13 Ls30
Gävlebukten S 13 Ls30
Gavorrano I 40 Ll48
Gavray F 22 Kt42
Gavrilov-Jam RUS 53 Mk17
Gávrio GR 49 Me53
Gávros GR 46 Mb50
Gavry RUS 17 Mh34
Gawachub NAM 216 Lj59
Gawa Island PNG 160 Sf50
Gawan IND (JKD) 109 Pc33
Gawa Obo CHN (QHI) 94 Pk28
Gawler AUS (SA) 152 Rk63
Gawler Ranges AUS 152 Rh62
Gaworzyce PL 36 Lq39
Gawu WAN 186 Ld41
Gaxun Nur CHN 92 Qa24
Gaya IND (BIH) 109 Pc33
Gaya MAL 122 Qj42
Gaya RN 186 Lb40
Gaya WAN 186 Le40
Gayam RI 129 Qh49
Gayam TCH 187 Lj41

Gayaza – Goa

Gayaza EAU 201 Mf46
Gayéri BF 185 La39
Gaylord USA (MI) 246 Fh23
Gaylord USA (MN) 241 Fc23
Gayna River CDN 231 Df13
Gayndah AUS (QLD) 151 Sf58
Gaysan SUD 197 Mh40
Gaza IL 64 Mh30
Gaz-Achak TM 71 Oa25
G'azalkent UZ 76 Oe25
Gazanak IR 72 Ng28
Gazandzhyk TM 71 Nh26
Gazaoua RN 186 Ld39
Gazara TJ 76 Oe26
Gaza Strip IL 64 Mh30
Gazelle Channel PNG 160 Sf47
Gazelle Peninsula PNG 160 Sf48
Gazi EAK 207 Mk48
Gaziantep TR 62 Mj27
Gazi-Husrev-begova džamija BIH 41 Lt47
Gazimağusa CY 51 Mo55
Gazimur RUS 91 Qk19
Gazimurskij Zavod RUS 91 Qk20
Gazipaşa TR 62 Mg27
Gazli UZ 76 Ob25
Gazligölakören TR 51 Ml52
Gbabam CI 193 Kh43
Gbaboua CAM 195 Lh42
Gbadikaha CI 193 Kh41
Gbadolite RDC 200 Ma43
Gbagba RCA 200 Ma43
Gbaïzera RCA 196 Lk42
Gbalatuai LB 192 Kf42
Gbambélédougou CI 193 Kh41
Gbananme DY 194 Lb42
Gbanbala CI/RG 192 Kf41
Gbanendji RCA 196 Ma42
Gbanga WAN 186 Ld41
Gbangbatok WAL 192 Kd42
Gbarnga LB 192 Kf42
Gbassa DY 186 Lb40
Gbassigbiri RCA 201 Md43
Gbatala LB 192 Kf42
Gbele Resource Reserve GH 193 Kj40
Gbéné DY 186 Lb40
Gbengué BF 193 Kj40
Gbentu WAL 192 Ke41
Gberia-Fotombu RG 192 Ke41
Gberia Fotombu WAL 192 Ke41
Gbéroubouay DY 186 Lb40
Gbesse LB 192 Ke42
Gbétitapéa CI 192 Kg42
Gbinti WAL 192 Kd41
Gbodonon CI 193 Kh41
Gboko WAN 194 Le42
Gboli LB 192 Kf43
Gbon CI 192 Kg41
Gbongan WAN 194 Lc42
Gbung GH 193 Kk41
Gbwado RDC 200 Ma44
Gcwihaba Caverns RB 213 Ma56
Gdańsk PL 36 Lt36
Gdov RUS 16 Mh32
Gdyel DZ 173 Kk28
Gdynia PL 36 Lt36
Geary USA (OK) 242 Fa28
Geba ETH 198 Mh41
Gebaswa WAN 186 Le39
Gebe RI 130 Re46
Gebeit SUD 191 Mj37
Gebeit Mine SUD 191 Mj36
Gebeledan CI 192 Kf41
Gebituolatuo CHN (QHI) 87 Pg26
Gebiz TR 51 Ml53
Gebre Guracha ETH 198 Mk41
Gebze TR 50 Mk50
Gecha ETH 197 Mh42
Gedaref SUD 190 Mh39
Gedi EAK 207 Mk47
Gediksaray TR 51 Mq50
Gedi National Monument EAK 207 Na47
Gediz TR 50 Mk51
Gedlegube ETH 199 Nc42
Gedo ETH 198 Mj41
Gedong CHN (GZH) 96 Qe32
Gedonghaji RI 125 Qc48
Gedongratu RI 125 Qc48
Gedong Songo Temple RI 128 Qf49
Gedongsurian RI 125 Qc48
Gedser DK 14 Lm36
Geel B 23 Lf39
Geelong AUS (VIC) 153 Sc65
Geelvink Channel AUS 144 Qg60
Geesaley SP 199 Nf40
Geeste D 32 Lh38
Geesthacht D 33 Ll37
Gefell D 33 Lm40
Gegentala Caoyuan CHN 93 Qf25
Geghard ARM 70 Nc25
Gê'gyai CHN (TIB) 88 Pa29
Geidam WAN 187 Lf39
Geifil SUD 197 Mf39
Geikie Gorge N.P. AUS 138 Rc55
Geikie Island CDN 239 Ff20
Geikie River CDN 233 Eh17
Geilenkirchen D 32 Lg40
Geilo N 12 Lj30
Geiranger N 12 Lh28
Geirangerfjorden N 12 Lg28
Geiro EAT 207 Mj49
Geiselhöring D 35 Ln42
Geisenfeld D 35 Lm42
Géiser el Tatio RCH 284 Gf57
Geisingen D 34 Lj43
Geislingen D 34 Lk42
Geita EAT 206 Mg47
Geithus N 12 Lk31
Geju CHN (YUN) 113 Qb34
Gekdepe TM 71 Nj26
Gekehn LB 192 Kg43
Gel SUD 197 Me42
Gel SUD 197 Mf43
Gela I 42 Lp53
Geladaindong CHN 89 Pf29
Geladi ETH 199 Nd42
Gelai EAT 204 Mj47
Gelai Bomba EAT 207 Mj47
Gelam RI 124 Qb45
Gelam RI 126 Qf47
Gelangchang CHN (CGQ) 95 Qd30
Gelati Monastery GE 70 Nb24
Geldern D 32 Lg39
Geldrop NL 32 Lf39
Gele RDC 200 Lk43
Geleen NL 32 Lf40
Gelembe TR 50 Mj51
Gelemso ETH 198 Na41
Gelendost TR 51 Mm52
Gelendžik RUS 55 Mk23
Gelgaudiškis LT 17 Mc35
Gelibolu TR 50 Mg50
Gelibolu Yarımadası Milli Parkı TR 50 Mg50
Gelila ETH 198 Mj41
Gelinggang RI 126 Qg47
Gelingüllü Barajı TR 51 Mq51
Gellab SUD 196 Mc41
Gellinsoor SP 199 Nd42
Gelnhausen D 34 Lk40
Gelsenkirchen D 32 Lh39
Gelting D 33 Lk36
Gelu RO 44 Mb44
Geluketapang RI 116 Ph44
Gelumbang RI 125 Qc47
Gemamudo GNB 183 Kc39
Gembi ETH 197 Mh41
Gembloux sur-Orneau B 23 Le40
Gembogl PNG 159 Sc48
Gembu WAN 195 Lf42
Geme RI 123 Rd43
Gemena RDC 200 Lk44
Gemeri Hayk ETH 198 Na40
Gemi ETH 197 Mh41
Gemini South Observatory RCH 288 Ge61
Gemla S 15 Lp34
Gemlik TR 50 Mk50
Gemlik Körfezi TR 50 Mj50
Gemmeiza SUD 190 Mh38
Gemmeiza SUD 197 Me42
Gemmeiza SUD 201 Mf43
Gemmell USA (MN) 241 Fc22
Gemona del Friuli I 41 Lo44
Gemsa ET 177 Mg32
Gemsbok N.P. RB 213 Ma58
Gemsbokvlakte ZA 213 Mc58
Gemünden D 32 Lj40
Gemünden D 34 Lk40
Genale Wenz ETH 198 Mk42
Gençay F 24 La44
Gencek TR 51 Mm53
Gendarme Barreto RA (SC) 294 Ge71
General Acha RA (LP) 292 Gh64
General Alvear RA (BA) 293 Gk64
General Alvear RA (MD) 288 Gg63
General Arenales RA (BA) 289 Gk63
General Ballivián RA (SA) 285 Gj57
General Belgrano RA (BA) 289 Ha63
General Bravo MEX (NL) 253 Fa33
General Cabrera RA (CD) 288 Gj62
General Camacho BOL 284 Gf54
General Carneiro BR (PR) 290 He59
General Cepeda MEX (COH) 253 Ek33
General Coffee S.P. USA 249 Fj30
General Conesa RA (BA) 293 Hb64
General Conesa RA (RN) 293 Gh66
General Daniel Cerri RA (BA) 293 Gj65
General Elizardo Aquino PY 285 Hb58
General Enrique Martínez ROU 289 Hd62
General Enrique Mosconi RA (FO) 285 Gj57
General Francisco Murguía (Nieves) MEX (ZCT) 253 Ej33
General Galarza RA (ER) 289 Ha62
General Güemes RA (SA) 285 Gh58
General Guido RA (BA) 293 Hb64
General José de San Martín RA (CH) 289 Ha59
General Juan Madariaga RA (BA) 293 Hb64
General Juan N. Álvarez, P.N. MEX 254 Fa37
General La Madrid RA (BA) 293 Gk64
General Lavalle RA (BA) 293 Hb64
General Levalle RA (CD) 288 Gj63
General Lucio Victorio Mansilla RA (FO) 289 Ha59
General Luna RP 123 Rd41
General Mansilla RA (BA) 289 Hb63
General M. Belgrano, Cerro RA 288 Gg60
General Mosconi RA (SA) 285 Gj57
General O'Brien RA (BA) 289 Gk63
General Pico RA (LP) 288 Gj63
General Pinedo RA (CH) 289 Gk59
General Pinto RA (BA) 289 Gk63
General Roca RA (RN) 292 Gg65
General Salgado BR (SP) 286 He56
General Sampaio BR (CE) 277 Ja48
General San Martín RA (BA) 289 Ha63
General San Martín RA (LP) 293 Gj64
General Santos RP 123 Rc42
Generalski Stol HR 41 Lq45
General Terán MEX (NL) 253 Fa33
General Toševo BG 47 Mj47
General Viamonte RA (BA) 289 Gk63
General Villegas RA (BA) 289 Gj63
Geneseo USA (NY) 247 Gb24
Geneva CH 34 Lg44
Geneva USA (AL) 249 Fh30
Geneva USA (GA) 249 Fh29
Geneva USA (NE) 240 Fb25
Geneva USA (NY) 247 Gb24
Genève CH 34 Lg44
Gengenbach D 34 Lj42
Gengis Khan Mausoleum CHN 93 Qe26
Gengis Khan Monument MNG 91 Qf21
Gengma Daizu CHN (YUN) 113 Pk34
Gengwa RDC 203 Mb47
Gen He CHN 91 Qk20
Genk B 23 Lf40
Genkainada J 103 Rf29
Genlis F 23 Lf43
Gennep NL 32 Lg39
Genoa AUS (VIC) 153 Se64
Genoa I 40 Lj46
Genoa USA (NE) 241 Fb25
Genohe J 101 Sa25
Génolhac F 25 Ld46
Génova I 40 Lj46
Gent B 23 Ld39
Genteng RI 129 Qh50
Genthin D 33 Ln38
Genting RI 116 Pk44
Genting Highlands Hill Resort MAL 117 Qa44
Gentio do Ouro BR (BA) 283 Hj51
Genyem RI 131 Sa47
Genzano di Lucánia I 43 Lr50
Geograph Channel AUS 140 Qg58
Geographe Bay AUS 144 Qh62
Geographical Center of the 48 Contiguous States USA 240 Fa26
Geographic Center of North America USA (ND) 238 Fa21
Geographic Center of U.S. USA 240 Ej23
Geological Exposure ZA 214 Mf58
George USA (WA) 232 Ea22
George ZA 216 Mb63
George VI Ice Shelf 296 Gc33
George Genescu RO 45 Mg42
George Gill Range AUS 142 Rf58
George Island GB 295 Ha72
George P. Cossar S.P. USA 248 Ff28
George Reservoir USA 249 Fh30
George River USA 229 Cb14
George R. Parks Highway USA 229 Ce14
Georges Bank 227 Gc10
George Sound NZ 155 Td68
Georgetown AUS (QLD) 148 Sb55
Georgetown AUS (TAS) 152 Sd66
George Town BS 251 Gc34
Georgetown GB 258 Fk36
Georgetown GUY 270 Ha42
Georgetown MAL 116 Qa43
Georgetown USA (DE) 247 Gc26
Georgetown USA (GA) 249 Fh30
Georgetown USA (KY) 249 Fh26
Georgetown USA (MS) 243 Fe30
Georgetown USA (SC) 249 Ga29
Georgetown USA (TX) 242 Fb30
Georgetown WAG 183 Kc39
Georgetown WV 261 Gk39
George V Land 297 Sb33
George Washington Birthplace Nat. Mon. USA 247 Gb26
George West USA (TX) 253 Fa31
Georgia GE 63 Nb24
Georgia USA 227 Fd12
Georgia USA 227 Fd12
Georgia Basin 267 Ja29
Georgiana USA (AL) 248 Fg30
Georgian Bay CDN 246 Fk23
Georgian Bay Islands N.P. CDN 247 Ga23
Georgievka KZ 84 Pa21
Georgievsk RUS 70 Nb23
Georgina Downs AUS (NT) 143 Rj56
Georgina River AUS (QLD) 148 Rk57
Georg von Neumayer ANT (D) 296 Kc33
Gera D 33 Ll40
Gera D 33 Ln40
Geraardsbergen B 23 Ld40
Gerace I 43 Lr52
Gerakaroú GR 46 Md50
Geráki GR 48 Mc53
Gerakiní GR 46 Md50
Geraldine NZ 155 Tf68
Geraldine USA (MT) 235 Ee22
Geraldo Toco Preto, T.I. BR 276 Hh48
Geraldton AUS (WA) 144 Qh60
Geraldton CDN (ON) 239 Fg21
Gerània Óri GR 48 Md52
Geranium AUS (SA) 152 Sa63
Gérardmer F 23 Lg42
Gerash IR 74 Nh32
Gerdau ZA 217 Md59
Gerdine, Mount USA 229 Cd15
Gerede TR 51 Mn50
Gerena E 28 Ko47
Gereshk AFG 78 Oc30
Gérgal E 29 Ks47
Gergi AFG 78 Ob29
Gergova RO 45 Mk46
Gerickes ZA 216 Mb63
Gerihun WAL 192 Ke42
Gering USA (NE) 240 Ej25
Geriş TR 51 Mm54
Gerisa SP 199 Nb40
Gerlach USA (NV) 234 Ea25
Gerlachovský štít SK 39 Ma41
Germa LAR 181 Lg32
Germakolo RI 130 Rg46
German Bight D 32 Lh36
German Creek AUS (QLD) 149 Se57
Germania RA (BA) 289 Gj63
Germansen Landing CDN (BC) 231 Dh18
Germany 7 La04
Germencik TR 49 Mh53
Germering D 35 Lm42
Germersheim D 34 Lj41
Germiston ZA 217 Me59
Gernika E 27 Ks53
Gernsheim D 34 Lj41
Gero J 101 Rj28
Gerolstein D 32 Lg40
Gerolzhofen D 34 Ll41
Gerona RP 120 Ra38
Gers F 24 La46
Gersfeld D 34 Lk40
Gersthofen D 35 Ll42
Gêrzê CHN (TIB) 88 Pc29
Gesäuse, N.P. A 35 Lp43
Gescher D 32 Lh39
Gesunda S 13 Lp30
Gèsves B 23 Lf40
Geta FIN 13 Lu30
Getafe E 29 Kr50
Geti RDC 201 Mf45
Getinge S 14 Ln34
Gettorf D 33 Lk36
Getty Center USA (CA) 236 Ea28
Gettysburg USA (PA) 247 Gb26
Gettysburg USA (SD) 240 Fa23
Gettysburg N.M.P. USA 247 Gb26
Getulina BR (SP) 286 Hf56
Getúlio Vargas BR (RS) 290 Hd59
Getxo E 27 Kr53
Getz Ice Shelf 296 Dd33
Geureudong, Mount RI 116 Pj43
Gevaş TR 63 Nb26
Gevgelija MK 46 Mc49
Gevrai IND (MHT) 108 Oh36
Gewandhaus in Zwickau D 33 Ln40
Gewane ETH 198 Na40
Gewane Wildlife Reserve ETH 198 Na40
Gex F 25 Lg44
Geyik Dağları TR 62 Mf27
Geyikli TR 50 Mg51
Geysir IS 10 Jk13
Geyve TR 50 Ml50
Gezhou Ba CHN 95 Qf30
Gezirat Dungunab SUD 191 Mj36
Gezirat Mukawwar SUD 191 Mj36
Geziret Halaib el Kebir SUD 177 Mj34
Geziret Mirear ET 177 Mh34
Geziret Rawabil SUD 177 Mj34
Geziret Siyal SUD 177 Mj34
Geziret Wadi Gemal ET 177 Mh33
Ghaba OM 69 Nj35
Ghabat al-'Arab SUD 197 Me41
Ghabda RN 186 Le37
Ghadamis LAR 174 Le30
Ghadduwah LAR 181 Lh32
Ghafargaon BD 112 Pf33
Ghaghara IND 107 Pa32
Ghaghe Island SOL 161 Sk49
Ghaghra IND (JKD) 109 Pc34
Ghaibi Dero PK 80 Od32
Ghairatganj IND (MPH) 109 Ok34
Ghallamane RIM 178 Kf34
Ghamid az Zenad KSA 66 Na36
Gham Shadzar IR 75 Oa31
Ghana 167 Kb09
Ghanem Ali SYR 65 Mk28
Ghangmi RI 131 Rk48
Ghanim KSA 69 Nh36
Ghantiali IND (RJT) 106 Og32
Ghanzi RB 213 Ma56
Ghanzi RB 213 Mb56
Ghanzi Farms RB 213 Ma56
Ghar Ali Sadr Sarab IR 72 Ne28
Gharb Binna SUD 190 Mf37
Ghard Abu Muharrik ET 177 Mf31
Ghardaïa DZ 173 Lb29
Ghardimaou TN 174 Le27
Gharghoda IND (CGH) 109 Pb34
Gharig SUD 197 Md40
Gharm TJ 76 Of26
Gharo PK 80 Od33
Ghârous RMM 185 La36
Gharyan LAR 174 Lg29
Ghat LAR 181 Lf33
Ghatal IND (WBG) 112 Pd34
Ghatampur IND (UPH) 107 Pa32
Ghatanji IND (MHT) 109 Ok35
Ghatgaon IND (ORS) 109 Pc35
Ghatprabha IND 108 Oh37
Ghats (Varanasi) IND 109 Pb33
Ghatsila IND (JKD) 112 Pd34
Ghaura IND (MPH) 109 Ok33
Ghauspur PK 81 Oe31
Ghayathi UAE 74 Ng34
Ghaydah YE 68 Nf38
Ghazali SUD 190 Mg37
Ghazali Cinema Town IR 72 Nf28
Ghazaouet DZ 173 Kk28
Ghaziabad IND (UPH) 107 Oj31
Ghazipur IND (UPH) 109 Pb33
Ghazni AFG 78 Oe29
Ghazzalah KSA 66 Na32
Ghedi I 40 Ll45
Gheorgheni RO 45 Mf44
Gherdi IND (MHT) 108 Oh37
Gherla RO 44 Md43
Ghermi IR 72 Ne26
Gherța Mică RO 44 Md43
Ghilarza I 31 Lj50
Ghimpați RO 45 Mf46
Ghion ETH 198 Mj41
Ghirza LAR 174 Lh30
Ghisonaccia F 31 Lk48
Ghisoni F 31 Lk48
Ghizar PK 79 Og27
Ghizar 79 Og27
Ghorahi NEP 88 Pb31
Ghorwal IND (UPH) 109 Pb33
Ghosia IND (UPH) 109 Pb33
Ghosla IND (MPH) 108 Oh34
Ghost Mining Town NAM 216 Lh59
Ghotanu IND (RJT) 106 Of32
Ghotki PK 81 Oe32
Ghoveo SOL 161 Sk50
Ghow-Gardan-Pass AFG 78 Od28
Ghowrayd Gharami AFG 79 Of27
Ghowrmach AFG 78 Ob28
Ghubaysh SUD 197 Md39
Ghubbat al Qamar YE 69 Ng37
Ghui IND (CGH) 109 Pa34
Ghura IND (MPH) 109 Ok33
Ghurian AFG 78 Oa28
Giali Truong Son VN/LAO 115 Qc36
Giamame = Jamaame SP 205 Nb45
Giang VN 115 Qd38
Giang Trung VN 115 Qe39
Gianitsá GR 46 Mc50
Giant Buddha CHN 94 Qb31
Giant's Causeway GB 18 Ko35
Giant's Playground NAM 216 Lk59
Gia Rai VN 117 Qc41
Giardini-Naxos I 42 Lq53
Giarmata RO 44 Mb45
Giáros GR 49 Me53
Giarre I 42 Lq53
Gia Vuc VN 115 Qe38
Gibagane SP 199 Nd41
Gibara C 259 Gb35
Gibbons CDN (AB) 233 Ed19
Gibbonsville USA (ID) 235 Ed23
Gibb River AUS (WA) 138 Rd54
Gibb River Road AUS 138 Rd54
Gibe ETH 198 Mj41
Gibellina Nuova I 42 Ln53
Gibeon NAM 212 Lj58
Gibeon Station NAM 212 Lj58
Gibraleón E 28 Ko47
Gibraltar AUS (SA) 152 Rh61
Gibraltar GB 28 Kp46
Gibraltar Ranges N.P. AUS 151 Sg60
Gibr Shet ETH 198 Mj42
Gibson AUS (WA) 144 Ra62
Gibson Desert AUS 136 Ra23
Gibson Desert Nature Reserve AUS 141 Rc58
Gibsons CDN (BC) 232 Dj21
Gibson Steps AUS 153 Sb65
Gibzde LV 17 Mc33
Gic H 38 Ls43
Gichigniy Nuruu MNG 90 Pj23
Gida WAN 195 Lf42
Gidam IND (CGH) 109 Pa36
Gidami ETH 197 Mh41
Gidar PK 80 Od31
Giddalur IND (APH) 111 Ok39
Gidda Plateau ETH 198 Mk42
Giddings USA (TX) 243 Fb30
Gidgee AUS (WA) 140 Qj59
Gidole ETH 198 Mj43
Gieboldehausen D 32 Ll39
Gien F 23 Lc43
Gienadga del Coro RA (CD) 288 Gh61
Giengen D 34 Ll42
Giens F 25 Lg47
Giera RO 44 Ma45
Gierłoż PL 37 Mb36
Gießen D 32 Lj40
Gieten NL 32 Lg38
Giethoorn NL 32 Lg38
Gietrzwałd PL 37 Ma37
Gifhorn D 33 Ll38
Gift Lake CDN (AB) 233 Ec18
Gifu J 101 Rj28
Gigant RUS 55 Na22
Gigante CO 272 Gc44
Gigante de Atacama RCH 284 Gf55
Gigha GB 18 Kp35
Gighera RO 46 Md47
Gightis TN 174 Lf29
Gignac F 25 Ld47
Giheina ET 177 Mf32
Gihofi BU 206 Mf47
G'ijduvon UZ 76 Oc25
Gijón E 26 Kp53
Gikongoro RWA 206 Me47
Gila USA (NM) 237 Ef29
Gila USA 237 Ef29
Gila Bend USA (AZ) 236 Ed29
Gila Cliff Dwellings Nat. Mon. USA 237 Ef29
Gila River Ind. Res. USA 237 Ee29
Gilău RO 44 Md44
Gilavë AL 46 Lu50
Gilbert Islands 134 Tb09
Gilberton AUS (QLD) 148 Sb55
Gilbert River AUS (QLD) 148 Sb55
Gilbert River AUS (QLD) 148 Sb55
Gilberts Dome AUS 149 Se57
Gilbués BR (PI) 282 Hh50
Gilé MOC 211 Mk54
Giles Meteorological Station AUS (WA) 141 Re58
Gilgai AUS (NSW) 151 Sf60
Gilgandra AUS (NSW) 151 Se61
Gilgil EAK 204 Mj46
Gilgit 79 Oh28
Gilgit 79 Oh28
Gilgit Mountains 79 Og27
Gilgunnia AUS (NSW) 153 Sd62
Gilimanuk RI 129 Qh50
Gil Island CDN 232 Df19
Gillam AUS (WA) 140 Qk56
Gillam CDN (MB) 238 Fb17
Gilleleje DK 14 Ln34
Gillette USA (WY) 235 Eh23
Gilliat AUS (QLD) 148 Sa56
Gillroyd AUS (WA) 140 Qh58
Gills Rock USA (WI) 246 Fg23
Gilmer USA (TX) 243 Fc29
Gilo ETH 197 Mg42
Gilort RO 44 Md46
Gilo Wenz ETH 197 Mg42
Gilroy USA (CA) 234 Dk27
Gilruth, Mount AUS 139 Rg52
Gima EC 272 Ga47
Gimåfors S 13 Lr28
Gimi WAN 186 Le41
Gimli CDN (MB) 238 Fb20
Gimo S 13 Lt30
Gimone F 24 La47
Gimone F 24 La47
Gimpil Darjaalan Monastery MNG 90 Qc23
Gimpu RI 127 Ra46
Ginchi ETH 198 Mk41
Ginda ER 191 Mk39
Gindalbie AUS (WA) 144 Ra61
Gindie AUS (QLD) 149 Se57
Ginduliai LT 17 Mb35
Gingee IND (TNU) 111 Ok40
Gingilup Swamps National Reserve AUS (WA) 144 Qh63
Gin Gin AUS (QLD) 151 Sf58
Gingin AUS (WA) 144 Qh61
Gingindlovu ZA 217 Mf60
Gingko Petrified Forest S.P. USA 232 Dk22
Gingoog RP 123 Rc41
Gingoog Bay RP 123 Rc41
Ginir ETH 198 Na42
Ginosa I 43 Lr50
Gintu RI 127 Ra46
Gióia del Colle I 43 Lr50
Gióia Táuro I 43 Lq52
Gioiosa Iónica I 43 Lr52
Gioúra GR 48 Me51
Gippsland AUS (VIC) 153 Sd64
Giraffenberge NAM 212 Lg55
Giralia AUS (WA) 140 Qh57
Giraltovce SK 39 Mb41
Girard USA (KS) 243 Fc27
Girardot CO 268 Gc43
Giraul ANG 208 Lg53
Girban SUD 197 Mf40
Girdawara IND (MHT) 109 Pa36
Girdwood USA (AK) 229 Cf15
Giresun TR 63 Mk25
Giresun Dağları TR 63 Mk25
Girgâ ET 177 Mf32
Giri PNG 159 Sc48
Giri RDC 195 Lk45
Giridih IND (JKD) 112 Pd33
Girilambone AUS (NSW) 151 Sd61
Girna IND 108 Oh35
Girna Dam IND 108 Oh35
Girne Keryneia CY 51 Mo55
Giro WAN 186 Lc40
Giromagny F 23 Lg43
Girón CO 268 Gd42
Girón EC 272 Ga47
Girona E 30 Lc49
Gironde F 24 Ku45
Girraween N.P. AUS 151 Sg60
Giru AFG 78 Od29
Giru AUS (QLD) 149 Sd55
Girvan GB 18 Kq35
Girvas RUS (KAR) 11 Mg14
Girvin USA (TX) 237 Ej30
Gisasa River USA 229 Ca13
Gisborne NZ 154 Tk65
Gisburn GB 21 Ks37
Gisenyi RWA 201 Me46
Gislaved S 15 Lo33
Gisors F 23 Lb41
Gissar TJ 76 Oe26
Gisuru BU 206 Mf47
Gitagum RP 123 Rc41
Gitarama RWA 206 Me47
Gitata WAN 186 Ld41
Gitega BU 206 Me47
Githio GR 48 Mc54
Giulianova I 42 Lo48
Giulvăz RO 44 Ma45
Giun-Dagi IR 72 Nc27
Giurgeni RO 45 Mh46
Giurgiu RO 47 Mf47
Giv IR 73 Nk29
Givar IR 73 Nh27
Give DK 14 Lk35
Givet F 23 Le40
Givors F 25 Le45
Givry F 25 Le44
Givry-en-Argonne F 23 Le42
Giwa WAN 186 Ld40
Giyani ZA 214 Mf57
Giza ET 177 Mf30
Gizab AFG 78 Od29
Giżałki PL 36 Ls38
Gizo SOL 160 Sj50
Giżycko PL 37 Mb36
Gjermundshamn N 12 Lf30
Gjerstad N 12 Lj32
Gjiri i Drinit AL 46 Lu49
Gjiri i Durrësit AL 46 Lu49
Gjiri i Karavastasë AL 46 Lu50
Gjiri i Rodonit AL 46 Lu49
Gjiri i Vlorës AL 46 Lu50
Gjirokastër AL 46 Ma50
Gjoa Haven CDN 224 Fa05
Gjøra N 12 Lk28
Gjøvik N 12 Ll30
Glace Bay CDN (NS) 245 Gk22
Glaciated Rocks and Engravings ZA 217 Mc60
Glacier Bay USA 231 Db16
Glacier Bay National Park and Preserve USA 231 Db16
Glacier Express CH 34 Lh44
Glacier Mount USA 229 Ck13
Glacier N.P. CDN 232 Eb20
Glacier N.P. (Montana) USA 233 Ec21
Glacier Peak USA 232 Dk21
Glacier Peak Wilderness Area USA 232 Dk21
Gladenbach D 32 Lj40
Gladewater USA (TX) 243 Fc29
Gladis Lake CDN 231 Dd16
Gladstad N 10 Lf13
Gladstone AUS (QLD) 149 Sf57
Gladstone AUS (SA) 152 Rk62
Gladstone AUS (TAS) 152 Se66
Gladstone CDN (MB) 238 Fa20
Gladstone USA (MI) 246 Fg23
Glad Valley USA (SD) 240 Ek23
Gladwin USA (MI) 246 Fh24
Glafsfjorden S 12 Ln31
Glåma N 12 Lm31
Glamis USA (CA) 236 Ec29
Glamis Castle GB 19 Ks34
Glamoč BIH 41 Lr46
Glamsbjerg DK 14 Ll35
Glan D 34 Lh41
Glan RP 123 Rc43
Glan S 13 Lq32
Glandore AUS (NSW) 151 Sd60
Glandorf D 32 Lj38
Glarner Alpen CH 34 Lk44
Glarus CH 34 Lk43
Glasgow GB 19 Kq35
Glasgow USA (KY) 248 Fh27
Glasgow USA (MO) 241 Fd26
Glasgow USA (MT) 235 Eg21
Glaslyn CDN (SK) 233 Ef19
Glassboro USA (NJ) 247 Gc26
Glasshouse Mountains AUS 151 Sg59
Glass Window Bridge BS 251 Gb33
Glastonbury GB 21 Ks39
Glauchau D 33 Ln40
Glaumbær IS 10 Ka13
Glavatićevo BIH 41 Lt47
Glavinica BG 47 Mg47
Glazaniha RUS 11 Mk14
Glazoue DY 194 Lb42
Głębokie PL 37 Md39
Gleïbat Boukenni RIM 184 Kf38
Gleibat El Foula DARS 178 Kd34
Gleichen CDN (AB) 233 Ed20
Gleinalpe A 35 Lq43
Gleisdorf A 35 Lq43
Glélé CI 192 Kg43
Glen AUS (WA) 140 Qj59
Glen ZA 217 Md60
Glenariff GB 18 Ko35
Glenarm GB 18 Kp36
Glenavon CDN (SK) 238 Ej20
Glenavy NZ 155 Tf68
Glenayle AUS (WA) 141 Rb58
Glenbeigh IRL 20 Kl38
Glenboro CDN (MB) 238 Fa21
Glenbow Mus. CDN 233 Ed20
Glenburgh AUS (WA) 140 Qj58
Glen Canyon USA 237 Ee27
Glen Canyon Dam USA 237 Ee27
Glen Canyon Nat. Rec. Area USA 237 Ee27
Glen Canyon Res. USA 237 Ee27
Glencoe AUS (QLD) 151 Sf58
Glen Coe GB 19 Kp34
Glencoe USA (MN) 241 Fc23
Glencoe ZA 217 Mf60
Glencolumbkille IRL 18 Km36
Glendale USA (AZ) 236 Ed29
Glendale USA (CA) 236 Ea28
Glendale USA (NV) 236 Ec27
Glendale ZW 210 Mf54
Glendalough IRL 20 Ko37
Glendambo AUS (SA) 152 Rh61
Glenden AUS (QLD) 149 Se56
Glendive USA (MT) 235 Eh22
Glendo USA (WY) 235 Eh24
Glenfiddich Distillery GB 19 Kr33
Glenfinnan GB 19 Kp34
Glen Florrie AUS (WA) 140 Qj57
Glengarriff IRL 20 Kl39
Glengarry Castle GB 19 Kq33
Glengorm Castle GB 18 Ko34
Glengyle AUS (QLD) 150 Rk58
Glenholme CDN (NS) 245 Gj23
Glenhope AUS (NSW) 151 Sd61
Gleniivet ZW 214 Mf56
Glen Innes AUS (NSW) 151 Sf60
Glenluce GB 18 Kq36
Glenlyon Peak CDN 231 Dc14
Glen More GB 19 Kq33
Glenmorgan AUS (QLD) 151 Se59
Glennallen USA (AK) 229 Ch14
Glenn Highway USA (AK) 229 Cj14
Glenn Highway USA 229 Cg14
Glenns Ferry USA (ID) 234 Ec24
Glennville USA (CA) 236 Ea28
Glennville USA (GA) 249 Fk30
Glenora AUS (QLD) 148 Sb55
Glen Orchard CDN (ON) 247 Ga23
Glenorchy NZ 155 Te68
Glenore AUS (QLD) 148 Sa54
Glenormiston AUS (QLD) 148 Rk57
Glenorn AUS (WA) 144 Ra60
Glenreagh AUS (NSW) 151 Sg61
Glenrothes GB 19 Kr34
Glenroy AUS (WA) 138 Rd54
Glens Falls USA (NY) 247 Gd24
Glenties IRL 18 Km36
Glenveagh N.P. IRL 18 Kn35
Glenwood USA (AR) 243 Fd28
Glenwood USA (IA) 241 Fc25
Glenwood USA (MN) 241 Fc23
Glenwood Canyon USA 235 Eg26
Glenwood Springs USA (CO) 235 Eg26
Glidden CDN (SK) 233 Ef20
Glifa GR 48 Mc52
Glifáda GR 48 Lu51
Glimåkra S 15 Lp34
Glimmingehus S 15 Lp35
Glina HR 41 Lr45
Glinojeck PL 37 Ma38
Glittertind N 12 Lj29
Gliwice PL 36 Lt40
Globe USA (AZ) 237 Ee29
Glodeanu-Siliștea RO 45 Mg46
Glodeni MD 45 Mh43
Gloggnitz A 35 Lq43
Glogovac SCG 46 Ma48
Głogów PL 36 Lr39
Głogówek PL 36 Ls40
Głogów Małopolski PL 37 Mb40
Gloie LB 192 Kf42
Glommen S 14 Ln34
Glommersträsk S 10 Lk13
Glória BR (BA) 283 Ja50
Gloria RP 121 Ra39
Glória de Dourados BR (MS) 286 Hc57
Glossa GR 48 Md51
Glöte S 13 Lo28
Gloucester AUS (NSW) 153 Sf62
Gloucester CDN (ON) 247 Gc23
Gloucester GB 21 Ks39
Gloucester USA (MA) 247 Ge24
Gloucester Island AUS 149 Se56
Gloucester Point USA (VA) 249 Gb27
Glovers Reef BH 255 Fg37
Glovertown CDN (NF) 245 Hc21
Główczyce PL 36 Ls36
Głowno PL 37 Lu39
Gloženski manastir BG 46 Me48
Głubczyce PL 36 Ls40
Glubokij RUS 55 Na21
Glubokoye KZ 85 Pb20
Głuchołazy PL 36 Ls40
Głuchowo PL 36 Lr38
Glücksburg D 32 Lk36
Glückstadt D 32 Lk37
Gluhove RUS 53 Nb18
Glyde River AUS 139 Rh52
Gmünd A 35 Lo44
Gmünd A 35 Lp42
Gmunden A 35 Lo43
Gnadenkapelle Altötting D 35 Ln42
Gnaraloo AUS (WA) 140 Qg57
Gnarp S 13 Ls28
Gnarrenburg D 32 Lj37
Gnayviyani Atoll MV 110 Og46
Gnemasson DY 193 La40
Gnesta S 13 Ls31
Gniazdowo PL 37 Mb38
Gniben DK 14 Lm34
Gnibi SN 183 Kc38
Gniechowice PL 36 Lr40
Gniew PL 36 Lt37
Gnieyien LB 192 Ke42
Gniezno PL 36 Ls38
G'nit SN 183 Kc37
Gnjilane SCG 46 Mb48
Gnoien D 33 Ln37
Gnonsamoridou RG 192 Kf41
Gnosjö S 15 Lo33
Gnowangerup AUS (WA) 144 Qk62
Goa IND 104 Oc16

Goa – Gran Chaco

Goa RP 121 Rb39
Goageb NAM 216 Lj59
Goal Mtn. USA 233 Ed22
Goalpara IND (ASM) 112 Pf32
Goaltor IND (WBG) 112 Pd34
Goan RMM 184 Kh39
Goari PNG 159 Sc49
Goaso GH 193 Kj42
Goat Fell GB 18 Kp35
Goat Horn Mosque (Chahar Borjak) AFG 78 Ob30
Goba ETH 198 Mk42
Goba MOC 217 Mg59
Gobabeb NAM 212 Lh57
Gobabis NAM 212 Lk57
Gobari RDC 203 Lk48
Gobe PNG 159 Se50
Gobele ETH 198 Na41
Gobernador Ayala RA (LP) 292 Gg64
Gobernador Costa RA (CB) 292 Ge68
Gobernador Duval RA (LP) 292 Gg65
Gobernador Gregores RA (SC) 294 Ge70
Gobernador Grespo RA (SF) 289 Gk61
Gobernador Mayano RA (SC) 294 Gf69
Gobesh AL 46 Ma50
Gobi Desert CHN 92 Qa25
Gobindpur IND (JKD) 112 Pd34
Gobindpur IND (ORS) 109 Pc34
Gobo J 101 Rh29
Gobo ZW 214 Mf55
Gobobosebberge NAM 212 Lh56
Gobra Nawapara IND (CGH) 109 Pa35
Gobur SUD 201 Mf43
Göçbeyli TR 50 Mh51
Goce Delčev BG 46 Md49
Goce Delčev BG 46 Md49
Goch D 32 Lg39
Gochang Dolmen Site ROK 100 Rd28
Gochas NAM 212 Lk58
Go Cong Dong VN 115 Qd40
Göd H 39 Lu43
Godar-e Alizak IR 73 Nj27
Godatair SUD 197 Md41
Godavari IND 104 Pa15
Godawarari NEP 88 Pa31
Godbout CDN (QC) 244 Gg21
Godby FIN 13 Lu30
Godda IND (JKD) 112 Pd33
Goddo SME 271 Hc43
Godé BF 185 Kj39
Gode ETH 199 Nb42
Godeanu RO 44 Mc46
Godeč BG 46 Md47
Godegode EAT 207 Mj49
Godeli ETH 199 Nb42
Goderich CDN (ON) 246 Fk24
Goderville F 22 La41
God-e Zere AFG 78 Oa31
Godh IND (UPH) 107 Pa32
Godhavn = Qeqertarsuaq DK 225 Hb05
Godhra IND (GUJ) 108 Og34
Godinlabe SP 199 Nd43
Godino SP 199 Ne41
Godofredo Viana BR (MA) 276 Hh46
Gödöllő H 39 Lu43
Godong RI 128 Qf49
Godøy N 12 Lf28
Godoy Cruz RA (MD) 288 Gf62
Gods Lake CDN 238 Fc18
Gods Lake Ind. Res. CDN 238 Fc18
Gods Lake Narrows CDN (MB) 238 Fc18
Gods River CDN 238 Fd17
Godthåb = Nuuk DK 225 Hb06
Godwin Austen, Mount PK 79 Oj28
Goe PNG 158 Sa50
Goegap Nature Reserve ZA 216 Lk60
Goëlettes SY 219 Nf51
Goes NL 32 Ld39
Gog ETH 197 Mh42
Gogango AUS (QLD) 149 Se57
Go-gawa J 101 Rg28
Gogo AUS (WA) 138 Rc55
Gogo BF 193 Kk40
Gogo WAN 194 Le41
Gogogogo RM 220 Nc58
Gogoi MOC 214 Mg56
Gogolin PL 36 Lt40
Gogore DY 194 Lb41
Gogorrón, P.N. MEX 254 Ek35
Gogounou DY 186 Lb40
Gogrial SUD 197 Me41
Gogui RMM 184 Kf38
Goh IND (BIH) 109 Pc33
Gohad IND (MPH) 107 Ok32
Gohana IND (HYA) 107 Oj31
Gohitafla CI 193 Kh42
Göhren D 33 Lo36
Goián E 26 Km51
Goiana BR (PE) 283 Jc49
Goiandira BR (GO) 286 Hf55
Goianésia BR (GO) 282 Hf53
Goianésia do Pará BR (PA) 276 Hf47
Goiânia BR (GO) 286 Hf54
Goianinha BR (RN) 277 Jc49
Goianorte BR (TO) 282 Hf50
Goiás BR (GO) 281 He53
Goiás BR 265 Hc21
Goiatins BR (TO) 276 Hg49
Goiatuba BR (GO) 286 Hf54
Goidhoo Atoll MV 110 Og43
Goilkera IND (JKD) 109 Pc34
Goio-En BR (RS) 290 Hd59
Goio-Erê BR (PR) 286 Hd58
Goi-Pula RDC 206 Md49
Göis P 26 Km50
Goito I 40 Ll45
Gojeb ETH 198 Mj42
Gojo ETH 198 Mk41
Gojra PK 79 Og30
Gójsk PL 37 Lu38
Gojyo J 101 Rh28
Gokak IND (KTK) 108 Oh37
Gokavaram IND (APH) 109 Pa37
Gökçeada TR 50 Mf50
Gökçebey TR 51 Mn49
Gökçedag TR 50 Mj51
Gökçek TR 63 Mk26
Gökçekaya Baraji TR 51 Mm50
Gökçeler TR 51 Ml50
Gökçen TR 49 Mh52
Gökçesu TR 51 Mm50
Gökırmak TR 62 Mg25
Gök Medrese TR 62 Mj26
Gökova TR 50 Mj53
Gökova Körfezi TR 49 Mh54
Göksu TR 63 Nb26
Göksu Milli Parkı TR 62 Mg27
Göksun TR 62 Mj26
Göktepe TR 50 Mj53
Gokwe ZW 214 Me55
Gol N 12 Lj30
Gola IND (JKD) 109 Pc34
Golaghat IND (ASM) 112 Ph32
Gola Hills WAL 192 Kd42
Golan IL/SYR 64 Mh29
Golana Gof EAK 205 Mk45
Golapalle IND (CGH) 109 Pa37
Golashkerd IR 75 Nj31
Golbaf IR 75 Nj31
Golbahar AFG 78 Oe28
Gölbaşı TR 51 Mn51
Gölbaşı TR 62 Mj27
Golbegui RN 185 La38
Golbin IR 73 Nk27
Golce PL 36 Lr37
Gol Choba EAK 204 Mj44
Golconda USA (NV) 234 Eb25
Golconda Fort IND 109 Ok37
Gölcük TR 50 Mh51
Gölcük TR 50 Mk50
Gölcük TR 51 Mp52
Gölcük TR 63 Mk26
Golčův Jenikov CZ 38 Lq41
Golczewo PL 36 Lp37
Gold USA (PA) 247 Gb25
Goldand Lake CDN 238 Ek17
Gołdap PL 37 Mc36
Gold Beach USA (OR) 234 Dh24
Goldberg D 33 Ln37
Gold Bridge CDN (BC) 232 Dj20
Gold Coast AUS (QLD) 151 Sg60
Gold Coast AUS 151 Sh59
Gold Coast GH 193 Kk43
Goldcreek USA (MT) 235 Ed22
Golddust USA (TN) 243 Ff28
Golden CDN (BC) 233 Eb20
Golden Bay NZ 155 Tg66
Golden Beach AUS (VIC) 153 Sd65
Goldendale USA (WA) 234 Dk23
Golden Ears Prov. Park CDN 232 Dj21
Golden Fleece GUY 270 Ha42
Golden Gate USA (FL) 250 Fk32
Golden Gate Bridge USA 234 Dj27
Golden Gate Highlands N.P. ZA 217 Me60
Golden Giant Mine CDN 239 Fh21
Golden Hinde CDN 232 Dh21
Golden Spike N.H.S. USA 235 Ed25
Golden Temple = Jindian CHN 113 Qb33
Golden Temple (Amritsar) IND 106 Oh30
Golden Triangle LAO/MYA/THA 113 Qa35
Golden Triangle Express MYA 113 Pj34
Golden Valley ZW 214 Me55
Goldfield USA (NV) 234 Eb27
Gold Mine Tours CDN 239 Fk21
Gold River CDN (BC) 232 Dg21
Goldsboro USA (NC) 249 Ga28
Goldsmith USA (TX) 237 Ej30
Goldsworthy AUS (WA) 140 Qk56
Goldthwaite USA (TX) 242 Fa30
Göle TR 63 Nb25
Golema Reka MK 46 Mb49
Goleniów PL 36 Lp37
Golestan AFG 78 Ob29
Golf de Sant Jordi E 30 La50
Golfe d'Ajaccio F 31 Lj49
Golfe de Cintra DARS 178 Kb34
Golfe de Gabès TN 174 Lf28
Golfe de Hammamet TN 174 Lf27
Golfe de la Gonâve RH 260 Gd36
Golfe de Porto F 31 Lj48
Golfe de Sagone F 31 Lj48
Golfe de Saint-Florent F 31 Lk48
Golfe de Saint-Malo F 22 Ks42
Golfe de Saint-Tropez F 25 Lg47
Golfe de Tadjoura DJI 199 Nb40
Golfe de Tunis TN 174 Lf27
Golfe de Valinco F 31 Lj49
Golfe du Lion F 25 Ld47
Golfe du Morbihan F 22 Ks43
Golfe du Saint-Laurent CDN 245 Gj21
Golfete de Coro YV 269 Gf40
Golfito CR 256 Fj41
Golfo Almirante Montt RCH 294 Gd71
Golfo Aranci I 31 Lk49
Golfo de Almería E 29 Ks46
Golfo de Ana María C 259 Ga35
Golfo de Ancud RCH 292 Gd66
Golfo de Arauco RCH 292 Gd64
Golfo de Batabanó C 258 Fj34
Golfo de Cádiz E 28 Kn46
Golfo de Cariaco YV 269 Gh40
Golfo de Cazones C 258 Fk35
Golfo de Chiriquí PA 256 Fj41
Golfo de Corcovado RCH 292 Gd67
Golfo de Cupica CO 268 Gb42
Golfo de Fonseca ES/HN/NIC 255 Fg39
Golfo de Guanacayabo C 259 Gb35
Golfo de Guayaquil EC 272 Fk47
Golfo de Honduras HN 255 Fg37
Golfo de Humboldt CO 268 Gb42
Golfo de la Masma E 26 Kn53
Golfo dell' Asinara I 31 Lj50
Golfo de los Mosquitos PA 257 Fk41
Golfo de Morrosquillo CO 268 Gc41
Golfo de Nicoya CR 256 Fh41
Golfo de Papagayo CR 256 Fh40
Golfo de Paria YV 270 Gj40
Golfo de Parita PA 257 Fk41
Golfo de Peñas RCH 294 Gc69
Golfo de San Blás PA 257 Ga41
Golfo de San Miguel PA 257 Ga41
Golfo de Tribugá CO 268 Gb43
Golfo de Urabá CO 268 Gb41
Golfo di Cágliari I 31 Lk51
Golfo di Follónica I 40 Ll48
Golfo di Gaeta I 42 Lo49
Golfo di Gioia I 43 Lq52
Golfo di Manfredónia I 43 Lr49
Golfo di Nápoli I 42 Lp50
Golfo di Ólbia I 31 Lk50
Golfo di Oristano I 31 Lj51
Golfo di Orosei I 31 Lk50
Golfo di Orosei e del Gennargentu, P.N. del I 31 Lk50
Golfo di Pálmas I 31 Lj52
Golfo di Policastro I 42 Lq51
Golfo di Salerno I 42 Lp50
Golfo di Sant'Eufémia I 43 Lr52
Golfo di Squillace I 43 Lr52
Golfo Dulce CR 256 Fj41
Golfo Nuevo RA 293 Gh67
Golfo San Esteban RCH 294 Gc69
Golfo San Jorge RA 292 Gg68
Golfo San José RA 293 Gh67
Golfo San Matías RA 293 Gh66
Golfo Trinidad RCH 294 Gc70
Golfo Triste YV 269 Gg40
Gölgeli Dağları TR 50 Mj53
Gol Gol AUS (NSW) 153 Sb62
Gol Gumbaz (Bijapur) IND 108 Oh37
Gölhisar TR 50 Mk53
Goli EAU 201 Mf44
Goliad USA (TX) 243 Fb31
Golica BG 47 Mh48
Golicyno RUS 52 Mj18
Goliševa LV 17 Mh34
Goljam Manastir BG 47 Mg48
Goljamo Kruševo BG 47 Mg48
Gölköy TR 63 Mj25
Golling A 35 Lo43
Göllü TR 51 Mp51
Gölmarmara TR 49 Mh52
Golmud CHN (QHI) 87 Ph27
Golmud He CHN 87 Ph27
Golog Shan CHN 94 Qa29
Golo Island RP 120 Ra39
Golokuati GH 193 La42
Golongosso RCA 196 Lk41
Gölören TR 51 Mo53
Golotl' RUS (DAG) 70 Nd24
Golovin USA (AK) 229 Bj13
Golovina RUS (YAO) 98 Rg21
Golovnia Bay USA 229 Bj13
Golovnino RUS 99 Sc24
Gölpasari TR 50 Ml50
Golpayegan IR 72 Nf29
Golri IND (RJT) 106 Og32
Golspie GB 19 Kr33
Golßen D 33 Lo39
Gol Tappeh IR 72 Nc27
Gol Tappeh IR 72 Ne28
Göltzschtalbrücke D 33 Ln40
Golubac SCG 44 Mb46
Golub-Dobrzyń PL 37 Lu37
Golumet' RUS 90 Qb19
Golungo Alto ANG 202 Lh50
Golweyn SP 205 Nc45
Gölyazı TR 51 Mo52
Gołymin-Ośrodek PL 37 Ma38
Goma RDC 201 Me46
Gomantong Caves MAL 122 Qj43
Gómara E 27 Ks51
Gomati IND 107 Pa31
Gombé G 194 Le45
Gombe WAN 187 Lf40
Gombela EAT 207 Mk48
Gombe-Matadi RDC 202 Lh48
Gombe Streams N.P. EAT 206 Me48
Gombo RG 183 Ke39
Gomboro BF 185 Kj39
Gomboussougou BF 193 Kk40
Gomes Carneivo, T.I. BR 281 Hc54
Gómez Farías MEX (CHH) 237 Eg31
Gomez Farías MEX (COH) 253 Ek33
Gómez Palacio MEX (DGO) 253 Ej33
Gómez Rendón = Progreso EC 272 Fk47
Gomishan IR 72 Nh27
Gommern D 33 Lm38
Gomon CI 193 Kh43
Gompa PK 79 Oj28
Gomulin PL 37 Lu39
Gomumu RI 130 Rd46
Gona CI 193 Kg41
Gonabad IR 73 Nk28
Gonaïves RH 260 Gd36
Gonarezhou N.P. ZW 214 Mf56
Gonaté CI 192 Kg42
Gonbad-e Ghaffarieh IR 72 Nd27
Gonbad-e-Qabus IR 72 Nh27
Gonçalves Dias BR (MA) 276 Hh48
Goncelin F 25 Lf45
Gonda IND (ORS) 109 Pc35
Gonda IND (UPH) 107 Pa32
Gondab-e-Kavus IR 72 Nh27
Gondal IND (GUJ) 108 Of35
Gonde ETH 198 Mk41
Gonder ETH 191 Mj40
Gondey TCH 196 Lk41
Gondia IND (MHT) 109 Pa35
Gondola MOC 214 Mg55
Gondolahun LB 192 Ke42
Gondomar P 26 Km51
Gondrecourt-le-Château F 23 Lf42
Gondwana ANT (D) 297 Tc33
Gönen TR 50 Mh50
Gonga CAM 195 Lg43
Gong'an CHN (HUB) 95 Qg30
Gongbogyamda CHN (TIB) 89 Pg31
Gongcheng CHN (GZG) 96 Qf33
Gonggar CHN (TIB) 89 Pf31
Gonggar Monastery CHN 89 Pf31
Gonghe CHN (QHI) 92 Qa27
Gonghui CHN (HBI) 93 Qh25
Gongliu CHN (XUZ) 84 Pb24
Gongo EAT 207 Mk49
Gongo TCH 196 Lk41
Gongogi BR 283 Ja53
Gongola WAN 187 Lf40
Gongolgon AUS (NSW) 151 Sd61
Gongpoquan CHN (GSU) 87 Pj25
Gongshan CHN (YUN) 113 Pk32
Gongshan CHN (YUN) 113 Qb33
Gong Xian CHN (HNN) 95 Qg28
Gong Xian CHN (SCH) 94 Qc31
Gongzhuling CHN (JLN) 100 Rc24
Goniądz PL 37 Mc37
Gonour IND (MPH) 109 Pa33
Gonoura J 103 Re29
Gonxi CHN (JGX) 102 Qh32
Gonzaga RP 121 Ra36
Gonzáles PY 285 Ha57
Gonzales USA (LA) 243 Fe30
Gonzales USA (TX) 243 Fb31
Gonzales Moreno RA (BA) 288 Gj63
González MEX (CHH) 252 Eg31
González MEX (TM) 253 Fa34
González Ortega MEX (ZCT) 253 Ej34
Gonzalez Videla, G. ANT (RCH) 296 Gd31
Gonzanamá EC 272 Ga48
Goobang N.P. AUS (NSW) 153 Se62
Goobies CDN (NF) 245 Hc22
Goodenough Bay PNG 159 Se50
Goodenough Island PNG 160 Sf50
Goodeve CDN (SK) 238 Ej20
Good Hope CDN (BC) 232 Dg20
Good Hope RB 213 Mc58
Goodhouse ZA 216 Lk60
Gooding USA (ID) 235 Ec24
Goodland USA (KS) 240 Ek26
Goodlands MS 221 Nj56
Goodnews Bay USA (AK) 228 Bk16
Goodnews Mining Camp USA (AK) 228 Bk16
Goodooga AUS (NSW) 151 Sd60
Goodpaster River USA 229 Ch13
Goodspeed Nunataks 297 Oa33
Goodwood AUS (NSW) 150 Sb61
Goodwood GB 21 Ku40
Goold Island AUS (QLD) 149 Sd55
Goole GB 21 Ku37
Goolgowi AUS (NSW) 153 Sc63
Goolis Mountains SP 199 Nc41
Goolma AUS (NSW) 153 Se62
Goomalling AUS (WA) 144 Qj61
Goomeri AUS (QLD) 151 Sg59
Goondiwindi AUS (NSW) 151 Sf60
Goondooblule AUS (NSW) 151 Se60
Goongarrie AUS (WA) 144 Ra61
Goongarrie N.P. AUS 144 Ra61
Goonyella Mine AUS (QLD) 149 Sd56
Goor NL 32 Lg38
Goose Bay CDN 225 Gd08
Goose Creek CDN 239 Fg18
Goose Creek USA (SC) 249 Ga29
Goose Creek USA 235 Ed24
Goose Lake CDN 233 Eg20
Goose Lake USA 234 Dk24
Goose River CDN 233 Eb18
Gooty IND (APH) 111 Oj39
Gooty Fort IND 111 Oj39
Gop IND (ORS) 112 Pd36
Gopalganj IND (BIH) 107 Pc32
Gopalpur BD 112 Pe33
Gopalpur-on-Sea IND (ORS) 109 Pc36
Gopat IND 109 Pb33
Gopichettipalaiyam IND (TNU) 111 Oj41
Göppingen D 34 Lk42
Góra PL 36 Lr39
Góra PL 37 Ma38
Gora Ačkasar ARM 70 Nb25
Gora Addala Šuhgel'meer RUS 70 Nd24
gora Ak-Ojuk RUS 85 Pe20
Gora Aragac ARM 70 Nc25
Gora Arlang TM 71 Nh26
gora Barun-Šabartuj MNG 91 Qf21
Gora Bazazbjuzi AZ/RUS 70 Nd25
Gora Bekmurat TM 71 Nh25
gora Beluha RUS/KZ 85 Pd21
Gora Blednaja RUS 58 Oa03
gora Čehova RUS 99 Sb22
gora Černaja RUS 99 Rh24
Gora Chokhrak TM 71 Nk26
gora Čingikan RUS 91 Qh19
Gora Cuguš RUS 55 Na24
Gora Dombaj RUS/GE 70 Na24
Gora Dyntau RUS 70 Nb24
Gora El'brus RUS 70 Nb24
Gora G'amys AZ 70 Nd25
Goragorskij RUS (CHE) 70 Nc24
gora Han-Ula RUS 90 Qb20
gora Huhak RUS 90 Qe19
Gorahun WAL 192 Ke42
Gora Kalwaria PL 37 Mb39
gora Kamuj RUS 99 Se23
Gora Karabil TM 73 Ob27
gora Karagoš RUS 85 Pe20
Gora Kazbek RUS/GE 70 Nc24
gora Kedrovaja RUS 98 Rf23
Gorakhpur IND (UPH) 107 Pb32
gora Ko RUS 99 Rj22
gora Komandnaja RUS 99 Rk20
gora Konžakovskij Kamen' RUS 58 Nd07
gora Krasnova RUS 99 Sb21
Gora Ledjanaja RUS 59 Tc06
gora Manas KS 76 Of24
gora Munku-Sardyk MNG/RUS 90 Qa20
gora Munku-Sasan RUS 90 Pk19
gora Narodnaja RUS 58 Oa05
Goráni GR 48 Mc54
gora Oblačnaja RUS 99 Rh24
gora Pajer RUS 58 Oa05
Gora Reza IR/TM 73 Nk27
Goras IND (MPH) 106 Oj33
Gora Skalistyj Golec RUS 59 Qd07
gora Snežnaja KS 77 Og25
gora Sohor RUS 90 Qc20
gora Stamberg RUS 99 Sb22
gora Stokan RUS 99 Sd23
Gora Tagarev TM/IR 71 Nj26
Gora Talgar KZ 77 Oj24
gora Tardoki Jani RUS 99 Rk21
gora Taskyl-Sajlyg RUS 90 Pj20
gora Tastau KZ 84 Pb22
gora Tel'posiz RUS 58 Nd06
Gorau IND (RJT) 106 Oh32
gora Vozvraščenija RUS 99 Sb21
Goražde BIH 46 Lt47
Gorban RO 45 Mj44
Gorbea RCH 292 Gd65
Gorbica RUS 91 Qk19
Gorbyl' RUS 98 Re20
Gorczański Park Narodowy PL 39 Ma41
Gördalen S 12 Ln29
Gorda Peak N.P. GB 261 Gh36
Gördes TR 50 Mj52
Gordion TR 51 Mn51
Gordon USA (NE) 240 Ej24
Gordon Downs AUS (WA) 138 Re55
Gordon Lake CDN 233 Ee17
Gordon, Mount AUS 144 Ra62
Gordon's Bay ZA 216 Lk63
Gordonvale AUS (QLD) 149 Sc54
Gore ETH 197 Mh41
Gore NZ 155 Te69
Goré TCH 195 Lj42
Gore Highway AUS 151 Sf59
Gorél BF 185 Kk38
Gorelki RUS 52 Mj18
Göreme TR 51 Mp52
Göreme Milli Parkı TR 51 Mp52
Gore Pt. USA 229 Ce16
Gorey IRL 20 Ko38
Gorgadji BF 185 Kk38
Gorgan IR 72 Nh27
Gorge d'Arak DZ 180 Lb33
Gorges DZ 173 Lb27
Gorges d'Aouli MA 172 Kh29
Gorges de Kola CAM 187 Lg41
Gorges de la Pipi RCA 196 Mb41
Gorges de l'Ardèche F 25 Le46
Gorges de la Restonica F 31 Lk48
Gorges de l'Asco F 31 Lk48
Gorges de l'Oued Seldja TN 174 Le28
Gorges de l'Oudingueur TCH 188 Lj35
Gorges de Lukwila RDC 203 Lk49
Gorges de Spelunca F 31 Lj48
Gorges de Talari RMM 183 Ke39
Gorges de Tighanimine DZ 174 Ld28
Gorges Diasso RCB 202 Lg48
Gorges du Dadès MA 172 Kh30
Gorges du Kadéi RCA 195 Lh44
Gorges du Keran TG 193 La41
Gorges du Prunelli F 31 Lk49
Gorges du Tarn F 25 Ld46
Gorges du Todra MA 172 Kh30
Gorges du Ziz MA 172 Kh29
Gorgol RIM 183 Kd37
Gorgol Blanc RIM 183 Kd37
Gorgol Noir RIM 183 Kd37
Gorgora ETH 191 Mj40
Gorgoram WAN 187 Lf39
Gori GE 70 Nc25
Gori PK 81 Of33
Gorica BG 47 Mh48
Goricë AL 46 Ma50
Goricy RUS 52 Mj17
Gori Hills WAL 192 Ke41
Gorinchem NL 32 Le39
Goris ARM 70 Nd26
Goritsá GR 48 Mc53
Gorizia I 41 Lo45
Gorizkij monastyr RUS 52 Mk17
Gorjačij Ključ RUS 55 Mk23
Gorjun RUS 98 Rj20
Gorkha NEP 88 Pc31
Gorkhi-Terelj Nature Reserve MNG 90 Qd21
Gørlev DK 14 Lm35
Gorlice PL 39 Mb41
Görlitz D 33 Lp39
Gorman USA (CA) 236 Ea28
Gormanstown IRL 20 Ko37
Gorna Beševica BG 46 Md47
Gorna Orjahovica BG 47 Mf47
Gorna Studena BG 47 Mf47
Gorni Okol BG 46 Md48
Gornjackij RUS 55 Na21
Gornja Radgona SLO 41 Lq44
Gornja Sabanta SCG 46 Ma47
Gornje Peulje BIH 41 Lr46
Gornji Jabolčište MK 46 Mb49
Gornji Milanovac SCG 46 Ma46
Gornji Vakuf = Uskoplje BIH 41 Ls47
Górno PL 37 Ma40
Gorno-Altajsk RUS (ALT) 85 Pc20
Gorno-Altay RUS 58 Pb08
Gornovodnoe RUS 99 Rh24
Gornozavodsk RUS 99 Sa22
Gornyak RUS 85 Pa20
Gornyj RUS 53 Ne20
Gornyj RUS 98 Rj20
Goro ETH 198 Na42
Goroch'an ETH 198 Mj41
Gorodec RUS 53 Nb17
Gorodišče RUS 53 Nc19
Gorodovikovsk RUS (KAL) 55 Na22
Gorogoro RI 130 Rd46
Goroka PNG 159 Sc49
Goroka Show PNG 159 Sc49
Gorom-Gorom BF 185 Kk38
Gorondema ZW 210 Me54
Gorong RI 130 Rf47
Gorongosa MOC 210 Mh55
Gorongoza MOC 214 Mh55
Gorongoza, P.N. de MOC 214 Mh55
Gorontalo RI 127 Rb45
Goronyo WAN 186 Lc39
Gorouol RN 185 La39
Goroubi RN 185 La38
Gorouol BF 185 La38
Górowo Iławeckie PL 37 Ma36
Gorrie AUS (NT) 139 Rg53
Gorron F 22 Ku42
Goršečnoe RUS 53 Mj20
Gór Stołowych, P.N. PL 36 Lr40
Gort IRL 20 Km37
Górtis GR 49 Me55
Görükle TR 50 Mj50
Gorumna Island IRL 20 Kl37
Gorutuba BR 282 Hj53
gory Byrranga RUS 58 Pc04
gory Koymatdag TM 71 Nh25
gory Prževal'skogo RUS 98 Rg24
Gorzkowice PL 37 Lu39
Gorzków-Osada PL 37 Md40
Gorzów Wielkopolski PL 36 Lq38
Gorzyń PL 36 Lq38
Gosau A 35 Lo43
Goschen Strait PNG 160 Sf51
Gościkowo Jordanowo PL 36 Lq38
Gosford AUS (NSW) 153 Sf62
Gosforth GB 19 Kr36
Goshogawara J 101 Sa25
Goshute Ind. Res. USA 235 Ec26
Goslar D 33 Ll39
Goşmanu RO 45 Mg44
Gospić HR 41 Lq46
Gossas SN 183 Kb38
Gossen N 12 Lg28
Gossi RMM 185 Kk38
Gossinga SUD 196 Mc41
Gostilja BG 46 Me47
Gostivar MK 46 Ma49
Göstling A 35 Lp43
Gostomia PL 36 Lr37
Gostyń PL 36 Ls39
Gostynin PL 37 Lu38
Göta älv S 14 Ln32
Göta kanal S 13 Lp32
Göta kanal S 13 Lr32
Göteborg S 14 Lm33
Gotel Mountains WAN 195 Lf42
Gotëne S 13 Lo32
Gotha D 33 Ll40
Goth Ahmad PK 80 Od33
Gothenburg USA (NE) 240 Ek25
Gothèye RN 185 La39
Gothiahalvøya N 11 Lk06
Gotia IND (CGH) 109 Pa36
Gotland S 15 Lt33
Götlunda S 13 Lq31
Goto-retto J 103 Re29
Gotska Sandön S 13 Lu32
Gotska Sandön n.p. S 13 Lu32
Gotsu J 101 Rg28
Göttingen D 32 Lk39
Gottskär S 14 Lm33
Gouandé DY 193 La40
Gouatchi RCA 200 Ma43
Gouaya BF 185 Kk39
Goubangzi CHN (LNG) 100 Ra25
Goubi TG 193 La41
Gouboua DY 193 La41
Goucester PNG 159 Se48
Gouchang CHN (GZH) 96 Qc33
Gouchi RN 186 Le39
Gouda NL 32 Le38
Gouda ZA 216 Lk62
Goudiri SN 183 Kd38
Goudomp SN 183 Kc39
Goudoumaria RN 187 Lf39
Gouéké RG 192 Kf41
Gouendo RMM 184 Kg39
Gouffre de Bogbaté RCA 196 Lk43
Gouffre de Friouato MA 173 Kh28
Gouga RCB 200 Lk44
Gouğaram RN 180 Ld36
Gough Island GB 167 Kb13
Gouiné CI 192 Kg42
Gouiret Moussa DZ 173 Lb30
Gouka DY 193 La41
Goulaonfla CI 192 Kg42
Goulburn AUS (NSW) 153 Se63
Gouldtown CDN (SK) 233 Eg20
Goulfey CAM 187 Lh39
Goulia CI 192 Kg40
Goulmina MA 172 Kh30
Goumbatou TCH 196 Mb40
Goumbi RN 186 Lc39
Goumbou RMM 184 Kg38
Gouménissa GR 46 Mc50
Gouméré CI 193 Kj42
Goúmero GR 48 Mb53
Gouna CAM 195 Lg41
Gounatolo SOL 161 Ta50
Gounda RCA 196 Ma41
Gounda RCA 196 Ma41
Goundam RMM 185 Kj37
Goundi TCH 187 Lj41
Gounou Gaya TCH 187 Lh41
Gourak AFG 78 Oc29
Goura, Mount WAN 186 Le40
Gourara DZ 173 La31
Gouray RIM 183 Kd38
Gouraya DZ 173 La27
Gouraya, P.N. de DZ 174 Lc27
Gourcy BF 185 Kj39
Gourdon F 24 Lb46
Gouré RN 187 Lf38
Goûr Ghaoua DZ 180 La33
Gourie JA 259 Gb36
Gourin F 22 Kr42
Gourits ZA 216 Ma63
Gouritsmond ZA 216 Ma63
Gourjhamar IND (MPH) 109 Ok34
Gourma RMM 185 Kk38
Gourma-Rharous RMM 185 Kk37
Gourmeur TCH 189 Ma37
Gournay-en-Bray F 23 Lb41
Gournia GR 49 Mf55
Gourrama MA 173 Kh29
Goush LAR 174 Lf29
Gouveia BR (MG) 287 Hj55
Gouveia P 26 Kn50
Gouvelândia BR (GO) 286 He55
Gouverneur USA (NY) 247 Gc23
Gouzé RCA 195 Lj42
Gouzon F 24 Lc44
Gov'-Altay MNG 85 Ph22
Gov' Altayn Nuruu MNG 82 Qa10
Govan River CDN 238 Fc18
Govedari HR 43 Ls48
Gove Peninsula AUS 139 Rj52
Goverdor Celso Ramos BR (SC) 291 Hf59
Goverdor Garmendia RA (TU) 288 Gh59
Goverdor Ingeniero V.Virasoro RA (CR) 289 Hb60
Governador Eugênio Barros BR (MA) 276 Hh48
Governador, T.I. BR 276 Hg48
Governador Valadares BR (MG) 287 Hk55
Government Point USA (CA) 236 Dk28
Governor Generoso RP 123 Rd42
Governor's Harbour BS 251 Gb33
Govindapalle IND (ORS) 109 Pb36
Govind Sagar IND 107 Oj30
Govurdak TM 73 Od27
Gowanda USA (NY) 247 Ga24
Gowhar Shad Mosque IR 73 Nk27
Gowhar Shar IR 75 Oa31
Gowidlino PL 36 Ls36
Gowmal Kalay AFG 78 Oe29
Gowran Park IRL 20 Kn38
Gowrie Park AUS (TAS) 152 Sd66
Goya RA (CR) 289 Ha60
Göyçay AZ 70 Nd25
Goyerkata IND (WBG) 112 Pe32
Goyllarisquizga PE 278 Gb51
Göynücek TR 51 Mq50
Göynük TR 51 Ml50
Goyo Kyauwo WAN 187 Lg40
Goyoum CAM 195 Lg43
Gozare AFG 78 Ob28
Goz-Beida TCH 196 Ma39
Gozdnica PL 36 Lq39
Gozha Co CHN 86 Pa28
Gözne TR 62 Mh27
Gozo M 42 Lp54
Goz Regeb SUD 190 Mk38
Graaff-Reinet ZA 217 Mc62
Graafwater ZA 216 Lk62
Grabarka PL 37 Mc38
Graben-Neudorf D 34 Lj41
Grabo CI 192 Kg43
Grăboc H 39 Lt44
Grabovica SCG 44 Lu46
Grabovica SCG 44 Mc46
Grabow D 33 Lm37
Grabów nad Prosną PL 36 Lt39
Grabowno PL 36 Lr37
Grabowo PL 37 Mc36
Graça Aranha BR (MA) 276 Hh48
Gračac HR 41 Lq46
Gračanica BIH 41 Ls47
Gračanica BIH 41 Lt46
Gračanica SCG 46 Mb48
Graçay F 22 Lb43
Gracefield CDN (QC) 244 Gb22
Gracemere AUS (QLD) 149 Sf57
Graceville USA (MN) 241 Fb23
Gračevka RUS 53 Ng19
Gračevka RUS 70 Nb23
Gracias HN 255 Ff38
Gradac HR 41 Lq45
Gradačac BIH 44 Lt46
Gradaús BR (PA) 275 He49
Gradec BG 46 Mc46
Gradešnica MK 46 Mb49
Gradgery AUS (NSW) 151 Sd61
Gradina BG 47 Mf47
Grădinari RO 44 Mb45
Grădište HR 41 Lt45
Grădiștea RO 44 Md46
Grădiștea RO 45 Mh46
Grădiștea de Munte RO 44 Md45
Grădiștea de Munte-Cioclovina, P.N. RO 44 Md45
Gradnica BG 47 Me48
Grado E 26 Ko53
Grado I 41 Lo45
Gradojević SCG 44 Lu46
Gradski bedemi SCG 46 Lt48
Grady USA (AR) 243 Fe28
Grady USA (NM) 237 Ej28
Grafenau D 35 Lo42
Gräfenberg D 35 Lm41
Gräfenhainichen D 33 Ln39
Grafenwöhr D 35 Lm41
Gråfjell N 12 Lk30
Grafton AUS (NSW) 151 Sg60
Grafton USA (ND) 238 Fb21
Grafton USA (WV) 247 Ga26
Graham CDN (ON) 239 Fe21
Graham USA (TX) 242 Fa29
Graham Island USA 231 Dd19
Graham Lake CDN 233 Ec17
Graham Land 296 Gd32
Graham River CDN 231 Dj17
Grahamstad ZA 217 Md62
Grahamstown ZA 217 Md62
Gråhøgda N 12 Lm28
Graiguenamanagh IRL 20 Ko38
Grain Coast LB 192 Ke43
Grainfield USA (KS) 240 Ek26
Grainton USA (NE) 240 Ek25
Grajagan RI 129 Qh50
Grajaú BR (MA) 276 Hg48
Grajaú BR 276 Hh48
Grajduri RO 45 Mh44
Grajewo PL 37 Mc37
Grajvoron RUS 52 Mh20
Gram DK 14 Lk35
Grama BR (MG) 286 He55
Gramado BR (RS) 290 He60
Graman AUS (NSW) 151 Sf60
Gramat F 24 Lb46
Grambling USA (LA) 243 Fd29
Grammichele I 42 Lp53
Gramphu IND (HPH) 107 Oj29
Grampian USA (PA) 247 Ga25
Grampianfjella N 11 Lf06
Grampian Mountains GB 19 Kq34
Grampians N.P. AUS 152 Sb64
Gramsh AL 46 Ma50
Gramzow D 33 Lo37
Gran N 12 Ll30
Granaatboskolk ZA 216 Lk61
Granada CO 268 Gc42
Granada CO 268 Gd44
Granada E 29 Kr47
Granada NIC 256 Fh40
Granada USA (CO) 242 Ej26
Gran Altiplanicie Central RA 294 Gf70
Granard IRL 18 Kn37
Gran Bajo del Gualicho RA 292 Gh66
Gran Bajo Oriental RA 294 Gf69
Granbori SME 271 Hc44
Granbury USA (TX) 242 Fb29
Granby CDN (QC) 247 Gd23
Granby USA (CO) 235 Eh25
Gran Caldera GQ 194 Le44
Gran Campo de Hielo Patagónico RA/RCH 294 Gd70
Gran Canaria E 178 Kc32
Gran Chaco RA/PY 265 Gd23

Guaporé BR 290 Hd60
Guaqui BOL 284 Gf54
Guará BR (SP) 286 Hg56
Guará BR 282 Hh52
Guara E 27 Ku52
Guaraci BR (SP) 286 Hf56
Guaraciaba BR (SC) 290 Hd59
Guaraciaba do Norte BR (CE) 277 Hk48
Guarai BR (TO) 282 Hf50
Guaramacal, P.N. YV 269 Ge41
Guarambaré PY 285 Hb58
Guaramirim BR (SC) 291 Hf59
Guaramuri GUY 270 Ha42
Guaranda EC 272 Ga46
Guaraní BOL 285 Gj56
Guaraniaçu BR (PR) 286 Hd58
Guarantã BR (SP) 286 Hf56
Guarantã do Norte BR (MT) 281 Hc50
Guarapari BR (ES) 287 Hk56
Guarapuava BR (MG) 287 Hg54
Guarapuava BR (PR) 286 He58
Guaraqueçaba BR (PR) 291 Hf58
Guararapes BR (SP) 286 He56
Guarariba BR (PB) 277 Jc49
Guaratinga BR (BA) 287 Ja54
Guaratingueta BR (SP) 287 Hh57
Guaratuba BR (PR) 291 Hf58
Guarayos BOL 279 Gf52
Guarda P 26 Kn50
Guardalavaca C 259 Gc35
Guardamar del Segura E 29 Ku48
Guarda-Mor BR (MG) 287 Hg54
Guardiagrele I 42 Lp48
Guardia Mitre RA (RN) 293 Gj66
Guardian Seamounts 256 Fg41
Guardo E 26 Kq52
Guareña E 28 Ko48
Guarento YV 270 Gj42
Guari PNG 159 Sd50
Guariba BR (SP) 286 Hf56
Guariba BR 280 Gk50
Guárico YV 269 Gg41
Guarita, T.I. BR 289 Hd59
Guarujá BR (SP) 287 Hg58
Guarulhos BR (SP) 287 Hg57
Guasave MEX (SL) 252 Ef33
Guasca CO 268 Gd43
Guasdualito YV 269 Ge42
Guasipati YV 270 Gk42
Guasizaco MEX (CHH) 252 Ef32
Guasopa PNG 160 Sg50
Guastalla I 40 Ll46
Guasuti, T.I. BR 286 Hc57
Guatacondo RCH 284 Gf56
Guataqui CO 268 Gc43
Guatemala 255 Fe38
Guatemala Basin 226 Fa16
Guatimape MEX (DGO) 253 Eh33
Guatire YV 269 Gg40
Guatopo, P.N. YV 269 Gg40
Guatraché RA (LP) 293 Gj64
Guaviare CO 269 Gf44
Guaxupé BR (MG) 287 Hg56
Guayabal C 259 Gb35
Guayabero CO 273 Gd44
Guayabones YV 268 Ge41
Guayaguayaré TT 270 Gk40
Guayama USA (PR) 261 Gg37
Guayapo YV 269 Gg43
Guayaquil EC 272 Ga47
Guayaquil MEX (BC) 236 Ec31
Guayaramerín BOL 279 Gh51
Guayas CO 272 Gc45
Guaycurú RA 289 Ha59
Guayllabamba EC 272 Ga45
Guayllabamba EC 272 Ga46
Guaymas MEX (SO) 252 Ee32
Guayquiraó RA 289 Ha61
Guayubin DOM 260 Ge36
Guayzimi EC 272 Ga48
Guba ETH 198 Mh40
Guba RDC 210 Md51
guba Buor-Haja RUS 59 Rc04
Guban SP 199 Nb40
Gubat RP 121 Rc39
Gubatsaa Hills RB 209 Mc55
Gúbbio I 40 Ln47
Gubed Rugguuda SP 199 Nd40
Guben D 33 Lp39
Gubi WAN 186 Le40
Gubin PL 36 Lp39
Gubio WAN 187 Lg39
Gubkin RUS 53 Mj20
Gubra IND (MPH) 109 Ok34
Guča SCG 46 Ma47
Gucheng CHN (HUB) 95 Qf29
Gucheng CHN (SAX) 95 Qf28
Guci Hot Water Spring RI 128 Qe49
Gudalur IND (TNU) 110 Oj41
Gudauta GE 70 Na24
Gudbrandsdalen N 12 Lk29
Gudenå DK 14 Lk34
Guder ETH 198 Mj41
Guder ETH 198 Mj41
Guder Falls ETH 198 Mj41
Gudermes RUS (CHE) 70 Nd24
Guderup DK 14 Lk36
Gudgaon IND (MPH) 109 Oj35
Gudha IND (RJT) 106 Oj32
Gudhjem DK 15 Lp35
Gudi WAN 186 Le41
Gudivada IND (APH) 109 Pa37
Gudiyattam IND (TNU) 111 Ok40
Gudong CHN (YUN) 113 Pk33
Güdül TR 51 Mn50
Gudur IND (APH) 111 Ok39
Gudvangen N 12 Lg30
Gudžal RUS 98 Rg20
Guéassou RG 192 Kf41
Guebwiller F 23 Lh43
Guechémé RN 185 Lb39
Guéckédou RG 192 Ke41
Guelb El Makhsar RIM 184 Kf36
Guelb El Rhein RIM 178 Kd34
Guelb er Richât RIM 178 Ke35
Guelb Makhrouga RIM 184 Kf36
Guelb Ragoum RIM 184 Kf36
Guelb Zednes RIM 178 Ke33
Guéléhé TCH 196 Lk41
Guélengdeng TCH 187 Lh40
Guellala TN 174 Lf29
Guelltat Sidi Saad DZ 173 La28
Guelma DZ 174 Ld27
Guelmim MA 172 Ke31
Guelta d'Archei TCH 189 Ma37
Guémar DZ 174 Ld29
Guémené-Penfao F 22 Kt43
Guémené-sur-Scorff F 22 Kr42
Güémez MEX (TM) 253 Fa34
Guemour DZ 173 Lc32
Guènt Paté SN 183 Kc38
Guépaouo CI 193 Kh42
Güeppí PE 272 Gc46
Guer F 22 Ks43
Güer Aike RA (SC) 294 Gf71
Guérande F 22 Ks43
Guerara DZ 173 Lc29
Guercif MA 173 Kj28
Guéréda TCH 189 Mb38
Guerende LAR 176 Ma34
Guéret F 24 Lb44
Guerguarat DARS 178 Kb35
Guérin-Kouka TG 193 La41
Guermessa TN 174 Lf29
Guerneville USA (CA) 234 Dj26
Guernsey GB 22 Ks41
Guernsey USA (WY) 235 Eh24
Guérou RIM 183 Ke37
Guerrero MEX (CHH) 237 Eg31
Guerrero MEX (COH) 253 Ek31
Guerrero, P. V. MEX 253 Fa34
Guerrero MEX 254 Ek36
Guerrero Negro MEX (BCS) 252 Ec32
Guerzim DZ 173 Kk31
Gueskérou RN 187 Lg39
Guéssabo CI 192 Kg42
Guéssého CI 192 Kg42
Guessou South DY 186 Lb40
Gueugnon F 25 Le44
Guéyo CI 192 Kg43
Guézaoua RN 186 Le38
Guffertspitze A 35 Lm43
Guge, Mount ETH 198 Mj42
Gugești RO 45 Mh45
Guglionesi I 42 Lq49
Guguan USA 119 Sb15
Guguang, Gunung RI 126 Qj44
Gugu, Mount ETH 198 Mk41
Gugurtli UZ 76 Ob25
Guhagar IND (MHT) 108 Og37
Guia Lopes da Laguna BR (MS) 285 Hb56
Guiana Basin 265 Hb16
Guiana Highlands 264 Gd17
Guiana Plateau 265 Hb17
Guiarote BOL 285 Gj55
Guibaré BF 185 Kk39
Guibéroua CI 192 Kg42
Guicán CO 268 Gd42
Guichi CHN (AHU) 102 Qj30
Guichón ROU 289 Hb62
Guidan-Roumji RN 186 Ld39
Guidari TCH 187 Lj41
Guider CAM 187 Lg41
Guidiguir RN 186 Le39
Guidiguis CAM 187 Lh40
Guidimaka RIM/RMM 183 Ke38
Guidimouni RN 186 Le39
Guiding CHN (GZH) 96 Qd32
Guidjiba CAM 195 Lg41
Guidong CHN (HUN) 97 Qg32
Guiembé CI 193 Kh41
Guiendana CI 193 Kh41
Guiengola MEX 255 Fc37
Guiffa RCA 196 Lk42
Guigang CHN (GZG) 96 Qe34
Guiglo CI 192 Kg42
Güigüe YV 269 Gg40
Guihua Temple CHN 94 Pk31
Guihuayuan CHN (SCH) 95 Qc30
Guihulñgan RP 123 Rb40
Guijuelo E 26 Kp50
Guilderton AUS (WA) 144 Qh61
Guildford GB 21 Ku39
Guiler Gol CHN 91 Ra22
Guilin CHN (GZG) 96 Qf33
Guillaumes F 25 Lg46
Guillestre F 25 Lg46
Guilmara DY 193 La40
Guilvinec F 22 Kq43
Guimarães BR (MA) 276 Hh47
Guimarães P 26 Km51
Guimaras Island RP 123 Rb40
Guimba RP 121 Ra38
Guimbalete MEX (COH) 253 Ej32
Guimiliau F 22 Kr42
Guinagourou DY 186 Lb41
Guinchos Cay BS 251 Ga34
Guindulman RP 123 Rc41
Guinea 167 Ka08
Guinea Basin 166 Kb10
Guinea-Bissau 167 Ka08
Güines C 258 Fj34
Guines F 23 Lb40
Guingamp F 22 Kr42
Guinguineo SN 183 Kc38
Guipavas F 22 Kq42
Guiping CHN (GZG) 96 Qf34
Guir RMM 185 Kj36
Güira de Melena C 258 Fj34
Guiratinga BR (MT) 286 Hd54
Guiri CAM 187 Lh40
Güiria YV 270 Gj40
Guiripa CO 268 Ge43
Guirwas SN 183 Kc38
Guisa C 259 Gb35
Guisborough GB 21 Kt36
Guiscard F 23 Ld41
Guise F 23 Ld41
Guishi Shuiku CHN 96 Qf33
Guissat RN 186 Le37
Guissèr MA 172 Kg29
Guissona E 30 Lb49
Guitiriz E 26 Kn53
Guitri CI 193 Kh43
Guiuan RP 123 Rc40
Guiyang CHN (GZH) 96 Qd32
Guiyang CHN (HUN) 96 Qg33
Gui Yuan Si CHN 102 Qh30
Guizhou CHN (HUB) 95 Qf30
Guizhou CHN 83 Qb13
Gujan-Mestras F 24 Kt46
Gujarat IND 104 Oc14
Gujar Khan PK 79 Og29
Gujba WAN 187 Lf40
Gujiao CHN (SAX) 93 Qg27
Gujranwala PK 79 Oh29
Gujrat PK 79 Oh29
Gujri IND (MPH) 108 Oh34
Gukovo RUS 55 Mk21
Gulabgarh 79 Oj29
Gulagambone AUS (NSW) 151 Se61
Gulang CHN (GSU) 92 Qb27
Gulangyu CHN 97 Qk33
Gulbarga IND (KTK) 108 Oj37
Gulbarga Fort IND 108 Oj37
Gulbene LV 17 Mg33
Gulbin Ka WAN 186 Lc40
Gul'ča KS 77 Og25
Gul'ča KS 77 Og26
Guldenløves Fjord DK 225 Ja06
Guledagud IND (KTK) 108 Oh38
Gulf Islands National Seashore USA 243 Ff30
Gulf of Aden 60 Nb16
Gulf of Alaska USA 224 Cc07
Gulf of Aqaba ET/KSA 64 Mh31
Gulf of Arab ET 177 Me30
Gulf of Bahrain KSA 67 Nf33
Gulf of Bone RI 127 Ra48
Gulf of Boothia CDN 225 Fc05
Gulf of Bothnia S/FIN 10 Lk15
Gulf of California MEX 226 Eb13
Gulf of Carpentaria AUS 136 Rd21
Gulf of Corinth GR 48 Mc52
Gulf of Darién PA/CO 257 Gb41
Gulf of Finland 16 Md31
Gulf of Gdansk PL 36 Lt36
Gulf of Genoa I 40 Lj46
Gulf of Guinea 168 La11
Gulf of Hikma ET 176 Me30
Gulf of Kachchh IND 108 Oe34
Gulf of Khambhat IND 108 Og35
Gulf of Liaotung CHN 100 Ra25
Gulf of Lingayan RP 120 Ra37
Gulf of Maine USA 247 Gf24
Gulf of Mannar IND/CY 111 Ok42
Gulf of Martaban MYA 114 Pj38
Gulf of Masirah OM 69 Nk35
Gulf of Mexico 227 Fb13
Gulf of Oman 60 Nd14
Gulf of Panama PA 257 Ga42
Gulf of Papua PNG 159 Sc50
Gulf of Paria YV 270 Gj40
Gulf of Riga EST/LV 17 Md33
Gulf of Saint Lawrence CDN 245 Gj21
Gulf of Sallum ET 176 Mc30
Gulf of Salonica GR 46 Mc50
Gulf of Santa Catalina USA 236 Ea29
Gulf of Sirte LAR 175 Lj30
Gulf of Suez ET 177 Mg31
Gulf of Taranto I 43 Ls50
Gulf of Tehuantepec MEX 255 Fc38
Gulf of Thailand T 118 Qa16
Gulf of Tolo RI 127 Rb47
Gulf of Tomini RI 127 Ra46
Gulf of Tonkin VN/CHN 96 Qd36
Gulf of Valencia E 30 La51
Gulf of Venezuela YV 268 Ge40
Gulf of Venice I 41 Ln45
Gulf of Zula ER 191 Mk39
Gulfport USA (MS) 243 Ff30
Gulf Saint Vincent AUS 152 Rk63
Gulfstream Park USA (FL) 250 Fk33
Gulganj IND (MPH) 109 Ok33
Gulgong AUS (NSW) 153 Se62
Gulioni EAT 207 Mk49
Gulir RI 130 Rf48
Guliston UZ 76 Oe25
Guljanci BG 47 Me47
Guljanic'ke UA 45 Ml43
Gul Kach PK 78 Oe30
Gul'kevići RUS 55 Na23
Gullbrandstorp S 14 Ln34
Gullfoss IS 10 Jk13
Gull Lake CDN (SK) 233 Ef20
Gull Lake CDN 233 Ed19
Gullspång S 13 Lp32
Güllü TR 50 Mk52
Güllü Dağları TR 63 Na25
Güllük TR 49 Mh53
Güllük Körfezi TR 49 Mh53
Gulmarg IND 79 Oh28
Gülpınar TR 50 Mg51
Gülşehir TR 51 Mp52
Gulshat KZ 84 Oh22
Gulsvik N 12 Lk30
Gulu EAU 204 Mg44
Gülük Dagı Milli Parkı TR 51 Ml54
Gulumba Gana WAN 187 Lh40
Gulwe EAT 207 Mj49
Guma = Pishan CHN (XUZ) 86 Ok27
Gumaca RP 121 Ra39
Gumare RB 213 Mb55
Gumba ANG 208 Lh51
Gumba RDC 200 Ma44
Gumbardo AUS (QLD) 151 Sc59
Gumbiro EAT 211 Mh51
Gumdag TM 71 Nh26
Gumel WAN 186 Le39
Gumgarhi NEP 88 Pb31
Gumi RI 130 Rd45
Gumiel de Hizán E 27 Kr51
Gumine PNG 159 Sc49
Gumla IND (JKD) 109 Pc34
Gumlu AUS (QLD) 149 Sd55
Gummersbach D 32 Lh39
Gummi WAN 186 Lc39
Gumsi WAN 187 Lf39
Gümüldür TR 49 Mh52
Gümüşçay TR 50 Mh50
Gümüşhane TR 63 Mk25
Gümüşkent TR 51 Mp52
Gümüşova TR 51 Ml50
Gümüşsu TR 50 Ml52
Gumu Uen SP 205 Nb45
Gumzai RI 131 Rh48
Guna IND (MPH) 109 Oj33
Guna Terara ETH 198 Mk40
Gunbad-e-Haruniyeh IR 73 Nk27
Gundabooka N.P. AUS (NSW) 151 Sc61
Gundardehi IND (CGH) 109 Pa35
Gundelfingen D 34 Ll42
Gundji RDC 200 Ma44
Gündoğmuş TR 51 Mn54
Gundulpet IND (KTK) 111 Oj41
Güneşli TR 51 Mq52
Güney TR 50 Mj52
Güney TR 50 Mk52
Güney Doğu Toroslar TR 62 Mj26
Gunga ANG 209 Lk53
Gungadei AUS (NSW) 153 Se63
Gungi RDC 203 Lk48
Gungo ANG 208 Lh51
Gungu RDC 203 Lk48
Gungure MOC 211 Mk51
Gunisao Lake CDN 238 Fb19
Gunisao River CDN 238 Fb19
Guniujiang Z.B. CHN 102 Qj31
Gunlom A.L. AUS 139 Rg52
Gunn CDN (AB) 233 Ec19
Gunna SUD 197 Md42
Gunnaur IND (UPH) 107 Ok31
Gunnebo S 15 Lr33
Gunnedah AUS (NSW) 151 Sf61
Gunnerus Ridge 297 Mc32
Gunning AUS (NSW) 153 Se63
Gunnison USA (CO) 235 Eg26
Gunnison USA (UT) 235 Ee26
Gunnison, Mount USA 235 Eg26
Gunpowder AUS (QLD) 148 Rk55
Guns NAM 212 Lk57
Günsang CHN (TIB) 88 Pb30
Gunt TJ 77 Og27
Gunta WAN 186 Le40
Guntakal IND (APH) 111 Oj39
Guntersville USA (AL) 248 Fg28
Guntin de Pallares E 26 Kn52
Guntur IND (APH) 109 Pa37
Gununa AUS (QLD) 148 Rk54
Gunungagung RI 125 Qc48
Gunung Ambang Reserve RI 127 Rc45
Gunung Angemuk RI 131 Rk47
Gunung Antares RI 131 Sa48
Gunung Api RI 130 Re48
Gunungapi RI 132 Rd49
Gunungapi RI 132 Rd49
Gunung Argopuro RI 128 Qg49
Gunung Bakayan RI 126 Qj44
Gunung Balease RI 127 Ra47
Gunung Basakan RI 126 Qj44
Gunung Batubrok RI 126 Qh45
Gunung Batukau RI 129 Qh50
Gunung Besar RI 128 Qg48
Gunung Bromo RI 128 Qg49
Gunung Butak RI 128 Qg49
Gunung Cemaru RI 126 Qh45
Gunung Chamah MAL 117 Qa43
Gunung Cirema RI 128 Qe49
Gunung Daku RI 127 Ra45
Gunung Dempo RI 125 Qb47
Gunung Dom RI 131 Rj47
Gunung Gading N.P. MAL 126 Qe45
Gunung Gagau MAL 117 Qb43
Gunung Gambuta RI 127 Rb45
Gunung Gandadiwata RI 127 Qk47
Gunung Guguang RI 126 Qj44
Gunung Halimun RI 128 Qd49
Gunung Harden RI 126 Qh43
Gunung Irau RI 130 Rg46
Gunung Kambuno RI 127 Ra47
Gunung Katoposo RI 127 Ra46
Gunung Kemal RI 126 Qj45
Gunungkembang RI 125 Qb47
Gunung Kerihun RI 126 Qh45
Gunung Kerinci RI 124 Qa46
Gunung Kinabalu MAL 122 Qj42
Gunung Kujat RI 126 Qj44
Gunung Kwoka RI 130 Rg46
Gunung Lawit RI 126 Qg45
Gunung Lawu RI 128 Qf49
Gunung Leuser N.P. RI 116 Pj44
Gunung Liangmangari RI 126 Qg46
Gunung Liangpran RI 126 Qh45
Gunung Liman RI 128 Qf49
Gunung Loi RI 126 Qg45
Gunung Lompobatang RI 129 Ra48
Gunung Lumaku MAL 122 Qh43
Gunung Lumut RI 126 Qh46
Gunung Malabar RI 128 Qd49
Gunung Malea RI 124 Pk45
Gunung Malino RI 127 Ra45
Gunung Masurai RI 124 Qa47
Gunung Mata Bia TLS 132 Rd50
Gunung Mebo RI 131 Rg46
Gunungmegang RI 125 Qb48
Gunung Meja Reserve RI 131 Rg46
Gunung Mekongga RI 127 Ra47
Gunung Menyapa RI 126 Qj45
Gunungmeraksa RI 125 Qc47
Gunung Merapi RI 128 Qf49
Gunung Merapi RI 129 Qh50
Gunung Mulu N.P. MAL 122 Qh43
Gunung Muria RI 128 Qf49
Gunung Mutis RI 132 Rc50
Gunung Nanti RI 125 Qb48
Gunung Niut RI 126 Qe45
Gunung Noring MAL 117 Qa43
Gunung Pancungapang RI 126 Qh45
Gunung Pangrango RI 128 Qd49
Gunung Payang RI 126 Qh45
Gunung Ranakah RI 129 Ra50
Gunung Rantemario RI 127 Ra47
Gunung Ratai RI 125 Qc48
Gunung Raung RI 129 Qh50
Gunung Raya RI 124 Qa47
Gunung Raya RI 126 Qg46
Gunung Rinjani RI 129 Qj50
Gunung Saran RI 126 Qf46
Gunung Sebayan RI 126 Qf46
Gunung Seblat RI 124 Qb47
Gunung Semeru RI 128 Qg50
Gunungsitoli RI 124 Pj45
Gunung Slamet RI 128 Qe49
Gunung Tahan MAL 117 Qa43
Gunung Takan RI 129 Qj50
Gunung Tamborra RI 129 Qj50
Gunung Tampu Inanajing RI 124 Pk45
Gunung Tata Mailau = Mount Ramelau TLS 132 Rc50
Gunung Tebak RI 125 Qc48
Gunung Tenamatua RI 127 Ra46
Gunung Tentolomatinan RI 127 Rb45
Gunung Tibau RI 126 Qh45
Gunung Trus Madi MAL 122 Qj43
Gunungtua RI 124 Pk45
Gunung Tuham RI 126 Qg45
Gunung Ubia RI 131 Rj48
Gunung Umsini RI 131 Rg46
Gunung Wanggamet RI 129 Ra51
Gunung Welirang RI 128 Qg49
Gunupur IND (ORS) 109 Pb36
Gunupur IND (ORS) 109 Pb36
Gunwara IND (MPH) 109 Pa33
Günyüzü TR 51 Mm51
Günzburg D 34 Ll42
Günzburg D 34 Ll42
Gunzenhausen D 35 Ll41
Guocheng CHN (GSU) 92 Qc27
Guodao CHN (SAX) 93 Qg27
Guo He CHN 102 Qj29
Guoquanyan CHN 94 Qb30
Guoyang CHN (AHU) 102 Qj29
Guozhen CHN (SAA) 95 Qd28
Gupeng CHN (GZG) 96 Qe34
Gupis 79 Og27
Guptapur IND (ORS) 109 Pc36
Gur RUS 99 Rj21
Guraghe, Mount ETH 198 Mk41
Gura Haitii RO 45 Mf43
Gurahonț RO 44 Mc44
Gura Humorului RO 45 Mf43
Gurais 79 Oh28
Gurampod IND (APH) 109 Ok37
Guran IR 75 Nh32
Gurasada RO 44 Mc45
Gurba RDC 197 Md43
Gurbantünggüt Shamo CHN 85 Pd23
Gurdaspur IND (PJB) 106 Oh29
Gurdim IR 75 Oa33
Gurdžaani GE 70 Nc25
Güre TR 50 Mk52
Gur'evsk RUS 17 Ma36
Gurgaon IND (HYA) 107 Oj31
Gurguéia BR 276 Hj49
Gurig N.P. & Cobourg Marine Park AUS 139 Rg51
Guri Hatnur IND (APH) 109 Ok36
Gurin WAN 187 Lg41
Gurinhatã BR (MG) 286 Hf55
Gurk A 35 Lo44
Gurk A 35 Lp44
Gurkovo BG 47 Mf48
Gurktaler Alpen A 35 Lo44
Gurlan UZ 71 Oa25
Gurmatkal IND (KTK) 108 Oj37
Gurner AUS (NT) 142 Rf57
Guro MOC 210 Mg54
Güroymak TR 63 Nb26
Gürpınar TR 50 Mj50
Gurramkonda IND (APH) 111 Ok40
Gurri SUD 196 Mb39
Gursahaiganj IND (UPH) 107 Ok32
Gursarai IND (UPH) 107 Ok33
Gurskoe RUS 99 Rj20
Guruapin RI 130 Rd45
Guru Chantal Monastery IND 107 Oj29
Gurué MOC 211 Mj53
Gurumaoa F 165 Cj53
Gurun MAL 116 Qa43
Gürün TR 62 Mj26
Gurupá BR (PA) 275 He46
Gurupi BR (TO) 282 Hf51
Gurupi BR 276 Hg46
Gurupizinho BR (PA) 276 Hg47
Guru Sai Baba IND 111 Oj39
Guru Shikhar IND 106 Og33
Guruve ZW 210 Mf54
Gurvan Saykhan MNG 92 Qb24
Gurvan Saykhan N.P. MNG 92 Qa24
Gury AUS (NSW) 151 Se60
Gurziwan AFG 78 Oc28
Gusau WAN 186 Ld39
Gusev RUS 17 Mc36
Gushan CHN (LNG) 100 Rb26
Gushan CHN 102 Qk32
Gushi CHN (HNN) 102 Qh29
Gushi CHN (TIB) 89 Pj30
Gushiago GH 193 Kk41
Gushikawa J 103 Rd32
Gush Laghar IR 73 Oa28
Gus'-Hrustal'nyj RUS 53 Na18
Gusi RI 131 Rg47
Gusinje SCG 46 Lu48
Gusinoozërsk RUS (BUR) 90 Qd20
Guskhara IND (WBG) 112 Pd34
Gúspini I 31 Lj51
Gusselby S 13 Lq31
Güssing A 35 Lr43
Gustavfjellet N 11 Lj06
Gustavia F 261 Gj37
Gustavsberg S 13 Lt31
Gustavus USA (AK) 231 Dc16
Gustav V Land N 11 Lk05
Gustine USA (CA) 234 Dk27
Güstrow D 33 Ln37
Gusum S 15 Lr32
Gus'-Železnyj RUS 53 Na18
Gutah CDN (BC) 231 Dk17
Gutcher GB 19 Ku30
Gutenberg RA (CD) 288 Gj60
Gutenko Mountains 296 Gd33
Gütersloh D 32 Lj39
Gutha AUS (WA) 144 Qh60
Guthalungra AUS (QLD) 149 Sd55
Guthrie USA (OK) 242 Fb28
Guthrie USA (TX) 242 Ek29
Guthrie Center USA (IA) 241 Fc25
Gutian CHN (FUJ) 102 Qk32
Gutierrez BOL 285 Gj55
Gutland L 23 Lf41
Gutsuo CHN (TIB) 88 Pd31
Gutu ZW 214 Mf55
Gutulia n.p. N 12 Ln28
Gützkow D 33 Lo37
Guuija MOC 214 Mg58
Guwahati IND (ASM) 112 Pf32
Guwayr SUD 190 Mg38
Guwer IRQ 65 Nb27
Guy CDN (AB) 233 Eb18
Guyana ZW 214 Me56
Guyana 263 Ha09
Guyang CHN (NMZ) 93 Qf25
Guyi ETH 197 Mh41
Guymon USA (OK) 242 Ek27
Guyra AUS (NSW) 151 Sf61
Guyuan CHN (HBI) 93 Qh25
Guyuan CHN (NHZ) 95 Qd28
Guyuyu River AUS 139 Rf52
Güzelbağ TR 51 Mm54
Güzelçamlı TR 49 Mh53
Güzelsu TR 51 Mm54
Güzelsu TR 63 Nb26
Güzelyurt = Morfou CY 51 Mo55
Güzelyurt TR 51 Mp52
Guzhang CHN (GZG) 96 Qc33
Guzhen CHN (AHU) 102 Qj29
Guzhou CHN (GZH) 96 Qe33
Guzmán MEX (CHH) 237 Eg30
G'uzor UZ 76 Od26
Gvardejsk RUS 17 Mb36
Gvarv N 12 Lk31
Gvasjugi RUS 99 Rj22
Gvozd HR 41 Lq45
Gwa MYA 114 Ph37
Gwaai ZW 213 Md55
Gwabazabuya ZW 213 Md55
Gwabegar AUS (NSW) 151 Se61
Gwadabawa WAN 186 Ld41
Gwadar PK 80 Ob33
Gwadar East Bay PK 80 Ob33
Gwagwalada WAN 186 Ld41
Gwaidam IND (UTT) 107 Ok30
Gwaii Haanas South Moresby National Park Reserve & Marine Conservation Area Reserve CDN 232 De19
Gwalior IND (MPH) 107 Ok32
Gwalior Fort IND 107 Ok32
Gwalishtap PK 80 Ob31
Gwamba WAN 186 Lc40
Gwambara WAN 186 Lc39
Gwanda ZW 214 Me56
Gwane RDC 201 Mc43
Gwara IND (MPH) 109 Pa34
Gwaram WAN 186 Le40
Gwarif RI 131 Rk47
Gwarzo WAN 186 Le40
Gwasero WAN 186 Lb41
Gwatar Bay PK 80 Oa33
Gwayi ZW 213 Md55
Gwayi River ZW 213 Md55
Gwda PL 36 Ls37
Gweebarra Bay IRL 18 Km36
Gwembe Z 210 Md54
Gweru ZW 214 Me55
Gweru ZW 214 Me55
Gweta RB 213 Mc56
Gwi WAN 186 Ld41
Gwillim River CDN 233 Eg17
Gwoza WAN 187 Lg40
Gy F 23 Lf43
Gyaca CHN (TIB) 89 Pg31
Gyál H 39 Lu43
Gyali GR 49 Mh54
Gyangze CHN (TIB) 89 Pe31
Gyaring Co CHN 88 Pe30
Gyaring Hu CHN 89 Pj28
Gydanskaja guba RUS 58 Od04
Gydanskij Poluostrov RUS 58 Od04
Gydanskiy Poluostrov RUS 58 Od04
Gyekiti GH 193 La41
Gyeongju ROK 100 Re28
Gyeongju Historic Areas ROK 100 Re28
Gyirong CHN (TIB) 88 Pc31
Gyitang CHN (TIB) 89 Pj30
Gyldenløvehøj DK 14 Lm35
Gylien S 11 Mb12
Gympie AUS (QLD) 151 Sg59
Gyobingauk MYA 114 Ph36
Gyokusendo J 103 Rd32
Gyomaendrőd H 39 Ma44
Gyömrő H 39 Lu43
Gyöngyös H 39 Lu43
Győr H 38 Ls43
Győrtelek H 39 Mc43
Gypsumville CDN (MB) 238 Fa20
Gyraspur IND 109 Ok34
Gysinge S 13 Lr30
Gysum Palace AUS (NSW) 153 Sc62
Gyttorp S 13 Lp31
Gyula H 39 Mb44
Gyumri ARM 70 Nb25
Gyzylarbat TM 71 Nj26
Gyzylsu TM 71 Ng26
Gžatsk RUS 52 Mh18

H

Haa-Alifu Atoll MV 110 Og42
Häädemeeste EST 16 Me32
Haa-Dhaalu Atoll MV 110 Og42
Haag am Hausruck A 35 Lo42
Haag in Oberbayern D 35 Ln42
Haag, Niederösterreich A 35 Lp42
Haag Nunataks 296 Ga34
Haakon VII Land N 11 Lg06
Haaksbergen NL 32 Lg38
Haalenberg NAM 216 Lh59
Ha'amonga Trilithon TO 164 Bc56
Haamstede NL 32 Ld39
Haanja kõrgustik EST 16 Mg33
Ha'ano Island TO 164 Bc55
Ha'apai Group TO 164 Bc55
Haapiti F 165 Cf54
Haapsalu EST 16 Md32
Haarlem NL 32 Le38
Haarlem ZA 216 Mb62
Haast NZ 155 Te67
Haastberget N 11 Ma06
Haast Bluff AUS (NT) 142 Rf57
Haasts Bluff A.L. AUS 142 Rf57
Haaway SP 205 Nb45
Hab PK 80 Od32
Habahe CHN (XUZ) 85 Pd21
Habalah Mountain Village KSA 68 Nb36
Ha Baroana Rock Paintings LS 217 Md60
Habarovsk RUS 98 Rh21
Habarut OM 69 Ng37
Habaswein EAK 205 Mk45
Habay-la-Neuve B 23 Lf41
Habban YE 68 Nd38
Habiganj BD 112 Pf33
Habirag CHN (NMZ) 93 Qh24
Habo S 15 Lp33
Habor Cirir SP 199 Nd43
Haboro J 99 Sa23
Habshan UAE 74 Ng34
Hachcholli IND (KTK) 108 Oj38
Hachenburg D 32 Lh40
Hachijo-jima J 101 Rk29
Hachinohe J 101 Sa25
Hachita USA (NM) 237 Ef30
Hacıbektaş TR 51 Mp52
Hacıfaklı TR 51 Mm52
Hacılar TR 51 Ml53
Hacılar TR 51 Mo51
Hacılar TR 51 Mq52
Hacıömer TR 63 Na26
Haci Zeynalabdin AZ 70 Ne25
Hackås S 13 Lp28
Hackettstown USA (NJ) 247 Gc25
Hack, Mount AUS 152 Rk61
Hackney GUY 270 Ha42
Haco ANG 208 Lh51
Hacufera MOC 214 Mg56
Haczów PL 39 Mb41
Hadaaftimo SP 199 Ne40
Hadagalli IND (KTK) 110 Oh39
Hadakta RUS 91 Qg20
Hadaluma ETH 199 Nb42
Hadamar D 32 Lj40
Hadar (site of Lucy) ETH 198 Na39
Hadashville CDN (MB) 238 Fc21
Hadat CHN (NMZ) 91 Qk21
Hadbin OM 69 Nh37
Hadda AFG 79 Of28
Hadda' KSA 66 Mk35
Hadda AFG 79 Of28
Haddad Bani Malik KSA 66 Na35
Had-des-Oulad-Frej MA 172 Kf29
Haddington GB 19 Ks35
Hadejia WAN 186 Lf39
Hadejia WAN 187 Lf39
Hadera IL 64 Mh29
Haderslev DK 14 Lk35
Hadgaon IND (MHT) 108 Oj36
Hadhah KSA 66 Na34
Hadh Bani Zaynan KSA 67 Ne35
Hadhdhunmathee Atoll = Laamu Atoll MV 110 Og45
Hadiboh YE 69 Ng39
Hadihui CHN (SAX) 93 Qf27
Hadilik CHN (XUZ) 86 Pd27
Hadım TR 62 Mg27
Hadımköy TR 50 Mj49
Hadjač UA 52 Mh20
Hadjer Bandala TCH 196 Ma40
Hadjer el Hamis TCH 187 Lh39
Hadong ROK 100 Rd28
Hadramawt YE 68 Ne38
Hadraniyah IRQ 65 Nb28
Hadrian's Wall GB 19 Ks36
Hadseløya N 10 Lh11
Hadsten DK 14 Ll34
Hadsund DK 14 Ll34
Haduyangratu RI 125 Qc48
Hadweezic River USA 229 Cg12
Hadžibejs'kij liman UA 45 Ml44
Hadžići BIH 41 Lt47
Hae THA 114 Qa36
Hægeland N 12 Lh32
Haeinsa Temple ROK 100 Re28
Haeju PRK 100 Rc26
Hae-nam ROK 103 Rd28
Haenertsburg ZA 214 Me57
Haéré Lao SN 183 Kc37
Hafar al 'Atk KSA 67 Nd32
Hafar al Batin KSA 67 Nc31
Hafford CDN (SK) 233 Eg19
Haffouz TN 174 Le28
Hafik TR 63 Mj26
Hafirat al Ayda KSA 66 Mk32
Hafirat Nisah KSA 67 Nd33
Hafizabad PK 79 Og29
Hafiz Sa'adi IR 74 Ng31
Hafjell alpincenter N 12 Ll29
Hafnarfjörður IS 10 Jj13
Haftgel IR 72 Ne30
Haft Tappeh IR 72 Ne29
Hag Abdullah SUD 190 Mg39
Hagadera EAK 205 Na45
Hagar Banga SUD 196 Mb40
Hagari IND 111 Oj39
Hagar Nish Plateau ER 191 Mj38
Hagelberg D 33 Ln38
Hagemeister Island USA 228 Bk16
Hagemeister Strait USA 228 Bk16
Hagen D 32 Lh39
Hagenow D 33 Lm37
Hage Qaltan Pir Gandom Beryan IR 73 Oa30
Hagere Hiywot ETH 198 Mj41
Hagerman USA (ID) 234 Ec24
Hagerman USA (NM) 237 Eh29
Hagerstown USA (MD) 247 Gb26
Hagetmau F 24 Ku47
Hagewood USA (LA) 243 Fd30
Hagfors S 13 Lo30
Häggenås S 10 Lh14
Hagi J 101 Rf28
Ha Giang VN 96 Qc34
Hagia Sophia TR 50 Mj49
Hagia Sophia (Trabzon) TR 63 Mk25
Hagondange F 23 Lg41
Hagonoy RP 120 Ra38
Hagonoy RP 123 Rc42
Haguenau F 23 Lh42
Hahndorf AUS (SA) 152 Rk63
Haho TG 193 La42
Hahót H 38 Lr44
Haia PNG 159 Sc49
Hai'an CHN (GDG) 96 Qf35
Hai'an CHN (JGS) 102 Ra29
Haib ZA 216 Lk60
Haibao Ta CHN 92 Qd26
Haibei CHN (HLG) 98 Rf22
Haibongo RMM 185 Kj37
Haicheng CHN (LNG) 100 Rb25
Haidargarh IND (UPH) 107 Pa32
Haidong CHN 92 Qb27
Hai Dong VN 96 Qc35
Haidra TN 174 Le28
Hai Duong VN 96 Qd35
Haifa IL 64 Mh29
Haifeng CHN (GDG) 97 Qh34
Haig AUS (WA) 145 Rd61
Haiger D 32 Lj40
Hai He CHN 93 Qj26
Haikang CHN (GDG) 96 Qf35
Haikou CHN (HAN) 96 Qf35
Ha'il KSA 66 Na32
Hailakandi IND (ASM) 112 Pg33
Hailar CHN (NMZ) 91 Qk21
Hailar He CHN 91 Qk21
Hailey USA (ID) 235 Ec24
Hailin CHN (HLG) 98 Re23
Hailing Dao CHN 96 Qf35
Hailun CHN (HLG) 98 Rd22
Hailuoto FIN 11 Mc13
Hailuoto FIN 11 Mc13
Haima OM 69 Nj36
Haimen CHN (JGS) 102 Ra30
Hainan CHN 83 Qb16
Hainan Dao CHN 96 Qf36
Hainan Strait CHN 96 Qe35
Hainburg A 35 Lr42
Haindi LB 192 Ke42
Haines USA (AK) 231 Dc16
Haines USA (OR) 234 Eb23
Haines City USA (FL) 250 Fk31
Haines Highway CDN 231 Db16
Haines Junction CDN (YT) 231 Db15
Hainfeld A 35 Lq42
Haingsisi RI 132 Rb51
Hainichen D 33 Lo40
Hainich, N.P. D 33 Ll39
Haining CHN (ZJG) 102 Ra30
Hainleite D 33 Ll39
Haiphong VN 96 Qd35
Haitan Dao CHN 97 Qk33
Haití C 259 Gb35

Haiti – Hawr as Sa'diyah

Haiti RH 259 Gd36
Haitou CHN (HAN) 96 Qe36
Hai Van VN 115 Qe37
Haiyan CHN (QHI) 92 Qa27
Haiyan CHN (ZJG) 102 Ra30
Haiyuan CHN (NHZ) 92 Qc27
Haizhou Wan CHN 102 Qk28
Hajar KSA 66 Mk34
Hajdarkan KS 77 Of26
Hajdúböszörmény H 39 Mb43
Hajdúnánás H 39 Mb43
Hajdúsámson H 39 Mb43
Hajdúszoboszló H 39 Mb43
Hajeb el Aïdun TN 174 Le28
Hájek CZ 38 Ln40
Hajiganj BD 112 Pf34
Haji Abad IR 73 Nk29
Haji Abad IR 75 Nh31
Haji Jafar Shahid PK 80 Oe32
Hajiki-saki J 101 Rk26
Hajin SYR 65 Na28
Hajipur IND (BIH) 109 Pc33
Hajjah YE 68 Nb37
Hajjah YE 68 Nb38
Hajnówka PL 37 Md38
Hajo IND (ASM) 112 Pf32
Hajo Do ROK 103 Rd28
Hajós H 39 Lu44
Hajrah KSA 66 Na35
Hajsyn UA 54 Me21
Hajyr RUS 59 Rc04
Hakahau F 165 Ck50
Hakai Recreation Area CDN 232 Df20
Hakefjord S 14 Lm33
Hakha MYA 112 Pg34
Hakkâri TR 63 Nb27
Hakkâri Dağlari TR 63 Nb27
Hakken-sen J 101 Rh28
Hakodate J 99 Sa25
Hakomis Lake CDN 238 Ej17
Hakskeenpan ZA 216 Ma59
Hakui J 101 Rj27
Hakupu NZ 164 Bf55
Haku-san J 101 Rj27
Hakusan N.P. J 101 Rj27
Hala PK 80 Oe33
Halab SYR 64 Mj27
Halab SYR 64 Mj28
Halaban KSA 67 Nc34
Halabiyeh SYR 65 Mk28
Halabja IRQ 65 Nc28
Halacho MEX (YT) 255 Fe35
Haladaukou CHN (NMZ) 93 Qk24
Halaib SUD 177 Mj34
Halali NAM 212 Lj55
Halástra GR 46 Mc50
Halat 'Ammar KSA 64 Mj31
Halawa USA (HI) 230 Cb35
Halberstadt D 33 Lm39
Halbrite CDN (SK) 238 Ej21
Halden N 12 Lm31
Haldensleben D 33 Lm38
Haldia IND (WBG) 112 Pe34
Haldibari IND (WBG) 112 Pe32
Haldikhora IND (BIH) 112 Pd32
Haldwani IND (UTT) 107 Ok31
Hale EAT 207 Mk48
Haleakala N.P. USA 230 Cb35
Halebid IND 110 Oj40
Haleji Bird Reserve PK 80 Od33
Halembe EAT 206 Me48
Hale, Mount AUS 140 Qj58
Hale River AUS 143 Rh58
Halesworth GB 21 Lb38
Half Assini GH 193 Kj43
Halfayat al-Muluk SUD 190 Mg39
Halfmoon Bay CDN (BC) 232 Dj21
Halfmoon Bay NZ 155 Te69
Half Moon Shoal 122 Qj41
Halfway Pt. CDN 239 Fk20
Halfway River CDN 231 Dj17
Halfweg ZA 216 Ma61
Halgen SP 199 Nc43
Halgeri IND (KTK) 110 Oh39
Haliburton Highlands CDN 247 Ga23
Halič UA 39 Me41
Halidon AUS (SA) 152 Sa63
Halifax AUS (QLD) 149 Sd55
Halifax CDN (NS) 245 Gj23
Halifax GB 21 Kt37
Halifax Bay AUS (QLD) 149 Sd55
Halikarnassos TR 49 Mh53
Halikko FIN 16 Md30
Hali Rud IR 75 Nj31
Halilulik RI 132 Rc50
Halimun, Gunung RI 128 Qd49
Haliyal IND (KTK) 108 Oh38
Haljala EST 16 Mg31
Halke Shan CHN 84 Pa24
Hálki GR 49 Mh54
Halkida GR 48 Md52
Halkir CDN (AB) 233 Ed19
Halkirk GB 19 Kr32
Halland S 14 Ln33
Hallandale USA (FL) 250 Fk33
Hallands Väderö S 14 Ln34
Hallasan ROK 103 Rd29
Hallasan N.P. ROK 103 Rd29
Hall Beach CDN 224 Fd05
Halle B 23 Le40
Halleck USA (NV) 234 Ec25
Hällefors S 13 Lp31
Hälleforsnäs S 13 Lr31
Hallein A 35 Lo43
Hällekis S 13 Lo32
Hallen S 10 Lh14
Hallersville USA (AK) 228 Cb16
Halle (Saale) D 33 Lm39
Hällesjö S 13 Lr28
Hallett AUS (SA) 152 Rk62
Hallettsville USA (TX) 243 Fb31
Halley ANT (UK) 296 Jc34
Halligen D 32 Lj36
Hallingdal N 12 Lk30
Hallingdalselv N 12 Lj30
Hällingsåfallet S 10 Lh13
Hall in Tirol A 35 Lm43
Hall Island USA 228 Bd15
Hall Islands FSM 156 Sc17
Halliste EST 16 Me32
Hällnäs S 10 Lk13
Hallock USA (MN) 238 Fb21
Hall Peninsula CDN 225 Gc06
Hall Point AUS 138 Rc53
Hall Point AUS 139 Rg51
Halls USA (TN) 243 Ff28
Halls Bay CDN 245 Hb21
Hallsberg S 13 Lq31
Halls Creek AUS (WA) 138 Rd55
Halls Gap AUS (VIC) 152 Sb64
Hållsta S 13 Lr31
Hallstahammar S 13 Lr31
Hallstatt A 35 Lo43
Hallstatt-Dachstein Salzkammergut A 35 Lo43
Hallstätter See A 35 Lo43
Hallstavik S 13 Lt30
Hallyo Haesang N.P. ROK 100 Re28
Halmahera RI 130 Re45
Halmahera Sea RI 130 Re46
Halmstad S 14 Ln34
Haloi IND (GUJ) 108 Og34
Halong Bay VN 96 Qd35
Halong City VN 96 Qd35
Hals DK 14 Ll34
Hal Saflieni Hypogeum M 42 Lp55
Hal'šany BY 17 Mg36
Hälsingland S 13 Lq29
Halsön FIN 13 Mb28
Halstead GB 21 La39
Halsteren NL 32 Le39
Halsur IND (KTK) 108 Oj37
Halsvik N 12 Lf30
Halten Bank 10 Le13
Haltern D 32 Lh39
Haltwhistle GB 19 Ks36
Haluaghat BD 112 Pf33
Halul Q 74 Ng33
Halvad IND (GUJ) 108 Of34
Halvarsgårdarna S 13 Lq30
Halvmåneøya N 11 Mb07
Ham F 23 Ld41
Ham TCH 187 Lh40
Hama SYR 64 Mj28
Hamab NAM 216 Lk60
Hamada J 101 Rg28
Hamada al Hamrah LAR 174 Lf31
Ham ada de la Dao ura DZ 173 Kj31
Hamada de Tindouf DZ 172 Kf32
Hamada deTinrhert DZ 174 Ld31
Hamada du Drâa DZ 172 Kg31
Hamada du Guir DZ 173 Kj30
Hamada ed Douakel DZ 172 Kg32
Hamada el Harich RMM 179 Kh34
Hamada Mangeni RN 181 Lg34
Hamada Marzuq LAR 181 Lg32
Hamadan IR 72 Ne28
Hamada Tounassine DZ 172 Kg31
Hamadat Tingarat LAR 174 Lf31
Hamada Zegher LAR 181 Lf32
Hamadet Bet Touadjine DZ 173 Kk30
Hamadet el Atchane DZ 173 Lc30
Hamaguir DZ 173 Kj30
Hamamah LAR 175 Ma29
Hamamasu J 99 Sa24
Hamamatsu J 101 Rj28
Haman CAM 195 Lg43
Hamar N 12 Lm30
Hamardomen N 12 Lm30
Hamarro Hadad ETH 198 Nb42
Hamasaka J 101 Rh28
Hama-Tombetsu J 99 Sb23
Hambidge Conservation Park AUS 152 Rh62
Hamburg D 33 Ll37
Hamburg USA (AR) 243 Fe29
Hamburg USA (CA) 234 Dj25
Hamburg USA (NY) 247 Ga24
Hamdah KSA 68 Nb36
Hamdallay RMM 184 Kh38
Hamdallay RN 185 Lb39
Hamdanah KSA 66 Na36
Hamdi TR 51 Mp50
Hamdıbey TR 50 Mh51
Häme FIN 16 Me29
Hämeenkyrö FIN 16 Md29
Hämeenlinna FIN 16 Me30
Hämeenselkä FIN 16 Me28
Hamelin AUS (WA) 140 Qh59
Hamelin Pool AUS 140 Qh59
Hameln D 32 Lk38
Hamen Wan CHN 97 Qj34
Hamersley Gorge AUS 140 Qk57
HamersleyRange AUS 140 Qj57
Hamhung PRK 100 Rd26
Hami CHN (XUZ) 87 Pg24
Hamid IR 72 Ne30
Hamid SUD 190 Mf36
Hamidiye TR 50 Mg49
Hamidiye TR 51 Ml51
Hamidiyeh IR 72 Ne30
Hamilton AUS (TAS) 152 Sd67
Hamilton AUS (VIC) 152 Sb64
Hamilton AUS 142 Rg59
Hamilton CDN (ON) 247 Ga24
Hamilton GB 19 Kq35
Hamilton NZ 154 Th64
Hamilton USA (AK) 229 Bj14
Hamilton USA (AL) 248 Fg28
Hamilton USA (IL) 241 Fe25
Hamilton USA (MT) 235 Ec22
Hamilton USA (OH) 246 Fh26
Hamilton USA (TX) 242 Fa30
Hamilton USA (WA) 232 Dj21
Hamilton Dome USA (WY) 235 Ef24
Hamilton Downs AUS (QLD) 148 Sb56
Hamilton Hotel AUS (QLD) 148 Sa57
Hamilton Island AUS 149 Se56
Hamilton, Mount USA 234 Ec26
Hamilton River AUS (QLD) 148 Sa57
Hamilton Sound CDN 245 Hc21
Hamim UAE 74 Nh34
Hamina FIN 16 Mh30
Hamiota CDN (MB) 238 Ek20
Hami Pendi CHN 87 Pf24
Hamirpur IND (HPH) 107 Oj30
Hamirpur IND (UPH) 107 Pa33
Hamju PRK 100 Rd26
Hamlin USA (TX) 242 Ek29
Hamlin USA (WV) 246 Fj26
Hamlin Bay AUS 144 Qh63
Hamm D 32 Lh39
Hammam al Alil IRQ 65 Nb27
Hammam Damt YE 68 Nc38
Hammamet TN 174 Lf27
Hammam Meskoutine DZ 174 Ld27
Hammam-Righa DZ 173 Lb27
Hammam Salahine DZ 174 Lc28
Hammar S 13 Lp32
Hammarön S 13 Lo31
Hammarslund S 15 Lp35
Hammel DK 14 Lk34
Hammelburg D 34 Lk40
Hammenhög S 15 Lp35
Hammerdal S 10 Lh14
Hammeren DK 15 Lp35
Hammerfest N 11 Mb10
Hamminkeln D 32 Lg39
Hammon USA (OK) 242 Fa28
Hammond USA (IL) 246 Fg25
Hammond USA (MT) 235 Eh23
Hammond Island AUS 146 Sb51
Hammonton USA (NJ) 247 Gc26
Hamnvik N 10 Lj11
Hamoud RIM 183 Ke38
Hampden CDN (NF) 245 Hb21
Hampenanperak RI 116 Pk44
Hampi IND 111 Oj39
Hampton CDN (NB) 245 Gh23
Hampton USA (AR) 243 Fd29
Hampton USA (IA) 241 Fd24
Hampton USA (SC) 249 Fk29
Hampton USA (VA) 249 Gb27
Hamra SUD 197 Me40
Hamra n.p. S 13 Lp29
Hamrat al-Wuzz SUD 190 Mf39
Hamrat as Shaykh SUD 189 Md38
Hamriya UAE 75 Nh33
Hamsara RUS 90 Pj19
Hämsön S 13 Lt28
Ham-Syra RUS 90 Pj19
Ham Tan VN 115 Qd40
Ham Thuam Nam VN 115 Qe40
Hamtic RP 123 Ra40
Hamuku RI 131 Rh47
Hamum-e-Chah Gheyb IR 75 Oa31
Hamum-e-Jazmurian IR 75 Nk32
Hamun-e Puzak AFG 78 Oa30
Hamun-e Saberi AFG 78 Oa30
Hamun-i Lora PK 80 Oc31
Hamun-i Mashkel PK 80 Ob31
Hamun-i Murgho PK 80 Oc32
Hamun N.P. IR 73 Oa30
Ham Yen VN 96 Qc34
Hamyški RUS (ADY) 55 Na23
Han TR 51 Ml51
Hana USA (HI) 230 Cc35
Hanagal IND (KTK) 111 Oj39
Hanahan PNG 160 Sh48
Hanak KSA 66 Mj33
Hanak TR 63 Nb25
Hanalei Bay USA (HI) 230 Ca34
Ha Nam VN 96 Qc35
Hanamaki J 101 Sa26
Hanami Plateau NAM 212 Lj58
Hanang, Mount EAT 204 Mh48
Hana Road USA 230 Cc35
Hanau D 34 Lj40
Hancăuți MD 45 Mh42
Hancavičy BY 52 Md19
Hâncești MD 45 Mj44
Hanceville CDN (BC) 232 Dj20
Hancheng CHN (SAA) 95 Qf28
Hanchuan CHN (HUB) 95 Qg30
Hancock USA (MI) 246 Ff22
Hancock USA (NY) 247 Gc25
Handa J 101 Rj28
Handagajty RUS (TUV) 85 Pg20
Handali EAT 207 Mh49
Handan CHN (HBI) 93 Qh27
Handapa IND (ORS) 109 Pc35
Handel CDN (SK) 233 Ef19
Handeni EAT 207 Mk48
Handewitt D 32 Lk36
Handha SP 199 Nf40
Handlová SK 39 Lt42
Handsworth AUS (QLD) 151 Sd58
Handwara 79 Oh28
Handyga RUS 59 Rd06
Hanestad N 12 Ll29
Hanford USA (CA) 236 Ea27
Hangal IND (KTK) 110 Oh39
Han Garaučića SCG 46 Lu48
Hanga Roa RCH 284 Ef59
Hang Chat THA 114 Pk36
Hanger ETH 198 Mj41
Hånger S 15 Lo33
Hanggin Houqi CHN (NMZ) 92 Qd25
Hanggin Qi CHN (NMZ) 92 Qe26
Hanging Rock AUS 140 Ra57
Hangingstone River CDN 233 Ee17
Hanging Trail LB 192 Kf43
Hangö = Hanko FIN 16 Mc31
Hangu CHN (TJN) 93 Qj26
Hangu PK 79 Of29
Hangzhou CHN (ZJG) 102 Ra30
Hangzhou Wan CHN 102 Ra30
Hanhowuz TM 73 Oa27
Hanhowuz sur hovdany TM 73 Oa27
Hani TR 63 Na26
Haniá GR 48 Md55
Hanidh KSA 67 Ne32
Haniótis GR 46 Md50
Han Island PNG 160 Sh48
Hanja ANG 208 Lg52
Han Jiang CHN 97 Qj33
Hankasalmi FIN 16 Mg28
Hankensbüttel D 33 Ll38
Hanker IND (CGH) 109 Pa35
Hankey ZA 217 Mc62
Hankinson USA (ND) 240 Fb22
Hanko = Hangö FIN 16 Mc31
Hanksville USA (UT) 235 Ee26
Hanley CDN (SK) 233 Eg20
Hanmer Springs NZ 155 Tg67
Hanna CDN (AB) 233 Ee20
Hanna USA (WY) 235 Eg25
Hannagan Meadow USA (AZ) 237 Ef29
Hannah Bay CDN 239 Ga20
Hannahville Ind. Res. USA 246 Fg23
Hannibal USA (MO) 241 Fe26
Hannik SUD 190 Mg37
Hann, Mount AUS 138 Rc53
Hannover D 32 Lk38
Hannoversch Münden D 32 Lk39
Hannur IND (MHT) 108 Oj37
Hannut B 23 Lf40
Hanö S 15 Lp35
Hanöbukten S 15 Lp35
Hanoi VN 96 Qc35
Hanover CDN (ON) 246 Fk23
Hanover ZA 217 Mc61
Hanover Road ZA 217 Mc61
Han Pijesak BIH 46 Lt46
Hansapark D 33 Ll36
Hanse IND (HPH) 107 Oj29
Hanshou CHN (HUN) 95 Qf31
Han Shui CHN 95 Qg30
Hansi IND (HYA) 106 Oh31
Hans Merensky Nature Reserve ZA 214 Mf57
Hanson Bay AUS 152 Rj64
Hansot IND (GUJ) 108 Og35
Hanstholm DK 14 Lj33
Han-sur-Nied F 23 Lg42
Hantai CHN (HUN) 95 Qf31
Hantamsberg ZA 216 Lk61
Hantau KZ 84 Og23
Hanti IND (BIH) 112 Pd33
Han Tombs CHN 96 Qf33
Hantoukoura BF 185 La39
Hanty-Mansijsk RUS 58 Ob06
Han Ul CHN (NMZ) 91 Qk23
Hanumangarh IND (RJT) 106 Oh31
Hanummana IND (MPH) 109 Pb33
Hanušovce nad Topl'ou SK 39 Mb41
Hanušovice CZ 38 Lr40
Hanwang CHN (SCH) 94 Qc30
Hanyin CHN (SAA) 95 Qe29
Hanyuan CHN (SCH) 94 Qb31
Hanzhong CHN (SAA) 95 Qd29
Hao Atoll F 303 Cb11
Haora IND (WBG) 112 Pe34
Haotan CHN (SAA) 92 Qe27
Haoud El Hamra DZ 174 Ld30
Haouich TCH 196 Ma39
Haoussa-Foulane RMM 185 La37
Haoxue CHN (HUB) 95 Qg30
Håøya N 11 Ma07
Hapai SOL 161 Sj50
Haparanda S 11 Mc13
Haparanda skärgårds n.p. S 11 Mb13
Hapčeranga RUS 91 Qg21
Hapo RI 130 Re44
Happy Camp USA (CA) 234 Dj25
Happy Corner USA (NH) 247 Ge23
Happy's Inn USA (MT) 233 Ec21
Happy Valley CHN (GDG) 97 Qh34
Hapur IND (UPH) 107 Oj31
Haputale CL 111 Pa43
Haql KSA 64 Mh31
Harabali RUS 53 Nd22
Harabarjan IR 74 Nh30
Harabeköy TR 51 Mn52
Harad KSA 67 Ne33
Harad YE 68 Nb37
Haradan KSA 67 Nd34
Haradok BY 52 Me18
Häradsbäck S 15 Lp34
Haradzďča BY 17 Mg37
Haradzeja BY 17 Mg37
Haraiki Atoll F 165 Cj54
Hárakas GR 49 Mf55
Haramachi J 101 Sa27
Haranor RUS 91 Qj20
Harappa PK 106 Og30
Harar ETH 198 Nb41
Harar (Elephant) Sanctuary ETH 198 Nb41
Harare ZW 210 Mf54
Harasiuki PL 37 Mc40
Harat ER 191 Mk38
Harat IR 74 Nh30
Harau Canyon RI 124 Qa46
Haraz-Djombo TCH 196 Lk39
Haraze Mangueigne TCH 196 Ma41
Harbang BD 112 Pg35
Harbel LB 192 Ke42
Harbin CHN (HLG) 98 Rd23
Harbo S 13 Ls30
Harbo WAN 186 Le39
Harbor Beach USA (MI) 246 Fj24
Harborg N 12 Lm28
Harbor Springs USA (MI) 246 Fh23
Harbour Breton CDN (NF) 245 Hc22
Harbour Deep CDN (NF) 245 Hb20
Harcourt AUS (VIC) 153 Sc64
Harcourt CDN (NB) 245 Gh22
Harda IND (MPH) 108 Oj34
Hardangerfjorden N 12 Lf31
Hardangervidda N 12 Lh30
Hardangervidda n.p. N 12 Lh30
Hardap NAM 212 Lj58
Hardap NAM 212 Lj58
Hardapdam NAM 212 Lj58
Hardapontspanningsoord NAM 212 Lj58
Hardap Recreational Resort NAM 212 Lj58
Hard Bargain BS 251 Gb32
Hardegsen D 32 Lk39
Hardelot-Plage F 23 Lb40
Hardenberg NL 32 Lg38
Harden, Gunung RI 126 Qh43
Harderwijk NL 32 Lf38
Hardheim D 34 Lk41
Hardin USA (IL) 241 Fe26
Hardin USA (MT) 235 Eg23
Harding ZA 217 Me61
Hardinsburg USA (KY) 248 Fg27
Hardisty CDN (AB) 233 Ee19
Hardoi IND (UPH) 107 Pa32
Hardtner USA (KS) 242 Fa27
Hardwicke Bay AUS 152 Rj63
Hare Bay CDN (NF) 245 Hd21
Hareid N 12 Lg28
Haren(Ems) D 32 Lh38
Hareto ETH 198 Mj41
Harewa ETH 198 Na41
Harewood GB 21 Kt37
Hargas nuur MNG 85 Pg21
Hargele ETH 198 Nb43
Hargeysa SP 199 Nc41
Hargigo ER 191 Mk39
Hargrave River CDN 238 Fa18
Hargshamn S 13 Lt30
Har Hu CHN 87 Pj26
Hari RI 125 Qb46
Haria E 178 Kd31
Harib YE 68 Nc38
Haribomo RMM 185 Kj37
Haridaspur IND (ORS) 112 Pd35
Haridwar IND (UTT) 107 Ok31
Harihar IND (KTK) 110 Oh39
Harihareshwar Beach IND 108 Og37
Harihari NZ 155 Tf67
Harikanassou RN 185 Lb39
Hari kurk EST 16 Md32
Harilek RI 125 Qb47
Harippad IND (KER) 110 Oj42
Haripur IND (APH) 109 Pc36
Harisal IND (MHT) 108 Oj35
Harjavalta FIN 16 Mc29
Härjedalen S 13 Ln28
Harkány H 41 Lt45
Harkidum IND (UTT) 107 Ok30
Har-ki-Pauri IND 107 Ok31
Harlan USA (IA) 241 Fc25
Harlan USA (KY) 249 Fj27
Hârlău RO 45 Mg43
Harlech Castle GB 20 Kq38
Harleigh Farm ZW 214 Mg55
Harlem USA (MT) 233 Ef21
Hårlev DK 14 Ln35
Harlin AUS (QLD) 151 Sg59
Harlingen NL 32 Lf37
Harlingen USA (TX) 253 Fb32
Harlow GB 21 La39
Harlowton USA (MT) 235 Ef22
Harmancık TR 50 Mk51
Harmånger S 13 Ls29
Härmänkylä FIN 11 Me13
Harmanli BG 47 Mf49
Harmil ER 191 Na38
Harmonia BR (RS) 290 Hb60
Harnai PK 78 Od30
Harnes F 23 Lc40
Harney Basin USA 234 Ea24
Harni BD 112 Pf34
Härnön S 13 Ls28
Härnösand S 13 Ls28
Har Nur CHN (NMZ) 91 Ra23
Har nuur MNG 85 Pg21
Haro E 27 Ks52
Haro SP 205 Na45
Haro Shikh SP 199 Nc41
Harøyfjorden N 12 Lg28
Harpanahalli IND (KTK) 110 Oh39
Harper LB 192 Kg43
Harper USA (KS) 242 Fa27
Harper USA (OR) 234 Eb24
Harper, Mount USA 229 Cj13
Harpers Ferry N.H.P. USA 247 Gb26
Harpersville USA (AL) 248 Fg29
Harpeth Narrows Historic Area USA 248 Fg27
Harpin RUS 98 Rj20
Harput Kalesi TR 63 Mk26
Harqin Qi CHN (NMZ) 93 Qk25
Harran TR 63 Mk27
Harrat al Buqum KSA 66 Na35
Harrat al Kishb KSA 66 Na34
Harrat al 'Uwayrid KSA 66 Mj32
Harrat ar Raha KSA 66 Mh32
Harrat Hadan KSA 66 Na35
Harrat Khaybar KSA 66 Mk33
Harrat Kurama KSA 66 Na33
Harrat Lunayyir KSA 66 Mj33
Harrat Nawasif KSA 66 Nb35
Harratola IND (MPH) 109 Pa34
Harrat Rahat KSA 66 Na34
Harrei IND (MPH) 109 Ok34
Harriburg LB 192 Ke42
Harriman USA (TN) 249 Fh28
Harrington AUS (NSW) 151 Sg61
Harrington USA (WA) 232 Ea22
Harrington Harbour CDN (QC) 245 Ha20
Harripur PK 79 Og29
Harris CDN (SK) 233 Eg20
Harris GB 18 Ko33
Harrisburg USA (AR) 243 Fe28
Harrisburg USA (IL) 243 Ff27
Harrisburg USA (PA) 247 Gb25
Harrismith ZA 217 Me60
Harris, Mount AUS 142 Re58
Harrison USA (AR) 243 Fd27
Harrison USA (NE) 240 Ej24
Harrisonburg USA (VA) 247 Ga26
Harrison Lake CDN 232 Dj21
Harrisonville USA (MO) 241 Fc26
Harrisville LB 192 Ke42
Harrisville USA (MI) 246 Fj23
Harrisville USA (NY) 247 Gc23
Harrodsburg USA (KY) 249 Fh27
Harrogate CDN (BC) 233 Eb20
Harrogate GB 21 Kt37
Harrow AUS (VIC) 152 Sa64
Harrström FIN 13 Mb28
Harry S. Truman S.P. USA 241 Fd26
Harsani IND (RJT) 106 Of33
Harsefeld D 32 Lk37
Harsin IR 72 Nd28
Harsor IND (RJT) 106 Oh32
Hârsova BG 47 Mg47
Hârsovo BG 47 Mh47
Harstad N 10 Lj11
Harsud IND (MPH) 108 Oj34
Harsum D 32 Lk38
Harsvika N 10 Le13
Hart USA (MI) 246 Fg24
Harta H 39 Lu44
Hartbeesfontein ZA 217 Md59
Hartberg A 35 Lq43
Hartebeest ZA 216 Ma60
Hårteigen N 12 Lh30
Hartford LB 192 Ke42
Hartford USA (CT) 247 Gd25
Hartford City USA (IN) 246 Fh25
Hartfort USA (SD) 240 Fb24
Hârtiești RO 45 Mf45
Hartington USA (NE) 240 Fb24
Hartland Covered Bridge CDN 244 Gg22
Hartland Point GB 20 Kq39
Hartlepool GB 21 Kt36
Hartley Bay CDN (BC) 232 Df19
Hartmannberge NAM 212 Lg54
Hart, Mount CDN 229 Ck14
Hart Mount CDN 238 Ek19
Hart Mtn. Nat. Antelope Refuge USA 234 Ea24
Hartola FIN 16 Mg29
Hart Ranges CDN 232 Dj18
Harts ZA 217 Mc59
Hartseer NAM 212 Lj56
Hartsel USA (CO) 235 Eh26
Hartselle USA (AL) 248 Fg28
Harts Range AUS (NT) 143 Rh57
Harts Range AUS 143 Rh57
Hartsville USA (SC) 249 Fk28
Hartville USA (MO) 243 Fd27
Hartwell USA (GA) 249 Fj28
Hartwell Lake USA 249 Fj28
Haruku RI 130 Re47
Haruku RI 130 Re47
Harun = Gunung Harden RI 126 Qh43
Harun TR 51 Mp50
Harunabad PK 81 Og31
Harur IND (TNU) 111 Ok40
Har us nuur MNG 85 Pg21
Harut YE 69 Ng38
Harvale IND (GOA) 108 Oh38
Harvest Home AUS (QLD) 149 Sd56
Harvey AUS (WA) 144 Qh62
Harvey USA (ND) 240 Fa22
Harwich GB 21 Lb39
Harwood AUS (NSW) 151 Sg60
Haryana IND 104 Od13
Harz D 33 Ll39
Harzgerode D 33 Lm39
Harz, N.P. D 33 Ll39
Hasa Abdal PK 79 Og29
Hašaat MNG 90 Qc23
Hasama J 101 Sa26
Hasan RUS 100 Rf24
Hasanabad IND (APH) 109 Ok36
Hasan Abad IR 72 Nf28
Hasan Abad IR 72 Ng29
Hasan Abad IR 73 Nk28
Hasançelebi TR 63 Mj26
Hasankale TR 63 Na26
Hasankale TR 63 Na27
Hasankeyf TR 63 Na27
Hasan Kuleh AFG 78 Oa29
Hasan Langi IR 75 Nj32
Hasanoğlan TR 51 Mo51
Hasan Paşa Kümbet TR 63 Nb26
Hasanpur IND (UPH) 107 Ok31
Hasarah KSA 67 Nb34
Hasardag Reserve TM 71 Nj26
Hasavjurt RUS (DAG) 70 Nd24
Hasayaz TR 51 Mo50
Hasbek TR 51 Mp51
Hase D 32 Lh38
Haselünne D 32 Lh38
Haser Gölü TR 63 Mk26
Hashab SUD 196 Mc39
Hashtrud IR 72 Nd27
Hasik OM 69 Nh37
Hasil RI 130 Re46
Hasilpur PK 81 Og31
Haskanit SUD 197 Md40
Haskell USA (TX) 242 Fa29
Haskovo BG 47 Mf49
Hasle DK 15 Lp35
Haslev DK 14 Lm35
Hasnabad IND (WBG) 112 Pe34
Hasnai BD 112 Pf33
Hasparren F 24 Kt47
Hassa TR 62 Mj27
Hassan IND (KTK) 110 Oj40
Hâssei Mbârek RIM 183 Ke37
Hassela S 13 Lr28
Hasselö S 15 Lr33
Hasselt B 23 Lf40
Hasselt NL 32 Lg38
Haßfurt D 35 Ll40
Hassi Bahbah DZ 173 Lb28
Hassi Barouda DZ 173 La31
Hassi Bel Guebbour DZ 174 Ld31
Hassi Berrekhem DZ 173 Lc29
Hassi-Bou-Allala DZ 173 Kj30
Hassi Daoula DZ 174 Lc29
Hassi Defla MA 173 Kj29
Hassi-Delaa DZ 173 Lb29
Hassi-el-Ahmar MA 173 Kj29
Hassi el Belrem DZ 180 Lb32
Hassi el Ghella DZ 173 Kk28
Hassi-el-Hadjar DZ 173 Lc30
Hassi el Khannfous DZ 173 Lb31
Hassi-el-Khenig DZ 180 Lb32
Hassi el Klebi DZ 172 Kh31
Hassi el Mounir DZ 172 Kg31
Hassi-Fahl DZ 173 Lb30
Hassi Fougani MA 172 Kh30
Hassi Fouini RIM 184 Kg37
Hassi Habadra DZ 180 Lc32
Hassi Hadhour DZ 173 Kk30
Hassi Hassane MA 173 Kj30
Hassi Ifertas LAR 174 Lf31
Hassi Inifel DZ 173 Lb31
Hassi Ismoulaye DZ 174 Le31
Hassi Issendjel DZ 180 Le32
Hâssi Karkabane RMM 185 Kk37
Hassi Kord Myriem DZ 173 Kj31
Hassi-Mahzez DZ 172 Kh31
Hassi Marraket DZ 173 Lb30
Hassi Messaoud DZ 174 Ld30
Hassi Moussa DZ 173 La31
Hassi Ntsel DZ 180 Ld32
Hassi Ramad DZ 174 Ld31
Hassi Ras el Erg DZ 173 Lb31
Hassi-R'Mel DZ 173 Lb29
Hassi Safiet Iniguel DZ 173 Lb30
Hassi Settafa DZ 173 Lb29
Hassi Tabankort DZ 174 Ld31
Hassi Tabelbalet DZ 180 Ld32
Hassi Tartrat DZ 179 Kg32
Hâssi Touil RIM 184 Kh37
Hässleholm S 15 Lo34
Hasslö S 15 Lq34
Hasslö S 15 Lq34
Hastings GB 21 La40
Hastings NZ 154 Tj65
Hastings USA (MI) 246 Fh24
Hastings USA (MN) 241 Fd23
Hastings USA (NE) 240 Fa25
Hastings Island MYA 116 Pk40
Hastings Island PNG 160 Sf51
Haštpar IR 72 Ne27
Hästveda S 15 Lo34
Haswayn YE 69 Ng38
Hasy Hague LAR 181 Lf32
Hasy in Agiuel LAR 181 Lf32
Hasy Tissan LAR 174 Lg31
Hata IND (UPH) 107 Pb32
Hatanga RUS 58 Qa04
Hatanga RUS 58 Qa04
Hatangskij zaliv RUS 58 Qb04
Hatay TR 62 Mj27
Hatch USA (NM) 237 Eg29
Hat Chao Mai N.P. THA 116 Pk42
Hatches Creek AUS (NT) 143 Rh56
Hatchie N.W.R. USA 248 Ff28
Hat Creek USA (WY) 235 Eh24
Hat Creek Hist. Ranch CDN 232 Dk20
Hateg RO 44 Mc45
Hatfield AUS 153 Sb62
Hat Gamaria IND (JKD) 109 Pc34
Hathazari BD 112 Pf34
Hat Head N.P. AUS 151 Sg61
Hatherleigh GB 20 Kq40
Hathras IND (UPH) 107 Ok32
Ha Tien VN 117 Qc40
Hatiheu F 165 Ck50
Hatiman J 101 Rj28
Ha Tinh VN 115 Qc36
Hatip TR 51 Mn53
Hatkhamba IND (MHT) 108 Og37
Hatkoli IND (CGH) 109 Pa36
Hatkoti IND (HPH) 107 Oj30
Hato Corozal CO 268 Ge42
Hato la Vergareña YV 270 Gj42
Hato Mayor DOM 260 Gf36
Hatpass RI 132 Rd49
Hatra IRQ 65 Nb28
Hatrik N 12 Lf30
Hatscher, Cerro RA 294 Gd70
Hatt UAE 75 Nh33
Hatta IND (MPH) 109 Ok33
Hattah AUS (VIC) 152 Sb63
Hattah Kulkyne N.P. AUS 152 Sb63
Hatteras USA (NC) 249 Gc28
Hatteras Abyssal Plain 227 Gb12
Hatteras Island USA 249 Gc28
Hattfjelldal N 10 Lh13
Hat Thai Muang N.P. THA 116 Pk41
Hattiesburg USA (MS) 243 Ff30
Hattigudur IND (KTK) 108 Oj37
Hattingen D 32 Lh39
Hatton-Dikoya CL 111 Pa43
Hattula FIN 16 Me29
Hattuşaş TR 51 Mp51
Hatu Iti F 165 Ck50
Hatunsaray TR 51 Mn53
Hatutaa F 165 Ck49
Hatvan H 39 Lu43
Hat Wanakon N.P. THA 116 Pk40
Hat Yai THA 116 Qa42
Hatzfeldhafen PNG 159 Sc48
Haud ETH 199 Nc41
Haugastøl N 12 Lh30
Hauge N 12 Lg32
Haugesund N 12 Lf31
Hauho FIN 16 Me29
Hauhui SOL 161 Ta50
Hauja BY 17 Mf36
Haukeligrend N 12 Lh31
Haukelisæter N 12 Lh31
Haukivesi FIN 16 Mj28
Haukivuori FIN 16 Mh28
Haultain River CDN 233 Eg17
Hauraha SOL 161 Ta51
Hauraki Gulf NZ 154 Th64
Hausach D 34 Lj42
Hausdiha IND (JKD) 112 Pd33
Hausruck A 35 Lo42
Hautajärvi FIN 11 Me12
Haut Atlas MA 172 Kf30
Haut Camopi F 271 Hd44
Hautefort F 24 Lb45
Hautes Fagnes B 23 Lf40
Haut-Kœnigsbourg F 23 Lh42
Hautmont F 23 Ld40
Hauts Plateaux DZ 173 Kk28
Hauts Plateaux de l'Ouest WAN 194 Le42
Hauzenberg D 35 Lo42
Havali AZ 70 Nd26
Havana C 258 Fj34
Havana USA (IL) 241 Fe25
Havant GB 21 Ku40
Havasupai Ind. Res. USA 236 Ed27
Havdhem S 15 Lt33
Havdrup DK 14 Ln35
Have Etoe GH 193 La42
Havel D 33 Ln38
Havelberg D 33 Ln38
Havelian PK 79 Og28
Haveli Lakkha PK 79 Og30
Havelland D 33 Ln38
Havelock USA (NC) 249 Gb28
Havelock Island IND 111 Pg40
Haven IND (KTK) 110 Oh39
Haverfordwest GB 20 Kq39
Haverhill GB 21 La38
Haverhill USA (MA) 247 Ge24
Håverud S 12 Ln32
Havilah AUS (QLD) 149 Sd56
Havířov CZ 38 Lt41
Havlíčkův Brod CZ 38 Lq41
Havneby DK 14 Lj35
Havøysund N 11 Mc10
Havran TR 50 Mh51
Havre USA (MT) 233 Ef21
Havre-Aubert CDN (QC) 245 Gk22
Havre-Saint-Pierre CDN (QC) 245 Gj20
Havrylivka UA 55 Mj21
Havsa TR 50 Mg49
Havza TR 62 Mh25
Hawaii USA (HI) 230 Cc36
Hawaii USA 230 Cb35
Hawaiian Islands USA 230 Ca34
Hawaiian Ridge 230 Bk34
Hawaii Volcanoes N.P. USA 230 Cc36
Hawal WAN 187 Lg40
Hawalli KWT 74 Nd31
Hawa Mahal IND 106 Oh32
Hawarden USA (IA) 241 Fb24
Hawar Islands BRN 74 Nf33
Hawera NZ 154 Th65
Hawesville USA (KY) 248 Fg27
Hawi USA (HI) 230 Cc35
Hawick GB 19 Ks35
Hawke Bay NZ 154 Tj65
Hawker AUS (SA) 152 Rk61
Hawke's Bay CDN (NF) 245 Hb20
Hawkes Bay Green Turtle Beach PK 80 Od33
Hawkesbury CDN (ON) 247 Gc23
Hawkesbury Island CDN 232 Df19
Hawkes Nest AUS (NSW) 153 Sg62
Hawk Inlet USA (AK) 231 Dc16
Hawkins Island USA 230 Cg15
Hawkinsville USA (GA) 249 Fj29
Hawks Head Lookout AUS 140 Qh59
Hawk Springs USA (WY) 235 Eh25
Hawr ad Dalmaj IRQ 65 Nc29
Hawrah YE 68 Ne38
Hawr al ,Awdah IRQ 65 Nd30
Hawr al Hammar IRQ 65 Nd30
Hawr ash Shubayjah IRQ 65 Nc29
Hawr as Sa'diyah IRQ 65 Nd29

Hawr as Suwayqiyah – Hohe Acht

Hawr as Suwayqiyah IRQ 65 Nc29
Hawr Limr Sawan IRQ 65 Nd30
Hawtat Sudayr KSA 67 Nc33
Hawthorne USA (NV) 234 Ea26
Hawza DARS 178 Ke32
Hawzen ETH 191 Mk40
Haxtun USA (CO) 240 Ej25
Hay AUS (NSW) 153 Sc63
Haya SUD 191 Mj37
Haya'er CHN (QHI) 87 Pg27
Hayang CHN (AHU) 102 Qk31
Hayange F 23 Lg41
Hayban SUD 197 Mf40
Haydarlı TR 51 Ml52
Hayden USA (CO) 235 Eg25
Haydere TR 62 Me27
Haydock Park GB 21 Ks37
Hayes Creek AUS (NT) 139 Rf52
Hayes Halvø DK 225 Gc03
Hayes, Mount USA 229 Cg14
Hayes River CDN 238 Fb18
Hayes River CDN 238 Fd17
Hayfield PNG 159 Sb49
Hayk' ETH 198 Mk40
Haykota ER 191 Mj39
Hay Lakes CDN (AB) 233 Ed19
Haymana TR 51 Mn51
Hay, Mount AUS 142 Rg57
Haynan YE 68 Ne38
Hayneville USA (AL) 248 Fg29
Hay Point AUS (QLD) 149 Se56
Hayrabolu TR 50 Mh49
Hay River AUS 143 Rj57
Hay River CDN 224 Ea06
Hays USA (KS) 240 Fa26
Hays USA (MT) 233 Ef22
Hays YE 68 Nb39
Hays Mountains 296 Cc36
Haystack Mount USA 229 Cd13
Haystack Peak USA 235 Ed26
Haysville USA (KS) 242 Fb27
Hayti USA (SD) 240 Fb23
Hayuliang IND (ARP) 113 Pj31
Hayward USA (CA) 234 Dj27
Hayward USA (WI) 241 Fe22
Haywards Heath GB 21 Ku39
Haywood Channel MYA 114 Pg36
Hazard USA (KY) 249 Fj27
Hazareh Castle IR 75 Nj32
Hazarganji Chiltan N.P. PK 78 Od30
Hazarganji N.P. Markhor Leopard PK 80 Od32
Hazaribagh IND (JKD) 109 Pc34
Hazaribagh N.P. IND 109 Pc33
Hazar Sum AFG 78 Oe27
Hazebrouck F 23 Lc40
Hazelton USA (ND) 240 Ek22
Hazelton Mtns. CDN 232 Dg18
Hazen USA (ND) 240 Ek22
Hazen Bay USA 228 Bh15
Hazen Strait CDN 225 Ec03
Hazlehurst USA (GA) 249 Fj30
Hazlet CDN (SK) 233 Ef20
Hazleton CDN (BC) 231 Dg18
Hazleton USA (PA) 247 Gc25
Hazmaba Duhaym KSA 66 Mk32
Hazor IL 64 Mh29
Hazoua TN 174 Ld29
Hazrat Khairuddin Mausoleum PK 81 Oe32
Hazur Sahib IND 108 Oj36
Hazyview ZA 214 Mf58
Headingly AUS (QLD) 148 Rk56
Headlands ZW 214 Mg55
Head of Bight AUS 145 Rf61
Head-Smashed-In Buffalo Jump CDN 233 Ed21
Healy USA (AK) 229 Cf14
Heanor GB 21 Kt38
Heany Junction ZW 214 Me56
Heard 301 Ob15
Hearne USA (TX) 243 Fb30
Hearst CDN (ON) 239 Fj21
Hearst San Simeon S.H.M. USA 236 Dk28
Heart's Content CDN (NF) 245 Hd22
Heath BOL/PE 279 Gf52
Heathcote AUS (VIC) 153 Sc64
Hebbe Falls IND 110 Oh40
Hebbronville USA (TX) 253 Fa32
Hebei CHN 83 Qc11
Hebel AUS (QLD) 151 Sd60
Hebera RI 130 Re46
Heber City USA (UT) 235 Ee25
Heberg S 14 Ln34
Heber Springs USA (AR) 243 Fe28
Hebi CHN (HNN) 93 Qh28
Hebo USA (OR) 234 Dj23
Hebrides GB 8 Kc07
Hebron CDN 225 Gd07
Hebron IL 64 Mh30
Hebron USA (ND) 240 Ej22
Hebron USA (NE) 240 Fb25
Heby S 13 Lr31
Hecate Strait CDN 232 De19
Hecelchakán MEX (CAM) 255 Fe35
Heceta Island USA 231 Dd18
Hechford Bank 116 Pj40
Hechi CHN (GZG) 96 Qe33
Hechingen D 34 Lj42
Hechuan CHN (CGQ) 95 Qd30
Hecla CDN (MB) 238 Fb20
Hecla/Grindstone Prov. Park CDN 238 Fb20
Hecla Island CDN 238 Fb20
Hector NZ 155 Tf66
Hectorspruit ZA 214 Mf58
Hector Tejada PE 279 Ge53
Hedalen N 12 Lk30
Heddal N 12 Lk31
Heddal stavkirke N 12 Lk31
Hédé F 22 Kt42
Hede S 13 Lo28
Hedemora S 13 Lq30
Hedensted DK 14 Lk35
Hedesunda S 13 Lr30
Hedeviken S 13 Lo28
Heek D 32 Lh38
Heerde NL 32 Lg38
Heerenveen NL 32 Lf38
Heerhugowaard NL 32 Le38
Heerlen NL 32 Lg40
Heetu ETH 198 Mj42
Heezen Fracture Zone ANT 296 Ea30
Hefa IL 64 Mh29
Hefei CHN (AHU) 102 Qj30
Hefeng CHN (HUB) 95 Qf31
Heffley Creek CDN (BC) 232 Dk20
Heflin USA (AL) 249 Fh29
Hegang CHN (HLG) 98 Rf22
Hegura-jima J 101 Rj27
Hegyfalu H 38 Lr43
Hehelek CHN (XUZ) 86 Pb27
Heho MYA 113 Pj35
Hehua CHN (HUB) 95 Qf30
Heide D 32 Lk36
Heidelberg D 34 Lj41
Heidelberg USA (MS) 243 Ff30
Heidelberg ZA 216 Ma63
Heidelberg ZA 217 Me59
Heidenau D 33 Lo40
Heidenheim D 34 Ll42
Heidenreichstein A 35 Lq42
Heidentor A 35 Lr42
Heide-Park D 32 Lk37
Heihe CHN (HLG) 98 Rd20
Hei He CHN 92 Qa26
Heijiang CHN (GZG) 96 Qf35
Heikendorf D 33 Ll36
Heilbron ZA 217 Md59
Heilbronn D 34 Lk41
Heiligenblut A 35 Ln43
Heiligenhafen D 33 Ll36
Heiligenstadt D 32 Ll39
Heilong Jiang CHN 98 Rf22
Heilongjiang CHN 83 Rb09
Heimaey IS 10 Jk14
Heimahe CHN (QHI) 92 Pk27
Heimerfrontfjella 296 Kb33
Heinävesi FIN 16 Mj28
Heinola FIN 16 Mg29
Heinsberg D 32 Lg39
Heinze Chaung MYA 114 Pj38
Heirane DZ 179 Kk32
Heishan CHN (LNG) 100 Rb25
Heishantou CHN (NMZ) 91 Qk20
Heishui CHN (SCH) 94 Qb29
Heitorai BR (GO) 282 Hf53
Heitske RI 158 Rk49
Heituinlahti FIN 16 Mh29
Hejanneh SYR 64 Mj29
Hejaz KSA 66 Mj32
Hejian CHN (HBI) 93 Qj26
Hejiang CHN (SCH) 95 Qc31
Hejin CHN (SAX) 95 Qf28
Hejing CHN (XUZ) 87 Pd24
Hekımdağ TR 51 Ml51
Hekimhan TR 63 Mj26
Hekla IS 10 Ka14
Hekou CHN (GSU) 92 Qb27
Hekou CHN (HUB) 102 Qh30
Hekou CHN (JGX) 102 Qj31
Heksem N 12 Lm28
Hel PL 36 Lt36
Hel Abad IR 72 Ne27
Helagsfjället S 13 Ln28
Helan CHN (NHZ) 92 Qd26
Helan Shan CHN 92 Qc26
Helanshan Z.B. CHN 92 Qd26
Heldrungen D 33 Lm39
Helechal E 28 Kp48
Helem IND (ASM) 112 Pg32
Helena USA (AR) 243 Fe28
Helena USA (MT) 235 Ed22
Helena USA (OK) 242 Fa27
Helen Falls CDN 246 Fk22
Helen Glacier 297 Pc32
Helen Reef PAL 121 Rf44
Helensburgh GB 19 Kq34
Helen Springs Roadhouse AUS (NT) 139 Rg55
Helensville NZ 154 Th64
Helgasjön S 15 Lp34
Helgeå S 15 Lo34
Helgoland D 32 Lh36
Helgoländer Bucht D 32 Lj36
Helgøya N 12 Ll30
Heli CHN (HLG) 98 Rf22
Helixi CHN (AHU) 102 Qk30
Hella IS 10 Jk14
Hella N 12 Lg29
Hell-Bourg F 221 Nh56
Helleland N 12 Lg32
Hellesvikan N 10 Le14
Hellesylt N 12 Lg28
Hellevoetsluis NL 32 Le39
Helligdomsklipperne DK 15 Lp35
Hellín E 29 Kt48
Hellisandur IS 10 Jj13
Hellnar IS 10 Jj13
Hells Canyon USA 234 Eb23
Hells Canyon Nat. Rec. Area USA 234 Eb23
Hells Gate Airtram CDN 232 Dk21
Hell's Gate N.P. EAK 204 Mj46
Hell Ville = Andoany RM 219 Ne52
Helme D 33 Lm39
Helmeringhausen NAM 212 Lj58
Helmond NL 32 Lf39
Helmsdale GB 19 Kr32
Helmsley GB 21 Kt36
Helmstedt D 33 Lm38
Helodrano Anantsono RM 220 Nb57
Helodrano Antongila RM 219 Ne53
Helodrano Antsiranana RM 219 Ne52
Helodrano Fanemotra RM 220 Nb57
Helodrano Mahajamba RM 218 Nd53
Helodrano Narinda RM 218 Nd53
Helong CHN (JLN) 100 Re24
Hel'pa SK 39 Lu42
Helper USA (UT) 235 Ee26
Helpter Berge D 33 Lo37
Helshan AL 46 Ma48
Helsingborg S 14 Ln34
Helsinge DK 14 Ln34
Helsingfors = Helsinki FIN 16 Me30
Helsingør DK 14 Ln34
Helsinki = Helsingfors FIN 16 Me30
Helston GB 20 Kp40
Heltermaa EST 16 Md32
Helvécia BR (BA) 287 Ja54
Helvecia RA (SF) 289 Gk61
Helvetinjärven kansallispuisto FIN 16 Md28
Hemau D 35 Lm41
Hemavan S 10 Lh13
Hemčik RUS 85 Pf20
Hemel Hempstead GB 21 Ku39
Hemer D 32 Lh39
Hemet USA (CA) 236 Eb29
Hemingford USA (NE) 240 Ej24
Hemis Monastery IND 79 Oj29
Hemling S 10 Lk14
Hemmoor D 32 Lk37
Hemnes N 12 Lm31
Hemnesberget N 10 Lg12
Hemphill USA (TX) 243 Fd30
Hempstead USA (TX) 243 Fb30
Hemse S 15 Lt33
Hemsedal N 12 Lj30
Hemsö S 13 Lt28
Henan CHN 83 Qc12
Henån S 14 Lm32
Hen and Chicken Islands NZ 154 Th63
Henasi-saki J 101 Rk25
Henbury AUS (NT) 142 Rg58
Henbury Meteorite Craters AUS 142 Rg58
Hendaye F 24 Kt47
Hendek TR 51 Ml50
Henderson RA (BA) 293 Gk64
Henderson USA (KY) 248 Fg27
Henderson USA (NC) 249 Ga27
Henderson USA (NE) 240 Fb25
Henderson USA (NV) 236 Ec27
Henderson USA (NY) 247 Gb24
Henderson USA (TN) 243 Ff28
Henderson USA (TX) 243 Fc29
Hendersonville USA (NC) 249 Fj28
Hendersonville USA (TN) 248 Fg27
Hendijan IR 74 Ne30
Hendon CDN (SK) 238 Ej19
Hendorabi IR 74 Ng32
Hendrina ZA 217 Me59
Hengam IR 75 Nk33
Henganofi PNG 159 Sc49
Hengchun RC 97 Ra34
Hengduan Shan CHN 113 Pk32
Hengelo NL 32 Lg38
Hengshan CHN (HUN) 96 Qg32
Heng Shan CHN 93 Qg26
Hengshan CHN 96 Qg32
Hengshan CHN 96 Qg32
Hengshui CHN (HBI) 93 Qh27
Heng Xian CHN (GZG) 96 Qe34
Hengyang CHN (HUN) 96 Qg32
Heničes'k UA 55 Mh22
Hénin-Beaumont F 23 Lc40
Hennan S 13 Lq28
Hennaya DZ 173 Kk28
Hennebont F 22 Kr43
Hennef D 32 Lh40
Hennenman ZA 217 Md59
Hennessey USA (OK) 242 Fb27
Hennigsdorf D 33 Lo38
Henningsvær N 10 Lh11
Henrichemont F 23 Lc43
Henrietta USA (TX) 242 Fa29
Henryetta USA (OK) 243 Fc28
Henry Ford Museum (Dearborn, MI) USA (MI) 246 Fj24
Henry Lawrence Island IND 111 Pg39
Hentei MNG 91 Qe21
Hentiesbaai NAM 212 Lh57
Henty AUS (NSW) 153 Sd63
Henvey Inlet Ind. Res. CDN 246 Fk23
Hen Xian CHN (HNN) 95 Qg28
Henzada MYA 114 Ph37
Hepburn CDN (SK) 233 Eg19
Heping CHN (GDG) 97 Qh33
Heping CHN (GZH) 95 Qe31
Heppner USA (OR) 234 Ea23
Hepu CHN (GZG) 96 Qe35
Heqing CHN (YUN) 113 Qa32
Heraclea MK 46 Mb50
Heradsbygd N 12 Lm30
Heraion GR 49 Mg53
Herakleia TR 49 Mh53
Heralds Cays AUS 149 Se54
Heraneny BY 17 Mf36
Herat AFG 78 Ob28
Hérault F 25 Ld47
Herbagat SUD 191 Mj37
Herbert CDN (SK) 233 Eg20
Herbert NZ 155 Tf68
Herberton AUS (QLD) 149 Sc54
Herbertpur IND (UTT) 107 Oj30
Herbert River AUS (QLD) 149 Sc54
Herbert River AUS 139 Rj55
Herbertsdale ZA 216 Ma63
Herbert Vale AUS (QLD) 148 Rk55
Herbert Wash AUS 141 Rc58
Herbignac F 22 Ks43
Herborn D 32 Lj40
Herbrechtingen D 34 Ll42
Herbstein D 32 Lk40
Herby PL 36 Lt40
Herceg-Novi SCG 46 Lt48
Hercegovina BIH 41 Ls47
Hercegszántó H 39 Lt45
Herchmer CDN (MB) 238 Fc17
Hercilópolis BR (SC) 290 He59
Hercules Bay PNG 159 Sd49
Herdla N 12 Le30
Herðubreið IS 10 Kb13
Hereford GB 21 Ks38
Hereford USA (CO) 235 Eh25
Hereford USA (TX) 237 Ej28
Herefoss N 12 Lj32
Hereke TR 50 Mk50
Herentals B 23 Le39
Hereroland NAM 212 Lk56
Herford D 32 Lj38
Hergla TN 174 Lf27
Héricourt F 23 Lg43
Heringsdorf D 33 Lp37
Herington USA (KS) 241 Fb26
Heriot Bay CDN (BC) 232 Dh20
Herisau CH 34 Lk43
Hérisson F 25 Lc44
Herl'any SK 39 Mb42
Herlen He CHN 91 Qj21
Herleshausen D 32 Ll40
Herlufsholm DK 14 Lm35
Herm GB 22 Ks41
Hermagor A 35 Lo44
Herman USA (MN) 240 Fb23
Hermando RA (CD) 288 Gj62
Herma Ness GB 19 Ku30
Hermannsburg AUS (NT) 142 Rg57
Hermannsburg D 33 Ll38
Hermannsdenkmal D 32 Lj39
Hermantown USA (MN) 241 Fd22
Hermanus ZA 216 Lk63
Hermanusdorings ZA 213 Md58
Hermel RL 64 Mj28
Hermidale AUS (NSW) 151 Sd61
Hermitage USA (AR) 243 Fd29
Hermitage Bay CDN 245 Hb22
Hermit Islands PNG 159 Sc46
Hermon ZA 216 Lk62
Hermon, Mount RL 64 Mh29
Hermopolis ET 177 Mf32
Hermosa USA (SD) 240 Ej24
Hermosillo MEX (BC) 236 Ec29
Hermosillo MEX (SO) 237 Ee31
Hermsdorf D 33 Lm40
Hernád H 39 Mb42
Hernandarias PY 286 Hc58
Hernandarias RA (ER) 289 Ha61
Hernandarias ROU 289 Hc62
Hernández MEX (SLP) 253 Ej34
Hernández Jovales MEX (CHH) 237 Ef30
Hernán M.Miraval RA (SE) 289 Gj59
Herne D 32 Lh39
Herne Bay GB 21 Lb39
Herning DK 14 Lj34
Héroes de la Independencia MEX (BC) 236 Ec30
Herold ZA 216 Mb62
Heroldsbaai ZA 216 Mb63
Herónia GR 48 Mc52
Heron Island AUS (QLD) 149 Sf57
Herradura RA (FO) 289 Ha59
Herrenberg D 34 Lj42
Herrenchiemsee D 35 Ln43
Herrera RA (SE) 288 Gj60
Herrera del Duque E 28 Kp49
Herrera de los Navarros E 27 Kt51
Herrera de Pisuerga E 26 Kq52
Herreruela E 28 Ko49
Herrestad S 12 Lm32
Herrick Creek CDN 232 Dk18
Herrljunga S 15 Lo32
Herrskog S 13 Ls28
Hersbruck D 35 Lm41
Herschel ZA 217 Md61
Hersónisos Akrotíri GR 49 Me55
Hersónisos Rodópou GR 48 Md55
Hersónisos Tiganis GR 48 Md55
Herstal B 23 Lf40
Hertford GB 21 Ku39
Herval BR (RS) 290 Hd62
Hervás E 28 Kp50
Hervey Bay AUS (QLD) 151 Sg58
Hervey Bay AUS 151 Sg58
Hervey Junction CDN (QC) 244 Gd22
Herzberg D 33 Ll39
Herzberg D 33 Lo39
Herzliya IL 64 Mh29
Herzogenaurach D 35 Ll41
Herzogenburg A 35 Lq42
Herzogville ZA 217 Mc60
Hesadi IND (JKD) 109 Pc34
Hešajin IR 72 Ne27
Hesdin F 23 Lc40
Hesel D 32 Lh37
Heshan CHN (GDG) 97 Qg34
Heshan CHN (GZG) 96 Qe34
Heshun CHN (SAX) 93 Qg27
Heskestad N 12 Lg32
Hesperia USA (CA) 236 Eb28
Hesselberg D 35 Ll41
Hesselø DK 14 Lm34
Hesselø Bugt DK 14 Lm35
Hessel Sound CDN 225 Fa03
Hessen D 34 Lj40
Hessisch Lichtenau D 32 Lk39
Hess Mts. CDN 231 De14
Hess River CDN 231 Dd14
Hestra S 15 Lo33
Hestra S 15 Lq33
Hetagima RI 131 Rk48
Hetauda NEP 88 Pc32
Hetényegyháza H 39 Lu44
Het Kruis ZA 216 Lk62
Hettinger USA (ND) 240 Ej23
Hettstedt D 33 Lm39
Hevelândia BR (AM) 274 Gk48
Heverstrom D 32 Lj36
Heves H 39 Ma43
Hevi GH 193 La42
Hévíz H 38 Ls44
Hevlin CZ 38 Lr42
Hevron IL 64 Mh30
Hewart Downs AUS (NSW) 150 Sa60
Hewitt USA (TX) 243 Fb30
Hexham GB 19 Ks36
Hexi CHN (SCH) 113 Qb32
He Xian CHN (AHU) 102 Qk30
He Xian CHN (GZG) 96 Qf33
Hexigten Qi CHN (NMZ) 93 Qj24
Hexrivierberge ZA 216 Lk62
Heyang CHN (SAA) 95 Qf28
Heydon ZA 217 Mc61
Heyrieux F 25 Lf45
Heysham GB 21 Ks36
Heyu CHN (HNN) 95 Qf29
Heyuan CHN (GDG) 97 Qh34
Heywood AUS (VIC) 152 Sa65
Heywood Islands AUS 138 Rc53
Heze CHN (SDG) 102 Qh28
Hezhang CHN (GZH) 96 Qc32
Hezuozhen CHN (GSU) 94 Qb28
Hhohho SD 214 Mf58
Hiagtin Gol CHN 87 Ph27
Hialeah USA (FL) 250 Fk33
Hian GH 193 Kj40
Hiawassee USA (GA) 249 Fj28
Hiawatha USA (CO) 235 Ef25
Hiawatha USA (KS) 241 Fc26
Hibbarah IRQ 65 Nb28
Hibberdene ZA 217 Mf61
Hibbing USA (MN) 241 Fd22
Hibernia Reef AUS 138 Rb52
Hickman, Mount CDN 231 De17
Hickmann RA (SA) 285 Gj57
Hickory USA (NC) 249 Fk28
Hickory USA 247 Gc24
Hickory Motor Speedway USA 249 Fk28
Hicks Bay NZ 154 Tk64
Hick's Cays BH 255 Fg37
Hickson Lake CDN 238 Ej17
Hickstead GB 21 Ku40
Hico USA (TX) 242 Fa30
Hico USA (WV) 249 Fk26
Hidaka J 99 Sb24
Hidalgo MEX (CHH) 237 Eg30
Hidalgo MEX (COH) 253 Fa32
Hidalgo MEX (TM) 253 Fa33
Hidalgo MEX (ZCT) 253 Ej34
Hidalgo MEX 253 Fa35
Hidalgo del Parral MEX (CHH) 253 Eh32
Hida-sanmyaku J 101 Rj27
Hidasnémeti H 39 Mb42
Hiddensee D 33 Lo36
Hidden Valley AUS (NT) 139 Rg54
Hidden Valley AUS (QLD) 149 Sd55
Hidden Valley AUS (QLD) 149 Sd56
Hidden Valley N.P. = Mirima National Park AUS 138 Re53
Hidra N 12 Lg32
Hidrelétrica Curuá-Una BR (PA) 275 Hc47
Hieflau A 35 Lp43
Hien VN 115 Qd38
Hienghène F 162 Tc56
Hien Luong Bridge VN 115 Qd37
Hierapolis TR 50 Mk53
Higashi-suido J 103 Re29
Higgins Bay USA (NY) 247 Gc24
Higginsville AUS (WA) 144 Ra61
Highbourn Cay BS 251 Gb33
Highbury AUS (QLD) 148 Sb54
Highbury AUS (QLD) 149 Sc57
Highbury GUY 271 Hb42
Highflats ZA 217 Mf61
High Hill River CDN 233 Ee17
High Island USA (TX) 243 Fc31
High Island USA 228 Bk16
Highland Plains AUS (NT) 139 Rj55
Highlands AUS (QLD) 150 Sc58
Highlands USA (NC) 249 Fj28
Highland Springs USA (VA) 249 Gb27
High Level CDN 224 Ea07
Highmore USA (SD) 240 Fa23
High Peak RP 120 Ra38
High Point USA (NC) 249 Fk28
High Prairie CDN (AB) 233 Eb18
High River CDN (AB) 233 Ed20
High Rock BS 251 Ga32
Highrock Ind. Res. CDN 238 Ek18
Highrock Lake CDN 233 Eh17
Highrock Lake CDN 238 Ek18
High Shoals USA 249 Fh28
High Springs USA (FL) 250 Fj31
Highway No. 1 USA 234 Dj26
Highwood USA (MT) 235 Ee22
High Wycombe GB 21 Ku39
Higuerillas MEX (TM) 253 Fb33
Higuerote YV 269 Gg40
Higueruela E 29 Kt48
Higüey DOM 260 Gf36
Hiidenportin kansallispuisto FIN 11 Me14
Hiiglet EAK 205 Na46
Hiiraan SP 199 Nc43
Hiiumaa EST 16 Mc32
Hijar E 27 Ku51
Hijtola RUS 16 Mk29
Hikkaduwa Beach CL 111 Pa43
Hikone J 101 Rj28
Hikueru Atoll F 165 Cj54
Hikurangi NZ 154 Tk64
Hilaricos RCH 284 Gf56
Hilbre CDN (MB) 238 Fa20
Hildburghausen D 33 Ll40
Hilden D 32 Lg39
Hildesheim D 32 Lk38
Hilf OM 69 Nk35
Hilialawa RI 124 Pj45
Hilibafunua RI 124 Pk46
Hilisimaetano RI 124 Pj45
Hili UAE 75 Nh33
Hillandale ZA 216 Ma62
Hillared S 15 Lo33
Hill City USA (ID) 234 Ec24
Hill City USA (KS) 240 Fa26
Hill City USA (MN) 241 Fd22
Hill Creek Extension Uintah and Ouray Ind. Res. USA 235 Ef26
Hilléket TCH 196 Ma39
Hill End AUS (NSW) 153 Se62
Hillerød DK 14 Ln35
Hilli IND (WBG) 112 Pe33
Hillosensalmi FIN 16 Mg29
Hill Resort Almora IND 107 Ok31
Hill Resort Coonoor IND 111 Oj41
Dalhousi IND 107 Oh29
Hill Resort Dalhousi IND 107 Oh29
Hill Resort Dehradun IND 107 Ok30
Hill Resort Kasauli IND (HPH) 107 Oj30
Hill Resort Kodaikanal IND 111 Oj41
Hill Resort Kullu IND (HPH) 107 Oj30
Hill Resort Manali IND 107 Oj29
Hill Resort Mount Abu IND 106 Og33
Hill Resort Mussourie IND 107 Ok30
Hill Resort Nainital IND 107 Ok31
Hill Resort Ootacamund IND 110 Oj41
Hill Resort Shimla IND 107 Oj30
Hill Resort Yercaud IND (TNU) 111 Ok41
Hillsboro USA (KS) 240 Fb26
Hillsboro USA (ND) 240 Fb22
Hillsboro USA (NM) 237 Eg29
Hillsboro USA (OH) 246 Fj26
Hillsboro USA (TX) 243 Fb29
Hillsborough GD 261 Gk39
Hillsborough Bay CDN 245 Gj22
Hillsdale USA (MI) 246 Fh25
Hillsdale USA (NY) 247 Gd24
Hillside AUS (WA) 140 Qk56
Hillside N.W.R. USA 248 Fe29
Hillsport CDN (ON) 239 Fh21
Hillston AUS (NSW) 153 Sc62
Hillswick GB 19 Kt30
Hilltop Ski Area USA 230 Ch15
Hilo USA (HI) 230 Cc36
Hilok RUS 91 Qf20
Hilok RUS 91 Qf20
Hilongos RP 123 Rc40
Hilpoltstein D 35 Lm41
Hiltaba AUS (SA) 152 Rh62
Hilton AUS (QLD) 148 Rk56
Hilton USA (NY) 247 Gb24
Hilton Head Island USA (SC) 249 Fk29
Hiltula FIN 16 Mj29
Hilvaro TR 63 Mk27
Hilvarenbeek NL 32 Lf39
Hilversum NL 32 Lf38
Hima KSA 68 Nc36
Himachal Pradesh IND 104 Od12
Himalaya 82 Od12
Himal Chuli NEP 88 Pc31
Himamaylan RP 123 Rb40
Himatnagar IND (GUJ) 108 Og34
Himba NAM 212 Lg54
Himbirti ER 191 Mk39
Himchari BD 112 Pg35
Himeji J 101 Rh28
Himeji-jo J 101 Rh28
Himi J 101 Rj27
Himki RUS 52 Mj18
Himmelbjerget DK 14 Lk34
Himmerfjärden S 13 Ls31
Himmerland DK 14 Lk34
Himmetdede TR 51 Mq52
Himo EAT 207 Mj47
Himora ETH 191 Mj39
Hinako RI 124 Pj45
Hinatuan RP 123 Rd41
Hin Bun LAO 115 Qc37
Hinche RH 260 Gd36
Hinchinbrook Entrance USA 230 Cg16
Hinchinbrook Island AUS (QLD) 149 Sd55
Hinchinbrook Island USA 230 Cg15
Hinchinbrook Island N.P. AUS (QLD) 149 Sd55
Hinckley GB 21 Kt38
Hinckley USA (MN) 241 Fd22
Hincks Conservation Park AUS 152 Rj62
Hinda RCB 202 Lg48
Hindaun IND (RJT) 107 Oj32
Hindol IND (ORS) 109 Pc35
Hinds Lake CDN 245 Hb21
Hindu Kush AFG 61 Ob12
Hindupur IND (APH) 111 Oj40
Hindu shrine (Kedarnath) IND 107 Ok30
Hines Creek CDN (AB) 233 Ea17
Hinesville USA (GA) 249 Fk30
Hinganghat IND (MHT) 109 Ok35
Hinganskij zapovednik RUS 98 Re21
Hingham USA (MT) 233 Ee21
Hinglaj = Hingol PK 80 Oc33
Hingol PK 80 Oc33
Hingol PK 80 Oc33
Hingoli IND (MHT) 108 Oj36
Hingorja PK 80 Oe32
Hinidan PK 80 Od33
Hinigaran RP 123 Rb40
Hinis TR 63 Na26
Hinituan Passage RP 123 Rc41
Hinkley, Mount AUS 141 Re59
Hinlopenstreet N 11 Lj05
Hin Nam No N.B.C.A. LAO 115 Qc37
Hinnøya N 10 Lh11
Hinoba-an RP 123 Rb41
Hinogyaung MYA 114 Ph37
Hinojosa del Duque E 28 Kp48
Hinomi-saki J 101 Rg28
Hinsdale USA (MT) 233 Eg21
Hin Taw MYA 113 Ph34
Hinton CDN (AB) 233 Eb19
Hinton USA (WV) 249 Fk27
Hınzır Dağı TR 62 Mj26
Hios GR 49 Mf52
Hios GR 49 Mg52
Hipolito Bouchard RA (CD) 288 Gj63
Hippodrome de la Cépière F 24 Lb47
Hippodrome de Montréal CDN (QC) 247 Gd23
Hippone DZ 174 Ld27
Hirado J 103 Re29
Hirado-jima J 103 Re29
Hirakud Reservoir IND 109 Pb35
Hiraman EAK 205 Mk46
Hiranai J 101 Sa25
Hirapur IND (MPH) 109 Ok33
Hiratsuka J 101 Rk28
Hiré CI 193 Kh42
Hirekerur IND (KTK) 110 Oh39
Hirfanlar TR 64 Mg26
Hirfanlı Barajı TR 51 Mo51
Hirfanlı Barajı TR 64 Mg26
Hirhafok DZ 180 Lc34
Hiriyur IND (KTK) 111 Oj40
Hirna ETH 198 Na41
Hiroo J 99 Sb24
Hirosaki J 101 Sa25
Hiroshima J 99 Sa24
Hiroshima J 101 Rg28
Hirschaid D 35 Lm41
Hirsholmene DK 14 Ll33
Hirson F 23 Le41
Hârșova RO 45 Mh46
Hirta GB 18 Km33
Hirtshals DK 14 Lk33
Hirvensalmi FIN 16 Mg29
Hisaka-jima J 103 Re29
Hisar IND (HYA) 106 Oh31
Hisarcık TR 50 Mk51
Hisarcık TR 51 Mq52
Hisarja BG 47 Me48
Hisingen S 14 Lm33
Hislaviči RUS 52 Mg18
Hisma KSA 64 Mh31
Hisn as Sahabi LAR 175 Ma30
Hisor tizmasi UZ 76 Od26
Hispaniola RH/DOM 260 Ge37
Historic Camden USA 249 Fk28
Histórico Santa Cruz la Vieja, P.N. BOL 285 Gj54
Historic Railway Station (Larrimah) AUS 139 Rg53
Historic Rugby USA 249 Fh27
Histria RO 45 Mj46
Hisua IND (BIH) 109 Pc33
Hisui PNG 159 Sd50
Hit IRQ 65 Nb29
Hita J 103 Rf29
Hitachi J 101 Sa27
Hitahiyamam J 99 Rk24
Hithadhoo MV 110 Og45
Hithadhoo MV 110 Og46
Hitia GUY 271 Hb43
Hitianau F 165 Ch54
Hiti Atoll F 165 Ch54
Hitoyoshi J 103 Rf29
Hitra N 10 Le14
Hittarp S 14 Ln34
Hitzacker D 33 Lm37
Hiva Oa F 165 Da50
Hivaro PNG 159 Sb49
Hiw ET 177 Mg33
Hiw VU 162 Td52
Hixon CDN (BC) 232 Dj19
Hiyoshi J 103 Rg29
Hizan TR 63 Nb26
Hjallerup DK 14 Ll33
Hjälmaren S 13 Lq31
Hjargas nuur MNG 85 Pg21
Hjärnarp S 15 Ln34
Hjelmeland N 12 Lg31
Hjelset N 12 Lh28
Hjeltefjorden N 12 Le30
Hjemmeluft N 10 Mb11
Hjerkinn N 12 Lk28
Hjerl Hede DK 14 Lk34
Hjo S 13 Lp32
Hjørring DK 14 Lk33
Hjortkvarn S 13 Lq32
Hkaingzi MYA 112 Pg35
Hkyenhpa MYA 113 Pj32
Hlabisa ZA 217 Mf60
Hlane Royal Game Reserve SD 217 Mf59
Hlegu MYA 114 Pj37
Hlevacha UA 54 Mf20
Hlinsko CZ 38 Lq41
Hlobyne UA 54 Mg21
Hlohovec SK 38 Ls42
Hlotse LS 217 Me60
Hluchiv UA 52 Mg20
Hluhluwe ZA 217 Mg60
Hluhluwe-Umfolozi Park ZA 217 Mf60
Hlusk BY 52 Me19
Hluthi SD 217 Mf59
Hlybokae BY 52 Md18
Hlynjany UA 39 Me41
HMAS Swan wreck diving AUS 144 Qh62
Hnathalo F 162 Td56
Hnivan' UA 54 Me21
Hnúšťa SK 39 Lu42
Ho GH 193 La42
Hoa Binh VN 96 Qc35
Hoa Binh VN 115 Qd37
Hoai Nhon VN 115 Qe38
Hoa Muc VN 96 Qc35
Hoang Lien Son VN 96 Qc35
Hoani COM 218 Nb52
Hoanib NAM 212 Lg55
Hoarusib NAM 208 Lg55
Hoback Junction USA (WY) 235 Ee24
Hoba Meteorite NAM 212 Lj55
Hoban PRK 100 Rd25
Hobart AUS (TAS) 152 Sd67
Hobart USA (OK) 242 Fa28
Hobatere Lodge NAM 212 Lh55
Hobbs USA (NM) 237 Ej29
Hobbs Coast 296 Db34
Hobetsu J 99 Sb24
Hobhouse ZA 217 Md60
Hobo CO 272 Gc44
Hoboksar CHN (XUZ) 85 Pc22
Hobro DK 14 Lk34
Hobucken USA (NC) 249 Gb28
Hoburgen S 15 Lt34
Hobyo SP 199 Ne43
Hocalar TR 50 Mk52
Hocalar TR 50 Mk52
Hochfeiler = Gran Pilastro A/I 40 Lm44
Hochfeld NAM 212 Lj56
Hochgölling A 35 Lo43
Hochharz, N.P. D 33 Ll39
Ho Chi Minh City = T.P. Ho Chi Minh VN 115 Qd40
Ho Chi Minh, T. P. VN 115 Qd40
Ho Chi Minh, T. P. VN 115 Qd40
Hochosterwitz A 35 Lp44
Hochreichhart A 35 Lp43
Hochschwab A 35 Lq43
Hochstadt D 35 Ll41
Hochstuhl A/SLO 35 Lp44
Hockenheimring D 34 Lj41
Hodal IND (HYA) 107 Oj32
Hodgenville USA (KY) 248 Fh27
Hodges Hill CDN 245 Hc21
Hodgeville CDN (SK) 233 Eg20
Hodgson CDN (MB) 238 Fb20
Hodgson Downs AUS (NT) 139 Rh53
Hodgson Downs A.L. AUS 139 Rh53
Hodgson River AUS 139 Rh53
Hodh RIM 184 Kg37
Hodma SP 199 Nd40
Hódmezővásárhely H 39 Ma44
Hodnanes N 12 Lf31
Hodo CDN (AB) 233 Ec18
Hodonín CZ 38 Ls42
Hodq Shamo CHN 92 Qd25
Hodulbaba Dağı TR 51 Mo53
Hodzana River USA 229 Cf12
Hoedic F 22 Ks43
Hoedspruit ZA 214 Mf58
Hoek van Holland NL 32 Le39
Hoelfjella 297 Ld33
Hoeryong PRK 100 Re24
Hoeyang PRK 100 Rd26
Hof D 35 Lm40
Hof N 12 Ll31
Hoffmans Cay BS 251 Gb33
Hofgeismar D 32 Lk39
Hofheim D 35 Ll40
Hofmeyr ZA 217 Mc61
Höfn IS 10 Kc13
Hofors S 13 Lr30
Hofsjökull IS 10 Ka13
Hofsós IS 10 Ka13
Hofu J 101 Rf28
Höga Kusten S 13 Lt28
Höganäs S 14 Ln34
Hogan Island AUS (VIC) 153 Sd65
Hogatza River USA 229 Cc12
Hog Cay BS 251 Gc34
Høgeloft N 12 Lj29
Hogem Ranges CDN 231 Dh18
Høgeset N 12 Lj29
Hoge Veluwe, N.P. de NL 32 Lf38
Hoggar DZ 180 Lc34
Hoggar, P.N. du DZ 180 Lc34
Hog Landing USA (AK) 229 Cc12
Hogoro EAT 207 Mj48
Högsäter S 12 Ln32
Hogsback ZA 217 Md62
Högsby S 15 Lr33
Högsjö S 13 Lq31
Hőgyész H 38 Lt44
Hohe Acht D 32 Lg40

Karu – Keriya

Karu PNG 160 Sg47
Karuah AUS (NSW) 153 Sf62
Karubaga RI 131 Rk47
Karubwe Z 210 Me53
Karufa RI 131 Rg47
Karula rahvuspark EST 16 Mg33
Karuma Game Reserve EAU 204 Mf44
Karumai J 101 Sa25
Karumba AUS (QLD) 148 Sa54
Karumbhar Island IND 108 Oe34
Karumwa EAT 206 Mg47
Karungi S 11 Mb12
Karungu EAK 204 Mh46
Karup DK 14 Lk34
Karur IND (TNU) 111 Ok41
Karvia FIN 16 Mc28
Karviná CZ 38 Lt41
Karwa IND (MPH) 109 Pa34
Karwai RI 131 Rh48
Karwar IND (KTK) 110 Oh39
Karwar Beach IND 110 Oh39
Karwendelgebirge A 35 Lm43
Karwi IND (UPH) 109 Pa33
Karymskoe RUS 91 Qh20
Karynzharyk KZ 71 Ng24
Kas SUD 196 Mc39
Kaş TR 62 Me27
Kasa CHN (SCH) 94 Qa30
Kasa RDC 200 Lk46
Kasaba EAT 206 Mf48
Kasaba Z 210 Me51
Kasaba Bay Z 206 Mf50
Kasabonika CDN (ON) 239 Ff19
Kasai J 101 Rh28
Kasai RDC 200 Lj47
Kasaji RDC 209 Mb51
Kasa Khurd IND (MHT) 108 Og36
Kasalu Z 210 Md53
Kasama Z 210 Mf51
Kasambule RDC 206 Md47
Kašan IR 72 Nf29
Kasan Bay USA 231 Dd18
Kasane RB 209 Mc54
Kasanga EAT 206 Mf50
Kasanga EAT 207 Mj49
Kasangulu RDC 202 Lh48
Kasanka N.P. Z 210 Mf52
Kasanza RDC 203 Mb49
Kasaragod IND (KER) 110 Oh40
Kasari J 103 Re31
Kasaro SUD 190 Mg40
Kašary RUS 53 Na21
Kasasi WAL 192 Ke41
Kasauli IND (HPH) 107 Oj30
Kasbah de Bizerte TN 174 Le27
Kasbah de Fès MA 173 Kh28
Kasba Tadla MA 172 Kg29
Kascjanevičy BY 17 Mh36
Kascjukovičy BY 52 Mg19
Kascjukovka BY 52 Mf19
Kasdir DZ 173 Kk29
Kasdol IND (CGH) 109 Pb35
Kåseberga S 15 Lp35
Kaseda J 103 Rf30
Kasempa Z 209 Mc52
Kasenga RDC 209 Mb51
Kasenga RDC 210 Me51
Kasenga Z 210 Md53
Kasenye RDC 201 Mf45
Kasese EAU 201 Mf45
Kasese RDC 201 Md46
Kaset Sombun THA 114 Qa37
Kaset Wisai THA 115 Qb38
Kasganj IND (UPH) 107 Ok32
Kashabowie CDN (ON) 239 Fe21
Kashambi ZW 214 Me56
Kashechewan CDN (ON) 239 Fk19
Kashi CHN (XUZ) 86 Oh26
Kashiba Z 210 Me51
Kashiji Plain Z 209 Mb52
Kashileshi RDC 203 Mb51
Kashima J 101 Sa28
Kashipur IND (ORS) 109 Pb36
Kashipur IND (UTT) 107 Ok31
Kashitu Z 210 Me52
Kashiwa J 101 Sa28
Kashiwazaki J 101 Rk27
Kashmar IR 73 Nk28
Kashmor PK 81 Oe31
Kashunuk River USA 228 Bh15
Kashwal SUD 197 Me42
Kasi LAO 114 Qb36
Kasia IND (UPH) 107 Pb32
Kasidishi RDC 203 Mb50
Kasigluk USA (AK) 228 Bj15
Kasimov RUS 53 Na18
Kašin RUS 52 Mj17
Kasinje MW 211 Mh53
Kasiruta RI 130 Rd46
Kasitu River MW 210 Mg51
Kasiui RI 130 Rf48
Kaskabulak KZ 84 Ok21
Kaskas SN 183 Kc37
Kaskasia River St. Fish and Wildlife Area USA 248 Ff26
Kaskasia R. St. Fish and Wildlife Area USA 241 Ff26
Kaskattama River CDN 238 Fe17
Kaskelen KZ 77 Oj24
Kaskelen KZ 77 Oj24
Kaskii FIN 16 Mj29
Kaskinen = Kaskö FIN 13 Mb28
Kaskö = Kaskinen FIN 13 Mb28
Kasompe Z 209 Mc52
Kasongan RI 126 Qg46
Kasongo RDC 206 Md48
Kasongo-Lunda RDC 202 Lj49
Kasonkomona Z 210 Md53
Kaspi GE 70 Nc25
Kaspijsk RUS (DAG) 70 Nd24
Kassa DY 186 Lb40
Kassala SUD 191 Mj39
Kassama RMM 183 Ke39
Kassandra GR 46 Md50
Kassari EST 16 Mc32
Kassarola RMM 184 Kh39
Kassel D 32 Lk39
Kasséré CI 193 Kg41
Kasserine TN 174 Le28
Kássos GR 49 Mg55
Kassou BF 193 Kj40
Kassoum BF 185 Kj39
Kastamonu TR 62 Mg25
Kastaniá GR 46 Mb51
Kastaniá GR 48 Mb51
Kastanitsa GR 48 Mc53
Kastelholman linna FIN 13 Ma30
Kastéli GR 49 Mf55
Kastellaun D 34 Lh40
Kastellorizo GR 62 Me27
Kaštel-Stari HR 41 Lr47
Kastl D 35 Lm41
Kastoriá GR 46 Mb50
Kastri GR 49 Me56
Kástro GR 48 Md52
Kástro GR 48 Mb53
Kastron Mefa'a = Umm al-Rasas JOR 64 Mh30
Kasuga J 101 Rh28
Kasui RI 125 Qc48
Kasuku RDC 201 Mc47
Kasulu EAT 206 Mf48
Kasumbalesa RDC 210 Md52
Kasumi J 101 Rh28
Kasumigaura-ura J 101 Sa27
Kasumkent RUS (DAG) 70 Ne25
Kasumpti IND (HPH) 107 Oj30
Kasungu MW 210 Mg52
Kasungu N.P. MW 210 Mg52
Kasur PK 79 Oh30
Kata THA 116 Pk42
Kataba Z 209 Mc54
Katagum WAN 186 Le40
Katagum WAN 187 Lf39
Katakakishi RDC 203 Mb50
Kataklik 79 Ok28
Katako-Kombe RDC 203 Mc47
Katákolo GR 48 Mb53
Katakwi EAU 204 Mg45
Katalla USA (AK) 230 Ch15
Katamatile AUS (VIC) 153 Sc64
Katana RDC 206 Me47
Katana RI 130 Re45
Katanda RDC 203 Mb49
Katanga RDC 203 Mc50
Katangagung RI 125 Qc47
Katangi IND (MPH) 109 Ok34
Katangi IND (MPH) 109 Ok35
Katanning AUS (WA) 144 Qj62
Kataouâne RIM 184 Kg37
Katapanga DY 193 La40
Katápola GR 49 Mf54
Katapoliani GR 49 Mf53
Katapuram IND (APH) 109 Pa36
Kataragama CL 111 Pa43
Katastári GR 48 Ma53
Kata Tjuta = The Olgas AUS 142 Rf58
Katavi N.P. EAT 206 Mf49
Katayan IR 72 Nf27
Katcha WAN 186 Ld41
Katchall Island IND 111 Pg42
Katchamba TG 193 La41
Katchirga BF 185 La38
Kate EAT 206 Mf49
Katedrala Sveti Jakov HR 41 Lq47
Katèn RUS 99 Rj22
Katende RDC 203 Mb49
Katenge RDC 203 Mb49
Katengo RDC 206 Me48
Katerini GR 46 Mc50
Katerloch A 35 Lq43
Katesh EAT 207 Mh48
Katete Z 210 Mg53
Katghora IND (CGH) 109 Pb34
Kathar MYA 113 Pj33
Katheni GR 48 Md52
Katherine AUS (NT) 139 Rg53
Katherine Gorge AUS (NT) 139 Rg53
Katherine River AUS 139 Rg52
Kathiawar Peninsula IND 108 Of34
Kathikas CY 51 Mn56
Kathleen Lake CDN 239 Fj22
Kathmandu NEP 88 Pc32
Kathoti IND (RJT) 106 Oh32
Kathu ZA 216 Mb59
Kathua 79 Oh29
Kati RMM 184 Kf39
Katiati PNG 159 Sc48
Katibunga Z 210 Mf51
Katiéna RMM 184 Kh39
Katiet RI 124 Pk47
Katihar IND (BIH) 112 Pd33
Katima Mulilo NAM 209 Mc54
Katimik Lake CDN 238 Fa19
Katingan RI 126 Qg47
Katini RDC 203 Lk49
Katiola CI 193 Kh41
Katipunan RP 123 Rb41
Katiti A.L. AUS 142 Rf58
Katiu Atoll F 165 Ch54
Katla SUD 197 Me40
Katlanovska Banja MK 46 Mb49
Katmai Bay USA 228 Cc17
Katmai, Mount USA 228 Cc16
Katmai National Park and Preserve USA 228 Cc16
Kato GUY 270 Ha43
Katoa TCH 187 Lh40
Káto Ahaia GR 48 Mb52
Káto Almiri GR 48 Mc53
Káto Asséa GR 48 Mc53
Katobo Z 209 Mc53
Katoda IND (RJT) 106 Oh33
Kato Deftera CY 51 Mo55
Katofio RDC 210 Me51
Kato Gialia CY 51 Mn55
Katojayo RI 124 Qa47
Káto Makrinoú GR 48 Mb52
Katombe RDC 203 Mb48
Katompi RDC 206 Md49
Katondwe Z 210 Mf53
Káto Nevrokópi GR 47 Md49
Katonga EAU 201 Mf45
Katonga Game Reserve EAU 204 Mf45
Katonkaraghaj KZ 85 Pc21
Katoomba AUS (NSW) 153 Sf62
Katoposo, Gunung RI 127 Ra46
Katorku hhoi Darvoz TJ 76 Of26
Katorkuhhoi Hisar TJ 76 Oe26
Katorkuhhoi Quarama TJ 76 Oe25
Katorkuhhoi Turkistan TJ 76 Od26
Katorkuhhoi Zarafšon TJ 76 Oe26
Katoto EAT 206 Mf48
Káto Vlassia GR 48 Mb52
Katowice PL 37 Lt40
Katranç Dağı TR 51 Mi53
Katrineholm S 13 Lr32
Katse EAK 205 Mk46
Katse Dam LS 217 Me60
Katse Dam LS 217 Me60
Katséna CAM 195 Lf42
Katsepy RM 218 Nd53
Katsina WAN 186 Ld39
Katsina-Ala WAN 194 Le42
Katsina-Ala WAN 194 Le42
Katsuba EAT 207 Mh48
Katsumoto J 103 Re29
Katsuta J 101 Sa27
Katsuura J 101 Sa28
Kattaqo'rg'on UZ 76 Od26
Kattavia GR 49 Mh55
Kattawagami Lake CDN 239 Fk21
Kattegat 14 Ll34
Kattegatcentret DK 14 Ll34
Katthammarsvik S 15 Lt33
Kattumavadi IND (TNU) 111 Ok41
Katueté PY 286 Hc58
Katukina, T.I. BR 279 Ge50
Katumbi MW 210 Mg51
Katun' RUS 85 Pd20
Katun Abad IR 74 Nh30
Katunayaka CL 111 Ok43
Katunda Z 209 Mc54
Katunguru EAU 201 Mf46
Katunskij hrebet RUS/KZ 85 Pd21
Katupa RI 129 Qk50
Katupat RI 127 Ra46
Katuria IND (BIH) 112 Pd33
Katwa IND (WBG) 112 Pe34
Katwe EAU 201 Me46
Katwe RDC 201 Me46
Katwijk aan Zee NL 32 Le38
Katy Wrocławskie PL 36 Lr39
Katzenbuckel D 34 Lk41
Kauai USA 230 Ca34
Kauai Channel USA 230 Ca35
Kaudom RB 209 Ma55
Kauehi Atoll F 165 Ch53
Kaufbeuren D 34 Ll43
Kaufman USA (TX) 243 Fb29
Kaufungen D 32 Lk39
Kauhajoki FIN 16 Mc28
Kauhanevan-Pohjankankaan kansallispuisto FIN 16 Mc28
Kauhava FIN 11 Mb14
Kaukauna USA (WI) 246 Ff23
Kaukaveld NAM/RB 213 Ma55
Kaukei KZ 71 Oa23
Kaukura Atoll F 165 Cg53
Kaula USA 230 Bk35
Kaulakahi Channel USA 230 Ca35
Kaulishishi Z 210 Me53
Kaulsdorf D 33 Lm40
Kaumalapau USA (HI) 230 Cb35
Kaunakakai USA (HI) 230 Cb35
Kaunas LT 17 Md36
Kaunos TR 49 Mj54
Kaup PNG 159 Sb49
Kaupanger N 12 Lh29
Kaupena PNG 159 Sc49
Kaurai PNG 160 Sg50
Kau Rainforest Museum PNG 159 Sc48
Kaura-Namoda WAN 186 Ld39
Kauri Museum NZ 154 Th64
Kauriram IND (UPH) 107 Pb32
Kaurissalo FIN 13 Ma30
Kausala FIN 16 Mg30
Kauske EST 16 Mh32
Kautokeino N 11 Mb11
Kau-Ye Island MYA 116 Pk40
Kavác YV 270 Gj43
Kavacık TR 50 Mj51
Kavadarci MK 46 Mc49
Kavajë AL 46 Lu49
Kavak TR 62 Mj25
Kavaklıdere TR 50 Mj53
Kavála GR 47 Me50
Kavalerovo RUS 99 Rh23
Kavali IND (APH) 111 Ok39
Kavar IR 74 Ng31
Kavaratti IND (LKW) 110 Og41
Kavaratti Island IND 110 Og41
Kavarna BG 47 Mj47
Kavarskas LT 17 Me35
Kavati EAK 204 Mj46
Kavendu RG 192 Kd40
Kaveripattinam IND (TNU) 111 Ok40
Kavieng PNG 160 Sf47
Kavinga Z 210 Mg52
Kavinga Z 210 Md53
Kavir-e Abarkuh IR 72 Ng30
Kavir-e Darre Angir IR 72 Nh30
Kavir-e Siyah Kuh IR 72 Nf29
Kavir-i Namak IR 73 Nj28
Kavir National Park IR 72 Nh28
Kavirondo Gulf EAK 204 Mh46
Kavital IND (KTK) 108 Oj37
Kavkazskij zapovednik RUS 55 Na24
Kävlinge S 15 Lo35
Kavu EAT 206 Mf49
Kavuluni EAK 207 Mk47
Kavumu RDC 206 Me47
Kaw F 271 Hd43
Kawagoe J 101 Rk28
Kawai IND (RJT) 108 Oj33
Kawaihae USA (HI) 230 Cc35
Kawaikini USA 230 Ca34
Kawajena SUD 197 Me42
Kawala EAT 206 Mf50
Kawalusu RI 123 Rc43
Kawambwa Z 206 Me50
Kawana Z 209 Mc52
Kawanoe J 101 Rg28
Kawant IND (GUJ) 108 Oh34
Kawardha IND (CGH) 109 Pa34
Kawarthas CDN 247 Ga23
Kawasa RDC 206 Me50
Kawasaki J 101 Rk28
Kawasi RI 130 Rd46
Kawatipoli MYA 114 Pj36
Kawauchi J 99 Sa25
Kawau Island NZ 154 Th64
Kawaya RDC 206 Me50
Kawayu J 99 Sc24
Kawe RI 130 Rf46
Kaweka NZ 154 Tj65
Kawembwe Z 210 Mf51
Kawemhakan SME 271 Hc44
Kawhia NZ 154 Th65
Kawich Peak USA 234 Eb26
Kawimbe Z 206 Mf50
Kawinaw Lake CDN 238 Fa19
Kawkpalut MYA 114 Pj37
Kawkwreik MYA 114 Pk37
Kawlinn MYA 113 Ph34
Kawteigo GH 193 Kj42
Kawula MW 210 Mh52
Kawungera EAU 201 Mf45
Kaxarari, T.I. BR 279 Gg50
Kaxgar He CHN 86 Oj26
Kax He CHN 84 Pc24
Kaxholmen S 15 Lp33
Kaxinawa Colônia Vinte e Sete, T.I. BR 279 Ge50
Kaxinawá do Rio Humaitá, T.I. BR 279 Ge50
Kaxinawá do Rio Jordão, T.I. BR 279 Gd50
Kaxinawá Nova Olinda, T.I. BR 279 Ge50
Kaya BF 185 Kk39
Kayaapu RI 124 Qb48
Kayabaşı TR 51 Mn51
Kayakent TR 51 Mm51
Kayak Island USA 230 Ch16
Kayaliköy Baraj TR 50 Mh49
Kayambi Z 206 Mf50
Kayan RI 127 Qj44
Kayan Bung IND 112 Ph33
Kayanga EAT 201 Mf46
Kayanga SN 183 Kc39
Kayankulam IND (KER) 110 Oj42
Kayan-Sungai Mentarang Reserve RI 126 Qh44
Kayanza BU 206 Me47
Kayapa TR 50 Mh51
Kayapó, T.I. BR 275 He49
Kayar IND (MHT) 109 Ok36
Kayar SN 183 Kb38
Kayasa RI 130 Rd45
Kayasan N.P. ROK 100 Re28
Kayattar IND (TNU) 111 Oj42
Kaycee USA (WY) 235 Eg24
Kayeli RI 130 Rd47
Kayembe Mukulu RDC 203 Mb50
Kaye, Mount AUS 153 Se64
Kayenta USA (AZ) 237 Ee27
Kayenze EAT 206 Mg47
Kayes RCB 202 Lg47
Kayes RCB 202 Lg48
Kayes RMM 183 Ke38
Kayima WAL 192 Ke41
Kaymakçı TR 50 Mj52
Kaymaz TR 51 Mm51
Kaymor SN 183 Kc39
Kayna-Bayonga RDC 201 Me46
Kaynarca TR 50 Mk50
Kaynarca TR 50 Ml49
Kaynaşlı TR 51 Mm50
Kayoa RI 130 Rd45
Kayogoro BU 206 Me48
Kayombo Z 209 Mb52
Kayonza RWA 201 Mf46
Kayrunnera AUS (NSW) 150 Sb61
Kaysergebergte SME 271 Hb44
Kayseri TR 51 Mq52
Kaysersberg F 23 Lh42
Kayuadi RI 129 Ra49
Kayuagung RI 125 Qc47
Kayuaro RI 124 Qa46
Kayunga EAU 204 Mg45
Kayuwaru RI 129 Qh49
Kayville CDN (SK) 233 Eh21
Kazačka RUS 53 Nb20
Kazakhstan KZ 57 Oa05
Kazakh Uplands KZ 58 Ob09
Kazak shyghanaghy KZ 70 Nf24
Kazaly KZ 76 Ob23
Kazan' RUS (TAR) 53 Ne18
Kazan TR 51 Mn50
Kazanka UA 54 Mg22
Kazanlăk BG 47 Mf48
Kazan-retto J 83 Sa13
Kazan-retto J 83 Sa13
Kazanskaja RUS 53 Na21
Kazarman KS 77 Oh25
Kazas RUS 90 Pj19
Kazaure WAN 186 Le39
Kaza Wenz ETH 191 Mj40
Kazbegi GE 70 Nc24
Kaz Dağı TR 50 Mg51
Kaz Dağı Milli Parkı TR 50 Mg51
Kazembe Z 206 Me50
Kazembe Z 210 Mg52
Kazer TCH 188 Lk36
Kazerun IR 74 Nf31
Kazi Kazi EAT 207 Mg48
Kazıklı TR 49 Mh53
Kazimierza Wielka PL 37 Ma40
Kazimierz Dolny PL 37 Mb39
Kazımkarabekir TR 62 Mg27
Kazincbarcika H 39 Ma42
Kaziranga N.P. IND 112 Pg32
Kaziza RDC 209 Mb51
Kaz'jany BY 17 Mg35
Kazlavščyna BY 17 Mf37
Kazlų Rūda LT 17 Md36
Kaznakovka KZ 85 Pb21
Kaznějov CZ 38 Lo41
Kaztalovka KZ 53 Ne21
Kazu MYA 113 Pj33
Kazuma Pan N.P. ZW 213 Mc55
Kazumba RDC 203 Mb49
Kazuno J 101 Sa25
Kazwama EAU 204 Mg45
Kazyghurt KZ 76 Oe25
Kbombole SN 183 Kb38
Kbor Roumia DZ 173 Lb27
Kcynia PL 36 Ls38
Kdyně CZ 38 Lo41
Kéa GR 48 Me53
Kéa GR 48 Me53
Keaau USA (HI) 230 Cc36
Keahole Point USA 230 Cb36
Keanae USA (HI) 230 Cb35
Kearney USA (NE) 240 Fa25
Keatchie USA (LA) 243 Fd29
Keating Point IND 111 Pg41
Kébaly RG 192 Kd40
Keban RI 125 Qb47
Keban TR 63 Mk26
Keban Bahar MAL 117 Qb44
Keban Baraji TR 63 Mk26
Kébara RCB 202 Lh47
Kebbe WAN 186 Lc39
Kébémèr SN 183 Kb38
Kébi CI 192 Kg41
Kébila RMM 192 Kg40
Kebili TN 174 Le29
Kebitigollewa CL 111 Pa42
Kebnekaise S 10 Lk12
Kébouya RCB 202 Lh46
Kebri Dehar ETH 199 Nc42
Kebumen RI 128 Qe49
Kéché RCA 196 Ma41
Kechika Ranges CDN 231 Dg16
Kechika River CDN 231 Dg16
Keçiborlu TR 51 Ml53
Keçiler TR 50 Mk52
Kecskemét H 39 Lu44
Kédainiai LT 17 Md35
Kedarnath IND (UTT) 107 Ok30
Kedarnath (Hindu shrine) IND 107 Ok30
Kedarnath Sanctuary IND 107 Ok30
Kedavur IND (KER) 110 Oh41
Keddie USA (CA) 234 Dk26
Kédédéssé TCH 187 Lj40
Kedgaon IND (MHT) 108 Oh36
Kedgwick CDN (NB) 244 Gg22
Kediet ej Jill RIM 178 Kd34
Ke Dinh VN 115 Qc36
Kedir RI 131 Rk47
Kediri RI 128 Qg49
Kedondong RI 125 Qc48
Kedong CHN (HLG) 98 Rd22
Kédougou SN 183 Kd39
Kédros GR 48 Mc51
Kędzierzyn-Koźle PL 36 Ls40
Keel IRL 18 Kk36
Keele River CDN 231 Df14
Keelung RC 97 Ra33
Keene USA (NH) 247 Gd24
Keeneland Race Course USA (KY) 249 Fh26
Keep River N.P. AUS 138 Re53
Keeroongooloo AUS (QLD) 150 Sb58
Keetmanshoop NAM 216 Lk59
Keewatin River CDN 238 Ek17
Keezhik Lake CDN 239 Ff20
Kefaloniá GR 48 Ma52
Kéfalos GR 49 Mg54
Kefamenanu RI 132 Rc50
Keffi WAN 186 Ld41
Kefken TR 50 Ml49
Kef Mimouna DZ 173 Lb29
Keftya ETH 191 Mj40
Kegalla CL 111 Pa43
Kēgart KS 77 Og25
Kégashka CDN (QC) 245 Gk20
Kegen KZ 77 Ok24
Kegen KZ 77 Ok24
Kegeyli UZ 71 Nk24
Kegum Kagati Lake USA 228 Bj15
Keheili SUD 190 Mg37
Kehiwin Ind. Res. CDN 233 Ee18
Kehl D 34 Lh42
Kehra EST 16 Mf31
Keibul Lam Jao N.P. IND 112 Pg33
Keighley GB 21 Kt37
Keila EST 16 Me31
Keila EST 16 Me31
Keila Island SOL 161 Sk48
Keili SUD 197 Mh40
Keimoes ZA 216 Ma60
Kei Mouth ZA 217 Me62
Keipene LV 17 Mf34
Kei Road ZA 217 Md62
Keïta RN 186 Lc38
Keith AUS (SA) 152 Sa64
Keith GB 19 Ks33
Keiyasi FJI 163 Tj54
Kejimkujik N.P. CDN 245 Gh23
Kekaha USA (HI) 230 Ca35
Kèkéjygr KS 77 Oh25
Kèk-Art KS 77 Oh25
Kékem CAM 194 Lf43
Kékes H 39 Ma43
Kekesu PNG 160 Sh48
Kek Lok Si MAL 116 Qa43
Kekova Adasi TR 62 Mf27
Kekri IND (RJT) 106 Oh33
Keku Strait USA 231 Dc17
Kel 79 Oh28
Kelai RI 127 Qj45
Kélakam RN 187 Lf39
Kelameili Shan CHN 85 Pe23
Kela Met ER 191 Mk38
Kelampok RI 128 Qe49
Kelan CHN (SAX) 93 Qf26
Kelang MAL 117 Qa44
Kelang MAL 117 Qa44
Kelang RI 130 Rd47
Kelanoa PNG 159 Sd49
Kelayang RI 124 Qb46
Kélbo BF 185 Kk39
Kelburn Castle GB 19 Kq35
Kèlcyrë AL 46 Ma50
Kélé G 202 Lg46
Keleft AFG 78 Od27
Kelekci TR 50 Mk53
Kelem ETH 197 Mh43
Keles KZ 76 Oe25
Keléya RMM 192 Kg40
Kelež RUS 85 Pg19
Kelheim D 35 Lm42
Kelibia TN 174 Lf27
Kelif TM 73 Od27
Kelifskiy Uzboy TM 73 Ob27
Keli Haji Ibrahim IRQ 65 Nc27
Kelimutu RI 129 Ra50
Keling RI 128 Qf49
Kelintobe KZ 76 Od24
Kelishom IR 72 Ne27
Kelkit TR 63 Mk25
Kelkit Çayı TR 63 Mk25
Kellaki CY 51 Mo56
Kéllé RCB 195 Lh46
Kéllé RN 186 Lf38
Kellerberrin AUS (WA) 144 Qj61
Kelleys Island S.P. USA 246 Fj25
Kellie's Castle MAL 117 Qa43
Kellinghusen D 32 Lk37
Kellogg USA (ID) 232 Eb22
Kellokoski FIN 16 Mf30
Kelloselkä FIN 11 Me12
Kells IRL 20 Ko37
Kelmė LT 17 Mc35
Kel'menci UA 45 Mg42
Kelmis B 23 Lg40
Kelmscott AUS (WA) 144 Qj62
Kelo TCH 187 Lh41
Kelongwa Z 210 Md52
Kelowna CDN (BC) 232 Ea21
Kelsey CDN (MB) 238 Fb17
Kelsey Bay CDN (BC) 232 Dh20
Kelso GB 19 Ks35
Kelso USA (CA) 236 Ec28
Kelso USA (WA) 232 Dj22
Kelton USA (UT) 235 Ed25
Kelu CHN (GDG) 96 Qf35
Kelua RI 126 Qh47
Kelume RI 125 Qc46
Kelvington CDN (SK) 238 Ej19
Kelvin Island CDN 239 Ff21
Kelwara IND (RJT) 108 Oj33
Kem' RUS (KAR) 11 Mh13
Kemah TR 63 Mk26
Kemal, Gunung RI 126 Qj45
Kemalpaşa TR 49 Mh52
Kemalpaşa TR 63 Na25
Kemaman MAL 117 Qb43
Kemano CDN (BC) 232 Dg19
Kemasik MAL 117 Qb43
Kemata I TCH 196 Lk41
Kembahi RI 127 Rb46
Kembangjanggut RI 126 Qj45
Kembapi RI 158 Sa50
Kembayan RI 126 Qf45
Kembé RCA 200 Ma43
Kembéra RG 192 Kd40
Kembolcha ETH 198 Mj41
Kembolcha ETH 198 Mk40
Kemdéré TCH 196 Lk41
Kemer TR 49 Mk54
Kemer TR 51 Ml54
Kemer TR 51 Ml53
Kemer TR 62 Mj26
Kemerburgaz TR 50 Mj49
Kemerhisar TR 51 Mp53
Kemerovo RUS 58 Pb07
Kemi FIN 11 Mc13
Kemijärvi FIN 11 Md12
Kemijärvi FIN 11 Md12
Kemijoki FIN 11 Mc12
Kemili RI 116 Pj43
Kemiö = Kimito FIN 16 Md30
Kemlja RUS (MOR) 53 Nc18
Kemmerer USA (WY) 235 Ee25
Kemnath D 35 Lm41
Kemondo EAT 201 Mf46
Kempele FIN 11 Mc13
Kemp Land 297 Nd32
Kemps Bay BS 251 Gb33
Kempsey AUS (NSW) 151 Sg61
Kempten D 34 Ll43
Kempton AUS (TAS) 152 Sd67
Kempton Park GB 21 Ku39
Kemptville CDN (NS) 245 Gh23
Kemubu MAL 117 Qb43
Kemumu RI 124 Qb47
Ken IND 109 Pa33
Kenabri AUS (NSW) 151 Se61
Kenadsa DZ 173 Kj30
Kenai USA (AK) 229 Ce15
Kenai Fjords N.P. USA 229 Ce16
Kenai Mts. USA 229 Ce16
Kenai National Wildlife Refuge USA 229 Ce15
Kenai Peninsula USA 229 Ce15
Kenalia PNG 158 Sb50
Kenamuke Swamp SUD 197 Mg42
Kenansville USA (NC) 249 Ga28
Kenapuru Head NZ 155 Th66
Kenar Darya IR 72 Ng27
Kenaston CDN (SK) 233 Eg20
Kenawa PNG 159 Sb50
Kencong RI 128 Qg50
Kendai IND (CGH) 109 Pb34
Kendal GB 21 Ks36
Kendall AUS (NSW) 151 Sg61
Kendall USA (FL) 250 Fk33
Kendall, Mount NZ 155 Tg66
Kendall River AUS (QLD) 146 Sb52
Kendari RI 127 Rb47
Kendawangan RI 126 Qf47
Kèndégué TCH 196 Lk40
Kenderes H 39 Ma43
Kendié G 202 Le46
Kendié RMM 185 Kj38
Kendisik RI 126 Qh46
Kendrapara IND (ORS) 112 Pd35
Kendrew ZA 217 Mc62
Kendu Bay EAK 204 Mh46
Kendujhargarh IND (ORS) 109 Pc35
Kenedy USA (TX) 242 Fb31
Kenel USA (SD) 240 Ek23
Kenema WAL 192 Ke42
Kénénkoun RMM 184 Kf39
Kenge RDC 203 Lj48
Keng Lon MYA 113 Pk35
Keng Tawng MYA 113 Pk35
Kengué RCB 202 Lg47
Kenhardt ZA 216 Ma60
Kéniéba RMM 183 Ke39
Keningau MAL 122 Qj43
Kénitra MA 172 Kg28
Kenli CHN (SDG) 93 Qk27
Kenmare IRL 20 Kl39
Kenmare USA (ND) 238 Ej21
Kenmare River IRL 20 Kk39
Kennacraig GB 18 Kp35
Kennebunk USA (ME) 247 Ge24
Kennedy AUS (QLD) 149 Sc55
Kennedy CDN (SK) 238 Ej20
Kennedy ZW 213 Md55
Kennedy Entrance USA 229 Cd16
Kennedy Peak MYA 112 Pg34
Kennedy Range AUS 140 Qh58
Kennedy Range N.P. AUS 140 Qh58
Kennedy Space Center USA 250 Fk31
Kenner USA (LA) 243 Fe31
Kenneth Range AUS 140 Qj58
Kennett USA (MO) 243 Fe27
Kennewick USA (WA) 234 Ea22
Kenney Dam CDN 232 Dh19
Keno City CDN (YT) 231 Dc14
Kenogami River CDN 239 Fh20
Kenora CDN (ON) 238 Fc21
Kenosha USA (WI) 246 Fg24
Kenozersky N.P. RUS 11 Mk15
Kensington CDN (PE) 245 Gj22
Kent CDN (BC) 232 Dk21
Kent USA (OR) 234 Dk23
Kent USA (TX) 237 Eh30
Kent USA (WA) 232 Dj22
Kent WAL 192 Kd41
Kentau KZ 76 Oe24
Ken Thao LAO 114 Qa37
Kenting N.P. RC 97 Ra34
Kent Junction CDN (NB) 245 Gh22
Kenton USA (OH) 246 Fj25
Kenton on Sea ZA 217 Mc62
Kent Peninsula CDN 224 Ec05
Kentucky USA 227 Fd11
Kentucky Derby USA (KY) 248 Fh26
Kentucky Diamond Caverns USA 248 Fg27
Kentucky Lake USA 243 Ff27
Kentucky Speedway USA (KY) 248 Fh26
Kentville CDN (NS) 245 Gh23
Kenya 167 Mb09
Kenya, Mount EAK 204 Mj46
Kenzou CAM 195 Lh43
Keokuk USA (MO) 241 Fe25
Keoladeo Ghana N.P. IND 107 Oj32
Keoladeo National Park IND 107 Oj32
Keonchi IND (MPH) 109 Pa34
Keonjhar Plateau IND 109 Pc35
Keo Pagoda VN 96 Qd35
Kep VN 96 Qd35
Kepahiang RI 124 Qb47
Kepala RI 125 Qc46
Kepelekese RDC 203 Ma49
Kepi RI 158 Rk49
Kępno PL 36 Ls39
Kepoh RI 125 Qd47
Keppel Bay AUS 149 Sf57
Keppel Bay Islands N.P. AUS 149 Sf57
Keppel Sands AUS (QLD) 149 Sf57
Kepsut TR 50 Mj51
Kepulauan Amboi RI 131 Rj47
Kepulauan Anambas RI 117 Qd44
Kepulauan Aru RI 131 Rh49
Kepulauan Aru RI 133 Rh49
Kepulauan Asia RI 130 Rf45
Kepulauan Ayu RI 130 Rf45
Kepulauan Babar RI 132 Re49
Kepulauan Bacan RI 130 Rd46
Kepulauan Badas RI 117 Qd45
Kepulauan Balabalangan RI 127 Qj47
Kepulauan Banda RI 130 Re48
Kepulauan Banggai RI 127 Rb46
Kepulauan Banyak RI 124 Pj45
Kepulauan Batu RI 124 Pk45
Kepulauan Boo RI 130 Re46
Kepulauan Bowokan RI 127 Rb47
Kepulauan Gorong RI 130 Rf48
Kepulauan Jin RI 131 Rh49
Kepulauan Kai RI 130 Rg48
Kepulauan Kangean RI 129 Qh49
Kepulauan Karakelong RI 123 Rd43
Kepulauan Karimata RI 126 Qe46
Kepulauan Karimunjawa RI 128 Qf48
Kepulauan Karlaralong RI 123 Rc43
Kepulauan Krakatau RI 125 Qc49
Kepulauan Kumamba RI 131 Rk46
Kepulauan Laut Kecil RI 129 Qh48
Kepulauan Lingga RI 125 Qc45
Kepulauan Macan RI 129 Ra49
Kepulauan Mapia RI 131 Rh45
Kepulauan Marabatua RI 129 Qh48
Kepulauan Moor RI 131 Rh47
Kepulauan Nanusa RI 123 Rd43
Kepulauan Natuna Selatan RI 117 Qe44
Kepulauan Natuna Utara RI 117 Qe43
Kepulauan Nusela RI 130 Rf46
Kepulauan Pabbiring RI 129 Qk48
Kepulauan Pandaidori RI 131 Rj46
Kepulauan Pasitallu RI 129 Ra49
Kepulauan Penyu RI 130 Rd48
Kepulauan Pisang RI 130 Rf47
Kepulauan Podena RI 131 Rk47
Kepulauan Sabalana RI 129 Qk49
Kepulauan Salabangka RI 127 Rb47
Kepulauan Sangihe RI 123 Rc44
Kepulauan Satengar RI 129 Qj49
Kepulauan Seribu RI 128 Qd48
Kepulauan Talaud RI 123 Rd44
Kepulauan Tanimbar RI 133 Rf50
Kepulauan Tayandu RI 130 Rf48
Kepulauan Tengah RI 129 Qj49
Kepulauan Toade RI 123 Rc44
Kepulauan Togian RI 127 Ra46
Kepulauan Tukangbesi RI 127 Rb48
Kepulauan Watubela RI 130 Rf48
Kepulauan Widi RI 130 Re46
Kerabai RI 126 Qf46
Kerak JOR 64 Mh30
Kerala IND 104 Od16
Kerama-retto J 103 Rd32
Keramidi GR 46 Mc51
Keramoti GR 47 Me50
Keram River PNG 159 Sc48
Kerang RI 126 Qj47
Kerangbolong RI 128 Qe49
Kéran, P.N. de la TG 193 La40
Kerar IND (MPH) 109 Pa34
Keratea GR 48 Md53
Kerava FIN 16 Mf30
Keravat PNG 160 Sg48
Kerawa WAN 187 Lg40
Kerč UA 55 Mj23
Kerčens'ka protoka RUS 55 Mj23
Kerchouél RMM 185 La37
Kerdem RUS 59 Rb06
Kéré RCA 196 Md43
Keré RCA 201 Mc43
Kerein Hills AUS (NSW) 153 Sd62
Kerema PNG 159 Sc49
Keremeos CDN (BC) 232 Ea21
Kérémou DY 186 Lb40
Kerempe Burnu TR 62 Mg24
Keren ER 191 Mk39
Kerend IR 72 Nd28
Keret' RUS (KAR) 11 Mg12
Keretang MAL 122 Qj42
Kerewan WAG 183 Kb39
Kergu EST 16 Me32
Kerguelen Islands 301 Oa14
Kerguelen Plateau 301 Ob14
Keri GR 48 Ma53
Kericho EAK 204 Mh46
Kericho EAK 207 Mh48
Kerihun, Gunung RI 126 Qh45
Keri Kera SUD 190 Mg40
Kerimäki FIN 16 Mk29
Kerimeri IND (APH) 109 Ok36
Kerinci, Gunung RI 124 Qa46
Kerinci Seblat N.P. RI 124 Qa46
Kerio EAK 204 Mj44
Kerio Valley National Reserve EAK 204 Mh45
Keriya = Yutian CHN (XUZ) 86 Pa27

Keriya He CHN 86 Pa27
Keriya Shankou CHN 86 Pa28
Kerké RMM 184 Kh38
Kerkebet ER 191 Mj38
Kerki TM 73 Oc27
Kerkichi TM 73 Oc27
Kérkira GR 48 Lu51
Kérkira GR 48 Lu51
Kerkouane TN 174 Lf27
Kerkrade NL 32 Lg40
Kermadec Islands NZ 137 Ua25
Kermadec Ridge 134 Tb13
Kermadec Trench 134 Ba13
Kerman IR 75 Nj30
Kermanshah IR 72 Nd28
Kermanshah IR 72 Nf30
Kermen BG 47 Mg48
Kermit USA (TX) 237 Ej30
Kermit USA (WV) 249 Fj27
Kermupass AFG 78 Od28
Kernavės LT 17 Me36
Kernersville USA (NC) 249 Fk27
Kernville USA (OR) 234 Dj23
Keroka EAK 204 Mh46
Kéros GR 49 Mf54
Kéros GR 49 Mf54
Kérou DY 186 Lb40
Kérouané RG 192 Kf41
Kerpen D 32 Lg40
Kerrobert CDN (SK) 233 Ef20
Kerrville USA (TX) 242 Fa30
Kerry Head IRL 20 Kl38
Kersa ETH 198 Na41
Kersadek ETH 198 Mk43
Kershaw USA (SC) 249 Fk28
Kersik Luwai RI 126 Qh46
Kersinіané RMM 183 Ke38
Kersley CDN (BC) 232 Dj19
Kertamulia RI 126 Qe46
Kerteminde DK 14 Ll35
Kertosono RI 128 Qg49
Kerumutan Nature Reserve RI 124 Qb45
Kerzaz DZ 173 Kk31
Kerženec RUS 53 Nc17
Kesagami Lake CDN 239 Fk20
Kesagami Lake Prov. Park CDN 239 Fk20
Kesagami River CDN 239 Fk20
Kesälahti FIN 16 Mk29
Keşan TR 50 Mg50
Kesem ETH 198 Mk41
Kesenuma J 101 Sa26
Kesh GB 18 Kn36
Keshan CHN (HLG) 98 Rc21
Keshem AFG 78 Of27
Keshendeh AFG 78 Od27
Keshgarh Sahib IND 107 Oj30
Keshod IND (GUJ) 108 Of35
Kesıkköpru TR 51 Mo51
Kesikköprü TR 51 Mp52
Kesinga IND (ORS) 109 Pb35
Keşiş Dağı TR 63 Mj25
Keskal IND (CGH) 109 Pa35
Keskin TR 51 Mo51
Kestell ZA 217 Me60
Kesteri LV 17 Mb34
Keswick GB 19 Kr36
Keszthely H 38 Ls44
Ket' RUS 58 Pa07
Keta GH 193 La43
Ketahun RI 124 Qa47
Keta Lagoon GH 193 La43
Ketama MA 173 Kh28
Ketapang RI 126 Qe46
Ketapang RI 126 Qh46
Ketapang RI 128 Qg49
Ketčenery RUS (KAL) 55 Nc22
Ketchikan USA (AK) 231 De18
Ketchum USA (ID) 235 Ec24
Kete Krachi GH 193 Kk42
Ketesso CI 193 Kj43
Ketiau RI 125 Qc47
Keti Bandar PK 80 Od33
Ketmen KZ/CHN 84 Pa24
Ketok Mtn. USA 228 Cb16
Ketomoknai PNG 158 Sa48
Kétou DY 194 Lb42
Kętrzyn PL 37 Mb36
Ketsko-Tymskaja ravnina RUS 58 Pa06
Ketta RCB 195 Lh45
Kétté CAM 195 Lh43
Kettering AUS (TAS) 152 Sd67
Kettering GB 21 Ku38
Kettering USA (OH) 246 Fh26
Kettle Falls USA (WA) 232 Ea21
Kettle Range USA 232 Ea21
Kettle River CDN 232 Ea21
Kettle River CDN 239 Ff17
Ketunga RI 126 Qf45
Keudemane RI 116 Pj43
Keuka Lake USA 247 Gb24
Keur Madiabel SN 183 Kb39
Keur Massène RIM 183 Kb37
Keur Momar Sar SN 183 Kc38
Keurusselkä FIN 16 Me28
Keuruu FIN 16 Me28
Kevastu EST 16 Mh32
Kévé TG 193 La42
Kevelaer D 32 Lg39
Kevington AUS (QLD) 151 Se58
Kevlavík IS 10 Jj13
Kewanee USA (IL) 246 Ff25
Kewasasap PNG 159 Se50
Kewaunee USA (WI) 246 Fg23
Keweenaw Bay Ind. Res. USA 246 Ff22
Keweenaw Peninsula USA 241 Fg22
Key After ETH 198 Mj43
Keyaluvik USA (AK) 228 Bh15
Key Biscayne USA (FL) 250 Fk33
Keyihe CHN (NMZ) 91 Rb20
Key Largo USA (FL) 250 Fk33
Key Like Mine CDN (SK) 233 Eh17
Keyport USA (NJ) 247 Gc25
Keyser USA (WV) 247 Ga26
Keystone USA (SD) 240 Ej24
Keytesville USA (MO) 241 Fd26
Key West USA (FL) 250 Fk33
Kezi ZW 214 Me56
Kežmarok SK 39 Ma41
Kgalagadi RB 213 Ma58
Kgalagadi Transfrontier Park RB/ZA 213 Ma58
Kgatleng RB 213 Md58
Kgolong RB 213 Mb58
Kgun Lake USA 228 Bj15
Khabou RIM 183 Kd38
Khabra al ,Arn KSA 66 Na34
Khadam KSA 67 Nd33
Khadarah KSA 68 Nb37
Khaga IND (UPH) 107 Pa33
Khagaria IND (BIH) 112 Pd33
Khahil OM 69 Nj36
Khai Bang Rachan Park THA 114 Qa38
Khair IND (UPH) 107 Oj32
Khaira IND (CGH) 109 Pa35
Khairabad IND (UPH) 107 Pa32
Khairagarh IND (CGH) 109 Pa35
Khairpur PK 80 Oe32
Khairpur PK 81 Og31
Khairpur Nathan Shah PK 80 Od32
Khajeh IR 72 Nd26
Khajiripada IND (ORS) 109 Pc36
Khajuraho IND 109 Ok33
Khajuri IND (JKD) 112 Pd33
Khajuu Us MNG 90 Qd22
Khakassia RUS 58 Pb08
Khakhea RB 213 Mb58
Khalabat PK 79 Og28
Khalach TM 73 Oc26
Khalari IND (CGH) 109 Pb35
Khalatse 79 Oj28
Khalban MNG 90 Pj21
Khalfallah DZ 173 La28
Khalij Dungunab SUD 191 Mj36
Khalilabad IND (UPH) 107 Pb32
Khalkhal IR 72 Ne27
Khalkhgol MNG 91 Qk22
Khalkhyn Gol MNG 91 Qk22
Khalkidhiki GR 46 Md50
Khallikot IND (ORS) 109 Pc36
Khaluf OM 69 Nj35
Khalzan Bürged Uul MNG 90 Qa21
Khalzan Sogootyn davaa MNG 90 Pk21
Khamar IND (ORS) 109 Pc35
Khama Rhino Sanctuary RB 213 Md57
Khamaria IND (MPH) 109 Pa34
Khambhaliya IND (GUJ) 108 Oe34
Khamgaon IND (MHT) 108 Oj35
Khamir YE 68 Nb38
Khami Ruins National Monument ZW 214 Me56
Khamis al Bahr KSA 68 Na36
Khamis Mushayt KSA 68 Nb36
Khamis Mutayr KSA 68 Nb36
Kham Khuan Kaeo THA 115 Qc38
Khammam IND (APH) 109 Pa37
Khammuan Limestone N.B.C.A. LAO 115 Qc37
Khampat MYA 112 Ph34
Kham Ta Kla THA 115 Qb37
Khamti MYA 113 Ph33
Khan NAM 212 Lh57
Khanabad AFG 78 Oe27
Khan al Baghdadi IRQ 65 Nb29
Khan al Hammad IRQ 65 Nc29
Khanapur IND (KTK) 108 Oh38
Khanaqin IRQ 65 Nc28
Khan ar Rahbah IRQ 65 Nc30
Khanaser SYR 64 Mj28
Khancoban AUS (NSW) 153 Se64
Khandagiri Caves IND 109 Pc35
Khandala IND (MHT) 108 Oj36
Khandpara IND (ORS) 109 Pc35
Khandwa IND (MPH) 108 Oj35
Khanewal PK 79 Of30
Khang Acheft RIM 183 Ke36
Khangai Mountains MNG 90 Pj22
Khangaiyn Nuruu MNG 90 Pj22
Khangarh PK 81 Of31
Khangat Sidi Nadji DZ 174 Ld28
Khania GR 48 Md55
Khankar IND (MPH) 107 Oj33
Khan Khenteyn Nature Reserve MNG 90 Qe21
Khan Khöhiy Nuruu MNG 85 Ph21
Khankhökhiy MNG 91 Qg22
Khanna IND (PJB) 107 Oj30
Khanom THA 116 Pk41
Khanozai PK 78 Od30
Khanpur PK 81 Of31
Khan Sheikhoun SYR 64 Mj28
Khansky Palats UA 55 Mg23
Khan's Palace UZ 76 Of25
Khan Takhti IR 72 Nc26
Khantayn Nuruu Uul MNG 90 Qb21
Khan Tengri peak KS 77 Pa24
Khanty-Mansi Autonomous District RUS 58 Ob06
Khanuy gol MNG 90 Qa21
Khân Yûnis IL 64 Mh30
Khao Kha Khaeng THA 114 Pk37
Khao Khieo Open Zoo THA 114 Qa39
Khao Kradong Park THA 115 Qb38
Khao Kriab Cave THA 116 Pk40
Khao Laem N.P. THA 114 Pk38
Khao Laem Reservoir THA 114 Pk38
Khao Luang N.P. THA 116 Pk41
Khao Nam Khang N.P. THA 116 Qa42
Khao Phra Vihan N.P. THA 115 Qc38
Khao Plara THA 114 Pk38
Khao Sam Roi Yot N.P. THA 114 Pk39
Khao Sok N.P. THA 116 Pk41
Khao Tha Phet Wildlife and Nature Education Centre THA 116 Pk41
Khaoui N'am MA 178 Kd32
Khao Yai N.P. THA 114 Qa38
Khapalu 79 Oj28
Khaptad N.P. NEP 88 Pa31
Kharaat MNG 90 Qd22
Kharagdiha IND (JKD) 112 Pd33
Kharagpur IND (WBG) 112 Pd34
Kharan PK 80 Oc31
Kharanah Q 74 Nf33
Kharanaq IR 72 Nh29
Kharar IND (PJB) 107 Oj30
Khar Balgasyn Tuur MNG 90 Qb22
Khar Bid AFG 78 Oc28
Kharchi IND (RJT) 106 Og33
Kharepatan IND (MHT) 108 Og37
Kharga Oasis ET 177 Mf33
Khargon IND (MPH) 108 Oh35
Kharian PK 79 Og29
Khariar IND (ORS) 109 Pb35
Khark IR 74 Nf31
Kharkhiraa Uul MNG 85 Pg21
Kharkhorin MNG 90 Qb22
Khar nuur MNG 90 Pj21
Kharora IND (CGH) 109 Pa35
Kharsia IND (CGH) 109 Pb35
Khartoum SUD 190 Mg39
Khartoum North SUD 190 Mg39
Kharupatia IND (ASM) 112 Pg32
Khar-Us MNG 85 Pg21
Kharvanaq IR 72 Nd26
Kharwar-i Baba Mausoleum PK 78 Od30
Kharyal IND (HYA) 106 Oh31
Kharzeb City IR 75 Nh32
Khasab OM 75 Nj32
Khas Alej SYR 65 Mk28
Khash IR 75 Oa31
Khashm al Jubayl LAR 181 Lj32
Khashm el Girba SUD 191 Mh39
Khashm el Girba Reservoir SUD 191 Mj39
Khas Konar AFG 79 Of28
Khasm Elmi SUD 197 Md39
Khasnar IND (MHT) 108 Oj35
Khasso RMM 183 Ke38
Khašuri GE 70 Nb25
Khaswan Mount CDN 231 Df18
Khatam UAE 74 Nh33
Khatansuudal MNG 92 Qa23
Khatauli IND (UPH) 107 Oj31
Khatavch MNG 91 Qg22
Khategaon IND (MPH) 108 Oj34
Khatgal MNG 90 Qa20
Khatmat Malahah OM 75 Nj33
Khatoon Bridge IR 72 Nc26
Khatt Atoui RIM 178 Kc35
Khaudom Game Park NAM 213 Ma55
Khaur PK 79 Og29
Khauxanas Ruins NAM 216 Lk59
Khaval AFG 78 Oc28
Khavda IND (GUJ) 108 Oe34
Khavirga MNG 91 Qg23
Khawasa IND (MPH) 109 Ok35
Khaw-bu-de MYA 113 Pk32
Khawr Adarmo SUD 190 Mh36
Khay' KSA 68 Na36
Khazar Abad IR 72 Ng27
Khazar Nature Reserve TM 71 Ng26
Khebuching IND (MNP) 112 Pg33
Khed IND (MHT) 108 Og36
Khed IND (MHT) 108 Og37
Kheda IND (GUJ) 108 Og34
Khed Brahma IND (GUJ) 108 Og34
Khelma IND (ASM) 112 Pg33
Khemis-des-Zémamra MA 172 Kf29
Khémis-Majdèn MA 172 Kg30
Khemis Miliana DZ 173 Lb27
Khemissa DZ 174 Ld27
Khemisset MA 172 Kg29
Khemmarat THA 115 Qc37
Khenchela DZ 174 Ld28
Khénifra MA 172 Kh29
Khenjan AFG 78 Oe28
Khenteyn Nuruu MNG 90 Qd21
Kherameh IR 74 Ng31
Kherba DZ 173 La27
Kherda IND (MHT) 108 Oj35
Kheri IND (MPH) 109 Oj35
Kherlen MNG 91 Qe22
Kherlen Gol MNG 91 Qg22
Kherrata DZ 173 Lc27
Kherwara IND (RJT) 108 Og34
Khe Sanh VN 115 Qd37
Khe Sanh Combat Base VN 115 Qd37
Khetri IND (RJT) 106 Oh31
Khe Ve VN 115 Qc37
Khewari PK 81 Oe32
Khewra PK 79 Og29
Kheyrabad AFG 78 Od27
Khezmir RIM 183 Ke36
Khezri IR 73 Nk28
Khilchipur IND (MPH) 108 Oj33
Khinwara IND (RJT) 106 Og33
Khipro PK 81 Oe33
Khiu PK 79 Of30
Khiva UZ 71 Oa25
Khlong Lan THA 114 Pk37
Khlong Lan N.P. THA 114 Pk37
Khlong Ngae THA 116 Qa42
Khlong Phrao N.P. THA 116 Pk41
Khlong Thom THA 116 Pk42
Khlong Wang Chao N.P. THA 114 Pk37
Khneiz Shamali SYR 65 Mk27
Khoda Afarin IR 72 Nd26
Khodala IND (MHT) 108 Og36
Khödrögö MNG 90 Pj21
Khodzhambaz TM 73 Oc26
Khogué Tobène SN 183 Kc38
Khojakpass PK 78 Od30
Khojd Tamir gol MNG 90 Qa22
Khok Chang THA 115 Qb37
Khökhöö MNG 90 Qa20
Khokhropar PK 81 Of33
Khokh Serkh Nature Reserve MNG 85 Pf21
Khökhtolgoy MNG 85 Pf21
Khok Kloi THA 116 Pk41
Khok Pho THA 116 Qa42
Khok Samrong THA 114 Qa38
Kholboo MNG 85 Ph21
Kholm AFG 78 Od27
Kholmuj IR 74 Nf31
Khomas NAM 212 Lj57
Khomas NAM 212 Lj57
Khomas Hochland NAM 212 Lh57
Khomeyn IR 72 Nf29
Khomeyni Shar IR 72 Nf29
Khon THA 114 Pk37
Khöndlön Uul MNG 90 Pj22
Khong Chiam THA 115 Qc38
Khong Khi Sua THA 114 Qa38
Khongor MNG 90 Qd21
Khongor MNG 91 Qf23
Khongor MNG 91 Qg23
Khong Phabeng Falls LAO/K 115 Qd38
Khong Sedon LAO 115 Qc38
Khonj IR 74 Ng32
Khon Kaen THA 115 Qb37
Khonsa IND (ARP) 113 Ph32
Khonsar IR 72 Nf29
Khon Sawan THA 115 Qb38
Khor IR 72 Ne26
Khor Abu Sunt SUD 190 Mf36
Khor Adar SUD 197 Mg41
Khor Anghar DJI 191 Nb40
Khorasgan IR 72 Nf29
Khor Atar SUD 197 Mf41
Khor Dulayb SUD 197 Mg40
Khor Fakkan UAE 75 Nj33
Khor Gandze CHN (SCH) 94 Pk30
Khorgo MNG 90 Pk21
Khorgo-Terkhiyn Tsagaan Nuur N.P. MNG 90 Pk21
Khoridul Saridag MNG 90 Pk20
Khorixas NAM 212 Lh56
Khor Nyanding SUD 197 Mg41
Khorramabad IR 72 Ne29
Khorram Shar IR 74 Ne30
Khor Rori OM 69 Nh37
Khorsabad IRQ 65 Nb27
Khor Tumat SUD 197 Mh41
Khorugh TJ 77 Of27
Khor Veveno SUD 197 Mg42
Khoshangan IR 75 Nj32
Khöshööt MNG 85 Pe21
Khöshööt MNG 90 Qb21
Khosrow Shahr IR 72 Nd27
Khossanto SN 183 Ke39
Khost PK 78 Od30
Khotol Mount USA 229 Ca13
Khoton nuur MNG 85 Pe21
Khouribga MA 172 Kg29
Khovd MNG 85 Pf21
Khovd MNG 92 Qb23
Khovd MNG 85 Pg22
Khovd gol MNG 85 Pf21
Khöviyn Am MNG 90 Pk22
Khövsgöl MNG 93 Qe24
Khövsgöl MNG 90 Pk20
Khövüün MNG 92 Qb24
Khowai IND (TRP) 112 Pf34
Khowang IND (ASM) 112 Ph32
Khowarib NAM 212 Lg55
Khowr-e Musa IR 74 Ne30
Khowr-e Soltani IR 74 Ng31
Khowst AFG 79 Oe29
Khoy IR 72 Nc26
Khrebet Dzhugdzhur RUS 59 Rd07
khrebet Karagëz TM 71 Nh26
khrebet Karatau KZ 76 Od23
khrebet Kopet dag TM 71 Nj26
Khreum MYA 112 Pg35
Khrisí GR 49 Mf56
Khuang Nai THA 115 Qc38
Khuan Kalong THA 116 Qa42
Khuan Khanun THA 116 Qa42
Khuan Niang THA 116 Qa42
Khubus ZA 216 Lj60
Khuchinarai THA 115 Qc37
Khudabad PK 80 Od32
Khudabad 79 Oh27
Khuff KSA 67 Nc33
Khujand TJ 76 Oe25
Khujirt MNG 90 Qa21
Khukhan THA 115 Qc38
Khulna BD 112 Pe34
Khulstay MNG 91 Qh21
Khulstayn Uul MNG 90 Qc22
Khulstayn Uul Nature Reserve MNG 90 Qc22
Khumbu NEP 88 Pd32
Khumrah KSA 66 Mk35
Khunaniwala PK 79 Of30
Khun Chae N.P. THA 114 Pk36
Khüngiy MNG 85 Ph21
Khüngiy Gol MNG 85 Ph21
Khunjerab N.P. PK 79 Oh27
Khunjerab Pass CHN/PK 86 Oh27
Khunti IND (JKD) 109 Pc34
Khun Yuam THA 114 Pj36
Khur IR 72 Nh29
Khur IR 73 Nk29
Khuraburi THA 116 Pk41
Khurai IND (MPH) 109 Ok33
Khuran IR 75 Nh32
Khurays KSA 67 Ne33
Khurayt SUD 196 Mc39
Khurda IND (ORS) 109 Pc35
Khurduraq IR 74 Ne30
Khurem MNG 90 Qb21
Khurja IND (UPH) 107 Oj31
Khushab PK 79 Og29
Khushareh IR 73 Oa30
Khutag MNG 90 Qb21
Khutse Game Reserve RB 213 Mc57
Khuwaimah OM 69 Nk35
Khuzdar PK 80 Od32
Khužjirt MNG 90 Qb22
Khvajeh Ghar AFG 78 Oe27
Khvet K 115 Qc40
Khwai River Lodge RB 213 Mb55
Khwane MYA 114 Pk38
Khwazakhela PK 79 Og28
Khwebe Hills RB 213 Mb56
Khyber Pass AFG/PK 79 Of28
Kia SOL 161 Sk49
Kiakalamu RDC 206 Me50
Kiama AUS (NSW) 153 Sf63
Kiamba RP 123 Rc42
Kiambi RDC 206 Me49
Kiambu EAK 204 Mj46
Kiampanjang RI 127 Qj44
Kiamsuuma SP 205 Nb45
Kiana USA (AK) 229 Bk12
Kiandarat RI 130 Rf47
Kiangara RM 220 Nd54
Kiangdom 79 Ok29
Kiangwe RDC 206 Md48
Kiang West N.P. WAG 183 Kc39
Kia Ora AUS (SA) 152 Rk62
Kiaradua RI 128 Qd49
Kiáto GR 48 Mc52
Kibæk DK 14 Lj34
Kibaha EAT 207 Mk49
Kibale EAU 201 Mf45
Kibale EAU 201 Mf46
Kibale Forest N.P. EAU 204 Mf45
Kibali RDC 201 Me44
Kibangou RCB 202 Lg47
Kibasira Swamp EAT 207 Mj50
Kibau EAT 207 Mh50
Kibawe RP 123 Rc42
Kibaya EAT 207 Mj48
Kibbanshalli IND (KTK) 111 Oj40
Kiberashi EAT 207 Mj48
Kiberege EAT 207 Mj49
Kiberie EAT 206 Mf48
Kibi GH 193 Kk42
Kibira, P.N. de la BU 206 Me47
Kibiti EAT 207 Mk49
Kibiya WAN 186 Le40
Kiboga EAU 201 Mf45
Kiboko EAK 207 Mj47
Kibombo RDC 206 Mc47
Kibondo EAT 206 Mf47
Kibre Mengist ETH 198 Mk43
Kıbrıscık TR 51 Mm50
Kibungu RWA 206 Mf47
Kibunzi RDC 202 Lg48
Kibuye RWA 206 Me47
Kibwana EAT 211 Mj51
Kibwesa EAT 206 Me49
Kibwezi EAK 207 Mj47
Kičevo MK 46 Ma49
Kichha IND (UTT) 107 Ok31
Kichi-Kichi TCH 187 Lj37
Kickapoo Ind. Caverns USA 246 Fe24
Kickapoo Ind. Res. USA 241 Fc26
Kicking Horse Pass CDN 232 Eb20
Kicman' UA 45 Mf42
Kidal RMM 185 La36
Kidapawan RP 123 Rc42
Kidatu EAT 207 Mj49
Kidderminster GB 21 Ks38
Kidd's Beach ZA 217 Md62
Kidekša RUS 53 Na17
Kidepo SUD 197 Mg43
Kidepo Valley N.P. EAU 204 Mg44
Kidira SN 183 Kd38
Kidston AUS (QLD) 148 Sc55
Kidugallo EAT 207 Mk49
Kiefersfelden D 35 Ln43
Kiekinkoski FIN 11 Mf13
Kiel D 33 Ll36
Kiel Bay D 33 Ll35
Kielce PL 37 Ma40
Kielder Water GB 19 Ks35
Kieler Förde D 33 Ll36
Kieler Woche D 33 Ll36
Kiembara BF 185 Kj39
Kien Duc VN 115 Qd40
Kienge RDC 210 Md51
Kien Luong VN 117 Qc40
Kierspe D 32 Lh39
Kieta PNG 160 Sh49
Kiev UA 54 Mf20
Kievka RUS 98 Rg24
Kifaya RG 183 Kd39
Kiffa RIM 183 Ke37
Kifinga RDC 206 Md50
Kifissós GR 48 Mc52
Kifri IRQ 65 Nc28
Kifunankese RDC 203 Mc48
Kifusa RDC 203 Mc49
Kigali RWA 201 Mf46
Kigalik River USA 229 Cc11
Kiganjo EAK 204 Mj46
Kigarama EAT 201 Mf46
Kigezi Game Reserve EAU 204 Me46
Kiğı TR 63 Na26
Kigille SUD 197 Mh41
Kigluaik Mts. USA 229 Bh13
Kigoma EAT 206 Me48
Kigonsera EAT 211 Mh51
Kigosi EAT 206 Mf47
Kigosi Game Reserve EAT 206 Mf47
Kigumba EAU 201 Mf45
Kigyósgárgyán H 39 Lu44
Kihei USA (HI) 230 Cb35
Kihelkonna EST 16 Mc32
Kihniö FIN 16 Md28
Kihnu EST 16 Md32
Kihnu EST 16 Md32
Kihti Skiftet FIN 13 Mb30
Kihurio EAT 207 Mk48
Kii-hanto J 101 Rh28
Kiikala FIN 16 Md30
Kiikoinen FIN 16 Mc29
Kii-Nagashima J 101 Rj28
Kii-suido J 101 Rh29
Kijevo HR 41 Lr47
Kijungu EAT 207 Mj48
Kika DY 186 Lb41
Kikai-jima J 103 Rf31
Kikale EAT 207 Mk49
Kikamba RDC 206 Md47
Kikegtek Island USA 228 Bh16
Kikinda SCG 44 Ma45
Kikiongolo RDC 202 Lh48
Kiknur RUS 53 Nd17
Kikoira AUS (NSW) 153 Sd62
Kikoka EAT 207 Mk49
Kikola EAT 207 Mj50
Kikonai J 99 Sa25
Kikondja RDC 206 Md50
Kikongo EAT 206 Mg47
Kikori River PNG 159 Sb49
Kikori-River-Region PNG 159 Sb49
Kikuyu EAK 204 Mj46
Kikwit RDC 203 Lk48
Kil N 12 Lk32
Kil S 13 Lo31
Kilafors S 13 Lr29
Kilaguni EAK 207 Mk47
Kilakkarai IND (TNU) 111 Ok42
Kilala EAK 204 Mj46
Kilal, Mount EAK 204 Mj44
Kilar IND (HPH) 107 Oj29
Kilauea Crater USA 230 Cc36
Kilbaha IRL 20 Kl38
Kilbrannan Sound GB 18 Kp35
Kilbuck Mountains USA 228 Ca15
Kilchoan GB 18 Ko34
Kilcolgan IRL 20 Km37
Kilcoy AUS (QLD) 151 Sg59
Kildare IRL 20 Ko37
Kildonan CDN (BC) 232 Dh21
Kildonan ZW 210 Mf54
Kilembe RDC 203 Lk48
Kilembe RDC 206 Md49
Kilembi RDC 206 Md48
Kilenclyukú híd H 39 Mb43
Kileo RDC 203 Mc48
Kilgore USA (NE) 240 Ek24
Kilgore USA (TX) 243 Fc29
Kilgoris EAK 204 Mh46
Kilia PNG 160 Sf50
Kilibo DY 186 Lb41
Kili Bulak CHN (QHI) 89 Pg29
Kilifas PNG 158 Sa47
Kilifi EAK 207 Mk47
Kili Island MH 157 Tb17
Kilija UA 45 Mk45
Kilim TCH 196 Lk40
Kilimanjaro EAT 204 Mj47
Kilimanjaro N.P. EAT 207 Mj47
Kilimatinde EAT 207 Mh48
Kilindoni EAT 207 Mk49
Kilingi-Nõmme EST 16 Me32
Kilíni GR 48 Mb53
Kilinochchi CL 111 Pa42
Kiliranjao RI 124 Qa46
Kilis TR 62 Mj27
Kilitbahir TR 50 Mg50
Kilju PRK 100 Re25
Kilkee IRL 20 Kl38
Kilkeel GB 18 Kp36
Kilkenny IRL 20 Kn38
Kilkhampton GB 20 Kq40
Kilkís GR 46 Mc50
Kilkivan AUS (QLD) 151 Sg59
Killala AUS (NSW) 151 Sc61
Killala Bay IRL 18 Kl36
Killaly CDN (SK) 238 Ej20
Killam CDN (AB) 233 Ee19
Killarney AUS (QLD) 148 Sc57
Killarney AUS (QLD) 151 Sg60
Killarney CDN (MB) 238 Fa21
Killarney CDN (ON) 246 Fk23
Killarney IRL 20 Kl38
Killarney N.P. IRL 20 Kl39
Killarney Park AUS (QLD) 151 Sd58
Killarney Prov. Park CDN 246 Fk22
Killbeggan IRL 20 Kn37
Killdeer USA (ND) 240 Ej22
Kill Devil Hills USA (NC) 249 Gc27
Killeen USA (TX) 242 Fb30
Killenaule IRL 20 Kn38
Killik River USA 229 Cc11
Killimer IRL 20 Kl38
Killin GB 19 Kq34
Killinkoski FIN 16 Md28
Killorglin IRL 20 Kl38
Killuda Bay USA 230 Cd17
Killybegs IRL 18 Km36
Kilmaine IRL 18 Kl37
Kilmarnock GB 19 Kq35
Kilmore AUS (VIC) 153 Sc64
Kilmore Quay IRL 20 Ko38
Kilogbe WAN 186 Lb40
Kilombero EAT 207 Mj50
Kilombero EAT 211 Mh51
Kilómetro 133 YV 269 Gh41
Kilometro 59 MEX (CAM) 255 Fe36
Kilómetro 80 MEX (VC) 253 Fb34
Kilómetro 88 YV 270 Gk42
Kilosa EAT 207 Mj49
Kilpisjärvi FIN 10 Ma11
Kilrush IRL 20 Kl38
Kilto AUS (WA) 138 Rb54
Kilttan Island IND 110 Og41
Kiluan RI 125 Qc48
Kilubi RDC 206 Md49
Kilubi RDC 206 Md48
Kilwa RDC 206 Me50
Kilwa Kisiwani EAT 207 Mk50
Kilwa Kivinje EAT 207 Mk50
Kilwa Masoko EAT 207 Mk50
Kilwat RI 130 Rg48
Kilyos TR 50 Mk49
Kim CAM 195 Lf43
Kim TCH 187 Lh41
Kim USA (CO) 237 Ej27
Kimaan RI 158 Rk49
Kimali EAT 207 Mh48
Kimamba EAT 207 Mj49
Kimambi EAT 207 Mk50
Kimana EAK 207 Mj47
Kiman el Mata'na ET 177 Mg33
Kimano II RDC 206 Me48
Kimba AUS (QLD) 146 Sb53
Kimba AUS (SA) 152 Rj62
Kimba RCB 202 Lh47
Kimball USA (NE) 240 Ej25
Kimball, Mount USA 229 Ch14
Kimbao RDC 203 Lj48
Kimbe PNG 160 Sf48
Kimbe Bay PNG 160 Sf48
Kimberley AUS (NSW) 152 Sa62
Kimberley Plateau AUS 138 Rc54
Kimberley ZA 217 Mc60
Kimberley Coast AUS 138 Rb53
Kimberley Downs AUS (WA) 138 Rc54
Kimberly CDN (BC) 233 Ec21
Kimberly USA (OR) 234 Ea23
Kimbiji EAT 207 Mk49
Kimbirilla Sud CI 192 Kg41
Kimbolton NZ 154 Th66
Kimchaek PRK 100 Re25
Kími GR 48 Me52
Kimilili EAK 204 Mh45
Kimito FIN 16 Mc30
Kimito = Kemiö FIN 16 Md30
Kimmirut CDN 225 Gb06
Kimobetsu J 99 Sa24
Kímolos GR 49 Me54
Kímolos GR 49 Me54
Ki Monastery IND 107 Ok29
Kimongo RCB 202 Lg48
Kimothon Cave EAK 204 Mh45
Kimovin River CDN 233 Ef17
Kimovsk RUS 53 Mk19
Kimpanga RDC 203 Mc49
Kimparana RMM 184 Kh39
Kimpata-Eku RDC 203 Lk48
Kimpelo RCB 202 Lh47
Kimpese RDC 202 Lh48
Kimry RUS 52 Mj17
Kimsambi EAT 201 Mf46
Kimuta Island PNG 160 Sg51
Kimvula RDC 202 Lh48
Kin J 103 Rd32
Kinabalu, Gunung MAL 122 Qj42
Kinabalu N.P. MAL 122 Qj42
Kinabatangan MAL 122 Qj43
Kinak Bay USA 228 Bh15
Kinali RI 124 Pk46
Kinambo EAT 206 Mf50
Kinango EAK 207 Mk48
Kinara AUS (QLD) 149 Sc55
Kinara RI 130 Rg47
Kínaros GR 49 Mg53
Kinbasket Lake CDN 233 Eb20
Kinbrace GB 19 Kr32
Kincaid CDN (SK) 233 Eg21
Kincardine CDN (ON) 246 Fk23
Kinchega N.P. AUS 152 Sa62
Kinchil MEX (YT) 255 Ff35
Kincolith CDN (BC) 231 Df18
Kinda RDC 203 Mc50
Kindamba RCB 202 Lh47
Kindang Bum MYA 113 Pj32
Kinder USA (LA) 243 Fd30
Kinderdijk NL 32 Le39
Kindersley CDN (SK) 233 Ef20
Kindi BF 185 Kj39
Kindi RDC 203 Lj48
Kindia RG 192 Kd40
Kindu RDC 206 Mc47
Kinel' RUS 53 Nf19
Kinesi EAT 204 Mg46
Kinešma RUS 53 Nb17
Kinga RDC 209 Mb51
Kinganga RDC 202 Lg48
Kingaon IND (MHT) 108 Oj36
Kingaroy AUS (QLD) 151 Sf59
King Ash Bay AUS (NT) 139 Rj53
King City USA (CA) 236 Dk27
King Cove USA (AK) 228 Bj18
King Edward River AUS 138 Rd53
King Edward VIII Gulf 297 Nd32
Kingfisher USA (OK) 243 Fb28
Kingfisher Island AUS 138 Rc54
King George USA (VA) 247 Gb26
King George Bay GB 295 Gk71
King George Island 296 Ha31
Kingisepp RUS 16 Mj31
King Island AUS 153 Sb65
King Island CDN 232 Dg19
King Island USA 229 Bf13
King John's Castle IRL 20 Km38
King Junction AUS (QLD) 146 Sb53
King Lear USA 234 Ea25
King Leopold Ranges AUS 138 Rc54
Kingman USA (AZ) 236 Ec28
Kingman USA (KS) 242 Fa27
Kingman Reef USA 157 Ud17
Kingnan RMM 192 Kg40
Kingolwira EAT 207 Mj49
Kingombe RDC 206 Md47
Kingombe RDC 206 Md47
Kingoonya AUS (SA) 152 Rh61
Kingoué RCB 202 Lh47
Kingri PK 79 Oe30
King River AUS (WA) 144 Qj63
King Salmon USA (AK) 228 Cb16
King Salmon River USA 228 Cb16
Kingsbridge GB 20 Kr40
Kingsburg ZA 217 Mf61
Kings Canyon AUS 142 Rf58
Kings Canyon N.P. USA 234 Ea27
Kingscliffe AUS 151 Sg60
Kingscote AUS (SA) 152 Rj63
King's Cove CDN (NF) 245 Hd21
King Sejong ANT (ROK) 296 Ha31
Kingsford USA (WI) 246 Ff23
Kings Highway JOR 64 Mh30
Kingsland USA (GA) 249 Fk30
Kings Landing Hist. Settlement CDN 245 Gg23
Kingsley ZA 217 Mf59
King's Lynn GB 21 La38
Kingsmill Group KIR 157 Tc19
Kings Mountain USA (NC) 249 Fk28
King Sound AUS 138 Rb54
Kings Peak USA 235 Ee25
Kingsport USA (TN) 249 Fj27
Kingston AUS (TAS) 152 Sd67
Kingston CDN (ON) 247 Gb23
Kingston JA 259 Gb37
Kingston USA (NY) 247 Gd25
Kingston USA (PA) 247 Gb25
Kingston Peak USA 236 Ec28
Kingston SE AUS (SA) 152 Rk64
Kingston upon Hull GB 21 Ku37
Kingstown WV 261 Gk39
Kingstree USA (SC) 249 Ga29
Kingsville LB 192 Ke42
Kingsville USA (TX) 253 Fb32
Kingswood ZA 217 Mc59
King Tongmyong's Mausoleum PRK 100 Rc26
Kingulube RDC 206 Me47
Kingungi RDC 203 Lj48
Kingussie GB 19 Kq33
Kingwaya RDC 203 Lk48
King William Island CDN 224 Fa05
King Williams Town ZA 217 Md62
Kingwood USA (WV) 247 Ga26
Kíni GR 49 Me53
Kiniama RDC 210 Me51
Kınık TR 49 Mk54
Kınık TR 50 Mh51
Kinipaghulghat Mts. USA 228 Bf14
Kinirapoort ZA 217 Me61
Kinishba Ruins USA 237 Ee29
Kinizsi H 38 Ls43
Kinjhar Lake PK 80 Od33
Kinkala RCB 202 Lh48
Kinkasan-jima J 101 Sa26
Kinkosi RDC 202 Lh48
Kinlochewe GB 19 Kp33
Kinna EAK 205 Mk45
Kinna S 14 Ln33
Kinnaird Head GB 19 Kt33
Kinnarp S 15 Lo32
Kinnear USA (WY) 235 Ef24
Kinnegad IRL 20 Kn37
Kinneviken S 13 Lo32
Kinniyai CL 111 Pa42
Kinomoto J 101 Rj28
Kino Nuevo MEX (SO) 236 Ed31
Kinoosao CDN (MB) 238 Ek17
Kinrola AUS (QLD) 149 Se57
Kinross GB 19 Kr34
Kinross ZA 217 Me59
Kinsale IRL 20 Km39
Kinsarvik N 12 Lg30
Kinsey USA (MT) 235 Eh22
Kinshasa RDC 202 Lh48
Kinsley USA (KS) 242 Fa27
Kinston USA (NC) 249 Gb28
Kintampo GH 193 Kk41
Kintampo Falls GH 193 Kk41
Kintap RI 126 Qh47
Kintinnian RG 192 Kf40
Kintore GB 19 Ks33
Kintyre GB 18 Kp35
Kinushseo River CDN 239 Fj18
Kinvarre IRL 20 Km37
Kinwat IND (MHT) 109 Ok36
Kinyanga EAU 201 Mf44
Kinyangiri EAT 207 Mh48
Kinyasungwe EAT 207 Mj48
Kinyéran RG 192 Kf40
Kinyeti SUD 204 Mg44
Kinyinya BU 206 Mf47
Kinzig D 34 Lj42
Kinzig D 34 Lk40

Kion – Kondio

Kion BF 185 Kj39
Kióni GR 48 Ma52
Kiowa USA (CO) 235 Eh26
Kiowa USA (KS) 242 Fa27
Kiowa National Grassland USA (NM) 242 Ej27
Kipaila RDC 206 Me49
Kipaka RDC 206 Md48
Kipanga EAT 207 Mh49
Kiparíssi GR 48 Md54
Kiparissía GR 48 Mb53
Kipchuk River USA 228 Ca15
Kipema RDC 202 Lh48
Kipembawe EAT 206 Mg49
Kipengere Range EAT 207 Mh50
Kipili EAT 206 Mf49
Kipinä FIN 11 Md13
Kipini EAK 207 Na47
Kipling CDN (SK) 238 Ej20
Kipnuk USA (AK) 228 Bj16
Kipséli GR 46 Mb50
Kipséli GR 46 Mc51
Kipti UA 52 Mf20
Kipumbwe EAT 207 Mk48
Kipushi RDC 210 Md51
Kipushia RDC 203 Mc49
Kipushia RDC 210 Me52
Kirakat IND (UPH) 109 Pb33
Kirakira SOL 161 Ta51
Kirandul IND (CGH) 109 Pa36
Kirané RMM 183 Ke38
Kiranomena RM 220 Nd55
Kiranur IND (TNU) 111 Ok41
Kirá Panagiá GR 48 Me51
Kiratpur IND (PJB) 107 Oj30
Kiratpur IND (UPH) 107 Ok31
Kirava UA 52 Mf20
Kiraz TR 50 Mj52
Kırbaşı TR 51 Mm51
Kirby USA (AR) 243 Fd28
Kirbyville USA (TX) 243 Fd30
Kirchberg D 34 Lh41
Kirchdorf A 35 Lp43
Kirchhain D 32 Lj40
Kirchheim-Bolanden D 34 Lj41
Kirchheim (Teck) D 34 Lk42
Kirchschlag A 35 Lr43
Kirdimi TCH 188 Lk36
Kireç TR 50 Mj51
Kirej RUS 90 Qa19
Kırelı TR 51 Mm53
Kiri RDC 200 Lk46
Kiriab RI 131 Rj46
Kiriáki GR 48 Mc52
Kiribati 135 Tb10
Kiriis West NAM 216 Lk59
Kırıkhan TR 62 Mj27
Kırıkkale TR 51 Mo51
Kirillov RUS 11 Mk16
Kirillovo RUS 99 Sb22
Kirillovskoe RUS 16 Mk30
Kirimati Atoll KIR 303 Ca09
Kirinda CL 111 Pa43
Kiringo EAT 207 Mk48
Kiriom N.P. K 115 Qc40
Kirishima-y. J 103 Rf30
Kirishima-Yaku N.P. J 103 Rf30
Kirit SP 199 Nd41
Kiritappu J 99 Sc24
Kiritiri EAK 204 Mj46
Kirit Rat Thanikhom THA 116 Pk41
Kiriwa PNG 158 Sa50
Kiriwina Island PNG 160 Sf50
Kırka TR 51 Ml51
Kırkağaç TR 50 Mh51
Kirkalocka AUS (WA) 144 Qj60
Kirkby Lonsdale GB 21 Ks36
Kirkcaldy GB 19 Kr34
Kirkcudbright GB 19 Kq36
Kirkenær N 12 Ln30
Kirkenes N 11 Mf11
Kirke Såby DK 14 Lm35
Kirkimbie AUS (NT) 139 Re54
Kırkışla TR 51 Mn52
Kirkjubæjarklaustur IS 10 Ka14
Kirkkonummi = Kyrkslätt FIN 16 Me30
Kirkkovo RUS 16 Mj31
Kirkland USA (TN) 248 Fg28
Kirkland Lake CDN (ON) 239 Fk21
Kırklareli TR 50 Mh49
Kırklareli Baraj TR 50 Mh49
Kirkliai LT 17 Mc35
Kirkøy N 12 Lm31
Kirkpatrick, Mount 297 Ta35
Kirksville USA (MO) 241 Fd25
Kirkuk IRQ 65 Nc28
Kirkun MNG 91 Qf21
Kirkwall GB 19 Ks32
Kirkwood ZA 217 Mc62
Kirn D 34 Lh41
Kirov RUS 52 Mh18
Kirovo-Čepeck RUS 58 Nc07
Kirovohrad UA 54 Mg21
Kirovsk RUS 52 Mf16
Kirovs'ke UA 55 Mh23
Kirovskij RUS 70 Ne23
Kirovskij RUS 98 Rg23
Kirovskij TJ 76 Oe27
Kirovskoe KS 76 Of24
Kirov = Vjatka RUS 58 Nc07
Kirriemuir GB 19 Kr34
Kirsanov RUS 53 Nb19
Kırşehir TR 51 Mp51
Kirsi BF 185 Kk39
Kirtachi RN 185 Lb39
Kirtaka PK 80 Oa31
Kirthar N.P. PK 80 Od33
Kirthar Range PK 80 Od32
Kiru EAU 204 Mg44
Kiru WAN 186 Le40
Kirua EAK 204 Mj45
Kiruna S 10 Ma12
Kirunavaara S 10 Ma12
Kirundo BU 206 Mf47
Kirundu RDC 201 Mc46
Kirwin N.W.R. USA 240 Fa26
Kiryu J 101 Rk27
Kiržač RUS 52 Mk17
Kisa S 15 Lq33
Kisabi RDC 206 Me50
Kisaki EAT 207 Mj49
Kisalaut RI 130 Rf47
Kisalföld H 38 Ls43
Kisangani RDC 201 Mc45
Kisangire EAT 207 Mk49
Kisantete RDC 203 Lj48
Kisantu RDC 202 Lh48
Kisar RI 132 Rd50
Kisaralik River USA 228 Bk15
Kisaran RI 116 Pk44
Kisarawe EAT 207 Mk49
Kisarazu J 101 Rk28
Kisatchie USA (LA) 243 Fd30
Kisatchie Hills Wilderness USA 243 Fd30
Kisaza EAT 207 Mk48
Kis-Balaton H 38 Ls44
Kisbér H 38 Lt43
Kisec RP 123 Rc42
Kiseljak BIH 41 Lt47
Kiseljak BIH 44 Lu46
Kisengi EAT 206 Mg48
Kisengwa RDC 206 Md48
Kisengwa RDC 206 Mc49
Kisessa EAT 206 Mg47
Kish IR 74 Nh32
Kishanganj IND (BIH) 112 Pd32
Kishangarh IND (MPH) 109 Ok33
Kishangarh IND (RJT) 106 Of32
Kishangarh IND (RJT) 106 Oh32
Kisha Shën Kollit AL 46 Ma49
Kishiwada J 101 Rh28
Kishni IND (UPH) 107 Ok32
Kishonrganj BD 112 Pe33
Kishorganj BD 112 Pf33
Kishtwar 79 Oh29
Kisi EAT 206 Mf49
Kisi WAN 186 Lb41
Kisielice PL 37 Lu37
Kisigo EAT 207 Mh49
Kisigo Game Reserve EAT 207 Mh49
Kisii EAK 204 Mh46
Kisiju EAT 207 Mk49
Kisima EAK 204 Mj45
Kisite Marine N.P. EAK 205 Mk48
Kisiwani EAT 207 Mj48
Kiskatinaw River CDN 232 Dk18
Kiskittogisu Lake CDN 238 Fa18
Kiskitto Lake CDN 238 Fa18
Kiskkunmajsa H 39 Lu44
Kisko FIN 16 Md30
Kisköre H 39 Ma43
Kiskőrös H 39 Lu44
Kiskunfélegyháza H 39 Lu44
Kiskunhalas H 39 Lu44
Kiskunlacháza H 39 Lt43
Kiskunsági N.P. H 39 Lu44
Kislovodsk RUS 70 Nb24
Kismaayo SP 205 Nb46
Kisomoro EAU 201 Mf45
Kisongo EAT 207 Mj47
Kisoro EAU 201 Me46
Kiso-sanmyaku J 101 Rj28
Kisose RDC 203 Mc49
Kisoshi RDC 206 Me48
Kispiox River CDN 231 Df18
Kissamos GR 48 Md55
Kissidougou RG 192 Ke41
Kissimmee USA (FL) 250 Fk31
Kississing Lake CDN 238 Ek18
Kisszentmiklós H 39 Lt44
Kist D 34 Lk41
Kistanje HR 41 Lq47
Kistelek H 39 Lu44
Kistha IND (APH) 108 Oj37
Kistigan Lake CDN 238 Fd18
Kisuki J 101 Rg28
Kisumu EAK 204 Mh46
Kisvárda H 39 Mc42
Kiswite EAT 206 Mf50
Kita RMM 184 Kf39
Kita-Daito-Jima J 103 Rf33
Kitaibaraki J 101 Sa27
Kitakami J 101 Sa26
Kitakami-koti J 101 Sa26
Kitakata J 101 Rk27
Kitakyushu J 103 Rf29
Kitala EAT 207 Mj49
Kitale EAK 204 Mh45
Kitami J 99 Sb24
Kitami-Yamato-tai J 99 Sc23
Kita-Nagato Q.N.P. J 101 Rf28
Kitanda RDC 206 Md49
Kitangari EAT 211 Mk51
Kitani EAK 207 Mj47
Kitaotao RP 123 Rc42
Kit Carson USA (CO) 240 Ej26
Kitchener AUS (WA) 145 Rc61
Kitchener CDN (ON) 247 Fk24
Kiteba RDC 203 Mc49
Kitee FIN 16 Ml28
Kitembé RCB 202 Lh47
Kitendwe RDC 206 Me49
Kitenga RDC 202 Lj48
Kitengo RDC 203 Mc49
Kiteto EAT 207 Mj48
Kitgum EAU 204 Mg44
Kithairónas Óros GR 48 Md52
Kíthira GR 48 Mc54
Kíthnos GR 48 Me53
Kíthnos GR 49 Me53
Kitika RCA 200 Mb43
Kitimat CDN (BC) 232 Df18
Kitimat Ranges CDN 232 Df19
Kitimat Village CDN (BC) 231 Df18
Kitiu GH 193 Kk40
Kitlope River CDN 232 Dg19
Kitmore Range AUS 142 Re57
Kitob UZ 76 Od26
Kitoj RUS 90 Qb19
Kitomanga EAT 207 Mk50
Kitou J 101 Rh29
Kítros GR 46 Mc50
Kitsuki J 103 Rf29
Kittelfjäll S 10 Lh13
Kittenning USA (PA) 247 Ga25
Kittilä FIN 11 Mc12
Kitt Peak Nat. Observatory USA 237 Ee30
Kitui EAK 204 Mj46
Kitumbia EAT 207 Mk50
Kitunda EAT 206 Mg49
Kitunga RDC 203 Mc50
Kitutu RDC 206 Me47
Kitwancool Totem Poles CDN 231 Dg18
Kitwanga CDN (BC) 232 Dg18
Kitwanga EAU 204 Mg45
Kitwe Z 210 Me52
Kitzbühel A 35 Ln43
Kitzbüheler Alpen A 35 Ln43
Kitzingen D 34 Ll41
Kiu Lom Reservoir MYA 114 Pk36
Kiumbila RDC 206 Md48
Kiunga EAK 205 Na46
Kiunga PNG 158 Sa49
Kiunga Marine National Reserve EAK 205 Na46
Kiuruvesi FIN 11 Md14
Kiverci UA 37 Mf40
Kivijärvi FIN 16 Mh30
Kivik S 15 Lp35
Kiviks marknad S 15 Lp35
Kiviöli EST 16 Mg31
Kivotós GR 46 Mb50
Kiwai Island PNG 159 Sb50
Kiwale EAT 207 Mg50
Kiwalik USA (AK) 229 Bk12
Kiwayu Island EAK 205 Na47
Kiwirrkurra A.L. AUS 141 Rd57
Kiworo RI 158 Rk49
Kiyamaki Dagh IR 72 Nd26
Kiyasar IR 72 Ng27
Kiyawa WAN 186 Le40
Kiyembwe RDC 206 Md47
Kıyıköy TR 50 Mj49
Kızbeyi TR 63 Mk27
Kizi-Hem RUS 90 Pj19
Kizilcadag TR 51 Mk53
Kızılcahamam TR 51 Mn50
Kızıldağ Milli Parkı TR 51 Mm53
Kızılırmak TR 51 Mp50
Kızılırmak TR 51 Mp50
Kiziljurt RUS (DAG) 70 Nd24
Kizil Kala TM 71 Nh25
Kızılkaya TR 51 Ml53
Kızılören TR 51 Ml52
Kızılören TR 51 Mn53
Kızılot TR 51 Mm54
Kizil Qianfo Dong CHN 86 Pb25
Kiziltašskij liman RUS 55 Mj23
Kızıltepe TR 63 Na27
Kizimbani EAT 207 Mk50
Kizimkazi EAT 207 Mk49
Kižinga RUS (BUR) 91 Qe20
Kiži Pogost RUS 11 Mh14
Kız Kalesi TR 62 Mh27
Kizljar RUS (DAG) 70 Nd24
Kizljarskij zaliv RUS 70 Nd23
Kizner RUS 53 Nf17
Kızören TR 51 Mo52
Kjahta RUS (BUR) 90 Qd20
Kjellerup DK 14 Lk34
Kjellmyra N 12 Ln30
Kjernmoen N 12 Lm29
Kjøllefjord N 11 Md10
Kjustendil BG 46 Mc48
Klaarbeck RI 130 Re46
Klaarstroom ZA 216 Mb62
Klabat RI 127 Rc45
Kladanj BIH 41 Lt46
Kladar RI 158 Rj50
Kladnica SCG 46 Ma47
Kladno CZ 38 Lp40
Kladovo SCG 44 Mc46
Klaeng THA 114 Qa39
Klagenfurt A 35 Lp44
Klaipėda LT 17 Mb35
Klakah RI 128 Qg49
Klamath USA (CA) 234 Dj25
Klamath USA 234 Dj25
Klamath Falls USA (OR) 234 Dk24
Klamath Mountains USA 234 Dj25
Klamono RI 130 Rf46
Klampa RI 127 Qj45
Klanac HR 41 Lq46
Klappen River CDN 231 Df17
Klarälven S 13 Lo31
Klaserie Nature Reserve ZA 214 Mf58
Klasies River Caves ZA 217 Mc63
Klášterec nad Ohří CZ 38 Lo40
Klasztor Paulinów PL 37 Lu40
Klasztor Świętej Anny PL 36 Lt40
Klatovy CZ 38 Lo41
Klausen = Chiusa I 40 Lm44
Klawer ZA 216 Lk61
Klawock USA (AK) 231 Dd18
Kle LB 192 Ke42
Kleck BY 17 Mg37
Kłecko PL 36 Ls38
Kleena CDN (BC) 232 Dh20
Klein Aub NAM 212 Lj57
Kleinbegin ZA 216 Ma60
Klein Karas NAM 216 Lk59
Klein Letaba ZA 214 Mf57
Kleinpoort ZA 217 Mc62
Kleinwalsertal D/A 34 Ll43
Kleinzee ZA 216 Lj60
Kleive N 12 Lh28
Klekovača BIH 41 Lr46
Kléla RMM 193 Kh40
Klembivka UA 45 Mj42
Klemtu CDN (BC) 232 Df19
Klenovac BIH 41 Lr46
Kleppe N 12 Lf32
Kleppestø N 12 Lf30
Klerksdorp ZA 217 Md59
Klerkskraal ZA 217 Md59
Klery Creek USA (AK) 229 Bk12
Klésso BF 193 Kj40
Kleszczele PL 37 Md38
Kletnja RUS 52 Mg19
Kletskij RUS 53 Nb21
Kleve D 32 Lg39
Klezevo RUS 16 Mh33
Kličav BY 52 Me19
Klička RUS 91 Qj20
Kličkinskij hrebet RUS 91 Qj20
Kliczków PL 36 Lq39
Klimavičy BY 52 Mf19
Klimovo RUS 52 Mg19
Klimovsk RUS 52 Mj18
Klin RUS 52 Mj17
Klinaklini Glacier CDN 232 Dg20
Klinaklini River CDN 232 Dh20
Klincovka RUS 53 Ne20
Klincy RUS 52 Mg19
Klingenthal D 35 Ln40
Klinghardtsberge NAM 216 Lh59
Klingnau CH 34 Lj43
Kliniča Sela HR 41 Lq45
Klintehamn S 15 Lt33
Klip ZA 217 Me59
Klipfontein ZA 217 Mc62
Klippan S 15 Lo34
Klipplaat ZA 217 Mc62
Kliprand ZA 216 Lk61
Kliprondawel NAM 216 Lk59
Klipskool ZA 214 Mf58
Klipvoor Dam ZA 213 Md58
Klissoúra GR 48 Ma51
Klisura BG 47 Me48
Klitmøller DK 14 Lj33
Klitoría GR 48 Mc53
Kljajićevo SCG 44 Lu45
Kljavica BY 17 Mf36
Kljavino RUS 53 Ng18
Ključ BIH 41 Lr46
Ključevskaja Sopka, vulkan RUS 59 Ta07
Kłobuck PL 36 Lt40
Kłodawa PL 36 Lt38
Kłodzko PL 36 Lr40
Kløfta N 12 Lm30
Klokkarvik N 12 Lf30
Kłomnice PL 37 Lu40
Klondike Highway CDN 231 Db14
Klondike Plateau CDN 231 Da14
Klos AL 46 Ma49
Kloštar Ivanić HR 41 Lr45
Kloster CH 34 Lk44
Kloster Corvey D 32 Lk39
Klosterkirche in Weingarten D 34 Lk43
Klosterkirche Jerichow D 33 Ln38
Kloster Lehnin D 33 Ln38
Kloster Lorsch D 34 Lj41
Kloster Maulbronn D 34 Lj41
Kloster Müstair CH 34 Ll44
Klosterneuburg A 35 Lr42
Klosterruine Chorin D 33 Lo38
Kloster Säben = Monastero di Sabiona I 40 Lm44
Kloster Sankt Gallen CH 34 Lk43
Klosterwappen A 35 Lq43
Kloster Zinna D 33 Lo38
Kloten CH 34 Lj43
Kloten S 13 Lq31
Klötze D 33 Lm38
Klouékanmé DY 193 La42
Klövsjö S 13 Lp28
Kluane Lake CDN 231 Da15
Kluane National Park CDN 231 Da15
Kluang MAL 117 Qb44
Kluczbork PL 36 Lt40
Klütz D 33 Lm37
Knäred S 15 Lo34
Knaresborough GB 21 Kt36
Knarvik N 12 Lf30
Knee Lake CDN 233 Eg18
Knewstubb Lake CDN 232 Dh19
Kneža BG 46 Me47
Knežev dvor HR 43 Lt48
Kneževici Sušica SCG 46 Lu47
Kneževi Vinogradi HR 44 Lt45
Knićanin SCG 44 Ma45
Knidos TR 49 Mh54
Knife R. Indian Villages N.H.S. USA 240 Ek22
Knight Inlet CDN 232 Dh20
Knight Island USA 229 Cg15
Knighton GB 21 Kr38
Knin HR 41 Lr46
Knislinge S 15 Lp34
Knittelfeld A 35 Lp43
Knivsta S 13 Ls31
Knjaževac SCG 46 Mc47
Knjaze-Volkonskoe RUS 98 Rh21
Knjažiha RUS 53 Nd18
Knocklong IRL 20 Km38
Knokke-Heist B 23 Ld39
Knollsgrund 15 Ls33
Knossós GR 49 Mf55
Knox Atoll MH 157 Tc17
Knox Coast 297 Qa32
Knoxville USA (GA) 249 Fj29
Knoxville USA (IA) 241 Fd25
Knoxville USA (TN) 249 Fj28
Knud Rasmussen Land DK 225 Hb02
Knüll D 32 Lk40
Knurów PL 36 Lt40
Knurowiec PL 37 Mb38
Knuthenborg DK 14 Lm36
Knutsford GB 21 Ks37
Knysna ZA 216 Mb63
Knysna National Lake Area ZA 216 Mb63
Knyszyn PL 37 Mc37
Koaba DY 193 La40
Ko Adang THA 116 Pk42
Koagas RI 130 Rg47
Koala BF 185 Kk39
Koamb CAM 195 Lg44
Koatinemo, T.I. BR 275 Hd48
Koba RI 125 Qd47
Koba RMM 183 Ke38
Kobadié RN 185 La39
Kobadja RCA 200 Lk43
Kobarid SLO 41 Lo44
Kobayashi J 103 Rf29
Kobe J 101 Rh28
Kobe RI 130 Rd45
Kobédaigouré CI 193 Kh43
Kobeljaky UA 54 Mh21
Kobenni RIM 184 Kf38
Kobero BU 206 Mf47
Kobi CAM 195 Lh43
Kobi WAN 187 Lg41
Koblagué TCH 187 Lj41
Koblenz D 32 Lh40
Kobli DY 193 La40
K'obo ETH 191 Mk40
Koboko EAU 201 Mf44
Kobona RUS 52 Mf15
Kobou RMM 185 Kk38
Koboža RUS 52 Mh16
Kobroor RI 131 Rh49
Kobryn BY 37 Me38
Kobuk USA (AK) 229 Cb12
Kobuk River USA 229 Ca12
Kobuk Valley National Park USA 229 Ca12
Kobuleti GE 70 Na25
Kobylin PL 36 Ls39
Kocaali TR 51 Ml49
Kocaaliler TR 51 Ml53
Kocaeli TR 50 Mk50
Kocaeli Yarımadası TR 50 Mk50
Kočani MK 46 Mc49
Koçarlı TR 62 Md27
Koceljevo SCG 44 Lu46
Kočerin BIH 41 Ls47
Kočetovka RUS 53 Na19
Kočevje SLO 41 Lp45
Koch'ang ROK 100 Rd28
Ko Chang THA 115 Qb40
Ko Chang THA 116 Pk41
Koch Bihar IND (WBG) 112 Pe32
Koch Creek CDN 232 Eb21
Kocher D 34 Lk42
Kochi IND (KER) 110 Oj42
Kochi J 101 Rg29
Kochkorka KS 77 Oh24
Kocjubyns'ke UA 54 Mf20
Kock PL 37 Mc39
Kočkarlej RUS 53 Nd19
Kočkor-Bazar-Korgon KS 77 Og25
Kocsola H 38 Lt44
Kócsújfalu H 39 Ma43
Kočubej RUS (DAG) 70 Nd23
Kodachad IND 110 Oh40
Kodad IND (APH) 109 Ok37
Kodaikanal IND (TNU) 111 Oj41
Kodala IND (ORS) 109 Pc36
Kodari NEP 88 Pc32
Kodarma IND (JKD) 109 Pc33
Kode S 14 Lm33
Kodeń PL 37 Md39
Kodiak USA (AK) 230 Cd17
Kodiak Island USA 230 Cd17
Kodiak National Wildlife Refuge USA 230 Cd17
Kodima UA 45 Ml43
Kodinar IND (GUJ) 108 Of35
Kodinsk RUS 58 Pd07
Kodjari BF 193 La40
Kodlipet IND (KTK) 110 Oh40
Kodok SUD 197 Mg41
Kodrąb PL 37 Lu39
Kodumuru IND (APH) 111 Oj39
Kodungallur IND (KER) 110 Oj41
Koduru IND (APH) 111 Ok40
Kodyma UA 45 Mk42
Koébonou CI 193 Kj41
Koegelbeen Caves ZA 216 Mb60
Koegelbeengrotte ZA 216 Mb60
Koekenaap ZA 216 Lk61
Koelwar IND (BIH) 109 Pc33
Koës NAM 212 Lk58
Kofa N.W.R. USA 236 Ed29
Kofarnihon TJ 76 Oe26
Kofças TR 50 Mh49
Kofele ETH 198 Mk42
Koffi-Amankro CI 193 Kj42
Koffiefontein ZA 217 Mc60
Kofiau RI 130 Re46
Kofinou CY 51 Mo56
Köflach A 35 Lq43
Koforidua GH 193 Kk42
Kofu J 101 Rg28
Kofu J 101 Rk28
Koga J 101 Rk27
Kogan AUS (QLD) 151 Sf59
Køge DK 14 Ln35
Køge Bugt DK 14 Ln35
Køge Bugt = Pikiutdleq DK 225 Ja06
Kogelberg Nature Reserve ZA 216 Lk63
Koghaly KZ 84 Ok23
Kogon RG 183 Kc40
Kogon UZ 76 Oc26
Kogula EST 16 Mc32
Koguryo, Capital Cities and Tombs of the Ancient Kingdom CHN 100 Rd25
Koguryo Tombs, Complex of PRK 100 Rd25/Rd26
Koguva EST 16 Md32
Kogyae Strict Nature Reserve GH 193 Kk42
Kohalpur NEP 88 Pa31
Kohan PK 80 Od32
Koh Ang Tong THA 116 Pk41
Kohat PK 79 Of29
Kohila EST 16 Me31
Kohima IND (NGL) 112 Ph33
Koh-i-Patandar PK 80 Oc32
Koh Kong K 115 Qb40
Kohler Glacier 296 Eb34
Kohler Range 296 Eb33
Kohlu PK 81 Oe31
Kohma RUS 53 Na17
Kohol RI 130 Rd47
Koh Phaluai THA 116 Pk41
Koh Phangan THA 116 Qa41
Kohrud IR 72 Ng27
Koh Rung K 115 Qb40
Koh Rung Samloem K 117 Qb40
Koh Samui THA 116 Qa41
Koh Tang K 117 Qb40
Koh Tao THA 116 Pk40
Koh Thmei K 117 Qb40
Kohtlajärve EST 16 Mh31
Kohung ROK 103 Rd28
Kohunlich MEX 255 Ff36
Koichabpan NAM 212 Lh59
Koidern CDN (YT) 231 Ck15
Koidu-Sefadu WAL 192 Ke41
Koila Kabé SN 183 Ke39
Koil Island PNG 159 Sc47
Koilkundla IND (APH) 111 Ok39
Koilovci BG 47 Me47
Koimbani COM 218 Nb51
Koindu WAL 192 Ke41
Koi Sanjaq IRQ 65 Nc27
Koito EAK 207 Mk47
Koivu FIN 11 Mc12
Kojandytau KZ 84 Ok23
Koje Do ROK 100 Re28
Kojetín CZ 38 Ls41
Kojin ROK 100 Re26
Kojonup AUS (WA) 144 Qj62
Kojtas KZ 85 Pc21
Koka ETH 198 Mk41
Kokand UZ 76 Of25
Kökar FIN 13 Ma31
Kökar FIN 13 Ma31
Kokaral tübegi KZ 71 Nk22
Kokas RI 130 Rg47
Kokatha AUS (SA) 152 Rh61
Kokcha UZ 71 Oa25
Kokemäki FIN 16 Mb29
Kokemäki FIN 16 Mc29
Kokemäkijoki FIN 16 Mc29
Kokenau RI 131 Rj48
Kokerboom Forest NAM 216 Lk59
Kokerboomwoud NAM 216 Lk59
Kokerit GUY 270 Ha42
Ko Kho Khao THA 116 Pk41
Kokinombléa GR 48 Md52
Kokish CDN (BC) 232 Dg20
Kok-Jangak KS 77 Og25
Kókkines Pétres GR 46 Md50
Kokkola FIN 11 Mb14
Koknese LV 17 Mf34
Koko ETH 198 Mj40
Koko WAN 186 Lc40
Koko WAN 194 Lc42
Kokoda PNG 159 Sd50
Kokofata RMM 184 Kf39
Kokologo BF 185 Kk39
Kokolopozo CI 192 Kg43
Kokomo USA (IN) 246 Fg25
Kokopo PNG 160 Sg48
Kokore DY 194 Lb41
Kokoro RG 183 Kf39
Kokosa ETH 198 Mk42
Kokoso GH 193 Kk43
Kokotí GR 48 Mc51
Kokoulo RG 192 Kd40
Kokpek KZ 77 Ok24
Kokpekti KZ 84 Pb21
Kökpınar TR 63 Na26
Kokqakam CHN (XUZ) 86 Pd26
Kokrajhar IND (ASM) 112 Pf32
Kokrines Hills USA 229 Cc13
Koksa RUS 85 Pc20
Kokšaga RUS 53 Nd17
Kokšajsk RUS (MEL) 53 Nd17
Koksan PRK 100 Rd26
Koksara IND (ORS) 109 Pb36
Koksarai KZ 76 Oe24
Köksengir tau KZ 71 Nj23
Köksengir tau KZ 76 Oc23
Kokstad ZA 217 Me61
Koksu KZ 84 Ok23
Koktal KZ 84 Ok23
Koktas KZ 84 Of22
Koktebel' UA 55 Mh23
Koktokay CHN (XUZ) 85 Pe22
Koktuma KZ 84 Pa23
Kokubo J 103 Rf30
Kokuj RUS 91 Qj19
Kokum Do ROK 103 Rd28
Ko Kut THA 115 Qb40
Kol PNG 159 Sc48
Kola LB 192 Kg42
Kola RI 131 Rh48
Kola RI 131 Rh48
Kolaba Fort IND 108 Og36
Kołacze PL 37 Md39
Kolaghat IND (WBG) 112 Pd34
Kolahun LB 192 Ke41
Kolaka RI 129 Ra48
Kolana RI 132 Rc50
Ko Lanta THA 116 Pk42
Ko Lanta Marine N.P. THA 116 Pk42
Kola Peninsula RUS 6 Mb03
Kolar IND (KTK) 111 Ok40
Kolari FIN 11 Mb12
Kolárovo SK 38 Ls43
Kolasava BY 17 Mg37
Kolåsen S 10 Lg14
Kolašin SCG 46 Lu48
Kolbäck S 13 Lr31
Kolbai KZ 84 Pa23
Kolbio EAK 205 Na46
Kolbu N 12 Ll30
Kolbudy Grn. PL 36 Lt36
Kolbuszowa PL 37 Mb40
Kol'čugino RUS 53 Mk17
Kolda SN 183 Kc39
Koldaga TCH 195 Lj41
kölder Zhaksykylysh KZ 71 Ob22
Kolding DK 14 Lk35
Koldinghus DK 14 Lk35
Kole RDC 201 Mc44
Kole RDC 203 Mb47
Kolebira IND (JKD) 109 Pc34
Kolen IR 72 Ne30
Kolenté RG/WAL 192 Kd41
Kolèntèn RG 192 Kd40
Kölesd H 39 Lt44
Kolga-Jaani EST 16 Mf32
Kolga laht EST 16 Mf31
Kolgaon IND (MHT) 108 Oh36
Kolgompja RUS 16 Mj31
Kolhan Upland IND 109 Pc34
Kolhapur IND (APH) 108 Ok37
Kolhapur IND (MHT) 108 Oh37
Kolhar IND (KTK) 108 Oh37
Kolho FIN 16 Me28
Kolhozabad TJ 76 Oe27
Kolhumadulu Atoll = Thaa Atoll MV 110 Og44
Kolia CI 192 Kg41
Koliba RG 183 Kd39
Ko Libong THA 116 Pk42
Koliganek USA (AK) 228 Cb16
Kölí Karasor KZ 84 Oh21
Kölí Kusmuryn KZ 58 Oa08
Kolimbiné RMM 183 Ke38
Kolín CZ 38 Lq40
Kolin kansallispuisto FIN 11 Me14
Kölí Siletiteniz KZ 58 Oc08
Kölí Tengiz KZ 58 Ob08
Koljučinskaja guba RUS 59 Ua05
Kolka LV 17 Mc33
Kolkasrags LV 17 Mc33
Kolkata IND (WBG) 112 Pe34
Kolkhetis Nakrdzali GE 70 Na24
Kolky UA 37 Mf39
Kollam IND (KER) 110 Oj42
Kölleda D 33 Lm39
Kollegal IND (KTK) 111 Oj40
Kolleru Lake IND 109 Pa37
Kollo RN 185 Lb39
Kollur IND (KTK) 110 Oh40
Kolmanskop NAM 216 Lh59
Kolmården S 13 Lr32
Köln D 32 Lg40
Kolno PL 37 Mb37
Kolo EAT 207 Mh48
Koło PL 36 Lt38
Kolobane SN 183 Kc38
Kolobeke RDC 200 Lk46
Kołobrzeg PL 36 Lq36
Koločava UA 39 Md42
Kolofata CAM 187 Lh40
Kolokani RMM 184 Kf39
Koloko BF 193 Kh40
Kolokolčovka RUS 53 Nc20
Kolokondé DY 193 La41
Kolombangara SOL 160 Sj49
Kolomenskye RUS 52 Mj18
Kolomna RUS 53 Mk18
Kolomonyi RDC 203 Mb48
Kolomyja UA 39 Mf42
Kolon CI 193 Kh41
Kolondiéba RMM 192 Kg40
Kolongotomo RMM 184 Kh39
Kolono RI 127 Rb48
Kolonodale RI 127 Ra46
Koloro, V. = Pamporovo BG 47 Me49
Kolosib IND (MZR) 112 Pg33
Koloveden kansallispuisto FIN 16 Mj28
Kolpaševo RUS 58 Pa07
Kolpino RUS 52 Mf16
Kolpny RUS 53 Mj19
Kólpos Agiou Órous GR 47 Md50
Kólpos Alkyonídon GR 48 Md52
Kólpos Hanión GR 48 Md55
Kólpos Ierissoú GR 47 Md50
Kólpos Kassándras GR 46 Md50
Kólpos Kaválas GR 47 Me50
Kólpos Kissámou GR 48 Md55
Kólpos Messarás GR 49 Me55
Kólpos Mirambélou GR 49 Me56
Kólpos Orfanoú GR 47 Md50
Kólpos Petalion GR 48 Me53
Kolpur PK 80 Od31
Kolskij Poluostrov RUS 58 Md05
Kolsva S 13 Lq31
Kolukısa TR 51 Mn52
Koluli ER 191 Na39
Kolur IND (CGH) 109 Pa36
Koluszki PL 37 Lu39
Kolwezi RDC 209 Mc51
Kolyčivka UA 52 Mf20
Kolyma RUS 59 Sc05
Kolyma Range RUS 59 Sc06
Kolymskaja nizmennost' RUS 59 Sd05
Kolyšlej RUS 53 Nc19
Kom CAM 195 Lf44
Koma ETH 198 Mj41
Komadougou Gana WAN 187 Lf40
Komadougou Yobe RN/WAN 187 Lg39
Komaio PNG 159 Sb49
Komaki J 101 Rj28
Komako PNG 159 Sc49
Komańcza PL 39 Mc41
Komanda RDC 201 Me45
Komandorskie ostrova RUS 59 Ta07
Komárno SK 38 Lt43
Komarno UA 39 Md41
Komárom H 38 Lt43
Komarówka Podlaska PL 37 Mc39
Komatipoort ZA 214 Mf58
Komatlapeta IND (ORS) 109 Pb36
Koma tou Gialou CY 51 Mp55
Komatsu J 101 Rj27
Komba RI 132 Rb49
Kombat NAM 212 Lj55
Kombe RDC 203 Mc48
Kombissiri BF 185 Kk39
Kombo ZW 214 Me55
Kombo-Itindi CAM 194 Le43
Kombone CAM 194 Le43
Kombong IND (ARP) 112 Ph31
Kombongou BF 193 La40
Komborodougou CI 193 Kh41
Koméayo CI 192 Kg42
Kome Island EAT 204 Mg47
Kome Island EAU 204 Mg46
Komejan IR 72 Ne28
Kom el Ahmar (Nekhen) ET 177 Mg33
Komenda GH 193 Kk43
Komering RI 125 Qc47
Komfane RI 131 Rh48
Komga ZA 217 Md62
Komha IND (ORS) 109 Pb35
Komi 9 Nc06
Kominternivs'ke UA 45 Ml44
Komin-Yanga BF 193 La40
Kôm Ishqaw ET 177 Mf32
Komiža HR 41 Lr47
Komló H 38 Lt44
Komniná GR 46 Mb50
Komo G 195 Lf45
Komo PNG 159 Sb49
Komodo RI 129 Qk50
Komodo RI 129 Qk50
Komodo N.P. RI 129 Qk50
Komodou RG 192 Kf41
Kôm Ombo ET 177 Mg33
Komono RCB 202 Lg47
Komoran RI 158 Rk50
Komoro J 101 Rk27
Komorzno PL 36 Lt39
Komosi RDC 200 Lk43
Komosomol'sk RUS 53 Na17
Komotini GR 47 Mf49
Kompia WAL 192 Kd41
Kompiam PNG 159 Sb48
Kompina PL 37 Ma38
Komponaone RI 127 Rb48
Kompong Cham K 115 Qc40
Kompong Chhnang K 115 Qc39
Kompong Som = Sihanoukville K 115 Qb40
Kompong Speu K 115 Qc40
Kompong Thom K 115 Qc39
Kompong Trach K 115 Qc40
Kompot RI 127 Rc45
Komsberge ZA 216 Ma62
Komsomolabad TJ 76 Oe26
Komsomol'sk RUS 17 Ma36
Komsomol'sk TM 71 Ob26
Komsomol'skaja ANT (RUS) 297 Pd33
Komsomol'skij RUS (DAG) 70 Nd24
Komsomol'skij RUS (KAL) 70 Nd23
Komsomol'skij RUS (MOR) 53 Nc18
Komsomol'skij zapovednik RUS 98 Rj20
Komsomol'sk-na-Amure RUS 98 Rj20
Komsomolskoye KZ 76 Oe25
Komsomol'sk Zapovednik RUS 17 Ma36
Komun Do ROK 103 Rd28
Kömür Burnu TR 49 Mg52
Kömürlimanı TR 50 Mf50
Kon CAM 195 Lf43
Kona BF 185 Kj39
Kôna RN 186 Le39
Kona WAN 187 Lf41
Konada IND (APH) 109 Pb36
Konak SCG 44 Ma45
Konakovo RUS 52 Mj17
Konakpınar TR 50 Mh51
Konandikro CI 193 Kh42
Konankro CI 193 Kh42
Konapeta IND (APH) 111 Ok39
Konarak IR 75 Oa33
Konare BG 47 Mj47
Konark IND (ORS) 112 Pd36
Konark Beach IND 109 Pd36
Konarzyny PL 36 Lr37
Konaweha RI 127 Ra47
Konch IND (UPH) 107 Ok33
Konda RI 130 Rf46
Konda RUS 91 Qg19
Kondagaon IND (CGH) 109 Pa36
Kondakamberu IND (ORS) 109 Pb36
Kondanar IND (CGH) 109 Pa36
Kondavidu IND 109 Pa37
Kondembia WAL 192 Ke41
Kondhali IND (MHT) 109 Ok35
Kondinin AUS (WA) 144 Qk62
Kondio = Kombongou BF 193 La40

Kondoa EAT 207 Mh48
Kondol' RUS 53 Nc19
Kondolovo BG 47 Mh48
Kondopoga RUS (KAR) 11 Mh14
Kondrovo RUS 52 Mh18
Kondue RDC 203 Mb48
Konduga WAN 187 Lg40
Koné F 162 Tc56
Koneng RI 116 Pj43
Koneurgench TM 71 Nk24
Kong CAM 195 Lg43
Kong CI 193 Kh41
Kongasso CI 192 Kg42
Kongbo RCA 200 Ma43
Kong Christian IX Land DK 225 Ja05
Kong Christian X Land DK 225 Jb4
Kongelai EAK 204 Mh45
Kong Frederik IX Land DK 225 Hc05
Kong Frederik VIII Land DK 225 Jc03
Kong Frederik VI Kyst DK 225 Hd06
Kongi He CHN 87 Pe25
Kong Karls Land N 11 Md06
Kong Krailat THA 114 Qa37
Konglong CHN (HUB) 102 Qh31
Kongo LB 192 Ke42
Kongolo NAM 209 Mb54
Kongolo RDC 206 Md48
Kongor SUD 197 Mf42
Kongoussi BF 185 Kk39
Kongsberg N 12 Lk31
Kongsøya N 11 Me06
Kongsten fort N 12 Ll31
Kongsvege Kongbreen N 11 Lg06
Kongsvinger N 12 Lm30
Kongtal IND (MNP) 112 Pg34
Kongur Shan CHN 86 Oh26
Kongwa EAT 207 Mj49
Kong Wilhelm Land DK 225 Jd03
Koni RDC 210 Md51
Konibodom TJ 76 Of25
Konice CZ 38 Lr41
Königsbrück D 33 Lo39
Königsbrunn D 35 Ll42
Königsee D 33 Lm40
Königstein D 33 Lp40
Königstein D 34 Lj40
Königswiesen A 35 Lp42
Königswinter D 32 Lh40
Königs Wusterhausen D 33 Lo38
Konimex UZ 76 Oc25
Konin PL 36 Lt38
Konina RMM 184 Kg39
Konio RMM 184 Kh39
Kónitsa GR 46 Ma50
Köniz CH 34 Lh44
Konj BIH 41 Lr47
Konjed Jan IR 72 Nf29
Konjic BIH 41 Ls47
Konkiep NAM 216 Lj59
Konko RDC 210 Md51
Konkoma ETH 198 Mk43
Konkouré RG 192 Kd40
Konkouré RG 192 Kd40
Konkwesso WAN 186 Lc40
Konna RMM 184 Kj38
Könnern D 33 Lm39
Konnevesi FIN 16 Mg28
Kono PNG 160 Sg47
Konobougou RMM 184 Kg39
Konodimini RMM 184 Kg39
Konopiště CZ 38 Lp41
Konopki PL 37 Ma38
Konos PNG 160 Sf47
Konoša RUS 58 Na06
Konosu J 101 Rk27
Konotop PL 36 Lq39
Konotop UA 52 Mg20
Kon Plong VN 115 Qe38
Konrra IND (JKD) 109 Pc34
Konsankoro RG 192 Kf41
Konséguéla RMM 184 Kh39
Końskie PL 37 Ma39
Konsmo N 12 Lh32
Konso ETH 198 Mj43
Konsotami RG 192 Kd40
Konstancin-Jeziorna PL 37 Mb38
Konstantin BG 47 Mg48
Konstantinovka RUS 98 Rd21
Konstantinovsk RUS 55 Na22
Konstantinovy Lázně CZ 38 Ln41
Konstantynów PL 37 Md38
Konstantynów Łódzki PL 37 Lu39
Konstanz D 34 Lk43
Konta IND (CGH) 109 Pa37
Konta WAL 192 Kd41
Kontagora WAN 186 Lc40
Kontagora WAN 186 Lc40
Kontcha CAM 195 Lg42
Kontilola Cave RI 131 Rk47
Kontiolahti FIN 11 Me14
Kon Tum VN 115 Qe38
Konuralp TR 51 Mm50
Konya TR 51 Mn53
Konya Ovası TR 62 Mg27
Konyrat KZ 84 Oh22
Konz D 34 Lg41
Konza EAK 204 Mj46
Konza RMM 185 Kj37
Konzi RDC 203 Lj48
Konzo CI 193 Kh42
Koobi Fora EAK 204 Mj43
Kookynie AUS (WA) 144 Ra60
Koolan Island AUS 138 Rb54
Koolatah AUS (QLD) 146 Sb53
Kooline AUS (WA) 140 Qj57
Koolpinyah AUS (NT) 139 Rf52
Koombooloombah AUS (QLD) 149 Sc54
Koonalda AUS (SA) 145 Re61
Koondoo AUS (QLD) 151 Sc58
Koongie Park AUS (WA) 138 Rd55
Kooniba AUS (SA) 152 Rg61
Koonmarra AUS (WA) 140 Qj59
Koopan Sud ZA 216 Ma59
Koopmansfontein ZA 217 Mc60
Koo Puay Noi THA 115 Qb38
Koor RI 130 Rg46
Koorawatha AUS (NSW) 153 Se63
Koorda AUS (WA) 144 Qj61
Koosa EST 16 Mh32
Kooskia USA (ID) 235 Ec22
Kootenay Bay CDN (BC) 233 Eb21
Kootenay Ind. Res. CDN 233 Ec21
Kootenay Lake CDN 233 Eb21
Kootenay N.P. CDN 233 Eb20
Kootenay River USA 233 Ec21
Kootingal AUS (NSW) 151 Sf61
Kootjieskolk ZA 216 Ma61
Koozata Lagoon USA 228 Be18
Kopa KZ 77 Oh24
Kopa Z 210 Mf51
Kopalnia Soli PL 37 Lu40
Kopaonik SCG 46 Ma47
Kopaonik, N.P. SCG 46 Ma47
Koparan TR 51 Mn51
Kopargo DY 193 La41
Koparnes N 12 Lf28
Kópasker IS 10 Kb12
Ko Payang THA 116 Pj41
Kopbirlik KZ 84 Oj22
Kopejsk RUS 58 Oa07
Koper SLO 41 Lo45
Kopervik N 12 Lf31
Ko Pha Yam THA 116 Pk41
Ko Phi THA 116 Pk42
Ko Phuket THA 116 Pk42
Kopiago PNG 159 Sb48
Kopidlno CZ 38 Lq40
Köping S 13 Lq31
Kopingue CI 193 Kj41
Koplik i Poshtëm AL 46 Lu48
Kopong RB 213 Mc58
Kopor'e RUS 16 Mk31
Koporokenié-Na RMM 185 Kj38
Koporskaja guba RUS 16 Mj31
Koppa IND (KTK) 110 Oh40
Koppal IND (KTK) 111 Oj39
Koppang N 12 Lm29
Kopparberg S 13 Lp31
Kopparstenarne S 13 Lu32
Koppe Dag IR/TM 73 Nj27
Kopperå N 10 Lf14
Koppi RUS 99 Sa21
Koppies ZA 217 Md59
Koppom S 12 Ln31
Ko Prah Thong THA 116 Pk41
Koprivna BIH 41 Lt46
Koprivnica HR 41 Lr44
Kopřivnice CZ 38 Lt41
Koprivštica BG 47 Me48
Köprübaşı TR 50 Mj52
Köprülü TR 51 Mn54
Köprülü Kanyon Milli Parkı TR 51 Mm53
Köprüören TR 50 Mk51
Kõpu EST 16 Md32
Koputh EAU 204 Mh44
Kopyčynci UA 54 Mc21
Kora IND (BIH) 112 Pd33
Ko Ra THA 116 Pk41
Korab SCG/AL 46 Ma49
Korablino RUS 53 Mk19
Ko Racha Noi THA 116 Pk42
Ko Racha Yai THA 116 Pk42
Koraghaty KZ 77 Og24
Koraghaty KZ 77 Og24
K'orahe ETH 199 Nc42
Korana HR 41 Lq45
Korand IR 73 Nh27
Korangal IND (APH) 108 Oj37
Korannaberg ZA 216 Mb59
Kora N.P. EAK 205 Mk46
Koraput IND (ORS) 109 Pb36
Korasa SOL 160 Sj49
Koratagere IND (KTK) 111 Oj40
Ko Rawi THA 116 Pk42
Korba IND (CGH) 109 Pb34
Korba TN 174 Lf27
Korbach D 32 Lj39
Korbenići HR 41 Lp45
Korbol TCH 187 Lj41
Korbous TN 174 Lf27
Korçe AL 46 Ma50
Korčevka RUS 53 Nd18
Korčula HR 41 Lr48
Korčula HR 41 Ls48
Kordai KZ 77 Oh24
Kordkuy IR 72 Nh27
Korea
Korea Bay 100 Rb26
Korean Folk Village ROK 100 Rd27
Korea Strait 83 Rb12
Korec' UA 54 Md20
Koregaon IND (MHT) 108 Oh37
Korem ETH 191 Mk40
Koré Maïroua RN 185 Lb39
Korenevo RUS 52 Mh20
Korenica HR 41 Lq46
Korenovsk RUS 55 Mk23
Koréra-Koré RMM 184 Kf38
Korf RUS 59 Tb06
Korfantów PL 36 Ls40
Korff Ice Rise 296 Gb34
Korgas KZ 84 Pa23
Korgen N 10 Lg12
Korgom RN 186 Le39
Korgun TR 51 Mo50
Körhasan TR 51 Mm51
Korhogo CI 193 Kh41
Koria FIN 16 Mg30
Koribundu WAL 192 Ke42
Korientzé RMM 184 Kj38
Korifási GR 48 Mb53
Korim RI 131 Rj46
Korinós GR 46 Mc50
Kórinthos GR 48 Mc53
Korioumé RMM 185 Kj37
Koripobi PNG 160 Sh49
Korita BIH 41 Lt47
Korita SCG 46 Lu48
Koriyama J 101 Sa27
Korjakskaja Sopka, vulkan RUS 59 Sd08
Korjukivka UA 52 Mg20
Korkuteli TR 51 Ml53
Korla CHN (XUZ) 87 Pd25
Körmen TR 49 Mh54
Körmend H 38 Lr43
Kornaka RN 186 Ld38
Kornat HR 41 Lq47
Kornati, N.P. HR 41 Lq47
Korneevka KZ 84 Oh20
Korneuburg A 35 Lr42
Kornik PL 36 Ls38
Kornofolia GR 47 Mg49
Kornwestheim D 34 Lk42
Koro CI 192 Kg41
Koro FJI 163 Tk54
Koro RMM 185 Kj38
Koroba PNG 159 Sb48
Korobo CI 193 Kh42
Koroča RUS 53 Mj20
Korodiga EAT 207 Mj48
Korodziba ZW 213 Md55
Köroğlu Dağları TR 51 Ml50
Köroğlu Tepe TR 51 Ml50
Korogwe EAT 207 Mk48
Korohane RN 186 Ld38
Korohouita CI 193 Kh41
Korolevu FJI 163 Tj55
Koroli Desert EAK 204 Mj44
Koromačno HR 41 Lp46
Koronadal RP 123 Rc42
Korondougou CI 192 Kg41
Koronga RMM 184 Kg38
Koróni GR 48 Mb54
Koronowo PL 36 Ls37
Korop UA 52 Mg20
Koror PAL 121 Rh42
Korort-Darasun RUS 91 Qg20
Körös H 39 Ma44
Koro Sea FJI 163 Tk54
Köröslådány H 39 Mb44
Körös-Maros N.P. H 39 Ma43
Korosten' UA 52 Me20
Korostyšiv UA 54 Me20
Koroth IND (KER) 110 Oh41
Koro Toro TCH 188 Lk37
Koroviha RUS 53 Nc17
Korovin Island USA 228 Bk18
Korovniki RUS 52 Mk17
Korovou FJI 163 Tk54
Korovou SOL 160 Sh49
Koroyanitu N.P. FJI 163 Tj54
Korpilahti FIN 16 Mf28
Korpo = Korppoo FIN 16 Mb30
Korppoo FIN 16 Mb30
Korppoo = Korpo FIN 16 Mb30
Korreh IR 74 Ng30
Korsakow RUS 99 Sb22
Korsberga S 15 Lq33
Korsfjorden N 12 Lf30
Korsimoro BF 185 Kk39
Korskrogen S 13 Lq29
Korsnäs FIN 13 Mb28
Korsør DK 14 Lm35
Korsun'-Ševčenkivs'kyj UA 54 Mf21
Korsze PL 37 Mb36
Kortala SUD 197 Mf39
Korten BG 47 Mf48
Kórthio GR 49 Me53
Kortrijk B 23 Ld40
Korucu TR 50 Mh51
Korup, P.N. de CAM 194 Le43
Koruyeh IR 72 Nf30
Koryak Autonomous District RUS 59 Tb06
Koryak Range RUS 59 Tb06
Koryčany CZ 38 Ls41
Korycin PL 37 Md37
Korzybie PL 36 Lr36
Kós GR 49 Mh54
Kós GR 49 Mh54
Kosa ETH 198 Mj42
Koš-Agač RUS (ALT) 85 Pe21
Kosaja Gora RUS 52 Mj18
Ko Samet N.P. THA 114 Qa39
Kosanica SCG 46 Lu47
Košarovce SK 39 Mb41
Kosava BY 37 Mf38
Kościan PL 36 Lr38
Kościelec PL 36 Lt38
Kościerzyna PL 36 Ls36
Kościół Mariacki PL 36 Lr36
Kościół Sytersów PL 36 Lr40
Kosciusko USA (MS) 243 Ff29
Kosciuszko, Mount AUS 153 Se64
Kosciuszko N.P. AUS (NSW) 153 Se63
Koš-Děbě KS 77 Oh25
Kose EST 16 Mf31
Köse TR 63 Mk25
Köse Dağları TR 63 Mj25
Kosgi IND (APH) 108 Oj37
Kosha SUD 190 Mf36
Koshi RDC 203 Lk48
Koshikijima-retto J 103 Re30
Koshk AFG 78 Ob28
Koshk-e Kohneh AFG 78 Ob28
Koshoba TM 71 Nh25
Ko Si THA 116 Pk42
Kosi Bay Nature Reserve ZA 217 Mg59
Košice SK 39 Mb42
Košická Belá SK 39 Mb42
Kosihovce SK 39 Lu42
Ko Similan THA 116 Pj41
Ko Similan N.P. THA 116 Pj41
Kosiv UA 39 Mf42
Kosjerić SCG 46 Lu46
Koška HR 41 Lt45
Koskaecodde Lake CDN 245 Hc22
Koskarkol KZ 84 Pa22
Koskenpää FIN 16 Mf28
Koski FIN 16 Md30
Koskolovo RUS 16 Mj31
Koskue FIN 16 Mc28
Koskue FIN 16 Mc28
Kosmás GR 48 Mc53
Koson UZ 76 Oc26
Kosong PRK 100 Re26
Kosonsoy UZ 77 Of25
Kosovska Mitrovica SCG 46 Ma48
Kosów Lacki PL 37 Mc38
Kosrae FSM 157 Ta17
Kosrayi IR 72 Nc28
Kosse USA (TX) 243 Fb30
Kosso CI 193 Kh43
Kossol Reef PAL 121 Rh42
Kossuth-Múzeum H 39 Lu43
Kosta S 15 Lq34
Kostanaj KZ 58 Oa08
Kostanjevica SLO 41 Lq45
Kostanjevica na Krki SLO 41 Lq45
Kostelec nad Černými Lesy CZ 38 Lp41
Kostelec na Hané CZ 38 Ls41
Kostenec BG 46 Md48
Koster ZA 213 Md58
Kosteröarna S 12 Lm32
Kostinbrod BG 46 Md48
Kostjantynivka UA 55 Mj21
Kostomłoty PL 36 Lr39
Kostomukša RUS (KAR) 11 Mf13
Kostopil' UA 54 Md20
Kostroma RUS 53 Na17
Kostryna UA 39 Mc42
Kostrzyn PL 36 Lp38
Kostuvate UA 45 Mm42
Kosubosu WAN 186 Lb41
Kosubuke RDC 203 Mb48
Ko Sukong THA 116 Pk42
Ko Surin Nua THA 116 Pj41
Ko Surin Tai THA 116 Pj41
Koszalin PL 36 Lr36
Kőszeg H 38 Lr43
Koszuty PL 36 Ls38
Kota IND (CGH) 109 Pb34
Kota IND (RJT) 106 Oh33
Kota Agung RI 125 Qc48
Kotabangun RI 126 Qj46
Kotabaru RI 124 Qa46
Kotabaru RI 124 Qa46
Kotabaru RI 126 Qj47
Kotabatu RI 125 Qb48
Kota Belud MAL 122 Qj42
Kota Bharu MAL 117 Qb42
Kotabumi RI 125 Qc48
Kot Addu PK 79 Of30
Kotagad IND (ORS) 109 Pb36
Kotagaroterminal RI 124 Qa45
Kotakapur RI 125 Qc47
Kota Kinabalu MAL 122 Qj43
Kota Lenggong MAL 116 Qa43
Kotamobagu RI 127 Rc45
Kota Nopan RI 124 Pk45
Kotanopan RI 124 Pk45
Kotapinang RI 124 Qa45
Kotaringin RI 124 Qb45
Ko Tarutao THA 116 Pk42
Kota Tinggi MAL 117 Qb45
Kota Tinggi Waterfalls MAL 117 Qb45
Kot Diji PK 80 Oe32
Kotdwara IND (UTT) 107 Ok31
Kotel BG 47 Mg48
Kotel'nikovo RUS 55 Nb22
Kotel'skij RUS 16 Mj31
Kotel'va UA 52 Mh20
Koteshwar IND (GUJ) 108 Oe34
Kotgajah RI 125 Qc48
Kotgal IND (MHT) 109 Pa35
Kothakota IND (APH) 108 Oj37
Kothapet IND (APH) 109 Oj36
Kothari IND (MHT) 109 Ok36
Köthen D 33 Lm39
Kothili IND (UPH) 107 Pb32
Kotiari Naoudé SN 183 Kd39
Kotido EAU 204 Mh44
Kotikawatta CL 111 Ok43
Kotira PK 80 Od32
Koti Strait RI 126 Qe44
Kotka FIN 16 Mg30
Kot Kapura IND (PJB) 106 Oh30
Kotlas RUS 58 Nb06
Kotlenski Prohod BG 47 Mg48
Kotli PK 79 Og29
Kotlik USA (AK) 229 Bj14
Kotly RUS 16 Mj31
Kot Mumin PK 79 Og29
Kotobi CI 193 Kh42
Kotongoro II TCH 196 Lk41
Koton-Karifi WAN 194 Ld41
Koton-Koro WAN 186 Lc40
Kotor SCG 46 Lt48
Kotoriba HR 41 Lr44
Kotor Katedrala SCG 46 Lt48
Kotorsko BIH 41 Lt46
Kotor Varoš BIH 41 Ls46
Kótosh PE 278 Gb50
Kotouba CI 193 Kj41
Kotoula CI 192 Kg40
Kotovo RUS 53 Nc20
Kotovsk RUS 53 Na19
Kotovs'k UA 45 Mk43
Kot Putli IND (RJT) 106 Oj32
Kotri IND 109 Pa35
Kotri PK 80 Oe33
Kötronas GR 48 Mc54
Kötschach A 35 Lo44
Kottagudem IND (APH) 109 Pa37
Kottai Malai IND 111 Oj42
Kottampatti IND (TNU) 111 Ok41
Kottappatti IND (TNU) 111 Ok41
Kottarakara IND (KER) 110 Oj42
Kottayam IND (KER) 110 Oj42
Kotto RCA 196 Ma43
Kottur IND (KTK) 111 Oj39
Kotuj RUS 58 Qa05
Koturdepe TM 71 Ng26
Kotwa ZW 210 Mg54
Kotzebue USA (AK) 229 Bj12
Kotzebue Sound USA 229 Bj12
Kötzting D 35 Ln41
Kouadio-Prikro CI 193 Kh42
Kouakourou RMM 184 Kh38
Kouandé DY 193 La40
Kouango RCA 200 Ma43
Kouankan RG 192 Kf41
Kouassikro CI 193 Kj42
Kouba Olanga TCH 188 Lk38
Koubia RG 192 Ke40
Koubo Abou Azraq TCH 196 Ma40
Kouchibouguac CDN (NB) 245 Gh22
Kouchibouguac N. P. CDN 245 Gh22
Koudougou BF 185 Kj39
Kouéré BF 193 Kh40
Koufália GR 46 Mc50
Koufey RN 187 Lg38
Kouffo DY 193 La42
Koufonisi GR 49 Mg56
Kouga ZA 216 Mb62
Kougaberge ZA 216 Mb62
Kougnohou TG 193 La42
Kougouleu G 194 Le45
Kouhezi CHN (NMZ) 100 Ra24
Kouibli CI 192 Kg42
Kouilou RCB 202 Lf48
Kouka BF 193 Kh40
Kouki RCA 195 Lj42
Koukia = Bentia RMM 185 La38
Kouklia CY 51 Mn56
Koukou TCH 196 Mb40
Koukourou RCA 196 Ma42
Koukourou RCA 196 Ma42
Koula RMM 184 Kg39
Koula RMM 184 Kh39
Koulbo TCH 196 Ma39
Koulbous SUD 189 Mb38
Koulé RG 192 Kf41
Koulé Ekou DY 193 Lb41
Koulikoro RMM 184 Kg39
Koulou RN 185 Lb39
Koulouan CI 192 Kg42
Koulountou SN 183 Kd39
Koum CAM 195 Lh41
Kouma RCA 196 Lk43
Kouma RCA 196 Lk42
Koumac F 162 Tc56
Koumaïra RMM 184 Kj38
Koumala AUS (QLD) 149 Se56
Koumameyong G 195 Lf45
Koumantou RMM 192 Kg40
Koumbal RCA 196 Mb41
Koumbala CI 193 Kh41
Koumbala RCA 196 Ma41
Koumbala RCA 196 Ma41
Koumbia BF 193 Kj40
Koumbia RG 192 Kd40
Koumbili BF 193 Kk40
Koumbi Saleh RIM 184 Kf38
Koumbri BF 185 Kj39
Koumia RMM 184 Kh39
Koumogo TCH 196 Lk41
Koumongou TG 193 La40
Koumou RCA 196 Mb42
Koumpentoum SN 183 Kc38
Koumra TCH 187 Lj41
Kounahiri CI 193 Kh42
Kounávi GR 49 Mf55
Koundara RG 183 Kd39
Koundé RCA 195 Lh42
Koundessong CAM 195 Lg44
Koundian RG 192 Kf40
Koundian RMM 183 Ke39
Koundjourou TCH 196 Lk39
Koundougou BF 193 Kh40
Koúndouros GR 48 Me53
Koun-Fao CI 193 Kj42
Koungheul SN 183 Kc39
Koungi BF 185 Kj39
Koungouri TCH 196 Lk40
Kouniana RMM 184 Kh39
Kounkane SN 183 Kc39
Kounoupítsa GR 48 Md53
Kounsitel RG 192 Kd40
Kountze USA (TX) 243 Fc30
Kouoro RMM 184 Kh39
Koup ZA 216 Ma62
Koupéla BF 185 Kk39
Kouraguè RMM 183 Ke39
Kouraï RG 192 Kf41
Kouré RN 185 Lb39
Kourémalé RMM 192 Kf40
Kourgou TCH 187 Lj40
Kouri BF 185 Kj39
Kouri RMM 184 Kh39
Kouri Kouri TCH 187 Lj39
Kourion CY 51 Mn56
Kourkéto RMM 183 Ke38
Kourou F 271 Hd43
Kourouba CI 192 Kg41
Kourouba RMM 184 Kf39
Kouroudjél RIM 183 Ke37
Kourougui BF 185 Kj39
Kouroukoto RMM 183 Ke39
Kourouma BF 193 Kh40
Kourouninkoto RMM 184 Kf39
Kouroussa RG 192 Kf40
Kousrosh Palace IR 74 Nf31
Koussa Arma RN 187 Lg37
Koussanar SN 183 Kc39
Koussané RMM 183 Ke38
Koussane SN 183 Kd38
Kousseri CAM 187 Lh39
Koussountou TG 193 La41
Koutaba CAM 195 Lf43
Koutalás GR 49 Me53
Koutammakou TG 193 La40
Koutia Gaïdi SN 183 Kc38
Koutiala RMM 184 Kh39
Kouto CI 193 Kg41
Koutougou TG 193 La40
Kouvola FIN 16 Mg30
Kouyou RCB 195 Lh46
Kovačevci BG 46 Md48
Kovačica SCG 44 Ma45
Kovada Gölü TR 51 Ml53
Kovada Gölü Milli Parkı TR 51 Ml53
Kovalam IND (KER) 110 Oj42
Kovalam Beach IND 110 Oj42
Kovancılar TR 63 Mk26
Kov-Ata TM 71 Nj26
Kovdor RUS 11 Mf12
Kovel' UA 37 Me39
Kovernino RUS 53 Nb17
Kovilpatti IND (TNU) 111 Oj42
Kovrov RUS 53 Na17
Kovvur IND (APH) 109 Pa37
Kovylkino RUS (MOR) 53 Nb18
Kowal PL 37 Lu38
Kowale Oleckie PL 37 Mc36
Kowangge RI 129 Qk50
Kowanyama AUS (QLD) 146 Sa53
Kowares NAM 212 Lh55
Kowary PL 36 Lq40
Kowkcheh AFG 78 Of27
Kowloon CHN (HKG) 97 Qh34
Kowon PRK 100 Rd26
Kowt-e Ashrow AFG 78 Oe28
Koxlax CHN (XUZ) 86 Pa26
Koya WAN 186 Ld39
Koyama RG 192 Kf42
Ko Yao Yai THA 116 Pk42
Koyasan sacred site (Koya) J 101 Rh28
Köyceğiz TR 49 Mj54
Köyceğiz Gölü TR 49 Mj54
Koygolo RN 185 Lb39
Koyna Reservoir IND 108 Og37
Koyuk USA (AK) 229 Bk13
Koyuk River USA 229 Bk13
Koyukuk USA (AK) 229 Cb13
Koyukuk National Wildlife Refuge USA 229 Cb13
Koyukuk River USA 229 Cb13
Koyulhisar TR 63 Mj25
Koyunağılı TR 51 Mm51
Koyyuru IND (APH) 109 Pb37
Koza CAM 187 Lg40
Kozac'ke UA 45 Ml44
Kozak TR 50 Mh51
Kozaklı TR 51 Mp51
Kozan TR 62 Mh27
Kozáni GR 46 Mb50
Kozanlı TR 51 Mn51
Kozara BIH 41 Lr45
Kozara, N.P. BIH 41 Lr46
Kozel'sk RUS 52 Mh19
Kozha Akhmed Yasaui Mausoleum KZ 76 Oe24
Kozhikode IND (KER) 110 Oh41
Koziegłowy PL 37 Lu40
Kozienice PL 37 Mb39
Koziki BY 37 Mf38
Kozjak German MK 46 Mc48
Kozjatyn UA 54 Me21
Kozloduj BG 46 Md47
Kozlovka RUS (TAR) 53 Ne18
Kozłów PL 37 Lu40
Kozlu TR 51 Mm49
Kozluk TR 63 Na26
Kozlupınar TR 63 Mk26
Koźmin PL 36 Ls39
Koźminek PL 36 Lt39
Koźminiec PL 36 Ls39
Koz'modem'jansk RUS (MEL) 53 Nd17
Kożuchów PL 36 Lq39
Kozu-jima J 101 Rk28
Kozyn UA 37 Mf40
Kpagto GH 193 Kk41
Kpako DY 185 Lb40
Kpalbusi GH 193 Kk41
Kpalimé TG 193 La42
Kpando GH 193 La42
Kparigu GH 193 Kk40
Kpaso GH 193 La41
Kpassa GH 193 La41
Kpassagon DY 194 Lb42
Kpatawe Falls LB 192 Kf42
Kpatinga GH 193 Kk41
Kpessi TG 193 La41
Kpetoe GH 193 La42
Kpetuo LB 192 Kf42
Kpeve GH 193 La42
Kraankuil ZA 217 Mc60
Krabbfjärden S 13 Ls32
Krabi THA 116 Pk41
Kra Buri THA 116 Pk40
Kräckelbäcken S 13 Lp29
Krafla IS 10 Kb13
Kraftstation S 10 Lk12
Kragenæs DK 14 Lm36
Kragerø N 12 Lk32
Kragujevac SCG 46 Ma46
Kraljište SCG 46 Mc48
Krajnovka RUS (DAG) 70 Nd24
Krakatau Island = Rakata RI 125 Qc49
Krakatau Volcano RI 125 Qc49
Kraké DY 194 Lb42
Krakhella N 12 Le29
Kråklingbo S 15 Lt33
Krakorum GH 193 Kj42
Krakovec' UA 39 Md41
Kraków PL 37 Lu40
Krakow am See D 33 Ln37
Kralendijk NL 269 Gf39
Kralický Sněžník PL 36 Lr40
Kraljevica HR 41 Lp45
Kraljevo SCG 46 Ma47
Kralovice CZ 38 Lo41
Kráľovský Chlmec SK 39 Mb42
Kralupy nad Vltavou CZ 38 Lp40
Kramators'k UA 55 Mj21
Kramfors S 13 Ls28
Kramjanica BY 37 Me37
Kranidi GR 48 Md53
Kranj SLO 41 Lp44
Kranji SGP 117 Qb45
Kranjska Gora SLO 41 Lo44
Kranovodskoye plato TM 71 Ng25
Kransfontein ZA 217 Me60
Kranskop ZA 217 Mf60
Kranuan THA 115 Qb37
Kraolândia BR (TO) 282 Hg50
Kraolândia, T.I. BR 276 Hg50
Krapina HR 41 Lq44
Krapinske Toplice HR 41 Lq44
Krapkowice PL 36 Ls40
Krasaesin THA 116 Qa42
Kraskino RUS 100 Rf24
Krāslava LV 17 Mh35
Kraslice CZ 38 Ln40
Krasnae BY 17 Mh36
Krásna Hôrka SK 39 Ma42
Krasnaja Gora RUS 52 Mf19
Krasnaja Gorbatka RUS 53 Na18
Krasnaja Jaruga RUS 52 Mh20
Krasnaja Poljana RUS 55 Na24
Krásna nad Hornádom SK 39 Mb42
Kraśnik PL 37 Mc40
Krasni Okny UA 45 Mk43
Krasnoarmejsk RUS 52 Mk17
Krasnoarmejsk RUS 53 Nc20
Krasnoarmijs'k UA 55 Mj21
Krasnobród PL 37 Md40
Krasnodar RUS 55 Mk23
Krasnodarskoe Vodohranilišče RUS 55 Mk23
Krasnodon UA 55 Mk21
Krasnoe RUS 17 Mb36
Krasnoe RUS 53 Mk19
Krasnogorsk RUS 99 Sb21
Krasnogvardejskoe RUS 55 Na23
Krasnohorivka UA 55 Mj21
Krásnohorské Podhradie SK 39 Ma42
Krasnohrad UA 55 Mh21
Krasnohvardijs'ke UA 55 Mh23
Krasnojarovo RUS 98 Re20
Krasnojarsk RUS 58 Pc07
Krasnojil's'k UA 45 Mf42
Krasnokamensk RUS 91 Qk20
Krasnokuts'k UA 52 Mh20
Krasnomajskij RUS 52 Mh17
Krasnopavlivka UA 55 Mj21
Krasnoperekops'k UA 54 Mg23
Krasnopillja UA 52 Mh20
Krasnopol'e RUS 99 Sb21
Krasnosel'e RUS 17 Mc36
Krasnosielc PL 37 Mb37
Krasnoslobodsk RUS (MOR) 53 Nb18
Krasnoslobodsk RUS 53 Nc21
Krasnotorovka RUS 37 Lu36
Krasnoye Znamya TM 73 Ob27
Krasnoznamensk RUS 17 Mc36
Krasny Aul KZ 84 Pa20
Krasnye Baki RUS 53 Nc17
Krasnye Barrikady RUS 70 Nd22
Krasnyj Holm RUS 52 Mj16
Krasnyj Jar RUS 53 Nf19
Krasnyj Jar RUS 70 Ne22
Krasnyj Kut RUS 53 Nd20
Krasnyj Luč UA 55 Mk21
Krasnyj Manyč RUS 55 Na22
Krasnystaw PL 37 Md40
Krastë AL 46 Ma49
Krasti LV 17 Me34
Krasyliv UA 54 Md21
Krathing Falls THA 115 Qb39
Kratie K 115 Qd39
Kratke Range PNG 159 Sc49
Kratovo MK 46 Mc48
Krau RI 131 Sa47
Kražiai LT 17 Mc35
Krėva BY 17 Mg36
Kreb Bekati el Báss RMM 179 La35
Krefeld D 32 Lg39
Kregbé CI 193 Kj42
Krek K 115 Qc40
Krekenava LT 17 Me35
Kremenčuc'ke vodoschovyšče UA 54 Mg21
Kremenčuk UA 54 Mg21
Kremenec' UA 54 Mc20
Kremidivka UA 45 Ml44
Kremikovci BG 46 Md48
Kreml RUS 52 Mj18
Kremlin USA (MT) 233 Ee21
Kreml Novgorod RUS 52 Mf16
Kremmen D 33 Lo38
Kremmling USA (CO) 235 Eg25
Kremna SCG 46 Lu47
Kremnický hrad SK 39 Lt42
Krems A 35 Lo44
Krems A 35 Lq42
Krenitzin Is. USA 228 Bh19
Krepoljin SCG 44 Mb46
Krepsko PL 36 Lr37
Kreševo BIH 41 Lt47
Kresk-Królowa PL 37 Mc38
Kresna BG 46 Md49
Krestcy RUS 52 Mg16
Kréstena GR 48 Mb53
Kretinga LT 17 Mb35
Kreuzeck A 35 Lo44
Kreuzenstein A 35 Lr42
Kreuztal D 32 Lj40
Kriátsi GR 48 Mc52
Kribi CAM 194 Le44
Krieglach A 35 Lq43
Kriel ZA 217 Me59
Kriens CH 34 Lj43
Krikelos GR 48 Mb52
Krim-Krim TCH 187 Lh41
Krimmler Fälle A 35 Ln43
Krini GR 48 Mc51
Krinides GR 47 Me49
Krishna IND 104 Od15
Krishnagiri IND (TNU) 111 Ok40
Krishnai IND (ASM) 112 Pf33
Krishnanagar IND (WBG) 112 Pe34
Krishnarajanagara IND (KTK) 110 Oj40
Krishnararja Sagar IND 110 Oj40
Kristdala S 15 Lr33
Kristiansand N 12 Lh32
Kristianstad S 15 Lp34
Kristiansund N 10 Ld14
Kristiinankaupunki = Kristinestad FIN 13 Mb28
Kristinehamn S 13 Lp31
Kristinestad = Kristiinankaupunki FIN 13 Mb28
Kriva Feja SCG 46 Mc48
Krivaja BIH 41 Lt46
Krivaja SCG 44 Lu45
Kriva Palanka MK 46 Mc48
Krivodol BG 46 Md47
Krivolak MK 46 Mc49
Krivoroz'e RUS 53 Na21
Kriz TN 174 Le28
Križanov CZ 38 Lr41
Križevci HR 41 Lr44
Križpolje HR 41 Lq45
krjaž Čekanovskogo RUS 59 Ra04
krjaž Vetrenyj pojas RUS 11 Mh14
Krk HR 41 Lp45
Krk HR 41 Lp46
Krka SLO 41 Lp45
Krka, N.P. HR 41 Lq47
Krkonošský N.P. CZ 38 Lq40
Krn SLO 41 Lo44
Krnja SCG 46 Lu48
Krnov CZ 38 Ls40
Krobia PL 36 Lr39
Krøderen N 12 Lk30
Krokek S 13 Lr32
Krokilio GR 48 Mc52
Krokom S 10 Lh14
Krolevec' UA 52 Mg20
Kromdraai ZA 217 Md59
Kroměříž CZ 38 Ls41
Kromy RUS 52 Mh19
Kronach D 35 Lm40
Kronauce LV 17 Md34
Kronborg DK 14 Ln34
Krong Buk VN 115 Qe39
Krong Koh Kong K 115 Qb40
Krong Pach VN 115 Qe39
Kronprins Christian Land DK 225 Jd02
Kronprins Olav kyst 297 Na32
Kronshagen D 33 Ll36
Kronštadt RUS 52 Me15
Kroonstad ZA 217 Md59
Kröpelin D 33 Ln36
Kropotkin RUS 55 Na23
Krośnice PL 36 Ls39
Krośniewice PL 37 Lu38
Krosno PL 39 Mb41
Krosnojarskoe vodohranilišče RUS 58 Pc08
Krosno Odrzańskie PL 36 Lq38
Krotoszyn PL 36 Ls39
Krotz Springs USA (LA) 243 Fe30
Krško SLO 41 Lq45
Krstac SCG 46 Lt47
Krueng Raya RI 116 Ph43
Kruger N.P. = Nasionale Krugerwildtuin ZA 214 Mf57
Krugersdorp ZA 217 Md59
Kruhla plošča UA 54 Mh21
Krui RI 125 Qb48
Kruidfontein ZA 216 Ma62
Krujë AL 46 Lu49
Krukenyči UA 39 Md41
Krukowo PL 37 Mb37
Krumbach D 34 Ll42
Krung Ching Waterfall THA 116 Pk41
Krung Thep = Bangkok THA 114 Qa39
Krupa na Vrbasu BIH 41 Ls46
Krupanj SCG 44 Lu46
Krupinská planina SK 39 Lu42
Krušari BG 45 Mh47
Krušari BG 47 Mh47
Krušedol Selo SCG 44 Lu45
Kruševac SCG 46 Mb47
Kruševo MK 46 Mb49
Krušné hory D/CZ 35 Ln40
Krušovene BG 47 Me47
Krušovica BG 46 Md47
Krustpils LV 17 Mf34
Kruszów PL 37 Lu39
Kruszwica PL 36 Lt38
Kruszyna PL 37 Lu40
Kruszyniany PL 37 Md37
Krutec RUS 53 Nc19
Kruzof Island USA 231 Dc17
Kryčav BY 52 Mf19
Krylovo RUS 17 Mb36
Krymsk RUS 55 Mj23
Kryms'ky hory UA 55 Mh23

La Paz HN 256 Fg38
La Paz MEX (BCS) 252 Ee33
La Paz RA (ER) 289 Ha61
La Paz RA (MD) 288 Gg62
La Paz ROU 289 Hb63
La Paz RP 121 Ra38
La Paz YV 268 Gd40
Lapchaura IND (MPH) 108 Oj33
La Pedrera CO 273 Gf46
La Pedrera MEX (TM) 253 Fb34
Lapeer USA (MI) 246 Fj24
Lapela BR (MA) 276 Hh47
La Peña MEX (DGO) 253 Eh34
La Peña MEX (TM) 253 Fa34
La Perla MEX (CHH) 253 Eh31
La Perouse Strait J/RUS 99 Sa23
La Pesca MEX (TM) 253 Fb34
La Piedad de Cabadas MEX (MHC) 254 Ej35
La Pine USA (OR) 234 Dk24
Lapinin Island RP 123 Rc40
La Pintada PA 257 Fk41
La Pintada (Rock paintings) MEX 252 Ed32
Laplace USA (LA) 243 Fe30
La Plagne F 25 Lg45
La Plaine WD 261 Gk38
Lapland S/FIN 10 Lj12
La Plant USA (SD) 240 Ek23
La Plata CO 272 Gc44
La Plata RA (BA) 289 Hb63
La Plata USA (MD) 247 Gb26
La Plata USA (MO) 241 Fd26
La Pobla de Segur E 30 La48
La Pocatière CDN (QC) 244 Gf22
La Poile River CDN 245 Ha22
La Pola de Gordón E 26 Kp52
Laponia S 10 Lj12
La Port USA (IN) 246 Fg25
La Portada RCH 284 Ge57
Laporte USA (PA) 247 Gb25
La Portera E 29 Kt49
Lapoş RO 45 Mg45
La Posta RA (CD) 288 Gj61
Lapovo SCG 46 Mb46
La Poyata CO 268 Gd43
Lappajärvi FIN 11 Mb14
Läppe S 13 Lq31
Lappeenranta FIN 16 Mj29
Lappersdorf D 35 Ln41
Lappfjärd = Lapväärtti FIN 13 Mb28
Lappi FIN 16 Mb29
Lappohja = Lappvik FIN 16 Md31
Lappoluobbal N 11 Mb11
Lappträsk = Laapinjärvi FIN 16 Mg30
Lappvik = Lappohja FIN 16 Md31
Laprida RA (BA) 293 Gk64
La Pryor USA (TX) 242 Fa31
Lâpseki TR 50 Mg50
Laptev Sea RUS 59 Qd03
Lapua FIN 11 Mb14
La Puebla de Cazalla E 28 Kp47
La Puebla del Río E 28 Ko47
La Puebla de Montalbán E 29 Kq49
La Puebla de Valverde E 29 Ku50
La Puerta MEX (BC) 236 Ec29
La Puerta RA (CD) 288 Gj61
La Puerta YV 269 Ge41
Lapu-Lapu RP 123 Rc40
La Punilla RCH 292 Ge64
La Punta EC 272 Gb45
La Punta RA (SE) 288 Gh60
La Purísma MEX (BCS) 252 Ed32
Lăpuş RO 44 Md43
La Push USA (WA) 232 Dh22
Lăpuşna MD 45 Mj44
Lapuşna MD 45 Mj44
Lăpuşna RO 45 Mf44
Lapväärtti = Lappfjärd FIN 13 Mb28
Lapwai USA (ID) 232 Eb22
Łapy PL 37 Mc38
Laqiyat Arba'in SUD 190 Me36
Laqiyat 'Umran SUD 190 Me37
La Quiaca RA (PJ) 284 Gh57
L'Àquila I 42 Lo48
Lar IND (UPH) 107 Pb32
Lar IR 74 Nh32
Lara AUS (VIC) 153 Sc64
Lara G 195 Lf45
Larabanga GH 193 Kk41
Laracha E 26 Km53
Larache MA 172 Kg28
Lara de los Infantes E 27 Kr52
Laragh IRL 20 Ko37
Laragne-Montéglin F 25 Lf46
La Ramada, Cerro BOL/RA 284 Gg57
Laramanay TCH 195 Lh41
Laramarca PE 278 Gc52
Laramate PE 278 Gc53
Laramie USA (WY) 235 Eh25
Laramie Mountains USA 235 Eh24
Laramie Peak USA 235 Eh24
Laranja BR (PI) 283 Hk50
Laranjeiras do Sul BR (PR) 286 Hd58
Laranjinha, T.I. BR 286 He57
Larantuka RI 132 Rb50
Larasara IND (ORS) 109 Pb35
La Rastra MEX (SL) 253 Eh34
Larat RI 133 Rg49
La Raya PE 279 Ge53
Larba DZ 173 Lb27
L'Arbresle F 25 Le45
Lärbro S 15 Lt33
Lärchenhof D 32 Lg39
Larde MOC 211 Mk54
Larderello I 40 Ll47
Larder Lake CDN (ON) 239 Ga21
l'Ardoukouba DJI 198 Nb40
Laredo E 27 Kr53
Laredo USA (TX) 253 Fa32
La Reforma C 258 Fj35
La Reforma MEX (SL) 252 Ef33
La Reforma MEX (SO) 236 Ee31
La Reforma RA (LP) 292 Gg64
La Reforma YV 270 Gk42
Laren CHN (GZG) 96 Qe33
La Réole F 24 Ku46
Largeau TCH 188 Lk37
Largentière F 25 Le46
L'Argentière-la Bessée F 25 Lg46
Largs GB 19 Kq35
la Rhune F 24 Kt47
Lariang RI 127 Qk46
Lariang RI 127 Qk46
La Ribera MEX (BCS) 252 Ef34
La Rica CO 268 Gc42
Lárimna GR 48 Md52
Larino I 42 Lp49
La Rioja E 27 Ks52
La Rioja RA (LR) 288 Gg60
La Rioja RA 267 Gc24
Lárissa GR 46 Mc51
Larkana PK 80 Oe32
Lark Harbour CDN (NF) 245 Ha21
Larkollen N 12 Ll31
Larmor-Plage F 22 Kr43
Larnach Castle NZ 155 Tf68
Larnaka CY 51 Mo56
Larnaka Gulf CY 51 Mo55
Lárnax CY 51 Mo56
Larne GB 18 Kp36
Larned USA (KS) 242 Fa26
Laro CAM 195 Lg41
La Robla E 26 Kp52
La Roca de la Sierra E 28 Ko49
La Rochebeaucourt-et-Argentine F 24 La45
La-Roche-Bernard F 22 Ks43
La Roche-Chalais F 24 La45
La Roche-en-Ardenne B 23 Lf40
La Rochefoucauld F 24 La45
La Rochelle CDN (MB) 238 Fb21
La Rochelle F 22 Kt44
La Roche-Posay F 22 La44
La Roche-sur-Foron F 25 Lg44
La Roche-sur-Yon F 22 Kt44
La Roda E 29 Ks49
La Roda de Andalucía E 28 Kq47
La Romana DOM 260 Gf36
Larón E 26 Ko52
La Ronge CDN (SK) 233 Eh18
Larop EAU 201 Mf44
Laroquebrou F 24 Lc46
Larose USA (LA) 243 Fe31
La Rosita CO 269 Ge43
La Rosita MEX (COH) 253 Ej31
La Rosita NIC 256 Fh39
Larrimah AUS (NT) 139 Rg53
Larrimah Historic Railway Station AUS (NT) 139 Rg53
Larroque RA (ER) 289 Ha62
Larry Point AUS 140 Qk55
Larry's River CDN (NS) 245 Gk23
Lars Christensen Coast 297 Ob32
Larsen Bay USA (AK) 230 Cc17
Larsen Ice Shelf 296 Gd32
Larto USA (LA) 243 Fe30
La Ruidosa GCA 255 Ff38
Laruns F 24 Ku48
Larvik N 12 Lk31
Larżanka UA 45 Mj45
Las 3 Matas YV 269 Gh41
Las Acequias RA (CD) 288 Gj62
Las Adjuntas MEX (JLC) 253 Ej34
Lasalimu RI 127 Rb48
La Salitrera MEX (GUR) 254 Ek37
La Sal Junction USA (UT) 235 Ef26
La Salle USA (IL) 246 Ff25
La Salvetat-sur-Agout F 24 Lc47
Las Aminas USA (CO) 242 Ej26
Lasanga Island PNG 159 Sd49
La Sanne CH 34 Lh44
Las Armas RA (BA) 293 Hb64
La Sarre CDN (QC) 239 Ga21
Las Arrias RA (CD) 288 Gj61
Las Bocas MEX (SO) 252 Ef32
Las Bonitas YV 269 Gh42
Las Breas RCH 288 Ge60
Las Breñas RA (CH) 289 Gk59
Las Cabezas de San Juan E 28 Kp46
Las Cabras MEX (SL) 252 Eh34
La Scala I 40 Lk45
Las Calenturas MEX (SO) 236 Ed30
Las Campanas Observatory RCH 288 Ge60
Las Cañas RA (CA) 288 Gh60
Lascano ROU 289 Hc62
Las Canoas MEX (DGO) 253 Eh34
Lascar, Volcán RCH 284 Gg57
Las Casuarinas RA (SJ) 288 Gf61
Las Catitas RA (MD) 288 Gf62
Lascelles AUS (VIC) 153 Sb63
Las Chapas RA (CB) 292 Gg67
Las Choapas MEX (VC) 255 Fc37
La Scie CDN (NF) 245 Hc21
la Scieri G 195 Lg45
Las Claritas YV 270 Gk42
Las Coloradas MEX (COH) 253 Ek32
Las Conchas BOL 285 Ha54
Las Conchas MEX (CHH) 237 Eh31
Las Cortaderas RA (NE) 292 Ge65
Las Cruces MEX (DGO) 253 Eh34
Las Cruces MEX (TM) 253 Fa34
Las Cruces USA (NM) 237 Eg29
Las Cuatas MEX (CHH) 237 Eh30
Las Dawaco SP 199 Ne40
Las Delicias CO 268 Ge43
Las Delicias RA (SE) 288 Gh59
La SelvaLacandona MEX 255 Fe37
Lasem RI 128 Qf49
la Sénia E 30 La50
La Serena E 28 Kp48
La Serena RCH 288 Ge60
Las Estrellas MEX (SO) 236 Ed31
La Seu de Palma de Mallorca E 30 Lc51
La Seu d'Urgell E 30 Lb48
La Seyne-sur-Mer F 25 Lf47
Las Flores MEX (TM) 253 Fb34
Las Flores RA (BA) 293 Ha64
Las Flores RA (SJ) 288 Gf61
Las Galeras DOM 260 Gf36
Las Gamas RA (SF) 289 Gk60
Las Gavias MEX (SLP) 253 Fa34
Las Glorias MEX (SL) 252 Ef33
Las Guacamayas MEX (MHC) 254 Ej36
Las Hacheras RA (CH) 285 Gk58
Lashburn CDN (SK) 233 Ef19
Lash-e Joveyn AFG 78 Oa30
Las Heras RA (SC) 294 Gf69
las Hermosas, P.N. CO 268 Gc44
Lashio MYA 113 Pj34
Lashkar Gah AFG 78 Oc30
Lashkari Bazar AFG 78 Oc30
Lasht PK 79 Og27
Las Huertas MEX (ZCT) 253 Ek33
Lasia RI 116 Pj44
Lasiana Beach RI 132 Rb51
Las Iglesias de Chiloé RCH 292 Gd67
L'Asile RH 260 Gd36
La Silla Observatory RCH 288 Ge60
Lasimuseo FIN 16 Me30
Łasin PL 36 Lu37
Lasjerd IR 72 Ng28
Łask PL 37 Lu39
Łaskarzew PL 37 Mb39
Laskó H 39 Ma43
Laskowice PL 36 Lt37
Las Lajas RA (NE) 292 Ge65
Las Lajitas MEX (SL) 252 Ef32
Las Lajitas RA (SA) 285 Gh58
Las Leñas RA (MD) 288 Ge63
Las Lisas GCA 255 Fe39
Las Lomas PE 272 Fk48
Las Lomitas RA (FO) 285 Gk58
Las Margaritas MEX (DGO) 253 Eh34
Las Marismas E 28 Ko47
Las Martinas C 258 Fh35
Las Médulas E 26 Ko52
Las Mercedes YV 269 Gg41
Las Minas PA 257 Fk42
Las Navas RP 121 Rc39
Las Navas de la Concepción E 28 Kp47
Las Negras E 29 Ks46
Las Nieves E 28 Ko47
Las Norias MEX (TM) 253 Fa33
Las Nutrias RA (BA) 293 Ha65
La Solana E 29 Kr48
La Soledad CO 268 Ge43
La Soledad MEX (DGO) 252 Eg33
La Soledad MEX (NL) 253 Ek33
La Soledad PA 257 Fk42
Lasolo RI 127 Ra47
Las Orquideas, P.N. CO 268 Gb42
La Sortija RA (BA) 293 Gk65
La Soufrière WV 261 Gk39
La Souterraine F 24 Lb44
Las Ovejas RA (NE) 292 Ge64
Lasovo SCG 46 Mc47
Las Palmas PE 278 Gc50
Las Palmas de Gran Canaria E 178 Kc31
Las Palomas MEX (CHH) 237 Eh30
Las Palomas MEX (COH) 253 Ek32
Las Pedroñeras E 29 Ks49
Las Perdices RA (CD) 288 Gj62
Las Petas BOL 280 Ha54
La Spézia I 40 Lk46
Las Piedras PE 279 Gf52
Las Piedras ROU 289 Hb63
Las Plumas RA (CB) 292 Gg67
Las Pulgas RA (CB) 292 Gf68
Las Ramadas RCH 288 Ge61
Las Rosas RA (SF) 289 Gk62
Lassance BR (MG) 287 Hh54
l'Assekrem DZ 180 Lc34
Lassen Volcanic N.P. USA (CA) 234 Dk25
Lassul PNG 160 Sf48
Las Tablas MEX (SLP) 253 Fa34
Las Tablas PA 257 Fk42
Låstad S 13 Lo32
Lastarria, Volcán RCH/RA 284 Gf58
Last Chance USA (CO) 240 Ej26
Las Tinajas RA (SE) 288 Gj59
Last Mountain Lake CDN 233 Eh20
Las Torolas, Cerro RA/RCH 288 Gf60
Las Toscas RA (BA) 289 Gk63
Las Toscas RA (SF) 289 Ha60
Las Toscas ROU 289 Hc62
Lastoursville G 202 Lg46
Lastovo HR 43 Lr48
Lastovo HR 43 Lr48
Las Trincheras YV 269 Gh42
Las Trojes HN 256 Fh38
Las Tunas C 259 Gb35
Las Tunitas MEX (BCS) 252 Ee33
La Suze-sur-Sarthe F 22 La43
Las Varas MEX (CHH) 237 Ef31
Las Varas MEX (CHH) 253 Eh31
Las Varas MEX (NYT) 253 Eh35
Las Varillas RA (CD) 289 Gj61
Las Vegas USA (NM) 237 Eh28
Las Vegas USA (NV) 236 Ec27
Las Vegas (La Tasajera) MEX (DGO) 253 Eh33
Las Ventas con Peña Aguilera E 29 Kq49
Las Vilos RCH 288 Ge61
Las Viñas E 29 Kr47
Las Virgenes, Volcán MEX 252 Ed32
La Tabatière CDN (QC) 245 Ha20
Latacunga EC 272 Ga46
Latady Island 296 Ga33
Latakia SYR 62 Mh28
Latalata RI 130 Rd46
La Tapera RCH 292 Ge68
La Tapoa RN 185 Lb39
Latas RCH 284 Gf57
La Tasajera MEX (SO) 237 Ef31
Latchford CDN (ON) 247 Ga22
Låtefossen N 12 Lg31
Latehar IND (JKD) 109 Pc34
Late Island TO 164 Bc55
Laterza I 43 Lr50
Latgale LV 17 Mg34
Latham AUS (WA) 144 Qj60
Lathen D 32 Lh38
Latheron GB 19 Kr32
La Ticla MEX 254 Ej36
La Tigra, P.N. HN 256 Fg38
Latik RIM 184 Kg37
Latimo Jong Mountain Reserve RI 127 Ra47
Latina I 42 Ln49
La Tina PE 272 Ga48
La Tinaja MEX (VC) 254 Fb36
La Tinaja de Bartolo MEX (DGO) 253 Eh33
La Tinidad RP 121 Ra37
Latisana I 41 Lo45
Látky SK 39 Lu42
Lato CI 193 Kh41
La Toba E 29 Kt50
Latoden BF 185 Kj39
La Tola EC 272 Ga45
La Tolita EC 272 Ga45
Latoma RI 127 Ra47
Latorycja UA 39 Mc42
Latou RI 127 Ra47
Latouche USA (AK) 229 Cg15
Latouche Island USA 230 Cf16
La Tour du-Pin F 25 Lf45
Látrabjarg IS 10 Jj13
La Trampa PE 278 Fk49
La Tranca RA (SL) 288 Gg62
La Tranche-sur-Mer F 22 Kt44
La Tremblade F 24 Kt45
La Trimouille F 24 Lb44
La Trinidad YV 269 Gf41
La Trinidad de Orichuna YV 269 Gf42
La Trinitaria MEX (CHP) 255 Fd37
La Trinité F 261 Gk38
La Trinité-Porhoët F 22 Ks42
Latrobe USA (PA) 247 Ga25
La Troncal EC 272 Ga47
Latrónico I 43 Lq50
La Troya RA 288 Gf60
Latundo-Lompo RI 129 Ra49
La Tunia CO 273 Gd45
La Tuque CDN (QC) 244 Gd22
Latur IND (MHT) 108 Oj36
Latvia LV 17 Mc34
Lat Yao THA 114 Pk38
Lau PNG 160 Sf48
Lau WAN 187 Lf41
Lau Basin 137 Ua22
Lauca, P.N. RCH 284 Gf55
Lauchhammer D 33 Lo39
Lauda-Königshofen D 34 Lk41
Lauder GB 19 Ks35
Lauderdale AUS (TAS) 152 Sd67
Laudio-Llodio E 27 Ks53
Laudona LV 17 Mg34
Lauenburg D 33 Ll37
Lauf D 35 Lm41
Laufen D 35 Ln43
Lauffen (Neckar) D 34 Lk41
Laugarbakki IS 10 Jk13
Laughlin USA (NV) 236 Ec28
Lauhanvuoren kansallispuisto FIN 16 Mc28
Laujar de Andarax E 29 Ks46
Laukaa FIN 16 Mf28
Laukuva LT 17 Mc35
Laun THA 116 Pk40
Launceston AUS (TAS) 152 Sd66
Launceston GB 20 Kq40
Launglon MYA 114 Pk38
La Union CO 268 Gb43
La Unión CO 272 Gb45
La Unión CO 273 Gd45
La Unión E 29 Ku47
La Unión EC 272 Fk46
La Unión HN 256 Fg38
La Unión MEX (DGO) 253 Ej33
La Unión MEX (GUR) 254 Ek37
La Unión MEX (QTR) 255 Ff37
La Unión PE 278 Gb50
La Unión RA (SA) 285 Gj57
La Unión RCH 292 Gd66
La Unión RCH 292 Gd66
La Unión YV 269 Gg41
Launlonbok Islands MYA 114 Pj39
Laupheim D 34 Lk42
Laura AUS (QLD) 147 Sc53
Laura AUS (SA) 152 Rk62
La Urbana YV 269 Gg42
Laurel USA (MS) 243 Ff30
Laurel USA (MT) 235 Ef23
Laureles MEX (COH) 253 Ej32
Laurel Park USA (MD) 247 Gb26
Laurencekirk GB 19 Ks34
Laurens USA (SC) 249 Fj28
Laurentians = Les Laurentides CDN 244 Gb22
Lauri IND (MPH) 109 Pa33
Lauria I 43 Lq50
La Uribe CO 268 Gb43
La Uribe CO 272 Gc44
Lau Ridge 134 Tb12
Laurie Lake CDN 238 Ej17
Laurinburg USA (NC) 249 Ga28
Lauriya Mandangarh IND (BIH) 107 Pc32
Lauro de Freitas BR (BA) 283 Ja52
Lauro Muller BR (SC) 291 Hf60
Lauro Sodré BR (AM) 274 Gj47
Lausanne CH 34 Lg44
Lausche D 33 Lp40
Lausitzer Neiße D 33 Lp39
Laussat F 271 Hd43
Laut RI 117 Qe43
Laut RI 126 Qe46
Laut RI 126 Qj47
Lautaporras FIN 16 Md30
Lautaro, Cerro RCH 294 Gd70
Lautaro RCH 292 Gd65
Lautem TLS 132 Rd50
Lauterbach (Hessen) D 32 Lk40
Lauterecken D 34 Lh41
Lautoka FJI 163 Tj54
Laut Strait RI 126 Qj47
Lauwersoog NL 32 Lg37
Lauzerte F 24 Lb46
Lava Beds Nat. Mon. USA (CA) 234 Dk25
Lavadáki GR 48 Mb53
Lavaderos MEX (TM) 253 Fa34
Laval CDN (QC) 247 Gd23
Laval F 22 Ku42
la Vall d'Uixó E 29 Ku49
Lavalle RA (MD) 288 Gf62
Lavalle RA (SE) 288 Gh60
Lavan IR 74 Ng32
Lavanono RM 220 Nc58
Lavara GR 47 Mg49
Lavaraty RM 220 Nd57
Lavardac F 24 La46
Lava Tubes AUS (QLD) 149 Sc55
Lavaur F 24 Lb47
Lávdas GR 46 Mb50
La Vega CO 272 Gb44
La Vega DOM 260 Ge36
La Vela de Coro YV 269 Gf40
Lavelanet F 24 Lb48
Lavello I 43 Lq49
Laveno I 40 Lj45
La Ventura MEX (COH) 253 Ek33
La Verendrye Mon. USA 240 Ek23
Laverton AUS (WA) 144 Rb60
Laverton Downs AUS (WA) 144 Rb60
Lavia FIN 16 Mc29
La Victoria MEX (SLP) 253 Ek34
La Victoria YV 268 Ge42
La Victoria YV 269 Gg40
La Vieille-Lyre F 22 La42
Lavik N 12 Lf29
La Vila Joiosa E 29 Ku48
La Viña RA (SA) 284 Gh58
Lavina USA (MT) 235 Ef22
La Violeta RA (BA) 289 Gk62
La Visite, P.N. RH 260 Gd36
La Viuda YV 270 Gj41
La Voulte-sur-Rhône F 25 Le46
Lavras BR (MG) 287 Hh56
Lavras de Mangabeira BR (CE) 277 Ja49
Lavras do Sul BR (RS) 290 Hd61
Lavre P 28 Km48
Lavrentija RUS 59 Ub05
Lavrio GR 48 Me53
Lavrovo RUS 11 Mj16
Lavry RUS 16 Mh33
Lavumisa SD 217 Mf59
Lavushi Manda N.P. Z 210 Mf52
Lawaki FJI 163 Tk54
Lawang RI 128 Qg49
Lawarai Pass PK 79 Of28
Lawas MAL 122 Qh43
Lawashi River CDN 239 Fj19
Lawdar YE 68 Nc39
Law Dome 297 Qc32
Lawe Sigalagala RI 116 Pj44
Laweueng RI 116 Ph43
Lawha IND (MHT) 108 Oj36
Lawik Reef PNG 160 Sg51
Lawit, Gunung RI 126 Qg45
Lawksawk MYA 113 Pj35
Lawley River N.P. AUS 138 Rc53
Lawn CDN (NF) 245 Hc22
Lawn Bay CDN 245 Hc22
Lawngmasu IND (MZR) 112 Pg34
Lawngngaw MYA 113 Ph32
Lawn Hill AUS (QLD) 148 Rk55
Lawn Hill N.P. AUS (QLD) 148 Rk55
Lawn Hill River AUS (QLD) 148 Rk55
Lawqah KSA 65 Nb31
Lawra GH 193 Kj40
Lawrence NZ 155 Te68
Lawrence USA (KS) 241 Fc26
Lawrence USA (MA) 247 Ge24
Lawrenceburg USA (TN) 248 Fg28
Lawrence House CDN 245 Gj23
Lawrenceville USA (GA) 249 Fj29
Lawrence Wells, Mount AUS 140 Ra59
Lawson AUS (NSW) 153 Sf62
Lawton USA (OK) 242 Fa28
Lawton USA (PA) 247 Gb25
Lawu, Gunung RI 128 Qf49
Laxå S 13 Lp32
Laxenburg A 35 Lr42
Laxford Bridge GB 19 Kq32
Laxi CHN (SDG) 100 Ra27
Laxman Jhoola IND 107 Ok30
Lay BF 185 Kk39
Lay F 22 Kt44
Laya RG 192 Kd41
Laya Dula RG 192 Ke41
Layang-Layang MAL 122 Qg42
La Yarada PE 284 Ge55
La Ye YV 269 Gf42
Layla KSA 67 Nd34
Layo PE 279 Ge53
Layshi MYA 112 Ph33
Layton USA (UT) 235 Ee25
Laytonville USA (CA) 234 Dj26
Laž RUS 53 Ne17
Lazarevac SCG 44 Ma46
Lazarevskoe RUS 55 Mk24
Lázaro Cárdenas MEX (BC) 236 Ec30
Lázaro Cárdenas MEX (MHC) 254 Ej37
Lazaropore MK 46 Ma49
Lazdijai LT 17 Md36
Lázio I 42 Ln48
Lazo RUS 59 Rd05
Lazo RUS 98 Rg24
La Zulema RA (SF) 289 Gk60
Lazuri de Beiuş RO 44 Mc44
Lead USA (SD) 240 Ej23
Leader CDN (SK) 233 Ef20
Leading Tickles CDN (NF) 245 Hc21
Leadore USA (ID) 235 Ed23
Leadville USA (CO) 235 Eg26
Leaf Rapids CDN (MB) 238 Fa17
Leahy USA (WA) 232 Ea22
Leakesville USA (MS) 243 Ff30
Leakey USA (TX) 242 Fa31
Lea Lea PNG 159 Sd50
Lealui Z 209 Mb53
Leamington CDN (ON) 246 Fj24
Le'an CHN (JGX) 102 Qh32
Leanchoil CDN (BC) 233 Eb20
Leander Point AUS 144 Qh60
Leandra ZA 217 Me59
Leandro N.Alem RA (MI) 289 Hc59
Leang-Leang RI 129 Qk48
Leaning Temple IND 109 Pc35
Leanja RM 218 Nd53
Le'an Jiang CHN 102 Qj31
Learmonth AUS (WA) 140 Qh57
Leavenworth USA (KS) 241 Fc26
Leavenworth USA (WA) 232 Dk22
Łeba PL 36 Ls36
Lebach D 34 Lg41
Lebak RP 123 Rc42
Lebaktebang RI 125 Qc48
Lébamba G 202 Lf47
Lebane SCG 46 Mb48
Lébango RCB 195 Lh45
Lébango RCB 195 Lh45
Lebanon RL 64 Mh29
Lebanon USA (FL) 250 Fj31
Lebanon USA (IN) 246 Fg25
Lebanon USA (KY) 248 Fh27
Lebanon USA (MO) 243 Fd27
Lebanon USA (NH) 247 Gd24
Lebanon USA (OR) 234 Dj23
Lebanon USA (PA) 247 Gb25
Lebanon USA (TN) 248 Fg27
Lebanon, Mount RL 64 Mh29
Lebap TM 71 Oa25
Le Barón MEX (CHH) 237 Eg30
Le Beausset F 25 Lf47
Lebed' RUS 85 Pd19
Lebedjan RUS 53 Mk19
Lebedyn UA 52 Mh20
Lebelau RI 132 Rd50
Lebelsur-Quévillon CDN (QC) 244 Gb21
Lébiri G 195 Lg46
Le Blanc F 22 Lb44
Lebo RDC 200 Mb43
Lebombo SD 217 Mf59
Lebongtandai RI 124 Qa47
Leboni RI 127 Ra47
Lebon Régis BR (SC) 290 He59
Le Borgne RH 260 Gd36
Lębork PL 36 Ls36
Le Bourg-d'Oisans F 25 Lg45
Lebowa Bochum ZA 214 Me57
Lebowakgomo ZA 214 Me58
Lebrija CO 268 Gd42
Lebrija E 28 Ko46
Lebu RCH 292 Gd64
Le Buisson-de-Cadouin F 24 La46
Le Castellet F 25 Lf47
Le Cateau-Cambrésis F 23 Ld40
Le Catelet F 23 Ld41
Le Caylar F 25 Ld47
Lecce I 43 Lt50
Lecco I 40 Lk45
Lécera E 27 Ku51
Lech A 34 Ll43
Lech D 35 Ll42
L'Echalp F 25 Lg46
Lechang CHN (GDG) 97 Qg33
Le Château-d'Oléron F 24 Kt45
Le Châtelet F 25 Lc44
Lechería YV 269 Gh40
Le Chesne F 23 Le41
Le Cheylard F 25 Le46
Lechința RO 44 Me43
Lechtaler Alpen A 34 Ll43
Leči LV 17 Mb33
Lecina E 30 La48
Leciñena E 27 Ku51
Leck D 32 Lj36
Le Conquet F 22 Kq42
Le Creusot F 25 Le44
Le Croisic F 22 Ks43
Le Crotoy F 23 Lb40
Lectoure F 24 La47
Łęczna PL 37 Mc39
Łęczyca PL 36 Lq37
Łęczyca PL 37 Lu38
Ledesma E 26 Kp51
Ledmore GB 19 Kq32
Lednice-Valtice CZ 38 Lr42
Ledong CHN (HAN) 96 Qe36
Le Donjon F 25 Ld44
Le Dorat F 24 Lb44
Le Doubs CH 34 Lh43
Ledu CHN (QHI) 92 Qb27
Leduc CDN (AB) 233 Ed19
Lędyczek PL 36 Lr37
Lee IRL 20 Km39
Leech Lake USA 241 Fc22
Leech Lake Ind. Res. USA 241 Fc22
Leedey USA (OK) 242 Fa28
Leeds GB 21 Kt37
Leeds GUY 271 Hb42
Leek GB 21 Ks37
Leek NL 32 Lg37
Leenane IRL 18 Kl37
Le Encrucijada YV 270 Gj41
Leeper USA (PA) 247 Ga25
Leer D 32 Lh37
Leerdam NL 32 Lf39
Leesburg USA (FL) 250 Fk31
Leesburg USA (GA) 249 Fh30
Leesburg USA (VA) 247 Gb26
Leesi EST 16 Mf31
Leesville USA (LA) 243 Fd30
Leeudoringstad ZA 217 Md59
Leeu-Gamka ZA 216 Ma62
Leeupoort ZA 213 Md58
Leeuw ZA 216 Mb62
Leeuwarden NL 32 Lf37
Leeuwin-Naturaliste N.P. AUS 144 Qh62
Lee Vining USA (CA) 234 Ea27
Leeward Islands 165 Cf54
Leeward Islands 227 Ha15
Le Faou F 22 Kq42
Le Faouët F 22 Kr42
Lefedža BG 47 Mf47
Lefellier CDN (MB) 238 Fb21
Léfini RDC 200 Lh47
Lefkáda GR 48 Ma52
Lefkáda GR 48 Ma52
Lefká Óri GR 48 Md55
Lefkimi GR 48 Ma51
Lefkógia GR 49 Me55
Lefkónas GR 46 Md49
Lefkoniko CY 51 Mo55
Lefkosia CY 51 Mo55
Lefor USA (ND) 240 Ej22
Léfoutou RCB 202 Lg47
Le François F 261 Gk38
Leganés E 29 Kr50
Legazpi RP 121 Rb39
Legden D 32 Lh38
Legé F 22 Kt44
Legendre Island AUS 140 Qj56
Leggett USA (CA) 234 Dj26
Legion Mine ZW 214 Me56
Legionowo PL 37 Ma38
Legkovo RUS 52 Mk16
Legkraal ZA 214 Me57
Legnago I 40 Lm45
Legnano I 40 Lj45
Legnica PL 36 Lr39
Legnickie Pole PL 36 Lr39
Legoland D 34 Ll42
Legoland DK 14 Lk35
Legoland California USA 236 Eb29
Legrad HR 41 Lr44
Le Grand- Lucé F 22 La43
Le Grand-Quevilly F 22 Lb41
Leguan Island GUY 270 Ha42
Legue City USA (TX) 243 Fc31
Le Guérouel RN 186 Ld38
Leguga RDC 201 Mc44
Legundi RI 125 Qc48
Legune AUS (NT) 139 Re53
Legutiano E 27 Ks52
Leh 79 Oj28
Le Havre F 22 La41
Lehigh Acres USA (FL) 250 Fk32
Lehliu-Gară RO 45 Mg46
Lehman Caves USA 234 Ec26
Lehnin D 33 Ln38
Lehre D 33 Ll38
Lehrte D 32 Lk38
Lehtimäki FIN 16 Md28
Lehua USA 230 Bk34
Lehututu RB 213 Ma57
Leiah PK 79 Of30
Leibnitz A 35 Lq44
Leibo CHN (SCH) 94 Qb31
Leicester GB 21 Kt38
Leichhardt, Mount AUS 142 Rg56
Leichhardt Range AUS (QLD) 149 Sd56
Leichhardt River AUS (QLD) 148 Rk55
Leichlingen D 32 Lh39
Leiden NL 32 Le38
Leie EST 16 Mg32
Leigh NZ 154 Th64
Leigh Creek AUS (SA) 143 Rk61
Leikanger N 12 Lf28
Leikanger N 12 Lg29
Leike IND (ASM) 112 Pg33
Leimebamba PE 278 Gb49
Leine D 32 Lk38
Leinefelde D 33 Ll39
Leinster AUS (WA) 140 Ra59
Leinster Downs AUS (WA) 140 Ra59
Leinster, Mount IRL 20 Ko38
Leipalingis LT 17 Md36
Leipzig D 33 Ln39
Leira N 10 Le14
Leira N 12 Lk30
Leiria P 28 Km49
Leirvåg N 12 Lf30
Leirvik N 12 Lf31
Leisi EST 16 Mc32
Leisler, Mount AUS 142 Re57
Leitai Han Mu CHN 92 Qb26
Leitchfield USA (KY) 248 Fg27
Leitchville AUS (VIC) 153 Sc63
Leiter USA (WY) 235 Eg23
Leithagebirge A 35 Lr43
Leitre PNG 158 Sa47
Leiva, Cerro CO 273 Gf44
Leivonmäen kansallispuisto FIN 16 Mf29
Leivonmäki FIN 16 Mg29
Leiyang CHN (HUN) 96 Qg32
Leiza E 27 Kt53
Leizhou Peninsula CHN 96 Qf35
Leizhou Wan CHN 96 Qf35
Le Jardin MA 172 Kf29
Lejkowo PL 36 Lr36
Lejone LS 217 Me60
Leka N 10 Lf13
Lékana RCB 202 Lh47
Lekeitio E 27 Ks53
Lekenik HR 41 Lr45
Lekeran AZ 70 Ne26
Lékéti RCB 202 Lh46
Lékéti RCB 202 Lh46
Lekhcheb RIM 183 Ke36
Lekhwair Oilfield OM 74 Nh34
Lekkersing ZA 216 Lj60
Lekki Lagoon WAN 194 Lc42
Leknes N 10 Lg11
Leknes N 12 Lg28
Łęknica PL 36 Lp39
Lekona RCB 195 Lh46
Lékoni G 202 Lg46
Lékoni G 202 Lh46
Leksand S 13 Lp30
Leland USA (MI) 246 Fh23
Leland USA (MS) 243 Fe29
Lelång S 12 Ln31
Le Lavandou F 25 Lg47
Lel'čycy BY 52 Me20
Leleasca RO 45 Me46
Léléhoy RMM 185 La38
Lelehudi PNG 160 Sf51
Leleque RA (CB) 292 Ge67
Leling CHN (SDG) 93 Qj27
Lelingluang RI 133 Rf49
Le Lion-d'Angers F 22 Ku43
Lelis PL 37 Mb37
Lellington USA (NC) 249 Ga28
Le Locle CH 34 Lg43
Lelogama RI 132 Rc50
Le Loroux-Bottereau F 22 Kt43
Lélouma RG 192 Kd40
Lelu FSM 157 Ta17
Le Lude F 22 La43
Lelydorp SME 271 Hc43
Lelygebergte SME 271 Hc43
Lelystad NL 32 Lf38
Le Malzieu-Ville F 25 Ld46
Leman Bank 21 Lb37
Lemang RI 124 Qb45
Le Mans F 22 La42
Le Mars USA (IA) 241 Fb24
Lema Shilindi ETH 198 Nb43
Lematang RI 125 Qb47
Le Maule F 261 Gk37
Lembar RI 129 Qj50
Lembé CAM 195 Lg43
Lemberg D 34 Lj42
Lembeye F 24 Ku47
Lembu, Mount RI 116 Pj43
Leme BR (SP) 286 Hg57
Le Medracen DZ 174 Ld28
Le Mêle-sur-Sarthe F 22 La42
Le Merlerault F 22 La42
Lemesos CY 51 Mo56
Lemförde D 32 Lj38
Lemfu RDC 202 Lh48
Lemgo D 32 Lj38
Lemhi USA 235 Ed23
Lemhi Range USA 235 Ed23
Lemieux CDN (BC) 231 Dd16
Lemland FIN 13 Ma30
Lemluia DARS 178 Kd32
Lemmenjoen kansallispuisto FIN 11 Mc11
Lemmer NL 32 Lf38
Lemmon USA (SD) 240 Ej23
Lemo RI 127 Ra46
Lemoenshoek ZA 216 Ma62
Lemolemo RI 130 Re46
Lemon Grove USA (CA) 236 Eb29
Le Mont-Dore F 25 Lc45
Lemoore USA (CA) 236 Ea27
Lempäälä FIN 16 Md29
Lemper RI 126 Qj46
Lemsford CDN (SK) 233 Ef20
Lemsid DARS 178 Kd32
Lemu WAN 186 Ld41
Lemukutan RI 126 Qe45

le Murge I 43 Lr50
Le Muy F 25 Lg47
Lemvig DK 14 Lj34
Lemyethna MYA 114 Ph37
Léna BF 193 Kj40
Lena N 12 Ll30
Lena RUS 59 Ra05
Lena USA (OR) 234 Ea23
Lena Delta RUS 59 Rb04
Lenakel VU 162 Te55
Lençóis BR (BA) 283 Hk52
Lençóis Maranhenses, P.N. dos BR 277 Hj47
Lençóis Paulista BR (SP) 286 Hf57
Lenda RDC 201 Me45
Léndas GR 49 Me56
Lendava SLO 41 Lr44
Lendepas NAM 212 Lk58
Lendery RUS (KAR) 11 Mf14
Le Neubourg F 22 La41
Lenger KZ 76 Oe24
Lengerich D 32 Lh38
Lenggries D 35 Lm43
Lengguru RI 131 Rh47
Lenghu CHN (QHI) 87 Pg26
Lenglong Ling CHN 92 Qa27
Lenglong Ling CHN 92 Qb27
Lengo RCA 200 Mb43
Lengoué RCB 195 Lh45
Lengshuijiang CHN (HUN) 96 Qf32
Lengshuitan CHN (HUN) 96 Qf32
Lengulu RDC 201 Md44
Lengulu RDC 201 Me44
Lengwe N.P. MW 210 Mh54
Lengyan Temple CHN 100 Rb25
Lengyeltóti H 38 Ls44
Lenhovda S 15 Lq34
Lenina BY 52 Mf19
Lenina RUS 70 Nc24
Lenine UA 55 Mh23
Leningradskaja ANT (RUS) 297 Sd32
Leningradskij TJ 76 Of26
Leninkent RUS (DAG) 70 Nd24
Leninogorsk KZ 85 Pb20
Leninogorsk RUS (TAR) 53 Ng18
Lenin Peak KS 77 Og26
Leninsk RUS 53 Nc21
Leninskij RUS 52 Mj18
Leninskij TJ 76 Oe26
Leninsk-Kuzneckij RUS 58 Pb08
Leninskoe KS 77 Og25
Leninskoe RUS (YAO) 98 Rg22
Lenkau PNG 159 Sc49
Lénkéring SN 183 Kd39
Lenkivci UA 54 Md21
Lenmalu RI 130 Rf46
Lenne D 32 Lj39
Lennestadt D 32 Lh39
Lennox Head AUS 151 Sg60
Leno-Angarskoe plato RUS 58 Qa07
Lenoir USA (NC) 249 Fk28
Lenoir City USA (TN) 249 Fh28
Lenore Lake CDN 233 Eh19
Lenox USA (SD) 240 Fb24
Lens F 23 Lc40
Lensk RUS 59 Qc06
Lent'evo RUS 52 Mj16
Lenti H 38 Lr44
Lentini I 42 Lq53
Lentsweletau RB 213 Mc58
Lentvaris LT 17 Mf36
Lenya MYA 116 Pk40
Lenzen D 33 Lm37
Léo BF 193 Kj40
Leoben A 35 Lq43
Leo Creek CDN (BC) 232 Dh18
Leogâne RH 260 Gd36
Leola USA (SD) 240 Fa23
Leominster GB 21 Ks38
Leominster USA (MA) 247 Ge24
León E 26 Kp52
León MEX (GJT) 254 Ek35
León NIC 256 Fg39
León, Cerro PY 285 Gk56
Leon USA (IA) 241 Fd25
Leona RA 294 Gd70
Léona SN 183 Kb38
Leonard USA (ND) 240 Fb22
Leonardville NAM 212 Lk57
Leona Vicario MEX (QTR) 255 Fg35
Leonding A 35 Lp42
Leone USA 164 Be53
Leones RA (CD) 289 Gj62
Leonessa I 42 Ln48
Leonforte I 42 Lp53
Leongatha AUS (VIC) 153 Sc65
Leonico Prado PE 272 Gc47
Leonídio GR 48 Mc53
Leonidovo RUS 99 Sb21
Leonora AUS (WA) 144 Ra60
Léon Viejo NIC 256 Fg39
Leopold and Astrid Coast 297 Pa32
Leopold Downs A.L. AUS 138 Rc54
Leopoldina BR (MG) 287 Hj56
Leopoldo de Bulhões BR (GO) 286 Hf54
Leopoldsburg B 23 Lf39
Leorda RO 45 Mg43
Leoti USA (KS) 240 Ek26
Léoua RCA 200 Ma43
Léoura BF 185 Kk39
Leova MD 45 Mj44
Lepakshi IND 111 Oj40
Le Palais F 22 Kr43
Lepanto USA (AR) 243 Fe28
Lepar RI 125 Qd47
Lepassaare EST 16 Mh33
Lepe E 28 Kn47
Lepel' BY 52 Me18
Lephepe RB 213 Mc57
Leping CHN (JGX) 102 Qj31
Lepoglava HR 41 Lr44
Lepokole Hills RB 214 Me56
Le Pont-de-Beauvoisin F 25 Lf45
Le Porge F 24 Kt46
Le Port F 221 Nh56
Le Portel F 23 Lb40
Leppävesi FIN 16 Mf28
Leppävirta FIN 16 Mh28
Lepşa RO 45 Mg45
Lepsi KZ 84 Ok22
Lepsi KZ 84 Ok22
Lepsi KZ 84 Pa23
Leptis Magna = Labdah LAR 174 Lh29
Le Puy-en-Velay F 25 Ld45
Leqceïba RIM 183 Kc37
Leqceïba RIM 183 Kd37
Lequena RCH 284 Gf56
Le Quesnoy F 23 Ld40
Lera MK 46 Mb49
Léraba BF/CI 193 Kh41
Léraba Occidentale BF/CI 193 Kh40
Lerbäck S 13 Lq32
Lercara Friddi I 42 Lo53
Léré RMM 184 Kh38
Léré TCH 187 Lh41
Lere WAN 186 Le40
Lere WAN 186 Le41
Lérici I 40 Lk46
Lerida AUS (NSW) 151 Sc61
Lerida AUS (QLD) 148 Sc57
Lérida CO 273 Ge45
Lerik AZ 70 Ne26
Lerín E 27 Kt52
Lerma E 27 Kr52
Lerma MEX (CAM) 255 Fe36
Lermontovo RUS 53 Nb19
Lérna GR 48 Mc53
Lerneb RMM 184 Kh37
Léros GR 49 Mg53
Leross CDN (SK) 238 Ej20
Le Rozier-Peyreleau F 25 Ld46
Lerum S 14 Ln33
Le Russey F 23 Lg43
Lervik N 12 Ll31
Lerwick GB 19 Kt30
Ler Zerai SUD 197 Md40
Les E 30 La48
Leş RO 44 Mb44
Les Abers F 22 Kq42
Les Abrets F 25 Lf45
Les Abymes F 261 Gk37
Les Aix-d'Angillon F 23 Lc43
Lešak SCG 46 Ma47
Les Andalouses DZ 173 Kk28
Les Andelys F 23 Lb41
Lešani MK 46 Ma49
Les Arcs F 25 Lg45
Les Arènes de Nimes F 25 Le47
Les Arènes de Saintes F 24 Ku45
Le Sauze F 25 Lg46
Les Baux-de-Provence F 25 Le47
les Borges Blanques E 30 La49
l'Escala E 30 Ld48
Les Calanche F 31 Lj48
Les Calanques F 25 Lf47
L'Escarène F 25 Lh47
Les Cayes RH 260 Gd36
Les Corniches F 25 Lh47
Lescun F 24 Ku48
Les Deux-Alpes F 25 Lg46
Les Echelles F 25 Lf45
Les Essarts F 22 Kt44
Les Eyzies-de-Tayac F 24 Lb46
Leshan CHN (SCH) 94 Qb31
Les Hattes F 271 Hd43
Les Herbiers F 22 Ku44
Lesjöfors S 13 Lp31
Lesko PL 39 Mc41
Leskovac SCG 46 Mb48
Leskovik AL 46 Ma50
Les Laurentides CDN 244 Ge21
Leslie USA (AR) 243 Fd28
Leslie USA (ID) 235 Ed24
Les Méchins CDN (QC) 244 Gg21
Lesneven F 22 Kq42
Lesnoe RUS 17 Ma36
Lesnoe RUS 52 Mh16
Lesnoj RUS 17 Ma35
Lesnoj Gorodok RUS 91 Qg20
Lesogorsk RUS 99 Sb21
Lesogorskij RUS 16 Mj29
Lesosibirsk RUS 58 Pc07
Lesotho 167 Ma12
Lesozavodsk RUS 98 Rg23
Lesozavodskij RUS 99 Sd23
Lesparre-Médoc F 24 Ku45
L'Esperance Rock NZ 137 Ua25
L'Esperou F 25 Ld46
Lespezi RO 45 Mg43
Les Ponts-de-Cé F 22 Ku43
Les Portes de Fer DZ 173 Lc27
Les Riceys F 23 Le43
Les Sables-d'Olonne F 22 Kt44
Lessau PNG 159 Sd47
Lessay F 22 Kt41
Lessebo S 15 Lq34
Lesse et Lomme, P.N. de B 23 Lf40
Lesser Antilles 227 Gc16
Lesser Caucasus 63 Nb25
Lesser Hinggan Range CHN 98 Rd20
Lesser Slave Lake CDN 233 Ec18
Lesser Slave Lake CDN 224 Eb07
Lesser Slave Lake Prov. Park CDN 233 Ec18
Lesser Slave River CDN 233 Ec18
Lesser Sunda Islands RI 118 Qb19
Lessini GR 48 Mb52
Le Sueur USA (MN) 241 Fd23
Lesueur, Mount AUS 144 Qh61
Les Ulis F 23 Lc42
Lésvos GR 49 Mg51
Leszno PL 36 Lr39
Letaba ZA 214 Mf57
Letälven S 13 Lp31
Létavértes H 39 Mb43
Letca RO 44 Md43
Letchworth Garden City GB 21 Ku39
Letchworth S.P. USA 247 Gb24
Letea RO 45 Mk45
Le Teil F 25 Le46
Letenye H 38 Lr44
Leteri IND (MPH) 109 Oj33
Letfata RIM 183 Kd37
Letha Taung MYA 112 Pg34
Lethbridge CDN (AB) 233 Ed21
Lethem GUY 270 Ha44
Lethen AUS (NSW) 152 Sb62
Lethiakane RB 213 Mc56
Le Thillot F 23 Lg43
Lethlhakeng RB 213 Mc58
Leti RI 132 Rd50
Letiahau RB 213 Mb56
Leticia CO 273 Gf48
Leting CHN (HBI) 93 Qk26
Letku FIN 16 Md30
Letnij bereg RUS 11 Mj13
Letoon TR 49 Mk54
Le Touquet-Paris-Plage F 23 Lb40
Letpadan MYA 114 Ph37
Letpan MYA 114 Ph36
Le Tréport F 23 Lb40
Letsibogo Dam RB 213 Md56
Letsitele ZA 214 Mf57
Letsok-Aw Island MYA 116 Pk40
Letta CAM 195 Lg43
Letterfrack IRL 18 Kl37
Letterkenny IRL 18 Kn36
Letyčiv UA 54 Md21
Leu K 115 Qd39
Léuá ANG 209 Ma51
Leuaniua Island SOL 161 Sk48
Leucate-Plage F 24 Ld48
Leukerbad CH 34 Lh44
Leupp USA (AZ) 237 Ee28
Leura AUS (QLD) 149 Se57
Leuser, Mount RI 116 Pj44
Leuser N.P., Gunung RI 116 Pj44
Leutkirch D 34 Ll43
Leuven B 23 Le40
Levang N 12 Lk32
Levanger N 10 Lf14
Levantine Basin 6 Ma06
Lévanto I 40 Lk46
Levasi RUS (DAG) 70 Nd24
Levelland USA (TX) 237 Ej29
Leven GB 21 Ks34
Lever BR 281 He51
Levera N.P. WG 261 Gk39
Le Verdon-sur-Mer F 24 Kt45
Leverett Glacier 296 Cb36
Leverkusen D 32 Lh39
Levet F 23 Lc44
Levican RCH 294 Ge69
Levice SK 38 Lt42
Lévico Terme I 40 Lm44
Levidi GR 48 Mc53
Levie F 31 Lk49
Levier F 25 Lg44
Le Vigan F 25 Ld47
Levin NZ 154 Th66
Levis CDN (QC) 244 Ge22
Levitha GR 49 Mg54
Levoča SK 39 Ma41
Le Voile de la Mariée RG 192 Kd41
Levroux F 22 Lb44
Levski BG 47 Mf47
Levuka FJI 163 Tk54
Levuo LT 17 Me35
Léwa CAM 195 Lg42
Lewa RI 129 Qk50
Lewe MYA 114 Ph36
Lewer NAM 212 Lj58
Lewes GB 21 La40
Lewes Plateau CDN 231 Db14
Lewis USA 232 Dj22
Lewisburg USA (PA) 247 Gb25
Lewisburg USA (TN) 248 Fg28
Lewisburg USA (WV) 249 Fk27
Lewis Hills CDN 245 Ha21
Lewisport CDN (NF) 245 Hc21
Lewis Range USA 233 Ed22
Lewis Smith Lake USA 248 Fg29
Lewiston USA (ID) 232 Eb22
Lewiston USA (IL) 241 Fe25
Lewiston USA (ME) 247 Ge23
Lewiston USA (UT) 235 Ee25
Lewistown USA (MT) 235 Ef22
Lewistown USA (PA) 247 Gb25
Lewisville USA (AR) 243 Fd29
Lexington USA (AL) 248 Fg28
Lexington USA (GA) 249 Fj29
Lexington USA (KY) 249 Fh26
Lexington USA (MS) 243 Fe29
Lexington USA (NC) 249 Fk28
Lexington USA (NE) 240 Fa25
Lexington USA (OR) 234 Ea23
Lexington USA (SC) 249 Fk29
Lexington USA (TN) 243 Ff28
Lexington USA (VA) 249 Ga27
Lexington Park USA (MD) 247 Gb26
Lexton AUS (VIC) 153 Sb64
Leybucht D 32 Lg37
Leyburn AUS (QLD) 151 Sf60
Leyburn GB 21 Kt36
Leye CHN (GZG) 96 Qd33
Leyte RP 123 Rc40
Leyte RP 123 Rc40
Leyte Gulf RP 123 Rc40
Ležajsk PL 37 Mc40
Lezama YV 269 Gg41
Lezay F 24 Ku44
Lezhë AL 46 Lu49
Lezhi CHN (SCH) 94 Qc30
Lézignan-Corbières F 24 Lc47
Lëzna BY 52 Mf18
Ležno PL 36 Lt36
Lezoux F 25 Ld45
L'gov RUS 52 Mh20
Lhari CHN (TIB) 89 Pg30
L'Haridon Bight AUS 140 Qg58
Lhasa CHN (TIB) 89 Pf31
Lhaviyani Atoll MV 110 Og43
Lhaze CHN (TIB) 88 Pd31
Lhokkruet RI 116 Ph43
Lhokseumawe RI 116 Pj43
Lhoksukon RI 116 Pj43
L'Hôpital Dr.Schweitzer G 202 Lf46
Lhorong CHN (TIB) 89 Ph30
L'Hospitalet E 30 Lc49
L'Hospitalet F 24 Lb48
Lhotse NEP/CHN 88 Pd32
Lhozhag CHN (TIB) 89 Pf31
Lhünzê CHN (TIB) 89 Pg31
Li THA 114 Pk37
Liak PNG 160 Sg51
Lian RP 120 Ra38
Liang RI 127 Rb46
Liang RI 130 Re47
Liang RP 123 Rd41
Lianga Bay RP 123 Rd41
Liangcheng CHN (NMZ) 93 Qg25
Liangcheng CHN (SDG) 93 Qk28
Lianghe CHN (CGQ) 95 Qe31
Lianghe CHN (GZH) 96 Qc33
Lianghe CHN (YUN) 113 Pk33
Lianghekou CHN (GSU) 94 Qc29
Liangmangari, Gunung RI 126 Qg46
Liangping CHN (CGQ) 95 Qd30
Liangpran, Gunung RI 126 Qh45
Liang Qu CHN 94 Qa31
Liangshan CHN (SDG) 93 Qj28
Liangshan CHN (SDG) 102 Qj28
Liangzi Hu CHN 102 Qh30
Lianhua CHN (JGX) 97 Qg32
Lianhua Shan CHN 97 Qh34
Lianjiang CHN (GDG) 96 Qf35
Lianjiang CHN (FJN) 102 Qk32
Lianokládi GR 48 Mc52
Lianping CHN (GDG) 97 Qh33
Lianshan CHN (GDG) 96 Qg33
Lianshui CHN (JGS) 102 Qk29
Liantang CHN (GZG) 96 Qf33
Liantang CHN (JGX) 102 Qj31
Lian Xian CHN (GDG) 96 Qg33
Lianyuan CHN (HUN) 96 Qf32
Lianyungang CHN (JGS) 102 Qk28
Lianyungang CHN (JGS) 102 Qk28
Liaocheng CHN (SDG) 93 Qh27
Liaodun CHN (XUZ) 87 Pg24
Liao He CHN 100 Rb24
Liaoning CHN 83 Ra10
Liaotung Peninsula CHN 100 Rb26
Liaoyang CHN (LNG) 100 Rb25
Liaoyuan CHN (JLN) 100 Rc24
Liaozhong CHN (LNG) 100 Rb25
Liaquatpur PK 81 Of31
Liard Highway CDN 231 Dj16
Liard Plateau CDN 231 Dg15
Liard River CDN 231 Dj16
Liard River Corridor CDN 231 Dh16
Liari PK 80 Od33
Liat RI 125 Qd47
Liatorp S 15 Lp34
Liawang Shan CHN 113 Qb33
Libagon RP 123 Rc40
Libano CO 268 Gc43
Líbano RA (BA) 293 Gk64
Libao CHN (JGS) 102 Ra29
Libau CDN (MB) 238 Fb20
Libba WAN 186 Lc40
Libby USA (MT) 233 Ec21
Libenge RDC 200 Lk44
Liberal USA (KS) 242 Ek27
Liberator General San Martin RA (SL) 288 Gh62
Liberdade BR 281 Hd51
Liberec CZ 38 Lp40
Liberia CR 256 Fh40
Liberia 167 Ka09
Libertad MEX (CAM) 255 Fe36
Libertad RA (CR) 289 Hb61
Libertad ROU 289 Hb63
Libertad YV 269 Gf41
Libertad YV 269 Gf41
Libertador RA (CR) 289 Ha61
Libertador General San Martín RA (PJ) 285 Gh57
Liberty USA (LA) 243
Liberty USA (NY) 247 Gc25
Liberty USA (TX) 243 Fc30
Libiąż PL 37 Lu40
Libina CZ 38 Ls41
Libjo RP 123 Rc40
Libmanan RP 121 Rb39
Libo CHN (GZH) 96 Qd33
Libode ZA 217 Me61
Libohovë AL 46 Ma50
Liboi EAK 205 Na45
Liboko RDC 200 Ma44
Libon RP 121 Rb39
Libona RP 123 Rc41
Libouemba G 195 Lg45
Libourne F 24 Ku46
Libramont-Chevigny B 23 Lf41
Libreville G 194 Le45
Libya 167 Lb07
Libyan Desert LAR/ET 176 Mc31
Licancábur, Volcán RCH 284 Gg57
Licata I 42 Lo53
Lice TR 63 Na26
Lich D 32 Lj40
Licheng CHN (JGS) 102 Qk29
Licheng CHN (SAX) 93 Qg27
Lichinga MOC 211 Mh52
Lichtenau D 32 Lj39
Lichtenburg ZA 217 Md59
Lichtenfels D 35 Lm40
Lichtenvoorde NL 32 Lg39
Lichuan CHN (HUB) 95 Qe30
Lichuan CHN (JGX) 102 Qj32
Liciro MOC 211 Mj54
Licking USA (MO) 243 Fe27
Lički Osik HR 41 Lq46
Ličko Lešće HR 41 Lq46
Lida BY 17 Mf37
Liden S 13 Lr28
Lidfontein NAM 212 Lk58
Lidhult S 15 Lo34
Lidia PE 279 Ge51
Lidingö S 13 Lt31
Lidjombo RCA 195 Lj44
Lidköping S 13 Lo32
Lido RN 185 Lb39
Lido di Jésolo I 41 Ln45
Lido di Metaponto I 43 Lr50
Lidoriki GR 48 Mc52
Lidzbark PL 37 Lu37
Lidzbark Warmiński PL 37 Ma36
Liebenburg D 33 Ll38
Liebenthal CDN (SK) 233 Ef20
Liebenwalde D 33 Lo38
Lieberose D 33 Lp38
Liebig, Mount AUS 142 Rf57
Liechtenstein FL 34 Lk43
Liechtensteinklamm A 35 Lo43
Liège B 23 Lf40
Lieksa FIN 11 Mf14
Lielauce LV 17 Mc34
Lielstraupe LV 17 Me33
Lielupe LV 17 Md34
Lielvārde LV 17 Me34
Liemianzhen CHN (SCH) 95 Qc30
Lienz A 35 Ln44
Liepāja LV 17 Mb34
Liepene LV 17 Mb33
Liepna LV 17 Mh33
Lier B 23 Le39
Lierbyen N 12 Ll31
Liesjärven kansallispuisto FIN 16 Md30
Liestal CH 34 Lh43
Lietnik USA (AK) 228 Bf14
Lieto FIN 16 Mc30
Lievestuore FIN 16 Mg28
Liévin F 23 Lc40
Liezen A 35 Lp43
Lifamatola RI 130 Rd46
Liffol-le-Grand F 23 Lf42
Lifford IRL 18 Kn36
Lifou F 162 Td56
Lifuka Island TO 164 Bc55
Lifune ANG 202 Lh50
Lifupa MW 210 Mg52
Liganga EAT 211 Mh51
Ligao RP 121 Rb39
Ligar TCH 187 Lj41
Ligera EAT 211 Mh51
Lighthouse Prov. H.S. CDN 245 Hd21
Lightning Ridge AUS (NSW) 151 Sd60
Lignano Sabbiadoro I 41 Lo45
Lignières F 23 Lc44
Ligny-en-Barrois F 23 Lf42
Ligny-le-Châtel F 23 Ld43
Ligowola EAT 211 Mj51
Ligueil F 22 La43
Ligui MEX (BCS) 252 Ee33
Ligunga EAT 211 Mj51
Ligúria I 40 Lj46
Ligurian Sea I/F 40 Lj47
Lihangwa EAT 207 Mk50
Lihás GR 48 Mc52
Lihir Group PNG 160 Sg47
Lihir Island PNG 160 Sg47
Lihoslavl' RUS 52 Mh17
Lihou Reefs and Cays AUS 149 Sg54
Lihovskoj RUS 55 Na21
Lihue USA (HI) 230 Ca35
Lihuél Calel, P.N. RA 292 Gh64
Lihula EST 16 Md32
Liinahamari RUS 11 Mf11
Lijiang CHN (YUN) 113 Qa32
Lijiang CHN 96 Qf33
Lijiang CHN 96 Qf33
Lijiang River cruises CHN 96 Qf33
Likala RDC 200 Lk45
Likame RDC 200 Ma44
Likasi RDC 210 Md51
Likati RDC 200 Mb44
Likati RDC 201 Mb44
Likely CDN (BC) 232 Dk19
Likely USA (CA) 234 Dk25
Likenäs S 13 Lo30
Likete RDC 200 Ma46
Likhmisar IND (RJT) 106 Og32
Liki RI 124 Qa46
Likiep Atoll MH 157 Tb16
Likisia TLS 132 Rc50
Liknes N 12 Lg32
Likódimo GR 48 Mb54
Likoma Island MW 211 Mh51
Likoto RDC 201 Mc46
Likouala RCB 195 Lh45
Likouala aux Herbes RCB 195 Lj45
Likovskoe RUS 16 Mj31
Liku RI 126 Qe45
Likum PNG 159 Sd47
Likupang RI 127 Rc45
Likuyu EAT 211 Mj51
Lilarea AUS (QLD) 149 Sc57
l'Île de Zembra, P.N. TN 174 Lf27
Lilienfeld A 35 Lq42
Lilienthal D 32 Lj37
Liling CHN (HUN) 97 Qg32
Liljendal FIN 16 Mg30
Lilla Creek AUS (NT) 142 Rh58
Lilla Edet S 14 Ln32
Lillärdal S 13 Lp29
Lille F 23 Ld40
Lillebonne F 22 La41
Lillehammer N 12 Ll29
Lillers F 23 Lc40
Lillesand N 12 Lj32
Lillestrøm N 12 Lm31
Lilli EST 16 Mf33
Lillie Marleen ANT (D) 297 Tc33
Lillo E 29 Kr49
Lillooet CDN (BC) 232 Dk20
Lillooet River CDN 232 Dj20
Lilo RDC 201 Mc46
Lilong IND (MNP) 112 Ph33
Lilongwe MW 210 Mg52
Liloy RP 123 Rb41
Lilydale AUS (SA) 152 Rk62
Lim RCA 195 Lh42
Lim SCG 46 Lu47
Lima PE 278 Gb52
Lima PY 285 Hb57
Lima S 13 Lo30
Lima USA (OH) 246 Fh25
Limache RA (CD) 289 Gj60
Lima Duarte BR (MG) 287 Hj56
Limah OM 75 Nj33
Liman RUS 70 Nd23
Limanáki GR 48 Mb52
Liman, Gunung RI 128 Qf49
Limanowa PL 39 Ma41
Limão do Curuá BR (AP) 275 He45
Limar RI 132 Rd49
Limas RI 125 Qc45
Limasawa Island RP 123 Rc41
Limassa RCA 200 Mb43
Limassol CY 51 Mo56
Limatambo PE 279 Gd52
Limavady GB 18 Ko35
Limay RA 292 Gf65
Limay RP 120 Ra38
Limay Mahuida RA (LP) 292 Gg64
Limba EAT 206 Mg49
Limbani PE 279 Gf53
Limbasa RDC 200 Mb43
Limbaži LV 17 Me33
Limbda IND (GUJ) 108 Of35
Limbdi IND (GUJ) 108 Of34
Limbé CAM 194 Le43
Limbe MW 211 Mh53
Limbé RH 260 Gd36
Limboto RI 127 Rb45
Limbuak MAL 122 Qj42
Limbung RI 127 Qk47
Limbunya AUS (NT) 139 Re54
Limburg D 32 Lj40
Lime Acres ZA 216 Mb60
Limeira BR (SP) 286 Hg57
Liménas Géraka GR 48 Md54
Liménas Hersonissou GR 49 Mf55
Limerick CDN (SK) 233 Eg21
Limerick IRL 20 Km38
Limes D 34 Lj40
Limestone Cliffs (Middle Caicos) GB 251 Ge35
Limestone Lake CDN 238 Fc17
Limestone Plateau ET 177 Mf33
Limestone Pt. CDN 238 Fa19
Limestone Rapids CDN 239 Ff18
Limestone River CDN 238 Fc17
Limfjorden DK 14 Lk34
Liminangcong RP 122 Qk40
Limingen N 10 Lg13
Limmared S 15 Lo33
Limmen Bay AUS 139 Rh53
Limmen Bight River AUS 139 Rh53
Limnes GR 48 Mc53
Límni GR 48 Md52
Limni Aliákmona GR 46 Mc50
Limni Ilíki GR 48 Md52
Limni Kastoriás GR 46 Mb50
Limni Kerkinis GR 46 Md49
Limni Korónia GR 46 Md50
Limni Mikri Préspa GR 46 Mb50
Limni Trihonida GR 48 Mb52
Limni Vegoritida GR 46 Mb50
Limni Vólvi GR 46 Md50
Limni Vouliagménis GR 48 Mc52
Limnos GR 47 Mf51
Limoeiro BR (PE) 283 Jc49
Limoeiro do Ajurú BR (PA) 276 Hf46
Limoeiro do Norte BR (CE) 277 Ja48
Limoges F 24 Lb45
Limón EC 272 Ga47
Limon USA (CO) 240 Ej26
Limone Piemonte I 40 Lh46
Limones EC 272 Ga45
Limones PA 256 Fj41
Limousin F 24 Lb45
Limousin F 24 Lb45
Limoux F 24 Lc47
Limpio PY 285 Hb58
Limpopo ZA 214 Me57
Limpopo ZA/ZW 214 Mf57
Limski kanal HR 41 Lo45
Limulunga Z 209 Mb53
Limuru EAK 204 Mj46
Lin AL 46 Ma49
Linah KSA 65 Nb31
Linao Bay RP 123 Rb42
Linapacan Island RP 122 Qk40
Linapacan Strait RP 122 Qk40
Linares E 29 Kr48
Linares MEX (NL) 253 Fa33
Linares RCH 292 Ge63
Linariá GR 48 Me52
Linbana S 10 Lk13
Lincang CHN (YUN) 113 Qa34
Lincan Ray RCH 292 Gd65
Linchang CHN (SAA) 95 Qe29
Linchuan CHN (JGX) 102 Qj32
Lincoln GB 21 Ku37
Lincoln RA (BA) 289 Gk63
Lincoln USA (CA) 234 Dk26
Lincoln USA (IL) 246 Ff25
Lincoln USA (ME) 244 Gf23
Lincoln USA (NE) 241 Fb25
Lincoln Birthplace N.H.S. USA 248 Fh27
Lincoln Caverns USA 247 Ga25
Lincoln City USA (OR) 234 Dj23
Lincoln Highway AUS 152 Rj62
Lincoln Island RP 120 Qg37
Lincoln Log Cabin S.H.S. USA 241 Ff26
Lincoln N.P. AUS 152 Rj63
Lincoln Sea CDN/DK 225 Ha02
Lincolnshire Wolds GB 21 Ku37
Lincoln's New Salem S.H.S. USA 241 Ff26
Lincoln's New Salem S.H.S. USA 246 Ff26
Lincoln Tomb S.H.S. USA 241 Ff26
Lincoln Tomb S.H.S USA 246 Ff26
Lincolnton USA (NC) 249 Fk28
Lind DK 14 Lj34
Lind USA (WA) 232 Ea22
Lindås N 12 Lf30
Lindau D 34 Lk43
Linde LV 17 Me34
Linde RUS 59 Ra05
Lindela MOC 214 Mh58
Lindelse DK 14 Ll36
Lindeman Group AUS 149 Se56
Lindeman Islands N.P. AUS 149 Se56
Linden CDN (AB) 233 Ed20
Linden D 32 Lj40
Linden GUY 270 Ha42
Linden USA (AL) 248 Fg29
Linden USA (TN) 248 Fg28
Linden USA (TX) 243 Fc29
Linderödsåsen S 15 Lo35
Lindesberg S 13 Lq31
Lindesnes N 12 Lh33
Lindesnes N 12 Lh33
Lindholm Høje DK 14 Lk33
Lindi EAT 207 Mk50
Lindi RDC 201 Md45
Lindian CHN (HLG) 98 Rc22
Lindi Bay EAT 207 Mk50
Lindis Valley NZ 155 Te68
Lindley ZA 217 Md59
Lindleyspoort ZA 213 Md58
Lindome S 14 Ln33
Lindos GR 49 Mj54
Lindoso P 26 Km51
Lindow D 33 Lo38
Lindsay CDN (ON) 247 Ga23
Lindsay USA (CA) 236 Ea27
Lindsay USA (MT) 235 Eh22
Lindsay USA (OK) 242 Fb28
Lindsborg USA (KS) 240 Fb26
Lindsdal S 15 Lr34
Linduri VU 162 Td53
Lineas de Nazca PE 278 Gc53
Line Islands 303 Bb09
Linevo RUS 53 Nc20
Linfen CHN (SAX) 93 Qf27
Lingadaw MYA 112 Ph35
Lingal IND (APH) 109 Ok37
Lingala IND (APH) 111 Ok39
Linga Linga MOC 214 Mh57
Linganamakki Reservoir IND 110 Oh39
Lingaraja Temple IND 109 Pc35
Lingayen RP 120 Ra38
Lingbao CHN (HNN) 95 Qf28
Lingbi CHN (AHU) 102 Qj29
Lingbim CAM 195 Lh43
Lingbo S 13 Lr29
Linge N 12 Lh28
Lingen D 32 Lh38
Lingga RI 125 Qc46
Lingga Karo Batak Village RI 116 Pk44
Linggi MAL 117 Qb44
Linghai CHN (LNG) 100 Ra25
Linghem S 13 Lq32
Lingig RP 123 Rd41
Lingi Point AUS 139 Rf51
Lingle USA (WY) 235 Eh24
Lingomo RDC 200 Mb45
Lingomo RDC 200 Mb46
Lingqi Dong CHN 102 Qk31
Lingqiu CHN (SAX) 93 Qh26
Lingshan CHN (GZG) 96 Qe34
Lingshan Dao CHN 100 Ra28
Lingshan Han Tombs CHN 93 Qh26
Lingshi CHN (SAX) 93 Qf27
Lingshui CHN (HAN) 96 Qf36
Ling Shui CHN 96 Qe34
Lingsugur IND (KTK) 108 Oj37
Lingtai CHN (GSU) 95 Qd28
Lingtou CHN (HAN) 96 Qe36
Linguaglossa I 42 Lq53
Linguère SN 183 Kc38
Lingwu CHN (NHZ) 92 Qd26
Ling Xian CHN (HUN) 97 Qg32
Lingyan Si CHN 93 Qj27
Lingyin Si CHN 102 Qk30
Lingyuan CHN (LNG) 93 Qk25
Lingyun CHN (GZG) 96 Qd33
Linhai CHN (HLG) 98 Rc20
Linhai CHN (ZJG) 102 Ra31
Linhares BR (ES) 287 Hk55
Linhe CHN (NMZ) 92 Qd25
Linhemo ANG 208 Lj52
Linia PL 36 Ls36
Linjiang CHN (JLN) 100 Rd25
Lin Jiang CHN 102 Ra31
Linji Temple CHN 93 Qh27
Linköping S 13 Lq32
Linkou CHN (HLG) 98 Rf23
Linkuva LT 17 Md34
Linli CHN (HUN) 95 Qf31
Linlithgow GB 19 Kr35
Linn USA (TX) 253 Fa32
Linna FIN 16 Mc30
Linnansaaren kansallispuisto FIN 16 Mj28
Linneus USA (MO) 241 Fd26
Linnoitus FIN 16 Mj30
Linping CHN (ZJG) 102 Ra30
Linqing CHN (SDG) 93 Qh27
Linqu CHN (SDG) 93 Qk27
Linquan CHN (AHU) 102 Qh29
Lins BR (SP) 286 Hf56
Linsan RG 192 Kd40
Linsell S 13 Lo28
Linshu CHN (SDG) 102 Qk28
Linshui CHN (SCH) 95 Qd30
Linshuize CHN (YUN) 96 Qc33
Linstead JA 259 Gb36
Linta RM 220 Nc58
Lintan CHN (GSU) 94 Qb28
Lintao CHN (GSU) 94 Qb28
Linté CAM 195 Lf43
Linton USA (IN) 248 Fg26
Linton USA (ND) 240 Ek22
Lintong CHN (SAA) 95 Qe28
Linxi CHN (HBI) 93 Qk26
Linxi CHN (NMZ) 93 Qk24
Linxia CHN (GSU) 94 Qb28
Lin Xian CHN (HNN) 93 Qg27
Lin Xian CHN (SAX) 93 Qf27
Linxiang CHN (HUN) 95 Qg31
Linyanti RB 213 Mc55
Linyanti Camp RB 213 Mb55
Linyanti Swamp NAM/RB 209 Mb55
Linyi CHN (SDG) 93 Qj27
Linyi CHN (SDG) 102 Qk28
Linying CHN (HNN) 95 Qg29
Linz A 35 Lp42
Linz D 32 Lh40
Linze CHN (GSU) 92 Qa26
Linzhen CHN (SAA) 93 Qe27
Linzolo RCB 202 Lh48
Linzor RCH 284 Gf57
Lioma MOC 211 Mj53
Lioni CO 269 Gf43
Lions Den ZW 210 Mf54
Lioppa RI 132 Rd49
Lioto RCA 200 Ma43
Lioua TCH 187 Lh39
Liouesso RCB 195 Lh45
Lipa RP 121 Ra39
Lipany SK 39 Ma41
Liparamba EAT 211 Mh51
Lipari I 42 Lp52
Lipari Islands I 42 Lp52
Lipcani MD 45 Mg42
Lipeck RUS 53 Mk19
Liperi FIN 11 Me14
Lipiany PL 36 Lp37
Lipica SLO 41 Lo45
Lipicy-Zybino RUS 52 Mj19
Lipik HR 41 Ls45
Lipin Bor RUS 11 Mk15
Lipka PL 36 Ls37
Lipki RUS 53 Mj19
Lipljan SCG 46 Mb48
Lipniak PL 37 Md36
Lipnica PL 36 Ls36
Lipnica Murowana PL 39 Ma41
Lipnidki BY 17 Mf37
Lipník nad Bečvou CZ 38 Ls41
Lipno PL 37 Lu38
Lipoba Z 209 Mb53
Lipoche Olivença MOC 211 Mh51
Lipolist SCG 44 Lu46
Lipova RO 44 Mb44
Lipovcy RUS 98 Rf23
Lipoven'ke UA 45 Ml42
Lipovljani HR 41 Lr45
Lippe D 32 Lh39
Lippstadt D 32 Lj39
Lipsi GR 49 Mg53
Lipsk PL 37 Md37
Lipsko PL 37 Mb39
Lipson AUS (SA) 152 Rj63
Lipton CDN (SK) 238 Ej20
Liptougou BF 185 La39
Liptovský Hrádok SK 39 Lu41
Lipu CHN (GZG) 96 Qf33
Liqen i Butrintit AL 46 Ma51
Liqeni i Banjës AL 46 Ma50
Lique, Cerro BOL 284 Gh56
Liqueni i Fierzës AL 46 Ma48
Lira EAU 204 Mg44
Liranga RCB 200 Lj46
Lirangwe MW 211 Mh53
Lircay PE 278 Gc52
Liri I 42 Lo49
Lisa Gora UA 45 Mm42
Lisala RDC 200 Ma44
Lisboa P 28 Kl48
Lisbon P 28 Kl48
Lisbon USA (ND) 240 Fb22
Lisbon Falls ZA 214 Mf58
Lisburn GB 18 Ko36

Liscannor Bay IRL 20 Kl38
Liscomb Game Sanctuary CDN 245 Gj23
Lisdoonvarna IRL 20 Kl37
Liseberg S 14 Ln33
Lishan CHN (SCH) 95 Qd30
Lishan Z.B. CHN 95 Qf28
Lishi CHN (SAX) 93 Qf27
Lishizhen CHN (CGQ) 95 Qd31
Lishu CHN (JLN) 100 Rc24
Lishui CHN (JGS) 102 Qk30
Lishui CHN (ZJG) 102 Qk31
Li Shui CHN 95 Qf31
Lisieux F 22 La41
Lisitu EAT 207 Mh50
Liskeard GB 20 Kq40
Liski RUS 53 Mk20
L'Isle-Adam F 23 Lc41
L'Isle-en-Dodon F 24 La47
L'Isle-Jourdain F 24 La44
L'Isle-Jourdain F 24 Lb47
L'Isle-sur-la-Sorgue F 25 Lf47
L'Isle-sur-le-Doubs F 23 Lg43
Lismore AUS (NSW) 151 Sg60
Lismore AUS (QLD) 151 Sf59
Lismore AUS (VIC) 153 Sb64
Lismore GB 18 Kp34
Lismore IRL 20 Kn38
Lisnaskea GB 18 Kn36
Lišov CZ 38 Lp41
Lissadell AUS (WA) 138 Re54
Lissenung Island Resort PNG 160 Sf47
Lissington AUS (NSW) 151 Sd60
List D 32 Lj36
Listafjorden N 12 Lg32
Lister, Mount 297 Ta34
Listowel CDN (ON) 246 Fk24
Listowel IRL 20 Kl38
Listvjanka RUS 90 Qc20
Lita EC 272 Ga45
Litang CHN (GZG) 96 Qe34
Litang CHN (SCH) 94 Qa31
Litawa Flats Z 209 Mb53
Litchfield USA (MN) 241 Fc23
Litchfield Beach USA (SC) 249 Ga29
Litchfield N.P. AUS 139 Rf52
Liteni RO 45 Mg43
Lithgow AUS (NSW) 153 Sf62
Lithuania LT 17 Mc35
Lití GR 46 Mc50
Litija SLO 41 Lp44
Litipara IND (JKD) 112 Pd33
Litóhoro GR 46 Mc50
Litoměřice CZ 38 Lp40
Litomyšl CZ 38 Lr41
Litoral RO 45 Mj46
Litovel CZ 38 Ls41
Litovko' RUS 98 Rh21
Little Abitibi Lake CDN 239 Fk21
Little Abitibi River CDN 239 Fk20
Little Aden = ,Adan as Sughra YE 68 Nc39
Little Andaman IND 111 Pg40
Little Avalon AUS 153 Sf62
Little Barrier Island NZ 154 Th64
Little Bay CDN (NF) 245 Ha22
Little Belt DK 14 Lk35
Little Belt Mts. USA 235 Ee22
Little Bighorn Nat. Battlefield USA 235 Ef23
Little Cadotte River CDN 233 Eb17
Little Cayman GB 259 Fk36
Little Churchill River CDN 238 Fc17
Little Coco Island MYA 111 Pg39
Little Colorado USA 237 Ee28
Little Current CDN (ON) 246 Fk23
Little Current River CDN 239 Fh20
Little Desert AUS 152 Sa64
Little Desert N.P. AUS 152 Sa64
Little Exuma Island BS 251 Gc34
Little Falls USA (MN) 241 Fc23
Littlefield USA (TX) 237 Ej29
Little Fort CDN (BC) 232 Dk20
Little Gombi WAN 187 Lg40
Little Grand Rapids CDN (MB) 238 Fc19
Little Halibut Bank 19 Kt32
Little Harbour BS 251 Gb33
Little Inagua Island BS 251 Gd35
Little Lake USA (CA) 236 Eb28
Little Mecatina River CDN 245 Gk19
Little Missouri USA 240 Ej22
Little Missouri Grassland N.P. USA 240 Ej22
Little Nicobar Island IND 111 Pg42
Little Ragged Island BS 251 Gc34
Little River Canyon USA 249 Fh28
Little River N.W.R. USA 243 Fc28
Little Rock USA (AR) 243 Fd28
Little Ruaha EAT 207 Mh50
Little Sachigo Lake CDN 238 Fd18
Little Sahara R.A. USA 235 Ed26
Little Salmon Lake CDN 231 Dc14
Little Salt Lake USA 235 Ed27
Little Sandy Desert AUS 140 Ra58
Little San Salvador Is. BS 251 Gc33
Little Scarcies WAL 192 Kd41
Little Smoky River CDN 233 Eb18
Littleton USA (CO) 235 Eh26
Littleton USA (NH) 247 Ge23
Little White House S.H.S. USA 249 Fh29
Little Zab IRQ 65 Nb27
Lituhu EAT 211 Mh51
Litunde MOC 211 Mh52
Lituya Bay USA 231 Db16
Litvínov CZ 38 Lo40
Liuba CHN (SAA) 95 Qd29
Liuchiu Yü RC 97 Ra34
Liuhe CHN (JLN) 100 Rc24
Liuheng Dao CHN (ZJG) 102 Rb31
Liujiachang CHN (HUB) 95 Qf30
Liujiang CHN (GZG) 96 Qe33
Liu Jiang CHN 96 Qe34
Liujing CHN (GZG) 96 Qf34
Liujixia Shiku CHN 92 Qb28
Liuku CHN (YUN) 113 Pk33
Liuli EAT 211 Mh51
Liulin CHN (SAX) 93 Qf27
Liuliu SOL 160 Sj49
Liupan Shan CHN 95 Qc28
Liupanshan Z.B. CHN 95 Qd28
Liupanshui CHN (GZH) 96 Qc32
Liupo MOC 211 Mk53
Liurongsi Huata CHN 97 Qg34
Liushi CHN (ZJG) 102 Ra31
Liushilipu CHN (AHU) 102 Qh29
Liuwa Plain Z 209 Mb53
Liuwa Plain N.P. Z 209 Mb53
Liuxu CHN (GZG) 96 Qe34
Liuyang CHN (HUN) 95 Qg31
Liuzhai CHN (GZG) 96 Qd33
Liuzhou CHN (GZG) 96 Qe33
Liuzhuang CHN (JGS) 102 Ra29
Livada RO 44 Md43
Livaderó GR 46 Mb50
Livaderó GR 47 Me49
Livádi GR 49 Me53
Livadiá GR 48 Mc52
Livadia Palats UA 55 Mh23
Livadohóri GR 47 Mf51
Līvāni LV 17 Mg34
Livari SCG 46 Lu48
Livarot F 22 La42
Lively CDN (ON) 246 Fk22
Lively Island GB 295 Ha72
Livengood USA (AK) 229 Cf13
Live Oak USA (FL) 249 Fj30
Livera CY 51 Mn55
Liverpool AUS (NSW) 153 Sf62
Liverpool CDN (NS) 245 Gh23
Liverpool GB 21 Ks37
Liverpool Bay GB 21 Kr37
Liverpool Range AUS 151 Sf61
Livezi RO 45 Mg44
Liv Glacier 296 Bc35
Livigno I 40 Ll44
Livikó Pélagos GR 49 Md55
Livingston CDN 225 Gc08
Livingston GB 19 Kr35
Livingston GCA 255 Ff38
Livingston USA (MT) 235 Ee23
Livingston USA (TN) 248 Fh27
Livingston USA (TX) 243 Fc30
Livingstone Z 209 Mc54
Livingstone Church ZA 216 Mb60
Livingstonegrot RB 213 Mc58
Livingstonekerk ZA 216 Mb60
Livingstone Memorial Z 210 Mf52
Livingstone Mountains EAT 207 Mh50
Livingstone's Cave RB 213 Mc58
Livingstonia MW 210 Mh51
Livingston Island 296 Gd31
Livizile RO 44 Md44
Livno BIH 41 Lr47
Livny RUS 53 Mj19
Livonia USA (MI) 246 Fj24
Livorno I 40 Ll47
Livramento do Brumado BR (BA) 283 Hk52
Livron-sur-Drôme F 25 Le46
Liw PL 37 Mb38
Liwa OM 75 Nj33
Liwa RI 125 Qc48
Liwale EAT 207 Mj50
Liwa Oasis UAE 74 Ng34
Imperial Tombs of the Ming and Qing Dynasties (Nanjing) CHN (JGS) 102 Qk29
Li Wenzhong, Tomb of = Imperial Tombs of the Ming and Qing Dynasties CHN (JGS) 102 Qk29
Liwiec PL 37 Mb38
Liwonde MW 211 Mh53
Liwonde N.P. MW 211 Mh53
Li Xian CHN (GSU) 95 Qc28
Li Xian CHN (HUN) 95 Qf31
Li Xian CHN (SCH) 94 Qb30
Lixin CHN (AHU) 102 Qj29
Lixoúri GR 48 Ma52
Lixus MA 172 Kg28
Liyang CHN (JGS) 102 Qk30
Li Yubu SUD 201 Md43
Lizarda BR (TO) 282 Hg50
Lizard Island AUS 147 Sc53
Lizard Point GB 20 Kp41
Līzespasts LV 17 Mg33
Lizotte CDN (QC) 244 Gd21
Lizums LV 17 Mg33
Ljachavičy BY 37 Mg37
Ljady RUS 52 Me16
Ljamca RUS 11 Mj13
Ljangar TJ 77 Og27
Ljaplëvka BY 37 Md39
Ljig SCG 46 Ma46
Ljørndalen N 13 Ln29
Ljuban' BY 52 Me19
Ljuban' RUS 52 Mf16
Ljubar UA 54 Md21
Ljubašivka UA 45 Ml43
Ljubča BY 17 Mg37
Ljubešiv UA 37 Mf39
Ljubija BIH 41 Lr46
Ljubim RUS 53 Na16
Ljubinje BIH 41 Lt48
Ljubiš SCG 46 Lu47
Ljubljana SLO 41 Lp44
Ljuboml' UA 37 Me39
Ljubovija SCG 46 Lu46
Ljubuški BIH 41 Ls47
Ljubymivka UA 55 Mj22
Ljubytino RUS 52 Mg16
Ljudinovo RUS 52 Mh19
Ljugarn S 15 Lt33
Ljukkum KZ 84 Oj22
Ljung S 15 Lo33
Ljunga S 13 Lr32
Ljungan S 13 Lr28
Ljungaverk S 13 Lq28
Ljungby S 15 Lp34
Ljungbyhed S 15 Lo34
Ljungbyholm S 15 Lr34
Ljungdalen S 13 Ln28
Ljunghusen S 15 Ln35
Ljungsbro S 13 Lq32
Ljungskile S 12 Lm32
Ljusdal S 13 Lr29
Ljusfallshammar S 13 Lq32
Ljusnan S 13 Lq29
Ljusterö S 13 Lt31
Ljustorp S 13 Ls28
Ljutomer SLO 41 Lr44
Lkhachinvandad Uul Nature Reserve MNG 91 Qh23
Llagostera E 30 Lc49
Llaima, Volcán RCH 292 Ge65
Llallagua BOL 284 Gg55
Llalli PE 279 Ge53
Llamellin PE 278 Gb50
Llampos RCH 288 Ge59
Llanberis GB 20 Kq37
Llandeilo GB 20 Kr39
Llandovery GB 20 Kr39
Llandrindod-Wells GB 21 Kr38
Llandudno GB 21 Kr37
Llanelli GB 20 Kq39
Llanes E 26 Kq53
Llanganates, P.N. EC 272 Ga46
Llangollen GB 21 Kr38
Llangurig GB 20 Kr38
Llanidloes GB 20 Kr38
Llano USA (TX) 242 Fa30
Llano USA 242 Fa30
Llanobajo CO 268 Gb44
Llano de Magdalena MEX 252 Ee33
Llano Estacado USA 237 Ej29
Llano Mariato PA 257 Fk42
Llanos de Challe, P.N. RCH 288 Ge60
Llanos de Chiquitos BOL 285 Gk55
Llanos de Guarayos BOL 280 Gj53
Llanos de la Rioja RA 288 Gg60
Llanos del Carmen MEX (SLP) 253 Ek34
Llanos del Orinoco CO/YV 269 Ge42
Llanos de Mojos BOL 279 Gh53
Llanquihue RCH 292 Gd66
Llanrheidol AUS (QLD) 148 Sa57
Llanrwst GB 21 Kr37
Llanwddyn GB 21 Kr38
Llanwrtyd Wells GB 20 Kr38
Llao Llao RA (RN) 292 Ge66
Llata PE 278 Gb50
Llaylla PE 278 Gc51
Llay-Llay RCH 288 Ge62
Lleida E 30 La49
Llera de Canales MEX (TM) 253 Fa34
Llerena E 28 Ko48
Lleyn GB 20 Kq38
Llica BOL 284 Gf55
Llico RCH 288 Gd63
Llifén RCH 292 Gd66
Llíria E 29 Ku49
Lliscaya, Cerro BOL/RCH 284 Gf55
Llivynci UA 45 Mg42
L'Ile-Rousse F 31 Lj48
Llorente RP 123 Rc40
Lloret de Mar E 30 Lc49
Lloyd Bay AUS 147 Sb52
Lloyd Lake CDN 233 Ef17
Lloydminster CDN (SK) 233 Ef19
Lloyd Rock BS 251 Gc35
Lloyds Camp RB 213 Mc55
Llucena E 29 Ku50
Llucmajor E 30 Lc51
Llullaillaco, P.N. RCH 284 Gf58
Llullaillaco, Volcán RCH/RA 284 Gf58
Lluta PE 284 Gd54
Lnáře CZ 38 Lo41
Loa RCH 284 Gf56
Loa USA (UT) 235 Ee26
Loaita Bank 122 Qh40
Loaita Island 122 Qh40
Loajanan RI 127 Qj46
Loakulu RI 127 Qj46
Loanda ANG 203 Lj50
Loanda G 202 Le46
Loandji RDC 203 Lk48
Loange RDC 203 Ma48
Loango RCB 202 Lf48
Loango RDC 202 Lg48
Loango, P.N. de G 202 Le47
Loanja Z 209 Mc54
Loano I 40 Lj46
Loay RP 123 Rc41
Lobatos MEX (ZCT) 253 Ej34
Lobatse RB 213 Mc58
Löbau D 33 Lp39
Lobay RCA 195 Lj43
Lobaye RCA 195 Lk44
Lobaye RDC 201 Mc45
Lobcovo RUS 53 Na17
Lobeke CAM 195 Lh44
Lobenstein D 33 Lm40
Lobería RA (BA) 293 Ha65
Löberöd S 15 Lo35
Łobez PL 36 Lq37
Lobi MW 210 Mh53
Lobira SUD 197 Mg43
Lobito ANG 208 Lg52
Lobitos PE 272 Fk48
Lobo CAM 195 Lg44
Lobo RI 131 Rh47
Lobo RP 121 Ra39
Lobo USA (TX) 237 Eh30
Loboko RCB 200 Lj46
Lobonäs S 13 Lq29
Lobos MEX 252 Eg33
Lobos RA (BA) 289 Ha63
Lobougoula RMM 193 Kh40
Loburg D 33 Ln38
Łobżenica PL 36 Ls37
Locarno CH 34 Lj44
Locas de Cahuinarí CO 273 Ge46
Lochaline GB 18 Kp34
Loch Awe GB 19 Kp34
Lochboisdale GB 18 Kn33
Loch Broom GB 19 Kp33
Loché MEX (YT) 255 Ff35
Loch Earn GB 19 Kq34
Lochearnhead GB 19 Kq34
Lochem NL 32 Lg38
Loch Ericht GB 19 Kq34
Loches F 22 Lb43
Loch Fyne GB 18 Kp35
Lochgilphead GB 18 Kp34
Lochiel ZA 217 Mf59
Lochinvar N.P. Z 210 Md53
Lochinver GB 19 Kp32
Loch Katrine GB 19 Kq34
Loch Ken GB 19 Kq35
Loch Lilly AUS (NSW) 152 Sa62
Loch Linnhe GB 19 Kp34
Loch Lochy GB 19 Kq34
Loch Lomond GB 19 Kq34
Loch Lomond and The Trossachs N.P. GB 19 Kq34
Loch Loyal GB 19 Kq32
Lochmaddy GB 18 Kn33
Loch Maree GB 19 Kp33
Loch Naver GB 19 Kq32
Loch Ness GB 19 Kq33
Łochów PL 37 Mb38
Loch Rannoch GB 19 Kq34
Lochranza GB 18 Kp35
Loch Roag GB 18 Ko32
Lochsa USA 235 Ec22
Loch Shin GB 19 Kq32
Loch Sport AUS (VIC) 153 Sd65
Loch Tay GB 19 Kq34
Lochvycja UA 52 Mg20
Lociel AUS (SA) 152 Rk62
Lock AUS (SA) 152 Rh62
Lockeport CDN (NS) 245 Gh24
Lockerbie GB 19 Kr35
Lockesburg USA (AR) 243 Fc29
Lockhart AUS (NSW) 153 Sd63
Lockhart USA (TX) 242 Fb31
Lockhart River AUS (QLD) 146 Sb52
Lockhart River A.L. AUS 146 Sb52
Lock Haven USA (PA) 247 Gb25
Lockichokio EAK 197 Mh43
Löcknitz D 33 Lp37
Lockwood USA (CA) 236 Dk28
Lockwood Hills USA 229 Cc12
Locminé F 22 Ks43
Loc Ninh VN 115 Qd40
Locri I 43 Lr52
Locri Epizefiri I 43 Lr52
Locronan F 22 Kq42
Loctudy F 22 Kq43
Locust CRiver USA 241 Fd26
Lod IL 64 Mh30
Lodein SUD 197 Mg42
Lodejenoe Pole RUS 11 Mg15
Löderup S 15 Lp35
Lodève F 25 Ld47
Lodge Corner USA (AR) 243 Fe28
Lodge Creek CDN 233 Ee21
Lodge Grass USA (MT) 235 Eg23
Lodhran PK 81 Of31
Lodi I 40 Lk45
Lodi RDC 203 Ma48
Lodi USA (CA) 234 Dk26
Løding N 10 Lh12
Lødingen N 10 Lj11
Lodja RDC 203 Mb47
Lodosa E 27 Ks52
Lödöse S 14 Ln32
Lodoyo RI 128 Qg50
Lodrani IND (GUJ) 108 Of34
Lodungokwe EAK 204 Mj45
Lodwar EAK 204 Mh44
Łódź PL 37 Lu39
Loei THA 114 Qa37
Loeka RDC 200 Mb44
Loémé RCB 202 Lg48
Loeng Nok Tha THA 115 Qc37
Loeriesfontein ZA 216 Lk61
Løfallstrand N 12 Lg30
Lofé SN 183 Kc38
Lofer A 35 Ln43
Loffa LB 192 Ke42
Lofoten N 10 Lg12
Lofoten Basin 6 La03
Lofsdalen S 13 Lo28
Loftahammar S 15 Lr33
Lofthus N 12 Lg30
Lofty Range AUS 140 Qk58
Lofty Ranges, Mount AUS 152 Rk63
Log RUS 53 Nb21
Loga RN 185 Lb39
Loga SUD 201 Mf43
Logan USA (IA) 241 Fc25
Logan USA (NM) 237 Ej28
Logan USA (OH) 246 Fj26
Logan USA (UT) 235 Ee25
Logan USA (WV) 249 Fk27
Logan Cave N.W.R. USA 243 Fc27
Logan Glacier CDN 231 Ck15
Logan, Mount CDN 231 Ck15
Logan Mountains CDN 231 Df15
Logan Pass USA 233 Ec21
Logansport USA (IN) 246 Fg25
Logatec SLO 41 Lp45
Loge ANG 202 Lh49
Logeloge EAT 207 Mk49
Logobou BF 193 La40
Logoforok SUD 204 Mg44
Logone CAM/TCH 187 Lh40
Logone Birni CAM 187 Lh40
Logone Gana TCH 187 Lh40
Logone Occidental TCH 195 Lh41
Logone Oriental TCH 195 Lj41
Lógos GR 48 Mc52
Logozohe DY 194 Lb42
Logroño E 27 Ks52
Logrosán E 28 Kp49
Løgstør DK 14 Lk34
Logtak Lake IND 112 Pg33
Løgumkloster DK 14 Lj35
Lohaghat IND (UTT) 107 Pa31
Lohals DK 14 Ll35
Lohara IND (CGH) 109 Pa35
Lohardaga IND (JKD) 109 Pc34
Lohatanjona Angadoka RM 218 Nd52
Lohatanjona Antsirakakambana RM 220 Nf54
Lohatanjona Fenambosy RM 220 Nc58
Lohatanjona Maromony RM 218 Nd53
Lohatanjona Vohibato RM 220 Ne54
Lohawat IND (RJT) 106 Og32
Lohikoski FIN 16 Mj29
Lohit IND 113 Ph32
Lohja FIN 16 Me30
Lohmar D 32 Lh40
Lohne D 32 Lj38
Lohr D 34 Lk40
Loi PNG 159 Sd47
Loibltunnel A/SLO 35 Lp44
Loiborsoit EAT 207 Mj48
Loi, Gunung RI 126 Qg45
Loi-kaw MYA 114 Pj36
Loikisale EAT 207 Mj47
Loi-lawm MYA 113 Pj34
Loile RDC 200 Ma46
Loimaa FIN 16 Md30
Loima Hills EAK 204 Mh44
Loimijoki FIN 16 Mc29
Loir F 22 Ku43
Loire F 22 Ku43
Loire F 22 Lb43
Loiro Poco BR (AM) 273 Gf45
Loi Sang MYA 113 Pj35
Loi Song MYA 113 Pj34
Loita Plains EAK 204 Mh46
Loi Tawngkyaw MYA 113 Pj34
Loitz D 33 Lo37
Loiyangalani EAK 204 Mj44
Loja E 28 Kq47
Loja EC 272 Ga47
Lojanice SCG 44 Lu46
Lojmola RUS (KAR) 11 Mf15
Lojsthajd S 15 Lt33
Lokači UA 37 Me40
Lokalema RDC 200 Mb45
Lokandu RDC 206 Mc47
Lokan tekojärvi FIN 11 Md12
Lokapur IND (KTK) 108 Oh37
Lokata RI 130 Rf46
Lökbetan AZ 70 Ne25
Løken N 12 Lm31
Lokeren B 23 Ld39
Loket CZ 38 Ln40
Lokgwabe RB 213 Ma58
Lokichar EAK 204 Mh44
Lokichar EAK 204 Mh44
Lokichar EAU 204 Mh44
Lokitanyaly EAK 204 Mh44
Lo Kitaung EAK 197 Mh43
Loknja RUS 52 Mf17
Loko WAN 194 Ld41
Lokofe RDC 201 Mb46
Lokoja WAN 194 Ld42
Lokolama RDC 203 Lk47
Lokolia RDC 200 Ma46
Lokolo RDC 200 Lk46
Lokomby RM 220 Nd57
Lokomo CAM 195 Lh44
Lokomo CAM 195 Lh44
Lokon RI 127 Rc45
Lokono PNG 160 Sf47
Lokori EAK 204 Mj45
Lokoro RDC 200 Lk46
Lőkösháza H 39 Mb44
Lokossa DY 193 La42
Lokot' RUS 52 Mh19
Lokoti CAM 195 Lh42
Loksa EST 16 Mf31
Loksado RI 126 Qh47
Lokutu RDC 201 Mb45
Lol SUD 196 Md41
Lol SUD 197 Me42
Lola ANG 208 Lg53
Lola RG 192 Kf42
Lolela USA (CA) 234 Dh25
Lolengi RDC 200 Ma45
Lolgorien EAK 204 Mh46
Loliondo EAT 207 Mh47
Lolland DK 14 Lm36
Lollar D 32 Lj40
Lolo G 202 Lg46
Lolo USA (MT) 235 Ec22
Loloata Resort PNG 159 Sd50
Lolobau Island PNG 160 Sf48
Lolodorf CAM 195 Lf44
Lolo Hot Springs USA (MT) 235 Ec22
Lolokadan IR 75 Oa31
Lolui Island EAU 204 Mg46
Lolwane ZA 216 Mb59
Lolworth AUS (QLD) 149 Sc56
Lom BG 46 Md47
Lom BG 46 Md47
Lom CAM 195 Lh43
Lom N 12 Lj29
Loma ETH 198 Mj42
Loma USA (MT) 233 Ee22
Loma Alta USA (TX) 242 Ek31
Loma Bonita MEX (VC) 254 Fc36
Loma de Cabrera DOM 260 Ge36
Lomako RDC 200 Ma45
Lomaloma FJI 163 Ua54
Lomami RDC 200 Mb46
Lomami RDC 201 Mc45
Loma Mountains Forest Reserve WAL 192 Ke41
Lomas PE 278 Gc53
Lomas Coloradas RA 292 Gg67
Lomas de Arena BOL 285 Gj54
Lomas de Arena MEX (CHH) 237 Eh30
Lomas del Real MEX (TM) 253 Fb34
Lomas de Zamora RA (BA) 289 Ha63
Lomaum ANG 208 Lh52
Lomba ANG 209 Ma53
Lombadina AUS (WA) 138 Rb54
Lombadina Point AUS 138 Rb54
Lombardía MEX (MHC) 254 Ej36
Lombardy I 40 Lk45
Lombe ANG 202 Lj50
Lombe RI 127 Rb48
Lombez F 24 La47
Lomblen RI 132 Rb50
Lombok RI 129 Qj50
Lombol SN 183 Kb38
Lombolo RCB 202 Lh48
Lomci BG 47 Mg47
Lomé TG 193 La42
Lomela RDC 200 Ma46
Lomela RDC 203 Mb47
Lomen N 12 Lj29
Lomen stavkirke N 12 Lj29
Łomianki PL 37 Ma38
Lomié CAM 195 Lg44
Loming SUD 197 Mg43
Lomma S 15 Lo35
Lommel B 23 Lf39
Lom nad Rimavicou SK 39 Lu42
Lomond CDN (AB) 233 Ed20
Lomonosov RUS 52 Me16
Lomonosov Ridge 298 Hb01
Lomo Plata PY 285 Ha57
Lomphat K 115 Qd39
Lomphat W.S. K 115 Qd39
Lompobatang, Gunung RI 129 Ra48
Lompoc USA (CA) 236 Dk28
Lom Sak THA 114 Qa37
Łomża PL 37 Mc37
Lonand IND (MHT) 108 Oh36
Lonar IND (MHT) 108 Oj36
Lonavala IND (MHT) 108 Og36
Lonavala Hill Resort IND 108 Og36
Lončakovo RUS 98 Rh22
Loncoche RCH 292 Gd65
Loncopue RA (NE) 292 Ge65
Londa IND (KTK) 108 Oh38
Londa Tana-Toraja RI 127 Qk47
Londela-Kayes RCB 202 Lg48
Londengo ANG 208 Lg52
Londiani EAK 204 Mh46
Londolovit PNG 160 Sg47
London CDN (ON) 246 Fk24
London GB 21 Ku39
London USA (KY) 249 Fh27
Londonderry GB 18 Kn36
London Reefs 122 Qg41
Londres RA (CA) 288 Gg59
Londrina BR (PR) 286 He57
Lone Butte CDN (BC) 232 Dk20
Lone Pine USA (CA) 236 Ea27
Lone Pine Ind. Res. USA 236 Eb27
Lone Star Park USA (TX) 243 Fb29
Lone ton MYA 113 Pj33
Lone Tree RB 213 Mb57
Lone Tree Borehole RB 213 Mb57
Lonevåg N 12 Lf30
Long THA 114 Pk36
Longa ANG 202 Lh51
Longa ANG 209 Lk54
Longa ANG 209 Lk53
Longá BR 277 Hj47
Longadambau RI 126 Qh45
Long'an CHN (GZG) 96 Qd34
Long'an CHN (SAA) 93 Qe27
Longana VU 162 Td53
Long'anqiao CHN (HLG) 98 Rc22
Longarone I 40 Ln44
Longaví RCH 292 Ge64
Longavi, Nevado de RCH 292 Ge64
Longbawan RI 126 Qh44
Long Bay Beach GB 261 Gh36
Long Bay Beach JA 259 Gb36
Long Beach USA (CA) 236 Ea29
Long Beach USA (MS) 243 Ff30
Long Beach USA (NC) 249 Ga29
Long Beach USA (NJ) 247 Gc26
Long Beach USA (NY) 247 Gd25
Long Beach Pen. USA 232 Dh22
Long Branch USA (NJ) 247 Gc25
Long Branch S.P. USA 241 Fd26
Long Cay BH 255 Fg37
Longchamp F 23 Lc42
Longchang CHN (GZH) 96 Qd32
Longchang CHN (SCH) 95 Qc31
Longchuan CHN (GDG) 97 Qh33
Longchuan CHN (YUN) 113 Pk33
Long Cove CDN (NF) 245 Hd22
Long Creek USA (OR) 234 Ea23
Long Dat VN 115 Qd40
Longe ANG 202 Lh49
Longeau F 23 Lf43
Longfellow USA (TX) 237 Ej30
Longfellow, Mount NZ 155 Tg67
Longfengshan Reservoir CHN 98 Rd23
Longford AUS (TAS) 152 Sd66
Longford IRL 18 Kn37
Long Gaij RI 126 Qh45
Longgang CHN (CGQ) 95 Qc31
Longgang Shan CHN 100 Rd24
Longgong Cave CHN 96 Qc32
Longgun CHN (HAN) 96 Qf36
Long Hai Beach VN 115 Qd40
Longhe CHN (HLG) 91 Rb19
Long Hu CHN 102 Qj31
Longhua CHN (HBI) 93 Qj25
Longhui CHN (HUN) 96 Qf32
Longhurst, Mount 297 Sd34
Longido EAT 207 Mj47
Longikis RI 126 Qj46
Longiram RI 126 Qh46
Long Island AUS 140 Qh56
Long Island AUS 149 Se57
Long Island BS 251 Gc34
Long Island CDN 239 Ga18
Long Island CDN 245 Gg23
Long Island PNG 159 Sd48
Long Island USA 247 Gd25
Long Island Sound CDN 239 Ga18
Longjiang CHN (HLG) 98 Rb22
Longjing CHN (JLN) 100 Re24
Longkou CHN (SDG) 100 Ra27
Longku IND (ASM) 112 Pg33
Longlac CDN (ON) 239 Fg21
Long Lake CDN 239 Fg21
Long Lake USA (NY) 247 Gc24
Long Lake USA 240 Fa22
Long Lake Ind. Res. CDN 239 Fg21
Long Lake N.W.R. USA 240 Fa22
Long Lama MAL 126 Qh44
Longleat House GB 21 Ks39
Long Lellang MAL 126 Qh44
Longli CHN (GZH) 96 Qd32
Longlin CHN (GZG) 96 Qc33
Longling CHN (YUN) 113 Pk33
Longlinjie CHN (GZG) 96 Qd34
Longmen CHN (GDG) 96 Qf35
Longmen CHN (GDG) 97 Qh34
Longmen Shan CHN 94 Qb30
Longmen Shiku CHN 95 Qg28
Long Men Xia CHN 95 Qe30
Longmont USA (CO) 235 Eh25
Longnah RI 126 Qj45
Longnan CHN (JGX) 97 Qh33
Longnawang RI 126 Qh45
Longo CI 193 Kh41
Longo G 195 Lg46
Longo RCB 195 Lj45
Longobucco I 43 Lr51
Longonjo ANG 208 Lh52
Longotea PE 278 Gb49
Longozabe RM 220 Ne55
Long Palai MAL 126 Qh44
Long Point CDN (ON) 247 Fk24
Long Point CDN 238 Fa19
Long Point CDN 245 Ha21
Long Point Bay CDN 247 Fk24
Long Point Prov. Park CDN 247 Fk24
Long Prairie USA (MN) 241 Fc23
Long Preston GB 21 Ks36
Longquan CHN (GZH) 96 Qd32
Longquan CHN (ZJG) 102 Qk31
Long Range Mountains CDN 245 Hb21
Longreach AUS (QLD) 148 Sc57
Longs Creek CDN (NB) 245 Gg23
Long Seridan MAL 122 Qh43
Longshan CHN (GDG) 97 Qg34
Longshan CHN (HUN) 95 Qe31
Long Shan CHN 92 Qa26
Long Shan Si CHN 97 Qk33
Longsheng CHN (GZG) 96 Qf33
Longtanshan Park CHN 100 Rd24
Long Thanh VN 115 Qd40
Longtian CHN (FJN) 97 Qk33
Long Tompas ZA 214 Mf58
Longton AUS (QLD) 149 Sc56
Longtown GB 19 Ks35
Longué-Jumelles F 22 Ku43
Longueuil CDN (QC) 247 Gd23
Longuyon F 23 Lf41
Long Valley USA (SD) 240 Ek24
Long Valley Junction USA (UT) 237 Ed27
Longview CDN (AB) 233 Ec20
Longview USA (TX) 243 Fc29
Longview USA (WA) 232 Dj22
Longwa EAT 207 Mj48
Longwangmiao CHN (HLG) 98 Rg23
Longwarry AUS (VIC) 153 Sc65
Longwy F 23 Lf41
Longxi CHN (GSU) 94 Qc28
Long Xian CHN (SAA) 95 Qd28
Longxing Temple CHN 93 Qh26
Long Xuyen VN 117 Qc40
Longyan CHN (FJN) 97 Qj33
Longyao CHN (HBI) 93 Qh27
Longyearbyen N 11 Lh06
Longyou CHN (ZJG) 102 Qk31
Longzhen CHN (HLG) 98 Rd21
Longzhou CHN (GZG) 96 Qd34
Löningen D 32 Lh38
Łoniów PL 37 Mb40
Lonja HR 41 Lr44
Lonkintsy RM 220 Ne54
Lonoke USA (AR) 243 Fe28
Lonquimay RA (LP) 293 Gj64
Lonquimay RCH 292 Ge65
Lonquimay, Volcán RCH 292 Ge65
Lonrong RI 129 Ra48
Lönsboda S 15 Lp34
Lons-le-Saunier F 25 Lf44
Lontar RI 130 Re48
Lontar RI 130 Rf48
Lontou RMM 183 Ke38
Lontra BR (PA) 275 He48
Lontra BR 276 Hf49
Lontra BR 286 Hd56
Lontué RCH 288 Ge63
Lontué RCH 288 Ge63
Lonua RDC 200 Mb45
Loogootee USA (IN) 248 Fg26
Lookout Mount USA 229 Cd12
Lookout Ridge USA 229 Ca11
Loolmalassin EAT 204 Mj47
Looma AUS (WA) 138 Rc55
Loon RP 123 Rb41
Loongana AUS (WA) 145 Rd61
Loon Lake CDN (SK) 233 Ef18
Loon Pt. CDN 239 Ga19
Loon River CDN 233 Ec17
Loonse en Drunense Duinen, N.P. NL 32 Lf39
Loop Head IRL 20 Kl38
Loosdrechtse Plassen NL 32 Lf38
Lop CHN (XUZ) 86 Pa27
Lopar HR 41 Lp46
Lopary RM 220 Nd57
Lopătari RO 45 Mg45
Lopatino RUS 53 Nc19
Lopatyn UA 37 Me40
Lop Buri THA 114 Qa38
Lopé, P.N. de la G 202 Lf46
Lopez CO 272 Gb44
Lopez RP 121 Rb39
Lop Nur = Yuli CHN (XUZ) 87 Pd25
Lop Nur CHN 87 Pf25
Lopori RDC 200 Ma45
Lopou CI 193 Kh43
Loppi FIN 16 Me30
Lora del Río E 28 Kp47
Lorain USA (OH) 246 Fj25
Loralai PK 78 Oe30
Lora River AUS 143 Rh60
Lorca E 29 Kt47
Lorch D 34 Lh40
Lordegan IR 72 Nf30
Lord Howe Island AUS 137 Sd25
Lord Howe Rise 134 Ta12
Lord Howe Seamounts 134 Sb12
Lord Loughborough Island MYA 116 Pj40
Lordsburg USA (NM) 237 Ef29
Lore TLS 132 Rd50
Lore Lindu N.P. RI 127 Ra46
Lorena BR (AM) 279 Ge49
Lorena BR (SP) 287 Hh57
Lorengau PNG 159 Sd47
Lorentz RI 131 Rk48
Lorentz N.P. RI 131 Rj48
Lorenzo Geyres ROU 289 Hb62
Loreto BOL 280 Gh53
Loreto BR (MT) 280 Ha51
Loreto CO 273 Ge47
Loreto EC 272 Gb46
Loreto I 41 Lo47
Loreto MEX (BCS) 252 Ee32
Loreto MEX (ZCT) 253 Ek34
Loreto RA (CR) 289 Hb59
Loreto RP 123 Rc40
Loreto Aprutino I 42 Lo48
Lorgues F 25 Lg47
Lorian Swamp EAK 205 Mk45
Lorica CO 268 Gc41
Lorient F 22 Kr43
Lőrinci H 39 Lu43
Loring USA (MT) 233 Eg21
Loriol-sur-Drôme F 25 Le46
Loris USA (SC) 249 Ga29
Lorlie CDN (SK) 238 Ej20
Lormes F 23 Ld43
Lormi IND (CGH) 109 Pa34
Lorna Glen AUS (WA) 140 Ra59
Lorne AUS (VIC) 153 Sb65
Lorneville CDN (NB) 245 Gg23
Loronyo SUD 197 Mg43
Loropéni BF 193 Kj40
Lörrach D 34 Lh43
Lorraine AUS (QLD) 148 Rk55
Lorraine F 23 Lf41
Lorraine F 23 Lf42
Lorris F 23 Lc43
Lort River AUS 144 Ra62
Loruk EAK 204 Mj45
Lorzot TN 174 Lf30
Los S 13 Lq29
Losai N.P. EAK 204 Mj45
Los Aldamos MEX (NL) 253 Fa32
Los Alerces, P.N. RA 292 Ge67
Los Almos USA (NM) 237 Eg28
Los Altos RA (CA) 288 Gh60
Los Americanos MEX (COH) 253 Ej32
Los Amores RA (SF) 289 Ha60
Los Andes = Sotomayor CO 272 Gb45

Luwombwa ⬜ Z 210 Me52
Luwuk ⬜ RI 127 Rb46
Luwumba ⬜ Z 210 Mg51
Luxembourg ● L 23 Lg41
Luxembourg ⬜● L 23 Lg41
Luxemburg ⬜ USA (IA) 241 Fe24
Luxeuil-les-Bains ⬜ F 23 Lg43
Luxi ⬜ CHN (YUN) 95 Qf31
Luxi ⬜ CHN (YUN) 113 Pk33
Lúxia ⬜ CHN (YUN) 113 Ob33
Lúxia ⬜ CHN (FJN) 102 Ra32
Luxikegongba ⬜ CHN (TIB) 88 Pd30
Luxor ⬜ ET 177 Mg33
Luxor ⬛ ET 177 Mg33
Luyando ⬜ PE 278 Gc50
Luyi ⬜ CHN (HNN) 102 Qh29
Luz ⬜ BR 278 Gc50
Lužajka ⬜ RUS 16 Mj30
Luz-Ardiden ▲ F 24 Ku48
Luzern ⬜ CH 34 Lj43
Luzhai ⬜ CHN (GZG) 96 Qe33
Luzhi ⬜ CHN (GZH) 96 Qc32
Luzhou ⬜ CHN (SCH) 95 Qc31
Luzi ⬜ ANG 209 Ma52
Luzi ⬜ RDC 203 Lk48
Luziânia ⬛ BR (GO) 286 Hg54
Luzilândia ⬜ BR (PI) 277 Hj47
Luzino ⬜ PL 36 Lt36
Luzon ▲ RP 121 Ra38
Luzon Strait ⬰ 118 Ra14
Luz-Saint-Sauveur ⬜ F 24 Ku48
Lužskaja guba ⬰ RUS 16 Mj31
Luzy ⬜ F 25 Ld44
L'viv ⬜ UA 39 Md41
Lwakhaka ⬜ EAK 204 Mh45
Lwanga ⬜ Z 206 Mg50
Lwela ⬜ Z 210 Me51
Lwówek Śląski ⬜ PL 36 Lg39
Lyall, Mount ▲ AUS 152 Td68
Lyantonde ⬜ EAU 201 Mf46
Lycan ⬜ USA (CO) 237 Ej27
Lychen ⬜ D 32 Lo38
Lycksele ⬜ S 10 Lk13
Lyddal ⬜ CDN (MB) 238 Fa18
Lydenburg ⬜▲ ZA 214 Mf58
Lydia ⬜ USA (KS) 242 Ek26
Lydiannasundet ⬰ N 11 Me06
Lydney ⬜ GB 21 Ks39
Lyell Island ▲ CDN 232 De19
Lygnern ⬰ S 14 Ln33
Lykso ⬜ ZA 217 Mc59
Lyle ⬜ USA (WA) 234 Dk23
Lyman ⬜ USA 45 Mk45
Lyman ⬜ UA 55 Mj21
Lyme Bay ⬰ GB 20 Kr40
Lyme Regis ⬜ GB 21 Kt40
Lymington ⬜ GB 20 Ks40
Łyna ⬜ PL 37 Ma36
Lynchburg ⬜ USA (SC) 249 Fk28
Lynchburg ⬜ USA (TN) 248 Fg28
Lynchburg ⬜ USA (VA) 248 Ga27
Lynden ⬜ USA (WA) 232 Dj21
Lyndhurst ⬜ AUS (QLD) 148 Sc55
Lyndhurst ⬜ AUS (SA) 143 Rk61
Lyndon ⬜ AUS (WA) 140 Qh57
Lyndon River ⬰ AUS 140 Qh57
Lyndonville ⬜ USA (VT) 247 Gd23
Lynd River ⬰ AUS (QLD) 148 Sb54
Lyngdal ⬜ N 12 Lh32
Lyngen ⬜ N 10 Ma11
Lyngør ⬜ N 12 Lk32
Lyngseidet ⬜▲ N 10 Ma11
Lynn ⬜ USA (MA) 247 Ge24
Lynn ⬜ USA (UT) 235 Ed25
Lynn Canal ⬰ USA 231 Dc16
Lynndyl ⬜ USA (UT) 235 Ed26
Lynn Haven ⬜ USA (FL) 249 Fh30
Lynn Lake ⬜ CDN (MB) 238 Ek17
Lynton ⬜ GB 20 Kr39
Lyntupy ⬜ BY 17 Mg35
Lyon ⬜⬛♦ F 25 Le45
Lyon Mountain ▲ USA (NY) 247 Gd23
Lyons ⬜ USA (GA) 249 Fj29
Lyons ⬜ USA (KS) 242 Fa26
Lyons ⬜ USA (NY) 247 Gd24
Lyons Falls ⬜ USA (NY) 247 Gc24
Lyons-la-Forêt ⬜ F 23 Lb41
Lyons River ⬰ AUS 140 Qh58
Lypci ⬜ UA 53 Mj20
Lypova Dolyna ⬜ UA 52 Mg20
Lyra Reef ▲ PNG 160 Sg46
Łyse ⬜ PL 37 Mb37
Lysefjorden ⬰ N 12 Lg32
Lysekil ⬜ S 12 Lm32
Lysi ⬜ CY 51 Mo55
Lyskovo ⬜ RUS 53 Nc17
Lysøysundet ⬜ N 10 Le14
Lyss ⬜ CH 34 Lh43
Lystrup ⬜ DK 14 Ll34
Lysvik ⬜ S 13 Lo31
Lysýcans'k ⬜ UA 55 Mk21
Lysye Gory ⬜ RUS 53 Nc20
Lytham Saint Anne's ⬜ GB 21 Ks37
Lyton ⬜ AUS (WA) 144 Qh60
Lytton ⬜ CDN (BC) 232 Dk20
Lyubimets ⬜ BG 47 Mg49

M

Ma ⬜ CAM 195 Lf42
Maala ⬜ Z 210 Md53
Ma'alaea Bay ⬰ USA 230 Cb35
Maalhosmadulu North = Raa Atoll ▲ MV 110 Og43
Maalhosmadulu South = Baa Atoll ▲ MV 110 Og43
Maamba ⬜ Z 210 Md54
Maam Cross ⬜ IRL 18 Kl37
Ma'an ⬜ CAM 195 Lf44
Ma'an ⬜ JOR 64 Mh30
Maanit ⬜ MNG 90 Qb21
Maanit ⬜ MNG 90 Qd22
Ma'an, Mount ▲ CHN 113 Pk33
Maanselkä ▲ FIN 11 Me12
Maanselkä ▲ FIN 11 Me14
Ma'anshan ⬜▲ CHN (AHU) 102 Qk30
Maardu ⬜ EST 16 Mf31
Ma'aret Mokhouz ⬜ SYR 64 Mj28
Maarianhamina = Mariehamn ⬜ FIN 13 Lu30
Maarja ⬜ EST 16 Mg32
Ma'arrat an-Nu'man ⬜ SYR 64 Mj28
Maas ⬰ NL 32 Lg39
Maasai Mara National Reserve ⬜☒ EAK 204 Mh46
Maasbracht ⬜ NL 32 Lf39
Maaseik ⬜ B 23 Lf39
Maasim ⬜ RP 123 Rc43

Maasin ⬜ RP 123 Rc40
Maasmechelen ⬜ B 23 Lf40
Maasstroom ⬜ ZA 214 Me57
Maastricht ⬜▲ NL 32 Lf39
Maatsuyker Islands ▲ AUS 152 Sd67
Maazaplateau ⬜▲ ET 177 Mf32
Mäaziz ⬜ MA 172 Kg29
Maba ⬜ RI 130 Re45
Mababe Depression ▲ RB 213 Mc55
Ma'bad ⬜ IR 72 Nh28
Mabaduam ⬜ PNG 158 Sa49
Mabaia ⬜ ANG 202 Lh49
Mabaké ⬜ SN 183 Kc38
Mabalacat ⬜ RP 120 Ra38
Mabalane ⬜ MOC 214 Mg57
Mabana ⬜ RDC 201 Me45
Mabanda ⬜ BU 206 Me48
Ma'bar ⬜ YE 68 Nc38
Mabarangandu ⬜ EAT 207 Mj50
Mabating ⬜ CHN (YUN) 94 Pk31
Mabdeitikra ⬜ IND (CGH) 109 Pb34
Mabein ⬜ MYA 113 Pj34
Mabélé ⬜ S 115 Lg42
Mabeleapudi ⬜ IND 109 Pa34
Mabelle ⬜ USA (TX) 242 Fa29
Mabenga ⬜ RDC 203 Lk47
Mabenge ⬜ RDC 201 Mc43
Mabian ⬜ CHN (SCH) 94 Qb31
Mabinay ⬜ RP 123 Rb41
Mablethorpe ⬜ GB 21 La37
Mabo ⬜ SN 183 Kc39
Mabokweni ⬜ EAT 207 Mk48
Mabole ⬜ WAL 192 Kd41
Maboleni ⬜ ZW 214 Me55
Mabopane ⬜ ZA 213 Me58
Mabote ⬜ MOC 214 Mh57
Mabou ⬜ CDN (NS) 245 Gk22
Mabrous ⬜ RN 181 Lg35
Mabton ⬜ USA (WA) 234 Dk22
Mabuasehube Game Reserve ⬜ RB 213 Mb58
Mabuhay ⬜ RP 123 Rb42
Mabuiag Island ▲ AUS 146 Sb50
Mabuki ⬜ EAT 206 Mf47
Mabura ⬜ GUY 270 Ha43
Mabuto ⬜ WAN 186 Lc40
Mabutsane ⬜ RB 213 Mb58
Macache ⬜ EC 272 Ga46
Macachin ⬜ RA (LP) 293 Gj64
Macaé ⬜ BR (RJ) 287 Hk57
Macaena ⬜ MOC 214 Mg58
Macaíba ⬜ BR (RN) 277 Jc48
Macajalar Bay ⬰ RP 123 Rc41
Macajuba ⬜ BR (BA) 283 Hk52
Macanda ⬜ MOC 211 Mh54
Macandze ⬜ MOC 214 Mg57
Macane ⬜ MOC 214 Mg56
Macao ⬜● CHN (MAC) 97 Qg34
Macao ⬜ CHN 97 Qg35
Macapá ⬜▲ BR (AP) 275 He45
Macará ⬜ EC 272 Ga48
Macará ⬜ RP 121 Ra36
Macaracas ⬜ PA 257 Fk42
Macarani ⬜ BR (BA) 283 Hk53
Macareo ⬰ YV 270 Gk41
Macari ⬜ PE 279 Ge53
Macaroca ⬜ BR (BA) 283 Hk50
Macaroni ⬜ AUS (QLD) 148 Sa54
Macarrão, T.I. ⬜ BR 273 Gg47
Macarrtane ⬜ MOC 214 Mg58
Macarthur ⬜ AUS (VIC) 152 Sb65
Macas ⬜ EC 272 Ga47
Macatanja ⬜ MOC 211 Mj54
Macaú ⬜ BR (RN) 277 Jb48
Macauá ⬰ BR 279 Gf50
Macauari ⬜ BR (AM) 274 Ha46
Macaúba ⬜ BR (TO) 276 Hg48
Macaúbas ⬜ BR (BA) 282 Hj53
Macaxeira ⬜ BR (AM) 273 Gg49
Macclenny ⬜ USA (FL) 249 Fj30
Macclesfield ⬜ GB 21 Ks37
Macclesfield Bank ▲ 120 Qh37
Macdiarmid ⬜ CDN (ON) 239 Ff21
Macdonald Downs ⬜ AUS (NT) 143 Rh57
Macdonald, Mount ▲ VU 162 Te54
Macdonnell Ranges ▲ AUS 142 Rg57
Macea ⬜ RO 44 Mb44
Maceda ⬜ E 26 Kn52
Macedo de Cavaleiros ⬜ P 26 Ko51
Macedonia ⬜ MK 46 Mb49
Maceió ⬜▲ BR (AL) 283 Jc50
Macenta ⬜ RG 192 Kf41
Macerata ⬜ I 41 Lo47
MacGrath ⬜ USA (AK) 229 Cc14
Mach ⬜ PK 80 Od31
Macha ⬜ BOL 284 Gg55
Macha ⬜ Z 210 Md54
Machacalis ⬜ BR (MG) 287 Hk54
Machacamarca ⬜ BOL 284 Gg55
Machachi ⬜ EC 272 Ga46
Machachuta ⬜ ZW 214 Me56
Machadinho ⬜ BR (RO) 280 Gj50
Machadinho ⬜ BR (SC) 280 Gg50
Machadinho ⬜ BR (MG) 287 Hh56
Machado ou Ji-Paraná ⬰ BR 280 Gk50
Machagai ⬜ RA (CH) 289 Gk59
Machaila ⬜ MOC 214 Mg57
Machakos ⬜ EAK 204 Mj46
Machala ⬜ EC 272 Ga47
Machali ⬜ RCH 288 Ge63
Machalilla ⬜ EC 272 Fk46
Machalilla, P.N. ⬜☒ EC 272 Fk46
Machanbwe ⬜ MYA 113 Pj32
Machaneng ⬜ RB 213 Md57
Machang ⬜ CHN (GZG) 96 Qd32
Machanga ⬜ MOC 214 Mh56
Machault ⬜ F 23 Le41
Machawaian Lake ⬰ CDN 239 Ff20
Machecoul ⬜ F 22 Kt44
Machemma Ruins ⬜ ZA 214 Mf57
Machemmaruines ⬜▲ ZA 214 Me57
Macheng ⬜ CHN (HUB) 102 Qh30
Macherla ⬜ IND (APH) 109 Ok37
Machesse ⬜ MOC 214 Mh55
Machhapuchare ▲ NEP 88 Pb31
Machias ⬜ USA (ME) 247 Gg23
Machichi River ⬰ CDN 238 Fe17
Machila ⬜ ZW 210 Me54
Machila Kuta ⬜ Z 209 Mc54

Machile ⬜ Z 209 Mc54
Machina ⬜ WAN 186 Lf39
Machinga ⬜ MW 211 Mh53
Machiques ⬜ YV 268 Gd40
Machu Picchu ⬜⬛ PE 279 Gd52
Machupo ⬰ BOL 279 Gh52
Machynlleth ⬜ GB 20 Kr38
Macia ⬜ MOC 214 Mg58
Maciana Marina ⬜ I 40 Ll48
Maciejowice ⬜ PL 37 Mb39
Măcin ⬜ RO 45 Mj45
Macinaggio ⬜ F 31 Lk48
Mackay ⬜ AUS (QLD) 149 Se56
Mackay ⬜ USA (ID) 235 Ed24
Mac Kean Island ▲ KIR 157 Ub19
Mackenzie ⬜ CDN (BC) 232 Dj18
Mackenzie ⬰ CDN 224 Dd06
Mackenzie Bay ⬰ CDN 224 Da05
Mackenzie Bay ⬰ 297 Oc32
Mackenzie King Island ▲ CDN 225 Ec03
Mackenzie Mountains ▲ CDN 231 Df14
Mackinac S.P. ⬜☒ USA 246 Fh23
Mackinaw City ⬜ USA (MI) 246 Fh23
Mackinnon Road ⬜ EAK 207 Mk47
Macklin ⬜ CDN (SK) 233 Ef19
Macks Inn ⬜ USA (ID) 235 Ee23
Macksville ⬜ AUS (NSW) 151 Sg61
Maclean ⬜ AUS (NSW) 151 Sg60
Maclean Strait ⬰ CDN 224 Ed03
Macleantown ⬜ ZA 217 Md62
Maclear ⬜ ZA 217 Me61
Macmillan Pass ⬜ CDN 231 Df14
Macmillan Plateau ▲ CDN 231 Dd14
Macmillan River ⬰ CDN 231 Dc14
Maco ⬜ RP 123 Rc42
Maçobere ⬜ MOC 214 Mg56
Macocola ⬜ ANG 202 Lj49
Macomb ⬜ USA (IL) 241 Fe25
Macomer ⬜ I 31 Lj50
Macomia ⬜ MOC 211 Na52
Mâcon ⬜ F 25 Le44
Macon ⬜ USA (GA) 249 Fj29
Macon ⬜ USA (MO) 241 Fd26
Macon ⬜ USA (MS) 243 Ff29
Macon ⬜ USA (GA) 246 Fh26
Macondo ⬜ ANG 209 Mb52
Macossa ⬜ MOC 210 Mg54
Macoun Lake ⬰ CDN 238 Ej17
Macovane ⬜ MOC 214 Mh56
Macquarie Harbour ⬰ AUS 152 Sc67
Macquarie Islands ▲ 134 Sb15
Macquarie Ridge ⬰ 134 Sb15
Mac Robertson Land ▲ 297 Nd33
Macroom ⬜ IRL 20 Km39
Macrorie ⬜ CDN (SK) 233 Eg20
Mactaris ⬜ TN 174 Le28
Mactún ⬜ MEX (TB) 255 Fe37
Macucauá ⬜ BR (AM) 279 Ge49
Macugnaga ⬜ I 40 Lh45
Macuira, P.N. ⬜☒ CO 268 Ge39
Macuma ⬜ EC 272 Gb47
Macumba ⬜ AUS (SA) 143 Rh59
Macura ⬜ BR (AM) 274 Gh46
Macuro ⬜ YV 270 Gk40
Macururé ⬜ BR (BA) 283 Ja50
Macusani ⬜ PE 279 Ge53
Macuspana ⬜ MEX (TB) 255 Fd37
Macuze ⬜ MOC 211 Mj54
Macwahok ⬜ USA (MA) 244 Gf23
Mada ▲ WAN 186 Le41
Madaba ⬜ IND 109 Ok32
Madaba ⬜ JOR 64 Mh30
Madadeni ⬜ ZA 217 Mf59
Madadi ⬜ ZW 210 Me54
Madagascar ▲ 167 Na11
Madagascar ⬜ 171 Nb23
Madagascar Basin ⬰ 171 Nc24
Madagascar Ridge ⬰ 171 Na25
Madagli ⬜ WAN 187 Lg40
Madagoi ⬜ SP 205 Nb45
Madain Salah ⬜⬛ KSA 66 Mj32
Madakasira ⬜ IND (APH) 111 Oj40
Madalena ⬜ BR (CE) 277 Ja48
Madama ⬜ RN 181 Lg35
Madampe ⬜ CL 111 Ok43
Madan ⬜ BG 47 Me49
Madana ⬜ TCH 187 Lj41
Madanapalle ⬜ IND (APH) 111 Ok40
Madang ⬜ PNG 159 Sc48
Madangawa ⬜ EAT 211 Mk51
Madang Resort ⬜ PNG 159 Sc48
Mädängsholm ⬜ S 15 Lo32
Madan Mahal Fort ⬜ IND (APH) 109 Ok33
Madaoua ⬜ RN 186 Le38
Madaripur ⬜ BD 112 Pf34
Madarounfa ⬜ RN 186 Le39
Madarski konnik ⬜⬛ BG 47 Mg47
Madau Island ▲ PNG 160 Sg50
Madawa ⬜ PNG 160 Sg51
Madawaska ⬜ USA (MA) 244 Gf22
Madbar ⬜ SUD 197 Mf47
Maddaloni ⬜ I 42 Lp49
Madded ⬜ IND (CGH) 109 Pa36
Maddela ⬜ RP 121 Ra37
Maddimadugu ⬜ IND (APH) 111 Ok39
Maddupur ⬜ IND (UPH) 109 Pb33
Maddur ⬜ IND (KTK) 111 Oj40
Madeira ▲ BR 274 Ha48
Madeira ⬜ P 8 Ka12
Madeira Islands ▲ P 8 Ka12
Madeirinha ⬰ BR 280 Gk51
Maden ⬜ TR 63 Na25
Madeniyet ⬜ KZ 84 Ok22
Madero ⬜ MEX (CHH) 237 Ej31
Madero ⬜ SP 205 Na44
Madgaon = Margao ⬜ IND (GOA) 108 Og38
Madgoul ⬜ DJI 191 Nd40
Madha ⬜ KSA 68 Nb36
Madh adh Dhahab ⬜ KSA 66 Na34
Madha N.P. ⬜☒ IND 107 Oj33
Madhavpur ⬜ IND (APH) 111 Ok39...
Madhepura ⬜ IND (BIH) 112 Pd33
Madhira ⬜ IND (APH) 109 Pa36
Madhogiri ⬜ IND (KTK) 111 Oj40
Madhubani ⬜ IND (JKD) 112 Pd33
Madhupur ⬜ IND (UPH) 109 Pb33
Madhupur Jungle N.P. ⬜☒ BD 112 Pf33
Madhya Pradesh ⬜ IND 104 Od14
Madibogo ⬜ ZA 214 Mc59
Madidi, P.N. ⬜☒ BOL 279 Gg52
Madidi ⬰ BOL 279 Gg52
Madikeri ⬜ IND (KTK) 110 Oh40
Madikwe Game Reserve ⬜☒ ZA 213 Mc58
Madill ⬜ USA (OK) 243 Fb28
Madimba ⬜ ANG 202 Lh49
Madimba ⬜ RDC 202 Lh48
Madina ⬜ CI 192 Kg40
Madina ⬜ RMM 184 Kf39
Madina ⬜ RMM 192 Kg40
Madina de Baixo ⬜ GNB 183 Kc40
Madina Junction ⬜ WAL 192 Kd41
Madinani ⬜ CI 192 Kg41
Madina-Oula ⬜ RG 192 Kd41
Madina-Sako ⬜ RMM 184 Kg39
Madina-Salambandé ⬜ RG 192 Ke40
Madinat al Abyar ⬜ LAR 175 Ma29
Madinat al 'bid ⬜ YE 68 Nc38
Madinat ash Sha'b ⬜ YE 68 Nc39
Madingo-Kayes ⬜ RCB 202 Lf48
Madingou ⬜ RCB 202 Lg48
Madinani ⬜ CAM 195 Lh41
Madi Opei ⬜ EAU 204 Mg44
Madirovalo ⬜ RM 220 Nd54
Madison ⬜ USA (AL) 248 Fg28
Madison ⬜ USA (FL) 249 Fj29
Madison ⬜ USA (GA) 249 Fj29
Madison ⬜ USA (IN) 246 Fh26
Madison ⬜ USA (MN) 240 Fb24
Madison ⬜ USA (MN) 240 Fb25
Madison ⬜ USA (NE) 240 Fb25
Madison ⬜ USA (SD) 241 Fb24
Madison ⬜ USA (WI) 246 Ff24
Madison ⬜ USA (WV) 249 Fk26
Madison ⬰ USA 235 Ee23
Madison Canyon Earthquake Area ⬜☒ USA 235 Ee23
Madisonville ⬜ USA (KY) 248 Fg27
Madisonville ⬜ USA (TX) 243 Fc30
Madiun ⬜ RI 128 Qf49
Madja ⬜ RCA 196 Mb40
Madjingo ⬜ G 195 Lh45
Madley, Mount ▲ AUS 141 Rb58
Madliena ⬜ LV 17 Mf34
Mado Derdetu ⬜ EAK 205 Mk45
Mado Gashi ⬜ EAK 205 Mk45
Madona ⬜ LV 17 Mg34
Madonna del Sasso ⬜⬛ CH 34 Lj44
Madonna di Campiglio ⬜⬛ I 40 Ll44
Madoonia Downs ⬜ AUS (WA) 144 Rb61
Madouagou ⬜ RMM 185 Kj38
Madovile ⬜ SP 205 Na44
Madrakah ⬜ KSA 66 Nc38
Madrakah ⬜ OM 69 Nj36
Madras = Chennai ⬜▲ IND (TNU) 111 Pa40
Madras ⬜ USA (OR) 234 Dk23
Madrasat Qasr Abu Hadi ⬜ LAR 175 Lj30
Mädrec ⬜ BG 47 Mg48
Madre de Deus de Minas ⬜ BR (MG) 287 Hh56
Madre de Dios ⬜ BOL 279 Gg55
Madre de Dios ⬰ PE 279 Ge52
Madrejón ⬜ RA (SA) 285 Gj57
Madrid ⬜▲⬛♦ E 29 Kr50
Madrid ⬜ RP 123 Rc41
Madridejos ⬜ E 29 Kr49
Madrigal ⬜ PE 279 Ge53
Madrigal de las Altas Torres ⬜ E 26 Kq51
Madrigalejo ⬜ E 28 Kp49
Mädrino ⬜ BG 47 Mg48
Madruga ⬜ C 258 Fk34
Madu ⬜ RI 129 Qf45
Madu ⬜ SUD 189 Md38
Madugula Kondas ▲ IND 109 Pb37
Madula ⬜ RDC 201 Mc45
Madula ⬜ RDC 202 Lg48
Madura ⬜ AUS (WA) 145 Rd61
Madura ▲ RI 128 Qg49
Madurai ⬜ IND (TNU) 111 Ok42
Madurantakam ⬜ IND (TNU) 111 Ok40
Madwa ⬜ EAT 207 Mh47
Madyan ⬜ PK 79 Og28
Madyo ⬜ EAT 207 Mk49
Madzilobge ⬜ RB 213 Md56
Madziwadzido ⬜ ZW 210 Me54
Madziwa Mine ⬜ ZW 210 Mf54
Madzuire ⬜ MOC 210 Mh54
Maebashi ⬜ J 101 Rk27
Mae Chaem ⬜ THA 114 Pk36
Mae Chai ⬜ THA 114 Pk36
Mae Charim ⬜ THA 114 Qa36
Mae Hong Son ⬜ THA 114 Pj36
Mae Khachan ⬜ THA 114 Pk36
Mae La Na ⬜ THA 114 Pj36
Mae La Noi ⬜ THA 114 Pj36
Maël-Carhaix ⬜ F 22 Kr42
Maella ⬜ E 30 La49
Mae Malai ⬜ THA 114 Pk36
Mãe Maria, T.I. ⬜ BR 276 Hf48
Mae Nam Mun ⬰ THA 115 Qc38
Mae Nam Ping ⬰ THA 114 Pk37
Mae Phrik ⬜ THA 114 Pk37
Mae Ping N.P. ⬜☒ THA 114 Pk37
Mae Pok ⬜ THA 114 Pk37
Mae Ramat ⬜ THA 114 Pj37
Mae Rang ⬜ THA 114 Pk37
Mae Rim ⬜ THA 114 Pk36
Mae Sai ⬜ THA 114 Pk35
Mae Sariang ⬜ THA 114 Pj36
Maes Howe ⬜⬛ GB 19 Kr31
Mae Sot ⬜ THA 114 Pj37
Maestre de Campo Island ▲ RP 121 Ra39
Mae Su ⬜ THA 114 Pj36
Mae Suai ⬜ THA 114 Pk36
Mae Suya ⬜ THA 114 Pj36
Mae Taeng ⬜ THA 114 Pk36
Mae Tub Reservoir ⬰ THA 114 Pk37
Mae Tun ⬜ THA 114 Pk37
Maevatanana ⬜⬛ RM 220 Nd54
Maewo ▲ VU 162 Te53
Mae Wong ⬜ THA 114 Pk38
Mae Wong N.P. ⬜☒ THA 114 Pk38...
Mafa ⬜ RI 130 Rd45
Mafa ⬜ WAN 187 Lg40
Maféré ⬜ CI 193 Kj43
Mafeteng ⬜ LS 217 Md60
Mafeteng Rock Paintings ⬜⬛ LS 217 Md60

Madhya Pradesh ⬜ IND 104 Od14
Madibogo ⬜ ZA 214 Mc59
Madidi, P.N. ⬜☒ BOL 279 Gg52
Madidi ⬰ BOL 279 Gg52
Madikeri ⬜ IND (KTK) 110 Oh40
Madikwe Game Reserve ⬜☒ ZA 213 Mc58
Madill ⬜ USA (OK) 243 Fb28
Madimba ⬜ ANG 202 Lh49
Madimba ⬜ RDC 202 Lh48
Madina ⬜ CI 192 Kg40
Madina ⬜ RMM 184 Kf39
Madina ⬜ RMM 192 Kg40
Madina de Baixo ⬜ GNB 183 Kc40
Madina Junction ⬜ WAL 192 Kd41
Madinani ⬜ CI 192 Kg41
Madina-Oula ⬜ RG 192 Kd41
Madina-Sako ⬜ RMM 184 Kg39
Madina-Salambandé ⬜ RG 192 Ke40
Madinat al Abyar ⬜ LAR 175 Ma29
Madinat al 'bid ⬜ YE 68 Nc38
Madinat ash Sha'b ⬜ YE 68 Nc39
Madingo-Kayes ⬜ RCB 202 Lf48
Madingou ⬜ RCB 202 Lg48
Madinani ⬜ CAM 195 Lh41
Madi Opei ⬜ EAU 204 Mg44
Madirovalo ⬜ RM 220 Nd54
Madison ⬜ USA (AL) 248 Fg28
Madison ⬜ USA (FL) 249 Fj29
Madison ⬜ USA (GA) 249 Fj29
Madison ⬜ USA (IN) 246 Fh26
Madison ⬜ USA (MN) 240 Fb24
Madison ⬜ USA (MN) 240 Fb25
Madison ⬜ USA (NE) 240 Fb25
Madison ⬜ USA (SD) 241 Fb24
Madison ⬜ USA (WI) 246 Ff24
Madison ⬜ USA (WV) 249 Fk26
Madison ⬰ USA 235 Ee23
Madison Canyon Earthquake Area ⬜☒ USA 235 Ee23
Madisonville ⬜ USA (KY) 248 Fg27
Madisonville ⬜ USA (TX) 243 Fc30
Madiun ⬜ RI 128 Qf49
Madja ⬜ RCA 196 Mb40
Madjingo ⬜ G 195 Lh45
Madley, Mount ▲ AUS 141 Rb58
Madliena ⬜ LV 17 Mf34
Mado Derdetu ⬜ EAK 205 Mk45
Mado Gashi ⬜ EAK 205 Mk45
Madona ⬜ LV 17 Mg34
Madonna del Sasso ⬜⬛ CH 34 Lj44
Madonna di Campiglio ⬜⬛ I 40 Ll44
Madoonia Downs ⬜ AUS (WA) 144 Rb61
Madouagou ⬜ RMM 185 Kj38
Madovile ⬜ SP 205 Na44
Madrakah ⬜ KSA 66 Nc38
Madrakah ⬜ OM 69 Nj36
Madras = Chennai ⬜▲ IND (TNU) 111 Pa40
Madras ⬜ USA (OR) 234 Dk23
Madrasat Qasr Abu Hadi ⬜ LAR 175 Lj30
Mädrec ⬜ BG 47 Mg48
Madre de Deus de Minas ⬜ BR (MG) 287 Hh56
Madre de Dios ⬜ BOL 279 Gg55
Madre de Dios ⬰ PE 279 Ge52
Madrejón ⬜ RA (SA) 285 Gj57
Madrid ⬜▲⬛♦ E 29 Kr50
Madrid ⬜ RP 123 Rc41
Madridejos ⬜ E 29 Kr49
Madrigal ⬜ PE 279 Ge53
Madrigal de las Altas Torres ⬜ E 26 Kq51
Madrigalejo ⬜ E 28 Kp49
Mädrino ⬜ BG 47 Mg48
Madruga ⬜ C 258 Fk34
Madu ⬜ RI 129 Qf45
Madu ⬜ SUD 189 Md38
Madugula Kondas ▲ IND 109 Pb37
Madula ⬜ RDC 201 Mc45
Madula ⬜ RDC 202 Lg48
Madura ⬜ AUS (WA) 145 Rd61
Madura ▲ RI 128 Qg49
Madurai ⬜ IND (TNU) 111 Ok42
Madurantakam ⬜ IND (TNU) 111 Ok40
Madwa ⬜ EAT 207 Mh47
Madyan ⬜ PK 79 Og28
Madyo ⬜ EAT 207 Mk49
Madzilobge ⬜ RB 213 Md56
Madziwadzido ⬜ ZW 210 Me54
Madziwa Mine ⬜ ZW 210 Mf54
Madzuire ⬜ MOC 210 Mh54
Maebashi ⬜ J 101 Rk27
Mae Chaem ⬜ THA 114 Pk36
Mae Chai ⬜ THA 114 Pk36
Mae Charim ⬜ THA 114 Qa36
Mae Hong Son ⬜ THA 114 Pj36
Mae Khachan ⬜ THA 114 Pk36
Mae La Na ⬜ THA 114 Pj36
Mae La Noi ⬜ THA 114 Pj36
Maël-Carhaix ⬜ F 22 Kr42
Maella ⬜ E 30 La49
Mae Malai ⬜ THA 114 Pk36
Mãe Maria, T.I. ⬜ BR 276 Hf48
Mae Nam Mun ⬰ THA 115 Qc38
Mae Nam Ping ⬰ THA 114 Pk37
Mae Phrik ⬜ THA 114 Pk37
Mae Ping N.P. ⬜☒ THA 114 Pk37
Mae Pok ⬜ THA 114 Pk37
Mae Ramat ⬜ THA 114 Pj37
Mae Rang ⬜ THA 114 Pk37
Mae Rim ⬜ THA 114 Pk36
Mae Sai ⬜ THA 114 Pk35
Mae Sariang ⬜ THA 114 Pj36
Maes Howe ⬜⬛ GB 19 Kr31
Mae Sot ⬜ THA 114 Pj37
Maestre de Campo Island ▲ RP 121 Ra39
Mae Su ⬜ THA 114 Pj36
Mae Suai ⬜ THA 114 Pk36
Mae Suya ⬜ THA 114 Pj36
Mae Taeng ⬜ THA 114 Pk36
Mae Tub Reservoir ⬰ THA 114 Pk37
Mae Tun ⬜ THA 114 Pk37
Maevatanana ⬜⬛ RM 220 Nd54
Maewo ▲ VU 162 Te53
Mae Wong ⬜ THA 114 Pk38
Mafa ⬜ RI 130 Rd45
Mafa ⬜ WAN 187 Lg40
Maféré ⬜ CI 193 Kj43
Mafeteng ⬜ LS 217 Md60
Mafeteng Rock Paintings ⬜⬛ LS 217 Md60

Maffin ⬜ RI 131 Rk46
Maffra ⬜ AUS (VIC) 153 Sd64
Mafia Channel ⬰ EAT 207 Mk49
Mafia Island ▲ EAT 207 Mk49
Mafia Marine Park ⬜☒ EAT 207 Mk50
Mafikeng ⬜ ZA 213 Mc58
Máfil ⬜ RCH 292 Gd65
Mafinji ⬜ EAT 207 Mj50
Mafou ⬰ RG 192 Ke41
Mafouné ⬜ RMM 184 Kh39
Mafra ⬜ BR (SC) 291 Hf59
Mafra ⬜ P 28 Kl48
Mafraq ⬜ JOR 64 Mj29
Mafunga-Busi-Plateau ▲ ZW 210 Me55
Maga ⬜ CAM 187 Lh40
Magadan ⬜ RM 220 Nd57
Magadi ⬜ IND (APH) 111 Ok40
Magadi ⬜ EAK 204 Mj46
Magadi ⬰ EAK 207 Mj46
Magalakwin ⬰ ZA 213 Me57
Magallanes, Cerro ▲ MEX 237 Ef30
Magamba ⬜ RCA 200 Mb43
Magana ⬜ WAN 186 Le41
Magandene ⬜ MOC 214 Mg57
Magangué ⬜ CO 268 Gc41
Maganik ▲ SCG (MLG) 254 Ej35
Maganja ⬜ MOC 211 Mj54
Maganoy ⬜ RP 123 Rc42
Maganoy ⬜ RP 123 Rc42
Maganza ⬜ EAT 206 Mf47
Magao ⬜ TCH 187 Lh40
Magara ⬜ BU 206 Me47
Magaria ⬜ RN 186 Le39
Magarida ⬜ PNG 159 Se51
Magaubo ⬜ PNG 159 Se51
Magazini ⬜ EAT 207 Mk48
Magba ⬜ CAM 195 Lf43
Magbakele ⬜ RDC 200 Mb44
Magburaka ⬜ WAL 192 Ke41
Magdagači ⬜ SP 205 Nc44
Magdalena ⬜ BOL 279 Gg51
Magdalena ⬜ BOL 280 Gg52
Magdalena ⬜ CO 268 Gd41
Magdalena ⬜ MEX (JLC) 254 Ej35
Magdalena ⬜ RA (BA) 289 Hb63
Magdalena ⬜ USA (NM) 237 Eg28
Magdalena de Kino ⬜ MEX (SO) 237 Ee30
Magdalena Tequisistlán ⬜ MEX (OAX) 254 Fc37
Magdeburg ⬜⬛ D 33 Lm38
Magdelaine Cays ▲ AUS 149 Sf54
Mage ⬜ BR (RJ) 287 Hj57
Magelang ⬜ RI 128 Qf49
Magellan Seamounts ⬰ 134 Sb08
Magén Gangri ▲ CHN 94 Pk28
Magenta ⬜ I 40 Lj45
Magetan ⬜ RI 128 Qf49
Maggánari ⬜ GR 49 Mf54
Maggieville ⬜ AUS (QLD) 148 Sa54
Maghagha ⬜ ET 177 Mf31
Maghama ⬜ RIM 183 Kd38
Maghera ⬜ GB 18 Ko36
Magherani ⬜ RO 45 Me44
Maghnia ⬜ DZ 173 Kk28
Maginge ⬜ EAT 211 Mh51
Magione ⬜ I 41 Ln47
Maglaj ⬜ BIH 41 Lt46
Maglavit ⬜ RO 45 Md46
Máglie ⬜ I 43 Lt49
Mäglič ▲ SCG 47 Mf48
Magna ⬜ USA (UT) 235 Ed25
Magnamana ⬜ BD 112 Pf35
Magnetawan ⬜ CDN (ON) 247 Ga23
Magnetic Island ⬜☒ AUS (QLD) 149 Sd55
Magnetic Island N.P. ⬜☒ AUS (QLD) 149 Sd55
Magnitogorsk ⬜ RUS 58 Nd08
Magnolia ⬜ USA (AR) 243 Fd29
Magnolia Plantation ⬜☒ USA 243 Fd30
Magnor ⬜ N 12 Ln31
Magny-Cours ⬜❋ F 23 Ld43
Magny-en-Vexin ⬜ F 23 Lb41
Mago ⬰ FJI 163 Ua54
Mágocs ⬜ H 38 Lt44
Magoebaskloof ⬜▲ ZA 214 Mf57
Magog ⬜ CDN (QC) 247 Gd23
Magogoni ⬜ EAT 207 Mk49
Mago, Mount ▲ ETH 198 Mj43
Mago N.P. ⬜☒ ETH 198 Mj43
Magoodhoo ⬜ MV 110 Og44
Magos ⬜ EAU 204 Mg44
Magou ⬜ DY 193 La40
Magoura ⬜ DZ 173 Kk28
Magowra ⬜ AUS (QLD) 148 Sa54
Magoye ⬜ Z 210 Md54
Magozal ⬜ MEX (VC) 254 Fb35
Magra ⬰ DZ 174 Lc28
Magrath ⬜ CDN (AB) 233 Ed21
Magrur ⬜ SUD 190 Md34
Magta Lahjar ⬜ RIM 183 Kd37
Magu ⬜ BR 277 Hj47
Magu ⬜ CHN (GZH) 96 Qc34
Maguan ⬜ CHN (YUN) 96 Qc34
Maguari ⬜ BR (AM) 274 Gh46
Maguarichic ⬜ MEX (CHH) 252 Eg32
Magude ⬜ MOC 214 Mg58
Mague ⬜ MOC 210 Mg54
Magueyal ⬜ MEX (COH) 253 Ej32
Maguiresbridge ⬜ GB 18 Kn36
Magumeri ⬜ WAN 187 Lg39
Magunge ⬜ ZW 210 Me54
Magura ⬜ BD 112 Pe34
Mãgura ⬜ RO 45 Mg47
Magurski P.N. ⬜☒ PL 39 Mb41
Magusheni ⬜ ZA 217 Me61
Magwe ⬜ SUD 197 Mg43
Magwe ⬰ RCB 202 Lh47
Mah ⬜ RCB 202 Lh47
Mahabad ⬜ IR 72 Nc27
Mahabaleshwar ⬜ IND (MHT) 108 Og37
Mahabaleshwar Hill Resort ⬜☒ IND 108 Og37
Mahabalipuram = Mamallapuram ⬜ IND 111 Pa40
Mahabe ⬜ RM 220 Nc56
Mahabo ⬜ RM 220 Nc56...

Mahabo ⬜ RM 220 Nd57
Mahaboboka ⬜ RM 220 Nc57
Mahackala ⬜ RUS (DAG) 70 Nd24
Mahad ⬜ IND (MHT) 108 Og36
Mahafaly ⬜ RM 220 Nd58
Mahagama ⬜ IND (JKD) 112 Pd33
Mahagaon ⬜ IND (MHT) 108 Oj36
Mahagi ⬜ RDC 201 Mf44
Mahaica Helena ⬜ GUY 271 Hb42
Mahajamba ⬰ RM 218 Nd53
Mahajan ⬜ IND (RJT) 106 Og33
Mahajanga ⬜▲ RM 218 Nd53
Mahajilo ⬰ RM 220 Nc55
Mahakaleshwar Temple ⬜⬛ IND 108 Oh34
Mahakam ⬰ RI 126 Qd45
Mahalapye ⬜ RB 213 Md57
Mahalchhari ⬜ BD 112 Pg34
Mahale Mountains ▲ EAT 206 Mf49
Mahale Mountains N.P. ⬜☒ EAT 206 Mf49
Mahalevona ⬜ RM 219 Ne53
Mahalingpur ⬜ IND (KTK) 108 Oh37
Mahallat ⬜ IR 72 Nf29
Mahalpur ⬜ IND (PJB) 107 Oj30
Maham ⬜ IND (HYA) 106 Oj31
Mahambo ⬜ RM 220 Ne54
Mahamuni Pagoda ▲ MYA 112 Pg35
Mahan ⬜ IND (MHT) 108 Oj33
Mahan ⬜ IR 75 Nj30
Mahanadi ⬰ IND 109 Pb35
Mahanadi Basin ▲ IND 109 Pa35
Mahanadi Delta ▲ IND 112 Pd35
Mahanewi ⬜ AUS (SA) 152 Rj61
Mahango Game Park ⬜☒ NAM 213 Ma55
Mahanoro ⬜ RM 220 Ne55
Maha Oya ⬜ CL 111 Pa43
Mahapleu ⬜ CI 192 Kg42
Maharadja Mausoleum ⬜⬛ PK 81 Og31
Maharashtra ⬜ IND 104 Od15
Mahasamund ⬜ IND (CGH) 109 Pb35
Maha Sarakham ⬜ THA 115 Qb37
Mahasoa ⬜ RM 220 Nd57
Mahasoa Atsinanana ⬜ RM 220 Nc57
Mahasolo ⬜ RM 220 Nd56
Mahassayweyne ⬜ SP 205 Nc44
Mahasthangarh ⬜⬛ BD 112 Pe33
Mahatalaky ⬜ RM 220 Nd57
Mahate ⬜ MOC 211 Na52
Mahatma Gandhi Marine N.P. ⬜☒ IND 111 Pg40
Mahatsinjo ⬜ RM 220 Nd57
Mahatsinjo ⬜ RM 220 Nd57
Mahattat 1 ⬜ SUD 190 Mf36
Mahattat 10 ⬜ SUD 190 Md36
Mahattat 3 ⬜ SUD 190 Mf36
Mahattat 6 ⬜ SUD 190 Mf36
Mahattat 8 ⬜ SUD 190 Mf36
Mahavavy ⬰ RM 219 Ne52
Mahavavy ⬰ RM 220 Nc54
Mahavelona ⬜⬛ RM 220 Ne54
Mahavelona ⬜ RM 220 Nc54
Mahaweli Ganga ⬰ CL 111 Pa42
Mahaxai ⬜ LAO 115 Qc37
Mahayag ⬜ RP 123 Rb41
Mahazoarivo ⬜ RM 220 Nd57
Mahazoarivo ⬜ RM 220 Nd57
Mahazoma ⬜ RM 220 Nd56
Mahbub ⬜ SUD 197 Me39
Mahbubabad ⬜ IND (APH) 109 Pa37
Mahbubnagar ⬜ IND (APH) 108 Oj37
Mahdah ⬜ OM 75 Nh33
Mahdalynivka ⬜ UA 54 Mh21
Mahdia ⬜ GUY 270 Ha43
Mahdia ⬜▲ TN 174 Lf29
Mahdija-Plage ⬜ MA 172 Kg28
Mahdi's Tomb ⬜⬛ SUD 190 Mg39
Mahé ⬜ IND (PND) 110 Oh41
Mahé ⬜ SY 219 Nh48
Mahébourg ⬜ MS 221 Nj56
Mahendragarh ⬜ IND (CGH) 109 Pb34
Mahendragarh ⬜ IND (HYA) 106 Oj31
Mahenge ⬜ EAT 207 Mj50
Mahé Pondicherry ⬜ IND 110 Oh41
Maheshwar ⬜ IND (MPH) 108 Oh34
Maheshkali Island ▲ BD 112 Pf35
Mahetika ▲ F (PYF) 165 Cj54
Mahfuzbhendaru ⬜ IND (APH) 109 Pb36
Mahgawan ⬜ IND (MPH) 107 Ok32
Mahi ⬰ IND 108 Og34
Mahia Peninsula ▲ NZ 154 Tj65
Mahibadhoo ⬜ MV 110 Og44
Mahidasht ⬜ IR 72 Nd27
Mahien ⬜ IND (MPH) 107 Ok32
Mahila ⬜ RDC 206 Me48
Mahilëv ⬜ BY 52 Mf19
Mahin ⬜ WAN 194 Lc42
Mahina ⬜ RMM 184 Ke39
Mahirija ⬜ MA 173 Kj29
Mahisa ⬜ IND (APH) 109 Ok33
Mahisma ⬜ IND (MPH) 109 Pb34
Mahoba ⬜ IND (UPH) 109 Ok33
Maholi ⬜ IND (UPH) 107 Ok32
Mahon = Maó ⬜▲ E 30 Le51
Mahone Bay ⬜ CDN (NS) 245 Gj23
Mahora ⬜ E 29 Kt49
Mahou ⬜ RMM 184 Kh39
Mahoua ⬜ TCH 196 Lk40
Mahrauni ⬜ IND (UPH) 109 Ok33
Mahrès ⬜ TN 174 Lf29
Mahri ⬜ PK 80 Od32
Mahrud ⬜ IR 73 Nk28
Mahsana ⬜ IR 72 Nd27
Mahnomen ⬜ USA (MN) 241 Fc22
Mahoba ⬜ IND (UPH) 109 Ok33
Maholi ⬜ IND (UPH) 107 Ok32
Mahon ⬜ E 30 Le51
Mahsud ⬜ IR 72 Nf29
Mahur ⬜ IND (MHT) 108 Oj35
Mahuva ⬜ IND (GUJ) 108 Of35
Mahwa ⬜ IND (RJT) 107 Oj32
Maials ⬜ E 30 La49
Maiama ⬜ PNG 159 Sd49
Maiana Atoll ▲ KIR 157 Tc18
Maiauatá ⬜ BR (PA) 276 Hf46
Maibo ⬜ TCH 196 Lk41
Mãicãneşti ⬜ RO 45 Mh45
Maicao ⬜ CO 268 Gd40
Mai Chau ⬜ VN 96 Qc35
Maiche ⬜ F 23 Lg43
Maici ⬰ BR (AM) 274 Gj49
Maicuru ⬰ BR 275 Hc46
Maidanshar = Kowt-e Ashrow ⬜ AFG 78 Oe28
Maidenhead ⬜ GB 21 Ku39
Maiden Island ▲ KIR 303 Ca10
Maiden, Mount ▲ AUS 141 Nb59
Maidi ⬜ RI 130 Rd45
Maidstone ⬜ CDN (SK) 233 Ef19
Maidstone ⬜ GB 21 La39
Maiduguri ⬜ WAN 187 Lg40
Maidukuru ⬜ IND (APH) 111 Ok39
Maielle, P.N.della ⬜☒ I 42 Lp48
Mäeruş ⬜ RO 45 Mf45
Maigatari ⬜ WAN 186 Le39
Maigudo, Mount ▲ ETH 198 Mj42
Maihar ⬜ IND (MPH) 109 Pa33
Maiinchi ⬜ WAN 186 Lc40
Maijishan Shiku ▲ CHN 95 Qc28
Maikala Range ▲ IND 109 Pa34
Maikapshaghai ⬜ KZ 85 Pc22
Maïko ⬜ RDC 201 Md46
Maikonkele ⬜ WAN 186 Ld41
Maïko, P.N.de la ⬜☒ RDC 201 Md46
Maikoro ⬜ TCH 195 Lj41
Mailani ⬜ IND (UPH) 107 Pa31
Mailepalli ⬜ IND (APH) 109 Ok37
Mailly-le-Camp ⬜ F 23 Le42
Mailsi ⬜ PK 81 Og31
Maimana = Meymaneh ⬜ AFG 78 Oe28
Maimón ⬜ DOM 260 Ge36
Main ⬰ D 34 Lk41
Mainaguri ⬜ IND (WBG) 112 Pe32
Mainamati ▲ BD 112 Pf34
Mainburg ⬜ D 35 Lm42
Main Camp ⬜ ZW 213 Md55
Main-Donau-Kanal ⬰ D 35 Lm41
Maine ⬜ D 22 Ku42
Maine ⬜ USA 225 Gc09
Maïné-Soroa ⬜ RN 187 Lg39
Maing Kwan ⬜ MYA 113 Pj32
Mainit ⬜ RP 123 Rc41
Mainland ⬜ CDN (NF) 245 Ha21
Mainland ▲ GB 19 Kr31
Mainland ▲ GB 19 Kr31
Mainling ⬜ CHN (TIB) 89 Ph31
Mainoru ⬜ AUS (NT) 139 Rh53
Mainpuri ⬜ IND (UPH) 107 Ok32
Main Range N.P. ⬜☒ AUS 151 Sg59
Main River ⬰ CDN 245 Hb21
Maintenon ⬜ F 23 Lb42
Maintirano ⬜ RM 220 Nc55
Mainz ⬜▲ D 34 Lj40
Maiparu ⬜ YV 270 Ga42
Maipo ⬜ RCH 288 Ge62
Maipo, Volcán ▲ RCH/RA 288 Gf63
Maipú ⬜ RA (BA) 293 Hb64
Maipu ⬜ RA (MD) 288 Gf62
Maipú ⬜ RCH 288 Ge62
Maiquetia ⬜ YV 269 Gg40
Maira ⬜ I 40 Lh46
Mairi ⬜ BR (BA) 283 Hk51
Mairiripotaba ⬜ BR (GO) 286 Hf54
Mairwa ⬜ IND (BIH) 107 Pc32
Maisandra ⬜ IND (KTK) 111 Oj40
Maisan-e-Jmam ⬜ IR 72 Nf29
Maisi ⬜ C 259 Gc35
Maïšiagala ⬜ LT 17 Mf36
Maisome Island ▲ EAT 204 Mg47
Maison Carrée de Nîmes ⬜⬛ F 25 Le47
Maisonnette ⬜ CDN (NB) 245 Gh22
Maisons de Champagne d'Épernay ⬜⬛ F 23 Ld41
Maitabi, Mount ▲ SOL 160 Sj49
Maitbhanga ⬜ BD 112 Pf34
Maitembge ⬜ RB 213 Md56
Maitioukoulou ⬜ RCA 195 Lj42
Maitland ⬜ AUS (NSW) 153 Sf62
Maitland ⬜ AUS (SA) 152 Rj63
Maitland Range ▲ AUS 138 Rd53
Maitri ▲ ANT (IND) 297 Lc33
Maitum ⬜ RP 123 Rc42
Maiurno ⬜ SUD 190 Mg40
Maizhokunggar ⬜ CHN (TIB) 89 Pf31
Maizuru ⬜ J 101 Rh28
Maja ⬰ RUS 59 Rd07
Majahual ⬜ MEX (QTR) 255 Fg36
Majak ⬜ RUS 98 Rj21
Majak Oktjabrja ⬜ RUS 53 Nc21
Majakly ⬜ UA 45 Mk43
Majdan ⬜ RUS 53 Ne18
Majdan ⬜ UA 39 Md42
Majdanpek ⬜ SCG 44 Mb46
Majenang ⬜ RI 128 Qe49
Majene ⬜ RI 127 Qk47
Majete Game Reserve ⬜☒ MW 210 Mh53
Majetu ⬜ BOL 280 Gh52
Majevica ▲ BIH 41 Lt46
Majgaon ⬜ IND (MPH) 109 Pb34
Majhaon ⬜ IND (JKD) 109 Pb33
Majholi ⬜ IND (MPH) 109 Pa33
Maji ⬜ ETH 197 Mh44
Majiahewan ⬜ CHN (NHZ) 92 Qc27
Majie ⬜ CHN (YUN) 113 Qb33
Majilovac ⬜ SCG 44 Mb46
Majimatu ⬜ EAT 207 Mk48
Maji Moto ⬜ EAT 204 Mh46
Majkop ⬜ RUS 55 Na25
Majki-Saj ⬜ KS 77 Og25
Majorski ⬜ RUS 55 Na22
Majors Place ⬜ USA (NV) 234 Ec26
Majski ⬜ RUS (KBA) 70 Nc24
Majskij ⬜ RUS 98 Re19
Majskij ⬜ RUS 98 Rb20
Majuba Hill ⬜ ZA 217 Me59

Manjeri – Mary Anne Group

Manjeri IND (KER) 110 Oj41
Manjhand PK 80 Oe33
Manjira Wildlife Sanctuary IND 108 Ok36
Manjlegaon IND (MHT) 108 Oj36
Manjo CAM 194 Le43
Manjola ZW 210 Md54
Manjou CAM 195 Lg43
Manjra IND 108 Oj36
Mankachar IND (ASM) 112 Pe33
Mankanza RDC 200 Lk45
Mankarbo S 13 Ls30
Man Kat MYA 113 Pk35
Mankato USA (KS) 240 Fa26
Mankato USA (MN) 241 Fd23
Mankera PK 79 Of30
Mankhan MNG 90 Qa20
Mankhan Nature Reserve MNG 85 Pg22
Manki CAM 195 Lf43
Mankim CAM 195 Lg43
Mankono CI 193 Kg41
Mankpan GH 193 Kk41
Mankrangso GH 193 Kk42
Mankulam CL 111 Pa42
Manley Hot Springs USA (AK) 229 Ce13
Man Li MYA 113 Pj34
Manlleu E 30 Lc49
Manmad IND (MHT) 108 Oh35
Manna RI 125 Qb48
Manna Hill AUS (SA) 152 Rk62
Man-Namlet MYA 113 Pk34
Mannar CL 111 Ok42
Mannemkonda IND (ORS) 109 Pa36
Manners Creek AUS (NT) 143 Rj57
Mannheim D 34 Lj41
Manni CHN (TIB) 88 Pd28
Manning USA (ND) 240 Ej22
Manning USA (SC) 249 Fk29
Manning Prov. Park CDN 232 Dk21
Manning Range, Mount AUS 144 Qk60
Manning Strait SOL 161 Sj49
Manningtree GB 21 Lb39
Mann Ranges AUS 142 Re58
Mann River AUS 139 Rh52
Mannum AUS (SA) 152 Rk63
Mannville CDN (AB) 233 Ee19
Mano LB/WAL 192 Ke42
Mano WAL 192 Kd41
Manoá Pium, T.I. BR 270 Gk44
Manogongu LB 192 Ke42
Manohardi BD 112 Pf33
Manokwari RI 131 Rh46
Manokwari RI 131 Rh47
Manole BG 47 Me48
Manoleasa RO 45 Mh43
Manolo Fortich RP 123 Rc41
Manoma RUS 99 Rj21
Manombo Atsimo RM 220 Nb57
Manometimay RM 220 Nc56
Manompana RM 220 Ne54
Manonga EAT 204 Mg47
Manono RDC 206 Md49
Manonwa RDC 203 Mc48
Manor IND (MHT) 108 Og36
Manorhamilton IRL 18 Km36
Manori Beach IND 108 Og36
Manosque F 25 Lf47
Manou RCA 196 Ma41
Manouane CDN (QC) 244 Gc22
Manova WAL 192 Ke41
Manp'o PRK 100 Rd25
Manpur IND (CGH) 109 Pa35
Manqabâd ET 177 Mf32
Manra KIR 157 Ub19
Manresa E 30 Lb49
Mansa IND (PJB) 106 Oh31
Mansa Z 210 Me51
Mansabá GNB 183 Kc39
Mansa Konko WAG 183 Kc39
Mansalay RP 121 Ra39
Man Sam MYA 113 Pj34
Mansar IND (MHT) 109 Ok35
Mansehra PK 79 Og28
Mansel Island CDN 225 Fd06
Mansfeld D 33 Lm39
Mansfield AUS (VIC) 153 Sd64
Mansfield GB 21 Kt37
Mansfield USA (AR) 243 Fc28
Mansfield USA (OH) 246 Fj25
Mansfield USA (PA) 247 Gb25
Mansfield Jetty USA (TX) 253 Fb32
Mansfiled USA (LA) 243 Fd30
Mansha Z 210 Mf51
Mansi MYA 113 Ph33
Mansiari IND (UTT) 107 Pa30
Mansidão BR (BA) 282 Hh51
Mansilla E 27 Kr52
Mansilla E 27 Ks52
Mansilla de las Mulas E 26 Kp52
Mansinha BR (TO) 282 Hg50
Mansión CR 256 Fh40
Mansle F 24 La45
Manso BR 281 Hc53
Mansôa GNB 183 Kc39
Manso au das Mortes BR 281 Hc53
Manson Creek CDN (BC) 231 Dh18
Manso-Nkwanta GH 193 Kk42
Mansoura DZ 173 Lc27
Mansourah DZ 173 Kk28
Mansur Abad IR 73 Nk29
Mansur Abad IR 74 Ng31
Mansura Ruins PK 81 Oe33
Manta DY 193 La40
Manta EC 272 Fk46
Mantadia-Andasibe, P.N.de RM 220 Ne55
Mantalinga RI 127 Ra47
Mantalingajan, Mount RP 122 Qj41
Mantamádos GR 49 Mg51
Mantanai Besar MAL 122 Qj42
Mantare EAT 206 Mg47
Mantaro PE 278 Gc51
Mantasoa RM 220 Nd55
Mantawa RI 127 Rb46
Manteca USA (CA) 234 Dk27
Mantecal YV 269 Gf42
Mantecal YV 269 Gh42
Mantehage RI 127 Rc45
Mantena BR (MG) 287 Hk55
Mantes-la-Jolie F 23 Lb42
Mantes-la-Ville F 23 Lb42
Manthani IND (APH) 109 Ok36
Manthiréa GR 48 Mc53
Manti USA (UT) 235 Ee26
Manticao RP 123 Rc41
Manto HN 256 Fg38
Manto PE 279 Gd52
Mantorp S 13 Lq32
Mantos Blancos RCH 284 Ge57
Mántova I 40 Ll45
Mantralayam IND (APH) 108 Oj38
Mäntsälä FIN 16 Mf30
Mänttä FIN 16 Me28
Mantua C 258 Fh34
Mantuan Downs AUS (QLD) 151 Sd58
Mantung AUS (SA) 152 Sa63
Mantup RI 128 Qg49
Manturovo RUS 53 Nc16
Mäntyharju FIN 16 Mg29
Mäntyluoto FIN 13 Mb29
Manu IND (TRP) 112 Pg34
Manú PE 279 Ge51
Manú PE 279 Ge52
Manu WAN 186 Lc39
Manuae Atoll F 165 Cc54
Manua Islands USA 164 Bf53
Manubepium RI 131 Rh46
Manuc Bei MD 45 Mj44
Manuel MEX (TM) 253 Fa34
Manuel Alves BR 282 Hf51
Manuel Alves Grande BR 276 Hg49
Manuel Alves Pequeno BR 276 Hg50
Manuel Antonio, P.N. CR 256 Fh41
Manuel Benavides MEX (CHH) 237 Ej31
Manuel Diaz ROU 289 Hc61
Manuel Emídio BR (PI) 276 Hj49
Manuel J.Cobo RA (BA) 293 Hb63
Manuel Ribas BR (PR) 286 He58
Manuel Tames C 259 Gc35
Manuel Urbano BR (AC) 279 Gf50
Manuel Vitorino BR (BA) 283 Hk53
Manui RI 127 Rb47
Manuk RI 130 Rf48
Manukan RP 123 Rb41
Manukau NZ 154 Th64
Manunda AUS (SA) 152 Rk62
Manunga Z 206 Me50
Manunui NZ 154 Th65
Manú, P.N. PE 279 Ge52
Manur IND (MHT) 108 Oh36
Manurimi BOL 279 Gg52
Manuripe BOL 279 Gf51
Manusela RI 130 Re47
Manusela N.P. RI 130 Re47
Manus Island PNG 159 Sd46
Manvi IND (KTK) 108 Oj38
Manville USA (WY) 235 Eh24
Manweng MYA 113 Pj34
Many USA (LA) 243 Fd30
Manyallaluk A.L. AUS 139 Rg53
Manyame ZW 210 Mf54
Manyani EAK 207 Mk47
Manyapadu IND (APH) 108 Oj38
Manyas TR 50 Mh50
Manyberries CDN (AB) 233 Ee21
Manych Depression RUS 55 Nb22
Manyelanong Game Reserve RB 213 Mc58
Manyeleti Game Reserve ZA 214 Mf58
Manyémen CAM 194 Le43
Many Farms USA (AZ) 237 Ef27
Manyikeni MOC 214 Mh57
Manyinga Z 209 Mc52
Manyoni EAT 206 Mf49
Manyoni EAT 207 Mh48
Manypeaks AUS (WA) 144 Qk63
Manzai PK 78 Oe30
Manzai PK 79 Of29
Manzanares CO 268 Gc43
Manzanares E 29 Kr48
Manzanilla Beach TT 270 Gk40
Manzanillo C 259 Gb35
Manzanillo MEX (COL) 253 Eh36
Manzengele RDC 203 Lj49
Manzhouli CHN (NMZ) 91 Qj21
Manzil PK 80 Ob31
Manzini SD 217 Mf59
Manzshir Monastery MNG 90 Qd22
Manzurka RUS 90 Qd19
Mao DOM 260 Ge36
Maó E 30 Le51
Mao EAT 206 Mf50
Mao TCH 187 Lh38
Maocaojie CHN (HUN) 95 Qg31
Mao'ershan CHN (HLG) 98 Rd23
Maogong CHN (GZH) 96 Qe32
Maohutang CHN (HUB) 95 Qf30
Maojing CHN (GSU) 92 Qd27
Maokeng ZA 217 Md59
Mao Ling CHN 95 Qe28
Maoming CHN (GDG) 96 Qf35
Maope RB 213 Md57
Maopora RI 132 Rd49
Mao Xian CHN (SCH) 94 Qb30
Mapagoro EAT 207 Mg50
Mapai MOC 214 Mf57
Mapamoiwa PNG 160 Sf50
Mapam Yumco CHN 88 Pa30
Mapanda RDC 203 Mc50
Mapane RI 127 Ra46
Mapangu RDC 203 Ma48
Mapanza Z 210 Md54
Mapari BR 273 Gg47
Mapastepec MEX (CHP) 255 Fd38
Mapat RI 127 Qj44
Mapatizi RCB 202 Lg47
Mapé RCA 200 Mb43
Mapelane Nature Reserve ZA 217 Mg60
Maphisa ZW 214 Me56
Mapi RI 158 Rk49
Mapi RI 158 Rk49
Mapiá BR 274 Ha48
Mapili RI 127 Qk47
Mapinhane MOC 214 Mh57
Mapire YV 269 Gh42
Mapiri BOL 279 Gg51
Mapiri BOL 279 Gf53
Mapiripán CO 273 Gd44
Maple Creek CDN (SK) 233 Ef21
Maple Ridge CDN (BC) 232 Dj21
Maplesville USA (AL) 248 Fg29
Mapleton USA (IA) 241 Fc24
Mapoon AUS (QLD) 146 Sa52
Mapoon A.L. AUS 146 Sb51
Mapor RI 125 Qc45
Mapor Beach RI 125 Qc45
Mapuera BR 275 Hb46
Mapulanguene MOC 214 Mg58
Mapunga Z 210 Md52
Mapungubwe ZA 214 Me57
Mapungubwe (Vhembe-Dongola) N.P. ZA 214 Me57
Mapusa IND (GOA) 108 Og38
Maputi RI 127 Qk45
Maputo MOC 214 Mg58
Maqên CHN (QHI) 94 Qa28
Maqna KSA 64 Mh31
Maqrat YE 69 Nf38
Maqteïr RIM 178 Ke35
Maqu CHN (GSU) 94 Qb29
Maquan He CHN 88 Pb31
Maquecha MOC 214 Mg56
Maqueda E 29 Kq50
Maqueda Channel RP 121 Rc39
Maquela do Zombo ANG 202 Lh49
Maqueze MOC 214 Mg58
Maquia PE 278 Gc49
Maquinchao RA (RN) 292 Gf66
Maquinchao RA 292 Gf66
Maquinista Levet RA (MD) 288 Gg62
Maquoketa USA (IA) 241 Fe24
Mara EAT 204 Mh46
Mara GUY 271 Hb42
Mara IND (MPH) 109 Pb34
Mara RI 130 Rf48
Mara ZA 214 Me57
Maraã BR (AM) 274 Gh46
Maraa Urubaxi, T.I. BR 274 Gh46
Marabá BR (PA) 276 Hf48
Marabadiassa CI 193 Kh41
Marabahan RI 126 Qh47
Marabidiyah IRQ 65 Nb29
Marabitanas BR (AM) 273 Gg45
Marabout Moulay Hassan DZ 180 Lc33
Marabouts TN 174 Ld29
Maracá BR (AP) 271 He44
Maracaçumé BR (MA) 276 Hh47
Maracaçumé BR 276 Hh46
Maracai BR (SP) 286 He57
Maracaibo YV 268 Ge40
Maracaju BR (MS) 286 Hc56
Maracanã BR (MA) 276 Hj47
Maracanã BR (PA) 276 Hg46
Maracanã BR 274 Ha49
Maracanaú BR (CE) 277 Ja47
Maracás BR (BA) 283 Hk52
Maracas Beach TT 270 Gk40
Maracay YV 269 Gg40
Maracoa CO 269 Gf44
Maracuni YV 269 Gf44
Maradah LAR 175 Lk31
Maradankadawala CL 111 Pa42
Maradi RN 186 Ld39
Maradun WAN 186 Ld39
Marafa EAK 207 Mk47
Marafa Depression (Hell's Kitchen) EAK 205 Mk47
Maragheh IR 72 Nd27
Maragogi BR (AL) 283 Jc50
Maragogipe BR (BA) 283 Ja52
Marah KSA 67 Nc33
Marahoue, P.N.de la CI 193 Kg42
Marais Poitevin F 22 Kt44
Marais Salants F 22 Ks43
Marais Vernier F 22 La41
Maraiwatsede, T.I. BR 281 He51
Marajai, T.I. BR 274 Gh47
Maraka RN 186 Ld39
Marakabei LS 217 Me60
Marakei Atoll KIR 157 Tc18
Marakele N.P. ZA 213 Md58
Marakesa RDC 201 Md45
Marakhayy YE 68 Nf38
Marakhi Reservoir IND 112 Pd33
Marakkanam IND (TNU) 111 Ok40
Maraku WAN 186 Le40
Maralal EAK 204 Mj45
Maralal Nature Sanctuary EAK 204 Mj45
Maraldy KZ 85 Pc21
Marale HN 256 Fg38
Marali RCA 196 Lk42
Maralinga AUS (SA) 145 Rf61
Maralinga Tjarutja A.L. AUS 142 Rf60
Maramag RP 123 Rc42
Maramasike SOL 161 Ta50
Marambio ANT (RA) 296 Ha31
Maramuni River PNG 159 Sb48
Maran MAL 117 Qb44
Marana USA (AZ) 237 Ee29
Maranalgo AUS (WA) 144 Qj60
Marand IR 72 Nc26
Marandala CI 193 Kh41
Marandet RN 186 Ld37
Maranello I 40 Ll46
Marang MAL 117 Qb43
Marango AUS (QLD) 151 Sd59
Maranguape BR (CE) 277 Ja47
Maranhão BR (AM) 275 Hb47
Maranhão BR 282 Hf53
Maranhão BR 265 Hc20
Maranhoto BR (AM) 274 Gj47
Marañón PE 272 Gc48
Marans F 22 Ku44
Maranura PE 279 Gd52
Marapa RA 288 Gh59
Marapanim BR (PA) 276 Hg46
Marapi BR 275 Hb45
Mar Argentino 295 Gh71
Marari BR 274 Gh45
Mara Rosa BR (GO) 282 Hf52
Marasende RI 129 Qk48
Mărășești RO 45 Mh45
Mărașu RO 45 Mh46
Marat UZ 76 Oc24
Marataizes BR (ES) 287 Hk56
Maratea I 43 Lq50
Marathon AUS (QLD) 148 Sb56
Marathon CDN (ON) 239 Fg21
Marathon USA (FL) 250 Fk33
Marathon USA (TX) 237 Ej30
Marathónas GR 48 Md52
Maratua RI 127 Qk44
Maraú BR (BA) 283 Ja53
Marau BR (RS) 290 Hd60
Maraudeur F (GF) 271 Hd44
Marauiá BR 274 Gh45
Maravatío de Ocampo MEX (MHC) 254 Ek36
Maravilha BR (AM) 274 Gk47
Maravilha BR (SC) 290 Hd59
Maravilhas BR (MG) 287 Hh55
Maravilla BOL 279 Gg51
Marawah LAR 175 Ma29
Marawaka PNG 159 Sc49
Marawi RP 123 Rc41
Marawi SUD 190 Mf37
Maraxo Patá BR (PA) 275 Hb45
Marayes RA (SJ) 288 Gg61
Marayoun RL 64 Mh29
Mar'ayt YE 69 Nf37
Marazion GB 20 Kp40
Marbach D 34 Lk42
Marbella E 28 Kq46
Marble Bar AUS (WA) 140 Qk56
Marble Bar Road AUS 140 Ra56
Marble Canyon USA (AZ) 237 Ee27
Marble Hall ZA 214 Me58
Marble Hill USA (MO) 243 Ff27
Marble Point ANT (USA) 297 Tb34
Marburg D 32 Lj40
Marcabeli EC 272 Ga47
Marcal H 38 Ls43
Marcala HN 256 Fg38
Marcali H 38 Ls44
Marcaltő H 38 Ls43
Marčana HR 41 Lo46
Marcapata PE 279 Ge52
Marcapomacocha PE 278 Gb51
Marcelândia BR (MT) 281 Hc51
Marcelino BR (AM) 273 Gg45
Marcelino BR (AM) 273 Gg46
Marcell USA (MN) 241 Fd22
Marcelo BR (PA) 275 He47
March A 35 Lr42
March GB 21 La38
Marchagee AUS (WA) 144 Qj61
Marche I 40 Lo47
Marche-en-Famenne B 23 Lf40
Marchena E 28 Kp47
Marchenoir F 22 Lb43
Marchinbar Island AUS 139 Rj51
Marciac F 24 La47
Marcigny F 25 Le44
Marcilla RP 120 Ra39
Marcillac-la-Croisille F 24 Lc45
Marcinkonys LT 17 Me36
Marcinkowice PL 39 Ma41
Marcionílio Sousa BR (BA) 283 Hk52
Marck F 23 Lb40
Marco USA (FL) 250 Fk33
Marco de Canaveses P 26 Km51
Marconi N.H.S. CDN 245 Ha22
Marco Rondon BR (RO) 280 Gk52
Marcos Juárez RA (CD) 289 Gj62
Marcos Parente BR (PI) 277 Hj49
Marcoux USA (MN) 241 Fb22
Marcus Baker, Mount USA (AK) 229 Cg15
Mard Abad IR 72 Nf28
Mardalen N 12 Lj28
Mardan PK 79 Og28
Mar de Ajó RA (BA) 293 Hb64
Mar de Espanha BR (MG) 287 Hj56
Mar del Plata RA (BA) 293 Hb65
Mardie AUS (WA) 140 Qh56
Mardie Island AUS 140 Qh56
Mardin TR 63 Na27
Mardin Dağları TR 63 Na27
Maré F (NCL) 162 Te56
Mare RI 129 Ra48
Marea del Portillo C 259 Gb36
Mare aux Crocodiles de Dounkou BF 185 Kj39
Mare aux Crocodiles de Sabou BF 185 Kj39
Marechal Cândido Rondon BR (PR) 286 Hc58
Marechal Deodoro BR (AL) 283 Jc50
Mare de Tizi RCA/TCH 196 Mb40
Mare d'Oursi BF 185 Kk38
Maree AUS (SA) 143 Rk60
Mareeba AUS (QLD) 149 Sc54
Mareeq SP 199 Nd44
Maremma I 42 Lm48
Maréna RMM 183 Ke38
Marenge RDC 206 Me48
Marengo USA (IA) 241 Fd25
Marengo Cave USA 248 Fg26
Marennes F 24 Kt45
Marerano RM 220 Nc56
Mareth TN 174 Lf29
Mareuil-sur-Lay F 22 Kt44
Mar'evka RUS 53 Ne19
Marevo RUS 52 Mg17
Marfa M 42 Lp55
Marfa USA (TX) 237 Eh30
Margao IND (GOA) 108 Og38
Margaree Forks CDN (NS) 245 Gk22
Margaret AUS (QLD) 150 Sb59
Margaret AUS 143 Rj60
Margaretville USA (NY) 247 Gc24
Margaret, Mount AUS 140 Qj57
Margaret River AUS (WA) 144 Qh62
Margaret River AUS 138 Rd55
Margarida BR (MS) 285 Hb56
Margarima PNG 159 Sb49
Margariti GR 48 Ma51
Margaritove RUS 55 Mk22
Margasari RI 126 Qh47
Margate GB 21 Lb39
Margate ZA 217 Mf61
Mărgău RO 44 Mc44
Margecany SK 39 Mb42
Margherita IND (ASM) 113 Ph32
Margherita di Savóia I 43 Lr49
Marghita RO 44 Mc43
Margiana TM 71 Oa26
Marg'ilon UZ 77 Of25
Margione I 40 Lh45
Margonin PL 36 Ls38
Margosatubig RP 123 Rb42
Marguerite CDN (BC) 232 Dj19
Marguerite Bay 296 Gc32
Margyang CHN (TIB) 89 Pe31
Marhamat UZ 77 Og25
Marhanec' UA 55 Mh22
Marhoum DZ 173 Kk28
Mari BR (AM) 274 Gh49
Mari PNG 158 Sa50
Mari SYR 65 Na28
Maria BR (PA) 276 Hf46
Maria MOC 211 Mj54
Maria PE 278 Gb49
Maria Aurora RP 121 Ra38
Maria Elena RCH 284 Gf57
Maria Eugenia RA (SF) 289 Gk61
Mariager DK 14 Lk34
Mariager Fjord DK 14 Ll34
Mariahan IND (UPH) 109 Pb33
María Ignacia RA (BA) 293 Ha64
Maria Island AUS 139 Rh53
Maria Island N.P. AUS 152 Se67
Mariakani EAK 207 Mk47
Maria Laach D 32 Lh40
Mariala N.P. AUS 151 Sc59
Marialva P 26 Kn50
Maria, Mount GB 295 Ha71
Marian AUS (QLD) 149 Se56
Mariana BOL 285 Gj55
Mariana BR (MG) 287 Hj56
Mariana Islands 134 Sa08
Mariana Trench 134 Sa08
Mariani IND (ASM) 112 Ph32
Marianna USA (AR) 243 Fe28
Marianna USA (FL) 249 Fh30
Mariannelund S 15 Lq33
Mariano I.Loza RA (CR) 289 Ha60
Marianópolis BR (MA) 276 Hh48
Mariánské Lázně CZ 38 Ln41
Mariarano RM 218 Nd53
Maria Saal A 35 Lp44
Maria Teresa ANG 202 Lh50
Maria Teresa RA (SF) 289 Gk63
Mariazell A 35 Lq43
Ma'rib YE 68 Nc38
Maribo DK 14 Lm36
Maribor SLO 41 Lq44
Marica BG 46 Md48
Marica BG 47 Mf48
Maricá BR (RJ) 287 Hj57
Maricaban Island RP 121 Ra39
Marical Caceres PE 278 Gc52
Maricao USA (PR) 261 Gg36
Marico ZA 213 Md58
Maridi SUD 197 Me43
Maridi SUD 201 Me43
Marié BR 273 Gf46
Marie Byrd Land ANT 296 Ed34
Mariefred S 13 Ls31
Marie-Galante F (GL) 261 Gk38
Mariehamn = Maarianhamina FIN 13 Lu30
Mariel C 258 Fj34
Mari-El RUS 53 Ne17
Marie Louise SY 219 Ng49
Marie Luise Bank 122 Qj40
Marielyst DK 14 Lm36
Marienberg D 33 Lo40
Mariental NAM 212 Lj58
Mariés GR 47 Me50
Mariestad S 13 Lo32
Marieta YV 269 Gg43
Marietta USA (GA) 249 Fh29
Marietta USA (OH) 247 Fk26
Mariga WAN 186 Ld40
Mariga WAN 186 Lc40
Marigat EAK 204 Mh45
Marignane F 25 Lf47
Marigot F (GL) 261 Gj36
Marigot RH 260 Gd36
Marigot WD 261 Gk38
Marihatag RP 123 Rd41
Marija Bistrica HR 41 Lr44
Marijampolė LT 17 Md36
Marikal IND (APH) 108 Oj37
Marikina RP 121 Ra38
Marilia BR (SP) 286 Hf57
Marimari BR 274 Ha48
Marimba ANG 203 Lj50
Marín E 26 Km52
Marina di Belvedere I 43 Lq51
Marina di Carrara I 40 Ll46
Marina di Cetraro I 43 Lq51
Marina di Grosseto I 40 Ll48
Marina di Léuca I 43 Lt51
Marina di Pisa I 40 Ll47
Marina di Ragusa I 42 Lp54
Marina di Ravenna I 40 Ln46
Marina Plains AUS (QLD) 147 Sb53
Mariñas E 26 Kn53
Marinduque Island RP 121 Ra39
Marine de Sisco F 31 Lk48
Marineland USA (FL) 250 Fk31
Marineland of Florida USA 250 Fk31
Marinella I 42 Ln53
Marineo I 42 Lo53
Mariner Glacier 297 Tb33
Marinette USA (WI) 246 Fg23
Maringá BR (PR) 286 He57
Maringa RDC 200 Ma45
Maringué MOC 210 Mh54
Maringues F 25 Ld45
Marinha Grande P 28 Km49
Marinho de Fernando de Noronha, P.N. BR 277 Jd47
Marinho dos Abrolhos, P.N. BR 287 Ja55
Marinka BG 47 Mh48
Marino de Punta Francés-Punta Pedernales, P.N. C 258 Fj35
Marino de Vallarta, P.N. MEX 252 Eh35
Marino Golfo de Chiriquí, P.N. PA 256 Fj41
Marino Isla Bastimentos, P.N. PA 257 Fk41
Marino Las Baulas, P.N. CR 256 Fh40
Marion USA (AL) 248 Fg29
Marion USA (AR) 243 Fe28
Marion USA (IA) 241 Fe24
Marion USA (IL) 243 Ff27
Marion USA (IN) 246 Fh25
Marion USA (KS) 241 Fb26
Marion USA (KY) 243 Ff27
Marion USA (NC) 249 Fk28
Marion USA (OH) 246 Fj25
Marion USA (SC) 249 Ga28
Marion USA (VA) 249 Fk27
Marion Downs AUS (QLD) 148 Rk57
Marion Reefs AUS 149 Sf55
Maripasoula F (GF) 271 Hd44
Maripipi Island RP 123 Rc40
Mariposa USA (CA) 234 Ea27
Mariposa Monarca MEX 254 Ek36
Mariquita CO 268 Gc43
Marisa RI 127 Ra45
Mariscala ROU 289 Hc63
Mariscal José Félix Estigarribia PY 285 Gk56
Mariscos GCA 255 Ff38
Marita Downs AUS (QLD) 148 Sb57
Maritime Alps F 25 Lg46
Maritime Museum (Geraldton) AUS 144 Qh60
Mariupol' UA 55 Mj22
Mariusa, P.N. YV 270 Gj41
Marivan IR 72 Nd28
Mariveles RP 120 Ra38
Mariveles Reef 122 Qg42
Märjamaa EST 16 Me32
Marka SP 205 Nc45
Markabougou RMM 184 Kg39
Markabygd N 10 Lf14
Markakasa IND (MHT) 109 Pa35
Markakol KZ 85 Pc21
Markakol Nature Reserve KZ 85 Pc21
Markala RMM 184 Kg39
Markapur IND (APH) 111 Ok39
Markaryd S 15 Lo34
Marken ZA 214 Me57
Markermeer NL 32 Lf38
Market Drayton GB 21 Ks38
Market Harborough GB 21 Ku38
Market Rasen GB 21 Ku37
Market Weighton GB 21 Ku37
Markham CDN (ON) 247 Ga24
Markham Bay PNG 159 Sd49
Markham, Mount 297 Tb35
Markham River PNG 159 Sd49
Markhun PK 79 Oh27
Marki PL 37 Mb38
Markik IND (APH) 109 Ok37
Markit CHN (XUZ) 86 Oj26
Markivka UA 45 Mk44
Markivka UA 53 Mk21
Markkleeberg D 33 Ln39
Markópoulo GR 48 Md53
Markounda RCA 195 Lj42
Markovo BG 47 Mh47
Markoy BF 185 Kk38
Marks USA (MS) 243 Fe28
Marksewo PL 37 Mb37
Marksville USA (LA) 243 Fe30
Marktheidenfeld D 34 Lk41
Markt Indersdorf D 35 Lm42
Marktoberdorf D 34 Ll43
Marktredwitz D 35 Ln40
Mark Twain Birthplace S.H.S USA 241 Fd26
Mark Twain Boyhood Home & Museum USA 241 Fe26
Mark Twain Lake USA 241 Fd26
Mark Twain National Forest USA 248 Fe27
Mark Twain N.W.R. USA 241 Fe26
Mark Twain N.W.R. USA 246 Fe25
Mark Twain S.P. USA 241 Fe26
Markundi SUD 196 Mb40
Markwassie ZA 217 Md59
Marl D 32 Lh39
Marla AUS (SA) 142 Rg59
Marlborough AUS (QLD) 149 Se57
Marlborough GB 21 Kt39
Marlborough GUY 270 Ha42
Marlborough Sounds NZ 155 Th66
Marle F 23 Ld41
Marlin USA (TX) 243 Fb30
Marlinton USA (WV) 249 Fk26
Marl Island PNG 159 Sc46
Marlo AUS (VIC) 153 Se64
Marloth Nature Reserve ZA 216 Ma62
Marlow GB 21 Ku39
Marlow USA (OK) 242 Fb28
Marma S 13 Ls30
Marma S 13 Lr29
Marmande F 24 La46
Marmara TR 50 Mh50
Marmara Adası TR 50 Mh50
Marmaraereglisi TR 50 Mh50
Marmara Gölü TR 50 Mj52
Marmaris TR 49 Mj54
Mármaro GR 49 Mg52
Mar Menor E 29 Ku47
Marmion Lake CDN 239 Fe21
Mármol MEX (SL) 252 Eg34
Marmolada I 40 Lm44
Marmot Bay USA 230 Cd16
Marmot Island USA 230 Ce16
Marmul OM 69 Nh36
Marnay F 23 Lf43
Marne D 32 Lk37
Marne F 23 Le42
Marneuli GE 70 Nc25
Marniu IND (ARP) 112 Ph32
Maro TCH 196 Lk41
Maroa YV 273 Gg44
Maroantsetra RM 219 Ne53
Marobi Raghza PK 79 Oe29
Marod IND (CGH) 109 Pa35
Maroda IND (CGH) 109 Pa36
Marofandilia RM 220 Nc56
Maroharatra RM 220 Nd56
Marojejy, P.N.de RM 219 Ne53
Marokau Atoll F 165 Cj54
Marol 79 Oj28
Marolambo RM 220 Ne56
Maromandia RM 219 Ne53
Maromandia RM 219 Nf53
Maromokotro RM 219 Ne53
Marondera ZW 214 Mf55
Maronga AUS (QLD) 151 Se59
Marongora ZW 210 Me54
Maroni F (GF) 271 Hc43
Maroochydore AUS (QLD) 151 Sg59
Maroona AUS (VIC) 153 Sb64
Maroonah AUS (WA) 140 Qh57
Maropaika RM 220 Nd57
Maros RI 129 Ra48
Maroseranana RM 220 Ne55
Marotandrano RM 220 Ne54
Marotolana RM 219 Ne53
Marotta I 41 Lo47
Maroua CAM 187 Lh40
Marouini F/SME 271 Hd44
Marova BR (AM) 274 Gj46
Marovac SCG 46 Mb48
Marovato RM 219 Ne52
Marovato RM 219 Ne53
Marovato RM 220 Nc58
Marovoay RM 220 Nd54
Marowijne SME 271 Hc43
Marowo RI 127 Ra46
Marqadeh Gharbiyeh SYR 65 Na28
Mar Qu CHN 94 Qa29
Marqua AUS (NT) 143 Rj57
Marquard ZA 217 Md60
Marquelia MEX (GUR) 254 Fa37
Marquesas Islands 303 Cb10
Marquesas Keys USA 250 Fj33
Marquette USA (MI) 246 Fg22
Marquez USA (TX) 243 Fb30
Marquise F 23 Lb40
Marquq SUD 197 Mf41
Marra A.L. AUS 139 Rh53
Marracua MOC 211 Mj54
Marracuene MOC 214 Mg58
Marradi I 40 Lm46
Marradong AUS (WA) 144 Qj62
Marrak KSA 68 Na37
Marrakech MA 172 Kf30
Marrakush MA 172 Kf30
Marrawah AUS (TAS) 152 Sc66
Marrecão BR (AM) 279 Gg49
Marrecas, T.I. BR 286 He58
Marrero USA (LA) 243 Fe31
Marromeu MOC 214 Mh55
Marron AUS (WA) 140 Qh58
Marrupa MOC 211 Mj52
Marsa Alam ET 177 Mh33
Marsa-Ben-Mehidi DZ 173 Kj28
Marsabit EAK 204 Mj44
Marsabit National Reserve EAK 205 Mk44
Marsa Darur SUD 191 Mj37
Marsa Delwein SUD 191 Mj36
Marsala I 42 Ln53
Marsa Matruh ET 176 Md30
Marsa Mubârak ET 177 Mh33
Marsa Salak SUD 191 Mj36
Marsa Shin'ab SUD 191 Mj36
Marsassoum SN 183 Kc39
Mars Bay BS 251 Gb34
Marsberg D 32 Lj39
Marsciano I 40 Ln48
Marsden AUS (NSW) 153 Sd62
Marseille F 25 Lf47
Marseille-en-Beauvaisis F 23 Lb41
Marsella CO 268 Gc43
Marsella PE 272 Gc47
Marsga al Burayqah LAR 175 Lk30
Marshall LB 192 Ke42
Marshall USA (AK) 228 Bj15
Marshall USA (AR) 243 Fd28
Marshall USA (MI) 246 Fh24
Marshall USA (MN) 241 Fc23
Marshall USA (MO) 241 Fd26
Marshall USA (NC) 249 Fj28
Marshall USA (TX) 243 Fc29
Marshall Islands 134 Ta08
Marshall Islands 135 Ta08
Marshall Seamounts MH 157 Tb17
Marshalltown USA (IA) 241 Fd24
Marshfield USA (MO) 243 Fd27
Marshfield USA (WI) 241 Fe23
Marsh Harbour BS 251 Gb32
Mars Hill USA (ME) 244 Gg22
Marsh Island USA 243 Fe31
Marsh Lake CDN 231 Dc15
Marsh Pt. CDN 238 Fd17
Mársico Nuovo I 43 Lq50
Marsoui CDN (QC) 244 Gg21
Märsta S 13 Ls31
Marstal DK 14 Ll36
Marstrand S 14 Lm33
Martaban MYA 114 Pj37
Martap CAM 195 Lg42
Martapura RI 125 Qc48
Martapura RI 126 Qh47
Marte WAN 187 Lg39
Martelange B 23 Lf41
Marten River CDN (ON) 247 Ga22
Martensøya N 11 Ma05
Martfű H 39 Ma43
Mártha GR 49 Mf55
Martha's Vineyard USA 247 Ge25
Martigné-Ferchaud F 22 Kt43
Martigny CH 34 Lh44
Martigues F 25 Lf47
Martil MA 172 Kh28
Martilla FIN 16 Mc30
Martin SK 39 Lt41
Martin USA (SD) 240 Ek24
Martin USA (TN) 243 Ff27
Martina Franca I 43 Ls50
Martinborough NZ 154 Th66
Martinésia BR (MG) 286 Hf55
Martínez de la Torre MEX (VC) 254 Fb35
Martinho Campos BR (MG) 287 Hh55
Martinique F 261 Gk38
Martinique Channel 261 Gk38
Martinópole BR (CE) 277 Hk47
Martinópolis BR (SP) 286 He57
Martinsburg USA (WV) 247 Ga26
Martinšćica HR 41 Lp46
Martin's Drift RB 213 Md57
Martinsicuro I 41 Lo48
Martinsville USA (IN) 246 Fg26
Martinsville USA (VA) 249 Ga27
Martins Well AUS (SA) 152 Rk61
Martna EST 16 Md32
Marton NZ 154 Th66
Martorell E 30 Lb49
Martos E 28 Kr47
Martti FIN 11 Me12
Martuni ARM 70 Nc25
Maru IND (AAN) 111 Pg41
Maru RI 133 Rf49
Maru WAN 186 Ld39
Maruanum BR (AP) 275 He45
Marudá BR (PA) 276 Hg46
Marudi MAL 122 Qh43
Maruf AFG 78 Od30
Marulan AUS (NSW) 153 Se63
Marum, Mount VU 162 Te54
Marungu EAT 206 Mf48
Marungua EAK 204 Mj46
Marupa BR 275 Hb49
Marutea Atoll F 165 Cj54
Maru'ura SOL 161 Ta50
Marvanthe Beach IND 110 Oh40
Marvão P 28 Kn49
Marv Dasht IR 74 Ng31
Marve Beach IND 108 Og36
Marvejols F 25 Ld46
Marvell USA (AR) 243 Fe28
Marvik N 12 Lg31
Marvine, Mount USA 235 Ee26
Marvo Lagoon SOL 161 Sk50
Marvyn USA (AL) 249 Fh29
Marwah AFG 78 Ob28
Marwan KSA 67 Nd34
Marwayne CDN (AB) 233 Ee19
Marwick Head GB 19 Kr31
Mary TM 73 Oa27
Maryal Bai SUD 197 Md41
Mary Anne Group AUS 140 Qh56

Meadow Lake – Middle America Trench

Meadow Lake Prov. Park CDN 233 Ef18
Meadowlands Racetrack USA (NJ) 247 Gc25
Meadow Valley Wash USA 236 Ec27
Meadville USA (MS) 243 Fe30
Meadville USA (PA) 247 Fk25
Meakan-dake J 99 Sb24
Meandarra AUS (QLD) 151 Se59
Meane Baba Mausoleum TM 73 Nk27
Mearim BR 276 Hg49
Meath Park CDN (SK) 233 Eh19
Meaux F 23 Lc42
Mebo, Gunung RI 131 Rg46
Mebridege ANG 202 Lh49
Mebsi IND (BIH) 107 Pc32
Mecanhelas MOC 211 Mh53
Mécatina CDN 245 Ha20
Mecaya CO 272 Gc45
Mecca KSA 66 Mk35
Mechang MAL 117 Qb43
Mechara ETH 198 Na41
Mechcheri IND (TNU) 111 Oj41
Mechelen B 23 Le39
Méchéria DZ 173 Kk29
Méchiméré TCH 187 Lh39
Mechra-Benâbbou MA 172 Kg29
Mechra-Ben-Ksiri MA 172 Kh28
Mechra-Hassi-Bouménienne DZ 173 Kj30
Mechroha DZ 174 Ld27
Mecidiye TR 50 Mg50
Mecito MOC 211 Mj54
Mecitözü TR 51 Mq50
Mečka BG 47 Mf47
Meckering AUS (WA) 144 Qj61
Mecklenburg Bay D 33 Lm35
Mecklenburgische Seenplatte D 33 Ln37
Mecklenburg-Vorpommern D 33 Ln37
Meconta MOC 211 Mk53
Mecubúri MOC 211 Mk53
Mecúfi MOC 211 Na52
Mecula MOC 211 Mj52
Medak IND (APH) 109 Ok36
Medak Church IND 108 Ok36
Medak Fort IND 109 Ok37
Medale ETH 198 Na42
Medan RI 116 Pk44
Medang RI 117 Qa44
Médanos RA (BA) 293 Gj65
Médanos de Coro, P.N. YV 269 Gf40
Medarametla IND (APH) 111 Ok39
Medart USA (FL) 249 Fh30
Medawachchiya CL 111 Pa42
Medd Allah RMM 184 Kh38
Mede I 40 Lj45
Médéa DZ 173 Lb27
Medeina TN 174 Le28
Medeiros BR (MG) 287 Hg56
Medeiros Neto BR (BA) 287 Hk54
Medellín CO 268 Gc42
Medelpad S 13 Lq28
Medeltidsbveckan S 15 Lt33
Medemblik NL 32 Lf38
Medenine TN 174 Lf29
Medenyči UA 39 Md41
Meder ER 191 Na39
Méderdra RIM 183 Kc37
Medeu KZ 77 Oj24
Medevi S 13 Lp32
Medford USA (OR) 234 Dj24
Medford USA (WI) 241 Fe23
Medgidia RO 45 Mj46
Medgyesegyháza H 39 Mb44
Medhane Alem ETH 198 Mj39
Medi SUD 201 Mf43
Media Luna RA (SL) 288 Gg63
Medianeira BR (PR) 286 Hc58
Mediaș RO 44 Me44
Medical Springs USA (OR) 234 Eb23
Medicina I 40 Lm46
Medicine Bow USA (WY) 235 Eg25
Medicine Bow Mts. USA 235 Eg25
Medicine Hat CDN (AB) 233 Ee20
Medicine Lake USA (MT) 233 Eh21
Medicine Lodge USA (KS) 242 Fa27
Medijana SCG 46 Mb47
Medina BR (MG) 287 Hk54
Medina KSA 66 Mk33
Medina USA (ND) 240 Fa22
Medina USA (NY) 247 Ga24
Medina USA (OH) 246 Fk25
Medinaceli E 27 Ks51
Medina del Campo E 26 Kq51
Medina de Pomar E 27 Kr52
Medina de Rioseco E 26 Kp51
Médina Gounas SN 183 Kd39
Médina Sidonia E 28 Kp46
Médina-Yorofoula SN 183 Kc39
Medinet el'Ameriya el Guedida ET 177 Me30
Medinet el-Faijûm ET 177 Mf31
Medinet Sahara ET 177 Mg34
Medininkai LT 17 Mf36
Medio RA 289 Gk62
Medio Rio Negro I, T.I. BR 273 Gg46
Medio Rio Negro I, T.I. BR 273 Gf46
Médiouna MA 172 Kg29
Mediterranean Sea 6 Lb06
Medje RDC 201 Md44
Medje RDC 201 Me44
Medjedel DZ 173 Lb28
Medjez el Bab TN 174 Le27
Medley CDN (AB) 233 Ee18
Medley River CDN 233 Ee18
Médoc F 24 Ku45
Medora USA (ND) 240 Ej22
Médouneu G 195 Lf45
Medrissa DZ 173 La28
Međugorje BIH 41 Ls47
Medulin HR 41 Lo46
Međurečje SCG 46 Ma47
Međuriječje SCG 46 Lu48
Medvedica RUS 53 Nc20
Medvedja SCG 46 Mb48
Medvenka RUS 52 Mj20
Medvež'egorsk RUS 11 Mh14
Medyka PL 39 Mc41
Medze LV 17 Mb34
Medžhid tabija BG 45 Mh46
Medzilaborce SK 39 Mb41
Meeberrie AUS (WA) 140 Qh58
Meekatharra AUS (WA) 140 Qj59
Meeker USA (CO) 235 Eg25
Meeladeen SP 199 Ne40
Meeline AUS (WA) 144 Qk60
Meelpaeg Lake CDN 245 Hb21
Meemu Atoll MV 110 Og44
Meenakshi Temple IND 111 Oj42
Meerane D 33 Ln40
Meersburg D 34 Lk43
Meerut IND (UPH) 107 Oj31
Meerzorg SME 271 Hc43
Mega ETH 205 Mk44
Mega IND (ARP) 112 Ph31
Mega RI 130 Rf46
Mega Escarpment ETH 198 Mk43
Megáli Panagía GR 47 Md50
Megáli Stérna GR 46 Mc49
Mégalithes (Bouar) RCA 195 Lh43
Mégalithes de Cauria F 31 Lj49
Megalithic Temples M 42 Lp55
Megáli Vrissi GR 46 Mc49
Megalo ETH 198 Na42
Megalohóri GR 46 Mb51
Megálo Horio GR 49 Mh54
Megalópoli GR 48 Mc53
Megalópoli GR 48 Mc53
Megamo RI 130 Rf46
Meganissi GR 48 Ma52
Mégara GR 48 Md52
Megasini IND 109 Pd35
Méga Spileo GR 48 Mc52
Megauda SUD 190 Mf37
Megeitia SUD 190 Mf39
Megève F 25 Lg45
Megezez ETH 198 Mk41
Meghalaya IND 104 Pc13
Meghri ARM 70 Nd26
Mégué BF 185 Kk39
Meguidene DZ 173 La31
Mehakit RI 126 Qh47
Mehal Meda ETH 198 Mk40
Mehamn N 11 Md10
Méhana RN 185 La38
Mehar PK 80 Od32
Meharry, Mount AUS 140 Qk57
Mehdawal IND (UPH) 107 Pb32
Mehdia DZ 173 La28
Mehdi Šahr IR 72 Ng28
Mehelata RI 132 Re50
Meherpur BD 112 Pe34
Mehesana IND (GUJ) 108 Og34
Mehetia F (PYF) 165 Cf54
Mehezangulu EAT 207 Mk48
Mehikoorma EST 16 Mh32
Mehkar IND (MHT) 108 Oj35
Mehrabpur PK 80 Od31
Mehran IR 72 Nd29
Mehran IR 74 Nh32
Mehrangarh Fort IND 106 Og32
Mehrawan IND (UPH) 109 Pb33
Mehrgarh PK 80 Od31
Mehring D 34 Lg41
Mehriz IR 72 Nh30
Mehtarlam AFG 79 Of28
Mehun-sur-Yèvre F 23 Lc43
Meia Meia EAT 207 Mh48
Meia Ponte BR 286 Hf55
Meicheng CHN (ZJG) 102 Qk31
Meidougou CAM 195 Lh42
Meiganga CAM 195 Lh42
Meigu CHN (SCH) 94 Qb31
Meihekou CHN (JLN) 100 Rc24
Meiktila MYA 113 Ph35
Meilen CH 34 Lj43
Meili CHN 94 Pk31
Meilleur River CDN 231 Dh15
Meinersen D 33 Ll38
Meinhardt D 34 Lk41
Meiningen D 33 Ll40
Meinmagwe MYA 114 Pg36
Meinmahla Kyun Wildlife Sanctuary MYA 114 Ph37
Meira E 26 Kn53
Meiringen CH 34 Lj44
Meishan CHN (AHU) 102 Qh30
Meishan CHN (SCH) 94 Qb30
Meishan Shuiku CHN 102 Qh30
Meißen D 33 Lo39
Meißner D 32 Lk39
Meister River CDN 231 De15
Meitan CHN (GZH) 96 Qd32
Meitingen D 35 Ll42
Mei Xian CHN (SAA) 95 Qd28
Meiyao CHN (JLN) 98 Ra23
Meiyu CHN (SCH) 113 Qa32
Meizhou CHN (GDG) 97 Qj33
Meizhou Dao CHN 97 Qk33
Meja Reserve, Gunung RI 131 Rg46
Mejia PE 284 Ge54
Mejillones RCH 284 Ge57
Mejo YV 269 Gg41
Meka AUS (WA) 140 Qj59
Mékambo G 195 Lg45
Mekane Selam ETH 198 Mk40
Mekdela ETH 198 Mk40
Meke Gölü TR 51 Mo53
Mékel CAM 195 Lh44
Mek'ele ETH 191 Mk40
Mékhé SN 183 Kb38
Mekhtar PK 79 Oe30
Meki ETH 198 Mk41
Mékié CAM 195 Lg43
Me-kin MYA 113 Pk35
Mekmene Ben Amar DZ 173 Kk29
Meknès MA 172 Kh29
Meko WAN 194 Lb42
Mekomo CAM 195 Lh44
Mekong 105 Qb16
Mekong Delta VN 117 Qd40
Mekongga, Gunung RI 127 Ra47
Mekongga Mountains RI 127 Ra47
Mekoryuk USA (AK) 228 Bg15
Mékrou DY 186 Lb40
Mekunde EAT 207 Mf48
Melá GR 48 Me52
Meladang RI 126 Qe46
Melado RCH 292 Ge63
Melaje SCG 46 Ma47
Melak RI 126 Qh46
Melaka MAL 117 Qa44
Melalap MAL 122 Qj43
Melalih RI 130 Rf46
Melanesia 134 Sa10
Melanesian Basin 134 Ta10
Melapi RI 126 Qg45
Melates GR 48 Mb51
Melawi RI 126 Qg46
Melbourne AUS (VIC) 153 Sc64
Melbourne USA (FL) 250 Fk31
Melchett Lake CDN 239 Fg20
Melchor Ocampo MEX (DGO) 253 Eh33
Meldorf D 32 Lk36
Mélé RCA 196 Ma41
Mele Bay VU 162 Te54
Melegnano I 40 Lk45
Meleiro BR (SC) 291 Hf60
Melenci SCG 44 Ma45
Melenki RUS 53 Na18
Melfi I 43 Lq50
Mélfi TCH 187 Lj40
Melfjorden N 10 Lg12
Melfort CDN (SK) 233 Eh19
Melfort ZW 214 Mf55
Melgaço BR (PA) 275 He46
Melgar de Fernamental E 26 Kq52
Melghat Wildlife Sanctuary IND 108 Oj34
Melhus N 10 Lf14
Melibocus D 34 Lj41
Melide E 26 Km52
Melides P 28 Km48
Meligalás GR 46 Mc50
Melilla E 173 Kj28
Melilla E 173 Kj28
Melilli I 42 Lq53
Melinești RO 44 Md46
Melinka RCH 292 Gd67
Melipeuco RCH 292 Ge65
Melipilla RCH 288 Ge62
Melíssa GR 46 Mc51
Melita CDN (MB) 238 Ek21
Mélito de Porto Salvo I 43 Lq54
Melitón Albañez MEX (BCS) 252 Ee34
Melitopol' UA 55 Mh22
Melivia GR 46 Mc51
Melk A 35 Lq42
Melka Guba ETH 198 Mk43
Melka Kuntre ETH 198 Mk41
Melka Mari ETH 198 Na43
Melka Teko = Gode ETH 199 Nb42
Melkrivier ZA 213 Me58
Mellakoski FIN 11 Mc12
Mellam SUD 196 Mc39
Mellan Fryken S 13 Lo31
Mellbystrand S 15 Ln34
Melle D 32 Lj38
Melle F 24 Ku44
Mellen USA (WI) 241 Fe22
Mellerud S 12 Ln32
Mellette USA (SD) 240 Fa23
Mellish Reef AUS 137 Sd22
Mellit SUD 189 Mc38
Mellita TN 174 Lf28
Melliyakarai IND (TNU) 111 Ok41
Mellizos RCH 284 Gf57
Mellizo Sur, Cerro RCH 294 Gd70
Mellrichstadt D 34 Ll40
Melmoth ZA 217 Mf60
Melnica SCG 44 Mb46
Mel'ničnoe RUS 99 Rh23
Mělník GB 46 Md49
Mělník CZ 38 Lp40
Mel'nikovo RUS 16 Mk30
Melnsils LV 17 Mc33
Melo G 195 Lf44
Melo PY 285 Ha56
Melo ROU 289 Hc62
Meloco MOC 211 Mk52
Mélong CAM 194 Le43
Melozitna River USA 229 Cc13
Melrose AUS (WA) 140 Ra59
Melrose CDN (NS) 245 Gj23
Melrose USA (MN) 241 Fc23
Melrose USA (NM) 237 Ej28
Melrose Abbey GB 19 Ks35
Melrose Plantation USA 243 Fd30
Mels CH 34 Lk43
Melstone USA (MT) 235 Eg22
Melsungen D 32 Lk39
Melton AUS (VIC) 153 Sc64
Melton Mowbray GB 21 Ku38
Meluco MOC 211 Mk52
Melun F 23 Lc42
Melun MYA 112 Pg35
Melunghi Gang CHN/BHT 89 Pf31
Melu Prey K 115 Qc39
Melur IND (TNU) 111 Ok41
Meluri IND (NGL) 112 Ph33
Melvich GB 19 Kr32
Melville CDN (SK) 238 Ej20
Melville Bay AUS 139 Rj52
Melville Bugt DK 225 Gd03
Melville Island AUS 139 Rf51
Melville Island CDN 225 Ec03
Melville Peninsula CDN 224 Fd05
Méma Farimaké RMM 184 Kh38
Memala RI 126 Qg46
Mé Maoya F (NCL) 162 Tc56
Memari IND (WBG) 112 Pe34
Memba CO 268 Gb43
Memba MOC 211 Na53
Membalong RI 125 Qd47
Membe PNG 159 Sc48
Membeca BR 281 Hb52
Memboro RI 129 Qk50
Membrío E 28 Kn49
Memel ZA 217 Me59
Memmingen D 34 Ll43
Memndee Lake AUS 152 Sb62
Mempawah RI 126 Qe45
Memphis ET 177 Mf31
Memphis USA (MO) 241 Fd25
Memphis USA (TN) 243 Ff28
Memphis USA (TX) 242 Ek28
Ména RMM 184 Kg39
Mena UA 52 Mg20
Mena USA (AR) 243 Fc28
Menâa DZ 174 Lc28
Menabe RM 220 Nc56
Menággio I 40 Lk44
Menai SY 218 Nd50
Menai Bridge GB 20 Kq37
Menai Strait GB 20 Kq37
Ménaka RMM 185 Lb38
Menamaty Iloto RM 220 Nc57
Mena Murtee AUS (NSW) 150 Sb61
Menanga RI 127 Rc46
Menangina AUS (WA) 144 Ra60
Mena Park AUS (QLD) 151 Sc58
Menarandra RM 220 Nc58
Menarbu RI 131 Rh47
Menard USA (TX) 242 Fa30
Menawashei SUD 196 Mc39
Menchia TN 174 Le29
Menčul UA 39 Md42
Mendala RI 125 Qf47
Mendam PNG 159 Sc49
Mendanau RI 125 Qd47
Mendanha BR (MG) 287 Hj55
Mendawai RI 126 Qe46
Mendawak RI 126 Qe46
Mende F 25 Ld46
Mende RDC 203 Mc47
Mendeleevsk RUS 53 Ng18
Menden D 32 Lh39
Mendenhall USA (MS) 243 Ff30
Mendenhall Glacier USA (AK) 231 Dc16
Méndez EC 272 Ga47
Méndez MEX (TM) 253 Fa33
Mendi ETH 197 Mh41
Mendi PNG 159 Sb49
Mendleyarri AUS (WA) 144 Ra60
Mendocino Fracture Zone 303 Ca05
Mendol RI 124 Qb45
Mendoorah AUS (NSW) 151 Se61
Mendopolo SUD 201 Mf43
Mendorah AUS (NT) 139 Rf52
Mendota USA (CA) 234 Dk27
Mendota USA (IL) 246 Ff25
Mendoza PE 278 Gb49
Mendoza RA (MD) 288 Gf62
Mendoza RA 267 Gc25
Mendrisio CH 34 Lj45
Mendung RI 124 Qb45
Mendut RI 128 Qf49
Mene de Mauroa YV 269 Ge40
Mene Grande YV 269 Ge41
Menemen TR 49 Mh52
Menen B 23 Ld40
Menengai Crater EAK 204 Mh46
Meneou CY 51 Mo56
Menesjärvi FIN 11 Md11
Menfi I 42 Ln53
Meng CAM 195 Lg42
Menga ANG 208 Lh51
Mengam, Mount PNG 159 Sc48
Mengcheng CHN (AHU) 102 Qj29
Mengen D 34 Lk42
Mengen TR 51 Mn50
Mengeš SLO 41 Lp44
Menggala RI 125 Qc48
Menggari RI 131 Rh46
Menghai CHN (YUN) 113 Qa35
Mengibar E 29 Kr47
Mengku CHN (YUN) 113 Pk34
Mengla CHN (YUN) 113 Pk34
Mengla CHN (YUN) 113 Qa35
Mengong CAM 195 Lf44
Mengshan CHN (GZG) 96 Qf33
Menguémé CAM 195 Lf44
Mengwi RI 129 Qh50
Mengyan CHN (GZH) 96 Qe32
Mengyin CHN (SDG) 93 Qj28
Mengyou CHN (YUN) 113 Pk33
Mengzi CHN (YUN) 113 Qb34
Menhir de Champ-Dolent F 22 Kt42
Menidi GR 48 Mb51
Menindee AUS (NSW) 152 Sb62
Meningie AUS (SA) 152 Rk63
Menkerja RUS 59 Ra05
Menku, T.I. BR 280 Ha52
Menna ETH 191 Mk40
Mennonite Colonies PY 285 Ha57
Menominee USA (MI) 246 Fg23
Menominee Ind. Res. USA 246 Ff23
Menomonee Falls USA (WI) 246 Ff24
Menomonie USA (WI) 241 Fe23
Menongue ANG 208 Lj53
Menorca E 30 Ld50
Mensa RUS 90 Qe20
Mentakab MAL 117 Qb44
Mentana I 42 Ln48
Mentasta Pass USA 229 Cj14
Mentawai Archipelago RI 124 Pk46
Mentawai Strait RI 124 Pk46
Menton F 25 Lh47
Mentone USA (TX) 237 Ej30
Mentor USA (OH) 246 Fk25
Menukung RI 126 Qg46
Menxing CHN (YUN) 113 Qa35
Menyamya PNG 159 Sd49
Menyapa, Gunung RI 126 Qj45
Menyuan CHN (QHI) 92 Qa27
Menza RUS 90 Qe21
Menzel Bourguiba TN 174 Le27
Menzel Chaker TN 174 Lf28
Menzelinsk RUS 53 Ng18
Menzel Temime TN 174 Lf27
Menzies AUS (WA) 144 Ra60
Menzies, Mount 297 Oa33
Meobbaai NAM 212 Lh58
Meoqui MEX (CHH) 253 Eh31
Meota CDN (SK) 233 Ef19
Meo Vac VN 96 Qc34
Mepala ANG 202 Lg49
Mepica MOC 211 Mj53
Mepina MOC 211 Mj53
Meponda MOC 211 Mh52
Mepozo ANG 202 Lg49
Meppel NL 32 Lg38
Meppen D 32 Lh38
Mê Qu CHN 94 Qb29
Mequens BR 280 Gk52
Mequinenza E 30 La49
Mequon USA (WI) 246 Fg24
Mer F 22 Lb43
Mera EC 272 Ga46
Merah RI 127 Qj45
Merai PNG 160 Sg48
Merak RI 128 Qd48
Merak Belantung Beach RI 125 Qc48
Meramec S.P. USA 241 Fe26
Meramec S.P. USA 248 Fe26
Merampi RI 123 Rd43
Meran = Merano I 40 Lm44
Merangin RI 124 Qa47
Merano = Meran I 40 Lm44
Merapah AUS (QLD) 146 Sb52
Merapi, Gunung RI 128 Qf49
Merapi, Gunung RI 129 Qh50
Meratswe RB 213 Mc57
Meratus Mountains RI 126 Qh47
Merauke RI 158 Sa49
Merauke RI 158 Sa50
Merawwah UAE 74 Ng33
Merbein AUS (NSW) 152 Sb63
Merca = Marka SP 205 Nc45
Mercaderes CO 272 Gb45
Mercantour F/I 25 Lh46
Mercantour, P.N.du F 25 Lh46
Mercato Saraceno I 40 Ln47
Merced USA (CA) 234 Dk27
Mercedario, Cerro RA 288 Ge61
Mercedes RA (BA) 289 Ha63
Mercedes RA (CR) 289 Hb60
Mercedes ROU 289 Ha62
Mercedes USA (TX) 253 Fb32
Mercuryeiland NAM 212 Lh58
Mercury Island NAM 212 Lh58
Merdrignac F 22 Ks42
Mereb Wenz ER/ETH 191 Mk39
Meredoua DZ 180 La33
Merefa UA 53 Mj21
Merei RO 45 Mg45
Merek RI 116 Pk44
Mereksen DZ 174 Le31
Mere Lava VU 162 Te53
Merenkurkku FIN/S 10 Ma14
Mererale ETH 199 Nc42
Meresichic MEX (SO) 237 Ee30
Mereuch K 115 Qd39
Merewa ETH 198 Mj42
Merga = Nukhayla SUD 189 Md36
Mergui MYA 114 Pk39
Mergui Archipelago MYA 114 Pk39
Meri CAM 187 Lh40
Méri SN 183 Kc37
Meriba AUS (SA) 152 Sa63
Méribel F 25 Lg45
Meriç TR 47 Mg49
Meričleri BG 47 Mf48
Mérida E 28 Ko48
Mérida MEX (YT) 255 Ff35
Mérida YV 268 Ge41
Meridan RI 124 Qa45
Meriden USA (CT) 247 Gd25
Méridiala RMM 184 Kg39
Meridian USA (MS) 243 Ff29
Meridian USA (TX) 242 Fb30
Méridja DZ 173 Kj30
Mérignac F 24 Ku46
Mérihas GR 48 Me53
Merikarvia FIN 13 Mb29
Merimbula AUS (NSW) 153 Se64
Meringa WAN 187 Lg40
Meringur AUS (VIC) 152 Sa63
Merino Downs AUS (QLD) 149 Sc57
Meri-Pori FIN 16 Mb29
Merir Island PAL 121 Rg43
Merit MAL 126 Qg44
Merivale AUS (QLD) 151 Se58
Merivale River AUS 151 Sd58
Merke KZ 77 Og24
Merkinė LT 17 Me36
Merkys LT 17 Me36
Merlo RA (SL) 288 Gh62
Merluna AUS (QLD) 146 Sb52
Merlung RI 124 Qb46
Mermerna Pecina SCG 46 Mb48
Merna USA (NE) 240 Fa25
Mernye H 38 Ls44
Meroe Temple and pyramids SUD 190 Mg38
Merolia AUS (WA) 144 Rb60
Meropoh MAL 117 Qa43
Merouana DZ 174 Lc28
Merpalli IND (MHT) 109 Pa36
Merpas RI 125 Qb48
Merredin AUS (WA) 144 Qk61
Merrick GB 19 Kq35
Merrill USA (OR) 234 Dk24
Merrill USA (WI) 246 Ff23
Merriman USA (NE) 240 Ek24
Merriman ZA 216 Mb61
Merritt CDN (BC) 232 Dk20
Merritt Island USA (FL) 250 Fk31
Merriwa AUS (NSW) 153 Sf62
Merriwagga AUS (NSW) 153 Sc62
Merry Island CDN 239 Gb18
Mersa Fatma ER 191 Na39
Mersa Gulbub ER 191 Mk38
Mersa Teklay ER 191 Mk38
Mersch L 23 Lg41
Merseburg D 33 Lm39
Mersin = İçel TR 62 Mh27
Mersing MAL 117 Qb44
Mērsrags LV 17 Md33
Merta IND (RJT) 106 Oh32
Merthyr Tydfil GB 20 Kr39
Merti EAK 205 Mk45
Merti Plateau EAK 205 Mk45
Mértola P 28 Kn47
Merton AUS (VIC) 153 Sc64
Mertondale AUS (WA) 144 Ra60
Mertoutek DZ 180 Lc33
Mertule Maryam ETH 198 Mk40
Mertvovid UA 45 Mm43
Merty Merty AUS (SA) 143 Sa60
Mertz Glacier 297 Sb32
Mertzon USA (TX) 242 Ek30
Meru EAK 204 Mj45
Méru F 23 Lc41
Merume Mountains GUY 270 Gk42
Meru, Mount EAT 204 Mj47
Meru N.P. EAK 205 Mk46
Merure, T.I. BR 281 Hd53
Merutai MAL 122 Qj43
Merv TM 73 Ob27
Merweville ZA 216 Ma62
Méry BY 17 Mh35
Meryemana TR 49 Mh53
Merzbacher Glacierlake CHN 84 Pa24
Merzifon TR 62 Mh25
Merzig D 34 Lg41
Merzouga MA 173 Kh30
Mesa MOC 211 Mk52
Mesa, Cerro RA 292 Gf65
Mesa USA (AZ) 237 Ee29
Mesa USA (CO) 235 Ef26
Mesa de Coloradas MEX (DGO) 252 Eg32
Mesa del Huracán MEX (CHH) 237 Ef31
Mesa del Seri MEX (SO) 237 Ee31
Mesagne I 43 Ls50
Mesai CO 273 Gd45
Mesaieed Q 74 Nf33
Mesanga RI 127 Qk46
Mesa Verde N.P. USA 237 Ef27
Mescalero Apache Ind.Res. USA 237 Eh29
Meschede D 32 Lj39
Mescit Dağlari TR 63 Na25
Meselefors S 10 Lj13
Meseta Baya RA 292 Gf65
Meseta Cascajos RA 294 Ge70
Meseta de Colitoro RA 292 Gf66
Meseta de Icutú YV 269 Gh42
Meseta de Jáua YV 269 Gh43
Meseta de Lago Buenos Aires RA 294 Ge69
Meseta del Canquel RA 292 Gf68
Meseta del Norte MEX 253 Ej31
Meseta de Montamayor RA 292 Gg68
Meseta de Somuncurá RA 292 Gg66
Meseta El Pedrero RA 294 Gf69
Meseta Vizcachas RA 294 Ge71
Mesfinto ETH 191 Mj40
Meshgin Shahr IR 72 Nd26
Meshkin IR 73 Nk27
Meshwa IND 108 Og34
Mesick USA (MI) 246 Fh23
Mesihovina BIH 41 Ls47
Mesilinka River CDN 231 Dh17
Mesklip ZA 216 Lj60
Meslay-du-Maine F 22 Ku43
Meslo ETH 198 Mk42
Mešnik SCG 46 Lu48
Mesohóri GR 46 Mc51
Mesopotamiá GR 46 Mb50
Mesopotamia IRQ 65 Nb29
Mesopótamo GR 48 Ma51
Mesquite USA (NV) 236 Ec27
Mesquite USA (TX) 243 Fb29
Messad DZ 173 Lb28
Messaména CAM 195 Lg44
Messelt N 12 Lm29
Messina I 42 Lq52
Messina ZA 214 Mf57
Messini GR 48 Mb53
Messíni GR 48 Mb53
Messiniakós Kólpos GR 48 Mc54
Messinó GR 48 Mc53
Meßkirch D 34 Lk43
Messok CAM 195 Lh44
Messolóngi GR 48 Mb52
Messondo CAM 195 Lf44
Messongi GR 48 Lu51
Messum Crater NAM 212 Lh56
Mesta BG 46 Md49
Mesta BG 46 Md49
Mestá GR 49 Mf52
Mestanza E 29 Kq48
Mesti GR 47 Mf50
Mestia GE 70 Nb24
Město Albrechtice CZ 38 Ls40
Město Touškov CZ 38 Lo41
Mestre I 40 Ln45
Mesuji RI 125 Qc47
Mesvres F 23 Le44
Mesyaf SYR 64 Mj28
Meta CO/YV 269 Gf42
Metagama CDN (ON) 246 Fk22
Metahara ETH 198 Mk41
Meta Incognita Peninsula CDN 225 Gc06
Metajna HR 41 Lq46
Metala IND (MHT) 108 Oj35
Meta Lake CDN 239 Fg20
Metaline Falls USA (WA) 232 Eb21
Metamorfósi GR 48 Mc54
Metán RA (SA) 285 Gh58
Metangula MOC 211 Mh52
Metapán ES 255 Ff38
Metar IL 64 Mh30
Metarica MOC 211 Mj53
Metáuro I 40 Ln47
Metchum CAM 194 Le42
Meteghan CDN (NS) 245 Gg23
Metema ETH 191 Mj40
Metengobalame MOC 210 Mh53
Metéora GR 46 Mb51
Meteor Crater USA 237 Ee28
Meteran PNG 159 Sf47
Meteti PA 257 Gb41
Méthana GR 48 Md53
Methóni GR 48 Mb54
Metil MOC 211 Mk54
Metionga Lake CDN 239 Fe21
Metković HR 41 Ls47
Metlakatla USA (AK) 231 De18
Metlaoui TN 174 Le28
Metlika SLO 41 Lq45
Metlili Chaamba DZ 173 Lb29
Metmarfag DARS 178 Kd32
Metóhi GR 48 Md52
Metohija SCG 46 Ma48
Metolola MOC 211 Mk54
Metonia MOC 211 Mh52
Metorica MOC 211 Mj52
Metoro MOC 211 Mk52
Metpalli IND (APH) 109 Ok36
Metro RI 125 Qc48
Metro Beach USA 246 Fj24
Metropolis USA (IL) 243 Ff27
Metsäkylä FIN 11 Me13
Metsera RDC 206 Md47
Metsküla EST 16 Mc32
Métsovo GR 46 Mb51
Metter USA (GA) 249 Fj29
Mettlach D 34 Lg41
Mettupalayam IND (TNU) 111 Oj41
Mettur IND (TNU) 111 Oj41
Metu ETH 197 Mh41
Metuge MOC 211 Na52
Metulang RI 126 Qh45
Metz F 23 Lg41
Metzingen D 34 Lk42
Metztitlán MEX (HDG) 254 Fa35
Meulaboh RI 116 Pj43
Meulan F 23 Lb42
Meurthe F 23 Lg42
Meuse B 23 Lf40
Meuselwitz D 33 Ln39
Meuseugit RI 116 Ph43
Mevlâna Monastery TR 51 Mn53
Mêwa CHN (SCH) 94 Qb29
Mexia USA (TX) 243 Fb30
Mexicali MEX (BC) 236 Ec29
Mexican Basin 250 Fg32
Mexican Plateau MEX 226 Ed13
Mexican Water USA (AZ) 237 Ef27
México MEX 254 Fa36
México MEX 223 Eb07
Mexico USA (MO) 241 Fe26
México City = Ciudad de México MEX (MEX) 254 Fa36
Mexico City MEX (MEX) 254 Fa36
Mexiko RP 121 Ra38
Meyanodas RI 133 Rf49
Meybod IR 72 Ng29
Meydancık TR 63 Nb25
Meyenburg D 33 Ln37
Meyer Range, H. PNG 160 Sg48
Meymac F 24 Lc45
Meymand IR 72 Nf30
Meymaneh AFG 78 Oc28
Meymeh IR 72 Nf29
Méyo Centre CAM 195 Lf44
Meyomessala CAM 195 Lg44
Meyrueis F 25 Ld46
Meyzieu F 25 Lf45
Mezali MYA 112 Ph35
Mezaligon MYA 114 Ph37
Mézapos GR 48 Mc54
Mezdra BG 46 Md47
Mezek BG 47 Mg49
Mezen' RUS 58 Na05
Mężenin PL 37 Mc37
Mézessé CAM 195 Lg44
Mežica SLO 41 Lp44
Mézières-en-Brenne F 22 Lb44
Mézières-sur-Issoire F 24 La44
Mézin F 24 La46
Mezőberény H 39 Mb44
Mezőcsát H 39 Ma43
Mezőkovácsháza H 39 Ma44
Mezőkövesd H 39 Ma43
Mézos F 24 Kt46
Mežotne LV 17 Me34
Mezőtúr H 39 Ma43
Mezquital MEX (DGO) 253 Eh34
Mezquital MEX 253 Eh34
Mezraa TR 63 Mk27
Mfango Island EAU 204 Mg46
Mfinga EAT 206 Mf49
Mfou CAM 195 Lf44
Mfouati RCB 202 Lg48
Mfum WAN 194 Le43
Mgahinga Gorilla N.P. EAU 204 Me46
Mgbidi WAN 194 Ld43
Mgeta EAT 207 Mj50
Mgodi Z 210 Mg51
Mgori EAT 207 Mh48
M'Guiden DZ 173 La31
Mhajjen SYR 64 Mj29
Mhamid MA 172 Kh31
Mhangura ZW 210 Mf54
Mhasvad IND (MHT) 108 Oh37
Mhemiedeh SYR 65 Na28
Mhow IND (MPH) 108 Oh34
Mhwala EAT 206 Mg48
Miagao RP 123 Rb40
Miahuatlán de Porfirio Díaz MEX (OAX) 254 Fb37
Miajadas E 28 Kp49
Miajlar IND (RJT) 106 Of32
Miamére RCA 196 Lk41
Miami USA (FL) 250 Fk33
Miami USA (OK) 243 Fc27
Miami Beach USA (FL) 250 Fk33
Mian Channun PK 79 Og30
Miandrivazo RM 220 Nc55
Mianduhe CHN (NMZ) 91 Ra21
Mianga G 195 Lf45
Miangas RI 123 Rd43
Miang Besar RI 127 Qk45
Miani Hor PK 80 Od33
Miankale IR 72 Ng27
Mianmin PNG 158 Sa48
Mianning CHN (SCH) 94 Qb31
Mianrud PK 80 Ob32
Mianwali PK 79 Of29
Mian Xian CHN (SAA) 95 Qd29
Mianyang CHN (SCH) 94 Qc30
Miao IND (ARP) 113 Pj32
Miao RDC 203 Mb49
Miaodao CHN 100 Ra26
Miaoergou CHN (XUZ) 84 Pb23
Miao Li RC 97 Ra33
Miarinarivo RM 220 Nd55
Miarinarivo RM 220 Ne54
Miary RM 220 Nb57
Miass RUS 58 Oa07
Miastko PL 36 Lr36
Mibalaie RDC 203 Ma48
Mica ZA 214 Mf58
Mica Creek CDN (BC) 232 Ea19
Micaela Cascallares RA (BA) 293 Gk65
Micaúne MOC 214 Mj55
Miccosukee Ind.Res. USA 250 Fk32
Micha EAT 206 Mg48
Michael, Mount PNG 159 Sc49
Michailovskij sobor RUS 17 Mb36
Michajlovskoe RUS 53 Nc17
Michalin PL 36 Lt38
Michalovce SK 39 Mb42
Michel Peak CDN 232 Dg19
Michelstadt D 34 Lk41
Michenjele EAT 211 Mk51
Miches DOM 260 Gf36
Michigan USA 227 Fc10
Michigan City USA (IN) 246 Fg25
Michigan International Speedway USA (MI) 246 Fh24
Michilla RCH 284 Ge57
Michimáhuida, Volcán RCH 292 Gd67
Michipicoten Bay CDN 239 Fh22
Michipicoten Island CDN 239 Fg22
Michoacán MEX 254 Ej36
Miclești RO 45 Mh44
Miconge ANG 202 Lg48
Micoud WL 261 Gk39
Micronesia 134 Sa08
Micronesia 135 Sa09
Mičurinsk RUS 53 Na19
Mida RI 117 Qd44
Midal RN 186 Lc37
Midale CDN (SK) 238 Ej21
Midar MA 173 Kj28
Midas USA (NV) 234 Eb25
Midas şehri TR 51 Ml51
Mid-Atlantic Ridge 300 Hb08
Middelburg NL 32 Ld39
Middelburg ZA 214 Me58
Middelburg ZA 217 Mc61
Middelfart DK 14 Lk35
Middelharnis NL 32 Le39
Middelpos ZA 216 Ma61
Middelwit ZA 213 Md58
Middle Alkali Lake USA 234 Ea25
Middle America Trench 226 Ed15

Modena USA (UT) 234 Ed27
Modesto USA (CA) 234 Dk27
Modesto Méndez GCA 255 Ff38
Modest Town USA (VA) 247 Gc27
Modhera Sun Temple IND 108 Og34
Módica I 42 Lp54
Modigliana I 40 Lm46
Modinagar IND (UPH) 107 Oj31
Modjigo RN 187 Lg37
Modlborzyce PL 37 Mc40
Mödling A 35 Lr42
Modong RI 125 Qc47
Modot MNG 91 Qe22
Modra špilja HR 41 Lr48
Modriča BIH 41 Lt46
Modugno I 43 Lr49
Moe AUS (VIC) 153 Sd65
Moebase MOC 211 Mk54
Moeko RDC 200 Lk44
Moelv N 12 Ll30
Moengo SME 271 Hc43
Moeraki Boulders NZ 155 Tf68
Moerkesung CHN (TIB) 88 Pc30
Moers D 32 Lg39
Moffat GB 19 Kr35
Moffen N 11 Lh05
Moffet Pt. USA 228 Bj18
Moffit USA (ND) 240 Ek22
Moftin RO 44 Mc43
Mofu Z 210 Mf51
Moga IND (PJB) 106 Oh30
Moga RDC 206 Md47
Mogadishu SP 205 Nc44
Mogadouro P 26 Ko51
Mogalu RDC 200 Lk44
Mogami-gawa J 101 Sa26
Moganshan CHN 102 Qk30
Mogao Ku CHN 87 Ph25
Mogapinyana RB 213 Md57
Mogaung MYA 113 Pj33
Mogdy RUS 98 Rg20
Mogee Bli LB 192 Kf43
Moghar IR 72 Ng29
Moghrar DZ 173 Kk29
Mogila EAK 197 Mh43
Mogilno PL 36 Ls38
Mogincual MOC 211 Na53
Moglenitsa GR 46 Mc50
Mogliano Véneto I 40 Ln45
Mogna RA (SJ) 288 Gf61
Mogoča RUS 59 Ra08
Mogojtuj RUS (AGB) 91 Qh20
Mogok MYA 113 Pj34
Mogorjelo BIH 41 Ls47
Mogoşoaia RO 45 Mf46
Mogosoaia RO 45 Mg46
Mogotio EAK 204 Mh45
Mogpog RP 121 Ra39
Mograt SUD 190 Mg37
Mogroum TCH 187 Lh40
Moguer E 28 Ko47
Mogumber AUS (WA) 144 Qj61
Mogwase ZA 213 Md58
Mogzon RUS 91 Qg20
Mohács H 39 Lt44
Mohács H 41 Lt45
Mohala IND (CGH) 109 Pa35
Mohale Dam LS 217 Md60
Mohale's Hoek LS 217 Md61
Mohall USA (ND) 238 Ek21
Mohammabad IR 73 Oa30
Mohammad Abad IR 72 Ng29
Mohammad Abad IR 74 Nh31
Mohammad Abad IR 75 Nj31
Mohammad Agha AFG 78 Oe28
Mohammad Hasan Khaan Bridge IR 72 Ng27
Mohammadia DZ 173 La28
Mohammedia MA 172 Kg29
Mohana IND (ORS) 109 Pc36
Mohanganj BD 112 Pf33
Mohania IND (BIH) 109 Pb33
Mohanlalganj IND (UPH) 107 Pa32
Mohanpur NEP 88 Pd32
Moharli IND (MHT) 109 Ok35
Mohdra IND (MPH) 109 Ok33
Mohe CHN (HLG) 91 Rb19
Mohe CHN (HLG) 91 Rb19
Mohean IND (AAN) 111 Pg42
Mohed S 13 Lr29
Moheda S 15 Lp34
Mohéli = Mwali COM 218 Nb52
Mohelnice CZ 38 Lr41
Mohen FSM 156 Sc17
Mohenjo Daro PK 80 Oe32
Mohgaon IND (MPH) 109 Pa34
Möhne D 32 Lj39
Möhnesee D 32 Lj39
Mohnyin MYA 113 Pj33
Moho PE 279 Gf53
Mohoda IND (MHT) 109 Ok35
Mohol IND (MHT) 108 Oh37
Mohora H 39 Lu43
Mohoro EAT 207 Mk50
Mohyliv-Podil's'kyj UA 45 Mh42
Moi N 12 Lg32
Moiben EAK 204 Mh45
Moi Hoa Binh Pagoda VN 117 Qc41
Moila Point PNG 160 Sh49
Moimba ANG 208 Lg54
Moincêr CHN (TIB) 88 Pa30
Moineşti RO 45 Mg44
Moinsi Hills GH 193 Kk42
Mo i Rana N 10 Lh12
Mõisaküla EST 16 Mf32
Moises Ville RA (SF) 289 Gk61
Moisie CDN (QC) 244 Gg20
Moison Lake CDN 238 Fb18
Moissac F 24 Lb46
Moïssala TCH 195 Lj41
Moitaco YV 269 Gh41
Möja S 13 Lt31
Mojácar E 29 Kt47
Mojados E 26 Kq51
Mojave USA (CA) 236 Ea28
Mojave Desert USA 236 Eb28
Mojave National Preserve USA 236 Ec28
Mojiang CHN (YUN) 113 Qa34
Moji das Cruzes BR (SP) 287 Hg57
Moji-Guaçu BR (SP) 286 Hg57
Mojikit Lake CDN 239 Ff20
Moji-Mirim BR (SP) 286 Hg57
Mojiquiçaba BR (BA) 287 Ja54
Mojo ETH 198 Na41
Mojo ETH 198 Mk41
Mojokerto RI 128 Qg49
Mojosari RI 128 Qg49
Moju BR 276 Hf47
Mojynkum KZ 76 Oe23
Mojynty KZ 84 Og22
Moka DY 194 Lb42
Moka IND (KTK) 111 Oj39
Moka J 101 Sa27
Mokalsar IND (RJT) 106 Og33
Mokambo RDC 210 Me52
Mokameh IND (BIH) 109 Pc33
Mokhotlong LS 217 Me60
Mokhpal IND (CGH) 109 Pa36
Mokil Atoll FSM 156 Sd17
Möklinta S 13 Lr30
Mokmine TN 174 Lf28
Moko RN 185 Lb39
Mokobody PL 37 Mc38
Mokokchung IND (NGL) 112 Ph32
Mokolo CAM 187 Lg40
Mokolo ZA 213 Md58
Mokolo Dam ZA 213 Md57
Mokolodi Nature Reserve RB 213 Mc58
Mokombe RDC 200 Mb46
Mo Ko Phi Phi N.P. THA 116 Pk42
Mokoreta NZ 155 Te69
Mokowe EAK 207 Na47
Mokp'o ROK 100 Rd28
Mokre PL 36 Ls37
Mokren BG 47 Mg48
Mokrous RUS 53 Nd20
Mokša RUS 53 Nb19
Mokšan RUS 53 Nc19
Moktama Kwe MYA 114 Pj38
Mokuti NAM 212 Lj55
Mokwa WAN 186 Lc41
Mol B 23 Lf39
Mola di Bari I 43 Ls49
Molalatau RB 214 Me57
Mo'lali botig'i UZ 76 Oc25
Molaly KZ 84 Ok23
Molaman IND (RJT) 106 Og31
Molas MEX (QTR) 255 Fg35
Molat HR 41 Lp46
Mold GB 21 Kr37
Moldava nad Bodvou SK 39 Mb42
Moldavia RO 45 Mg43
Molde N 12 Lh28
Moldefjorden N 12 Lg28
Moldo-Too KS 77 Oh25
Moldova MD 45 Mh43
Moldova RO 45 Mg43
Moldoveanu RO 45 Me45
Moldray KZ 84 Ok20
Mole GH 193 Kk41
Molecreek AUS (TAS) 152 Sd66
Molegbe RDC 200 Ma43
Molem N.P. IND 108 Oh38
Mole N.P. GH 193 Kk41
Molepolole RB 213 Mc58
Môle-SaintNicolas RH 260 Gd36
Molesworth AUS (QLD) 150 Sb60
Molėtai LT 17 Mf35
Molfetta I 43 Lr49
Molibagu RI 127 Rb45
Molières F 24 Lb46
Molina E 29 Kt50
Molina RCH 288 Ge63
Molina de Segura E 29 Kt48
Moline USA (IL) 241 Fe25
Moline USA (KS) 243 Fb27
Molinella I 40 Lm46
Molinggapoto RI 127 Rb45
Molinos RA (SA) 284 Gg58
Moliro RDC 206 Mf50
Molise I 42 Lp49
Molkom S 13 Lo31
Mollafeneri TR 50 Mk50
Mollendo PE 284 Gd54
Mollerin Lake AUS 144 Qj61
Mollerussa E 30 La49
Mollisfossen N 10 Ma11
Mölln D 33 Ll37
Mölltorp S 13 Lp32
Molo MYA 113 Pj34
Molobala RMM 184 Kh39
Molobog RI 127 Rc45
Molocopote BR (PA) 275 Hc45
Molodežnaja ANT (RUS) 297 Na33
Molodo RMM 184 Kg38
Molokai USA 230 Cb35
Molong AUS (NSW) 153 Se62
Molong IND (ASM) 112 Pg33
Molopo RB/ZA 213 Mb58
Moloporivier ZA 213 Mc58
Mólos GR 48 Mc52
Moloskovicy RUS 16 Mk31
Moloundou CAM 195 Lh44
Molsheim F 23 Lh42
Molteno ZA 217 Md61
Molu RI 133 Rf49
Molucca Islands RI 119 Rb19
Molucca Sea RI 119 Ra19
Molumbo MOC 211 Mj53
Molunat HR 43 Lt48
Molwe RDC 209 Mc51
Moma MOC 211 Mk54
Moma RDC 203 Mb49
Momaligi WAL 192 Kd42
Momats RI 131 Rk48
Momba AUS (NSW) 150 Sb61
Momba EAT 206 Mg50
Mombaça BR (CE) 277 Ja48
Mombasa EAK 207 Mk48
Mombasa Marine N.P. EAK 205 Mk48
Mombenzélé RCB 195 Lj45
Mombetsu J 99 Sb23
Mombetsu J 99 Sb24
Mombo ANG 203 Ma51
Mombo Camp RB 213 Mb55
Mombongo RDC 200 Mb45
Mombongo RDC 201 Mc45
Momboyo RDC 200 Lk46
Mombuey E 26 Ko52
Mombum RI 158 Rk50
Momčilgrad BG 47 Mf49
Mommark DK 14 Ll36
Momote PNG 159 Sd47
Momotombo, Volcán NIC 256 Fg39
Mompiche EC 272 Fk45
Mompog Passage RP 121 Rb39
Mompono RDC 200 Ma45
Momskij hrebet RUS 59 Sb05
Møn DK 14 Ln35
Mon IND (NGL) 112 Ph32
Mon MYA 112 Ph35
Monach Islands GB 18 Kn33
Monaco MC 25 Lh47
Monaco Deep 168 Jd12
Monadyr KZ 84 Of21
Monaghan IRL 18 Ko36
Monahans USA (TX) 237 Ej30
Mona Passage DOM/USA 260 Gf36
Monapo MOC 211 Na53
Mona Quimbundo ANG 203 Lk50
Monarch Mtn. CDN 232 Dh20
Monari AFG 78 Oe29
Monaši UA 45 Ml44
Monasterace Marina I 43 Lr52
Monasterio de Guadalupe E 28 Kp49
Monasterio de Leyre E 27 Kt52
Monasterio de Piedra E 27 Kt51
Monasterio de San Juan de la Peña E 27 Ku52
Monasterio de Veruela E 27 Kt51
Monasterio de Yuste E 28 Kp50
Monastero di Sabiona = Kloster Säben I 40 Lm44
Monastery of Saint Anthony ET 177 Mg31
Monastery of Saint Catherine ET 177 Mg31
Monastery of Saint Paul ET 177 Mg31
Monastery of Saint Simeon ET 177 Mg33
Monastir I 31 Lk51
Monastir TN 174 Lf28
Monastyrščina RUS 52 Mf18
Monastyryšče UA 54 Me21
Monastyrys'ka UA 39 Mf41
Monastyrys'ka UA 54 Mc21
Monatélé CAM 195 Lf43
Monboré CAM 187 Lh41
Monção BR (MA) 276 Hh47
Monção P 26 Km52
Mončegorsk RUS 58 Mc05
Mönchengladbach D 32 Lg39
Monchique P 28 Km47
Monchy CDN (SK) 233 Eg21
Moncks Corner USA (SC) 249 Fk29
Monclova MEX (COH) 253 Ek32
Moncontour F 22 Ks42
Moncton CDN (NB) 245 Gh22
Mondai BR (SC) 290 Hd59
Mondéjar E 29 Kr50
Mondello I 42 Lo52
Mon Desir NAM 212 Lh55
Mondim de Basto P 26 Kn51
Mondjamboli RDC 200 Mb44
Mondjuku RDC 200 Ma46
Mondo EAT 207 Mh48
Mondo TCH 187 Lh39
Mondocino USA (CA) 234 Dj26
Mondolfo I 41 Lo47
Mondombe RDC 200 Mb46
Mondomo CO 272 Gb44
Mondoñedo E 26 Kn53
Mondoro CI 192 Kg41
Mondoro RMM 185 Kk38
Mondoubleau F 22 La43
Mondovi I 40 Lh46
Mondovi USA (WI) 241 Fe23
Mondragone I 42 Lo49
Mondrian Island AUS 145 Rb63
Mondriz E 26 Kn53
Mondsee A 35 Lo43
Mondy RUS (BUR) 90 Qa20
Moné CAM 194 Le42
Moneague JA 259 Gb36
Moneasa RO 44 Mc44
Monein F 24 Ku47
Monemvassiá GR 48 Md54
Monemvassiá Kástro GR 48 Md54
Monesterio E 28 Ko48
Monestir de Montserrat E 30 Lb49
Monestir de Sant Cugat E 30 Lc49
Monestir Santes Creus E 30 Lb49
Moneta USA (WY) 235 Eg24
Monett USA (MO) 243 Fd27
Moneyingyi Wetland Wildlife Sanctuary MYA 114 Pj37
Moneymore GB 18 Ko36
Monfalcone I 41 Lo45
Monforte P 28 Kn49
Monga I 40 Lm47
Monga RDC 200 Mb43
Mongala RDC 200 Ma44
Mongalla SUD 201 Mf43
Mongalla Game Reserve SUD 197 Mf43
Mongbwalu RDC 201 Mf45
Mong Cai VN 96 Qd35
Mongemputu RDC 203 Ma47
Mongeri WAL 192 Ke41
Mongers Lake AUS 144 Qj60
Mongge RI 130 Rg46
Monggui RI 131 Rh46
Möng Hpayak MYA 113 Pk35
Möng Hsat MYA 113 Pk35
Möng Hsu MYA 113 Pk34
Mongkaing MYA 113 Pj35
Mongla BD 112 Pe34
Möng Long MYA 113 Pj34
Möng Mit MYA 113 Pj34
Mongne MYA 113 Pj35
Mongo TCH 196 Lk39
Mongo WAL 192 Kd41
Mongol Dagurian Nature Reserve MNG 91 Qh21
Mongol Èls MNG 85 Ph22
Mongolia MNG 57 Pb05
Mongomo GQ 195 Lf45
Mongonu WAN 187 Lg39
Mongororo TCH 196 Mb39
Mongotong CHN (TIB) 94 Pk31
Mongoumba RCA 200 Lk44
Möng Pan MYA 113 Pk35
Möng Ping MYA 113 Pk35
Möng Ton MYA 113 Pk35
Mongu Z 209 Mb53
Mongua ANG 208 Lh54
Mônguel RIM 183 Kd37
Möng Yai MYA 113 Pk34
Möng Yang MYA 113 Pk35
Möng Yawng MYA 113 Qa35
Möng Yu MYA 113 Pk34
Monheim D 35 Ll42
Mönh Hajrhan MNG 85 Pf22
Moni RI 129 Ra50
Moni Agios Ioanni Theologou GR 49 Mg53
Moní Arkádi GR 49 Me55
Moniatis CY 51 Mn56
Monico USA (WI) 246 Ff23
Monida USA (MT) 235 Ed23
Moni Dochiariu GR 47 Me50
Monimpébougou RMM 184 Kh38
Moni Simonos Pétras GR 47 Me50
Möniste EST 16 Mg33
Monistrol-d'Allier F 25 Ld46
Monistrol-sur-Loire F 25 Le45
Moni Timiou Prodromou GR 46 Md49
Monitor CDN (AB) 233 Ee19
Monitor Range USA 234 Eb26
Monitos CO 268 Gb41
Monje RA (SF) 289 Gk62
Monkaringa GH 193 Kk40
Monkayo RP 123 Rd42
Monkey Bay MW 211 Mh53
Monkey Mia AUS (WA) 140 Qg58
Mönkhbulag MNG 90 Qb22
Mońki PL 37 Mc37
Monkira AUS (QLD) 150 Sa58
Monkoto RDC 200 Ma46
Monmouth GB 21 Ks39
Monmouth Park USA (NJ) 247 Gc25
Monnow Bridge GB 21 Ks39
Mono CO 269 Gf43
Mono TG 193 La42
Monobamba PE 278 Gc51
Mono Lake USA 234 Ea26
Monolithio GR 48 Mb51
Monólithos GR 49 Mh54
Monolon AUS (NSW) 150 Sb61
Monopamba CO 272 Gb45
Monópoli I 43 Ls50
Monou TCH 189 Mb37
Monóvar E 29 Ku48
Monowai NZ 155 Td68
Monreal del Campo E 29 Kt50
Monreale I 42 Lo52
Mon Repos Conservation Park AUS 151 Sg58
Monroe USA (GA) 249 Fj29
Monroe USA (LA) 243 Fd29
Monroe USA (MI) 246 Fj25
Monroe USA (NC) 249 Fk28
Monroe USA (NY) 247 Gc25
Monroe USA (OR) 234 Dj23
Monroe USA (UT) 235 Ed26
Monroe USA (WA) 232 Dk22
Monroe USA (WI) 246 Ff24
Monroe City USA (MO) 241 Fe26
Monroeville USA (AL) 248 Fg30
Monrou DY 186 Lb40
Monrovia LB 192 Ke42
Monroy E 28 Ko49
Monroyo E 29 Ku50
Mons B 23 Ld40
Monsanto P 26 Kn50
Monsaraz P 28 Kn48
Monschau D 32 Lg40
Monsélice I 40 Lm45
Monsenhor Gil BR (PI) 277 Hj48
Møns Klint DK 14 Ln36
Mönsterås S 15 Lr33
Mont Abourak RMM 185 La37
Montagnac F 25 Ld47
Montagnana I 40 Lm45
Montagne Azul Paulista BR (SP) 286 Hf56
Montagne d'Ambre, P.N.de la RM 219 Ne52
Montagne de Lure F 25 Lf46
Montagne de Nganha CAM 195 Lh42
Montagne du Lubéron F 25 Lf47
Montagne Noire F 24 Lc47
Montagnes Arawa F 271 Hd44
Montagnes del'Affolé RIM 183 Ke37
Montagnes Trinité F 271 Hd43
Mont Agou TG 193 La42
Montagu ZA 216 Ma62
Montague CDN (PE) 245 Gj22
Montague Island AUS (QLD) 153 Sf64
Montague Island USA 230 Cg16
Montague Sound AUS 138 Rc53
Montague Strait USA 230 Cg16
Mont Aigoual F 25 Ld46
Montaigu F 22 Kt44
Montaitas KZ 76 Oe24
Montalbán E 29 Ku50
Montalcino I 40 Lm47
Montalegre ANG 203 Lj50
Montalegre P 26 Kn51
Montalivet-les-Bains F 24 Kt45
Montalto I 43 Lq52
Montalto di Castro I 42 Lm48
Montalto Uffogo I 43 Lr51
Montalvânia BR (MG) 282 Hh53
Montalvo EC 272 Ga46
Montalvo EC 272 Gb47
Montamarta E 26 Kp51
Montana BG 46 Md47
Montana USA 226 Eb09
Montaña de Celaque HN 255 Ff38
Montaña de Comayagua HN 255 Fg38
Montaña Punta Piedra HN 256 Fh38
Montañas de Colón HN 256 Fh38
Montañas de Comayagua HN 256 Fg38
Montañas de Convento EC 272 Ga46
Montañas del Norte de Chiapas MEX 255 Fd37
Montañas de Onzole EC 272 Ga45
Montañas de Patuca HN 256 Fh38
Montanas de Yoro HN 255 Fg38
Montanas de Yoro HN 256 Fg38
Montanha BR (ES) 287 Hk55
Montargil P 28 Km49
Montargis F 23 Lc43
Montashee Mtns. CDN 232 Ea20
Montauban F 24 Lb47
Montauban-de-Bretagne F 22 Ks42
Montauk USA (NY) 247 Gd25
Montbard F 23 Le43
Mont Bata RCA 195 Lh43
Montbazillac F 24 La46
Montbazon F 22 La43
Montbéliard F 23 Lg43
Mont Bellevue de l'Inini F 271 Hd44
Mont Bélo RCB 202 Lg48
Mont Birougou G 202 Lg46
Mont Birougou, P.N.de G 202 Lg46
Montblanc E 30 Lb49
Mont Blanc F/I 25 Lg45
Montbrison F 25 Le45
Montbron F 24 La45
Montceau-les-Mines F 25 Le44
Montchanin F 25 Le44
Mont Cottica F 271 Hc43
Montcuq F 24 Lb46
Mont-de-Marsan F 24 Ku47
Mont de Niangbo CI 193 Kh41
Montdidier F 23 Lc41
Mont-Dore F (NCL) 162 Td57
Mont Douan CI 192 Kg42
Mont du Métal DZ 180 Le35
Monteagle AUS (QLD) 149 Sd57
Monteagudo BOL 285 Gj55
Monte Alban MEX 254 Fb37
Monte Albo I 31 Lk50
Monte Alegre BR (PA) 275 Hc46
Monte Alegre de Goiás BR (GO) 282 Hg52
Montealegre del Castillo E 29 Kt48
Monte Alegre de Minas BR (MG) 286 Hf55
Monte Alén, P.N.de GQ 194 Lf45
Monte Amaro I 42 Lp48
Monte Amiata I 40 Lm48
Monte Argentário I 42 Lm48
Monte Argentário-Porto San Stéfano I 42 Lm48
Monte Azul BR (MG) 282 Hj53
Montebello Islands AUS 140 Qh56
Montebelluna I 40 Ln45
Monte Belo ANG 208 Lh52
Monte Binga MOC/ZW 214 Mg55
Monte Botte Donato I 43 Lr51
Monte Buckland RA 295 Gh73
Monte Burney RCH 294 Gd72
Monte Calvo I 43 Lq49
Monte Campana RA 295 Gh73
Montecarlo RA (MI) 289 Hc59
Monte Carmelo BR (MG) 286 Hg55
Monte Caseros RA (CR) 289 Hb61
Montecatini Terme I 40 Ll47
Montécchio Emilia I 40 Ll46
Montècchio Maggiore I 40 Lm45
Monte Cervati I 42 Lq50
Montech F 24 Lb47
Monte Chiperone MOC 211 Mh54
Monte Christo ZA 213 Md57
Monte Cimone I 40 Ll46
Monte Cinto F 31 Lk48
Monte Comán RA (MD) 288 Gg63
Monte Creek CDN (BC) 232 Ea20
Monte Cristi DOM 260 Ge36
Montecristi EC 272 Fk46
Monte Cristi, P.N. RH 260 Ge36
Monte Cristo BR (AM) 273 Gg48
Montecristo, P.N. ES 255 Ff38
Monte d'Accoddi I 31 Lj50
Monte Darwin RCH 294 Gf73
Monte die Sette Fratelli I 31 Lk51
Monte Dinero RA (SC) 294 Gf72
Monte di Prunu F 31 Lk48
Monte Dourado BR (PA) 275 Hd46
Montefalco I 40 Ln48
Monte Falterona I 40 Lm47
Montefiascone I 42 Ln48
Monte Fitz Roy RA 294 Gd70
Monteforte de Lemos E 26 Kn52
Montefrío E 28 Kq47
Monte Gariglione I 43 Lr51
Montego Bay JA 259 Gb36
Monte Grande BOL 280 Gj54
Monte Greco I 42 Lp49
Monte Hacho MA 28 Kp45
Monte Hart Dyke RCH 294 Gc72
Montehermoso E 28 Ko50
Monte Hermoso RA (BA) 293 Gk65
Monte Inés RA 294 Gf70
Monteiro BR (PB) 277 Jb49
Monte is Caràvius I 31 Lj51
Monte Jervis RCH 294 Gc70
Monte Ladrillero RCH 294 Gd72
Monte León, Cerro RA 294 Gf71
Montelibano CO 268 Gc42
Montélimar F 25 Le46
Montelimar NIC 256 Fg40
Monte Limbara I 31 Lk50
Monte Línas I 31 Lj51
Monte Lindo PY 285 Ha57
Monte Lindo Grande RA 285 Ha58
Montella I 42 Lq50
Montellano E 28 Kp46
Montello USA (NV) 235 Ec25
Monte Mabu MOC 211 Mj54
Monte Maca RCH 292 Gd68
Monte Maiz RA (CD) 289 Gj62
Monte Mariana MEX (ZCT) 253 Ej34
Monte Melimoyu RCH 292 Gd68
Montemorelos MEX (NL) 253 Fa33
Montemor-o-Novo P 28 Km48
Monte Namuli MOC 211 Mj53
Montendre F 24 Ku45
Montenegro BR (RS) 290 He60
Monte Nieddu I 31 Lk50
Monte Núria I 42 Lo48
Monte Pascoal BR 287 Ja54
Monte Pascoal, P.N.de BR 287 Ja54
Monte Patria RCH 288 Ge61
Monte Perdido E 30 La48
Monte Petroso I 42 Lo49
Monte Philippi RA 294 Gf71
Monte Pio MEX (VC) 255 Fc36
Monte Plata DOM 260 Gf36
Monte Pollino I 43 Lr51
Montepuez MOC 211 Mk52
Montepulciano I 40 Lm47
Monte Quemado RA (SE) 285 Gj58
Monterado RI 126 Qe45
Monte Rasu I 31 Lk50
Montereau F 23 Lc42
Monte Rei BR (MG) 282 Hh53
Monterey USA (CA) 234 Dk27
Monterey USA (VA) 247 Ga26
Monterey Bay USA 234 Dj27
Montería CO 268 Gc41
Monteriggioni I 40 Lm47
Montero BOL 285 Gj54
Monteros RA (TU) 288 Gh59
Monte Rosa I/CH 34 Lh45
Monterosso al Mare I 40 Lk46
Monterotondo I 42 Ln48
Monterrey MEX (NL) 253 Ek33
Monterrico GCA 255 Fe39
Montes Altos BR (MA) 276 Hg48
Monte San Giorgio CH 34 Lj45
Monte San Lorenzo o Cocharane RCH 294 Gd69
Monte San Savino I 40 Lm47
Monte Sant'Àngelo I 43 Lq49
Monte Santo BR (BA) 283 Ja51
Monte Santo de Minas BR (MG) 287 Hg56
Monte Sarmiento RCH 294 Ge73
Montes Claros BR (MG) 287 Hj54
Montes de León E 26 Ko52
Montes de Oca RA (BA) 293 Gj65
Montes de Toledo E 29 Kq49
Monte Senes I 31 Lk50
Monte Sholl RA 294 Gg70
Monte Sigfried RCH 294 Gc70
Montesilvano I 42 Lp48
Monte Sirino I 43 Lq50
Monte Skyring RCH 294 Gd73
Montesquieu-Volvestre F 24 Lb47
Monte Stewart RCH 294 Ge73
Monte Tetris RA 294 Gd70
Monte Triste RA 292 Gh67
Monte Urtigu I 31 Lj50
Montevarchi I 40 Lm47
Monte Velino I 42 Lo48
Monte Vettore I 41 Lo48
Monte Victoria RCH 294 Ge72
Montevideo ROU 289 Hb63
Montevideo USA (MN) 241 Fc23
Montevidiu BR (GO) 286 He54
Monte Viso I 40 Lh46
Monte Vista USA (CO) 237 Eg27
Monte Volturino I 43 Lq50
Monte Vúlture I 42 Lq50
Monte Warton RCH 294 Gd72
Monte Wilson PE 278 Gb53
Monte Zeballos RA 294 Ge69
Montezuma BR (MG) 282 Hj53
Montezuma USA (GA) 249 Fj29
Montezuma USA (IA) 241 Fd25
Montezuma Castle Nat. Mon. USA 237 Ee28
Montfaucon-d'Argonne F 23 Lf41
Montfaucon-en-Velay F 25 Le45
Montgomery USA (AL) 248 Fg29
Montgomery USA (TX) 243 Fc30
Montgomery Island AUS 138 Rc53
Montgomery Pass USA 234 Ea26
Mont Guédi TCH 187 Lk39
Mont Guimbiri CAM 195 Lg43
Montguyon F 24 Ku45
Monthey CH 34 Lg44
Mont Hoyo RDC 201 Me45
Mont Hoyo, P.N. RDC 201 Mf45
Monti I 31 Lk50
Monti Aurunci I 42 Lo49
Mont Iboundji G 202 Lf46
Monticello USA (AR) 243 Fe29
Monticello USA (FL) 249 Fj30
Monticello USA (GA) 249 Fj29
Monticello USA (IA) 241 Fe24
Monticello USA (IN) 246 Fg25
Monticello USA (KY) 249 Fh27
Monticello USA (MN) 241 Fd23
Monticello USA (MS) 243 Fe30
Monticello USA (NY) 247 Gc25
Monticello USA (UT) 237 Ef27
Monticello USA 247 Ga26
Montichiari I 40 Ll45
Monticiano I 40 Lm47
Monti del Gennargentu I 31 Lk50
Monti della Laga I 42 Lo48
Montier-en-Der F 23 Le42
Montignac F 24 Lb45
Montigny F 23 Lg41
Montigny-le-Roi F 23 Lf43
Montigny-sur-Aube F 23 Le43
Monti Jesi MOC 211 Mh52
Montijo E 28 Ko48
Montijo P 28 Km48
Montilla E 28 Kq47
Montima RDC 200 Ma44
Montipa ANG 208 Lg53
Monti Sibillini I 41 Lo48
Monti Sibillini, P.N.dei I 41 Lo47
Monti Simbruini I 42 Lo49
Montivilliers F 22 La41
Mont Joli CDN (QC) 244 Gf21
Mont Kopé CI 192 Kg43
Mont Koronga TG 193 La41
Mont-Laurier CDN (QC) 244 Gc22
Mont-Louis F 24 Lc48
Montluçon F 25 Lc44
Montluel F 25 Lf45
Mont Mabanda G 202 Lf47
Montmagny CDN (QC) 244 Ge22
Montmarault F 25 Lc44
Montmarte CDN (SK) 238 Ej20
Montmédy F 23 Lf41
Mont Méla RCA 196 Mb41
Mont Mimongo G 202 Lg46
Montmirail F 23 Ld42
Montmoreau-Saint-Cybard F 24 La45
Montmorency F 23 Lc42
Montmorillon F 24 La44
Mont Moubolo RN 181 Lf36
Mont Mounier F 25 Lg46
Mont Ngaoui CAM/RCA 195 Lh42
Mont Niénokoue CI 192 Kg43
Mont Nimba CI/RG 192 Kf42
Monto AUS (QLD) 151 Sf58
Montoire-sur-le-Loir F 22 La43
Mont Oku CAM 195 Lf42
Montón E 27 Kt51
Montoro E 28 Kq48
Mont Péko CI 192 Kg42
Mont Péko, P.N.du CI 192 Kg42
Mont Pelat F 25 Lg46
Mont Pelé G 202 Lf47
Montpelier USA (ID) 235 Ee24
Montpelier USA (VT) 247 Gd23
Montpellier F 25 Ld47
Mont Pelvoux F 25 Lg46
Montpon-Ménestérol F 24 La45
Montréal CDN (QC) 247 Gd23
Montreal CDN 239 Fj22
Montreal Lake CDN (SK) 233 Eh18
Montréal Lake CDN 233 Eh18
Montreal L. Ind. Res. CDN 233 Eh19
Montreal River CDN 239 Fk22
Montréjeau F 24 La47
Montreuil F 23 Lb40
Montreuil-Bellay F 22 Ku43
Montreux CH 34 Lg44
Montreux CH 34 Lg44
Montrevel-en-Bresse F 25 Lf44
Montrichard F 22 La43
Montrond-les-Bains F 25 Le45
Montrose CDN (BC) 232 Eb21
Montrose GB 19 Ks34
Montrose USA (AR) 243 Fe29
Montrose USA (CO) 235 Eg26
Montrose Wildlife Area USA 241 Fd26
Montrouis RH 260 Gd36
Montroy E 29 Ku49
Mont-Saint-Aignan F 22 Lb41
Mont-Saint-Michel F 22 Kt42
Montsalvy F 24 Lc46
Mont Sangbé, P.N.du CI 192 Kg42
Monts Bagzane RN 186 Le37
Monts Bambouto CAM 194 Lf43
Monts Bleus RDC 201 Mf44
Monts Boutourou CI 193 Kj41
Monts Chic-Chocs CDN 244 Gh21
Monts de Belezma DZ 174 Lc28
Monts de Beni-Snassen MA 173 Kj28
Monts de Cristal G 195 Lf45
Monts de Cristal, P.N.des G 194 Lf45
Monts de Daïa DZ 173 Kk28
Monts de la Medjerda DZ/TN 174 Le27
Monts de Ouled Naïl DZ 173 Lb28
Monts des Ksour DZ 173 Kk29
Monts des Nementcha DZ 174 Ld28
Monts des Traras DZ 173 Kk28
Monts de Tébessa DZ 174 Ld28
Monts de Tlemcen DZ 173 Kk28
Monts du Cantal F 25 Lc45
Monts du Hodna DZ 173 Lc28
Monts du Hombori RMM 185 Kj38
Monts du Mouydir DZ 180 Lb33
Monts du Zab DZ 173 Lc28
Montségur F 24 Lb48
Montseny E 30 Lc49
Montserrat E 30 Lb49
Montserrat GB 261 Gj37
Montserrat GB 261 Gj37
Monts Grouix CDN 244 Gg20
Montsinery F (GF) 271 Hd43
Monts Kabyé TG 193 La41
Monts Manding RMM 183 Kf39
Monts Marungu RDC 206 Me49
Monts Mitumba RDC 206 Me48
Monts Mugila RDC 206 Me49
Monts Notre-Dame CDN 244 Gf22
Monts Otish CDN 244 Ge19
Monts Totomaï RN 181 Lh35
Montsûrs F 22 Ku42
Mt Tendre CH 34 Lg44
Mont Ténibre F 25 Lg46
Mont Teza BU 201 Me47
Mont Tonkoui CI 192 Kg42
Mont Toussoro RCA 196 Mb41
Mont Tremblant CDN 244 Gc22
Montuïri E 30 Lc51
Mont Ventoux F 25 Lf46
Monument Hill S.H.S. USA 243 Fb31
Monument Natural Alerce Costero RCH 292 Gd66
Monumento ao Padre Cícero BR (CE) 283 Ja49
Monumento Batalla de Junín PE 278 Gc51
Monumento Natural Ballena Franca Austral RA 293 Gj67
Monumento Natural Bosques Petrificados RA 294 Gf69
Monumento Natural Cerro Ñielol RCH 292 Gd65
Monumento Natural Contulmo RCH 292 Gd64
Monumento Natural Dos Lagunas RCH 294 Ge68
Monumento Natural Dunas d.C.Polonio y Costa Atlántica ROU 289 Hd63
Monumento Natural El Morado RCH 288 Ge62
Monumento Natural Isla Cachagua RCH 288 Ge62
Monumento Natural Laguna de los Cisnes RCH 294 Ge72
Monumento Natural Laguna de los Pozuelos RA 284 Gh57
Monumento Natural Los Pingüinos RCH 294 Ge72
Monumento Natural Pichasca RCH 288 Ge61
Monumento Natural Salar de Surire RCH 284 Gf55
Monumento Natural Valle del Encantado RCH 288 Ge61
Monument Rocks USA 240 Ek26
Monuments intérieurs et romans d'Arles F 25 Le47
Monument Valley Navajo Tribal Park USA 237 Ee27
Monywa MYA 113 Ph34
Monza CHN (TIB) 89 Pg29
Monza I 40 Lk45
Monze Z 210 Md54
Monzón E 30 La49
Monzon PE 278 Gb50
Mooi ZA 213 Md59
Mooirivier ZA 217 Me60
Moojeeba AUS (QLD) 147 Sb53
Mooketsi ZA 214 Mf57

Mount Patullo – Murphy

Mount Patullo CDN 231 Df17
Mount Peale USA 235 Ef26
Mount Pearl CDN (NF) 245 Hd22
Mount Penot VU 162 Td54
Mount Perry AUS (QLD) 151 Sf58
Mount Petras 296 Dc34
Mount Peuetsagoe RI 116 Pj43
Mount Peulik USA 228 Cb17
Mount Pfizner AUS 142 Rh57
Mount Pinapan RI 116 Pk44
Mount Pinatubo RP 120 Ra38
Mount Pinos USA 236 Ea28
Mount Pleasant USA (MI) 246 Fh24
Mount Pleasant USA (MO) 241 Fe25
Mount Pleasant USA (SC) 249 Ga29
Mount Pleasant USA (TX) 243 Fc29
Mount Pleasant USA (UT) 235 Ee26
Mount Plummer USA 228 Ca15
Mount Popa MYA 113 Ph35
Mount Popomanaseu SOL 161 Ta50
Mount Pulog N.P. RP 121 Ra37
Mount Pye NZ 155 Te69
Mount Queen Bess CDN 232 Dh20
Mount Ragang RP 123 Rc42
Mount Rainier N.P. USA 232 Dk22
Mount Ramelau TLS 132 Rc50
Mount Ranai RI 117 Qe43
Mount Ratz CDN 231 Dd17
Mount Rebecca AUS (WA) 140 Qh59
Mount Remarkable AUS (QLD) 148 Rk56
Mount Remarkable AUS 138 Rd54
Mount Remarkable N.P. AUS 152 Rk62
Mount Revelstoke N.P. CDN 232 Eb20
Mount Robe AUS 150 Sa61
Mount Robinson AUS 140 Qk57
Mount Robson CDN 232 Ea19
Mount Robson Prov. Park CDN 232 Ea19
Mount Rogers N.R.A. USA 249 Fk27
Mount Roosevelt CDN 231 Dh16
Mount Roraima GUY/YV 270 Gk43
Mount Ruapehu NZ 154 Th65
Mount Rungwe EAT 207 Mh50
Mount Rupert ZA 217 Mc60
Mount Rushmore Nat. Memorial USA 240 Ej24
Mount Russell USA (AK) 229 Ce14
Mount Ryan AUS 153 Se62
Mount Sage N.P. GB 261 Gh36
Mount Saint Gregory CDN 245 Ha21
Mount Saint Helens Nat. Volcanic Mon. USA 232 Dj22
Mount Sandiman AUS (WA) 140 Qh58
Mount Sandiman AUS 140 Qh58
Mount Sanford USA (AK) 229 Ch14
Mount Sankanbiaiwa WAL 192 Ke41
Mount Sasari SOL 161 Sk50
Mount Saunders 297 Tb36
Mount's Bay GB 20 Kp40
Mount Seelig 296 Ed35
Mount Selinda ZW 214 Mg56
Mount Selous CDN 231 Dd14
Mount Sembuang RI 116 Pj43
Mount Shasta USA (CA) 234 Dj25
Mount Shasta USA 234 Dj25
Mount Sherrick CDN 239 Ga20
Mount Sicapoo RP 121 Ra37
Mount Sidley 296 Dc34
Mount Silisili WS 164 Bd52
Mount Siple 296 Dc33
Mount Sir James MacBrien CDN 231 Dg14
Mount Skinner AUS (NT) 142 Rh57
Mount Somers NZ 155 Tf67
Mount Spokane S.P. USA 232 Eb22
Mount Stanley EAU/RDC 201 Mf45
Mount Steele CDN 231 Ck15
Mount Sterling USA (IL) 241 Fe25
Mount Sterling USA (KY) 249 Fj26
Mount Sterling USA (OH) 246 Fj26
Mount Stevens NZ 155 Tg66
Mount Stewart AUS (QLD) 149 Sc56
Mount Stewart CDN 229 Da14
Mount Stinear 297 Ob33
Mount Strong PNG 159 Sd49
Mount Stuart AUS (WA) 140 Qj57
Mount Sturgeon AUS (QLD) 148 Sc56
Mount Suckling PNG 159 Se50
Mount Sulen PNG 158 Sb47
Mount Sullivan AUS 139 Rf54
Mount Surprise AUS (QLD) 148 Sc55
Mount Tabletop AUS 149 Sd57
Mount Takahe 296 Eb34
Mount Taknan PNG 160 Sh49
Mount Taranaki NZ 154 Th65
Mount Tavani VU 162 Te54
Mount Thuillier IND 111 Pg42
Mount Tipton USA 236 Ec28
Mount Tip Tree AUS (QLD) 149 Sc54
Mount Tobin USA 234 Eb25
Mount Tom White USA 230 Cj15
Mount Tops AUS 142 Rg56
Mount Trumbull USA 236 Ed27
Mount Tutoko NZ 155 Te68
Mount Ulbanep PNG 159 Sb47
Mount Unbunmaroo AUS (QLD) 148 Sa57
Mount Vangunu SOL 161 Sj50
Mount Vernon AUS (WA) 140 Qk58
Mount Vernon USA (AL) 248 Fg30
Mount Vernon USA (IL) 241 Ff26
Mount Vernon USA (KY) 249 Fh27
Mount Vernon USA (MO) 241 Fe25
Mount Vernon USA (MO) 243 Fd27
Mount Vernon USA (OH) 246 Fj25
Mount Vernon USA (OR) 234 Ea23
Mount Vernon USA (WA) 232 Dj21
Mount Victor 297 Mc33
Mount Victoria MYA 112 Pg35
Mount Victoria NZ 155 Tg67
Mount Victoria PNG 159 Sd50
Mount Victory PNG 159 Se50
Mount Waddington CDN 232 Dh20
Mount Walton AUS 144 Qk61
Mount Warning AUS 151 Sg60
Mount Washington USA (KY) 248 Fh26
Mount Wechecha ETH 198 Mk41
Mount Wedge AUS (SA) 152 Rh62
Mount Wells AUS 138 Rd54
Mount Wharton 297 Ta35
Mount Whitney USA 236 Ea27
Mount Wilhelm PNG 159 Sc48
Mount Will CDN 231 Df17
Mount William AUS 152 Sb64
Mount William N.P. AUS 152 Se66
Mount Wiloughby AUS (SA) 143 Rh59
Mount Wilson CDN 231 Df14
Mount Windsor AUS (QLD) 148 Sa57
Mount Wittenoon AUS (WA) 140 Qj59
Mount Wood USA 235 Ee23
Mount Woodroffe AUS 142 Rf59
Mount Yawatoutou GH/TG 193 La42
Mount Zeil AUS 142 Rg57
Mouping CHN (SDG) 100 Ra27
Moura AUS (QLD) 151 Se58
Moura BR (AM) 274 Gk46
Moura P 28 Kn48
Mourão P 28 Kn48
Mouray TCH 196 Ma40
Mourdiah RMM 184 Kg38
Mourenx F 24 Ku47
Mouri Mountains WAN 187 Lf41
Mourmelon-le-Grand F 23 Le41
Mourne Mountains GB 18 Kp36
Mouroungoulay TCH 187 Lj41
Mousa GB 19 Kt30
Mousa Broch GB 19 Kt30
Mouscron B 23 Ld40
Mousgougou TCH 187 Lj40
Moussa Castle RL 64 Mh29
Moussafoyo TCH 196 Lk41
Moussaya RG 192 Kd41
Moussaya RG 192 Ke40
Moussoro TCH 187 Lj39
Moustiers-Sainte-Marie F 25 Lg47
Moutamba RCB 202 Lg47
Mouthe F 25 Lg44
Mouth of the Shannon IRL 20 Kl38
Mouths of the Amazon BR 276 Hf45
Mouths of the Ganges IND 112 Pe35
Mouths of the Indus PK 80 Od33
Mouths of the Irrawaddy MYA 114 Ph38
Mouths of the Krishna IND 111 Pa39
Mouths of the Mekong 117 Qd41
Moutier CH 34 Lh43
Moûtiers F 25 Lg45
Moutindi G 202 Lf47
Moutong RI 127 Ra45
Mouton Rothschild F 24 Ku45
Moutourous CAM 187 Lh40
Moutsamoudou COM 218 Nc52
Moutsoúna GR 49 Mf53
Mouy F 23 Lc41
Mouyondzi RCB 202 Lg47
Mouzáki GR 48 Mb51
Mouzarak TCH 187 Lh39
Mouzon F 23 Lf41
Movie World AUS 151 Sg59
Movila Miresii RO 45 Mh45
Moviliţa RO 45 Mg46
Mowanjum AUS (WA) 138 Rb54
Mowanjum A.L. AUS 138 Rb54
Mowasi GUY 270 Ha43
Möwe Bay NAM 212 Lg55
Moxotó BR 283 Jb50
Moya COM 218 Nc52
Moyale EAK 205 Mk44
Moyale ETH 205 Mk44
Moyamba WAL 192 Kd41
Moyen Atlas MA 172 Kh29
Moyeni LS 217 Md61
Moyenne Sido RCA 196 Lk41
Moyhu AUS (VIC) 153 Sd64
Moyie CDN (BC) 233 Ec21
Moyie Springs USA (ID) 233 Eb21
Mo'ynoq UZ 71 Nk24
Moyo EAU 201 Mf44
Moyo RI 129 Qj50
Moyobamba PE 278 Gb49
Moyogalpa NIC 256 Fh40
Moyowosi EAT 206 Mf48
Moyowosi Game Reserve EAT 206 Mf48
Moyto TCH 187 Lj39
Moyu CHN (XUZ) 86 Ok27
Moyuela E 27 Kt51
Mozăceni RO 45 Mf46
Mozaffar Abad-e Kur Gol IR 72 Nf28
Možajsk RUS 52 Mj18
Mozambique 167 Mb11
Mozambique Basin 171 Md24
Mozambique Channel 171 Na22
Mozambique Plateau 171 Md22
Mozambique Ridge 171 Md25
Mozdok RUS (SOA) 70 Nc24
Mozduran IR 73 Oa27
Mozia I 42 Ln53
Mozirje SLO 41 Lp44
Mozogo-Gokoro, P.N.de CAM 187 Lg40
Mpaathutlwa Pan RB 213 Mb58
Mpaathutlwapan RB 213 Mb58
Mpagwe EAT 206 Mf48
Mpaha GH 193 Kk41
Mpakani EAT 207 Mk49
Mpal SN 183 Kb38
Mpala RDC 206 Me49
Mpama RDC 200 Lh47
Mpanda EAT 206 Mf49
Mpandaamatenga RB 213 Mc55
Mpanga EAT 207 Mj49
Mpanta Z 210 Me51
Mpase RDC 200 Ma46
Mpataba GH 193 Kj43
Mpatora EAT 207 Mk50
Mpé RCB 202 Lh47
Mpesao Hills GH 193 Kj42
Mpessoba RMM 184 Kh39
Mphaki LS 217 Me61
Mphoengs ZW 213 Md56
Mphwayungu EAT 207 Mh49
Mpiéla RMM 184 Kg39
Mpigi EAU 204 Mg45
Mpika Z 210 Mf51
Mpili Z 210 Md53
Mpo RDC 203 Lk48
Mpoko RCA 195 Lk43
Mpomgwe Z 210 Me52
Mponde EAT 207 Mh48
Mponela MW 210 Mg52
Mporokoso Z 206 Mf50
Mpouya RCB 202 Lj47
Mpraeso GH 193 Kk42
Mpui EAT 206 Mf50
Mpulungu Z 206 Mf50
Mpumalanga ZA 217 Me59
Mpumalangao ZA 217 Mf60
Mpume RDC 203 Lk48
Mpurukasese EAT 211 Mj51
Mpwapwa EAT 207 Mj49
Mragowo PL 37 Mb37
M'Rara DZ 174 Lc29
Mrauk-U MYA 112 Pg35
Mrčajevci SCG 46 Ma47
Mrežičko MK 46 Mc49
Mrikula Devi Temple IND 107 Oj29
Mrirt MA 172 Kh29
Mrkonjić Grad BIH 41 Ls46
Mrkopalj HR 41 Lp45
Mrohaung = Mrauk-U MYA 112 Pg35
Mrzeżyno PL 36 Lq36
M'Saken TN 174 Lf28
Msak Mallat LAR 181 Lf33
Msalalo EAT 207 Mh48
Mšanec' UA 39 Mc41
Msanga EAT 207 Mk49
Msangasi EAT 207 Mk48
Msanzara Z 210 Mf52
Msanzi EAT 206 Mf50
Msata EAT 207 Mk49
Mscislav BY 52 Mf19
Mšenélázně CZ 38 Lp40
Msechela EAT 211 Mj51
Msesia EAT 206 Mg49
M'Sied MA 172 Ke31
M'Sila DZ 173 Lc28
Msima EAT 206 Mf49
Msimbati EAT 211 Na51
Msoro Z 210 Mf52
Msuna ZW 213 Md55
Mswebe Z 210 Md53
Mswega EAT 207 Mj50
Mszczonów PL 37 Ma39
Mt Aburassein RCA/SUD 196 Mc41
Mtakataka MW 210 Mh53
Mtakuja EAT 206 Mf49
Mtama EAT 211 Mk51
Mtamble EAT 207 Mk48
Mtambo EAT 206 Mf49
Mta Mepists'karo GE 70 Nb25
Mtamvuna ZA 217 Me61
Mtan SYR 64 Mj29
Mtandawala EAT 207 Mk50
Mtandura EAT 207 Mk50
Mtanila EAT 206 Mg49
Mtarazi Falls ZW 214 Mg55
Mt Dangoura RCA/SUD 197 Md42
Mtembwe EAT 207 Mj50
Mtera Reservoir EAT 207 Mh49
Mt Gaoun RCA 195 Lh42
Mtito Andei EAK 207 Mk47
Mtondo EAT 207 Mk50
Mtongwe EAT 207 Mk48
Mto wa Mbu EAT 207 Mh47
Mts du Fazao TG 193 La41
Mts Karé RCA 195 Lj42
Mtskheta GE 70 Nc25
Mtubatuba ZA 217 Mg60
Mtuga Z 210 Me53
Mtukula EAT 211 Mj51
Mtwapa EAK 207 Mk47
Mtwara EAT 211 Na51
Mu F (NCL) 162 Td56
Muabanama MOC 211 Mj53
Muadiala RDC 203 Ma49
Muaguide MOC 211 Na52
Mualadzi MOC 210 Mg53
Mualama MOC 211 Mk54
Muaná BR (PA) 276 Hf46
Muanda RDC 202 Lg48
Muangai ANG 209 Lk52
Muang Beng LAO 113 Qa35
Muang Boran THA 114 Qa39
Muang Houn LAO 113 Qa35
Muang Huang LAO 115 Qb36
Muang Kham LAO 115 Qb36
Muang Khong LAO 115 Qc38
Muang Khua LAO 113 Qa35
Muang Khun LAO 115 Qb36
Muang Long LAO 113 Qa35
Muang Nan LAO 114 Qa36
Muang Ngoi LAO 113 Qb35
Muang Pa LAO 114 Qa36
Muang Pak-Cay LAO 114 Qa36
Muang Phin LAO 115 Qd37
Muang Phu Khoun LAO 114 Qb36
Muang Pon THA 114 Pj36
Muang Samsip THA 115 Qc38
Muang Sing LAO 113 Qa35
Muang Singh Historical Park THA 114 Pk38
Muang Sui LAO 115 Qb36
Muang Xai LAO 113 Qb35
Muanza MOC 214 Mh55
Muanzanza RDC 203 Ma49
Muapula MOC 211 Mj52
Muaquia MOC 211 Mj52
Muar MAL 117 Qb44
Muara BRU 122 Qh43
Muaraaman RI 124 Qb47
Muarabadak RI 127 Qj46
Muarabeliti RI 125 Qb47
Muara Binuangeun RI 128 Qc49
Muarabungo RI 124 Qb46
Muaradua RI 125 Qc48
Muaraenim RI 125 Qb47
Muara Hiu RI 126 Qh46
Muarainu RI 126 Qh46
Muaraklingi RI 125 Qb47
Muara Koman RI 126 Qh46
Muarakuwis RI 124 Qb47
Muaranayan RI 126 Qj46
Muarapangean RI 126 Qj44
Muarapantai RI 124 Qa46
Muarapupit RI 125 Qb47
Muarasaibi RI 124 Pk46
Muarasaung RI 125 Qb48
Muarasiberut RI 124 Pk46
Muarasigep RI 124 Pk46
Muarasikabaluan RI 124 Pk46
Muarasimatalu RI 124 Pk46
Muarasoma RI 124 Pk45
Muaratalang RI 124 Qb47
Muaratebo RI 124 Qb46
Muaratembesi RI 125 Qb46
Muarateweh RI 126 Qh46
Muarawahau RI 127 Qj45
Muari RI 130 Rd46
Muatua MOC 211 Mk53
Mubambe RDC 210 Md51
Mubanzi EAU 201 Mf46
Mubayira ZW 214 Mf55
Mubende EAU 201 Mf45
Mubi WAN 187 Lg40
Mubo CHN (GSU) 92 Qd27
Muborak UZ 76 Oc26
Mubrani RI 131 Rg46
Mubur RI 117 Qd44
Mucajaí BR (RR) 270 Gk44
Mucajaí BR 270 Gk44
Mucambi Z 209 Mc52
Mucari ANG 203 Lj50
Muchaze MOC 214 Mg56
Muchea AUS (WA) 144 Qh61
Mucheve MOC 214 Mh56
Muchinga Mountains Z 210 Mf52
Muchinka Z 210 Mf52
Muchówka PL 39 Ma41
Muchuchu Ruins ZW 214 Mf55
Muck GB 18 Ko34
Muckadilla AUS (QLD) 151 Se59
Mučkapskij RUS 53 Nb20
Muckross IRL 20 Kl38
Mucojo MOC 211 Na52
Muconda ANG 209 Ma51
Mucondo ANG 202 Lh50
Mucope ANG 208 Lh54
Mucuali MOC 211 Mk54
Mucuaso ANG 209 Ma54
Mucubela MOC 211 Mj54
Mucuchies YV 269 Ge41
Mucucuaú BR 274 Gk45
Mucugê BR (BA) 283 Hk52
Mucuim BR 274 Gh49
Mucumbura MOC 210 Mf54
Mucumbura ZW 210 Mf54
Mucupia MOC 215 Mj55
Mucur TR 51 Mp51
Mucure YV 269 Gh41
Mucuri BR (BA) 287 Ja55
Mucuri BR 287 Ja55
Mucurici BR (ES) 287 Hk55
Mucuripi BR (AM) 273 Gf47
Mucussueje ANG 209 Ma51
Mudabidri IND 110 Oh40
Mudang Jiang CHN 98 Re23
Mudanjiang CHN (HLG) 98 Re23
Mudan Jiang CHN 98 Rf22
Mudanthurai Tiger Sanctuary IND 111 Oj42
Mudanya TR 50 Mj50
Mud Butte USA (SD) 240 Ej23
Muddanuru IND (APH) 111 Ok39
Muddebihal IND (KTK) 108 Oj37
Muddus n.p. S 10 Ma12
Muddy Gap USA (WY) 235 Eg24
Mudgal IND (KTK) 108 Oj37
Mudgee AUS (NSW) 153 Se62
Mudgod IND (KTK) 110 Oh39
Mudhai OM 69 Ng37
Mudhol IND (KTK) 108 Oh37
Mudigere IND (KTK) 110 Oh40
Mudigubba IND (APH) 111 Oj39
Mudjatik River CDN 233 Eg17
Mudon MYA 114 Pj37
Mudukulattur IND (TNU) 111 Ok42
Mudumalai Sanctuary IND 110 Oj41
Mudumu N.P. NAM 213 Mb55
Mudun SP 205 Nb45
Mudurnu TR 51 Mm50
Muecate MOC 211 Mk53
Mueda MOC 211 Mk51
Muel E 27 Kt51
Mueller Range AUS 138 Rd55
Muembe MOC 211 Mh52
Muende MOC 210 Mg53
Muftah SUD 190 Mg36
Mufulira Z 210 Me52
Mufu Shan CHN 95 Qg31
Mufu Shan CHN 102 Qh31
Mugambo = Lagosa EAT 206 Me48
Mugang CHN (YUN) 96 Qc34
Mugango EAT 204 Mg46
Muganskaja ravnina AZ 70 Ne26
Mugeba MOC 211 Mj54
Mugello I 40 Lm46
Mügeln D 33 Lo39
Muger ETH 198 Mk41
Muger ETH 198 Mk41
Muger Falls ETH 198 Mk41
Muggon AUS (WA) 140 Qh59
Mughal Sarai IND (UPH) 109 Pb33
Mughayra KSA 64 Mj31
Mughsayl OM 69 Ng37
Mugina BU 206 Me48
Muğla TR 50 Mj53
Mugling NEP 88 Pc32
Müglitztal D 33 Lo40
Mugota EAK 204 Mj45
Mug Qu CHN 89 Pg29
Muguia MOC 211 Mk52
Mugumu EAT 204 Mh46
Muhagiria SUD 196 Mc40
Muhairiqah KSA 67 Nc34
Muhala RDC 206 Me48
Muhammad Qol SUD 191 Mj36
Muhavura EAU/RWA 206 Me46
Muhayil KSA 68 Nb36
Muhaywir IRQ 65 Na29
Muheza EAT 207 Mj48
Muheza EAT 207 Mk48
Muhinji Chini EAT 207 Mk50
Muhino RUS 98 Rd19
Mühlacker D 34 Lj42
Mühldorf D 35 Ln42
Mühlhausen D 33 Ll39
Mühlig-Hofmann-fjella 297 Lb33
Mühlviertel A 35 Lp42
Muhoi Kondui RUS 91 Qg19
Muhoršibir RUS (BUR) 90 Qd20
Muhovo BG 46 Md48
Muhu EST 16 Md32
Muhula = Namiroa MOC 211 Mk53
Muhulu RDC 201 Md46
Muhuwesi EAT 211 Mj51
Mui Ca Mau VN 117 Qc41
Mui Chan May Dong VN 115 Qe37
Muico MOC 211 Mk52
Mui Doc VN 115 Qd37
Muidumbe MOC 211 Mk51
Muié ANG 209 Ma53
Mui Ke Ga VN 115 Qe40
Mui La Gan VN 115 Qe40
Mui Lai VN 115 Qd37
Mui Nai VN 117 Qc40
Mui Nam Tram VN 115 Qe38
Muine ANG 209 Ma54
Mui Ne VN 115 Qe40
Mui Ne Beach VN 115 Qe40
Mui Ron VN 115 Qd36
Mui Rong Quèn VN 115 Qc36
Muiron Islands AUS 140 Qh56
Muisné EC 272 Fk45
Mui Sot VN 115 Qc36
Muite MOC 211 Mk53
Muizenberg ZA 216 Lk63
Mujšin RUS 91 Qh19
Muju ROK 100 Rd27
Mujui dos Campos BR (PA) 275 Hc47
Muka Z 210 Md54
Mukačeve UA 39 Mc42
Mukah MAL 126 Qg44
Mukala RDC 203 Lj48
Mukana RDC 206 Md50
Mukandakunda Z 209 Mb52
Mukanga RDC 203 Ma49
Mukanya EAT 207 Mj50
Mukawa PNG 159 Se50
Mukawwa Island ET 177 Mh34
Mukdahan THA 115 Qc37
Mukdahan N.P. THA 115 Qc37
Mukebo RDC 206 Md49
Muke Turi ETH 198 Mk41
Mukilteo USA (WA) 232 Dj22
Mukinbudin AUS (WA) 144 Qk61
Mukinge Hill Z 209 Mc52
Mu Ko Chang N.P. THA 115 Qb39
Mu Koh Angthong N.P. THA 116 Pk41
Mukomuko RI 124 Qa47
Mukono EAU 204 Mg45
Mu Ko Phetra N.P. THA 116 Pk42
Mukosa ZW 210 Mg54
Mu Ko Surin N.P. THA 116 Pj41
Mukošyn UA 37 Mf39
Mu Ko Tarutao N.P. THA 116 Pk42
Mukpalli IND (MHT) 109 Pa36
Mukrian IND (PJB) 106 Oh30
Mukry TM 73 Oc27
Muk Sukhteh IR 75 Ob31
Muktsar IND (PJB) 106 Oh30
Mukuku Z 210 Me52
Mukulaikwe Z 210 Md53
Mukulushi RDC 209 Mc51
Mukunsa Z 206 Me50
Mukupa Kaoma Z 206 Mf50
Mukur = Moqor AFG 78 Od29
Mukutawa River CDN 238 Fb19
Mukutungu EAT 207 Mj50
Mul IND (MHT) 109 Ok35
Mula E 29 Kt48
Mula PK 80 Od31
Mulaku Atoll = Meemu Atoll MV 110 Og44
Mulaley AUS (NSW) 151 Se61
Mulalika Z 210 Me53
Mulan CHN (HLG) 98 Re23
Mulanay RP 121 Rb39
Mulanje MW 211 Mh54
Mulanje Mountains MW 211 Mh53
Mulanur IND (TNU) 111 Oj41
Mulatos CO 268 Gb41
Mulayjah KSA 67 Ne32
Mulbagal IND (KTK) 111 Ok40
Mulchatna River USA 229 Cc15
Mulchen RCH 292 Gd64
Mulda D 33 Lo39
Muleba EAT 201 Mf46
Mule Creek Junction USA (WY) 235 Eh24
Mulegé MEX (BCS) 252 Ed32
Mulele Z 209 Mb54
Mulembe RDC 206 Me47
Mulenda RDC 203 Mc48
Muleshoe USA (TX) 237 Ej28
Muleta ETH 198 Na41
Mulevala MOC 211 Mj54
Mulga Park AUS (NT) 142 Rf58
Mulgathing AUS (SA) 152 Rg61
Mulgildie AUS (QLD) 151 Sf58
Mulgrave CDN (NS) 245 Gk23
Mulgrave Hills USA (AK) 229 Bj12
Mulgul AUS (WA) 140 Qk58
Mulhacén E 29 Kr47
Mulhalli IND (KTK) 111 Oj40
Mülheim (Ruhr) D 32 Lg39
Mulhouse F 23 Lh43
Muli CHN (SCH) 113 Qa32
Muli MV 110 Og44
Mulia RI 131 Rj47
Muli Channel RI 158 Rk49
Mulika Lodge EAK 205 Mk45
Mulilo Z 210 Mg51
Muling CHN (HLG) 98 Rf23
Muling He CHN 98 Rg23
Mulka AUS (SA) 143 Rk60
Mullaittivu CL 111 Pa42
Mullen USA (NE) 240 Ek24
Muller Range PNG 158 Sb48
Müller Range RI 126 Qg45
Mullet Peninsula IRL 18 Kk36
Mullewa AUS (WA) 144 Qh60
Müllheim D 34 Lh43
Mullingar IRL 20 Kn37
Mullins USA (SC) 249 Ga28
Mull of Galloway GB 18 Kq36
Mull of Kintyre GB 18 Kp35
Müllrose D 33 Lp38
Mullsjö S 15 Lo33
Mulobezi Z 209 Mc54
Mulock Glacier 297 Sd34
Mulondo ANG 208 Lh53
Mulonga Plain Z 209 Mb54
Mulongo RDC 206 Md49
Muloorina AUS (SA) 143 Rj60
Mulshi IND (MHT) 108 Og36
Mulshi Lake IND 108 Og36
Multai IND (MPH) 109 Ok35
Multan PK 79 Of30
Multan Fort PK 79 Of30
Multia FIN 16 Me28
Mulu ETH 198 Na41
Mulu MAL 126 Qh44
Muluala Z 209 Mb54
Mulu Caves MAL 122 Qh43
Mulungu RDC 203 Mb50
Mulungushi Z 210 Me53
Mulu N.P., Gunung MAL 122 Qh43
Mulyungarie AUS (SA) 152 Sa61
Muma RDC 200 Mb44
Mumalla SUD 196 Mc40
Muman IR 75 Oa33
Mumbai IND (MHT) 108 Og36
Mumbeji Z 209 Mb52
Mumbleberry Lake AUS 150 Rk58
Mumbondo ANG 208 Lh51
Mumbué ANG 208 Lj52
Mumbwa Z 210 Md53
Mumena RDC 210 Md51
Mumeng PNG 159 Sd49
Mumfor RI 131 Rh46
Mumias EAK 204 Mh45
Mummballup AUS (WA) 144 Qj62
Mumoma RDC 203 Mb49
Mun RI 131 Rg48
Muna MEX (YT) 255 Ff35
Muna RI 127 Rb48
Muna RUS 59 Qd05
Munabao IND (RJT) 106 Of33
Munai CHN (YUN) 113 Pk34
Munaishy KZ 70 Ng24
Munamägi EST 16 Mh33
Munaya CAM 194 Le43
Muncakkabau RI 125 Qc48
Münchberg D 35 Lm40
Müncheberg D 33 Lp38
München D 35 Lm42
München-Riem D 35 Lm42
Munchique, P.N. CO 272 Gb44
Muncho Lake CDN (BC) 231 Dh16
Muncho Lake Prov. Park CDN 231 Dh16
Muncie USA (IN) 246 Fh25
Munda PK 79 Of30
Munda SOL 160 Sj50
Mundabullangana AUS (WA) 140 Qk56
Mundare CDN (AB) 233 Ed19
Mundargi IND (KTK) 110 Oh39
Mundaú BR (CE) 277 Ja47
Munday USA (TX) 242 Fa29
Mundemba CAM 194 Le43
Mundesley GB 21 Lb38
Mundford GB 21 La38
Mundi IND (MPH) 108 Oj34
Mundico Coelho BR (PA) 275 Hb49
Mundiwindi AUS (WA) 140 Ra57
Mundo Marino RA 293 Hb64
Mundo Novo BR (BA) 283 Hk51
Mundo Novo BR (MS) 286 Hc57
Mundra IND (GUJ) 108 Oe34
Mundrabilla Motel AUS (WA) 145 Re61
Mundri SUD 201 Mf43
Mundubbera AUS (QLD) 151 Sf58
Mundul AFG 79 Of28
Mundwa IND (RJT) 106 Og32
Mundy River AUS 143 Rk61
Munenga ANG 208 Lh51
Munera E 29 Ks49
Mungaa EAT 207 Mh48
Mungallala AUS (QLD) 151 Sd59
Mungana AUS (QLD) 148 Sc54
Mungaoli IND (MPH) 109 Ok33
Mungári MOC 210 Mg54
Mungeli IND (CGH) 109 Pa34
Mungeranie AUS (SA) 143 Rk60
Mungia E 27 Ks53
Mungilli A.L. AUS 141 Rc58
Mungindi AUS (NSW) 151 Se60
Mungkarta A.L. AUS 139 Rh56
Munglinup AUS (WA) 144 Ra62
Mungo ANG 203 Lk49
Mungo ANG 208 Lj51
Mungo N.P. AUS 153 Sb62
Mungo Park Memorial WAG 183 Kc39
Mungra Badshahpur IND (UPH) 109 Pb33
Munhango ANG 209 Lk52
Munich D 35 Lm42
Munieng RDC 210 Me52
Muniesa E 27 Ku51
Munim BR 276 Hj47
Munising USA (MI) 246 Fg22
Muniungu RDC 202 Lj48
Muniz Freire BR (ES) 287 Hk56
Munjola IND (CGH) 109 Pa36
Munka-Ljungby S 15 Ln34
Munkebo DK 14 Ll35
Munkedal S 12 Lm32
Munkfors S 13 Lo31
Munkumpu Z 210 Md52
Munmarlary AUS (NT) 139 Rg52
Munnar IND (KER) 111 Oj41
Munsan ROK 100 Rd27
Munshiganj BD 112 Pf34
Munshir Hat BD 112 Pf34
Münsingen D 34 Lk42
Münster CH 34 Lj44
Münster D 32 Lh39
Münster D 33 Ll38
Munster F 23 Lh42
Münster zu Ulm D 34 Lk42
Muntaiwani RI 126 Qh46
Munteni RO 45 Mh45
Muntgatsi EAK 204 Mh45
Munții Apuseni, P.N. RO 44 Mc44
Munții Bistriței RO 45 Mf43
Munții Călimani RO 45 Me43
Munții Codru-Moma RO 44 Mc44
Munții Făgărașului RO 45 Me45
Munții Gilău RO 44 Md44
Munții Goșmanului RO 45 Mg44
Munții Gurghiu RO 45 Mf44
Munții Harghita RO 45 Mf44
Munții Lăpușului RO 44 Md43
Munții Lotrului RO 44 Md45
Munții Măcinului, P.N. RO 45 Mj45
Munții Maramureșului RO 44 Me43
Munții Meseș RO 44 Md43
Munții Metaliferi RO 44 Mc44
Munții Semenic RO 44 Mc45
Munții Tarcului RO 44 Mc45
Munții Vâlcanului RO 44 Md45
Munții Zarndului RO 44 Mc44
Muntok RI 125 Qc47
Muntu RDC 203 Lk47
Munukata J 103 Rf29
Mununga Z 210 Me51
Munyamadzi Z 210 Mf52
Munyati ZW 214 Mf55
Münzkirchen A 35 Lo42
Munzur Dağları TR 63 Mk26
Munzur Vadisi Milli Parkı TR 63 Mk26
Muoco MOC 211 Mj52
Muodoslompolo S 11 Mb12
Muong Lan VN 115 Qc36
Muong Lay VN 113 Qb35
Muong Man VN 115 Qe40
Muong Tei VN 113 Qb34
Muonio FIN 11 Mb12
Mupa ANG 208 Lh54
Mu Pagoa Falls WS 164 Bd52
Mupamadzi Z 210 Mf52
Mupa, P.N.da ANG 208 Lh53
Mupfure ZW 210 Me54
Muqakoori SP 199 Nd43
Muqaybirah YE 68 Nd39
Muqaynimah KSA 67 Ne34
Muqdisho SP 205 Nc44
Muqshin OM 69 Nh36
Muquém BR (GO) 282 Hf53
Muqui BR (ES) 287 Hk56
Mur A 35 Lo43
Mura BR (AM) 274 Ha47
Muradıye TR 49 Mh52
Muradiye TR 63 Nb26
Muradiye Camii TR 49 Mh52
Murakami J 101 Rk26
Muralgarra AUS (WA) 144 Qj60
Muralla Romana de Lugo E 26 Kn52
Murallón, Cerro RA/RCH 294 Gd70
Muramgaon IND (MHT) 109 Pa35
Muramvya BU 206 Me47
Muranga EAK 204 Mj46
Murangering EAK 204 Mh44
Muránska planina, N.P. SK 39 Lu42
Murarai IND (WBG) 112 Pd33
Murat F 25 Lc45
Murat Dağı TR 50 Mk52
Muratlı TR 50 Mh49
Murato F 31 Lk48
Murau A 35 Lp43
Muravera I 31 Lk51
Murberget S 13 Ls28
Murça P 26 Kn51
Murchison Range AUS 139 Rh55
Murchison AUS (VIC) 153 Sc64
Murchison NZ 155 Tg66
Murchison Falls EAU 204 Mf44
Murchison Falls N.P. = Kabalega Falls N.P. EAU 204 Mf44
Murchison Island CDN 239 Ff21
Murchison River AUS (WA) 140 Qh59
Murchison Roadhouse AUS (WA) 140 Qh59
Murcia E 29 Kt47
Murcia E 29 Kt47
Mur-de-Barrez F 25 Lc46
Mur-de-Bretagne F 22 Ks42
Murdo USA (SD) 240 Ek24
Murdochville CDN (QC) 245 Gh21
Murdock Point AUS 147 Sc53
Mureck A 35 Lq44
Mürefte TR 50 Mh50
Murehwa ZW 210 Mf54
Mureibit SYR 64 Mk27
Mureș RO 44 Me44
Muret F 24 Lb47
Murfreesboro USA (AR) 243 Fd28
Murfreesboro USA (NC) 249 Gb27
Murfreesboro USA (TN) 248 Fg28
Murg D 34 Lj42
Murgab TJ 77 Oh26
Murgan AUS (QLD) 151 Sf59
Murgap TM 73 Ob27
Murgap TM 73 Ob27
Murgaš BG 46 Md48
Murgenella AUS (NT) 139 Rg51
Murgeni RO 45 Mj44
Murgești RO 45 Mg45
Murgha Kibzai PK 79 Oe30
Murghob TJ 77 Og26
Murgia E 27 Ks52
Murgoo AUS (WA) 140 Qj59
Muri CHN (QHI) 92 Qa27
Muriaé BR (MG) 287 Hj56
Muriaé BR 287 Hj56
Muria, Gunung RI 128 Qf49
Muribeca BR (CE) 277 Ja48
Muricilândia BR (TO) 276 Hf49
Muricizal BR 276 Hf49
Muridke PK 79 Oh30
Muriege ANG 203 Ma50
Muriel Lake CDN 233 Ee18
Murighiol RO 45 Mk45
Murilo Atoll FSM 156 Sc17
Murin Bridge AUS (NSW) 153 Sd62
Murindó CO 268 Gb42
Muritiba BR (BA) 283 Ja52
Müritz D 33 Ln37
Müritz, N.P. D 33 Ln37
Murizidié Pass LAR 181 Lh34
Murliganj IND (BIH) 112 Pd33
Murmansk RUS 58 Mc05
Murnau D 35 Lm43
Murnpeowie AUS (SA) 143 Rk60
Muro E 30 Ld51
Muro del Alcoy E 29 Ku48
Muro Lucano I 42 Lq50
Murom RUS 53 Nb18
Murongo EAT 201 Mf46
Muroran J 99 Sa24
Muros E 26 Kl52
Muroto J 103 Rh29
Murphy USA (ID) 234 Eb24

Murphysboro – Nanarup

Murphysboro USA (IL) 243 Ff27
Murqushi 79 Oh27
Murramarang National Park AUS (NSW) 153 Sf63
Murra Murra AUS (QLD) 151 Sd60
Murray USA (KY) 243 Ff27
Murray USA (UT) 235 Ee25
Murray Bridge AUS (SA) 152 Rk63
Murray Downs AUS (NT) 143 Rh56
Murray Fracture Zone 303 Ca07
Murray Harbour CDN (PE) 245 Gj22
Murray Island AUS 147 Sb50
Murray River AUS 144 Qj62
Murray River AUS 153 Sc63
Murray River Basin AUS 152 Sa62
Murraysburg ZA 216 Mb61
Murray's Falls GUY 270 Ha44
Murray Sunset N.P. AUS 152 Sa63
Murrayville AUS (VIC) 152 Sa63
Murree PK 79 Og29
Murrhardt D 34 Lk42
Murri CO 268 Gb42
Murroa MOC 211 Mj54
Murrua MOC 211 Mj54
Murrumateman AUS (NSW) 153 Se63
Murrumbidgee River AUS 153 Sd63
Murrumburrah AUS (NSW) 153 Se63
Murrupula MOC 211 Mk53
Murrurundi AUS (NSW) 151 Sf61
Murska Sobota SLO 41 Lr44
Mursko Središće HR 41 Lr44
Murtajapur IND (MHT) 108 Oj35
Murten CH 34 Lh44
Murter HR 41 Lq47
Murter HR 41 Lq47
Murtle Lake CDN 232 Ea19
Muru BR 279 Ge50
Murua PNG 159 Sc49
Muruasigar EAK 198 Mh44
Murud IND (MHT) 108 Og36
Murud IND (MHT) 108 Oj36
Murud Beach IND 108 Og36
Murudeshwar IND 110 Oh39
Murung RI 126 Qh45
Murupara NZ 154 Tj65
Murupu BR (RR) 270 Gk44
Mururoa 303 Da12
Murwara IND (MPH) 109 Pa34
Murwillumbah AUS (NSW) 151 Sg60
Mürz A 35 Lq43
Mürzzuschlag A 35 Lq43
Muş TR 63 Na26
Musa LT 17 Me34
Musa Z 209 Mc53
Musa Z 209 Mc53
Musa Ali Terara DJI/ER/ETH 191 Nb40
Musaaroole SP 205 Nc44
Musadi RDC 203 Mb47
Musafirkhana IND (UPH) 107 Pa32
Musaia WAL 192 Ke41
Musa Khel PK 79 Of29
Musa Khel Bazar PK 79 Oe30
Musala BG 46 Md48
Musala RI 124 Pk45
Musale Z 210 Md53
Musallam IRQ 65 Nd30
Musan PRK 100 Re24
Musandam Peninsula OM 75 Nj32
Musa Qal'eh AFG 78 Oc29
Musa River PNG 159 Se50
Musashi J 103 Rf29
Musawa WAN 186 Ld39
Musbat SUD 189 Mc38
Muscat OM 75 Nk34
Muscatine USA (MO) 241 Fe25
Musée de Bretagne F 22 Kt42
Musée de Tahiti et des Îles F (PYF) 165 Cf54
Musée Fech F 31 Lj49
Musée Gauguin F (PYF) 165 Cf54
Musée Gauguin F (PYF) 165 Da50
Musenge RDC 201 Me46
Musenge RDC 203 Mb50
Museo Archeologico I 42 Lq53
Museo del Oro CO 268 Gc43
Museo Guggenheim E 27 Ks53
Museo Playa Girón (Bay of Pigs Inv. Mus.) C 258 Fk34
Museu do Indio (Cuiabá) BR 281 Hb53
Museu Goeldi (Belém) BR (PA) 276 Hf46
Museum Het Princessehof NL 32 Lf37
Museum of Automobiles (Morrilton, AK) USA 243 Fd28
Museum of Cape Breton Heritage CDN 245 Gk22
Museum of Central Australia AUS 142 Rg57
Museum of Northern British Columbia CDN 231 De18
Museum of Tropical Queensland AUS (QLD) 149 Sd55
Museum Rég. des Mines CDN 244 Ga21
Museumsinsel in Berlin D 33 Lo38
Museumsmeile D 32 Lh40
Musgrave Harbour CDN (NF) 245 Hd21
Musgrave Range AUS 142 Rf59
Mushabani IND (JKD) 112 Pd34
Mushayfat SUD 197 Mf40
Mushenge RDC 203 Ma48
Mushie RDC 202 Lj47
Mushima Z 209 Mc53
Mushipashi Z 210 Mf51
Mushota Z 206 Me50
Mushrefah KSA 68 Nb36
Mushu Island PNG 159 Sb47
Mushumbi Pools ZW 210 Mf54
Musi RI 125 Qc47
Musin WAN 194 Lb42
Musiri IND (TNU) 111 Ok41
Muskauer Park D 33 Lp39
Muskeg Lake CDN 239 Ff21
Muskegon USA (MI) 246 Fg24
Muskegon Heights USA (MI) 246 Fg24
Muskeg River CDN 231 Dj15
Muskira IND (UPH) 107 Ok33
Muskö S 13 Lt31
Muskogee USA (OK) 243 Fc28
Muskratdam Lake CDN 238 Fd19
Muskwa River CDN 231 Dh16
Muslimabagh PK 78 Od30
Muslim Pilgrimage site of Shek Husen ETH 198 Na42
Musofu Z 210 Me52
Musoma EAT 204 Mg46
Musombe EAT 207 Mh49
Musondweji Z 209 Mc52
Musone I 41 Lo47
Musorka RUS 53 Ne19
Musoro Z 210 Mf52
Musoshi RDC 210 Md51
Musquodoboit Harbour CDN (NS) 245 Gj23
Mussau Island PNG 159 Se46
Musselburgh GB 19 Kr35
Musselshell USA 235 Ef22
Mussende ANG 208 Lj51
Musserra ANG 202 Lg49
Mussidan F 24 La45
Mussolo ANG 208 Lj51
Mussomeli I 42 Lo53
Mussoorie IND (UTT) 107 Ok30
Mussuma ANG 209 Ma53
Mussuma ANG 209 Ma53
Mussy-sur-Seine F 23 Le43
Mustafabad IND (UPH) 107 Pa33
Mustafa Kara Paşa Camii TR 62 Mh25
Mustafakemalpaşa TR 50 Mj50
Mustafa-paša džamija MK 46 Mb49
Mustahil ETH 199 Nc43
Mustang NEP 88 Pb31
Mustang Island USA 253 Fb32
Mustér = Disentis CH 34 Lj44
Mustique WV 261 Gk39
Mustjala EST 16 Mc32
Mustla EST 16 Mf32
Mustvee EST 16 Mg32
Musu Dan PRK 100 Re25
Musungwa Z 209 Mc53
Muswellbrook AUS (NSW) 153 Sf62
Muszyna PL 39 Ma41
Mut ET 177 Me33
Mut TR 62 Mg27
Mutala MOC 211 Mj53
Mutalau NZ 164 Bf55
Mutale ZA 214 Mf57
Mutamba dos Macombes MOC 211 Mk51
Mutambara BU 206 Me48
Mutambara ZW 214 Mg55
Mutampet IND (APH) 109 Ok36
Mutaralam RI 125 Qc48
Mutarara MOC 211 Mh54
Mutare ZW 214 Mg55
Mutarnee AUS (QLD) 149 Sd55
Mutatá CO 268 Gb42
Mutawintji N.P. (Mootwingee) AUS 150 Sb61
Mutha EAK 205 Mk46
Mutianyu CHN 93 Qj25
Mutiene RDC 202 Lh48
Mutinde EAT 206 Mf48
Muting RI 158 Sa49
Mutinlupa RP 121 Ra38
Mutir EAU 201 Mf44
Mutis, Gunung RI 132 Rc50
Mutiweshiri ZW 214 Mf55
Mutoko ZW 210 Mg54
Mutombo Mukulu RDC 203 Mc50
Mutomo EAK 205 Mk46
Muto One F (PYF) 165 Ck49
Mutooroo AUS (SA) 152 Sa62
Mutorashanga ZW 210 Mf54
Mutoto RDC 203 Mb48
Mutoto RDC 206 Me49
Mutoto-saki J 103 Rh29
Mutrah OM 75 Nk34
Mutshatsha RDC 209 Mc51
Mutsu J 99 Sa25
Muttaburra AUS (QLD) 148 Sc57
Muttalıp TR 51 Ml51
Muttapuram IND (APH) 109 Pa37
Muttonbird Island NZ 155 Td69
Muttukuru IND (APH) 111 Pa39
Mutúali MOC 211 Mj53
Mutuati EAK 205 Mk45
Mutukula EAU 201 Mf46
Mutukula IND (APH) 109 Ok37
Mutum BR (AM) 274 Gk49
Mutum BR (MG) 287 Hk55
Mutum BR (MS) 286 Hd56
Mutum BR 273 Gf48
Mutumbi RDC 206 Me49
Mutum Biyu WAN 187 Lf41
Mutumbu ANG 208 Lj52
Mutumbwe Z 209 Mc52
Mutum Daya WAN 187 Lf41
Mutum ou Madeira BR 281 Hc54
Mutum Paraná BR (RO) 280 Gh50
Mutungu-Tari RDC 203 Lj49
Mutur CL 111 Pa42
Mutu-wan J 101 Sa25
Muurame FIN 16 Mf28
Mu us Shamo CHN 92 Qd26
Muvattupuzha IND (KER) 110 Oj42
Muxi CHN (SCH) 94 Qb31
Muxía E 26 Kl53
Muxian CHN (YUN) 96 Qc34
Muxima ANG 202 Lg50
Muyange BU 206 Mf47
Muyinga BU 206 Mf47
Muy Muy NIC 256 Fh39
Muyombe Z 210 Mg51
Muyuka CAM 194 Le43
Muyumba RDC 206 Md49
Muzaffarabad PK 79 Og28
Muzaffargarh PK 79 Of30
Muzaffarnagar IND (UPH) 107 Oj31
Muzaffarpur IND (BIH) 107 Pc32
Muzambinho BR (MG) 287 Hg56
Muzarabani ZW 210 Mf54
Muze MOC 210 Mf53
muzej-usad ba „Tarhany“ RUS 53 Nb19
Muzeul Satului RO 45 Mf46
Muzhen CHN (AHU) 102 Qj30
Muzhllit të Skënderbeut AL 46 Lu49
Muzillac F 22 Ks43
Muzizi EAU 201 Mf45
Muzo CO 268 Gc43
Muzo CO 268 Gd42
Múzquiz MEX (COH) 253 Ek32
Muztag CHN 86 Pa27
Muztag CHN 87 Pd27
Muztagata CHN 86 Oh26
Mvangan CAM 195 Lf44
Mveng CAM 195 Lg44
Mvengué CAM 195 Lf44
Mvomero EAT 207 Mj49
Mvoung G 195 Lg45
Mvouti RCB 202 Lg48
Mvuma ZW 214 Mf55
Mvurwi ZW 210 Mf54
Mwabvi Game Reserve MW 211 Mh54
Mwadi Kalumbu RDC 203 Lk49
Mwadingusha RDC 210 Md51
Mwadui EAT 206 Mg47
Mwaga EAK 207 Mk47
Mwagné, P.N.de G 195 Lg45
Mwai EAT 206 Mf49
Mwakilunga EAT 207 Mg47
Mwala EAT 207 Mh50
Mwali COM 218 Nb52
Mwamagembe EAT 207 Mg49
Mwambo EAT 211 Na51
Mwana RDC 206 Me47
Mwana-Ndeke RDC 206 Md48
Mwanangumune Z 209 Mb53
Mwangalala RDC 210 Md51
Mwango RDC 203 Mc49
Mwanza EAT 206 Mg47
Mwanza MW 210 Mh53
Mwanza RDC 206 Md49
Mwanza Gulf EAT 204 Mg47
Mwanzangoma RDC 203 Mb48
Mwatate EAK 207 Mk47
Mwatwe Z 209 Mc52
Mwea National Reserve EAK 204 Mj46
Mweelrea IRL 18 Kl37
Mweka RDC 203 Ma48
Mwela and Sumina Rocks Z 210 Mf51
Mwelemu Z 210 Md52
Mwendi EAT 207 Mk50
Mwene-Biji RDC 203 Mb50
Mwene-Ditu RDC 203 Mb49
Mwenezi ZW 214 Mf56
Mwenezi ZW 214 Mf56
Mwenga RDC 206 Me47
Mweru Wantipa N.P. Z 206 Me50
Mwilambwe RDC 203 Mc50
Mwimbi EAT 206 Mf50
Mwingi EAK 205 Mk46
Mwingi National Reserve EAK 205 Mk46
Mwinilunga Z 209 Mc51
Mwini Lunga Z 210 Mg51
Mwinilunga Petroglyphs Z 209 Mc51
Mwisi EAT 206 Mg48
Mwitika EAK 205 Mk46
Mwitikiri EAT 207 Mh49
Mwombezhi Z 209 Mc52
Myakka City USA (FL) 250 Fj32
Myall Lakes N.P. AUS 153 Sg62
Myalup AUS 144 Qh62
Myanaung MYA 114 Ph36
Myangan Ugalfat Uul MNG 90 Qa22
Myanmar MYA 57 Pb07
Mychajlivka UA 55 Mh22
Mychla MYA 114 Pj36
Myczków PL 39 Mc41
Mye, Mount CDN 231 Dd14
Myingyan MYA 113 Ph35
Myinmoletkat MYA 114 Pk39
Myinmu MYA 113 Ph35
Myitkyina MYA 113 Pj33
Myittha MYA 113 Pj35
Myjava SK 38 Ls42
Mykénai GR 48 Mc53
Mykolajiv UA 39 Md41
Mykolajiv UA 54 Mf22
Mykolajivka UA 55 Mg23
Mykulyči UA 37 Me40
My Lai VN 115 Qe38
Myllykoski FIN 16 Mg30
Mymensingh BD 112 Pf33
Mynamäki FIN 16 Mc30
Mynaral KZ 84 Og23
Mynfontein ZA 216 Mb61
Myo gyi MYA 113 Pj35
Myola AUS (QLD) 148 Sa55
Myolo SUD 197 Me42
Myoshi J 101 Rg28
Myotha MYA 113 Ph35
Myoyang San PRK 100 Rd25
Myra TR 62 Mf27
Myrdal N 12 Lh30
Mýrdalsjökull IS 10 Ka14
Myre N 10 Lh11
Myres Castle GB 19 Kr34
Myrhorod UA 54 Mg21
Myrmoen N 12 Lm28
Myronivka UA 54 Mf21
Myrskylä = Mörskom FIN 16 Mf30
Myrtle Beach USA (SC) 249 Ga29
Myrtle Creek USA (OR) 234 Dj24
Myrtle Point USA (OR) 234 Dh24
Myrtou CY 51 Mo55
Myrviken S 13 Lp28
Mys Alevina RUS 59 Sc07
Mys Aniva RUS 99 Sb22
Myšanka BY 37 Mf38
Mys Buor-Haja RUS 59 Rc04
Mys Elizavety RUS 59 Sa08
Mysen N 12 Lm31
Mys Gamova RUS 100 Rf24
Mysingen S 13 Lt32
Mys Južnyj RUS 59 Sd07
Mys Kamčatskij RUS 59 Ta07
Mys Kanin Nos RUS 58 Na05
mys Kolgompja RUS 16 Mj31
Mys Kril'on RUS 99 Sb23
mys Kronockij RUS 59 Ta08
mys Kurgolskij RUS 16 Mj31
Myślenice PL 39 Lu41
Myślibórz PL 36 Lp38
Myslivka UA 39 Md42
Mys Lopatka RUS 59 Sd08
Mys Lovcova RUS 99 Sd23
mys Navarin RUS 59 Td06
Mys Neupokoeva RUS 58 Pd03
mys Oljutorskij RUS 59 Tc07
My Son VN 115 Qd38
Mysore IND (KTK) 111 Oj40
Mysore Palace IND 111 Oj40
Mysovka RUS 17 Mb35
Mys Ozernoj RUS 59 Ta07
Mys Rikorda RUS 99 Sd23
Mys Sjurkum RUS 99 Sa20
mys Šmidta RUS 59 Ua05
Mys Tajgonos RUS 59 Sd06
Mys Terpenija RUS 99 Sc21
Mystery Caves USA 241 Fd24
Mystic Caverns USA 243 Fd27
Mys Tolstoj RUS 59 Sd07
Mys Želanija RUS 58 Ob03
Myszków PL 37 Lu40
Myszyniec PL 37 Mb37
My Tho VN 115 Qd40
Mytilíni GR 49 Mg51
Mytišči RUS 52 Mj18
Mýtna SK 39 Lu42
Mývatn IS 10 Kb13
M'Zab DZ 173 Lb29
Mže CZ 38 Ln41
Mzenga EAT 207 Mk49
Mziha EAT 207 Mj48
Mzimba MW 210 Mg51
Mzimkulu ZA 217 Mf61
Mzimvuba ZA 217 Me61
Mzuzu MW 210 Mh51

N

Naab D 35 Ln41
Naala TCH 187 Lh39
Naalehu USA (HI) 230 Cc36
Na'am SUD 197 Me41
Na'am SUD 197 Me43
Naama DZ 173 Kk29
Naantali = Nådendal FIN 16 Mc30
Naas IRL 20 Ko37
Nababeep ZA 216 Lj60
Nabadeed SP 199 Nb41
Nabadwip IND (WBG) 112 Pe34
Nabalat SUD 190 Mf39
Nabar TCH 189 Ma36
Nabas RP 123 Rb40
Nabavatu FJI 163 Tk54
Nabburg D 35 Ln41
Naberera EAT 207 Mj48
Naberežny Čelny RUS 53 Ng18
Nabesna River USA 229 Cj14
Nabeul TN 174 Lf27
Nabha IND (PJB) 107 Oj30
Nabiac AUS (NSW) 153 Sg62
Nabi Ayoub OM 69 Ng37
Nabiélianayou BF 193 Kj40
Nabiganj BD 112 Pf33
Nabilatuk EAU 204 Mh44
Nabileque BR 285 Hb56
Nabire RI 131 Rh47
Nabk Anu Qasr KSA 64 Mk30
Nabogo GH 193 Kk41
Naboomspruit ZA 213 Me58
Naboulgou TG 193 La40
Nabouwalu FJI 163 Tk54
Nabq ET 177 Mh31
Nabq Reserve ET 177 Mh31
Nabu MYA 113 Pj34
Nabua RP 121 Rb39
Nabulus IL 64 Mh29
Nabunturan RP 123 Rc42
Nabuvoll N 12 Lm28
Nabuyango Island EAT 204 Mg46
Nacala MOC 211 Na53
Nacala Velha MOC 211 Na53
Nacaroa MOC 211 Mk53
Nacavala MOC 211 Mk53
Nacebe BOL 279 Gg51
Nachacachi MEX (CHH) 252 Eg32
Nachindundo MOC 211 Na51
Nachingwea EAT 211 Mk51
Nachna IND (RJT) 106 Of32
Náchod CZ 38 Lr40
Na Chuak THA 115 Qb38
Nachuge IND (AAN) 111 Pg40
Nacimiento RCH 292 Gd64
Nacional'nyj park Pričlbrus'e RUS 70 Nb24
Nackara AUS (SA) 152 Rk62
Naco MEX (SO) 237 Ef30
Naco USA (AZ) 237 Ef30
Nacogdoches USA (TX) 243 Fc30
Nacori Chico MEX (SO) 237 Ef31
Nacozari Viejo MEX (SO) 237 Ef30
Nacuñán RA (MD) 288 Gg63
Nad Al Sheba UAE 74 Nh33
Nadamu Dahui CHN 93 Qh24
Nadarzyce PL 36 Lr37
Nadawli GH 193 Kj40
Nadbużański Park Krajobrazowy PL 37 Mb38
Nådendal = Naantali FIN 16 Mc30
Nadežda UA 45 Mk44
Nadi FJI 163 Tj54
Nadi SUD 190 Mg37
Nadiad IND (GUJ) 108 Og34
Nădlac RO 44 Ma44
Nadmorski Park Krajobrazowy PL 36 Lt36
Nadoba TG 193 La40
Nador MA 173 Kj28
Nadria IND (MPH) 109 Pa33
Naduk RI 125 Qd47
Nadvirna UA 39 Me42
Nadym RUS 58 Oc05
Nadzab PNG 159 Sd49
Na'ebabad AFG 78 Od27
Naejangsan N.P. ROK 100 Rd28
Nærbø N 12 Lf32
Nærøyfjorden N 12 Lg30
Næstved DK 14 Lm35
Nafada WAN 187 Lf40
Nafadji SN 183 Ke39
Náfpaktos GR 48 Mb52
Náfplio GR 48 Mc53
Naft Khaneh IRQ 65 Nc28
Nafud ad Dahl KSA 67 Nc35
Nafud al Ghuwaytah KSA 64 Mk31
Nafud al Mazhur KSA 67 Nb32
Nafud al Urayq KSA 66 Nb33
Nafud as Sirr KSA 67 Nc33
Nafud ath Thuwayrat KSA 67 Nc32
Nag PK 80 Oc32
Naga DZ 172 Kg31
Naga GH 193 Kk40
Naga RP 121 Rb39
Naga RP 123 Rb40
Nagabulik RI 126 Qf47
Nagai Island USA 228 Bk18
Nagaj IND (MHT) 108 Oh37
Nagajbakovo RUS 53 Ng18
Naga-jima J 103 Rf29
Nagaland IND 105 Pc13
Nagamangala IND (KTK) 111 Oj40
Nagami Lake CDN 239 Fh21
Nagano J 101 Rk27
Nagaoka J 101 Rk27
Nagaon IND (ASM) 112 Pg32
Nagappattinam IND (TNU) 111 Ok41
Nagapur IND (MHT) 108 Oj36
Nagar IND (RJT) 107 Oj32
Nagara RMM 183 Ke38
Nagarhole IND (KTK) 110 Oj40
Nagarhole N.P. IND 110 Oh41
Nagari IND (TNU) 111 Ok40
Nagarjunakonda IND 109 Ok37
Nagarjunasagar IND 109 Ok37
Nagarjunasagar-Srisailam Sanctuary IND 109 Ok37
Nagar Karnul IND (APH) 108 Ok37
Nagarote NIC 256 Fg39
Nagar Parkar PK 81 Of33
Nagarze CHN (TIB) 89 Pf31
Nagasaki J 103 Re29
Nagasamudram IND (APH) 111 Oj39
Nagasari IND (GUJ) 108 Of35
Nagash Mosque ETH 191 Mk40
Nagato J 101 Rf28
Nagatsugawa J 101 Rj28
Nagaur IND (RJT) 106 Og32
Nagbhir IND (MHT) 109 Ok35
Nagbo GH 193 Kk40
Nagda IND (MPH) 108 Oh34
Nagda IND (MPH) 108 Oh34
Nageezi USA (NM) 237 Eg27
Nag el Ma'mariya ET 177 Mg33
Nagercoil IND (TNU) 111 Oj42
Naggen S 13 Lq28
Nag Hammâdi ET 177 Mg32
Naghan IR 72 Nf30
Naghsh-e-Rostam IR 74 Ng30
Nagichot SUD 197 Mg43
Nagina IND (UPH) 107 Ok31
Nagłowice PL 37 Ma40
Nago J 103 Rd32
Nagod IND (MPH) 109 Pa33
Nagoda CL 111 Pa43
Nagomba EAT 211 Mk51
Nagor'e RUS 52 Mk17
Nagorno-Karabakh ARM 63 Nc26
Nagornyj RUS 59 Td06
Nagothana IND (MHT) 108 Og36
Nagoya J 101 Rj28
Nagpur IND (MHT) 109 Ok35
Nagqu CHN (TIB) 89 Pg30
Nagreg RI 128 Qd49
Nagu = Nauvo FIN 16 Mb30
Nagua DOM 260 Gf36
Nagum PNG 159 Sb49
Nagurunguru A.L. AUS 139 Re54
Nagyatád H 38 Ls44
Nagybajom H 38 Ls44
Nagyhalász H 39 Mb42
Nagyigmánd H 38 Lt43
Nagykanizsa H 38 Lr44
Nagykáta H 39 Lu43
Nagykőrös H 39 Lu43
Nagykunság H 39 Ma43
Nagylak H 39 Ma44
Nagyszénás H 39 Ma44
Naha J 103 Rd32
Nahačiv UA 37 Md40
Na Haeo THA 114 Qa37
Nahan IND (HPH) 107 Oj30
Na Hang VN 96 Qc34
Nahanni Butte CDN (NWT) 231 Dj15
Nahanni National Park CDN 231 Dh15
Nahanni Range CDN 231 Dj15
Nahariya IL 64 Mh29
Nahavand IR 72 Ne28
Nahavand IR 72 Ne28
Nahe D 34 Lh41
Naheleg ER 191 Na38
Nahlin CDN (BC) 231 De16
Nahlin Plateau CDN 231 Dd16
Nahodka RUS 101 Rg24
Nahoon Reef ZA 217 Md62
Nahoria IND (MPH) 109 Pb33
Nahoro EAT 211 Mj51
Nahr al Khabour SYR 65 Na27
Nahr al-Qash SUD 191 Mj39
Nahr al Uzaym IRQ 65 Nc28
Nahr az Zab al Kabir IRQ 65 Nb28
Nahr az Zab as Saghir IRQ 65 Nb27
Nahr Diyala IRQ 65 Nc28
Nahrin AFG 78 Oe27
Nahuelbuta, P.N. RCH 292 Gd64
Nahuel Huapí RA (RN) 292 Ge66
Nahuel Huapí, P.N. RA 292 Ge66
Nahuel Mapá RA (SL) 288 Gg63
Nahunta USA (GA) 249 Fk30
Nahuo CHN (GDG) 96 Qf35
Nai PNG 159 Se46
Naica MEX (CHH) 253 Eh32
Naicam CDN (SK) 233 Eh19
Naij Tal CHN (QHI) 89 Ph28
Naikliu RI 132 Rb50
Naikoon Prov. Park CDN 232 De19
Naila D 35 Lm40
Naiman Qi CHN (NMZ) 100 Ra24
Nain CDN 225 Gd07
Na'in IR 72 Ng29
Nainital IND (UTT) 107 Ok31
Nainpur IND (MPH) 109 Pa34
Naiopue MOC 211 Mj53
Naipé MOC 211 Mk53
Naiqu CHN (SCH) 94 Qa31
Nairai FJI 163 Tk54
Nairn GB 19 Kr33
Nairobi EAK 204 Mj46
Nairobi N.P. EAK 204 Mj46
Naissaar EST 16 Me31
Naitaba FJI 163 Ua54
Naivasha EAK 204 Mj46
Naivos RI 116 Pj44
Najac F 24 Lb46
Najaf Abad IR 72 Nd28
Najaf Abad IR 72 Nf29
Na'jan KSA 67 Nd33
Najba RUS 99 Sb22
Najbere RUS (CHE) 70 Nd24
Najd KSA 66 Na33
Nájera E 27 Ks52
Najibabad IND (UPH) 107 Ok31
Najitun CHN (NMZ) 98 Rb22
Najran KSA 68 Nc37
Naj Tunich GCA 255 Ff37
Nakachenje Z 210 Md53
Nakadori-jima J 103 Re29
Nakagawa J 99 Sb23
Nakagusuku Castle J 103 Rd32
Naka Kharai PK 80 Od33
Nakambe = Volta Blanche BF 185 Kk39
Nakambe GH 193 Kk39
Nakamura J 103 Rg29
Nakanai Mountains PNG 160 Sf48
Nakanno RUS 59 Qb06
Nakano-jima J 101 Rg27
Nakano-jima J 103 Re31
Nakapalle IND (APH) 109 Pb37
Nakapanya EAT 211 Mj51
Nakapiripirit EAU 204 Mh45
Nakartiaganj IND (BIH) 107 Pc32
Nakasato J 101 Sa25
Naka-Shibetsu J 99 Sc24
Nakasongola EAU 204 Mg45
Naka-Tane J 103 Rf30
Nakatsu J 103 Rf29
Nakawale EAT 211 Mh51
Nakchamik Island USA 228 Cb17
Naked Island USA (AK) 229 Cg15
Nakfa ER 191 Mk38
Nakfa Wildlife Reserve ER 191 Mk38
Nakhl OM 75 Nj34
Nakhl Shahbah KSA 66 Na35
Na Khoang VN 113 Qb35
Nakhola IND (ASM) 112 Pg32
Nakhon Nayok THA 114 Qa38
Nakhon Pathom THA 114 Qa39
Nakhon Phanom THA 115 Qc37
Nakhon Ratchasima THA 115 Qb38
Nakhon Sawan THA 114 Qa38
Nakhon Si Thammarat THA 116 Pk41
Nakhon Thai THA 114 Qa37
Nakhtarana IND (GUJ) 108 Oe34
Naki-Est TG 193 La40
Nakifuma EAU 204 Mg45
Nakiloro EAU 204 Mh44
Nakina CDN (ON) 239 Fg20
Nakitoma EAU 204 Mg45
Nakla EAT 207 Mk50
Na Klang THA 114 Qb37
Naklik PL 37 Mc40
Nakło nad Notecią PL 36 Ls37
Naknek USA (AK) 228 Cb16
Naknek Lake USA (AK) 228 Cc16
Nako IND 107 Ok30
Nako IND 107 Ok30
Nakodar IND (PJB) 106 Oh30
Nakonde Z 206 Mg50
Nakop NAM 216 Lk60
Nakpanduri GH 193 Kk40
Nakpayili GH 193 La41
Nakrekal IND (APH) 109 Ok37
Nakskov DK 14 Lm36
Näkten S 13 Lp28
Nakuru EAK 204 Mj46
Nakusp CDN (BC) 232 Eb20
Naku-Tombetsu J 99 Sb23
Nakwehe EAK 198 Mh44
Nal PK 80 Od32
Nalatale Ruins ZW 214 Me55
Nalaykh MNG 90 Qd22
Nalázi MOC 214 Mg58
Na'lbandan IR 72 Nf28
Nalbant RO 45 Mj45
Nalbara AUS (WA) 144 Qj60
Nalbari IND (ASM) 112 Pf32
Nal'čik RUS (KBA) 70 Nb24
Naldurg IND (MHT) 108 Oj37
Nałęczów PL 37 Mc39
Naledi RB 213 Mc58
Nálepkovo SK 39 Ma42
Nalgonda IND (APH) 109 Ok37
Nalhati IND (WBG) 112 Pd33
Nalhiapur IND (UPH) 107 Pb32
Nali CHN (GZG) 96 Qe35
Nal Lake IND 108 Of34
Nallıhan TR 51 Mm50
Nalong MYA 113 Pj33
Nalusanga Z 210 Md53
Nalusuku Pool Z 209 Mb54
Nalut LAR 174 Lf30
Nalwangaa EAT 207 Mk50
Nalžovské Hory CZ 38 Lo41
Nama RI 130 Rf48
Namaacha MOC 214 Mg58
Namacunde ANG 208 Lh54
Namacurra MOC 211 Mj54
Namadgi N.P. AUS (ACT) 153 Se63
Namakgale ZA 214 Mf57
Namakia RM 218 Nc53
Namakkal IND (TNU) 111 Ok41
Namaklwe MYA 114 Pk36
Namakzar-e Shadad IR 75 Nj30
Namaland NAM 212 Lj59
Namalatu Beach RI 130 Re47
Namanga EAK 207 Mj47
Namangan UZ 77 Of25
Namanjavira MOC 211 Mj54
Namanyere EAT 206 Mf49
Namapa MOC 211 Mk52
Namaponda MOC 211 Mk53
Namaqualand ZA 216 Lj61
Namaqua N.P. ZA 216 Lj60
Namaro RN 185 La39
Namarrói MOC 211 Mj53
Namas RI 131 Sa48
Namasagali EAU 204 Mg45
Namasale EAU 204 Mg45
Namassi CI 193 Kj42
Namatanai PNG 160 Sg47
Namatele EAT 207 Mk50
Namatote RI 131 Rg47
Na Maw LAO 113 Qa35
Namazga Depe TM 73 Nk27
Namba ANG 208 Lh51
Nam Bai VN 113 Qb34
Nambala Z 210 Md53
Nambazo MW 211 Mh53
Nam Beng LAO 113 Qa35
Namber RI 131 Rh46
Nambi AUS (WA) 144 Ra60
Nambikwara, T.I. BR 280 Ha52
Nambinda EAT 207 Mj50
Nambol IND (MNP) 112 Pg33
Nambonkaha CI 193 Kh41
Nambour AUS (QLD) 151 Sg59
Nambuangongo ANG 202 Lh50
Nambucca Heads AUS (NSW) 151 Sg61
Nambung N.P. AUS 144 Qh61
Namche Bazar NEP 88 Pd32
Nam Chon Reservoir THA 114 Pk38
Namco CHN (TIB) 89 Pf30
Nam Co CHN 89 Pf30
Namdalen N 10 Lg13
Namdhapa N.P. IND 113 Pj32
Nam Dinh VN 96 Qd35
Nämdö S 13 Lt31
Nämdöfjärden S 13 Lt31
Namehumba EAT 207 Mk50
Na Meo LAO 96 Qc35
Nameri N.P. IND 112 Pg32
Náměšť nad Oslavou CZ 38 Lr41
Námestovo SK 39 Lu41
Nametil MOC 211 Mk53
Nam Et N.B.C.A. LAO 113 Qb35
Namew Lake CDN 238 Ej18
Namhae Do ROK 100 Rd28
Nam Ha N.B.C.A. LAO 113 Qa35
Namhan Gang PRK 100 Rd27
Namhkan MYA 113 Pj34
Namhpakka MYA 113 Pj34
Namhsan MYA 113 Pj35
Namhta MYA 113 Ph33
Nami MAL 116 Qa42
Namialo MOC 211 Mk53
Namib Desert ANG 208 Lf54
Namib Desert NAM 212 Lg55
Namibe ANG 208 Lg53
Namibia 167 Lb12
Namibia Abyssal Plain 170 Lb24
Namib Naukluft Park NAM 212 Lh57
Namidode MOC 211 Mj54
Namie J 101 Sa27
Namies ZA 216 Lk60
Namina MOC 211 Mk53
Namioka J 101 Sa25
Namipit RP 121 Ra37
Namiquipa MEX (CHH) 237 Eg31
Namir MNG 85 Pf21
Namiroa MOC 211 Mk53
Namissiguima BF 185 Kj39
Namitete MW 210 Mg53
Namjagbarwa CHN 89 Ph31
Nam Kading N.B.C.A. LAO 115 Qc36
Nam Khao LAO 115 Qc36
Nam Khap Ban Tang VN 96 Qc34
Namlan MYA 113 Pj34
Namlea RI 130 Rd47
Namling CHN (TIB) 88 Pe31
Nam-mawng MYA 113 Pk35
Nam Nao N.P. THA 114 Qa37
Nam Ngum Reservoir LAO 115 Qc36
Nam Noen LAO 113 Qb35
Namoi River AUS 151 Se61
Namoluk Island FSM 156 Sc17
Namonuito Atoll FSM 156 Sb17
Namor BR (AM) 274 Gj49
Namorik Atoll MH 157 Tb17
Namoroka, P.N.de RM 220 Nc54
Namorona RM 220 Ne56
Nam Ou LAO 113 Qb35
Namounou BF 193 La40
Nampa USA (ID) 234 Eb24
Nampagan MYA 113 Ph33
Nampala RMM 184 Kh38
Nam Pat THA 114 Qa37
Nampawng MYA 113 Pj34
Nampevo MOC 211 Mj54
Nam Phoui N.B.C.A. LAO 114 Qa36
Nampingo EAT 207 Mj50
Nämpnäs FIN 13 Mb28
Nampo PRK 100 Rc26
Nampuécha MOC 211 Na52
Nampula MOC 211 Mk53
Nam Pun THA 114 Qa36
Nampungu EAT 211 Mj51
Namrole RI 130 Rd47
Namru CHN (TIB) 88 Pa30
Namsê La NEP/CHN 88 Pb31
Namsham MYA 113 Pj34
Namsos N 10 Lf13
Namsskogan N 10 Lg13
Namtabung RI 133 Rf50
Nam Taung MYA 113 Pj35
Nam Tha LAO 113 Qa35
Nam Theun LAO 115 Qc37
Nam Theun N.B.C.A. LAO 115 Qc37
Nam Tok Chattrakan N.P. THA 114 Qa37
Namtok Khlong Kaeo National Park THA 115 Qb39
Nam Tok Mae Surin N.P. THA 114 Pk36
Namtu MYA 113 Pj34
Namu CDN (BC) 232 Dg20
Namu Atoll MH 157 Tb17
Namudi PNG 159 Se50
Namuka-i-lau FJI 163 Ua55
Namukumbo Z 210 Md53
Namuno MOC 211 Mk52
Nam Un Reservoir THA 115 Qb37
Namur B 23 Le40
Namuruputh EAK 197 Mh43
Namutoni NAM 212 Lj55
Namwala Z 210 Md53
Namwon ROK 100 Rd28
Nam Xam N.B.C.A. LAO 96 Qc35
Nam Xeng LAO 113 Qb35
Namyit Island 122 Qh40
Namysłów PL 36 Ls39
Namyunn MYA 113 Pj32
Nan THA 114 Qa36
Nana CAM 195 Lh42
Nana RCA 195 Lh43
Nana Bakassa RCA 195 Lj42
Nana Bakassa RCA 195 Lj42
Nana Barya RCA 195 Lj42
Nana Candundo ANG 209 Mb51
Nanae J 99 Sa25
Nanaimo CDN (BC) 232 Dj21
Nanambinia AUS (WA) 145 Rb62
Nana Museum of the Arctic USA (AK) 229 Bj12
Nanango AUS (QLD) 151 Sg59
Nanania Plateau NAM 212 Lj58
Nanao J 101 Rj27
Nan'ao Dao CHN 97 Qj34
Nanaputa EAT 211 Mk51
Nanarup AUS (WA) 144 Qk63

Nanay – Nereta

Nanay PE 272 Gc47
Nanbai CHN (GZH) 96 Qd32
Nanbu CHN (SCH) 95 Qd30
Nancha CHN (HLG) 98 Re22
Nanchang CHN (JGX) 102 Qh31
Nanchan Si CHN 93 Qg26
Nancheng CHN (JGX) 102 Qj32
Nanchititla, P.N. MEX 254 Ek36
Nanchong CHN (SCH) 95 Qd30
Nanchuan CHN (CGQ) 95 Qd31
Nancowry Island IND 111 Pg42
Nancy F 23 Lg42
Nanda Devi IND 107 Pa30
Nanda Devi National Park IND 107 Ok30
Nandaime NIC 256 Fg40
Nandaly AUS (VIC) 153 Sb63
Nandan CHN (GZG) 96 Qd33
Nandankanan Biological Park IND 109 Pc35
Nandavaram IND (APH) 111 Ok39
Nanded IND (MHT) 108 Oj36
Nandewar Range AUS 151 Sf61
Nandgaon IND (MHT) 109 Oj35
Nandgaon Kaji IND (MHT) 108 Oj35
Nandghat IND (CGH) 109 Pa35
Nandi ZW 214 Mf56
Nandian CHN (YUN) 113 Qb34
Nandi Hills IND 111 Oj40
Nandikotkur IND (APH) 108 Ok38
Nandom GH 193 Kj40
Nandowrie AUS (QLD) 151 Sd58
Nandura IND (MHT) 108 Oj35
Nandurbar IND (MHT) 108 Oh35
Nandyal IND (APH) 111 Ok39
Nanfeng CHN (JGX) 102 Qj32
Nanga AUS (WA) 140 Qg59
Nangade MOC 211 Mk51
Nanga Eboko CAM 195 Lg43
Nangai Ketunga RI 126 Qf45
Nangal IND (PJB) 107 Oj30
Nanga Mahap RI 126 Qf46
Nanga Mau RI 126 Qf46
Nangandu EAT 207 Mj49
Nanganga EAT 211 Mk51
Nanga Parbat PK 79 Oh28
Nanga Pinoh RI 126 Qf46
Nangaroro RI 129 Ra50
Nangaru EAT 207 Mk50
Nanga Sokan RI 126 Qf46
Nanga Suruk RI 126 Qg45
Nanga Tamin MAL 126 Qg44
Nanga Tayap RI 126 Qf46
Nangazê Co CHN 88 Pd30
Nanggun Bum MYA 113 Pk32
Nangin MYA 116 Pk40
Nangis F 23 Ld42
Nango J 103 Rf29
Nangola RMM 184 Kg39
Nangolet SUD 197 Mg43
Nangong CHN (HBI) 93 Qh27
Nangqên CHN (QHI) 89 Pj29
Nang Rong THA 115 Qb38
Nanguruwe EAT 211 Na51
Nangwarry AUS (SA) 152 Sa64
Nangwashi Z 209 Mb54
Nang Xian CHN (TIB) 89 Pg31
Nanhua CHN (YUN) 113 Qa33
Nan Hua CHN 97 Qg33
Nanhui CHN (SHG) 102 Ra30
Nanjangud IND (KTK) 111 Oj40
Nanjiang CHN (SCH) 95 Qd29
Nanjian Yizu Zizhixian CHN (YUN) 113 Qa33
Nanjiao CHN (YUN) 113 Qa34
Nanjing CHN (JGS) 102 Qk29
Nanjing CHN (JGS) 102 Qk29
Nanjinji EAT 207 Mk50
Nankang CHN (JGX) 97 Qh33
Nanking CHN (JGS) 102 Qk29
Nankoku J 101 Rg29
Nankova ANG 209 Lk54
Nankunshan CHN 97 Qg34
Nanle CHN (HNN) 93 Qh27
Nanling CHN (AHU) 102 Qk30
Nan Ling CHN 96 Qg33
Nanlixa MOC 211 Mj52
Nanning CHN (GZG) 96 Qe34
Nannup AUS (WA) 144 Qh63
Nano DY 186 Lb41
Na Noi THA 114 Qa36
Nanoro BF 185 Kj39
Nanpara IND (UPH) 107 Pa32
Nanpeng Liedao CHN 97 Qj34
Nanping CHN (FJN) 102 Qk32
Nanping CHN (HUB) 95 Qg31
Nanping CHN (SCH) 94 Qc29
Nanpur IND (MPH) 108 Oh34
Nanri Dao CHN 97 Qk33
Nanripo MOC 211 Mk53
Nansebo ETH 198 Mk42
Nansei Islands J 103 Rc33
Nansen, Mount CDN 231 Db14
Nansen Sound CDN 225 Fc03
Nan Shan CHN 85 Pd24
Nanshan Island 122 Qh40
Nanshui Shuiku CHN 97 Qg33
Nansio EAT 206 Mg47
Nantamba PNG 160 Sf48
Nanterre F 23 Lc42
Nantes F 22 Kt43
Nanteuil-le-Haudouin F 23 Lc41
Nanti, Gunung RI 125 Qb48
Nantilla AUS (NSW) 150 Sb61
Nanton CDN (AB) 233 Ed20
Nanton GH 193 Kk41
Nantong CHN (JGS) 102 Ra29
Nantou RC 97 Ra34
Nantua F 25 Lf44
Nantucket USA (MA) 247 Ge25
Nantucket Island USA 247 Gf25
Nantucket Shoals USA 247 Ge25
Nantucket Sound USA 247 Gf25
Nantula MOC 211 Mk52
Nantuto MOC 211 Mj53
Nantwich GB 21 Ks37
Nanuku Passage FJI 163 Ua54
Nanumanga TUV 157 Td20
Nanumea Atoll TUV 157 Td20
Nanuque BR (MG) 287 Hk54
Nanusa RI 123 Rc44
Nanutarra AUS (WA) 140 Qh57
Nanvakfak Lake USA (AK) 228 Bk16
Nanwan Reservoir CHN 95 Qg29
Nanxi CHN (SCH) 94 Qc31
Nan Xian CHN (HUN) 95 Qg31
Nanxiao CHN (GZG) 96 Qe34
Nanxiong CHN (GDG) 97 Qh33
Nanxu CHN (GZG) 96 Qf33
Nanyamba EAT 211 Mk51
Nanyang CHN (HNN) 95 Qg29
Nanyangdian Shan CHN 102 Ra32
Nanyang Hu CHN 102 Qj28
Nan-yo J 101 Sa26
Nanyuki EAK 204 Mj46
Nanzamu CHN (LNG) 100 Rc25
Nanzhai CHN (GZH) 96 Qe32
Nanzhang CHN (HUB) 95 Qf30
Nanzhao CHN (HNN) 95 Qg29
Nanzheng CHN (SAA) 95 Qd29
Nanzhila Rest Camp Z 209 Mc54
Naogaon BD 112 Pe33
Naoli He CHN 98 Rg22
Naolinco MEX (VC) 254 Fb36
Não-me-Toque BR (RS) 290 Hd60
Naora PNG 160 Sf48
Náousa GR 49 Mf53
Náoussa GR 46 Mc50
Napa, Cerro BR/RCH 284 Gf56
Napa USA (CA) 234 Dj26
Napabale Lake RI 127 Rb48
Napadogan CDN (NB) 245 Gg22
Napaha MOC 211 Mk52
Napaiskak USA (AK) 228 Bk15
Na Pali Coast USA 230 Ca34
Napanwainam RI 131 Rh47
Napan-yaur RI 131 Rh47
Napata and Djebel Barkal Temples SUD 190 Mf37
Napeitom EAK 204 Mj45
Napido RI 131 Rh46
Napier NZ 154 Tj65
Napier ZA 216 Lk63
Napier Downs AUS (WA) 138 Rc54
Napier Mountains 297 Nc32
Naples I 42 Lp50
Naples USA (FL) 250 Fk32
Napo CHN (GZG) 96 Qc34
Napo PE 272 Gc46
Napoleon AUS (QLD) 150 Sc59
Napoleon USA (ND) 240 Fa22
Napoleon USA (OH) 246 Fh25
Nápoli I 42 Lp50
Nappamerrie AUS (QLD) 150 Sa59
Nappanee USA (IN) 246 Fh25
Napperby AUS (NT) 142 Rg57
Napuka Atoll F 165 Ck53
Naqāda ET 177 Mg33
Naqb al-Hadjar YE 68 Nd38
Naqadeh IR 72 Nc27
Naqil al Farda YE 68 Nc38
Naqš-e-Šapur IR 74 Nh31
Nār S 15 Lt33
Nara J 101 Rh28
Nara RMM 184 Kg38
Narač BY 17 Mg36
Nara Canal PK 81 Oe32
Naracoorte AUS (SA) 152 Sa64
Naracoorte Caves Conservation Park AUS 152 Sa64
Naraha IND (BIH) 112 Pd32
Naraini IND (UPH) 109 Pa33
Narainpur IND (CGH) 109 Pa36
Narajiv UA 39 Me41
Naran PK 79 Og28
Narang AFG 79 Of28
Narangmor EAK 198 Mh43
Naranjal EC 272 Ga47
Naranjal PY 289 Hc58
Naranjito EC 272 Ga47
Naranjos BOL 285 Ha55
Naranjos MEX (VC) 254 Fb35
Narao J 103 Re29
Narasannapeta IND (APH) 109 Pc36
Narasapur IND (APH) 109 Pa37
Narasaraopet IND (APH) 109 Pa37
Narasimharajapura IND (KTK) 110 Oh40
Narasinghpur IND (ORS) 109 Pc35
Naratasty RUS 53 Ng18
Narathiwat THA 117 Qa42
Nara Visa USA (NM) 237 Ej28
Naravuka FJI 163 Tk54
Narayanganj BD 112 Pf34
Narayanganj IND (MPH) 109 Pa34
Narayangaon IND (MHT) 108 Og36
Narayanpet IND (APH) 108 Oj37
Narayan Sarovar IND 108 Oe34
Narberth GB 20 Kq39
Narbonne F 25 Lc47
Narborough = Isla Fernandina EC 272 Fe46
Narcondan Island IND 114 Ph39
Nardò I 43 Lt50
Nardoo AUS (NSW) 150 Sc60
Narečenski bani BG 47 Me49
Narellen AUS (NSW) 153 Sf63
Narembeen AUS (WA) 144 Qk62
Naréna RMM 184 Kf39
Nares Abyssal Plain 227 Gc14
Nares Strait 225 Gb03
Naretha AUS (WA) 145 Rc61
Narew PL 37 Mb38
Narew PL 37 Md38
Narewka PL 37 Md38
Nargund IND (KTK) 108 Oh38
Nari PK 80 Od31
Na Ri VN 96 Qd34
Narib NAM 212 Lj58
Narijn gol MNG 85 Pg20
Narimanov RUS 70 Nd22
Narin Gol CHN 87 Pf27
Narin Nur CHN (NMZ) 92 Qe26
Narita J 101 Sa28
Nar'jan-Mar RUS 58 Nc05
Narlı TR 62 Mj27
Narmada IND 104 Oc14
Narman TR 63 Na25
Narnaul IND (HYA) 106 Oj31
Narni I 42 Ln48
Narob NAM 212 Lj58
Narochanski N.P. BY 17 Mg36
Naro-Fominsk RUS 52 Mj18
Naro Island RP 123 Rb40
Narok EAK 204 Mh46
Naro Moru EAK 204 Mj46
Narooma AUS (NSW) 153 Sf64
Naro Sura EAK 204 Mh46
Narovlja BY 52 Me20
Narowal PK 79 Oh29
Närpes = Närpiö FIN 13 Mb28
Narphung BHT 112 Pf32
Närpiö = Närpes FIN 13 Mb28
Narra RP 122 Qk41
Narrabri AUS (NSW) 151 Se61
Narragansett Bay USA 247 Ge25
Narrandera AUS (NSW) 153 Sd63
Narran Lake AUS 151 Sd60
Narrawallee Beach AUS 153 Sf63
Narraway River CDN 232 Dk18
Narrogin AUS (WA) 144 Qj62
Narromine AUS (NSW) 153 Se62
Narrow C. USA 230 Cd17
Narrowsburg USA (NY) 247 Gc25
Narsampet IND (APH) 109 Ok37
Narsapur IND (APH) 108 Ok37
Narsarsuaq DK 225 Hc06
Narsi IND (MHT) 108 Oj36
Narsinghgarh IND (MPH) 108 Oj34
Narsinghpur IND (MPH) 109 Ok34
Narsipatnam IND (APH) 109 Pb37
Nart CHN (NMZ) 93 Qh24
Nart MNG 90 Qc21
Nartkala RUS (KBA) 70 Nb24
Naru-jima J 103 Re29
Narupa EC 272 Gb46
Naruto J 101 Rh28
Narva EST 16 Mj31
Narvacan RP 120 Ra37
Narva-Jõesuu EST 16 Mj31
Narva laht EST/RUS 16 Mh31
Närvijoki FIN 13 Mb28
Narvik N 10 Lj11
Narvskij zaliv EST/RUS 16 Mh31
Narvskoje vodohranilišče RUS 16 Mj31
Narwai IND (MPH) 107 Oj33
Narwana IND (HYA) 106 Oj31
Narwiańs P.N. PL 37 Mc37
Narwinbi Aboriginal Reserve AUS 139 Rj53
Naryilco AUS (QLD) 150 Sa60
Naryn KS 77 Oh25
Naryn KS 77 Oj25
Naryn KZ 84 Oh23
Naryn RUS (TUV) 85 Ph20
Narynkol KZ 77 Pa24
Naryškino RUS 52 Mh19
Nås S 13 Lp30
Năsăud RO 44 Me43
Nasavrky CZ 38 Lq41
Nasbinals F 25 Ld46
Nascentes do Rio Parnaiba, P.N.das BR 282 Hh51
Nash Harbor USA (AK) 228 Bg15
Nashiño EC 272 Gb46
Nashua USA (NH) 247 Ge24
Nashu Bum MYA 113 Pj33
Nashville USA (AR) 243 Fd29
Nashville USA (GA) 249 Fj30
Nashville USA (NC) 249 Ga28
Nashville USA (TN) 248 Fg27
Nashville Superspeedway USA (TN) 248 Fg27
Nashwaak Bridge CDN (NB) 245 Gg22
Nasia GH 193 Kk40
Nasia GH 193 Kk40
Nasibāt Timāna ET 177 Mg34
Našice HR 41 Lt45
Nasielsk PL 37 Ma38
Näsijärvi FIN 16 Md29
Nasik IND (MHT) 108 Og36
Nasik RI 125 Qd47
Nasik Road IND (MHT) 108 Og36
Nasi, Mount ETH 198 Mh41
Nasionale Addo Olifantpark ZA 217 Mc62
Nasionale Augrabieswatervalpark ZA 216 Ma60
Nasionale Krugerwildtuin = Kruger N.P. ZA 214 Mf57
Nasipit RP 123 Rc41
Nasir SUD 197 Mg41
Nasirabad IND (RJT) 106 Oh32
Nasirabad PK 80 Oe31
Nasiriyan IR 72 Nd29
Nasmah LAR 174 Lg30
Naso I 42 Lp52
Nasolot EAK 204 Mh45
Nasolot National Reserve EAK 204 Mh45
Nason SME 271 Hc43
Nasondoye RDC 209 Mc51
Naso Point RP 123 Ra40
Nasorolevu FJI 163 Tk54
Nasrapur IND (MHT) 108 Og36
Nasrullahganj IND (MPH) 108 Oj34
Nassarawa WAN 186 Ld41
Nassau BS 251 Gb33
Nassau D 32 Lh40
Nassau Island NZ 157 Uc21
Nass Basin CDN 231 Df17
Nassian CI 193 Kh41
Nassian CI 193 Kj41
Nässjö S 15 Lp33
Nassoukou DY 193 La40
Nassoumfou BF 185 Kk38
Nass River CDN 231 Df18
Nastola FIN 16 Mf30
Nasugbu RP 120 Ra38
Nasuraghena SOL 161 Tb51
Näsviken S 13 Lr29
Nata PA 257 Fk41
Nata RB 213 Md56
Nataja MW 211 Mh53
Natal BR (RN) 277 Jc48
Natal BR (TO) 276 Hf48
Natal RI 124 Pk45
Natal Downs AUS (QLD) 149 Sd56
Natal Felicidade, T.I. BR 274 Ha47
Natalinci SCG 46 Ma46
Natalicio PY 289 Hc59
Natanz IR 72 Nf29
Nataraja Temple IND 111 Ok41
Nata Sanctuary RB 213 Md56
Natchez USA (MS) 243 Fe30
Natchez Trace Parkway (Mississippi) USA 248 Fe29
Natchez Trace Parkway (Tennessee) USA 248 Fg28
Natchez Trace Resort S.P. USA 248 Ff28
Natchitoches USA (LA) 243 Fd30
Natewa Bay FJI 163 Tk54
Nathahu MYA 114 Ph37
Nathan River AUS (NT) 139 Rh53
Na Thawi THA 116 Qa42
Nathdwara IND (RJT) 106 Og33
Nathenje MW 210 Mg53
Na Thon THA 116 Pk41
Nathorst Land N 11 Lh07
Nathrop USA (CO) 235 Eg26
Na-ti MYA 113 Pk34
Natiboani BF 193 La40
Natimuk AUS (VIC) 152 Sa64
Natinga = Garu GH 193 Kk40
National Botanical Gardens (Pyin U Lwin) MYA 113 Ph35
National Chambal Wildlife Sanctuary IND 106 Oj33
National Hall of Fame for Famous A. Ind. USA 242 Fa28
National Hist. District (Bentonsport) USA 246 Fe25
Nationalpark CH 34 Ll44
National Park NZ 154 Th65
Nationalpark Eifel D 32 Lg40
National Radio Astronomy Observatory USA 247 Ga26
National Radio Astronomy Observatory VLA Telescope (Socorro NM) USA 237 Eg29
National Railroad Museum USA 249 Ga28
National West Coast Tourist Recreation Area NAM 212 Lg56
National Wool Museum AUS (VIC) 153 Sc65
Nation River CDN 232 Dh18
Natitingou DY 193 La40
Natividade BR (TO) 282 Hg51
Natla River CDN 231 Df14
Nat ma taung N.P. MYA 112 Pg35
Natmauk MYA 113 Ph35
Natore BD 112 Pe33
Natrona USA (WY) 235 Eg24
Nattai N.P. AUS 153 Sf63
Nättarö S 13 Lt32
Nattaung MYA 114 Pj36
Nättraby S 15 Lq34
Natuco MOC 211 Mj52
Natukanaoka Pan NAM 208 Lh55
Natuna Besar RI 117 Qe43
Natuna Sea RI 117 Qd45
Natural Arch USA 249 Fh27
Natural Bridge USA (AL) 248 Fg28
Naturaliste Channel AUS 140 Qg58
Naturaliste Plateau 136 Qc25
Naturita USA (CO) 235 Ef26
Naturno = Naturns I 40 Ll44
Naturns = Naturno I 40 Ll44
Naturpark Brownsberg SME 271 Hc43
Natuurreservaat Boven Coesewijne SME 271 Hc43
Natuurreservaat Brinckheuvel SME 271 Hc43
Natuurreservaat Centraal Suriname SME 271 Hb43
Natuurreservaat Copi SME 271 Hc43
Natuurreservaat Coppename Monding SME 271 Hc43
Natuurreservaat Galibi SME 271 Hc43
Natuurreservaat Hertenrits SME 271 Hb42
Natuurreservaat Peruvia SME 271 Hc43
Natuurreservaat Sipaliwini SME 271 Hb44
Natuurreservaat Wane Kreek SME 271 Hc43
Natuurreservaat Wia-Wia SME 271 Hc43
Nau TJ 76 Oe25
Nauabu PNG 160 Sf51
Nauari BR (PA) 275 Hc45
Naubise NEP 88 Pc32
Nauchas NAM 212 Lj57
Nauders A 34 Ll44
Nauela MOC 211 Mj53
Nauen D 33 Ln38
Naugachhia IND (BIH) 112 Pd33
Naujan RP 121 Ra39
Naujoji Akmenė LT 17 Mc34
Naukluft NAM 212 Lj58
Naukot PK 81 Oe33
Naulila ANG 208 Lh54
Naumatang RI 132 Rd49
Naumburg D 33 Lm39
Naumovskij RUS 55 Na22
Naungmo MYA 112 Ph33
Naung-Mon MYA 113 Pj32
Naupada IND (APH) 109 Pc36
Naupara IND (CGH) 109 Pb34
Nauroz Kalat PK 80 Oc31
Nauru NAU 157 Tb19
Nauru 135 Ta10
Naushahro Firoz PK 80 Oe32
Nausori FJI 163 Tk55
Naustdal N 12 Lf29
Nauta PE 273 Gd48
Nautanwa IND (UPH) 107 Pb32
Naute Recreation Area NAM 216 Lk59
Nautla MEX (VC) 254 Fb35
Nautsi RUS 11 Me11
Nauvo = Nagu FIN 16 Mb30
Nauvo FIN 16 Mb30
Nava E 26 Kp53
Navacerrada E 29 Kr50
Navael'nja BY 17 Mf37
Navahermosa E 29 Kq49
Navahrudak BY 17 Mf37
Navahrudskae uzvyšša BY 17 Mf37
Navajo Ind. Res. USA 237 Ef27
Navajo Reservoir USA (NM) 237 Eg27
Naval RP 123 Rc40
Navalcarnero E 29 Kq50
Navalgund IND (KTK) 108 Oh38
Navalmanzano E 26 Kq51
Navalmoral de la Mata E 28 Kp49
Navalvillar de Pela E 28 Kp49
Navan IRL 20 Ko37
Navapolack BY 52 Me18
Navapur IND (MHT) 108 Og35
Navarcles E 30 Lb49
Navarra E 27 Kt52
Navarre USA (FL) 248 Fg30
Navarrenx F 24 Ku47
Navarrés E 29 Ku49
Navarro RA (BA) 289 Ha63
Navarro USA (CA) 234 Dj26
Navascués E 27 Kt52
Navas del Madroño E 28 Ko49
Navasëlki BY 37 Mg38
Navasëlki BY 52 Me19
Navašino RUS 53 Nb18
Navasota USA (TX) 243 Fb30
Navassa Island C 259 Gc36
Navegantes BR (SC) 291 Hf59
Navegaon N.P. IND 109 Pa35
Nävekvarn S 13 Lr32
Navelgas E 26 Ko53
Naveslândia BR (GO) 286 He55
Navia E 26 Ko53
Navio BR 283 Jb50
Navios MEX (DGO) 253 Eh34
Navirai BR (MS) 286 Hc57
Naviti FJI 163 Tj54
Navlakhi IND (GUJ) 108 Of34
Navlja RUS 52 Mh19
Năvodari RO 45 Mj46
Navoiy UZ 76 Oc25
Navojoa MEX (SO) 252 Ef32
Navolato MEX (SL) 252 Eg33
Navoloki RUS 53 Na17
Navrongo GH 193 Kk40
Navsari IND (GUJ) 108 Og35
Navua FJI 163 Tk55
Nawa SYR 64 Mj29
Nawabganj BD 112 Pe33
Nawabshah PK 80 Oe32
Nawada IND (BIH) 109 Pc33
Nawagai PK 79 Of28
Nawah AFG 78 Od29
Na Wai THA 114 Pk36
Nawakshut RIM 183 Kb36
Nawani GH 193 Kk41
Nawapara BD 112 Pe34
Nawapara IND (ORS) 109 Pb35
Nawinda Kuta Z 209 Mc54
Nawng-awn MYA 113 Pk35
Nawnghkio MYA 113 Pj34
Nawngleng MYA 113 Pk34
Nawngpuawng MYA 112 Ph33
Na Wong THA 116 Pk42
Naxçivan AZ 70 Nc26
Naxçivan AZ 63 Nd26
Náxos GR 49 Mf53
Náxos GR 49 Mf53
Naxos I 42 Lq53
Nay F 24 Ku47
Naya Chor PK 81 Oe33
Nayagarh IND (ORS) 109 Pc35
Nayagram IND (WBG) 112 Pd34
Nayakanhatti IND (KTK) 111 Oj39
Nayarit MEX 253 Eh35
Nayau FJI 163 Ua54
Nayband IR 73 Nj29
Nayé SN 183 Kd38
Naylowr AFG 78 Od28
Nayoro J 99 Sb23
Nayouri BF 185 La39
Nayudupeta IND (APH) 111 Ok40
Nazaré BR (AP) 271 He44
Nazaré BR (BA) 283 Ja52
Nazaré BR (PA) 276 Hf46
Nazaré BR (TO) 276 Hg49
Nazaré P 28 Kl49
Nazareth BOL 280 Gh53
Nazareth CO 268 Gc43
Nazareth IL 64 Mh29
Nazareth Speedway USA (PA) 247 Gc25
Nazas MEX (DGO) 253 Eh33
Nazca PE 278 Gc53
Nazca Ridge 264 Fd23
Naze J 103 Re31
Nazerat IL 64 Mh29
Nazilli TR 50 Mj53
Nazko CDN (BC) 232 Dj19
Nazko River CDN 232 Dj19
Nazomba MOC 211 Mk51
Nazran' RUS (ING) 70 Nc24
Nazret ETH 198 Mk41
Nbâk RIM 183 Kc37
Nbeïket Dlim RIM 184 Kg37
Ncanaha ZA 217 Mc62
Nchelenge Z 206 Me50
Ncue GQ 195 Lf44
Ndaba RWA 201 Me46
Ndaki RMM 185 Kk38
Ndala EAT 206 Mg48
N'Dalatando ANG 202 Lh50
Ndali DY 186 Lb41
Ndanda RCA 200 Mb43
Ndandu Z 209 Mb53
Ndangane SN 183 Kb38
Ndarapo Swamp EAK 205 Mk47
Ndarassa RCA 196 Mb42
Ndébougou RMM 184 Kh38
Ndeji WAN 186 Lc41
Ndékebalandji G 195 Lg46
Ndekesha RDC 203 Mb49
Ndélé RCA 196 Ma41
Ndélélé CAM 195 Lh43
Ndemba CAM 195 Lg43
Ndendé G 202 Lf47
Ndere EAK 204 Mh45
Ndere Island N.P. EAK 204 Mh46
N'dhala Gorge N.P. AUS 143 Rh57
Ndia SN 183 Kd38
Ndiago RIM 183 Kb37
Ndiguina CAM 187 Lh40
Ndigwa EAK 204 Mh46
Ndikiniméki CAM 195 Lf43
Ndikoko CAM 195 Lf43
Ndim RCA 195 Lh42
Ndindi G 202 Lf47
Ndindi SN 183 Kb38
Ndioum SN 183 Kc37
Ndioum Guènt SN 183 Kc38
Nditam CAM 195 Lf43
Ndiya WAN 194 Ld43
N'Djaména TCH 187 Lh39
Ndji RCA 196 Mb42
Ndjim CAM 195 Lf43
Ndjolé CAM 195 Lf43
Ndjolé G 195 Lf46
Ndjoundou RCB 200 Lj46
Ndjounou G 195 Lg46
Ndjwé CAM 195 Lh44
Ndoba Z 210 Me51
Ndofane SN 183 Kc39
Ndok CAM 195 Lh42
Ndokama CAM 194 Le43
Ndokayo CAM 195 Lh43
Ndoki RCB 195 Lj45
Ndokouassikro CI 193 Kh42
Ndola Z 210 Me52
Ndole EAT 207 Mj49
Ndole Bay Z 206 Mf50
Ndolwane ZW 213 Md55
Ndom CAM 195 Lf43
Ndondo SOL 161 Ta50
Ndongolo G 195 Lf45
Ndop CAM 194 Lf43
Ndora Mountains WAN 195 Lf42
Ndorola BF 193 Kh40
Ndoto Mountains EAK 204 Mj45
Ndougou G 202 Le46
Ndoukou RCA 200 Ma43
Ndoumbou RCA 195 Lj42
Ndroq AL 46 Lu49
Ndu CAM 195 Lf42
Ndu RDC 200 Mb43
Nduli EAT 207 Mh49
Ndumo ZA 217 Mg59
Ndumo Game Reserve ZA 217 Mg59
Ndundu EAT 207 Mk50
Ndundu Rufiji EAT 207 Mk49
Nduye RDC 201 Me45
Ndzuani COM 218 Nc52
Néa Aghialos GR 48 Mc51
Néa Artáki GR 48 Md52
Néa Epidavros GR 48 Md53
Néa Fókea GR 46 Md50
Neah Bay USA (WA) 232 Dh21
Néa Ionia GR 48 Mc51
Néa Kalikrátia GR 46 Md50
Neale Junction AUS (WA) 145 Rc60
Neale Junction Nature Reserve AUS 145 Rc60
Neales River AUS 143 Rh59
Néa Mihanióna GR 46 Mc50
Néa Moni GR 49 Mg52
Néa Moudania GR 46 Md50
Neamț RO 45 Mg43
Néa Péramos GR 47 Me50
Neápoli GR 46 Mb50
Neápoli GR 48 Md54
Neápoli GR 49 Mf55
Nearchus Passage MYA 114 Pj40
Neath GB 20 Kr39
Néa Triglia GR 46 Md50
Néa Zihni GR 47 Md49
Nebbou BF 193 Kk40
Nebe RI 132 Rb50
Nebelat el Hagana SUD 197 Me39
Nebelhorn D 34 Ll43
Nebiler TR 50 Mg51
Nebine River AUS 151 Sd60
Neblina, Cerro de la EC 272 Fk46
Nebo AUS (QLD) 149 Se56
Nebolči RUS 52 Mg16
Nebo, Mount JOR 64 Mh30
Nebraska USA 226 Ed10
Nebraska City USA (NE) 241 Fc25
Nébrodi I 42 Lp53
Necaise USA (MS) 243 Ff30
Nece F (NCL) 162 Td56
Necedah USA (WI) 241 Fe24
Nechako River CDN 232 Dh19
Nechi CO 268 Gc42
Nechi CO 268 Gc41
Nechisar N.P. ETH 198 Mj43
Neckar D 34 Lj42
Neckargemünd D 34 Lj41
Neckarsulm D 34 Lk41
Necochea RA (BA) 293 Ha65
Necoclé CO 268 Gb41
Nécropoles de Bourzanga BF 185 Kk39
Necropoli Ànghelu Rùiu I 31 Lj50
Necropoli di Sulcis I 31 Lj51
Necropoli etrusca Cervéteri I 42 Ln48
Necropoli etrusca Tarquinia I 42 Lm48
Necropoli Sant'Andria Priu I 31 Lj50
Necropolis Deffufa SUD 190 Mf37
Necungas MOC 210 Mh54
Nédéley TCH 188 Lk38
Nedelišće HR 41 Lr44
Nederweert NL 32 Lf39
Nedrata ETH 198 Mk40
Nedryhajliv UA 52 Mg20
Nedstrand N 12 Lf31
Nedumangad IND (KER) 110 Oj42
Needles CDN (BC) 232 Ea21
Needles USA (CA) 236 Ec28
Neepawa CDN (MB) 238 Fa20
Nefasit ER 191 Mk39
Nefas Mewch'a ETH 198 Mk40
Nefta TN 174 Ld29
Neftejugansk RUS 58 Oc06
Neftekumsk RUS 70 Nc23
Nefza TN 174 Le27
Negage ANG 202 Lh49
Négala RMM 184 Kf39
Nega Nega Z 210 Me53
Negānzi DY 186 Lb40
Negar IR 75 Nj31
Negara RI 126 Qh47
Negara RI 129 Qh50
Negaunee USA (MI) 246 Fg22
Negele ETH 198 Mk43
Negerilama RI 116 Qa44
Negev Desert IL 64 Mh30
Negginan CDN (MB) 238 Fb19
Neghele ETH 198 Mk42
Negola ANG 208 Lh53
Negomano MOC 211 Mk51
Negombo CL 111 Ok43
Negombo Beach CL 111 Ok43
Negotin SCG 46 Mc46
Negotino MK 46 Mc49
Negrași RO 45 Mf46
Nègrepelisse F 24 Lb46
Negrești RO 45 Mh44
Negrești-Oaș RO 44 Md43
Negrete RCH 292 Gd64
Negribreen N 11 Lk06
Negril JA 259 Ga36
Negril Beach JA 259 Ga36
Negril Point JA 259 Ga36
Negrine DZ 174 Ld28
Negro, Cerro RA 292 Ge65
Negro, Cerro RA 292 Gf68
Negros RP 123 Rb41
Negru Vodă RO 45 Mj47
Neguac CDN (NB) 245 Gh22
Nehaevskij RUS 53 Na20
Nehaj HR 41 Lp46
Nehalem USA (OR) 234 Dj23
Nehalem USA 232 Dj23
Neharelae BY 17 Mh37
Nehbandan IR 73 Oa30
Nehe CHN (HLG) 98 Rc21
Nehone ANG 208 Lj54
Neiafu TO 164 Bd55
Neiba DOM 260 Ge36
Neifaru MV 110 Og43
Neihart USA (MT) 235 Ee22
Neijiang CHN (SCH) 94 Qc31
Neil Armstrong Air & Space Mus. USA 246 Fh25
Neilburg CDN (SK) 233 Ef19
Neilersdrif ZA 216 Ma60
Neill Island IND 111 Pg40
Neillsville USA (WI) 241 Fe23
Neilton USA (WA) 232 Dj22
Nei Mongol Gaoyuan CHN 92 Qa25
Neina NAM 212 Lj55
Neinsberg NAM 212 Lj56
Neišapur IR 73 Nk27
Neiva CO 272 Gc44
Neixiang CHN (HNN) 95 Qf29
Neja RUS 53 Nb16
Neja RUS 53 Nb16
Nejdek CZ 38 Ln40
Neji MEX (BC) 236 Eb29
Nejime J 103 Rf30
Nejo ETH 197 Mh41
Nejsvětější Trojice CZ 38 Ls41
Neka IR 72 Ng27
Nekemte ETH 198 Mj41
Nekla PL 36 Ls38
Nekmard BD 112 Pe33
Nekob MA 172 Kh30
Nekrasovskoe RUS 53 Na17
Nekró Manteíon GR 48 Ma51
Nelamangala IND (KTK) 111 Oj40
Nelaug N 12 Lj32
Nelia AUS (QLD) 148 Sb56
Nelidovo RUS 52 Mg17
Neligh USA (NE) 240 Fa24
Neligh Mill S.H.S USA 240 Fa24
Nellie, Mount AUS 138 Rc54
Nelligere IND (KTK) 111 Oj40
Nellore IND (APH) 111 Ok39
Nel'ma RUS 99 Rk22
Nelson CDN (BC) 232 Eb21
Nelson GB 21 Ks37
Nelson NZ 155 Tg66
Nelson RA (SF) 289 Gk61
Nelson Bay AUS (NSW) 153 Sg62
Nelson Forks CDN (BC) 231 Dh16
Nelson House CDN (MB) 238 Fa18
Nelson Island USA 228 Bh15
Nelson Lakes N.P. NZ 155 Tg67
Nelson River CDN 238 Fc17
Nelspoort ZA 216 Mb62
Nelspruit ZA 214 Mf58
Néma RIM 184 Kg37
Nemaiah Valley CDN (BC) 232 Dj20
Neman BY 17 Md37
Neman RUS 17 Mc35
Nemanva ZW 214 Mf56
Nembrala RI 132 Rb51
Nemenčinė LT 17 Mf36
Nemours F 23 Lc42
Nemrut Dağı TR 63 Mk26
Nemrut Dağı Milli Parkı TR 63 Mk27
Nemšová SK 38 Lt42
Nemunas 17 Mc35
Nemunelis LV/LT 17 Me34
Nemuro J 99 Sc24
Nemuro-hanto J 99 Sc24
Nemuro-kaikyo J/RUS 99 Sc24
Nemyriv UA 37 Md40
Nemyriv UA 54 Me21
Nenagh IRL 20 Kn38
Nenana USA (AK) 229 Cf13
Nenana River USA 229 Cf13
Nendo SOL 157 Tb21
Nene GB 21 La38
Nenets Autonomous District RUS 58 Nd05
Nenggiri MAL 117 Qa43
Nengo ANG 209 Ma53
Nengone Village F (NCL) 162 Td56
Nenitoúria GR 49 Mf52
Nenjiang CHN (HLG) 98 Rc21
Nen Jiang CHN 98 Rc20
Neno MW 211 Mh53
Nenoksa RUS 11 Mk13
Neo J 101 Rj28
Néo Erásmio GR 47 Me50
Neohóri GR 46 Mb51
Neola USA (UT) 235 Ee25
Néo Monastiri GR 48 Mc51
Néo Petritsi GR 46 Md49
Neopolis BR (SE) 283 Jb51
Neosho USA (MO) 243 Fc27
Néos Marmarás GR 47 Md50
Néos Skopós GR 46 Md49
Nepal NEP 104 Pa13
Nepalganj NEP 88 Pa31
Nepara NAM 208 Lk54
Nepean CDN (ON) 247 Gc23
Nepeña PE 278 Ga50
Nephi USA (UT) 235 Ee26
Nephin IRL 18 Kl37
Nephin Beg Range IRL 18 Kl36
Nepisiguit Bay CDN 245 Gh22
Nepisiguit River CDN 245 Gg22
Nepoko RDC 201 Me44
Nepolje SCG 46 Ma48
Nepomuk CZ 38 Lo41
Neptun RO 45 Mj47
Neptune Beach USA (FL) 249 Fk30
Neptune Islands AUS 152 Rj63
Nera I 42 Ln48
Nera RO 44 Mb46
Nérac F 24 La46
Nerang AUS (QLD) 151 Sg59
Neratovice CZ 38 Lp40
Neravailu IND (APH) 111 Ok40
Nerča RUS 91 Qj19
Nerčinsk RUS 91 Qj20
Nerčugan RUS 91 Qj19
Nerehta RUS 53 Na17
Nereju RO 45 Mg45
Neresheim D 34 Ll42
Nereta LV 17 Mf34

Neretva – Niwas

Neretva BIH 41 Ls47
Neringa-Nida LT 17 Ma35
Neriquinha ANG 209 Ma53
Neris LT 17 Me36
Nerja E 28 Kr46
Nerjungri RUS 59 Ra07
Nerka Lake USA (AK) 228 Ca16
Nerl' RUS 52 Mj17
Nérondes F 23 Lc44
Nerópolis BR (GO) 286 Hf54
Nerpič'e RUS 99 Sc21
Nerpio E 29 Ks48
Nerren Nerren AUS (WA) 140 Qh59
Nerrima AUS (WA) 138 Rc55
Nerušaj UA 45 Mk45
Nerva E 28 Ko47
Nerva RUS 16 Mh30
Nervi I 40 Lk46
Nes N 12 Lk30
Nes N 12 Lh29
Nesbyen N 12 Lk30
Nesebăr BG 47 Mh48
Nesflaten N 12 Lg31
Nesgo PNG 160 Sf47
Nesheim N 12 Lg30
Neskaupstaður IS 10 Kd13
Neslandsvatn N 12 Lk32
Nesle F 23 Lc41
Nesna N 10 Lg12
Nesodden N 12 Ll31
Ness City USA (KS) 240 Fa26
Nessona MOC 214 Mh55
Nestáni GR 48 Mc53
Nestavoll N 12 Lk28
Nesterov RUS 17 Mc36
Nesterovo RUS (BUR) 90 Qd19
Nestiary RUS 53 Nc17
Néstos GR 47 Me49
Néstos Délta GR 47 Me50
Nesttun N 12 Lf30
Nesvik N 12 Lg31
Netaar RI 131 Sa47
Netanya IL 64 Mh29
Netarhat IND (JKD) 109 Pc34
Nétéboulou SN 183 Kd39
Netergueat RIM 183 Kd36
Nethang-Temple CHN 89 Pf31
Netherlands NL 32 Ld38
Netherlands Antilles NL 260 Gf39
Netia MOC 211 Mk53
Netivot IL 64 Mh30
Neto I 43 Lr51
Netrakona BD 112 Pf33
Nettetal D 32 Lg39
Nettiling Lake CDN 224 Gb05
Nettuno I 42 Ln49
Neubrandenburg D 33 Lo37
Neubukow D 33 Lm36
Neuburg an der Donau D 35 Lm42
Neuchâtel CH 34 Lg44
Neuenhagen D 33 Lo38
Neuenhaus D 32 Lg38
Neuenkirchen D 32 Lk37
Neuf-Brisach F 23 Lh42
Neufchâteau B 23 Lf41
Neufchâteau F 23 Lf42
Neufchâtel-en-Bray F 23 Lb41
Neufchâtel-sur-Aisne F 23 Le41
Neufundland and Labrador CDN 225 Ha07
Neu-Halbstadt PY 285 Gk57
Neuhaus (Amt Neuhaus) D 33 Ll37
Neuhaus am Rennweg D 33 Lm40
Neuhof D 34 Lk40
Neuillé-Pont-Pierre F 22 La43
Neukirchen A 35 Ln43
Neukirchen D 32 Lk40
Neulengbach A 35 Lq42
Neum BIH 41 Ls48
Neumarkt A 35 Lo43
Neumarkt A 35 Lp43
Neumarkt in der Oberpfalz D 35 Lm41
Neumarkt-Sankt Veit D 35 Ln42
Neumünster D 33 Lk36
Neunburg D 35 Ln41
Neung-sur-Beuvron F 22 Lb43
Neunkirchen A 35 Lr43
Neunkirchen D 34 Lh41
Neuquén RA (NE) 292 Gf65
Neuquén RA 292 Gf64
Neuquén RA 267 Gb26
Neuruppin D 33 Ln38
Neusiedl A 35 Lr43
Neusiedler See A 35 Lr43
Neusiedler See-Seewinkel, N.P. A 35 Lr43
Neuss D 32 Lg39
Neustadt bei Coburg D 35 Lm40
Neustadt (Aisch) D 35 Ll41
Neustadt am Rübenberge D 32 Lk38
Neustadt (Donau) D 35 Lm42
Neustadt/Dosse D 33 Ln38
Neustadt-Glewe D 33 Lm37
Neustadt (Holstein) D 33 Ll36
Neustadt (Orla) D 33 Lm40
Neustadt (Weinstraße) D 34 Lj41
Neustift A 35 Lm43
Neustrelitz D 33 Lo37
Neutral Junction AUS (NT) 142 Rg56
Neutraubling D 35 Ln42
Neu-Ulm D 34 Ll42
Neuvic F 24 Lc45
Neuville-aux-Bois F 23 Lc42
Neuville-de-Poitou F 22 La44
Neuville-sur-Saône F 25 Le45
Neuvy-sur-Barangeon F 23 Lc43
Neuwerk D 32 Lj37
Neuwied D 32 Lh40
Nevada USA (MO) 243 Fc27
Nevada USA 226 Ea11
Nevada City USA (CA) 234 Dk26
Nevado, Cerro el RA 288 Gf63
Nevado, Cerro RCH 292 Gd67
Nevado Anchohuma BOL 279 Gf53
Nevado Chorolque BOL 284 Gh56
Nevado Coropuna PE 279 Gd53
Nevado de Acay RA 284 Gg58
Nevado de Cachi RA 284 Gg58
Nevado de Chañi RA 284 Gh58
Nevado de Colima, P.N. MEX 254 Ej36
Nevado de Incahuasi RA/RCH 288 Gf59
Nevado del Candado RA 288 Gg59
Nevado del Huila CO 272 Gc44
Nevado del Huila, P.N. CO 272 Gc44
Nevado del Illimani BOL 284 Gg54
Nevado de Longavi RCH 292 Ge64
Nevado de Poquis RA/RCH 284 Gg57
Nevado de Ruiz CO 268 Gc43
Nevado de Tolima CO 268 Gc43
Nevado de Toluca, Volcan MEX (MEX) 254 Fa36
Nevado Huayna Potosi BOL 279 Gf54
Nevado Ojos del Salado RCH/RA 288 Gf59
Nevado Queva RA 284 Gg58
Nevado Sajama BOL 284 Gf55
Nevado Salcantay PE 279 Gd52
Nevado Tres Cruces RA/RCH 288 Gf59
Nevado Tres Cruces, P.N. RCH 288 Gf59
Nevaišiu LT 17 Mg35
Nevasa IND (MHT) 108 Oh36
Neveklov CZ 38 Lp41
Nevel' RUS 52 Me17
Nevel'sk RUS 99 Sa22
Nevers F 23 Ld44
Nevertire AUS (NSW) 151 Sd61
Neves BR 276 Hh49
Nevesinje BIH 41 Lt47
Nevestino BG 46 Mc48
Nevežis LT 17 Me35
Neville CDN (SK) 233 Eg21
Nevinnomyssk RUS 55 Na23
Nevlunghavn N 12 Lk32
Nevşehir TR 51 Mp52
Nevskoe RUS 17 Mc36
New Adubiase GH 193 Kk42
New Aiyansh CDN (BC) 231 Df18
Newala EAT 211 Mk51
New Albany USA (IN) 248 Fh26
New Albany USA (MS) 243 Ff28
New Alton Downs AUS (SA) 143 Rk59
New Amsterdam GUY 271 Hb42
Newark USA (DE) 247 Gc26
Newark USA (NJ) 247 Gc25
Newark USA (OH) 246 Fj25
Newark-on-Trent GB 21 Ku37
New Bataan RP 123 Rd42
New Bedford USA (MA) 247 Ge25
Newberg USA (OR) 234 Dj23
New Bern USA (NC) 249 Gb28
Newberry USA (SC) 249 Fk28
Newberry Nat. Vol. Mon. USA 234 Dk24
New Bight BS 251 Gc33
New Boston USA (TX) 243 Fc29
New Braunfels USA (TX) 242 Fa31
Newbridge IRL 20 Ko37
New Britain PNG 156 Sb20
New Britain USA (CT) 247 Gd25
New Britain Trench PNG 156 Sc20
Newbrook CDN (AB) 233 Ed18
New Brunswick CDN 225 Gc09
New Brunswick USA (NJ) 247 Gc25
Newburgh USA (NY) 247 Gc25
Newbury GB 21 Kt39
Newburyport USA (MA) 247 Ge24
New Bussa WAN 186 Lc41
New Caledonia F 135 Ta12
New Caledonia 137 Ta23
New Caledonia Basin 134 Ta12
Newcastle AUS (NSW) 153 Sf62
Newcastle CDN (NB) 245 Gh22
Newcastle GB 18 Kp36
New Castle USA (IN) 246 Fh26
New Castle USA (PA) 247 Fk25
New Castle USA (VA) 249 Fk27
Newcastle USA (WY) 235 Eh24
Newcastle ZA 217 Me59
Newcastle Bay AUS 146 Sb51
Newcastle Range AUS (QLD) 148 Sb55
Newcastle-under-Lyme GB 21 Ks38
Newcastle upon Tyne GB 19 Kt36
Newcastle Waters AUS (NT) 139 Rg54
Newcastle West IRL 20 Kl38
New Corella RP 123 Rc42
Newdale CDN (MB) 238 Ek20
New Debiso GH 193 Kj42
Newdegate AUS (WA) 144 Qk62
New Delhi IND (DEL) 107 Oh31
New Denver CDN (BC) 232 Eb21
New Dixie AUS (QLD) 146 Sb53
Newell USA (SD) 240 Ej23
Newell Highway AUS 151 Se61
Newellton USA (LA) 243 Fe29
New England USA (ND) 240 Ej22
New England N.P. AUS 151 Sg61
New England Plateau AUS (NSW) 151 Sg61
New England Seamounts 227 Gd11
Newe Zohar IL 64 Mh30
Newfolden USA (MN) 238 Fb21
New Forest AUS (WA) 140 Qh59
Newfound Gap USA 249 Fj28
Newfoundland CDN 225 Ha09
Newfoundland Basin 300 Hb05
Newfoundland Evaporation Basin USA 235 Ed25
New Georgia SOL 161 Sj50
New Georgia Group SOL 160 Sj50
New Georgia Sound SOL 160 Sj49
New Germany CDN (NS) 245 Gh23
New Glasgow CDN (NS) 245 Gj23
New Guinea RI/PNG 158 Rj47
New Guinea Trench 134 Rb09
Newhalem USA (WA) 232 Dk21
Newhalen USA (AK) 229 Cc16
New Halfa SUD 190 Mh39
New Hamilton USA (AK) 229 Bj14
New Hampshire USA 247 Ge24
New Hampton USA (IA) 241 Fd24
New Hanover PNG 159 Se47
New Hanover ZA 217 Mf60
Newhaven GB 21 La40
New Haven USA (CT) 247 Gd25
New Hazleton CDN (BC) 231 Dg18
New Hebrides 137 Tb22
New Hebrides Basin 137 Ta22
New Hebrides Trench 134 Ta11
New Iberia USA (LA) 243 Fe31
New Ireland PNG 156 Sc19
New Jersey USA 247 Gc25
New Kalala Z 209 Mc53
New Kapedmai LB 192 Kf41
Newkirk USA (NM) 237 Eh28
New Knockhock USA (AK) 228 Bh14
New Lanark GB 19 Kr35
New Leipzig USA (ND) 240 Ek22
New Lexington USA (OH) 246 Fj26
New Liskeard CDN (ON) 247 Ga22
New London USA (CT) 247 Gd25
New Longoro GH 193 Kj41
New Madrid USA (MO) 243 Ff27
Newman AUS (WA) 140 Qk57
Newmarket GB 21 La38
New Martinsville USA (WV) 247 Fk26
New Meadows USA (ID) 234 Eb23
New Mexico USA 226 Ec12
New Mirpur 79 Og29
Newnan USA (GA) 249 Fh29
New Norcia AUS (WA) 144 Qj61
New Norfolk AUS (TAS) 152 Sd67
New Orleans USA (LA) 243 Fe31
New Orleans USA (LA) 243 Fe31
New Paltz USA (NY) 247 Gc25
New Philadelphia USA (OH) 247 Fk25
New Pine Creek USA (OR) 234 Dk24
New Plymouth NZ 154 Th65
New Plymouth USA (ID) 234 Eb24
Newport CDN (NS) 245 Gh23
Newport GB 21 Ks38
Newport GB 21 Ks39
Newport GB 21 Kt40
Newport USA (AR) 243 Fe28
Newport USA (MA) 247 Gf23
Newport USA (NH) 247 Gd24
Newport USA (OR) 234 Dh23
Newport USA (RI) 247 Ge25
Newport USA (TN) 249 Fj28
Newport USA (VT) 247 Gd23
Newport USA (WA) 232 Eb21
Newport News USA (VA) 249 Gb27
Newport Pagnell GB 21 Ku38
New Port Richey USA (FL) 250 Fj31
New Providence Island BS 251 Gb33
Newquay GB 20 Kp40
New Richmond CDN (QC) 245 Gh21
New Richmond USA (WI) 241 Fd23
New Ringold USA (OK) 243 Fc28
New River Gorge Natl. River USA 249 Fk27
New Roads USA (LA) 243 Fe30
New Rochelle USA (NY) 247 Gd25
New Rockford USA (ND) 240 Fa22
New Romney GB 21 La40
New Ross IRL 20 Ko38
Newry AUS (NT) 138 Re54
Newry GB 18 Ko36
Newry USA (ME) 247 Ge23
New Schwabenland 297 Lb33
New Siberian Islands RUS 59 Sa03
New Smyrna Beach USA (FL) 250 Fk31
New South Wales AUS 136 Sa25
Newstead AUS (VIC) 153 Sc64
New Stuyahok USA (AK) 228 Cb16
Newton USA (IA) 241 Fd25
Newton USA (KS) 242 Fb26
Newton USA (MS) 243 Ff29
Newton USA (NJ) 247 Gc25
Newton USA (TX) 243 Fd30
Newton Abbot GB 20 Kr40
Newton Hills CDN (NS) 245 Gj23
Newtonmore GB 19 Kq33
Newton Peak NZ 155 Tf67
Newton Stewart GB 19 Kq36
Newtontoppen N 11 Lj06
Newtown GB 21 Kr38
New Town USA (ND) 240 Ej22
Newtownabbey GB 18 Kp36
Newtownards GB 18 Kp36
Newtown Saint Boswells GB 19 Ks35
Newtownstewart GB 18 Kn36
New Ulm USA (MN) 241 Fc23
New Waterford CDN (NS) 245 Gk22
New Westminster CDN (BC) 232 Dj21
New York PE 272 Gc48
New York USA (NY) 247 Gd25
New York USA 227 Ga10
New York USA 227 Ga10
New Zealand NZ 135 Ta14
Nexø DK 15 Lq35
Neyestanek IR 72 Ng29
Neyriz IR 74 Nh31
Neyveli IND (TNU) 111 Ok41
Neyzar IR 72 Nf28
Nezam Abad IR 72 Nf29
Nezam-ol-Molk BakraviTomb IR 73 Nk27
Nez de Jobourg F 22 Kt41
Nez Perce Ind. Res. USA 234 Eb22
Nezvys'ko UA 39 Mf42
Ngaanyatjarra Land Council A.L. AUS 141 Rd57
Ngabang RI 126 Qe45
Ngabé RCB 202 Lj47
N'gabu MW 211 Mh54
Ngabwe Z 210 Md52
Ngadda WAN 187 Lg39
Ngadza RCA 200 Ma43
Ngai Giao VN 115 Qd40
Ngajira EAT 207 Mh49
Ngala WAN 187 Lh39
Ngalau Indah Caves RI 124 Qa46
Ngali RDC 203 Lk47
Ngali RI 129 Ra50
Ngaliwurru/Nungali A.L. AUS 139 Rf53
Ngalo RDC 200 Mb43
Ngalurrtja A.L. AUS 142 Rf57
Ngam CAM 195 Lh42
Ngam TCH 187 Lj40
Ngama TCH 187 Lj40
Ngamakwe ZA 217 Md62
Ngamba EAT 206 Mg50
Ngambé CAM 195 Lf43
Ngambé Tikar CAM 195 Lf43
Ngamdu WAN 187 Lg40
Ngamiland NAM 213 Ma55
Ngamo ZW 213 Md55
Ngamring CHN (TIB) 88 Pd31
Nganda MW 210 Mg51
Nganda SN 183 Kc39
Ngandane CI 193 Kh40
Ngangala SUD 201 Mf43
Ngangerabeli Plains EAK 205 Na46
Ngangganawili AUS (WA) 140 Ra59
Ngangla Rinco CHN 88 Pb30
Nganglong Kangri CHN 88 Pa29
Nganji RDC 206 Md47
Nganjuk RI 128 Qf49
Ngan So'n VN 96 Qd34
Nganzi ANG 202 Lg48
Ngao THA 114 Pk36
Ngaoundal CAM 195 Lg42
Ngaoundéré CAM 195 Lg42
Ngapa MOC 211 Mk51
Ngapali MYA 114 Ph36
Ngara EAT 206 Mf47
Ngarangou TCH 187 Lh39
Ngarimbi EAT 207 Mk50
Ngarkat Conservation Park AUS 152 Sa63
Ngasamo EAT 207 Mg47
Ngaso Plain EAK 198 Mk44
Ngassao Noum CAM 195 Lh42
Ngathainggyaung MYA 114 Ph37
Ngatik Atoll FSM 156 Sd17
Ngato CAM 195 Lh44
Ngawi RI 128 Qf49
Ngawihi NZ 154 Th66
Ngaywa EAT 206 Mg48
Ngbala RCB 195 Lh44
N'Gelewa RDC 200 Mb46
Ngerengere EAT 207 Mk49
Nggatokae SOL 161 Sk50
Nggela Pile SOL 161 Ta50
Nggela Sule SOL 161 Ta50
Nghia Dan VN 115 Qc36
Nghia Hung VN 96 Qd35
Nghi Har VN 115 Qc36
Ngiapanda EAT 207 Mk49
Ngidinga RDC 202 Lh48
Nginyang EAK 204 Mh45
Ngo RCB 202 Lh47
Ngoasé CAM 195 Lg44
Ngoc Co Rinh VN 115 Qe38
Ngoc Hien VN 117 Qc41
Ngoc Linh VN 115 Qd38
Ngog Mapubi CAM 195 Lf44
Ngoïla CAM 195 Lh44
Ngoko RCB 195 Lh46
Ngola CAM 195 Lh43
Ngol Kedju WAN 194 Le42
Ngolo RDC 200 Lk45
Ngolo Z 206 Mf50
Ngoma EAU 201 Mf45
Ngoma NAM 209 Mc54
Ngoma Z 209 Mc53
Ngoma Bridge RB 209 Mc54
Ngoma Tsé-Tsé RCB 202 Lh48
Ngombé RCA 200 Mb43
Ngomedzap CAM 195 Lf44
Ngong CAM 187 Lg41
Ngong EAK 204 Mj46
Ngonga CAM 194 Lf43
Ngongo RCB 195 Lh46
Ngonye Falls Z 209 Mb54
Ngora EAU 204 Mg45
Ngorengore EAK 204 Mh46
Ngoring Hu CHN 89 Pj28
Ngorkou RMM 185 Kj38
Ngoro CAM 195 Lf43
Ngorongoro EAT 207 Mh47
Ngorongoro Conservation Area EAT 207 Mh47
Ngorongoro Crater EAT 207 Mh47
Ngoso RDC 203 Lk48
Ngote RDC 201 Mf44
Ngoto RCA 195 Lj43
Ngotwane RB 213 Md58
Ngouanga RCA 196 Ma43
Ngoulemakong CAM 195 Lf44
Ngoulonkila RCB 202 Lh47
Ngouma RMM 185 Kj38
Ngoumgbi G 202 Le46
Ngounié G 202 Lf46
Ngoura CAM 195 Lh43
Ngoura CAM 195 Lh43
Ngoura TCH 187 Lj39
Ngouri TCH 187 Lj39
Ngourti RN 187 Lg38
N'Goussa DZ 173 Lc29
Ngoutchey TCH 187 Lj37
Ngouye Pété SN 183 Kd37
Ngouyo RCA 201 Mc43
Ngovayang CAM 195 Lf44
Ngoyeboma RCB 195 Lh45
Ngozi BU 206 Me47
Ngudu EAT 206 Mg47
Nguélémendouka CAM 195 Lg43
Nguema RDC 203 Mb49
Ngugha RB 213 Mb55
Ngui RCA 196 Mb42
Nguia Bouar RCA 195 Lh43
Nguigmi RN 187 Lg38
Nguila CAM 195 Lf43
Nguiu AUS (NT) 139 Rf51
Ngukurr AUS (NT) 139 Rh53
Ngulakula EAT 207 Mk49
Ngulu Atoll FSM 156 Rd17
Nguna VU 162 Te54
Ngundu ZW 214 Mf56
Nguni EAK 205 Mk46
Ngunut RI 128 Qg50
Nguroje WAN 195 Lf42
Ngurore WAN 187 Lg41
Nguru WAN 187 Lf39
Nguruka EAT 206 Mf48
Nguru Mountains EAT 211 Mj51
Ngut CAM 194 Le43
Nguyakro CI 193 Kh42
Ngwaketse RB 213 Mc58
Ngwale EAT 211 Mj51
Ngwedaung MYA 114 Pj36
Ngwena ZW 214 Me55
Ngweze NAM/RB 209 Mc54
Ngweze Pool Z 209 Mb54
Ngwezumba RB 209 Mc55
Ngwo CAM 194 Le42
Nhabe RB 213 Mb56
Nhachengue MOC 214 Mh57
Nhacoa GNB 183 Kc40
Nhacra GNB 183 Kc40
Nhamassonge MOC 210 Mg54
Nhamatanda MOC 214 Mh55
Nhamayabué MOC 211 Mh54
Nhamundá BR (PA) 275 Hb47
Nhamundá BR 275 Hb46
Nhamundá Mapuera, T.I. BR 274 Ha46
Nhandeara BR (SP) 286 He56
Nhandu BR 281 Hc50
Nharêa ANG 208 Lj51
Nha Trang VN 115 Qe39
Nhembа MOC 210 Mg53
Nhia ANG 208 Lh51
Nhill AUS (VIC) 152 Sa64
Nhlangano SD 217 Mf59
Nho Quan VN 96 Qc35
Nhulunbuy AUS (NT) 139 Rj52
Niablé CI 193 Kj42
Niada RCA 200 Ma43
Niafounké RMM 184 Kh38
Niagara USA (ND) 240 Fb22
Niagara Falls CDN (ON) 247 Ga24
Niagara Falls USA (NY) 247 Ga24
Niagara Falls USA/CDN 247 Ga24
Niagué CI 192 Kg43
Niah MAL 126 Qg44
Niah Caves MAL 126 Qg44
Niah N.P. MAL 126 Qg44
Niakaramandougou CI 193 Kh41
Niakhar SN 183 Kb38
Nialaha'u Point SOL 161 Ta50
Niambézaria CI 193 Kh43
Niamey RN 185 Lb39
Niamina RMM 184 Kg39
Niamtougou TG 193 La41
Niamvoudou CAM 195 Lg43
Niandan RG 192 Kf40
Niandankoro RG 192 Kf40
Nianfissa CI 192 Kg41
Nianfors S 13 Lr29
Niangara RDC 201 Md44
Niangara RDC 201 Me44
Niangoloko BF 193 Kh40
Niani CI 192 Kg43
Nia-Nia RDC 201 Md45
Niantanina RMM 192 Kf40
Nianyu IND (ARP) 112 Ph32
Nianzishan CHN (HLG) 98 Rb22
Niao Dao CHN 92 Pk27
Niaoshu Shan CHN 94 Qc28
Niapidou CI 192 Kg43
Niapu RDC 201 Md44
Niapu RDC 201 Me44
Niara RCB 202 Lg47
Niari RCB 202 Lh47
Niaro SUD 197 Mf40
Nias RI 124 Pj45
Niasar fire temple IR 72 Nf28
Nibe DK 14 Lk34
Nibinamik Lake CDN 239 Ff19
Nibong Tebal MAL 116 Qa43
Nicage MOC 211 Mk52
Nicaj-Shalë AL 46 Lu48
Nicaragua 256 Fg39
Nicasio PE 279 Ge53
Nice F 25 Lh47
Niceville USA (FL) 248 Fg30
Nicgale LV 17 Mg34
Nichinan J 103 Rf30
Nichlaul IND (UPH) 107 Pb32
Nicholas Channel BS 250 Ga34
Nicholasville USA (KY) 249 Fh27
Nichole BD 112 Pe33
Nicholson AUS (WA) 138 Re55
Nicholson, Mount AUS (QLD) 151 Se58
Nicholson Range AUS 140 Qj59
Nicholson River AUS (QLD) 148 Rk54
Nicholls Town BS 251 Ga33
Nickerie SME 271 Hb43
Nickerson Ice Shelf 296 Cc34
Nickol Bay AUS 140 Qj56
Nicman CDN (QC) 244 Gg20
Nicobar Islands IND 104 Pc17
Nicola Mameet Ind. Res. CDN 232 Dk20
Nicola River CDN 232 Dk20
Nicolás Bruzzone RA (CD) 288 Gh63
Nicosia CY 51 Mo55
Nicosia I 42 Lp53
Nicótera I 43 Lq52
Nicoya CR 256 Fh40
Nictau CDN (NB) 244 Gg22
Nicuadala MOC 211 Mj54
Niculițel RO 45 Mj45
Nicupa MOC 211 Na53
Nidadavole IND (APH) 109 Pa37
Nidda D 34 Lk40
Nidderau D 34 Lj40
Nidelva N 12 Lj32
Nídri GR 48 Ma52
Nidzica PL 37 Ma37
Niéboré RG 192 Ke40
Niebüll D 32 Lj36
Niedalino PL 36 Lr36
Niederaula D 32 Lk40
Niederbronn-les-Bains F 23 Lh42
Niedere Tauern A 35 Lp43
Niederlausitz D 33 Lo39
Niedersachsen D 32 Lj38
Niedersächsisches Wattenmeer, N.P. D 32 Lh37
Niedrzwica Duża PL 37 Mc39
Niefang GQ 194 Lf45
Niéga BF 185 Kk39
Niégo BF 193 Kj40
Niekershoop ZA 216 Mb60
Nielisz PL 37 Md40
Niéllé CI 193 Kh40
Niellim TCH 187 Lj41
Niem RCA 195 Lh42
Niemba RDC 206 Me49
Niemba RDC 206 Me48
Niemce PL 37 Mc39
Niemelane RIM 183 Ke36
Niemisel S 10 Mb13
Niéna RMM 193 Kg40
Nienburg D 32 Lk38
Nierstein D 34 Lj41
Niesen A CH 34 Lh44
Niesky D 33 Lp39
Nieu-Bethesda ZA 217 Mc61
Nieuw Amsterdam SME 271 Hc43
Nieuwegein NL 32 Lf38
Nieuw Nickerie SME 271 Hb43
Nieuwoudtville ZA 216 Lk61
Nieuwpoort B 23 Lc39
Nieuwpoort NL (NA) 269 Gf39
Nieva PE 272 Gb48
Niewęgłosz PL 37 Mc39
Niezabyszewo PL 36 Ls36
Nifi KSA 67 Nb33
Niğde TR 51 Mp53
Niğde Kalesi TR 51 Mp53
Nigel ZA 217 Me59
Niger WAN 168 La16
Niger 167 La08
Niger Delta WAN 194 Lc43
Niger Fan 168 La16
Nigeria 167 La09
Nighasan IND (UPH) 107 Pa31
Night Hawk Lake CDN 239 Fk21
Nightmote USA (AK) 228 Bh15
Nigrangombe EAT 207 Mj50
Nigrita GR 46 Md50
Nigua 260 Ge36
Niha Caves RL 64 Mh29
Nihada OM 75 Nj34
Nihessiue MOC 211 Mk53
Nihing PK 80 Oc31
Nihiru Atoll F 165 Cj54
Nihoa USA 230 Bk34
Nihonmatsu J 101 Sa27
Niigata J 101 Rk27
Niihama J 101 Rg29
Niihau USA 230 Bk35
Niijima J 101 Rk28
Niimi J 101 Rg28
Niitsu J 101 Rk27
Nijar E 29 Ks46
Nijiao CHN (YUN) 113 Qb33
Nijkerk NL 32 Lf38
Nij Laluk IND (ASM) 112 Pg32
Nijmegen NL 32 Lf39
Nijverdal NL 32 Lg38
Nikea GR 46 Mc51
Nikel' RUS 11 Mf11
Nikiforos GR 47 Me49
Nikiniki RI 132 Rc50
Nikitas GR 47 Md50
Nikitskij monastyr RUS 52 Mk17
Nikkaluokta S 10 Lk12
Nikki DY 186 Lb41
Nikko J 101 Rk27
Nikko N.P. J 101 Rk27
Nikoemvon CAM 195 Lf44
Nikolaevka RUS 53 Nd19
Nikolaevo BG 47 Mf48
Nikolaevsk RUS 53 Nc21
Nikolaevsk-na-Amure RUS 59 Sa08
Nikolo-L'vovskoe RUS 98 Rf24
Nikol'sk RUS 53 Nd19
Nikonga EAT 206 Mf47
Nikopol BG 47 Me47
Nikopol' UA 54 Mh22
Nikópoli GR 48 Ma51
Nikópoli GR 48 Ma51
Nikopolis ad Istrum BG 47 Mf47
Niksar TR 62 Mj25
Nikshar IR 75 Oa32
Nikšić SCG 46 Lt48
Nikumaroro KIR 157 Ub19
Nikunau Island KIR 157 Td19
Nilanga IND (MHT) 108 Oj36
Nilaveli Beach CL 111 Pa42
Nile ET 169 Mc13
Nile SUD 190 Mg37
Nile Delta ET 177 Mf30
Niles USA (MI) 246 Fg25
Nilgiri IND (ORS) 112 Pd35
Nilgiri Mtn. Railway IND (KTK) 111 Oj41
Nili AFG 78 Od29
Nilka CHN (XUZ) 84 Pb24
Nillpass AFG 78 Od28
Nilphamari BD 112 Pe33
Nilt 79 Oh27
Nimach IND (MPH) 108 Oj33
Niman RUS 98 Rg20
Nimbahera IND (RJT) 108 Oh33
Nimbin AUS (NSW) 151 Sg60
Nimbotong RI 131 Sa47
Nîmes F 25 Le47
Nimiuktuk River USA 229 Ca11
Nimjat RIM 183 Kc37
Nim Ka Khera IND (RJT) 106 Oh33
Nimmitabel AUS (NSW) 153 Se64
Nimrod Glacier 297 Sd35
Nimrud IRQ 65 Nb27
Nimule SUD 204 Mg44
Nimule N.P. SUD 204 Mg44
Nin HR 41 Lq46
Nina NAM 212 Lk57
Nin Bay RP 123 Rd40
Ninda ANG 209 Ma53
Nindigully AUS (QLD) 151 Se60
Nine Degree Channel IND 110 Og42
Ninette CDN (MB) 238 Fa21
Ninette NAM 212 Lk57
Nineteyeast Ridge 301 Pa12
Ninety Mile Beach AUS 153 Sd65
Ninety Mile Beach NZ 154 Tg63
Ningaloo AUS (WA) 140 Qg57
Ningaloo Reef Marine Park AUS 140 Qg57
Ning'an CHN (HLG) 98 Re23
Ningari RMM 185 Kj38
Ningau Island PNG 159 Se48
Ningbo CHN (ZJG) 102 Ra31
Ningcheng CHN (NMZ) 93 Qk25
Ningde CHN (FJN) 102 Qk32
Ningdu CHN (JGX) 102 Qh32
Ningera PNG 158 Sa47
Ningerum PNG 158 Sa48
Ningguo CHN (AHU) 102 Qk30
Ninghai CHN (ZJG) 102 Ra31
Ninghe CHN (TJN) 93 Qj26
Ninghua CHN (FJN) 102 Qj32
Ningi WAN 186 Le40
Ningjing Shan CHN 94 Pj30
Ningming CHN (GZG) 96 Qd34
Ningnan CHN (SCH) 113 Qb32
Ningqiang CHN (SAA) 95 Qd29
Ningshan CHN (SAA) 95 Qe29
Ningwu CHN (SAX) 93 Qg26
Ningxia Huizu Zizhiqu CHN 83 Qb11
Ning Xian CHN (GSU) 95 Qd28
Ningxiang CHN (HUN) 95 Qg31
Ningyuan CHN (HUN) 96 Qf33
Ninh Binh VN 96 Qc35
Ninh Hoa VN 115 Qe39
Ninh Son VN 115 Qe40
Ninia RI 131 Rk48
Ninigo Group PNG 159 Sc46
Ninilchik USA (AK) 229 Ce15
Ninive IRQ 65 Nb27
Ninjin CHN (SDG) 93 Qj27
Ninohe J 101 Sa25
Ninole USA (HI) 230 Cc36
Niños Héroes MEX (SL) 252 Ef32
Ninotsminda GE 70 Nb25
Ninove B 23 Le40
Nioaque BR (MS) 286 Hc56
Nioaque, T.I. BR 286 Hc56
Niobrara USA (NE) 240 Fa24
Niobrara USA 240 Ek24
Niodior SN 183 Kb39
Niofoin CI 193 Kg41
Nioka RDC 201 Mf44
Nioka RDC 203 Mb49
Nioki RDC 203 Lj47
Niokolo Koba SN 183 Kd39
Niokolo-Koba SN 183 Kd39
Niokolo-Koba, P.N.du SN 183 Kd39
Niono RMM 184 Kh38
Nioro du Rip SN 183 Kc39
Nioro du Sahel RMM 184 Kf38
Niort F 22 Ku44
Niou BF 185 Kk39
Nioût RIM 184 Kg37
Nipa PNG 159 Sb49
Nipahpanjang RI 125 Qc46
Nipani IND (KTK) 108 Oh37
Nipawin CDN (SK) 233 Eh19
Nipawin Prov. Park CDN 233 Eh19
Nipekamew River CDN 233 Eh18
Nipepe MOC 211 Mj52
Niphad IND (MHT) 108 Oh35
Nipigon CDN (ON) 239 Ff21
Nipigon Bay CDN 239 Ff21
Nipin River CDN 233 Ef18
Nipiodi MOC 211 Mj54
Nipomo USA (CA) 236 Dk28
Nippur IRQ 65 Nc29
Niquelândia BR (GO) 282 Hf53
Niquero C 259 Gb35
Nir IR 72 Nd26
Nira IND (MHT) 108 Oh36
Nirgua YV 269 Gf40
Nirmal IND (APH) 109 Ok36
Nirwana Beach RI 127 Rb48
Niš SCG 46 Mb47
Nisa P 28 Kn49
Nisa TM 73 Nk27
Nisab KSA 65 Nc31
Nisab YE 68 Nd38
Nisai RI 129 Qk50
Nišava SCG 46 Mc47
Niscemi I 42 Lp53
Niseko Shakotan Otaru-kaigan Q.N.P. J 99 Sa24
Nish AFG 78 Oc29
Nishi CHN (HUN) 95 Qf31
Nishi-Chugokusanchi Q.N.P. J 101 Rg28
Nishino-jima J 101 Rg27
Nishi-no-Omote J 103 Rf30
Nishi-Okoppe J 99 Sb23
Nishi-Sonogi-hanto J 103 Re29
Nishon UZ 76 Oc26
Nisiá Petalíi GR 48 Me53
Nisío Strofádhes GR 48 Ma53
Niška Banja SCG 46 Mc47
Niskibi River CDN 239 Ff17
Nisko PL 37 Mc40
Nisling River CDN 231 Da14
Nisou CY 51 Mo55
Nisporeni MD 45 Mj43
Nissan S 15 Lo33
Nissan Island PNG 160 Sh48
Nissedal N 12 Lj31
Nisséko BF 193 Kj40
Nisser N 12 Lj31
Nissi EST 16 Me31
Nissi Ioanínon GR 48 Ma51
Nissiros GR 49 Mh54
Nissum Bredning DK 14 Lj34
Nissum Fjord DK 14 Lj34
Nistru MD 45 Mk44
Nisutlin River CDN 231 Dd15
Nisut Plateau CDN 231 De15
Nita'a KSA 67 Ne32
Nita Downs AUS (WA) 138 Ra55
Nitaure LV 17 Mf33
Nitchequon CDN (QC) 244 Ge19
Niterói BR (RJ) 287 Hj57
Nith GB 19 Kr35
Nitinat CDN (BC) 232 Dh21
Niti Pass CHN/IND 88 Ok30
Nitmiluk N.P. AUS 139 Rg53
Nitra SK 38 Ls42
Nitra SK 38 Lt42
Nitrianske Pravno SK 38 Lt42
Nitriansky hrad SK 38 Lt42
Nittambuwa CL 111 Pa43
Nittedal N 12 Ll30
Nittenau D 35 Ln41
Nittur IND (KTK) 111 Oj40
Nituj RUS 99 Sb21
Niuafo'ou TO 164 Bc53
Niuatoputapu TO 164 Bd53
Niuchang CHN (GZH) 96 Qc33
Niuchang CHN (YUN) 96 Qc34
Niue NZ 164 Bf55
Niulakita TUV 157 Td21
Niumi N.P. WAG 183 Kb39
Niutahi F (PYF) 165 Cg53
Niutao TUV 157 Td20
Niut, Gunung RI 126 Qe45
Niutoushan CHN (AHU) 102 Qk30
Niuzhuang CHN (LNG) 100 Rb25
Nivala FIN 11 Mc14
Nivano PK 80 Ob32
Nivelles B 23 Le40
Nivenskoe RUS 17 Ma36
Nivernais F 23 Ld43
Niwai IND (RJT) 106 Oh32
Niwas IND (MPH) 109 Pa34

Oktjabr'sk – Osmancık

Oktjabr'sk KZ 58 Nd09
Oktjabr'sk RUS 53 Ne19
Oktjabr'skij RUS 53 Nb22
Oktjabr'skij RUS 53 Ng18
Oktwin MYA 114 Pj36
Oktyah'sk TM 71 Nk24
Oku CAM 195 Lf42
Oku J 103 Rc32
Okubie WAN 194 Lc43
Okučani HR 41 Ls45
Okuchi J 103 Rf29
Okulovka RUS 52 Mg16
Okundi WAN 194 Le42
Okurcalar TR 51 Mm54
Okushiri J 99 Rk24
Okushiri-to J 99 Rk24
Okuta WAN 186 Lb41
Okwa RB 213 Ma57
Okwa RB 213 Mb57
Okwa WAN 194 Ld41
Olá PA 257 Fk41
Ola USA (AR) 243 Fd28
Ólafsfjörður IS 10 Ka12
Olaf V Land N 11 Lk06
Olaine LV 17 Md34
Olancha USA (CA) 236 Eb27
Olanchito HN 256 Fg38
Öland S 15 Lr34
Ölands norra udde S 15 Ls33
Ölands södra grund 15 Lr35
Ölands södra udde S 15 Lr34
Olargues F 24 Lc47
Olaria BR (PI) 277 Hk47
Olary AUS (SA) 152 Sa62
Olascoaga RA (BA) 289 Gk63
Olathe USA (KS) 241 Fc26
Olavarría RA (BA) 293 Gk64
Olavinlinna FIN 16 Mj29
Oława PL 36 Ls40
Olbernhau D 33 Lo40
Olbia I 31 Lk50
Old Bulawayo ZW 214 Me56
Old Coralie AUS (QLD) 148 Sa55
Old Cork AUS (QLD) 148 Sa57
Old Crow CDN 224 Da05
Old Dongola SUD 190 Mf37
Oldeani EAT 207 Mh47
Oldeide N 12 Lf29
Olden N 12 Lg29
Oldenburg D 32 Lj37
Oldenburg in Holstein D 33 Ll36
Oldenzaal NL 32 Lg38
Olderfjord N 11 Mc10
Old Factory Bay CDN 239 Ga19
Old Faithful Geysir USA 235 Ee23
Old Forge USA (NY) 247 Gc24
Old Fort NAM 216 Lj59
Old Fort Hays USA 240 Fa26
Old Fort & Jail F (PYF) 165 Da50
Old Fort Niagara S.H.S. & Fort Niagara L.H. USA 247 Ga24
Old Fort William CDN 239 Ff21
Old Ft. Henry CDN 247 Gb23
Old Ft. Parker S.H.S. USA 243 Fb30
Old Gold Mine NZ 155 Tf67
Oldham GB 21 Ks37
Old Harbor USA (AK) 230 Cd17
Old Head of Kinsale IRL 20 Km39
Old Irontown Ruins USA 236 Ed27
Old Man of Hoy GB 19 Kr32
Oldman River CDN 233 Ec21
Old Maswa EAT 207 Mg47
Oldmeldrum GB 19 Ks33
Old Minto USA (AK) 229 Cf13
Old Mkushi Z 210 Me53
Old Mosque RI 128 Qf49
Old Nariam EAU 204 Mh45
Old Numery AUS (NT) 143 Rh58
Ol Doinyo Lengai EAT 207 Mh47
Ol-Doinyo N.P. EAK 204 Mj46
Oldonyo Orok EAK 204 Mj47
Oldonyo Sambu EAT 207 Mj47
Old Orchard Beach USA (ME) 247 Ge24
Old Oyo WAN 186 Lc41
Old Oyo N.P. WAN 186 Lc41
Old Perlican CDN (NF) 245 Hd21
Old Petauke Z 210 Mf53
Olds CDN (AB) 233 Ec20
Old Sitka USA (AK) 231 Dc17
Old Spanish Treasure Cave USA 243 Fc27
Old Suakin coral stone houses SUD 191 Mj37
Oldtidsveien N 12 Lm31
Oldtimer's Mus. (Maple Creek) CDN (SK) 233 Ef21
Old Town USA (ME) 247 Gf23
Olduvai Gorge EAT 207 Mh47
Old Village USA (AK) 229 Cc15
Old wagon bridge ZA 217 Mc60
Old Wives Lake CDN 233 Eh20
Öldziyt gol MNG 90 Pk22
Olean USA (NY) 247 Ga24
Olecko PL 37 Mc36
Oléggio I 40 Lj45
Oleiros P 28 Kn49
Olëkma RUS 59 Ra07
Olëkminsk RUS 59 Ra06
Olëkminskij Stanovik RUS 59 Qd08
Oleksandrija UA 54 Mf21
Oleksandrivka UA 45 Mm43
Oleksandrivka UA 54 Mg21
Oleksandrivka UA 54 Mh21
Oleksandrivka UA 54 Mg22
Oleksandrivka UA 55 Mj21
Ølen N 12 Lf31
Olenëk RUS 59 Qc05
Olenëk RUS 59 Qd04
Olenëkskij zaliv RUS 59 Qd04
Olengui RUS 91 Og20
Olenguruone EAK 204 Mh46
Olenino RUS 52 Mg17
Olenivka UA 54 Mg23
Oléron F 24 Kt45
Oles'ko UA 39 Me41
Oleśnica PL 36 Ls39
Olesno PL 36 Lt40
Oleszno PL 37 Ma40
Oleszyce PL 37 Md40
Olevs'k UA 52 Md20
Olevu I EAU 201 Mf44
Olex USA (OR) 234 Dk23
Olfen D 32 Lh39
Ol'ga RUS 99 Rh24
Olga, Mount AUS 142 Rf58
Olgastretet N 11 Mb06
Ölgiy MNG 85 Pf21
Ølgod DK 14 Lj35
Olhão P 28 Kn47
Ol'hi RUS 53 Na19
Olho d'Agua das Flores BR (AL) 283 Jb50
Ol'hovatka RUS 53 Mk20
Ol'hovka RUS 53 Nc21
Oli DY 186 Lb40
Oli WAN 186 Lc41
Olib HR 41 Lp46
Oliena I 31 Lk50
Olifants NAM 212 Lk58
Olifants ZA 214 Mf57
Olifants ZA 216 Lk61
Olifants ZA 216 Mb62
Olifants Game Reserve ZA 214 Mf58
Olifantshoek ZA 216 Mb59
Olimarao Atoll FSM 156 Sb17
Olimbia GR 48 Mb53
Olimje Samostan SLO 41 Lq44
Olimp RO 45 Mj47
Olimpia BR (SP) 286 Hf56
Olimpiáda GR 47 Md50
Olimpos Beydağları Milli Parkı TR 51 Ml54
Olinalá MEX (GUR) 254 Fa37
Olinda BR (PE) 283 Jc49
Olinda BR (PI) 277 Hj48
Olindina BR (BA) 283 Ja51
Olinga = Maganja MOC 211 Mj54
Olio AUS (QLD) 148 Sb56
Olioserri EAK 207 Mj47
Olite E 27 Kt52
Oliva E 29 Ku48
Oliva RA (CD) 288 Gj62
Oliva de la Frontera E 28 Ko48
Olive USA (MT) 235 Eh23
Oliveça-a-Nova ANG 208 Lg53
Oliveira BR (MG) 287 Hh56
Oliveira de Azeméis P 26 Km50
Oliveira do Hospital P 26 Kn50
Oliveira dos Brejinhos BR (BA) 282 Hj52
Olivenza E 28 Kn48
Oliver Lake CDN 238 Ej17
Olivet F 22 Lb43
Olivet USA (SD) 240 Fb24
Olivia USA (MN) 241 Fc23
Olivine Range NZ 155 Te68
Oljeitu Khudabanda IR 72 Ne27
Oljutorskij zaliv RUS 59 Tb07
Ol Kalou EAK 204 Mj46
Olkusz PL 37 Lu40
Ollagüe RCH 284 Gf56
Ollagüe, Volcán BOL/RCH 284 Gf56
Ollantaytambo PE 279 Gd52
Ollerton GB 21 Kt37
Ollombo RCB 202 Lh46
Olmaliq UZ 76 Oe25
Olmedo E 26 Kq49
Olmedo EC 272 Fk46
Olmesutye EAK 204 Mh46
Olmeto F 31 Lj49
Olmos PE 278 Ga48
Olney USA (TX) 242 Fa29
Oloči RUS 91 Qk20
Olodio CI 192 Kg43
Olofström S 15 Lp34
Ologbo Game Reserve WAN 194 Lc42
Oloibiri WAN 194 Ld43
Oloitokitok EAK 207 Mj47
Oloj RUS 59 Ta05
Olojskij hrebet RUS 59 Ta05
Ololdou SN 183 Kd38
Olombuni SOL 161 Ta50
Olomouc CZ 38 Ls41
Olonec RUS 11 Mg15
Olongapo RP 120 Ra38
Olongliko RI 126 Qh46
Olonki RUS (UOB) 90 Qb19
Olono RCB 202 Lh47
Olorgesailie EAK 204 Mj46
Oloron-Sainte-Marie F 24 Ku47
Olosega Island USA 164 Bf53
Olot E 30 Lc48
Olovjannaja RUS 91 Qh20
Olovo BIH 41 Lt46
Olpad IND (GUJ) 108 Og35
Olpe D 32 Lh39
Ol'ša RUS 52 Mf18
Olsberg D 32 Lj39
Olshammar S 13 Lp32
Olskirke DK 15 Lp35
Olszamy PL 37 Ma39
Olszanka PL 37 Mc36
Olsztyn PL 37 Ma37
Olsztynek PL 37 Ma37
Olszyna PL 36 Lp39
Olt RO 44 Me45
Olta RA (LR) 288 Gg61
Oltedal N 12 Lg32
Olten CH 34 Lh43
Oltenița RO 45 Mg46
Olteț RO 44 Me46
Oltina RO 45 Mh46
Oltinko'l UZ 71 Nk24
Oltu TR 63 Na25
Ol Tukai EAK 207 Mj47
Oltuš BY 37 Md39
Oluanpi RC 97 Ra35
Oluanpi RC 97 Ra35
Ölü Deniz TR 49 Mk54
Olukanda National Monument NAM 212 Lh54
Olukbaşı TR 51 Mq51
Oluku WAN 194 Lc42
Olu Malua = Three Sisters Islands SOL 161 Tb51
Olumo Rock WAN 194 Lb42
Olur TR 63 Nb25
Olustvere EST 16 Mf32
Olutanga Island RP 123 Rb42
Olvega E 27 Kt51
Olvera E 28 Kp46
Ólymbos GR 49 Mh55
Olympia GR 48 Mb53
Olympia USA (WA) 232 Dj22
OlympicMountains USA 232 Dj22
Olympic N.P. USA 232 Dj22
Olympos CY 51 Mn56
Ólympos GR 46 Mc50
Ólympos N.P. GR 46 Mc50
Olympus, Mount USA 232 Dj22
Ölynthos GR 46 Md50
Ölziyt MNG 90 Qa21
Oma CHN (TIB) 88 Pb29
Oma J 99 Sa25
Omachi J 101 Rj27
Omae-saki J 101 Rk28
Omagari J 101 Sa26
Omagh GB 18 Kn36
Omaha USA (GA) 249 Fh29
Omaha USA (NE) 241 Fc25
Omaha Ind. Res. USA 241 Fb24
Omaheke NAM 212 Lk56
Omak USA (WA) 232 Ea21
Omakau NZ 155 Te68
Omakwia GUY 270 Ha43
Omali GR 46 Mb50
O'Malley AUS (SA) 145 Rf61
Omalur IND (TNU) 111 Ok41
Oman OM 57 Nb07
Omapere NZ 154 Tg63
Omar Ali Saiffudien Mosque BRU 122 Qh43
Omarama NZ 155 Te68
Omarolluk Sound CDN 239 Ga17
Omarska BIH 41 Lr46
Omaruru NAM 212 Lh56
Omaruru NAM 212 Lh56
Omas PE 278 Gb52
Oma-saki J 99 Sa25
Omatako NAM 212 Lj56
Omatako NAM 212 Lj56
Omate PE 284 Ge54
Omati PNG 159 Sb49
Omawewozonyanda NAM 212 Lk56
Omba = Uruma RI 131 Rh48
Ombalantu = Uutapi NAM 208 Lh54
Ombella RCA 195 Lk43
Ombika NAM 212 Lh55
Ombo N 12 Lf31
Ombotozu NAM 212 Lj56
Omboué G 202 Le46
Ombrone I 40 Lm48
Ombu RA (SF) 289 Gk61
Ombúes de Lavalle ROU 289 Hb62
Ombuku NAM 208 Lg54
Omchi TCH 181 Lj35
Omdurman SUD 190 Mg39
Omegna I 40 Lj45
Omeo AUS (VIC) 153 Sd64
Ömerli Baraj TR 50 Mk49
Ometepec MEX (GUR) 254 Fa37
Om Hajer ER 191 Mj39
Omicron AUS (QLD) 150 Sa60
Omidiyeh IR 72 Nd30
Omi-Hachiman J 101 Rj28
Omineca Mountains CDN 231 Dg17
Omineca River CDN 231 Dh18
Omirzak KZ 70 Nf24
Omiš HR 41 Lr47
Omitara NAM 212 Lk57
Omkareshwar IND 108 Oj34
Omkoi THA 114 Pk37
Ommen NL 32 Lg38
Ömnögov' MNG 92 Qb24
Omo ETH 198 Mj42
Omoa F (PYF) 165 Da51
Omoku WAN 194 Ld43
Omolon RUS 59 Sd05
Omolon RUS 59 Ta05
Omono-gawa J 101 Sa26
Omo N.P. ETH 198 Mh43
Omo Strict Nature Reserve WAN 194 Lc42
Omo Valley ETH 198 Mh43
Ompomouéna G 202 Lf46
Ompupa ANG 208 Lg54
Omsk RUS 58 Oc08
Omu J 99 Sb23
Omu-Aran WAN 194 Lc41
Omuo WAN 194 Lc42
Omura-wan J 103 Re29
Omurtag BG 47 Mg47
Omusati NAM 212 Lh55
Omuta J 103 Rf29
Oña EC 272 Ga47
Ona RUS 85 Pe19
Ona RUS 91 Qf19
Onaisin RCH 294 Gf72
Onakawana CDN (ON) 239 Fk20
Onaman Lake CDN 239 Fg20
Onang RI 127 Qk47
Onaping Lake CDN 239 Fk22
Onawa USA (IA) 241 Fb24
Onaway USA (MI) 246 Fh23
Onbimisan TR 63 Nb27
Oncativo RA (CD) 288 Gj61
Oncócua ANG 208 Lg54
Onda E 29 Ku49
Ondangwa NAM 208 Lh54
Ondarroa E 27 Ks53
Ondava SK 39 Mb41
Ondaw MYA 113 Ph34
Onder IND (MPH) 109 Oj33
Onderstedorings ZA 216 Ma61
Ondjiva ANG 208 Lh54
Ondo WAN 194 Lc42
Ondores PE 278 Gb51
Öndörkhaan MNG 91 Qf22
One and Half Degree Channel MV 110 Og45
One Ete RI 127 Rb47
Onega RUS 11 Mk14
Onega RUS 11 Mk14
Önege KZ 53 Nd21
Oneida USA (NY) 247 Gc24
Oneida USA (TN) 249 Fh27
Oneida Ind. Res. USA 246 Fk24
O'Neill USA (NE) 240 Fa24
Onema Okolo RDC 203 Mb47
Onema Ututu RDC 203 Mb47
Oneonta USA (AL) 248 Fg29
Oneonta USA (NY) 247 Gc24
Oner RUS 99 Sb20
Onești RO 45 Mg44
Onetangi NZ 154 Th64
One Tree AUS (NSW) 153 Sc63
Onežskaja guba RUS 11 Mh13
Onga G 202 Lh46
Onganjera NAM 208 Lh54
Ongarue NZ 154 Th65
Ongava Lodge NAM 212 Lh55
Ongeri RDC 203 Mc48
Ongerup AUS (WA) 144 Qk62
Onggunoi RI 127 Rc45
Ongi MNG 90 Qb23
Ongi gol MNG 90 Qb22
Ongiyn Monastery MNG 90 Qc23
Ongjin PRK 100 Rc27
Ongkaw RI 127 Rc45
Ongkharak THA 114 Qa38
Ong Lang Beach VN 117 Qb40
Ongniud Qi CHN (NMZ) 93 Qk24
Ongoka RDC 201 Md46
Ongole IND (APH) 111 Ok39
Ongonyi RCB 200 Lj46
Ongoro Gotjari NAM 212 Lj57
Onhne MYA 114 Pj37
Oni GE 70 Nb24
Oni WAN 194 Lc42
Onich GB 19 Kp34
Onida USA (SD) 240 Ek23
Onilahy RM 220 Nc57
Onin Peninsula RI 130 Rf47
Onion Lake CDN (SK) 233 Ef19
Onion Lake Ind. Res. CDN 233 Ef19
Onitsha WAN 194 Ld42
Ono FJI 163 Tk55
Ono J 101 Rj28
Onofio HN 256 Fg38
Ono-i-Lau FJI 137 Ua23
Onoko TCH 187 Lh40
Onolimbu RI 124 Pj45
Onomichi J 101 Rg28
Onon MNG 91 Qf21
Onon RUS 91 Qg20
Onon-Bal'džinskij hrebet MNG 91 Qf21
Onondaga Cave S.P. USA 241 Fe26
Onondaga Cave S.P. USA 248 Fe26
Onon Gol MNG 91 Qf21
Onoto YV 269 Gh41
Onotoa Atoll KIR 157 Td19
Onseepkans NAM 216 Lk60
Onslow AUS (WA) 140 Qh56
Ontake-san J 101 Rj28
Ontar VU 162 Td53
Ontario CDN 225 Fb08
Ontario USA (CA) 236 Eb28
Ontario USA (OR) 234 Eb23
Ontario USA (WI) 241 Fe24
Ontario Peninsula CDN 246 Fk24
Ontario Place CDN 247 Ga24
Ontimitta IND (APH) 111 Ok39
Ontinyent E 29 Ku48
Ontmoeting ZA 216 Ma59
Ontonagon USA (MI) 246 Ff22
Ontong Java Atoll SOL 161 Sk48
Ontong-Java Rise 156 Sd19
Ontur E 29 Kt48
Onuma Q.N.P. J 99 Sa24
Onuškis LT 17 Mf34
Onverwacht SME 271 Hc43
Onward USA (MS) 243 Fe29
Onwul WAN 194 Le42
Onyx Cave USA 243 Fd27
Onzaga CO 268 Gd42
Onze-Lieve-Vrouwekerk B 23 Le39
Oobagooma AUS (WA) 138 Rc54
Oodnadatta AUS (SA) 143 Rh59
Oodweyne SP 199 Nc41
Oog van Kuruman ZA 216 Mb59
Ooldea AUS (SA) 145 Rf61
Oolloo AUS (NT) 139 Rf52
Oombulgurri A.L. AUS 138 Rd53
Oona River CDN (BC) 231 De18
Oopmyn ZA 217 Mc60
Oorindi AUS (QLD) 148 Sa56
Oos-Londen ZA 217 Md62
Oostburg NL 32 Ld39
Oostende B 23 Lc39
Oosterend NL 32 Lf37
Oosterhout NL 32 Le39
Oostermoed ZA 213 Md58
Oosterschelde NL 32 Ld39
Oosterscheldedam NL 32 Ld39
Oosterwolde NL 32 Lg38
Oostkapelle NL 32 Ld39
Oost-Vlieland NL 32 Lf37
Ootacamund IND (TNU) 110 Oj41
Ootsa Lake CDN (BC) 232 Dg19
Ootsa Lake CDN 232 Dh19
Ooty = Ootacamund IND (TNU) 110 Oj41
Opachuanau Lake CDN 238 Fa17
Opactwo Cystersów Sulejów PL 37 Lu39
Opaka BG 47 Mg47
Opala RDC 201 Mc46
Opal Deposit AUS 143 Rh60
Opanözü TR 50 Mk51
Opari SUD 204 Mg44
Oparić SCG 46 Mb47
Opasatika CDN (ON) 239 Fj21
Opasatika Lake CDN 239 Fj21
Opasquia Prov. Park CDN 238 Fd19
Opatija HR 41 Lp45
Opatów PL 36 Lt39
Opatów PL 37 Mb40
Opava CZ 38 Ls41
Opelika USA (AL) 249 Fh29
Opelousas USA (LA) 243 Fd30
Opémiska, Mount CDN 244 Gc20
Open Bay PNG 160 Sf48
Opernhaus Bayreuth D 35 Lm41
Opheim USA (MT) 233 Eg21
Ophir USA (AK) 229 Cb14
Ophir USA (OR) 234 Dh24
Opi WAN 194 Ld42
Opienge RDC 201 Md45
Opin RI 130 Re47
Opinnagau River CDN 239 Fj18
Opišnja UA 54 Mh21
Opličići BIH 41 Ls47
Opobo WAN 194 Ld43
Opočka RUS 52 Me17
Opoczno PL 37 Ma39
Opole PL 36 Ls40
Opol'e RUS 16 Mj31
Opole Lubelskie PL 37 Mb39
Opono Lake NAM 212 Lh55
Opotiki NZ 154 Tj65
Opovo SCG 44 Ma45
Opp USA (AL) 249 Fg30
Oppdal N 12 Lk28
Oppenheim D 34 Lj41
Oppicherla IND (APH) 109 Ok37
Opportunity USA (WA) 232 Eb22
Opsa BY 17 Mg35
Opthalmia Range AUS 140 Qk57
Optic Lake CDN (MB) 238 Ek18
Optikeigen Lake CDN 239 Ff20
Optima N.W.R. USA 242 Ek27
Opunake NZ 154 Tg65
Opuwo NAM 212 Lg55
Opuzen HR 41 Ls48
Op Xian CHN (JGS) 102 Qj28
Oqbaytal UZ 76 Oc24
Oqtosh UZ 76 Oc26
Oqtov tizmasi UZ 76 Oc25
Oqtov tizmasi UZ 76 Od25
Ora = Auer I 40 Lm44
Ora PNG 160 Sf48
Oraba EAU 201 Mf44
Oracle USA (AZ) 237 Ee29
Oracle Junction USA (AZ) 237 Ee29
Oradea RO 44 Mb43
Orah WAN 194 Lc42
Orahova BIH 41 Ls45
Orahovac SCG 46 Ma48
Orahovačko Polje BIH 41 Ls46
Orahovica BIH 41 Lt46
Orahovica HR 41 Ls45
Orai IND (UPH) 107 Ok33
Oraison F 25 Lf47
Oral KZ 53 Nf20
Orami PNG 160 Sh49
Oran DZ 173 Kk28
Oranapai GUY 270 Ha42
Orang IND (ASM) 112 Pg32
O Rang K 115 Qd39
Orange AUS (NSW) 153 Se62
Orange F 25 Le46
Orange NAM 216 Lj60
Orange USA (TX) 243 Fd30
Orange USA (VA) 247 Ga26
Orangeburg USA (SC) 249 Fk29
Orange Cay BS 251 Ga33
Orange City USA (IA) 241 Fb24
Orange Creek AUS (NT) 142 Rg58
Orange Fan 170 Lc25
Orange Park USA (FL) 249 Fk30
Orangerie Bay PNG 159 Se51
Orangeville CDN (ON) 247 Fk24
Orange Walk BH 255 Ff36
Orange Walk BH 255 Ff36
Orani RP 120 Ra38
Orania ZA 217 Mc60
Oranienburg D 33 Lo38
Oranje NAM/ZA 216 Lj60
Oranjegebergte SME 271 Hc44
Oranjemund NAM 216 Lj60
Oranjestad NL (AR) 269 Ge39
Oranjestad NL (NA) 261 Gj37
Oranjeville ZA 217 Me59
Oranmore IRL 20 Km37
Oransbari RI 131 Rh46
Oranzeri RUS 70 Nd23
Orapa RB 213 Mc56
Oras RP 121 Rc39
Oras Bay RP 121 Rc39
Orăștie RO 44 Md45
Orașu Nou RO 44 Md43
Oratia, Mount USA 228 Bk16
Oravița RO 44 Mb45
Oravská Lesná SK 39 Lu41
Oravská Polhora SK 39 Lu41
Oravský Podzámok SK 39 Lu41
Orb F 25 Ld47
Orbaf CI 193 Kh43
Orbassano I 40 Lh45
Orbeasca RO 45 Mf46
Orbec F 22 La41
Orbetello I 42 Lm48
Orbost AUS (VIC) 153 Se64
Örbyhus S 13 Ls30
Orce E 29 Ks47
Orchard City USA (CO) 235 Eg26
Orchha IND 109 Ok33
Orchid Beach AUS (QLD) 151 Sg58
Orchid Island FJI 163 Tk55
Orchowo PL 36 Lt38
Orcières F 25 Lg46
Orco I 40 Lh45
Orcopampa PE 279 Gd53
Ord USA (NE) 240 Fa25
Orda KZ 53 Nd21
Orda TCH 181 Lj35
Ordes E 26 Km53
Ordesa y Monte Perdido, P.N.de E 30 La48
Ord, Mount AUS 138 Rc54
Ordos CHN 92 Qd26
Ord River AUS (WA) 138 Re54
Ord River AUS 138 Re53
Ordu TR 63 Mj25
Orduña E 27 Kr52
Ordway USA (CO) 242 Ej26
Ordžonikidze UA 54 Mh22
Ordžonikidzevskij RUS (KCH) 70 Na24
Ore WAN 194 Lc42
Orea E 29 Kt50
Oreälven S 13 Lq29
Orebić HR 41 Ls48
Örebro S 13 Lq31
Oredež RUS 52 Mf16
Oregon USA (MO) 241 Fc26
Oregon USA 226 Dd10
Oregon Caves Nat. Mon. USA 234 Dj24
Oregon City USA (OR) 234 Dj23
Oregon Dunes N.R.A. USA 234 Dh24
Öregrund S 13 Lt30
Öregrundsgrepen S 13 Lt30
Öreg-tó H 38 Lt43
Orehovo-Zuevo RUS 53 Mk18
Orel RUS 16 Mh32
Orel RUS 52 Mj19
Orel' UA 54 Mh21
Orellana PE 272 Ga48
Orellana PE 278 Gc49
Orem USA (UT) 235 Ee25
Ören TR 49 Mh53
Orenburg RUS 58 Nd08
Örencik TR 50 Mk51
Orense = Ourense E 26 Kn52
Orense RA (BA) 293 Ha65
Orerokpe WAN 194 Lc43
Orestes Pereyra MEX (DGO) 253 Eh32
Orestiada GR 47 Mg49
Öresundsbro DK 14 Ln35
Orfejev spomenik SLO 41 Lq44
Orford GB 21 Lb38
Organabo F (GF) 271 Hd43
Organ Pipe Cactus Nat. Mon. USA 236 Ed29
Organ Pipes NAM 212 Lh56
Organyà E 30 Lb48
Orgaz E 29 Kr49
Orgelet F 25 Lf44
Órgiva E 29 Kr46
Örgön MNG 90 Qa23
Orgósolo I 31 Lk50
Orgun-e Kalan AFG 78 Oe29
Orhaneli TR 50 Mk51
Orhangazi TR 50 Mk50
Orhanlı TR 50 Mk53
Orhei MD 45 Mj43
Orhei MD 45 Mj43
Orhomenós GR 48 Mc52
Orhon gol MNG 90 Qc21
Oria E 29 Ks47
Orialen RG 192 Kf40
Orichiv UA 55 Mh22
Orick USA (CA) 234 Dh25
Orient USA (TX) 242 Ek30
Orient USA (WA) 232 Ea21
Oriental MEX (PUE) 254 Fb36
Oriente RA (BA) 293 Gk65
Oriente Novo BR (RO) 280 Gj50
Orientos AUS (QLD) 150 Sa60
Orient Point USA (NY) 247 Gd25
Orihuela E 29 Ku48
Orijahovo BG 46 Md47
Orillia CDN (ON) 247 Ga23
Orimattila FIN 16 Mf30
Orin USA (WY) 235 Eh24
Orinduik GUY 270 Ha43
Orinduik Falls GUY 270 Gk43
Orinoco YV/CO 264 Gc17/Gc18
Orinoco Delta YV 270 Gk41
Ório GR 48 Me52
Oriolo I 43 Lr50
Oriomo PNG 159 Sb50
Orissa IND 104 Pa14
Orissaare EST 16 Md32
Oristano I 31 Lj51
Oriszentpéter H 38 Lr44
Orito CO 272 Gb45
Orituco YV 269 Gg41
Oritupano YV 270 Gj41
Orivesi FIN 16 Mk28
Orivesi FIN 16 Me29
Oriximiná BR (PA) 275 Hc46
Orizaba MEX (VC) 254 Fb36
Ørje N 12 Lm31
Orkadiéré SN 183 Kd38
Orkanger N 10 Le14
Örkelljunga S 15 Lo34
Orkhon gol MNG 90 Qb22
Orkhon Valley Cultural Landscape MNG 90 Qa23
Orkhon Waterfall MNG 90 Qa22
Orkney CDN (SK) 233 Eg21
Orkney ZA 217 Md59
Orkney Islands GB 19 Ks31
Orla PL 36 Lt39
Orla USA (TX) 237 Ej30
Orlamesh AFG 78 Od27
Orland USA (CA) 234 Dj26
Orlândia BR (SP) 286 Hg56
Orlando USA (FL) 250 Fk31
Orlea RO 47 Me47
Orléanais F 22 Lb43
Orleans BR (SC) 291 Hf60
Orléans F 23 Lb43
Orleans USA (MA) 247 Ge25
Orleans Farms AUS (WA) 145 Rb62
Orle River Game Reserve WAN 194 Ld42
Orlești RO 44 Me46
Orlík CZ 38 Lp41
Orlik RUS (BUR) 90 Pk19
Orlivka UA 45 Mj45
Orlja BY 17 Me37
Orlov Gaj RUS 53 Ne20
Orlovka RUS 98 Re19
Orlovskij RUS 55 Nb22
Orlu WAN 194 Ld43
Orly F 23 Lc42
Ormanlı TR 51 Mm49
Orman Reef AUS 146 Sb50
Ormara PK 80 Oc33
Ormea I 40 Lh46
Ormoc RP 123 Rc40
Ormond Beach USA (FL) 250 Fk31
Ormond-by-the-Sea USA (FL) 250 Fk31
Órmos Almirou GR 49 Me55
Órmos Panórmou GR 49 Mf53
Órmos Sagiádas GR 48 Ma51
Ormož SLO 41 Lr44
Ormskirk GB 21 Ks37
Ormtjernkampen n.p. N 12 Lk29
Ornans F 23 Lg43
Orne F 22 Ku42
Ørnes N 10 Lg12
Orneta PL 37 Ma36
Örnö S 13 Lt31
Örnsköldsvik S 10 Lk14
Oro RA 289 Ha59
Orobayaya BOL 280 Gj52
Oro Blanco PE 273 Gd47
Orocea RO 44 Mc44
Orocó BR (PE) 283 Ja50
Orocue CO 268 Ge43
Orocuina HN 256 Fg39
Orodara BF 193 Kh40
Orog Nuur MNG 90 Pk23
Orogrande USA (NM) 237 Eg29
Orohena, Mount F (PYF) 165 Cf54
Oroi PNG 159 Sd50
Oroluk Atoll FSM 156 Sd17
Orom EAU 204 Mg44
Oromocto CDN (NB) 245 Gg23
Oron WAN 194 Le43
Orona KIR 157 Ub19
Orondo USA (WA) 232 Dk22
Oroners AUS (QLD) 146 Sb53
Oronga PNG 159 Sc48
Oronkua BF 193 Kj40
Orono USA (ME) 247 Gf23
Oropesa E 28 Kp49
Oropesa PE 279 Gd53
Oroqen Zizhiqi CHN (NMZ) 98 Rb20
Oroquieta RP 123 Rb41
Orós BR (CE) 277 Ja49
Óros Díkti GR 49 Mf55
Orosei I 31 Lk50
Orosháza H 39 Ma44
Óros Ídi GR 49 Me55
Óros Íti GR 48 Mc52
Óros Panahaikó GR 48 Mb52
Oroszlány H 38 Lt43
Orovada USA (NV) 234 Eb25
Oro Valley USA (AZ) 237 Ee29
Oroville USA (CA) 234 Dk26
Oroville USA (WA) 232 Ea21
Orpesa E 30 La50
Orpheus Island AUS (QLD) 149 Sd55
Orqohan CHN (NMZ) 91 Ra21
Orr USA (MN) 238 Fd21
Orrefors S 15 Lq34
Orrliden S 13 Ln29
Orrorroo AUS (SA) 152 Rk62
Orša BY 52 Mf18
Orsa S 13 Lp29
Oršac BIH 41 Lr46
Orsa Grönklitt S 13 Lp29
Orsasjön S 13 Lp29
Örségi N.P. H 38 Lr44
Orsk RUS 58 Nd08
Orșova RO 44 Mc46
Ørsta N 12 Lg28
Örsundsbro S 13 Ls31
Orta TR 51 Mo50
Ortaca TR 49 Mj54
Ortaderesin KZ 84 Oh22
Ortahisar TR 51 Mp52
Ortakaraören TR 51 Mn53
Ortakent TR 49 Mh53
Ortaklar TR 49 Mh53
Ortakonak TR 62 Mg26
Ortaköy TR 50 Mg50
Ortaköy TR 51 Mo52
Ortaköy TR 51 Mq50
Ortaköy TR 62 Mh26
Ortaköy TR 63 Nb25
Orta Nova I 43 Lq49
Orta San Giulio I 40 Lj45
Ortasu KZ 84 Oh22
Orta Toroslar TR 62 Mg27
Ortau KZ 84 Og21
Orte I 42 Ln48
Ortega CO 268 Gc44
Orteguaza CO 272 Gc45
Orthez F 24 Ku47
Ortho BOL 279 Gg51
Ortigueira BR (PR) 286 He58
Ortigueira E 26 Kn53
Orting USA (WA) 232 Dj22
Ortisei = Sankt Ulrich I 40 Lm44
Ortiz MEX (SO) 252 Ee31
Ortiz YV 269 Gg41
Ortler = Ortles I 40 Ll44
Ortles = Ortler I 40 Ll44
Ortnevik N 12 Lg29
Orto F 31 Lj48
Orto Botanico I 40 Lm45
Ortona I 42 Lp48
Ortonville USA (MN) 241 Fb23
Ortrand D 33 Lo39
Örtze D 32 Ll38
Orumiyeh IR 72 Nc27
Orumiyeh IR 63 Nc27
Orumiyeh Bazaar IR 72 Nc27
Orumo EAU 204 Mg44
Orungo EAU 204 Mg44
Orуro BOL 284 Gg54
Orust S 14 Lm32
Oruwanje NAM 212 Lg55
Oruzgan AFG 78 Od29
Orvault F 22 Kt43
Orvieto I 42 Ln48
Orvin Land N 11 Mc05
Orzesze PL 36 Lt40
Orzinuovi I 40 Lk45
Orživ UA 54 Md20
Orzuiyeh IR 75 Nj31
Orzyc PL 37 Ma37
Orżycja UA 54 Mg21
Orzysz PL 37 Mb37
Oš KS 77 Og25
Os N 12 Lm28
Osa RUS (UOB) 90 Qb19
Osa RUS 90 Qc19
Osada prasłowiańska PL 36 Ls38
Osage USA (IA) 241 Fd24
Osage Beach USA (MO) 243 Fd26
Osage City USA (KS) 241 Fc26
Osage Ind. Res. USA 243 Fb27
Osaka J 101 Rh28
Osăm BG 47 Me47
Osawatomie USA (KS) 241 Fc26
Osborn USA (SC) 249 Fk29
Osborne USA (KS) 240 Fa26
Osby S 15 Lo34
Osca BOL 280 Gh54
Oscar F (GF) 271 Hd44
Oscar II-Land N 11 Lg06
Oscar Soto Maynes MEX (CHH) 237 Eg31
Osceola USA (AR) 243 Ff28
Osceola USA (IA) 241 Fd25
Osceola USA (MO) 243 Fd26
Osceola USA (NE) 240 Fb25
Oschatz D 33 Lo39
Oschersleben D 33 Lm38
Oschiri I 31 Lk50
Oscoda USA (MI) 246 Fj23
Ose N 12 Lh32
Osečina SCG 44 Lu46
Osen N 10 Lf13
Osenovlag BG 46 Md48
Oshakati NAM 208 Lh54
Oshamambe J 99 Sa24
Oshana NAM 212 Lh55
Oshawa CDN (ON) 247 Ga24
Oshikango NAM 208 Lh54
Oshikoto NAM 212 Lj55
Oshikuku NAM 208 Lh54
Oshima J 101 Rk28
Oshima-hanto J 99 Sa24
Oshivelo NAM 212 Lj55
Oshkosh USA (NE) 240 Ej25
Oshkosh USA (WI) 246 Ff23
Oshtoran Kuh IR 72 Ne29
Oshun WAN 194 Lc42
Oshwe RDC 203 Lk47
Osieczna PL 36 Lr39
Osieczno PL 36 Lq37
Osiek PL 36 Lt37
Osijek HR 41 Lt45
Osilinka River CDN 231 Dh17
Ósimo I 41 Lo47
Osino GH 193 Kk42
Osinów PL 36 Lp38
Ósios Loukás GR 48 Mc52
Osjaków PL 36 Lt39
Osječenica BIH 41 Lr46
Osječenica SCG 46 Lt48
Oskaloosa USA (IA) 241 Fd25
Oskarshamn S 15 Lr33
Oskarström S 15 Ln34
Oskélanéo CDN (QC) 244 Gc21
Öskemen KZ 85 Pb21
Os'kino RUS 53 Mk20
Öskjuvatn IS 10 Kb13
Oskol RUS 53 Mj20
Osku IR 72 Nd27
Öşk Vank TR 63 Na25
Ösling L 23 Lf41
Oslo N 12 Ll31
Oslo USA (MN) 238 Fb21
Oslofjorden N 12 Ll31
Osmanabad IND (MHT) 108 Oj36
Osmancık TR 62 Mh25

Pafuri Gate – Paraná

Pafuri Gate ZA 214 Mf57
Pag HR 41 Lq46
Pag HR 41 Lq46
Pagadenbaru RI 128 Qd49
Pagadian RP 123 Rb42
Pagadian Bay RP 123 Rb42
Pagai Selatan RI 124 Qa47
Pagai Utara RI 124 Qa47
Pagan USA 119 Sb15
Pagancillo RA (LR) 288 Gf60
Paganzo RA (LR) 288 Gg61
Pagaralam RI 125 Qb48
Pagas Divisas BR (AP) 275 Hd46
Pagassitikós Kólpos GR 48 Mc51
Pagatan RI 126 Qh47
Pagawyun MYA 114 Pk38
Page USA (AZ) 237 Ee27
Page USA (OK) 243 Fc28
Pagėgiai LT 17 Mb35
Pageland USA (SC) 249 Fk28
Pagelaziai LT 17 Me35
Pagergunung RI 125 Qc47
Pagimana RI 127 Rb46
Paglugaban Island RP 122 Qk40
Pagny-sur-Mosur F 23 Lg42
Pagodas (Monywa) MYA 113 Ph34
Pagodas (Pakokku) MYA 112 Ph35
Pago Pago USA 164 Be53
Pagosa Springs USA (CO) 237 Eg27
Pagou BF 185 La39
Pagsanjan RP 121 Ra38
Paguilou G 202 Le46
Paguyaman RI 127 Rb45
Pagwachuan CDN 239 Fh21
Pagwa River CDN (ON) 239 Fh20
Pagwi PNG 159 Sb48
Pahala USA (HI) 230 Cc36
Pahalgam 79 Oh28
Pahari IND (MPH) 109 Ok34
Paharikhera IND (MPH) 109 Pa33
Paharpur BD 112 Pe33
Paharpur PK 79 Of29
Pahaska Tepee USA (WY) 235 Ee23
Pahepa RI 123 Rc44
Pahiatua NZ 154 Th66
Pa Hin Ngam N.P. THA 114 Qa38
Páhnes GR 48 Me55
Pahoa USA (HI) 230 Cc36
Pahokee USA (FL) 250 Fk32
Pahoturi River PNG 159 Sb50
Pahraničny BY 37 Md37
Pahrump USA (NV) 236 Ec27
Pahsien Cave RC 97 Ra34
Pahue F (PYF) 165 Cf53
Pahur IND (MHT) 108 Oh35
Pahute Peak USA 234 Ea25
Pai MYA 113 Pj34
Pai THA 114 Pk36
Pai WAN 187 Lf41
Paia USA (HI) 230 Cb35
Paiçandu BR (PR) 286 Hd57
Paide EST 16 Mf32
Paignton GB 20 Kr40
Paihia NZ 154 Th63
Paijan PE 278 Ga49
Päijänne FIN 16 Mf29
Päijänteen kansallispuisto FIN 16 Mf29
Paiko WAN 186 Ld41
Pail PK 79 Og29
Paila BOL 280 Gj54
Pailin K 115 Qb39
Paillaco RCH 292 Gd66
Pailón BOL 285 Gj54
Pailou CHN (HBI) 93 Qj25
Paimbœuf F 22 Ks43
Paimio FIN 16 Mc30
Paimionjoki FIN 16 Mc30
Paimpol F 22 Kr42
Paim Vilho BR (RS) 290 He59
Painan RI 124 Qa46
Pain de Sucre RM 219 Ne52
Paine RCH 288 Ge62
Paine Grande, Cerro RCH 294 Gd71
Painel BR (SC) 291 He59
Painesville USA (OH) 247 Fk25
Pains BR (MG) 287 Hh56
Painted Churches CY 51 Mn56
Painted Desert USA 237 Ee28
Painted Desert USA 237 Ef28
Paint Lake CDN 238 Fb18
Paint Lake Prov. Park CDN 238 Fa18
Paint Rock USA (TX) 242 Fa30
Paintsville USA (KY) 249 Fj27
Paipa CO 268 Gd43
Paipote RCH 288 Ge59
Pai River Rafting THA 114 Pk36
Paisagem Cultural de Sintra P 28 Kl48
Paisha RC 97 Qk34
Paisley GB 19 Kq35
Paisley USA (OR) 234 Dk24
País Vasco E 27 Ks53
Paita F (NCL) 162 Td57
Paita PE 272 Fk48
Paithan IND (MHT) 108 Oh36
Paiton RI 128 Qg49
Păiuşeni RO 44 Mc44
Pajal GCA 255 Ff38
Pajala S 11 Mb12
Paján EC 272 Fk46
Pajapita GCA 255 Fd38
Pajarito CO 268 Gd43
Paje EAT 207 Mk49
Paje RB 213 Md57
Pajeczno PL 37 Lt39
Pajeú BR 283 Ja50
Pajón MEX 255 Fd38
Pajonal, Cerro RCH 284 Gf56
Pajule EAU 204 Mg44
Páka H 38 Lr44
Pakabong PNG 160 Sg47
Pakala IND (APH) 111 Ok40
Pakaraima Mountains GUY 270 Gk43
Pakashkan Lake CDN 239 Fe21
Pakaur IND (WBG) 112 Pd33
Pakbeng LAO 114 Qa36
Pak Charang THA 115 Qb38
Pak Chom THA 115 Qb37
Pak Chong THA 114 Qa38
Pa Kham THA 115 Qb38
Paki WAN 186 Le40
Pakima RDC 203 Mc47
Pakin Atoll FSM 156 Sd17
Pakistan PK 57 Oa07
Pak Kading LAO 115 Qc36
Pakkat RI 116 Pk44
Pak Khat THA 115 Qb36
Paklenica, N.P. HR 41 Lq46
Pak Mong LAO 113 Qb35
Pakokku MYA 112 Ph35
Pakouabo CI 193 Kh42
Pak Ou Caves LAO 113 Qb35
Pakowki Lake CDN 233 Ee21
Pakpattan PK 79 Og30
Pak Phayun THA 116 Qa42
Pakrac HR 41 Ls45
Pakruojis LT 17 Md35
Paks H 39 Lt44
Paksan LAO 115 Qb36
Pakse LAO 115 Qc38
Paksong LAO 115 Qd38
Pak Tha LAO 113 Qa35
Pak Tho THA 114 Pk39
Pak Thong Chai THA 115 Qb38
Paku RI 124 Qa46
Pakuanaji RI 125 Qc48
Pakuli RI 127 Qk46
Pakwach EAU 201 Mf44
Pakwash Lake CDN 238 Fd20
Pakwash Prov. Park CDN 238 Fd20
Pak Xeng LAO 113 Qb35
Pala TCH 187 Lh41
Palabaka RCB 195 Lh46
Palabeck EAU 204 Mg44
Palačany BY 17 Mg36
Palace of Abbasi ET 177 Mf30
Palace on Wheels IND 106 Oh32
Palacio de la Granja de San Ildefonso E 26 Kq50
Palacios BOL 279 Gg52
Palacios HN 256 Fh38
Palacios RA (SF) 289 Gk61
Palacios USA (TX) 243 Fb31
Pałac Krasiczyn PL 39 Mc41
Pałac Nieborow PL 37 Ma38
Pałac Rogalin PL 36 Lr38
Pałac Walicki PL 37 Ma39
Palafrugell E 30 Ld49
Palagonia I 42 Lp53
Palagruža HR 43 Lr48
Palaichori CY 51 Mo56
Palais des Ducs F 23 Lf43
Palais des Papes F 25 Le47
Palais des Rois de Majorque F 24 Lc48
Palaiseau F 23 Lc42
Palaiyam IND (TNU) 111 Ok41
Palakkad IND (KER) 110 Oj41
Palakollu IND (APH) 109 Pb37
Palala LB 192 Kf42
Palala ZA 213 Me57
Palala ZA 213 Me58
Palamakoloi RB 213 Mb57
Palamás GR 46 Mc51
Palamau = Daltonganj IND (JKD) 109 Pc33
Palamau N.P. IND 109 Pc34
Palamea RI 130 Rd46
Palamós E 30 Ld49
Palana AUS (TAS) 153 Sd65
Palana IND (RJT) 106 Og32
Palanan RP 121 Rb37
Palanan Bay RP 121 Rb37
Palanan Point RP 121 Rb37
Palanas RP 121 Rb39
Palanga LT 17 Mb35
Palangkaraya RI 126 Qg47
Palani IND (TNU) 111 Oj41
Palani Hills IND 111 Oj41
Palanok UA 39 Mc42
Palanpur IND (GUJ) 108 Og33
Palanro RI 129 Ra48
Palantak PK 80 Oc32
Palapag RP 121 Rc39
Palapye RB 213 Md57
Palárikovo SK 38 Lt42
Palasa RI 127 Ra45
Palasamudram IND (APH) 111 Oj40
Palas de Rei E 26 Kn52
Palashbari BD 112 Pe33
Palaspal IND (ORS) 109 Pc35
Palatae RI 129 Ra48
Palatka KS 77 Ok24
Palatka USA (FL) 250 Fk31
Palatna SCG 46 Mb47
Palattsy KZ 85 Pb21
Palau I 31 Lk49
Palau MEX (COH) 253 Ek32
Palau 135 Rb09
Palau de la Música Catalana E 30 Lc49
Palau Güell E 30 Lc49
Palaui Island RP 121 Rb36
Palau Islands PAL 121 Rg42
Palauk MYA 114 Pk39
Palaw MYA 114 Pk39
Palawan RP 122 Qk41
Palawan Passage RP 122 Qj41
Palawan Trough 122 Qh42
Palayankottai IND (TNU) 111 Oj42
Palazzina di Caccia di Stupinigi I 40 Lh46
Palazzo Ducale di Mántova I 40 Ll45
Palazzo Ducale d'Urbino I 40 Ln47
Palazzolo Acréide I 42 Lp53
Palazzolo sull'Oglio I 40 Lk45
Palazzo Madama I 40 Lh45
Palazzo Reale di Caserta I 42 Lp49
Palca PE 278 Gc51
Palca PE 279 Ge53
Palca PE 284 Gf54
Palca RCH 284 Gf55
Palcamayo PE 278 Gc51
Palcazú PE 278 Gc51
Paldiski EST 16 Me31
Pale BIH 41 Lt47
Paleh RUS 53 Na17
Palékastro GR 49 Mg55
Paleleh RI 127 Ra45
Paleleh Mountains RI 127 Ra45
Palembang RI 125 Qc47
Palena I 42 Lp49
Palena RCH 292 Gd67
Palencia E 26 Kq51
Palenque MEX (CHP) 255 Fe37
Palenque MEX 255 Fd37
Palenque PA 257 Ga41
Paleo Frourio GR 48 Lu51
Paleohóra GR 48 Md55
Paleohóri GR 48 Mb51
Paleokastritsa GR 48 Lu51
Paleópoli GR 47 Mf50
Paleópoli GR 49 Me53
Palermo CO 272 Gc44
Palermo I 42 Lo52
Palesse BY 37 Md39
Palesse BY 52 Md19
Palestina CO 268 Gb43
Palestina EC 272 Ga46
Palestine USA (TX) 243 Fc30
Palestrina I 42 Ln49
Paletwa MYA 112 Pg35
Palé MYA 112 Ph35
Palgarup AUS (WA) 144 Qj63
Palghar IND (MHT) 108 Og36
Palghat = Palakkad IND (KER) 110 Oj41
Palgrave, Mount AUS 140 Qh57
Palhana IND (UPH) 109 Pa33
Pálháza H 39 Mb42
Palheta BR (AM) 274 Gh47
Palhoça BR (SC) 291 Hf59
Pali IND (CGH) 109 Pb34
Pali IND (MPH) 109 Pa34
Pali IND (RJT) 106 Og33
Palia IND (UPH) 107 Pa31
Pali-Aike, P.N. RCH 294 Gf72
Palian THA 116 Pk42
Palianawa IND (GUJ) 108 Of34
Paliat RI 129 Qh49
Paligrad MK 46 Mb49
Palikir FSM 156 Sd17
Palimbang RP 123 Rc42
Palin H 38 Lr44
Palindi RI 129 Ra51
Palinuro I 42 Lq50
Paliochori GR 49 Me54
Palio di Siena I 40 Lm47
Palioúri GR 47 Md51
Paliouriá GR 46 Mb51
Páliros GR 48 Mc54
Palisades Res. USA 235 Ee24
Palitana IND (GUJ) 108 Of35
Paliūniškis LT 17 Me35
Palizada MEX (CAM) 255 Fd36
Paljavaam RUS 59 Tc05
Pälkäene FIN 16 Me29
Palk Bay CL 111 Ok42
Palkino RUS 16 Mj33
Palkonda IND (APH) 109 Pb36
Palk Strait IND/CY 111 Ok42
Pal Lahara IND (ORS) 109 Pc35
Pallamadu CL 111 Pa42
Pallasca PE 278 Gb50
Pallas-Ounastunturi kansallispuisto FIN 11 Mb11
Pallina BOL 284 Gf54
Pallipatu IND (APH) 111 Ok40
Pallisa EAU 204 Mg45
Palliser Bay NZ 154 Th66
Pallu IND (RJT) 106 Oh31
Palma BR 282 Hg52
Palma MOC 211 Na51
Palma Del Rio E 28 Kp47
Palma de Mallorca E 30 Lc51
Palma di Montechiaro I 42 Lo53
Palmales EC 272 Fk47
Palmaner IND (APH) 111 Ok40
Palmanova I 41 Lo45
Palmar EC 272 Fk46
Palmar YV 268 Gd40
Palmarejo YV 268 Ge40
Palmares BR (PE) 283 Jc50
Palmar Grande BOL 285 Gj56
Palmarin SN 183 Kb39
Palmarito YV 268 Ge42
Palmarito de Cauto C 259 Gc35
Palmas BR (PR) 290 He59
Palmas BR (RS) 290 Hd61
Palmas de Cocalán, P.N. RCH 288 Ge63
Palmas de Monte Alto BR (BA) 282 Hj53
Palmas do Tocantins BR (TO) 282 Hf51
Palma Sola MEX (VC) 254 Fb36
Palma Sola RA (PJ) 285 Gh57
Palma Soriano C 259 Gb35
Palmas, T.I. BR 290 Hd59
Palma Sur CR 256 Fj41
Palm Bay USA (FL) 250 Fk32
Palm Beach USA (FL) 250 Fk32
Palm Cove AUS (QLD) 149 Sc54
Palmdale USA (CA) 236 Ea28
Palmdale USA (FL) 250 Fk32
Palmeira BR (PR) 286 He58
Palmeira CV 182 Jj37
Palmeira das Missões BR (RS) 290 Hd59
Palmeira d'Oeste BR (SP) 286 He56
Palmeira dos Indios BR (AL) 283 Jb50
Palmeirais BR (PI) 276 Hj49
Palmeirândia BR (MA) 276 Hh47
Palmeirante BR (TO) 276 Hg49
Palmeiras BR (BA) 283 Hk52
Palmeiras BR (MS) 286 Hc56
Palmeiras BR 281 He53
Palmeiras BR 282 Hg51
Palmeiras de Goiás BR (GO) 286 Hf54
Palmeiras do Javari BR (AM) 273 Gd48
Palmeirópolis BR (TO) 282 Hf52
Palmela P 28 Km48
Palmer USA (AK) 229 Cf15
Palmeral de Elche E 29 Ku48
Palmeral d'Elx E 29 Ku48
Palmer Land 296 Gc33
Palmer River AUS (QLD) 148 Sb54
Palmer Station ANT (USA) 296 Gd31
Palmerston NZ 155 Tf68
Palmerston Atoll NZ 157 Ud22
Palmerston North NZ 154 Th66
Palmerville AUS (QLD) 147 Sc53
Palmgrove N.P. AUS (QLD) 151 Se58
Palm Harbor USA (FL) 250 Fj31
Palmi I 43 Lq52
Palmillas MEX (TM) 253 Fa34
Palmira CO 268 Gb44
Palmira EC 272 Ga47
Palmira RA (MD) 288 Gf62
Palm Islands AUS (QLD) 149 Sd55
Palmiste RH 260 Gd35
Palmital BR (PR) 286 He58
Palmital BR (SP) 286 He57
Palmitas ROU 289 Hb62
Palmópolis BR (MG) 287 Hk54
Palmse EST 16 Mf31
Palm Springs USA (CA) 236 Eb29
Palm Valley AUS (NT) 142 Rg58
Palm Valley USA (FL) 249 Fk30
Palmwag NAM 212 Lh55
Palmyra SYR 64 Mk28
Palmyra Atoll USA 157 Ud17
Palo RP 123 Rc40
Palo Alto USA (CA) 234 Dj27
Palo Blanco RA (CA) 288 Gg59
Palo Duro Canyon USA 242 Ek28
Palo Duro Canyon S.P. USA 242 Ek28
Paloeloeimenepeu BR/SME 271 Hc44
Paloemeu SME 271 Hc44
Palo Grande PA 256 Fj41
Paloh MAL 117 Qb44
Paloich SUD 197 Mg40
Paloje IND (MHT) 108 Og36
Palojoensuu FIN 11 Mb11
Palokastër AL 46 Ma50
Palolo RI 127 Ra46
Palomares MEX (OAX) 255 Fc37
Palomas E 28 Ko48
Palomas MEX (SLP) 253 Fa34
Palomas Viejo MEX (CHH) 237 Eg30
Palomeras E 29 Kr49
Palometas BOL 285 Gj54
Palometillas BOL 280 Gh54
Palomino CO 268 Gd40
Palompon RP 123 Rc40
Paloncha IND (APH) 109 Pa37
Palo Pinto USA (TX) 242 Fa29
Palopo RI 127 Ra47
Palora EC 272 Gb46
Palos C 258 Fk34
Palo Santo RA (FO) 285 Ha58
Palos Blancos BOL 285 Gj56
Palotina BR (PR) 286 Hd58
Palouse USA (WA) 232 Eb22
Palo Verde, P.N. CR 256 Fh40
Palpa PE 278 Gc53
Palpalá RA (PJ) 285 Gh58
Palparara AUS (QLD) 150 Sa58
Palpite C 258 Fk34
Pålsboda S 13 Lq31
Păltiniş RO 44 Mc45
Păltiniş RO 44 Md45
Palu RI 127 Qk46
Palu RI 129 Ra50
Palu TR 63 Mk26
Palung N.P. RI 126 Qf46
Palwal IND (HYA) 107 Oj31
Pama BF 193 La40
Pama RCA 195 Lj43
Pama RCA 200 Ma43
Pamalap RG 192 Kd41
Pamangkat RI 126 Qe45
Pamanukan RI 128 Qd49
Pamatata RI 129 Ra48
Pamban Island IND 111 Ok42
Pambarra MOC 214 Mh56
Pambeguwa WAN 186 Le40
Pambuka ZW 214 Me56
Pambula Beach AUS 153 Sf64
Pamdai RI 131 Rj47
Pamekasan RI 128 Qg49
Pameungpeuk RI 128 Qd49
Pamgarh IND (CGH) 109 Pb35
Pamiers F 24 Lb47
Pamir AFG/TJ 79 Og27
Pamir TJ 77 Of26
Pamlico Sound USA 249 Gb28
Pamoni YV 270 Gh44
Pampa BR 287 Hk54
Pampa USA (TX) 242 Ek28
Pampa Apeleg RA 292 Ge68
Pampa Aullagas BOL 284 Gg55
Pampa Cerro Morro RA 294 Gg69
Pampachiri PE 278 Gd53
Pampa de Agnia RA (CB) 292 Gf67
Pampa de Chalia RA 294 Ge68
Pampa de Chunchanga PE 278 Gb53
Pampa de Cortaderas PE 278 Gd53
Pampa de Huayuri PE 278 Gc53
Pampa del Agua Amarga RA 292 Gf65
Pampa de las 3 Hermanas RA 294 Gg69
Pampa de las Salinas RA 288 Gg61
Pampa de la Varita RA 288 Gg63
Pampa de la Yoya PE 284 Ge54
Pampa del Castillo RA (CB) 294 Gf68
Pampa del Castillo RA 294 Gf68
Pampa del Diamante RA 288 Gf63
Pampa del Indio RA (CH) 289 Ha59
Pampa del Infierno RA (CH) 289 Gk59
Pampa de los Guanacos RA (SE) 289 Gk59
Pampa del Salado RA 288 Gg62
Pampa del Setenta RA 294 Gf69
Pampa del Tamarugal RCH 284 Gf56
Pampa de Talagapa RA 292 Gf67
Pampa El Toro PE 272 Fk47
Pampa Hermosa PE 278 Gc49
Pampa Húmeda RA 293 Gk64
Pampamarca PE 278 Gd53
Pampanua RI 129 Ra48
Pampa Pelada RA 292 Gg68
Pampas PE 278 Gd52
Pampas PE 278 Gb50
Pampas PE 278 Gc52
Pampas RA 267 Gc26
Pampa Salamanca RA 292 Gg68
Pampas de Sacramento PE 278 Gc49
Pampa Seca RA 288 Gh63
Pampa Verde RA (CH) 289 Gk59
Pampa Verdún RA 294 Ge69
Pampilhosa da Serra P 26 Kn50
Pamplemousses MS 221 Nj56
Pampliega E 27 Kr52
Pamplona CO 268 Gd42
Pamplona E 27 Kt52
Pamplona RP 121 Ra36
Pampoenpoort ZA 216 Mb61
Pamporovo = Koloro, V. BG 47 Me49
Pamucak TR 49 Mh53
Pamukkale TR 50 Mk53
Pamukova TR 50 Ml50
Pamuru IND (APH) 111 Ok39
Pamūšis LT 17 Md34
Pana G 202 Lg46
Pana USA (IL) 241 Ff26
Panaba MEX (YT) 255 Ff35
Panabo RP 123 Rc42
Panaca USA (NV) 234 Ec27
Pañacocha EC 272 Gb46
Panaeati Island PNG 160 Sg51
Panagia GR 46 Mb51
Panagia Halkeon GR 46 Md50
Panagia Parigorítissa GR 48 Ma51
Panagjurište BG 47 Me48
Panaji IND (GOA) 108 Og38
Panaikkudi IND (TNU) 111 Oj42
Panaitan RI 128 Qc49
Panajachel GCA 255 Fe38
Panamá PA 257 Ga41
Panama 257 Fk41
Panama Canal PA 257 Ga41
Panama City USA (FL) 249 Fh30
Panama City Beach USA (FL) 249 Fh30
Panambi BR (RS) 290 Hd60
Panambi RA (MI) 289 Hc59
Panamericana (Arizona) USA 236 Ed29
Panamericana (British Columbia) CDN 232 Ee22
Panamericana (California) USA 234 Dj26
Panamericana (Coahuila) MEX 253 Ek33
Panamericana (El Salvador) ES 255 Ff39
Panamericana (Montana) USA 235 Ee22
Panamericana (Nicaragua) NIC 256 Fh39
Panamericana (Oaxaca) MEX 254 Fb37
Panamericana (Oregon) USA 234 Dj23
Panamericana (Panamá) PA 257 Fk41
Panamericana (San Luis Potosi) MEX 253 Fa34
Panamericana (Sonora) MEX 252 Ef32
Panamint Range USA 236 Eb27
Panamint Springs USA (CA) 236 Eb27
Pan'an CHN (ZJG) 102 Ra31
Panao PE 278 Gc50
Panaon Island RP 123 Rc41
Panar MAL 122 Qh43
Panare THA 117 Qa42
Panareh-Chalai Beach THA 117 Qa42
Panarik RI 117 Qe44
Panaro I 40 Ll46
Panatinane Island PNG 160 Sg51
Panawina Island PNG 160 Sg51
Panay RP 123 Ra40
Panay Gulf RP 123 Rb40
Panban AUS (NSW) 153 Sb62
Pancake Rocks and Blowholes NZ 155 Tf67
Pančarevo BG 46 Md48
Pancas BR (ES) 287 Hk55
Pančevo SCG 44 Ma46
Panchgani IND (MHT) 108 Og37
Panchgani Hill Resort IND 108 Og37
Panchori IND (RJT) 106 Og32
Pancho Villa MEX (CHH) 237 Ef30
Panciu RO 45 Mh45
Pâncota RO 44 Mb44
Pançudo BR (AP) 275 He46
Pancuma RI 127 Ra46
Pancungapang, Gunung RI 126 Qh45
Panda MOC 214 Mh58
Pandambili EAT 207 Mj49
Pandan RP 121 Rc38
Pandan RP 123 Rb40
Pandanan Island RP 122 Qj41
Pandan Bay RP 123 Ra40
Pandan Beach RI 124 Pk45
Pandane MOC 214 Mh58
Pandanus AUS (QLD) 149 Sc55
Pandany RUS 11 Mg14
Pandaria IND (CGH) 109 Pa34
Pan de Azúcar, Cerro RA 294 Gf70
Pan de Azucár RCH 288 Ge59
Pan de Azúcar ROU 289 Hc63
Pan de Azúcar, P.N. RCH 288 Ge59
Pandegelang RI 128 Qd49
Pandeiros BR 282 Hh53
Pandėlys LT 17 Mf34
Pandhana IND (MPH) 108 Oj35
Pandharkawada IND (MHT) 109 Ok36
Pandharpur IND (MHT) 108 Oh37
Pandhurna IND (MPH) 109 Ok35
Pandi CO 268 Gc43
Pandie Pandie AUS (SA) 143 Rk59
Pandiri RI 127 Ra46
Pandivere kõrgustik EST 16 Mg31
Pando ROU 289 Hc63
Pandogari WAN 186 Ld40
Pandora CR 256 Fj41
Pandrup DK 14 Lk33
Pandu IND (ASM) 112 Pf32
Pandu RDC 200 Lk43
Pandzhikent TJ 76 Od26
Panelas BR (MT) 280 Gk50
Panelas BR (PE) 283 Jb50
Panem IND (APH) 111 Ok39
Panemunė LT 17 Mb35
Paneri IND (ASM) 112 Pf32
Panes E 26 Kq53
Panetólio GR 48 Mb52
Panevėžys LT 17 Me35
Pang 79 Oj29
Panga RDC 201 Md45
Pangai TO 164 Bc55
Pangala RCB 202 Lh48
Pangandaran RI 128 Qe49
Pangani EAT 207 Mk48
Pangani EAT 207 Mk48
Pangantocan RP 123 Rc42
Panganuran RP 123 Rb42
Panga pank EST 16 Mc32
Pangar CAM 195 Lg43
Pangeo RI 130 Re44
Panggoe SOL 160 Sj49
Pangi RDC 206 Md47
Pangia PNG 159 Sc49
Pangkajene RI 127 Qk47
Pangkajene RI 129 Ra48
Pangkalanbrandan RI 116 Pk44
Pangkalanbun RI 126 Qf47
Pangkalandurian RI 125 Qb46
Pangkalanpanduk RI 124 Qb45
Pangkalansusu RI 116 Pk43
Pang Kalong LAO 113 Qa35
Pangkalpinang RI 125 Qd47
Pangkor MAL 116 Qa43
Pangkyehtu MYA 113 Pj35
Pang La THA 114 Pk36
Panglao Beach RP 123 Rb41
Panglao Island RP 123 Rb41
Panglong MYA 113 Pj35
Pangnirtung CDN 224 Gc05
Pango PNG 160 Sg47
Pangoa PNG 158 Sa49
Pango Aluquem ANG 202 Lh50
Pangonda RCA 196 Ma42
Pangquangou Z.B. CHN 93 Qf27
Pangrango, Gunung RI 128 Qd49
Pang Sida N.P. THA 115 Qb38
Pangu CHN (HLG) 91 Rb19
Panguipulli RCH 292 Gd65
Panguitch USA (UT) 235 Ed27
Panguma WAL 192 Ke41
Panguruan RI 116 Pk44
Pangutaran Group RP 122 Ra42
Pangutaran Island RP 122 Ra42
Panhala IND 108 Oh37
Panhandle USA 249 Fh30
Panićkovo BG 47 Mf49
Panihati IND (WBG) 112 Pe34
Panikhar 79 Oj28
Panipat IND (HYA) 107 Oj31
Paniqui RP 120 Ra38
Panitan RP 123 Rb40
Panitian RP 122 Qk41
Panjab AFG 78 Od28
Panjabungan Tonga RI 124 Pk45
Panjakent TJ 76 Od26
Panjang RI 125 Qc48
Panjang RI 126 Qe44
Panjang RI 130 Rf48
Panjgur PK 80 Oc32
Panji RI 116 Pj44
Panjin CHN (LNG) 100 Rb25
Panjpai PK 80 Od31
Panjshir-Valley AFG 78 Oe28
Panka BHT 112 Pf32
Pankshin WAN 186 Le41
Pankulam CL 111 Pa42
Panlong CHN (SCH) 95 Qd30
P'anmunjom ROK 100 Rd27
Panna IND (MPH) 109 Pa33
Panna N.P. IND 109 Pa33
Pannawonica AUS (WA) 140 Qj56
Panngi VU 162 Te53
Panniar IND (MPH) 107 Oj32
Pannonhalma H 38 Ls43
Panopah RI 126 Qf46
Pano Panagia CY 51 Mn56
Panorama BR (SP) 286 He56
Pánormos GR 49 Mg53
Panrutti IND (TNU) 111 Ok41
Panshan, Mount CHN 93 Qj25
Panshanu Pass WAN 186 Le41
Panshi CHN (JLN) 100 Rd24
Panskura IND (WBG) 112 Pd34
Pantà de Camarasa E 30 La49
Pantà de Canelles E 30 La48
Pantà de Rialb E 30 Lb49
Pantà de Sant Antoni E 30 La48
Pantà d'Escales E 30 La48
Pantà de Terradets E 30 La48
Pantà d'Oliana E 30 Lb48
Pantai RI 126 Qj47
Pantai koka RI 129 Rb50
Pantai Remis MAL 116 Qa43
Pantalam IND (KER) 110 Oj42
Pantalica I 42 Lq53Pantanal BR 275 Hb49
Pantanal de Nabileque BR 285 Hb56
Pantanal do Rio Negro BR 285 Hb55
Pantanal do São Lourenço BR 281 Hb54
Pantanal do Taquari BR 285 Hb55
Pantanal Matogrossense BR 281 Hb54
Pantanal Matogrossense, P.N.do BR 285 Hb54
Pântano do Sul BR (SC) 291 Hf59
Pântano Grande BR (RS) 290 Hd61
Pantar RI 132 Rc50
Pantekra RI 116 Pj43
Pantemakassar TLS 132 Rc50
Pantha MYA 112 Ph34
Panther Huk NAM 216 Lh59
Panther Swamp N.W.R. USA 248 Fe29
Panti RI 124 Qa45
Panticeu RO 44 Md43
Panticpaeum UA 55 Mj23
Pantijan A.L. AUS 138 Rc54
Pantoja PE 272 Gc46
Pantoloan RI 127 Qk46
Pantu MAL 126 Qf45
Pantukan RP 123 Rc42
Pantzarané CI 193 Kj41
Panu RDC 203 Lk47
Panwari IND (UPH) 107 Ok33
Panxi CHN (YUN) 113 Qb33
Panxian CHN (GZH) 96 Qc33
Panyam WAN 186 Le41
Panzhihua CHN (SCH) 113 Qa32
Panzi RDC 203 Lj49
Paoay RP 120 Ra36
Paola I 43 Lr51
Paoli USA (IN) 248 Fg26
Paomaping CHN (YUN) 113 Qa32
Paonia USA (CO) 235 Eg26
Paonta Sahib IND (HPH) 107 Oj30
Paopao F (PYF) 165 Cf54
Paopao Island PNG 160 Sh47
Paoua RCA 195 Lj42
Paouignan DY 194 Lb42
Pápa H 38 Ls43
Papagaio BR (MA) 276 Hh48
Papagaios BR (MG) 287 Hh55
Papago Ind. Res. USA 236 Ed29
Papaikou USA (HI) 230 Cc36
Papakura NZ 154 Th64
Papallacta Pass RA 273 Gf46
Papalutla MEX (GUR) 254 Fa36
Papanasam Beach IND 110 Oj42
Papanduva BR (SC) 291 He59
Papantla MEX (VC) 254 Fb35
Paparoa N.P. NZ 155 Tf67
Paparoa Range NZ 155 Tf67
Papa Stour GB 19 Kt30
Papa Westray GB 19 Ks31
Papayato RI 127 Ra45
Pape LV 17 Mb34
Papeete F (PYF) 165 Cf54
Papela RI 132 Rb51
Papenburg D 32 Lh37
Papenoo F (PYF) 165 Cf54
Papera BR (AM) 274 Gh46
Papey IS 10 Kc13
Paphos CY 51 Mn56
Papilė LT 17 Mc34
Papillion USA (NE) 241 Fb25
Papilys LT 17 Mf34
Papiniseri IND (KER) 110 Oh41
Papollo NIC 256 Fg40
Paposo PE 284 Ge58
Pappadahandi IND (ORS) 109 Pb36
Paprenda IND (UPH) 107 Pa33
Papua New Guinea 135 Sa10
Papuk HR 41 Ls45
Papulankutja AUS (WA) 141 Re58
Papun MYA 114 Pj36
Papunauá CO 273 Gf45
Papunya AUS (NT) 142 Rf57
Papuri CO 273 Gf45
Papuri YV 268 Ge40
Paqiu SUD 197 Mf42
Paquera CR 256 Fh41
Paquiçamba BR (PA) 275 He47
Paquiçamba, T.I. BR 275 He47
Paquisha EC 272 Ga47
Par IND (ARP) 112 Pg32
Pará BR 275 Hf46
Pará BR 287 Hh55
Pará BR 265 Hb19
Para RI 123 Rc44
Parabubure, T.I. BR 281 Hd53
Paraburdoo AUS (WA) 140 Qj57
Paracale RP 121 Rb38
Paracanã, T.I. BR 275 He48
Paračany BY 17 Mf37
Paracas PE 278 Gb52
Paracatu BR (MG) 287 Hg54
Paracatú BR 287 Hg54
Paracel Islands CHN 120 Qg37
Parachilna AUS (SA) 152 Rk61
Parachinar PK 79 Of29
Paracho MEX (MHC) 254 Ej36
Paraćin SCG 46 Mb47
Paracuhuba, T.I. BR 274 Ha47
Paracuru BR (CE) 277 Ja47
Parada BR (PA) 275 He47
Paradela P 26 Kn51
Para de Minas BR (MG) 287 Hh55
Paradip IND (ORS) 112 Pd35
Paradise USA (CA) 234 Dk26
Paradise Island BS 251 Gb33
Paradise Valley USA (NV) 234 Eb25
Paradisi GR 49 Mj54
Paradisia GR 48 Mc53
Paradji RG 192 Kd40
Parado BR 281 Hc51
Parado RI 129 Qk50
Pará do Mamori BR 274 Ha47
Paradonparp Beach THA 116 Pk40
Pará do Ramos BR 275 Hb47
Paragominas BR (PA) 276 Hg47
Paragoula USA (AR) 243 Fe27
Paraguá BOL 280 Gk52
Paragua YV 269 Gj42
Paraguaçu BR 283 Hk52
Paraguaçu Paulista BR (SP) 286 He57
Paraguai BR 285 Hb56
Paraguaipoa YV 268 Ge40
Paraguarí PY 285 Hb58
Paraguay PY 285 Hb58
Paraguay 263 Ha12
Paraíba BR 277 Jc49
Paraíba BR 265 Ja20
Paraíba do Sul BR (RJ) 287 Hj57
Paraíba do Sul BR 287 Hk56
Paraibano BR (MA) 276 Hj49
Paraim BR 282 Hh50
Parainen = Pargas FIN 16 Mc30
Paraíso BOL 280 Gk53
Paraíso BR (AM) 274 Ha49
Paraíso BR (MS) 286 Hd55
Paraíso CR 256 Fh40
Paraíso MEX (TB) 255 Fd36
Paraíso do Leste BR (MT) 286 Hc54
Paraíso do Norte BR (PR) 286 Hd57
Paraíso do Tocantins BR (TO) 282 Hf51
Paraisópolis BR (MG) 287 Hh57
Paraitepui YV 270 Gk43
Paraiyanalankulam CL 111 Pa42
Parajuru BR (CE) 277 Jb48
Parakan RI 128 Qf49
Parakou DY 186 Lb41
Parakylia AUS (SA) 152 Rj61
Paralia GR 48 Mc52
Paralia Porovitsis GR 48 Mc52
Paralimni CY 51 Mo55
Paralkote IND (CGH) 109 Pa36
Parama Island PNG 159 Sb50
Paramakudi IND (TNU) 111 Ok42
Paramaribo SME 271 Hc43
Paramatti IND (TNU) 111 Oj41
Parambu BR (CE) 277 Hk49
Paramillo CO 268 Gc42
Paramillo, P.N. CO 268 Gb42
Paramirim BR (BA) 283 Hj52
Paramirim BR 282 Hj51
Paramithiá GR 48 Ma51
Páramo Frontino CO 268 Gb42
Paramonga PE 278 Gb51
Páramos del Angel EC 272 Gb45
Páramos del Batallón y La Negra, P.N. YV 268 Ge41
Paramoti BR (CE) 277 Ja48
Paran RI 126 Qh47
Paraná BR (TO) 282 Hg52
Paranã BR 282 Hg52
Paraná BR 286 He56
Paraná BR 267 Hb23

Pobedino – Port of Ness

Pobedino RUS 17 Mc36
Pobedy peak KS 77 Pa24
Pobé Mengao BF 185 Kk39
Pobězovice CZ 38 Ln41
Pobiedziska PL 36 Ls38
Pobierowo PL 36 Lp36
Pobitite kamani BG 47 Mh47
Población RCH 288 Ge63
Poča RUS 11 Mk14
Pocahontas CDN (AB) 233 Eb19
Pocahontas USA (AR) 243 Fe27
Pocahontas USA (IA) 241 Fc24
Pocahontas S.P. USA (VA) 249 Gb27
Počajiv UA 37 Mf40
Počajiv UA 54 Mc20
Pocatello USA (ID) 235 Ed24
Poccha PE 278 Gb50
Počep RUS 52 Mg19
Pochomil NIC 256 Fg40
Počinok RUS 52 Mg18
Počitelj BIH 41 Ls47
Pocking D 35 Lo42
Pocklington Reef PNG 160 Sh51
Poço BR 282 Hj51
Poço BR 283 Hk50
Poço de Fora BR (BA) 283 Ja50
Poçoes BR (BA) 283 Hk53
Pocola RO 44 Mc44
Poconé BR (MT) 285 Hb54
Poço Redondo BR (SE) 283 Jb50
Poços BR (BA) 283 Hj50
Poços de Caldas BR (MG) 287 Hg56
Pocosin Lakes N.W.R. USA 249 Gb28
Poço Verde BR (SE) 283 Ja51
Pocrane BR (MG) 287 Hk55
Pocri PA 257 Fk42
Pocrovca MD 45 Mh42
Pocsaj H 39 Mb43
Podalakur IND (APH) 111 Ok39
Podari RO 44 Md46
Podbereze'e RUS 52 Mf16
Podbereze'e RUS 52 Mf17
Podbořanský Rohozec CZ 38 Lo40
Podbořany CZ 38 Lo40
Podborov'e RUS 52 Me17
Podbožur SCG 46 Lt48
Poddor'e RUS 52 Mf17
Poděbrady CZ 38 Lq40
Podgora HR 41 Ls47
Podgorac SCG 46 Mb47
Podgorenskij RUS 53 Mk20
Podgorica SCG 46 Lu48
Podi RI 127 Ra46
Podil UA 54 Mg21
Podile IND (APH) 111 Ok39
Podil's'ka Vysočyna UA 45 Mk42
Podil's'ka vysočyna UA 54 Md21
Podil's'ke UA 45 Mg42
Podil's'kyj Tovtry N.P. UA 54 Md21
Podkamennaja Tunguska RUS 58 Pd06
Podkova BG 47 Mf49
Podlasie PL 37 Mc38
Podlesnoje RUS 53 Nd20
Podocarpus, P.N. EC 272 Ga48
Podoleš'e RUS 16 Mj32
Podol'sk RUS 52 Mj18
Podor SN 183 Kc37
Podorožnje UA 39 Me41
Podporož'e RUS 11 Mh15
Podrašnica BIH 41 Lr46
Podravina HR 41 Ls45
Podromanija BIH 46 Lt47
Podsnežnoe RUS 53 Nc19
Podu Iloaiei RO 45 Mh43
Podujevo SCG 46 Mb48
Podu Turcului RO 45 Mh44
Podyji, N.P. CZ 38 Lr42
Poe Bank 116 Pj41
Poechos PE 272 Fk48
Poel D 33 Lm36
Poeppel's Corner AUS 150 Rk58
Poesoegroenoe SME 271 Hc43
Pofadder ZA 216 Lk60
Pogana RO 45 Mh44
Poganovski manastir SCG 46 Mc48
Pogar RUS 52 Mg19
Poggibonsi I 40 Lm47
Pòggio Mirteto I 42 Ln48
Pognoa BF 193 La40
Pogo CI 193 Kh40
Pogo RMM 184 Kh39
Pogoanele RO 45 Mg46
Pogost RUS 11 Mh15
Pogradec AL 46 Ma50
Pograničnyj RUS 98 Rf23
Pogromnoe RUS 53 Ng19
Poh RI 127 Rb46
P'ohang ROK 100 Re27
Pohénegamook CDN (QC) 244 Gf22
Pohja = Pojo FIN 16 Md30
Pohja - Eesti klint EST 16 Mg31
Pohjanmaa FIN 11 Mb14
Pohoarna MD 45 Mj43
Pohokura NZ 154 Th65
Pohong CHN (GZG) 96 Qd34
Pohořelice CZ 38 Lr42
Pohoří na Šumavě CZ 38 Lp42
Pohorje SLO 41 Lq44
Pohrebyšče UA 54 Me21
Pohri IND (MPH) 107 Oj33
Pohutu Geysir NZ 154 Tj65
Pohvistnevo RUS 53 Ng19
Poiana Lacului RO 45 Me45
Poiana Largului RO 45 Mf43
Poiana Mare RO 46 Md47
Poiana Stampei RO 45 Mf43
Poibrene BG 46 Md48
Põide EST 16 Md32
Poie RDC 203 Mb47
Poienile de Sub Munte RO 44 Me43
Poigar RI 127 Rc45
Poindimié F (NCL) 162 Tc56
Point Adam USA (AK) 229 Cd16
Point Alexander AUS 139 Rj52
Point Angeles USA (WA) 232 Dj21
Point Arena USA (CA) 234 Dj26
Point Arrowsmith AUS 139 Rj52
Point au Fer Island USA 243 Fe31
Point-au-Père Lighthouse CDN 244 Gf21
Point Baker USA (AK) 231 Dd17
Point Banks USA (AK) 229 Cd16
Point Barrow USA 224 Cb04
Point Bell AUS 152 Rg62
Point Berliet RN 180 Le35
Point Blaze AUS 139 Rf52
Point Bridget USA (AK) 231 Dc16
Point Brown AUS 152 Rg62
Point Bugui RP 121 Rb39
Point Calimere IND 111 Ok41
Point Cloates AUS 140 Qg57
Point Culver AUS 145 Rc62
Point d'Entrecasteaux AUS 144 Qh63
Point Dover AUS 145 Rc62
Point Drummond AUS 152 Rh63
Point Dume Beach USA 236 Ea28
Pointe a la Hache USA (LA) 243 Ff31
Pointe à Michel CDN 244 Gf21
Pointe-à-Pitre F (GL) 261 Gk37
Pointe Béhague F 271 He43
Pointe de Barfleur F 22 Kt41
Pointe-de-l'Est Nat. Wildlife Area CDN 245 Gk22
Pointe de l'Ouest CDN 244 Gh21
Pointe de Penhir F 22 Kq42
Pointe de Saint- Mathieu F 22 Kq42
Pointe de Souellaba CAM 194 Le44
Pointe du Raz F 22 Kq42
Pointe Edward Casino USA 246 Fj24
Pointe Heath CDN 245 Gk21
Pointe Kakachischuan CDN 239 Ga18
Pointe Lefèvre F (NCL) 162 Td56
Pointe Longue CDN 239 Ga19
Pointe-Noire F (GL) 261 Gk37
Pointe-Noire RCB 202 Lf48
Pointe-Parent CDN (QC) 245 Gk20
Pointe Pongara G 194 Le45
Pointe Quest RH 251 Gd35
Point Escarpada RP 121 Rb36
Point Escuminac CDN 245 Gh22
Pointe Snape CDN 239 Ga20
Pointe Swayan CDN 239 Ga20
Point Harbor USA (NC) 249 Gc27
Point Hibbs AUS 152 Sc67
Point Hicks AUS 153 Se64
Point Hillier AUS 144 Qj63
Point Hope USA 224 Bc05
Point Isabel Lighthouse S.H.P. USA 253 Fb32
Point Jahleel AUS 139 Rf51
Point Malcolm AUS 145 Rb62
Point Maud AUS 140 Qg57
Point McNeill CDN (BC) 232 Dg20
Point Mellon CDN (BC) 232 Dj21
Point Nuyts AUS 144 Qj63
Point of Ayre GB 19 Kq36
Point Pedro CL 111 Pa42
Point Pedro CL 111 Pa42
Point Pelee N.P. CDN 246 Fj25
Point Pleasant USA (NJ) 247 Gc25
Point Pleasant USA (WV) 249 Fj26
Point Renfrew CDN (BC) 232 Dh21
Point Reyes USA 234 Dj27
Point Reyes Nat. Seashore USA 234 Dj26
Point Riou USA 230 Ck16
Point Salvation AUS 145 Rb60
Point Salvation A.L. AUS 145 Rc60
Point Samson AUS (WA) 140 Qj56
Point Sir Issac AUS 152 Rh63
Point Spencer USA (AK) 229 Bg13
Point Stuart AUS (NT) 139 Rf52
Point Sur USA 234 Dk27
Point Torment AUS 138 Rb54
Point Townsend USA (WA) 232 Dj21
Point Westhall AUS 152 Rg62
Point Whidbey AUS 152 Rh63
Poissonnier Point AUS 140 Qk55
Poissy F 23 Lc42
Poitiers F 22 La44
Poitou F 22 Ku44
Poitou-Charente F 24 Ku44
Poivre SY 219 Ng48
Poix-de-Picardie F 23 Lb41
Pojarkovo RUS 98 Re21
Pojezierze Bytowskie PL 36 Ls36
Pojezierze Ełckie PL 37 Mc36
Pojezierze Iławskie PL 37 Lu37
Pojezierze Mrągowskie PL 37 Mb37
Pojezierze Pomerskie PL 36 Lr37
Po Jiang CHN 102 Qj31
Pojuca BR 283 Ja52
Pokaran IND (RJT) 106 Of32
Pokataroo AUS (NSW) 151 Se60
Pokemouche CDN (NB) 245 Gh22
Pokeno NZ 154 Th64
Pokenui NZ 154 Tg63
Pokhara NEP 88 Pc31
Pokigron SME 271 Hc43
Po-kil Do ROK 103 Rd28
Pokka FIN 11 Mc11
Poko RDC 201 Md44
Pokok Sena MAL 116 Qa42
Pokrov RUS 53 Mk18
Pokrovka KS 76 Of24
Pokrovka KZ 77 Oh24
Pokrovsk RUS 53 Nd20
Pokrovskaja Arčada RUS 53 Nc19
Pokrovs'ke UA 53 Mk21
Pokrovs'ke UA 55 Mj22
Pokuma Z 210 Md54
Pola RP 121 Ra39
Polacca USA (AZ) 237 Ee28
Polack BY 52 Me18
Polackaja Nižina BY 52 Md18
Pola de Laviana E 26 Kp53
Pola de Lena E 26 Kp53
Pola de Siero E 26 Kp53
Pola de Somiedo E 26 Ko53
Poladpur IND (MHT) 108 Og37
Polaia Kalan IND (MPH) 108 Oj34
Połajewo PL 36 Lr38
Poland USA (NY) 247 Gc24
Poland 7 Lb04
Połaniec PL 37 Mb40
Połanów PL 36 Lr36
Polar Bear Express CDN 239 Fk20
Polar Bear Provincial Park CDN (ON) 239 Fj18
Polar Plateau ANT 296 Eb36
Polatlar TR 51 Mn51
Polatlı TR 51 Mn51
Polavaram IND (APH) 109 Pa37
Połczyn-Zdrój PL 36 Lr37
Poldasht IR 72 Nc26
Pole Abyssal Plain 299 Lc01
Pol-e'Alam AFG 78 Oe28
Polebridge USA (MT) 233 Ec21
Polee RI 130 Rf47
Pol-e Fasa IR 74 Ng31
Pol-e Khomri AFG 78 Oe28
Pol-eSefid IR 72 Ng27
Polesella I 40 Lm46
Polésine I 40 Lm46
Poleski P.N. PL 37 Md39
Polessk RUS 17 Mb36
Polewali RI 127 Qk47
Pol-e Zal IR 72 Ne29
Polgár H 39 Mb43
Polgárdi H 38 Lt43
Poli CAM 195 Lg41
Poli RC 97 Ra33
Polia RO 45 Mg44
Poličan AL 46 Ma50
Police PL 36 Lp37
Policemans Point AUS (SA) 152 Rk63
Polička CZ 38 Lr41
Policoro I 43 Lr50
Polidámio GR 48 Mc51
Poliegos GR 49 Me54
Poligiros GR 46 Md50
Polignano a Mare I 43 Ls49
Poligny F 25 Lf44
Polihnitos GR 49 Mg51
Polikastro GR 46 Mc50
Polillo Island RP 121 Ra38
Polillo Islands RP 121 Ra38
Polimilos GR 46 Mc50
Poliochni GR 47 Mf51
Polis CY 51 Mn55
Polis'ke UA 52 Me20
Polistena I 43 Lr52
Poljana BG 47 Mg48
Poljany RUS 16 Mk30
Poljice BIH 41 Lt46
Polkowice PL 36 Lr39
Polla I 42 Lq50
Pollachi IND (TNU) 111 Oj41
Pollença E 30 Ld51
Pollilo RP 121 Ra38
Pollilo Strait RP 121 Ra38
Pollino, P.N.del I 43 Lr51
Pollo USA (TX) 243 Fc30
Pollock USA (LA) 243 Fd30
Polmak N 11 Me10
Polna RUS 16 Mj32
Polobaya Grande PE 284 Ge54
Polochic GCA 255 Ff38
Pologi RO 45 Mf46
Pologoe Zajmišče RUS 53 Nc21
Polohy UA 55 Mj22
Polokwane = Pietersburg ZA 214 Me57
Polom SCG 46 Ma46
Polomolok RP 123 Rc42
Poloniny, Národný park SK 39 Mc41
Polonnaruwa CL 111 Pa43
Polonne UA 54 Md20
Pôlo Norte BR (AM) 279 Gf49
Polonyna Runa UA 39 Mc42
Polonyns'kyj chrebet UA 39 Mc42
Polovragi RO 44 Md45
Polski Trămbeš BG 47 Mf47
Polson USA (MT) 233 Ec22
Poltava UA 54 Mh21
Põltsamaa EST 16 Mf32
Põltsamaa EST 16 Mf32
Poluostrov Cheleken TM 71 Ng26
Poluostrov Jamal RUS 58 Ob04
Poluostrov Kanin RUS 58 Na05
poluostrov Kanin RUS 9 Na05
Poluostrov Rybačij RUS 11 Mf11
Poluostrov Svjatoi Nos RUS 90 Qe19
Poluostrov Terpenija RUS 99 Sc21
Polur IND (TNU) 111 Ok40
Põlva EST 16 Mh32
Polvora PE 278 Gb49
Polyantho GR 47 Mf49
Polynesia 302 Ba10
Polyuc MEX (QTR) 255 Ff36
Poma RDC 201 Mc46
Pomabamba PE 278 Gb50
Pomahuaca PE 272 Ga48
Pomán RA (CA) 288 Gg60
Pomarance I 40 Ll47
Pomarkku FIN 16 Mc29
Pomasi, Cerro de PE 279 Ge53
Pombal BR (PB) 277 Jb49
Pombal P 28 Km49
Pombas BR (AM) 274 Gj46
Pombuige ANG 208 Lh51
Pomene MOC 214 Mh57
Pomeranian Bay D 33 Lp36
Pomeroy USA (OH) 246 Fj26
Pomeroy USA (WA) 234 Eb22
Pomeroy ZA 217 Mf60
Pomézia I 42 Ln49
Pomfret ZA 213 Mb58
Pomio PNG 160 Sf48
Pomona AUS (QLD) 151 Sg59
Pomona RA (RN) 292 Gh65
Pomonaeiland NAM 216 Lh59
Pomona Island NAM 216 Lh59
Pomorie BG 47 Mh48
Pomorjany UA 39 Me41
Pomos CY 51 Mn55
Pompano Beach USA (FL) 250 Fk32
Pompei I 42 Lp50
Pompéia BR (SP) 286 He57
Pompeu BR (MG) 287 Hh55
Pompey F 23 Lg42
Pompeys Pillar USA (MT) 235 Eg23
Pompeys Pillar USA 235 Ef23
Pom Phra Chunlachomkiao THA 114 Qa39
Pomun Temple ROK 100 Rd27
Pomuq UZ 76 Oc26
Ponape Island FSM 156 Sd17
Ponass Lake CDN 233 Eh19
Ponca USA (NE) 241 Fb24
Ponca City USA (OK) 243 Fb27
Ponce USA (PR) 261 Gg36
Poncha Springs USA (CO) 235 Eg26
Ponchatoula USA (LA) 243 Fe30
Ponda EAT 207 Mk50
Pond Creek USA (OK) 242 Fb27
Pond Creek N.W.R. USA 243 Fc29
Pondicherry IND (PND) 111 Ok41
Pondicherry IND 111 Ok41
Pond Inlet CDN 225 Ga04
Pondosa USA (CA) 234 Dk25
Pondung Lamanggang RI 124 Qa47
Poneloya NIC 256 Fg39
Ponérihouen F (NCL) 162 Tc56
Ponferrada E 26 Ko52
Pong THA 114 Qa36
Pongai BR (SP) 286 Hf56
Pongara, P.N.de G 194 Le45
Pong Chi THA 114 Qa37
Pong Gua Waterfalls VN 115 Qe40
Pong Nam Ron THA 115 Qb39
Pongo SUD 197 Md42
Pongo de Paquipachango PE 278 Gc51
Pongola ZA 217 Mf59
Pongola Bush Nature Reserve ZA 217 Mf59
Pongolapoort Dam ZA 217 Mg59
Pongore ZW 213 Md55
Poni BF 193 Kj40
Poniatowa PL 37 Mc39
Ponikiew Mała PL 37 Mb38
Ponikovica SCG 46 Lu47
Ponio TG 193 La40
Ponley K 115 Qc39
Ponnaiyar IND 111 Ok40
Ponnampet IND (KTK) 110 Oh40
Ponnani IND (KER) 110 Oh41
Ponneri IND (TNU) 111 Pa40
Ponoarele RO 44 Mc46
Ponoj RUS 58 Md05
Ponoj RUS 58 Na05
Ponoka CDN (AB) 233 Ed19
Ponondougou CI 193 Kg41
Ponorogo RI 128 Qf49
Ponoševac SCG 46 Ma48
Ponot RP 123 Rb41
Pons F 24 Ku45
Ponson Island RP 123 Rc40
Ponta Albina ANG 208 Lf53
Ponta Barra MOC 214 Mh57
Pontacq F 24 Ku47
Ponta da Baleia BR 287 Ja54
Ponta da Juatinga BR 287 Hh57
Ponta da Mota BR (SE) 283 Jb51
Ponta da Piedade P 28 Km47
Ponta da Serra, T.I. BR 270 Gk44
Ponta das Palmeirinhas ANG 202 Lg50
Ponta de Corumbaú BR 287 Ja54
Ponta Delgada P 8 Jc11
Ponta de Mucuripe BR 277 Ja47
Ponta de Pedras BR (PA) 276 Hf46
Ponta de Porto Belo BR 291 Hf59
Ponta de Sagres P 28 Km46
Ponta do Arpoador BR 286 Hg58
Ponta do Boi BR 287 Hh57
Ponta do Calcanhar BR 277 Jc48
Ponta do Mutá BR 283 Ja52
Ponta do Ouro MOC 217 Mg59
Ponta do Rapa BR 291 Hf59
Ponta do Seixas BR 277 Jc49
Ponta dos Indios BR 271 He43
Ponta dos Naufragados BR 291 Hf59
Ponta do Sol CV 182 Jh37
Ponta Freitas Morna ANG 202 Lg49
Ponta Grande CV 182 Jh37
Ponta Grossa BR (PR) 286 He58
Pontailler-sur-Saône F 23 Lf43
Ponta Jericoacoara BR 277 Hk47
Pontal BR (SP) 286 Hf56
Pontal do Manguinha BR 283 Jb51
Pontalina BR (GO) 286 Hf54
Ponta Lipobane MOC 211 Mk54
Ponta Macacos MOC 214 Mj55
Ponta Macovane MOC 214 Mh56
Ponta Malongane MOC 217 Mg59
Ponta Maunhane MOC 211 Na52
Ponta Moreia CV 182 Jj38
Pont-à-Mousson F 23 Lg42
Pontão P 28 Km49
Ponta Paza BR 283 Jb51
Ponta Pelindã GNB 183 Kb40
Ponta Porã BR (MS) 286 Hc57
Ponta Rebordelo BR 275 Hf45
Pontarion F 24 Lb45
Pontarlier F 25 Lg44
Ponta Santo António BR 283 Ja54
Ponta São Sebastião MOC 214 Mh57
Pontassieve I 40 Lm47
Ponta Tarafo CV 182 Jj38
Pont-Audemer F 22 La41
Pontaumur F 25 Lc45
Pontcharra F 25 Lg45
Pontchateau F 22 Ks43
Pont-d'Ain F 25 Lf44
Pont de Normandie F 22 La41
Pont-de-Roide F 23 Lg43
Pont-de-Vaux F 25 Le44
Pont du Gard F 25 Le47
Ponte Alta do Bom Jesus BR (TO) 282 Hg52
Ponteareas E 26 Km52
Ponte Branca BR (GO) 286 Hd54
Pontecorvo I 42 Lo49
Ponte da Barca P 26 Km51
Ponte del Diavolo I 41 Lo44
Ponte de Lima P 26 Km51
Pontedera I 40 Ll47
Ponte de Sor P 28 Km49
Pontedeume E 26 Km53
Ponte do Rio Verde BR (MS) 286 Hd55
Ponte Firme BR (MG) 287 Hg55
Pontefract GB 21 Kt37
Ponte Leccia F 31 Lk48
Ponte Nova BR (MG) 287 Hj56
Pontenova Villaodriz E 26 Kn53
Pont-en-Royans F 25 Lf45
Pontes e Lacerda BR (MT) 280 Ha53
Ponte Serrada BR (SC) 290 He59
Ponte Tresa I 40 Lj45
Pontevedra E 26 Km52
Pontgibaud F 25 Lc45
Ponthieu F 23 Lb40
Pontiac USA (IL) 246 Ff25
Pontianak RI 126 Qe46
Pontian Kechil MAL 117 Qb45
Pontic Mountains TR 60 Mc10
Pontivy F 22 Ks42
Pont-l'Abbé F 22 Kq43
Pont-l'Evêque F 22 La41
Ponto Alta do Tocantins BR (TO) 282 Hg51
Pontoise F 23 Lc41
Pontokerasiá GR 46 Md49
Ponton AUS 145 Rb61
Ponton CDN (MB) 238 Fa18
Pontorson F 22 Kt42
Pontotoc USA (MS) 243 Ff28
Pontrémoli I 40 Lk46
Pontresina CH 34 Lk44
Ponts E 30 Lb49
Pont-Sainte-Maxence F 23 Lc41
Pont-Saint-Esprit F 25 Le46
Pont-Saint-Vincent F 23 Lg42
Pont-sur-Yonne F 23 Ld42
Pont Valentré F 24 Lb46
Pontypool GB 21 Kr39
Ponuga PA 257 Fk42
Pony Express Station USA 241 Fb26
Ponza I 42 Ln50
Poochera AUS (SA) 152 Rh62
Poole GB 21 Kt40
Pool Malebo RDC 202 Lh48
Poolowanna Lake AUS 143 Rj59
Pool's Cove CDN 245 Hc22
Pooncarie AUS (NSW) 153 Sb62
Poopó BOL 284 Gg55
Poor Knights Islands NZ 154 Th63
Poorman USA (AK) 229 Cc13
Poor Man Ind. Res. CDN 233 Eh20
Põõsaspea neem EST 16 Md31
Poowong AUS (VIC) 153 Sc65
Pop UZ 76 Of25
Popa G 202 Lg46
Popa Falls NAM 213 Ma55
Popagaon NEP 88 Pb31
Popa, Mount MYA 113 Ph35
Popa Mountain Park MYA 113 Ph35
Popayán CO 272 Gb44
Popčevo MK 46 Mc49
Pope LV 17 Mb33
Popenguine SN 183 Kb38
Poperinge B 23 Lc40
Popești RO 44 Mc43
Popielów PL 36 Ls40
Poplar Bluff USA (MO) 243 Fe27
Poplarfield CDN (MB) 238 Fb20
Poplar Point CDN 238 Fb19
Poplar River CDN 233 Eg21
Poplar River CDN 238 Fb19
Poplar River Power Station and Strip Mine CDN 233 Eh21
Poplarville USA (MS) 243 Ff30
Popocatépetl MEX 254 Fa36
Popodara RG 192 Kd40
Popof Island USA 228 Bk18
Popoh RI 128 Qf50
Popo-kabaka RDC 202 Lj48
Pópoli I 42 Lo48
Popomanaseu, Mount SOL 161 Ta50
Popondetta PNG 159 Se50
Popovača HR 41 Lr45
Popovići BIH 41 Ls46
Popovo BG 47 Mg47
Popovyči UA 39 Mc41
Popow PL 36 Lt39
Poppi I 40 Lm47
Poprad SK 39 Ma41
Poprad SK 39 Ma41
Popšica SCG 46 Mb47
Popsko BG 47 Mf49
Poptún GCA 255 Ff37
Popular Point CDN (MB) 238 Fb20
Populónia I 40 Ll48
Poquis, Nevado de RA/RCH 284 Gg57
Porangahau NZ 154 Tj66
Porangatu BR (GO) 282 Hf52
Porata IND (ORS) 109 Pb36
Porazava BY 37 Me38
Porbandar IND (GUJ) 108 Oe35
Porcher Island CDN 232 De19
Porcuna E 28 Kq47
Porcupine USA (AK) 231 Db16
Porcupine Abyssal Plain 8 Ka09
Porcupine Gorge N.P. AUS (QLD) 148 Sc56
Porcupine Hills CDN 238 Ek19
Porcupine Prov. Forest CDN 238 Ek19
Pordenone I 41 Ln45
Pordim BG 47 Me47
Pore CO 268 Ge43
Porebada PNG 159 Sd50
Porebeni MD 45 Mj43
Poreč HR 41 Lo45
Porecatu BR (PR) 286 He57
Poreč'e RUS 16 Mj32
Porédaka RG 192 Kd40
Porga DY 193 La40
Porgera PNG 159 Sb48
Porhov RUS 52 Me17
Pori FIN 16 Mb29
Pori PRK 100 Rd25
Pori Jazz FIN 16 Mb29
Porirua NZ 154 Th66
Þórisvatn IS 10 Ka13
Porjus S 10 Lk12
Porkkala FIN 16 Me31
Þorlákshöfn IS 10 Jk14
Porlamar YV 270 Gj40
Pormpuraaw AUS (QLD) 146 Sa53
Pornic F 22 Ks43
Poro Island RP 123 Rc40
Poroma PNG 159 Sb49
Poronaj RUS 99 Sb20
Poronajsk RUS 99 Sb21
Porongurup AUS (WA) 144 Qj63
Póros GR 48 Md53
Póros GR 48 Ma52
Porosozero RUS 11 Mg14
Porozina HR 41 Lp45
Porpoise Bay 297 Rb32
Porquinhos-Aldeia Chinela, T.I. BR 276 Hh49
Porquis Junction CDN (ON) 239 Fk21
Porras FIN 16 Md30
Porrentruy CH 34 Lh43
Porretta Terme I 40 Ll46
Porriño E 26 Km52
Porsangenfjorden N 11 Mc10
Porsea RI 116 Pk44
Porsgrunn N 12 Lk31
Þórshöfn IS 10 Kc12
Þórsmörk IS 10 Ka14
Portachuelo BOL 285 Gj54
Portadown GB 18 Ko36
Portaferry GB 18 Kp36
Portage USA (AK) 229 Cf15
Portage USA (WI) 246 Ff24
Portage Glacier USA 229 Cf15
Portage la Prairie CDN (MB) 238 Fa20
Portal BR 283 Hk50
Port Alberni CDN (BC) 232 Dh21
Port Albert AUS (VIC) 153 Sd65
Portalegre P 28 Kn49
Portales USA (NM) 237 Ej28
Port Alexander USA (AK) 231 Dc17
Port Alfred ZA 217 Md62
Port Alice CDN (BC) 232 Dg20
Port Alma AUS (QLD) 149 Sf57
Porta Nigra D 34 Lg41
Port Antonio JA 259 Gb36
Portara GR 49 Mf53
Portarlington IRL 20 Kn37
Port Arthur AUS (TAS) 152 Sd67
Port Arthur = Lüshun CHN (LNG) 100 Ra26
Port Arthur USA (TX) 243 Fd31
Port Askaig GB 18 Ko35
Port au Choix N.H.S. CDN 245 Hb20
Port Augusta AUS (SA) 152 Rj62
Port au Port Bay CDN 245 Ha21
Port-au-Prince RH 260 Gd36
Port Austin USA (MI) 246 Fj23
Port aux Choix CDN (NF) 245 Hb20
Portavadie GB 18 Kp35
Port Aventura E 30 Lb49
Porta Westfalica D 32 Lj38
Port Barton RP 122 Qk40
Port Bickerton CDN (NS) 245 Gk23
Port Blair IND (AAN) 111 Pg40
Port Blandfort CDN (NF) 245 Hc21
Port Bradshaw AUS 139 Rj52
Port Broughton AUS (SA) 152 Rj62
Port Burwell Prov. Park CDN 247 Fk24
Port Campbell AUS (VIC) 153 Sb65
Port Campbell National Park AUS (VIC) 153 Sb65
Port -Cartier CDN (QC) 244 Gg20
Port Charlotte USA (FL) 250 Fj32
Port Chilkoot USA (AK) 231 Dc16
Port Clarence USA 229 Bg13
Port Clements CDN (BC) 232 Dd19
Port Clinton USA (OH) 246 Fj25
Port Colborne CDN (ON) 247 Ga24
Port Curtis AUS 149 Sf57
Port d'Addaia E 30 Le50
Port-Daniel CDN (QC) 245 Gh21
Port Davey AUS 152 Sc67
Port-de-Bouc F 25 Le47
Port-de-Paix RH 260 Gd36
Port de Pollença E 30 Ld51
Port d'es Torrent E 30 Lb52
Port Dickson MAL 117 Qa44
Port Douglas AUS (QLD) 149 Sc54
Port Edward CDN (BC) 232 De18
Port Edward ZA 217 Mf61
Porteira BR (PA) 275 Hb46
Porteirinha BR (MG) 282 Hj53
Portél BR (PA) 275 He46
Portel P 28 Kn48
Portelândia BR (GO) 286 Hd54
Port Elgin CDN (ON) 246 Fk23
Port Elizabeth ZA 217 Mc62
Port Ellen GB 18 Ko35
Port Elliot AUS (SA) 152 Rk63
Portena RA (CD) 288 Gj61
Port-en-Bessin F 22 Ku41
Port Erin GB 18 Kq36
Porters Corner USA (MT) 235 Ed22
Porterville USA (CA) 236 Ea27
Porterville ZA 216 Lk62
Portes d'Enfer RDC 206 Md48
Port Essington CDN (BC) 232 Df18
Port Fairy AUS (VIC) 152 Sb65
Port Fitzroy NZ 154 Th64
Port Fourchon USA (LA) 243 Fe31
Port Fuâd ET 177 Mg30
Port-Gentil G 194 Le46
Port Germein AUS (SA) 152 Rk62
Port Gibson USA (MS) 243 Fe30
Port Gregory AUS (WA) 144 Qh60
Port Grimaud F 25 Lg47
Port Grosvenor ZA 217 Me61
Port Hacking AUS 153 Sf63
Port Harcourt WAN 194 Ld43
Port Hardy CDN (BC) 232 Dg20
Port Harrison = Inukjuak CDN 225 Ga07
Port Hastings CDN (NS) 245 Gk23
Porthcawl GB 20 Kr39
Port Hedland AUS (WA) 140 Qk56
Port Heiden USA (AK) 228 Ca17
Port Heiden USA (AK) 228 Ca17
Porthill USA (ID) 233 Eb21
Port Hope CDN (ON) 247 Ga24
Port Hope Simpson CDN 225 Ha08
Port Howard GB (GBF) 295 Ha71
Port Howe BS 251 Gc33
Port Huron USA (MI) 246 Fj24
Portile de Fier, P.N. RO 44 Mc46
Portillo RCH 288 Ge62
Portimão P 28 Km47
Portinatx E 30 Lb51
Port Jackson AUS 153 Sf62
Port Jackson NZ 154 Th64
Port Jervis USA (NJ) 247 Gc25
Port-Joinville F 22 Ks44
Port Kembla AUS (NSW) 153 Sf63
Port Kenny AUS (SA) 152 Rh62
Portland AUS (VIC) 152 Sa65
Portland USA (IN) 246 Fh25
Portland USA (ME) 247 Ge24
Portland USA (OR) 234 Dj23
Portland USA (TN) 248 Fg27
Portland USA (TX) 253 Fb32
Portland Bay AUS 152 Sa65
Portland Bigth JA 259 Gb37
Portland Channel USA 231 De18
Portland Creek Pond CDN 245 Hb20
Portland Inlet CDN 231 De18
Portland Island NZ 154 Tj65
Portland Point JA 259 Gb37
Portland Roads AUS (QLD) 146 Sb52
Port Langdon AUS 139 Rj52
Port-la-Nouvelle F 25 Ld47
Port Laoise IRL 20 Kn37
Port Latta AUS (TAS) 152 Sc66
Port Lavaca USA (TX) 243 Fb31
Port Lincoln AUS (SA) 152 Rh63
Portlock USA (AK) 229 Ce16
Portlock Reefs PNG 159 Sc50
Port Loins USA (AK) 230 Cd17
Port Loko WAL 192 Kd41
Port Loring CDN (ON) 246 Fk23
Port-Louis F (GL) 261 Gk37
Port-Louis F 22 Kr43
Port Louis MS 221 Nj56
Port MacDonnell AUS (VIC) 152 Sa65
Port Macquarie AUS (NSW) 151 Sg61
Port Mansfield USA (TX) 253 Fb32
Port Maria JA 259 Gb36
Port Mayaca USA (FL) 250 Fk32
Port McArthur AUS 139 Rj53
Portmeirion GB 20 Kq38
Port-Menier CDN (QC) 245 Gh21
Port Moller USA (AK) 228 Bk18
Port Moller USA (AK) 228 Bk18
Portmore JA 259 Gb37
Port Moresby PNG 159 Sd50
Port Musgrave AUS 146 Sa51
Portnacroish GB 19 Kp34
Portnahaven GB 18 Ko35
Port-Navalo F 22 Ks43
Port Neill AUS (SA) 152 Rj63
Port Nelson BS 251 Gc34
Port Nelson CDN 238 Fd17
Port Nelson (abandoned) CDN 238 Fd17
Port Neville CDN (BC) 232 Dg20
Port Noarlunga AUS (SA) 152 Rk63
Port Nolloth ZA 216 Lj60
Porto BR (PI) 277 Hj47
Porto F 31 Lj48
Porto P 26 Km51
Porto Acre BR (AC) 279 Gg50
Porto Alegre BR (PA) 275 Hb48
Porto Alegre BR (RS) 290 He61
Porto Alegre STP 194 Ld45
Porto Alegre do Norte BR (MT) 281 He51
Porto Alencastro BR (MG) 286 He55
Porto Alto P 28 Km48
Porto Amboim ANG 208 Lg51
Porto Amelia = Pemba MOC 211 Na52
Porto Antunes BR (AM) 273 Gg47
Porto Arari BR (AP) 275 He45
Porto Azzurro I 40 Ll48
Portobelo PA 257 Ga41
Portobelo, P.N. PA 257 Ga41
Porto Bicentenário BR (RO) 280 Gj51
Porto Braga BR (AM) 274 Gh47
Porto Braga BR (MS) 285 Hb56
Porto Caiuá BR (MS) 286 Hd57
Porto Calvo BR (AL) 283 Jc50
Porto Camargo BR (PR) 286 Hd57
Porto Cervo I 31 Lk49
Porto Cesáreo I 43 Ls50
Porto Chique BR (MG) 287 Hh54
Port O'Connor USA (TX) 253 Fb31
Portocristo E 30 Ld51
Porto da Balsa P 26 Kn50
Porto da Folha BR (SE) 283 Jb50
Porto de Galinhas BR (PE) 283 Jc50
Porto de Pedras BR (AL) 283 Jc50
Porto do Mangue BR (RN) 277 Jb48
Porto do Moz BR (PA) 275 Hd46
Porto dos Gaúchos BR (MT) 281 Hb51
Porto do Son E 26 Km52
Porto Empédocle I 42 Lo53
Porto Esperança BR (MS) 285 Hb55
Porto Esperidião BR (MT) 280 Ha53
Porto Estrella BR (MT) 281 Hb53
Portoferráio I 40 Ll48
Porto Ferreira BR (SP) 286 Hg56
Portofino I 40 Lk46
Port of Ness GB 19 Ko32

R

Río Sorbe – Rowena

Río Sorbe E 29 Kr51
Río SouthJuan DOM 260 Ge36
Riosucio CO 268 Gb42
Riosucio CO 268 Gc43
Río Tajo E 29 Kr50
Río Tajo E/P 28 Kn49
Río Tajuña E 29 Ks50
Rio Teá, T.I. BR 273 Gg46
Río Tejo E/P 28 Kn49
Río Tercero RA (CD) 288 Gh62
Río Tiétar E 26 Kq50
Río Tigre EC 272 Gb47
Rio Tinto BR (PB) 277 Jc49
Río Tirón E 27 Kr52
Río Tocuyo YV 269 Gf40
RioTombali GNB 183 Kc40
Río Torío E 26 Kp52
Río Tormes E 26 Kp51
Rio Tuba RP 122 Qj41
Río Turia E 29 Kt50
Rioug RIM 183 Ke37
Río Valderaduey E 26 Kp51
Rio Verde BR (GO) 286 He54
Rio Verde BR 281 Hb52
Rio Verde BR 281 He54
Rio Verde BR 283 Hj51
Rio Verde BR 286 Hd56
Rio Verde BR 286 He55
Rio Verde BR 286 Hg54
Río Verde EC 272 Ga45
Río Verde MEX (QTR) 255 Ff36
Rioverde MEX (SLP) 254 Ek35
Río Verde PY 285 Ha57
Río Verde RA 292 Gh66
Rio Verde de Mato Grosso BR (MS) 286 Hc55
Rio Verde Grande BR 282 Hj53
Rio Verde Pequeno BR 282 Hj53
Rio Vermelho BR (MG) 287 Hj55
Río Viejo, P.N. YV 268 Ge42
Rio Villegas RA (RN) 292 Ge66
Rio Vista USA (CA) 234 Dk26
Río Xévora P 28 Kn49
Río Xipembe MOC 214 Mg56
Rioz F 23 Lg43
Rio Zêzere P 28 Kn49
Riozinho BR 273 Gg47
Riozinho BR 275 Hd49
Río Zújar E 28 Kp48
Ripač BIH 41 Lq46
Ripanj SCG 44 Ma46
Ripky UA 52 Mf20
Ripley USA (MS) 243 Ff28
Ripley USA (TN) 243 Ff28
Ripley USA (WV) 247 Fk26
Ripoll E 30 Lc48
Ripon GB 21 Kt36
Riponpet IND (KTK) 110 Oh40
Riposto I 42 Lq53
Ripplebrook USA (OR) 234 Dj23
Riquewihr F 23 Lh42
Rireibo do Pombal BR (BA) 283 Ja51
Risalpur PK 79 Og28
Risbäck S 10 Lh13
Riscal de Catavina MEX 236 Ec31
Riscle F 24 Ku47
Rishikesh IND (UTT) 107 Ok30
Rishiri J 99 Sa23
Rishirifuji J 99 Sa23
Rishiri-Rebun-Sarobetsu N.P. J 99 Sa23
Rishiri-to J 99 Sa23
Rishton UZ 77 Of25
Rising Star USA (TX) 242 Fa29
Riska N 12 Lf32
Riske Creek CDN (BC) 232 Dj20
Risnes N 12 Lg32
Risnjak, N.P. HR 41 Lp45
Rison USA (AR) 243 Fd29
Risør N 12 Lk32
Risoul 1850 F 25 Lg46
Rissani MA 172 Kh30
Risti EST 16 Me32
Ristiina FIN 16 Mh29
Ristilä FIN 16 Mg28
Ristna neem EST 16 Mc32
Rita Blanca National Grassland USA (TX) 242 Ej27
Ritchie ZA 217 Mc60
Rithi IND (MPH) 109 Pa34
Ritlite BG 46 Md47
Rito ANG 209 Lk54
Rito Gompar CHN (TIB) 89 Pg31
Ritsem S 10 Lj12
Ritter USA (OR) 234 Ea23
Ritter Hot Springs USA (OR) 234 Ea23
Ritterhude D 32 Lj37
Ritzville USA (WA) 232 Ea22
Riumar E 30 La50
Rivadavia RA (BA) 289 Gj63
Rivadavia RA (SA) 285 Gj58
Rivadavia RA (SJ) 288 Gf61
Rivadavia RCH 288 Ge60
Riva del Garda I 40 Ll45
Rivalensundet N 11 Md06
Rivas CR 256 Fj41
Rivas NIC 256 Fh40
Rive-de-Gier F 25 Le45
Rivera EC 272 Ga47
Rivera RA (BA) 293 Gj64
Rivera ROU 289 Hc61
Riverboat Cruises (Murray River) AUS (NSW) 152 Sb63
River Cess LB 192 Kf43
River Falls USA (WI) 241 Fd23
River Gambia N.P. WAG 183 Kc39
Riverhead USA (NY) 247 Gd25
Riverina AUS (WA) 144 Ra60
River Jordan CDN (BC) 232 Dh21
River Kwai Bridge THA 114 Pk38
River Rafting (Devaprayag) IND 107 Ok30
River Rafting (Tanakpur) IND 107 Pa31
Rivers CDN (MB) 238 Ek20
Riversdal ZA 216 Ma63
Riversdale BH 255 Ff37
Riversdale NZ 155 Te68
Riversdale ZA 216 Ma63
Riversdale Beach NZ 154 Tj66
Riverside AUS (QLD) 149 Se56
Riverside USA (CA) 236 Eb29
Riverside USA (NM) 237 Eh29
Riverside USA (OR) 234 Ea24
Riverside USA (WY) 235 Eg25
Rivers Inlet CDN 232 Dg20
Riversleigh AUS (QLD) 148 Rk55
Riverton CDN (MB) 238 Fb20
Riverton NZ 155 Td69
Riverton USA (WY) 235 Ef24
Riverview CDN (NB) 245 Gh22
Rivesaltes F 24 Lc48
Riviera USA (TX) 253 Fb32
Riviera di Levante I 40 Lk46
Riviera di Ponente I 40 Lj47
Rivière Aguanus CDN 245 Gj20
Rivière à la Marte CDN 244 Gc20
Rivièrea-Pièrre CDN (QC) 244 Gd22
Rivière au Phoque CDN 239 Ga18
Rivière-au-Renard CDN (QC) 245 Gh21
Rivière-au-Tonnerre CDN (QC) 244 Gh20
Rivière-aux-Graines CDN (QC) 244 Gh20
Rivière aux Outardes CDN 244 Gf21
Rivière aux Sables CDN 244 Ge21
Rivière-auxSaumons CDN (QC) 245 Gj21
Rivière Baskatong CDN 244 Gc22
Rivière Batiscan CDN 244 Gd22
Rivière Bell CDN 244 Gb21
Rivière Betsiamites CDN 244 Gf21
Rivière Bleue CDN (QC) 244 Gf22
Rivière Broadback CDN 244 Gb20
Rivière Cabonga CDN 244 Gb22
Rivière Cascapédia CDN 244 Gg21
Rivière Chamouchouane CDN 244 Gd21
Rivière Chaudière CDN 244 Ge22
Rivière Chibougamau CDN 244 Gc21
Rivière Corvette CDN 244 Gc19
Rivière Coulonge CDN 244 Gb22
Rivière Decelles CDN 244 Ga22
Rivière des Outaouais CDN 244 Ga22
Rivière Dozois CDN 244 Gb22
Rivière du Lièvre CDN 244 Gc22
Rivière-du-Loup CDN (QC) 244 Gf22
Rivière Dumoine CDN 244 Gb22
Rivière du Petit CDN 245 Ha20
Rivière du Vieux Comptoir CDN 239 Ga19
Rivière Eastmain CDN 244 Gd19
Rivière Gatineau CDN 244 Gc22
Rivière Harricanaw CDN 239 Ga20
Rivière-Héva CDN (QC) 244 Ga21
Rivière Jupiter CDN 245 Gj21
Rivière Kanaaupscow CDN 244 Gd18
Rivière Kapsaouis CDN 239 Ga18
Rivière Kitchigama CDN 239 Ga20
Rivière la Ronde CDN 244 Gg19
Rivière Magpie CDN 244 Gh20
Rivière Maica CDN 244 Gb20
Rivière Manicouagan CDN 244 Gf21
Rivière Manicrois CDN 244 Gf20
Rivière Manitou CDN 244 Gh20
Rivière Matapédia CDN 244 Gg21
Rivière Matawin CDN 244 Gd22
Rivière Mégiscane CDN 244 Gb21
Rivière Missisicabi CDN 239 Ga20
Rivière Mistassibi CDN 244 Gd20
Rivière Mistawak CDN 239 Ga21
Rivière Moisie CDN 244 Gg20
Rivière Mouchalagane CDN 244 Gf19
Rivière Natashquan CDN 245 Gk20
Rivière Némiscau CDN 244 Gb20
Rivière Nestaocan CDN 244 Gd20
Rivière Nottaway CDN 239 Ga20
Rivière Obamska CDN 239 Ga20
Rivière Olomane CDN 245 Gk20
Rivière Opinaca CDN 239 Gb19
Rivière Outardes Quatre CDN 244 Gf20
Rivière Pentecôte CDN (QC) 244 Gg21
Rivière Péribonka CDN 244 Ge21
Rivière-Pilote F (MT) 261 Gk38
Rivière Pipmuacan CDN 244 Ge21
Rivière Portneuf CDN 244 Gf21
Rivière Romaine CDN 244 Gj20
Rivière Rupert CDN 239 Gb20
Rivière Saguenay CDN 244 Ge21
RivièreSaint Jean CDN (QC) 244 Gh20
Rivière Saint-Jean CDN 244 Gh20
Rivière Saint-Maurice CDN 244 Gd21
Rivière Sakami CDN 244 Gc19
Rivière St-Augustin CDN 245 Ha20
Rivière Ste-Marguerite CDN 244 Gg20
Rivière St-Maurice CDN 244 Gd22
Rivière Sud-Est MS 221 Nj56
Rivière Taureau CDN 244 Gd22
Rivière Temiscamie CDN 244 Gd20
Rivière Toulnustouc CDN 244 Gf21
Rivière Trenche CDN 244 Gd21
Rivière Turgeon CDN 239 Ga21
Rivière Vermillon CDN 244 Gd22
Rivière Waswanipi CDN 244 Gb21
Riviersonderend ZA 216 Lk63
Rivne UA 54 Md20
Rivne UA 54 Mf21
Rivoli I 40 Lh45
Rivungo ANG 209 Ma54
Riwat PK 79 Og29
Riwoqê CHN (TIB) 89 Pj30
Riyadh KSA 66 Nd33
Riyadh al Khabra KSA 67 Nb32
Rizal RP 121 Ra37
Rizal RP 121 Ra39
Rize TR 63 Na25
Rizhao CHN (SDG) 93 Qk28
Rizokarpaso = Dipkarpaz CY 51 Mp55
Rjabovskij RUS 53 Na20
Rjasnopil' UA 45 Mm43
Rjazan' RUS 53 Mk18
Rjazanka RUS 53 Nb19
Rjažsk RUS 53 Na19
Rjukan N 12 Lj31
Rkiz RIM 183 Kc37
Roa E 26 Kr51
Roa N 12 Ll30
Road Town GB (VI) 261 Gh36
Roan Cliffs USA 235 Ef26
Roanne F 25 Le44
Roanoke USA (AL) 249 Fh29
Roanoke USA (VA) 249 Ga27
Roanoke Rapids USA (NC) 249 Gb27
Roans Prairie USA (TX) 243 Fc30
Roaringwater Bay IRL 20 Kl39
Roastbeefeiland NAM 216 Lh59
Roastbeef Island NAM 216 Lh59
Robat IR 75 Nj30
Robat-e Ja'li AFG 78 Oa31
Robat-e-Khoshab IR 73 Nj29
Robat-e Khoshk Aveh AFG 78 Ob29
Robat-e-Posht Badam IR 73 Nh29
Robat-e-Qarah Bil IR 73 Nj27
Robatkarim IR 72 Nf28
Robat Khan IR 73 Nj29
Robat Kur IR 73 Nj29
Robat Sang IR 73 Nk28
Robb CDN (AB) 233 Eb19
Robben Island ZA 216 Lk62
Robbies Pass NAM 208 Lg55
Robbins Island AUS (TAS) 152 Sc66
Robbinsville USA (NC) 249 Fj28
Robe AUS (SA) 152 Rk64
Robe ETH 198 Na42
Röbel D 33 Ln37
Robe, Mount AUS 150 Sa61
Robe River AUS 140 Qh56
Robert Lee USA (TX) 242 Ek30
Robert's Arm CDN (NF) 245 Hc21
Roberts Creek Mtn. USA 234 Eb26
Robertsfors S 10 Ma13
Robertsganj IND (UPH) 109 Pb33
Robertson ZA 216 Lk62
Robertson Bay CDN 239 Ga17
Robertson Bay 297 Tb33
Robertsport LB 192 Ke42
Robertstown AUS (SA) 152 Rk62
Roberval CDN (QC) 244 Gd21
Robi ETH 198 Mk42
Robinhood AUS (QLD) 148 Sb55
Robins Camp ZW 213 Mc55
Robinson USA (IL) 248 Fg26
Robinson, Mount AUS 140 Qk57
Robinson Range AUS 140 Qk58
Robinson River AUS (NT) 139 Rj54
Robinson River AUS 139 Rj54
Robinson River CDN 245 Ha21
Robinson River PNG 159 Se51
Robledo E 29 Ks48
Robles La Paz CO 268 Gd40
Roblin CDN (MB) 238 Ek20
Röblingen D 33 Lm39
Robooksibia RI 131 Rh46
Roboré BOL 285 Ha55
Robsart CDN (SK) 233 Ef21
Robson, Mount CDN 232 Ea19
Robstown USA (TX) 253 Fb32
Roby USA (TX) 242 Ek29
Roca Bruja CR 256 Fg40
Rocafuerte EC 272 Fk46
Rocamadour F 24 Lb46
Rocanville CDN (SK) 238 Ek20
Roca Redonda EC 272 Fe45
Roça Tapirapé BR (PA) 281 He50
Roccadáspide I 42 Lq50
Rocca Imperiale I 43 Lr50
Roccamena I 42 Lo53
Roccaraso I 42 Lp49
Roccastrada I 40 Lm47
Roccella Iónica I 43 Lr52
Rocha ROU 289 Hc63
Rochdale GB 21 Ks37
Roche Cabrit F (GF) 271 Hd43
Rochechouart F 24 La45
Rochedo BR (MS) 286 Hc55
Rochefort B 23 Lf40
Rochefort F 24 Ku45
Rochelle USA (IL) 246 Ff25
Rocher Ako'akas CAM 195 Lf44
Rocher Corneille F 25 Ld46
Rocher d'Ifandana RM 220 Nd56
Rocher du Mézessé CAM 195 Lg44
Rocheservière F 22 Kt44
Rochester GB 21 La39
Rochester USA (IN) 246 Fg25
Rochester USA (MN) 241 Fd23
Rochester USA (NH) 247 Ge24
Rochester USA (NY) 247 Gb24
Roche Tado F (GF) 271 Hd43
Rochlitz D 33 Ln39
Rockall 8 Kb07
Rockall Plateau 8 Ka07
Rockall Trough 8 Ka08
Rock Creek CDN (BC) 232 Ea21
Rockdale USA (TN) 248 Fg28
Rockdale USA (TX) 243 Fb30
Rockefeller Plateau 296 Da34
Rock Engravings NAM 216 Lk59
Rock Engravings ZA 217 Mc59
Rock Falls USA (IL) 246 Ff25
Rockford USA (AL) 248 Fg29
Rockford USA (IL) 246 Ff24
Rock Fort Temple (Trichy) IND 111 Ok41
Rockglen CDN (SK) 233 Eh21
Rockhampton AUS (QLD) 149 Sf57
Rockhampton Downs AUS (NT) 139 Rh55
Rock Hill USA (SC) 249 Fk28
Rockingham AUS (WA) 144 Qh62
Rockingham USA (NC) 249 Ga28
Rockingham Bay AUS (QLD) 149 Sd55
Rocklake USA (ND) 238 Fa21
Rockland CDN (QC) 247 Gc23
Rockland USA (MA) 247 Gf23
Rock 'n' Roll Hall of Fame (Cleveland) USA 246 Fk25
Rock of Cashel IRL 20 Kn38
Rock Paintings LS 217 Me61
Rock Paintings RB 213 Mc58
Rock Paintings ZA 216 Ma61
Rock Port USA (MO) 241 Fc25
Rockport USA (TX) 253 Fb31
Rockport USA (WA) 232 Dk21
Rock Rapids USA (IA) 241 Fb24
Rock River CDN 231 Dg15
Rock River USA (WY) 235 Eh25
Rock Sound BS 251 Gb33
Rock Springs USA (MT) 235 Eg22
Rocksprings USA (TX) 242 Ek31
Rock Springs USA (WY) 235 Ef25
Rockstone GUY 270 Ha42
Rockton AUS (NSW) 153 Se64
Rockville USA (IN) 246 Fg26
Rockville USA (MD) 247 Gb26
Rockwood USA (MA) 244 Gf23
Rockwood USA (TN) 249 Fh28
Rocky Boy USA (MT) 233 Ef21
Rocky Boy Ind. Res. USA 233 Ef21
Rocky Ford USA (CO) 242 Ej26
Rocky Gully AUS (WA) 144 Qj63
Rocky Island ET 177 Mj34
Rocky Island Lake CDN 239 Fj22
Rocky Lake CDN 238 Ek18
Rocky Mount USA (NC) 249 Gb28
Rocky Mount USA (VA) 249 Ga27
Rocky Mountain House CDN (AB) 233 Ec19
Rocky Mountain N.P. USA 235 Eh25
Rocky Mountains CDN/USA 222 Db04
Rocky Mountains Forest Reserve CDN 233 Ec20
Rocky Mtn. House N.H.S. CDN 233 Ec19
Rocky Mtns. Forest Reserve CDN 233 Eb19
Rocky Point USA (AK) 229 Bj13
Ročov CZ 38 Lo40
Rocroi F 23 Le41
Roda Velha BR (BA) 282 Hh52
Rødberg N 12 Lj30
Rødbyhavn DK 14 Lm36
Rödeby S 15 Lq34
Rødekro DK 14 Lk35
Rodel GB 18 Ko33
Roden NL 32 Lg37
Rodeo RA (SJ) 288 Gf61
Rodeo USA (NM) 237 Ef30
Roderick River AUS 140 Qj59
Rodez F 24 Lc46
Rodi Garganico I 42 Lq49
Rodina Mat UA 54 Mf20
Roding D 35 Ln41
Rodna RO 44 Me43
Rodna, P.N. RO 44 Me43
Rodniki RUS 53 Na17
Rodolívos GR 47 Md50
Ródos GR 49 Mj54
Ródos GR 49 Mj54
Rodovia Perimetral Norte BR 275 Hb45
Rødvig DK 14 Ln35
Roebourne AUS (WA) 140 Qj56
Roebuck Bay AUS 138 Rb55
Roebuck Plains AUS (WA) 138 Rb54
Roedtan ZA 213 Me58
Roela EST 16 Mg31
Roermond NL 32 Lg39
Roeselare B 23 Ld40
Roeseveltpiek SME 271 Hc44
Roești RO 44 Me46
Roes Welcome Sound CDN 224 Fc06
Roetgen D 32 Lg40
Rofia WAN 186 Lc40
Rogač HR 41 Lr47
Rogačevka RUS 53 Mk20
Rogačica SCG 46 Lu46
Rogaguado BOL 280 Gh52
Rogaliński Park Krajobrazowy PL 36 Lr38
Rogaška Slatina SLO 41 Lq44
Rogatica BIH 46 Lu47
Rogen S 12 Ln28
Rogers USA (AR) 243 Fc27
Rogers City USA (MI) 246 Fj23
Rogerson USA (ID) 235 Ec24
Rogers Pass CDN (BC) 232 Eb20
Rogersville CDN (NB) 245 Gh22
Roggeveen Basin 266 Fa24
Roggeveldberge ZA 216 Ma62
Rogliano I 43 Lr51
Rogne N 12 Lk29
Rogo WAN 186 Ld40
Rogone MOC 211 Mj53
Rogowo PL 36 Ls38
Rogoz RO 44 Md43
Rogoźniczka PL 37 Mc38
Rogożno PL 36 Lr38
Rogun WAN 186 Lc41
Rohan F 22 Ks42
Rohat IND (RJT) 106 Og33
Rohatyn UA 39 Me41
Rohožník SK 38 Ls42
Rohrbach A 35 Lo42
Rohrbach-lès-Bitche F 23 Lh41
Rohri PK 81 Oe32
Rohru IND (HPH) 107 Oj30
Rohtak IND (HYA) 107 Oj31
Rohtas IND 109 Pb33
Rohtas Fort PK 79 Og29
Rohuküla EST 16 Md32
Rohuneeme EST 16 Me31
Roi Et THA 115 Qb37
Roismala FIN 16 Mc29
Roissy F 23 Lc42
Roja LV 17 Mc33
Rojão P 26 Km50
Rojas RA (BA) 289 Gk63
Röjdåfors S 13 Ln30
Rojhan PK 81 Oe31
Roka EAK 207 Mk47
Rokan RI 124 Qa45
Rokan RI 124 Qa45
Rokan-Kanan RI 124 Qa45
Rokan-Kiri RI 124 Qa45
Rokeby AUS (QLD) 146 Sb52
Rokeby N.P. AUS 146 Sb52
Rokewood AUS (VIC) 153 Sb64
Rokiciny PL 37 Lu39
Rokiškis LT 17 Mf35
Rokkasho J 99 Sa25
Rokom SUD 201 Mf43
Rokoroko RI 127 Rb48
Rokuan kansallispuisto FIN 11 Md13
Rokycany CZ 38 Lo41
Rokytne UA 52 Md20
Roland CDN (MB) 238 Fb21
Rolândia BR (PR) 286 He57
Roland in Bremen D 32 Lj37
Røldal N 12 Lg31
Roldan RA (SF) 289 Gk62
Rolde NL 32 Lg38
Rolfstorp S 14 Ln33
Rolim de Moura BR (RO) 280 Gk51
Roll USA (OK) 242 Fa28
Rolla USA (MO) 243 Fe27
Rolla USA (ND) 238 Fa21
Rolleston AUS (QLD) 151 Se58
Rollet CDN (QC) 247 Ga22
Rolleville BS 251 Gc34
Rolling Fork USA (MS) 243 Fe29
Rolling Hills CDN (AB) 233 Ee20
Rolling R. Ind. Res. CDN 238 Ek20
Rollingstone AUS (QLD) 149 Sd55
Rollo BF 185 Kk39
Roluos Group K 115 Qc39
Roma AUS (QLD) 151 Se59
Roma I 42 Ln49
Roma I 42 Lm49
Roma LS 217 Md60
Roma S 15 Lt33
Roma USA (TX) 253 Fa32
Romaine CDN (QC) 245 Gk20
Romallo RA (BA) 289 Gk62
Roman BG 46 Md47
Roman RO 45 Mg44
Roman Baths GB 21 Ks39
Romanche Gap 300 Ka09
Romăneşti RO 45 Mh43
Romang RA (SF) 289 Ha60
Romang RI 132 Rd49
Romania RO 44 Md44
Romanovka RUS (BUR) 91 Qg19
Romanshorn CH 34 Lk43
Romans-sur-Isère F 25 Lf45
Romantische Straße D 34 Lk41
Romaria BR (MG) 286 Hg55
Romaškino RUS 53 Nf19
Romblon RP 121 Rb39
Romblon Island RP 121 Rb39
Romblon Strait RP 121 Rb39
Rome I 42 Ln49
Rome USA (GA) 249 Fh28
Rome USA (NY) 247 Gc24
Romilly-sur-Seine F 23 Ld42
Romiton UZ 76 Oc26
Romlott-vár H 38 Ls44
Rommani MA 172 Kg29
Romney USA (WV) 247 Ga26
Romny RUS 98 Re20
Romny UA 52 Mg20
Rømø DK 14 Lj35
Romo RI 126 Qe45
Romodan UA 54 Mg21
Romorantin-Lanthenay F 22 Lb43
Rømø Sommerland DK 14 Lj35
Romsdalen N 12 Lh28
Romsey GB 21 Kt40
Rómulo Calzada MEX (TB) 255 Fd37
Ron IND (KTK) 108 Oh38
Ronan USA (MT) 233 Ec22
Roncador BR (PR) 286 Hd58
Roncador Reef SOL 161 Sk49
Roncesvalles E 27 Kt53
Ronchamp F 23 Lg43
Ronciglione I 42 Ln48
Ronda E 28 Kp46
Ronda Alta BR (RS) 290 Hd59
Rondane n.p. N 12 Lk29
Rønde DK 14 Ll34
Ronde WG 261 Gk39
Rondeador, T.I. BR 276 Hh48
Rondeau Prov. Park CDN 246 Fk24
Rondon BR (PR) 286 Hd57
Rondon do Pará BR (PA) 276 Hf48
Rondônia BR 264 Gd21
Rondonópolis BR (MT) 286 Hc54
Rond-Point de Gaulle TCH 181 Lj36
Rondslottet N 12 Lk29
Ronehamn S 15 Lt33
Rongai EAK 204 Mh46
Rong'an CHN (GZG) 96 Qe33
Rongbon Cave THA 114 Qa39
Rongbuk Monastery CHN 88 Pd31
Rongcheng CHN (SDG) 100 Rb27
Rongelap Atoll MH 157 Tb16
Rongerik Atoll MH 157 Tb16
Rongjenj IND (MGA) 112 Pf33
Rong Kat THA 114 Pk36
Rongkop RI 128 Qf50
Rong Kwang THA 114 Qa36
Rongo EAK 204 Mh46
Rongshui CHN (GZG) 96 Qe33
Rõngu EST 16 Mg32
Rong Xian CHN (GZG) 96 Qf34
Rong Xian CHN (SCH) 94 Qc31
Ronien Daun Sam K 115 Qb39
Ron Morel Mus. CDN 239 Fj21
Rønne DK 15 Lp35
Ronne Bay 296 Gb33
Ronneby S 15 Lq34
Ronne Ice Shelf ANT 296 Gd34
Ronnenberg D 32 Lk38
Rönnöfors S 10 Lg14
Ron Phibun THA 116 Pk41
Ronse B 23 Ld40
Ronuro BR 281 Hc52
Roodepoort ZA 217 Md59
Rooibergdam ZA 216 Mb60
Rooiberge LS 217 Me60
Rooibokkraal ZA 213 Md58
Rooibokkraal NAM 212 Lh57
Rooikraal ZA 214 Me58
Rooin RI 131 Rh47
Rooirand NAM 212 Lj58
Roorkee IND (UTT) 107 Oj31
Roosendaal NL 32 Le39
Roosevelt BR 280 Gk50
Roosevelt USA (UT) 235 Ef25
Roosevelt Campobello Internat. Park CDN 245 Gg23
Roosevelt Island 296 Bc34
Roosevelt, Mount CDN 231 Dh16
Roosevelt N.P. Nth. Unit USA 240 Ej22
Roosevelt N.P. Sth. Unit USA 240 Ej22
Roosevelt, T.I. BR 280 Gk51
Roossenekal ZA 214 Me58
Roosville CDN (BC) 233 Ec21
Root Lake CDN (MB) 238 Ek18
Root River CDN 231 Dh14
Ropar IND (PJB) 107 Oj30
Ropczyce PL 37 Mb40
Roper Bar AUS (NT) 139 Rh53
Roper River AUS 139 Rh53
Roper Valley AUS (NT) 139 Rh53
Ropotovo MK 46 Mb49
Roquefort F 24 Ku46
Roque Gonzales BR (RS) 290 Hc60
Roque Pérez RA (BA) 289 Ha63
Roquesteron F 25 Lh47
Roquetaillade F 24 Ku46
Roquetas de Mar E 29 Ks46
Roquetes E 30 La50
Roraima BR 265 Gd18
Roraima, Mount GUY/YV 270 Gk43
Rore BIH 41 Lr46
Rori IND (PJB) 106 Oh31
Rori RI 131 Rj46
Rorke's Drift ZA 217 Mf60
Røros N 12 Lm28
Rorschach CH 34 Lk43
Rørvik N 10 Lf13
Ros' BY 17 Me37
Ros' UA 54 Mf21
Rošal' RUS 53 Mk18
Rosal de la Frontera E 28 Kn47
Rosales RP 121 Ra38
Rosalia USA (WA) 232 Eb22
Rosalindbank 259 Fk37
Rosamorada MEX (NYT) 253 Eh34
Rosana BR (SP) 286 Hd57
Rosans F 25 Lf46
Rosário BR (MA) 276 Hh47
Rosario DOM 260 Ge36
Rosario MEX (SO) 252 Ef32
Rosario PE 284 Ge58
Rosario PY 285 Hb58
Rosario RA (SF) 289 Gk62
Rosario ROU 289 Hb63
Rosario RP 120 Ra37
Rosario RP 121 Ra39
Rosario YV 268 Gd40
Rosario de la Frontera RA (SA) 285 Gh58
Rosario de Lerma RA (SA) 284 Gh58
Rosario del Tala RA (ER) 289 Ha62
Rosário do Sul BR (RS) 290 Hc61
Rosario Izapa MEX 255 Fd38
Rosario Oeste BR (MT) 281 Hb53
Rosarito MEX (BC) 236 Ec31
Rosarito MEX (BC) 236 Eb29
Rosarito MEX (BCS) 252 Ee32
Rosarno I 43 Lq52
Rosa Seamount 252 Ec32
Rosa Zárate EC 272 Ga45
Rosburg USA (WA) 232 Dj22
Roscales E 26 Kq52
Roščino RUS 52 Mf15
Roscoff F 22 Kr42
Roscommon IRL 18 Km37
Roscrea IRL 20 Kn38
Rose SCG 46 Lt48
Rose USA (NE) 240 Fa24
Roseau USA (MN) 238 Fc21
Roseau WD 261 Gk38
Rose BlacheHarbour Le Cou CDN (NF) 245 Ha22
Rosebud AUS (VIC) 153 Sc65
Rosebud USA (SD) 240 Ek24
Rosebud Ind. Res. USA 240 Ek24
Rosebud River CDN 233 Ed20
Roseburg USA (OR) 234 Dj24
Rose Creek CDN 233 Ec19
Rosedale AUS (QLD) 149 Sf57
Rosedale USA (MS) 243 Fe29
Rosedown Plantation USA 243 Fe30
Rose Harbour CDN (BC) 232 De19
Rose Hill = Beau-Bassin MS 221 Nj56
Rosehill Gardens AUS (NSW) 153 Sf62
Roseires Reservoir SUD 197 Mh42
Rosemont Plantation USA 243 Fe30
Rosenberg USA (TX) 243 Fc31
Rosendal N 12 Lg31
Rosendal ZA 217 Md60
Rosengarten D 32 Lk37
Rosenheim D 35 Ln43
Rose Point CDN 231 De18
Rose Prairie CDN (BC) 231 Dk17
Rose River AUS 139 Rh52
Roses E 30 Ld48
Roseto degli Abruzzi I 42 Lp48
Rosetown CDN (SK) 233 Eg20
Rosetta ET 177 Mf30
Rose Valley CDN (SK) 238 Ej19
Rosewood AUS (NT) 138 Re54
Rosh Pinah NAM 216 Lj59
Roshtkhar IR 73 Nk28
Roșia RO 44 Mc44
Roșia de Secaș RO 44 Md44
Roșia Nouă RO 44 Mc44
Rosica BG 45 Mh47
Rosice CZ 38 Lr41
Rosignano Marittimo I 40 Ll47
Rosignano Solvay I 40 Ll47
Rosignol GUY 271 Hb42
Roșiori RO 44 Mb43
Roșiori de Vede RO 45 Me46
Roskilde DK 14 Ln35
Roskilde Rockfestival DK 14 Ln35
Roslagen S 13 Lt30
Roslavl' RUS 52 Mg19
Rosman USA (NC) 249 Fj28
Rosmead ZA 217 Mc61
Rosolini I 42 Lp54
Rosoman MK 46 Mb49
Rosporden F 22 Kr43
Rossano I 43 Lr51
Rossan Point IRL 18 Km36
Rossarden AUS (TAS) 152 Sd66
Ross Bay Jtn. CDN (NF) 244 Gg19
Ross-Bethio SN 183 Kb37
Ross Ice Shelf ANT 296 Bd35
Rössing NAM 212 Lh57
Rössing Uranium Mine NAM 212 Lh57
Ross Island CDN 238 Fb18
Ross Lake USA 232 Dk21
Rosslare IRL 20 Ko38
Rosslare Harbour IRL 20 Ko38
Roßlau D 33 Ln39
Rosso RIM 183 Kc37
Ross-on-Wye GB 21 Ks39
Rossoš' RUS 53 Mk20
Rossouw ZA 217 Md61
Rossport CDN (ON) 239 Fg21
Ross River CDN (YT) 231 Dd15
Ross River CDN 231 De14
Ross Sea ANT 296 Bd33
Rosston USA (AR) 243 Fd29
Rosston USA (OK) 242 Fa27
Røssvatnet N 10 Lh13
Rossville AUS (QLD) 147 Sc53
Rosswood CDN (BC) 231 Df18
Rosswood Plantation USA 243 Fe30
Røst N 10 Lg12
Rostaq AFG 78 Oe27
Rostaq IR 74 Ng32
Rosthern CDN (SK) 233 Eg19
Roštkala TJ 77 Of27
Rostock D 33 Ln36
Rostov RUS 52 Mk17
Rostov-na-Donu RUS 55 Mk22
Rostrenen F 22 Kr42
Røsvik N 10 Lh12
Roswell USA (GA) 249 Fh28
Roswell USA (NM) 237 Eh29
Rot S 13 Lp29
Rota E 28 Ko46
Rota USA 119 Sb16
Rot am See D 34 Ll41
Rotenburg D 32 Lk39
Rotenburg (Wümme) D 32 Lk37
Roth D 35 Lm41
Rothenburg (Tauber) D 34 Ll41
Rothera ANT (UK) 296 Gc32
Rotherham GB 21 Kt37
Rothesay GB 19 Kp35
Rothschild USA (WI) 246 Ff23
Rothwell GB 21 Kt37
Roti RI 132 Rb51
Roti RI 132 Rb51
Rotifunk WAL 192 Kd41
Roto AUS (NSW) 153 Sc62
Rotoava F (PYF) 165 Ch54
Rotondella I 43 Lr50
Rotorua NZ 154 Tj65
Rotsskildery ZA 216 Ma61
Rotsskilderye RB 213 Mc58
Rott D 35 Ln42
Rotten CH 34 Lj44
Rottenburg D 34 Lj42
Rottenburg D 35 Ln42
Rotterdam NL 32 Le39
Rottnaälven S 12 Ln30
Rottne S 15 Lp33
Rottnen S 15 Lq34
Rottneros S 13 Lo31
Rottnest Island AUS 144 Qh61
Rottumeroog NL 32 Lg37
Rottumerplaat NL 32 Lg37
Rottweil D 34 Lj42
Rotuma FJI 157 Td21
Rötz D 35 Ln41
Roualist Bank 117 Qc41
Roubaix F 23 Ld40
Roudnice nad Labe CZ 38 Lp40
Rouen F 22 Lb41
Rougemont F 23 Lg43
Rough Rock USA (AZ) 237 Ef27
Rouhia TN 174 Le28
Rouillac F 24 Ku45
Roulans F 23 Lg43
Round Mountain AUS 151 Sg61
Round Mountain USA (TX) 242 Fa30
Round Pd. CDN 245 Hb21
Round Rock USA (AZ) 237 Ef27
Round Rock USA (TX) 242 Fb30
Roundup USA (MT) 235 Ef22
Round Valley Ind. Res. USA 234 Dj26
Roura F (GF) 271 Hd43
Rousay GB 19 Kr31
Roussillon F 25 Le45
Roussillon F 25 Lf47
Route 62 ZA 216 Lk62
Route 66 USA 241 Ff26
Route 66 (Missouri) USA 243 Fd27
Route 66 Mus. USA 242 Fa28
Route 66 (New Mexico) USA 237 Eh28
Route 66 (New Mexico) USA 242 Eh28
Route 66 S.P. USA 241 Fe26
Route des Crêtes F 23 Lg43
Route des Grandes Alpes F 25 Lg46
Route des Kasbahs MA 172 Kg30
Route Napoléon F 25 Lg47
Route transsaharienne DZ/RN 180 Lc35
Rouxville ZA 217 Md61
Rouyn-Noranda CDN (QC) 239 Ga21
Rova d'Antongona RM 220 Nd55
Rovaniemi FIN 11 Mc12
Rovato I 40 Lk45
Roveň SK 39 Mb41
Roven'ki RUS 53 Mk21
Rover USA (AR) 243 Fd28
Rovereto I 40 Lm45
Röverhagen D 33 Ln36
Roverud N 12 Ln30
Rovigo I 40 Lm45
Rovinari RO 44 Md46
Rovine di Roselle I 40 Lm48
Rovinj HR 41 Lo45
Rovnoe RUS 53 Nd20
Rów PL 36 Lp38
Rowena AUS (NSW) 151 Se60

Rowley Shoals – Saint Charles

Rowley Shoals AUS 136 Qd22
Rowy PL 36 Ls36
Roxas RP 121 Ra37
Roxas RP 121 Ra39
Roxas RP 122 Qk40
Roxas RP 123 Rb40
Roxboro USA (NC) 249 Ga27
Roxborough Downs AUS (QLD) 148 Rk57
Roxby Downs AUS (SA) 152 Rj61
Roxen S 13 Lq32
Roy USA (MT) 235 Ef22
Roy USA (NM) 237 Eh28
Roy USA (UT) 235 Ed25
Royal Bardia N.P. NEP 88 Pa31
Royal Botanic Gardens GB 21 Ku39
Royal Canal IRL 20 Kn37
Royal Chitwan N.P. NEP 88 Pc32
Royal Citadel (Polonnaruwa) CL 111 Pa43
Royal City USA (WA) 232 Ea22
Royal Exhibition Building and Carlton Gardens AUS (VIC) 153 Sc64
Royal Gorge USA 235 Eh26
Royal Manas N.P. BHT 112 Pf32
Royal N.P. AUS 153 Sf63
Royal Palace RI 129 Qk50
Royal Palm Beach USA (FL) 250 Fk32
Royal Pavilion GB 21 Ku40
Royal Randwick AUS (NSW) 153 Sf62
Royal Sukla Phanta N.P. NEP 88 Pa31
Royal Tombs VN 115 Qd37
Royal Tunbridge Wells GB 21 La39
Royan F 24 Kt45
Roye F 23 Lc41
Roy Hill AUS (WA) 140 Qk57
Røyken N 12 Ll31
Røykfossen N 10 Ma11
Røyrvik N 10 Lg13
Royston GB 21 Ku38
Royston USA (GA) 249 Fj28
Roza BG 47 Mg48
Rozafa AL 46 Lu48
Rožaj SCG 46 Ma48
Różan PL 37 Mb38
Rozay-en-Brie F 23 Lc42
Rozdeevka RUS 98 Re20
Rozdil'na UA 45 Ml44
Rozdol'ne UA 54 Mg23
Rožencovo RUS 53 Nd17
Rozengain RI 130 Rf48
Roženski manastir BG 46 Md49
Rozivka UA 55 Mj22
Rožmitál pod Třemšínem CZ 38 Lo41
Rožňava SK 39 Ma42
Rožnov pod Radhoštěm CZ 38 Lt41
Rozogi PL 37 Mb37
Rožok RUS 53 Nb18
Rozoy-sur-Serre F 23 Le41
Rozprza PL 37 Lu39
Roztoczański P.N. PL 37 Md40
Roztoky CZ 38 Lp40
Rozvadov CZ 38 Ln41
Rožyšče UA 37 Mf40
Rrogozhinë AL 46 Lu49
Rtiščevo RUS 53 Nb19
Rt Kamenjak HR 41 Lo46
Rt Ploča HR 41 Lq47
Ruacana NAM 208 Lh54
Ruacana Falls NAM 212 Lh54
Ruaha N.P. EAT 207 Mh49
Ruahine Range NZ 154 Tj66
Ruang RI 130 Rc44
Ruangwa EAT 211 Mk51
Ruapehu, Mount NZ 154 Th65
Ruapuke Island NZ 155 Te69
Ruatoria NZ 154 Tk64
Ruba BY 52 Mf18
Rubafu EAT 201 Mf46
Rubbestadneset N 12 Lf31
Rubcovsk RUS 85 Pa20
Rubeho Mountains EAT 207 Mj49
Rubengera RWA 206 Me47
Rubens RA 294 Ge71
Rubeshibe J 99 Sb24
Rubi RDC 201 Mc44
Rubi RDC 201 Mc44
Rubiás E 26 Kn53
Rubiataba BR (GO) 282 Hf53
Rubinéia BR (SP) 286 He56
Rubino CI 193 Kh42
Rubío YV 268 Gd42
Rubondo N.P. EAT 206 Mf47
Rubuga EAT 206 Mg48
Ruby USA (AK) 229 Cc13
Ruby USA (WA) 232 Eb21
Ruby USA 235 Ed23
Ruby Lake USA 234 Ec25
Ruby Mts. USA 234 Ec25
Ruby Mts. Scenic Area USA 234 Ec25
Ruby Range CDN 231 Da15
Rubys Inn USA (UT) 236 Ed27
Rubyvale AUS (QLD) 149 Sd57
Ruby Valley USA (NV) 234 Ec25
Rucachoroi, Cerro RA 292 Ge65
Rucăr RO 45 Mf45
Rucava LV 17 Mb34
Rucheng CHN (HUN) 97 Qg33
Ruciane-Nida PL 37 Mb37
Rud IR 73 Oa28
Ruda S 15 Lr33
Rudall AUS (SA) 152 Rj62
Rudall River N.P. AUS 141 Rb57
Rudarpur IND (UPH) 107 Pb32
Ruda Śląska PL 36 Lt40
Rudauli IND (UPH) 107 Pa32
Rudayba SUD 190 Mf39
Rudbar AFG 78 Ob30
Rudbar IR 72 Ne27
Rude HR 41 Lq45
Rud-e Atrak IR 73 Nh27
Rud-e Bampur IR 75 Nk32
Rud-e Dez IR 72 Ne29
Rud-e Helle IR 74 Ng31
Rud-e Helmand AFG 78 Ob30
Rudehen IR 72 Nf28
Rud-e Kal-e Šur IR 73 Nj27
Rud-e Karun IR 72 Ne29
Rud-e Koja IR 75 Oa33
Rud-e Kor IR 74 Ng30
Rud-e Kul IR 75 Nh32
Rud-e Marun IR 74 Ne30
Rud-e Mehran IR 74 Nh32
Rud-e Mond IR 74 Ng31
Rud-e Polvar IR 74 Ng30
Rud-e Qesel Owzan IR 72 Ne27
Rüdersdorf D 33 Lo38
Rüdesheim D 34 Lh41
Rudhauli IND (UPH) 107 Pb32
Rudi MD 45 Mh42
Rudilla E 29 Kt50
Rudinka HR 41 Lq46
Rūdiškės LT 17 Me36
Rudka UA 37 Mf39
Rudka-Červyns'ka UA 37 Mf39
Rudkøbing DK 14 Ll36
Rudky UA 39 Md41
Rudna Glava SCG 44 Mc46
Rudnaja Pristan' RUS 99 Rh23
Rudnichnyi KZ 84 Ok23
Rudnik BG 47 Mh48
Rudnik SCG 46 Ma46
Rudniki PL 36 Lt39
Rudnja RUS 52 Mf18
Rudnyj KZ 58 Oa08
Rudo BIH 46 Lu47
Rudolstadt D 33 Lm40
Rudong CHN (JGS) 102 Ra29
Rudrapur IND (UTT) 107 Ok31
Rud Sar IR 72 Nf27
Rue F 23 Lb40
Rueda E 26 Kq51
Ruen BG 47 Mh48
Ruente Nacional CO 268 Gd43
Ruetz A 35 Lm43
Rufa'a SUD 190 Mg39
Ruffec F 24 La44
Rufiji EAT 207 Mk49
Rufino BR (PA) 275 Hb46
Rufino RA (SF) 289 Gj63
Rufisque SN 183 Kb38
Rufrufua RI 130 Rg47
Rufunsa Z 210 Me53
Rugaga EAT 207 Mj48
Rugāji LV 17 Mh33
Ruganga EAT 207 Mh50
Rugao CHN (JGS) 102 Ra29
Rugby GB 21 Kt38
Rugby USA (ND) 238 Ek21
Rügen D 33 Lo36
Rugheiwa SUD 190 Mf38
Rugles F 22 La42
Rugombo BU 206 Me47
Rugovska klisura SCG 46 Ma48
Rugozi EAT 206 Mg47
Rugufu EAT 206 Mf48
Ruguj RUS 52 Mg16
Ruhan' RUS 52 Mg19
Ruhengeri RWA 201 Me46
Ruhland D 33 Lo39
Ruhner Berg D 33 Lm37
Ruhnu saar EST 17 Md33
Ruhr D 32 Lh39
Ruhudji EAT 207 Mh50
Ruhuhu EAT 207 Mh50
Rui'an CHN (ZJG) 102 Ra32
Rui Barbosa BR (BA) 283 Hk52
Ruichang CHN (JGX) 102 Qh31
Ruicheng CHN (SAX) 95 Qf28
Ruidera E 29 Ks48
Ruidosa USA (TX) 237 Eh30
Ruidoso USA (NM) 237 Eh29
Ruijin CHN (JGX) 97 Qj33
Ruiki RDC 201 Mc46
Ruili CHN (YUN) 113 Pj33
Ruines d'Assodé RN 180 Le36
Ruines de Loropéni BF 193 Kj40
Ruïnes d'Empúries E 30 Ld48
Ruines de Ouara TCH 189 Ma38
Ruins of Aksum ETH 191 Mk39
Ruins of Fort Craig USA 237 Eg29
Ruins of Sambor K 115 Qc39
Ruins of Windsor USA 243 Fe30
Ruiru EAK 204 Mj46
Ruitersbos ZA 216 Mb62
Ruiz, Nevado de CO 268 Gc43
Ruiz MEX (SL) 252 Ef33
Ruiz Cortines, P. A. MEX 252 Ef32
Rūjiena LV 17 Mf33
Rukanga EAK 207 Mk47
Ruki RDC 195 Lh46
Rukube EAT 206 Mg47
Rule USA (TX) 242 Fa29
Rulenge EAT 206 Mf47
Ruleville USA (MS) 243 Fe29
Rum GB 18 Ko33
Ruma SCG 44 Lu45
Ruma WAN 186 Ld39
Rumah KSA 67 Nd33
Rumah Anyi MAL 126 Qg45
Rumah Kulit MAL 126 Qh44
Rumah Layang MAL 126 Qf45
Rumah Maya MAL 126 Qg44
Rumahtinggih RI 158 Sa49
Ruma N.P. EAK 204 Mh46
Rumayn YE 68 Nb37
Rumbek SUD 197 Me42
Rumberpon RI 131 Rh46
Rumboci BIH 41 Ls47
Rumburk CZ 33 Lp40
Rum Cay BS 251 Gc34
Rumeila SUD 190 Mh40
Rumford USA (ME) 247 Ge23
Rumia PL 36 Lt36
Rumilly F 25 Lf45
Rumoi J 99 Sa24
Rumphi MW 210 Mg51
Rumpi Hills CAM 194 Le43
Rumšiškės LT 17 Me36
Rumuruti EAK 204 Mj45
Run RI 130 Re48
Runan CHN (HNN) 102 Qh29
Runcorn GB 21 Ks37
Runde N 12 Lf28
Runde ZW 214 Mf56
Rundfloen N 12 Ln29
Rundu NAM 209 Lk54
Runduma RI 127 Rc48
Runesten DK 14 Lk35
Rungsted DK 14 Ln35
Rungu RDC 201 Md44
Rungu RDC 201 Me44
Rungwa EAT 206 Mg49
Rungwa EAT 206 Mf49
Rungwa EAT 206 Mg49
Rungwa Game Reserve EAT 207 Mh49
Rungwe, Mount EAT 207 Mh50
Runiz IR 74 Ng31
Runmarö S 13 Lt31
Runn S 13 Lq30
Runni IND (BIH) 107 Pc32
Runtuna S 13 Ls32
Runzewe EAT 206 Mf47
Ruokojärvi FIN 11 Mc12
Ruokolahti FIN 16 Mj29
Ruoqiang CHN (XUZ) 87 Pe26
Ruo Shui CHN 92 Pk25
Ruovesi FIN 16 Me29
Rupanyup AUS (VIC) 153 Sb64
Rupat RI 124 Qa45
Rupawati IND (GUJ) 108 Og34
Rupe HR 41 Lq47
Rupea RO 45 Mf44
Rupert USA (ID) 235 Ed24
Rupia EAT 207 Mj50
Rupia EAT 207 Mj50
Ruppert Coast 296 Cd34
Rupsi ZW 214 Mg56
Rur D 32 Lg40
Rura IND (UPH) 107 Ok32
Rurópolis Presidente Médici BR (PA) 275 Hc48
Rurrenabaque BOL 279 Gg53
Rurum WAN 186 Le40
Rušan TJ 77 Of27
Rusape ZW 214 Mg55
Rusava UA 45 Mj42
Ruse BG 47 Mf47
Rusenski Lom, N.P. BG 47 Mg47
Rusera IND (BIH) 112 Pd33
Rushan CHN (SDG) 100 Ra27
Rushden GB 21 Ku38
Rushinga ZW 210 Mg54
Rushungi EAT 207 Mk50
Rushville USA (NE) 240 Ej24
Rusizi, P.N.de BU 206 Me47
Rusk USA (TX) 243 Fc30
Rusken S 15 Lp33
Rusnė LT 17 Mb35
Ruso THA 117 Qa42
Ruso USA (ND) 240 Ek22
Russas BR (CE) 277 Jb48
Russell CDN (MB) 238 Ek20
Russell NZ 154 Th63
Russell USA (KS) 240 Fa26
Russell Fiord USA 231 Da16
Russell Islands SOL 161 Sk50
Russell Lake CDN 238 Ek17
Russell Lake USA 249 Fj28
Russell, Mount USA (AK) 229 Ce14
Russell Springs USA (KS) 240 Ek26
Russellville USA (AL) 248 Fg28
Russel Range AUS 145 Rb62
Rüsselsheim D 34 Lj41
Russelville USA (AR) 243 Fd28
Russia RUS 57 Oa03
Russkaja ANT (RUS) 296 Da33
Russkij Kameškir RUS 53 Nd19
Russkiy Sever N.P. RUS 11 Mk15
Russlleville USA (KY) 248 Fg27
Rust A 35 Lr43
Rustavi GE 70 Nc25
Rust de Winter ZA 213 Me58
Rust de Winterdam ZA 213 Me58
Rust de Winter Nature Reserve ZA 214 Me58
Rust de Winter Nature Reserve ZA 217 Me58
Rustenburg GUY 271 Hb43
Rustenburg ZA 213 Md58
Rustenburg Nature Reserve ZA 217 Md58
Rusterfjelbma N 11 Me10
Ruston USA (LA) 243 Fd29
Rusumu EAT 206 Mf47
Rusumu Falls EAT 206 Mf47
Ruszów PL 36 Lq39
Rutana BU 206 Me47
Rute E 28 Kq47
Ruteng RI 129 Ra50
Rutenga ZW 214 Mf56
Rutete EAT 207 Mj50
Rutford Ice Stream 296 Fd34
Rüthen D 32 Lj39
Rutherfordton USA (NC) 249 Fj28
Ruthin GB 21 Kr37
Ruti PNG 159 Sc48
Rutigliano I 43 Lr49
Rutka-Tartak PL 37 Mc36
Rutland USA (VT) 247 Gd24
Rutland Island IND 111 Pg40
Rutland Plains AUS (QLD) 146 Sa53
Rutledalen N 12 Lf29
Rutog CHN (TIB) 88 Ok29
Rutshuru RDC 201 Me46
Rutukira EAT 207 Mh51
Rutul RUS (DAG) 70 Nd25
Ruunaankosket FIN 11 Mf14
Ruvo di Púglia I 43 Lr49
Ruvu EAT 207 Mk49
Ruvu EAT 207 Mk49
Ruvubu EAT 201 Mf47
Ruvubu, P.N.de la BU 206 Mf47
Ruvuma EAT/MOC 211 Mj51
Ruvu Remiti EAT 207 Mj48
Ruwais UAE 74 Ng33
Ruwenzori RDC/EAU 204 Me45
Ruwenzori Mountains N.P. EAU 204 Me45
Ruya ZW 210 Mf54
Ruyang CHN (HNN) 95 Qg28
Ru-ye Sang AFG 78 Od28
Ruyigi BU 206 Mf47
Ruyuan CHN (GDG) 97 Qg33
Ruza RUS 52 Mj18
Ruzaevka RUS 53 Nc18
Ružany BY 37 Me38
Ruzhou CHN (HNN) 95 Qg28
Ružomberok SK 39 Lu41
Rwanda 167 Ma10
Rwindi RDC 201 Me46
Ry DK 14 Lk34
Ryan USA (OK) 242 Fb29
Ryan, Mount AUS 153 Se62
Rybachye KZ 84 Pa22
Rybačij RUS 17 Ma35
Rybczewice PL 37 Mc39
Rybinsk RUS 52 Mk16
Rybinsk Reservoir RUS 52 Mk16
Rybnik PL 36 Lt40
Rybnik PL 37 Md37
Rybno PL 37 Mb37
Rybnoe RUS 53 Mk18
Rybreka RUS 11 Mh15
Rychłocice PL 36 Lt39
Rychnowo PL 37 Ma37
Rychtal PL 36 Ls39
Rychwał PL 36 Lt38
Ryd S 15 Lp34
Rydaholm S 15 Lp34
Rydberg Peninsula 296 Ga33
Ryde GB 21 Kt40
Rydet S 14 Lm33
Rydsnäs S 15 Lq33
Rydzewo PL 37 Mb37
Rye GB 21 La40
Ryegate USA (MT) 235 Ef22
Ryggsteinhavet N 12 Le29
Rykene N 12 Lj32
Ryke Yseøyane N 11 Mc07
Ryki PL 37 Mb39
Ryl'sk RUS 52 Mh20
Rymań PL 36 Lq37
Rymanów PL 39 Mb41
Rymanów-Zdrój PL 39 Mb41
Rýmařov CZ 38 Ls41
Rymättylä FIN 16 Mb30
Ryn PL 37 Mb37
Ryn-kum KZ 53 Nd21
Ryohakusanchi J 101 Rj27
Ryongthong Temple PRK 100 Rd26
Ryotsu J 101 Rk26
Rypin PL 37 Lu37
Rysjedalsvika N 12 Lf29
Rytterknægten DK 15 Lp35
Ryukyu Islands J 83 Ra13
Ryukyu Trench J 83 Rb14
Rząśnik PL 37 Mb38
Rzecznica PL 36 Ls37
Rzepin PL 36 Lp38
Rzeszów PL 37 Mb40
Ržev RUS 52 Mh17
Ržyščiv UA 54 Mf21

S

Sa PNG 159 Sc48
Sa RMM 184 Kh38
Saa CAM 195 Lf43
Sa'a SOL 161 Ta50
Saacow = Jilib SP 205 Nb45
Saadani National Park EAT 207 Mk48
Saaifontein ZA 216 Ma61
Saalbach A 35 Ln43
Saalburg D 34 Lj40
Saale D 33 Lm40
Saalfeld D 33 Lm40
Saalfelden am Steinernen Meer A 35 Ln43
Saam IR 75 Oa31
Saan SYR 64 Mj28
Saanich CDN (BC) 232 Dj21
Saar D 34 Lg41
Saaraaray SP 205 Nc44
Saarbrücken D 34 Lg41
Saarburg D 34 Lg41
Sääre EST 17 Mc33
Saaremaa EST 16 Mc32
Saari FIN 16 Mk29
Saarijärvi FIN 11 Mc14
Saaristomeren kansallispuisto = Skärgårdshavets n.p. FIN 16 Mb31
Saarland D 34 Lg41
Saarlouis D 34 Lg41
Saarschleife D 34 Lg41
Šaartuz TJ 76 Oe27
Saas Fee CH 34 Lh44
Saatli AZ 70 Ne26
Saba NL (NA) 261 Gj37
Šabac SCG 44 Lu46
Sabadell E 30 Lc49
Sabah MAL 122 Qj43
Sabaiya SUD 196 Md42
Sabak MAL 117 Qa44
Sabalana RI 129 Qk49
Sabalanung RI 126 Qj44
Sabalgarh IND (MPH) 107 Oj32
Sabaluka Game Reserve SUD 190 Mg38
Saba Marine Park NL (NA) 261 Gj37
Sabana C 259 Gc35
Sabana CO 273 Gd46
Sabana SME 271 Hc43
Sabana de Cardona YV 269 Gg42
Sabana de la Mar DOM 260 Gf36
Sabana Grande YV 269 Ge41
Sabanalarga CO 268 Gc40
Sabanalarga CO 268 Gc42
Sabanalarga CO 268 Gd43
Sabana San Francisco MEX (QTR) 255 Ff36
Sabancaya, Volcán PE 279 Ge53
Sabancuy MEX (CAM) 255 Fe36
Sabaneta CO 268 Gd42
Sabaneta DOM 260 Ge36
Sabaneta YV 269 Gf40
Sabaneta YV 269 Gf41
Sabang RI 116 Ph43
Sabang RI 127 Qk45
Sabang RP 122 Qk40
Sabang Beach RP 123 Rc41
Sabanillas MEX (COH) 253 Ek33
Şabanözü TR 51 Mo50
Şabanözü TR 51 Mn51
Sabará BR (MG) 287 Hj55
Sabarat F 24 Lb47
Sabarei EAK 198 Mj43
Sabari GH 193 La41
Sabari IND 109 Pa36
Sabarmati IND 108 Og34
Sabaru RI 129 Qk49
Sabatinivka UA 45 Ml42
Sabatti RI 124 Pk46
Sabáudia I 42 Lo49
Sabaya BOL 284 Gf55
Saba Yoi THA 116 Qa42
Sabbioneta I 40 Ll45
Sabena Desert EAK 205 Mk45
Saberania RI 131 Rk47
Sabeugukgung RI 124 Qa47
Sabha LAR 181 Lh32
Sabidug RP 121 Ra35
Sabie MOC 214 Mg58
Sabie ZA 214 Mf58
Sabi Island MYA 116 Pk40
Sabile LV 17 Mc33
Sabiñánigo E 27 Ku52
Sabinas MEX (COH) 253 Ek32
Sabinas Hidalgo MEX (NL) 253 Ek32
Sabine USA 243 Fd30
Sabine Land N 11 Lk06
Sabine N.F. USA 243 Fc30
Sabine N.W.R. USA 243 Fd31
Sabine Pass USA (TX) 243 Fd31
Sabine Peninsula CDN 225 Eb03
Sabino BR (SP) 286 Hf56
Sabinópolis BR (MG) 287 Hj55
Sabinosa E 178 Ka32
Sabinov SK 39 Mb41
Sabirabad AZ 70 Ne26
Sabkhat ad Dabbiyah KSA 67 Ne32
Sabkhat al Hayshah LAR 175 Lh30
Sabkhat ar Riyas KSA 67 Ne32
Sabkhat el Bardawil ET 177 Mg30
Sabkhat Ghuzayyil LAR 175 Lk31
Sabkhat Hawaza KSA 64 Mk30
Sabkhat Matti UAE 74 Nf34
Sabkhat Mujazzam LAR 174 Lf30
Sabkhat Shunayn LAR 175 Ma30
Sabkhat Tawurgha LAR 175 Lh29
Sabkhat Umm al 'Izam LAR 175 Lh30
Šabla BG 47 Mj47
Sablayan RP 121 Ra39
Sable Island CDN 245 Gk23
Sable Island Bank 245 Gk24
Sablé-sur-Sarthe F 22 Ku43
Sa Boat THA 114 Qa38
Saboba GH 193 La41
Saboeiro BR (CE) 277 Ja49
Sabomi WAN 194 Lc42
Sabonagri RN 185 Lb39
Sabon Birni RN 186 Lb40
Sabon-Birni WAN 186 Ld39
Sabon Birnin Gwari WAN 186 Ld40
Sabongari CAM 195 Lf42
Sabongida WAN 194 Lc42
Sabon Kafi RN 186 Le38
Saborna crkva SCG 44 Ma46
Saborsko HR 41 Lq46
Sabou BF 185 Kj39
Sabratah LAR 174 Lg29
Sabres F 24 Ku46
Sabrina Coast 297 Ra32
Sabsé BF 185 Kk39
Sabtaev KZ 58 Ob09
Sabtang Island RP 121 Ra35
Sabuda RI 130 Rf47
Sabugal P 26 Kn50
Sabulubbek RI 124 Pk46
Sabuncupınar TR 50 Ml51
Säby S 15 Lp33
Sabya KSA 68 Nb37
Sabzakpass AFG 78 Ob28
Sabzevar IR 73 Nj27
Sacaba BOL 284 Gg54
Sacacama ANG 209 Ma52
Sacado do Humaitá BR (AM) 279 Gf49
Sacama CO 268 Gd42
Sacambanda ANG 209 Ma54
Sacambunge ANG 209 Mb51
Sacanche PE 278 Gb49
Sac and Fox Ind. Res. USA 241 Fd24
Sacandia ANG 202 Lh48
Sacanta RA (CD) 288 Gj61
Sacapulas GCA 255 Fe38
Sacco Uein SP 205 Nb45
Sacecorbo E 29 Ks50
Sacedón E 29 Ks50
Săcel RO 44 Me43
Săcele RO 45 Mf45
Săcele RO 45 Mj46
Săceni RO 45 Mf46
Sachang CHN (GZH) 96 Qd32
Sachayoj RA (SE) 289 Gk59
Sachida IND (ARP) 112 Pg32
Sachigo CDN (ON) 238 Fd19
Sachigo Lake CDN 238 Fd19
Sachigo River CDN 238 Fe18
Sachna BD 112 Pf33
Sachojere BOL 280 Gh53
Sachsen D 33 Lo39
Sachsen-Anhalt D 33 Lm38
Sachsenring D 33 Ln40
Sachs Harbour CDN 224 Dd04
Sächsische Schweiz, N.P. D 33 Lp40
Sachula ANG 209 Ma51
Saçıkara TR 62 Mg26
Sacile I 40 Ln45
Šack BY 52 Md19
Šack RUS 53 Na18
Šac'k UA 37 Md39
Sacks USA (AL) 248 Fh29
Šac'kyj pryrodnyj n.p. UA 37 Md39
Saco USA (ME) 247 Ge24
Saco USA (MT) 233 Eg21
Sacol Island RP 123 Rb42
Sacoşu Turcesc RO 44 Mb45
Sacramento BR (MG) 286 Hg55
Sacramento USA (CA) 234 Dk26
Sacramento USA 234 Dj25
Sacre ou Timalacia BR 280 Ha52
Sacro Monte di Ghiffa I 40 Lj45
Sacro Monte di Oropa I 40 Lh45
Sacro Monte di Serralunga di Crea I 40 Lj45
Sacro Monte di Soccorso I 40 Lk45
Sacro Monte di Valperga Canavese I 40 Lh45
Sacta BOL 280 Gh54
Săcueni RO 44 Mc43
Sacuriuina ou Ponte de Pedra BR 281 Hb52
Sacuunda ANG 209 Mb51
Sada E 26 Km53
Sada ZA 217 Md62
Sádaba E 27 Kt52
Sadabad IND (UPH) 107 Ok32
Sadabe RM 220 Nd55
Sadad SYR 64 Mj28
Sad Ad Dokan IRQ 65 Nc27
Sa'dah YE 68 Nb37
Sadai RI 125 Qd47
Sadala EST 16 Mg32
Sadam OM 75 Nj34
Sada-misaki J 103 Rg29
Sadani EAT 207 Mk49
Sadao THA 116 Qa42
Sadaseopet IND (APH) 108 Oj37
Sâdât City ET 177 Mf30
Sadau RI 126 Qf47
Sadaung MYA 113 Ph34
Sadda PK 79 Of29
Sadd-e Eskandar IR 72 Nh27
Saddle L. Ind. Res. CDN 233 Ee18
Saddle Mount USA 235 Ed24
Saddle Peak IND 111 Pg39
Saddle-Peaks VU 162 Te56
Sadd Malky KSA 68 Nb37
Sa Dec VN 117 Qc40
Sadh OM 69 Nh37
Sadi ETH 197 Mh41
Sadi ETH 198 Na43
Sadich IR 75 Nk33
Sadio SN 183 Kc38
Sadiola RMM 183 Ke39
Sadiqabad PK 81 Of31
Sadiya IND (ASM) 113 Ph32
Sadjoavato RM 219 Ne52
Sado-jima J 101 Rk27
Sadolangang RI 129 Qk49
Sadova RO 46 Md47
Sadovo BG 47 Me48
Sadovoe RUS 53 Nc22
Sado Yahiko Q.N.P. J 101 Rk27
Sadr el Hiltan ET 177 Mg30
Sadri IND (RJT) 106 Og33
Sadriddin-Aini-Park TJ 76 Oe26
Šadrinsk RUS 58 Oa07
Sadus KSA 67 Nd33
Sæbø N 12 Lg28
Sæby DK 14 Ll33
Săedinenie BG 47 Me48
Săedinenie BG 47 Mf48
Saelices E 29 Ks49
Saerra de São Domingos BR 282 Hg53
Sævareid N 12 Lf30
Safad ETH 191 Mj40
Safaha SUD 197 Md41
Safané BF 185 Kj39
Safara P 28 Kn48
Safed Koh PK 79 Of29
Saffaqah KSA 67 Nc33
Saffar Kalay AFG 78 Oc30
Säffle S 13 Ln31
Safford USA (AL) 248 Fg29
Safford USA (AZ) 237 Ef29
Saffron Walden GB 21 La38
Safi MA 172 Kf29
Safi TCH 187 Lj38
Safia PNG 159 Se50
Safipur IND (UPH) 107 Pa32
Safir YE 68 Nd38
Safita SYR 64 Mj28
Safonovo RUS 52 Mg18
Safotu WS 164 Bd52
Safranbolu TR 62 Mg25
Safwan IRQ 65 Nd30
Sâg RO 44 Mc43
Saga CHN (TIB) 88 Pc31
Saga J 103 Rf29
Saga RI 130 Rg47
Sagabari RMM 184 Kf39
Sagadi EST 16 Mg31
Sagadi SUD 190 Mg40
Sagai PK 78 Od30
Sagaing MYA 113 Ph35
Sagala RMM 184 Kg39
Sagalassos TR 51 Ml53
Sâgallou DJI 198 Nb40
Sagami-wan J 101 Rk28
Sagamu WAN 194 Lb42
Sagan CHN (XUZ) 86 Ok27
Šagan KZ 84 Ok20
Sagana EAK 204 Mj46
Sagar IND (KTK) 110 Oh39
Sagar IND (MPH) 109 Ok34
Sagaranten RI 128 Qd49
Sagard D 33 Lo36
Sagaredžo GE 70 Nc25
Sagaria BD 112 Pf34
Sagarmatha = Mount Everest NEP/CHN 88 Pd31
Sagarmatha N.P. NEP 88 Pd32
Sagarpara IND (WBG) 112 Pe33
Sagastyr RUS 59 Rb04
Sagata SN 183 Kb38
Sagauli IND (BIH) 107 Pc32
Sagay RP 123 Rb40
Sagd KSA 68 Na37
Sage USA (WY) 235 Ee25
Saggrenda N 12 Lk31
Saghand IR 72 Nh29
Saginaw USA (MI) 246 Fj24
Saginaw Bay USA 246 Fj24
Sagleipie LB 192 Kf42
Saglek Bay CDN 225 Gd07
Sagne RIM 183 Kd38
Šagonar RUS (TUV) 85 Pg20
Sagone F 31 Lj48
Sağpazar TR 51 Mp50
Sagra E 29 Ks47
Sagrada Família E 30 Lc49
Sagres P 28 Km46
Sagsag PNG 159 Se48
Sagu MYA 112 Ph35
Saguache USA (CO) 237 Eg26
Sagua deTánamo C 259 Gc35
Sagua la Grande C 258 Fk34
Saguaro N.P. USA 237 Ee29
Sagunt E 29 Ku49
Sagunto = Sagunt E 29 Ku49
Sagure ETH 198 Mk42
Sagvåg N 12 Lf31
Sagwara IND (RJT) 108 Oh34
Sa'gya CHN (TIB) 88 Pd31
Sahaba SUD 190 Mf37
Sahabad IND (UPH) 107 Ok31
Sahagún CO 268 Gc41
Sahagún E 26 Kp52
Saham OM 75 Nj33
Sahara 168 Kc14
Saharabedi IND (ORS) 112 Pd35
Sahara City = Medinet Sahara ET 177 Mg34
Saharanpur IND (UPH) 107 Oj31
Saharna Nouă MD 45 Mj43
Saharsa IND (BIH) 112 Pd33
Sahasinaka RM 220 Nd56
Sahaswan IND (UPH) 107 Ok31
Sahavato RM 220 Ne56
Sahave RM 220 Nd56
Sahawa IND (RJT) 106 Oh31
Sahechores E 26 Kp52
Saheib SUD 196 Mc40
Sahel 168 Lb15
Sahib PK 81 Of31
Sahibganj IND (JKD) 112 Pd33
Sahin TR 50 Mg49
Sahiwal PK 79 Og30
Sahiwal PK 79 Og30
Sah Kuh IR 72 Nh27
Sahl Abad IR 73 Nk29
Sahneh IR 72 Nd28
Sahoba UZ 76 Oc26
Sahoué G 194 Le45
Sahra' Marzuq LAR 181 Lg33
Sahra Surt LAR 175 Lj30
Šahr-e-Suhte IR 73 Oa30
Šahristan TJ 76 Oe26
Sahtaneh River CDN 231 Dk16
Šahtersk RUS 99 Sb21
Šahty RUS 55 Na22
Sahuaripa MEX (SO) 237 Ef31
Sahuaro MEX (SO) 236 Ed30
Sahuayo de J.Ma. Morelos MEX (MHC) 254 Ej35
Šahun'ja RUS 53 Nd17
Šahy SK 39 Lt42
Sai J 99 Sa25
Saibai Island AUS 146 Sb50
Sai Buri THA 117 Qa42
Sai-Cinza, T.I. BR 274 Ha49
Saïda DZ 173 La28
Saida RL 64 Mh29
Saidabad IND (UPH) 109 Pb33
Said Abu Bakr al-Mirgani ER 191 Mk39
Saidapuram IND (APH) 111 Ok39
Saïdia MA 173 Kj28
Saidor PNG 159 Sd48
Saidpur BD 112 Pe33
Saidpur IND (UPH) 109 Pb33
Saidu Sharif PK 79 Og28
Saidu stupas PK 79 Og28
Saidu stupas PK 79 Og28
Saigo J 101 Rg27
Saiha IND (MZR) 112 Pg34
Saihan Toroi CHN (NMZ) 92 Qa25
Sai Island Temple SUD 190 Mf36
Saikanosy Ampasindava RM 218 Nd52
Saikanosy Masoala RM 219 Nf53
Saikhoa Ghat IND (ASM) 113 Ph32
Saiki J 103 Rf29
Saillans F 25 Lf46
Sailolof RI 130 Rf46
Sailu IND (MHT) 109 Ok35
Saimaa FIN 16 Mj29
Saimenski kanal FIN/RUS 16 Mj29
Sain Alto MEX (ZCT) 253 Ej34
Saindak PK 80 Oa31
Sai Ngam THA 114 Pk37
Sainsbury Pt. CDN 239 Ga18
Saïnsoutou SN 183 Ke39
Saint Abb's Head GB 19 Ks35
Saint Adolphe CDN (MB) 238 Fb21
Saint-Affrique F 25 Lc47
Saint-Agrève F 25 Le46
Saint-Aignan F 22 Lb43
Saint Alban's CDN (NF) 245 Hc22
Saint Albans GB 21 Ku39
Saint Albans USA (VT) 247 Gd23
SaintAlbans USA (WV) 249 Fk26
Saint Albert CDN (AB) 233 Ed19
Saint Albert Dome PNG 158 Sb48
Saint-Alexandre CDN (QC) 244 Gf22
Saint-Amand-en-Puisaye F 23 Ld43
Saint-Amand-les-Eaux F 23 Ld40
Saint-Amand-Montrond F 23 Lc44
Saint-Ambroise CDN (QC) 244 Ge21
Saint-Ambroix F 25 Le46
Saint-Amé F 23 Lg42
Saint-Amour F 25 Lf44
Saint-André F (RE) 221 Nh56
Saint-André-de-Cubzac F 24 Ku45
Saint-André-de-l'Eure F 22 Lb42
Saint-André-les-Alpes F 25 Lg46
Saint Andrew CDN (NB) 245 Gg23
Saint Andrew's CDN (NF) 245 Ha22
Saint Andrews GB 19 Ks34
Saint Andrews GB 19 Ks34
Saint Anne GB 22 Ks41
Saint Anne Marine N.P. SY 219 Nh48
Saint Ann's Bay CDN 245 Gk22
Saint Anthony CDN 225 Ha08
Saint Anthony USA (ID) 235 Ee24
Saint-Antoine F 31 Lk48
Saint Arnaud AUS (VIC) 153 Sb64
Saint Arnaud NZ 155 Tg66
Saint-Aubin-d'Aubigné F 22 Kt42
Saint-Aubin-du-Cormier F 22 Kt42
Saint-Augustin CDN (QC) 245 Ha20
Saint Augustine USA (FL) 250 Fk31
Saint Augustine Beach USA (FL) 250 Fk31
Saint Austell GB 20 Kq40
Saint-Austremoine d'Issoire F 25 Ld45
Saint-Avold F 23 Lg41
Saint Barthélemy F (GL) 261 Gj37
Saint Bathans NZ 155 Te68
Saint-Beat F 24 La48
Saint Bees Head GB 19 Kr36
Saint Bees Islands AUS 149 Se56
Saint-Benoit F (RE) 221 Nh56
Saint-Benoît-du-Sault F 24 Lb44
Saint Bernard F (GF) 271 Hd43
Saint-Bertrand-de-Comminges F 24 La47
Saint-Bonnet F 25 Lg46
Saint Brendan's CDN (NF) 245 Hd21
Saint-Brévin-les-Pins F 22 Ks43
Saint-Brice-en-Cógles F 22 Kt42
Saint Bride's CDN (NF) 245 Hc22
Saint Bride's Bay GB 20 Kp39
Saint-Brieuc F 22 Ks42
Saint Brieux CDN (SK) 233 Eh19
Saint-Bruno CDN (QC) 244 Ge21
Saint-Calais F 22 La43
Saint-CaSaint-le-Guildo F 22 Ks42
Saint Catharines CDN (ON) 247 Ga24
Saint Catherine's Point GB 21 Kt40
Saint-Céré F 24 Lb46
Saint-Chamond F 25 Le45
Saint Charles USA (AR) 243 Fe28

Sankt Gilgen – Santiago Papasquiaro

Sankt Gilgen A 35 Lo43
Sankt Goar D 34 Lh40
Sankt Gotthard CH 34 Lj44
Sankt Ingbert D 34 Lh41
Sankt Jakob A 35 Ln44
Sankt Johann A 35 Ln43
Sankt Johann A 35 Lo43
Sankt Leon-Rot D 34 Lj41
Sankt Margrethen CH 34 Lk43
Sankt Martin CH 34 Lk44
Sankt Michael BY 52 Md19
Sankt Michaelisdonn D 32 Lk36
Sankt Moritz CH 34 Lk44
Sankt-Peterburg RUS 52 Mf16
Sankt Peter-Ording D 32 Lj36
Sankt Pölten A 35 Lq42
Sankt Sophia BY 52 Me18
Sankt Ulrich = Ortisei I 40 Lm44
Sankt Valentin A 35 Lp42
Sankt Veit an der Glan A 35 Lp44
Sankt Vika S 13 Ls32
Sankt Wendel D 34 Lh41
Sankuru RDC 203 Ma48
San Leo I 40 Ln47
San Leonardo de Yagüe E 27 Kr51
Sanlifan CHN (HUB) 102 Qh30
Şanlıurfa TR 63 Mk27
San Lorenzo BOL 285 Ha54
San Lorenzo EC 272 Fk46
San Lorenzo EC 272 Ga45
San Lorenzo HN 256 Fg39
San Lorenzo Tenochtitlan MEX 255 Fc37
San Lorenzo, Cerro PE 278 Ga49
San Lorenzo PE 279 Gf51
San Lorenzo PY 285 Hb58
San Lorenzo RA (CR) 289 Ha60
San Lorenzo RA (SF) 289 Gk62
San Lorenzo de Calatrava E 29 Kr48
San Lorenzo de El Escorial E 29 Kq50
San Lorenzo de El Escorial E 29 Kq50
San Lorenzo de la Parrilla E 29 Ks49
San Lourdes BOL 279 Gf51
Sanlúcar de Barrameda E 28 Ko46
Sanlúcar de Guadiana E 28 Kn47
San Lucas BOL 284 Gh56
San Lucas MEX (BCS) 252 Ef34
San Lucas USA (CA) 236 Dk27
San Lucas de Abajo MEX (ZCT) 253 Ej33
San Lúcido I 43 Lr51
San Luis C 259 Gc35
San Luis CO 268 Gc42
San Luis GCA 255 Ff37
San Luis MEX (BC) 236 Ec31
San Luis PE 278 Gb50
San Luis RA (SL) 288 Gg62
San Luis RA 267 Gc25
San Luis RCH 288 Gf59
San Luis USA (AZ) 236 Ec29
San Luis USA (CO) 237 Eh27
San Luis al Medio ROU 289 Hd62
San Luis de la Loma MEX (GUR) 254 Ek37
San Luis de la Paz MEX (GJT) 254 Ek35
San Luis del Cordero MEX (DGO) 253 Eh33
San Luis de Montagnes Belos BR (GO) 286 He54
San Luis de Palmar RA (CR) 289 Ha59
San Luis de Shuaro PE 278 Gc51
San Luis Gonzaga MEX (BCS) 252 Ee33
San Luis Obispo USA (CA) 236 Dk28
San Luis Potosí MEX (SLP) 253 Ek34
San Luis Potosí MEX 253 Ek34
San Luis Río Colorado MEX (SO) 236 Ec29
San Luis Valley USA 237 Eh27
Sanluri I 31 Lj51
San Manuel USA (AZ) 237 Ee29
San Marcelino RP 120 Ra38
San Marco I 40 Ln45
San Marco MEX (TB) 255 Fe37
San Marco in Lámis I 43 Lq49
San Marcos BR (PA) 276 Hf46
San Marcos CO 268 Gc41
San Marcos MEX (GUR) 254 Fa37
San Marcos MEX (GUR) 254 Fa37
San Marcos PE 278 Ga49
San Marcos USA (TX) 242 Fb31
San Mariano RP 121 Rb37
San Marino AUS (SA) 143 Rh60
San Marino RSM 40 Ln47
San Marino RSM 40 Ln47
San Martín BOL 280 Gj52
San Martín RA (CA) 288 Gh60
San Martín RA (MD) 288 Gf62
Sânmartin RO 45 Mf44
San Martín ANT (RA) 296 Gc32
San Martín 1 RA (FO) 285 Ha58
San Martín 2 RA (FO) 285 Ha58
San Martín de Frómista E 26 Kq52
San Martín de los Andes RA (NE) 292 Ge66
San Martín del Pimpollar E 26 Kp50
San Martín de Montalbán E 29 Kq49
San Martín de Valdeiglesias E 29 Kq50
San Martino di Castrozza I 40 Lm44
San Martín Texmelucan MEX (PUE) 254 Fa36
San Mateo CR 256 Fh41
San Mateo EC 272 Fk46
San Mateo USA (CA) 234 Dj27
San Mateo USA (NM) 237 Eg28
San Mateo YV 269 Gh41
San Mateo Ixtatán GCA 255 Fe38
San Matías BOL 285 Ha54
Sanmaur CDN (QC) 244 Gd22
Sanmen CHN (ZJG) 102 Ra31
Sanmen Wan CHN 102 Ra31
Sanmenxia CHN (HNN) 95 Qf28
San Miguel BOL 280 Gj54
San Miguel BOL 285 Gk54
San Miguel CO 272 Gb45
San Miguel CO 273 Ge45
San Miguel CO/EC 272 Gb45
San Miguel ES 255 Ff39
San Miguel MEX (COH) 253 Ej31
San Miguel MEX (JLC) 254 Ej35
San Miguel PA 257 Ga41
San Miguel PE 278 Ga49
San Miguel PE 278 Gd52
San Miguel RA (BA) 289 Ha63
San Miguel RA (CR) 289 Hb59
San Miguel RA (MD) 288 Gg62
San Miguel RP 121 Ra38
San Miguel RP 123 Rd41
San Miguel USA (AZ) 237 Ee30
San Miguel USA 236 Dk28
San Miguel Bay RP 121 Rb39
San Miguel de Allende MEX (GJT) 254 Ek35
San Miguel de Azapa RCH 284 Ge55
San Miguel de Baga C 259 Gb35
San Miguel de Huachi BOL 279 Gg53
San Miguel del Cantil MEX (DGO) 252 Eg33
San Miguel del Monte RA (BA) 289 Ha63
San Miguel de Salinas E 29 Ku47
San Miguel de Temoaya MEX (DGO) 253 Eh34
San Miguel de Tucumán RA (TU) 288 Gh59
San Miguel do Araguaia BR (GO) 281 He52
San Miguelito HN 255 Ff38
San Miguelito MEX (SO) 237 Ef30
San Miguelito NIC 256 Fh40
San Miguelito PA 257 Ga41
San Miguel Palmas MEX (QRT) 254 Fa35
San Miguel Suchixtepec MEX (OAX) 254 Fb37
Sânmihaiu de Câmpie RO 44 Me44
Sanming CHN (FJN) 102 Qj32
San Miniato I 40 Ll47
Sänna EST 16 Mg33
Sanna IND (CGH) 109 Pb34
San Narciso RP 121 Rb39
Sannaspos ZA 217 Md60
San Nicandro Gargánico I 42 Lq49
San Nicolás BOL 280 Gh53
San Nicolás MEX (SO) 252 Ef31
San Nicolás de la Joya MEX (CHH) 252 Eg32
San Nicolas de los Arrocos RA (BA) 289 Gk62
San Nicolás de los Garza MEX (NL) 253 Ek33
San Nicolas Island USA 236 Ea29
Sânnicolau Mare RO 44 Ma44
Sannieshof ZA 217 Mc59
Sanniki PL 37 Lu38
Sannohe J 101 Sa25
Sannou RG 192 Kd40
Sanok PL 39 Mc41
Sanokwelle LB 192 Kf42
San Onofre CO 268 Gc41
San Onofre USA (CA) 236 Eb29
Šanovo BG 47 Mf48
Sanoyie LB 192 Kf42
San Pablo BOL 280 Gj53
San Pablo CO 268 Gd42
San Pablo CO 272 Gb45
San Pablo EC 272 Ga46
San Pablo PE 278 Ga49
San Pablo RP 121 Ra38
San Pablo YV 269 Gg42
San Pablo de Huacareta BOL 285 Gj56
San Pablo de Lipez BOL 284 Gg56
San Paolo fuori le Mura I 42 Ln49
San Pascual RP 121 Rb39
San Pedro BH 255 Fg37
San Pedro CI 192 Kg43
San Pedro E 29 Ks48
San Pedro GCA 255 Fe37
San Pedro MEX (BC) 236 Ed31
San Pedro PE 272 Ga48
San Pedro PE 279 Ge51
San Pedro RA (BA) 289 Ha62
San Pedro RA (MI) 289 Hc59
San Pedro RA (PJ) 285 Gh58
San Pedro RA (SE) 288 Gh59
San Pedro RCH 284 Gf56
San Pedro RCH 292 Gd64
San Pedro YV 269 Gg43
San Pedro Amuzgos MEX (OAX) 254 Fa37
San Pedro Channel USA 236 Ea29
San Pedro de Atacama RCH 284 Gf57
San Pedro de Buena Vista BOL 284 Gh55
San Pedro de Cachi PE 278 Gc52
San Pedro de Colaloa RA (TU) 288 Gh59
San Pedro de Coris PE 278 Gc52
San Pedro de la Roca Castle = El Morro C 259 Gc35
San Pedro de las Colonias MEX (COH) 253 Ej33
San Pedro de la Soledad MEX (BCS) 252 Ef34
San Pedro de Lloc PE 278 Ga49
San Pedro del Norte NIC 256 Fh39
San Pedro del Paraná PY 289 Hb59
San Pedro del Pinatar E 29 Ku47
San Pedro de Quemez BOL 284 Gf56
San Pedro de Ycuamandiyú PY 285 Hb58
San Pedro d.M. DOM 260 Gf36
San Pedro Juchatengo MEX (OAX) 254 Fb37
San Pedro Norte RA (CD) 288 Gh61
San Pedro Sula HN 255 Ff38
San Pedro Tapanatepec MEX (OAX) 255 Fc37
San Pedro Totolapan MEX (OAX) 254 Fb37
San Pedro, Volcán RCH 284 Gf56
San Pellegrino Terme I 40 Lk45
Sanpoil River USA 232 Ea21
Sanpoku J 101 Rk26
San Policarpio RP 121 Rc39
Sanquhar GB 19 Kr35
Sanquianga, P.N. CO 272 Ga44
San Quintín MEX (BC) 236 Ec30
San Quintín MEX (CHP) 255 Fe37
San Quirico d'Orcia I 40 Lm47
San Rafael BOL 279 Gf52
San Rafael BOL 284 Gh54
San Rafael BOL 285 Gk54
San Rafael CO 273 Gg45
San Rafael CR 256 Fh40
San Rafael EC 272 Gb46
San Rafael MEX (BCS) 252 Ec32
San Rafael MEX (NL) 253 Ek33
San Rafael PE 278 Gb51
San Rafael RA (MD) 288 Gf63
San Rafael YV 268 Ge40
San Rafael de Atamaica YV 269 Gg42
San Rafael de Canagua YV 269 Ge41
San Rafael de Imataca YV 270 Gk42
San Rafael Desert USA 235 Ee26
San Rafael Glacier RCH 294 Gd69
San Rafael Knob USA 235 Ee26
San Ramón BOL 280 Gh53
San Ramón BOL 280 Gh52
San Ramón BOL 280 Gj53
San Ramón C 259 Gb35
San Ramón CR 256 Fh40
San Ramón MEX (QTR) 255 Ff35
San Ramón PE 272 Gb48
San Ramón PE 278 Gc51
San Ramón RA (LR) 288 Gg61
San Ramón ROU 289 Hc63
San Ramon RP 123 Ra42
San Ramón de la Nueva Orán RA (SA) 285 Gh57
San Remigio RP 123 Rb40
San Remo AUS (VIC) 153 Sc65
San Remo I 40 Lh47
San Rolando MEX (TM) 253 Fa34
San Roque E 28 Kp46
San Roque RA (CR) 289 Ha60
San Roque RP 121 Rc39
Sans Souci, Citadelle/ RH 259 Gd36
San Saba USA (TX) 242 Fa30
Sansalé RG 192 Kc40
San Salvador BS 251 Gc33
San Salvador ES 255 Ff39
San Salvador PE 273 Ge47
San Salvador RA (ER) 289 Ha61
San Salvador ROU 289 Hb62
San Salvador de Jujuy RA (PJ) 284 Gh58
San Salvador El Seco MEX (PUE) 254 Fb36
San Salvo I 42 Lp48
Sansanding RMM 184 Kh39
Sansanne-Mango TG 193 La40
Sansarpur IND (UPH) 107 Pa31
San Sebastián = Donostia E 27 Ks53
San Sebastián MEX (JLC) 253 Eh35
San Sebastián MEX (VC) 254 Fa35
San Sebastián RA (TF) 294 Gf72
San Sebastián USA (PR) 261 Gg36
San Sebastián de la Gomera E 178 Kb31
San Sebastián de los Reyes E 29 Kr50
San Sebastián Zinacatepec MEX (PUE) 254 Fb36
Sansepolcro I 40 Ln47
San Severino Marche I 41 Lo47
San Severo I 42 Lq49
Sansha CHN (FJN) 102 Ra32
Sansha Wan CHN 102 Qk32
Sanshui CHN (GDG) 97 Qg34
San Silvestre BOL 279 Gf51
San Silvestre YV 269 Ge41
San Simón BOL 280 Gj52
Sansing Most BIH 41 Lr46
Sanso RMM 192 Kg40
San Stéfano di Camastra I 42 Lp52
Sansui CHN (GZH) 96 Qe32
Sansundi RI 131 Rh46
Sansu-ri PRK 100 Rd25
Santa PE 278 Ga50
Santa PE 278 Ga50
Santa USA (ID) 232 Eb22
Santa Albertina BR (SP) 286 He55
Santa Amalia E 28 Ko49
Santa Ana BOL 280 Gh52
Santa Ana BOL 285 Gk54
Santa Ana BOL 285 Gh56
Santa Ana C 259 Ga35
Santa Ana CO 268 Gc41
Santa Ana EC 272 Fk46
Santa Ana EC 272 Ga47
Santa Ana ES 255 Ff38
Santa Ana MEX (SO) 237 Ee30
Santa Ana PE 273 Gd48
Santa Ana PE 278 Gc53
Santa Ana RA (MI) 289 Hc59
Santa Ana RP 121 Rb36
Santa Ana USA (CA) 236 Eb29
Santa Ana YV 268 Gd41
Santa Ana YV 269 Gh41
Santa Ana Island SOL 161 Tb51
Santa Anita MEX (BCS) 252 Ef34
Santa Anita MEX (COH) 253 Ej31
Santa Anita Park USA (CA) 236 Eb28
Santa Anna USA (TX) 242 Fa30
Santa Barbara BOL 280 Gk54
Santa Barbara BR (AM) 273 Gg48
Santa Barbara BR (MG) 287 Hj55
Santa Barbara CO 268 Gc43
Santa Bárbara E 29 Ks47
Santa Bárbara HN 255 Ff38
Santa Bárbara MEX (CHH) 252 Eh32
Santa Barbara RCH 292 Gd64
Santa Barbara USA (CA) 236 Ea28
Santa Bárbara YV 268 Ge42
Santa Bárbara YV 269 Gg44
Santa Bárbara YV 270 Gj41
Santa Barbara Channel USA 236 Dk28
Santa Bárbara de Casa E 28 Kn47
Santa Bárbara d'Oeste BR (SP) 286 Hg57
Santa Barbara Island USA 236 Ea29
Santa Birgitta Kapell S 15 Lr34
Santa Brigida BR (BA) 283 Ja50
Santa Catalina CO 268 Gc40
Santa Catalina PA 257 Fk42
Santa Catalina PE 278 Ga49
Santa Catalina PE 278 Gc49
Santa Catalina RA (PJ) 284 Gg56
Santa Catalina RA (SE) 288 Gh60
Santa Catalina RP 123 Rb41
Santa Catalina YV 269 Gf42
Santa Catalina YV 270 Gk41
Santa Catalina Island USA 236 Ea29
Santa Catarina BR 267 Hb24
Santa Catarina MEX (BC) 236 Ec31
Santa Catarina MEX (NL) 253 Ek33
Santa Cecília BR (SC) 290 He59
Santa Cecilia CR 256 Fh40
Santa Cesárea Terme I 43 Lt50
Santa Clara BR (AP) 275 He46
Santa Clara C 259 Ga34
Santa Clara MEX (DGO) 253 Ej33
Santa Clara RA (PJ) 285 Gh58
Santa Clara USA (UT) 236 Ed27
Santa Clara YV 269 Gh41
Santa Clara-a-Velha P 28 Km47
Santa Clara de Olimar ROU 289 Hc62
Santa Clara do Ingaí BR (RS) 290 Hd60
Santa Clara Ind. Res. USA 237 Eg28
Santa Clotilde PE 273 Gd47
Santa Coloma de Queralt E 30 Lb49
Santa Comba E 26 Km53
Santa Croce Camarina I 42 Lp54
Santa Cruz BOL 279 Gf53
Santa Cruz BR (ES) 287 Hk55
Santa Cruz BR (PA) 275 Hb47
Santa Cruz BR (PA) 275 Hd47
Santa Cruz BR (PE) 283 Hk50
Santa Cruz BR (RN) 277 Jb49
Santa Cruz BR (RO) 280 Gj50
Santa Cruz CR 256 Fh40
Santa Cruz MEX (NYT) 252 Eh35
Santa Cruz MEX (NYT) 253 Eh35
Santa Cruz PE 272 Gc48
Santa Cruz PE 278 Gb51
Santa Cruz RA 294 Gf71
Santa Cruz RA 267 Gb28
Santa Cruz RCH 288 Ge63
Santa Cruz RP 120 Qk38
Santa Cruz RP 121 Ra38
Santa Cruz RP 121 Ra39
Santa Cruz RP 121 Rb39
Santa Cruz RP 123 Rc42
Santa Cruz USA (CA) 234 Dj27
Santa Cruz YV 270 Gk42
Santa Cruz Cabrália BR (BA) 287 Ja54
Santa Cruz das Palmeiras BR (SP) 286 Hg56
Santa Cruz de Bucaral YV 269 Gf40
Santa Cruz de Campezo E 27 Ks52
Santa Cruz de la Palma E 178 Kb31
Santa Cruz de la Sierra BOL 285 Gj54
Santa Cruz del Norte C 258 Fk34
Santa Cruz del Quiché GCA 255 Fe38
Santa Cruz del Sur C 259 Ga35
Santa Cruz de Mompox CO 268 Gc41
Santa Cruz de Mudela E 29 Kr48
Santa Cruz de Succhabamba PE 278 Ga49
Santa Cruz de Tenerife E 178 Kb31
Santa Cruz d.J.R. MEX (GJT) 254 Ek35
Santa Cruz do Arari BR (PA) 276 Hf46
Santa Cruz do Rio Pardo BR (SP) 286 Hf57
Santa Cruz dos Milagres BR (PI) 277 Hj48
Santa Cruz do Sul BR (RS) 290 Hd60
Santa Cruz Island USA 236 Ea29
Santa Cruz Islands SOL 157 Tb21
Santa Cruz Verapaz GCA 255 Fe38
Santadi I 31 Lj51
Santa Eduwiges MEX (SO) 237 Ee31
Santa Elena EC 272 Fk47
Santa Elena MEX (COH) 253 Ej32
Santa Elena RA (ER) 289 Ha61
Santa Elena, Cerro RA 292 Gh68
Santa Elena RP 121 Rb38
Santa Elena YV 270 Gj41
Santa Elena de Uairén YV 270 Gk43
Santa Eleodora RA (BA) 289 Gj63
Santa Eufemia E 28 Kq48
Santa Eugenia E 26 Km52
Santa Eulalia E 29 Kt50
Santa Eulalia MEX (COH) 242 Ek31
Santa Eulália P 28 Kn48
Santa Eulària des Riu E 30 Lb52
Santa Fé BR (AM) 273 Gd48
Santa Fé BR (AM) 279 Gf50
Santa Fé C 258 Fj34
Santa Fe CO 268 Ge42
Santa Fé E 29 Kr47
Santa Fe MEX (BCS) 252 Ee33
Santa Fe MEX (CHH) 253 Ej31
Santa Fe PA 257 Fk41
Santa Fe PA 257 Ga41
Santa Fé RA (SF) 289 Gk61
Santa Fé RA 267 Gd25
Santa Fe RP 121 Rb39
Santa Fe USA (NM) 237 Eh28
Santa Fe de Antioquia CO 268 Gc42
Santa Fé de Minas BR (MG) 287 Hh54
Santa Fé do Sul BR (SP) 286 He56
Santa Filomena BR (PE) 283 Hk50
Santa Filomena BR (PI) 282 Hh50
Sant'Àgata di Militello I 42 Lp52
Santa Helena BR (AC) 279 Ge50
Santa Helena BR (MA) 276 Hh47
Santa Helena BR (PR) 286 Hc58
Santa Helena de Cusima CO 268 Ge43
Santa Helena de Goiás BR (GO) 286 He54
Santai CHN (SCH) 94 Qc30
Santa Ines BR (BA) 283 Ja52
Santa Inês BR (MA) 276 Hh47
Santa Inés CO 273 Gd45
Santa Inés YV 269 Gf40
Santa Inez, T.I. BR 270 Gk43
Santa Isabel EC 272 Ga47
Santa Isabel MEX (SLP) 253 Ek34
Santa Isabel NIC 256 Fh40
Santa Isabel PA 257 Ga41
Santa Isabel PE 272 Gc48
Santa Isabel SOL 161 Sk49
Santa Isabel do Araguaia BR (PA) 276 Hf49
Santa Isabel do Rio Negro BR (AM) 274 Gh46
Santa Isabella RA (LP) 292 Gg64
Santa Juana RCH 292 Gd64
Santa Juana YV 269 Gg42
Santa Júlia BR (AM) 274 Gk49
Santa Juliana BR (MG) 286 Hg55
Santa Lucia C 258 Fh34
Santa Lucia C 259 Gb35
Santa Lucía EC 272 Ga46
Santa Lucía PE 279 Ge53
Santa Lucía RA (CR) 289 Ha60
Santa Lucía ROU 289 Hb63
Santa Lucía YV 269 Gf41
Santa Lucia Bank USA 236 Dk28
Santa Lucia Range USA 236 Dk28
Santaluz BR (BA) 283 Ja51
Santa Luz BR (PI) 282 Hh50
Santa Luzia BR (BA) 283 Ja53
Santa Luzia BR (MA) 276 Hh47
Santa Luzia BR (MG) 287 Hj55
Santa Luzia BR (PA) 276 Hg46
Santa Luzia BR (PB) 277 Jb49
Santa Luzia do Paruá BR (MA) 276 Hh47
Santa Magdalena RA (CD) 288 Gj63
Santa Margherita I 31 Lj52
Santa Maria ANG 208 Lg52
Santa Maria BR (AM) 274 Gh49
Santa Maria BR (AM) 274 Ha48
Santa Maria BR (BA) 283 Ja53
Santa Maria BR (PA) 275 He46
Santa Maria BR (RS) 290 Hd60
Santa Maria BR 275 Hf49
Santa Maria CH 34 Ll44
Santa Maria CO 268 Gd43
Santa Maria CV 182 Jj37
Santa Maria HN 256 Fg38
Santa María MEX (BC) 236 Ec30
Santa María MEX (CAM) 255 Fe36
Santa María MEX (SO) 236 Ee31
Santa María RA (CA) 288 Gg59
Santa Maria RP 123 Rc42
Santa Maria USA (CA) 236 Dk28
Santa María YV 268 Ge41
Santa María YV 269 Gg42
Santa María Asunción Tlaxiaco MEX (OAX) 254 Fb37
Santa María Ayoquezco MEX (OAX) 254 Fb37
Santa Maria Càpua Vétere I 42 Lp49
Santa Maria da Boa Vista BR (PE) 283 Ja50
Santa Maria da Vitória BR (BA) 282 Hh52
Santa María de Ipire YV 269 Gh41
Santa María de Jetibá BR (ES) 287 Hk56
Santa María de la Peña E 27 Ku52
Santa María del Azogue E 26 Km53
Santa Maria del Camí E 30 Lc51
Santa Maria delle Grazie I 40 Lk45
Santa María del Oro MEX (DGO) 253 Eh33
Santa María del Oro MEX (NYT) 253 Eh35
Santa María de Los Guaicas YV 270 Gh44
Santa María del Páramo E 26 Kp52
Santa Maria del Regno I 31 Lj50
Santa María del Río MEX (SLP) 254 Ek35
Santa María de Nanay PE 273 Gd47
Santa María de Nieva PE 272 Gb48
Santa Maria do Oeste BR (PR) 286 He58
Santa Maria do Suaçuí BR (MG) 287 Hj55
Santa Maria do Tocantins BR (TO) 282 Hg50
Santa María Ecatepec MEX (OAX) 254 Fc37
Santa María Huatulco MEX (OAX) 254 Fb38
Santa María Huazolotitlán MEX (OAX) 254 Fb37
Santa Maria Island VU 162 Td53
Santa Maria la Real de Nieva E 26 Kq51
Santa Marinella I 42 Lm48
Santa Mario do Pará BR (PA) 276 Hg46
Santa Marta ANG 208 Lg52
Santa Marta CO 268 Gc40
Santa Marta E 28 Ko48
Santa Martha MEX (BCS) 252 Ed33
Santa Martha MEX (MEX) 254 Fa36
Santa Mónica MEX (COH) 253 Ek31
Santa Monica USA (CA) 236 Ea28
Santan RI 127 Qj46
Santana BR (AM) 274 Gj46
Santana BR (AM) 279 Gg50
Santana BR (AP) 275 He45
Santana BR (AP) 275 He46
Santana BR (BA) 282 Hh52
Santana BR (MA) 276 Hg48
Santana BR 281 He50
Santana CO 268 Gc44
Santana CO 268 Gd42
Santana da Boa Vista BR (RS) 290 Hd61
Santana da Serra P 28 Km47
Santana de Pirapama BR (MG) 287 Hh55
Santana do Acaraú BR (CE) 277 Hk47
Santana do Araguaia BR (PA) 281 He50
Santana do Cariri BR (CE) 277 Ja49
Santana do Ipanema BR (AL) 283 Jb50
Santana do Livramento BR (MT) 281 Hb53
Santana do Livramento BR (RS) 290 Hc61
Santana do Matos BR (RN) 277 Jb48
Santana, T.I. BR 281 Hc53
Santander E 27 Kr53
Santander RP 123 Rb41
Santander Jiménez MEX (TM) 253 Fa33
Sant'Andrea Frius I 31 Lk51
Sant'Angelo dei Lombardi I 42 Lq50
Sant'Angelo Lodigia I 40 Lk45
Sant'Antioco I 31 Lj51
Sant Antoni de Portmany E 30 Lb52
Sant'Antonio di Santadi I 31 Lj51
Santanyí E 30 Ld51
Santa Olalla del Cala E 28 Ko47
Santa Pau E 30 Lc48
Santa Paula USA (CA) 236 Ea28
Santa Pola E 29 Ku48
Sant' Apollinare Nuovo di Ravenna I 40 Ln46
Santa Quitéria BR (CE) 277 Hk48
Santa Quitéria do Maranhão BR (MA) 277 Hj47
Sant'Arcàngelo I 43 Lr50
Santarcàngelo di Romagna I 40 Ln46
Santarém BR (PA) 275 Hc47
Santarém P 28 Km49
Santarém Novo BR (PA) 276 Hg46
Santaren Channel BS 251 Ga33
Santa Rita BR (AM) 273 Gf47
Santa Rita BR (MA) 276 Hh47
Santa Rita BR (PB) 277 Jc49
Santa Rita CO 268 Gf43
Santa Rita CO 273 Gd45
Santa Rita HN 256 Fg38
Santa Rita MEX (BCS) 252 Ee33
Santa Rita NIC 256 Fg39
Santa Rita YV 268 Ge40
Santa Rita YV 269 Gg41
Santa Rita de Cássia BR (BA) 282 Hh51
Santa Rita de Catuna RA (LR) 288 Gg61
Santa Rita do Araguaia BR (GO) 286 Hd54
Santa Rita do Pardo BR (MS) 286 Hd56
Santa Rita do Passa Quatro BR (SP) 286 Hg56
Santa Rita do Sapucaí BR (MG) 287 Hh57
Santa Rosa BOL 279 Gg53
Santa Rosa BR (RO) 280 Gk52
Santa Rosa BR (RR) 270 Gj44
Santa Rosa BR (RS) 290 Hc59
Santa Rosa BR (TO) 282 Hf51
Santa Rosa CO 268 Gc42
Santa Rosa CO 272 Gb45
Santa Rosa CO 273 Ge45
Santa Rosa CO 273 Gf44
Santa Rosa EC 272 Ga47
Santa Rosa MEX (QTR) 255 Ff36
Santa Rosa MEX (SO) 252 Ef31
Santa Rosa PE 278 Ga49
Santa Rosa PE 279 Ge52
Santa Rosa PE 279 Ge53
Santa Rosa RA (CR) 289 Ha60
Santa Rosa RA (LP) 293 Gh64
Santa Rosa RA (SA) 285 Gh57
Santa Rosa USA (AZ) 236 Ed29
Santa Rosa USA (CA) 234 Dj26
Santa Rosa USA (NM) 237 Eh28
Santa Rosa YV 268 Gd41
Santa Rosa YV 269 Gf41
Santa Rosa YV 269 Gh41
Santa Rosa Beach USA (FL) 249 Fg30
Santa Rosa da Vigia BR (PA) 276 Hf46
Santa Rosa de Abuná BOL 279 Gg51
Santa Rosa de Amonadona YV 273 Gg45
Santa Rosa de Copán HN 255 Ff38
Santa Rosa de las Misiones PY 289 Hb59
Santa Rosa del Conlara RA (SL) 288 Gh62
Santa Rosa de Lima BR (SC) 291 Hf60
Santa Rosa de Lima ES 256 Fg39
Santa Rosa del Monday PY 286 Hc58
Santa Rosa del Río Primera RA (CD) 288 Gj61
Santa Rosa de Mbutuy PY 285 Hb58
Santa Rosa de Ocopa PE 278 Gc51
Santa Rosa de Socco PE 278 Gb51
Santa Rosa de Viterbo BR (SP) 286 Hg56
Santa Rosa Island USA 236 Dk29
Santa Rosa Island USA 248 Fg30
Santa Rosalía MEX (BCS) 252 Ed32
Santa Rosalía YV 269 Gh42
Santa Rosalita MEX (BC) 236 Ec31
Santa Rosa, P.N. CR 256 Fh40
Santarskie ostrova RUS 59 Rd07
Santa Severa F 31 Lk48
Santa Sylvina RA (CH) 289 Gk59
Santa Teresa BR 282 Hf52
Santa Teresa MEX (NYT) 253 Eh34
Santa Teresa MEX (TM) 253 Fa33
Santa Teresa MEX (TM) 253 Fb33
Santa Teresa PE 272 Gc48
Santa Teresa RA (SF) 289 Gk62
Santa Teresa YV 269 Gg40
Santa Teresa de Goiás BR (GO) 282 Hf52
Santa Teresa di Riva I 42 Lq53
Santa Teresa do Tocantins BR (TO) 282 Hg51
Santa Teresa Gallura I 31 Lk49
Santa Teresa, P.N. ROU 289 Hd62
Santa Teresinha de Goiás BR (GO) 282 Hf53
Santa Teresita RA (BA) 293 Hb64
Santa Terezinha BR (MT) 281 He51
Santa Terezinha BR (SC) 291 He59
Santa Theresa AUS (NT) 143 Rh58
Santa Victoria RA (SA) 284 Gh57
Santa Victoria RA (SA) 285 Gj57
Santa Vitória BR (MG) 286 He55
Santa Vitória do Palmar BR (RS) 290 Hd62
San-Ta-Wani Safari Camp RB 213 Mb55
Santaworld S 13 Lp30
Sant Carles de la Ràpita E 30 La50
Sant Carles de Peralta E 30 Lb51
Sant Celoni E 30 Lc49
Sante Bennur IND (KTK) 110 Oh39
Santee Ind. Res. USA 240 Fb24
Santee N.W.R. USA 249 Fk29
Sant'Elia a Pianisi I 42 Lp49
Santemarahalli IND (KTK) 111 Oj41
San Teodoro I 31 Lk50
Santéramo in Colle I 43 Lr50
Santerno I 40 Lm46
Santerre F 23 Lc41
Santesteban E 27 Kt53
Sant'Eufémia Lamézia I 43 Lr52
Sant Feliu de Guíxols E 30 Ld49
Sant Francesc de Formentera E 30 Lb52
Santhe MW 210 Mg52
Santhià I 40 Lj45
Santiago BR (RS) 290 Hc60
Santiago CR 256 Fh41
Santiago EC 272 Ga47
Santiago GCA 255 Fe38
Santiago MEX (NL) 253 Ek33
Santiago PA 257 Fk41
Santiago PE 272 Gb47
Santiago RCH 288 Ge62
Santiago RP 121 Ra37
Santiago Astata MEX (OAX) 254 Fc38
Santiago Choapan MEX (OAX) 254 Fc37
Santiago de Alcántara E 28 Kn49
Santiago de Anchucaya PE 278 Gb52
Santiago de Andamarca BOL 284 Gg55
Santiago de Cao PE 278 Ga49
Santiago de Chiquitos BOL 285 Ha55
Santiago de Chocorvos PE 278 Gc52
Santiago de Chuco PE 278 Ga50
Santiago de Compostela E 26 Km52
Santiago de Cotagaita BOL 284 Gh56
Santiago de Cuba C 259 Gc35
Santiago de Huari BOL 284 Gg55
Santiago de las Vegas C 258 Fj34
Santiago del Estero RA (SE) 288 Gh59
Santiago del Estero RA 267 Gd24
Santiago de los Caballeros MEX (SL) 252 Eg33
Santiago de los Cabelleros DOM 260 Ge36
Santiago del Teide E 178 Kb31
Santiago de Machaca BOL 284 Gf54
Santiago de Pacaguaras BOL 279 Gf52
Santiago do Cacém P 28 Km48
Santiago Ixcuintla MEX (NYT) 253 Eh35
Santiago,James = Isla San Salvador EC 272 Fe46
Santiago Juxtlahuaca MEX (OAX) 254 Fb37
Santiago Mts. USA 237 Ej31
Santiago Papasquiaro MEX (DGO) 253 Eh33

Santiago Pinotepa – Sauce Blanco

Santiago Pinotepa Nacional MEX (OAX) 254 Fa37
Santiago Tuxtla MEX (VC) 255 Fc36
Santiaguillo MEX (ZCT) 253 Ej34
Santibánez de la Sierra E 26 Kp50
San Tiburico MEX (ZCT) 253 Ek33
Santiguila RMM 184 Kg39
Santillana del Mar E 27 Kq53
San Timoteo YV 268 Ge41
Santipur IND (CGH) 109 Pa35
Säntis CH 34 Lk43
Santissima Trinità di Saccàrgia I 31 Lj50
Santisteban del Puerto E 29 Kr48
Santi Suk THA 114 Qa36
Sant Joan d'Alacant E 29 Ku48
Sant Llorenç de Morunys E 30 Lb48
Sant Mateu E 30 La50
Santo Amaro BR (AM) 279 Ge49
Santo Amaro BR (BA) 283 Ja52
Santo Anastácio BR (SP) 286 He56
Santo André ANG 208 Lh52
Santo André BR (PA) 276 Hf46
Santo André BR (SP) 287 Hg57
Santo Ângelo BR (RS) 290 Hc60
Santo Antonio BR (AM) 274 Gk47
Santo Antônio BR (MA) 276 Hh46
Santo Antônio BR (PA) 275 Hb46
Santo Antônio BR (RN) 277 Jc49
Santo Antonio BR (RO) 279 Gg50
Santo Antonio BR 282 Hf51
Santo António STP 194 Ld45
Santo Antônio da Barra BR (GO) 286 He54
Santo Antônio da Platina BR (PR) 286 He57
Santo Antonio de Leverger BR (MT) 281 Hb53
Santo Antônio do Içá BR (AM) 273 Gg47
Santo Antônio do Jacinto BR (MG) 287 Hk54
Santo Antônio do Sudoeste BR (PR) 290 Hd59
Santo Augusto BR (RS) 290 Hd59
Santo Corazón BOL 285 Ha54
Santo Cristo BR (RS) 290 Hc59
Santo Domingo C 258 Fk34
Santo Domingo DOM 260 Gf36
Santo Domingo MEX (BC) 236 Ec31
Santo Domingo MEX (BCS) 252 Ee33
Santo Domingo MEX (DGO) 253 Eh33
Santo Domingo MEX (SLP) 253 Ek34
Santo Domingo MEX 236 Ec30
Santo Domingo NIC 256 Fh39
Santo Domingo RA (SA) 285 Gj58
Santo Domingo YV 268 Gd42
Santo Domingo de Acobamba PE 278 Gc51
Santo Domingo de la Calzada E 27 Ks52
Santo Domingo de los Colorados EC 272 Ga46
Santo Domingo de Silos E 27 Kr51
Santo Domingo Pueblo USA (NM) 237 Eg28
Santo Domingo Tehuantepec MEX (OAX) 255 Fc37
Santo Estevão BR (BA) 283 Ja52
Santo Expedito BR (SP) 286 He56
Santo Inácio BR (BA) 282 Hj51
Santo Inácio BR (PR) 286 He57
San Tomé YV 269 Gh41
Santoña E 27 Kr53
Santonia F (GF) 271 Hc43
Santo Niño RP 123 Rc42
Santo Onofre BR 282 Hj52
Santópolis do Aguapú BR (SP) 286 He56
Santos AUS (QLD) 150 Sa60
Santos BR (SP) 287 Hg57
Santos Dumont BR (MG) 287 Hj56
Santos Lugares RA (SE) 288 Gj59
Santos Mercado BOL 279 Gg50
Santos Reyes Nopala MEX (OAX) 254 Fb37
Santo Tirso P 26 Km51
Santo Tomás MEX (BC) 236 Eb30
Santo Tomás MEX (CHH) 237 Eg31
Santo Tomás NIC 256 Fh39
Santo Tomas PE 279 Gd53
Santo Tomás PE 279 Gd53
Santo Tomas RP 123 Rc42
Santo Tomé RA (CR) 289 Hb60
Santo Tome RA (SF) 289 Gk61
Sant Pere de Rodes E 30 Ld48
Santpur IND (KTK) 108 Oj36
Santuari de Lluc E 30 Lc51
Santuari de Sant Salvador E 30 Ld51
Santuario de las Lajas CO 272 Gb45
Santuario delle Santa Casa I 41 Lo47
Santuario de Loyola E 27 Ks53
Santuario di San Michele I 43 Lq49
Santuário do Bom Jesus BR 287 Hj56
Santuario Laguna El Peral RCH 288 Ge62
Santuario Nacional Calipuy PE 278 Ga50
Santuario Nacional de Ampay PE 279 Gd52
Santuario Nacional Huayllay PE 278 Gb51
Santuario Nacional Lagunas de Mejía PE 284 Ge54
Santuario Nacional Manglares de Tumbes PE 272 Fk47
Santuario Nacional Tanaconas Namballes PE 272 Ga48
Santubong MAL 126 Qf45
Santu Lussùrgiu I 31 Lj50
Sant Vicenç E 30 Lb49
San Ubaldo NIC 256 Fh40
Sanup Plateau USA 236 Ed28
Sanur Beach RI 129 Qh50
San Valentín, Cerro RCH 294 Gd69
San Vicente BOL 284 Gg56
San Vicente CO 268 Gd42
San Vicente EC 272 Fk46
San Vicente ES 255 Ff39
San Vicente MEX (BC) 236 Eb30
San Vicente RA (BA) 289 Ha63
San Vicente RA (MI) 289 Hc59
San Vicénte YV 269 Gg43
San Vicente de Alcántara E 28 Kn49
San Vicente de Caguan CO 272 Gc44
San Vicente de Cañete PE 278 Gb52
San Vicente de la Barquera E 27 Kq53
San Vicente Tancuayalab MEX (SLP) 254 Fa35
San Victor GUY 270 Gk42
San Vincente MEX (SLP) 253 Ek33
San Vincenzo I 40 Ll47
San Vitale di Ravenna I 40 Ln46
San Vito CR 256 Fj41
San Vito I 31 Lk51
San Vito al Tagliamento I 41 Ln45
San Vito dei Normanni I 43 Ls50
San Vito lo Capo I 42 Ln52
Sanxenxo = Sangenjo E 26 Km52
Sanya CHN (HAN) 96 Qe36
Sanya Juu EAT 207 Mj47
Sanyang CHN (AHU) 102 Qk30
Sanyati ZW 210 Me54
Sanyati ZW 210 Me54
Sanying CHN (NHZ) 92 Qd27
Sanying CHN (YUN) 113 Qa32
Sanyuan CHN (SAA) 95 Qe28
Sanza I 42 Lq50
Sanza Pombo ANG 202 Lh49
São Antônia BR (RR) 270 Gk44
São Antonio BR (AM) 274 Gk49
São Antonio BR (AP) 275 He45
São Antonio BR (PA) 275 Hc49
São Antônio da Abunari BR (AM) 274 Gk46
São Antônio das Missões BR (RS) 290 Hc60
São Antonio de Jesus BR (BA) 283 Ja52
São Antônio de Padua BR (RJ) 287 Hj56
São Antônio do Amparo BR (MG) 287 Hh56
São Antônio do Monte BR (MG) 287 Hh56
São Antônio dos Lopes BR (MA) 276 Hh48
São Bartolomeu BR 282 Hg54
São Benedito BR (CE) 277 Hk48
São Benedito BR (MT) 285 Hb54
São Benedito BR 281 Hb50
São Benedito do Rio Preto BR (MA) 276 Hj47
São Bento BR (MA) 276 Hh47
São Bento BR 283 Jc49
São Bento do Norte BR (RN) 277 Jb48
São Bento do Sul BR (SC) 291 Hf59
São Bernardo BR (AM) 279 Gg50
São Bernardo BR (MA) 277 Hj47
São Bernardo do Campo BR (SP) 287 Hg57
São Borja BR (RS) 290 Hc60
São Brás BR (AM) 273 Gf49
São Brás de Alportel P 28 Kn47
São Caetano BR (PE) 283 Jb50
São Caetano de Odivelas BR (PA) 276 Hf46
São Carlos BR (RO) 280 Gh51
São Carlos BR (SC) 290 Hd59
São Carlos BR (SP) 286 Hg57
São Cosme BR (PA) 275 He46
São Cristóão ANG 208 Lg52
São Cristóvão BR (SE) 283 Jb51
São Cristóvão do Sul BR (SC) 290 He59
São Desidério BR (BA) 282 Hh52
São Desidério BR 282 Hh52
São Domingos BR (GO) 282 Hg52
São Domingos BR (GO) 286 Hf54
São Domingos BR (MA) 276 Hh49
São Domingos BR (MS) 285 Hb55
São Domingos GNB 183 Kb39
São Domingos do Capim BR (PA) 276 Hg46
São Domingos do Capim Novo BR (PA) 276 Hg47
São Domingos do Maranhão BR (MA) 276 Hh48
São Domingos do Prata BR (MG) 287 Hj55
São Domingos, T.I. BR 281 He51
São Felicio BR (AP) 275 Hd45
São Felix do Araguaia BR (MT) 281 He51
São Felix do Coribe BR (BA) 282 Hh52
São Felix do Xingu BR (PA) 275 He49
São Fidelis BR (RJ) 287 Hk56
São Filipe CV 182 Jh38
São Francisco BR (MG) 282 Hh53
São Francisco BR 279 Gf50
São Francisco BR 283 Jb50
São Francisco das Chagas BR (AM) 275 Hb47
São Francisco das Chagas BR (PI) 282 Hh50
São Francisco das Chagas BR 277 Ja48
São Francisco de Assis BR (RS) 290 Hc60
São Francisco de Paula BR (RS) 290 He60
São Francisco de Sales BR (MG) 286 Hf55
São Francisco do Maranhão BR (MA) 277 Hj49
São Francisco do Sul BR (SC) 291 Hf59
São Gabriel BR (RS) 290 Hc61
São Gabriel da Cachoeira BR (AM) 273 Gg46
São Gabriel da Palha BR (ES) 287 Hk55
São Gabriel de Goiás BR (GO) 282 Hg53
São Gabriel do Oeste BR (MS) 286 Hc55
São Geraldo do Araguaia BR (PA) 276 Hf49
São Gonçalo do Abaeté BR (MG) 287 Hh55
São Gonçalo do Amarante BR (CE) 277 Ja47
São Gonçalo dos Campos BR (BA) 283 Ja52
São Gotardo BR (MG) 287 Hg55
São Hill EAT 207 Mh50
São Ifigênia de Minas BR (MG) 287 Hj55
São Jerônimo BR (RS) 290 He60
São Jerônimo da Serra BR (PR) 286 He57
São Jerônimo, T.I. BR 286 He57
São João BR (AM) 274 Gk48
São João BR (PR) 290 Hd58
São João Batista BR (MA) 276 Hh47
São João Batista BR (SC) 291 Hf59
São João da Barra BR (RJ) 287 Hk56
São João da Barra BR 280 Ha50
São João da Boa Vista BR (SP) 287 Hg56
São João d'Aliança BR (GO) 282 Hg53
São João da Madeira P 26 Km50
São João da Ponte BR (MG) 282 Hh53
São João da Pracajuba BR (PA) 275 He46
São João da Serra BR (PI) 277 Hk48
São João del Rei BR (MG) 287 Hh56
São João de Pirbas BR (PA) 276 Hg46
São João de Rio Pardo BR (SP) 287 Hg56
São João do Araguaia BR (PA) 276 Hf48
São João do Caiuá BR (PR) 286 Hd57
São João do Paraiso BR (MG) 283 Hk53
São João do Paraná BR (PA) 281 Hb50
São João do Piauí BR (PI) 283 Hj50
São João dos Patos BR (MA) 276 Hj49
São João dos Poleiros BR (MA) 276 Hj48
São João do Tigre BR (PB) 277 Jb50
São João do Triunfo BR (PR) 291 He58
São João Evangelista BR (MG) 287 Hj55
São Joaquim BR (AM) 273 Gg45
São Joaquim BR (SC) 291 Hf60
São Joaquim da Barra BR (SP) 286 Hg56
São Joaquim, P.N.de BR 291 Hf60
São José BR (AC) 279 Gf50
São José BR (PA) 276 Hf47
São José BR (RS) 290 Hd61
São José BR (SC) 291 Hf59
São José das Laranjeras BR (SP) 286 He57
São José da Tapera BR (AL) 283 Jb50
São José de Anaua BR (RR) 274 Gk45
São José de Belmonte BR (PE) 283 Ja49
São José de Mipibu BR (RN) 277 Jc49
São José de Piranhas BR (PB) 277 Ja49
São Jose de Ribamar BR (MA) 276 Hh47
São José do Caciporé BR (AP) 271 He44
São José do Cerrito BR (SC) 290 He59
São José do Egito BR (PE) 283 Jb49
São José do Norte BR (RS) 290 Hd61
São José do Peixe BR (PI) 277 Hj49
São José do Piria BR (PA) 276 Hg46
São José do Rio Claro BR (MT) 281 Hb52
São José do Rio Preto BR (SP) 286 Hf56
São José dos Ausentes BR (RS) 291 He60
São José dos Campos BR (SP) 287 Hh57
São José dos Dourados BR 286 He56
São José dos Martirios BR (TO) 276 Hf49
São José dos Pinhais BR (PR) 291 Hf58
São José do Xingu BR (MT) 281 Hd51
São Julio do Jurupari BR (PA) 275 He45
São Leopoldo BR (RS) 290 He60
São Leopoldo, T.I. BR 273 Gf48
São Lourenço BR (MG) 287 Hh57
São Lourenço BR 285 Hb54
São Lourenço do Oeste BR (SC) 290 Hd59
São Lourenço do Sul BR (RS) 290 He61
São Lucas ANG 208 Lj51
São Luís BR (AM) 274 Gh46
São Luís BR (AM) 274 Gk47
São Luís BR (MA) 276 Hh47
São Luís BR (RR) 274 Gk45
São Luís do Quitunde BR (AL) 283 Jc50
São Luis do Tapajós BR (PA) 275 Hb48
São Luís Gonzaga BR (MA) 276 Hh48
São Luís Gonzaga BR (RS) 290 Hc60
São Luiza do Oeste BR (RO) 280 Gk51
São Luzia do Pacui BR (AP) 275 He45
São Manuel BR (MT) 281 Hc53
São Manuel BR (SP) 286 Hf57
São Manuel ou Teles Pires BR 281 Hb50
São Marcos BR (RS) 290 He60
São Marcos BR 286 Hg54
São Marcos da Serra P 28 Km47
São Marcos, T.I. BR 270 Gk44
São Marcos, T.I. BR 281 Hd53
São Martinho BR (RS) 290 Hd59
São Martinho de Angueira P 26 Ko51
São Mateus BR (ES) 287 Ja55
São Mateus BR 287 Hk55
São Mateus do Maranhão BR (MA) 276 Hh48
São Mateus do Sul BR (PR) 291 He58
São Miguel BR (AP) 275 He45
São Miguel BR (MT) 281 Hd52
São Miguel BR (RN) 277 Ja49
São Miguel BR 280 Gj51
São Miguel BR 281 Hb52
São Miguel BR 282 Hg53
São Miguel Arcanjo BR (SP) 286 Hg57
São Miguel das Missões BR (RS) 290 Hc60
São Miguel das Missões BR 289 Hc60
São Miguel d'Oeste BR (SC) 290 Hd59
São Miguel do Guamá BR (PA) 276 Hg46
São Miguel do Iguaçu BR (PR) 286 Hc58
São Miguel dos Campos BR (AL) 283 Jb50
São Miguel dos Macacos BR (PA) 275 He46
São Miguel do Tapuio BR (PI) 277 Hk48
Saône F 25 Le44
Saoner IND (MHT) 109 Ok35
São Nicolau ANG 208 Lg53
São Nicolau BR 277 Hk48
Saonli IND (MPH) 109 Ok35
São Paulo BR (SP) 286 Hg57
São Paulo BR 265 Hb23
São Paulo do Potengi BR (RN) 277 Jc48
São Pedro BR (AM) 273 Gg46
São Pedro BR (AM) 273 Gg48
São Pedro BR (AM) 274 Gj47
São Pedro BR (PA) 275 He47
São Pedro BR (PR) 290 Hd59
São Pedro BR (SP) 286 Hg57
São Pedro BR 277 Ja50
São Pedro CV 182 Jh37
São Pedro da Aldeia BR (RJ) 287 Hj57
São Pedro do Ico BR (AC) 279 Gf50
São Pedro do Piauí BR (PI) 277 Hj48
São Pedro dos Crentes BR (MA) 276 Hg49
São Pedro do Sepatini, T.I. BR 274 Gh49
São Pedro do Sul BR (RS) 290 Hc60
São Pedro, T.I. BR 274 Ha47
São Perdo da Quilemba ANG 202 Lh50
São Pualo de Olivença BR (AM) 273 Gf47
São Raimundo das Mangabeiras BR (MA) 276 Hh49
São Raimundo Nonato BR (PI) 283 Hj50
Saorge F 25 Lh47
São Romão BR (AM) 273 Gg48
São Romão BR (MG) 287 Hh54
São Roque BR (SP) 286 Hg57
São Roque de Minas BR (MG) 287 Hg56
São Sebastião BR (AL) 283 Jb50
São Sebastião BR (SP) 287 Hh57
São Sebastião da Amoreira BR (PR) 286 He57
São Sebastião da Boa Vista BR (PA) 276 Hf46
São Sebastião do Paraiso BR (MG) 287 Hg56
São Sebastião do Tocantins BR (TO) 276 Hf48
São Sebastião do Uatumã BR (AM) 275 Hb47
São Sepé BR (RS) 290 Hd61
São Simão BR (GO) 286 He55
São Simão BR (RS) 290 He61
São Simão BR (SP) 286 Hg56
São Teotónio P 28 Km47
São Tomé BR (AP) 275 He46
São Tomé STP 194 Ld45
São Tomé STP 194 Ld45
São Tomé and Príncipe 167 La09
Saourikro CI 193 Kh42
São Valentim BR (RS) 290 Hd59
São Vendelino BR (RS) 290 He60
São Vicente BR (AC) 279 Ge49
São Vicente BR (MT) 281 Hc53
São Vicente BR (PA) 275 He46
São Vicente BR (SP) 287 Hg57
São Vicente do Sul BR (RS) 290 Hc60
São Vicente Ferrer BR (MA) 276 Hh47
Sapa VN 113 Qb34
Sápai GR 47 Mf49
Sapajou F (GF) 271 Hd43
Sapanca Gölü TR 50 Ml50
Sapanjang RI 129 Qh49
Sapão BR 282 Hh51
Saparua RI 130 Re47
Saparua RI 130 Re47
Sapat RI 125 Qb46
Sapé BR (PB) 277 Jc49
Sapele WAN 194 Lc43
Sapelo Island National Estuarine Research Reserve USA 249 Fk30
Sapernoe RUS 52 Me15
Sapidan IR 74 Nf30
Sapiénza GR 48 Mb54
Sapinero USA (CO) 235 Eg26
Sapiranga BR (RS) 290 He60
Sapi Safari Area ZW 210 Me53
Sápmi N 11 Mc11
Sapoaga Falls WS 164 Be52
Sapoba WAN 194 Lc42
Sapodilla Cays BH 255 Ff37
Saponé BF 185 Kk39
Sapo N.P. LB 192 Kf43
Sapo Sapo RDC 203 Mb48
Saposoa PE 278 Gb49
Sapouí BF 193 Kk40
Sapožok RUS 53 Na19
Sapphir Mts. USA 235 Ed22
Sappho USA (WA) 232 Dh21
Sapporo J 99 Sa24
Sapri I 43 Lq50
Sapšal'skij hrebet RUS 85 Pe20
Sapt al Ulaya KSA 66 Na36
Sapucaia BR (AM) 275 Hb47
Sapucaia BR (RJ) 287 Hj57
Sapucaia do Sul BR (RS) 290 He60
Sapuka-Besar RI 129 Qk49
Sapulpa USA (OK) 243 Fb28
Sapulu RI 128 Qg49
Sapulut MAL 122 Qj43
Saqim YE 68 Nb37
Saqiyah IRQ 65 Nb28
Saqqez IR 72 Nd27
Saqr YE 69 Nf38
Saquia el Hamra DARS 172 Ke32
Saquisili EC 272 Ga46
Sara BF 193 Kj40
Sara FIN 16 Mc28
Sara RI 131 Rg47
Sara RP 123 Rb40
Sarab IR 72 Nd27
Sarab Dowreh IR 72 Ne29
Sarab-e Jahangir IR 72 Nd29
Sarabikulovo RUS 53 Nf18
Sarâbit el Khâdim ET 177 Mg31
Saraburi THA 114 Qa38
Sarad IND (MHT) 108 Og35
Sarafara SUD 197 Mf40
Sarafchegan IR 72 Nf28
Saraf Doungous TCH 196 Lk39
Saraféré RMM 185 Kj38
Saragt TM 73 Oa27
Saraguro EC 272 Ga47
Sara Hahan SP 199 Nd40
Sarai RUS 53 Na19
Saraidana IND (MPH) 109 Pa34
Sarai Gambila PK 79 Of29
Sar'ain IR 72 Nd26
Saraipali IND (CGH) 109 Pb35
Säräisniemi FIN 11 Md13
Saraiu RO 45 Mj46
Sarajevo BIH 41 Lt47
Saraj-Gir RUS 53 Ng19
Sara-Kawa TG 193 La41
Sarakhs IR 73 Oa27
Sarakina GR 46 Mb50
Sarakina GR 46 Mb51
Sarakini GR 46 Mb50
Sara Koyra RN 185 La38
Saralžyn KZ 53 Ne21
Saramacca SME 271 Hc43
Saramati MYA 112 Ph33
Sarameriza PE 272 Gb48
Saramon F 24 La47
Saran IR 72 Ng28
Saranac Lake USA (NY) 247 Gc23
Saranci BG 46 Md48
Sáránd H 39 Mb43
Sarandë AL 46 Ma51
Sarandi BR (PR) 286 He57
Sarandi BR (RS) 290 Hd58
Sarandi BR (RS) 290 Hd59
Sarandi RA 289 Ha60
Sarandi del Yi ROU 289 Hc62
Sarandi Grande ROU 289 Hb62
Sarangani Island RP 123 Rc43
Sarangarh IND (CGH) 109 Pb35
Sarangpur IND (MPH) 108 Oj34
Saran, Gunung RI 126 Qf46
Saransk RUS 53 Nc18
Sarantáporo GR 46 Mc50
Sarapali IND (ORS) 109 Pc35
Sarapul RUS 58 Nc07
Sarare BR 280 Ha53
Sarare, T.I. BR 280 Ha53
Saraskheri IND (MPH) 109 Oj33
Sarasota USA (FL) 250 Fj32
Šarašova BY 37 Me38
Sarata UA 45 Mk44
Sarata UA 45 Mk44
Sarat Abidah KSA 68 Nb36
Šara-Tagot RUS 90 Qd19
Sarateni MD 45 Mj44
Sarath IND (JKD) 112 Pd33
Saratoga Hot Springs USA 235 Eg25
Saratoga N.H.P. USA 247 Gd24
Saratoga Racetrack USA (NY) 247 Gd24
Saratoga Springs USA (NY) 247 Gd24
Saratov RUS 53 Nc20
Saratovskoe vodohranilišče RUS 53 Ne19
Saravah IR 72 Ne27
Saravan IR 75 Ob32
Sarawak MAL 126 Qg44
Sarawak Cultural Village MAL 126 Qf45
Saray TR 50 Mh49
Saraya SN 183 Ke39
Sarayan IR 73 Nk29
Saraykent TR 51 Mq51
Sarayköy TR 50 Mj53
Sarayköy TR 51 Mm51
Sarayönü TR 51 Mn52
Sarbaz IR 75 Oa32
Sarbaz IR 75 Oa32
Sarbinowo PL 36 Lq36
Sar Bisheh IR 73 Nk29
Sárbogard H 39 Lt44
Sarbulak CHN (XUZ) 85 Pe22
Sarco RCH 288 Ge60
Sarda NEP 88 Pa31
Sárdara I 31 Lj51
Sardarshahr IND (RJT) 106 Oh31
Sardasht IR 74 Nf30
Sarde Band AFG 78 Oe29
Sardes TR 50 Mj52
Sardhana IND (UPH) 107 Oj31
Sardinas EC 272 Gb46
Sardinata CO 268 Gd41
Sardinia I 31 Lj50
Sardinia I 31 Lj50
Sardis USA (GA) 249 Fk29
Sardrud IR 72 Nd27
Sarege RI 129 Qk49
Sarékali RG 192 Kd40
Sareks n.p. S 10 Lj12
Sarektjåkka S 10 Lj12
S'Arenal E 30 Lc51
Saré Ndiaye SN 183 Kc39
Šarengrad HR 44 Lu45
Sar-e Pol AFG 78 Oc27
Sar-e-Pol-e-Sahab IR 72 Nc28
Sar-e Raqowl AFG 78 Od28
Saréyamou RMM 185 Kj37
Sarfayt OM 69 Ng37
Sargapur IND (KTK) 108 Oj37
Sargasso Sea 227 Gb12
Sargodha PK 79 Og29
Sargur IND (KTK) 110 Oj41
Sarh TCH 196 Lk41
Sarhad AFG 79 Og27
Sarhad IR 75 Oa31
Sarhala CI 193 Kg41
Šarhorod UA 54 Me21
Sari IR 72 Ng27
Sariä BR 273 Gh49
Saria GR 49 Mh55
Saria GR 49 Mh55
Saria 79 Oh29
Sariba Island PNG 160 Sf51
Saric MEX (SO) 237 Ee30
Sarıcakaya TR 50 Ml50
Sarie Marais Base ANT (SA) 296 Kd33
Sariet ez Zit TN 174 Lf28
Sarif YE 69 Nf37
Sarigan USA 119 Sb15
Sarıgöl TR 50 Mj52
Sarigua, P.N. PA 257 Fk41
Sarika Falls THA 114 Qa38
Sarıkamış TR 63 Nb25
Sarıkaya TR 51 Mq51
Sarikei MAL 126 Qf44
Sariko'l UZ 76 Od26
Sarikorola RMM 184 Kg39
Sarıköy TR 50 Mh50
Sarimoy UZ 71 Oa25
Sarimoy UZ 76 Ob25
Sarina AUS (QLD) 149 Se56
Sariñena E 27 Ku51
Sarioba TR 51 Mn51
Sar-i-Parom PK 80 Ob32
Sarıpınar TR 63 Mk26
Saripoi RI 126 Qh46
Sariq UZ 76 Od27
Sariqamish ko'li UZ 71 Nj24
Sarir al Qattusah LAR 181 Lh32
Sariri PNG 159 Se50
Sarir Kalanshiyū LAR 175 Ma32
Sarir Tibesti LAR 181 Lj34
Sarir Umm 'Illah LAR 181 Lh32
Sariska Tiger Reserve IND 107 Oj32
Šarišský hrad SK 39 Mb41
Sarita USA (TX) 253 Fb32
Sariwon PRK 100 Rc26
Sariyahsi TR 51 Mo52
Sarıyar TR 51 Mm50
Sarıyar Barajı TR 51 Mm50
Sariyer TR 50 Mk49
Šar'ja RUS 52 Nd16
Šar'ja RUS 53 Nc16
Sark GB 22 Ks41
Sarkadkeresztúr H 39 Mb44
Sarkala IND 108 Of35
Sarkan KZ 84 Ok23
Šarkavščyna BY 17 Mh35
Sarkhej IND (GUJ) 108 Og34
Şarkikaraağaç TR 51 Mm52
Sarkin Kudin WAN 194 Le41
Şarkışla TR 62 Mj26
Şarköy TR 50 Mh50
Sarlat-la-Canéda F 24 Lb46
Särmäşag RO 44 Mc43
Sarmette USA 167 Td54
Sarmi RI 131 Rk46
Sarmiento RA (CB) 292 Gf68
Sarmiento RA (CD) 288 Gh61
Sarmizegetusa Regia RO 44 Md45
Särna S 13 Lo29
Sarnaki PL 37 Mc38
Sarnano I 41 Lo47
Sarnath IND 109 Pb33
Sarnen CH 34 Lj44
Sarner See CH 34 Lj44
Särnevo BG 47 Mf48
Sarnia CDN (ON) 246 Fj24
Sárnico I 40 Lk45
Sarno I 42 Lp50
Sarny UA 52 Md20
Särö S 14 Lm33
Saroako RI 127 Ra47
Sarolangun RI 124 Qb47
Saroma J 99 Sb23
Saroma-ko J 99 Sb23
Saromoana RM 220 Ne54
Saronida GR 48 Md53
Saronida GR 48 Md53
Saronikós Kólpos GR 48 Md53
Saronno I 40 Lj45
Sarore RI 158 Sa50
Sárosd H 39 Lt43
Saros Körfezi TR 50 Mg50
Sárospatak H 39 Mb42
Sarot TR 51 Mm50
Šarovce SK 38 Lt42
Sarowbi AFG 78 Oe28
Sarowbi AFG 78 Oe29
Sarpinskie ozera RUS 53 Nc21
Šar Planina MK/SCG 46 Ma48
Šar Planina, N.P. SCG 46 Mb48
Sarpsborg N 12 Ll31
Sarralbe F 23 Lh42
Sarrapio YV 269 Gh42
Sarrebourg F 23 Lh42
Sarreguemines F 23 Lh41
Sarre-Union F 23 Lh42
Sarria E 26 Kn52
Sarro RMM 184 Kh39
Sarstoon N.P. BH 255 Ff38
Sartam IND (ARP) 112 Pg31
Sartell USA (MN) 241 Fc23
Sartène F 31 Lj49
Sarteneja BH 255 Ff36
Sarteneja BH 255 Ff36
Sarthe F 22 Ku43
Sārti GR 47 Md50
Sarubetsu J 99 Sb24
Sarufutsu J 99 Sb23
Saruhanlı TR 49 Mh52
Sarulla RI 124 Pk45
Sarumatinggi RI 116 Pk44
Sarumatinggi RI 124 Pk45
Sarungga RI 126 Qh47
Saru Pathar IND (ASM) 112 Pg32
Saruq IR 72 Ne28
Saruwaged Range PNG 159 Sd49
Sarvada IND (MHT) 108 Oh37
Sárvár H 38 Lr43
Sarvestan IR 74 Ng31
Särvsjön S 13 Lo28
Sarwan IND (MPH) 108 Oh34
Saryaghash KZ 76 Oe25
Sary-Bulak KS 77 Oh25
Saryesik - Atyrau KZ 84 Oj23
Saryg-Sep RUS (TUV) 85 Ph20
Sarykamyshskoye ozera TM 71 Nj25
Sarykemer KZ 76 Of24
Saryolen KZ 85 Pc22
Saryozek KZ 84 Oj23
Saryshaghan KZ 84 Og22
Sarysu KZ 76 Od23
Sarysu KZ 84 Of21
Sary-Taš KS 77 Og26
Saryzhal KZ 84 Ok21
Sarzana I 40 Lk46
Sarzeau F 22 Ks43
Sarzedas P 28 Kn49
Sasabe USA (AZ) 237 Ee30
Sasak RI 124 Pk46
Sasan caravanserai IR 72 Nf28
Sasan Gir N.P. IND 108 Of35
Sasaram IND (BIH) 109 Pc33
Sasari, Mount SOL 161 Sk50
Sa Savina E 30 Lb52
Sasbeneh ETH 199 Nb42
Sasd H 38 Lt44
Sasebo J 103 Re29
Sasino PL 36 Ls36
Saskal' RUS 98 Rd20
Saskatchewan CDN 224 Ec07
Saskatchewan Landing Prov. Park CDN 233 Ef20
Saskatchewan River CDN 238 Ej19
Saskatchewan River Crossing CDN (AB) 233 Eb19
Saskatoon CDN (SK) 233 Eg19
Saskylah RUS 59 Qc04
Sasolburg ZA 217 Md59
Sasoma 79 Oj28
Sason TR 63 Na26
Sasovo RUS 53 Na18
Sassandra CI 192 Kg43
Sassandra CI 193 Kg43
Sàssari I 31 Lj50
Sassélé RCA 195 Lj43
Sassie Island AUS 146 Sb51
Sassnitz D 33 Lo36
Sassoferrato I 41 Ln47
Sasso Lungo = Langkofel I 40 Lm44
Sasso Marconi I 40 Lm46
Sassoumbouroum RN 186 Le39
Sassuolo I 40 Ll46
Sástago E 27 Ku51
Šaštín-Stráže SK 38 Ls42
Sastown LB 192 Kf43
Sastre RA (SF) 289 Gk61
Sastyg-Hem RUS (TUV) 85 Ph19
Sasu RI 130 Rd45
Sasvad IND (MHT) 108 Oh36
Sasykkul' TJ 77 Og27
Sasykol KZ 84 Pa22
Sata J 103 Rf30
Satadougou RMM 183 Ke39
Satama-Sokoro CI 193 Kh42
Satama-Sokoura CI 193 Kh42
Sata misaki J 103 Rf30
Satana IND (MHT) 108 Oh35
Satanta USA (KS) 242 Ek27
Sataplia Nakrdzali GE 70 Nb24
Satara IND (MHT) 108 Og37
Satara ZA 214 Mf58
Satawal Island FSM 156 Sb17
Satawan Atoll FSM 156 Sc17
Satellite Beach USA (FL) 250 Fk31
Satéma RCA 200 Ma43
Såtenäs S 12 Ln32
Satengar RI 129 Qj49
Säter S 13 Lq30
Säter S 13 Lq28
Satevó MEX (CHH) 252 Eg32
Sathing Phra THA 116 Qa42
Šatili GE 70 Nc24
Sātiņi LV 17 Mc34
Satipo PE 278 Gc51
Satiri BF 193 Kh40
Satiwala PK 79 Og30
Satkania BD 112 Pg34
Satkhira BD 112 Pe34
Satna IND (MPH) 109 Pa33
Sato J 103 Re30
Šatoj RUS (CHE) 70 Nc24
Šator BIH 41 Lr46
Sátoraljaújhely H 39 Mb42
Šatorina HR 41 Lq46
Satovča BG 47 Md49
Satpura Range IND 108 Oh35
Şatra RO 44 Md43
Satrokala RM 220 Nc57
Satsuma USA (AL) 243 Ff30
Satsuma-hanto J 103 Rf30
Satsuma-Iwojima J 103 Rf30
Satsunan Islands J 103 Re32
Sattahip THA 114 Qa39
Satt-e Sur IR 72 Ng28
Satthwa MYA 114 Ph36
Satti 79 Oj28
Satui RI 126 Qh47
Satuk THA 115 Qb38
Satu Mare RO 44 Mc43
Satun THA 116 Qa42
Satur IND (TNU) 111 Oj42
Šatura RUS 53 Mk18
Saturnino Maria Laspiur RA (CD) 289 Gj61
Satwas IND (MPH) 108 Oj34
Saty KZ 77 Ok24
Satyamangalam IND (TNU) 111 Oj41
Saucats F 24 Ku46
Sauce RA (CR) 289 Ha61
Sauce Blanco RA (RN) 293 Gj66

Sauce de la Luna – Senta

Sauce de la Luna RA (ER) 289 Ha61
Saucillo MEX (CHH) 253 Eh31
Sauclières F 25 Ld47
Sauda N 12 Lg31
Saudade BR (AM) 274 Gh48
Saudainu RI 124 Pk46
Saudakent KZ 76 Oe24
Sauðárkrókur IS 10 Ka13
Saudável BR (BA) 283 Hj52
Saúde BR (AM) 279 Ge49
Saúde BR (BA) 283 Hk51
Saudi Arabia KSA 57 Na07
Saue EST 16 Me31
Sauer D 34 Lg41
Sauer ZA 216 Lk62
Sauerland D 32 Lh39
Sauêruiná ou Papagaio BR 280 Ha52
Saugues F 25 Ld46
Saujil RA (CA) 288 Gg60
Saujon F 24 Ku45
Sauk Centre USA (MN) 241 Fc23
Saukorem RI 131 Rg46
Sauk Rapids USA (MN) 241 Fc23
Saul F (GF) 271 Hd44
Saula BR (PA) 275 Hb46
Sauland N 12 Lj31
Săulești RO 44 Md46
Saulieu F 23 Le43
Saulkrasti LV 17 Me33
Sault F 25 Lf46
Saulteaux River CDN 233 Ec18
Sault Sainte Marie CDN (ON) 246 Fh22
Sault Sainte Marie USA (MI) 246 Fh22
Saum USA (MN) 241 Fc22
Saumarez Reefs AUS 149 Sg56
Saumlakki RI 133 Rf49
Saumur F 22 Ku43
Saundatti IND (KTK) 108 Oh38
Saunders, Mount AUS 297 Tb36
Sauren PNG 159 Se48
Sauri Hill WAN 186 Ld40
Saurimo ANG 203 Ma50
Sauriwaunawa GUY 270 Ha44
Sausar IND (MPH) 109 Ok35
Sausu RI 127 Ra46
Sautar ANG 208 Lk51
Sautatá CO 268 Gb42
Saut de Doubs F 25 Lg43
Saut Sabbat F (GF) 271 Hd43
Sautso-canyon N 11 Mb11
Sauveterre-de-Béarn F 24 Ku47
Sauveterre-de-Guyenne F 24 Ku46
Sauvo FIN 16 Mc30
Sauxillanges F 25 Ld45
Sauzé-Vaussais F 24 Ku44
Sav IR 72 Ng29
Sava HN 256 Fg38
Sava HR/BIH 41 Ls45
Savage USA (MT) 235 Eh22
Savage River AUS (TAS) 152 Sc66
Savage River N.P. AUS (TAS) 152 Sc66
Savai'i Island WS 164 Bd52
Savalou DY 193 La42
Savalou Mts DY 193 La41
Savane MOC 214 Mh55
Savanna USA (OK) 243 Fc28
Savannah USA (GA) 249 Fk29
Savannah USA (MO) 241 Fc26
Savannah USA (TN) 243 Ff28
Savannah Downs AUS (QLD) 148 Sa55
Savannah Sound BS 251 Gb33
Savannakhét LAO 115 Qc37
Savanna-la-Mar JA 259 Ga36
Savant Lake CDN (ON) 239 Fe20
Savant Lake CDN 239 Fe20
Savantvadi IND (MHT) 108 Og38
Savanur IND (KTK) 110 Oh39
Savarkundla IND (GUJ) 108 Of35
Săvârșin RO 44 Mc44
Savaștepe TR 50 Mh51
Savate ANG 208 Lj54
Savazy RM 220 Nc57
Savcılı TR 51 Mo51
Savé DY 194 Lb41
Save F 24 Lb47
Save MOC 214 Mh56
Save ZW 214 Mf55
Saveh IR 72 Nf28
Savelugu GH 193 Kk41
Savenay F 22 Kt43
Săveni RO 45 Mg43
Saverdun F 24 Lb47
Saverne F 23 Lh42
Savigliano I 40 Lh46
Savignano sul Rubicone I 40 Ln46
Savinja SLO 41 Lp44
Savinskij RUS 11 Na14
Săvirii Vechi MD 45 Mh42
Savitaipale FIN 16 Mh29
Savitri Temple IND 106 Oh32
Šavnik SCG 46 Lu48
Savoie F 25 Lg45
Savo Island SOL 161 Sk50
Savona CDN (BC) 232 Dk20
Savona I 40 Lj46
Savonlinna FIN 16 Mj29
Savonranta FIN 16 Mk28
Savran UA 45 Ml42
Såvsjö S 15 Lp33
Savu RI 129 Ra51
Savu RI 129 Ra51
Savusavu FJI 163 Tk54
Savusavu Bay FJI 163 Tk54
Savu Sea RI 129 Ra50
Savute RB 213 Mc55
Savute Marsh RB 209 Mb55
Saw MYA 112 Ph35
Sawabi PK 79 Og28
Sawahan RI 128 Qf49
Sawahlunto RI 124 Qa46
Sawai Madhopur IND (RJT) 106 Oj33
Sawaleke FJI 163 Tk54
Sawang Daen Din THA 115 Qb37
Sawankhalok THA 114 Pk37
Sawara J 101 Sa28
Sawarangan RI 126 Qh48
Sawatch Mts. USA 235 Eg26
Sawbill CDN (NF) 244 Gg19
Sawe LB 192 Kg43
Sawin PL 37 Md39
Sawinnu LAR 175 Ma30
Sawknah LAR 175 Lh31
Sawla GH 193 Kj41
Sawmills ZW 214 Me55
Sawt-Law MYA 113 Pk32
Sawtooth Mts. USA 235 Ec24
Saxby Downs AUS (QLD) 148 Sb56
Saxby River AUS (QLD) 148 Sa55
Saxman USA (AK) 231 De18
Saxmundham GB 21 Lb38
Saxnäs S 10 Lh13
Say RMM 184 Kh39
Say RN 185 Lb39
Sayabec CDN (QC) 244 Gg21
Sayak KZ 84 Oj22
Sayalkudi IND (TNU) 111 Ok42
Sayán PE 278 Gb51
Sayang RI 130 Re45
Sayat TM 71 Ob26
Sayaxché GCA 255 Fe37
Saydnaya SYR 64 Mj29
Sayé CI 193 Kj41
Sayengga RI 131 Rg47
Sayhut YE 69 Nf38
Saylac SP 199 Nb40
Säyneinen FIN 11 Me14
Saynshand MNG 91 Qf23
Saynshand MNG 92 Qb24
Sayram Hu CHN 84 Pa23
Sayre USA (OK) 242 Fa28
Sayre USA (PA) 247 Gb25
Sayrob UZ 76 Od26
Say Tha Ni LAO 115 Qb36
Sayula MEX (JLC) 254 Ej36
Say'un YE 68 Ne38
Saza EAT 206 Mg50
Saza'i Kalan AFG 78 Od27
Sazan AL 46 Lu50
Sazılar TR 51 Mm51
Sazin PK 79 Og28
Sazlijka BG 47 Mf48
Šazud TJ 77 Og27
Sbaa DZ 173 Kk31
Sbeïtla TN 174 Le28
Scaddan AUS (WA) 144 Ra62
Scaër F 22 Kr42
Scăeşti RO 44 Md46
Scafell Pike GB 19 Kr36
Scaife Mountains 296 Gc33
Scalasaig GB 18 Ko34
Scalea I 43 Lq51
Scalloway GB 19 Kt30
Scammon Bay USA (AK) 228 Bg15
Scammon Bay USA (AK) 228 Bh15
Scandia CDN (AB) 233 Ed20
Scandinavia 6 Lb03
Scanno I 42 Lo49
Scansano I 40 Lm48
Scanzano Ionico I 43 Lr50
Scapa Flow GB 19 Kr32
Šćara BY 17 Mf37
Scarborough AUS 144 Qh61
Scarborough GB 21 Ku36
Scarborough TT 270 Gk40
Scarborough Reef RP 120 Qj38
Scarborough Shoal 120 Qj38
Scarinish GB 18 Ko34
Scărișoara RO 44 Mc44
Scarp GB 18 Kn32
Scarriff IRL 20 Km38
Scawfell Bank 117 Qd42
Scawfell Island AUS 149 Se56
Ščedrohir UA 37 Me39
Ščekino RUS 52 Mj19
Scenic USA (SD) 240 Ej24
Schaalsee D 33 Ll37
Schaffhausen CH 34 Lj43
Schagen NL 32 Le38
Schakalskuppe NAM 216 Lj59
Scharbeutz D 33 Ll36
Schärding A 35 Lo42
Scharhörn D 32 Lj37
Scharmützelsee D 33 Lp38
Scheeßel D 32 Lk37
Schefferville CDN 225 Gc08
Scheibbs A 35 Lq42
Scheifling A 35 Lp43
Schell Creek Range USA 234 Ec26
Schenectady USA (NY) 247 Gc24
Schesaplana CH/A 34 Lk43
Scheßlitz D 35 Lm41
Scheveningen NL 32 Le38
Schiermonnikoog NL 32 Lg37
Schiermonnikoog NL 32 Lg37
Schiermonnikoog, N.P. NL 32 Lg37
Schiffdorf D 32 Lj37
Schifffahrtsmuseum D 32 Lj37
Schiffshebewerk Rothensee D 33 Lm38
Schiltach D 34 Lj42
Schio I 40 Lm45
Schirmeck F 23 Lh42
Schitu Duca RO 45 Mh43
Schitu Golești RO 45 Mf45
Schkeuditz D 33 Ln39
Schladen D 33 Ll38
Schladming A 35 Lo43
Schlanders = Silandro I 40 Ll44
Schlei D 32 Lk36
Schleiden D 32 Lg40
Schleinitz Range PNG 160 Sf47
Schleiz D 33 Lm40
Schleswig D 32 Lk36
Schleswig-Holstein D 33 Lk36
Schleswig-Holsteinisches Wattenmeer, N.P. D 32 Lj36
Schleusingen D 33 Ll40
Schlieben D 33 Lo39
Schlitz D 32 Lk40
Schloss Altenburg D 33 Ln40
Schloss Aschaffenburg D 34 Lk41
Schloss Augustusburg D 32 Lg40
Schloss Clemenswerth D 32 Lh38
Schloss Duwisib NAM 212 Lj58
Schloss Dyck D 32 Lg39
Schloss Esterházy A 35 Lr43
Schlossgarten in Ludwigslust D 33 Lm37
Schloss Gottorf bei Schleswig D 32 Lk36
Schloss Güstrow D 33 Ln37
Schloss Hartenfels in Torgau D 33 Ln39
Schloss Jever D 32 Lh37
Schloss Linz A 35 Lp42
Schloss Ludwigsburg D 34 Lk42
Schloss Neuschwanstein D 35 Ll43
Schlosspark Neustrelitz D 33 Lo37
Schloss Porcia in Spittal an der Drau A 35 Lo44
Schloss Schwerin D 33 Lm37
Schloss und Park von Sanssouci D 33 Ln38
Schloss Wilhelmsburg Schmalkalden D 33 Ll40
Schloss Wilhelmshöhe D 32 Lk39
Schloss zu Gotha D 33 Ll40
Schlüchtern D 34 Lk40
Schlüsselfeld D 35 Ll41
Schmalkalden D 33 Ll40
Schmallenberg D 32 Lj39
Schmidt RCH 292 Gd65
Schmidtsdrift ZA 217 Mc60
Schmölln D 33 Ln40
Schmücke D 33 Lm39
Schneeberg D 33 Ln40
Schneverdingen D 32 Lk37
Schoberspitze A 35 Lp43
Schokland NL 32 Lf38
Schönberg D 33 Ll36
Schönberg D 33 Ll37
Schönbrunn A 35 Lr42
Schönebeck D 33 Lm38
Schongau D 35 Ll43
Schöningen D 33 Ll38
Schönsee D 35 Ln41
Schoombee ZA 217 Mc61
Schopfheim D 34 Lh43
Schörfling A 35 Lo43
Schorndorf D 34 Lk42
Schouten Islands PNG 159 Sc47
Schramberg D 34 Lj42
Schreiber CDN (ON) 239 Fg21
Schrobenhausen D 35 Lm42
Schruns A 34 Lk43
Schubert Inlet 296 Gb33
Schuckmansburg NAM 209 Mc54
Schurz USA (NV) 234 Ea26
Schuyler USA (NE) 241 Fb25
Schwaan D 33 Ln37
Schwabach D 35 Lm41
Schwäbische Alb D 34 Lk42
Schwäbisch Gmünd D 34 Lk42
Schwäbisch Hall D 34 Lk41
Schwabmünchen D 35 Ll42
Schwaigern D 34 Lj41
Schwalmstadt D 32 Lk40
Schwalmtal D 32 Lk40
Schwandorf D 35 Ln41
Schwaner Range RI 126 Qf46
Schwanewede D 32 Lj37
Schwarmstedt D 32 Lk38
Schwarze Elster D 33 Lo39
Schwarzenbek D 33 Ll37
Schwarzenberg D 35 Ln40
Schwarzrand NAM 212 Lj58
Schwatka Mts. USA (AK) 229 Cb12
Schwaz A 35 Lm43
Schwechat A 35 Lr42
Schwedt D 33 Lp37
Schweich D 34 Lg41
Schweinfurt D 34 Ll40
Schweizer Jura CH 34 Lg44
Schweizer Reneke ZA 217 Mc59
Schwerin D 33 Lm37
Schweriner See D 33 Lm37
Schwerin Mural AUS 141 Re58
Schwerte D 32 Lh39
Schwetzingen D 34 Lj41
Schwielochsee D 33 Lp38
Schwyz CH 34 Lj43
Sciacca I 42 Lo53
Scicli I 42 Lp54
Ščigry RUS 53 Mj20
Scilla I 43 Lq52
Ščinawa PL 36 Lr39
Scoarța RO 44 Md45
Scobey USA (MT) 233 Eh21
Scone AUS (NSW) 153 Sf62
Scooba USA (MS) 243 Ff29
Scoresby Land DK 225 Jd04
Scoresby Sound DK 225 Jd04
Scoresbysund = Ittoqqortoormiit DK 225 Jd04
Scornicești RO 45 Me46
Scorpion Bight AUS 145 Rd62
Ščors UA 52 Mf20
Ščorsy BY 17 Mg37
Scotia USA (CA) 234 Dh25
Scotia Bay CDN (BC) 231 Dd16
Scotia Ridge 267 Hb29
Scotia Sea 267 Hb30
Scotland GB 19 Kq34
Scotland Neck USA (NC) 249 Gb27
Scott Base ANT (NZ) 297 Tb34
Scott Canyon ANT 297 Td33
Scott Channel CDN 232 Df20
Scott City USA (KS) 240 Ek26
Scott Coast 297 Ta34
Scott Mountains 297 Nc32
Scott Reef AUS 138 Ra53
Scottsbluff USA (NE) 240 Ej25
Scotts Bluff Nat. Mon. USA 240 Ej25
Scottsboro USA (AL) 248 Fg28
Scottsburg USA (IN) 246 Fh26
Scottsburgh ZA 217 Mf61
Scottsdale AUS (TAS) 152 Sd66
Scottsdale USA (AZ) 237 Ee29
Scottsville USA (KY) 248 Fg27
Scottsville USA (VA) 249 Ga27
Scotty's Castle USA 236 Eb27
Scotty's Junction USA (NV) 236 Eb27
Scourie GB 19 Kp32
Scrabster GB 19 Kr32
Scranton USA (KS) 241 Fc26
Scranton USA (ND) 240 Ej22
Scranton USA (PA) 247 Gc25
Ščučyn BY 17 Me37
Sculeni MD 45 Mh43
Scunthorpe GB 21 Ku37
Scuol CH 34 Ll44
Scutaru RO 45 Mg44
Ščyrec' UA 39 Md41
Seabra BR (BA) 283 Hk52
Seabreeze Amusement Park USA 247 Gb24
Seacow ZA 217 Mc61
Seaford USA (DE) 247 Gc26
Seaforth AUS (QLD) 149 Se56
Seagaia Ocean Dome J 103 Rf30
Sea Gardens RI 116 Ph43
Seahouses GB 19 Kt35
Sea Isle City USA (NJ) 247 Gc26
Sea Lake AUS (VIC) 153 Sb63
Seal C. USA 228 Ca18
Seal Cay BS 251 Gb34
Seal Cove CDN (NF) 245 Hb21
Sea Lion Island GB 295 Ha72
Seal Is. USA 228 Ca17
Seal Point ZA 217 Mc63
Sealy USA (TX) 243 Fb31
Seamer GB 21 Ku36
Sea of Azov UA/RUS 55 Mj22
Sea of Galilee IL 64 Mh29
Sea of Heat CHN 113 Pk33
Sea of Japan 83 Rc11
Sea of Marmara TR 50 Mj50
Sea of Okhotsk RUS 59 Sb07
Sea of the Hebrides GB 18 Ko34
Sea Park ZA 217 Mf61
Seara BR (SC) 290 Hd59
Searchlight USA (NV) 236 Ec28
Searchmont CDN (ON) 246 Fh22
Searcy USA (AR) 243 Fe28
Seaside USA (OR) 234 Dj23
Seaside Point USA (OR) 232 Dh23
Seaspray AUS (VIC) 153 Sd65
Sea Temple RI 129 Qh50
Seattle USA (WA) 232 Dj22
Seaview Range AUS (QLD) 149 Sc55
Seaward Kaikoura Range NZ 155 Tg67
Sea World AUS 151 Sg59
Sea World USA 250 Fk31
Sea World of San Antonio USA 242 Fa31
Seba RI 129 Ra51
Sébaco NIC 256 Fg39
Sebakung RI 126 Qj46
Šebalino RUS (ALT) 85 Pc20
Se Bangfai LAO 115 Qc37
Sebangka RI 125 Qc45
Sebaring RP 122 Qj41
Sebastian USA (FL) 250 Fk32
Sebastian Inlet USA (FL) 250 Fk32
Sebastopol USA (CA) 234 Dj26
Sebastopol USA (MS) 243 Ff29
Sebatik RI 127 Qj43
Sebauh MAL 126 Qg44
Sebayan, Gunung RI 126 Qf46
Sebba BF 185 La39
Sebderat ER 191 Mj39
Sebdou DZ 173 Kk28
Sébé G 195 Lh46
Šebekino RUS 53 Mj20
Sébékoro RMM 184 Kf39
Seben TR 51 Mm50
Seberi BR (RS) 290 Hd59
Seberida RI 124 Qb46
Sebeș RO 44 Md45
Sebeș RO 44 Md45
Sebesi RI 125 Qc48
Sebeta ETH 198 Mk41
Sébété RMM 184 Kg38
Sebež RUS 52 Me17
Sebežskij N.P. RUS 52 Me17
Şebinkarahisar TR 63 Mk25
Sebis RO 44 Mc44
Sebit EAK 204 Mh45
Sebkha Aïn Belbela DZ 172 Kh32
Sebkha Azzel-Matti DZ 180 La33
Sebkha de Timimoun DZ 173 La31
Sebkha de Tindouf DZ 172 Kg32
Sebkha el Mellah DZ 173 Kk31
Sebkha Mekerrhane DZ 180 La32
Sebkha Ndrhamcha RIM 183 Kc36
Sebkha Tah DARS 172 Kd32
Sebkhat El Kébira DZ 173 Kk28
Sebkhet Afouidich DARS 178 Kc35
Sebkhet Aghzoumal DARS 178 Kd33
Sebkhet Chemchâm RIM 178 Kd35
Sebkhet el Jill RIM 178 Kd34
Sebkhet En Nou TN 174 Le28
Sebkhet Ghallamane RIM 178 Kf34
Sebkhet Grinnah DARS 178 Kc34
Sebkhet Iguetti RIM 178 Kf33
Sebkhet Oumm ed Droûs Guebli RIM 178 Ke34
Sebkhet Oumm ed Droûs Telli RIM 178 Ke33
Sebkhet Sidi El Hani TN 174 Lf28
Sebkhet Tanouzkka DARS 178 Kc34
Sebkhet Tidsit DARS 178 Kc34
Seblat, Gunung RI 124 Qb47
Sebnitz D 33 Lp40
Sebol GCA 255 Ff38
Sebonpopo RI 130 Re45
Sebring USA (FL) 250 Fk32
Sebta = Ceuta E 172 Kh28
Sebt-des-Gzoula MA 172 Kf29
Sebuku RI 125 Qc48
Sebuku RI 126 Qj47
Sebuku RI 127 Qj44
Sebuku RI 128 Qc48
Šebunino RUS 99 Sa22
Secador BR (MS) 286 Hc57
Sécchia I 40 Ll46
Secemin PL 37 Lu40
Sečenovo RUS 53 Nc18
Sechin PE 278 Ga50
Sechura PE 272 Fk48
Seclin F 23 Ld40
Secondigny F 22 Ku44
Seco ó Yaminue RA 292 Gg66
Sečoveljske soline SLO 41 Lo45
Secretary Island NZ 155 Td68
Secunderabad IND (APH) 109 Ok37
Sécure BOL 279 Gh53
Security USA (CO) 235 Eh26
Seda LT 17 Mc34
Seda LV 17 Mf33
Sedalia USA (MO) 241 Fd26
Sedan AUS (QLD) 150 Sb58
Sedan F 23 Le41
Sedan USA (KS) 243 Fb27
Sedan USA (NM) 237 Ej27
Sedanau RI 117 Qd44
Sedanka Island USA 228 Bg19
Seddon NZ 155 Th66
Seddonville NZ 155 Tf66
Sedeh IR 72 Ng30
Sedeh IR 72 Ng30
Sedeh IR 73 Nk29
Sedeinga Temple SUD 190 Mf36
Séderon F 25 Lf46
Sedgefield ZA 216 Mb63
Sédhiou SN 183 Kc39
Sédini I 31 Lj50
Sedjenane TN 174 Le27
Sedlčany CZ 38 Lp41
Sedlyšče UA 37 Me39
Sedoa RI 127 Ra46
Sedona USA (AZ) 237 Ee28
Sedrata DZ 174 Le27
Sedrata DZ 174 Ld27
Sedro Wolley USA (WA) 232 Dj21
Šeduva LT 17 Md35
Sędziszów PL 37 Ma40
Seebe CDN (AB) 233 Ec20
Seeberg A/SLO 35 Lp44
Seefeld A 35 Lm43
Seehausen D 33 Lm38
Seeheim NAM 216 Lj59
Seeis NAM 212 Lj57
Seekoegat ZA 216 Mb62
Seekwa GH 193 Kj42
Seeley Lake USA (MT) 235 Ed22
Seelig, Mount 296 Ed35
Seelow D 33 Lp38
Seemore Downs AUS (WA) 145 Rc61
Seenu Atoll = Addoo Atoll MV 110 Og46
Seer MNG 85 Pg21
Sées F 22 La42
Şefaatli TR 51 Mp51
Sefar DZ 181 Le33
Seferihisar TR 49 Mg52
Seferihisar Baraj TR 49 Mg52
Séféto RMM 184 Kf38
Sefid Abeh IR 73 Oa30
Sefid Rud IR 72 Ne27
Sefophe RB 213 Md57
Sefoula MA 173 Kj29
Sefrou MA 172 Kh29
Segag ETH 198 Nb42
Segah RI 127 Qj44
Segala ER 191 Na39
Ségala RMM 183 Ke38
Segama MAL 122 Qk43
Segamat MAL 117 Qb44
Segangane MA 173 Kj28
Şegarcea RO 44 Md46
Ségbana DY 186 Lb40
Segbwema WAL 192 Ke42
Segesta I 42 Ln53
Seget RI 130 Rf46
Segeža RUS 11 Mh14
Seghe SOL 161 Sj50
Segorbe E 29 Ku49
Ségou RMM 184 Kg39
Segovia CO 268 Gc42
Segovia E 26 Kq50
Segozero RUS 11 Mg14
Segré F 22 Ku43
Segrun RI 116 Pj44
Ségué RMM 184 Kj39
Seguedine RN 181 Lg35
Séguéla CI 192 Kg42
Séguéla RMM 184 Kg38
Séguéla RMM 184 Kg39
Séguélon CI 192 Kg41
Séguénéga BF 185 Kj39
Seguin USA (TX) 242 Fb31
Segunda RA 288 Gj61
Segunda USA (VI) 261 Gh36
Segura P 28 Kn49
Segura de la Sierra E 29 Ks48
Segura de León E 28 Ko48
Segurola RA (BA) 293 Hb64
Sehithwa RB 213 Mb56
Sehlabathebe N.P. LS 217 Me60
Sehnkwehn LB 192 Kf43
Seho RI 127 Rc47
Sehonghong LS 217 Me60
Sehore IND (MPH) 108 Oj34
Sehulea PNG 160 Sf50
Sehwan PK 80 Od32
Seia P 26 Kn50
Seibert USA (CO) 240 Ej26
Șeica Mare RO 44 Me44
Seikakap RI 126 Qe46
Seikan Tunnel J 99 Sa25
Seikpyu MYA 112 Ph35
Seilhac F 24 Lb45
Seiling USA (OK) 242 Fa27
Seinäjoki FIN 16 Mc28
Seine F 23 Ld42
Seini RO 44 Md43
Seinma RI 131 Rk48
Seira RI 133 Rf49
Seirijai LT 17 Md36
Seitsemisen kansallispuisto FIN 16 Md29
Sejeli EAT 207 Mj49
Sejerø DK 14 Lm35
Sejerø Bugt DK 14 Lm35
Sejm UA 52 Mg20
Sejmčan RUS 59 Sc06
Sejny PL 37 Md36
Sejorong RI 129 Qj50
Seka ETH 198 Mj42
Seka THA 115 Qb37
Seka Banza RDC 202 Lg48
Sekadau RI 126 Qf45
Sekak RI 130 Rg46
Sekatak RI 127 Qj44
Sekayan RI 127 Qk45
Sekayu RI 125 Qb47
Sekenke EAT 207 Mh48
Sekhutlane RB 213 Mc58
Šeki AZ 70 Nd25
Seki J 101 Rj28
Seki TR 50 Mk54
Sekibisho Shima J 103 Rc33
Sekigahara-Oro Q.N.P. J 101 Rj28
Sekili TR 51 Mp51
Sekodi RI 124 Qb45
Sekoma RB 213 Mb58
Sekoma Pan RB 213 Mb58
Sekomapan RB 213 Mb58
Sekondi GH 193 Kk43
Sekong LAO 115 Qd38
Sek'ot'a ETH 191 Mk40
Șekowa PL 39 Mb41
Sekpiegu GH 193 Kk41
Šeksna RUS 52 Mk16
Sekuau MAL 126 Qg44
Sekulovo BG 47 Mh47
Sekupang RI 125 Qb45
Sela BF 193 Kk40
Se La IND 112 Pg32
Selalang MAL 126 Qf44
Selama MAL 116 Qa43
Selangan MAL 126 Qg44
Selaön S 13 Ls31
Selaphum THA 115 Qb37
Selárgius I 31 Lk51
Selaru RI 133 Rf50
Șelaru RO 45 Mf46
Selassi RI 130 Rg47
Selat Alas RI 129 Qj50
Selatan RI 130 Rd48
Selat Aruri RI 131 Rh46
Selat Bangka RI 125 Qc47
Selat Bengkalis RI 124 Qa45
Selat Berhala RI 125 Qc46
Selat Bungalaut RI 124 Pk46
Selat Dampier RI 130 Rf46
Selat Durian RI 125 Qb45
Selat Gaspar RI 125 Qd47
Selat Jailolo RI 130 Re45
Selat Lombok RI 129 Qh50
Selat Nautilus RI 131 Rg48
Selat Ombai 132 Rc50
Selatpanjang RI 124 Qb45
Selat Rupat RI 124 Qa45
Selat Sanding RI 124 Qa47
Selat Sape RI 129 Qk50
Selat Siberut RI 124 Pk46
Selat Woinui RI 131 Rh46
Selat Yapen RI 131 Rj46
Selawik USA (AK) 229 Ca12
Selawik Lake USA 229 Bk12
Selawik National Wildlife Refuge USA 229 Ca12
Selawik River USA 229 Ca12
Selayar RI 125 Qc46
Selayar RI 129 Ra49
Selb D 35 Ln40
Sélba BF 185 Kk38
Selbekken N 10 Le14
Selbitz D 35 Lm40
Selbjørnsfjorden N 12 Lf31
Selbu N 10 Lf14
Selby GB 21 Kt37
Selby USA (SD) 240 Ek23
Selco RUS 16 Mj32
Selçuk TR 49 Mh53
Selde DK 14 Lk34
Seldovia USA (AK) 229 Ce16
Sele I 42 Lq50
Selebi-Phikwe RB 213 Md57
Šelehov RUS 90 Qa19
Selehovskaja RUS 11 Mk15
Selemdža RUS 98 Re20
Selendi TR 50 Mj52
Selenga RUS 90 Qd19
Selenge MNG 90 Qa21
Selenge MNG 90 Qc21
Selenge MNG 90 Qc21
Selenge RDC 200 Lk46
Selenge Gol MNG 90 Qc21
Selengei EAK 207 Mj47
Selenginsk RUS (BUR) 90 Qd20
Sélestat F 23 Lh42
Séléti SN 183 Kb39
Selevac SCG 44 Ma46
Selfoss IS 10 Jk14
Selge TR 51 Mm53
Seli WAL 192 Kd41
Sélibabi RIM 183 Kd38
Seligenstadt D 34 Lj40
Selihino RUS 98 Rj20
Sélim RCA 201 Md43
Selim Caravanserai ARM 70 Nc26
Selimiye TR 49 Mh53
Selimpaşa TR 50 Mj49
Seling IND (MZR) 112 Pg34
Sélinkégni RMM 183 Ke38
Selinunte I 42 Ln53
Selište SCG 46 Mc47
Seliu RI 125 Qd47
Seližarovo RUS 52 Mg17
Seljaküla EST 16 Md31
Seljatyn UA 45 Mf43
Selje N 12 Lf28
Seljebø N 12 Lj28
Seljord N 12 Lj31
Selkirk CDN (MB) 238 Fb20
Selkirk GB 19 Ks35
Selkirk Mountains CDN 232 Eb20
Sellâourich DARS 178 Kd34
Sellers USA (SC) 249 Ga28
Selles-sur-Cher F 22 Lb43
Sells USA (AZ) 236 Ee30
Selma USA (AL) 248 Fg29
Selma USA (CA) 236 Ea27
Selmer USA (TN) 243 Ff28
Selokolela RB 213 Mc58
Selokolela RB 213 Mc58
Sélo Kouré RG 192 Ke40
Selongey F 23 Lf43
Šelopugino RUS 91 Qj20
Sélouma RG 192 Ke40
Selous ZW 214 Mf55
Selous Game Reserve EAT 207 Mj50
Selous, Mount CDN 231 Dd14
Selpel RI 130 Rf46
Selsele-ye Kuh-e Tirband-e Torkestan AFG 78 Oc28
Selsele-ye Safid Kuh AFG 78 Ob28
Selsele-ye Siyah Kuh AFG 78 Ob29
Selsey Bill GB 21 Ku40
Seltz F 23 Lj42
Selu IND (MHT) 108 Oj36
Seluan RI 117 Qd43
Selva RA (SE) 289 Gj60
Selva Alegre EC 272 Ga45
Selvas BR 264 Gb20
Selviria BR (MS) 286 He56
Selwyn AUS (QLD) 148 Sa56
Selwyn Mountains CDN 231 De14
Selwyn Range AUS (QLD) 148 Rk56
Semacueza MOC 214 Mh55
Seman AL 46 Lu50
Semana RMM 192 Kg40
Semangka RI 125 Qc48
Semanu RI 126 Qj44
Semarang RI 128 Qf49
Semarsot IND (CGH) 109 Pb34
Semarwara IND (RJT) 108 Og34
Sematan MAL 126 Qe45
Sematang RI 127 Ra45
Semau RI 132 Rb51
Semaya RI 129 Qh50
Sembabule EAU 201 Mf46
Sembadeh IND (MHT) 108 Oj35
Sembakung RI 127 Qj44
Sembé RCB 195 Lh45
Sembehun WAL 192 Ke42
Semberang RI 127 Qk45
Sembuang, Mount RI 116 Pj43
Şemdinli TR 63 Nc27
Semei SUD 197 Mf39
Semenic-Cheile Carașului, P.N. RO 44 Mb45
Semenivka UA 52 Mg19
Semenov RUS 53 Nc17
Semenovka KZ 84 Ok20
Semënovka RUS 53 Nc21
Semënovka RUS 98 Rd20
Semera MAL 126 Qf45
Semerdžievo BG 47 Mg47
Semeru, Gunung RI 128 Qg50
Semeteh RI 125 Qb47
Semey KZ 84 Pa20
Sémien CI 192 Kg42
Semikarakorsk RUS 55 Na22
Semiliguda IND (ORS) 109 Pb36
Semiluki RUS 53 Mk20
Seminoe Reservoir USA 235 Eg24
Seminole USA (OK) 243 Fb28
Seminole USA (TX) 237 Ej29
Seminole Canyon S.P. USA 242 Ek31
Seminole Nation Mus. USA 243 Fb28
Semirara Island RP 123 Ra40
Semirara Islands RP 121 Ra39
Semirom IR 72 Nf30
Semitau RI 126 Qf45
Semliki RDC 201 Me45
Semliki Wildlife Reserve EAU 204 Mf45
Semmeringbahn A 35 Lq43
Semna SUD 190 Mf36
Semnan IR 72 Ng28
Semna West Temple SUD 190 Mf36
Semois B 23 Lf41
Semolale RB 214 Me56
Šemordan RUS 53 Nf17
Semox GCA 255 Ff38
Sempacher See CH 34 Lj43
Šempeter SLO 41 Lq44
Semporna MAL 122 Qk43
Semri IND (MPH) 109 Ok34
Semuliki N.P. EAU 204 Mf45
Semur-en-Auxois F 23 Le43
Sena BOL 279 Gg52
Sena BOL 279 Gg51
Senador Firmino BR (MG) 287 Hj56
Senador José Porfírio BR (PA) 275 He47
Senador Pompeu BR (CE) 277 Ja48
Senafe ER 191 Mk39
Senaki GE 70 Nb24
Señal Canoas PE 278 Gb51
Señal Huascarán PE 278 Gb50
Señal Mongon PE 278 Ga50
Sena Madureira BR (AC) 279 Gf50
Senanga Z 209 Mb54
Senatobia USA (MS) 243 Ff28
Senayang RI 125 Qc46
Senchi GH 193 La42
Sendafa ETH 198 Mk41
Sendai J 101 Sa26
Sendai J 103 Rf30
Sendai-wan J 101 Sa26
Sendangbiro RI 128 Qg50
Sendelingsfontein ZA 217 Md59
Senden D 34 Ll42
Sendhwa IND (MPH) 108 Oh35
Șendreni RO 45 Mh45
Senec SK 38 Ls42
Seneca USA (OR) 234 Ea23
Seneca USA (SC) 249 Fj28
Seneca USA (SD) 240 Fa23
Seneca Caverns USA 247 Ga26
Seneca Lake USA 247 Gb24
Seneca Rocks USA (WV) 247 Ga26
Sénégal RIM/SN 183 Kc37
Senegal 167 Ka08
Senekal ZA 217 Md60
Seney USA (MI) 246 Fh22
Seney N.W.R. USA 246 Fg22
Senftenberg D 33 Lo39
Senga MW 211 Mh52
Sengan WAN 194 Lc43
Sengata RI 127 Qj45
Sengeti RI 125 Qb46
Sênggê Zangbo = Indus CHN 88 Pa30
Senggigi Beach RI 129 Qj50
Sengkamang RI 124 Qa45
Sengkang RI 129 Ra48
Senguer RA 294 Gf68
Senguerr RA 292 Ge68
Sengwa ZW 210 Me55
Senhor do Bonfim BR (BA) 283 Hk51
Senhoro do Porto BR (MG) 287 Hj55
Senica SK 38 Ls42
Senigállia I 41 Lo47
Senirkent TR 51 Mf52
Senj HR 41 Lp46
Senja N 10 Lj11
Senji = Gingee IND (TNU) 111 Ok40
Senjit Khad MNG 91 Qf23
Senkaya TR 63 Nb25
Senkele Swayne's Hartebeest Sanctuary ETH 198 Mk42
Senkobo Z 209 Mc54
Senlis F 23 Lc41
Sen Monorom K 115 Qd39
Sennar SUD 190 Mg40
Sennecey-le-Grand F 25 Le44
Sennen GB 20 Kp40
Senneterre CDN (QC) 244 Gb21
Sennybridge GB 20 Kr39
Seno Aisén RCH 294 Gd68
Seno Almirantazgo RCH 294 Gf73
Sénoba SN 183 Kc39
Seno de Reloncaví RCH 292 Gd66
Senohrad SK 39 Lu42
Senoia USA (GA) 249 Fh29
Senokos BG 47 Mj47
Senonches F 22 Lb42
Seno Otway RCH 294 Ge72
Senorbì I 31 Lk51
Senorong RI 127 Rb46
Seno Skyring RCH 294 Gd72
Senoudébou SN 183 Kd38
Senovo BG 47 Mg47
Senqua ZA 217 Me61
Senquanyana LS 217 Me60
Sens F 23 Ld42
Sensuntepeque ES 255 Ff39
Senta SCG 44 Ma45

Sherborne – Simiyu

Sherborne ZA 217 Mc61
Sherbro Island WAL 192 Kd42
Sherbrooke CDN (QC) 247 Ge23
Sherbrooke Vill. CDN 245 Gj23
Sherbro River WAL 192 Kd42
Sherburne USA (NY) 247 Gc24
Sherburne N.W.R. USA 241 Fd23
Sherburne Reef PNG 159 Se47
Sherda TCH 181 Lj35
Shereiq SUD 190 Mg37
Shergarh IND (RJT) 106 Og32
Sherghati IND (BIH) 109 Pc33
Sheridan USA (AR) 243 Fd28
Sheridan USA (WY) 235 Eg23
Sheridan Lake USA (CO) 240 Ej26
Sheringa AUS (SA) 152 Rh62
Sheringham GB 21 Lb38
Sherlock AUS (SA) 152 Rk63
Sherlock River AUS 140 Qj56
Sherman USA (MA) 244 Gf23
Sherman USA (TX) 243 Fb29
Sherman Mtn. USA 234 Ec25
Sherobod UZ 76 Od27
Sherpur BD 112 Pf33
Sherrick, Mount CDN 239 Ga20
Sherridon CDN (MB) 238 Ek18
,s-Hertogenbosch NL 32 Lf39
Sherwood CDN (AB) 233 Ed19
Sherwood Ranch RB 213 Md57
Sheshalik USA (AK) 229 Bj12
Shesh Deh IR 74 Ng31
Sheslay River CDN 231 Dd16
Shetland Islands GB 19 Ku30
Shetpe KZ 71 Ng23
Shetrawa IND (RJT) 106 Og32
Shetrunjaya Hill IND 108 Of35
Shetrunji IND 108 Of35
Shëvasija AL 46 Lu51
Shevchenko shyghanaghy KZ 71 Oa22
Shevgaon IND (MHT) 108 Oh36
She Xian CHN (HBI) 93 Qg27
Sheyang CHN (JGS) 102 Ra29
Sheyenne USA (ND) 240 Fa22
Sheyenne Grassland N.P. USA 240 Fb22
Sheykhabad AFG 78 Oe28
Sheykh Farid ad-Din Attar IR 73 Nk27
Shey Phoksundo N.P. NEP 88 Pb31
Shezongo Z 210 Md54
Shiant Islands GB 18 Ko33
Shibam YE 68 Nb38
Shibam YE 68 Ne38
Shibao CHN 113 Pk32
Shibaozhai CHN 95 Qe30
Shibata J 101 Rk27
Shibecha J 99 Sc24
Shibetsu J 99 Sb23
Shibetsu J 99 Sc24
Shibin el-Kôm ET 177 Mf30
Shibogama Lake CDN 239 Ff19
Shib Yak AFG 78 Oa29
Shicheng CHN (JGX) 102 Qj32
Shiel Bridge GB 19 Kp33
Shieldaig GB 19 Kp33
Shields USA (ND) 240 Ek22
Shieli KZ 76 Od23
Shigu CHN (YUN) 113 Qa32
Shihan YE 69 Ng37
Shihezi CHN (XUZ) 85 Pc23
Shihuajie CHN (HUB) 95 Qf29
Shijiazhuang CHN (HBI) 93 Qh26
Shikabe J 99 Sa24
Shikarpur IND (KTK) 110 Oh39
Shikarpur PK 80 Oe32
Shikine-jima J 101 Rk28
Shikohabad IND (UPH) 107 Ok32
Shikoku J 101 Rh29
Shikoku-sanchi J 101 Rg29
Shikongkong CHN 97 Qg33
Shikotsu-ko J 99 Sa24
Shikotsu-Toya N.P. J 99 Sa24
Shilabo ETH 199 Nc42
Shilah UAE 74 Ng34
Shilik KZ 77 Ok24
Shilik KZ 77 Ok24
Shiliktí KZ 85 Pc22
Shilipu CHN (HUB) 95 Qg30
Shillong IND (MGA) 112 Pf33
Shiloango RDC 202 Lg48
Shima SYR 65 Mk28
Shimabara J 103 Rf29
Shimba Hills National Reserve EAK 205 Mk48
Shimbiris SP 199 Nd40
Shimen CHN (HUN) 95 Qf31
Shimen CHN (SCH) 94 Qb31
Shimizu J 99 Sb24
Shimizu J 101 Rk28
Shimla IND (HPH) 107 Oj30
Shimoda J 101 Rk28
Shimodate J 101 Rk27
Shimoga IND (KTK) 110 Oh40
Shimokita-hanto J 99 Sa25
Shimokita Q.N.P. J 99 Sa25
Shimo-Koshiki J 103 Re30
Shimo-koshiki-jima J 103 Re30
Shimoni EAK 207 Mk48
Shimoni Caves EAK 205 Mk48
Shimono-jima J 100 Re28
Shimonoseki J 103 Rf29
Shimunenga Z 210 Md53
Shimuwini Bushveld Camp ZA 214 Mf57
Shinak Pass IRQ 65 Nc27
Shinan CHN (GZG) 96 Qe34
Shinano-gawa J 101 Rk27
Shinas OM 75 Nj33
Shindand AFG 78 Ob29
Shinga RDC 203 Mc47
Shingbwiyang MYA 113 Pj32
Shingletown USA (CA) 234 Dk25
Shingu J 101 Rh29
Shingwedzi ZA 214 Mf57
Shingwedzi ZA 214 Mf57
Shinjo J 101 Sa26
Shinkafe WAN 186 Ld39
Shinkay Hills AFG 78 Oe29
Shino-saki J 101 Rh29
Shinoúsa GR 49 Mf54
Shinyanga EAT 206 Mg47
Shiogama J 101 Sa26
Shiojiri J 101 Rj27
Shipasbamba PE 272 Gb48
Shiping CHN (YUN) 113 Qb34
Shipkila CHN/IND 88 Ok30
Shippagan CDN (NB) 245 Gh22
Shippensburg USA (PA) 247 Gb25
Shiprock USA (NM) 237 Ef27
Shipu CHN (ZJG) 102 Ra31
Shiqian CHN (GZH) 96 Qe32
Shiquan CHN (SAA) 95 Qe29
Shiquanhe CHN (TIB) 88 Ok29
Shira'ayn KSA 66 Na35
Shir Abad IR 72 Ne26
Shirahama J 101 Rh29
Shirakami-dake J 101 Sa25
Shirakami-Sanchi J 101 Sa25
Shirakawa J 101 Sa27
Shirame-san J 101 Rk27
Shirane-san J 101 Rk28
Shiranuka J 99 Sc24
Shiraroi J 99 Sa24
Shirase Coast 296 Cb34
Shirati EAT 204 Mh46
Shiraton J 101 Rj28
Shiraz IR 74 Ng31
Shirdi IND (MHT) 108 Oh36
Shiree MNG 90 Pj22
Shiree MNG 90 Qb23
Shireet MNG 91 Qg23
Shiretoko-hanto J 99 Sc23
Shiretoko-misaki J 99 Sc23
Shiretoko N.P. J 99 Sc23
Shirgah IR 72 Ng27
Shirin IR 72 Nc27
Shirin Su IR 72 Ne28
Shirinthorn Reservoir THA 115 Qc38
Shiripuno EC 272 Gb46
Shir Khan AFG 78 Oe27
Shir Kuh IR 72 Nh30
Shirley NAM 212 Lk58
Shiroishi J 101 Sa27
Shirpur IND (MHT) 108 Oh35
Shirvan IR 73 Nj27
Shirwan Mazin IRQ 65 Nc27
Shirya-saki J 99 Sa25
Shishaldin Volcano USA 228 Bh18
Shishi CHN (FJN) 97 Qk33
Shishinda ETH 197 Mh42
Shishked Gol MNG 90 Pk20
Shishmaref Inlet USA 229 Bh12
Shishou CHN (HUB) 95 Qg31
Shisur OM 69 Ng36
Shitai CHN (AHU) 102 Qj30
Shit Bay EC 272 Fk47
Shittaung-Temple MYA 112 Pg35
Shiuji BHT 112 Pe32
Shiura J 101 Sa25
Shiv IND (RJT) 106 Of32
Shivpuri IND (MPH) 107 Oj33
Shiwa Ngandu Z 210 Mf51
Shiwa Ngandu Z 210 Mf51
Shiwulidun CHN (NHZ) 92 Qd27
Shixing CHN (GDG) 97 Qh33
Shiyan CHN (HUB) 95 Qf29
Shiyang He CHN 92 Qb26
Shiza GR 48 Mb54
Shizhenjie CHN (JGX) 102 Qj31
Shizilu CHN (GZG) 96 Qe35
Shizong CHN (YUN) 113 Qb33
Shizu CHN (CGQ) 95 Qe31
Shizu CHN (ZJG) 102 Ra31
Shizuishan CHN (NHZ) 92 Qd26
Shizuizi CHN (YUN) 113 Qb32
Shizunai J 99 Sb24
Shizuoka J 101 Rk28
Shkodër = Skutari AL 46 Lu48
Shkumbin AL 46 Ma49
Shmetiyeh SYR 65 Mk28
Shoal Bay IND (AAN) 111 Pg40
Shoal Cape AUS 144 Ra62
Shoal Lake CDN (MB) 238 Ek20
Shoal Point AUS 144 Qh60
Shoal Water Bay AUS 149 Sf57
Shobara J 101 Rg28
Shofirkon UZ 76 Oc25
Shofuku-ji J 103 Rf29
Shoja Abad IR 72 Nf29
Shol IND (ARP) 112 Ph31
Sholakkorghan KZ 76 Oe24
Sholapur IND (MHT) 108 Oh37
Sholinghur IND (TNU) 111 Ok40
Shonzhy KZ 77 Ok24
Shoqan IR 73 Nj27
Shoranur IND (KER) 110 Oj41
Shorap PK 80 Oc33
Shorapur IND (KTK) 108 Oj37
Sho'rchi UZ 76 Od27
Shoreacres CDN (BC) 232 Eb21
Shoreham USA (NY) 247 Gd25
Shorkot PK 79 Og30
Shorobe RB 213 Mb55
Shortland Island SOL 160 Sh49
Shortland Islands SOL 160 Sh49
Shoshone USA (CA) 236 Eb28
Shoshone USA (ID) 235 Ec24
Shoshone Ice Caves USA 235 Ec24
Shoshone Mountains USA 234 Eb26
Shoshong RB 213 Md57
Shoshong Hills RB 213 Md57
Shoshoni USA (WY) 235 Ef24
Shotor-Khun-Pass AFG 78 Oc28
Shouning CHN (FJN) 102 Qk32
Shoup USA (ID) 235 Ec23
Shouten Islands AUS 152 Se67
Shouxian CHN (AHU) 102 Qj29
Shouyang CHN (SAX) 93 Qg27
Shovot UZ 71 Oa25
Showil SUD 190 Mf39
Show Low USA (AZ) 237 Ee28
Shree Meenakshi Sundareswarwar Temple = Meenakshi Temple IND 111 Oj42
Shreveport USA (LA) 243 Fd29
Shrewsbury GB 21 Ks38
Shri Nathji Temple IND 106 Og33
Shrine of Hazrate Masumeh IR 72 Nf28
Shrine of Imam Reza IR 73 Nk27
Shrines of Ise J 101 Rj28
Shrirampur IND (MHT) 108 Oh36
Shriwardhan IND (MHT) 108 Og36
Shriwardhan Beach IND 108 Og36
Shtugara AL 46 Ma51
Shu KZ 76 Oe23
Shu KZ 77 Og24
Shuagpai Shuiku CHN 96 Qf33
Shuajingsi CHN (SCH) 94 Qb30
Shuanfeng CHN (HUN) 96 Qg32
Shuangbai CHN (YUN) 113 Qa33
Shuangcheng CHN (HLG) 98 Rd23
Shuangfeng CHN (HLG) 98 Rd22
Shuanggou CHN (HUB) 95 Qg29
Shuangliao CHN (JLN) 100 Rb24
Shuanglin Si CHN 93 Qg27
Shuangliu CHN (SCH) 94 Qb30
Shuangpai CHN (HUN) 96 Qf33
Shuangpaishan CHN (HUN) 97 Qg32
Shuangtaihekou Z.B. CHN 100 Ra25
Shuangtaizi He CHN 100 Rb25
Shuangyashan CHN (HLG) 98 Rf22
Shuanhhe CHN (SCH) 95 Qd30
Shubenacadie Prov. Park CDN 245 Gj23
Shucheng CHN (AHU) 102 Qj30
Shudanzhuang CHN (XUZ) 86 Pc27
Shufu CHN (XUZ) 86 Oh26
Shuganu IND (MNP) 112 Pg33
Shuheit SUD 190 Mh40
Shuiba CHN (HUN) 95 Qe31
Shuicheng CHN (GZH) 96 Qc32
Shuiji CHN (FJN) 102 Qk32
Shuijiang CHN (CGQ) 95 Qd31
Shuikou CHN (GZH) 96 Qe33
Shuitutue CHN (CGQ) 95 Qd31
Shujaabad PK 81 Of31
Shujalpur IND (MPH) 108 Oj34
Shulan CHN (JLN) 98 Rd23
Shulbinsk KZ 84 Pa20
Shule CHN (XUZ) 86 Oj26
Shule He CHN 87 Ph25
Shule He CHN 92 Pk26
Shule Nanshan CHN 87 Pj26
Shulgareh AFG 78 Od27
Shumagin Islands USA 228 Bk18
Shumanay UZ 71 Nk24
Shume EAT 207 Mk48
Shunchang CHN (FJN) 102 Qj32
Shunde CHN (GDG) 97 Qg34
Shungnak USA (AK) 229 Cb12
Shungyang CHN (JLN) 100 Rc24
Shunyi CHN (BJG) 93 Qj25
Shuozhou CHN (SAX) 93 Qg26
Shuqra YE 68 Nc39
Shur Ab IR 72 Nf28
Shur Ab IR 72 Nf29
Shurbarkol KZ 84 Oe21
Shuru IR 75 Oa31
Shurugwi ZW 214 Mf55
Shushicë AL 46 Lu50
Shushtar IR 72 Ne29
Shushufindi Central EC 272 Gb46
Shuswap Lake CDN 232 Ea20
Shut ,bat ad Daybaban LAR 174 Lf31
Shute Harbour AUS (QLD) 149 Se56
Shuttleworth AUS (QLD) 149 Sd57
Shu Xi CHN 102 Qk30
Shuyak Island USA (AK) 229 Cd16
Shuyang CHN (JGS) 102 Qk28
Shwebo MYA 113 Ph34
Shwedaung MYA 114 Ph36
Shwegu MYA 113 Pj33
Shwegyin MYA 114 Pj37
Shweli MYA 113 Pj34
Shwemyo MYA 113 Pj35
Shyghanak KZ 84 Og23
Shymbulak CHN 84 Pa24
Shymbulak KZ 77 Oj24
Shymkent KZ 76 Oe24
Shynghanak KZ 76 Of23
Shynkozha KZ 84 Pa22
Shyok 79 Oj28
Shyok 79 Oj28
Shyok 79 Ok28
Si RMM 184 Kh39
Sia RI 131 Rh49
Siabu RI 124 Pk45
Siabun RI 124 Qb47
Siabuwa ZW 210 Me54
Siaeb G 202 Lg47
Siahan Range PK 80 Ob32
Siak RI 124 Qa45
Siakinderapura RI 124 Qb45
Siak-Kecil RI 124 Qa45
Sialangonan RI 116 Pk44
Sialivakou RCB 202 Lf48
Sialkot PK 79 Oh29
Sialum PNG 159 Sd49
Siaman PNG 160 Sg48
Siamsa Tire IRL 20 Kl38
Siana CI 192 Kg41
Siang IND 112 Ph31
Sianhala CI 192 Kg40
Sianok Canyon RI 124 Qa46
Sianów PL 36 Lr36
Siantan RI 117 Qd44
Sião o Matapire YV 273 Gh45
Siara PNG 160 Sh48
Siare CO 268 Ge44
Siare Guajibos CO 273 Ge44
Siargao Island RP 123 Rd41
Siasi RP 123 Ra43
Siasikabole Z 210 Md54
Sias Island RP 123 Ra43
Siassi PNG 159 Sd48
Siatlai MYA 112 Pg34
Siaton RP 123 Rb41
Siau RI 123 Rc44
Šiaulėnai LT 17 Md35
Šiauliai LT 17 Md35
Siavonga Z 210 Me54
Sibaboh RI 116 Pj44
Sibaibai RI 124 Qa47
Sibalay BD 112 Pe34
Sibalom RP 123 Rb40
Sibande RI 116 Pk44
Sibanicú C 259 Gb35
Sibari I 43 Lr51
Sibau RI 126 Qg45
Sibayameer = Lake Sibaya ZA 217 Mg59
Sibay Island RP 123 Ra40
Sibayo PE 279 Ge53
Sibayu RI 127 Qk45
Sibbo = Sipoo FIN 16 Mf30
Šibenik HR 41 Lq47
Siberia RUS 58 Pa06
Siberimanua RI 124 Pk47
Siberut RI 124 Pk46
Sibi PK 80 Od31
Sibi RMM 184 Kf39
Sibidiri PNG 158 Sb50
Sibigo RI 116 Ph44
Sibiloi N.P. EAK 204 Mj44
Sibircevo RUS 98 Rg23
Sibirskie uvaly RUS 58 Oc06
Sibiti EAT 204 Mh47
Sibiti RCB 202 Lg47
Sibiu RO 44 Me45
Sib Kuh IR 74 Ng32
Sibley USA (IA) 241 Fc24
Siboa RI 127 Ra45
Sibolga RI 124 Pk45
Siboluton RI 127 Ra45
Siborongborong RI 116 Pk44
Šibot RO 44 Md45
Sibr OM 69 Nh37
Sibsagar IND (ASM) 112 Ph32
Sibu MAL 117 Qc44
Sibu MAL 126 Qf44
Sibuco RP 123 Rb42
Sibuguey Bay RP 123 Rb42
Sibundoy CO 272 Gb45
Si Bun Ruang THA 115 Qb37
Sibushi J 103 Rf30
Sibut RCA 200 Lk43
Sibutu Island RP 122 Qk43
Sibuyan Island RP 121 Rb39
Sibuyan Sea RP 121 Rb39
Sicamous CDN (BC) 232 Ea20
Sicapoo, Mount RP 121 Ra37
Sichinoe J 101 Sa25
Sichnice PL 36 Ls39
Si Chomphu THA 115 Qb37
Sichuan CHN 82 Qa13
Sicily I 42 Lo53
Sicily I 42 Lp53
Sicily Island USA (LA) 243 Fe30
Siciska PL 37 Lu39
Sico HN 256 Fh38
Sicogon Island RP 123 Rb40
Sicuani PE 279 Ge53
Sicunusa SD 217 Mf59
Šid SCG 44 Lu45
Sid Ahmed RIM 184 Kf37
Sidao CHN (SDG) 100 Rb27
Sidareja RI 128 Qe49
Sidar Hat BD 112 Pf34
Sidas RI 126 Qe45
Siddapur IND (KTK) 110 Oh39
Siddhapur IND (GUJ) 108 Og34
Siddharthanagar NEP 88 Pb32
Siddipet IND (APH) 109 Ok36
Side TR 51 Mm54
Sideby = Siipyy FIN 13 Mb28
Sideia Island PNG 160 Sf51
Sideni EAT 207 Mk48
Sidensjö S 10 Lk14
Sidéradougou BF 193 Kh40
Siderno I 43 Lr52
Sidhauli IND (UPH) 107 Pa32
Sidhi IND (MPH) 109 Pa33
Sidhi SP 199 Nb40
Sidi IND (MPH) 109 Pa34
Sidi RDC 200 Lk43
Sidi-Abdallah-des-Rhiata MA 173 Kh28
Sidi Abed MA 172 Kf29
Sidi Aïssa DZ 173 Lb28
Sidi Akhfennir MA 178 Kd31
Sidi Ali DZ 173 La27
Sidi-Allal-el-Bahraoui MA 172 Kg29
Sidi-Allal-Tazi MA 172 Kg28
Sidi as Sayd LAR 174 Lg29
Sidi Barani ET 176 Mc30
Sidi Bel Abbès DZ 173 Kk28
Sidi-Bennour MA 172 Kf29
Sidi-Bettache MA 172 Kg29
Sidi Boubekeur DZ 173 La28
Sidi-Bou-Othmane MA 172 Kg30
Sidi Bouzid MA 172 Kf29
Sidi Bou Zid TN 174 Le28
Sidi el Mokhtâr RMM 185 Kj36
Sidi Hamadouche DZ 173 Kk28
Sidi-Harazem MA 172 Kh29
Sidi Hasseur DZ 173 La28
Sidi Ifni MA 172 Ke31
Sidi-Kacem MA 172 Kh28
Sidikalang RI 116 Pk44
Sidi Khaled DZ 173 Lc28
Sidi Khalifah LAR 175 Ma29
Sidikidougou RG 192 Kf41
Sidikila RG 192 Kf40
Sidi Ladjel DZ 173 Lb28
Sidi Moktar MA 172 Kf30
Sidi Moussa DZ 180 Lc32
Sidi-Moussa MA 172 Kf29
Siding Spring Observatory AUS 151 Se61
Sidirókastro GR 46 Md49
Sidi-Slimane MA 172 Kh28
Sidi-Smaïl MA 172 Kf29
Sidi Toui, P.N. TN 174 Lf29
Sidi-Yahya-du Rharb MA 172 Kg28
Sidlaghatta IND (KTK) 111 Oj40
Sidlaw Hills GB 19 Kr34
Sidley, Mount 296 Dc34
Sidmouth GB 20 Kr40
Sidney CDN (BC) 232 Dj21
Sidney USA (IA) 241 Fc25
Sidney USA (MT) 235 Eh22
Sidney USA (NE) 240 Ej25
Sidney USA (NY) 247 Gc24
Sidney USA (OH) 246 Fh25
Sido RMM 192 Kg40
Sidoan RI 127 Ra45
Sidoarjo RI 128 Qg49
Sidon = Saida RL 64 Mh29
Sidra = Surt LAR 175 Lj30
Sidrolândia BR (MS) 286 Hc56
Siduk RI 126 Qf46
Siedlce PL 37 Mc38
Sieg D 32 Lh40
Siegburg D 32 Lh40
Siegen D 32 Lj40
Siékorolé RMM 192 Kf40
Sielezavanga SOL 160 Sj49
Sielpia Wielka PL 37 Ma39
Siembra RI 130 Rg47
Siemiatycze PL 37 Mc38
Siemień PL 37 Mc39
Siempang K 115 Qd38
Siem Reap K 115 Qb39
Siena I 40 Lm47
Sieniawa PL 37 Mc40
Šienlaukis LT 17 Mb35
Siennica PL 37 Mb38
Sieradz PL 36 Lt39
Sieraków PL 36 Lr38
Sierentz F 23 Lh43
Sierpc PL 37 Lu38
Sierra Añueque RA 292 Gf66
Sierra Apas RA 292 Gg66
Sierra Baoruco, P.N. DOM 260 Ge36
Sierra Blanca RA 292 Gg66
Sierra Blanca USA (TX) 237 Eh30
Sierra Cabrera Baja E 26 Ko52
Sierra Cañadón Grande RA 292 Gf68
Sierra Chica RA (BA) 293 Gk64
Sierra City USA (CA) 234 Dk26
Sierra Colmena MEX 255 Fe37
Sierra Colorada RA (RN) 292 Gg66
Sierra Colorada RA 292 Gg67
Sierra Coyote MEX 252 Ee32
Sierra Cuntamana PE 278 Gd50
Sierra de Agalta HN 256 Fh38
Sierra de Agalta HN 256 Fh38
Sierra de Aguas Calientes RA 284 Gg58
Sierra de Amambay BR 286 Hc57
Sierra de Antonio MEX 237 Ee30
Sierra de Auca Mahuida RA 292 Gf64
Sierra de Ávila E 26 Kp50
Sierra de Calalaste RA 284 Gg58
Sierra de Carmen Silva RCH 294 Gf72
Sierra de Catán Lil RA 292 Ge65
Sierra de Cazorla E 29 Ks48
Sierra de Choique Mahuida RA 292 Gh65
Sierra de Columbia MEX 236 Ec31
Sierra de Cuma Malal RA 293 Gj64
Sierra de Famatina RA 288 Gg60
Sierra de Gata E 28 Ko50
Sierra de Guadalupe E 28 Kp49
Sierra de Guadarrama E 26 Kq50
Sierra de Guampí YV 269 Gh42
Sierra de Gúdar E 29 Ku50
Sierra de Guecomea MEX 237 Ee30
Sierra de Juarez MEX 236 Ec29
Sierra de la Giganta MEX 252 Ee33
Sierra de la Punilla RA 288 Gf60
Sierra de las Minas GCA 255 Ff38
Sierra de las Quijadas, P.N. RA 288 Gg62
Sierra de la Ventana RA (BA) 293 Gk65
Sierra de la Ventana RA 293 Gk64
Sierra del Huantraico RA 292 Gf64
Sierra del Huesco MEX 237 Eh30
Sierra de Lihuél Calel RA 292 Gh64
Sierra del Lacandón GCA 255 Fe37
Sierra del Lacandón, P.N. GCA 255 Fe37
Sierra del Morro RA 288 Gh62
Sierra del Nevado RA 292 Gf63
Sierra de los Cuchumatanes GCA 255 Fe38
Sierra del Tandil RA 293 Ha64
Sierra del Teleno E 26 Ko48
Sierra del Viejo MEX 236 Ed30
Sierra del Zamuro YV 269 Gj43
Sierra de Maigualida YV 269 Gh43
Sierra de Miahuatlán MEX 254 Fb37
Sierra de Mulegé MEX 252 Ed32
Sierra de Neiba DOM 260 Ge36
Sierra de Palauco RA 292 Gf63
Sierra de Perijá CO/YV 268 Gd41
Sierra de Perijá, P.N. YV 268 Gd41
Sierra de Quilmes RA 288 Gg59
Sierra de San Pedro E 28 Ko49
Sierra de San Pedro Mártir MEX 236 Ec30
Sierra de Tontal RA 288 Gf61
Sierra de Tunuyan RA 288 Gf62
Sierra de Unturán YV 270 Gh45
Sierra de Urbión E 27 Ks51
Sierra de Valle Fertil RA 288 Gg61
Sierra de Varela RA 288 Gg63
Sierra de Velasco RA 288 Gg60
Sierra El Batatete MEX 252 Ee32
Sierra Gorda RCH 284 Gf57
Sierra Grande MEX 237 Eh31
Sierra Grande RA (RN) 292 Gh66
Sierra Grande RA 292 Gh66
Sierra Huacache RA 292 Ge67
Sierra La Asamblea MEX 236 Ed31
Sierra la Culata, P.N. YV 268 Ge41
Sierra La Esperanza HN 256 Fh38
Sierra La Esperanza HN 256 Fh38
Sierra La Laguna MEX 252 Ee34
Sierra Leone 167 Ka09
Sierra Leone Basin 166 Ka09
Sierra Leone Rise 300 Jb09
Sierra Lipetrén RA 292 Gf66
Sierra Los Órganos MEX 253 Ej34
Sierra Madre RP 121 Rb37
Sierra Madre de Chiapas MEX 255 Fd38
Sierra Madre del Sur MEX 254 Ek37
Sierra Madre Mts. USA 236 Ea28
Sierra Madre Occidental MEX 226 Ec13
Sierra Madre Oriental MEX 226 Ed13
Sierra Maestra C 259 Gb35
Sierra Maestra, Gran P.N. C 259 Gb35
Sierra Mojada MEX (COH) 253 Ej32
Sierra Morena E 29 Ko47
Sierra Nevada E 29 Kr47
Sierra Nevada RA 292 Gf67
Sierra Nevada, Cerro RCH/RA 288 Gf59
Sierra Nevada USA 234 Dk26
Sierra Nevada del Cocuy CO 268 Gd42
Sierra Nevada de Santa Marta CO 268 Gd40
Sierra Nevada de Santa Marta, P.N. CO 268 Gd40
Sierra Nevada, P.N. YV 269 Ge41
Sierra Nevada, P.N.de E 29 Kr47
Sierra Olte RA 292 Gf67
Sierra Pacaraima YV 270 Gj43
Sierra Pailemán RA (RN) 292 Gh66
Sierra Pailemán RA 292 Gg66
Sierra Peyuami YV 269 Gj43
Sierra San Luis, P.N. YV 269 Gf40
Sierras Bayas RA (BA) 293 Gk64
Sierras de Córdoba RA 288 Gh61
Sierra Tapirapeco YV 274 Gh45
Sierra Vieja MEX (ZCT) 253 Ej34
Sierraville USA (CA) 234 Dk26
Sierra Vista USA (AZ) 237 Ee30
Sierra Vizcaíno MEX 252 Ec32
Sierre CH 34 Lh44
Siete Puntas PY 285 Hb57
Șieu RO 44 Me43
Sieuleni RO 45 Mf44
Sif YE 68 Ne38
Sifahandra RI 124 Pj45
Sifeni ETH 191 Na40
Sif-Fatima DZ 174 Le30
Sifié CI 192 Kg41
Sífnos GR 49 Me54
Sig DZ 173 Kk28
Si Galangang RI 124 Pk45
Sigatoka FJI 163 Tj55
Sigatoka Sand Dunes N.P. FJI 163 Tj55
Sigean F 24 Lc47
Sigenti RI 127 Ra45
Siggerud N 12 Lm31
Sighetu Marmației RO 44 Md43
Sighișoara RO 45 Me44
Sigici RI 124 Pk47
Sigiriya CL 111 Pa43
Sigli RI 116 Ph43
Siglufjörður IS 10 Ka12
Sigmaringen D 34 Lk42
Signal Hill N.H.S. CDN 245 Hd22
Signal Peak USA 236 Ec29
Sigoisooinan RI 124 Pk47
Sigony RUS 53 Ne19
Sigor EAK 204 Mh45
Sigourney USA (IA) 241 Fd25
Sigri GR 49 Mf51
Sigsbee Deep 226 Fb14
Sigsig EC 272 Ga47
Sigtuna S 13 Ls31
Siguanea C 258 Fj35
Siguatepeque HN 256 Fg38
Sigueira Campos BR (PR) 286 Hf57
Sigüenza E 29 Ks51
Sigües E 27 Kt52
Siguiri RG 192 Kf40
Sigulda LV 17 Me33
Sigulu Island EAU 204 Mg45
Siguri Falls EAT 207 Mj50
Sihanoukville K 115 Qb40
Šihany RUS 53 Nd19
Sihaung Ashe MYA 112 Ph34
Sihong CHN (JGS) 102 Qk29
Sihora IND (MPH) 109 Pa34
Sihuas PE 278 Gb50
Sihui CHN (GDG) 97 Qg34
Siikainen FIN 16 Mb29
Siilinjärvi FIN 11 Md14
Siipyy = Sideby FIN 13 Mb28
Siirt TR 63 Na27
Sijungjung RI 124 Qa46
Sik MAL 116 Qa43
Sikancing RI 124 Qb47
Sikandapur IND (UPH) 107 Pc32
Sikandapur IND (UPH) 109 Pc32
Sikandra IND (BIH) 112 Pd33
Sikandra IND (UPH) 107 Ok32
Sikandrabad IND (UPH) 107 Oj31
Sikandra Rao IND (UPH) 107 Ok32
Sikang IND 113 Ph31
Sikanni Chief River CDN 231 Dj17
Sikao THA 116 Pk42
Sikar IND (RJT) 106 Oh32
Sikarakara RI 124 Pk45
Sikasso RMM 193 Kh40
Sikaunda Petroglyphs (paintings) Z 213 Md54
Sikaw MYA 113 Pj34
Sika water mills IR 72 Ne29
Sikeli RI 129 Ra48
Sikensi CI 193 Kh43
Sikereti NAM 213 Ma55
Sikerkupa IND (ORS) 109 Pb36
Sikeston USA (MO) 243 Ff27
Sikhoraphum THA 115 Qb38
Sikhote-Alin RUS 98 Rg24
Sikiés GR 46 Mc51
Sikilang RI 124 Pk45
Sikinos GR 49 Mf54
Sikinos GR 49 Mf54
Sikire BF 185 Kk38
Sikitico EAT 206 Mf49
Sikkal IND (TNU) 111 Ok42
Sikkim IND 104 Pb13
Sikonge EAT 206 Mg48
Sikongo Z 209 Mb53
Sikourió GR 46 Mc51
Sikovicy RUS 16 Mj32
Siktjah RUS 59 Ra05
Sikwane RB 213 Md58
Sila PNG 159 Se50
Silago RP 123 Rc40
Sila Grande I 43 Lr51
Sila Greca I 43 Lr51
Šilalė LT 17 Mc35
Silandro = Schlanders I 40 Ll44
Silang RP 121 Ra38
Silango PNG 160 Sf48
Si Lanna N.P. THA 114 Pk36
Silao MEX (GJT) 254 Ek35
Sila Piccola I 43 Lr51
Silavatturai CL 111 Ok42
Silay RP 123 Rb40
Silba HR 41 Lp46
Silbaš SCG 44 Lu45
Silchar IND (ASM) 112 Pg33
Silda IND (WBG) 112 Pd34
Sildegapet N 12 Lf28
Šile TR 50 Mk49
Sileia SUD 189 Mb38
Silene LV 17 Mg35
Silent Valley N.P. IND 110 Oj41
Siles E 29 Ks48
Silesia USA (MT) 235 Ef23
Silet DZ 180 Lc34
Silgadhi NEP 88 Pa31
Silheti IND (CGH) 109 Pa35
Silhouette SY 219 Nh48
Sili IND (JKD) 109 Pc34
Silian A 35 Ln44
Siliana TN 174 Le27
Silifke TR 62 Mg27
Siliguri IND (WBG) 112 Pe32
Silil SP 199 Nb40
Silin CHN (GZG) 96 Qd34
Siling CHN (TIB) 88 Pc31
Siling Co CHN 89 Pe30
Silisili, Mount WS 164 Bd52
Silistra BG 45 Mh46
Silivaşu de Câmpie RO 44 Me44
Silivri TR 50 Mj49
Siljan N 12 Lk31
Siljan S 13 Lp30
Siljansnäs S 13 Lp30
Šilka RUS 91 Qj20
Šilka RUS 91 Qj20
Silkaatskop ZA 213 Md58
Silkeborg DK 14 Lk34
Šilkinskij hrebet RUS 91 Qj19
Silk Market UZ 77 Of25
Silk Road UZ 76 Oe25
Silkwood AUS (QLD) 149 Sd54
Silla E 29 Ku49
Sillajhuay BOL/RCH 284 Gf55
Sillamäe EST 16 Mh31
Sillanwali PK 79 Og30
Sille TR 51 Mn53
Silleda E 26 Km52
Sillé-le-Guillaume F 22 Ku42
Sillerud S 12 Ln31
Silli BF 193 Kj40
Sillustani PE 279 Ge53
Sillod IND (MHT) 108 Oh35
Silloth GB 19 Kr36
Silmi ETH 198 Na41
Šil'naja Balka KZ 53 Ne20
Silong CHN (GZG) 96 Qe34
Silongo Z 209 Mb53
Šilovo RUS 53 Mk19
Šilovo RUS 53 Na18
Silowana Plains Z 209 Mb54
Silozwane Cave ZW 214 Me56
Silsbee USA (TX) 243 Fc30
Silsby Lake CDN 238 Fc18
Silte ETH 198 Mk42
Siltou TCH 187 Lh37
Siluas RI 126 Qe45
Siluko WAN 194 Lc42
Siluko WAN 194 Lc42
Šilutė LT 17 Mb35
Silutshana ZA 217 Mf60
Silván E 26 Ko52
Silvan TR 63 Na26
Silvan Baraj TR 63 Na26
Silvani IND (MPH) 109 Ok34
Silvânia BR (GO) 286 Hf54
Silva Porto Gare ANG 208 Lj52
Silva Sánchez MEX (TM) 253 Fa33
Silvassa IND (DNH) 108 Og35
Silver Bank 260 Gf35
Silver Bank Passage DOM 260 Ge35
Silver City USA (ID) 234 Eb24
Silver City USA (MI) 246 Ff22
Silver City USA (NM) 237 Ef29
Silverdalen S 15 Lq33
Silver Dollar CDN (ON) 239 Fe21
Silver Lake USA (OR) 234 Dk24
Silver Lake USA (WA) 232 Dj22
Silvermine Mountains IRL 20 Km38
Silvermuseet S 10 Lj12
Silver Park CDN (SK) 233 Eh19
Silver Peak USA (NV) 234 Eb27
Silver Plains AUS (QLD) 147 Sb52
Silversand NAM 212 Lj57
Silver Springs USA (FL) 250 Fj31
Silver Springs USA (NV) 234 Ea26
Silver Star Mine AUS (QLD) 148 Rk55
Silverstone GB 21 Kt38
Silverthrone Mtn. CDN 232 Dg20
Silverton AUS (NSW) 150 Sa61
Silverton USA (CO) 237 Eg27
Silverton USA (TX) 242 Ek28
Silver Waterfall = Thac Bac VN 113 Qb34
Silves BR (AM) 274 Ha47
Silves P 28 Km47
Silvi I 42 Lp48
Silvia CO 272 Gb44
Silwa Bahari ET 177 Mg33
Sima COM 218 Nc52
Simakalo RI 124 Qa47
Simakivka UA 54 Me20
Şimal UAE 75 Nh33
Simamba Z 209 Mc54
Simanbadi IND (ORS) 109 Pc35
Simanindo RI 116 Pk44
Šimanovsk RUS 98 Rd20
Simao CHN (YUN) 113 Qa34
Simão Dias BR (SE) 283 Jb51
Simara NEP 88 Pc32
Simara Island RP 121 Rb39
Simaria IND (JKD) 109 Pc33
Simaria IND (MPH) 109 Pa33
Simav TR 50 Mj51
Simba RDC 200 Mb45
Simbach D 35 Ln42
Simbai PNG 159 Sc48
Simberi Island PNG 160 Sf47
Simbirsk = Uljanovsk RUS 53 Ne18
Simbo EAT 206 Me48
Simbo EAT 206 Mg48
Simbol Pozo RA (SA) 285 Gj58
Simbol Pozo RA (SE) 288 Gh60
Simen Mountains ETH 191 Mk40
Simenti SN 183 Kd39
Simeria RO 44 Md45
Simeto I 42 Lp53
Simeulue RI 116 Ph44
Simferopol' UA 55 Mh23
Simga IND (CGH) 109 Pa35
Simi GR 49 Mh54
Simi GR 49 Mh54
Simien Mountains N.P. ETH 191 Mk40
Similajau N.P. MAL 126 Qg44
Similipal N.P. IND 112 Pd35
Similot NEP 88 Pa31
Simindou RCA 196 Mb42
Siminiout F (GF) 271 Hd44
Simiri RN 185 Lb38
Simiriundui GUY 270 Gk42
Simiti CO 268 Gd42
Simi Valley USA (CA) 236 Ea28
Simiyu EAT 204 Mg47

Socavão – Spin Buldak

Socavão BR (PR) 286 Hf58
Sochaczew PL 37 Ma38
Sochinsky nacional'nyj park RUS 55 Mk23
Soči RUS 55 Mk24
Society Hill USA (SC) 249 Ga28
Society Islands 303 Ca11
Socodor RO 44 Mb44
Socompa PE 284 Gf58
Socompa RA (SA) 284 Gf58
Socompa, Volcán RCH/RA 284 Gf58
Socorro BR (PR) 286 He58
Socorro BR (SP) 287 Hg57
Socorro CO 268 Gd42
Socorro RP 123 Rc41
Socorro USA (NM) 237 Eg28
Socorro USA (TX) 237 Eg30
Socota CO 268 Gd42
Socota PE 278 Ga49
Socotra YE 69 Nh39
Soc Trang VN 117 Qc41
Socuéllamos E 29 Ks49
Soda Creek CDN (BC) 232 Dj19
Sodakor IND (RJT) 106 Of32
Sodankylä FIN 11 Md12
Soda Springs USA (ID) 235 Ee24
Söderåkra S 15 Lr34
Söderarm S 13 Lu31
Söderåsens n.p. S 15 Lo35
Söderbärke S 13 Lq30
Söderfors S 13 Ls30
Söderhamn S 13 Ls29
Söderköping S 13 Lq32
Södermanland S 13 Lr31
Södertälje S 13 Ls31
Södertörn S 13 Ls31
Södervik S 13 Lt31
Sodi RI 127 Qk46
Sodiri SUD 190 Me39
Sodium ZA 216 Mb61
Sodo ETH 198 Mj42
Sodore ETH 198 Mk41
Södra Kvarken S 13 Lu30
Södra Midsjöbanken 15 Ls35
Södra Ölands odlingslandskap S 15 Lr34
Södra Vi S 15 Lq33
Sodwana Bay N.P. ZA 217 Mg59
Soe RI 132 Rc50
Soekmekaar ZA 214 Me57
Soela väin EST 16 Mc32
Soeng San THA 115 Qb38
Soesdyke GUY 270 Ha42
Soest D 32 Lj39
Soetdoring Nature Reserve ZA 217 Md60
Sofádes GR 48 Mc51
Sofara RMM 184 Kh38
Sofia BG 46 Md48
Sofia RM 219 Ne53
Sofija BG 46 Md48
Sofijivka UA 54 Mg21
Sofijskij sobor RUS 52 Mf16
Sofiyskiy sobor UA 54 Mf20
Sof Omar Caves ETH 198 Na42
Sofporog RUS 11 Mf13
Sofular TR 51 Mp52
Sogakofe GH 193 La42
Sogamoso CO 268 Gd43
Soğanlı Valley TR 51 Mp52
Sogda RUS 98 Rg20
Sögel D 32 Lh38
Sogeri PNG 159 Sd50
Sogndal N 12 Lh29
Sognefjellsvegen N 12 Lj29
Sognefjorden N 12 Lf29
Sognesjøen N 12 Le29
Sogod RP 123 Rc40
Sogolle TCH 187 Lh38
Sogoot MNG 90 Pk21
Sogossagasso BF 193 Kh40
Soguip'o ROK 103 Rd29
Soğukpınar TR 50 Mk50
Soğuksu TR 50 Ml50
Soğuksu Milli Parkı TR 51 Mn50
Söğüt TR 50 Ml50
Söğüt TR 51 Mk53
Söğüt Dağı TR 50 Mk53
Söğütlü TR 50 Ml50
Söğütlü TR 63 Na26
Sog Xian CHN (TIB) 89 Pg30
Sohâg ET 177 Mf32
Sohagi IND (MPH) 109 Pa33
Sohar OM 75 Nj33
Sohela IND (ORS) 109 Pb35
Sohey IR 72 Ng29
Sohna IND (HYA) 107 Oj31
Sohós GR 46 Md50
Sohuksan Do ROK 103 Rc28
Soignies B 23 Le40
Soila IND (RJT) 106 Og32
Şoimi RO 44 Mc44
Soin BF 184 Kj39
Soini FIN 11 Mc14
Sointula CDN (BC) 232 Dg20
Soissons F 23 Ld41
Soja J 101 Rg28
Sojat IND (RJT) 106 Og33
Sojol RI 127 Ra45
Sojoson Man PRK 100 Rc26
Sojoton Point RP 123 Rb41
Sojuz ANT (RUS) 296 Gc33
Sokal' UA 37 Me40
Sokch'o ROK 100 Re26
Söke TR 49 Mh53
Sokele RDC 203 Mc50
Sokhumi GE 70 Na24
Sokhumi GE 63 Na24
Sokna N 12 Lk30
Soknedal N 12 Ll28
Soko CI 193 Kj42
Soko Banja SCG 46 Mb47
Sokodé TG 193 La41
Sokoiyo RI 127 Ra47
Sokol RUS 99 Sb22
Sokolac BIH 46 Lt47
Sokoliv UA 39 Mf41
Sokółka PL 37 Md37
Sokollu Camii TR 50 Mh49
Sokolo RMM 184 Kg38
Sokolov CZ 38 Ln40
Sokołów Małopolski PL 37 Mc40
Sokołów Podlaski PL 37 Mc38
Sokolski manastir BG 47 Mf48
Sokoły PL 37 Mc38
Sokorbey RN 185 Lb39
Sokoto WAN 185 Lc40
Sokoto WAN 186 Lc39
Sokoulama RG 192 Kf41
Sokoura RMM 184 Kj39
Soksok RN 186 Ld38
Sokyrjany UA 45 Mh42
Sola C 259 Gb35
Sola N 12 Lf32
Sola VU 162 Td52
Sola de Vega MEX (OAX) 254 Fb37
Solahpet IND (KTK) 108 Oj37
Solan IND (HPH) 107 Oj30
Solana RP 121 Ra37
Solana USA (FL) 250 Fk32
Solana del Pino E 29 Kq48
Solander Island NZ 155 Td69
Solânea BR (PB) 277 Jc49
Solano RP 121 Ra37
Solano YV 273 Gg45
Solar de Mateus P 26 Kn51
Solares E 27 Kr53
Solat RI 130 Rd45
Solberg S 10 Lj14
Solca RO 45 Mf43
Sol'cy RUS 52 Mf16
Soldado Monge EC 272 Gb47
Şoldănești MD 45 Mj43
Sol de Julio RA (SE) 288 Gj60
Sol de Mañana BOL 284 Gg57
Sölden A 35 Lm44
Soldotna USA (AK) 229 Ce15
Solé BF 185 Kj38
Soleb Temple SUD 190 Mf36
Solec Kujawski PL 36 Lt37
Soledad CO 268 Gc40
Soledad USA (CA) 234 Dk27
Soledad YV 270 Gj41
Soledad de Doblado MEX (VC) 254 Fb36
Soledad de G. Sánchez MEX (SLP) 253 Ek34
Soledade BR (PB) 277 Jb49
Soledade BR (RS) 290 Hd60
Solemar BR (SP) 286 Hg58
Sølen N 12 Lm29
Solënoe RUS 55 Nb22
Solenyj RUS 70 Nd22
Solenzara F 31 Lk49
Solenzo BF 184 Kh39
Sole Pit 21 Lb37
Solh Abad IR 73 Nj28
Solhan TR 63 Na26
Soli RN 186 Ld38
Solihull GB 21 Kt38
Solikamsk RUS 58 Nd07
Soliman TN 174 Lf27
Solimões = Amazon BR 274 Gk47
Solingen D 32 Lh39
Solis de Mataojo ROU 289 Hc63
Solita CO 272 Gc45
Solitaire NAM 212 Lj57
Sölktäler A 35 Lo43
Sollebrunn S 14 Ln32
Sollefteå S 10 Lj14
Sollentuna S 13 Ls31
Sóller E 30 Lc51
Sollidén S 15 Lr34
Sollihøgda N 12 Ll31
Solna BF 185 La39
Solncevo RUS 53 Mj20
Solnečnogorsk RUS 52 Mj17
Solnečnyj RUS 98 Rj20
Solnice CZ 38 Lr40
Solo RI 128 Qf49
Šolohovskij RUS 55 Na21
Solok RI 124 Qa46
Sologo EAK 205 Mk44
Soloma GCA 255 Fe38
Solomon Islands 135 Ta10
Solomon Islands 156 Sc20
Solomon Sea PNG 156 Sc20
Solomon's Wall RB 214 Me57
Solon CHN (NMZ) 91 Ra22
solonchakovyye vpadiny Unguz TM 71 Nk26
Solone UA 54 Mh21
Solonešnoe RUS 85 Pc20
Solongtyn davaa MNG 90 Pk21
Solonópole BR (CE) 277 Ja48
Solonţ RO 45 Mg44
Solor RI 132 Rb50
Solothurn CH 34 Lh43
Solotvyn UA 39 Me42
Solotvyna UA 39 Md43
Soloveckie RUS 11 Mh13
Solovetsky monastyr RUS 11 Mh13
Solov'evsk RUS 91 Qh21
Solsnes N 12 Lh28
Solsona E 30 Lb49
Solsvik N 12 Le30
Solt H 39 Lu44
Šolta HR 41 Lr47
Soltan Abad IR 73 Nj27
Soltan Bagh AFG 78 Oe29
Soltaniyeh IR 72 Ne27
Soltau D 32 Lk38
Solti-lapály H 39 Lu44
Soltvadkert H 39 Lu44
Solusi ZW 214 Me56
Solvang USA (CA) 236 Dk28
Solvarbo S 13 Lq30
Sölvesborg S 15 Lp34
Solway Firth GB 19 Kr36
Solwezi Z 210 Md52
Soly BY 17 Mg36
Solymar ROU 289 Hc63
Sol y Nieve E 29 Kr47
Som IND (RJT) 108 Og33
Soma J 101 Sa27
Soma TR 50 Mh51
Somabhula ZW 214 Me55
Somadougou RMM 184 Kh38
Somaén E 27 Ks51
Somain F 23 Ld40
Somalia 167 Na09
Somali Basin 301 Nb09
Somali Plateau ETH 198 Na41
Somalomo CAM 195 Lg44
Somavaram IND (APH) 109 Pb37
Somba RI 127 Qk47
Sombo ANG 203 Ma50
Sombo ANG 203 Ma50
Sombor SCG 44 Lu45
Sombrerete MEX (ZCT) 253 Ej34
Sombrero KNA 261 Gj36
Sombrero RCH 294 Gf72
Sombrero Channel IND 111 Pg42
Sombrero Negro RA (FO) 285 Gk57
Sombrio BR (SC) 291 Hf60
Şomcuta Mare RO 44 Md43
Somdet THA 115 Qb37
Somero FIN 16 Md30
Somers AUS (VIC) 153 Sc65
Somerset AUS (QLD) 146 Sb51
Somerset AUS (TAS) 152 Sc66
Somerset CDN (MB) 238 Fa21
Somerset USA (KY) 249 Fh27
Somerset USA (PA) 247 Ga26
Somerset-East ZA 217 Mc62
Somerset Island CDN 225 Fb04
Somerset Oos ZA 217 Mc62
Somerset West ZA 216 Lk63
Somerton AUS (NSW) 151 Sf61
Someș RO 44 Md43
Someșul RO 44 Md44
Someșul Mare RO 44 Me43
Somianki PL 37 Mb38
Somil ANG 209 Ma53
Somina BIH 41 Lt48
Somina SCG 46 Lt48
Somme F 23 Lb40
Sommen S 15 Lq33
Sömmerda D 33 Lm39
Sommerdown NAM 212 Lk56
Sommesous F 23 Le42
Sommières F 25 Le47
Somo RMM 184 Kh39
Somogyvár H 38 Ls44
Somonino PL 36 Lt36
Somosomo FJI 163 Ua54
Somotillo NIC 256 Fg39
Sompeta IND (APH) 109 Pc36
Som Poi THA 115 Qb38
Sompolno PL 36 Lt38
Somra MYA 112 Ph33
Son IND 109 Pb33
Son IND 112 Pg33
Soná PA 257 Fk41
Sonaco GNB 183 Kc39
Sonagiri IND 107 Ok33
Sonai-Rupa N.P. IND 112 Pg32
Sonamukhi BD 112 Pe33
Sonamukhi IND (WBG) 112 Pd34
Sonapur IND (ORS) 109 Pb35
Sonar IND 109 Ok34
Sonari IND (ASM) 112 Ph32
Sonarigaon IND (ASM) 112 Ph32
Sonbong PRK 100 Rf24
Sonch'on PRK 100 Rc26
Soncillo E 27 Kr52
Sonda PK 80 Oe33
Søndalo I 40 Ll44
Søndeled N 12 Lk32
Sønderborg DK 14 Lk36
Sønder Nissum DK 14 Lj34
Sønder Omme DK 14 Lj35
Sondershausen D 33 Ll39
Søndersø DK 14 Ll35
Søndervig DK 14 Lj34
Sondi RI 116 Pk44
Sondo IND (MHT) 109 Ok36
Son Dong VN 96 Qd35
Søndrestrømfjord = Kangerlussuaq DK 225 Hb05
Søndrio I 40 Lk44
Sondu EAK 204 Mh46
Son en Breugel NL 32 Lf39
Sonepat IND (HYA) 107 Oj31
Song MAL 126 Qg45
Song THA 114 Qa36
Song WAN 187 Lg41
Songa MOC 210 Mg53
Songa RDC 203 Mc50
Songa RI 130 Rd46
Songaw Lagoon GH 193 La43
Song Ba VN 115 Qe39
Songbu CHN (HUB) 102 Qh30
Song Ca VN 115 Qd36
Song Cau VN 115 Qe39
Song Da VN 96 Qb35
Song Da Reservoir VN 96 Qc35
Song Dong Nai VN 115 Qd40
Songea EAT 211 Mh51
Songgwangsa Temple ROK 100 Rd28
Song Hong VN 96 Qc34
Songhua Hu CHN 100 Rd24
Songhua Jiang CHN 98 Re22
Songjiang CHN (SHG) 102 Ra30
Songir IND (GUJ) 108 Og34
Songir IND (MHT) 108 Oh35
Songjiang CHN (JLN) 100 Re24
Songjianghe CHN (JLN) 100 Rd24
Songkan CHN (GZH) 95 Qd31
Songkhla THA 116 Qa42
Songkhon LAO 115 Qc37
Song Khwae THA 114 Qa36
Song-Köl KS 77 Oh25
Songkou CHN (FJN) 97 Qk33
Songling CHN (NMZ) 91 Ra22
Song Ling CHN 93 Qk25
Song Luy VN 115 Qe40
Songmen CHN (ZJG) 102 Ra31
Songming CHN (YUN) 113 Qb33
Songnim PRK 100 Rc26
Songnisan N.P. ROK 100 Rd27
Songo ANG 202 Lh49
Songo SUD 196 Mc41
Songo-lolo RDC 202 Lh48
Songo Mnara EAT 207 Mk50
Songpan CHN (SCH) 94 Qb29
Song Phinong THA 114 Qa38
Songsha CHN (TIB) 88 Pa30
Songshan CHN 95 Qg28
Songshan Z.B. CHN 93 Qh25
Songtao CHN (GZH) 95 Qe31
Songxi CHN (FJN) 102 Qk32
Song Xian CHN (HNN) 95 Qg28
Songyang CHN (ZJG) 102 Qk31
Songyu ROK 100 Re27
Songyuan CHN (JLN) 98 Rc23
Songzi CHN (HUB) 95 Qf30
Songzi He CHN 95 Qf30
Sonhat IND (CGH) 109 Pb34
Son Hiep VN 115 Qe39
Son Hoa VN 115 Qe39
Sonid Youqi CHN (NMZ) 93 Qg24
Sonid Zuoqi CHN (NMZ) 93 Qg24
Sonjo EAT 207 Mh47
Sonkovo RUS 52 Mj17
Sonkwale Mountains WAN 194 Le42
Son La VN 113 Qb35
Son Mbong CAM 195 Lf44
Sonmiani PK 80 Od33
Sonmiani Bay PK 80 Od33
Sonneberg D 33 Lm40
Sonnenjoch A 35 Lm43
Sono BR 287 Hh54
Sonoita USA (AZ) 237 Ee30
Sonoma Range USA 234 Eb25
Sonora BR (MS) 286 Hc54
Sonora MEX 226 Eb13
Sonora USA (CA) 234 Dk27
Sonora USA (TX) 242 Ek30
Sonoran Desert USA 236 Ec29
Sonora Pass USA 234 Ea26
Sonoumom DY 186 Lb41
Sonoyta MEX (SO) 236 Ed30
Sonozo CI 193 Kg41
Sonpar Hills IND 109 Pb33
Sonpuri IND (GUJ) 108 Of35
Sonqor IR 72 Nd28
Sonseca E 29 Kr49
Sonsón CO 268 Gc43
Sonsonate ES 255 Ff39
Sonsorol Islands PAL 121 Rg43
Sonstraal ZA 216 Mb59
Sonta RDC 210 Me51
Sontang RI 124 Qa45
Son Tay VN 96 Qc35
Sonthofen D 34 Ll43
Sontra D 32 Lk39
Soomaa rahvuspark EST 16 Mf32
Sooya SP 205 Nb45
Sopachuy BOL 285 Gh55
Sopchoppy USA (FL) 249 Fh30
Soperton USA (GA) 249 Fj29
Sophie F (GF) 271 Hd43
Sop Huai THA 114 Pk36
Sopianae H 38 Lt44
Sopinusa RI 130 Rg47
Soplin PE 272 Gb47
Sop Moei THA 114 Pj37
Sopo SUD 196 Md41
Sopore 79 Oh28
Sopot PL 36 Lt36
Sopot SCG 44 Ma46
Sopotnica MK 46 Mb49
Sop Prap THA 114 Pk37
Sopron H 38 Lr43
Soprtrán CO 268 Gc42
Soputan RI 127 Rc45
Sora I 42 Lo49
Sorab IND (KTK) 110 Oh39
Sorada IND (ORS) 109 Pc36
Sorah PK 81 Oe32
Soråker S 13 Ls28
Soraksan ROK 100 Re26
Soraksan N.P. ROK 100 Re26
Sora Mboum CAM 195 Lh42
Soran KZ 84 Og21
Sorano I 42 Lm48
Sorapa PE 284 Gf54
sor Arys KZ 76 Od23
sor Ashchkol KZ 76 Od23
Sorata BOL 279 Gf53
Sorati-gawa J 99 Sc24
Sorau WAN 187 Lg41
Søraust-Svalbard naturreservat N 11 Ma07
Sorbas E 29 Ks47
Sörbygden S 13 Lr28
Sördellen S 13 Lr29
Sore F 24 Ku46
Sorel CDN (QC) 244 Gd22
Sorell AUS (TAS) 152 Sd67
Soresina I 40 Lk45
Sør-Flatanger N 10 Lf13
Sørfonna N 11 Mb06
Sörforsa S 13 Lr29
Sörgono I 31 Lk50
Sorgues-l'Ouvèze F 25 Le46
Sorgun TR 51 Mq51
Sør-Gutvika N 10 Lf13
Sori DY 186 Lb40
Soria E 27 Ks51
Soriano ROU 289 Ha62
sor Kajdak KZ 71 Ng23
Sørkappøya N 11 Lj07
Sorkh Ab AFG 78 Ob29
Sørland N 12 Lg32
Sor Laspur PK 79 Og27
Sørli N 10 Lg13
Sornac F 24 Lc45
Sorø DK 14 Lm35
Soro IND (ORS) 112 Pd35
Soro PK 78 Od30
Soro = Bahr el Ghazal TCH 187 Lj38
Sorobango CI 193 Kj41
Soroca MD 45 Mj42
Sorocaba BR (SP) 286 Hg57
Soroč'i Gory RUS 53 Nf18
Sorol Atoll FSM 156 Sa17
sor Oli Kultyk KZ 71 Ng23
Sorombéo CAM 195 Lh41
Sorondideri RI 131 Rh46
Sorong RI 130 Rf46
Sororó BR 276 Hf48
Sororó, T.I. BR 276 Hf48
Soroti EAU 204 Mg45
Søroyane N 12 Lf28
Sorrento CDN (BC) 232 Ea20
Sorrento I 42 Lp50
Sorriso BR (MT) 281 Hc52
Sorsakoski FIN 16 Mh28
Sorsan Grasslands IND 108 Oj33
Sorsele S 10 Lj13
Sorso I 31 Lj50
Sorsogon RP 121 Rc39
Sør-Spitsbergen n.p. N 11 Lj07
Sørstraumen N 10 Ma11
Sort E 30 Lb48
Sortavala RUS 11 Mf15
Sortland N 10 Lh11
Sørumsand N 12 Lm31
Sørvågen N 10 Lg12
Sörvattnet S 13 Ln28
Sørvika N 12 Lm28
Sosan ROK 100 Rd27
Sosan Haean N.P. ROK 100 Rd27
Sösdala S 15 Lo34
Sos del Rey Católico E 27 Kt52
Sosedka RUS 53 Nb19
Sosneado, Cerro RA 288 Gf63
Sosnenskij RUS 52 Mj19
Sosnogorsk RUS 58 Nc06
Sosnove UA 54 Md20
Sosnovka RUS 53 Na19
Sosnovka RUS 53 Nf17
Sosnovo-Ozërskoe RUS (BUR) 91 Qf19
Sosnovyj Bor RUS 16 Mk31
Sosnowica PL 37 Md39
Sosnowiec PL 37 Lu40
Soso Bay FJI 163 Tk55
Sosolo SOL 160 Sj49
Sosonpal IND (CGH) 109 Pa36
Sospel F 25 Lh47
Sosso RCA 195 Lh44
Sossobé RMM 184 Kh38
Sossusvlei NAM 212 Lh58
Sossusvlei Lodge NAM 212 Lh58
Sossusvlei Pan NAM 212 Lh58
Šoštanj SLO 41 Lq44
Šostka UA 52 Mg20
Sosúa DOM 260 Ge36
Sošyčne UA 37 Me39
Sota DY 186 Lb40
Sotara, Volcán CO 272 Gb44
Sotasæter N 12 Lh29
Soteapan MEX (VC) 255 Fc36
Sotian RMM 193 Kg40
Sotik EAK 204 Mh46
Sotillo de la Adrada E 26 Kq50
Sotla SLO/HR 41 Lq44
Soto RA (CD) 288 Gh61
Soto del Barco E 26 Ko53
Sotogrande E 28 Kp46
Sotok RI 126 Qf45
Soto La Marina MEX (TM) 253 Fa34
Sotomayor CO 272 Gb45
Sotouboua TG 193 La41
Sotra N 12 Lf30
Sottunga FIN 13 Ma30
Sottunga FIN 13 Ma30
Sotuta MEX (YT) 255 Ff35
Souanké RCB 195 Lh44
Souassi TN 174 Lf28
Soubakaniédogou BF 193 Kh40
Soubakpérou DY 193 La41
Soubané RG 192 Kc40
Soubéira BF 185 Kk39
Soubré CI 192 Kg43
Souchang CHN (ZJG) 102 Qk31
Soudan AUS (NT) 139 Rj56
Soudan Bank 221 Nk55
Soudougui BF 193 La40
Souf DZ 174 Ld29
Soufflenheim F 23 Lh42
Soufli GR 47 Mg49
Soufrière WL 261 Gk39
Sougueur DZ 173 La28
Souhoulé RG 192 Kf42
Souillac F 24 Lb46
Souillac MS 221 Nj56
Souilly F 23 Lf41
Souk-Ahras DZ 174 Ld27
Souk-el-Arba-des-Beni-Hassan MA 172 Kh28
Souk-el-Arba-du-Rharb MA 172 Kg28
Souk-Jemâa-de-Oulad-Abbou MA 172 Kg29
Soukoukoutane RN 185 Lb38
Souk Tenadjeleline RMM 185 La38
Soul ROK 100 Rd27
Soul ROK 100 Rd27
Soulabali SN 183 Kc39
Soulac-sur-Mer F 24 Kt45
Soúli GR 48 Mc53
Souliou GR 48 Ma51
Soulis Pond CDN 245 Hc21
Soulópoulo GR 48 Ma51
Sounding Creek CDN 233 Ee20
Sound of Barra IRL 18 Kn33
Sound of Harris GB 18 Kn33
Sound of Jura GB 18 Kp35
Sound of Monach GB 18 Kn33
Sound of Mull GB 18 Kp34
Sound of Sleat GB 19 Kp33
Sounds of Starlight Theatre AUS 142 Rg57
Soungrougrou SN 183 Kc39
Souq al-Milh YE 68 Nc38
Source Bleu de Meski MA 173 Kh30
Source chaude de Déssikou RCA 196 Lk42
Source chaude de Soborom TCH 188 Lj35
Source du Nil BU 206 Me47
Sour-el-Ghozlane DZ 173 Lb27
Souris CDN (MB) 238 Ek21
Souris CDN (PE) 245 Gj22
Souris USA 238 Ek21
Sourou RMM 185 Kj39
Souroukaha CI 193 Kh41
Sourountouna RMM 184 Kh39
Sourpi GR 48 Mc51
Sousa BR (PB) 277 Ja49
Sousceyrac F 24 Lc46
Sousel P 28 Kn48
Sous-Massa, P.N. MA 172 Kf30
Sousse TN 174 Lf28
Soustons F 24 Kt47
Sout ZA 216 Lk61
Sout ZA 216 Ma60
South Africa 167 Ma13
South Alligator River AUS 139 Rg52
Southampton GB 21 Kt40
Southampton USA (NY) 247 Gd25
Southampton Island CDN 225 Fd06
South Andaman IND 111 Pg39
South Australia AUS 136 Rc24
South Australian Basin 134 Ra14
Southaven USA (MS) 243 Ff28
South Banda Basin RI 132 Rd49
South Banggi Strait MAL 122 Qj42
Southbank CDN (BC) 232 Dh18
South Bay CDN (ON) 238 Fd20
South Bay USA (FL) 250 Fk32
South Baymouth CDN (ON) 246 Fj23
South Bend USA (IN) 246 Fg25
South Bimini BS 251 Ga33
South Boston USA (VA) 249 Ga27
South Brahmaputra Hills IND 112 Pg33
South Branch CDN (NF) 245 Ha22
Southbridge NZ 155 Tg67
South Brook CDN (NF) 245 Hb21
South Brookfield CDN (NS) 245 Gh23
South Bruny Island AUS 152 Sd67
South Bruny N.P. AUS 152 Sd67
South Carolina USA 227 Fd12
South Carolina USA 227 Fd12
South Cay CO 257 Fk38
South Channel RP 120 Ra38
South China Basin 118 Qc15
South China Mountains CHN 96 Qd33
South China Sea 118 Qc15
South Coast Highway AUS 144 Ra62
South Dakota USA 226 Ed10
South Downs GB 21 Ku40
South East RB 213 Mc58
South East Aru Marine Reserve RI 131 Rh49
South East Cape AUS 152 Sd67
Southeast Cape USA 228 Bf14
Southeast Forests N.P. AUS 153 Se64
Southeast Indian Ridge 134 Qa14
South East Pacific Basin 266 Ed30
South East Point AUS 153 Sd65
Southeast Point BS 251 Gd35
Southend CDN (SK) 238 Ej17
Southend-on-Sea GB 21 La39
Southerland Falls NZ 155 Td68
Southern Alps NZ 155 Te68
Southern Altay Gobi Nature Reserve MNG 92 Pj24
Southern Central Reserve A.L. AUS 141 Rc59
Southern Cross AUS (WA) 144 Qk61
Southern Indian Lake CDN 238 Fa17
Southern Laos Cruise LAO/K 115 Qc38
Southern Lau Group FJI 163 Ua55
Southern Lueti Z 209 Mb53
Southern N.P. SUD 197 Me42
Southern Pines USA (NC) 249 Ga28
Southern Sporades GR 49 Mf52
Southern Uplands GB 19 Kq35
Southey CDN (SK) 233 Eh20
South Fiji Basin 134 Tb12
South Foreland GB 21 Lb39
South Fork USA (CO) 237 Eg27
South Fork Kuskokwim River USA 229 Cd14
SouthFrancisco de Macoris DOM 260 Ge36
South Galway AUS (QLD) 150 Sb58
Southgate River CDN 232 Dh20
South Georgia GB 267 Ja29
South Georgia GB 267 Ja29
South Goulburn Island AUS 139 Rg51
South Gut Saint Ann's CDN (NS) 245 Gk22
South Harbour CDN (NS) 245 Gk22
South Hatia Island BD 112 Pf34
South Haven USA (MI) 246 Fg24
South Heart River CDN 233 Eb18
South Hill USA (VA) 249 Ga27
South Honshu Ridge 83 Rd12
South Horr EAK 204 Mj45
South Huvadhoo Atoll = Gaafu-Dhaalu Atoll MV 110 Og45
South Indian Lake CDN (MB) 238 Fa17
South Island AUS 149 Sf56
South Island EAK 204 Mj44
South Island NZ 155 Te67
South Island N.P. EAK 204 Mj44
South Junction CDN (MB) 238 Fc21
South Kinangop EAK 204 Mj46
South Kitui National Reserve EAK 205 Mk46
South Korea ROK 57 Ra06
South Lake Rukwa EAT 206 Mg50
South Lake Tahoe USA (NV) 234 Ea26
South Luangwa N.P. Z 210 Mf52
South Luconia Shoals 122 Qg43
South Male Atoll MV 110 Og44
South Miladhunmadulu Atoll = Noonu Atoll MV 110 Og43
South Molton GB 20 Kr39
South Moose Lake CDN 238 Ek19
South Mtn. USA 234 Eb24
South Nahanni River CDN 231 Dh15
South Nilandhoo Atoll = Dhaalu Atoll MV 110 Og44
Southold USA (NY) 247 Gd25
South Orkney Islands GB 267 Hc30
South Orkney Islands GB 267 Hc30
South Ossetia GE 63 Nc24
South Padre Island USA (TX) 253 Fb32
South Padre Island USA (TX) 253 Fb32
South Pass City USA (WY) 235 Ef24
South Pole ANT 296 Ga36
South Porcupine CDN (ON) 239 Fk21
Southport AUS (QLD) 151 Sg59
Southport AUS (TAS) 152 Sd67
Southport CDN (NF) 245 Hd21
Southport GB 21 Kr37
Southport USA (NC) 249 Ga29
South Prince of Wales Wilderness USA 231 Dd18
South Pt. BS 251 Gc34
South Point = Ka Lae USA 230 Cc36
South River of Georgia CDN 232 Dh21
South Ronaldsay GB 19 Ks32
South Rukuru River MW 210 Mg51
South Salmara IND (ASM) 112 Pf33
South Sandwich Islands GB 267 Jc31
South Sandwich Islands GB 267 Jc31
South Sandwich Trench 267 Jc29
South Saskatchewan River CDN 233 Ef20
South Scotia Ridge 267 Hb31
South Shetland Islands ANT 296 Ha31
South Shields GB 19 Kt36
South Sioux City USA (NE) 241 Fb24
South Solomon Trench 156 Ta21
South Stradbroke Island AUS 151 Sg59
South Taranaki Bight NZ 154 Th66
South Tasman Rise 134 Sa14
South Thiladhunmathee Atoll = Haa-Dhaalu Atoll MV 110 Og42
South Thompson River CDN 232 Ea20
South Trap NZ 155 Td69
South Tucson USA (AZ) 237 Ee29
South Turkana National Reserve EAK 204 Mh45
South Twin Island CDN 239 Ga19
South Twin Lake CDN 245 Hc21
South Tyne GB 19 Ks36
South Uist GB 18 Kn33
South Wabasca Lake CDN 233 Ed18
South West Cape AUS 152 Sc67
Southwest Cape NZ 155 Td69
Southwest Cay 122 Qh40
Southwest Gander River CDN 245 Hc21
Southwest Indian Ridge 301 Na14
Southwest Miramichi River CDN 245 Gg22
Southwest N.P. AUS 152 Sd67
Southwest Pacific Basin 303 Cb13
Southwest Point BS 251 Gb33
Southwest Point BS 251 Gc34
Southwest Point BS 251 Gd35
South West Rocks AUS (NSW) 151 Sg61
Southwold GB 21 Lb38
South Yandaminta AUS (NSW) 150 Sa60
Souto Soares BR (BA) 283 Hk52
Soutpan NAM 212 Lk57
Soutpan ZA 217 Md60
Soutpansberg ZA 214 Me57
Souvigny F 25 Ld44
Sovata RO 45 Mf44
Soverato I 43 Lr52
Sovereign Hill AUS (VIC) 153 Sb64
Sovetsk RUS 17 Mb35
Sovetskaja ANT (RUS) 297 Pb34
Sovetskaja RUS 53 Nb21
Sovetskaja RUS 55 Na23
Sovetskaja Gavan' RUS 99 Sa21
Sovetskij RUS 16 Mj30
Sovetskij RUS 53 Ne17
Sovetskoe RUS (KBA) 70 Nb24
Sowa Pan RB 213 Mc56
Sowczyce PL 36 Lt40
Soweto ZA 217 Md59
Sowia Góra PL 36 Lq38
Sowma'eh Sara IR 72 Ne27
Soy EAK 204 Mh45
Soyaló MEX (CHP) 255 Fd37
Soya-misaki J 99 Sb23
Soyet IND (MPH) 108 Oj33
Soyo ANG 202 Lg49
Sozak KZ 76 Oe23
Sozopol BG 47 Mh48
Sozu J 101 Rj27
Spa B 23 Lf40
Spain 7 Kb06
Spalding AUS (SA) 152 Rk62
Spalding GB 21 Ku38
Spálené Poříčí CZ 38 Lo41
Spaniard's Bay CDN (NF) 245 Hd22
Spanish Fork USA (UT) 235 Ee25
Spanish Head GB 18 Kq36
Spanish Town JA 259 Gb37
Spanwerk ZA 213 Md58
Sparks USA (NV) 234 Ea26
Sparreholm S 13 Lr31
Sparta USA (GA) 249 Fj29
Sparta USA (NC) 249 Fk27
Sparta USA (TN) 248 Fh28
Sparta USA (WI) 241 Fe24
Spartanburg USA (SC) 249 Fk28
Spárti GR 48 Mc53
Sparwood CDN (BC) 233 Ec21
Spas-Klepiki RUS 53 Na18
Spaso Jakovlenskij monastyr RUS 52 Mk17
Spasovo BG 47 Mj47
Spassk-Dal'nij RUS 98 Rg23
Spassk-Rjazanskij RUS 53 Na18
Spatsizi Plateau CDN 231 Df17
Spatsizi Plateau Wilderness Prov. Park CDN 231 Df17
S.Paulo e S.Pedro BR 265 Jc18
Spean Bridge GB 19 Kq34
Spearfish USA (SD) 240 Ej23
Spearman USA (TX) 242 Ek27
Speculator USA (NY) 247 Gc24
Speedwell Island GB 295 Ha72
Speightstown BDS 261 Ha39
Speke Gulf EAT 204 Mg47
Spello I 40 Ln47
Spencer USA (IA) 241 Fc24
Spencer USA (IN) 248 Fg26
Spencer USA (NE) 240 Fa24
Spencer USA (TN) 249 Fh28
Spencer USA (WV) 247 Fk26
Spencer Bay NAM 212 Lh58
Spencer Bridge CDN (BC) 232 Dk20
Spencer Gulf AUS 152 Rj63
Spentrup DK 14 Ll34
Speos of Horemheb ET 177 Mg33
Sperrin Mountains GB 18 Kn36
Spessart D 34 Lk41
Spétses GR 48 Md53
Spétses GR 48 Md53
Spey GB 19 Kr33
Speyer D 34 Lj41
Speyside Beach TT 270 Gk40
Spezand PK 78 Od30
Spezzano Albanese I 43 Lr51
Spezzano della Sila I 43 Lr51
Spiddle IRL 20 Kl37
Spiekeroog D 32 Lh37
Spielcasino Baden-Baden D 34 Lj42
Spiez CH 34 Lh44
Spijkenisse NL 32 Le39
Špilberk CZ 38 Lr41
Spileon Diroú GR 48 Mc54
Spileo Stalaktiton GR 49 Mf53
Spilimbergo I 41 Ln44
Spiljani SCG 46 Ma48
Spilsby GB 21 La37
Spinazzola I 43 Lr50
Spin Buldak AFG 78 Od30

Špindlerův Mlýn – Sucuiu

Špindlerův Mlýn CZ 38 Lq40
Spioenkop ZA 217 Me60
Spirit Lake USA (IA) 241 Fc24
Spirit Lake Ind. Res. USA 240 Fa22
Spirit River CDN (AB) 233 Ea18
Spiritwood CDN (SK) 233 Eg19
Spirovo RUS 52 Mh17
Spišská Belá SK 39 Ma41
Spišský hrad SK 39 Ma42
Spitak ARM 70 Nc25
Spitsbergen N 11 Lg06
Spitskopvlei ZA 217 Mc61
Spittal an der Drau A 35 Lo44
Spitz A 35 Lq42
Spitzkoppe NAM 212 Lh56
Spitzkoppe Rock Paintings NAM 212 Lh56
Spiveys Corner USA (NC) 249 Ga28
Spjelkavik N 12 Lg28
Split HR 41 Lr47
Split Lake CDN (MB) 238 Fb17
Split Lake CDN 238 Fb17
Split Lake Ind. Res. CDN 238 Fb17
Splügen CH 34 Lk44
Splügenpass = Passo dello Spluga I/CH 34 Lk44
Spodsbjerg DK 14 Ll36
Spofford USA (TX) 242 Ek31
Spoggies AUS 152 Rg62
Špogi LV 17 Mg34
Spokane USA (WA) 232 Eb22
Spokane House USA 232 Eb22
Spokane Ind. Res. USA 232 Eb22
Špola UA 54 Mf21
Spoleto I 42 Ln48
Spook Cave USA 246 Fe24
Spookmyndorp NAM 216 Lh59
Spooner USA (WI) 241 Fe23
Sporades GR 9 Mb11
Spotorno I 40 Lj46
Spotted House USA (WY) 235 Eh23
Spøttrup DK 14 Lj34
Sprague USA (WA) 232 Eb22
Sprague USA 234 Dk24
Spratly Islands 122 Qh40
Spray USA (OR) 234 Ea23
Spreča BIH 44 Lt46
Spree D 33 Lp39
Spreewald D 33 Lp39
Spremberg D 33 Lp39
Sprengisandur IS 10 Ka13
Şpring RO 44 Md45
Springbok ZA 216 Lj60
Spring Creek AUS (QLD) 148 Sc55
Spring Creek USA (NV) 234 Ec25
Springdale CDN (NF) 245 Hb21
Springdale USA (AR) 243 Fc27
Springe D 32 Lk38
Springer USA (NM) 237 Eh27
Springerville USA (AZ) 237 Ef28
Springfield USA (CO) 237 Ej27
Springfield USA (GA) 249 Fk29
Springfield USA (IL) 241 Ff26
Springfield USA (KY) 248 Fh27
Springfield USA (MA) 247 Gd24
Springfield USA (MO) 243 Fd27
Springfield USA (OH) 246 Fj26
Springfield USA (OR) 234 Dj23
Springfield USA (TN) 248 Fg27
Springfield USA (VT) 247 Gd24
Springfield Plateau USA 243 Fd27
Springfontein ZA 217 Mc61
Spring Garden GUY 270 Ha42
Springhill CDN (NS) 245 Gh23
Spring Hill USA (FL) 250 Fj31
Springhill USA (LA) 243 Fd29
Springrale AUS (QLD) 148 Sa57
Spring Ridge AUS (NSW) 151 Sf61
Springs ZA 217 Me59
Springside CDN (SK) 238 Ej20
Springs Junction NZ 155 Tg67
Springsure AUS (QLD) 151 Se58
Springvale AUS (WA) 138 Rd54
Springvale USA (ME) 247 Ge24
Springvale Homestead AUS (NT) 139 Rg53
Spring Valley ZA 217 Md62
Springview USA (NE) 240 Fa24
Springville USA (NY) 247 Ga24
Springville USA (UT) 235 Ee25
Springwater CDN (SK) 233 Ef19
Sproge S 15 Lt33
Spruce Grove CDN (AB) 233 Ed19
Spruce Home CDN (SK) 233 Eh19
Spruce Island USA 230 Cd17
Spruce Meadows CDN (AB) 233 Ec20
Spruce Pine USA (NC) 249 Fj28
Spruce Woods Prov. Park CDN 238 Fa21
Spur USA (TX) 242 Ek29
Spurn Head GB 21 La37
Spuž SCG 46 Lu48
Squamish CDN (BC) 232 Dj21
Squarnish River CDN 232 Dj20
Squaw Creek N.W.R. USA 241 Fc25
Squaw Lake USA (MN) 241 Fc22
Squaw Valley USA (CA) 234 Dk26
Squillace I 43 Lr52
Squinzano I 43 Lt50
Squires Mem. Prov. Park CDN 245 Hb21
Squirrel River USA 229 Bk12
Sragen RI 128 Qf49
Sravanabelgola IND 110 Oj40
Sravasti IND 107 Pb32
Srb HR 41 Lr46
Srbac BIH 41 Ls45
Srbica SCG 46 Ma48
Srbobran SCG 44 Lu45
Srbovac SCG 46 Ma48
Srdiečko SK 39 Lu42
Sre Ambel K 115 Qb40
Srebărna BG 45 Mh46
Srebărna Nature Reserve BG 45 Mg47
Srebrenica BIH 46 Lu46
Srebrenik BIH 44 Lt46
Sredec BG 47 Mf48
Sredec BG 47 Mh48
Sredinnyj hrebet RUS 59 Ta07
Sredna Gora BG 47 Me48
Srednebelaja RUS 98 Re20
Srednerusskaja vozvyšennost' RUS 53 Mj19
Sre Koki K 115 Qd39
Śrem PL 36 Ls38
Sremska Mitrovica SCG 44 Lu46
Sremski Karlovci SCG 44 Lu45
Sre Noy K 115 Qc39
Sre Peang K 115 Qb39
Sretensk RUS 91 Qj19
Sribawono RI 125 Qc48
Sribne UA 52 Mg20
Sri Dungargarh IND (RJT) 106 Oh31
Srigiripadu IND (APH) 109 Ok37
Sri Jayewardenepura CL 111 Ok43
Srikakulam IND (APH) 109 Pb36
Sri Kalahasti IND (APH) 111 Ok40
Sri Karanpur IND (RJT) 106 Og31
Sri Krishna Mutt (Udupi) IND 110 Oh40
Sri Lanka CL 104 Pa17
Srimangal BD 112 Pf33
Sri Mohangarh IND (RJT) 106 Of32
Srinagar IND (UTT) 107 Ok30
Srinagar 79 Oh28
Srinagarindra N.P. THA 114 Pk38
Srinakarin Reservoir THA 114 Pk38
Sringeri IND 110 Oh40
Srinivaspur IND (KTK) 111 Ok40
Srirangam IND (TNU) 111 Ok41
Srirangapatna IND (KTK) 111 Oj40
Srisailam IND (APH) 109 Ok37
Srivilliputtur IND (TNU) 111 Oj42
Środa Wielkopolska PL 36 Ls38
Srokowo PL 37 Mb36
Srostki RUS 85 Pc19
Sr'reenshamali SYR 65 Mk27
Ssese Islands EAU 204 Mg46
Staaten River AUS (QLD) 148 Sb54
Staaten River N.P. AUS (QLD) 148 Sb54
Stabbursdalen n.p. N 11 Mc10
Stachanov UA 55 Mk21
Stachy CZ 38 Lo41
Stack Skerry GB 19 Kq31
Stad N 12 Lf28
Stade D 32 Lk37
Staderton ZA 217 Me59
Stadskanaal NL 32 Lh38
Stadthagen D 32 Lk38
Stadtlohn D 32 Lg38
Staffa GB 18 Ko34
Staffanstorp S 15 Lo35
Staffelberg D 35 Lm40
Stafford GB 21 Ks38
Stagira GR 47 Md50
Stahnsdorf D 33 Lo38
Staicele LV 17 Me33
Stajki BY 17 Mg37
Staked Plains = Llano Estacado USA 237 Ej29
Stakliškės LT 17 Me36
Stalbe LV 17 Mf33
Stalker Castle GB 19 Kp34
Ställdalen S 13 Lp31
Staller Sattel I/A 35 Ln44
Staloluokta S 10 Lj12
Staloluokta fjällstation S 10 Lj12
Stalowa Wola PL 37 Mc40
Stambolijski BG 47 Me48
Stamford AUS (QLD) 148 Sb56
Stamford GB 21 Ku38
Stamford USA (CT) 247 Gd25
Stamford USA (TX) 242 Fa29
Stamford Bridge GB 21 Ku37
Stamnes N 12 Lf30
Stampriet NAM 212 Lk58
Stamsund N 10 Lg11
Stânceni RO 45 Mf44
Standing Rock Ind. Res. USA 240 Ek23
Standing Stone S.P. USA 248 Fh27
Standish USA (MI) 246 Fj24
Stanford USA (KY) 249 Fh27
Stanford USA (MT) 235 Ee22
Stånga S 15 Lt33
Stangån S 15 Lq33
Stange N 12 Lm30
Stanger ZA 217 Mf60
Stanhope AUS (VIC) 153 Sc64
Stanhope GB 19 Ks36
Staniard Creek BS 251 Gb33
Stanica Bagaevskaja RUS 55 Na22
Staniel Cay Beach BS 251 Gb33
Stanišić SCG 44 Lu45
Staňkov CZ 38 Lo41
Stanley AUS (TAS) 152 Sc66
Stanley GB (GBF) 295 Hb71
Stanley USA (ND) 238 Ej21
Stanley Mission CDN (SK) 233 Eh18
Stanley, Mount EAU/RDC 201 Mf45
Stanley Reservoir IND 111 Oj41
Stanmore ZW 214 Me56
Stanovoe RUS 53 Mk19
Stanovoye Nagor'ye RUS 59 Qc07
Stanovoy Khrebet RUS 59 Ra07
Stans CH 34 Lj44
Stansbury AUS (SA) 152 Rj63
Stansmore Range AUS 141 Rd56
Stanthorpe AUS (QLD) 151 Sf60
Stanton Bank GB 18 Kn34
Stanwell AUS (QLD) 149 Sf57
Stanwell Park AUS (NSW) 153 Sf63
Stanwood USA (WA) 232 Dj21
Stanyčno-Luhans'ke UA 55 Mk21
Staphorst NL 32 Lg38
Stapleford ZW 214 Mg55
Staples USA (MN) 241 Fc22
Stapleton USA (NE) 240 Ek25
Stąporków PL 37 Ma39
Stara PL 37 Lu39
Stara Caryčanka UA 45 Mk44
Starachowice PL 37 Mb39
Staraja Russa RUS 52 Mf17
Stara Kiszewa PL 36 Lt36
Stara Moravica SCG 44 Lu45
Stara Novalja HR 41 Lp46
Stara Pazova SCG 44 Ma46
Stara Rečka BG 47 Mg47
Stara Reka BG 47 Mg48
Stara Sajmyrzino RUS 53 Nd18
Stara Ušycja UA 45 Mh42
Stara Vyživka UA 37 Me39
Stara Zagora BG 47 Mf48
Starbuck Island KIR 303 Ca10
Star City USA (AR) 243 Fe29
Stare Dolistowo PL 37 Mc37
Stare Jeżewo PL 37 Mc37
Stare Kiełbonki PL 37 Mb37
Stare Strącze PL 36 Lr39
Stargard Szczeciński PL 36 Lq37
Stårheim N 12 Lf29
Starica RUS 52 Mh17
Starica RUS 52 Mh19
Starigrad HR 41 Lr47
Stari grad Mostar BIH 41 Ls47
Stari grad Sarajevo BIH 41 Lt47
Stari Ras SCG 46 Ma47
Starke USA (FL) 250 Fj31
Starkville USA (MS) 243 Ff29
Starkweather USA (ND) 238 Fa21
Starnberg D 35 Lm42
Starnberger See D 35 Lm43
Starobil's'k UA 53 Mk21
Starobin BY 52 Md19
Starodub RUS 52 Mg19
Starogard PL 36 Lq37
Starogard Gdański PL 36 Lt37
Starojur'evo RUS 53 Na19
Starokostjantyniv UA 54 Md21
Starominskaja RUS 55 Mk22
Staro Nagoričane MK 46 Mb48
Staro Petrovo Selo HR 41 Ls45
Starosel BG 47 Me48
Staro Selo BG 47 Mg47
Starotitarovskaja RUS 55 Mj23
Starožilovo RUS 53 Mk18
Start Point GB 20 Kr40
Stary Dvor RUS 53 Na17
Stary Dzierzgoń PL 37 Lu37
Staryi Oskol RUS 53 Mj20
Stary Ivanovka RUS 53 Nf18
Staryja Darohi BY 52 Me19
Staryj Bajsarovo RUS 53 Ng18
Staryj Kulatka RUS 53 Nd19
Staryj Račejka RUS 53 Ne19
Staryj Sambir UA 39 Mc41
Starý Smokovec SK 39 Ma41
Staßfurt D 33 Lm39
Staszów PL 37 Mb40
State College USA (PA) 247 Gb25
State Line USA (MS) 243 Ff30
State Mosque MAL 117 Qa44
Statenville USA (GA) 249 Fj30
Statesboro USA (GA) 249 Fk29
Statesville USA (NC) 249 Fk28
Stathelle N 12 Lk31
Station de capture d'Epulu RDC 201 Me45
Statue of Liberty USA 247 Gd25
Staume N 12 Lf29
Staunton USA (VA) 247 Ga26
Staunton River S.P. USA 249 Ga27
Stavanger N 12 Lf32
Stave SCG 46 Lu46
Stave Lake CDN 232 Dj21
Stavelot B 23 Lf40
Stavern N 12 Lk32
Stavki UA 45 Mm43
Stavky UA 37 Me39
Stavre S 13 Lq28
Stavrodrómi GR 48 Mb53
Stavropol' RUS 55 Na23
Stavrós GR 47 Md50
Stavroskiádi GR 46 Ma50
Stavroúpoli GR 47 Me49
Stawiski PL 37 Mc37
Stawiszyn PL 36 Lt39
St-CharlesGarnier CDN (QC) 244 Gf21
Steamboat USA (OR) 234 Dj24
Steamboat Springs USA (CO) 235 Eg25
Stebbins USA (AK) 229 Bj14
Stebnyk UA 39 Md41
Steele USA (MO) 243 Ff27
Steele USA (ND) 240 Fa22
Steele, Mount CDN 231 Ck15
Steelpoort ZA 214 Mf58
Steelville USA (MO) 243 Fe27
Steenbergen NL 32 Le39
Steens Mountain USA 234 Ea24
Steenstrup Gletscher DK 225 Ha03
Steenvoorde B 23 Lc40
Steenwijk NL 32 Lg38
Steepbank River CDN 233 Ee17
Steephill Lake CDN 238 Ej18
Steep Point AUS 140 Qg59
Steese Highway USA (AK) 229 Ch13
Stefan Karadža BG 47 Mg47
Stefansson Island CDN 225 Ec04
Ştefan-Vodă MD 45 Mk44
Steffen, Cerro RA/RCH 292 Ge68
Steffisburg CH 34 Lh44
Stege DK 14 Ln36
Stegna PL 36 Lu36
Ştei RO 44 Mc44
Steigen N 10 Lh12
Steillopsbrug ZA 214 Me57
Steilrand ZA 217 Mf59
Steilrandberge NAM 208 Lg54
Stein D 35 Lm41
Steinach A 35 Lm43
Steinach D 33 Lm40
Stein am Rhein CH 34 Lj43
Steinau D 34 Lk40
Steinbach CDN (MB) 238 Fb21
Steine N 10 Lh11
Steinen BR 281 Hc52
Steinfeld D 32 Lj38
Steinfeld NAM 212 Lj58
Steinfurt D 32 Lh38
Steinhagen D 33 Ln36
Steinhatchee USA (FL) 250 Fj31
Steinhausen NAM 212 Lk56
Steinheim D 32 Lk39
Steinhuder Meer D 32 Lk38
Steinkjer N 10 Lf14
Steinkopf ZA 216 Lj60
Steinsdalsfossen N 12 Lg30
Steins Ghost Town USA (AZ) 237 Ef29
Steinshamn N 12 Lg28
Stekenjokkvägen S 10 Lh13
Steķi LV 17 Mg34
Stella ZA 217 Mc59
Stella Maris BS 251 Gc34
Stellarton CDN (NS) 245 Gj23
Stellenbosch ZA 216 Lk62
Stelling van Amsterdam NL 32 Le38
Stelmužė LT 17 Mg35
Stélvio, P.N.delle = Stilfser Joch, N.P. I 40 Ll44
Stená Foúrkas GR 48 Mc52
Stenay F 23 Lf41
Stendal D 33 Lm38
Stende LV 17 Mc33
Stenen CDN (SK) 238 Ej20
Stenhouse AUS (SA) 152 Rj63
Stenó Andikíthira GR 48 Md55
Stenó Kafiréa GR 49 Me52
Stenó Kéas GR 48 Me53
Steno Kimolou Sifnou GR 49 Me54
Stenó Kithira GR 48 Md54
Stenó Koufonisi GR 49 Mg56
Stenón Kithnou GR 48 Me53
Stenó Petási GR 48 Md53
Stenó Políegou Folégandrou GR 49 Me54
Stenó Serifou GR 49 Me53
Steno Sifnou GR 49 Me53
Štěnovice CZ 38 Lo41
Stenshuvuds n.p. S 15 Lp35
Stenstorp S 15 Lo32
Stenungsund S 14 Lm32
Stepanakert = Xankendi AZ 70 Nd26
Step'anavan ARM 70 Nc25
Stepanci MK 46 Mb49
Stephanie Wildlife Reserve ETH 198 Mj43
Stephens Passage USA 231 Dd17
Stephenville CDN (NF) 245 Ha21
Stephenville USA (TX) 242 Fa29
Stephenville Crossing CDN (NF) 245 Ha21
Štepivka UA 52 Mh20
Stepnica PL 36 Lp37
Stepnoe Matjunico RUS 53 Nd19
Stepojevac SCG 44 Ma46
Stepovak Bay USA (AK) 228 Bk18
Stepp Rock CDN (MB) 238 Fa20
Sterdyń-Osada PL 37 Mc38
Sterkfontein ZA 217 Md59
Sterkfontein Dam Nature Reserve ZA 217 Me60
Sterkspruit ZA 217 Md61
Sterkstroom ZA 217 Md61
Sterling USA (CO) 240 Ej25
Sterling ZA 216 Ma61
Sterling City USA (TX) 242 Ek30
Sterling Highway USA (AK) 229 Ce16
Sterling Hts. USA (MI) 246 Fj24
Sterling Landing USA (AK) 229 Cc14
Sterlitamak RUS 58 Nd08
Sternberg D 33 Lm37
Šternberk CZ 38 Ls41
Stérnes GR 49 Me55
Steroh YE 69 Ng39
Sterzing = Vipiteno I 40 Lm44
Stęszew PL 36 Lr38
Stettin Lagoon D/PL 33 Lp37
Stettler CDN (AB) 233 Ed19
Steubenville USA (OH) 247 Fk25
Stevenage GB 21 Ku39
Stevens, Mount NZ 155 Tg66
Stevenson Lake CDN 238 Fc19
Stevensons Peak AUS 142 Rf58
Stevens Pass USA 232 Dk22
Stevens Point USA (WI) 246 Ff23
Stevens Village USA (AK) 229 Cf12
Stevensville USA (MT) 235 Ec22
Stevns Klint DK 14 Ln35
Stewart CDN (BC) 231 Df18
Stewart Crossing CDN (YT) 231 Db14
Stewart Island NZ 155 Te69
Stewart Island NZ 155 Te69
Stewart Islands SOL 161 Tb50
Stewart, Mount AUS (QLD) 149 Sc56
Stewart, Mount CDN 229 Da14
Stewart Plateau CDN 231 Dc14
Stewart River CDN 231 Dd13
Stewarts Point USA (CA) 234 Dj26
Stewart Valley CDN (SK) 233 Eg20
Stewartville USA (MN) 241 Fd24
Steynsburg ZA 217 Mc61
Steynsrus ZA 217 Md59
Steyr A 35 Lp42
Steytlerville ZA 217 Mc62
Stężyca PL 36 Ls36
Stiegler's Gorge EAT 207 Mk49
Stift Admont A 35 Lp43
Stift Altenburg A 35 Lq42
Stift Göttweig A 35 Lq42
Stift Klosterneuburg A 35 Lr42
Stift Kremsmünster A 35 Lp42
Stift Melk A 35 Lq42
Stift Sankt Paul A 35 Lp44
Stift Seckau A 35 Lp43
Stiftskirche Innichen I 40 Ln44
Stift Zwettl A 35 Lq42
Stigen S 12 Ln32
Stigler USA (OK) 243 Fc28
Stigliano I 43 Lr50
Stigtomta S 13 Lr32
Stikine Plateau CDN 231 De16
Stikine Ranges CDN 231 De16
Stikine River CDN 231 De17
Stikine Strait USA 231 Dd17
Stile DZ 174 Lc28
Stiles USA (TX) 242 Ek30
Stilfontein ZA 217 Md59
Stilfser Joch, N.P. = Stélvio, P.N.delle I 40 Ll44
Stilída GR 48 Mc52
Stillwater USA (NV) 234 Ea26
Stillwater USA (OK) 243 Fb27
Stilo I 43 Lr52
Stilwell USA (OK) 243 Fc28
Štimlje SCG 46 Mb48
Stinăpari RO 44 Mb46
Stinear, Mount 297 Ob33
Stinnett USA (TX) 242 Ek28
Štip MK 46 Mc49
Stíra GR 48 Me52
Stirling AUS (NT) 142 Rg56
Stirling AUS (QLD) 148 Sa54
Stirling GB 19 Kr34
Stirling Castle GB 19 Kr34
Stirling Creek AUS 139 Re54
Stirling North AUS (SA) 152 Rj62
Stirling Range N.P. AUS 144 Qk63
Štítary CZ 38 Lq42
Štítnik SK 39 Ma42
Stjørdal N 10 Lf14
Saint Joseph WD 261 Gk38
Stob BG 46 Md48
Stobi MK 46 Mb49
Stockach D 34 Lk43
Stockaryd S 15 Lp33
Stockbridge GB 21 Kt39
Stockbridge Ind. Res. USA 246 Ff23
Stockdale USA (TX) 242 Fb31
Stockerau A 35 Lr42
Stockholm S 13 Ls31
Stockman's Hall of Fame AUS (QLD) 148 Sc57
Stockport GB 21 Ks37
Stockport ZA 213 Md57
Stockton USA (CA) 234 Dk27
Stockton USA (GA) 249 Fj30
Stockton USA (KS) 240 Fa26
Stockton-on-Tees GB 21 Kt36
Stockton Plateau USA 237 Ej30
Stockton S.P. USA 243 Fd27
Stoczek Lukowski PL 37 Mb39
Stod CZ 38 Lo41
Stöde S 13 Lr28
Stødi N 10 Lh12
Stoffberg ZA 214 Me58
Stoholm DK 14 Lk34
Stoke-on-Trent GB 21 Ks37
Stokes N.P. AUS 144 Ra62
Stokes Point AUS 153 Sb66
Stokkvågen N 10 Lg12
Stokmarknes N 10 Lh11
Stolac BIH 41 Ls47
Stolin BY 52 Md20
Stolkertsijver SME 271 Hc43
Stollberg D 33 Ln40
Stöllet S 13 Lo30
Stoloiceni MD 45 Mj44
Stómio GR 46 Mc51
Stondansi-stuwmeer SME 271 Hb43
Stone GB 21 Ks38
Stone Circles WAG 183 Kc39
Stone Forest CHN 113 Qb33
Stoneham USA (CO) 240 Ej25
Stonehaven GB 19 Ks34
Stonehenge AUS (QLD) 150 Sb58
Stonehenge GB 21 Kt39
Stone Ind. Res. CDN 232 Dj19
Stone Mtn. Park USA (GA) 249 Fh29
Stone Mtn. Prov. Park CDN 231 Dh16
Stone Rondavel NAM 216 Lk59
Stonewall CDN (MB) 238 Fb20
Stone-walled ruins RB 213 Md57
Stonglandet N 10 Lj11
Stonhoekoe SME 271 Hc44
Stony Creek Ind. Res. CDN 232 Dh19
Stony Ind. Res. CDN 233 Ec20
Stony Plain CDN (AB) 233 Ed19
Stony Rapids CDN 225 Ed07
Stony River USA 229 Cc15
Stooping River CDN 239 Fj20
Stopnica PL 37 Ma40
Stör D 32 Lk37
Storå S 13 Lq31
Stora Askö S 15 Lr33
Stora Le S 12 Lm31
Stora Sjöfallets n.p. S 10 Lj12
Storavan S 10 Lk13
Storby FIN 13 Lu30
Stordalen N 12 Lg28
Storebæltsbro DK 14 Ll35
Storebro S 15 Lq33
Store Hånosi N 12 Lh30
Store Heddinge DK 14 Ln35
Store mosse n.p. S 15 Lo33
Støren N 10 Lf14
Storfjorden N 11 Lk07
Storfors S 13 Lp31
Storforsen S 10 Ma13
Storjord N 10 Lh12
Storjorda N 10 Lg12
Storkerson Peninsula CDN 225 Ec04
Storkow D 33 Lo38
Stormberg ZA 217 Md61
Stormberg ZA 217 Md61
Storm Lake USA (IA) 241 Fc24
Stormrivier ZA 216 Mb62
Stormsvlei ZA 216 Ma63
Stornoway GB 19 Ko32
Storøya N 11 Me05
Storožynec' UA 45 Mf42
Storsjön S 13 Lp28
Storsjön S 13 Lr30
Storsudret S 15 Lt33
Storuman S 10 Lj13
Storvorde DK 14 Ll34
Storvreta S 13 Ls31
Story USA (AR) 243 Fd28
Story USA (WY) 235 Eg23
Story City USA (IA) 241 Fd24
Stöten S 13 Ln29
Stoughton CDN (SK) 238 Ej21
Stoughton USA (WI) 246 Ff24
Stour GB 21 La38
Stourhead GB 21 Ks39
Stout Lake CDN 238 Fc19
Stovbcy BY 17 Mg37
Stovbcy BY 52 Md19
Støvring DK 14 Lk34
Stowięcino PL 36 Ls36
Stowmarket GB 21 La38
Stow-on-the-Wold GB 21 Kt39
Strabane GB 18 Kn36
Stradella I 40 Lk45
Straelen D 32 Lg39
Strahan AUS (TAS) 152 Sc67
Straight Lake CDN 239 Ff19
Strait of Belle Isle CDN 225 Ha08
Strait of Canso CDN 245 Gk23
Strait of Dover 23 Lb40
Strait of Gibraltar 28 Kp45
Strait of Hormuz 75 Nj32
Strait of Jubal ET 177 Mg32
Strait of Jubal ET 177 Mg32
Strait of Magellan RA 294 Ge72
Strait of Malacca MAL/RI 116 Pk43
Strait of Messina I 42 Lq52
Strait of Otranto I/AL 43 Lt50
Straits of Florida 251 Fk34
Strakonice CZ 38 Lo41
Straldža BG 47 Mg48
Stralsund D 33 Lo36
Strambino I 40 Lh45
Strâmtura RO 44 Me43
Strand ZA 216 Lk63
Stranda N 12 Lg28
Strandby DK 14 Ll33
Strandebarm N 12 Lg30
Strandfontein ZA 216 Lk61
Strangford GB 18 Kp36
Strangford Lough GB 18 Kp36
Strängnäs S 13 Ls31
Strångsjö S 13 Lr32
Stranraer GB 18 Kp36
Strasbourg CDN (SK) 233 Eh20
Strasbourg F 23 Lh42
Strasburg D 33 Lo37
Străşeni MD 45 Mj43
Straßwalchen A 35 Lo43
Stratford NZ 154 Th65
Stratford USA (TX) 237 Ej27
Stratford-upon-Avon GB 21 Kt38
Strathalbyn AUS (SA) 152 Rk63
Strathburn AUS (QLD) 146 Sb53
Strathcona Prov. Park CDN 232 Dh21
Strathfillan AUS (QLD) 148 Sb57
Strathgordon AUS (QLD) 146 Sb53
Strathgordon AUS (TAS) 152 Sd67
Strathhaven AUS (QLD) 146 Sb53
Strathmay AUS (QLD) 146 Sb53
Strathmerton AUS (VIC) 153 Sc63
Strathmore AUS (QLD) 148 Sb54
Strathmore AUS (QLD) 148 Sc57
Strathmore AUS (QLD) 149 Sd56
Strathmore CDN (AB) 233 Ed20
Strathroy AUS (QLD) 148 Sc56
Strathroy CDN (ON) 246 Fk24
Stratínista GR 48 Ma51
Stratinska BIH 41 Lr46
Stratóni GR 47 Md50
Stratonikeia TR 50 Mj53
Strátos GR 48 Mb52
Stratton GB 20 Kq40
Stratton USA (ME) 247 Ge23
Straubing D 35 Ln42
Straumnes IS 10 Jj12
Strausberg D 33 Lo38
Strawberry Mountain USA 234 Dk23
Stražica BG 47 Mf47
Strážný CZ 38 Lo42
Štrba SK 39 Ma41
Štrbské Pleso SK 39 Ma41
Streaky Bay AUS (SA) 152 Rh62
Streaky Bay AUS 152 Rh62
Streatfield Lake CDN 239 Fh19
Streator USA (IL) 246 Ff25
Strečno SK 39 Lt41
Streeter USA (ND) 240 Fa22
Strehaia RO 44 Md46
Strekov SK 38 Lt43
Strelča BG 47 Me48
Strenči LV 17 Mf33
Stresa I 40 Lj45
Strešer SCG 46 Mc48
Strevell USA (ID) 235 Ed24
Strezimirovci SCG 46 Mc48
Strezovce SCG 46 Mb48
Stříbro CZ 38 Ln41
Strickland Bay AUS 138 Rb54
Strickland River PNG 158 Sb49
Strilky UA 39 Mc41
Strimónas GR 46 Md50
Strimonikó GR 46 Md49
Strjama BG 47 Me48
Strmica HR 41 Lr46
Stroeder RA (BA) 293 Gj66
Strofiliá GR 48 Md52
Strogonof Point USA 228 Ca17
Strokkur IS 10 Jk13
Strómboli I 42 Lq52
Stromeferry GB 19 Kp33
Stromiec PL 37 Mb39
Stromness GB 19 Kr32
Strömsbruk S 13 Ls29
Strömsnäsbruk S 15 Lo34
Strömstad S 12 Lm32
Strömsund S 10 Lh14
Ströms Vattudal S 10 Lh13
Strong USA (AR) 243 Fd29
Strong, Mount PNG 159 Sd49
Stróngoli I 43 Ls51
Stronsay GB 19 Ks31
Strontian GB 19 Kp34
Stropkov SK 39 Mb41
Strošinci SCG 44 Lu46
Stroud AUS (NSW) 153 Sf62
Stroud GB 21 Ks39
Stroud USA (OK) 243 Fb28
Stroumpi CY 51 Mn56
Struan CDN (SK) 233 Eg19
Struer DK 14 Lj34
Struga MK 46 Ma49
Struisbaai ZA 216 Ma63
Struma BG 46 Mc48
Strumica MK 46 Mc49
Struve Geodetic Arc BY 37 Me37
Struve Geodetic Arc EST 16 Mg32
Struve Geodetic Arc FIN 16 Mg30
Struve Geodetic Arc LT 17 Mf36
Struve Geodetic Arc LV 17 Mf34
Struve Geodetic Arc N 11 Mb11
Struve Geodetic Arc S 11 Mb12
Struve Geodetic Arc UA 54 Md21
Strydenburg ZA 216 Mb60
Strydoortberge ZA 214 Me58
Stryi UA 39 Md41
Stryj UA 39 Md41
Stryker USA (MT) 233 Ec21
Stryn N 12 Lg29
Strzegom PL 36 Lr40
Strzegowo-Osada PL 37 Ma38
Strzelce Krajeńskie PL 36 Lq38
Strzelce Opolskie PL 36 Lt40
Strzelecki National Park AUS (TAS) 152 Se66
Strzelecki Regional Reserve AUS 143 Rk60
Strzelecki River AUS 143 Sa60
Strzelin PL 36 Ls40
Strzelno PL 36 Lt38
Stuart USA (FL) 250 Fk32
Stuart USA (VA) 249 Fk27
Stuart Bluff Range AUS 142 Rg57
Stuartburn CDN (MB) 238 Fb21
Stuart Highway (Northern Territory) AUS 139 Rg53
Stuart Highway (South Australia) AUS (SA) 142 Rh59
Stuart Island USA (AK) 229 Bj14
Stuart Lake CDN 232 Dh18
Stuart Range AUS 143 Rh60
Stuart River CDN 232 Dh18
Stuart Rocks USA (FL) 250 Fk32
Stubaier Alpen A 35 Lm43
Stubbekøbing DK 14 Ln36
Stubbenkammer D 33 Lo36
Stubičke Toplice HR 41 Lq45
Stubline SCG 44 Ma46
Studenci HR 41 Ls47
Studénka CZ 38 Lt41
Studina RO 47 Me47
Study Butte USA (TX) 237 Ej31
Studzieniczna PL 37 Md37
Stugufläten N 12 Lj28
Stugun S 10 Lh14
Stuhr D 32 Lj37
Stuibenfall A 35 Ll43
Stuie CDN (BC) 232 Dg19
Stull Lake CDN 238 Fd18
Stumholmen S 15 Lq34
Stung Treng K 115 Qc39
Stupava SK 38 Ls42
Stupino RUS 52 Mk18
Stupnik HR 41 Lq45
Stur IND (UPH) 109 Pb33
Sturgeon CDN 239 Fk22
Sturgeon Bay CDN 238 Fb19
Sturgeon Bay USA (WI) 246 Fg23
Sturgeon Falls CDN (ON) 247 Ga22
Sturgeon Lake CDN 233 Eb18
Sturgeon Lake CDN 239 Fe21
Sturgeon L. Ind. Res. CDN 233 Eb18
Sturgeon River CDN 233 Eg19
Sturgis USA (MI) 246 Fh25
Sturgis USA (SD) 240 Ej23
Sturkö S 15 Lq34
Šturlić BIH 41 Lq45
Štúrovo SK 39 Lt43
Sturt Bay AUS 152 Rj63
Sturt Creek AUS (WA) 138 Re55
Sturt Highway (South Australia) AUS 152 Rk63
Sturt Highway (New South Wales) AUS 153 Sb63
Sturt N.P. AUS 150 Sa60
Stutterheim ZA 217 Md62
Stuttgart D 34 Lk42
Stuttgart USA (AR) 243 Fe28
Stuurmansfontein Corbelled House ZA 216 Ma61
Stuurmansfontein Karbeelde huise ZA 216 Ma61
Stuyahok USA (AK) 229 Bk14
Stykkishólmur IS 10 Jj13
Styr BY 52 Md19
Styr UA 37 Mf40
Suaçuí Grande BR 287 Hj55
Suai TLS 132 Rc50
Suain PNG 159 Sb49
Šuakhevi GE 70 Nb25
Suakin SUD 191 Mj37
Suakin Archipelago SUD 191 Mk37
Suakoko LB 192 Kf42
Suam EAK 204 Mh45
Suana RDC 203 Ma49
Suan Phung THA 114 Pk39
Suao RC 97 Ra33
Suapi BOL 279 Gg53
Suaqui Grande MEX (SO) 252 Ef31
Suara ER 191 Mk38
Suardi RA (SF) 289 Gk61
Suarmar IND (CGH) 109 Pb35
Sua-Sua YV 270 Gk42
Suatala IND (MPH) 109 Ok34
Suay Rieng K 115 Qc40
Subah RI 128 Qe49
Subanburung RI 125 Qb47
Suban Hot Springs RI 124 Qb47
Subansiri IND 112 Pg31
Subarnagiri IND (ORS) 109 Pb36
Subashi CHN 86 Pb25
Subaşı TR 62 Me25
Subate LV 17 Mf34
Subcarpaţii Buzăului RO 45 Mg45
Subei CHN (GSU) 87 Ph26
Subiaco I 42 Lo49
Subi Besar RI 126 Qe44
Subic RP 120 Ra38
Subi Kecil RI 126 Qe44
Subi Reef 122 Qh40
Subiyah KWT 74 Ne31
Sublett USA (ID) 235 Ed24
Sublette USA (KS) 242 Ek27
Subotica SCG 44 Lu44
Subrahmanya IND (KTK) 110 Oh40
Subteniente Perín RA (FO) 285 Gk58
Subugo EAK 204 Mh46
Subway Caves USA (CA) 234 Dk25
Sucatinga BR (CE) 277 Jb48
Suceava RO 45 Mf43
Suceava RO 45 Mg43
Sucesso BR (CE) 277 Hk48
Suceviţa RO 45 Mf43
Sucha Beskidzka PL 39 Lu41
Suchań PL 36 Lq37
Súchil MEX (DGO) 253 Ej34
Suchorze PL 36 Ls36
Suchowola PL 37 Md37
Sucio CO 268 Gb42
Suciu de Sus RO 44 Me43
Suck IRL 20 Km37
Sucker River CDN (SK) 233 Eh18
Suckling, Mount PNG 159 Se50
Sucre BOL 284 Gh55
Sucre CO 268 Gc41
Sucre EC 272 Fk46
Sucúa EC 272 Ga47
Sucuba, T.I. BR 270 Gk44
Sucuiu RO 45 Mg45

Sucunduri – Tabocal

Sucunduri BR 274 Ha49
Sucupira do Norte BR (MA) 276 Hh49
Sućuraj HR 41 Ls47
Sucuriju BR (AP) 275 Hf45
Sucuriú BR 286 Hd56
Sudak UA 55 Mh23
Sudan 167 Ma08
Sudan 168 La16
Sudbury CDN (ON) 246 Fk22
Sudbury GB 21 Kt38
Sudbury GB 21 La38
Sudd SUD 197 Mf41
Sude D 33 Lm37
Süderbrarup D 32 Lk36
Sudest Island PNG 160 Sg51
Sudetes PL 36 Lq40
Sudislavl' RUS 53 Na17
Sudogda RUS 53 Na18
Sudova Vyšnja UA 39 Md41
Südtirol I 40 Lm44
Sudvala Caves ZA 217 Mf58
Sudvalagrotte ZA 217 Mf58
Sudža RUS 52 Mh20
Sue SUD 197 Me43
Sueca E 29 Ku49
Suemez Island USA 231 Dd18
Sueno's Stone GB 19 Kr33
Suez ET 177 Mg31
Suez ET 177 Mg31
Suez Bay ET 177 Mg31
Suez Canal ET 177 Mg30
Sufaynah KSA 66 Na34
Sufetula TN 174 Le28
Suffield CDN (AB) 233 Ee20
Suffolk USA (VA) 249 Gb27
Sufiyan IR 72 Nc26
Şugag RO 44 Md45
Sug al Khamis LAR 174 Lg29
Sugarloaf Mtn. USA 228 Cb16
Sugbai Passage RP 122 Ra43
Suggi Lake CDN 238 Ej18
Sugihwaras RI 125 Qb48
Suğla Gölü TR 51 Mm53
Sugoj RUS 59 Sd06
Sugu WAN 195 Lg41
Sugun CHN (XUZ) 86 Oj26
Sugut MAL 122 Qj42
Suguta EAK 204 Mj45
Suguti EAT 204 Mg46
Suhai Hu CHN 87 Pg26
Suhait CHN (NMZ) 92 Qc26
Suhaja RUS (BUR) 90 Qd19
Suhell Island IND 110 Og41
Suhindol BG 47 Mf47
Suhiniči RUS 52 Mh18
Suhl D 33 Ll40
Suhlendorf D 33 Ll38
Suhodol RUS 53 Nf19
Suho Polje BIH 44 Lu46
Suhopolje HR 41 Ls45
Suhorečka RUS 53 Ng19
Suhostrel BG 46 Md49
Suhoton N.P. RP 123 Rc40
Suhum GH 193 Kk42
Şuhut TR 51 Ml52
Sui DY 186 Lb41
Sui PNG 159 Sb50
Suiá-Miçu BR 281 Hd51
Suibin CHN (HLG) 98 Rf22
Šuica BIH 41 Ls47
Suichang CHN (ZJG) 102 Qk31
Suichuan CHN (JGX) 97 Qh32
Suide CHN (SAA) 93 Qf27
Suifenhe CHN (HLG) 98 Rf23
Suigam IND (GUJ) 108 Of33
Suihua CHN (HLG) 98 Rd22
Suileng CHN (HLG) 98 Rd22
Suining CHN (HUN) 96 Qf32
Suining CHN (JGS) 102 Qj29
Suining CHN (SCH) 95 Qc30
Suipacha BOL 284 Gh56
Suiping CHN (HNN) 95 Qg29
Suiping CHN (HNN) 102 Qh29
Suippes F 23 Le41
Suir IRL 20 Kn38
Suiti burnu AZ 70 Nf25
Suixi CHN (GDG) 96 Qf35
Sui Xian CHN (HNN) 102 Qh28
Suiyang CHN (GZH) 96 Qd32
Suiyang CHN (HLG) 98 Rf23
Suizhong CHN (LNG) 100 Ra25
Suizhou CHN (HUB) 95 Qg30
Suj PK 81 Oe31
Šuja RUS 53 Na17
Sujangarh IND (RJT) 106 Oh32
Sujawal PK 80 Oe33
Sujindik KZ 53 Nd21
Sukabumi RI 128 Qd49
Sukadana RI 125 Qc48
Sukadana RI 126 Qe46
Sukagawa J 101 Sa27
Sukajadi RI 116 Pk44
Sukamade RI 129 Qg50
Sukamara RI 126 Qf47
Sukamenang RI 124 Qb47
Sukanegara RI 128 Qd49
Sukaraja RI 125 Qb48
Sukaraja RI 126 Qf47
Sukarame RI 125 Qc47
Sukau MAL 122 Qk43
Sükhbaatar MNG 90 Qd20
Sükhbaatar MNG 91 Qg22
Sukhothai THA 114 Pk37
Sukhothai Historical Park THA 114 Pk37
Sukhuma LAO 115 Qc38
Suki PNG 158 Sa50
Sukkertoppen = Manitsoq DK 225 Hb05
Sukkur PK 80 Oe32
Sukkwan Island USA 231 Dd18
Sukma IND (CGH) 109 Pa36
Sukna SYR 65 Mk28
Sukorejo RI 128 Qe49
Sükösd H 39 Lu44
Sukses NAM 212 Lj56
Sukumo J 103 Rg29
Sukunka River CDN 232 Dk18
Sukur Cultural Landscape WAN 187 Lg40
Sukuro EAT 207 Mj48
Sula N 12 Le29
Šula = Šunlja Stijena SCG 46 Lu47
Sula UA 54 Mg21
Sulagiri IND (TNU) 111 Oj40
Sulaiyimah KSA 67 Nc35
Sulak RUS 70 Nd24
Sulakyurt TR 51 Mo50
Sula Sgeir GB 19 Ko31
Sulatna River USA 229 Cc13
Sulawesi RI 118 Ra19
Sulaymiyah KSA 67 Nb35
Sulechów PL 36 Lq38
Sulęcin PL 36 Lq38
Sulęczyno PL 36 Ls36
Suleja WAN 186 Ld41
Sulejówek PL 37 Mb38
Sulen, Mount PNG 158 Sb47
Sule Skerry GB 19 Kq31
Sulevkent RUS (DAG) 70 Nd24
Süleymanli TR 51 Mo51
Sulgura IND (ORS) 109 Pc35
Sulia RDC 201 Md46
Suliki RI 124 Qa46
Sulików PL 36 Lq39
Sulima WAL 192 Ke42
Sulina RO 45 Mk45
Sulingen D 32 Lj38
Suliszewo PL 36 Lq37
Sulitjelma N 10 Lj12
Sulitjelma N/S 10 Lj12
Suljukta KS 76 Oe26
Sulkava FIN 16 Mj29
Sullana PE 272 Fk48
Sullivan USA (IN) 248 Fg26
Sullivan USA (MO) 241 Fe26
Sullivan Bay CDN (BC) 232 Dg20
Sullivan, Mount AUS 139 Rf54
Sullom Voe GB 19 Kt30
Sullorssuaq Vaigat DK 225 Hb04
Sully-sur-Loire F 23 Lc43
Sulmierzyce PL 36 Ls39
Sulmona I 42 Lo48
Süloğlu TR 50 Mg49
Sulphur USA (LA) 243 Fd30
Sulphur USA (NV) 234 Ea25
Sulphur USA (OK) 243 Fb28
Sulphur Springs USA (TX) 243 Fc29
Sultan CDN (ON) 246 Fj22
Sultan LAR 175 Ma30
Sultandaği TR 51 Mm52
Sultan Dağları TR 51 Mm52
Sultan-e Bakwah AFG 78 Ob29
Sultanganj IND (BIH) 112 Pd33
Sultan Hamud EAK 207 Mj47
Sultanhanı TR 51 Mo52
Sultanhanı TR 62 Mh26
Sultanhanı Caravanserai TR 51 Mo52
Sultani Mosque IR 72 Ng28
Sultaniyazbiy-kalasy TM 73 Oc26
Sultan Kudarat RP 123 Rc42
Sultanpur IND (UPH) 107 Pb32
Sultansazlığı Milli Parkı TR 51 Mq52
Sultan's Palace BRU 122 Qh43
Sultan's Palace MAL 116 Qa42
Sultan's Palace RI 127 Qj46
Sultan's Palace (Say'un) YE 68 Ne38
Sultan Tekesh TM 71 Nk24
Sulu RDC 203 Mc48
Suluan Island RP 123 Rc40
Sulu Archipelago RP 123 Ra43
Sulu Basin RP 123 Ra42
Suluistyk TJ 77 Oh27
Suluk RUS 98 Rh20
Sülüklü TR 51 Mn52
Sulults ETH 198 Mk41
Suluntah LAR 175 Ma29
Suluq LAR 175 Ma30
Sulusaray TR 51 Mr51
Sulu Sea RP 122 Qk41
Sulutöbe KZ 76 Od23
Sulya IND (KTK) 110 Oh40
Sülz D 32 Lh39
Sulzbach-Rosenberg D 35 Lm41
Sulzberger Bay 296 Cb34
Sulzberger Ice Shelf 296 Cc34
Sumaco EC 272 Gb46
Sumaco, P.N. EC 272 Gb46
Sumaco, Volcán EC 272 Gb46
Sumadija SCG 44 Ma46
Sumampa RA (SE) 288 Gj60
Sumanga RI 129 Qk49
Suman Khayrkhan MNG 92 Pj23
Sumapaz, P.N. CO 268 Gc43
Sumar IR 72 Nc29
Sumara Pass YE 68 Nc38
Sumaré BR (SP) 286 Hg57
Sumas USA (WA) 232 Dj21
Sumatra RI 118 Pd18
Sumatra USA (MT) 235 Eg22
Sumaúma BR (AM) 274 Gk49
Sumaúma BR (AM) 274 Gk49
Šumava CZ 38 Lo41
Šumava, N.P. CZ 38 Lo41
Sumayr YE 68 Nb37
Sumba ANG 202 Lg49
Sumba RI 129 Qk51
Sumba Strait RI 129 Qk50
Sumbawa RI 129 Qk50
Sumbawa Besar RI 129 Qj50
Sumbawanga EAT 206 Mf49
Sumbe ANG 208 Lg51
Sumbe KZ 77 Pa24
Sumbi RDC 202 Lg48
Sumburgh GB 19 Kt31
Sumburgh Head GB 19 Kt31
Sumbuya WAL 192 Ke42
Sumda 79 Ok28
Sumdo CHN (SCH) 94 Qa31
Sumé BR (PB) 277 Jb49
Sume Z 206 Mf50
Sumedang RI 128 Qd49
Sümeg H 38 Ls44
Sumela TR 63 Mk25
Šumen BG 47 Mg47
Sumenep RI 128 Qg49
Šumenska krepost BG 47 Mg47
Šumensko Plato, N.P. BG 47 Mg47
Šumerlja RUS 53 Nd18
Sümiyn Bulag MNG 91 Qh21
Summerdell AUS (QLD) 149 Sd57
Summerford CDN (NF) 245 Hc21
Summer Lake USA (OR) 234 Dk24
Summer Lake USA 234 Dk24
Summerland CDN (BC) 232 Ea21
Summer Palace CHN 93 Qj26
Summerside CDN (PE) 245 Gj22
Summerstrand ZA 217 Mc63
Summersville USA (WV) 249 Fk26
Summerton USA (SC) 249 Fk29
Summerville USA (GA) 249 Fh28
Summerville USA (SC) 249 Fk29
Summit USA (SD) 240 Fb23
Summit Lake CDN (BC) 231 Dh16
Summit Lake CDN (BC) 232 Dj18
Summit Lake Ind. Res. USA 234 Ea25
Sumner Strait USA 231 Dd17
Sumoto J 101 Rh28
Sumpangbinangae RI 129 Ra48
Šumperk CZ 38 Lr41
Sumprabum MYA 113 Pj32
Sumqayit AZ 70 Ne25
Šumskas LT 17 Mf36
Sumter USA (SC) 249 Fk29
Sumuna PNG 160 Sf47
Sumur RI 128 Qc49
Sumurbungkar RI 129 Qh49
Sumxi CHN (TIB) 86 Pa28
Sumy UA 52 Mh20
Sumzom CHN (TIB) 89 Pj31
Sun USA 233 Ed22
Sunag IND (KTK) 108 Oh37
Sunah YE 68 Ne38
Sunakhalla IND (ORS) 109 Pc35
Sunam IND (PJB) 106 Oh30
Sunan CHN (GSU) 92 Pk26
Sunan PRK 100 Rc26
Sunbay Beach USA 261 Gh36
Sunbeam USA (ID) 235 Ec23
Sunburry AUS (VIC) 153 Sc64
Sunburst USA (MT) 233 Ee21
Sunbury USA (NC) 249 Gb27
Sunbury USA (PA) 247 Gb25
Sunchales RA (SF) 289 Gk61
Suncho Corral RA (SE) 288 Gj59
Sunch'on PRK 100 Rc26
Sunch'on ROK 100 Rd28
Sun City USA (AZ) 236 Ed29
Sun City USA (CA) 236 Eb29
Sun City ZA 213 Md58
Sun City Center USA (FL) 250 Fj32
Suncun CHN (SDG) 93 Qj28
Sundagarh IND (ORS) 109 Pc34
Sundance USA (WY) 235 Eh23
Sundarbans IND/BD 112 Pe34
Sundarbans National Park IND 112 Pe34
Sundarnagar IND (HPH) 107 Oj30
Sunda Shelf RI 125 Qd45
Sunda Strait RI 125 Qc49
Sundays ZA 217 Mc62
Sunday Strait AUS 138 Rb54
Sundborn S 13 Lq30
Sundby DK 14 Lj34
Sunde N 12 Lf31
Sunderland GB 19 Kt36
Sundern D 32 Lj39
Sündiken Dağları TR 51 Ml51
Sundi-Lutete RDC 202 Lh48
Sundown N.P. AUS 151 Sf60
Sundre CDN (AB) 233 Ec20
Sundsbruk S 13 Ls28
Sundsvall S 13 Ls28
Sundvallsbukten S 13 Ls28
Sungaiaya RI 126 Qf45
Sungaibali RI 126 Qj47
Sungaibamban RI 116 Pk44
Sungaibelidah RI 125 Qc47
Sungaibengkali RI 124 Qb46
Sungaibilut RI 124 Qa45
Sungai Buluh RI 125 Qc46
Sungaibuntu RI 125 Qc47
Sungaibuntu RI 128 Qd49
Sungaidareh RI 124 Qa46
Sungaiguntung RI 125 Qb45
Sungai Kolok THA 117 Qa42
Sungailiat RI 125 Qd46
Sungailurus RI 116 Qa44
Sungai Padi THA 117 Qa42
Sungaipakning RI 124 Qb45
Sungaipenuh RI 124 Qa47
Sungaiperak RI 124 Qb46
Sungai Petani MAL 116 Qa43
Sungaisarik RI 124 Qa45
Sungaiselan RI 125 Qc47
Sungai Sinput MAL 117 Qa43
Sungaitapang RI 126 Qf45
Sungbo's Eredo WAN 194 Lb42
Sungguminasa RI 129 Ra48
Sungikai SUD 197 Me39
Sungkup RI 126 Qh47
Sung Men THA 114 Qa36
Sung Noen THA 114 Qa38
Sungo MOC 210 Mg54
Sungsang RI 125 Qc47
Sungurlare BG 47 Mg48
Sungurlu TR 51 Mp50
Suni SUD 196 Mc39
Sunizona USA (AZ) 237 Ef30
Sunja HR 41 Lr45
Sun Kosi NEP 88 Pd32
Sun Kosi Reservoir NEP 88 Pd32
Sun Kosi River Rafting NEP 88 Pd32
Šunlja Stijena = Šula SCG 46 Lu47
Sun Moon Lake RC 97 Ra34
Sunndal N 12 Lg30
Sunndalen N 12 Lj28
Sunndalsøra N 12 Lj28
Sunne S 13 Lo31
Sunnemo S 13 Lo31
Sunnmøre N 12 Lg28
Sunnyside USA (NV) 234 Ec26
Sunnyside USA (WA) 234 Ea22
Sunnyvale USA (CA) 234 Dj27
Sun Prairie USA (WI) 246 Ff24
Sunrise Park Ski Resort USA (AZ) 237 Ef29
Sunset Beach USA 230 Ca35
Sunset Country AUS 152 Sa63
Sunset Crater Nat. Mon. USA 237 Ee28
Sunshine Coast AUS 151 Sg59
Suntai WAN 194 Lf42
Suntai WAN 195 Lf42
Suntaži LV 17 Me34
Sun Temple (Konark) IND 112 Pd36
Suntsar PK 80 Oa33
Suntu ETH 198 Mj41
Su Nuraxi I 31 Lj51
Sun Valley USA (ID) 235 Ec24
Sunwi Do PRK 100 Rc27
Sunwu CHN (HLG) 98 Rd21
Sunyani GH 193 Kj42
Sun Yat-sen CHN 102 Qk29
Suoi Rut VN 96 Qc35
Suojarvi RUS 11 Mg14
Suolahti FIN 16 Mf28
Suomenlinna FIN 16 Me30
Suomenniemi FIN 16 Mh29
Suomenselkä FIN 11 Mc14
Suomusjärvi FIN 16 Md30
Suomussalmi FIN 11 Me13
Suo-nada J 103 Rf29
Suonenjoki FIN 11 Md14
Suong K 115 Qc40
Suontee FIN 16 Mg29
Suoqiao CHN (SCH) 94 Qb30
Supamo YV 270 Gj42
Supas BOL 285 Gh56
Supaul IND (BIH) 112 Pd32
Supe ETH 197 Mh41
Supe IND (MHT) 108 Oh36
Superagui, P.N.do BR 286 Hf58
Superbagnères F 24 La48
Superior USA (MT) 235 Ec22
Superior USA (NE) 240 Fa25
Superior USA (WI) 241 Fd22
Superior USA (WY) 235 Ef25
Super Tubes USA (CA) 236 Ea29
Supetar HR 41 Lr47
Suphanburi THA 114 Qa38
Süphan Dağı TR 63 Nb26
Supia CO 268 Gc43
Supiori RI 131 Rh46
Suplac RO 44 Me44
Suplee USA (OR) 234 Ea23
Supplejack Downs AUS (NT) 139 Rf55
Supply USA (NC) 249 Ga29
Support Force Glacier 296 Hd35
Supraśl PL 37 Md37
Supu RI 130 Rd44
Suq ,Abs YE 68 Nb37
Suq al Ahad KSA 68 Nb37
Suq ar Rubu KSA 66 Na35
Suq ash Shuyukh IRQ 65 Nd30
Suqian CHN (JGS) 102 Qk29
Suqrah OM 69 Nj36
Suqrah Bay OM 69 Nj36
Suq Suwayd KSA 66 Mk33
Suqutra YE 69 Nh39
Sur OM 75 Nk34
Sur RL 64 Mh29
Sura ETH 198 Na42
Sura RUS 53 Nd18
Surab PK 80 Od31
Surabaya RI 125 Qc48
Surabaya RI 128 Qg49
Surahammar S 13 Lr31
Surallah RP 123 Rc42
Surami GE 70 Nb25
Suranam IND (APH) 109 Ok36
Šurany SK 38 Lt42
Surat AUS (QLD) 151 Se59
Surat IND (GUJ) 108 Og35
Suratgarh IND (RJT) 106 Og31
Suratkai IND (KTK) 110 Oh40
Surat Thani THA 116 Pk41
Šur Av AFG 78 Od30
Suraž RUS 52 Mg19
Surbiton AUS (QLD) 149 Sd57
Surdești RO 44 Md43
Surdulica SCG 46 Mc48
Surendranagar IND (GUJ) 108 Of34
Surf USA (CA) 236 Dk28
Surf City USA (NC) 249 Gb28
Surf City USA (NJ) 247 Gc26
Surfers Paradise AUS (QLD) 151 Sg59
Surfing Beaches AUS (WA) 144 Qk63
Surgères F 24 Ku44
Surgura IND (ORS) 109 Pb34
Surgut RUS 58 Oc06
Surhob TJ 77 Of26
Súria E 30 Lb49
Surian RI 124 Qa46
Suriapet IND (APH) 109 Ok37
Surigao RP 123 Rc41
Surigao Strait RP 123 Rc40
Surik IR 72 Nc26
Surin THA 115 Qb38
Suriname 263 Ha09
Suripá YV 269 Gf42
Šurlane SCG 46 Mb48
Surlangun RI 124 Qb47
Surman LAR 174 Lg29
Surmaq IR 72 Ng30
Surmaq IR 72 Ng30
Surovikino RUS 53 Nb21
Surrey CDN (BC) 232 Dj21
Sursand IND (BIH) 107 Pc32
Sursee CH 34 Lj43
Surskoe RUS 53 Nd18
Surt LAR 175 Lj30
Surtanahu PK 81 Oe32
Surtsey IS 10 Jk14
Surubim BR (PE) 283 Jc49
Surubiú BR 276 Hf47
Sürüç TR 51 Mo52
Suruç TR 63 Mk27
Suruga-wan J 101 Rk28
Surumu BR 270 Gk44
Surup RP 123 Rd42
Surviliškis LT 17 Me35
Surwaya IND (MPH) 107 Oj33
Šuš IR 72 Ne29
Şuşa AZ 70 Nd26
Susa CO 268 Gd43
Susa I 40 Lh45
Susa Danial-e-Nabi IR 72 Ne29
Susah LAR 175 Ma29
Susak HR 41 Lp46
Susaki J 103 Rg29
Susangerd IR 72 Ne30
Susanville USA (CA) 234 Dk25
Suşat TR 62 Mj27
Suşehri TR 63 Mk25
Susēja LV 17 Mf34
Susek SCG 44 Lu45
Sušice CZ 38 Lo41
Susitna River USA 229 Ce15
Suslonger RUS 53 Ne17
Susong CHN (AHU) 102 Qj30
Susques RA (PJ) 284 Gg57
Sussex CDN (NB) 245 Gh23
Sussex USA (VA) 249 Gb27
Sussex USA (WY) 235 Eg24
Sussuarana BR (BA) 283 Hk53
Sustut Peak CDN 231 Dg17
Sustut River CDN 231 Dg17
Susuka SOL 160 Sj49
Susulatna River USA 229 Cc14
Susuman RUS 59 Sb06
Susunu RI 131 Rg47
Susurluk TR 50 Mj51
Susuz TR 51 Ml50
Šušve LT 17 Md35
Suswe ZW 210 Mg54
Susz PL 37 Lu37
Sutay Uul MNG 85 Pg22
Sutcliffe USA (NV) 234 Ea26
Sütçüler TR 51 Ml53
Sutherland USA (NE) 240 Ek25
Sutherland ZA 216 Ma62
Sutherland Observatory ZA 216 Ma62
Sutherland Sterrewag ZA 216 Ma62
Sutherlin USA (OR) 234 Dj24
Sutjeska klisura BIH 46 Lt47
Sutjeska, N.P. BIH 46 Lt47
Sutlej PK 81 Of31
Sutti WAN 186 Lc39
Sutton AUS (NSW) 153 Se63
Sutton USA (WV) 247 Fk26
Sutton Downs AUS (QLD) 148 Sc56
Sutton Lake CDN 239 Fh18
Sutton River CDN 239 Fj18
Suttsu J 99 Sa24
Sutukoba WAG 183 Kc39
Sutvik Island USA 228 Cb17
Sutyr' RUS 98 Rg20
Suugaant MNG 90 Qd23
Süüj MNG 90 Qc22
Suure-Jaani EST 16 Mf32
Suur-Pakri EST 16 Md31
Suur Pellinki FIN 16 Mf30
Suur väin EST 16 Md32
Suusamyr KS 77 Og24
Suva FJI 163 Tk55
Suva Planina SCG 46 Mc47
Suva Reka SCG 46 Ma48
Suvorov RUS 52 Mj18
Suvorove UA 45 Mj45
Suvorovo BG 47 Mh47
Suvorovskaja RUS 70 Nb23
Suvut PNG 160 Sf47
Suwałki PL 37 Mc36
Suwannaphum THA 115 Qb38
Suwannee USA (FL) 250 Fj31
Suwanose-jima J 103 Re31
Suwarrow Atoll NZ 157 Ud21
Suwasra IND (MPH) 108 Oj33
Suwayr KSA 65 Na30
Suweida SYR 64 Mj29
Suwon ROK 100 Rd27
Suxianling CHN 97 Qg33
Suxu CHN (GZG) 96 Qe34
Suyapa HN 256 Fg38
Suycutambo PE 279 Ge53
Suye müyis KZ 70 Ng25
Suykbulak KZ 84 Pa21
Suyo PE 272 Ga48
Suzaka J 101 Rk27
Suzdal' RUS 53 Na17
Suzhou CHN (AHU) 102 Qj29
Suzhou CHN (JGS) 102 Ra30
Suzuka J 101 Rj28
Suzu-misaki J 101 Rj27
Suzzara I 40 Ll46
Svabensverk S 13 Lq29
Svågan S 13 Lr28
Svalbard N 11 Mc06
Svalbard N 6 Lb01
Svalbarðseyri IS 10 Kb13
Svaljava UA 39 Mc42
Svanberga S 13 Lt31
Svaneke DK 15 Lq35
Svaneti GE 63 Nb24
Svängsta S 15 Lp34
Svanøy N 12 Lf29
Svanskog S 12 Ln31
Svappavaara S 10 Ma12
Svardsjö S 13 Lq30
Svarstad N 12 Lk31
Svartå S 13 Lp31
Svartån S 15 Lp32
Svartnäs S 13 Lr30
Svatá Hora CZ 38 Lp41
Svatá Kateřina CZ 38 Lo41
Svatove UA 53 Mk21
Svatsum N 12 Lk29
Svea ANT (S) 296 Kb33
Sveagruva N 11 Lj07
Svedala S 15 Lo35
Svėdasai LT 17 Mf35
Sveg S 13 Lp28
Svegssjön S 13 Lp28
Sveio N 12 Lf31
Švėkšna LT 17 Mb35
Svelgen N 12 Lf29
Svelvik N 12 Ll31
Švenčionėliai LT 17 Mf35
Švenčionys LT 17 Mg35
Svendborg DK 14 Ll35
Svenes N 12 Lj32
Svenljunga S 15 Lo33
Svensby N 10 Lk11
Svenska Högarna 13 Lu31
Svenskøya N 11 Md06
Svenstavik S 13 Lp28
Šventoji LT 17 Me35
Sverdlove UA 54 Mf22
Sverdlovs'k UA 55 Mk21
Sverdrup Channel CDN 225 Fa03
Sverdrupfjella 297 La33
Sverdrup Islands CDN 225 Fa03
Sveštari BG 47 Mg47
Svetac HR 41 Lq47
Sveta Eufemija HR 41 Lo45
Sveta Marija na Škriljinah HR 41 Lo45
Sveti Danijela SLO 41 Lq44
Sveti Donat HR 41 Lq46
Sveti Ivan Žabno HR 41 Lr45
Sveti Ivan Zelina HR 41 Lr45
Sveti Kostantin i Elena BG 47 Mj47
Sveti Križ HR 41 Lq46
Sveti Lovro HR 41 Lr47
Sveti Marko HR 41 Ls48
Sveti Nikola BG 47 Mj47
Sveti Nikole MK 46 Mb49
Sveti Rok SLO 41 Lq44
Sveti Stefan SCG 46 Lt48
Sveti Tskhoveli GE 70 Nc25
Svetlahorsk BY 52 Me19
Svetlaja RUS 99 Rk22
Svetlice SK 39 Mc41
Svetlogorsk RUS 17 Ma36
Svetlograd RUS 70 Nb23
Svetlovodnaja RUS 99 Rj22
Svetlyi Jar RUS 53 Nc21
Svetlyj RUS 37 Ma36
Svetogorsk RUS 16 Mj29
Sviby EST 16 Md32
Sviča UA 39 Md41
Svidník SK 39 Mb41
Svijaga RUS 53 Ne18
Svilajnac SCG 46 Mb46
Svilengrad BG 47 Mg49
Svinndal N 12 Ll31
Svir BY 17 Mg36
Svir' RUS 11 Mh15
Svirsk RUS 90 Qb19
Svislač BY 37 Me37
Svislač BY 52 Me19
Svištov BG 47 Mf47
Svitava CZ 38 Lr41
Svitavy CZ 38 Lr41
Svitlovods'k UA 54 Mg21
Svobodnyj RUS 98 Re20
Svobody RUS 70 Nb24
Svodna BIH 41 Lr45
Svoge BG 46 Md48
Svoge BG 46 Md47
Svolvær N 10 Lh11
Svorkmo N 10 Le14
Svrljig SCG 46 Mc47
Svullrya N 12 Ln30
Svyati Gory N.P. UA 55 Mj21
Swaershoek ZA 217 Mc62
Swaffham GB 21 La38
Swain Reefs AUS 149 Sf56
Swains Atoll USA 157 Ub21
Swainsboro USA (GA) 249 Fj29
Swakop NAM 212 Lj56
Swakopmund NAM 212 Lh57
Swale GB 21 Ks36
Swallow Grotto CHN 113 Qb34
Swallow Reef = Layang-Layang MAL 122 Qg42
Swamis USA (CA) 236 Eb29
Swanage GB 21 Kt40
Swana-Mume RDC 210 Md51
Swan Hill AUS (VIC) 153 Sb63
Swan Hills CDN (AB) 233 Ec18
Swan Hills CDN 233 Ec18
Swan Lake CDN 238 Ek19
Swan Lake N.W.R. USA 241 Fd26
Swannell Range CDN 231 Dg17
Swanquarter USA (NC) 249 Gb28
Swanquarter N.W.R. USA 249 Gb28
Swan River CDN (MB) 238 Ek19
Swan River CDN 233 Ec18
Swan River CDN 238 Ej19
Swan River CDN 239 Fj19
Swan River USA (MN) 241 Fd22
Swansea AUS (TAS) 152 Se67
Swansea GB 20 Kr39
Swans Island USA 245 Gf23
Swanton USA (VT) 247 Gd23
Swan Vale AUS (QLD) 150 Sb58
Swan Valley USA (ID) 235 Ee24
Swarożyn PL 36 Lt36
Swartberg ZA 217 Me61
Swartdoorn ZA 216 Lk61
Swart Kei ZA 217 Md62
Swartkolkvloer ZA 216 Lk61
Swartkops ZA 217 Mc62
Swartkrans ZA 217 Md59
Swartmodder ZA 216 Ma60
Swart-Nossob NAM 212 Lk57
Swartplaas ZA 217 Md59
Swartrots NAM 216 Lh59
Swartruggens ZA 213 Md58
Swartruggens ZA 216 Lk62
Swarzędz PL 36 Ls38
Swat PK 79 Og28
Swate WAN 186 Lb40
Swaziland 167 Mb12
Swazi Market SD 217 Mf59
Sweden 7 Lb03
Sweeney Mountains 296 Gb33
Sweers Island AUS (QLD) 148 Rk54
Sweetgrass USA (MT) 233 Ed21
Sweetgrass Ind. Res. CDN 233 Ef19
Sweet Home USA (OR) 234 Dj23
Sweetwater USA (OK) 242 Fa28
Sweetwater USA (TN) 249 Fh28
Sweetwater USA (TX) 242 Ek29
Sweetwater USA 235 Ef24
Sweetwater Station USA (WY) 235 Ef24
Sweihan UAE 74 Nh33
Swellendam ZA 216 Ma63
Świdnica PL 36 Lr40
Świdnik PL 37 Mc39
Świdwin PL 36 Lq37
Świebodzice PL 36 Lr40
Świebodzin PL 36 Lq38
Świecie PL 36 Lt37
Świekatowo PL 36 Lt37
Świeradów-Zdrój PL 36 Lq40
Świerczów PL 36 Ls40
Świerzawa PL 36 Lq39
Święta Anna PL 37 Lu40
Święta Lipka PL 37 Mb36
Świętno PL 36 Lr38
Świętokrzyski Park Narodowy PL 37 Ma40
Swift Current CDN (SK) 233 Eg20
Swift Current Creek CDN 233 Ef21
Swift River CDN (BC) 231 De16
Swift River CDN 231 De16
Swift River USA 229 Cc15
Swifts Creek AUS (VIC) 153 Sd64
Swift Trail Junction USA (AZ) 237 Ef29
Świgtajno PL 37 Mc36
Swindon GB 21 Kt39
Swinford IRL 18 Km37
Świnoujście PL 36 Lp37
Swiss Hist. Vill. USA 246 Ff24
Switzerland CH 34 Lh44
Syakotan-hanto J 99 Sa24
Syängja NEP 88 Pb31
Syčevka RUS 52 Mh18
Syców PL 36 Ls39
Sycowice PL 36 Lq38
Sydney AUS (NSW) 153 Sf62
Sydney CDN (NS) 245 Gk22
Sydney = Manra KIR 157 Ub19
Sydney Mines CDN (NS) 245 Gk22
Syeri RI 131 Rh46
Syghyndy müyis KZ 70 Nf23
Syke D 32 Lj38
Sykes Bluff AUS 141 Rd59
Sykkylven N 12 Lg28
Syktyvkar RUS 58 Nc06
Sykvan Lake CDN (AB) 233 Ec19
Sylacauga USA (AL) 248 Fg29
Sylhet BD 112 Pf33
Sylt D 32 Lj36
Sylva USA (NC) 249 Fj28
Sylvania CDN (SK) 238 Ej19
Sylvania USA (GA) 249 Fk29
Sylvania USA (OH) 246 Fj25
Sylvester USA (GA) 249 Fj30
Sylvester River AUS (QLD) 148 Rk57
Synel'nykove UA 55 Mh21
Synevyr, N.P. UA 39 Md42
Synnot Range AUS 138 Rc54
Syötekylä FIN 11 Md13
Syötteen kansallispuisto FIN 11 Md13
Syowa ANT (J) 297 Md32
Syracuse USA (KS) 242 Ek27
Syracuse USA (NY) 247 Gb24
Syrdarja KZ 76 Ob23
Syre USA (MN) 241 Fb22
Syria SYR 60 Md11
Syriam MYA 114 Pj37
Syrian Desert 64 Mk29
Šyrjajeve UA 45 Ml43
Šyroke UA 54 Mg22
Šyščycy BY 52 Md19
Sysmä FIN 16 Mf29
Sysslebäck S 13 Ln30
Syston GB 21 Kt38
Systyg-Hem RUS 85 Ph19
Syvulja UA 39 Me42
Syzran' RUS 53 Ne19
Szabadszállás H 39 Lu44
Szadek PL 37 Lt39
Szamotuły PL 36 Lr38
Szarvas H 39 Ma44
Szatmári-Tiszahát H 39 Mc42
Százhalombatta H 39 Lt43
Szczawne PL 39 Mc41
Szczawnica PL 39 Ma41
Szczebrzeszyn PL 37 Mc40
Szczecin PL 36 Lp37
Szczecinek PL 36 Lr37
Szczekociny PL 37 Lu40
Szczerców PL 37 Lu39
Szczuczyn PL 37 Mc37
Szczurowa PL 37 Ma40
Szczyrk PL 39 Lu41
Szczytno PL 37 Ma37
Szécsény H 39 Lu42
Szederkény H 41 Lt45
Szeged H 39 Ma44
Székely H 39 Mb42
Székesfehérvár H 38 Lt43
Székkutas H 39 Ma44
Szekszárd H 39 Lt44
Szendrő H 39 Ma42
Szentendre H 39 Lu43
Szentes H 39 Ma44
Szentlőrinc H 38 Ls44
Szepietowo PL 37 Mc38
Szerencs H 39 Mb42
Szigetvár H 38 Ls44
Szilvásvárad H 39 Ma42
Szin H 39 Ma42
Szklarska Poręba PL 36 Lq40
Szolnok H 39 Ma43
Szombathely H 38 Lr43
Szozurkowo PL 37 Ma36
Szprotawa PL 36 Lq39
Sztabin PL 37 Md37
Sztum PL 36 Lu37
Szubin PL 36 Ls38
Szydłów PL 37 Ma40
Szydłowiec PL 37 Ma39
Szypliszki PL 37 Md36

T

Taabo CI 193 Kh42
Taalintehdas = Dalsbruk FIN 16 Mc30
Taal Lake RP 121 Ra39
Taam RI 130 Rg48
Taba ET 177 Mh31
Tabaco RP 121 Rb39
Tabaconas PE 272 Ga48
Tabah KSA 66 Nb32
Tabahanyar RI 124 Qb47
Tabajara BR (MG) 287 Hk55
Tabajara BR (RO) 280 Gj50
Tabakkentatyr KZ 84 Oh22
Tabala MEX (SL) 252 Eg33
Tabalo PNG 159 Se46
Tabalosos PE 278 Gc49
Tabang RI 126 Qj45
Tabankort RMM 185 La37
Tabapuã BR (SP) 286 Hf56
Tabaquén CO 273 Gf44
Tábara E 26 Kp51
Tabar Island PNG 160 Sg47
Tabar Islands PNG 160 Sg47
Tabarka TN 174 Le27
Tabas IR 73 Nj29
Tabasco MEX (ZCT) 254 Ej35
Tabasco MEX 255 Fd36
Tabasin IR 73 Oa30
Tabaskwia Channel CDN 239 Fg19
Tabatinga BR (AM) 273 Gf48
Tabatinga BR (SP) 286 Hf56
Tabay YV 268 Ge41
Tabelbala DZ 173 Kj31
Taber CDN (AB) 233 Ed21
Taberfane RI 131 Rh49
Taberg S 15 Lp33
Tabergda DZ 174 Ld28
Tabernas E 29 Ks47
Tabibug PNG 159 Sc48
Tabina RP 123 Rb42
Tabing RI 124 Qa46
Tabingbulang RI 125 Qb47
Tabin Wildlife Reserve MAL 122 Qk43
Tabiona USA (UT) 235 Ee25
Tabir RI 124 Qb46
Tabiteuea Atoll KIR 157 Tc19
Tab Khon Falls THA 116 Pk41
Tabkin Kouka RN 185 Lb38
Tabla RN 185 Lb39
Tablas BOL 284 Gg54
Tablas de Daimiel, P.N.de las E 29 Kr49
Tablas Island RP 121 Rb39
Tablas Strait RP 121 Ra39
Tablate E 29 Kr46
Tablazo de Ica PE 278 Gc53
Table Mountain N.P. ZA 216 Lk63
Table Cape NZ 154 Tj65
Tableland AUS (WA) 138 Rd54
Table Mountain ZA 216 Lk62
Table Rock Lake USA 243 Fd27
Table Rock S.P. USA 243 Fd27
Table Rock S.P. USA 249 Fj28
Tabletop, Mount AUS 149 Sd57
Tabligbo TG 193 La42
Taboada RA (SE) 288 Gj60
Taboca BR (AM) 274 Gk47
Tabocal BR (AM) 274 Gj46
Tabocal BR 274 Gj49

Tsiombe RM 220 Nc58
Tsiribihina RM 220 Nc55
Tsiroanomandidy RM 220 Nd55
Tsitondroina RM 220 Nd56
Tsitsikamma N.P. ZA 216 Mb63
Tsivory RM 220 Nd58
Tsodilo RB 213 Ma55
Tsodilo Hills RB 213 Ma55
Tsoe RB 213 Mc56
Tsogstsalu 79 Ok28
Tsolo ZA 217 Me61
Tsomo ZA 217 Md61
Tsomo ZA 217 Md62
Tso Morari 79 Ok29
Tsondab NAM 212 Lh57
Tsondabvlei NAM 212 Lh58
Tsonjiyn Chuluu MNG 91 Qf23
Tsqaltubo GE 70 Nb24
Tsu J 101 Rj28
Tsubata J 101 Rj27
Tsuchiura J 101 Sa27
Tsugaru Q.N.P. J 101 Sa25
Tsugaru Strait J 99 Sa25
Tsujima J 100 Re28
Tsuli ZW 213 Md55
Tsumbiri RDC 202 Lj47
Tsumeb NAM 212 Lj55
Tsumis Park NAM 212 Lj57
Tsumkwe NAM 213 Ma55
Tsundupalle IND (APH) 111 Ok40
Tsuruga J 101 Rj28
Tsurugi-san J 101 Rh29
Tsurui J 99 Sc24
Tsuruoka J 101 Rk26
Tsuyama J 101 Rh28
Tswaane RB 213 Mb57
Tswalu Private Desert Reserve ZA 216 Mb59
Tswapong Hills RB 213 Md57
T-Tree Bay AUS 151 Sg59
Tual RI 130 Rg48
Tuam IRL 18 Km37
Tua Marine National Park = Bunaken-Manado Tua Marine National Park RI 127 Rc45
Tuamotu Archipelago 303 Cb11
Tuamotu Ridge 303 Cb12
Tuanake Atoll F 165 Ch54
Tuanan RI 126 Qh47
Tuan Giao VN 113 Qb35
Tuangku RI 116 Pj44
Tuao RP 121 Ra37
Tuapse RUS 55 Mk23
Tuaran MAL 122 Qj42
Tua River PNG 159 Sc49
Tuba City USA (AZ) 237 Ee27
Tubai-Manu F 165 Ce54
Tuban RI 128 Qg49
Tubarão BR (SC) 291 Hf60
Tubarão Latunde, T.I. BR 280 Gk52
Tubarjal KSA 64 Mk30
Tubau MAL 126 Qg44
Tubbataha Reef National Marine Park RP 122 Qk41
Tubbergen NL 32 Lg38
Tubeya RDC 203 Mb49
Tubigon RP 123 Rb41
Tübingen D 34 Lk42
Tubisyimita RI 131 Rg46
Tubize B 23 Le40
Tübkaraghan müyis KZ 70 Nf23
Tubo WAN 186 Ld40
Tubod RP 123 Rb41
Tubou FJI 163 Ua55
Tubruq LAR 175 Mb29
Tubruq War Cemeteries LAR 175 Mb29
Tubuai Islands 303 Ca12
Tuburan RP 123 Rb40
Tubutama MEX (SO) 237 Ee30
Tucacas YV 269 Gf40
Tucano BR (BA) 283 Ja51
Tucavaca BOL 285 Ha55
Tuchan F 24 Lc48
Tucheng CHN (GZH) 96 Qc32
Tuchita CDN (YT) 231 Df15
Tuchola PL 36 Ls37
Tucholski Park Krajobrazowy PL 36 Lt37
Tuchów PL 39 Mb41
Tuckanarra AUS (WA) 140 Qj59
Tucker Glacier 297 Tb33
Tučovo RUS 52 Mj18
Tucson USA (AZ) 237 Ee29
Tucumã BR (AM) 274 Ha49
Tucumã BR (PA) 275 He49
Tucumán RA 267 Gc24
Tucumcari USA (NM) 237 Ej28
Túcume PE 278 Ga49
Tucuña CO 273 Ge45
Tucunaré BR (AM) 274 Gh45
Tucupido YV 269 Gh41
Tucupita YV 270 Gj41
Tucuriba BR (AM) 274 Ha48
Tucuruí BR (PA) 276 Hf47
Tucu-Tucu RA (SC) 294 Ge70
Tuczna PL 37 Md39
Tuczno PL 36 Lq38
Tuczno PL 36 Lr37
Tudela E 27 Kt52
Tudela de Duero E 26 Kq51
Tudu EST 16 Mg31
Tudulinna EST 16 Mh31
Tudun Wada WAN 186 Le40
Tuéjar E 29 Kt49
Tuékta RUS (ALT) 85 Pc20
Tuena AUS (NSW) 153 Se63
Tu-Endie-Wei S.P. USA 247 Fk26
Tueré BR 275 He47
Tuerjishan Reservoir CHN 100 Rb24
Tufeni RO 45 Me46
Tufi PNG 159 Se50
Tufi Dive Resort PNG 159 Se50
Tug CHN (NMZ) 93 Qe26
Tug Der SP 199 Nd41
Tugela ZA 217 Mf60
Tugela ZA 217 Mf60
Tugela Ferry ZA 217 Mf60
Tughyl KZ 85 Pc22
Tugidak Island USA 230 Cc17
Tugu GH 193 Kk41
Tuguegarao RP 121 Ra37
Tugyi MYA 114 Ph37
Tuhala EST 16 Me31
Tuham, Gunung RI 126 Qg45
Tuherahera F (PYF) 165 Cf53
Tui E 26 Km52
Tuichi BOL 279 Gf53
Tuilibigeal AUS (NSW) 153 Sd62
Tuin MK 46 Mb49
Tuina RCH 284 Gf57
Tuineje E 178 Kc31
Tuiué BR (AM) 274 Gj48
Tuiyk KZ 77 Ok24
Tūja LV 17 Me33
Tujmazy RUS 53 Ng18
Tujn gol MNG 90 Qa23
Tujun RUS 98 Rg20
Tujuwe RI 129 Ra48
Tukarak Island CDN 239 Ga17
Tukayel ETH 199 Nc41
Tûkh ET 177 Mf30
Tuki SOL 160 Sj49
Tukola Tolha CHN (QHI) 89 Ph29
Tukosmera VU 162 Te55
Tukrah LAR 175 Ma29
Tuktoyaktuk CDN 224 Db05
Tukuhora F (PYF) 165 Ch54
Tukums LV 17 Md34
Tukuna Porto Espiritual, T.I. BR 273 Gf48
Tukuna Santo Antonio, T.I. BR 273 Gf48
Tukuna Umariaçu, T.I. BR 273 Gf48
Tukuyu EAT 206 Mg50
Tula EAK 205 Mk46
Tula EAK 205 Mk46
Tula MEX (TM) 253 Fa34
Tula MEX 254 Fa35
Tula RUS 52 Mj18
Tula USA 164 Be53
Tula de Allende MEX (HDG) 254 Fa35
Tulak AFG 78 Ob29
Tulameen CDN (BC) 232 Dk21
Tulancingo MEX (HDG) 254 Fa35
Tulare SCG 46 Mb48
Tulare USA (CA) 236 Ea27
Tulare USA (SD) 240 Fa23
Tularosa USA (NM) 237 Eg29
Tulate GCA 255 Fe38
Tulayhah IRQ 65 Na29
Tula Yiri WAN 187 Lf41
Tulbagh ZA 216 Lk62
Tulcán EC 272 Gb45
Tulcea RO 45 Mj45
Tul'čyn UA 54 Me21
Tule RI 123 Rd43
Tulebaevo KZ 84 Ok22
Tüledy araldary KZ 70 Nf23
Tulehu RI 130 Re47
Tulga AUS (QLD) 148 Sb57
Tulgheş RO 45 Mf44
Tulia USA (TX) 242 Ek28
Tuli Block RB 213 Md58
Tuligbeni UA 45 Mf43
Tuliguil'nic'kij liman UA 45 Mm44
Tulihe CHN (NMZ) 91 Ra20
Tulijá MEX 255 Fd37
Tuliszków PL 36 Lt38
Tuljupur IND (MHT) 108 Oj37
Tullah AUS (TAS) 152 Sc66
Tullahoma USA (TN) 248 Fg28
Tullamore AUS (NSW) 153 Sd62
Tullamore IRL 20 Kn37
Tulle F 24 Lb45
Tulln A 35 Lr42
Tullos USA (LA) 243 Fd30
Tullow IRL 20 Ko38
Tullus SUD 196 Mc40
Tully AUS (QLD) 149 Sc54
Tułowice PL 36 Ls40
Tulsa USA (OK) 243 Fb27
Tulsipur IND (UPH) 107 Pb32
Tulsipur NEP 88 Pb31
Tulsk IRL 18 Km37
Tulu PNG 159 Sd46
Tuluá CO 268 Gb43
Tulu Bobo ETH 198 Mk41
Tuluca BR (AM) 273 Gf45
Tulu Deemtu ETH 198 Mk42
Tuluksak USA (AK) 228 Bk15
Tulul Al Ashaqif JOR 64 Mj29
Tulum MEX (QTR) 255 Fg35
Tulum MEX 255 Fg35
Tulumayo PE 278 Gc51
Tulume RDC 203 Mb49
Tulum, Parque Nacional MEX 255 Fg35
Tulun RUS 58 Qa08
Tulungagung RI 128 Qf50
Tulungselapan RI 125 Qc47
Tulun Islands PNG 160 Sh48
Tulu Welel ETH 197 Mh41
Tulyčiv UA 37 Me39
Tuma RUS 53 Na18
Tumaco CO 272 Ga45
Tuman PE 278 Ga49
Tumauini RP 121 Ra37
Tumba RDC 203 Mb47
Tumba S 13 Ls31
Tumbangjul RI 126 Qf46
Tumbangkiran RI 126 Qg46
Tumbangmirih RI 126 Qg46
Tumbangsamba RI 126 Qg46
Tumbangtalaken RI 126 Qg46
Tumbanlahung RI 126 Qh46
Tumbarumba AUS (NSW) 153 Sd63
Tumbes PE 272 Fk47
Tumbiscatio de Ruiz MEX (MHC) 254 Ej36
Tumbler Ridge CDN (BC) 232 Dk18
Tumbukut MYA 113 Pj33
Tumbwe RDC 210 Md51
Tumby Bay AUS (SA) 152 Rj63
Tumd Youyi CHN (NMZ) 93 Qf25
Tumd Zuoqi CHN (NMZ) 93 Qf25
Tumen CHN (JLN) 100 Re24
Tumen Gang PRK/CHN 100 Re24
Tumen Jiang CHN/PRK 100 Re24
Tumeremo YV 270 Gk42
Tumgaon IND (CGH) 109 Pb35
Tumia, T.I. BR 279 Gg49
Tumindao Island RP 122 Qk43
Tumkur IND (KTK) 111 Oj40
Tumlingtan NEP 88 Pd32
Tumnar IND (CGH) 109 Pa36
Tumnin RUS 99 Sa21
Tumpat MAL 117 Qb42
Tumsar IND (MHT) 109 Ok35
Tumu GH 193 Kk40
Tumucumaque, P.N. do BR 275 Hd45
Tumupasa BOL 279 Gg53
Tumut AUS (NSW) 153 Se63
Tuna GH 193 Kj41
Tuna IND (GUJ) 108 Of34
Tunaca YV 269 Gg42
Tunadal S 13 Ls28
Tuna Gain RI 130 Rg47
Tunapa, Cerro BOL 284 Gg55
Tunapuna TT 270 Gk40
Tunari, P.N. BOL 284 Gg54
Tunas de Zaza C 259 Ga35
Tunaydiba SUD 190 Mh40
Tunçbilek TR 50 Mk51
Tunceli TR 63 Mk26
Tunchang CHN (HAN) 96 Qf36
Tuncurry AUS (NSW) 153 Sg62
Tundavala ANG 208 Lg53
Tundi IND (JKD) 112 Pd33
Tundik KZ 84 Oj20
Tundla IND (UPH) 107 Ok32
Tundulu Z 206 Me50
Tunduma EAT 206 Mg50
Tunduru EAT 211 Mj51
Tundža BG 47 Mf48
Tunga WAN 194 Le41
Tungabhadra IND 108 Oj38
Tungabhadra Reservoir IND 110 Oj39
Tungaru SUD 197 Mf40
Tungaztarim CHN (XUZ) 86 Pb27
Tungho RC 97 Ra34
Tungkai RI 125 Qb46
Tungkaranasam RI 126 Qj47
Tungku MAL 122 Qk43
Tungokočen RUS 91 Qh19
Tungsha Islands CHN 97 Qj35
Tungshih RC 97 Ra33
Tungsten CDN (NWT) 231 Df15
Tungting Lake CHN 95 Qg31
Tungurahua, Volcán EC 272 Ga46
Tunguwatu RI 131 Rh48
Tuni IND (APH) 109 Pb37
Tunica USA (MS) 243 Fe28
Tunis TN 174 Lf27
Tunisia TN 167 La06
Tunja CO 268 Gd43
Tunka La IND 112 Pf32
Tunkas MEX (YT) 255 Ff35
Tünkhel MNG 90 Qd21
Tunku Abdul Rahman Park MAL 122 Qj42
Tunnel Creek N.P. AUS 138 Rc54
Tunnel de Tende F/I 25 Lh46
Tunnel du Fréjus F/I 25 Lg45
Tunnel du M Blanc F 25 Lg45
Tunnel las Raíces RCH 292 Ge65
Tunnels USA (HI) 230 Ca34
Tunqiu CHN (GZG) 96 Qe33
Tunstall GB 21 Ks36
Tunta Topocalma RCH 288 Gd63
Tuntum BR (MA) 276 Hh48
Tuntutuliak USA (AK) 228 Bj15
Tununak USA (AK) 228 Bh15
Tunungua EAT 207 Mj49
Tunuyán RA (MD) 288 Gf62
Tunuyán RA 288 Gg62
Tunzam MYA 112 Pg34
Tuolo CHN (GZG) 96 Qd34
Tuol Tel K 115 Qb39
Tuol Toteong K 115 Qb39
Tuong Duong VN 115 Qc36
Tuotuo He CHN 89 Pf28
Tuotuo Heyan CHN (QHI) 89 Pg28
Tüp KS 77 Ok24
Tupã BR (SP) 286 He56
Tupaceretã BR (MS) 285 Hb55
Tupaciguara BR (MG) 286 Hf55
Tupai Atoll F 165 Ce54
Tupana BR 274 Gk48
Tupanatinga BR (PE) 283 Jb50
Tupanciretã BR (RS) 290 Hd60
Tuparrito CO 269 Gf43
Tuparro CO 269 Gf43
Tupelo USA (MS) 243 Ff28
Tupelo USA (OK) 243 Fb28
Tupi RP 123 Rc42
Tupicino RUS 16 Mj32
Tupilco MEX (TB) 255 Fd36
Tupi Paulista BR (SP) 286 He56
Tupiratins BR (TO) 282 Hf50
Tupiza BOL 284 Gh56
Tüpkaraghan tübegi KZ 70 Nf23
Tupoko YV 270 Gj42
Tupper CDN (BC) 232 Dk18
Tupper Lake USA (NY) 247 Gc23
Tupran IND (APH) 109 Ok37
Tupungato RA (MD) 288 Gf62
Tupungato, Cerro RA/RCH 288 Gf62
Tuquan CHN (NMZ) 91 Ra23
Túquerres CO 272 Gb45
Tuqu Gang CHN 96 Qe36
Tura CHN (XUZ) 86 Pd27
Tura CHN (MO) 241 Fd26
Tura IND (MGA) 112 Pf33
Tura RUS 58 Qa06
Turabah KSA 66 Na35
Turabah KSA 67 Nb31
Turagua, Cerro YV 269 Gh42
Turaida LV 17 Me33
Turaiyur IND (TNU) 111 Ok41
Turama River PNG 159 Sb49
Turan RUS (TUV) 85 Pg19
Turangi NZ 154 Th65
Turan Lowland 60 Oa10
Turar KZ 76 Of24
Turayf KSA 64 Mk30
Turbaco CO 268 Gc40
Turbah YE 68 Nb39
Turbat PK 80 Ob33
Turbeville USA (SC) 249 Ga29
Turbio RA 294 Ge71
Turbjo RCH 288 Ge60
Turbo CO 268 Gb41
Turbo EAK 204 Mh45
Turčianske Teplice SK 39 Lt42
Turco BOL 284 Gf55
Turda RO 44 Md44
Turda SUD 197 Me40
Turee Creek AUS (WA) 140 Qk57
Turee Creek AUS 140 Qj57
Turégano E 26 Kq51
Tureh IR 72 Ne28
Tureia Atoll 303 Da12
Turek PL 36 Lt38
Turen RI 128 Qg50
Tureni RO 44 Md44
Turfan Depression CHN 87 Pe24
Turga RUS 91 Qj20
Turgajskoe plato KZ 56 Oa04
Turgan KZ 77 Oj24
Türgen Uul MNG 85 Pg21
Türgen Uul Nature Reserve MNG 85 Pf21
Turgut TR 51 Mm52
Turgutlu TR 49 Mh52
Turgutreis TR 49 Mh53
Turhal TR 51 Mm50
Turi BR 273 Gf46
Türi EST 16 Mf32
Turiaçu BR (MA) 276 Hh46
Turiaçú BR 276 Hh47
Turicato MEX (MHC) 254 Ek36
Turija UA 37 Me39
Turijs'k UA 37 Me39
Turilari RA (PJ) 284 Gg57
Turin CDN (AB) 233 Ed21
Turin I 40 Lh45
Turis E 29 Ku49
Turiščevo RUS 52 Mh19
Turjak SCG 46 Ma48
Turjak SLO 41 Lp45
Turka RUS (BUR) 90 Qe19
Turka RUS 91 Qe19
Turka UA 39 Md41
Turkana EAK 204 Mh44
Türkeli TR 50 Mh50
Türkeve H 39 Ma43
Turkey TR 60 Mc11
Turkey USA 241 Fe24
Turkey Creek AUS (WA) 138 Re54
Turkistan KZ 76 Oe24
Turkmenabat TM 71 Ob26
Turkmenbashi TM 71 Ng25
Turkmenbashi Bay TM 71 Ng26
Turkmengala TM 73 Ob27
Turkmenistan TM 57 Nb06
Turkmenskiy zaliv TM 71 Ng26
Türkoğlu TR 62 Mj27
Turksad RUS 70 Nc23
Turks and Caicos Islands GB 259 Ge34
Turks Island Passage BS 251 Ge35
Turks Islands GB 259 Ge35
Turku = Åbo FIN 16 Mc30
Turkwel Gorge Reservoir EAK 204 Mh45
Turlock USA (CA) 234 Dk27
Turmalina BR (MG) 287 Hj54
Turmi ETH 198 Mj43
Turnagain Arm USA 229 Ce15
Turnagain River CDN 231 Df16
Turneffe Islands BH 255 Fg37
Turner AUS (WA) 138 Re54
Turner USA (MT) 233 Ef21
Turner Falls Park USA 242 Fb28
Turner Lake CDN 233 Ef17
Turner River AUS 140 Qk56
Turners Peninsula WAL 192 Kd42
Turnhout B 23 Le39
Türnitz A 35 Lq43
Turnor Lake CDN (SK) 233 Ef17
Turnov CZ 38 Lq40
Turnu RO 44 Mb44
Turnu Măgurele RO 47 Me47
Turocak RUS (ALT) 85 Pd19
Turoś PL 37 Mb37
Turpan CHN (XUZ) 87 Pe24
Turrialba CR 256 Fj41
Turriff GB 19 Ks33
Tursaq IRQ 65 Nc29
Tursunzade TJ 76 Oe26
Turt MNG 90 Qa20
Turtel MK 46 Mc49
Turtle Beach USA (FL) 250 Fj32
Turtle Beach YE 69 Ng39
Turtleford CDN (SK) 233 Ef19
Turtle Harbour HN 256 Fg37
Turtle Islands RP 122 Qk42
Turtle Islands Marine Park MAL 122 Qk42
Turtle Lake CDN 233 Ef19
Turtle Lake USA (ND) 240 Ek22
Turuépano, P.N. YV 269 Gj40
Turuhansk RUS 58 Pb05
Turu/Mariquita, T.I. BR 276 Hf47
Turuntaevo RUS (BUR) 90 Qd19
Tururu BR (CE) 277 Ja47
Turuvekere IND (KTK) 111 Oj40
Turvânia BR (GO) 286 He54
Turvelândia BR (GO) 286 He54
Turvo BR (PR) 286 He58
Turvo BR (SC) 291 Hf60
Turvo BR 281 He54
Turvo BR 286 Hf56
Turzovka SK 38 Lt41
Tus IR 73 Nk27
Tusaquilla RA (PJ) 284 Gg57
Tuscaloosa USA (AL) 248 Fg29
Tuscánia I 42 Lm48
Tuscany I 40 Ll47
Tuscola USA (TX) 242 Fa29
Tuscumbia USA (AL) 248 Fg28
Tuscumbia USA (MO) 241 Fd26
Tusen-øyane N 11 Ma07
Tushchybas shyghanagh KZ 71 Nk22
Tushkadi BD 112 Pe34
Tuskegee USA (AL) 249 Fh29
Tušnica BIH 41 Ls47
Tustumena Lake USA 229 Ce15
Tutaev RUS 52 Mk17
Tutak TR 63 Nb26
Tuticorin IND (TNU) 111 Ok42
Tutin SCG 46 Ma48
Tutira NZ 154 Tj65
Tutóia BR (MA) 277 Hj47
Tutoko, Mount NZ 155 Te68
Tutova RO 45 Mh44
Tutova RO 45 Mh44
Tutrakan BG 45 Mg46
Tuttlingen D 34 Lj43
Tutuaca MEX 237 Ef31
Tutuala TLS 132 Rd50
Tutubu EAT 206 Mg48
Tutuila Island USA 164 Be53
Tutume RB 213 Md56
Tutupaca, Volcán PE 284 Ge54
Tutut RI 116 Pj43
Tutwiler USA (MS) 243 Fe29
Tutyaka TR 51 Mo52
Tuul Gol MNG 90 Qc22
Tuulos FIN 16 Me29
Tuusniemi FIN 11 Me14
Tuusula FIN 16 Mf30
Tuva RUS 58 Pd08
Tuvalu 135 Tb10
Tuvalu Islands TUV 157 Td20
Tuvana-i-Ra FJI 137 Ua23
Tuvuca FJI 163 Ua54
Tuwayq KSA 67 Nc33
Tuwwal KSA 66 Mk34
Tuxcueca MEX (JLC) 254 Ej35
Tuxedni Bay USA 229 Cd15
Tuxford CDN (SK) 233 Eh20
Tuxpam (Tuxpan) MEX (VC) 254 Fb35
Tuxpan MEX (JLC) 254 Ej36
Tuxpan MEX (NYT) 253 Eh35
Tuxpan = Tuxpam MEX (VC) 254 Fb35
Tuxtepec MEX (OAX) 254 Fb36
Tuxtla Gutiérrez MEX (CHP) 255 Fd37
Tuya River CDN 231 De16
Tuy Duc VN 115 Qd39
Tuyen Quang VN 96 Qc35
Tuy Hoa VN 115 Qe39
Tuy Phong VN 115 Qe40
Tuysarkan IR 72 Ne28
Tuža RUS 53 Nd17
Tuzantla MEX (MHC) 254 Ek36
Tuzantlán MEX (GUR) 254 Fa36
Tuz-Ashuue KS 77 Og24
Tuz Gölü TR 51 Mo52
Tuzi SCG 46 Lu48
Tuzigoot Nat. Mon. USA 237 Ee28
Tuz Khurmatu IRQ 65 Nc28
Tuzla BIH 44 Lt46
Tuzla TR 51 Mp52
Tuzla Gölü TR 51 Mq52
Tuzluca TR 63 Nb25
Tuzlukçu TR 51 Mm52
Tuzly UA 45 Ml45
Tuzule RDC 203 Mb49
Tvååker S 14 Ln33
Tvărdica BG 47 Mf48
Tvardiţa MD 45 Mj44
Tvedestrand N 12 Lj32
Tveitsund N 12 Lj31
Tver' RUS 52 Mh17
Tving S 15 Lq34
Tvrđa HR 41 Ls45
Tvrđava SCG 46 Mb47
Tvrdošín SK 39 Lu41
Twardogóra PL 36 Ls39
Tweed GB 19 Ks35
Tweed Heads AUS (NSW) 151 Sg60
Tweedsmuir Prov. Park CDN 232 Dg19
Tweefontein ZA 216 Lk62
Tweeling ZA 217 Me59
Twee River NAM 212 Lk58
Twee Rivieren ZA 216 Ma59
Tweespruit ZA 217 Md60
Twello NL 32 Lg38
Twelve Apostles AUS 153 Sb65
Twelve Foot Davis Prov. Hist. Site CDN 233 Eb17
Twentynine Palms USA (CA) 236 Ec28
Twifo-Praso GH 193 Kk43
Twilight Cove AUS 145 Rd62
Twin Bridges USA (MT) 235 Ed23
Twin Falls AUS 139 Rg52
Twin Falls USA (ID) 235 Ec24
Twingi Z 210 Me51
Twin Lakes CDN (AB) 233 Eb17
Twin Mount USA (AK) 229 Cj13
Twin Peaks AUS (WA) 140 Qh59
Twin Ring Motegi J 101 Sa27
Twin Wells AUS (NSW) 152 Sa62
Twistringen D 32 Lj38
Twitya River CDN 231 Df13
Twizel NZ 155 Tf68
Two Fold Bay AUS (NSW) 153 Se64
Two Harbors USA (MN) 241 Fe22
Two Hills CDN (AB) 233 Ee19
Two Rivers USA (WI) 246 Fg23
Two Rocks AUS (WA) 144 Qh61
Two Wells AUS (SA) 152 Rk63
Twyfelfontein Rock Engraving NAM 212 Lh56
Tychowo PL 36 Lr37
Tychy PL 37 Lu40
Tyczyn PL 39 Mc41
Tyélé RMM 184 Kg39
Tyfors S 13 Lp30
Tygda RUS 98 Rd19
Tygda RUS 98 Rd19
Tyin N 12 Lj29
Tykocin PL 37 Mc37
Tylawa PL 39 Mb41
Tyler USA (TX) 243 Fc29
Tylertown USA (LA) 243 Fe30
Tylisos GR 49 Mf55
Tylkowo PL 37 Ma37
Tylösand S 14 Ln34
Tymkove MD 45 Mk43
Tyndall USA (SD) 240 Fb24
Tyndrum GB 19 Kq34
Tynemouth GB 19 Kt35
Tyner CDN (SK) 233 Ef20
Tyngsjö S 13 Lo30
Tyniec PL 37 Lu40
Týniště nad Orlici CZ 38 Lr40
Týn nad Vltavou CZ 38 Lp41
Tynset N 12 Ll28
Tyoplye Klyuchi KS 77 Oh24
Tyre RL 64 Mh29
Tyresta n.p. S 13 Ls31
Tyrifjorden N 12 Ll30
Tyringe S 15 Lo34
Tyringham AUS (NSW) 151 Sg61
Tyristrand N 12 Ll30
Tyrma RUS 98 Rg20
Tyrma RUS 98 Rf20
Tyrnyauz RUS (KBA) 70 Nb24
Tyrol Basin Ski Area USA 246 Ff24
Tyrrhenian Sea 6 Lb06
Tysa UA 39 Md42
Tyškivka UA 54 Mf21
Tysnes N 12 Lf30
Tyssebotn N 12 Lf30
Tyssedal N 12 Lg30
Tystberga S 13 Ls32
Tyszowce PL 37 Md40
Tytuvėnai LT 17 Md35
Tywi GB 20 Kr38
Tywyn GB 20 Kq38
Tzaneen ZA 214 Mf57
Tzasar 79 Oj29
Tzermiádo GR 49 Mf55
Tzintzuntzan MEX 254 Ek36
Tziscao MEX (CHP) 255 Fe37
Tzucacab MEX (YT) 255 Ff35

U

Uaçá, T.I. BR 271 He44
Uaco Cungo ANG 208 Lh51
Ua Huka F (PYF) 165 Da50
Uamba ANG 202 Lj49
Uanda AUS (QLD) 149 Sc56
Uangando ANG 208 Lj54
Uanle Uen = Wanlaweyn SP 205 Nc44
Uape MOC 211 Mk54
Ua Pou F (PYF) 165 Ck50
Uar Addoi SP 205 Na44
Uarges EAK 204 Mj45
Uar Igarore SP 205 Nb45
Uarini BR (AM) 274 Gh47
Uarini BR 274 Gh47
Uati-Paraná, T.I. BR 273 Gf47
Uatumã BR 274 Ha47
Uauá BR (BA) 283 Ja50
Uauaretê BR (AM) 273 Gf45
Uaupes BR 273 Gf45
Uavala ANG 208 Lj54
Uaxactún GCA 255 Ff37
Ub SCG 44 Ma46
Uba BR (MG) 287 Hj56
Uba KZ 85 Pb20
Uba WAN 187 Lg40
Ubaí BR (MG) 287 Hh54
Ubai PNG 160 Sf48
,Ubaid SUD 196 Mc39
Ubaira BR (BA) 283 Ja52
Ubaitaba BR (BA) 283 Ja53
Ubajara BR (CE) 277 Hk47
Ubajay RA (ER) 289 Ha61
Ubangi RCB/RDC 195 Lj45
Ubar OM 69 Ng36
Ubatã BR (BA) 283 Ja53
Ubate CO 268 Gd43
Ubatuba BR (SP) 287 Hh57
Ubauru PK 81 Oe31
Ubay RP 123 Rc40
Ubaye F 25 Lg46
Ube J 103 Rf29
Úbeda E 29 Kr48
Ubehebe Crater USA 236 Eb27
Uberaba BR (MG) 286 Hg55
Uberaba BR 286 Hf55
Uberlândia BR (MG) 286 Hf55
Überlingen D 34 Lk43
Ubia, Gunung RI 131 Rj48
Ubiaja WAN 194 Ld42
Ubieszyn PL 37 Mc40
Ubiratã BR (PR) 286 Hd58
Ubirr Rock AUS 139 Rg52
Ubl'a SK 39 Mc42
Ubli SCG 46 Lt48
Ubol Rat Reservoir THA 115 Qb37
Ubombo ZA 217 Mg59
Ubon Ratchathani THA 115 Qc38
Ubovka RUS 98 Rh23
Ubrique E 28 Kp46
Ubudiah Mosque MAL 116 Qa43
Ubundu RDC 201 Mc46
Ucacha RA (CD) 288 Gj62
Ucapinima CO 273 Gf45
Ucar AZ 70 Nd25
Ucayali PE 272 Gc49
Ucero E 27 Kr51
Učës BY 37 Mf38
Uch PK 81 Of31
Uch-Adzhi TM 71 Ob26
Uchalon IND (WBG) 112 Pd34
Ucharonidge AUS (NT) 139 Rh54
Uchiza PE 278 Gb50
Uchqo'rg'on UZ 77 Og25
Uchquduq UZ 76 Ob24
Uchsoy UZ 71 Nk24
Uchte D 32 Lj38
Uckermark D 33 Lo37
Uckfield GB 21 La40
Ucluelet CDN (BC) 232 Dh21
Üçpınar TR 51 Mn53
Ucross USA (WY) 235 Eg23
Úcua ANG 202 Lh50
Uda RO 45 Me46
Uda RUS 90 Qe20
Uda RUS 90 Pj19
Udačnoe RUS 53 Nd22
Udačnyj RUS 59 Qc05
Udaigiri IND 112 Pd35
Udainagar IND (MPH) 108 Oj34
Udaipur IND (RJT) 108 Og33
Udaipur IND (TRP) 112 Pf34
Udaipura IND (MPH) 109 Ok34
Udakatla IND (APH) 108 Oj37
Udala IND (ORS) 112 Pd35
Udaquiola RA (BA) 293 Ha64
Udayagiri Caves IND 109 Oj34
Udayagiri Caves IND 109 Pc35
Udayd SUD 190 Mh39
Udaypur IND 109 Ok34
Udbina HR 41 Lq46
Uddevalla S 12 Lm32
Uddheden S 13 Ln31
Uddjaure S 10 Lj13
Udegi WAN 194 Ld41
Uden NL 32 Lf39
Udgir IND (MHT) 108 Oj36
Udhagamandalam = Ootacamund/Ooty IND 110 Oj41
Udhampur 79 Oh29
Udi IND (UPH) 107 Ok32
Udi WAN 194 Ld42
Údine I 41 Lo44
Udinsk RUS (BUR) 90 Qe19
Udmurtia 9 Nc07
Udomlja RUS 52 Mh17
Udong K 115 Qc40
Udon Thani THA 115 Qb37
Udumalaippettai IND (TNU) 111 Oj41
Udupi IND (KTK) 110 Oh40
Udu Point FJI 163 Tj54
Udu Point FJI 163 Ua54
Udzungwa Mountains N.P. EAT 207 Mj49
Udzungwa Range EAT 207 Mh50
Ueca ETH 198 Mj41
Uecker D 33 Lo37
Ueckermünde D 33 Lp37
Ueda J 101 Rk27
Uegit = Waajid SP 205 Nb44
Uele RDC 200 Mb44
Uelen RUS 59 Ub05
Uelzen D 33 Ll38
Uepi Island Resort SOL 161 Sk50
Uere RDC 196 Mc43
Uetersen D 32 Lk37
Uetze D 33 Ll38
Ufa RUS 58 Nd07
Ufa RUS 58 Nd08
Ufeyn SP 199 Ne40
Uffenheim D 34 Ll41
Ugab NAM 212 Lj55
Ugab Rock Finger NAM 212 Lh56
Ugab Vingerklip NAM 212 Lh56
Ugāle LV 17 Mc33
Ugalla EAT 206 Mf48
Ugalla EAT 206 Mf48
Ugalla River Game Reserve EAT 206 Mf48
Uganda 167 Mb09
Uganik Island USA 228 Cd16
Ugao SCG 46 Ma47
Ugărčin BG 47 Me47
Ugarit SYR 64 Mh28
Ugashik Bay USA (AK) 228 Ca17
Ugashik Lake USA (AK) 228 Cb17
Ugba WAN 194 Le42
Ugbala WAN 194 Le42
Ugbenu WAN 194 Lc42
Ugep WAN 194 Le43
Ughelli WAN 194 Ld43
Ugie ZA 217 Me61
Ugijar E 29 Kr46
Ugine F 25 Lg45
Ugjut KS 77 Oh25
Uglegorsk RUS 99 Sb21
Uglekamensk RUS 98 Rg24
Uglič RUS 52 Mk17
Ugljan HR 41 Lq46
Ugljan HR 41 Lq46
Uglovoe RUS 98 Re20
Ugo WAN 194 Ld42
Ugol'nye Kopi RUS 59 Td06
Ugoofaaru MV 110 Og43
Ugra RUS 52 Mh18
Ugtam Nature Reserve MNG 91 Qg21
Ugumji WAN 186 Lf40
Uğurlu TR 62 Mf27
Uğurlu Baraj TR 63 Mj25
Uğurludağ TR 51 Mp50
Uhaymir SUD 190 Mg39
Uhekera EAT 207 Mg48
Uhen WAN 194 Lc42
Uherské Hradiště CZ 38 Ls41
Uherský Brod CZ 38 Ls41
Uhi WAN 194 Ld42
Uhiere WAN 194 Ld42
Uhlenhorst NAM 212 Lj57
Uhly UA 37 Mf39
Uhniv UA 37 Md40
Uhrichsville USA (OH) 247 Fk25
Uhta RUS 58 Nc06
Uibai BR (BA) 283 Hj51
Uig GB 18 Ko33
Uige ANG 202 Lh49
Uiha Island TO 164 Bc55
Uijongbu ROK 100 Rd27
Uiju PRK 100 Rc25
Uinta USA 235 Ee25
Uintah and Ouray Ind. Res. USA 235 Ee25
Uinta Mountains USA 235 Ee25
Uiraponu BR (MT) 280 Ha53
Uiraúna BR (PB) 277 Ja49
Uiseb Caves NAM 212 Lj55
Uis Myn NAM 212 Lh56
Uisong ROK 100 Re27
Uitenhage ZA 217 Mc62
Uithoorn NL 32 Le38
Uithuizen NL 32 Lg37
Uitkyk ZA 216 Lk60
Uitsakpan ZA 216 Ma59
Uitsigpunt (Fish River Canyon) NAM 216 Lj59
Uivar RO 44 Ma45
Ujae Atoll MH 157 Tb17
Ujali WAN 194 Ld42
Ujaly KZ 71 Nh23
Ujanmas RI 125 Qb47
Ujar RUS 58 Pc07
Ujdah MA 173 Kk28
Ujelang Atoll MH 156 Ta17
Ujeździec Mały PL 36 Ls39
Újfehértó H 39 Mb43
Ujhani IND (UPH) 107 Ok32
Uji J 101 Rh28
Uji-gunto J 103 Re30
Ujiji EAT 206 Me48
Ujir RI 131 Rh48
Ujjain IND (MPH) 108 Oh34
Ujma PL 36 Lt38
Ujmen' RUS 85 Pd20
Ujohbilang RI 126 Qh45
Ujście PL 36 Lr37
Ujście Warty, P.N. PL 36 Lp38
Ujungbatu RI 124 Qa45
Ujungkulon N.P. RI 128 Qc49
Ujung Pandang RI 129 Ra48
Ujung Pandang RI 127 Qk48
Ukal Sagar IND 108 Og35
Ukata WAN 186 Lc40
Ukdungle 79 Ok29
Ukenyengi EAT 207 Mg47
Ukerewe Island EAT 204 Mg46
uKhahlamba ZA 217 Me60
uKhahlamba-Drakensberg N.P. ZA 217 Me60
Ukhia BD 112 Pg35
Ukhrul IND (MNP) 112 Ph33
Ukiah USA (CA) 234 Dj26
Ukiah USA (OR) 234 Ea23
Ukiernica PL 36 Lq37
Uki Ni Masi Island SOL 161 Ta51
Ukkamba IND (ORS) 109 Pb36
Ukmergė LT 17 Me35
Ukora Island EAT 204 Mg46
Ukraine 7 Ma05
Ukrainian Cultural Heritage Village CDN 233 Ed19
Ukui RI 124 Qb46
Uku-jima J 103 Re29
Ukwatutu RDC 201 Md43
Ukwi Pan RB 213 Ma57
Ukwipan RB 213 Ma57
Ula TR 50 Mj53
Ulaanbaatar MNG 90 Qd22
Ulaanbulag MNG 90 Qc22
Ulaandel MNG 91 Qg22
Ulaan-Ereg MNG 91 Qe22
Ulaangom MNG 85 Pg21
Ulaan nuur MNG 92 Qb23
Ulaan Tayga MNG/RUS 90 Pk20
Ulaan-Uul MNG 93 Qf23
Ulaanžirėm MNG 90 Qc23
Ulakmakam RI 124 Qb46
Ulamona PNG 160 Sf48
Ulan CHN (QHI) 92 Pk27
Ulana NIC 256 Fj38
Ulan Bator MNG 90 Qd22
Ulanbel KZ 76 Of23
Ulan Erge RUS 55 Nc22
Ulanhot CHN (NMZ) 98 Rb22
Ulanlinggi CHN (XUZ) 87 Pd24
Ulanów PL 37 Mc40
Ulansuhai Nur CHN 93 Qe25
Ulan Tohoi CHN (NMZ) 92 Qa25
Ulan-Udė RUS (BUR) 90 Qd20
Ulan Ul Hu CHN 89 Pf28
Ulapara BD 112 Pe33
Ularbemban RI 125 Qb45
Ulaş TR 62 Mj26
Ulawa Island SOL 161 Ta50

Ulaya – Valea Ursului

Ulaya EAT 207 Mj49
Ulbanep, Mount PNG 159 Sb47
Ulbi KZ 85 Pb20
Ulbroka LV 17 Me34
Ulcinj SCG 46 Lu49
Ulco ZA 217 Mc60
Ul' durga RUS 91 Qh19
Uledi MW 210 Mg51
Ulefoss N 12 Lk31
Uleila del Campo E 29 Ks47
Ulete EAT 207 Mh50
Ulfborg DK 14 Lj34
Ulft NL 32 Lg39
Ulgai CHN (NMZ) 91 Qk23
Ulianópolis BR (PA) 276 Hg47
Uliastay MNG 90 Pj22
Ulibice CZ 38 Lq40
Ulieş RO 45 Mf44
Ulindi RDC 201 Md46
Ulithi Atoll FSM 156 Rd16
Ul'janovka UA 45 Ml42
Ul'janovka UA 45 Ml43
Uljanovo RUS 17 Mc36
Uljanovsk RUS 53 Ne18
Uljutuj RUS 91 Qj20
Uljin ROK 100 Re27
Ülken KZ 84 Og23
Ülken Borsyk kumy KZ 71 Nk22
Ülken Özen KZ 53 Ne21
Ülken sor KZ 71 Ng23
Ulladulla AUS (NSW) 153 Sf63
Ullal IND (KTK) 110 Oh40
Ullal Beach IND 110 Oh40
Ullapool GB 19 Kp33
Ullared S 14 Ln33
Ullatti S 10 Ma12
Ulla Ulla BOL 279 Gf53
Ullawarra AUS (WA) 140 Qj57
Ulldecona E 30 La50
Ullerslev DK 14 Ll35
Ulloma BOL 284 Gf54
Ullún RA (SJ) 288 Gf61
Ullung ROK 101 Rf27
Ullung Do ROK 101 Rf27
Ulm D 34 Ll42
Ul'ma RUS 98 Rf20
Ulmara AUS (NSW) 151 Sg60
Ulmen D 32 Lg40
Ulmu RO 45 Mh46
Ulongwe MOC 210 Mh53
Ulricehamn S 15 Lo33
Ulrika S 15 Lq32
Ulsan ROK 100 Re28
Ulsta GB 19 Kt30
Ulsteinvik N 12 Lf28
Ulster D 32 Lk40
Ulster IRL/GB 18 Kn36
Ultima AUS (VIC) 153 Sb63
Ulu MYA 116 Pk40
Ulu RI 123 Rc44
Ulu RUS 59 Rb06
Ulu SUD 197 Mg40
Ulubat Gölü TR 50 Mj50
Ulubey TR 50 Mk52
Uluborlu TR 51 Ml52
Ulu Camii (Aksaray) TR 51 Mo52
Ulu Camii (Bolu) TR 51 Mm50
Ulu Camii (Çorum) TR 51 Mp50
Ulu Camii (Divriği) TR 63 Mk26
Ulu Camii (Diyarbakır) TR 63 Na26
Uluçınar TR 62 Mh27
Uludağ Milli Parkı TR 50 Mk50
Uludağ Tepe TR 50 Mk50
Uluderbent TR 50 Mj52
Uludere TR 63 Nb27
Uluggat CHN (XUZ) 86 Oh26
Ulug-Hen = Verhnij Enisej RUS 85 Pg20
Uluguru Mountains EAT 207 Mj49
Ulu Kiran MAL 126 Qf45
Ulukışla TR 51 Mp53
Uluköy TR 50 Mg51
Ulu Layar MAL 126 Qf45
Ulundi ZA 217 Mf60
Ulungur He CHN 85 Pe22
Ulungur Hu CHN 85 Pd22
Uluru AUS 142 Rf58
Uluru = Ayers Rock AUS 142 Rf58
Uluru N.P. AUS 142 Rf58
Ulu-Ulu RI 126 Qj44
Ulva AUS (QLD) 149 Sc56
Ulva GB 18 Ko34
Ulvåker S 13 Lo32
Ulveah VU 162 Te54
Ulverston GB 21 Kr36
Ulverstone AUS (TAS) 152 Sd66
Ulvik N 12 Lg30
Ulvila FIN 16 Mb29
Ulvsvåg N 10 Lh11
Ulyanovskii KZ 84 Og20
Ulysses USA (KS) 242 Ek27
Ulz MNG 91 Qg21
Ulz gol MNG 91 Qg21
Uma CHN (NMZ) 91 Ra19
Uma RDC 201 Md45
Uma Daro MAL 126 Qf44
Umag HR 41 Lo45
Umaid-Bahwan-Palace IND 106 Og32
Umaish WAN 194 Ld41
Umán MEX (YT) 255 Ff35
Uman' UA 54 Mf21
Umanak Fjord DK 225 Hb04
Umarga IND (MHT) 108 Oj37
Umari BR 279 Gh50
Umaria IND (MPH) 109 Pa34
Umarkhed IND (MHT) 108 Oj36
Umarkot IND (ORS) 109 Pb36
Umarkot PK 81 Oe33
Umatilla USA (OR) 234 Ea23
Umatilla Ind. Res. USA 234 Ea23
Umba EAT 205 Mk48
Umba Game Reserve EAT 207 Mk48
Umbakumba AUS (NT) 139 Rj52
Umbar Depe TM 73 Od27
Umbarpada IND (GUJ) 108 Og35
Umbe PE 278 Gb50
Umbeara AUS (NT) 142 Rg58
Umbeb Bay VU 162 Td54
Umbelasha SUD 196 Mb41
Umbele RI 127 Rb47
Umbertide I 40 Ln47
Umboi Island PNG 159 Sd48
Umbraj IND (MHT) 108 Oh37
Umbria I 40 Ln47
Umbukul PNG 159 Se49
Umbulan Balam RI 125 Qb48
Umbulan Gayohpecoh RI 125 Qc47
Umbulan Sumurkucing RI 125 Qc48
Umbumbulu ZA 217 Mf61
Umburanas BR (BA) 283 Hk51
Umbuzeiro BR (PB) 277 Jc49
Umčari SCG 44 Ma46
Ume ZW 210 Me54
Umeå S 10 Ma14
Umeälven S 10 Lj13
Umera RI 130 Re46
Um er-Rasas = Umm al-Rasas JOR 64 Mh30
Umfurudzi Safari Area ZW 210 Mf54
Umiat USA (AK) 229 Cd11
Umiray RP 121 Ra38
U'mista Cult. Centre CDN 232 Dg20
Umka SCG 44 Ma46
Umkomaas ZA 217 Mf61
Umlazi ZA 217 Mf60
Umling IND (MGA) 112 Pf33
Umm al Aranib LAR 181 Lh32
Umm Al-Ashtan UAE 74 Ng34
Umm al Jamajim KSA 67 Nc32
Umm al Khashab KSA 68 Nb37
Umm al-Qaiwain UAE 74 Nh33
Umm al Qalban KSA 66 Na32
Umm al-Rasas JOR 64 Mh30
Umm an-Nar UAE 74 Nh33
Ummanz D 33 Lo36
Umm ar Rizam LAR 175 Mb29
Umm Ashar Ash Sharjim KSA 67 Nc32
Umm as-Samim OM 69 Nh35
Umm Az-Zumul UAE 74 Nh34
Umm Badr SUD 189 Md38
Umm Barbit SUD 197 Mg40
Umm Bel SUD 197 Me39
Umm Buru SUD 189 Mb38
Umm Busha SUD 197 Mf39
Umm Dafag SUD 196 Mb40
Umm Dam SUD 197 Mf39
Umm Defeis SUD 197 Me39
Umm Digulgulaya SUD 196 Mc40
Umm Dubban SUD 190 Me39
Umm Durman SUD 190 Mg39
Umm el-Jimal JOR 64 Mj29
Umm Gamala SUD 197 Me40
Umm Gederri SUD 196 Mb40
Umm Haraz SUD 196 Mb40
Umm Hawsh SUD 197 Md39
Umm Hisin UAE 74 Ng34
Umm Hitan SUD 197 Mf40
Umm Inderaba SUD 190 Mf39
Umm Kaddada SUD 197 Md39
Umm Lajj KSA 66 Mj33
Umm Marahik SUD 196 Mc39
Umm Qais JOR 64 Mh29
Umm Qasr IRQ 65 Nd30
Umm Qozein SUD 189 Md38
Umm Qurein SUD 190 Me38
Umm Rahaw SUD 190 Mf37
Umm Rumeila SUD 190 Mh38
Umm Rumetia SUD 190 Mf38
Umm Ruwaba SUD 197 Mf39
Umm Sa'ad LAR 176 Mc30
Umm Sagura SUD 197 Me41
Umm Said = Mesaieed Q 74 Nf33
Umm Sayyala SUD 190 Mf39
Umm Segelti SUD 197 Mf39
Umm Urumah KSA 66 Mj33
Umniati ZW 214 Me55
Umpaqua USA 234 Dh24
Um Phang THA 114 Pk37
Umpire USA (AR) 243 Fc28
Umpuhua MOC 211 Mj53
Umraniye TR 51 Mm51
Umrer IND (MHT) 109 Ok35
Umri IND (MHT) 108 Oj36
Umri IND (MPH) 107 Ok32
Umsini, Gunung RI 131 Rg46
Umsning IND (MGA) 112 Pf33
Umtamvuna Nature Reserve ZA 217 Mf61
Umtata ZA 217 Me61
Umtata Dam ZA 217 Me61
Umtentu ZA 217 Mf61
Umuahia WAN 194 Ld43
Umuarama BR (PR) 286 Hd57
Umu-Duru WAN 194 Ld43
Umunede WAN 194 Ld42
Umurbey TR 50 Mg50
Umurga LV 17 Me33
Umurlu TR 49 Mh53
Umutina, T.I. BR 281 Hb53
Umutombuko Z 206 Me50
Umutu WAN 194 Ld43
Umwukwe Range ZW 210 Mf54
Umzimkulu ZA 217 Me61
Umzingwani ZW 214 Me56
Umzinto ZA 217 Mf61
Una BIH 41 Lq46
Una BR (BA) 283 Ja53
Una BR 283 Jc50
Una IND (GUJ) 108 Of35
Una IND (HPH) 107 Oj30
Unai BR (MG) 287 Hg54
Unaipass AFG 78 Oe28
Unalakleet USA (AK) 229 Bk14
Unalakleet River USA 229 Bk14
Unalaska USA (AK) 228 Bg19
Unalaska Bay USA (AK) 228 Bg19
Unalaska Island USA 228 Bg19
Unalga Island USA 228 Bh19
Unango MOC 211 Mh52
Unari FIN 11 Mc12
Unauna RI 127 Ra46
Unawari RI 131 Rh47
Unawatuna Beach CL 111 Pa44
Unayzah KSA 67 Nb32
Unbunmaroo, Mount AUS (QLD) 148 Sa57
Uncastillo E 27 Kt52
Uncompahgre Plateau USA 235 Ef26
Unda RUS 91 Qj20
Undaima SP 199 Nf40
Undara Volcanic N.P. AUS (QLD) 148 Sc55
Undaunda Z 210 Me53
Unden S 13 Lp32
Undenäs S 13 Lp32
Underberg ZA 217 Me60
Underåker S 10 Lg14
Underwater Caves BS 251 Gb33
Unduma BOL 279 Gg52
Undva neem EST 16 Mb32
Unea Island PNG 159 Se48
Unecha RUS 52 Mg19
Unei BR 273 Gg46
Uneiuxi BR 273 Gg46
Uneiuxi, T.I. BR 273 Gg46
Úněšov CZ 38 Lo41
UNEXSO BS 251 Ga32
Ungalik Island USA 228 Bk18
Ungalik USA (AK) 229 Bk13
Ungalik River USA 229 Ca13
Ungarra AUS (SA) 152 Rj63
Unga Strait USA (AK) 228 Bk18
Ungava Bay CDN 225 Gc07
Ungerem PNG 158 Sa49
Ungheni MD 45 Mh43
Ungheni RO 45 Me46
Ungo RUS 91 Qe20
Unguja EAT 207 Mk48
Unguriņi LV 17 Mf33
Ungwana Bay EAK 205 Na47
Ungwatiri SUD 190 Mh38
Unhe ANG 209 Ma54
Uniab NAM 212 Lg56
União BR (AM) 273 Gf47
União BR (PI) 277 Hj48
União da Vitória BR (PR) 290 He59
União de Minas BR (MG) 286 He55
União dos Palmares BR (AL) 283 Jc50
Uniara IND (RJT) 106 Oj33
Unica BOL 284 Gg55
Unichowo PL 36 Ls36
Uničov CZ 38 Ls41
Uniejów PL 36 Lt39
Unije HR 41 Lp46
Unimak USA (AK) 228 Bh18
Unimak Bay USA (AK) 228 Bh18
Unimak Island USA 228 Bh18
Unimak Pass USA (AK) 228 Bh18
Unini BR 274 Gj46
Unión RA (SL) 288 Gh63
Union USA (MO) 241 Fe26
Union USA (OR) 234 Eb23
Union USA (SC) 249 Fk28
Union WV 261 Gk39
Union Center USA (SD) 240 Ej23
Union City USA (PA) 247 Ga25
Union City USA (TN) 243 Ff27
Union Creek USA (OR) 234 Dj24
Uniondale ZA 216 Mb62
Unión de Tula MEX (JLC) 253 Eh36
Unión Hidalgo MEX (OAX) 255 Fc37
Union Juárez MEX (CHP) 255 Fd38
Union Springs USA (AL) 249 Fh29
Uniontown USA (PA) 247 Ga26
Unionville USA (MO) 241 Fd25
Unionville USA (NV) 234 Ea25
Unipouheos Ind. Res. CDN 233 Ee19
Uniśław PL 36 Lt37
United Arab Emirates UAE 74 Ng34
United Kingdom 7 Kb04
United States USA 223 Ea06
Unity CDN (SK) 233 Ef19
Unity USA (OR) 234 Ea23
Universal City USA (TX) 242 Fa31
Universal Studios USA 250 Fk31
University Park USA (NM) 237 Eg29
University Place USA (WA) 232 Dj22
Unmet VU 162 Td54
Unna D 32 Lh39
Unnamed Conservation Park AUS 142 Re60
Unnao IND (UPH) 107 Pa32
Unnaryd S 15 Lo34
Uno GNB 183 Kb40
Unpongko VU 162 Te55
Unryul PRK 100 Rc26
Unsan PRK 100 Rc25
Unst GB 19 Ku30
Unstrut D 33 Ll39
Unteres Odertal, N.P. D 33 Lp38
Unterhaching D 35 Lm42
Unterluckersee D 33 Lo37
Unuk River CDN 231 De17
Ünye TR 63 Mj25
Unzen J 103 Rf29
Uoro o Mbini GQ 195 Lf45
Uotsuri Jima J 103 Rb33
Uozo J 101 Rj27
Upa EST 16 Mc32
Upala CR 256 Fh40
Upalco USA (UT) 235 Ee25
Upanema BR (RN) 277 Jb48
Upang RI 125 Qc47
Upata YV 270 Gj41
Upemba, P.N.de l' RDC 206 Md50
Upernavik DK 225 Ha04
Upham USA (ND) 238 Ek21
Upi RP 123 Rc42
Upington ZA 216 Ma60
Upinniemi = Obbnäs FIN 16 Me30
Upleta IND (GUJ) 108 Of35
'Upolu Island WS 164 Be52
Upolu Point USA 230 Cc35
Uppalapadu IND (APH) 111 Ok39
Upper Arrow Lake CDN 232 Ea20
Upper Canada Vill. CDN 247 Gc23
Upper Daly A.L. AUS 139 Rf53
Upper Forster Lake CDN 233 Eh17
Upper Guinea 166 Kb09
Upper Karoo ZA 216 Ma61
Upper Klamath Lake USA 234 Dj24
Upper Lake USA 234 Ea25
Upper Lough Erne IRL 18 Kn36
Upper Mississippi N.W.R. USA 246 Fe24
Upper-Normandie F 22 La41
Upper Peninsula USA 241 Fh22
Upper Red Lake USA 238 Fc21
Upper Sandusky USA (OH) 246 Fj25
Upper Sioux Ind. Res. USA 241 Fc23
Upper Soda USA (OR) 234 Dj23
Upper Svaneti GE 70 Nb24
Upper Twin Lake CDN 239 Fg20
Uppinangadi IND (KTK) 110 Oh40
Uppland S 13 Ls31
Upplands-Väsby S 13 Ls31
Uppsala S 13 Ls31
Upsala CDN (ON) 239 Fe21
Upsala Glacier RA 294 Gd70
Upshi 79 Oj29
Upton USA (WY) 235 Eh23
Uqban YE 68 Nb38
Uqlat as Suqur KSA 66 Nb33
Ur IRQ 65 Nd30
Uracoa YV 270 Gj41
Urad Houqi CHN (NMZ) 92 Qd25
Urad Qianqi CHN (NMZ) 92 Qe25
Urad Zhongqi CHN (NMZ) 92 Qe25
Urahoro J 99 Sb24
Uraim BR 276 Hg47
Urakawa J 99 Sb24
Ural RUS 58 Nd08
Uralla AUS (NSW) 151 Sf61
Ural Mountains 9 Oa06
Urambo EAT 206 Mg48
Uran IND (MHT) 108 Og36
Urana AUS (NSW) 153 Sd63
Urandangi AUS (QLD) 148 Rk56
Urandi BR (BA) 282 Hj53
Uranga AUS (NSW) 151 Sg61
Uranium City CDN 224 Ec07
Uran-Togoo Tulga Mountain Nature Reserve MNG 90 Qb21
,Uraq SUD 190 Mg39
Uraricuera BR 270 Gk44
Ura-Vajgurore AL 46 Lu50
Uravakonda IND (APH) 111 Oj39
Urayirah KSA 67 Ne33
Urbana USA (IL) 246 Ff25
Urbana USA (OH) 246 Fj25
Urbandale USA (IA) 241 Fd25
Urbánia I 40 Ln47
Urbano Noris C 259 Gb35
Urbano Santos BR (MA) 276 Hj47
Urbi SUD 190 Mf37
Urbinasopon RI 130 Rf46
Urbino I 40 Ln47
Urcos PE 279 Ge52
Urdampilleta RA (BA) 293 Gk64
Urdaneta RP 120 Ra38
Urdgol MNG 85 Pg22
Urdinarrain RA (ER) 289 Ha62
Urd Tamir Gol MNG 90 Qa22
Ure GB 21 Kt36
Ure WAN 194 Ld41
Ureca GQ 194 Le44
Urema RI 131 Rh47
Uren RUS 53 Nc17
Ureña RA 288 Gh59
Ureparapara VU 162 Td52
Ures MEX (SO) 237 Ee31
Urewera N.P. NZ 154 Tj65
Urgal RUS 98 Rg20
Urgal RUS 98 Rg20
Urganch UZ 71 Oa25
Urganlı TR 49 Mh52
Urgench = Urganch UZ 71 Oa25
Urgoma Mountains ETH 198 Mk42
Ürgüp TR 51 Mp52
Urgut UZ 76 Od26
Urho CHN (XUZ) 85 Pc22
Urho Kekkosen kansallispuisto FIN 11 Me11
Uri TCH 189 Lk35
Uria RO 44 Me43
Uriah USA (AL) 248 Fg30
Uribe CO 272 Gb44
Uribia CO 268 Gd40
Uribicha BOL 280 Gj53
Urica YV 269 Gh41
Uri Hauchab Mountains NAM 212 Lh58
Urik RUS 90 Qa19
Uriman YV 270 Gj43
Urique MEX (CHH) 252 Eg32
Urisirima GUY 270 Ha42
Uritiyacu PE 272 Gc48
Uriuk RUS 90 Qd20
Uri Wenz ETH 191 Mk40
Uriž UA 39 Md41
Urjala FIN 16 Md29
Urjumkan RUS 91 Qk20
Urjumkanskij hrebet RUS 91 Qk20
Urjupino RUS 91 Qk19
Urjupinsk RUS 53 Na20
Urk NL 32 Lf38
Urla TR 49 Mg52
Urlaţi RO 45 Mg46
Urlingford IRL 20 Kn38
Urmary RUS 53 Nd18
Urmi RUS 98 Rg21
Urnes N 12 Lh29
Uromi WAN 194 Ld42
Uroševac SCG 46 Mb48
Uroteppa TJ 76 Oe26
Urov RUS 91 Ra20
Urrampinyu Jiljiltjarri A.L. AUS 142 Rg58
Urrao CO 268 Gb42
Ursus Cove USA 229 Cd16
Urszulewo PL 37 Lu38
Urt MNG 92 Qa24
Urt Moron CHN (QHI) 87 Pg27
Uru BR 281 Hf53
Uruachic MEX (CHH) 252 Ef32
Uruaçu BR (GO) 282 Hf53
Uruanã BR (GO) 282 Hf53
Uruapan MEX (BC) 236 Eb30
Uruapan del Progreso MEX (MHC) 254 Ej36
Uruara BR 275 Hd47
Urubamba PE 279 Gd52
Urubamba PE 279 Gd52
Urubaxi BR 274 Gh46
Urubici BR (SC) 291 Hf60
Urubu Branco, T.I. BR 281 He51
Urubu Grande BR 281 Hf51
Urucara BR (AM) 275 Hb47
Urucu BR 274 Gh48
Uruçuca BR (BA) 283 Ja53
Uruçuí BR (PI) 276 Hh49
Urucuia BR (MG) 287 Hh54
Urucuia BR 282 Hh54
Uruçuí Preto BR 276 Hh50
Urucu Juruá, T.I. BR 276 Hh48
Urucuriana BR 275 Hc45
Uru-Eu-Wau-Wau, T.I. BR 280 Gj51
Urugu EAT 207 Mh48
Uruguai BR 290 Hd59
Uruguaiana BR (RS) 289 Hb60
Uruguay BR/RA 289 Hb60
Uruguay 263 Ha13
Uruguinha BR (AP) 275 He45
Uruk = Erech IRQ 65 Nc30
Urukthapel PAL 121 Rh42
Uruma RI 131 Rh48
Urumaco YV 269 Ge40
Ürümqi CHN (XUZ) 85 Pd24
Ürünlü TR 62 Mf27
Uruoca BR (CE) 277 Hk47
Urupadi BR 275 Hb47
Urupês BR (SP) 286 Hf56
Uruq al Avarik KSA 68 Nd36
,Uruq al Mawarid KSA 68 Ne36
,Uruq al Mundafin KSA 68 Nc36
Uruq ar Rumaylah KSA 67 Nd35
Uruq Subay KSA 66 Nb34
Ürür gol MNG 90 Qa20
Urussanga BR (SC) 291 Hf60
Urussu RUS 53 Ng18
Uruwira EAT 206 Mf49
Uryzhar KZ 84 Pa22
Urzędów PL 37 Mc39
Urziceni RO 45 Mg46
Us RUS 85 Pg19
Usa J 103 Rf29
Ušaćy BY 52 Me18
Usadišće RUS 52 Mg16
Usagari EAT 206 Mg48
Usagre E 28 Ko48
Uşak TR 50 Mk52
Usakos NAM 212 Lh56
Ušakovskoe RUS 59 Ua04
Usambara Mountains EAT 205 Mk48
U.S. Army Aviation Mus. USA 249 Fh30
Usarp Mountains 297 Ta33
,Usaylay KSA 67 Nc33
Uš-Bel'dir RUS (TUV) 90 Pk20
Uschodni BY 52 Md19
Usedom D 33 Lo37
Usedom D 33 Lp36
Useless Loop AUS (WA) 140 Qg59
Usen RUS 53 Nh18
Usengi EAK 204 Mh46
Usfan KSA 66 Mk35
Ushaa Z 209 Mb53
Usharal KZ 76 Of24
Usharal KZ 84 Pa22
,Ushayrah KSA 67 Nc33
Ushetu EAT 206 Mg48
Ushibuka J 103 Rf29
Ushirombo EAT 206 Mf47
Ushtobe KZ 84 Oj23
Ushuaia RA (TF) 294 Gf73
Usib NAM 212 Lh57
Usilampatti IND (TNU) 111 Oj42
Usim RI 130 Rg46
Usina Apiacás BR (MT) 281 Hb51
Usina São Francisco BR (AM) 274 Ha48
Usingen D 34 Lj40
Usino PNG 159 Sc48
Usk CDN (BC) 232 Df18
Usk GB 21 Ks39
Uska IND (UPH) 107 Pb32
Uskoplje BIH 41 Ls47
Uslar D 32 Lk39
Usman' RUS 53 Mk19
Usmas ezers LV 17 Mc33
Usmat UZ 76 Od26
Usoke EAT 206 Mg48
Usol'e-Sibirskoe RUS 90 Qb19
Uson RP 121 Rb39
Usovo RUS 53 Nb19
Uspallata RA (MD) 288 Gf62
Uspenie manastir BG 46 Mc47
Uspenskij sobor RUS 52 Mf18
Uspenskij sobor Rjazan' RUS 53 Mk18
Uspenskij sobor Tver' RUS 52 Mh17
Usquil PE 278 Ga49
Usran KSA 68 Nb36
Ussel F 24 Lc45
U.S. Space & Rocket Center USA 248 Fg28
Ussuri RUS 98 Rh22
Ussurijsk RUS 98 Rf24
Usta RUS 53 Nd17
Usta USA (SD) 240 Ej23
Usta Muhammad PK 80 Oe31
Ust'-Barguzin RUS (BUR) 90 Qe19
Ust'-Cil'ma RUS 58 Nc05
Ust'-Džeguta RUS (KCH) 70 Na23
Ust'-Džilinda RUS (BUR) 91 Qf19
Ust'-Élegest RUS (TUV) 85 Ph20
Uster CH 34 Lj43
Ustibar BIH 46 Lu47
Ustikolina BIH 46 Lt47
Ust'-Ilimsk RUS 58 Qa07
Ústí nad Labem CZ 38 Lp40
Ústí nad Orlicí CZ 38 Lr41
Ustipraća BIH 46 Lu47
Ustjurt Plateau KZ/UZ 60 Nd10
Ustjužna RUS 52 Mj16
Ustka PL 36 Lr36
Ust'-Kamčatsk RUS 59 Ta07
Ust'-Kan RUS (ALT) 85 Pc20
Ust'-Karsk RUS 91 Qk19
Ust'-Koksa RUS (ALT) 85 Pc20
Ust'-Kujga RUS 59 Rd04
Ust'-Kut RUS 58 Qb07
Ust'-Labinsk RUS 55 Mk23
Ust'-Luga RUS 16 Mj31
Ust'-Maja RUS 59 Rc06
Ust'-Nera RUS 59 Sa06
Ust'-Omčug RUS 59 Sb06
Ust'-Ordynsk Buryat Autonomous District RUS 58 Qa08
Ust'-Ordynskij RUS (UOB) 90 Qc19
Ustovo BG 47 Me49
Ustrem BG 47 Mg48
Ustroń PL 39 Lt41
Ustronie Morskie PL 36 Lq36
Ustrzyki Dolne PL 39 Mc41
Ust'-Sobolevka RUS 99 Rk22
Ust'-Ulagan RUS (ALT) 85 Pe20
Ust'-Umal'ta RUS 98 Rg20
Ust'-Varga RUS 58 Na06
Ustyluh PL 37 Me40
Ust-Zolotaja RUS 85 Pg19
Usu CHN (XUZ) 85 Pc23
Usuki J 103 Rf29
Usuktuk River USA 229 Cb10
Usulutan ES 255 Ff39
Usumacinta GCA/MEX 255 Fe37
Usur IND (CGH) 109 Pa36
Usutu ZA 214 Me57
Usu-zan J 99 Sa24
Usvjaty RUS 52 Mf18
Uta RI 131 Rj48
Utah USA 226 Eb11
Utah Lake USA 235 Ed25
Utajärvi FIN 11 Md13
Utåker N 12 Lf31
Utambalila EAT 206 Mg50
Utangala RI 127 Rb45
Utansjö S 13 Ls28
Utar RI 129 Qj50
Utara Baliem RI 131 Rk48
Utcubamba PE 272 Ga48
Utegi EAT 204 Mh46
Utembo ANG 209 Ma54
Ute Mountain Ind. Res. USA 237 Ee27
Utena LT 17 Mf35
Utete EAT 207 Mk50
U Thai LAO 113 Qa34
Uthai Thani THA 114 Qa38
Uthal PK 80 Od33
Uthompho LAO 115 Qc37
U Thong THA 114 Pk38
Uthumph on Phisai THA 115 Qc38
Utiariti BR (MT) 280 Ha52
Utiariti, T.I. BR 280 Ha52
Utica CO 268 Gc43
Utica TN 174 Lf27
Utica USA (MS) 243 Fe29
Utica USA (NY) 247 Gc24
Utica USA (OH) 246 Fj25
Utiel E 29 Kt49
Utik Lake CDN 238 Fb18
Utikuma Lake CDN 233 Ec18
Utikuma River CDN 233 Ec17
Utila HN 256 Fg37
Utinga BR (BA) 283 Hk52
Utinga BR 283 Hk52
Utlängan S 15 Lq34
Utne N 12 Lg30
Utnur IND (APH) 109 Ok36
Utö FIN 16 Mb31
Utö S 13 Lt32
Utraula IND (UPH) 107 Pb32
Utrecht NL 32 Lf38
Utrecht ZA 217 Mf59
Utrera E 28 Kp47
Utria, P.N. CO 268 Gb43
Utroja RUS 17 Mh34
Utsira N 12 Le31
Utsjoki FIN 11 Md11
Utstein Kloster N 12 Lf31
Utsunomiya J 101 Rk27
Uttamapalaiyam IND (TNU) 111 Oj42
Uttangarai IND (TNU) 111 Ok40
Uttaradit THA 114 Qa37
Uttaranchal IND 104 Od12
Uttarkashi IND (UTT) 107 Ok30
Uttarkashi Ski area IND 107 Ok30
Uttar Pradesh IND 104 Pa13
Uttar Pradesh State Astronomical Observatory IND 107 Ok31
Uttoxeter GB 21 Kt38
Uttukkotta IND (APH) 111 Ok40
Utuado USA (PR) 261 Gg36
Utuana EC 272 Ga48
Utubulak CHN (XUZ) 85 Pd22
Utupua SOL 157 Tb21
Uturoa F (PYF) 165 Ce54
Uturuncu, Cerro BOL 284 Gg57
Utvin RO 44 Mb45
Uukuniemi FIN 16 Mk29
Uummannaq = Dundas DK 225 Gc03
Uummannarsuaq = Kap Farvel DK 225 Hd07
Uurainen FIN 16 Mf28
Üüreg MNG 85 Pf20
Üüreg nuur MNG 85 Pf20
Uusikaupunki = Nystadt FIN 13 Mb30
Uutapi NAM 208 Lh54
Uvá CO 269 Gf44
Uvalde USA (TX) 242 Fa31
Úvaly CZ 38 Lp40
Uvarovo RUS 53 Nb20
Uvdal N 12 Lj30
Uvdal stavkirke N 12 Lj30
Uvinza EAT 206 Mf48
Uvira RDC 206 Me47
Uvol PNG 160 Sf49
Uvs MNG 85 Pg21
Uvs nuur MNG 85 Pg20
Uvs Nuur Nature Reserve MNG 85 Pg20
Uvungu RDC 203 Mc47
Uwajima J 103 Rg29
Uwa-kai J 103 Rg29
Uwakeka RI 132 Rd49
Uwanda Game Reserve EAT 206 Mg49
Uwanza EAT 207 Mh48
Uwapa RI 131 Rh47
Uwaynat Wannin LAR 174 Lg31
Uwekuli RI 127 Ra47
Uwi RI 117 Qd45
Uwimmerah RI 158 Sa49
Uxal MEX 255 Ff37
Uxin Ju CHN (NMZ) 93 Qe26
Uxin Qi CHN (NMZ) 92 Qe26
Uxmal MEX 255 Ff35
Uyak Bay USA (AK) 228 Cc17
Uyluk Tepe TR 49 Mk54
Uyo WAN 194 Ld43
Uyowa EAT 206 Mf48
Uyuali = Mutúali MOC 211 Mj53
Uyugan RP 121 Ra35
Uyun KSA 67 Ne33
Uyuni BOL 284 Gg56
Üyzen MNG 92 Qd23
Uzbekistan UZ 57 Oa05
Uzdowo PL 37 Ma37
Uzebba WAN 194 Lc42
Uzerche F 24 Lb45
Uzès F 25 Le47
Uzgen KS 77 Og25
Užhorod UA 39 Mc42
Užice SCG 46 Lu47
Uzlovaja RUS 53 Mk19
Užovka RUS 53 Nc18
Üzümlü TR 49 Mk54
Üzümlü TR 51 Mm53
Üzümlü TR 63 Mk26
Uzuncaburç TR 62 Mg27
Uzunköprü TR 50 Mg49
Uzunpınar TR 51 Ml52
Užventis LT 17 Mc35
Uzyn UA 54 Mf21
Uzynaghash KZ 77 Oj24

V

Vaal ZA 217 Mc60
Vaalbos N.P. ZA 217 Mc60
Vaaldam ZA 217 Me59
Vaaldam Nature Reserve ZA 217 Me59
Vaalimaa FIN 16 Mh30
Vaalkop Dam ZA 213 Md58
Vaalwater ZA 213 Me58
Vaasa FIN 11 Ma14
Vaavu Atoll = Felidhoo Atoll MV 110 Og44
Vabalninkas LT 17 Me35
Vabre F 24 Lc47
Vác H 39 Lu43
Văča BG 47 Me48
Vaca Guzmán BOL 285 Gj55
Vacaria BR (RS) 290 He60
Vacaria BR 282 Hj54
Vacaville USA (CA) 234 Dj26
Vache D 32 Ll40
Vache MOC 211 Mj53
Väckelsång S 15 Lp34
Vada IND (MHT) 108 Og36
Vadakkevila IND (KER) 110 Oj42
Väddö S 13 Lt30
Vadehavet DK 14 Lj35
Vader USA (WA) 232 Dj22
Vadheim N 12 Lf29
Vadodara IND (GUJ) 108 Og34
Vado del Yeso C 259 Gb35
Vadsø N 11 Me10
Vadstena S 13 Lp32
Vadu Crişului RO 44 Mc44
Vaduz FL 34 Lk43
Vadvetjåkka n.p. S 10 Lk11
Værøy N 10 Lg12
Vaga RCB 202 Lh46
Vågaholmen N 10 Lg12
Vågåmo N 12 Lk29
Vaganski vrh HR 41 Lq46
Vagator Beach IND 108 Og38
Vaggeryd S 15 Lp33
Vaghena SOL 161 Sj49
Vagnhärad S 13 Ls32
Vägsele S 10 Lk13
Vågsøy N 12 Lf29
Váh SK 38 Ls42
Váh SK 39 Lu41
Vahs TJ 76 Oe27
Vahto FIN 16 Mc30
Vaíaau F (PYF) 165 Ce54
Vaiaku TUV 157 Td20
Vaiden USA (MS) 243 Ff29
Vaihingen (Enz) D 34 Lj42
Vai Island PNG 159 Sc47
Vaikam IND (KER) 110 Oj42
Väike-Pakri EST 16 Md31
Vaikuntha Perumal Temple IND 111 Ok40
Vail USA (CO) 235 Eg26
Vailala River PNG 159 Sc49
Vailly-sur-Sauldre F 23 Lc43
Vainikkala FIN 16 Mj30
Vaiņode LV 17 Mb34
Vaisala WS 164 Bd52
Vaishali IND (BIH) 109 Pc33
Vaishnav Devi Shrine IND 79 Oh29
Vaison-la-Romaine F 25 Lf46
Vaitahu F (PYF) 165 Da50
Vaitape F (PYF) 165 Ce54
Vaitupu TUV 157 Td20
Vajszló H 41 Ls45
Vakaga RCA 196 Mb41
Vakfıkebir TR 63 Mk25
Vakhsh TJ 76 Oe26
Vakıf TR 50 Mg50
Vakil Abad IR 75 Nk31
Vaku RDC 202 Lg48
Vakuta PNG 160 Sf50
Vakuta Island PNG 160 Sf50
Valaam monastyr RUS 11 Mf15
Valadim MOC 211 Mj52
Valamon luostari FIN 11 Me14
Valandovo MK 46 Mc49
Valappadi IND (TNU) 111 Ok41
Valaská Belá SK 38 Lt42
Valašská Polanka CZ 38 Ls41
Valašské Meziříčí CZ 38 Ls41
Valavanni IND (PND) 111 Ok41
Valayat IR 74 Nf31
Vålberg S 13 Lo31
Valbo S 13 Lr30
Valbonë AL 46 Lu48
Vălčedrăm BG 46 Md47
Valcheta RA (RN) 292 Gg66
Valcheta RA 292 Gg66
Vălčidol BG 47 Mh47
Valdagno I 40 Lm45
Val d'Agri e Lagonegrese, P.N. I 43 Lr50
Valdahon F 23 Lg43
Valdaisky N.P. RUS 52 Mg17
Valdaj RUS 52 Mg17
Valdayskaya Vozvyshennost' RUS 52 Mg17
Valdefuentes E 28 Ko49
Valdelagua E 29 Kr49
Valdeltormo E 30 La50
Valdemārpils LV 17 Mc33
Valdemars Slot DK 14 Ll35
Valdemarsvik S 15 Lr32
Valdemeca E 29 Ks50
Valdemoro E 29 Kr50
Valdenoceda E 27 Kr52
Valdepeñas E 29 Kr48
Valdepeñas de Jaén E 29 Kr47
Valderas E 26 Kp52
Val de Reuil F 22 Lb41
Valderrobres E 30 La50
Valdés RA (BA) 289 Gk63
Valdez RP 122 Qj41
Valdez USA (AK) 229 Cg15
Val d'Isère F 25 Lg45
Valdivia RCH 292 Gd65
Valdivia Fracture Zone 266 Fc27
Valdobbiádene I 40 Ln45
Val-d'Or CDN (QC) 244 Gb21
Val d'Orcia I 40 Lm48
Valdosta USA (GA) 249 Fj30
Valdres N 12 Lj29
Vale USA (OR) 234 Eb24
Valea Argovei RO 45 Mg46
Valea Ierii RO 44 Md44
Valea lui Mihai RO 44 Mc43
Valea Mare-Pravăţ RO 45 Mf45
Valea Mărului RO 45 Mh45
Valea Perjei MD 45 Mj44
Valea Sării RO 45 Mg45
Valea Ursului RO 45 Mh44

Valea Uzului – Victoria West

Valea Uzului RO 45 Mg44
Valea Viilor RO 44 Me44
Vale do Guaporé, T.I. BR 280 Gk52
Valejkidki BY 17 Mf36
Valemount CDN (BC) 232 Ea19
Valença BR (BA) 283 Ja52
Valença do Minho P 26 Km52
Valença do Piauí BR (PI) 277 Hk49
Valençay F 22 Lb43
Valence F 24 La46
Valence F 25 Le46
Valence-sur-Baïse F 24 La47
València E 29 Kt49
València E 30 Ku51
Valencia RP 123 Rc42
Valencia YV 269 Gg40
Valencia de Alcántara E 28 Kn49
Valencia de Don Juan E 26 Kp52
Valenciennes F 23 Ld40
Vălenii de Munte RO 45 Mg45
Valeni-Stânişoara RO 45 Mf43
Valensole F 25 Lf47
Valentano I 42 Lm48
Valente BR (BA) 283 Ja51
Valentia Island IRL 20 Kk39
Valentim Gentil BR (SP) 286 He56
Valentin ROU 289 Hb61
Valentin RUS 99 Rh24
Valentine USA (NE) 240 Ek24
Valentine N.W.R. USA 240 Ek24
Valenza I 40 Lj45
Våler N 12 Lm30
Valera PE 278 Gb49
Valera YV 269 Ge41
Valeria E 29 Ks49
Valerio MEX (CHH) 252 Eg32
Valesdir VU 162 Te54
Valevåg N 12 Lf31
Vale Verde BR (RS) 290 Hd60
Valevka BY 17 Mf37
Valga EST 16 Mg33
Val Grande, P.N.della I 40 Lj44
Valguarnera Caropepe I 42 Lp53
Valhalla Prov. Park CDN 232 Eb21
Vali Abad IR 72 Nf27
Valier USA (MT) 233 Ed21
Valira GR 48 Mb53
Vălişoara RO 44 Mc44
Väliug RO 44 Mc45
Val-Jalbert CDN 244 Gd21
Valjevo SCG 46 Lu46
Valka LV 17 Mf33
Valkeakoski FIN 16 Me29
Valkeala FIN 16 Mg30
Valkenswaard NL 32 Lf39
Valkmusan kansallispuisto FIN 16 Mg30
Valko = Valkom FIN 16 Mg30
Valkom = Valko FIN 16 Mg30
Valky UA 53 Mh21
Valkyrjedomen 297 Md33
Valla S 13 Lr31
Valladolid E 26 Kq51
Valladolid EC 272 Ga48
Valladolid MEX (YT) 255 Ff35
Vallargärdet S 13 Lo31
Vall de Boí E 30 La48
Vall del Madriu-Perafita-Claror AND 30 Lb48
Valldemossa E 30 Lc51
Valle N 12 Lh31
Valle Altares RA 292 Gf67
Valle Castor RCH 294 Gf73
Valle d'Aosta I 40 Lh45
Valle de Allende MEX (CHH) 253 Eh32
Valle de Bravo MEX (MEX) 254 Ek36
Valle de Cabuérniga E 27 Kq53
Valle de Calingasta RA 288 Gf61
Valle de Chapalcó RA 292 Gh64
Valle de Guanape YV 269 Gh41
Valle dei Templi I 42 Lo53
Valle de la Luna BOL 284 Gf54
Valle de la Luna = Parque Provincial Ischigualasto RA 288 Gg61
Valle de la Luna RCH 284 Gf57
Valle de la Pascua YV 269 Gh41
Valle del Río Deseado RA 294 Gf69
Valle del Río Elqui RCH 288 Ge60
Valle de Santiago MEX (GJT) 254 Ek35
Valle de Viñales C 258 Fj34
Valle de Zaragoza MEX (CHH) 252 Eh32
Valle do Douro P 26 Kn51
Valledupar CO 268 Gd40
Vallée de la Lufira RDC 210 Md51
Vallée de l'Azaough RMM/RN 185 Lc37
Vallée de l'Azar RMM 185 Lb38
Vallée de l'Ourika MA 172 Kg30
Vallée de Mai N.P. SY 219 Nh48
Valle Edén ROU 289 Hb61
Vallée du Dadès MA 172 Kg30
Vallée du Drâa MA 172 Kg30
Vallée du Ferlo SN 183 Kd38
Vallée du M'Zab DZ 173 Lb29
Valléedu Saloum SN 183 Kc38
Vallée du Serpent RMM 184 Kf38
Vallée du Tilemsi RMM 185 La36
Vallée du Ziz MA 172 Kh30
Valle Encantado RA 292 Ge66
Valle Fertil RA 288 Gg61
Valle General Racedo RA 292 Gf67
Vallegrande BOL 285 Gh55
Valle Gran Rey E 178 Kb31
Vallehermoso E 178 Kb31
Valle Hermoso MEX (QTR) 255 Ff36
Valle Hermoso MEX (TM) 253 Fb33
Vallei van Verlatheid ZA 216 Mb62
Vallejo USA (CA) 234 Dj26
Valle Las Palmas MEX (BC) 236 Eb29
Valle Maracó Grande RA 292 Gh64
Valle-mi PY 285 Hb57
Valle Nacional MEX (OAX) 254 Fb37
Vallenar RCH 288 Ge60
Valle Nerecó RA 292 Gh64
Valle Nevado RCH 288 Ge62
Vallentuna S 13 Lt31
Valletta M 42 Lp55
Valle Ucal RA 293 Gh64
Valley USA (AL) 249 Fh29
Valley USA (WY) 235 Ef23
Valley City USA (ND) 240 Fb22
Valley Falls USA (OR) 234 Dk24
Valley Mills USA (TX) 242 Fb30
Valley of Desolation ZA 216 Mb62
Valley of Fire S.P. USA 236 Ec27
Valley of Fires S.P. USA 237 Eg29
Valley of Flowers N.P. IND 107 Ok30
Valley of Lagoons AUS (QLD) 149 Sc55
Valley of the Kings ET 177 Mg33
Valley of wild elephants = Yexianggu CHN 113 Qa34
Valley of Willow USA (AK) 229 Cc11
Valley R. Ind. Res. CDN 238 Ek20
Valley River CDN 238 Ek20
Valley Station USA (KY) 248 Fh26
Valleyview CDN (AB) 233 Eb18
Valli di Comàcchio I 40 Ln46
Vallières RH 260 Ge36
Vallon-Pont-d'Arc F 25 Le46
Vallorbe CH 34 Lg44
Valls E 30 Lb49
Vallsta S 13 Lr29
Vallvik S 13 Ls29
Valmanya F 24 Lc48
Val Marie CDN (SK) 233 Eg21
Valmiera LV 17 Mf33
Valognes F 22 Kt41
Valøy N 10 Lf13
Valožyn BY 17 Mg36
Valpaços P 26 Kn51
Val-Paradis CDN (QC) 239 Ga21
Valparai IND (TNU) 111 Oj41
Valparaíso BR (AC) 278 Gd49
Valparaíso BR (SP) 286 He56
Valparaíso CO 272 Gc45
Valparaíso MEX (ZCT) 253 Ej34
Valparaíso RCH 288 Ge62
Valparaiso USA (IN) 246 Fg25
Valpovo HR 41 Lt45
Valréas F 25 Le46
Vals ZA 217 Md59
Valsad IND (GUJ) 108 Og35
Valsbaai ZA 216 Lk63
Valset N 10 Le14
Valsjöbyn S 10 Lh13
Vals-les-Bains F 25 Le46
Valtellina I 40 Lk44
Valterlândia BR (AM) 279 Gg50
Val-Thorens F 25 Lg45
Valtournenche I 40 Lh45
Valujki RUS 53 Mk20
Valul lui Traian MD 45 Mj44
Valverde E 178 Kb32
Valverde de Júcar E 29 Ks49
Valverde del Camino E 28 Ko47
Valverde de Leganés E 28 Ko48
Valverde del Fresno E 28 Ko50
Vama RO 45 Mf43
Vamberk CZ 38 Lr40
Vamdrup DK 14 Lk35
Våmhus S 13 Lp29
Vamlingbo S 15 Lt33
Vammala FIN 16 Mc29
Vampula FIN 16 Mc29
Van TR 63 Nb26
Vanadzor ARM 70 Nc25
Vanajavesi FIN 16 Me29
Vana-Kuuste EST 16 Mg32
Vanalphensvlei ZA 213 Me58
Vanån S 13 Lo29
Vanapa River PNG 159 Sd50
Van Asch van Wijckgebergte SME 271 Hc44
Vânatori RO 44 Mc46
Vânatori RO 45 Me44
Vanavara RUS 58 Qa06
Van Blommesteinmeer = Brokopondostuwmeer SME 271 Hc43
Van Buren USA (AR) 243 Fc28
Van Buren USA (ME) 244 Gg22
Van Canh VN 115 Qe39
Vanceboro USA (ME) 245 Gg23
Vanceburg USA (KY) 249 Fj26
Vancouver CDN (BC) 232 Dj21
Vancouver USA (OR) 234 Dj23
Vancouver Island CDN 232 Dh21
Vancouver Island Range CDN 232 Dh21
Vanda = Vantaa FIN 16 Me30
Vanda ANT (NZ) 297 Tb34
Van Daalen RI 131 Rj47
Vandalur IND (TNU) 111 Pa40
Vandavasi IND (TNU) 111 Ok40
Vandekerckhove Lake CDN 238 Ek17
Vanderbijlpark ZA 217 Md59
Vandergrift USA (PA) 247 Ga25
Vanderhoof CDN (BC) 232 Dh18
Vanderkloof ZA 217 Mc61
Vanderkloof Dam ZA 217 Mc61
Vanderlei BR (BA) 282 Hj52
Vanderlin Island AUS 139 Rj53
Van de Wal RI 131 Rk47
Van Diemen Gulf AUS 139 Rf51
Vändra EST 16 Mf32
Vandyksdrif ZA 217 Me59
Vandžiogala LT 17 Md35
Vāne LV 17 Mc34
Vanegas MEX (SLP) 253 Ek34
Vänern S 13 Ln32
Vänersborg S 12 Ln32
Vangaindrano RM 220 Nd57
Vangaži LV 17 Me33
Van Gölü TR 63 Nb26
Vangsnes N 12 Lg29
Vangunu SOL 161 Sk50
Vangunu, Mount SOL 161 Sj50
Vang Vieng LAO 115 Qb36
Vanh Ninh VN 115 Qe39
Van Horn USA (TX) 237 Eh30
Vani GE 70 Nb24
Vani IND (MHT) 108 Oj35
Vanikolo SOL 157 Tb21
Vanimo PNG 158 Sa47
Vanino RUS 59 Sa09
Vanivilasa Sagara IND 111 Oj40
Vaniyambadi IND (TNU) 111 Ok40
Vânju Mare RO 44 Mc46
Van Lan VN 115 Qe40
Van Mijenfjorden N 11 Lh07
Vanna N 10 Lk10
Vannareid N 10 Lk10
Vännäs S 10 Lk14
Vannes F 22 Ks43
Vannsjø N 12 Ll31
Vanoise, P.N.de la F 25 Lg45
Vanovano SOL 160 Sj50
Van Reenen ZA 217 Me60
Vanrhynsdorp ZA 216 Lk61
Vanrook AUS (QLD) 148 Sa54
Vansbro S 13 Lp30
Vänsjö S 13 Lq29
Vanstadensrus ZA 217 Md60
Vantaa FIN 16 Me30
Vantaa = Vanda FIN 16 Me30
Vantage CDN (SK) 233 Eh21
Vantage USA (WA) 232 Dk22
Van Tassell USA (WY) 235 Eh24
Vanthli IND (GUJ) 108 Of35
Vant's Drift ZA 217 Mf60
Vanttauskoski FIN 11 Md12
Vanua Balavu FJI 163 Ua54
Vanua Lava VU 162 Td52
Vanua Levu FJI 163 Tk54
Vanuatu 135 Ta11
Vanuire, T.I. BR 286 He56
Vanvikan N 10 Lf14
Van Wert USA (OH) 246 Fh25
Van Wyksdorp ZA 216 Ma62
Van Wyksvlei ZA 216 Ma61
Van Zylsrus ZA 216 Mb59
Vao F (NCL) 162 Td57
Vapi LAO 115 Qc38
Vaquería MEX (NL) 253 Fa33
Var F 25 Lg47
Vara S 13 Ln32
Varadero C 258 Fk34
Varades F 22 Kt43
Varakallu IND (APH) 108 Ok38
Varakļāni LV 17 Mg34
Varalé CI 193 Kj41
Varallo I 40 Lj45
Varamin IR 72 Nf28
Varanasi IND (UPH) 109 Pb33
Vărăncău MD 45 Mk43
Varangerbotn N 11 Me10
Varangerfjorden N 11 Mf10
Varangerhalvøya N 11 Me10
Varapaeva BY 17 Mh35
Varar IND 108 Oe34
Varatec RO 44 Mc43
Varaždin HR 41 Lr44
Varaždinske Toplice HR 41 Lr44
Varazze I 40 Lj46
Varberg S 14 Ln33
Vărbica BG 47 Mg48
Varbola EST 16 Me31
Várda GR 48 Mb52
Vardannapet IND (APH) 109 Ok37
Vardar MK 46 Mc49
Vardar klisura MK 46 Mc49
Vardarski Rid MK 46 Mc49
Varde DK 14 Lj35
Vardenis ARM 70 Nc25
Vardin IR 72 Nd26
Vardö FIN 13 Ma30
Vårdö FIN 13 Ma30
Vardø N 11 Mf10
Vardzya GE 70 Nb25
Varekil S 14 Lm32
Varel D 32 Lj37
Varela GNB 183 Kb39
Varela RA (SL) 288 Gg63
Varėna LT 17 Me36
Varena I LT 17 Me36
Varengeville-sur-Mer F 22 La41
Varennes-en-Argonne F 23 Lf41
Varennes-sur-Allier F 25 Ld44
Vareš BIH 41 Lt46
Varese I 40 Lj45
Varese Lígure I 40 Lk46
Vârfu Câmpului RO 45 Mg43
Vârfurile RO 44 Mc44
Vårgårda S 15 Ln32
Vargem BR 283 Ja50
Vargem Grande BR (MA) 276 Hj47
Varginha BR (MG) 287 Hh56
Vargön S 12 Ln32
Varhaug N 12 Lf32
Varilhes F 24 Lb47
Varillas PE 284 Ge58
Varirata N.P. PNG 159 Sd50
Váris GR 46 Mb50
Varjota BR (CE) 277 Hk48
Varkala IND (KER) 110 Oj42
Varkan IR 72 Nf29
Varkaus FIN 16 Mh28
Varmahlið IS 10 Ka13
Värmeln S 13 Ln31
Värmland S 13 Ln30
Värmlandsbro S 13 Lo31
Värmlandsnäs S 13 Lo31
Varna BG 47 Mh47
Värnamo S 15 Lp33
Varniai LT 17 Mc35
Varnja EST 16 Mh32
Varnjany BY 17 Mg36
Varnsdorf CZ 33 Lp40
Varoška Rijeka BIH 41 Lr45
Várpalota H 38 Lt43
Vărşag RO 45 Mf44
Vărşand RO 44 Mb44
Varšec BG 46 Md47
Văršilo BG 47 Mh48
Vartdal N 12 Lg28
Varto TR 63 Na26
Vârtop RO 44 Md46
Vartun IR 72 Ng29
Varva UA 52 Mg20
Varvara BG 47 Me48
Varzaneh IR 72 Ng29
Várzea Alegre BR (CE) 277 Ja49
Várzea da Palma BR (MG) 287 Hh54
Várzea do Poço BR (BA) 283 Hk51
Varzea Grande BR (MT) 281 Hb53
Várzea Grande BR (PI) 276 Hj49
Várzeas BR (BA) 282 Hh52
Varzelândia BR (MG) 282 Hh53
Varzi I 40 Lk46
Varzy F 23 Ld43
Vasa Barris BR 283 Ja50
Vasalemma EST 16 Me31
Vasaloppet S 13 Lp29
Vásárosnamény H 39 Mc42
Vasco da Gama IND (GOA) 108 Og38
Vasconcelos MEX (VC) 255 Fc37
Vasil'evka RUS 98 Rh22
Vasil'evo RUS 16 Mh33
Vasil'evo RUS 53 Ne18
Vasilíki GR 48 Ma52
Vasjuganskaja ravnina RUS 58 Od07
Vaškai LT 17 Me34
Vaskivesi FIN 16 Md28
Vasknarva EST 16 Mh32
Vas'kovo RUS 11 Na13
Vaslui RO 45 Mh44
Vaslui RO 45 Mh44
Väsman S 13 Lp30
Vassilika GR 46 Md50
Vassilikó GR 48 Md52
Vassilikós GR 48 Ma53
Västansjö S 13 Lp28
Västbacka S 13 Lp29
Västerås S 13 Lr31
Västerbotten S 10 Ma13
Västerdalälven S 13 Lo30
Väster-Götland S 14 Lo32
Västerhaninge S 13 Lt31
Västervik S 15 Lr33
Vasto I 42 Lp48
Västra S 13 Ls31
Västra Ämtervik S 13 Lo31
Vasvár H 38 Lr43
Vasylivka UA 55 Mh22
Vasyl'kiv UA 54 Mf20
Vasyl'kivka UA 55 Mj21
Vasyšćeve UA 53 Mj21
Vața de Jos RO 44 Mc44
Vatan F 22 Lb43
Vatersay GB 18 Kn34
Váthi GR 46 Mc49
Vathí GR 49 Mg54
Vatican City V 42 Ln49
Vatla EST 16 Md32
Vatnajökull IS 10 Kb13
Vatne N 12 Lg28
Vatoa FJI 137 Ua22
Vatolatsaka RM 220 Nc57
Vatomandry RM 220 Ne55
Vatra MD 45 Mj43
Vatra Dornei RO 45 Mf43
Vatra Moldoviței RO 45 Mf43
Vattaikundu IND (TNU) 111 Oj41
Vattanam IND (TNU) 111 Ok42
Vattaru Channel MV 110 Og44
Vättern S 13 Lp32
Vättlax FIN 16 Mc31
Vatu-i-ra Channel FJI 163 Tk54
Vatulele FJI 163 Tj55
Vatutine UA 54 Mf21
Vaucouleurs F 23 Lf42
Vaudrey F 25 Lf44
Vaughan Springs AUS (NT) 142 Rf57
Vaughn USA (NM) 237 Eh28
Vau i Dejës AL 46 Lu49
Vaukalata BY 17 Mh36
Vaupés CO 273 Ge45
Vauvert F 25 Le47
Vauxhall CDN (AB) 233 Ed20
Vavatenina RM 220 Ne54
Vava'u Group TO 164 Bd55
Vava'u Island TO 164 Bd55
Väversunda S 13 Lp32
Vavkavysk BY 37 Me37
Vavkavyskae vzvyšša BY 37 Me37
Vavoua CI 192 Kg42
Vavuniya CL 111 Pa42
Vaxholm S 13 Lt31
Växjö S 15 Lp34
Våxtorp S 15 Lo34
Vayittiri = Vythiri IND (KER) 110 Oj41
Vayrac F 24 Lb46
Vazante BR (MG) 287 Hg54
Vazobe RM 220 Nd55
Vazvan IR 72 Nf29
Veal Rinh K 115 Qb40
Vechelde D 33 Ll38
Vechta D 32 Lj38
Vecinos E 26 Kp50
Veclaicene LV 17 Mg33
Vecpiebalga LV 17 Mf33
Vecses H 39 Lu43
Vecumnieki LV 17 Me34
Vedaranyam IND (TNU) 111 Ok41
Veddige S 14 Ln33
Vedea RO 45 Mf46
Vedea RO 47 Mf47
Vedevåg S 13 Lq31
Vedia RA (BA) 289 Gk63
Vedrovo RUS 53 Nb17
Vedshir IND (MHT) 108 Oh36
Veendam NL 32 Lg37
Veenendaal NL 32 Lf39
Veere EST 16 Mc32
Vega N 10 Lf13
Vega USA (TX) 237 Ej28
Vega Baja USA (PR) 261 Gg36
Vega de Alatorre MEX (VC) 254 Fb35
Vegadeo E 26 Kn53
Vegamót IS 10 Jj13
Vegaøyan N 10 Lf13
Vegarienza E 26 Ko52
Vegårshei N 12 Lj32
Veghel NL 32 Lf39
Véglie I 43 Ls50
Vegreville CDN (AB) 233 Ed19
Végueta PE 278 Gb51
Vegusdal N 12 Lj32
Vehmaa FIN 16 Mb30
Vehu FIN 16 Me28
Veiru PNG 159 Sc49
Veisiejai LT 17 Md36
Ve Javis AUS (QLD) 150 Sb58
Vejdelevka RUS 53 Mk20
Vejen DK 14 Lk35
Vejer de la Frontera E 28 Kp46
Vejle DK 14 Lk35
Vejle Fjord DK 14 Lk35
Vejprty CZ 38 Lo40
Vekilski BG 47 Mh47
Velacruz EC 272 Ga47
Vela Luka HR 41 Lr48
Velanganni IND (TNU) 111 Ok41
Velanídia GR 48 Md54
Velapur IND (MHT) 108 Oh37
Velasco Ibarra EC 272 Ga46
Velasco Ibarra = Empalmé EC 272 Ga46
Vel'aty SK 39 Mb42
Velavadar N.P. IND 108 Og34
Velázquez ROU 289 Hc63
Velbert D 32 Lh39
Velden A 35 Lp44
Veldhoven NL 32 Lf39
Veldrif ZA 216 Lk62
Velduri IND (APH) 111 Oj39
Velebit HR 41 Lq46
Velēna LV 17 Mg33
Velencei-tó H 39 Lt43
Velenje SLO 41 Lq44
Veles MK 46 Mb49
Velestino GR 48 Mc51
Velež BIH 41 Ls47
Vélez CO 268 Gd42
Vélez Blanco E 29 Ks47
Vélez-Málaga E 28 Kq46
Vélez Rubio E 29 Ks47
Vélia I 42 Lq50
Velika GR 48 Mb53
Velika HR 41 Ls45
Velika Gorica HR 41 Lr45
Velikaja RUS 16 Mj33
Velikaja Guba RUS 11 Mh14
Velikaja Kema RUS 99 Rj23
Velika Kladuša HR 41 Lq45
Velika Paklenica HR 41 Lq46
Velika Plana SCG 44 Mb46
Velika Plana SCG 46 Mb47
Velika Planina SCG 46 Mb48
Velika Slatina SCG 46 Ma48
Veliki Dal'nik UA 45 Ml44
Velikie Luki RUS 52 Mf17
Veliki Gradište SCG 44 Mb46
Veliki Grđevac HR 41 Ls45
Veliki kanal SCG 44 Lu45
Veliki Kupci SCG 46 Mb47
Veliki Morava SCG 46 Mb46
Veliki Novosilka UA 55 Mj22
Veliki Preslav BG 47 Mg47
Veliki Radinci SCG 44 Lu45
Veliki Šiljegovac SCG 46 Mb47
Veliki Zdenci HR 41 Ls45
Veliko Tărnovo BG 47 Mf47
Velille PE 279 Ge53
Velimlje SCG 46 Lt48
Vélingara SN 183 Kc38
Vélingara SN 183 Kc39
Velingrad BG 47 Me48
Veliž RUS 52 Mf18
Veljun HR 41 Lq45
Velká Bíteš CZ 38 Lr41
Vel'ké Kapušany SK 39 Mc42
Velké Losiny CZ 38 Ls40
Velké Meziříčí CZ 38 Lq41
Velkomstpynten N 11 Lg06
Velký Bor CZ 38 Lo41
Veľký Krtíš SK 39 Lu42
Veľký Šariš SK 39 Mb41
Veľký Tribeč SK 38 Lt42
Vella Lavella SOL 160 Sj49
Vellankulam CL 111 Pa42
Velletri I 42 Ln49
Vellinge S 15 Lo35
Vellmar D 32 Lk39
Vellore IND (TNU) 111 Ok40
Velloso RA (BA) 293 Ha64
Velmerstot D 32 Lj39
Velneshwar Beach IND 108 Og37
Vel'sk RUS 58 Na06
Velugodu IND (APH) 108 Ok38
Veluwezoom, N.P. NL 32 Lg38
Velventós GR 46 Mc50
Velyka Hluša UA 37 Mf39
Velyka Horodnycja UA 37 Mf40
Velyka Lepetycha UA 54 Mg22
Velyka Mychajlivka UA 45 Mk43
Velyka Pysarivka UA 52 Mh20
Velyki Dederkaly UA 54 Md21
Velyki Mosty UA 37 Me40
Velykoploske UA 45 Mk43
Velykyj Bereznyj UA 39 Mc42
Velykyj Burluk UA 53 Mj21
Veman S 13 Lo28
Vemb DK 14 Lj34
Vembanad Lake IND 110 Oj42
Vemdalen S 13 Lo28
Vemork N 12 Lj31
Vempalle IND (APH) 111 Ok39
Vemulavada IND 109 Ok36
Ven S 14 Ln35
Venable Ice Shelf 296 Fc33
Venado MEX (SLP) 253 Ek34
Venado Tuerto RA (SF) 289 Gk62
Venafro I 42 Lp49
Venâncio Aires BR (RS) 290 Hd60
Venarey-les Laumes F 23 Le43
Venčane SCG 44 Ma46
Vence F 25 Lh47
Venda Nova P 26 Kn51
Venda Nova do Imigrante BR (ES) 287 Hk56
Vendas Novas P 28 Km48
Vendée F 22 Kt44
Vendée F 22 Kt44
Vendeuvre-sur-Barse F 23 Le42
Vendôme F 22 Lb43
Venec BG 47 Mg47
Venetie USA (AK) 229 Cg12
Véneto I 40 Lm45
Venev RUS 53 Mk18
Veneza BR (PE) 283 Ja50
Veneza BR (PI) 277 Hj48
Venézia I 40 Ln45
Venezuela 263 Gb09
Venezuela Basin 260 Gf37
Vengurla IND (MHT) 108 Og38
Vengurla Beach IND 108 Og38
Veniaminof Volcano USA 228 Ca17
Venice I 40 Ln45
Venice USA (FL) 250 Fj32
Venice USA (LA) 243 Ff31
Vénissieux F 25 Le45
Venjan S 13 Lo30
Venjanssjön S 13 Lo30
Venkatagiri IND (APH) 111 Ok40
Venkatagirikota IND (APH) 111 Ok40
Venkatapuram IND (APH) 109 Pa36
Venlo NL 32 Lg39
Vennesla N 12 Lh32
Venosa I 43 Lq50
Venray NL 32 Lg39
Venta LT 17 Mc34
Venta LV 17 Mb33
Venta de Ballerias E 27 Ku51
Venta de Baños E 26 Kq51
Ventanas EC 272 Ga46
Ventania BR (PR) 286 He58
Vente LT 17 Mb35
Ventersburg ZA 217 Md60
Ventersdorp ZA 217 Md59
Venterstad ZA 217 Mc61
Ventilla BOL 284 Gg55
Ventimiglia I 40 Lh47
Ventisquero, Cerro RA 292 Ge66
Ventisquero Sur, Cerro RCH 292 Ge67
Ventspils LV 17 Mb33
Ventuari YV 269 Gg43
Ventura USA (CA) 236 Ea28
Venturosa BR (PE) 283 Jb50
Venu IND 108 Oe35
Veppur IND (TNU) 111 Ok41
Vera BR (MT) 281 Hc52
Vera E 29 Kt47
Vera RA (SF) 289 Gk60
Vera Cruz BR (BA) 283 Ja52
Veracruz MEX (VC) 254 Fb36
Veracruz MEX 254 Fb35
Veracruz NIC 256 Fg40
Vera Cruz do Oeste BR (PR) 286 Hd58
Veranópolis BR (RS) 290 He60
Veraval IND (GUJ) 108 Of35
Verbania I 40 Lj45
Verbeek Mountains RI 127 Ra47
Verbier CH 34 Lh44
Vercelli I 40 Lj45
Verchnjadzvinsk BY 52 Md18
Verchnje Syn'ovydne UA 39 Md41
Verchn'odniprovs'k UA 54 Mh21
Verdalsøra N 10 Lf14
Verde MEX 252 Eg32
Verde Island RP 121 Ra39
Verden (Aller) D 32 Lk38
Verdigre USA (NE) 240 Fa24
Verdon F 25 Lg47
Verdun F 23 Lf41
Verdún ROU 289 Hc62
Verdun-sur-le-Doubs F 25 Lf44
Vereeniging ZA 217 Md59
Verena ZA 213 Me58
Verenal CO 272 Gb44
Vergara ROU 289 Hd62
Vergato I 40 Lm46
Vergeleë ZA 213 Mc58
Vergemont AUS (QLD) 148 Sb57
Vergennes USA (VT) 247 Gd23
Vergina GR 46 Mc50
Vergt F 24 La45
Verhneimbatsk RUS 58 Pb06
Verhnetulomskoe Vodohranilišče RUS 11 Mf11
Verhnezejskaja ravnina RUS 59 Rb08
Verhnje Usugh RUS 91 Qh19
Verhnij Baskunčak RUS 53 Nd21
Verhnij Enisej RUS 85 Pg20
Verhnij Mel'gin RUS 98 Rf20
Véria GR 46 Mc50
Verila BG 46 Md48
Verín E 26 Kn51
Verinsko BG 46 Md48
Veriora EST 16 Mh32
Verkehrshaus CH 34 Lj43
Verkhoyanskiy Mountains RUS 59 Rb05
Verkykerskop ZA 217 Me59
Verl D 32 Lj39
Verla FIN 16 Mg29
Verlegenhuken N 11 Lj05
Vermandois F 23 Ld41
Vermelho BR 275 Hf49
Vermelho BR 276 Hg50
Vermelho BR 281 He53
Vermenton F 23 Ld43
Vermilion CDN (AB) 233 Ee19
Vermilion Bay CDN (ON) 238 Fd21
Vermilion Bay USA 243 Fe31
Vermilion Falls CDN 238 Fd23
Vermilion River CDN 233 Ed19
Vermillion USA (SD) 241 Fb24
Vermont USA 247 Gd23
Vernadsky ANT (UA) 296 Gc32
Vernal USA (UT) 235 Ef25
Vernazza I 40 Lk46
Vernești RO 45 Mg45
Verneuil-sur-Avre F 22 La42
Verneuk Pan ZA 216 Ma60
Vernoe RUS 98 Re20
Vernon CDN (BC) 232 Ea20
Vernon F 23 Lb41
Vernon USA (TX) 242 Fa28
Vernon USA (UT) 235 Ed25
Vernon Islands AUS 139 Rf52
Vero F 31 Lk48
Vero Beach USA (FL) 250 Fk32
Verona I 40 Lm45
Véronica RA (BA) 289 Hb63
Ver-o-Peso (Belém) BR (PA) 276 Hf46
Versailles F 23 Lc42
Versailles USA (MO) 241 Fd26
Versailles USA (IN) 246 Fh26
Versailles USA (KY) 249 Fh26
Versalles CO 268 Gb43
Veršino-Darasunskij RUS 91 Qh19
Versmold D 32 Lj38
Vertelim RUS 53 Nc18
Vertentes BR (PE) 283 Jc49
Vertijivka UA 52 Mf20
Vertintes C 259 Ga35
Vertisko GR 46 Md50
Vértiz RA (LP) 288 Gj63
Vertjačij RUS 53 Nb21
Vertus F 23 Le42
Verulam ZA 217 Mf60
Verviers B 23 Lf40
Vervins F 23 Ld41
Vesanka FIN 16 Mf28
Ves'egonsk RUS 52 Mj16
Vesele UA 55 Mh22
Veselí Kut UA 45 Mk44
Veselí nad Lužnicí CZ 38 Lp41
Veselí nad Moravou CZ 38 Ls42
Veseloe RUS 37 Lu36
Veselovskoe Vodohranilišče RUS 55 Na22
Veselynove UA 54 Mf22
Vešenskaja RUS 53 Na21
Vesoul F 23 Lg43
Vespaciano BR (MG) 287 Hj55
Vessigebro S 14 Ln34
Vestby N 12 Ll31
Veste Coburg D 35 Ll40
Vesterålen N 10 Lh11
Vesterli N 10 Lh12
Vesterø Havn DK 14 Ll33
Vesterøy N 12 Ll31
Vestfjorden N 10 Lg12
Vestfonna N 11 Lk06
Vestiges préhistoriques et Peintures rupestres RN 180 Le35
Vestmannaeyjar IS 10 Jk14
Vestnes N 12 Lh28
Vestvågøy N 10 Lg11
Vesúvio I 42 Lp50
Veszprém H 38 Ls43
Vețel RO 44 Mc45
Vetlanda S 15 Lq33
Vetluga RUS 53 Nc17
Vetluga RUS 53 Nd17
Vetrişoaia RO 45 Mj44
Větrný Jeníkov CZ 38 Lq41
Veulettes-sur-Mer F 22 La41
Veurne B 23 Lc39
Vevelstad = Forvika N 10 Lg13
Vevey CH 34 Lg44
Vévi GR 46 Mb50
Veymandhoo MV 110 Og44
Veymandhoo Channel MV 110 Og44
Veynes F 25 Lf46
Veys IR 72 Ne30
Vézelay F 23 Ld43
Vézère F 24 Lb45
Vezirköprü TR 62 Mh25
V. Guerrero MEX (BC) 236 Ec29
V. Guerrero MEX (ZCT) 253 Ej34
Vi S 13 Ls28
Via Áppia I 42 Ln49
Viacha BOL 284 Gf54
Viadana I 40 Ll46
Viaduc-de-Garabit F 25 Ld46
Viaducto la Polvorilla RA 284 Gg58
Viadutos BR (RS) 290 Hd59
Vialadougou CI 192 Kg41
Viale RA (ER) 289 Ha61
Via Lemovicensis F 24 La45
Via Mala CH 34 Lk44
Viamonte RA (CD) 288 Gj62
Viana ANG 202 Lg50
Viana BR (ES) 287 Hk56
Viana BR (MA) 276 Hh47
Viana BR (PA) 275 He46
Viana E 27 Ks52
Viana de Bolo E 26 Kn52
Viana do Alentejo P 28 Kn48
Viana do Castelo P 26 Km51
Vianden L 23 Lg41
Vianen NL 32 Lf39
Viangchan LAO 115 Qb36
Vianópolis BR (GO) 286 Hf54
Via Podiensis F 24 Lb46
Viaréggio I 40 Ll47
Vias F 25 Ld47
Viaté G 195 Lf45
Via Tolosana F 24 Lc47
Via Turonensis F 22 La44
Vibble S 15 Lt33
Viborg DK 14 Lk34
Vibo Valéntia I 43 Lr52
Vibraye F 22 La42
Vic E 30 Lc49
Vicam MEX (SO) 252 Ee32
Vicdessos F 24 Lb48
Vic-en-Bigorre F 24 La47
Vicente Guerrero MEX (BC) 236 Ec30
Vicente Guerrero MEX (DGO) 253 Ej34
Vicentinópolis BR (GO) 286 Hf54
Vicenza I 40 Lm45
Vichada CO 269 Gf43
Vichadero ROU 289 Hc61
Viche EC 272 Ga45
Vichina RA 288 Gf60
Vichy F 25 Ld44
Vichy-Bellerive F 25 Ld44
Vici USA (OK) 242 Fa27
Vicksburg USA (MS) 243 Fe29
Vic-le-Comte F 25 Ld45
Vic-le-Fesq F 25 Le47
Vico F 31 Lj48
Viçosa BR (AL) 283 Jb50
Viçosa BR (MG) 287 Hj56
Viçosa do Ceará BR (CE) 277 Hk47
Vicovu de Jos RO 45 Mf43
Vic-sur-Cère F 25 Lc46
Victor USA (ID) 235 Ee24
Victor Harbour AUS (SA) 152 Rk63
Victoria AUS 136 Sa26
Victoria = Limbé CAM 194 Le43
Victoria CDN (BC) 232 Dj21
Victoria CO 268 Gc43
Victoria M 42 Lp54
Victoria RA (ER) 289 Gk62
Victoria RA (LP) 292 Gh64
Victoria RCH 292 Gd65
Victoria RO 45 Me45
Victoria RO 45 Mh43
Victoria RP 121 Ra39
Victoria SY 219 Nh48
Victoria USA (TX) 243 Fb31
Victoria Terminus = Chhatrapati Shivaji Station IND (MHT) 108 Og36
Victoria Beach CDN (MB) 238 Fb20
Victoria Bryant S.P. USA 249 Fj28
Victoria Falls Z/ZW 213 Mc54
Victoria Falls ZW 209 Mc54
Victoria Highway AUS 139 Re53
Victoria Island CDN 224 Eb04
Victoria Lake CDN 245 Hb21
Victoria Land ANT 297 Tb33
Victoria Memorial IND 112 Pe34
Victoria, Mount MYA 112 Pg35
Victoria, Mount NZ 155 Tg67
Victoria, Mount PNG 159 Sd50
Victoria Nile EAU 204 Mg45
Victoria Nile EAU 204 Mf44
Victoria Park Racecourse (SA) 152 Rk63
Victoria River AUS (NT) 139 Rf53
Victoria River AUS 139 Rf53
Victoria River CDN 245 Hb21
Victoria River Downs AUS (NT) 139 Rf54
Victorias RP 123 Rb40
Victoria Strait CDN 224 Ed05
Victoriaville CDN (QC) 244 Ge22
Victoria West ZA 216 Mb61

Victorino – Völklinger Hütte

Victorino C 259 Gb35
Victor, Mount 297 Mc33
Victor Rosales MEX (ZCT) 253 Ej34
Victorville USA (CA) 236 Eb28
Victory, Mount PNG 159 Se50
Vičuga RUS 53 Na17
Vicuña RCH 288 Ge61
Vicuña Mackenna RA (CD) 288 Gh62
Vicus PE 272 Fk48
Vida USA (MT) 235 Eh22
Vida USA (OR) 234 Dj23
Vidal PE 273 Gd47
Vidal USA (CA) 236 Ec28
Vidalia USA (GA) 249 Fj29
Vidal Junction USA (CA) 236 Ec28
Vidamlja BY 37 Md38
Vidauban F 25 Lg47
Videbæk DK 14 Lj34
Videira BR (SC) 290 He59
Videle RO 45 Mf46
Videsæter N 12 Lh29
Vidice CZ 38 Ln41
Vidigueira P 28 Kn48
Vidin BG 46 Mc47
Vidisha IND (MPH) 109 Oj34
Vidiškiai LT 17 Me35
Vidneva BY 17 Mg36
Vidsel S 10 Ma13
Viduša BIH 41 Lt48
Vidzeme LV 17 Mf33
Vidzy BY 17 Mg35
Viechtach D 35 Ln41
Viedgesville ZA 217 Me61
Viedma RA (RN) 293 Gj66
Viedma, Volcán RA 294 Gd70
Vieille Chapelle (Tadoussac) CDN 244 Gf21
Viejo RA 288 Gj60
Viejo, Volcán NIC 256 Fg39
Viekšniai LT 17 Mc34
Vielha E 30 La48
Vielsalm B 23 Lf40
Vienenburg D 33 Ll39
Vieng Kham LAO 113 Qb35
Vieng Phukha LAO 113 Qa35
Vieng Thong LAO 113 Qb35
Vieng Xai LAO 96 Qc35
Vienna A 35 Lr42
Vienna USA (IL) 243 Ff27
Vienna USA (MO) 241 Fe26
Vienna USA (OH) 247 Fk26
Vienne F 22 La43
Vienne F 25 Le45
Vieques USA 261 Gh36
Viernheim D 34 Lj41
Viersen D 32 Lg39
Vierwaldstätter See CH 34 Lj44
Vierzehnheiligen D 35 Lm40
Vierzon F 23 Lc43
Viesca MEX (COH) 253 Ej33
Viesīte LV 17 Mf34
Vieste I 43 Lr49
Vietas S 10 Lk12
Vietnam VN 57 Qa08
Viet Tri VN 96 Qc35
Vieux Bordeaux F 24 Ku46
Vieux Fort WL 261 Gk39
View Point (Fish River Canyon) NAM 216 Lj59
Vif F 25 Lf45
Viga RP 121 Rc39
Vigala EST 16 Me32
Vigan RP 120 Ra37
Vigeland N 12 Lh32
Vigévano I 40 Lj45
Vigia BR (PA) 276 Hf46
Vigía Chico MEX (QTR) 255 Fg36
Vignola I 40 Ll46
Vigo E 26 Km52
Vigra N 12 Lg28
Vigrestad N 12 Lf32
Vihanti FIN 11 Mc13
Vihari PK 79 Og30
Vihiers F 22 Ku43
Vihotraivo RM 220 Ne54
Vihtari FIN 16 Mk28
Vihti FIN 16 Me30
Viiala FIN 16 Md29
Viira EST 16 Md32
Viisarimäki FIN 16 Mg28
Viișoara RO 45 Mg44
Viitasaari FIN 11 Mc14
Viitna EST 16 Mg31
Viivikonna EST 16 Mh31
Vijayapuri North IND (APH) 109 Ok37
Vijayawada IND (APH) 109 Pa37
Vijaydurg IND (MHT) 108 Og37
Vijaydurg Beach IND 108 Og37
Vijosë AL 46 Ma50
Vik IS 10 Ka14
Vik S 15 Lp35
Vika S 13 Lp30
Vikajärvi FIN 11 Md12
Vikanes N 12 Lf30
Vikarabad IND (APH) 108 Oj37
Vikarbyn S 13 Lq30
Vikedal N 12 Lf31
Vikeke TLS 132 Rd50
Viken S 14 Ln34
Vikenara Point SOL 161 Sk50
Vikersund N 12 Lk31
Vikevåg N 12 Lf31
Vikindu EAT 207 Mk49
Viking CDN (AB) 233 Ee19
Vikingskipet N 12 Lm30
Vikna N 10 Lf13
Vikno UA 45 Mf42
Vikos-Aoos N.P. GR 48 Ma51
Vikran N 10 Lk11
Viksjö S 13 Ls28
Viksøyri N 12 Lg29
Vila Aurora BR (PA) 276 Hg47
Vila Bela da São Trinidade BR (MT) 280 Ha53
Vila Capixabas BR (AC) 279 Gg51
Vila Conceição BR (PA) 276 Hg47
Vila de Manica MOC 214 Mg55
Vila de Rei P 28 Km49
Vila de Sena MOC 211 Mh54
Vila do Bispo P 28 Km47
Vila do Maio CV 182 Jj38
Vila dos Remédios BR (RN) 277 Jd47
Vila Flor ANG 208 Lh52
Vila Flor P 26 Kn51
Vilafranca del Maestrat E 29 Ku50
Vilafranca del Penedès E 30 Lb49
Vila Franca de Xira P 28 Km48
Vilagarcía de Arousa E 26 Km52
Vilaine F 22 Ks43
Viļaka LV 17 Mh33
Vilakalaka VU 162 Td53
Vilalba = Villalba E 26 Kn53
Vila Martins BR (AM) 279 Gf49
Vila Meriti BR (AM) 274 Ha48
Vila Mouzinho MOC 210 Mh53
Vila Nazaré BR (AM) 274 Gh47
Viļāni LV 17 Mg34
Vilankulo MOC 214 Mh57
Vilano Beach USA (FL) 250 Fk31
Vila Nova ANG 208 Lj52
Vila Nova da Fronteira MOC 211 Mh54
Vila Nova de Famalição P 26 Km51
Vila Nova de Foz Côa P 26 Kn51
Vila Nova de Milfontes P 28 Km47
Vila Nova de Paiva P 26 Kn50
Vila Nova do Piauí BR (PI) 277 Hk49
Vila Nova do Seles ANG 208 Lh51
Vilanova i la Geltrú E 30 Lb49
Vila Nova Sintra CV 182 Jh38
Vila Palestina BR (PA) 276 Hg48
Vila Porto Franco BR (AM) 274 Ha49
Vila Pouca de Aguiar P 26 Kn51
Vilar P 26 Kn50
Vila-real E 29 Ku49
Vila Real P 26 Kn51
Vila Real de Santo Antonio P 28 Kn47
Vilar Formoso P 26 Ko50
Vila Rica BR (MS) 286 Hc57
Vila Rica BR (MT) 281 He51
Vilarinho do Monte BR (PA) 275 Hd46
Vila Sagrado Coração de Jesus BR (AM) 274 Ha48
Vila Tambaquí BR (AM) 274 Gh47
Vila Tepequem BR (RR) 270 Gk44
Vilattikulam IND (TNU) 111 Ok42
Vila Tugendhat CZ 38 Lr41
Vila Valério BR (ES) 287 Hk55
Vila Velha BR (AP) 271 He44
Vila Velha BR (ES) 287 Hk56
Vila Velha BR 286 He58
Vila Velha de Ródão P 28 Kn49
Vila Verde de Ficalho P 28 Kn47
Vila Viçosa P 28 Kn48
Vilcabamba EC 272 Ga48
Vilcabamba Viejo PE 278 Gd52
Vilcashuamán PE 278 Gd52
Vilcas Huaman PE 278 Gd52
Vilches E 29 Kr48
Vilcún RCH 292 Gd65
Vilcún RCH 292 Gd65
Vildbjerg DK 14 Lj34
Vilejka BY 17 Mg36
Vilelas RA (SE) 289 Gj59
Vilhelmina S 10 Lj13
Vilhena BR (RO) 280 Gk52
Viligili MV 110 Og45
Vilija BY 17 Mg36
Viljandi EST 16 Mf32
Viljoenskroon ZA 217 Md59
Viljuj RUS 59 Ra06
Viljujsk RUS 59 Ra06
Viljujskoe plato RUS 59 Qc05
Viljujskoe vodohranilišče RUS 59 Qc06
Vilkaviškis LT 17 Md36
Vilkija LT 17 Md35
Villa Abecia BOL 284 Gh56
Villa Adriana I 42 Ln49
Villa Ahumada MEX (CHH) 237 Eg30
Villa Alegre RCH 292 Ge63
Villa Alemana RCH 288 Ge62
Villa Alhué RCH 288 Ge62
Villa Amengual RCH 292 Gd68
Villa Ana RA (SF) 289 Ha60
Villa Angela RA (CH) 289 Gk59
Villa Atamisqui RA (SE) 288 Gj60
Villa Atuel RA (MD) 288 Gg63
Villa Azueta MEX (VC) 254 Fc36
Villaba RP 123 Rc40
Villa Berthet RA (CH) 289 Gk59
Villablino E 26 Ko52
Villa Bruzual YV 269 Gf41
Villa Bustos RA (LR) 288 Gg60
Villacañas E 29 Kr49
Villa Cañas RA (SF) 289 Gk63
Villacarillo E 29 Kr48
Villa Carlos Paz RA (CD) 288 Gh61
Villacarriedo E 27 Kr53
Villacastín E 26 Kq50
Villach A 35 Lo44
Villacidro I 31 Lj51
Villa Constitución RA (SF) 289 Gk62
Villada E 26 Kq52
Villadama MEX (NL) 253 Ek32
Villa de Arista MEX (SLP) 253 Ek34
Villa de Cura YV 269 Gg40
Villa de Guadelupe MEX (CAM) 255 Fe36
Villa del Carmén ROU 289 Hb62
Villa de Leyva CO 268 Gd43
Villa del Río E 28 Kq47
Villa del Rosario RA (CD) 288 Gj61
Villa del Totoral RA (CD) 288 Gh61
Villa de Maria RA (CD) 288 Gj60
Villa de Reyes MEX (SLP) 254 Ek35
Villa d'Este I 42 Ln49
Villa de Zaachila MEX (OAX) 254 Fb37
Villadiego E 27 Kq52
Villa Dolores RA (CD) 288 Gh61
Villa Dos Trece RA (FO) 289 Ha59
Villa El Chocón RA (NE) 292 Gf65
Villa Elisa RA (ER) 289 Ha62
Villa Escalante MEX (MHC) 254 Ek36
Villa Figueroa RA (SE) 288 Gj59
Villaflores MEX (CHP) 255 Fd37
Villa Florida PY 289 Hb59
Villa Foscari I 40 Ln45
Villa Franca PY 289 Ha59
Villafranca del Bierzo E 26 Ko52
Villafranca de los Barros E 28 Ko48
Villafranca de los Caballeros E 29 Kr49
Villafranca di Verona I 40 Ll45
Villafranco del Guadalquivir E 28 Ko47
Villa General Belgrano RA (CD) 288 Gh62
Villa General Güemes RA (FO) 285 Ha58
Villa General M.Belgrano RA (FO) 285 Ha58
Villa General Roca RA (SL) 288 Gg62
Villages de Pygmés RDC 201 Me45
Villa Gesell RA (BA) 293 Hb64
Villa Gobernador Gálvez RA (SF) 289 Gk62
Villa González Ortega MEX (ZCT) 253 Ek34
Villa Guadelupe MEX (SO) 236 Ed30
Villaguay RA (ER) 289 Ha61
Villa Guillermina RA (SF) 289 Ha60
Villaharta E 28 Kq48
Villahermosa E 29 Ks48
Villahermosa MEX (CAM) 255 Ff37
Villa Hermosa MEX (SO) 236 Ed30
Villahermosa MEX (TB) 255 Fd36
Villa Hidalgo MEX (JLC) 254 Ej35
Villahoz E 27 Kr52
Villa Huidobro RA (CD) 288 Gh63
Villa Hvitträsk FIN 16 Me30
Villa Iris RA (BA) 293 Gj65
Villa Jesús Maria MEX (BC) 236 Ed31
Villa Jovis I 42 Lp50
Villajoyosa = La Vila Joiosa E 29 Ku48
Villa Juárez MEX (AGS) 253 Ej34
Villa Juárez MEX (SO) 252 Ef32
Villa Junqueiro MOC 211 Mj53
Villa Krause RA (SJ) 288 Gf61
Villa La Angostura RA (NE) 292 Ge66
Villa Larca RA (SL) 288 Gh62
Villalba = Vilalba E 26 Kn53
Villa Lola YV 270 Gj42
Villalón de Campos E 26 Kp52
Villalonga RA (BA) 293 Gj65
Villa López MEX (CHH) 253 Eh32
Villalpando E 26 Kp51
Villa Madero MEX (CAM) 255 Fe36
Villa Mainero MEX (TM) 253 Fa33
Villamalea E 29 Kt49
Villamanrique E 29 Kr48
Villa María RA (CD) 288 Gj62
Villa Martín BOL 284 Gg56
Villamartín E 28 Kp46
Villa Mascardi RA (RN) 292 Ge66
Villa Matamoros MEX (CHH) 253 Eh32
Villamayor E 27 Ku51
Villamayor de Santiago E 29 Ks49
Villa Mazán RA (LR) 288 Gg60
Villa Media Agua RA (SJ) 288 Gf61
Villa Mercedes RA (SL) 288 Gh62
Villa Minetti RA (SF) 289 Gk60
Villa M.Moreno RA (TU) 288 Gh59
Villa Montes BOL 285 Gj56
Villandraut F 24 Ku46
Villandry F 22 La43
Villa Nova de Cerveira P 26 Km51
Villanubla E 26 Kq51
Villanueva BOL 279 Gh51
Villanueva CO 268 Gd40
Villanueva HN 256 Fg38
Villanueva MEX (ZCT) 253 Ej34
Villanueva NIC 256 Fg39
Villa Nueva RA (MD) 288 Gf62
Villa Nueva RA (SJ) 288 Gf61
Villanueva de Alcorón E 29 Ks50
Villanueva de Argaño E 27 Kr52
Villanueva de Córdoba E 28 Kq48
Villanueva de Gállego E 27 Ku51
Villanueva de la Fuente E 29 Ks48
Villanueva de la Jura E 29 Kt49
Villanueva de la Serena E 28 Kp48
Villanueva de la Sierra E 28 Ko50
Villanueva de las Torres E 29 Kr47
Villanueva del Campo E 26 Kp51
Villanueva del Fresno E 28 Kn48
Villanueva del Huerva E 27 Kt51
Villanueva de los Castillejos E 28 Kn47
Villanueva de los Infantes E 29 Kr48
Villanueva del Río y Minas E 28 Kp47
Villány H 41 Lt45
Villa Ocampo RA (SF) 289 Ha60
Villa O'Higgins RCH 295 Gd70
Villa Ojo de Agua RA (SE) 288 Gj60
Villa Ortega RCH 292 Ge68
Villapalacios E 29 Ks48
Villa Paranacito RA (ER) 289 Ha62
Villapinzon CO 268 Gd43
Villaputzu I 31 Lk51
Villard RH 260 Gd36
Villard-de-Lans F 25 Lf45
Villardeciervos E 26 Ko51
Villar de Domingo Garcia E 29 Ks50
Villardefrades E 26 Kp51
Villar del Arzobispo E 29 Ku49
Villar del Rey E 28 Ko49
Villareal de los Infantes = Vila-real E 29 Ku49
Villa Reducción RA (CD) 288 Gj62
Villa Regina RA (RN) 292 Gg65
Villarejo de Fuentes E 29 Ks49
Villarejo de Salvanés E 29 Kr50
Villarente E 26 Kp52
Villarmayor E 26 Kp51
Villa Romana del Casale I 42 Lp53
Villarpando DOM 260 Ge36
Villarrica PY 285 Hb58
Villarrica RCH 292 Gd65
Villarrica, P.N. RCH 292 Ge65
Villarrica, Volcán RCH 292 Gd65
Villarrín de Campos E 26 Kp51
Villarrobledo E 29 Ks49
Villarroya de la Sierra E 27 Kt51
Villarrubia de los Ojos E 29 Kr49
Villars CH 34 Lh44
Villars-les-Dombes F 25 Lf45
Villarta de los Montes E 28 Kq49
Villarti IND (APH) 109 Pa37
Villasalto I 31 Lk51
Villasana de Mena E 27 Kr53
Villa Sánchez Magallanes MEX (TB) 255 Fd36
Villa San Giovanni I 43 Lq52
Villa San José de Vinchina RA (LR) 288 Gf60
Villa San Martin = Cuidad de Loreto RA (SE) 288 Gh60
Villa Santa Maria I 42 Lp49
Villa Serano BOL 285 Gh55
Villasimius I 31 Lk51
Villa Trinidad RA (SF) 289 Gk61
Villa Tunari BOL 284 Gh54
Villa Unión MEX (DGO) 253 Eh34
Villa Unión MEX (SL) 252 Eg34
Villa Unión RA (LR) 288 Gf60
Villa Valeria RA (CD) 288 Gh63
Villa Vásquez DOM 260 Ge36
Villavicencio CO 268 Gd43
Villaviciosa E 26 Kp53
Villaviciosa RP 121 Ra37
Villaviciosa de Córdoba E 28 Kp48
Villa Viscarra BOL 284 Gh54
Villa Ygatimi PY 286 Hc58
Villazón BOL 284 Gh57
Villedieu-les-Poêles F 22 Kt42
Villedieu-sur-Indre F 22 Lb44
Villefort F 25 Ld46
Villefranche-de-Conflent F 24 Lc48
Villefranche-de-Lauragais F 24 Lb47
Villefranche-de-Rouergue F 24 Lc46
Villefranche-du-Périgord F 24 Lb46
Villefranche-sur-Cher F 22 Lb43
Villefranche-sur-Mer F 25 Lh47
Villefranche-sur-Saône F 25 Le45
Ville-Marie CDN (QC) 247 Ga22
Villena E 29 Ku48
Villeneuve F 24 Lc46
Villeneuve-lès-Avignon F 25 Le47
Villeneuve-sur-Lot F 24 La46
Villeneuve-sur-Yonne F 23 Ld42
Ville Platte USA (LA) 243 Fd30
Villeréal F 24 La46
Villeroy CDN (QC) 244 Ge22
Villers-Bocage F 22 Ku41
Villers-Bocage F 23 Lc41
Villers- Bretonneux F 23 Lc41
Villers-Cotterêts F 23 Ld41
Villersexel F 23 Lg43
Villerupt F 23 Lf41
Villeurbanne F 25 Le45
Villiers ZA 217 Me59
Villiers-Saint-Georges F 23 Ld42
Villingen-Schwenningen D 34 Lj42
Villupuram IND (TNU) 111 Ok41
Vilnius LT 17 Mf36
Vil'njans'k UA 55 Mh22
Vil'nohirs'k UA 54 Mh21
Vilppula FIN 16 Me28
Vils D 35 Lm41
Vils D 35 Ln42
Vilsandi rahvuspark EST 16 Mb32
Vil'šanka UA 45 Mj42
Vil'šany UA 53 Mh20
Vilsbiburg D 35 Ln42
Vilshofen D 35 Lo42
Vimianzo E 26 Km53
Vimioso P 26 Ko51
Vimmerby S 15 Lq33
Vimoutiers F 22 La42
Vina CAM 195 Lh42
Vinac BIH 41 Ls46
Viña del Mar RCH 288 Ge62
Vinanivao RM 219 Nf53
Vinaròs E 30 La50
Vinay F 25 Lf45
Vincennes USA (IL) 248 Fg26
Vincennes Bay 297 Qb32
Vincent USA (TX) 242 Ek29
Vicente Noble DOM 260 Ge36
Vinces EC 272 Ga46
Vindeln S 10 Lk13
Vinderup DK 14 Lj34
Vindex AUS (QLD) 148 Sb57
Vindhya Range IND 108 Oj34
Vindö S 13 Lt31
Vindrej RUS 53 Nb18
Vinegar Hill USA 234 Dk23
Vineland USA (CO) 237 Eh26
Vineland USA (NJ) 247 Gc26
Vinga RO 44 Mb44
Vingåker S 13 Lq31
Vinh VN 115 Qc36
Vinhais P 26 Ko51
Vinh Cam Ranh VN 115 Qe40
Vinh Chao VN 115 Qe39
Vinh Da Nang VN 115 Qe37
Vinh Duang Quat VN 115 Qe38
Vinh Hy VN 115 Qe40
Vinh Loc VN 96 Qc35
Vinh Long VN 117 Qc40
Vinh Moc Tunnel VN 115 Qd37
Vinh Padaran VN 115 Qe40
Vinh Phan Ri VN 115 Qe40
Vinh Phan Thiet VN 115 Qe40
Vinh Rach Gia VN 117 Qc41
Vinh Son VN 115 Qe38
Vinh Trang Pagoda VN 115 Qd40
Vinh Van Phong VN 115 Qe39
Vinica MK 46 Mc49
Vinište BG 46 Md47
Vinita USA (OK) 243 Fc27
Vinje N 12 Lg30
Vinkovci HR 44 Lt45
Vinnycja UA 54 Me21
Vinograd BG 47 Mf47
Vinön S 13 Lq31
Vinon-sur-Verdon F 25 Lf47
Vinslöv S 15 Lo34
Vinson Massif 296 Fd34
Vinstra N 12 Lk29
Vintar RP 121 Ra36
Vintermarknad S 10 Lk12
Vinukonda IND (APH) 109 Ok37
Vinza RCB 202 Lh47
Violet Town AUS (VIC) 153 Sc64
Violet Valley A.L. AUS 138 Rd54
Vioolsdrif ZA 216 Lj60
Viphya Mountains MW 210 Mg51
Vipiteno = Sterzing I 40 Lm44
Vir HR 41 Lq46
Virac RP 121 Rc39
Virachey K 115 Qd39
Virachey N.P. K 115 Qd38
Viralimalai IND (TNU) 111 Ok41
Viramgam IND (GUJ) 108 Og34
Viranşehir TR 63 Mk27
Virar IND (MHT) 108 Og36
Virarajendrapet IND (KTK) 110 Oh40
Virawah PK 81 Of33
Virazon RA 293 Ha65
Virazon RA 293 Ha65
Virbalis LT 17 Mc36
Virden CDN (MB) 238 Ek21
Vire F 22 Ku42
Virei ANG 208 Lg53
Vireši LV 17 Mg33
Virf Cindrel RO 44 Md45
Virf Fâncelul RO 45 Mf44
Virf Svinecea RO 44 Mc46
Virgem da Lapa BR (MG) 287 Hj54
Virgin Gorda GB 261 Gh36
Virginia AUS (SA) 152 Rk63
Virginia IRL 18 Kn37
Virginia USA (MN) 241 Fd22
Virginia USA 227 Ga11
Virginia USA 227 Ga11
Virginia ZA 217 Md60
Virginia Beach USA (VA) 249 Gb27
Virginia City USA (MT) 235 Ee23
Virginia City USA (NV) 234 Ea26
Virgin Islands GB 261 Gh36
Virgin Islands GB/USA 261 Gh36
Virgin Is. N.P. USA 261 Gh36
Virginópolis BR (MG) 287 Hj55
Virgin Passage USA 261 Gh36
Virihaure S 10 Lj12
Virkby = Virkkala FIN 16 Md30
Virkkala = Virkby FIN 16 Md30
Virklund DK 14 Lk34
Virojoki FIN 16 Mh30
Virolahden FIN 16 Mh30
Viroqua USA (WI) 241 Fe24
Virovitica HR 41 Ls45
Virpazar SCG 46 Lu48
Virrat FIN 16 Md28
Virsbo S 13 Lq31
Virserum S 15 Lq33
Virsko More HR 41 Lp46
Virtasalmi FIN 16 Mh28
Virton B 23 Lf41
Virtsu EST 16 Md32
Virttaa FIN 16 Mc30
Virú PE 278 Ga50
Viruá, P.N. do BR 274 Gk45
Virudó CO 268 Gb43
Virudunagar IND (TNU) 111 Oj42
Virunga, P.N.des RDC 201 Me46
Vis HR 41 Lr47
Vis HR 41 Lr48
Visaginas LT 17 Mg35
Visalaukė LT 17 Mf36
Visalia USA (CA) 236 Ea27
Visarwari IND (MHT) 108 Oh35
Visayan Sea RP 123 Rb40
Visayas RP 119 Ra16
Visby S 15 Lt33
Vischering D 32 Lh39
Visconde do Rio Branco BR (MG) 287 Hj56
Viscount Melville Sound CDN 225 Ec04
Viscri RO 45 Mf44
Visé B 23 Lf40
Višegrad BIH 46 Lu47
Viseisei FJI 163 Tj54
Viseu BR (PA) 276 Hg46
Viseu P 26 Kn50
Vișeu RO 44 Me43
Vișeu de Sus RO 44 Me43
Vishakhapatnam IND (APH) 109 Pb37
Vishalla Village IND 108 Og34
Vishnupur IND (WBG) 112 Pd34
Vishwa Shanti Stupa IND 109 Pc33
Vișina RO 47 Me47
Visingö S 15 Lp32
Visita BR (MT) 274 Ha49
Viskafors S 15 Ln33
Viskån S 14 Ln33
Vislanda S 15 Lp34
Visočica HR 41 Lq46
Viso del Marqués E 29 Kr48
Visoki Dečani SCG 46 Ma48
Visoko BIH 41 Lt47
Visp CH 34 Lh44
Vis Rivier NAM 212 Lj58
Vis Rivier NAM 216 Lj60
Visrivier ZA 217 Mc61
Vissannapeta IND (APH) 109 Pa37
Vissefjärda S 15 Lq34
Visselhövede D 32 Lk38
Vista Alegre BR (AM) 273 Gg46
Vista Alegre BR (AM) 274 Gh46
Vistabella del Maestrat E 29 Ku50
Viste Alegre ANG 202 Lh50
Vistula PL 37 Lu38
Vistula Lagoon PL/RUS 37 Lu36
Vištytis LT 17 Mc36
Visuvesi FIN 16 Md28
Visvisu Point SOL 161 Sj49
Vit BG 47 Me47
Vita IND (MHT) 108 Oh37
Vitalo F (GF) 271 Hd44
Vitebsk BY 52 Mf18
Viterbo I 42 Ln48
Vitez BIH 41 Ls46
Vi Thanh VN 117 Qc41
Vithkuq AL 46 Mb50
Vitiaz I Deep 302 Sa08
Vitiaz II Deep 137 Ub23
Vitiaz III Deep 137 Ua25
Vitiaz Strait PNG 159 Sd48
Vitiaz Trench 134 Ta10
Vitichi BOL 284 Gh56
Vitigudino E 26 Ko50
Viti Levu FJI 163 Tj55
Vitim RUS 59 Qc08
Vitim RUS 91 Qg19
Vitimskoe ploskogo RUS 91 Qg19
Vitina SCG 46 Mb48
Vitolište MK 46 Mb49
Vitor PE 284 Ge54
Vitória BR (ES) 287 Hk56
Vitoria BR (PA) 275 Hd47
Vitória da Conquista BR (BA) 283 Hk53
Vitória de Santo Antão BR (PE) 283 Jc50
Vitoria do Mearim BR (MA) 276 Hh47
Vitoria-Gasteiz E 27 Ks52
Vitória Seamount 265 Ja23
Vitorino BR (PR) 290 Hd59
Vitorino Freire BR (MA) 276 Hh48
Vitoša, N.P. BG 46 Md48
Vitré F 22 Kt42
Vitrolles F 25 Lf47
Vitry-le-François F 23 Le42
Vitshumbi RDC 201 Me46
Vitteaux F 23 Le43
Vittel F 23 Lf42
Vittória I 42 Lp54
Vittorio Véneto I 40 Ln45
Vittsjö S 15 Lo34
Viù I 40 Lh45
Viv RUS 58 Pd05
Vivario F 31 Lk48
Viveiro E 26 Kn53
Vivian CDN (MB) 238 Fb21
Vivian USA (SD) 240 Ek24
Viviers F 25 Le46
Vivo ZA 214 Me57
Vivonne F 22 La44
Viwa FJI 163 Tj54
Vizcaino MEX (BCS) 252 Ed32
Vize TR 50 Mh49
Vizianagaram IND (APH) 109 Pb36
Vizille F 25 Lf45
Viziru RO 45 Mh45
Vizovice CZ 38 Ls41
Vizzini I 42 Lp53
Vjalikija Matykaly BY 37 Md38
Vjartsilja RUS 11 Mf14
Vjatka RUS 53 Nf17
Vjatskie Poljany RUS 53 Nf17
Vjatskoe RUS 53 Na17
Vjazemskij RUS 98 Rh22
Vjaz'ma RUS 52 Mh18
Vjazniki RUS 53 Nb17
Vlădeni RO 45 Mg43
Vlădeni RO 45 Mh43
Vladikavkaz RUS (SOA) 70 Nc24
Vladimir RUS 53 Na17
Vladimir SCG 46 Lu48
Vladimirovo BG 46 Md47
Vladimirovo RUS 99 Sb21
Vladivostok RUS 100 Rf24
Vlad Tepeș RO 45 Mh46
Vlagtwedde NL 32 Lh37
Vlaháta GR 48 Ma52
Vlaháva GR 46 Mb51
Vlahiá GR 48 Md52
Vlăhița RO 45 Mf44
Vlaming Head Lighthouse AUS 140 Qh56
Vlasenica BIH 46 Lt46
Vlašim CZ 38 Lp41
Vlașin RO 45 Mf46
Vlasotince SCG 46 Mc48
Vlieland NL 32 Lf37
Vlissingen NL 32 Ld39
Vlkolinec SK 39 Lu41
Vlorë AL 46 Lu50
Vlotho D 32 Lj38
Vltava CZ 38 Lp41
Vobkent UZ 76 Oc25
Vöcklabruck A 35 Lo42
Vodice HR 41 Lq47
Vodil UZ 77 Of25
Vodlozersky N.P. RUS 11 Mj14
Vodňany CZ 38 Lp41
vodní nádrž Hracholusky CZ 38 Lo41
vodní nádrž Lipno CZ 38 Lp42
Vodnjan HR 41 Lo46
vodoschovyšče Sjalec BY 37 Me38
Vodskov DK 14 Ll33
Voerde D 32 Lg39
Vogan TG 193 La42
Vogar CDN (MB) 238 Fa20
Vogatsikó GR 46 Mb50
Vogelkop RI 130 Rf46
Vogelkop RI 130 Rf46
Vogelsberg D 32 Lk40
Vogelweide NAM 212 Lk58
Voghera I 40 Lk46
Voh F (NCL) 162 Tc56
Võhandu EST 16 Mh33
Vohburg D 35 Lm42
Vohemar = Iharana RM 219 Ne52
Vohenstrauß D 35 Ln41
Vohidiala RM 220 Ne54
Vohilava RM 220 Ne56
Vohilengo RM 220 Ne54
Vohimasina RM 220 Ne56
Vohimena RM 220 Ne54
Vohipeno RM 220 Nd57
Vohitrambo RM 220 Nd57
Võhma EST 16 Mf32
Võhma EST 16 Mc32
Voi EAK 207 Mk47
Voi VN 115 Qd36
Voikoski FIN 16 Mg29
Voineasa RO 44 Md45
Voineasa RO 44 Me46
Voinești RO 45 Mf45
Voinjama LB 192 Kf41
Voiron F 25 Lf45
Vöiste EST 16 Me32
Voiteg RO 44 Mb45
Voitsberg A 35 Lq43
Vojens DK 14 Lk35
Vojinka UA 55 Mg23
Vojnić HR 41 Lq45
Vojnica BIH 41 Ls46
Vojnika BG 47 Mg48
Vojnovo BG 45 Mh47
Vojutyči UA 39 Md41
Vojvodina SCG 44 Lu45
Vokeo Island PNG 159 Sc47
Volary CZ 38 Lo42
Volborg USA (MT) 235 Eh23
Volcán PA 256 Fj41
Volcán RA (PJ) 284 Gh57
Volcán Alcedo EC 272 Fe46
Volcán Altar EC 272 Ga46
Volcán Antisana EC 272 Ga46
Volcán Antofalla RA 284 Gg58
Volcán Antuco RCH 292 Ge64
Volcán Aracar RA 284 Gg58
Volcán Arenal, P.N. CR 256 Fh40
Volcán Atitlan GCA 255 Fe38
Volcán Barú, P.N. PA 256 Fj41
Volcán Calbuco RCH 292 Gd66
Volcán Callaqui RCH 292 Ge64
Volcán Cayambe EC 272 Ga45
Volcán Chachani PE 284 Ge54
Volcán Chiguana BOL 284 Gg56
Volcán Chillán RCH 292 Ge64
Volcán Chimborazo EC 272 Ga46
Volcán Choshuenco RCH 292 Gd65
Volcán Concepción NIC 256 Fh40
Volcán Copahue RA/RCH 292 Ge64
Volcán Copiapó RCH 288 Gf59
Volcán Corcovado RCH 292 Gd67
Volcán Cotopaxi EC 272 Ga46
Volcán Cumbal CO 272 Gb45
Volcán Darwin EC 272 Fe46
Volcán de Colima MEX 254 Ej36
Volcán de Fuego GCA 255 Fe38
Volcán Domuyo RA 292 Ge64
Volcán Doña Juana CO 272 Gb45
Volcán Fernandina EC 272 Fe46
Volcán Galeras CO 272 Gb45
Volcán Guagua Pichincha EC 272 Ga46
Volcán Gualtatiri RCH 284 Gf55
Volcán Huequi RCH 292 Gd67
Volcán Illiniza EC 272 Ga46
Volcán Ipala HN 255 Ff38
Volcán Isluga RCH 284 Gf55
Volcán Isluga, P.N. RCH 284 Gf55
Volcán Lanín RCH 292 Ge65
Volcán Lascar RCH 284 Gg57
Volcán Lastarria RCH/RA 284 Gf58
Volcán Las Virgenes MEX 252 Ed32
Volcán Licancábur RCH 284 Gg57
Volcán Llaima RCH 292 Ge65
Volcán Llullaillaco RCH/RA 284 Gf58
Volcán Lonquimay RCH 292 Ge65
Volcán Maipo RCH/RA 288 Gf63
Volcán Masaya, P.N. NIC 256 Fg39
Volcán Michimáhuida RCH 292 Gd67
Volcán Misti PE 284 Ge54
Volcán Momotombo NIC 256 Fg39
Volcano USA (HI) 230 Cc36
Volcán Ollagüe BOL/RCH 284 Gf56
Volcano Mayon RP 121 Rb39
Volcán Osorno RCH 292 Gd66
Volcán Parinacota RCH 284 Gf55
Volcán Peteroa RCH/RA 288 Ge63
Volcan Pico de Orizaba MEX 253 Fb36
Volcán Poás, P.N. CR 256 Fh40
Volcán Puracé CO 272 Gb44
Volcán Puyehue RCH 292 Gd66
Volcán Reventador EC 272 Gb46
Volcán Sabancaya PE 279 Ge53
Volcán Sangay EC 272 Ga47
Volcán San José RA/RCH 288 Gf62
Volcán San Pedro RCH 284 Gf56
Volcán Socompa RCH/RA 284 Gf58
Volcán Sotara CO 272 Gb44
Volcans, P.N.des RWA 206 Me46
Volcán Sumaco EC 272 Gb46
Volcán Tacaná GCA/MEX 255 Fd38
Volcán Tacora RCH 284 Gf54
Volcán Tajumulco GCA 255 Fe38
Volcán Tenorio, P.N. CR 256 Fh40
Volcán Ticsani PE 284 Ge54
Volcán Tinguiririca RCH 288 Ge63
Volcán Tremen RA 292 Ge64
Volcán Tungurahua EC 272 Ga46
Volcán Tutupaca PE 284 Ge54
Volcán Viedma RA 294 Gd70
Volcán Viejo NIC 256 Fg39
Volcán Villarrica RCH 292 Gd65
Volcán Wolf EC 272 Fe45
Volčki RUS 53 Na19
Volda N 12 Lg28
Volda RUS 11 Mj14
Volga RUS 52 Mk17
Volga RUS 9 Na07
Volga-Baltijskij kanal RUS 52 Mk16
Volga Upland RUS 53 Nc20
Volgodonsk RUS 55 Nb22
Volgograd RUS 53 Nc21
Volgogradskoe Vodohranilišče RUS 53 Nc20
Volgorečensk RUS 53 Na17
Volhov RUS 52 Mf16
Volhov RUS 52 Mg16
Volintiri MD 45 Mk44
Volissós GR 49 Mf52
Volkach D 34 Ll41
Völkermarkt A 35 Lp44
Völkerschlachtdenkmal D 33 Ln39
Völklinger Hütte D 34 Lg41

Volkovo – Warmbad

Volkovo RUS 17 Mh33
Volkspelemonument ZA 217 Mc60
Volksrust ZA 217 Me59
Vollsjö S 15 Lo35
Vol'noe RUS 53 Nd22
Volnovacha UA 55 Mj22
Voločaevskij RUS 55 Nb22
Voločanka RUS 58 Pc04
Voločys'k UA 54 Md21
Volodarka UA 54 Me21
Volodarsk RUS 53 Nb17
Volodymyrec' UA 52 Md20
Volodymyr-Volyns'kyj UA 37 Me40
Vologda RUS 52 Mk16
Volokolamsk RUS 52 Mh17
Volokonovka RUS 53 Mj20
Voloma RUS 11 Mf14
Volop ZA 216 Mb60
Vólos GR 48 Mc51
Vološča UA 39 Md41
Volosjanka UA 39 Mc42
Volosovo RUS 52 Me16
Volotovo RUS 53 Mk20
Volovec' UA 39 Md42
Völs A 35 Lm43
Vol'sk RUS 53 Nd19
Volstruisleegte ZA 216 Mb62
Volta Redonda BR (RJ) 287 Hh57
Volterra I 40 Ll47
Voltri I 40 Lj46
Volturno I 42 Lp49
Volubilis MA 172 Kh28
Volvic F 25 Ld45
Volyně CZ 38 Lo41
Volyns'ka vysočyna UA 37 Me40
Volžsk RUS 53 Ne18
Volžskij RUS 53 Nc21
Vom WAN 186 Le41
Vomano I 42 Lo48
Von Bachontspanningsoord NAM 212 Lj57
Von Bach Recreational Resort NAM 212 Lj57
Vondrove RM 220 Nc56
Vondrozo RM 220 Nd57
Vonešta Voda BG 47 Mf48
Von François Fort NAM 212 Lj57
Von Frank Mountain USA (AK) 229 Cc14
Vónitsa GR 48 Ma52
Võnnu EST 16 Mh32
Von Otterøyane N 11 Ma06
Voortrekker fort ZA 214 Mf58
Vopnafjörður IS 10 Kc13
Vopnafjörður IS 10 Kc13
Voranava BY 17 Mf36
Vorbasse DK 14 Lk35
Vordingborg DK 14 Lm36
Vorey F 25 Ld45
Voria Pindos GR 46 Ma50
Vöring Plateau 8 La05
Vøringsfossen N 12 Lh30
Vórion Stenón Kérkiras GR 48 Lu51
Vorjing IND 112 Ph31
Vorkuta RUS 58 Oa05
Vorma N 12 Lm30
Vormsi EST 16 Md32
Vorniceni RO 45 Mg43
Vorochta UA 39 Me42
Vorona RUS 53 Nb19
Vorona UA 39 Me42
Voronet RO 45 Mf43
Voronež RUS 53 Mk20
Voronjaky UA 39 Me41
Voronovo RUS 16 Mj31
Vorotynec RUS 53 Nc17
Vorožba UA 52 Mh20
Vorpommersche Boddenlandschaft, N.P. D 33 Lo36
Vorskla UA 54 Mh21
Vorsma RUS 53 Nb18
Vorstershoop ZA 213 Mb58
Võrtsjärv EST 16 Mf32
Võru EST 16 Mh33
Vosburg ZA 216 Mb61
Vose TJ 76 Oe27
Vosges F 23 Lg43
Voshod RUS 53 Nc22
Voskopojë AL 46 Ma50
Voskresensk RUS 53 Mk18
Voskresenskoe RUS 52 Mj17
Voskresenskoe RUS 53 Nc17
Vosktesenovka RUS 98 Re20
Voss N 12 Lg30
Vostočnyj RUS 99 Sb21
Vostok ANT (RUS) 297 Qb34
Vostok RUS 99 Rh22
Võsu EST 16 Mf31
Vota do Jurem BR (PI) 277 Hk47
Votice CZ 38 Lp41
Votorantim BR (SP) 286 Hg57
Votuporanga BR (SP) 286 Hf56
Voúdia GR 49 Me54
Vouga ANG 208 Lj52
Vouillé F 22 La44
Vouka RCB 202 Lg47
Vouliagméni GR 48 Md53
Vourkári GR 48 Me53
Vouzela P 26 Km50
Vouziers F 23 Le41
Vovčans'k UA 53 Mj20
Voves F 22 Lb42
Vovodo RCA 196 Mc42
Voxna S 13 Lq29
Voxnan S 13 Lq29
Voyageurs National Park USA 238 Fd21
vozera Narač BY 17 Mg36
vozera Snudy BY 17 Mh35
vozera Vyhanaščanskae BY 37 Mf38
Voznesens'k UA 45 Mm43
Voznesenskoe RUS 53 Nb18
Vozroždenija otasi UZ 71 Nk23
vozvyshennost' Karabil TM 73 Ob27
vpadiny Akchakaya TM 71 Nk25
Vrå DK 14 Lk33
Vrå S 15 Lo34
Vráble SK 38 Lt42
Vraca BG 46 Md47
Vračanski Balkan, N.P. BG 46 Md47
Vrácevšnica SCG 46 Ma46
Vrådal N 12 Lj31
Vradiïvka UA 45 Ml43
Vrangfoss sluser N 12 Lk31
Vranje SCG 46 Mb48
Vranov CZ 38 Lq42
Vranov nad Topl'ou SK 39 Mb42
Vransko jezero HR 41 Lq47
Vrapce Polje SCG 46 Lu47
Vratcata BG 46 Md47
Vratěnín CZ 38 Lq42
Vratnica MK 46 Mb48
Vražji prolaz HR 41 Lp45
Vrbanja BIH 41 Ls46
Vrbanja HR 44 Lt46
Vrbas BIH 41 Ls46
Vrbovec HR 41 Lr45
Vrbovsko HR 41 Lq45
Vrchlabí CZ 38 Lq40
Vrede ZA 217 Me59
Vredefort ZA 217 Md59
Vredefort Dome ZA 217 Md59
Vredenburg ZA 216 Lk62
Vredendal ZA 216 Lk61
Vredeshoop NAM 216 Lk59
Vreed en Hoop GUY 270 Ha42
Vrésthena GR 48 Mc53
Vretstorp S 13 Lp31
Vrgorac HR 41 Ls47
Vrhnika SLO 41 Lp45
Vrhopolje BIH 41 Lr46
Vrh Tresta SCG 46 Mb46
Vridachalam IND (TNU) 111 Ok41
Vriezenveen NL 32 Lg38
Vrigstad S 15 Lp33
Vrindavan IND 107 Oj32
Vrises GR 49 Me55
Vrissohóri GR 46 Ma50
Vrlika HR 41 Lr47
Vrnjačka Banja SCG 46 Ma47
Vrpolje HR 41 Lt45
Vršac SCG 44 Mb45
Vrsar HR 41 Lo45
Vrtoče BIH 41 Lr46
Vrulja SCG 46 Lu47
Vryburg ZA 217 Mc59
Vryheid ZA 217 Mf59
Vsetín CZ 38 Ls41
Vsevoložsk RUS 52 Mf15
V-shaped Stone WAG 183 Kc39
Vuaqava FJI 163 Ua55
Vube RDC 201 Md44
Vube RDC 201 Me44
Vučitrn SCG 46 Ma48
Vui-Uata-In, T.I. BR 273 Gf47
Vuka HR 41 Lt45
Vuka HR 41 Lt45
Vukovar HR 44 Lt45
Vuladdore Reef RP 120 Qg37
Vulavu SOL 161 Sk50
Vulcan CDN (AB) 233 Ed20
Vulcan RO 44 Md45
Vulcan RO 45 Mf45
Vulcănești MD 45 Mj45
Vulci I 42 Lm48
vulkan Ključevskaja Sopka RUS 59 Ta07
vulkan Korjakskaja Sopka RUS 59 Sd08
vulkan Tjatja RUS 99 Sd23
Vultureni RO 44 Md44
Vultureni RO 45 Mh44
Vulturu RO 45 Mh45
Vumba Mountains ZW 214 Mg55
Vumba Rock Paintings MOC 214 Mg55
Vumbwe MW 210 Mg52
Vung Cay Duong VN 117 Qc40
Vung Tau VN 115 Qd40
Vunisea FJI 163 Tk55
Vuohijärvi FIN 16 Mg29
Vuoksa RUS 16 Mj29
Vuollerim S 10 Ma12
Vuottas S 10 Ma12
Vurnary RUS 53 Nd18
Vuyyuru IND (APH) 109 Pa37
Vwawa EAT 206 Mg50
Vwaza Marsh Game Reserve MW 210 Mg51
Vyaparla IND (APH) 108 Ok37
Vyara IND (GUJ) 108 Og35
Vybor RUS 52 Me17
Vyborg RUS 16 Mj30
Vyborgskij zamok RUS 16 Mj30
Vyčegda RUS 58 Nb06
Vydrino RUS (BUR) 90 Qc20
Vydryči UA 37 Me39
Vygoniči RUS 52 Mh19
Vygozero RUS 11 Mh14
Vyhanaščy BY 37 Mf38
Vyksa RUS 53 Nb18
Vylkove UA 45 Mk45
Vynnyky UA 39 Me41
Vynohradiv UA 39 Mc42
Vypolzovo RUS 52 Mg17
Vyrica RUS 52 Mf16
Vyša RUS 53 Nb19
Vyšhorod UA 54 Mf20
Vyška UA 39 Mc42
Vyškov CZ 38 Lr41
Vyšné Nemecké SK 39 Mc42
Vyšné Ružbachy SK 39 Ma41
Vyšnij Voloček RUS 52 Mh17
Vysock RUS 16 Mj30
Vysokaje BY 37 Md38
Vysoké Mýto CZ 38 Lr41
Vysokogornyj RUS 99 Rk20
Vysokovsk RUS 52 Mj17
Vyšší Brod CZ 38 Lp42
Vytegra RUS 11 Mj15
Vythiri IND (KER) 110 Oj41
Vyžnycja UA 39 Mf42
Vyžnyc'kyj N.P. UA 45 Mf42

W

Wa CI 192 Kf42
Wa GH 193 Kj40
Waaciye SP 199 Ne40
Waaheen SP 199 Nc40
Waajid SP 205 Nb44
Waal NL 32 Lf39
Waala F (NCL) 162 Tb55
Waalre NL 32 Lf39
Waalwijk NL 32 Lf39
Waanje WAL 192 Ke42
Waanyi Garawa A.L. AUS 139 Rj55
Waar RI 131 Rh47
Waat SUD 197 Mg41
Wabag PNG 159 Sb48
Wabakimi Lake CDN 239 Ff20
Wabakimi Prov. Park CDN 239 Ff20
Wabamun Lake CDN 233 Ec19
Wabasca-Desmarais CDN (AB) 233 Ed18
Wabasca Ind. Res. CDN 233 Ed18
Wabasca River CDN 233 Ed17
Wabash USA (IN) 246 Fh25
Wabasha USA (MN) 241 Fd23
Wabassi River CDN 239 Fg20
Wabe Gestro ETH 198 Na42
Wabe Mena ETH 198 Na43
Wabe Shebele SP 199 Nc43
Wabe Shebele Wenz ETH 199 Nb43
Wabigoon Lake CDN 238 Fd21
Wabimeig Lake CDN 239 Fh20
Wabinosh Lake CDN 239 Ff20
Wabi Shebele ETH 198 Na42
Wabo PNG 159 Sc49
Wabowden CDN (MB) 238 Fa18
Wąbrzeźno PL 36 Lt37
Wabuda PNG 159 Sb50
Wabuk Point CDN 239 Fh18
Wachapreague USA (VA) 247 Gc27
Wachau A 35 Lq42
Wachile ETH 198 Mk43
Wąchock PL 37 Ma39
Wächtersbach D 34 Lk40
Wacker USA (AK) 231 De18
Waco CDN (QC) 244 Gh20
Waco USA (TX) 243 Fb30
Wad PK 80 Od32
Wada'ah SUD 196 Mc39
Wadalei PNG 160 Sf50
Wadau PNG 159 Sd48
Wadayama J 101 Rh28
Wad Banda SUD 197 Md39
Wad Ban Naqa SUD 190 Mg38
Wadbilliga N.P. AUS (NSW) 153 Se64
Waddan LAR 175 Lj31
Waddenzee NL 32 Lf37
Waddikee AUS (SA) 152 Rj62
Waddington, Mount CDN 232 Dh20
Waddy Point AUS 151 Sg58
Wadebridge GB 20 Kq40
Wad el Haddad SUD 190 Mg40
Wadena CDN (SK) 238 Ej20
Wadena USA (MN) 241 Fc22
Wad en Nail SUD 190 Mh40
Wädenswil CH 34 Lj43
Wadesboro USA (NC) 249 Fk28
Wadeye AUS (NT) 139 Re53
Wad Hassib SUD 197 Md40
Wadhwan IND (GUJ) 108 Of34
Wadi IND (KTK) 108 Oj37
Wadi Abu Dawn SUD 190 Mg37
Wadi Abu Khinzir SUD 190 Mf39
Wadi ad Dawasir KSA 66 Nb35
Wadi ad Dumran LAR 181 Lh32
Wadi Adhanah YE 68 Nc38
Wadi Agwampt SUD 190 Mh37
Wadi Akash IRQ 65 Na29
Wadi al 'Aqiq KSA 66 Na34
Wadi al 'Atfayn YE 68 Nc37
Wadi al Athl LAR 181 Lk33
Wadi al 'Atk KSA 67 Nd33
Wadi al Awra LAR 175 Lj31
Wadi al Bayadah LAR 181 Lk32
Wadi al Farigh LAR 181 Lj33
Wadi al Fat LAR 174 Lh31
Wadi al Ghadaf IRQ 65 Nb29
Wadi al-Ghalla SUD 197 Me40
Wadi al Ghiran KSA 67 Nd35
Wadi al Hadh LAR 181 Lj33
Wadi al Hamd KSA 66 Mj33
Wadi al Hamim LAR 175 Mb30
Wadi al Hasan JOR 64 Mj30
Wadi al-Hayat LAR 181 Lg32
Wadi Al-Hitan (Whale Valley) ET 177 Me30
Wadi al Jadwal KSA 67 Nd35
Wadi al Jarir KSA 66 Nb33
Wadi al Jawf YE 68 Nc37
Wadi al Jifr KSA 67 Nc34
Wadi al Jizi KSA 66 Mj32
Wadi al Khirr KSA 65 Nb31
Wadi al Ku SUD 196 Mc39
Wadi al Lith KSA 66 Na35
Wadi al Magran KSA 67 Nd35
Wadi al Masilah YE 68 Nf38
Wadi al-Milk SUD 190 Mf38
Wadi al Mirah IRQ 65 Na29
Wadi al Qaha KSA 66 Mk34
Wadi al Tided TCH 181 Lk35
Wadi al Ubayyid IRQ 65 Nb29
Wadi al Ugayb LAR 175 Lj31
Wadi al Wa'ir LAR 181 Lk32
Wadi al-Warriya UAE 75 Nj33
Wadi Amij IRQ 65 Na29
Wadi Amur SUD 190 Mh37
Wadi Andam OM 75 Nk34
Wadi Aoual LAR 174 Lf31
Wadi Araba ET 177 Mg31
Wadi Araba JOR/IL 64 Mh30
Wadi Armah YE 69 Nf37
Wadi ar Ratqah IRQ 65 Na29
Wadi ar Rika KSA 67 Nc34
Wadi ar Rimah KSA 66 Na32
Wadi ar Risha KSA 67 Nc33
Wadi ar Ru'ays LAR 181 Lk32
Wadi ash Sha'ban KSA 66 Na32
Wadi ash Sharmah KSA 64 Mh31
Wadi ash Shati LAR 181 Lg32
Wadi ash Shitab KSA 67 Nd34
Wadi ash Shubah LAR 175 Mb30
Wadi ash Shubayrimah LAR 181 Lj32
Wadi Aslam KSA 67 Nc34
Wadi as Sirhan KSA 64 Mj30
Wadi as Sulaymaniyah KSA 65 Na30
Wadi ath Tharthar IRQ 65 Nb28
Wadi at Turmus KSA 66 Nb32
Wadi Azum SUD 196 Mb39
Wadi az Zimam LAR 175 Lh31
Wadi Bana YE 68 Nc39
Wadi Barjuj LAR 181 Lg33
Wadi Bayir JOR 64 Mj30
Wadi Baysh KSA 68 Nb37
Wadi Bayy al Kabir LAR 174 Lh30
Wadi Bishain KSA 66 Nb35
Wadi Bu al Ghiraf LAR 175 Lj32
Wadi Bu al Hidan LAR 181 Lk32
Wadi Dabl KSA 64 Mj31
Wadi Dahyan YE 69 Nf36
Wadi Derbeikan SUD 190 Mh37
Wadi Dhayqah OM 75 Nk34
Wadi Doan YE 68 Ne38
Wadi Eidukal SUD 190 Mh37
Wadi el 'Allâqi ET 177 Mg34
Wadi el Asyûti ET 177 Mf32
Wadi el Miyâh ET 177 Mg33
Wadi el Tarfa ET 177 Mf31
Wadi Fajr KSA 64 Mj31
Wadi Faysal LAR 174 Lg30
Wadi Gabgaba ET 177 Mg34
Wadi Gabgada SUD 190 Mg36
Wadi Garâra ET 177 Mg34
Wadi Habob SUD 190 Mh37
Wadi Hadramaut YE 68 Ne37
Wadi Hajr YE 68 Nd38
Wadi Halfa SUD 190 Mf36
Wadi Hamir IRQ 65 Na30
Wadi Harawah LAR 175 Lj30
Wadi Harjib KSA 68 Nb36
Wadi Hawashiya ET 177 Mg31
Wadi Hawran IRQ 65 Mk29
Wadi Hayyan KSA 66 Mj32
Wadi Howar SUD 190 Mf38
Wadi Huwar SUD 189 Mc37
Wadi Ibra SUD 196 Mc40
Wadi Idimah KSA 68 Nc36
Wadi Irawan LAR 181 Lf32
Wadi Jarif LAR 175 Lj30
Wadi Jiz YE 69 Nf37
Wadi Kaja SUD/TCH 196 Mb39
Wadi Khabb YE 68 Nc37
Wadi Khasab ET 177 Mh33
Wadi Khirr IRQ 65 Nb30
Wadi Kunayr LAR 175 Lh32
Wadi Langeb SUD 191 Mj38
Wadi Majrur SUD 189 Md37
Wadi Makhyah YE 68 Ne37
Wadi Mathendous LAR 181 Lf33
Wadi Mawr YE 68 Nb37
Wadi Mimoun LAR 174 Lf30
Wadi Muheit SUD 190 Mg38
Wadi Mujib JOR 64 Mh30
Wadi Muqaddam SUD 190 Mf39
Wadi Musa JOR 64 Mh30
Wadi Nabi SUD 190 Mg36
Wadi Nahr OM 75 Nj34
Wadi Najran KSA 68 Nc37
Wadi Nayyal KSA 64 Mk31
Wadi Nisah KSA 67 Nd33
Wadi Oko SUD 190 Mh36
Wadi Qarzah LAR 174 Lh30
Wadi Qena ET 177 Mg32
Wadi Qinab YE 68 Ne37
Wadi Qitbit OM 69 Nh36
Wadi Rabigh KSA 66 Mk34
Wadi Rafash OM 75 Nj34
Wadi Rakhawt YE 69 Nf37
Wadi Ranyah KSA 66 Nb35
Wadi Rawawais LAR 175 Lh30
Wadi Rum JOR 64 Mh31
Wadi Sahuq KSA 66 Na33
Wadi Sannur ET 177 Mf31
Wadi Sha'it ET 177 Mg33
Wadi Shihan OM 69 Ng37
Wadi Shubram KSA 66 Nb33
Wadi Shurshut LAR 174 Lf30
Wadi Tamat LAR 175 Lj30
Wadi Tanarut LAR 174 Lf31
Wadi Tanezzruft LAR 181 Lf33
Wadi Tarib KSA 68 Nb36
Wadi Tarut LAR 174 Lg32
Wadi Tathlith KSA 66 Nb35
Wadi Tinis LAR 181 Lf33
Wadi Turabah KSA 66 Na35
Wadi Umm al-Hait OM 69 Ng36
Wadi Wouri TCH 181 Lh35
Wadi Yadat SUD 190 Mh38
Wadi Zabid YE 68 Nb38
Wadi Zahawn YE 69 Nf37
Wadi Zamzam LAR 174 Lh30
Wadi Zazamt LAR 174 Lf30
Wadlew PL 37 Lu39
Wadley USA (GA) 249 Fj29
Wad Madani SUD 190 Mg39
Wadomari J 103 Re32
Wadowice PL 39 Lu41
Wad Rawa SUD 190 Mg39
Wadwani IND (MHT) 108 Oj36
Waeng THA 117 Qa43
Waenhuiskrans ZA 216 Ma63
Waeplau RI 130 Rd47
Wafangdian CHN (LNG) 100 Ra26
Wafra KWT 74 Nd31
Wagait Aboriginal Reserve AUS 139 Rf52
Wagan PNG 159 Sd49
Waganella AUS (NSW) 153 Sc63
Wagau PNG 159 Sd49
Wageningen NL 32 Lf39
Wageningen SME 271 Hb43
Wagga Wagga AUS (NSW) 153 Sd63
Waghai IND (GUJ) 108 Og35
Waghete RI 131 Rj48
Wagiman A.L. AUS 139 Rf53
Wagin AUS (WA) 144 Qj62
Waglisa CDN (BC) 232 Df19
Wagner BR (BA) 283 Hk52
Wagner USA (SD) 240 Fa24
Wagon Mound USA (NM) 237 Eh27
Wagontire USA (OR) 234 Ea24
Wagrain A 35 Lo43
Wągrowiec PL 36 Ls38
Waha RI 127 Rb48
Wahai RI 130 Re47
Wahala TG 193 La42
Wahat al Jufra LAR 175 Lj31
Wahat Salima SUD 190 Me36
Wah Cantonment PK 79 Og29
Wahiawa USA (HI) 230 Cb35
Wahibah Sands OM 75 Nk35
Wahlbergøya N 11 Lk06
Wahoo USA (NE) 241 Fb25
Wahpeton USA (ND) 241 Fb22
Wahran DZ 173 Kk28
Wahroonga AUS (WA) 140 Qh58
Wai IND (MHT) 108 Og37
Wai RI 130 Re46
Waialua USA (HI) 230 Ca35
Waian RC 97 Qk34
Waiāpi, T.I. BR 275 Hd45
Waiblingen D 34 Lk42
Waibula PNG 160 Sf50
Waidhan IND (MPH) 109 Pb33
Waidhaus D 35 Ln41
Waidhofen an der Thaya A 35 Lq42
Waidhofen an der Ybbs A 35 Lp43
Waigama RI 130 Re46
Waigeo RI 130 Rf45
Waihau Bay NZ 154 Tj64
Waihi NZ 154 Th64
Waikabubak RI 129 Qk50
Waikaia NZ 155 Te68
Waikanae NZ 154 Th66
Waikaremoana NZ 154 Tj65
Waikato River NZ 154 Th65
Waikawa NZ 155 Te69
Waikelo RI 129 Qk50
Waikerie AUS (SA) 152 Sa63
Waikiki USA (HI) 230 Cb35
Waikopai River NZ 155 Tg66
Waikouaiti NZ 155 Tf68
Wailapa VU 162 Td53
Wailuku USA (HI) 230 Cb35
Waimarama NZ 154 Tj65
Waimate NZ 155 Tf68
Waimea USA (HI) 230 Cc35
Waimea Bay USA (HI) 230 Ca35
Waimes B 23 Lg40
Waimiri Atroari, T.I. BR 274 Gk46
Wainganga IND 109 Ok35
Waingapu RI 129 Ra50
Waini GUY 270 Ha42
Wainono Lagoon NZ 155 Tf68
Wainui NZ 154 Tk65
Wainwright CDN (AB) 233 Ee19
Waiotapu NZ 154 Tj65
Waiouru NZ 154 Th65
Waipa RI 131 Rj47
Waipara NZ 155 Tg67
Waipawa NZ 154 Tj65
Waipoua Kauri Forest NZ 154 Tg63
Waipukang RI 132 Rb50
Waipukurau NZ 154 Tj66
Wair RI 131 Rg48
Wairoa NZ 154 Tj65
Waisa PNG 159 Sc49
Waisai RI 130 Rf46
Waitaki River NZ 155 Tf68
Waitangi National Reserve NZ 154 Th63
Waitara NZ 154 Th65
Waitomo Caves NZ 154 Th65
Waitpinga Beach AUS 152 Rk63
Waitsburg USA (WA) 234 Ea22
Waiwa PNG 159 Se50
Waiwai GUY 274 Ha45
Waiwera NZ 154 Th64
Waiwerang RI 132 Rb50
Waje WAN 186 Ld41
Wajima J 101 Rj27
Wajir Bor EAK 205 Na45
Waka ETH 198 Mj42
Waka RDC 200 Ma45
Wakaf Tapai MAL 117 Qb43
Wakamoek RI 130 Rf46
Waka, P.N.de la G 202 Lf46
Wakasa-wan J 101 Rh28
Wakasawan Q.N.P. J 101 Rh28
Wakatin RI 130 Rd47
Wakatobi Marine N.P. RI 127 Rb48
Wakaw CDN (SK) 233 Eh19
Wakayama J 101 Rh28
Wake USA 135 Ta08
WaKeeny USA (KS) 240 Fa26
Wakefield GB 21 Kt37
Wake Forest USA (NC) 249 Ga28
Waki F (GF) 271 Hd44
Wakinosawa J 99 Sa25
Wakkanai J 99 Sa23
Wakkerstroom ZA 217 Mf59
Waklarok USA (AK) 228 Bh14
Wako PNG 159 Se49
Wakomata Lake CDN 246 Fj22
Wakooka AUS (QLD) 147 Sc53
Wakool AUS (NSW) 153 Sc63
Wakulla Sprs. S.P. USA 250 Fh30
Wakunai PNG 160 Sh48
Wal EAT 206 Mg48
Walachia RO 44 Md46
Walagonya Aboriginal Reserve AUS 140 Ra57
Walamba Z 210 Me52
Walanae RI 129 Ra48
Walandi IND (MHT) 108 Oj36
Wal Athiang SUD 197 Me42
Wałbrzych PL 36 Lr40
Walbundrie AUS (NSW) 153 Sd63
Walburton River AUS 143 Rk59
Walcha AUS (NSW) 151 Sf61
Walcheren NL 32 Ld39
Walch River AUS (QLD) 149 Sc54
Walcott USA (WY) 235 Eg25
Wałcz PL 36 Lr37
Waldbröl D 32 Lh40
Waldburg AUS (WA) 140 Qj58
Waldburg Range AUS 140 Qj58
Waldeck D 32 Lk39
Waldegrave Island AUS 152 Rh62
Walden USA (CO) 235 Eg25
Waldenburg USA (AR) 243 Fe28
Waldkirch D 34 Lh42
Waldkirchen D 35 Lo42
Waldkraiburg D 35 Ln42
Waldo USA (FL) 250 Fj31
Waldport USA (OR) 234 Dh23
Waldron USA (AR) 243 Fc28
Waldshut-Tiengen D 34 Lj43
Waldviertel A 35 Lq42
Waleabahi RI 127 Rb46
Waleakodi RI 127 Rb46
Walembele GH 193 Kk40
Walensee CH 34 Lk43
Wales GB 20 Kq39
Wales USA 224 Bd13
Walewale GH 193 Kk40
Walgett AUS (NSW) 151 Se61
Walgoolan AUS (WA) 144 Qk61
Walgra AUS (QLD) 148 Rk56
Walgreen Coast 296 Ed33
Walhalla D 35 Ln41
Walhalla USA (ND) 238 Fb21
Walhalla USA (SC) 249 Fj28
Walikale RDC 201 Me46
Walindi Plantation Resort PNG 160 Sf48
Walir RI 130 Rg48
Walis Island PNG 159 Sb47
Walkaway AUS (WA) 144 Qh60
Walker USA (MN) 241 Fc22
Walker USA 234 Ea26
Walkerbaai ZA 216 Lk63
Walker Bay ZA 216 Lk63
Walker Lake CDN 238 Fb18
Walker Lake USA 229 Cc12
Walker Lake USA 234 Ea26
Walker Mountains 296 Fa33
Walker River Ind. Res. USA 234 Ea26
Walker's Cay BS 251 Ga32
Walkerston AUS (QLD) 149 Se56
Walkerville AUS (VIC) 153 Sc65
Wall USA (SD) 240 Ej24
Wallabi Island AUS 144 Qg60
Wallace USA (ID) 233 Ec22
Wallace USA (NC) 249 Ga28
Wallace USA (NE) 240 Ek25
Wallaceburg CDN (ON) 246 Fj24
Wallal Downs AUS (WA) 140 Ra55
Wallaman Falls AUS (QLD) 149 Sc55
Wallam River AUS 151 Sd59
Wallan AUS (VIC) 153 Sc64
Wallangara AUS (NSW) 151 Sf60
Wallanthery AUS (NSW) 153 Sc62
Wallara Ranch Roadhouse AUS (NT) 142 Rg58
Wallaroo AUS (SA) 152 Rj62
Wallasey GB 21 Kr37
Walla Walla USA (WA) 234 Ea22
Wall diving (Caicos Islands) GB 251 Ge35
Wall Doxey S.P. USA 248 Ff28
Walldürn D 34 Lk41
Walled City of Ma'in YE 68 Nc37
Wallekraal ZA 216 Lj61
Wallenfels D 35 Lm40
Wallennbeen AUS (NSW) 153 Se63
Wallingford GB 21 Kt39
Walling Rock AUS 144 Ra60
Wallis and Futuna F 135 Tb11
Wallis Islands F 164 Bb52
Wall of Gengis Khan MNG 91 Qg21
Wallowa USA (OR) 234 Eb23
Wallowa Mountains USA 234 Eb23
Walls GB 19 Kt30
Walls of China AUS 153 Sb62
Wallumbilla AUS (QLD) 151 Se59
Walney Island GB 21 Kr36
Walnut USA (CA) 234 Dj27
Walnut USA (MS) 243 Ff28
Walnut Canyon Nat. Mon. USA 237 Ee28
Walnut Grove USA (MN) 241 Fc23
Walnut Ridge USA (AR) 243 Fe27
Walong IND (ARP) 113 Pj31
Walosi RI 127 Rb48
Walpole AUS (WA) 144 Qj63
Walpole-Nornalup N.P. AUS 144 Qj63
Walrus Is. USA 228 Bk16
Walrus Island USA 228 Bf17
Walrus Island USA 228 Bk17
Walsall GB 21 Kt38
Walsenburg USA (CO) 237 Eh27
Walsh USA (CO) 237 Ej27
Walsrode D 32 Lk38
Waltair IND (APH) 109 Pb37
Walterboro USA (SC) 249 Fk29
Walters USA (OK) 242 Fa28
Waltham CDN (QC) 247 Gb23
Waltman USA (WY) 235 Eg24
Walton CDN (NS) 245 Gj23
Walton, Mount AUS 144 Qk61
Walton-on-the-Naze GB 21 Lb39
Waltzing Matilda Center AUS (QLD) 148 Sb57
Walu Besa RI 130 Rd47
Walungu RDC 206 Me47
Walungurru AUS (NT) 142 Re57
Walvis Bay NAM 212 Lh57
Walvis Bay NAM 212 Lj57
Walvis Bay Nature Reserve NAM 212 Lh57
Walvis Ridge 170 La24
Wały Chrobrego PL 36 Lp37
Wamal RI 158 Rk50
Wamanfo GH 193 Kj42
Wamar RI 131 Rh48
Wamaza RDC 206 Md48
Wamba EAK 204 Mj45
Wamba RDC 203 Lj48
Wamba WAN 186 Le41
Wamba Luadi RDC 203 Lj49
Wamba Mountains WAN 195 Lf42
Wambiana AUS (QLD) 149 Sd56
Wamboin AUS (NSW) 151 Sd61
Wamdé Tabal BF 185 Kk38
Wamego USA (KS) 241 Fb26
Wamena RI 131 Rk48
Wami EAT 207 Mk49
Wamis LAR 174 Lg30
Wampana-Karlantijpa A.L. AUS 139 Rf54
Wampaya Aboriginal Reserve AUS 139 Rh54
Wamsutter USA (WY) 235 Eg25
Wana PK 78 Oe29
Wanaaring AUS (NSW) 150 Sc60
Wanadou RG 192 Kf41
Wanaka NZ 155 Te68
Wanapitei RI 130 Rd47
Wanapitei Lake CDN 239 Fk22
Wanasabari RI 127 Rb48
Wanau RI 130 Rg46
Wanblee USA (SD) 240 Ek24
Wanda RA (MI) 289 Hc58
Wandai RI 131 Rj47
Wandammen Peninsula RI 131 Rh47
Wandammen / Wondiwoi Mountains Reserve RI 131 Rh47
Wanda Shan CHN 98 Rf23
Wandering AUS (WA) 144 Qj62
Wandering River CDN 233 Ed18
Wanderlândia BR (TO) 276 Hg49
Wando PNG 158 Sa50
Wando ROK 103 Rd28
Wandoan AUS (QLD) 151 Se59
Waneroo AUS (WA) 144 Qh61
Wanesabe RI 129 Qj50
Wang PL 36 Lq40
Wang PNG 160 Sg47
Wangamana AUS (NSW) 150 Sc60
Wanga Mountains WAN 194 Lf42
Wanganui NZ 154 Th65
Wanganui River NZ 154 Th65
Wangaratta AUS (VIC) 153 Sd64
Wangary AUS (SA) 152 Rh63
Wangasi-Turu GH 193 Kk41
Wangben CHN (JLN) 100 Rb24
Wangcang CHN (SCH) 95 Qd29
Wang Chan THA 114 Qa39
Wangcheng CHN (HUN) 95 Qg31
Wang Chin THA 114 Pk37
Wang Chomphu THA 114 Qa37
Wangdue Phodrang BHT 112 Pe32
Wangen D 34 Lk43
Wangerooge D 32 Lh37
Wanggamet, Gunung RI 129 Ra51
Wanggao CHN (GZG) 96 Qf33
Wanggar RI 131 Rh47
Wang Hin THA 114 Qa37
Wangi Falls AUS 139 Rf53
Wangiwangi RI 127 Rb48
Wangjiang CHN (AHU) 102 Qj30
Wangkui CHN (HLG) 98 Rd22
Wangmo CHN (GZH) 96 Qd33
Wang Nam Yen THA 115 Qb39
Wang Noi THA 114 Qa38
Wang Nua THA 114 Pk36
Wangon RI 128 Qe49
Wangpang Yang CHN 102 Ra30
Wangqing CHN (JLN) 100 Re24
Wang Sam Mo THA 115 Qb37
Wang Saphung THA 114 Qa37
Wang Thong THA 114 Qa37
Wang Wiset THA 116 Pk42
Wang Zhaojun CHN 93 Qf25
Wangziguan CHN (GSU) 95 Qc29
Wanham CDN (AB) 233 Ea18
Wan Hsa-la MYA 113 Pk35
Wanhuayan CHN 97 Qg33
Wani IND (MHT) 109 Ok35
Wanie-Rukula RDC 201 Mc45
Wanigela PNG 159 Se50
Wanimiyn A.L. AUS 139 Rf53
Wanjarri Nature Reserve AUS 140 Ra59
Wanjiabu CHN (JGX) 102 Qh31
Wankaner IND (GUJ) 108 Of34
Wankawayn SP 205 Nc44
Wan Kongmöng MYA 113 Pk35
Wan Long MYA 113 Pk34
Wanna AUS (WA) 140 Qj57
Wannaska USA (MN) 238 Fc21
Wannian CHN (JGX) 102 Qj31
Wanning CHN (HAN) 96 Qf36
Wanparti IND (APH) 108 Ok37
Wan Pong MYA 113 Pk35
Wanquan CHN (HBI) 93 Qh25
Wanshan Qundao CHN 97 Qh35
Wansheng CHN (CGQ) 95 Qd31
Wansra RI 131 Rh46
Wantage GB 21 Kt39
Wantoat PNG 159 Sd49
Wanuskewin Heritage P. CDN 233 Eg19
Wan Xian CHN (CGQ) 95 Qe30
Wanyuan CHN (SCH) 95 Qe29
Wanzai CHN (JGX) 102 Qh31
Wapakoneta USA (OH) 246 Fh25
Wapato USA (WA) 232 Dk22
Wapawekka Hills CDN 233 Eh18
Wapawekka Lake CDN 233 Eh18
Wapella CDN (SK) 238 Ek20
Wapenamanda PNG 159 Sb48
Wapi IND (GUJ) 108 Og35
Wapikopai Lake CDN 239 Ff19
Wapi Pathum THA 115 Qb38
Waplewo PL 37 Ma37
Wapoga RI 131 Rj47
Wapotih RI 130 Rd47
Waprak RI 131 Rh47
Wapsa Khani NEP 88 Pd32
Wapuli GH 193 La41
Wapumba Island PNG 159 Sb50
Wapweelah AUS (NSW) 151 Sc60
Waqên CHN (SCH) 94 Qb29
Wara WAN 186 Lc40
Warakurna AUS (WA) 141 Re58
Warambif PNG 160 Sg48
Warandab ETH 199 Nc42
Warandji DY 186 Lb40
Warangal IND (APH) 109 Ok36
Warao Indians YV 270 Gk44
Waraseoni IND (MPH) 109 Pa35
Waratah AUS (TAS) 152 Sc66
Waratah Bay AUS 153 Sd65
Wara Wara Mountains WAL 192 Ke41
Warbreccan AUS (QLD) 150 Sb58
Warburg D 32 Lk39
Warburton AUS (WA) 141 Rd59
Warburton A.L. AUS 141 Rd59
Warburton Range AUS 141 Rd59
Ward NZ 155 Th66
Wardang Islands AUS 152 Rj63
Wardé RMM 184 Kg38
Warden ZA 217 Me59
Wardenburg D 32 Lj37
Warder ETH 199 Nc42
Wardha IND (MHT) 109 Ok35
Wardha IND 109 Ok35
Ward Hunt Strait PNG 160 Sf50
Wardo RI 131 Rh46
Ward River AUS 151 Sd58
Ware CDN (BC) 231 Dh17
Ware USA (MA) 247 Gd24
Waregem B 23 Ld40
Waregem Mine AUS (NT) 139 Rh55
Wareham GB 21 Ks40
Waremme B 23 Lf40
Waren D 33 Ln37
Waren RI 131 Rj47
Waren RI 131 Rj47
Warenbayne AUS (QLD) 151 Sf59
Warenda AUS (QLD) 148 Sa57
Warendorf D 32 Lj39
Wargaadhi SP 199 Nd44
War Galon SP 199 Nd42
Warialda AUS (NSW) 151 Sf60
Waria River PNG 159 Sd50
Wari Godri IND (MHT) 108 Oh36
Warilau RI 131 Rh48
Warin Chamrap THA 115 Qc38
Waring Mountains USA (AK) 229 Ca12
Wario River PNG 158 Sb48
Waritchaphum THA 115 Qb37
Warka PL 37 Mb39
Warkopi RI 131 Rh46
Warkworth NZ 154 Th64
Warlubie PL 36 Lt37
Warman CDN (SK) 233 Eg19
Warmandi RI 130 Rg46
Warmbad NAM 216 Lk60

X

Xiangyun – Yola

Xiangyun CHN (YUN) 113 Qa33
Xianju CHN (ZJG) 102 Ra31
Xianling Tomb CHN (HUB) 95 Qg30
Xianning CHN (HUB) 102 Qh31
Xianshan Gang CHN 102 Rb31
Xiantao CHN (HUB) 95 Qg30
Xiantong Si CHN 93 Qg26
Xianxia Ling CHN 102 Qk31
Xianyang CHN (SAA) 95 Qe28
Xianyou CHN (FJN) 97 Qk33
Xianzhou CHN (GZG) 96 Qe34
Xiaochang CHN (HUB) 102 Qh30
Xiaodianzi CHN (HUB) 95 Qf29
Xiaogan CHN (HUB) 95 Qg30
Xiaoguanxi CHN (YUN) 113 Qb32
Xiaohe CHN (SAA) 95 Qe29
Xiaojiahe CHN (HLG) 98 Rg22
Xiaojin CHN (SCH) 94 Qb30
Xiaoling Tomb = Imperial Tombs of the Ming and Qing Dynasties CHN (JGS) 102 Qk29
Xiaomei Guan CHN 97 Qh33
Xiaonanchuan CHN (QHI) 89 Ph28
Xiao San Xia CHN 95 Qe30
Xiaoshan CHN (ZJG) 102 Ra30
Xiaoshi CHN (LNG) 100 Rc25
Xiaotian CHN (AHU) 102 Qj30
Xiaowutai Shan CHN 93 Qh25
Xiao Xian CHN (AHU) 102 Qj28
Xiaoxita CHN (HUB) 95 Qf30
Xiaoyangjie CHN (YUN) 113 Qb33
Xiapu CHN (FJN) 102 Qk32
Xiasi CHN (GZH) 96 Qd33
Xiatai CHN (XUZ) 84 Pa24
Xia Xian CHN (SAX) 95 Qf28
Xiaxiyu CHN (HBI) 93 Qg26
Xiayi CHN (HNN) 102 Qj28
Xiazha CHN (YUN) 96 Qc33
Xiazhuang CHN (HNN) 102 Qh29
Xichang CHN (GZG) 96 Qe35
Xichang CHN (SCH) 113 Qb32
Xichong CHN (SCH) 95 Qc30
Xichou CHN (YUN) 96 Qc34
Xichú MEX (GJT) 254 Ek35
Xichuan CHN (HNN) 95 Qf29
Xicoténcatl MEX (TM) 253 Fa34
Xicotepec de Juarez MEX (PUE) 254 Fb35
Xidi CHN 102 Qk31
Xie BR 273 Gg45
Xieng Ngeun LAO 114 Qb36
Xien Hon LAO 114 Qa36
Xiezhou Guandimiao CHN 95 Qf28
Xifeng CHN (GSU) 95 Qd28
Xifeng CHN (GZH) 96 Qd32
Xifeng CHN (LNG) 100 Rc24
Xigangzi CHN (HLG) 98 Rd21
Xigaze CHN (TIB) 88 Pe31
Xihan Shui CHN 95 Qc29
Xi He CHN 92 Qa24
Xiheying CHN (HBI) 93 Qh26
Xi Hu CHN 102 Ra30
Xihua CHN (HNN) 102 Qh29
Xiis SP 199 Nd40
Xiji CHN (NHZ) 95 Qc28
Xi Jiang CHN 96 Qf34
Xijin Shuiku CHN 96 Qe34
Xijir Ulan Hu CHN 89 Pf28
Xijishui CHN (GSU) 92 Qc27
Xikou CHN (ZJG) 102 Ra31
Xikouzi CHN (NMZ) 91 Ra19
Xikrin do Rio Cateté, T.I. BR 275 He49
Xilamuren Caoyuan CHN 93 Qf25
Xi Liao He CHN 100 Rb24
Xilin CHN (GZG) 96 Qc33
Xi Ling Xia CHN 95 Qf30
Xilinhot CHN (NMZ) 93 Qj24
Xilinji = Mohe CHN (HLG) 91 Rb19
Xıllı AZ 70 Ne26
Xilókastro GR 48 Mc52
Xilong-Shan Z.B. CHN 94 Qb28
Xime GNB 183 Kc40
Ximeng CHN (YUN) 113 Pk34
Ximucheng CHN (LNG) 100 Rb25
Xin CHN 102 Qj31
Xin'anjiang Sk. CHN 102 Qk31
Xin'ansuo CHN (YUN) 113 Qb34
Xinavane MOC 214 Mg58
Xin Barag Youqi CHN (NMZ) 91 Qj21
Xin Barag Zuoqi CHN (NMZ) 91 Qk21
Xinbin CHN (LNG) 100 Rc25
Xincai CHN (HNN) 102 Qh29
Xinchang CHN (GZH) 96 Qd33
Xinchang CHN (ZJG) 102 Ra31
Xincheng CHN (HBI) 93 Qh26
Xincheng Weijin Mu CHN 92 Pk26
Xinchuan Gang CHN 102 Ra29
Xindeng CHN (ZJG) 102 Qk31
Xindian CHN (HLG) 98 Rd23
Xindu CHN (SCH) 94 Qc30
Xinduqiao CHN (SCH) 94 Qa30
Xinfeng CHN (JGX) 97 Qh33
Xinfengjiang Shuiku CHN 97 Qh34
Xingalool SP 199 Ne41
Xing'an CHN (GZG) 96 Qf33
Xingan CHN (JGX) 102 Qh32
Xingcheng CHN (LNG) 100 Ra25
Xinge ANG 203 Lk50
Xingfeng CHN (GDG) 97 Qh33
Xingguo CHN (JGX) 97 Qh32
Xinghe CHN (NMZ) 93 Qg25
Xinghua CHN (JGS) 102 Qk29
Xingkai Hu CHN 98 Rg23
Xinglong CHN (HAN) 96 Qf36
Xinglong CHN (HBI) 93 Qj25
Xingning CHN (GDG) 97 Qh33
Xingod SP 199 Ne42
Xingou CHN (HUB) 95 Qg30
Xingpan CHN (GZG) 96 Qe35
Xingren CHN (GZH) 96 Qc33
Xingrenbu CHN (NHZ) 92 Qc27
Xingshan CHN (HUB) 95 Qf30
Xingtai CHN (HBI) 93 Qh27
Xingtang CHN (HBI) 93 Qh26
Xingu BR 265 Hb20
Xinguara BR (PA) 276 Hf49
Xingwen CHN (SCH) 95 Qc31
Xing Xian CHN (SAX) 93 Qf26
Xingxingxia CHN (XUZ) 87 Ph25
Xingyi CHN (GZH) 96 Qc33
Xinhe CHN (XUZ) 86 Pb25
Xinhuang CHN (HUN) 96 Qe32
Xining CHN (QHI) 92 Qa27
Xiniujiao CHN (GZG) 96 Qe35
Xinji CHN (HBI) 93 Qh27
Xinjian CHN (JGX) 102 Qh31
Xin Jiang CHN 102 Qj31
Xinjie CHN (YUN) 96 Qc34
Xinjie CHN (YUN) 113 Qb33
Xinjin CHN (SCH) 94 Qb30
Xinkai He CHN 100 Ra24
Xinlicheng CHN 100 Rc24
Xinlong CHN (SCH) 94 Qa30
Xinmin CHN (LNG) 100 Rb25
Xinning CHN (HUN) 96 Qf32
Xinqing CHN (HLG) 98 Re21
Xinshizhen CHN (SCH) 94 Qb31
Xintai CHN (SDG) 93 Qj28
Xintian CHN (HUN) 96 Qg33
Xin Xian CHN (HNN) 102 Qh30
Xinxiang CHN (HNN) 95 Qg28
Xinxing CHN (GDG) 96 Qg34
Xinxing CHN (HAN) 96 Qe36
Xinxu CHN (GZG) 96 Qd34
Xinyang CHN (HNN) 102 Qh29
Xinye CHN (HNN) 95 Qg29
Xinyi CHN (GDG) 96 Qf34
Xinyi CHN (JGS) 102 Qk28
Xinying CHN (HAN) 96 Qe36
Xinyu CHN (JGX) 102 Qh32
Xinyuan CHN (XUZ) 84 Pb24
Xinzhan CHN (GZH) 95 Qd31
Xinzhan CHN (HLG) 98 Rc23
Xinzhao Shan CHN 92 Qd26
Xinzhelin Shuiku CHN 102 Qh31
Xinzheng CHN (HNN) 95 Qg28
Xinzhou CHN (GZG) 96 Qd33
Xinzhou CHN (SAX) 93 Qg26
Xinzhu CHN (HUB) 102 Qh30
Xinzo de Limia E 26 Kn52
Xinzuotang CHN (GDG) 97 Qh34
Xiongyuecheng CHN (LNG) 100 Rb25
Xiping CHN (HNN) 95 Qf29
Xiping CHN (HNN) 102 Qh29
Xi Qiao CHN 97 Qg34
Xiqu CHN (SCH) 113 Qa32
Xique-Xique BR (BA) 283 Hj51
Xirdalan AZ 70 Ne25
Xishaqundao CHN 120 Qg37
Xishui CHN (GZH) 95 Qd31
Xishui CHN (HUB) 102 Qh30
Xi Shui CHN 102 Qh30
Xi Taijnar Hu CHN 87 Pg27
Xitole GNB 183 Kc40
Xi Ujimqin Qi CHN (NMZ) 91 Qj23
Xiushui CHN (JGX) 102 Qh31
Xiu Shui CHN 102 Qh31
Xiuwen CHN (GZH) 96 Qd32
Xiuwu CHN (HNN) 95 Qg28
Xiuyan CHN (LNG) 100 Rb25
Xiuying CHN (HAN) 96 Qf36
Xiwu CHN (QHI) 89 Pj29
Xixabangma Feng CHN 88 Pc31
Xixia CHN (HNN) 95 Qf29
Xi Xian CHN (HNN) 102 Qh29
Xi Xian CHN (SAX) 93 Qf27
Xixiang CHN (SAA) 95 Qd29
Xixia Wangling CHN 92 Qd26
Xixona E 29 Ku48
Xiyang CHN (SAX) 93 Qg27
Xizang Zizhiqu CHN 83 Pb12
Xmaben MEX (CAM) 255 Ff36
Xocavand AZ 70 Nd26
Xochiapa MEX (VC) 254 Fc37
Xochicalco MEX 254 Fa36
Xochimilco MEX (MEX) 254 Fa36
Xochob MEX 255 Ff36
Xo'jayli UZ 71 Nk24
Xom Tang VN 96 Qc35
Xovos UZ 76 Oe25
Xpujil MEX (CAM) 255 Ff36
Xpujil MEX 255 Ff36
Xuan'en CHN (HUB) 95 Qe31
Xuanhan CHN (SCH) 95 Qd30
Xuanhua CHN (HBI) 93 Qh25
Xuankong Monastery CHN 93 Qg26
Xuan Loc VN 115 Qd40
Xuan Mai VN 96 Qc35
Xuanwei CHN (YUN) 96 Qc32
Xuanzhong Si CHN 93 Qg27
Xuanzhou CHN (AHU) 102 Qk30
Xuchang CHN (HNN) 95 Qg28
Xudat AZ 70 Ne25
Xu Da, Tomb of = Imperial Tombs of the Ming and Qing Dynasties CHN (JGS) 102 Qk29
Xuddur SP 199 Nb43
Xudun SP 199 Nd41
Xuebao Ding CHN 94 Qb29
Xuefeng Shan CHN 95 Qf32
Xuejiadao CHN (SDG) 100 Ra28
Xueshan CHN 92 Qc27
Xugui CHN (QHI) 89 Pj28
Xultún GCA 255 Ff37
Xumishan Shiku CHN 92 Qc27
Xunantunich BH 255 Ff37
Xundian CHN (YUN) 113 Qb33
Xungru CHN (TIB) 88 Pc31
Xun He CHN 95 Qe29
Xun He CHN 98 Re21
Xunhua CHN (QHI) 92 Qb28
Xun Jiang CHN 96 Qf34
Xunke CHN (HLG) 98 Re21
Xunwu CHN (JGX) 97 Qh33
Xun Xian CHN (HNN) 93 Qh28
Xunyang CHN (SAA) 95 Qe29
Xunyi CHN (SAA) 95 Qe28
Xupu CHN (HUN) 96 Qf32
Xushui CHN (HBI) 93 Qh26
Xuwen CHN (GDG) 96 Qf35
Xuyi CHN (JGS) 102 Qk29
Xuyong CHN (SCH) 95 Qc31
Xuzhou CHN (JGS) 102 Qj28
Xylofagou CY 51 Mo55
Xylóskalo GR 48 Md55

Y

Yaak USA (MT) 233 Ec21
Yaamba AUS (QLD) 149 Sf57
Ya'an CHN (SCH) 94 Qb31
Yaaq Braaway SP 205 Nb45
Yaba RI 130 Rd46
Yaba-Hita-Hikosan N.P. J 103 Rf29
Yabassi CAM 194 Le43
Yabayo CI 192 Kg43
Yabebyry PY 289 Hb59
Yabello ETH 198 Mk43
Yabello Sanctuary ETH 198 Mk43
Yabia RDC 200 Mb44
Yablonovyy Range RUS 59 Qc08
Yabroud SYR 64 Mj29
Yabucoa USA (PR) 261 Gh36
Yabuli CHN (HLG) 98 Re23
Yabus ETH 197 Mh41
Yabuyanos PE 273 Gd46
Yacambú, P.N. YV 269 Gf41
Yacaré Norte PY 285 Ha57
Yacata FJI 163 Ua54
Yachats USA (OR) 234 Dh23
Yacheng CHN (HAN) 96 Qe36
Yacimiento Río Turbio RA (SC) 294 Gd71
Yacuiba BOL 285 Gj56
Yacuma BOL 279 Gg53
Yadagiri Gutta IND 109 Ok37
Yadavindra Gardens IND 107 Oj30
Yadgir IND (KTK) 108 Oj37
Yadibikro CI 193 Kh42
Yadkinville USA (NC) 249 Fk27
Yadmah KSA 68 Nc36
Yafase RI 131 Sa47
Yafran LAR 174 Lg29
Yagaba GH 193 Kk40
Yagaji RN 186 Le38
Yagasa Cluster FJI 163 Ua55
Yago CAM 187 Lh40
Yagradagzê Shan CHN 89 Ph28
Yaguachi Nuevo EC 272 Ga47
Yaguajay C 259 Ga34
Yaguaraparo YV 270 Gj40
Yaguarón PY 285 Hb58
Yaguarón ROU 289 Hd62
Yaguas CO 273 Ge47
Yaha THA 116 Qa42
Yahekou CHN (HNN) 95 Qg29
Yahk CDN (BC) 232 Eb21
Yaho BF 193 Kj40
Yahşiham TR 51 Mo51
Yahşiyan TR 51 Mo51
Yahualica de González Gallo MEX (JLC) 254 Ej35
Yahuma RDC 200 Mb45
Yahyalı TR 51 Mq52
Yaibrai CHN (NMZ) 92 Qb26
Yaita J 101 Rk27
Yajalón MEX (CHP) 255 Fd37
Yajiang CHN (SCH) 94 Qa30
Yaka RCA 200 Lk43
Yakana RDC 200 Mb45
Yakarra AUS (QLD) 150 Sb60
Yakassé-Attobrou CI 193 Kj42
Yakassé Mé CI 193 Kj43
Yakeshi CHN (NMZ) 91 Ra21
Yakima USA (WA) 232 Dk22
Yakima Ind. Res. USA 232 Dk22
Yakkabog UZ 76 Od26
Yakmach PK 80 Ob31
Yako BF 185 Kj39
Yakoma RDC 200 Mb43
Yakote J 101 Sa26
Yaku J 103 Rf30
Yaku-jima J 103 Rf30
Yakumo J 99 Sa24
Yakushima N.P. J 103 Rf30
Yakutat USA (AK) 231 Da16
Yakutat Bay USA 231 Da16
Yakutia RUS 59 Qc05
Yala EAK 204 Mh45
Yala GH 193 Kk40
Yala THA 117 Qa42
Yalagüina NIC 256 Fg39
Yalakdere TR 50 Mk50
Yalaki RDC 200 Mb45
Yalama AZ 70 Ne25
Yala N.P. CL 111 Pa43
Yalape PE 278 Gb49
Yalardy AUS (WA) 140 Qh59
Yalata AUS (SA) 145 Rf61
Yalata A.L. AUS 145 Rf61
Yalbalgo AUS (WA) 140 Qh58
Yale CDN (BC) 232 Dk21
Yale EAK 204 Mh45
Yale USA (WA) 232 Dj22
Yaleko RDC 201 Mc45
Yalgar River AUS 140 Qk59
Yalgo BF 185 Kk39
Yalgoo AUS (WA) 144 Qj60
Yalgorup N.P. AUS 144 Qh62
Yali BF 185 La39
Yalí NIC 256 Fg39
Yaligimba RDC 200 Mb44
Yalıhüyük TR 51 Mn53
Yalıkavak TR 49 Mh53
Yalıköy TR 50 Mj49
Yalinga RCA 196 Mb42
Yallalong AUS (WA) 140 Qh59
Yalleroi AUS (QLD) 151 Sc58
Yallingup AUS (WA) 144 Qh62
Yallo BF 184 Kj39
Yalock AUS (NSW) 153 Sc62
Yaloké RCA 195 Lj43
Yalong Jiang CHN 94 Pk29
Yalong Jiang CHN 113 Qa32
Yalongwa RDC 200 Mb45
Yaloupi F (GF) 271 Hd44
Yalova TR 50 Mk50
Yalpirakinu A.L. AUS 142 Rg57
Yalsihón MEX (YT) 255 Ff35
Yalta UA 55 Mh23
Yalufi RDC 201 Mc45
Yalu Jiang CHN/PRK 100 Rd25
Ya'lujiang Kou PRK 100 Rc26
Yalvaç TR 51 Mm52
Yamada J 101 Sa26
Yamagata J 101 Sa26
Yamaguchi J 101 Rf28
Yamakawa J 101 Rh28
Yamal Nenets Autonomous District RUS 58 Oc05
Yamal Poluostrov RUS 58 Ob04
Yamanashi J 101 Rk28
Yamanlar TR 50 Mk52
Yamara YV 269 Gg43
Yamarna AUS (WA) 141 Rb59
Yamasa DOM 260 Ge36
Yamasaki J 101 Rh28
Yamatan CHN (QHI) 94 Pk28
Yamato Rise 83 Rc11
Yamatsun J 101 Sa27
Yamba AUS (NSW) 151 Sg60
Yamba BF 185 La39
Yambala RCA 196 Ma42
Yambala Koudouvélé RCA 196 Ma42
Yambarran Range AUS 139 Rf53
Yambata RDC 200 Ma44
Yamba-Yamba RDC 206 Md48
Yambéring RG 192 Kd40
Yambio SUD 201 Me43
Yambol BG 48 Mg48
Yambuya RDC 201 Mc45
Yamdena RI 133 Rf49
Yamethin MYA 113 Pj35
Yamnotri IND (UTT) 107 Ok30
Yamoussoukro CI 193 Kh42
Yampa USA (CO) 235 Eg25
Yampa USA 235 Ef25
Yamparaez BOL 284 Gh55
Yamuna IND 107 Pa33
Yamunanagar IND (HYA) 107 Oj30
Yamzho Yumco CHN 89 Pf31
Yan MAL 116 Qa43
Yanaba Island PNG 160 Sf50
Yanac AUS (VIC) 152 Sa64
Yanac PE 278 Gb50
Yanachaga Chemillén, P.N. PE 278 Gc51
Yanacu Grande PE 272 Gc48
Yanadani J 103 Rg29
Yanahuanca PE 278 Gb51
Yanai J 101 Rg29
Yanam IND (PND) 109 Pb37
Yanam Pondicherry IND 109 Pb37
Yanan CHN (GDG) 96 Qf34
Yan'an CHN (SAA) 93 Qe27
Yanaoca PE 279 Ge53
Yanatil PE 279 Gd52
Yanbian CHN (SCH) 113 Qa32
Yanbu al Bahr KSA 66 Mk33
Yancannia AUS (NSW) 150 Sb61
Yanchang CHN (SAA) 93 Qf27
Yancheng CHN (JGS) 102 Ra29
Yanchi CHN (NHZ) 92 Qd27
Yanco AUS (NSW) 153 Sd63
Yanco Glen AUS (NSW) 150 Sa61
Yancun CHN (GDG) 97 Qh34
Yandal AUS (WA) 140 Ra59
Yandang shan CHN 102 Ra32
Yandaran AUS (QLD) 151 Sg58
Yandaxkak CHN (XUZ) 87 Pe26
Yandev WAN 194 Le42
Yandil AUS (WA) 140 Qj59
Yandina SOL 161 Sk50
Yandina Plantation Resort SOL 161 Sk50
Yandja RDC 200 Lj46
Yandon MYA 114 Ph37
Yandongi RDC 200 Mb44
Yandun CHN (XUZ) 87 Pf24
Yanfolila RMM 192 Kf40
Yanga CAM 195 Lh44
Yanga TCH 196 Lk41
Yangalia RCA 196 Ma42
Yangambi RDC 201 Mc45
Yangara TCH 188 Lk35
Yangas PE 278 Gb51
Yangasso RMM 184 Kh39
Yangbajain CHN (TIB) 89 Pf30
Yangchang CHN (YUN) 96 Qc32
Yangcheng CHN (SAX) 95 Qg28
Yangchuan CHN (GZH) 96 Qd32
Yangchun CHN (GDG) 96 Qf34
Yangcun CHN (TJN) 93 Qj26
Yangdok PRK 100 Rd26
Yangga RI 158 Sa50
Yang He CHN 93 Qh25
Yangi Qal'eh AFG 78 Oe27
Yangiqishloq UZ 76 Od25
Yangirabot UZ 76 Oc25
Yangiyer UZ 76 Oe25
Yangiyo'l UZ 76 Oe25
Yangizang UZ 76 Od27
Yangjiang CHN (GDG) 96 Qf35
Yanglin CHN (YUN) 113 Qb33
Yangling CHN (SAA) 95 Qd28
Yangluo CHN (HUB) 102 Qh30
Yangmingshan N.P. RC 97 Ra33
Yangon MYA 114 Pj37
Yangon MYA 114 Pk37
Yangpingguan CHN (SAA) 95 Qd29
Yangpu Gang CHN 96 Qe36
Yangquan CHN (SAX) 93 Qg27
Yangquangu CHN (SAX) 93 Qf27
Yangqu Shan CHN 93 Qg27
Yangshan CHN (GDG) 96 Qg33
Yangshuo CHN (GZG) 96 Qf33
Yangtouyan CHN (YUN) 113 Qa33
Yangtze CHN 83 Qb12
Yangudi Rassa N.P. ETH 198 Na40
Yangxi CHN (GDG) 96 Qf35
Yangxin CHN (HUB) 102 Qh31
Yang-Yang SN 183 Kc38
Yangyuan CHN (HBI) 93 Qh25
Yangzhou CHN (JGS) 102 Qk29
Yangzi'e Z.B. CHN 102 Qk30
Yanhu CHN (TIB) 88 Pb29
Yanhuitlán MEX 254 Fb37
Yanji CHN (JLN) 100 Re24
Yanjin CHN (YUN) 94 Qc31
Yanjing CHN (CGQ) 95 Qd31
Yankari NationalPark WAN 187 Lf41
Yankton USA (SD) 240 Fb24
Yankton Ind. Res. USA 240 Fa24
Yanling CHN (HNN) 102 Qh28
Yanmen CHN (YUN) 94 Pk31
Yanmen G CHN 93 Qg26
Yanonge RDC 201 Mc45
Yanqi CHN (XUZ) 87 Pd24
Yanqing CHN (BJG) 93 Qh25
Yanqul OM 75 Nj34
Yanrey AUS (WA) 140 Qh57
Yanshan CHN (HBI) 93 Qj26
Yanshan CHN (YUN) 96 Qc34
Yanshou CHN (HLG) 98 Re23
Yansoribo RI 131 Rg46
Yantabulla AUS (NSW) 151 Sc60
Yantai CHN (SDG) 100 Ra27
Yantou CHN (ZJG) 102 Ra31
Yantzaza EC 272 Ga47
Yanxi CHN (HUN) 95 Qf31
Yanyuan CHN (SCH) 113 Qa32
Yanzikou CHN (GZH) 96 Qc32
Yao RCA 200 Lk43
Yao TCH 187 Lj39
Yao'an CHN (YUN) 113 Qa33
Yaodian CHN (GSU) 95 Qd28
Yaodian CHN (SAA) 93 Qe27
Yaolin Dong CHN 102 Qk31
Yaoundé CAM 195 Lf44
Yaowang Shan CHN 95 Qe28
Yao Xian CHN (SAA) 95 Qe28
Yapacana, P.N. YV 269 Gg44
Yapacani BOL 280 Gh54
Yapei GH 193 Kk41
Yapen RI 131 Rj46
Yapero RI 131 Rj48
Yapeyú RA (CR) 289 Hb60
Yapıldak TR 51 Ml51
Yap Islands FSM 156 Rd17
Yappar River AUS (QLD) 148 Sb55
Yapraklı TR 51 Mo50
Yap Trench 156 Rd17
Yapuparra A.L. AUS 141 Rd59
Yaqui MEX 237 Ef31
Yara C 259 Gb35
Yaraka AUS (QLD) 150 Sc58
Yaraligöz Dağı TR 62 Mh25
Yarawin AUS (NSW) 151 Sd61
Yarbasan TR 50 Mj52
Yarda TCH 188 Lk36
Yardea AUS (SA) 152 Rh62
Yardımcı Burnu TR 62 Mf27
Yardimli AZ 70 Ne26
Yare GB 21 Lb38
Yaré Lao SN 183 Kc37
Yaren NAU 157 Tb19
Yargatenga BF 193 Kk40
Yargatti IND (KTK) 108 Oh38
Yari CO 273 Gd45
Yarıkkaya TR 51 Mm52
Yarim YE 68 Nc38
Yaringa North AUS (WA) 140 Qh58
Yarışlı Gölü TR 51 Mk53
Yaritagua YV 269 Gf40
Yarkant CHN (XUZ) 86 Oj26
Yarkant He CHN 86 Oj27
Yarlarweelor AUS (WA) 140 Qj58
Yarloop AUS (WA) 144 Qh62
Yarlung Zangbo Jiang CHN 89 Pf31
Yarma TR 51 Mn53
Yarmouth CDN (NS) 245 Gg24
Yarmouth USA (ME) 247 Ge24
Yaro Lund PK 81 Oe32
Yarpuz TR 51 Mm53
Yarra DY 186 Lb40
Yarrabubba AUS (WA) 140 Qj59
Yarraden AUS (QLD) 146 Sb53
Yarram AUS (VIC) 153 Sd65
Yarra Ranges N.P. AUS (VIC) 153 Sc64
Yarrie AUS (WA) 140 Ra56
Yarronvale AUS (QLD) 151 Sc59
Yarrowitch AUS (NSW) 151 Sg61
Yarrowmere AUS (QLD) 149 Sc56
Yarrum AUS (QLD) 148 Rk54
Yarumal CO 268 Gc42
Yarvicoya, Cerro RCH 284 Gf56
Yasa RDC 203 Ma47
Yasawa FJI 163 Tj54
Yasawa Group FJI 163 Tj54
Yashi WAN 186 Ld39
Yashikela WAN 186 Lb41
Yashiro-jima J 101 Rg29
Yasinza'i Kalay AFG 78 Oc30
Yasothon THA 115 Qc38
Yass AUS (NSW) 153 Se63
Yasuj IR 72 Nf30
Yasun Burnu TR 63 Mj25
Yasuni EC 272 Gb46
Yasuni PE 272 Gc46
Yasuni, P.N. EC 272 Gc46
Yat RN 181 Lg35
Yata BOL 279 Gh52
Yata BOL 279 Gg52
Yata RCA 196 Mb41
Yatağan TR 50 Mj53
Yatako BF 185 La38
Yatang CHN (YUN) 113 Pk32
Yate F (NCL) 162 Td57
Yates Center USA (KS) 243 Fc27
Yatha MYA 113 Ph34
Yathon AUS (NSW) 153 Sc62
Yathon Nature Reserve AUS 153 Sc62
Yati CO 268 Gc42
Yatolema RDC 201 Mc45
Yatsushiro J 103 Rf29
Yatsu-take J 101 Rk28
Yatta EAK 204 Mj46
Yatta Plateau EAK 204 Mj46
Yatúa YV 273 Gg45
Yatung CHN (TIB) 88 Pe32
Yauca PE 278 Gc53
Yauco USA (PR) 261 Gg36
Yauhannah USA (SC) 249 Ga29
Yauli PE 278 Gc52
Yaupita BOL 285 Gh56
Yauri PE 279 Ge53
Yauyos PE 278 Gc52
Yauyupe HN 256 Fg39
Yaval IND (MHT) 108 Oh35
Yavari BR/PE 273 Ge48
Yavaros MEX (SO) 252 Ef32
Yavaşlar TR 62 Me26
Yavatmal IND (MHT) 109 Ok35
Yavero ó Paucartambo PE 279 Gd52
Yavineto PE 272 Gc46
Yavita YV 273 Gg44
Yaviza PA 257 Gb41
Yavsan Tuzlası TR 51 Mo52
Yavuzeli TR 62 Mj27
Yawatahama J 103 Rg29
Yawatongguzlangar CHN (XUZ) 86 Pb27
Yawatoutou, Mount GH/TG 193 La42
Yawgu GH 193 La40
Yawimu RI 158 Rk49
Yawngo MYA 113 Pk34
Yawri Bay WAL 192 Kd41
Yaxcabá MEX (YT) 255 Ff35
Yaxchilán MEX (CHP) 255 Fe37
Yayama RDC 200 Mb46
Yaygölü TR 51 Mq52
Yaylacık TR 51 Mn53
Yayvantepe TR 63 Na27
Yazd IR 72 Nh30
Yazdan IR 73 Oa29
Yazhou CHN (GZH) 96 Qd33
Yazıçayırı TR 51 Mo51
Yazıhan TR 63 Mk26
Yazılıkaya TR 51 Mp51
Yazıtepe TR 51 Mr50
Yazman PK 81 Of31
Yazoo City USA (MS) 243 Fe29
Ybbs A 35 Lp43
Ybbs A 35 Lq42
Ybycuí PY 289 Hb59
Ybycuí, P.N. PY 285 Hb58
Ybytyruzú, P.N. PY 285 Hb58
Yby-Yaú PY 285 Hb57
Ydby Hede DK 14 Lj34
Ye MYA 114 Pj38
Yea AUS (VIC) 153 Sc64
Yeadon GB 21 Kt37
Yebawmi MYA 113 Ph33
Yebbi-Bou TCH 188 Lk35
Yebbi Souma TCH 181 Lj35
Yebok MYA 114 Pg36
Yebya MYA 112 Ph35
Yecheng CHN (XUZ) 86 Oj27
Yecla E 29 Kt48
Yécora MEX (SO) 252 Ef31
Yedisu TR 63 Na26
Yedseram WAN 187 Lg40
Yeehaw Junction USA (FL) 250 Fk32
Yeelanna AUS (SA) 152 Rh63
Yeelirrie AUS (WA) 140 Ra59
Yegguebo RN 188 Lg36
Yeghegnadzor ARM 70 Nc26
Yégué TG 193 La41
Yegyi MYA 114 Ph37
Yeha ETH 191 Mk39
Yei SUD 197 Mf43
Yei SUD 201 Mf43
Yeji CHN (AHU) 102 Qh30
Yeji GH 193 Kk41
Yekaterinburg RUS 58 Oa07
Yekepa LB 192 Kf42
Yekia TCH 187 Lj37
Yekokora RDC 200 Ma45
Yek Shaba IR 72 Nd27
Yelahanga IND (KTK) 111 Oj40
Yela Island PNG 160 Sh51
Yelbarsli TM 73 Oa27
Yelcho RCH 292 Gd67
Yelcho ANT (RCH) 296 Gd31
Yele WAL 192 Ke41
Yeleğen TR 50 Mj52
Yelerbon AUS (QLD) 151 Sf60
Yélimané RMM 183 Ke38
Yelkaturti IND (APH) 109 Ok36
Yell GB 19 Kt30
Yellabinna Regional Reserve AUS 145 Rg61
Yellandu IND (APH) 109 Pa37
Yellapur IND (KTK) 110 Oh39
Yellareddi IND (APH) 108 Ok36
Yellowdine AUS (WA) 144 Qk61
Yellowdine Nature Reserve AUS (WA) 144 Qk61
Yellow Grass CDN (SK) 233 Eh21
Yellowhead Pass CDN 232 Ea19
Yellowknife CDN 224 Eb06
Yellow Pine USA (ID) 234 Ec23
Yellow River CHN 83 Qc11
Yellow Sea 83 Ra11
Yellowstone USA 235 Eg22
Yellowstone National Park USA 235 Ee23
Yell Sound GB 19 Kt30
Yellville USA (AR) 243 Fd27
Yelma AUS (WA) 141 Ra59
Yeloten TM 73 Ob27
Yelvertoft AUS (QLD) 148 Rk56
Yelwa WAN 186 Lc40
Yelwa WAN 186 Le41
Yema RDC 202 Lg48
Yema Nanshan CHN 87 Ph26
Yema Shan CHN 87 Ph26
Yemassee USA (SC) 249 Fk29
Yembo ETH 197 Mh41
Yemen YE 57 Na08
Yemnu PNG 158 Sb47
Ye-myet-ni MYA 112 Ph35
Yen CAM 195 Lg44
Yenagoa WAN 194 Ld43
Yenan-gyaung MYA 112 Ph35
Yen Bai VN 96 Qc35
Yenchang CHN (TIB) 89 Pe30
Yen Chau VN 96 Qc35
Yendé Milimou RG 192 Ke41
Yendéré BF 193 Kh40
Yendi GH 193 Kk41
Yénéganou RCB 202 Lg47
Yenge RDC 200 Ma46
Yengema WAL 192 Ke41
Yengi Kand IR 72 Nd27
Yengisar CHN (XUZ) 86 Oj26
Yengo RCB 195 Lh45
Yengo N.P. AUS 153 Sf62
Yenibaşak TR 63 Na26
Yeniçağa TR 51 Mn50
Yenice TR 50 Mj53
Yenice TR 51 Mn49
Yenice TR 51 Mn51
Yeniceoba TR 51 Mn52
Yeniçubuk TR 62 Mj26
Yenifakılı TR 51 Mq51
Yenifoça TR 49 Mg52
Yenihisar TR 49 Mh53
Yenikent TR 51 Mn51
Yenikent TR 51 Mo52
Yeniköy TR 50 Mj51
Yeniköy TR 50 Mj52
Yenimehmetli TR 51 Mn51
Yenipazar TR 50 Mj53
Yenipazar TR 50 Mi50
Yenipazar TR 51 Mq51
Yenişarbademli TR 51 Mm53
Yenişehir TR 50 Mk50
Yenişehir TR 50 Mk52
Yeniyıldız TR 51 Mp53
Yen Ly VN 115 Qc36
Yenne F 25 Lf45
Yéno G 202 Le46
Yeno G 202 Lf46
Yentna River USA 229 Ce14
Yeola IND (MHT) 108 Oh35
Yeo Lake AUS 141 Rc59
Yeo Lake Nature Reserve AUS 145 Rc60
Yeoval AUS (NSW) 153 Se62
Yeovil GB 21 Ks40
Yepachic MEX (CHH) 252 Ef31
Yepes E 29 Kr49
Yeppoon AUS (QLD) 149 Sf57
Yeraltı şehri (Derinkuyu) TR 51 Mp52
Yerba Loca RCH 288 Ge62
Yercaud IND (TNU) 111 Ok41
Yeremarou DY 186 Lb41
Yerevan ARM 63 Nc25
Yergara IND (KTK) 108 Oj37
Yeriho IL 64 Mh30
Yerilla AUS (WA) 144 Ra60
Yerington USA (NV) 234 Ea26
Yerköprü TR 51 Mn52
Yerköprü TR 62 Mg27
Yerköy TR 51 Mp51
Yermala IND (MHT) 108 Oh36
Yeröö gol MNG 90 Qd21
Yerupaja, Cerro PE 278 Gb51
Yerville F 22 La41
Yesagyo MYA 113 Ph35
Yesan ROK 100 Rd27
Yeshin MYA 112 Ph34
Yeshwant Sagar IND 108 Oh34
Yesilbağ TR 51 Mm53
Yeşil Camii (Bursa) TR 50 Mk50
Yeşil Camii (İznik) TR 50 Mk50
Yeşildağ TR 51 Mm53
Yeşilhisar TR 51 Mq52
Yeşilırmak TR 62 Mh25
Yeşilova TR 50 Mk53
Yeşilova TR 51 Mo52
Yeşilöz TR 51 Mn51
Yeşilvadi TR 50 Mk49
Yeşilyurt TR 51 Mn51
Yeşilyurt TR 51 Mr51
Yeste E 29 Ks48
Yesterday River CDN 239 Fk20
Yet ETH 199 Nb43
Yetla de Juárez MEX (OAX) 254 Fb37
Yetman AUS (NSW) 151 Sf60
Ye-u MYA 113 Ph34
Yevlax AZ 70 Nd25
Ye Xian CHN (HNN) 95 Qg29
Yexianggu CHN 113 Qa34
Yeyik CHN (XUZ) 86 Pb27
Yeyungou CHN (XUZ) 86 Pc25
Yhú PY 286 Hc58
Yi ROU 289 Hb62
Yi'an CHN (HLG) 98 Rc22
Yibin CHN (SCH) 94 Qc31
Yichang CHN (HUB) 95 Qf30
Yicheng CHN (HUB) 95 Qg30
Yicheng CHN (SAX) 95 Qf28
Yichuan CHN (HNN) 95 Qg28
Yichuan CHN (SAA) 95 Qf28
Yichun CHN (HLG) 98 Re22
Yichun CHN (JGX) 102 Qh32
Yidun CHN (SCH) 94 Pk30
Yiew RI 130 Re45
Yifag ETH 198 Mj40
Yifeng CHN (JGX) 102 Qh31
Yığılca TR 51 Mm50
Yihuang CHN (JGX) 102 Qj32
Yijun CHN (SAA) 95 Qe28
Yilan CHN (HLG) 98 Re22
Yildirim Camii TR 50 Mh51
Yıldız Dağları TR 50 Mh49
Yıldızeli TR 62 Mj26
Yilehuli Shan CHN 98 Rc20
Yiliang CHN (YUN) 96 Qc32
Yiliang CHN (YUN) 113 Qb33
Yilingyan CHN 96 Qe34
Yilong CHN (SCH) 95 Qd30
Yilou BF 185 Kk39
Yilui PNG 158 Sb47
Yima CHN (HNN) 95 Qf28
Yimen CHN (SAA) 95 Qd28
Yimin CHN (NMZ) 91 Qk21
Yimni River PNG 159 Sb48
Yimuhe CHN (NMZ) 91 Ra19
Yinan CHN (SDG) 93 Qk28
Yinchuan CHN (NHZ) 92 Qd26
Yindi AUS (WA) 144 Rb61
Yingcheng CHN (HUB) 95 Qg30
Yingchengzi Tomb CHN 100 Ra26
Yingde CHN (GDG) 97 Qg33
Yinggehai CHN (HAN) 96 Qe36
Yinghe CHN (AHU) 102 Qj29
Ying He CHN 102 Qj29
Yingjiang CHN (YUN) 113 Pj33
Yingjin He CHN 93 Qk24
Yingkou CHN (LNG) 100 Rb25
Yingkou CHN (LNG) 100 Rb25
Yingpanshan CHN (SCH) 96 Qc32
Yingshan CHN (AHU) 102 Qj29
Yingshan CHN (SCH) 95 Qd30
Yingtan CHN (JGX) 102 Qj31
Yingui CAM 194 Lf43
Ying Xian CHN (SAX) 93 Qg26
Yingxian Mu Ta CHN 93 Qg26
Yingxiuwan CHN (SCH) 94 Qb30
Yining CHN (XUZ) 84 Pa24
Yiningarra A.L. AUS 142 Re56
Yinjiang CHN (GZH) 95 Qe32
Yinjiang CHN (GZH) 96 Qe32
Yinma He CHN 98 Rc23
Yin Shan CHN 93 Qe25
Yinxu CHN 93 Qh27
Yipinglang CHN (YUN) 113 Qa33
Yiqikai CHN (QHI) 94 Pk28
Yirba Muda ETH 198 Mk42
Yirga Chefe ETH 198 Mk42
Yirié RG 192 Kf41
Yirol SUD 197 Mf42
Yirrkala AUS (NT) 139 Rj52
Yirshi CHN (NMZ) 91 Qk22
Yishui CHN (SDG) 93 Qk28
Yitong CHN (JLN) 100 Rc24
Yitong He CHN 98 Rc23
Yitulihe CHN (NMZ) 91 Ra20
Yiwu CHN (XUZ) 87 Ph24
Yiwu CHN (ZJG) 102 Ra31
Yiwulu Shan CHN (LNG) 100 Ra25
Yi Xian CHN (HBI) 93 Qh26
Yixing CHN (JGS) 102 Qk30
Yiyang CHN (HUN) 95 Qg31
Yiyang CHN (JGX) 102 Qj31
Yiyu IND (ARP) 112 Ph31
Yiyuan CHN (SDG) 93 Qk27
Yizhang CHN (HUN) 97 Qg33
Yizheng CHN (JGS) 102 Qk29
Yizhou CHN (GZG) 96 Qe33
Yizhou CHN (LNG) 100 Ra25
Ylakiai LT 17 Mb34
Ylämaa FIN 16 Mj30
Yläne FIN 16 Mc30
Yli-Kitka FIN 11 Me12
Ylimarkku = Övermark FIN 13 Mb28
Ylitornio FIN 11 Mb12
Ylivieska FIN 11 Mc13
Ylöjärvi FIN 16 Md29
Yngaren S 13 Lr32
Yngen S 13 Lp31
Yoakum USA (TX) 243 Fb31
Yoboki DJI 199 Nb40
Yocalla BOL 284 Gh55
Yof SN 183 Kb38
Yofor RI 131 Rj48
Yogoum TCH 189 Lk37
Yogyakarta RI 128 Qf49
Yohaltún MEX (CAM) 255 Fe36
Yoho N.P. CDN 233 Eb20
Yohualichan MEX 254 Fb35
Yoichi J 99 Sa24
Yokadouma CAM 195 Lh44
Yok Don N.P. VN 115 Qd39
Yokkaichi J 101 Rj28
Yoko CAM 195 Lg43
Yokoate-jima J 103 Re31
Yokoboué CI 193 Kh43
Yokohama J 99 Sa25
Yokohama J 101 Rk28
Yokosuka J 101 Rk28
Yola CAM 195 Lh43

Yola – Zhi Jin Cave

Yola WAN 187 Lg41
Yolande F (GF) 271 Hd43
Yolcular TR 63 Nb26
Yoliati MEX (SLP) 253 Ek34
Yolombo RDC 200 Mb46
Yolüstü TR 63 Na26
Yomou RG 192 Kf42
Yomuka RI 158 Rk49
Yonago J 101 Rg28
Yoneshiro-gawa J 101 Sa25
Yonezawa J 101 Sa27
Yong'an CHN (FJN) 97 Qj33
Yongchang CHN (GSU) 92 Qa26
Yongcheng CHN (HNN) 102 Qj29
Yongcheng CHN (JGX) 102 Qk31
Yongchuan CHN (CGQ) 95 Qc31
Yongde CHN (YUN) 113 Pk34
Yongdeng CHN (GSU) 92 Qb27
Yongding CHN (FJN) 97 Qj33
Yongdok ROK 100 Re27
Yongfeng CHN (JGX) 102 Qh32
Yongfeng CHN (JGX) 102 Qh32
Yongfu CHN (GZG) 96 Qf33
Yonghung PRK 100 Rd26
Yongjia CHN (ZJG) 102 Ra31
Yongjing CHN (GSU) 92 Qb28
Yongju ROK 100 Re27
Yongkang CHN (ZJG) 102 Qk31
Yongle CHN (GZH) 96 Qe32
Yonglegong CHN 95 Qf28
Yongling Tomb CHN 100 Rb25
Yongning CHN (GZG) 96 Qe34
Yongning CHN (NHZ) 92 Qd26
Yongofondo RCA 200 Mb43
Yong Peng MAL 117 Qb44
Yongping CHN (JGX) 102 Qj31
Yongping CHN (SAA) 93 Qe27
Yongping CHN (YUN) 113 Pk33
Yong Quan Si CHN 102 Qk32
Yongren CHN (YUN) 113 Qa32
Yongshan CHN (YUN) 94 Qb31
Yongsheng CHN (YUN) 113 Qa32
Yongshun CHN (HUN) 95 Qe31
Yongxin CHN (HUN) 97 Qg32
Yongxin CHN (JGX) 97 Qh32
Yongxiu CHN (JGX) 102 Qh31
Yongzhou CHN (HUN) 96 Qf32
Yonibana WAL 192 Kd41
Yonkers USA (NY) 247 Gd25
Yonne F 23 Ld43
Yontai CHN (FJN) 97 Qk33
Yopal CO 268 Gd43
Yopie Podogle LB 192 Kf42
Yopurga CHN (XUZ) 86 Oj26
Yorazlar TR 51 Mm52
Yorito HN 256 Fg38
York AUS (WA) 144 Qj61
York GB 21 Kt37
York USA (NE) 240 Fb25
York USA (PA) 247 Gb26
York USA (SC) 249 Fk28
York WAL 192 Kd41
Yorke Peninsula AUS 152 Rj63
Yorketown AUS (SA) 152 Rj63
Yorkeys Knob AUS (QLD) 149 Sc54
York Factory (abandoned) CDN 238 Fd17
Yorkshire USA (NY) 247 Ga24
Yorkshire Dales N.P. GB 21 Ks36
Yorkshire Downs AUS (QLD) 148 Sa56
Yorkshire Wolds GB 21 Ku36
Yorkton CDN (SK) 238 Ej20
Yorktown USA (TX) 242 Fb31
Yornaning AUS (WA) 144 Qj62
Yoro HN 256 Fg38
Yoro RMM 185 Kj38
Yorobougoula RMM 192 Kg40
Yoron J 103 Re32
Yoron-jima J 103 Re32
Yorosso RMM 184 Kh39
Yorubaland Plateau WAN 194 Lb41
Yosemite N.P. USA (CA) 234 Ea27
Yosemite Village USA (CA) 234 Ea27
Yoshino-gawa J 101 Rg28
Yoshino-Kumano N.P. J 101 Rh29
Yoshino sacred site J 101 Rh28
Yosu ROK 100 Rd28
Yosua PNG 158 Sb48
Yotai-santi J 99 Sa24
Youangarra AUS (WA) 144 Qk60
Youanmi Downs AUS (WA) 144 Qk60
Yoube ETH 199 Nc42
Youdunzi CHN (QHI) 87 Pf26
Youghal IRL 20 Kn39
Youghal Bay IRL 20 Kn39
Youkounkoun RG 183 Kd39
You Le Yuan CHN 94 Qc30
Youllemmedene RMM 185 La37
Young AUS (NSW) 153 Se63
Young CDN (SK) 233 Eh20
Young ROU 289 Hb62
Youngerina AUS (NSW) 151 Sc60
Younghusband Peninsula AUS 152 Rk63
Youngstown CDN (AB) 233 Ee20
Youngstown USA (OH) 247 Fk25
Youssoufia MA 172 Kf29
Youvarou RMM 184 Kh38
You Xian CHN (HUN) 97 Qg32
Youyang CHN (CGQ) 95 Qe31
Youyi Feng CHN 85 Pd21
Youzhou CHN (HNN) 95 Qg28
Yowa RDC 200 Ma44
Yowergabbie AUS (WA) 144 Qj60
Yo Yo Park AUS (QLD) 151 Sd59
Yozgat TR 51 Mp51
Yozgat Camlığı Milli Parkı TR 51 Mp51
Ypacaraí, P.N. PY 285 Hb58
Ypäjä FIN 16 Md30
Ypané PY 285 Hb57
Ype Jhú PY 286 Hc57
Ypsilanti USA (MI) 246 Fj24
Yreka USA (CA) 234 Dj25
Ysabel Channel PNG 159 Se46
Yset N 12 Ll28
Yssingeaux F 25 Le45
Ystad S 15 Lo35
Ytyk KS 77 Ok25
Ytre Arna N 12 Lf30
Ytre Oppedal N 12 Lf29
Ytre Sula N 12 Le29
Ytterhogdal S 13 Lp28
Yttermalung S 13 Lo30
Yu RI 130 Re46
Yuanbao Shan CHN 96 Qe33
Yuanjiang CHN (YUN) 113 Qb34
Yuan Jiang CHN 95 Qf31
Yuan Jiang CHN 113 Qa34
Yuanlin CHN (NMZ) 91 Ra21
Yuanlin RC 97 Ra34
Yuanling CHN (HUN) 95 Qf31
Yuanmou CHN (YUN) 113 Qa33
Yuanping CHN (SAX) 93 Qg26
Yuanqu CHN (SAX) 95 Qf28
Yuantan CHN (AHU) 102 Qj30
Yuantouzhu CHN 102 Ra30
Yuanyang CHN (YUN) 113 Qb34
Yuba USA (OK) 243 Fb29
Yuba City USA (CA) 234 Dk26
Yubari J 99 Sa24
Yubdo ETH 197 Mh41
Yubetsu J 99 Sb23
Yubetu-dake J 99 Sa24
Yucatán MEX (YT) 255 Fg35
Yucatán MEX 255 Ff35
Yucatán Basin 258 Fh35
Yucatán Channel 258 Fh35
Yucatán Peninsula MEX 255 Ff35
Yucca House Nat. Mon. USA 237 Ef27
Yucca Valley USA (CA) 236 Eb28
Yücebağ TR 63 Na26
Yuchán RA (SE) 288 Gj59
Yuci CHN (SAX) 93 Qg27
Yucumo BOL 279 Gg53
Yudi Shan CHN 91 Rb19
Yudu CHN (JGX) 97 Qh33
Yuechi CHN (SCH) 95 Qd30
Yueliang He CHN 98 Rb23
Yuelushan CHN 95 Qg31
Yuendumu AUS (NT) 142 Rf57
Yuendumu A.L. AUS 142 Rf57
Yueqing CHN (ZJG) 102 Ra31
Yuexi CHN (AHU) 102 Qj30
Yueyang CHN (HUN) 95 Qg31
Yueyang CHN (SCH) 95 Qc30
Yueya Quan CHN 87 Ph26
Yueya Quan CHN 87 Ph26
Yufle SP 199 Nd40
Yugan CHN (JGX) 102 Qj31
Yugia CHN (QHI) 87 Ph26
Yuğluk Dağı TR 62 Mg27
Yuhe CHN (SAA) 93 Qe27
Yuhe CHN (SDG) 102 Qj28
Yuhomae J 103 Rf29
Yuhong CHN (GZG) 96 Qd33
Yuhuan CHN (ZJG) 102 Ra31
Yuhuan Dao CHN 102 Ra31
Yuin AUS (WA) 140 Qj59
Yuinmery AUS (WA) 144 Qk60
Yu Jiang CHN 96 Qe34
Yukarıçamozü TR 63 Mj26
Yukarı Sakarya Ovaları TR 51 Mm51
Yuki RDC 203 Lk47
Yuki River USA 229 Cb13
Yukon Charley Rivers Nat. Preserve USA (AK) 229 Cj13
Yukon Delta USA 228 Bj14
Yukon Delta National Wildlife Refuge USA (AK) 228 Bh15
Yukon Flats National Wildlife Refuge USA 229 Cg12
Yukon Plateau CDN 231 Db14
Yukon River USA 229 Cd13
Yukon Territory CDN 224 Da06
Yüksekova TR 63 Nc27
Yukuhashi J 103 Rf29
Yulara AUS (NT) 142 Rf58
Yuleba AUS (QLD) 151 Se59
Yulee USA (FL) 249 Fk30
Yule River AUS 140 Qk56
Yuli CHN (XUZ) 87 Pd25
Yuli RC 97 Ra34
Yuli WAN 186 Lf41
Yulin CHN (GZG) 96 Qf34
Yulin CHN (SAA) 93 Qe26
Yulinsi Shiku CHN 87 Ph25
Yulong Xueshan CHN 113 Qa32
Yuma USA (AZ) 236 Ec29
Yuma USA (CO) 240 Ej25
Yumare YV 269 Gf40
Yumariba YV 270 Gj43
Yumbarra Conservation Park AUS 152 Rg61
Yumbe EAU 201 Mf44
Yumbel RCH 292 Gd64
Yumbi RDC 200 Lj46
Yumbi RDC 201 Md46
Yumbo CO 268 Gb44
Yumen CHN (GSU) 87 Pj26
Yumenguan CHN (GSU) 87 Pg25
Yumen Guan CHN 87 Pg25
Yumen Zhen CHN (GSU) 87 Pj25
Yumin CHN (XUZ) 84 Pb22
Yuna AUS (WA) 144 Qh60
Yunak TR 51 Mm52
Yunchara BOL 284 Gh56
Yuncheng CHN (SAX) 95 Qf28
Yuncheng CHN (SDG) 93 Qj28
Yundamindra AUS (WA) 144 Rb60
Yunday RCH 292 Ge64
Yunfu CHN (GDG) 96 Qg34
Yungaburra AUS (QLD) 149 Sc54
Yungang Grottoes CHN 93 Qg25
Yungas BOL 280 Gh54
Yungay PE 278 Gb50
Yungay PE 284 Gf58
Yunguyo PE 284 Gf54
Yunhe CHN (ZJG) 102 Qk31
Yunkai Dashan CHN 96 Qf34
Yunkanjini A.L. AUS 142 Rf57
Yunlong CHN (YUN) 113 Pk33
Yunmeng CHN (HUB) 95 Qg30
Yunnan CHN 82 Qa13
Yunta AUS (SA) 152 Rk62
Yuntaishan CHN 102 Qk28
Yuntdağ TR 49 Mh52
Yunt Dağı TR 49 Mh52
Yunusemre TR 51 Mm51
Yunuslar TR 62 Mf27
Yunwu CHN (GZH) 96 Qd32
Yunwu Shan CHN 93 Qj25
Yunwu Shan CHN 96 Qf34
Yunxi CHN (SCH) 95 Qc30
Yun Xian CHN (HUB) 95 Qf29
Yun Xian CHN (YUN) 113 Qa33
Yunxiao CHN (FJN) 97 Qj34
Yunyang CHN (CGQ) 95 Qe30
Yunyang CHN (HNN) 95 Qg29
Yuolong CHN (HUN) 95 Qg31
Yuping CHN (GZH) 96 Qe32
Yuqian CHN (ZJG) 102 Qk30
Yuqing CHN (GZH) 96 Qd32
Yuquan CHN (HLG) 98 Rd23
Yu Quan Guan CHN 95 Qc28
Yura BOL 284 Gh56
Yura PE 284 Ge54
Yurayaco CO 272 Gb45
Yuraygir N.P. AUS 151 Sg60
Yurimaguas PE 272 Gb48
Yuriria MEX (GJT) 254 Ek35
Yurua PE 279 Gd50
Yuruari YV 270 Gk42
Yurubí, P.N. YV 269 Gf40
Yushan CHN (JGX) 102 Qk31
Yu Shan RC 97 Ra34
Yushan N.P. RC 97 Ra34
Yushanzhen CHN (CGQ) 95 Qe31
Yushe CHN (GZH) 96 Qc32
Yushe CHN (SAX) 93 Qg27
Yushu CHN (JLN) 98 Rd23
Yushu CHN (QHI) 89 Pj29
Yushutun CHN (HLG) 98 Rb22
Yusufeli TR 63 Na25
Yusun Shoal 115 Qe40
Yusupalik Tag CHN 87 Pe26
Yutian CHN (XUZ) 86 Pa27
Yuto RA (PJ) 285 Gh57
Yuty PY 289 Hb59
Yuwang CHN (NHZ) 92 Qd27
Yuxi CHN (GZH) 95 Qd31
Yuxi CHN (YUN) 113 Qb33
Yuxia CHN (YUN) 96 Qc33
Yu Xian CHN (SAX) 93 Qg26
Yuxikou CHN (AHU) 102 Qk30
Yuyao CHN (ZJG) 102 Ra30
Yuzawa J 101 Sa26
Yuzhuduq UZ 76 Ob24
Yverdon CH 34 Lg44
Yvetot F 22 La41
Ywa Ngan MYA 113 Pj35
Ywathike MYA 112 Pg35
Ywathit MYA 114 Ph36
Ylanly TM 71 Nk25
Yzetfontein ZA 216 Lk62

Z

Zaachila MEX 254 Fb37
Zâafrane TN 174 Le29
Zaamar Uul MNG 90 Qc21
Zaangarskoe plato RUS 58 Pc07
Zaankhoshuu MNG 90 Qa22
Zaanstad NL 32 Le38
Zabadani SYR 64 Mj29
Zabajkal'sk RUS 91 Qj21
Zabala RO 45 Mg45
Zabalj SCG 44 Ma45
Zabalocce BY 52 Mf19
Zabata RCB 202 Lh47
Zab-e Kuchek IR 72 Nc27
Zabid YE 68 Nb38
Zabierzów PL 37 Lu40
Zabinka BY 37 Md38
Ząbkowice Śląskie PL 36 Lr40
Žabljak SCG 46 Lu47
Žabłudów PL 37 Md37
Žabno PL 37 Ma40
Zabol IR 73 Oa30
Zaboli IR 75 Oa32
Zabolova LV 17 Mh33
Zaborski Park Krajobrazowy PL 36 Ls37
Zăbrani RO 44 Mb44
Zabré BF 193 Kk40
Zabriskie Point USA 236 Eb27
Zabrze PL 36 Lt40
Zaburunje KZ 70 Nf22
Zaburunje shyghanaghy KZ 70 Nf22
Zabzugu GH 193 La41
Zabzuni AL 46 Ma49
Zacapa GCA 255 Ff38
Zacapa HN 255 Ff38
Zacapu MEX (MHC) 254 Ek36
Zacapuato MEX (GUR) 254 Ek36
Zacatecas MEX (ZCT) 253 Ej34
Zacatecas MEX 253 Ej34
Zacatecoluca ES 255 Ff39
Zacatepec MEX (MOR) 254 Fa36
Zacatlán MEX (PUE) 254 Fb36
Zachary USA (LA) 243 Fe30
Zachidnyj Buh UA/PL 37 Me40
Zachlorou GR 48 Mc52
Zacoalco de Torres MEX (JLC) 254 Ej35
Zacualtipan MEX (HDG) 254 Fa35
Zadar HR 41 Lq46
Zadarski kanal HR 41 Lq46
Zadetkale Island MYA 116 Pj40
Zadetkyi Island MYA 116 Pj41
Zadgay MNG 90 Pk22
Zadié G 195 Lg45
Zadoj CHN (QHI) 89 Ph29
Zadonsk RUS 53 Mk19
Zadunajvka UA 45 Mk45
Zafarana ET 177 Mg31
Zafar Qand IR 72 Ng29
Zafarwal PK 79 Oh29
Zafferana Etnea I 42 Lq53
Zafra E 28 Ko48
Zag MA 172 Kf31
Zag MNG 90 Pk22
Zagai Island AUS 146 Sb50
Zagań PL 36 Lq39
Zagaoua TCH 189 Mb38
Zagare LT 17 Md34
Zagastayn Davaa MNG 90 Pj21
Zaghouan TN 174 Lf27
Zagnańsk PL 37 Ma40
Zagné CI 192 Kg42
Zagora MA 172 Kh30
Zagorje ob Savi SLO 41 Lq44
Zagóra PL 39 Mc41
Zagreb HR 41 Lq45
Zagros Mountains IR 60 Nb12
Zagubica SCG 46 Mb46
Zaguinasso CI 193 Kg40
Zagustaj RUS 91 Qf20
Zagvozd HR 41 Ls47
Zagzig ET 177 Mf30
Zahamena, P.N.de RM 220 Ne54
Zaháro GR 48 Mb53
Zaharoddze BY 37 Mf38
Zaharovka KZ 84 Of21
Zaharovo RUS 91 Qe20
Zahedan IR 75 Oa31
Zahirabad IND (APH) 108 Oj37
Zahlé RL 64 Mh29
Záhony H 39 Mc42
Zahran KSA 68 Nb37
Zahrat al Batn IRQ 65 Nb30
Zahrez Chergui DZ 173 Lb28
Zahrez Gharbi DZ 173 Lb28
Zaïda MA 172 Kh29
Zaidín E 30 La49
Zaigraevo RUS (BUR) 90 Qe20
Zaila RDC 203 Mc50
Zaili Alatau KZ 77 Oj24
Zaimovo SCG 46 Ma48
Zai N.P. JOR 64 Mh29
Zainsk RUS 53 Ng18
Zaïo MA 173 Kj28
Zaj RUS 53 Nf18
Zajač'e RUS 53 Mj20
Zaječar SCG 46 Mc47
Zajsan KZ 85 Pc22
Zajsan köli KZ 85 Pb21
Zaka ZW 214 Mf56
Zakamenska RUS (BUR) 90 Qb20
Zákány H 38 Lr44
Zakarpats'ka nyzovyna UA 39 Mc42
Zakhmet TM 73 Ob27
Zakho IRQ 65 Nb27
Zaki Biam WAN 194 Le42
Zákinthos GR 48 Ma53
Zákinthos GR 48 Ma53
Zakliczyn PL 39 Ma41
Zakobjakino RUS 53 Na16
Zakopane PL 39 Lu41
Zakouma TCH 196 Lk40
Zakouma, P.N.de TCH 196 Lk40
Zakou Shankou CHN 92 Pk27
Zakroczym PL 37 Ma38
Zákros GR 49 Mg55
Zákros GR 49 Mg55
Zaksybutaly tau KZ 71 Nk22
Zala ANG 202 Lh49
Zala H 38 Lr44
Zalaa MNG 92 Pk23
Zalaapáti H 38 Ls44
Zalabaska H 38 Lr44
Zalabiyeh SYR 65 Mk28
Zaladanki IND (APH) 111 Ok39
Zalaegerszeg H 38 Lr44
Zalakomár H 38 Ls44
Zalamea de la Serena E 28 Kp48
Zalamea la Real E 28 Ko47
Zalanga WAN 186 Lf40
Zalantun CHN (NMZ) 98 Rb22
Zalari RUS 90 Qb19
Zalaszentgrót H 38 Ls44
Zalău RO 44 Md43
Zalesie PL 37 Md38
Zalim KSA 66 Nb34
Zalingei SUD 196 Mb39
Zaliouan CI 192 Kg42
Zališčyky UA 45 Mf42
zaliv Aniva RUS 99 Sb22
zaliv Mordvinova RUS 99 Sb22
zaliv Prostor RUS 99 Se23
zaliv Šelihova RUS 59 Sd06
zaliv Terpenija RUS 99 Sb21
Zalizci UA 39 Mf41
Zalizci UA 54 Mc21
Zalki IND (KTK) 108 Oh37
Zaltan LAR 175 Lk31
Zaltbommel NL 32 Lf39
Zaluč'e RUS 52 Mf17
Žaludok BY 17 Me37
Zalut MYA 114 Pk39
Zam BF 185 Kk39
Zama RN 185 Lb38
Zamakh YE 68 Nd37
Zamanajrykty tau KZ 71 Nh23
Zamania IND (UPH) 109 Pb33
Zamárdi H 38 Ls44
Zamarte PL 36 Ls37
Zamatobgwe ZW 214 Mf55
Zamay CAM 187 Lg40
Zambejiti KZ 58 Nc08
Zambeke RDC 201 Mc44
Zambezi Z 209 Mb52
Zambezi 210 Me53
Zambezi Deka ZW 213 Md55
Zambezi Escarpment Z/ZW 210 Md54
Zambezi N.P. ZW 213 Mc55
Zambezi Source Z 209 Mc51
Zambia 167 Ma11
Zamboanga RP 123 Rb42
Zamboanga Peninsula RP 123 Rb42
Zambrano CO 268 Gc41
Zambrano HN 256 Fg38
Zambrów PL 37 Mc38
Zambué MOC 210 Mf53
Zámek CZ 38 Lr42
Zamek A.Wazówny PL 36 Lt37
Zamek Biskupów PL 37 Ma36
Zamek Dębińskich PL 39 Ma41
Zámek Kroměříž CZ 38 Ls41
Zamek Książ PL 36 Lr40
Zamek Książęcy PL 36 Lq39
Zámek Litomyšl CZ 38 Lr41
Zamek Malbork PL 36 Lt36
Zamek obronny PL 36 Lr40
Zamek Wedlów Tuczyńskich PL 36 Lr37
Zamfara WAN 185 Lc39
Zaminan IR 75 Ob32
Zamkova Hora UA 54 Md20
Zamlat Amagraj DARS 178 Kc33
Zamora E 26 Kp51
Zamora EC 272 Ga47
Zamora EC 272 Ga48
Zamora de Hidalgo MEX (MHC) 254 Ej36
Zamość PL 37 Md40
Zamyn-Üüd MNG 93 Qf24
Zamza RCA 196 Ma42
Zan TCH 196 Lk40
Zanaaul KZ 85 Pc21
Žanaga RCB 202 Lg47
Žanaortalyk KZ 84 Oh22
Zanarač BY 17 Mg36
Zanda CHN (TIB) 88 Ok30
Zandamela MOC 214 Mh58
Zanderij SME 271 Hc43
Zandvoort NL 32 Le38
Zane Hills USA (AK) 229 Cc12
Zanesville USA (OH) 246 Fj26
Zanfla CI 193 Kh42
Zangarediguedim IND (APH) 109 Pa37
Zangasso RMM 184 Kh39
Zangdo CHN (TIB) 88 Pd30
Zangla 79 Oj29
Zanglivéri GR 46 Md50
Zangnanadon DY 194 Lb42
Zango WAN 186 Le39
Zanjan IR 72 Ne27
Zanjan Bazaar IR 72 Ne27
Zanjitas RA (SL) 288 Gg62
Zánka H 38 Ls44
Zanskar 79 Oj29
Zanskar 79 Oj28
Zanskar 79 Oj29
Zanthus AUS (WA) 145 Rb61
Zantiébougou RMM 192 Kg40
Zanybek KZ 53 Nd21
Zanzibar EAT 207 Mk49
Zanzibar Channel EAT 207 Mk48
Zanzibar Island EAT 207 Mk48
Zanzra CI 192 Kg42
Zaokskij RUS 52 Mj18
Zao Q.N.P. J 101 Sa26
Zaoro-Songou RCA 195 Lj43
Zao-san J 101 Sa26
Zaoshi CHN (HUB) 95 Qg30
Zaouia-s Moussa DZ 174 Ld31
Zaoyang CHN (HUB) 95 Qg29
Zaozhuang CHN (SDG) 102 Qj28
Zapadnaja Dvina RUS 52 Mg17
Zapadna Morava SCG 46 Ma47
Zapadni Rodopi BG 47 Me49
Zapadnoe KZ 58 Ob08
Zapadno-Karel'skaja vozvyšennost RUS 11 Mf13
Zapadno Sahalinskie gory RUS 99 Sb21
Zapai RDC 201 Mc43
Zapala RA (NE) 292 Ge65
Zapaleri, Cerro BOL/RA/RCH 284 Gg57
Zapallar RCH 288 Ge61
Zapallar RCH 288 Ge62
Zapata RA (MD) 288 Gf62
Zapata USA (TX) 253 Fa32
Zapfendorf D 35 Ll40
Zapién MEX (CHH) 253 Eh32
Zapoljarnyj RUS 11 Mf11
Zapopan MEX (JLC) 254 Ej35
Zaporižžja UA 55 Mh22
Zaporožskoe RUS 52 Mf15
Zapotillo EC 272 Fk48
Zapotitlic MEX (JLC) 254 Ej36
Zapovednyj RUS 98 Rg24
Zaprešić HR 41 Lq45
Zaprudnja RUS 52 Mj17
Zaprudy BY 37 Me38
Zaqatala AZ 70 Nd25
Zar RIM 183 Kc37
Zara TR 63 Mj26
Zarafshon UZ 76 Ob26
Zarafshon UZ 76 Oc25
Zarafšon TJ 76 Oe26
Zaragoza CO 268 Gc42
Zaragoza E 27 Ku51
Zaragoza MEX (CHH) 237 Eg31
Zaragoza MEX (COH) 253 Ek31
Zaragoza MEX (NL) 253 Fa34
Zarajsk RUS 53 Mk18
Zarand IR 73 Nj28
Zaranj AFG 78 Oa30
Zaranou CI 193 Kj42
Zarasai LT 17 Mg35
Zárate RA (BA) 289 Ha63
Zarautz E 27 Ks53
Zaraza YV 269 Gh41
Zard PK 80 Oc31
Zarečka BY 37 Mf38
Zareh Sharan AFG 78 Oe29
Zarembo Island USA 231 Dd17
Zarghat KSA 66 Na32
Zarghun PK 78 Od30
Zarghun Shahr AFG 78 Oe29
Zari WAN 187 Lg39
Zaria WAN 186 Ld40
Zarin Abad IR 72 Ne27
Zarisberg NAM 212 Lj58
Žarki PL 37 Lu40
Zărnești RO 45 Mf45
Žarnovica SK 39 Lt42
Zaroko CI 193 Kh42
Žarošice CZ 38 Lr41
Zarqa JOR 64 Mj29
Zarqa SUD 197 Me39
Zarqa' Hadida SUD 197 Md40
Zarqan IR 74 Ng31
Zarrentin D 33 Ll37
Zarrin IR 72 Nh29
Zarrin Abad IR 72 Ne28
Zarrine Rud IR 72 Nd27
Zarrin Shar IR 72 Nf29
Zarskoe Selo RUS 52 Mf16
Zaruma EC 272 Ga47
Zarumilla PE 272 Fk47
Žary PL 36 Lq39
Zaryanovsk KZ 85 Pc21
Zarza de Granadilla E 28 Ko50
Zarzaïtine DZ 174 Le31
Zarzal CO 268 Gb43
Zarzis TN 174 Lf29
Zasa LV 17 Mf34
Zasieki PL 36 Lp39
Žaškiv UA 54 Mf21
Zasos'e RUS 16 Mj31
Zastron ZA 217 Md61
Žatec CZ 38 Lo40
Zatoka Pucka PL 36 Lt36
zatoka Syvaš UA 55 Mh22
Zătreni RO 44 Md46
Zatyšša UA 45 Mk43
Zaunguzskiye Karakumy TM 71 Nk25
Zavala BIH 41 Ls48
Zavalinë AL 46 Ma50
Zavalla RA (SF) 289 Gk62
Zavalla USA (TX) 243 Fc30
Zavareh IR 72 Ng29
Zave ZW 210 Mf54
Zavet BG 47 Mg47
Zavetvoe RUS 55 Nb22
Zavety Il'iča RUS 99 Sa21
Zavidovići BIH 41 Lt46
Zavitaja RUS 98 Re20
Zavitinsk RUS 98 Re20
Zavitne UA 55 Mj23
Zavizan HR 41 Lp46
Zavkhan MNG 90 Pj21
Zavkhan Gol MNG 85 Ph21
Zavodoukovsk RUS 58 Ob07
Zavoj MK 46 Ma49
Zavolž'e RUS 53 Nb17
Zawady PL 37 Ma39
Zawidów PL 36 Lq39
Zawiercie PL 37 Lu40
Zawilah LAR 181 Lh32
Zawita IRQ 65 Nb27
Zawiyat al Izziyat LAR 175 Mb29
Zawiyat al Murassas LAR 175 Mb29
Zawiyat Masus LAR 175 Ma30
Zawoja PL 39 Lu41
Zayaki Jangal PK 80 Oc32
Zayat MYA 112 Ph34
Zayat-koun MYA 113 Ph35
Zaymah KSA 66 Na35
Zayni OM 75 Nj33
Zaza RUS 91 Qf19
Zazafotsy RM 220 Nd57
Zazhong CHN (TIB) 89 Pj31
Zaziatou RN 185 Lb39
Zázrivá SK 39 Lu41
Zbaraž UA 54 Mc21
Zbąszyń PL 36 Lq38
Zbečno CZ 38 Lo40
Zbiroh CZ 38 Lo41
Zblewo PL 36 Lt37
Zbójna PL 37 Mb37
Zbójno PL 37 Lu37
Zboriv UA 39 Mf41
Zborov SK 39 Mb41
Zborowice PL 39 Ma41
Zbruč UA 45 Mg42
Zbuczna PL 37 Mc38
Žď'ár CZ 38 Lo40
Žď'ár nad Sázavou CZ 38 Lq41
Ždirec nad Doubravou CZ 38 Lq41
Zdolbuniv UA 54 Md20
Zdunje MK 46 Mb49
Zduńska Wola PL 36 Lt39
Zduny PL 37 Lu38
Zdzieszowice PL 36 Lt40
Zebak AFG 79 Of27
Zeballos CDN (BC) 232 Dg21
Zebediela ZA 214 Me58
Zé Biel BR (TO) 276 Hg49
Zebilla GH 193 Kk40
Žebrak PL 37 Mc38
Zebreira P 28 Kn49
Zediyn Nuruu MNG 90 Qb20
Zé Doca BR (MA) 276 Hh47
Zéé DY 194 Lb42
Zeebrugge B 23 Ld39
Zeehan AUS (TAS) 152 Sc66
Zeekoegat ZA 214 Me58
Zeerust ZA 213 Md58
Zeewyk Channel AUS 144 Qg60
Zefat IL 64 Mh29
Zefreh IR 72 Ng29
Zegbé CI 193 Kh43
Zeghamra DZ 173 Kj31
Zegon MYA 113 Pj34
Zégoua RMM 193 Kh40
Zegstey MNG 90 Qb22
Zéguédéguen BF 185 Kk39
Zehdenick D 33 Lo38
Zeil, Mount AUS 142 Rg57
Žeimelis LT 17 Md34
Žeimena LT 17 Mf35
Žeimiai LT 17 Md35
Zeist NL 32 Lf38
Zeitz D 33 Ln39
Zeja RUS 98 Rd20
Zejsko-Bureinkaja ravnina RUS 98 Re20
Zejskoe vodohranilišče RUS 59 Rb08
Zêkog CHN (QHI) 94 Qa28
Želazna PL 36 Ls36
Želča RUS 16 Mh32
Żelechów PL 37 Mb39
Zelená Hora CZ 38 Lo41
Zelenaja Rošča RUS 16 Mk30
Zelenbreg MK 46 Mc49
Zelenčukskaja RUS (KCH) 70 Na24
Zelenivka UA 55 Mj22
Zelenodol'sk RUS 53 Ne18
Zelenodol's'k UA 54 Mg22
Zelenogirs'ke UA 45 Ml43
Zelenograd RUS 52 Mj17
Zelenogradsk RUS 17 Ma36
Zelenokumsk RUS 70 Nb23
Železná Ruda CZ 38 Lo41
Železnodorožnyj RUS 17 Mb36
Železnogorsk RUS 52 Mh19
Zelfana DZ 173 Lc29
Želiezovce SK 38 Lt42
Želju Vojoda BG 47 Mg48
Zella-Mehlis D 33 Ll40
Zell am See A 35 Ln43
Zell an der Pram A 35 Lo42
Žel'tau Ajtau KZ 84 Og23
Zelter MNG 90 Qc20
Zeltini LV 17 Mg33
Zeltweg A 35 Lp43
Žel'va BY 37 Me37
Želva LT 17 Mf35
Zelzate B 23 Ld39
Žemaičių Kalvarija LT 17 Mc34
Žemaičių Naumiestis LT 17 Mb35
Žemaitija LT 17 Mc35
Žemaitijos n.p. LT 17 Mb34
Žemberovce SK 39 Lt42
Zemblak AL 46 Ma50
Zembra TN 174 Lf27
Zemen BG 46 Mc48
Zemenskiya prolom BG 46 Mc48
Zemgale LV 17 Me34
Zemio RCA 201 Mc43
Zemite LV 17 Mc34
Zemlja Aleksandry RUS 58 Nb02
Zemlja Georga RUS 58 Nc02
Zemmora DZ 173 La28
Zemmour DARS 178 Kd33
Zemo Ažara GE 70 Na24
Zemplénagárd H 39 Mc42
Zempléni-hegység H 39 Mb42
Zempoala MEX 254 Fb36
Zemurray Gardens Lodge Complex USA 243 Fe30
Zendeh Jan AFG 78 Oa28
Zenguele ANG 202 Lh49
Zenica BIH 41 Ls46
Zenkoji J 101 Rk27
Zentsuji J 101 Rg28
Zenza do Itombe ANG 202 Lh50
Žepče BIH 41 Lt46
Zephyrhills USA (FL) 250 Fj31
Zepita PE 284 Gf54
Zepu CHN (XUZ) 86 Oj26
Zéralda DZ 173 Lb27
Zerauk AFG 78 Oe29
Žeravna BG 47 Mg48
Zerbst D 33 Ln39
Žerdevka RUS 53 Na20
Žerebkove UA 45 Mk43
Zeribet el Oued DZ 174 Ld28
Zerkov Bogojavlenija RUS 53 Na17
Zerkov Borisa i Gleba RUS 53 Na17
Zerkov pokrova na Nerli RUS 53 Na17
Zermatt CH 34 Lh44
Zernograd RUS 55 Na22
Zerouilet MA 173 Kj29
Zerqan AL 46 Ma49
Žeskazgan KZ 58 Ob09
Zestaponi GE 70 Nb24
Zeta SCG 46 Lu48
Zêtang CHN (TIB) 89 Pf31
Zetel D 32 Lh37
Žetikara KZ 58 Oa08
Žetikonyr kum KZ 84 Oe22
Zeulenroda D 33 Lm40
Zeuthen D 33 Lo38
Zeven D 32 Lk37
Zevenaar NL 32 Lf39
Zevenbergen NL 32 Le39
Zeyn-od Din IR 72 Nh30
Zeytinbağı TR 50 Mj50
Zeytindağ TR 49 Mh52
Zeytinlı TR 50 Mg51
Zgierz PL 37 Lu39
Zgniłoche PL 37 Ma37
Zgorzelec PL 36 Lq39
Zgozhd AL 46 Ma49
Zgurița MD 45 Mj42
Zhairan KZ 84 Of21
Zhaksykylysh KZ 71 Ob22
Zhalaghash KZ 76 Oc23
Zhalanash KZ 77 Ok24
Zhalong Lake Sanctuary CHN 98 Rc22
Zhambyl KZ 84 Of22
Zhambyl KZ 84 Og23
Zhamshi KZ 84 Oh22
Zhanaakshiman KZ 84 Oj20
Zhanadariya KZ 76 Oc23
Zhanakala KZ 76 Ob23
Zhanakorghan KZ 76 Od24
Zhanang CHN (TIB) 89 Pf31
Zhanaozen KZ 71 Ng24
Zhanatas KZ 76 Oe24
Zhanbay aral KZ 70 Ne22
Zhangbei CHN (HBI) 93 Qh25
Zhangcunpu CHN (AHU) 102 Qh29
Zhang Fei Ci CHN 95 Qe30
Zhangguangcai Ling CHN 98 Re23
Zhanghe Shuiku CHN 95 Qf30
Zhang Hua CHN 95 Qg30
Zhanghuang CHN (GZG) 96 Qe35
Zhanghyztobe KZ 84 Pa21
Zhangjiachuan CHN (GSU) 95 Qd28
Zhangjiajie CHN (HUN) 95 Qf31
Zhangjiakou CHN (HBI) 93 Qh25
Zhangjialing CHN (JGX) 102 Qj31
Zhangjiang CHN (JGS) 102 Ra30
Zhangla CHN (SCH) 94 Qb29
Zhangping CHN (FJN) 97 Qj33
Zhangpu CHN (FJN) 97 Qj33
Zhangqiu CHN (SDG) 93 Qj27
Zhangshu CHN (JGX) 102 Qh31
Zhangwu CHN (LNG) 100 Rb24
Zhangye CHN (GSU) 92 Qa26
Zhangzhou CHN (FJN) 97 Qj33
Zhanjiang CHN (GDG) 96 Qf35
Zhansugirov KZ 84 Ok23
Zhanyi CHN (YUN) 113 Qb33
Zhaodong CHN (HLG) 98 Rc22
Zhaojue CHN (SCH) 94 Qb31
Zhaokua CHN (YUN) 113 Qb33
Zhao Ling CHN 95 Qe28
Zhaolin Gongyuan CHN 98 Rd23
Zhaoling Tomb CHN 100 Rb25
Zhaoping CHN (GZG) 96 Qf33
Zhaoqing CHN (GDG) 96 Qg34
Zhaosu CHN (XUZ) 84 Pa24
Zhaotong CHN (YUN) 113 Qb32
Zhao Xian CHN (HBI) 93 Qh27
Zhaoxing CHN (HLG) 98 Rf22
Zhaoyuan CHN (HLG) 98 Rc23
Zhaozhen CHN (SCH) 94 Qc30
Zhaozhou CHN (HLG) 98 Rc23
Zhaozhou Qiao CHN 93 Qh27
Zha po Gang CHN 96 Qf35
Zhapu CHN (ZJG) 102 Ra30
Zhari Namco CHN 88 Pc30
Zharkent KZ 84 Pa23
Zharma KZ 84 Pa21
Zharyk KZ 84 Pa21
Zharykbas KZ 76 Of24
Zhaxigang CHN (TIB) 88 Ok29
Zhazuo CHN (GZH) 96 Qd32
Zhdanovo KZ 76 Of24
Zhecheng CHN (HNN) 102 Qh28
Zhefang CHN (YUN) 113 Pk33
Zhejiang CHN 83 Qd13
Zhejue CHN (GZH) 113 Qb32
Zhelang CHN (GDG) 97 Qh34
Zhen'an CHN (SAA) 95 Qe29
Zhenba CHN (SAA) 95 Qd29
Zhenbao Ding CHN 96 Qf32
Zhenfeng CHN (GZH) 96 Qc33
Zhengcheng CHN (GDG) 97 Qg34
Zhenghe CHN (FJN) 102 Qk32
Zhengxiangbai Qi CHN (NMZ) 93 Qh24
Zhengyang CHN (HNN) 102 Qh29
Zhengzhou CHN (HNN) 95 Qg28
Zhenhai CHN (FJN) 97 Qk33
Zhenhai CHN (ZJG) 102 Ra31
Zhenjiang CHN (JGS) 102 Qk29
Zhenkang CHN (YUN) 113 Pk34
Zhenlai CHN (JLN) 98 Rb23
Zhenning CHN (GZH) 96 Qc32
Zhenping CHN (HNN) 95 Qg29
Zhenping CHN (SAA) 95 Qe30
Zhenqian CHN (FJN) 102 Qk32
Zhenxiong CHN (YUN) 96 Qc32
Zhenyuan CHN (GSU) 95 Qd28
Zhenyuan CHN (GZH) 96 Qe32
Zhenyuan CHN (YUN) 113 Qa33
Zherong CHN (FJN) 102 Qk32
Zhesang CHN (YUN) 96 Qc34
Zhetibai KZ 71 Ng24
Zhetisai KZ 76 Oe25
Zhexi Shuiku CHN 95 Qf31
Zhicheng CHN (HUB) 95 Qf30
Zhidan CHN (SAA) 92 Qe27
Zhidoi CHN (QHI) 89 Ph29
Zhigan CHN (TIB) 88 Pb30
Zhijiang CHN (HUB) 95 Qf30
Zhijiang CHN (HUN) 96 Qe32
Zhijin CHN (GZH) 96 Qc32
Zhi Jin Cave CHN 96 Qc32

CREDITS/CONTRIBUTORS

© 2006 Verlag Wolfgang Kunth GmbH & Co KG, Munich
Innere Wiener Straße 13
81667 Munich
Telephone +49.89.45 80 20-0
Fax +49.89.45 80 20-21
info@geographicmedia.de
www.kunth-verlag.de

©Cartography: GeoGraphic Publishers GmbH & Co. KG

Map relief 1 : 2,250,000/1 : 4,500,000/1 : 18,000,000/1 : 27,000,000/1 : 45,000,000/ 1 : 54,000,000/1 : 63,000,000/1 : 85,000,000 MHM ® Copyright © Digital Wisdom, Inc.

English language distribution:

GeoCenter International Ltd
The Viables Centre, Harrow Way
Basingstoke, Hants RG22 4BJ
England
Tel: (44) 1256 817 987
Fax: (44) 1256 817 988
e-mail: sales@geocenter.co.uk
www.insightguides.com

Concept: Wolfgang Kunth
Cartography and Editorial Staff: GeoKarta – Ralf van den Berg, geoinformatics specialist, Stuttgart; Jens Ewers, cartographer (UAS), Stuttgart; Bernd Hilberer, cartographer (UAS), Leonberg; Doris Kordisch, cartographer (UAS), Markkleeberg; Peter Krause, graduate geographer, Stuttgart; Gabriele Luber, graduate geographer (M.A.), Kufstein; Karen Morlok, cartographer, Renningen-Malmsheim; Heiner Newe, graduate geographer, Altensteig; Beate Reußnach, cartographer (UAS), Schwabach; Bernhard Spachmüller, cartographer (UAS), Schwabach; Karin Stemmer, cartographer, Gäufelden
Coordination: Heiner Newe, Claus-Peter Waider, Michael Kaiser
Text Translation: Demetri Lowe
Cover design: Derrick Lim
Layout: Um|bruch, Munich
Prepress: Dorothea Happ
Litho (title pages): Fotolito Varesco, Auer (Italy)
Printing: Appl, Wemding
Printed in Germany

Pictures:
II–III large picture: Satellite picture of Arab peninsula; small pictures, left to right: Atacama Desert, Chile; San Francisco, USA; Iceland; Chambord Castle, France; Nambung NP, Australia; Marrakesh, Morocco; Wat Phra Kaeo in Bangkok, Thailand; Moorèa, French-Polynesia.
IV: Gulf of Aqaba
VI top to bottom: Mont-Saint-Michel, France; Angkor, Cambodia; Milford Sound, New Zealand; gnus and zebras in the Ngorongoro Crater, Tanzania; Glacier Bay, Alaska; Machu Picchu, Peru; icebergs in the Antarctic.
XII–XIII left to right: Garden Route, »Outeniqua Choo-Tjoe«train, South Africa; Dolomites, Italiy; Hoggar Mountains, Algeria; Mount Egmont, New Zealand; Iguaçu Falls, Brazil; Dresden, Germany; Guggenheim Museum in Bilbao, Spain.
XIV–XV left to right: Varanasi, India; Himeji-jo, Japan; Borobudur, Indonesia; rocks in Kakadu NP, Australia; monastery at Popocatépetl, Mexico; pyramid in Chichén Itzá, Mexico; Las Vegas, USA; Caribbean impressions.
XVI–XVII large picture: Hurricane cloud formations over Pacific; satellite pictures, left to right: Amazon; Patagonia; Simpson Desert; Lesser Antilles; Andes; Sahara; Bali and Lombok; Tassili n'Ajjer.

Picture credits:
II.1 dv/Woodhouse; II.2 Premium; II.3,4 Getty; III.1 Premium; III.2 Huber/ Orient; III.3 Premium/Lawton; III.4 Getty; VI, VII.1,3,4 Premium; VII.2 Pix/Masterfile; XII.1 Christoph & Friends; XII.2 Premium; XII.3 Getty; XIII.1,2 Premium, XIII.3 Huber; XIV.1 Getty/Harris; XIV.2 Huber/Orient; XIV.3 Premium/Marr/Panoramic Images; XIV.4 Transglobe/Schmitz; XV.1 Premium/Brimberg/NGS; XV.2 Getty/Cosmo Condina; XV.3 Premium; XV.4 Getty/Giles; XVI, XVII © Geospace/Eurimage/Spotimage.

Cover photograph © NASA